THE LAW REPORTS

OF THE

INCORPORATED COUNCIL OF LAW REPORTING
FOR IRELAND

1984—1988

INCORPORATED COUNCIL OF LAW REPORTING
FOR NORTHERN IRELAND
1984—1985

AND

THE IRISH LAW REPORTS MONTHLY

1976—1979, 1984—1988

DIGEST OF CASES

DECIDED BY THE

SUPERIOR AND OTHER COURTS IN IRELAND AND NORTHERN IRELAND

AND REPORTED FROM 1984 to 1988

EDITED BY
JULITTA M. CLANCY,
B.A., Dip. Archival Stds., R.I.
AND
EDWARD F. RYAN,
M.A. Barrister-at-Law,
Of the King's Inns and Middle Temple

CONSULTANT EDITOR
GERARD HOGAN,
B.C.L., LL.M. (N.U.I.), LL.M. (Penn.), M.A., Barrister-at-Law, King's Inns

COMPILED AND INDEXED BY
JULITTA M. CLANCY

DUBLIN:
INCORPORATED COUNCIL OF LAW REPORTING
FOR IRELAND
LAW LIBRARY, FOUR COURTS, DUBLIN 7.

ISBN 0 946738 02 5

Printed in the Republic of Ireland by
Cahill Printers Limited
East Wall Road, Dublin 3.

CONTENTS

JUDGES AND LAW OFFICERS

DURING THE PERIOD OF THESE REPORTS

IRELAND

Chief Justice:

The Hon. THOMAS F. O'HIGGINS
The Hon. THOMAS A. FINLAY

The Supreme Court:

The Hon. THOMAS F. O'HIGGINS, C.J.
The Hon. THOMAS A. FINLAY, C.J.
The Hon. BRIAN WALSH
The Hon. SEAMUS HENCHY
The Hon. FRANK GRIFFIN
THE HON ANTHONY J. HEDERMAN
The Hon. NIALL MCCARTHY

The High Court:

The Hon. THOMAS A. FINLAY *President*
The Hon. LIAM HAMILTON *President*
The Hon. JOHN M. GANNON
The Hon. THOMAS A. DOYLE
The Hon. JAMES G. MCMAHON
The Hon. HERBERT R. MCWILLIAM
The Hon. DECLAN D. COSTELLO
The Hon. JAMES A. D'ARCY
The Hon. RONAN C. KEANE
The Hon. DONAL P. BARRINGTON
The Hon. MELLA E. CARROLL
The Hon. RODERICK J. O'HANLON
The Hon. HENRY D. BARRON
The Hon. FRANCIS D. MURPHY
The Hon. KEVIN LYNCH
The Hon. SEAMUS F. EGAN
The Hon. ROBERT BARR
The Hon. GERARD J. W. LARDNER
The Hon. JOHN J. BLAYNEY
The Hon. JOHN J. MCKENZIE
The Hon. RICHARD P. JOHNSTON

Ex officio — President of the Circuit Court

The Hon. THOMAS JOSEPH NEYLON
The Hon. THOMAS F. ROE

Attorney General:

PETER D. W. SUTHERLAND, S.C.
JOHN ROGERS, S.C.
JOHN MURRAY, S.C.

NORTHERN IRELAND

Lord Chief Justice:

The Right Hon. LORD LOWRY

Lords Justices of Appeal:

The Right Hon. SIR EDWARD WARBURTON JONES
The Right Hon. SIR MAURICE WHITE GIBSON
The Right Hon. TURLOUGH O' DONNELL
The Right Hon. SIR JOHN WILLIAM B. KELLY

Queen's Bench Division:

The Right Hon. JOHN WILLIAM B. KELLY
The Hon. JOHN BRIAN E. HUTTON
The Hon. JOHN PATRICK B. HIGGINS
The Hon. ROBERT DOUGLAS CARSWELL

Chancery Division:

The Hon. DONALD BRUCE MURRAY

Family Division:

The Hon. JOHN CLARKE MACDERMOTT

Attorney General:

The Right Hon. SIR MICHAEL HAVERS, Q.C., M.P.

INCORPORATED COUNCIL OF LAW REPORTING FOR IRELAND

DURING THE PERIOD OF THESE REPORTS

EDITORS AND REPORTERS

THE IRISH REPORTS

Editors:

Reporters:

THE NORTHERN IRELAND REPORTS

Editor:

Assistant Editors:

THE IRISH LAW REPORTS MONTHLY

Editor:

Reporters:

LIST OF ABBREVIATIONS

A.G.	Attorney General
Art.	Article
C.A.	Court of Appeal
C.C.A.	Court of Criminal Appeal
C.J.	Chief Justice
Ch. D.	Chancery Division
Cir. Ct.	Circuit Court
Co. Ct.	County Court
Crown. Ct.	Crown Court
D.P.P.	Director of Public Prosecutions
Dist. Ct.	District Court
E.A.T.	Employment Appeals Tribunal
E.C.J.	European Court of Justice
Fam. D.	Family Division
H.C.	High Court
H.L.	House of Lords
ILRM	Irish Law Reports Monthly
I.L.T.R.	Irish Law Times Reports
I.R.	Irish Reports
Ir. Jur. Rep.	Irish Jurist Reports
J.	Justice
L.C.J.	Lord Chief Justice
L.J.	Lord Justice of Appeal
Lab. Ct.	Labour Court
Mag. Ct.	Magistrate's Court
N.I.	Northern Ireland Northern Ireland Reports
O.	Order
P.	President of the High Court
Q.B.D.	Queen's Bench Division
Q.S.	Quarter Sessions
r.	Rule
R.S.C.	Rules of the Superior Courts
R.S.C. (N.I.)	Rules of the Supreme Court (Northern Ireland)
Rec. Ct.	Recorder's Court
S.C.	Supreme Court
Sch.	Schedule
S.I.	Statutory Instrument
S.R.& O.	Statutory Rules and Orders
Sect. or s.	Section
Sp. Crim. Ct.	Special Criminal Court
Sub-s.	Sub-section

TABLE OF CASES

Name of Case	Volume and page	Column of Digest
,, ,, *v.* Sun Alliance and London Insurances Ltd.	[1985] ILRM 522	1164
Attorney General (*ex rel.* Society for the Protection of Unborn Children Ltd.) *v.* Open Door Counselling Ltd.	[1988] I.R.593; [1987] ILRM 477	180
Attorney General, Brennan *v.*	[1984] ILRM 355	991
,, ,, Cafolla *v.*, *see* Cafolla *v.* O'Malley		
,, ,, Curtis *v.*	[1985] I.R.458; [1986] ILRM 428	235
,, ,, Draper *v.*	[1984] I.R.277; [1984] ILRM 643	211
,, ,, Madigan *v.*	[1986] ILRM 136	229
,, ,, Norris *v.*	[1984] I.R.36	214
,, ,, O'G.(T.) *v.*	[1985] ILRM 61	15
,, ,, Private Motorists' Provident Society Ltd. *v.*	[1984] ILRM 88	227
,, ,, Representative Church Body *v.*	[1988] I.R.19	88
,, ,, Sunshine Radio Productions Ltd. *v.*	[1984] ILRM 170	69
,, ,, Tormey *v.*, *see* Tormey *v.* Ireland		
Attorney General for England and Wales *v.* Brandon Book Publishers Ltd.	[1986] I.R.597; [1987] ILRM 135	171
Attorney General for Northern Ireland, Northern Bank Executor and Trustee Co. Ltd. *v.*, *In re* Dunlop	[1984] N.I. 408	86
Aughey *v.* Ireland	[1986] ILRM 206	594
Avonmore Creameries Ltd., Daly *v.*	[1984] I.R.131	807
B		
B. (E.), *In re*	[1985] N.I.128	9
B.(R.), S.(A.) *v.*	[1984] ILRM 66	546
Bairead *v.* Maxwells of Donegal Ltd.	[1986] ILRM 508	1036
Baker, *In the Goods of*	[1985] I.R.101	1157
,, *v.* Cohn-Vossen; *In the Estate of* Mieth ...	[1986] ILRM 175	1139
Balkan Tours Ltd. *v.* Minister for Communications	[1988] ILRM 101	1182
Ballagh, State (Lynch) *v.*	[1986] I.R.203; [1987] ILRM 65	339
Banco Ambrosiano S.P.A. *v.* Ansbacher & Co.	[1987] ILRM 669	63
Bank of Ireland *v.* O'Keeffe...	[1987] I.R.47	64
,, ,, *v.* Purcell	[1988] ILRM 480	568
,, ,, L.(H.) *v.*	[1978] ILRM 160	1142
Bank of Ireland Finance Ltd., Browne *v.*	[1987] I.R.346	1017
,, ,, ,, Corran Construction Co. *v.*	[1976-7] ILRM 175	105
Bannerton, *In re*	[1986] I.R.758; [1986] ILRM 471; [1984] ILRM 662	732
Bannon *v.* Craigavon Development Commission	[1984] N.I.387	918
Barrett *v.* Independent Newspapers Ltd.	[1986] I.R.13; [1986] ILRM 601	427
Barrett Apartments Ltd., *In re*	[1985] I.R.350; [1985] ILRM 679	1100
Barrington's Hospital, *see* Governors of Barrington's Hospital *v.* Minister for Health		
Barry *v.* Secretary of State	[1984] N.I.39	288
Bates, Reddy *v.*	[1984] ILRM 197	417
Bayzana Ltd. *v.* Galligan	[1987] I.R.238	640
Beara Fisheries and Shipping Ltd. *v.* Minister for the Marine	[1987] I.R.413; [1988] ILRM 221	625
Beckmann Instruments (Galway) Inc., Brady *v.*	[1986] ILRM 361	795
Beecham Group Ltd. *v.* Goodalls of Ireland Ltd.	[1978] ILRM 106	1171
Beechpark Estates Ltd., Ó hArgain *v.*	[1979] ILRM 57	1058
Begley, O'Donnell *v.*	[1987] ILRM 105	794
Belenos Publications Ltd., Holloway *v.* (No. 1)	[1987] I.R.405; [1987] ILRM 790	946

Name of Case	Volume and page	Column of Digest
(F.J.) & Sons Ltd.	[1985] N.I.50	960
Carlisle Trust Ltd., White *v.*	[1976-7] ILRM 311	702
Carmody, People *v.*	[1988] ILRM 370	389
Carr *v.* Phelan	[1976-7] ILRM 149	708
Carrigan (P.J.) Ltd. *v.* Norwich Union Fire Society Ltd.	[1987] I.R.618	949
Carroll *v.* Sheridan	[1984] ILRM 451	997
,, Coras Iompair Éireann *v.*	[1986] ILRM 312	826
,, Dublin Corporation *v.*	[1987] I.R.401; [1988] ILRM 86	293
,, Irish Distributive and Administrative Trade Union *v.*	[1988] ILRM 713	1178
,, MacDaibheid *v.*	[1978] ILRM 14	1049
Carroll Industries plc *v.* O'Cúlacháin	[1988] I.R.705	1033
Cartmill *v.* Ireland	[1987] I.R.192; [1988] ILRM 430	239
Carthy, Reeves *v.*	[1984] I.R.348	799
Carty Builders & Co. Ltd., Dublin County Council *v.*	[1987] I.R.355	890
Cassidy Electrical Supply Co. Ltd., Uniacke *v.*, *In re* W.J. Hickey Ltd.	[1988] I.R. 126	1082
Castlemahon Poultry Products Ltd., *In re*	[1987] ILRM 222	120
Caudron *v.* Air Zaire	[1985] I.R.716; [1986] ILRM 10	632
Cavern Systems Dublin Ltd. *v.* Clontarf Residents Association	[1984] ILRM 24	913
Central Bank of Ireland, Irish Trust Bank Ltd. *v.*	[1976-7] ILRM 50	941
Central Trust Investment Society Ltd., Coyle *v.*	[1978] ILRM 211	1096
Centreline Ltd., Kavanagh *v.*	[1987] ILRM 306	29
Chambers *v.* Department of the Environment ...	[1985] N.I.181	798
Chariot Inns Ltd., Robinson *v.*	[1986] ILRM 621	883
Charlton *v.* Ireland	[1984] ILRM 39	236
Chemise Lacoste S.A., La, *v.* Controller of Patents, Designs and Trade Marks	[1978] ILRM 8	1172
Chief Constable, McKee *v.*	[1984] N.I.169	297
Chief Electoral Officer, McCartney *v.*	[1984] N.I.240	471
Childers Heights Housing Ltd. v. Molderings ...	[1987] ILRM 47	45
Circuit Court Judge for Western Circuit, Joyce *v.*	[1987] ILRM 316	154
Clancy *v.* Commissioners of Public Works in Ireland	[1988] ILRM 268	805
,, *v.* Ireland	[1988] I.R.326	230
,, D.P.P. *v.*	[1986] ILRM 268	1077
,, Tennent *v.*	[1987] I.R.15; [1988] ILRM 214	998
Clarets Ltd., *In re*, *see* Spain *v.* McCann		
Clarke *v.* Roche, *see* State (Clarke)*v.* Roche		
Cleary, Minister for Agriculture *v.*	[1988] ILRM 294	325
Clifford, Feeney *v.*	[1988] I.R.499	449
,, Hannigan *v.*, *see* O'Flynn v. Clifford		
,, O'Flynn *v.*	[1988] I.R.740	373
,, State (Payne) *v.*	[1985] ILRM 70	382
Cliftonville Football and Athletic Club Ltd., Johnston *v.*	[1984] N.I.9	1009
Clinch *v.* Connellan, *see* State (Clinch) *v.* Connellan		
Clinton, *In re*; O'Sullivan *v.* Dunne	[1988] ILRM 80	1151
,, D.P.P. *v.*	[1984] ILRM 127	1075
Clontarf Residents Association, Cavern Systems Dublin Ltd. *v.*	[1984] ILRM 24	913
Coffey *v.* McDonagh, *see* O'Neill *v.* Butler		
,, People *v.*	[1987] ILRM 727	295
Cohn-Vossen, Baker *v.*, *In the Estate of* Mieth ...	[1986] ILRM 175	1139
Cole *v.* Webb Caravan Services Ltd.	[1985] ILRM 1	923
Collins *v.* Ruane, *see* State (Collins) *v.* Ruane		

Name of Case	Volume and page	Column of Digest
Daly *v.* Avonmore Creameries Ltd....	[1984] I.R.131	807
,, *v.* Minister for Agriculture, *see* State (Daly) *v.* Minister for Agriculture		
,, *v.* Ruane, *see* State (Daly) *v.* Ruane		
,, MacCarthaigh *v.*	[1985] I.R.73; [1986] ILRM 116	1044
,, Meath County Council *v.*	[1987] I.R.391; [1988] ILRM 274	891
Damen and Zonen *v.* O'Shea	[1976-7] ILRM 275	956
Darragh, O'Kelly *v.*	[1988] ILRM 309	845
Dataproducts (Dublin) Ltd., Murphy *v.*	[1988] I.R. 10	1033
Davidson, Lamb Brothers Dublin Ltd. *v.*	[1978] ILRM 226	501
De Valera, State (Gallagher Shatter & Co.) *v.*	[1987] I.R.55; [1987] ILRM 555	943
,, ,, ,, ,, ...	[1986] ILRM 3	939
Deasy, Horgan *v.*	[1979] ILRM 71	1091
Defence, Minister for, *see under* Minister		
Deighan, *In re*, *see* Kelly, *In re*		
,, *v.* Hearne	[1986] I.R. 603	203
,, *v.* Sunday Newspapers Ltd.	[1985] N.I.9	937
Delap, Rainey *v.*	[1988] I.R.470; [1988] ILRM 620	350
Dent (A.) & Co. Ltd. *v.* Controller of Patents	[1978] ILRM 172	1173
Department of the Environment, Allen *v.*	[1985] N.I.195	905
,, ,, ,, Chambers *v.*	[1985] N.I.181	798
,, ,, ,, McInerney Properties Ltd. *v.*	[1984] N.I.1	741
Desmond and Boyle *v.* Brophy	[1985] I.R.449; [1986] ILRM 547	817
Dillon, Donohue *v.*	[1988] ILRM 654	916
,, R. *v.*	[1984] N.I.292	320
Diners Club Ltd. *v.* Revenue Commissioners ...	[1988] I.R.158	1059
Director of Consumer Affairs *v.* Sunshine Holidays Ltd.	[1984] ILRM 551	254
,, ,, ,, *v.* Walsh (Joe) Tours Ltd.	[1985] ILRM 273	254
Director of Public Prosecutions *v.* Clancy	[1986] ILRM 268	1077
,, ,, ,, ,, ,, *v.* Clinton	[1984] ILRM 127	1075
,, ,, ,, ,, ,, *v.* Corrigan ...	[1986] I.R.290; [1987] ILRM 575	1070
,, ,, ,, ,, ,, *v.* Donoghue ...	[1986] I.R.188; [1987] ILRM 129	1070
,, ,, ,, ,, ,, *v.* Flahive	[1988] ILRM 133	1074
,, ,, ,, ,, ,, *v.* Gaffney ...	[1987] I.R.173; [1988] ILRM 39; [1986] ILRM 657	302
,, ,, ,, ,, ,, *v.* Greeley ...	[1985] ILRM 320	1067
,, ,, ,, ,, ,, *v.* Grey	[1986] I.R.317; [1987] ILRM 4	360
,, ,, ,, ,, ,, *v.* Independent Newspapers Ltd., *see* State (D.P.P.) *v.*—		
,, ,, ,, ,, ,, *v.* Johnson ...	[1988] ILRM 747	368
,, ,, ,, ,, ,, *v.* Joyce	[1985] ILRM 206	1066
,, ,, ,, ,, ,, *v.* Kelso	[1984] ILRM 329	329
,, ,, ,, ,, ,, *v.* Littlejohn ...	[1978] ILRM 147	338
,, ,, ,, ,, ,, *v.* McCutcheon	[1986] ILRM 433	311
,, ,, ,, ,, ,, *v.* McLoughlin	[1986] I.R.355; [1986] ILRM 493	1054
,, ,, ,, ,, ,, *v.* McMahon	[1986] I.R.393; [1987] ILRM 87	312
,, ,, ,, ,, ,, *v.* Nangle	[1984] ILRM 171	337
,, ,, ,, ,, ,, *v.* O'Connor ...	[1985] ILRM 333	1069
,, ,, ,, ,, ,, *v.* Olympic Amusements	[1987] ILRM 320	588
,, ,, ,, ,, ,, *v.* Roberts ...	[1987] I.R.268	736
,, ,, ,, ,, ,, *v.* Roe, *see* State		

Name of Case	Volume and page	Column of Digest
E.(W.), E.(I.) *v.*	[1985] ILRM 691	564
ESB, *see* Electricity Supply Board		
Eamonn Andrews Productions Ltd., *see* Andrews (Eamonn) Productions		
Eastern Health Board, Glow Heating Ltd. *v.* ...	[1988] I.R.110	116
,, ,, ,, H. *v.*	[1988] I.R.747	1126
,, ,, ,, Murphy *v.*	[1979] ILRM 100	479
,, ,, ,, State (Kershaw) *v.*	[1985] ILRM 235	1113
,, ,, ,, State (McLoughlin) *v.*	[1986] I.R.416	1114
Eccles *v.* Ireland	[1985] I.R.545; [1986] ILRM 343	232
Economic and Social Research Institute, Tormey *v.*	[1986] I.R.615	930
Education, Minister for, *see under* Minister		
Edwards, Berkeley *v.*	[1988] I.R.217	377
,, Northern Bank Ltd. *v.*	[1985] I.R.284; [1986] ILRM 167	144
Egan Electric Co.Ltd., *In re*	[1987] I.R.398	128
Egan (William) & Sons Ltd. *v.* Sisk (John) & Sons Ltd	[1986] ILRM 283	412
Electoral (Amendment) Bill, 1983, *In re*	[1984] I.R.268; [1984] ILRM 539	153
Electricity Supply Board *v.* Gormley	[1985] I.R.129; [1985] ILRM 494	224
Elf Investments Ltd., Maloney *v.*	[1979] ILRM 253	1087
Elliott (P.) & Co.Ltd. *v.* Minister for Education	[1987] ILRM 710	37
Elm Motors Ltd., Irish Shell Ltd. *v.*	[1984] I.R.200; [1984] ILRM 595	638
Elton Homes Ltd., Dublin County Council *v.* ...	[1984] ILRM 297	878
Employment Appeals Tribunal, Nova Colour Graphic Supplies Ltd. *v.*	[1987] I.R.426	484
,, ,, ,, State (IBM Ireland Ltd.) *v.*	[1984] ILRM 31	483
,, ,, ,, State (Irish Pharmaceutical Union) *v.*	[1987] ILRM 36	777
Environment, Department of, *see* Department of the Environment		
Ergas Ltd., Flogas Ltd. *v.*	[1985] ILRM 221	265
Everard (F.J.) & Sons Ltd., Carlingford Lough Harbour Commissioners *v.*	[1985] N.I.50	960
F		
F.(F.) *v.* F.(C.)	[1987] ILRM 1	693
F.(P.), O'H.(A.) *v.*	[1986] ILRM 489	562
F.P.H. Properties S.A. *v.* An Bord Pleanála, *see* State (F.P.H. Properties S.A.) *v.* An Bord Pleanála		
Faberge Incorporated *v.* Controller of Patents, Designs and Trade Marks	[1976-7] ILRM 335	1176
Fallon *v.* Gannon	[1988] ILRM 193	814
,, Airlie *v.*	[1976-7] ILRM 1	1095
Fanning, Harte *v.* (No.1)	[1988] ILRM 70	525
,, ,, ,, (No.2)	[1988] ILRM 75	526
,, Russell *v.*	[1988] I.R.505; [1988] ILRM 333; [1986] ILRM 401	534
,, Shannon *v.*	[1984] I.R.569; [1985] ILRM 385	529
Farm Machinery Distributors Ltd., *In re, see* Tempany *v.* Royal Liver Trustees Ltd.		
Farrell *v.* Farrelly	[1988] I.R.201	381
Farrelly, Farrell *v.*	[1988] I.R.201	381
Fawsitt, State (O'Connell) *v.*	[1986] I.R.362; [1986] ILRM 639	370
Feeley *v.* O'Dea, *see* State (Feeley) *v.* O'Dea		
Feeney *v.* Clifford	[1988] I.R.499	449
,, Sauerzweig *v.*	[1986] I.R.224	716

Name of Case	Volume and page	Column of Digest
Fegan, Traynor *v.*	[1985] I.R.586	739
Finance, Minister for, *see under* Minister		
Finnegan *v.* An Bord Pleanála	[1979] ILRM 134	216
First National Building Society, Gale *v.*	[1985] I.R.609; [1987] ILRM 30	999
Fisheries and Forestry, Minister for, *see under* Minister		
Fisons Pharmaceuticals Ltd., *In re*	[1984] ILRM 393	847
Fitzgerald *v.* An Bord Pleanála, *see* State (Fitzgerald) *v.* An Bord Pleańala		
,, *v.* Limerick Corporation	[1985] ILRM 445	291
Fitzgibbon St. Garda Station, State (Bouzagou) *v.*	[1985] I.R.426; [1986] ILRM 98	25
,, ,, ,, ,, State (Kugan) v., *see* State (Kugan) *v.* O'Rourke		
Fitzpatrick *v.* Collins	[1978] ILRM 244	1150
,, *v.* DAF Sales Ltd.	[1988] I.R.464	597
,, *v.* Independent Newspapers plc	[1988] I.R.132; [1988] ILRM 707	946
,, *v.* McCormack	[1986] I.R.380	722
,, *v.* McGivern (Frank) Ltd.	[1976-7] ILRM 239	71
,, State (Bowes) *v.*	[1978] ILRM 195	172
Flaherty *v.* Martin, *see* State (O'Rourke) *v.* Martin		
Flahive, D.P.P. *v.*, ...	[1988] ILRM 133	1074
Flanagan *v.* Mulhall	[1985] ILRM 134	995
,, *v.* University College Dublin	[1988] I.R.724	779
Flannery *v.* Governor of the Military Detention Barracks, *see* State (Flannery) *v.* —		
Fleming, *In re Estate of* , ...	[1987] ILRM 638	1157
Flint, O'Hara *v.*	[1979] ILRM 156	1088
Flogas Ltd. *v.* Ergas Ltd.	[1985] ILRM 221	265
Flynn *v.* An Post	[1987] I.R.68	497
,, *v.* D.P.P.	[1986] ILRM 290	366
,, *v.* Power	[1985] I.R.648; [1985] ILRM 336	485
,, D.P.P. (Nagle) *v.*	[1987] I.R.534	344
Folens & Co. Ltd. *v.* Minister for Education... ...	[1984] ILRM 265	267
Foley *v.* Johnson	[1988] I.R. 7	711
Folio Homes Ltd., Quirke *v.*	[1988] ILRM 496	712
Fortune *v.* Jacob (P.E.) and Co. Ltd.	[1976-7] ILRM 277	793
Foundries Du Lion S.A. *v.* International Factors (Ire.) Ltd.	[1985] ILRM 66	
Freeman *v.* Connellan, *see* State (Freeman) *v.* Connellan		
French, *In re*	[1985] N.I.310	749
Friendly Societies, Registrar of, *see under* Registrar		
Furey *v.* Minister for Defence, *see* State (Furey) *v.* Minister for Defence		
G		
G. *v.* G.	[1984] I.R.368	146
G.(M.) *v.* H.(A.), *see* State (M.G.) *v.* H.(A.); H. *v.* An Bord Uchtála		
Gaelcrann Teoranta *v.* Payne	[1985] ILRM 109	645
Gaffney, D.P.P. *v.*	[1987] I.R.173; [1986] ILRM 657; [1988] ILRM 39	302
,, O'Mahony *v.*	[1986] I.R.36	264
Gaiety Theatre, Andrews (Eamonn) Productions Ltd. *v.*	[1976-7] ILRM 119	704
Galdan Properties Ltd., *In re*	[1988] I.R.213; [1988] ILRM 559	1118
Gale *v.* First National Building Society	[1985] I.R.609; [1987] ILRM 30	999
Gallagher *v.* Governor of Portlaoise Prison, *see* State		

Name of Case	Volume and page	Column of Digest
O'Mahoney & Co. Manufacturing Ltd.	[1978] ILRM 116	1170
Industry and Commerce, Minister for, *see under* Minister		
Inland Revenue, Commissioners of, *see under* Commissioners		
Inspector of Taxes, Insulation Products Ltd. *v.*	[1984] ILRM 610	1023
Inspector of Taxes' Association *v.* Minister for the Public Service	[1986] ILRM 296	93
Insulation Products Ltd. *v.* Inspector of Taxes ...	[1984] ILRM 610	1023
Insurance Corporation of Ireland Ltd., Aro Road and Land Vehicles Ltd. *v.*	[1986] I.R.403	649
,, ,, ,, Rohan Construction Ltd. *v.*	[1988] ILRM 373; [1986] ILRM 419	648
Insurance Officer *v.* McCaffrey	[1984] N.I.108	1111
International Factors (Ire.) Ltd., S.A.Foundries du Lion MV *v.*	[1985] ILRM 66	1084
International Factors (N.I.) Ltd. v. Streeve Construction Ltd.	[1984] N.I.245	113
Inver Resources Ltd. *v.* Limerick Corporation ...	[1987] I.R.159; [1988] ILRM 47	873
Ireland, Arnold and Kennedy *v.*, *see* Kennedy *v.* Ireland		
,, Aughey *v.*	[1986] ILRM 206	594
,, Cafolla *v.*, *see* Cafolla *v.* O'Malley		
,, Cartmill *v.*	[1987] I.R.192; [1988] ILRM 430	239
,, Charlton *v.*	[1984] ILRM 39	236
,, Clancy *v.*	[1988] I.R.326	230
,, Dowman *v.*	[1986] ILRM 111	543
,, Eccles *v.*	[1985] I.R.545; [1986] ILRM 343	232
,, Garvey *v.*	[1979] ILRM 266	410
,, Hayes *v.*	[1987] ILRM 651	407
,, Kelly *v.*	[1986] ILRM 318	951
,, Kennedy *v.*	[1987] I.R.587; [1988] ILRM 472	177
,, Kostan *v.*	[1978] ILRM 12	232
,, L'Henreyenat *v.*	[1984] ILRM 249	219
,, McGimpsey *v.*	[1988] I.R.567	188
,, McKevitt *v.*	[1987] ILRM 541	421
,, McMahon *v.*	[1988] ILRM 610	828
,, Muckley *v.*	[1985] I.R.472; [1986] ILRM 364	213
,, Muldoon *v.*	[1988] ILRM 367	829
,, Murray *v.*	[1985] I.R.532; [1985] ILRM 542	178
,, Ormond *v.*	[1988] ILRM 490	938
,, Osheku *v.*	[1986] I.R.733; [1987] ILRM 330	23
,, Pok Sun Shum *v.*	[1986] ILRM 593	22
,, Shannon *v.*	[1984] I.R.548; [1985] ILRM 449	217
,, Tormey *v.*	[1985] I.R.289; [1985] ILRM 375; [1984] ILRM 657	205
,, Webb *v.*	[1988] I.R.353; [1988] ILRM 565	59
Ireland, Government of, State (Sheehan) *v.* ...	[1987] I.R. 550; [1988] ILRM 437	678
Irish Agricultural Machinery Ltd. *v.* Ó Cúlacháin	[1987] I.R.458	1037
Irish Agricultural Wholesale Society Ltd., Reno Engrais et Produits Chemiques S.A. *v.*	[1976-7] ILRM 179	626
Irish Association of Distributive Trades Ltd. *v.* 3 Guys Ltd.	[1979] ILRM 269	1011
Irish Civil Service Building Society *v.* Registrar of Friendly Societies	[1985] I.R.167	76
Irish Commercial Society Ltd. *v.* Plunkett	[1986] I.R.258	617
,, ,, ,, ,, ,, ...	[1987] ILRM 504; [1986] ILRM 624	936

Name of Case	Volume and page	Column of Digest
,, ,, ,, ,, ,, ...	[1988] I.R. 1	937
Irish Distributive and Administrative Trade Union *v.* Carroll	[1988] ILRM 713	1178
Irish Grain Board Ltd., Tradax (Ireland) Ltd. *v.*	[1984] I.R.1; [1984] ILRM 471	1079
Irish Land Commission, Dreher *v.*	[1984] ILRM 94	138
,, ,, ,, State (Callaghan) *v.* ...	[1978] ILRM 201	692
Irish Leathers Ltd. *v.* Minister for Labour	[1986] I.R.177	495
Irish Life Assurance Co. Ltd. *v.* Dublin Land Securities Ltd.	[1986] I.R.332	268
,, ,, ,, ,, ,, Lift Manufacturers Ltd. *v.*	[1979] ILRM 277	621
Irish National Insurance Co. Ltd., Brady *v.*	[1986] I.R.698; [1986] ILRM 669	653
Irish Permanent Building Society *v.* Caldwell (No. 1) (Registrar of Building Societies)	[1979] ILRM 273	920
Irish Pharmaceutical Union *v.* Employment Appeals Tribunal, *see* State (Irish Pharmaceutical Union) *v.*—		
Irish Shell and B.P. Ltd. *v.* Costello (John) Ltd.	[1984] I.R.511; [1985] ILRM 554	714
Irish Shell Ltd. *v.* Elm Motors Ltd	[1984] I.R.200; [1984] ILRM 595	638
Irish Shipping Ltd., *In re*	[1986] ILRM 518	118
,, ,, ,, *v.* Byrne	[1987] I.R.468	496
Irish Transport and General Workers' Union, Rodgers *v.*	[1978] ILRM 51	1180
Irish Trust Bank Ltd. *v.* Central Bank of Ireland	[1976-7] ILRM 50	941
Ivory *v.* Ski-Line Ltd.	[1988] I.R.399	485
J		
Jacob (P.E.) and Co. Ltd., Fortune *v.*	[1976-7] ILRM 277	793
Jacob International Ltd. Inc. *v.* Ó Cléirigh	[1985] ILRM 651	1040
Jaggers Restaurant Ltd. *v.* Ahearne	[1988] I.R.308; [1988] ILRM 553	724
John Costello Ltd., *see under* Costello		
Johnson *v.* Longleat Properties (Dublin) Ltd. ...	[1976-7] ILRM 93	72
,, D.P.P. *v.*	[1988] ILRM 747	368
,, Foley *v.*	[1988] I.R. 7	711
,, McCarthy *v.*	[1988] I.R.23	756
Johnson & Johnson (Ireland) Ltd. *v.* C.P. Security Ltd.	[1985] I.R.362; [1986] ILRM 559	502
Johnston *v.* Cliftonville Football and Athletic Club Ltd.	[1984] N.I.9	1009
Jordan *v.* Commissioner of An Garda Síochána, *see* State (Jordan) *v.* —		
Joyce *v.* Circuit Court Judge for Western Circuit	[1987] ILRM 316	154
,, D.P.P. *v.*	[1985] ILRM 206	1066
Judge *v.* D.P.P., *see* O'Reilly and Judge *v.* D.P.P.		
Justice, Minister for, *see under* Minister		
K		
K. *v.* K.	[1988] I.R.161	563
K., N. (Otherwise K.) *v.*	[1985] I.R.733; [1986] ILRM 75	558
Kane *v.* Governor of Mountjoy Prison	[1988] I.R.757; [1988] ILRM 724	175
Kavanagh, *In the Goods of,* Healy *v.* MacGillicuddy	[1978] ILRM 175	1159
,, *v.* Centreline Ltd	[1987] ILRM 306	29
Keane, Maguire *v.*	[1986] ILRM 235	534
Kearney *v.* Minister for Justice	[1986] I.R.116; [1987] ILRM 52	166
Keegan *v.* Stardust Victims Compensation Tribunal, *see* State (Keegan and Lysaght) *v.* —		
Keenan *v.* Shield Insurance Co. Ltd.	[1987] I.R.113	650
,, ,, ,, ,, ,, ,, ...	[1988] I.R.89	35
,, P.M.P.A. Insurance Co. Ltd. *v.*	[1985] ILRM 173	491

Name of Case	Volume and page	Column of Digest
Keenan Bros. Ltd., *In re*	[1985] I.R.401; [1985] ILRM 254, 641	101
Keeney *v.* O'Malley, *see* State (Keeney) *v.* O'Malley		
Kehoe, People *v.*	[1985] I.R.444; [1986] ILRM 690	303
Kelleher, State (McEldowney) *v.*	[1985] ILRM 10	200
Kelly, *In re*	[1984] ILRM 424	256
,, *v.* Board of Governors of St. Laurence's Hospital	[1988] I.R.402	800
,, *v.* Breen	[1978] ILRM 63	941
,, *v.* Crowley	[1985] I.R.212	818
,, *v.* Ireland	[1986] ILRM 318	951
,, Brennan *v.*	[1988] ILRM 306	919
,, Kenny *v.*	[1988] I.R.457	681
,, People *v.*	[1987] I.R.596	326
,, State (Crothers) *v.*	[1978] ILRM 167	713
,, State (Rollinson) *v.*	[1984] I.R. 248; [1984] ILRM 625	237
Kelly's Carpetdrome Ltd., *In re*; Byrne *v.* UDT Bank Ltd.	[1984] ILRM 418	1001
Kellystown Co. *v.* Hogan (Inspector of Taxes) ...	[1985] ILRM 200	1025
Kelso, D.P.P. *v.*	[1984] ILRM 329	329
Kennedy *v.* Hearne	[1988] I.R.481; [1987] I.R.120; [1988] ILRM 52, 531	202
,, *v.* Ireland	[1987] I.R.587; [1988] ILRM 472	177
,, State (O'Donoghue) *v.*	[1979] ILRM 109	376
Kenny *v.* An Post	[1988] I.R.285	478
,, *v.* Kelly	[1988] I.R.457	681
,, *v.* Minister for Social Welfare, *see* State (Kenny) *v.* Minister for Social Welfare		
Kent, Siebel *v.*	[1976-7] ILRM 127	1093
Kent County Council *v.* S., *In re* S.	[1984] ILRM 292	544
Kerrane *v.* Hanlon (N.) (Ireland) Ltd.	[1987] I.R.259	1029
,, Knockhall Piggeries *v.*	[1985] ILRM 655	1052
Kerry County Council, Ahern *v.*	[1988] ILRM 392	751
,, ,, ,, O'Connor *v.*	[1988] ILRM 660	877
Kershaw *v.* Eastern Health Board, *see* State (Kershaw) *v.* —		
Kett *v.* Shannon	[1987] ILRM 364	20
Kielt, State (Murphy) *v.*	[1984] I.R. 458; [1985] ILRM 141	978
Kildare County Council, McKone Estates Ltd. *v.*	[1984] ILRM 313	856
Kilkenny County Council, Walsh *v.*	[1978] ILRM 1	821
Killiney and Ballybrack Development Association Ltd. *v.* Minister for Local Government	[1978] ILRM 78	867
Kinahan Electrical Ltd., Ward *v.*	[1984] I.R.292	207
King *v.* Minister for Justice, *see* State (King) *v.* Minister for Justice		
Kirby, Dublin County Council *v.*	[1985] ILRM 325	880
Knockhall Piggeries *v.* Kerrane	[1985] ILRM 655	1052
Kostan *v.* Ireland	[1978] ILRM 12	232
Kotsonouris, O'Driscoll (Gay) Ltd. *v.*	[1987] I.R.265	923
Kugan *v.* O'Rourke, *see* State (Kugan) *v.* O'Rourke		
Kutchera *v.* Buckingham International Holdings Ltd.	[1988] I.R.61; [1988] ILRM 1, 501	142
Kylemore Bakery Ltd. *v.* Minister for Trade, Commerce and Tourism	[1986] ILRM 529	257
L		
L. *v.* L.	[1984] ILRM 607	1145
L.(F.M.) *v.* An tArd Chláraitheoir na bPósadh	[1984] ILRM 667	563

NAME OF CASE	VOLUME AND PAGE	Column of Digest
L.(H.) *v.* Bank of Ireland	[1978] ILRM 160	1142
LRC International Ltd. *v.* the Controller of Patents, Designs and Trade Marks	[1976-7] ILRM 164	1173
Labour Court, Cadwell *v.*	[1988] I.R.280	491
Labour Court, State (Aer Lingus Teo.) *v.*	[1987] ILRM 373	488
Labour Court, State (Polymark (Ireland) Ltd.) *v.*	[1987] ILRM 357	666
Labour, Minister for, *see under* Minister		
Lackagh Rock Ltd., Galway County Council *v.*	[1985] I.R.120	888
Lally *v.* Meath County Council	[1985] ILRM 269	292
Lamb Brothers Dublin Ltd. *v.* Davidson	[1978] ILRM 226	501
Lambert *v.* Lambert...	[1987] ILRM 390	928
Lansing Bagnall & Co.Ltd., Henley Forklift (Ireland) Ltd. *v.*	[1979] ILRM 257	99
Larkins *v.* National Union of Mineworkers	[1985] I.R.671	147
Lavery *v.* Ministry of Defence	[1984] N.I.99	411
Lavery Ltd., Wine Inns Ltd. *v.*	[1985] N.I.427	727
Lawlor *v.* Minister for Agriculture	[1988] ILRM 400	209
Lawter Products, Sisk (John) and Son Ltd. *v.* ...	[1976-7] ILRM 204	73
Leahy, McMahon *v.*	[1984] I.R.525; [1985] ILRM 423	527
Leinster Importing Co.Ltd. *v.* Dublin County Council	[1984] ILRM 605	140
Leitrim County Council, Moran *v.*	[1985] I.R.111	293
Leonard *v.* Leonard...	[1988] ILRM 245	1197
L'Henreyenat *v.* Ireland	[1984] ILRM 249; [1983] I.R. 193	219
Lift Manufacturers Ltd. *v.* Irish Life Assurance Co.Ltd.	[1979] ILRM 277	621
Limerick Corporation, Fitzgerald *v.*	[1985] ILRM 445	291
Limerick Corporation, Inver Resources Ltd. *v.*	[1987] I.R.159; [1988] ILRM 47	873
,, ,, Reid *v.*	[1987] ILRM 83; [1984] ILRM 366	137
Limerick Prison, Governor of, *see under* Governor		
Linden, R. *v.*	[1984] N.I.251	309
Littlejohn, D.P.P. *v.*	[1978] ILRM 147	338
Livingstone *v.* Ministry of Defence	[1984] N.I.356	55
Local Government, Minister for, *see under* Minister		
Lombard & Ulster Banking Ltd. *v.* Amurec Ltd.	[1976-7] ILRM 222	105
,, ,, ,, ,, *v.* Murray ...	[1987] ILRM 522	65
Londonderry Port and Harbour Commissioners, Moyne *v.*	[1986] I.R.299	1128
Longleat Properties (Dublin) Ltd., Johnson *v.*	[1976-7] ILRM 93	72
Loughnane *v.* Hogan	[1987] I.R.322	881
Lowe, Dublin Corporation *v.*, *see* Dublin Corporation *v.* Ashley		
Lunham Brothers Ltd., Cronin *v.*	[1986] ILRM 415	1031
Lynch *v.* Ballagh, *see* State (Lynch) *v.* Ballagh		
Lyons *v.* Thomas	[1986] I.R.666	1094
Lysaght *v.* Stardust Victims Compensation Tribunal, *see* State (Keegan and Lysaght) *v.*—		
,, O'Mahony *v.*	[1988] I.R.29	48
M		
M., a doctor, *In re*	[1984] I.R.479	779
M., *In re*, M.(J.) and M.(G.) *v.* An Bord Uchtála	[1987] I.R.510; [1988] ILRM 203	13
M. *v.* M.	[1979] ILRM 160	556
M. *v.* The Medical Council	[1984] I.R.485	199
M.(C.) *v.* M.(T.)	[1987] I.R.152; [1988] ILRM 262	551
,, ,, ...	[1988] ILRM 456	150
M.(G.), M.(S.) *v.*	[1985] ILRM 186	14
M.(J.) and M.(G.) *v.* An Bord Uchtála; *In re* M.	[1987] I.R.510; [1988] ILRM 203	13

Name of Case	Volume and page	Column of Digest
Madigan *v.* Attorney General	[1986] ILRM 136	229
,, Whelan *v.*	[1978] ILRM 136	696
Magee, State (Pletzer) *v.*	[1986] ILRM 441	364
Magill T.V. Guide Ltd., Radio Telefís Éireann *v.*	[1988] I.R.97	637
Maguire *v.* D.P.P.	[1988] ILRM 166	365
,, *v.* Keane	[1986] ILRM 235	534
,, *v.* O'Hanrahan	[1988] ILRM 243	367
Maher *v.* Maher	[1987] ILRM 582	17
Mahon, State (Brennan) *v.*	[1978] ILRM 17	355
Maloney *v.* Elf Investments Ltd.	[1979] ILRM 253	1087
Mangan, State (Cuddy) *v.*	[1988] ILRM 720	369
Margan Ltd., Neville *v.*	[1988] I.R.734	924
Marine, Minister for the, *see under* Minister		
Marley, People *v.*	[1985] ILRM 17	308
Marren, Dublin County Council *v.*	[1985] ILRM 593	875
Marshall, Stud Managers Ltd. *v.*	[1985] I.R.83	914
Martin, R. *v.*	[1985] N.I.324	327
,, State (Dixon) *v.*	[1985] I.R.106; [1985] ILRM 240	384
,, State (Flaherty) *v.*, *see* State (O'Rourke) *v.* Martin		
,, State (Gleeson) *v.*	[1985] ILRM 577	383
,, State (McKeon) *v.* *see* State (Gleeson) *v.* Martin		
,, State (O'Flaherty) *v.* *see* State (O'Rourke) *v.* Martin		
,, State (O'Rourke) *v.*	[1984] ILRM 333	387
Martin (R.F.) Ltd. *v.* Duffy	[1985] N.I.417	1085
Martyn, North Western Health Board *v.*	[1987] I.R.565; [1988] ILRM 519; [1985] ILRM 226	487
Masser (A.H.) Ltd., *In re*; McCann v. Revenue Commissioners	[1986] I.R.455	103
Maxwells of Donegal Ltd., Bairead *v.*	[1986] ILRM 508	1036
Maye *v.* Revenue Commissioners	[1986] ILRM 377	1060
Maynooth College, McGrath and Ó Ruairc *v.* ...	[1979] ILRM 166	182
Mayo County Council, Rabbette *v.*	[1984] ILRM 156	839
Meagher *v.* Blount	[1984] ILRM 671	1102
Mealiffe *v.* Walsh (G.N.) Ltd.	[1986] I.R.427; [1987] ILRM 301	706
Meath County Council *v.* Daly	[1987] I.R.391; [1988] ILRM 274	891
,, ,, Lally *v.*	[1985] ILRM 269	292
Medical Council, The, M. *v.*	[1984] I.R.485	199
Medical Incorporated, Grehan *v.*	[1986] I.R.528; [1986] ILRM 627	960
Meehan, Commodity Broking Co.Ltd. *v.*	[1985] I.R.12	263
Meenaghan *v.* Dublin County Council	[1984] ILRM 616	40
Melbarien Enterprises Ltd. *v.* Revenue Commissioners, *see* State (Melbarien Enterprises Ltd.) *v.* —		
Merchant Banking Ltd., *In re*	[1987] ILRM 260	126
Merck Sharp & Dohme (Ireland) Ltd., Hanrahan *v.*	[1988] ILRM 629	835
Merrick, O Domhnaill *v.*	[1984] I.R.151; [1985] ILRM 40	962
Mespil Ltd. *v.* Capaldi	[1986] ILRM 373	267
Midland Health Board, *In re, see* D., *In re*		
Mieth, *In the Estate of;* Baker *v.* Cohn-Vossen	[1986] ILRM 175	1139
Millen *v.* Brown	[1984] N.I.328	957
Miller Brewing Co. *v.* Controller of Patents, Designs and Trade Marks	[1987] I.R.434; [1988] ILRM 259	1175
Minister for Agriculture *v.* Cleary	[1988] ILRM 294	325
,, ,, ,, Lawlor *v.*	[1988] ILRM 400	209
,, ,, ,, Silver Hill Duckling Ltd. *v.*	[1987] I.R.289; [1987] ILRM 516	949

Name of Case	Volume and page	Column of Digest
Ó Cúlacháin, Carroll Industries plc *v.*	[1988] I.R.705	1033
,, Irish Agricultural Machinery Ltd. *v.*	[1987] I.R.458	1037
,, McCann (Charles) Ltd. *v.*	[1986] I.R.196; [1985] I.R.298; [1986] ILRM 229	1028
,, Navan Carpets Ltd. *v.*	[1988] I.R.164	1055
O'D. *v.* O'D.	[1976-7] ILRM 142	546
O'Dare *v.* Sheehy, *see* State (O'Dare) *v.* Sheehy		
O'Dea, State (Feeley) *v.*	[1986] I.R.687	451
Ó Dómhnaill *v.* Merrick	[1984] I.R.151; [1985] ILRM 40	962
O'Donnell *v.* Begley	[1987] ILRM 105	794
,, State (Gartlan) *v.*	[1986] ILRM 588	347
O'Donoghue *v.* Kennedy, *see* State (O'Donoghue) *v.* Kennedy		
O'Driscoll, Hynes-O'Sullivan *v.*	[1988] I.R.436	428
O'Driscoll (Gay) Ltd. *v.* Kotsonouris	[1987] I.R.265	923
O'Flaherty *v.* Martin, *see* State (O'Rourke) *v.* Martin		
O'Flynn *v.* Clifford	[1988] I.R.740	373
O'G.(T.) *v.* Attorney General	[1985] ILRM 61	15
O'H.(A.) *v.* F.(P.)	[1986] ILRM 489	562
O'H.(N.) *v.* R.(G.)	[1986] ILRM 563	1147
O'Hanrahan, Dublin Corporation *v.*	[1988] I.R.121	584
" Maguire *v.*	[1988] ILRM 243	367
,, State (Hughes) *v.*	[1986] ILRM 218	663
O'Hara *v.* Flint	[1979] ILRM 156	1088
Ó hArgáin *v.* Beechpark Estates Ltd.	[1979] ILRM 57	1057
Ó hÚallacháin *v.* Burke	[1988] ILRM 693	459
O'K.(C.) *v.* P.(W.)	[1985] I.R.279	560
O'Kane *v.* Campbell	[1985] I.R.115	838
O'Keeffe *v.* McMenamin, *see* State (O'Keeffe) *v.* McMenamin		
,, Bank of Ireland *v.*	[1987] I.R.47	64
O'Kelly *v.* Darragh	[1988] ILRM 309	845
O'Leary *v.* Dublin County Council	[1988] I.R.150	876
,, *v.* Neilan, *see* State (O'Leary) *v.* Neilan		
O'Looney *v.* Minister for the Public Service	[1986] I.R.543	593
O'Loughlin, *In re*	[1985] N.I.421	731
,, *v.* Teeling	[1988] ILRM 617	414
O'Loughran, Hegarty *v.*	[1987] I.R.135; [1987] ILRM 603	742
Olympic Amusements, D.P.P. *v.*	[1987] ILRM 320	588
O'Mahony *v.* Gaffney	[1986] I.R.36	264
,, *v.* Lysaght	[1988] I.R.29	48
,, People *v.*	[1985] I.R.517; [1986] ILRM 245	332
O'Malley, Cafolla *v.*	[1985] I.R.486; [1986] ILRM 177	220
,, Comerford *v.*	[1987] ILRM 595	83
,, State (Keeney) *v.*	[1986] ILRM 31	362
Ó Monacháin *v.* An Taoiseach	[1986] ILRM 660	161
O'Mullane *v.* Riordan	[1978] ILRM 73	1098
O'Neill *v.* Butler	[1979] ILRM 243	359
,, Byrne *v.*	[1979] ILRM 47	702
,, R. *v.*	[1984] N.I.264	386
O'Neill (Charles) & Co. Ltd., Three Stripe International Ltd. *v.*	[1988] I.R.144	280
Open Door Counselling Ltd., Attorney General (*ex rel.* S.P.U.C.) *v.*	[1988] I.R.593; [1987] ILRM 477	180
O'R., Revenue Commissioners *v.*	[1984] ILRM 406	1052
O'R. *v.* O'R.	[1985] I.R.367	158
O'Regan *v.* Plunkett, *see* State (O'Regan) *v.* Plunkett		
O'Reilly and Judge *v.* D.P.P.	[1984] ILRM 224	374

Name of Case	Volume and page	Column of Digest
,, *v.* Kehoe	[1985] I.R.444; [1986] ILRM 690	303
,, *v.* Kelly	[1987] I.R.596	326
,, *v.* McCaffrey	[1986] ILRM 687	298
,, *v.* McCormack	[1984] I.R.177	450
,, *v.* McGinley...	[1987] I.R.340	305
,, *v.* McMahon	[1984] ILRM 461	324
,, *v.* Marley	[1985] ILRM 17	308
,, *v.* Mulvey	[1987] I.R.502	323
,, *v.* O'Mahony	[1985] I.R.517; [1986] ILRM 245	332
,, *v.* Prunty	[1986] ILRM 716	310
,, *v.* Quilligan	[1986] I.R.495; [1987] ILRM 606	316
,, *v.* Tiernan	[1988] I.R.250	390
,, *v.* Towson	[1978] ILRM 122	296
,, *v.* Walsh	[1986] I.R.722; [1988] ILRM 137	300
Pesca Valentia Ltd. *v.* Minister for Fisheries and Forestry	[1985] I.R.193; [1986] ILRM 68	622
Phelan, Carr *v.*	[1976-7] ILRM 149	708
Philpott *v.* Registrar of Titles, *see* State (Philpott) *v.* Registrar of Titles		
Pierce, Dowd *v.*	[1984] ILRM 653	710
Pine Valley Developments Ltd. *v.* Dublin Co. Council, *see* State (Pine Valley Developments Ltd.) *v.* —		
,, ,, ,, ,, *v.* Minister for the Environment	[1987] I.R.23; [1987] ILRM 747	868
Pletzer *v.* Magee, *see* State (Pletzer) *v.* Magee		
Plunkett, Irish Commercial Society Ltd. *v.*	[1986] I.R.258	617
,, ,, ,, ,, ,, ,, ...	[1987] ILRM 504; [1986] ILRM 624	936
,, ,, ,, ,, ,, ,, ...	[1988] I.R. 1	937
,, State (O'Regan) *v.*	[1984] ILRM 347	1072
Point Blank Ltd., House of Spring Gardens Ltd. *v.*	[1984] I.R.611	259
Pok Sun Shum *v.* Ireland	[1986] ILRM 593	22
Polymark (Ireland) Ltd. *v.* Labour Court, *see* State (Polymark (Ireland) Ltd.) *v.* ———		
Portlaoise Prison, Governor of, *see under* Governor		
Post, An, Flynn *v.*	[1987] I.R.68	497
,, ,, Kenny *v.*	[1988] I.R.285	478
Posts and Telegraphs, Minister for, *see under* Minister		
Power *v.* Minister for Social Welfare	[1987] I.R.307	1109
,, *v.* Moran, *see* State (Power) *v.* Moran		
,, Flynn *v.*	[1985] I.R.648; [1985] ILRM 336	485
Power Supermarkets Ltd., *In re*	[1988] I.R.206	729
Powerscourt Estates *v.* Gallagher	[1984] ILRM 123	631
Powerscourt Shopping Centre Ltd., Sweeney (F.G.) Ltd. *v.*	[1984] I.R.501; [1985] ILRM 442	707
Price, Ó Coindealbháin *v.*	[1988] I.R. 14	1020
Prison Service Credit Union Ltd. v. Registrar of Friendly Societies	[1987] ILRM 367	616
Private Motorists Protection Association, *see* P.M.P.A.		
Private Motorists Provident Society Ltd. *v.* Attorney General	[1984] ILRM 88	227
,, ,, ,, ,, ,, *v.* Moore	[1987] I.R.472; [1988] ILRM 526	264
Prunty, People *v.*	[1986] ILRM 716	310
Public Lighting Services Ltd., S.E.E. Co. Ltd. *v.*	[1987] ILRM 255	930
,, ,, ,, ,, ,, ,,	[1988] ILRM 677	791
Public Service, Minister for, *see under* Minister		

Name of Case	Volume and page	Column of Digest
,, Travers *v.*	[1985] ILRM 343	336
S		
S. *v.* S.	[1976-7] ILRM 156	560
S. *v.* S., *see* S.(A.) *v.* B.(R.)		
S., H. *v.*	[1979] ILRM 105	567
S., Kent County Council *v.*, *In re* S.	[1984] ILRM 292	544
S., O'B. *v.*	[1984] I.R.316; [1985] ILRM 86	169
S., O'Brien *v.*, *In re* Walker, *see* O'B. *v.* S.		
S., S. *v.*	[1976-7] ILRM 156	560
S.(A.) *v.* B.(R.); S. *v.* S.	[1984] ILRM 66	546
S.(S.), *In re*, *see* Kent County Council *v.* S.		
S.A. Foundries du Lion MV *v.* International Factors (Ire.) Ltd.	[1985] ILRM 66	1084
S.E.E. Co.Ltd. *v.* Public Lighting Services Ltd.	[1987] ILRM 255	930
,, ,, ,, ,, ,, ,,	[1988] ILRM 677	791
S.H. Ltd., Grangeford Structures Ltd. *v.*	[1988] ILRM 129	34
Sachs *v.* Standard Chartered Bank (Ireland) Ltd.	[1987] ILRM 297	549
St.Alban's Investment Co. *v.* Sun Alliance and London Insurance Co.Ltd.	[1984] ILRM 501	647
St.Kevin's Company, Hogan *v.*	[1986] I.R.80; [1987] ILRM 17	47
St. Laurence's Hospital, Kelly *v.* Board of Governors of,	[1988] I.R. 402	800
Salih *v.* The General Accident Fire and Life Assurance Corporation Ltd.	[1987] I.R.628	929
Sauerzweig *v.* Feeney	[1986] I.R.224	716
Savage *v.* Nolan	[1978] ILRM 151	1191
Savage Brothers Ltd. *v.* Shillington (Heating and Plumbing) Ltd.	[1985] N.I.85	38
Scully, State (McKeown) *v.*	[1986] I.R.524; [1986] ILRM 133	282
Secretary of State, Barry *v.*	[1984] N.I.39	288
,, ,, ,, McCloskey *v.*	[1984] N.I.365	289
Sepia Ltd. *v.* Hanlon (M.& P.) Ltd.	[1979] ILRM 11	1086
Serge Caudron *v.* Air Zaire, *see* Caudron *v.* Air Zaire		
Seum *v.* Kent, *see* Siebel *v.* Kent		
Shalaine Modes Ltd., Green Property Co. Ltd. *v.*	[1978] ILRM 222	700
Shannon *v.* Fanning	[1984] I.R.569; [1985] ILRM 385	529
,, *v.* Ireland	[1984] I.R.548; [1985] ILRM 449	217
,, Kett *v.*	[1987] ILRM 364	20
Sheehan *v.* Government of Ireland, *see* State (Sheehan) *v.* —		
,, *v.* McMahon, *see* State (Sheehan) *v.* McMahon		
Sheehy, Attorney General *v.*	[1988] I.R. 226	574
,, D.P.P. *v.*	[1987] ILRM 138	1068
,, State (O'Dare) *v.*	[1984] ILRM 99	342
Sheeran, D.P.P. *v.*	[1986] ILRM 579	346
Shennick Lodge Ltd. *v.* Monaghan County Council	[1986] I.R.442; [1986] ILRM 273	289
Sheridan, Carroll *v.*	[1984] ILRM 451	997
Sherry *v.* Wine, *see* State (Sherry) *v.* Wine		
Sherry-Brennan, *In re*	[1979] ILRM 113	721
Shiel, *In re*; Browne *v.* Mulligan	[1976-7] ILRM 327	476
Shield Insurance Co. Ltd., Keenan *v.*	[1987] I.R.113	650
,, ,, ,, ,, ,, ...	[1988] I.R.89	35
,, ,, ,, Walsh *v.*	[1976-7] ILRM 218	50
,, ,, ,, Zurich Insurance Co. *v.*	[1988] I.R.174	652
Shillington (Heating and Plumbing) Ltd., Savage		

Name of Case	Volume and page	Column of Digest
,, (Divito) *v.* Arklow Urban District Council	[1986] ILRM 123	585
,, (Dixon) *v.* Martin	[1985] I.R.106; [1985] ILRM 240	384
,, (Donegal V.E.C.) *v.* Minister for Education	[1985] I.R.56	461
,, (Duffy) *v.* Minister for Defence	[1979] ILRM 65	434
,, (F.P.H. Properties S.A.) *v.* An Bord Pleanála	[1987] I.R.698	863
,, (Feeley) *v.* O'Dea	[1986] I.R.687	451
,, (Fitzgerald) *v.* An Bord Pleanála	[1985] ILRM 117	852
,, (Flaherty) *v.* Martin, *see* State (O'Rourke) *v.* Martin		
,, (Flannery) *v.* Governor of the Military Detention Barracks	[1976-7] ILRM 13	389
,, (Freeman) *v.* Connellan	[1986] I.R.433; [1987] ILRM 470	357
,, (Furey) *v.* Minister for Defence	[1988] ILRM 89	664
,, (Gallagher Shatter & Co.) *v.* de Valera ...	[1986] ILRM 3	939
,, ,, ,, ,, ,, ,,	[1987] I.R.55; [1987] ILRM 555	943
,, (Gallagher) *v.* Governor of Portlaoise Prison	[1987] ILRM 45	164
,, (Gartlan) *v.* O'Donnell	[1986] ILRM 588	347
,, (Gilliland) *v.* Governor of Mountjoy Prison	[1987] I.R.201; [1987] ILRM 278; [1986] ILRM 381	191
,, (Gleeson) *v.* Connellan	[1988] I.R.559	331
,, (Gleeson) *v.* Martin	[1985] ILRM 577	383
,, (Harrington) *v.* Wallace	[1988] I.R.290	755
,, (Haverty) *v.* An Bord Pleanála	[1987] I.R.485; [1988] ILRM 545	850
,, (Hughes) *v.* O'Hanrahan	[1986] ILRM 218	663
,, (IBM Ireland Ltd.) *v.* Employment Appeals Tribunal	[1984] ILRM 31	483
,, (Irish Pharmaceutical Union) *v.* Employment Appeals Tribunal	[1987] ILRM 36	777
,, (Jordan) *v.* Commissioner of An Garda Síochána	[1987] ILRM 107	480
,, (Keegan and Lysaght) *v.* Stardust Victims Compensation Tribunal	[1986] I.R.642; [1987] ILRM 202	672
,, (Keeney) *v.* O'Malley	[1986] ILRM 31	362
,, (Kenny) *v.* Minister for Social Welfare ...	[1986] I.R.693	1116
,, (Kershaw)*v.* Eastern Health Board	[1985] ILRM 235	1113
,, (King) *v.* Minister for Justice	[1984] I.R. 169	284
,, (Kugan) *v.* O'Rourke (Fitzgibbon St. Garda Station)	[1985] I.R.658; [1986] ILRM 95	26
,, (Lynch) *v.* Ballagh	[1986] I.R.203; [1987] ILRM 65	339
,, (M.G.) *v.* H.(A.); H. *v.* An Bord Uchtála	[1984] ILRM 237	16
,, (McCaud) *v.* Governor of Mountjoy Prison	[1985] I.R.68; [1986] ILRM 129	191
,, (McCormack) *v.* Curran	[1987] ILRM 225	356
,, (McCoy) *v.* Dún Laoghaire Corporation ...	[1985] ILRM 533	899
,, (McEldowney) *v.* Kelleher	[1985] ILRM 10	200
,, (McInerney & Co.Ltd.) *v.* Dublin County Council	[1985] I.R.1; [1985] ILRM 513	904
,, (McKeon) *v.* Martin, *see* State (Gleeson) *v.* Martin		
,, (McKeown) *v.* Scully	[1986] I.R.524; [1986] ILRM 133	282
,, (McLoughlin) *v.* Eastern Health Board ...	[1986] I.R.416	1114
,, (Melbarien Enterprises Ltd.) *v.* Revenue Commissioners	[1985] I.R.706; [1986] ILRM 476	1015
,, (Multiprint Label Systems Ltd.) *v.* Neylon	[1984] ILRM 545	1017
,, (Murphy) *v.* Kielt (Governor of St. Patrick's Institution)	[1984] I.R. 458; [1985] ILRM 141	978
,, (Murray) *v.* Roe, *see* State (Gleeson) *v.* Martin		
,, (N.C.E.Ltd.) *v.* Dublin County Council ...	[1979] ILRM 249	853
,, (O'Connell) *v.* Fawsitt	[1986] I.R.362; [1986] ILRM 639	370

NAME OF CASE	VOLUME AND PAGE	Column of Digest
(Trimbole) *v.* Governor of Mountjoy Prison		
Trinity College Dublin, Dublin Corporation *v.*	[1985] ILRM 283; [1984] ILRM 84	994
Trustee Savings Bank *v.* Incorporated Law Society of Ireland	[1987] I.R.430; [1988] ILRM 541	1119
Tuite *v.* Tuite	[1978] ILRM 197	1153
,, McLoughlin *v.*	[1986] I.R.235; [1986] ILRM 304	233
Tylers Ltd., Macey Ltd. *v.*	[1978] ILRM 82	713
U		
UDT Bank Ltd., Byrne v., *In re* Kelly's Carpetdrome Ltd.	[1984] ILRM 418	1001
Údarás na Gaeltachta, Comhlucht Páipéar Ríomhaireachta Teo. *v.*	[1987] I.R.684	934
Ulster Bank Ltd. *v.* McCullough	[1985] N.I.288	1153
,, ,, ,, Towey *v.*	[1987] ILRM 142	811
Uniacke *v.* Cassidy Electrical Supply Co. Ltd., *see* Hickey (W.J.) Ltd., *In re*		
University College Dublin, Flanagan *v.*	[1988] I.R.724	779
Uyttewaal *v.* Commissioners of Public Works in Ireland	[1987] I.R.439	997
V		
Valley Pines Associates, *see* Grehan *v.* Medical Incorporated		
Valuation, Commissioner of, *see under* Commissioner		
Van Raaj, Griffiths *v.*	[1985] ILRM 582	420
Vehicle Buildings and Insulations Ltd. *In re*	[1986] ILRM 239	131
W		
W.(D.), C.(D.) *v.*	[1987] ILRM 58	555
W.(J.) *v.* W.(M.)	[1978] ILRM 119	545
Walker, *In re*; *see* O'B. v.S		
,, MacNaughton *v.*	[1976-7] ILRM 106	1141
Wallace, State (Harrington) *v.*	[1988] I.R.290	755
Walsh *v.* Kilkenny County Council	[1978] ILRM 1	821
,, *v.* Ministry of Defence	[1985] N.I.62	411
,, *v.* Registrar of Companies, *see* Oakthorpe Holdings Ltd., *In re*		
,, *v.* Shield Insurance	[1976-7] ILRM 218	50
,, Cooke *v.*	[1984] I.R.710	207
,, ,, ...	[1984] ILRM 208	415
,, Director of Public Prosecutions *v.*	[1985] ILRM 243	1073
,, People *v.*	[1986] I.R.722; [1988] ILRM 137	300
Walsh (G.N.) Ltd., Mealiffe *v.*	[1986] I.R.427; [1987] ILRM 301	706
Walsh (Joe) Tours Ltd., Director of Consumer Affairs *v.*	[1985] ILRM 273	254
Walshe *v.* Córas Iompair Éireann	[1985] ILRM 180	959
Ward *v.* Kinahan Electrical Ltd.	[1984] I.R.292	207
,, *v.* McMaster	[1985] I.R.29; [1986] ILRM 43	787
,, ,, ,, ...	[1988] I.R.337	824
,, Bolands Ltd. *v.*	[1988] ILRM 382	496
Waring's Will Trusts, *In re*; Harnett *v.* Calvert ...	[1985] N.I.105	1190
Warnock *v.* Revenue Commissioners	[1985] I.R.663; [1986] ILRM 37	1041
Waterford County Council, Agra Trading Ltd. *v.*	[1985] ILRM 249	291
Waterford Glass Ltd. *v.* Controller of Patents, Designs and Trade Marks	[1984] ILRM 565	1177
Waterford Harbour Commissioners v. British Railways Board	[1979] ILRM 296	271

Name of Case	Volume and page	Column of Digest
Wayte (Holdings) Ltd., *In re*; Burns v. Hearne	[1986] I.R.448	1035
Webb *v*. Ireland	[1988] I.R.353; [1988] ILRM 565	59
Webb Caravan Services Ltd., Cole *v*.	[1985] ILRM 1	923
Weeland *v*. Radio Telefís Éireann	[1987] I.R.662	255
Weir *v*. Dun Laoghaire Corporation...	[1984] ILRM 113	797
Welltrade (Middle East) Ltd., Hartery *v*.	[1978] ILRM 38	477
Wesley College, Governors of, *v*. Commissioner of Valuation	[1984] ILRM 117	993
Western Health and Social Services Board, Monteith *v*.	[1984] N.I.257	964
Western Potato Co-Operative Ltd. *v*. Durnan ...	[1985] ILRM 5	266
Western Regional Fisheries Board, Heneghan *v*.	[1986] ILRM 225	482
Wexford North Slob Commissioners, Stelzer *v*.	[1988] ILRM 279	823
Whelan *v*. Madigan	[1978] ILRM 136	696
,, *v*. Tobin	[1976-7] ILRM 199	730
White *v*. Carlisle Trust Ltd.	[1976-7] ILRM 311	702
,, *v*. McCooey	[1976-7] ILRM 72	1090
White-Spunner, O'Brien *v*.	[1979] ILRM 240	1089
Whitecross Potatoes (International) Ltd. *v*. Coyle	[1978] ILRM 31	258
Williams Group Tullamore Ltd., *In re*	[1985] I.R.613	109
Wilson *v*. Neilan, *see* State (Wilson) *v*. Neilan		
Wine, State (Sherry) *v*.	[1985] ILRM 196	363
Wine Inns Ltd. *v*. Lavery Ltd.	[1985] N.I.427	727
Wislang, *In re*, ...	[1984] N.I.63	466
Woodward (Joseph) & Sons Ltd., O'Sullivan *v*.	[1987] I.R.255	42
Wren, Harris *v*.	[1984] ILRM 120	536
,, McGowan *v*.	[1988] ILRM 744	665
,, Quinn *v*.	[1985] I.R.322; [1985] ILRM 410	532
Wymes *v*. Tehan	[1988] I.R.717	627
X		
X.J.S. Investments Ltd., *In re*	[1986] I.R.750; [1987] ILRM 659	861
X.J.S. Investments Ltd. *v*. Dun Laoghaire Corporation, *see* X.J.S. Investments Ltd., *In re*		
Y		
Yeates *v*. Minister for Posts and Telegraphs	[1978] ILRM 22	94
Youghal Carpets (Yarns) Ltd., Cronin *v*.	[1985] I.R.312; [1985] ILRM 666	1026
Z		
Zurich Insurance Co. *v*. Shield Insurance Co.Ltd.	[1988] I.R.174	652

CASES FOLLOWED, OVERRULED, OR SPECIALLY CONSIDERED

Brennan v. **Dorney,** (1888) 21 L.R. Ir. 353
applied
see LICENSING ACTS, 1

Brewer Street Investments Ltd. v. **Barclay's Woollen Co. Ltd.,** [1954] 1 Q.B. 428
applied
see CONTRACT, 10

Brightside Kilpatrick Engineering Services v. **Mitchell Construction Ltd.,** [1975] 2 Lloyd's Rep. 493
followed
see ARBITRATION, 5

British Eagle International Airlines v. **Compagnie Nationale Air France,** [1975] 1 W.L.R. 758; [1975] 2 All E.R. 390
considered
see COMPANY, 16

British Insulated and Helsby Cables v. **Atherton,** [1926] A.C. 205
applied
see REVENUE, 8

Broome v. **Agar,** (1928) 138 L.T. 698; 44 T.L.R. 339
considered
see DEFAMATION, 1

Broomfield v. **Minister for Justice,** (H.C., unreported, 10 April, 1981)
not followed
see CIVIL SERVICE, 1

Brown's Estate, *In re*, **Brown** v. **Brown,** [1893] 2 Ch. 300
followed
see BANKING, 2

Browns Transport Ltd. v. **Kropp,** (1958) 100 C.L.R 263
considered
see EUROPEAN COMMUNITIES, 1

Brunsden v. **Humphrey,** (1884) 14 Q.B.D. 141; 53 L.J.Q.B. 476
explained and distinguished
see PRACTICE AND PROCEDURE, 42

Buchanan Ltd. and Anor. v. **McVey,** [1954] I.R. 89; 90 I.L.T.R. 121
applied
see CONFLICT OF LAWS, 5

Buckley and Ors. (Sinn Fein) v. **Attorney General,** [1950] I.R. 67
applied
see CONSTITUTION, 23, 29
considered
see GAMING AND LOTTERIES, 3

Bucks v. **Bowers,** [1970] Ch. 431; [1970] 2 W.L.R. 676
considered
see REVENUE, 13

Burdett v. **Abbot,** (1811) 14 East 1; 104 E.R. 501
applied
see ROAD TRAFFIC OFFENCES, 6

Burdle v. **Secretary of State for the Environment,** [1972] 1 W.L.R. 1207; [1972] 3 All E.R. 240
dictum approved
see PLANNING, 26

Burke v. **John Paul & Co. Ltd.,** [1967] I.R. 277
applied
see NEGLIGENCE, 13

Burt v. **Claude Cousins,** [1971] 2 Q.B. 426; [1971] 2 W.L.R. 930
considered
see NEGLIGENCE, 24

Byrne v. **Ireland,** [1972] I.R. 241
applied
see BAILMENT
CONSTITUTION, 20
considered
see CONSTITUTION, 11
COURTHOUSES
followed
see CONSTITUTION, 10

C. v. **C.,** [1921] P. 399
followed
see FAMILY LAW, 19

C. v. **C.,** [1976] I.R. 254; 111 I.L.T.R. 133
applied
see FAMILY LAW, 6, 27

CL Nye Ltd., *In re*, [1971] 1 Ch. 442
followed
see COMPANY, 6

Cahill v. **Sutton,** [1980] I.R. 269
applied
see CONSTITUTION, 22, 34, 39, 47
considered
see CONSTITUTION, 22, 23, 34
DAMAGES, 9
JUDICIAL REVIEW, 14
LOCAL GOVERNMENT, 9
followed
see CONSTITUTION, 47

Caldwell v. **Sumpters,** [1972] Ch. 478; [1972] 2 W.L.R. 412
considered
see SOLICITOR, 1

Church and General Insurance Co. v. **Connolly and McLoughlin,** (H.C., unreported, 7 May 1981)
considered
see ARBITRATION, 3

Churchward v. **Churchward,** [1895] P. 7
applied
see FAMILY LAW, 17

Cityview Press v. **An Chomhairle Oiliúna,** [1980] I.R. 381
applied
see CONSTITUTION, 25
considered
see CONSTITUTION, 25

Clarke v. **Ramuz,** [1891] 2 Q.B. 456
followed
see SALE OF LAND, 9

Clayton's Case, (1816) 1 Mer. 572; [1814-23] 35 All E.R. 1
rule applied
see COMPANY, 20

Clegg v. **Metcalfe,** [1914] 1 Ch. 808
considered
see LOCAL GOVERNMENT, 9

Cleveland Petroleum Co. Ltd. v. **Dartstone Ltd.,** [1969] 1 W.L.R. 116
considered
see INJUNCTION, 12

Clough Mill Ltd. v. **Martin,** [1985] 1 W.L.R. 111
approved
see SALE OF GOODS, 3

Coco v. **A.N. Clark (Engineers) Ltd.,** [1969] R.P.C. 41
considered and applied
see CONTRACT, 3

Cohane v. **Cohane,** [1968] I.R. 176
considered
see PRACTICE AND PROCEDURE, 17

Coleman's Depositories Ltd., *In re*, [1907] 2 K.B. 798
dicta applied
see REVENUE, 4

Colgan v. **Connolly Construction Co. (Ireland) Ltd.,**[1980] ILRM 33
considered
see NEGLIGENCE, 2, 3
followed
see NEGLIGENCE, 3

Collins v. **County Cork V.E.C.,** (S.C., unreported, 18 March 1983)
applied
see EDUCATION, 2

Collins v. **Doyle,** [1982] ILRM 495
considered
see PRACTICE AND PROCEDURE, 17

Combe v. **Combe,** [1951] 2. K.B. 215; [1951] 1 All E.R. 767
considered
see CONTRACT, 4

Comhlucht Páipéar Ríomhaireachta Teo. (In vol. Liquidation) v. **Údarás na Gaeltachta,** [1987] I.R. 684
followed
see PRACTICE AND PROCEDURE, 24

Commissioners of Inland Revenue v. **Dalgety & Co.,** [1930] 1 K.B. 1; (1929) 15 T.C. 216
considered
see REVENUE, 39

Commonwealth of Australia v. **John Fairfax & Sons Ltd.,** (1980) 147 C.L.R. 39
approved
see CONSTITUTION, 14

Connelly v. **D.P.P.,** [1964] A.C. 1254
followed
see CRIMINAL LAW, 38

Conole v. **Redbank Oyster Co.,** [1976] I.R. 191
principles affirmed and applied
see NEGLIGENCE, 17

Conroy v. **Attorney General,** [1965] I.R. 411
applied
see CONSTITUTION, 2, 56
considered
see CONSTITUTION, 56
distinguished
see CONSTITUTION, 49

Convey v. **Regan,** [1952] I.R. 56
applied
see LIMITATION OF ACTIONS, 1

Cook and Ors., *In re*, [1986] 1 NIJB 43
applied
see LOCAL GOVERNMENT, 5

Cook v. **Whellock,** (1890) 24 Q.B.D. 658; 59 L.J.Q.B. 329
followed
see PRACTICE AND PROCEDURE, 18

Cooke v. **Walsh,** [1984] I.R. 710; [1984] ILRM 208
considered
see NEGLIGENCE, 15
referred to
see DAMAGES, 11, 12

O'Brien v. **Keogh,** [1972] I.R. 144
explained
see CONSTITUTION, 47

O'C. v. **D.,** [1985] I.R. 265; [1985] ILRM 123
considered
see CONFLICT OF LAWS, 5

Odeon Assoc. Theatres v. **Jones,** [1971] 1 W.L.R. 442; [1971] 2 All E.R. 407
considered
see REVENUE, 18
dicta applied
see REVENUE, 23

O'Donovan v. **Cork County Council,** [1967] I.R. 373; 102 I.L.T.R. 169
considered
see NEGLIGENCE, 26

O Laighléis, *In re*, [1960] I.R. 93; 95 I.L.T.R. 92
applied
see CONSTITUTION, 39
CRIMINAL LAW, 2

O'R. v. **O'R.,** [1985] I.R. 367
applied
see CONSTITUTION, 31

Ord v. **Ord,** [1923] 2 K.B. 432; [1923] All E.R. 206
considered
see PRACTICE AND PROCEDURE, 42

O'Reilly v. **Granville,** [1971] I.R. 90
considered
see LIMITATION OF ACTIONS, 2

O'Sullivan v. **P. Ltd.,** (1962) 3 I.T.C. 355
considered
see REVENUE, 7
followed
see REVENUE, 7

O'Toole (Jack) Ltd. v. **MacEoin Kelly Associates,** [1986] I.R. 277; [1987] ILRM 269
applied
see PRACTICE AND PROCEDURE, 21, 22
cited
see PRACTICE AND PROCEDURE, 23
considered
see PRACTICE AND PROCEDURE, 21
followed
see PRACTICE AND PROCEDURE, 21

Overseas Tankship (U.K.) Ltd. v. **Morts Dock & Engineering Co. Ltd., (The Wagon Mound) (No. 1),** [1961] A.C. 388
applied
see DAMAGES, 7
NEGLIGENCE, 13

Owners of Dredger Liebosch v. **Owners of S.S. Edison,** [1933] A.C. 499
considered
see NUISANCE, 3
disapproved
see DAMAGES, 7

P.(H.) v. **P.(W.),** [1985] ILRM 527
applied
see PRACTICE AND PROCEDURE, 27

Padfield v. **Minister of Agriculture, Fisheries and Food,** [1968] A.C. 997; [1968] 2 W.L.R. 924
considered
see JUDICIAL REVIEW, 14

Palmer v. **Day & Son,** [1895] 2 Q.B. 618
distinguished
see COMPANY, 17

Parker v. **British Airways Board,** [1982] Q.B. 1004
considered
see BAILMENT

Parmiter v. **Coupland,** (1840) 151 E.R. 340
considered
see DEFAMATION, 1

Patrick and Lyon Ltd., [1933] Ch. 786
followed
see COMPANY, 8

Patrick v. **Broadstone Mills Ltd.,** [1954] 1 W.L.R. 158; [1954] 1 All E.R. 163
approved
see REVENUE, 18

Pavia & C. S.P.A. v. **Thurmann-Nielson,** [1952] 2 Q.B. 84
distinguished
see SALE OF GOODS, 1

Pearn v. **Sargent,** [1973] 2 Lloyd's Rep. 141; [1974] Crim. L.R. 34
considered
see STATUTE, 3

Pearson v. **Naydler,** [1977] 1 W.L.R. 899; [1977] 3 All E.R. 531
applied
see PRACTICE AND PROCEDURE, 21

Pembroke U.D.C. v. **Commissioner of Valuation,** [1904] 2 I.R. 429
distinguished
see RATING AND VALUATION, 4

Petrotim Securities Ltd. v. **Ayres,** [1964] 1 W.L.R. 190; [1964] 1 All E.R. 269
applied
see REVENUE, 14
considered
see REVENUE, 28

Phillips v. **Eyre,** (1870) L.R. 6 Q.B. 1
not followed
see PRACTICE AND PROCEDURE, 52

Phipps v. **Earl of Anglesea,** (1721) 5 Vin Abr. 209 part 8
considered and applied
see CONFLICT OF LAWS, 2

Pigs Marketing Board v. **Donnelly (Dublin) Ltd.,** [1939] I.R. 413
approved
see CONSTITUTION, 25

Pine Valley Developments Ltd. v. **Minister for the Environment,** [1987] I.R. 23; [1987] ILRM 747
applied
see NEGLIGENCE, 33

Pioneer Aggregates (U.K.) Ltd. v. **Secretary of State for the Environment,** [1985] A.C. 132; [1984] 3 W.L.R. 32
distinguished
see PLANNING, 31

Pok Sun Shum v. **Ireland,** [1986] ILRM 593
considered
see ALIENS, 2

Power Securities Ltd. v. **Daly,** (H.C., unreported, 27 Feb. 1984)
considered
see ARBITRATION, 11

Prince Albert v. **Strange,** (1849) 1 H. & Tw. 1
considered and applied
see CONTRACT, 3

Private Motorists Provident Society Ltd. v. **A.G.,** [1983] I.R. 339; [1984] ILRM 88
applied
see CONSTITUTION, 43

Purcell v. **F.C. Trigell Ltd.,** [1971] 1 Q.B. 358
applied
see PRACTICE AND PROCEDURE, 23

Purtill v. **Athlone U.D.C.,** [1968] I.R. 205
considered
see NEGLIGENCE, 28

Quinn v. **Wren,** [1985] I.R. 322; [1985] ILRM 410
applied
see EXTRADITION, 8

Quinn's Supermarket v. **Attorney General,** [1972] I.R. 1
considered
see CONSTITUTION, 39
RATING AND VALUATION, 1
followed
see CONSTITUTION, 47

R. v. **Ball,** [1911] A.C. 47
distinguished
see CRIMINAL LAW, 26

R. v. **Belfon,** [1976] 1 W.L.R. 741
applied
see CRIMINAL LAW, 32

R. v. **Board of Visitors of Hull Prison,** *ex parte* **St. Germain (No. 1),** [1979] Q.B. 425
not followed
see JUDICIAL REVIEW, 12

R. v. **Boardman,** [1975] A.C. 421
applied
see CRIMINAL LAW, 26

R. v. **Bow Street Magistrates,** *ex parte* **Mackeson,** (1981) 75 Cr. App. R. 24
considered
see CONSTITUTION, 16

R. v. **British Broadcasting Corp.,** *ex parte* **Lavelle,** [1983] 1 W.L.R. 23; [1983] 1 All E.R. 241
doubted
see EMPLOYER AND EMPLOYEE, 23

R. v. **Byrne,** [1960] 2 Q.B. 396; [1960] 3 W.L.R. 440
considered
see CRIMINAL LAW, 30

R. v. **Cardiff Coroner,** *ex parte* **Thomas,** [1970] 1 W.L.R. 1975; [1970] 3 All E.R. 469
considered
see CORONER

R. v. **Cleere,** [1983] 5 Crim. App. R. (S.) 465
distinguished
see PRISONS, 1

R. v. **Collister and Warhurst,** (1955) 39 Cr. App. R. 100
considered and applied
see CRIMINAL LAW, 25

R. v. **Criminal Injuries Compensation Board,** *ex parte* **Lain,** [1967] 2 Q.B. 864; [1967] 3 W.L.R. 348
followed
see REVENUE, 2

Siskina (Cargo Owners) v. **Distos S.A.,** [1979] A.C. 210; [1977] 3 W.L.R. 532
considered
see INJUNCTION, 9

Smith v. **Ireland and Ors.,** [1983] ILRM 300
considered
see LIMITATION OF ACTIONS, 2

Smith v. **Lloyd,** (1854) 9 Ex. 562
distinguished
see LIMITATION OF ACTIONS, 1

Smith v. **Morgan,** [1971] 1 W.L.R. 803
considered and applied
see SUCCESSION, 15

Solicitors' Act, 1954, *In re*, [1960] I.R. 239
considered
see CONSTITUTION, 28

Solosky v. **The Queen,** (1980) 1 S.C.R. 821
considered
see CONSTITUTION, 10

Somers v. **W.,** [1979] I.R. 94
applied
see FAMILY LAW, 29

Somjee v. **Minister for Justice,** [1981] ILRM 324
considered
see CONSTITUTION, 37

Sorrell v. **Finch,** [1977] A.C. 728; [1976] 2 W.L.R. 833
considered
see NEGLIGENCE, 24

Spiller v. **Spiller,** (1819) 3 Swan. 556
applied
see SALE OF LAND, 3

Stagg v. **Wyatt,** (1838) 2 Jur. 892
distinguished
see LANDLORD AND TENANT, 19

State v. **Treanor,** [1924] 2 I.R. 193
followed
see CRIMINAL LAW, 17

State (A.G.) v. **Fawsitt,** [1955] I.R. 30
distinguished
see CRIMINAL LAW, 48

State (A.G.) v. **Roe,** [1951] I.R. 172
approved
see DISTRICT COURT, 3
distinguished
see CRIMINAL LAW, 62

State (Abenglen Properties Ltd.) v. **Dublin Corporation,** [1984] I.R. 381; [1982] ILRM 590
applied
see DISTRICT COURT, 1
JUDICIAL REVIEW, 4, 9

State (Aherne) v. **Governor of Limerick Prison,** [1983] ILRM 17
applied
see CRIMINAL LAW, 78

State (Alf-A-Bet Promotions Ltd.) v. **Bundoran U.D.C.,** 112 I.L.T.R. 9
applied
see PLANNING, 16

State (Bloomfield) v. **Neylon,** [1985] ILRM 602
overruled
see CRIMINAL LAW, 29

State (Bowes) v. **Fitzpatrick,** [1978] ILRM 195
considered
see CRIMINAL LAW, 6
distinguished
see CRIMINAL LAW, 18

State (Browne) v. **Feran,** [1967] I.R. 147
considered
see CONSTITUTION, 25

State (Burke) v. **Garvey,** [1979] ILRM 232
considered
see CIVIL SERVICE, 1

State (C.) v. **Minister for Justice,** [1967] I.R. 106
considered
see CONSTITUTION, 26

State (Clarke) v. **Roche,** [1986] I.R. 619; [1987] ILRM 309; [1986] ILRM 565
cited
see CRIMINAL LAW, 39
considered
see CRIMINAL LAW, 44

State (Collins) v. **Ruane,** [1984] I.R. 105; [1985] ILRM 349
followed
see CRIMINAL LAW, 49

State (Córas Iompair Éireann) v. **An Bord Pleanála,** (S.C., unreported, 12 Dec. 1984)
considered
see PLANNING, 1

State (Cronin) v. **Circuit Court Judge of the Western Circuit,** [1937] I.R. 34; 71 I.L.T.R. 3
considered
see CRIMINAL LAW, 46

State (Minister for Lands and Fisheries) v. **Sealy,** [1939] I.R. 21; 73 I.L.T.R. 21
applied
see PRACTICE AND PROCEDURE, 15

State (Modern Homes (Ireland) Ltd.) v. **Dublin Corporation** [1953] I.R. 202; 88 I.L.T.R. 79
considered
see JUDICIAL REVIEW, 14

State (Murphy) v. **Governor of St. Patrick's Institution,** *see* **State (Murphy)** v. **Kielt**

State (Murphy) v. **Johnston,** [1983] I.R. 235
considered
see CONSTITUTION, 55

State (Murphy) v. **Kielt, (Governor of St. Patrick's Institution),** [1984] I.R. 458; [1985] ILRM 141
applied
see PRISONS, 4
followed
see JUDICIAL REVIEW, 5

State (Nicolaou) v. **An Bord Uchtála,** [1966] I.R. 567; 102 I.L.T.R. 1
applied
see CONSTITUTION, 13

State (O'Callaghan) v. **O'hUadhaigh,** [1977] I.R. 42
considered
see JUDICIAL REVIEW, 11

State (O'Connell) v. **Fawsitt,** [1986] I.R. 362; [1986] ILRM 639
considered
see CRIMINAL LAW, 65
followed
see CRIMINAL LAW, 57

State (O'Flaherty) v. **O'Floinn,** [1954] I.R. 295; 90 I.L.T.R. 179
applied
see CRIMINAL LAW, 44
considered
see PRACTICE AND PROCEDURE, 36
followed
see CRIMINAL LAW, 36

State (O'Hagan) v. **Delap,** [1982] I.R. 213; [1983] ILRM 241
applied
see DISTRICT COURT, 2

State (O'Rourke) v. **Kelly,** (S.C., unreported, 28 July 1980)
distinguished
see CONSTITUTION, 29

State (Pheasantry Ltd.) v. **Donnelly,** [1982] ILRM 512
applied
see CONSTITUTION, 56

State (Pine Valley Developments) v. **Dublin Co. Council,** [1984] I.R. 407; [1982] ILRM 169
considered
see PLANNING, 36

State (Quinn) v. **Ryan,** [1965] I.R. 70; 100 I.L.T.R. 105
followed
see CONSTITUTION, 20
principles affirmed
see CONSTITUTION, 16

State (Roche) v. **Delap,** [1980] I.R. 170
applied
see DISTRICT COURT, 1
considered
see JUDICIAL REVIEW, 8

State (Rollinson) v. **Kelly,** [1984] I.R. 248; [1984] ILRM 625
applied
see CRIMINAL LAW, 29
considered
see CONSTITUTION, 56
DISTRICT COURT, 1

State (Royle) v. **Kelly,** [1974] I.R. 259
considered
see ALIENS, 4
CRIMINAL LAW, 50

State (Shanahan) v. **Attorney General,** [1964] I.R. 239
applied
see CONSTITUTION, 26
CRIMINAL LAW, 66
not followed
see CONSTITUTION, 26

State (Sheerin) v. **Kennedy,** [1966] I.R. 379
considered
see CASE STATED, 3
CONSTITUTION, 25
PRACTICE AND PROCEDURE, 14

State (Stanford) v. **Dun Laoghaire Corporation,** (S.C., unreported, 20 Feb. 1981)
considered
see PLANNING, 1

State (Thornhill) v. **Minister for Defence,** [1986] I.R 1
applied
see DEFENCE FORCES, 3, 4

TABLE OF ARTICLES OF THE CONSTITUTIONS OF SAORSTÁT ÉIREANN (THE IRISH FREE STATE) AND OF IRELAND

CITED AND JUDICIALLY INTERPRETED

1922, **Constitution of the Irish Free State (Saorstát Éireann), 1922**

Article	
2	*see* BAILMENT
11	*see* BAILMENT
51	*see* BAILMENT
61	*see* CONSTITUTION, 25
64	*see* CONSTITUTION, 3
66	*see* CONSTITUTION, 6
73	*see* BAILMENT CONTRACT, 12

1937, **Constitution of Ireland, 1937**

Article	
	see INJUNCTION, 6
Preamble	*see* CONSTITUTION, 23
1	*see* CONSTITUTION, 22, 23
2	*see* CONSTITUTION, 23
3	*see* CONSTITUTION, 23
5	*see* BAILMENT CONSTITUTION, 22
6	*see* CONSTITUTION, 1, 20, 22, 26 EXTRADITION, 8
9	*see* ALIENS, 2
10	*see* BAILMENT
11	*see* CONSTITUTION, 25
12	*see* CONSTITUTION, 1
15	*see* CONSTITUTION, 20, 23, 25, 34, 39 EXTRADITION, 6
15.4	*see* SOCIAL WELFARE, 8
15.5	*see* EUROPEAN COMMUNITIES, 1
16	*see* CONSTITUTION, 1, 36, 37
25	*see* CONSTITUTION, 25
28	*see* CONSTITUTION, 22, 23, 25, 41
29	*see* CONSTITUTION, 13, 22, 23, 24, 25, 39, 41 INJUNCTION, 2
29.4.3	*see* CONSTITUTION, 22, 35
30	*see* CONSTITUTION, 26 CRIMINAL LAW, 46
33	*see* CRIMINAL LAW, 70
34	*see* CONSTITUTION, 3, 4, 12, 26, 27, 28, 29, 31, 33, 41, 50 CRIMINAL LAW, 71
34.1	*see* CONSTITUTION, 30 FAMILY LAW, 4
34.2	*see* CONSTITUTION, 32
34.3	*see* PRACTICE AND PROCEDURE, 42
34.3.1	*see* CONSTITUTION, 32
34.3.2	*see* CASE STATED, 3
34.3.4	*see* CONSTITUTION, 32, 53
34.4.3	*see* CONSTITUTION, 2, 6 PRACTICE AND PROCEDURE, 19
35	*see* CONSTITUTION, 50
36	*see* CONSTITUTION, 3, 4, 5, 32, 33
37	*see* CONSTITUTION, 31

TABLE OF STATUTES OF IRELAND, GREAT BRITAIN AND THE UNITED KINGDOM

CITED AND JUDICIALLY INTERPRETED OR ENFORCED

1542

1542, 33 Hen.8 c. 10 (Ir.)—Act for Joint Tenants, 1542
see LAND, 3

1695

1695, 7 Wm. 3 c. 12 (Ir.)—Statute of Frauds, 1695
see SALE OF LAND, 5
s. 2
see SALE OF LAND, 7, 14

1795

1795, 35 Geo. 3 c. 21—Maynooth College Establishment Act, 1795
s. 3
see CONSTITUTION, 21

1827

1827, 7 & 8 Geo. 4 c. 53—Excise Management Act, 1827
s. 78
see CRIMINAL LAW, 52

1828

1828, c. 54—Criminal Law (Ireland) Act, 1828
s. 20
see CRIMINAL LAW, 75

1833

1833, 3 & 4 Wm.4 c. 68—Licensing (Ireland) Act, 1833
s. 4
see LICENSING ACTS, 4
s. 15
see LICENSING ACTS, 2

1836

1836, 6 & 7 Wm. 4 c. 32—Building Societies Act, 1836
see BUILDING SOCIETY, 1

1836, 6 & 7 Wm. 4 c. 38—Licensing (Ireland) Act, 1836
s. 16
see LICENSING ACTS, 2

1836, 6 & 7 Wm. 4 c.116—Grand Jury (Ireland) Act, 1836
s.77
see DISTRICT COURT, 4

1837

1837, 7 Wm. 4 & 1 Vict. c. 26—Wills Act, 1837
s. 18
see SUCCESSION, 21

1838

1838, 1 & 2 Vict. c. 56—Poor Relief (Ireland) Act, 1838
s.63
see RATING AND VALUATION, 4

1841

1841, 4 & 5 Vict. c. 20—Excise Collection and Management Act, 1841
s. 24
see SURETY

1844

1844, 7 & 8 Vict. c.81—Marriages (Ireland) Act, 1844
s. 49
see FAMILY LAW, 25

1845

1845, 8 & 9 Vict. c. 18—Lands Clauses Consolidation Act, 1845
see COMPULSORY ACQUISITION, 1

1845, 8 & 9 Vict. c. 20—Railway Clauses Consolidation Act, 1845
s. 49
see NEGLIGENCE, 31

1845, 8 & 9 Vict. c.113—Evidence Act, 1845
see CRIMINAL LAW, 24

1847

1847, 10 & 11 Vict. c. 27—Harbours, Docks and Piers Clauses Act, 1847
see STATUTE, 3

1849

1849, 12 & 13 Vict. c. 53—Attorneys and Solicitors (Ireland) Act, 1849
ss. 2, 6
see PRACTICE AND PROCEDURE, 27

1851

1851, 14 & 15 Vict. c. 93—Petty Sessions (Ireland) Act, 1851
s.8, para.1
see DISTRICT COURT, 4

1877

1877, 40 & 41 Vict. c. 49—General Prisons (Ireland) Act, 1877
ss. 12, 13(2)
see PRISONS, 2

1878

1878, 41 & 42 Vict. c. 52—Public Health (Ireland) Act, 1878
s. 23
see ARBITRATION, 6
s. 24
see ARBITRATION, 6
PLANNING, 5
s. 65A
see LOCAL GOVERNMENT, 1, 2
s. 174
see LOCAL GOVERNMENT, 9
ss. 181, 185, 193
see NEGLIGENCE, 28
ss. 216, 217
see PLANNING, 5
s. 234
see NEGLIGENCE, 28

1879

1879, 42 & 43 Vict. c. 11—Bankers' Books Evidence Act, 1879
s. 9
see REVENUE, 26

1879, 42 & 43 Vict. c. 50—Bills of Sale (Ireland) Act, 1879
see SALE OF GOODS, 4

1880

1880, 43 & 44 Vict. c. 13—Births and Deaths Registration (Ireland) Act, 1880
s. 7
see FAMILY LAW, 4

1880, 43 and 44 Vict. c. 20—Inland Revenue Act, 1880
s. 43(4)
see NEGLIGENCE, 25

1881

1881, 44 & 45 Vict. c. 41—Conveyancing and Law of Property Act, 1881
s. 2, para.(iii)
see REAL PROPERTY, 7
s. 7
see PLANNING, 13
s. 14
see LANDLORD AND TENANT, 10
ss. 19(1)(iii), 24(3), 24(8)
see REAL PROPERTY, 7
s. 65
see SUCCESSION, 12

1882

1882, 45 & 46 Vict. c. 38—Settled Land Act, 1882
ss. 51, 58(1)
see SUCCESSION, 12

1883

1883, 46 & 47 Vict. c. 7—Bills of Sale (Ireland) Act (1879) (Amendment) Act, 1883
s. 8
see SALE OF GOODS, 4

1885

1885, 48 & 49 Vict. c. 69—Criminal Law Amendment Act, 1885
s. 11
see CONSTITUTION, 39

1889

1889, 52 & 53 Vict. c. 45—Factor's Act, 1889
s. 9
see SALE OF GOODS, 6

1890

1890, 53 & 54 Vict. c. 39—Partnership Act, 1890
see REVENUE, 38
s. 2(3)
see PARTNERSHIP

1891

1891, 54 & 55 Vict. c. 39—Stamp Act, 1891
ss. 54, 62
see REVENUE, 42

1893

1893, 56 & 57 Vict. c. 39—Industrial and Provident Societies Act, 1893
s. 10(3)
see INDUSTRIAL AND PROVIDENT SOCIETIES, 1

1893, 56 & 57 Vict. c. 61—Public Authorities Protection Act, 1893
s. 1(a)
see LIMITATION OF ACTIONS, 4

1893, 56 & 57 Vict. c. 71—Sale of Goods Act, 1893
s. 1
see SALE OF GOODS, 3, 4
s. 4
see SALE OF GOODS, 1
s. 17
see SALE OF GOODS, 3, 4
s. 51
see CONTRACT, 2

1898

1898, 61 & 62 Vict. c. 37—Local Government (Ireland) Act, 1898
see DISTRICT COURT, 4
s.10
see COMPULSORY ACQUISITION, 6

1956

1956, c. 74—Copyright Act, 1956
ss. 1, 3, 4, 10, 11, 17, 18, 49, Sch.3
see COPYRIGHT, 1

1968

1968, c. 68—Design Copyright Act, 1968
s.1
see COPYRIGHT, 1

1973

1973, c. 36—Northern Ireland Constitution Act, 1973
s. 21(1)
see LOCAL GOVERNMENT, 3

1975

1975, c. 14—Social Security (Northern Ireland) Act, 1975
ss. 36, 79
see SOCIAL WELFARE, 5

1978

1978, c. 5—Northern Ireland (Emergency Provisions) Act, 1978
s. 8.
see CRIMINAL LAW, 21
ss. 11(1), 31(1)
see CRIMINAL LAW, 3

1978, c. 23—Judicature (Northern Ireland) Act, 1978
s. 62
see PRACTICE AND PROCEDURE, 57
s. 62(2)
see PRACTICE AND PROCEDURE, 56
s. 86(1)
see PRACTICE AND PROCEDURE, 6

1979

1979, c. 54—Sale of Goods Act, 1979
s. 25(1)
see SALE OF GOODS, 6

PRIVATE AND LOCAL ACTS

1830

1830, 11 Geo. 4 c. 72—Barrington's Hospital Act, 1830
s. 1
see STATUTE, 2

1852

1852, 15 & 16 Vict. c. cli—Wexford Harbour Embankment Act, 1852
ss. 25, 26, 45
see NEGLIGENCE, 29

1854

1854, 17 & 18 Vict. c. 177—Londonderry Port and Harbour Act, 1854
see STATUTE, 3

1874

1874, 37 & 38 Vict. c. 144—Londonderry Port and Harbour Act, 1874
see STATUTE, 3

1882

1882, 45 & 46 Vict. c. 162—Londonderry Port and Harbour Act, 1882
see STATUTE, 3

1898

1898, 61 & 62 Vict. c. cclii—Fishguard and Rosslare Railways and Harbours Act, 1898
s. 70
see CONTRACT, 12

TABLE OF THE STATUTES OF SAORSTÁT ÉIREANN (THE IRISH FREE STATE) AND OF IRELAND

CITED AND JUDICIALLY INTERPRETED OR ENFORCED

1979

1980

TABLE OF STATUTES OF NORTHERN IRELAND

CITED AND JUDICIALLY INTERPRETED OR ENFORCED

1953

1953, c. 18—Prison Act (Northern Ireland), 1953
s.16(1)
see ELECTORAL LAW, 2

1958

1958, c. 10—Statute of Limitations (Northern Ireland), 1958
s. 9A, 9D
see PRACTICE AND PROCEDURE, 45, 57

1958, c. 23—Trustee Act (Northern Ireland), 1958
s. 57(1)(b)
see TRUSTS, 4

1960

1960, c. 22—Companies Act (Northern Ireland), 1960
s. 114, table A, art. 7
see COMPANY, 13

1962

1962, c. 14—Electoral Law Act (Northern Ireland), 1962
s.65(6)
see ELECTORAL LAW, 2

1964

1964, c. 21—Magistrates' Court Act (Northern Ireland), 1964
s. 15
see NEGLIGENCE, 32

1965

1965, c. 35—Adoption Act (Northern Ireland), 1965
s.5(1)
see ADOPTION, 1

1968

1968, c. 32—Criminal Justice (Committal for Trial) Act (Northern Ireland), 1968
ss. 3, 7
see CRIMINAL LAW, 38

1968, c. 34—Children and Young Persons Act (Northern Ireland), 1968
ss. 66, 68
see CRIMINAL LAW, 68

1969

1969, c. 15—Grand Jury (Abolition) Act (Northern Ireland), 1969
s. 2(1)
see CRIMINAL LAW, 38

1971

1971, c. 13—Licensing Act (Northern Ireland), 1971
s. 5(2)
see LICENSING ACTS, 6, 7, 8
s. 5(5)
see LICENSING ACTS, 7
Sch. 1, Part 1, para. 1
see LICENSING ACTS, 11
Sch. II
see LICENSING ACTS, 7

1971, c. 30—Payments for Debt (Emergency Provisions) Act (Northern Ireland), 1971
s. 1
see LANDLORD AND TENANT, 12

1972

1972, c. 9—Local Government Act (Northern Ireland), 1972
s. 7(1)
see LOCAL GOVERNMENT, 3
s. 18(1)
see LOCAL GOVERNMENT, 4

ORDERS IN COUNCIL HAVING EFFECT AS ACTS OF THE PARLIAMENT OF NORTHERN IRELAND

1972

1972, S.I. No. 1263, N.I.12—Education and Libraries (Northern Ireland) Order, 1972
arts. 5, 6(1), 11(1), 34, 35 Sch.9, paras. 1, 2
see EDUCATION, 4
art. 41, Sch.9, para.3
see EDUCATION, 3

1972, S.I. No. 1634, N.I. 17—Planning (Northern Ireland) Order, 1972
art. 22
see PLANNING, 15

art. 30
see PLANNING, 14
arts. 70, 71, 73
see PLANNING, 40

1977

1977, S.I. No. 1248, N.I.15—Criminal Injuries (Compensation) (Northern Ireland) Order, 1977
art. 6 (10)
see CRIMINAL INJURIES, 1
art. 9(a)
see CRIMINAL INJURIES, 2

1977, S.I. No. 2157, N.I. 28—Rates (Northern Ireland) Order, 1977
art.13(1)(c)(ii)
see GAMING AND LOTTERIES, 2

1978

1978, S.I. No. 1042, N.I. 12—Companies (Northern Ireland) Order, 1978
art. 129
see COMPANY, 14

1979

1979, S.I. No.924, N.I.8—Inheritance (Provision for Family and Dependants) (Northern Ireland) Order, 1979
arts. 2, 5
see SUCCESSION, 3

1981

1981, S.I. No. 154, N.I.1—Road Traffic (Northern Ireland) Order, 1981
art. 2
see ROAD TRAFFIC OFFENCES, 15
art. 194(3)
see ROAD TRAFFIC OFFENCES, 7

1981, S.I. No. 1675, N.I. 26—Magistrates' Courts (Northern Ireland) Order, 1981
art. 19
see CRIMINAL LAW, 40
art. 20
see CRIMINAL LAW, 45
art. 33
see CRIMINAL LAW, 38
art. 42(3)
see CRIMINAL LAW, 26

TABLE OF EUROPEAN COMMUNITIES LEGISLATION TABLE OF HUMAN RIGHTS CONVENTIONS

CITED AND JUDICIALLY INTERPRETED OR ENFORCED

EUROPEAN COMMUNITIES

Treaty of Rome, 1957,
- Art. 30
  - *see* INJUNCTION, 10
- Art. 31
  - *see* INJUNCTION, 10
- Art. 36
  - *see* INJUNCTION, 10
- Art. 48
  - *see* INJUNCTION, 4
- Art. 85
  - *see* INJUNCTION, 10, 11
- Art. 86
  - *see* INJUNCTION, 10, 11
- Art. 90
  - *see* INJUNCTION, 10
- Art. 119
  - *see* EMPLOYER AND EMPLOYEE, 18
- Art. 177
  - *see* EUROPEAN COMMUNITIES, 2

EC Council Directives
- 79/7/EEC, Art. 4(1)
  - *see* SOCIAL WELFARE, 4

EC Council Regulations
- 17/62
  - *see* INJUNCTION, 11
- 804/84, 856/84, 857/84
  - *see* CONSTITUTION, 35

EC Commission Regulations
- 1371/84
  - *see* CONSTITUTION, 35

HUMAN RIGHTS CONVENTIONS

European Convention for the Protection of Human Rights and Fundamental Freedoms,
- art. 17
  - *see* LOCAL GOVERNMENT, 4

TABLE OF STATUTORY RULES AND ORDERS ETC.

CITED AND JUDICIALLY INTERPRETED OR ENFORCED

ACKNOWLEDGEMENTS

The Incorporated Council of Law Reporting for Ireland gratefully acknowledges the permission given by the under-mentioned for the use of copyright material in their respective reports:

The Incorporated Council of Law Reporting for England and Wales.
The Incorporated Council of Law Reporting for Northern Ireland.
The proprietor of the *Irish Law Reports Monthly*.

GUIDE TO ARRANGEMENT OF CASES

Cases included in the *Digest* are arranged according to their principal subject-matter under the following headings:

THE IRISH REPORTS

THE IRISH REPORTS
1984-1988
THE NORTHERN IRELAND REPORTS
1984-1985
THE IRISH LAW REPORTS MONTHLY
1976-1979, 1984-1988

DIGEST OF CASES

A

ABATTOIR

—— Intensification of use — Absence of planning permission.
see **Planning,** 29

ABORTION INFORMATION

—— Right to life of unborn — Pregnancy counselling services — Abortion considered as an option — Referral to medical clinic in Great Britain — Whether the giving of such assistance unlawful — Whether admitted activities of defendants amounted to conspiracy to corrupt public morals.
see **Constitution,** 20

ABUSE OF PROCESS
see **Practice and Procedure,** 1, 2

—— Action — Estoppel — *Res judicata* — Civil action for damages for assault — Criminal proceedings involving same issue finding no assault took place — Whether plaintiff estopped from bringing civil proceedings.
see **Practice and Procedure,** 41

—— Complaint — Time limit — Delay — Magistrates Court — Offence triable summarily or on indictment — Complaints laid three years after offence — Summons defective — Whether magistrates have a discretion to refuse to hear a summons.
see **Criminal Law,** 40

—— Evidence — Admissibility — Statement of accused — Ruling of inadmissibility — Inadmissible statement accidentally given to jury — Retrial — Whether High Court entitled prior to retrial to restrain prosecution from adducing same statement — Whether such attempt an abuse of process of court.
see **Judicial Review,** 11

—— Extradition — State acquiescing in orders refusing extradition — Subsequent attempt to extradite person in respect of identical circumstances — Whether State precluded from denying person relief identical to that previously obtained — Equality of treatment.
see **Extradition,** 4

ADMINISTRATION OF ESTATES—*continued.*

—— Will — Revocation — Subsequent marriage — Will executed in 1951 — Marriage by testator in 1954 — Death of testator in 1983 — Act of 1965 prima facie applicable to will — Nevertheless will revoked by subsequent marriage as provided by s.18 of repealed Wills Act, 1837 — Executor named in will without status to seek assistance of court.

see **Succession,** 21

ADMINISTRATION OF JUSTICE

see **Constitution,** 2-7, 26-33

see also **Courts** *and individual courts*

ADMINISTRATIVE LAW

see **Civil Service; Delegated Legislation; Government; Health Service; Judicial Review; Local Government; Minister of the Government; Natural and Constitutional Justice; Planning; Prisons; Social Welfare; State-Sponsored Bodies; Tribunal; Ultra Vires**

ADMISSIBILITY OF EVIDENCE

see **Criminal Law,** 2, 6, 11-21, 26, 33
Evidence, 1

ADMISSION — Accused — Statement — Admissibility.

see **Criminal Law,** 2, 6, 18-21, 33
Judicial Review, 11

ADOPTION

1. —— **Consent** — *Refusal — Children wards of court — Application for leave to place children for adoption — Parents refused consent — Whether consent witheld unreasonably — Whether consent issue to be considered on application for leave — Adoption Act (Northern Ireland)* 1965, (*c*.35), *s*.5(1).] The Northern Health and Social Services Board applied for leave to place the respondents' five children for adoption. The Board had previously obtained an order making the children wards of court and at the time of the hearing they were living with foster parents. The respondents, being the natural parents, refused to consent to the application. **Held**, refusing the application that, 1, it would be wrong to grant leave for the children to be placed for adoption where the court concluded that it would not dispense with the consent of the parents on the final application for adoption. *F.* v. *S.* [1973] Fam. 203 distinguished. 2. Where the natural parents do not give their consent to adoption the court can only dispense with that consent on one of the grounds stated in section 5(1) of the Adoption Act (Northern Ireland), 1967. 3. In applying section 5(1) of the 1967 Act the court has to satisfy itself first as to one of the grounds in sub-paragraphs (*a*) to (*e*); secondly, the court has to consider whether the consent of the parent should be dispensed with, and it is in relation to the second matter that it is stated that the welfare of the child shall be the paramount consideration. 4. In this case, while the respondents left much to be desired as parents, their marriage appeared to be stable; they had a satisfactory home and a genuine love of their children; the father was in steady employment and he realised the need to change his past pattern of drunken and criminal behaviour. Accordingly, the parents' decision not to consent fell within the band of reasonable decisions which parents in their section of society and their circumstances might make. Therefore their withholding of consent was not unreasonable. *In re E.B.*

(H.C.) [1985] N.I.128

2. —— **Consent** — *Refusal — Infant placed for adoption — Marriage of parents subsequent to placement for adoption — Consequent legitimisation of infant — Parents seeking re-registration of child — Consent of mother to adoption — Whether consent to be dispensed with — Constitution — Family and education — Presumption of constitutionality — Statute — Interpretation — Welfare of infant — Whether infant's welfare presumptively to be found within the family — Legitimacy Act,* 1931, (*No.* 13), *Schedule — Adoption Act,* 1964, (*No.* 2), *s.2 — Adoption Act,* 1974, (*No. 24), s.3 — Guardianship of Infants Act,* 1964, (*No.* 7), *ss.* 2, 3, — *Constitution of Ireland,* 1937, *Arts.* 41, 42.5.] The infant girl who was the subject of these proceedings was placed in foster care by her natural mother one week after her birth on the 25th September, 1982. The mother took this course because at the time she was worried about the effect on the child of being brought up by an unmarried mother. Although the mother knew the infant's father, a widower with grown-up children, she did not wish to marry him solely because of her pregnancy. The infant was placed for adoption within three months of birth. The adopting parents, both in their twenties, already had one adopted child. The natural mother later married the father of the infant, and they then applied pursuant to the provisions of the Legitimacy Act, 1931, for the infant's birth to be re-registered. The natural mother, in correspondence with the adoption society, refused to give her consent to an order for the infant's adoption. The adopting parents issued proceedings claiming that the natural mother's consent to adoption should be dispensed with pursuant to the provisions of the Adoption Act, 1974. The natural parents issued further proceedings pursuant to the provisions of the Guardianship of Infants Act, 1964, in which they sought custody of the infant; the adopting parents issued cross-claims seeking similar relief. The High

ADOPTION—*continued.*

Court (Lynch J.) granted an order, pending determination of the proceedings, restraining re-registration of the infant's birth. The natural parents did not challenge the suitability of the adopting parents to provide a secure and stable home for the infant, and it was established in evidence that the infant and the adopting parents' other child had formed a close relationship. The adopting parents presented medical evidence relating to the natural parents, indicating that the father suffered from blood pressure and a partially detached retina, while the mother suffered from overstrain which was occasioned by her care for her own ageing mother whom she had nursed up to her death, which was prior to her becoming pregnant with the infant. Psychiatric evidence at the trial indicated that there was a risk of long-term psychological harm to the infant if custody was transferred from the adopting parents to the natural parents. At the date of the hearings in the High Court the natural mother was expecting another child.

Section 3 of the Guardianship of Infants Act, 1964, provides that in any proceedings where the custody, guardianship or upbringing of an infant is in question the court "shall regard the welfare of the infant as the first and paramount consideration." Section 2 of the Act defines the word "welfare" as comprising "the religious and moral, intellectual, physical and social welfare of the infant." Section 3 of the Adoption Act, 1974, provides that in any case where a person has applied for an adoption order and where the consent of any person is required for such an order to be made, the court may dispense with the consent of that person "if it is satisfied that it is in the best interests of the child so to do." This provision allows the court to dispense with the consent of the mother to the making of an adoption order. Section 2 of the Adoption Act, 1964, provided for the adoption of a child whose birth had been legitimised by the subsequent remarriage of its parents where re-registration had not taken place pursuant to the Legitimacy Act, 1931, and, when read in conjunction with s. 3 of the Act of 1974, it granted power to the court to dispense with the consent of the natural father where the natural father consented to the placing of the infant for adoption. **Held** by Lynch J., in granting custody of the infant to the adopting parents, but refusing to dispense with the parents' consent to adoption, 1, it would not be clearly necessary for the welfare, or in the best interests, of the infant for the court to dispense with the consent to adoption of the natural mother in view of the existence of a stable and prosperous home for her with the natural parents, since the provisions of s. 3 of the Act of 1974 must be read in the light of the natural mother's continuing right to refuse or withdraw

ADOPTION—*continued.*

her consent, and in the circumstances the court should take account of the fact that the marriage of the natural parents resulted in the infant forming part of a family within the meaning of Articles 41 and 42 of the Constitution. 2. Having regard to the limited ability of the natural father to object to the placement of the child for adoption, there was a heavy onus on the adopting parents to prove such consent in order to invoke the jurisdiction of the court arising under the combined effects of s. 2 of the Adoption Act, 1964 and s. 3 of the Adoption Act, 1974, and in view of the father's constant willingness to be responsible for the infant, an assertion of acquiescence in the mother's original decision to place the child was not sufficient to discharge this onus of proof. 3. Having regard to the test of the primacy of the welfare of the child stated in s. 3 of the Guardianship of Infants Act, 1964, custody of the infant should remain with the adopting parents because the evidence presented to the court as to the risk of long term psychological harm if custody was awarded to the natural parents was sufficiently proximate to outweigh the contrary factors such as the anomalous legal position of the infant as the legitimised child of the natural parents.

On appeal by the natural parents as to the custody issue, it was **Held** by the Supreme Court (Finlay C.J., Griffin, Hederman, McCarthy and O'Hanlon JJ.), in remitting the custody issue to the High Court, 1, the test as to the welfare of the child, stated in s. 3 of the Guardianship of Infants Act, 1964, must, if possible, be given a meaning consistent with the infant's rights as stated in Articles 41 and 42 as a member of the family, in view of the subsequent marriage of her parents. 2. Notwithstanding the presumption of validity attaching to its provisions or the absence of a challenge to the constitutional validity of s. 3 of the Act of 1964, the court cannot supplant the right to education by the family and parents conferred on the infant by Article 42, s. 1 unless there is established to the satisfaction of the court the exceptional circumstances referred to in Article 42, s. 5, arising from a failure for moral or physical reasons on the part of the parents to provide that education, and in the circumstances s. 3 ought to be construed as involving a constitutional presumption that the welfare of the child, as defined in s. 2 of the Act, is to be found within the family unless there are compelling reasons why this cannot be achieved, or the evidence establishes an exceptional case as envisaged by Article 42. s. 5, and in this light the matter should be reconsidered on the basis of this test. *Dicta* of Henchy J. in *In re J., an Infant* [1966] I.R. 295 approved. *Dicta* of O'Higgins C.J. in *J.* v. *D.* (Unreported, Supreme Court, 22nd June, 1977) considered. On the re-hearing

ADOPTION—*continued.*

of the custody matter in the High Court, when additional evidence regarding the effects of transferring custody of the infant to the parents was given in the context, *inter alia,* of the passage of time, it was **Held** by Lynch J., in awarding custody to the natural parents, having regard to the evidence that the natural parents could provide a good home for the infant if custody was transferred to them, it had not been established in evidence that any possible adverse effects would arise such as to rebut the constitutional presumption that the infant's welfare was to be found within the family or as to amount to compelling reasons why this could not be achieved by the parents, even accepting that they might understimate the difficulties involved in this. *In re J.H., an infant; K.C.* v. *An Bord Uchtála*

(H.C., S.C.) [1985] I.R.375; [1986] ILRM 65; [1985] ILRM 302

3. —— **Consent** — *Validity — Full and free knowledge — Evidence — Appeal — Findings of fact — Oral hearing — Transcript of evidence — Primary and secondary facts — Whether appellate court entitled to substitute own inference of fact — Adoption Act,* 1974, (*No.* 24), *s.*3.] M. was born in March, 1980. M.'s mother was married but separated and her husband was not M.'s father. Upon advice and counsel from an adoption society the mother, shortly after the birth, signed a form consenting to M.'s placement for adoption. Upon her discovery in July, 1980, that M. had been placed with the plaintiffs, the mother took measures and made representations to the adoption society, the plaintiffs and the defendant for the return of the child. In April, 1982, she attended upon the defendant and gave evidence as to the circumstances of M.'s birth and informed the defendant that she had no intention of consenting to adoption. In January, 1985, the defendant deemed M. eligible for adoption. Upon request made to her through the adoption society in May, 1985, the mother refused to consent to the legalisation of the adoption order. The plaintiffs, by special summons, sought orders under s. 3 of the Adoption Act, 1974, granting them an adoption order and dispensing with the mother's consent for such order. Upon full plenary hearing on oral evidence in the High Court it was **Held** by Barron J., in refusing the orders sought, that on the evidence the mother's agreement to place for adoption, which freely made, was without full knowledge of its consequences and this deprived her of the capacity to make a fully informed, free decision. *S.* v. *Eastern Health Board* (Unreported, High Court, Finlay P., 28 February, 1979) applied.

On appeal by the plaintiffs, it was **Held** by the Supreme Court (Henchy, Griffin and Hederman JJ., McCarthy and Gannon JJ. dissenting), in allowing the appeal and granting the orders sought, 1, that on appeal while it would not normally disturb the findings of primary or basic facts, which depended on the assessment made by the trial judge of the credibility and quality of witnesses and the weight to be attached to their evidence in the oral hearing, the court might substitute its own findings of secondary facts, being findings made by evaluations of and inferences from the primary facts, if it considered the inferences made by the trial judge to be incorrect.

Principles in *Northern Bank Finance* v. *Charlton* [1979] I.R. 149 and *Benmax* v. *Austin Motor Co. Ltd.* [1955] A.C. 370 followed. 2. That the mother's state of mind at the relevant time was to be inferred from what was said or done or left unsaid or undone having regard to the proximate relevant circumstances before and after the signing of the form for placement. 3. That the proper conclusion from the undisputed primary facts was that the mother at the time of the placement had given her full and free consent to adoption. *Per* McCarthy, J. (dissenting): That the state of a person's mind is itself a primary fact and the court on appeal should not interfere with the trial judge's finding. *Per* Gannon J. (dissenting): That the issues of free and full knowledge essential to consent were so personal to the mother and witnesses to those facts that the judicial findings upon them were particularly dependent upon the *voir dire.* The transcript of the evidence could reasonably support the findings of the trial judge. *In re M.; J.M. and G.M.* v. *An Bord Uchtála*

(H.C., S.C.) [1987] I.R.510; [1988] ILRM 203

4. —— **Documents** — *Discovery — Prospective parents applying for an order dispensing with consent of mother — Prospective parents seeking discovery of certain documents — Such documents being subject to a claim of privilege — Whether in best interests of child to disclose — Whether adoption society entitled to rely on s.*8 *— Adoption Act,* 1976, (*No.* 29), *s.*8.] The proceedings in this case involved, *inter alia,* a claim by the plaintiffs, who were prospective adoptive parents, for an order dispensing with the consent of the mother, who was one of the defendants, and an order for interim custody, and a claim by the mother for custody. The Adoption Board and the Adoption Society were amongst the other defendants. In affidavits of discovery filed on behalf of the Board and the Society privilege was claimed in relation to certain documents based on s. 8 of the Adoption Act, 1976. This section prohibits an order for the discovery, inspection, production or copying of any book, document or record of the Board unless a court is satisfied that it is in the best interests of any child concerned to

ADOPTION—*continued.*

do so. **Held** by Finlay P. making an order for the discovery of certain documents which were both relevant and non-privileged s. 8 of the Act of 1976 requires that the confidentiality of the Adoption Board's papers should be maintained unless it is established to the satisfaction of the court as a matter of probability that the best interests of a child concerned in a particular case require their discovery or production. Once that has been established there cannot arise any question of balancing the interests of an individual child concerned in a particular case against the general proceedings and efficiency of the activities of the Board. The only documents which should be discovered were those which would enable either the prospective adopters or the natural mother to be aware of evidence relevant to the issues, i.e. suitability as custodians of the child, which could be adduced or which would enable either of the parties concerned to adequately cross-examine witnesses. It was unnecessary for the court to examine documents which constituted a form of hearing because they could not be used to obtain admissible evidence or for cross-examination of possible witnesses. The argument by the Adoption Society that they were covered by s. 8 of the 1976 Act and that documents prepared by them for submission to the Board were also so covered were rejected. It was not necessary to decide upon the claim to privilege made by the Society in reliance on confidentiality because any such privilege would be in the plaintiffs who had waived it. *S.M.* v. *G.M.*

(H.C.) [1985] ILRM 186

5. —— **Exclusion** — *Widower — Infant placed for adoption — Final consent signed — Death of prospective adoptive mother before adoption order made — Legislation providing that, whereas a widow could obtain the adoption order, widower could not — Whether such provision constitutionally valid — Constitution of Ireland,* 1937, *Arts.* 40.1, 40.2.1 — *Adoption Act,* 1952, (*No.* 25), *s.*13(1) — *Adoption Act,* 1974, (*No.* 24), *s.*5 (1).] The plaintiff and his wife obtained custody of a little boy in March, 1983, in expectation of the making of an adoption order once the consent of the boy's mother had been obtained. Six months later, and before the adoption order could be made, the plaintiff's wife died in a motoring accident. By virtue of s. 5(1) of the Adoption Act, 1974, the plaintiff, as a childless widower, was no longer a person in whose favour an adoption order could then be made. Even if he had had another child in his custody, his right to an adoption order would have been subject, according to a further proviso in s. 5(1) of the 1974 Act, to renewed consent from the boy's

ADOPTION—*continued.*

mother. Evidence was given that the little boy's welfare was emphatically best served by his remaining with the plaintiff. The boy's mother was, after initial contrary indications, in favour of her child being adopted by the plaintiff. The plaintiff accordingly sought a declaration that s. 5(1) of the 1974 Act was invalid having regard to Article 40.1 of the Constitution. **Held** by McMahon J., 1, that the ineligibility of a childless widower to adopt a child already in his custody was unreasonable and unjust, and that the priviso in that behalf in s. 5(1) of the Adoption Act, 1974, was repugnant to Article 40.1 of the Constitution. 2. That the requirement in sub-para. (ii) of the same section requiring special consent to precede the making of an adoption order in favour of a widower was similarly repugnant. 3. That the offending provisions could lawfully be severed from the rest of the section in which they occurred. *T. O'G. v. Attorney General*

(H.C.) [1985] ILRM 61

6. —— **Placement** — *Location — Mother consenting to put child up for adoption — Fosterage arranged — Foster parents seeking order of custody — Mother wanting child placed for adoption outside the county in which she was residing — Foster parents living short distance from the mother — Mother applying for an order of habeas corpus — Welfare of infant — Constitution of Ireland,* 1937, *Art.* 40.4.2. — *Guardianship of Infants Act,* 1964, (*No.* 7), *s.*3.] The mother of an illegitimate child, expecting that her child would be placed for adoption outside the county in which she was living, as had been explained to her by a social worker of the Health Board, consented to having her child fostered. The Health Board arranged fosterage with foster parents who lived in the same rural community. Almost two months after the birth of the child and after the child had been fostered, the mother gave her consent to the placement of her child for adoption but made it clear that she did not want the child adopted in the county in which she resided. At the beginning of January, 1982, the foster parents applied to the Health Board to have the child adopted but the Health Board at the time neglected to forward the application to An Bord Uchtála. In April, 1982, the mother learned of this adoption application and objected. Subsequently, the Health Board unsuccessfully tried to recover custody of the child from the foster parents so that the child could be placed for adoption in another county in accordance with the wishes of the mother. The mother applied to the High Court for an absolute order of habeas corpus on the ground that the foster parents were unlawfully detaining the child. In the second action the foster parents sought an order pursuant to s. 3 of the Adoption

ADOPTION—*continued.*

Act, 1974, granting them custody of the child and authorising An Bord Uchtála to dispense with the consent of the mother required by the Adoption Acts 1952 to 1976, to the making of an adoption order in favour of the foster parents. **Held** by McWilliam J. in refusing the order of habeas corpus and making an order disposing with the mother's consent:—

In considering an application for an order of habeas corpus it is essential to consider on whose behalf it was made. In the instant case it was made on behalf of the child. The rights of the mother to have the care of the child and of the child to be with its mother which were emphasised in *G.* v. *An Bord Uchtála* [1980] I.R. 32 did not arise since the mother was rejecting her right to personal custody of the child. Since she had abdicated her rights and duties with regard to the child, the court was only concerned with ascertaining what was best for the welfare of the child as provided by section 3 of the Guardianship of Infants Act, 1964. The medical evidence established that the child was well assimilated in the family of the foster parents and to move the child away from the family would have an adverse effect on the child. The rights of the foster parents were not prejudiced by the failure of the Health Board to forward their adoption application to An Bord Uchtála at the appropriate time, since they had applied for an adoption order by completing all the requisite forms for the Health Board. *State (M.G.)* v. *A.H., H.* v. *An Bord Uchtála*

(H.C.) [1984] ILRM 237

ADVERSE POSSESSION

—— **Joint tenants** — *Next-of-kin of deceased owner remaining in possession — Whether interest of other next-of-kin defeated by adverse possession — Whether shares of those excluded from possession acquired as joint tenants or as tenants in common — Administration of Estates Act,* 1959 (*No.*8), *ss.*13, 22 — *Succession Act,* 1965, (*No.* 27), *s.* 125(1).] M.M. was the registered owner of the lands comprised in three folios of the Register, County Kilkenny. Her husband, who may have been the actual owner of these lands, died on 11 June, 1913, his wife M.M. and six children (namely J.M., Ph.M., A.M., P.M., E.M., and the plaintiff) surviving him. M.M., J.M., P.M., and A.M., left the lands sometime prior to 1940 leaving Ph. M., K.M., and the plaintiff in occupation of the lands. M.M. died testate in 1961 having made a will purporting to leave her interest in the lands to her son Ph.M. Ph.M. died on 29 April, 1983, having made a will purporting to leave his interest in the lands to the defendant, the sole executor named therein. K.M. died intestate in 1986. **Held** The interest which M.M. had in these lands, and any interest

ADVERSE POSSESSION—*continued.*

which J.M., P.M., and A.M. might have had in these lands was barred by the adverse possession of Ph.M., K.M., and the plaintiff over the long period of years from c. 1935 on. Ph.M., K.M., and the plaintiff acquired the shares of M.M., J.M., P.M., and A.M. in these lands as *joint tenants.* Accordingly by right of survivorship, the plaintiff has now acquired title to those interests, i.e. the interests of M.M., J.M., P.M., and A.M. who were excluded from the lands for the statutory period. Further, and contrary to the weight of legal authority, Ph.M., A.M., and the plaintiff also occupied the lands as *joint tenants* in relation to their own shares. Accordingly Ph.M., K.M., and the plaintiff became entitled by long possession to be registered as full owners of these lands as joint tenants and not as tenants in common, and on the death of Ph.M. and K.M. without having severed their respective joint tenancies, the plaintiff became entitled, by right of survivorship, to the entire interest in these lands. *Maher* v. *Maher*

(H.C.) [1987] ILRM 582

—— *Animus possidendi* — Intended user by owner to build upon lands — Whether defendant knew intended user — Whether title of plaintiff defeated.
see **Limitation of Actions,** 1

—— Limitation of actions — Documentary tenancy from week to week — Tenant paying no rent for 24 years — Negotiations for purchase by tenant of landlord's interest in property — Landlord's demands for payment of rent ignored by tenant — Landlord serving notice to quit — Limitation of actions — Ejectment — Accrual of right of action — Abandonment of tenancy — Whether determination of tenancy could be presumed from landlord's conduct — Whether landlord's action for recovery of possession statute barred.
see **Landlord and Tenant,** 19

ADVERTISEMENT

—— Betting licence — Certificate of suitability advertised in newspaper — Whether a newspaper circulating in the area.
see **Gaming and Lotteries,** 2

—— Planning application
see **Constitution,** 45
Planning, 3

ADVOCATE
see **Counsel**

AFFIDAVIT — Admissibility as evidence —

AFFIDAVIT—*continued.*

Northern Ireland — Affidavits sworn for use in Republic.
see **Criminal Law,** 11

AGE LIMITS — Appointment to post — Discrimination — Sex or marital status.
see **Employer and Employee,** 13

AGENCY
see also **Partnership**

1. —— **Agreement** — *Sole selling agent — Whether principal entitled to refuse to pay commission where sale completed without assistance of agent — Whether agent acting solely in connection with sale — Whether agency arose only in future on happening of certain events — Whether intention of parties to be taken from documents only — Whether term to be implied into agreement — Whether consistent with expressed intention of parties.*

Restitution — Quasi-contract- Quantum meruit — Reasonable sum for services rendered — Whether relief possible where parties have entered into concluded agreement.] In 1980 the defendants entered into a written agreement with the plaintiffs giving them the 'sole selling agency' for the sale of their land. The plaintiffs held themselves out to be lobbyists and estate agents and the parties hoped that the land would be rezoned for industrial purposes by Dublin County Council which was then reviewing the county development plan. The agreement stated that it was the defendants' intention 'to market these lands at the earliest possible date after the hoped-for rezoning', the defendants accepting this 'subject to the land being and remaining rezoned "industrial"'. In 1982 the defendants sold their land without any assistance from the plaintiffs. In 1983 the Council passed a motion incorporating a provisional decision to rezone the lands for industrial use but this decision was not confirmed, as required, by a second motion. The plaintiffs claimed a commisison on the sale and alternatively a sum as reasonable remuneration for their services. **Held** by Costello J. in dismissing the claim, 1, the contract between the parties, which consisted of the written terms agreed in 1980, envisaged that the plaintiffs' agency would arise only when the lands were rezoned, and so long as they so remained, and not before; and that it would arise on the passing of the first motion by the Council rather than on the passing of the final motion confirming the rezoning. 2. While the fact that the plaintiffs were 'sole selling agents' would not automatically prevent the defendants from selling the land without any obligation to pay the plaintiffs a commission, the parties must have intended that such a sale could not defeat the plaintiffs' claim

AGENCY—*continued.*

to a commission through their efforts to seek a rezoning of the land. *Murphy Buckley and Keogh Ltd.* v. *Pye (Ireland) Ltd* [1971] I.R. 57 discussed. 3. It would not be consistent with the expressed intention of the parties to imply into the agreement a term that the defendants would not sell the land without the plaintiffs' consent prior to the land being rezoned where, as happened, there was a two year delay in considering the rezoning. 4. The plaintiffs were not entitled to a sum for their services since the courts would only make such awards on a *quantum meruit* where work was done at the request of one party to a contemplated contract which was never in fact entered into. *Folens & Co. Ltd.* v. *Minister for Education* [1984] ILRM 265 distinguished. *G.F. Galvin Estates Ltd.* v. *Hedigan*
(H.C.) [1985] ILRM 295

2. —— **Authority** — *Ostensible authority — Whether principal made representation to third party — Whether agency in existence — Third party given use of motor vehicle by employee of owner — Third party involved in motor accident — Third party negligent — Whether owner liable.*] The second defendant, a garage owner (the seller) sold to the first defendant (the buyer) a motor car which, after proving defective, was taken back for repairs. The buyer was given the use of a Renault car until his own car was repaired. A few days later he returned the car but the seller was not present in the garage. A mechanic on duty informed the buyer that the Fiat would be ready that evening and when he said he required a car immediately the mechanic let him have a Mini car which was standing in the garage. Two days later the buyer, driving the Mini, negligently collided with the plaintiff as she was walking on the public road and she suffered severe injuries. The plaintiff sued the seller and the buyer for damages. Her claim against the buyer was settled but as his driving of the Mini was not covered by insurance the issue arose as to whether she was confined to recovering damages under the Motor Insurance Bureau scheme or whether she could recover against the seller's insurance. At the trial of a separate issue in the High Court the jury found that at the time of the accident the buyer was driving with the consent of the seller. The seller appealed and the net question was whether the mechanic was acting as agent for the vendor when he allowed the purchaser to take the Mini. **Held** by the Supreme Court (Henchy, Griffin and Hederman JJ.) in allowing the appeal, 1, the mechanic was without actual authority to lend the Mini to the buyer. 2. On the question as to whether the mechanic had ostensible authority to lend the car, there was no representation of any kind by the seller to the buyer that the

AGENCY—*continued.*

mechanic had authority to lend the car. 3. In lending the car to the buyer the mechanic was not the vendor's agent and the vendor could not be held liable for the purchaser's negligent driving. *Dicta* in *Armagas Ltd v Mundogas SA* [1985] 3 All E.R. 795 applied. *Kett* v. *Shannon* **(S.C.) [1987] ILRM 364**

—— Agreement — Auctioneer — Public auction — Fees — Auction cancelled — Vendor subsequently selling premises by private treaty — Whether auctioneer entitled to fees.
see **Auctioneers and Estate Agents**

—— Contract — Privity — Renewal — Option to renew agreement — Agent claiming privity with party to separate agreement — Whether separate agreements to be considered as single arrangement — Whether agency terminated on reasonable notice.
see **Company,** 2

AGRICULTURE
see also **Animals**

—— Abattoir — Intensification of use — Absence of planning permission.
see **Planning,** 29

—— Agricultural land — Valuation — Constitution — Statute — Validity — Valuation carried out between 1852 and 1866 — Valuation unrelated to present-day circumstances — Whether unjust attack on property rights — Whether arbitrary and unjust discrimination.
see **Rating and Valuation,** 1

—— Contract — Breach — Supply of potatoes to UK — Whether contract void for illegality — Clause providing that in the event of import/export controls the potatoes would be supplied from Northern Ireland.
see **Contract,** 2

—— Contract — Mistake — Supply of seed potatoes — Crop failure — Whether contract rendered void — Whether implied obligations remaining.
see **Contract,** 8

—— Excise duty on livestock — European Communities — Whether measure having effect equivalent to a customs duty — Common organisation of the markets — Whether duty *ultra vires* as

AGRICULTURE—*continued.*

unreasonable — Whether decision on European law required.
see **European Communities,** 1

—— European Communities — Milk levy — Regulations giving effect to EC milk levy — Such regulations having retrospective effect — Whether unjust — Whether unjustified attack on property rights — Whether any such infringement necessitated by membership of the European Community.
see **Constitution,** 35

—— Revenue — Farming — Capital gains tax — Land purchased by taxpayer and let on conacre — Land sold and proceeds used by taxpayer to purchase other land — Whether taxpayer entitled to postponement of liability to capital gains tax.
see **Revenue,** 6

—— Revenue — Farming — Income tax — Animal husbandry — Exemption — Partnership — Fattening of pigs in purpose-built housing — Whether constitutes farming — Whether exempt.
see **Revenue,** 36

ALIENS
Deportation order. Nos. 1, 2
Landing permission. Nos. 3, 4
Settlement permission. No. 5

1. —— **Deportation order** — *Alien marrying before order took effect — Extension to permission to stay — Constitution — Family — Whether order in conflict with rights of family — Whether aliens entitled to benefit of provisions of Constitution relating to family — Whether order must comply with natural justice — Aliens Order,* 1946 *(S.R. & O. No.* 395) — *Aliens (Amendment) Order,* 1975 (*S.I. No.* 128) — *Aliens Act,* 1935 (*No.* 14) — *Irish Nationality and Citizenship Act,* 1956, (*No.* 26), *ss.* 15, 16 — *Constitution of Ireland,* 1937, *Arts.* 41, 42.] The first-named plaintiff, a native of China, arrived in this country in 1978 and worked in a restaurant. As a result of a serious incident in 1979, the Department of Justice on behalf of the Minister informed the first-named plaintiff that he must leave the country. Later that year the first-named plaintiff married the second-named plaintiff. They had three children and his wife was expecting a fourth child. Steps to implement the decision in relation to permission for the first-named plaintiff to remain in this country as an alien were not taken. No decision was taken to request him to leave the country and, instead, from time to time, he obtained permits which were granted to him

ALIENS—*continued.*

by the Department of Labour allowing him to continue to work. In 1981, the first-named plaintiff made a formal application to the Minister for a certificate of naturalisation in addition to an application to carry on business as a self-employed person. Meetings between him and officials of the Department of Justice took place followed by correspondence. His application for a certificate of naturalisation was refused and he was informed that he must leave the country but a stay for a further three months was allowed to enable him to wind up his business affairs. Proceedings were instituted by the plaintiffs and a number of declarations were sought, *inter alia,* that, 1, the 1946 and 1975 Aliens Orders did not empower the Minister in view of Articles 40, 41 and 42 of the Constitution to control the duration of stay and/or engagement in business of the first-named plaintiff within the State and otherwise control or prohibit his movements within and/or departure from and re-entry into the State. 2. The second-named plaintiff had a right under Article 41 to have her family unit protected in its constitution and in particular to be allowed to cohabit with her husband and to reside within the State. 3. The first-named plaintiff, as the lawful spouse of the second-named plaintiff and father of the third and fourth-named plaintiffs was entitled to the protection of Articles 9, 40, 41 and 42. 4. Ss. 15 and 16 of the Irish Nationality and Citizenship Act, 1956, were repugnant to Article 9. 5. The action of the Minister in refusing the permission of the first-named plaintiff violated the principles of the Constitution and natural justice. **Held** by Costello J. in dismissing the action, 1, the rights given to the 'family' were not absolute and the decisions of the Minister and the provisions of the Aliens Act and the orders made under it were permissible restrictions. 2. If the Minister had the power to order an alien's departure from the State, then if he was married to an Irish citizen, no entitlement to the declaration sought could exist. 3. The court did not need to decide whether aliens could claim constitutional protection of their rights because the claim was based on a misunderstanding of the first-named plaintiff's rights. 4. No right of the second-named plaintiff was being infringed by ss. 15 and 16 of the Act of 1956. 5. The Minister was required to carry out the rules of natural justice and to adopt fair procedures and he had done so. *Pok Sun Shum* v. *Ireland*

(H.C.) [1986] ILRM 593

2. —— **Deportation order** — *Ministerial discretion — Alien married to Irish citizen — Personal rights — Family — Aliens Order,* 1946 (*S.R. and O. No.* 395) — *Aliens (Amendment) Order,* 1975, (*S.I. No.* 128), *reg.* 13 — *Aliens Act,* 1935

ALIENS—*continued.*

(*No.* 14) — *Constitution of Ireland,* 1937, *Arts.* 40, 41, 42. *Constitution — Equality — Discrimination on basis of sex — Naturalisation — Irish Nationality and Citizenship Act,* 1956 (*No.* 26), *ss.* 8, 16 — *Constitution of Ireland,* 1937, *Arts.* 9, 40.] Regulation 13 of the Aliens Order, 1946 (as amended) provides, *inter alia,* that the Minister for Justice may, if he deems it conducive to public good so to do, make a deportation order requiring an alien to leave and remain out of the State. On the 11th June, 1979, the first plaintiff, an alien, was permitted entry to the State for one month, provided he did not take up employment. He remained in the State after 11th July, 1979, and engaged in employment until August, 1982, when he registered for unemployment assistance. The second plaintiff, an Irish citizen, married the first plaintiff on 26th June, 1981. On the 15th March, 1983, pursuant to the above regulation the Minister made an order refusing the first plaintiff permission to stay in the jurisdiction beyond 30th April, 1983, unless he could produce documentary proof of his ability to maintain himself and any dependants from his own resources. The plaintiffs sought an order prohibiting the first plaintiff's deportation relying in essence on the proposition that the first plaintiff had changed his status of alien by marriage. They argued *inter alia,* that the second plaintiff and third plaintiff were entitled to the society of the first plaintiff in the State, that the Aliens Act, 1935, was inconsistent with Articles 40, 41 and 42 of the Constitution insofar as it applied to male aliens who had married Irish citizens and who, *bona fide,* intended to continue to reside with their families within the State, that an order for the deportation of the first plaintiff and the exercise of the powers to make such an order under the Aliens Orders of 1946 and 1975 was *ultra vires* the powers conferred by the Aliens Act, 1935, because it infringed the constitutional rights of all three plaintiffs under Articles 40, 41 and 42. The defendants disputed the *locus standi* of the plaintiffs and their entitlement to challenge the constitutionality of the above Acts and Orders. **Held** by Gannon J., in dismissing the plaintiffs' claim, 1, that the interests of the common good of the State necessitates that the State should have control of the entry of aliens, their departure, their activities and their duration of stay within the State. The protection of such fundamental right of the State permits restrictions on the exercise of an individual's personal rights and consequently such rights are not capable of consideration entirely independently of the overall provisions of the Constitution. Accordingly the State's fundamental rights could prevail over the related constitutional rights of members of a family. 2. That the right to reside in a particular

ALIENS—*continued.*

place of the individual's choice was not a fundamental or constitutional right of a citizen, whether married or single. 3. That although the first plaintiff was by virtue of s. 4 of the Aliens Act, 1935, amenable to the laws of the State in like manner as was a citizen and his marital and familial status would be recognised and protected by the State, nonetheless while being so amenable the State would apply to him sanctions for non-compliance with the law. *Pok Sun Shum* v. *Ireland* [1986] ILRM 593 considered. 4. That, since the first plaintiff was in breach of the laws of the State an order by the Minister deporting the first plaintiff, if made in due exercise of the discretion vested in him by the Aliens Act, 1935, and the statutory orders thereunder, would not infringe the constitutional rights of the plaintiffs, as the scope of the discretion was expressed in sufficiently wide terms as to take into account the marital status of the alien and the statutory orders of 1946 and 1975 and any implementation thereof by the Minister were not *ultra vires* the authority conferred by the Aliens Act, 1935, nor inconsistent with the Constitution. *Osheku* v. *Ireland*

(H.C.) [1986] I.R.733; [1987] ILRM 330

3. —— **Landing Permission** — *Refusal of leave to land — Absence of visa — Alien married in Ireland — Alien barred from matrimonial home — Constitution — Personal rights — Habeas corpus — Procedure specified by Constitution — Aliens Order,* 1946 (*S.R. and O. No.* 395), *art.* 5, *clause* 2 — *Aliens (Amendment) Order,* 1975 (*S.I. No.* 128), *art.* 3 — *Aliens Act,* 1935 (*No.* 14) — *Constitution of Ireland,* 1937, *Arts.* 40.4.2, 41, 42.] Article 5, clause 2, of the Aliens Order, 1946, as inserted by article 3 of the Aliens (Amendment) Order, 1975, provides that an immigration officer may refuse leave to land to an alien, provided that the officer is satisfied that the alien came from a place outside the State other than Great Britain or Northern Ireland, in circumstances where *inter alia* the alien is not in a position to support himself and is not in possession of a valid Irish visa. Article 40 s. 4, sub-s. 2 of the Constitution provides that where any person makes complaint to the High Court, alleging that he is being unlawfully detained, the High Court shall forthwith enquire into the said complaint, and may order the custodian of such person to produce the body of such person before the court, and to certify in writing the grounds of his detention. The said Article further provides that, unless satisfied that such person is being detained in accordance with the law, the High Court, upon production of his body before the court, shall order his release. Article 41 of the Constitution guarantees, *inter alia,* to protect the family in its constitution and authority, and to

ALIENS—*continued.*

guard with special care the institution of marriage. Article 42 of the Constitution acknowledges the family as the primary and natural educator of the child. The prosecutor was a Moroccan national, married to an Irish citizen. Pursuant to the provisions of the said order he was served with a notice of refusal of leave to land at Dublin Airport and accordingly, was detained in Fitzgibbon Street Garda Station, pending his removal from the State. The grounds for refusal were stated in the notice to be the prosecutor's lack of a valid Irish visa and his inability to support himself. Pursuant to the provisions of Article 40, s. 4, sub-s. 2 of the Constitution, the prosecutor made complaint to the High Court, alleging that his detention was not in accordance with the law. He stated on affidavit that his reason for coming to this country was in order to reside here permanently with his wife and family and that he owned the family residence at Coolock, Co. Dublin. An order of habeas corpus was made requiring the respondent to produce the body of the prosecutor before the Court. Upon compliance with the said order, it emerged in evidence, *inter alia,* that the family home of the prosecutor was the property of Dublin Corporation, and further, that the prosecutor's wife possessed a barring order against him. **Held** by Barrington J., in ruling that the prosecutor's detention was in accordance with the law, 1, that the reasons given by the immigration officer were valid and sufficient reasons for refusal of leave to land. 2. That the fact that the prosecutor did not own the family residence and that his wife had obtained a barring order against him was relevant in considering whether the prosecutor could support himself. 3. That a non-citizen is entitled to rely upon Articles 41 and 42 of the Constitution. *Northampton County Council* v. *A.B.F.* [1982] ILRM 164 considered. 4. That the prosecutor could not automatically claim the rights guaranteed to the family under Article 41 of the Constitution, since his family was divided. *State (Bouzagou)* v. *Fitzgibbon St. Garda Station*

(H.C.) [1985] I.R.426; [1986] ILRM 98

4. —— **Landing permission** — *Refusal of leave to land — Absence of visa — Discretion of immigration officer — Refusal based on language deficiency and absence of visa — Discretion improperly exercised — Constitution — Personal rights — Habeas corpus — Aliens (Amendment) Order,* 1975 (*S.I. No.* 128), *art.* 3, *Sixth Schedule — Aliens (Amendment) Order,* 1985 (*S.I. No.* 154) — *Constitution of Ireland,* 1937, *Art.* 40.4.2.] Article 3 of the Aliens (Amendment) Order, 1975, provides that an immigration officer may refuse leave to land to an alien, coming from a place outside the State other than Great Britain

ALIENS—*continued.*

or Northern Ireland, where the alien is not a citizen of a State specified in the sixth schedule of the order and is not in possession of a valid Irish visa. Under the Aliens (Amendment) Order, 1985, the sixth schedule to the Order of 1975 was amended by the deletion of Sri Lanka. The result of this was that as from the 31 May, 1985, a citizen of Sri Lanka could be refused leave to land if not in possession of a valid Irish visa. The prosecutors were citizens of Sri Lanka. They arrived at Dublin Airport on the 23 June, 1985, and did not possess valid Irish visas. Pursuant to the provisions of the Order of 1985 they were each served with a notice of refusal of leave to land at Dublin Airport and, accordingly, were detained in Fitzgibbon Street Garda Station, pending their removal from the State. The grounds for refusal were stated in the notice to be the lack of valid Irish visas. Pursuant to the provisions of Article 40, s. 4, sub-s. 2 of the Constitution, the prosecutors sought orders of habeas corpus, alleging that their detention was not in accordance with the law. An order of habeas corpus was made. It was argued by the respondent that the remedy of habeas corpus was not available to the prosecutors. The prosecutors argued that the provisions of s. 3, sub-s. 4 of the Order of 1975 had not been complied with as there was no evidence of any 'arrest' as required by the sub-section. The respondent argued that where jurisdiction to detain has been established, relief by way of habeas corpus is not available unless the procedure has been so flawed by basic defect as to render the detention one which is not 'in accordance with law.' It emerged in evidence, *inter alia,* that the prosecutors had been booked to study and had paid fees to two different schools for the purpose of learning English. The immigration officer in his affidavit averred to the fact that in his opinion, neither of the prosecutors was likely to benefit from this projected course of study as they understood very little English. **Held** by Egan J. in finding that the detention of the prosecutors was not in accordance with law and ordering their release, 1, that the remedy of habeas corpus can be sought by 'any person' whether a citizen of the State or not, under Article 40, s. 4, sub-s. 2 of the Constitution. 2. That even though the words 'arrest' and 'detain' are separate words in the sub-section, once an involuntary detention has been proved it must necessarily have been preceded by an arrest. 3. That is was not necessary for a prosecutor to establish a procedural defect in the detention before relief by way of habeas corpus could be sought. *The State (Royle)* v. *Kelly* [1974] I.R. 259 considered. 4. That although the Order of 1975 gave a discretionary power of detention to an immigration officer, the law could not justify an exercise of such discretion based on an opinion

ALIENS—*continued.*

that the detainees have a poor knowledge of the English language. *State (Kugan)* v. *O'Rourke (Fitzgibbon St. Garda Station)*

(H.C.) [1985] I.R.658; [1986] ILRM 95

5. —— **Settlement permission** — *Refusal of leave to settle in the State — Male alien married to Irish citizen — Aliens Registration Office refusing to permit alien to settle — Permission granted for fourteen days only — Whether endorsement on alien's passport the exercise of statutory powers without fair procedures — Entitlement to fair procedures — Whether denial of wife's constitutional rights to the company and society of her spouse — Constitution of Ireland,* 1937, *Arts.* 40.3, 41.1 — *Aliens (Amendment) Order,* 1975 (*S.I. No.* 128), *art.*3.] The first named plaintiff (M.A.) was born in Tunisia in 1949. On Tunisia gaining its independence he left with his mother and went to France but still remained a Tunisian citizen. In 1968 he went to England and in 1976 set up business in England and advertised in this country. He decided to set up business in this country and contacted the Aliens Registration Office to obtain the necessary permission. In 1978 he provided himself with a home in Dublin. In 1979 he went to Paris but on return to Ireland was refused entry. Being a Tunisian citizen he was not entitled to a French passport and was only entitled to a Tunisian one which he obtained in 1979. He returned to Ireland on this passport in October 1979 and handed his passport to the Aliens Registration Office. In December, 1979, he went to England and was involved in proceedings there. His passport was forwarded to him and he returned to Tunisia and then to Paris. As a result of communications with the Aliens Registration Office he obtained permission to return to this country for fourteen days only. On his return however, his passport was endorsed for a three-month stay, the official who did so presumably being unaware of the arrangements which had been made. He brought his passport to the Aliens Registration Office on 12 March, 1980, and it was altered to enable him to have a further fourteen days from the aforesaid date. He did not honour this. In July, 1980, he married the second named plaintiff (S.A.), an Irish citizen, in Dublin. A prosecution was initiated under the Aliens Act, 1935, but was adjourned as the plaintiffs wished to issue these proceedings. It was contended on behalf of the plaintiffs, firstly, that the alteration of the stamp on the first named plaintiff's passport was invalid as having been made without giving M.A. the opportunity of a fair hearing, and secondly, that S.A. has a constitutional right to the company of her husband whenever she comes to, and remains within the State. **Held** in dismissing the claim, the first named plaintiff made no effort to challenge the

ALIENS—*continued.*

decision at the time and did not ask for reasons. No question of fair procedures strictly arose, since the first named plaintiff was not seeking to acquire a right under a statutory power, nor was he threatened with the loss of a right so granted. There was no denial of the second-named plaintiff's constitutional rights, the fulfilment of a desire to visit her immediate family in the company of her husband is not a fundamental right guaranteed by the Constitution. The decision by the Aliens Registration Office does not weaken the family as an institution nor does it undermine the status of marriage. *Abdelkefi v. Minister for Justice*

(H.C.) [1984] ILRM 138

—— Voting rights — Dáil Éireann — Right to vote restricted by Constitution to citizens — Bill conferring franchise upon resident British citizens — Whether Bill repugnant to the Constitution — Whether constitutional provisions exclude aliens from voting rights.

see **Constitution,** 1

AMUSEMENT HALLS — Gaming licences.

see **Gaming and Lotteries,** 3-7

ANCIENT MONUMENT

see **National Monument**

ANGLO-IRISH AGREEMENT — Constitution — Validity — Whether Agreement contrary to Arts. 2 and 3 of the Constitution.

see **Constitution,** 23

ANIMALS

see also **Agriculture**
Fisheries

1. —— **Guard dog** — *Injury to plaintiffs — Liability — Propensity to attack — Whether owner strictly liable — Whether defence to show that its escape was caused by the wrongful act of a third party.*] Both plaintiffs sought damages for injuries they sustained in two separate incidents as a result of being attacked by the defendant's Doberman Pincher dog. There was evidence before the court that the said dog was a guard dog and had been specially trained to attack and hold people in certain circumstances. The defendants in defending the plaintiff's claim relied on the fact that the said dog had been stolen and therefore its escape was caused by the wrongful act of a third party and further that the dog's behaviour could not reasonably have been anticipated. **Held** by Barron J. in holding defendants liable, since the animal was trained to attack, it had a known propensity to cause damage and the owner was therefore strictly liable for the injuries sustained and it was not a defence that its escape had been caused by the wrongful act of a third party. *Behrens* v. *Bertram Mills Circus Ltd.* [1975] 1 ALL E.R. 583 approved. *Kavanagh* v. *Centreline Ltd.*

(H.C.) [1987] ILRM 306

2. —— **Negligence** — *Road traffic accident — Cattle straying — Driver colliding with cattle which had strayed onto main road — Whether cattle constituted a public nuisance — Whether defendants negligent — Whether under a duty to prevent cattle straying onto public road.*] The plaintiff was injured when his motor-car collided at night on a main road with a bullock owned by the defendant. The animal was one of a herd that had strayed on to the road through an open gate. The evidence did not establish who had left the gate open. The collision occurred as the cattle, having been found by the defendant's neighbour, were being guided back along the road by him and another man. The plaintiff asserted that the two men were acting as servants of the defendant, and sued in nuisance and in negligence. The defendant contended that there was no liability for cattle escaping on the road, and that the men herding the cattle were acting as volunteers. **Held** by McWilliam J. in dismissing the case, 1, that the presence of cattle on a highway could constitute a nuisance: *Cunningham* v. *McGrath Brothers* [1964] I.R. 209, *Hall* v. *Wightman* [1926] N.I. 72, and *Cunningham* v. *Whelan* 52 I.L.T.R. 67 considered. 2. That the test of liability in nuisance is akin to that in negligence and is the doing or permitting of something of which the natural and probable consequence is the creation of a nuisance: *dictum* of Kingsmill-Moore J. in *Cunningham* v. *McGrath Brothers* applied. 3. That there is no general duty to fence lands adjoining the highway, but failure to prevent animals straying onto a modern main motor road running through fenced farm land may constitute negligence: *Cunningham* v. *Whelan (supra)* considered, rule in *Searle* v. *Wallbank* doubted. 4. That, in the instant case, the plaintiff had failed to establish that there was any breach of duty by the defendant, who was not liable for the acts of the two men who undertook to pursue the escaped herd. *Gillick* v. *O'Reilly*

(H.C.) [1984] ILRM 402

—— Horses — Showjumping — Prohibition on use of non-Irish horses by Irish showjumpers in international competion — Whether unreasonable restraint of trade.

see **European Communities,** 2.

—— Injury — Factory emissions — Whether

1. —— **Award** — *Enforcement* — *Foreign*

ARBITRATION—*continued.*

award — New York Convention — Whether arbitral procedure in accordance with agreement of parties to contract — Ambiguity of documentation — Whether court has jurisdiction to investigate facts on which defence to enforcement based — Matters appropriate for consideration as defence to enforcement — Arbitration Act, 1980 (*No.* 7), *ss.*2, 6(1), 9(2), *Schedule.*] The applicants had entered into two contracts for the supply of cane molasses to the respondents. Each contract was negotiated through a series of letters and telexes. In negotiating the first contract the applicants suggested that any disputes would be arbitrated 'amicably in Hamburg'. The respondents replied that arbitration should take place in London and the parties ultimately agreed that arbitration take place in London under the rules of the Grain and Feed Trade Association (GAFTA). The first contract was performed satisfactorily. In negotiating the second contract the applicants stated in a telex that all conditions other than price and date of arrival were to be as per the first contract. In a subsequent letter the applicants confirmed these terms and added that any disputes would be arbitrated 'amicably in Hamburg'. The respondents did not respond to either of these communications. After further correspondence in which the respondents sought to vary the amount of delivery and price and the applicants refused to do so, the respondents purported to repudiate the contract, the applicants submitted the dispute to arbitration in London under GAFTA rules, the respondents refused to recognise the jurisdiction of the arbitrators to hear the matter and the arbitrators awarded the applicants damages for breach of contract. The applicants sought to have the award enforced pursuant to Part III of the Arbitration Act, 1980. The respondents disputed that there was any binding contract in existence and that if there was the arbitration could only have taken place in Hamburg. Part III of the 1980 Act provides for the enforcement of foreign arbitral awards made under the New York Convention (which forms a Schedule to the Act). S. 2 of the Act defines an arbitration agreement as an agreement in writing to submit disputable matters to arbitration. S.6 of the Act defines 'award' as an award made in pursuance of an arbitration agreement in the territory of a state, other than this State, which is a party to the Convention. Both this State and the United Kingdom are party to the Convention. S. 9 (2) (*e*) of the 1980 Act provides that enforcement of an arbitral award made under the New York Convention may be refused if it is proved that 'the composition of the arbitral authority or the arbitral procedure was not in accordance with the agreement of the parties'. S. 9 (2) (*d*) and (*f*) also provide defences to enforcement where the arbitration deals with matters not contemplated by a reference and the

ARBITRATION—*continued.*

award has not become binding on the parties. **Held** by Costello J. in enforcing the award, the parties had agreed under the first contract that arbitration of disputes should take place in London under GAFTA rules, this had been confirmed in the telex negotiating the terms of the second contract, and the reference to arbitration in Hamburg in the subsequent letter confirming the terms could not, as an error in the preparation of a formal contract, affect the legal consequences following from what had actually been agreed, and in these circumstances the respondents had failed to discharge the onus resting on them to prove that the arbitration did not take place in accordance with what had been agreed, as envisaged by s. 9 (2) (*e*) of the 1980 Act. *Per* Costello J., once a point is raised by a respondent seeking to resist enforcement of an award by relying on s. 9 of the 1980 Act, the court is not bound by the arbitrator's conclusion that it has been composed in accordance with the parties' agreement. **Held** by the Supreme Court (Finlay C.J., Henchy and Griffin JJ.) in dismissing the respondents' appeal, 1, it was not appropriate that the question of whether there was a binding agreement between the parties be raised as a defence to enforcement under s. 9 (2) (*d*) or (*f*) of the 1980 Act, but was a matter which fell to be determined under the Act by a court considering whether, pursuant to ss. 2 and 6 (1) of the Act, there was in existence an arbitration agreement and award to which the Act applied, and in considering this issue the court was not to be affected by the existence of a decision of the arbitral authority. 2. The evidence established that there was an agreement in existence between the parties and that the parties had agreed that arbitration take place in London under GAFTA rules, particularly in view of the fact that the alteration from the original proposal of arbitration in Hamburg to arbitration in London was at the instance of the respondents, and the High Court was entitled to conclude that the patent error in the applicants' letter referring to arbitration in Hamburg did not affect the correctness of the general provision that all conditions, other than those specifically altered in the telex, should be as per the first contract. *Cremer (Peter) GmbH* v. *Co-operative Molasses Traders Ltd.*

(H.C., S.C.) [1985] ILRM 564

2. —— **Award** — *Enforcement — Misconduct — Whether established — Building contract — Dispute referred to arbitration — Award made but payment not forthcoming — Application for liberty to enforce the award — Whether arbitrator guilty of misconduct — Arbitration Act,* 1954 (*No.* 26), *s.*41.] The plaintiff, the main contractor

ARBITRATION—*continued.*

in the construction of a large shopping centre, had entered into a sub-contract with the defendant. A dispute having arisen between the parties, an arbitrator was appointed in accordance with the terms of the contract, and the plaintiff was awarded a sum of money together with the costs of arbitration. When payment was not forthcoming, the plaintiff instituted proceedings seeking to enforce the award. The defendant, for its part, issued separate proceedings seeking to have the award set aside and claiming that the arbitration was a nullity due to the misconduct of the arbitrator. The alleged misconduct was the refusal of the arbitrator to adjourn the hearing in order to allow the defendant to file details of a counterclaim. Some time previously, following the filing of a defence, the defendant had notified the arbitrator that it would be filing a substantial counterclaim. When the arbitrator had heard nothing further for two months, he wrote to the defendant, giving 21 days for the filing of an amended defence and counterclaim. When this was not done, the arbitrator appointed a date for the arbitration, which, on the day, he refused to adjourn further. The defendant's solicitors walked out in protest, and the arbitrator continued the proceedings in their absence. Both sets of proceedings were heard together in the High Court. **Held** by Costello J. in making an order enforcing the award, and in finding that the arbitrator had not been guilty of any misconduct, 1, a reasonable period had been granted to the defendant for the filing of the amended defence and counterclaim. No explanation was given either to the arbitrator or to the court as to why the documents were not forthcoming within the specified time. 2. In the circumstances, reasonable notice of the arbitration having been given, the arbitrator had jurisdiction to continue the hearing in the absence of the defendant. To hold otherwise would mean that a party could frustrate the proceedings by mere inaction. *Grangeford Structures Ltd.* v. *S.H.Ltd.*

(H.C.) [1988] ILRM 129

3. —— **Award** — *Finality — Mistake of law — Error on face of award — Jurisdiction of courts to review awards — Power of court to remit award for reconsideration by arbitrator — Circumstances in which award will be remitted — Power of court to direct arbitrator to state special case — Arbitration Act,* 1954 (*No.* 26), *ss.*35, 36. *Practice — Appeal — Supreme Court — Issue not argued before High Court — Issue as to jurisdiction of High Court to have entertained proceedings — Whether Supreme Court will decide issue not argued in court below.*] The plaintiff applied to the defendant insurer for insurance cover. In reply to a question on the proposal form whether the plaintiff had ever sustained

ARBITRATION—*continued.*

loss by any of the risks he wished to insure against, he replied "No". He signed a declaration at the foot of the proposal form that the particulars therein contained were "true and complete in every respect and that no material fact had been suppressed or withheld" and agreed that the declaration and the answers given on the proposal form should be the basis of the contract between the parties. The plaintiff was issued with a policy and soon after suffered a loss by fire in respect of which he claimed to be idemnified by the defendant. The defendant disputed its liability to pay the plaintiff on the grounds that he had failed to disclose the fact that he had within the previous year been paid £53 in respect of fire damage to a pump. The dispute was referred to arbitration and the arbitrator found (1) that the declaration signed by the plaintiff and his agreement that the answers given should be the basis of the contract constituted a condition precedent of the contract; (2) that the plaintiff's answer was not true or complete; (3) that the inaccuracy or incompleteness did not amount to a misrepresentation or concealment of a material fact; and (4) that the defendant was under no liability to the plaintiff under the policy. The plaintiff applied to the High Court for an order setting aside the award on the grounds that the arbitrator had erred in law in arriving at his determination. Blayney J. held that the arbitrator had not erred in law and dismissed the claim. (See the report at [1987] I.R. 113). On appeal by the plaintiff to the Supreme Court the Court raised the issue, which had been neither argued nor decided below, as to whether the High Court had had jurisdiction to entertain the proceedings. **Held** by the Supreme Court (Finlay C.J., Walsh, Griffin, Hederman and McCarthy JJ.), in dismissing the appeal, 1, that although the issue had not been taken in the High Court, the Supreme Court was entitled to raise a question as to the jurisdiction of the High Court to have heard the proceedings. 2. That while the High Court had jurisdiction at common law to set aside an award where there was an obvious or fundamental error of law on the face of the award, this was not such a case. *Church and General Insurance Co.* v. *Connolly and McLoughlin* (Unreported, High Court, Costello J., 7th May, 1981); *Ex parte Strabane R.D.C.* [1910] 1 I.R. 135 and *The Honourable the Irish Society* v. *Ministry for Finance* [1958] N.I. 170 considered. 3. That once the arbitrator had made his award without qualification and in the absence of any request that he should state any question of law or any part of his award in the form of a special case, the power under s. 35 of the Arbitration Act, 1954, to state a special case for the determination of the High Court, was spent. 4. That the power of the High Court,

ARBITRATION—*continued.*

under s. 36 of the Act of 1954, to remit an award or part of an award for reconsideration by the arbitrator might be appropriate to cases involving a patent error of calculation; awards which on their face were ambiguous or uncertain; cases where the arbitrator himself sought to rectify an error and, perhaps, cases where new evidence had become available, but it was not appropriate to this case. *Keenan* v. *Shield Insurance Co. Ltd.*
(S.C.) [1988] I.R.89

Editor's note: For High Court judgment on Insurance issue, reported at [1987] I.R. 113, *see* **Insurance,** 5.

4. —— **Building contract** — *Architect's certificate — Architect issuing final certificate for payment — Contractor subsequently making claim for additional payments — Whether contractor barred from pursuing these claims — Interpretation of building contract — General conditions.*] Cl. 29 (*g*) of the General Conditions of a Building Contract issued by the Royal Institute of Architects of Ireland provides: 'The said final certificate shall be conclusive in any proceedings arising out of this contract (whether by arbitration under clause 31 of these conditions or otherwise) that the works have been properly carried out and completed in accordance with the terms of this contract and *that any necessary effect has been given to all terms of this contract which require an adjustment to be made to the contract sum*'. Cl. 24 (*b*) provides that 'If any act or default of the employer delays progress of the works then the contractor shall within seven days of the act or default give notice in writing to the architect to this effect and any time lost from this cause shall be ascertained and certified by the architect, and the employer shall pay or allow to the contractor such damages as the contractor shall have incurred by the delay'. The claimant respondent, a building contractor, entered into two separate building contracts with the Minister for Education, the appellant, to build two post-primary schools in accordance with the terms of Articles of Agreement and the General Conditions of a Building Contract issued by the Royal Institute of Architects of Ireland. Subsequent to the issue of the final certificate for payment in respect of each contract a dispute arose between the parties on the interpretation of cls. 29 (*f*) and (*g*) and 24 (*b*) of the General Conditions. The dispute was submitted to arbitration. The arbitrator stated the following question in the case stated to the High Court pursuant to the Arbitration Acts: 'Is the claimant barred by cl. 29 (*f*) and (*g*) of the said general conditions from pursuing in arbitration claims for compensation for delay and disruption made under cls. 2, 12, or 24 (*b*) of the said general conditions and for

ARBITRATION—*continued.*

breach of contract'. Gannon J. in answering the question in the case stated concluded that the claimant was barred by cl. 29 (*f*) and (*g*) from pursuing in arbitration claims other than for delay provided for in cl. 24 (*b*) of the said general conditions. The Minister for Education appealed the decision to the Supreme Court. The net issue the court had to decide having regard to the terms of cls. 29 (*f*) and (*g*) and a large number of other clauses in the conditions which expressly provide for variations or adjustments to the contract sum was whether the provisions of cl. 24 (*b*) could properly be described as a term of a contract which require an adjustment to be made to the contract sum. **Held** by Gannon J., 1, the clauses providing for arbitration should be construed not merely according to the ordinary meaning of the words used but also consistently with the implementation of the agreement, and the overall scheme devised by the conditions. 2. In construing cl. 29 (*g*) the final certificate is conclusive as to all matters of work, materials, quality, quality standards and values with respect to which the architect had to exercise his judgment in determining that it was appropriate to issue the final certificate and in calculating the amount of final payment on foot of the contract sum with adjustments permitted under the condition of agreement. 3. The provisions of cl. 29 (*g*) do not make the final certificate conclusive between the parties on matters such as damages or penalties for which no guidance or measurement is provided and with respect to which no adjustment to the contract sum is required or may be made. On appeal it was **Held** by the Supreme Court (Finlay C.J., Henchy, Griffin, Hederman and McCarthy JJ.) in dismissing the appeal, a final certificate when issued does not bar a claim under cl. 24 (*b*) either by way of ordinary claim or arbitration as such claims do not fall within the definition of a term of the contract which requires adjustment to the contract sum in view of the fundamental difference between the form of this clause and other clauses in the contract which expressly require variations or adjustments to the contract sum. *P. Elliott & Co. Ltd.* v. *Minister for Education*
(H.C., S.C.) [1987] ILRM 710

5. —— **Building contract** — *Delay — Claim by main contractor against sub-contractor for delay — Certificate issued by architect exonerating contractor — Certificate did not state when in architect's opinion sub-contracting work ought to have been completed — Whether certificate adequate — Whether contractor can recover from sub-contractor in absence of certificate.*] The claimant, who had entered into a contract to build a geriatric unit at a hospital, entered into a sub-con-

ARBITRATION—*continued.*

tract with the respondent for the installation of certain mechanical services. Clause 27 (*d*) (ii) of the contract provided: "If any nominated sub-contractor fails to complete the sub-contract works . . . within the period specified in the sub-contract or within any extended time granted by the contractor . . . then if the same ought reasonably so to have been completed the architect . . . shall certify in writing accordingly; any such certificate shall be issued to the contractor and immediately upon issue the architect shall send a duplicate copy thereof to the nominated sub-contractor." Clause 8 (*a*) of the sub-contract provided: ". . . provided that the contractor shall not be entitled to claim any loss or damage under this clause unless the architect shall have issued to the contractor (with a duplicate copy to the sub-contractor) a certificate in writing stating that in his opinion the sub-contract works . . . ought reasonably to have been completed within the specified period or within any extended period or periods as the case may be." Practical completion of the main contract was achieved 42 weeks in delay and the architect issued two certificates of extension of time amounting in total to 42 weeks to the claimant. In relation to that extension of time, the architect sent a letter dated 19 January, 1977, to the claimant which stated (*inter alia*): ". . . we enclose a certificate giving our awards. (1) Mechanial subcontract, *Claim* , 15 weeks; *Award,* 12 weeks; *Contract clause,* 23 (*g*) . . ." That letter also enclosed a copy of a letter also dated 19 January, 1977, sent by the architect to the respondent stating: "In accordance with clause 27 (*d*) (ii) of the contract conditions . . . we would inform you that in the recent certificate of extension of time granted to the [plaintiff] the period set against your work was [12 weeks]." The claimant claimed damages against the respondent for alleged delay by the respondent in completing the sub-contract and the claim was referred to arbitration. Before the arbitrator, the claimant argued that by virtue of the reference in it to clause 27 (*d*) (ii) the letter was a certificate under clause 8 (*a*) of the sub-contract, alternatively that, in the absence of such a certificate, the claimant was entitled to recover compensation for the failure of the respondent to complete the sub-contract on time and that the terms of the arbitration clause empowered the arbitrator to disregard the absence of such a certificate.

The arbitrator stated a case for the High Court under section 22 (1) (*a*) of the Arbitration Act (Northern Ireland), 1937, in these terms: "1. Are the [certificates extending time and the letter dated 19 January, 1977, from the architect to the respondent] annexed hereto validly and lawfully issued certificates, which are binding on the arbitrator, for the purposes of, and according to

ARBITRATION—*continued.*

the procedure stipulated in clause 8 (*a*) of the nominated sub-contract (or any other relevant clause) made between the parties dated April 1974? 2. In the absence of validly and lawfully issued certificates from the architect, can the claimant sustain any claim for damages arising out of alleged delay by or on the respondent's part?" **Held,** that, 1, the architect's letter was not a certificate under clause 8 (*a*), which required the architect to express in writing his opinion that the sub-contract works ought reasonably to have been completed within the specified period. The language used by the architect was so ambiguous that it was difficult even to infer that the architect did hold the required opinion. It was not a sufficient compliance with the clause to declare merely that the sub-contractor was in delay. 2. While clause 8 (*a*) did impose on the sub-contractor a duty to proceed with due expedition, the claimant had only one right of claim under that clause which was subject to the proviso which made an architect's certificate a condition precedent to a claim under the clause. *Ellis Mechanical Construction* v. *Wates Construction Ltd.* [1978] 1 Lloyd's Rep. 33 considered. 3. The right to set off under clause 13 did not entitle the claimant to deduct any loss resulting from the delay from any money due to the respondent as that right was limited to sums which the respondent was liable to pay to the claimant. 4. The arbitrator could not disregard the absence of a certificate under clause 8 (*a*). If an arbitration clause is in general terms. as it was in this case, the arbitrator must give effect to the provisions of the contract between the parties and he cannot waive or override those provisions unless special powers have been conferred to enable him so to do. *Brightside Kilpatrick Engineering Services* v. *Mitchell Construction Ltd.* [1975] 2 Lloyd's Rep. 493 followed.*Savage Brothers Ltd.* v. *Shillington (Heating and Plumbing) Ltd.*

(Q.B.D.) [1985] N.I. 85

6. —— **Compulsory acquisition** — *Valuation — Dispute as to value — Arbitrator stating case to High Court — Power of court to remit — Arbitration Act,* 1954 (*No.* 26), *s.* 36. — *Compulsory acquisition — Dispute as to value — Valuation going to arbitration — Factors to be taken into account — Sewerage facilities — Public Health (Ireland) Act,* 1878, (*c.* 25), *ss.* 23, 24 — *Acquisition of Land (Assessment of Compensation) Act,* 1919, (*c.* 57), *s.* 2 — *Local Government (Planning and Development) Act, 1963 (No.* 28), ss. 55, 56, 69.] The County Council ('the acquiring authority') had made a compulsory purchase order in respect of land ('the

ARBITRATION—*continued.*

subject land') in the Dodder Valley area owned by Mr. Meenaghan ('the claimant'). The subject land had been zoned 'Q' and 'T' for certain non-developmental purposes and the acquiring authority had decided to reserve the existing capacity of the Dodder Valley main sewer for future developments on other lands. The arbitrator made an interim award for £400,000, which was not paid, and stated that the assessment of a larger sum would depend on the answers to certain questions submitted by him to the court. The questions were as follows: 1. Is the designation 'Q' in the County Dublin Development Plan 1972 equivalent to a reservation for a particular purpose? 2. Is the designation 'T' in the County Dublin Development Plan equivalent to a reservation for a particular purpose? 3. Could the acquiring authority, as the sanitary authority, have refused to allow effluent from the foul water sewers of a scheme of development on the subject land to be discharged into the Dodder Valley main sewer? 4. Would a decision, made at the time of the service of a notice to treat, by the acquiring authority as planning authority, to refuse to grant a planning permission for a scheme of development on the subject land for the reason that the capacity of the Dodder Valley main sewer was pre-empted to provide capacity for a scheme of development on other lands some of which scheme was probably or possibly undertaken by a local authority, confer a right to compensation? On the hearing of the case stated counsel for the acquiring authority asked to have the case stated remitted to the arbitrator to hear evidence about the connection of the Dodder Valley sewer with the sewers of Dublin Corporation so that the acquiring authority could make submissions about the legal considerations applicable to any possible connection from the subject land to the Dodder sewer. **Held** by O'Hanlon J. on remitting the case to the arbitrator for considering the replies to the questions. The designations 'T' and 'Q' amounted to a reservation for a particular purpose within Rule 11 of the statutory rules for the assessment of compensation, contained in the Fourth Schedule to the Local Government (Planning and Development) Act, 1963, and inserted into s. 2 of the Acquisition of Land (Assessment of Compensation) Act, 1919, by s. 69 of the 1963 Act. *Dublin County Council* v *Shortt* [1982] ILRM 117 and [1983] ILRM 377 (Supreme Court) followed. The court should only exercise its power under s. 36 of the Arbitration Act, 1954, to remit the case to the arbitrator if one of the following conditions were satisfied: (i) Defect or error patent or on the face of the award. (ii) Where the arbitrator has admitted he made some mistake which he desired to correct by having the award remitted to him for that purpose. (iii) Where material evidence which could not with reasonable diligence have been discovered before the award was made had since been obtained. (iv) Where there has been misconduct on the part of the arbitrator. None of these conditions applied and therefore the case would not be remitted. Question 3 would be answered 'Yes'. *Dublin County Council* v *Shortt* followed. In relation to Question 4 it is a moot point whether such a decision can give rise to a claim for compensation under s. 55 of the 1963 Act without the applicant being first required to take steps to quash the decision and proceed with the development. Therefore the question would be answered by stating that such a decision to pre-empt the sewage capacity would not entitle the acquiring authority to refuse planning permission while at the same time barring any claim for compensation by the claimant by reason of the exclusion referred to in s. 56(1) (b) (i) of the Local Government (Planning and Development) Act, 1963. In relation to the complaint that the interim award of £400,000 had not been paid it would appear that such interim award would be enforceable under s. 41 of the Arbitration Act, 1954, before the final determination of the case stated. *Meenaghan v. Dublin County Council*
(H.C.) [1984] ILRM 616

7. —— **Misconduct** — *Additional evidence — Arbitrator's award in writing — Arbitrator requesting additional evidence after oral hearing but prior to making his award — Additional evidence not admitted — Award expressed to be "in the absence of and because of the absence of" additional evidence — Whether arbitrator has power or jurisdiction to admit such evidence — Whether award could be remitted to arbitrator to hear additional evidence — Whether misconduct of the proceedings.*] An arbitration, arising out of a dispute between the plaintiff landlords and the defendant tenant as to who was liable for the cost of works to be carried out by the fire oficer in Cork, was held on the 24 April, 1986. On the 22 May, 1986, the arbitrator requested certain additional evidence, which he felt was necessary to enable him to make a determination on the issue. At a meeting on this issue counsel for the defendant submitted that the arbitrator had no power or jurisdiction to re-open the proceedings and that the plaintiffs should not be given an opportunity to present further evidence that could have been made available at the original hearing. Counsel for the plaintiffs submitted that the arbitrator had full jurisdiction to hear further evidence and that the arbitrator was not *functus officio* until the award was made. Without hearing any additional evidence the arbitrator made his award which was expressed to be made "in the absence of and because of the absence of"

ARBITRATION—*continued.*

the additional evidence sought. On the plaintiffs' application to have the award remitted to the arbitrator for the purpose of allowing him to hear the additional evidence it was **Held** by Carroll J., in deciding that the matter came within the ground of misconduct of the proceedings by refusing to hear evidence material to the issues to be decided, 1, that an arbitrator was not *functus officio* until he made an award and until such time it was within his power and jurisdiction to hear further evidence; particularly so in the instant case as the proceedings had not been formally closed and further the arbitrator had stated he required the evidence to enable him to decide the issue. *In re Maunder* (1883) 49 L.T. 535 applied. 2. That the award made should be set aside and the matter remitted to the arbitrator to hear such additional evidence as both parties might now wish to tender and the arbitrator should then make his award accordingly. *O'Sullivan* v. *Joseph Woodward & Sons Ltd.*

(H.C.) [1987] I.R.255

8. —— **Misconduct** — *Hearing — Arbitration Act,* 1954 (*No.* 26), *s.* 38 — *Contract — Sale of land — Conditions — Particulars — Misdescription — Materiality — Registered land — Recorded folio acreage greater than acreage actually held in possession — Land Registry practice — Registration of Title Act,* 1964 (*No.* 16), *ss.* 31, 85.] Section 38, sub-s. 1 of the Arbitration Act, 1954, provides:- "Where (a) an arbitrator or umpire has misconducted himself or the proceedings, or (b) an arbitration or award has been improperly procured, the court may set the award aside." By contract in writing the plaintiff vendor agreed to sell and the defendant purchaser to purchase lands totalling in area 54.804 acres comprised in Folios 754 and 882 of the Register of Freeholders, County Dublin. Clause 21 of the general conditions of sale provided that any dispute arising as to "any error, omission or mis-statement in the particulars of these conditions or in the course of any representations or negotiations leading up to the sale . . . shall be settled by arbitration." Upon a dispute as to the extent of the lands actually sold, the plaintiff instituted High Court proceedings for rescission and damages. These were stayed on the defendant's application pending reference of the dispute to arbitration. After hearing both parties the arbitrator wrote to them requiring further evidence and submissions on the plaintiff's contention that the sale related to the contents of the folios rather than their alleged acreage and that the purchaser at the time of the sale had examined and surveyed the lands and was well aware of their extent. After some further evidence the arbitrator made his award, the recitals of which stated that there was a discrepancy

ARBITRATION—*continued.*

between the greater acreage on the folios and the lesser acreage on their accompanying Land Registry maps. This was accounted for by a Land Registry practice whereby, while the total acreage on the face of each folio was computed by subtraction of the particular acreage expressed by the registered owner in each transfer away from the folio, the accompanying official Land Registry maps recorded an additional deduction of land *ad medium filum* of any road border in favour of the transferee unless there were express words to the contrary in the transfer itself. The plaintiff applied to the High Court to set aside the award of the arbitrator on the grounds that there was an error on the face of the award which found in effect that Land Registry practice had reduced the area of land comprised in the folios; that there had been misconduct under s.38 of the Arbitration Act, 1954, in that his decisions upon the materiality of an error, omission or misstatement and in the particulars or conditions of sale and upon compensation and its quantum were made without affording the plaintiff any opportunity of adducing evidence or making submissions on those issues. **Held** by Carroll J., in granting the reliefs sought and remitting the dispute to arbitration, 1, that since the scheme of registration of title was founded upon the conclusiveness of the register by s. 31 of the Registration of Title Act, 1964, as opposed to the registry map (s. 85), and by s. 32 of the same Act any errors on the folio originating from the Land Registry might be rectified by the Registrar of Titles only with the consent of the registered owner and other interested parties thereby affected, there was an error of law on the face of the arbitrator's award in holding that the vendor could not give title in accordance with the acreage stated in the particulars of the agreement for sale. 2. That even if the arbitrator were correct on the law, there had been misconduct of the proceedings in that the plaintiff was not afforded sufficient opportunity of adducing evidence or making submissions on the materiality of any discrepancy of acreage nor, in the event of a ruling against the plaintiff on that issue, upon the appropriate form or quantum of compensation prior to the making of his final award. *The State (Hegarty)* v. *Winters* [1956] I.R. 320 applied. Upon appeal by the defendant it was **Held** by the Supreme Court (Finlay C.J., Hederman and McCarthy JJ.), in allowing the appeal and restoring the award of the arbitrator, 1, that the findings and decision of the arbitrator accorded precisely with the original interlocutory order of the High Court, which specifically remitted the dispute to arbitration to determine the total acreage of land for which the plaintiff could have been in a position to give vacant possession to

ARBITRATION—*continued.*

the defendant. 2. That since s. 38 of the Arbitration Act, 1954, did not make it mandatory to set aside an arbitration award on the grounds of alleged misconduct, the court would refuse to set aside the award even though the vendor had not been heard on those issues of materiality, compensation and quantum, as no valid argument could have been advanced at the hearing to alter the award made. *Geraghty* v. *Rohan Industrial Estates Ltd.*

(H.C., S.C.) [1988] I.R.419

9. —— **Misconduct** — *Whether established — Whether objection made to arbitrator's conduct at time of arbitration — Whether parties entitled to complain later — Whether arbitrator took all matters between parties into account — Whether court would exercise discretion to extend leave for appealing to court — Rules of the Superior Courts,* 1962 (*S.I. No.* 72), *O.* 56 *r.* 4.] The defendants engaged the plaintiff to build a dwellinghouse for them. Following disputes between the parties certain issues were referred for determination by an arbitrator who paid two visits to the site, on one occasion, at her own request, unaccompanied. The arbitrator made her award, which was taken up by the plaintiff two days later and sent to the defendants. After the defendants indicated their dissatisfaction with the award they sought by notice of motion, an order pursuant to 0.56 r. 4 of the Rules of the Superior Courts, 1962, extending the time within which they would apply to the court to set aside the award and challenged the award on the ground that the arbitrator was guilty of misconduct in that she (a) inspected the premises on her own; (b) did not allow sufficient time to the defendants to make their submissions and (c) did not answer all the questions put to her. The plaintiff claimed an order pursuant to s.41 of the Arbitration Act, 1954, giving them liberty to enforce the award. **Held** by Barron J. in granting the plaintiff's claim and making no order on the defendant's motion, 1, when the arbitrator indicated her desire to make the inspection on her own and no objection was made, it was not now open to either party to complain of the manner in which the inspection took place. 2. There was no ground of complaint with regard to the time allowed by the arbitrator to the defendants to make their submissions. 3. The real issue between the parties was the sum ultimately payable by one or other of them and, in relation to which the arbitrator answered all the questions put to her, it was clear that she took all matters in dispute into account. *Stillorgan Orchard Ltd* v. *McLoughlin & Harvey Ltd.* [1978] ILRM 128 applied. *Childers Heights Housing Ltd.* v. *Molderings*

(H.C.) [1987] ILRM 47

ARBITRATION—*continued.*

10. —— **Practice** — *Question of law — Refusal of arbitrator to state case — Building contract — Dispute referred to arbitration — Award — Application for an order to set aside award — Arbitrator refusing to state a case — Whether misconduct — Arbitration Act,* 1954 (*No.* 26), *ss.* 35(1), 36(1), 38(1).] S. 35(1) of the Arbitration Act, 1954, provides that: "An arbitrator or umpire may, and shall if so directed by the court state — (a) any question of law arising in the course of the reference, or (b) any award or any part of an award in the form of a special case for the decision of the court." S. 38(1) provides that: "where (a) an arbitrator or umpire has misconducted himself or the proceedings or (b) an arbitration or award has been improperly procured, the court may set the award aside." By an agreement in writing dated 3 September, 1974, the plaintiff agreed to carry out certain alterations and renovations to the plaintiff's premises. A dispute arose between the parties and in accordance with the aforesaid agreement the matter was referred to arbitration. Prior to the hearing the defendants caused to be served on the plaintiff a document entitled 'Points of Claim' in which their claim was set forth. The plaintiff in reply delivered a document entitled 'Points of Defence & Counterclaim' and the defendants delivered a document entitled 'Points of Reply to the defence and counterclaim.' The plaintiff's counsel in his opening and closing submissions to the arbitration referred the arbitrator to the possibility of stating a case for the decision of the High Court on the legal question of the interpretation of the relevant conditions in the contract. The arbitrator did not state a case to the court on the question of law that arose in the course of the reference and made an award in favour of the defendants. By his said award he made no ruling on the respondent's/plaintiff's counterclaim. The plaintiff instituted proceedings in the High Court claiming that the arbitrator's award should be set aside in accordance with s. 38 of the Arbitration Act, 1954, the arbitrator having misconducted himself or the proceedings in: (1) failing to state a case for the decision of the court on the points of law raised in the proceedings and; (2) failing to make any ruling/award upon the counterclaim included in the pleadings on behalf of the respondent/plaintiff herein, or alternatively an order remitting the said reference to arbitration to the arbitrator for his further award and determination. **Held** by Hamilton J. in refusing to grant the relief sought, 1, on the facts of this case the court is not satisfied that a formal application was made to the arbitrator in this case that he should state a special case for the decision of the court. 2. The failure of an arbitrator to state any question of law in the form of a special case for

ARBITRATION—*continued.*

the decision of the court does not of itself amount to misconduct because s. 35 of the Arbitration Act, 1954, is permissive and not mandatory. 3. An award of an arbitrator will be sustained although he has omitted in his award to notice some claim put forward by a party if according to a fair interpretation on the award, as in this case, it is to be presumed that the arbitrator is taking the claim into consideration in making the award. 4. Having regard to the manner in which the claim and counterclaim were set forth to the arbitrator this award amounts to an adjudication that the plaintiff's claim and counterclaim has not been established and is therefore good on its face. *Stillorgan Orchard Ltd.* v. *McLoughlin and Harvey Ltd.*

(H.C.) [1978] ILRM 128

11. —— **Practice** — *Question of law — Refusal of arbitrator to state case — Landlord and tenant — Dispute — Arbitration — Finding on a point of law — Refusal of arbitrator to state a case to the High Court — Application by unsuccessful party to the court to direct the arbitrator to state a case — Arbitration Act,* 1954 (*No.* 26), *s.* 35.] Section 35 of the Arbitration Act, 1954, provides that an arbitrator may, and shall if so directed by the court, state any question of law arising in the course of the reference in the form of a special case for the decision of the court. The plaintiffs were tenants of various units in a shopping centre under a uniform lease from the first defendant, which provided that the tenants were to pay a sum in respect of maintenance and services provided by the landlord. The costs of providing the services were to be ascertained by the landlord's auditors or accountants, who were to issue certificates specifying the total of such costs and the amount of each tenant's contribution. The certificates were expressed in the lease to be final and binding on the parties. There was also a covenant in the lease providing for a reference to arbitration of any dispute between the parties. In 1982 a dispute arose between the plaintiffs and the first defendant as to the amount of money payable by the plaintiffs in respect of contribution to the costs of providing the services. The plaintiffs wished to dispute the certificates issued by the defendant's accountants. The defendant maintained that the certificates were final and binding and could not be questioned by the plaintiffs. The parties chose an accountant to act as arbitrator and the matter was referred to arbitration. After extensive argument on the question whether the certificates could be questioned, the arbitrator held that the plaintiffs could impugn the certificates in the circumstances of the case. The plaintiffs requested the arbitrator to state a case to the High Court under s. 35 of the Arbitration Act, 1954. The

arbitrator refused. The plaintiffs applied to the High Court for an order directing the arbitrator to state a case on the point of law to the High Court. At the hearing of the application it was **Held** by Murphy J., in refusing the plaintiffs' application, 1, that the real issue in dispute at the arbitration was a question of law, namely, whether or not the accountant's certificates were final and binding or whether the plaintiffs could dispute the findings implicit in those certificates. 2. That it appeared from the extensive correspondence between the parties and from the arguments addressed to the arbitrator that the parties had chosen to have the point of law decided by the arbitrator. 3. Section 35 of the Act of 1954 confers on the court and on an arbitrator a discretion in relation to the statement of a case even where a point of law arises and the court should be slow to usurp the functions of the chosen tribunal by directing a case to be stated. *Halfdan Grieg & Co.* v. *Sterling Coal* [1973] Q.B. 843 and *Power Securities Ltd.* v. *Daly* (Unreported, High Court, Murphy J., 27 February, 1984) considered. 4. That in the circumstances it would be unjust and unfair to permit the unsuccessful party to assert a right to have the decision of the High Court substituted for that of the arbitrator, when they had already agreed that the question of law should be decided by the arbitrator. 5. That the decision of the arbitrator in relation to the point of law did not terminate his duties as arbitrator and therefore he was not *functus officio*. *Hogan* v. *St.Kevin's Company*

(H.C.) [1986] I.R.80; [1987] ILRM 17

12. —— **Practice** — *Stay on proceedings — Agreement — Arbitration clause — Proceedings to enforce an agreement for the sale of solicitor's practice — Application to stay proceedings pending arbitration — Whether Court should stay proceedings — Whether Court's discretion curtailed — Whether delay rendering the arbitration agreement inoperative or incapable of being performed — Arbitration Act,* 1954 (*No.* 26), *s.* 12 — *Arbitration Act,* 1980 (*No.* 7), *ss.* 4, 5.] Section 5, sub-s. 1 of the Arbitration Act, 1980, provides: "If any party to an arbitration agreement, or any person claiming through or under him, commences any proceedings in any court against any other party to such agreement, or any person claiming through or under him, in respect of any matter agreed to be referred to arbitration, any party to the proceedings may at any time after an appearance has been entered, and before delivering any pleadings or taking any other steps in the proceedings, apply to the court to stay the proceedings, and the court, unless it is satisfied that the arbitration agreement is null and void, inoperative or incapable

ARBITRATION—*continued.*

of being performed, or that there is not in fact any dispute between the parties with regard to the matter agreed to be referred, shall make an order staying the proceedings." The plaintiffs brought proceedings to enforce an agreement for the sale of a solicitor's practice to the defendant. The defendant applied pursuant to s. 5 of the Act of 1980 to stay the said proceedings on the basis that the parties had agreed to have all matters of dispute arising out of the alleged agreement resolved by arbitration. The plaintiffs argued that the defendant's excessive delay in bringing the issues in dispute before the arbitrator amounted to a repudiation of the arbitration agreement. **Held** by O'Hanlon J., in granting a stay on the proceedings, 1, that as none of the excluding circumstances referred to in s. 5 applied, the court was obliged to grant the relief sought. *Per* O'Hanlon J. If the defendant continued to delay the arbitration in the future the arbitration agreement could be regarded as having become inoperative or incapable of being performed and in such circumstances the plaintiffs would be entitled to ask to have the stay on the present proceedings removed. *O'Mahony v. Lysaght*

(H.C.) [1988] I.R.29

13. —— **Practice** — *Stay on proceedings — Agreement — Arbitration clause — Disputes — Injunctions to enforce compliance — Appearance — Interlocutory order — Plaintiff subsequently seeking to refer all disputes to arbitration — Whether "taking any other steps in the proceedings" — Whether plaintiff estopped from staying proceedings — Arbitration Act,* 1980 (*No.* 7), *s.* 5.] By agreement in writing made in March, 1979, the defendant agreed to supply exclusively to the plaintiff 50,000 gallons of skim milk per day at a price fixed by the terms of the agreement. Clause 10 provided that all disputes arising out of the agreement be referred to arbitration. Following changes in market circumstances the defendant threatened to withdraw supplies from the plaintiff and sell to a competitor. The plaintiff obtained in the High Court interim injunctions compelling the defendant to continue supplies in accordance with the agreement. The defendant entered an appearance and the plaintiff obtained interlocutory injunctions in the same terms. The defendant sought an early hearing of the dispute and pressed the plaintiff to file its statement of claim. The plaintiff applied to have its proceedings stayed to allow all issues to be referred to arbitration under clause 10 of the agreement. **Held** by O'Hanlon J., in refusing to stay proceedings, that the plaintiff in applying for and obtaining interlocutory injunctions pending the hearing of the action, had taken "steps in the proceedings" within the meaning of s. 5 of the Arbitration Act, 1980, and had thereby elected to exclude its option under the arbitration clause. *MacCormac Products Ltd. v. Monaghan Co-operative Society Ltd.*

(H.C.) [1988] I.R.304

14. —— **Practice** — *Time limit — Agreement to refer disputes to arbitration — Time limit — Whether undue hardship caused by refusal to extend time — Arbitration Act,* 1954 (*No.* 26), *ss.* 3(1), 42, 45.] S. 45 of the Arbitration Act, 1954, provides that where an agreement to refer future disputes to arbitration limits the time in which arbitration may be commenced, the court if it thinks undue hardship would otherwise be caused, may extend such time. The applicant was the holder of a policy of insurance with the respondent, condition 15 of which provided that all differences arising from the policy were to be referred to arbitration, and claims not referred to arbitration within twelve months from disclaimer of liability were to be deemed to have been abandoned. Liability on foot of a claim made by the applicant was repudiated by the respondent on 13 October, 1970. Further correspondence ensued between the parties, and on 17 January, 1973, the applicant's solicitor notified the respondent by letter that the matter was being referred to arbitration. The respondent replied by referring the applicant to condition 15 of the insurance policy, and advised the applicant that it would be necessary to apply to the court for permission to extend time in which to do arbitration, pursuant to s. 45 of the Arbitration Act, 1954. S. 3(1) of the 1954 Act provides that arbitration shall be deemed to have commenced when one party serves on the other a written notice requiring him to appoint or concur in the appointing of an arbitrator. The applicant applied to the High Court for relief pursuant to s. 45. **Held** by Hamilton J. in granting the relief sought, and in deeming arbitration proceedings to have been commenced by the letter of 17 January, 1973: the respondent having repudiated on the grounds set forth in its letter of 13 October, 1970, will not suffer prejudice if those grounds are valid, and undue hardship would be caused to the applicant by refusing relief, notwithstanding the inexcusable delay of the applicant both in commencing arbitration and in making the instant application. *Walsh* v. *Shield Insurance Co. Ltd.*

(H.C.) [1976-7] ILRM 218

—— Compulsory acquisition.
see **Compulsory Acquisition,** 1-3

—— Lease — Option to furnish fee simple — Whether refusal of county registrar to deal with matter subject to arbitration.
see **Landlord and Tenant,** 11

ARREST AND DETENTION—*continued.*
see **Criminal Law,** 1-8, 18

—— Legality — Drunken driving — Whether necessary that accused be brought to Garda station as an arrested person.
see **Road Traffic Offences,** 2

—— Legality — Gardai trespassers on private property — Arrest affected through non-violent trespass not unlawful *per se.*
see **Road Traffic Offences,** 6

—— Legality — Overt surveillance — Manner and purpose — Whether amounts to continuing detention — Whether amounts to unlawful harassment.
see **Constitution,** 17

—— Legality — Road traffic offences.
see **Road Traffic Offences,** 1-6

—— Legality — Second arrest — Validity of second arrest without release from custody.
see **Criminal Law,** 8

—— Legality — Suspicion of Garda — Suspicion of commission of scheduled offence — Unauthorised possession of firearm — Detention — Suspicion not genuine — Deliberate violation of right to liberty — Subsequent extradition proceedings tainted with illegality.
see **Constitution,** 16

—— Legality — Statutory power — Whether removal to a second Garda station made arrest unlawful.
see **Road Traffic Offences,** 3

—— Misuse of powers — Whether a conscious or deliberate violation of constitutional rights.
see **Constitution,** 16

—— Offences against the State Act.
see **Criminal Law,** 4-6, 8

—— Personal injuries — Damages — Liability — Plaintiff detained in Garda station — Plaintiff setting fire to cell and suffering extensive burns — Negligence — Contributory negligence.
see **Damages,** 13

—— Place — Dwelling of citizen — Garda Síochána entering dwelling house — Whether entry by Gardai lawful —

ARREST AND DETENTION—*continued.*
Whether arrest lawful — Inviolability of dwelling.
see **Criminal Law,** 7

—— Released prisoner — Order for re-arrest of released prisoner following breach of a condition of his release — Failure to make arrest until after the expiry of the prisoner's sentence — Whether subsequent imprisonment lawful or fair.
see **Prisons,** 4

—— Statement of admission by accused while in detention — Admissibility.
see under **Accused**

—— Statutory power — Motive — Arrest in respect of scheduled offence — Questioning in respect of non-scheduled offence — Whether arrest lawful.
see **Constitution,** 15
Criminal Law, 1, 6, 18

—— Suspicion — Emergency powers — Arrest on suspicion of being a terrorist — Whether constable had honest suspicion.
see **Criminal Law,** 3

—— Suspicion — Offences against the State — Whether suspicion of arresting officer required — Whether suspicion of other person, communicated to arresting officer, sufficient.
see **Criminal Law,** 4

—— Wrongful arrest — Damages — Plaintiff arrested in army raid and held for several hours — Assessment of damages — Whether exemplary damages should be awarded.
see **Damages,** 5

ARSON
see **Criminal Injuries,** 6

ARTERIAL DRAINAGE — Fishery — Interference — Spawning beds upstream beyond fishery area — Reduction in fish stock — Whether injury to fishery — Compensation — Assessment — Rules.
see **Real Property,** 4

ARTISTIC WORKS
—— Copyright — Infringement — Reproduction.
see **Contract,** 3
Copyright, 1

—— Income tax — Exemption — Work to be

ARTISTIC WORKS—*continued.*

"original and creative" — Exemption not granted for later works — Whether later works "original and creative".
see **Revenue,** 34

ASBESTOS WASTE — Planning appeal — Whether injurious to health — Whether oral hearing required.
see **Constitution,** 20

ASSAULT

—— **Battery** — *Plaintiff struck by baton round deliberately fired by soldier — No specific defence pleaded justifying firing of baton round — Whether plaintiff struck intentionally. Practice — Pleadings — Application to amend pleadings for purpose of appeal hearing.*] The plaintiff was struck and injured by a baton round fired by a soldier after the security forces had been attacked by rioters. The plaintiff claimed damages from the defendants pleading two causes of action viz. negligence and assault and battery. It was not disputed that the plaintiff had been struck by a baton round deliberately fired by a soldier. The defendants did not plead any specific defence justifying the firing of the baton round. The trial judge delivered his judgment only in relation to the claim of negligence dismissing the claim on the ground that the plaintiff had not proved negligence on the part of the defendants. The plaintiff appealed arguing that the trial judge failed to consider and adjudicate upon the claim of assault and battery. The defendant argued that the tort of battery was not committed unless a baton round was deliberately fired with the intention of striking the plaintiff. The defendant also applied for leave to amend the defence. **Held** allowing the appeal and ordering a new trial, that, 1, a battery is the intentional and direct application of force to another person even although the person directly struck may not be the person whom the assailant intended to strike. 2. The soldier who fired the baton round which struck the plaintiff was guilty of battery to the plaintiff and the plaintiff was entitled to damages unless the defendants could establish the defence that the firing was justified. The defendant would not have been entitled at the trial to raise this defence as it had not been pleaded and for this reason an application to amend the defence for the purpose of the appeal hearing to include justification was refused. However, the defendants were given leave to amend the defence for the purpose of the new trial. *Livingstone* v. *Ministry of Defence*

(C.A.) [1984] N.I.356

—— Damages — Plaintiff assaulted by a member of an army patrol — Awarded aggravated damages — Whether

ASSAULT—*continued.*

exemplary damages should be awarded — Whether soldier a "servant of the government" — Whether aggressive conduct.
see **Damages,** 4

ASSOCIATION
see **Freedom of Association**

ATHLETE — Suspension.
see **Natural and Constitutional Justice,** 2

ATHLETIC CLUB — Income Tax — Exemption.
see **Revenue,** 35

ATTACHMENT
see **Contempt of Court**

ATTACHMENT OF DEBTS
see **Garnishee**

ATTORNEY GENERAL

—— Function — High Court — Constitutional issue — Challenge to validity of pre-1937 statute — Requirement by rules of court that Attorney General be notified of proceedings challenging the validity of law having regard to the provisions of the Constitution — Whether requirement extended to challenge to validity of pre-1937 statute.
see **Practice and Procedure,** 14

—— Guardian of public rights — Company operating in breach of a statutory monopoly — Attorney General, acting as guardian of public rights, seeking an injunction — Whether proceedings misconceived.
see **Postal Service**

—— Guardian of public rights — Private assertion — Whether common law limitations on private assertion of public rights carried over from common law by Constitution.
see **Practice and Procedure,** 8

AUCTIONEERS AND ESTATE AGENTS

—— **Contract** — *Fees — Auction cancelled — Vendor subsequently selling premises by private treaty — Whether auctioneer entitled to fees.*] The plaintiffs, a firm of auctioneers, were engaged by the defendants to offer their premises for sale by public auction. By agreement in writing, the plaintiffs' fees were set at the rate of 2.5% payable by the defendants. The defendants were also liable for advertising expenses. The auction was subsequently cancelled, and some months later, the defendants sold their premises by private treaty to one R., who had initially contacted the plaintiffs to make an offer upon seeing the notice of postponement of the auction in a newspaper. The plaintiffs claimed, in breach of contract, the sum of £2,650, being 2.5% of the proceeds of sale of the defendants' premises, on the ground that it was an implied term of their agreement that the fee would be paid in the event of a sale to any person introduced. **Held** by Gannon J. in dismissing the plaintiffs' claim, 1, a contract made with an agent to conduct a public auction is one whereby the agent is promised his commission upon completion of the transaction which he is endeavouring to bring about. *Luxor (Eastbourne) Ltd.* v *Cooper* [1941] A.C. 108 applied. 2. The plaintiffs were not bound by the terms of the contract to convey to the defendants any offers which they might have received prior to the proposed auction, nor were the defendants obliged to accept any such offers. 3. The provision in the contract for payment to the plaintiffs

of advertising expenses is consistent with the proposition that there would be no remuneration if an auction were not held. *Daniel Morrissey & Sons Ltd.* v. *Nalty*

(H.C.) [1976-7] ILRM 269

—— Agreement — Sole selling agent — Whether principal entitled to refuse to pay commission where sale completed without assistance of agent.
see **Agency,** 1

—— Duty of care — Defective premises — Whether auctioneer valuing dwelling on behalf of housing authority owed the purchaser a common law duty of care.
see **Negligence,** 2

AUTREFOIS ACQUIT, PLEA OF — Whether the quashing of an order amounts to an acquittal.
see **Criminal Law,** 53

B

BAIL

—— Extradition — Tests applicable — Likelihood of accused absconding — Onus of proof lying on person resisting application.

see **Extradition,** 1

—— Station bail — Recognisance returnable for four days later — Intervening sitting of the District Court — Validity of procedure — Whether "appropriate time" — Jurisdiction of District Court.

see **Criminal Law,** 36

BAILMENT

—— **Detinue** — *Implied term as to title of bailor — Plaintiffs discovering property at national monument — Property having been buried with the object of concealing it — Delivery of property to the State — Plaintiffs demanding return of property — State alleging that property unlawfully in possession of plaintiffs prior to bailment — State seeking to assert its own subsequently acquired title — Obligation of bailee to account for property to bailor — Whether State estopped from denying title of plaintiffs — National Monuments Act,* 1930 (*No.* 2), *ss.* 8, 14.

Constitution — The State — Prerogative — Treasure trove — Whether the State entitled to former royal prerogative of treasure trove — Constitution of Saorstát Éireann, 1922, *Arts.* 2, 73 — *Constitution of Ireland,* 1937, *Art.* 49.

Constitution — The State — Sovereignty — Incidents of sovereignty — Antiquities of national importance — Treasure trove — Bona vacantia — Lost or mislaid chattels — "Natural resources" — "Royalties and franchises" — Personal rights — Property rights — Constitution of Saorstát Éireann, 1922, *Arts. 2, 11, 51 — Constitution of Ireland,* 1937, *Arts.* 5, 10, 40.3, 49.

Equity — Estoppel — Reasonable expectation — Plaintiffs discovering valuable antiquities at national monument — Property delivered into custody of State — Assurance that plaintiffs would be honourably treated — Whether plaintiffs entitled to a reward.] On the 17 February, 1980, the plaintiffs visited a ruined abbey where, using a metal detector, they discovered and dug up a hoard of treasure. From the circumstances of its discovery the hoard had clearly been buried with the object of concealing it. The plaintiffs had the implied permission of the owners of the land on which the ruins stood to visit the site but they had no permission to dig on the lands. A preservation order had been made in respect of the ruin under the National Monuments Act, 1930, so that it was an offence to injure or to interfere with the site. The plaintiffs took possession of the hoard and later brought it to the National Museum where it was delivered to the director with a letter stating that it was given into his care '. . . for the present and pending the determination of the legal ownership or status thereof.' The director received the hoard and promised the plaintiffs that they would be honourably treated. The National Museum, with the consent of the landowners, carried out excavations on the site and found a number of missing components of the objects and carried out restoration work on them. In November, 1981, the plaintiffs' solicitors wrote to the Chief State Solicitor asking for the return of the hoard but the Chief State Solicitor replied that it was the property of the State. The plaintiffs then brought proceedings for the return of the treasures. Meanwhile, following negotiations with the National Museum, each of the landowners had conveyed all rights, property and interest which they might have in the hoard to the Minister for Education. In their defence to the plaintiffs' proceedings the defendants pleaded that the treasures, insofar as they consisted of treasure trove were the property of the State and insofar as they did not, that they were the property of the Minister for Education by virtue of the conveyances from the landowners. **Held** by Blayney J., in giving judgment for the plaintiffs, 1, that the action was not concerned with and would not determine the ownership of the hoard but was an action between a bailor and a bailee in which the only issue was whether the plaintiffs, as bailors, were entitled to the return of the hoard. 2. That it was an implied term of the bailment that the bailor had title to the goods bailed. Accordingly, the defendants were estopped from denying the title of the plaintiffs or from claiming that the plaintiffs' possession was unlawful. 3. That a person who has received property from another as his bailee, agent or servant must, as a general rule, restore or account for that property to the person from whom he received it. The only defences available to a bailee in an action for non-delivery were for the bailee either to show that he had delivered the goods to the order of the bailor or to allege and prove the title of a third party; but the State, as bailee, was not entitled to attempt to set up any title it might have in the property. *Rogers, Sons & Co.* v. *Lambert & Co.* [1891] 1 Q.B. 318 and *Biddle* v. *Bond* (1865) 6 B. & S. 225 followed. 4. That the right to treasure trove had been part of the royal prerogative of the Crown which had not been carried over into the law of Saorstát Éireann by Article 73 of the 1922 Constitution and so was not part of the law of

BAILMENT—*continued.*

Saorstát Éireann at the time of passing of the Constitution of Ireland, 1937, and was not part of current law. *Byrne* v. *Ireland* [1972] I.R. 241 applied. 5. That the work done on the hoard while it was in the possession of the National Museum had greatly added to its value so that it would be inequitable to order the return of the hoard without requiring the plaintiffs to make a fair and just allowance to the State commensurate with the expenditure which had been incurred by the State in preserving and restoring the hoard. *Munro* v. *Wilmott* [1949] 1 K.B. 295 and *Greenwood* v. *Bennett* [1973] Q.B. 195 followed. *Peruvian Guano Co.* v. *Dreyfus Brothers & Co.* [1982] A.C. 166 distinguished. 6. That when the plaintiffs' solicitors demanded the return of the hoard the National Museum had notice of the plaintiffs' claim and so were no longer in the position of innocent purchasers. In spending further monies on the hoard the National Museum, even if it honestly believed the State to be the owner of the hoard, must necessarily have accepted the risk that the plaintiffs' claim was valid and accordingly, the allowance should not take account of work done after that date. *Greenwood v. Bennett* [1973] Q.B. 195 considered. 7. That in the absence of any evidence of actual damage suffered by the plaintiffs the award of damages for detention should be nominal only. 8. That the plaintiffs were entitled to an order for the return of the hoard conditional upon payment of the allowance or, at their option, to recover its value less the amount of the allowance, together with £1 damages for its detention. On appeal by the defendants it was **Held** by the Supreme Court (Finlay C.J., Walsh, Henchy, Griffin and McCarthy JJ.), in allowing the appeal and in substituting an order for the payment of a reward to the plaintiffs, 1, that no royal prerogative in existence prior to the enactment of the Constitution of Saorstát Éireann wsas by virtue of the provisions of that Constitution vested in the Irish Free State and accordingly could not be captured by Article 49, s. 1 of the Constitution of Ireland. *Byrne v. Ireland* [1972] I.R. 241 applied. 2. That while in general a bailment involved an implied term as to the title of the bailor to the goods, it could do so only where such an implied term was not excluded by the express terms of the bailment. *Rogers, Sons & Co. v. Lambert & Co.* [1891] 1 Q.B. 318 considered. 3. (Walsh and McCarthy JJ. dissenting). That the terms of the plaintiffs' solicitors' letter which accompanied the delivery of the hoard were wholly inconsistent with implying into any bailment arising from that delivery any acknowledgment or admission of the plaintiffs' title. 4. That, where a bailee asserted and established a good title in himself to the goods, he established the termination of the bailment and, by reason of such termination, any estoppel which would otherwise operate between bailor and bailee ceased to operate. *Rogers, Sons & Co.* v. *Lambert & Co.* [1891] 1 Q.B. 318 and *Biddle v. Bond* (1865) 6 B. & S. 225 considered. 5. (McCarthy J. *dubitante*). That the owner of a fee simple interest in land can assert a good claim to possession, as distinct from ownership, of any chattels which may be found in the land as against a finder of those chattels (trespasser or otherwise) whose claim is based simply on unearthing and removing the chattels. *Elwes* v. *Brigg Gas Co.* (1886) 33 Ch. D. 562 and *Parker* v. *British Airways Board* [1982] Q.B. 1004 considered. 6. (Per Finlay C.J.; Henchy and Griffin JJ. concurring). That in any event the fact that the plaintiffs were finders by an act of trespass would disentitle them to any rights in the object found; certainly as between them and the owners of the lands. 7. (Walsh J. dissenting). That by the conveyances of the landowners of their rights in the hoard the State became entitled to ownership and possession of the hoard subject only to the rights of any person capable of proving a title as "true owner". 8. (Walsh and McCarthy JJ. dissenting). That the expression "all royalties" in Article 10, s. 1 of the Constitution, construed in the light of Article 5, must be widely construed and must include the sovereignty or sovereign rule of the State. 9. That it is a necessary ingredient of sovereignty in a modern State and certainly in the State having regard to the provisions of the Constitution of Ireland with an emphasis on its historical origins and a constant concern for the common good, that there should be ownership in the State of all objects which constitute antiquities of importance and are discovered to have no known owner. 10. That it would be inconsistent with the framework of the society created and protected by the Constitution if such objects could become the exclusive property of those who by design or chance might discover them or of the owners of the lands on which they might be found. 11. *Per* Walsh J. That this applied to all antiquities of national importance, not only those made of gold and silver. 12. *Per* Walsh and McCarthy JJ. That the right of the State to exercise dominion over all artefacts forming part of the national heritage derived not from Article 10 which was concerned with natural resources but from the declaration of the sovereignty of the State contained in Article 5. 13. That the unqualified assurance given to the plaintiffs by the director or of the National Museum that they would be honourably treated was an integral part of the transaction under which the hoard was deposited in the Museum and accepted on behalf of the State. It would be inequitable and unjust if the State were allowed to repudiate that assurance and give only a

BAILMENT—*continued.*

meagre and disproportionate reward. *Amalgamated Property Co.* v. *Texas Bank* [1982] Q.B. 84 considered. 14. That in the circumstances of the case it was proper that the Supreme Court should assess the appropriate reward. 15. That having regard to the value and importance of the objects found, the circumstances of their finding, the nature and extent of past rewards and the attitude and conduct of the plaintiffs after the find, the court would assess £25,000 each as the appropriate reward. *Webb* v. *Ireland*

(H.C., S.C.) [1988] I.R.353; [1988] ILRM 565

BANKING

see also **Industrial and Provident Societies; Negotiable Instruments**

1. —— **Fraudulent misappropriation** — *Foreign company — Money lodged to account — Claim that this money consisted of funds fraudulently misappropriated — Whether sufficient inference of fraud — Obligation of receiving bank — Whether required to repay the funds actually advanced.*] Following the compulsory liquidation of the first-named plaintiff, an Italian company based in Milan, the second, third and fourth-named plaintiffs were appointed liquidating commissioners. They sought a declaration that they were entitled to possession of monies lodged in an account in Ansbacher Bank in Dublin. These monies were in the name of the last-named defendant and under the control of the second-named defendant. The plaintiffs alleged that the said monies had been fraudulently misappropriated by the second-named defendant, who, they alleged, had utilised, in conspiracy with three other named persons, an opportunity presented by the recapitalisation of a large Italian publishing company in order to perpetrate a fraud upon the first-named plaintiff. The alleged fraud involved a transfer of large sums of money from the first-named plaintiff to Banco Ambrosiano Overseas Ltd (B.A.O.L.), which sums the plaintiffs said were never repaid. Records of the first-named plaintiff company were examined by an independent expert witness, who gave evidence that two sums deposited with B.A.O.L. were repaid with interest on the due date. The said sums were identical with the sums which the plaintiffs alleged had not been repaid. The plaintiffs did not attempt to establish that these records did not represent the true position. However, they alleged that the monies used to repay the advance were not the identical monies that had been advanced, and that the monies which had been advanced had been fraudulently misappropriated. **Held** by Hamilton P. in refusing to make the declaration sought, 1, where money is deposited with a bank, the receiving

BANKING—*continued.*

bank fulfils its obligations if it repays an equivalent amount, plus the agreed interest, to the depositor. 2. The actual monies deposited with B.A.O.L. ceased on the date of the deposit to be the property of the depositor. (3) The plaintiffs, therefore, have failed to discharge the onus of proof that funds were fraudulently misappropriated, or that the sum claimed herein formed a portion of funds fraudulently misappropriated from the plaintiff company. On appeal it was **Held** by the Supreme Court in allowing the appeal, in finding that the removal of the monies the subject-matter of the proceedings from Banco Ambrosiano was fraudulent, and in making a declaration in favour of the plaintiffs in respect of the said monies, 1, there is no rational or cogent reason why fraud in civil cases should require a higher standard of proof than that of the balance of probabilities. Where, however, such proof is largely a matter of inference, such inference must not be drawn lightly, or without regard to all the circumstances, including the circumstances of the consequences of a finding of fraud. *Per* Henchy J. — in considering an allegation of fraud, evidence cannot be ignored which tends to show that the person accused of fraud has acted in an apparently dishonest manner in other matters relating to the same general transaction. 2. The evidence established that the second named defendant had obtained the money through a series of transactions which could only be interpreted as a dishonest appropriation. 3. An appellate court hearing an appeal from a decision of a judge sitting without a jury will be at liberty to disagree with such decision if it depended upon the judge's view of the evidence, or inferences he had drawn from it, since the competence of the appellate court to evaluate the questions in issue is no less than that of the tribunal of fact, the evidential data being essentially the same in both courts. *Northern Bank Finance v Charlton* [1979] I.R. 149 applied. *Banco Ambrosiano S.P.A.* v. *Ansbacher & Co.*

(H.C., S.C.) [1987] ILRM 669

2. —— **Guarantee** — *Guarantee to bank payable on demand — Continuing security — Accrual of cause of action — Necessity of demand.*

Limitation of actions — Survival of cause of action — Guarantee payable on demand — Continuing security — Demand made after death of guarantor — Proceedings against estate of guarantor — Whether cause of action subsisting at time of death of deceased — Proceedings commenced 3 years after death of guarantor — Whether claim statute barred — Civil Liability Act, 1961 (*No.* 41), *ss.* 8, 9.] Section 9, sub-s. 2 of the Civil Liability Act, 1961, provides *inter alia* that:- "(2). No proceedings shall be maintainable in respect

BANKING—*continued.*

of any cause of action whatsoever which has survived against the estate of a deceased person unless . . . (*b*) proceedings are commenced in respect of that cause of action within . . . the period of two years after his death . . .". On the 19 February, 1985, proceedings were instituted against the defendant as legal personal representative of M.O'K. for monies due on foot of a continuing guarantee dated the 18 November, 1980, whereby M.O'K. had guaranteed to pay on demand the debts of B. Ltd. M.O'K. had died on the 11 February, 1982, and a demand for payment on foot of the guarantee had been made against his estate on the 6 May, 1982. The defendant disputed the plaintiff's claim arguing that it was statute barred by s. 9, sub-s. 2 of the Act of 1961. **Held** by Barron J., in giving judgment for the plaintiffs, 1, that the plaintiffs' cause of action on foot of the guarantee did not arise until after the demand was made. 2. That since the plaintiffs' demand had not been made until after the death of the deceased, there was no cause of action subsisting against him at the time of his death and, accordingly, s. 9, sub-s. 2 of the Act of 1961 was not applicable. *In re J. Brown's Estate. Brown* v. *Brown* [1893] 2 Ch. 300 followed. *Bank of Ireland v. O'Keeffe*

(H.C.) [1987] I.R.47

3. —— **Guarantee** — *Charge to bank to secure loan to company — Associated company acting as surety — Directors also guaranteeing loan and charging property — Default in repayments — Proceedings against corporate surety — Decree for possession of property — Appeal to Supreme Court pending — Proceedings also instituted against directors — Whether bank entitled to exercise its rights to possession of directors' property until they have exercised their rights against the principal debtor and co-surety — Whether doctrine of marshalling applicable.*] The defendants were directors of V.I. Co., which had granted a licence to an associate company, A.I., to develop lands, the property of V.I., at Bullock Harbour, Dun Laoghaire. In pursuit of this end, the plaintiff advanced sums of money to both companies. As security for the V.I. debt, the plaintiff obtained a legal mortgage of four penthouse apartments on the Bullock Harbour site, and a joint and several guarantee from the defendants. This guarantee was supported by a mortgage on a house in Kilcroney and one in Drumcondra, the property of the defendants. The Kilcroney house was later released from the mortgage, and the plaintiff accepted instead an equitable mortgage upon a house in Santry. As security for the loan granted to A.I., the plaintiff obtained a first legal mortgage of the building licence, and a guarantee from V.I., supported by a mortgage

of the four penthouse apartments already mentioned, and a mortgage of the freehold site on which the apartments were built. The defendants and a third party also jointly and severally guaranteed the loan, which guarantee was supported by a charge on the houses at Kilcroney and Drumcondra. Both companies defaulted on their repayments. In earlier proceedings, the plaintiff had sued both companies jointly for possession of the site at Bullock Harbour. An order for possession was made, and at the date of the instant proceedings, an appeal to the Supreme Court was pending. The instant proceedings comprised two separate actions. In the first, the plaintiff sued the defendants as sureties of the A.I. debt, claiming possession of the Kilcroney property. The defendants argued that if the two companies were unsuccessful in their Supreme Court appeal, the proceeds of sale of the Bullock Harbour site would be sufficient to discharge A.I.'s debt. The second action was a claim by the plaintiff against the defendants as sureties of the debt owed by V.I., in which the plaintiff sought a well-charging order and the sale of the Santry property. The defendants contended that if the Supreme Court confirmed the High Court order for possession of the Bullock Harbour site, the plaintiff could expect to realise a sum greater than the debt owed by V.I. **Held** by Costello J. in finding for the plaintiff and making the orders sought, 1, the doctrine of marshalling cannot be relied upon as a defence to proceedings instituted by a creditor against one or more of several co-sureties, where they have separately mortgaged different properties as securities for their separate guarantees. 2. The plaintiff is not estopped from maintaining its action against the defendants, notwithstanding that its action against the defendants' co-surety is unresolved. 3. The defence to the plaintiff's claim against V.I. is based on an error of fact, as the Bullock Harbour site was not charged with any liability in respect of the debt of V.I. *Lombard & Ulster Banking Ltd.* v. *Murray*

(H.C.) [1987] ILRM 522

—— Bank — Negligence — Customer involved in business with relative making payment by cheque to customers — Customer allowed to maintain account beyond overdraft — Customer's relative's business collapsed — Customer requesting information from bank on relative's creditworthiness — Customer's business collapsing — Whether bank liable.

see **Negligence,** 20

—— Banker — Books — Power of the High Court to order the production for

BROADCASTING

1. —— **Radio broadcasting station** — *Unlicensed possession and use of apparatus for wireless telegraphy — Apparatus seized — Constitution — Fair procedures — Whether seizure procedure inconsistent with guarantee of fair procedures — Application for a mandatory injunction requiring return of apparatus — Wireless Telegraphy Act,* 1926 (*No.* 45), *ss.*3, 5, 8, 12.

BROADCASTING—*continued.*

Injunction — Interlocutory — Unlicensed possession and use of apparatus for wireless telegraphy — Apparatus seized — Constitutional challenge to the seizure procedure — Application for an injunction restraining interference with the broadcasting — Application for a mandatory injunction requiring return of apparatus — Whether injunctions be granted.] The plaintiffs owned and operated radio broadcasting stations. At no time had they applied for a licence to possess or use apparatus for wireless telegraphy to the defendant Minister who, under the Wireless Telegraphy Act, 1926, had sole power to grant or refuse such licences. Acting under a search warrant granted pursuant to s. 8 of the Act, officials of the Department of Posts and Telegraphs seized the plaintiffs' broadcasting equipment. The plaintiffs issued proceedings claiming the relevant provisions of the Act to be inconsistent with the Constitution and in violation of the EEC Treaty. They then applied to court for interlocutory relief restraining the defendants from interfering with their ability to broadcast and seeking the return of their equipment pending trial of the full action. The plaintiffs contended that: (i) the defendant Minister had abused his power under the Act to the extent of creating a broadcasting monopoly in favour of the State broadcasting station; (ii) the Act was in violation of Articles 38, 40.6.1°.i and 45 of the Constitution; and (iii) they would suffer irreparable loss to their business if the interlocutory relief they sought was refused. **Held** by Murphy J. in refusing the applications, 1, the evidence had not established that the Minister had abused his regulatory power under the 1926 Act. 2. The plaintiffs' constitutional claims made out a stateable case involving difficult quesions of law calling for detailed consideration. *Dicta* of Lord Diplock in *American Cyanamid Co.* v. *Ethicon Ltd.* [1975] A.C. 396, 407 applied. 3. While the defendants might not suffer financial loss if the plaintiffs were successful in their applications, it would only be in extraordinary cases that the courts would restrain a Minister from performing a duty laid on him by legislation passed for the common good. The implicit representations over a number of years that the plaintiffs' activities would be regularised did not amount to such an extraordinary case. *Nova Media Services Ltd.* v. *Minister for Posts and Telegraphs*

(H.C.) [1984] ILRM 161

2. —— **Radio broadcasting station** — *Unlicensed possession and use of apparatus for wireless telegraphy — Apparatus seized — Application for a mandatory injunction requiring return of apparatus.*] Murphy J. delivered his judgment on 10 June 1983 saying: The facts of this case, the arguments made and the relief sought are similar to those dealt with in the judgment just delivered (*Nova Media Services & Anor* v. *The Minister for Posts & Telegraphs & Ors* [1984] ILRM 161). It is perhaps proper to note that in this matter the defendants did seek to establish with greater certainty that the plaintiff company had been responsible for certain radio interference caused at Dublin Airport. On the other hand the plaintiffs produced detailed evidence on affidavit in refutation of this charge. All that can be said at this stage is that the conflict in this area has been heightened. Clearly it cannot be resolved until the various witnesses can be heard and cross-examined in their evidence. Another feature of this case which to some extent distinguishes it from the *Radio Nova* proceedings is the fact that the plaintiff company has not resumed broadcasting since its equipment was seized by the Minister. It is not clear whether this is due to the absence of appropriate equipment or a policy decision made by the plaintiffs. However as I understand it the plaintiffs in these proceedings — unlike the plaintiffs in the *Radio Nova* case — are pressing an application for a mandatory injunction for the return of the equipment. As I have already indicated in the *Radio Nova* case on facts which are substantially the same as those in the present case I do not accept that this is a proper case in which to grant a negative injunction. A *fortiori* it would be wholly inappropriate to make a positive order. Indeed, whatever might be said in favour of restraining further action by the defendants I would find it impossible to see how a court set up under the Constitution could, on an interlocutory application, direct a Government Minister to return equipment to a plaintiff to enable that plaintiff to commit what is on the face of it a criminal offence. Accordingly, the application will be refused. *Sunshine Radio Productions Ltd.* v. *Attorney General*

(H.C.) [1984] ILRM 170

—— Freedom of expression — Broadcast of television programme concerning Circuit Court proceedings under appeal — Plaintiff alleging programme critical of Circuit Court judgment — Right to a fair trial — Whether programme brought administration of justice into disrepute — Whether unbalanced programme amounts to contempt of court.
see **Contempt of Court,** 1

BUILDER
see also **Building Contract.**

—— Building company — Sale of land —

BUILDER—*continued.*

Deposits — Building company intending to build apartment block — "Booking" deposits paid — Neither building agreements nor contracts for the sale of land executed — Insolvency of company — Depositors claiming lien over site of proposed development — Booking deposit held not to confer on prospective purchaser a lien on building site or an equitable estate.
see **Sale of Land,** 15

—— Duty of care — Defective premises — Dwelling built on land owned by builder — Whether builder owed a common law duty of care to purchaser.
see **Negligence,** 2, 3

—— Negligence — Defective premises — Contribution — Engineer's certificate as to structural stability — Architect's certificate based on such certificate — Whether builder or architect negligent.
see **Negligence,** 1

—— Negligence — Demolition work — Adjoining premises.
see **Negligence,** 5

BUILDING CONTRACT

1. —— **Breach** — *Defects in premises — Computation of damages — Whether purchaser entitled to loss in letting value or loss of interest on capital.*

Landlord and tenant — Covenant — Premises being authorised structure — Failure to obtain planning permission — Whether breach of covenant for quiet enjoyment — Landlord and Tenant Law Amendment (Ireland) Act, 1860 (*c.* 154), *s.* 41.] The plaintiff purchased, by way of lease for a term of nine hundred years, an unfinished house from the defendant, a firm of builders. Her action against the defendant was based on two separate claims. She claimed firstly that no valid planning permission had been obtained for the house, which was, therefore, an unauthorised structure within the meaning of the Local Government (Planning and Development) Act, 1963. In this regard, the plaintiff sought an order awarding her the estimated cost of rectifying alleged defects if proper planning permission was secured and the house put in order. Secondly, the plaintiff claimed that the house was so poorly constructed and finished that the defendant had failed to give her what she had contracted to buy, namely, a house of high quality. Evidence was adduced to show that the house was of superior design, but that the workmanship, finish and materials left much to be desired. The plaintiff claimed further a sum equivalent to the loss to her in letting value, as it had been her intention to instal a tenant in the house when it was completed, and she also claimed a sum equivalent to the loss of interest on capital to date. **Held** by Parke J. in awarding damages in compensation for defects in the premises, and in making a declaration that no proper planning permission had been obtained, with liberty to either party to apply, 1, the relief claimed in relation to the lack of planning permission was based on a hypothesis, and the court could not make such an order. 2. Damages for breach of contract are assessed as being such as may fairly and reasonably be considered to arise naturally from the breach itself, or may reasonably be supposed to have been in the contemplation of the parties. *Hadley* v. *Baxendale* (1854) 9 Exch. 341 followed. 3. There was no evidence to show that the plaintiff's intention to produce an income by letting had ever been communicated to the defendant so as to put him on notice that a claim might arise under this head. Neither had evidence been adduced, nor any legal basis demonstrated, as to loss of interest on capital being a measure of damages in the circumstances. *Fitzpatrick* v. *Frank McGivern Ltd.*
(H.C.) [1976-77] ILRM 239

2. —— **Breach** — *Defects in premises — Exclusion clause — Further clause that purchaser not deprived of his common law rights — Claim for damages for remedying defects and for diminution in value — Whether caught by exclusion clause — Whether purchaser entitled to damages for inconvenience and loss of engagement.*] The plaintiff, the purchaser of a dwellinghouse built by the defendant, sued the defendant for breach of an agreement in writing whereby the house was to be built in accordance with certain specifications. The plaintiff claimed damages in respect of certain defects in the dwellinghouse and for inconvenience and anxiety caused to him as a consequence of the said defects. The contract between the parties contained a clause excluding any liability of the defendant for structural defects arising from materials and workmanship not being in accordance with the specifications, unless notice in writing were given within a period of eighteen months from the date of completion and within one month from the date on which the defects became apparent. However, at the instance of the plaintiff, a further clause was added to the agreement, providing that nothing in the contract was to deprive the purchaser of his common law rights. The defendant argued that the exclusion clause operated to prevent liability for any defects not notified within the specified time. **Held** by McMahon J. in giving judgment for the plaintiff, 1, since the plaintiff had a common law right to recover damages for

BUILDING CONTRACT—*continued.*

breach of contract, the effect of the additional clause was to deprive the defendant of the benefit of the exclusion clause in the contract. 2. Damages may be awarded for inconvenience or loss of enjoyment when these are in the presumed contemplation of the parties as being likely to result from the breach of contract. *Johnson* v. *Longleat Properties (Dublin) Ltd.*

(H.C.) [1976-7] ILRM 93

3. —— **R.I.A.I. Standard Form** — *Practice — Set off — Summary judgment — Whether defendant entitled to set off — R.I.A.I. Standard Form building contract,* 1966 *edition — Whether provisions of same inconsistent with right of set off.*] The plaintiff sought to enter summary judgment for the sum of £168,537 on foot of three interim architect's certificates issued under a contract for the erection by the plaintiff of a factory for the defendant. The defendant sought to resist judgment on the basis that it was entitled to set off against the said sum certain quantified claims as yet unproved against the plaintiff, relating to alleged breaches of contract. Clause 29 of the contract provided for payment of the amount specified in an interim certificate within fourteen days, subject only to any default in payment of sub-contractors, and to the right of the employer to retain a specified amount. Clause 28 envisaged the suspension of works upon failure to pay upon the interim certificate, and clause 31 provided for arbitration of all disputes after completion of the works. **Held** by Finlay P. in finding the plaintiff entitled to enter judgment in the amount claimed, 1, the true test as to whether a common-law right of set-off exists in relation to payment on foot of an interim certificate in a building contract is whether all the relevant terms of the said contract are in any particular event inconsistent with the exercise of such right. *Gilbert-Ash (Northern) Ltd.* v. *Modern Engineering (Bristol) Ltd.* [1974] A.C. 689 considered. 2. The exercise of a right to set-off is not consistent with the provisions of clauses 28 and 29 of the instant contract, and, in particular, it would deprive the plaintiff of the right to refer the dispute to arbitration, this effectively frustrating clause 31. *John Sisk & Son Ltd.* v. *Lawter Products B.V.*

(H.C.) [1976-7] ILRM 204

4. —— **R.I.A.I. Standard Form** — *Practice — Set off — Architect's certificate of sum due to contractor — Interim certificate — Final certificate — Set off — Employer claiming damages for negligence and delay — Whether employer entitled to withold sums certified as payable and due to contractor pending determination of cross-claim — R.I.A.I. Standard Form Contract,* 1977 *ed., cl.* 38.] The plaintiff building contractor claimed against the defendant employer the sum of £101,799.23 arising out of a building contract,

BUILDING CONTRACT—*continued.*

in the R.I.A.I. Standard Form (1977 edition), between the parties. That sum was made up of a sum due on foot of an architect's interim certificate, a sum due on foot of an architect's final certificate, and a sum in respect of interest on those two sums calculated in accordance with the provisions of the contract. On a motion for summary judgment, the defendant admitted that the sums claimed had been duly certified for payment but claimed a right to set off an unliquidated claim, substantially in excess of that amount, for damages for negligence and delay on the part of the plaintiff in executing the works. The plaintiff claimed that the provisions of the articles of agreement between the parties precluded any right of set-off by the defendant and that the monies were immediately payable. **Held** by Murphy J., in refusing the plaintiff's application to enter final judgment, 1, that the amount included in an architect's certificate, whether interim or final, does not constitute a debt of a particular character and enjoys no special immunity from any cross-claims or right of set-off to which the debtor may be entitled. 2. That there is a presumption that each party to a building contract is entitled to all those remedies for its breach as would arise by operation of law, including the remedy of setting up a breach of warranty in diminution or extinction of the price of materials supplied or work executed under the contract. 3. That the parties to building contracts or sub-contracts, like the parties to any other type of contract, are entitled to incorporate in their contract any clause they please, in particular a clause extinguishing, curtailing or enlarging the ordinary rights of set-off. 4. That the question whether the parties have in fact curtailed or restricted the common law or equitable right of set-off depends on the construction of the agreement between them. *Modern Engineering* v. *Gilbert-Ash* [1974] A.C. 639 and *John Sisk and Son Limited* v. *Lawter Products B.V.* [1976-7] ILRM 204 considered. 5. That the test to be applied in determining whether the parties have in fact excluded the right of set-off is not whether the right has been unequivocally excluded by the terms of the contract but is rather whether all the relevant terms of the building contract are in any particular event inconsistent with the exercise in that event of such right. *John Sisk and Son Limited* v. *Lawter Products B.V.* [1976-7] ILRM 204, followed. 6. That, as a matter of construction, the terms of the R.I.A.I. (1977 edition) form of articles of agreement between the parties were not inconsistent with the right of set-off and counterclaim. *P.J. Hegarty & Sons Ltd.* v. *Royal Liver Friendly Society*

(H.C.) [1985] I.R.524

BUILDING CONTRACT—*continued.*

—— Action for specific performance — Sub-contractor — Nomination of alternative sub-contractor — Application for interlocutory injunction — Balance of convenience — Whether prejudice likely to result.
see **Injunction,** 1

—— Arbitration — Architect's certificate — Architect issuing final certificate for payment — Contractor subsequently making claim for additional payments — Whether contractor barred from pursuing these claims — Interpretation of building contract — General conditions.
see **Arbitration,** 4

—— Arbitration — Award — Application for an order to set aside award — Arbitrator refusing to state a case — Whether misconduct.
see **Arbitration,** 10

—— Arbitration — Award — Enforcement — Award made but payment not forthcoming — Application for liberty to enforce the award.
see **Arbitration,** 2

—— Defective premises — Damages — Measure of damages.
see **Damages,** 2

—— Delay in completion — Claim by main contractor against sub-contractor for delay — Arbitration — Certificate issued by architect exonerating contractor — Certificate did not state when in architect's opinion sub-contracting work ought to have been completed — Whether certificate adequate — Whether contractor can recover from sub-contractor in absence of certificate.
see **Arbitration,** 5

—— Execution — Title — Investigation — Solicitor — Investigation not made until after completion of building and making of payments — Discovery of pre-existing equitable mortgage.
see **Negligence,** 26

—— Main contractor in liquidation — Application of property — Monies paid to main contractor to meet its liability to sub-contractor — Winding up before payment to sub-contractor.
see **Company,** 16

—— Specific performance — Whether specific performance lies — Whether contract requiring constant supervision by court — Whether basis for refusal of order in existence.

BUILDING CONTRACT—*continued.*

see **Injunction,** 1

BUILDING SOCIETY

1. —— **Alteration of rules** — *Registration of alterations by Registrar of Building Societies — Function of Registrar — Alterations "in accordance with" the Act — Statutory definition of building society — Rule making powers of building society — Separate classes of shares with different voting rights — Separate categories of directors — Alternate directors — Proposed Merger or Takeover Conditional Order,* 1984 (*S.I. No.* 217) — *Building Societies Act,* 1836 (*c.* 32) — *Building Societies Act,* 1976 (*No.* 38), *s.*12 — *Mergers, Takeovers and Monopolies (Control) Act,* 1978 (*No.* 17), *s.*5.] The capital of the plaintiff building society was made up of approximately £20m. in investment shares, to which voting rights attached, and £87m. in savings shares, to which no voting rights attached. In February, 1984, an offer was made by Bank of Ireland to purchase all the investment shares, which was referred to the Minister for Industry, Trade, Commerce and Tourism pursuant to the Mergers, Takeovers and Monopolies (Control) Act, 1978. The Minister prohibited the proposed takeover except on terms that the rules of the plaintiff were amended in the manner in the schedule to his order. The plaintiff, by special resolution, altered its rules in accordance with the schedule and the alterations were forwarded to the defendant for registration under s. 12 of the Building Societies Act, 1976. The defendant took the view that the alterations were not in accordance with the 1976 Act and refused to register them. The plaintiff applied to the High Court, by way of appeal from the defendant's decision, for a declaration that the defendant was not entitled to refuse to register the alterations. **Held** by Murphy J., in granting the relief sought, 1, that the only feature of the definition of a building society in the Act of 1976 is that it should be incorporated for the limited or special purpose of raising money and advancing it to members or to persons deemed to be members upon a particular form of security. 2. That the only limit of the rule-making power of a building society, as to matters not governed by the general law or by any express prohibition in the Act, was that it could not be exercised so as to make the society a thing different from a building society formed for the purposes and in the manner defined by the Act. *Murphy* v. *Scott* (1884) 9 App. Cas. 519 followed. 3. That the Act of 1976, properly construed, permitted the issue of shares having a wide range of differing rights, both as to voting and otherwise. *Irish Permanent Building Society* v. *Cauldwell* [1981] ILRM 242 considered. 4. That there was nothing in the Act of 1976 which prevented the adoption of rules

BUILDING SOCIETY—*continued.*

alowing for two categories of directors and conferring on one class of shareholders the exclusive right to elect directors to one of those categories. 5. That there was nothing in the Act of 1976 to prevent rules being adopted empowering the directors to appoint alternate directors. On appeal by the defendant it was **Held** by the Supreme Court (Walsh, Henchy and Griffin JJ.), in disallowing the appeal, 1, that the duty of the Registrar of Building Societies in his examination of alterations to rules was only to ensure that rules made were not in conflict with the provisions of the Act. 2. That the Act of 1976 should be regarded as setting out a general framework but not as legislating in detail for the government of each society so that a society was free, within that general framework, to make such rules as were thought best for the administration and management of the society. 3. That, the Act having particularly provided that the plaintiff society could issue shares to which no voting rights attached, the plaintiff could issue shares which had only qualified or no voting rights and that the voting rights which attached to some shares could be more weighty than others. 4. That there was nothing in the Act which required that all directors must be of the same class or that the method of appointing or removing them should be uniform for all directors. 5. That the use of alternate directors was not in principle contrary to the basic structure or legal concept of building societies, nor was it prohibited by the statute. *Irish Civil Service Building Society* v. *Registrar of Friendly Societies*

(H.C., S.C.) [1985] I.R.167

2. —— **Prior mortgage** — *Premises subject to a charge to secure apportioned rent — Whether society precluded from lending money on such premises — Whether such charge a "prior mortgage" — Building Societies Act,* 1976 (*No.* 38), *s.* 80.

Statute — Interpretation — Meaning of "prior mortgage" — Teleological approach — Whether justified — Whether wholly unreasonable result — Alternative approaches open to legislature — Building Societies Act, 1976 (*No.* 38), *s.* 80.] The Building Societies Act, 1976, s. 80 prohibits a building society from making advances on property subject to a prior mortgage, unless the prior mortgage is its own. The plaintiff and defendant

BUILDING SOCIETY—*continued.*

were respectively the vendor and purchaser of a house subject to a small rent reserved in a lease created in 1904 but 'primarily liable' to an apportioned part of that rent by virtue of an assignment executed in 1962. The plaintiff denied the defendant's contention that a covenant to pay such rent constituted a mortgage. Though in form, a vendor and purchaser summons seeking completion of a sale, the action was essentially a test case taken to establish the effect of s. 80 of the Building Societies Act, 1976. **Held** by Murphy J., a charge to secure an apportioned part of a leasehold rent does constitute a prior mortgage within the menaing of s. 80. *Rafferty* v. *Crowley*

(H.C.) [1984] ILRM 350

BURGLARY
see **Criminal Injuries,** 3
Criminal Law, 33

BURIAL GROUND
—— Cattle wandering onto cemetery — Cattle poisoned by eating yew leaves — Wall between pastureland and cemetery damaged — Whether local authority negligent or in breach of statutory duty in not having wall repaired.
see **Negligence,** 28

—— Land acquired by trustees of Church of Ireland church for use as burial ground — Land situate within 100 yards of plaintiff's premises — Whether consent in writing of plaintiff required for use of land as burial ground.
see **Local Government,** 9

BUSINESS LAW
see **Agency; Banking; Company; Contract; Guarantee; Partnership; Revenue; Trade and Industry**

BUSINESS PREMISES — Lease — Restrictive covenant as to user.
see **Landlord and Tenant,** 2-5

BYE-LAWS — Definition — Whether regulations constitute bye-laws.
see **Local Government,** 8

C

CANAL — Nuisance — Lack of maintenance — Flooding — Breach of statutory duty.
see **Negligence,** 29

CAPITAL ACQUISITIONS TAX
see **Revenue,** 5

CAPITAL GAINS TAX
see **Compulsory Acquisition,** 1
Revenue, 6, 7

CASE STATED

1. —— Case Stated under Summary Jurisdiction Act, 1857 — *Applications to District Court for gaming certificate — Objection by local authority — Objection challenging jurisdiction of court — Applications struck out — Application for case stated on question of jurisdiction — Whether questions of jurisdiction may be subject of case stated — Whether court entitled to refuse to state case requested by party asserting jurisdiction of court — Summary Jurisdiction Act,* 1857 (*c.* 43), *s.* 2 — *Gaming and Lotteries Act,* 1956 (*No.* 2), *ss.* 15, 16 (1)(a) — *Courts (Supplemental Provisions) Act,* 1961 (*No.* 39), *s.* 51 (1).] The applicant, which was the holder of licences under the Gaming and Lotteries Act, 1956, in respect of two premises, applied to the District Court for the renewal of certificates authorising the issue of those licences. The relevant local authority objected to the grant of certificates on the grounds, *inter alia,* that the applicant had failed to give to the authority 28 days notice in writing of its intention to apply, as required by s. 16, sub-s. 1 (a) of the Act of 1956. The respondent District Justice ruled that, as that requirement had not been complied with, the applications were not properly before him, and he accordingly struck them out. The applicant subsequently applied to the respondent to state a case setting out the facts and the grounds of his decision for the opinions thereon of the High Court; this application was refused and no grounds for that refusal were given to the applicant. On the applicant's application to the High Court by way of judicial review for a rule pursuant to s. 5 of the Summary Jurisdiction Act, 1857, calling upon the respondent to show cause why he should not state and sign a case for the opinion of the High Court, and for an order of mandamus directing the respondent to state and sign a case as requested, it was **Held** by Blayney J. in granting the relief sought, 1, that there is no rule of law which prohibits the District Court from raising questions as to its own jurisdictions for the opinion thereon of the High Court by way of case stated. 2. That where a District Justice strikes out a case before him on the grounds that he has no jurisdiction to hear it, he is not entitled to refuse

CASE STATED—*continued.*

to state a case which is applied for by the party seeking to challenge that decision. *Attorney General* v. *Beirne* [1943] I.R. 480 explained. 3. That, since the respondent had not offered any reason to the applicant for his refusal to state a case, it must be assumed that he had been of opinion that the application was merely frivolous. 4. That it was open to the High Court to form its own opinion as to whether the application for a case stated was frivolous. In the instant case the application raised a substantial point of law and could not be considered frivolous. *The State (Turley)* v. *Ó Floinn* [1968] I.R. 248 applied. *Sports Arena Ltd.* v. *O'Reilly*

[1987] I.R.185

2. —— **Consultative case stated** — *Circuit Court — Jurisdiction — Whether Circuit Court required to hear evidence before case is stated to Supreme Court — Courts of Justice Act,* 1936 (*No.* 48), *s.* 38 (3) — *Courts of Justice Act,* 1947 (*No.* 20), *s.* 16.

Circuit Court — Jurisdiction — Case stated — Consultative case stated from Circuit Court to Supreme Court — Evidence not completed in Circuit Court — Whether Circuit Court had jurisdiction to state a case — Courts of Justice Act, 1947 (*No.* 20), *s.* 16.

Precedent — Stare decisis — *Previous decisions of Supreme Court — Jurisdiction of Supreme Court to review its previous decisions.]* The jurisdiction of a Circuit Court judge to refer a question of law to the Supreme Court by way of case stated for the determination of the Supreme Court, pursuant to s. 16 of the Courts of Justice Act, 1947, is exercisable at any time during the hearing of the matter before the Circuit Court notwithstanding that all the facts have not been found nor all the evidence heard. So **Held** by the Supreme Court (Finlay C.J., Walsh and McCarthy JJ.; Henchy and Griffin JJ. dissenting). *Corley* v. *Gill* [1975] I.R. 313 overruled. *Dolan* v. *Corn Exchange* [1975] I.R. 315 considered. *Doyle* v. *Hearne* (No. 1)

(S.C.) [1987] I.R.601; [1988] ILRM 318

3. —— **Criminal prosecution in District Court** — *Penalty in excess of District Court jurisdiction in civil matters — Whether offence a minor offence — Attempt to raise constitutionality of statute by way of case stated — Courts (Supplemental Provisions) Act,* 1961 (*No.* 39), *s.* 52 — *Constitution of Ireland,* 1937, *Art.* 34.3.2.

Statutory minimum wage — Power of District Court to order payment of arrears — Whether

CASE STATED—*continued.*

payment of minimum wage a statutory condition of employment — Industrial Relations Act, 1946 (*No.* 26), *s.* 45.] The defendant was prosecuted in the District Court by the Minister for Labour for, *inter alia,* failure to pay his employee remuneration of not less than the statutory minimum on the 19 July, 1986, contrary to the Employment Regulation Order (Catering Joint Labour Committee), 1986, and to s. 45, sub-s. 1, of the Industrial Relations Act, 1946. On the evidence the district justice was satisfied that a breach of s. 45, sub-s. 1, of the Act had taken place. The complainant applied to the district justice to order payment of the sum of £8,874 to the employee, that sum representing the amount by which the employee had been underpaid by the defendant during the course of her employment from the 18 March, 1981, to the 19 July, 1986. The district justice stated a case for the opinion of the High Court on the question of whether he had jurisdiction to order payment of this sum which exceeded the jurisdiction of the District Court in a civil action. The defendant argued that such an order could not be made on the grounds, *inter alia,* that if the statute allowed the District Court to award arrears of the magnitude claimed, it took the offence out of the category of "minor offence" triable by the District Court and was, therefore, unconstitutional. **Held** by O'Hanlon J., in answering the case stated, 1, that it was not open to the defendant to plead that the provisions of the statute were unconstitutional before the Distrct Court having regard to the provisions of Article 34, s. 3, sub-s. 2 of the Constitution which provides that no question as to the validity of any law having regard to the Constitution shall be raised in any court other than the High Court or the Supreme Court. *The State (Sheerin)* v. *Kennedy* [1966] I.R. 379 considered. 2. That it was not permissible to raise the issue of the constitutionality of a statute by way of case stated from the District Court. *Foyle Fisheries Commission* v. *Gallen* [1960] Ir. Jur. Rep. 35 applied. 3. That powers conferred on the District Court by a statute enacted subsequent to the Constitution of 1937 may be lawfully and validly exercised unless and until the statute has been successfully impugned in proceedings appropriate for that purpose. *The People (Attorney General)* v. *McGlynn* [1967] I.R. 232 considered. 4. That s. 45, sub-s. 2, of the Industrial Relations Act, 1946, which empowers the District Court to order payment of the difference between the statutory minimum wage and the wage actually paid, refers only to payment of wages made on the date on which the offence charged under s. 45, sub-s. 1, was committed. 5. That in s. 45, sub-s. 3, of the Act of 1946 the term "statutory conditions of employment" means the statutory conditions of employment other than the condition requiring payment

CASE STATED—*continued.*

of the minimum wage. 6. That the only power of the District Court to order payment of arrears arose under s. 45, sub-s. 4 (a) of the Act of 1946 and could not be invoked unless notice of intention to avail of s. 45, sub-s. 4 (a) was served on the defendant together with the summons. *Minister for Labour* v. *Costello*
(H.C.) [1988] I.R.235

—— Appeal — Acquittal — Whether D.P.P. had validly invoked the jurisdiction of the High Court — Whether possible to state case against acquittal.
see **Criminal Law,** 34

—— Arbitration — Question of law — Refusal of arbitrator to state case.
see **Arbitration,** 10, 11

—— Consultative case stated to Supreme Court — Approach of Supreme Court to case stated — Whether arguments not made before Circuit Court would be entertained.
see **Local Government,** 2

—— Interest — Award — Case stated by Appeal Commissioners — Decision by High Court on interpretation of Income Tax Acts — Consequential order for repayment of overpaid tax — Order for payment of a sum of money — Whether court had jurisdiction to order payment of interest.
see **Revenue,** 39

—— Practice — Interpretation of statutory provisions — Whether reference must be on basis of particular circumstances arising.
see **Criminal Law,** 51

—— Revenue appeal — Point of law — Principles applicable — Finding of fact by Circuit Court — Inferences drawn from facts — Jurisdiction of High Court — Function of High Court in hearing revenue cases stated.
see **Revenue,** 3

CASUAL TRADING

1. —— **Market right** — *Whether defendants selling at a market held in pursuance of a market right — Case stated — Courts (Supplemental Provisions) Act,* 1961 (*No.* 39), *s.* 52 — *Casual Trading Act,* 1980 (*No.* 43), *ss.* 1, 2.] Section 2, sub-s. 2 (h) of the Act of 1980, provides that

CASUAL TRADING—*continued.*

casual trading does not include selling at a market or fair held in pursuance of a market right. A "market right" is defined in s. 1 of the Act as a right conferred by franchise or statute to hold a fair or market, that is to say, a concourse of buyers and sellers to dispose of commodities. In 1949 the complainant bought the franchise to hold markets and fairs on Wednesdays and Saturdays in the town of Skibbereen. Since that date they did not hold or promote any markets in the area, except for the years 1968 to 1972 when they collected tolls from two persons trading in the area on Saturdays. Summonses were issued by the complainants against the defendants charging them with offences contrary to ss. 2 and 5 of the Casual Trading Act, 1980, alleging that the defendants had carried on casual trading in a casual trading area without a licence or permit or (in the case of some of the defendants) in contravention of the conditions contained in the permits that had been granted to them. The defendants argued that they were not engaged in casual trading within the meaning of the Act of 1980 because they were selling at a market held in pursuance of a market right and were therefore within the exception provided for in s. 2, sub-s 2 (h) of the Act. At the trial of the action in the District Court the district justice, on his own motion, stated a case for the determination by the High Court of certain questions of law raised in the action. **Held** by Lynch J., in ruling the points of law, 1, that the franchise created by the charter was not terminated by the lack of exercise of it by the complainant but that there was no obligation on the complainant to hold markets in accordance with the terms of the charter. 2. That whether or not the complainant held markets under the charter those members of the public wishing to trade had rights, which were in the nature of proprietary rights, to attend at the market places on the dates specified in the charter to engage in trading and such trading was within the exception provided for in s. 2, sub-s. 2 (h) of the Act of 1980. *Skibbereen Urban District Council* v. *Quill*

(H.C.) [1986] I.R.123; [1986] ILRM 170

2. —— **Validity of certain bye-laws** — *Proposal to designate land as casual trading area subject to conditions — Whether decision perverse — Jurisdiction of Circuit Court on appeal from Urban District Council resolution — Casual Trading Act,* 1980 (*No.* 43), *ss.* 5(1)(4)(7), 7(2)(8) — *Rules of the Superior Courts, O.*84 (4).] S. 7(2) of the Casual Trading Act, 1980, sets out a number of matters to which the local authority must give consideration prior to designating any lands as a casual trading area. The Tullamore UDC after considering the matters outlined in s. 7(2) of the Act passed a resolution in accordance with the Casual Trading Act, 1980, designating O'Connor Square, Tullamore a designated trading area 'to be regulated in accordance with the proposed Casual Bye-laws annexed to this Resolution or such amended Bye-laws as may be made by the Council from time to time in accordance with the provisions of s. 7(8) of the said Act.' The applicants appealed the aforesaid resolution to the respondent who dismissed the appeal and authorised the said proposal without making it subject to any conditions. The applicants sought and obtained leave to apply for an order of certiorari in respect of the respondent's order. The applicants submit that in view of the evidence and reports from the planning officer, gardai and engineer before the local authority the decision was perverse. The respondent did not file any affidavit but an affidavit was sworn on behalf of the Tullamore UDC by their town clerk. Also the issue arose whether draft Bye-law no. 11 and Bye-law no. 12 annexed to the said resolution were *ultra vires* the Casual Trading Act, 1980. **Held** by Egan J. in making an order quashing the respondent's order and remitting the matter to the respondent with a direction to him to reconsider it and reach a decision in accordance with the findings of this court, 1, the local authority by virtue of the Casual Trading Act, 1980, has been invested with the power to designate an area and not the Circuit Court and therefore it would be wrong for the Circuit Court to attempt to nullify that power save in very exceptional circumstances, which said circumstances do not exist in this case. 2. There was evidence to indicate that the Tullamore UDC gave consideration as was their statutory duty to the matters set forth in s. 7(2) of the 1980 Act. 3. Subss. (iv) and (v) of the draft Bye-laws no. 11 are *ultra vires* s. 5(4) and (7) of the Casual Trading Act, 1980, as they invest the council with unlimited power to refuse applications to persons who hold a current licence. 4. Bye-law no. 12 which authorises the requirement of an additional sum in respect of the 'over all management of the area' is *ultra vires* the powers confered by s. 5(1) of the Act which only authorises a charge for a permit to licence holders. 5. The respondent was fully entitled to authorise the proposal in so far as it consisted of the designation of O'Connor Square, but after that he ought to have stated that the proposal was subject to the condition that subss. (iv) and (v) of the draft Bye-law no. 11 and the entire Bye-law no. 12 would be excluded. *Comerford* v. *O'Malley*

(H.C.) [1987] ILRM 595

CATTLE

—— Bovine export levy.

see **European Communities,** 1

CATTLE—*continued.*

—— Milk levy.
see **Constitution,** 35

—— Straying onto highway — Road traffic accident — Whether owner negligent — Whether under a duty to prevent cattle straying onto public road.
see **Animals,** 2

—— Trespass — Cemetery — Cattle poisoned by eating yew leaves.
see **Negligence,** 28

CEMETERY
see **Burial Ground**

CENTRAL CRIMINAL COURT — Validity of exclusion of jurisdiction of High Court sitting as Central Criminal Court.
see **Constitution,** 32

CERTIORARI
see under **Judicial Review**

CHARGE
see also **Mortgage**

—— Company.
see **Company,** 3-8

—— Guarantee — Charge to bank to secure loan to company — Default — Decree for possession of property.
see **Banking,** 3

—— Registered land — Deed of charge.
see **Real Property,** 6, 7

CHARGE (CRIMINAL)
see **Criminal Law,** 48

CHARITIES

1. —— **Cy-près** — *Gift in will to Hall Building Fund — Fund used in purchase of new building — Balance of fund held for maintenance of same at testator's death — Whether purposes of fund completed before testator's death — Whether general charitable intent.*] The testator who died in 1981 by his will, executed in 1974, bequeathed a fourth share of his residuary estate to "The treasurer for the time being of the Building Fund in connection with Victoria Memorial Hall, May Street, Belfast, and the receipt of such treasurer shall be a sufficient discharge to my executor." Victoria Memorial Hall was the place of worship of a self-governing congregation known as the Victoria Memorial Hall Assembly. In 1967 the Assembly established a building committee which at its first meeting resolved that, "[t]he building fund . . . be established at once; . . . [and] if a new building had not been proceeded with by the end of five years . . . all gifts would be returned. . . ." The Assembly members then envisaged that a new hall would be built either by demolition and rebuilding on the site of the existing hall or on a nearby site. The building of a new hall had not been put in hand by 1972, but the building fund remained in existence and in 1975, after consent for the demolition of the building, which had been listed as a building of special architectural or historic interest, had been refused, the Assembly resolved to purchase and adapt the Crescent Church, University Road, Belfast. In 1976 the Assembly resolved to sell the Victoria Hall and use the proceeds to assist in the purchase of the Crescent Church. After completion of the purchase and renovation of the latter, the credit remaining in the building fund was carried forward to a fund called the Crescent Church Building Fund to be used for the renovation or repair of the Crescent Church. On an originating summons to determine whether the residuary bequest should go to the Crescent Church Building Fund, **Held,** that, 1, the gift was a gift for the purposes for which the building fund was to be applied at the date of the will. The essential purpose of the fund was the replacement of the Victoria Memorial Hall and while that purpose might have included the replacement of the Hall by the purchase of other premises, it did not include the future maintenance of those premises when purchased. Accordingly the gift failed. 2. A cy-près scheme was directed, however, as there was a general charitable intention. Although there was merely a single gift to charity, the paramount intention of the testator was the advancement of religion by making provision in his will for the assistance of the Victoria Memorial Hall Assembly in what was then its most pressing need, viz. the obtaining of a new place of worship and that contributing to the cost of a new building was not the only object which animated the testator. *In re Currie; McClelland* v. *Gamble*
(Ch.D.) [1985] N.I. 299

2. —— **Cy-près** — *Public benefit — Gift to found a home for old Presbyterian persons — Whether charitable — Whether for relief of aged — Whether sufficiently certain — Whether a sufficient section of the public.*] The testator, who died in 1971, left his residuary estate on trust for his sisters during their lives and then directed his trustees, "to hold the remainder of my residuary estate for the Presbyterian Residential Trust, Adelaide House, to found or to help to found a home for old Presbyterian persons and I would ask them to consider whether the block of houses and grounds numbered 476, 478 and 480 Antrim Road, Belfast, could be put to this use as it is my

CHARITIES—*continued.*

strong desire that if at all possible these houses should be used for that purpose." The Presbyterian Residential Trust admitted persons of limited means or who, owing to infirmity or advancing years were unable to maintain their own homes; such admittance was offered in the first place to members of the Presbyterian Church. At the time of the testator's death, his residuary estate would have been sufficient to help found a home under the auspices of the trust. However on the death of his surviving sister in 1980, it was not practicable to use the houses in Antrim Road and the funds available were insufficient to found or help found a home. On an originating summons to determine various matters arising from the will **Held,** that, 1, on the true construction of the will, the testator's object was not merely to support the Presbyterian Residential Trust, but to found or help to found a home and the testator had specified the class of persons qualified to benefit from that object, viz. old Presbyterian persons, who are in need of such housing by reason of the decline in their powers and independence brought about by advancing years. This object is, subject to the satisfaction of the requirement of public benefit, a valid charitable gift for the relief of the aged, as it relieves a need attributable to the aged condition of the person to be relieved. *Joseph Rowntree Memorial Trust Housing Association Ltd.* v. *Attorney General* [1983] 1 All E.R. 288 followed. 2. The public benefit requirement was satisfied in this case. The question whether or not potential beneficiaries can fairly be said to constitute a section of the public is a question of degree and a distinction is drawn between the different heads of charity when considering this question. The relief of poverty (including help for the aged and impotent) necessarily confers individual benefits on the recipients of the donor's bounty. In order for it to constitute a public, as opposed to a merely private, benefaction it has to include a public element, so that it transcends the conferring of benefit upon individuals selected by the donor and serves the wider purpose of benefiting the public weal by the provision of material assistance to classes of persons who require it by reason of their particular disability. Here the testator's gift cannot be regarded as being a private benefaction; it was designed to serve the wider purpose of benefiting the public by providing accommodation for the relief of a class of persons requiring it by reason of their age. The fact that the persons selected to occupy the accommodation were to be Presbyterians rather than any other denomination does not negative the paramountcy of the public purpose of assistance for the aged. *Dingle* v. *Turner* [1972] A.C. 601

CHARITIES—*continued.*

applied. Alternatively, if it was necessary to consider whether the Presbyterian Church in Ireland constituted a section of the public as distinct from a fluctuating body of individuals united only by a common personal bond of voluntary association, the members of that church are sufficiently defined and identified by a common quality of a public nature: membership of any branch of the Christian Church is a quality which does not depend on the members' relationship to any individual propositus. *Dicta* of MacDermott J. and Andrews L.C.J. in *Trustees of the Londonderry Presbyterian Church House* v. *Commissioners of Inland Revenue* [1946] N.I. 178; 27 T.C. 431 applied. 3. As the testator's intention would have been practicable at the date of his death, the gift was subject to an indefeasible charitable trust and consequently the preparation of a cy-près scheme was directed. *In re Dunlop; Northern Bank Executor and Trustee Company Ltd.* v. *A.G. for N.I.*

(Ch.D.) [1984] N.I. 408

3. —— **Cy-près** — *Trusts — Objects — Failure — Books in old library of St.Canice's Cathedral — Bequests to establish a library as an adjunct to the Cathedral — Original purposes ceasing to provide suitable and effective method of using property — Whether Court could alter original purposes of the charitable gift to allow the property to be given cy-près — Proceeds of sale of the books to be applied towards the maintenance and upkeep of the Cathedral — Cultural asset — Whether elaborate cy-près scheme necessary — Irish Church Act,* 1869 (*c.* 42) — *Charities Act,* 1961 (*No.* 17), *s.* 47.] Section 47 of the Chairities Act, 1961, sets out the circumstances in which the original purposes of a charitable gift may be altered to allow the property given or part of it to be applied cy-près. The plaintiff claimed ownership of the collection of books contained in the old and new libraries attached to St. Canice's Cathedral in the city of Kilkenny, and claimed a cy-près order under s. 47 of the Charities Act, 1961, authorising the sale of the books comprised in the old library and the application of the proceeds of sale towards the maintenance and upkeep of the Cathedral. Most of the books contained in the old library were made up of bequests under the wills of Bishop Otway and Bishop Maurice and were affected by the trusts of these wills. The plaintiff alleged that the books in the old library were no longer used and for many years past no librarian had been employed for either the old or the new libraries. The plaintiff further alleged that the Cathedral had fallen into a serious state of disrepair and he averred to the fact that 'considerably more money would have to be spent on the Cathedral to carry out

CHARITIES—*continued.*

the full restoration of the building.' The application was opposed by the defendant on the grounds that the old library was an important cultural asset for Kilkenny and for Ireland, and if put up for sale the books would leave the country as there was no effective legal restriction on the export of old books. **Held** by O'Hanlon J., in making the order in the terms sought by the plaintiff, 1, that although Bishop Otway and Bishop Maurice in donating their collections of books to St. Canice's Cathedral intended that a library in the true sense of the word would be established as an adjunct to the cathedral, it was clear that no such use had been made of the old library on any regular basis for many years past. 2. That the original purposes of the charitable gift of the collections of books had ceased to provide a suitable and effective method of using the property available by virtue of the gift, regard being had to the spirit of the gift. 3. That in the circumstances of the present case, it was permissible to alter the original purposes of the charitable gift (in the case of both bequests) to allow the property given to be applied cy-près. 4. That the collections of books comprised in the old library should be sold in whatever manner the plaintiff might be advised to effect such sale and the proceeds thereof applied towards the repair and maintenance of St. Canice's Cathedral. *Representative Church Body* v. *The Attorney General*

(H.C.) [1988] I.R. 19

—— Rates — Exemption — Private fee paying school — Charitable purposes — Whether school of a public nature — Basis of exemption.
see **Rating and Valuation,** 4

CHATTEL

—— Lost or mislaid chattels — Treasure trove — Antiquities of national importance — Chattel found in land — Finder trespassing — Rights of ownership and possession as between landowner and finder — Chattel part of ancient hoard — Whether finder entitled to reward — Promissory estoppel — Whether finder had legitimate expectation — Reasonable reward — Factors to be taken into consideration.
see **Bailment**

—— Personal chattels — Passing of property — Retention of title — Power to take possession.
see **Sale of Goods,** 4

—— Real property — Charge — Default — Receiver attempting to claim proceeds

CHATTEL—*continued.*

of sale of chattels — Chattels not part of property charged.
see **Real Property,** 7

CHEQUE
see under **Negotiable Instruments**

CHILD
see **Infant**
see also **Illegitimate Child; Young Offender**

CHOICE OF LAW
see **Conflict of Laws**

CHURCH
see also **Ecclesiastical Courts; Religious Institution; Seminary**

—— Charitable gift — Cy-près.
see **Charities,** 3

—— Churchyard — Burial ground.
see **Local Government,** 9

—— Occupier's liability — Licensor and licensee — Infant plaintiff lighting candle as devotional exericse — Plaintiff's clothing catching fire — Foreseeability — Factors to be considered — Absence of warning — Personal injuries — Damages — Whether excessive.
see **Negligence,** 19

CIRCUIT COURT

—— Action triable without jury — Right of plaintiff to proceed — Cross claim pending and triable with jury in High Court.
see **Practice and Procedure,** 10

—— Jurisdiction — Appeal from District Court — Costs — Jurisdiction of the Circuit Court to award costs of appeal — Whether limitation of costs under rule 67, District Court Rules, 1948, applicable.
see **Practice and Procedure,** 15

—— Jurisdiction — Case stated — Consultative case stated — Whether Circuit Court required to hear evidence before case is stated to Supreme Court.
see **Case Stated,** 2

—— Jurisdiction — Criminal appeal — Sentence — Power of Circuit Court judge to increase sentences.
see **Criminal Law,** 78

CIRCUIT COURT—*continued.*

—— Jurisdiction — Criminal appeal — Summonses issued on foot of invalid complaint — No appearance by defendant in District Court — Conviction — Appeal to Circuit Court — Whether issue of complaint could be raised in Circuit Court — Whether Circuit Court having jurisdiction to hear appeal.
see **Criminal Law,** 39

—— Jurisdiction — Criminal jurisdiction — Statutory provision for exercise of jurisdiction in circuit where offence committed or where accused resided or was arrested — Provision allowing for transfer of trial to Dublin Circuit Court — Transfer of trial mandatory if 7 days notice given by prosecution or defence — Whether criminal jurisdiction of Circuit Court a local and limited jurisdiction — Whether mandatory transfer of trial contrary to natural justice.
see **Constitution,** 3

—— Procedure — Appeal from District Court against conviction — Offence of possession of a controlled drug — Sentence — Obligation to obtain medical or probation report before sentence — Hearing on sentence only — Change of circumstances of convict — Whether Circuit Court obliged to obtain further medical reports before sentence.
see **Criminal Law,** 79

CITIZEN
—— Non-citizen
see **Aliens**

—— Rights
see **Rights and Freedoms**

CIVIL EVIDENCE
see **Evidence**

CIVIL PROCEDURE
see **Practice and Procedure**

CIVIL SERVICE
1. —— **Dismissal** — *Office-holder — Probationer — Prosecutor appointed to probationary position — Minister empowered by statute to dismiss where satisfied of certain matters — Prosecutor dismissed without warning — Reasons for dismissal and material upon which decision based not disclosed — Whether summary dismissal permissible — Whether Minister's decision reviewable — Constitutional limitations on exercise of power — Effect of non-disclosure of reasons for dismissal — Civil Service Regulation Act,* 1956

CIVIL SERVICE—*continued.*

(*No.* 46), *ss.* 5, 7 — *Civil Service Regulation (Amendment) Act,* 1958 (*No.* 34), *s.* 3.] Section 7 of the Civil Service Regulation Act, 1956, as amended by s. 3 of the Civil Service Regulation (Amendment) Act, 1958, provides that where in respect of a civil servant who has been appointed to an established position and who under his conditions of service is serving in a probationary capacity, the appropriate authority is, at any time during the civil servant's probationary period, satisfied that he has failed to fulfil the conditions of probation attaching to his probationary position, then the appropriate authority shall terminate the services of that civil servant. The prosecutor was appointed by the respondent as an established veterinary inspector in the Department of Agriculture subject to the regulations and conditions that had already been supplied to him. Condition 2 of those conditions stated that the prosecutor was required to serve a probationary period of two years duration and if during that period his services were satisfactory as regards health, conduct and efficiency generally, he could expect to be finally appointed on the completion of the two years but if during that period his services were unsatisfactory his appointment could be terminated at any time. Near the end of his probationary period (during which time he never received complaint about his services) the prosecutor was informed by the respondent that he had decided to terminate his appointment because the conditions of probation attaching to his probationary position had not been satisfied. Despite requests made of the respondent the prosecutor was not informed of the grounds upon which the respondent's decision was based. The prosecutor obtained a conditional order of certiorari in the High Court quashing the respondent's decision on the ground that his dismissal was contrary to natural justice in that he was not notified of the reason for his dismissal nor afforded the opportunity to make submissions in relation there. The respondent showed cause, contending, *inter alia,* that he was entitled by virtue of s. 7 of the Act of 1956 (as amended) to terminate the prosecutor's services on satisfying himself, as he contended he had, that the prosecutor had failed to fulfil the conditions of service attaching to his probationary tenure. On the prosecutor's motion to make the conditional order absolute, wherein neither the reasons for the respondent's decision nor the material upon which it was based were disclosed to the court, it was **Held** by Barron J., in making the conditional order absolute 1, that the respondent was entitled to dispense with the services of the prosecutor without warning him that he proposed to act in that manner. *Hynes* v. *Garvey* [1978] I.R. 174; *The State (McGarrity)* v. *Deputy Commissioner of the Garda Síochána* 112

CIVIL SERVICE—*continued.*

I.L.T.R. 25 and *The State (Burke)* v. *Garvey* [1979] ILRM 232 considered. 2. That, nevertheless, s. 7 of the Act of 1956 (as amended) could not be construed as giving to the respondent a power to act in any manner he pleased; that power could only be exercised in conformity with the Constitution and the view of the respondent as to the matters in question must be seen to be *bona fide* held, to be factually sustainable and not unreasonable. *The State (Lynch)* v. *Cooney* [1982] I.R. 337 applied. 3. That as the respondent had failed to disclose the material upon which he had acted or the reasons for his action there was no matter from which the court could determine whether or not such material was capable of supporting his decision. 4. That since the respondent continued to refuse to supply this material it must be presumed that there was no such material and, accordingly, the respondent had failed to show that he had acted *intra vires. Broomfield* v. *The Minister for Justice* (High Court, Costello J., *Ex tempore,* 10 April, 1981) not followed. *The State (Daly)* v. *The Minister for Agriculture*

(H.C.) [1987] I.R. 165; [1988] ILRM 173

2. —— **Staff association** — *New staff association seeking negotiation recognition from Minister for the Public Service — Refusal of recognition — Nature of decision — Whether administrative or judicial — Whether refusal of recognition supported by evidence before Minister — Judicial review — Administrative act — Civil Service Regulation Act,* 1956 (*No.* 46), *s.* 17.] Upon its formation in 1980 the Inspector of Taxes' Association (ITA) sought recognition from the Minister for the Public Service as a staff association entitled to operate the Civil Service Conciliation and Arbitration Scheme. It was refused on grounds that it was the settled policy of the operation of the scheme that no grade of civil servant could be represented by two staff associations at the same time and as a corollary that no staff association who did not admit to membership all the members of the grade which it sought to represent could obtain recognition. Another staff association, formed from members of the staff of the Revenue Commissioners and known as the Association of Inspectors of Taxes (AIT), existed since prior to 1952. Up to 1960, the membership of the AIT was confined to Inspectors of Taxes (Technical). In 1952 the AIT had been granted recognition as a staff association entitled to take part in the operation of the scheme. Following the refusal of the Minister to grant recognition to the ITA, they instituted proceedings claiming that the Inspector of Taxes (Technical) were, in fact, a separate grade and that the Minister should, therefore, have recognised them as such and properly considered the

CIVIL SERVICE—*continued.*

application of the ITA for recognition as representing that grade. The High Court dismissed the plaintiffs' action and they appealed at the hearing of which the officers of the ITA were added as plaintiffs. **Held** by the Supreme Court (Finlay C.J., Hamilton P., Walsh, Henchy and Griffin JJ.), in dismissing the appeal, 1, the function the Minister was performing in deciding to classify or refusing to classify particular persons as a separate grade was an administrative function. 2. It was open to the Minister, having regard to his responsibility with regard to re-grading, to the regulation of the Civil Service and to the matters which he could properly take into consideration in deciding the topic of grading in any particular area, to have reached the conclusion that he did. 3. It could not be said that differences established between the work-load, responsibility, qualification and training of Inspectors of Taxes (Technical) and Inspectors of Taxes (Non-Technical) were such that having regard to other considerations it was not open to the Minister to decide to leave both these categories in the same grade. 4. The trial judge's decision, that the application for recognition in which was subsumed an implied application for a review of the grading was fairly considered by the Minister, was supported by the evidence and could not and should not be disturbed. *Inspector of Taxes Association* v. *Minister for the Public Service*

(S.C.) [1986] ILRM 296

3. —— **Suspension** — *Application for injunction restoring plaintiffs to their position — Whether suspension in breach of natural justice — Whether suspension a breach of the constitutional right to earn a livelihood — Whether injunction be granted — Civil Service Regulation Act,* 1956 (*No.* 46), *s.* 13.] S. 13 of the Civil Service Regulation Act, 1956, provides that a civil servant may be suspended from duty if it appears to the suspending authority that the civil servant has been guilty of grave misconduct or grave irregularity warranting disciplinary action. A trade dispute had arisen between the first-named defendant and the members of his department. The plaintiffs were civil servants employed as fitters in that department, and the Irish Post Office Engineering Union, to which many of the plaintiffs belonged, had placed a picket on premises used by the first-named defendant at Mill Street. The plaintiffs were ordered to report for duty at the Mill Street premises, but when they refused to pass the picket they were suspended without pay under s. 13 of the 1956 Act. Pending the trial of their action seeking injunctions, the plaintiffs sought interlocutory injunctions restoring them to their positions and giving them the right of remuneration. **Held** by Kenny J. in refusing the relief sought, 1, the

CIVIL SERVICE—*continued.*

order given to the plaintiffs was a lawful one, and the motives behind it were not relevant to its validity. 2. The suspension imposed upon the plaintiffs was not a breach of their constitutional right to earn a livelihood, as it was the plaintiffs themselves who deprived themselves of a livelihood by refusing to obey the order given. 3. There was no breach of natural or constitutional justice in suspending the plaintiffs without a hearing, since each of the plaintiffs knew the reason for the suspension. 4. An injunction ordering the defendants to restore the plaintiffs to their former positions would amount to the specific enforcement of a contract for personal services. The court will not order the specific performance of such a contract. 5. An injunction will be granted prior to the trial of an action only when damages would not be an adequate remedy. In this case, the damages would be the amount of wages lost by the plaintiff. This would be an adequate remedy. *Yeates* v. *Minister for Posts and Telegraphs*

(H.C.) [1978] ILRM 22

—— Employment — Labour Court — Ordinary member — Employment insurance — Whether employed in civil service — Whether employment under a contract of service.

see **Social Welfare,** 2, 3

—— Employment — Suspension — Transfer of civil servant to employment of state-sponsored body — Suspension — Authority to suspend — Natural justice — Permissible duration of suspension.

see **Employer and Employee,** 23

CLUB

1. —— **Negligence** — *Private members' club — Member injured at dance at club premises — Member having paid admission charge to dance — Liability of club — Common interest — Common liability — Whether member could maintain action for damages against representatives of club.*] The plaintiff was a member of an unincorporated members' club which was managed by a committee which worked without remuneration. While attending a dance at the club premises, to which he had paid an admission fee, the plaintiff was injured as a result of a fall which he attributed to the negligence of the persons who organised and ran the dance. The monies collected for admission to the dance were applied to the general purposes of the club. The plaintiff commenced proceedings for damages against the defendants as representing the club. The defendants were the trustees of the club in whom its property was vested and the plaintiff did not

CLUB—*continued.*

attribute any personal responsibility for negligence to any one of them. The defendants disputed the plaintiff's claim on the grounds, *inter alia,* that the plaintiff, as a member of the club, could not maintain an action against the club. By order of the Supreme Court (see the report at [1987] I.R. 106) a preliminary issue of law was directed to be tried as to whether the plaintiff could maintain an action against the representatives of the club of which he was a member in respect of his accident. **Held** by Gannon J., in deciding the issue in the negative, 1, that the club had no separate legal character distinct from its members. 2. That the duty, upon which the plaintiff's action was founded, to observe suitable standards of care in the organisation and running of the dance, was a duty shared equally by all the members of the club, including the plaintiff. 3. That the only liability which might attach to the club for a breach of that duty was the vicarious liability of all the members, including the plaintiff, as principals, for the wrongful acts or defaults of their agent, whether a member or servant of the club. 4. That the plaintiff's contribution to the admission receipts did not avoid his share of the responsibility for observing suitable standards of care. 5. That, accordingly, the plaintiff's action was not maintainable at law. *Murphy* v. *Roche* (*No.* 2)

(H.C.) [1987] I.R. 656

Editor's note: For the decision of the Supreme Court on the preliminary issue of law, reported in [1987] I.R. 106, *see* **Practice and Procedure,** 58

2. —— **Renewal of licence** — *Club being a limited company — Whether supply of exciseable liquor under the control of the members — Registration of Clubs (Ireland) Act,* 1904 (*No.* 9), *s.* 4.] At the hearing of an application for a renewal of a club licence an objection was made by a member of the Garda Síochána on the ground that the club, being a limited company, was a separate entity from its members and therefore the supply of exciseable liquor was not under the control of the members or of a committee appointed by the members. The President of the District Court stated a case for the opinion of the High Court as to whether this ground of objection was one upon which the club must be refused a renewal of its certificate of registration under the provisions of the Registration of Clubs (Ireland) Act, 1904. **Held** by McWilliam J. in answering the question in the case stated in the negative, 1, it was clear that the directors of the company constituted the 'governing body' of the club within the meaning of s. 4 of the Registration of Clubs (Ireland) Act, 1904, and that the

CLUB—*continued.*

members of club and of the company were identical. Furthermore under the articles of association of the company it did not appear to be possible to have a member of the company who was not a member of the club. Accordingly the ground of objection was not one upon which the club must be refused a renewal of its certificate of registration. *National Sporting Club Ltd.* v. *Cope* [1900] 82 L.T. 352 distinguished, since the company in that case was limited by shares and not by guarantee. *In re Parnell G.A.A. Club Ltd.* **(H.C.) [1984] ILRM 246**

—— Change of use — Unlicensed to licensed.
see **Planning,** 14

—— Income tax — Exemption — Club to promote athletic sport — Whether legitimate avoidance of payment of tax — Funds provided by one person — Total control in two trustees — Whether two persons can constitute a "body of persons".
see **Revenue,** 35

—— Sports club.
see also under **Sporting Activities**

COERCION
see **Duress; Undue Influence**

COLLECTIVE AGREEMENT — Employment — Whether intention to enter into legal relations — Onus of proof.
see **Employer and Employee,** 2

COMMERCIAL LAW
see **Agency; Arbitration; Banking; Company; Contract; Guarantee; Insurance; Mortgage; Negotiable Instruments; Partnership; Patents; Restraint of Trade; Sale of Goods; Trade and Industry; Trade Mark**

COMMISSIONERS OF PUBLIC WORKS

—— Arterial drainage — Fishery — Interference — Compensation — Assessment.
see **Real Property,** 4

—— Preservation order — National monument.
see **Constitution,** 44

COMMITTAL FOR TRIAL
see also **Return for Trial**

—— Delay — Remand in custody — Whether delay unreasonable — Observations on delay in holding committal proceedings.
see **Habeas Corpus**

—— Depositions not endorsed — Whether endorsement mandatory.
see **Criminal Law,** 38

COMMON INFORMER

—— Complaint — Withdrawal — Power of

COMMON INFORMER—*continued.*

D.P.P. — Complaint made by policeman as common informer — Whether D.P.P. has power to compel withdrawal of the complaint.
see **Criminal Law,** 46

—— Extent of distinction between police officers and other common informers.
see **Criminal Law,** 46

COMMUNICATE, RIGHT TO,
see **Constitution,** 8, 10

COMMUNICATIONS
see **Broadcasting; Postal Service; Telephone Calls; Transport**

COMPANY
see also **Partnership**

Administration. No. 1
Agreement. No.2
Charge. Nos. 3-8
Fraudulent trading. No. 9
Receivership. No. 10
Shareholder — oppression of minority. No. 11
Shares. Nos. 12, 13
Ultra vires. Nos. 14, 15
Winding up. Nos. 16-31

ADMINISTRATION

1. —— **Insurance company** — *Appointment of administrator — Administrator appointed receiver and manager of the property and assets of a body connected with the insurance company — Administrator's appointment ceasing upon appointment of liquidator — Administrator retaining certain funds to defray expenses — Whether certain items of expenditure be paid out of retained funds — Insurance* (*No.*2) *Act,* 1983 (*No.* 29), *ss.* 1, 2(2), 2(3), 3(1)(*a*), 3(4)(*a*), 4.] S.4 of the Insurance (No. 2) Act, 1983, provides that the administrator of an insurer may be appointed by the court to be receiver and manager of the property and assets of a 'body connected with the insurer', conferring upon him such powers as the court may think fit. S. 2(2) of the Act provides for the appointment of such an administrator of an insurer, and s. 3(4)(*a*) provides that the costs and expenses incurred by such administrator in the exercise of his functions shall be paid out of the revenue of the business of the insurer. The appellant, the administrator of PMPA Insurance Co. Ltd. ('the Company'), had been appointed receiver of PMPS ('the Society') pursuant to s. 4 of the 1983 Act. His position as receiver and manager ceased upon the appointment of a liquidator to the Society on the 5 December, 1983. Upon ceasing to be

receiver, the administrator handed over to the liquidator all the property and assets of the Society, except certain funds which he retained 'to defray any expenses which the court might determine he was properly entitled to meet by deduction out of the funds of the Society, and on trust for the Society in respect of any excess.' Eight separate items of expenditure were in issue, and the High Court ordered that four of these should not be paid out of the retained funds. The basis of the decision of the High Court was that the administrator had been appointed receiver for the benefit of the Company, not of the Society, and that his work as receiver therefore formed part of his functions as administrator of the Company. **Held** by the Supreme Court (Finlay C.J., Henchy and Griffin JJ. concurring) in allowing the appeal in part and in varying the order of the High Court, 1, the combined definitions of 'administrator' and 'functions' contained in s. 1 of the Act must be construed as meaning that 'functions' include powers and duties conferred by the Act, but not those otherwise conferred. 2. The powers conferred on the administrator by the court in appointing him receiver and manager of the Society cannot be described as powers or functions conferred by the Act. Expenses incurred in the exercise of such powers can therefore be retained from the funds of the Society. *In re P.M.P.A. Insurance Co. Ltd.*
(S.C.) [1988] ILRM 109; (H.C.) [1986] ILRM 524

AGREEMENT

2. —— **Execution** — *Requirement of writing — Agreement to be for number of years — Initialling of agreement — Whether sufficient compliance with requirement that agreements be executed in writing — Companies Act,* 1963 (*No.* 33), *s.* 38.

Contract — Privity — Agency — Renewal — Option to renew agreement — Agent claiming privity with party to separate agreement — Whether separate agreements to be considered as single arrangement — Whether agency terminated on reasonable notice.] The first defendant (the English company) was a manufacturer of forklift trucks. Its sole agent in Northern Ireland was the second defendant (the Northern company). In 1973 it was decided that the sole agency in the Republic should be transferred to a new company, the plaintiff (the Irish company), subject to guarantees to the English company regarding the creditworthiness of the Irish company. Detailed correspondence took place between the managing directors of the English and Northern companies and the managing director of the Irish company to ensure that these guarantees were met. The Northern company agreed that it would underwrite the Irish company's debts. The arrangement between the parties was formalised

in two documents of August, 1973. The first document was called the 'head agreement' and was between the English company and the Northern company. The second was called the 'scheduled agreement' and was between the Northern company and the Irish company. The head agreement provided that the Northern company was to have exclusive agency for the whole of Ireland 'on its own account and risk', and that the Irish company would distribute the English company's forklifts in the Republic. The scheduled agreement provided that the Northern company would grant sole agency in the Republic to the Irish company and that the agreement was to continue for five years with a renewal option for a further five years. The scheduled agreement was expressed to have been approved by the English company and was initialled by its managing director and the managing director of the Northern company. The Northern company provided the working capital for the Irish company. For the duration of the agreement the English company shipped forklifts direct to the Irish company and invoiced the Northern company who then invoiced the Irish company. The make up of the English company altered during the course of the agreement, and some differences arose between the Irish and English companies. In 1975, the Irish company proposed a new exclusive agency agreement, and the English company forwarded its standard form agreement for the perusal of the Irish company. Nothing further occurred in connection with this agreement, but the English company continued to supply forklifts to the Irish company. The Irish company sought renewal of the 1973 agreement, but the Northern company refused. The Irish company instituted proceedings against the Northern and English companies. In the High Court, McWilliam J. held that the Irish company was entitled to the benefit of the head agreement, on the basis that the two agreements formed part of a tripartite agreement between the parties. The English company appealed. **Held** by the Supreme Court, in allowing the appeal: the purpose of the head agreement was to interpose between the English and Irish company a creditworthy company, and by having two separate agreements to confer contractual rights and obligations only on the English company without conferring any rights or obligations on the Irish company who were not privy to the head agreement. The intention of the parties was that the two documents were only binding as between the respective parties to each, and the manner in which they were performed until 1975 indicated that this was the understanding of the parties, so that the Irish company was not entitled to claim that it was the exclusive agent of the English company for five years from the date of the agreement. *Per* O'Higgins C.J.: it was doubtful if the initialling of the scheduled agreement complied with the provisions of s. 38 of the Companies Act, 1963. *Per* Griffin J.: from 1975, the Irish company was agent for the English company on an *ad hoc* basis, and since it was a commercial arrangement it was determinable on reasonable notice, and in the circumstances the 12 months notice which the Irish company received was reasonable. *Henley Forklift (Ireland) Ltd.* v. *Lansing Bagnall & Co. Ltd.*

(S.C.) [1979] ILRM 257

CHARGE

3. —— **Book debts** — *Winding up — Charge and debenture over present and future book debts expressed to be a "first fixed charge" — Words not inclusive — Intention of instrument as a whole — Monies received from debtors to be paid into special bank account by company — Restrictions on company's use of charged assets — Whether company could carry on business in the ordinary way — Whether fixed or floating charges created — Companies Act,* 1963 (*No.* 33), *s.* 285 (7), *s.* 288.] In May, 1983, Keenan Brothers Limited ("the company") was in serious financial difficulties. The banks were prepared to lend financial assistance and on the 3 May, 1983, the company created a charge in favour of A.I.B. Ltd., and on the 5 May, 1983, the company created a debenture in favour of A.I.I.B. Ltd. The charge was stated to be a "first fixed charge" over all book debts and other debts present and future, as was the debenture. Both deeds provided that "(1) the company collect and pay all monies received in respect of book debts, present and future, into a special bank account designated for that purpose; (2) all withdrawals, transfers and payments from the book debts account to be approved in writing by one of the chargees; (3) if requested by the chargee(s) the company would execute a legal assignment of its book debts in favour of the chargee(s); (4) the company could not, without the consent in writing of the chargee(s) charge, waive, assign, discount or otherwise diminish or dispose of its book debts." Clause 7.3 of the debenture provided that the company could not, without the consent in writing of the chargee(s), "carry on its business other than in the ordinary and normal course." On the 31 August, 1983, an agreement was entered into between the company and A.I.B. Ltd., stated to be supplemental to the deed of charge, which provided for the opening of a "Book Debts Receivable Account" in the joint names of the bank and the company whereby the bank had absolute discretion to allow the company to transfer money from this account to the company's working account.

Clause 4 of this agreement provided that the bank could, on the happening of any of the events rendering the money secured immediately payable, terminate the agreement; no further monies could then be withdrawn and the account would then be closed and a receiver could be appointed over the book debts. From the 4 October, 1983, until the appointment of the provisional liquidator all receipts of the company were lodged to the book debts receivable account. Pursuant to s. 280 of the Companies Act, 1963, the liquidator applied to the court for directions as to whether the charge and debenture created fixed or floating charges. **Held** by Keane, J. in giving directions, 1, the statement in both deeds that the securities thereby created were fixed charges was not conclusive and the question whether the charges were fixed or floating had to be determined by the intention of the parties inferred from the deeds read as a whole. Subsequent conduct of the parties is inadmissible as an aid to construction. *In re Yorkshire Woolcombers' Association Ltd.* [1903] 2 Ch. 284; *Evans* v. *Rival Granite Quarries Ltd.* [1910] 2 K.B. 979; *Stave Falls Lumber Company* v. *Westminster Trust Company* (1940) 4 D.L.R. 382; *Welch* v. *Bowmaker (Ireland) Ltd.* [1980] I.R. 251, *In re Armagh Shoes Ltd.* [1982] N.I. 59 and *Whitworth Street Estates Ltd.* v. *Miller* [1970] A.C. 583, considered. 2. The provision in the deeds requiring the company to lodge the proceeds of the book debts to the special bank account was not inconsistent with an intention to create a floating charge since the company was empowered to collect the debts itself and the effect of the deeds allowed the company's debtors to set off the company's debts to them without notice to the bank. A fixed charge would automatically vest all debts in the bank. 3. The company was not prohibited from dealing with the charged assets in the course of its business. The deeds provided for a cash flow from the special account and, although this was restricted, it was nevertheless consistent with an intention to create a floating charge. *Illingworth* v. *Houldsworth* [1904] A.C. 355, considered. *Siebe Gorman* v. *Barclays Bank* [1979] 2 Lloyds Rep. 142 not followed. 4. A floating charge does not have to embrace the entire undertaking of a company. It may be confined to a class of assets such as company book debts present and future. 5. Accordingly, the charges created were floating charges. The banks appealed to the Supreme Court which **Held** (Finlay C.J., Walsh, Henchy, Hederman and McCarthy JJ.), in allowing the appeal, 1, a fixed charge may be created in respect of a company's book debts and other debts both present and future. 2. The use of the word "fixed charge" in the deeds is not conclusive. One must look also to the intention

COMPANY—Charge.

of the parties and the effect of the deeds in so far as they purported to carry out that intention. 3. The company could not carry on business in the ordinary course as regards the charged assets. The mandatory lodgement of the proceeds of all book debts to a special account under the control of the banks was intended to and did in fact deprive the company of the free use of the proceeds of such book debts such as it would have been entitled to under a floating charge. Furthermore, the assets were withdrawn from ordinary trade use, put in the keeping of the debenture holder, sterilized and made indisposable save at the absolute discretion of the debenture holder. Accordingly, the charges created were fixed charges. *Siebe Gorman* v. *Barclays Bank* [1979] 2 Lloyds Rep. 142, considered. *In re Keenan Bros. Ltd.*

(H.C., S.C.) [1985] I.R.401; [1985] ILRM 641

4. —— **Book debts** — *Receivership — Priority between creditors — Charge over book debts of company — Restriction on use of charged assets — Whether floating charge or fixed charge created — Companies Act,* 1963 (*No.* 33), *s.* 316.] By a debenture made on 30th March, 1981, between M. Ltd., W. I. Ltd. and W.I.E. Ltd. and a number of banks, the companies agreed to create a charge over the book debts of M. Ltd. Receivers were subsequently appointed under the provisions of the debenture over the assets of the companies. The applicants applied to the High Court for directions as to whether the charge created by the debenture was a floating charge or a fixed charge. **Held** by Barron J., in giving directions, 1, that a floating charge over property enables the chargor to use that property freely. A fixed charge creates an immediate assignment in equity of the property charged; that assignment does not occur with a floating charge unless and until it crystallises. Accordingly, the nature of a charge may be ascertained by determining whether or not the instrument of charge permits unrestricted use, or, in the alternative, it may be ascertained by determining when if ever the equitable assignment takes place. *Re Keenan Bros. Ltd.* [1985] I.R. 401 followed; *Siebe Gorman & Co. Ltd.* v. *Barclays Bank Ltd.* [1979] 2 Lloyd's Rep 142 applied. 2. That the deed of charge effectively acknowledged that the debts were in equity the property of the chargee, and were not available in the ordinary course of business. Accordingly, notwithstanding the fact that certain sub-clauses of the deed suggested that the execution of the deed did not effect such an assignment, the clear intention of the parties as expressed in the deed and the effect of the deed was to create a fixed charge over the book debts of M. Ltd. *In re*

COMPANY—*continued.*

A.H.Masser Ltd; McCann v. *Revenue Commissioners*

(H.C.) [1986] I.R.455

5. —— **Prior mortgage** — *Liquidation — Debenture granted subject to rights of a prior mortgagee — Particulars registered — Failure to register particulars of mortgagee — Mortgagee obtaining order extending time for registration — Sale of property — Whether debenture holder priority over mortgagee — Companies Act,* 1963 (*No.* 33), *ss.* 99, 106, 316.] Pursuant to a debenture dated 17 January, 1977, granted by Clarets Ltd. (the company) to the second named defendant (the bank) it was expressly provided that the bank's security was subject to the rights of a prior mortgagee (the defendant). Particulars of the bank's mortgage debenture were registered on 7 February, 1977, under s. 99 of the Companies Act, 1963. However, particulars of the defendant's earlier mortgage dated 28 February, 1975, had not by then been registered and when the defendant became aware of the non-registration he applied successfully under s. 106 of the Act of 1963 for an extension of time in which to register the particulars. Registration took place on 23 August, 1977, the court order of 29 July, 1977, having recited that the failure to register within the time required by the section was 'accidental.' The bank appointed a receiver and the company's property was sold subsequent to which the receiver instituted proceedings under s. 316 of the Act of 1963 in which the bank claimed priority over the defendant in relation to the proceeds of sale. The defendant opposed the claim. **Held** by Costello J. in deciding that the bank's mortgage debenture did not rank in priority to the earlier mortgage, 1, the effect of an order under s. 106 of the Act of 1963 was that the charge became a valid charge *ab initio* from the date of registration subject to such conditions as the court might impose when it extended the time. *Ehrmann Brothers Ltd. In re* [1906] 2 Ch. 697 and *Watson* v. *Duff Morgan & Vermont (Holdings) Ltd.* [1974] 1 W.L.R. 450 applied. 2. The effect of the court's order of 29 July, 1977, was that the defendant's security became a valid one when registration was effected without prejudice in the bank's rights under their mortgage debenture. Those rights were subject at all times to those of the first mortgagee. 3. The bank was bound by the words of their agreement and they could not now obtain priority which they expressly agreed they would not have. *Spain* v. *McCann; In re Clarets Ltd.*

(H.C.) [1978] ILRM 215

6. —— **Registration** — *Certificate of Registrar — Conclusiveness — Liquidation — Right to*

COMPANY—Charge.

enforce security — Validity of mortgage — Mortgage not registered within twelve days of creation — Mortgage subsequently registered — Whether certificate of registration conclusive evidence that requirements complied with — Companies Act, 1963 (*No.* 33), *ss.* 99, 104.] The plaintiff company provided the defendant company with credit loan facilities for the purpose of purchasing property. The purchase was completed in November, 1972, and, as agreed between the parties, the defendant company deposited the indentures of mortgage and conveyance, which were undated, together with documents of title, with the plaintiff company. The defendant company's solicitor gave an undertaking at the time of depositing the documents to provide the sum of £3,500 to enable the solicitor for the plaintiff company to have the indentures stamped prior to registration. By January, 1974, the solicitor for the plaintiff company had still not received the sum of £3,500 and decided that his firm would pay the stamp duty to enable registration of the mortgage. The indentures of conveyance and mortgage were duly stamped, signed and the dates, 21 March and 22 March respectively were inserted on the hitherto undated indentures. The necessary papers were lodged with the Registrar of Companies who, on 10 April, 1974, certified the date of creation of the charge as 22 March, 1974, and certified that the charge was registered on 10 April, 1974, pursuant to s. 99 of the Companies Act, 1963. The liquidator contested the plaintiff company's right to enforce their security on the grounds that the mortgage was void by reason of the plaintiff company's failure to register the charge within 21 days of its creation, as required by s. 99 of the Companies Act, 1963. **Held** by Hamilton J. in holding that the charge was a valid charge, the Registrar of Companies issued his certificate of registration pursuant to s. 104 of the Companies Act, 1963, which states that the certificate shall be conclusive evidence that the registration requirements of the Act have been complied with. *Eric Holmes (Property) Ltd., In re* [1965] Ch. 1052 and *CL Nye Ltd., In re* [1971] Ch. 442 followed. *Lombard & Ulster Banking (Ir.) Ltd.* v. *Amurec Ltd.*

(H.C.) [1976-7] ILRM 222

7. —— **Validity** — *Liquidation — Charge registered one month before winding up — Whether charge void as being fraudulent preference — Companies Act,* 1963 (*No.* 33), *s.* 286.] The combined effect of s. 286 of the Companies Act, 1963, and s. 53 of the Bankruptcy (Ireland) (Amendment) Act, 1872, is that if a company which is unable to pay its debts creates a charge over property in favour of a creditor within six months of its winding-up, such charge will be deemed a fraudulent preference and invalid. The

COMPANY—*continued.*

plaintiff company had deposited the title deeds of its premises with the defendant as security for a loan in December, 1974, but this charge was not registered in accordance with s. 99 of the 1963 Act. Some time after February, 1975, the defendant became apprehensive about the company's account, and also became aware of the unregistered charge. As a result of representations made by the defendant, a fresh deposit of title deeds was made in October, 1975. This charge was registered some days later, less than a month before the winding-up of the company. The liquidator brought the instant action, claiming that the charge was void as being a fraudulent preference of the defendant. **Held** by McWilliam J. in refusing the plaintiff's claim, 1, in order to establish a fraudulent preference, a liquidator must prove that the dominant intention of the company was to prefer the creditor in question. 2. On the evidence, the intention of the company in creating the charge appeared to be that of keeping the company going for as long as possible. This intention falls short of an intention to prefer the defendant over other creditors. *Corran Construction Co.* v. *Bank of Ireland Finance Ltd.*

(H.C.) [1976-7] ILRM 175

8. —— **Validity** — *Liquidation — Company creating a floating charge within twelve months before the commencement of the winding up — Whether company solvent immediately after creation of the charge — Companies Act,* 1963 (*No.* 33), *s.* 288.] The plaintiff, as liquidator of Creation Printing Co. Ltd. (the company) instituted proceedings to have determined whether a floating charge created in favour of the first defendant (the bank) by a debenture dated 4 June, 1975, was valid pursuant to s. 288 of the Companies Act, 1963. The second defendant, representing the unsecured creditors, submitted that the company was not solvent immediately after the creation of the floating charge. The company was, with other companies, a subsidiary of the Creation Group Ltd. (the parent company) and all accounts for the companies were kept by the parent company which owed sums amounting to £305,000 to Foir Teo., the bank and the Northern Bank Ltd., all of which loans were guaranteed by the company which itself owed £324,000 to the parent company. The debenture was given to the bank by the company to secure the repayment to the bank of money previously advanced by the bank to the parent company. The consideration for the guarantee to the bank was that the bank would not demand immediate payment from the parent company. If the assets of the company, mainly consisting of the premises and the very valuable printing machines, had been realised at the end of May, 1975, the company

would have had to discontinue its business. **Held** by McWilliam J. in ruling that the company was insolvent within the meaning of s. 288 of the 1963 Act, 1, it was clear from the wording of the section that the onus of establishing the solvency of the company was on the bank. 2. So far as the accounts of the company were concerned it was not material whether the debts had to be paid to the parent company or to the bank and the other guaranteed creditors of the parent company. 3. The company could not pay its debts without going out of business at the time the debenture was issued. *Patrick and Lyon Ltd.* [1933] Ch. 786 and *Ex Parte Russell* (1882) 19 Ch. D. 588 followed. *Crowley* v. *Northern Bank Finance Corporation Ltd.*

(H.C.) [1978] ILRM 219

[*Editor's Note:* Supreme Court judgment reported at [1981] I.R. 353]

FRAUDULENT TRADING

9. —— **Debts** — *Whether transaction constituted carrying on business — Whether fraudulent intent proved in each of participants — Test for determining extent of liability of participants — Companies Act,* 1963 (*No.* 33), *s.* 297.] The liquidator of Hunting Lodges Ltd. applied pursuant to s. 297 of the Companies Act, 1963, to have its two directors, Mr. and Mrs. Porrit, and a Mr. O'Connor and Plage Services Ltd. declared personally responsible for the debts of the company. In 1981 the company owed substantial amounts in tax and the Revenue began investigations into its affairs. At a meeting in December 1982 a Revenue official warned the company's auditor about any attempt to dispose of assets without paying the Revenue. In January 1983 the Revenue issued a summons claiming over £200,000 in arrears of tax plus interest. In March 1983 Mr. Porrit met Mr. O'Connor to begin negotiations on the sale of the company's property known as Durty Nelly's, and Mr. Porrit also wishing to have £200,000 as money on the side as part of the deal. At a meeting with the Revenue in April, which Mr. Porrit attended, the company's auditor stated that the company was then hopelessly insolvent; the Revenue official stated he would advise that the company be liquidated. In early May the Revenue sent a notice to the company requiring payment of the tax debt, in default threatening liquidation. The sale of Durty Nelly's was completed in early June, Mr. O'Connor operating through Plage Services Ltd. to avoid liability for VAT. Mr. and Mrs. Porrit both signed the conveyance to acknowledge the affixing of the seal of Hunting Lodges Ltd. Part of the purchase price was lodged by Mr. Porrit in a building society account under a false name, the mandate documents for

which were signed by himself and his wife also using false names. Two days later the Revenue successfully applied for the appointment of a provisional liquidator and the company was wound up later in June. S. 297 (1) of the Companies Act, 1963, provides that where 'it appears that any business of the company has been carried on with intent to defraud creditors . . . the court . . . may . . . declare that any persons who are knowingly parties . . . shall be personally responsible, without any limitation of liability, for all or any of the debts or other liabilities of the company . . .' **Held** by Carroll J. determining the application, 1, since carrying on business was not synonymous with trading, it was not necessary that all the company's business be carried on with fraudulent intent for s. 297 to operate on a single transaction committed with fraudulent intent was sufficient. 2. Each of the four respondents were parties to the sale of the property within the meaning of s. 297 in that each took positive steps of some nature relating to the transaction and it was not necessary to show a common fraudulent intent provided each of the participants acted for a fruadulent purpose. 3. In determining the extent to which each participant should be liable, it was important to look at the entire circumstances; that Mr. Porrit should be personally responsible for all the company's debts as he had directed all his efforts to getting as much money out of the company as he could before the Revenue moved against it; that Mrs. Porrit, as a married woman, could not escape responsibility and should be personally liable for all amounts advanced to her since 1976; and that Mr. O'Connor and Plage Services Ltd. should be jointly and severally liable for the amount of unaccounted-for cash which Mr. O'Connor had given to Mr. Porrit. *In re Hunting Lodges Ltd.*

(H.C.) [1985] ILRM 75

RECEIVERSHIP
see also **No. 4**

10. —— **Reservation of title** — *Suppliers claiming to be entitled to trace the proceeds of their goods — Whether reservation of title clause effective.*] Four companies, the claimants, who supplied goods to Stokes & McKiernan Ltd. (hereinafter referred to as the company) which were still in their possession on 4 April, 1978, when a receiver was appointed to it, claimed to be entitled to trace the proceeds of their goods sold by the company and to recover such money as held by the company on their behalf. Although the conditions of sale relied on by each claimant is different, each condition in one form or another contained a provision that the property in the goods shall not pass to the company until

COMPANY—Fraudulent Trading.

the full price had been paid for them. One of the claimants conditions of sale Oerlikon Electrodes (Ireland) Ltd. (hereinafter referred to as Oerlikon) expressly provided where full payment had not been received by them in the case of the re-sale by the company, Oerlikon's beneficial entitlement would attach to the proceeds of the re-sale or to the claim for such proceeds. Two of the claimants also claimed to be entitled to goods fully paid for by the company in the hands of the receiver on foot of an express condition in their condition of sale. The receiver brought an application seeking specific answers to questions raised relating to the ownership and the right to trace the proceeds of the aforementioned goods of the claimant to the company or to the receiver. **Held** by McWilliam J. in answering the questions raised, 1, the claimants are entitled to the return of the goods in the possession of the company at the time of the appointment of the receiver which had not been paid for or the price for which he may have sold them. *Aluminium Industries Vaassen B.V. v. Romalpa Aluminium Ltd.* [1976] 1 W.L.R. 676 considered. 2. In view of the express conditions of sale relating to the rights of Oerlikon to the purchase money on a resale by the company, the company is bound to hold the proceeds of the resale of the goods on trust for Oerlikon and Oerlikon is entitled to follow the proceeds of this sale. *Aluminium Industries Vaassen B.V.* v. *Romalpa Aluminium Ltd.* [1976] 1 W.L.R. 676 approved and followed. 3. The claimants are entitled to trace the purchase price of their goods into the hands of the receiver. *Aluminium Industries Vaassen B.V.* v. *Romalpa Aluminium Ltd.* [1976] 1 W.L.R. 676 considered. 4. The claims made under the two conditions relating to goods in the hands of the receiver which have been fully paid for must fail as the conditions are not strong and clear enough and further such conditions should be construed more strongly against the parties who have prepared it for their own advantage. *In re Stokes & McKiernan Ltd.*

(H.C.) [1978] ILRM 240

SHAREHOLDER — OPPRESSION OF MINORITY
see also **Nos. 12, 30**

11. —— **Oppression of minority** — *Share capital divided into ordinary non-voting shares and 8% non-participating voting preference shares — Directors deciding to allow preference shareholders to participate in profits — Ordinary shareholders objecting — Resolution passed by preference shareholders — "Oppression" — Conduct not burdensome, harsh or wrongful — Individual transaction — Affairs of company being conducted in disregard of interests of members —*

COMPANY—Oppression.

Companies Act, 1963 (*No.* 33), *s.* 205.] At the time of its incorporation in 1966 the share capital of W. Ltd. was £250,000 divided into 250,000 shares of £1 each of which 133,540 were issued and fully paid. The founder members, two brothers, had run the business in effect as a partnership but when their children inherited their shares confusion arose and the business suffered. The business was reorganised by the appointment of a managing director and in 1972 the capital structure of the company was reorganised by providing for a capital of £400,000, divided into 250,000 ordinary shares of £1 each and 150,000 8% preference shares of £1 each. Of both the ordinary and the preference shares 133,540 were issued and fully paid. The preference shares carried a right to a fixed 8% noncumlative dividend and voting rights; the ordinary shares, so long as any preference shares were outstanding, conferred no voting rights. The company prospered and the ordinary shareholders received very substantial dividends and fared very much better than the preference shareholders. The board of directors decided that it would be fair to allow the preference shareholders to participate in the accrued profits earned from a particular part of the company's business. To this end a scheme was devised and passed in general meeting (at which the ordinary shareholders were not entitled to attend) to allow the distribution of a sum of £267,000 between all the shareholders. A number of the ordinary shareholders objected, claiming that the action of the preference shareholders was oppressive and had been taken in disregard of their rights, and petitioned the High Court for relief under s. 205 of the Act of 1963. **Held** by Barrington J., in granting the relief sought, 1, that while this case involved an individual transaction rather than a course of conduct, an isolated transaction could give rise to relief under s. 205. *In re Westwinds Holding Company Ltd.* (Unreported, High Court, Kenny J., 21st May, 1974) considered. 2. That s. 205 of the Act of 1963 offers relief not only when the affairs of the company are being conducted in an oppressive manner but also where they are being conducted in disregard of the interests of some member or members. 3. That, while the preference shareholders had acted within their formal powers and honestly, and while there was no conduct that was burdensome, harsh, wrongful or that involved any lack of probity or fair dealing towards any of the members, the proposed action was in objective disregard of the interests of the ordinary shareholders in that so much of the monies as would be paid to the preference shareholders would not be available for distribution to the ordinary

COMPANY—Oppression.

shareholders or for purposes of which the ordinary shareholders might approve and, accordingly, that to persist in implementing the scheme would be oppressive to the ordinary shareholders. *Semble* that in view of the diferences in the wording of s. 210 of the English Act of 1948 and s. 205 of the Act of 1963, the authorities on s. 210 of the English Act must be treated with some reserve when interpreting the Irish section. *In re Williams Group Tullamore Ltd.*

(H.C.) [1985] I.R.613

SHARES

12. —— **Acquisition** — *Dissenting shareholder — Whether acquisition unfair — Whether acquisition oppressive — Whether company advancing money for the purpose of its own shares — Companies Act,* 1963 (*No.* 33), *ss.* 60, 204.] S. 204 of the Companies Act, 1963, makes provision for the acquisition of the shares of one company (the transferor) by another (the transferee). Where this has been approved in respect of not less than four-fifths in value of the shares affected, the transferee may within certain time limits give notice to any dissenting shareholder that it desires to acquire the beneficial ownership of his shares. Unless the dissenting shareholder applies to the court within one month from the date of such notice, the transferee shall be entitled and bound to acquire beneficial ownership of the shares of the dissenting shareholder. S. 60 of the said Act provides that it shall not be lawful for a company, directly or indirectly, to make financial provision for the purchase of its own shares. The applicants were the personal representatives of a deceased shareholder in D. and C. Co. Ltd. (the transferor), and were dissenting shareholders in a scheme within the terms of s. 204 of the 1963 Act, whereby the respondent wished to acquire their shares. Evidence was given that a loan of £800,000 had been made by the transferor to the respondent, and this sum was due and owing at the date of the notice given to the applicants pursuant to s. 204. The applicants alleged that the acquisition of the shares was unfair to them, that it was oppressive in that the shares were being expropriated by a company with a majority shareholding, and that the loan of £800,000 had not been called in due to the controlling interest of the respondent in the transferor company, and finally that the scheme was effectively in breach of s. 60 of the Act in that the money owed by the respondent to the transferor was being used to purchase its own shares. Evidence was given on behalf of the respondent that a third party was advancing the money for the purchase of the shares. **Held** by McWilliam J. in refusing to make the order sought, 1, where the statutory provisions have been complied with, the onus is on an applicant

COMPANY—Shares.

to establish unfairness, *Re Hoare and Co. Ltd.* (1933) 150 L.T. 374; *Grierson, Oldham and Adams Ltd.* [1968] 1 Ch. 17, followed. 2. The making by directors of an unsatisfactory decision in the context of the business of a company does not constitute oppression. 3. Since the money for the purchase of the shares was being advanced by a third party, there was no breach of the provisions of s. 60 of the 1963 Act. *McCormick v. Cameo Investments Ltd.*

(H.C.) [1978] ILRM 191

13. —— **Voting** — *Trust — Shares transferred to directors to secure loan — Loan repaid — No re-transfer of shares — Whether shares held in bare trust — General meeting — Vote by show of hands — Whether trust shares voted with personal shares — Shares voted against interest of beneficiary — Whether equitable owner precluded from setting aside resolution — Companies Act (Northern Ireland),* 1960, (*c.* 22) *s.* 114, *table A, art.* 7.] E. was registered as the holder of 250 shares in a private company of which he was the governing director. The remaining shares were held as follows: E.'s brothers J., G. and P. held 250, 200 and 200 respectively and F., an employee, held 1 share. In 1960 E. borrowed a sum from J. and G. and he transferred 160 shares to J. and 80 to G., to secure the loan. The loan was repaid in or about 1965, but E.'s shares were not transferred back to him and remained registered in the names of J. and G. After dissension between E., J. and G., the latter two requisitioned an extraordinary general meeting of the company for purposes of revoking the articles of association with conferred on E. the position of governing director. At that meeting J. and G. voted, on a show of hands, for the resolution. E. did not attend as he had been advised that as the registered owner of only 10 shares he could not prevent its passing: if, however, the shares transferred to J. and G. by way of security had been transferred back to E., he could have defeated the resolution. In an action by E., Gibson L.J. declared that the resolution was null and void. On appeal by J. it was argued that J. and G. were not trustees of the voting rights attaching to the shares transferred to them by way of security; that there had been no breach of trust as the value of those shares had not been detrimentally affected; and that the court should not set the resolution aside as the company was not affected by an equitable interest in the shares. **Held,** dismissing the appeal, that, 1, when the debt was repaid the mortgagees, J. and G., became bare trustees for the mortgagor, E. Consequently, at the material time, J. was a trustee in respect of the voting rights attached to the shares originally transferred to him by E. as security. 2. As on a show

of hands a shareholder can cast only one vote, J. was deemed to have voted not only his own shares but also the shares he held on trust: in so doing he placed himself in a position where his interest and his duty as a trustee conflicted for the resolution, by depriving E. of his position, was clearly to E.'s detriment and J.'s duty to E. was not limited merely to protecting the value of the trust shares. 3. Section 114 and article 7 of Table A of the Companies Act (Northern Ireland), 1960, are intended to protect the company if it deals with the registered holder of shares (for example by paying dividends to him), even if it has notice that the shares are held on trust for a third party, but do not operate to prevent an equitable owner of shares obtaining an order from the court to protect his equitable interests, even if that order operates against the company as well as the trustee of the shares. *McGrattan* v. *McGrattan*

(C.A.) [1985] N.I.28

ULTRA VIRES

14. —— **Dealing with company** — *Defendant engaged in dealings with other company — Defendant alleged to owe debt to other company — Other company indebted to plaintiff — Third party director to both companies — Cheques drawn on defendant in favour of plaintiff — Cheques dishonoured — Whether the plaintiff dealt with defendant in good faith — Companies (Northern Ireland) Order,* 1978 (*S.I. No.* 1042, *N.I.* 12), *art.* 129.] The defendant company's business was that of a building contractor. It was closely linked with L., a company which manufactured building materials. In 1981 L. entered into a factoring arrangment with the plaintiff and the plaintiff was indemnified against any loss resulting from the agreement by the third party, a director of both the defendant company and L., and by another company controlled by the third party. The plaintiff incurred losses arising from the factoring agreement and demanded payment from the guarantors. At a meeting between the plaintiff's manager and the third party, the business dealings between all the third party's companies were discussed and it appeared that the defendant company was indebted to L. The defendant company had been indebted to L. but, unknown to the plaintiff, this debt had been discharged. After this meeting the third party drew three post-dated cheques on the defendant company's account in favour of the plaintiff, for an amount less than the debt the plaintiff believed was due to L. By the time the cheques were presented, the third party had ceased to be a director of the defendant company and payment on the cheques was refused on the grounds that they were no longer in accordance with the defendant company's mandate. In an

action it was argued by the defendant company that the cheques could not be sued on as they were drawn for an unauthorised purpose and were *ultra vires* the company. **Held,** that as the plaintiff had no actual knowledge that the cheques were *ultra vires* the defendant company and in view of the relations between the third party's companies, the plaintiff had acted in good faith in receiving the defendant company's cheques. Accordingly the transactions were deemed to be within the defendant company's capacity and binding on it by virtues of section 129 of the Companies (Northern Ireland) Order, 1978. *International Factors (N.I.) Ltd.* v. *Streeve Construction Ltd.*

(Q.B.D.) [1984] N.I.245

15. —— **Notice** — *Guarantee and mortgage by company of third party debt — Transaction ultra vires company — Creditor reading company's memorandum and articles before guarantee executed — Creditor failing to understand effect of memorandum and articles — Whether creditor had actual notice of guarantee being ultra vires company — Subsequent resolution amending memorandum and empowering company to execute guarantee and mortgage for third party debts — Whether resolution having retrospective effect — Whether company estopped from relying on ultra vires nature of guarantee — Estoppel in pais — Companies Act,* 1963 (*No.* 33), *ss.* 7, 8(1), 10(1).] The plaintiff bank agreed to advance a sum of money by way of loan to the first defendant on the security of a mortgage to be executed by the second defendant company (an unlimited company having share capital) over certain property owned by the company. The solicitor acting for the bank sent the necessary documentation to the company for execution, and this included a draft resolution approving the execution of the mortgage. The company's solicitor sent a copy of the company's memorandum and articles of association to the bank's solicitor. In evidence the bank's solicitor was unable to recall having read the memorandum and articles but stated that it was his practice to do so. He also stated that, at the time, he did not consider that the transaction was *ultra vires* the company and that the first indication of this had occurred after execution of the guarantee. The first defendant defaulted on the loan from the bank, which began proceedings against both defendants, seeking judgment for the sum outstanding as against the first defendant, and a well charging order on the property concerned as against the company. The company argued that the memorandum did not authorise the execution of a guarantee and mortgage in connection with the debts of a third party since the primary object of the company was to operate as an investment company and any

COMPANY—Ultra Vires.

borrowing powers could only be exercised as incidental to those objects. The bank submitted that the transaction was not *ultra vires* the company, but that if it was, they were protected by the provisions of s. 8 (1) of the Companies Act, 1963, which had modified the *ultra vires* rule. The bank also submitted that a subsequent resolution of the company had been passed authorising the company executing guarantees in respect of third party debts and that this had retrospective effect. S. 8 (1) of the Companies Act, 1963, provides that any act done by a company which if it had been empowered to do the same would have been lawful "shall, notwithstanding that the company had no power to do such act or thing, be effective in favour of any person relying on such act or thing who is not shown to have been actually aware, at the time when he relied thereon, that such act or thing was not within the powers of the company." The company submitted also that the bank was actually aware of the fact that the transaction in question was *ultra vires* the company in view of the bank's solicitor having possession of the memorandum and articles of the company. **Held** by Keane J. in refusing to grant the plaintiff a well charging order against the company, 1, the memorandum of associaiton of the company clearly envisaged that it would operate as an investment, and not a trading company, and any of the powers as to borrowing could only be exercised validly having regard to that primary object and for its own purposes as opposed to guaranteeing advances made to other persons; and the power, specified in a paragraph of the memorandum, to do such things as might be deemed by the company to be incidental or conducive to the attainment of the objects already specified in the memorandum could not be interpreted as applying to the guarantee and mortgage in question since only the bank and the first plaintiff could possibly derive any benefit from the transaction, and so it could not be deemed conducive to the attainment of any of the company's objects. *Quaere:* whether if such a transaction was authorised by the memorandum it would nevertheless be *ultra vires* as no conveivable benefit could result to the company *Dicta* of Bower L.J. in *Hutton* v. *West Cork Railway Co.* (1883) 23 Ch. D. 654 mentioned. *In re Lee, Behrens & Co.* [1932] 2 Ch. 46 doubted in light of *Charterbridge Corp. Ltd.* v. *Lloyd's Bank Ltd.* [1970] Ch. 62. 2. The evidence indicated that the bank's solicitor read the company's memorandum and came to the conclusion that the guarantee and mortgage was *intra vires* the company, so that in the light of the true interpretation of the memorandum he mistakenly believed that the transaction was authorised; but

COMPANY—*continued.*

since the bank had possession of the memorandum and articles there were no further facts which they could have been made aware of and what they had failed to do was draw the correct inference from those facts and in these circumstances the bank had "actual notice" within the meaning of s. 8 (1) of the Companies Act, 1963, and therefore could not rely on its provisions. Discussion of the modification of the *ultra vires* rule and the inapplicability of the constructive notice to commercial transactions. 3. The subsequent resolution of the company authorising it to execute guarantees and mortgages such as the one in this case did not operate retrospectively; the provision of s. 10 (1) of the 1963 Act stating that any alterations of the memorandum "shall be as valid as if originally contianed therein" must be read in the light of s. 7 of the Act as relieving the company from the necessity of having the memorandum in its altered from signed again by the subscribers and attesting witnesses and then reprinted. 4. The company was not estopped from relying on the *ultra vires* nature of the transaction since the bank had not relied on any representation the company may have made as to the guarantee and mortgage, and since the bank at all times considered that the transaction was valid it had not altered its position in any way in reliance on a representation, if any was made by the company; the sending of the company's memorandum and articles to the bank did not amount to a representation that the company had the power in question, but was no more than an invitation to the bank to satisfy itself that the transaction was *intra vires*.

Reporter's Note: the judgment in this case makes reference to the further modification of the *ultra vires* rule in England by virtue of that country's European Communities Act, 1972. A similar provision is contained in Reg. 6 of the European Communities (Companies) Regulations, 1973 (S.I. No. 163). These regulations apply only to limited liability companies. The company in this case was not a limited company: see Keane, *Company Law in the Republic of Ireland* (London, 1985). *Northern Bank Finance Corp. Ltd.* v. *Quinn*

(H.C.) [1979] ILRM 221

WINDING UP

see also **Nos. 3, 5-8**

16. ——**Application of property** — *Building contract — Main contractor in liquidation — Monies paid to main contractor to meet its liabilities to sub-contractor — Winding up of main contractor before payment to sub-contractor — Provision in main contract requiring payment by employer direct to sub-contractor in certain*

COMPANY—Winding Up.

circumstances — Provision in sub-contract that monies paid to main contractor in respect of work done by sub-contractor be held in trust for sub-contractor — Retention monies in hands of employer — Effect of contracts — Whether retention monies the property of main contractor — Whether sub-contractor entitled to payment out of retention monies — Whether scheme to secure payment for sub-contractor contrary to public policy — Companies Act, 1963 (*No.* 33), *s.* 275.] The third defendant, the main contractor to a building contract, was insolvent and in liquidation. The plaintiff, a nominated sub-contractor, sought a declaration that it was entitled to be paid out of retention monies in the hands of the employer, the first defendant, a sum which had been certified as due to it by the architect, the second defendant, and which had been paid by the employer to the main contractor but which had not been paid over to the plaintiff. Clause 55 (*a*) of the main contract provided that: "On application to the Architect . . . the Contractor shall be entitled to receive . . . a certificate from the Architect of the amount due to him from the employer including sums due (if any) in respect of nominated sub-contractors (which sums shall be shown separately on each certificate) and before issuing any such certificate the Architect shall require the Contractor to furnish him reasonable proof that all nominated sub-contractor's accounts in previous certificates have been duly discharged . . . and in default of such proof . . . the employer shall himself pay such accounts upon the certificate of the Architect and deduct the amount so paid from any sums otherwise payable to the Contractor." The liquidator of the main contractor resisted the plaintiff's claim on the grounds that the retention monies were the property of the main contractor and that clause 55 (*a*) which sought to defeat the *pari passu* provisions of s. 275 of the Act of 1963 was void as being contrary to public policy. **Held** by Costello J., in giving judgment for the plaintiff, 1, that where the effect of a contract is that an asset which is actually owned by a company at the commencement of its liquidation would be dealt with otherwise than in accordance with s. 275 of the Act of 1963, then and to that extent the contract, as a matter of public policy, is void. *British Eagle International Airlines* v. *Compagnie Nationale Air France* [1975] 1 W.L.R 758 considered. *Carreras Rothmans Limited* v. *Freeman Mathews Treasure Limited* [1985] Ch. 207 approved. 2. That in the instant case the effect of the contracts was not to dispose of the contractor's asset but to impose a contingent liablilty on the retention fund to suffer a reduction in the event of a specified default by the contractor. 3. That the liquidator of the third defendant took the company's property subject to the liabilities

COMPANY—*continued.*

which affected it in the company's hands. *Glow Heating Ltd.* v. *Eastern Health Board*

(H.C.) [1988] I.R.110

17. —— **Assets** — *Money paid by mistake to company prior to liquidation — Whether constituting assets of company subsequent to liquidation — Whether subject to right of set-off — Whether company holding money as trustee — Purpose of constructive trust — Estoppel — Whether arising — Whether person acted to his detriment.*

Equity — Tracing — Money paid in error — Claim for repayment — Whether tracing available — Mixed fund — Whether money held in trust — Whether subject to set-off — Constructive trust — Purpose of such trust — Estoppel — Whether person claiming set-off acting to his detriment.] The former bankers of Irish Shipping Ltd. claimed a right of set-off pursuant to s. 251 of the Irish Bankrupt and Insolvent Act, 1857, and this general right was not disputed by the liquidator. What was disputed was (*a*) whether certain monies had been held in trust by Irish Shipping, and if so, whether these monies were subject to set-off; (*b*) whether monies ordered by Irish Shipping on the day before the liquidation to be transferred to the bankers on the day following the liquidation were subject to set-off; (*c*) whether the amount contained in a draft drawn by the payer prior to the liquidation but received by the bank after the liquidation was subject to set-off, and (*d*) whether a duplicate payment made in error and paid into the account of Irish Shipping in credit, was subject to set-off. **Held** by Carroll J., 1, a right of set-off can only apply to monies actually in the account of the debtor at the date of the liquidation, unless the party claiming the right is party to a contract remaining to be performed at that date. *Palmer* v. *Day & Son* [1895] 2 Q.B. 618 distinguished. 2. Where monies are paid by mistake into the account of a company, such monies do not form part of the assets of that company at the date of its liquidation. *Chase Manhattan Bank NA* v. *Israel-British Bank (London) Ltd.* [1981] Ch. 105 followed. 3. Monies paid by mistake must be regarded as being akin to lost property rather than trust property, and in the absence of a defence of equitable estoppel, may be traced by the payer. Purpose of constructive trust and remedy of tracing discussed. *In re Hallett's Estate* (1880) 13 Ch. D. 698 applied. *In re Irish Shipping Ltd.*

(H.C.) [1986] ILRM 518

18. —— **Creditors** — *Classification — Preferential debts — Test applicable — Unpaid wages or salary of servants or employees — Whether employee engaged under a contract of service or a*

COMPANY—Winding Up.

contract for services — Claimants in first category entitled to be paid as preferential creditors — Companies Act, 1963 (*No.* 33), *s.* 285.] On the 15th November, 1982, the High Court made an order directing that The Sunday Tribune Ltd. be wound up by the court, and appointing an official liquidator. During the winding up of the company, the official liquidator applied to the court for the determination of the proper classification of the debts proved by three creditors of the company in respect of wages or salary owed to each of them by the company for services rendered to the company by each of those creditors. The three creditors claimed that the sums so due to them were debts payable in the winding up in accordance with the priority specified in s. 285, sub-s. 2, of the Act of 1963. It is provided by sub-s. 2 (*b*) of that section that, in the winding up of a company, there shall be paid in priority to all other debts all wages or salary (whether or not earned wholly or in part by way of commission) of "any clerk or servant" in respect of services rendered to the company during the four months before the relevant date. The first claimant had been employed by the company on a shift basis as sub-editor of the newspaper published by the company. He was required to attend at the company's premises at a specified time and he had worked under the guidance of the chief sub-editor and to his instructions. The second claimant had been paid a fixed sum each week as a journalist for writing the material for a weekly column published in the company's newspaper; she was required to attend and particpate at the company's editorial conferences. The third claimant had furnished regularly articles for the company's newspaper but each article had been commissioned separately by the company. The official liquidator had refused to enter the names of the three claimants in the list of preferential creditors because of the independent nature of their work and because income tax had not been deducted by the company from their remuneration in accordance with the PAYE system. At the hearing of the official liquidator's application it was **Held** by Carroll J., in determining the issues, 1, that the proper test to apply was to ascertain whether or not the services rendered to the company by each claimant had been rendered pursuant to a contract of service. 2. That the evidence established that the services so rendered to the company by each of the first two claimants had been rendered pursuant to contracts of service and that, accordingly, the debts proved by those two claimants qualified for the priority specified in s. 285, sub-s 2, of the Act of 1963. *Beloff* v. *Pressdram Ltd.* [1973] 1 All E.R. 241 and *Stevenson, Jordan & Harrison Ltd.* v. *MacDonald* [1952] 1 T.L.R. 101 considered. 3. That the services rendered to the company

COMPANY—*continued.*

by the third claimant had not been rendered pursuant to a contract of service and, accordingly, the debt proved by that claimant did not qualify for such priority. *In re Sunday Tribune Ltd.*

(H.C.) [1984] I.R.505

19. —— **Creditors** — *Classification — Preferential debts — Wages due to employees — Wages having preferential status — Employment contributions under social welfare legislation in respect of such wages due — Whether "employer's contribution" having similar preferential status — Companies Act,* 1963 (*No.* 33), *s.* 285(2)(*e*) — *Social Welfare (Consolidation) Act,* 1981, (*No.* 33) *ss.* 9(1)(*a*), 10(1)(*b*).] S. 285 (2) of the Companies Act, 1963, provides:— "In a winding up there shall be paid in priority to all other debts . . . (*e*) . . . all amounts due in respect of contributions payable during the twelve months next before the relevant date by the company as the employer of any person under the Insurance (Intermittent Unemployment) Act, 1952, or the Social Welfare Acts, 1952-1961 . . ." S.10(1)(*b*) of the Social Welfare (Consolidation) Act, 1981, provides:— ". . . where in any contribution year a payment is made to or for the benefit of an employer contributor in respect of reckonable earnings of that employer contributor, there shall be payable an employment contribution comprising . . ." Costello J., in a judgment delivered on 6 May 1986 held that such contributions were to be treated as preferential debts under s.285 (2) (*e*). The liquidator appealed and submitted that the employer's contributions did not comprise of "amounts due in respect of contributions payable during the 12 months next before the relevant date" pursuant to s. 285 (2) (*e*) of the Companies Act, 1963. **Held** by the Supreme Court (Finlay C.J., Walsh, Henchy, Griffin and McCarthy JJ.) in allowing the appeal, by virtue of s.10 of the 1981 Act no liability to pay employment contributions arose until reckonable earnings were paid. As reckonable earnings due to the Company's employers were only paid since the liquidation, liability to pay the employer's contribution only arose after that date. The contributions therefore were not "payable" in the twelve months prior to the liquidation appointment and so they did not enjoy the benefit of s.285 (2) (*e*) of the 1963 Act. *In re Castlemahon Poultry Products Ltd.*

(S.C.) [1987] ILRM 222

20. —— **Creditors** — *Fraudulent preference — Bank account — Lodgments of £23,000 made by director between decision to wind up and date of winding up — Intention of director to prefer bank and reduce his guarantee liability — Whether bank*

COMPANY—Winding Up.

entitled to priority in regard to company's wages payments made from overdrawn account — Whether monies advanced for the payment of wages — No wages account — Whether rule in Clayton's Case applied to lodgments — Bankruptcy (Ireland) Amendment Act, 1872 (*c*.58), *s.* 53 — *Companies Act,* 1963 (*No.* 33), *ss. 285,* 286, 399.] The plaintiff company was effectively controlled by two directors; W.M. and his wife M.M. On the 16th June, 1980, by joint and several guarantee W.M. and M.M. guaranteed the obligations of the company to the defendant on foot of its current account up to £75,000 with interest. On the 15 September, 1980, an extraordinary general meeting of the company was called for 3 October, 1980, to consider a resolution to wind up the company as the company had become insolvent. The company went into liquidation on 3 October, 1980. A wages account was opened with the defendant on 17 September, 1980. On the 30 September, 1980, the wages account was debited with the sum of £32,519.11 and the company's current account was credited in the same sum. Between the 17 September and the 3 October, a further sum of £4,348.72 was debited to the wages account. An additional sum of £23,278.13 was lodged to the company's current account between the 15 September, 1980, and the 3 October, 1980. On the plaintiff's application for a determination, pursuant to s. 280 of the Companies Act, 1963, as to whether the crediting of the latter sum constituted a fraudulent preference and whether the preferential claim under s. 285, sub-s. 6 of the same Act made by the defendant against the plaintiff for £47,027.66 (for monies paid by the company for wages for four months prior to liquidation), was a valid one, it was **Held** by Carroll J., 1, that the lodgments made to the current account after the 15 September, 1980, amounted to a fraudulent preference as they preferred the defendant directly and the guarantors indirectly as it was to be inferred from the circumstances that such was the dominant purpose of the lodgments. *Re M. Kushler Ltd.* [1943] Ch. 248 considered. 2. That the defendant was entitled to the benefit of subrogation provided for in s. 285, sub-s. 6 of the Companies Act, 1963, which section should be given a benevolent construction. *Re Rampgill Mill Ltd.* [1967] Ch. 1138 considered. 3. That subrogation could be claimed within the limits laid down by s. 285, sub-s. 3 in relation to any cheques debited to the bank account within the period prior to the passing of the resolution for the winding-up of the company to which priority is to be given in accordance with the provisions of that section. The rule in *Clayton's Case* (1816) 1 Mer. 572 applied. *Station Motors Ltd.* v. *Allied Irish Banks Ltd.*

COMPANY—*continued.*

(H.C.) [1985] I.R.756

21. —— **Deposit interest** — *Liability to tax — Whether deposit interest earned by money in the hands of the liquidator liable to tax — Whether tax payable a "necessary disbursement" — Whether tax payable ranks as a preferential payment or an unsecured debt — Companies Act,* 1963 (*No.* 33), *ss.* 244, 285 — *Finance Act,* 1983 (*No.* 15), *s.* 56 — *Winding Up Rules 1966, r.* 129.] The liquidator of three companies which had been wound up thirteen years previously raised certain questions by motion concerning how the admitted liability of the companies to pay income tax, corporation profits tax and cororation tax on deposit interest accrued on monies held by the liquidator since the winding up was to be discharged: (1) Whether the tax payable in respect of the deposit interest was a necessary disbursement of the liquidator under the third heading of rule 129 (1) of the Winding Up Rules, 1966; (2) If the tax were found to be payable but not under rule 129, whether the tax payable would rank as a preferential payment under s. 285 of the Companies Act, 1963; (3) Whether the tax if payable but not under either of the above provisions would rank as an unsecured debt in the winding up of the companies. Rule 129 made provision for the priority of certain payments in the winding up of an insolvent company, and the third heading gave priority to "necessary disbursements" of the official liquidator "other than expenses properly incurred in preserving, realising or getting in the assets hereinbefore provided." It was submitted on behalf of the liquidator that those provisions of rule 129 had no application to this case following the interpretation of the rule in *Revenue Commissioners* v. *Donnelly* [1983] ILRM 329. On behalf of the Revenue it was contended that under the combined effect of the obligation to pay tax provided in the Corporation Tax Act, 1976, and the provisions of s. 244 of the Companies Act, 1963, whereby the court could make an order for payments out of the assets of an insolvent company of the costs, charges and expenses incurred in the winding up in such priority as the court thought just, the court in this instance could find that the tax liability was payable under rule 129. **Held** by Costello J., 1, liability to pay tax in this case could not be regarded as a necessary disbursement under rule 129 in the light of the specific interpretation of that rule by the Supreme Court in *Revenue Commissioners* v. *Donnelly,* where it was held that the rule was intended to deal with liabilities of the company, and the third heading of which did not include liability for corporation tax. The question of an order under s. 244 of the Companies Act, 1963, did not arise as the Revenue had based their case only on the Winding Up

COMPANY—Winding Up.

Rules. 2. The tax payable did not rank as a preferential payment as s. 285 gave priority to taxes due before the winding up and not as in this instance since that event. 3. Nor did the tax payable rank as an unsecured debt as the duties of the liquidator did not include payment of debts to the Revenue for liabilites incurred in the post liquidation period. Although s. 56 of the Finance Act, 1983, had cured that defect its effect was not retroactive. Therefore, the tax was not recoverable by the Revenue under rule 129 on the accrued interest notwithstanding the statutory obligation on the company to pay taxes. *In re Hibernian Transport Companies Ltd.*

(H.C.) [1984] ILRM 583

22. —— **Deposit interest** — *Liability to tax — Interest accruing on monies placed on deposit by liquidator — Liability to corporation tax — Whether tax due part of the "costs, charges and expenses properly incurred in the winding up" — Companies (Winding-Up) Rules* 1909, *r.* 187(2); *Rules of Superior Courts,* 1966 (*S.I. No.* 28), O.74, *r.* 129 *(Winding Up Rules) — Companies (Consolidation) Act,* 1908 (*c.*69), *s. 171 — Companies Act,* 1963 (*No.* 33), *ss.* 244, 281.] Section 281 of the Companies Act, 1963, provides, *inter alia,* that ". . . costs, charges and expenses properly incurred in the winding up . . . shall be payable . . . in priority to all other claims." The applicant was the liquidator of N. Ltd., a company in voluntary liquidation. During the course of the liquidation he placed some of the company's funds on deposit. Interest accrued on the funds in respect of which corporation tax was payable. The applicant sought directions from the High Court, as to whether tax arising on the interest was payable in priority to other claims by virtue of the provisions of s. 281 of the Act of 1963. The High Court (Carroll J.), in a judgment reported at [1986] I.R. 183, answered the above question in the affirmative. On appeal, by the applicant, it was **Held** by the Supreme Court (Finlay C.J., Henchy and Griffin JJ.), in dismissing the appeal, 1, that rule 129 of the Winding-up Rules, 1966, did not apply to voluntary winding-up and was in narrower terms than s.281 of the Act of 1963. Accordingly, different tests were applicable in determining whether a debt was payable pursuant to s. 281 of the Act of 1963 in a voluntary winding-up from those which would be applicable in a winding up by the High Court. *In Re Van Hool McArdle Ltd.* [1982] ILRM 340, *Revenue Commissioners* v. *Donnelly* [1983] ILRM 329 distinguished. 2. That the word "charges' used in s. 281 of the Act of 1963 was additional to rather than synonymous with "costs and expenses", and the section therefore applied to a wider category of payments than fees and similar sums. 3. That since it was proper for the

COMPANY—*continued.*

liquidator to put the monies on deposit, the tax that arose on the interest which accrued was "properly incurred", and being so incurred subsequent to the winding-up commencing was a charge properly incurred therein within the meaning of s. 281 of the Act of 1963. *In re Beni-Felkai Mining Company Ltd.* [1934] 1 Ch. 406 considered. *In re Noyek (A.) & Sons Ltd; Burns* v. *Hearne*

(H.C.) [1986] I.R.183; [1987] ILRM 508; (S.C.) [1988] I.R.772

23. —— **Disclaimer of onerous property** — *Application to disclaim a lease — Whether lease "onerous" — Position of guarantors — Whether the disclaimer would end the liability of the guarantors — Companies Act,* 1963 (*No.* 33), *s.* 290.] In 1976 the respondent granted to Massey Ferguson (Eire) Ltd. a 35-year lease of factory premises at Naas Road, Dublin. Massey Ferguson Holdings Ltd., a third party to the lease, guaranteed to the respondent the due payment of the rent and the performance of the usual leasehold covenants. In 1979 the T.M.G. Group acquired the issued share capital of Massey Ferguson (Eire) Ltd. (which was then re-named Farm Machinery Distributors Ltd.) and agreed to assume liability for the guarantee given to the respondent by Massey Ferguson Holdings Ltd. In January, 1983, Farm Machinery Distributors Ltd. went into voluntary liquidation and the applicant in these proceedings was appointed liquidator. The applicant discovered that the lease of the Naas Road property represented a liability of some £1,250,000, the rent being above the going rate, a schedule of dilapidations having been served, and there being no prospect of assigning the lessee's interest other than at a "reverse premium." The applicant accordingly sought, pursuant to section 290 of the Companies Act, to disclaim the lease as onerous. The disclaimer was opposed by the respondent, and the court also entertained submissions from the two parties liable under the guarantee. It fell to the court to consider the position of the latter and to decide whether a disclaimer would put an end to the liability of the guarantors. **Held** by Keane J., granting the applicant leave to disclaim the lease, 1, that the court's exclusive concern was with the interests of parties involved in the liquidation, but the court would consider the rights of third parties where that was necessary in order to release a company from liability. 2. That, in connection with leases, the release of an original lessee or surety was not necessary for the purpose of releasing a company from liability. 3. That, in the instant case, disclaimer of the onerous lease would facilitate the liquidation and be in the general interest. 4. That the rights *inter se* of the respondent, Massey Ferguson Holdings Ltd. and

the T.M.G. Group would not be affected by the disclaimer. 5. That the respondent was entitled to receive rent from the applicant from the date of his appointment as liquidator until that of his notice of disclaimer. *Tempany* v. *Royal Liver Trustees Ltd., In re Farm Machinery Distributors Ltd.*

(H.C.) [1984] ILRM 273

24. —— **Disclaimer of onerous property** — *Hiring contract — Power of liquidator to disclaim — Whether properly burdened with onerous covenant — High Court order giving liberty to disclaim — Effect of section — Whether other party to the contract entitled to prove for the injury sustained — Measure of damages — Companies Act,* 1963 (*No.* 33), *s.* 290(1), (3), (9).] Under three agreements made between 1976 and 1979 Irish Telephone Rentals Ltd. (Rentals) agreed with Ranks (Ireland) Ltd. (the company) to instal and let for a period of 14 years certain telephone equipment. The rent was to be paid quarterly in advance during the currency of the agreements. All of the agreements contained the following clause: "If the subscriber shall repudiate this contract and the company (Rentals) shall accept such repudiation so as to terminate this contract the company may thereupon remove the installation and the subscriber shall pay to the company all payments then accrued due and also a sum equal to the present value of a 5% basis of the remaining rentals that would have been payable under this contract if not so terminated less an allowance of 25% to cover the estimated cost of the maintenance and value of recovered material. The said sum shall be payable as liquidated damages it being an agreed estimate of the loss the company would suffer." On 5 December, 1983, an order was made for the winding up of the company and the appointment of an official liquidator. The liquidator subsequently sought liberty in the High Court to disclaim the hire contracts and by order dated 8 February, 1985, Barr J. acceded to the application and also gave liberty to the liquidator to pay to Rentals the sum of £11,272.03 which represented the amount of rental due on foot of the hire contracts for the period in which the liquidator occupied the premises in which the equipment was installed. The liquidator then asked the court for a decision on the interpretation and effect of s. 290 of the Companies Act, 1963, which entitles a liquidator, in certain circumstances, to disclaim property burdened with onerous covenants. **Held** by Murphy J. in answering the questions raised, 1, the essence of s. 290 of the Act was that the company was relieved of the continuing onerous obligations but only on the terms that the other party to the contract had the right to prove the injury it

sustained. 2. The entitlement to prove in the winding up pertained not only to creditors but to all persons who had entered into contracts which were beneficial to them and onerous to the company whose rights are affected by a disclaimer permitted by the court. 3. The appropriate measure of damages was not that provided for under Clause 11. That method was only appropriate where the hirer repudiated the contract. A disclaimer was not the same as a repudiation in that a disclaimer is effective without the acceptance and in spite of the opposition of Rentals. *In re Ranks (Ireland) Ltd.*

(H.C.) [1988] ILRM 751

25. —— **Liquidator** — *Remuneration — Liquidator making application for interim payment of fees — Inquiry by examiner — Examiner's report coming before the court — Liquidator not afforded an opportunity to submit evidence establishing the necessity of the work undertaken — Court ruling against liquidator — Appeal to Supreme Court — Whether liquidator entitled to remuneration — Companies Act,* 1963 (*No.* 33), *s.* 228 — *RSC O.*74, *r.* 47.] The official liquidator who was appointed on 24 May, 1982, in all made five applications for interim payment of fees, grounding each application on an affidavit exhibiting a report covering the relevant period in respect of which the fees were claimed. The fifth application (which is the subject of this appeal) was originally brought by notice of motion before Costello J. on 3 December, 1984, who ordered that an inquiry be made by the examiner and a report to be duly furnished. After the inquiry was held the assistant examiner furnished a report dated 20 February, 1985, approving a sum of £266,782.84 to be paid to the liquidator in discharge of his fee, and two further sums for out of pocket expenses plus VAT. The report came before Costello J. on 11 March and 29 April, 1985. On neither occasion did the revenue solicitor representing the general body of creditors submit any recommendation on the reduction in quantum. Counsel for the liquidator had intended to submit evidence establishing the necessity to carry out the work undertook on the report on 29 April, 1985. However due to a misunderstanding as to the manner in which the learned judge was approaching the application, counsel for the liquidator was not afforded such an opportunity as Costello J. delivered his judgment on the 29 April ruling against the right of the liquidator to recover anything for his report save a nominal charge. The liquidator appealed this decision and sought an order restoring the amount certified in the examiner's certificate on a number of grounds in particular that he was not afforded an opportunity of making a case in respect of the fee claimed. **Held**

COMPANY—Winding Up.

by the Supreme Court (Finlay C.J., Hederman and McCarthy JJ.) in allowing the appeal and varying part of the High Court's order, 1, the liquidator must be afforded an opportunity of making his case in respect of the fees claimed for the preparation of the report. 2. The function of the examiner in holding an enquiry into the liquidator's fee is to consider quantum only and not liability. *In re Merchant Banking Ltd.*

(S.C.) [1987] ILRM 260

26. —— **Proceedings** — *Liquidator seeking to impose personal responsibility on directors of company — Whether entitled to use the transcript of evidence on oath taken from the directors in the course of their examinations in the winding-up proceedings — Companies Act,* 1963 (*No.* 33), *ss.* 245(4), 297, 298.] The liquidator in the course of proceedings to wind up a company brought an application under ss. 297-298 of the Companies Act, 1963, seeking to impose unlimited personal liability on the former directors of the company for its debts and liabilities, and to compel payment by them of monies or restoration of company property. The liquidator claimed to be entitled to use the transcripts of evidence on oath taken from the directors in the course of their examination pursuant to an order of the court in the winding up proceedings under the provisions of s. 245 of the 1963 Act. It was contended for the directors that such evidence was not admissible by virtue of s. 245(4) of the Act which disallowed the use of such evidence against a person examined under the section 'in any other proceedings civil or criminal except in the case of any criminal proceedings for perjury in respect of such answer.' The proceedings for the winding up of the company was not 'other proceedings' and the provisions of s. 245 of the Act do not create a new and separate set of proceedings. The examination under that section form part of those proceedings and the answers given in the course of such examination might be used for the purposes of any application to the court in the course of such proceedings, but not in any other proceedings. Therefore the liquidator was entitled to have the answers of the directors given in examination admitted in evidence for the purpose of the application under ss. 297-298. *In re Aluminium Fabricators Ltd.*

(H.C.) [1984] ILRM 399

27. —— **Stamp duty** — *Proceeds of sale of charged assets received by liquidator — Examiner's certificate of liquidator's account — Stamp duty payable on certificate — Whether stamp duty payable out of funds recovered before payment of creditors — Whether payable when fund insufficient to meet secured claims — Whether stamp duty payable as a cost or expense of the liquidation*

COMPANY—*continued.*

— Supreme Court and High Court (Fees) Order, 1984 (*S.I. No.* 19) *as amended by the Supreme Court and High Court (Fees) Order,* 1985 (*S.I. No.* 36), *part* 3, *para.* 34 — *Companies Act,* 1963 (*No.* 33), *ss.* 231(1)(*d*), 280(1).] Stamp duty is payable out of the actual funds recovered by the liquidator before payment of the secured creditors' debts and is not a cost or expense of the liquidation generally. If the proceeds of sale of a company's assets are more than sufficient to meet the claims of the secured creditors, the unsecured creditors must pay stamp duty on the remaining funds coming to them out of the proceeds of sale. Stamp duty is payable on every £100.00 recovered by the liquidator regardless of whether the amount recovered or proceeds of sale is sufficient to meet the claims of the secured creditors. So **held** by O'Hanlon J. *In re Michael Orr (Kilternan) Ltd.; In re Thornberry Construction (Ireland) Ltd.*

(H.C.) [1986] I.R.273

28. —— **Voluntary winding up** — *Liquidator subletting charged asset — Whether liquidator acting as a receiver/manager of debenture holders in so doing — Deficiency — Whether rental income received on behalf of general creditors.*] Where a debenture holder has not exercised its powers under the debenture to appoint a receiver and an insolvent company is wound up and the liquidator subsequently sublets the premises the subject of the debenture holder's fixed charge with its approval the liquidator is not acting as a receiver or manager on behalf of the debenture holder and the rents and profits of the subletting must be applied to satisfy the debts of the general body of creditors. So **held** by Costello J. *In re London Windsor and Greenwich Hotels Limited* [1892] 1 Ch. 639 distinguished. *In re Egan Electric Co. Ltd.*

(H.C.) [1987] I.R.398

29. —— **Voluntary winding up** — *Whether court has power to annul winding-up resolution — Whether court has power to extend time to call a creditors' meeting — Whether liquidator validly appointed — Companies Act,* 1963 (*No.* 33), *ss.* 234, 256, 266, 267, 280 — *Companies (Amendment) Act,* 1982 (*No.* 10), *s.* 9.] Section 280, sub-s. 1 of the Companies Act, 1963, provides that in relation to every voluntary winding up of a company "the liquidator or any contributory or creditor may apply to the court to determine any question arising in the winding up, or to exercise . . .all or any of the powers which the court might exercise if the company were being wound up by the court." Sub-section 3 of that section provides, *inter alia,* that "an office copy of an order

COMPANY—Winding Up.

made by virtue of this section annulling the resolution to wind up . . . shall forthwith be forwarded by the comany to the registrar of companies for registration." Section 234 of the Act of 1963 empowers the court to annul a winding up order where the company is being wound up by the court. O.H. had never traded and had no creditors. By special resolution passed at an extraordinary general meeting of its members it was resolved that O.H. be wound up voluntarily and that the applicant be appointed liquidator. The directors of O.H. failed to make and deliver to the registrar of companies a statutory declaration of solvency in accordance with s. 256 of the Act of 1963. Accordingly, and by virtue of sub-s. 7 of that section, the winding up fell to be governed by the provisions of the Act relating to a creditors' voluntary winding up and in particular by ss. 266 and 267. In default of the requirements of s. 266, O.H. failed to summon a creditors' meeting at which a liquidator might have been appointed in accordance with the provisions of s. 267 and O.H. was accordingly unable to proceed in the winding up. The applicant applied to the High Court for an order annuling the resolution to wind up the company voluntarily or, in the alternative, for an order extending and fixing the time for the holding of a creditors' meeting pursuant to s. 266. **Held** by Carroll J., in granting the relief sought, 1, that, by analogy with the power of the court under s. 234 of the Companies Act, 1963, to annul a winding up order in a court winding up, and by virtue of the reference at sub-s. 3 of s. 280 of the Act of 1963 to "an order . . . annulling the resolution to wind up", the court was empowered by s.280 of the Act of 1963, in an appropriate case, to annul the resolution to wind up a company voluntarily. 2. That in the circumstances of this case where the company was not trading and had no creditors it was appropriate for the court to make such an order. 3. That the court did not have power to extend the time to call a creditors' meeting as the time limit was provided by statute and there was no discretion given to the court to extend it; nor was there any analogous power given to the court in a winding up by the court. 4. That no liquidator having been appointed in accordance with the provision of sub-s. 1 of s. 267 of the Act of 1963, the appropriate person to make the application under s.280 of that Act was a contributory and the matter would be adjourned to allow a contributor to be substituted for the applicant. *Per* Carroll J. in the case of a trading company with creditors it might be necessary to require that a petition to wind up be presented. *In re Oakthorpe Holdings Ltd.; Walsh* v. *Registrar of Companies*

(H.C.) [1987] I.R.632

COMPANY—*continued.*

30. —— **Whether just and equitable** — *Oppression — Company conducted in informal manner — Equivalent to partnership — Three directors being equal owners — One director claiming oppression — Whether order for winding up of company appropriate — Whether alternative order to remedy oppression and end dispute appropriate — Discretion of court — Whether activities complained of brought basis of informal arrangement to an end — Companies Act,* 1963 (*No.* 33), *ss.* 205, 213, 215.] S. 205 of the Companies Act, 1963, provides that where the court is satisfied that the affairs of the company are being conducted or the directors' powers are being exercised in a manner oppressive to any member of the company, the court may, on the application of such member, make such order as it thinks fit with a view to bringing to an end the matters complained of. S. 215 provides for applications for the winding-up of a company to be made by petition to the court of any person entitled to bring proceedings under s. 205. S. 213 provides that a company may be wound up by the court where, *inter alia,* the court is of opinion that it just and equitable to do so, and where the court is satisfied that the powers of the directors are being exercised in a manner oppressive to any member. The section provides further that the court may dismiss a petition where it is of opinion that proceedings under s. 205 would be more appropriate. B.S. was one of three directors and equal shareholders in the company. The company was run in an informal manner. On 3 February, 1979, the two other directors, by notice in writing, informed B.S. that a resolution removing him from the office of director would be moved at a general meeting to be held on 12 March, 1979. No meeting of the board of directors had been convened at which a decision was taken to hold a meeting on 12 March, or to propose the resolution. In the event, no meeting was held on 12 March. Following the notification in writing to B.S. on 3 February, he was told by the other directors that they were relieving him of his responsibilities as a working director, and they offered to pay him three months salary in lieu of notice. B.S. petitioned the High Court for the winding-up of the company under s. 213 of the Companies Act, 1963. The company sought to restrain the petitioner from advertising the petition, on the grounds that it was not presented in good faith, and that proceedings under s. 205 would be more appropriate. McWilliam J., in refusing the order sought, held that ss. 205 and 213 (*g*) of the Companies Act, 1963, apply to members of a company in their capacity as members. The petition of B.S. was based on his office of director. He had been deprived of all his functions in that capacity, and thus had a *bona fide* claim to have the company wound up.

COMPANY—Winding Up.

On the same basis, it would not be open to the court to dismiss the petition on the grounds that proceedings under s. 205 would be more appropriate. **Held** by Gannon J. in making an order under s. 213 of the Companies Act, 1963, 1, proceedings under s. 205 would not be appropriate, in that there was no form of order capable of being made by the court under that section which would bring to an end the matters complained of by the petitioner. 2. The nature of the relationship between the three directors was in substance, though not in form, that of a partnership, based on mutual confidence. The action of the other directors on the 3 February, 1979, amounted to a repudiation of the relationship on which the company was founded. *Ebrahimi* v. *Westbourne Galleries* [1973] A.C. 360 applied.3. The purported removal of the petitioner from the office of director was irregular and ineffective in law. *In re Murph's Restaurants Ltd.*

(H.C.) [1979] ILRM 141

31. —— **Whether just and equitable** — *Company with two directors — Test applicable — Whether administration of company practicable — Whether oral hearing required — Whether petitioner guilty of misconduct disentitling relief — Companies Act,* 1963 (*No.* 33), *s.* 213 (*f*).] A petition to wind up Vehicle Building and Insulations Ltd., a company incorporated in 1972 for the purpose of repairing and dealing in motor vehicles, was presented to the High Court on the grounds that it was just and equitable so to do. The petitioner and Mr. H. were the only shareholders and directors of the company, each holding 50% of the issued share capital. On behalf of the petitioner it was alleged that there was a state of deadlock in the management of the business of the company and that, in substance the relationship between the petitioner and Mr. H. being that of partners, it would be just and equitable to wind up the company in the same circumstances in which a partnership would be wound up. She further alleged that the company would become insolvent if the assessments to tax which had been raised against the company, were not successfully contested or might become insolvent if Mr. H. was permitted to continue the management of the business in an inefficient manner. Mr. H. filed a replying affidavit in which he denied the petitioner's allegations of incompetence and harrassment and attributed the rift to the 'highly dubious manner' in which he alleged the petitioner had managed the company's financial affairs. He averred that the affairs of the company had been under investigation for some time by the Investigation Department of the Revenue Commissioners and in addition that the Fraud Squad of the Garda Síochána had also been called in to investigate

COMPANY—*continued.*

certain aspects of the dealings with the assets of the company. He claimed that an order to wind up the company should not be made because the lack of confidence between the directors was caused by the petitioner. A motion for directions was brought by the petitioner and an order of the High Court was made directing that the petition be advertised. Four creditors indicated an intention of appearing on the hearing of the petition, of which three supported the petition. **Held** by Murphy J. in ordering the company be wound up, 1, the objective fact was that the shareholders/directors could not legally or practically administer the company without the cooperation of each other and that in practice neither party was able or willing to cooperate with the other. 2. Although there was no means by which the guilt of either party could be established on affidavit, the court was apprehensive that a protracted oral hearing might not solve the problem in view. 3. Whilst the court was not by any means prepared to exculpate the petitioner from any wrongdoing, the court would not be justified either in concluding that she was guilty of such misconduct as would disentitle her or the particular circumstances of the case to have an order made which seemed to be required not only in her interest but in the interests of the creditors of the company. 4. The court could and would bear in mind that of the four creditors who had indicated an intention of appearing on the hearing of the petition, three had supported it and in all of the circumstances it seemed that it was an appropriate case in which to make an order for the winding up of the company on the grounds that it was just and equitable so to do. *In re Vehicle Buildings and Insulations Ltd.*

(H.C.) [1986] ILRM 239

—— Action — Security for costs — Limited company — Corporate plaintiff's action dismissed with costs — Appeal to Supreme Court — Plaintiff insolvent — Defendant seeking security of costs — Whether order discretionary.
see **Practice and Procedure,** 19

—— Action — Security for costs — Limited company — Liquidation
see **Practice and Procedure,** 22, 23, 24

—— Action — Security for costs — Limited company — Plaintiff company unable to meet any order for costs — Whether plaintiff's impecunious state caused by wrong the subject matter of claim — Onus of proof on plaintiff.
see **Practice and Procedure,** 20, 21

—— Affairs — Oppression — Director's powers

COMPULSORY ACQUISITION

1. —— **Compensation** — *Assessment — Capital gains tax — Land to be acquired compulsorily by the Minister for Communications — Compensation assessed by an arbitrator — Additional amount awarded to compensate for capital gains tax arising on the transfer of the lands — Whether arbitrator entitled to award such additional compensation — Acquisition of Land (Assessment of Compensation) Act,* 1919 (*c.* 57) — *Property Values (Arbitration and Appeals) Act,* 1960 (*No.* 45) — *Land Clauses Consolidation Act,* 1845 (*c.* 18) — *Capital Gains Tax Act,* 1975 (*No.* 20).] The claimants were the owners of certain lands in County Dublin which were to be acquired compulsorily by the Minister for Communications. The value of the lands was assessed by an arbitrator. In addition to assessing the value of the lands, the arbitrator heard evidence in relation to the capital gains tax which would be payable by the claimants upon the acquisition of the lands by the Minister. The arbitrator then awarded an additional amount of compensation calculated by reference to the capital gains tax which would arise. Counsel for the Minister objected to this additional award and the arbitrator agreed to state a case for the opinion of the High Court as to whether he was entitled to award the additional amount of compensation. **Held** by Gannon J., in answering the case stated in the negative, 1, that liability to capital gains tax does not arise as a consequence of ownership of property but on the disposal of an interest in property and by virtue of s. 8 of the Capital Gains Tax Act, 1975, the compulsory acquisition of land is a disposal for capital gains tax purposes. 2. That capital gains tax is chargeable on a person in respect of gains accruing to him in the tax year, and in order to calculate the tax which would arise on the compulsory acquisition of property it would be necessary to consider matters relevant to the personal tax liability of claimants. Such an investigation is not within the function or duties of an arbitrator under the Acquisition of Land (Assessment of Compensation) Act, 1919, and the Property Values (Arbitrations and Appeals) Act, 1960. 3. That the rules set out in s. 2 of the Act of 1919 are consistent with the principle that compensation should be such an amount as would put the claimants as far as possible in the same position as they would have been in if the events giving rise to the payment of compensation had not occurred. *Re Lucas and Chesterfield Gas and Water Board* [1909] 1 K.B. 16, considered. 4. That the liability to capital gains tax arises after the assessment of compensation and the acquisition of the property, and the rules of s. 2 of the Act of 1919 do not provide for an adjustment of compensation by reference to claims which may

COMPULSORY ACQUISITION—*continued.*

subsequently arise in respect of the compensation received by the claimants. *In re Heron*
(H.C.) [1985] I.R.623

2. —— **Compensation** — *Assessment — Factors to which arbitrator had regard — Acquisition of Land (Assessment of Compensation) Act,* 1919 (*c.* 57), *s.* 2 — *Local Government (Planning and Development) Act,* 1963 (*No.* 28), *s.* 69 — *Housing Act,* 1966 (*No.* 21), *s.* 84(1).] S. 84(1)(*b*) of the Housing Act, 1966, provides that the value of land subject to a compulsory acquisition order must be assessed as at the date of service of the notice to treat. S. 2(11) of the Acquisition of Land (Assessment of Compensation) Act, 1919, provides that regard shall not be had to any depreciation or increase in value attributable to the land, or any land in its vicinity, being reserved for any purpose in a development plan. The respondent had compulsorily acquired land the property of the claimant, and the arbitrator appointed to assess compensation stated a case for the opinion of the High Court as to whether (1) regard should be had to the fact that a nearby by-pass was nearing completion at the date of the notice to treat, (2) regard should be had to the claimant's loss due to the statutory rate of interest being lower than the commercial rate, and (3) the claimant was entitled to compensation in respect of costs incurred in objecting to the confirmation of the compulsory acquisition order. **Held** by McWilliam J. in answering the questions in the case stated as follows: No. 1: Yes; No. 2: No; No. 3: No:, 1, the date at which land ceases to be subject to a development plan is the earliest date at which there is no reasonable possibility of the work undertaken thereon being discontinued. 2. Where the legislature had declared a rate of interest on purchase money, an arbitrator is not entitled effectively to increase this to the commercial rate by increasing the purchase price for this purpose. 3. Where a claimant does not succeed in opposing a compulsory acquisition order, the cost of the objection cannot be allowed as part of the purchase price. *Holiday Motor Inns Ltd.* v. *Dublin County Council*
(H.C.) [1976-7] ILRM 343

3. —— **Compensation** — *Assessment — Valuation date — Property at valuation date subject to rent control — Whether subsequent declaration of invalidity of rent control legislation operates retrospectively to affect the assessment of compensation — Acquisition of Land (Assessment of Compensation) Act,* 1919 (*c.* 57), *s.* 2.] Rent-controlled dwellings owned by the claimant appellant were compulsorily acquired by the respondent. The resultant compensation, which stood to be determined as of the date of a notice

COMPULSORY ACQUISITION—*continued.*

to treat served in 1977, was the subject of arbitration in 1982. Because of the intervening decision of the Supreme Court in *Blake and Ors* v. *The Attorney General* [1982] I.R. 117; [1981] ILRM 34, which declared Parts II and IV of the Rent Restrictions Act, 1960, to be invalid, the arbitrator stated a special case to the High Court as to: "whether in respect of the relevant premises I ought to value the claimant's interest therein on the valuation date as though Parts II and IV of the Rent Restrictions Act, 1960, as amended were valid and in force at that date." On 5 March, 1984, Finlay P. (as he then was) answered that question in the affirmative. From this judgment (reported at [1984] ILRM 366) the claimant appealed to the Supreme Court. **Held** by Walsh J. (Henchy, Griffin, Hederman and McCarthy JJ. concurring) dismissing the appeal, that, 1, in accordance with s. 2 of the Acquisition of Land (Assessment of Compensation) Act, 1919, the case must be governed by the actual circumstances prevailing at the valuation date. 2. The hardship resulting from the effects of invalid legislation did not fall within the scope of the arbitration. 3. The present case did not concern anything done pursuant to the void provisions of the Rent Restrictions Act, 1960; it concerned solely the market value of property at a particular moment in history which was affected by considerations then actually in existence in the minds of prospective buyers and sellers. *Reid v. Limerick Corporation*
(S.C.) [1987] ILRM 83

4. —— **Land Acts** — *Price fixed at sum payable in Land Bonds equal in nominal value to the sum fixed — Whether the statutory provisions enabling the price to be paid in such a way instead of cash ceased to be part of the law on the coming into force of the Constitution — Whether provision inconsistent with Articles 40 or 43 — Constitution of Ireland,* 1937. *Arts.* 40.3, 43, 50 — *Land Act,* 1923 (*No.* 42), *ss.* 3, 25 — *Land Bond Act,* 1934 (*No.* 11), *ss.* 2, 4(3) — *Land Act,* 1950 (*No.* 16), *ss.* 5(1), 27.] In 1967 the Land Commission made a compulsory acquisition of lands, the property of the plaintiff. The price of the lands was fixed at £24,000 payable in 8% Land Bonds valued at £24,000. The appellant appealed against the order and the judicial commissioner fixed the price of the land at £30,000 payable in 9¾% Land Bonds equal in nominal value to £30,000. The plaintiff did not want to take the Land Bonds and wanted cash instead. On his refusal to give up possession litigation was undertaken on behalf of the Land Commission resulting in an order for possession being given to the latter. The Land Commission is only empowered to purchase for cash where land is offered to them for sale under s. 27 of the Land Act, 1950, and when there is

COMPULSORY ACQUISITION—*continued.*

right to vacant possession and the Land Commission requires the land for the provision of new holdings. The acquisition in this case did not fall within the terms of s. 27 so the Land Commission had no power to pay cash for the applicant's interest. On 6 August, 1971, the Bonds stood at 98 with a realisable value of £29,400. The plaintiff contended, (i), that he was entitled either to £30,000 in cash or to sufficient land bonds to realise £30,000 instead of £29,400. (ii) An order that the statutory provisions enabling the price to be paid by the Land Commission in land bonds equal in nominal value to the sum fixed by the judicial commissioner are repugnant to or inconsistent with Articles 40 and 43 of the Constitution which he claimed protect him against compulsory acquisition save at a just price i.e. that fixed by the judicial commissioner. **Held** by O'Higgins C.J., Walsh, Henchy, Griffin, Hedermann JJ. concurring, 1, that the provisions of s. 2 of the Land Bond Act, 1934, are not inconsistent with the provisions of Article 40.3. 2. There was no evidence to suggest that the Minister for Finance failed to do everything that was reasonable for the purpose of endeavouring to secure that the market price of the land bonds should remain at or near par as required by s. 4 of the Land Bonds Act, 1934, as amended by the Land Act, 1953. 3. That the plaintiff was not entitled to be paid any purchase price other than the £30,000 nominal value 9¾% land bonds issued to him in 1971. *Dreher* v. *Irish Land Commission* **(S.C.) [1984] ILRM 94**

5. —— **Planning authority** — *Planning application refused in view of compulsory acquisition — Whether order made in compliance with housing legislation — Effect of order — Housing Act,* 1966 (*No.* 21), *s.* 55 — *Local Government (Planning and Development) Act,* 1963 (*No.* 28), *s.* 26.] The prosecutor obtained a conditional order of certiorari to quash the order made by the respondents on 22 September, 1978, refusing to grant outline planning permission to the prosecutor for the development of certain lands. The application was refused on the grounds that a compulsory purchase order was made by Limerick County Council in respect of the lands and that the proposal for development was therefore premature pending the determination of the order of the Minister for the Environment. The prosecutor submitted that s. 26 of the Local Government (Planning and Development) Act, 1963, confined the planning authority in considering an application for permission to considerations concerning the planning and development of an area, and that the planning authority neglected to consider these in making a compulsory purchase order which had the effect

COMPULSORY ACQUISITION—*continued.*

of being a mere change of ownership. They further submitted that the precise terms of the refusal did not even indicate that the compulsory acquisition order referred to was for the purpose of the Housing Acts and in particular neglected to set out for which of the many purposes of the Housing Acts it is intended by the Council to use the lands if they finally acquire them. **Held** by Finlay J. in discharging the conditional order,1, the planning authority set out the precise terms of the refusal and the reasons that led to the decision in the notification of refusal; thus the prosecutor knew precisely what the compulsory purchase order referred to. 2. The making of a compulsory purchase order is not just a mere change of ownership, as s. 55(3) of the Housing Act, 1966, provided that the planning authority must come within the statutory objectives when they are acquiring the land compulsorily and these objectives in themselves clearly affect the planning and development of the lands concerned. 3. The present refusal is on the basis that the application for outline planning permission was premature having regard to the service of the compulsory purchase order and therefore in no way would prejudge a subsequent application were the order not to be confirmed. 4. The prosecutor would not be prejudiced by the issue of this refusal by the planning authority should he wish to seek compensation in the event of the compulsory purchase order being confirmed. *The State (Sweeney)* v. *Minister for the Environment* **(H.C.) [1979] ILRM 35**

6. —— **Powers** — *Local authority — Residential and recreational development — County council also planning authority — Whether Council can only acquire lands for recreational purposes in its capacity as planning authority — Local Government (Irl.) Act,* 1898 (*c.* 37), *s.* 10 — *Local Government* (*No.* 2) *Act,* 1960 (*No.* 40), *ss.* 10, 11 — *Local Government (Planning and Development) Act,* 1963 (*No.* 28), *s.* 2—*Housing Act,* 1966 (*No.* 21), *s.* 86.] Dublin County Council made a compulsory purchase order acquiring land for the purpose of providing residential and recreational facilities. The council was local authority and planning authority for the area on which the land was situate. The order was made pursuant to the provisions of, *inter alia,* s. 10 of the Local Government (Irl.) Act, 1898, the Local Government (No. 2) Act, 1960, the Housing Act, 1966, (conferring powers of compulsory acquisition on local authorities) and the Local Government (Planning and Development) Act, 1963, (conferring powers of compulsory acquisition on planning authorities). The plaintiff owners of the land challenged the order on the ground that the council's powers under the 1963 Act were confined to acquisition for recreational

COMPULSORY ACQUISITION—*continued.*

purposes and that its powers as local authority under the other Acts could not be used for the purposes of the 1963 Act. The council relied on the provisions of s. 10 of the 1898 Act as adapted by s. 11 of the 1960 Act. S. 10(1) of the 1898 Act states that a county council 'for the purpose of any of their powers and duties, may acquire . . . any land . . . or rights over or in land.' S. 11(1)(*c*) of the 1960 Act states that powers and duties shall refer to 'all such powers, functions and duties as may at any material time stand exercisable or performable' by a county council or local authority. **Held** by McWilliam J. in refusing the plaintiff's claim, s. 11(1)(*c*) of the 1960 Act, read in conjunction with s. 10 of the 1898 Act, conferred a comprehensive power of compulsory acquisition on the defendant as a county council, which could be effected under s. 10 of the 1960 Act (as amended by s. 86 of the Housing Act, 1966) for the purposes of its functions as planning authority under the 1963 Act. *Movie News Ltd.* v. *Galway County Council* 1970 No. 25 Sp., High Court (Kenny J.), 30 March 1973 not followed. *Leinster Importing Co. Ltd.* v. *Dublin County Council*

(H.C.) [1984] ILRM 605

—— Commissioners of Public Works — Drainage scheme — Statutory powers — Fishery — Compulsory interference — Spawning beds upstream beyond fishery area — Interference — Reduction in fish stock — Whether injury to fishery — Compensation — Assessment — Rules.
see **Real Property,** 4

—— Compensation — Planning decisions.
see **Planning,** 5, 7.

—— Dispute as to value — Valuation going to arbitration — Factors to be taken into account — Sewerage facilities.
see **Arbitration,** 6

—— Land Acts — Vesting — Building ground excepted from scheme of general vesting — Application by tenant to have Land Commission acquire landlord's interest — Whether acquisition in the interest of the country.
see **Land,** 2

—— Land Commission — Sale of land — Condition of sale that contract dependent on Land Commission approval — Whether prospective purchaser has standing to object to compulsory acquisition of the land.
see **Land,** 1

CONCURRENT WRONGDOERS
see **Damages,** 7
Negligence, 1-3, 31
Practice and Procedure, 12, 13

CONFESSION — Accused — Admissibility.
see **Criminal Law,** 6, 18-21, 33

CONFIDENCE, BREACH OF

—— Equitable principles — Absence of contractual liability — Proposals for commercial partnership — Plaintiffs divulging to defendants details of design of bullet-proof vest — Information misused by defendants — Effect of publication on plaintiffs' patent — Springboard doctrine — Plaintiffs entitled to damages.
see **Contract,** 3

—— Interlocutory injunction sought to restrain alleged breach of confidence — Confidential information shared between foreign government and private individual — Principles governing the protection of such information — Effect of constitutional provisions on duty of confidentiality.
see **Constitution,** 14

CONFLICT OF LAWS
Contract. Nos. 1,2
Foreign judgment — enforcement. Nos. 4, 5
Marriage — dissolution. Nos. 6, 7

1. —— **Contract** — *Proper law* — *Contract expressed to be "construed and governed by the laws of the Republic of Ireland . . . and subject only to the jurisdiction of the Irish Courts"* — *Subject matter of, and parties to, contract unconnected with Ireland* — *Service out of the jurisdiction of plenary summons* — *Application to set aside service* — *Whether contract "by its terms to be governed by Irish Law"* — *Whether parties' choice of law binding on court* — *Rules of the Superior Courts,* 1986 (*S.I. No.* 15), *O.* 11, *r.* 1(e)(iii), *O.* 12, *r.* 26.] The plaintiff, who resided in South Africa, entered into an agreement through Bahamian agents to lend a sum of Canadian dollars to the defendant, a public company incorporated under the laws of Alberta, Canada. The agreement was executed in Canada. The repayment of the sum borrowed was to be made to the plaintiff's London bankers. Further provisions of the loan agreement entitled the plaintiff, in the event of default, to demand of the defendant company that it allot to him a number of shares in the company and to nominate a number of persons to be appointed to its board of directors. A clause of the loan agreement provided that it was to be construed and governed by the laws of the Republic of Ireland, to be

CONFLICT OF LAWS—*continued.*

deemed to have been made in the Republic of Ireland and to be subject only to the jurisdiction of the Irish courts. The plaintiff applied *ex parte* to the High Court and obtained an order giving him liberty to serve notice of a plenary summons on the defendant out of the jurisdiction, pursuant to O. 11, r. 1 (e) (iii) of the Rules of the Superior Courts, 1986, on the ground that it concerned an action in respect of a contract which by its terms was to be governed by Irish law. The relief sought included, *inter alia,* declarations and injunctions related to the plaintiff's claim that he was entitled to have shares in the defendant allotted to him and to nominate directors to the board of the defendant. The defendant entered a conditional appearance to the summons, for the purpose of contesting jurisdiction only. On the defendant's application to the High Court for an order discharging the order authorising service out of the jurisdiction, it was **Held** by Carroll J., in discharging the order, 1, that the proper law of the contract was the law governing its essential validity. 2. That the provisions of the contract which the plaintiff sought to enforce were concerned with the internal management and control of a public company and raised the question whether the company was entitled to enter into and was bound by the contract. 3. That the law of Alberta and not of Ireland must be applied to decide whether the defendant company, a creature of Albertan statute, had capacity to enter into the contract. 4. That Albertan law, as the law determining the defendant's contractual capacity, was the system of law to be applied to determine the contract's essential validity. 5. That, accordingly, notwithstanding the choice of law clause in the contract, Albertan law was the proper law of the contract and that the contract was not one which was, by its terms, to be governed by Irish law. On appeal from the judgment and order of the High Court, it was **Held** by the Supreme Court (Finlay C.J., Walsh, Hederman and McCarthy JJ.; Henchy J. dissenting), in allowing the plaintiff's appeal, 1, that regardless of the fact that it might be necessary for a court to apply Albertan law to determine the capacity of the defendant to enter into the contract, the proper law of the contract itself was Irish law, as the parties had expressly chosen it. 2. That, even if Irish law had not been chosen as the proper law of the contract, the defendant should not be permitted to evade the express contractual provision whereby it agreed that the Irish courts should have exclusive jurisdiction, unless it could advance strong reasons to the contrary. 3. That an Irish court should not decline to entertain an action for declaratory relief against a defendant outside the jurisdiction simply on the grounds that any order which it made could not be enforced or supervised by the court, or was unlikely to be obeyed; it was a matter for the plaintiff to endeavour to enforce his judgment in a foreign jurisdiction, according to the remedies available in that jurisdiction. *Per* Walsh and Hederman JJ.: That, since it was a well established principle of law in several countries that a contractual agreement to submit to the jurisdiction of a foreign court amounted to an unequivocal acceptance of the jurisdiction of that court, the fact that the parties had agreed to submit to the jurisdiction of the Irish courts would be an important factor in securing the enforcement abroad of any judgment obtained in Ireland.* *Per* Henchy J., dissenting: That the plaintiff's claim was in effect one for an order to compel the specific performance of the contract; that Irish courts should refuse to entertain the claim since to grant the relief sought would be to make an order which the court was incapable of enforcing. *Kutchera* v. *Buckingham International Holdings Ltd.*
(H.C., S.C.) [1988] I.R.61; [1988] ILRM 1, 501

Editors note: Corrigendum to report: In addition to agreeing with the judgment of McCarthy J., Finlay C.J. agreed wth the judgment of Walsh J. Accordingly the *dictum* expressed by Walsh and Hederman JJ. is supported by a majority of the court.

2. —— **Contract** — *Proper law — Judgment mortgage — Domestic immovable property — European Monetary System — Whether repayment of remainder of debt be in sterling — Currency Act, 1927 (No.* 32), *s.* 45 (1) — *Central Bank Act,* 1971 (*No.* 24), *s.* 43.] The plaintiff obtained a declaration in the High Court on 10 July, 1978, that the sum of £163,291.74p was well charged on the defendant's interest in certain lands situate in Co. Donegal and on the 2 July, 1979, a further declaration that the sum of £170,000.00 was declared well charged on lands in Co. Kildare. The direction of the High Court was sought as to the proper currency for calculating the balance due to the plaintiff. By order of the 31 January, 1983, Carroll J. declared that the defendant was entitled to have any payments made by him to the plaintiff on foot of the primary orders credited to him in the currency of the Republic of Ireland. At the time the primary order was made Ireland had not entered the European Monetary System and it was later, in March, 1979, that the parity link between sterling and Irish currency was broken. Taking account of the prevalent exchange rates between sterling and Irish currency the effect of the further declaration was to reduce the defendant's outstanding liability to a far lesser sum than that which would have obtained if the payments by the defendant were credited against his indebtedness in sterling. The plaintiff appealed to the

CONFLICT OF LAWS—*continued.*

Supreme Court from the latter declaration on the grounds that the contract for the advances that made up the total debt was made in Derry, where the currency was sterling, the proper law of the contract was Northern Ireland law and that the manner of enforcement of a judgment debt should be construed in the light of the overriding contract. **Held** by McCarthy J. (Finlay C.J. and Griffin J. concurring) in dismissing the appeal and affirming the High Court order, that, while the proper law of the contract was the law prevailing in Northern Ireland and the plaintiffs could have expressed the amount of the judgments obtained in sterling, where money advanced is secured and charged on immovable property within the State, then it must be construed, failing the use of some totally inapposite description, as being in the currency of the State wherein the lands are situate. *Lansdowne* v. *Lansdowne and Others* (1820) 2 Bligh 60 and *Phipps* v. *Earl of Anglesea* (1721) 5 Vin. Abr. 209 part 8 considered and applied. *Northern Bank Ltd.* v. *Edwards*

(S.C.) [1985] I.R.284; [1986] ILRM 167

3. —— **Domicile** — *Irish domicile of origin — Whether acquisition of a foreign domicile of choice — Evidence — Relevance of statement by deceased that he was domiciled in Ireland.*] The plaintiff, the brother of the deceased, raised the question in the proceedings before the court as to whether the deceased had abandoned his domicile of origin and acquired a domicile of choice in France. The defendants, the deceased's wife and children, submitted that the deceased had acquired a domicile of choice in France. A similar issue had been litigated in France where it was held, and confirmed on appeal, that according to French law the deceased had died domiciled in France. Evidence was adduced that the deceased had resided in France from 1949 to his death on 22 April, 1984. The deceased never had an Irish residence although he retained his Irish passport and driving licence. He had insisted that his children acquired French citizenship. He suffered from bad health and although he came to Ireland in 1967 in search of a doctor he returned to Paris where he eventually found a doctor with whom he visited on a regular monthly basis. The plaintiff submits in support of his contention that the deceased in 1982 made his will in Ireland rather than in France and in doing so he declared that Ireland was his domicile. The plaintiff further submitted that the deceased intended in 1983 to spend his remaining years in Ireland, as he had transferred £100,000 to a bank account in Ireland, made enquiries about a nursing home in Dalkey and finally made arrangements that he would be buried in County Westmeath. **Held** by Costello J. in finding that the deceased died domiciled in France, 1, the plaintiff's evidence did not displace the conclusion to be drawn from the evidence before the court that the deceased had obtained a domicile of choice in France. 2. Although there was evidence to suggest that the deceased had formed the intention in 1983 to return to live in Ireland, that intention to abandon his French domicile was ineffective as the deceased had not in fact changed his residence before he died in April, 1984. 3. The deceased's own statement that he was domiciled in Ireland is a conclusion of law rather than a statement of what his past intentions had been and does not disprove the evidence which shows the deceased had previously decided to reside permanently in France. *In re Rowan; Rowan* v. *Rowan*

(H.C.) [1988] ILRM 65

4. —— **Foreign judgment** — *Enforcement — Maintenance order — Foreign divorce — Maintenance of child — Order of foreign court directing provision of maintenance by defendant — Whether maintenance order part of divorce proceedings — Whether a final order — Constitution of Ireland,* 1937, *Art.* 41.] The plaintiff and defendant had been wife and husband but a divorce *a vinculo matrimonii* was granted on the 15 May, 1980, by a Massachusetts court at the hearing of a petition filed in that court by the plaintiff. The plaintiff claimed in the High Court in Ireland an order directing the defendant to pay to the plaintiff the sum of $3,230 (or the equivalent in Irish pounds) being the unpaid balance of a sum payable by the defendant to the plaintiff on foot of (a) an agreement made between the parties on the 2 April, 1979, and (b) an order of a Massachusetts court of that date directing the defendant to comply with the terms of that agreement. The parties were married in Ireland in 1958 and had gone to live in the United States of America. On the 8 April, 1978, the plaintiff had filed in the Massachusetts court a petition for divorce *a vinculo matrimonii.* On the 12 February, 1979, in separate proceedings in that court, the plaintiff had claimed an order directing the defendant to pay to her certain maintenance payments for the support of a child of the marriage. The order of the Massachusetts court dated 2 April, 1979, was made in those maintenance proceedings. In accordance with the standard practice of the Massachusetts court, its divorce decree dated the 15 May, 1980, contained an order directing the defendant to make such maintenance payments to the plaintiff for the support of the said child; and the maintenance proceedings were discontinued. The defendant contended that the plaintiff was asking the court to implement divorce proceedings and so to act in violation of the provisions of Article

CONFLICT OF LAWS—*continued.*

41, s. 3, of the Constitution and that, in any event, the order directing the payment of maintenance for the child was unenforceable as it lacked finality. **Held** by Finlay P., in giving judgment for the plaintiff, 1, that the evidence of the law of the Commonwealth of Massachusetts, adduced on behalf of the plaintiff, established that the order directing payment of maintenance for the named child was the product of proceedings which were distinct from the plaintiff's divorce proceedings, notwithstanding the incorporation of that maintenance relief in the decree of divorce, and that, accordingly, the provisions of Article 41 of the Constitution did not preclude the plaintiff from obtaining the relief sought by her. *Mayo-Perrott* v. *Mayo-Perrott* [1958] I.R. 336 distinguished. 2. That such evidence of the foreign law applicable also established that the court which had made the maintenance order had no power to vary, rescind or alter that order with retrospective effect and that, accordingly, the maintenance order was a final order for the purposes of the plaintiff's claim. *McDonnell* v. *McDonnell* [1921] 2 I.R. 148 distinguished; *Keys* v. *Keys* [1919] 2 I.R. 160, *Nouvion* v. *Freeman* (1889) 15 App. Cas. 1 and *Beatty* v. *Beatty* [1924] 1 K.B. 807 considered. 3. That, accordingly, the plaintiff was entitled to judgment for the sum claimed by her. *G.* v. *G.*

(H.C.) [1984] I.R.368

5. —— **Foreign judgment** — *Enforcement — Mareva injunction — Foreign trade union — Foreign court imposing fine for trade union's contumacious civil contempt — Union's funds transferred to Irish bank — Foreign sequestrators seeking vesting of union funds — Irish bank and union restrained from transferring funds — Foreign court removing union's trustees and appointing receiver — Foreign receiver seeking vesting of funds — Whether sequestration on receivership enforceable in this jurisdiction — Whether either a penal process — Whether order appointing receiver final and conclusive — Whether court should make an inspection order ex parte — Power of the High Court to order the production or inspection of a bank's books, documents or computer printouts — Bankers' Books Evidence (Amendment) Act,* 1959 (*No.* 21).] Proceedings had been commenced in the English High Court against the first defendant, being a trade union set up, organised and carrying on its affairs in England in accordance with the law of that country. The English High Court had made an order restraining the first defendant from doing certain acts, including instructing or urging any of its members to strike or not to work or not to pass any picket-line in the Yorkshire area of the union. The first defendant was subsequently adjudicated to be in contempt of that court for failing to

CONFLICT OF LAWS—*continued.*

comply with certain parts of its order and was fined £200,000 with 14 days to pay. The first defendant having failed to pay the fine, the English High Court appointed the first, second, third and fourth plaintiffs as sequestrators over the real and personal property of the first defendant, the writ of sequestration to remain in force until the first defendant should purge its contempt or until further order. The order of sequestration expressly authorised the sequestrators to prosecute proceedings in Ireland seeking the recovery of funds of the first defendant currently on account with the second defendant, and to apply in such proceedings for whatever interlocutory relief might be appropriate. The sequestrators applied to the High Court (Barrington J.) and were granted an interim injunction, *inter alia,* restraining the first and second defendants or any person acting in concert with them or any person with notice of the making of the order, in particular, any financial institution or bank, within the jurisdiction of the court, from disposing of or otherwise dealing in any manner whatsoever with any monies held to the account of the first defendant, and ordering the second defendant to produce for the inspection of the first four plaintiffs, the bankers' books, including correspondence or computer printouts from electronic recordings relating to any account of the first defendant held by the second defendant. The second defendant, having complied with the interim order, applied *ex parte* to the High Court and was granted an order dismissing it from the action. By interlocutory order in a further set of proceedings commenced in the English High Court, the three existing trustees of the first defendant's assets were removed from their positions and the fifth plaintiff was appointed receiver pending the trial of the action, with express authority to institute proceedings in any jurisdiction for the purpose of recovering any of the assets, save in so far as the assets might from time to time be in the possession or control of any sequestrator appointed by the English High Court. The receiver applied to this High Court to be joined as a fifth plaintiff in these proceedings, and the second defendant applied to be rejoined as a second defendant, both of which applications were granted. At the trial of the action in which the first four plaintiffs acting as sequestrators and the fifth plaintiff acting as receiver claimed to be entitled to the monies the property of the first defendant on deposit with the second defendant it was **Held** by Barrington J., in dismissing the claims of the sequestrators and continuing the interim injunction, 1, that the contempt of which the union was convicted fell into the category of contumacious civil contempt, having ceased to be a mere matter between private litigants but having called into question the

CONFLICT OF LAWS—*continued.*

authority of the English High Court. 2. That the sequestration process whether civil or criminal in nature and whether coercive or punitive in purpose was penal in effect, being a process for establishing the authority of the court against a recalcitrant litigant and punishing it for its contempt. 3. That the High Court would not entertain a suit brought for the purpose of enforcing within this State a penal law or process of a foreign State. *Buchanan Ltd. and Another* v. *McVey* [1954] I.R. 89, applied. 4. That there were independent grounds for the appointment of the receiver and that the receivership was not simply an indirect method of enforcing the sequestration and thus an indirect attempt to enforce within this State the penal law or process of a foreign State. 5. That the foreign order appointing the receiver, being interlocutory in nature, and the union (the owner of the funds) opposing the payment of the funds to the receiver, it was doubtful whether there were any trustees entitled to hold the union funds on behalf of the union at the present time. 6. That accordingly, the funds were to be preserved with the second defendant until permanent trustees of the union's property were identified or appointed in accordance with the provisions of English law. *Semble:* In the normal course there would be no justification for making an inspection order *ex parte* such as the one made against the bank in this case and a freezing order would be sufficient to maintain the *status quo,* but the necessity for the *ex parte* order in this case arose from the fear that a portion of the funds had already been transferred to other financial institutions in the State, the identities of which were unknown to the sequestrators. *Semble:* That the purpose of the Bankers' Books Evidence Acts, 1879-1959, was merely to facilitate bankers by allowing them in certain circumstances to prove the contents of some of their books by secondary evidence and that there was nothing in these Acts or in the decision of Murphy J. in *O'C.* v. *D.* [1985] I.R. 265 to circumscribe the power of the High Court in an appropriate case to order the production or inspection of any of the bank's books, documents or computer printouts. *O'C.* v. *D.* [1985] I.R. 265 considered. *Larkins* v. *National Union of Mineworkers*

(H.C.) [1985] I.R.671

6. —— **Marriage** — *Dissolution — Foreign decree of divorce — Validity — Test applicable — Appeal to Supreme Court — Alternative test suggested — Whether Supreme Court may consider arguments not raised in High Court — Whether findings of fact in High Court sufficient to enable Supreme Court to consider new arguments.*] The respondent husband married in Ireland on the 28 November, 1946. The couple resided in Ireland until 1955 when they separated and the wife went to live in England. The respondent continued to live in Ireland with his two children until 1961, when he was dismissed from his employment. The respondent then went to London, in September 1961, to seek employment. His wife instituted divorce proceedings in England in 1959, and, on fulfilling the English statutory requirement of being not less than three years continuously resident in England, she obtained an English divorce on 25 April, 1962. The respondent married the petitioner on 21 June, 1962. The petitioner sought a decree of nullity on the ground that the purported marriage between the petitioner and the respondent was bigamous, as the respondent on the aforesaid date was still married to another party under Irish law. The High Court (Carroll J.) held that the marriage of 21 June, 1962, was null and void on the grounds that the respondent lacked the capacity to marry the petitioner as on the aforesaid date he was a party to a valid subsisting marriage in Ireland. The court, in refusing to recognise the English divorce, found that the respondent was domiciled in Ireland at the date of divorce and had not acquired a domicile of choice in England. The respondent appealed to the Supreme Court on the grounds that domicile was not the only appropriate test to be applied by the courts with regard to the recognition of a foreign divorce decree, but that the alternative test of whether a real and substantial connection existed between the parties and the law of the country of the court granting the divorce should be applied as laid down in *Indyka* v. *Indyka* [1969] A.C. 33. **Held** by the Supreme Court (Finlay C.J., Henchy, Griffin, McCarthy and McMahon JJ.), in dismissing the appeal, 1, that since the evidence before the court did not show a real and substantial connection between the parties and England, the court would be deciding a point of law upon theoretical facts which the court should decline to do. 2. That notwithstanding the anomalies existing in the law of domicile, the test as laid down in *Indyka's Case* could not be considered as an alternative to the domicile test, when the domicile test was the only test raised in the High Court and arising on the facts of the case. *Indyka* v. *Indyka* [1969] A.C. 33 distinguished. *Per* Finlay C.J.: as a fundamental principle the court should not hear and determine an issue which has not been raised in the High Court. *K.D. (otherwise C.)* v. *M.C.*

(S.C.) [1985] I.R. 697; [1987] ILRM 189

7. —— **Marriage** — *Dissolution — Recognition of foreign decree absolute — Domicile of husband — Parties divorced in the U.K. — Whether husband domiciled in Britain — Parties resident for time in Ireland — Parties both British*

CONFLICT OF LAWS—*continued.*

citizens — Whether domicile of origin displaced — Onus of proof — Whether legislation abolishing dependent domicile retrospective in effect — Whether dependent domicile concept existed up to enactment of legislation — Wife's application for maintenance — Motion to stay proceedings — Whether motion should be granted before decree made absolute — Domicile and Recognition of Foreign Divorces Act, 1986 (*No.* 24), *s.* 5 — *Family Law (Maintenance of Spouses and Children) Act,* 1976 (*No.* 11), *s.* 5 — *Guardianship of Infants Act,* 1964 (*No.* 7), *s.* 11. *Constitution — Family — Recognition of divorces — Whether concept of dependent domicile survived enactment of Constitution — Constitution of Ireland,* 1937, *Arts.* 40.1, 40.3, 41.] The applicant wife and respondent husband were both British citizens. The husband's income derived primarily from writing and producing pop records. In the late 1960s he incurred large income tax bills while living in England and to avoid future income tax the couple moved with their children to Ireland where such income was exempt from income tax. The marriage broke down, and the husband returned to England, where he instituted divorce proceedings. A decree *nisi* had been granted when the wife applied for interim maintenance for herself and her children, and the husband applied for a stay on proceedings. **Held** by Egan J. refusing the stay and making an interim award to the wife, 1, if the decree absolute issued, and the divorce was one recognised in Irish law by the Domicile and Recognition of Foreign Divorces Act, 1986, the wife would no longer be entitled to claim maintenance for herself pursuant to the Family Law (Maintenance of Spouses and Children) Act,1976, although she would be entitled to claim maintenance for her children as guardian under s. 11 of the Guardianship of Infants Act, 1964. *B.* v. *B.* [1980] ILRM 257 and *T.* v. *T.* [1983] I.R. 29; [1982] ILRM 217 discussed. 2. Although on the affidavits the husband might have acquired a domicile of choice in Ireland when the couple came to live here, the issue should only be determined after a full oral hearing; and it was inadvisable to address the matter prior to the divorce decree becoming absolute; and in the circumstances the stay would be refused and interim maintenance awarded to the wife and children.

At the trial of the action, based on oral evidence, and after the divorce decree had become absolute, **Held** by Barr J. in holding the divorce decree should be recognised in Irish law: 3. Bearing in mind the parties had come to reside in Ireland primarily for financial reasons, it could not be said that the husband had acquired a domicile of choice in Ireland; and in this context there was a crucial difference between setting up home for an indefinite period and setting up a permanent home. *T.* v. *T.* [1983] I.R. 29; [1982] ILRM 217 and *In re Sillar* [1956] I.R. 344 applied. 4. While statements made during a lifetime may be a factor in determining domicile, they cannot prevail against facts indicating a contrary outcome, and the statement by the husband in his will that he was domiciled in Ireland may have been made in ignorance of its significance and in the false belief that domicile in Ireland was required to gain the relevant tax advantages. 5. The English divorce decree came within the ambit of s. 5 of the Domicile and Recognition of Foreign Divorces Act, 1986, which provided that its terms were to apply in relation to divorces granted after the commencement of the Act, even where as in this case the divorce proceedings had been initiated before the commencement of the Act. *Per* Barr J.: The 1986 Act contained an apparent lacuna in relation to divorces initiated before the Act's commencement, but granted afterwards. The wife had argued that the Act allowed for a husband to apply for a divorce before the Act's commencement and, provided he was domiciled in England at the time, it would be recognized under the 1986 Act; whereas if the wife applied for a divorce in the same circumstances the decree would not be recognised if the husband's domicile was Irish, by virtue of the dependent domicile rule which the 1986 Act had abolished; and therefore the 1986 Act should not be given this retrospective effect since it operated in a discriminatory manner. This argument was based on the false premise that the dependent domicile doctrine had survived up to the enactment of the 1986 Act, but since it was not consistent with the principles of equality before the law and equal rights in marriage contained in Articles 40.1, 40.3 and 41 of the Constitution, it did not continue as part of Irish law until 1986; and thus the retrospective effect of the 1986 Act did not operate in the discriminatory manner alleged by the wife. And although some decisions of the courts prior to the 1986 Act may have assumed the validity of the dependent domicile rule, these could not now be challenged. *Murphy* v. *Attorney General* [1982] I.R. 241 applied. *C.M.* v. *T.M.*
(H.C.) [1988] ILRM 456

Editor's note: For High Court judgment on maintenance issue reported at [1987] I.R. 152 and [1988] ILRM 262, *see* **Family Law,** 9.

—— Choice of law — Whether significant connection with jurisdiction — Appropriate choice of law to proceedings in question — Negligence — Fitting of heart valve manufactured in United States.

see **Practice and Procedure,** 52

CONFLICT OF LAWS—*continued.*

—— Evidence — Evidence of expert on provisions of English statute — Whether courts bound to accept evidence — Whether evidence contradicted.
see **Contract,** 12

—— Marriage — Dissolution — Recognition of foreign decree absolute — Domicile of husband.
see **Family Law,** 9

CONSECUTIVE SENTENCE
see **Criminal Law,** 74-6

CONSPIRACY
—— Inducement of breach of contract — Plaintiff offered position as principal of primary school — Pressure exerted on manager to cancel appointment — Appointment subsequently cancelled — Whether manager in breach of contract — Whether defendants induced such breach — Whether defendants engaged in an actionable conspiracy.
see **Employer and Employee,** 1

—— Offence — Conspiracy to corrupt public morals — Whether established — Non-directive counselling regarding abortion.
see **Constitution,** 20

CONSTITUTION
Bill — validity. No. 1
Courts. Nos. 2-7, 26-33
Fundamental rights. Nos. 8-21, 38-48
International relations. Nos. 22-5
Statute — validity. Nos. 26-51
Trial of offences. Nos. 49-51, 52-6

BILL — VALIDITY

1. —— **Elections** — *Dáil Éireann — Extension of franchise — Right to vote restricted by Constitution to citizens — Bill conferring franchise upon resident British citizens — Repugnancy — Constitution of Ireland,* 1937, *Arts.* 6, 12, 16, 47.] Section 16, sub-s. 2, of the Constitution stated that "every citizen" without distinction of sex who had reached the age of 18 years, who was not disqualified by law and complied with the provisions of the law relating to elections, should have the right to vote at an election for members of Dáil Éireann. By Article 12, s. 2, sub-s. 2, every such citizen is given a right to vote at an election for President and, by Article 47, s. 3, he is given a right to vote at a referendum. The Electoral (Amendment) Bill, 1983, as passed by

CONSTITUTION—Bill.

both Houses of the National Parliament, contained provisions which would entitle a British citizen to be registered in a constituency as a Dáil elector if ordinarily resident in that constituency, and thus become entitled to vote at a Dáil election in that constituency. Pursuant to Article 26 of the Constitution the President of Ireland referred the Bill of 1983 to the Supreme Court for a decision on the question whether the Bill, or any provision or provisions thereof, was or were repugnant to the Constitution or to any provision thereof. In pronouncing its decision on the question so referred, it was **Held** by the Supreme Court, 1, that any repugnancy with the provisions of the Constitution must be clearly established by the opponents of the Bill. *The Criminal Law (Jurisdiction) Bill,* 1975 [1977] I.R. 129 applied. 2. That, in declaring that all powers of government derive, under God, from "the people" whose right it is "to designate the rulers of the State" and, in final appeal, to "decide all questions of national policy", the provisions of Article 6, s. 1, of the Constitution showed (with Articles 12 and 47) that the right to vote at elections for members of Dáil Éireann conferred on every citizen by Article 16 was a right which was restricted to citizens who formed part of the people of Ireland. 3. That, accordingly, the Bill of 1983 was repugnant to the Constitution. *In re Electoral (Amendment) Bill,* 1983
(S.C.) [1984] I.R.268; [1984] ILRM 539

Bodily integrity, right to, *see* No. 39
Communicate, right to, *see* Nos. 8, 10

COURTS
see also Nos. 26-33

2. —— **Administration of justice** — *Summons — Peace Commissioner signing summons — Whether invalid as being an exercise of judicial power — Whether defect cured by attendance in court — Constitution of Ireland,* 1937, *Art.* 34.4.3.
Road traffic — Disqualification — Whether factors to be considered taken into account in judicial manner — Whether necessary to reconsider evidence presented to convict — Road Traffic Act, 1961 (*No.* 24), *s.* 106.] The applicant was convicted by the respondent of offences under the Road Traffic Act, 1961, as amended, and a driving disqualification was imposed. He sought judicial review on the grounds that the respondent did not act judicially in imposing the disqualification and that the summons was a nullity in that it purported to be signed by a Peace Commissioner who in the process was exercising a judicial function. **Held** by Barr J. in refusing the relief sought, 1, the evidence necessary for the respondent to make the judicial finding that

CONSTITUTION—Courts.

the applicant should be disqualified was already before him once he had convicted the applicant and it was not necessary to re-consider that evidence in making the judicial determination on disqualification; and the applicant had an opportunity to present evidence as to whether the qualification should have been made under s. 106 of the 1961 Act. *Dictum* in *Conroy* v. *Attorney General* [1965] I.R. 411 applied. 2. Since the defect in the summons related to the process for procuring the attendance of the accused before the court, the actual attendance of the accused (subject to a case of a conscious and deliberate violation of constitutional rights in securing attendance) cured that defect, as well as his failure to take the point before the respondent. *The People* v. *Kehoe* [1985] I.R. 444; [1986] ILRM 690 and *dicta* in *The State (Lynch)* v. *Ballagh* [1987] ILRM 65 applied. *Joyce* v. *Circuit Court Judge for the Western Circuit*

(H.C.) [1987] ILRM 316

3. —— **Jurisdiction** — *Courts of local and limited jurisdiction — Criminal jurisdiction of Circuit Court — Statutory provision for exercise of jurisdiction in circuit where offence committed or where accused resided or was arrested — Provision allowing for transfer of trial to Dublin Circuit Court — Transfer of trial mandatory if 7 days notice given by prosecution or defence — Whether criminal jurisdiction of Circuit Court a local and limited jurisdiction — Whether mandatory transfer of trial contrary to natural justice — Courts of Justice Act,* 1924 (*No.* 10), *s.* 52 — *Courts (Establishment and Constitution) Act,* 1961 (*No.* 38), *ss.* 4, 5 — *Courts (Supplemental Provisions) Act,* 1961 (*No.* 39), *s.* 25 — *Courts Act,* 1981 (*No.* 11), *s.* 31(1) — *Constitution of Saorstát Éireann,* 1922, *art.* 64 — *Constitution of Ireland,* 1937, *Arts.* 34, 36.] The prosecutor, a resident of County Wicklow, was arrested in County Wicklow and charged with several offences alleged to have been committed in County Wicklow and was returned for trial to Wicklow Circuit Court. On the application of the Director of Public Prosecutions the prosecutor's trial was transferred, pursuant to s. 31, sub-s. 1(*a*) of the Courts Act, 1981, to the Dublin Circuit Court. The prosecutor pleaded guilty to several counts and was sentenced to a term of imprisonment. The prosecutor obtained a conditional order of certiorari quashing those convictions on the grounds firstly, that s. 31, sub-s. 1(*a*) of the Act of 1981 did not confer jurisdiction on the Dublin Circuit Court to try matters arising from acts committed, arrests made or where defendants resided outside the Dublin Circuit; secondly, that if s. 31, sub-s. 1(*a*) did purport to confer such jurisdiction, it was not a local and limited jurisdiction and so was unconstitutional

CONSTITUTION—*continued.*

and thirdly, that s. 31, sub-s. 1(*a*) was unconstitutional in that it gave no right of objection to an accused person whom it was sought to transfer from one jurisdiction to another. It was argued on behalf of the respondents in showing cause that s. 31, sub-s. 1(*a*) of the Act of 1981 did confer jurisdiction on the Dublin Circuit Court to try such matters when application had been duly made to the judge before whom the accused was triable to transfer the trial and further that the jurisdiction conferred was a jurisdiction which could be exercised by a court of local and limited jurisdiction and that s. 31, sub-s. 1(*a*) was not invalid having regard to the provisions of the Constitution. Gannon J. in the High Court allowed the cause shown and discharged the conditional order ([1986] ILRM 337.) On appeal by the prosecutor it was **Held** by the Supreme Court (Finlay C.J., Walsh, Griffin, Hederman and McCarthy JJ.), in disallowing the appeal, 1, that the object of Article 34, s. 3, sub-s. 4 of the Constitution which required the establishment of courts of local and limited jurisdiction was the provision of local, cheaper and more convenient venues to litigants than the High Court. It was left to the Oireachtas to decide how this would be achieved. *Hosie* v. *Lawless* [1927] I.R. 464 considered. 2. That the Circuit Court, which was established by s. 4, sub-s. 1 of the Courts (Establishment and Constitution) Act, 1961, was a single court for the whole State but its jurisdiction was exercised in accordance with statute, and in particular in accordance with the Courts (Supplemental Provisions) Act, 1961, on a local basis. *Grimes and Others* v. *Owners of S.S. Bangor Bay* [1948] I.R. 350 considered. 3. That while the structure of the Circuit Court was based on the exercise of its jurisdiction locally, experience had shown that it was necessary to allow for the transfer of trials to avoid injustice to either party by reason of local conditions or circumstances; such provision did not alter the essential local exercise of the jurisdiction of the court. 4. That where 7 days notice had been given of an application under s. 31, sub-s. 1(*a*) of the Act of 1981 the Circuit Court judge had no discretion in the matter but had to transfer the trial to the Dublin Circuit Court. The section gave no right of argument to the notice party, whether it was the prosecution or the defence, so there was no inequality between them. *The State (Boyle)* v. *Neylon*

(S.C.) [1986] I.R.551; [1987] ILRM 535

4. —— **Jurisdiction** — *High Court — Enactments conferring jurisdiction on Circuit Court and District Court — Whether jurisdiction of High Court ousted — Whether enactments valid — Rules of the Superior Courts,* 1962 (*S.I. No.* 72), *O.* 60 — *Guardianship of Infants Act,* 1964 (*No.*

CONSTITUTION—Courts.

7), *s.* 5 — *Family Law (Maintenance of Spouses and Children) Act,* 1976 (*No.* 11), *s.* 23 — *Courts Act,* 1981 (*No.* 11), *ss.* 12, 15 — *Family Law (Protection of Spouses and Children) Act,* 1981 (*No.* 21), *ss.* 1, 2 — *Constitution of Ireland,* 1937, *Arts.* 34, 36.] Section 2 of Article 34 of the Constitution states that the courts shall comprise courts of first instance and a court of final appeal. Section 3, sub-s. 1, of that Article states that the courts of first instance shall include a High Court invested with "full original jurisdiction in and power to determine all matters and questions whether of law or fact, civil or criminal." Article 36 of the Constitution states (*inter alia*) that, subject to the preceding provisions of the Constitution, the constitution and and organization of the Courts, the distribution of jurisdiction and business among the Courts and the judges and all matters of procedure, shall be regulated "in accordance with law." The plaintiff, being the wife of the defendant, issued a summons in the High Court in which she claimed certain reliefs under (*inter alia*) the Acts of 1964 and 1976, and the second Act of 1981. Section 5 of the Act of 1964, as enacted originally, stated that the jurisdiction conferred on a court by Part II of that Act might be exercised by the High Court; but the s. 5 substituted therefor by the Courts Act, 1981, contained no reference to the High Court in declaring that the said jurisdiction may be exercised by the Circuit Court or the District Court. Section 23 of the Act of 1976, as originally enacted, stated that the High Court, the Circuit Court (on appeal from the District Court) and the District Court might exercise concurrently jurisdiction to determine proceedings under ss. 5, 6, 7 and 9 of the Act of 1976; but the s. 23 substituted therefor by the Courts Act, 1961, contained no reference to the High Court in declaring that the Circuit Court and the District Court shall have jurisdiction to determine those proceedings. Section 2, sub-s. 1, of the second Act of 1981 states that "the Court" may make a barring order and by s. 1 defines "the Court"as the Circuit Court or the District Court. The plaintiff served on the Attorney General a notice which informed him that issues concerning the validity of the Acts of 1964 and 1976 and the second Act of 1981 "may arise in this action" and that the plaintiff would contend that, if the said sections of those Acts purported to restrict or remove the jurisdiction of the High Court to hear the claims made in her summons, those sections were unconstitutional. At the hearing of the plaintiff's motion seeking a ruling of the issues so raised, it was **Held** by Gannon J., in determining the said issues, 1, that the jurisdiction of the High Court to hear the claims made by the plaintiff had not been removed or restricted. 2. That the court might either accept or decline to accept for hearing, in accordance with its own procedures, the claims made by the plaintiff. 3. That the said sections of the Acts of 1964 and 1976 and of the second Act of 1981 were valid enactments having regard to the Constitution. *R.* v. *R.*

(H.C.) [1984] I.R.296

5. —— **Jurisdiction** — *High Court — Practice direction — Family law — Enactments conferring jurisdiction on Circuit Court and District Court — Concurrent jurisdiction vested in the High Court by the Constitution — Whether High Court may decline to exercise its jurisdiction — Whether discretion to decline jurisdiction derives from the Rules of the Superior Courts,* 1962 (*S.I. No.* 72), *O.* 49, *r.* 7 — *Guardianship of Infants Act,* 1964 (*No.* 7), *s.* 11 — *Family Law (Maintenance of Spouses and Children) Act,* 1976 (*No.* 11), *ss.* 5, 6, 7, 9, 23 — *Family Law (Protection of Spouses and Children) Act,* 1981 (*No.* 21), *s.* 1 — *Constitution of Ireland,* 1937, *Art.* 36.] A practice direction of the High Court requires that in any case where relief is sought in the High Court under the Guardianship of Infants Act, 1964, Family Law (Maintenance of Spouses and Children) Act, 1976, or the Family Law (Protection of Spouses and Children) Act, 1981, the parties should attend before the High Court and submit evidence or arguments as to whether the case is one appropriate for the High Court to exercise its jurisdiction or whether it was one which should be remitted to the Circuit Court or District Court. The plaintiff issued a special summons in the High Court in which she claimed certain reliefs under the Acts of 1964, 1976 and 1981. Section 23 of the Act of 1976, as originally enacted, provided that the High Court, the Circuit Court and the District Court should concurrently have jurisdiction to hear applications under ss. 5, 6, 7 and 9 of that Act. However, s. 1, sub-s. 1 of the amending Act of 1981 defined "the Court" for the purposes of such applications as being the Circuit Court or the District Court, and made no reference to any express jurisdiction of the High Court to deal concurrently with those matters. At the hearing of the application pursuant to the practice direction, it was **Held** by Murphy J., in declining to exercise the inherent or constitutional jurisdiction of the High Court to determine the issues between the parties, 1, that the jurisdiction of the High Court to accept or to decline to entertain certain matters was alternative to and independent of its right to remit proceedings to the Circuit Court or District Court pursuant to the Rules of the Superior Courts, O. 49, r. 7. *R.* v. *R.* [1984] I.R. 296, applied. 2. That the Act of 1981 indicates a clear intention on the part of the Oireachtas that applications under ss. 5, 6, 7 and 9 of the Act of

CONSTITUTION—Courts.

1976 should be made in the first instance to the court of limited and local jurisdiction. *Dicta* of Gannon J. in *R.* v. *R.*, considered. 3. That, there being no special question of fact or law which would distinguish this case from many others, the refusal of the High Court to exercise its jurisdiction would not result in a denial of justice. *O'R.* v. *O'R.*

(H.C.) [1985] I.R.367

6. —— **Jurisdiction** — *Supreme Court — Appellate jurisdiction from High Court — Damages — Whether award excessive — Whether Supreme Court may assess damages in absence of consent from parties — Whether jurisdiction to substitute assessment in lieu of re-trial limited by legislation — Courts of Justice Act,* 1924 (*No.* 10), *s.* 96 — *Courts (Supplemental Provisions) Act,* 1961 (*No.* 39), *s.* 48 — *Constitution of Saorstát Éireann,* 1922, art. *66 — Constitution of Ireland,* 1937, *Art.* 34.4.3.] The Constitution of Saorstát Éireann provided, in article 66, that the then Supreme Court "shall, with such exceptions . . . and subject to such regulation as may be prescribed by law, have appellate jurisdiction from all decisions of the High Court." Article 34, s. 4, sub-s. 3, of the Constitution, provides that the Supreme Court "shall with such exceptions and subject to such regulations as may be prescribed by law, have appellate jurisdiction from all decisions of the High Court." Section 96 of the Courts of Justice Act, 1924, provides that every appeal from a judgment of the High Court founded on the verdict of a jury in a civil case "shall be by way of motion before the appellate tribunal for a new trial", and that "the appellate tribunal may, in lieu of ordering a new trial, set aside the verdict, findings and judgment appealed against and enter such judgment as the court considers proper." The provisions of the Act of 1924 were carried over by s. 48 of the Courts (Supplemental Provisions) Act, 1961. The plaintiff recovered damages in the High Court from the defendants in respect of personal injuries suffered as a result of their negligence. Included in the award of the High Court jury were the sum of £30,000 in respect of pain and suffering to the date of the hearing and the sum of £55,000 in respect of pain and suffering in the future. The defendants appealed to the Supreme Court against the award of these sums on the ground that they were excessive, and submitted that the Supreme Court should substitute such sums as appeared appropriate. The plaintiff submitted that the Supreme Court did not have jurisdiction to substitute its own assessment of damages for that of the High Court, and that a new trial should be ordered if the Court considered the award to be excessive. Alternatively, the plaintiff argued that the court's jurisdiction

CONSTITUTION—*continued.*

was limited to those cases where the parties consented to jurisdiction. **Held** by the Supreme Court (Finlay C.J., Henchy, Griffin and Hederman JJ.; McCarthy J. dissenting) in allowing the appeal and varying the award of the High Court, 1, the jurisdiction of the Supreme Court to hear appeals from decisions of the High Court derived from Article 34, s. 4, sub-s. 3, of the Constitution, and any exception or regulation by law of the court's jurisdiction must be clearly and unambiguously stated. *Dicta* of Walsh J. in *The People* v. *Conmey* [1975] I.R. 341 applied. 2. Section 96 of the Courts of Justice Act, 1924, did not amount to an exception to the appellate jurisdiction of the Supreme Court, as it must have been intended to carry over the jurisdiction of the Supreme Court operating under the Saorstát Éireann Constitution which in article 66 conferred similar jurisdiction to that conferred by Article 34, s. 4, sub-s. 3 of the Constitution, and therefore the court had jurisdiction to substitute its own assessment of damages for that of a jury. *Gahan* v. *Engineering Products Ltd.* [1971] I.R. 30 discussed. 3. The Supreme Court would only substitute its own assessment where the justice of the case so required, and while the wishes of the parties to the case must be taken into consideration when the court exercised its discretion in the matter, it would be inconsistent with the obligation of the court to administer justice between the parties on the facts before it if one party could exercise a veto over the exercise of the discretion. *Per* McCarthy J. (dissenting): in substituting its own assessment of damages, the Supreme Court would be substituting its own findings of fact for that of the High Court; the Supreme Court's jurisdiction was confined to an assessment of the correctness of verdicts appealed against, and to fail to order a re-trial in circumstances such as in the present case was to deny the plaintiff the right to a jury verdict conferred by ss. 94 and 96 of the Courts of Justice Act, 1924. 4. Where, as in this case, there was no conflict between the medical witnesses as to the injuries suffered and the plaintiff's prognosis, where the plaintiff had put forward no reason why the case should be remitted to the High Court, and there was now a substantial lapse of time between the time of the accident and the possible date for a re-trial, the Supreme Court should bring the litigation to a conclusion and exercise its discretion by substituting its own award for that of the jury. 5. While the award for past pain and suffering was somewhat generous, it would not be interfered with, but the amount for future pain and suffering was excessive considering that the plaintiff's condition was likely to remain stable and she had been able to return to work. *Holohan* v. *Donohoe*

CONSTITUTION—Courts.

(S.C.) [1986] I.R.45; [1986] ILRM 250

7. —— **Úsáid sa chúirt** — *An tAcht Cúirteanna Breithiúnais,* 1924, *alt* 71 — *Forléiriú — "Sa mhéid gur féidir é agus gach ní a bhaineann leis an scéal d'áireamh" — Ceartas Aiceanta — Gan dualgas reachtúil ar Bhreitheamh Dúiche de réir ailt* 71 *den Acht Cúirteanna Breithiúnais,* 1924 *cúis a éisteacht gan fear teangan.*] Cúisíodh an gearánaí sa Chúirt Dúiche, An Bhun Bheag, ceantar Gaeltachta, ar an 2ú Feabhra, 1976, ós comhair an Bhreithimh Dúiche Patrick Keenan Johnson faoi fhorálacha alt 24 den Acht Rialtais Áitiúil (Pleanáil agus Forbairt), 1963, a shárú. Comhairle Chontae Dhún na nGall a thug an t-ionchúiseamh ar aghaidh. D'fhógair atúrnae na Comhairle Contae gur i mBéarla a bhí sé leis an ionchúiseamh a chur i láthair. Dúirt an gearánaí go raibh ar intinn aige é féin a chosaint ar an ionchúiseamh sa teanga náisiúnta. Shocraigh an Breitheamh úsáid a bhaint as ateangaire. Chuir an gearánaí in aghaidh an chúis do dhul ar aghaidh ar an mbonn sin agus d'agair sé nach raibh oiread eolais ar an nGaeilge ag an mBreitheamh Dúiche agus a chuirfeadh ar a chumas déanamh in éamais conganta ó fhear teangan agus fianaise á thabhairt sa teangain sin, agus d'iarr sé go gcuirfí an chúis ar athló go dtí go mbeadh Breitheamh ar fáil len í éisteacht go mbeadh an t-eolas riachtanach aige ar an nGaeilge. Diúltaíodh don iarratas san: leanadh den chúis, agus gearradh fineáil £5 ar an ghearánaí, móide £23.75 costais: an t-iomlán le híoc laistigh de thrí mhí: muna ndéanfaí amhlaidh, mí sa phríosún a bheith le fulaingt ag an gearánaí. Cúisíodh an gearánaí in athuair sa Chúirt Dúiche, An Bhun Bheag, ar an 11ú Bealtaine, 1976, ós comhair an Bhreithimh Dúiche Michael Larkin faoi fhorálacha alt 24 den Acht Rialtais Áitiúil (Pleanáil agus Forbairt), 1963, a shárú. Nuair glaodh an chúis dhein an Breitheamh Dúiche ateangaire a cheapadh chun aon fhianaise a thabharfaí as Gaeilge a aistriú go Béarla. Arís, chuir an gearánaí in aghaidh Breithimh Dúiche do dhul i mbun na cúise agus gan oiread eolais ar an nGaeilge aige agus a chuirfeadh ar a chumas déanamh in éamais conganta ó fhear teangan agus fianaise á thabhairt sa teangain sin, agus d'iarr go gcuirfí an chúis ar athló go dtí go mbeadh Breitheamh ar fáil len í éisteacht go mbeadh an t-eolas riachtanach aige ar an nGaeilge. Diúltaíodh don iarratas san. Chomh mhaith chéanna, dhiúltaigh an Breitheamh Dúiche glacadh le haragóint an ghearánaí nach raibh dlínnse aige an cás d'éisteacht agus leanadh den chúis le cabhair an ateangaire. Ciontaíodh an gearánaí. Gearradh fineáil £8.80 air ndéanfaí amhlaidh, trí mhí príosúntachta a bheith le fulaingt ag an ngearánaí. Dhiúltaigh an gearánaí na suimeanna a luadh san ordú a dhein an Breitheamh Dúiche Patrick Keenan Johnson

CONSTITUTION—*continued.*

dár dáta an 2ú Feabhra, 1976, a íoc. Gabhadh é agus cuireadh i bPríosún Mountjoy é ar an 21ú Meitheamh, 1976, agus coinníodh fá choimeád é sa phríosún go dtí an 25ú Meitheamh, 1976, nuair a scaoileadh amach ar bhannaí é go n-éistfí imeachta a bhí le tionscnamh aige d'fhonn breith na cúirte d'fháil faoi'n phríosúntacht san do bheith dleathach nó neamhdhleathach. Ina Ráiteas Éilimh d'iarr an gearánaí (1) Ordú á dhearbhú gur theip ar an Rialtas agus ar an Aire Dlí agus Cirt na dualgais a leagtar orthu faoi alt 71 den Acht Cúirteanna Breithiúnais, 1924, a chomhlíonadh; (2) Ordú i bhfoirm *mandamus* a chuirfeadh iachall ar an Rialtas agus ar an Aire Dlí agus Cirt na dualgais sin a chomhlíonadh; (3) Ordú i bhfoirm *certiorari* chun an dá chiontú a chur ar neamhní; agus (4) damáistí i leith na tréimhse a chaith sé i bpríosún toisc nár íoc sé na suimeanna airgid a luadh in ordú an Bhreithimh Johnson. Tar éis an chúis a éisteacht san Ard Chúirt, dhiúltaigh an Breitheamh Ó hUrmholtaigh do gach éileamh ón ngearánaí agus do dhein ordú ag díbeadh na cúise. Dhein an gearánaí achomharc chun na Cúirte Uachtaraí. **Breith** na Cúirte Uachtaraí (Walsh, Ó hInnse agus Ó Gríofa Brmh.) agus an t-achomharc á dhíbeadh, 1, níl aon dualgas iomlán leagtha ar Bhreitheamh Dúiche ag alt 71 den Acht Cúirteanna Breithiúnais, 1924, cúis a éisteacht gan fear teangan. 2. Má cheaptar Breitheamh do Dhúiche ina bhfuil liomatáiste ina bhfuil an Ghaeilge in úsáid ghinearálta, ní mór dó bheith cáilithe de réir alt 71 den Acht Cúirteanna Breithiúnais chun feidhmiú in éamais ateangaire nuair a tugtar fianaise trí Ghaeilge. Ach níl éifeacht leis an dualgas san ach 'sa mhéid gur féidir é agus gach ní a bhaineann leis an scéal d'áireamh.' 3. Tá ceart i gcónaí ag gearánaí nó ag finné ar bith a chuid fianaise féin a thabhairt as Gaeilge, ach níl cead ag gearánaí, faoi alt 71 ná aon fhoráil dlí eile, iallach a chur ar an mBreitheamh an cás ar fad éisteacht as Gaeilge má tá finné nó duine ar bith eile atá páirteach sa chás nach dtuigeann Gaeilge. *Per* Walsh Brmh.: 'Theip ar an Rialtas agus ar an tAire Dlí agus Cirt a ndualgais reachtúla faoi alt 71 den Acht (Cúirteanna Breithiúnais, 1924) a chomhlíonadh ar an 11ú lá de Bhealtaine, 1976.'

(**Irish language** — *Use in court — Courts of Justice Act,* 1924, *s.* 71 — *Interpretation — "So far as may be practicable having regard to all relevant circumstances" — Natural right — No statutory obligation on a District Justice according to s.* 71 *of the Courts of Justice Act,* 1924, *to hear a case without an interpreter.*)] The Plaintiff was charged in the District Court, Bunbeg, a Gaeltacht District on 2 February, 1976, before District Justice Johnson for contravention of the provisions of section 24 of the Local Government

CONSTITUTION—Courts.

(Planning and Development) Act, 1963. Donegal County Council brought on the prosecution. The solicitor for the County Council announced that he was going to present the case in English. The plaintiff said that it was his intention to defend himself on the charge in the national language. The Justice decided to use an interpreter. The plaintiff objected to the case going ahead on that basis and submitted that the District Justice did not possess sufficient knowledge of the Irish language as to enable him to dispense with the assistance of an interpreter while evidence was being given in that language and applied that the case be adjourned until a Justice with the necessary knowledge of the Irish language would be available to hear the case. That application was refused: the case proceeded and the plaintiff was fined £5.00 together with £23.75 costs: the total amount to be paid within three months: in default of payment the plaintiff to be imprisoned for one month. The plaintiff was again charged in the District Court, Bunbeg, on 11 May, 1976, before District Justice Larkin for contravention of the same provisions of the Act of 1963. When the case was called the District Justice appointed an interpreter to translate into English any evidence that would be given in Irish. Again the plaintiff objected to the District Justice entering on the case without his possessing such knowledge of the Irish language as would enable him to dispense with the assistance of an interpreter when evidence was being given in that language, and he applied that the case be adjourned until a Justice with the necessary knowledge of the Irish language would be available to hear the case. That application was refused. The District Justice refused to accept the argument of the plaintiff that the District Justice did not have the jurisdiction to hear the case and the case proceeded with the assistance of an interpreter. The plaintiff was convicted. He was fined £8.80 together with £23.85 costs: the total to be paid within one month and if not paid accordingly the plaintiff to be imprisoned for 3 months. The plaintiff refused to pay the amounts specified in the order of 2 February, 1976. He was arrested and imprisoned in Mountjoy Prison on 21 June, 1976, and he was kept in prison until 25 June, 1976, when he was released on bail pending the hearing of these proceedings. In his Statement of Claim the plaintiff claimed (1) an order declaring that the Government and the Minister for Justice failed to fulfil the obligations imposed on them by section 71 of the Act of 1924; (2) an order in the form of mandamus to compel the Government and the Minister for Justice to fulfil these obligations; (3) an order in the form of certiorari to quash the two convictions and (4) damages for the period he spent in prison by reason of his non-payment of the

CONSTITUTION—*continued.*

sums of money specified in the order of Justice Johnson. Having heard the case in the High Court, Mr. Justice Hamilton refused each of the plaintiff's claims. On appeal to the Supreme Court it was **Held,** 1, there is no absolute obligation imposed on a District Justice by section 71 of the Courts of Justice Act, 1924, to hear a case without an interpreter. 2, If a District Justice is appointed to a district in which there is an area in which the Irish language is in general use, he must be qualified in accordance with section 71 of the Courts of Justice Act to act without an interpreter when evidence is given in Irish. However that obligation is effective only "so far as may be practicable having regard to all the relevant circumstances." 3. A plaintiff or any witness has the right always to give his own evidence in Irish but a plaintiff is not entitled under section 71 or under any other statutory provision to compel a Justice to hear the whole case in Irish if there is a witness or any other person taking part in the case who does not understand Irish. *Per* Walsh J. "The Government and the Minister for Justice failed to fulfil their obligations under section 71 of the Act (Courts of Justice Act, 1924) on the 11 May, 1976." *Ó Monacháin* v. *An Taoiseach*

(S.C.) [1986] ILRM 660

Delegated legislation, *see* Nos. 34, 35
Elections, *see* Nos. 1, 36, 37
Equality, *see* Nos. 12, 13, 36, 37, 39, 40
Extradition, *see* Nos. 16, 17, 24, 25, 41
Fair procedures, *see* Nos. 11, 28, 40, 42, 51
Family, *see* Nos. 8, 9, 19, 38
Freedom of expression, *see* No. 14

FUNDAMENTAL RIGHTS
see also Nos. 38-48

Family. Nos. 8, 9, 19, 38
Personal rights. Nos. 10-20
Religion. No. 21

8. —— **Family** — *Convicted prisoner — Effect of imprisonment on rights of family — Right to communicate — Inquiry into legality of detention — Constitution of Ireland,* 1937, *Art.* 40.4.2. *Prisons — Prisoner — Subsisting rights of convicted prisoner's family — Right to communicate — Rules for the Government of Prisons,* 1947 (*S.R. & O. No.* 320), *Rules* 59, 60.] The applicant was a convicted prisoner. He applied for mandamus and habeas corpus on the ground that the provisions of the Rules for the Government of Prisons, 1947, were in breach of the constitutional rights of his wife and son, who had not been convicted of any criminal offence. The application was treated as one for an enquiry under Article 40.4.2· of the Constitution. **Held** by

CONSTITUTION—Fundamental Rights.

Lynch J. in refusing the application, 1, the diminution of the constitutional rights of the applicant's family was clearly envisaged by the Constitution which recognises the requirement for the trial of offences and imposition of punishments, including capital punishment, which have consequential effects in relation to any rights associated with the prisoner; and the Prison Rules regulating visits were not invalid in this light. 2. Since there was no requirement for the court to hear arguments from the respondent, it was not necessary to have the applicant in court to respond to any submissions or replies by the respondent. *The State (Gallagher)* v. *Governor of Portlaoise Prison*

(H.C.) [1987] ILRM 45

9. —— **Family** — *Whether any right to protection from a negligent act which interferes with its constitution or authority — Education — Whether children have the right to be educated by their father — Whether children have any right to protection from a negligent act which interferes with the right to be educated by their father — Constitution of Ireland,* 1937, *Arts.* 41, 42. *Damages — Negligence — Loss of non-pecuniary benefits deriving from parent-child relationship — Whether recoverable at common law.*] The plaintiff's father suffered severe personal injuries in the course of his employment with the defendant at the defendant's factory premises. Proceedings instituted on his behalf against the defendant alleging that his injuries were caused by the defendant's negligence were settled. Due to the severe nature of his injuries the plaintiffs' father was made a ward of court. The infant plaintiffs, suing by their mother, instituted proceedings against the defendant claiming, *inter alia,* damages in tort and breach of constitutional duty for the loss of the non-pecuniary benefits which the father of a family bestows on his children. The defendant denied liability and was granted an application to have the following preliminary issues determined prior to the trial of the action: (1) whether the defendant owed to the plaintiffs or any of them in the circumstances as pleaded by the plaintiffs any duty of care or any statutory duty, (2) whether the damages as pleaded were too remote in law, (3) whether the plaintiffs' claim was bad in law and whether it disclosed a cause of action against the defendant and (4) if the plaintiffs' claim did disclose a cause of action whether such cause of action was satisfied and barred by virtue of the amends in compensation paid by the defendant to the plaintiffs' father. At the trial of the preliminary issues it was **Held** by Costello J., in answering Q.1 in the negative and Q.3 in the affirmative and finding it unnecessary to answer Qs. 2 or 4, 1, that damages are not recoverable at common law for the loss

CONSTITUTION—*continued.*

of the non-pecuniary benefits deriving from the parent-child relationship. *McLoughlin* v. *O'Brian* [1983] 1 A.C. 410 considered. 2. That Article 41, s. 1, sub-ss. 1 and 2 of the Constitution confers on the family the right to protection from legislation and from the deliberate acts of State officials which attack or impair its constitution or authority. It does not confer on the family any right to protection from a negligent act which attacks or impairs its constitution or authority. *Dictum* of Kenny J. in *Ryan* v. *A.G.* [1965] I.R. 294 at 309 applied. 3. That Article 42, s. 1 of the Constitution impliedly confers on the children of a family the right to be educated by their father. It does not confer on the children of a family any right to protection from a negligent act which interferes with their right to be educated by their father. *P.H.* v. *John Murphy & Sons Ltd.*

(H.C.) [1987] I.R. 621; [1988] ILRM 300

10. —— **Personal rights — Communication** — *Plaintiff prisoner — Prison Rules — Inspection and censorship of plaintiff's mail — Whether breach of constitutional right to communicate — Whether plaintiff entitled to damages for non-delivery of letters addressed to him — Rules for the Government of Prisons,* 1947 (*S.I. No.* 320) *— Constitution of Ireland,* 1937, *Art.* 40.] Rule 63 of the Rules for the Government of Prisons, 1947, provides for *inter alia* the compulsory inspection and, if the contents are objectionable, the censorship of prisoners' letters. The plaintiff was a convicted prisoner. As a result of certain unauthorised actions taken by prison officers in the prison, certain letters which were addressed to the plaintiff, and the contents of which were agreed not to have been objectionable, were not delivered to the plaintiff. The plaintiff sought *inter alia* a declaration that rule 63 was invalid having regard to the provisions of the Constitution and damages for breach of his constitutional rights. The plaintiff also sought an injunction restraining the defendants from opening, reading, destroying or interfering with his correspondence. **Held** by Costello J., 1, that when a citizen is lawfully deprived of his liberty one of the consequences is that he is deprived of the right to exercise many constitutionally protected rights and that the constitutional rights that may still be exercised are those which do not depend on the continuance of his personal liberty and which are compatible with the reasonable requirements of the place of imprisonment. *The Attorney General* v. *Paperlink Ltd.* [1984] ILRM 373 and *Murray* v. *The Attorney General* [1985] I.R. 532, applied. 2. That Article 40, s. 3, sub-s. 1, of the Constitution includes the right to communicate as one of the unspecified personal rights included in that article but that right is not an absolute one and its exercise may be regulated

CONSTITUTION—Fundamental Rights.

by law. Prison security is endangered by unrestricted correspondence and the evidence established that, in practice, the only matters which were regarded by the prison authorities as being subject to rule 63, were matters relating to security; therefore the restriction on the right to communicate could reasonably be justified and was not contrary to the provisions of the Constitution. *Solosky* v. *The Queen* (1980) 1 S.C.R. 821 considered. 3. That the plaintiff suffered an unjustified infringement of his constitutional right to communicate as certain letters which had been passed under the Prison Rules were not delivered to him but he would be awarded nominal damages only as he had suffered no pecuniary loss and there was insufficient evidence that an award for exemplary damages would be justified. 4. That the State is vicariously liable for the wrongful actions of the prison officers in respect of the non-delivery of correspondence to the plaintiff which was found to be unobjectionable under the Prison Rules, because although unauthorised, the wrongful act was performed within the scope of the prison officers' employment. *Byrne* v. *Ireland* [1972] I.R. 241 followed. *Quaere:* Whether the State may be liable for acts of a servant of the State which amount to an infringement of a right protected by the Constitution even though performed outside the scope of the State's servant's employment. *Kearney* v. *Minister for Justice*

(H.C.) [1986] I.R.116 ; [1987] ILRM 52

—— Communication.
see also No.8 (*above*)

11. —— **Personal rights — Constitutional torts** — *Constitutional obligations of State — Commissioner of Garda Síochána purportedly dismissed by Government — Government purporting to appoint successor — Declaration by High Court that purported dismissal invalid — Purported commissioner directing sworn enquiry into allegations of breach of discipline against plaintiff — Plaintiff attending and being represented at enquiry — Enquiry conceded to have been a nullity — Duty of purported commissioner to avoid putting plaintiff to unnecessary expense — Whether plaintiff entitled to recover legal costs and expenses of attending and being represented at enquiry — Garda Síochána (Discipline) Regulations,* 1971.] On the 19 January, 1978, the Government purported to dismiss G. from the office of Commissioner of the Garda Síochána and purported to appoint McL. in his place. On the 31 October, 1978, in proceedings brought by G. against Ireland, the purported dismissal of G. was declared void by the High Court and on the 9 March, 1979, that decision was affirmed by the Supreme Court. On the 16 November, 1978,

CONSTITUTION—*continued.*

McL., purporting to act as Commissioner of the Garda Síochána, directed the holding of a sworn enquiry into allegations of breach of discipline against the plaintiff and such enquiry was held in January, 1979, In February, 1979, McL. purported to confirm the decision of the enquiry and to dismiss the plaintiff from the force. On the 15 December, 1980, the plaintiff brought High Court proceedings claiming to have the purported action of McL. declared invalid and claiming damages for those acts. Before the trial of the action in the High Court it was conceded on behalf of the defendants that McL.'s action was a nullity but no award of damages was made ([1985] ILRM 606). The plaintiff claimed before the Supreme Court to be entitled to the costs and expenses of attending and being legally represented at the purported enquiry. **Held** by the Supreme Court (Finlay C.J., Walsh, Henchy, Griffin and McCarthy JJ.), in varying the order of the High Court, 1, that at the time when the purported order directing the holding of a sworn enquiry was made, the High Court decision to the effect that the purported dismissal of G. was void had already been delivered. It followed from that the purported appointment of McL. as Commissioner was invalid and that the enquiry ordered by him was a nullity. 2. That it must be presumed that the defendants were aware that unless the legal position was reversed by the Supreme Court, it was probable that the plaintiff would have incurred expense in attending an enquiry which would not avail him. 3. That the second defendant, McL., and vicariously the State, owed a duty to the plaintiff in protection of his property rights, not to initiate an enquiry which might result in being a nullity and thereby put him to wholly unnecessary expense. If the defendants did decide for good reason to initiate such an enquiry, they owed him an obligation to recoup the expense to which he had been unnecessarily put. *Byrne* v. *Ireland* [1972] I.R. 241 considered. 4. That the plaintiff was entitled to the costs and expenses of his representation and attendance at the purported enquiry, taxed on a solicitor and client basis. *McHugh* v. *Commissioner of An Garda Síochána*

(S.C.) [1986] I.R.228 ; [1987] ILRM 181

12. —— **Personal rights — Equality** — *Prize bonds — Whether inflation has rendered the statutory prize bond competition unfair — Whether injustice resulted — Finance (Miscellaneous Provisions) Act,* 1956 (*No.* 47), *Constitution of Ireland, Arts.* 34, 40.1.] The Minister for Finance was sued as the administrator of the Prize Bond lottery established by the Finance (Miscellaneous Provisions) Act, 1956. Under the Prize Bond scheme redeemable bonds purchased for £5 participate in periodic draws for prizes.

CONSTITUTION—Fundamental Rights.

The plaintiff, who sued in person, had purchased a prize bond in 1961. He established that £5 in 1961 was equivalent to £50 at current values, and he asserted that it was unfair that bonds currently purchased for £5 should have the same chance of winning a prize as his longstanding investment. He contended that the scheme in its present form could not be reconciled with the equality provisions of the Constitution, and he invited the court, with reference to its duty under Article 34 to administer justice and to intervene to restrain the Minister from issuing new bonds. **Held** by Murphy J., dismissing the claim, 1, Article 34 of the Constitution did not vest in judges the power to substitute for the enactment of the legislature their view of what was fair and just. 2. The plaintiff had not in reality suffered injustice: his bond had participated in many past draws, and it was a fallacy to compare his position with that of current purchasers. 3. In the circumstances it would not be appropriate to comment on the equality provisions of the Constitution which under existing case law appeared to be confined to a guaranteed of equality of citizens as human persons. *Heaney* v. *Minister for Finance*

(H.C.) [1986] ILRM 164

13. —— **Personal rights — Equality** — *Property rights — Succession — Intestacy — Claim of illegitimate child — Whether "issue" of intestate — Statute — Interpretation — Succession Act,* 1965 (*No.* 27), *ss.* 67, 69 — *Constitution of Ireland,* 1937, Arts. 29, 40, 41, 43.] Section 1, sub-s. 1, of Article 41 of the Constitution declares that the State recognises the family as the natural primary and fundamental unit group of society, and as a moral institution possessing inalienable and imprescriptible rights, antecedent and superior to all positive law. Sub-section 2 of that section declares that the State guarantees to protect the family in its constitution and authority, as the necessary basis of social order and as indispensable to the welfare of the nation and the State. Section 3, sub-s, 1, of that Article declares that the State pledges itself to guard with special care the institution of marriage, on which the family is founded, and to protect it against attack. The defendant was the natural child of her father and her mother, who were not married to each other. The defendant's father died on 5 May, 1975, a bachelor and intestate, leaving him surviving the plaintiff (his sister), a second sister, his brother, the defendant's mother, and his natural daughter, the defendant. Section 67, sub-s. 3, of the Act of 1965, provides that if an intestate dies "leaving issue" and no spouse, his estate shall be distributed "among the issue" as specified therein. The Act of 1965 does not contain a definition of the word "issue." Section 69, sub-s. 1, of the Act of 1965 provides

CONSTITUTION—*continued.*

that if an intestate dies, without leaving a spouse, issue or a parent, his estate shall be distributed between his brothers and sisters in the manner therein specified. The plaintiff's application for a grant of letters of administration of the estate of the deceased was opposed by the defendant, who claimed to be the issue of the deceased and who lodged a caveat. The plaintiff instituted an action in the High Court in which she claimed an order setting aside the caveat and giving her liberty to proceed with her application. The defendant claimed, in the alternative, a declaration that ss. 67 and 69 of the Act of 1965 were invalid having regard to the provisions of the Constitution. **Held** by D'Arcy J., in giving judgment for the plaintiff, 1, that the legislature, before and after the enactment of the Constitution in 1937, had enacted legislation which conferred expressly some property rights on illegitimate children and that, in view of the apparently deliberate refusal of the legislature to state in the Act of 1965 that the word "issue", when used therein, included illegitimate children, there were no grounds to justify the court in interpreting that word so as to include such children. 2. That no right to succeed to the estate of her father was conferred on the defendant by virtue of the acknowledgment in Article 43, s. 1, of the Constitution that man has the natural right to the private ownership of goods, or by the guarantee therein by the State not to abolish the right of private ownership or the general right to inherit property, or by the guarantee by the State in Article 40, s. 3, to protect and vindicate the personal and property rights of the citizen. 3. That the "family" mentioned in Article 41 of the Constitution is the family founded on a valid marriage in accordance with the law of the State. *The State (Nicolaou)* v. *An Bord Úchtála* [1966] I.R. 567 applied. 4. That, in view of the provisions of Article 41 of the Constitution, the terms of ss. 67 and 69 of the Act of 1965 were not in breach of the qualified declaration in article 40, s. 1, that all citizens shall, as human persons, be held equal before the law; and that, accordingly, the provisions of ss. 67 and 69 of the Act of 1965 were not invalid having regard to the provisions of the Constitution.

On appeal by the defendant it was **Held** by the Supreme Court, in disallowing the appeal, 1, that the meaning of the word issue in ss. 67 and 69 of the Act of 1965 was governed by the context in which it appeared, being an Act providing for succession to property on intestacy and providing expressly in s. 110 for some succession rights of illegitimate children, without extending the meaning of that word to include such children. 2. That, accordingly, the meaning of that word in those sections did not include children who were not issue of a lawful marriage. 3. That the

CONSTITUTION—Fundamental Rights.

provisions of s. 1, sub-s. 2, of Article 43 of the Constitution did not confer upon the defendant a right to intestate succession in respect of the estate of her father. 4. That, as no right of intestate succession in respect of that estate was vested in the defendant either by the Act of 1965 or by the Constitution, she had failed to establish a personal right which required to be protected and vindicated pursuant to Article 40, s. 3, of the Constitution. 5. That the "family" recognised in Article 41 of the Constitution is the family which is based on a valid marriage in accordance with the law of the State. 6. That the main issue was whether the discrimination in favour of legitimate issue effected by s. 67 of the Act of 1965 was a contravention of the provisions of Article 40, s. 1, of the Constitution which states that "all citizens shall, as human persons, be held equal before the law" but which adds the proviso "this shall not be held to mean that the State shall not in its enactments have due regard to differences of capacity, physical and moral, and of social function." 7. That the said discrimination could not be justified as being due to any of the differences of capacity or of social function mentioned in the said proviso. 8. That, nevertheless, the said discrimination, although not justified by the proviso to Article 40, s. 1, f the Constitution, was justified by ss. 1 and 3 of Article 41 of the Constitution since ss. 67 and 69 of the Act of 1965 form part of an Act which is designed to strengthen the protection of the family in accordance with the provisions of Article 41. 9. That, therefore, the said discrimination was not an invidious discrimination in the sense of being unjust, unreasonable or arbitrary and, accordingly, the provisions of ss. 67 and 69 of the Act of 1965 were not invalid having regard to the provisions of the Constitution. *O'B.* v. *S.*

(H.C., S.C.) [1984] I.R.316; [1985] ILRM 86

14. —— **Personal rights — Freedom of expression** — *Tort — Breach of confidence — Interlocutory injunction sought to restrain alleged breach of confidence — Confidential information shared between foreign government and private individual — Principles governing the protection of such information — Effect of constitutional provisions on duty of confidentiality — Constitution of Ireland,* 1937, *Art.* 40.6.1.] Article 40, s. 6, sub-s. 1 (i) of the Constitution provides, *inter alia,* that the right of citizens to express freely their convictions and opinions guaranteed therein is subject to public order and morality and further provides that the State shall endeavour to ensure that organs of public opinion while preserving their rightful liberty of expression, including criticism of Government policy, shall not be used to undermine public order or morality or the authority of the State. The plaintiff as

CONSTITUTION—*continued.*

chief law officer of England and Wales obtained an interim injunction in the High Court restraining the defendant from publishing a book written by a deceased member of the British secret service which publication the plaintiff contended would be in breach of that member's life long obligation of confidentiality to her employer in respect of each and every aspect of her employment. On the plaintiff's motion on notice to the defendant seeking an interlocutory injunction further restraining publication of the said book it was **Held** by Carroll J., in refusing the plaintiff's application, 1, that since there was no question of public order or morality or the authority of the State being undermined in this case the defendant had a *prima facie* constitutional right under Article 40, s. 6, sub-s. 1 (i) to publish information and the onus rested on the plaintiff to establish, in the context of an interlocutory application, that the constitutional right of the defendant should not be exercised. 2. That the public interest in this jurisdiction would not be affected by publication of the book and, therefore, the consideration which would move courts in the United Kingdom in the matter were different to those to be applied by the courts here. *Attorney General* v. *The Observer Limited and Others; Attorney General* v. *Guardian Newspapers Limited and Others* (unreported, English Court of Appeal, 25 July, 1986) distinguished. 3. That the principles governing the protection of confidences originating in private or commercial settings, as expounded by the High Court and Supreme Court in *House of Spring Gardens* v. *Point Blank* [1984] I.R. 611, had no application to a case such as this. 4. That there was no absolute confidentiality in relation to information shared between a government and a private individual. *Dicta* of Mason J. in *The Commonwealth of Australia* v. *John Fairfax & Sons Ltd.* (1980) 147 C.L.R. 39 at pp. 51-52 approved. 5. That, the plaintiff had no cause of action and accordingly the balance of convenience lay with permitting the defendant to exercise its constitutional right to publish. *Attorney General for England and Wales* v. *Brandon Book Publishers Ltd.*

(H.C.) [1986] I.R.597; [1987] ILRM 135

15. —— **Personal rights — Liberty** — *Inquiry into legality of detention — Requirement of immediate inquiry — Detention in police custody — Effect of order for release — Constitution of Ireland,* 1937, *Art.* 40.4.2.

Criminal law — Arrest — Statute — Offences against the State — Motive — Arrest in respect of scheduled offence — Questioning in respect of non-scheduled offence — Whether arrest lawful — Whether colourable device — Whether

CONSTITUTION—Fundamental Rights.

exclusion of murder as scheduled offence anomalous — Offences Against the State Act, 1939 (*No.* 13), *s.* 30.] The applicant had been arrested under s. 30 of the Offences against the State Act, 1939, in relation to a murder which had been committed with the use of firearms. In the course of the killing, it appeared that damage was done to the weapon used, and the applicant had been arrested on suspicion of having committed an offence under the Malicious Damage Act, 1861. The applicant applied for an inquiry under Article 40.4 into the legality of his detention, in the course of which the Gardaí stated that the ultimate or real purpose of arresting the applicant under s. 30 had been to interrogate him in respect of the killing. **Held** by Finlay P. in ordering the applicant's release: since the real purpose of the arrest had been to interrogate the applicant in respect of the killing, the arrest on suspicion of having committed an offence of malicious damage was a colourable device to bring what was in reality and in plain truth a murder investigation within the ambit of s. 30 of the Offences against the State Act, 1939, and since the malicious damage offence was not serious, grave or substantial there was no lawful justification for continuing to detain the applicant without bringing him before a court; and the order under Article 40.4, while not forming any barrier to an arrest for murder, required that the applicant, if charged, be brought before the appropriate tribunal and charged without delay. *The People* v. *Towson* [1978] ILRM 122 distinguished. *Per curiam:* it appears to be a legal anomaly that murder, a very grave offence, is not a scheduled offence under the Offences against the State Act, 1939. *The State (Bowes)* v. *Fitzpatrick*

(H.C.) [1978] ILRM 195

16. —— **Personal rights** — **Liberty** — *Inquiry into legality of detention — Invasion of constitutional rights — Deliberate violation — Invasion by persons on behalf of the Executive — Planned results of such invasion — Inherent jurisdiction — Abuse of process — Scheme of courts within Constitution.*

Practice and procedure — Appeal to Supreme Court — Stay on order of High Court — Power of appellate court — Constitution — Liberty — High Court order releasing from detention — Exercise of appellate powers in conflict with Constitution.

Criminal law — Arrest — Suspicion — Arrest without proper suspicion — Detention — Illegal arrest and detention — Legality of subsequent extradition proceedings — Extradition Act, 1965 (*Part II*) (*No.* 19) *Order,* 1984 (*S.I. No.* 271) — *Extradition Act,* 1965 (*No.* 17) — *Constitution of Ireland,* 1937, *Art.* 40.] At 2.00 p.m. on 25 October, 1984, the prosecutor was arrested in

CONSTITUTION—*continued.*

purported pursuance of s. 30 of the Offences Against the State Act, 1939. Early next afternoon the detention period was extended by another twenty-four hours. At about the same time (1.15 p.m.) the Government made an order applying Part II of the Extradition Act, 1965, in relation to the Commonwealth of Australia as and from that date. That same afternoon the prosecutor applied to the High Court to have the legality of his detention ascertained, which hearing was fixed for 7.00 p.m. that evening. At 6.00 p.m. a provisional warrant pursuant to s. 27 of the Extradition Act, 1965, was issued by District Justice Ballagh. At the High Court hearing Egan J. found that no genuine suspicion that the prosecutor had committed a firearms offence could have been formed by the arresting Garda; that the arrest and detention were illegal and accordingly ordered the prosecutor's release. A short while later, at approximately 10.00 p.m. outside the immediate precincts of the Four Courts the prosecutor was arrested on foot of the provisional warrant just issued by District Justice Ballagh. He was then brought to the District Court and remanded in custody. On 2 November, 1984, a habeas corpus application challenging the remand orders was refused by Egan J. On 8 November the Minister for Justice addressed an order to District Justice Kotsonouris pursuant to s. 26 of the Extradition Act, 1965, signifying that he had received from the Commonwealth of Australia a request for the extradition of the prosecutor. Application was then made on 17 November to District Justice Kotsonouris for orders committing the prosecutor to prison, there to await the order for his extradition or until the High Court or Supreme Court should order his release. On 4 November the prosecutor applied to the High Court pursuant to Article 40 of the Constitution for an inquiry as to the legality of his detention, at the end of which hearing it was **Held** by Egan J., that the object of the arrest, pursuant to s. 30 of the Offences Against the State Act, 1939, of the prosecutor was to ensure that he would be available for the provisional warrant arrest; that such arrest amounted to a deliberate and conscious violation of constitutional rights; that there were no extraordinary excusing circumstances; that his detention in subsequent proceedings was tainted by the illegality of his original arrest and accordingly the prosecutor was to be immediately released. The respondent then applied to the Supreme Court for a stay on the order of the High Court pending appeal. **Held** by the Supreme Court (Finlay C.J., Walsh, Henchy, Hederman and McCarthy JJ.) that whatever powers the court may have to make its ordinary appellate jurisdiction effective, such powers would not be exercised in a manner inconsistent with the Constitution. On appeal by the respondent from the order of the High Court it was **Held** by the Supreme Court (Finlay C.J., Henchy, Griffin, Hederman and McCarthy JJ.) in dismissing the appeal and affirming the judgment of Egan J., 1, the courts have not only an inherent jurisdiction but a positive duty (*a*) to protect persons against the invasion of their constitutional rights; (*b*) if invasion has occurred, to restore as far as possible the person so damaged to the position in which he would have been if his rights had not been invaded; and (*c*) to ensure as far as possible that persons acting on behalf of the executive who consciously and deliberately violate the constitutional rights of citizens do not for themselves or their superiors obtain the planned results of that invasion. Principles in *The State* (*Quinn*) v. *Ryan* [1965] I.R. 70; *The People* (*Attorney General*) v. *O'Brien* [1965] I.R. 142 and *The People* v. *Lynch* [1982] I.R. 64 affirmed. 2. The well recognised jurisdiction of the courts at common law to prevent an abuse of their own process is amplified and reinforced by the position of the courts within the framework of the Constitution and a direct duty arises to prevent such abuse of their process. *R.* v. *Bow Street Magistrates, ex p. Mackeson* (1981) 75 Cr. App. R. 24 considered. *The State (Trimbole)* v. *Governor of Mountjoy Prison*

(H.C., S.C.) [1985] I.R.550; [1985] ILRM 465

17. —— **Personal rights** — **Liberty** — *Inquiry into legality of detention — Detention — Privacy — Surveillance — Overt surveillance — Whether applicant's liberty interfered with — Whether surveillance justified — Duties of Garda Síochána — Investigation of crime — Execution of extradition warrant — Extradition Act,* 1965 (*No.* 17), *Part III — Constitution of Ireland,* 1937, *Art.* 40.

Criminal law — Criminal investigation — Garda Síochána — Suspect kept under close overt surveillance — Garda Síochána anticipating request for extradition warrant — Whether surveillance interfered with liberty of subject — Whether surveillance justifiable — Whether justified — Harrassment — Conspiracy and Protection of Property Act, 1875 (*c.* 86), *s.* 7 — *Extradition Act,* 1965 (*No.* 17), *Part III — Constitution of Ireland,* 1937, *Art.* 40.] At 1.12 p.m. on the 23 November, 1987, the applicant was arrested pursuant to s. 30 of the Offences Against the State Act, 1939, on suspicion of being a member of an unlawful organisation. On the following morning a cache of arms was found near where he had been arrested and the period of his detention was lawfully extended to 1.12 p.m. on the 25 November. Shortly before the applicant was released the gardaí learned that a request would be made by the R.U.C. for a

provisional extradition warrant and at 1.45 p.m. a formal request was made. However the application to the District Court could not be made until a district justice would become available at 8.00 p.m. that evening. Following his release from detention the applicant was subject to intense surveillance by members of the Garda and the army. He was openly followed by several gardaí on foot and by at least two patrol cars, first to a solicitor's office and later to a private house where he met a number of persons known to be sympathetic to him. At about 6.15 p.m. the applicant was driven away from the house at speed and was pursued by a patrol car. The garda car ultimately caught up with and over took the car in which the applicant was travelling and stopped it, the intention of the garda driver being to arrest the driver for dangerous driving. The applicant fled from the car and through a hedge and fell into a ditch. A garda who followed fell on top of him and after a struggle the applicant was arrested for causing a breach of the peace. He was taken to Cavan Garda station and charged before a district justice with assault and malicious damage to the garda's watch. He was remanded in custody until the following day. By this time a provisional extradition warrant had been obtained under s. 49 of the Extradition Act, 1965, but it was decided not to execute it. On the following day, 26 November, the applicant was released on bail on the assault and malicious damage charges but immediately after leaving court was rearrested on foot of the provisional warrant and was remanded in custody. The applicant complained to the High Court that he was being unlawfully detained and an enquiry was ordered under Article 40, s. 4 of the Constitution. In particular he complained that the level of surveillance to which he had been subjected was a breach of his constitutional rights, was unjustified and was so close as to amount to unlawful detention. **Held** by Egan J., in refusing the application for release, 1, that the applicant's liberty had not been curtailed while he was on foot. 2. That the purpose of stopping the car in which the applicant was travelling was not to detain the applicant but to restrain the driver from driving dangerously. 3. That the surveillance of the applicant would have been objectionable in the absence of justification. 4. That the surveillance in the instant case was justified either by the expectation of the provisional warrant or by the hope that evidence would be obtained against the applicant in relation to the arms which had been found. 5. That the gardaí had been entitled to charge the applicant with the alleged assault in priority to executing the provisional extradition warrant. On appeal by the applicant it was **Held** by the Supreme Court (Finlay C.J., Henchy, Griffin, Hederman and

CONSTITUTION—Fundamental Rights.

McCarthy JJ.), in dismissing the appeal, 1, (Hederman and McCarthy JJ. dissenting) that from the time of his release from s. 30 detention until his arrest for causing a breach of the peace, the applicant was free to go and to be where he wished. 2. That in the absence of specific justification the overt surveillance of an individual could constitute an infringement of his constitutional right to privacy and could be unlawful. 3. That in determining whether such surveillance was unlawful the court would have regard to the nature of the surveillance, the nature and importance of the police duty being discharged and to all the circumstances of the case. 4. (Hederman and McCarthy JJ. dissenting) That there were no grounds for distinguishing the duties of investigating and detecting crime from the duty of executing an extradition warrant. 5. That having regard to the nature of the duty being performed by the Garda Síochána and to the fact that covert surveillance was most unlikely to keep the gardaí aware of the applicant's whereabouts, the nature and extent of the surveillance were justified. *Per* McCarthy J. dissenting, (Hederman J. concurring) That overt surveillance differed from covert surveillance in that in the former case the subject's freedom of choice of movement was restricted. *Kane* v. *Governor of Mountjoy Prison*

(H.C., S.C.) [1988] I.R.757; [1988] ILRM 724

18. —— **Personal rights — Privacy** — *Unenumerated rights — Right to privacy in telephone conversations — Unjustified tapping of telephone by State — Action for damages for breach of constitutional rights — Constitution of Ireland,* 1937, *Art.* 40.3.

Damages — Aggravated or exemplary damages — Breach of constitutional rights — Unconstitutional action on the part of servants of the State — Civil Liability Act, 1961 (*No.* 41), *ss.* 7, 14.] Between May and Novermber, 1982, by authority of a warrant issued by the Minister for Justice, the private telephones of the plaintiffs, who were political journalists, were tapped. In January, 1983, the Minister for Justice issued a public statement in which he admitted the tapping. He further admitted that there had been no justification for the tapping and that what had occurred went beyond anything that could be explained as an error of judgment. The plaintiffs brough proceedings for damages for the unlawful tapping of their telephones. In particular, they claimed that the actions of the servants of the State amounted to a breach of their personal right to privacy and freedom from unlawful and unwarranted intrusion guaranteed by Article 40 of the Constitution. The defendants admitted the fact of the tapping but denied that there had been any illegality or that the plaintiffs' constitutional

CONSTITUTION—*continued.*

rights had been infringed. **Held** by Hamilton P., in giving judgment for the plaintiffs, 1, that the right to privacy, though not specifically guaranteed by the Constitution, was one of the personal rights of the citizen which flowed from the Christian and democratic nature of the State. *Ryan* v. *The Attorney General* [1965] I.R. 294 and *Norris* v. *The Attorney General* [1984] I.R. 36 considered. 2. That the constitutional right to privacy included the right to hold private telephone conversations without deliberate, conscious and unjustified intrusion by servants of the State. 3. That the right to privacy was not an unqualified right but was subject to the constitutional rights of others and to the requirements of public order, public morality and the common good. 4. That the tapping of the plaintiffs' telephones had been deliberate, conscious and unjustifiable and was an actionable infringement of their constitutional rights. *Meskell* v. *Córas Iompair Éireann* [1973] I.R. 121 applied. 5. That while the reputations of the plaintiffs had been vindicated by the statement of the Minister for Justice, the damage suffered by them had been aggravated by the fact that the tapping had been done by an organ of state which was constitutionally obliged to defend their rights. *Rookes* v. *Barnard* [1946] A.C. 1129 considered. *Kennedy* v. *Ireland*

(H.C.) [1987] I.R.587; [1988] ILRM 472

19. —— **Personal rights — Procreation** — *Prisoner — Opportunity to beget children — Deprivation — Husband and wife each serving sentence of imprisonment for life — Wife aged 37 years — No children of marriage — Basis for restriction on prisoners' rights by the State — Whether husband and wife constitute family — Constitutional rights of prisoners not infringed by conditions of imprisonment — Constitution of Ireland,* 1937, *Arts.* 40, 41.] The plaintiffs, who were husband and wife, were both serving sentences of penal servitude for life. They had no children, and conjugal visits were denied to them while in prison. The plaintiffs claimed that as a married couple they had a right to beget children; that this right was protected by the Constitution and that it was being unconstitutionally infringed. They sought a declaration *inter alia* that they were entitled to bail so that they could exercise this right outside prison or, alternatively, a declaration that the prison authorities were obliged to provide facilities that would enable them to exercise this right within the confines of the prison. The plaintiffs argued that each, as a married person, had a basic human right to procreate children and that this right was protected by Article 41 of the Constitution. They argued that there was a hierarchy of constitutionally protected rights and Article 41, by describing the rights of the family as being

CONSTITUTION—Fundamental Rights.

inalienable and imprescriptible and superior to all positive law, places the right to procreate children very high on the scale of values. Alternatively, it was one of the unspecified personal rights in Article 40 which the State was required to defend and vindicate. The plaintiffs' case was not that every married prisoner could claim to exercise the right to beget children, but that an invalid restriction occurred when the combined effect of the term of imprisonment and the age of the wife renderd it unlikely that a child could be conceived on the expiry of the prison term, and that in the particular circumstances of this case where the first named plaintiff was 37 years of age, the right claimed must override the consequences of the lawful deprivation of their liberty. **Held** by Costello J., in dismissing the plaintiffs' claim, 1, that a married couple without children is a "family", within the meaning of Article 41 and is entitled to the same constitutional protection under Article 41 as a married couple with children. 2. The right to beget children is one of the unspecified personal rights which by Article 40 the State is required to defend and vindicate and this right is distinct from the right to privacy. *Ryan* v. *The Attorney General* [1965] I.R. 294 and *McGee* v. *The Attorney General* [1974] I.R. 284 considered. 3. The rights accorded to the family in Article 41, s. 1, sub-s. 1 belong to the institution itself and are distinct from the personal rights which each individual enjoys by virtue of membership of the family. 4. The rights of the family and its integrity as a unit group can be validly restricted by the State in the exercise of the powers lawfully conferred on it in spite of the fact that there is no reference in Article 41 of the Constitution to any restrictive power to delimit the exercise of these rights. 5. In construing the Constitution, the courts should adopt a purposive approach to interpretation which would examine the text of the Constitution as a whole and identify its purpose and objectives in protecting human rights, in order to achieve a harmonious interpretation and to avoid a strict construction which would allow the imperfection of words to defeat or pervert any of the Constitution's fundamental purposes. *The Attorney General* v. *Paperlink Ltd.* [1984] ILRM 373 and *Tormey* v. *Ireland* [1985] I.R. 289 considered. 6. In order to evaluate the right to beget children, the court should consider its innate qualities and nature and this right should not be devalued because it is a personal right protected by Article 40, s. 3, sub-s. 1, without the benefit of the more explicit language employed by Article 40, s. 1, sub-section 1. *People* v. *Shaw* [1982] I.R. 1 considered. 7. In the instant case, the restriction on the plaintiffs' rights to beget children is a reasonable consequence of the State's power to imprison and is constitutionally permissible. The

CONSTITUTION—*continued.*

State, as guardian of the common good, is empowered by the Constitution to restrict rights in certain circumstances. The rights which may be exercised by a prisoner are those which do not depend on the continuation of his liberty and which are compatible with the reasonable requirements of the prison service or which do not impose unreasonable demands on it. *Murray* v. *Ireland*

(H.C.) [1985] I.R.532 ; [1985] ILRM 542

20. —— **Personal rights — Right to life of the unborn** — *Pregnancy counselling services — Abortion considered as an option — Referral to medical clinic in Great Britain — Whether the giving of such assistance unlawful — Whether admitted activities of defendants amounted to conspiracy to corrupt public morals.*

Locus standi — Locus standi *of relator — Whether constitutional provisions self-executing in the absence of legislation — Offences Against the Person Act,* 1861 (*c.* 100), *ss.* 58, 59 — *Health (Family Planning) Act,* 1979 (*No.* 20), *s.* 10 — *Constitution of Ireland,* 1937, *Arts.* 6, 15, 38, 40.] The defendants provided a service to pregnant women which *inter alia* included counselling women who had an unwanted pregnancy and who sought assistance on the options open to them. Termination of pregnancy might be one of the options discussed and if the pregnant woman wished to consider this further the defendants would refer her to a medical clinic in Great Britain where abortions were performed. The plaintiff commenced proceedings which sought *inter alia* (1) a declaration that the activities of the defendants were unlawful having regard to the provisions of Article 40, s. 3, sub-s. 3 of the Constitution; (2) a declaration that the activities of the defendants amounted to a conspiracy to corrupt public morals; and (3) an injunction prohibiting the defendants from carrying on such activities. **Held** by Hamilton P., in granting the first declaration, in refusing the second declaration and in granting an injunction, 1, that the plaintiff had the *locus standi* to maintain the proceedings. That the public interest was committed to the care of the plaintiff and it was his function to represent the public in litigation. He was entitled to sue to restrain the commission of an unlawful act, to protect and vindicate a right acknowledged by the Constitution and to prevent the corruption of public morals. When the Attorney General sues with a relator, the relator need have no personal interest in the subject except his interest as a member of the public. *Moore* v. *The Attorney General & Ors.* [1930] I.R. 471 and *The Attorney General* v. *Logan* [1891] 2 Q.B. 100 applied. 2. That the right to life of the unborn had always been recognised in Ireland at common law, by statute law, and also

CONSTITUTION—Fundamental Rights.

by the Constitution as one of the unenumerated personal rights which the State guaranteed to protect and since the passing of the Eight Amendment to the Constitution, specific recognition has been given to such right. *G.* v. *An Bord Uchtála* [1980] I.R. 32; *McGee* v. *The Attorney General* [1974] I.R. 284; and *Norris* v. *The Attorney General* [1984] I.R. 36 considered. 3. That the judicial organ of government was obliged to lend its support, if sought, to the enforcement of the right to life of the unborn, to defend and vindicate that right and, if there was a threat to that right from whatever source, to protect that right from such threat. 4. That a right guaranteed by the Constitution carried with it its own right to a remedy, and did not require legislation for its enforcement unless expressly stated by the Constitution. *Educational Company of Ireland Ltd.* v. *Fitzpatrick* (*No.* 2) [1961] I.R. 345; *Byrne* v. *Ireland* [1972] I.R. 241; *Meskell* v. *C.I.E.* [1973] I.R. 121 and *In re Mead* (Unreported, Supreme Court, 26 July, 1972) applied. 5. That the offence of conspiracy to corrupt public morals could be committed even when the agreement between two or more persons was to assist in the commission of a lawful act. The giving of assistance to obtain an abortion in another jurisdiction where it was not a crime, could constitute a conspiracy to corrupt public morals however the declaration sought on this ground would not be granted as it was an offence triable on indictment and it was for a jury to decide in each case whether or not persons were likely to be corrupted. *Knuller* v. *Director of Public Prosecutions* [1973] A.C. 435 and *Attorney General* v. *Able* [1984] Q.B. 795 considered. 6. That the activities of the defendants amounted to counselling and assisting pregnant women to travel abroad to obtain further advice on abortion and to secure an abortion and, as such, were unlawful having regard to the provisions of Article 40, s. 3, sub-s. of the Constitution and as such constituted a violation of the fundamental law of the State and if damage had been suffered such activities would amount to an actionable conspiracy. 7. That the qualified right to privacy, the rights of association and freedom of expression and the right to disseminate information cannot be invoked to interfere with the fundamental right to life of the unborn. 8. That the provisions of the law of the European Communities were not applicable because the relevant activities took place within the State.

On appeal by the defendants it was **Held** by the Supreme Court (Finlay C.J., Walsh, Henchy, Griffin and Hederman JJ.) in dismissing the appeal and varying the orders of the High Court, 1, that the jurisdiction of the courts could be invoked by a party who had a *bona fide* concern

CONSTITUTION—*continued.*

and interest for the protection of the constitutionally guaranteed right to life of the unborn and it was not necessary that any specific pregnant woman and her unborn child be represented before the courts. The Attorney General was an especially appropriate person to invoke the jurisdiction of the court. *The State (Quinn)* v. *Ryan* [1965] I.R. 70 followed. 2. That it was not necessary in order to assist in the destruction of the life of the unborn for the defendants to advise or encourage the procuring of abortions, it was enough that their admitted activities were assisting pregnant women to travel outside the jurisdiction in order to have an abortion. 3. That there was no implied or unenumerated constitutional right to information about the availability of abortion outside the State, the purpose of which was to defeat the constitutional right to life of the unborn child. 4. That the order of the High Court was directed to the giving of assistance to a pregnant woman to have an abortion in another jurisdiction and did not prevent a pregnant woman herself from becoming aware of the existence of abortion outside the State accordingly no question arose as to the interpretation of the Treaty of the European Economic Community. *Attorney General (ex rel. Society for the Protection of Unborn Children Ireland Ltd.)* v. *Open Door Counselling Ltd.*

(H.C., S.C.) [1988] I.R.593 ; [1987] ILRM 477

21. —— **Religious discrimination** — *Seminary — Employment — Dismissal — Whether discrimination in dismissing teacher — Teacher also priest — Seminary obtaining funds from State but applied for lay purposes as recognised college of university — Whether primarily seminary or university — Domestic tribunal — Natural justice — Whether dismissal in breach of rules of natural justice — Bias — Whether tribunal prejudiced — Whether powers conferred on trustees of college* ultra vires *powers conferred by statute — Constitution of Ireland,* 1937, *Arts.* 44.2.3, 44.2.5 — *Maynooth College Establishment Act,* 1795 (c. 21), *s.* 3 — *Irish Universities Act,* 1908 (*c.*38), *s.* 2(4) — *Higher Education Authority Act,* 1971 (*No.* 22), *s.* 1(*c*). *Judicial review — Administrative tribunal — Discretion — Whether discretion exercised* ultra vires — *Nature of judicial review — Whether court entitled to review exercise of discretion where tribunal acted honestly and reasonably.*] The plaintiffs were lecturers in Maynooth College, and also priests of the Catholic Church. Maynooth College was established in 1795 for the purpose of better providing for the education of Catholics in Ireland. It had been a seminary only for many years, but in the 1960s began to accept lay students as well as seminarians. Pursuant to the Irish Universities Act,

CONSTITUTION—Fundamental Rights.

1908, Maynooth became a constituent college of the National University of Ireland, and under the Higher Education Act, 1971, funds were disbursed to the college by the Higher Education Authority to fund the salaries of teaching staff in the college. In 1969 the first plaintiff published an article in a newspaper which the college trustees considered to be prejudicial to ecclesiastical authority and the interests of the college. He was instructed to desist from writing such articles, but he continued to publish material which the college authorities considered prejudicial. In 1975, after the first plaintiff returned from a year's sabbatical leave, he informed the college authorities of his intention to seek laicisation and he also adopted lay, non-clerical attire. He was directed to resume clerical dress, but refused on the basis that he was seeking laicisation and that the wearing of clerical dress was not required under the college statutes. The second plaintiff also returned from sabbatical leave in 1975 wearing lay attire and also informed the college authorities of his intention to seek laicisation. He also informed them of his intention to reside outside the college. The authorities instructed the second plaintiff to resume clerical dress and that he was required under the college statutes to reside within the college, but the second plaintiff refused to accept these instructions. The trustees instituted the procedure for dismissing the plaintiffs from the college, and pursuant to this the plaintiffs were dismissed from their posts. The plaintiffs did not attend the meetings of the trustees which led to their dismissal, as they had been refused permission to attend with representatives of their trade union. The plaintiffs instituted proceedings claiming that their dismissals were invalid on the ground that the defendants were biased in their decision to dismiss since they had arrived at their decision long before the resolutions dismissing had been passed and also that, in relation to the first plaintiff, the defendants had acted *ultra vires* the statutes of the college in that the real reason for dismissing him had been his application for laicisation. In the High Court, Hamilton J. held that the dismissal of the first plaintiff was invalid for the reason alleged but found that the dismissal of the second plaintiff was valid. On appeal by the defendants against the verdict in relation to the first plaintiff and by the second plaintiff against the dismissal of his claim. **Held** by the Supreme Court (O'Higgins C.J., Henchy, Griffin, Kenny and Parke JJ.) in allowing the defendants' appeal and dismissing the second plaintiff's appeal, 1, a preconceived idea or strong view on a matter did not invalidate a decision made by an administrative body such as the trustees, provided the body concerned was willing to hear what had to be said on both sides,

CONSTITUTION—*continued.*

had resolved not to make up its mind beforehand and afforded the affected party an opportunity of making his defence, so that even though the trustees were determined in advance to see the matter through to the end this did not affect the validity of the decision to dismiss the plaintiffs. The nature of a court's jurisdiction to review the decisions of domestic tribunals discussed. *Dicta* in *White* v. *Kuzych* [195] A.C. 585 applied. 2. The fact that some of the statutes of the college had been in disuse for some time did not affect the validity of the dismissal procedure under those statutes, and since the plaintiffs had accepted the statutes when taking up their appointments they were bound by their provisions, and while Maynooth was also a pontifical university this status was one under common law only and was not cognisable or enforceable in a court of law. 3. The allegation by the plaintiffs that the trustees had contrived to dismiss them on spurious grounds required strong evidence in support, and having regard to the contents of the articles they had written and their refusal to obey the directions of the college authorities regarding dress, there was evidence before the court which justified the decisions to dismiss. 4. The trial judge's inference that the first plaintiff's application for laicisation had been a factor in the trustees' decision to dismiss him was not apparent from the evidence from which the inference was drawn and, having regard to the presumption against *mala fides* and the expertise of the trustees in the requirements of canon law, the actual grounds stated by the defendants should be accepted by the court in the absence of an alternative probable, as opposed to possible, explanation. 5. Assuming that since the college administered grants from the State they might act in contravention of the prohibition on religious discrimination in Article 44.2.3° of the Constitution, the requirement that the plaintiffs comply with the requirements of the laicisation procedure did not amount to such discrimination, and since Article 44.2.5° conferred on every religious denomination the right to manage its own affairs and maintain institutions for religious purposes the trustees were acting within this provision and were not acting in breach of any of the plaintiffs' constitutional rights. *Per* Henchy J.: the prohibition on religious discrimination must be interpreted in the light of its general objective of giving vitality to freedom of religion, and in this context the State might be required to buttress internal disabilities and discrimination within particular religions. *Quaere per* Henchy J.: whether, in view of Maynooth continuing essentially as a seminary it is constitutionally permissible for the State to be involved in its financing. *McGrath and O'Ruairc* v. *Maynooth College*

(S.C.) [1979] ILRM 166

CONSTITUTION

INTERNATIONAL RELATIONS

22. —— **Executive power** — *Government — State sovereignty — Derivation of powers of government — Requirements of the common good — People — Treaty binding upon State — Single European Act — Title III — European Political Co-operation — Foreign policy referrable to common position adopted by High Contracting Parties — Whether sovereignty fettered — Whether executive powers alienated — Government — Ratification — Scheme of constitutional powers — Breach of Constitution — Judicial review — Whether ratification proposed by Government amenable to judicial review — Constitution of Ireland,* 1937, *Arts.* 1, 5, 6, 28, 29.

Constitution — Statute — Validity — European Communities — Accession — Amendment of Constitution — Licence — Scope — Treaties establishing European Communities — Objectives — Amendment of Treaties — Whether amendment of Treaties authorised by original licence for accession — Single European Act — European Communities Act, 1972 (*No.* 27) — *European Communities (Amendment) Act,* 1986 (*No.* 37) — *Constitution of Ireland,* 1937, *Art.* 29.4.3.

Locus standi — *Treaty — Not part of domestic law — Constitutional infringement alleged — Plaintiff suffering no injury — Ratification — Reliefs — Declaration and injunction — Whether plaintiff entitled to challenge treaty ratification in absence of injury — Whether exceptional circumstances established — Single European Act.*

Injunction — Interlocutory relief — Breach of Constitution — Presumption — Whether fair question of law to be tried — Balance of convenience — Treaty — Ratification — Effect — Status quo — Preservation — Whether injunction necessary to preserve constitutional status quo — Exceptional considerations.] Article 29, s.4,sub-s. 3 of the Constitution states: "3° The State may become a member of the European Coal and Steel Community (established by Treaty signed at Paris on the 18th day of April, 1951), the European Economic Community (established by Treaty signed at Rome on the 25th day of March, 1957) and the European Atomic Energy Community (established by Treaty signed at Rome on the 25th day of March, 1957). No provision of this Constitution invalidates laws enacted, acts done or measures adopted by the State necessitated by the obligations of membership of the Communities or prevents laws enacted, acts done or measures adopted by the Communities, or institutions thereof, from having the force of law in the State." By treaties made at Luxembourg on the 17 February, 1986, and The Hague on the 28 February, 1986, and known collectively as the

Single European Act ("the SEA") the twelve Member States resolved to amend and in general expand the scope of the treaties of and governing the European Communities. Article 33 of the SEA provided: "1. This Act will be ratified by the High Contracting Parties in accordance with their respective constitutional requirements. The instruments of ratification will be deposited with the Government of the Italian Republic. 2. This Act will enter into force on the first day of the month following that in which the instrument of ratification is deposited of the last Signatory State to fulfil that formality." Title III of the SEA embodied a separate treaty whereby each of the High Contracting Parties agreed to adopt its foreign policy positions to those of the others and refrain from impeding a consensus and joint action within a structured framework known as European Political Cooperation. Title II embodied structural changes to the treaties of and governing the European Communities and, in the case of the European Economic Community, provided for increased use of voting by qualified majority in the European Council; the enumeration of detailed objectives of the European Economic Community; and a new court of first instance inferior to the Court of Justice of the European Communities. By the European Communities (Amendment) Act, 1986, most of the provisions of the SEA, with the exception *inter alia* of Title III, were inserted into the European Communities Act, 1972, whereby they became part of the domestic law of the State. Section 3, sub-s. 3 of the Act of 1986 provided that the Act should come into operation on such date as the Minister for Foreign Affairs appointed, although the Act itself was enacted on the 23 December, 1986. The plaintiff issued a plenary summons on the 22 December, 1986 seeking essentially declarations that any purported ratification of the SEA would be void having regard to the provisions of the Constitution and injunctions restraining such ratification. In addition he sought a declaration that the European Communities (Amendment) Bill, 1986, (enacted the following day) would, if enacted, be repugnant to the Constitution and null and void in purporting to enact certain parts of the SEA into domestic law. Upon a hearing for interlocutory injunctions it was contended by the defendants that there was no fair question of law raised for trial on the issues and objected that the plaintiff lacked *locus standi* for interlocutory relief and that his application amounted to an abuse of the process of the court. **Held** by Barrington J., in granting the interlocutory injunctions, that the plaintiff had raised a fair question of law to be tried on the issues for which there were weighty and countervailing considerations justifying a departure from the received rule of practice

CONSTITUTION—International Relations.

regarding *locus standi* and in addition the plaintiff had standing to the extent that he claimed that the Constitution itself was being amended in the absence of the consultation by referendum with the plaintiff and the electorate specifically provided by the Constitution. *Campus Oil Ltd.* v. *Minister for Industry and Energy* (*No.* 2) [1983] I.R. 88 and *Cahill* v. *Sutton* [1980] I.R. 269 considered. Upon full hearing on the substantive issues, it was **Held** by the High Court (Hamilton P., Barrington and Carroll JJ.) in refusing the reliefs sought and discharging the interlocutory injunctions, 1, that those parts of the SEA enacted into domestic law by the European Communities (Amendment) Act, 1986, were within the scope of the constitutional licence for accession to the European Communities granted by the Third Amendment to the Constitution and embodied in Article 29, s. 4, sub-s. 3 thereof. 2. The plaintiff lacked the required *locus standi* to challenge the remainder of the SEA, being Title III, as it had not been incorporated into domestic law and he was unable to show any special injury or infringement of his rights. *Cahill* v. *Sutton* [1980] I.R. 269 applied. *Per Curiam:* That the acts of the Government are entitled to a presumption of constitutional validity, in the same way as legislation passed by the Oireachtas. The plaintiff appealed to the Supreme Court from the judgment and order of the High Court and then obtained in the Supreme Court similar interim and interlocutory injunctions pending the hearing of the appeal. On the issue of the constitutionality of the European Communities (Amendment) Act, 1986, it was **Held** by the Supreme Court (Finlay C.J., Walsh, Henchy, Griffin and Hederman JJ.), in refusing to declare the Act invalid having regard to the provisions of the Constitution, 1, that the plaintiff had *locus standi* to challenge the Act in the particular circumstances where its coming into force would affect every citizen notwithstanding the plaintiff's failure to prove the threat of any special injury or prejudice peculiar to him arising from the Act. Principles in *Cahill* v. *Sutton* [1980] I.R. 269 considered. 2. That so much of the SEA which was to become law by the Act of 1986 was properly within the constitutional licence of Article 29, s. 4, sub-s. 3, which authorised the State's accession to a living, dynamic Community, and the proposed changes to qualified voting in the European Council had already been anticipated in the establishing Treaties after the transitional period; the allegedly new objectives of the SEA brought into Irish law amounted to no more than a more specific enumeration of the objectives of the establishing Treaties; and the proposed new court of first instance did not in any way extend the primacy of the Court of Justice of the European Communities over the

CONSTITUTION—*continued.*

Irish courts beyond that already authorised by Article 29, s. 4, sub-s. 3 of the Constitution. On the issue of Title III, being the treaty whereby Ireland agreed to adopt its foreign policy positions within the framework of European Political Cooperation, not being part of the domestic law incorporated by the Act of 1986, it was **Held** by the Supreme Court (Walsh, Henchy and Hederman JJ.; Finlay C.J. and Griffin J. dissenting), in allowing the appeal and declaring the ratification of Title III unconstitutional, 1, (Finlay C.J. and Griffin J. concurring) that the Constitution vested in the Government the executive power of the State in its external relations, subject to the provisions of the Constitution, and the Government's conduct of foreign policy was beyond the purview of the courts. *Boland* v. *An Taoiseach* [1974] I.R. 338 followed. 2. That where, however, in its conduct of foreign policy the Government purported to alienate any powers of government or fetter the sovereignty of the State, then the Government acted beyond the powers entrusted by the Constitution to it, and the courts, as sole arbiters upon breaches of constitutional restraints, were obliged to restrain the Government from so acting. 3. That since Title III of the SEA would bind the State to concede part of its sovereignty in its relations with other states and to conduct foreign policy without regard to the requirements of the common good, the ratification proposed by the Government was impermissible in the absence of authorisation by the Constitution. *Per* Finlay C.J. and Griffin J., dissenting: Title III did not oblige the State to cede any sovereignty in its foreign policy. The courts would have a right and duty to intervene only where the Government's conduct of foreign relations constituted an actual or threatened invasion of the constitutional rights of the citizen. *Crotty* v. *An Taoiseach*

(H.C., S.C.) [1987] I.R.713 ; [1987] ILRM 400

23. —— **Executive power** — *Government — Anglo-Irish Agreement — Status of Northern Ireland — Whether Agreement contrary to Articles 2 and 3 of the Constitution.*

Constitution — Executive — International relations — Separation of powers — Judicial review of international treaty — Presumption of constitutionality of international treaty — Interpretation of international treaty — Whether agreement constitutes an unconstitutional fettering of the executive power to deal with international relations.

Locus standi — *Whether plaintiffs entitled to challenge international agreement. Constitution of Ireland,* 1937, *Preamble, Arts.* 1, 2, 3, 15, 28, 29.] On the 15 November, 1985, an agreement, known as the Anglo-Irish Agreement, was reached between the respective governments of

CONSTITUTION—International Relations.

Ireland and the United Kingdom. This agreement contained, *inter alia,* provisions affirming the existing status of Northern Ireland and recognising that this status would only be changed with the consent of the majority of the population of Northern Ireland: provisions establishing an intergovernmental conference and a secretariat to deal with matters covered by the agreement; and provisions allowing the Irish government to put forward its views on devolution and major legislative and policy proposals within Northern Ireland in relation to the interests of the minority community in Northern Ireland. Other provisions related to security and legal matters, cross-border co-operation and economic development. The plaintiffs, who were both born in and resident in Northern Ireland, sought a declaration that the Anglo-Irish Agreement was contrary to the provisions of the Constitution of Ireland, 1937. In particular, they argued that, in recognising the legitimacy of the present status of Northern Ireland, the agreement violated Articles 2 and 3 of the Constitution and that the intergovernmental conference and its secretariat established by the agreement restricted the government of Ireland in the exercise of the external relations power of the state, contrary to Articles 28 and 29 of the Constitution. The defendants argued, *inter alia,* that the plaintiffs did not have the *locus standi* necessary to challenge the agreement. **Held** by Barrington J., in dismissing the plaintiffs' constitutional challenge to the Anglo-Irish Agreement, 1, that, having regard to the Preamble to the Constitution of 1937 and to Articles 2 and 3 thereof, it would be inappropriate for the court to refuse to hear the plaintiffs' case on the grounds of lack of *locus standi,* particularly since the plaintiffs were acting sincerely and raised an important constitutional issue. *Cahill* v. *Sutton* [1980] I.R. 269 and *Crotty* v. *An Taoiseach* [1987] I.R. 713 considered. 2. That the formulation of national policy by the government must be free from judicial interference but the government, in exercising the executive power of the state in the area of international relations, is subject to the Constitution of 1937 and, therefore, to judicial review by the courts. However, the conduct of foreign policy did not easily lend itself to judicial review and the courts should exercise appropriate restraint in this area. *Crotty* v. *An Taoiseach* [1987] I.R. 713; *Boland* v. *An Taoiseach* [1974] I.R. 338 and *The State (Gilliland)* v. *Governor of Mountjoy Prison* [1987] I.R. 201 considered. 3. That there was a presumption that in entering into a particular treaty, the government did not violate the Constitution of 1937. The onus rested on the plaintiffs to establish that the treaty complained of expressly contradicted some provision of the Constitution. *Buckley and*

CONSTITUTION—*continued.*

Others (Sinn Féin) v. *The Attorney General* [1950] I.R. 67 applied. 4. That an international treaty must be interpreted having regard to international law and such interpretation should not be coloured by reference to the Constitution. *East Donegal Co-Operative Society* v. *The Attorney General* [1970] I.R. 317 distinguished. 5. That the territorial claim to "the whole island of Ireland" contained in Article 2 of the Constitution was a political claim and not a legal right. Article 3 of the Constitution placed a temporary constitutional limit on the jurisdiction of the national parliament to legislate for the whole of Ireland pending the re-integration of the national territory. Accordingly, Article 1 of the Anglo-Irish Agreement, which recognised the present status of Northern Ireland, did not offend against Articles 2 and 3 of the Constitution. *Russell* v. *Fanning* [1988] I.R. 505 and *In Re The Criminal Law (Jurisdiction) Bill,* 1975 [1977] I.R. 129 approved. *The People* v. *Ruttledge* [1978] I.R. 376; *The State (Gilsenan)* v. *McMorrow* [1978] I.R. 360 and *Boland* v. *An Taoiseach* [1974] I.R. 338 considered. 6. That Article 29 of the Constitution guides the government towards a pacific settlement of the dispute with the United Kingdom over the partition of Ireland, in accordance with the generally recognised principles of international law. 7. That the Anglo-Irish agreement did not involve an unconstitutional fettering of the executive powers of the government. Article 29, s. 5 of the Constitution, clearly implies that the State may enter into international agreements and, in so doing, may commit itself to dealing with some aspect of its foreign policy in a particular manner. The intergovernmental conference was merely a forum in which the representatives of the two governments met on a regular basis to discuss matters relating to Northern Ireland and did not involve the transfer of any matters relating to the conduct of foreign policy to a supranational authority. *Crotty* v. *An Taoiseach* [1987] I.R. 713 distinguished. 8. That the concept of the common good of the Irish people did not exclude special concern for minority interests within the community and, therefore, it was constitutionally acceptable for the government to enter into a treaty whereby it committed itself to have particular regard and concern for the rights of the minority in Northern Ireland. 9. That the failure of the Irish government to consult with the Unionist population of Northern Ireland and the system of "direct rule" of Northern Ireland by the Parliament of the United Kingdom, were both political matters which were not subject to review by the courts. *McGimpsey* v. *Ireland*

(H.C.) [1988] I.R.567

24. —— **Extradition treaty** — *International*

CONSTITUTION—International Relations.

agreement involving a charge upon public funds — Extradition treaty between Ireland and the United States of America — Whether treaty a charge upon the public funds — Meaning of "charge" — Approval of Dáil Éireann — Means by which treaty expenses approved by Dáil Éireann — Constitution of Ireland, 1937, *Art.* 29 — *Extradition Act,* 1965 (*No.* 17) — *Extradition Act,* 1965 (*Part II*) (*No.* 20) *Order,* 1984 (*S.I. No.* 300).

Extradition — Extraditable offence — Correspondence with offence under Irish law — Defence of provocation to murder charge — Whether murder charge corresponds if ambit of defence varies — Defence of provocation not actually open to prosecutor — whether relevant to extradition — Extradition Act, 1965 (*No.* 17), (*Part II*).] Dáil Éireann approval of an international agreement involving a charge upon public funds is sufficiently satisfied, in the case of an extradition treaty, where such treaty is adopted pursuant to Part II of the Extradition Act, 1965, and Dáil Éireann by s. 5 of the same Act has made a provision for expenses arising out of the Act. **So held** by Egan J. *Quaere* whether an offence under Irish law corresponds for the purpose of extradition proceedings with an offence under foreign law, where the ambit of a defence to a charge of that offence does not similarly correspond. *The State (McCaud)* v. *Governor of Mountjoy Prison*

(H.C.) [1985] I.R. 68; [1986] ILRM 129

25. —— **Extradition treaty** — *Whether treaty binding on State — Whether treaty charge on public funds — Meaning of "costas" or "charge" — Language in Constitution — Interpretation — Whether common meaning to prevail over distinct meaning — Conflict between Irish and English text — Public funds — Statutory provisions — Treaty terms — Whether obligation of assistance of Attorney General a charge on public funds — Whether expenses of extradition to be borne by the State a charge on public funds — Whether Dáil Éireann approval necessary to bind State — Whether the terms of the treaty or the nature or extent of the charge to be approved by Dáil Éireann — Application of extradition provisions — Government order — Whether Government order "a law" — Detention arising from combination of statute and Government order — Application of non-binding treaty — Legality of detention pending extradition — Whether law authorising detention consistent with the provisions of the Constitution — Case stated by High Court to Supreme Court — Extradition Act,* 1965 (*Part II*) (*No.* 20) *Order,* 1984 (*S.I. No.* 300) — *Extradition Act,* 1965 (*No.* 17), *Part II, ss.* 5, 8, 10, 25, 26, 29, 47, 50 — *Constitution (Consequential Provisions) Act,* 1937 (*No.* 40), *s.* 6 —

CONSTITUTION—*continued.*

Appropriation Act, 1984 (*No.* 26) — *Exchequer & Audit Department Act,* 1866 (*c.* 39) — *Constitution of Saorstát Éireann,* 1922, *art.* 61 — *Constitution of Ireland,* 1937, *Arts.* 11, 15, 25, 29, 40, 50.

Constitution — Statute — Construction — Extradition treaty — Incorporation into domestic law — State not bound by treaty — Whether statutory sub-section automatically incorporating treaty into domestic law — Legislative powers — Delegation — Whether delegation constitutional — Presumption of constitutionality of sub-section — Extradition Act, 1965 (*No.* 17), *ss.* 4, 8 — *Constitution of Ireland,* 1937, *Arts.* 15, 28, 29.

Extradition — Procedure — District Court hearing under Part II of Extradition Act, 1965 — *Whether statement of offences disclosed corresponding offences in Irish law — Extradition orders of District Court — Contents of orders — Failure to specify corresponding Irish offences — Error in recitals — Rule of specialty — Whether face of order discloses want or excess of jurisdiction — Extradition Act,* 1965 (*No.* 17), *Part II.*] The prosecutor, a U.S. citizen, was arrested on foot of a provisional warrant and committed to prison pending the execution of an order for his extradition to the U.S.A, made after the statutory hearing in the District Court pursuant to Part II of the Extradition Act, 1965. He obtained in the High Court conditional orders of habeas corpus challenging the legality of his detention pursuant to Article 40 of the Constitution on the grounds *inter alia:* (*a*) that the statement of offences furnished by the United States of America in compliance with s. 25, sub-s. 1 (*b*) of the Extradition Act, 1965, did not disclose any offence under Irish law; (*b*) that the District Court order of extradition was bad on its face and invalid in that it (i) failed to specify the offences in Irish law which corresponded to the charges on foot of which the prosecutor's extradition was sought; (ii) failed to disclose whether the District Justice had conducted the proper statutory enquiry to determine if the charges corresponded to offences in Irish law; (iii) failed to satisfy the requirements as to speciality contained in the treaty of extradition; (*c*) that the treaty of extradition between Ireland and the United States of America, being an international agreement involving a charge on public funds, was not binding on the State in the absence of the approval of Dáil Éireann of the terms of the said treaty in accordance with the requirements of Article 29, s. 5, sub-s. 2 of the Constitution and therefore that the prosecutor's detention on foot of a government order applying a non-binding extradition treaty was illegal. On the respondent showing cause, it was **Held** by Barrington J., in agreeing to state a case to the

CONSTITUTION—International Relations.

Supreme Court on the validity of the law detaining the prosecutor, 1, that the extradition orders of the District Court did not have to specify the particular offences in Irish law to which the extradition charges corresponded in proceedings under Part II of the Extradition Act, 1965. *The State (Trimbole)* v. *The Governor of Mountjoy Prison* [1985] I.R. 550 approved. 2. That such errors as were found in the recitals to the orders for extradition did not disclose want or excess of jurisdiction or that the hearing in the District Court was not conducted other than in accordance with the requirements of law. 3. That the failure to specify corresponding offences in Irish law on the face of the extradition orders did not infringe any rule of specialty. It was sufficient that the order specified the American offences charged since specialty is a matter for the requesting state after extradition has been effected. 4. That the terms of the treaty of extradition between Ireland and the United States of America imposed a charge on public funds and, in the absence of the approval of Dáil Éireann required by Article 29, s.5, sub-s.2 of the Constitution, the treaty was not binding on the State. *The State (McCaud)* v. *The Governor of Mountjoy Prison* [1985] I.R. 68 considered. 5. That the Extradition Act, 1965 (Part II) (No. 20) Order, 1984, made by the Government pursuant to s. 8 of the Act, in purporting to apply the provisions of Part II of the Act in relation to the United States of America on foot of a treaty not binding on the State was accordingly invalid having regard to the provisions of Article 29, s. 5, sub-s. 2 of the Constitution. 6. That while the prosecutor was being detained by a law, namely the application of Part II of the Extradition Act, 1965, by Government order in relation to the United States of America, such law was invalid having regard to the provisions of the Constitution and accordingly the question of the validity of such law would be referred to the Supreme Court by way of case stated in accordance with the provisions of Article 40, s. 4, sub-s. 3 of the Constitution. Pending settlement of the case stated to the Supreme Court the prosecutor was permitted to make a further submission to the High Court. He submitted that if the effect of s. 8, sub-s. 5 of the Extradition Act, 1965, was that any extradition treaty concluded by the State was therefore automatically incorporated into the domestic law, then that subsection was repugnant to Article 15, s. 2 of the Constitution. Article 15, s. 2 vests the sole and exclusive power of making laws in the Oireachtas. If s. 8, sub-s. 5 of the Extradition Act, 1965, was self-executing it involved an unconstitutional delegation of legislative powers to the executive and was therefore invalid. Therefore the prosecutor's detention if based on

CONSTITUTION—*continued.*

such automatic incorporation of the treaty of extradition between Ireland and the United States of America into Irish domestic law was illegal. In rejecting the submission and refusing to include it in the case stated it was **Held** by Barrington J., 1, that the submission that s. 8, sub-s. 5 of the Extradition Act, 1965, automatically incorporated all extradition treaties into domestic law was not supported by construction of the whole of s. 8, which provided that extradition treaties are only incorporated into domestic law by Government order only, pursuant to s. 8, sub-section 1. This delegation to the executive of powers otherwise reserved to the legislature is nevertheless constitutional in that by the procedure enacted by s. 4 of the same Act every such Government order still remained subject to Oireachtas scrutiny and annulment. *Cityview Press* v. *An Chomhairle Oiliúna* [1980] I.R. 381 applied. 2. Accordingly the prosecutor had failed to rebut the presumption that s. 8, sub-s. 5 of the Extradition Act, 1965, does not violate the Constitution. On the issue of jurisdiction for the case stated from the High Court, it was **Held** by the Supreme Court (Finlay C.J., Henchy and Griffin JJ.; Hederman and McCarthy JJ. dissenting) in deciding to hear the case stated, 1, that the prosecutor's detention arose from a combination of s. 29 of the Extradition Act, 1965, together with the specific application by the Government order of Part II of the Act to the United States of America, and such particular application was subject to scrutiny and annulment by the Oireachtas. The effect of such combination was that the Extradition Act, 1965, (Part II) (No. 20) Order,1984, was a law within the meaning of Article 40, s. 4, sub-s. 3 of the Constitution and accordingly the High Court had jurisdiction to refer the question of the validity of such law to the Supreme Court by way of case stated. *The State (Sheerin)* v. *Kennedy* [1966] I.R. 379 considered. 2. That since the case stated involved the question of the validity of a law having regard to the provisions of the Constitution it was therefore subject to the requirements of Article 34, s. 4, sub-s. 5 directing that the decision of the Supreme Court shall be pronounced by a single judgment. 3. (*Per* Hederman and McCarthy JJ. dissenting) Article 15, s. 2 of the Constitution vests the sole and exclusive power of making laws in the Oireachtas. The Government order was made pursuant to a law already enacted and was not a law for the purposes of Article 40, s. 4, sub-section 3. Therefore, the High Court did not have jurisdiction granted by Article 40, s. 4, sub-s. 3 to refer the question of the validity of such a Government order to the Supreme Court by way of case stated. *Pigs Marketing Board* v. *Donnelly (Dublin) Ltd.* [1939] I.R. 413 approved. *The*

CONSTITUTION—International Relations.

State (Sheerin) v. *Kennedy* [1966] I.R.379; *The State (Browne)* v. *Feran* [1967] I.R. 147 and *Cityview Press* v. *An Chomhairle Oiliúna* [1980] I.R. 381 considered. On the substantive issue of the case stated, it was **Held** by the Supreme Court in deciding against the validity of the Government order, 1, that an international agreement the terms of which imposed a charge on public funds, became binding on the State in accordance with the requirements of art. 29, s. 5, sub-s. 2 only where such terms were approved by Dáil Éireann. 2. That the terms of the treaty of extradition between Ireland and the United States of America included in art. XVII provisions that Ireland as a requested State should bear all the expenses of the United States of America arising out of the arrest, detention, extradition proceedings and surrender of the person sought under the treaty. In addition where Ireland was the requesting State it should bear all expenses arising out of document translation of documents and the transportation of the person sought from the place of extradition to Ireland, and accordingly these terms constituted a charge upon public funds. 3. That in the absence of Dáil Éireann approval of its terms required by Article 29, s. 5, sub-s. 2 of the Constitution, the treaty of extradition was not binding on the State and the Extradition Act, 1965, (Part II) (No. 20) Order, 1984, which applied the provisions of Part II of the Extradition Act, 1965, to the United States of America on foot of such treaty, was a law which was invalid having regard to the provisions of the Constitution. *The State (Gilliland)* v. *Governor of Mountjoy Prison.*
(H.C., S.C.) [1987] I.R. 201; [1987] ILRM 278; [1986] ILRM 381

Liberty, right to, *see* Nos. 15, 16, 17, 41
Locus standi, *see* Nos. 20, 22, 23, 34, 39, 42, 45, 47, 53
Personal rights, *see* Nos. 10-20, 39-43
Privacy, right to, *see* Nos. 18, 39
Procreate, right to, *see* No. 19
Property rights, *see* Nos. 13, 44-8
Religion, *see* No. 21
Right to earn livelihood, *see* Nos. 42, 43

STATUTE — VALIDITY

Courts. Nos. 26-33
Delegated legislation. Nos. 34, 35
Elections. Nos. 36, 37
Family. No. 38
Personal rights. Nos. 39-43
Property rights. Nos. 44-8
Trial of offences. Nos. 49-51

26. —— **Courts** — *Administration of justice — Interference — Criminal law — Indictable offence*

CONSTITUTION—Statute.

— Preliminary examination — Refusal of judge to send accused forward for trial — Director of Public Prosecutions sending accused forward for trial — Enactment invalid — Stare decisis *— Courts of Justice Act,* 1936 (*No.* 48), *s.* 62 *— Criminal Procedure Act,* 1967 (*No.* 12), *ss.* 5-8 *— Prosecution of Offences Act,* 1974 (*No.* 22), *s.* 3 *— Constitution of Ireland,* 1937, *Arts.* 6, 30, 34, 50.] The plaintiff was arrested and charged before the District Court with the commission of two indictable offences. In performance of the duty expressly imposed on him by s. 5 of the Act of 1967, the District Justice conducted a preliminary examination of those charges and at the conclusion of that examination, being of the opinion that there was insufficient evidence to put the plaintiff on trial on those charges, the District Justice ordered, pursuant to s. 8, sub-s. 5, of the Act of 1967, that the plaintiff be discharged. After the plaintiff had been discharged, the first defendant, in purported exercise of the powers conferred by s. 62 of the Act of 1936, directed that the plaintiff be sent forward to the Circuit Court for trial on indictment on the same charges. The plaintiff claimed in the High Court a declaration that the relevant provisions of s. 62 of the Act of 1936 (*inter alia*) were repugnant to the provisions of the Constitution and had no legal effect. **Held by** Gannon J., in refusing to make the declarations sought by the plaintiff, 1, that an order of a District Justice pursuant to s. 8, sub-s. 5, of the Act of 1967 does not constitute a determination of a justiciable controversy *inter partes.* 2. That a direction given by the Director of Public Prosecutions pursuant to s. 62 of the Act of 1936 is the initiation of a criminal prosecution which is authorised by Article 30, s. 3, of the Constitution and s. 3 of the Act of 1974. 3. That the provisions of s. 62 of the Act of 1936 did not infringe either the personal rights of the plaintiff under the Constitution or the provisions of the Constitution relating to the administration of justice. *The State (Shanahan)* v. *The Attorney General* [1964] I.R. 239 (S.C.) applied. On appeal by the plaintiff it was **Held** by the Supreme Court, in allowing the appeal, 1, that a District Justice, in conducting a preliminary examination pursuant to s. 5, sub-s. 1, of the Act of 1967 and in determining whether an accused should be sent forward for trial on indictment or should be discharged, is exercising the judicial power of the State as conferred on the District Court by law in accordance with the Constitution of Ireland, 1937. *The State (C.)* v. *Minister for Justice* [1967] I.R. 106 considered. 2. That s. 62 of the Act of 1936 — having been applied by s. 48 of the Courts (Supplemental Provisions) Act, 1961, to the present courts established by the Courts (Constitution and Establishment) Act, 1961, as if s. 62 had

CONSTITUTION—Statute.

been enacted by the former Act of 1961 — must be treated as a section of a statute passed by the National Parliament after the enactment of the Constitution. 3. That the only, and the intended, effect of a direction given pursuant to s. 62 of the Act of 1936 is to render a judicial determination made by a District Justice nugatory and, thereby, to frustrate an order of the District Court. 4. That, accordingly, the provisions of s. 62 of the Act of 1936 constitute an interference by the executive in the judicial domain and are invalid having regard to the provisions of the Constitution. *The State (Shanahan)* v. *The Attorney General* [1964] I.R. 239 (S.C.) not followed. 5. That it had not been established that the provisions of s. 3 of the Act of 1974 were similarly invalid. *Costello* v. *D.P.P.*

(H.C., S.C.) [1984] I.R.436; [1984] ILRM 413

27. —— **Courts** — *Administration of justice — Interference — Statutory power — Validity — Indictable offence — Preliminary examination — Accused sent forward for trial by District Justice — Indictment subsequently framed by D.P.P. — Indictment containing substituted counts charging other offences — Whether substitution of counts rendered nugatory a judicial determination — Whether procedure unfair or discriminatory — Criminal Procedure Act,* 1967 (*No.* 12), *s.* 18 — *Constitution of Ireland,* 1937, *Art.* 34.] Section 8, sub-s. 2 of the Criminal Procedure Act, 1967, provides that if a District Justice conducting a preliminary examination of an indictable offence is of opinion that there is a sufficient case to put the accused on trial for some indictable offence other than that charged, he shall cause him to be charged with that offence. By s. 18 of the Act, where a person has been sent forward by a District Justice for trial for an indictable offence, the indictment against him may include, either in substitution for or in addition to counts charging the offence for which he has been sent forward, any counts founded on any of the documents and exhibits considered by the Justice at the preliminary examination, being counts which may lawfully be joined in the same indictment. The applicant was charged with an indictable offence. He elected for trial in the Circuit Court and, following a preliminary examination before a District Justice, was sent forward for trial on that charge. The first respondent, exercising the power conferred by s. 18 of the Act of 1967, framed an indictment containing counts charging two other offences, in substitution for the count charging the offence for which the applicant had been sent forward for trial. The substituted counts were founded on the documents and exhibits considered by the Justice at the preliminary examination. On the plaintiff's

CONSTITUTION—*continued.*

application by way of judicial review for a declaration that s. 18 was invalid having regard to the provisions of the Constitution on the grounds that it permitted an interference by the executive in the administration of justice it was **Held** by Lardner J., in refusing the application, 1, that, since the order made by the District Justice sending the applicant forward for trial was not a final determination of the guilt or innocence of the applicant but merely a determination that there was a sufficient case to put him on trial, it did not constitute an administration of justice. *Costello* v. *Director of Public Prosecutions* [1984] I.R. 436 distinguished. 2. That it followed that the substitution in the indictment of two fresh counts for that on which the applicant had been sent forward for trial was not an interference with the exercise of the judicial power of the State. On appeal by the applicant it was **Held** by the Supreme Court (Finlay C.J., Hamilton P., Walsh, Griffin and Hederman JJ.), in disallowing the appeal, 1, that the power of the first respondent to add or substitute counts after the applicant had been sent forward for trial was not an unfair or discriminatory procedure since any such additional or substituted counts had to be founded on the documents and exhibits considered by the District Justice. 2. That the right of a person charged with an indictable offence to a preliminary examination before a District Justice was not a constitutional but rather a statutory right. 3. That the fact that the District Justice did not exercise his power under s. 8, sub-s. 2 of the Act of 1967 to cause the applicant to be charged with additional offences and to send him forward for trial for those offences, did not constitute a finding by him that the offence in respect of which he did sent the applicant forward for trial was the only offence supported by the evidence. 4. That it followed that the substitution of counts in the indictment by the respondent did not conflict with or render nugatory the order of the District Justice. *Costello* v. *Director of Public Prosecutions* [1984] I.R. 436 distinguished. 5. That it was an inherent part of the function of the first respondent in the prosecution of indictable offences, and an administrative rather than a judicial function, to frame the precise form of the indictment, thereby ensuring that the true issue between the people and the accused was properly and fairly put before the court. 6. That the judge presiding over the trial retained an ultimate discretion as to whether the procedure of trying an accused on substituted counts, or any counts included in an indictment, was lawful and fair. *O'Shea* v. *D.P.P.*

(H.C., S.C.) [1988] I.R.655

28. —— **Courts** — *Administration of justice —*

CONSTITUTION—Statute.

Judicial function — Exception — Limited functions and powers of a judicial nature — Tribunal — Fair procedures — Natural justice — Professions — Disciplinary code — Medical practitioners — Publication of finding of tribunal — Review by High Court — Personal rights — Vindication — Medical Practitioners Act, 1978 (*No.* 4), *ss.* 45-8 — *Constitution of Ireland,* 1937, *Arts. 34, 40.*] Upon an allegation of professional misconduct being made against a medical practitioner, it is provided by s. 45 of the Act of 1978 that the Fitness to Practise Committee may enquire into that allegation and report their findings to the Medical Council. Section 46 provides that, having considered that report, the Council may decide (*inter alia*) that the practitioner's name should be erased from the general register of medical practitioners and, in that event, the practitioner may apply to the High Court under s. 46 for an order cancelling the decision of the Council; if no such application is made by the practitioner, the Council may apply to the High Court for an order affirming its decision. Under sub-s. 5 of s. 46 the findings of the Committee and the decision of the Council on any report made to it by the Committee may be made public if the medical practitioner has been found, as a result of such enquiry, to have been guilty of professional misconduct. An allegation was made that the plaintiff, a medical practitioner, was guilty of professional misconduct. The Committee enquired into that allegation and the plaintiff was represented by solicitor and counsel at the enquiry. When the Committee, at the conclusion of their enquiry, reported their finding on the allegation to the defendant Council, that defendant decided that the plaintiff's name should be removed from the general register of medical practitioners. The plaintiff applied to the High Court under s. 46 for an order cancelling the decision of the defendant Council but, before that application had been determined, the plaintiff brought this action in the High Court and claimed therein declarations that ss. 45 and 46 of the Act of 1978 were invalid having regard to the provisions of the Constitution and that the decision of the defendant Council was null and void. At the trial of the plaintiff's action it was **Held** by Finlay P., in dismissing the plaintiff's claims, 1, that, at the hearing by the High Court of the plaintiff's application for the cancellation of the decision of the defendant Council made pursuant to s. 46 of the Act of 1978, the true construction of that Act would require (*a*) that an onus of proof should lie upon the defendant Council to establish (i) the correctness of the finding that the plaintiff had been guilty of an act or acts of professional misconduct and (ii) the correctness of the defendant Council's decision that the plaintiff's name should be erased from

CONSTITUTION—*continued.*

the said register and (*b*) that, in the event of the court affirming the finding of professional misconduct, the plaintiff be given an opportunity to address the court upon the appropriate penalty to be imposed on him. *In re M. a Doctor* [1984] I.R. 479 considered. 2. That, apart from the power to publish the finding of the Committee or the decision of the Council and the power of the Council under s. 48 to advise, admonish, or censure a medical practitioner, neither the Committee nor the Council was invested by the impugned enactments with any powers that were final and binding on the medical practitioner whose conduct had been investigated under s. 45 of the Act and that, accordingly, the exercise of those powers (apart from the two exceptions) did not constitute the administration of justice within the meaning of Article 34, s. 1, of the Constitution. *In re the Solicitors Act, 1954* [1960] I.R. 239 considered. 3. That the powers mentioned in those two exceptions, even if they involved the administration of justice, were limited functions and powers of a judicial nature and, as such, were permitted by the exemption provided by Article 37 of the Constitution. 4. That, in view of the onus of proof to be discharged by the defendant Council at the hearing of the plaintiff's application for cancellation of that defendant's decision, the fact that the plaintiff would make that application as a person already condemned by the Committee and the Council did not constitute a lack of fair procedures, nor did the fact that the plaintiff had no opportunity to make submissions to the defendant Council before it made its decision. *East Donegal Co-Operative* v. *The Attorney General* [1970] I.R. 317 considered. 5. That, when permitted by s. 46 of the Act of 1978, the publication of a finding of the Committee adverse to a medical practitioner, or the publication of an adverse decision of the Council affecting him, would not constitute an unjust attack on the good name of the practitioner contrary to the provisions of Article 40, s. 3, sub-s.2, of the Constitution. *M.* v. *The Medical Council*

(H.C.) [1984] I.R.485

29. —— **Courts** — *Administration of justice — Judicial function — Invasion — Street and house-to-house collection — Application for collections permit refused — Chief Superintendent of opinion that proceeds would benefit an unlawful organisation — Unsuccessful appeal to District Court — Issue of fact as to whether Chief Superintendent was correct in the opinion he arrived at excluded from District Justice's appellate jurisdiction — Whether appeal procedure constitutionally invalid — Whether unwarranted invasion of judicial power — Whether open to prosecutor, on an*

CONSTITUTION—Statute.

application for certiorari, to challenge the constitutionality of legislation — Constitution of Ireland, 1937, *Art.* 34 — *Street and House-to-House Collections Act,* 1962 (*No.* 13), *s.* 13(4).] S. 3 of the Street and House-to-House Collections Act, 1962, makes it a criminal offence to hold or be concerned in the holding of a collection of money from the public by means of collections in the public streets or in the course of house to house visits save in accordance with a collection permit granted under the Act. Applications for permits are required to be made to the chief superintendent of the garda station for any locality in which it is proposed to hold such a collection. S. 9 provides that a chief superintendent shall not grant a collection permit if he is of the opinion that the proceeds of the collection would be used for any one of a number of specified and objectionable purposes. S. 13 provides that where an application for a permit is refused by a chief superintendent the applicant may appeal to the District Court against the refusal and if, on the hearing of the appeal, the court is satisfied, having regard to all the circumstances of the case, that the application should not have been refused the court may direct the chief superintendent to grant the collection permit in accordance with the application. S. 13(4) provides however, that if a member of the Garda Síochána not below rank of Inspector states on oath that he has reasonable grounds for believing that the proceeds of the collection to which the collection permit relates will be used for an unlawful object or contrary to public morality or for the benefit of an unlawful organisation such an appeal shall be disallowed. The prosecutor was chairman of a local national H-block umbrella committee, and was refused a permit by a garda superintendent pursuant to s. 9(*b*) of the Act. The prosecutor appealed to the District Court. The chief superintendent then gave evidence that he had reasonable grounds to believe that the proceeds of the collection would be used for an unlawful object or contrary to public morality or for the benefit of an organisation the membership of which was unlawful. The District Justice then stated that he had no alternative but to disallow the appeal because of the provisions of s. 13(4). The prosecutor sought to quash the District Court order on certiorari alleging, *inter alia,* that the s. 13(4) procedure was constitutionally invalid. The application was refused by Costello J. (see [1982] ILRM 568) and the prosecutor appealed to the Supreme Court. **Held** by the Supreme Court (Walsh, Henchy, Griffin, Hederman and McCarthy JJ.) allowing the appeal, s. 13(4) was invalid having regard to the provisions of the Constitution because it constituted an impermissible invasion of the judicial power in that it requires in the

CONSTITUTION—*continued.*

circumstances outlined therein that judicial proceedings within the exclusive competence of the courts are to be determined by the Oireachtas. Principles in *Buckley* v. *Attorney General* [1950] I.R. 67 and *Maher* v. *Attorney General* [1973] I.R. 140 applied; *The State (O'Rourke)* v. *Kelly,* Supreme Court, unreported, 28 July 1980, distinguished. *Per curiam* It is well established that a challenge to the constitutionality of provisions of an Act of the Oireachtas may be raised on an application of certiorari. *The State (McEldowney)* v. *Kelleher*

(S.C.) [1985] ILRM 10

30. —— **Courts** — *Administration of justice — Judicial function — Revenue — Pay as You Earn — Duty of employer to remit tax witheld — Employer omitting to remit tax in time — Assessments issued — Enforcement proceedings commenced notwithstanding late payment of tax by employer — Whether assessment a judicial function — Whether assessment and enforcement procedures operated unfairly — Income Tax (Employments) Regulations,* 1960 (*S.I. No.* 28) — *Income Tax Act,* 1967 (*No.* 6), *s.* 485 — *Finance Act,* 1968 (*No.* 33), *ss.* 7, 8 — *Constitution of Ireland,* 1937, *Arts.* 34.1, 40.3.

Defamation — libel — damages — quantum — nature of defence — aggravated damages.] The plaintiff was an employer who remitted tax to the Collector General on 19 July, 1984, in respect of emoluments paid to his employees in the income tax month ended 5 May, 1984. Under the Income Tax (Employment) Regulations, 1960, this remittance should have been made on or before 14 May, 1984. Section 7 of the Finance Act, 1968, provides that where the Revenue Commissioners have reason to believe that an employer has failed to remit tax due in respect of an income tax month they may issue an estimated assessment in respect of that month and where the employer fails to reply within a specified time the sum assessed becomes recoverable in the normal way. On the 2 July, 1984, an estimated assessment in relation to the month ending 5 May, 1984, was issued and sent to the plaintiff. On 25 July, 1984, the assessment not having been answered an enforcement notice was issued by the Revenue Commissioners and sent to the city sheriff. In August, 1984, the plaintiff commenced an action in the High Court challenging the constitutionality of certain sections of the Income Tax Act, 1967, and the Finance Act, 1968, and claiming damages for breach of his constitutional rights and libel. In the High Court Murphy J. rejected the constitutional challenge but awarded the plaintiff £500 damages and £2,000 aggravated damages for libel. (See the report at [1987] I.R. 120). On appeal by the plaintiff it was **Held** by the Supreme Court (Finlay C.J.,

CONSTITUTION—Statute.

Henchy, Griffin, Hederman and McCarthy JJ.), in refusing to declare s. 7 of the Act of 1968 invalid having regard to the provisions of the Constitution, 1, that a feature of a justiciable controversy was that two parties were contesting some matter, whether of law or of fact, and had conflicting assertions concerning such matters. Furthermore a characteristic of the exercise of a judicial function was that by its determination the tribunal or court concerned imposed liabilities or affected rights. *Reg. (Wexford County Council)* v. *Local Government Board* [1902] 2 I.R. 349 considered. 2. That, accordingly, it was the fact of default of payment of a levied tax which amounted to a judicial determination and not a determination under s. 7 of the Act of 1968 that the tax had not been paid and since there was no default in payment in the instant case the issue of the certificate to the sheriff was a nullity. 3. That the power vested in the first defendant by s. 7 did not oust the functions vested in judges under Article 34 of the Constitution. Where the first defendant exceeded the scope of his powers under s. 7 the courts were empowered to intervene and resolve the issue between a taxpayer and the first defendant. 4. That, accordingly, s. 7 of the Act of 1968 was not invalid having regard to the provisions of the Constitution. On further issues in the appeal it was **Held** by the Supreme Court, in increasing the amount awarded for aggravated damages and disallowing the appeal on all other issues, 1, that as the prescribed procedures observed by the defendants were not unfair or insufficient to vindicate the plaintiff's constitutional rights there had been no invasion of the plaintiff's constitutional rights under the Constitution. 2. That a person seeking a declaration of *ultra vires* must show he has a *bona fide* interest and that there is a practical advantage to the making of such a declaration, and, the plaintiff being unable to show such interest or advantage, the court would decline to consider whether the issue of a notice, which was admittedly a nullity, was *ultra vires* the powers of the defendants. 3. That the sum of £2,000 for aggravated damages in addition to a sum of £500 ordinary damages was inadequate to compensate the plaintiff, a solicitor acting as a solicitor, for harm to his character and reputation arising from the conduct of the proceedings in the High Court by the defendants and a sum of £10,000 would be awarded for aggravated damages making a total award of £10,500. *Kennedy* v. *Hearne*
(S.C.) [1988] I.R.481 ; [1988] ILRM 52, 531; (H.C.) [1987] I.R.120

31. —— **Courts** — *Administration of justice — Judicial function — Revenue — Income tax — Assessment — Schedule D — Taxpayer not appealing assessments — Assessments becoming*

CONSTITUTION—*continued.*

"final and conclusive" — Tax not paid — Certificate issued by Collector General — County sheriff instructed to levy tax in default — Notice of seizure served on plaintiff — Whether assessment a judicial function — Whether legislation empowering execution in the absence of court order constitutional — Income Tax Act, 1967 (*No.* 6), *ss.* 184, 416, 485 — *Constitution of Ireland,* 1937, *Arts.* 34, 37, 40.3, 40.5.] Section 184 of the Income Tax Act, 1967, empowers an Inspector of Taxes to raise an estimated assessment to income tax on a person who has failed to make a return of income when required to do so. Section 416 provides that in default of a notice of appeal against the assessment it shall become final and conclusive. The Collector General is empowered by s. 485 to issue a certificate setting out that a taxpayer has made a default in paying income tax and the county registrar or sheriff is required to levy the sum certified to be in default. The plaintiff had been sent notices of assessment to income tax in relation to a number of tax years. The assessments had stated that the plaintiff carried on a particular trade and had estimated the amount of income arising in that trade and tax payable thereon in the years 1980/81 to 1983/84 inclusive. The plaintiff did not appeal any of the assessments and they became final and conclusive. The Collector General issued a certificate specifying that a sum of money, being the tax charged in each of those years together with interest, was unpaid. Arising from that certificate the county sheriff caused a notice of seizure to be issued and served on the plaintiff claiming the sum of £33,056.68. The plaintiff commenced proceedings in the High Court seeking declarations that the actions of the Collector General and county sheriff together with certain provisions of the Income Tax Act, 1967, were in breach of Articles 34, 37 and 40, ss. 3 and 5 of the Constitution of Ireland, 1937. **Held** by Murphy J., in dismissing the plaintiff's claim, 1, that the task of an Inspector of Taxes in making assessments was to compute the amount of tax to be paid having regard to the information provided by the taxpayer. So described, his function was a purely administrative one. The fact that the taxpayer failed to provide necessary information meant that the assessment was of necessity an estimated one, however, this merely made the Inspector's task more difficult, it did not alter the essential nature of his function. *Murphy* v. *Corporation of Dublin* [1972] I.R. 215 considered. 2. That the taxpayer was precluded from disputing an assessment which had become final and conclusive by virtue of something more akin to statutory estoppel resulting from the inaction of the taxpayer than to a judicial order or decree purporting to have been made by the Inspector. 3. That the recovery of amounts due by distress

CONSTITUTION—Statute.

levied by the county sheriff and the right to break into and enter the dwelling house of a citizen was not an integral part of the judicial function, nor did it derive from the judicial function. Such a power could be conferred by statute on an authorised officer without the necessity of invoking the judicial process. *Deaton* v. *The Attorney General and Others* [1963] I.R. 270 and *Abbey Films* v. *The Attorney General* [1981] I.R. 158 considered. 4. That the proposition that the High Court had a general jurisdiction to set aside an assessment on the ground that it was erroneous in some material respect was not established by the plaintiff. The alleged misdescription of the taxpayer in the notice of assessment was not sufficient to render the assessment invalid. *Dictum* of Denning L.J. in *Royal Court Derby Porcelain Co. Ltd.* v. *Raymond Russell* [1949] 2 K.B. 417 distinguished. 5. That the High Court had an inherent jurisdiction to decline to entertain issues where legislation had provided other suitable and appropriate machinery to resolve them. Where there was a valid and effective determination of tax payable by the taxpayer there was no justiciable issue to refer to the court. *R.* v. *R.* [1984] I.R. 296 and *O'R.* v. *O'R.* [1985] I.R. 367 applied. 6. In order for the plaintiff to re-open assessments which have become final and binding on him in accordance with the provisions of statute he would have to show that the procedure by which the assessments were made was invalid or unconstitutional. *Deighan* v. *Hearne*

(H.C.) [1986] I.R. 603

32. —— **Courts** — *Jurisdiction — High Court — Personal rights — Accused returned for trial on indictment to Circuit Court in Dublin — Right to trial in Central Criminal Court — Former legislation repealed — "Full" original jurisdiction of High Court — Courts of first instance under the Constitution — Courts of local and limited jurisdiction under the Constitution — Courts of Justice Act,* 1924 (*No.* 10), *s.* 54 — *Courts Act,* 1964 (*No.* 11), *s.* 6 — *Courts Act,* 1981 (*No.* 11), *ss.* 31(1), 32(1) — *Constitution of Ireland,* 1937, *Arts.* 34.2, 34.3.1, 34.3.4, 36, 38.2, 40.1.] The plaintiff was arrested and charged with a serious offence under the Larceny Act, 1916. Having been sent forward for trial on indictment to the Dublin Circuit Court pursuant to s. 8 of the Criminal Procedure Act, 1967, he sought a transfer of his trial to the Central Criminal Court or, alternatively, to a circuit outside Dublin. Section 31, sub-s. 31, sub-s. 1, of the Courts Act, 1981, permits the transfer of a criminal trial from a Circuit Court judge sitting outside Dublin to the Dublin Circuit but not *vice versa.* Section 32, sub-s. 1, of the Courts Act, 1981, repealed s. 6 of the Courts Act, 1964, which allowed for the

CONSTITUTION—*continued.*

transfer of trials in criminal cases by judges of the Circuit Court to the Central Criminal Court. The plaintiff brought an action in the High Court challenging the constitutionality of s. 31, sub-s. 1, on the ground that it infringed Article 34, s. 3, sub-s. 1 of the Constitution which provides that the "Courts of First Instance shall include a High Court invested with full original jurisdiction in and power to determine all matters and questions whether of law or fact, civil or criminal." Costello J. dismissed the plaintiff's action. The plaintiff appealed to the Supreme Court in relation to s. 32, sub-s. 1 of the aforesaid Act only. **Held** by the Supreme Court in holding that s. 32, sub-s. 1 was not invalid having regard to the provisions of the Constitution, 1, Article 34, s. 3, sub-s. 1 was not to be read literally as to do so would produce absurdity and bring that provision into conflict with other constitutional provisions. 2. Article 34, s. 3, sub-s. 4 recognises that the High Court is not expected to be a suitable forum for determining at first glance all justiciable matters. Furthermore to divert every justiciable matter to the High Court for trial would not be in accordance with the due administration of justice having regard especially to fundamental fairness, the right to equality before the law and compliance with the basic purpose of Article 38, s. 2 of the Constitution. 3. The rule of literal interpretation must give way to the more fundamental rule of constitutional interpretation that the Constitution must be read as a whole and not simply as the sum of its parts. This means that where two constructions of a provision are open in the light of the Constitution as a whole, despite the apparent unambiguity of the provision itself, the court should adopt the construction which will achieve the smooth and harmonious operation of the Constitution. 4. Accordingly, the "full" original jurisdiction of the High Court must be deemed to be full in the sense that all justiciable matters (save those removed by the Constitution itself from the original jurisdiction of the High Court) shall be within the original jurisdiction of the High Court in one form or another. If, in exercise of its powers under Article 34, s. 3, sub-s. 4, parliament commits certain matters to the jurisdiction of the District Court or Circuit Court, the functions of hearing and determining those matters may, expressly or by necessary implication, be given exclusively to those courts. 5. The inter-relation of Article 34, s. 3, sub-s. 1 and Article 34, s. 3, sub-s. 4 ensures that the full original jurisdiction of the High Court can be invoked so as to ensure that justice will be done. Where there has been a statutory devolution of jurisdiction to a lower court the full jurisdiction of the High Court can be involved in proceedings such as habeas corpus, certiorari, prohibition,

CONSTITUTION—Statute.

mandamus, *quo warranto,* injunction or a declaratory action so as to ensure that the hearing and determination will be in accordance with law. Furthermore every person tried in the Circuit Court may seek leave to appeal to the Court of Criminal Appeal and may also invoke the jurisdiction of the High Court to prevent the trial being entered on or being conducted in violation of his fundamental rights. *Tormey* v. *Ireland* **(S.C.) [1985] I.R.289; [1985] ILRM 375; (H.C.) [1984] ILRM 657**

33. —— **Courts** — *Practice — Action — Transfer — Power of High Court to transfer action to Circuit Court — Courts of Justice Act,* 1924 (*No.* 10), *s.* 25 — *Courts of Justice Act,* 1936 (*No.* 48), *s.* 11 — *Constitution of Ireland,* 1937, *Arts.* 34, 36, 50.] The provisions of s. 25 of the Act of 1924 and s. 11 of the Act of 1936, stating the circumstances in which the High Court may transfer to the Circuit Court an action instituted in the High Court but which could have been commenced in the Circuit Court, are not inconsistent with the provisions of the Constitution and, therefore, continued to be of full force and effect pursuant to Article 50 of the Constitution. So **Held** by McMahon J. *Ward* v. *Kinahan Electrical Ltd.*

(H.C.) [1984] I.R. 292

34. —— **Delegated legislation** — *Ministerial order — Whether made* ultra vires — *Statute conferring powers on Minister — Victims of road traffic accidents excluded by ministerial order from provision of free health services — Such exclusion not stated in statute as part of its policy — Ministerial order made* ultra vires — *Health Services Regulations,* 1971 (*S.I. No.* 105), *art.* 6 — *Health Services (Limited Eligibility) Regulations,* 1979 (*S.I. No.* 110), *art.* 1 — *Health Act,* 1970 (*No.* 1), *ss.* 45-6, 51-3, 56, 72 — *Constitution of Ireland,* 1937, *Arts.* 15, 40.] The scheme of the Health Act, 1970, is to provide free medical services for persons who are unable to afford such services themselves. Section 72, sub-ss. 1-2, authorise the Minister for Health to regulate the manner or extent to which health services are provided free of charge under the Act. Article 6, sub-art. 3, of the Health Services Regulations, 1971, provides that a person who requires treatment for injuries received in a road traffic accident should not be entitled to avail of the services under the Health Act, 1970, unless he can establish that he is not entitled to receive damages or compensation in respect of the injuries from a third party. The infant plaintiff suffered severe brain damage as a result of injuries he received in a road traffic accident when he was nine years old. Suing by his father and next friend he

CONSTITUTION—*continued.*

instituted proceedings in which he sought damages *inter alia* for charges made for his stay in hospital. The defendant contended that as the plaintiff was a person with full eligibility under the Health Act, 1970, his exclusion from free medical services by virtue of art. 6, sub-art. 3, of the Health Services Regulations, 1971, was unconstitutional and, further, that the Minister acted *ultra vires* in excluding persons who would otherwise be eligible from the benefits of the Health Act,1970. In the trial of the constitutional issue Hamilton J. directed that the defendant, Patrick Walsh, [hereinafter called "the defendant"] be the plaintiff and that the Attorney General and the infant plaintiff [hereinafter called "the plaintiffs"] be the defendants. **Held** by Hamilton J. in giving judgment for the plaintiffs, 1, s. 72,sub-s. 1, of the Health Act,1970, was not invalid having regard to the provisions of the Constitution. There was a presumption that the Oireachtas intended a constitutional construction of the section and therefore the powers conferred on the Minister could only be for the purpose of giving effect to principles and policies which are contained in the Act. *McDonald* v. *Bord na gCon* [1965] I.R. 217 applied. 2. Section 72, sub-s. 2, of the Health Act, 1970, was not invalid having regard to the provisions of the Constitution. The power given to the Minister was to differentiate between *classes* of persons and not between individuals and therefore the provisions of Art. 40, s. 1, of the Constitution did not apply. 3. The provisions of art. 6, sub-art. 3, of the Health Services Regulations, 1971, were not invalid having regard to the provisions of the Constitution. It was within the competence of the Oireachtas to vest in the Minister the power of deciding what class of persons, who had eligibility for health services under the Health Acts, were entitled to avail of same. *East Donegal Co-Operative* v. *The Attorney General* [1970] I.R. 317 applied. 4. The Minister acted *ultra vires* in making the regulation. 5. The defendant had *locus standi* to raise the issues. On appeal by the defendant it was **Held** by the Supreme Court, (O'Higgins C.J., Henchy, Griffin, Hederman and McCarthy JJ.) in allowing the appeal, 1, because of the presumption of constitutionality in its favour, s. 72 of the Health Act, 1970, should be interpreted to mean that the Oireachtas did not intend to delegate its power of lawmaking to the Minister. Accordingly, s. 72 only authorises such exclusions as the Act itself contemplates. 2. Article 6, sub-art. 3, of the Health Services Regulations, 1971, in purporting to exclude a category of persons from the benefits of the Health Act, 1970, (which exclusion is not authorised by the Act) was seeking to amend the Act by ministerial regulation rather than by appropriate legislation. Since the Oireachtas did not intend to give such a power to the Minister art. 6, sub-art. 3, is *ultra vires* the Minister and therefore void. 3. (*Per* O'Higgins C.J., Henchy, Griffin and Hederman JJ. concurring). The defendant had *locus standi* to raise the issues. *Cahill* v. *Sutton* [1980] I.R. 269 applied. 4. *Per* McCarthy J.: A defendant subjected to a claim for the plaintiff's hospital expenses is entitled to challenge the validity of those charges in the same way as the plaintiff is entitled. It is unnecessary to apply any principle derived from *Cahill* v. *Sutton. Cahill* v. *Sutton* [1980] I.R. 269 considered. *Cooke* v. *Walsh*

(H.C., S.C.) [1984] I.R. 710

see also [1984] ILRM 208 — **Damages,** 9

35. —— **Delegated legislation** — *Regulations giving effect to EC milk levy — Such regulations having retrospective effect — Whether unjust — Whether unjustified attack on property rights — Whether any such infringement necessitated by membership of the European Community — Council regulations* 804/84, 856/84, 857/84 — *Commission Regulation* 1371/84 — *European Communities (Milk levy) Regulations,* 1985 (*S.I.No.* 416), *reg.* 4, 12 — *Constitution of Ireland,* 1937, *Arts.* 29.4.3, 40.3.2, 43.] The EEC Superlevy Regulations fixed an EEC limit for the production of milk and milk products and determined a national reference quantity (or the milk quota as more commonly known). Where formula (B) was adopted the competent authority (in Ireland the Minister for Agriculture) fixed the reference quantity for every purchaser (the co-operative) by reference to the deliveries taken by them in the calendar year 1983. Any purchasers who took deliveries after 2 April, 1984, in excess of the quantities allocated to them became liable to pay the levy to the Minister but the purchaser/co-operative could then penalise the farmer who over-produced by recovering the levy from him. Article 5(1) and (2) of EEC Regulation 1371/84 provided that where an entire holding or several parts of a holding is sold, leased or transferred by inheritance the corresponding reference quantity shall be transferred in the former case in full to the producer who takes over the holding and in the latter case distributed among the producers operating the holding in proportion to the areas used for milk production. Article 5(3) provides that Article 5(1) and (2) might have retrospective effect. Regulation No. 1371/84 was implemented by S.I. No. 416 of 1985. The plaintiff, the owner of two dairy farms of relatively the same size namely Burtonstown farm and Brownstown farm sold the Burtonstown farm on 28 November, 1983, to the second and third defendants. The said defendants wished to sell the milk they produced

from Burtonstown farm to Tir Laighen Co-op and not Bailieborough Co-op as had been the case with the plaintiff. A dispute arose between the parties as to what extent the purchasers' milk quota passed with the sale of Burtonstown farm. At this point the Minister for Agriculture became involved as it is his duty to ascertain the appropriate fraction of milk quota to be transferred from Bailieborough Co-op to Tir Laighen Co-op. The plaintiff presented to officials of the Department a number of arguments in an effort to retain as large a fraction of his original quota as possible. The Minister after carrying out an investigation made adjustments to the reference quantities allocated to the purchasers/co-operatives. The plaintiff rejected these adjustments and in challenging the validity of the superlevy regulations submitted: (1) that the domestic regulations in so far as they purport to give retrospective effect to the provisions of Article 5(1) and (2) of Regulation 1371/84 are firstly unconstitutional as they constitute an unjust attack on the property rights of the plaintiff in so far as their milk quota was a valuable property right and secondly are *ultra vires* the Minister as they are not within the terms and objects of the enabling legislation or in accordance with constitutional propriety; (2) Article 29.4.3 of the Constitution does not exempt the domestic regulation from the purview of the Constitution as those regulations were not 'necessitated by the obligations of membership of the communities'; (3) that Article 5(3) of EEC Regulation 1371/84 was null and void because it was made without sufficient reason or adequate motivation. **Held** by Murphy J. in dismissing the plaintiff's claim, 1, the Minister in ascertaining the appropriate fraction of milk quota to be transferred from the Bailieborough Co-op to Tir Laighean Co-op carried out the task competently and fairly and the particular decision implicit in the final conclusion was correct and as accurate as one could possibly hope to achieve. 2. The scheme and purpose of the regulations is such that where holdings have changed hands or been sub-divided between the basis year and the coming into operation of the superlevy regulations the person acquiring the holdings should acquire also quotas appropriate to the amount and the nature of the lands acquired by them. 3. The superlevy regulations in no way attempt to abolish the right of private ownership or the general right to transfer, bequeath or inherit property. Although they do delimit the exercise of certain rights of ownership, this delimitation is clearly with a view to reconciling the exercise of ownership rights with the exigencies of the common good. 4. The general limitation or curbing of the right to enter into or expand dairy production is not a limitation on ownership rights

CONSTITUTION—Statute.

such as calls for monetary compensation. 5. The interference with the property rights of dairy farmers in general conforms with Article 43 and does not require to be examined by reference to Article 40.3 of the Constitution. Even if the regulations were considered under that Article the court is satisfied the retrospective operation of the regulations was in no sense unjust as it created a careful balance between the rights of the vendors and purchasers and further the regulations were neither capricious or arbitrary. 6. Even if contrary to the view already expressed the view was taken that the domestic regulations offended Articles 40 or 43 of the Constitution this infringement would fall within the exception provided by Article 29.4.3 of the Constitution by virtue of the word 'necessitated' in that Article which must extend to and include acts or measures which are consequent upon membership in the community and in general fulfilment of the obligations of such membership. *Lawlor* v. *Minister for Agriculture*

(H.C.) [1988] ILRM 400

36. —— **Elections** — *Ballot papers — Listing of candidates' names in alphabetical order — Voting bias — Constitution — Fairness of procedure — Equality before the law — Right to vote and stand in elections — Electoral Act,* 1963 (*No.* 19), *s.* 16 — *Constitution of Ireland,* 1937, *Arts.* 16, 40.] The plaintiff, who intended to present himself as a candidate in the local elections and afterwards for Dáil Éireann, sought a declaration that the procedure provided by s. 16 of the Electoral Act, 1963, whereby candidates' names on ballot papers were listed in alphabetical order, offended Article 40 of the Constitution in failing to provide fairness of procedures or to hold the plaintiff equal before the law, and was therefore repugnant to the Constitution and invalid. **Held** by Murphy J., in dismissing the claim, that such system of alphabetical listing significantly favoured those candidates who took alphabetical precedence and were placed higher up on the ballot paper, but that such bias for higher placed candidates reflected not a defect in the system itself but rather an indifference of the electorate, and accordingly the plaintiff had failed to establish that the legislation providing such system was unreasonable. *Draper* v. *the Attorney General* [1984] I.R. 286 considered. *O'Reilly* v. *Minister for the Environment*

(H.C.) [1986] I.R.143; [1987] ILRM 290

37. —— **Elections** — *National Parliament — Dáil Éireann — Right to vote — Disabled citizen — Inability to attend at polling station — Absence of statutory provision for postal vote in national elections — Personal rights — Electoral Act,* 1923 (*No.* 12), *s.* 21, *4th and 5th schedules — Electoral*

CONSTITUTION—*continued.*

Act, 1960 (*No.* 43), *s.* 8 — *Electoral Act,* 1963 (*No.* 19), *ss.* 7, 22, 23, 26, 27 — *Constitution of Ireland,* 1937, *Arts.* 16, 40.] Article 16, s. 1, sub-s. 2, of the Constitution of Ireland, 1937, stated:— "Every citizen without distinction of sex who has reached the age of eighteen years who is not disqualified by law and complies with the provisions of the law relating to the election of members of Dáil Éireann, shall have the right to vote at an election for members of Dáil Éireann." Article 16, s. 1. sub-s. 4, states that no voter may exercise more than one vote at an election for Dáil Éireann, and that the voting shall be by secret ballot. Section 7 of Article 16 states that, subject to the preceding provisions of the Article, elections for membership of Dáil Éireann, including the filling of casual vacancies, shall "be regulated in accordance with law." Section 26 of the Electoral Act, 1963, states that every person whose name is on the register of Dáil electors for the time being in force for a constituency, and no other person, shall be entitled to vote at the poll at a Dáil election in that constituency. The provisions of the Electoral Acts and the regulations made thereunder require all such electors, other than members of the police and defence forces, to cast their votes at polling stations. The plaintiff, a citizen of Ireland, was entitled to vote at the poll at an election for members of Dáil Éireann. She suffered from multiple sclerosis and, because of her chronic physical disability, she was unable to go to a polling station to cast her vote at Dáil elections. The plaintiff claimed in the High Court declarations that she was entitled to be provided with facilities to enable her to cast her vote, and that various provisions of the Electoral Acts were inconsistent with, or repugnant to, the Constitution. **Held,** by McMahon J., in rejecting the claim of the plaintiff, 1, that the right of a citizen to vote at an election of members of Dáil Éireann is a personal right which is guaranteed by Article 40, s. 3, of the Constitution. 2. That, nevertheless, it was the responsibility of the National Parliament to make laws governing the manner in which the right to vote at such elections must be exercised and, in doing so, to strike a balance between the rights of the physically disabled to vote and the risks of abuse inherent in postal voting. 3. That the plaintiff had failed to rebut the presumption that the provisions of the Act of 1963 were in accordance with the Constitution, and had not established that the provisions of the Act of 1923 were inconsistent with the Constitution. *Somjee* v. *The Minister for Justice* [1981] ILRM 324 considered. On appeal by the plaintiff it was **Held** by the Supreme Court, in disallowing the appeal, 1, that the right of a citizen to vote at elections for members of Dáil

CONSTITUTION—Statute.

Éireann (declared in Article 16 of the Constitution) is conferred by that Article on citizens who comply with the provisions of the law relating to such elections. 2. That the present statute law provides a reasonable regulation of such elections, having regard to the obligation of secrecy, the need to prevent abuses and other requirements of the common good. 3. That the failure to provide facilities to enable the plaintiff to vote at those elections did not amount to an interference by the State in the exercise of the right to vote declared in s. 1, sub-s. 2, of Article 16 of the Constitution; nor did that failure constitute a breach by the State of the provisions of s. 1 of Article 40 of the Constitution relating to the equality of citizens before the law. 4. That, even if the plaintiff's right to vote at such elections were a personal right within the meaning of s. 3. sub-s. 1, of Article 40 of the Constitution, the Court was not satisfied that the State had failed to defend and vindicate that right. *Draper* v. *Attorney General*
(H.C., S.C.) [1984] I.R.277 ; [1984] ILRM 643

38. —— **Family** — *Revenue — Income tax — Husband and wife — Assessment — Statute declared to be invalid — Effect — Subsequent enactment — Married taxpayers to pay as much tax under new enactment, in respect of tax years prior to new enactment as they would have done under former enactment — Validity — Recovery from taxpayer of tax not paid — Income Tax Act,* 1967 (*No.* 6), *ss.* 192-7 — *Finance Act,* 1980 (*No.* 14), *s.* 21 — *Constitution of Ireland,* 1937, *Arts.* 40.3, 41.] In *Murphy* v. *The Attorney General* [1982] I.R. 241, the Supreme Court declared that ss. 192 to 197 of the Income Tax Act, 1976, were invalid having regard to the provisions of the Constitution. The Supreme Court by a majority also held that the tax collected under the impugned provisions was not recoverable by the taxpayer. Section 21 of the Finance Act, 1980 provided for a system under which the tax collected from married persons, in respect of the tax years prior to 1979/80, would not be any less than would have been collected under the impugned provisions. The plaintiffs, a husband and wife, were assessed in respect of the tax years 1975/76 to 1979/80 under the provisions of s. 21 of the Act of 1980. On the 29 April, 1982, the plaintiffs issued a plenary summons seeking a declaration that the provisions of s. 21 were repugnant to the Constitution. **Held** by Barrington J., in declaring s. 21 of the Finance Act, 1980, to be repugnant to the Constitution, 1, that s. 21 re-imposes a tax on married persons which the Supreme Court has already declared to be invalid having regard to the provisions of the Constitution. 2. That the imposition of that tax by s. 21 is not justifiable on the grounds that it

CONSTITUTION—*continued.*

places those affected in the same position as those affected by the earlier impugned provisions. 3. That s. 21 is therefore invalid having regard to the provisions of Article 41 and Article 40, s. 3 of the Constitution. 4. That the State may not rely on the provisions of s. 21 in attempting to determine a taxpayer's liability to income tax. On appeal by the defendants it was **Held** by the Supreme Court, in dismissing the appeal, 1, that the essence of the decision in the *Murphy Case* is that the relevant sections were invalid having regard to the provisions of the Constitution by virtue of the fact that they penalised the married state. 2. That s. 21 has the same effect as the earlier impugned provisions, and, accordingly, in the light of the decision in *Murphy's Case,* it is invalid having regard to the provisions of Article 41 of the Constitution. *Murphy* v. *The Attorney General* [1982] I.R. 241 applied. *Muckley* v. *Ireland*
(H.C., S.C.) [1985] I.R.472 ; [1986] ILRM 364

39. —— **Personal rights** — **Bodily integrity** — *Privacy — Freedom of expression — Homosexual plaintiff* — Locus standi — *Equality before the law — Enactments imposing punishments for commission of acts of buggery, indecent assault and gross indecency — Whether enactments inconsistent with Constitution — Offences Against the Person Act,* 1861 (*c.* 100), *ss.* 61, 62 — *Criminal Law Amendment Act,* 1885 (*c.* 69), *s.* 11 — *Constitution of Ireland,* 1937, *Arts.* 15, 29, 40, 50.] Section 61 of the Act of 1861 states that a person convicted of the crime of buggery shall be liable to be sentenced to penal servitude. Section 62 of that Act states that a person who attempts to commit that crime, or who is guilty of an assault with intent to commit it or of any indecent assault upon a male person, shall be guilty of a misdemeanour and liable to be sentenced to penal servitude. Section 11 of the Act of 1885 provides that a male person who commits, or attempts to procure the commission by a male person of, an act of gross indecency with another male person shall be guilty of a misdemeanour and liable to imprisonment for a term not exceeding two years. The plaintiff, an Irish citizen, claimed in the High Court a declaration that the provisions of ss. 61 and 62 of the Act of 1861 were inconsistent with the provisions of the Constitution of Ireland, 1937, and had not been continued in force by Article 50 thereof as part of the law of the State. He also claimed a similar declaration in respect of the provisions of s. 11 of the Act of 1885. At the trial of his action, the plaintiff stated in his evidence that he was exclusively, congenitally and irreversibly homosexual; it was submitted on his behalf that the impugned provisions were inconsistent with the declaration in Article 40, s. 1, of

CONSTITUTION—Statute.

the Constitution that all citizens be held equal before the law, and an infringement of the personal rights of citizens guaranteed by s. 3 of that Article. **Held** by McWilliam J., in dismissing the plaintiff's claims, 1, that the plaintiff lacked *locus standi* to challenge the constitutionality of the impugned enactments on grounds relating solely to the effect of those provisions on the rights or interests of married citizens. *Cahill* v. *Sutton* [1980] I.R. 269 applied. 2. That neither s. 61 nor s. 62 of the Act of 1861 made any distinction between men and women or between homosexuals and heterosexuals and that, accordingly, neither of those sections contravened the equality before the law postulated in Article 40, s. 1, of the Constitution. 3. That the discrimination effected by s. 11 of the Act of 1885, by confining the offences there defined to those for which only men were liable to be punished, was not a discrimination which was contrary to the equality proclaimed in Article 40, s. 1, of the Constitution. 4. That none of the plaintiff's claims to rights of privacy and bodily integrity and to freedoms of expression and association was a claim recognised by the Constitution and guaranteed by Article 40, s. 3, thereof. 5. That, accordingly, the impugned enactments had been continued in force as part of the law of the State under Article 50 of the Constitution. *Ryan* v. *The Attorney General* [1965] I.R. 294; *Quinn's Supermarket* v. *The Attorney General* [1972] I.R. 1; *McGee* v. *The Attorney General* [1974] I.R. 284 and *de Burca* v. *The Attorney General* [1976] I.R. 38 considered. On appeal by the plaintiff it was **Held** by the Supreme Court (O'Higgins C.J., Finlay P., Henchy, Griffin and McCarthy JJ.), in disallowing the appeal, 1, that the issues raised would be determined on the assumption that the impugned sections of the Acts of 1861 and 1885 formed part of the law of the State immediately prior to the enactment of the Constitution in 1937. 2. (*a*) That the plaintiff, in challenging the validity of the sections under the Constitution, lacked *locus standi* to invoke the effect of the sections on the rights and interests of married citizens (McCarthy J. dissenting). *Cahill* v. *Sutton* [1980] I.R. 269 applied. (*b*) That the plaintiff had *locus standi* to challenge otherwise the validity of the sections under the Constitution although he had not been prosecuted under any of the sections. 3. *Per* O'Higgins C.J., Finlay P., Henchy and Griffin JJ. — That the function of the court was not to reform the law but to ascertain whether any of the sections was inconsistent with the provisions of the Constitution so that it was not continued in force, pursuant to Article 50, after the enactment of the Constitution in 1937. 4. That the issue of inconsistency under Article 50 should be determined in the light of the current state of the law and of the principles

CONSTITUTION—*continued.*

of interpretation of the Constitution that had been evolved since its enactment. 5. *Per* O'Higgins C.J., Finlay P. and Griffin J. — That the onus of proving inconsistency under Article 50 lay on the party seeking to establish it, and that there was no presumption that the impugned sections were consistent with the provisions of the Constitution. 6. *Per* O'Higgins C.J., Finlay P., Henchy and Griffin JJ. — That, for the reasons stated by the trial judge, the terms of ss. 61 and 62 of the Act of 1861 did not contain an invidious discrimination contrary to Article 40, s. 1, of the Constitution. 7. *Per* O'Higgins C.J., Finlay P., Henchy and Griffin JJ. — That neither the omission from the Acts of 1861 and 1885 of offences relating to acts of gross indecency by females nor the omission therefrom of offences relating to the sexual activities of heterosexuals outside marriage constituted invidious discrimination contrary to Article 40, s. 1, of the Constitution. 8. *Per* O'Higgins C.J., Finlay P. and Griffin J. — That the exigencies of the common good prevailed over any complaints the plaintiff might have about the ill effects of the existence of the impugned sections upon his health, or about any impairment of his freedom of expression or his freedom of association. 9. That, having regard to the Christian nature of the State, the immorality of the deliberate practice of homosexuality, the damage that such practice causes to the health of citizens and the potential harm to the institution of marriage, there was no inconsistency between the terms of any of the impugned sections and the provisions of the Constitution and that, therefore, the right to privacy claimed by the plaintiff could not prevail against the sanctions imposed by those sections (Henchy and McCarthy JJ. dissenting). 10. *Per* O'Higgins C.J., Finlay P., Henchy and Griffin JJ. — That the Convention for the Protection of Human Rights and Fundamental Freedoms (signed at Rome on the 4 November, 1950, and ratified by the Government of Ireland on the 18 February, 1953) does not form part of the domestic law of the State. *In re Ó Laighléis* [1960] I.R. 93 applied; *Dudgeon* v. *United Kingdom* (1981) 4 E.H.R.R. 149 mentioned. *Norris* v. *Attorney General*

(H.C., S.C.) [1984] I.R.36

40. —— **Personal rights** — **Equality** — *Planning — Appeals — Requirement of lodgment of deposit — Whether arbitrary discrimination — Permission — Asbestos waste — Whether injurious to health — Whether relevant to constitutionality of planning legislation — Hearing — Whether oral hearing required — Fair procedures — Constitution of Ireland,* 1937, *Arts.* 40.1, 40.3 — *Local Government (Planning and Development) Act,* 1976 (*No.*28), *ss.* 15, 16, 18.] The

CONSTITUTION—Statute.

appellant had failed to obtain in the High Court a declaration that the Local Government (Planning and Development) Act, 1976, was unconstitutional. By his notice of appeal to the Supreme Court, he confined himself to seeking a declaration that ss. 15, 16 and 18 of the Act were repugnant to the Constitution. S. 15 provides that a deposit shall be lodged with any appeal to the Planning Board. S. 16 gives the Board an absolute discretion to hold an oral hearing of any reference or appeal to the Board, except where the Minister shall otherwise direct. S. 18 provides that where the Board is of opinion that a reference or appeal is vexatious, or is being unnecesarily delayed by any person, the Board may determine such reference or appeal after service of a notice in that regard upon that party, notwithstanding that no submission has been made by that party to the Board in relation to the reference or appeal. **Held** by the Supreme Court (O'Higgins C.J., Henchy, Griffin, Kenny and Parke JJ.) in disallowing the appeal, 1, the purpose of s. 15 is to prevent appeals or references which are without reality or substance. Since the amount of the deposit was returnable, and is not so high as to prevent genuine appeals being brought, there was no unconstitutional discrimination involved in the section. 2. Although under the Local Government (Planning and Development) Act, 1963, any person bringing an appeal had an absolute right to an oral hearing, it was open to the Oireachtas to alter the law in this regard in the manner provided for in s. 16 of the 1976 Act. 3. The powers given to the Board under s. 18 of the 1976 Act can only be exercised after an opportunity has been afforded to the appellant to put forward his case. *Finnegan* v. *An Bord Pleanála*

(H.C., S.C.) [1979] ILRM 134

41. —— **Personal rights — Extradition** — *Warrant for arrest of plaintiff issued in Northern Ireland — Warrant endorsed for execution within the State — Order directing delivery of plaintiff to authorities in Northern Ireland — Procedure — Admission of evidence by affidavit during course of trial — R.S.C.,* 1962, *O.* 39, *r.* 1 — *Extradition Act,* 1965 (*No.* 17), *Part III — Constitution of Ireland,* 1937, *Arts.* 29, 34, 40.] Pursuant to Part III of the Extradition Act, 1965, the plaintiff, a citizen of Ireland, was arrested in the State on foot of two warrants issued by a judicial authority in Northern Ireland, charging him with murder contrary to common law. The warrants were endorsed for execution within the State by the Assistant Commissioner of the Garda Síochána, and the plaintiff was brought before the District Court, which made two orders directing that the plaintiff be delivered into the custody of the Northern Ireland police. The plaintiff applied to

CONSTITUTION—*continued.*

the High Court for a declaration, *inter alia,* that Part III of the Extradition Act, 1965, is invalid having regard to the provisions of the Constitution. At the trial in the High Court of the issues raised in the plaintiff's summons, the plaintiff sought to introduce evidence by affidavit without the consent of the defendants, under order 39, rule 1 of the Rules of the Superior Courts. The High Court (Finlay P.) admitted the evidence by affidavit, but dismissed the plaintiff's claim as to the declarations sought. *Per* Finlay P. — In any ordinary litigation between parties, it would not be in the interests of justice to permit, in the absence of agreement, the introduction of evidence by affidavit during the course of the trial, and applications for a direction under order 39, r.1, must be made as a preliminary application before the trial of an action. *R.*v. *Milne* [1978] N.I. 110 and *Wyatt* v. *McLoughlin* [1974] I.R. 395 considered. The plaintiff appealed against the dismissal of his claim. **Held** by the Supreme Court, in dismissing the appeal and affirming the order of the High Court, 1, that the plaintiff had failed to establish that the law, procedure or practice relating to the interrogation, detention or trial of the plaintiff in Northern Ireland would, on their due application, subject the plaintiff to what would be less than his entitlement under Art. 40, s. 3, of the Constitution in a corresponding prosecution in this State. 2. That there was no evidence that any person charged with a criminal offence had been prejudiced or endangered in his trial by reason of public discord, sectarian conflict or other factional aspects of society in Northern Ireland; that the plaintiff had therefore failed to establish that, if extradited, he would be exposed to physical danger or the risk of an unfair trial by reason of conditions generally in Northern Ireland, such as to be deprived of his personal rights under Art. 40, s. 3, of the Constitution. 3. That the exception from extradition provided by s. 11, sub-s. 2, of Part II of the Act of 1965, had no application to the facts of this case. 4. That the court was not satisfied by the evidence that a requirement of scrutiny by the District Court of the basis of the charges in the extradition warrant is a generally recognised principle of international law. 5. That, in the absence of any evidence in this or any previous case of extradition to Northern Ireland of a lack of good faith or of evidential basis for the charges set out in the warrants, the plaintiff had failed to establish that he was being deprived of his personal rights under Art. 40, s.3. of the Constitution. 6. That the reciprocity which is necessarily implicit in the Extradition Act, 1965, justifies the presumption that fundamental fairness of procedures will be exercised by the requesting State, after extradition has taken

CONSTITUTION—Statute.

place; in particular, that upon delivery into the custody of the Northern Ireland police on foot of an extradition warrant, a person will be brought as soon as practicable before a Magistrates Court. In the absence of sufficient evidence to rebut this presumption, the plaintiff had failed to establish that, if extradited, he would be denied his personal rights under Art. 40, s. 3, of the Constitution. *Quaere:* whether the scope and application of Article 29, s. 3, of the Constitution may be used by the plaintiff to test the constitutionality of Part III of the Extradition Act, 1965. *Shannon* v. *Ireland*

(H.C., S.C.) [1984] I.R.548 ; [1985] ILRM 449

42. —— **Personal rights — Fair procedures** — *Fisheries — Arrest of foreign fishing vessel — Detention order made — Vessel released upon provision of security — Whether requirement to give security amounted to a requirement to give bail — If so, whether such bail oppressive — Major or minor offence — Constitution of Ireland,* 1937, *Arts.* 38.1, 40.3 — *Fisheries Consolidation Act,* 1959 (*No.* 14), *ss.* 221, 222(A), 232, 235(2)(A), (B) — *Fisheries Amendment Act,* 1978 (*No.* 18), *ss.* 2(2), 5, 7, 14.

Constitution — Arrest of foreign fishing vessel — Detention order made — Vessel released upon provision of security — Challenge to the constitutionality of the relevant legislation — Whether open to the Master of the vessel to argue that the legislation affected the constitutional rights of the vessel's owner — Locus standi — *Whether detention of the vessel amounted to a deprivation of the right to earn a livelihood — Whether physical presence of plaintiff necessary — Constitution of Ireland,* 1937, *Art.* 40.3 — *Fisheries Consolidation Act,* 1959(*No.* 14), *ss.* 221, 222(A), 232, 232(A), 234(1), 235(2) — *Fisheries Amendment Act,* 1978 (*No.*18), *ss.* 2(2), 12, 13, 14.

Practice — Barristers and solicitors — Presumption that counsel and solicitor appear on express instructions of the client.] The plaintiff was the Master of a French fishing boat which was arrested by an Irish naval vessel. He was charged with various offences. The plaintiff was subsequently released on bail under the provisions of s. 234(2) of the Fisheries (Consolidation) Act, 1959. The District Court order also provided for the detention of the boat but contained a provision allowing security for its release of £134,000. This sum was subsequently reduced in the High Court to £34,000. When an order for detention of a boat has been made pursuant to the 1959 Act, s. 235(2) (*a*) and (*b*) of the Fisheries (Consolidation) Act, 1959, (inserted by s. 14 of the Fisheries (Amendment) Act, 1978) may apply. The section provides that a District Justice may order and fix such security of a sum that in his opinion is sufficient to provide

CONSTITUTION—*continued.*

for: (1) payment of the maximum fines which may be ordered, (2) the estimated amount of costs, (3) the estimated value of any forfeiture which may be made, (4) that the security provided for is in addition to and not in substitution for any other bond or recognisance which the defendant concerned may be required to enter into by the District Justice. The plaintiff claimed that the requirement to give additional security amounted to requirement to give additional bail and that such bail was oppressive and contrary to fair procedure as implicitly required by the Constitution. In the High Court it was held by Carroll J. that the security requirement did amount to bail and as such it was oppressive and that so much of paragraph (a) as related to the preconviction attendance of the defendant and all of paragraph (b) were invalid. The defendants appealed. **Held** by O'Higgins C.J., (Walsh, Griffin, McCarthy and O'Hanlon JJ. concurring) in allowing the appeal, the provision of security referred to in sub-paragraphs (*a*) and (*b*) does not amount to bail but is intended and designed to permit an application by the owner and other interested parties for the release of the boat pending the trial of the defendant. *Per curiam.* An examination of paragraph (*a*) of s. 235(2) indicates the following: (i) The District Justice is given power, at his discretion, to order the release of the boat prior to any adjudication of the proceedings against the defendant. (ii) This power is exercisable if satisfactory security is given. (iii) The security must be such as to provide in the event of the conviction of the defendant, or his prior disappearance or absconding, for the payment of the maximum fine, the costs of the proceedings and the estimated value of any forfeiture. (iv) The required security must be given by any one who seeks the release of the boat and the failure to give it prevents the release, not of the defendant, but of the boat. *L'Henreyenat* v. *Ireland*

(H.C., S.C.) [1984] ILRM 249

43. —— **Personal rights — Right to earn livelihood** — *Gaming machines — Proprietor — Act of 1956 restricting player's stake to two and a half pence — Subsequent 950% increase in cost of living — Original stake restriction unaltered — Plaintiff failing to establish infringement of personal rights — Effect of statute increased substantially by events subsequent to enactment — Gaming and Lotteries Act,* 1956(*No.*2), *ss.* 2, 4, 12-15, 19 — *Gaming and Lotteries Act,* 1970 (*No.*6), *ss.* 1-2 — *Decimal Currency Act,* 1970 (*No.*21), *s.* 9(1) — *Finance Act,* 1975 (*No.*6), *s.* 43 — *Gaming and Lotteries Act,* 1979 (*No.* 6), *ss.* 1-2 — *Constitution of Ireland,* 1937, *Art.* 40.3.1, 40.3.2.] Section 4 of the Gaming and Lotteries Act, 1956, as amended by the Gaming

CONSTITUTION—Statute.

and Lotteries Act, 1979, prohibits, *inter alia,* the provision of facilities for gaming by means of any slot-machine. However, Part III of the Act of 1956 permits this business to be carried out at an amusement hall or funfair provided that an excise licence has been granted by the Revenue Commissioners pursuant to s. 19 of the Act of 1956. However, such a licence may only be obtained on production of a certificate granted by the District Court pursuant to s. 15 of the Act of 1956. Section 14 of the Act of 1956, as amended by s. 9, sub-s. 1 of the Decimal Currency Act, 1970, imposes maximum amounts on the stake to be wagered and the prizes to be won of two and a half pence and 50 pence, respectively. The plaintiff was the proprietor of an amusement hall where he operated a number of slot-machines. He was convicted in the District Court of exceeding the limits permitted by s. 14 of the Act of 1956, as amended, and he appealed to the Circuit Court. The appeal was adjourned to enable the plaintiff to bring proceedings by which the plaintiff sought a declaration that s. 14 of the Act of 1956, as amended, was invalid having regard to the provisions of Article 40, s. 3, sub-ss. 1 and 2 of the Constitution of Ireland, 1937. The plaintiff accepted that s. 14 of the Act of 1956, as amended, was valid when enacted but submitted that due to events which had occurred subsequently, the section now operated to infringe his constitutional rights, in particular his right to earn a livelihood. The plaintiff had commenced business in 1963 since when outgoings on the premises in respect of wages, rates, light, heat, insurance and telephone had increased greatly. Between 1956 and 1984 the cost of living increased by 950%. By virtue of s.. 43 of the Finance Act, 1975, the plaintiff became liable to apply for a "gaming machine licence" in respect of every slot-machine in the premises, on an annual basis, and to pay an annual excise duty of £50 in respect of each licence. The duty payable had been increased by successive Finance Acts to £300. In addition the excise duty payable on the issue of "gaming machine licences" in respect of his premises, pursuant to s. 19 of the Act of 1956 had increased from £40 in 1963 to £300 at the time of the commencement of proceedings. **Held** by Costello J., in dismissing the plaintiff's claim, 1, that the right to earn a livelihood is protected by Article 40, s. 3, sub-s. 1 and 2 of the Constitution. *The Attorney General* v. *Paperlink Ltd.* [1984] ILRM 373 applied. 2. That the plaintiff had failed to show that because of events which had occurred subsequently to the enactment of the Act of 1956 the restriction placed on his right to earn a livelihood constituted an unjust attack on that right because he had not proved that these restrictions are not reasonably required by the exigencies of the

CONSTITUTION—*continued.*

common good. *Brennan* v. *The Attorney General* [1984] ILRM 355 and *Blake* v. *The Attorney General* [1982] I.R. 117, considered. *Private Motorists Provident Society* v. *The Attorney General* [1983] I.R. 339, applied. 3. That the court has no jurisdiction to decide the level of restrictions that are reasonably necessary to curb gaming in licensed amusement halls since these are matters peculiarly within the jurisdiction and competence of the Oireachtas but the court can consider whether such restrictions are capable of being so justified. *Brennan* v. *The Attorney General* [1984] ILRM 335, applied. 4. That the plaintiff had failed to show that it would be unreasonable for the Oireachtas to conclude that present day social conditions required the maintenance of the limits set by the Act of 1956 despite the decline in the value of money since that time. On appeal by the plaintiff it was **Held** by the Supreme Court, in dismissing the appeal, 1, that the Act of 1956, as amended by the Acts of 1970 and 1979, clearly indicates a continuing view on the part of the Oireachtas that the exigencies of the common good required a strict control on the provision of facilities for gaming in amusement halls. 2. That, if instead of exercising a right absolutely to prohibit the use of slot-machines, the Oireachtas permits it subject even to very rigid restrictions which make both the use of the machine unattractive and the profitability of its operation small or minimal that cannot be inconsistent with the Constitution. 3. That, even if the imposition of these restrictions on the operation of gaming had been proved to be such as to make it wholly unprofitable as part of the business of an amusement hall proprietor, such restrictions would not be an unjust attack on the plaintiff's property rights as they were so clearly imposed with due regard to the exigencies of the common good. *Private Motorists Provident Society Ltd.* v. *The Attorney General* [1983] I.R. 339, applied. *Cafolla* v. *O'Malley*
(H.C., S.C.) [1985] I.R. 486; [1986] ILRM 177

44. —— **Property rights** — *National monument — Preservation order — Validity of relevant legislation — Whether unjust attack on property rights — Constitution of Ireland,* 1937, *Arts.* 40, 43 — *National Monuments Act,* 1930 (*No.*2), *ss.* 8, 14 — *National Monuments Act,* 1954 (*No.* 37), *s.* 3.

National Monument — Preservation order — Validity — Whether order ultra vires — *Whether order made in accordance with principles of natural justice — National Monuments Act,* 1930 (*No.*2), *ss.* 8, 14 — *National Monuments Act,* 1954 (*No.* 37), *s.* 3.] In 1977 the plaintiff bought land at Loughshinny on the coast of County Dublin which included a 38½-acre site occupied by a prehistoric promontory fort. In 1970 the

CONSTITUTION—Statute.

latter had been listed for preservation under s. 8 of the National Monuments (Amendment) Act, 1954, a section which also prohibited the owner from interfering with the site without giving prior notice to the Commissioners of Public Works. Soon after acquiring the land the plaintiff, who knew through his predecessor-in-title that the land contained an ancient monument, employed contractors to plough part of the area occupied by the fort. He failed to notify the Commissioners of his intention to undertake this work, and could not at the relevant time be found by the Commissioners and warned to desist. Accordingly the Commissioners, defendants in the action, made a preservation order under s. 8 of the National Monuments Act, 1930 (as amended by s. 3 of the 1954 Act), the effect of which was to apply to the site the extensive prohibitions listed in s. 14 of the 1930 Act. In correspondence subsequently, the defendants declined an application from the plaintiff to revoke the preservation order. The plaintiff proceeded to seek from the High Court a declaration that the defendants, by failing to consult him prior to the making of the preservation order, had acted *ultra vires*; and that s.8 of the 1930 Act, which includes no provision for the payment of compensation to owners of land containing national monuments, was an unjust attack on the property rights of citizens within the meaning of Article 40.3.2° of the Constitution. In the High Court McWilliam J. refused to grant the declarations sought. From this judgment (reported in [1983] ILRM 391) the plaintiff appealed to the Supreme Court. **Held** by O'Higgins C.J., in two judgments, the first a judgment of the court (pronounced in accordance with its practice when adjudicating on constitutional matters) that the impugned legislation was valid, and the second a unanimous decision that there had been no breach of natural justice, that, 1, the defendants were entitled, by reason of the emergency created by the plaintiff's unlawful ploughing operation, to act promptly to protect the national monument. 2. The defendants had treated the plaintiff's subsequent protest as an application to revoke the preservation order, and duly dealt with his submissions in accordance with the principles of natural justice. 3. The rights of property guaranteed by the Constitution are subject to regulation with reference to the common good, which plainly requires that national monuments be preserved, and to social justice, which may or may not according to circumstances require the payment of compensation: *Dreher* v. *Irish land Commission* [1984] ILRM 94 considered. 4. S. 8 of the National Monuments Act, 1930, delimits not the right of private ownership but the user to which land, in the interests of the common good, may be put. 5. The preservation of national

CONSTITUTION—*continued.*

monuments should be regarded as the common duty of all citizens. *O'Callaghan* v. *Commissioners of Public Works in Ireland*

(S.C.) [1985] ILRM 364

45. —— **Property rights** — *Public utility — Private property — Interference — Common good — Electricity supply cables — National grid — Statutory power of plaintiff board to erect pylons on defendant's land — No right to compensation — Statute unconstitutional — Local government — Planning — Permission — Application — Advertisement — Inadequate description of location — Permission invalid — Owner of registered land affected by exercise of statutory power — Local Government (Planning and Development) Regulations,* 1964 (*S.I. No.* 221), *art.* 9 — *Electricity Supply Act, 1927 (No.* 27), *ss.* 53(5), 98 — *Electricity (Supply) (Amendment) Act, 1941 (No.* 1), *s.* 5 — *Electricity (Supply) (Amendment) Act,* 1945 (*No.* 12), *s.* 46 — *Local Government (Planning and Development) Act,* 1963 (*No.* 28), *ss.* 25, 26 — *Registration of Title Act,* 1964 (*No.* 6), *ss.* 52(1), 69, 72 — *Constitution of Ireland,* 1937, *Arts.* 40.3, 43.] Section 53, sub-s. 5, of the Electricity (Supply) Act, 1927, as amended by s. 46 of the Electricity (Supply) (Amendment) Act, 1945, provides that, if an owner or occupier of land fails to give her consent within 7 days after the service on her of a notice stating the intention of the Electricity Supply Board to place an electric line across her land, the Board may place such line across her land in the position and manner stated in the notice. Section 98 of the Act of 1927, as amended by s. 5 of the Electricity (Supply) (Amendment) Act, 1941, authorises the Board, on giving 7 days written notice of its intention, to lop or cut any tree, shrub, or hedge which obstructs or interferes with the erection or laying of any electric wires of the Board with the survey of the proposed routes of any transmission or distribution lines of the Board. The defendant was the owner of registered land which she had purchased without notice that the plaintiff had obtained planning permission for the erection of an electricity transmission line, a portion of which the plaintiff intended to run across her land, and without notice of the advertisement pursuant to which the application for planning permission had been made. This advertisement had described the location of the land to which the application related by naming the two townlands at which the transmission line was to commence and terminate in the county where the defendant's land was situate. Pursuant to s. 53, sub-s. 3, of the Electricity (Supply) Act, 1927, the plaintiff served a notice on the defendant of its intention to erect an electric line and three electricity pylons on her land and of its intention, pursuant

CONSTITUTION—Statute.

to s. 98 of the Act of 1927, as amended, after a period of 7 days, to lop or cut certain trees, shrubs, or hedges which obstructed or interfered with the electric line or with the erection of the line. When the plaintiff's represenatives attended at the defendant's land for the purpose of carrying out these works they were refused entry by the defendant. The plaintiff issued a plenary summons in the High Court seeking an injunction restraining the defendant from preventing the plaintiff from entering and carrying out these works upon her land. Pending the trial of the action the plaintiff sought and was refused an interlocutory injunction by the High Court. At the trial of the plaintiff's action in the High Court it was **held** by Carroll J. in granting the injunction sought (subject to the proviso that the defendant be given another opportunity to choose between the three options provided by the plaintiff for the siting of the electricity pylons), 1, that as the substantive effect of the entire of ss. 53 and 98 of the Act of 1927 was considered by the Oireachtas when amending them post 1937, both sections as amended were entitled to the presumption of constitutionality. 2. That s. 53, sub-s. 5 and s. 98, as amended, did not constitute an unjust attack on the defendant's property rights and were not invalid having regard to the provisions of Articles 40, s. 3 and 43, s. 2 of the Constitution. 3. That the planning permission obtained by the plaintiff was valid, as the plaintiff had sufficient interest to support its application for planning permission, and it was not open to the defendant to argue that the advertisement was inadequate, as she had acquired the lands after planning permission was granted and was therefore unaffected by any shortcomings the advertisement may have had. *Frescati Estates* v. *Walker* [1975] I.R. 177 applied. 4. That the defendant had not purchased the land free from the plaintiff's right to do what the planning permission allowed, as a grant of planning permission was not included in the phrase "all other rights, including the rights of the State", contained in s. 52, sub-s. 1, of the Registration of Title Act, 1964. 5. That the defendant had not purchased the land free from the way-leave that would be created by the placing of an electricity line across her land, as this was a burden to which her land was subject by virtue of s. 52, sub-s. 1 (*b*) of the Act of 1964, being an easement which was not created by express grant after first registration and which did not require registration by virtue of s. 72, sub-s. 1 (*h*) of the Act of 1964. 6. That the decision where to place the pylons was not bad for want of fairness.

On appeal by the defendant it was **Held** by the Supreme Court in allowing the appeal and in granting a declaration that s. 53, sub-s. 5, of the

CONSTITUTION—*continued.*

Electricity (Supply) Act, 1927, as amended, is invalid having regard to the provisions of Article 40, s. 3, of the Constitution, 1, that the nature and extent of the amendments to ss. 53 and 98 of the Act of 1927 by s. 46 of the Act of 1945 and by s. 5 of the Act of 1941, respectively, were such that they had the effect of re-enacting those sections as part of a post-Constitution statute which attracted the presumption of constitutionality. 2. That the power to lay an electricity transmission line compulsorily was a power to impose a burdensome right over land, which in this instance was a requirement of the common good. 3. That whether the granting of such powers to the plaintiff without the provision of any obligation to pay adequate compensation constituted an infringement of Article 40, s. 3, sub-ss. 1 or 2, was governed by the principle that any State action that is authorised by and conforms to Article 43 of the Constitution cannot be unjust for the purposes of Article 40, s. 3, sub-section 2. *Dictum* of Walsh J. in *Dreher* v. *Irish Land Commission* [1984] ILRM 94 at 96, applied. 4. That the *ex gratia* payment of compensation in an amount determined by the plaintiff was not the same as an obligation to pay adequate compensation, which obligation implied the right to have the amount assessed by an independent arbiter or tribunal. 5. That the right to sue for and obtain damages in compensation for the violation of a person's constitutional rights did not amount to the protection of those rights by the State, as required by Article 40, s. 3, sub-s. 2, of the Constitution. *Meskell* v. *C.I.E.* [1973] I.R. 121, considered. 6. That having regard to the fact that the plaintiff provided *ex gratia* payments of compensation, which it asserted to be reasonable, and to the fact that the plaintiff, in order to acquire the right over the defendant's land which it sought to enforce under s. 53 of the Act of 1927, could have availed of s. 45 of that Act, which section provides an express right to compensation, the protection of the defendant's property rights, by providing the right to compensation, was clearly practicable. 7. That, s. 53, sub-s. 5, of the Act of 1927, as amended, is invalid having regard to the provisions of Article 40, s. 3, of the Constitution, as the powers contained therein to compulsorily impose a burdensome right over land without providing a corresponding right to adequate compensation are not necessitated by the principles of social justice nor by the exigencies of the common good. *Dictum* of Walsh J. in *Dreher* v. *Irish Land Commission* [1984] ILRM 94 at 96, applied. 8. That the imposition of the relatively minor burden on landowners of the cutting or lopping of trees, shrubs or hedges so as to make and keep safe the existence of a major electricity transmission line was not an unjust attack on the

CONSTITUTION—Statute.

plaintiff's property rights and that the defendant had failed to establish that s. 98 of the Act of 1927, as amended, was invalid having regard to the provisions of Article 40, s. 3, of the Constitution. 9. That, as a member of the public who was affected by the planning permission granted, the defendant was entitled to challenge the validity of that permission on the basis of non-compliance with the permission regulations made pursuant to s. 25 of the Local Government (Planning and Development) Act, 1963. *Crodaun Homes Ltd.* v. *Kildare County Council* [1983] ILRM 1, applied. 10. That in the absence of any suggestion that the planning authority could have made any submissions not made by the plaintiff, there was no procedural requirement or requirement of justice which prevented the defendant from challenging the validity of planning permission which directly affected her, on the grounds of having been made without authority, without joining the planning authority as a party to the action. 11. That assuming, without so deciding, that the Planning Acts are applicable to the plaintiff, the advertisement pursuant to which the application for planning permission was made did not comply with Article 9, s. 4 (*a*) of the permission regulations applicable, in that the location of the land in respect of which the permission was sought was not adequately identified, and that the permission obtained by the plaintiff pursuant to s. 26 of the Act of 1963 was therefore invalid. *Crodaun Homes Ltd.* v. *Kildare County Council* [1983] ILRM 1, applied. *Electricity Supply Board* v. *Gormley*

(H.C., S.C.) [1985] I.R.129; [1985] ILRM 494

46. —— **Property rights** — *Shareholders — Registered provident society engaged in the business of banking — Legislation enacted prohibiting such societies from accepting or holding deposits — Whether legislation invalid — Whether unjust attack on property rights of shareholders — Whether shareholder has property rights capable of being invoked — Whether prohibition infringed shareholders' right of association — Constitution of Ireland,* 1937, *Arts.* 40.3, 40.6.1(iii) — *Industrial and Provident Societies (Amendment) Act,* 1978 (*No.* 23), *s.* 5(2).] S. 5(2) of the Industrial and Provident Societies (Amendment) Act, 1978, prohibited industrial and provident societies from accepting or holding deposits after the end of a period of five years commencing on the passing of the Act. The first named plaintiff was a society registered under the Industrial and Provident Societies Act, 1893, which engaged in the business of banking in accordance with its powers as a society so registered and the second named plaintiff was a shareholder in the first named plaintiff. The plaintiffs sought a declaration that the Act of 1978 was invalid having

CONSTITUTION—*continued.*

regard to the provisions of the Constitution contending *inter alia* that the Act of 1978 contravened the provisions of Art. 40.3 of the Constitution as an unjust attack on property rights and that the Act of 1978 interfered with the freedom of association guaranteed by Art. 40.6.1(iii). The defendant contended *inter alia* that the first named plaintiff was not entitled to the constitutional protection afforded by the personal rights guaranteed by the Constitution to citizens and that the second named plaintiff had no property rights in the assets or business of the first named plaintiff. The defendant adduced evidence in the High Court that at the time of passing of the Act of 1978 a large number of industrial and provident societies were engaged in the business of banking free from the restrictions imposed on persons other than licensed banks carrying on banking businesses, but were outside the control of the Central Bank. The High Court held in dismissing the plaintiffs' claim that since the general public who placed money on deposit were therefore at risk the Minister had a legitimate concern to protect members of the general public who would not have the commercial awareness of banking institutions in relation to making deposits. The plaintiffs appealed. **Held** (O'Higgins C.J., Finlay P., Walsh, Henchy and McCarthy JJ.), 1, since the second named plaintiff was entitled to complain if the impugned legislation interfered with any of his personal rights it was unnecessary to consider the question of the rights of the first named plaintiff. 2. As a shareholder the second named plaintiff had to the extent of his investment an interest in the first named plaintiff and contactual rights arising therefrom which were property rights capable of being harmed by injury done to the first named plaintiff and of being invoked for the purposes of Art. 40.3. 3. The prohibition in the impugned section was not an expropriation of the business of the first named plaintiff or of the property rights of its shareholders but was a regulation of the range of business which the first named plaintiff might lawfully transact and since on the evidence the regulations affected by the legislation were reasonable and in the public interest it could not be regarded as an unjust attack on property rights. 4. The exercise of the right of the second named plaintiff to associate with others was not prevented by a law controlling in the public interest what such an association might do and such regulation was not an infringement of Art. 40.6.1 (iii). *Private Motorists Provident Society Ltd.* v. *Attorney General*

(S.C.) [1984] ILRM 88

47. —— **Property rights** — *Taxation — Residential property tax levied on properties over certain value — Whether unjust attack on property*

CONSTITUTION—Statute.

and family rights — Whether constituting invidious discrimination — Presumption of constitutionality in taxation matters — Locus standi — *Constitution of Ireland,* 1937, *Arts.* 40.1, 40.3, 41, 43 — *Finance Act,* 1983 (*No.* 15).] Part VI of the Finance Act, 1983, imposed a residential property tax on persons owning and occupying dwellings with an aggregate net market value exceeding £65,000. The tax was levied at the rate of 1½% on the amount by which the net market value exceeded £65,000. Exempted from payment of the tax were persons whose aggregated household income did not exceed £20,000. To the income of the owner was added the incomes of persons (other than servants) normally resident with him. The plaintiffs sought a declaration that the tax was invalid because it infringed rights of the person and family, and of property and privacy, to be found in Articles 40.1, 40.3 and 41 of the Constitution. The plaintiffs in the first action, a husband and wife, contended that the criterion of 'net market value' ignored the fact that an owner might possess only a limited or, as in their case, a mortgage-encumbered interest in the property. The plaintiffs in the second action, a mother and son, objected to the principle of aggregating the incomes of the household. The mother, who was the owner, had an income of only £1,400. She did not know the incomes of those with whom she shared her house, her husband and five children, but surmised that it exceeded £20,000. The son who was co-plaintiff objected to disclosing his income to his mother. They argued that the tax, by requiring knowledge of the income of others, was an intrusion upon their alleged constitutional right to privacy; and, by rendering it disadvantageous for certain persons to reside together, tended to the break-up of families. **Held** by O'Hanlon J., dismissing the two actions, 1, the plaintiffs had no *locus standi* to advance hypothetical arguments, and were limited to showing how they themselves were prejudiced by the impugned tax. *Cahill* v. *Sutton* [1980] I.R. 269 and *King* v. *Attorney General* [1981] I.R. 233 followed; *dicta* in *O'Brien* v. *Keogh* [1972] I.R. 144 explained. 2. Article 40.1 of the Constitution guarantees citizens their equality as human persons, and the plaintiffs could not establish that a tax on the ownership and occupation of land discriminated against them as human persons: *Quinn's Supermarket Ltd.* v. *Attorney General* [1972] I.R. 1 and *Murtagh Properties Ltd.* v. *Cleary* [1972] I.R. 330 followed; *Brennan & Ors* v. *Attorney General* [1983] ILRM 449 discussed. 3. Taxation statutes enjoy an especially strong presumption of constitutionality and have been struck down as an 'unjust attack' on rights of property only where

CONSTITUTION—*continued.*

they can be regarded as 'unreasonable', 'arbitrary', or 'hostile' or 'invidious' in their discrimination against particular persons or classes. 4. It is legitimate to impose a tax on the occupation of property, even if the occupier is not the freehold owner and enjoys only a small income, for taxation is inherently an interference with property and frequently discriminatory, though not unreasonable or arbitrary. 5. The 1983 Act did not authorise any invasion of the privacy of other members of a household, and it was doubtful whether a provision for the compulsory disclosure of information about income would infringe any constitutional right of privacy. 6. It was improbable that the tax would impose such hardship as would lead to the break-up of families. The plaintiffs appealed to the Supreme Court. **Held** (O'Higgins C.J., Henchy, Griffin, Hederman and McCarthy JJ.), dismissing the appeal, 1, the court would consider the actual circumstances of the plaintiffs and would disregard hypothetical arguments, but another plaintiff with sufficient *locus standi* might in the future successfully challenge the Act. *Cahill* v. *Sutton* [1980] I.R. 269 applied. 2. When examining the constitutionality of a taxation law the court does not enquire into the policy or effectiveness of the statute, but recognises the duty of the State to impose taxation, which necessarily interferes with the property rights of affected citizens. 3. A tax on the occupation of property does not infringe any personal right to equality, nor is such a tax, imposed with reference to a high market value, offensive to principles of justice or fair play. 4. The provisions of the Act which require the aggregation of the income of the taxpayer with that of other members of a household is not the basis on which the tax is imposed by a criterion for exemption from it; and in providing for aggregation the State is merely recognising the reality that members of a common household generally contribute to the expenses of the home. 5. Even if a tax produces hardship, difficulty in making payment is not a ground for challenging its validity. *Madigan* v. *Attorney General*

(H.C., S.C.) [1986] ILRM 136

48. —— **Property rights** — *Unlawful organisation — Suppression order — Forfeiture of organisation's property — Minister empowered to freeze monies in bank without notice to account-holder — Procedures — Fair hearing — Owner establishing monies not property of unlawful organisation entitled to repayment and compensation — Whether forfeiture and money freezing procedure unjust attack on property rights — Interest of the common good — Offences Against the State Act,* 1939 (*No.* 13), *ss.* 19, 22 — *Offences Against the State (Amendment) Act,* 1985 (*No.*

CONSTITUTION—Statute.

3) — *Constitution of Ireland,* 1937, *Arts.* 40.3, 43.] Section 19 of the Offences Against the State Act, 1939, provides that where the Government is of opinion that any particular organisation is an unlawful organisation it shall be lawful for the Government by order ("suppression order") to declare that such organisation is an unlawful organisation and ought, in the public interest, to be suppressed. By s. 22 immediately upon the making of such a suppression order "all the property (whether real, chattel real, or personal and whether in possession or in action) of such organisation shall become and be forfeited to and vested in the Minister for Justice." By s. 2 of the Offences Against the State (Amendment) Act, 1985, where the Minister is of opinion that certain monies held by a bank would, but for the operation of s. 22 of the Act of 1939, be the property of an unlawful organisation, he is empowered to freeze those monies and cause the bank to pay them into the High Court, whence, after 6 months, they might be paid out to the Minister on his *ex parte* application and paid into the Exchequer. Section 3 provides for payment out of the monies by the High Court to any party claiming within 6 months to be entitled to them "if that court is satisfied that s. 22 . . . has not had effect in relation to the monies and that the person is the owner of the monies." Section 4 provides, *inter alia,* for compensation to be paid by the Minister to the owner for loss incurred by him by reason of the payment of the monies into and their retention in the High Court. The Act of 1985 was enacted on the 19 February, 1985. On the following day the Minister for Justice directed the Bank of Ireland, Navan, County Meath, to pay into the High Court the sum of £1,750,816.27 held at that time upon a joint account in the names of the plaintiffs. By plenary summons dated the 29 March, 1985, the plaintiffs sought declarations in the High Court that s. 22 of the Act of 1939 and ss. 2, 3, 5, 6, 7 and 8 of the Act of 1985 were invalid having regard to the provisions of the Constitution. **Held** by Barrington J., in refusing the declarations sought, that despite reversing the ordinary onus of proof, by placing it upon the owner of property seeking to establish his entitlement to it, the machinery of the Act of 1985 nevertheless provided for a fair hearing and compensation in cases of error, and thus constituted no more than a permissible delimitation of property rights in the interests of the common good and was not therefore an unjust attack upon private property contrary to Articles 40, s. 3 and 43 of the Constitution. *Calero-Toledo* v. *Pearson Yacht Leasing Co.* (1974) 416 U.S. 663 and *Dreher* v. *The Irish Land Commission* [1984] ILRM 94 considered. *Clancy* v. *Ireland*

CONSTITUTION—*continued.*

(H.C.) [1988] I.R.326

49. —— **Trial of offences** — *Minor offence — Fisheries — Summary conviction — Fine and forfeiture of equipment — Whether offence minor offence — Severity of punishment — Whether forfeiture primary punishment — Constitution of Ireland,* 1937, *Art.* 38 — *Fisheries (Consolidation) Act,* 1959 (*No.* 14), *s.* 221.] S. 221(1) of the Fisheries (Consolidation) Act, 1959, as amended, provides that where a foreign fishing boat enters within the exclusive fishery limits of the State in contravention of the section, the master of such boat will be liable on summary conviction to a fine not exceeding £100. Sub-s. 2 provides that if fishing had taken place while the boat was within the said limits, the court must order the forfeiture of all fish and fishing gear on the boat. The plaintiff having contravened both sub-sections was fined the maximum penalty, and his equipment, worth £102,040, was confiscated. The plaintiff claimed that the forfeiture of his property constituted a penalty, and that this penalty was so severe that the offence could not be a minor offence triable summarily. For this reason, the plaintiff sought a declaration that s. 221 was unconstitutional. **Held** by McWilliam J. in granting the declaration sought: the forfeiture of the fish and fishing gear was both a penalty and a direct consequence of a conviction under the section, and removed the offence from the category of minor offences triable summarily. *Melling* v. *Ó Mathghamhna* [1960] I.R. 1, and *Re Haughey* [1971] I.R. 217 followed: *Conroy* v. *Attorney General and Keaveney* [1965] I.R. 411 distinguished. *Kostan* v. *Ireland*

(H.C.) [1978] ILRM 12

50. —— **Trial of offences** — *Right to trial in due course of law — Courts — Judicial independence — Special Criminal Court — Appointment and removal of members — Remuneration of members — Enactment valid — Offences Against the State Act,* 1939 (*No.* 13), *s.* 39 — *Constitution of Ireland,* 1937, *Arts.* 34, 35, 38.] Section 39, sub-s. 2 of the Offences Against the State Act, 1939, states that each member of a Special Criminal Court shall be appointed, and be removeable at will, by the Government. Section 39, sub-s. 4 of the Act states, *inter alia,* that the remuneration of members of Special Criminal Courts shall be such as the Minister for Finance thinks proper. The plaintiffs were charged, *inter alia,* with capital murder. They were tried before the Special Criminal Court, convicted and condemned to death. Proceedings were commenced seeking a declaration that s. 39 of the Offences Against the State Act, 1939, was invalid having regard to Articles 34 and 35 of the Constitution and that the Special Criminal Court

was unconstitutionally constituted, together with consequential declarations that the convictions and sentences imposed on the plaintiffs were invalid and of no effect. The High Court (Barrington J.) refused the relief sought. On appeal by the plaintiffs it was **Held** by the Supreme Court in disallowing the appeal, 1, that by virtue of Article 38, s. 6, of the Constitution, the impugned sub-sections of s. 39 of the Act of 1939 could not be invalidated merely by reason of any inconsistency with the provisions of Articles 34 and 35 of the Constitution. 2. That the impugned sub-sections of s. 39 of the Act of 1939 were not to be interpreted as giving the Government and Minister for Finance, respectively, unfettered power to interfere with, or influence, the proceedings and decisions of the Special Criminal Court. If the Government or Minister sought to exercise the powers conferred on them by these sub-sections in a manner capable of interfering with the judicial independence of the Special Criminal Court, such attempt would be prevented and corrected by the courts. *East Donegal Co-Operative* v. *The Attorney General* [1970] I.R. 317 considered. *Eccles* v. *Ireland*
(S.C.) [1985] I.R.545; [1986] ILRM 343

51. —— **Trial of offences** — *Whether criminal offence — Revenue — Requirement to make a return of income — Failure to comply with requirement — Penalties — Whether penalties of a criminal nature — Whether indicative of a criminal offence — Income Tax Act, 1967 (No.* 6), *ss.* 172, 500 — *Constitution of Ireland,* 1937, *Art.* 38.] Section 500 of the Income Tax Act, 1967, imposes a fixed monetary penalty on any person who fails to comply with a notice served upon him which requires him to deliver any document or furnish any particulars. Section 508 of that Act empowers any duly authorised officer of the Revenue to sue by civil proceedings for the recovery of that penalty. The plaintiff was required by notice issued by the first defendant (an Inspector of Taxes) to deliver returns of income for certain income tax years. The plaintiff failed to comply with the notice within the time specified. The first defendant sued the plaintiff, claiming penalties which arose under s. 500 of the Income Tax Act, 1967, by virtue of the plaintiff's failure to comply with the terms of the notice. Judgment was duly entered in favour of the first defendant. The plaintiff issued proceedings seeking a declaration that s. 500 of the Income Tax Act, 1967, was repugnant to the Constitution in that it imposed a criminal penalty other than in a manner permitted by the Constitution. **Held** by Carroll J., in dismissing the plaintiff's claim, 1, that the concept of a penalty under the Income Tax Act, 1918, the Act on which the Income Tax Act, 1967, was based, was that of a statutory

debt recoverable by the State in civil proceedings and not a punishment for a criminal offence. 2. That apart from the imposition of a penalty, all the indicia of a criminal offence are absent from s. 500 of the Income Tax Act, 1967. 3. That the requirement that a person who fails to make a return of income when required to do so should pay a penalty into the Central Fund is not indicative of a criminal offence and is not repugnant to the Constitution. *Melling* v. *Ó Mathghamhna* [1962] I.R. 1 applied. *Attorney General* v. *Casey* [1930] I.R. 163 considered. *McLoughlin* v. *Tuite*
(H.C.) [1986] I.R.235 ; [1986] ILRM 304

TRIAL OF OFFENCES
see also Nos. 3, 49-51

52. —— **Fair procedures** — *Trial — Delay — Trial abandoned — Proposed re-trial — Whether prejudice arising — Whether interlocutory injunction to restrain said trial be granted — Constitution of Ireland,* 1937, *Arts.* 38.1, 40.3.] The plaintiff applied for an interlocutory injunction restraining the defendant, originally the prosecutor in a case entitled *D.P.P.* v. *O'Connor,* from proceeding with the aforesaid case on the grounds that to proceed with the said case would involve an injustice to the plaintiff and would breach his constitutional right to have fair procedures at his trial. The plaintiff was charged in October, 1985, with receiving a large number of items of jewellery contary to s. 31(1) of the Larceny Act, 1916. The trial judge dismissed the jury when the case came up for hearing in February, 1985, on the grounds that the inclusions by the defendant of a large number of items of jewellery in relation to which there was no evidence of theft was prejudicial to the trial of the remaining allegations. The Director of Public Prosecutions prepared a fresh indictment against the plaintiff in April, 1985, and served a notice dated 20 July, 1985, on the plaintiff in November, 1985, notifying him of the two witnesses that proposed to give additional evidence at the trial on the second indictment scheduled to begin in December, 1985. The plaintiff applied for an interlocutory injunction restraining the Director of Public Prosecutions from proceeding with the trial on the ground that to proceed would involve an injustice to the plaintiff and would breach his constitutional right to fair procedure. The plaintiff relied on a number of grounds, in particular: (i) That despite a letter of 25 January, 1985, sent by the plaintiff's solicitors to the defendant requesting the defendant not to proceed with the first trial on substantially the grounds on which the trial judge discharged the jury, the defendant ignored the request; (ii) due to the extent of the matters charged in the indictment the cost of the plaintiff's defence was greatly increased thus causing the plaintiff to exhaust his financial

CONSTITUTION—Trial of Offences.

resources and lose his business; (iii) the plaintiff is 60 years of age and has been suffering from a serious illness for several months past; (iv) it was two and a half years since the plaintiff was charged. **Held** by Lardner J. making the order sought, 1, the plaintiff's right to fair procedure would be infringed by a further trial by reason of the circumstances outlined by the plaintiff's counsel together with the element of delay. 2. The element of fairness in relation to the right to fair procedure is a matter of degree which is determined by the circumstances in each case. *O'Connor* v. *D.P.P.*

(H.C.) [1987] ILRM 723

53. —— **Jury trial** — *Whether jury must try issues of fact — Whether court of trial may be precluded from assessing issues relating to guilt or innocence of accused — Customs offences — Evasion of customs duties — Statute — Determination of value of goods — Final and unappealable determination by District Court — Offence triable with jury — Fairness of procedures — Whether fair appeal possible — Whether statute inconsistent with Constitution —* Locus standi — *Determination of District Court not yet made — Finance Act,* 1963 (*No.* 23), *ss.* 34(4)(*d*)(i),(iii) — *Constitution of Ireland,* 1937, *Arts.* 34.3.4, 38.1, 38.2, 38.5.] The plaintiff was charged with offences relating to the fraudulent evasion of customs duties contrary to s. 186 of the Customs Consolidation Act, 1876, as amended by s. 34 of the Finance Act, 1963. Section 34 of the Act of 1963 provided that, in the event of a defendant to such a charge challenging the estimated value of the goods in question, he may give notice to the prosecution of such challenge; and the District Justice with carriage of the preliminary proceedings in the matter shall, pursuant to sub-s. 4(*d*)(i) of s. 34 determine the value of the goods "and the value so determined shall be final and not appealable." Sub-section 4 (*d*)(iii) of s. 34 provided that at the trial of the offence "the value so determined shall be taken conclusively as being the value of the goods, without further evidence." The plaintiff served notice disputing the estimated value of the goods in relation to the charges against him and, before the District Court determined the value of the goods, he initiated proceedings in which he challenged the constitutionality of sub-s. 4(*d*)(i) and sub-s. 4(*d*)(iii) of s. 34 of the Act of 1963. Section 34, sub-s. 4(*d*)(ii) of the Act of 1963 provided that, in the event of the value of the goods exceeding £100 (increased to £500 by s. 44 of the Finance Act, 1976) the offence should be tried on indictment. **Held** by Carroll J., in granting the relief sought, 1, the plaintiff had the *locus standi* to

CONSTITUTION—*continued.*

challenge the constitutionality of the provisions in question as he was in imminent danger of a determination affecting his rights, and this need not necessarily be a decision which would adversely affect his rights. 2. Where the trial of offences pursuant to s. 34 of the Act of 1963 took place with a jury, it was the role of the jury alone to determine disputed issues of fact, and the issue of the value of the goods was material to the question as to whether a defendant had the fraudulent intent necessary to constitute an offence under the legislation in question, so that the provisions of s. 34, which precluded the jury from determining these matters, were in breach of Article 38, ss. 1 and 5 of the Constitution. *Dicta* in *The People* v. *Lynch* [1982] I.R. 64 applied. 3. The provisions of s. 34 of the Act of 1963 were repugnant to Article 38, ss. 1 and 2, of the Constitution in assigning to the District Court the power to decide an issue of fact relative to an offence which was not a minor offence, and also in the fragmenting of issues in a criminal trial between two courts of equal jurisdiction insofar as an offence would be triable in the District Court. *Corporation of Dublin* v. *Flynn* [1980] I.R. 357 and *Deaton* v. *The Attorney General* [1963] I.R. 170 applied. 4. There would be an absence of fair procedures where, on appeal, the court of appeal would be precluded from reducing a fine because the finding as to value was unappealable where the court would otherwise have reached the conclusion that the value was excessive and not warranted by the evidence. *Curtis* v. *Attorney General*

(H.C.) [1985] I.R.458 ; [1986] ILRM 428

54. —— **Minor offence** — *Bookmaker — Infringement of betting duty regulations — Whether minor offence capable of being tried summarily — Matters to which the court is to have regard — Constitution of Ireland,* 1937, *Art.* 38.2 — *Finance Act,* 1926 (*No.* 35), *ss. 24, 25 — Betting Duty (Certified Returns) Regulations,* 1934 (*S.R. & O. No.* 113), *regs.* 8, 18, 23, 29.] S. 24 of the Finance Act, 1926, provides *inter alia* that an excise duty should be paid by every bookmaker on every bet entered by him (after 1 November, 1926) and s. 24(4) provides that every person who fails to pay any such sum payable by him shall be guilty of an offence and liable on summary conviction to an excise penalty of £500. Between 1977 and 1978 sixty-four summonses were issued by the third named defendant (D.P.P.) against the plaintiff alleging offences under s. 24 (of the Finance Act, 1926) and alleging failure to comply with regulations made under s. 25 of the Act which offences were subject to a similar penalty. The plaintiff contended *inter alia* (i) that none of the offences were minor offences within the meaning of Art. 38.2 of the

Constitution and accordingly could not be tried summarily and (ii) if the offences did constitute minor offences the plaintiff was entitled to be furnished in advance of the hearing with a statement of the evidence to be called on the hearing of the summons. **Held,** 1, the matters to which the court must have regard in determining whether an offence is a minor offence as set out in the decision of Lavery J. in *Melling* v. *Ó Mathghamhna* [1962] I.R. 1, include the severity of the penalty involved (which while the most important consideration was not a primary consideration in all cases). 2. Where the court is required to determine (otherwise than for the purpose of the Criminal Justice Act, 1951) whether an offence created by statute passed before the Constitution is a minor offence and for that purpose has regard to the monetary penalty which might be imposed the relevant date for evaluating the penalty is the date on which the Constitution came into operation and not the date on which the summons is directed to be heard by the District Court. 3. The gravity of the offence as charged could best be gauged in the instant case by the monetary penalty stipulated which in 1937 would have represented a very significant amount and accordingly did not constitute the offence a minor offence within the meaning of Art. 38.2 of the Constitution. In the circumstances the court was not required to make a determination on the plaintiff's second contention. *Charlton* v. *Ireland*

(H.C.) [1984] ILRM 39

55. —— **Minor offence** — *Test applicable — Mitigation of statutory penalty — Statute — Interpretation — Mistake — Enactment inoperative — Revenue — Excise duty — Bookmaker's records of bets accepted — False returns furnished — Whether single or multiple offences — Betting Duty (Certified Returns) Regulations,* 1934 (*S.R. & O. No.* 113), *regs.* 8, 9, 26-9 — *Finance Act,* 1926 (*No.* 35), *ss.* 24, 25 — *Constitution of Ireland,* 1937, *Art.* 38.] Section 25, sub-s. 1, of the Act of 1926 confers on the Revenue Commissioners power to make regulations for securing the payment by bookmakers of excise duty on bets accepted by them, and sub-s. 2 of that section states that every person who contravenes or fails to comply with a regulation made under that section "shall be guilty of an offence under this section and shall be liable on summary conviction thereof to an excise penalty of five hundred pounds." The Revenue Commissioners made the Regulations of 1934 pursuant to the power conferred on them by s. 25 of the Act of 1926. Regulation 29 of those regulations states that a bookmaker, being authorised to pay excise duty in that manner, shall forward to the Collector of Customs and Excise not later than the

Thursday next following the week ending Saturday "to which the daily returns required by number 27 of these regulations relate" a certified summary of such daily returns in the prescribed form and the amount of the excise duty payable in respect of the bets accepted by him during that week. Regulation 30 of those regulations states that a bookmaker having more than one office shall make separate returns and forward separate remittances of duty for each of his offices. The prosecutor was a bookmaker who carried on his business at two offices. He was prosecuted summarily in the District Court as defendant on 56 complaints charging him with contraventions of regulation 29 of the Regulations of 1934 by failing, in respect of each of seven consecutive weeks and each of his offices, to furnish with the weekly return (i) a return of two specified bets accepted by him and (ii) the excise duty payable on each of those bets. The prosecutor was convicted by the respondent District Justice of each of the 56 offences and the respondent imposed in respect of each offence the statutory penalty of £500, but he mitigated that sum to £125. The prosecutor obtained in the High Court a conditional order of certiorari quashing, unless cause were shown to the contrary, his convictions on the grounds (1) that regulation 29 was inoperative by reason of the fact that regulation 27, mentioned therein, did not require any daily returns; (2) that, even if regulation 29 imposed a duty to make returns, only 14 offences had been proved and (3) that the offences so charged were not minor offences and that, accordingly, they should have been tried on indictment before a jury. In granting an order absolute, notwithstanding the cause shown by the respondent, the trial judge held in favour of the prosecutor on the second and third grounds but against him on the first ground. At the hearing of an appeal by the respondent and a cross-appeal by the prosecutor, it was **Held** by the Supreme Court (O'Higgins C.J., Henchy, Griffin, Hederman and McCarthy JJ.), in disallowing the appeal and allowing the cross-appeal, 1, that having regard to the contemporary value of the sum of £500, the offences created by s. 25, sub-s. 2, of the Act of 1926 were minor offences within the meaning of Article 38, s. 2, of the Constitution (O'Higgins C.J. dissenting). 2. That the mistaken reference to regulation 27 (instead of regulation 26) in regulation 29 could not be remedied by the court and that, accordingly, the convictions, being based upon alleged contraventions of regulation 29, were not valid convictions (Henchy and Griffin JJ. dissenting). *The State (Murphy)* v. *Johnston* [1983] I.R. 235 considered. 3. *Per* O'Higgins C.J., Hederman and McCarthy JJ. — That, if regulation 29 had referred to the regulation which required the daily returns, a trial of the 56

CONSTITUTION—Trial of Offences.

charges could not have resulted in more than 28 convictions, being two convictions in respect of each of the seven weekly returns made by each of the prosecutor's offices. *The State (Rollinson)* v. *Kelly*

(S.C.) [1984] I.R. 248; [1984] ILRM 625

56. —— **Minor offence** — *Plaintiff charged with gaming offences triable summarily — Plaintiff owning gaming equipment of considerable value — Such equipment liable to forfeiture upon conviction — Whether gaming offences minor offences — Distinction between primary and secondary punishment — Gaming and Lotteries Act,* 1956 (*No.* 2), *ss.* 4, 47 — *Gaming and Lotteries Act,* 1979 (*No.* 6), *s.* 1 — *Constitution of Ireland,* 1937, *Arts.* 38.2, 38.5.] Article 38, s. 5 of the Constitution provides that save in the case of, *inter alia,* the jurisdiction of summary courts to try minor offences, no person shall be tried on any criminal charge without a jury. The plaintiff, an amusement caterer, was the defendant to a number of summonses brought by the third defendant which alleged that he had committed a number of offences under s. 4, sub-s. 1(*c*) of the Gaming and Lotteries Act, 1956, (as amended) which makes it an offence, triable summarily, to promote or assist in promoting or providing facilities for any kind of gaming by means of any slot-machine. In addition to the penalties provided by the Act of rendering a person found guilty of such offence to a fine not exceeding £100 or to imprisonment for a term not exceeding 3 months, or to both such fine and imprisonment (s. 44) and to the possible revocation of his gaming licence or permit (s. 46), the Act provides at s. 47, sub-s. 1 that the court may order the forfeiture of any gaming instrument used in the commission of the offence. That section further provides that in the case of a conviction under s. 5 of the Act which, *inter alia,* makes it an offence to use any premises or place for unlawful gaming, the court may order the forfeiture of any gaming instrument found on the premises or at the place concerned. Pending the hearing of the summonses in the District Court, the plaintiff commenced proceedings in the High Court seeking a declaration that s. 4, sub-s. 1(*c*) and s. 47 of the Act were invalid having regard to the provisions of the Constitution on the basis that the power of forfeiture conferred upon the District Court constituted, or would constitute where exercised in relation to the plaintiff's machines which were of considerable value, a penal deprivation of property of such proportions as would remove the offences with which the plaintiff was charged from the category of minor offences. **Held** by Murphy J., in dismissing the plaintiff's claim, 1, that the primary criterion for determining whether an offence was a minor one related to the primary punishment provided which, in this case, was the financial and custodial penalties prescribed by s. 44, and not to any secondary punishment such as to the liability to forfeiture provided under section 47. *Conroy* v. *The Attorney General* [1965] I.R. 411 and *The State (Pheasantry Ltd.)* v. *Donnelly* [1982] ILRM 512 applied. 2. That the classification of the consequence of forfeiture as secondary punishment was reinforced in the instant case by consideration of the need for an administrative or executive power to deprive a citizen of equipment, for example gaming instruments, which were inherently designed for the commission of a criminal offence. *Conroy* v. *The Attorney General* [1965] I.R. 411 considered. 3. That even if the power of forfeiture had any bearing in determining the gravity of the offences, its value in that regard could only be determined in the circumstances of the present case when the District Justice before whom the summonses would come had had an opportunity of hearing evidence as to the value of the equipment which he was empowered to forfeit and had reached his decision having regard to that evidence and all of the other relevant factors. *L'Henryenat* v. *The Attorney General* [1983] I.R. 193 and *dicta* of Henchy J. in *The State (Rollinson)* v. *Kelly* [1984] I.R. 248 considered. 4. That, accordingly, having regard to the primary punishment for the offence in question and the nature of the offence itself, viewed on a commonsense basis, the offence was a minor one only. *Cartmill* v. *Ireland*

(H.C.) [1987] I.R.192 ; [1988] ILRM 430

Minor offence, *see also* Nos. 42, 49
Unborn, Right to life of, *see* No. 20

—— Adaptation of enactments — Enactment of Parliament of Great Britain and Ireland — Provision of ferry service from Ireland to Wales — Suspension of service by decision of English government minister — Whether decision having extra-territorial effect — Whether statutory obligation suspended by Oireachtas.
see **Contract,** 12

—— Administration of justice — Due course of law — Peace Commissioner — Power of peace commissioner to issue search warrant — Whether a judicial function.
see **Criminal Law,** 70, 71

—— Adoption — Infant placed for adoption — Final consent signed — Death of prospective adoptive mother before adoption order made — Legislation

CONSTITUTION—*continued.*

providing that, whereas a widow could obtain the adoption order, widower could not — Whether such provision constitutionally valid.
see **Adoption,** 5

—— Aliens — Family rights — Extent of entitlement.
see **Aliens,** 1-3

—— Constitutional justice.
se **Natural and Constitutional Justice**

—— Courts — Validity of any law — Inconsistency — Pre-Constitution enactment — Whether enactment continued in force — Relevant point of time for assessment of inconsistency — No presumption that enactment consistent with Constitution — Onus of proof.
see **Constitution,** 39

—— Education — Right to free primary education — Interference with this right — Claim for damages — Whether such claim a claim in tort — Assessment of damages.
see **Damages,** 1

—— Elections — Extension of franchise — Dáil Éireann — Right to vote restricted by Constitution to citizens — Bill conferring franchise upon resident British citizens — Whether bill repugnant to the Constitution — Whether constitutional provisions exclude aliens from voting rights.
see **Constitution,** 1

—— Executive — International relations.
see **Constitution,** 22-5

—— Executive power — Government — State sovereignty — Derivation of powers of government — Requirements of the common good — People — Treaty binding upon State — Single European Act — Title III — European Political Co-operation — Foreign policy referrable to common position adopted by High Contracting Parties — Whether sovereignty fettered — Whether executive powers alienated — Government — Ratification — Breach of Constitution — Judicial review — Whether ratification proposed by Government amenable to judicial review.
see **Constitution,** 22

—— Fair procedures,

CONSTITUTION—*continued.*

see **Constitution,** 11, 28, 40, 42, 51
for full references, see **Fair Procedures**

—— Family — Alien — Marriage to female Irish citizen — Deportation order — Ministerial discretion — Whether deportation order would infringe plaintiff's constitutional rights
see **Aliens,** 2

—— Family — Alien — Marriage to female Irish citizen — Refusal of leave to stay in State — Applicant not holding Irish visa — Previous residence with family in State — Evidence of domestic problems — Whether domestic problems to be considered in refusing leave to stay.
see **Aliens,** 3

—— Family — Aliens — Order to leave country — Alien marrying before order took effect — Extension to permission to stay — Whether order in conflict with rights of family — Whether aliens entitled to benefit of provisions of Constitution relating to family — Whether order must comply with natural justice.
see **Aliens,** 1

—— Family and education — Child — Custody — Infant placed for adoption — Subsequent marriage of natural parents legitimising infant — Consent of mother to adoption — Whether consent to be dispensed with — Welfare of infant — Whether infant's welfare presumptively to be found within the family — Whether interests of child to be paramount consideration in determining custody dispute — Whether State may interfere with parental right of education within the family other than in exceptional cases — Presumption of constitutionality.
see **Adoption,** 2

—— Family — Child — Custody — English Court ordering that infant be placed in the custody of a county council — Father removing infant from jurisdiction of the English courts — Father being an Irish citizen domiciled in England — Council seeking an order of habeas corpus — Legality of infant's detention — Whether father and infant entitled to be regarded as "family" — Appropriate forum for the determination of the infant's future welfare.
see **Family Law,** 1

CONSTITUTION—*continued.*

—— Family — Marriage — Divorce — Recognition of divorces — Whether concept of dependent domicile survived enactment of Constitution.
see **Conflict of Laws,** 7

—— Family — Marriage — Foreign divorce.
see **Conflict of Laws,** 4

—— Family — Married persons — Right of married persons to be treated no less favourably than unmarried persons in similar circumstances — Social welfare payments — Disabled persons' maintenance allowance — Provision requiring account to be taken of income of spouse — Whether requirement extended to social welfare income of spouse in his own right.
see **Statute,** 1

—— Interpretation — Language of Constitution — Conflict between Irish and English texts — Whether common meaning to prevail over distinct meaning.
see **Constitution,** 25

—— Interpretation — Personal rights — Right to procreate — Married couple within prison — Whether right protected and recognised under provisions of Constitution relating to family or relating to personal (unenumerated) rights — Whether absence of expressive language relating to right related to value to be placed on the right.
see **Constitution,** 19

—— Interpretation — Purposive or literal approach — Whether court precluded from considering the principles of social policy.
see **Postal Service**

—— *Locus standi* — Apprehension of breach of rights — Whether sufficient *locus standi.*
see **Constitution,** 53

—— *Locus standi* — International agreement — Whether plaintiffs entitled to challenge international agreement.
see **Constitution,** 23

—— *Locus standi* — Non-citizen.
see **Aliens,** 2, 3

—— *Locus standi* — Planning permission — Challenge to validity.
se **Constitution,** 45

CONSTITUTION—*continued.*

—— *Locus standi* — Public right — Attorney General — Intervention — Assertion of public right by private citizen — Whether common law limitations on private assertion of public right carried over from common law by the Constitution — Whether private citizen has *locus standi* to assert breach of public right without showing particular loss or damage.
see **Practice and Procedure,** 8

—— *Locus standi* — Relator proceedings — *Locus standi* of relator — Whether constitutional provisions self-executing in the absence of legislation.
see **Constitution,** 20

—— *Locus standi* — Statutory offence — Validity — Plaintiff challenging constitutionality of enactment — Plaintiff neither prosecuted nor threatened with prosecution — Challenge restricted by plaintiff's circumstances.
see **Constitution,** 39

—— *Locus standi* — Taxation statute — Validity — Whether hypothetical arguments may be considered.
see **Constitution,** 47

—— *Locus standi* — Treaty — Not part of domestic law — Constitutional infringement alleged — Plaintiff suffering no injury — Ratification — Reliefs — Declaration and injunction — Whether plaintiff entitled to challenge treaty ratification in absence of injury — Whether exceptional circumstances established — Single European Act.
see **Constitution,** 22

—— Natural justice.
see **Natural and Constitutional Justice**

—— Personal rights — Dwelling — Inviolability — Criminal law — Arrest — Trespass by Garda Síochána in dwelling of arrested person — Whether arrest unlawful.
see **Criminal Law,** 7

—— Personal rights — Dwelling — Inviolability — Power of Peace Commissioner to issue search warrant — Requirement that Peace Commissioner be satisfied by information on oath that reasonable grounds exist for suspecting the commission of an offence — Whether power consistent with inviolability of dwelling.
see **Criminal Law,** 70, 71

CONSTITUTION—*continued.*

—— Personal rights — Equality — Adoption — Exclusion — Widower.
see **Adoption,** 5

—— Personal rights — Equality — Criminal trial — Venue — Whether provision for the transfer of criminal trial pending before the Circuit Court outside Dublin in violation of the guarantee of equality before the law.
see **Constitution,** 32

—— Personal rights — Equality — Discrimination on basis of sex — Naturalisation.
see **Aliens,** 2

—— Personal rights — Equality — Extradition — State acquiescing in orders refusing extradition — Subsequent attempt to extradite person in respect of identical circumstances — Whether State precluded from denying person relief identical to that previously obtained — Whether attempt to extradite an abuse of the processes of the court.
see **Extradition,** 4

—— Personal rights — Equality — Franchise — Invalid's right to vote — Inability to attend polling station — Absence of statutory provision for postal vote in national elections.
see **Constitution,** 37

—— Personal rights — Equality — Right to vote and stand in elections — Ballot papers — Listing of names in alphabetical order — Voting bias.
see **Constitution,** 36

—— Personal rights — Freedom of association — Garda Síochána — Promotion — Proposed changes in system of promotion — Powers of Garda Commissioner — Powers of Minister for Justice — Rights of members of Garda Representative Association and Association of Garda Sergeants and Inspectors — Limitations of ranks within the Garda Síochána — Right of freedom of association for members of Garda Síochána — Limitations on extent to which members of the force may organise.
see **Garda Síochána,** 5

—— Personal rights — Freedom of association — Plaintiff offered position as principal of a primary school — Plaintiff not being a member of trade union — Pressure exerted on manager to cancel appointment — Whether defendants engaged in actionable conspiracy to cause plaintiff to abandon his constitutional right to dissociate.
see **Employer and Employee,** 1

—— Personal rights — Freedom of the press — Right to communicate — Criminal law — Conviction — Pending appeal — Publication of a magazine article based on material supplied by sole witness for the prosecution — Injunction application to restrain publication — Whether article likely to prejudice the appeal — Freedom of the press.
see **Injunction,** 14

—— Personal rights — Interpretation of Constitution — Right to procreate — Married couple within prison — Whether right protected and recognised under provisions of Constitution relating to family or relating to personal (unenumerated) rights — Whether absence of expressive language relating to right related to value to be placed on the right.
see **Constitution,** 19

—— Personal rights — Legal advice — Access to solicitor — Garda custody — Whether detained person has constitutional right of access to solicitor — Whether arises when detained person requests access or before.
see **Criminal Law,** 17

—— Personal rights — Legal aid — Right of poor person charged with serious offence to free legal aid — Fair procedures — Trial in due course of law — Statutory implementation of constitutional right.
see **Criminal Law,** 50

—— Personal rights — Liberty — Habeas corpus.
see **Constitution,** 15-17

—— Personal rights — Liberty — Habeas corpus — Alien — Refusal of leave to stay in the State — Discretion of immigration officer — Refusal based on absence of visa and language deficiency — Whether discretion improperly exercised.
see **Aliens,** 4

—— Personal rights — Liberty — Habeas corpus — Detention — Grounds — Certificate — Special Criminal Court — Appointment and composition — Conviction —

CONSTITUTION—*continued.*
Whether detention vitiated by events prior to charge of applicant.
see **Special Criminal Court**

—— Personal rights — Liberty — Habeas corpus — Procedures specified by Constitution — Alien — Refusal of leave to land.
see **Aliens,** 3

—— Personal rights — Privacy — Freedom of expression — Homosexual plaintiff — Equality before the law — Enactments imposing punishments for acts of buggery, indecent assault and gross indecency — Whether enactments inconsistent with Constitution.
see **Constitution,** 39

—— Personal rights — Right of access to courts — Whether right to compel suit or prosecution — Extra- territorial offence — Prosecutor seeking to be tried in the Republic — D.P.P. indicating that proceedings would not be instituted — Whether prosecutor deprived of his constitutional rights of access to the courts of this jurisdiction.
see **Criminal Law,** 49

—— Personal rights — Right of action — Recourse to courts — High Court — Unlimited jurisdiction — Power to transfer action — Action transferred to Circuit Court — Whether power of transfer inconsistent with Constitution.
see **Constitution,** 33

—— Personal rights — Right to communicate — Right to earn a livelihood — Whether such a right a personal or a property right — Postal monopoly — Whether violative of personal and property rights.
see **Postal Service**

—— Personal rights — Right to earn livelihood.
see **Constitution,** 42, 43

—— Personal rights — Right to earn a livelihood — Employment — Suspension — Civil servants — Application for injunction restoring plaintiffs to their position — Natural justice — Whether suspension a breach of the constitutional right to earn a livelihood.
see **Civil Service,** 3

—— Personal rights — Right to earn a livelihood — Breach of statutory duty — Whether amounts to breach of constitutional rights.
see **Statute,** 3

CONSTITUTION—*continued.*
—— Personal rights — Right to work — Trade union — Resolution for the introduction of a compulsory retirement scheme — Plaintiff not present when vote taken — Whether resolution valid — Whether natural justice infringed — Whether infringement of plaintiff's right to work.
see **Trade Union,** 2

—— Property rights — National monument — Preservation order — Validity of relevant legislation — Whether unjust attack on property rights.
see **Constitution,** 44

—— Property rights — Private property — Interference — Common good — Electricity supply cables — National grid — Statutory power of plaintiff board to erect pylons on defendant's land — No right to compensation — Statute unconstitutional.
see **Constitution,** 45

—— Property rights — Purchase of land with benefit of planning permission — Such permission granted by Minister of State — Supreme Court subsequently ruling such permission *ultra vires* — Whether State had failed to vindicate the property rights of the plaintiff.
see **Planning,** 13

—— Property rights — Regulations giving effect to EC milk levy — Such regulations having retrospective effect — Whether unjust — Whether unjustified attack on property rights — Whether any such infringement necessitated by membership of the European Community.
see **Constitution,** 35

—— Property rights — Shareholders — Registered provident society engaged in the business of banking — Legislation enacted prohibiting such societies from accepting or holding deposits — Whether legislation invalid — Whether unjust attack on property rights of shareholders.
see **Constitution,** 46

—— Property rights — Taxation — Residential property tax levied on properties over certain value — Whether unjust attack on property and family rights — Whether constituting invidious discrimination — Presumption of constitutionality in taxation matters.
see **Constitution,** 47

CONSTITUTION—*continued.*

—— Property rights — Unlawful organisation — Suppression order — Forfeiture of organisation's property — Minister empowered to freeze monies in bank without notice to account-holder — Procedures — Fair hearing — Owner establishing monies not property of unlawful organisation entitled to repayment and compensation — Whether forfeiture and money freezing procedure unjust attack on property rights — Interest of the common good.
see **Constitution,** 48

—— State — Prerogative — Treasure trove — Whether the State entitled to former royal prerogative of treasure trove.
see **Bailment**

—— State — Sovereignty — Incidents of sovereignty — Antiquities of national importance — Treasure trove — *Bona vacantia* — Lost or mislaid chattels — "Natural resources" — "Royalties and franchises" — Personal rights — Property rights.
see **Bailment**

—— State — Subversive organisation — Aims and objectives — Attack upon Constitution and organs of State — Criteria for extradition.
see **Extradition,** 8

—— State — Vicarious liability — Wrongful actions of servant.
see **Constitution,** 10

—— Statute — Construction — Extradition treaty — Incorporation into domestic law — State not bound by treaty — Whether statutory sub-section automatically incorporating treaty into domestic law — Legislative powers — Delegation — Whether delegation constitutional — Presumption of constitutionality of sub-section.
see **Constitution,** 25

—— Statute — Validity — Agricultural land — Valuation — Valuation carried out between 1852 and 1866 — Valuation unrelated to present day circumstances — Whether unjust attack on property rights — Whether arbitrary and unjust discrimination — Whether constitutional challenge includes a challenge to the validity of a section of a post-constitutional statute.
see **Rating and Valuation,** 1

CONSTITUTION—*continued.*

—— Statute — Validity — Attorney General — Function — Challenge to validity of pre-1937 statute — Requirement by rules of court that Attorney General be notified of challenge to validity of law — Whether requirement extended to challenge to validity of pre- 1937 statute — Whether court would consider issue in the absence of notification.
see **Practice and Procedure,** 14

—— Statute — Validity — Courts — Jurisdiction — Circuit Court — Criminal jurisdiction — Transfer of trial to Dublin Circuit Court.
see **Constitution,** 3

—— Statute — Validity — Courts — Jurisdiction — Enactment conferring jurisdiction on Circuit Court and District Court — Whether High Court without jurisdiction.
see **Constitution,** 4

—— Statute — Validity — Criminal prosecution in District Court — Penalty in excess of District Court jurisdiction in civil matters — Whether offence a minor offence — Attempt to raise constitutionality of statute by way of case stated.
see **Case Stated,** 3

—— Statute — Validity — Criminal statute — Presumption of constitutionality — Injunction — Balance of convenience — Whether presumption of constitutionality precluded court from deciding the interlocutory issue on the balance of convenience.
see **Injunction,** 2, 4

—— Statute — Validity — Delegated legislation — Family — Married persons — Right of married persons to be treated no less favourably than unmarried persons in similar circumstances — Social welfare payments — Disabled person's maintenance allowance — Provision requiring account to be taken of income of spouse — Whether requirement extended to social welfare income of spouse in his own right — Validity of provision — Disabled Persons (Maintenance Allowances) Regulations, 1984, art. 4.
see **Statute,** 1

—— Statute — Validity — Delegated legislation — Fisheries — Offshore licence — Ministerial regulations — Employee

CONSTITUTION—*continued.*

—— Trial of offences — Minor offence — Whether minor offence triable summarily.
see **Constitution,** 42

—— Trial of offences — Personal rights — Right to fair procedures — Due course of law — Right to a speedy trial.
see **Criminal Law,** 63

—— Trial of offences — Right to trial in due course of law — Courts — Judicial independence — Special Criminal Court — Appointment and removal of members — Remuneration of members — Validity.
see **Constitution,** 50

—— Trial of offences — Whether criminal offence — Revenue — Requirement to make a return of income — Failure to comply with requirement — Penalties — Whether penalties of a criminal nature.
see **Constitution,** 51

CONSTITUTIONAL JUSTICE
see **Natural and Constitutional Justice**

CONSTITUTIONAL RIGHTS
see under **Constitution**
see also **Rights and Freedoms**

—— Alleged breach — Judgment — Execution — *Fieri facias* — Seizure of property — Injunction — Principles applicable.
see **Injunction,** 6

—— Interference — Claim for damages — Whether such claim a claim in tort — Assessment of damages.
see **Damages,** 1

—— Restriction on exercise — Conflict with State's fundamental rights.
see **Aliens,** 2

—— Violation — Effect of violation on securing attendance in court.
see **Constitution,** 2

CONSTITUTIONAL TORTS — Garda disciplinary enquiry — Plaintiff attending — Enquiry conceded to have been a nullity — Whether plaintiff entitled to recover legal costs and expenses of attending and being represented.
see **Constitution,** 11

CONSTRUCTIVE TRUST —— Company — Winding up — Money paid by mistake to company prior to liquidation — Whether company holding money as trustee — Purpose of constructive trust

CONSTRUCTIVE TRUST—*continued.*

— Estoppel — Whether person claiming set off acting to its detriment.
see **Company,** 17

CONSULTATIVE CASE STATED
see under **Case Stated**

CONSUMER PROTECTION
see also **Defective Premises; Defective Products; Hire Purchase**

1. —— **Information** — **False statements** — *False statements as to the provision of services, accommodation or facilities — Whether defendant knew statements to be false — Whether defendant reckless — Penalty — Whether court should provide for the payment of compensation — Consumer Information Act,* 1978 (*No.* 1), *ss.* 6, 17(3)(*a*), 22(2).] S. 6 of the Consumer Information Act, 1978, provides that a person shall be guilty of an offence who, in the course or for the purposes of a trade, business or profession, makes a statement which he knows to be false or recklessly makes a statement which is false. The maximum penalty when a prosecution is brought in the District Court is £500. The Director of Consumer Affairs issued three summonses alleging that the defendant had made such statements to eight named persons concerning the availability of holiday accommodation in Spain when it knew that its contractual arrangements with the Spanish owners of the accommodation had broken down. The defendant maintained that the problem of overbooking arose from the default of a third party, and sought to avail of a defence provided by s. 22 of the Act; *viz,* that the offence was due to a mistake, accident, or the default of another, and that it had taken all reasonable precautions to avoid the commission of the offence. S. 22 (2) provides that a defendant intending to rely on such defence shall serve notice of his intention to do so at least seven clear days before the hearing. This requirement had not been met. S. 17 (3) of the Act allows the court to award to an injured party (who has not taken other proceedings) the whole or part of any fine that may be imposed on a defendant. **Held** Justice Wine refused to permit the defendant to defend in the terms of s. 22, and convicted the defendant on foot of the three summonses. The greater part of the fines imposed was awarded as compensation to the eight adults who had been affected by the commission of the offences. *Director of Consumer Affairs* v. *Sunshine Holidays Ltd.*

(Dist. Ct.) [1984] ILRM 551

2. —— **Investigative procedure** — *Powers conferred on "authorised officers" — Authorisation required to indicate the matters in respect of which the officer may act — Whether provision satisfied by a recital in the authorisation of the powers which he is authorised to exercise — Consumer*

CONSUMER PROTECTION—*continued.*

Information Act, 1978 (*No.* 1), *s.* 16.] S. 16 of the Consumer Information Act, 1978 (which is reproduced below in the judgment of McCarthy J.) creates an offence of obstructing or impeding an officer authorised to conduct investigations under the Act. Such an officer is required to produce his authorisation, if asked, and s. 16(2) requires that the authorisation indicate 'the matters' in respect of which the officer may act. The Director of Consumer Affairs had been complainant, in a District Court prosecution, in which it was alleged that the defendants, a tour-operating company and its secretary, had comitted an offence by failing to supply information about a Spanish holiday booking to an authorised officer, one Robert McLean. The defendants had sought to inspect McLean's authorisation, which, upon production, proved no more than a recital of the powers conferred by the Consumer Information Act, 1978. The defendants contended that this form of authorisation, which was silent about the specific matters into which inquiry was to be made, failed to comply with the Act. Upon conviction in the District Court the defendants appealed to the Circuit Court, urging before Judge O'Hanrahan the insufficiency of the form of authorisation. Judge O'Hanrahan, at the defendants' request, by way of a consultative case stated, sought the opinion of the Supreme Court on the validity of Robert McLean's authorisation. The case stated and the form of authorisation appear in the judgment of Hederman J. **Held** by the Supreme Court answering the question in the case stated in the negative, 1, that the form of authorisation was insufficient, and that the defendants in the absence of a valid authorisation had committed no offence under s. 16(4). 2. That the 'matters' required to be indicated by s. 16(2) are the particular investigation or investigations. *Director of Consumer Affairs* v. *Jœ Walsh Tours Ltd.*

(S.C.) [1985] ILRM 273

CONSUMER SUBSIDIES — Standard bread subsidy scheme — Whether retailer in breach of terms — Whether subsidy may be recouped.
see **Contract,** 1

CONTEMPT OF COURT

1. —— **Criminal contempt** — *Freedom of expression — Broadcast of television programme concerning Circuit Court proceedings under appeal — Plaintiff alleging programme critical of Circuit Court judgment — Right to a fair trial — Whether programme brought administration of justice into disrepute — Whether unbalanced programme amounts to contempt of court.*] The plaintiff was the successful defendant in a Circuit Court action which was the subject matter of a

CONTEMPT OF COURT—*continued.*

television programme produced and broadcast by the defendants. The plaintiff sought an interlocutory injunction to prevent the further broadcast of the programme pending the determination of an appeal of the Circuit Court order to the High Court. The plaintiff alleged that the programme was in contempt of court in that it was critical of the Circuit Court judgment; attempted to surround the judgment with a wall of criticism and innuendo and advocated a result other than that sustained in the proceedings. He further alleged that the programme prejudiced his right to a fair trial in the High Court because it made the presentation of his defence more difficult. **Held** by Carroll J. in refusing the interlocutory injunction, 1, that to go beyond the acceptable limits of freedom of expression, criticism of a judgment must bring the administration of justice into disrepute. 2. That in the instant case the programme, although unbalanced, did not go beyond the acceptable limits of reasonable criticism and accordingly the criticisms alleged did not amount to contempt of court. *In re Kennedy and McCann* [1976] I.R. 382 applied. 3. That furthermore the plaintiff had failed to establish that he was prejudiced in the presentation of his defence to the High Court and, accordingly, was not denied his right to a fair trial. *Weeland* v. *Radio Telefís Éireann*

(H.C.) [1987] I.R. 662

2. —— **Criminal contempt in the face of the court** — *Whether triable summarily — Necessity to protect proper administration of justice — Whether contempt trial necessary where alleged contempt involved witness in civil action who proceeded to testify in the action.*] In the course of an application by the liquidator of Kelly's Carpetdrome Ltd. under s. 297 of the Companies Act, 1963, a Mr. McGoldrick who the liquidator proposed to call as a witness stated that he had been approached by Mr. Kelly and Mr. Deighan, that they had attempted to suborn him and also suggested that he not attend to give evidence in the application. The judge hearing the s. 297 application, Costello J., ordered the arrest of Mr. Kelly and Mr. Deighan and proceeded to try them summarily for contempt of court. **Held** by Costello J. in convicting Mr. Kelly and Mr. Deighan, the evidence established that a contempt in the fact of the court had been committed which, in the interests of the proper administration of justice, required to be tried summarily and immediately at the instance of the trial judge without reference to the Director of Public Prosecutions. *The State (D.P.P.)* v. *Walsh and Conneely* [1981] I.R. 412 considered. On appeal by Mr. Kelly and Mr. Deighan to the Supreme Court (O'Higgins C.J., Walsh, Henchy, Griffin and Hederman JJ.) it was: **Held**

CONTEMPT OF COURT—*continued.*

in reversing the High Court, while a trial judge had power to try summarily a contempt in the face of the court where this was necessary to protect the administration of justice, having regard to the fact that Mr. McGoldrick proceeded to give evidence in the s. 297 application the necessity to try the contempt matter did not arise. *In re Kelly*

(H.C., S.C.) [1984] ILRM 424

3. —— **Newspaper publication** — *Article stating that Director of Public Prosecutions intended to bring charges against a local authority councillor — Political party to which councillor belonged referred to — Name of councillor not given — Whether publication could tend to prejudice the trial of proceedings that were pending.*] An *ex parte* application was made by counsel for the D.P.P. for a conditional order of attachment against the publisher and editors of the *Evening Herald* and a journalist on that paper arising out of an article on 30 March, 1984, which stated that the D.P.P. intended to bring indecency charges against an un-named local authority councillor. The councillor's political party was named but not the local authority. No charge had been brought at that time but on 1 April, 1984, a charge of indecency was brought against a named person and the affidavit grounding the application linked that charge with the article. **Held** (O'Hanlon J.) refusing the application, the court had not been referred to any case in this or any other common law jurisdiction where attachment for contempt of court had been grounded upon material published when no court had actually had seisin of the case in respect of which contempt was alleged. Furthermore having regard to the preservation of press freedom the facts disclosed in the grounding affidavit did not justify the extension in the law sought by the D.P.P. Also the criminal proceedings for indecency were still pending and it is preferable that contempt proceedings should not be dealt with until after the pending criminal proceedings. *State (D.P.P.)* v. *Independent Newspapers Ltd.*

(H.C.) [1985] ILRM 183

CONTRACEPTIVES

see **Family Planning**

CONTRACT

see also **Building Contract; Hire Purchase; Insurance; Sale of Goods; Sale of Land**

1. —— **Breach** — *Agreement to provide subsidy on retail price of bread — Whether retailer in breach of terms — Whether subsidy may be recouped.*] On 20 August, 1982, the first-named defendant sent to all registered bakeries including the plaintiff a copy of an amended bread subsidy scheme in a document headed 'standard bread subsidy scheme.' The explanatory notes contained the terms and conditions under which the scheme would be operated from that date. They also stated that the subsidy payable on bread was a consumer subsidy and that the purpose of the subsidy was to reduce the price of bread at the point of sale for the benefit of the consumer. The type of bread to which the subsidy would attach was set out in the notes. Claims for payment of subsidies were to be made on official application forms, a condition being that a separate application form was required to be submitted after the end of each specified two week accounting period. Where monies had been paid in respect of incorrect claims and/or it transpired that the bread on which the subsidy was claimed was not eligible for subsidy, reimbursement of overpayments would be effected by refunds from the bakery concerned or by deductions from the bakery's subsequent claims. From early September, 1982, the plaintiff claimed and was paid subsidy under the scheme but subsidy was refused in respect of the period 12 February, 1983, to 21 May, 1983, the first-named defendant alleging that the plaintiff had made incorrect claims. The plaintiff instituted proceedings and claimed, *inter alia,* that they were not obliged to pass on some of the subsidy to the consumer. **Held** by Costello J. in granting to the first-named defendant a number of declarations, 1, the case was a matter for the determination of the parties' rights and duties on a breach of contract being established. Manufacturers who received the subsidy were required to pass it on in full to the consumer and such requirement was a term of the contract entered into between the parties. The evidence established that this term was breached by the plaintiff. 2. The first-named defendant was entitled to be recouped any overpayments made by him to the plaintiff by the difference between the prices actually charged for certain of the plaintiff's bread products and those which should have been charged had the full benefit of the scheme been passed on to the consumer from August, 1982 to 12 February, 1983. The first-named defendant was entitled also to deduct from unpaid claims of the plaintiff the amount of the subsidy not passed on and the sums which the said defendant was entitled to withhold by way of deductions under the claims made after 12 February, 1983. *Kylemore Bakery Ltd.* v. *Minister for Trade, Commerce and Tourism*

(H.C.) [1986] ILRM 529

2. —— **Breach** — *Claim for damages for breach of contract — Sale of goods — Whether contract void for illegality — Onus of proof — Sale of Goods Act,* 1893 (*c.* 71), *s.* 51.] The plaintiff claimed damages for breach of contract

CONTRACT—*continued.*

from the defendant. The parties had entered into a contract that the defendant would supply potatoes from his farm in County Meath to the plaintiff company in the United Kingdom. Clause 11 of the contract provided that in the event of import/export controls on the part of either Government, the potatoes would be supplied from Northern Ireland. The defendant alleged that the intention of the parties in drafting the said clause was that potatoes from his farm should be smuggled across the border and thence exported to the plaintiff in the United Kingdom, and that the contract was thus void for illegality. **Held** by Finlay P. in giving judgment for the plaintiff, that the onus of proving the illegality of a contract is on the party alleging it, and that the defendant had not proved an illegal intention on the part of the plaintiff. *Whitecross Potatoes (International) Ltd.* v. *Coyle* **(H.C.) [1978] ILRM 31**

3. —— **Breach** — *Implied term — Necessity — Compromise agreement — Applicable to sales of specified article and any variation of article agreed in writing by licensor — Variation sold without knowledge of licensor — Term implied to effect that licensee obliged to obtain approval of licensor for variation.*

Confidence — Breach — Equitable principles — Method of cutting and assembling bullet proof vest — Manufacturing process for bullet proof vest — Proposals for commercial partnership — Plaintiffs divulging information to defendants — Information misused by defendants — Effect of publication in plaintiffs' patent — Spring-board doctrine — Plaintiffs entitled to damages.

Copyright — Infringement — Reproduction — Authorisation — Artistic works — Cutting patterns for body armour — Redesign exercise carried out — Whether redesign exercise independent — Whether causal connection between copyright works and first defendant's product — Prior publication of drawings in patent specification not fatal to claim — Defendant's product printed in England — Whether distributed in Ireland — Jurisdiction — Industrial and Commercial Property (Protection) Act, 1927 (*No.* 16), *s.* 176 — *Copyright Act,* 1963 (*No.* 10), *ss.* 3(2), 7(3), 9(8), 22, 24, 60 — *Patents Act,* 1964 (*No.* 12).

Directors — Liability for commission of torts — Authorising infringement — Civil Liability Act (No. 41), 1961, *s.* 21.

Damages — Assessment — Compromise agreement — Plaintiff entitled to damages for breach of contract to pay royalties — Damages arising from surreptitious repeat contract — Plaintiffs electing for an account of profits accruing to defendants pursuant to repeat contract and claiming payment for amount so found — Copyright Act, 1963 (*No.* 10), *ss.* 22, 24 — *Courts Act, 1981 (No.* 11), *s.* 22.] M.S., the third plaintiff, began

CONTRACT—*continued.*

to interest himself in the design and manufacture of bullet-proof vests in about 1975. He had no scientific knowledge or specialist training other than as a tailor and cutter. However, he succeeded in developing a unique type of vest based on the use of a new and remarkable fibre, Kevlar. He had developed this side of the first plaintiff's business, of which he was a director, with a fair degree of success by the time he met W.W., the third defendant, late in 1978. W.W. had substantial business interests, controlling a group of companies in the United Kingdom, including one with a subsidiary, M. Ltd. As a result of W.W.'s commercial contacts with Libya, M. Ltd. received an enquiry in 1978 about the provision of protective clothing for the Libyan army. Neither W.W. nor any of the other defendants knew anything about ballistics or bullet proof vests at that time. W.W. contacted M.S. because of the latter's expertise in this area. W.W. was the father of the fourth defendant and the father-in-law of the seventh defendant, MacL. A series of meetings between M.S. and W.W. and the latter's associates led to a consensus on a joint venture on a fifty-fifty basis, the vests to be manufactured by M. Ltd., and in May, 1979, M.S. went to Libya to submit his products for testing by the Libyan army. The Libyans decided to purchase a particular version of M.S.'s vest. The joint venture agreement was finalised in June, 1979. In the meanwhile M.S. was supplying full technical information about his product to the defendants. A revised memorandum of 7 July, 1979, set out most detailed information on the component parts of the vest; its mode of manufacture, the materials used, the sources of the materials, preliminary costings and a list of the plant and equipment required. On the 11 August, 1979, the first Libyan contract was signed with the Libyan authorities. It provided for the manufacture and supply of 15,000 of M.S.'s vests, worth over £5 million, by an Isle of Man company under W.W.'s control, E. Ltd., the second defendant. E. Ltd. was in voluntary liquidation at the time of the commencement of this action. Relations between M.S. and the defendants broke down completely over the succeeding months. In November, 1979, the first defendant, P.B. Ltd., a wholly-owned subsidiary of E. Ltd., was formed and it began manufacture of the vests at a premises in Cork in January, 1980. When M.S. came to learn of the existence of P.B. Ltd. and of its activities, he obtained Anton Piller orders against P.B. Ltd. and other defendants, both in Ireland and in England, on the basis of misuse of confidential information and breach of copyright. These proceedings were settled and compromised and an agreement was signed on 10 September, 1980, which *inter alia* provided for royalty payments to be made to M.S. or his companies on the first Libyan con-

CONTRACT—*continued.*

tract which was then nearing completion. It also provided for the payment of royalties, in certain circumstances, in respect of any further contracts for the manufacture of armoured vests entered into with the Libyan authorities. The term, "armoured vest", was defined with reference to a sample annexed to the agreement and as "any variation as might be mutually agreed in writing" thereto. Royalties in respect fo the first contract were duly paid to M.S. In July, 1981, P.B. Ltd. recommenced the manufacture of vests for the Libyan army. Again by chance this came to M.S.'s knowledge and he instituted fresh proceedings, commencing with Anton Piller orders, in Ireland, in England and in the Channel Islands, claiming damages for misuse of the same confidential information and for infringement of copyright in the cutting patterns for the vest and in a brochure. Damages were also claimed for breach of the agreement of 10 September, 1980. The claim against the second defendant was only in respect of breach of contract. During the proceedings details came to light of a second contract concluded with the second defendant by the Libyan authorities on 22 January, 1981, for the supply of a further 15,000 vests worth over £5 million. In relation to the breach of contract claim, the defendants argued that the vest manufactured under the second Libyan contract was not a "variation" of the vest as defined in the contract and also that the existence of an implied term, as pleaded by the plaintiffs, that the defendants would seek their approval for any "variation" was not required to give business efficacy to the agreement. The defendants further pleaded that the vests manufactured under the second contract had been the product of independent design work under professional legal guidance. The defendants further pleaded that the confidential information at issue was in any event in the public domain and that the copyright infringement claim could not be sustained since various drawings relating to the products in question had been published in M.S.'s U.K. patent specifications.

Held by Costello J., in granting the relief sought by the plaintiffs, 1, in relation to the claim for damages for breach of contract; the product manufactured for the second Libyan contract was an armoured vest as defined in the agreement of 10 September, 1980. Since there had been no notification of this second contract as required by the agreement the first, second, third and fourth defendants were in breach of the agreement. It was necessary to imply into the agreement a requirement that the defendants should submit for approval to the third plaintiff any armoured vest of theirs which could be regarded as a variation of the armoured vest as defined. *Liverpool City Council* v. *Irwin* [1977] A.C. 229 applied. 2. In relation to the breach of confidence

CONTRACT—*continued.*

claim; in such an action the court is asked to enforce what is essentially a moral obligation. In so doing it must firstly decide whether there exists from the relationship between the parties an obligation of confidence regarding the information which had been imparted and it must then decide whether the information which was communicated could properly be regarded as confidential. *Prince Albert* v. *Strange* (1849) 1 H. & Tw. 1; *Morrison* v. *Moat* (1851) 9 Hare 241; *Saltman Engineering Co.* v. *Campbell Engineering Co. Ltd.* (1948) 65 R.P.C. 203; *Terrapin Ltd.* v. *Builders Supply Co. (Hayes) Ltd.* [1960] R.P.C. 128; *Cranleigh Precision Engineering Ltd.* v. *Bryant* [1965] 1 W.L.R. 1317; *Seager* v. *Copydex Ltd.* [1967] 1 W.L.R. 923; *Fraser* v. *Evans* [1969] 1 Q.B. 349; *Argyll* v. *Argyll* [1967] Ch. 302; *Coco* v. *A.N. Clark (Engineers) Ltd.* [1969] R.P.C. 41 and *Thomas Marshall Ltd.* v. *Guiner* [1979] Ch. 237 considered and applied. 3. Once it is established that an obligation of confidence exists and that the information is confidential, then the person to whom it is given has the duty to act in good faith, and this means that he must use the information for the purpose for which it was imparted to him and cannot use it to the detriment of the informant. *A.B. Consolidates* v. *Europe Strength Food Co.* [1978] 2 N.Z.L.R. 515 considered. 4. Information which if contained in a patent specification might lack novelty because it had been published in an earlier specification may nonetheless be imparted in circumstances which impose an obligation to treat it in confidence; and similarly information which is known to persons in the relevant art might be communicated to some other person so as to impose a like obligation. 5. It follows that a duty of good faith had been imposed on the first, third, fourth and seventh named defendants; the information which M.S. communicated to the defendants could properly be regarded as confidential information; the defendants had been guilty of a breach of confidence in relation to the second Libyan contract as M.S.'s information had been used for their own purposes and to the detriment of M.S. 6. In relation to the claim for breach of copyright; there was a substantial degree of objective similarity, as regards both design and component parts, between the "new" vest of the first defendant and M.S.'s vest. Accordingly a *prima facie* case of infringement had been made out. The first defendant, having reproduced and published the vest was liable for copyright infringement. The third, fourth and seventh defendants had "authorised" the first defendant's infringing acts within the meaning of s. 7, sub-s. 3, of the Copyright Act, 1963. 7. Parliament had conferred two separate and distinct sets of rights on those who possessed patents and copyrights. There was nothing in either code which suggested that the

CONTRACT—*continued.*

rights conferred by the Copyright Act, 1963, were affected by an application for a patent under the Patent Act, 1964, and ought to be construed accordingly. *Catnic Components Ltd.* v. *Hill and Smith Ltd.* [1982] R.P.C. 183 not followed. 8. In relation to the brochure, infringement may have taken place by the importation of brochures into Ireland. 9. In relation to assessment of damages; the plaintiffs were entitled to damages for breach of the agreement to pay royalties at the rate specified in the agreement together with statutory interest; the plaintiffs were further entitled to damages for the surreptitious repeat contract and were entitled to elect, as they did, for an account of profits accruing to the defendants pursuant to the repeat contract and to claim the amount so found. The plaintiffs would be entitled to an order for the payment of the difference between what the defendants expended upon manufacturing the goods and the price accruing to them for their sale. *Peter Pan Manufacturing Corporation* v. *Corsets Silhouette Ltd.* [1964] 1 W.L.R. 96 applied. **Held** by the Supreme Court (O'Higgins C.J., Griffin and McCarthy JJ.) in dismissing the appeal of first, third, fourth and seventh defendants, 1, the trial judge was entitled on the evidence to reach the findings he did and had properly determined the issues before him. 2. *Per* McCarthy J. in a claim for breach of confidence the obligation of secrecy, whilst enforced by equitable principles, depends more upon commercial necessity than moral duty. *House of Spring Gardens Ltd.* v. *Point Blank Ltd.*

(H.C., S.C.) [1984] I.R.611

4. —— **Breach** — *Indemnity — Consideration — Forebearance.*] In February, 1981, Pistola Investments Limited (the company) opened an account with the plaintiff. The defendant was the sole beneficial owner of the company. The company traded in the futures market through the agency of the plaintiff and by 8 October, 1981, owed some Stg.£36,000 to the plaintiff. Calls were made on the company which it did not meet. At a meeting with the plaintiff's managing director the defendant acknowledged the company's indebtedness and intimated that the company was insolvent and said that he would try to repay the debt of the company at the rate of Stg.£1,000 per month. The defendant refused to sign a guarantee of the company's liability. The defendant made a total of two payments of Stg.£1,000 each. The plaintiff claimed *inter alia* that there was an agreement with the defendant and/or it was represented by the defendant that the defendant would indemnify the plaintiff in respect of the money owed by the company to the plaintiff and that the plaintiff acting on that agreement and/or the faith of the representations forebore to sue the company. **Held** by Barron J., in dismissing the plaintiff's claim, 1, the agreement between the plaintiff and the defendant amounted to an indemnity by the defendant and not a guarantee as the defendant agreed to pay the money in any event and not only if the principal debtor did not. 2. However, the indemnity was unenforceable as it was not given for consideration. There was no request express or implied to forebear from bringing proceedings, which if it induced such forebearance would amount to good consideration. *Alliance Bank Ltd.* v. *Broom* 2 Dr. & Sm. 289; *Miles* v. *New Zealand Alford Estate Company* 32 Ch.D. 266; *Fullerton* v. *Provincial Bank of Ireland* [1903] A.C. 309; *Combe* v. *Combe* [1951] 2 K.B. 215; [1951] 1 All E.R. 767, considered. *Commodity Broking Co. Ltd.* v. *Meehan*

(H.C.) [1985] I.R.12

5. —— **Consideration** — *Action — Settlement of action — Sale of land part of settlement agreement — Absence of note or memorandum — Sale of land unenforceable — Whether original action discharged.*] A plaintiff's cause of action remains discharged by a settlement agreement even though the defendant is precluded from enforcing it. **So held** by Lynch J. *O'Mahony* v. *Gaffney*

(H.C.) [1986] I.R. 36

6. —— **Debt** — *Cheque — Money owing on foot of loan — Subsequent sale of shares by debtor to lender — Cheque drawn by lender in favour of debtor in payment for shares — Endorsement by debtor of cheque in favour of lender — Acceptance by lender of cheque — Cheque dishonoured by lender's bank — Whether acceptance of cheque by lender an unconditional discharge of debtor's obligations.*] The defendant was indebted to the plaintiff in the sum of £306,308.60 arising from a loan to him by the plaintiff. On 19 October, 1983, he sold his shares in the P.M.P.A. Insurance Company to the plaintiff for a price of £400,000. The shares were paid for by the plaintiff with a cheque drawn on its bank account in favour of the defendant. On receipt of the cheque the defendant endorsed it and delivered it back to the plaintiff in discharge of his debt to the plaintiff in respect of the loan. On the same day the plaintiff was put into official liquidation under the terms of the Insurance (No. 2) Act, 1983. On 20 October, 1983, the plaintiff's cheque was lodged in its bank account and it was subsequently dishonoured by the bank. The plaintiff commenced proceedings against the defendant claiming repayment of the loan together with interest. The defendant claimed that his endorsement and delivery of the plaintiff's cheque constituted a discharge of his indebtedness, and he counterclaimed for the difference between the amount due on foot of the loan and the amount of the cheque. **Held** by Murphy J., in dismissing the plaintiff's claim, that where payment is made

CONTRACT—*continued.*
to a creditor by endorsing back to him his own cheque there is no justification for implying into the transaction a condition that the discharge or release of the original debt is conditional upon the cheque being honoured by the creditor's bank. *Marreco* v. *Richardson* [1908] 2 K.B. 584 distinguished. *Private Motorists' Provident Society Ltd.* v. *Moore*
(H.C.) [1987] I.R. 472 ; [1988] ILRM 526

7. —— **Inducement of breach** — *Exclusive supply contract — Purchaser subsequently entering into similar contract with another supplier — Whether inducement of breach of contract — Position of person who innocently enters into contract without knowledge of prior inconsistent contract — Whether under duty to cease supplies.*] In January, 1982, Flogas Ltd. entered into a contract with Shannon Dairies Ltd. whereby Flogas Ltd. agreed to supply and Shannon Dairies Ltd. agreed to buy its total requirements of liquified petroleum gas for a period of five years. In March Flogas entered into a similar contract with Crosstown Services Ltd. In February, 1982, Flogas Ltd.'s competitor Irish National Gas Ltd., an associate company of the first named defendants, Ergas Ltd., entered into a similar exclusive supply arrangement with Shannon Dairies Ltd. In May, 1982, Irish National Gas entered into a similar agreement with Crosstown Services, but for a period of three years only. Flogas, on hearing that its customers had entered into inconsistent contracts with Ergas instituted proceedings claiming damages for procuring a breach of contract. Both companies denied that they had any binding contract with the plaintiff. The plaintiff claimed that once the defendants had been informed of the prior inconsistent contracts with the plaintiff it was the defendant's duty to cease to supply the two companies in question and that their failure to do so was an actionable interference in those contracts. The defendants argued that they entered into valid legal contracts with the two companies without notice of the plaintiff's prior inconsistent contracts and that they could not be said to commit a tort by carrying out their contracts in accordance with their terms. **Held** by Barrington J. dismissing the plaintiff's action, although the plaintiff had entered into binding contracts with the two companies, the defendants did not induce or procure a breach of these contracts. The defendants entered into contracts with the two companies in question without knowledge, actual or constructive, of the prior inconsistent contracts between those companies and the plaintiff. The law could not place the defendants, innocent parties, in a position in which they must, on inadequate information, make a decision as to the respective rights of the plaintiff and the two

CONTRACT—*continued.*
companies in question, a decision which could lead to their being sued by either party. The only safe and proper course for the defendants was to observe their own contracts which they knew to be valid and legally binding, with the two companies. *Flogas Ltd.* v. *Ergas Ltd.*
(H.C.) [1985] ILRM 221

8.—— **Mistake** — *Both parties contracting on assumption which proved false — Supply of seed potatoes — Crop failure — Whether contract rendered void — Whether implied obligations remaining.*] The plaintiff brought an action for the price of seed potatoes supplied to the defendant. The defendant counterclaimed on the ground that the seed failed to produce the expected crop. The contract between the parties stated, *inter alia,* that the defendant was to produce and sell to the plaintiff 80 tons of potatoes, that these were to be produced from seed potatoes supplied exclusively by the plaintiff, that the plaintiff would supply seed certified as suitable by Department of Agriculture inspectors, that such certification would be conclusive evidence of their purity and health and that the plaintiffs would supply the seed without warranty of germination or crop result. An agricultural scientist stated that the defendant's crop failure could have been caused either by direct contact with fertiliser, 'fertiliser burn', or by reduced vitality of the seeds, 'physiological age.' The seed potatoes sold to the defendant were originally part of a larger lot another farmer had rejected. The remainder of this lot was sold to two other farmers who gave evidence of crop failure also. **Held** by Judge Clarke, 1, on the evidence, the more consistent explanation of the defendant's crop failure was reduced seed vitality. 2. Insofar as the terms of the contract were contradictory or ambiguous they were to be interpreted *contra proferentem,* against the plaintiff in this instance. 3. Although the plaintiff's refusal to provide a warranty of quality regarding the seeds might be considered as an exemption clause, the fact that the contract as a whole related to the production of 80 tons of potatoes and that the evidence established the seeds were not capable of producing such a crop necessitated the construction that both parties had entered into the contract on the basis of a mistake causing the basic purpose of the contract to collapse and rendering it void. *Bell* v. *Lever Bros. Ltd.* [1932] A.C. 161 and *Sheikh Bros. Ltd.* v. *Odisner* [1957] A.C. 136 discussed. 4. The defendant would be deemed impliedly liable for the fair price of such of the seed potatoes as produced a crop and of which he took the benefit. *Western Potato Co-Operative Ltd.* v. *Durnan*
(Circ. Ct.) [1985] ILRM 5

9. —— **Mistake** — *Mutual mistake — Compro-*

CONTRACT—*continued.*

mise of litigation — Document authenticated by signatures of counsel — Lack of consensus ad idem *— Whether compromise enforceable — Whether agreement a nullity.*] Two actions for possession of land and recovery of arrears of rent, brought by connected plaintiffs against common defendants, were purported to be settled. The settlement was in writing and authenticated by the signatures of counsel. Subsequently the parties failed to agree on the scope of the settlement. On the plaintiff's motion to enforce the settlement both of the counsel involved gave oral evidence. The High Court judge hearing the motion accepted that there was an element of mutual mistake in the transaction, but felt bound to order that the terms of the settlement be enforced. From this decision the defendants appealed to the Supreme Court. **Held** by the Supreme Court (Finlay C.J., Henchy and Griffin JJ.) allowing the appeal and ordering that the actions proceed to trial, 1, the settlement, reached in limited time that did not allow the reduction of its terms to unambiguous written expression, rested on a mutual mistake, for which no blame attached to the counsel involved. 2. The general rule is that a person who enters into an agreement, giving the other person the impression that he understands the nature and effect of the agreement, will not afterwards be allowed to say that he should not be bound by it because he did not at the time understand its import; but the agreement in the present case was surrounded by circumstances of latent ambiguity and mutual misunderstanding such as indicated that there was no *consensus ad idem,* and the seeming agreement was a nullity. *Mespil Ltd.* v. *Capaldi*

(S.C.) [1986] ILRM 373

—— Mistake.
see also No. 11

10. —— **Quasi contract** — *Discussion co. cerning publication of an encyclopaedia — Publishing company expending money on project — Claim for indemnity against money expended and damages for breach of contract — Whether contract agreed as to publication — Claim in quasi contract — Assessment — Whether interest in sum payable allowed — Whether inflation to be taken into account.*] Between 1970 and 1975 the managing director of the plaintiff company carried on discussions and negotiations with the Department of Education over the production by the plaintiff of a children's encyclopaedia in Irish for the Department. Subsequently the plaintiff did certain preliminary work all of which was approved of or directed by officials of the Department. No contract was ever agreed on and the Department made it clear that approval would have to be obtained from the Government Contracts Commission before there could be a contract for production of the encyclopaedia. No such approval had been given when, in January, 1975, the Department wrote to the plaintiff saying that no further commitments could be made in relation to the production of the encyclopaedia as there were no funds available for the project. The plaintiff claimed that although no contract had been entered into an undertaking to complete the project had been given by the Department which the plaintiff was entitled to treat as binding. In the alternative it was claimed that the Department was liable to recoup the expenditure actually incurred by the plaintiff on the work together with a reasonable profit. Furthermore, if damages were awarded, it was submitted that interest on the sum payable should be allowed from the date by which it should have been paid and that allowance should be made for the rate of inflation. **Held** by McWilliam J. in giving a decree for £57,000, there was no concluded contract for the production of the encyclopaedia, and no representation binding the Department to pay for the production of the encyclopaedia. Nevertheless both parties proceeded on the basis that such a contract would be made between them and the plaintiff went ahead with the preliminary work. Such work although expected to make a profit for the plaintiff was being done for the benefit of the Department. In these circumstances an action could be founded on quasi-contract. Looking at the facts a promise to pay for the work done should be implied, irrespective of the actual views or intentions of the parties at the time when the work was done. *William Lacy (Hounslow) Ltd.* v. *Davis* [1957] 1 W.L.R. 932 and *Brewer Street Investments Ltd.* v. *Barclay's Woollen Co. Ltd.* [1954] 1 Q.B. 428, principles applied. As there was no contract to publish the encyclopaedia no sum, calculated on the basis of the loss of the profits which would have been made by completing the work, would be allowed. The plaintiff was entitled to interest since it must have suffered from loss of interest on, or from loss of the use of, the money that should have been paid. No allowance for inflation would be made because the claim did not relate to property or repairs to property and there was no evidence that any definite intended use of the money due had been affected by inflation. *Folens & Co. Ltd.* v. *Minister for Education*

(H.C.) [1984] ILRM 265

11. —— **Rectification** — *Contract for sale of ground rents — Alleged term not embodied in contract — Notice of term to purchaser's agent — Whether notional assent to term by purchaser — Whether mutual mistake — Whether conduct of purchaser such as to permit rectification for unilateral mistake — Notice to treat served on vendor*

CONTRACT—*continued.*

— *Whether notice vested vendor's estate or interest in acquiring authority.*] The plaintiff company owned a substantial portfolio of ground rents in and around Dublin which portfolio it placed on the market. It also owned certain lands in Palmerstown, Co. Dublin, the subject of compulsory purchase orders of the County Council and Corporation of Dublin, together with other adjoining lands the acquisition of which had been agreed with the authorities and two local residential properties. W., an auctioneer, communicated an offer from F., a property developer, to buy the portfolio to the plaintiff which offer the plaintiff's board accepted and a contract for sale was drawn up. The plaintiff had no intention of including the Palmerstown properties in the sale to F. and despite N., the plaintiff's property portfolio manager, having furnished the plaintiff's legal department with a list of the properties the plaintiff wished to have excluded from the contract, that department, due to an oversight, included all but a portion of the Palmerstown properties in the contract. F. retained M., a solicitor, to act on his behalf in the transaction and the defendant company was formed by F. to take the conveyance of the ground rents. On the day the draft contracts were due to be exchanged between the parties M. was not satisfied that the draft contract proffered by the plaintiff's legal department included all the properties F. was entitled to acquire, but it was indicated to him by that legal department that the transaction would be at an end if the contract were not signed that day and having informed F. of the situation, F. advised him to proceed as he thought best and M. therefore executed and exchanged contracts on behalf of the defendant. Subsequent to that date, the schedules to the contract were altered by agreement of the parties to include and exclude certain properties which were and were not regarded as forming part of the sale but on the plaintiff discovering the error that had been made with regard to the Palmerstown properties and seeking their exclusion from the contract, F. refused to take that course, his attitude being that he had been required to accept the contract in the form presented to M. with whatever consequences that might entail for him, and therefore the plaintiff should adopt the same approach. N. had told W., some time prior to the execution of the contract, that a "significant holding of land the subject of a C.P.O. at Palmerstown" was not being included in the contract; W., however, never informed F. of this. In the circumstances the plaintiff contended that the contract was drawn up and signed under a mutual mistake of fact and instituted proceedings in the High Court seeking rectification of the contract so as to exclude the Palmerstown properties and an order of specific performance of the contract as so rectified. The defendant

CONTRACT—*continued.*

counterclaimed for, *inter alia,* an order of specific performance of the contract as it stood. It was proved at the trial of the plaintiff's action that the total amount of compensation then payable in respect of the Palmerstown properties which were the subject of compulsory purchase orders or the acquisition of which had been agreed was, together with interest accrued, £594,761. **Held** by Keane J., in dismissing the plaintiff's claim and granting the defendant the order of specific performance sought by it, 1, that a written contract will be rectified to carry out the common true intention of the parties thereto where that common intention has continued up to the execution of the contract and has been reflected in some outward expression of accord of the parties, whether constituting a binding enforceable agreement or not. The onus on the party seeking rectification to prove such an intention is a heavy one. *Joscelyne* v. *Nissen* [1970] 2 Q.B. 86; *Rooney & McParland* v. *Carlin* [1981] N.I. 138; *Monaghan County Council* v. *Vaughan* [1948] I.R. 306; *Shipley U.D.C.* v. *Bradford Corporation* [1936] Ch. 375 and *Nolan* v. *Graves and Hamilton* [1946] I.R. 376, considered and applied. 2. That there was no such intention on the part of the palintiff and F. in this case. Although W. must on the facts be considered to have been the agent of F. it did not follow that because W.'s knowledge of the plaintiff's intention to exclude the Palmerstown properties could be imputed to F. as principal, there had , therefore, been a notional asent on F.'s part to the inclusion in the contract of a term to that effect. Statement in Bowstead on Agency, 15th ed. at p. 412 explained; *dicta* of Clauson J. in *Shipley U.D.C.* v. *Bradford Corporation* [1936] Ch. 375 at p. 396 and *Fowler* v. *Scottish Equitable Life Insurance Society* [1858] 28 L.J. Ch. 225 considered. 3. That even if W.'s knowledge could be treated as an adequate basis for F.'s notional assent to the inclusion of the disputed term, it was not clear what that term was since N.'s statement did not specify whether it was the land the subject matter of the County Council or Corporation compulsory purchase order or both which it was intended to exclude from the contract and whether this exclusion extended to the land that had been acquired by agreement and the two residential properties. Such uncertainty was fatal to the plaintiff's claim for rectification on the basis of mutual mistake having regard to the heavy burden of proof that lies on a plaintiff in a rectification case. 4. That notwithstanding the absence of mutual mistake, a court could nevertheless order rectification of a contract where there had been a unilateral mistake and it would be inequitable in the circumstances to allow the party against whom the relief is sought to retain a benefit derived from the mistake. F.,

CONTRACT—*continued.*

however, was not aware that a mistake was being made in the execution of the contract and there was accordingly neither "sharp practice" on his part nor anything in his conduct prior to or at the time of the execution of the contract which rendered it unconscionable for him to resist rectification on the alternative ground of unilateral mistake. *Roberts (A.) & Co. Ltd.* v. *Leicestershire County Council* [1961] Ch. 555 and *Bates (Thomas) & Son Ltd.* v. *Wyndham's (Lingerie) Ltd.* [1981] 1 W.L.R. 505, distinguished. *Riverlate Properties Ltd.* v. *Paul* [1975] Ch. 133 considered. *Gun* v. *M'Carthy* (1884) 13 L.R. Ir. 304 not followed. 5. That a notice to treat served by Dublin County Council in respect of part of the plaintiff's Palmerstown lands before the execution of the contract did not operate to vest in that Authority any estate or interest in those lands, which lands could, therefore, be as much the subject matter of the order of specific performance granted in the defendant's favour as the other Palmerstown properties. *Dicta* of Henchy J. in *In re Green Dale Building Co.* [1977] I.R. 256 at p. 265 applied. *Irish Life Assurance Company Ltd.* v. *Dublin Land Securities Ltd.*

(H.C.) [1986] I.R.332

12. —— **Statutory duty** — *Substitution by agreement of parties for statutory obligations — Estoppel — Party to agreement estopped from insisting on enforcement of statutory obligations — Statute providing for ferry service — Party providing facilities for ferry — Facilities not used — Breach of contract — Measure of damages — Fishguard and Rosslare Railways and Harbours Act,* 1898 (*c.* cclii), *s.* 70

Constitution — Adaptation of enactments — Enactment of Parliament of Great Britain and Ireland — Provision of ferry service from Ireland to Wales — Suspension of service by decision of English government minister — Whether decision having extra-territorial effect — Whether statutory obligation suspended by Oireachtas — Constitution of Saorstát Éireann, 1922, *Art.* 73 — *Constitution of Ireland,* 1937, *Art.* 50 — *Adaptation of Enactments Act,* 1922 (*No.* 2), *s.* 5.

Conflict of laws — Evidence — Evidence of expert on provisions of English statute — Whether courts bound to accept evidence — Whether evidence contradicted.

Damages — Contract — Measure of damages — Loss of income — Whether claim sustainable for loss in provision of unused capital asset — Whether claim amounts to seeking double compensation — Whether loss of income reasonably in contemplation of parties.] The Fishguard and Rosslare Railways and Harbours Act provides that the Great Western Railway Company shall afford a daily steamer service between Waterford and New Milford or Fishguard, and that the

CONTRACT—*continued.*

service shall be as efficient as that provided by the company at the date of the passing of the Act. The section provides further that the provisions shall continue until Parliament otherwise determines. and that the Railway and Canal Commission shall have power to enforce these provisions in the same manner in which they were enabled to enforce s. 2 of the Railway and Canal Traffic Act, 1854. The enforcement machinery of the latter Act provides that complaints be made by summons to the superior courts in Dublin. By virtue of the provisions of the Railway and Canal Act, 1888, jurisdiction in this matter passed to the Railway and Canal Commission, which was empowered to award damages to any aggrieved party, provided a claim was made within one year from the discovery of the matter complained of. Finally, by virtue of the provisions of the Railway Act, 1924, and the Transport Act, 1947, the powers of the Railway and Canal Commission became vested in the High Court. By virtue of the provisions of s. 31 (2)(*b*) of the Transport Act, 1962, all the rights and liabilities of the British Transport Commission comprised in the shipping services provided by that Commission pursuant to the Railway Shipping Acts transferred to the defendant, and the closing words of the subsection transfer to the defendant 'any property, rights and liabilities not falling to be transferred under any other provision in this Act.' The Great Western Railway Company carried on the service provided in the 1898 Act, affording, however, two sailings weekly, rather than the daily service specified. In 1939, an agreement was entered into between the company of the one part, and the plaintiffs, of the other part, by which it was agreed that the company would maintain a minimum of three sailings weekly. The company expressly covenanted not to seek parliamentary modification of the terms imposed by s. 70 of the said Act, in consideration of the plaintiffs' covenating not to seek to enforce those terms. In 1940, by order of the British Minister for Transport, the operation of s. 70 was suspended. After the war years, the service was resumed, and in 1959 a new agreement was entered into between the British Transport Commission as successor of the company, and the plaintiffs, which agreement was essentially the same as that of 1939. The British Transport Commission carried on the service until 1962. In that year, the defendant board was established pursuant to the provisions of the Transport Act, 1962, and thereafter the service was operated and maintained by them. In 1978, the defendant, having notified the plaintiffs, discontinued the service. The plaintiffs claimed damages for breach of the statutory duty imposed by the 1898 Act. During the 1950's and early 1960's, the Waterford-Fish-

CONTRACT—*continued.*

guard service had been operated from a terminal at Adelphi Quay, Waterford. At a meeting between the parties in December, 1964, the defendant proposed to replace the existing sailing vesel with a new steamer, with a weekly minimum of three round trips. The defendant indicated at this meeting that if the plaintiffs would provide new port facilities, the defendant would require safeguards against their being made available to their competitiors. By mid-1966, the plaintiffs were considering a major new development at the North Wharf. The general manager of the defendant board visited Waterford at this time and proposed the establishment of a working-party to report on the most suitable site for the providing of accommodation for container traffic. The report of the working party, which was submitted in November, 1966, recommended the development of the North Wharf in line with the plaintiffs' proposals, and further recommended that on completion of this development Adelphi Quay should be abandoned by the defendant. Upon receipt of this report, the general manager of the defendant board wrote to the plaintiffs by letter dated 7 December, 1966, announcing that the new steamer had been chartered, and approving the recommendations of the working-party. In particular, he stated that he would be glad to learn that these 'will be acted on by all concerned'. The plaintiffs proceeded with the development of the North Wharf, but the proposed move of the defendant never took place. As part of the instant proceedings, the plaintiffs sought to claim damages for breach of contract, which they alleged had been made by the letter of 7 December, 1966. The plaintiffs also claimed damages for failure to fulfil an alleged obligation to provide an annual through-put of 10,000 containers per annum on the Waterford-Fishguard route. Finally, the plaintiffs claimed damages for breach of the 1959 agreement, alleging that the defendant, as successor to the Commission, had failed to maintain the shipping service which they were required to maintain pursuant to the said agreement.

Held by Costello J. in giving judgment for the plaintiffs, 1, that the Fishguard and Rosslare Railways and Harbours Act, 1898, became part of the law of the Irish Republic by virtue of Article 73 of the Constitution of 1922, and that the obligations imposed by s. 70 of the said Act were not discontinued under Irish law by the Ministerial Order of 1940, which did not have extra-territorial effect. 2. That the said statutory obligations were imposed on the defendant by virtue of s. 31 subs. 2(*b*) of the Transport Act, 1962, since the shipping services provided by the British Transport Commission were supplied in exercise of the powers conferred on that body by the Railway Shipping Acts. 3. That the plaintiffs were a 'party aggrieved' within the meaning of the Railway and Canal Act, 1888, and were thus statutorily entitled to maintain an action for damages; 4. That, although the statutory obligations imposed by s. 70 of the 1898 Act had been broken previously, the claim of the plaintiffs was not statute-barred, since each new breach gave rise to a new cause of action. In the instant case, the plaintiffs had brought proceedings within one year from the notification to them of the defendant's intention to withdraw the service. 5. That on the evidence adduced, the defendant had entered into a contractual relationship with the plaintiffs on 7 December, 1966, and was in breach of this obligation, but that no contract had been entered into in respect of an annual through-put of containers. 6. That the defendant, by suspending sailings for three months during 1977, was in breach of the 1959 agreement. 7. That in assessing damages, the plaintiff could rely on the number of sailings which the defendant had contracted to provide per annum, rather than the number of actual sailings in a given year, where that number was lower. 8. That a claim for damages for breach of the North Wharf contract, and a claim to damages for breach of statutory duty were two separate claims, and the plaintiffs were entitled to be compensated in respect of each. *Cullinane* v. *British 'Rema' Manufacturing Co. Ltd.* [1954] 1 Q.B. 292, distinguished. The defendant appealed from the order of the High Court insofar as it related to breach of statutory duty and breach of the North Wharf contract, and it was **Held** by the Supreme Court (O'Higgins C.J., Henchy, Griffin, Kenny, Parke JJ.) in dismissing the appeal, but remitting the case to the High Court for reassessment of damages, 1, that the successive contracts entered into by the parties in 1939, 1959 and 1966 replaced the rights and duties of the parties under s. 70 of the 1898 Act. The plaintiffs were not therefore entitled to an award of damages for breach of the said section, and were estopped from reverting to the position which had prevailed prior to 1939 (O'Higgins C.J. and Kenny J. dissenting). *Per:* Henchy J. — the aim of the 1966 agreement was to provide a shipping service which would be accepted by both parties as a substitute for the defendant's obligations under s. 70. 2. That in assessing damages for breach of the North Wharf contract, the measure of damages is the sum which may reasonably supposed to have been in the contemplation of the parties — which in this case was the loss of profit to the plaintiffs which would result from the breach. The plaintiffs could not be allowed to be doubly compensated by an award of damages on the basis of their capital expenditure also (O'Higgins C.J. and Kenny J. dissenting). *Per:* O'Higgins C.J. — there are two rights and two claims. A claim in respect of

COPYRIGHT

see also **Patents; Trade Marks; Trade Names and Designs**

1.—— **Design** — *Engineering drawings — Artistic works — Non-registrable design — Reproduction in three-dimensional form in a series of machines — Statute-barred copying of first machines — Whether defendant's modifications to subsequent machines avoided infringement — Duration of copyright — Whether copyright limited to 15 years — Whether "conversion" or "flagrancy" damages recoverable — Registered Designs Act,* 1949 (*c.* 88), *s.* 7(1) — *Copyright Act,* 1956 (*c.* 74), *ss.* 1, 3, 4, 10, 11, 17, 18, 49, *Sch.* 3 — *Design Copyright Act,* 1968 (*c.* 68), *s.*1 — *Copyright (Industrial Designs) Rules,* 1957 (*S.I. No.* 867).] The first plaintiff, an engineer who controlled the second and third plaintiff companies, developed an automatic machine for weighing and bagging coal in 1966. From 1969 to 1971 the defendant, who had a small engineering workshop in Co. Antrim, did a considerable amount of work for the plaintiff in connection with the construction and installation of the plaintiff's machines at various coal-yards in Northern Ireland. In 1971 the defendant was asked to supply machines "similar" to the plaintiff's to a coal-yard in Belfast. It was conceded that in making these machines the defendant infringed many aspects of the copyright in the plaintiff's machine. The plaintiff was aware of this breach and in 1972 his solicitors wrote to the defendant requiring him to cease the manufacture of the machines. However this letter was written on behalf of a company unknown to the defendant. From 1975 to 1982 the second defendant, a company controlled by the defendant, made some 130 machines. These machines, referred to in the action as "marks 2 to 6", all incorporated various improvements and modifications to the machines made by the defendant in 1971. In 1981 a letter was written on behalf of the plaintiff listing certain drawings in which the plaintiff claimed copyright and which it was alleged that the defendant had breached. Proceedings were commenced the following year for an injunction to restrain the defendants from reproducing the plaintiff's designs and damages for infringment of copyright. The defendant argued, *inter alia,* (i) that, as the designs had been applied industrially by the plaintiff in 1968, the copyright period was the 15 years period specified by section 10 (3) of the Copyright Act, 1956, as amended by the Design Copyright Act, 1968, even though those designs were not registrable under the Registered Design Acts; (ii) that there was no actionable infringement of the plaintiff's copyright, as any infringement by the defendant's mark 1 machines in 1971 was statute barred and the making of the mark 2 to 6 machines merely amounted to the permissible taking of a concept which was then applied in ways of the taker's own devising, and (iii) that there was no case for conversion or flagrancy damages. **Held** that, 1, the amendments made by the Design Copyright Act, 1968, to the Copyright Act, 1956, which allow ordinary artistic copyright to the owner of a registrable design during the period of 15 years after that design has been industrially applied, whether or not the design has been registered under the Registered Designs Act, 1949, but which limit the artistic copyright in such cases to 15 years, do not apply to the artistic copyright in a drawing which has been applied industrially, but which did not constitute a design registrable under the 1949 Act. *Hoover plc* v. *George Hulme (Stockport) Ltd.* (1982) F.S.R. 565 *not followed.* 2. While the defendant had made a number of modifications to the plaintiff's machine, all the defandant's machines reproduced the heart of the plaintiff's machine — the single screen feeder with an efficient dribble feed device — which ensured that the correct weight was automatically fed into the weight hopper and distinguished the plaintiff's machine from other coal bagging machines, and this amounted, looking to the quality rather than the quantity of the part reproduced, to a reproduction by the defendant of a substantial part of the copyright work. 3. Conversion or "flagrancy" damages were not awarded as the defendant did not know that copyright subsisted in the machines and in view of the misleading nature of the letter sent to the plaintiff in 1972, the absence of any concealment of the defendant's activities and the plaintiff's familiarity with same, the defendant had no reasonable grounds for suspecting that copyright existed. *Smith v. Greenfield*

(Ch.D.) [1984] N.I.125

2. —— **Design** — *Registered design — Infringement — Sportswear — Whether defendant's sportswear an "obvious imitation" of plaintiff's registered design — Publication prior to registration — Whether publication such as to make further publication contrary to good faith — Whether "textile design" — Industrial and Commercial Property (Protection) Act,* 1927 (*No.* 16), *ss.* 64, 72, 75.

Injunction — Interlocutory — Claim and counterclaim — Principles applicable — Whether serious question to be tried.] Section 64, sub-s. 1 of the Industrial and Commercial Property (Protection) Act, 1927, provides that "the controller may . . . on the application . . . of any person claiming to be the proprietor of any new or original design not previously published . . . register such design under this Act." Section 72 of the Act of 1927 provides that "the disclosure

COPYRIGHT—*continued.*

of a design by the proprietor to any other person, in such circumstances as would make it contrary to good faith for that other person to use or publish the design, and the disclosure of a design in breach of good faith by any person other than the proprietor of the design and the acceptance of a first and confidential order for goods bearing a new or original textile design intended for registration, shall not be deemed to be a publication of the design sufficient to invalidate the copyright thereof if registration thereof is obtained subsequently to the disclosure or acceptance." Section 75 of the Act of 1927 provides that any interested party may apply for the cancellation of the registration of a design on the grounds *inter alia* that the design had been published prior to its registration. The plaintiff was the exclusive supplier of certain sportswear to the Football Association of Ireland. In February, 1988, it completed a design for a jersey to be worn by the Irish team at the European Championships in June, and showed the design to at least two buyers. Thereafter (in early March, 1988) the plaintiff applied for registration of the design pursuant to the Act of 1927. The application was granted on the 14 April, 1988, giving the plaintiff copyright in the design for a period of five years from the date of its application. The defendant was a trade rival of the plaintiff and designed and marketed between March and May, 1988, "supporters' jerseys" intended to be as close as possible to the team jersey in appearance. One of these designs was similar to the plaintiff's design. The plaintiff sought an interlocutory injunction restraining the defendant from allegedly infringing the plaintiff's copyright by marketing these jerseys. The defendant responded that there had been no imitation of the plaintiff's product and that, in any case, the court would accede to a proposed counterclaim that the plaintiff's design should be deleted from the register as having been published prior to the plaintiff's application. **Held** by Costello J., in granting the interlocutory order, 1, although the life of the rival products was likely to have expired by the time the case came to trial, nevertheless the court would reach its decision in accordance with the long established principle applicable to a motion for an interlocutory injunction namely that the plaintiff had to show that there was a serious question to be considered by a court of trial both in respect of its claim and the defendant's counterclaim. 2. That to succeed in its claim it was unnecesary for the plaintiff to show deliberate copying of their design by the defendant, it being sufficient that, on comparision of the rival jerseys, the defendant's should appear to be an obvious imitation of the plaintiff's. 3. That, on applying the test as to whether the eye would confuse the two designs

COPYRIGHT—*continued.*

under normal conditions, it was clear that the plaintiff had shown a serious question to exist for the consideration of a trial court in this regard. 4 That, with respect to the counterclaim, it was open to the plaintiff to argue that, in the circumstances, disclosure of its design by a buyer would amount to a breach of faith on his part. Accordingly there was a serious issue to be tried in relation to the counterclaim. *Gunston* v. *Winox Ltd.* [1921] 1 Ch. 664 considered. 5. That, were the plaintiff to succeed at the trial of the action, it would be granted an injunction as damages would be an inadequate remedy, there being an unquantifiable loss of goodwill to the plaintiffs. Accordingly the balance of convenience favoured granting an interlocutory injunction. *Three Stripe International Ltd.* v. *O'Neill (Charles) & Co.Ltd.*

(H.C.) [1988] I.R.144

—— Infringement — Authorisation — Artistic works — Cutting patterns for body armour — Prior publication of drawings in patent specification not fatal to claim — Defendant's product printed in England — Whether distributed in Ireland — Jurisdiction.

see **Contract,** 3

CORONER

—— **Inquest** — *Verdict — Suicide — Statutory exclusions of questions of civil or criminal liability — Whether verdict available — Notice of inquest not served on next-of-kin — Whether breach of natural and constitutional justice — Certiorari — Coroner Act,* 1962 (*No.* 9), *s.*30.] Section 30 of the Coroners Act, 1962, provides that "questions of civil or criminal liability shall not be considered or investigated at an inquest" and accordingly every inquest is confined to ascertaining the identity of the deceased and how, when, and where the death occurred. An inquest jury found the cause of death of the deceased husband of the prosecutrix to be:— (*a*) multiple injuries, (*b*) accident on railway line, (*c*) suicide." The next of kin received no notification of the date of the holding of the inquest. The prosecutrix obtained a conditional order of certiorari to quash the verdict of suicide on the grounds that (*a*) the coroner and his jury acted in excess and without jurisdiction in recording a verdict of suicide, and (*b*) the inquest offended the principles of natural justice in failing to give the next-of-kin notice of its holding and arriving at a verdict with no evidence of the mental state of the deceased prior to his death. **Held** by O'Hanlon J. in making absolute the order notwithstanding cause shown, 1, the coroner and jury exceeded the jurisdiction conferred on them by s. 30 of the Coroners Act, 1962, by finding that the deceased had unlawfuly

CORONER—*continued.*

brought about his own death by suicide. Even if it were within their powers to bring in such a verdict the evidence in this case was not adequate to support a finding of suicide. *Reg.* v. *London Coroner, Ex p. Barber* [1975] 1 W.L.R. 1310; *Rex* v. *Huntbach* [1944] I K.B. 606 and *Reg.* v. *Cardiff Coroner, Ex p. Thomas* [1970] 1 W.L.R. 1975 considered. 2. That there had been a breach of the rules of natural and constitutional justice in failing to afford the next-of-kin an opportunity of being heard or represented at the inquest. *The State (McKeown)* v. *Scully*

(H.C.) [1986] I.R.524; [1986] ILRM 133

CORPORATION TAX
see **Revenue,** 3, 4, 8-24

CORPOREAL HEREDITAMENT

—— Fishery rights — Interference — Riparian owner — Whether fishery rights of plaintiffs corporeal or incorporeal hereditaments — Whether plaintiffs entitled to order to restrain defendant's activities.
see **Real Property,** 5

—— Fishing rights — Interference — Arterial drainage scheme.
see **Real Property,** 4

CORRESPONDING OFFENCE
see **Constitution,** 24, 25
Extradition, 9

CORROBORATION

—— Evidence — Accomplice.
see **Criminal Law,** 9

—— Evidence — Rape.
see **Criminal Law,** 22

COSTS
see **Practice and Procedure,** 15-33

—— Award — Appeal from the District Court — Conviction by the District Justice under the Road Traffic Act, 1961, *s.* 53 — Jurisdiction of the Circuit Court to award costs of appeal — Whether limitation of costs under rule 67 of the District Court Rules, 1948, applicable.
see **Practice and Procedure,** 15

—— Interest — Award of costs — Dispute as to the period in relation to which the interest thereon should be calculated — Whether interest payable from date of High Court order or from when costs were taxed.
see **Practice and Procedure,** 16

COSTS—*continued.*

—— Representation — Police officer — Dismissal inquiry.
see **Constitution,** 11

—— Security for,
see **Practice and Procedure,** 17-25

—— Solicitor — Lien — Title deeds.
see **Solicitor,** 1

—— Taxation
see **Practice and Procedure,** 26-33

COUNSEL

—— Action — compromise.
see under **Action**

—— Appearance — Presumption that counsel and solicitor appear on express instruction of the client.
see **Constitution,** 42

—— Barrister — Income tax — Assessment — Cessation of profession — Outstanding fees paid after cessation.
see **Revenue,** 30

—— Barrister — Income tax — Capital expenditure — Provision of plant — Allowance for wear and tear — Purchase of law books — Whether entitled to allowance.
see **Revenue,** 29

—— Fees — Taxation.
see **Practice and Procedure,** 26, 28, 29

COURTHOUSES

—— **Repair** — *Minister of State — Statutory power — Enforcement of repairs to courthouse — Mandamus — Minister directed to exercise his powers — Courthouses (Provision and Maintenance) Act,* 1935 (*No.* 18), *ss.*3, 6.] By s. 3 of the Act of 1935 it is the duty of a council of a county or of a county borough to provide and maintain in its functional area courthouse accommodation in the manner there stated. Whenever a council fails or neglects to maintain in proper repair and condition any such accommodation which it is so required to maintain, it is provided by s. 6, sub-s. 1, of that Act that the Minister for Justice, after consultation with the Minister for Finance, shall direct the Commissioners of Public Works in Ireland "to execute such repairs and to do such other work as may be necessary or proper" to put such courthouse accommodation into proper repair and condition. The courthouse in Waterford was allowed to fall into a very bad state of disrepair and in the year 1967 the

COURTHOUSES—*continued.*

solicitors of the Waterford Law Society complained to the Corporation of Waterford about the condition of the courthouse. In the year 1970 the judges of the High Court refused to sit in the courthouse and the Minister for Justice urged the Corporation to effect the necessary repairs. Alternative accommodation, provided by the Corporation, proved to be unsatisfactory, and in 1973 the prosecutors, being solicitors practising in Waterford, obtained in the High Court a conditional order of mandamus commanding the respondent Minister to exercise the powers conferred on him by s. 6 of the Act of 1935, unless cause were shown to the contrary. In 1974 the prosecutors applied for an order absolute, notwithstanding the case shown by the respondent. **Held** by Doyle J., in disallowing the cause shown, 1, that the alternative accommodation provided by the Corporation was unsuitable and inadequate. 2. That the repair of the courthouse, although involving extensive renewal work, was feasible and that the prosecutors were entitled to an order absolute. *Byrne* v. *Ireland* [1972] I.R. 241 considered. *The State (King)* v. *Minister for Justice*

(H.C.) [1984] I.R. 169

—— District Court — Licensed premises — Statutory provision allowing room to be rented for holding of petty sessions — Prohibition on renting room where spiritous or fermented liquors sold — Prosecutrix summoned to appear before District Court sitting in licensed premises — Jurisdiction.
see **District Court,** 4

COURTS
see also **Judge; Locus Standi; Tribunal**
For individual courts see under name of court.

—— Abuse of process.
see **Abuse of Process**

—— Administration of justice.
see **Constitution,** 2-7, 26-33

—— Administration of justice — Interference — Statutory power — Validity — Indictable offence — Preliminary examination — Accused sent forward for trial by District Justice — Indictment subsequently framed by D.P.P. — Indictment containing substituted counts charging other offences — Whether substitution of counts rendered nugatory a judicial determination — Whether procedure unfair or discriminatory.

COURTS—*continued.*
see **Constitution,** 27

—— Administration of justice — Interference — Statutory power — Validity — Indictable offence — Preliminary examination — Refusal of judge to send accused forward for trial — D.P.P. sending accused forward for trial — Enactment invalid — *Stare decisis.*
see **Constitution,** 26

—— Administration of justice — Judicial function — Revenue — Pay as You Earn — Duty of employer to remit tax witheld — Employer omitting to remit tax in time — Assessments issued — Enforcement proceedings commenced notwithstanding late payment of tax by employer — Whether assessment a judicial function.
see **Constitution,** 30

—— Administration of justice — Judicial function — Exception — Limited functions and powers of a judicial nature.
see **Constitution,** 28

—— Administration of justice — Judicial function — Revenue — Income tax — Assessment — Schedule D — Taxpayer not appealing assessments — Assessments becoming "final and conclusive" — Tax not paid — Certificate issued by Collector General — County sheriff instructed to levy tax in default — Notice of seizure served on plaintiff — Whether assessment a judicial function — Whether legislation empowering execution in the absence of court order constitutional.
see **Constitution,** 31

—— Administration of justice — Judicial function — Invasion — Street and house-to-house collection — Application for collections permit refused — Chief Superintendent of opinion that proceeds would benefit an unlawful organisation — Unsuccessful appeal to District Court — Whether appeal procedure constitutionally invalid — Whether unwarranted invasion of judicial power.
see **Constitution,** 29

—— Central Criminal Court — Validity of exclusion of jurisdiction of High Court sitting as Central Criminal Court.
see **Constitution,** 32

COURTS—*continued.*

—— Constitution — Jurisdiction — Statute — Validity — Accused returned for trial on indictment to Circuit Court in Dublin — Right to trial in Central Criminal Court — Former legislation repealed — "Full" original jurisdiction of High Court — Courts of first instance under the Constitution — Courts of local and limited jurisdiction under the Constitution.
see **Constitution,** 32

—— Contempt.
see **Contempt of Court**

—— Ecclesiastical.
see **Ecclesiastical Courts**

—— Irish language — Use in court.
see **Constitution,** 7

—— Jurisdiction.
see **Constitution,** 3-6

—— Right of access to,
see **Criminal Law,** 49

—— Special Criminal Court — Establishment — Validity.
see **Special Criminal Court**

COVENANT

—— Lease.
see **Landlord and Tenant,** 1-5, 10

—— Restrictive covenant.
see **Injunction,** 12
Restraint of Trade, 1

CREDIT UNION — Amendment to rules — Registrar of Friendly Societies refusing to register such amendment — Whether Registrar so entitled.
see **Industrial and Provident Societies,** 1

CRIME PREVENTION — Habitual criminals — Sentence — Lengthy sentence imposed — Whether amounting to preventative detention — Whether attempt to reform by prevention appropriate basis for sentence.
see **Criminal Law,** 81

CRIMINAL APPEAL
see **Criminal Law,** 14, 21, 34, 35, 79

CRIMINAL CONTEMPT
see **Contempt of Court**

CRIMINAL EVIDENCE
see under **Criminal Law**

CRIMINAL INJURIES

Criminal injury to persons. Nos.1, 2
Criminal injury to property. Nos. 3-7
Limitation of actions. No. 8

1. —— **Criminal injury to persons** — *Compensation — Refusal — Appeal — Compensation awarded by court — Respondent decided to withold payment until appellant complied with request for information — Whether power to withold compensation — Crown Proceedings Act,* 1947 (*c.* 35), *s.* 25(3) — *Criminal Injuries (Compensation) (Northern Ireland) Order,* 1977 (*S.I. No.* 1248, N.I. 15), *art.* 6 (10).] The appellant was attacked and sustained personal injuries. In a statement to police describing the incident he said that he did not want to name his assailant. An application for compensation under the Criminal Injuries (Compensation) (Northern Ireland) Order, 1977, was refused by the respondent on the ground, *inter alia,* that there had been provocative or negligent conduct, within the meaning of article 5(2) of the 1977 Order, which contributed to the criminal injury. The appellant appealed to the High Court and compensation was assessed at £2,000, but reduced to £1,000 by virtue of the said article 5(2). After the appellant's solicitor inquired as to the payment of the compensation awarded by the court the respondent replied that the position was being considered under article 6(10) of the 1977 Order. The respondent later stated that compensation would be withheld under the said article 6(10) until the appellant supplied the full names and addresses of certain persons. The appellant sought declarations that he was entitled to immediate payment of the compensation and that the said article 6(10) did not authorise the respondent to withhold payment of an award made by the court. **Held,** that the decision to withhold compensation under article 6(10) of the 1977 Order is a decision for the Secretary of State; the court cannot of its own motion decide to withhold compensation and the question of withholding compensation cannot arise until a decision has been reached that compensation is payable, for until compensation is awarded and assessed there is little point in the Secretary of State making a request for information because there is no machinery which enables the Secretary of State to withhold all or any part of compensation until the request is complied with. The provision in section 25 of the Crown Proceedings Act, 1947, for payment by a Government department of sums under court orders is a general provision which is overridden by the later and particular provision in article 6(10) of the 1977 Order. *Barry* v. *Secretary of State*
(C.A.) [1984] N.I.39

CRIMINAL INJURIES—*continued.*

2. —— **Criminal injury to persons** — *Compensation — Refusal — Appeal to Recorder's Court — Judgment in favour of respondent — Part of compensation paid — Respondent died otherwise than as result of criminal injury — Whether balance of compensation payable — Whether respondent "entitled" — Criminal Injuries (Compensation) (Northern Ireland) Order,* 1977 (*S.I. No.* 1248, N.I. 15), *art.* 9(*a*) — *Crown Proceedings Act,* 1947 (*c.* 44), *s.* 25 (3).] The respondent's wife sustained a criminal injury in 1978. The Secretary of State decided that she was not entitled to compensation and she appealed to the Additional Recorder of Belfast who held that she was entitled to compensation amounting to £50,000. An order for the payment of that sum was made in 1980. At her request payments amounting to £22,500 were made in that year. She died in 1981, otherwise than as a result of the criminal injury, leaving a balance outstanding of £27,500 plus interest. The Secretary of State, in reliance on article 9(a) of the Criminal Injuries (Compensation) (Northern Ireland) Order, 1977, declined to pay the balance of the compensation. In the Queen's Bench Division MacDermott J. held that section 25(3) of the Crown Proceedings Act, 1947, imposed a statutory obligation to pay the entire sum which was not affected by the said article 9(a). On appeal to the Court of Appeal, **Held** that the balance of the compensation was payable. Section 25 of the 1947 Act is a general provision which does not provide for payment of the balance of the compensation in this case as it is overridden by the 1977 Order, which is a later and more particular provision. *Barry* v. *Secretary of State* [1984] N.I. 34 followed. However the word "entitled" in article 9(*a*) of the 1977 Order refers to a person who has a right to compensation before the compensation has been awarded by a court and accordingly the article does not apply to justify nonpayment where a court has made an order for the payment of compensation. *McCloskey* v. *Secretary of State*

(C.A.) [1984] N.I.365

3. —— **Criminal injury to property** — *Malicious injury — Crime against property — Burglary — Burglar entering premises with intent to steal — Burglar starting fire by carelessly discarding cigarette — Property stolen — Premises damaged by fire — Whether burglary a crime against the premises — Statute — Interpretation — Crime against the property damaged — Larceny Act,* 1916 (*c.* 50), *s.* 23A — *Criminal Law (Jurisdiction) Act,* 1976 (*No.* 14), *s.* 6. — *Malicious Injuries Act,* 1981 (*No.* 9), *s.* 5.] Section 23A, sub.s. 1 of the Larceny Act, 1916, as inserted by s. 6 of the Criminal Law (Jurisdiction) Act, 1976, provides, *inter alia,* that:— "A person is guilty of burglary if — (*a*) he enters any building or part of a building as a trespasser and with intent to [*steal anything in the building*]; or (*b*) having entered any building or part of a building as a trespasser, he steals or attempts to steal anything in the building or that part of it, or inflicts or attempts to inflict on any person therein any grievous bodily harm." The applicant's hotel was damaged by fire. A man who had entered the hotel as a trespasser, with the intention of stealing a tape recorder, started a fire by discarding a cigarette without extinguishing it. He did not intend to set fire to the hotel or its contents and his behaviour was not wanton. He took the tape recorder and a stereo cassette and left without noticing the fire. The applicant claimed copmpensation under the Malicious Injuries Act, 1981, and was awarded £9,650 in the Circuit Court. On appeal by the respondent to the High Court, Barron J. stated a case for the determination of the Supreme Court as to (1) whether the burglary, as defined by either paragraph (*a*) or (*b*) of s. 23A, sub-s. 1 of the Act of 1916, was a crime against the hotel premises; and (2) whether the fire had been started in the course of the commission of a burglary. It was argued on behalf of the respondent that the crime against s. 23A, sub-s. 1 was a crime against the property intended to be stolen or stolen and not against the hotel premises. It was argued on behalf of the applicant that a 'crime against property damaged' within the meaning of s. 5, sub-s. 2 (*d*) of the Act of 1981, was any crime in which the property damaged was involved. **Held** by the Supreme Court (Finlay C.J., Walsh, Henchy and Hederman JJ.), 1, that the correct test to be applied in determining whether a crime was a 'crime against the property damaged' was to ascertain firstly, whether the crime in general was a crime against property as distinct from a crime against the person; and secondly, what property the particular penal section was intended to protect. 2. That s. 23A of the Act of 1916 was clearly a section intended to protect buildings and the persons and goods therein; so that an offence contrary to that section was a crime against both the buildings and the contents. 3. That the offence, created by s. 23A, sub-s. 1(*a*), of entering a building with intent to steal, was completed as soon as the burglar entered the premises; but the offence, created by sub-s. 1(*b*), of stealing after entering a building as a trespasser, was not complete until the goods were stolen. Therefore the act of discarding the lighted cigarette had occurred during the course of committing a crime of burglary contrary to s. 23A, sub-s. 1(*b*) of the Act of 1916. *Shennick Lodge Ltd.* v. *Monaghan County Council*

(S.C.) [1986] I.R.442 ; [1986] ILRM 273

CRIMINAL INJURIES—*continued.*

4. —— **Criminal injury to property** — *Malicious injury — Crime against property — Unauthorised taking and user of motor vehicle — Damage to vehicle — Whether caused in the course of committing a crime against the property damaged — Road Traffic Act,* 1961 (*No.* 24), *s.* 112 (1) — *Malicious Injuries Act,* 1981 (*No.* 9), *s.* 5 (2) (*d*) — *Road Traffic Act,* 1968 (*No.* 25), *s.* 65.] The applicant's motor car was taken without his permission by a person unknown and was later found abandoned and crashed. The car appeared to be unrepairable. The applicant sought compensation, claiming the damage had been caused maliciously within the meaning of the Malicious Injuries Act, 1981. The Circuit Court awarded the applicant damages under the 1981 Act, but stated a case to the Supreme Court as to the correctness of that decision. S. 5 (2) (*d*) of the 1981 Act provides that an act is done maliciously if done 'in the course of, whether or not for the purpose of, the committing of a crime against the property damaged.' **Held** by the Supreme Court (O'Higgins C.J., Henchy and Griffin JJ.) in affirming the Circuit Court: since the act of taking the car without permission constituted a criminal offence under s. 112 (1) of the Road Traffic Act, 1961, as amended, and since the driver of the car at the time of the crash was committing the continuing offence of using the car without the owner's permission, the damage caused by the crash was caused in the course of committing a crime against the property damaged within the extended meaning of 'maliciously' in s. 5 (2) of the 1981 Act. *Fitzgerald* v. *Limerick Corporation*

(S.C.) [1985] ILRM 445

5. —— **Criminal injury to property** — *Malicious injury — Damage by fire — Application for compensation — Fire caused by employee — Whether fire caused deliberately or by an act of wanton recklessness — Onus of proof — Whether employee knew what he did was likely to cause damage.*] The applicant in a malicious injury claim sought to establish that Joseph Morrissey, a fifteen year-old employee, had maliciously caused a fire in the box-room of QK Cold Stores Ltd. at Kilmacthomas. The evidence was that Morrissey had discarded a lighted match, and that fire resulted from the ignition of waxed backing paper from a roll of adhesive labels. There was further evidence that Morrissey had been out late the night before the fire, and had arrived without apology or explanation two hours late for his day's work. The applicant's contention was that Morrissey had deliberately caused the fire or, at the least, that he had left the box-room knowing that a fire had broken out. **Held** by McCarthy J, on appeal from the Circuit Court in County Waterford, in the course

CRIMINAL INJURIES—*continued.*

of two judgments, 1, that there was a presumption against the commission of a crime, which presumption the applicant had not rebutted. 2. That Joseph Morrissey had shown wanton disregard for the consequences of throwing away his lighted match. 3. That an initial careless act and a subsequent deliberate abstention from action represented grossly wanton and reckless conduct constituting malice within the meaning of the malicious injury code: *Wexford Timber Company* v. *Wexford Corporation and Another* 88 I.L.T.R. 137 followed. 4. That a finding of malicious damage was justified. *Agra Trading Ltd.* v. *Waterford County Council*

(H.C.) [1985] ILRM 249

6. —— **Criminal injury to property** — *Malicious injury — Damage by fire — Fire started carelessly by employee — No intention to injure — Whether act malicious — Malicious Injuries Act,* 1981 (*No.* 9), *s.* 5(2).] A fifteen year old stable boy, employed by the applicant, set fire to some loose straw which he had gathered in a heap some six or seven feet from the applicant's tack room in which were kept riding equipment and hay. The boy left the fire unattended and some of the flaming straw reached the tack room and destroyed its contents. It was found as fact that the straw was carelessly lit, that the stable boy had no intention of injuring the applicant or his property and that the fire in the tack room was a direct but unforeseen consequence of setting the loose straw alight. It was also found that the stable boy merely intended to set fire to the heap of straw and was quite unconscious of the possible effects. **Held** by McCarthy J., sitting as a judge of the High Court on Circuit dismissing an application for compensation under the Malicious Injuries Act, 1981, 1, the stable boy's action, in setting fire to the straw, fell far short of amounting to a 'wanton act' on his part. Furthermore it had not been established that this act was a 'wrongful act' within the meaning of the Malicious Injuries Act, 1981, s. 5 (2) of, if technically a wrongful act, that it was done without just cause or excuse. *Artificial Coal Co.* v. *Minister for Finance* [1928] I.R. 238 and *Wexford Timber Co.* v. *Wexford Corporation and Wexford County Council* 88 I.L.T.R. 137 considered. 2. 'Caused' in s. 5 (2) of the Act connotes 'caused as a reasonable and probable consequence.' In the circumstances, the stable boy's action did not 'cause' the fire in the tack room. *Lally* v. *Meath County Council*

(H.C.) [1985] ILRM 269

7. —— **Criminal injury to property** — *Malicious injury — Whether damage caused "wantonly" — Motor car unlawfully taken by two*

CRIMINAL INJURIES—*continued.*

youths — Collision with applicant's car — Incompetent and erratic driving causing collision — Malicious Injuries Act, 1981 (No. 9), *s.* 5.] Section 5 of the Malicious Injuries Act, 1981, provides *inter alia* that damage shall be taken to be maliciously caused if caused wantonly. A motor car was unlawfully taken by two youths and while being driven by one of them, an inexperienced driver, at excessively high speed, went out of control when the driver failed to negotiate a bend in the road and collided with the applicant's car. On an application to the Circuit Court for compensation under the provisions of the said Act the Circuit Court Judge awarded compensation in respect of the damage caused to the applicant's car. On appeal by the respondents to the High Court it was **Held** by Barron J. in disallowing the appeal, that the car was driven in such a manner, without regard for the consequences, that the driver must have known that it was highly probable that he would crash, and the taking of such a risk being totally unjustifiable, the damage had therefore been caused wantonly. *McDowell* v. *Dublin Corporation* [1903] 2 I.R. 541; *Boyd* v. *Antrim County Council* [1941] N.I. 127 and *The People* v. *Murray* [1977] I.R. 360 considered. The statutory meaning of the word "wantonly" considered. *Moran* v. *Leitrim County Council*
(H.C.) [1985] I.R. 111

8. —— **Limitation of actions** — *Statutory construction — Accrual of cause of action — Proceedings commenced outside this period — Whether court power to extend time — Malicious Injuries Act (No.* 9), 1981, *ss.* 8, 14, 23.] Section 8, sub-s. 1 of the Malicious Injuries Act, 1981, provides that "A person seeking compensation under this Act shall, within fourteen days after . . . the damage was caused . . . serve . . . preliminary notice . . . of his intention to apply for compensation." Section 23 of the Act of 1981 provides:— "(1) Proceedings under this Act shall not be commenced after the expiration of three years from the date on which the cause of action accrued. (2) A cause of action under this Act shall accrue on the date of the service of a preliminary notice under section 8." Section 14, sub-s. 3 of the Act of 1981 provides that "The court may, in relation to any act or proceedings under this Act . . . extend the time for, set aside either wholly or in part, amend or otherwise deal with in such manner and on such terms as the court may think just, such act or proceedings." On the 12 April, 1983, M. Ltd. served preliminary notice of intention to claim compensation for damage done to its property on the 6 April, 1983. On the 9 May, 1986, the company commenced its proceedings under the Act. More than 3 years had elapsed since the accrual of the cause of

CRIMINAL INJURIES—*continued.*

action but an order was made by the Circuit Court judge, pursuant to s. 14 of the Act of 1981, extending the time for commencement of proceedings. The applicant applied to the High Court for an order for certiorari by way of judicial review of the order of the Circuit Court on the grounds that s. 14 of the Act did not confer jurisdiction on the court to extend the time limit of 3 years prescribed by s. 23. **Held** by Carroll J., in quashing the order of the Circuit Court, 1, that the time limit of 3 years for commencement of proceedings prescribed by s. 23 was — subject to the saver for persons under a disability — an absolute bar to the commencement of proceedings under the Act. 2. That the power conferred by s. 14 did not confer jurisdiction on the Circuit Court judge to extend that time limit. *Dublin Corporation* v. *Carroll*
(H.C.) [1987] I.R.401; [1988] ILRM 86

—— Compensation Tribunal — Tribunal required to award compensation to dependants of persons killed in attempting to save human life — Claim by widow — Burden of proof — Primary facts not in dispute — Rejection of claim by Tribunal — Whether failure to infer from facts that deceased was attempting to save a life was at variance with reason and common sense.
see **Judicial Review,** 10

—— Personal injuries — Garda Síochána — Compensation — Assessment — Principles applicable — Future economic loss — Mitigation of loss by award of pension — Whether value of pension to be deducted from value of future economic loss proved.
see **Garda Síochána,** 4

—— Property — Motor car — Unauthorised and inexperienced driver — Collision with applicant's car — Whether driver had acted wantonly.
see **Criminal Injuries,** 7

CRIMINAL INVESTIGATION
see also **Arrest and Detention**

—— Search warrant — Absence — Evidence — Admissibility.
see **Criminal Law,** 15, 16

—— Search warrant — Issue — Validity.
see **Criminal Law,** 70-2

—— Surveillance — Garda Síochána — Suspect kept under close overt surveillance —

CRIMINAL INVESTIGATION—*continued.*

Whether surveillance interfered with liberty of subject — Whether justified. *see* **Constitution,** 17

CRIMINAL LAW

see also **Criminal Injuries; Extradition; Road Traffic Offences**

Arrest Nos. 1-8
Evidence. Nos. 9-26
Miscellaneous offences. Nos. 27-29
Offences against the person. Nos. 30-32
Offences against property. No. 33
Practice and procedure. Nos. 34-69
Search warrant. Nos. 70-72
Sentence. Nos. 73-82

ARREST

see also No. 18

1. —— **Detention in Garda station** — *Whether lawful — Whether detained person free to leave — Whether under arrest — Whether detained for purpose of questioning — Whether detained person entitled to leave — Onus of proof.*] The defendant had driven in his own car to a garda station when requested or invited to do so by members of the Garda Síochána, and at the station had given information as to his movements around the time of a murder which the Gardaí were investigating. The Gardaí who had obtained the information from the defendant left the station to verify his account, and from then until their return he was further questioned by other Gardaí. On the return of the first set of Gardaí, who intimated to the defendant that they did not believe his account, he was further questioned, and he was asked for his car keys, which he gave them and which were not returned. The defendant subsequently made an incriminating statement in relation to the murder and was charged with that offence. At his trial, counsel objected to the admissibility of the statement on the ground the defendant was not lawfully detained at the time since he was not free to leave the station nor was he told he was free to leave. **Held** by Hamilton J. in ruling the detention unlawful and the evidence inadmissible, while the defendant, on the evidence, went voluntarily to the garda station in the first instance, when the Gardaí had returned from checking his account, he had become a very real suspect in respect of the crime being investigated and at this stage should have been told he was free to go if he so wished, and although in some instances an accused person might be aware of his right to leave in such circumstances, the onus was on the State to prove that and, in the absence of such evidence in the present case, that onus had not been discharged. Observations in *Dunne* v. *Clinton* [1930] I.R. 366, *The People* v. *Walsh* [1980] I.R. 294 and *The People* v. *Lynch* [1982] I.R. 64 applied. *The People* v. *Coffey*
(C.C.A.) [1987] ILRM 727

2. —— **Emergency powers** — *Motive — Arrest in respect of scheduled offence — Questioning in respect of non-scheduled offence — Whether arrest lawful — Whether arrest effected for spurious purpose unconnected with offence authorised by statutory power — Whether sufficient reasons and explanation given for arrest — Emergency Powers Act,* 1976 (*No.* 33), *s.* 2.

Evidence — Circumstantial — Murder — Statement of accused — Whether sufficient to convict — Absence of body of victim.

Evidence — Statement — Admissibility — Breach of Judges' Rules — Discretion to exclude — Whether discretion should be exercised to introduce — Purpose of particular rule — Judges' Rules, rule 9.] The applicant had been arrested in relation to the murder of a person which had involved firearms, pursuant to s. 2 of the Emergency Powers Act, 1976. The arrest was made in respect of the firearms matter, which was authorised under s. 2 of the Act, and he was questioned in relation to the murder, which was not an offence in respect of which an arrest could be made under s. 2. The applicant made a verbal incriminating statement regarding the murder, and was charged with and convicted of the offence. On application for leave to appeal: **Held** by the Court of Criminal Appeal (O'Higgins C.J., Finlay P. and Costello J.) in dismissing the application, 1, since the suspicion that the applicant had been involved in the shooting in question also involved inevitably a suspicion that he had been involved in an offence of being in possession of a firearm with intent to endanger life, there had not been a spurious invention of an imagined offence, and since the correctly held suspicion arose directly out of the matter being investigated, the arrest was lawful; and it could not be the case that in the investigation of a matter under s. 2 where some other offence, in respect of which a common law arrest only could have been effected, was also discovered, only a common law arrest could be made; and in making an arrest under s. 2 rights which would otherwise be protected could not be abrogated or set aside. *Christie* v. *Leachinsky* [1947] A.C. 573 discussed. 2. There was no requirement that the applicant be informed of the precise length of his proposed detention under s. 2 once he had been told that he was being arrested under that section in relation to a particular offence. *In re O Laighleis* [1960] I.R. 93 applied. 3. While the statement had not been recorded pursuant to rule 9 of the Judge's Rules, the trial court could, in the exercise of its discretion, admit the statement

CRIMINAL LAW—Arrest.

where there was a reasonable explanation of the failure to comply with rule 9, and in this light and the particular mischief which rule 9 was aimed at, namely the adducing of invented or planted oral statements, the trial court had correctly exercised its discretion. 4. The trial court was entitled to act on the statement made by the applicant, even in the absence of other evidence indicating that a killing had taken place. *The People* v. *Towson* **(C.C.A.) [1978] ILRM 122**

3. —— **Emergency powers** — *Plaintiff arrested on suspicion of being a terrorist — Constable acted on instructions from superior officer — Whether constable had honest suspicion that plaintiff a "terrorist" — Northern Ireland (Emergency Provisions) Act,* 1978 (*c.* 5), *ss.* 11(1), 31(1).] The plaintiff was summarily arrested at his home on the morning of 8 September, 1981, by a constable of the Royal Ulster Constabulary. The arrest was made under section 11(1) of the Northern Ireland (Emergency Provisions) Act, 1978, which reads: "Any constable may arrest without warrant any person whom he suspects of being a terrorist." The previous evening the arresting constable had been told by his section sergeant that the plaintiff was a suspect terrorist and instructed to arrest him: the constable had no other knowledge of the plaintiff. The plaintiff was released on the evening of 8 September and later brought an action for damages for, *inter alia,* wrongful arrest. The trial judge held that the arrest was lawful and on appeal the Court of Appeal, Jones L.J. dissenting, reversed the decision holding that the Act required a *bona fide* suspicion of a certain form of terrorist activity, as defined in section 31 of the Act, on the part of the person to be arrested, and that the constable's suspicion that the plaintiff was a member of a proscribed organisation fell short of that requirement. The Chief Constable appealed to the House of Lords. **Held** allowing the appeal, that the arrest was lawful because the constable had honestly suspected the plaintiff of being a terrorist. The definitions of "terrorism" and "terrorist" in section 31 (1) of the Act were broad and on the true construction of section 11 (1) of that Act what mattered was the state of mind of the arresting officer. That state of mind could legitimately be derived from the instruction given to the arresting officer by his superior officer. The arresting officer was not bound and would not have been entitled to question those instructions or ask on what information they were founded. *Per curiam* The powers of arrest under section 11 are not qualified by any words of "reasonableness." The suspicion has to be honestly held but it need not in addition be a reasonable suspicion. *McKee* v. *Chief Constable*

(C.A., H.L.) [1984] N.I. 169

CRIMINAL LAW—*continued.*

4. —— **Offences against the State** — *Suspicion — Whether suspicion of arresting officer required — Whether suspicion of other person, communicated to arresting officer, sufficient — Offences Against the State Act,* 1939 (*No.* 13), *s.* 30.] The applicant was arrested pursuant to s. 30 of the Offences Against the State Act, 1939. During his trial it was argued that his arrest was invalid, on the ground that the arresting officer in evidence stated that he had formed a personal suspicion that the applicant had committed a scheduled offence under the Act. He stated that the basis for the suspicion had been communicated to him by a superior officer. The applicant was convicted of a number of offences. On appeal by the applicant: **Held** by the Court of Criminal Appeal (Henchy, Gannon and Egan JJ.) in dismissing the application, 1, the arresting officer, in stating in evidence that his arrest under s. 30 of the 1939 Act was on suspicion that a scheduled offence had been committed, had sufficiently complied with the requirements of s. 30, and it was irrelevant that the suspicion derived from the mental processes of a superior officer rather than from the arresting officer's. 2. To construe s. 30 as requiring communication of the superior officer's information to the arresting officer would be inconsistent with the declared objective of the Offences Against the State Act, 1939. *The People* v. *McCaffrey*

(C.C.A.) [1986] ILRM 687

5. —— **Offences against the State** — *Statutory power — Detention of arrested person — Extension by direction of Chief Superintendent — Death of Chief Superintendent prior to trial of respondent — Whether necessary to have evidence from Chief Superintendent — Whether evidence as to state of mind required — Whether evidence from Garda officer present at time of making of extension order sufficient — Offences Against the State Act,* 1939 (*No.* 13), *s.* 30(3).] The respondent was arrested pursuant to the provisions of s. 30 of the Offences Against the State Act, 1939, on suspicion of having been involved in the commission of robbery with firearms, which was a scheduled offence under the Act of 1939. He was detained in Garda custody for a period of 24 hours, during which time a Chief Superintendent of the Garda Síochána authorised his detention for a further period of 24 hours commencing at the expiration of the first 24 hour period. This extension was made pursuant to the provisions of s. 30, sub-s. 3 of the Act of 1939, which provides that "[w]henever a person is arrested under this section, he may be removed to and detained in custody in a Garda Síochána station, a prison, or some convenient place for a period

CRIMINAL LAW—Arrest.

of twenty-four hours from the time of his arrest and may, if an officer of the Garda Síochána not below the rank of Chief Superintendent so directs, be so detained for a further period of twenty-four hours." In the course of the second 24 hour period, the respondent made a statement to the Garda Síochána. He was subsequently charged with a number of offences and at his trial in the Central Criminal Court, his counsel objected to the manner in which the validity of the extension order was proved by the prosecution. The Chief Superintendent who had signed the extension order had died prior to the trial. The trial judge ruled that, in the absence of the Chief Superintendent, there was no evidence that the respondent's detention beyond the expiration of the first 24 hour period was lawful, since the document signed by him was not evidence in itself of a valid extension. The trial judge therefore ruled the respondent's statement inadmissible, since it was obtained during unlawful custody, and there being no other evidence directed the jury to return a verdict of not guilty. On appeal by the Director of Public Prosecutions against the verdict of not guilty it was **Held** by the Supreme Court (Finlay C.J., Walsh, Griffin, Hederman and McCarthy JJ.), in dismissing the appeal, 1, that the trial judge had been correct in ruling that, in the absence of direct evidence from the Chief Superintendent as to his state of mind when making the extension order, the prosecution had failed to establish that the continued detention of the respondent after the expiration of the initial 24 hour period was lawful; and the evidence of the Garda officer who was present when the Chief Superintendent issued the authorisation under s. 30, sub-s. 3 of the Act of 1939 was irrelevant to the validity of the respondent's further period of detention. *Per* Finlay C.J., Griffin and Hederman JJ.: since the validity of the respondent's original arrest under s. 30 of the Act of 1939 had not been raised at the trial or in the appeal to the Supreme Court, no view should be expressed by the court on that matter. *Per* Walsh J.: the transcript of the trial was ambiguous as to the words used by the arresting officer in effecting the original arrest, but it was necessary for the arrest to be valid that he would have specified the particular scheduled offence in respect of which the requisite suspicion existed in the mind of the arresting officer. *Per* McCarthy J.: if the arresting officer had stated that he was arresting the accused under s. 30 of the Act of 1939 for possession, the arrest would have been lawful since in the context in which the words occurred this would have meant unlawful possession. *The People* v. *Byrne*

(S.C.) [1987] I.R. 363

6. —— **Offences against the State** — *Validity of arrest — Scheduled offence — Minor amount of malicious damage done in the course of the commission of a murder — Arrest on suspicion of having committed offence of malicious damage — No evidence of terrorist or subversive motive — Arresting officer anxious to interrogate suspect with regard to murder — Suspicion justified — Arrest and detention lawful — Malicious damage part of* actus reus *of murder — Admissibility of statement made by accused — Scope of questioning permitted — Offences Against the State (Scheduled Offences) Order,* 1972 (*S.I. No.* 142), — *Offences Against the State Act,* 1939 (*No.* 13), *ss.* 30, 36.] Sub-section 1 of s. 30 of the Offences Against the State Act, 1939, empowers a member of the Garda Síochána to arrest and interrogate any person whom the member suspects of having committed an offence scheduled for the purposes of the Act. By the Order of 1972 the Government declared offences under the Malicious Damage Act, 1861, to be scheduled offences. An elderly lady was found murdered in the kitchen of her home. She had suffered multiple injuries and a severe head wound which was the cause of her death. The kitchen was connected to a small shop by a glass door. The door had been in good repair the previous evening but a pane of glass was found to be broken. Outside the premises a heavy metal pot, which was probably the main murder weapon, was found to be broken. Subsequently, the appellant was arrested by a member of the Garda Síochána, under s. 30 of the Offences Against the State Act, 1939, on suspicion of having committed a scheduled offence, namely malicious damage to the pane of glass and the pot. It was not contested that the member had grounds for suspecting the appellant of having been involved in that crime. The arresting member gave evidence that while the appellant was arrested on that suspicion, he was anxious to question him concerning the killing of the old lady. No evidence was given of any subversive or terrorist motive in the crime. Pursuant to that arrest the accused was detained and questioned and made statements, some of which were admitted in evidence. He was charged with murder and malicious damage but was indicted and tried only for murder. The appellant appealed from his conviction in the Central Criminal Court to the Court of Criminal Appeal pursuant to a certificate of leave to appeal granted by the trial judge, on the grounds, firstly, that s. 30 of the Act of 1939 should be interpreted having regard to the long title and other provisions of the Act to the effect that the right of arrest only arose when a person was suspected of having committed a scheduled offence for subversive motives; and secondly, that having regard to the seriousness of the crime of murder being

CRIMINAL LAW—Arrest.

investigated and the relatively trivial amount of malicious damage, the exercise of the power under s. 30 of the Act of 1939 was a colourable device only and rendered the arrest unlawful. On the hearing of the appeal it was further argued on behalf of the appellant that a person arrested under s. 30 on suspicion of having committed a scheduled offence could only be questioned about that precise offence and not any other offence. **Held** by the Court of Criminal Appeal (Finlay C.J., Egan and Barr JJ.), in dismissing the appeal, 1, that while it was clear from the terms of s. 36, sub-s. 1 of the Act of 1939 that it would have been open to the Government to declare that a particular class or kind of offence, such as an offence with a particular terrorist or other motive, would be a scheduled offence; or to declare that offences against the Malicious Damage Act, 1861, which were carried out with a subversive or terrorist motive, would be scheduled offences; what in fact was scheduled under the Act of 1939 were all offences under the Act of 1861. 2. That an offence against the Act of 1861 came within the precise and unequivocal definition of an offence scheduled for the purposes of the Act of 1939 and that, as such, it was coercive to construe s. 30 as entitling a member of the Garda Síochána to arrest, without warrant, a person whom he suspected of having committed such an offence. 3. That the terms of s. 30 were clear and unambiguous and that there was no room for interpolating into that meaning and definition of a scheduled offence a qualification arising either from the long title or other provisions of the Act. 4. That, having regard to the amount of the damage caused and to the place, circumstances and time at which it was alleged to have been caused, the offence of malicious damage suspected was a real offence and was necessarily involved as part and parcel of the same incident or transaction as the murder and, accordingly, the arrest was justified. *The State (Bowes)* v. *Superintendent Fitzpatrick* [1978] ILRM 195; *The People (D.P.P.)* v. *Towson* [1978] ILRM 122 considered. 5. That in a case where the act of malicious damage on suspicion of which the accused was arrested clearly formed part and parcel of the series of incidents involved in the murder of the deceased, at least, there were no grounds for inhibiting or restricting the right of the Gardaí to interrogate the appellant with regard to the entire transaction, including the murder. On appeal by the appellant, the Court of Criminal Appeal having certified that its decision involved points of law of exceptional public importance, it was **Held** by the Supreme Court (Walsh, Henchy, Griffin, Hederman and McCarthy JJ.), in dismissing the appeal, 1, that the power of arrest conferred by s. 30 of the Act of 1939 was exercisable against any person *bona*

CRIMINAL LAW—*continued.*

fide suspected of having committed a scheduled offence, whether or not such offence was suspected to have been political or subversive in motive. *The People (D.P.P.)* v. *Quilligan* [1986] I.R. 495 applied. 2. That neither the disproportion between the nature of two offences nor the concentration of the investigation on the more serious was, by itself, sufficient to establish a reasonable probability that the arrest in respect of the malicious damage was simply a colourable device to hold the accused in custody to question him in relation to the murder. 3. That the true test to be applied in determining the validity of the arrest under s. 30 of the Act of 1939 was whether, on the evidence, the Garda Síochána had a genuine interest in the malicious damage and a desire to pursue it. 4. That while the alleged offence of malicious damage was very insignificant in comparison with the murder, the two offences were so closely connected that it was clear that the author of the malicious damage was, more than likely, connected in some way with the murder. *The People* v. *Walsh*
(C.C.A., S.C.) [1986] I.R.722; [1988] ILRM 137

7. —— **Place — Dwelling of citizen** — *Garda Síochána entering dwelling house — Whether permission to enter granted — Whether Gardaí trespassing at time of arrest — Whether arrest unlawful — Meaning of responses to Garda request to enter premises — Inviolability of dwelling — Road Traffic Act,* 1961 (*No.* 24), *s.* 107 — *Constitution of Ireland,* 1937, *Art.* 40.5.

Constitution — Personal rights — Dwelling — Inviolability — Criminal law — Arrest — Trespass by Garda Síochána in dwelling of arrested person — Whether arrest unlawful — Constitution of Ireland, 1937, *Art.* 40.5.] Article 40, s. 5 of the Constitution provides: "The dwelling of every citizen is inviolable and shall not be forcibly entered save in accordance with law." The defendant was charged with a number of offences under the Road Traffic Act, 1961. At his trial in the District Court it was stated by the prosecution that the defendant had driven a car through a garda check point. The car was followed by the gardaí and eventually stopped in the driveway of a dwelling house. The defendant was requested to stop by a garda but he refused and continued into the house. The gardaí made two requests to enter the house, but were refused on both occasions by the defendant's brother. On the second occasion, the defendant's brother was arrested for assault. The gardaí returned a third time to the front door of the house, and enquired if anybody was inside; a male voice answered "Yes, in here." The gardaí then entered the premises and effected the arrest of the defendant. At his trial, the defendant argued that the arrest which took place was not lawful since it

CRIMINAL LAW—Arrest.

took place in violation of the provisions of Article 40, s. 5, of the Constitution. The District Justice found that there was no invitation to the gardaí to enter the premises. On a consultative case stated to the High Court as to whether in the light of these findings the arrest was lawful, it was **Held** by MacKenzie J., that although there was no invitation, in the ordinary sense of the word, to enter the premises there was certainly no refusal or indication that the gardaí were trespassers; nor was there a request to leave or a rejection of the opportunity for the gardaí to make a common law arrest of the defendant and, accordingly, the arrest was lawful. *Morris* v. *Beardmore* [1981] A.C. 446 distinguished. *Director of Public Prosecutions* v. *Closkey* (Unreported, High Court, O'Hanlon J., 6 February, 1984) applied. On appeal by the defendant, pursuant to leave granted by the High Court under s. 52, sub-s. 2 of the Courts (Supplemental Provisions) Act, 1961, it was **Held** by the Supreme Court (Finlay C.J., Walsh, Henchy, Hederman and McCarthy JJ.), in allowing the appeal, 1, that in light of the particular circumstances and the trial judge's finding that there was no invitation to enter, the defendant's arrest was in violation of Article 40, s. 5, of the Constitution, because in view of the fact that the gardaí had twice been refused entry there could be no presumption that there was an invitation to enter, either as a matter of fact or law merely because there was no express refusal. *Morris* v. *Beardmore* [1981] A.C. 446 discussed; *Director of Public Prosecutions* v. *Closkey* (Unreported, High Court, O'Hanlon J., 6 February, 1984) distinguished and doubted. *Per* Henchy J. (dissenting in part): that it was for the trial judge to determine whether the gardaí entered the dwelling as licensees, since his finding that there was no invitation to enter did not necessarily make the gardaí trespassers at the time of arrest. 2. That s. 107 of the Road Traffic Act, 1961, did not authorise the gardaí to enter a dwelling without the owner's consent, since its terms only authorised arrest without warrant where there was a refusal to give specified information. *Director of Public Prosecutions* v. *Gaffney*

(H.C., S.C.) [1987] I.R. 173; [1988] ILRM 39; (H.C.) [1986] ILRM 657

8. —— **Second arrest** — *Validity of second arrest without release from custody — Detention — Duration — Extension order — Special Criminal Court — Jurisdiction — Whether manner in which attendance of accused before court was procured was relevant to jurisdiction — Objection to jurisdiction of court — Time to take objection — Content of extension order — Offences Against the State Act,* 1939 (*No.* 13), *ss.* 30, 43.] At 8.10 a.m. on the morning of the 7 August, 1983, in

CRIMINAL LAW—*continued.*

the course of a shoot out between gardaí and a number of armed men, of whom the applicant was one, the applicant was arrested and handcuffed. At 8.50 a.m., when the gardaí were satisfied that the situation had stabilised, the applicant was formally arrested under s. 30 of the Offences Against the State Act, 1939. An order was subsequently made extending the period of his detention for a further period of 24 hours from 8.50 a.m. on the 8 August, 1983. At 4.00 p.m. on the 8 August, 1983, the applicant was charged before the Special Criminal Court with a number of offences arising out of the events of the previous day, and was convicted on three counts. The applicant applied to the Court of Criminal Appeal for leave to appeal against those convictions, arguing that his restraint at 8.10 a.m. constituted an arrest and that his purported arrest at 8.50 a.m. and the extension order made on foot of that arrest, were invalid. Accordingly, it was argued, the applicant had been in unlawful custody at the time when he was charged before the Special Criminal Court and that court, therefore, had had no jurisdiction to deal with him. **Held** by the Court of Criminal Appeal (McCarthy, O'Hanlon and Barron JJ.), in refusing the application, 1, that the jurisdiction of the Special Criminal Court under s. 43 of the Act of 1939 is lawfully invoked when, in regard to a scheduled offence, the Director of Public Prosecutions directs that a person be brought before that court, and does not depend on the technical validity of the manner in which an individual may be present before the court. 2. That, while there may be circumstances in which unfair procedures or breach of constitutional rights might invalidate a trial, ordinarily, the time to take such a point is when the accused is first brought before the court; if the point is not then taken, it is spent. 3. *Semble* that, where a common law arrest is made, a garda officer who then discovers grounds for arrest under s. 30 of the Act of 1939, is entitled to effect a further arrest without going through the colourable manoeuvre of an apparent release from custody. *Dictum* of Henchy J. in *The State (Walsh)* v. *Maguire* [1979] I.R. 372, considered. *The People* v. *Kehoe*

(C.C.A.) [1985] I.R.444; [1986] ILRM 690

Autrefois acquit. *see* No. 53
Bail *see* No. 36
Complaint *see* Nos. 39-46
Confession — admissibility *see* Nos. 18-21
Corroboration *see* Nos. 9, 22

EVIDENCE

Accomplice. Nos. 9, 10
Admissibility. Nos. 10, 11-21
Corroboration. Nos. 9, 22

CRIMINAL LAW—Evidence.

Prejudicial evidence. Nos. 11, 23
Sufficiency. No. 24
Witness. Nos. 25, 26

9. —— **Accomplice** — *Corroboration — Whether matters found by trial judge to be corroboration capable of so being — Whether trial judge erred in considering credibility of witness.*] The appellant, a Detective Sergeant in the Special Branch of the Royal Ulster Constabulary, was charged with a series of crimes which included bank and post office robberies and the hijacking of cars. The principal witness for the Crown was a paid police informer called O'Doherty. The Crown alleged that the appellant and O'Doherty had jointly planned and, through O'Doherty, committed the crimes. O'Doherty had previously been convicted and sentenced for his role in the crimes. The learned trial judge decided that it would be wrong to convict the appellant of any of the crimes on the evidence of O'Doherty unless that evidence was corroborated. The judge then acquitted the appellant on all except four charges, which related to a bank robbery, and for which he found other evidence corroborating O'Doherty's evidence. On appeal, the appellant contended that the evidence of corroboration found by the learned trial judge was not capable of being corroboration and that he had misdirected himself in law as to the test of creditworthiness and was wrong in finding O'Doherty's evidence a fit subject for corroboration. **Held,** allowing the appeal and quashing the convictions, that, 1, the evidence of corroboration as found by the learned trial judge did not connect or tend to connect the appellant with the crimes and therefore the cogent and compelling corroboration which he found to be indispensable to a finding of guilt in this case was absent. 2. The evidence of an accomplice was capable of being corroborated only if it was credible and in assessing its credibility the court must have regard to the character of the accomplice giving the evidence. The assessment is to be made at the end of a trial and must have regard to the credibility of the witness himself and all other relevant factors when viewed with any corroboration. *R.* v. *McCormick* **(C.A.) [1984] N.I.50**

10. —— **Accomplice** — *Cross-examination — Whether evidence from accomplice's previous trial relevant — Whether going to motive or credit — Test of admissibility — Dangers of convicting on evidence of accomplice — Whether trial judge's direction correct in law — Procedure — Defect in book of evidence — Whether trial unsatisfactory.*] The appellant was charged with larceny of cattle. At his trial, the primary evidence tendered by the prosecution was that of an alleged accomplice

CRIMINAL LAW—*continued.*

of the appellant. The book of evidence contained a composite statement from the accomplice, who had made a number of statements to the Garda Síochána, but the composite statement did not include all the information disclosed by the accomplice. In addition, certain forensic evidence was not revealed until the trial was in progress. Counsel for the appellant referred to these gaps in evidence in the course of the trial. In the course of the cross-examination of the accomplice by counsel for the appellant, counsel attempted to introduce evidence of a newspaper account of the accomplice's own trial in relation to the same events as those involved in the appellant's trial. The trial judge ruled that such newspaper accounts were not admissible as evidence of what occurred during the accomplice's trial. He further ruled that only the official transcript of the trial would be admissible as evidence as to what occurred during the trial, and that evidence from a member of the Garda Síochána who was present at the accomplice's trial (and which the appellant's counsel wished to introduce) was also not admissible. The trial judge directed the jury on the dangers involved in convicting an accused on the evidence of an accomplice. The appellant was found guilty of the charges. On the appellant's application for leave to appeal to the Court of Criminal Appeal (Finlay C.J., Costello and Barrington JJ.), it was **Held** in granting the application and ordering a re-trial, 1, that although there had been some errors and omissions from the book of evidence as served on the appellant, in that not all evidence was revealed to the defence prior to the trial, effective use had been made by counsel for the appellant of these errors and omissions, and these errors did not constitute an unfair procedure, nor make the trial unsatisfactory. 2. That the trial judge's direction to the jury on the danger of convicting on the evidence of an accomplice, which drew attention to the fact that an accomplice may have something to gain from giving evidence and that there was a danger of convicting without independent corroboration, was a full and correct direction to the jury. 3. That although the trial judge was correct in ruling out the use of newspaper reports of the accomplice's trial, he was not correct in law in ruling that only the official transcript of that trial was admissible as to what occurred during that trial since the transcript was only of evidential value for the purposes of an appeal; and evidence of a member of the Garda Síochána who was present at the trial would have been admissible. 4. That the line of questioning followed by counsel for the appellant as to what occurred at the accomplice's trial fell into the category of questioning which might lead to establishing the accomplice's bias or partiality, as distinct from a general assertion of lack of

CRIMINAL LAW—Evidence.

credit; and the line of questioning was therefore one of the exceptions to the rule prohibiting contradiction of collateral matters. *The People* v. *McGinley*

(C.C.A.) [1987] I.R. 340

11. —— **Admissibility** — **Documents** — *Affidavits sworn for use in courts in the Republic of Ireland — Whether admissible — Whether prejudicial — Fingerprints — Whether correct inference drawn — Whether fair trial — Whether abuse of process — Whether verdict unsafe or unsatisfactory — Evidence Act,* 1851 (*c.* 93), *ss.* 7, 9 — *Ireland Act,* 1949 (*c.* 41), *s.* 3(2).] The appellant was convicted of murder. The evidence at the trial consisted of two of the appellant's fingerprints found on the car used in the fatal attack, forensic evidence that weapons used in the attack had been used in a number of other terrorist attacks in Counties Antrim and Londonderry, affidavits sworn by the appellant for the purpose of resisting his extradition from the Republic of Ireland to Northern Ireland in which he said that he was an active member of the Provisional I.R.A. and a member of the active service unit of the Provisional I.R.A. which operated in the South Derry area. At the trial evidence proposed to be given to the effect that the Provisional I.R.A. was the only terrorist organisation attacking the security forces in the area in the period in question was ruled inadmissible. On appeal it was argued that copies of affidavits filed in courts in the Republic of Ireland were not admissible under section 7 of the Evidence Act, 1851, as that section had not been specifically adapted following the creation of the Irish Free State, that the statements in the affidavits had not been made voluntarily and that admission of the affidavit evidence was contrary to the rule that evidence of previous discreditable behaviour by an accused was not to be admitted for the purpose of proving that the accused committed the crime charged. **Held,** allowing the appeal that, 1, the statements made for the purposes of proceedings in the Republic of Ireland were admissible. There was no technical difficulty in the notion that before 1922 section 7 of the 1851 Act did not apply to the courts in the part of Ireland which became the Irish Free State, yet did so apply after 1922. The Irish Free State (Consequential Adaptation of Enactments) Order, 1923, adapted section 10 of the 1851 Act, which provides for the admissibility of documents within the United Kingdom, so as to make it inapplicable to the courts in the Irish Free State. Once that had been done the way was clear for holding that since the courts in the Irish Free State were not covered by section 10, they were covered by section 7 as were the courts of any other British colony or any foreign state.

CRIMINAL LAW—*continued.*

The rule as to the admission of statements made to persons in authority did not apply to these affidavits. 2. Once the evidence which proposed to establish that the Provisional I.R.A. was the only active terrorist organisation in the area at that time was ruled inadmissible there was no evidence which specifically connected either the murder or any of the other incidents in which the same guns were used with the Provisional I.R.A. or with the South Derry active service unit of that organisation. There was no evidence to exclude the existence of other active republican terrorist organisations or groups in the area or the possibility that the attack had been perpetrated by one such organisation or group; still less was there a correspondence between the areas in which the guns were used on other occasions with the description by the appellant of his group. *R.* v. *Martin* [1985] N.I. 324 considered. *R.* v. *McGlinchey*

(C.A.) [1985] N.I. 435

12. —— **Admissibility** — **Documents** — *Reconstructed records from damaged originals — Unavailability of person compiling records — Whether documents admissible.*

Evidence — Identification parade — Objection by accused to participation — Requirement as to jury direction.

Trial — Jury — Absence of some members during direction by judge — Whether trial unsatisfactory.

Trial — Procedure — Interventions by judge during conduct of defence — Whether excessive — Whether injustice resulted.] The applicant was convicted in the Circuit Court on eleven counts of obtaining money on forged documents and three counts of uttering forged documents. The applicant sought leave to appeal on the grounds, *inter alia,* (i) that evidence of cheque journals which had been in a fire and had been reconstructed by a person who was unable to give evidence at the trial should not have been admitted in evidence; (ii) that evidence of an identification parade, to which the applicant had objected at the time because of the absence of his solicitor, should not have been admitted; (iii) that the trial was seriously prejudiced by the disclosure that he was wanted on a charge of murder; (iv) that some jurors had been absent during the course of the judge's direction; and (v) that the judge interrupted his cross-examinations so often as to make it impossible to conduct his defence properly. **Held** by the Court of Criminal Appeal (Henchy, Keane and Murphy JJ.) in quashing the convictions of obtaining money on forged documents and ordering a new trial in respect of the counts of uttering forged documents, 1, in the absence of the person who compiled the cheque journals, it would not be

CRIMINAL LAW—Evidence.

possible for a jury to reach a safe conclusion as to the reliability of the entries made in them and they should not have been admitted in evidence. *Myers* v. *Director of Public Prosecutions* [1965] A.C. 1001 discussed. 2. The admissibility of the evidence of the identification parade, notwithstanding the applicant's objections, was a matter for the trial judge to determine, but once admitted the jury should have been directed that he was not obliged to take part, even though in lawful custody, and that his refusal to consent reduced its probative value. *The People* v. *Martin* [1956] I.R. 22 applied. 3. While the jury was informed that the applicant had been acquitted by direction of the High Court on the charge of murder, a verdict of guilty reached after the jury heard that he was wanted for murder could not safely be allowed to stand, and the jury should have been discharged at this stage. 4. The procedure whereby some jurors were absent during the course of the judge's direction was irregular and unsatisfactory, and having regard to the principle that the jury must not separate once they retire to consider their verdict and may not communicate with any person other than their bailiff, a verdict reached in these circumstances could not be allowed to stand. 5. While the interruptions by the judge were prompted by a desire to ensure that the jury grasped the evidence, they were excessive in number, but no injustice resulted to the applicant and he was in no way inhibited in presenting his case. *The People* v. *Marley*

(C.C.A.) [1985] ILRM 17

13. —— **Admissibility** — **Hearsay** — Res gestae — *Burglary — Car used for escape — Husband saw car and told wife registration number — Wife transmitted number on telephone to police — Telephone conversation tape recorded — Whether tape recording admissible as part of* res gestae.] From their home a couple observed two men breaking into a jeweller's shop. While the husband looked out the window, his wife telephoned the police. He saw a car draw up at the shop and two men get into it. He observed the number of the car and informed his wife of it. She transmitted the number on the phone. The conversation was recorded at the police station. The registration number was that of the appellant's car. At the trial neither the husband nor his wife could remember the full registration number of the car and the trial judge admitted the tape recording of the telephone conversation as part of the *res gestae*. The appellant was convicted and appealed. **Held,** quashing the conviction, that the tape recording should not have been admitted in evidence. While evidence of the husband's words may have been admissible

CRIMINAL LAW—*continued.*

as part of the *res gestae*, because they were sufficiently contemporaneous with the burglary, were those of a bystander indirectly indicating the identity of a wrongdoer, and may have been made under the pressure of the events; the tape recording merely contained the words of his wife and her words relating to the car number could not be part of the *res gestae*. *R.* v. *Linden*

(C.A.) [1984] N.I. 251

14. —— **Admissibility** — **Hearsay** — *Telephone calls — Tracing of calls — Whether evidence as to voice on telephone established by hearsay — Whether admissible — Whether retrial should be ordered — Proviso.*

Evidence — Admissibility — Tape recordings — Telephone calls — Whether admissible — Whether defect in quality affects admissibility — Factors affecting weight to be given to evidence — Whether recording of telephone call made to person not then on trial admissible if part of transaction as a whole.

Appeal — Defect in trial — Proviso — Whether miscarriage of justice actually occurred — Whether shown that court disregarded inadmissible evidence.] The applicant was charged with various offences, based partly on evidence of telephone calls relating to the payment of a ransom. His voice was identified at the trial from recordings made; and the process of tracing these calls was also put in evidence. Objection was taken to the method of proof of these tracings, on the ground that part of the proof of such tracings was established by hearsay evidence. The trial judge ruled the evidence was admissible. The applicant subsequently gave evidence accounting for his movements, but was convicted. On appeal: **Held** by the Court of Criminal Appeal (McCarthy, D'Arcy and Egan JJ.) in allowing the appeal and ordering a re-trial, 1, the evidence as to tracing involved an element of hearsay in the chain of proof, and as there was no question of an essential witness being unavailable it was not admissible. *Myers* v. *Director of Public Prosecutions* [1965] A.C. 1001 distinguished. 2. There was ample and clear independent proof to support the conviction made, and the supportive evidence of tracing was not vital, but the court could not be satisfied that the trial jury had not taken account of inadmissible evidence, and the defence had been required to go into evidence, so that the court could not apply the provision in s. 5 (1) of the Courts of Justice Act, 1928, but would order a re-trial. *The People* v. *Ruttledge* [1946] 1 Frewen 75 applied. 3. In a trial where a significant part of the evidence consists of a tape recording, and the tape is shown to be authentic, defects in sound quality, disputes as to the identity of the speakers or the fact that there were available

CRIMINAL LAW—Evidence.

more persons to give evidence as to the identity of the speakers are no grounds for excluding it from evidence; but the trial judge should always direct the jury as to sound quality if evidence on this point has been given by the defence. 4. Where an offence is alleged to have been committed by two or more persons, there is no rule of evidence excluding personal accounts of recipients of telephone calls or mechanical recordings of them on the ground merely that they were not made by the person then on trial, if it is shown that they were made as part of the transaction as a whole. *The People* v. *Prunty*

(C.C.A.) [1986] ILRM 716

15. —— **Admissibility** — **Procured by unlawful means** — *Entry on premises — No order authorising entry — Whether evidence admissible — Family planning — Unlawful sale of contraceptives — Discretion to exclude evidence — Health Act,* 1947 (*No.* 28), *s.* 96(1) — *Health (Family Planning) Act,* 1979 (*No.* 20), *s. 4(4).*

Criminal law — Health — Family planning — Unlawful sale of contraceptives — Authority to enter premises — Whether in force — Whether evidence obtained without warrant admissible — Whether judge must exercise discretion to admit evidence — Nature and substance of evidence — Health Act, 1947 (*No.* 28), *s.* 96(1) — *Health Family Planning) Act,* 1979 (*No.* 20), *s.* 4(4).] The respondents were charged, in the District Court, with supplying contraceptives contrary to s. 4 (4) of the Health (Family Planning) Act, 1979, to a garda sergeant. The sergeant gave evidence that he went to the Family Planning Services Ltd. clinic, in plain clothes, that he entered the premises and saw the respondents and that he spoke to each of them. Counsel for the first-named respondent at this point objected that unless an order made by the Minister for Health pursuant to s. 96 (1) of the Health Act, 1947, was produced, authorising the garda sergeant to enter the premises, all his intended evidence relating to conversations or events during his presence on the premises was inadmissible and should be excluded. Counsel for the appellant admitted that no such order was in force on the date in question and that he had no evidence other than that of the garda sergeant in support of the charge. The District Justice ruled that any evidence intended to be given by the sergeant as to what transpired in the premises during his visit was inadmissible and dismissed the charge in each case. At the request of counsel for the appellant, the District Justice submitted a case stated in each case, as to whether he was correct (1) in ruling that members of the Gardaí had no lawful authority to enter onto the premises in question, no order under s. 96 (1) of the Health Act 1947, being in force on the date in

CRIMINAL LAW—*continued.*

question; (2) in ruling that the evidence obtained by any garda during such a visit to the premises was inadmissible; (3) in dismissing the charge. The respondents argued, in the High Court, that the District Justice, in deciding to exclude the sergeant's intended evidence, did so in the exercise of a judicial discretion which should not be interfered with. **Held** by Gannon J. in allowing the appeal, 1, if the circumstances arise which require a District Justice to exercise his discretion as to whether or not to admit relevant probative evidence, he must be sufficiently informed of the nature and substance of the intended evidence to put its probative value in the balance of fair trial in the public interest as against that of prejudice or unfairness. *People (A.G.)* v. *O'Brien* [1965] I.R. 142 and *R.* v. *Sang* [1980] A.C. 402 discussed. 2. A District Justice, in order to exercise his discretion in a judicial manner, must find, as a fact, that the circumstances requiring the exercise of such discretion have arisen, and make the enquiry and assessment of the intended evidence in a judicial manner. The circumstances for the exercise of that discretion did not arise in these cases. 3. The District Justice did not, in fact, exercise any discretion, as he did not have before him the matter for his consideration for the purpose of so doing. The intervention and rejection by anticipation of probative evidence relevant and pertinent to the issue for trial by the court was insupportable. *Director of Public Prosecutions* v. *McCutcheon*

(H.C.) [1986] ILRM 433

16. —— **Admissibility** — **Procured by unlawful means** — *Summary trial — Defendants charged with gaming and lottery offences — Gardaí having no search warrant — Gardaí trespassers — Objection to their evidence — Evidence admissible — Court's discretion to exclude — Balancing of public interests — Relevant factors to consider.*

Evidence — Search warrant — Gaming and lottery offences — Licensed premises — Whether Gardaí trespassers in absence of search warrant — Licensing Act (Ireland), 1874 (*c.* 69), *s.* 23 — *Intoxicating Liquor Act,* 1927 (*No.* 15), *s.* 22 — *Gaming and Lotteries Act,* 1956 (*No.* 2), *ss.* 9, 38, 39.] The defendants were charged with offences involving gaming machines on licensed premises contrary to s. 9 of the Gaming and Lotteries Act, 1956. In the District Court and on their appeal to the Circuit Court evidence was adduced of observations made by a Garda on the licensed premises. The Garda had entered the premises in plain clothes, without a search warrant under s. 39 of the Act, and for the specific purpose of discovering if offences under the Act were being committed. Objection was taken to the admissibility of this evidence on the ground

CRIMINAL LAW—Evidence.

that the evidence had been procured by unlawful means. At the request of the prosecution the Circuit Court judge stated a case to the Supreme Court on the questions, firstly, of whether a Garda must have a search warrant under s. 39 of the 1956 Act before entering a licensed premises for the purpose of detecting possible offences under the Act and, secondly, of whether evidence procured by a Garda present on licensed premises for this purpose, and without a search warrant, was admissible. **Held** by the Supreme Court (Finlay C.J., Walsh, Henchy, Hederman and McCarthy JJ.), 1, that members of the Garda Síochána must have a search warrant under s. 39 of the Gaming and Lotteries Act, 1956, before entering a licensed premises for the purpose of detecting possible offences under the Act. That in the absence of such lawful authority the Gardaí were trespassers. 2. That where evidence has been obtained by unlawful means, but without any conscious and deliberate violation of a constitutional right, it shall be admissible unless the court excludes it in the exercise of its discretion. The exercise of this discretion involves the balancing of the public interest in the detection and punishment of crime and the public interest in ensuring that individuals are not subjected to illegal or inquisitorial methods of investigation and that the state does not attempt to advance its ends by utilising the fruits of such methods. *The People (Attorney General)* v. *O'Brien* [1965] I.R. 142 followed. *Director of Public Prosecutions* v. *McMahon*

(S.C.) [1986] I.R.393; [1987] ILRM 87

17. —— **Admissibility** — **Procedure** — *Onus of disproving alleged inadmissibility — Accused alleging detention in custody unlawful — Whether State must disprove allegation — Whether issue of fact raised requiring determination by trial court — Appeal — Whether trial unsatisfactory.*

Trial — Voir dire *— Evidence — Admissibility — Whether issue to be tried on* voir dire *by judge or by jury — Whether accused prejudiced by having issue determined by jury on* voir dire *— Function of jury under the Constitution — Whether jury impartiality on ultimate issue likely to be affected — Criminal Justice Act,* 1984 (*No.* 22), *s.* 25 *— Constitution of Ireland,* 1937, *Arts.* 38.1, 38.5.

Constitution — Personal rights — Legal advice — Access to solicitor — Garda custody — Whether detained person has constitutional right of access to solicitor — Whether arises when detained person requests access or before — Criminal Justice Act, 1984 (*No.* 22), *s.* 4 *— Constitution of Ireland,* 1937, *Art.* 40.3.] The appellant had been brought to a Garda station and had been questioned in relation to the events surrounding a killing which the Garda Síochána were investigating. The appellant, while in custody, made inculpatory statements in which he admitted participation in the killing. The appellant was charged with murder. In the course of his trial in the Central Criminal Court (Gannon J. and a jury), counsel acting for the appellant intimated to the trial judge that his client would challenge the admissibility of the inculpatory statements on a number of grounds, among them being that the appellant had requested, but was denied, access to a solicitor, and that he was not told he was free to leave the Garda station at a time when he had not yet been arrested or charged with any offence. Counsel requested the trial judge to put these issues to the jury in accordance with the views expressed in the Supreme Court in *The People* v. *Lynch* [1982] I.R. 64. The trial judge declined to leave the issue of the admissibility of the statements to the jury, and determined the matter in the jury's absence on the *voir dire.* The trial judge ruled that the statements were admissible in evidence; and also ruled that in relation to the issue as to whether the appellant was in unlawful detention at the time he made the statements, the appellant had failed to make out a *prima facie* case and on this basis rejected the argument put forward. The appellant applied for leave to appeal to the Court of Criminal Appeal on the ground, *inter alia,* that the trial judge was in error in not leaving the issue of admissibility to the jury. **Held** by the Court of Criminal Appeal (McCarthy, Costello and Murphy JJ.) in dismissing the application, 1, that the trial judge was not obliged to submit every issue as to the admissibility of evidence to a trial jury, since this requirement related only to the issue of the admissibility of evidence obtained in conscious and deliberate violation of an accused person's constitutional rights where an issue of conflict of fact arose for determination. *The People* v. *Lynch* [1982] I.R. 64 explained. 2. That the trial judge had not erred since he determined that there was no real conflict of fact which required resolution and, in light of the evidence presented before him, he was entitled to reject the submission that the admissibility of the statements be determined by the jury. On further appeal to the Supreme Court pursuant to certificate of leave to appeal granted by the Court of Criminal Appeal under s. 29 of the Courts of Justice Act, 1924, it was **Held** by the Supreme Court (Finlay C.J., Walsh, Henchy, Griffin and Hederman JJ.) in quashing the convictions and order a re-trial (Finlay C.J., Henchy, Griffin, Hederman JJ.; Walsh J. dissenting), that the procedure adopted in criminal trials of having the trial judge determine on the *voir dire* the issue of the admissibility of evidence in the absence of the jury was the proper

CRIMINAL LAW—Evidence.

approach to such matters in accordance with Article 38 of the Constitution, since the alternative of having the issue determined as a preliminary matter by the jury could act as an inhibiting factor in the conduct by the accused's counsel of cross-examination of witnesses for the prosecution, who would be giving evidence in the trial proper, and could also result in prejudice on the part of the jury in determing the guilt or innocence of the accused. *The State* v. *Treanor* [1924] 2 I.R. 193 followed. *Jackson* v. *Denno* (1964) 378 U.S. 368 and *The People* v. *McGlynn* [1967] I.R. 232 considered. *Dicta* in *The People* v. *Lynch* [1982] I.R. 64 not followed. *Per* Henchy J.: if the jury was informed of the content of evidence on the *voir dire,* it would be unfit to try the issue of guilt or innocence since it would lack the requirement of impartiality, and the alternative procedure of having different juries determine the issues of admissibility and weight would not be consistent with the guarantee of a unitary and unbroken trial contained in Article 38, s. 5 of the Constitution. *Per* Griffin J.: the advantages to the accused person, in being allowed challenge the prosecution witnesses on the *voir dire* in the absence of the jury without the prosecution being allowed subsequently to adduce substantive evidence of what was said on the *voir dire,* and in this way retaining his right to silence at the trial itself where imputations as to character might arise on the *voir dire,* were important safeguards which ought not be abandoned, particularly in the light of a uniform practice in this jurisdiction. *Per* Walsh J. (dissenting): the question of prejudicing the jury could be overcome by having it determine the matter of admissibility without being informed of the contents of the evidence in question, and by the trial judge directing specific questions requiring answer; experience since the introduction of this procedure in Irish courts had not indicated any difficulty in adapting to such a method of determining the matter. 2. That once the appellant's counsel had indicated to the trial judge that his client would be giving evidence that he had been under the impression that he was not free to leave the Garda station, the trial judge had erred in law in not requiring the prosecution to adduce evidence which would establish either that at the time the appellant's detention was lawful or that he was not in custody. *Per* Walsh J.: the issue raised by counsel, as to whether the appellant had requested to see his solicitor, fell to be considered in the context of the obligation on the Garda Síochána to observe fair procedures in accordance with Article 40, s. 3 of the Constitution, regardless of whether an arrested person has a constitutional right to be asked if he wishes to see a solicitor. *Per* Henchy J.: the trial judge's determination

CRIMINAL LAW—*continued.*

that a person detained by the police has no constitutional right to consult with a solicitor was in accordance with the decided cases and should not be disturbed. *The People* v. *Farrell* [1978] I.R. 13 and *The People* v. *Shaw* [1982] I.R. 1 considered. *The People* v. *Conroy*

(C.C.A., S.C.) [1986] I.R. 460

18. —— **Admissibility — Statement of accused** — *Admission — Detention of suspect — Grounds — Power of police to interrogate suspect while detained — Stated grounds for detention — Not corresponding with primary ground for interrogation — None of suspected offences of a political or subversive nature — Extended powers of interrogation — Whether applicable — Offences Against the State (Scheduled Offences) Order,* 1972 (*S.I. No.* 142) — *Offences Against the State Act,* 1939 (*No.* 13), *ss.* 30, 36, 52.] Section 30, sub-s. 1 of the Offences Against the State Act, 1939, empowers a member of the Garda Síochána *inter alia* to interrogate and arrest any person whom the member suspects of being concerned, as principal or accessory, in the commission of an offence under the Act, or an offence which is for the time being a scheduled offence under Part V of the Act; sub-s. 3 of that section states that the suspect may be detained in custody in a police station for a period of 24 hours from the time of his arrest and, if a certain direction is given, for a further period of 24 hours. Section 36 of that Act empowers the government, while Part V of the Act is in force, by order to declare offences of any particular type to be scheduled offences whenever it is "satisfied that the ordinary courts are inadequate to secure the effective administration of justice and the preservation of public peace and order" in relation to that particular type of offence. Section 52 of that Act provides, by sub-s. 1, that a member of the Garda Síochána may demand of a suspect, while so detained, a full account of his movements and actions during any specified period and all information in his possession in relation to the commission by another person of any scheduled offence. Sub-section 2 of s. 52 provides that a suspect who fails or refuses to give a policeman any such information or who gives information which is false or misleading shall be guilty of an offence under that section. The accused were suspected of having been concerned in the breaking into the house of two elderly brothers, as a result of which both brothers had been injured, one fatally, and damage had been done to the brothers' property. There was no ground for believing the offences to have had any political or subversive connotations. The accused could not have been arrested or detained under s. 30 of the Act of 1939 on suspicion of murder, assault or robbery with violence; they could, however,

CRIMINAL LAW—Evidence.

be so arrested or detained on suspicion of malicious damage contrary to the Malicious Damage Act, 1861, which was one of the types of offence which was declared to be a scheduled offence for the purposes of Part V of the Act of 1939 by the Offences against the State (Scheduled Offences) Order, 1972. While so detained under s. 30, both accused made statements of an incriminatory nature. The successful prosecution of the accused on any charge connected with the burglary depended on the admission in evidence of those statements by the trial judge. On the trial of the accused for murder, the trial judge (Barr J.) held that Part V of the Act of 1939, was intended to deal only with crimes of a subversive nature, and that, as no subversive element had been shown to exist in the crime imputed to the accused, their arrest and detention under s. 30 of that Act had been illegal, and the statements obtained during such detention were therefore inadmissible; the trial judge accordingly directed the jury to record a verdict of not guilty in favour of each of the accused. The Director of Public Prosecutions appealed to the Supreme Court against the verdicts. **Held** by the Supreme Court (Walsh, Henchy, Griffin, Hederman and McCarthy JJ.), in allowing the appeals, 1, that where an offence is declared by order under s. 36 of the Act of 1939 to be a scheduled offence for the purposes of that Act, the provisions of ss. 30 and 52 of that Act become applicable in relation to such offence, and the police powers conferred by the sections become exercisable against any person *bona fide* suspected of being involved in the commission of such offence, whether such suspected offence is or is not believed to have been political or subversive in its motive. 2. That, as the evidence in this case showed the existence of a genuine suspicion on the part of the police officers concerned that the accused had been involved in a scheduled offence, namely malicious damage to property, the police had been justified in arresting the accused and in interrogating them about the background to that offence. 3. That as the arrest and interrogation had been genuinely directed towards the investigation of a scheduled offence, the fact that the police had come to be more concerned with the more serious, though not scheduled, offence of murder which was closely linked with the related offence of malicious damage did not render illegal the detention and interrogation of the accused or render inadmissible as evidence at their trial for murder the admissions which they had made in the course of the investigation of the malicious damage charge. *The People* v. *Towson* [1978] ILRM 122 applied. *The State (Bowes)* v. *Fitzpatrick* [1978] ILRM 195 distinguished. *The People* v. *Quilligan*

CRIMINAL LAW—*continued.*

(S.C.) [1986] I.R.495; [1987] ILRM 606

19. —— **Admissibility — Statement of accused** — *Admission — Statement of admission by accused in answer to question by member of An Garda Síochána — Whether question an inducement or threat — Effect of inducement — Offences Against the State Act,* 1939 (*No.* 13), *s.* 30.] The applicant was convicted before the Special Criminal Court of possession of firearms and ammunition contrary to s. 15 (*a*) of the Firearms Act, 1925, as amended. The only evidence against the accused was a statement of admission of responsibility made by him to a member of an Garda Síochána while in custody. The applicant applied for leave to appeal against his conviction on the ground that his statement of admission was inadmissible as evidence because it was made as a result of a question asked by a member of an Garda Síochána which operated as an inducement to make the statement and therefore the statement was not voluntary. **Held** by the Court of Criminal Appeal (Finlay C.J., Lynch and Egan JJ.), in refusing the application for leave to appeal, 1, that while the question asked by the detective inspector induced the applicant to admit responsibility for the offence, the question was not a threat or an improper inducement by threat. 2. That an interview with a prime suspect by the gardaí must involve an attempt to induce the suspect to make a statement in which he will either admit his guilt or establish his innocence. It is only an improper inducement which involves a threat or promise of temporal disadvantage or advantage which will render a statement thus obtained inadmissible. 3. That for the gardaí to state that they may have to make further inquiries which may inconvenience or upset other persons, cannot in itself be regarded as a threat or an improper inducement by threat if it is a fact and not a threat to harass others whom the gardaí did not believe were involved. *Attorney General* v. *Cleary* 72 I.L.T.R. 84 and *Attorney General* v. *McCabe* [1927] I.R. 129 applied. The Court of Criminal Appeal certified that its decision involved points of law of exceptional public importance and on appeal by the applicant it was **Held** by the Supreme Court (Walsh, Henchy, Griffin, Hederman and McCarthy JJ.), in allowing the appeal and setting aside the conviction, 1, that the incriminating statement of the appellant had not been proved to have been free and voluntary and that therefore evidence of the statement ought not to have been received. The appellant was unwilling to make any form of admission until the question was put to him by the detective inspector and it was clear beyond all reasonable doubt that the effect of the question was to cause him to make the confession. 2. That the onus was on the prosecution to prove

CRIMINAL LAW—Evidence.

that the statement was voluntary, the test being whether or not the question was calculated to induce the appellant to admit the offence because of fear of prejudice or hope of advantage. The test was an objective one and it was irrelevant to consider the intention or motive of the person who posed the question. 3. That the effect of the words used, irrespective of what they were intended to mean, were calculated to convey that the appellant's family would not be interrogated by the Garda Síochána if the appellant admitted responsibility. In the circumstances of the case, that amounted to an improper inducement which produced a confession. *The People* v. *Hoey*
(C.C.A., S.C.) [1987] I.R.637 ;[1988] ILRM 666

20. —— **Admissibility — Statement of accused** — *Confession — Jury trial — Accused held at Castlereagh Police Office and interviewed in same manner as persons suspected of terrorist offences — Arrest and detention of accused alleged to be unlawful — Whether accused's statement voluntary — Whether "oppressive circumstances" — Whether court should exercise discretion to exclude evidence because of unfairness to accused.*] The accused was arrested for the non-scheduled offence of the murder of her husband. The accused was interviewed on five occasions over three days by police officers at Castlereagh Police Office. The accused made two written statements and a number of verbal admissions. During the subsequent trial, the Crown sought to tender the admissions in evidence. The accused argued that the admissions should be excluded on the following grounds. (i) That because of her physical and nervous condition she was not fit to be interviewed; that the length, frequency, nature and manner of the interviews coupled with the circumstances of Castlereagh Police Office amounted to oppression and were such as to sap her will and caused her to make the admissions and thus rendered them involuntary. In particular the accused contended that during the interviews she was urged by her son to make a statement whereby he would gain an amnesty from prosecution thereby undermining her will. (ii) That the judge should exercise his discretion to exclude the admissions as having been obtained unfairly because her arrest under section 12 of the Prevention of Terrorism (Tempory Provisions) Act, 1976, was invalid and her consequent detention was therefore unlawful and unfair. (iii) That the police were in breach of the Judges' rules in failing to charge her when there was sufficient evidence to do so and in not bringing her before a Magristrate's Court as soon as possible after the expiry of 24 hours from her arrest. A *voir dire* was held to determine the admissibility of the statements. **Held** admitting the statements in evidence, 1, the Crown had

CRIMINAL LAW—*continued.*

proved beyond all reasonable doubt that the accused's written and verbal statements were voluntary in the sense that they were not obtained by fear of prejudice or hope of advantage excited or held out by a person in authority or by oppressive conduct. Although the accused was nervous and emotional, her condition was not at any stage such as to make it oppressive to continue to interview her. The length, frequency and nature of the interviews did not cause her excessive strain and/or undermine her will to keep silent, but were conducted in a proper and restrained manner. The interviewing of persons suspected of non-scheduled offences at Castlereagh Police Office was not in itself oppressive but provided protection to persons being detained there and guarded the police agaisnt unfounded allegations being made by prisoners. The accused's son did not urge his mother to make a statement or refer to his gaining an amnesty from prosecution. 2. The court has a discretion to exclude otherwise admissible evidence if, in all the circumstances, it woud operate unfairly against the accused. In considering whether to exercise this discretion with regard to a voluntary confession statement, regard may be had to causation, viz whether the accused would have been likely to make the statement if the circumstances or actions complained of had not been permitted to exist or take place, and to the voluntariness of the statement. Breaches of the Judges' rules may also be relevant and while it is not the function of the court in trying a criminal case to discipline policemen, factors such as the unlawfulness of detention should not be excluded altogether from consideration. 3. However, in the present case the police had not broken the Judges' rules or deliberately deferred charging the accused in order to gain an improper or unfair advantage and therefore did not cause any unfairness requiring the exclusion of the admissions; even on the assumption that the arrest and subsequent detention was invalid there was not a sufficient degree of prejudice as to make if unfair to admit the statements; the allegations of unfairness advanced by the accused were not sufficiently borne out to constitute oppression which operated so as to induce her to make the statements *R.* v. *McBrien*
(Crown Ct.) [1984] N.I.280

21. —— **Admissibility — Statement of accused** — *Confession — Lengthy and persistent interviewing of accused — One interview commenced after midnight — Some admissions retracted — Oppressive circumstances — Whether discretion to exclude should be exercised — Whether improper to show post-mortem photographs to accused — Northern Ireland (Emergency Provisions) Act,* 1978 (*c.* 5), *s.* 8.

CRIMINAL LAW—Evidence.

Criminal procedure — Appeal — Whether verdict unsafe or unsatisfactory — Confession — Probative value — Whether judge failed to give weight to circumstances in which it was obtained — Parts of confession inconsistent with other evidence and contradictory — Whether judge failed to deal with inconsistencies — Accused acquitted on certain counts — Whether whole confession unreliable.] The accused were arrested and while in police custody made a number of oral and written statements of admission relating to terrorist offences. At the conclusion of a *voir dire* the accused submitted that while the statements were admissible under section 8 of the Northern Ireland (Emergency Provisions) Act, 1978, the court should exercise its discretion to exclude the statements. The accused, Dillon, contended that the court should exclude his statements in the exercise of its discretion as he had retracted his confessions on a number of occasions whilst in custody; that the length and times of the interviews were excessive and in particular one interview commenced after midnight contrary to a recommendation of the Bennett Report; that the police conduct of the interviews was improper; that the police had told untruths to induce him to make the statements and that it would be unsafe to admit the statements because of the obvious untruths and inconsistencies they contained. The accused, Gorman, contended that his mental condition at the time of the interviews was such that no reliance could be placed upon them and that the police had been guilty of improprieties during the interviews in particular by showing post-mortem photographs to the accused. **Held,** admitting the statements of the accused that, 1, the discretion to exclude statements which are admissible under section 8 should not be exercised so as to defeat the will of Parliament as expressed in the section. In considering that will it was permissible for the court to look at the report of the Commission which preceded it to see what was the mischief at which the section was directed. The intent of Parliament in enacting the section was that provided there had not been torture or inhuman or degrading treatment, statements made by a suspected member of a terrorist organisation after periods of searching questioning should not be admitted, notwithstanding that at the outset the suspect did not wish to confess and that the interrogation caused him to speak when otherwise he would have stayed silent. However, there may be cases where, although there has been no torture or inhuman or degrading treatment, the condition of the suspect brought about, it may be unintentionally, by the questioning was such that the court considers that it should exercise its discretion to exclude the statement. 2. At all times while in custody the doctors who examined

CRIMINAL LAW—*continued.*

the accused, Dillon, found him to be in good physical and mental condition. The accused made a statement of admission at an early stage in the interviews which made clear that he had not been subjected to any great pressure from the police before he began to make confessions. The fact that the accused retracted his confessions was not a ground to exclude the statements as the reason for the retraction was the accused's realisation the he would be prosecuted for crimes in which he had admitted involvement. The lengths and times of the interviews were not such as to exclude the statements. Save in exceptional circumstances interviews should not be conducted after midnight but in the special circumstances of this case there was no good reason for excluding statements on this ground. In exercising its discretion the court shall not exclude statements as a means of controlling police conduct in interrogating suspects. The inconsistencies and untruths in the statements was not a ground for excluding them but went to the reliability of the statements if they were admitted in evidence. 3. The involuntariness at common law of the statements of the accused, Gorman, was not a reason for excluding them. The accused's oral and written statements were so detailed and coherent that this was not a case where the mental state of the accused rendered them unreliable. The showing of post-mortem photographs to the accused was undesirable conduct by the police but did not constitute torture or inhuman or degrading treatment or affect the reliability of the accused's statements and was not a ground for excluding them. The accused, Dillon, was found guilty on 18 of 25 charges and sentenced to various concurrent terms of imprisonment including a term of 20 years for the attempted murder of members of the Royal Ulster Constabulary. The accused appealed to the Court of Appeal against conviction and sentence contending (1) that the trial judge having exercised his discretion to admit the appellant's statements failed to give proper weight to the circumstances in which they were obtained; (2) that the trial judge failed to deal with and resolve contradictions and inconsistencies in the appellant's statements; and (3) that it was unsafe and unsatisfactory to rely on certain of the appellant's statements and admissions particularly as the trial judge was unable to and did not rely on a number of other statements and admissions by the appellant. **Held,** dismissing the appeal, 1, that the trial judge in admitting the statements considered the circumstances in which they were obtained in order to assess the weight and probative value of the admissions and had regard to the evidence of the *voir dire* in deciding his verdict. 2. The appellant's case that it was logically irreconcilable to find the appellant guilty on

CRIMINAL LAW—Evidence.

certain counts while acquitting him on others was not sound: the trial judge, having seen and heard the evidence, assessed the reliability of the appellant's self-inculpating statements but without speculating against him refused to convict on any charge in regard to which those statements left any room for doubt. 3. The offence was a cold-blooded and deliberate assassination attempt and the sentence of 20 years was completely in line with sentences imposed for similar offences. *R.* v. *Dillon*

(Crown Ct., C.A.) [1984] N.I. 292

—— **Admissibility — Statement of accused.**
see also Nos. 1, 2, 6, 33, 47

22. —— **Corroboration** — *Rape — Evidence relied on as corroboration — Distress coincided with the complaint — Whether distressed condition of complainant capable of constituting corroboration — Judge's direction to jury.*] The applicant was convicted of rape. As corroboration of the complaint the prosecution tendered the evidence of certain witnesses to whom the prosecutrix complained, as to her distressed condition at the time that she made the complaint of rape. The defence case was that the prosecutrix consented to sexual intercourse with the applicant and that her subsequent distress was due to the fact that she had lost her virginity unexpectedly and this was not corroboration because, as the complaint was not corroborative of itself, the description of a distressed condition could not be treated as corroboration if it was part of the complaint or must be given so little weight as to be of no significance. The trial judge left to the jury the question of whether or not the distressed condition constituted corroboration of the evidence of the prosecutrix, but did not state to the jury that the alleged corroboration was a description of a distressed condition apparent at the time of making a complaint of rape. On the applicant's application for leave to appeal against conviction and sentence it was **Held** by the Court of Criminal Appeal (McCarthy, Gannon and Barr JJ.), in dismissing the application, 1, that the distressed condition of a complainant in a case of rape, might depending on the circumstances, amount to corroboration of the offence but the jury should be wary of relying upon it. 2. That the trial judge was bound to warn the jury of the need for corroboration, the weakness of evidence of a distressed condition as corroboration in cases of rape and the danger of convicting in the absence of corroboration. *Attorney Gerneral* v. *Cradden* [1955] I.R. 130; *Attorney General* v. *O'Sullivan* [1930] I.R. 552 and *Reg.* v. *Knight* [1966] 1 W.L.R. 230 followed. 3. That in the instant case the jury was told of its role in assessing what was corroboration and,

CRIMINAL LAW—*continued.*

putting the defence case to the jury, the trial judge made it clear that the jury should consider the issue of whether or not there was corroboration in the light of the defence submissions as to the cause of the distress. *The People* v. *Mulvey*

(C.C.A.) [1987] I.R.502

—— **Corroboration.**
see also No. 9

23. —— **Prejudicial evidence** — *Procedure — Conviction in Special Criminal Court — Whether inadmissible prejudicial evidence given during the trial — Whether trial held in accordance with statute — Forensic evidence — Whether findings based in inferences capable of more than one interpretation — Offences Against the State Act,* 1939 (*No.* 13), *s.* 41(4).] Earl Mountbatten of Burma was killed by an explosion on board his lobster boat, *Shadow V,* off Mullaghmore in the County of Sligo at 11.45 a.m. on 27 August 1979. Two men apprehended by the police at Granard two hours before the explosion, Thomas McMahon and John Joe McGirl, were tried for his murder before the Special Criminal Court. McMahon alone was convicted. He applied to the Court of Criminal Appeal for leave to appeal against his conviction. The application was grounded on (1) the alleged impropriety of the Special Criminal Court in proceeding with the trial after hearing a detective offer evidence that the accused was a bomb maker; and (2) the insufficiency of forensic evidence establishing that the accused had been in contact with the explosives used in the murder or with paint from Earl Mountbatten's boat. The arguments advanced by the appellant's counsel are set out below in the judgment. **Held** by the Court of Criminal Appeal (Hederman, Ellis and Murphy JJ.) refusing leave to appeal, 1, that, where prejudical evidence is heard, the Special Criminal Court has a discretion whether to disqualify itself from continuing with the trial: *The State (Healy)* v. *Donoghue* [1976] I.R. 325 applied. 2. That the Special Criminal Court was in the instant case composed of three experienced judges who recognised the prejudical nature of the evidence and were capable of excluding it from their minds. 3. That the Special Criminal Court had applied the proper standards in examining the circumstantial and forensic evidence in the case, and was entitled to draw the conclusion it did. *The People* v. *McMahon*

(C.C.A.) [1984] ILRM 461

24. —— **Sufficiency** — *Certificate of appointment — Offences contrary to European Community regulations — Authorised officers of the Minister for Agriculture — Whether certificate that*

CRIMINAL LAW—Evidence.

officer had been appointed sufficient evidence of the fact of appointment — Whether oral evidence sufficient — Evidence Act, 1845 (*c.* 113) — *Ministers and Secretaries Act,,* 1924 (*No.* 16), *ss.* 15(4), 17(c) — *Documentary Evidence Act,* 1925 (*No.* 24), s. 7(2) — *European Communities (Marketing of Fertiliser) Regulations* 1978 (*S.I. No.* 13), *regs. 2,* 4, 6, 7(4).] On 22 July, 1985, two senior agricultural officers of the Department of Agriculture attended at the defendant's premises where the defendant had for sale fertilizer designated as E.E.C. fertilizer. The officers gave evidence that they were officers of the Department of Agriculture and they produced certificates furnished to them pursuant to Regulation 7 (4) of European Communities (Marketing of Fertilizers) Regulations, 1978, as evidence that they were authorised to act for the purposes of the said regulations. The defendant was subsequently charged with a number of offences under the said regulations. When the matter came before the District Court, the District Justice held that the certificates tendered by the two officers were not evidence of the fact of their appointment in writing as authorised officers and, furthermore, that the oral evidence given on oath by the officers was not sufficient without the production of the actual appointment in writing itself. The Minister appealed by way of case stated by the District Justice in the following terms: (1) Is a statement on oath by a witness that he was on the date of an alleged offence duly appointed and authorised in writing by the complainant to act as an authorised officer for the purposes of the European Communites (Marketing of Fertilizers) Regulations, 1978, of itself and without more *prima facie* evidence for the purpose of a prosecution under these Regulations which I am bound to accept in the absence of evidence to the contrary on the grounds that there is a presumption in law that persons acting in an official capacity pursuant to statute or statutory regulation have been regularly and properly appointed. (2) Are certificates purporting to be signed by an Assistant Secretary of the Department of Agriculture in the form annexed to this case stated *prima facie* evidence which I am bound to accept that the persons named therein are authorised officers and were duly appointed by the Minister for Agriculture for the purpose of the European Communities (Marketing of Fertilizers) Regulations, 1978, (S.I. No. 13 of 1978). **Held** by Lynch J. answering the first question in the affirmative and remitting the case to the District Court, 1, in this case, the sort of powers purported to be exercised by the two officers of the Department of Agriculture could not be regarded as extraordinary powers but rather as the sort of powers which such officers might normally be expected to have and to

CRIMINAL LAW—*continued.*

execute in the course of their duties. In the circumstances, the evidence given on oath by the officers tht they were duly appointed in writing by the Minister was sufficient *prima facie* evidence of that fact: *The People* v. *Farrell* [1978] I.R. 13 and *Martin* v. Quinn [1980] I.R. 245 discussed. 2. An answer to the second question was unnecessary given an affirmative answer to the first. Nevertheless, it should be answered in the negative for the following reasons: the certificate actually produced in court was neither the original appointment in writing nor did it purport to be a copy of or an extract from such appointment in writing. Moreover, there was nothing in the Ministers and Secretaries Act, 1924, or the Documentary Evidence Act, 1925, which would make this form of certificate evidence of the truth of its contents in so far as it is purported to certify that the officer had been appointed to be an authorised officer by another instrument in writing. The Evidence Act, 1845, did not apply to this certificate either. *Minister for Agriculture* v. *Cleary*

(H.C.) [1988] ILRM 294

25. —— **Witness** — *Character of witness — Previous convictions of prosecution witness — Record unknown to defence or prosecution — Whether material to credibility of witness — Extent of duty on prosecution to inform defence.*] The applicant was convicted, *inter alia,* of wounding with intent to do grievous bodily harm, contrary to s. 18 of the Offences Against the Person Act, 1861. He denied the charges and denied being at the scene when the offences took place. The prosecution witness, who identified the applicant as being present at the scene, was not cross-examined as to his credibility, however, unknown to both the prosecution and defence, he had a number of serious convictions recorded against him. It was argued on behalf of the applicant that there could have been a different verdict by the jury if this evidence had been available. **Held** by the Court of Criminal Appeal (Finlay C.J., Lynch and Lardner JJ.), in allowing the application and directing a new trial, 1, that, where the prosecution was aware of a previous conviction of a prosecution witness, they should so inform the defence before the trial. 2. That if the trial judge was satisfied that the conviction could go to the credit of that witness he could permit it to be put to him. 3. That the prosecution did not have a duty to make exhaustive or widespread enquiries about every prosecution witness so as to ascertain if convictions had been recorded against him or her. 4. That if, unknown to the prosecution and defence, there was a serious or significant conviction recorded against a prosecution witness, and if this fact was discovered after the trial, the Court of Appeal may,

CRIMINAL LAW—Evidence.

upon being satisfied as to the fact of such conviction and being also satisfied that it was material to the credibility of the witness, allow an appeal and direct a new trial. *R.* v. *Collister and Warhurst* (1955) 39 Cr. App. R. 100; *R.* v. *Parks* [1961] 1 W.L.R. 1484 and *R.* v. *Paraskeva* (1983) 76 CR. App. R. 162 considered and applied. *The People* v. *Kelly*

[1987] I.R.596

26. —— **Witness** — *Written statements made by Crown witnesses at committal — Witnesses refused to attend trial — Statement read at trial — Whether reasonable efforts made to secure attendance — Magistrates' Courts (Northern Ireland) Order,* 1981 (*S.I. No.* 1675, N.I. 26), *art.* 42(3).

Evidence — Admissibility — Similar fact — Accused charged with murder of members of security forces in bomb incident — Convicted of attempted murder in shooting incident in same area — Whether evidence of similar facts — Whether evidence of motivation — Whether prejudicial.] The appellant was charged with a number of offences arising out of two incidents. In one incident in June, 1973 (the Johnston incident), a car containing four men drove into the farmyard of Mr. Johnston, a member of the Ulster Defence Regiment, at Tullygallaghan, Newtownhamilton, Co. Armagh and opened fire on and wounded Mr. Johnston and four others. In the other incident in April, 1973 (the Carrickovaddy incident) a bomb was detonated in a culvert on the Carrickovaddy Road, Tullygallaghan, Newtownhamilton, killing two soldiers and wounding a third. The evidence against the accused with regard to the Johnston incident consisted of fingerprints found inside the Johnston home and on the car used in the incident and the statements of five witnesses who failed to appear at the trial. With regard to the Carrickovaddy incident the sole evidence against the accused was a fingerprint on a lemonade bottle found with some other food and drink in a derelict farmhouse close to the detonation point of the bomb. In convicting the appellant, the trial judge said that the evidence for the Carrickovaddy incident was not sufficient by itself to satisfy him beyond reasonable doubt, but, being satisfied of the appellant's guilt in the Johnston incident, he took that into account as similar fact evidence which also showed a motive which tended to rebut the appellant's innocent explanation for the presence of his fingerprint on the bottle. The appellant appealed to the Court of Appeal on the grounds that the trial judge should not have allowed the statements of evidence of the absent witnesses to be read at the trial as evidence and that he had erred in applying the doctrine of similar

CRIMINAL LAW—*continued.*

facts. **Held,** that, 1, article 42 (3) of the Magistrates' Courts (Northern Ireland) Order, 1981, which provides that statements may be read as evidence at the trial "if the court is satisfied . . . that all reasonable efforts to find or secure his attendance have been made without success" does not require exhaustive efforts to secure attendance in every case; what constitutes reasonable efforts may vary from case to case. In this case the court was satisfied that all reasonable efforts had been made to secure attendance. The article was sufficiently wide to include a witness who refused to attend for any reason provided all reasonable efforts to find him or to secure his attendance have been made. The fact that a witness genuinely fears for his life and that there is a reasonable basis for this belief may be relevant in assisting the court to determine whether "all reasonable efforts" have been made. 2. The evidence about the Johnston incident did not in any way qualify to be treated as similar fact evidence with a view to proving the appellant's participation in the Carrickovaddy incident. The common features of both crimes were, in the context of the prolonged terrorist activity in Northern Ireland, sadly commonplace and were not sufficiently striking in similarity to help prove that the appellant committed the crimes in the Carrickovaddy incident. *Per* Lord Lowry L.C.J. in order to be admissible, the crimes committed must share with the crime charged common features which were variously stated as being "strikingly similar" or having an "underlying link" or "positive probative value." In choosing one of these tests it was difficult to ignore either of the others or their implications for the full application of the test as all three were intimately related if not interdependent. There could hardly be an "underlying link" if there was no "strikingly similar evidence" to prove it. And the underlying link was not provided by commonplace similarities but by similarities that were "striking." Further, evidence became the more "positively probative" the more striking the similarities and the more obvious the underlying link. *R.* v. *Boardman* [1975] A.C. 421 and *R.* v. *Scarrott* [1978] Q.B. 1016 applied. 3. The appellant's motivation to kill members of the security forces, proved by his participation in the Johnston incident did not negative the defence of his innocent contact with the lemonade bottle as there was nothing in that evidence to indicate more than a general hostility to the security forces. *R.* v. *Ball* [1911] A.C. 47 distinguished. *R.* v. *Martin*

(C.A.) [1985] N.I.324

Excise offence — penalty *see* No. 52
Extra-territorial offence *see* No. 49

Legal aid *see* Nos. 50, 51

MISCELLANEOUS OFFENCES

27. —— **Firearms** — *Possession — Accused being constables in R.U.C. — Whether possession for a lawful purpose — Accused believing that their lives would be in danger — Whether such belief honest and reasonable — Firearms Act,* 1964 (*No.* 1), *s.* 27A — *Criminal Law Jurisdiction Act,* 1976 (*No.* 14), *s.* 8.] The three defendants were all R.U.C. members. One night, when they were off duty, they crossed the border into this State and went to a public house in Castleblayney, County Monaghan because the public houses in Northern Ireland were at that time closed. They all carried regulation issue R.U.C. hand guns, which were loaded, for use if necessary to protect their lives. They had no firearms certificates under the Firearms Acts. A hostile crowd attacked them in Castleblayney. One of the defendants brandished his gun to ward off the crowd. Each of the defendants was indicted before the Special Criminal Court on counts of two offences; one, possession of a firearm without a certificate and two, an offence contrary to s. 27 (*a*) (1) of the 1964 Act as inserted by the 1976 Act. S. 27 (*a*) (1) provides that 'A person who has a firearm or ammunition in his possession or under his control in such circumstances as to give rise to a reasonable inference that he has not got it in his possession or under his control for a lawful purpose shall, unless he has it in his possession or under his control for a lawful purpose, be guilty of an offence . . .' The accused all pleaded guilty to the first offence. **Held,** unlawful possession of a firearm may be for a lawful purpose. Although the circumstances gave rise to a reasonable inference that the defendants had the loaded guns for an unlawful purpose it would be a good defence if they could prove, on the balance of probabilities, that they had had an honest and reasonable belief that their lives might be in danger and that protection of their lives required them to carry their guns. The defendants had discharged this onus. The defendants were therefore all acquitted on the second count. *Director of Public Prosecutions* v. *Kelso*

(Sp. Crim. Ct.) [1984] ILRM 329

28. —— **Misuse of drugs** — *Offence — Possession of controlled drug — Cannabis resin — Whether possession for personal use or some other purpose — Whether indictment must distinguish between purposes for which drug is possessed — Whether triable summarily or on indictment — Misuse of Drugs Act,* 1977 (*No.* 12), *ss.* 3, 15, 27.] The prosecutor was tried on indictment on a number of charges under the

Misuse of Drugs Act, 1977. He pleaded guilty to the charge of unlawful possession of the controlled drug cannabis resin, contrary to s. 3 of the 1977 Act. The Director of Public Prosecutions entered a *nolle prosequi* in relation to the other charges, which included unlawful possession for the purpose of supplying, contrary to s. 15 of the 1977 Act and the Misuse of Drugs Regulations, 1979. The prosecutor was convicted by the respondent. He applied for certiorari to quash the conviction on the ground that there was no power to convict or sentence for possession of a controlled drug where that possession is for personal use. S.3 of the 1977 Act provides that 'a person who has a controlled drug in his possession . . . shall be guilty of an offence', but that the Minister for Health may by order declare that this shall not apply to a controlled drug specified in the order. S.5. of the Act sets out the basis on which the Minister may make regulations to prevent the misuse of controlled drugs. The Minister made the 1979 regulations on this basis. S.15 of the Act states that any person 'who has in his possession, whether lawfully or not, a controlled drug for the purpose of selling or otherwise supplying it to another in contravention of regulations under s. 5 of this Act, shall be guilty of an offence.' S. 27 (1) (*a*) provides a scale of sentences as to offences under s. 3, in relation to cannabis, where the court is satisfied that the person had possession for his personal use; and s. 27 (1) (*b*) provides for a scale of sentences as to offences under s.3 in any other case. **Held** by O'Hanlon J. in granting the order, 1, although the proper course for the prosecutor would have been to move to quash the count to which he pleaded guilty, rather than submit to the jurisdiction of the trial court, his failure to challenge the validity of the indictment at the proper time was not in itself sufficient to defeat his claim. *The State (Williams)* v. *Kelly (No. 2)* [1970] I.R. 271 applied. 2. The combined effect of ss. 3 and 27 of the 1977 Act was to create a summary offence of unlawful possession of controlled drugs where possession was for personal use, and a further offence which may be prosecuted as a summary or indictable offence at the option of the Director of Public Prosecutions where possession was for a purpose other than personal use, an essential ingredient of the indictable offence being the establishing that possession was for other than personal use, that this appeared on the indictment and also formed part of the court order. 3. Although the evidence disclosed that the trial judge dealt with the case on the basis that the accused was in possession of the controlled drug for a purpose other than personal use, the order of the court failed to disclose jurisdiction on its face by not referring to the purpose for which the drug was

CRIMINAL LAW—Miscellaneous Offences.

in the accused's possession. *The State (Bloomfield)* v. *Neylon*

(H.C.) [1985] ILRM 602

29. —— **Misuse of drugs** — *Offence — Possession of controlled drug — Cannabis resin — District Court — Sentence — Reduced sentence where possession for personal use — Whether enactment created two offences — Whether order of court must show that possession found to be for personal use — Whether order must set out that offence found to be minor offence — Misuse of Drugs Act,* 1977 (*No.* 12), *ss.* 3, 27 — *Misuse of Drugs Act,* 1984 (*No.* 18), *s.* 6.] Section 3 of the Misuse of Drugs Act, 1977, creates the offence of unlawful possession of a controlled drug. By s. 27, sub-s. 1 of the Act, as amended by s. 6 of the Misuse of Drugs Act, 1984, every person found guilty of an offence under s. 3 shall be liable: "(*a*) where the relevant controlled drug is cannabis or cannabis resin and the court is satisfied that the person was in possession of such drug for his personal use: (i) in the case of a first offence, (I) on summary conviction, to a fine not exceeding £300, or (II) on conviction on indictment, to a fine not exceeding £500, (ii) in the case of a second offence, (I) on summary conviction, to a fine not exceeding £400, or (II) on conviction on indictment, to a fine not exceeding £1,000, (iii) in the case of a third or subsequent offence, (I) on summary conviction, to a fine not exceeding £1,000 or, at the discretion of the court, to imprisonment for a term not exceeding twelve months, or to both the fine and the imprisonment, or (II) on conviction on indictment, to a fine of such amount as the court considers appropriate or, at the discretion of the court, to imprisonment for a term not exceeding three years, or to both the fine and the imprisonment; (*b*) in any other case— (i) on summary conviction, to a fine not exceeding £1,000 or, at the discretion of the court to imprisonment for a term not exceeding twelve months, or to both the fine and the imprisonment, or (ii) on conviction on indictment, to a fine of such amount as the court considers appropriate or, at the discretion of the court, to imprisonment for a term not exceeding seven years, or to both the fine and the imprisonment." The prosecutor was convicted by the respondent District Justice of "[unlawful possession of] a controlled drug, to wit, cannabis resin, contrary to s. 3 of the Misuse of Drugs Act, 1977," and was fined the sum of £150. The prosecutor obtained an absolute order of certiorari in the High Court quashing the respondent's order of conviction, on the grounds that the order was bad on its face and void for failing to show whether the court had found that such possession was for the personal use of the prosecutor, whether the sentence was imposed pursuant to s. 27, sub-s. 1 (*a*) or (*b*) of the Act, and whether the court had determined the offence to be a minor offence.

CRIMINAL LAW—*continued.*

On the respondent's appeal to the Supreme Court against the judgment and order of the High Court it was **Held** by the Supreme Court (Finlay C.J., Griffin and Hederman JJ.) in allowing the appeal discharging the order and allowing the cause shown, 1, that s. 3 of the Act of 1977 created only one offence of possession *simpliciter;* the question of use of the drug was not an ingredient of the offence and arose only in relation to the penalty to be imposed under section 27. *The State (Bloomfield)* v. *Neylon* [1985] ILRM 602 overruled. 2. That the respondent's failure to set out in the order of conviction that he had determined the offence to be a minor offence did not invalidate the order; the fine of £150 which was imposed by him marked the offence as a minor one, as would the maximum fine of £300 had it been imposed. *The State (Rollinson)* v. *Kelly* [1984] I.R. 248 applied. 3. That the respondent's order of conviction was good on its face, since it had set out the offence of possession contrary to s. 3 of the Act, and it was not necessary for the order to set out the section or sub-section of the Act under which the penalty was imposed. *Per* Griffin J. That were a District Justice to impose a fine exceeding £300 in the case of a second, third or subsequent offence of unlawful possession of cannabis for personal use the order of the court should state the facts found which conferred jurisdiction to impose such a fine. *The State (Gleeson)* v. *Connellan*

(S.C.) [1988] I.R.559

Misuse of drugs, *see also* Nos. 60, 71, 79

OFFENCES AGAINST THE PERSON

30. —— **Murder** — *Defence of diminished responsibility — Issues determinable by jury — Relevance of medical evidence — Refusal of trial judge to leave to the jury a defence of diminished responsibility in formula suggested — Appeal against conviction in the Central Criminal Court — Criminal Justice Act,* 1964 (*No.* 5), *s.* 4.] The accused was arraigned in the Central Criminal Court on an indictment for murder. At the trial of the accused before a judge and a jury, the defence was that the accused was suffering from such abnormality of mind as substantially impaired his mental responsibility for his acts as to entitle the jury to consider the alternative of finding a verdict of manslaughter instead of murder. The defence of insanity was not raised on behalf of the accused. Medical evidence was adduced to the effect that the accused suffered from a condition of psychotic intensity, which

prevented him from stopping or withdrawing from violent acts and that this was what occurred in the instant case. The trial judge refused to leave to the jury the defence of diminished responsibility in the formula contended for on behalf of the accused. However he directed the jury that if they were not satisfied beyond a reasonable doubt, having regard to the medical and other evidence, that the accused was capable of forming the necessary intent for murder, then their verdict should be not guilty of murder but guilty of manslaughter. The accused was convicted of murder and sentenced to penal servitude for life. He appealed directly to the Supreme Court against his conviction. **Held** by the Supreme Court (Finlay C.J., Walsh, Griffin, Hederman, and McCarthy JJ.), in disallowing the appeal and affirming the conviction, 1, that the defence of diminished responsibility in the formula contended for on behalf of the accused does not form part of Irish law and could not exist side by side with the present law concerning the defence of insanity. 2. That, accordingly, the trial judge had acted correctly in refusing to leave such a defence to the jury and had correctly charged the jury concerning the necessary intent which must be established as a matter of law for the offence of murder. *Reg.* v. *Byrne* [1960] 2 Q.B. 396 considered. *The People* v. *O'Mahony*
(S.C.) [1985] I.R.517; [1986] ILRM 245

31. —— **Murder** — *Self-defence — Accused a soldier — Deceased shot while running away from scuffle — Whether accused honestly believed he was acting in self-defence — Inference drawn from accused's failure to give explanation — Whether infringement of right to silence — Whether trial judge failed to consider possibility that accused was attempting to arrest deceased — Whether verdict of manslaughter should have been considered.*] On the afternoon of 9 August, 1983, two army foot patrols, each consisting of four soldiers, were in the vicinity of Springfield Road and Whiterock Road in West Belfast. The appellant was a member of one patrol. The second patrol passed a group of young men who had been drinking beer and cider. The deceased, a member of that group, ran over to a member of the second patrol and punched him on the face and then pulled at his riot gun, causing him to stagger and to go down on his knees. A minor fracas then commenced between other members of the group and the patrol. A this point the appellant's patrol arrived at the scene. The deceased then ran off. The leader of the first patrol shouted "stop him" or "get him" and the appellant gave chase. The appellant shouted on three occasions to the deceased to stop, all without success. On the third occasion, the appellant aimed and fired his rifle and the bullet struck and

killed the deceased who had at all times been running forward. The appellant was charged with murder. At his trial he put forward the defence that he fired in self-defence or in defence of another soldier behind him because he believed the deceased was turning to fire at him with a pistol. The appellant stated that he did not fire at the deceased for the purpose of arresting him. The trial judge rejected the defence and convicted the appellant, although he found as a fact that the appellant had decided that if the deceased did not stop in response to any of his calls, the appellant would let him go and would not shoot at him. The appellant appealed to the Court of Appeal on the grounds that, (*a*) the conviction was unsafe and unsatisfactory because the trial judge failed to reconcile some of his findings of fact, which were consistent with the appellant's case, with his finding of guilt, and in particular had failed to establish the appellant's motive, and the trial judge had erred in drawing adverse inferences from the appellant's failure after the shooting to put forward his belief that the deceased had been about to fire at him; (*b*) the appellant was entitled to use force to effect an arrest, notwithstanding that he had been purporting to act in self-defence; and (*c*) the crime was one of manslaughter and not murder, because the circumstances justified some action by the appellant and he had merely acted beyond the necessity of the occasion. **Held,** dismissing the appeal, that, 1, the trial judge's findings of fact could not be challenged. Motive is not an ingredient which the Crown had to prove in order to prove the crime of murder. If the Crown proves that the accused killed the deceased, that the accused acted with the intent to kill or cause grievious bodily harm to the deceased, and the Crown further disproves any defence which is or could on the evidence be raised, such as self-defence or the exercise of reasonable force in effecting an arrest, then the Crown has proved that the accused is guilty of murder, and the motive with which the accused carried out the act which killed the deceased is irrelevant. Consequently, once the defence that the appellant might have been shooting to effect an arrest was out of the case and the trial judge was satisfied that the Crown had eliminated the reasonable possibility of self defence, the appellant's intentional shooting to kill or seriously injure could only mean a finding of murder. *Per curiam:* Where the trial is conducted and the factual conclusions are reached by the same person, one need not expect every step in the reasoning to be spelt out expressly, nor is the reasoning carried out in sealed compartments with no intercommunication or overlapping. It can safely be inferred that a judge who is himself the tribunal of fact will recognise the issues and

CRIMINAL LAW—Offences Against the Person.

view in its entirety a case where one issue is interwoven with another. 2. The inferences which the trial judge drew from the appellant's failure to give an earlier explanation for his action did not infringe the right to silence. In this trial the judge was also the jury and, provided he did not misdirect himself, was at liberty to draw inferences from the conduct of the accused. 3. It is the duty of the judge to put such questions as appear to him to arise properly on the evidence, whatever the line of defence adopted. Here the trial judge did consider the defence under section 3 of the Criminal Law Act (Northern Ireland), 1967, of using reasonable force to effect an arrest, and, in his capacity as judge of fact, made findings based on evidence which destroyed the possibility of a section 3 defence. *R.* v. *Hooper* [1915] 2 K.B. 431 distinguished. 4. That as the trial judge found that if self defence was justified, the force used was not excessive, the issue of whether the crime was one of manslaughter and not murder where the accused acted beyond the necessity of the occasion did not arise on the facts. *R.* v. *Thain*

(C.A.) [1985] N.I.457

32. —— **Shooting with intent to commit murder** — Mens rea — *Whether necessary to establish intention to commit murder — Whether reckless disregard of risk of killing as a likely outcome sufficient to constitute required intent — Offences Against the Person Act,* 1861 (*c.* 100), *s.* 14.] The applicants were convicted of shooting with intent to commit murder contrary to s. 14 of the Offences Against the Person Act, 1861. The court of trial held that it was sufficient to constitute the offence where the natural consequence of shooting would be to kill or seriously injure and that the shots were fired with reckless disregard of the risk of killing, in the sense that it would be likely, but not necessarily the desired, outcome of shooting. S. 14 of the 1861 Act provides that whosoever 'shall shoot at any person . . . with intent . . . to commit murder, shall, whether any bodily injury be affected or not, be guilty of a felony.' The applicants sought leave to appeal on the ground that the necessary intent to constitute the offence had not been established. **Held** by the Court of Criminal Appeal (O'Higgins C.J, McWilliam and Barron JJ.) in granting leave to appeal and quashing the convictions, 1, while it was anomalous that where a person shoots at another intending to cause serious injury and that person dies, the offence of murder has been committed, while if he does not die the offence of shooting with intent to murder has not been committed, s. 14 of the 1861 Act specifically required proof of an intent to kill and it was irrevelant that the court of trial was

CRIMINAL LAW—*continued.*

satisfied that those who fired the shots would have been guilty of murder had any person been killed. *Cawthorne* v. *H.M. Advocate* 1968 JC 32 considered. 2. In order to determine whether an intent to kill existed, a court may take into account that a reasonable man would have foreseen that the natural and probable consequence of the acts was to cause death and that the accused acted in reckless disregard of that likely outcome of the acts, but such factors of themselves would not constitute proof of such intent. *Dicta* of Wien J. in *Reg.* v. *Belfon* [1976] 1 W.L.R 741 applied. *Reg.* v. *Smith* [1961] A.C. 290 and *Reg.* v. *Hyam* [1975] A.C. 55 considered. *The People* v. *Douglas*

(C.C.A.) [1985] ILRM 25

OFFENCES AGAINST PROPERTY

33. —— **Entering premises as trespasser and stealing therein** — *Evidence of owner of the premises — Whether offence established — Whether accused entered as trespasser — Distinction between breaking and entering — Larceny Act,* 1916 (*c.* 50), *s.* 23 — *Criminal Law (Jurisdiction) Act,* 1976 (*No.* 14), *s.* 6.

Evidence — Admissibility — Statement by accused in Garda custody — Young person — Whether obligation to have parent or guardian present during questioning — Whether fear of obstruction of course of justice justifies refusal to have parent present — Whether trial judge has discretion to admit evidence.] The defendant, then aged 14, was charged with having entered premises as a trespasser and stolen property therein, contrary to s. 23 of the Larceny Act, 1916, as inserted by s. 6 of the Criminal Law (Jurisdiction) Act, 1976. At his trial in the District Court, the owner of the premises stated he had given 'no one permission to break in.' The defendant had been arrested in his father's presence, was then brought to a Garda station and questioned and made a statement relating to the alleged offence. At no stage during questioning was the defendant in the presence of his parents. The District Justice stated a case to the High Court as to whether the evidence of the owner of the premises was sufficient to support a conviction on the charge and as to the admissibility of the statment made by the defendant. **Held** by Finlay P., 1, although the offence of entering a building as trespasser and stealing therein was different from the offence of breaking and entering, and while precise legal meanings had been given to breaking and entering, the evidence of a lay witness must be construed by a trial judge in accordance with common sense and with the reasonable inference from the words used, and in this context the evidence given was capable of supporting a conviction, though not necessarily demanding that a conviction must be entered. 2. It was most desirable in the interests of justice that a young person suspected of a criminal offence should be questioned in the presence of a parent or guardian, unless this is a practical impossibility; that this was not an inflexible rule, but was more akin to one of the Judges' Rules and non-compliance could not in any circumstances automatically make a statement inadmissible. *D.P.P.* v. *W.F.* 114 I.L.T.R. 110 applied. 3. Since the defendant was taken to the Garda station as a suspected person, the advice of his father to exercise his undoubted right of silence could not be construed as an obstruction of the course of justice, but where there might be grounds on which the Gardaí could validly decide that the presence of one parent might obstruct the course of justice, they should endeavour to secure the attendance of another parent or guardian. *Travers* v. *Ryan*

(H.C.) [1985] ILRM 343

Offences Against the State Act *see* Nos. 4-6, 18, 19, 23, 66

PRACTICE AND PROCEDURE

Appeal. Nos. 34, 35, 79
Bail. No. 36
Certificate of conviction. No. 37
Committal for trial. No. 38
Complaint. Nos. 39-46
Disclosure of information. No. 47
Emergency powers. No. 48
Extra-territorial offence. No. 49
Legal aid. Nos. 50, 51
Penalty — excise offence. No. 52
Plea — autrefois acquit. No. 53
Preliminary examination. Nos. 54-6
Prosecution. Nos. 57, 58
Remand. No. 59
Return for trial. No. 60
Summons. Nos. 39-44, 61, 62, 68
Trial. Nos. 63-7
Young offender. Nos. 68, 69

34. —— **Appeal** — *Case stated — Acquittal — Whether D.P.P. had validly invoked the jurisdiction of the High Court — Necessary steps — Whether complied with — Whether possible to state case against acquittal — Summary Jurisdiction Act,* 1857 (*c.* 43), *s.* 2 — *Courts of Justice Act,* 1924 (*No.* 10), *ss.* 36, 91 — *Courts (Supplemental Provisions) Act,* 1961 (*No.* 39), *s.* 51 — *R.S.C. O.* 62, *r.* 5 — *District Court Rules,* 1948, *r.* 201.] The respondent was tried and acquitted by the District Court on a charge of assault occasioning actual bodily harm. He admitted striking the injured party but said that it was done in the course of defending himself from what he felt was an imminent blow from

the injured party. Three witnesses had seen the respondent turn and strike the injured party. The District Justice acquitted on the basis that the respondent's evidence raised a doubt as to whether the offence had been proved and the respondent was entitled to benefit of that doubt. The appellant appealed against the acquittal, contending that the respondent's evidence was so incredible that it was a perverse decision in law for the District Justice to allow it to raise a doubt in his mind. It was conceded by the respondent that where a District Justice reaches a determination which is unsupported by any evidence before him, his decision whether to acquit or convict may be set aside on appeal by way of case stated. **Held** by Finlay P. although there was a clear air of implausibility about the evidence of the respondent it would be an unwarranted interference by the High Court in a proceeding which is exclusively confined to correcting errors of law by an inferior court to hold that the evidence of the respondent could not have raised a doubt in the mind of the District Justice. The appeal by way of case stated against the acquittal would be dismissed. *Director of Public Prosecutions* v. *Nangle*

(H.C.) [1984] ILRM 171

35. —— **Appeal** — *Court of Criminal Appeal — Whether point of law of exceptional public importance — Whether desirable in public interest that appeal be carried to Supreme Court — Courts of Justice Act,* 1924 (*No.* 10), *s.* 29.

Extradition — Specialty rule — Whether rule infringed by trying defendant in Special Criminal Court — Extradition Act, 1965 (*No.* 17), *s.* 39.] The appellant applied for a certificate under s. 29 of the Courts of Justice Act, 1924, to take a further appeal to the Supreme Court and he based it on four grounds including, *inter alia,* that the charge on which he had been tried in the Special Criminal Court was contrary to what had been warranted by the then Attorney General in his affidavit to the court in England which dealt with the extradition proceedings. He also claimed he should not have been tried in the Special Criminal Court, that the Court of Criminal Appeal had incorrectly dismissed his appeal on 22 January, 1974, and that the copy of the indictment which he was provided with incorrectly bore the stamp of the Dublin Circuit Court and a reference to a trial by jury. **Held** by the Court of Criminal Appeal (Henchy J., Gannon and McMahon JJ.) in refusing the application, 1, for the purpose of granting a certificate under s. 29 of the Act of 1924, the onus was on the appellant to show two points — that there was a point of law of exceptional public importance and, secondly, that it was desirable in the public interest that an appeal be carried from the Court

CRIMINAL LAW—Practice.

of Criminal Appeal to the Supreme Court. 2. Contrary to what had been submitted by the appellant, the Rule of Specialty contained in s. 39 of the Extradition Act, 1965, had been precisely observed and the fact that he had been tried in the Special Criminal Court did not change in any way the offence as described in the Attorney General's affidavit. 3. His plea that the Special Criminal Court did not have jurisdiction to try him was an unsound proposition in law. 4. The Court of Criminal Appeal had dismissed his appeal on 22 January, 1974, after being informed by his counsel that it was the appellant's intention that, in lieu of proceeding with the appeal, proceedings would be instituted by way of prohibition or certiorari in the High Court. Even if there was a point of law of exceptional public importance involved, it could not be said that it would be desirable in the public interest that a further appeal should be taken, particularly as the appellant had allowed about three years to pass without taking any step in the matter. 5. While the indictment that was used in the Special Criminal Court had the two defects referred to, they were only peripheral or superficial defects and the appellant was not misled in any possible way. The indictment that was used in the trial was correct in every substantive respect. *Director of Public Prosecutions* v. *Littlejohn*

(C.C.A.) [1978] ILRM 147

—— **Appeal.**

see also Nos. 14, 21, 79

36. —— **Bail** — *Station bail — Prosecutor arrested in Dublin Metropolitan District and charged with summary offence — Duties of Garda Síochána following arrest — Prosecutor granted bail by member in charge of Garda station — Recognisance taken for appearance of prosecutor five days later before Dublin Metropolitan District Court — Member in charge of Garda station having regard to District Court Rules,* 1985, *purporting to empower Gardaí to allow arrested persons station bail for up to thirty days — District Court Rules — Powers of District Court Rules Committee — Whether granting of station bail part of the practice and procedure of the District Court — Whether purported rule* ultra vires — *Prosecutor appearing before District Court on day fixed by recognisance — Whether laying of charge sheet before court sufficient to confer jurisdiction to deal with prosecutor — District Court (Criminal Procedure Act, 1967) Rules,* 1985 (*S.I. No.* 23) — *Courts of Justice Act,* 1924 (*No.* 10), *s.* 91 — *Courts of Justice Act,* 1936 (*No.* 48), *s.* 72 — *Criminal Justice Act,* 1951 (*No.* 2), *s.* 15 — *Criminal Procedure Act,* 1967 (*No.* 12), *s.* 31(1) — *Criminal Justice Act, 1984 (No.* 22), *s.* 26.] Section 31, sub-s. 1 of the Criminal Procedure

CRIMINAL LAW—*continued.*

Act, 1967, provides that:— "Whenever a person is brought in custody to a Garda Síochána station by a member of the Garda Síochána, the sergeant or other member in charge of the station may, if he considers it prudent to do so and no warrant directing the detention of that person is in force, release him on bail and for that purpose take from him a recognisance, with or without sureties, for his due appearance before the District Court at the appropriate time and place." Rule 39, sub-rule 1 of the District Court Rules, 1948, as substituted by the District Court (Criminal Procedure Act, 1967) Rules, 1985, purported to provide that:— ". . . where a person is being released on bail from a Garda Síochána station under [*s. 31 of the Act of 1967*] the recognisance to be taken from him may be conditioned for his appearance at the next sitting of the court for the court area in which he has been arrested or at any subsequent sitting thereof to be held not later than 30 days after such next sitting." On the 1 March, 1985, the prosecutor was arrested in the Dublin Metropolitan District and taken to C. Garda station where he was charged with a summary offence. The duty sergeant considered it prudent to release him on bail pursuant to s. 31, sub-s. 1 of the Act of 1967. The next sitting of the Dublin Metropolitan District Court would have been on the 4 March, but the recognisance was conditioned for his appearance on the 6 March, at 2.00 p.m., which was the next time that the arresting member was rostered for duty and which the sergeant considered was 'the appropriate time and place.' The sergeant considered that he had thirty days within which to act in accordance with the District Court (Criminal Procedure Act, 1967) Rules, 1985. On the 6 March, 1985, the prosecutor appeared before the District Court. His solicitor objected to the jurisdiction of the court on the grounds that the prosecutor had not been brought before the court at the earliest possible sitting to be charged. The District Justice adjourned the case. The prosecutor obtained an absolute order of certiorari in the High Court quashing the remand order on the grounds that the Rules of 1985 were *ultra vires* the District Court Rules Committee in that they dealt with a function of the Garda Síochána rather than with the practice and procedure of the District Court.

On appeal by the respondent it was **Held** by the Supreme Court (Walsh, Henchy, Griffin, Hederman and McCarthy JJ.) in allowing the appeal and discharging the order, 1, that the fact that the prosecutor had appeared before the District Court on the 6 March, when the complaint was made to the District Justice by formally laying the charge sheet before the court, was sufficient to give jurisdiction to the District Justice in respect of the summary offence with

CRIMINAL LAW—Practice.

which the prosecutor had been charged. 2. (Henchy J. dissenting) that the only function of the District Court Rules Committee was to make rules to enable the District Court to function, to carry out its duties, to exercise its jurisdiction and to regulate its practice and procedure. It had no power to legislate for any other purpose and, in particular, had no power to regulate the performance of the functions of the Garda Síochána. *Woolf* v. *Ó Griobhta* [1953] I.R. 276 and *The State (O'Flaherty)* v. *Ó Floinn* [1954] I.R. 295 followed. 3. (Henchy J. dissenting) that the jurisdiction of the District Court to enter on the hearing of an alleged offence triable summarily depended on the making of a complaint to a person authorised to receive such a complaint. What happened before a complaint was made depended on the exercise of some discretion by the Garda officer concerned and this could not in any sense be regarded as falling under the heading of the pleading, practice and procedure of the District Court any more than the arrest itself could. 4. (Henchy J. dissenting) that the 1985 Rules did not purport to deal with any matter of which the court was seised but rather sought to vest the Garda officer concerned with a discretion, which he did not have under s. 31, sub-s. 1 of the Act of 1967, to postpone the appearance of a person released on station bail for up to thirty days. 5. (Henchy J. dissenting) that the provision of the 1985 Rules which purported to substitute a new rule 39, sub-rule 1 of the District Court Rules, 1948, were *ultra vires* the District Court Rules Committee and void. 6. *Per* Henchy J. (dissenting) the power of the District Court Rules Committee to make rules for the 'practice and procedure of the District Court generally' was not confined to practice and procedure in court but also covered matters preliminary to and consequential on what might take place in court. The enlargement of the period of release on bail was a procedural or administrative convenience and not a prejudicial change in substantive law and therefore did not go beyond the modification or adaptation of a statute. 7. *Per* Walsh J. *Semble:* that the functions purportedly conferred on peace commissioners to hear evidence and exercise a discretion whether prisoners should be remanded in custody or on bail were judicial functions. As peace commissioners in the exercise of those functions were not within the provisions of either Article 34 or Article 37 of the Constitution of Ireland, their position was somewhat dubious having regard to the provisions of the Constitution. *The State (Lynch)* v. *Ballagh*
(S.C.) [1986] I.R.203; [1987] ILRM 65

37. —— **Certificate of conviction** — *Conviction in District Court on various charges —*

CRIMINAL LAW—*continued.*

Appeal to Circuit Court — Circuit Court judge allowing two appeals but dismissing the others and confirming the convictions and sentences — Certificates of conviction not correctly recording the orders spoken by the judge — Application for certiorari — Courts of Justice (District Court) Act, 1946 (*No.* 21), *s.* 23.] The prosecutors, two gardaí, were each convicted of two charges of common assault and assault causing actual bodily harm on two successive days against the prisoner in custody. They appealed the convictions and sentence to the Circuit Court; the respondent disallowed the appeals, except on one charge each of 'actual bodily harm.' The County Registrar's certificate disclosed that the respondent dismissed the appeal and varied the charge to one of common assault and that sentence was affirmed. This was an erroneous certificate, the prosecutors obtained a conditional order of certiorari and cause was shown by the respondent. **Held** by Gannon J, refusing to make absolute the conditional order, that as there was no evidence that the Circuit Court had issued any instrument necessary to enforce its decision, the District Court orders in relation to the 'actual bodily harm' convictions subsisted. Though the certificate was erroneous, no order of certiorari was necessary to protect the prosecutors from excessive punishment. *The State (O'Dare)* v. *Sheehy*
(H.C.) [1984] ILRM 99

38. —— **Committal for trial** — *Depositions not endorsed — Whether endorsement mandatory — Insufficiency of evidence — Whether magistrate acted within jurisdiction — Whether committal and subsequent conviction null — Grand Jury (Abolition) Act (Northern Ireland),* 1969 (*c.* 15), *s.* 2(1) — *Criminal Justice (Committal for Trial) Act (Northern Ireland),* 1968 (*c.* 32), *ss.* 3, 7 — *Magistrates' Courts (Northern Ireland) Order,* 1981 (*S.I. No.* 1675, N.I. 26), *art.* 33.

Conviction quashed on appeal — Retrial — Whether judge in retrial should have access to judgment quashing conviction.] Each of the three appellants were committed for trial by the use of written statements at a preliminary enquiry. Many of the statements put in evidence did not comply with section 3 of the Criminal Justice (Committal for Trial) Act (Northern Ireland), 1968, and its replacement, article 33 of the Magistrates' Courts (Northern Ireland) Order, 1981, because they were not endorsed by the person who recorded the statement or to whom the statement was delivered for the purposes of the proceedings. In none of the cases would the evidence have sufficed to commit the accused for trial without resort to the statements which were not endorsed. At each trial no order, under section 2(3) of the Grand Jury (Abolition) Act (Northern Ireland), 1969, to enter "No Bill"

CRIMINAL LAW—Practice.

was made. Each defendant was arraigned, one pleaded guilty and two not guilty. The latter were tried and found guilty. All three were sentenced and then appealed. On appeal all three argued that the statements were defective, that the committals for trial, the Bills of Indictment and the trials were all nullities. For the Crown it was argued that the provisions requiring endorsement were not mandatory, but merely directory. One appellant had been convicted at an earlier trial, but the convictions had been quashed and a new trial ordered. He also appealed on the ground that the judge at the second trial should not have had before him a copy of the judgment of the Court of Appeal ordering the new trial. **Held** that, 1, the endorsement of a witness's declaration required by the 1968 Act and the 1981 Order was mandatory as the legislation clearly and unambiguously laid down conditions for the admission of statements; statutes enlarging an inferior court's jurisdiction, as these did, must be construed strictly; the power to admit statements was to the accused's prejudice and should be strictly construed and the requirement in question was in addition to those laid down in the equivalent legislation for England and Wales and so was presumably considered important. Consequently the unendorsed statements had been inadmissible at the preliminary enquiries. 2. The validity of a committal for trial, however, could not be challenged on the ground of want of evidence. *Connelly* v. *D.P.P.* [1964] A.C. 1254 and *R. (Blakeney)* v. *Roscommon JJ.* [1894] 2 I.R. 158 followed. Moreover, to convict a person summarily, or commit him for trial on evidence which does not support the charge, is an error of law in the exercise of jurisdiction and not an example of the absence or excess of jurisdiction. Therefore the committals were not void and it was of no avail for the appellants to challenge the committals after they had been convicted. *R.* v. *Governor of Brixton Prison, ex parte Armah* [1964] A.C. 556 and *R. (Martin)* v. *Mahony* [1910] 2 I.R. 695 followed. *Quaere* If there had been no admissible written statements it might be argued that a committal had been made without complying with a prerequisite to jurisdiction. *per curiam* It would be open to a presiding judge faced with irregularily admitted statements to refrain from ordering "No Bill", if that was the sole defect, as he could see that when the hearing commenced, the Crown would be able to present a case. Alternatively, the Crown could serve notice, when the defect was discovered, of intention to give evidence in the terms of the statements. 3. On a new trial it may be very desirable for the judge at the new trial to know the reasoning of the Court of Appeal in order to avoid an error which was held to have occurred during the first trial. It was undesirable

CRIMINAL LAW—*continued.*

for the Court of Appeal, if it was minded to order a new trial, to express any opinion as to the credibility of the evidence or as to how any factual issue should or might be resolved, but, as judgments are delivered in open court, it would be virtually impossible to ensure that the judge on the new trial had not read, in whole or in part, the judgment of the appellate court. If it appeared that he had done so and the judgment contained seriously prejudicial matter, appropriate steps should be taken to safeguard the accused. In this case there was no prejudice to the appellant concerned as the Court of Appeal had done no more than draw specific attention to the fact that there was a conflict of evidence that had to be resolved. *R.* v. *Campbell*
(C.A.) [1985] N.I.354

39. —— **Complaint** — *Invalidity — Summary jurisdiction — District Court — Summonses issued on foot of invalid complaint — No appearance by defendant in District Court — Defendant convicted and appealing to Circuit Court — Whether issue of complaint could be raised in Circuit Court — Whether Circuit Court having jurisdiction to hear appeal — Whether hearing of summonses in District Court constituted valid complaint — Petty Sessions (Ireland) Act,* 1851 (*c.* 93), *s.* 10 — *Statute of Limitations,* 1957 (*No.* 6), *Schedule, part II.*] Summonses were issued against the defendant in the District Court on foot of a complaint made in accordance with a procedure which the Supreme Court subsequently held in other proceedings to be invalid — see *The State (Clarke)* v. *Roche* [1986] I.R. 619 [No. 43 *below*]. The defendant did not appear in the District Court on the date specified in the summonses for their hearing and which hearing was within six months from the time when the cause for the complaint had arisen. The prosecuting garda proceeded in his absence and the defendant was convicted. On his appeal to the Circuit Court against those convictions, it was argued on the defendant's behalf that the complaint upon which the summonses had been issued was invalid for the purposes of s. 10 of the Petty Sessions (Ireland) Act, 1851. It was submitted on behalf of the complainant that it was not open to the defendant on an appeal to take any point as to the validity of a complaint and the Circuit Court judge stated five questions for the opinion of the Supreme Court relating (*a*), to that issue, (*b*), to the jurisdiction of the Circuit Court to entertain an appeal when the validity of a complaint was in issue and (*c*), to the issue as to whether there was evidence of a valid complaint having been made in the matter. **Held** by the Supreme Court (Finlay C.J., Walsh, Henchy, Hederman and McCarthy JJ.) in answering the questions raised in the case stated,

CRIMINAL LAW—Practice.

1, that a defence based on s. 10 of the Act of 1851 could be raised on an appeal from the District Court to the Circuit Court since the appeal in the Circuit Court takes the form of a hearing *de novo*. The fact that the defendant did not take the point on the statute in the District Court did not preclude him from taking it in the Circuit Court. *Minister for Agriculture* v. *Norgro Ltd.* [1980] I.R. 155 considered. 2. That the jurisdiction of the Circuit Court to enter upon a hearing of the appeal was not affected by the fact that the defendant was raising a defence based on s. 10 of the Act of 1851. 3. That although the complaint upon which the summonses had been issued was invalid, the actual prosecution of the charges in the summonses in the District Court on the date in question itself constituted a valid complaint for the purposes of section 10. 4. That whatever artificiality attached to treating the hearing in the District Court as amounting to a complaint when the prosecuting garda was himself unaware of any legal frailty in the initial complaint, there could be no injustice to the defendant in this result as there was no suggestion that the defendant was otherwise than fully aware that the summonses would be proceeded with in the District Court on the date in question. *Per* Finlay C.J. If, as occurred in this case, a defendant relies on a purely technical point without merit or substance with regard to the real justice of the case, the complainant must be entitled equally to rely on a purely technical point. The treating of the initiation of the proceedings in the District Court as the making of a complaint is a purely technical point but is one which in the circumstances of this case the complainant is entitled to rely upon. *Director of Public Prosecutions (Nagle)* v. *Flynn*

(S.C.) [1987] I.R. 534

40. —— **Complaint** — *Time limit — Magistrates' Court — Delay — Abuse of process — Offence triable summarily or on indictment — Complaints laid three years after offence — Summons defective — Whether defects remediable — Whether question of delay should be considered as a preliminary point — Whether magistrates have a discretion to refuse to hear a summons — Magistrates' Courts (Northern Ireland) Order,* 1981 (*S.I. No.* 1675, *N.I.* 26), *art.* 19.] The applicants appeared at a magistrates' court to answer summonses, issued on 12 December, 1984, on foot of complaints made the same day and returnable on 28 January, 1985, which alleged that each of them on 8 September, 1981, planted a hoax bomb, contrary to article 3(1)(*a*) of the Criminal Law (Amendment) (Northern Ireland) Order, 1977. At the hearing counsel for the applicants objected that the court had no jurisdiction to hear the matter on the grounds that the offence

CRIMINAL LAW—*continued.*

was a summary offence no longer capable of being tried upon indictment and the complaint had not been made to a justice of the peace within six months of the offence, that the excessive delay in making a complaint was an abuse of the process of the court and that the summons was defective because it proceeded on the basis that the offence was an indictable offence triable summarily. No evidence was called and no amendment was either sought or made. The court ruled that as the offence charged was triable upon indictment, the six month time limit did not apply: it declined to rule on the submission concerning delay being an abuse of process until all the evidence was heard and ruled that the summons was not inappropriate as there was power to refer the matter at any time to the Crown Court under article 45 of the Magistrate's Courts (Northern Ireland) Order, 1981. The case was then adjourned generally to enable the applicants to apply to the High Court for orders of prohibition and certiorari to prevent the Resident Magistrate from inquiring into the complaints. **Held,** refusing relief, that as the offence was triable either on indictment or summarily, the time limit did not apply by reason of article 19(2) of the 1981 Order, and assuming, without so deciding, that a magistrates' court had power to refuse jurisdiction on the ground of excessive delay, the application was premature as the court had not yet had an opportunity of considering whether the delay was inexcusable and the erroneous references in the summons were remediable and not a ground for judicial review. *Per* Lord Lowry L.C.J.: It could be argued that if a magistrate declines jurisdiction to hear proceedings on the ground that they are oppressive and an abuse of the process of the court, the High Court can in a suitable case give effect to his decision by refusing an order of mandamus and thereby leaving the aggrieved party without a remedy. *Mills* v. *Cooper* [1967] 2 Q.B. 459 considered. *In re Simmons*

(Q.B.D.) [1985] N.I. 490

41. —— **Complaint** — *Time limit — Summary jurisdiction — Summons — Issue — Whether complaint made within statutory period — Whether evidence before courts as to valid issue of summons — Nature of summons — Petty Sessions (Ireland) Act,* 1851 (*c.* 93), *s.* 10(4).] S. 10 of the Petty Sessions (Ireland) Act, 1851, provides that where a complaint has been made to a justice as to any matter arising within his jurisdiction, he shall have power to proceed in respect of such complaint, provided that in all cases of summary jurisdiction, the complaint has been made within six months of the date on which the cause of the complaint arose. The respondent had been charged with four offences contrary to the Road

CRIMINAL LAW—Practice.

Traffic Act, 1961, as amended. The charges were contained in four summonses, dated eight months later than the date on which the offences were alleged to have occurred. During the hearing of the charges in the District Court, evidence was adduced to show that the original complaint had been made within the six month period, and summonses had issued on foot thereof. The summonses were produced to the court, and were found to be dated within the six month period, and to have been signed by the peace commissioner who had received the complaint. This was not the same peace commissioner who had signed the later summonses. The District Justice dismissed the charge against the respondent on the ground that a second complaint had been made to a different peace commissioner, outside the statutory period, and that it was the basis of the charges. The District Justice then stated a case for the High Court, at the request of the appellant, as to whether his determination was correct in law. **Held** by Gannon J. in finding that the District Justice was wrong in law in dismissing the charges, 1, a summons is a notification that a complaint has been made to an authorised person, and is itself merely a process by which an accused person is compelled to attend court. *Director of Public Prosecutions* v. *Gill* [1980] I.R. 263 followed. 2. A complaint relating to the offences with which the respondent was charged had been made to an authorised person within the statutory period and there had been no evidence before the District Court upon which it could be held that the charges against the respondent related to a new complaint made outside the statutory period. *Director of Public Prosecutions* v. *Sheeran*

(H.C.) [1986] ILRM 579

42. —— **Complaint** — *Time limit — Summary jurisdiction — Summons — Issue — Whether complaint made within statutory period — Whether evidence before court as to valid issue of summons — Nature of summons — Petty Sessions (Ireland) Act,* 1851 (*c.* 93), *s.* 10(4).] The prosecutor was charged with dangerous driving and also an offence contrary to the Road Traffic Act, 1961, on 28 January, 1984, at Miltverton, Skerries, County Dublin. He was served with two summonses requiring his attendance in the District Court for summary trial. The first summons related to the charge of dangerous driving, was dated 17 October, 1984, and was issued by S. Ó Braonáin, a District Justice clerk. The second summons related to the alleged offence contrary to s. 49 of the Road Traffic Act, 1961, was dated 8 May, 1984, and was issued by Denis O'Neill, a District Court clerk. The respondent on hearing both charges on 22 March, 1985, convicted the

CRIMINAL LAW—*continued.*

prosecutor in respect of each charge. The prosecutor obtained a conditional order of certiorari on the ground that the respondent exceeded his jurisdiction as required by s. 10 (4) of the Petty Sessions (Ireland) Act, 1851, in failing to hear any evidence as to whether the complaint was made within six months of the offence. The prosecutor did not challenge the competency of the persons who issued the summons. **Held** by Gannon J. in allowing the cause shown: although one of the summonses was not issued until 17 October, 1984, the respondent had evidence before him on the day of the trial that on 8 May, 1984 (being a date within six months from 28 January, 1984), the initiating complaint has been made by a garda pursuant to s. 10 (4) of the Petty Sessions (Ireland) Act, 1851. *Director of Public Prosecutions* v. *Sheeran* [1986] ILRM 579 followed. *The State (Gartlan)* v. *O'Donnell*

(H.C.) [1986] ILRM 588

43. —— **Complaint** — *Time limit — Summary jurisdiction — Summons — Issue — District Court — Six months time limit for making of complaint in summary offences — Whether complaint must within six months be brought to attention of person authorised to receive it — Whether consideration of complaint and issue of summons are administrative acts capable of being delegated — Rules of the District Court,* 1948 (*S.R. & O. No.* 431 *of* 1947), *s.* 66 — *Petty Sessions (Ireland) Act,* 1851 (*c.* 93), *ss.* 10(4), 21.] The prosecutor garda applied to the Dublin District Court clerk's office for the issue of a summons charging the defendant with an offence under the Road Traffic Acts. The summons which was issued recited on its face that a complaint had been made to the clerk, and purported to be signed by him. On this summons being struck out without prejudice to its being re-entered, due to bad service, a fresh summons was applied for and issued, grounded upon the original complaint but purporting to be signed by a successor to the first District Court clerk. The face of this summons had been altered so that it did not recite that a complaint had been made to the issuing clerk. The respondent District Justice held that this summons was bad on its face and dismissed it, on the ground that it was not issued by the person to whom the complaint was made. The prosecutor obtained conditional orders of certiorari and mandamus quashing the respondent's order and commanding her to hear and determine the complaint. The defendant was made a notice party to the action and, at the hearing, challenged the validity of the summons on the additional ground that, owing to the manner in which the office of the Dublin District Court clerk was organised, no summons issuing therefrom could be shown to have been considered and signed by the clerk

CRIMINAL LAW—Practice.

himself, rather than by some member of his staff whom he had authorised to affix his signature to summonses. On the motion to make absolute the conditional orders of certiorari and mandamus, notwithstanding cause shown, it was **Held** by Barron J., in allowing the cause shown and discharging the conditional orders, 1, that if a complaint has been validly made and it becomes necessary to issue a fresh summons through inability to proceed on foot of the first summons, it is not necessary that the fresh summons be issued by the person to whom the complaint was made. *D.P.P.* v. *Gill* [1980] I.R. 263 considered. 2. That it is not necessary to recite on the face of a summons that a complaint was made to the person signing the summons, or to any person lawfully entitled to receive it. *Minister for Agriculture* v. *Norgro* [1980] I.R. 155 considered. 3. That the question whether delay in the issue of a summons would prejudice the defendant in the presentation of his defence is one to be considered by the District Justice hearing the matter, and not by the person issuing the summons. 4. That, where a summons is dismissed without prejudice to the complaint being again made, the prosecution may be brought again, by the complainant applying for the issue of a fresh summons grounded upon the original complaint. 5. That an order of dismiss without prejudice may in appropriate cases be quashed on certiorari notwithstanding that the matter could in any event be re-entered in the District Court. *R. (Bridges and Ram)* v. *Armagh Justices* [1897] 2 I.R. 236 approved. 6. That, if it cannot be shown that a District Court clerk (or other authorised person) has personally considered a complaint made to him, any summons which may subsequently be issued on foot of such complaint is invalid and the jurisdiction of the District Court cannot become exercisable. *D.P.P.* v. *McQuaid* (Unreported, High Court, Murphy J., 26 October, 1984) approved. 7. That, for a complaint to be validly made, it must, within six months of the date of the cause of complaint, come to the attention of a person authorised to receive it; it is not sufficient that the complaint be delivered to his office within that period. *Hill* v. *Anderton* [1982] 2 All E.R. 963 not followed. *Attorney General (McDonnell)* v. *Higgins* [1964] I.R. 374 considered. On appeal by the prosecutor from the judgment and order of the High Court it was **Held** by the Supreme Court (Finlay C.J., Walsh, Griffin, Hederman and McCarthy JJ.) in dismissing the appeal and affirming the judgment of Barron J., 1, that for a complaint to be validly made, it must, within six months of the date of the cause of complaint, come to the attention of a person authorised to receive it and to issue a summons in respect thereof. 2. That the issue of a summons on foot of a complaint is a judicial

CRIMINAL LAW—*continued.*

act, as distinct from an administrative act capable of being lawfully delegated. *Quaere* whether the power given to District Court clerks to receive and consider complaints and to issue summonses was an unconstitutional administration of justice in a criminal matter by a non-judicial body. *The State (Clarke)* v. *Roche*
(H.C., S.C.) [1986] I.R.619; [1987] ILRM 309; [1986] ILRM 565

44. —— **Complaint** — *Time limit — Summary jurisdiction — Summons — Issue — Complaint made to District Court clerk within six months of alleged offence — Summons issued by District Justice outside six months — Whether complaint validly made — Whether District Court clerk entitled to receive complaint — District Court Rules,* 1948 (*S.R. & O. No.* 431 *of* 1947), *rr.* 29, 30 — *Petty Sessions (Ireland) Act,* 1851 (*c.* 93), *s.* 10 — *Courts of Justice Act,* 1924 (*No.* 10), *s.* 91.

Practice and Procedure — District Court — District Court Rules Committee — Power to make rules including "the adaptation or modification of any statute" — Statute authorising district justice to receive complaint and issue summons — Rule of court permitting District Court clerk to receive complaint and issue summons — Whether rule validly made — Whether power to receive complaint and issue summons — District Court Rules, 1948 (*S.R. & O. No.* 431 *of* 1947), *rr.* 29, 30 — *Petty Sessions (Ireland) Act,* 1851 (*c.* 93), *s.* 10 — *Courts of Justice Act,* 1924 (*No.* 10), *s.* 91 — *Court Officers Act,* 1926 (*No.* 27), *s.* 48 — *Courts of Justice Act,* 1936 (*No.* 48), *s.* 71.] Section 10 of the Petty Sessions (Ireland) Act, 1851, provides *inter alia* that: "Whenever Information shall be given to any Justice that any Person has committed or is suspected to have committed any . . . Offence, within the Limits of the Jurisdiction of such Justice, . . . it shall be lawful for such Justice to receive such Information or Complaint, and to proceed in respect of the same, subject to the following Provisions: 4. In all Cases of Summary Jurisdiction the Complaint shall be made . . . within Six Months from the Time when the Cause of Complaint shall have arisen . . ." Section 91 of the Courts of Justice Act, 1924, provides that the District Court Rules Committee "may . . . make . . . District Court Rules . . . for . . . the practice and procedure of the District Court generally . . . including . . . the adaptation or modification of any statute that may be necessary for any of the purposes aforesaid and all subsidiary matters." Rules 29 and 30 of the District Court Rules, 1948, provide *inter alia* that: "29. When it is intended that a summons . . . only shall be issued to require the attendance before the court of a person against whom a complaint is made, the complaint may

CRIMINAL LAW—Practice.

be made to a Justice, a Peace Commissioner or a Clerk . . . 30. In all cases of summary jurisdiction — (1)(*c*) a Clerk may issue a summons (i) in cases where a defendant is charged with an offence, if the offence is stated to have been committed or the defendant resides within the limits of the Court Area . . . for which he acts as Clerk." On the 22 September, 1986, a District Court clerk received a complaint from a Garda O'D. alleging that the applicant had, on the 19 May, 1986, committed an offence contrary to s. 49 of the Road Traffic Act, 1961. The District Court clerk considered that complaint and decided to issue a summons, which he purported to do, but that summons was not served on the applicant. On the 4 February, 1987, the respondent District Justice issued a further summons in respect of the same alleged offence. The applicant applied for an order of prohibition by way of judicial review of the prosecution on the grounds that no valid complaint had been made to and received by a person entitled to do so within six months of the alleged offence. It was argued on behalf of the respondent in opposition to the application, that the complaint which had been made to the District Court clerk had been validly made within the prescribed time. **Held** by Barr J., in refusing the application, 1, that while a decision by a District Court clerk to act on a complaint by issuing a summons on foot of it was a judicial act, the mere receipt of a complaint was not. *The State (Clarke)* v. *District Justice Roche* [1986] I.R. 619 considered. 2. That the complaint, upon which the summons which had been served on the applicant was based, had been duly made within the period specified by the Act of 1851 to a person entitled to receive it. *Director of Public Prosecutions* v. *Gill* [1980] I.R. 263 considered. On appeal by the applicant it was **Held** by the Supreme Court (Finlay C.J., Walsh, Griffin, Hederman and McCarthy JJ.), in allowing the appeal and in prohibiting the further prosecution of the applicant, 1, that rr. 29 and 30 of the District Court Rules, 1948, in purporting to confer on a District Court clerk the power of receiving a complaint and deciding whether or not to issue a summons on foot of it which theretofore had been confined by statute to a District Justice, went far beyond the adaptation or modification of a statute authorised by s. 91 of the Courts of Justice Act, 1924. *The State (O'Flaherty)* v. *O'Floinn* [1954] I.R. 295 applied. 2. That the power conferred on a District Court clerk by r. 29 of the Rules of 1948 to receive a complaint would be meaningless apart from the power conferred by r. 30 to decide whether or not to issue a summons and, accordingly, was not severable. *The State (Clarke)* v. *District Justice Roche* [1986] I.R. 619 considered. 3. That rr. 29 and 30 of the Rules of 1948 in so

CRIMINAL LAW—*continued.*

far as they are purported to grant to a District Court clerk power to receive a complaint or to issue a summons were *ultra vires* the District Court Rules Committee and were invalid. 4. That no valid complaint had been made with regard to the alleged offence within the statutory limitation period and, accordingly, that the proceedings against the applicant were barred. *Rainey* v. *Delap*
(H.C., S.C.) [1988] I.R.470 ; [1988] ILRM 620

45. —— **Complaint** — *Warrants — Complaints made to justice and warrants issued — Complaints placed before another justice and fresh warrants issued — Whether complaints made to other justice — Whether fresh warrants valid — Magistrates' Courts (Northern Ireland) Order,* 1981 (*S.I. No.* 1675, *N.I.* 26), *art.* 20.] In May, 1983, 15 warrants for the arrest of the applicant were issued in respect of complaints made to a justice of the peace. The warrants were issued for the purpose of obtaining the extradition of the applicant from the Republic of Ireland. In February, 1984, the police officer who made the complaints went to another justice of the peace for the purpose of obtaining fresh warrants and placed before him the original complaints. The justice of the peace then considered the complaints, without signing them or being asked to sign them, and then signed and issued new warrants. On an application for judicial review for an order of certiorari to quash the fresh warrants, **Held,** granting the relief sought, that complaints must be in writing and substantiated on oath and that the police officer had not proved that he made complaints when he placed the original complaints before the second justice. *In re Burns*
(Q.B.D.) [1985] N.I. 279

46. —— **Complaint** — *Withdrawal — Power of D.P.P. — Common informer — Summary trial in District Court — Complaint made by policeman as common informer — Defendant not represented — Fair procedures — Ministers and Secretaries Act,* 1924 (*No.* 16), *s.* 6 — *Criminal Justice (Administration) Act,* 1924 (*No.* 44), *s.* 9 — *Prosecution of Offences Act,* 1974 (*No.* 22), *s.* 3 — *Constitution of Ireland,* 1937, *Arts.* 30, 40.] The prosecutor, Collins, was charged, as defendant, in the District Court on a complaint that he had committed a summary offence. The complaint had been made by a policeman acting on his own as a common informer. The hearing of the complaint, at which the prosecutor was represented by solicitor and counsel, was adjourned. At the resumed hearing of the complaint, the Director of Public Prosecutions sought leave to withdraw the complaint but his

CRIMINAL LAW—Practice.

application was refused by the respondent District Justice. The prosecutor's solicitor and counsel, anticipating that the complaint would be withdrawn, failed to attend the court at the resumed hearing of the complaint. Being confronted with that situation, the prosecutor failed to seek an adjournment and undertook his own defence; he was convicted of the offence. The prosecutor obtained in the High Court a conditional order of certiorari quashing his conviction, unless cause were shown to the contrary. Cause was shown by the complainant policeman and the prosecutor then applied for an order absolute, notwithstanding the cause shown. **Held** by Gannon J., in allowing the cause shown and discharging the conditional order, 1, that the Director of Public Prosecutions had no power to compel the withdrawal of a complaint charging a defendant with the commission of a summary offence when that complaint had been made by a common informer and was being duly prosecuted in accordance with the law. *The People* v. *Roddy* [1977] I.R. 177; *Wedick* v. *Osmond & Son* [1935] I.R. 820 and *The State (Cronin)* v. *Circuit Court Judge of the Western Circuit* [1937] I.R. 34 considered. 2. That, as the prosecutor had not sought an adjournment of the hearing of the complaint, the District Justice had acted correctly in proceeding with the determination of the complaint. On appeal by the prosecutor it was **Held** by the Supreme Court (O'Higgins C.J., Walsh, Henchy, Griffin and McCarthy JJ.), in allowing the appeal, 1, that the Director of Public Prosecutions had no power to compel the withdrawal of the complaint made by the common informer. 2. That, in the circumstances confronting the defendant at the resumed hearing of the complaint, the District Justice had acted in excess of jurisdiction in proceeding with the determination of the complaint without giving the defendant an opportunity to be represented by his legal advisers. 3. That the defendant had been justified in bringing certiorari proceedings instead of appealing to the Circuit Court against his conviction. *The State (Collins)* v. *Ruane*.
(H.C., S.C.) [1984] I.R.105; [1985] ILRM 349; [1984] ILRM 443

47. —— **Disclosure of information to defence** — *Statements by accused to police* — Voir dire — *Attorney General's guidelines — Whether Crown should furnish statements to defence — Accused an informer — Whether Crown under a duty to inform court at outset of trial.*] The accused was charged with a number of serious terrorist offences. The accused, on a *voir dire*, gave evidence in support of his application that the court should exercise its discretion to exclude from evidence, oral and written statements made by

CRIMINAL LAW—*continued.*

him after his arrest implicating him in the numerous serious offences with which he was charged. In the course of the *voir dire* the accused gave evidence that he had been acting as a police informer having given information regarding the criminal activities of other persons. The accused stated that the reason he had made the admissions was because he had accepted an offer made to him by a police officer that if he turned Queen's evidence he would get a good deal. The accused contended he was entitled to see all the documents held by the Crown or the police containing details of meetings between the accused and police officers and of information which the accused furnished at the meetings. The accused submitted that it was relevant to the case being made on the *voir dire* that he had been a police informer that any document which related to such information was relevant and therefore the defence was entitled to see such documents. The accused further submitted that although the defence was aware before the trial that the accused acted as a police informer prior to his arrest, the Crown was under a duty to inform the court at the commencement of the trial that the accused had acted as a police informer and the defendant had been seriously prejudiced by the failure of the Crown to carry out this duty and therefore the trial judge should discharge himself from the further conduct of the trial. **Held,** refusing the applications that, 1, there was no rule of law that the defence in a criminal case has the right prior to the trial, to see documents in the possession of the Crown or the police, which were relevant to issues which might arise in the trial and especially in relation to issues which may arise on the *voir dire* as to the admissibility of a statement. 2. In accordance with the principle in *R.* v. *Foxford* [1974] N.I. 188 the procedure whereby the defence became aware of information in the possession of the Crown, relevant to an issue in the trial, is that either the Crown itself will call a witness who will give the information in the course of his evidence, subject to the point that the Crown ought to offer the statement to the defence if the statement is materially at variance with the maker's evidence in court, or the Crown will make that person available to the defence as a witness. 3. The trial judge had a discretion to direct the Crown to furnish the documents to the accused and in exercising this discretion should have regard to the Attorney-General's guidelines on *Disclosure of Information to the Defence in Cases to be Tried on Indictment* 74 Crim. App. R. 302. Documents which would have a bearing on issues arising on a *voir dire* were probably not within the contemplation of those who prepared the guidelines but once the issues in the *voir dire* became clear in the course of the trial it was appropriate

CRIMINAL LAW—Practice.

to apply the guidelines by way of an analogy to the *voir dire*. 4. At the end of the accused's evidence in chief, the Crown should furnish details of the information given to the police by the accused of his own involvement in criminal activities and furnish an edited version of the information given by him about the criminal activities of other persons. It was desirable that the court should supervise the editing. It was not appropriate for the Crown to furnish such documents to the defence until the accused had completed his evidence in chief on the *voir dire* as the accused might tailor his evidence in chief to conform with the information contained in the documents. 5. The defence knew before the commencement of the trial that the accused was a police informer. There was no obligation on the Crown to inform the court at the commencement of the trial that the accused had been a police informer as in the present case there was no attempt to conceal the information from the court as it was quite clear to both the prosecution and defence at some stage in the trial this fact would emerge, as it had. The defence had not been prejudiced and there was no reason for the trial judge to discharge himself. *R.* v. *McAllister*

(Crown Ct.) [1985] N.I. 407

48. —— **Emergency powers legislation** — *Procedure — Accused charged in Garda station — Whether lawful to charge accused otherwise than in District Court or Special Court — Emergency Powers Act,* 1976 (*No.* 33), *s.* 2.] This is an application to have a conditional order of certiorari made absolute. The prosecutor was arrested pursuant to s. 2 of the Emergency Powers Act,1976, and held in custody for more than 48 hours before being charged at a Garda station with three offences including one of possession of firearms. He was then immediately brought to the District Court but he was not recharged. After a number of remands the District Justice returned him for trial. The Emergency Powers Act,1976, provides for special and stringent powers of arrest and detention for persons suspected of offences against the Offences Against the State Act, 1939, or scheduled offences. S. 2 (4) of the Act provides that: 'a person in custody under sub-section 3 of this section may at any time during such custody be charged before the District Court or a Special Court established under Article 38.3.10 with an offence or be released by direction of a member of the Garda Síochána not below the rank of superintendent and shall if not so charged or released be released at the expiration of the custody.' **Held** by Finlay P. in making absolute the conditional order, 1, it is not lawful to charge a person who has been arrested pursuant to the provisions of s. 2 of the Emergency Powers Act,

CRIMINAL LAW—*continued.*

1976, otherwise than in the District Court or in a Special Court. 2. He must be validly and lawfully charged with an indictable offence before the District Justice can conduct a preliminary examination. *A.G.* v. *Burke* and *State (A.G.)* v. *Judge Fawsitt* [1955] I.R. 30 distinguished. *The State (Brennan)* v. *Mahon*

(H.C.) [1978] ILRM 17

49. —— **Extra-territorial offence** — *Irish citizen in custody in Northern Ireland — Application to Garda Superintendent to seek a warrant — Prosecutor seeking to be delivered into the custody of the Garda Síochána — Director of Public Prosecutions indicating that proceedings would not be instituted in this jurisdiction — Garda Superintendent declining to seek a warrant — Application for orders of certiorari and mandamus — Whether decision of Garda Superintendent reviewable — Role of D.P.P. — Whether D.P.P.'s decision reviewable — Whether* prima facie *case of* mala fides *made out — Whether prosecutor deprived of his constitutional rights of access to the courts of this jurisdiction.*] The Criminal Law (Jurisdiction) Act, 1976, provides that where a person has been charged with an extra-territorial offence in Northern Ireland, he may elect to be tried in the Republic, provided that a judge of the High Court of Northern Ireland, or the court of trial, is satisfied that a warrant for the arrest of the accused man has been issued in the Republic for a corresponding offence, based on an information laid by a member of the Garda Síochána. The prosecutor had been returned for trial in the Crown Court at Belfast, charged with an extra-territorial offence within the meaning of the 1976 Act. The acts of which he was accused constituted offences under Irish law also, and rendered him liable to arrest, charge and trial within this jurisdiction. The prosecutor wished to opt for trial within the Republic, and accordingly, he requested the respondents to issue a warrant for his arrest. The second-named respondent decided not to issue a warrant, and the prosecutor obtained conditional orders of certiorari and mandamus in the High Court in Dublin. **Held** by Barr J. in allowing the cause shown by the respondents, and in discharging the conditional orders, 1, the function of the Director of Public Prosecutions in deciding whether or not to prosecute an individual for the alleged commission of a criminal offence is an executive one, and it is not reviewable by the courts, as this would interfere with his independence. *Savage and McOwen* v. *Director of Public Prosecutions* [1982] ILRM 385 applied. 2. The fact that the laws of evidence relating to the admissibility of confessions made while in police

custody differ substantially in the two Irish jurisdictions, obliges the Director to make an independent assessment as to whether or not an individual should be prosecuted in this jurisdiction. 3. The extent of the right of an accused charged with an extra-territorial offence in Northern Ireland to be tried in this jurisdiction is an option exercisable only where the Director of Public Prosecutions has caused a warrant to be issued for his arrest for a corresponding offence under Irish law, and where the Director has decided against the issue of such a warrant, the exercise of the option by an accused does not arise. 4. It would be contrary to public policy to interpret the constitutional right of an accused to trial in due course of law as including a right to compel the Director of Public Prosecutions to bring him to trial in the Republic, or cause his arrest within the Republic on any charge. **Held** by the Supreme Court (Finlay C.J., Walsh, Henchy, Griffin and Hederman JJ.) in dismissing the appeal, 1, members of the Garda are completely independent of the Director of Public Prosecutions in the exercise of their duty. *The State (Collins)* v. *Ruane* [1985] ILRM 349, followed. 2. In the instant case, the evidence before the court indicated only that the first-named respondent consulted with the Director of Public Prosecutions before deciding not to proceed, and not that he had abdicated his discretion in this regard. 3. The decisions of the Director of Public Prosecutions can in certain circumstances be reviewed by the courts. In the instant case, the evidence did not exclude the possibility of a proper and valid decision by the Director, which was not reviewable by the court. *Per* Walsh J.: The actions of the Director of Public Prosecutions cannot properly be the subject of certiorari. A failure on the D.P.P.'s part to perform a statutory duty could be the subject of mandamus. 4. The constitutional right of access to the courts is a right to initiate litigation, not a right to compel suit or prosecution. 5. The statutory right of an individual to select the jurisdiction for his trial does not arise until a warrant for his arrest has been issued by the appropriate authority in this State. *The State (McCormack)* v. *Curran*

(H.C., S.C.) [1987] ILRM 225

50. —— **Legal aid** — *Right of poor person charged with serious offence to free legal aid — Whether accused entitled to nominate solicitor from panel — Procedure to be followed by court in assigning solicitor — Duty of court to hear and consider representations of accused — Duty of court to enquire why a particular solicitor sought.*

Constitution — Personal rights — Legal aid — Right of poor person charged with serious offence to free legal aid — Fair procedures — Trial in

due course of law — Statutory implementation of constitutional right — Criminal Justice (Legal Aid) Regulations, 1965 (*S.I. No.* 12), *reg.* 7(1) — *Criminal Justice (Legal Aid) Act,* 1962 (*No.* 12), *s.* 2 — *Constitution of Ireland,* 1937, Art. 40.] The prosecutor, an unemployed 20 year old who had left school at the age of 15 years and who had no formal or technical qualifications, appeared before the first respondent charged with two offences each of which carried possible sentences of imprisonment. The prosecutor sought legal aid and asked that S., a solicitor on the legal aid panel, be assigned to represent him. The respondent, however, refused to assign S. and adjourned the charges. At the adjourned hearing the prosecutor renewed his application for legal aid. The respondent, having enquired into the prosecutor's circumstances, agreed to grant legal aid and intimated his intention to assign a solicitor alphabetically from the legal aid panel. The prosecutor again asked for S. The respondent enquired whether S. was representing the prosecutor on any other charges and was told that he was not. No further representations were made by the prosecutor and the respondent made no further enquiries. The prosecutor was not willing to accept a solicitor assigned in accordance with the respondent's practice so no solicitor was assigned to him. The prosecutor obtained a conditional order of prohibition prohibiting the second respondent from hearing the charges against him until he should be granted legal aid, on the grounds that the first respondent had failed to comply with the Criminal Justice (Legal Aid) Regulations, 1965, and with the constitutional guarantee of fair procedures and trial in due course of law, in failing to consider any representations made by the prosecutor and by refusing to assign to him the solicitor of his choice. It was argued on behalf of the respondent, in showing cause, that the respondent had acted within his jurisdiction and discretion and that the respondent's practice in assigning solicitors alphabetically was necessary for the proper and orderly conduct of the business of his court. The prosecutor moved to have the conditional order made absolute notwithstanding cause shown. **Held** by Barr J., in disallowing the cause shown and making absolute the conditional order of prohibition, 1, that reg. 7(1) of the Criminal Justice (Legal Aid) Regulations, 1965, requires that a court, which was granted a certificate for free legal aid pursuant to s. 2 of the Criminal Justice (Legal Aid) Act, 1962, should, before assigning a solicitor, hear any representations which the accused wishes to make as to which solicitor he wishes to represent him. 2. That, having regard to the constitutional rights of the accused and the spirit and intention of the Act of 1962, a meaningful operation of the

CRIMINAL LAW—Practice.

Regulations of 1965 required that if the court had any reservations about the assignment of the solicitor nominated by the accused it should consider any reasons put forward by him, and if necessary enquire of the applicant, as to why he wished to have a particular solicitor represent him. *The State (Healy)* v. *Donoghue* [1976] I.R. 325 and *The State (Royle)* v. *Kelly* [1974] I.R. 259 considered. 3. That the court should be very slow to refuse to assign the applicant's choice of solicitor and should do so only if there is good and sufficient reason. 4. That where the court, having considered the representations of the applicant, is satisfied that there is a compelling reason for refusing to assign the solicitor of the applicant's choice, it should state that reason and enquire whether the applicant wishes to nominate another solicitor. 5. That the court should choose a solicitor for the applicant only where he has not nominated one himself or where any nominated by him are unable to accept the nomination or are unacceptable to the court for good and sufficient reason. 6. That, in the instant case, the respondent should have enquired of the applicant as to why he wanted the services of a particular solicitor and should, at the very least, have considered those reasons before assigning a solicitor to act for him. *Per curiam.* A judge has the right, subject to the law and the principles of natural justice, to organise and conduct the business of his court in such a way as he deems most conducive to the efficient administration of justice. *Per curiam.* It is undesirable in cases of judicial review for persons exercising judicial functions to rely on affidavits made by themselves as this exposes them to the risk of being cross examined. It would be more judicious if the affidavit were made by the court clerk or registrar. *The State (Freeman)* v. *Connellan*
(H.C.) [1986] I.R.433 ; [1987] ILRM 470

51. —— **Legal aid** — *Whether essential in the interests of justice — Exceptional circumstances — Whether onus on defendant to establish existence of exceptional circumstances — Whether defendant to be informed by District Justice of right to legal aid — Whether defendant to be invited to put forward exceptional circumstances — Criminal Justice (Legal Aid) Act,* 1962 (*No.* 12), *s.* 2.

Practice — Case stated — Interpretation of statutory provisions — Whether reference must be on basis of particular circumstances arising.

Words and phrases — "Exceptional circumstances" — "Gravity of the charge" — Criminal Justice (Legal Aid) Act, 1962 (*No.* 12), *s.* 2.] Pursuant to s. 52(1) of the Courts (Supplemental Provisions) Act, 1961, three cases were referred to the High Court by way of cases stated. The cases were stated prior to the District Justice

CRIMINAL LAW—*continued.*

hearing any evidence in the proceedings and they contained no findings of fact in relation to any offences charged. The issues in the cases related to the manner in which the District Justice should exercise the power of granting or refusing legal aid certificates under s. 2 of the Criminal Justice (Legal Aid) Act, 1962, which provided that such certificates be granted where it appears that by 'reason of the gravity of the charge or of exceptional circumstances it is essential in the interests of justice' that the defendant be granted legal aid. **Held** by McMahon J. in answering the questions, 1, the District Justice, on making a reference on the meaning of statutory expressions, must make the said reference on the basis of the particular facts arising in the proceedings before him. 2. In determining whether the defendant should receive legal aid the onus of establishing the exceptional circumstances necessary under s. 2 of the Criminal Justice (Legal Aid) Act, 1962, is not upon the defendant. 3. Where upon facts alleged by the prosecution a District Justice might consider a sentence of imprisonment appropriate, it is not open to him to treat the offence as a minor one. 4. The defendant should be informed of his right to obtain legal aid by the District Justice where it appears to the District Justice that his means are sufficient to enable him to obtain legal aid. *O'Neill* v. *Butler*
(H.C.) [1979] ILRM 243

52. —— **Penalty** — *Excise offence — Mandatory penalty on conviction — Power to mitigate penalty incurred in excise cases — General power of court in criminal cases to take other offences into consideration in awarding punishment — Whether court has discretion as to size of fine in excise cases — Whether court may take other offences into consideration in imposing penalty in excise cases — Betting Duty (Certified Returns) Regulations,* 1934 (*S.R. & O. No.* 113 *of* 1934), *regs.* 15 *and* 18 — *Excise Management Act,* 1827 (*c.* 53), *s.* 78 — *Finance Act,* 1926 (*No.* 35), *s.* 25(1), (2) — *Criminal Justice Act,* 1951 (*No.* 2), *s.* 8 — *Finance Act,* 1982 (*No.* 14), *ss.* 69(1)(*b*), 70.] Section 8 of the Criminal Justice Act, 1951, provides that where a person, on being convicted of an offence, admits himself guilty of any other offence and asks to have it taken into consideration in awarding punishment, the court may take such other offence into consideration accordingly. A note of that fact shall then be made and the accused person shall not subsequently be prosecuted for that offence. The respondent, a bookmaker, was charged with 18 breaches of the Betting Duty (Certified Returns) Regulations, 1934. The offences each carried a mandatory excise penalty of £800, but the court could mitigate such penalty to a sum not less than £400, pursuant to s. 78 of the Excise Management

CRIMINAL LAW—Practice.

Act, 1827, as amended. When these charges came on for hearing before the District Court the respondent submitted that it was open to the court to convict him of one offence and, in imposing the penalty, to take into consideration his admissions of guilt to the other charges. On behalf of the appellant it was submitted to the District Court that, upon conviction of a person charged with an excise offence, the court had no discretion as to the imposition of a penalty, or as to the size of such penalty; there was merely a power to direct a mitigation of the penalty once it had been imposed. The appellant further submitted that since the imposition of the specified penalty was mandatory, the court could not purport to take any matters into consideration in awarding such punishment and, consequently, the provisions of s. 8 of the Act of 1951 could not apply. The District Justice held that the Act of 1951 was applicable to the proceedings and accordingly fined the respondent the sum of £800, in relation to the charge on which he had originally pleaded guilty, and noted the other offences as taken into consideration. At the request of the appellant the District Justice stated a case for the opinion of the High Court as to whether he was correct in point of law so to decide. On appeal to the Supreme Court from the decision of the High Court that the District Justice had been correct in point of law, it was **Held** by the Supreme Court (Finlay C.J., Henchy, Griffin and Hederman JJ.; McCarthy J. dissenting) in allowing the appeal, 1, (per Finlay C.J.; Hederman and Griffin JJ. concurring) that s. 8 of the Criminal Justice Act, 1951, is only applicable to an award of punishment in respect of an offence where the court can genuinely and *bona fide* take into consideration an admission of guilt to other offences in deciding what level of punishment to award. 2. (*Per* Finlay C.J.; Hederman and Griffin JJ. concurring) That where a court has no discretion with regard to the imposition of a mandatory penalty, as was here the case, an accused person's admission of guilt to other offences could not be taken into consideration. *Per* Henchy J., that excise penalties are in reality a form of penal taxation for the benefit of the Exchequer and, as special provisions of the customs and excise code, the procedures for their imposition and mitigation are unaffected by subsequent statutory provisions of general application, such as s. 8 of the Criminal Justice Act, 1951. *R.* v. *Poor Law Commissioners* (1838) 6 Ad. & El. 56; *Westham (Churchwardens, etc.)* v. *Fourth City Mutual Building Society* [1892] 1 Q.B. 654 and *The Vera Cruz* (1884) 10 App. Cas. 59 approved. *Per* McCarthy J., dissenting — that s. 8 of the Act of 1951 is, on its face, unrestricted in its application and the fact that excise offences are not

CRIMINAL LAW—*continued.*

expressly excluded from its operation indicates that the Act was intended to apply to such offences. *Director of Public Prosecutions* v. *Grey* **(S.C.) [1986] I.R.317; [1987] ILRM 4**

53. —— **Plea** — Autrefois acquit — *Whether the quashing of an order amounts to an acquittal — Grounds for granting an order of certiorari — Distinction between a proceeding commenced without jurisdiction and one validly commenced during which jurisdiction is exceeded.*] The prosecutor had appealed to the respondent's court from a District Court conviction for refusal to furnish a sample of blood or urine to a registered medical practitioner. The respondent had affirmed the conviction despite a submission by the prosecutor's counsel that the State had omitted an essential element of the case, the proof that its doctor was a registered medical practitioner. Subsequently, in certiorari proceedings, the submission made on the prosecutor's behalf was upheld. The State, however, on the view that a District Court conviction subsisted, sought to re-enter the appeal that had first brought the matter into the respondent's court. On 10 April, 1984, the respondent ruled that the appeal was properly before him, but gave the prosecutor leave to seek an order of prohibition in the High Court. On 19 September, 1984, Lynch J. granted the prosecutor a conditional order of prohibition on the grounds that he had previously been acquitted and that a re-entry of the appeal, after considerable lapse of time and the suffering of a period of disqualification from driving, would be in breach of natural justice. The State showed cause against the making of the conditional order, and the matter came back to Lynch J. upon motion to make the conditional order absolute. **Held** by Lynch J., allowing the cause shown in part, but granting an absolute order of prohibition, 1, the prosecutor was entitled to enter a plea of *autrefois acquit* at the second hearing of his appeal in the Circuit Court; the respondent would accordingly be prohibited from entertaining the appeal save for the purpose of making an order reversing the District Court conviction. 2. An order of certiorari may issue in two types of case: where there has been a want of jurisdiction, and where lawful jurisdiction has been vitiated by a fundamental error; only in the second type of case has an accused person lawfully been in peril, and only here is a plea of *autrefois acquit* permissible; the instant case was within the second category, in that the respondent had not lacked jurisdiction but had erred in admitting evidence; and the prosecutor's contention that a renewed trial of his appeal involved a breach of natural justice could not be upheld: lapse of time, occasioned by the litigation, did

CRIMINAL LAW—Practice.

not bar the rights of the parties. *The State (Keeney)* v. *O'Malley*

(H.C.) [1986] ILRM 31

54. —— **Preliminary examination** — *Cross-examination — District Justice not permitting cross-examination of witness — Prosecutor sent forward for trial — Whether denial of fair procedures — Criminal Procedure Act,* 1967 (*No.* 12), *ss.* 5, 6, 7, 8, 12, 14, 15.] The prosecutor, Sherry, was the defendant in a rape trial. At the preliminary hearing in the District Court held under the Criminal Procedure Act, 1967, the prosecutor's solicitor demanded the attendance of the woman allegedly raped so that he might examine her by way of sworn deposition pursuant to s. 7(2) of the Act. The respondent District Justice directed the solicitor to confine his questioning of the woman to direct evidence, on the ground that he represented the party calling for the attendance of the witness. The solicitor asserted that he was entitled to cross-examine the witness, and his client sought an order of certiorari on this basis. A conditional order granted by Gannon J. was, after cause shown, discharged by O'Hanlon J. From the latter's ruling the prosecutor appealed to the Supreme Court. **Held** by McCarthy J. affirming the decision of O'Hanlon J.: that justice did not require an accused person to have a right of cross-examination at the preliminary stage unless the deposition was being made at the instance of the prosecution itself. *The State (Sherry)* v. *Wine*

(S.C.) [1985] ILRM 196

55. —— **Preliminary examination** — *Depositions — Use of statements from Book of Evidence — Identification of accused — Additional witnesses — Refusal of adjournment — Extent of review on certiorari — Criminal Procedure Act,* 1967 (*No.* 12), *ss.* 6, 7.] The prosecutor applied for certiorari to quash the respondent's order sending him forward for trial. The prosecutor objected to a number of matters arising on the preliminary examination, including the putting to witnesses of the statement of evidence in the Book of Evidence rather than their original statements; that objections made were not noted by the respondent; that the witnesses should not have been asked to identify any person in court; that original exhibits were not examined by the respondent; that an adjournment to hear additional witnesses should have been allowed; that the copy of the sworn information served on the prosecutor did not contain the signature of the Justice before whom it was sworn; and that there was no evidence to support the authority of the superintendent who endorsed the warrant for arrest. **Held** by O'Hanlon J. refusing the relief sought, 1, certiorari should not be used as a

CRIMINAL LAW—*continued.*

method of appealing decisions of inferior courts to the High Court, and should only be granted where the inferior court or tribunal acted without, or in excess of, jurisdiction or in disregard of fair procedures; and in the case of an order sending an accused person forward for trial the court would be reluctant to extend the existing categories for grounds for relief. *R. (Blakeney)* v. *Roscommon JJ.* [1884] 2 I.R. 158 and *The State (Healy)* v. *Ballagh* (Unreported. High Court, 22 April 1983) approved and applied. 2. There was no obligation to put original statements rather than the statements in the Book of Evidence; the failure to note some objections would not, standing alone, entitle the prosecutor to relief; the respondent acted within jurisdiction in asking witnesses to identify persons in court; there was no absolute obligation on the respondent to examine all exhibits although in some instances such a course might be relevant to the decision whether to send a person forward for trial, but in this instance was not required; the respondent had a discretion to refuse an adjournment to hear additional witnesses and in the circumstances had exercised that discretion within jurisdiction; the failure to comply with s. 6(1) of the 1967 Act in relation to the copy information served on the prosecutor was a technical non-compliance and there was substantial compliance at the very least; and the respondent must be taken to have reached the conclusion that the superintendent who authorised the arrest was duly authorised to do so or that this was not a matter which required to be proved before making the order. *The State (Williams)* v. *Kelleher* [1983] I.R. 112 discussed. *The State (Daly)* v. *Ruane*

(H.C.) [1988] ILRM 117

56. —— **Preliminary examination** — *Exhibits — Whether accused person entitled to inspect exhibits to be produced at trial — Theft of exhibits — Whether accused deprived of right to inspect — Criminal Procedure Act,* 1967 (*No.* 12), *s.* 6(1).

Judicial review — Certiorari — Delay — Technical flaws — Discretion.] The respondent ordered the prosecutor to be sent forward for trial on a charge of receiving certain property, mainly silverware, knowing it to have been stolen. The prosecutor obtained a conditional order of certiorari to quash the order of the respondent contending that there was a failure by the respondent to comply with the requirements of the Criminal Procedure Act, 1967, on the grounds that he was entitled under the Act to be given a list of the exhibits in the case and an opportunity to inspect the exhibits if he so desired. The statement of evidence of a detective garda described the recovery of the stolen goods from the custody of the prosecutor and referred to 'Exhibit 1' and 'Exhibit 2' and stated: 'I have

CRIMINAL LAW—Practice.

retained the plastic bag, pillow slip, items of silverware, scales, gauge and and magnifying glass in my possession and I will produce them in court when required.' In the course of the preliminary inquiry in the District Court it emerged for the first time that the exhibits were no longer available for production or inspection as they had been stolen from Tallaght garda station during a burglary. When the application to make absolute the conditional order came before the court the issue was whether the requirements of the Act of 1967 had been complied with. **Held** by O'Hanlon J. in allowing the cause shown and discharging the conditional order of certiorari: the respondent had complied with the requirements of the Act. The respondent was in a position to make a valid decision under the Act and did so when sending the prosecutor forward for trial. There were no longer exhibits available for production at the trial and once that was made clear and an adequate explanation was given for their disappearance there was no infringement of the right of the prosecutor under the Act to inspect all the exhibits. *Semble:* In an application for certiorari where the prosecutor is outside the normal time limit, such delay may ground the exercise of the court's discretion to refuse relief in respect of technical defects in a preliminary examination. *The State (Pletzer)* v. *Magee*
(H.C.) [1986] ILRM 441

57. —— **Prosecution** — *Delay — Delay in prosecuting charges — Whether such delay excessive — Whether defendant deprived of his right to a fair trial.*] The applicant had been arrested on criminal charges on 11 December, 1984. The case was adjourned several times, and was finally struck out on the 27 March, 1985, as the Book of Evidence was not ready. The arresting officer having sworn a new information in relation to the same alleged offences, he obtained a warrant from the District Court on 16 September, 1985, for the arrest of the applicant. Fearing a repetition of the events of March, 1985, the arresting officer waited until he had received an assurance from the office of the Chief State Solicitor that the Book of Evidence was ready before arresting the applicant. The arrest was finally effected on 13 March, 1986. The applicant was remanded to the District Court on 20 March and 9 April. On the latter date he did not appear. A bench warrant for his arrest was issued, and he was re-arrested on 23 May and brought before the District Court where he was served with the Book of Evidence. On 23 June he was sent forward for trial to the Circuit Criminal Court by the second-named respondent. The applicant sought an order of prohibition directed to the first-named respondent and an order of certiorari directed to the second-named respondent, on the ground

CRIMINAL LAW—*continued.*

that the delay in prosecuting the charges had been so excessive that it amounted to a deprivation of his constitutional right to trial with all due and reasonable expedition. **Held** by Barr J. in refusing the relief sought, 1, in all cases involving delay in criminal proceedings the test must be whether or not it has been shown to be prejudicial to the fair trial of the accused. *The State (O'Connell)* v. *Fawsitt* [1986] ILRM 639, followed. 2. The breach of duty of the arresting officer in not immediately acting upon the arrest warrant did not of itself vitiate the arrest and subsequent prosecution. *Maguire* v. *D.P.P.*
(H.C.) [1988] ILRM 166

58. —— **Prosecution** — *Indictable offence — Director of Public Prosecutions delegating carriage of prosecution to solicitor being whole-time employee of company making criminal complaint against defendant — Whether delegation of power* ultra vires *the director — Whether risk of unfairness inherent in delegation — Prosecution of Offences Act,* 1974 (*No.* 22), *ss.* 4, 7.

Post Office — Employee — Criminal law — Prosecution — Indictable charge against employee of Post Office — Solicitor employed by Post Office having carriage of prosecution — Whether delegation of carriage of case by D.P.P. ultra vires — *Whether likely to create unfairness in procedure — Postal and Telecommunications Services Act,* 1983 (*No.* 24), — *Prosecution of Offences Act,* 1974 (*No.* 22), *ss.* 4, 7.] The plaintiff appellant claimed a series of declarations and an injunction against the defendant arising out of the appointment by the defendant of a solicitor, Mr. S., in the whole-time employment of the Post Office to be the solicitor acting in a prosecution of the plaintiff on indictable charges contrary to the provisions of the Post Office Act, 1908, as amended by the Postal and Telecommunications Services Act, 1983. The plaintiff was a postman in the employment of the Post Office and formerly had been a postman in the employment of the Department of Posts and Telegraphs. He was suspended from his duties without pay by the Post Office and arising out of the incident in question he brought proceedings against the Post Office seeking declarations, *inter alia,* that his suspension was invalid. Those civil proceedings were issued the day before the criminal proceedings were brought against him. The plaintiff was brought before the District Court pursuant to the summons for preliminary examination of the criminal charges against him and a book of evidence was served upon him by the prosecution, while Mr. S. was acting as solicitor in the case. Subsequent to the hearing of this action in the High Court, the plaintiff was returned for trial to the Circuit Criminal Court. The case was tried in the High Court on the pleadings

CRIMINAL LAW—Practice.

and by order of the High Court made by Gannon J. the action was dismissed. The plaintiff appealed to the Supreme Court and argued on two grounds that a mis-trial had occurred in the High Court in the procedures adopted in that court. The other grounds of appeal were substantive issues of law. **Held** by the Supreme Court (Finlay C.J., Henchy, Griffin, Hederman and McCarthy JJ.) in dismissing the appeal, 1, having regard to the legal issues which arose in the case, the refusal by the trial judge at the commencement of the action either to allow the plaintiff to amend his pleadings to include a plea that he had suffered prejudice resulting from the manner in which the prosecution had been conducted or, to allow the plaintiff to give evidence in support of that plea, did not create any injustice or could not have contributed to a wrong decision. The absence from the book of evidence of matter which the plaintiff considered might be favourable to him, was not connected with the question of the appointment of the solicitor to conduct the prosecution and in any event could have been corrected on behalf of the plaintiff in the preliminary investigation procedure in the District Court under the Criminal Procedure Act, 1967. 2. The nomination of the appointment by the defendant of Mr. S., who was not employed in the public service, as the solicitor to conduct a prosecution on an indictable charge was not *ultra vires*. The Director of Public Prosecution, like the Attorney General in the prosecution of offences prior to the Prosecution of Offences Act, 1974, was not confined in his appointment or nomination of a solicitor to conduct a charge on an indictable offence to solicitors employed in the public service. 3. The learned trial judge was correct in holding that there was no possibility of an actual injustice flowing from the decision of the defendant of nominating or appointing Mr. S. as the solicitor for the prosecution. Furthermore, there could not be any reasonable belief on the part of members of the public that the selection of Mr. S. to conduct the proceedings on indictment on the instructions of and as agent for the Director of Public Prosecutions created an injustice. *Flynn* v. *D.P.P.*

(S.C.) [1986] ILRM 290

59. —— **Remand** — *Conviction in District Court — Appeal to Circuit Court — Applicant remanded in custody in accordance with Circuit Court procedure — Judicial review — Whether valid remand — Criminal Procedure Act,* 1967 (*No.* 1), *s.* 24.] The applicant on appeal from a District Court criminal case was remanded in custody from 19 May, 1987, to 17 June, 1987, in accordance with the procedure of the Circuit Court and not the District Court. The applicant

CRIMINAL LAW—*continued.*

sought an order for judicial review on the grounds that his remand had not been a valid remand as it had not been in accordance with the procedure of the District Court by virtue of the provisions of s. 24 of the Criminal Procedure Act, 1967, which provides for periods of remand of the accused in the District Court. **Held** by Carroll J. in refusing to make the order sought, 1, the provisions of the Criminal Procedure Act, 1967, do not apply to the Circuit Court when hearing an appeal against an order of conviction or sentence made in a District Court criminal case. 2. As the procedure of the Circuit Court rather than that of the District Court applies to the Circuit Court when it hears an appeal from the District Court in a criminal case the remand of the applicant in custody had been properly made. *The State (D.P.P.)* v. *Kennedy* Unreported. High Court (Barron J.) 11 July, 1985. *Maguire* v. *O'Hanrahan*

(H.C.) [1988] ILRM 243

Remand *see also* No. 69

60. —— **Return for trial** — *Delay — Misuse of drugs — Return to wrong Circuit Court — Circuit Court having no jurisdiction — Error due to fault of the D.P.P. — Charges hanging over accused for a longer period — Whether a ground for setting aside proceeding — No contention that the accused was hindered in the conduct of his defence — R.S.C.,* 1986, *O.* 84 — *Courts (Supplemental Provisions) Act,* 1961 (*No.* 39), *s.* 25.] The notice party, a resident of County Dublin, was arrested on 14 June, 1986, for offences contrary to the Misuse of Drugs Act, 1977. The alleged offences were committed in County Dublin. On 14 November, 1986, he was returned for trial, in error, to Wicklow Circuit Court. He was arraigned on 10 February, 1987. Subsequently the error in the return for trial came to light and the applicant applied to the High Court on 13 May, 1987, for liberty to apply for judicial review. The applicant obtained liberty to apply for judicial review on the ground that the order returning the notice party for trial was made without or in excess of jurisdiction in that it purported to return the said notice party for trial to a court which had no jurisdiction to embark on such a trial. The application was opposed by the notice party on the grounds that the applicant was guilty of delay. **Held** by Keane J. in granting the relief sought by the applicant, 1, the delay was relatively short and there would have to be a more substantial period of delay to deprive the applicant of the relief sought. 2. As a result of an error which was no responsibility of the notice party he has had charges hanging over him for a longer period. This is an insufficient ground by itself for setting aside all further proceedings. 3.

CRIMINAL LAW—Practice.

There was no allegation that the notice party was hindered in the conduct of his defence. *Director of Public Prosecutions* v. *Johnson*

(H.C.) [1988] ILRM 747

61. —— **Summons** — *Issue — Delay — Summary offence — Delay in issuing and serving summonses — Whether such delay excessive — Whether such as to prejudice accused's right to fair trial — Whether delay caused by actions of defendants — Whether delay by State culpable — Natural justice — Petty Sessions Act,* 1851 (*c.* 93), *s.* 10(4) — *Road Traffic Act,* 1961 (*No.* 24), *s.* 49.] The prosecutor was alleged to have committed an offence contrary to s. 49 of the Road Traffic Act, 1961 — as amended by s. 13 of the Road Traffic (Amendment) Act of 1978 — on 8 December, 1982. A complaint was made within the statutory six month period. A summons was issued in December, 1984 and was served on the prosecutor in January, 1985, over two years after the alleged offence. The prosecutor sought to make absolute a conditional order of certiorari on the grounds that the delay in bringing the matter to trial had the effect of depriving him of the opportunity of producing reliable evidence in his defence. **Held** by D'Arcy J. in making the order of certiorari absolute, 1, where delay in the prosecution of a criminal offence is so long as to produce substantial prejudice to the accused or where it was of such length of time as to be unconscionable in any way, a court of trial has a judicial discretion to decline to proceed to hear the case *Regina* v. *Watford Justices, ex parte Outrim* [1983] R.T.R. 26 applied. 2. In order to support an application alleging excessive delay, there must be not only a lapse of time sufficient to lay the foundations of such an allegation, but also there must be an absence of any evidence that the accused person has contributed to the delay by his own negligence or by any attempt to avoid service of the proceedings. 3. In certain circumstances, delay alone by its nature and its length must inevitably lead to prejudice, unfairness and injustice to an applicant. *The State (Cuddy)* v. *Mangan*

(H.C.) [1988] ILRM 720

62. —— **Summons** — *Sufficiency — Signature — District Court Clerk affixing signature to the summons by use of a rubber stamp — Conviction — Certiorari — Whether open to prosecutor to challenge sufficiency of summons — Prosecutor acquiescing in adjournments of his case — Validity of concept of "representation without prejudice" questioned.*] The prosecutor was convicted by the respondent at Tralee District Court of two offences involving drunken driving. The trial had been adjourned on five occasions because the local District Justice knew the prosecutor and

CRIMINAL LAW—*continued.*

wished the case to be heard by another. The prosecutor's solicitor purported to be appearing for his client 'without prejudice' and to be holding merely a 'watching brief.' When the case finally came to be heard, the solicitor submitted *inter alia* that the summons was bad by reason of a discrepancy between the signature of the District Court Clerk as found in the form of a rubber stamp facsimile on the summons and as observed in holograph elsewhere. The District Justice rejected this submission, and convicted. The prosecutor, relying on the decision in *The State (Attorney-General)* v. *Judge Roe* [1951] I.R. 172, sought and obtained a conditional order of certiorari. **Held** by Finlay P., discharging the conditional order, 1, that the prosecutor had failed in the District Court to make a clear and unequivocal challenge to the summons and had acquiesced in numerous adjournments and was thereby precluded from relying on any want of form: *D.P.P.* v. *Clein* [1983] ILRM 76 applied. 2. That the prosecutor had not raised in the District Court a defence based on the time for the prosecution of offences: *The State (Attorney-General)* v. *Judge Roe* [1951] I.R. 172 distinguished; *Minister for Agriculture* v. *Norgro Ltd.* [1980] I.R. 155 followed. 3. That a solicitor representing an accused person did not appear 'without prejudice' or hold a 'watching brief', and that it was undesirable and inappropriate for an officer of the court to attend a summary prosecution for the purpose of gathering evidence for a subsequent State Side application. *The State (O'Leary)* v. *Neilan*

(H.C.) [1984] ILRM 35

63. —— **Trial** — *Delay — Trial on indictment — Due course of law — Prohibition — Right of accused to trial with reasonable expedition — Delay of 5 years since alleged offence — Delay of 3 years since return for trial — Delay due to workload of trial court — Whether delay excessive — Factors relevant to assessing whether delay excessive — Evidence against accused comprising evidence of identification — Material defence witness untraceable due to lapse of time — Whether question of delay should be left to trial judge.*

Constitution — Trial of offences — Personal rights — Right to fair procedures — Due course of law — Right to a speedy trial — Constitution of Ireland, 1937, *Art.* 38.1.] On the 8 July, 1982, the prosecutor was returned for trial to the Cork Circuit Court on two charges of assault occasioning actual bodily harm arising out of an incident which had occurred on the 25 January, 1981. A substantial part of the evidence against the prosecutor was evidence of identification. On several occasions between November, 1982, and June, 1984, he appeared before that court but his case was never listed for hearing. His counsel

CRIMINAL LAW—Practice.

objected to these adjournments with increasing force as they became more frequent. In July, 1984, the prosecutor's case was listed for trial but was not reached and was adjourned to the next sessions with a direction from the judge that it was to be given priority immediately after the custody cases. The State obtained a date for trial for the 6 November, 1984, which was the second week of the Michaelmas criminal sessions but the prosecutor, who had by then taken up employment in England and who had been present for the first week of the sessions, was unable to remain in the country. The prosecutor appeared before the court again in January, 1985, and after a series of short adjournments the trial was listed for the 30 April, 1985. The prosecutor obtained a conditional order of prohibition restraining the respondents from dealing further with the prosecution on the grounds that he had been denied due process of law and had not been afforded a speedy trial and had thereby been prejudiced. In particular the prosecutor relied on the fact that an important alibi witness could not be traced and that his employment in England was jeopardised. The respondents, in showing cause, argued that the delay had resulted from the inability of the Circuit Court to deal with the great volume of criminal business before it; and from the failure of the prosecutor to appear on the 6 November, 1984. On the prosecutor's motion to make the conditional order absolute notwithstanding cause shown, it was **Held** by Murphy J., in allowing the cause shown and discharging the conditional order, 1, that the Constitution guarantees to every citizen that the trial of a person charged with a criminal offence will not be delayed excessively. Regard must be had not only to delay caused by intentional abuse of the rights of an accused or the failure to make use of available facilities to prosecute the charge, but to the whole period of delay. *In the Matter of Paul Singer* (*No.* 2) 98 I.L.T.R. 112 considered. 2. That the period of delay must be considered having regard to all the circumstances of the case so as to achieve a fair and just balance between the exercise of individual freedoms and the requirements of an ordered society. *The Criminal Law (Jurisdiction) Bill,* 1975 [1977] I.R. 129 followed. 3. That the delay which had occurred in this case could be left to the discretion of the trial judge who would be conscious of the problems which arise with regard to evidence of identification after a lapse of time and with regard to the availability of witnesses; and who would have the power to administer the appropriate warnings or directions to a jury to prevent injustice arising and, if the delay was excessive or unduly prejudicial, to dismiss the charges. On appeal by the prosecutor, it was **Held** by the Supreme Court (Finlay C.J., Walsh, Henchy, Griffin and McCarthy JJ.), in allowing the appeal and granting the order of prohibition sought, 1, that a person charged with a criminal offence is entitled, as part of his right to be tried in due course of law, to a trial with reasonable expedition. 2. That where the trial of a person charged with an indictable offence has been excessively delayed so as to prejudice his chance of obtaining a fair trial, the appropriate remedy by which his constitutional rights might be defended and protected was by order of prohibition. Such a person should not be put to the risk of being arraigned and pleading before a jury. 3. That having regard to all the circumstances of the case, and in particular to the unavailability of a defence witness who would have been available earlier, the delay in this case was both excessive and prejudicial. *The State (O'Connell)* v. *Fawsitt*

(H.C., S.C.) [1986] I.R.362; [1986] ILRM 639

64. —— **Trial** — *Delay — Whether such as to prejudice accused's right to fair trial — Whether delay caused by actions of defendants — Whether delay by the State culpable — Constitution of Ireland,* 1937, *Art.* 38.1.] The prosecutor had been charged with various offences arising out of an incident involving a motor car driven by him at the time. On remand to the District Court, the prosecutor did not appear, as, unknown to the court, he was then in custody on another charge. A warrant was issued for his arrest, and following his release from custody, he was arrested on foot of the warrant and remanded on continuing bail until 14 January. On that date, he elected for trial before judge and jury for one of the offences, malicious damage and assault. All the other offences with which he had been charged were summary offences. From 11 February to 30 April, there were five adjournments, the first as a result of the non-appearance of the prosecutor, and the others because the book of evidence was not ready. On 30 April, the indictable charges were struck out, but the State mentioned that they would probably be re-entered. The summary matters came before the court on 7 May, and were adjourned until 25 June, and again until 23 July. The first adjournment was in favour of the prosecutor's solicitor and the second in favour of the State. On 23 July, fresh charges were preferred with respect to the indictable offences, and the District Justice accepted jurisdiction. The prosecutor was remanded on continuing bail until 30 July. A conditional order of prohibition was granted on 31 July, on the ground, *inter alia,* that the delay had been such that the prosecutor's constitutional right to a fair trial in due course of law had been prejudiced. **Held** by Carroll J., in refusing to make absolute the conditional order,

CRIMINAL LAW—Practice.

1, where an accused person is in custody on another charge at the date of his remand, it is for the said accused to ensure that the court is made aware of that fact. 2. The prosecutor had himself contributed to the delay by his non-attendance, and by the seven week adjournment granted to facilitate his solicitor. 3. The delay on the part of the State was not such culpable delay as would entitle the prosecutor from immunity from trial on the indictable charges. *The State (O'Keeffe)* v. *McMenamin*

(H.C.) [1986] ILRM 653

65. —— **Trial** — *Delay — Trial on indictment — Due course of law — Right of accused to trial with reasonable expedition — Delay of 18 months from commission of offence to charge — Whether suspect in commission of a crime has a right to have a charge preferred against him expeditiously — Factors relevant to assessing whether delay excessive — Criminal Procedure Act,* 1967 (*No.* 12) — *Constitution of Ireland,* 1937, *Art.* 40.] Each of the applicants was, in February, 1988, charged with the commission of an offence in August, 1986. When the matters first came before the respondent District Justice, he expressed the opinion that the delay was unreasonable and inexcusable and he rejected as unsatisfactory reasons which were offered for the delay. He was not, however, given any assistance as to what effect, if any, the delay had had or could have on the trial of the accused, should they be returned for trial. The respondent District Justice, accordingly, proceeded with the preliminary examination required by s. 5 of the Criminal Procedure Act, 1967, and returned the accused for trial by orders made pursuant to s. 8 of that Act (as amended) dated the 15 March, 1988. The applicants each sought leave to apply for judicial review by way of certiorari directed to the first respondent in respect of the said orders returning them for trial, and orders of prohibition directed to the second respondent and the third respondent prohibiting the arraignment of the applicants on the charges upon which they had been returned for trial, and prohibiting the trial of the applicants on those charges. No evidence was adduced before either the District Court or the High Court that the delay which had taken place might reasonably have had the effect of depriving the applicants of a fair trial. **Held** by the High Court (Gannon J.) in refusing to grant the relief sought, 1, that there was an important distinction between the stage before charge, when a matter of a suspected crime was being investigated, and the stage after an accused person had been charged and so was subject to the directions of a court. Before any charge of a criminal offence was preferred against a person there was a presumption of innocence and a

CRIMINAL LAW—*continued.*

constitutional protection of his liberty and good name, accorded to him by Article 40 of the Constitution. 2. That a person who was a mere suspect (and therefore presumed to be innocent) had no legal right to have a charge made against him nor to have some legal process diligently or expeditiously pursued, by arrest or by summons, to bring him before a court. It was no part of the function of the courts to participate either in the investigation of criminal offences or in the supervisory direction of those engaged in that work. 3. That once before the courts, the courts would not adopt nor approve or assist any procedure, seemingly lawful in form, for invoking their jurisdiction if found to be in fact illegal or in breach of any constitutional right of an accused person. If it appeared to a court that an accused person had been deprived of the right and opportunity of a fair trial or put to an unfair disadvantage in facing his trial by reason of circumstances within the control of the prosecution such as by unwarranted delay in bringing a charge, the constitutional obligation on the courts to vindicate the rights of the citizen would require dismissal of the charges or other refusal to adopt the unwarranted procedures. 4. That in the instant case the applicants had not given any grounds upon which a court could arrive at a conclusion that the period of delay was such as might have been expected to prejudice the chances of either of them obtaining a fair trial. *The State (O'Connell)* v. *Fawsitt* [1986] I.R. 362, considered. *O'Flynn* v. *Clifford; Hannigan* v. *Clifford*

(H.C.) [1988] I.R.740

66. —— **Trial — Special Criminal Court** — *D.P.P. directing trial in Special Criminal Court — Whether power unconstitutional — Opinion of D.P.P. that ordinary courts inadequate — Whether reviewable by the courts — Offences Against the State Act,* 1939 (*No.* 13), *ss.* 47, 48 — *Prosecution of Offences Act,* 1974 (*No.* 22), *s.* 3.] The plaintiff was tried and convicted of certain offences in the Special Criminal Court on foot of certificates issued by the Director of Public Prosecutions (D.P.P.) under the Offences Against the State Act, 1939, directing his trial in that court. In respect of one offence, the D.P.P. directed under s. 47(1) of the Act that the plaintiff be charged before and tried by the Special Criminal Court. In respect of another, the D.P.P. directed under s. 48 of the Act that the trial of the plaintiff be transferred from the Central Criminal Court to the Special Criminal Court, because in his opinion the ordinary courts were inadequate to secure the effective administration of justice and the preservation of public peace and order in relation to the trial of the plaintiff. The plaintiff challenged the validity

CRIMINAL LAW—Practice.

of his trial and conviction on the grounds that the power of the D.P.P. was not constitutionally permissible, the certificate under s. 47 deprived him of meaningful procedures prior to his trial, the opinion on which the D.P.P. exercised his power under s. 48 should be reviewed by the courts and his power under s. 48 was an unconstitutional intrusion into the judicial powers of the High Court. The defendants did not contravert the evidence of the plaintiff that he was not a member of or associated with any illegal organisation but asserted that his claims disclosed no cause of action. **Held** by Carroll J. in dismissing the claims, 1, since the Constitution authorised the legislature to choose the method of determining the inadequacy of the ordinary courts and it did not require a judicial determination, the choice of the D.P.P. was not unconstitutional. *In re MacCurtain* [1941] I.R. 83 and *In re Criminal Law (Jurisdiction) Bill, 1975* [1977] I.R. 129 applied. 2. There was no constitutional requirement for any preliminary investigation by the District Court and therefore the direct return for trial to the Special Criminal Court was not unconstitutional. *The State (Shanahan)* v. *Attorney General* [1964] I.R. 239 applied. 3. The courts could not investigate the reasonableness of the opinion of the D.P.P. in open court or in private since to do so would render impossible the operation of the Act. *Savage* v. *Director of Public Prosecutions* [1982] ILRM 385 applied. *In re the Criminal Law (Jurisdiction) Bill, 1975* [1977] I.R. 129 considered. 4. The power of the D.P.P. was not an unwarranted intrusion into the functions of the High Court since its function to try an offence would have ceased once the D.P.P. had made his determination. *O'Reilly* v. *D.P.P.; Judge* v. *D.P.P.*

(H.C.) [1984] ILRM 224

67. —— **Trial** — *Voir dire — Witnesses — Accused requested presence of jury during* voir dire — *Whether trial judge erred in refusing request — Whether trial judge failed to consider accused's request that other witnesses be excluded while one witness giving evidence — Whether new trial should be ordered.*] *R.* v. *Brinkley*. [*Note*]

(C.A.) [1984] N.I.48

68. —— **Young offender** — *Juvenile court — Jurisdiction — Summons signed before defendant was 17 — Served afterwards — Whether juvenile court had jurisdiction — Whether proceedings had commenced — Children and Young Persons Act (Northern Ireland)* 1968 (*c.* 34), *ss.* 66, 68.] In its legal sense the word "proceedings" is ambiguous. It can mean an entire action or steps in an action commencing, in a criminal case, from the date of the complaint and including everything that happens at the trial or hearing. In section

CRIMINAL LAW—*continued.*

66(2) of the Children and Young Persons Act (Northern Ireland), 1968, which provides that where any proceedings in respect of a young person are commenced before a juvenile court and the young person attains the age of 17 before the conclusion of the proceedings the court may continue to deal with the case, the critical time is the beginning of the original juvenile court hearing and the court was therefore right to decline jurisdiction in a case where the defendant became 17 after a complaint was made but before the summons was served on him. *Dixon* v. *McCann*

(C.A.) [1985] N.I. 257

69. —— **Young offender** — *Remand — Whether of an unruly character — Imprisonment — Evidence on which decision made — Whether evidence of unruly character must be tested by cross-examination — Children's Act,* 1908 (*c.* 67), *s.* 102(3).] S. 102(3) of the Children's Act, 1908, provides that a young person shall not be sentenced to imprisonment for an offence unless the court certifies that he is of so unruly a character that he cannot be detained in a place of detention provided under the Act. The prosecutor, a 15-year old boy, appeared before the respondent charged with a number of offences. Upon hearing evidence that the prosecutor had persistently absconded from St. Lawrence's Children Centre in Finglas, the respondent remanded him in custody in Mountjoy Prison. On the return date, upon application of the solicitor for the prosecutor, the respondent remanded the prosecutor for a further week, and indicated that she would have to do so again in Mountjoy Prison. The solicitor consented to this. At the hearing of the case the prosecutor pleaded guilty to certain of the charges against him. The respondent then certified the prosecutor to be of unruly character, having considered a report from St. Lawrence's School, Finglas, and she remanded him by order in Mountjoy Prison. The report was not read in open court nor was it read by either the prosecutor or his solicitor. The only sworn evidence before the court as to the character of the prosecutor tended to show that he was of co-operative disposition. A conditional order of certiorari quashing the order of the respondent was granted to the prosecutor on the grounds that the order was made without jurisdiction and in breach of the rules of natural justice. **Held** by Finlay P. in disallowing the cause shown and making absolute the conditional order, 1, the decision to certify a young offender as being of unruly character can be reached only upon sworn admissible evidence, and the offender must be given the opportunity to test that evidence in cross-examination. 2.

Some of the material relied upon by the respondent in reaching the conclusion that the prosecutor was of unruly character was not sworn evidence and was not known to either the prosecutor or his solicitor and the procedure whereby the respondent reached the conclusion that the prosecutor was of unruly character was not in accordance with the principles of natural justice. *The State (O'Donoghue)* v. *Kennedy*

(H.C.) [1979] ILRM 109

Preliminary examination *see* Nos. 54-6
Remand *see* Nos. 59, 69
Summons *see* Nos. 39-44, 61, 62, 68

SEARCH WARRANT

70. —— **Issue** — *Validity — Powers of peace commissioner — Arrest — Issue of peace commissioner of search warrant upon receiving sworn information of garda — Information required to show "reasonable cause to believe" that offence committed — Applicant's dwelling entered by garda acting on authority of warrant — Warrant purporting to confer power of arrest — Applicant charged with offence and returned for trial — Whether information sworn by garda required to show grounds for reasonable belief — Whether issue of warrant an administration of justice and reserved to judges — Whether conferring of power of arrest rendered warrant bad in law on its face — Whether certiorari should issue to quash warrant prior to trial — Rules of the Superior Courts,* 1986, *O.* 84, *r.* 21(1) — *Larceny Act,* 1916 (*c.* 11), *s. 42 (1)* — *Courts of Justice Act,* 1924 (*No.* 10), *s.* 88(3)(b) — *Constitution of Ireland,* 1937, *Arts.* 33, 40.5.] Section 42, sub-s. 1 of the Larceny Act, 1916, provides that a justice of the peace may, if it is made to appear by an information on oath before him that there is reasonable cause to believe that any person has in his possession or on his premises any property with respect to which an offence under the Act has been committed, issue a warrant to search for and seize the same. By s. 88, sub-s. 3 (b) of the Courts of Justice Act, 1924, the powers of justices of the peace with respect to the issue of warrants are vested in peace commissioners. The first respondent, a peace commissioner, issued to a member of the Garda Síochána a warrant under s. 42, sub-s. 2 of the Act of 1916, to search premises occupied by the applicant. The warrant was issued on foot of a sworn information in which the garda recited that he had reasonable cause for suspicion, from information which he had received and which he believed to be true, that certain stolen property would be found on those premises. The warrant also purported to confer on the searching garda a power of arrest. A search of the premises was subsequently carried

out and the property recovered. The applicant was arrested, charged and returned for trial before the Dublin Circuit Court. The applicant applied to the High Court (Blayney J.) and obtained leave to apply for judicial review in respect of the search warrant. The grounds relied upon by the applicant included, *inter alia,* that the first respondent had not been furnished with sufficient information to satisfy himself that there was reasonable cause to believe that there was stolen property on the premises, that the issue of a search warrant was a judicial rather than an administrative act and could not be performed by a person other than a judge, and that the unlawful inclusion of a power of arrest in the warrant rendered it bad in law on its face. On the applicant's application for an order of certiorari by way of judicial review of the warrant, it was **Held** by the High Court (Hamilton P.), in refusing the application, 1, that the issue of a warrant authorising the entry and search of the dwelling house of a citizen was not inconsistent with Article 40, s. 5 of the Constitution. 2. That the issue of search warrants did not amount to an administration of justice in a criminal matter, such as could only be performed by judges. *Ryan* v. *O'Callaghan* (Unreported, High Court, Barr J., 22 July, 1987) applied. 3. That the information on oath of the garda was sufficient to make it appear to the first respondent that there was reasonable cause to believe that stolen property was to be found on the premises occupied by the applicant. 4. That the power of arrest which the warrant purported to confer, and which the applicant sought to impugn, had not been relied on by the Gardaí; it could be severed from the power to search, which was not thereby invalidated. 5. That the discretionary remedy of certiorari should in any event be refused since the object in seeking it was to have excluded the evidence obtained on foot of the search; the proper forum for the determination of the issue of admissibility of evidence was at the forthcoming trial of the applicant. *The State (Glover and Mulligan)* v. *McCarthy* [1981] ILRM 47 considered. *Berkeley v. Edwards*

(H.C.) [1988] I.R.217

71. —— **Issue** — *Validity — Powers of peace commissioner to issue search warrant — Requirement that peace commissioner be satisfied by information on oath of reasonable grounds for suspecting that an offence was committed — Information deposing to garda having reasonable grounds for suspecting that an offence was committed — Whether warrant validly issued — Misuse of Drugs Act,* 1977 (*No.* 12), *s.* 26 — *Misuse of Drugs Act,* 1984 (*No.* 18), *s.* 13.

Constitution — Administration of justice — Due course of law — Peace Commissioner — Power

CRIMINAL LAW—Search Warrant.

of peace commissioner to issue search warrant — Whether a judicial function — Misuse of Drugs Act, 1977 (*No.* 12), *s.* 26 — *Misuse of Drugs Act,* 1984 (*No.* 18), *s.* 13 — *Constitution of Ireland,* 1937, *Arts.* 34, 38.

Constitution — Personal rights — Inviolability of dwelling — Search warrant — Power of peace commissioner to issue search warrant — Requirement that peace commissioner be satisfied by information on oath that reasonable grounds exist for suspecting the commission of an offence — Whether power consistent with inviolabilty of dwelling — Misuse of Drugs Act, 1977 (*No.* 12), *s.* 26 — *Misuse of Drugs Act,* 1984 (*No.* 18), *s.* 13 — *Constitution of Ireland,* 1937, *Art.* 40.5.

Judicial review — Certiorari — Discretion — Alternative procedure available to applicant — Rules of the Superior Courts, 1986, (O.84.] Section 26, sub-s. 1 of the Misuse of Drugs Act, 1977, as amended by s. 13 of the Misuse of Drugs Act, 1984, provides *inter alia* that:— "(1) If a Justice of the District Court or a Peace Commissioner is satisfied by information on oath of a member of the Garda Síochána that there is reasonable ground for suspecting that— (aa) . . . a plant of the genus *Cannabis* . . . is being cultivated contrary to section 17 of this Act on any premises or other land . . . such Justice or Peace Commissioner may issue a search warrant mentioned in subsection (2) of this section." The first respondent issued a warrant pursuant to s. 26 of the Misuse of Drugs Acts, 1977 and 1984, authorising Garda D. to enter and search a house in Dublin. The warrant recited that the first respondent was satisfied by the information on oath of Garda D. that there was reasonable ground for suspecting that cannabis was being cultivated at the premises. The information on oath of Garda D. on foot of which the warrant was issued stated : 'I am a member of the Garda Síochána and I have reasonable grounds for suspecting that a plant of the genus *Cannabis* is being cultivated at [the premises].' Following the issue of the warrant the house was searched and some heroin was found. The applicant, who was visiting the house, was also searched and was charged with offences contrary to the Misuse of Drugs Acts. The applicant obtained leave to apply for an order of certiorari by way of judicial review to quash the search warrant on the grounds, firstly, that the respondent could not have been satisfied that there were reasonable grounds for suspecting any of the matters referred to in s. 26 of the Acts of 1977 and 1984, because no sufficient or proper information had been laid before him; and secondly, that the power to issue search warrant conferred on peace commissioners by s. 26 of the Acts of 1977 and 1984, was invalid having regard to the provisions of the Constitution in that (*a*) it was a judicial

CRIMINAL LAW—*continued.*

function reserved by Article 34 to judges; (*b*) the respondent was embarking on part of the trial of the applicant, and (*c*) the power was inconsistent with the inviolability of the dwelling guaranteed by Article 40, s. 5. **Held** by Hamilton P., in refusing the relief sought, 1, that statutory powers encroaching on the liberty of the citizen and the inviolability of the dwelling should be construed in the manner which is least restrictive of individual rights. *Dictum* of Lord Diplock in *Reg.* v. *I.R.C., Ex p. Rossminster* [1980] A.C. 952, 1008 approved. 2. That it was a condition precedent to the exercise of the power to issue a search warrant conferred by s. 26 of the Acts of 1977 and 1984, that the District Justice or Peace Commissioner should himself be satisfied that facts existed which constituted reasonable grounds for suspecting that an offence was being committed. *Reg.* v. *I.R.C., Ex.p. Rossminster* [1980] A.C. 952 considered. 3. That in deciding whether or not to issue a warrant the first respondent was obliged to act judicially. *Rex* v. *Electricity Commissioners. London Electricity Joint Committee Co. (1920), Ex parte* [1924] 1 K.B. 171 considered. 4. That the first respondent had acted without jurisdiction in issuing the search warrant because he personally had no information before him which would have enabled him to be satisfied that there were reasonable grounds for suspecting that an offence was being committed. 5. That the applicant's object in seeking to have the search warrant quashed, which was to have the evidence obtained as a result of the search rendered inadmissible in the course of his trial, was properly a matter to be dealt with by the trial judge. Accordingly, that the court would refuse to make an order of certiorari. *The State (Glover)* v. *District Justice McCarthy* [1981] ILRM 47 considered. 6. That the issue of a search warrant prior to the commencement of a prosecution was part of the process of criminal investigation and was an executive rather than a judicial function. *Ryan* v. *O'Callaghan* (Unreported, High Court, Barr J., 22 July, 1987) and *Berkeley* v. *Edwards* [1988] I.R. 217 applied. 7. That the power conferred on a peace commissioner by s. 26 of the Acts of 1977 and 1984 to issue a search warrant, in providing a simple procedure readily available to the police in appropriate cases while at the same time stipulating that an independent person must be satisfied that the issue of a search warrant was appropriate, represented a balance between the requirements of the common good and the protection of individual rights and was not unconstitutional. *Ryan* v. *O'Callaghan* (Unreported, High Court, Barr J., 22 July, 1987) and *Berkeley* v. *Edwards* [1988] I.R. 217 applied. *Byrne* v. *Grey*

CRIMINAL LAW—Search Warrant.

(H.C.) [1988] I.R.31

72. —— **Issue** — *Validity — Powers of peace commissioner — Arrest warrants — Accused suspected to be in house with stolen property — Search and arrest warrants obtained by garda from peace commissioner — House entered and searched — Accused arrested — Accused charged and convicted of receiving — Whether issue of arrest warrant a judicial act — Whether peace commissioner competent to issue warrants — Whether arrest warrants required where gardai lawfully on premises and suspect accused of having committed felony — Whether invalidity in arrest vitiated subsequent trial and conviction — Larceny Act,* 1916 (*c.* 50), *s.* 42(1) — *Courts of Justice Act,* 1924 (*No.* 10), *s.* 88(3).] C., a member of the Garda Síochána, received information that the owner of certain stolen property had chased the applicants into their house while they carried his property, and that they and the stolen property remained therein. Later on the same day C. applied by way of complaint made on oath and in writing to the first respondent, a peace commissioner, and received warrants for the arrest of the applicants. Before executing these warrants he returned to the first respondent and obtained a warrant to search the premises. Early the next day C., accompanied by fellow members of the Garda Síochána, entered the premises, read over the warrants of arrest to the applicants, arrested them and removed them to a local Garda Station. In the station the applicants were charged, cautioned and made no reply. Later that day they were duly brought before the District Court and remanded. When the charges were ultimately dealt with by the second respondent, a District Justice, each of the applicants was convicted of receiving stolen property, and orders of detention were made in respect of each applicant. The applicants applied to the High Court for leave to apply by way of judicial review for orders of certiorari quashing the convictions made by the second respondent and quashing the search warrant and warrants for arrest issued by the first respondent. Leave was granted only in respect of the warrant for arrest in each case, on the ground that the first respondent, not being a judge appointed under the Constitution and having no power to administer justice in a criminal matter, had no jurisdiction to issue warrants of arrest and was acting *ultra vires* in so doing. On the applicant's application by way of judicial review for orders of certiorari quashing the said warrants of arrest, it was **Held** by O'Hanlon J., in refusing the applications, 1, that as the exercise by a peace commissioner of the power to issue a search warrant pursuant to the provisions of the Larceny Act, 1916, and the Courts of Justice Act, 1924, was not unconstitutional, notwithstanding

CRIMINAL LAW—*continued.*

that he was not a judge appointed under the Constitution, it followed that C. and his colleagues were lawfully entitled to enter into and to search the premises, and were lawfully on the premises when they arrested the applicants. *Ryan* v. *O'Callaghan* (Unreported, High Court, Barr J., 22 July, 1987) applied. 2. That, as C. suspected each of the applicants of having comitted the felony of receiving stolen goods and had arrested them for the purpose of charging them with that offence, he had a common law power of arrest and it was unnecessary for him to apply for arrest warrants. 3. That, accordingly, it was unnecessary to decide whether the arrest warrants were validly issued by the respondent peace commissioner since they were in any event superfluous. 4. That, even if there were an unconstitutional invalidity in the procedure whereby the applicants were arrested and brought before the District Court, the respondent District Justice had lawful seisin of the case as the procedure did not involve a deliberate and conscious violation of the constitutional rights of the applicants. *The State (Lynch)* v. *Ballagh* [1986] I.R. 203 considered. 5. That it followed from the fact that the applicants had been tried and convicted in due course of law that, even if the initial arrests were invalid, any invasion of their personal rights preceding such trials was minimal in character and discretionary relief by way of certiorari in respect of those arrests should be refused. *Farrell* v. *Farrelly*

(H.C.) [1988] I.R.201

SENTENCE

73. —— **Aggregate sentences exceeding 12 months** — *Convictions for larceny and malicious damage — Accused already serving a sentence — Whether District Justice acting in excess of jurisdiction — Criminal Justice Act,* 1951 (*No.* 2), *ss.* 5, 41.] The prosecutor, who had been lodged in prison on 28 June, 1983, to serve a sentence of twelve months imposed by the District Court, was convicted by the respondent District Justice on 26 July, 1983, of further offences and sentenced to another period of twelve months. The effect of the second twelve-month sentence was to imprison the prosecutor from June 1983 to July 1984, a period of thirteen months. Relying on s. 5 of the Criminal Justice Act, 1951, (which provides that 'where two or more sentences passed by the District Court are ordered to run consecutively the aggregate term of imprisonment shall not exceed twelve months') and on *obiter dicta* of Henchy J. in *The State (White)* v. *Martin* 111 I.L.T.R. 21, decrying the apparent inability of a District Justice to impose a new sentence on a person already serving a twelve-month sentence, the prosecutor sought an order

CRIMINAL LAW—Sentence.

of certiorari challenging his second sentence. **Held** by Finlay P., discharging a conditional order of certiorari, that the respondent had not ordered the impugned sentence to run consecutively, and that neither s. 5 of the Criminal Justice Act, 1951, nor any other provision restricted the right of the District Court to impose sentence of up to twelve months by reason of sentences being served by a convicted person. *The State (Payne)* v. *Clifford*

(H.C.) [1985] ILRM 70

74. —— **Consecutive sentence** — *Accused already serving sentence of imprisonment — Sentence to run from legal expiration of sentence at present being served — Whether void for uncertainty — Power to impose consecutive sentences.*

Judicial review — Certiorari — Delay — Criminal law — Application to quash sentence — Out of time — Whether delay in seeking order a ground for refusal — Whether order issues ex debito justitiae.] The prosecutors were, on different occasions, sentenced to periods of imprisonment and penal servitude. Subsequently, each of them received further sentences which were to commence at the legal expiration of the sentences each of them were then serving. In the case of the first and third prosecutor, the consecutive sentence referred to the length of the sentence already being served; in the case of the second prosecutor the consecutive sentence referred to the court and the date on which the sentence already being served was imposed. The prosecutors challenged the validity of the orders imposing the consecutive sentences on the ground that they were void for uncertainty in failing to specify the sentence from which they were to commence. The first and third prosecutors also contended that the expression 'legal expiration' was uncertain since they could not predict in advance the remission, if any, which they would receive on any sentence then being served and the third prosecutor contended that a consecutive sentence could only be imposed in respect of an offence committed subsequently to that in respect of which the earlier sentence was imposed. The respondents, in addition to denying these claims contended that the delay by the prosecutors in claiming relief disentitled them to absolute orders of certiorari. **Held** by Barron J. in declining to grant absolute orders of certiorari, 1, since the prosecutors were alleging that the orders concerned were bad on their face for uncertainty, they would be entitled to certiorari *ex debito justitiae* and accordingly delay was no bar to them claiming relief. *The State (Walsh)* v. *Maguire* [1979] I.R. 372 applied. 2. Where a consecutive sentence is imposed, the convicted person must know which sentence already imposed on him is the sentence to which

CRIMINAL LAW—*continued.*

his fresh sentence is to run consecutively, and if there is a reasonable doubt as to this the sentence will be bad for uncertainty. 3. There was no doubt as to the meaning to be accorded to each of the consecutive sentences imposed on the three prosecutors since in the case of the first and third prosecutors it was clear that there was only one sentence which could have been referred to and in the case of the second prosecutor the consecutive sentence must have referred to a particular sentence then being served by him since there would have been no point in imposing a consecutive sentence in respect of the other terms he was then serving. *The State (Keating)* v. *Ó hUadhaigh* High Court, unreported, (Finlay P.) 11 May, 1984, discussed. 4. The phrase 'legal expiration' in the consecutive sentences imposed on the first and third prosecutors was not void for uncertainty since it referred to the actual determination of the sentence whenever that legally occurs, taking account of remission. 5. The power to impose consecutive sentences exists whether the offence in respect of which it is imposed was committed prior, or subsequent, to the offence in respect of which the earlier offence was committed, and as there was no distinction in practice between penal servitude and imprisonment as forms of punishment it would be unreasonable that the indication of the imposition of one rather than the other should attract a different legal result. *R.* v. *Greenberg* [1943] 1 K.B. 381 applied. *The State (Gleeson)* v. *Martin*

(H.C.) [1985] ILRM 577

75. —— **Consecutive sentence** — *Jurisdiction to impose consecutive sentences for a felony — Sentence to commence at the conclusion of the last of any sentence being served — Uncertainty — Certiorari — Criminal Law (Ireland) Act,* 1828 (*c.* 54), *s.* 20 — *Criminal Law (Jurisdiction) Act,* 1976 (*No.* 14), *s.* 5 — *Statute Law Revision Act, 1983 (No.* 11), *s.* 1.] The prosecutor was convicted in the Circuit Court before the respondent Circuit Court Judge of robbery and was sentenced to five years imprisonment "to commence at the legal expiration of the last of any sentence at present being served by the accused." The prosecutor was then serving four sentences of imprisonment. He obtained a conditional order of certiorari in the High Court quashing his conviction, unless cause were shown to the contrary. At the hearing of the motion for an order absolute, notwithstanding cause shown, the prosecutor argued that a sentence of five years imprisonment to commence at the legal expiration of the last of any sentence then being served by him, was void for uncertainty as the date of commencement of the sentence could be construed as being the expiration of either the

CRIMINAL LAW—Sentence.

most recently imposed sentence or the sentence that would be the last to expire. The prosecutor further argued that the respondent had no jurisdiction to impose a consecutive sentence on the conviction of more than one felony, by reason of the repeal of the Act of 1828 by the Act of 1983. **Held** by Lynch J., in allowing cause shown and discharging the conditional order, 1, that, there was no uncertainty as to the date on which the sentence would commence because either construction referred to the same sentence of imprisonment. 2. That the purpose of the Act of 1983 is merely to repeal enactments which have ceased to be in force or have become unnecessary and does not intend to make any changes in the law; accordingly the power conferred in the Act of 1828 to impose consecutive sentences in respect of a felony remains. *The State (Jones)* v. *O'Donovan* [1973] I.R. 329 considered. *The State (Dixon)* v. *Martin*

(H.C.) [1985] I.R.106; [1985] ILRM 240

76. —— **Consecutive sentence** — *Validity — Detention — Youthful offender — Two convictions and sentences — Each sentence being 12 months detention in St. Patrick's Institution — Second sentence being a consecutive sentence — Whether second sentence imposed validly by District Justice — Criminal Justice Act, 1951 (No.* 2), *s.* 5 — *Criminal Justice Act,* 1960 (*No.* 27), *s.* 13(1).] Section 5 of the Criminal Justice Act, 1951, provides that where a sentence of imprisonment is passed on any person by the District Court, the court may order that the sentence shall commence at the expiration of any other term of imprisonment to which that person has been previously sentenced, however that where two or more sentences passed by the District Court are ordered to run consecutively the aggregate term of imprisonment shall not exceed twelve months. Section 13, sub-s. 1 of the Criminal Justice Act, 1960, provides that where a person who is not less than seventeen and not more than twenty-one years of age is convicted of an offence for which he is liable to be sentenced to a term of penal servitude or imprisonment, he may, in lieu of being so sentenced, be sentenced to be detained in Saint Patrick's Institution for a period not exceeding the term for which he might have been sentenced to penal servitude or imprisonment, as the case may be. The prosecutor, when he was 18 years of age, was convicted in the District Court of larceny contrary to s. 2 of the Larceny Act, 1916, and of burglary contrary to s. 23A of the Larceny Act, 1916, as inserted by s. 6 of the Criminal Law (Jurisdiction) Act, 1976. In respect of the first offence the District Justice imposed a sentence of twelve months detention in St. Patrick's Institution,a juvenile detention centre, and in respect

CRIMINAL LAW—*continued.*

of the second charge he was also sentenced to twelve months detention in St.Patrick's Institution, the sentence to commence on the expiration of the twelve months imposed on the first charge. The prosecutor obtained a conditional order of certiorari in the High Court to quash the second sentence. Notwithstanding cause shown, an absolute order of certiorari was granted by D'Arcy J. on 8 October, 1984, on the basis that it was not within the jurisdiction of the District Justice to impose upon the prosecutor two consecutive periods of detention in St. Patrick's Institution which aggregated to more than twelve months. On appeal by the respondent it was **Held** by the Supreme Court (Henchy, Griffin and McCarthy JJ.; Finlay C.J. and Hederman J. dissenting) in allowing the appeal, allowing the cause shown and discharging the order, that the consecutive sentence imposed by the District Justice was not invalid. *Per* Henchy and Griffin JJ. — there was no statutory prohibition to limit the aggregate of terms of detention to twelve months. Section 5 of the Criminal Justice Act, 1951, applied only to terms of imprisonment and had no application to terms of detention in St. Patrick's Institution. *Per* McCarthy J. — the date of commencement of a term of imprisonment is not an integral part of the term of imprisonment itself and, accordingly, the postponed operation of the second sentence of detention was not invalid. *Per* Finlay C.J. and Hederman J. dissenting — Section 13, sub-s.1 of the Criminal Justice Act, 1960, could not be construed as permitting a District Justice to impose on a person convicted before him a period of detention at Saint Patrick's Institution which exceeds either what he would or could have imposed upon the same person in the same circumstances, had he been imposing a sentence of imprisonment. *The State (Clinch)* v. *Connellan*

(S.C.) [1985] I.R.597; [1986] ILRM 455

77. —— **Disparity of sentence** — *Armed robbery — Co-accused treated leniently — Whether ground for reducing accused's sentence — Observations on sentencing.*] The appellant pleaded guilty to a charge of armed robbery and was sentenced to seven years imprisonment. The appellant appealed against the sentence on the ground that it was excessive and that there was such a disparity between the sentence and that of one of his co-accused, who was tried on a different occasion before another judge and received a sentence of four years imprisonment, that his sentence should be reduced. **Held,** dismissing the appeal that, 1, the sentence of seven years was not excessive. Armed robbery was a very serious crime which must be visited with an

CRIMINAL LAW—Sentence.

immediate and lengthy custodial sentence including a considerable element of deterrence. A sentence within the range of 10 to 13 years was an appropriate starting point. A sentence may be increased if there was a high degree of planning; if force was actually used or the accused has been involved in more than one such crime. It would be appropriate to reduce the sentence if the degree of preparation or efficiency of performance was low; if the money and weapons were recovered or the accused pleaded guilty. Those who acted in a secondary role as accessories ought not to receive the same term as principals. 2. Disparity of sentences for the same offence is a proper ground of appeal even when imposed by different judges. A sentence of four years for armed robbery was clearly inadequate. However, the fact that a judge in sentencing a co-accused has passed a sentence below the range which the court has laid down or would consider justified is not in itself a valid ground for reducing a sentence, which was in no way excessive, imposed on another accused. *R.* v. *O'Neill*

(C.A.) [1984] N.I.264

78. —— **District Court appeals** — *Power of Circuit Court judge to increase sentences — Whether absence of fairness in the procedure.*] The prosecutors, O'Rourke and White, had been convicted in the District Court of an assault and had each been fined £50. The prosecutor, O'Flaherty, had been convicted of receiving stolen goods and had been fined £10. Upon appeal to the Circuit Court, the respondent had affirmed these convictions and imposed prison sentences in place of the fines: three months in the case of assault and twelve months in that of receiving stolen goods. The prosecutors, in affidavits grounding applications for orders of certiorari, sought to establish *inter alia* that the imposition of the more severe penalties constituted an infringement of natural or constitutional justice. It was submitted on their behalf that the prosecutors had appealed in an effort to clear their names and that they had no warning that the appellate court might increase their sentences. **Held** by Gannon J. discharging conditional orders of certiorari, that, 1, the Circuit Court judge was entitled to vary or increase a penalty imposed by the District Court (*The State (Aherne)* v. *Governor of Limerick Prison* [1983] ILRM 17 applied). 2. The prosecutors had failed to establish a lack of fairness or justice or an excess of jurisdiction by the respondent. *The State (O'Rourke)* v. *Martin; The State (O'Flaherty)* v. *Martin*

(H.C.) [1984] ILRM 333

79. —— **Misuse of drugs** — *Appeal — Offence of possession of a controlled drug — Obligation*

CRIMINAL LAW—*continued.*

to obtain medical or probation report before sentence — Appeal from the District Court — Appeal against conviction — Hearing on sentence only — Change of circumstances of convict — Whether Circuit Court obliged to obtain further medical reports before sentence — Misuse of Drugs Act, 1977 (*No.* 12).] Sub-section 1(*a*) of s. 28 of the Misuse of Drugs Act, 1977, provides *inter alia:—* "Where a person is convicted of an offence . . . under s. 15 of this Act . . . the Court shall remand the person . . . and request a health board, court welfare officer or other body or person . . . to— (i) cause to be furnished to the court a medical report in writing on the convicted person together with such recommendations (if any) as to medical treatment which the person making the report considers appropriate to the needs of the convicted person, and (ii) furnish to the court a report in writing as to the vocational and educational circumstances and social background of the convicted person together with such recommendations (if any) as to care which the body or person making the report considers appropriate to the said needs." Further provisions of s. 28 allow the court, in lieu of penal sentence, to permit the convict to enter into a recognisance with conditions that he attend specified medical treatment or educational/vocational training courses. The prosecutor was convicted in the District Court of possession of a controlled drug under s. 15 of the Misuse of Drugs Act, 1977. Pursuant to the requirements of s. 28 of the same Act the District Justice considered a medical and a probation officer's report before sentencing the prosecutor to 12 months imprisonment. On appeal against sentence only, the Circuit Court judge considered the same two reports, but did not require further reports, before affirming the sentence of the District Court. The prosecutor sought and obtained in the High Court a conditional order of certiorari quashing the order of the respondent. On motion to make the conditional order absolute the prosecutor contended that the respondent had been obliged by s. 28 to cause to be furnished with and consider up to date medical and other reports before deliberating on and imposing sentence. **Held** by Barr J. and affirmed on appeal by the Supreme Court (Henchy, Griffin and Hederman JJ.), that the penological intent and scheme of s. 28 necessitated that the reports required by the section be comprehensive and up to date and reflect the essential circumstances of the convict as they existed at the time when they were being considered by the sentencing court. Where the circumstances had changed radically and these would have been reflected in fresh reports the sentencing judge acted beyond jurisdiction in imposing sentence without consideration of those reports and this

CRIMINAL LAW—Sentence.

applied on appeal also, whether such appeal be against conviction or sentence only. *The State (Slattery)* v. *Roe*

(H.C., S.C.) [1986] I.R.768; [1986] ILRM 511

80. —— **Penal servitude in military custody** — *Whether sentence imposed laid down by law — Prisons Act,* 1972 (*No.* 7), *ss.* 2, 4.] The appellant had been charged with the offence of wounding with intent to cause grievous bodily harm, and had been transferred to military custody pursuant to s. 2(3) of the Prisons Act, 1972. S. 2(4) of the said Act provides that upon conviction in such circumstances, any sentence which the court might lawfully impose may be served in military custody. The appellant was convicted in the Special Criminal Court to seven years' penal servitude in military custody. However, this was stated in the warrant to be detention 'in military custody for a period of seven years.' In fact the only sentence which a court could lawfully impose for the offence of wounding with intent was seven years' penal servitude. The applicant unsuccessfully sought an order of habeas corpus in the High Court, on the ground, *inter alia,* that the sentence imposed was not laid down by law. On the appellant's *ex parte* appeal, it was **Held** by the Supreme Court (Henchy J., Griffin and Parke JJ. concurring) in dismissing the appeal, the sentence as recorded in the warrant was ambiguous. In such case, where the correct sentence had been imposed by the court, the warrant must be interpreted so as to give effect to the lawful sentence. *The State (Flannery)* v. *Governor of Military Detention Barracks*

(S.C.) [1976-7] ILRM 13

81. —— **Preventative detention** — *Habitual criminals — Lengthy sentence imposed — Whether amounting to preventative detention — Whether attempt to reform by prevention appropriate basis for sentence — Prevention of Crime Act,* 1908 (*c.* 50), *s.* 10.] The applicants were habitual criminals, the first applicant having convictions beginning in 1968 and the second applicant having convictions dating back to 1961. Primarily the convictions were for burglary. They had served numerous terms of imprisonment imposed by the District Court, primarily for periods of up to 12 months. In the instant case, they were charged with burglary, and pleaded guilty to the charges in the Circuit Court. The trial judge (Judge Murphy) imposed a sentence of six years imprisonment on each applicant, stating that the applicants were 'not amenable in any manner to the ordinary constrictions of the society in which they live and they are preying on innocent people and my primary duty is to protect those people.' The applicants applied for leave to appeal against the sentence. **Held** by the

CRIMINAL LAW—*continued.*

Court of Criminal Appeal (McCarthy, Barron and Egan JJ.) in allowing the application, the only justification for the radical departure by the trial judge from the previous measures of imprisonment which had been imposed on the applicants was an understandable attempt to procure reform by prevention, but in the absence of appropriate statutory provisions this was an unacceptable basis for the particular sentence, and a sentence of three years imprisonment would be substituted in respect of each of the applicants. *Per curiam:* there are apparently no facilities in the State for preventative detention, as envisaged by s. 10 of the Prevention of Crime Act, 1908. *The People* v. *Carmody*

(C.C.A.) [1988] ILRM 370

82. —— **Rape** — *Appeal from Court of Criminal Appeal — Whether Supreme Court should set out sentencing guidelines for rape — Effect of plea of guilty in mitigation of sentence.*] The appellant was one of three men who forcibly entered a car where the complainant was in the company of her boyfriend. The car was driven for some distance until, while her boyfriend was locked into the boot of the car, the complainant was taken to a nearby field and raped by two of the men; she was also subjected to acts of sexual perversion. Later on the same day two men, including the appellant, were interviewed by members of the Garda Síochána and made statements admitting the crime. The appellant pleaded guilty to rape and was sentenced to serve twenty-one years' penal servitude. The appellant appealed to the Court of Criminal Appeal against the severity of his sentence and his sentence was affirmed. The Attorney General issued a certificate pursuant to s. 29 of the Courts of Justice Act, 1924, certifying that the decision of that court involved a point of law of exceptional public importance *viz.*, the guidelines which the courts should apply in relation to sentences for the crime of rape, and certifying that it was desirable in the public interest that an appeal should be taken to the Supreme Court. The appellant filed a notice setting out the grounds of appeal against his sentence. It was **Held** by the Supreme Court (Finlay C.J.; Walsh, Henchy and Griffin JJ. concurring; McCarthy J. dissenting) in allowing the appellant's appeal, 1, that, having regard to its appellate jurisdiction, the Court should deal only with issues arising on grounds of appeal submitted in individual cases and should not set down a standard or tariff of penalties of general application. 2. That, accordingly, the Attorney General's certificate must be read as stating the point of law to be whether, on the application of correct principles, the sentence in this particular case was appropriate. 3. That the character of rape was such, even when committed without any

CRIMINAL LAW—Sentence.

aggravating circumstance, as to make the appropriate sentence, in the absence of wholly exceptional circumstances, a substantial immediate period of detention or imprisonment. 4. That the lack of any element of premeditation on the part of the accused should be considered as the absence of an additional aggravating circumstance, rather than as a mitigating factor. 5. That since the maximum sentence provided by statute for rape was penal servitude for life, the fact that the sentence imposed in this case was in excess of any which had heretofore been imposed could not of itself be considered wrong in principle. 6. That the fact that the sentence imposed in this case was in excess of the conventional period which a person who was sentenced to life imprisonment might expect to serve could not be taken into consideration by a court in imposing sentence, since the extent of that period was a matter of policy to be decided by the Executive. 7. That an admission of guilt made at an early stage and followed by a subsequent plea of guilty is a significant mitigating factor in the case of rape, since it provides the complainant with an early assurance that she will not have to describe in detail her rape and face the ordeal of cross-examination at a trial. 8. That an admission of guilt may, depending on the circumstances of the case and the strength of the evidence against an accused, also be taken as an indication of remorse and as a ground for a trial judge to have some expectation that the accused may be rehabilitated into society. 9. That while the court would have upheld the sentence of twenty-one years had the appellant put the complainant through the ordeal of a trial, the sentence imposed did not have sufficient regard to the appellant's admission of guilt and plea of guilty. Accordingly the sentence would be reduced to one of seventeen years' penal servitude. *Per* McCarthy J. (dissenting): That it was inconceivable that the trial judge had not taken into account the defendant's admission of guilt and subsequent plea of guilty; the sentence imposed was not inappropriate. *Per curiam:* that neither a victim's previous sexual experience nor the fact that she could be considered to have exposed herself by imprudence to the danger of being raped, could be considered mitigating circumstances in any rape. *The People* v. *Tiernan*
(S.C.) [1988] I.R.250

CRIMINAL LAW—*continued.*

—— Accused.
see **Accused**

—— Appeal — Acquittal — Whether D.P.P. had validly invoked the jurisdiction of the High Court — Whether possible to state case against acquittal.
see **Criminal Law,** 34

—— Appeal — Defect in trial — Proviso — Whether miscarriage of justice actually occurred — Whether shown that court disregarded inadmissible evidence.
see **Criminal Law,** 14

—— Appeal — Offence of possession of a controlled drug — Obligation to obtain medical or probation report before sentence — Appeal from the District Court — Appeal against conviction — Hearing on sentence only — Change of circumstances of convict — Whether Circuit Court obliged to obtain further medical reports before sentence.
see **Criminal Law,** 79

—— Appeal — Severity of sentence — Rape — Attorney General certifying point of law of exceptional public importance — Guidelines for sentencing in rape cases.
see **Criminal Law,** 82

—— Appeal — Whether point of law of exceptional public importance — Whether desirable in public interest that appeal be carried to Supreme Court.
see **Criminal Law,** 35

—— Appeal — Whether verdict unsafe or unsatisfactory — Confession — Probative value — Whether judge failed to give weight to circumstances in which it was obtained — Parts of confession inconsistent with other evidence and contradictory — Whether judge failed to deal with inconsistencies — Accused acquitted on certain counts — Whether whole confession unreliable.
see **Criminal Law,** 21

—— Armed robbery — Appropriate sentence.
see **Criminal Law,** 77

—— Arrest.
see **Criminal Law,** 1-8

for further references, see **Arrest and Detention**

D

DÁIL ÉIREANN

—— Election — Franchise — Disabled citizen — Inability to attend at polling station — Absence of statutory provision for postal vote in national elections — Constitutional validity of statutory provisions.
see **Constitution,** 37

—— Election — Franchise — Extension — Right to vote restricted by Constitution to citizens — Bill conferring franchise upon resident British citizens — Constitution — Repugnancy.
see **Constitution,** 1

—— Extradition treaty between Ireland and the United States of America — Whether treaty a charge upon the public funds — Approval of Dáil Éireann — Means by which treaty expenses approved by Dáil Éireann.
see **Constitution,** 24

—— Extradition treaty — Whether treaty binding on State — Whether treaty charge on public funds — Whether Dáil Éireann approval necessary to bind State — Whether the terms of the treaty or the nature or extent of the charge to be approved by Dáil Éireann.
see **Constitution,** 25

DAMAGE TO PROPERTY
see **Criminal Injuries,** 3-7

DAMAGES

Constitutional right — interference. No.1
Defective premises. No.2
Exemplary damages. Nos. 3-5
Foreseeability — remoteness. Nos. 6, 7
Personal injuries. Nos. 8-13

1. —— *Constitutional right — Interference — Right to free primary education — Interference with this right — Claim for damages — Whether such claim a claim in tort — Assessment of damages — Constitution of Ireland,* 1937, *Art.* 42.2 — *Trade Disputes Act,* 1906 (*c.* 47), *s.* 4.] The plaintiff was in fifth class in Castledonovan National School in Drimoleague, County Cork, one of the three schools affected by the teacher's strike in April, 1976. He attended school till June, 1976. In August, 1976, the I.N.T.O. issued a directive to all their members in the schools adjoining Drimoleague parish directing them not to enrol pupils from the affected schools. The

DAMAGES—*continued.*

plaintiff's father submitted that he attempted to enrol the plaintiff in other schools in January, 1977, but was refused by the defendants who were the principals in the other schools in the vicinity. The plaintiff's father gave evidence that he did not know that the I.N.T.O. directive was withdrawn in June, 1977. The plaintiff enrolled in Togher School in January, 1978, and attended there till June. He was then 13 years of age and he was put into fifth class with his brother who was two years younger. In 1982, the plaintiff sat and failed the intermediate certificate after which he left school and became an apprentice butcher. Evidence was given by a clinical psychologist who assessed him as having an I.Q. of 76 and maintained he was equipped for the ordinary business of life with manual skills rather than intellectual ones. The plaintiff claimed damages for unlawful interference with the constitutional right to free primary education pursuant to Article 42.4 of the Constitution. The case of *Crowley* v. *Ireland* [1980] I.R. 102 which arose out of the same strike established that a cause of action existed. In that case McMahon J. held that the said directive was an unlawful inteference with the constitutional right of the plaintiff and the other pupils affected to free primary education, however he left open the question of whether any of them were entitled to damages. The plaintiff only proceeded against the I.N.T.O., the individual members of the union's national executive and certain named teachers who had refused to enrol him in their schools and the teachers whom his father had heard had refused to enrol his friends on the grounds that his father presumed that they would have refused to enrol the plaintiff also. **Held** by Carroll J. in making an award of damages against all save one of the remaining named defendants, 1, this is not an action based on tort and therefore the defendant union cannot rely on the protection of s. 4 of the Trade Disputes Act, 1906. 2. The plaintiff is entitled to recover in full the damages sustained by him for the period the directive was in existence, and also general damages for foreseeable mental distress, anxiety and inconvenience. *Cosgrove* v. *Ireland* [1982] ILRM 48 applied. 3. The plaintiff failed to satisfy the court that he was entitled to recover future general damages. *Hayes* v. *Ireland*

(H.C.) [1987] ILRM 651

2. —— *Defective premises — Measure of damages — Agreement to build house — Dispute as to alleged defects in workmanship and materials — Repairs deferred while liability disputed —*

DAMAGES—*continued.*

Decision in accordance with commercial good sense — Date by reference to which damages should be assessed — Plaintiff's financial stringency — Whether relevant.] The plaintiff by an agreement in writing contracted to buy from the defendant a bungalow for the sum of £36,000 which was being built by the defendant. The home was virtually complete when the contract was signed. The plaintiff claimed that serious defects appeared in the house from an early stage after the sale was closed in mid 1979; that he repeatedly brought these matters to the notice of the first-named defendant but that nothing was done to remedy them. The plaintiff commenced proceedings for damages by plenary summons dated 6 November, 1980. The statement of claim was delivered on 14 August, 1981, and claimed damages of £13,731.56 being the amount of the lowest tender submitted to the plaintiff to remedy the defects. A defence was delivered on 24 May, 1982, which traversed the entire of the plaintiff's claim save for the fact that an agreement for sale had been made between the parties. By the time the action came on for hearing in February, 1984, the cost of the remedial works had increased to £21,685 as a result of inflation. At the commencement of the action the defendant conceded for the first time that the plaintiff was entitled to damages but argued firstly that the tender of £13,731.56 was excessive and secondly that the damages to which the plaintiff was entitled should be measured by reference to the cost of remedial works at the time the tender of the builder was received and not by reference to the cost at the time of the action. **Held** by O'Hanlon J. finding for the plaintiff, 1, the tender of £13,731.56 was not excessive and the architect of the plaintiff had over-stated neither the defects in the house nor the nature of the remedial works which would be required to remedy them. 2. It was appropriate to enquire whether the plaintiff could be regarded as having acted in a reasonable manner in postponing the carrying out of the remedial works until he knew the outcome of his action for damages against the defendants. *Dodd Properties (Kent) Ltd.* v. *Canterbury City Council* [1980] 1 All E.R. 928 approved. 3. The plaintiff could not be faulted for delaying the carrying out of remedial works which were at all times going to cost a massive amount by comparison with the original purchase price of the house. Furthermore the purchaser was faced with a denial of legal liability by the builder and could not be certain that any expenditure on the property would be recouped until the issue had been decided by litigation. Accordingly he should not be penalised by receiving only an award of damages which would fall short of making good his loss at the time of the action. 4. Damages would be awarded by reference to the up-dated cost of making good the defects in the house as of the time of the action and the plaintiff would be compensated for the other loss that he had sustained. This sum of £26,686.47 would be increased to £27,000 so as to allow the plaintiff a nominal sum by way of general damages for inconvenience and upset. *Corrigan* v. *Crofton*

(H.C.) [1985] ILRM 189

3. —— **Exemplary damages** — *Dismissal — Officeholder — Dismissal held invalid — Failure to pay salary on due dates — Loss of availability of salary — Whether dismissal resulted in injury to health — Whether due to unlawful nature of dismissal — Exemplary damages — Loss arising from arbitrary nature of dismissal.*] The plaintiff was Commissioner of An Garda Síochána when he was dismissed by the Government. The plaintiff instituted proceedings in which it was determined that the dismissal was invalid for being in breach of the rules of natural justice: [1981] I.R. 75; 113 I.L.T.R. 61. The plaintiff was paid his salary for the period between the date of his purported dismissal and the date when he resigned his office. The plaintiff's claim for damages on foot of his wrongful dismissal was in respect of (1) special damage arising from the failure to receive his pay at the appointed times; (2) general damages arising from injury to health and reputation; and (3) exemplary damages for the arbitrary nature of the Government's dismissal. **Held** by McWilliam J., in assessing damages, 1, the plaintiff had suffered loss by not receiving his pay at the appropriate times since he either had to borrow money at interest to replace his salary or was deprived of the opportunity of making investments or otherwise so as to make a profit. 2. The plaintiff was not entitled to general damages in relation to injured feelings or frustration, since there was no injury to the plaintiff's health in the normally accepted sense, and the other matters complained of would have been applicable to a greater or lesser extent had he been lawfully removed from office. *Addis* v. *Gramophone Co. Ltd.* [1909] A.C. 488 applied; *Cox* v. *Phillips Industries Ltd.* [1976] 1 W.L.R. 638 considered. 3. The plaintiff was entitled to exemplary damages in respect of the injury suffered arising from the arbitrary and oppressive conduct of the Government taking account that similar injury would, to a large extent, have been sustained by the plaintiff had he been lawfully removed from office. *Garvey* v. *Ireland*

(H.C.) [1979] ILRM 266

4. —— **Exemplary damages** — *Plaintiff assaulted by a member of an army patrol —*

DAMAGES—*continued.*

Awarded aggravated damages — Whether exemplary damages should be awarded — Whether soldier a "servant of the government" — Whether aggressive conduct.] The appellant who was then aged 16 years was assaulted by a member of an Army patrol who shoved a knee against the appellant's private parts and struck him with the butt of a rifle on the head. The appellant's head was cut and bled freely. The soldier and another member of the patrol then fastened "plastic type" handcuffs around the appellant's ankles and feet. A sizeable crowd gathered and showed hostility to the Army patrol. Fifteen minutes later vehicles arrived and the appellant was taken to hospital and discharged that evening. The appellant sued the respondent for damages for assault and battery. The respondent admitted liability and the nature and degree of the assault was not challenged. The appellant suffered no serious or permanent physical consequences. The learned Additional Recorder of Belfast awarded the appellant damages of £1,000 which sum included an amount for aggravated damages but not for exemplary damages. The appellant appealed against the award contending that the case was a proper one for exemplary damages and that the award should be significantly increased. **Held,** allowing the appeal, that the appellant's entitlement to damages could be considered under the following heads, 1, general damages in respect of pain and suffering and loss of amenities and enjoyment in life. 2. Aggravated damages as compensation for injury to a person's feelings. In the case of assault and battery they may be properly awarded if in addition to the physical injury the victim also suffered indignity or humiliation, here the appellant's youth, his reserved personality and the nature of the assault were relevant considerations, it was also relevant that the crowd were hostile to the soldiers and sympathetic to the appellant and so any humiliation felt would have been less. 3. Exemplary damages which are in essence punitive, they may be awarded when the actions of a servant of the Government, such as a soldier acting in aid of the civil power are oppressive and when the punitive element was not sufficiently met within the compensatory award. The conduct of the soldier was a deliberate and unjustifiable abuse of the lawful power to stop and question persons and a proper award to include exemplary damages was £2,500. *Lavery* v. *Ministry of Defence*

(Q.B.D.) [1984] N.I.99

5. —— **Exemplary damages** — *Wrongful arrest — Plaintiff arrested in army raid and held for several hours — Assessment of damages — Whether exemplary damages should be awarded.*] In 1980 the plaintiff was arrested by an army

DAMAGES—*continued.*

patrol which entered her home at 6.30 a.m. She was taken to a police station where she was questioned and photographed and released after two hours. No suggestion was made that she had committed any offence and no comment was made to her on release, except a phrase indicating mistaken identity. The plaintiff had not been subjected to physical or verbal harassment. In 1982 she commenced an action for damages and in its defence the defendant alleged, *inter alia,* that the plaintiff had been lawfully arrested. At the trial of the action the defendant conceded that the arrest was unlawful, and the only issue was that of damages. The plaintiff was a schoolteacher and at the time of the incident had been substituting for absent teachers at various schools. As a result of the arrest she had not been asked back for some time to the school she went to that morning. She had also subsequently suffered from nervousness and bad dreams. The witness for the defendant said that the arrest was part of a "screening" operation and that at the briefing before the arrest it was said that she was thought to be associating with a member of an illegal organisation. **Held,** awarding the plaintiff £4,000 damages, that the conduct of the defendant's agents at the briefing rendered it liable to pay exemplary damages for oppressive and arbitrary conduct by the servants of the Government. *Walsh* v. *Ministry of Defence*

(Q.B.D.) [1985] N.I.62

6. —— **Foreseeability** — *Remoteness — Future loss of profits — Destruction of brochures used in mail order business — Foreseeability of loss — Remoteness — Test — Assessment of damages.*] The plaintiff's warehouse was flooded due to the negligence of the first-named defendant. Stored there were brochures which the plaintiffs had planned to use in their sales campaign in the mail order market in the U.S. Preliminary leaflets had been posted inviting interested persons to send for the brochures. As a result of the flood these brochures were destroyed. The plaintiffs were unsuccessful in getting the brochures re-printed in time to post them in order to exploit the Christmas market. The action having been discontinued as against the second-named defendant the plaintiff claimed damages from the first-named defendants under various heads, including, in particular, future loss of profits arising from the destruction of the brochures. The defendant contended (1) that no one could have anticipated that the loss of the brochures would have resulted in such a large claim for loss of profits; (2) that no one could have foreseen that the plaintiffs would not have succeeded in getting the brochures reprinted in time to exploit the Christmas market. **Held** by Carroll J. in giving judgment for the plaintiffs, 1, if a defendant

DAMAGES—*continued.*

through its negligence injures property in a warehouse, it must take the responsibility for damaging whatever goods are there. It is also foreseeable that, because a warehouse is part of the world of commerce, there will be economic loss and possible loss of profits. If the goods cannot be replaced, then the economic loss, including loss of profits is foreseeable. 2. The economic consequences of the loss of the brochures was immediately predictable at the time of the damage. 3. If the court is satisfied that the plaintiff has fulfilled its duty to mitigate its losses, then the fact that the plaintiff's inability to do so was unforeseeable, is not relevant. 4. In all the circumstances the plaintiff made all reasonable attempts to mitigate loss and the fact that it failed to do so did not count against it. *William Egan & Sons Ltd.* v. *John Sisk & Sons Ltd.*

(H.C.) [1986] ILRM 283

7. —— **Foreseeability** — *Remoteness — Loss of premises — Interest on loan for premises — Whether recoverable — Whether reasonably foreseeable — Award — Apportionment — Concurrent wrongdoers — Each defendant responsible for event causing loss to plaintiff — Whether appropriate to apportion damage between defendants — Civil Liability Act,* 1961 (*No.* 41), *s.* 11.] The plaintiffs leased a premises for a term of 21 years from 1 July, 1964. The first-named defendant owned the premises, and also two adjoining premises which it wished to demolish and re-develop. It employed the second-named defendant to carry out this work under the direction of its architect. The second-named defendant employed the third-named defendant to carry out the demolition work. In January, 1972, the plaintiffs commenced a travel agency business in the premises. As a result of the demolition and excavation work being carried out in the adjoining premises the side of the premises collapsed, depriving the plaintiffs of the use of the premises for eighteen months and destroying and damaging some of their property. The plaintiff claimed damages under the following headings: (1) the value of the equipment damaged and destroyed; (2) the rent of alternative accommodation from the time of the collapse until their return to the new offices; (3) loss of profits from their being deprived of the use of their premises. McWilliam J., in granting the plaintiffs' damages, made the decree against all the defendants and did not apportion damages as between them. The case was then re-entered for argument on an item of damage. The question the court was required to decide was whether the plaintiffs were entitled to recover interest on the money they had borrowed in order to pay for alternative premises. **Held** by McWilliam J. in allowing the plaintiffs recover the interest: the plaintiffs were entitled to recover such interest on the money they borrowed for the alternative premises as they could establish was reasonable in the circumstances; it was a question of fact whether the plaintiffs in mitigating their loss acted reasonably; and a reasonable man would have foreseen that the plaintiffs would have been put out of business had they been unable to obtain alternative premises to enable them to continue their business. *Overseas Tankship (U.K.) Ltd.* v. *Morts Dock & Engineering Co. Ltd.; The Wagon Mound (No. 1)* [1961] A.C. 388 applied; *Owners of Dredger Liebosch* v. *Owners of SS Edison* [1933] A.C. 499 disapproved. *Riordan's Travel Ltd.* v. *Acres and Co.Ltd.*

(H.C.) [1979] ILRM 3

8. —— **Personal injuries** — *Award — Deductions — Social Welfare disability benefit — Pay related benefit — Whether possible future social welfare payments deductible from damages — Road traffic accident — Social Welfare Act,* 1984 (*No.* 5), *s.* 12.] On 17 September, 1985, a collision occurred between the plaintiff cyclist and a car owned by the second named defendant and driven by the first named defendant. The plaintiff suffered injuries to his right shoulder, neck and back. He further complained of the onset of psoriasis and clinical depression. He did no work from the date of his accident to the date of hearing in April, 1988. He was made redundant by his employer as part of a scheme of redundancy in December, 1986. There was evidence that his redundancy was due to his particular skills being no longer required and not to his being out from work due to the injury; therefore his redundancy payment of approximately £17,000 was not deductible from his damages. The jury found the defendants responsible for the accident and awarded damages as follows: (*a*) agreed special damages £922.93; (*b*) loss of earnings to date £14,423; (*c*) future loss of earnings £5,000; (*d*) pain and suffering to date £7,500; (*e*) pain and suffering in the future £6,000. Total £33,845.93. The amount allowed by the jury for loss of earnings to date was less than the amount agreed between the parties as the probable earnings of the plaintiff from the date of accident to the date of hearing if he had continued to be employed by the same employer during that period *viz.* £24,493. It was conceded by the plaintiff that the total social welfare disability benefit paid to the plaintiff to the date of hearing *viz.* £16,800 should be deducted from the damages awarded. The defendants contended that a further amount of £14,040 should also be deducted, being the amount which would be paid in disability benefit to the plaintiff from the date of hearing to the expiry of five years from the date of

DAMAGES—*continued.*

accident, assuming that he continued to receive such benefit. **Held** by MacKenzie J., 1, on the evidence he could not say it was probable that the plaintiff would receive disability benefit in the future. 2. Therefore he would not deduct any amount for disability benefit from the amount awarded by the jury for future loss of earnings and future pain and suffering. *O'Loughlin* v. *Teeling*

(H.C.) [1988] ILRM 617

9. —— **Personal injuries** — *Future economic loss — Road traffic accident — Appropriate multiplier — Risk of umemployment — Rate of interest — Cost of future care — General damages — Whether account to be taken of plaintiff's lack of awareness or appreciation of his condition.*

Delegated legislation — Health services — Exclusion of certain road traffic accident victims from class of persons entitled to hospital services free of charge — Whether ultra vires *— Intention of legislature — Presumption of constitutionality — Health Act,* 1970 (*No.* 1), *s.* 72 *— Health Services Regulations,* 1971 (*S.I. No.* 105), *art.* 6.] The plaintiff suffered severe brain damage in a road traffic accident, as a result of which it was stated that his mental age would at no time be more than two years. In proceedings against the defendant, his claim for damages included hospitalisation charges which had been imposed on the plaintiff pursuant to Art. 6 (3) of the Health Services Regulations, 1971. This regulation excluded from the class of persons with full eligibility for hospital in-patient and out-patient services provided for in ss. 52 and 56 of the Health Act, 1970, those who required treatment for injuries received in a road traffic accident, unless it appeared that such persons would not be entitled to receive damages or compensation from another person in respect of the injuries. The regulation was purportedly made pursuant to s. 72 of the Health Act, 1970, which empowered the Minister for Health to make regulations in which any of the health services described in the Act would be 'made available only to a particular class of the persons who have eligibility for that service.' It was conceded that but for the regulation the plaintiff would have been entitled to the hospital services free of charge. The defendant contended that the regulation was *ultra vires* the Minister and, if not, that it was unconstitutional. In the High Court, Hamilton J. rejected both these claims and awarded the plaintiff damages totalling £757,538.92. The defendant appealed on the same grounds as had been put forward in the High Court and also that the damages awarded were excessive. **Held** by the Supreme Court (O'Higgins C.J., Henchy, Griffin, Hederman and McCarthy JJ.) in reversing the High Court

DAMAGES—*continued.*

on the issue of *ultra vires*, 1, the defendant had standing to challenge the validity of the regulation because it was his only means of disputing the imposition of hospital charges on the plaintiff which the defendant was expected to meet. *Per* O'Higgins C.J. (Henchy, Griffin and Hederman JJ. concurring; McCarthy J. reserving the question) the decision in *Cahill* v. *Sutton* [1980] I.R. 269 could equally apply to an issue of *ultra vires* as to an issue of constitutionality. 2. While s. 72 may have envisaged excusing a particular health board from the obligation to provide a particular service for a particular class of those with limited eligibility, the regulation was *ultra vires* the Minister in purporting to exclude from the benefit of the services in ss. 52 and 56 a category of persons whose exclusion was in no way authorised or contemplated by the Act, and in a manner which attempted to amend the two sections by ministerial regulation instead of by appropriate legislation. *Per* O'Higgins C.J. (Henchy, Griffin, Hederman and McCarthy JJ. concurring): in determining the issue of *ultra vires,* it is necessary, in accordance with the presumption of constitutionality, to interpret the provisions of the Act in a manner which would absolve the Oireachtas from any intention to delegate its exclusive power of making or changing laws. **Held** further by the Supreme Court *per* Griffin J. (O'Higgins C.J., Henchy and Hederman JJ. concurring; McCarthy J. dissenting) in ordering a new trial on the issue of damages. 3. In ascertaining damages for future loss of earnings the trial judge had not taken into account the risk of unemployment or redundancy which economic forecasts indicated as likely for the present and foreseeable future, or that the plaintiff would have been required to pay income tax and that other deductions would have been made from his wages. *Dicta* of Griffin J. in *Reddy* v. *Bates* [1984] ILRM 197 applied. *Per* McCarthy J.: an assumption that high unemployment levels would continue to the end of the plaintiff's anticipated working life could not necessarily be made, and since the discounts for income tax and other deductions in assesment had not been argued before the court, they should not form the basis for a decision on this part of the assessment. *Per curiam:* the rate of interest ($2\frac{1}{2}$%) chosen by the trial judge in calculating damages for future loss of earnings would not be interfered with, but in future cases a different rate might be justified. 4. The sum awarded to the plaintiff's mother for care and attention was excessive in not taking into account that the plaintiff would be cared for in a day centre for the foreseeable future and that she could not take care of him for the whole of his anticipated lifetime. The amount for transport to, and therapy in, the day centre was also

DAMAGES—*continued.*

excessive as were the hospitalisation charge damages. *Per* McCarthy J.: only the amount for hosital charges should be set aside. 5. The general damages did not take into account the plaintiff's lack of awareness or appreciation of his condition, and since a jury, or trial judge, should also consider whether the total or global sum awarded is a fair and reasonable compensation to the injured person, the amounts awarded were excessive. *Per* McCarthy J.: the issue of the awareness or appreciation of his condition should be reserved for further consideration, and since there was no error patent on the trial judge's assessment it should not be interfered with on appeal. Decision of Hamilton J. [1983] ILRM 429 reversed. *Cooke* v. *Walsh*

(S.C.) [1984] ILRM 208

Editor's note: see also **Constitution,** 34 — [1984] I.R.710

10. —— **Personal injuries** — *General damages — Road traffic accident — Award of jury — Appeal to Supreme Court — Whether damages excessive — Principles applicable.*] In 1979, at the age of 24, the plaintiff, a clerk, suffered brain damage due to a car crash caused by the defendant's negligence. The brain damage caused severe physical loss of capacity and impairment of memory and concentration. The plaintiff spent over a year in hospital and rehabilitation centres and had a number of important operations. The brain damage resulted in a rare form of disabling bony growth which made walking difficult even after operations and rehabilitation. The plaintiff needed someone to help her in her flat. Her expert evidence was to the effect that she would never work again. In the plaintiff's action for damages in the High Court actuarial evidence was given in relation to the future special damages. As regards the future loss of earnings the actuary took into account the possibility of death and changing interest rates. Using the actuarial figures for age 65 as a multiplier, the plaintiff's capitalised loss of future earnings would have been £123,000.000. The jury in the High Court awarded, *inter alia,* general damages to date £100,000.00, general damages for future £150,000.00, special damages for the future (*a*) loss of earnings £144,000.00 (*b*) cost of housekeeper £115,000.00. The total of the award was £551,354.00. The defendant appealed. Both parties consented to an assessment by the Supreme Court of any item of damages set aside by the court. **Held** (Griffin and Hederman JJ.: McCarthy J. dissenting in parts) allowing the appeal and reducing the damages to £400,354.00. In a case where the damages have been assessed under several headings the total sum and the income it could generate should be considered by the jury to ascertain whether such sum is out of all proportion to the circumstances of the case. A jury's verdict on damages can only be set aside if, on the view of the facts which is most favourable to the plaintiff, no reasonable proportion exists between the amount awarded and the facts of the case. The total award of £551,354.00 was excessive. *Foley* v. *Thermocement Ltd.* 90 I.L.T.R. 92 applied. In assessing the amount to award for future loss of earnings actuarial figures are only a guideline. In making such assessments the jury should have to consider evidence relating to the risk of unemployment, redundancy, illness, accident or marriage prospects. The amount for future loss of earnings would be reduced to £123,000.00. The amount for a housekeeper would not be interfered with, although it was higher than appeared correct, because it was in the range of damages which on the evidence the jury could have found. The general damages were excessive and the amount for the past would be reduced to £50,000.00 and for the future to £70,000.00. Juries should be directed, in cases where sufficient damages have been awarded to cover all losses and bodily needs and to enable the plaintiff to live in comparative comfort having regard to the disability, that this fact should be reflected in the amount of general damages to be awarded. *Per* McCarthy J. The total of the amount calculated under the various headings, though it may be high, is not of itself a ground for interference. *Foley* v. *Thermocement Ltd.* only applies to general damages. The income which may be generated by the total award is irrelevant. In reviewing general damages, the awards for past and future should be considered both separately and as a whole. As a general rule, awards for general damages should only be interfered with if the disparity between the views of the Supreme Court and each item of the award is not less than 25%. *Reddy* v. *Bates*

(S.C.) [1984] ILRM 197; [1983] I.R. 141

11. —— **Personal injuries** — *General damages — Road traffic accident Failure to wear seat belt — Proportion of fault appropriate — Factors to be considered in compensating victim.*

Negligence — Indemnity — Concurrent wrongdoer — Employer and employee — Road traffic accident — Employer seeking indemnity from employee using vehicle in course of employment — Employee guilty of negligence — Civil Liability Act, 1961 (*No.* 41), *s.* 21 — *Road Traffic Act,* 1961 (*No.* 24), *s.* 118.] The plaintiff suffered severe personal injuries in a road traffic accident when a passenger in a car owned by Quinnsworth and driven by its employee, Durning, was in collision with a bus owned by CIE. As a result the plaintiff became a quadriplegic, totally

DAMAGES—*continued.*

dependent on others. His family provided for his needs up to and after the trial of his action against the three defendants. In the trial the drivers of the bus and car both gave evidence that they were on the correct side of the road at the time of the collision. The High Court jury found the driver of the car negligent in that he was on the right hand side of the road at the time of the collision. It also found, in answering another question on the issue paper, which had been agreed by all parties, that although the bus driver was on the correct side he was negligent in failing to drive as close as possible to the left hand side. The car driver was found 78% at fault, the bus driver 20% and, for failing to wear his seat belt, the plaintiff 2%. Damages totalling £1,484,591.72 were awarded, comprising *inter alia,* £439,674 for future care, £48,768 for future out of pocket expenses and £800,000 for general damages. Appealed as to the apportionment of blame to CIE, the degree of fault apportioned to the plaintiff for failing to wear a seat belt, the amount of damages awarded and the indemnity awarded to Quinnsworth as against Durning. **Held** by the Supreme Court (O'Higgins C.J., Henchy, Griffin, Hederman and McCarthy JJ.), 1, although the jury was answering an agreed question in apportioning blame to the bus driver, there was no evidence to support such a conclusion and in these circumstances the court would set aside that finding and apportion total blame to the car driver. *Semble:* had there been evidence to justify the finding the parties would have been bound by their conduct at the trial. 2. The 2% fault apportionment to the plaintiff for failure to wear a seat belt was unjustifiably low and, on the evidence adduced, a figure of 15% fault should be substituted. 3. The sum awarded for future care was wholly unreal and unreasonable in overproviding for the nursing requirements of the plaintiff and would be reduced to £203,454 to include a part-time housekeeper and orderly to assist his family and further allowance. 4. The sum for future out of pocket expenses should be increased to £131,064 to take account of the need for a part-time nurse, medical appliances including wheelchairs and partial liability for hospital care. *Cooke* v. *Walsh* [1984] ILRM 208 referred to. 5. The sum for general damages should represent fair and reasonable compensation for the loss and injury sustained by the plaintiff, taking account of the total sum awarded in respect of past and future loss or expense, ordinary living standards prevailing in the country, the general level of incomes and the things on which the plaintiff might reasonably be expected to spend money, and since in the light of such factors the jury's award was wholly unrealistic, it should be reduced to £150,000. *Dicta* of Griffin J. in *Reddy* v. *Bates* [1983] I.R. 141 applied. *Per* O'Higgins C.J., (Henchy, Griffin and Hederman JJ. concurring): in a case of this nature unless particular circumstances suggest otherwise, general damages should not exceed a sum in the region of £150,000. *Per* McCarthy J. (concurring): settlements of personal injuries claims involving sums of over £150,000 for general damages do not necessarily mirror the true measure of damages. 6. Durning was not entitled to be indemnified by Quinnsworth and, since Quinnsworth had seen to it that Durning was protected by insurance from third party liability arising from his driving, Quinnsworth was not barred from claiming an indemnity from Durning. Those insuring against Road Traffic Act liability should pay the damages in respect of such liability. *Lister* v. *Romford Ice and Cold Storage Co. Ltd.* [1957] A.C. 555 and *Morris* v. *Ford Motor Co.* [1973] 1 Q.B. 792 considered; *Harvey* v. *R. G. O'Dell Ltd.* [1958] 2 Q.B. 78 doubted. *Per* McCarthy J.: It is not for the Supreme Court to express a view on whether decisions of foreign courts were wrongly decided but merely, where relevant to express agreement or otherwise with a legal principle stated in such decisions. *Quaere,* per McCarthy J., whether the decision in *Reddy* v. *Bates* laid down a principle that those items of the award which comprise past special damage and future identifiable and concrete loss are to be added together for the purpose of calculating the income that prudent investment might realise therefrom. *Sinnott* v. *Quinnsworth Ltd.*

(S.C.) [1984] ILRM 523

12. —— **Personal injuries** — *General damages — Road traffic accident — Negligence — High Court award — Appeal to Supreme Court — Whether damages excessive.*] At the age of 14 the plaintiff was severely injured in a road accident, in which she sustained, besides a serious leg injury, brain damage resulting in permanent intellectual and emotional impairment and in the physical handicaps of unsteady balance and intermittent tremors. At a trial without a jury Hamilton J. assessed damages at £683,000, made up as follows: care and attention for life, £350,000; future loss of earnings, £125,000; agreed special damages, £48,000; general damages for pain and suffering, £160,000 — Total £683,000. The figures for care and attention and for future loss of earnings represented the capitalised values of annual sums of £12,000 and £4,000 respectively. The actuarial calculation assumed that the plaintiff would live for more than fifty years, that a real rate of interest of 5% could be obtained, and that taxation would diminish that yield by half. The defendant appealed to the Supreme Court on the basis that the total award as well as the component parts

DAMAGES—*continued.*

(other than the agreed figure for special damages) were excessive. In the months following Hamilton J.'s award, which was made on 10 February, 1983, the Supreme Court delivered its judgments in *Reddy* v. *Bates* [1984] ILRM 197, *Cooke* v. *Walsh* [1984] ILRM 208, and *Sinnott* v. *Quinnsworth* [1984] ILRM 523. In *Reddy* v. *Bates* the majority held that, in a case where damages were assessed under several heads, it was proper to consider whether the total sum and the income it could generate were proportionate to the circumstances. In that case, and in *Cooke* v. *Walsh,* it was held that actuarial figures were only a guideline, and that such figures might be discounted to allow for the uncertainties of future economic prospects, levels of taxation and changed personal circumstances. In *Sinnott* v. *Quinnsworth* it was held that general damages should not as a rule exceed £150,000. **Held** (Griffin and Hederman JJ., McCarthy J. dissenting in part), allowing the appeal, that, 1, *per* Griffin and Hederman JJ.: the global figure for damages and the three disputed items were excessive. 2. *Per* Griffin and Hederman JJ.: the plaintiff's injuries were severe, but were not comparable with those involved in a case of quadriplegia. 3. *Per* Griffin and Hederman JJ.: the figure of £350,000 and £125,000 reached on actuarial evidence should be reduced respectively to £290,000 and £85,000, on the principle that actuarial multipliers should be discounted to allow for future uncertainties, such as the possibility that the after-tax return on the invested capital will exceed the posited rate of 2½%. 4. *Per curiam:* the figure for general damages should be reduced from £160,000 to £100,000. 5. *Per* Griffin and Hederman JJ.: the plaintiff's damages should be reduced in total by £160,000 from £683,000 to £523,000. 6. *Per* McCarthy J. (dissenting): the evidence and argument did not warrant reductions in the sums awarded for care and attention and future loss of earnings; arbitrary reductions should be avoided; and, as the function of the Supreme Court was to review, rather than to assess, damages, the case should be referred back to the trial judge. *Griffiths* v. *Van Raaj*

(S.C.) [1985] ILRM 582

13. —— **Personal injuries** — *Liability — Arrest and detention in Garda station — Plaintiff alleging that he was left with matches — Plaintiff setting fire to cell and suffering extensive burns — Whether defendants negligent — Whether defendant contributorily negligent and, if so, to what extent — Whether damages awarded excessive.*] The plaintiff was arrested and brought to a garda station after being found drunk and incapable by members of the Garda Síochána. He was searched and his belt and at least one box of matches were taken from him before he was locked in a cell on his own. The plaintiff alleged that he was in fact left with two boxes of matches in one of his trouser pockets following the search of his person and that after being in the cell for 15 or 20 minutes when he shouted to the gardaí to bring him a cigarette, threatening to set the cell on fire unless they did so, they failed to do so and he then lit a pillow in the centre of the cell. The fire spread rapidly over the floor and up the walls. The plaintiff suffered extensive burns and instituted proceedings against the defendants. The evidence for the defence denied the plaintiff's account of the events. It was that after two hours during which the plaintiff appeared to be settling down and during which period he was inspected every quarter of an hour, suddenly he was heard to be shouting and the cell was found to be on fire. He was released as soon as possible. A jury in the High Court found that the defendants' servants or agents were negligent, that the plaintiff was 15% to blame and assessed damages of £161,500 in favour of the plaintiff. Judgment for the plaintiff was entered by the court and the defendants appealed both against the findings of liability and against the assessment of damages. **Held** *Per* Finlay C.J., Walsh and McCarthy JJ., 1, the defendants' appeal in so far as it sought a finding that there was no evidence of negligence would be rejected. 2. There would be a re-trial on the issue of liability on the basis that the trial already had was unsatisfactory. The trial judge left only one general question with regard to the defendants' negligence to the jury. For the trial to be satisfactory a specific question on whether the search failed to reveal one or more boxes of matches in the plaintiff's possession and, subject to any objection with regard to the pleadings, a specific question on whether the defendants' servants heard the warning given by the plaintiff and ignored it would have to left to the jury. *Per* Henchy and Griffin JJ. dissenting. 3. The trial judge should have acceded to the application of the defendants to have the case withdrawn from the jury. Having regard to the evidence any finding that the plaintiff had been left with two boxes of matches would be perverse. The appeal should be allowed and the plaintiff's claim dismissed. *Per* Finlay C.J., Walsh, Henchy and Griffin JJ. (McCarthy J. expressing no view). 4. On the evidence a finding of only 15% proportion of fault against the plaintiff was so unreasonable that it should be set aside. *Per* Finlay C.J., Walsh, Henchy and Griffin JJ. 5. (i) Having regard to the jury award of £42,000 for loss of earnings to date, the jury was entitled to make an award under this head but not at the rate at which they did. The amount would be set aside. (ii) The jury award of £80,000 for loss of earnings

DAMAGES—*continued.*

in the future should be set aside. A separate figure under this head was not warranted by the evidence. (iii) The award of £39,000 for general damages to date, while generous, was not so excessive as to require intevention by the court. (iv) The award of £29,000 for general damages in the future was excessive and should be set aside. *McKevitt* v. *Ireland*

(S.C.) [1987] ILRM 541

DAMAGES—*continued.*

DECEASED PERSON—*continued.*

see **Adverse Possession**

DECLARATION

see cross-references under **Judicial Review**

DEED

—— Repugnancy — Subsequent provision only qualifying earlier one.

see **Landlord and Tenant,** 2

—— Transfer of land — Reservation of right of residence, care and support — Application to cancel transfer — Whether undue influence — Whether deed improvident.

see **Undue Influence**

DEFAMATION

1.—— **Libel** — *Ordinary meaning of words — Teachta Dála — National daily newspaper — Whether words published capable of bearing other than a defamatory meaning — Trial judge directing jury that words defamatory — Functions of judge and jury.*

Damages — Libel — Assessment — Compensatory purpose of damages — Damages to be fair and reasonable and bear correspondence with injury suffered — Factors to be considered in making an award of damages for libel — Review by appellate court of jury's assessment of damages.] The plaintiff was a member of the Fianna Fáil party and a Teachta Dála representing a Dublin constituency. The defendant was the publisher of the *Evening Herald* newspaper. On the 7 February, 1983, a meeting of the Fianna Fáil parliamentary party was held at Leinster House to consider a resolution that Mr. Charles Haughey be removed from the leadership of the party. The meeting lasted approximately twelve hours and ended with the defeat of the resolution. The members of the Fianna Fáil parliamentary party leaving Leinster House had to pass through the foyer, where a group of journalists had gathered awaiting news or comment. On the 8 February, 1983, the *Evening Herald* newspaper reported that "There were savage scenes as TDs left Leinster House early today. Michael Barrett TD, a Dublin Haugheyite leaned over and pulled at my beard and said 'You thought you'd dance on his grave'." The plaintiff brought proceedings against the defendant for damages for libel. The defendant admitted publishing the words complained of but claimed justification. At the trial of the action no evidence was called on behalf of the defendant. The trial judge refused to leave a question to the jury as to whether the words were defamatory, but ruled as a matter of law that they were. Accordingly the case went to the jury only for assessment of damages, which were assessed at

DEFAMATION—*continued.*

£65,000. The defendant appealed to the Supreme Court on the grounds, firstly, that the trial judge was wrong in law to direct the jury that the words were defamatory and had thereby produced a mistrial; and secondly, that the jury's award of damages was excessive. **Held** by the Supreme Court (Finlay C.J., Henchy, Griffin, Hederman and McCarthy JJ.), in allowing the appeal, 1, that where in a libel action the nature of the words complained of was in issue, it was for the judge in the first instance to decide whether the words were reasonably capable of bearing the defamatory meaning alleged. If the judge answered that question in the negative the case could not go to the jury: but (Finlay C.J. and McCarthy J. dissenting) if the judge ruled that the words were capable of bearing the defamatory meaning alleged, it was always a matter for the jury to decide whether the words did in fact carry that meaning. *Parmiter* v. *Coupland* (1840) 151 E.R. 340; *Broome* v. *Agar* (1928) 138 L.T. 698 considered. 2. That while appellate courts might be extremely slow to interfere with the assessment by a jury of damages for defamation, such assessments were subject to review. 3. That the plaintiff was entitled to be compensated not only for the damage to his reputation but also for the anxiety, distress and injury to his feelings from the time of publication right up until the time of assessment of damages. 4. That in all the circumstances of the case the jury's award was excessive and must be set aside. *Per* Finlay C.J. and McCarthy J. (dissenting), that if an appellate court could set aside the verdict of a jury finding words not to be defamatory on the grounds that it was perverse and unreasonable, it followed as a necessary consequence that a trial judge had a right and a duty in an appropriate case to prevent such a perverse or unreasonable result by directing the jury. *Berry* v. *Irish Times* [1973] I.R. 368; *Lockhart* v. *Harrison* (1928) 139 L.T. 521 considered. *Per* Finlay C.J. and McCarthy J. (dissenting), that on the facts of a finding by a jury that the words were not defamatory would have been perverse and, accordingly, that the re-trial should be confined to the issue of damages. *Barrett* v. *Independent Newspapers Ltd.*

(S.C.) [1986] I.R.13; [1986] ILRM 601

2.—— **Libel** — *Privilege — Qualified privilege — Complaint to professional body — Professional body not having interest or duty in receiving complaint — Defendant's honest and reasonable belief that professional body had such interest — Whether occasion thereby one of qualified privilege — Malice — Essentials of malice for case to go to jury.*] The plaintiff was a consultant psychiatrist and the defendant a solicitor both practising in Cork. The defendant required the plaintiff to give evidence on behalf of his client

DEFAMATION—*continued.*

at family law proceedings in Dublin. The plaintiff objected to attending and the defendant eventually served a subpoena upon her, enclosing viaticum of £20. She complied and the case settled after lunchtime without having commenced. About a week later the defendant received a bill from the plaintiff for £300 and he wrote to her and demanded a breakdown of her fees. She wrote a fortnight later to the Incorporated Law Society of Ireland, enquiring as to whether the Society had laid down any guidelines for compelling professional people to attend court by subpoena at extremely short notice, complaining that the defendant had treated her badly and seeking the Society's assistance in obtaining her fee. The Law Society sent a copy of her letter to the defendant and asked him for his comments. He replied in a very lengthy letter of criticism and described her as a person "who holds scant regard for professional ethics and even less for the solemnity of the law." The letter further stated that when told that the defendant would be obliged to serve a subpoena, the plaintiff said she could send a"sick note", and that she had attempted to avoid service of the subpoena and that she was obsessed with payment of her fees. On the following day the defendant sent a copy of that letter together with a covering letter to the secretary of the Irish Medical Association ("I.M.A."). The covering letter formally complained that she was willing alone or with members of the medical profession to falsify a medical certificate on her behalf; that she was lacking in integrity in making a misleading complaint to the Law Society; and that she charged exorbitant fees and expenses for a court appearance. The secretary to the I.M.A. by letter replied that the I.M.A. had no function in relation to such complaints and referred him to the Medical Council. The defendant then made an identical complaint to the Medical Council, enclosing also a copy of his original letter to the Law Society. The plaintiff in the High Court claimed damages for libel in respect of all three letters. The defendant pleaded denial, justification and qualified privilege; the plaintiff in reply alleged malice. At the trial, before judge and jury, the defendant applied at the close of the evidence for the plaintiff for a direction of no case to answer. The trial judge (Johnson J.) ruled that while the letters to the Law Society and Medical Council were made on occasions of qualified privilege, since it had not been established that the plaintiff was a member of the I.M.A., the letter to it could not be privileged unless the defendant in evidence established he had honestly believed it to be the appropriate body to address a complaint concerning the plaintiff's conduct. At the conclusion of the defendant's case, the defendant repeated his

DEFAMATION—*continued.*

application for a dismiss. The trial judge then ruled that since the defendant had honestly believed the I.M.A. to be the appropriate body, therefore the letter was published on an occasion of qualified privilege. He further ruled that there was no evidence, in any of the letters complained of, from which a jury could conclude malice more likely than not, and dismissed the plaintiff's claim. The plaintiff appealed to the Supreme Court against the judgment and order of the High Court on the grounds: (1) that, in the absence of proof of the I.M.A.'s interest or duty in receiving complaints concerning the plaintiff, the letter was not published on an occasion of qualified privilege and that the defendant's honest belief could not render the occasion privileged; (2) that the trial judge erred in law in ruling that the plaintiff had failed to establish sufficient malice to go to the jury. The defendant cross-appealed on the trial judge's refusal to give a direction at the close of the plaintiff's evidence, and submitted in the Supreme Court that the defendant's honest and reasonable belief had rendered the occasion privileged. **Held** by the Supreme Court (Finlay C.J., Henchy, Griffin, Hederman and McCarthy JJ.) in dismissing the defendant's cross-appeal and allowing the plaintiff's appeal and directing a new trial, 1, that the defendant's mere honest belief that the party addressed had an interest or duty in receiving the publication in issue could not render the occasion privileged and the trial judge erred in law in so ruling and withdrawing the case from the jury. *Reilly* v. *Gill and Others* 85 I.L.T.R. 165; *Kirkwood Hackett* v. *Tierney* [1952] I.R. 185 and *Hebditch* v. *MacIlwaine* [1894] 2 Q.B. 54 followed. 2. That on the evidence, even if the defendant's belief that the I.M.A. had the appropriate interest or duty to receive the complaint had been honest, it could not have been reasonable, as a simple preliminary inquiry, without complaint of the plaintiff in particular, could have confirmed the I.M.A.'s absence of duty or interest in the matter, and thus even on his own submissions the defendant had failed to establish the occasion as privileged. 3. That in the circumstances it was unnecessary to decide on the submissions made to the court that a defendant's honest and reasonable belief that the party addressed had an interest or duty in receiving the publication in issue was capable, by itself, of rendering the occasion privileged. *London Association for Protection of Trade* v. *Greenlands Limited* [1916] 2 A.C. 15 considered. *Per* Henchy and Hederman JJ. The court should not depart from well-established precedents limiting occasions of qualified privilege unless ordained by statute or required by justice. *Per* McCarthy J. An occasion of qualified privilege is a legal conclusion to be drawn from established

DEFAMATION—*continued.*

facts: it would hardly be desirable that a party suffering injury to his reputation would be unable to determine from objective facts whether his legal remedy was denied by evidence to be revealed only at the trial of the action that the defendant had honestly and reasonably believed the occasion of publication to have been privileged. 4. That where the plaintiff can point to instances of malice, the trial judge must allow the case to go to the jury if it could reasonably hold as a matter of probability that any one of those instances represents malice. However, mere multiplicity of alleged instances, none of which, by itself, could be evidence of malice, did not amount to malice. *Dicta* in *Kirkwood Hackett* v. *Tierney* [1952] I.R. 185 and *Turner* v. *Metro-Goldwyn-Mayer Pictures Ltd.* [1950] 1 All E.R. 449 approved. *Per* McCarthy J. There may be circumstances where a series of items of evidence no one of which would be sufficient to displace the burden of proof of malice may have the cumulative effect of so doing. 5. That the trial judge erred in law in ruling that there was not sufficient evidence from which the jury could conclude the probability of the existence of malice, having regard in particular to the length, scope, occasional violent tone and continued publication of the letter to the Law Society and the fact that it was written in response to the plaintiff's letter concerning the defendant, and the issues of malice should not have been withdrawn from the jury. *Hynes-O'Sullivan* v. *O'Driscoll*

(S.C.) [1988] I.R.436

—— Libel — Damages — Quantum — Nature of defence — Aggravated damages.
see **Constitution,** 30

—— Libel — Defence — Particulars — Rolled-up plea — Further and better particulars — Compliance with court order — Whether sufficient compliance.
see **Practice and Procedure,** 49

—— Libel — Defence — Particulars — Statement of claim reproducing alleged libel — Libel including statements of fact, opinions and comments — Statement of facts alleged to be true — Plaintiff entitled to further particulars of (*a*) what part of alleged libel consists of statements of fact (*b*) the facts on which defendant relies as establishing truth of alleged libel and (*c*) the matters relied on as supporting truth of libel.
see **Practice and Procedure,** 48

—— Privilege — Qualified privilege — Whether evidence of malice.

DEFAMATION—*continued.*

see **Employer and Employee,** 4

DEFECTIVE PREMISES

—— Building contract — Breach — Defects in premises — Computation of damages — Whether purchaser entitled to loss in letting value or loss of interest on capital.
see **Building Contract,** 1

—— Building contract — Breach — Defects in premises — Exclusion clause — Further clause that purchaser not deprived of his common law rights — Claim for damages for remedying defects and for diminution in value — Whether caught by exclusion clause — Whether purchaser entitled to damages for inconvenience and loss of engagement.
see **Building Contract,** 2

—— Contribution — Engineer's certificate as to structural stability — Architect's certificate based on such certificate — Whether builder or architect negligent — Contribution as between defendants — Damages.
see **Negligence,** 1

—— Damages — Measure of damages — Agreement to build house — Dispute as to alleged defects in workmanship and materials — Repairs deferred while liability disputed — Decision in accordance with commercial good sense — Date by reference to which damages should be assessed — Plaintiff's financial stringency — Whether relevant.
see **Damages,** 2

—— Damages — Whether damages payable for defective workmanship and inconvenience as well as in respect of dangerous defects — Joint tortfeasors — Contribution or indemnity.
see **Negligence,** 2

—— Duty of care — Architect — Architect carrying out visual inspection of property — Scope and terms of engagement — Inspection — Survey — Extent of duty of care.
see **Negligence,** 3

—— Duty of care — Builder — Dwelling built on land owned by builder — Whether builder owed a common law duty of care to purchaser.
see **Negligence,** 2, 3

DEFENCE FORCES

1. —— **Dismissal** — *Navy — Natural justice — Notification of decision given but postponed to allow representation — No representations made — Whether sufficient compliance with rules of natural justice —* Audi alteram partem.

Natural justice — Employment — Dismissal — Office — Office dependent on obtaining specified qualification — Failure to obtain qualification — Repeated warnings given — Dismissal notified but postponed to allow representations — No representations made — Whether sufficient compliance with audi alteram partem *rule.*] The prosecutor enlisted as a petty officer in the Irish navy, for a period of four years in 1977 subject to the conditions in the Defence Acts, 1954 and 1960 and the regulations made thereunder. He failed to qualify for the engine room artificer (E.R.A.) certificate (which was an essential qualification to enable him to stand watch on his own in the ship's engine room) due to his ineptitude, indifference and inability to perform routine duties efficiently and safely. The authorities after due consideration decided to discharge the prosecutor pursuant to the aforesaid regulations for 'not being likely to become efficient.' They informed him on 23 February, 1978, that they were about to discharge him, and actually discharged him on 6 March, 1978, giving him opportunity to make representations to them which he failed to do. In August, 1978, he instituted certiorari proceedings to quash his discharge on the grounds that he had not been informed of his discharge until after his discharge. The High Court granted an absolute order of certiorari. On appeal **Held** by the Supreme Court (Henchy, Kenny and Parke JJ.) in allowing the appeal, 1, the principles of natural justice were complied with as the respondent was repeatedly told prior to his discharge of the reason for his discharge and so was given an adequate opportunity to meet the case against him. *The State (Gleeson)* v. *Minister for Defence* [1976] I.R. 280 distinguished. 2. The purpose of the *audi alteram partem* rule in this situation was to ensure that the prosecutor was in full knowledge of his impending discharge and the reason for it, and that he could make representations as he thought fit. 3. The rule of *audi alteram partem* had been observed as prior to his discharge if the prosecutor had had a good case to make he still had time and opportunity to make it efficiently. *The State (Duffy)* v. *Minister for Defence*
(S.C.) [1979] ILRM 65

DEFENCE FORCES—*continued.*

2. —— **Pension** — *Disability pension — Deduction — Injury to serving soldier in road traffic accident — Award of damages in civil action — Award reflecting loss of difference between private's pay and sergeant's pay — Award not reflecting total loss of soldier's pay — Appeal against jury's award settled for gross sum for damages — Premature retirement due to injury — Disability pension awarded — Provision in pensions Acts allowing Minister to take into consideration compensation received by soldier — Pension nullified by deduction of annual value of capital sum paid in compensation — Obligation of Minister in considering compensation paid — Intent of provision — Effect of provision — Whether compensation in respect of wounding other than wounding on active service could be taken into account — Army Pensions Act,* 1923 (*No.* 26), *s.* 13 — *Army Pensions Act,* 1927 (*No.* 12), *s.*12.] Section 13, sub-s. 2 of the Army Pensions Act, 1923, as amended by s. 3 of the Army Pensions Act, 1927, and by s. 3 of the Army Pensions Act, 1946, provides *inter alia* as follows: "Any compensation which may be received from or on behalf of the person alleged to be responsible for the act which caused the wounding or death of a person . . . may be taken into consideration in fixing the amount of any pension, allowance or gratuity, which might be awarded under this Act to or in respect of such person . . ." In 1975, the prosecutor, who was then a serving private soldier, was injured when the army car in which he was travelling as a passenger crashed. In High Court proceedings brought against the Minister for Finance for the alleged negligence of the army driver of the car, the prosecutor was awarded £98,213.84 damages by a jury. Of that award a sum of £20,300 was in respect of potential loss of earnings in the future and represented the capital value of the difference between a private's pay and a sergeant's pay to the maximum age to which the prosecutor might have remained in the army. The prosecutor would probably have been promoted to sergeant but for his injuries, but at the time of the award no assessment had been made of his suitability to remain in the army. The Minister for Finance appealed that award to the Supreme Court on the grounds that it was excessive in respect of general damages and in April, 1982, by which time both parties were aware that the prosecutor would not be retained in the army, the appeal was settled for a sum of £90,000. It was not specified what part of that sum represented loss of earnings. In May, 1982, the prosecutor was discharged from the army and the Army Pensions Board recommended the payment to him of a disability pension. The respondent awarded the pension recommended but abated it by £5,301 per annum, which was an actuarial conversion of the yearly value of the capital sum paid on foot of the aforesaid settlement. The prosecutor objected to the deduction and obtained a conditional order of certiorari quashing it on the grounds that the respondent had misconstrued his powers under the Army Pensions Acts, 1923-1977. It was argued on behalf of the prosecutor that the statutory power in s. 13, sub-s. 2 of the Act of 1923 to take compensation into account in fixing the amount of a pension was limited to compensation for loss of earnings and did not extend to damages for personal injuries. The jury's award, it was argued, did not take account of the loss of his private's pay and because the respondent was aware of how the jury's award was made up, he could not now treat the prosecutor as if compensation for loss of pay had been awarded. It was argued for the respondent showing cause that the meaning of s. 13, sub-s. 2 of the Act of 1923 was clear and unambiguous and that there was nothing in the Acts to exclude general damages or to confine its application to special damages for loss of pay; and, in any event, that the sum agreed in settlement of the appeal had not been subdivided. On the prosecutor's motion to make absolute the conditional order notwithstanding cause shown it was **Held** by Gannon J., in allowing the cause shown and discharging the conditional order, 1, that the effect of s. 13 of the Act of 1923 was that a pension under the Army Pensions Acts would not be paid to a person who was otherwise adequately provided for in respect of the matter giving rise to his entitlement. 2. That, in the context in which s. 13 of the Act of 1923 was enacted and applied, the word "compensation" clearly had the same meaning as damages assessed and awarded by a jury in a civil action whether such award related only to personal injuries or to pay related loss or to both. On appeal by the respondent it was **Held** by the Supreme Court (Finlay C.J., Walsh, Henchy, Griffin and McCarthy JJ.), in allowing the appeal and quashing the entire of the award certificate, 1, that on the proper construction of s. 13, sub-s. 2 of the Act of 1923 as amended, the respondent might, before fixing the amount of any pension, either initially or by review, take into consideration any compensation received by the applicant; but was not entitled to subject a pension which had been approved by him on the recommendation of the Army Pensions Board to an automatic abatement by a sum calculated to be the annual value of the lump sum of compensation. 2. That the statutory function of the respondent under s. 13, sub-s. 2 of the Act of 1923 was to make a *bona fide* individual decision on the merits of each case, having due regard for

DEFENCE FORCES—*continued.*

the terms of the Army Pensions Act. *Quaere* whether, while the amendments to s. 13, sub-s. 2 of the Act of 1923 by the Army Pensions Act, 1946, were clearly intended to allow the Minister to take into consideration awards made in respect of road traffic injuries, it might, having regard to the definition of "wound" in s. 16 of the Act of 1923, be a necessary construction of the Act that the only compensation which could properly be considered was compensation in respect of wounding on active service. *The State (Thornhill)* v. *Minister for Defence*

(H.C., S.C.) [1986] I.R.1

3. —— **Pension** — *Disability pension — Deduction — Injury to serving soldier in accident — Award of damages in civil action — Provision in Pensions Acts allowing Minister to take into consideration compensation received by soldier — Obligation of Minister to consider the merits of each individual case — Fair procedures in review process — Guidelines for the exercise of ministerial discretion in review process — Army Pensions Act,* 1923 (*No.* 26), *s.* 13 — *Army Pensions Act,* 1927 (*No.* 12), *s.* 12 — *Army Pensions Act,* 1946 (*No.* 3), *s.* 3.] Section 13, sub-s. 2, of the Army Pensions Act, 1923, as amended, provides, *inter alia,* as follows: "Any compensation which may be received from or on behalf of the person alleged to be responsible for the act which caused the wounding . . . of . . . a soldier may be taken into consideration when fixing the amount of any pension, allowance or gratuity which might be awarded under this Act to or in respect of such . . . soldier and if such compensation is received after the award of any such pension or allowance the Minister may review the award and, having regard to the amount of such compensation, either terminate the pension or allowance or reduce the amount thereof." The plaintiff, a serving private soldier, was seriously injured in an accident in February, 1981. Consequently the plaintiff was discharged from the army and was awarded a pension under the Army Pensions Acts, 1923-1973. High Court proceedings taken against the Minister for Defence for the alleged negligence of members of the defence forces in causing the accident were settled for £220,000.00 damages paid to the plaintiff. Subsequently the plaintiff was informed by letter that his pension was being totally abated in view of the compensation awarded, as the compensation, when actuarially assessed, converted into an annuity that exceeded the amount of the pension payable. The plaintiff commenced High Court proceedings seeking to invalidate the decision of the Minister to abate his pension. After the commencement of these proceedings the Minister proposed to review the plaintiff's case in the light of the decision of the Supreme Court in *The State (Thornhill)* v. *The Minister for Defence* [1986] I.R. 1. The Minister sought representations from the plaintiff which the plaintiff refused to make and as a result of this refusal it was decided not to interfere with the original review of the pension. **Held** by Costello J., in granting the declarations sought, 1, that in reviewing the amount of any pension under s. 13, sub-s. 2, of the Army Pensions Act, 1923, the Minister must make a valid decision on the merits of the particular case and not merely subject the pension to an actuarial calculation. A decision not to interfere with the original review did not constitute a valid review. *The State (Thornhill)* v. *The Minister for Defence* [1986] I.R. 1 applied. 2. That the plaintiff was entitled to payment of his unabated pension until a valid review under s.13, sub-s. 2 of the Act took place. 3. That the Minister was constitutionally obliged to adopt fair procedures when carrying out a review under s. 13, sub-s. 2, of the Act. *Per* Costello J. In carrying out a review the Minister is entitled to take into account the proportion of damages attributable to general damages, to special damages and to loss of earnings; whether the damages represent the full value of the plaintiff's claim; and to make an actuarial calculation to assess the weekly value to the plaintiff of the whole or part of the award. *McKinley* v. *Minister for Defence*

(H.C.) [1988] I.R.139

4. —— **Pension** — *Disability pension — Deduction — Injury to soldier in course of his duties — Award of damages in civil action — Premature retirement due to injury — Disability pension awarded — Provision in Pension Acts allowing Minister to take into consideration compensation received by soldier — Pension nullified by deduction of annual value of capital sum paid in compensation — Whether compensation in respect of wounding other than wounding on active service could be taken into account — Whether Minister entitled to reduce pension by reference only to compensation received for future loss of earnings — Army Pensions Act,* 1923 (*No.* 26), *ss.* 13(2), 16 — *Army Pensions Act,* 1927, (*No.* 12), *ss.* 1, 12, 26 — *Army Pensions Act,* 1946 (*No.* 3), *s.* 3(1).] The Army Pensions Act, 1923, (the Principal Act) makes provision for the grant by the Minister for Defence of a "wound pension" to soldiers discharged from the defence forces as disabled. By s. 16 of that Act "wound" means a wound or injury received in the course of duty while attached to or forming part of a force engaged in operations against the enemy or engaged in military operations in a place wholly or partly occupied by the enemy. By s.

DEFENCE FORCES—*continued.*

13, sub-s. 2, as amended by s. 3, sub-s. 1 of the Act of 1946, any compensation received from the person responsible for the act which caused the wounding of a soldier may be taken into consideration in fixing the amount of a pension awarded "under this Act" and, where such compensation is received after the award of a pension, the Minister may review the award and reduce the amount thereof. Section 12 of the Act of 1927 enlarged the scope for granting pensions to soldiers suffering from disablements due to wounds attributable to service in the defence forces; by s. 1 the word "wound", for the purposes of that Act but not for the purposes of the Principal Act, is defined as meaning an interruption of the normal continuity of body tissue caused by direct or indirect violence. By s. 26 the expression "under this Act" in, *inter alia,* s. 13 of the Principal Act is defined to mean "under the Principal Act or under the Principal Act as amended by this present Act or under this present Act." The applicant was disabled by injuries which he suffered in a road traffic accident in the course of his duty as a member of the defence forces. He was discharged from the Army and was awarded a pension under the provisions of the Act of 1927. He subsequently succeeded in proceedings against the State in respect of those injuries and was awarded damages. The award included sums in respect of pain and suffering and loss of earnings to date and for the future. The respondent then reviewed the applicant's pension and terminated it, on the grounds that the annual value of the award for damages, calculated on an actuarial basis, exceeded the amount payable to the applicant as a pension. The applicant applied for judicial review of the respondent's decision and argued that the entitlement of the respondent under the Act of 1923 to take into account any compensation received in fixing the amount of a pension arose only in relation to wound pensions granted under and within the meaning of that Act, and also that the respondent was entitled to take into consideration only that proportion of the award which represented compensation for future loss of earnings. **Held** by O'Hanlon J. in refusing the application, 1, that although the applicant had not been wounded within the meaning of the Principal Act, the respondent could apply s. 13, sub-s. 2 of that Act to the pension granted under the Act of 1927, and that the word "wounding" in that sub-section must be interpreted in accordance with the wider definition of "wound" set out in the later Act. 2. That as so applied, the respondent was entitled to take into account the compensation awarded in the civil proceedings, the defendant in that case being the person responsible for wounding the applicant. 3. That "compensation" in s. 13,

DEFENCE FORCES—*continued.*

sub-s. 2 of the Act of 1923 was not confined to compensation for loss of earnings or to any particular heading of damages. *The State (Thornhill)* v. *Minister for Defence* [1986] I.R. 1 applied. 4. That a wide discretion was conferred on the respondent as to the principles which he should apply in the review of pensions where compensation had been awarded, and that no invalidity in the exercise of his jurisdiction had been demonstrated. *McKinley* v. *Minister for Defence* [1988] I.R. 139 approved. *Breen* v. *Minister for Defence*

(H.C.) [1988] I.R.242

—— Arrest — Army raid — Wrongful arrest — Damages — Whether exemplary damages should be awarded — Oppressive and arbitrary conduct by servants of the Government.
see **Damages,** 5

—— Assault — Plaintiff assaulted by member of army patrol — Damages — Whether exemplary damages should be awarded — Whether soldier a "servant of the Government" — Whether aggressive conduct.
see **Damages,** 4

—— Dismissal — Fair procedures — Natural justice — Certiorari — Delay — Lack of candour — Whether disentitling to relief.
see **Judicial Review,** 2

DEFINITIONS
see **Words and Phrases**

DELAY
see also **Limitation of Actions**

—— Action — Dismissal for want of prosecution.
see **Practice and Procedure,** 5-7, 54

—— Building contract — Delay in completion — Claim by main contractor against sub-contractor.
see **Arbitration,** 5

—— Certiorari — Delay in claiming relief — Whether delay in seeking order a ground for refusal — Whether order issues *ex debito justitiae.*
see **Criminal Law,** 74

—— Certiorari — Lack of candour — Whether disentitling prosecutor to relief — Whether delay excessive — Whether certiorari would have any effect.

DISCRIMINATION
see **Equal Treatment; Equality before the Law**

—— Employment.
see **Employer and Employee,** 13-18

DISMISSAL
see **Employer and Employee,** 7-12 *and cross-references following*

—— Office holder.
see under **Office Holder**

—— Teacher.
see **Employer and Employee,** 12

—— University lecturer.
see **Constitution,** 21
Education, 5

DISTRICT COURT

1. —— **Jurisdiction** — *Criminal case — Minor offences — Number of similar offences charged in the one summons — Effect — Offence of making false statements to obtain unemployment benefit — Location of offence's commission — Certiorari — Discretion to refuse remedy — Adequacy of alternative relief — District Court Rules,* 1948 (*S.R. & O. No.* 431 *of* 1947), *rr.* 25, 44 — *Courts of Justice Act,* 1924 (*No.* 10), *s.* 79 — *Social Welfare (Consolidation) Act,* 1981 (*No.* 1), *s.* 115.] Rule 25(*b*) of the Rules of 1948, provides that the jurisdiction of a District Justice in cases of summary jurisdiction shall be exercised by him within his district in the court area of that district wherein the offence charged (or, if more than one offence is stated to have been committed within that district, any one of such offences) is stated to have been committed or the court area of that district wherein the accused has been arrested or resides. The prosecutor was tried by the respondent District Justice sitting in the District Court area of Letterkenny on foot of a summons charging him with having made on a number of dates in 1982, and within the said court area, a statement for the purpose of obtaining unemployment benefit which was false and misleading in a material respect, namely, that he was unemployed on certain dates in that year when he was not so unemployed, contrary to s.115, sub-s. 1, of the Act of 1981. The penalty provided by the sub-section on summary conviction of an offence thereunder is a fine not exceeding £500, or, at the discretion of the court, imprisonment for a term not exceeding one year, or both such fine and such imprisonment. Evidence was given at the trial of the prosecutor (who resided in the District Court area of Raphoe), that, on each of the dates in question,

DISTRICT COURT—*continued.*

he had completed the official form provided for applications for unemployment benefit, and had then presented it to the Gardaí stationed at Carrigans in the District Court area of Newtown Cunningham who had in turn transmitted it by post to the unemployment exchange situate in the District Court area of Letterkenny. The respondent convicted the prosecutor of an offence in respect of every date set out in the summons, but imposed a penalty in relation to only two of the offences, which in each case was a fine of £250 and a term of imprisonment for 6 months. The prosecutor filed a notice of appeal to the Circuit Court against those convictions and obtained a conditional order of certiorari in the High Court quashing, unless cause was shown to the contrary, the conviction order of the respondent on the grounds, 1, that the respondent had no jurisdiction to try the offences charged against the prosecutor because they had not been committed within the District Court area of Letterkenny; 2, that the effect of charging each of the offences in the one summons was to take them out of the category of minor offences and, 3, on a number of further grounds related to the manner in which the convictions were recorded against the prosecutor. At the hearing of the prosecutor's motion for an order absolute, notwithstanding the cause shown, it was **Held** by Carroll J., in allowing the cause shown and discharging the conditional order, 1, that the offences were committed within the District Court area of Letterkenny since s. 115, sub-s. 1, of the Act of 1981 only proscribes false statements directed to some person who has power under that Act to decide whether unemployment benefit will be given, and, accordingly, the offences were not complete until the official forms were received by the unemployment exchange in Letterkenny. 2. That in determining whether a number of offences charged against a person in the one proceedings constitute minor offences, the nature and gravity of each offence must be considered separately and each offence here, when so considered, could not be classed as other than a minor one. *Charlton* v. *Ireland and Others* [1984] ILRM 39 and *The State (Rollinson)* v. *Kelly* [1984] I.R. 248 considered. 3. That, as any errors contained in the respondent's conviction order did not go to the jurisdiction of the District Court and could be remedied on the prosecutor's appeal to the Circuit Court, the Court would exercise its discretion to refuse an order of certiorari in respect of them. *The State (Roche)* v. *Delap* [1980] I.R. 170 and *The State (Abenglen Properties)* v. *Corporation of Dublin* [1984] I.R. 381 applied. *The State (Wilson)* v. *Neilan*

(H.C.) [1985] I.R. 89; [1987] ILRM 118

DISTRICT COURT—*continued.*

2. —— **Practice and procedure** — *Criminal case — Minor offence — Indictable offence triable summarily — Whether offence a minor offence fit to be tried summarily — No objection by accused to summary trial — Plea of guilty by accused — Jurisdiction accepted — Emergence of new facts — Accused already serving prison sentence — Court unable to impose intended sentence — Court of opinion that offences not fit to be tried summarily — Jurisdiction refused — Accused sent forward for trial to Circuit Court — Whether an absence of fair procedures — Criminal Justice Act,* 1951 (*No.* 2), *s.* 2.] Section 2, sub-s. 2 of the Criminal Justice Act,1951, provides that the District Court may try summarily a person charged with an indictable offence scheduled to that Act if, *inter alia,* the court is of opinion that "the facts proved or alleged constitute a minor offence fit to be so tried." The applicant appeared before the respondent District Justice charged with four scheduled offences. The facts relating to the offences were minor and fit to be tried summarily. The applicant acceded to the jurisdiction of the court and pleaded guilty to each offence. The respondent was informed that the applicant was currently serving two sentences of imprisonment, the longer of which would not expire for seventeen months. The respondent was of opinion that the charges before him merited a sentence of two years' imprisonment. He decided that since he was unable to impose the sentences which he had intended, as he had no power to impose a two year sentence to commence on the expiry of the existing sentences, the offences, though minor, were not fit to be tried summarily and that the applicant should be sent forward for trial to the Circuit Court. He therefore refused jurisdiction and adjourned proceedings for service of a book of evidence. On the applicant's application by way of judicial review for an order of prohibition prohibiting the respondent from proceeding to a preliminary hearing of the charges and from sending the applicant forward for trial, and for an order of mandamus compelling him to deal with the matter on the basis of the convictions recorded by him, it was **Held** by Barr J., in refusing the application, 1, that where a District Justice in the course of the summary trial of an indictable offence comes to the conclusion on proper grounds that the matter is not fit to be tried summarily, he is entitled to discontinue the summary trial and send the accused forward for trial to the Circuit Court, notwithstanding that he had previously formed the opinion referred to in s. 2 of the Act of 1951. *The State (O'Hagan)* v. *Delap* [1982] I.R. 213 applied. 2. That when the respondent heard evidence that the applicant was serving a two year sentence of imprisonment, most of which was unexpired, and found himself inhibited from imposing the sentence which he believed the offences merited, he was entitled to form the opinion that the offences, though minor, were not fit to be tried summarily and to send the applicant forward for trial to a court which would not be similarly inhibited in relation to sentence. 3. That the applicant had suffered no prejudice by the procedure adopted by the respondent as he would not be bound by his plea of guilty when sent forward to the Circuit Court. *Per* Barr J. That had the applicant pleaded not guilty and a trial on the merits taken place in the District Court, the respondent would not have been entitled to refuse jurisdiction having heard evidence of the applicant's previous convictions and to send the applicant forward to the Circuit Court, as that would have created a situation of double jeopardy which would have deprived the applicant of his constitutional right to fair procedures. *Feeney* v. *Clifford*

(H.C.) [1988] I.R.499

3. —— **Practice and procedure** — *Criminal case — Order — Signature — Rubber stamp — Return for trial — Rules of court — Non-compliance — Transmission of documents to court of trial — Transmission after period allowed — Motion to quash indictment — Case stated — District Court Rules,* 1948, (*S.R. & O. No.* 431 *of* 1947), *rr.* 13, 23 — *District Court (Criminal Procedure Act,* 1967) *Rules,* 1967 (*S.I. No.* 181), *rr.* 2, 38 — *Courts of Justice Act,* 1947 (*No.* 20), *s.* 16 — *Criminal Procedure Act,* 1967 (*No.* 12), *s.* 8.] Section 8, sub-s. 6, of the Act of 1967 provides that an order of a District Justice sending an accused person forward to the Circuit Court for trial on indictment shall be "in writing signed by the justice" and rule 38 of the Rules of 1967 states that the relevant District Court clerk shall transmit the order (*inter alia*) to the appropriate County Registrar within 10 days after the date of the order. After a District Justice had conducted a preliminary examination of certain charges brought against the accused, the District Justice made an order returning the accused for trial on indictment in the Circuit Court. The signature of the District Justice on the order was an ink impression of the signature resulting from the use of a rubber stamp. The order was not transmitted to the Circuit Court within the period specified in r. 38 of the Rules of 1967. Before the accused was arraigned in the Circuit Court, he brought a motion in that court to quash the indictment on the ground that the proceedings had been invalidated by a failure to comply with the rules of court and that the Circuit Court lacked jurisdiction to conduct the trial of the accused. The Circuit Court judge adjourned

DISTRICT COURT—*continued.*

the hearing of that motion when, at the request of the accused, he stated a Case for the determination by the Supreme Court of the points of law raised by the accused. **Held** by the Supreme Court (O'Higgins C.J., Henchy and McCarthy JJ.), in ruling the points of law, 1, that a signature made by means of a rubber stamp was as valid as a manuscript signature and that, in the absence of any evidence to the contrary, the presumption that the District Justice's signature had been duly affixed by him to the order prevailed. *The State (Attorney General)* v. *Roe* [1951] I.R. 172 approved. 2. That the failure to transmit the order of the District Justice to the Circuit Court within the period prescribed by the Rules of 1967 did not invalidate the order or affect the jurisdiction of the Circuit Court in the proceedings before it. *The People* v. *McCormack*

(S.C.) [1984] I.R. 177

4. —— **Venue** — *Licensed premises — Statutory provision allowing room to be rented for holding of petty sessions — Prohibition on renting room where spiritous or fermented liquors sold — Prosecutrix summoned to appear before District Court sitting at licensed premises — Whether District Justice had jurisdiction to deal with complaint against prosecutrix — Statute — Interpretation — Legislative intent.*

Statute — Interpretation — Effect — Legislative intent — Whether statute repealed by subsequent legislation — Disappearance of subject matter of statute — Desuetude — Grand Jury Presentments (Ireland) Act, 1836 (*c.* 116), *s.* 77 — *Petty Sessions (Ireland) Act,* 1851 (*c.* 93), *s.* 8, *para.*1 — *Local Government (Ireland) Act,* 1898 (*c.* 37) — *Courthouses (Provision and Maintenance) Act,* 1935 (*No.* 18) — *Courts of Justice Act,* 1953 (*No.* 32) — *Courts (Establishment and Constitution) Act,* 1961 (*No.* 38).] Section 8 of the Petty Sessions (Ireland) Act, 1851, provides *inter alia* that: "The Places where Justices shall sit in the Discharge of their Duties shall be subject to the following Provisions: 1. Wherever a public Court House shall be maintained by County Presentment at any Place fixed for the holding of Petty Sessions the Petty Sessions shall be held therein, if not inconvenient to the Public; but whenever no such public Court House shall be so maintained, or the holding of Petty Sessions therein would be inconvenient to the Public, it shall be lawful for the Grand Jury of the County to present an annual sum not exceeding Ten Pounds for the Rent of a public Justice Room . . . provided that such Room shall not be in a House where spirituous or fermented liquors are sold . . ." The prosecutrix was summoned to appear before the District Court sitting at premises which were licensed for the sale of intoxicating liquor to answer a complaint of larceny. Her solicitor objected to the jurisdiction of the respondent to deal with the complaint arguing that the District Court was prohibited by s. 8 of the Petty Sessions (Ireland) Act, 1851, from sitting in licensed premises. The respondent adjourned the proceedings. The prosecutrix obtained a conditional order of certiorari quashing the adjournment on the grounds that the adjournment order had been made without power or authority by reason of s. 8 of the Act of 1851. The respondent showed cause on the grounds firstly, that s. 8 of the Act of 1851 did not affect the jurisdiction of the District Court and secondly, that s. 8 had been repealed by implication by subsequent legislation. The prosecutrix applied for an order absolute notwithstanding cause shown. **Held** by Keane J., in allowing the cause shown and in discharging the conditional order, 1, that while s. 8, para. 1 of the Act of 1851 prohibited the expenditure of public monies for renting courtroom accommodation in licensed premises, it did not affect the validity of any proceedings. 2. That, accordingly, it was unnecessary to express any opinion on the question as to whether s. 8, para. 1 of the Act of 1851 had been repealed by implication by later legislation. *Per curiam.* That s. 8, para. 1 of the Act of 1851 had no purpose and was inoperable independently of the statutory scheme for the financing of courtroom accommodation by county cess of which it had been part and which had long since been repealed. *The State (Feeley)* v. *O'Dea*

(H.C.) [1986] I.R. 687

—— Case stated under Summary Jurisdiction Act, 1857 — Applications to District Court for gaming certificate — Objection challenging jurisdiction of court — Applications struck out — Application for case stated on question of jurisdiction — Whether questions of jurisdiction may be subject of case stated — Whether court entitled to refuse to state case requested by party asserting jurisdiction of court.

see **Case Stated,** 1

—— Hearing — Landlord and tenant — Corporation flat — Notice to quit — Tenant not represented — Tenant not invited to give evidence — Possession awarded to corporation — Whether hearing in breach of natural justice.

see **Landlord and Tenant,** 17

—— Jurisdiction — Criminal case — Indictable

E

EEC
see **European Communities**

EASEMENT — Right of way.
see **Real Property,** 1-3

ECCLESIASTICAL COURTS
—— Annulment of marriage.
see **Family Law,** 11, 12, 20, 24

—— Annulment of marriage — Effect of decision on claim in civil courts.
see **Family Law,** 12

EDUCATION
see also **School**

1. —— **Admission of students to school** — *School board of management — Criteria applied — Whether arbitrary — Obligations of board of management — Whether decision subject to judicial review.*] In September, 1986, the respondents, the board of management of Portmarnock Community School (which operated under a deed of trust) in response to more than 200 enquiries from students seeking enrolment to their school for the academic year commencing September, 1987, dispatched to the parents of these children an application form and a letter dated 3 November, 1986, which clearly indicated that places could not be guaranteed but did not disclose the criteria by which the candidates would be selected for enrolment. The board of management met on 20 November, 1986, and decided that 160 first year pupils would be taken in for September, 1987, but this was later increased to 165. The board of management appointed a sub-committee to investigate and assess each application form and to make recommendations to the board at its next meeting. The sub-committee at a meeting of the full board on 26 November, 1986, recommended a set of criteria for acceptance which was unanimously agreed upon by the board. The sub-committee met on 27 November and the issue later arose as to which criteria they had applied in view of the fact that the members of the board had been circulated with a document dated 27 November setting out the criteria which was actually different from those adopted at the meeting 26 November. The respondent submitted that the document of 27 November contained the draft proposals of the criteria which were subsequently modified and altered by the meeting of 26 November. The students' names which did not fall within the criteria were included in a ballot drawn by the local curate. Nine of the parents whose childrens' application for admission to

EDUCATION—*continued.*

the school for academic year 1987/88 had been rejected, applied for certiorari quashing the decision made by the respondent on or about 27 November, 1986. **Held** by Murphy J. in dismissing the application, 1, it was within the board of management's power to limit the intake of students as the power of government and direction expressly conferred on the board necessarily implied the right and indeed the duty to limit admission when capacity was exceeded. 2. It would be irresponsible of the board of management to admit an excessive number of students as to do so would involve a decline in educational standards, a danger to health and a very real risk to the safety of the students, and the decision of the board of management to limit the intake to 165 new students was a fair and reasonable decision based on sound argument. 3. The criteria adopted by the board on 26 November, 1986, were the relevant material criteria and in fact those applied by the sub-committee in their meeting on 27 November. 4. The court recognised that a valid argument existed for postponing the determination of criteria until the problem had been identified. 5. The obligations of the board of management in the deed of trust were expressed in the widest terms to control and manage the school and there was nothing to prevent them from having regard to appropriate and reasonable factors based on educational requirements and family circumstances in seeking to resolve the problem of limiting the enrolment. 6. It was part of the function of the board of management to try to design a rational, fair and logical scheme to give a logical coherence to those students whom they admitted enrolment and those whom they must regrettably reject. 7. There was no basis for the suggestion that the parents were misled or that they had any well founded legitimate expectation that the1984 criteria would be applied as the evidence was that criteria when made were made for one year and on an *ad hoc* basis. 8. As there was no suggestion that the board of management were dissatisfied with the actions of the sub-committee in the circumstances it would be quite wrong to attempt to parse and analyse in a legalistic way these criteria and challenge them on those grounds when the court is satisfied that on the evidence that the spirit and intent of the criteria were observed with honesty and integrity by the sub-committee. *Per Curiam:* although there was a doubt as to whether certiorari lay to quash the board's design, the court would proceed on the basis that it did lie. *Ó hUallachain* v. *Burke*
(H.C.) [1988] ILRM 693

EDUCATION—*continued.*

2. —— **Employment** — *Vocational teacher — Suspension by Vocational Education Committee — Ministerial inquiry refused — Whether Minister has discretion to refuse to hold inquiry — Nature of inquiry — Whether Vocational Education Committee has* locus standi *to challenge refusal to hold inquiry — Vocational Education Act,* 1930 (*No.* 29), *ss.* 30, 105 — *Vocational Education (Amendment) Act,* 1944 (*No.* 9), *ss.* 7, 8.] The prosecutor, County Donegal Vocational Education Committee, determined in November, 1983, to suspend a vocational teacher from the performance of his duties, without remuneration, in accordance with the provisions of s. 7 of the Vocational Education (Amendment) Act, 1944. Pursuant to the provisions of the same section, the Committee reported the suspension to the Minister for Education. That report was accompanied by documentation relating to the conduct by the teacher of his duties over a number of years, and the material was also forwarded to the teacher concerned. At the hearing of the meeting of the Committee which decided to suspend the teacher, he was represented by a member of his trade union and was given an opportunity to speak on his own behalf but he chose not to do so. The material on which the Committee took its decision disclosed repeated records of absence without permission by the teacher and refusals by him to co-operate in administrative work in connection with the work requested of him by the school principal. The Committee also considered the contents of reports conducted by vocational school inspectors which were highly critical of his work as a teacher. In April, 1984, the Committee was informed by letter from the Department of Education that as the Minister was not satisfied that the teacher had been appraised with sufficient precision of the grounds for his suspension the Minister had decided to terminate the suspension, that the teacher's remuneration for the period of suspension should be paid to him and that it was a matter for the Committee to determine if it wished to proceed further with the matter. The Committee sought an order of mandamus requiring the Minister to inquire into the allegations that the teacher had failed to perform satisfactorily the duties imposed on him. **Held** by O'Hanlon J., in refusing to grant the order sought, 1, while the Minister was under an obligation to inquire into the alleged misconduct of a teacher once a properly constituted Vocational Education Committee had taken a decision to suspend a teacher pursuant to s. 7 of the Act of 1944, and since in this case there was no irregularity in the proceedings before the Committee, the Minister had not complied with the duty imposed by the statutes to hold an inquiry, it was however not clear that termination of the

EDUCATION—*continued.*

suspension could not take place at the same time as the holding of an inquiry, and having regard to the delays involved, the proper course would be for the Committee to consider whether to re-commence the suspension procedure afresh. *Collins* v. *Co. Cork Vocational Education Committee* (Unreported, Supreme Court — 18 March, 1983) applied; observations in *Ní Bheoláin* v. *City of Dublin Vocational Education Committee* (Unreported, High Court — 28 January, 1983) explained and followed. 2. *Prima facie,* a Vocational Education Committee has standing to bring proceedings against any person it considers to be wrongfully impeding the fulfilling of its duties, under s. 30, of the Vocational Education Act, 1930, to establish and maintain a suitable system of continuation education and to supply technical education in its area. *Per curiam:* an amendment to the legislation empowering a Vocational Education Committee or the Minister to suspend a teacher with pay would ameliorate the hardship which may be unnecessarily and unjustifiably caused to some office holders having regard to the length of time which may be absorbed in the conduct of an inquiry. *The State (Donegal V.E.C.)* v. *Minister for Education*

(H.C.) [1985] I.R.56

3. —— **School transport** — *Applicant registered and attending school nearest home — Education Board refused transport to school — Offered transport to alternative school — Education Board's policy to maintain existing school bus routes — Whether Board under duty to provide transport to school actually attended — Mandamus — Education and Libraries (Northern Ireland) Order,* 1972 (*S.I. No.* 1263, *N.I.* 12), *art.* 41, *sch.* 9, *para.* 3.] The applicant's son was a registered pupil attending a primary school which was 5.9 miles from his home. The applicant requested the Western Education and Library Board to provide transport to the school pursuant to its duty under article 41 of the Education and Libraries (Northern Ireland) Order, 1972. The Board refused and offered transport to another primary school which was 6.1 miles from the applicant's home, on the grounds that the nearest school bus collection service to the first school was over three miles away and, although the second school was further from the applicant's home, it was served by a bus service which passed the applicant's home. The applicant argued that as his son was a registered pupil attending the first school, which was the nearest to his home, the Board was under a duty to provide him with transport to that school. The Board contended that (*a*) it was entitled to adopt and give effect

EDUCATION—*continued.*

to a policy set out in a Department of Education circular in deciding what transport to offer to a child and could have regard to existing bus routes and the relative costs of transporting children to different schools and it was not obliged to transport a child to the school nearest his home if there was a cheaper transport available to another school which the child could attend; (*b*) article 5 of the 1972 Order imposed a duty on the Board to have regard to the needs of the area as a whole and article 41 should be construed accordingly; and (*c*) to grant the applicant's request would have disrupted existing bus routes, inconvenienced other pupils thereby causing unreasonable and excessive expense to the Board. **Held,** granting an order of mandamus requiring the Board to make arrangements for the provision of transport of the applicant's son to the first school that, 1, the decisions of the Board in relation to the provision of school transport must be governed by the provisions of the 1972 Order and not by a circular from the Department of Education in which the guidance set out may be based upon a mistaken apprehension of the law. 2. The inclusion of the word "shall" in article 41(1) imposed upon the Board a duty to make arrangements for the provision of transport for pupils living more than a certain distance from the school at which they were registered to attend the school. If a statute imposed a duty on a public authority to provide transport to facilitate the attendance of persons at a place the ordinary and natural meaning of that provision was that the transport was to take those persons to the place to which they wanted to go or in the case of children, to which their parents wanted them to go, and not to a place which the public authority wanted them to go. 3. In construing article 41 it was necessary to have regard to paragraph 3 of schedule 9 to the 1972 Order, which related to the criminal liability of a parent failing to secure the regular attendance of his child at school. In stating the defences open to a parent when his child did not regularly attend school, paragraph 3 of schedule 9 by implication specified the circumstances in which the Board was under a duty to make arrangements for the provision of transport and confirmed the construction that the article imposed a duty to provide transport to facilitate attendance at the school nearest to the pupil's home. 4. While article 5 imposed a duty on the Board to provide an effective system of education for the community there was nothing inconsistent with the general scheme if the 1972 Order in article 41 imposed a duty on the Board to provide transport (subject to the limitations imported by paragraph 3 of schedule 9) to facilitate the attendance of individual pupils at the schools they attended.

EDUCATION—*continued.*

The Board had failed to establish that the provision of the transport to the applicant's son to the school at which he was a registered pupil would have involved it in unreasonable expenditure or ran counter to a reasonable transport policy. *In re Brownlee*

(Q.B.D.) [1985] N.I. 339

4. —— **Transfer provisions** — *Choice of school — Parental wishes — Policy of Education Board — Whether Board bound by parental wishes — Whether Board had regard to parental wishes — School attendance order — Application to Department for direction naming school to be attended — Whether application defective — Whether parental choice of school involved unreasonable expense.*

Statute — Construction — Conflict between provisions in articles and schedule — Whether words should be read into schedule — Education and Libraries (Northern Ireland) Order, 1972 (*S.I. No.* 1263, *N.I.* 12), *arts.* 5, 6(1), 11(1), 34, 35, *sch.* 9, *paras.* 1, 2.] The applicant lived in County Fermanagh about 7 miles from Lisnaskea and 9 miles from Enniskillen. In a transfer report relating to the transfer of the applicant's daughter E. from primary to secondary school, the applicant's wife gave as the parents' preferences of school, two schools in Enniskillen. The Western Education and Library Board inserted on the form, as a third choice, a school in Lisnaskea because E. lived within that school's traditional intake area. The applicant was later informed that a place was available for E. at the Lisnaskea school. Before the beginning of the school year E.'s mother informed the Board that they would be moving to live in Enniskillen and requested a place for E. at an Enniskillen school. This request was granted. Shortly after E. commenced attendance at the Enniskillen school, the Board formed the view that there had not been a genuine move to Enniskillen and instructed the Enniskillen school not to admit E. and requested E.'s parents to send her to the school in Lisnaskea. E.'s parents did not comply with this request, however, with the result that E. ceased to attend any school. The applicant said that the move by his wife and E. to Enniskillen occurred when he and his wife were temporarily estranged and that she had since returned to his home. He also appealed against the Board's decision to refuse to permit E. to go to school in Enniskillen on the ground that school transport was readily available and E.'s elder brother and sister travelled to school in Enniskillen by bus. The Board, however, confirmed E.'s placement at the Lisnaskea school, stated that it was about to make a School Attendance Order, and invited the applicant to select a school to be named in the order in accordance with schedule 9, paragraph

EDUCATION—*continued.*

1(3) of the Education and Libraries (Northern Ireland) Order, 1972. The applicant selected the Enniskillen school as the school to be named in the order, but the Board applied to the Department that the Lisnaskea school be named in the order on the grounds that the school selected by the applicant would involve unreasonable expense to the Board. On an application for judicial review the applicant argued that by virtue of article 34 of and schedule 9 to the 1972 Order, the wishes of the parents as to the choice of school were paramount. For the Board it was argued that there was no duty for education to be conducted in accordance with the wishes of the parent; that the Board was under a duty of providing an efficient system of education, which entitled the Board to have a policy that looked at their area as a whole; that the applicant's suggested construction of article 34 had been rejected by the Court of Appeal in England and that the qualifications to article 34 relating to efficiency and avoidance of unreasonable expense should be given a broad interpretation. **Held,** that, 1, the primary duty laid on the Board is the duty in article 5 to provide an efficient system of education for the community in its area. The requirement in article 34 to have regard to the principle that pupils should be educated in accordance with the wishes of their parents did not mean that the Board could not have regard to other considerations relating to its primary duty such as the desirability of ensuring that a school is supported by an adequate intake of pupils from its surrounding area. *Watt* v. *Kesteven County Council* [1955] 1 Q.B. 408 followed. *Semble* the qualifications to article 34 relate to the efficient instruction of an individual pupil and the avoidance of unreasonable public expenditure in respect of that individual: the Board's right to support a school by requiring pupils from its traditional intake area to attend it does not arise from these provisos but from article 5. 2. Paragraphs 1 and 2 of schedule 9 to the 1972 Order, which appear to give the parents a right to select the school to be named in a school attendance order, are in conflict with articles 5 and 34 of that Order and, as these paragraphs, being in a schedule, are clearly subordinate to articles 5 and 34, they cannot operate to alter the true construction of article 34. Consequently the words "or would be in conflict with the policy of the board" should be read into paragraphs 1(4) and 2(1) after the words "would involve unreasonable expense to the board." *Federal Steam Navigation Co.* v. *Department of Trade and Industry* [1974] 1 W.L.R. 505; [1974] 2 All E.R. 97 C.A. and *Wills* v. *Bowley* [1982] 2 All E.R. 654 applied. 3. On the facts of the case the Board did have regard to the wishes of E.'s parents. The Board is entitled to have a policy and to prefer that policy to the wishes of the parents of an individual child, it is only obliged to have regard to those wishes and, after having such regard, it is entitled not to give effect to them if they run counter to its policy. 4. E.'s attendance at the Enniskillen school would not involve any unreasonable expense for the Board and as "unreasonable expense to the Board" in paragraph 1(14) of schedule 9 clearly refers to unreasonable expense in relation to the individual child who has not been attending school, the court had jurisdiction to hold that the Board's application to the Department for a direction that the Lisnaskea school should be named in the school attendance order was defective. On a further hearing to determine whether the application to the Department for a direction relating to the school attendance order was a nullity, it was conceded by counsel that as notice had been given to the applicant of the application after it had been made and the Department was fully aware of the applicant's views, the application was not a nullity notwithstanding the failure to give notice to the applicant before the application for a direction. Counsel for the Board, however, argued that although the Board's application was based on unreasonable expense, the Department could decide the application for a direction by reference to policy matters of which it was aware from other correspondence. **Held,** prohibiting the Department from naming the Lisnaskea school in the school attendance order, that an application for a direction under paragraph 1(3) of schedule 9 was separate from other proceedings and the Department could only give a direction if it considers that the ground, being one of the grounds specified in the paragraph, advanced by the Board was valid. Here the ground on which the Board applied for a direction was invalid as E.'s attendance at the Enniskillen school would not involve unreasonable expense. Therefore E. would attend the Enniskillen school. *Rootkin* v. *Kent County Council* [1981] 1 W.L.R. 1186 and *Maritime Electric Company Limited* v. *General Dairies Limited* [1937] 1 All E.R. 748 distinguished. *In re Bogue* **(Q.B.D.) [1985] N.I.218**

5. —— **University** — *Visitor — Judicial review — Jurisdiction — Applicant a probationary lecturer — Not confirmed in post — Appealed to Board of Visitors — Applied for judicial review — Whether issues concerned private rules of University — Whether issues of public law or private law — Whether undue delay — Constitution of Board — Bias — Oral hearing — Legal representation.*] In 1981 the applicant was appointed by the Senate of the Queen's University of Belfast to a lectureship (medical) in Anatomy,

EDUCATION—*continued.*

subject to a period of probation until 30 September, 1983. His conditions of appointment provided for an annual assessment of his "teaching, research and scholarly ability" by an ad hoc group consisting of his Head of Department and senior colleagues. The ad hoc group made, in September, 1982, an adverse assessment of the applicant's progress and, in February, 1983, reported that it was unable to recommend to the Board of Curators that he be confirmed in post. The Board of Curators invited the applicant to attend for interview but he failed to do so. In his absence the Board decided that it could not recommend to the Senate that he be confirmed in post and informed him of their decision. In April, 1983, the applicant exercised his right of appeal to a committee appointed by the Senate. The appeal committee, after considering the oral and written submissions of the applicant, dismissed the appeal and so reported to the Senate which in May, 1983, resolved to terminate the applicant's employment with effect from 27 May 1983, informing him that his salary up to the end of the academic year (30 September, 1983) would be paid to him in a lump sum. The applicant appealed to the Visitor and in July, 1983, a Board of Visitors was appointed, taking up office on 1 October, 1983. In November the Board informed the applicant that it proposed to consider the appeal on the documents submitted to it. The applicant sought an oral hearing and also legal representation but in January, 1984, this was refused. The applicant then sought, and, on appeal, was granted leave to apply for judicial review. It was contended for the University that the matters in dispute were within the exclusive jurisdiction of the Board of Visitors. The applicant contended that the Board had no jurisdiction because (*a*) the Board had not been in existence at the time of the appeal and had subsequently delayed unduly, (*b*) that the Board, containing a member of the Convocation of the University and a former Secretary of the University, was improperly constituted and had acted unfairly by refusing an oral hearing and legal representation, (*c*) the issues in dispute involved questions of contract and the legality of the proceedings of several bodies of the University, and (*d*) the Board could not grant effective remedies. **Held,** that the matters in dispute were exclusively within the visitorial jurisdiction, 1, before the visitorial jurisdiction can be invoked it must be shown that the applicant was a member of the University and that the matters in dispute were matters within the jurisdiction of the Visitor. Here the applicant, as a lecturer, was a member of the University and his dismissal did not take him outside the Visitor's jurisdiction with regard to the matters in dispute which related to the regularity and propriety of his non-confirmation in and removal from his post of probationary lecturer. 2. These matters came within the jurisdiction of the Visitor as expressed in Chapter XXIII of the Statutes of the University and in any event came within the general powers of the Visitor as they were matters of an internal domestic character or touched upon the interpretation or execution of private rules of regulations of the University. 3. The applicant had a right under his contract of employment to have the criteria relating to the assessment of his fitness as a lecturer observed and the special procedures of the relevant University bodies regularly and fairly followed: but this right related to the regular and fair execution of procedures in accordance with the internal rules and regulations of the University, if the matters in dispute related purely to common law or statutory rights and not to private or special rights of the University then the visitorial jurisdiction would be excluded. 4. If the matters in dispute did not fall within the exclusive jurisdiction of the Visitor they would be issues of contract for which the appropriate remedy was an action for damages, injunction or declaration and not an application for judicial review which was inappropriate because no issue of public law was involved. 5. The Board of Visitors had sufficient powers to grant relief for the purpose of the applicant's appeal. 6. The appointment of a Board of Visitors after the applicant lodged his appeal did not deprive the Board of jurisdiction: visitorial jurisdiction never fails through lack of a visitor. 7. There was no unreasonable delay on the part of the Board. 8. There was neither reasonable suspicion nor likelihood of bias in the membership of the Board. 9. An oral hearing or legal representation were not a necessary part of natural justice, in any event the Board's decision not to give an oral hearing or legal representation was not a final one. *In re Wislang*

(Q.B.D.) [1984] N.I. 63

—— Constitutional right — Right to free primary education — Interference with this right — Teachers — Trade dispute — Claim for damages — Whether such claim a claim in tort — Assessment of damages.

see **Damages,** 1

—— Employment — Teacher — Dismissal — Pregnancy — Unmarried woman teacher living with married man — Teacher employed at secondary convent school for girls — Whether dismissal resulted from pregnancy — Whether substantial grounds justifying dismissal.

EDUCATION—*continued.*

see **Employer and Employee,** 12

—— Employment — Teacher — Dismissal — Seminary — Teacher also priest — Whether discrimination.
see **Constitution,** 21

—— University — Disciplinary procedures — Breach of academic discipline — Natural justice — Fair procedures — Whether disciplinary regulations adequate to ensure fair hearing.
see **Natural and Constitutional Justice,** 5

—— University — Seminary — Pontifical university — Seminary obtaining funds from State but applied for lay purposes as recognised college of university — Whether primarily seminary or university — Dismissal of teacher — Whether discriminatory.
see **Constitution,** 21

—— University — Undergraduate course — Offer of place — Acceptance — Deferral by college of place offer to next academic year — Whether enforceable by candidate — Remedies — Judicial review.
see **Judicial Review,** 15

EJECTMENT
see also **Adverse Possession**

—— Action for recovery of land.
see **Limitation of Actions,** 1, 5

—— Tenancy.
see **Landlord and Tenant,** 12, 17, 19

ELECTORAL LAW

1. —— **Local election** — *Election petition — Whether notice to be served on D.P.P. — Whether actions of returning officer an irregularity — Whether request for recount could only be made by candidate or his agent — Electoral Act,* 1963 (*No.* 19), *s.* 82 — *Local Elections (Petitions and Disqualifications) Act,* 1974 (*No.* 8), *ss.* 2, 5, 7 — *Prosecution of Offences Act,* 1974 (*No.* 22), *ss.* 3(1), 4(4) — *Local Elections Regulations,* 1965 (*S.I. No.* 128), *arts.* 11, 71.] The local election to Clonmel Corporation of June, 1979, was questioned by a petition to the Circuit Court and the hearing was fixed for October, 1979. The petitioner, the first-named respondent, and the Attorney General were the only parties at this stage. The Director of Public Prosecutions had not been served. Evidence was heard and judgment reserved. On the resumption in November, 1979, of the hearing for the delivery of the judgment (1) an application was made on behalf of the other respondents to be joined in the proceedings and (2) it was intimated that notice of the petition should have been served on the D.P.P. pursuant to s. 3 (1) of the Prosecution of Offences Act, 1974. It was then contended by the second, third, fourth, fifth and sixth-named respondents that the entire proceedings were avoided by reason of failure to serve the D.P.P. in the first instance. **Held** by Judge Sheridan in ordering a new hearing of the petition. 1, for the purposes of having full representation before the court liberty was given to add the other respondents. The hearing would have to commence afresh as the first hearing had taken place in their absence. 2. While the failure to serve the D.P.P. did not avoid the proceedings, it was not the function of the court to pre-judge any submissions which might be adduced by the D.P.P. from the moment of service of the petition on him. The result of the last count in the local election led to a tie between the petitioner and the sixth-named respondent and to the election of the sixth-named respondent on the basis of his first preference votes. There was evidence of there having been no pause between the declaration by the returning officer of the final count and the final declaration by him of the result of the election. A person who was not the official agent of the petitioner attempted to request a recount on behalf of the petitioner. No recount was requested by the petitioner or his agent. **Held** by Judge Sheridan in dismissing the application for a non-suit. 3. The returning officer should have anticipated a recount. To rush through a declaration of the count and a declaration of the result without giving an opportunity to the unsuccessful candidate or his agent to request a recount amounted to a denial of natural justice. The announcement of the last count should have been independent of any other announcement. A considerable pause should then have been allowed. 4. The Local Elections Regulations, 1965, allow informal agents to be appointed and the person who applied for the recount was at least an informal agent of the petitioner and, so, in spite of Article 71 of the Regulations providing for official agents, her request had the same effect as if delivered by the petitioner or his officially appointed agent. 5. The action of the returning officer relating to the last count was an irregularity. There was an onus on the petitioner to show that such an irregularity was likely to have affected the result. In this case the election could not have been closer and so that onus had been discharged. **Held** further by Judge Sheridan in ordering a recount. 6. Once the petition was presented in time the failure to serve a party 'as soon as may be' if that party is not prejudiced

ELECTORAL LAW—*continued.*

does not avoid the proceedings. *Dicta* in *Williams* v. *Tenby Corporation* (1879) 5 C.P.D. 135 not followed. 7. Having deemed the sixth-named respondent to have been elected the returning officer should have allowed a considerable pause to elapse to enable the parties to digest this announcement and to make clear to him their requirements, and his failure to do so in the circumstances of this poll was a non-observance of the rules relating to recounts as to affect the outcome of the election. *Woodward* v. *Sarsons* (1875) L.R. 10 C.P. 733 applied. *Boyle* v. *Allen*
(Circ.Court) [1979] ILRM 281

2. —— **Voting facilities** — *Remand prisoner — Plaintiff on electoral register for constituency of Foyle — Detained as remand prisoner in Belfast — Whether power or duty to provide voting facilities in Belfast — Whether duty to take plaintiff to his constituency — Electoral Law Act (Northern Ireland),* 1962 (*c.* 14), *s.* 65(6) — *Prison Act (Northern Ireland),* 1953 (*c.* 18), *s.* 16(1).] The plaintiff was detained in H.M. Prison, Belfast while being tried at Belfast Crown Court. His home address was within the parliamentary constituency of Foyle and he wished to vote in the European Assembly election held on 14 June, 1984. He sought a declaration that the defendants should provide such facilities as would have enabled him to vote in person or by post as an absent voter. **Held,** that, 1, the plaintiff was legally entitled to vote in the election: however, as he did not fall within the categories or persons entitled to vote as absent voters, he would have to vote in person. 2. The plaintiff could only vote in person at a polling place within the parliamentary constituency of Foyle: the Chief Electoral Officer did not have the power to situate a polling station within Belfast Prison as the provision in section 65(6) of the Electoral Law Act (Northern Ireland) Act, 1962 (as amended), enabling him to add to the polling stations designated in the polling scheme such stations as he considers necessary, refers to what are commonly known as ballot boxes rather than polling places. 3. Section 16(1) of the Prison Act (Northern Ireland), 1953, which confers a power to direct the attendance of a detained person at any place if such attendance is desirable in the interests of justice, does not extend to attendance for the purpose of voting in an election. *McCartney* v. *Chief Electoral Officer*
(Ch.D.) [1984] N.I.240

—— Elections — Ballot papers — Listing of candidates' names in alphabetical order — Voting bias — Constitution — Fairness of procedure — Equality before the law — Right to vote and stand in elections.

ELECTORAL LAW—*continued.*

see **Constitution,** 36

—— Franchise — Dáil Éireann — Right to vote — Disabled citizen — Inability to attend at polling station — Absence of statutory provision for postal vote in national elections — Constitutional validity of statutory provisions.
see **Constitution,** 37

—— Franchise — Extension — Dáil Éireann — Right to vote restricted by Constitution to citizens — Bill conferring franchise upon resident British citizens — Constitution — Repugnancy.
see **Constitution,** 1

—— Local elections — Vacancy — County council — Vacancy arising on death of member — Standing orders providing that such vacancies be filled by co-option — Standing orders further providing that co-option be of a person from the same electoral area — Council meetings — Whether vacancy remained unfilled — Whether standing order *ultra vires.*
see **Local Government,** 7

ELECTRICITY SUPPLY BOARD — National grid — Private property — Interference — Statutory power to erect pylons on defendant's land — Use of land restricted — Absence of compensation for restriction — Constitution — Statute — Validity.
see **Constitution,** 45

EMERGENCY POWERS
see also **Offences against the State**

—— Arrest — Legality.
see **Criminal Law,** 2, 3

—— Procedure — Accused charged in Garda station — Whether lawful to charge accused otherwise than in District Court or Special Court.
see **Criminal Law,** 48

EMPLOYER AND EMPLOYEE
see also **Civil Service; Employer's Liability; Employment Appeals Tribunal; Labour Court; Trade Union**

Contract. Nos. 1-6
Dismissal. Nos. 7-12
Employment equality. Nos. 13-15
Equal pay. Nos. 16-18

Minimum notice. Nos. 19-22
Suspension. No. 23
Trade dispute. Nos. 24, 25
Vicarious liability. No. 26

CONTRACT OF EMPLOYMENT

1. —— **Breach** — *Cancellation of appointment — Plaintiff offered position as principal of a primary school — Plaintiff not being a member of trade union — Pressure exerted on manager to cancel appointment — Appointment subsequently cancelled — Whether manager in breach of contract — Whether defendants induced or procured such breach.*

Constitution — Personal rights — Freedom of association — Plaintiff offered position as principal of a primary school — Plaintiff not being a member of trade union — Pressure exerted on manager to cancel appointment — Whether defendants engaged in actionable conspiracy to cause plaintiff to abandon his constitutional right to dissociate.

Tort — Conspiracy — Inducement of breach of contract — Plaintiff offered position as principal of primary school — Pressure exerted on manager to cancel appointment — Appointment subsequently cancelled — Whether manager in breach of contract — Whether defendants induced such breach — Whether defendants engaged in an actionable conspiracy.] The plaintiff, a primary school teacher of considerable experience and a member of the Irish National Teachers Organisation (INTO) obtained an appointment as assistant at a primary school in Glanmire, Co. Cork, where, after a short period, the manager offered him the position of vice-principal. Rule 115F of the INTO provides that no member of that organisation can accept appointment as vice-principal unless he is the longest standing teacher in the school other than the principal. However, the Irish National Teachers Organisation may exempt a member from the application of this rule. The plaintiff asked the INTO for a ruling as to whether he should accept the position which had been offered to him, since there was at the school another teacher with longer service in that school. The INTO in reply merely referred the plaintiff to the aforesaid rule 115F. The plaintiff accepted the appointment and subsequently resigned his membership of INTO. The second, third, fourth and fifth-named defendants, who were members of INTO made repeated but unsuccessful representations to the Bishop of Cork seeking to have the plaintiff removed from his position. Some two years later, the first-named defendant, the manager of Ovens National School, advertised the post of principal in the daily newspapers, to which advertisment the plaintiff, among others, replied. The plaintiff, with seven others, was shortlisted for the position by the Department of Education. The first-named defendant subsequently appointed the plaintiff to the post. Some dissatisfaction was felt among the members of the INTO at the appointment, as a result of which the second to fifth-named defendants called upon Canon Ahern and made representations to that effect. Upon hearing that Canon Ahern had not yet sought the customary approval of the Bishop of Cork to the plaintiff's appointment, the other defendants informed the canon that they would go to the Bishop and make representations against the plaintiff's appointment. Canon Ahern then said he would cancel the appointment if the other defendants made their representations to him in writing, which was duly done, and the plaintiff was so notified. The plaintiff sought other appointments in the Cork area, but was unsuccessful because of his dispute with the INTO, and he was ultimately obliged to move with his wife and family to Bray, Co. Wicklow. The plaintiff sought damages for breach of contract against the first-named defendant and damages for procuring a breach of contract against the other named defendants. **Held** by Finlay P. in awarding damages for breach of contract against the first named defendant, damages for procuring a breach of contract and for conspiracy against the other named defendants, and in ordering the other named defendants to fully indemnify the first-named defendant in respect of his liability to the plaintiff, 1, the agreement made between the first-named defendant and the plaintiff was an agreement to appoint the plaintiff as principal of Ovens National School, and for that purpose to seek the approval of the Bishop of Cork. By failing to seek such approval, or the sanction of the Minister for Education, the defendant was in breach of contract. 2. The other-named defendants were fully aware of the existence of the said agreement and by the pressure they exerted upon the first-named defendant were instrumental in procuring its breach. 3. An agreement by two or more persons to prevent the appointment or promotion of a primary teacher as part of a general campaign to ensure that all teachers in that part of the country will become and remain members of a trade union is a coercion of the said teacher to abandon his constitutional right to dissociate and is an actionable conspiracy. *Meskell* v. *Córas Iompair Éireann* [1973] I.R. 121 applied. 4. The damages awarded to the plaintiff in respect of breach of contract would be equal to the difference in salary for the entire school year. Damages would not be recoverable from the first-named defendant in respect of the plaintiff's move to Bray,

EMPLOYER AND EMPLOYEE—Contract.

since this could not have been within the reasonable contemplation of the parties. The other named defendants, would however, be liable for loss flowing from the said move, since the material and probable consequence of their conspiracy was the prevention of the appointment of the plaintiff as principal at any school in Cork city. 5. The real and effective cause of the breach of contract by the first-named defendant was the action taken by the other named defendants. *Cotter* v. *Ahern*

(H.C.) [1976-7] ILRM 248

2. —— **Collective agreement** — *Employees dismissed for redundancy — Employees seeking declaration that the company gave them a guarantee that they would not be made redundant before a certain date — Company denying that such guarantee contemplated legal relations — Whether intention to enter into legal relations — Onus of proof.*] The plaintiffs were employed as foremen by the defendant company, which in 1979 was engaged in motor assembly. The plaintiffs' union entered into productivity agreements with the company from time to time, but the plaintiffs as foremen also formed a committee to discuss with the company matters of common interest. In 1979, the company ran into financial difficulties and secured agreement on the redeployment of foremen in its business. In return, the foremen asked for an assurance in writing from the company that their jobs would be secure. A document giving "an assurance that compulsory redundancy" would not be introduced if market conditions necessitated changes in manning and staffing arrangements was produced by the company for the plaintiffs. On the plaintiffs' insistence the company agreed in a further document to "guarantee" protection for them against compulsory redundancy up to 1984. The company's business deteriorated in 1980 and they made the plaintiffs redundant. The plaintiffs claimed that the company was thereby in breach of the 1979 agreements, but the company alleged that the agreements did not contemplate any legal relations. **Held** by Barrington J. that the defendant was in breach of their agreements with the plaintiffs. While the company may not have intended by the agreements to create legal relations, they had not made this known to the plaintiffs; that the plaintiffs were seeking a legally binding agreement and the company knew this; that in the circumstances there was a presumption, based on an objective legal test, that the parties intended to create legal relations; and that the company had failed to discharge the heavy onus on them to rebut that presumption. *Edwards* v. *Skyways Ltd.* [1964] 1 W.L.R. 349 approved. *Ford Motor Co. Ltd.* v. *Amalgamated Union of Engineering and Foundry Workers*

EMPLOYER AND EMPLOYEE—*continued.*

[1969] 2 Q.B. 303 considered. *O'Rourke* v. *Talbot (Ireland) Ltd.*

(H.C.) [1984] ILRM 587

3. —— **Frustration** — *Appointment terminated for stated or other reasons — Whether circumstances required to terminate appointment had arisen — Whether contract frustrated.*] The appellant had been appointed as physician to the Sheil Hospital, which has been established pursuant to the will of one S. The funds for the maintenance of the hospital were held by trustees and by the Commissioners of Charitable Donations and Bequests for Ireland. The terms of the contract between the appellant and the Board of Governors of the hospital provided, *inter alia,* that his appointment was terminable by the governors "if it should happen at any time that there are insufficient funds available to enable the hospital to continue in operation or it should have to close down for any other reason, such termination to be by three months previous notice in writing . . ." The financial position of the hospital deteriorated, and, on 11 February, 1974, the High Court acceded to the application of the Board of Governers to a create a scheme *cyprès,* whereby the hospital would be closed, and a lease thereof would be granted to the North-Western Health Board for a term of twelve years. On 22 February, 1974, the appellant was informed by letter in writing that his appointment would terminate on the 28th of the same month. The hospital closed on that day, and reopened under the management of the health board two days later. The appellant sought compensation in respect of the termination of his appointment, and, upon trial of the issue in the High Court, was awarded an amount equivalent to three months salary, less income tax. The applicant appealed the amount of the award, submitting that the circumstances required to justify termination of his appointment had not arisen. He contended that, in construing the relevant term of his contract, the *ejusdem generis* rule should be applied, and the closing of the hospital had to be connected with insufficiency of funds before his appointment could be terminated. The respondent contended that the contract had been frustrated by the High Court order of 11 February, or, alternatively, that the appellant was entitled only to three months loss of earnings. **Held** by the Supreme Court (Kenny J.; O'Higgins C.J. and Parke J. concurring) in varying the amount of the High Court award downwards, 1, the doctrine of frustration of contract cannot apply where the terms of an agreement show that the parties contemplated the possibility of the event upon which reliance is placed as terminating the contract. *Cricklewood Property Trust Ltd.* v. *Leighton Investment Trust*

EMPLOYER AND EMPLOYEE—Contract.

Ltd. [1945] A.C. 221 applied. 2. The words "for any other reason" contained in the relevant term of the contract indicate that the *ejusdem generis* rule of construction does not apply. The appellant's contract could be terminated if the governors decided to close the hospital and the High Court approved this step. 3. The appellant was entitled to damages for the breach of that part of the contract which required that he receive three months' notice of termination of his appointment. However, damages would be limited to the amount of salary and fees which he would have received if he had been served with a valid notice. *Per curiam* Where a respondent also seeks a variation of a High Court order, he must serve a notice to that effect upon the appellant, on pain of an adjournment or penalisation in costs. *Browne* v. *Mulligan; In re Shiel*

(S.C.) [1976-7] ILRM 327

4. —— **Termination** — *Employee on holiday — Serious situation developing requiring employee's attention — Whether lawful and reasonable of employer to require employee to interrupt his holiday.*

Defamation — Qualified privilege — Whether evidence of malice.] The plaintiff, an accountant, had been employed by the first-named defendant in its office in Libya. His wife and only child had left Ireland in order to reside there with him. His contract of employment provided that he should be entitled to four weeks leave per annum. In the summer of 1973, the plaintiff's wife returned to Ireland to give birth to their second child, which was expected at the end of July or beginning of August. The plaintiff arranged to take three weeks holidays in Ireland, commencing on 6 August and ending on 27 August, on which date he planned to return to Libya with his wife and family. During this period, serious tax problems requiring the plaintiff's attention arose at the Libyan office, and he was requested to return as soon as possible. He did so on 20 August, with an agreement that he could return to Ireland at a later date to complete his holidays. On 23 September he left Libya and flew to London. A conflict of evidence arose at this point, the plaintiff alleging that he brought with him a completed set of accounts relating to the said tax problems, the defendants alleging that he did not, but had been summoned to London to discuss the accounts and the problems that had arisen. A meeting followed between the plaintiff and representatives of the defendant company and further work was done on the accounts. The following day, the plaintiff returned to Ireland to resume his holiday. A day later, he received an urgent message from the company to return to the office. He did not do so. His employment was terminated forthwith, and the

EMPLOYER AND EMPLOYEE—*continued.*

plaintiff initiated the instant proceedings seeking damages for wrongful dimissal and breach of contract. He also claimed damages for defamation against the company and the second-named defendant, its chairman. This claim was based on a misunderstanding by the defendants of a paragraph in a letter written to them by the plaintiff's solicitor on his behalf, which they took to be an attempt to blackmail the company. They alleged blackmail in letters written by the second-named defendant to the Incorporated Law Society and the Garda Síochána. **Held** by Finlay P. in dismissing the plaintiff's claims, 1, in view of the gravity and urgency of the problems requiring the plaintiff's attention, and in view of the fact that the plaintiff was aware of his importance in the resolution of those problems, it was not unreasonable for the defendant to request the plaintiff to interrupt his holiday. 2. The plaintiff was bound by his contract of employment to accede to the reasonable requests of his employers, and his failure to do so, given the gravity of the situation, justified his dismissal. The cancellation and rearrangement of the plaintiff's holiday did not constitute a breach of contract on the part of the defendant. 3. The interpretation made by the defendants of the letter written by the plaintiff's solicitor, although wrong, was reasonable in the circumstances, and the allegations, subsequently made did not bear any aspect of reckless exaggeration constituting evidence of malice. *Hartery* v. *Welltrade (Middle East) Ltd.*

(H.C.) [1978] ILRM 38

Termination of contract, *see also* Nos. 7-12 (Dismissal)

5. —— **Terms** — *Contract of service — Postal sorters — Overtime period — Fifteen minute break during three and a half hour overtime shift — Whether term of contract of service — Whether enforceable by postal sorters — Consideration — Postal and Telecommunications Services Act,* 1983 (*No.* 24), *s.* 45.] The plaintiffs were postal sorters employed by the defendant. They regularly worked an overtime shift from 8 p.m. to 11.30 p.m. at the defendant's Sheriff St. office in Dublin. In 1969 a superintendent suggested a fifteen minute break around 9.30 p.m. for all postal sorters to minimise disruption of work caused by small groups leaving at irregular intervals for purposes of nature. This was discussed and agreed to by union representatives and became the practice. In 1983 a different superintendent decided to discontinue the practice. The plaintiffs in High Court proceedings sought *inter alia* declarations that the fifteen minute break was a term of their contracts of service and orders for payment of any monies deducted by

EMPLOYER AND EMPLOYEE—Contract.

the defendant in respect of such break period. Upon plenary hearing the defendant applied to the trial judge at the conclusion of the evidence for the plaintiffs for a direction that the defendant had no case to answer. **Held** by O'Hanlon J., in granting the direction sought and dismissing the plaintiffs' claims, that on the evidence the practice relied upon by the plaintiffs was never incorporated as a term into their contracts of service in that the arrangement was more akin to the process of collective bargaining and was never intended to create legal relations or be legally enforceable, and moreover even if there had been such an intention, any purported promise on behalf of the defendant to release the plaintiffs from their work obligations for 15 minutes was not met by any new consideration. *Semble* the guarantee of "conditions of service" of staff of the former Department of Posts and Telegraphs and transferred by s. 45 of the Postal and Telecommunications Act, 1983, to An Post and Telecom Éireann relates to such conditions of service as were legally enforceable. *Kenny* v. *An Post*

(H.C.) [1988] I.R.285

6. —— **Terms** — *Health board officers — Salary — Increment on transfer to new post — Calculation of salary requiring approval of Minister — Approval not granted — Increased salary granted prior to seeking approval — Refusal resulting in decreased salary — Whether Minister acting* intra vires *— Whether officers entitled to receive payments in accordance with original determination prior to Minister's refusal — Health Act,* 1970, (*No.* 1) *s.* 14.] S. 14 of the Health Act, 1970 provides, *inter alia,* that officers of the Health Board shall be appointed by the Board in accordance with the directions of the Minister for Health and Social Welfare, and that they shall be paid such remuneration and allowances as the chief executive officer of the board shall determine, in accordance with the directions of the Minister. By circular No. 10/71, the Minister gave certain directions in this regard. *Inter alia,* he directed at para. 14, sub-para. 1, that 'where the same salary scale applies to the officer's existing office and the office to which he has been newly appointed he shall remain on the same point of the scale, and may retain his existing incremental date." And at sub-para. 6: "where the minimum of the new salary scale is less than existing pay, the officer may enter the new scale at the point nearest but not below existing pay plus one increment." The plaintiffs had been appointed senior executive officers of the board. Prior to their appointments they had held the positions of section officers with the board. During that time, they had been assigned to organisations and method duties, which carried

EMPLOYER AND EMPLOYEE—*continued.*

an annual allowance over and above their salaries as section officers. The starting pay of the plaintiffs in their new appointment was calculated by the chief executive officer, taking into account the O and M allowance, thus bringing them within para. 14, sub-para. 6 of circular No. 10/71. However, he subsequently sought the approval of the Minister for this determination. By letter dated 18 August, 1972, the Minister refused his approval. The chief executive officer thereupon recalculated the plaintiffs' salary, not taking into account the O and M allowances, thus bringing the salaries within sub-para. 1 of para. 14 above. The plaintiffs were thereafter paid at this reduced rate. The plaintiffs claimed that the O and M allowances should have been added to their salaries as section officers for the purpose of calculating their new rates of pay as senior executive officers, and they sought a declaration that their starting pay should be thus calculated. They also claimed arrears of salary. **Held** by Costello J, in refusing the relief sought, 1, the letter of 18 August, 1972, was a direction made *intra vires* by the Minister in accordance with s. 14 of the Health Act, 1970, and the chief executive officer was statutorily bound to act upon it. 2. A new determination within the meaning of s. 14 of the Health Act, 1970, was made by the chief executive officer in accordance with the Minister's directions after 18 August, 1972, and from that time the plaintiffs became legally entitled only to remuneration in accordance with that determination. 3. Prior to the new determination, the plaintiffs had been legally entitled to receive payment in accordance with calculations made under para. 14, sub-para. 6 of Circular No. 10/71. *Murphy* v. *Eastern Health Board*

(H.C.) [1979] ILRM 100

DISMISSAL

see also 3, 4

7. —— **Natural justice** — *Garda Síochána — Summary dismissal by Commissioner — Absence of formal inquiry — Limitations of rules of natural justice in context of certain State services — Acquittal of dismissed Garda at trial on charge of assault on suspect — Counsel for dismissed Garda seeking admission that witness at trial committed the assault — Absence of such allegation in statement of dismissed Garda — Dismissal by Commissioner on ground that statement contained falsehood or prevarication — Opportunity given to advance reasons against dismissal — Garda Síochána (Discipline) Regulations,* 1971, (*S.I. No.* 316) *Regs.* 6, 34.] Reg. 34(*a*) of the Garda Síochána (Discipline) Regulations, 1971, confers on the Commissioner of the Garda Síochána a power to dismiss a member of the force without

EMPLOYER AND EMPLOYEE—Dismissal.

holding an inquiry "where the Commissioner is not in any doubt as to the material facts and the relevant breach of discipline [being a breach as defined in the 1971 Regulations] is of such gravity that the Commissioner has decided that the facts and the breach merit dismissal and that the holding of an inquiry could not affect his decision." The regulation also provides that this power of summary dismissal shall not be exercised without the member's being given an opportunity of advancing to the Commissioner reasons against the proposed dismissal. Following an incident at a Garda station in which a suspect who was being questioned died as a result of an assault, the prosecutor, a member of the Garda Síochána who had been present at the station, made a statement in the course of a Garda investigation of the events leading to the death of the suspect. His statement did not disclose any assault on the suspect in his presence. The prosecutor was subsequently tried and acquitted on a charge of an asault on the suspect. At his trial, counsel for the prosecutor, in the course of his cross-examination of a fellow garda who was a witness for the prosecution, had sought to elicit an admission that the witness had committed the assault. No allegation of this nature had been made by the prosecutor in his statement. The Commissioner, invoking Reg. 34, then notified the prosecutor that he proposed to dismiss him summarily on the ground that he had made a statement which contained a falsehood or prevarication, in breach of regulation 6 of the 1971 Regulations. In accordance with Reg. 34, the prosecutor was given an opportunity to advance reasons against his proposed dismissal. In so doing he stated that he stood over his original statement but he made no attempt to explain the inconsistency between his statement and the case made on his behalf in the course of his trial. Notwithstanding the representations made by the prosecutor, the Commissioner, with the consent of the Minister for Justice made an order purporting to dismiss the prosecutor under Reg. 34. The Order recited the fact that the Commissioner had carefully examined the reasons advanced by the prosecutor against his dismissal. The prosecutor thereupon initiated proceedings challenging the validity of the dismissal order. Having obtained conditional orders of certiorari and mandamus against the respondents quashing the dismissal order and compelling his reinstatement as a member of the Garda Síochána pending the holding of an inquiry under the 1971 Regulations, the prosecutor applied to the High Court to make absolute the conditional orders notwithstanding the cause shown by the respondents. The prosecutor contended that the dismissal order was made without regard to the principles of natural and constitutional justice and that he was entitled

EMPLOYER AND EMPLOYEE—*continued.*

to demand that the conventional inquiry under the 1971 Regulations should take place before a decision to dismiss him could validly be made. **Held** by O'Hanlon J. in discharging the conditional orders of certiorari and mandamus and allowing the cause shown, 1, special considerations apply in relation to the power of the State to dispense with the services of members of the armed forces, of the Garda Síochána, and of the prison service, because it is of vital concern to the community as a whole that the members of these services should be completely trustworthy. Accordingly, it was permissible to confer on the Commissioner of the Garda Síochána the exceptional powers contained in Reg. 34 of the 1971 Regulations, although the scope for making use of these powers must be very limited in character. 2. If a member of the Garda Síochána, against whom it was proposed to exercise the power of dismissal, admitted that he was guilty of a serious breach of discipline, the Commissioner could lawfully act upon the faith of such admission without resorting to the inquiry process. In such circumstances, there could not be said to be a denial of natural or constitutional justice, since the member concerned has an opportunity to deal with the facts which are regarded as constituting a grave breach of discipline and makes it clear by his own admission that these facts apply to his case. 3. The allegations made against the garda witness on behalf of the prosecutor in the course of his trial, should be regarded as an admission, by the prosecutor, that an assault had been committed on the suspect by the garda witness, in his presence, on the night that the suspect met his death. Thus it was clear that the prosecutor had deceived the Garda investigators whilst purporting to give a full and accurate account of all that had occurred in the station, in his presence, on the night of the fatality. 4. In the circumstances, the Commissioner was entitled to invoke the provisions of Reg. 34 of the 1971 Regulations. There had been a sufficient compliance with the requirements of natural and constitutional justice and, accordingly, the dismissal of the prosecutor was valid. *The State (Jordan)* v. *Commissioner of the Garda Síochána* **(H.C.) [1987] ILRM 107**

8. —— **Natural justice** — *Office-holder — Delegation of power to dismiss — Whether* ultra vires *or whether dismissal in breach of principles of natural justice.*] The plaintiff held statutory office with the defendant Board. His terms of employment provided that he could not be dismissed without full investigation by the Board. The Board delegated its functions of 'deployment and control of staff' to its regional manager. A dispute arose between the plaintiff and the

EMPLOYER AND EMPLOYEE—Dismissal.

regional manager: purporting to exercise his power of control, the manager suspended, and then dismissed the plaintiff. The Board refused to intervene. The plaintiff sought a declaration that his dismissal was void. **Held** by Carroll J. in granting the declaration, 1, the plaintiff's contract required an investigation by the Board itself, not a delegate, before he could be dismissed; since no such investigation had taken place, the dismissal was void. *Quaere,* whether the manager's power to control staff included power to dismiss. 2. The dismissal was also void for want of natural justice (to which the plaintiff, as an office-holder, was entitled) as a party to the dispute had acted as prosecutor and judge. *Heneghan* v. *Western Regional Fisheries Board*
(H.C.) [1986] ILRM 225

9. —— **Unfair dismissal** — *Claim — Time limit — Whether mandatory requirement on employee to notify employer — Unfair Dismissals Act,* 1977 (*No.* 10), *s.* 8.] The second named respondent was dismissed by the prosecutor for alleged misconduct. He initiated a claim for redress under the Unfair Dismissals Act, 1977, and gave the first respondent a notice in writing in accordance with the provisions of s. 8(2) of the Act within the time specified. However, the first named respondent then furnished to the prosecutor a copy of the notice in writing within the time specified in the Act. At the hearing of the second named respondent's claim before the first named respondent, the prosecutor as employer, submitted that the first named respondent had no jurisdiction to hear and determine the claim made under the Act by the second named respondent in view of the latter's failure to give the requisite notice in writing to the prosecutor. The first-named respondent held that it did have such jurisdiction to hear the claim. The prosecutor then obtained conditional orders of mandamus, certiorari and prohibition. The second named respondent by affidavit purported to show cause against the making of the said orders. For determination of the court was whether s. 8(2) of the Act requires that a copy notice, required to be served on the employer concerned should be served by the employee or his agent, or whether the requirements of s. 8(2) were met once the employer concerned was served with a copy of the notice in writing by any person, such as the first-named respondent? **Held** by Hamilton J. that the first named respondent had jurisdiction to determine the claim of the second named respondent against the prosecutor, 1, the requirements of s. 8(2) are complied with once (*a*) the notice in writing claiming redress is given to the rights commissioner or tribunal within six months of the date of the relevant dismissal and, (*b*) a copy of the notice was given to the employer

EMPLOYER AND EMPLOYEE—*continued.*

concerned within the same period. 2. Once the latter notice is served on the employer concerned within the statutory period it does not matter whether it is served by the claimant or by the tribunal. *The State (IBM Ireland Ltd.)* v. *Employment Appeals Tribunal*
(H.C.) [1984] ILRM 31

10. —— **Unfair dismissal** — *Continuity of service — Transfer of undertaking — Employee in service of company — Change of employment to new company — Transfer of majority of customers to new company — Test to be applied in finding transfer of business — Whether a finding of continuity of service by Employment Appeals Tribunal open to challenge to judicial review — Minimum Notice and Terms of Employment Act,* 1973 (*No.* 4), 1*st Sched., para.* 7 — *Unfair Dismissals Act,* 1977 (*No.* 10), *s.* 20.] Section 2, sub-s. 1 (*a*) of the Unfair Dismissals Act, 1977, provides that the Act shall not apply in relation to an employee who, at the date of his dismissal, had less than one year's continuous service with the employer who dismissed him; the First Schedule to the Minimum Notice and Terms of Employment Act, 1973, as amended by the Act of 1977, applies for the purpose of ascertaining such continuity of service. Paragraph 7 of that Schedule provides:— "Where the whole or part of a trade, business or undertaking was or is transferred to another person either before or after the passing of this Act, the service of an employee in the trade, business or undertaking, or the part thereof, so transferred, shall be reckoned as part of the service of the employee with the transferee and the transfer shall not operate to break the continuity of the service of the employee." The second respondent was employed by a company which became unable to continue in business. On behalf of that company he negotiated an agreement with the applicant company and, pursuant to that agreement, changed employment and entered the service of the applicant. During a transitional period before the first company went out of business, sales enquiries were directed to the offices of the applicant and, as a result, the majority of trade customers transferred their business to it. The second respondent was dismissed by the applicant eleven months after he commenced employment with it, and he sought redress for unfair dismissal. It was held by the first respondent that the transfer of employment did not amount to a breach of continuity of service and that the second respondent was accordingly entitled to compensation. The applicant instituted an appeal to the Circuit Court against that decision. On the applicant's application by way of judicial review for an order of certiorari quashing the first respondent's award, on the ground that it

had acted in excess of jurisdiction, it was **Held** by Barron J. in refusing the application, 1, that there had been sufficient evidence before the first respondent to justify the findings that the applicant had been put in possession of a going concern and that the second respondent had continued to work as if no change of ownership had occurred. *Kenmir Limited* v. *Frizzel* [1968] 1 W.L.R. 329 and *Woodhouse* v. *Peter Brotherhood Limited* [1972] 1 W.L.R. 401 considered. *Per* Barron J. That whether there has been continuity of service of an employee is a question of fact to be determined by the Tribunal and that an error in such a finding of fact should be remedied by way of appeal; in the circumstances no useful purpose would be served by the granting of discretionary relief. *Nova Colour Graphic Supplies Ltd.* v. *The Employment Appeals Tribunal*

(H.C.) [1987] I.R.426

11. —— **Unfair dismissal** — *Maternity rights — Return to work — Statutory requirement that employer be notified in writing of intention to return to work — Whether statutory requirement mandatory — Whether employee unfairly dismissed — Unfair Dismissals Act,* 1977 (*No.* 10) *— Maternity Protection of Employees Act,* 1981 (*No.* 2), *ss.* 15, 22, 26.] Section 22, sub-s. 1 of the Maternity Protection of Employees Act, 1981, provides, *inter alia,* that ". . . the entitlement to return to work in accordance with s. 20 . . . shall be subject to an employee who has been absent from work while on maternity leave or additional maternity leave in accordance with this Act having, not later than four weeks before the date on which she expects to return to work, notified in writing (or caused to be so notified) her employer . . . of her intention to return to work and of the date on which she expects to return to work." The requirement in that subsection is mandatory and if an employee is subsequently dismissed for failure to comply with its provisions, such dismissal is not unfair. So **Held** by Egan J. *Ivory* v. *Ski-Line Ltd.*

(H.C.) [1988] I.R.399

12. —— **Unfair dismissal** — *Reasons for dismissal — Whether substantial grounds justifying dismissal — School teacher — Pregnancy — Unmarried woman teacher living with married man — Teacher employed at secondary convent school for girls — School managed by order of nuns — Whether dismissal resulted from pregnancy — Whether substantial grounds to justify dismissal — Jurisdiction of the High Court — Unfair Dismissals Act,* 1977 (*No.* 10), *s.* 6.] The appellant was a teacher in a Roman Catholic denominational secondary convent school at Rabercon, New Ross, County Wexford, which

was managed and controlled by the second respondents. During 1980-81 the school principal, who was the first respondent, received complaints from parents of children attending the school alleging that the appellant was having an association with a married man living in the town, whose wife had left him. In August, 1981, the first respondent informed the appellant of these complaints, reminded her of her obligations stemming from the denominational nature of the school and told her unless this unsatisfactory situation improved the appellant's contract of employment would be terminated. The appellant did not deny the complaints but took the view that she had not openly rejected the school's norms as her private life was a matter of her own private concern. In November, 1981, the appellant went to live with the married man in his home. In April, 1982, the school principal learned that the appellant was pregnant. On 6 August, 1982, the appellant was informed that she would have to resign or be dismissed. She did not resign and her employment with the school was terminated by letter from the school manager dated 22 August, 1982. The appellant brought an appeal to the Employment Appeals Tribunal under the Unfair Dismissals Act, 1977. The Tribunal ruled that the dismissal had not been unfair. From that decision the appellant appealed to the Circuit Court which upheld the decision of the Tribunal. The appellant appealed to the High Court. **Held** by Costello J., in dismissing the appeal on the grounds that the respondents had substantial grounds for dismissing the appellant, 1, the appellant's dismissal did not result from her pregnancy, which merely confirmed the nature of the relationship; warning of dismissal having been given to the appellant prior to such confirmation. 2. The respondents were entitled to take into account that the appellant was employed in a religious school with well known aims and objectives as well as requirements for its lay staff different to those of a secular institution. 3. The evidence established that the dismissal occurred not as a punishment for a breach of code of conduct taught in the school but from an assessment made of the effect on the school and its pupils of a continued breach of that code by the appellant. 4. In making such an assessment the respondents were entitled to take into account that the appellant's association was carried on openly and publicly in a country town of quite a small population; that within a short period of time it would have been common knowledge in the town (*a*) that the appellant was associating on a regular basis with a member of the town's business community whose wife had recently left him, (*b*) that she had commenced to live with him as man and wife and (*c*) that she had a child by him. 5. The respondents were

EMPLOYER AND EMPLOYEE—Dismissal.

entitled to conclude that such conduct amounted to a rejection of the norms of behaviour and the ideals which the school was endeavouring to instil in and set for its pupils and was capable of damaging their efforts to foster in their pupils norms of behaviour and religious tenets which the school had been established to promote. In the circumstances there were substantial grounds for dismissing the appellant. 6. The fact that the conduct relied on to justify the dismissal was not prohibited either expressly or by implication in the appellant's contract of employment is only part of the overall circumstances to be considered by a court under the Act of 1977 where the test is whether in all the circumstances there were substantial grounds to justify the dismissal. *Flynn* v. *Power*

(H.C.) [1985] I.R.648; [1985] ILRM 336

EMPLOYMENT EQUALITY

13. —— **Age requirement** — *Discrimination — Sex or marital status — Requirement not essential for such employment — Evidence — Unchallenged assertions — Admissions — Labour Court — Appeal — Limitation — Review by High Court of evidence before Labour Court — Employment Equality Act,* 1977 (*No.* 16), *s.* 2 (*c*).] Section 2 (*c*) of the Employment Equality Act, 1977, provides:— "discrimination shall be taken to occur . . . where because of his sex or marital status a person is obliged to comply with a requirement, relating to employment . . ., which is not an essential requirement for such employment . . . and in respect of which the proportion of persons of the other sex or (as the case may be) of a different marital status but of the same sex able to comply is substantially higher." The respondent had been employed for twelve years as a clerical officer when in 1967 she was required upon marriage to give up her job. From 1975 to 1981 she was employed intermittently on a temporary basis by the appellant. In 1980 her application for the permanent and pensionable post of grade IV clerk was refused in that one of the specifications for the grade was that candidates be 27 years of age or younger. By complaint to the Labour Court she contended that the 27 year age barrier contravened s. 2, sub-s. (*c*) of the Act of 1977 in that its effect was to discriminate against married women as opposed to men or unmarried women, and yet it was not an essential requirement for the grade. The appellant contended that the 27 year age barrier was justified for various reasons, including that the appellant was bound by ministerial regulation pursuant to s. 18 of the Health Act, 1970. The respondent was referred to an equality officer who accepted her contentions. On appeal essentially the same arguments were advanced and

EMPLOYER AND EMPLOYEE—Equality.

the Labour Court upheld the equality officer's determination and further awarded £3,000 compensation. The appellant by special summons pursuant to s. 21, sub-s. 4 of the Act of 1977 appealed the Labour Court's decision on a point of law to the High Court where it was **Held** by Barron J., in allowing the appeal and declaring the Labour Court's determination bad in law, that in the absence of evidence, whether statistical or otherwise, that the age requirement did discriminate against the respondent because of her "sex or marital status", the Labour Court was not entitled to find such age requirement discriminatory. On appeal by the respondent it was **Held** by the Supreme Court (Finlay C.J., Hederman and McCarthy JJ.) in allowing the appeal and restoring the determination of the Labour Court, that in the absence of evidence proving the age requirement discriminatory, this was established by the appellant's admission of unchallenged assertions, and it was not thereafter open to the appellant to challenge those assumptions of fact after declining in the High Court to have the matter remitted to the Labour Court to make specific findings of fact. *Per* Finlay C.J.: It is desirable that the equality officer and the Labour Court should in their conclusions set out their findings of fact and the evidence upon which they were so found. Parties appealing findings of fact should unequivocally so state in their notice of appeal. *North Western Health Board* v. *Martyn*

(H.C., S.C.) [1987] I.R.565; [1988] ILRM 519; (H.C.) [1985] ILRM 226

14. —— **Reference of disputes to Labour Court** — *Time limit — Alleged general practice of discrimination — Reference to Labour Court by Employment Equality Agency — Whether reference caught by statutory time-bar — Employment Equality Act,* 1977 (*No.* 16), *ss.* 2(b), 3, 19, 20, 27(2), 34.

Judicial review — Certiorari and prohibition — Labour Court determination — Application to quash — Whether error of law as to jurisdiction — Employment Equality Act, 1977 (*No.* 16), *ss.* 19, 20.

Statute — Interpretation — Employment equality — Statutory time-bar for reference of "disputes" — Employment Equality Agency making a reference — Statute providing that such reference be "dealt with as if it were a reference" of a dispute — Whether time-bar applicable to such reference — Employment Equality Act, 1977 (No. 16), *ss.* 19, 20.] S.19(5) of the Employment Equality Act, 1977, provides that reasonable cause must be shown why a reference under s. 19 has not been lodged within the six months: s. 20 (*a*) provides

EMPLOYER AND EMPLOYEE—Equality.

where the Minister considers discrimination has been practised against persons or that a practice referred to in s.3 (2) is being applied or operated he may refer the matter to the court and it will be dealt with as if it were a reference under s. 19. Prior to August, 1970, female employees, including cabin crew or air hostesses, employed by Aer Lingus retired on marriage. In 1980, Aer Lingus entered into an agreement with the Union to re-employ 28 former cabin crew or air hostesses that had retired on marriage subject to their suitability. A fundamental term of this agreement was that their seniority ranked as and from 19 May, 1980. They worked the 1980 and 1981 seasons and in August, 1982, 27 out of the 28 complained to Aer Lingus of discrimination under ss. 2 and 3 of the Employment Equality Act, 1977, by virtue of the non-recognition by Aer Lingus of their service both permanent and temporary prior to their re-employment in 1980. The reference was referred to the Labour Court pursuant to s. 19 of the Act. The complainants sought the assistance of the Employment Equality Agency (the Agency) in the preparation of their case. Following written submissions from both sides and an oral hearing before the Labour Court on 27 June, 1983, the court held that reasonable cause had not been shown why the reference relating to the alleged act of discrimination of 1 July, 1977, had not been lodged within the six months pursuant to s. 19(5) of the Act. The Agency then sought to make a fresh reference under s. 20 of the Act; s. 20(*a*) providing where the Agency considers discrimination has been practised against persons or that a practice referred to in s. 3(2) is being applied or operated it may refer the matter to the Labour Court and it will be dealt with as if it were a reference under s. 19. There commenced a series of lengthy correspondence and the Labour Court on consideration of the correspondence recommended that the complaint be referred to an Equality Officer for investigation. Aer Lingus applied for a conditional order of certiorari which was granted by Keane J. along with a conditional order of prohibition, on 29 July, 1985. Lardner J. allowed the cause shown and dismissed the application for orders of certiorari and prohibition. Aer Lingus appealed the High Court decision on the grounds that a reference made under s. 20 of the 1977 Act was caught by the time bar of six months contained in s. 19 (5). **Held** by the Supreme Court in allowing the appeal, in interpreting the Employment Equality Act, 1977, in the natural and ordinary meaning of the words and sentences contained therein, s. 19 (5) applies to references under s. 20 of the Act. *The State (Aer Lingus Teo.)* v. *Labour Court*

(H.C., S.C.) [1987] ILRM 373

EMPLOYER AND EMPLOYEE—*continued.*

15. —— **Reference of disputes to Labour Court** — *Time limit — Presumption of adequate grounds for decision — Compensation — Statute — Discretion — Whether Labour Court erred in law — Employment Equality Act,* 1977 (*No.* 16), *ss.* 3, 19, 21, 22, 23.] The respondents were employed by the appellants as female attendants at the appellant's swimming pools and were all members of the I.T.G.W.U. The I.T.G.W.U. entered into an agreement with the appellants in relation to the rostering of male and female attendants at the appellants' swimming pools approximately one year prior to the date of commencement of the Act of 1977. More than six years after this agreement was made the respondents complained to the appellants that it discriminated against them contrary to s. 3, sub-s. 4 of the Act of 1977. The respondents referred the dispute to the Labour Court pursuant to s. 19, sub-s. 1 of the Act of 1977, sub-s. 5 of which section provides that save only where a reasonable cause can be shown such a reference shall be lodged not later than six months from the date of first occurrence of the act alleged to constitute the discrimination. The Labour Court decided that a reasonable cause had been shown by the respondents for the delay in lodging the reference and, on appeal by the respondents from the recommendation of an equality officer, held that there was discrimination and awarded compensation to each of the respondents. The appellants appealed to the High Court where it was **Held** by Murphy J. in dismissing the appeal, 1, that in the absence of an appropriate record of the proceedings before the Labour Court or of a direct and immediate challenge to the manner in which it had exercised its jurisdiction the High Court was compelled to assume that the Labour Court had before it the appropriate facts on which to base its conclusion that a reasonable cause had been shown by the respondents pursuant to s. 19, sub-s. 5 of the Act of 1977. 2. That the Court would not circumscribe the wide discretion conferred on the Labour Court by s. 23, sub-s. 1 of the Act of 1977 to calculate the appropriate amount of compensation to award nor would it identify the material circumstances to which regard should be had. 3. That it had not been shown that the Labour Court erred in law in deciding that a reasonable cause had been shown by the respondents pursuant to s. 19, sub-s. 5 of the Act of 1977 and in computing the amount of compensation to award to the respondents pursuant to sub-s. 1 of section 23. *Cork Corporation* v. *Cahill*

(H.C.) [1987] I.R.478

EMPLOYER AND EMPLOYEE—*continued.*

EQUAL PAY

16. —— **Appeal from Labour Court** — *Entitlement to equal pay — Collective agreement providing for the implementation of a new unisex salary structure — Agreement proposed and accepted as being "in full and final settlement of claims" — Whether employees estopped from claiming arrears of equal pay — Whether Labour Court erred in law — Anti-Discrimination (Pay) Act,* 1974 (*No.* 15), *ss.* 2(1), 4, 5, 7.] The defendants who were female employees of P.M.P.A. claimed that for the years 1976 and 1977 they were underpaid the difference between their actual remuneration and what male employees were paid for performing similar work. The High Court upheld the recommendation of the Labour Court which had upheld the defendants' claim. The plaintiffs appealed to the Supreme Court on the grounds, *inter alia,* that the Labour Court had erred in law in upholding the defendants' claim despite the acceptance of a settlement sum which dealt with a number of claims made against the company by the defendants. The settlement included the following passage: "The proposals are made on the understanding that they are in full and final settlement of all claims, and that no claims of a cost increasing nature will be made for the duration of the 1978 National Wage Agreement." Counsel for the P.M.P.A. contended that the words 'all claims' should be construed as including the defendants' claim. **Held** by Henchy J. (Griffin and McCarthy JJ. concurring) in dismissing the appeal, 1, that there was no evidence that the defendants' claim was included in the settlement which covered other claims. 2. The plaintiff's submissions involved points of fact which had not been established, and there was no issue of law on which the Labour Court's decision could be challenged. *P.M.P.A. Insurance Co. Ltd.* v. *Keenan*

(H.C., S.C.) [1985] ILRM 173

17. —— **Equality officer** — *Investigation — Finding of discrimination — "Recommendation" — Appeal to Labour Court — Whether Labour Court entitled to allow appeal without reference to equality officer's finding of discrimination and consequent recommendation — Anti-Discrimination (Pay) Act,* 1974 (*No.* 15), *ss.* 2, 3, 4, 7, 8.] Section 8, sub-s. 1 of the Anti-Discrimination (Pay) Act, 1974, as amended by s. 18 of the Employment Equality Act, 1977, provides as follows:— "(*a*) A party to a dispute in relation to which an equality officer has made a recommendation may appeal to the [Labour] Court against the recommendation or may appeal to the Court for a determination that the recommendation has not been implemented."

EMPLOYER AND EMPLOYEE—Equal Pay.

The applicants, who were female factory operatives employed by the notice party, requested through their trade union an investigation by an equality officer pursuant to s. 7 of the Act of 1974 of their dispute with the notice party as to their entitlement to pay equal to that of equivalent male employees of the notice party. The equality officer found that there was unequal pay for like work and issued a recommendation accordingly. The respondent allowed an appeal by the notice party on the grounds that the equality officer had misinterpreted certain provisions of the Act, notably its concepts of "equal value", "like work" and "remuneration", but did not refer to his findings of fact or to his recommendation. The applicants applied in the High Court for relief by way of judicial review and sought an order quashing the order made by the respondent on the grounds that it had acted beyond the jurisdiction conferred by s. 8 of the Act in allowing an appeal upon issues raised by the notice party without determining upon the reocmmendation made by the equality officer. **Held** by Egan J., in granting the orders sought and remitting the matter to the Labour Court for full rehearing, that, upon proper construction of s. 8 and the provisions of the Anti-Discrimination (Pay) Act, 1974, where an equality officer has made findings of discrimination and issued a recommendation upon such findings, then an appeal upon that decision must include an investigation of and decision upon the merits of such findings of discrimination and consequent recommendation. *Cadwell* v. *The Labour Court*

(H.C.) [1988] I.R.280

18. —— **"Like work"** — *Work of higher value — Legislation providing equal pay for like work — Employees making comparison with different work — Determination that employees' work of higher value — Other workers being paid more — Legislation not allowing for equal pay determination in such circumstances — Intention of legislature — Anti-Discrimination (Pay) Act,* 1974 (*No.* 15), *ss.* 2, 3.

European Communities — Equal pay — Legislation lacuna allowing employee to be paid lower wage in respect of male employee whose work was of lesser value — Whether consistent with Treaty of Rome — Article 177 reference — Anti-Discrimination (Pay) Act, 1974 (*No.* 15), *ss. 2, 3 — Treaty of Rome,* 1957, *Art.* 119.

Statute — Interpretation — Legislation lacuna — Legislature not addressing point now arising — Whether court may impute intention of legislature — Anti-Discrimination (Pay) Act, 1974 (*No.* 15), *ss.* 2, 3.] S.2 of the Anti-Discrimination (Pay) Act, 1974, provides that a female employee shall be entitled to the same rate of pay as a male employee under the same employer, where both are engaged in 'like work.' S. 3 (c) of the said Act provides that 'two persons shall be regarded as employed in like work' where 'the work performed by one is equal in value to that performed by the other in terms of the demands it makes in relation to such matters as skill, physical or mental effort, responsibility and working conditions.' Article 119 of the EEC Treaty provides that men and women shall receive equal pay for equal work. The appellants, all female, were employed by the respondent in the dismantling, cleaning, oiling and reassembling of telephones and other equipment. They had brought proceedings in the Labour Court, claiming the same rate of pay as a male employee of the respondent, who was employed as a stores labourer. Although the work of the appellants was different in kind to that of the male employee, they sought to argue that it was 'like work' within the meaning of s. 3 (*c*) above. It was found by the Labour Court that the work of the appellants was superior in value to that of the male employee, and that it was not, therefore, 'like work' within the maning of s. 3 (*c*). The appellants appealed to the High Court. In the course of argument, counsel for the appellants submitted that s. 3 (*c*) of the 1974 Act should be construed as though the words 'at least' appeared before the words 'equal in value.' **Held** by Keane J. in staying the proceedings pending the outcome of a referral to the European Court of Justice, 1, the construction of s. 3 (*c*) of the 1974 Act urged by the appellants would result in equal pay for unequal work, an outcome which could not have been intended by the legislature. 2. An intention to partly remedy an injustice cannot be imputed to the legislature, where by the use of different language the injustice could have been remedied in its entirety. 3. Where the legislature in drafting a statute has not addressed itself to a particular issue, it is not for the court to impute to the legislature the intention of dealing with that issue, or to construe the statute accordingly. *Director of Public Prosecutions* v. *Flanagan* [1979] I.R. 265 applied. 4. A possible outcome of s. 3 (*c*) is that the appellants may lawfully be paid lower wages than male employees whose work is of lesser value. It is a question of Community as well as national law whether such an outcome is reconcilable with Article 119 of the EEC Treaty. *Murphy* v. *Bord Telecom Eireann* **(H.C.) [1986] ILRM 483**

MINIMUM NOTICE

19. —— **Lay off** — *Claim for compensation — Employees laid off — Notice of intention to claim redundancy payment — Effect on contract of employment — Whether employment ceased due to termination by employer — Whether waiver of*

right to notice — Whether employees estopped — Redundancy Payments Act, 1967 (*No.* 21), *ss.* 11, 12, 13 — *Redundancy Payments Act,* 1971 (*No.* 20), *s.* 11 — *Minimum Notice and Terms of Employment Act,* 1973 (*No.* 4), *ss.* 4, 5, 7, 1*st Sched.* — *Unfair Dismissals Act,* 1977 (*No.* 10), *s.* 20.] The appellant company entered into an agreement with it's employees' union representatives in July, 1980, in settlement of an industrial dispute. The agreement provided *inter alia* that the union would provide the company with a list of employees who would prefer to be made redundant rather than work at the rates offered by the company and that upon resumption of work the company would lay off such persons thereby enabling them after four weeks to apply to be made redundant. Approximately 60 employees were laid off by the appellant and each duly applied for and received payments under the Redundancy Payment Acts, 1967-1979. The printed form used by the employees to institute such applications contained two parts, one comprising a notice of intention to terminate employment and the other a notice of intention to claim redundancy payment. The employees concerned applied on the latter part of the form, and subsequently made claims under the Minimum Notice and Terms of Employment Act, 1973, for compensation for loss arising from the plaintiff's failure to give them notice of its intention to terminate their contract of employment. The Employment Appeals Tribunal held that the employees' claims for compensation were valid. The plaintiff appealed contending *inter alia* (i) that as a matter of law it did not terminate its employees' contracts of employment and was therefore not required to give the notice specified by the 1973 Act; (ii) The employees had waived their rights to notice, and (iii) That they were now estopped from exercising such rights. **Held,** 1, although the plaintiff purported to avail of the statutory lay-off procedures it could not reasonably have believed that the suspension of the employment of those on the list would not be permanent and since the statutory precondition for the initiation of the lay off procedure under the Act did not exist,the employees were entitled to treat the resulting repudiation by the plaintiff of its employees' contracts of employment as having terminated those contracts. 2. Before an employee could be said to have waived his right to notice, the waiver must be clear and unambiguous. 3. There was nothing on the facts to suggest that the employees waived their rights to minimum notice under s. 7 of the 1973 Act, and it could not be said that in accepting the plaintiff's proposals that they thereby represented to the plaintiff that they would not enforce the statutory rights which arose as a consequence of such acceptance.

EMPLOYER AND EMPLOYEE—Notice.

Appeal dismissed. *Industrial Yarns Ltd.* v. *Greene*

(H.C.) [1984] ILRM 15

20. —— **Lay off** — *Employee on lay off — Employer serving notice of dismissal by reason of redundancy — Employee claiming payment in respect of period of notice — Whether employee suffered loss in respect of period of notice — Effect of notice of dismissal on lay off — Cessation of employment no longer temporary — Duty of employee to mitigate loss — Employee claiming unemployment benefit — Whether payment in respect of notice period should be reduced by reference to social welfare benefits received — Redundancy Payments Act,* 1967 (*No.* 21), *s.* 11 — *Minimum Notice and Terms of Employment Act,* 1973 (*No.* 4), *s.* 5.] The plaintiff company, which was in financial difficulties, reduced its workforce and temporarily laid off a number of its employees, including the second defendant. Some months later it became apparent that there was no longer any prospect of recalling the second defendant to work and he was given six weeks notice of dismissal by reason of redundancy. During the period of lay off and the period of notice the second defendant had been in receipt of unemployment benefit and was paid a redundancy payment by the plaintiff. The second defendant claimed to be entitled to be paid his wages by the plaintiff in respect of the period of notice. The plaintiff argued that because the second defendant had been on lay off when the notice of dismissal was served, he would not have been earning in any event and consequently had suffered no loss. The plaintiff further argued that, even if the second defendant had suffered loss, he was obliged to mitigate that loss: and had done so to the extent of the social welfare payments which he had received. The Employment Appeals Tribunal rejected both the plaintiff's arguments and held that the second defendant was entitled to be paid for the notice period without deduction. The plaintiff brought these proceedings in the High Court by way of appeal from the decision of the Employment Appeals Tribunal. **Held** by Barrington J., in dismissing the plaintiff's action, 1, that having regard to the definition of 'lay off' in the Redundancy Payments Act, 1967, an essential element of a lay off was the employer's belief that the cessation of employment would not be permanent. 2. That once notice of dismissal was served, the second named defendant was no longer laid off but was an employee under notice of dismissal and the rights of the parties were then governed by the provisions of the Minimum Notice and Terms of Employment Act, 1973. 3. That the second defendant had a right under the Act of 1973 to be paid by the plaintiff in respect

EMPLOYER AND EMPLOYEE—*continued.*

of any time during his normal working hours when he was ready and willing to work but when no work was provided for him. Accordingly, his loss under s. 12 of the Act of 1973 was the money he was by statute entitled to receive and did not receive. 4. That the plaintiff's obligation to pay the statutory sum was antecedent to any obligation on the part of the State to pay unemployment benefit, so the plaintiff was obliged to pay the full statutory sum without reduction by reference to the employee's entitlement under the social welfare code. *Irish Leathers Ltd.* v. *Minister for Labour*

(H.C.) [1986] I.R.177

21. —— **Liquidation of employer company** — *Liquidator serving notice of dismissal by reason of redundancy — Employee claiming payment in respect of period of notice — Employee employed by liquidator on a day to day basis at the same wages for a period longer than the prescribed period of notice subsequent to notice of dismissal being served — Whether employee suffered loss by virtue of lack of statutory notice — Redundancy Payments Acts,* 1967-79 — *Minimum Notice and Terms of Employment Act,* 1973 (*No.* 4), *ss.* 4, 5, 11, 12, *2nd Sched.*] Section 12 of the Minimum Notice and Terms of Employment Act, 1973, concerns actual loss relating to breach of contract or failure to comply with s. 5 and the Second Schedule of that Act and consequently the Employment Appeals Tribunal may only award compensation for lack of statutory notice where there is evidence of actual loss. So **held** by Lardner J. *Irish Shipping Ltd.* v. *Byrne.*

(H.C.) [1987] I.R.468

22. —— **Receivership** — *Termination of employment — Notice — Continuance of business — Purported extension of notice — Whether permissible — Whether employees received their statutory entitlement — Minimum Notice and Terms of Employment Act,* 1973 (*No.* 4), *ss.* 7(1), 11(2).] The plaintiff company having gone into receivership in 1984, the receiver gave notice to each of the defendants, who were employed by the company, that their employment would terminate on a given date. In each case, the period of notice given was that provided for by the Minimum Notice and Terms of Employment Act, 1973. However, before the expiration of the notice, this period was extended from week to week by means of a notification typed on each defendant's pay-packet. The employment of the defendants finally terminated on 12 October, 1984, one week after the final extension notice to each defendant. The Employment Appeals Tribunal held that the final notification was the relevant notice of termination for the purposes of the 1973 Act, and that the defendants had

not therefore received the minimum statutory notice, and it awarded them compensation accordingly. The plaintiff appealed to the High Court pursuant to s. 11 (2) of the 1973 Act, submitting that the notice required by the Act was a minimum period, and that any extension complied in law with the requirements of the Act. The High Court dismissed the appeal, holding that a statutory notice, in order to comply with the Act, must nominate a date on which the employment is to terminate, and that if the employer does not terminate the notice on that date, he must be seen as having either waived the notice or re-employed the employee. On appeal from this decision, it was **Held** by the Supreme Court (Henchy J., Hederman J. concurring, and McCarthy J.) in allowing the appeal and setting aside the decision of the Employment Appeals Tribunal, 1, the notice required by the Act must not be stringently and technically construed, as though it were analogous to a Notice to Quit. The Act is not concerned with the form of the notice, but only with the length. The provisions of the Act are complied with once the notice conveys to the employee that he will lose his employment at the end of a period expressed or necessarily implied in the notice, once that period is not less than the statutory minimum. 2. An employer may rely upon the cumulative period created by extensions of an original notice of termination, so long as a plurality of notices is not used to mislead the employee or subvert the operation of the Act. *Bolands Ltd.* v. *Ward* **(H.C., S.C.) [1988] ILRM 382**

SUSPENSION

23. —— **Validity** — *Natural justice — Act transferring plaintiff civil servant into employment of State sponsored body — Plaintiff liable to suspension under his former civil service regime — Delegation of power of suspension permissible — Plaintiff's new employer purporting to delegate such power to officer — Officer suspending plaintiff — Whether officer had authority to suspend — Conditions under which power exercisable — Natural justice — Permissible duration of suspension — Criminal and civil proceedings arising out of suspension — Full hearing by employer into suspension postponed until proceedings determined — Whether such postponement reasonable — Relevant factors — Postal and Telecommunications Services Act,* 1983 (*No.* 24), *s.* 45 — *Postal and Telecommunications Services (Amendment) Act,* 1984 (*No.* 10), *s.* 5 — *Civil Service Regulation Act,* 1956 (*No.* 46), *ss.* 13, 14, 15.] The Postal and Telecommunications Services Act, 1983, transferred the control and operation of the national postal service from the Minister for Posts and Telegraphs to the defend-

ant company. By virtue of s. 45 of the Act of 1983, as amended, persons including the plaintiff who were serving in the Department of Posts and Telegraphs as of the 1 January, 1984, were transferred into the employment of the defendant. Sub-sections 2, 3 and 4 of that section provided, *inter alia,* that the conditions of service to which those employees were subject before they were transferred would continue to apply to them and that the conditions in regard to tenure of office which the defendant would grant to them were to be no less favourable than those prevailing for the time being in the civil service. Prior to his transfer, the plaintiff had the status of an established civil servant; as such he was liable to be suspended from his duties under s. 13 of the Civil Service Regulation Act, 1956, where it appeared to the suspending authority that he had been guilty of grave misconduct or grave irregularity warranting disciplinary action or where such a charge was made and it appeared to that suspending authority that the charge warranted investigation. Before the transfer of functions to the defendant, the Minister of State at the Department of Posts and Telegraphs had pursuant to the relevant statutory provisions and regulations delegated his power of suspension to C. Subsequent to the 1 January, 1984, the Chief Executive of the defendant re-nominated C. as a suspending authority for the defendant. On the 9 May, 1984, C. suspended the plaintiff from his duties without pay on suspicion of the plaintiff having, amongst other things, stolen letters or packages in the course of post. The plaintiff was informed of the reason for his suspension and afforded an opportunity to explain his alleged misconduct. The plaintiff instituted proceedings on the 17 July, 1984, seeking, *inter alia,* a declaration that his suspension was void on the grounds that there was no jurisdiction vested in the defendant to delegate the power of suspension and that the suspension was contrary to natural justice. Two days later the plaintiff was charged with offences relating to interference with mail; nevertheless he requested that a full hearing by the defendant be held into the complaint of misconduct on which his suspension rested as soon as was reasonably practicable and sought, but was refused, an interlocutory injunction in the High Court directing that such a hearing be held. In November of the following year a jury acquitted the plaintiff of all the offences with which he had been charged. During all this time and thereafter until the determination of these proceedings the plaintiff remained suspended without pay. At the trial of his action in the High Court the plaintiff also sought to impugn the validity of his suspension on the ground that even if it was initially valid it ceased to be so after the date on which it would

EMPLOYER AND EMPLOYEE—Suspension.

have been reasonably practicable to have held a full hearing into his suspension. The High Court (Costello J.) dismissed all the plaintiff's claims and he appealed. **Held** by the Supreme Court (Finlay C.J., Walsh, Henchy, Hederman and McCarthy JJ.) in allowing the appeal in relation to the plaintiff's claim that his suspension had become invalid by the passage of time, 1, that C. had authority to suspend the plaintiff because (*per* McCarthy J.; Finlay C.J., Walsh and Hederman JJ. concurring) the delegation to C. which had been effected by the Minister of State was made applicable with respect to the defendant's employees by s. 45 of the Act of 1983 and also because (Henchy J. concurring) that statutory provision vested a power of delegation in the Chief Executive thereby enabling him to nominate C. afresh. 2. That natural justice had been complied with in respect of the plaintiff having been informed of the reason for his suspension and having been afforded an opportunity to answer the charge of misconduct upon which the suspension rested. 3. That the power of suspension must be construed as permitting the suspension to have been continued only for the period of time in which it would not have been reasonably practicable to have held a full hearing into the suspension. 4. (Henchy J. dissenting) That as the plaintiff had at all times desired that a full hearing into his suspension be proceeded with notwithstanding the pending criminal and civil proceedings, his suspension became invalid as of the earliest date on which such a hearing would have been ready to proceed, viz., the 1 August, 1984. Such a hearing would have in no way impinged on the issues in the instant proceedings. *Dicta* of Woolf J. in *Reg.* v. *British Broadcasting Corpn., Ex parte Lavelle* [1983] 1 W.L.R. 23 at p. 36 doubted. *Per* McCarthy J. The real point was that the matters about which an enquiry into the suspension would be concerned were wholly removed from the matters under consideration in the present action. The action formed no ground for not proceeding with the enquiry, no more than did the existence of this appeal from the decision in the High Court. *Per* Henchy J. dissenting. The issues which would have arisen at the enquiry could not have been segregated from the issues raised in these proceedings. Not alone was it not open to the plaintiff to claim that the fundamental requirements of justice meant that the defendant was bound to hold an enquiry into the suspension while the High Court proceedings were pending, but it would not have been in accordance with legal propriety to have done so, primarily because the defendant would thereby have knowingly trespassed on the High Court jurisdiction which the plaintiff had invoked. *Flynn* v. *An Post*

(S.C.) [1987] I.R.68

EMPLOYER AND EMPLOYEE—*continued.*

TRADE DISPUTE

24. —— **Connection with employer** — *Employment or non-employment — Meaning of non-employment — Dispute concerning refusal of employer to employ some but not all members of trade union — Trade Disputes Act,* 1906 (*c.* 47), *ss.* 3, 5.

Trade dispute — Contract of employment — Whether contract in existence — Sub-contractor — Trade union in dispute with employer of sub-contractor — Whether protection of trade disputes legislation available — Trade Disputes Act, 1906 (*c.* 47), *s.* 3.

Injunction — Interlocutory — Trade dispute — Inducement of breach of contract — Contract terminated — Whether appropriate to grant injunction in respect of continuing picketing.] The plaintiff was the builder of flats for which Brian Flynn was subcontracted to do bricklaying and blockwork. He employed a number of block-workers who were members of the Incorporated Brick and Stone Layers Trade Union. The first-named defendant was general secretary and the second-named defendant was shop steward in the trade union. The union discovered that Brian Flynn was employed as a sub-contractor by the plaintiff contrary to the union's policy which requires their bricklayers to be employed directly by the main contractors. The union, by letter, requested the plaintiff to employ directly their members. The plaintiff, by letter, informed the union that they had terminated their contract with Brian Flynn. A number of meetings followed between the parties but the plaintiff refused to employ all the union members who had been employed by Brian Flynn and advertised for blocklayers. The plaintiff employed five men, all members of the union, as a result of this advertisement but two members of the union who had previously been employed by Brian Flynn still remained unemployed. The union then threatened strike action unless the plaintiff employed these remaining two men. The plaintiff refused to comply with the union's request and as a result industrial action followed. The plaintiff sought (1) an injunction restraining the defendants from conspiring to induce a breach of contract between the plaintiff and Brian Flynn; (2) an injunction restraining the defendants from conspiring to cause a withdrawal of labour from the plaintiff or from picketing the plaintiff's site or taking any strike action against the plaintiff. The defendants argued that their conduct was justifiable on the grounds that a trade dispute existed and therefore they were protected by the provisions of the Trade Disputes Act, 1906. Hamilton J. granted an interim injunction to the plaintiff. On application for interlocutory injunctions, **Held** by McWilliam J. in refusing to

EMPLOYER AND EMPLOYEE—Dispute.

grant the injunctions, 1, the contract between Brian Flynn and the plaintiff had terminated prior to any industrial action being taken, so that it was not appropriate to grant an injunction regarding it. *Semble:* The contract between the plaintiff and Brian Flynn was not a contract of employment within the meaning of s. 3 of the Trade Disputes Act, 1906, so that the trade union would have no protection under the Act regarding that contract. 2. A trade dispute within the meaning of the provisions of the 1906 Act existed between the plaintiff and the defendants relating to the non-employment of the defendants. *J. Bradbury Ltd.* v. *Duffy*

(H.C.) [1979] ILRM 51

25. —— **Picketing** — *Dispute over termination of contract — Application for injunction to restrain picketing — Whether picketing entitled to statutory protection — Whether picketer an employee of the plaintiff — Whether plaintiff the employer of the picketer — Trade Disputes Act,* 1906 (*c.* 47), *ss.* 2, 5(3) — *Constitution of Ireland,* 1937, *Art.* 40.] The Trade Disputes Act, 1906, permits picketing of an employer's premises in furtherance of a trade dispute between the employer and a workman. The defendant, a painter and decorator, had for many years worked regularly for the plaintiff. Up to the year 1976, no written agreement existed between the parties, but at no time was PAYE tax or PRSI paid by the plaintiff in respect of the defendant. During that period, the defendant was considered by himself and by the plaintiff as liable for the payment of VAT arising from the weekly payments made to him by the plaintiff. In 1976, a written agreement was entered into by the parties providing that the rate at which the defendant would be paid would be related to the current National Wage Agreement, with a 25% increase to allow for PRSI contributions to be borne by the defendant when he employed people to assist him in work on the plaintiff's premises, and to allow for insurance premiums to be paid by the defendant in relation to his employees. This agreement was signed by the plaintiff and by the defendant using his trading name. Prior to the agreement, discussions had taken place between the parties as to the possibility of the defendant becoming a regular employee of the plaintiff, but the defendant had elected not to change his status. In 1978, the plaintiff terminated its contract with the defendant, who then commenced to picket the plaintiff's premises. The plaintiff obtained an interim injunction restraining the picketing. Subsequently the plaintiff instituted proceedings against the defendant, and brought a motion seeking interlocutory relief. By consent the motion was treated as the trial of the action.

EMPLOYER AND EMPLOYEE—*continued.*

Held by Costello J. in granting an injunction restraining the defendant from picketing the premises of the plaintiff, 1, the contractual relationship between the parties was one in which the defendant was in the position of an independent contractor. 2. An independent contractor is not entitled to the protection of the Trade Disputes Act, 1906, since the person for whom he contracts to work cannot be regarded as his employer for the purposes of the Act. *Lamb Brothers Dublin Ltd.* v. *Davidson*

(H.C.) [1978] ILRM 226

Unfair dismissals, *see* Nos. 9-12, 19

VICARIOUS LIABILITY

26. —— **Criminal act of employee** — *Vicarious liability of employer — Measure of damages.*] By agreement between the plaintiff and the defendant, a specialist security protection service was provided for the plaintiff's premises by the defendant. A security officer in the employment of the defendant was convicted of having taken goods from the premises of the plaintiff and the fact of the theft was not disputed by the defendant. The plaintiff company contended that the defendant was vicariously liable for the act of its employee and issued proceedings seeking damages for breach of agreement, negligent misrepresentation, negligence and conversion. **Held** by Egan J., in giving judgment for the plaintiff, 1, that where the employer is specifically engaged to safeguard the property of another, he is under a duty to take due care to protect it. 2. That, where an employer delegates such duty to his employee, he is vicariously liable for the act of that employee, notwithstanding that the act is a criminal one. *Morris* v. *C.W. Martin and Sons Ltd.* [1966] 1 Q.B. 716 applied. *Cheshire* v. *Bailey* [1905] 1 K.B. 237, not followed. 3. That, in assessing damages, the plaintiff should be entitled to recover the value of the stolen goods assessed at their replacement value together with the costs incurred in investigating the theft and interest. *Johnson & Johnson (Ireland) Ltd.* v. *C.P.Security Ltd.*

(H.C.) [1985] I.R.362 ; [1986] ILRM 559

—— Age limits — Entry to post — Discrimination — Sex or marital status.
see **Employer and Employee,** 13

—— Civil Service employment.
see **Civil Service**

—— Collective agreement — Whether intention

to enter into legal relations — Onus of proof.
see **Employer and Employee,** 2

—— Company — Winding up — Creditors — Classification — Preferential debts — Test applicable — Unpaid wages or salary of servants or employees — Whether employee engaged under a contract of service or a contract for services — Claimants in first category entitled to be paid as preferential creditors.
see **Company,** 18

—— Company — Winding up — Creditors — Classification — Preferential debts — Wages due to employees — Wages having preferential status — Employment contributions under social welfare legislation in respect of such wages due — Whether "employer's contribution" having similar preferential status.
see **Company,** 19

—— Contract — Contract of service or partnership — Employer's annual obligation to provide information relating to employees — Fishing vessel owned and operated by skipper — Crew engaged prior to each voyage — Remuneration based on value of catch — Whether employment or partnership in existence — Whether skipper an employer.
see **Revenue,** 38

—— Contract — Termination — Trade dispute — Whether contract of employment — Independent contractor.
see **Employer and Employee,** 25

—— Contract of employment — Trade dispute — Whether contract in existence — Sub-contractor — Trade union in dispute with employer of sub-contractor — Whether protection of trade disputes legislation available.
see **Employer and Employee,** 24

—— Dismissal — Defence forces — Constitution — Fair procedures — Certiorari — Delay — Lack of candour — Whether disentitling to relief.
see **Judicial Review,** 2

—— Dismissal — Garda — Probationer — Natural justice — Dismissal for not being likely to become efficient and well-conducted guard — Previous

EMPLOYER AND EMPLOYEE—*continued.*

breaches of discipline as basis for dismissal — Pending enquiry into breach of discipline discontinued — Whether dismissal *ultra vires.*
see **Natural and Constitutional Justice,** 1

—— Dismissal — Natural justice — Officer in naval service — Office dependent on obtaining specified qualification — Failure to obtain qualification — Repeated warnings given — Dismissal notified but postponed to allow representations — No representations made — Whether sufficient compliance with *audi alteram partem* rule.
see **Defences Forces,** 1

—— Dismissal — Office holder — Probationer — Natural justice — Whether reasons required — Whether reasons be disclosed.
see **Civil Service,** 1

—— Dismissal — Officeholder — Wrongful dismissal — Damages — Failure to pay salary on due dates — Loss of availability of salary — Whether dismissal resulted in injury to health — Whether due to unlawful nature of dismissal — Exemplary damages — Loss arising from arbitrary nature of dismissal.
see **Damages,** 3

—— Dismissal — University lecturer — Probationer — Board of Visitors — Jurisdiction.
see **Education,** 5

—— Dismissal — University lecturer — Seminary — Whether religious discrimination in dismissing teacher — Teacher also priest — Seminary obtaining funds from State but applied for lay purposes as recognised college of university.
see **Constitution,** 21

—— Employee — Dishonesty — Liability of employer — Theft of third party's goods — Defendant employers contracting as security firm to protect plaintiff's premises — Thieves gaining access to premises with help of defendant's employee.
see **Employer and Employee,** 26

—— Employer's liability.
see **Employer's Liability**

—— Employment equality — Labour Court —

ESTOPPEL—*continued.*

Whether trial of first action in lower court should be stayed.
see **Practice and Procedure,** 10

—— Issue estoppel — *Res judicata.*
see **Practice and Procedure,** 41, 42

—— Landlord and tenant — New tenancy — Decontrolled premises — Statutory tenancy — Death of tenant — Whether dependants entitled to tenancy — Estoppel — Whether acceptance by landlord of dependant as tenant precluded landlord from denying statutory tenancy.
see **Landlord and Tenant,** 6

—— Minister — Statutory authority — Whether extendable by estoppel.
see **Social Welfare,** 3

—— Planning — Exempted development — Agent of planning authority representing that development exempt — Whether authority estopped from denying the development exempt — Whether representation *ultra vires.*
see **Planning,** 33

—— Promissory estoppel — Legitimate expectation — University — Undergraduate course — Offer of place — Acceptance — Deferral by college of place offer to next academic year — Whether enforceable by candidate — Remedies — Judicial review.
see **Judicial Review,** 15

—— Promissory estoppel — Reasonable expectation — Plaintiffs discovering valuable antiquities at national monument — Property delivered into custody of State — Assurance that plaintiffs would be honourably treated — Whether plaintiffs entitled to a reward.
see **Bailment**

—— Proprietary estoppel — Lease — Agreement for lease — Licence — Conditions to be satisfied before equity can be enforced against the owner of the land — Claimant acting to his detriment — Claimant's belief or expectation that he had interest in the land — Encouragement or acquiescence of landowner — Onus of proof on claimant — Special circumstances.
see **Real Property,** 9

ESTOPPEL—*continued.*

—— Reasonable expectation.
see **Bailment**
see also **Legitimate Expectation**

—— *Res judicata* — Distinction between cause of action estoppel and issue estoppel.
see **Family Law,** 11

—— Road traffic accident — Personal injury action — Claim made against driver of vehicle — Driver dying from injuries received in accident — Liberty sought to join insurers as defendants in place of deceased — Whether insurers estopped from opposing such an order.
see **Practice and Procedure,** 43

—— Road traffic accident — Plaintiff passenger — Personal injuries — Summons not issued within limitation period — Defendant outside jurisdiction — Failure to issue summons within period caused by absence of solicitor so authorised — Defendant prevented from pleading Statute of Limitations.
see **Limitation of Actions,** 2

EUROPEAN COMMUNITIES

1. —— **Agriculture** — *Excise duty on livestock — Whether measure having effect equivalent to a customs duty — Common organisation of the markets — Whether duty* ultra vires *as unreasonable — Whether decision on European law required — Imposition of Duties* (*No.* 239) *Agricultural Produce (Cattle and Milk) Order,* 1979 (*S.I. No.* 152) — *Agricultural Produce (Cattle and Milk) Regulations,* 1979 (*S.I. No.* 160).

Statute — Delegated legislation — Whether arbitrary or unreasonable — Whether confirmed by subsequent enactment — Presumption against retrospection — Agriculture — Levy on livestock — Imposition of Duties Act, 1957 (*No.* 7), *ss.* 1,2 — *Finance Act,* 1966 (*No.* 17), *s.* 15(2)(*d*) — *Finance (Excise Duty on Tobacco Products) Act,* 1977 (*No.* 32) — *Finance Act,* 1980 (*No.* 14), *s.* 79 — *Imposition of Duties* (*No.* 239) *Agricultural Produce (Cattle and Milk) Order,* 1979 (*S.I. No.* 152) — *Agricultural Produce (Cattle and Milk) Regulations,* 1979 (*S.I. No.* 160) — *Constitution of Ireland,* 1937, *Art.* 15.5.] In 1979, the Government introduced a temporary excise duty or levy of 2% in respect of, *inter alia,* bovine animals which were slaughtered in, or exported from the State. The duty was payable by the proprietor of the premises in the case of animals slaughtered at the premises, and by the exporter in the case of animals exported from the State. The Revenue Commissioners were empowered to regulate the system of collecting the duty. Regulation 8 of S.I. No. 160 of 1979 allowed the proprietor of a premises in which the animals were slaughtered, or an exporter, to withhold from the amount to

EUROPEAN COMMUNITIES—*continued.*

be paid by him to the seller of animals a sum equal to the amount of duty payable. The plaintiffs, three butchers and an exporter of livestock, challenged the validity of the duty on the ground that it amounted to the imposition of a customs duty contrary to the provisions of the Treaty of Rome. The issue was referred to the European Court of Justice, which ruled ([1981] E.C.R. 735) that an indirect tax on the value of agricultural products subject to common organisations of the markets was not, in principle, incompatible with the Treaty; that such a duty would be incompatible if it had the effect of impeding the proper functioning of the relevant common organisations; and that these were questions of fact to be determined by the national court. At the resumed High Court hearing, the plaintiffs asserted that: the duty had the effect of encouraging smuggling between Northern Ireland and the Republic and of distorting the legal trade between those parts of Ireland also; in view of farmer resistance to the duty, butchers and exporters found it impossible to pass on the levy to the seller of animals as had been envisaged by the levy, and it was thus unreasonable and invalid; that as a result it operated as a customs duty rather than an excise duty; and that S.I. No. 152 of 1979 and S.I. No. 160 of 1979 were *ultra vires* the rule-making authority conferred by the Imposition of Duties Act, 1957. **Held** by Barrington J. in granting the relief sought, 1, since the court was concerned with the legality of the duty, and not with its wisdom, the incidence of smuggling, even if it had occurred, could not affect the validity of the duty; and that the changes in the legal movement of cattle between Northern Ireland and the Republic in 1979 were caused by factors other than the imposition of the duty. Effects of the Common Agricultural Policy in Ireland considered. 2. Because in practice it was impossible for exporters to shift the duty back to producers, it operated as a duty on exports contrary to the provisions of the Treaty of Rome. Nature of the distinction between customs duty and excise duty discussed. *Browns Transport Ltd.* v. *Kropp* (1958) 100 C.L.R. 263 considered. 3. The statutory instruments were *ultra vires* the 1957 Act in purporting to adapt legislation dealing with specific impositions of duties on wine and tobacco products to the duty on bovine animals, and S.I. No. 160 of 1979 was also unreasonable and unworkable. *Per* Barrington J.: it is doubtful if s. 2 of the 1957 Act, providing for confirmation of certain orders made under s. 1 of the Act, has any application to orders suggested to be, in whole or in part, void *ab initio*. **Held** by the Supreme Court (Finlay C.J., Walsh, Henchy, Griffin and Gannon JJ.) in dismissing the appeal, 1, S.I. No. 152 of 1979 was *ultra vires* the Finance Act, 1966, since it operated in an untargeted, indiscriminate and unfair manner by imposing the primary liability which fell on the exporter or butcher rather than on the producer of live cattle and was therefore made in excess of the impliedly intended scope of the delegation under the 1966 Act. *Cassidy* v. *Minister for Industry and Commerce* [1978] I.R. 297 applied. 2. The confirmation of S.I. No. 152 of 1979 by s. 79 of the Finance Act, 1980, was not relevant, in that it must presumptively have been intended to operate prospectively only, since otherwise it would have infringed Article 15.5 of the Constitution by making non-payment of the levy in 1979 an infringement of the law. *Hamilton* v. *Hamilton* [1982] I.R. 466 applied. 3. Since the case could be determined by reference to domestic law, it was not necessary for the court to have regard to a decision as envisaged by Article 177 of the Treaty of Rome, having regard to the paramount force and effect of community law. *Doyle* v. *An Taoiseach*
(H.C.) [1986] ILRM 693

2. —— **Procedure** — *Reference to European Court of Justice — Supreme Court — Issue arising for first time — Consideration of mandatory reference — Treaty of Rome,* 1957, *Art.* 177.

Judicial review — Ultra vires — *Administrative body — Regulation — Restraint of trade — Prohibition on use of non-Irish horses by Irish showjumpers in international competition — Fair and equal position to be given in competitive arena — Whether regulation* ultra vires.

Restraint of trade — Rule-making body — Prohibition on use of non-Irish horses by Irish showjumpers in international competition — Whether unreasonable restraint on individual showjumper's trade — Whether contrary to public policy — Protection of Irish half-bred horse industry.] The defendants, members of the Equestrian Federation of Ireland ('the Federation'), had passed a resolution preventing Irish competitors in international competitions from being mounted on other than Irish-bred horses. The federation was affiliated to the Fédération Equestre Internationale, the Rules and General Regulations of which were binding upon it. Article 100, rule 1 of the General Regulations provided that the Regulations were established in order that competitors from different nations might compete against each other under fair and equal conditions. The plaintiff, a professional showjumper of world class, alleged that the resolution was in unreasonable restraint of trade, and that it was *ultra vires* the powers of the defendants. He also contended that a resolution which had the effect that only competitors riding Irish-bred horses could compete in international competitions meant that those affected by the resolution could not compete under fair and

EUROPEAN COMMUNITIES—*continued.*

equal conditions, in accordance with Article 100 of the General Regulations. It was held by Hamilton J. in the High Court that the resolution was void as being an unreasonable restraint of trade. The defendants appealed against the order of the High Court. **Held** by the Supreme Court (O'Higgins C.J., Griffin and Parke JJ.; Henchy and Kenny JJ. dissenting) in allowing the appeal, 1, the resolution of the federation was not *ultra vires* its powers, because where the federation was of opinion that the encouragement of the Irish horse-breeding industry was essential for the future of the equestrian sport in Ireland, it was the duty of the federation to encourage such industry. Conversely, where the federation was of opinion that the spectacle of Irish competitors mounted upon foreign-bred horses would be harmful to the sport in Ireland, it was the duty of the federation not to authorise such competitors; and it was within the federation's powers to make a judgment in the form of the resolution which it passed. 2. (*Per* O'Higgins C.J.) Art 100, rule 1 of the General Regulations referred to the conditions under which competitors, once selected, shall compete, and not to the manner in which individuals were selected to be competitors. (*Per* Griffin and Parke JJ. (concurring) the reference to fair and equal conditions in Art. 100, rule 1, was confined to matters provided for in the regulations and rules of the Fédération Equestre Internationale, which provide, in effect, a charter for international showjumping competitions. (*Per* Henchy and Kenny JJ. (dissenting): the resolution passed by the defendants was *ultra vires* their powers in its application to the plaintiff, and was therefore invalid, since its effect was to impose a pre-competition restriction which placed the plaintiff in an unfair and unequal position in the competition arena, contrary to the provisions of Art. 100, rule 1 of the General Regulations. 3. (*Per* O'Higgins C.J., Griffin and Parke JJ.): although the plaintiff is inhibited in his efforts to maintain his superior position in showjumping by reason of the resolution passed by the defendants, his interests must be balanced against that section of the public concerned with horse-breeding and showjumping, and accordingly the resolution did not amount to an unreasonable restraint of trade. (*Per* O'Higgins C.J.): where an allegation that a decision or resolution is contrary to certain provisions of the Treaty of Rome is relied upon before the Supreme Court, being the court of final appeal, the question of a mandatory reference to the Court of Justice of the European Communities would arise. *Macken* v. *O'Reilly*

(H.C., S.C.) [1979] ILRM 79

—— Accession — Amendment of Constitution — Licence — Scope — Treaties establishing European Communities — Objectives — Amendment of Treaties — Whether amendment of Treaties authorised by original licence for accession — Single European Act.
see **Constitution,** 22

—— Agriculture — Milk levy — Regulations giving effect to EC milk levy — Such regulations having retrospective effect — Whether unjust — Whether unjustified attack on property rights.
see **Constitution,** 35

—— Council directive — Effect — Failure of member state to fully implement directive — Whether directive has direct effect — Whether directive sufficiently unconditional and precise — Equality of treatment.
see **Social Welfare,** 4

—— Equal pay — Legislation lacuna allowing employee to be paid lower wage in respect of male employee whose work was of lesser value — Whether consistent with Treaty of Rome.
see **Employer and Employee,** 18

—— Equal treatment.
see **Social Welfare,** 4
Statute, 1

—— Law — Supremacy — Relationship of European Communities law to domestic law — Application to High Court for interlocutory injunction — Plaintiff claiming breach of Irish law — Defendant having complained to Commission of European Communities of breach by plaintiff of community law — Investigation by Commission in progress — Whether existence of investigation should influence Irish court in deciding whether to grant injunction.
see **Injunction,** 11

—— Single European Act — Title III — European political cooperation — Foreign policy referrable to common position adopted by High Contracting Parties — Government — Ratification — Breach of Constitution.
see **Constitution,** 22

—— Statute alleged to be in breach of Community law — Effect on presumption of constitutionality.
see **Injunction,** 2

EUROPEAN COMMUNITIES—*continued.*

—— Supply and distribution of fuel — Government powers to regulate acquisition, supply, distribution and marketing — Whether incompatible with Community obligations — Whether mandatory regime a quantitative restriction or measure having equivalent effect — Whether restriction on competition — Application for interlocutory injunction — Whether injunction be granted.
see **Injunction,** 10

—— Treaty of Rome — Free movement of workers — Conformity — Offshore fishing licences — Ministerial regulations — New conditions — Employee nationality specifications — Injunction application.
see **Injunction,** 4

EVIDENCE
see also **Criminal Law — Evidence.**

1. —— **Admissibility** — *Communication between members of the Gardaí — Claim of privilege — Whether such communications inadmissible in evidence because, as a class, their admission would be against the public interest — Whether claim for privilege should be rejected.*] At the hearing in the District Court of a charge of unlawful assault contrary to common law, the defence called upon the Garda who it was alleged had been assaulted to produce his original report in respect of the incident. The District Justice upheld the State's claim that the report was privileged and did not need to be produced. The District Justice did, however, grant the request made by the defence to state a case for the opinion of the High Court whether his determination was correct in point of law. **Held,** 1, executive privilege cannot be claimed in respect of a class of documents as such. In light of the principles enunciated in *Murphy* v. *Dublin Corporation* [1972] I.R. 215 the claim that communications between one member of the Gardaí and another are inadmissible as evidence because, as a class, their admission would be against the public interest was not sustainable. (*Attorney General* v. *Simpson* [1959] I.R. 105 not followed). 2. Since the State had not advanced specific grounds of possible damage to the public interest which might result from disclosure the claim to privilege should have been rejected. If specific grounds had been advanced it would have been necessary for the District Justice himself to read the document privately and determine its admissibility in accordance with the principles enunciated in *Murphy* v. *Dublin Corporation. Director of Public Prosecutions (Hanley)* v. *Holly*
(H.C.) [1984] ILRM 149

EVIDENCE—*continued.*

2. —— **Estoppel** — *Issue estoppel* — Res judicata — *Whether issue raised in defence had been determined in previous proceedings — Negligence — Contributory negligence — Duty owed by plaintiff to take care for his own safety — Contributory negligence dependent on finding of negligence.*] The parties were involved in a motor accident in September, 1984. The defendant in these proceedings (McL.) had sued the plaintiff (G.) in negligence in an earlier action arising out of the same incident. McL. had been successful in the Circuit Court but the decision was overturned on appeal to the High Court and the action dismissed on the grounds that McL. had failed to discharge the onus of proof of negligence. While the latter case was pending before the Circuit Court G. instituted these proceedings alleging that the accident was caused by McL.'s negligence. McL. denied the claim on the grounds, *inter alia,* of G.'s contributory negligence. G. claimed that the earlier proceedings had decided that he was not negligent and therefore the issue of his negligence was *res judicata* and McL. was estopped from raising it. McL. argued that the High Court had not made any specific finding as to the issue of negligence and that therefore the estoppel did not arise. By order of the High Court a preliminary issue of law was directed to be tried as to whether such an estoppel arose. **Held** by Blayney J., in deciding the issue in the negative, 1, that in order for an issue estoppel to arise there must have been a final determination by a court of competent jurisdiction of the same issue in earlier proceedings between the same parties. *Shaw* v. *Sloan* [1982] N.I. 393 applied. 2. That the High Court had not found that the plaintiff had not been negligent, the appeal having been decided on other grounds. *Donohoe* v. *Browne* [1986] I.R. 90 distinguished. 3. That the issue raised by the plea of contributory negligence was whether the accident was caused or contributed to by the plaintiff's failure to take reasonable care for his own safety, a plea which only arises where there has been a finding of negligence against the other party. That issue had not been determined in the earlier proceedings and accordingly the estoppel pleaded did not arise. *Gilroy* v. *McLoughlin*
(H.C.) [1988] I.R. 44

—— Admissibility.
see **Criminal Law,** 10, 11-21, 33

—— Admissibility — Affidavit — Practice — Objection to introduction of evidence at trial without prior notice — Case involving constitutional rights of citizen

EVIDENCE—*continued.*

plaintiff — *Prima facie* case — Discharge of onus — Whether bald statement sufficient.
see **Practice and Procedure,** 20, 21

—— Onus of proof — Oireachtas — Bill — Constitution — Repugnancy — Reference by President to Supreme Court — Opponents to bill to establish repugnancy.
see **Constitution,** 1

—— Onus of proof — Statute — Validity — Pre-Constitution enactment — Whether enactment continued in force — Onus on plaintiff challenger — No presumption that enactment consistent with Constitution.
see **Constitution,** 39

—— Power — Exercise — Condition precedent — Proof — Failure — Revenue omitting proof that tax payer duly required to make return of income.
see **Revenue,** 26

—— Practice — Privilege — *Subpoena duces tecum* issued requiring officer of the Central Bank to produce documents — Oath of secrecy — Statutory privilege — Whether summons be set aside.
see **Practice and Procedure,** 44

—— Signature — Proof — Rubber stamp — *Prima facie* evidence.
see **District Court,** 3

—— Tape recording — Admissibility.
see **Criminal Law,** 13, 14.

—— Telephone calls — Tracing — Voice established by tracing.
see **Criminal Law,** 14

EXCISE DUTY
see **Customs and Excise**

EXCISE OFFENCE
see **Constitution,** 54, 55

—— Penalty — Mandatory penalty on conviction — Power to mitigate penalty incurred in excise cases — Whether court has discretion as to size of fine in excise cases — Whether court may take other offences into consideration in imposing penalty in excise cases.
see **Criminal Law,** 52

EXCISE OFFENCE—*continued.*

EXCLUSIVE SUPPLY CONTRACT
see **Contract,** 7

EXECUTIVE POWER
see **Government**

EXECUTIVE PRIVILEGE
see **Evidence,** 1

EXECUTION — *Fieri facias.*
see **Injunction,** 6

EXECUTOR
see **Personal Representative**

EXEMPLARY DAMAGES
see **Damages,** 3-5

EXEMPTED DEVELOPMENT
see **Planning,** 32-4

EXPORT SALES RELIEF — Corporation tax.
see **Revenue,** 11-13

EXPRESSION, FREEDOM OF,
see **Freedom of Expression**

EXTENSION OF TIME
see **Practice and Procedure,** 53, 54

EXTRA-TERRITORIAL OFFENCE — Irish citizen in custody in Northern Ireland — Prosecutor wishing to be tried in the Republic — D.P.P.indicating that proceedings would not be instituted in this jurisdiction — Application for orders of certiorari and mandamus — Role of D.P.P. — Whether D.P.P.'s decision reviewable — Whether prosecutor deprived of his constitutional rights of access to the courts of this jurisdiction.
see **Criminal Law,** 49

EXTRADITION
see also **Constitution,** Nos. 24, 25, 41

1. —— **Bail** — *Tests applicable — Likelihood of accused absconding — Onus of proof lying on person resisting application — Same test applicable to application for bail in extradition proceedings as in other criminal proceedings — Extradition Act,* 1965 (*No.* 17), *s.* 29 — *Constitution of Ireland,* 1937, *Art.* 40.] The prisoner was committed to prison on foot of an order for his extradition to the United States of America. He obtained a conditional order of habeas corpus and applied for bail pending the final determination of the habeas corpus proceedings. In

EXTRADITION—*continued.*

deciding to grant bail the judge applied the test of whether or not it was probable that the prisoner would abscond and therefore be unavailable for extradition. The decision was appealed on the ground that that particular test should be applied differently in an extradition case, namely, that the court should have adopted a stricter approach than in an ordinary criminal case and that it was for the prisoner to satisfy the court that there was no real or reasonable possibility that if granted bail he would not be available for extradition and furthermore that the obligations of the State under an extradition treaty curtailed the court's power to grant bail. On appeal by the Attorney General it was **Held** by the Supreme Court (Finlay C.J., Henchy, Griffin, Hederman and McCarthy JJ.) in dismissing the appeal, 1, one of the obligations of the State under an extradition treaty is to take all reasonable steps to ensure the prisoner is available for extradition but this does not curtail the power of the High Court to grant bail in such circumstances. 2. There is no reason for applying the absconding test any differently in extradition cases as compared with ordinary criminal cases. It is always for the party opposing the bail application to satisfy the court of the probability of the prisoner absconding if granted bail. Accordingly the absconding test had been applied properly. *The People* v. *Gilliland*

(S.C.) [1985] I.R.643; [1986] ILRM 357

2. —— **Delay** — *Arrest on foot of warrants relating to offences committed seven years previously — Whether excessive delay — Whether unfair discrimination.*] The applicant, who had been arrested and remanded in custody in Northern Ireland in 1979, charged with certain offences, escaped some time later and came to live in the Republic. He was then aged sixteen. Two years later, he was convicted of another offence within the Republic and sentenced to five years imprisonment. In September, 1982, a request for his extradition to Northern Ireland was made by the R.U.C., but the warrant was returned to them as not containing an offence corresponding to any charge under Irish law. A fresh warrant was also returned, with the information that the applicant was due for release from prison on 5 August, 1986, and that if extradition was still required, the warrant should be re-submitted three months prior to that date. Eleven warrants were received in July, 1986, and returned with legal queries. On 29 August, the applicant was arrested on foot of fresh warrants received the previous day. Three other persons involved with the applicant in the commission of the original offences had been dealt with by the Northern Ireland courts in 1980, and had since served their sentences. The

EXTRADITION—*continued.*

applicant sought judicial review in order to prevent his extradition. Since the granting of the order permitting judicial review, he had been out on bail, and had got married. He submitted that extradition should be refused on the ground of excessive delay. **Held** by Carroll J. in refusing to grant the relief sought, 1, the fact that the applicant was not dealt with by the Northern Ireland courts in 1980 was due to his own fault, as was the delay between 1982 and 1986. Any question of prejudice due to delay could be raised at first instance in the Northern Ireland courts. *Hanlon* v. *Fleming* [1981] I.R. 489 followed. 2. The applicant had not shown that the State had unfairly discriminated against him. *McMahon* v. *Leahy* [1984] I.R. 525 distinguished. *Harte* v. *Fanning (No.1)*

(H.C.) [1988] ILRM 70

3. —— **Political offence** — *Damage to property — Possession of firearms — Whether political offence — Onus of proof.*] The District Court in Portlaoise made five separate orders on 5 September, 1986, ordering the plaintiff to be delivered into the custody of the R.U.C. on foot of 5 warrants issued in Northern Ireland on 28 August, 1986. The first three warrants related to the offences of setting fire to specific buildings in Northern Ireland and the fourth and fifth warrant referred to the offences of theft and possession of a shotgun and cartridges contrary to the relevant statutes in Northern Ireland. The plaintiff seeks an order for his release pursuant to s. 50 of the Extradition Act, 1965, on the grounds that the offences to which the warrants relate are political offences and therefore accordingly he is entitled to be released. He submitted in support of his claim that he was a member of Na Fianna Éireann which opposed the state of Northern Ireland and whose objectives were to damage property in the North in order that they would render the maintenance of the Union prohibitively expensive due to the Government's obligation to pay compensation for malicious damage to property. He further submitted that the shotgun was stolen because it would be useful in training within Fianna Éireann. Evidence was also adduced that one of the premises had been set on fire because the firm had been supplying materials to the British Army and the other premises had been attacked because it was the meeting place of Loyalist groups and the railway station had been attacked because it was a railway station. **Held** by Blayney J. in refusing to make the order sought, 1, the onus of establishing that the offences to which the warrants relate are political offences is upon the plaintiff who is seeking asylum here which in this case he failed to do. *McGlinchy* v. *Wren* [1983] ILRM 169 applied. 2. In view of the inconsistencies in the plaintiff's

EXTRADITION—*continued.*

affidavit and the evidence before the court regarding the stated objectives of Na Fianna Éireann and the other objectives that were adduced in evidence, the plaintiff failed to discharge the onus of proof that the offences to which the warrant related involving damage to property were political offences. 3. The plaintiff's submissions that the stealing of the shotgun and the cartridges would be useful in training within Fianna Éireann was insufficient to discharge the onus of proof as it left open the question of what the training was for and so failed to establish that the offences had a political character. *Harte* v. *Fanning (No. 2)*

(H.C.) [1988] ILRM 75

4. —— **Political offence** — *Equality before the law — Group escape from foreign custody — Escapers entering the State — Extradition of four escapers sought — Successful defences based on political nature of escape — Extraditions refused — Extradition of fifth escaper sought — Defence based on allegation of political nature of escape — The State inhibited from controverting claim of fifth escaper — Extradition Act,* 1965 (*No.* 17), *ss.* 44, 50 — *Constitution of Ireland,* 1937, *Art.* 40.] The plaintiff was found guilty in Northern Ireland on counts of robbery and the unlawful possession of a firearm; he was sentenced to eight years imprisonment. While serving his sentence, the plaintiff made an unsuccessful attempt to escape from prison. On the 10 March, 1975, the plaintiff was brought in custody to a courthouse in Northern Ireland to answer a charge that he had attempted to escape from prison; he escaped from the courthouse with four other prisoners and, having crossed the border, he came to reside within the State. On the 4 April, 1975, the four co-escapers were arrested within the State on the strength of warrants issued in Northern Ireland which recited their escapes from the courthouse, and proceedings were instituted under the Extradition Act, 1965, for orders directing them to be delivered into the custody of the Northern Ireland authorities. Each of those four escapers claimed and obtained in the High Court an order directing his release under s. 50 of the Act of 1965 on the ground that his escape from the courthouse in Northern Ireland was a political offence or an offence connected with a political offence. The defendants in those four High Court actions were represented by counsel who were instructed by the Chief State Solicitor; in two of those actions the claim of the escaper to exemption from extradition on the ground of the political nature of his escape was not opposed and, in the other two actions, that claim of the escaper, if opposed, was opposed unsuccessfully. On the 4 February, 1983, a warrant (which recited the plaintiff's escape from the courthouse on the 10

EXTRADITION—*continued.*

March, 1975) was issued in Northern Ireland for the arrest of the plaintiff and it was endorsed by the defendant for execution within the State. On the 31 March, 1983, the plaintiff was arrested in the State and on the same date the District Court made an order directing that he be delivered into the custody of the Northern Ireland authorities. The plaintiff issued a summons in the High Court and claimed an order directing his release from custody pursuant to s. 50 of the Act of 1965; in his affidavit he averred that the offences for which he was sentenced to eight years imprisonment had been committed by him at the command of an unlawful organisation in order to raise funds in furtherance of its aims, which included the overthrow of the system of government in Northern Ireland, and he averred that his escape from the courthouse was a political offence or an offence connected with a political offence. At the trial in the High Court of the issues raised by the plaintiff's summons, there was no firm evidence of the nature or the results of the proceedings instituted under s. 50 of the Act of 1965 by the plaintiff's four co-escapers. **Held** by Keane J., in dismissing the plaintiff's claim, 1, that there was an onus on the plaintiff to establish that the offence to which the warrant of the 4 February, 1983, related was a political offence or an offence connected with a political offence, and that he had failed to discharge that onus. *Bourke* v. *The Attorney General* [1972] I.R. 36; *Hanlon* v. *Fleming* [1981] I.R. 489 and *McGlinchey* v. *Wren* [1982] I.R. 154 considered. The plaintiff appealed against the dismissal of his claim and, at the hearing of his appeal, he obtained leave from the Supreme Court to adduce further evidence of the nature and the results of the proceedings that had been instituted by his four co-escapers. **Held** by the Supreme Court (O'Higgins C.J., Henchy, Griffin, Hederman and McCarthy JJ.), in allowing the appeal after considering such further evidence, 1, that the circumstances of the plaintiff's escape from the courthouse in Northern Ireland did not differ materially from the escapes of the other four escapers from that courthouse. 2. That the declaration that all citizens shall, as human persons, be held equal before the law (contained in Article 40, s. 1, of the Constitution) was a relevant factor in determining the plaintiff's appeal in view of the fact that the Chief State Solicitor had either acquiesced in, or had opposed unsuccessfully, the grant of an order of release under s. 50, sub-s. 1, of the Act of 1965 to each of the other four escapers on the ground that his escape from the courthouse was a political offence or an offence connected with a political offence. 3. That, in the special circumstances, the court would not permit the

EXTRADITION—*continued.*

defendant (who represented the State) to controvert the plaintiff's claim to an order for release under s. 50 of the Act of 1965. *McMahon* v. *Leahy*

(H.C., S.C.) [1984] I.R.525; [1985] ILRM 423

5. —— **Political offence** — *Onus of proof — Warrant for arrest of plaintiff — Warrant issued in Northern Ireland — Warrant endorsed for execution within the State — Order directing delivery of plaintiff to authorities in Northern Ireland — Warrant reciting charge of murder — Application for release — Failure of applicant to establish that offence designated in warrant was a political offence or connected with such offence — Extradition Act,* 1965 (*No.* 17), *ss.* 43(1), 50 — *Criminal Law (Jurisdiction) Act,* 1976 (*No.* 14), *ss.* 2(2)(*a*), 20(4)(*b*) — *Constitution of Ireland,* 1937, *Art.* 40.] Section 50, sub-s. 1, of the Act of 1965 states that where a person has been arrested under Part III of the Act he shall be released if the High Court so directs. Subsection 2 of that section states *inter alia* that such direction may be given where the High Court is of opinion (*a*) that the offence to which the warrant relates is "a political offence or an offence connected with a political offence" or (*b*) that there are substantial reasons for believing that the person named in the warrant would, if removed from the State, be prosecuted or detained for such an offence. On the 6 July, 1983, two warrants were issued by a justice of the peace in Northern Ireland charging the plaintiff with the murder in Northern Ireland, contrary to common law, of an 84 year old man, who had many years before been a member and the Speaker of the Northern Ireland House of Commons, and of his son, who had also previously been a member of the Northern Ireland House of Commons and of the Northern Ireland Assembly. The warrants were endorsed for execution within the State by the defendant, the Assistant Commissioner of the Garda Síochána, pursuant to s. 43, sub-s. 1, of the Act of 1965. The plaintiff was brought before the District Court, which made two orders directing that the plaintiff be delivered into the custody of the Northern Ireland police. The plaintiff issued two special summonses in the High Court seeking orders directing his release under s. 50 of the Act of 1965. At the hearing of both actions concurrently in the High Court the plaintiff submitted that the offences to which the warrants related were political offences or offences connected with political offences; alternatively, that there were substantial reasons for believing that the plaintiff, if removed from the State, would be prosecuted or detained for such an offence. The plaintiff further submitted that his extradition to Northern Ireland, where the procedures

EXTRADITION—*continued.*

and constitution of the courts differed from those of this State, would constitute a failure to vindicate his personal rights contrary to Art. 40 of the Constitution. **Held** by the High Court (McWilliam J.) in dismissing the plaintiff's claim, 1, that the extradition of the plaintiff to Northern Ireland, the procedures or constitution of whose courts differed from those of this State, did not constitute a failure to vindicate the plaintiff's personal rights contrary to Art. 40 of the Constitution. 2. That the offences to which the warrants related were not political offences or offences connected with a political offence. *McGlinchey* v. *Wren* [1982] I.R. 154, applied. 3. That the plaintiff had failed to establish that there were substantial reasons for believing that, if removed from the State under Part III of the Act of 1965, he would be prosecuted or detained for a political offence or an offence connected with a political offence. *Per curiam:* That the offence of membership of Fianna Éireann was a political offence in Northern Ireland, but it was unlikely that the plaintiff, if extradited, would be prosecuted or detained for this much less serious offence. *McGlinchey* v. *Wren* [1982] I.R. 154; *McMahon* v. *Leahy* [1984] I.R. 525 and *Bourke* v. *Attorney General* [1972] I.R. 36, considered.

The plaintiff appealed to the Supreme Court. At the hearing of the appeal by the Supreme Court the plaintiff submitted a further claim that the charges in the warrants could embrace the offence of counselling or procuring in this State the offence of murder in Northern Ireland, and that these were offences for which the plaintiff might not be extradited according to s. 20, sub-s. 4 (*b*), of the Criminal Law (Jurisdiction) Act, 1976. **Held** by the Supreme Court (O'Higgins C.J., Henchy, Griffin, Hederman and McCarthy JJ.), in disallowing the appeal, 1, that the offences to which the warrants related were not political offences or offences connected with a political offence. *McGlinchey* v. *Wren* [1982] I.R. 154, applied; *McMahon* v. *Leahy* [1984] I.R. 525 considered. *Per* O'Higgins C.J.; Henchy and Griffin JJ. concurring: What constitutes a political offence falls to be determined in each case having regard to the act done and the facts and circumstances which surrounded its commission — the onus being on the person claiming the political exception to establish that the offence to which the warrant relates comes within its protection. The test is whether the person charged was at the relevant time engaged, either directly or indirectly, in what reasonable, civilised people would regard as policital activity. The circumstances disclosed of the murders in question here were so brutal, cowardly and callous that it would be a distortion of language if they were to be accorded the status of political

EXTRADITION—*continued.*

offences. *Per* Hederman J.: The decisive criterion to determine whether an ordinary criminal offence becomes a relative political offence is whether the perpetrator acted with a political motive or for a political purpose. There was no evidence here upon which the court could hold that the plaintiff was a participant or probably a participant in the crimes committed. It followed therefore, that the court had no material upon which it could seek to examine the motives attributable to the plaintiff for offences with which, he says, he had no connection. Therefore the court could not be of the opinion that the offences charged were either political offences or offences connected therewith. *Per* McCarthy, J.: The determination of whether or not an offence charged is a political offence, or an offence connected with a political offence, should rest primarily upon the assessment of the true motivation of the individual committing the offence, the true nature of the offence itself and the identity of the victim. In assessing these factors the proximity of each to the alleged political aim is critically important and capable of objective assessment. In order to assess motive it is not necessary for the individual charged to admit his involvement in the crime. 2. That the plaintiff had failed to discharge the onus of proving that there were substantial reasons for believing that, if removed to Northern Ireland, he would be prosecuted or detained for a political offence or an offence connected with a political offence. *Bourke* v. *Attorney General* [1972] I.R. 36, considered. *Per* O'Higgins C.J.; Henchy and Griffin JJ. concurring: That even if it were accepted that membership of Fianna Éireann constituted a political offence in Northern Ireland, there was no basis for believing that the plaintiff would be prosecuted for such, if removed to face the more serious charges of murder. *Per* O'Higgins C.J.: Henchy, Griffin and McCarthy JJ. concurring: The affidavit of detective inspector McCann was not an undertaking proferred on behalf of the appropriate authority in Northern Ireland that if extradition were granted, the plaintiff would not be prosecuted except for those offences for which extradition was sought, but was evidence of a decision, already taken, not to mount any such prosecution. 3. (O'Higgins C.J., Henchy and Griffin JJ. concurring). That there was no substantial reason for believing that the plaintiff, if extradited, would be charged with counselling or procuring in this State the murders in Northern Ireland of the persons named in the warrants, which were offences other than those to which the warrants related. *Reg.* v. *Smyth* [1982] N.I. 271, applied. *Per* O'Higgins C.J. Henchy and Griffin JJ. concurring: Extradition proceeds on the assumption that the Rule of Speciality will

EXTRADITION—*continued.*

operate. 4. (O'Higgins C.J., Henchy and Griffin JJ. concurring). That counselling or procuring in this State the offence of murder in Northern Ireland was not an offence by reason only of a provision of Northern Ireland law corresponding to s. 2, sub-s. 2(*a*), of the Criminal Law (Jurisdiction) Act, 1976, such that it came within the exception from extradition provided by s.20, sub-s. 4(*b*), of that Act, as it was also an offence contrary to the common law in Northern Ireland. *Reg.* v. *Smyth* [1982] N.I. 271, applied. *Shannon* v. *Fanning*

(H.C., S.C.) [1984] I.R.569; [1985] ILRM 385

6. —— **Political offence** — *Offence connected with political offence — Warrant issued in England — Offence of fraudulent deception specified in warrant — Offence committed to assist aims of organisation of which defendant was a member — Those aims including the setting aside of the Constitution by unconstitutional means — Political offence exception interpreted so as not to embrace offence facilitating such objective — Constitutional construction preferred — Accused not entitled to release — Extradition Act,* 1965 (*No.* 17), *ss.* 47, 50 — *Constitution of Ireland,* 1937, *Arts.* 15, 39.] Article 15, s. 6, sub-ss. 1 and 2, of the Constitution provide that the right to raise and maintain military or armed forces is vested exclusively in the Oireachtas and that no military or armed force shall be raised or maintained (other than by the Oireachtas) for any purpose whatsoever. Article 39 defines treason as consisting of, *inter alia,* attempting by force of arms or other violent means to overthrow the organs of government established by the Constitution, or taking part or being concerned in, or inciting or conspiring with any person to make or to take part or be concerned in any such attempt. An order was made in the District Court pursuant to s. 47 of the Extradition Act, 1965, directing that the plaintiff be delivered into the custody of a member of the English police force in London, England on foot of a warrant which had been issued by a judicial authority there, and which warrant had been duly endorsed by the defendant for execution within the State pursuant to s. 43 of the Act. That warrant recited a complaint alleging that the plaintiff had dishonestly obtained by false pretences the sum of £600 in cash from a bank in London, contrary to s. 15, sub-s. 1, of the (English) Theft Act, 1968. The plaintiff sought an order in the High Court directing his release pursuant to s. 50 of the Act of 1965 on the basis that the offence specified in the warrant was either a political offence or an offence connected with a political offence. In an affidavit sworn by the plaintiff for those proceedings, he deposed, *inter alia,* that he had committed the offence

EXTRADITION—*continued.*

specified in the warrant on behalf of an illegal organisation which styled itself as the Irish National Liberation Army (the I.N.L.A.), the aims and objectives of which were the establishment of a "thirty-two county workers Republic by force of arms" and by other means, including the waging of "a military campaign against the forces of the Crown within the six counties of Northern Ireland, and the United Kingdom and elsewhere." He further deposed that he was a member of the I.N.L.A. at the time of the offence's commission and had given the £600 to one whom he believed to be a fellow member of that organisation. **Held** by Gannon J., in dismissing the application, 1, that, although it was a necessary inference from the evidence that the offence to which the warrant related was of the same quality and was committed with the same motivation and to achieve the same objectives as the acts perpetrated by the I.N.L.A. with the arms, weapons or instruments of violence procured through its commission, the offence was neither in fact, nor in its nature, a political offence. *Shannon* v. *Fanning* [1984] I.R. 548; *McGlinchey* v. *Wren* [1982] I.R. 154 and *Bourke* v. *The Attorney General* [1972] I.R. 36, considered. 2. That, as the plaintiff's evidence only showed that the offence to which the warrant related was connected with all the activities of the I.N.L.A., and did not establish any of those activities to be a political offence, the plaintiff had failed to discharge the onus cast upon him by s. 50 of the Act of 1965 of proving the commission of a political offence with which the offence specified in the warrant was connected. *Bourke* v. *The Attorney General* [1972] I.R. 36 and *Shannon* v. *Fanning* [1984] I.R. 548, further considered. On appeal by the plaintiff, it was **Held** by the Supreme Court (Finlay C.J., Henchy, Griffin, Hederman and McCarthy JJ.), in disallowing the appeal, 1, that the plaintiff had failed to establish that the offence specified in the warrant was either a political offence or an offence connected with a political offence. 2. (*Per* Finlay C.J., Henchy, Griffin and Hederman JJ.), that the attainment of the objectives of the I.N.L.A. necessarily involved the destruction and setting aside of the Constitution by means expressly or impliedly prohibited by it, viz., Article 39 and (Hederman J. dissenting), Article 15, s. 6. Accordingly, an interpretation of s. 50 of the Act of 1965 which conferred immunity from extradition on a person in relation to an offence committed by him with the intention of directly furthering such an objective would not be in conformity with the Constitution and, therefore, was one which the Oireachtas must be presumed not to have intended. *McDonald* v. *Bord na gCon* [1965] I.R. 217 and *East Donegal Co-Operative* v. *The Attorney General* [1970] I.R. 317, applied. 3. (*Per* Finlay C.J., Henchy, Griffin, Hederman and McCarthy JJ.), that whilst it is possible and of assistance to identify factors which should be assessed in reaching a decision as to whether any particular offence is or is not a political offence, it is probably neither possible, nor desirable, to attempt a precise or comprehensive definition of that term. *Bourke* v. *The Attorney General* [1972] I.R. 36; *McGlinchey* v. *Wren* [1982] I.R. 154 and *Shannon* v. *Fanning* [1984] I.R. 548, considered. *Per* McCarthy J. The proposition that the courts should grant protection to a person charged with an offence stamped with the purpose of over-throwing the organs of the State, including the courts, is a ludicrous one. *Quinn* v. *Wren*

(H.C., S.C.) [1985] I.R.322; [1985] ILRM 410

7. —— **Political offence** — *Robbery — Motive — No evidence upon which trial judge could have held robbery instigated on behalf of I.R.A. or motivated by desire to assist I.R.A. — Burden of proof — Extradition Act,* 1965 (*No.* 17), *s.* 50.] The plaintiff, whose extradition to England was ordered by the District Court, instituted High Court proceedings claiming that the offence of robbery to which the warrant related was a political offence or an offence connected with a political offence and that he was entitled to be discharged under s. 50 of the Extradition Act, 1965. The trial judge, in granting the plaintiff the order sought, said that the plaintiff had persuaded him that the crime was carried out for the Provisional I.R.A. The defendants appealed. **Held** by the Supreme Court (Finlay C.J., Walsh, Henchy, Griffin and McCarthy JJ.) in allowing the appeal, 1, the basis of the trial judge's finding appeared to be the evidence given by the plaintiff, both initially on affidavit and the subsequent cross-examination on his affidavit. The statement made by the plaintiff to the police clearly contradicted the account put in his affidavit and what he said in court. 2. There was no evidence upon which the trial judge could have held that the robbery was instigated on behalf of the I.R.A. or motivated by a desire to assist the I.R.A., and since the burden of proof of establishing political motivation lay upon the plaintiff and he failed to discharge that burden he was not entitled to the relief sought. *Maguire* v. *Keane*

(S.C.) [1986] ILRM 235

8. —— **Political offence** — *Subversive organisation — Aims and objectives — Attack upon Constitution and organs of State — Criteria for extradition — Extradition Act,* 1965 (*No.* 17), *s.* 50 — *Constitution of Ireland,* 1937, *Art.* 6.

Extradition — Evidence — Foreign warrant — "Judicial authority" — Proofs — Statutory requirements — Whether satisfied — Extradition Act,

EXTRADITION—*continued.*

1965 (*No.* 17), *Part III.*] The plaintiff, a member of the Irish Republican Army, was convicted at Belfast Crown Court of attempted murder and sentenced to 20 years imprisonment. He subsequently escaped from prison. Some time later he was arrested in Dublin on foot of nineteen warrants from Northern Ireland backed for execution in the State by the first defendant. Upon an order by the Dublin Metropolitan District Court for his delivery to Northern Ireland the plaintiff applied to the High Court for release on divers grounds, including that the offences for which he was sought to be extradited were political offences or offences connected with political offences. **Held** by O'Hanlon J., in refusing to order his release, 1, that the protection afforded by s. 50, sub-s. 2(*a*) of the Extradition Act, 1965, could not extend to offences which, albeit otherwise political, were committed on behalf of the Irish Republican Army, whose stated aims necessarily involved an attack upon the Constitution and its organs of State. *Quinn* v. *Wren* [1985] I.R. 322 applied. 2. That although the plaintiff could be prosecuted in this jurisdiction for the same offences by virtue of the provisions of the Criminal Law (Jurisdiction) Act, 1976, such prosecution was not mandatory and there was nothing in that Act to limit or qualify the provisions of Part III of the Extradition Act, 1965. The plaintiff appealed to the Supreme Court against the judgment and order of the High Court. Pending the hearing of his appeal the plaintiff in certiorari proceedings challenged the jurisdiction of the District Court to make the extradition orders on the grounds that the original warrants for arrest upon which they were based were not issued by a "judicial authority" in accordance with the requirements of Part III of the Extradition Act, 1965. **Held** by Barr J. and affirmed on appeal by the Supreme Court (Finlay C.J., Henchy, Griffin, Hederman and McCarthy JJ.) that for the purposes of Part III of the Act of 1965, the question as to whether the authority which issued and verified an extradition warrant was a 'judicial authority' within the meaning of the Act, was a question to be determined by the law of the requesting state. Accordingly where a judicial authority was appointed and its warrant was verified by the law of the requesting state the requirements of Part III of the Act were satisfied. *Gillespie* v. *Attorney General* [1976] I.R. 233 applied. Upon the plaintiff's appeal from the decision of O'Hanlon J. it was **Held** by the Supreme Court (Finlay C.J., Henchy and Griffin JJ.; Hederman and McCarthy JJ. dissenting) in dismissing the appeal and affirming the decision of O'Hanlon J., that the presumption of constitutionality of the Extradition Act, 1965, being a statute passed after the coming into force of the Constitution of Ireland, 1937, necessarily required that the expression "political offence" in s. 50 thereof could not be construed so as to grant immunity to a person charged with an offence the purpose of which was to subvert the Constitution or usurp the functions of its organs of State. *Quinn* v. *Wren* [1985] I.R. 322 applied. *Per* Finlay C.J.; Henchy and Griffin JJ. concurring: Where a person loses the immunity of the "political offence" exception granted by s. 50 of the Extradition Act, 1965, because the offence for which he is sought to be extradited was committed under the aegis of an organisation the aims and objectives of which are an attack upon the Constitution and a subversion of its organs of State, that person does not regain the same immunity by falling back upon some personal mental reservation incompatible with the stated aims and objectives of the organisation. *Per* McCarthy J.: Article 6 of the Constitution, properly construed, does not take away the protection of s. 50 of the Extradition Act, 1965, from offences committed for the purpose of pursuing a particular policy which may be opposed to that expressed by the government of the day, whether or not expressly endorsed by the legislature. That expressed policy might change between the date of the commission of the act and the application for extradition: the government itself may change with a like consequence. *Per* McCarthy J.: The requirement of reciprocity in extradition arrangements necessitates the requesting state's compliance after extradition with the constitutional fair procedures that apply in this jurisdiction. It is a vital ingredient of such arrangements that constitutional rights will not be disregarded, that fundamental fairness of procedures will not be violated; and the making of the reciprocal arrangement must presume accordingly. Where, however, there have been cases in which those rights were violated, that presumption is negatived. *Russell* v. *Fanning*

(H.C., S.C.) [1988] I.R.505; [1988] ILRM 333; [1986] ILRM 401

9. —— **Warrant** — *Uncertainty* — *Whether warrant void for uncertainty* — *Whether sufficient correspondence of offences* — *Offences against the Person Act,* 1861 (*c.* 100), *s.* 62 — *Criminal Law (Amendment) Act,* 1935 (*No.* 6), *s.* 14 — *Extradition Act,* 1965 (*No.* 6), *s.* 50.] A warrant was issued in March, 1982, from the Magistrate's Court Aberdare, Wales for the arrest of the plaintiff on the following charge: "for that he (the defendant) sometime between the 1 January 1981 and 26 October 1981 at Mountain Ash in the County of Glamorgan did indecently assault Paul Armstrong born 7.3.1965 a male person under the age of 16 years (in that he tied the said Paul Armstrong to bedroom furniture removed

EXTRADITION—*continued.*

his clothing and struck him several blows across the bare buttocks) contrary to section 15 (1) of the Sexual Offences Act, 1956." The warrant was executed by the defendant Deputy Commissioner on 1 April, 1982, pursuant to the Extradition Act, 1965. The plaintiff was arrested on 4 May, 1982, and brought the same day to Kilrush District Court whereupon the District Justice ordered him to be delivered into the custody of the South Wales Constabulary at Shannon Airport for conveyance to Aberdare. The plaintiff instituted these proceedings by special summons seeking an order under s. 50 of the Extradition Act, 1965, directing his release and alternatively for a declaration that the warrant was void for uncertainty. The plaintiff contended that in addition to the claim of uncertainty of the warrant the order directing his extradition was invalid as the alleged offence did not correspond with an offence in this jurisdiction. He submitted that, since the alleged victim was over the age of 15 years at all times material to the offence, it would have been necessary for the particulars of the offence to have shown that the assault took place without the consent of the male person concerned. S. 14 of the Criminal Law (Amendment) Act, 1935, (amending s. 62 of the Offences Against the Person Act, 1861) provides that consent shall not be a defence where the person assaulted was under the age of 15 years whereas 16 is the relevant age in England and Wales. Therefore, it was submitted, the plaintiff was deprived of a possible defence of consent under Irish law. **Held** by Finlay P. in dismissing the plaintiff's claim, the identification of the offence of assault was in itself sufficiently clear and unambiguous, and the particulars of the offence of indecent assault were such as to indicate to the accused the charge he had to face. The fact that there might be differences between English law (which had not been formally proved in court) and Irish law to the nature and extent of the defence available to the accused upon a final proof of the facts was insufficient to render the recital of the offence void for uncertainty. Correspondence of the offence was sufficiently established in the warrant, and it was not necessary to establish total identity. Plaintiff's claim was dismissed. (An appeal to the Supreme Court was dismissed.) *Harris* v. *Wren*

(H.C.) [1984] ILRM 120

—— Arrest — Imprisonment — Legality — U.S.A. — Murder — Drug dealing — Committal warrant — Applicant arrested and imprisoned.
see **Constitution,** 24

EXTRADITION—*continued.*

—— Constitution — Personal rights — Foreigner — Liberty — Deliberate violation of person's constitutional right — Detention obtained by unwarrantable arrest and misuse of s. 30 of the Offences Against the State Act, 1939 — Subsequent *prima facie* valid arrest of accused and initiation of extradition proceedings under Extradition Act, 1965 — Subsequent extradition proceedings tainted by illegality of arrest and detention under Act of 1939.
see **Constitution,** 16

—— Constitution — Personal rights — Liberty — Suspect kept under close surveillance — Garda Síochána anticipating request for extradition warrant — Whether surveillance justified.
see **Constitution,** 17

—— Evidence — Foreign warrant — "Judicial authority" — Proofs — Statutory requirements — Whether satisfied.
see **Extradition,** 8

—— Extraditable offence — Correspondence with offence under Irish law — Defence of provocation to murder charge — Whether murder charge corresponds if ambit of defence varies — Defence of provocation not actually open to prosecutor — Whether relevant to extradition.
see **Constitution,** 24

—— Procedure — Constitution — Personal rights — Whether extradition arrangements safeguard personal rights of citizen — Whether procedures in courts of Northern Ireland meet minimum standards applicable in the State.
see **Constitution,** 41

—— Procedure — District Court hearing under Part II of Extradition Act, 1965 — Whether statement of offences disclosed corresponding offences in Irish law — Extradition orders of District Court — Contents of orders — Failure to specify corresponding Irish offences — Error in recitals — Rule of specialty — Whether face of order discloses want or excess of jurisdiction.
see **Constitution,** 25

—— Specialty rule — Whether rule infringed by trying defendant in Special Criminal Court.
see **Criminal Law,** 35

EXTRADITION—*continued.*

—— Statute — Validity — Foreign warrant — Charge of murder in Northern Ireland — Reciprocal legislation — Fair procedures — Part III of Extradition Act, 1965 not invalid.
see **Constitution,** 41

EXTRADITION—*continued.*

—— Treaty — Whether binding on State — Whether charge on public funds.
see **Constitution,** 24, 25

F

FAIR PROCEDURES—*continued.*

—— Tribunal — Natural justice — Exercise of power — Duty to act judicially — Includes duty to furnish reasons for decision.
see **Judicial Review,** 13

—— Tribunal — Professional discipline — Medical practitioner — Removal of doctor's name from register — Validity of enactment under Constitution.
see **Constitution,** 28

FAIR TRADE
see **Restrictive Practices**

FAIRS AND MARKETS — Casual trading.
see **Casual Trading**

FALSE IMPRISONMENT

—— **Arrest** — *Reasonable use of force — Garda in scuffle with young person — Whether acting in the course of duty — Whether reasonable force used.*] The plaintiff was caught by the assistant manager of a supermarket on 22 April, 1981, when he attempted to steal a four stone bag of potatoes. He was accompanied by two little girls, his sister and a cousin, aged three and four respectively. The assistant manager kept him in the shop while he called the guards. The two guards on arrival arrested the plaintiff. The defendant guard led the plaintiff out of the shop holding the plaintiff's wrist loosely in his left hand while the second guard followed behind them with the two children. On reaching the patrol car the plaintiff feared that the two children would be left behind. He tried to refuse to get into the car and a scuffle then occurred. The defendant guard remaining on the pavement tightened his grip on the plaintiff and in so doing forced the plaintiff's wrist to go up behind him as the plaintiff entered the car. They all then travelled in the car to the plaintiff's home. At the plaintiff's home his mother leaned in through the open door and hit her son a number of times. The plaintiff was then brought to the Garda Station where he was not charged but was dealt with under the Juvenile Liaison Scheme. He was detained for about an hour and a half and released when his older brother arrived. When outside, he complained to his brother that his wrist hurt, who in turn brought him back in and a formal complaint was made. That evening he was brought to the family doctor who referred him the next day to Jervis Street Hospital, where they applied plaster of paris. This was removed about two weeks later and strapping was then applied and kept on for a further two weeks. The plaintiff's claim was dismissed in the Circuit Court, and he appealed to the High Court. **Held**

FALSE IMPRISONMENT—*continued.*

by Barron J. in allowing the appeal, 1, the plaintiff sustained the injury in the course of the scuffle with the defendant guard, induced by his belief that the children would be left behind. 2. The defendant guard was not acting in the course of his duty when the injury to the plaintiff was caused in denying him the right to concern himself with the welfare of his charges and consequently the use of force by him was an unlawful act. 3. An arresting officer is entitled to use such force as is reasonably necessary to effect an arrest and such force as is necessary to ensure that the arrest is maintained. *Dowman* v. *Ireland*
(H.C.) [1986] ILRM 11

—— Magistrates — Liability — Jurisdiction — Juvenile court made training school order in respect of plaintiff — Plaintiff not informed of right to legal aid — Order quashed — Action against members of juvenile court — Whether liable in civil action for damages.
see **Negligence,** 32

FALSE STATEMENTS

—— Consumer Information Act.
see **Consumer Protection,** 1

FAMILY HOME
see **Family Law,** 6, 10, 27-30

—— Joint tenancy — Jurisdiction to order sale.
see **Land,** 3

FAMILY LAW
see also **Adoption**

Child. Nos. 1-4
Maintenance. Nos. 5-9
Marriage. Nos. 10-26
Property — family home. Nos. 27-30

CHILD

1. —— **Custody** — *English Court ordering that infant be placed in the custody of a county council — Father removing infant from jurisdiction of the English courts — Father being an Irish citizen domiciled in England — Council seeking an order of habeas corpus — Legality of infant's detention — Whether father and infant entitled to be regarded as "family" — Appropriate forum for the determination of the infant's future welfare — Constitution of Ireland,* 1937, *Arts.* 40, 41, 42.] The applicant, an English local authority responsible *inter alia* for the welfare of children entrusted to its care by the courts, sought an

order for the return to its custody of the three-year old son of the respondent. The latter, a 47-year old, unemployed and twice-divorced Irishman, who had resided in England since 1956 and had there been married and divorced, had brought the boy to Ireland to prevent the applicant obtaining custody of the child pursuant to an order of an English court. The respondent contended that he and his infant son were a 'family' entitled to protection under Articles 41 and 42 of the Constitution; and that his child, if returned to England, would be in danger of being given to adoptive parents. **Held** by Finlay P, making an order for the return of the child, 1, that the child's family had broken up, and that it was not possible for the court to provide for his upbringing and education as part of a unified family. 2. That, on the facts, there was no plan to give the child to adoption: *Northampton County Council* v. *A.B.F. and M.B.F.* [1982] ILRM 164 distinguished. 3. That the respondent's marriage, his divorce and the subsequent arrangements for the care of his son, had taken place in England, where the majority of the child's relatives resided; and that, having regard to the principle appropriate to the comity between courts, it was appropriate to make the order sought by the applicant. *In re S.; Kent County Council* v. *S.*

(H.C.) [1984] ILRM 292

2. —— **Custody** — *Separation of parents — Husband seeking custody of the children — Domicile of the parties — Whether husband abandoned Irish domicile of origin — Factors to be taken into account in awarding custody — Whether age a weighty factor — Guardianship of Infants Act,* 1964 (*No.* 6).] Unhappy differences having arisen between the parties, a married couple, the plaintiff husband sought custody of their two children. His wife resisted the application on the ground that the court had no jurisdiction to deal with the matter, since both parties and their children were domiciled in England. Both parties had been born and brought up in Ireland, but had lived in England for more than twenty years, both before and after their marriage. Some years after their marriage, they returned to Ireland and bought a home there. Following their separation the wife returned to England with the children. Pursuant to an order of the High Court in the nature of habeas corpus, the children were returned to the jurisdiction where, at the time of the instant application, they were residing with their father and his married sister. **Held** by Doyle J. in awarding custody to the defendant wife, 1, the plaintiff had never abandoned his Irish domicile of origin, and his right of access to the Irish courts remained unimpaired. 2. The tender age of the children was a weighty factor in the decision to award custody to their mother. The decision, however, was made in the context of present circumstances and may be varied when conditions, especially the ages of the children, alter. *J.W.* v. *M.W.*

(H.C.) [1978] ILRM 119

3. —— **Custody** — *Welfare of child — Both parents considered suitable — Whether children of tender years should remain in custody of mother — Guardianship of Infants Act,* 1964 (*No.* 7), *s.* 3.] S. 3 of the Guardianship of Infants Act, 1964, provides that in considering questions of guardianship and custody, the court shall regard the welfare of the child as the first and paramount consideration. The plaintiff had two children, aged six and three years respectively. Unhappy differences having arisen between the parties, the plaintiff husband sought custody of both children. During the hearing, the learned trial judge indicated that he considered both parents suitable to have custody. **Held** by Hamilton J. in refusing the application, and in awarding custody to the defendant wife: Where both parents are equally suitable to have custody, children of tender years should remain in the custody of their mother, and removal of children from such custody can be justified only where the mother has failed in her duty towards them. *O'D.* v. *O'D.*

(H.C.) [1976-7] ILRM 142

4. —— **Paternity** — *Evidence admissible to prove paternity — Evidence of wife that child not the child of the marriage — Whether admissible — Rule in* Russell v. Russell — *Whether part of the common law of Ireland — Whether incompatible with the provisions of the Constitution — Constitutional entitlement to fair procedures — Obligations of the Registrar of Births and Deaths — Constitution of Ireland,* 1937, *Arts.* 34.1, 38.1, 40.3, 50 — *Registration of Births and Deaths (Ireland) Act,* 1863 (*c.* 11) — *Births and Deaths Registration Act (Ireland),* 1880 (*c.* 13), *s.* 7 — *Guardianship of Infants Act,* 1964 (*No.* 7), *ss.* 6(4), 11(4).] A.S., the first named plaintiff, wife of the first named defendant (W.S.), sought an order declaring that the second named plaintiff (R.B.) with whom she had lived, was the father of a male child born during her marriage to W.S. and for an order directing the name of R.B. be registered by the Registrar General as father of the infant. W.S. elected not to defend the proceedings and the Registrar General sought formal proof of paternity and pleaded the presumption of law that the father of the child was W.S. The proceedings were amended to include a claim for the appointment of the plaintiffs (A.S. and R.B.) as guardians of the infant. The plaintiffs (A.S. and R.B.) and W.S. sought to

establish paternity by oral evidence of A.S. relating to non-access at the relevant time and counsel for the Registrar General drew the attention of the court to the Rule in *Russell* v. *Russell* [1924] A.C. 687 i.e. the rule of law excluding evidence of non-access by husband or wife tending to prove the illegitimacy of the child born during their marriage. Counsel for the plaintiffs contended that this rule never became part of the law of the State or if it did that it was no longer part of the law due to incompatibility with the Constitution and the requirements of public policy. Medical evidence indicated that W.S. could not have been the father of the child and that it was probable that R.B. was the father. **Held** by O'Hanlon J., 1, on the medical evidence W.S. could not have been the father whereas there was a high degree of probability that R.B. was the father of the infant. 2. Although the rule in *Russell* v. *Russell* formed part of the law of the State up to the enactment of the Constitution in 1937, Articles 34.1, 38.1 and 40.3 guaranteed to citizens a constitutional entitlement to fair procedures when they get to court and the concept that a spouse could not be allowed to rebut the presumption of legitimacy existing in favour of all issue born during the subsistence of the marriage by proving non-access at the relevant time by his or her own direct evidence was inconsistent with this constitutional guarantee. Accordingly the rule in *Russell* v. *Russell* ceased to have legal effect in the State after the enactment of the Constitution in 1937. 3. The Registrar General would be directed to register the birth in the usual manner and to register R.B. as the father of the child. 4. Custody of the child would be awarded to the plaintiffs. *A.S.* v. *R.B.*

(H.C.) [1984] ILRM 66

MAINTENANCE

5. —— **Agreement** — *Index-linked maintenance payments — Absence of a provision allowing for the future variation of the terms of the agreement — Agreement made a rule of court — Whether the court has jurisdiction to vary the terms — Family Law (Maintenance of Spouses and Children) Act,* 1976 (*No.* 11), *ss.* 6, 8.] The plaintiff wife, the beneficiary of an index-linked maintenance agreement that had been made a rule of court pursuant to s. 8 of the Family Law (Maintenance of Spouses and Children) Act, 1976, sought to commit her husband, the defendant, to prison, or to have his earnings attached, because of his failure to make the agreed payments. Apart from its provision that the maintenance payments should be increased annually in accordance with the Consumer Price Index, the agreement contained no other mechanism for varying the amount of the payments. The

husband established that his circumstances had altered adversely, and that his wife had obtained employment, and he sought to have the amount of the payments reduced. S. 8 of the Family Law (Maintenance of Spouses and Children) Act, 1976, which permits the court to receive maintenance agreements that are fair and reasonable and in the interests of both spouses and any dependent children, provides that such agreements shall be deemed to be maintenance orders for the purposes of enforcement. The question arose whether the court had the jurisdiction to vary the terms of such agreements as if they were maintenance orders made under s. 5 of the Act. **Held** by Carroll J. that, 1, in interpreting s. 8 of the Family Law (Maintenance of Spouses and Children) Act, 1976, the specific power to enforce maintenance agreements as maintenance orders excluded any general power to vary such agreements. 2. *Semble,* a maintenance agreement not containing a provision enabling application to be made to the court to vary it, is not a fair and reasonable one and should not be received as a rule of court. 3. The husband would not be committed to prison for failure to observe an agreement that was unjust in view of his changed circumstances and the husband's earnings would not be attached because the court must have regard to the protected earnings rate defined in s. 10 (4) (*b*) of the 1976 Act. *J.D.* v. *B.D.*

(H.C.) [1985] ILRM 688

6. —— **Application** — *Application by wife for maintenance — Whether wife's action in leaving family home amounted to desertion.*

Matrimonial property — Family home built directly under supervision of husband — Husband paying for site and obtaining loan — Wife contributing some money towards construction costs — Whether wife entitled to an interest in the family home — Whether trust to be imposed in wife's favour.] The plaintiff, a wife who had parted from her husband in 1971 and was later divorced in England, sought from the defendant, her former husband, an order for maintenance; an order regulating access to the five children of the marriage, then aged between 14 and 20 and living with their father; and a declaration of her interest in the old matrimonial home, a house which the defendant had himself laboured to build, and of which he was sole owner at law. The plaintiff's claim for maintenance was refused on the ground of her desertion, and access to the children was held not to be of benefit to them. In considering the property rights of the parties it was found that the plaintiff had contributed to the building costs of the family home in the ratio of £1,200 to £1,950. She had provided £900 in cash and £300

FAMILY LAW—Maintenance.

indirectly. The defendant had contributed £250 from his earnings, arranged for a loan of £1,500, and put in work valued at £500. From the total of these sums, £2,250, £300 was deducted in recognition of the plaintiff's indirect contributions to the project through her maintenace of the defendant's children and household. It fell to be considered whether the plaintiff's contribution, given towards the improvement rather than acquisition of the defendant's land, gave her either a proportionate share of the beneficial ownership or a charge for the amount of her contribution. **Held** by Barron J., 1, that the plaintiff's claim fell to be considered in accordance with the law of trusts and not of contract: *Heavy* v. *Heavy* 111 I.L.T.R. 1 and *C.* v. *C.* [1976] I.R. 254 applied. 2. That where a wife expends monies in the improvement of her husband's property she will have no claim to be recompensed unless there was an agreement to that effect or unless the husband had led her to act to her detriment, in which case her recompense would be in money and not in a finding that she had an equitable estate in the property: *W* v. *W* [1981] ILRM 202 applied. 3. That in the instant case there was no evidence to show that the defendant had caused the plaintiff to act to her detriment and consequently no reason to impose a trust in her favour. *N.A.D.* v. *T.D.*

(H.C.) [1985] ILRM 153

7. —— **Foreign domicile** — *Wife obtaining a divorce — Order requiring husband to pay a lump sum in lieu of maintenance — Husband avoiding being made amenable to pay — Monies lodged in an Irish bank — Whether contrary to public policy for the court to grant aid in the execution of this payment.*] The plaintiff and the claimant were husband and wife domiciled in England. The claimant succeeded in obtaining a decree of divorce a *vinculo matrimonii* which was made absolute on 5 October, 1984. The claimant subsequently on 3 January, 1985, applied to the Registrar of the Family Division of the English High Court and was granted an order directing the plaintiff to pay her a lump sum of £35,000 sterling within seven days in lieu of maintenance. The plaintiff failed to discharge the monies due to the claimant whereupon the claimant sought to execute the aforesaid order and decree of the English Court in Ireland by applying to the High Court on the basis that the plaintiff had monies lodged in an Irish bank (the defendants in the original action). The High Court granted judgment to the claimant against the plaintiff for the sum of £45,307.44. The plaintiff appealed this decision. **Held** by the Supreme Court (Finlay C.J., Hederman and McCarthy JJ.) in dismissing the appeal, 1, the plaintiff's obligation to his wife arose directly from the marriage itself rather than

FAMILY LAW—*continued.*

from a dissolution of the marriage. *Mayo Perrot* v. *Mayo Perrot* [1958] I.R. 336 applied. 2. Since the courts in Ireland recognise a divorce based on foreign domicile, it would be an anomalous position if the courts were deemed to be incapable of executing a final judgment for maintenance. 3. A provision of maintenance recoverable within the law of this country and therefore the requirements of public policy would clearly favour the enforcement of this judgment. *Sachs* v. *Standard Chartered Bank (Ireland) Ltd.*

(S.C.) [1987] ILRM 297

8. —— **Principles to be applied** — *Enquiries required by court — Income potential of spouse and minimum reasonable requirements of children — True take-home pay and minimum standard of living requirements of spouse making maintenance payments — Family Law (Maintenance of Spouses and Children) Act,* 1976 (*No.* 11), *s.* 5.] The plaintiff wife sought a mandatory order directing the defendant husband to comply with the terms of a deed of settlement, an order for judgment for £675 by way of arrears of maintenance and an order that the defendant should pay the monthly sum due in accordance with the terms of the order of the court. The settlement had been negotiated following proceedings taken by the plaintiff in which she claimed, *inter alia,* custody of the three children and maintenance for herself and the children. The deed provided, *inter alia,* for the payment of a total sum of £357 per month maintenance to be tied to an index of the defendant's employers. It also provided that the defendant was to retain the normal tax-free allowance with the related children's allowance and that the £357 had to be calculated accordingly. Pursuant to s. 5 of the Family Law (Maintenance of Spouses and Children) Act, 1976, Costello J. made an order directing the defendant to pay to the plaintiff a sum of £800 per month in respect of the maintenance of herself and the three children. The defendant appealed. **Held** by the Supreme Court (Finlay C.J., Henchy and Hederman JJ.) in allowing the appeal, 1, the court must have regard to the somewhat pathetic fact that upon separation of a husband and wife and particularly, a husband and wife with children, it is inevitable that all the parties will suffer a significant diminution in the overall standard of living. 2. In determining a case pursuant to s. 5 of the 1976 Act, the court must ascertain: (i) the income earned or capable of being earned by the wife, apart from the maintenance for which the husband is responsible; (ii) the true net take-home pay or income of the husband; (iii) the minimum reasonable requirements of, in this case, the wife and the children for whose upkeep she is responsible; and (iv) reasonable living

expenses of the husband, bearing in mind the general consideration of the economy affecting all the parties concerned, but leaving him with a reasonable standard of living. 3. There existed a distinct possibility that the amount of maintenance fixed by the trial judge on the evidence then adduced before him, was not properly related to the capacity of the defendant to pay and provide for his own living expenses and therefore the matter should be remitted to the High Court for trial by Costello J, having regard to the findings of the Supreme Court, maintenance to be fixed for the future on the basis of evidence concerning the present situation and circumstances of the parties and with a power retrospectively to review the maintenance provided for in the original order of Costello J. and make any consequential financial adjustments between the parties. *R.H.* v. *N.H.*

(S.C.) [1986] ILRM 352

9. —— **"Spouse"** — *Meaning — Whether right of spouse to apply ceases after recognition of foreign divorce — Family Law (Maintenance of Spouses and Children) Act,* 1976 (*No.* 11), *s.* 5.

Conflict of laws — Marriage — Dissolution — Recognition of foreign decree absolute — Domicile of husband — Domicile and Recognition of Foreign Divorces Act, 1986 (*No.* 24), *s.* 5.] The plaintiff wife and defendant husband were married in London in 1975, when both were resident and domiciled in England. In 1979 they took up residence in Ireland. The marriage broke down in 1985 and the husband returned to England. On the 19 January, 1987, he obtained an English decree *nisi* on foot of his petition for divorce. A cross-petition for dissolution of the marriage by the wife was out of time and was disallowed. That refusal was not appealed by the wife who had, in June, 1986, commenced proceedings against her husband in the High Court claiming, *inter alia,* maintenance for herself and for the two children of the marriage under s. 5 of the Family Law (Maintenance of Spouses and Children) Act, 1976. At the hearing on the 30 January, 1987, of a motion by the plaintiff for interim maintenance the defendant sought to have the proceedings against him stayed on the ground that as an application would be made by him to have the decree *nisi* made absolute on the expiry of the minimum period of six weeks laid down in English law, and as this application would be unopposed, the plaintiff would by the 2 March, 1987, have ceased to be a "spouse" within the meaning of the Act of 1976 for the purposes of applying for maintenance. **Held** by Egan J., in refusing to stay the proceedings and in granting the plaintiff interim maintenance, that if an English court did make absolute the decree *nisi* and the decree absolute were recognised by the

State, the plaintiff's claim for maintenance on her own behalf and that of the children would have to dismissed. However, that did not preclude the Court from making an interim order as the plaintiff was currently a "spouse" within the meaning of the Act. Nor did it preclude an application for maintenance by the plaintiff on behalf of the children under s. 11 of the Guardianship of Infants Act, 1964. *Per* Egan J. The question of the recognition by the State of any decree absolute between the parties depended in this case on the domicile of the husband. This was a matter too important to be decided on correspondence and affidavits and could only fairly be resolved at plenary hearing with oral evidence. *C. M.* v. *T.M.*

(H.C.) [1987] I.R.152; [1988] ILRM 262

Editor's note: For later High Court judgment on the divorce issue, reported at [1988] ILRM 456, *see* **Conflict of Laws,** 7.

MARRIAGE

Barring order. No. 10
Nullity. Nos. 11-22
Separation agreement. No. 23
Validity. Nos. 24-6

10. —— **Barring order** — *Exclusion of husband from matrimonial home — Whether warranted by circumstances — Breakdown of marriage — Welfare of wife and children — Evidence — Estoppel — Family Law (Maintenance of Spouses and Children) Act,* 1976 (*No.* 11), *s.* 22 — *Family Law (Protection of Spouses and Children) Act,* 1981 (*No.* 21), *ss.* 2, 17.] Section 2, sub-s. 1, of the Act of 1981 states that a court, on the application of a spouse, may make an order (called a barring order) directing the other spouse to leave the matrimonial home and prohibiting that spouse from entering it for a specified period. The sub-section states that the order may be made if the court is of opinion that there are reasonable grounds for believing that "the safety or welfare" of the applicant spouse or of any child so requires. Sub-section 2 of s. 2 states that such order may also prohibit the other spouse from using or threatening to use violence against, molesting or putting in fear the applicant spouse or any child. By s. 6 of the Act contravention of the terms of a barring order constitutes a criminal offence. Section 11 of the Act enables the court, on the application of either spouse, to discharge a barring order if the court is satisfied that the safety or welfare of the spouse does not require that the order should continue in force. In February, 1981, the plaintiff wife obtained in the District Court (pursuant to s. 22 of the Act of 1976) a barring order which directed

FAMILY LAW—Marriage.

her husband, the defendant, to leave their matrimonial home; on appeal by the defendant husband, that order was set aside by the Circuit Court on the 23 June, 1981, and the defendant returned to his home soon afterwards. On the 23 March, 1981, the plaintiff had instituted this action in the High Court claiming (*inter alia*) a barring order against the defendant pursuant to s. 22 of the Act of 1976. The Act of 1981 came into operation on the 24 July, 1981. At the trial of an interlocutory motion brought by the plaintiff, the trial judge made an order on the 24 June, 1982, pursuant to s. 2 of the Act of 1981 directing the defendant to leave, and prohibiting him from re-entering, the matrimonial home until further order. The trial judge, who heard the oral evidence of the parties, held that the defendant had behaved in an extremely reprehensible manner towards the plaintiff, that the marriage of the parties had broken down irretrievably and that the defendant had neither acted violently towards the plaintiff or their children nor threatened them with violence. On appeal by the defendant it was **Held** by the Supreme Court (O'Higgins C.J., Griffin and McCarthy JJ.), in allowing the appeal, 1, that, by reason of s. 17, sub-s. 3, of the Act of 1981, the appeal raised an issue relating to the proper application of s. 2, sub-s. 1, of the Act of 1981. 2. That the grounds which justify a barring order made pursuant to s. 2, sub-s. 1, of the Act of 1981 must be related to conduct of the respondent spouse which affects the health or welfare of the applicant spouse or a child. 3. That the irretrievable breakdown of the marriage of the parties did not furnish, *per se,* grounds for making a barring order pursuant to s. 2, sub-s. 1, of the Act of 1981. 4. That the evidence disclosed circumstances which were insufficient to furnish reasonable grounds for believing that the safety or welfare of the plaintiff or the children of the marriage required that a barring order be made (Griffin J. dissenting). 5. *Per* Griffin and McCarthy JJ. — The trial judge had acted correctly in rejecting a plea by the defendant of *res judicata* based upon the decision of the Circuit Court made on the 23 June, 1981. *O'B.* v. *O'B.*

(S.C.) [1984] I.R. 182; [1984] ILRM 1

11. —— **Nullity** — *Capacity — Psychiatric illness — Whether petitioner entitled to decree of nullity on basis of respondent's inability to enter into and sustain normal marriage relationship due to psychiatric illness — Whether marriage void or voidable — Whether petitioner approbated marriage — Whether petitioner estopped by earlier matrimonial proceedings against respondent — Matrimonial Causes and Marriage Law (Ireland) Amendment Act, 1870* (*c.* 110).] The petitioner and the respondent were married in 1974. In

FAMILY LAW—*continued.*

1978 the respondent was diagnosed as a manic depressive. Evidence was given that the respondent both before and after the marriage had undergone a number of serious mood changes each lasting for a considerable time. In early 1981 the respondent seriously assaulted the petitioner twice and the petitioner obtained a High Court order barring the respondent from the family home. The petitioner took the present proceeding seeking a decree of nullity of the marriage claiming (*a*) that by reason of his mental capacity and state of mind at the time of their marriage the respondent was unable to understand the nature, purpose and consequences of the marriage contract and (*b*) that at the time of the marriage the respondent was suffering from such disease of the mind that he was unable to maintain or sustain a normal relationship with her or with any children there might be of the marriage. The respondent contended, *inter alia,* (i) that since the Ecclesiastical Courts of the Church of Ireland did not grant decrees of nullity on the grounds advanced by the petitioner the High Court had no jurisdiction under the Matrimonial Causes and Marriage Law (Ireland) Amendment Act, 1870, now to do so, (ii) that even if the petitioner was correct in asserting her claim for a nullity decree on these grounds the alleged illness rendered the marriage merely voidable and since the petitioner by her action in 1981 had approbated the marriage she had disentitled herself to a decree. **Held,** 1, on the facts the respondent suffered from a psychiatric illness both before his marriage, at the time of his marriage and subsequent to his marriage. 2. Marriage was a lifelong union and the law recognised that there was more to marriage than physical consummation, and that a marriage required for its maintenance the creation of an emotional and psychological relationship between the spouses, and that advances in psychiatric medicine since 1870 allowed the identification of psychiatric illnesses which in some cases might be so severe as to make it impossible for one of the parties to the marriage to enter into and to sustain the relationship which should exist between married couples. 3. The statutory obligation created in 1870 to apply the principles and rules of the Ecclesiastical Courts of the Church of Ireland did not prevent civil courts from developing those principles in the light of the developments in modern medicine (*dicta* of Kenny J. in *S.* v. *S.,* Barrington J. in *R.S.J.* v. *J.S.J.* applied). 4. On the facts the petitioner was entitled to have her marriage declared null and void. 5. The illness established in this case was one which rendered the marriage voidable and not void: (*A.* v. *B.* applied). 6. The defence of approbation could not succeed since the petitioner did not know that her husband

FAMILY LAW—Marriage.

suffered from a psychiatric illness at the time of the marriage until several years after the ceremony and until she obtained legal advice she was never aware that her husband's illness entitled her to a nullity decree. 7. Since the validity of the petitioner's marriage was not put in issue in the 1981 proceedings and was not determined by the court no estoppel of any sort arose resultant upon those proceedings *Gaffney* v. *Gaffney* [1975] I.R. 133 distinguished. *D.* v. C.

(H.C.) [1984] ILRM 173

12. —— **Nullity** — *Capacity — Psychiatric illness — Petitioner suffering from schizophrenia — Inability to form and sustain normal marriage relationship — Respondent obtained nullity decree from ecclesiastical court — Whether relevant to the determination of civil court.*] The petitioner and respondent met when they were both under 16. After a period of time they began to have sexual intercourse every time they met. The petitioner began to feel guilty about this, and felt that people were talking about her and looking at her strangely. She was referred by her family doctor to a psychiatrist. The petitioner was found to improve initially but, after six months had a relapse at which time it was discovered she was pregnant. As the parties were engaged at this time, the petitioner wanted to get married but the respondent did not. The parties married and within two weeks the petitioner went back to live with her parents. That was the end of the relationship. Some time later the petitioner met a man whom she found warm and loving. She went to live with him and had two children by him. The petitioner sought a decree of nullity on two separate grounds. Firstly that she did not fully and properly consent to the marriage in that through her psychiatric illness she was incapable of understanding the nature, duties and responsibilities of marriage. Secondly that because of the illness, she was incapable of entering into a permanent and meaningful relationship with the respondent. **Held** by Blayney J. in declaring the marriage with the respondent null and void, 1, the petitioner was at the date of her marriage suffering from a psychotic illness and as a result was unable to enter and sustain a normal marriage relationship with the respondent. The petitioner has, accordingly, shown a *prima facie* case entitling her to a decree of nullity. The ground on which the petitioner relies made the marriage voidable only. *D* v. *C* [1984] ILRM 173 followed. 2. The petitioner could not rely on this ground as avoiding the marriage unless she could establish that the respondent had previously repudiated the marriage. This requirement did not create any obstacle, as the respondent by seeking and

FAMILY LAW—*continued.*

obtaining a decree of nullity from the ecclesiastical courts had clearly repudiated the marriage. 3. The relevant date for the purpose of forming a permanent and meaningful relationship with the respondent was the date of the petitioner's marriage and her capacity to form such a relationship at any other time was not relevant to this issue. *D.C.(otherwise D.W.)* v. *D.W.*

(H.C.) [1987] ILRM 58

13. —— **Nullity** — *Capacity — Psychiatric illness — Respondent suffering from psychiatric illness — Whether respondent capable of understanding nature, purpose and consequences of marriage — Whether capable of entering into and sustaining marriage relationship or of giving valid consent to marriage.*] The petitioner and respondent, a Catholic priest ordained in 1979, met at a time when he had experienced a number of profoundly depressing and unsettling events. Despite the advice of friends and colleagues that he should postpone any decision to marry until his state of mind had improved, the petitioner and respondent were married in August, 1982. In February, 1983, the respondent was diagnosed as suffering from paranoid schizophrenia and a consultant psychiatrist gave evidence that the condition probably existed at the time of the marriage. The respondent at no stage sought laicisation and terminated the relationship abruptly in 1985. **Held** by O'Hanlon J., in granting the petition, 1, that the purported marriage of the petitioner and respondent was null and void on the ground that at the time of its solemnisation the respondent was incapable by reason of psychiatric illness of giving a full, free and informed consent to the marriage and was also incapable by reason of such psychiatric condition of entering into and sustaining a normal marriage relationship. *M.E.* v. *A.E.*

(H.C.) [1987] I.R.147

14. —— **Nullity** — *Collusion — Evidence — Non-consummation — Evidence indicating that marriage was not consummated — Trial judge inferring collusion between parties — Whether inference open to judge — Whether in accordance with natural justice — Whether decree of nullity should be granted on the basis of evidence presented only — Whether rehearing of issues required.*

Judgment — Evidence — Nullity — Non-consummation — Evidence indicating marriage was not consummated — Trial judge inferring collusion between parties — Whether inference open to judge — Whether in accordance with natural justice — Whether rehearing required in view of evidence presented.] The petitioner applied for a

FAMILY LAW—Marriage.

decree of nullity on the grounds of non-consummation of the marriage. The evidence presented on her behalf, which was not challenged, was that the marriage had not in fact been consummated by virtue of a psychological incapacity on the part of the husband. The trial judge reserved judgment and when he delivered judgment he refused the petitioner relief on the grounds that he considered the parties had acted in collusion in bringing the petition and was not satisfied that the marriage had not been consummated. The petitioner appealed to the Supreme Court. **Held** by the Supreme Court (Henchy, Kenny and Parke JJ.) in allowing the appeal: on the basis of the evidence presented in the High Court, it was not open to the trial judge to refuse the relief sought, since it was not in accordance with the proper administration of justice or the principles of natural justice to cast aside the corroborated and unquestioned evidence of witnesses, and in the circumstances since a rehearing of the matter would be unlikely to produce any verdict other than the granting of a decree of nullity, the court would order a decree of nullity. *M.* v. *M.*

(S.C.) [1979] ILRM 160

15. —— **Nullity** — *Delay — Approbation — Whether delay excessive — Whether party approbated — Party subsequently obtaining church annulment and marrying another party in church — Party having children and then separating from second partner — Party denying second marriage — Whether approbation of first marriage — Whether public policy requires legislation of second marriage to establish legitimacy of children — Non-consummation of first marriage — Whether impotence of one party established.*] The parties were married on 18 March, 1968. The petitioner wife before and after their marriage sought unsuccessfully to have sexual intercourse with the respondent husband, who was repulsed by all her efforts. In December, 1970, the petitioner left the respondent and applied for a church annulment which she obtained in December, 1971. There was medical evidence that in December, 1971, the petitioner was found to be *virgo intacta,* and was capable of sustaining normal sexual intercourse. On 31 July, 1976, the petitioner married C.S. in a Roman Catholic Church under the mistaken belief that she was free to marry. Unhappy differences arose in 1982, and the petitioner left C.S. taking with her their two children. Sometime later C.S. located their whereabouts, and sought access to the two children. The petitioner sought legal advice and learned for the first time that she had not been married to C.S. and was advised that C.S. had no right to see the two children. C.S. successfully

FAMILY LAW—*continued.*

brought proceedings for access to his two children. The petitioner seeks a decree of nullity on the grounds of the respondent's inability to consummate the marriage. C.S. submits that the petitioner should be denied the relief on the grounds: (1) that there is excessive delay; (2) that by denying her marriage to C.S. she approbated her marriage to the respondent. **Held** by Barron J. in granting the decree of nullity, 1, the marriage between the petitioner and respondent was never consummated due to psychological reasons on the respondent's behalf. 2. The petitioner had been unaware that her marriage had not been annulled in civil law and on becoming so aware she acted promptly this excusing her excessive delay in seeking the relief she now seeks. 3. The court is satisfied that the petitioner in denying her marriage to C.S. did not intend to return to the respondent but rather was under the mistaken belief that this denied C.S. a right of access to his children. 4. It is in the public interest that the petitioner should be granted the relief sought as it will legalise the marriage between the petitioner and C.S. and also establish that the two children are and always have been legitimate. *A.M.N.* v. *J.P.C.*

(H.C.) [1988] ILRM 170

16. —— **Nullity** — *Duress — Grounds on which relief will be granted — Absence of real consent on the part of the petitioner — Duress — Matrimonial Causes and Marriage Law (Ireland) Amendment Act,* 1870 (*c.* 110), *s.* 13.] The petitioner became pregnant as a result of a short and casual relationship with the respondent, when she was nineteen years of age. The petitioner's parents took the view that the petitioner should marry the respondent. The petitioner was a quiet, unassertive and obedient girl and had no view as to what course she should take. She acceded to her parents' wishes in the belief that they knew what was best for her. At no time before the marriage ceremony six weeks later did she express any contrary view. The petitioner sought a decree of nullity in the High Court based on the ground that she was forced to go through the ceremony of marriage by such duress as made the marriage void for absence of real consent. **Held** by Carroll J., in refusing to grant a decree of nullity, that while the parties would not have got married but for the pregnancy, they nevertheless intended to marry. There was no evidence of coercion or persuasion such as to destroy the reality of the petitioner's consent or overbear her will thus amounting to duress. *M.K. (otherwise McC.)* v. *McC.* [1982] ILRM 277 distinguished. On appeal by the petitioner it was **Held** by the Supreme Court (Finlay C.J., Griffin, Hederman and McCarthy JJ.; Henchy J. dissenting) in allowing the appeal, 1, that consent

FAMILY LAW—Marriage.

to the making of a valid marriage must be a free exercise of the independent will of the parties. The concept of duress is not restricted to threats of physical harm or of other harmful consequences. If the decision to marry has been caused by external pressure or influence, whether falsely or honestly applied, to such an extent as to lose the character of a fully free act of that person's will, no valid marriage has occurred. *Singh* v. *Singh* [1971] 2 W.L.R. 963 not followed. *M.K. (Otherwise McC.)* v. *McC.* [1982] ILRM 277 approved. 2. That while the court should enquire into the validity of a marriage in accordance with defined legal concepts, these concepts and their legal definition must remain subservient to the objective of ascertaining whether the consent of the petitioning party was real or apparent. 3. That in the instant case, the petitioner was acting in obedience to the wishes of her parents, accordingly her consent was not the full and free consent required for marriage but was apparent only and no valid marriage occurred. *N. (otherwise K.)* v. *K.*

(H.C., S.C.) [1985] I.R.733; [1986] ILRM 75

17. —— **Nullity** — *Duress* — *Marriage in consequence of pregnancy and wife's threat to procure an abortion* — *Whether marriage contracted under duress* — *Refusal of wife to cohabit in normal relationship with husband* — *Whether indicative of disease of mind* — *Absence of wife from trial after previous correspondence about the intended proceedings* — *Whether evidence of collusion.*] The petitioner, a young husband, sought a declaration of the nullity of his marriage to the respondent on the grounds of duress and her inability to contract. He alleged that he had been induced to marry the respondent by reason of her prior pregnancy and her threat to procure an abortion of the foetus. He further alleged that his wife had shown no readiness to live with him in a normal relationship and that her unwillingness to do so was evidence of a disease of the mind rendering her incapable of contracting a valid marriage. The marriage had been duly celebrated and consummated. The wife declined to appear at the trial, but two letters *inter partes* revealed that the couple had previously considered the course of the intended proceedings. **Held** by Barron J., refusing the petition, 1, that the petitioner had not discharged the burden of proving that the case came before the court without collusion: *Churchward* v. *Churchward* [1985] P. 7 applied. 2. That there was no sufficient evidence of duress. 3. That there was no evidence of illness negativing consent: *R.S.J.* v. *J.S.J.* [1982] ILRM 263 and *D.* v. *C.* [1984] ILRM 173 considered. *Per curiam.* If the petitioner had given his consent solely for the purpose of saving the life of his unborn child, this would have

FAMILY LAW—*continued.*

constituted a ground for a decree of nullity. *E.P.* v. *M.C.*

(H.C.) [1985] ILRM 34

18. —— **Nullity** — *Duress* — *Undue influence* — *Wife's emotional bondage to husband at date of marriage amounting to duress* — *Subjective test applied* — *Petition granted.*] The petitioner wife first met the respondent husband in 1966, when she was under sixteen years of age and he was eighteen years old. From the outset the respondent showed himself to be extremely jealous, possessive and domineering. Their relationship was marked by constant fighting and arguments on both their parts. At the insistence of the respondent the petitioner acquiesced in sexual intercourse with him and subsequently felt an obligation to remain with him because of the sexual relationship between them. The respondent on occasions threatened to expose details of this relationship. During the course of their courtship the respondent went to extreme lengths to restore the relationship, on occasions it was broken off, by resorting to an intensive campaign of watching and besetting the petitioner's home and place of work and by following her to and from work in his car. In November, 1972, the parties had a major disagreement and separated. After this the petitioner strenuously resisted seeing the respondent. In February, 1973, the respondent, after consistent efforts to see the petitioner, called to her home where he threatened to commit suicide if the petitioner wouldn't marry him. The petitioner finally relented and the parties were married in November, 1974. **Held** by McMahon J. in granting the petition, 1, that the petitioner lacked the free will required to enter into a valid contract of marriage due to the duress and undue influence the respondent exercised over the petitioner, thus their purported marriage was null and void. 2. That the duress need not be restricted to violence or threats thereof and any pressure improperly brought to bear may amount to duress. *K.* v. *McC.* [1982] ILRM 277 and *Scott* v. *Sebright* (1885) 12 P.D. 21 applied. 3. That the subjective test must be applied when considering the effect of pressure on the mind of the petitioner. Any degree of duress which in fact causes a person to agree to a marriage to which he or she would not otherwise have agreed invalidates the marriage. *C.O'K.* v. *W.P.*

(H.C.) [1985] I.R.279

19. —— **Nullity** — *Impotence* — *Respondent refusing to have intercourse* — *Respondent not impotent generally* — *Whether marriage null and void* — *Matrimonial Causes and Marriage Law (Ireland) Amendment Act,* 1870 (*c.* 110), *s.* 13.] The appellant was the wife of the respondent, to

FAMILY LAW—Marriage.

whom she was married for some seven years. They had known each other for two years prior to the marriage, during which period they had frequent sexual intercourse. However, the marriage itself was never consummated, the respondent refusing to have intercourse and saying that his wife 'revolted' him. The appellant attempted on one occasion to effect sexual intercourse, but her husband proved unresponsive. It subsequently transpired that he had met another woman shortly before the marriage, and had fallen in love with her. She subsequently became pregnant by the respondent, although she apparently miscarried the child. The respondent then left his wife and went to live with the other woman. The appellant failed in the High Court to obtain a decree of nullity based on the fraudulent behaviour of the respondent. On appeal, the case was argued primarily on the ground that the respondent was impotent *vis-à-vis* the appellant. **Held** by the Supreme Court (Henchy and Griffin JJ., Kenny J. dissenting in part) in reversing the order of the High Court and declaring the marriage to be null and void, 1, where a husband, although not impotent generally, is incapable of sexual intercourse with his wife, the wife is entitled to a declaration that the marriage is null and void, *C.* v. *C.* [1921] P 399 followed. 2. In the light of the respondent's pre-marital sexual relationship with the appellant, and his on-going sexual relationship with his mistress after the marriage, the only reasonable inference to be drawn is that after the marriage he developed a complete incapacity in relation to his wife. *Per* Kenny J.: The evidence does not justify a finding of *impotentia quod hanc.* However, the appellant is entitled to a decree on the ground that the respondent had determined at the date of the marriage not to have sexual intercourse with her. Where the other spouse is unaware of such determination, or has not agreed to it, the consent necessary to a valid marriage does not exist. *S.* v. *S.*

(S.C.) [1976-7] ILRM 156

20. —— **Nullity** — *Impotence — Failure to inseminate — Whether ground for granting nullity — Whether ground recognised by Ecclesiastical Courts — Matrimonial Causes and Marriage Law (Ireland) Amendment Act,* 1870 (*c.* 110), *s.* 13.] The petitioner who married the respondent in December, 1979, sought a decree of nullity of their marriage on the alleged impotence of the respondent, pleading that he was able to achieve erection and penetration but not the emission of seed. This was not disputed by the respondent who had been unable to achieve emission in sexual relationships he had with other women including the petitioner before their marriage. As a consequence the marriage relationship

FAMILY LAW—*continued.*

became progressively less. The petitioner left the family home in November, 1980, and the petition was issued in February, 1982. The petitioner submitted that the law of this jurisdiction should recognise inability to inseminate as constituting impotence and rendering a marriage null and void. **Held** by McMahon J. in refusing the petition: To treat insemination as a necessary element in the consummation of a marriage would amount to adding a new ground of nullity to those recognised in the ecclesiastical law as administered before the Matrimonial Causes and Marriage Law (Amendment) Act, 1870, and it was not open to the High Court to depart from the statute by admitting a new ground of nullity. *M. M. (otherwise G.)* v. *P. M.*

(H.C.) [1986] ILRM 515

21. —— **Nullity** — *Impotence — Failure to consummate marriage — Impotence of one partner to another — Whether ground for declaring marriage a nullity — Whether impotence of both parties required to be shown.*] The parties married on 28 September, 1974. Both the petitioner husband and the respondent wife made several unsuccessful attempts prior to and after their marriage to have sexual intercourse. The petitioner was unable to penetrate the respondent and for this reason the respondent underwent a minor gynaecological operation. Medical evidence was given that at this particular time the respondent was found to be *virgo intacta.* Despite the operation they failed after continuous efforts to consummate the marriage. In 1981, both parties separated and later formed relationships which included successful sexual relationships with other partners, and the respondent recently had a child by her present partner. The petitioner instituted nullity proceedings on the grounds of alleged impotence or incapacity on the part of the respondent. **Held** by Lynch J. in declaring the marriage to be null and void, 1, the marriage between the husband and the wife was never consummated due to the fact that the wife was impotent relative to the husband, although not generally or absolutely impotent. 2. Once the court is satisfied that the wife was and is impotent relative to the husband, it is not necessary for it to find whether or not the husband was and is impotent relative to the wife. *L.C.* v. *B.C. (otherwise B.L.).*

(H.C.) [1986] ILRM 618

22. —— **Nullity** — *Non-consummation — Whether incapable — Presumption — Refusal to consummate — Whether incapacity to be presumed.*] The petitioner married the respondent in 1970, and the marriage was never consummated. Initially, this stemmed from a physical inability on the part of the petitioner. Apart

from this problem, relations between the parties were good. Over a period of some years, the petitioner sought help from books dealing with the subject, but the respondent showed little interest in reading them, and on one occasion accused the petitioner of putting pressure on him. In 1979, the petitioner sought help from a family planning clinic, and was advised to carry out certain relaxation exercises, in which, it was suggested, the respondent should also participate. He refused to do so. The relationship between the parties deteriorated from that time, and following a visit to Canada during which the petitioner achieved full sexual intercourse with another man, she and the respondent separated. The petitioner sought a decree of nullity from the High Court. Medical evidence adduced at the hearing disclosed no physical reason why either party should be unable to consummate the marriage. **Held** by Barron J. in declaring the marriage null and void: The respondent was unable to consummate the marriage because of his impotence towards the petitioner, and where an affectionate husband, otherwise capable of performing the sexual act, refuses to do so, it is presumed that he is psychologically incapable of doing so. *A. O'H. (otherwise F.)* v. *P.F.*

(H.C.) [1986] ILRM 489

23. —— **Separation agreement** — *Subsequent proceedings for divorce* a mensa et thoro — *Whether separation agreement a bar to such proceedings — Succession Act,* 1965 (*No.* 27), *s.* 120(2).] A husband and wife separated by virtue of a separation agreement made between the parties. This agreement did not affect the wife's rights of inheritance under the Succession Act, 1965. The husband subsequently brought proceedings for a divorce *a mensa et thoro* on the grounds of his wife's adultery, the object of which was to alter the separation agreement so as to deprive his wife of her inheritance rights under s.120, sub-s. 2 of the Succession Act, 1965. **Held** by MacKenzie J., in refusing the petition, that the separation agreement entered into between the parties was a bar to subsequent proceedings for divorce *a mensa et thoro. Courtney* v. *Courtney* [1923] 2 I.R. 31 followed; *Lewis* v. *Lewis* [1940] I.R. 42 distinguished. *K.* v. *K.*

(H.C.) [1988] I.R.161

24. —— **Validity** — *Church annulment — Husband marrying again before obtaining civil annulment of first marriage — First marriage voidable — Whether second marriage valid — Constitution of Ireland,* 1937, *Art.* 41.3 — *Offences Against the Person Act,* 1861 (*c.* 100), *s.* 57.] F.M.L. married O'C. in 1972. In 1978 a papal dispensation was granted which in canon law entitled each party to re-marry. It did not, and

did not purport to, affect the status of the marriage in civil law. In 1979 F.M.L. and A.L. (the plaintiffs in this action) went through a ceremony in a Roman Catholic Church. In 1980 the High Court granted a decree of nullity in respect of the 1972 marriage on the ground of non consummation due to O'C.'s impotence. The plaintiffs then sought to have their marriage registered by the defendant who refused to do so. The plaintiffs brought this action seeking a declaration that their marriage was a lawful and valid marriage and an order compelling the defendant to register it. **Held** by Lynch J.: even though the 1972 marriage was voidable and not void, the decree of nullity in 1980 was retroactive and made the 1972 marriage void *ab initio* to all intents and purposes. *Semble:* The chronology of the steps taken by the first named plaintiff is so far as the criminal and civil law are concerned, very undesirable. A marriage which is voidable for impotence is not voidable, nor consequently void *ab initio,* unless and until the High Court shall have pronounced it so. In the meantime the spouse remains apparently validly married and open to prosecution for bigamy. *F.M.L.* v. *An tArd Chláraitheoir na bPósadh*

(H.C.) [1984] ILRM 667

25. —— **Validity** — *Failure to comply with formalities — Marriage (Ireland) Act,* 1844 (*c.* 81), *s.* 49.] The parties, an estranged German couple, underwent a ceremony of marriage at the Lutheran Church in Dublin in 1963. The husband, here the respondent in a maintenance application brought by the wife, sought to establish that he and his wife had not been lawfully married. The record of the Dublin marriage showed that a certificate had been produced to the officiating pastor stating (in accordance with the German legal requirement) that the parties had previously been married by a civil act in East Berlin. By producing his passport and otherwise, the husband showed that he had not been in East Germany at the date of the alleged civil marriage. It was further established that the Dublin Lutheran Church was not, at the date of the Irish ceremony registered for the celebration of marriages; that no statutory licence or certificate was issued to authorise the ceremony; and that no banns were published. The record did not establish that the Dublin marriage was duly witnessed, although the wife asserted it had been. **Held** by Murphy J., adjourning the appeal to allow the parties to consider their positions following his findings, that, 1, the husband had discharged the heavy onus of proving that there had been no civil ceremony of marriage in East Berlin. 2. The failure to comply with the German requirement that a civil marriage must precede a religious ceremony was not relevant to the

FAMILY LAW—Marriage.

validity of the Irish marriage. 3. The Dublin marriage was undertaken without a statutory licence in an unregistered building and without publication of banns, but, on the balance of probability, in the presence of the requisite witnesses; that the applicant wife was not aware of defects in the Irish ceremony; that both parties had honestly believed that they had contracted a valid marriage; and that it was settled law that to invalidate a marriage for non-compliance with the statutory formalities it was necessary to prove a conscious disregard of the statute and that both parties had been aware of a defect. *I.E.* v. *W.E.*
(H.C.) [1985] ILRM 691

26. —— **Validity** — *Moslem marriage ceremony in South Africa joining persons of different race — Marriage without formal validity in South Africa — Moslem marriage potentially polygamous — Subsequent exchange of marriage vows — Whether the parties thereby intended a monogamous union — Whether such an exchange may be recognised as a valid marriage at common law.*] The plaintiff, an Irish girl, sought to recover possession of her Dublin home from the defendant, a South African Asian to whom she had been united in a Moslem marriage ceremony in South Africa. The outcome of the ejectment proceedings, taken in the Circuit Court, and on appeal to the High Court, depended on whether the parties had contracted a marriage that could be recognized in Ireland as valid at common law. The evidence established that the plaintiff, after an engagement lasting several years, had travelled to South Africa to be with the defendant; that they agreed to get married; that a wedding (at which the plaintiff was represented but at which she was not present) was celebrated in a mosque; that such an inter-racial marriage lacked formal validity under South African law; that a moslem marriage was regarded as potentially polygamous; and that at a reception following the ceremony in the mosque there was an exchange of marriage vows in English. The parties, conscious of the deficiencies in their arrangements, intended to undergo a civil ceremony of marriage in Dublin. That this never took place and that the parties broke up was attributed to the improper influence of the plaintiff's family. **Held** by Barron J., finding that the parties were not husband and wife according to the law of this jurisdiction, that, 1, the existence of a common law marriage must be determined by the nature of the ceremony and the intention of the parties in relation to that ceremony and not as to their belief as to its effect: *Wolfenden* v. *Wolfenden* [1945] 2 All E.R. 539, *Penhas* v. *Eng* [1953] A.C. 304; and *Ussher* v. *Ussher* [1912] 2 I.R. 445 considered. 2. The parties intended to be bound by their South African marriage, even though they believed they could not be legally married in South Africa. 3. The Moslem marriage ceremony being potentially polygamous, it fell to examine the significance of the subsequent exchange of married vows. 4. The latter ceremony was explicable as an extension and explanation of the proceedings at the mosque, and the evidence did not establish that it was held for the purpose of confirming that the parties intended a monogamous union. *Conlan* v. *Mohamed*
(H.C.) [1987] ILRM 172

PROPERTY

27. —— **Family home** — *Beneficial interest — Husband purchasing house in own name — Wife contributing to household expenses — Whether wife entitled to beneficial share of ownership by virtue of contributions.*] The defendant husband purchased a house in his own name by means of a mortgage, paying a deposit of £500 by the sale of the mobile home he and his wife, the plaintiff, had lived in for the first year of their marriage, and by borrowing from a credit union. In 1973, five years after their marriage, the plaintiff and the defendant separated. Proceedings were instituted by the plaintiff claiming a declaration under s. 12 of the Married Womens Status Act, 1957, that she was entitled to the sole beneficial interest in the family home or alternatively determining the extent of her beneficial interest in the premises. The plaintiff, who continued to work after her marriage, claimed the money she earned was spent on her own necessaries and on meeting the expenses of the household and in that way her earnings helped to meet the mortgage repayments thereby entitling her to a beneficial interest in the proceeds of the sale of the home. The defendant alleged that most of the plaintiff's earnings were spent on herself. **Held** by McMahon J., 1, had the wife not been earning, the husband would not have been able to keep up the mortgage repayments, run a car and maintain their standard of living. 2. So far as the money was spent on the wife's needs, these were expenses which the husband would have been bound to meet if she was not able to pay for them herself. If there was a saving to the husband which entitled him *pro tanto* to meet the mortgage repayments the wife should be regarded as contributing towards those repayments. *C.* v. *C.* [1976] I.R. 254 applied. 3. On the evidence, the net proceeds of sale should be distributed in a proportion of 100 to 18 as between the husband and the wife. *R.* v. *R.*
(H.C.) [1979] ILRM 1

28. —— **Family home** — *Beneficial interest — Wife seeking a declaration of interest in husband's house.*] A wife, the plaintiff and appellant, who

FAMILY LAW—Property.

had contributed to the cost of a previous matrimonial home, was agreed to have been entitled to one-third of the net proceeds of its sale, which had been £1,800. The husband went on to acquire another house for £9,000, but under an arrangement with his employer he did not pay for the acquisition but merely discharged the mortgage repayments on a loan. The sum of £1,800 was, with the wife's consent, expended on furniture. The wife sought a declaration that she was entitled to a share of one-eighteenth in the new house, a fraction that was a simplification of the calculation 600/10,800, where the numerator represented her share of the proceeds of sale and the denominator the addition of the costs of the new house and its furniture. In the High Court [1981 No. 357 Sp], Costello J. rejected this contention and found that the wife's interest was confined to a one-third share in the furniture. From this decision she appealed to the Supreme Court. **Held** by Henchy J. (Griffin and Hederman JJ. concurring) dismissing the appeal, that the wife's £600 was not applied to the purchase of the second house either directly or indirectly, and had not been part of a general family fund, the existence of which could have been held to have relieved the husband of the burden of house purchase. *D. McC.* v. *M. McC.*

(S.C.) [1986] ILRM 1

29. —— **Family home** — *Consent to sale — Spouse not informed of sale — Purchaser making no inquiries — Vendor spouse making statutory declaration that house not a family home — Whether purchaser deemed to have notice — Whether desertion avoids necessity to obtain consent to sale — Family Home Protection Act,* 1976 (*No.* 27), *ss.* 3, 4.] The defendant and her husband held a weekly tenancy in a dwelling since 1968. The defendant left the dwelling in 1973, with their two children, and went to live in America from where she carried on a desultory correspondence with the husband up to May, 1979. In November, 1978, the husband purchased the dwelling from the landlord, and the next day sold the dwelling to the plaintiffs. The husband made a statutory declaration that the dwelling was not a family home within the meaning of the Family Home Protection Act, 1976, and that his wife had never contacted him since she left him. The plaintiffs later sought to resell the dwelling, but the new purchasers challenged the validity of the statutory declaration made by the husband. The husband commenced proceedings claiming that the plaintiffs were purchasers for full value within the meaning of s. 3 of the Family Home Protection Act, 1976, or alternatively an order dispensing with the consent of the defendant to

FAMILY LAW—*continued.*

a sale to the plaintiffs. The husband died suddenly in May, 1979, and the plaintiffs were substituted as the plaintiffs in these proceedings. **Held** by McWilliam J. in refusing to make an order dispensing with the consent of the defendant to the sale to the purchaser, 1, it was not unreasonable for the defendant to withhold her consent. 2. Applications for orders dispensing with the consent of the defendant to the sale to the purchaser must be made before the execution of the conveyance and not after, otherwise the contract is void and unenforceable. 3. The plaintiffs were not purchasers for full value within the meaning of s. 3 of the Family Home Protection Act, 1976, as no enquiries were made by them from the defendant that ought reasonably to have been made. 4. Desertion does not avoid the necessity for obtaining the consent required by s. 3 of the Family Home Protection Act, 1976, unless a court order was obtained under s. 4 of the Act. *Somers* v. *W.* [1979] I.R. 94 applied. *H. v. S.*

(H.C.) [1979] ILRM 105

30. —— **Family home** — *Equitable mortgage — Advances made on foot of deposit of title deeds — Deposit made prior to Act coming into effect — Further advances — Whether consent of spouse required — Family Home Protection Act,* 1976 (*No.* 27), *ss.* 2, 3(1).] The plaintiff held an equitable charge over the defendant's lands by virtue of the deposit of title deeds in 1975 to secure present and future advances. The said lands included the family home of the defendant and his wife since the passing of the Family Home Protection Act, 1976, within the meaning of the said Act. Further advances were made to the defendant on foot of the deposit of title deeds after the 1976 Act came into force but no consents to these advances were obtained from the defendant's wife. S. 3 of the 1976 Act requires a consent where there is a conveyance of an 'interest' in the family home. The Act defines interest as meaning "any estate, right, title or other interest, legal or equitable." It was accepted at all times that the defendant had notice at all material times that the said lands comprised the family home of the defendant. **Held** by Barron J. in making a declaration that no security was created in favour of the plaintiff over the family home of the defendant in respect of advances made after the date upon which the Act came into force, 1, all the advances made after the 1976 Act came into force required the consent of the defendant's wife since, although the bank obtained an estate in the lands, the word 'interest' in the 1976 Act is defined more widely than a reference to an estate and the fact that an estate had been conveyed need not prevent a subsequent transaction from conveying

FAMILY LAW—*continued.*

an 'interest' in the lands. 2. Future further advances are the conveyance of an interest in the lands for the purpose of s. 3 of the 1976 Act as each time there is a further advance the interest of the mortgagor in those lands is being altered and the value of the equity of redemption is also being altered. 3. As the plaintiff had notice that the lands were a family home for the purpose of the Act, the rights of the spouse are not subordinate to the right of the plaintiff and therefore the plaintiff should have obtained the consent of the spouse prior to making any further advances after the date upon which the Act came into force. *Bank of Ireland* v. *Purcell*
(H.C.) [1988] ILRM 480

—— Child — Custody — Adoption.
see **Adoption**

—— Child — Custody — Protection — Court order committing infant to care of health board — Validity — Whether made in accordance with law — Whether health board had capacity to take infant in care.
see **Practice and Procedure,** 14

—— Family — Constitutional rights — Alien — Marriage to female Irish citizen — Refusal of leave to settle in State.
see **Aliens,** 1-3, 5

—— Family — Constitutional rights — Conflict with exercise of State's fundamental rights — Whether State's fundamental rights could prevail over related constitutional rights of members of a family.
see **Aliens,** 2

—— Family — Constitutional rights — Convicted prisoner — Effect of imprisonment on rights of family — Right to communicate — Inquiry into legality of detention.
see **Constitution,** 8

—— Family — Constitutional rights — Dwelling — Taxation — Residential property tax.
see **Constitution,** 47

—— Family — Constitutional rights — Husband and wife — Procreation — Husband and wife each serving sentence of imprisonment for life — No children of marriage — Basis for restriction on prisoners' rights by State — Whether husband and wife constitute family —

FAMILY LAW—*continued.*

Whether right to procreate a personal right.
see **Constitution,** 19

—— Family — Constitutional rights — Meaning of "family".
see **Constitution,** 13
Family Law, 1

—— Family — Constitutional rights — Whether any right to protection from a negligent act which interferes with its constitution or authority — Education — Whether children have the right to be educated by their father — Whether children have any right to protection from a negligent act which interferes with the right to be educated by their father.
see **Constitution,** 9

—— Family — Constitutional rights — Whether possible to automatically claim rights guaranteed where family divided.
see **Aliens,** 3

—— Maintenance — Parties divorced in the U.K. — Whether husband domiciled in Britain — Parties resident for time in Ireland — Parties both British citizens — Whether domicile of origin displaced — Onus of proof — Whether legislation abolishing dependent domicile retrospective in effect — Whether dependent domicile concept existed up to enactment of legislation — Wife's application for maintenance — Motion to stay proceedings — Whether motion should be granted before decree made absolute.
see **Conflict of Laws,** 7

—— Maintenance — Practice — High Court — Jurisdiction.
see **Constitution,** 4, 5

—— Marriage — Dissolution — Foreign decree of divorce — Validity — Test applicable — Appeal to Supreme Court — Alternative test suggested — Whether Supreme Court may consider arguments not raised in High Court — Whether findings of fact in High Court sufficient to enable Supreme Court to consider new arguments.
see **Conflict of Laws,** 6

—— Marriage — Dissolution — Recognition of foreign decree absolute — Domicile of husband — Parties divorced in the U.K. — Whether husband domiciled in

FEES
see also **Costs**

—— Auctioneer — Auction cancelled — Vendor subsequently selling premises by private treaty — Whether auctioneer entitled to fees.
see **Auctioneers and Estate Agents**

—— Liquidator — Application for interim payment of fees — Inquiry by examiner — Appeal to Supreme Court.
see **Company,** 25

—— Taxation of costs.
see **Practice and Procedure,** 26-33

FIERI FACIAS
see **Injunction,** 6

FINANCE
—— Local government — Service charges.
see **Local Government,** 1, 2

—— Local government — Rating.
see **Rating and Valuation**

—— Taxation.
see **Revenue**

FINANCIAL INSTITUTIONS
see **Banking; Building Society; Credit Union; Hire Purchase; Industrial and Provident Societies**

FINGERPRINTS
see **Criminal Law,** 12

FIRE
—— Malicious damage claims.
see **Criminal Injuries,** 3, 5, 6

—— Stardust dancehall — Compensation tribunal.
see **Judicial Review,** 9

FIRE INSURANCE
—— Contract — Interpretation — Destruction of premises by fire — Whether contract of insurance contained a reinstatement clause — Assessment of loss.
see **Insurance,** 2

—— Contract — *Uberrima fides* — Breach of warranty — Incomplete answer.
see **Insurance,** 5

FIRE SERVICES

—— **Fire safety notice** — *Service — Terms of notice intended to impose continuing obligations on occupier — Occupier appealing to District Court — Compliance by occupier with terms before hearing of appeal — Nature of court's order — Confirmation of safety notice — Fire*

FIRE SERVICES—*continued.*

Services Act, 1981 (*No.* 30), *ss.* 20, 21.] Where the owner or occupier of a building upon whom a fire authority has, pursuant to s. 20 of the Fire Services Act, 1981, served a fire safety notice intended to impose obligations of a continuing nature appeals to the District Court pursuant to s. 21 of that Act against such notice, the fact that the appellant owner or occupier has effected the precautions specified in the notice to the satisfaction of the fire authority before the hearing of the appeal does not *per se* warrant the District Court in annulling the said notice under s. 21, sub-s. 3, of that Act. In particular, the statutory ground of appeal specified at paragraph (*b*) of s. 21, sub-s. 1, of the Act of 1981 viz., that the building is not a potentially dangerous building, is not made out by showing that, subsequent to the service of the notice of appeal, the appellant has carried out works to the building such that the fire authority is able to conclude that it is no longer a potentially dangerous building. So **held** by Murphy J. *Per* Murphy J., it would be helpful if the fire authority were to distinguish in any fire safety notice it might serve between obligations addressed to the owners and occupiers and those imposed on the buildings and, also, to draw a clear distinction between continuing obligations and those being imposed once and for all. *Transactus Investments Ltd.* v. *Dublin Corporation*

(H.C.) [1985] I.R.501

FIREARMS
—— Possession — Whether political offence.
see **Extradition,** 3

—— Possession — Whether possession for a lawful purpose — Accused being constables in R.U.C.
see **Criminal Law,** 27

FISCAL NULLITY — Doctrine.
see **Revenue,** 7

FISHERIES
see also **Harbours and Piers**

—— **Fisheries Acts** — *Offence — Detention of boat by sea fisheries protection officer — Order of District Court releasing boat on payment into court of security for costs, fines and forfeitures — Defendant convicted — Order for fine and costs to be deducted from money lodged — Balance returned to defendant — Order for forfeiture of catch and fishing gear — Whether court had power to order additional sum to be deducted from security in lieu of order of forfeiture — Fisheries (Consolidation) Act, 1959 (No.* 14), *s.* 235 (2) (*a*) — *Fisheries (Amendment) Act,* 1978 (*No.* 18), *ss.* 2 (5), 14.] Section 235, sub-s. 2 (*a*) of the Fisheries

FISHERIES—*continued.*

(Consolidation) Act, 1959, as inserted by s. 14 of the Fisheries (Amendment) Act, 1978, provides that a District Justice may require a boat which has been detained pending charges under the Act to be released upon payment into court of a sum of money which is sufficient security for payment of the fine and award of costs which may be ordered and for the estimated value of any catch and gear which may be forfeited upon the determination of those proceedings. The notice party, who was charged with an offence under the Acts and whose boat was detained by a sea fisheries protection officer, obtained from the District Court an order releasing the boat upon lodgment of security. He was subsequently convicted of that offence by the respondent in the Circuit Court and was fined and ordered to pay the costs of the proceedings. The court also made an order under s. 2, sub-s. 5 of the Act of 1978 for the forfeiture of the catch and fishing gear of the notice party. On behalf of the applicant, the prosecuting authority under the Acts, it was submitted to the Circuit Court that the value of the catch and gear forfeited, together with a sum in respect of fine and costs, should be deducted from the security lodged in court, and that such sums should be paid to the applicant in lieu of an order of forfeiture. The ground for this application was that an order for forfeiture could not be executed, as the notice party's catch and gear had been removed from the jurisdiction. The respondent held that there was no provision in the Acts for the deduction of a sum from the monies lodged in court in lieu of an order of forfeiture, and ordered that a sum in respect of fine and costs only be deducted from the lodgment, the balance to be returned to the notice party. On the applicant's application by way of judicial review for an order of certiorari quashing the respondent's order and for an order of mandamus directing the respondent to make an order that a sufficient sum be paid out of the security in lieu of forfeiture, it was **Held** by Murphy J. in refusing the application, 1, that the respondent had no power upon conviction, in lieu of an order for forfeiture of catch and gear, to estreat that part of the security provided by a boat owner equal to the value of the catch and gear released on foot of such security. 2. *Semble.* That it might have been open to the respondent, having made an order for forfeiture of catch and gear, to decline to release any part of the security lodged in court until he was satisfied that the forfeiture order had operated effectively. 3. That the respondent had statutory power to release the security lodged in court; the fact a different course might have been taken if different arguments had been addressed to the court did not mean that the respondent had acted without or in excess of jurisdiction. *The State (Holland)* v. *Kennedy* [1977] I.R. 193 and *Gill* v. *Connellan* [1987] I.R.541 considered. *Attorney General* v. *Sheehy*

(H.C.) [1988] I.R. 226

—— Employment — Contract of service or partnership — Employer's annual obligation to provide information relating to employees — Fishing vessel owned and operated by skipper — Crew engaged prior to each voyage — Remuneration based on value of catch — Whether employment or partnership in existence — Whether skipper an employer.
see **Revenue,** 38

—— Fishing rights — Interference — Arterial drainage scheme — Compensation — Assessment.
see **Real Property,** 4

—— Fishing rights — Interference — Rights of riparian owner — Interference with plaintiffs' fishing rights by canoes — Whether fishery rights of plaintiffs corporeal or incorporeal hereditaments — Whether plaintiffs entitled to order to restrain defendant's activities.
see **Real Property,** 5

—— Offence — Arrest of foreign fishing vessel — Detention order made — Vessel released upon provision of security — Whether requirement to give security amounted to a requirement to give bail — If so, whether such bail oppressive — Major or minor offence.
see **Constitution,** 42

—— Offence — Summary conviction — Fine and forfeiture of equipment — Trial of offence — Whether offence minor offence.
see **Constitution,** 49

—— Offshore fishing licences — Conditions of nationality attaching to licences — Challenge to validity of statutory provisions under which licence granted — Whether plaintiffs entitled to injunction restraining enforcement of conditions.
see **Injunction,** 4

—— Offshore fishing licences — Conditions of nationality attaching to licences — Vessel arrested for fishing in breach of conditions — Plaintiff seeking order restraining enforcement of conditions.

G

GAMING AND LOTTERIES

1. —— **Betting licence** — *Certificate of personal fitness required for licence to issue — Statute — Interpretation — Companies excluded from Act's definition of licensed bookmaker — Companies also prohibited from applying for certificate of personal fitness — Company authorising agent to apply for licence on its behalf — Whether agent entitled to certificate in those circumstances — Betting Act,* 1931 (*No.* 27), *ss.* 2, 4 and 6.] A certificate of personal fitness to hold a betting licence under the Betting Act, 1931, may be issued to a natural person even though that person is acting as agent for a company and will hold the betting licence on its behalf. Such a construction of the Act of 1931 does not conflict with either the Act's definition of the term "licensed bookmaker" which expressly excludes companies from its scope or with s. 4 of the Act which imposes a similar limitation on the persons who may apply for a certificate of personal fitness since it is the agent and not the company who makes the application for the certificate and who will become the licensed bookmaker. So **held** by Barron J. *McDonnell* v. *Reid*

(H.C.) [1987] I.R. 51

2. —— **Betting licence** — *Certificate of suitability — Application advertised in* Irish News *— Whether a newspaper circulating in area — Valuation of premises less than £200 at hearing of application — Certificate granted but not issued until revised certificate of valuation produced — Valuation list revised after hearing — Whether court erred in granting certificate.*

Rating and valuation — Date at which alteration to list takes effect — Rating (Northern Ireland) Order, 1977 (*S.I. No.* 2157, *No.* 28), *art.* 13(1)(*c*)(ii).

Judicial review — Practice — Application to add grounds of relief to statement more than three months after event — R.S.C. (N.I.), O. 53, *r.* 4, 6(2).

Certiorari — Whether error going to jurisdiction — Whether error on face of record — Whether affidavit filed by notice party part of record.] The prosecutors applied for judicial review of an order of a magistrate's court granting a certificate of suitability in respect of premises of 61 Castle Street, Comber, under section 6 of the Betting and Lotteries (Northern Ireland) Act, 1957, to the notice party F. F. had advertised the application for a certificate in the *News Letter* and

GAMING AND LOTTERIES—*continued.*

Irish News in compliance with the requirement in section 6(3) of the 1957 Act that notice of the application be inserted in at least two newspapers circulating in the area. The application was heard on 29 May, 1984, and, there being no objections, a certificate was granted, subject to the condition that it would not issue until a certificate of valuation was produced. At the date of the application the rateable value of the premises was £135. Section 7(1)(*j*) of the 1957 Act required the court hearing the application to refuse a certificate if the net annual value of the premises was less than £200. The valuation list was revised on 18 June, 1984, and the premises valued at £270. On 19 June, 1984, a certificate of suitability was issued. The prosecutors sought to quash the certificate on the ground that the *Irish News* was not a newspaper circulating in the area in which the premises are situated as required by section 6(3) of the 1957 Act, and also sought to rely upon the additional ground that the valuation of the premises was less than £200 on 29 May, 1984, so that the Magistrate's Court had acted without jurisdiction in granting the certificate. It was argued on behalf of F. that order 53, rule 4 of the Rules of the Supreme Court (Northern Ireland), 1980, prevented the prosecutors relying upon additional grounds as it would unfairly prejudice his rights and he had altered his position to his detriment by carrying out alterations on the strength of the certificate. He also argued that the failure to comply with section 7(1)(*j*) of the 1957 Act at most disclosed an error of law which did not appear on the face of the record so as to entitle the prosecutors to relief. The only evidence of the rateable value of the premises on date of the issue of the certificate was contained in an affidavit on F.'s behalf. **Held,** quashing the certificate, that, 1, it was desirable that all matters which can properly be put forward should be before the court. In considering whether to exercise the discretion to allow the amendments it was relevant that F. commenced the alterations to the previous before the time limit for commencing proceedings for judicial review and it was unlikely that notice of the additional grounds would have deterred him from completing the alterations. Moreover, the prosecutors had no means of knowing the date of the certificate of valuation until after the hearing granting the certificate. Accordingly, the prosecutors were permitted to amend their statement to include the additional grounds. 2. The requirement of advertising in two newspapers under section 6(3) was to ensure proper publication for application under the 1957 Act. A newspaper

GAMING AND LOTTERIES—*continued.*

circulating in an area is intended to mean something more than the mere fact that a newspaper may be available in the area; it should be sold or read on a scale which will contribute materially to the prospect that local government electors residing in the electoral division will be informed of the application. The sale of two copies per day of the *Irish News* in the area and the addition of two imported copies did not come within the concept of a newspaper circulating in the area. 3. On the date of granting the certificate of suitability the valuation of the premises was less than £200 and under section 7(1)(*j*) the application for a certificate should have been refused. By article 13 of the Rates (Northern Ireland) Order, 1977, the subsequent alteration of valuation did not take effect until 18 June, 1984, when it was made in the list. As the list was not altered until after the hearing of 29 May, 1984, the magistrate had fallen into an error of law in granting the certificate. 4. Although the error of law did not appear on the record, it was deposed to be an affidavit filed on behalf of F., and it was permissible for the court to look at an affidavit filed by a notice party and he was taken to consent to it being used to supplement the record. *In re Stevenson*

(Q.B.D.) [1984] N.I.373

3. —— **Gaming licence** — *Amusement halls — Annual renewal — Slot machines — Application to District Court — Application made after expiry of licence — Refusal of court to authorise issue of new licence — Right of appeal — Whether expired licence continues in force pending determination of appeal — Resolution of local authority required to permit gaming — Resolution rescinded after date of application — Whether rescission could prevent grant where application already before court — Whether invasion of judicial process — Gaming and Lotteries Act,* 1956 (*No.* 2), *Part III, ss.* 12, 13, 14, 15, 18.] Section 12 of the Gaming and Lotteries Act, 1956, provides that Part III of the Act, permitting the licensing of amusement halls for the purpose of providing facilities for gaming which would otherwise be unlawful, shall not have effect in any area unless there is for the time being in force a resolution of the local authority adopting the Part for that area; s. 13 provides, *inter alia,* that a local authority may rescind the adoption of Part III of the Act. Section 15 of the Act provides for the granting by the District Court of a certificate authorising the issue by the Revenue Commissioners of a gaming licence in respect of a particular year, while by s. 18, sub-s. 3, it is enacted that where the holder of a subsisting licence is refused a certificate by the District Court and appeals against that refusal to the Circuit Court, "the licence shall continue in force

GAMING AND LOTTERIES—*continued.*

pending the determination of an appeal against such refusal." The applicant, the owner of an amusement hall, was the holder of a gaming licence in respect of premises situate within the administrative area of Dublin Corporation. Fourteen days after the expiry of that licence, he applied to the District Court for the grant of a certificate authorising the issue of a new licence for the forthcoming year. On his application being refused, he filed notice of appeal against that decision; the appeal was from time to time adjourned by the Circuit Court and was ultimately re-entered two and a half years after the date of the decision of the District Court. During that period successive annual licences were issued to the applicant by the Revenue Commissioners in purported reliance upon s. 18, sub-s. 3. Immediately prior to the re-entry of the appeal Dublin City Council rescinded the adoption of Part III of the Act of 1956. The Circuit Court judge stated a consultative case for the opinion of the Supreme Court as to whether the rescission of the adoption of Part III of the Act by the City Council could prevent the court from entertaining an existing application which was then before it and whether, by virtue of s. 18, sub-s. 3, the applicant was to be deemed the holder of a subsisting licence which had continued in force pending the determination of his appeal. **Held** by the Supreme Court (Griffin, Walsh and Hederman JJ.) in answering the case stated, 1, that since the period specified in the applicant's previous licence had expired prior to his application, the applicant was not, on the date of the decision of the District Court, "the holder of a subsisting licence" and s. 18, sub-s. 3 of the Act had no application to him. 2. That, as the resolution of the City Council rescinding the adoption of Part III of the Act applied to the entire community in the whole of the county borough of Dublin, it could not be regarded as an intervention in a particular application then before the court and thus as an unconstitutional invasion of the judicial process. *Buckley and Others (Sinn Féin)* v. *Attorney General* [1950] I.R. 67 considered. 3. That the court had no jurisdiction to grant a certificate unless it was satisfied that the local authority had adopted Part III of the Act and that that resolution was still in force at the time when the application was made. *In re Camillo*

(S.C.) [1988] I.R.104 ; [1988] ILRM 738

4. —— **Gaming licence** — *Amusement halls — Certificates under Part III of Act of 1956 — District Court — Jurisdiction — Resolution by local authority — Resolution rescinded — Effects — Gaming and Lotteries Act,* 1956 (*No.* 2), *Part III.*] The District Court has jurisdiction to grant certificates authorising the issue of licences for

GAMING AND LOTTERIES—*continued.*

amusement halls and funfairs under Part III of the Gaming and Lotteries Act, 1956, only upon resolution by the appropriate local authority, and the certificates thereby granted are not of unlimited duration but annual only. So **held** by Johnson J. and affirmed by the Supreme Court (Finlay C.J., Henchy and Griffin JJ.). *Dublin Corporation* v. *O'Hanrahan*

(H.C., S.C.) [1988] I.R.121

5. —— **Gaming licence** — *Amusement halls — Local authority resolution permitting gaming halls in authority's area — Applicant seeking licence — Application refused by District Court — Local authority giving notice of intention to rescind resolution allowing gaming — Local authority restricting gaming — Whether applicant carried out business — Whether decision of local authority* ultra vires *by reason of bad faith — Gaming and Lotteries Act,* 1956 (*No.* 2), *Part III.*] The prosecutor is a restaurant owner and carries on business with his wife at Upper Main Street, Arklow. The first named respondent is a Local Authority within the meaning of the Gaming and Lotteries Act, 1956. The prosecutor wished to extend his business and applied to Arklow Urban District Council (the council) for planning permission for a change of user of part of his premises to use as an amusement centre. The application was refused by the council but, on appeal, was granted by An Bord Pleanála on 25 February, 1982. The prosecutor applied to the District Court for a certificate authorising the issue of a gaming licence pursuant to the 1956 Act. The District Court granted such a certificate but it was refused by the Circuit Court on appeal by the council. The council objected, *inter alia,* on the ground that there were enough licences in the locality and that the premises were unsuitable. Under Part III of the 1956 Act a certificate for a licence can be granted only for one year at most and a new application must be made each year, and, in considering an application for a certificate the District Court shall have regard to, *inter alia,* the number of gaming licences in force in the locality, the suitability of the premises and the class of persons likely to resort thereto. Part III shall not have effect in any area unless there is a resolution by the local council. Such a resolution was passed by the council in 1956 in respect of the whole of its administrative area. The prosecutor, having modified his premises, made another application to the District Court and notice of this was published in a newspaper on 5 February, 1983, and was posted to the council on 3 February. In October, 1982, the council had published a notice of intention to rescind Part III. The resolution was passed at a meeting on 9 February, 1983, rescinding Part III. At the same meeting the council resolved to adopt Part III in respect of certain areas which did not include the street in which the prosecutor carried on business but did include areas in which there were four premises licensed for gaming. On 7 March, 1983, the prosecutor's application was adjourned in view of the resolution of 9 February. The prosecutor then applied for an order of certiorari to quash the resolution of 9 February. The prosecutor obtained a conditional order of certiorari. Cause against making absolute of the conditional order was shown by the council. On the hearing of the application to have the conditional order made absolute, McWilliam J. allowed the cause shown and discharged the conditional order. The prosecutor appealed. The prosecutor's challenge to the validity of the resolution was put forward on four main grounds (1) that the council's conduct amounted to an unconstitutional interference with the administration of justice, (2) that the resolution was made in bad faith, (3) that the resolution was made as a result of bias or interest, (4) that the resolution was made in disregard to the essentials of justice. **Held** by Henchy J. (Griffin and Hederman JJ.) in dismissing the appeal, 1, there was no *lis* before the District Court when the council intervened nor was there pending proceedings of which the District Court was seised. Consequently the council's resolution did not constitute an unconstitutional invasion of the judicial process. 2. The onus was upon the prosecutor to show that the council acted in bad faith or were unfairly discriminating and the prosecutor failed to discharge such onus. 3. No grounds were found to substantiate the prosecutor's claim that the council's resolutions were made as a result of bias or interest between the council and other parties. 4. The council's attitude reflected responsible public opinion in the area to which the application to convert his premises into a licensed amusement hall applied and the council had not departed from the requirements of natural justice. *The State (Divito)* v. *Arklow Urban District Council*

(S.C.) [1986] ILRM 123

6. —— **Gaming licence** — *Amusement halls — Local authority resolution to permit licensing — Rescission by subsequent resolution — One month's notice of resolution to be given to every councillor — Notice of passing of resolution to be published in newspaper — Copy of newspaper notice to be "evidence of the passing" of resolution — Whether newspaper notice evidence that resolution was validly passed — Whether onus on local authority to prove one month's notice given to every councillor — Gaming and Lotteries Act,* 1956 (*No.* 2), *s.* 13(1), (3), (4), (5).] The applicants applied to the Dublin Metropolitan District Court for a certificate pursuant to Part III of the

GAMING AND LOTTERIES—*continued.*

Act of 1956, authorising the issue of a gaming licence in respect of premises within the administrative area of Dublin Corporation. At the hearing of the application the court was satisfied that Part III of the Act had been adopted by resolution of Dublin City Council in 1956, and that that resolution had been in force for many years. There was produced to the court a copy of a newspaper, dated five months prior to the application, which contained a public notice of the rescinding of the original resolution. It was argued on behalf of the Corporation that, as the application for the renewal of the certificate was dated subsequent to the passing of the rescinding resolution, the court had no jurisdiction to entertain the application. On behalf of the applicants it was argued that while the production of a copy of the newspaper containing the notice of rescission was sufficient to prove that the Corporation had purported to pass that resolution, it was not sufficient evidence that one month's notice had been given to each member of the Council. On being placed on strict proof by the court that notice had been given to each council member in compliance with the provisions of s. 13, sub-s. 3 of the Act, the Corporation adduced evidence which showed that the sending of notices to members of the City Council was the responsibility of the secretary of the City Manager; that the secretary was assisted by several employees of the Corporation and also made use of a computer which had stored on it the names and addresses of the members of the Council; that a procedure was adopted by his staff which, if correctly followed, would result in notices being served to each of the current members of the Council; but that the secretary was not able to state positively which staff member had posted notices to Council members on the relevant occasion, or whether the correct procedure had been properly followed. There was no evidence produced to the court to show that any Council member had not received the notice. The District Justice stated a consultative case for the opinion of the High Court as to whether in those circumstances there was an onus on the Corporation to establish that notice of the resolution on which it relied had been validly served on every member of the City Council. **Held** by Barrington J., 1, that the purpose of sub-s. 5 of s. 13 was to provide a simple method of adducing evidence to the court that the relevant resolution had been passed as an effective resolution of the local authority and in compliance with the requirements as to notice contained in sub-section 3. 2. That the production of a copy of a newspaper containing the requisite public notice was merely *prima facie* evidence that the resolution had been validly passed, and was capable of being rebutted by evidence showing that any one councillor had not in fact received the notice. 3. That in the present case there was no evidence to rebut the evidence produced in accordance with sub-s. 5 of s. 13, which was therefore sufficient to demonstrate compliance with the requirements of the Act. *In re Murphy*

(H.C.) [1987] I.R.667

7. —— **Gaming licence** — *Offences — Gaming machines in which both the stake to be hazarded and amount to be won exceeded statutory limits — Owners of machines holding gaming and gaming machine licences — Effect of subsequent legislation — Whether operation of machine a criminal offence — Gaming and Lotteries Act,* 1956 (*No.* 2), *ss.* 4, 14, 15, 19 — *Finance Act,* 1975 (*No.* 6), *s.* 43.] The applicant, an owner of an amusement hall, was charged with offences of having gaming machines on his premises in which both the stakes to be hazarded and the amount which could be won exceeded the statutory limits. The applicant at the time of the alleged offences was the holder of both a gaming licence and a gaming machine licence granted pursuant to respectively the provisions of the Gaming and Lotteries Act, 1956, and s. 43 of the Finance Act, 1975. The applicant was convicted in the District Court of the alleged offences and appealed to the Circuit Court whereupon Judge Sheehy stated a consultative case to the Supreme Court and raised the following question: whether the holder of a gaming machine licence pursuant to s. 43 of the 1975 Act could commit a criminal offence under s. 4 of the 1956 Act where the alleged offence is in respect of a gaming machine the subject matter of the gaming machine licence? The applicant submitted that the effect of s. 43 of the 1975 Act was to make lawful the operation of a gaming machine in respect of which a licence had been issued by a Revenue Commissioner even though it was in breach of the provisions of the 1956 Act or any conditions attached to the certificate. **Held** by the Supreme Court (Finlay C.J., Walsh, Griffin, Hederman and McCarthy JJ. concurring) in answering the case stated in the affirmative: s. 43 of the 1975 Act is not an affirmative provision making lawful the use of a gaming machine, it is a negative provision by virtue of s. 43(3) prohibiting the use of a gaming machine unless an excise licence has been obtained and revenue duty has been paid. *Director of Public Prosecutions* v. *Olympic Amusements*

(S.C.) [1987] ILRM 320

—— Gaming certificate — Application — Objection by local authority — Objection challenging jurisdiction of court — Applicant applying for case stated on question of jurisdiction — Whether court entitled to refuse to state case

GAMING AND LOTTERIES—*continued.*

requested by party asserting jurisdiction of court.
see **Case Stated,** 1

—— Offences — Bookmaker — Betting duty regulations — Infringement.
see **Constitution,** 54, 55
Criminal Law, 52

—— Offence — Licensed premises — Whether Gardaí trespassers in absence of search warrant — Objection to Gardaí's evidence.
see **Criminal Law,** 16

—— Offences — Whether minor offences capable of being tried summarily — Plaintiff owning gaming equipment of considerable value — Such equipment liable to forfeiture upon conviction.
see **Constitution,** 56

—— Statute — Validity — Gaming machines — Proprietor — Personal rights — Right to earn livelihood — Act of 1956 restricting player's stake to two and a half pence — Subsequent 950% increase in cost of living — Original stake restriction unaltered.
see **Constitution,** 43

GARDA SÍOCHÁNA
see also **Arrest and Detention**
Criminal Investigation

1. —— **Disciplinary inquiry** — *Details of alleged breach of discipline not disclosed — Whether violation of fair procedures — Whether regulations unconstitutional — Constitution of Ireland,* 1937, *Art.* 40 — Garda Síochána Act, 1924 (*No.* 25), *ss.* 4(2), 5 — *Police Forces Amalgamation Act,* 1925 (*No.* 7), *s.* 14(1) — *Garda Síochána (Discipline) Regulations* 1971 (*S.I. No.* 316), *regs.* 6, 8(2), 9, 11, 12, 13, 14, 15, 31, 34.] Regulation 34 of the Garda Síochána (Discipline) Regulations, 1971, makes provision for the dismissal from the force of any member whom the Commissioner considers unfit for retention therein. The regulation further provides at subsection (2)(*b*) thereof that the said power of dismissal can be exercised only where, *inter alia,* the disclosure of facts relating to the breach of discipline would be liable to affect the security of the State, or do serious and unjustifiable damage to some other person, provided that 'the Commissioner shall consider whether . . . some special inquiry can be held', and the dismissal can only take place with the consent of the Minister for Justice, and after the member concerned has been given an opportunity of

GARDA SÍOCHÁNA—*continued.*

advancing to the Commissioner his reasons against the proposed dismissal. The plaintiff, a member of the Garda Síochána, was served with a notice by the Commissioner, relating to an alleged breach of discipline, informing him that the Commissioner proposed to dismiss him from the force. A subsequent notice from the third-named defendant informed the plaintiff of the date of a special inquiry to investigate the alleged breach of discipline, pursuant to regulation 34 as aforesaid. Neither notice gave details of the alleged breach of discipline, or of the matters to be dealt with at the inquiry, and a request by the plaintiff's solicitor for further information was refused by the Commissioner. The plaintiff challenged the constitutionality of regulation 34 on the basis that it accorded the Commissioner an unrestricted power of dismissal, and failed to vindicate the plaintiff's right to hold office as a member of the Garda Síochána, which he alleged to be a property right protected by Article 40.3 of the Constitution. The plaintiff further submitted that the Commissioner was not entitled to form the opinion that disclosure of the facts relating to the alleged breach of discipline would be liable to affect the security of the State, or do serious and unjustifiable damage to the rights of other persons. The plaintiff claimed, finally, that the notice from the Commissioner was *ultra vires* on the ground, *inter alia,* that it failed to notify him of the reasons for which he was considered unfit for retention in the force. **Held** by Hamilton J. in finding that regulation 34 was not inconsistent with the Constitution, but in finding that the plaintiff, prior to the inquiry, was entitled to full notice of the grounds upon which the Commissioner relied in forming the opinion that he was unfit for retention in the force, full notice of the essential facts constituting the reason for so doing, and particulars of the alleged breach of discipline, 1, insofar as regulation 34 refers to the opinion of the Commissioner, the court was not entitled to substitute its own opinion. 2. The plaintiff, while not giving any right, either constitutional or statutory, to remain in office as a member of the Garda Síochána, had a right to remain in office until such time as his position was terminated in accordance with the relevant statutory provisions and the rules of natural justice. 3. It was implicit in regulation 34 that the power conferred on the Commissioner therein must be exercised by him fairly and in accordance with the principles of natural justice. *East Donegal Co-operative Livestock Marts Ltd.* v. *Attorney General* [1970] I.R. 317 applied. 4. The notices received by the plaintiff failed to disclose reasons why he was considered unfit for retention in the force, and thus did not give him a reasonable opportunity of presenting his response. *Hogan* v. *Minister for Justice*

GARDA SÍOCHÁNA—*continued.*

(H.C.) [1976-7] ILRM 184

2. —— **Disciplinary inquiry** — *Two-stage procedure — Matter being referred to Appeal Board — Board deciding that it had no jurisdiction to hear appeal — Whether jurisdictional error — Whether invalidated finding at initial stage — Garda Síochána (Discipline) Regulations* 1971 (*S.I. No.* 316), *regs.* 16, 20.] Regulation 20(4) of the Garda Síochána (Discipline) Regulations, 1971, provides that where application is made to the Garda Commissioner for review of the decision of an inquiry, he shall affirm or set aside the decision. Where application is 'for a review of his decision in relation to disciplinary action, [he shall] affirm or revoke the decision in relation to disciplinary action, or . . . refer the application to the Appeal Board.' The appellant, a member of the Garda Síochána, had been found guilty, by an unsworn inquiry, of two breaches of discipline; (*a*) falsehood or prevarication in stating, on an application form for use of his car for official purposes, that the car was properly taxed, and (*b*) falsehood or prevarication in making a similar statement on an application form for travelling expenses. The appellant was penalised, and appealed against the finding that he had been in breach of discipline, and against the disciplinary action, by way of application for review. The Commissioner referred the matter to the Appeal Board, which took the view that it had no jurisdiction to hear the appeal against the finding of breach of discipline, and referred the matter back to the Commissioner, who subsequently affirmed the decision of the inquiry. The appellant sought orders of certiorari quashing the initial decision of the inquiry, on the ground that the charges were bad for duplicity, and also the decision of the Appeal Board to send the matter back to the Commissioner. In the High Court, McWilliam J. held, in granting the orders sought, that the appellant had not been charged with two different offences, but with one offence, which could be committed in different ways, and that it must be stated in which way it was alleged to have been committed, as had been done in the instant case. The learned judge held further that on the true construction of regulation 20(4) of the 1971 Regulations, the Commissioner was entitled to refer the application for review to the Appeal Board. Since the matter was properly before the board, it was bound to decide it, and had no jurisdiction to refer it to anyone else. The respondents appealed against so much of the High Court order as quashed the decision of the unsworn inquiry. **Held** by the Supreme Court (Henchy J., Kenny and Parke JJ. concurring) in allowing the appeal, 1, the findings of the inquiry rested on facts which the appellant never sought to controvert. Since

GARDA SÍOCHÁNA—*continued.*

the correct procedure was adopted, and the facts were not in dispute, the said findings cannot be successfully impugned. 2. The jurisdictional error which occurred at the appeal stage cannot reasonably be held to invalidate what had gone before. *The State (Sheehan)* v. *McMahon*

(H.C., S.C.) [1976-7] ILRM 305

3. —— **Fatal injury** — *Compensation — Member of Garda Síochána fatally injured in the course of his duty — Dependents' claim for compensation — Assessment — Whether court should take into consideration the value of the pension and gratuity payable to dependents by reason of the death of the deceased in the course of his duty, from an unlawful act — Garda Síochána (Compensation) Act,* 1941 (*No.* 19), *ss.* 9, 10 — *Garda Síochána (Compensation) (Amendment) Act,* 1945 (*No.* 1), *s.* 2.] Section 10, sub-s. 3 of the Garda Síochána (Compensation) Act, 1941, provides *inter alia* that a judge of the High Court in fixing the sum to be awarded as compensation, shall take into consideration the fact that the applicant is entitled to a pension or gratuity out of public funds by reason of the death of the deceased. In contrast, s. 10, sub-s. 1(*a*), of that Act (as inserted by the Act of 1945) provides that a judge in assessing the amount of compensation payable, shall not take into account any property to which the applicant has become entitled by reason of the death of the deceased. The plaintiffs were the widow and children of a garda fatally injured in the course of his duty. At the hearing in the High Court of the plaintiffs' claim for compensation under the Garda Síochána (Compensation) Acts, 1941-1945, the defendant submitted that the full value of the pension and gratuities payable to the widow and children of the deceased should be deducted from the amount of compensation payable to the plaintiffs. The plaintiffs contended that the only sum which should be deducted was the difference between the ordinary pension payable under the contributory pension scheme and the special pension payable by reason of the death of the deceased from a non-accidental injury. The President stated a case for the determination by the Supreme Court of that question of law. **Held** by the Supreme Court (Henchy, Griffin, McCarthy JJ.), 1, that no part of the value of the special pension and allowances was to be taken into account in fixing the amount of the compensation. 2. That even if there is a lack of congruity between the two statutory provisions, s. 10, sub-s. 1(*a*), should prevail as it represented the later thinking of the Oireachtas. *McLoughlin* v. *Minister for the Public Service*

(S.C.) [1985] I.R. 631; [1986] ILRM 28

4. —— **Personal injuries** — *Maliciously*

GARDA SÍOCHÁNA—*continued.*

inflicted — Discharge from force as result of injuries — Special pension awarded on discharge — Claim for compensation — Assessment — Principles applicable — Future economic loss — Mitigation of loss by award of pension — Whether value of pension to be deducted from value of future economic loss proved — Garda Síochána (Compensation) Act, 1941 (*No.* 19), *s.* 10(2), (3) — *Garda Síochána (Compensation) (Amendment) Act,* 1945 (*No.* 1), *s.* 2(2).] The Garda Síochána (Compensation) Acts, 1941-1945, provide, *inter alia,* for the granting of compensation out of public monies to members of the Garda Síochána on whom personal injuries have been maliciously inflicted. By s. 10, sub-s. 2 of the Act of 1941, the court, in fixing compensation under the Act: "(*a*) shall have regard to any medical or surgical expenses incurred or likely to be incurred by the applicant in respect or in consequence of the injuries, and (*b*) shall take into consideration the detrimental effect which the injuries might reasonably be expected to have on the future earning power generally of the applicant and, in particular (if the injuries do not preclude the applicant from continuing to be a member of the Garda Síochána), on his future career in that force, and (*c*) shall have regard to the pain and suffering caused by the injuries to the applicant and also, in a proper case, to any disease or tendency to disease caused by the injuries." By s. 10, sub-s. 3, para (*a*) of the Act of 1941, the court, in fixing the amount of compensation payable under the Act, "shall take into consideration the fact, if it is a fact, that the applicant is entitled . . . to a pension, allowance, or gratuity out of public funds in respect of the . . . injuries which is or are the subject of the application, but shall not regard the amount of such pension, allowance, or gratuity (if any) as a measure or standard by reference to which the amount of the compensation is to be fixed." The applicant applied to the High Court, pursuant to the provisions of the Acts of 1941-1945, for compensation for personal injuries maliciously inflicted on him in the course of the performance of his duties as a member of the Garda Síochána. As a result of his injuries he had been discharged from the force and had been awarded a special pension. It was argued in the High Court on behalf of the respondent that the court should take into consideration, by way of deduction from the actuarial calculation of the loss of salary, an actuarial calculation of the value of the special pension being paid to the applicant, as not to do so would be to compensate the applicant twice for the financial loss which he would incur in the future. The High Court (Hamilton P.) stated a case for the opinion of the Supreme Court on the question whether, in assessing compensation payable in respect of

GARDA SÍOCHÁNA—*continued.*

financial loss, the court should have regard to the special pension payable to the applicant, and deduct the value of the same from the value of the loss proved. **Held** by the Supreme Court (Walsh J., Henchy, Griffin and Hederman JJ. concurring; McCarthy J. dissenting), that, since payment to the applicant of a special pension as from the date of his discharge reduced the economic loss which he would suffer in respect of future earning capacity, the value of that pension should be deducted from the value of the economic loss proved. *O'Looney* v. *Minister for the Public Service*

(S.C.) [1986] I.R. 543

5. —— **Promotion** — *Proposed changes in system of promotion — "Vertical" and "horizontal" promotions — Powers of Garda Commissioner — Powers of Minister for Justice — Rights of members of Garda Representative Association and Association of Garda Sergeants and Inspectors — Limitations of ranks within the Garda Síochána — Right of freedom of association for members of Garda Síochána — Limitations on extent to which members of the force may organise — Garda Síochána Act,* 1977 (*No.* 24), *s.* 1 — *Constitution of Ireland,* 1937, *Art.* 40.6.1(iii) — *Garda Síochána (Promotion) Regulations,* 1960 (*S.I. No.* 203), *regs.* 5, 8, 9, 10 — *Garda Síochána (Promotion) Regulations,* 1962 (*S.I. No.* 97).] The case originated in a dispute concerning proposed changes in the system of promotion in the Garda Síochána. Promotion to sergeant, station sergeant and inspector were governed by the Garda Síochána (Promotion) Regulations, 1960, as amended in 1962. Regulation 5 provided that promotion to sergeant was by passing examinations, unless exempted or by showing special zeal and ability on duty, better known as 'special promotion.' Promotion to station sergeant and inspector (Regs. 8, 9, 10) was also by examination, unless exempted, or by giving consistently meritorious service to the detective branch and showing special zeal in his duties — also known as 'special promotion.' In 1979 the Ryan Report, commissioned by the Government to examine, *inter alia,* the system of promotions in the force, found that 'special promotions' bred mistrust and jealousy and eroded confidence in the procedures, and recommended instead a single system supervised by a promotions board. A working party on the report, on which the Garda Representative Association and the Association of Garda Sergeants and Inspectors were represented, recommended further that on promotion all Gardaí should spend at least one year in uniform before being allocated to specialised duties, with some exceptions in highly technical areas. The effect of this would be to end 'vertical' promotions, under which a detective

GARDA SÍOCHÁNA—*continued.*

garda could make his way to inspector without leaving the detective branch, and replace it with a 'horizontal' system under which a detective garda would have to leave the detective branch for at least a year to go back into uniform. The plaintiffs claimed this was an unnecessary break in their careers and placed them at a disadvantage for further promotion because they had to compete with members who had more experience in the uniformed branch; that they were not adequately represented by their associations or properly consulted, and when they sought to form a new association to represent the detective branch, permission was refused by the Garda Commissioner under s. 13 of the Garda Síochána Act, 1924 (as inserted by the Garda Síochána Act, 1977). The plaintiffs asked the court to make permanent an interlocutory injunction to restrain the Garda Commissioner from making promotions under the proposed new system. They sought a declaration that s. 13 of the 1924 Act was invalid having regard to the Constitution, and other ancillary relief. **Held** by Barrington J. dismissing the applications, 1, the plaintiffs had an adequate opportunity to influence the policies of the respective associations in relation to promotion; no effort was made by those associations to disguise from them what was going on. 2. The Garda Síochána Act, 1972, provides for ten separate ranks in the force but there is no rank of detective garda or detective sergeant. 3. S. 13 of the Garda Síochána Act, 1924 (as inserted by s. 1 of the Garda Síochána Act, 1977) authorised the establishment of one association for all ranks below that of sergeant, or a number of associations for one or more of those ranks, but not for more than one association for any particular rank. 4. The right of association in Article 40.6.1°(iii) of the Constitution is 'subject to public order' and because of their close connection with the security of the State, Gardaí may have to accept limitations on their right to form associations and unions which other citizens would not have to accept. *Aughey* v. *Ireland*

(H.C.) [1986] ILRM 206

—— Communications between members — Admissibility as evidence — Claim of privilege — Whether admission would be against the public interest.
see **Evidence,** 1

—— Detention of person in custody — Legal advice — Whether detained person has constitutional right of access to solicitor — Duty to observe fair procedures.
see **Criminal Law,** 17

—— Discipline — Inquiry — Discontinuance — Garda Commissioner directing that a new inquiry be held into same allegations — Certiorari — Whether appointment of new board of inquiry be quashed.
see **Judicial Review,** 3

—— Dismissal — Garda — Probationer — Natural justice — Dismissal for not being likely to become efficient and well-conducted guard — Previous breaches of discipline as basis for dismissal — Pending enquiry into breach of discipline discontinued — Whether dismissal *ultra vires.*
see **Natural and Constitutional Justice,** 1

—— Dismissal — Natural justice — Summary dismissal — Absence of formal inquiry — Limitations of rules of natural justice in context of certain State services — Acquittal of dismissed Garda at trial on charge of assault on suspect — Counsel for dismissed Garda seeking admission that witness at trial committed the assault — Absence of such allegation in statement of dismissed Garda — Dismissal by Commissioner on ground that statement contained falsehood or prevarication — Opportunity given to advance reasons against dismissal.
see **Employer and Employee,** 7

—— Employment — Discipline — Commissioner of Garda Síochána purportedly dismissed by Government — Government purporting to appoint successor — Declaration by High Court that purported dismissal invalid — Purported commissioner directing sworn enquiry into allegations of breach of discipline against plaintiff — Enquiry conceded to have been a nullity — Duty of purported commissioner to avoid putting plaintiff to unnecessary expense — Whether plaintiff entitled to recover legal costs and expenses of attending and being represented at enquiry.
see **Constitution,** 11

—— Investigation of crime.
see **Criminal Investigation**

—— Powers — Search warrant — Gaming and lottery offences — Licensed premises — Whether Gardaí trespassers in absence of search warrant — Objection to their evidence — Evidence admissible — Court's discretion to exclude

GARDA SÍOCHÁNA—*continued.*

it — Balancing of public interests — Relevant factors to be considered.
see **Criminal Law,** 16

—— Station bail — District Court Rules empowering Gardaí to allow arrested persons station bail for up to 30 days — Powers of District Court Rules Committee — Whether purported rule *ultra vires* — Validity of procedure.
see **Criminal Law,** 36

GARNISHEE

—— **Attachment of debts** — *Garnishee — Judgment creditor — Judgment debtor obtaining bank loan on foot of solicitor's undertaking to discharge loan out of monies due to judgment debtor on foot of judgment — Judgment creditor seeking attachment of said judgment — Whether undertaking gave rise to equitable assignment or charge in favour of the bank — Whether bank had priority over judgment creditor — Whether solicitor's lien for costs had priority over judgment creditor.*

Solicitor — Undertaking — Effect — Solicitor undertaking to pay proceeds of judgment to bank — Judgment creditor seeking to attach proceeds — Whether undertaking created equitable assignment of proceeds of judgment — Whether bank entitled to priority over judgment creditor.

Solicitor — Costs — Lien — Solicitor claiming against proceeds of judgment for costs — Judgment creditor obtaining conditional order of garnishee against proceeds — Judgment creditor applying for absolute order before solicitor had applied for charging order — Whether solicitor entitled to priority over judgment creditor.] The plaintiff obtained judgment in the High Court on foot of a hire purchase agreement against the first defendant who had supplied certain goods the subject matter of the said agreement. The judgment for £24,000 was stayed on condition that the first defendant paid the sum in two instalments of £12,000 by specified dates. In the same action the second defendant, who was the hire purchase company, succeeded in its counterclaim against the plaintiff in the sum of £18,000. This judgment was stayed on condition that monthly instalments were paid by the plaintiff. The plaintiff defaulted in the said payments and the second defendant entered judgment against the plaintiff and obtained a conditional order of garnishee to attach the £12,000 still owing by the first defendant to the plaintiff. The plaintiff resisted the second defendant's application to make the conditional order of garnishee absolute on the grounds that he had negotiated a loan from his bank on an undertaking from his solicitor to discharge his liability to the bank out of the

GARNISHEE—*continued.*

monies due to the plaintiff from the first defendant. The plaintiff argued that the effect of this arrangement was to create an equitable assignment or charge in favour of the bank, giving the bank priority over the second defendant as judgment creditor. In addition, the plaintiff's solicitor claimed that an agreement with the plaintiff to discharge his costs out of the monies due from the first defendant took priority over the claim of the second defendant as judgment creditor. **Held** by O'Hanlon J., in making the conditional order absolute subject to the bank's claim, 1, that in order to give the bank's claim priority over that of the judgment creditor, the plaintiff had to prove a specific agreement with the bank that his liability to the bank would be discharged out of a particular fund. In the circumstances, the arrangement was sufficient to give rise to an equitable assignment in favour of the bank of that part of the funds referred to in the correspondence creating the agreement. *Field* v. *Megaw* (1869) L.R. 4 C.P. 660 and *F.B. Warren, In Re A.M. Wheeler* v. *The Trustee in Bankruptcy* [1938] 1 Ch. 725 followed. 2. That a solicitor's lien for costs gives a solicitor the right to go to court to have property charged in his favour. In the absence of an application for a charging order made before the hearing of the application to have a conditional order of garnishee made absolute, the claim of the judgment creditor under the garnishee order takes priority over the solicitor's claim for costs. *James Bibby Ltd.* v. *Woods and Howard* [1949] 2 K.B. 449 followed. 3. That, accordingly, the conditional order of garnishee should be made absolute in favour of the second defendant as against so much of the sum due and owing by the first defendant to the plaintiff remaining after satisfaction of the claim of the bank. *Fitzpatrick* v. *DAF Sales Ltd.*

(H.C.) [1988] I.R. 464

GIFT

—— Charity — Cy-près.
see **Charities,** 1-3

—— Will — Construction of will.
see **Succession,** 12-17

GIFT TAX — Relief — Nephew or niece — Gift of farm to niece — Whether niece worked substantially full time on the farm.
see **Revenue,** 5

GOOD ESTATE MANAGEMENT — Lease of retail unit — Restrictive covenant as to user — Refusal of landlord to consent to change of user.
see **Landlord and Tenant,** 4, 5

H

HABEAS CORPUS
see also **Constitution,** 15-17

—— **Remand in custody** — *Delay in committal proceedings — Applicant charged on basis of information given by accomplice — Applicant remanded in custody — No committal proceedings — Ten months since first remand — Whether evidence against the application — Whether delay in committal proceedings unreasonable — Whether Court has jurisdiction to issue writ — Whether mandamus appropriate remedy — Observations on delay in holding committal proceedings.*] The applicant was arrested on 15 March, 1984, and on 21 March, 1984, he was charged with murder. The applicant denied the charge. On 22 March, 1984, the applicant was ordered by a magistrate to be remanded in custody to the Crumlin Road prison from week to week until the date of this hearing in January, 1985, when he applied for a writ of habeas corpus. He had previously been refused bail by a High Court Judge on 19 April, 1984. On that occasion the Crown revealed that the evidence against the applicant would be the evidence of an accomplice. On 26 November the Crown revealed that no direction to prosecute the applicant would issue until after the trial of the accomplice. No witness statement had been taken from the accomplice. The applicant argued that there was no evidence against him and that the delay in holding committal proceedings was unreasonable. **Held,** refusing the application, that, 1, the written statement under caution made by the accomplice and his replies to police questions constituted evidence against the applicant which justified his arrest and remands in custody. 2. In view of the great volume of terrorist crime and the particular circumstances of this case, the delay in holding committal proceedings was not unreasonable. 3. The court has no jurisdiction to issue a writ of habeas corpus to overrule the decision of a magistrate made within jurisdiction that there was evidence against an accused which justified his being remanded in custody. This is so even if the court found that there was no evidence against the applicant which justified his remand in custody. 4. The decision whether to adjourn the proceedings and remand the accused in custody or to hold the committal proceedings is always a matter for the discretion of the magistrate, which discretion must be exercised judicially and for a proper purpose. If, however, the magistrate, in the exercise of his discretion, continued to remand the accused in custody from week to week without taking steps to fix a date for the committal hearing, then the appropriate remedy was to apply to the court for an order of mandamus directing that a committal hearing take place, rather than seeking a writ of habeas corpus. *Per curiam.* Delay in holding committal proceedings is not a proper ground for an application to the High Court for bail. *In re McAleenan*

(Q.B.D.) [1985] N.I.496

—— Constitution — Alien — Refusal of leave to stay in the State — Discretion of immigration officer — Refusal based on absence of visa and language deficiency — Whether discretion improperly exercised.
see **Aliens,** 4

—— Constitution — Alien — Refusal of leave to land — Procedures specified by Constitution.
see **Aliens,** 3

—— Detention — Grounds — Certificate — Special Criminal Court — Appointment and composition — Conviction — Whether detention vitiated by events prior to charge of applicant.
see **Special Criminal Court**

—— Extradition — U.S.A. — Murder — Drug dealing — Committal warrant — Applicant arrested and imprisoned — Lawful imprisonment.
see **Constitution,** 24

—— Infant — Custody — English court ordering that infant be placed in care of county council — Father removing infant from jurisdiction — Council seeking order of habeas corpus — Legality of infant's detention.
see **Family Law,** 1

—— Inquiry under Constitution.
see **Constitution,** 15-17

—— *Locus standi* — Whether remedy available to non-citizens.
see **Aliens,** 4

HARBOURS AND PIERS

—— Harbour Commissioners — Pier vested in Commissioners — Powers — Duty to maintain pier — Power to make byelaws — Restriction on user of pier — Whether harbour master empowered to restrict user permanently — Whether Commissioners in breach of statutory duty.
see **Statute,** 3

HARBOURS AND PIERS—*continued.*

—— Harbour dues — Summons — Service out of jurisdiction.
see **Practice and Procedure,** 51

HEALTH AND SAFETY

see also **Accidents; Health Services; Medical Practitioner; Medical Negligence; Mental Treatment; Public Health**

—— Asbestos waste — Whether injurious to health — Planning appeal — Whether oral hearing required.
see **Constitution,** 20

—— Family planning — Unlawful sale of contraceptives — Authority to enter premises — Whether in force — Whether evidence obtained without warrant admissible.
see **Criminal Law,** 15

—— Fire prevention — Fire safety notices — Terms.
see **Fire Services**

—— Health and safety at work.
see **Negligence,** 6-10, 18

HEALTH SERVICES

see **also Medical Practitioner; Medical Negligence; Mental Treatment; Social Welfare**

1. —— **County home** — *Institution similar thereto — Voluntary patient — Chargeability of services involved — Whether inmates receiving more than shelter and maintenance — Mental Treatment Act,* 1945 (*No.* 19), *s.* 158 — *Health Act,* 1947 (*No.* 28), *s.* 2 — *Health Act,* 1953 (*No.* 26), *ss.* 6, 54 — *Health Act,* 1970 (*No.* 1), *ss.* 3, 51.] S. 54 of the Health Act, 1953, defines 'institutional assistance' as 'shelter and maintenance in a county home or similar institution.' S. 51 of the Health Act, 1970, defines 'in-patient servies' as 'institutional services provided for persons while maintained in a hospital, convalescent home or home for persons suffering from physical or mental disability. . . .' In 1956, by ministerial direction, the former Crooksling Sanatorium became a home for the nursing care of senile patients from Grangegorman Mental Hospital who could not be discharged because they had no relatives. In pursuance of this arrangement, the ward in the instant case was transferred to Crooksling, where she was certified by the medical officer to require 'continual accommodation and nursing care in a geriatric

HEALTH SERVICES—*continued.*

institution.' The appellants (the Eastern Health Board) claimed that it had been wrongly decided in the High Court that the ward was receiving in-patient services in Crooksling. **Held** by the Supreme Court (Henchy J., Griffin and Kenny JJ. concurring) in dismissing the appeal, the ward receives nursing care requisite for a patient of her age and state of health, and this goes beyond the range of mere shelter and maintenance, and amounts to the provision of in-patient services. *In re McInerney*

(H.C.) [1976-7] ILRM 229

2. —— **Hospital** — *Discontinuance of services — Minister directing health board to discontinue certain in-patient services in particular hospital — Whether decision* ultra vires — *Whether discontinuance of service amounted to direction relating to the arrangements for providing services in a hospital — Health Act, 1970 (No.* 1), *s.* 38.] The Minister for Health issued a direction to the North Eastern Health Board to discontinue the provision of in-patient gynaecological services in a hospital within the board's area. The direction was made in purported compliance with the provisions of s. 38 (2) of the Health Act, 1970, which provides that the Minister 'may give to a health board such direction as he thinks fit in relation to the provision or maintenance of any premises provided and maintained [by the board] and in relation to the arrangements for providing services therein, and the health board shall comply with any such direction.' The plaintiffs were residents of the area in which the hospital was situated and they challenged the validity of the direction issued by the Minister. The High Court determined that the Minister had acted *intra vires* in making the direction. On appeal by the plaintiffs: **Held** by the Supreme Court (O'Higgins C.J., Griffin and Hederman JJ.) in allowing the appeal: while the provisions of s. 38 of the 1970 Act extended to a hospital, as here, which was in existence prior to the coming into force of the Act, the words allowing the Minister to make directions concerning 'arrangements for providing services' in hospitals contemplated positive action and not the cessation or the discontinuance of what was being done, and therefore the Minister has acted *ultra vires* the powers conferred on him by s. 38 (2). *Semble:* the Minister would have been entitled, after holding a local inquiry, to have directed the closure of the entire hospital pursuant to s. 38 (3). *McMeel* v. *Minister for Health*

(S.C.) [1985] ILRM 616

—— Free health services — Eligibility — Victims of road accidents excluded by Ministerial order — Such exclusions not

HEALTH SERVICES—*continued.*

stated in statute as being part of its policy — *Ultra vires.*
see **Constitution,** 34
Damages, 9

—— Health board — Employee — Personal injuries — Home help employed in the community — Defective condition of patient's house — Home help injured in patient's house — Responsibility of health board.
see **Negligence,** 10

—— Health board — Employees — Salary — Increments — Minister refusing approval.
see **Employer and Employee,** 6

—— Health board — Infant — Custody — Court order committing infant to care of health board — Whether health board had capacity to take infant.
see **Practice and Procedure,** 14

—— Hospital — Discontinuance of services — Minister directing health board to discontinue certain in-patient services in particular hospital — Whether decision *ultra vires.*
see **Health Services,** 2

—— Hospital — Duty of care — Standard of care — In-patient subject to epileptic fits and automatism — Fall from window in toilet room — Standards of nursing or custodial care — Whether injury foreseeable — Whether hospital in breach of duty.
see **Negligence,** 14

—— Hospital — Private hospital — Public funds — Discontinuance — Executive decision — Legality.
see **Statute,** 2

HEARSAY EVIDENCE — Admissibility.
see **Criminal Law,** 13, 14

HIGH COURT

—— **Jurisdiction** — *Appeal — Ministerial order — Person aggrieved — Scope of court's appellate jurisdiction — Minister purporting to protect fisheries of the State — Order removing prohibition against use of drift nets for taking salmon — Order annulled — Fisheries (Consolidation) Act,* 1959 (*No.* 14), *ss.* 8, 9, 11.] Section 9 of the Act of 1959 confers on the Minister for Fisheries and Forestry power to

HIGH COURT—*continued.*

make such bye-laws as are in his opinion expedient "for the more effectual government, management, protection and improvement of the fisheries of the State." Section 8 of the Act states that the Minister may cause an inquiry to be held in any fishery district in relation to the fisheries therein and "the best means to be adopted for the regulation, improvement or protection thereof." The respondent Minister caused an inquiry to be held by a senior inspector of his department concerning salmon fishing off the coast of the county of Kerry, with particular reference to the justification for certain bye-laws, made in the year 1913, which prohibited taking salmon with drift nets in the tidal waters of a specified area off that coast. In his report to the respondent Minister, the senior inspector who had conducted the inquiry strongly advised the respondent against revoking the said bye-laws which prohibited salmon fishing with drift nets in that area. Nevertheless, on the 3 June, 1981, the respondent made an order pursuant to s. 9 of the Act of 1959 revoking the said bye-laws and thus removing the prohibition against such fishing in most of the Kerry District Fishery. The appellants, claiming to be persons aggrieved by the effect of the respondent's revocation order, appealed to the High Court against that order and claimed an order pursuant to s. 11 of the Act of 1959 annulling the revocation order. At the hearing of the appeal the respondent refused to admit the report of the senior inspector and the judge then allowed the appellants to call the inspector to give evidence; in his oral evidence the inspector proved his report and two memoranda which he had also furnished to the respondent before the revocation order was made. The appellants gave evidence in support of their claims to be persons aggrieved. **Held** by Costello J., in allowing the appeal, 1, that s. 11 of the Act of 1959 conferred jurisdiction on the court to determine the appeal on the merits. *Dodd* v. *Minister for Fisheries* [1934] I.R. 291; *Carltona Ltd.* v. *Commissioners of Works* [1943] 2 All E.R. 560 and *Minister of National Revenue* v. *Wrights' Canadian Ropes Ltd.* [1947] A.C. 109 considered. 2. That the issue raised by the appeal was whether the terms of the respondent's revocation order were expedient for "the more effectual government, management, protection and improvement of the fisheries of the State." 3. That the court would normally determine that issue upon the evidence and other relevant material which had been available to the respondent when he made the revocation order. 4. That the court would have regard to the probable consequences of the revocation order, including its effect upon fishery areas outside the area immediately affected by its provisions. 5. That, contrary to the averment in the affidavit filed on

HIGH COURT—*continued.*

behalf of the respondent, there had been no "volume of expert technical advice" available to the respondent before he made the revocation order, apart from the report and advice of his senior inspector; and that the suggestion in that affidavit that the opinion formed by the respondent had been supported by expert technical advice was contrary to the fact. 6. That the overwhelming weight of the scientific evidence led to the conclusion that the revocation order was not expedient for the more effectual government, management, protection and improvement of the fisheries of the State; and that, accordingly, that bye-law should be annulled. 7. That the appellants were persons aggrieved, within the meaning of that term in s. 11 of the Act of 1959, by the revocation order. *Dunne* v. *Minister for Fisheries and Forestry*
(H.C.) [1984] I.R. 230

—— Jurisdiction — Action — Transfer — Transfer to Circuit Court — Whether power of transfer inconsistent with provisions of Constitution.
see **Constitution,** 33

—— Jurisdiction — Case stated by Appeal Commissioners — Interest — Award — Whether court had jurisdiction to order payment of interest.
see **Revenue,** 39

—— Jurisdiction — Case stated — Revenue appeal — Point of law — Principles applicable — Finding of fact by Circuit Court — Inferences drawn from facts — Jurisdiction of High Court — Function of High Court in hearing revenue cases stated.
see **Revenue,** 3

—— Jurisdiction — Constitution — Statute — Validity — "Full" original jurisdiction — Statute effectively barring High Court action on basis akin to issue estoppel — Whether provision valid.
see **Practice and Procedure,** 42

—— Jurisdiction — Limitations — Absence — Enactments conferring jurisdiction on Circuit Court and District Court — Jurisdiction of High Court not ousted.
see **Constitution,** 4

—— Jurisdiction — Limits — Constitution — Courts of limited jurisdiction — Enactment conferring jurisdiction in respect of specified subject — Criminal law — Trial — Venue — Indictable offence — Accused sent forward for trial in Circuit Court — Accused formerly entitled to obtain order transferring trial to High Court — Abolition of that right — Whether lawful exclusion of High Court jurisdiction.
see **Constitution,** 32

—— Jurisdiction — Limits — Practice direction — Enactments conferring jurisdiction on Circuit Court and District Court — Concurrent jurisdiction vested in the High Court by the Constitution — Whether High Court may decline to exercise its jurisdiction — Whether discretion to decline jurisdiction derives from the Rules of the Superior Courts 1962.
see **Constitution,** 5

—— Jurisdiction — Planning enforcement — s. 27 applications.
see **Planning,** 22, 23

—— Jurisdiction — Wards of court — Whether possession of property a condition precedent to exercise of wardship jurisdiction.
see **Mental Treatment**

—— Practice — Constitutional issue — Attorney General — Function — Requirement by rules of court that Attorney General be notified of challenge to validity of law — Whether requirement extended to challenge to validity of pre-1937 statute — Whether court would consider issue in the absence of notification.
see **Practice and Procedure,** 14

HIGHWAY — Authority — Duty of care.
see **Negligence,** 11, 12

HIRE PURCHASE

—— **Hire purchase agreement** — *Vendor in breach of contract — Action for damages against vendor and finance company — No privity of contract between plaintiff and finance company — Whether action against finance company be dismissed.*] The plaintiff averred that, by an agreement made on 16 January, 1978, between himself and the defendants, he bought a motor lorry for £4,500. He also averred that, at or before the making of the agreement, the defendants and each of them expressly warranted and represented to him that the lorry was a 1971 lorry and the same was a term of the agreement. Alternatively he alleged that the first named defendant, in so warranting and representing, was acting as the servant or agent of the second

HIRE PURCHASE—*continued.*

named defendant. The plaintiff also averred that it was an implied term of the agreement that the lorry was not subject to any other charges and liabilities and, in particular, that no sum was then due to the Revenue Commissioners for customs and excise duties in respect of the lorry. The plaintiff then averred that, in breach of the agreement, the lorry was not a 1971 lorry as stated in the Hire Purchase Agreement between the defendants and that there was a sum of money due for customs to the Revenue Commissioners in respect thereof which the defendants knew, or ought to have known, and which they wrongfully failed to disclose to the plaintiff at or before the making of the agreement. He claimed rescission of the agreement and damages for breach of contract and fraud. The defendants denied the various averments. At the end of the plaintiff's case counsel for the second named defendant applied for a direction that the court should dismiss the action against the said defendant at that stage as there was no privity of contract between it and the plaintiff. **Held** In dismissing the action against the second named defendant, the second named defendant could have no authority or title to sell the lorry to the plaintiff on the day when the property passed to him. While that defendant was the legal owner of the lorry prior to the sale to the plaintiff the first named defendant was the hire-purchaser with an entitlement to become the owner by complying with the provisions of his agreement with the second named defendant. The first named defendant did this with the aid of funds provided by the plaintiff. When his title to the lorry was thus perfected the first named defendant completed his agreement to sell and deliver the lorry to the plaintiff. Accordingly there was no privity of contract between the plaintiff and the second named defendant. *Halpin* v. *Rothwell*
(H.C.) [1984] ILRM 613

HISTORIC MONUMENT
see **National Monument**

HOMOSEXUALITY — Legislation — Validity — Offences against the Person Act.
see **Constitution,** 39

HOSPITAL
see under **Health Services**

HOTEL

—— Intoxicating liquor licence — Renewal — Premises licensed as a hotel after 1960 — Premises having been previously licensed as a hotel — Obligation to register premises as a hotel with Bord Failte Eireann — Premises not so registered — Objection by garda to renewal

HOTEL—*continued.*

of licence — Licence having previously been renewed without objection — Nature of obligation to register premises as a hotel — Whether objector precluded by previous renewals from relying on non-registration.
see **Licensing Acts,** 12

—— Valuation — Annual value — Calculation — Decrease in profitability.
see **Rating and Valuation,** 2

HOUSING
see also **Builder; Building Contract; Defective Premises; Dwelling; Family Home; Planning**

1. —— **House** — *Change of user — Permission refused — Applicant aggrieved — Remedy — Declaratory order — Applicant seeking declaration that refusal of housing authority void — Discretion of court — Alternative appellate procedure available to applicant — Declaration refused — Housing Act,* 1969 (*No.* 16), *ss.* 4, 10.] On the 3 June, 1975, the plaintiff applied pursuant to ss. 2 and 3 of the Housing Act, 1969, to the defendant housing authority for permission to use her house at No. 30 Dartmouth Square, Dublin, otherwise than for human habitation; she wanted to use her house as offices for the purposes of her husband's practice as an architect. She stated that, if she obtained such permission, she would erect a mews residence at the rear of her house and that she would thus provide residential accommodation in excess of that which would be displaced by the change in the use of her house. On the 1 July, 1975, the defendants refused to give such permission on the ground that "such change of use would result in a reduction in the supply of housing in the functional area of the Corporation." The plaintiff did not appeal to the Minister for Local Government against that refusal pursuant to s. 4, sub-s. 6(*a*), of the Act of 1969 but she claimed in the High Court declarations that the grounds for the refusal were contrary to the facts and that the refusal was unreasonable and contrary to natural justice; she also claimed an order setting aside the refusal and a declaration that permission was deemed to have been given to her by the expiry of five weeks from the 3 June, 1975, and by the provisions of s. 4, sub-s. 5, of the Act of 1969. At the trial of her action the judge dismissed her claims. On appeal by the plaintiff it was **Held** by the Supreme Court (O'Higgins C.J., Hederman and McCarthy JJ.), in disallowing the appeal, 1, that the declarations sought by the plaintiff were discretionary remedies which the court would grant only in appropriate circumstances. 2. That, even if the defendants' refusal had been invalid, the court would not make an order declaring that invalidity

HOUSING—*continued.*

at the suit of a party who (*a*) had not chosen to avail of the statutory appellate procedure provided for persons aggrieved by such refusals and (*b*) would acquire, by means of such declaration, default permissions under the Housing Act, 1969, and under the Local Government (Planning and Development) Act, 1963. *Creedon* v. *Dublin Corporation*

(S.C.) [1984] I.R.428

2. —— **Housing authority** — *Allocation of houses to person residing outside housing authority's functional area — Whether authority acting* ultra vires — *Housing Act,* 1966 (*No.* 21), *ss.* 53, 60, 109.] Under s. 53 of the Housing Act, 1966, each housing authority has a duty to inspect houses in their functional area and ascertain to what extent there are houses unfit for human habitation in the area. They must then assess the adequacy of the supply of houses and the supply of housing and must prepare and adopt a programme setting out the work they propose having regard to the housing needs of their functional area. By virtue of s. 60 the housing authority is required to make the scheme determining the priority to be accorded to categories of persons specified under the scheme. Under sub-s. (2) the housing authority has power to review the scheme. Buncrana U.D.C. adopted a scheme on 10 September, 1969, and by resolution dated 18 September, 1978, they eliminated condition 3 of that scheme which provided as follows: 'No preference shall be given to any person who has not been resident in the town for a period of less than two years.' The deletion was to take effect from 1 September, 1979. When Buncrana U.D.C. proposed to provide housing for applicants residing outside its functional area the plaintiff sought an order declaring that the respondents were acting *ultra vires.* In his replying affidavit the county manager for Donegal stated he was obliged to house applicants residing outside of the functional area and relied on a ruling of the Chief Justice in the case of *McDonald* v. *Feeley and Dublin County Council* (Unreported, Supreme Court 23 July, 1980), and which formed the basis of a directive from the Minister for the Environment that housing authorities were obliged to house applicants residing outside their functional area. In the High Court it was held by Carroll J. that the defendants' contention was based on a misapprehension of the judgment of the Supreme Court, and that the housing authority was not entitled to house persons residing outside its functional area. The defendants appealed. **Held** by the Supreme Court (O'Higgins C.J., Griffin and McCarthy JJ.) in dismissing the appeal, 1, the appellants as housing authority are not entitled to house people who are not resident in their functional area. 2. The duty of the appellants is to allocate the houses which they have provided in accordance with its scheme of priorities enabling them to house suitable applicants who fit within the designated category who are domiciled within the functional area of the Council. *McNamee* v. *Buncrana Urban District Council*

(H.C., S.C.) [1984] ILRM 77

—— Compulsory acquisition of land.
see **Compulsory Acquisition,** 2, 5

—— Dwelling — Constitution — Inviolability.
see **Dwelling**

—— House — Defects in construction.
see **Defective Premises**

—— Housing authority — Duty of care — Statutory power of housing authority to make loans to persons of limited means to enable purchase of dwelling — Requirement that housing authority be satisfied as to value of house — Plaintiff applying for loan — House valued by valuer on behalf of housing authority — No structural inspection carried out by local authority — House valued at £25,000 — Loan granted to plaintiff — House seriously defective — Whether housing authority owed purchaser a common law duty of care in valuing house.
see **Negligence,** 2, 30

—— Rent — Private dwellings.
see **Landlord and Tenant,** 13-16

—— Termination of tenancy — Corporation flat — Notice to quit and Demand for Possession — District Court hearing — Tenant not represented — Tenant not invited to give evidence — Possession awarded to Corporation — Whether hearing in breach of natural justice.
see **Landlord and Tenant,** 17

HUMAN RIGHTS CONVENTION
see **Local Government,** 4

HUSBAND AND WIFE
see **Family Law**

—— Barring order.
see **Family Law,** 10

—— Child — Paternity — Dispute.
see **Family Law,** 4

—— Children — Custody.

I

ILLEGAL ORGANISATION

—— Aims and objectives — Attack upon Constitution and organs of State — Criteria for extradition.
see **Extradition,** 8

—— Member — Offence — Extradition — Political offence — Robbery — Motive — No evidence upon which trial judge could have held robbery instigated on behalf of I.R.A. or motivated by desire to assist I.R.A. — Burden of proof.
see **Extradition,** 7

—— Offence — Extradition — Offence committed to assist aims of organisation of which defendant was a member — Those aims including the setting aside of the Constitution by unconstitutional means — Political offence exception interpreted so as not to embrace offence facilitating such objective.
see **Extradition,** 6

—— Property rights — Suppression order — Forfeiture of organisation's property — Minister empowered to freeze monies in bank without notice to account-holder — Whether forfeiture and money freezing procedure unjust attack on property rights — Interest of the common good.
see **Constitution,** 48

—— Street and house-to-house collection — Refusal of permit — Chief Superintendent of opinion that proceeds would benefit illegal organisation — Constitutionality of legislation.
see **Constitution,** 29

ILLEGITIMATE CHILD
see also **Adoption**

—— Placement for adoption — Marriage of parents subsequent to placement — Consequent legitimisation — Parents seeking re-registration of child.
see **Adoption,** 2

—— Registration of birth — Paternity — Evidence admissible to prove paternity — Evidence of wife that child not the child of the marriage — Whether admissible — Rule in *Russell* v. *Russell* — Whether part of the common law of Ireland — Whether incompatible with the provisions of the Constitution — Obligations of the Registrar of Births and Deaths.
see **Family Law,** 4

—— Succession — Intestacy — Whether "issue" of intestate — Statute — Interpretation — Succession Act, 1965, ss. 67, 69.
see **Constitution,** 13

—— Unmarried mother's allowance — Entitlement.
see **Social Welfare,** 9

IMMIGRATION *see* **Aliens**

IMPLIED TERM — Contract.
see **Building Contract,** 4
Contract, 3, 6, 8, 10
Landlord and Tenant, 18
Sale of Goods, 1

IMPOTENCE
—— Nullity application.
see **Family Law,** 19-21

IMPRISONMENT
see **Arrest and Detention; False Imprisonment; Prisons; Sentence.**

INCOME TAX
see **Revenue,** 1, 27-41

INCORPORATED LAW SOCIETY — Compensation fund.
see **Solicitor,** 2

INDEMNITY INSURANCE
see **Insurance,** 3, 5, 6

INDUCEMENT OF BREACH OF CONTRACT
see **Contract,** 7
Employer and Employee, 1, 24
Injunction, 5

INDUSTRIAL AND PROVIDENT SOCIETIES

1. —— **Credit union** — *Amendment to rules — Registrar of Friendly Societies refusing to register such amendment — Whether Registrar so entitled — Function and jurisdiction of Registrar — Industrial and Provident Societies Act,* 1893 (*c.* 39), *s.* 10(3) — *Credit Union Act,* 1966 (*No.* 19), *ss.* 1, 2(3), 2(4), 3, 6, 13, 17, 27, 33, 35 — *Industrial and Provident Societies (Amendment) Act,* 1978 (*No.* 23).] The appellant appealed to the District Court against a decision of the respondent not to register an amendment to the rules of the appellant's Industrial and Provident Societies.

INDUSTRIAL AND PROVIDENT SOCIETIES *—continued.*

Roche D.J. stated a case to the High Court and raised a number of points on the interpretation of the Industrial and Provident Societies Acts, 1893-1978, and questioned particularly the extent of the Registrar of Friendly Societies' jurisdiction and function in relation to this decision to register or refuse to register any proposed amendments to the rules of the Credit Union. **Held** by Barrington J. in answering the first question in the affirmative: The sole function of the Registrar of Friendly Societies is to enquire whether or not a proposed amendment would result in the breach of the Industrial and Provident Societies Acts, 1893-1978, and where he is satisfied that no breach would occur he is under a mandatory duty to register the proposed amendment to the rules. *Prison Service Credit Union Ltd.* v. *Registrar of Friendly Societies* **(H.C.) [1987] ILRM 367**

2. —— **Winding up** — *Order for winding up of plaintiff society made by High Court — Winding up governed by Companies Act,* 1963, *Part VI — Effect of winding up order on property of plaintiff — Investigation of affairs of plaintiff by Registrar of Friendly Societies — Statutory power of Registrar to bring proceedings in name of society — Whether power affected by winding up order — Whether Registrar entitled to bring proceedings in name of plaintiff after winding up order without leave of the court — Companies Act,* 1963 (*No.* 33), *ss.* 170, 215, 229, 231 — *Industrial and Provident Societies (Amendment) Act,* 1978 (*No.* 23), *ss.* 11-17, 19.] The plaintiff was one of a number of industrial and provident societies and companies controlled by the first defendant. On the 27 February, 1985, on the plaintiff's own petition, an order was made for the winding up of the plaintiff. The official liquidator, having first obtained the leave of the court pursuant to s.231 of the Companies Act, 1963, commenced proceedings against several of the defendants in the instant proceedings for a declaration that the plaintiff and those defendants had carried on business as a single entity and for ancilliary relief with a view to preserving the defendants' assets. Those proceedings were compromised subject to the approval of the court. On the 3 February, 1985, the Registrar of Friendly Societies, who had for some time been dissatisfied with the management of the group's affairs, appointed an inspector pursuant to the provisions of the Industrial and Provident Societies (Amendment) Act, 1978, to investigate the affairs of the group. When the Registrar received the inspector's report he instituted these proceedings for a declaration that the defendants' assets were the property of the plaintiff, for damages and for injunctive relief similar to that

INDUSTRIAL AND PROVIDENT SOCIETIES *—continued.*

claimed in the liquidator's proceedings. The defendants brought a motion to have the instant proceedings dismissed and by agreement between the parties a preliminary legal issue was argued, *inter alia,* as to whether the Registrar had power to institute proceedings under s. 14, sub-s. 8 of the Act of 1978, notwithstanding that the society in whose name the proceedings were issued was in the course of being wound up by the court. It was argued on behalf of the defendants that since the plaintiff, by virtue of s. 19 of the Act of 1978, was to be wound up as if it was a company, no proceedings could be brought in its name once it was in liquidation otherwise than by leave of the court in accordance with s. 231 of the Act of 1963. It was argued on behalf of the Registrar that his power under s. 14, sub-s. 8 of the Act of 1978, was independent of whether or not the plaintiff was in liquidation; that s.231 of the Act of 1963 did not apply to him and that the instant proceedings differed from the liquidator's proceedings and were brought against different parties. **Held** by Barron J., in determining that the Registrar did not have power to institute the proceedings, 1, that the power given to the Registrar by s. 14, sub-s. 8 of the Act of 1978 to bring proceedings in the name of a society, could only be exercised in respect of a cause of action vested in a society. 2. That by s. 299 of the Act of 1963, which, by s. 19 of the Act of 1978 applied to the plaintiff, once the plaintiff went into liquidation the cause of action passed into the control of the liquidator who alone, with the sanction of the court, had authority to bring proceedings in the name of the plaintiff. 3. That, on construction of s. 14, sub-s. 8 of the Act of 1978, no new cause of action was created which was not available to the liquidator in similar circumstances. 4. That to construe s. 14, sub-s. 8 of the Act of 1978 otherwise than as being subordinated to the general provisions of the Act of 1963 could lead, in a case where the court had refused to sanction the commencement of proceedings and the Registrar had decided otherwise, to a situation where an administration officer would effectively be reversing a decision of the High Court. Such a construction would make the power invalid having regard to the provisions of the Constitution. *Costello* v. *Director of Public Prosecutions* [1984] I.R. 436, considered. On appeal by the Registrar it was **Held** by the Supreme Court (Finlay C.J., Hederman and McCarthy JJ.), in dismissing the appeal, 1, that the power contained in s. 14, sub-s. 8 of the Act of 1978, was purely procedural in nature. It enabled the Registrar to pursue certain causes of action which existed in a society in circumstances in which he

INDUSTRIAL AND PROVIDENT SOCIETIES *—continued.*

was satisfied that the society had not or was unwilling to institute the appropriate proceedings but it did not create any new cause of action. 2. That while the existence in s. 14, subs. 8 of the Act of 1978 of a right in the Minister for Industry and Commerce to indemnify the plaintiff against costs and expenses involved in proceedings instituted by the Registrar would, if exercised, be a factor in the propriety of instituting proceedings which would be absent in the case of a claim brought by the liquidator, this did not make the Registrar's proceedings fundamentally different; nor did it prevent the power being one which could be operated so as to reverse a decision of the court. 3. That subject only to the exceptions contained in s. 19 of the Act of 1978, the application of the provisions of Part VI of the Act of 1963, to the winding up of societies was clear and unconditional. To hold that the Registrar's power under s. 14, sub-s. 8 of the Act of 1978 survived a winding up order would be a fundamental alteration of the machinery of Part VI of the Act of 1963, which envisaged that every winding up by the court should be under the control and direction of the court. *Irish Commercial Society Ltd.* v. *Plunkett*
(H.C., S.C.) [1986] I.R.258

—— Insolvency — Minister of Government — Duty of care — Depositor lodging money with industrial and provident society — Society subsequently going into liquidation — Depositor receiving a dividend of only part of sum lodged — Whether Minister owed duty of care
see **Negligence,** 33

—— Shareholder — Property rights — Registered provident society engaged in the business of banking — Legislation enacted prohibiting such societies from accepting or holding deposits — Whether legislation invalid — Whether unjust attack on property rights of shareholders.
see **Constitution,** 46

INDUSTRIAL PROPERTY PROTECTION
see **Copyright; Patents; Trade Mark; Trade Names and Designs**

INDUSTRIAL RELATIONS
see **Employer and Employee**
Trade Union

—— Statutory minimum wage — Power of District Court to order payment of arrears — Whether payment of minimum wage a statutory condition of employment.
see **Case Stated,** 3

INDUSTRIAL TRAINING GRANTS — Corporation tax — Whether revenue or capital receipts.
see **Revenue,** 24

INDUSTRIAL TRIBUNAL
see **Employment Appeals Tribunal**
Labour Court

INDUSTRY
see **Trade and Industry**

INFANT
see also **Adoption; Illegitimate Child; Young Offender**

—— Children — Wards of court — Adoption — Consent — Refusal — Parents refused consent — Whether consent witheld unreasonably — Whether consent issue to be considered on application for leave.
see **Adoption,** 1

—— Custody — Guardianship
see **Adoption**
Family Law, 1-3

—— Custody — Infant placed for adoption — Subsequent marriage of natural parents legitimising infant — Whether parental right of education within the family to be considered in determining welfare of child in custody dispute.
see **Adoption,** 2

—— Custody — Protection — Court order committing infant to care of health board — Validity — Whether made in accordance with law — Whether health board had capacity to take infant in care.
see **Practice and Procedure,** 14

—— Illegitimate child
see **Illegitimate Child**

—— Paternity — Birth — Registration — Evidence of wife that child not the child of the marriage — Whether admissible — Rule in *Russell* v. *Russell* — Whether part of the common law of Ireland — Whether incompatible with the provisions of the Constitution.
see **Family Law,** 4

—— Personal injuries — Licensee — Roman Catholic church — Candelabra — Plaintiff lighting candle as devotional exercise — Plaintiff's clothing catching fire — Whether candelabra a concealed

INJUNCTION
INTERLOCUTORY

1. —— **Building contract** — *Action for specific performance — Balance of convenience — Whether prejudice likely to result — Sub-contractor — Nomination of alternative sub-contractor.*

Specific performance — Building contract — Whether specific performance lies — Whether contract requiring constant supervision by court — Whether basis for refusal of order in existence.] The plaintiff was a sub-contractor of the second-named defendant, who was the builder and main contractor of a large complex, of which the first-named defendant was the developer. The plaintiff tendered for the supply and installation of lifts in the complex, and the second-named defendant accepted the tender, subject to certain conditions, by letter dated 4 January, 1979. One of the conditions provided that a sub-contract agreement would be entered into in accordance with the terms of the main contract. Condition 16 of the main contract provided that a sub-contractor must agree to indemnify the main contractor against the same obligations in respect of the sub-contract as those for which the main contractor was liable in respect of the main contract. Negotiations followed, and the plaintiff agreed to provide a guarantee bond. Owing to a delay in auditing the plaintiff's accounts, the plaintiff's insurance company would not immediately furnish this. However, by letter dated 13 June, the plaintiff confirmed that a bond was being obtained. The delay continued, and on 5 October the second-named defendant informed the plaintiff that a new nomination had been made for the sub-contract. The plaintiff, meanwhile, had finally obtained confirmation of the issue of a bond on 3 October. The plaintiff sought an interlocutory injunction restraining the second-named defendant from making a new nomination pending the hearing of an action for specific performance of the contract. The defendants contended that an injunction should be refused, as specific performance of a contract for services cannot be decreed, and because damages would be an adequate remedy. **Held** by McWilliam J. in granting an injunction, 1, since the basis of the rule refusing specific performance of a contract for services is that the court cannot oversee the performance of the contract, where such supervision is unnecessary the rule is not applicable. 2. In the instant case, since the defendants had not averred that they would be prejudiced by the delay involved in the plaintiff obtaining the guarantee bond, the balance of convenience lay in granting the injunction. *Educational Co. of Ireland* v. *Fitzpatrick* [1961] I.R. 323 and *American Cyanamid Co.* v. *Ethicon Ltd.* [1975] A.C. 396 applied. *Lift Manufacturers Ltd.* v. *Irish Life Assurance Co. Ltd.*

(H.C.) [1979] ILRM 277

2. —— **Fisheries** — *Offshore fishing licences — Conditions of nationality attaching to licences — Plaintiff seeking to restrain enforcement of conditions pending hearing of action — Effect of such injunction to prevent Executive from exercising powers vested by statute — Balance of convenience — No special principles applicable — Case made out for interlocutory relief — Plaintiff granted interlocutory injunction — Fisheries (Consolidation) Act,* 1959 (*No.* 14), *s.* 222B — *Fisheries (Amendment) Act,* 1983 (*No.* 27), *s.* 2 — *Constitution of Ireland,* 1937, *Art.* 29.] The plaintiff company was the owner of three sea-fishing vessels formerly registered in Spain, but since May of 1981, registered in the State. In December, 1983, the first defendant, issued licences in respect of the plaintiff's boats, pursuant to the provisions of s. 222B of the Fisheries

(Consolidation) Act, 1959, inserted by s. 2 of the Fisheries (Amendment) Act, 1983. The licences contained a condition that the boats should not be used for sea-fishing within the exclusive fishing limits of the State, or otherwise, unless 75 per cent or more of the members of the crew were Irish citizens, or nationals of another Member-State of the E.E.C. The operation of this condition became effective on the issue of the licences in 1984, following an initial postponement. On the 11 September, 1984, one of the plaintiff's boats was arrested and the master thereof charged with the offence of fishing otherwise than in accordance with the licence in that the entire crew of the boat were Spanish nationals. The master was returned for trial in the Cork Circuit Court and the vessel was released from detention upon the lodgment of a security. On the 12 March, 1985, in the High Court, Lardner J. granted an interlocutory injunction to the plaintiff, restraining the defendants, pending trial of the action, *inter alia,* from enforcing the condition attaching to the licences. **Held** by the Supreme Court (Finlay C.J., Walsh, Griffin, Hederman and McCarthy JJ.), in dismissing the appeal, 1, that the application for an injunction fell to be decided in accordance with the ordinary principles governing interlocutory injunctions. 2. That no special principle applied with regard to an application for an interlocutory injunction where the consequence arising from the granting of the injunction was to postpone the bringing to trial of a criminal charge or was to prevent the Executive from carrying out powers vested in them by a statute which enjoyed a presumption of constitutional validity. *The State (Llewellyn)* v. *Ua Donnchadha* [1973] I.R. 151, considered. 3. That accordingly: (i) (McCarthy J. dissenting) the presumption of constitutionality which applied to the impugned statute was material as to whether the plaintiff had established a fair question to be tried, and; (ii) the consequences arising from the granting of the interlocutory injunction, (the prevention of the Executive from carrying out powers vested by the statute enjoying such a presumption and the postponing of the bringing to trial of a criminal offence created by such a statute), were matters for consideration on the balance of convenience. *Per* McCarthy J.: The constitutional presumption attaching to the impugned statute is irrelevant since the Constitution itself, by sub-s. 3 of s. 4 of Art. 29, envisages some freedom from constitutional scrutiny of laws enacted, acts done or measures adopted by the European Economic Communities or institutions thereof. 4. That, notwithstanding the presumption of constitutionality which attached to the statute, the plaintiff had clearly established that there was a fair question to be tried and that the balance

of convenience lay in favour of the plaintiff, notwithstanding also that the operation of the statute was suspended. 5. That, accordingly, the plaintiff was entitled to an injunction pending trial of the action, but that it was inappropriate that the injunction be granted against the second defendant, Ireland. *Pesca Valentia Ltd.* v. *Minister for Fisheries and Forestry*
(S.C.) [1985] I.R.193 ; [1986] ILRM 68

3. —— **Fisheries** — *Offshore fishing licence — Conditions as to nationality attaching — Vessel arrested for fishing in breach of condition — Plaintiff seeking order restraining enforcement of condition — Whether plaintiff came to court with clean hands — Balance of convenience — Whether order be refused.*] The plaintiff company obtained a temporary Irish fishing licence to fish for hake in March, 1986, and registered their two vessels, the *Itxaso* and the *Saladina* as Irish vessels in April, 1986. They informed the first named defendant that they would be operating from Castletownbere and would land their catch in Castletownbere or Killybegs or Galway. The plaintiff was aware from the very beginning that restrictions would be imposed regarding the composition of their crew in particular by a letter of 11 March, 1986. In July, 1986, they were informed of the condition which was to be attached to their licence which stated that the upper limit of Spanish crew members of each of the plaintiff's vessels could not exceed 25% of the complete crew. Evidence was adduced that the plaintiff crew was an all Spanish crew, that they operated out of a Spanish port, where they also landed their catch and the *de facto* result of the plaintiff's operation was to increase the Spanish hake quota by the amount that the plaintiff's vessels caught and landed in Spain and correspondingly reduce the Irish hake quota by the same amount. The plaintiff company's vessel, the *Itxaso,* was arrested for fishing in breach of the condition attached to their licence on 27 August, 1986. The plaintiff sought an interlocutory injunction restraining the defendants from enforcing the condition pending the hearing of the action on a number of grounds including that the condition was contrary to EEC treaties and law, and that if the relief was not granted the plaintiff company would go into liquidation. The defendants resisted the application on a number of grounds including the equitable principle that 'he who seeks equity must come to court with clean hands.' **Held** by Lynch J. in refusing the order sought, 1, the plaintiff company has not 'come into court with clean hands' as they have dishonoured the assurances they gave resulting in their operation not benefiting the Irish economy. 2. The plaintiff company obtained their licence to fish with full notice that some condition regarding the composition of the

INJUNCTION—*continued.*

crew would be imposed. *Pesca Valentia Ltd.* v. *Minister for Fisheries & Forestry, Ireland and The Attorney General* [1985] I.R. 193 distinguished. 3. The plaintiff has failed to satisfy the court that it is in danger of going into liquidation if the relief sought is refused in view of the fact that it took in excess of two months from the date of the arrest of the *Itxaso* before taking steps to seek information and further evidence was adduced that it may be able to find alternative uses for the vessels. *Ardent Fisheries Ltd.* v. *Minister for Tourism, Fisheries and Forestry*

(H.C.) [1987] ILRM 528

4. —— **Fisheries** — *Offshore fishing licence — Ministerial regulation — New conditions — Employee nationality specifications — Non-compliance made a criminal offence — Statutory instrument — Constitutionality — Presumption — Treaty of Rome,* 1957 — *Free movement of workers — Conformity — Reference of identical issue to Court of Justice of the European Communities — Balance of convenience — Status quo — Fisheries (Consolidation) Act,* 1959 (*No.* 14), *s.* 222B, *as inserted by s.* 2 *of the Fisheries (Amendment) Act,* 1983 (*No.* 27) — *Treaty of Rome,* 1957, *Art.* 48.] Section 222B of the Fisheries (Consolidation) Act, 1959, as inserted by s. 2 of the Fisheries (Amendment) Act, 1983, makes it a criminal offence to engage a boat in sea-fishing save in accordance with the licence granted by the Minister for the Marine. By the same section one of the conditions attaching to the licence may require the boat's crew members to "be of a nationality specified in the condition." The plaintiff was the owner and operator from Castleberehaven in Co. Cork of a sea-fishing boat, the *Johnny Ruth,* engaged in long-line fishing, the techniques for which were relatively new to Ireland but much practised and well developed in Spain. A new licence for the *Johnny Ruth,* issued on the 10 July, 1986, by the first defendant to the plaintiff, contained new conditions requiring the boat thenceforth to be crewed by members 75% of which were to be either Irish or EEC nationals other than nationals of Spain or Portugal. On the 1 May, 1987, the *Johnny Ruth* was arrested and charged with offences of non-compliance with the conditions of its licence. The ship's master, a Spaniard, was returned for trial in the Circuit Criminal Court in Cork, where he was remanded on bail and the ship was released on the plaintiff's bond of £16,750. On the 16 June, 1987, the plaintiff issued a summons in the High Court seeking declarations that s. 222B of the Act of 1959 and the fishing licence conditions were unlawful, void and of no effect having regard to Article 48 of the Treaty of Rome and beyond the law-making and regulatory competences of the defendants and injunctions restraining the first and third defendants from enforcing the same conditions in the licence. At the hearing on affidavit of an application for an interlocutory injunction the defendants contended that the presumption of constitutionality of the ministerial regulations and the primacy of the criminal law precluded the court from deciding the interlocutory issue on the balance of convenience. **Held** by Carroll J., in granting the interlocutory injunctions sought, 1, that the presumption of constitutionality was material to the court's determination as to whether the plaintiff had made out a fair question to be tried at the full hearing. 2. Where such fair question for full hearing concerned the validity of a law, then the court should consider that factor among others in deciding the balance of convenience but should not be precluded from such consideration merely because the law challenged was criminal. *Pesca Valentia* v. *Minister for Fisheries* [1985] I.R. 193 applied. 3. On the facts the balance of convenience favoured the granting of an interlocutory injunction, which moreover restored the *status quo. Beara Fisheries and Shipping Ltd.* v. *Minister for the Marine*

(H.C.) [1987] I.R.413 ; [1988] ILRM 221

5. —— **Inducement of breach of contract** — *Whether fair* prima facie *case — Whether damages adequate remedy — Balance of convenience.*] In May, 1974, the plaintiff, by contract in writing, agreed to purchase from Granuphos, a Tunisian based company, and it in turn agreed to sell to the plaintiff, all granulated and ground phosphatic products manufactured or dealt with by Granuphos, other than for domestic consumption. The duration of the contract was for a period of ten years from 1 January, 1974. In February, 1976, the second named defendant decided to place an order with Granuphos for a cargo of phosphate and the first named defendant agreed to purchase the said cargo from them and distribute it to retail outlets. On 15 March, 1976, Granuphos purported to determine the agreement with the plaintiff, by way of telex, alleging that the plaintiff was in breach of the agreement. On the same day the second named defendant entered into an agreement with Granuphos for the sale and purchase of phosphatic products. The cargo was shipped to the second named defendant on 26 March, 1976. On 1 April, 1976, the plaintiff informed them of the existence of the alleged exclusive contract of 1974 and thereafter initiated proceedings alleging that the defendants had induced a breach of the said contract. In an application brought by the second named defendant, it sought an order releasing it from certain undertakings give by each party to the

INJUNCTION—*continued.*

proceedings in a written consent dated 5 April, 1976. Under the terms of the consent the company was entitled to be so discharged by the court, if satisfied that there had been unreasonable delay on the part of the plaintiff in prosecuting the action, or, that the plaintiff was not entitled to an interlocutory injunction. **Held** by Hamilton P. in granting the order sought, 1, there was no unreasonable delay and such delay as did occur was occasioned by the defendants and not the plaintiff. 2. If the plaintiff was to succeed in an application for an interlocutory injunction it must be able to show (i) a fair *prima facie* case in support of its rights, (ii) that damages are not an adequate remedy and (iii) that the balance of convenience lies with the granting of the injunction rather than the refusal thereof. The plaintiff has shown a fair *prima facie* case. Even if there was a violation of the plaintiff's rights, damages are an adequate remedy. Although the ascertainment of damages may create problems, that of itself, is no reason why an injunction should be granted. The balance of convenience, having regard to the large quantity of product imported by the second named defendant and now in storage, lies with the said defendant. Consequently, if the plaintiff had applied for an interlocutory injunction in the first instance, the same would have been refused. *Reno Engrais et Produits Chemiques S.A.* v. *Irish Agricultural Wholesale Society Ltd.*

(H.C.) [1976-7] ILRM 179

6. —— **Judgment** — *Execution* — Fieri facias — *Seizure — Interlocutory injunction — Principles applicable — Fair question to be tried — Balance of convenience — Compensation in damages — Injunction to prohibit sale under writ of* fieri facias.

Practice — Procedure — Fieri facias — *Renewal — Breach of statute — Constitutional rights — Legality of seizure — Whether orders of* fieri facias *valid — Whether renewal of* fieri facias *orders before expiry can be done* ex parte — *Whether new orders must be sought when partial execution has taken place — Whether partial execution on original order is a bar to issue of new order after a year — Whether certificate of solicitor necessary — Whether new order will result in the loss of priority gained with original — Whether movement of cattle was in breach of Diseases of Animals Act,* 1966, *and regulations made thereunder — Whether permits valid — Whether invalidity of permits would involve the return of the goods — Remedy for breach of Act of* 1966 *and regulations — Whether trespass prior to seizure would invalidate it — Whether necessary to give judgment debtor prior notice of execution — Rules of the Superior Courts,* 1986 (*S.I. No.* 15), *O.* 42, *rr.* 17, 20, *O.* 63, *r.* 1(32), *r.* 4 — *Enforcement of Court Orders Act,* 1926 (*No.* 18), *s.* 8 — *Diseases of Animals Act,* 1966 (*No.* 6) — *Constitution of Ireland,* 1937.] The defendant, in her capacity as sheriff for County Meath, seized goods (91 head of cattle, 2 tractors and a bucket) belonging to the plaintiff on foot of orders of *fieri facias* at the instance of judgment creditors who had recovered judgments against the plaintiff for sums in excess of £400,000. She informed the plaintiff that unless the full sum due on foot of the execution orders was paid within 48 hours from the time of seizure, the goods might be sold without further notice to him. Payment not having been received within the prescribed time, the defendant made arrangements for the sale of the goods by auction. The plaintiff issued a plenary summons and applied for interlocutory relief by way of injunction to restrain the defendant from proceeding with the sale and a mandatory injunction compelling her to restore the property seized. The plaintiff sought to establish that the defendant's seizure of the goods was unlawful on the grounds that the orders of *fieri facias* were invalid; that the movement of the cattle which were seized was in breach of the Diseases of Animals Act, 1966, and the regulations made thereunder and that the seizure was carried out with a disregard for his constitutional rights. In relation to the *fieri facias* orders, the plaintiff submitted that they could only be renewed by order of the court and on notice to the plaintiff. Alternatively he contended that if new orders were issued, this could only be done on a solicitor's certificate that nothing had been levied under the first writ and as execution had previously taken place under the original orders, the present orders were invalid. The plaintiff claimed that the defendant committed trespass on his lands and failed to give him notice of the intention to carry out the execution process and that these were breaches of his constitutional rights which invalidated the seizure. **Held** by O'Hanlon J., in refusing to grant an interlocutory injunction, 1, that an applicant for an interlocutory injunction must establish that there is a fair question to be determined; that the balance of convenience favours its granting and that it may not be possible to compensate him by an award in damages. *Campus Oil* v. *Minister for Industry (No 2)* [1983] I.R. 88 followed. 2. That the Rules of the Superior Courts, 1986, permit an application *ex parte* for the renewal of orders of *fieri facias* before the expiration of one year from their issue. 3. That new orders can be issued even if partial execution has already taken place on foot of the original writs and a solicitor's certificate that nothing has been levied on the original orders is not necessary and they are not to be regarded as renewals of original orders but rather as new orders ranking in priority according

INJUNCTION—*continued.*

to the dates they bear. 4. That the defendant was in duty bound to proceed on the orders of *fieri facias* which appeared regular on their face and there was no evidence of an application being made to the court without notice to the plaintiff to renew orders which had expired or of any substantial case for challenging their validity. 5. That the plaintiff had failed to establish a substantial issue to be tried in relation to the validity of the permits granted for the movement of the cattle and even if they were invalid, the remedy for any breach of the regulations made under the Diseases of Animals Act, 1966, is provided for by the Act of 1966 and the regulations and would not involve a compulsory return of the cattle. 6. That a trespass committed by the defendant prior to the seizure and not sufficiently linked to it to be justifiable would not invalidate the subsequent seizure in obedience to execution orders. Nor was the defendant under any obligation to give notice to the plaintiff of her intention to levy execution. *Wymes* v. *Tehan*

(H.C.) [1988] I.R.717

7. —— **Mandatory interlocutory injunction** — *Action for unlawful interference with economic interests — Mandatory interlocutory injunction sought — Whether grant of such relief dependent on plaintiff's prospects of success at trial of action — Whether terms of injunction sought certain enough to enable court to ensure compliance with its order — Whether grant of relief would prejudge one of the issues in the case.*] The first plaintiff and the first defendant owned adjoining orebodies in Nevinstown, County Meath. The first defendant's orebody was held under a State mining lease granted in 1975 and made with amongst other persons the defendant Minister's predecessor-in-title. One of the provisions of that lease, clause f., provided that the lessee, the first defendant, undertook to co-operate with the lessor so as to ensure that the minerals thereby demised and any privately owned minerals in Nevinstown would be exploited in the most efficient and most economical manner with consequent benefit to all concerned and also provided that the lessee undertook to act reasonably in all negotiations to achieve such end. The lease further provided that should any dispute arise between the lessor and lessee concerning, *inter alia,* clause f. or as to any action taken by a party to the lease in purported execution of or compliance with clause f., the dispute was to be referred to artibration in the manner therein provided. The defendant Minister's predecessor-in-title had also in 1975 entered into an agreement with the first plaintiff whereby it was agreed, amongst other things, that the parties thereto would procure that the first plaintiff

INJUNCTION—*continued.*

would actively proceed to develop and exploit its mine "in as expeditious a business manner as is possible . . ." The first plaintiff's orebody had not as yet been exploited and the plaintiffs commenced these proceedings against the defendants claiming damages for, *inter alia,* inflicting economic loss and damage on them by unlawful means, the plaintiffs claiming that it was the strategy of the first defendant to acquire the first plaintiff's orebody at a gross under-value through a variety of tactics including, it was alleged, the refusal or failure of the first defendant to negotiate as required by clause f. of the State mining lease and also by procuring a breach by the defendant Minister of his obligations owed to the first plaintiff under the 1975 agreement. Those proceedings also included claims for relief by way of injunction based on an allegation that the defendant Minister was a trustee for the plaintiffs of the obligations which it was said the first defendant owed to him by virtue of clause f. in the mining lease. In relation to the claims for relief by way of injunction, the plaintiffs applied to the High Court for the grant of those reliefs in interlocutory form — one order which was sought being to direct the first defendant to meet with the plaintiffs "at such times and with such frequency as may be necessary for the purpose of discussing what arrangements may be made" between the first plaintiff and the first defendant as regards the use of the first defendant's facilities in the exploitation of the mineral assets of the first plaintiff and for certain other specified purposes. **Held** by Murphy J., in refusing the plaintiffs interlocutory injunctions in the terms sought or any other relief to like effect, 1, that whilst the plaintiffs might have difficulty in establishing at the trial of their action liability for unlawful interference with their economic interests or in establishing that the defendant Minister was a trustee for them of the obligations contained in clause f. or that that provision was not in any event void for uncertainty or incapable of having contractual force, their right to a mandatory interlocutory injunction did not necessarily depend on the court evaluating the strength of their cause of action. *Dicta* of Megarry J. in *Shepherd Homes Ltd.* v. *Sandham* [1971] Ch. 340 at p. 349 and of O'Higgins C.J. in *Campus Oil Ltd.* v. *Minister for Industry (No. 2)* [1983] I.R. 88 at pp. 106-107 considered. Observations of Murphy J. on liability for unlawful interference with economic interests; the creation of trusts over contractual obligations and the legal status of "agreements to agree." 2. That, nevertheless, the injunctions sought by the plaintiffs or any injunctions to like effect would not, if granted, be certain enough in their terms to enable it to be ascertained whether the defendants were complying with the order of the court.

INJUNCTION—*continued.*

It was immaterial that if a dispute arose as to whether the defendants were acting reasonably in the negotiations the arbitration procedure in the mining lease could be invoked since the issue of compliance was something which the court itself had to determine. *Redland Bricks Ltd.* v. *Morris* [1970] A.C. 652 and *Fishenden* v. *Higgs & Hill Ltd.* (1935) 153 L.T. 128 applied. 3. That the relief sought would also be refused on the ground that to direct that a meeting be held for the purposes of clause f. would not be merely to maintain the *status quo* but would be to prejudge one of the issues in the case by compelling the parties to decide, at least on some temporary or conditional basis, the legal framework within which that provision was to be operated. *Bula Ltd.* v. *Tara Mines Ltd. (No. 2)*

(H.C.) [1987] I.R.95; [1988] ILRM 157

8. —— **Mareva injunction** — *Whether jurisdiction to grant such an injunction — Whether confined to cases where defendant is resident outside the State — Whether real risk of removal or disposal of defendant's assets.*] The plaintiff sued the defendants, who were directors of the Gallagher Group of companies, on foot of a deed of guarantee dated 21 December, 1981, by virtue of which the defendants undertook jointly and severally to guarantee the repayment to the plaintiff by a third party, Lambert Jones Estates Ltd., of £500,000 lent by the plaintiff to the third party together with interest on that amount. Despite being requested to do so, the third party failed to discharge any part of the sum by the due date. The plaintiff then called on the defendants to pay the outstanding sum, which on 4 May, 1982, amounted to £588,046.97 including interest. No part of the sum was discharged by the defendants. The plaintiff, having obtained an interim injunction, sought an interlocutory injunction restraining the defendants from disposing of their assets up to the value of the plaintiff's claim, whether the assets were within or outside the jurisdiction, so as to defeat the plaintiff's chances of executing on a judgment. The plaintiff alleged that the defendants owned substantial amounts of property, and that there were substantial grounds for believing that the defendants would charge their personal assets in such a manner that certain other of the defendants' creditors might be preferred to the plaintiff; amounting to fraudulent preference. The defendants contended that the plaintiff had agreed to defer repayment of the loan to a later agreed date, on condition that the Gallagher Group also deferred repayment of the latter's loan to the third party and subordinated it to all other loans due by the third party. They also alleged that an injunction restraining disposal of assets could only be granted where a defendant

INJUNCTION—*continued.*

outside the jurisdiction had property inside the jurisdiction, or where it was shown that a defendant, because of his foreign nationality or domicile or otherwise, was likely to take his property out of the jurisdiction and that such a remedy should not be confused with fraudulent preference in a bankruptcy matter. **Held** by McWilliam J. in granting the injunction sought, 1, the plaintiff was *prima facie* entitled to payment of the money guaranteed by the defendants. 2. An injunction might be granted where it appeared to the court that dispositions were likely to be made for the purpose of preventing a plaintiff from recovering the amount of his award, as distinct from the purpose of conducting the normal business or personal affairs of the defendant. This jurisdiction was not confined to foreign defendants. 3. In the present case, the reluctance of the defendants to disclose their assets and their dispositions and proposed dispositions of them, combined with the fact their businesses are not personal but conducted by a group of companies, indicated that they were probably mainly interested to deprive the plaintiff of the opportunity of recovering. 4. The injunction could be removed on application by the defendants showing grounds of hardship, either to themselves or to anyone else, including creditors of the defendants who are entitled to be paid in the ordinary course of business. *Powerscourt Estates* v. *Gallagher*

(H.C.) [1984] ILRM 123

9. —— **Mareva injunction** — *Whether injunction should issue — Practice — Summons — Service — Service out of jurisdiction — Provision by rule of court where any injunction is sought as to anything to be done within the jurisdiction — Plaintiffs claiming right to a "mareva injunction" — Whether such right sufficient to entitle plaintiff to serve notice of summons outside jurisdiction — Rules of the Superior Courts,* 1962 (*S.I. No.* 72), *O.* 4, *r.* 2, *O.* 11, *r.* 1(*g*), *O.* 12, *r.* 36.] Order 4, r. 1 of the Rules of the Superior Courts,1962, provides *inter alia* that the indorsement of claim on a plenary summons shall be an indorsement of relief claimed and the grounds thereof expressed in general form in such one of the forms in Appendix B, Part 11, of the Rules as shall be applicable to the case, or such other similarly concise form as the nature of the case may require. Order 11, r. 1(*g*) provides that service out of the jurisdiction of an originating summons or notice may be allowed by the court when any injunction is sought as to anything to be done within the jurisdiction or any nuisance within the jurisdiction is sought to be prevented or removed, whether damages are or are not also sought in respect thereof. The plaintiffs were ex-employees or the representatives of deceased

INJUNCTION—*continued.*

employees of the defendant, the national airline of Zaire, which had no place of business or agency within the jurisdiction. They sought damages against the defendant for breaches of contracts which were made and which breaches occurred outside the jurisdiction. An aeroplane, the property of the defendant was delivered to Dublin Airport for the purposes of having repairs carried out. In a draft plenary summons the plaintiffs claimed (1) an injunction restraining the defendant, its servants or agents from moving out of the jurisdiction or in any way dealing with the aeroplane so as to reduce the value thereof to a sum less than 113,887,939 Belgian Francs; (2) judgment for the said sum; (3) further and other relief and (4) costs. On the *ex parte* application of the plaintiffs the High Court (Costello J.) granted them liberty to issue and serve a plenary summons in terms of the aforesaid draft on the defendant outside the jurisdiction on the grounds that the action fell within the class of action set out in Order 11, r. 1(*g*) and further granted an interim injunction on the terms of para. (1) thereof. The defendant applied by notice of motion pursuant to Order 12, r. 26 of the aforesaid Rules for an order setting aside that order which was heard together with the plaintiffs' motion for an interlocutory injunction. The High Court (Barr J.) refused the defendant's application and granted the application of the plaintiff. On appeal by the defendant against both orders it was **Held** by the Supreme Court (Finlay C.J., Henchy and Hederman JJ.) in allowing the appeal, 1, that to come within Order 11, r. 1(*g*) the injunction sought in the action had to be part of the substantive relief to which the plaintiffs' cause of action entitled them and had to be properly and necessarily sought in the indorsement of claim contained in the originating summons. 2. That, since the relief sought by the plaintiffs by way of injunction was an interlocutory injunction pending the determination of the action and not part of the substantive relief sought at the determination of the action, the order granting liberty to the plaintiffs to issue and serve notice of the originating summons out of the jurisdiction should be set aside. 3. Accordingly, since the plaintiffs did not have a subsisting action within the jurisdiction, the interlocutory injunction should be set aside. *Siskina (Cargo Owners)* v. *Distos S.A.* [1979] A.C. 210 considered. *Caudron* v. *Air Zaire*

(S.C.) [1985] I.R.716; [1986] ILRM 10

10. —— **Principles to be applied** — *Disputed facts — Serious questions of law raised demanding detailed argument — Balance of convenience — Whether injunction be granted.*

European Communities — Supply and distribution of fuel — Government powers to regulate

INJUNCTION—*continued.*

acquisition, supply, distribution and marketing — Whether incompatible with Community obligations — Whether mandatory regime a quantitative restriction or measure having equivalent effect — Whether restriction on competition — Application for interlocutory injunction — Whether injunction be granted — Treaty of Rome, 1957, *Arts.* 30, 31, 36, 85, 86, 90 — *Fuels (Control of Supplies) Act,* 1971 (*No.* 3), *ss.* 2, 3 — *Fuels (Control of Supplies) Act,* 1982 (*No.* 18), *s.* 3(1) — *Fuels (Control of Supplies) Order,* 1982.] The plaintiffs are a group of Irish owned and controlled companies engaged in the business of importing petroleum products for resale in the Republic of Ireland. They supplied approximately 14% of the gasoline market in the State and a somewhat higher percentage of other petroleum products. The entire of the balance of the Irish market is supplied by multinational petroleum companies. The fourth named defendant is a company established by the State for the purposes of purchasing and importing oil products and which, on behalf of the State, owns and operates the oil refinery at Whitegate, in the County of Cork. By Statutory Instrument entitled Fuels (Control of Supplies) Order, 1982, made by the first named defendant on 25 August, 1982, pursuant to the provisions of the Fuels (Control of Supplies) Acts, 1971-1982, the plaintiffs were required to purchase 35% of their fuel oil requirements from the Whitegate Oil Refinery at prices and terms fixed by the fourth named defendant. This scheme or directive is known as the 'mandatory regime.' The plaintiffs instituted proceedings by way of plenary summons on 1 September, 1982, claiming a declaration that the Fuel (Control of Supplies) Order, 1982, was invalid, first on the ground that it was incompatible with Articles 30, 31, 85, 86 and 90 of the Treaty of Rome, and secondly on the ground that it contravened the provisions of Articles 40 and 43 of the Constitution of Ireland. Having instituted proceedings against the defendants, the plaintiffs applied in the High Court for an interlocutory injunction restraining the defendants, pending the trial of the action, from implementing the mandatory regime. The plaintiffs' application was refused by Murphy J. (reported at [1983] ILRM 258). On the close of pleadings the proceedings were then re-listed in the High Court before Murphy J. for the purposes of considering an application by the plaintiffs, which was opposed by the defendants, that the court should seek a preliminary ruling from the Court of Justice of the European Community as to whether Articles 30 and 31 of the Treaty of Rome were to be interpreted as applying to the mandatory regime as established by the Fuels (Control of Supplies) Order, 1982. Although the defendants opposed the plaintiffs' application

INJUNCTION—*continued.*

they suggested that if such a preliminary question was to be put a further question should also go as to whether, in the event of the first question being answered in the affirmative, the application of Article 36 of the Treaty applied to the mandatory regime. Having heard the application, Murphy J. availing of the procedure laid down in Article 177 of the Treaty of Rome, decided to seek a preliminary ruling on both questions from the Court of Justice. The defendants' appeal against this decision to the Supreme Court was dismissed. Subsequently the defendants decided to seek full observance of the mandatory regime, which was resisted by all but one of the plaintiffs who continued to import their fuel oil requirements without taking a percentage from the oil refinery at Whitegate. Whilst the multinational oil companies complied with the mandatory regime the defendants considered that the refusal by all but one of the plaintiffs to do so would lead to the multinational oil companies deciding not to take 35% of their fuel oil requirements from the Whitegate refinery. The defendants, therefore, sought leave to amend their defence by adding a counter claim and applied to the High Court for interlocutory injunctions against the five plaintiffs who were refusing to comply with the mandatory regime. The application was heard by Keane J. who granted the interlocutory injunctions sought by the defendants holding that the plaintiffs had established that there was a fair question to be tried and the balance of convenience and the preservation of the *status quo* favoured the award of the judgments sought. The plaintiffs appealed to the Supreme Court contending that in granting the interlocutory relief on the defendants' application, the High Court had failed to have regard to the correct criteria to be applied in considering an application for an interlocutory injunction and in particular in considering an application for an injunction which was of a mandatory nature. The appellants contended, *inter alia,* that a court of first instance entertaining an application for an interlocutory injunction should require the party applying to establish a substantial question to be tried and a probability that the party against whom the injunction was sought would fail at the trial of the action in relation to such a question.

Held (High Court) by Keane J., granting both injunctions, 1, that the party seeking an interlocutory injunction need not establish on the balance of probabilities that his case will succeed but merely that there is a fair question to be tried: *Educational Company of Ireland* v. *Fitzpatrick* [1961] I.R. 323 explained; *Esso Petroleum Company (Ireland) Ltd.* v. *Fogarty* [1965] I.R. 531 *Dictum* approved; *American Cyanamid* v. *Ethicon Ltd.* [1975] A.C. 396 approved. 2. Although mandatory injunctions should not in the absence of special circumstances be granted on motion, their award or withholding is a matter of discretion: *London Borough of Hounslow* v. *Twickenham Garden Developments Ltd.* [1970] 3 All E.R. 326 and *Shepherd Homes Ltd.* v. *Sandham* [1970] 3 All E.R. 402 considered. 3. Although the court had a duty to uphold the provisions of the Treaty of Rome, that obligation did not alter its traditional jurisdiction in relation to interlocutory injunctions: *Hoffman La Roche* v. *Centrafarm Vertriebsgesellschaft Pharmazeutischer Erzeugnisse GmbH* [1977] E.C.R. 957 applied. 4. The defendants had established that there was a fair question to be tried and the balance of convenience and the preservation of the *status quo* favoured the award of the injunctions sought. **Held** (Supreme Court) (O'Higgins C.J. and Griffin J.; Hederman J. concurring with O'Higgins C.J. and adopting the comments of Griffin J.) dismissing the appeal, 1, in cases where the rights of the party applying for interlocutory relief are disputed and challenged and where a significant period must elapse before the trial, the court hearing the application must exercise its discretion whether or not to grant such relief with due regard to established principles. The test to be applied by the court in exercising its discretion as to granting or refusing an interlocutory injunction is whether a fair *bona fide* or serious question has been raised to be decided at the trial by the party seeking relief. The court ought not to weigh up the relative strengths of the parties' cases on the evidence available at the interlocutory stage, that evidence being then necessarily incomplete. Once a fair or serious question has been raised the court should then go on to consider whether the balance of convenience lies in favour of granting or refusing the interlocutory injunction sought. There is no rule that the court is not entitled to take account of the balance of convenience unless the party seeking the interlocutory injunction satisfies the court that the probability is in favour of the case of the party against whom the relief is sought ultimately failing in the final issue of the suit. The trial judge applied the correct test in considering whether the applicants had raised a fair question as to whether their rights had been violated. (*Educational Co. of Ireland* v. *Fitzpatrick* [1961] I.R. 323 explained; *Esso Petroleum Co. (Ireland)* v. *Fogarty* [1965] I.R. 531 *Dictum* approved; *American Cyanamid Co.* v. *Ethicon Ltd.* [1975] A.C. 396 approved). 2. A mandatory injunction may be granted by way of interlocutory relief in exceptional cases. In the circumstances of the case it was proper that it should have been granted by way of interlocutory relief. *Campus Oil Ltd.* v. *Minister for Industry and Energy*

(H.C., S.C.) [1984] ILRM 45

11. —— **Principles to be applied** — *Factors to be considered by court in deciding whether to grant interlocutory injunction — Serious question to be tried — Adequacy of damages — Public interest — Statutory duty of plaintiff to promote national culture — Defendant having complained to Commission of European Communities of breach by plaintiff of community law — Investigation in progress by Commission — Whether existence of investigation should influence court in deciding whether to grant injunction — Broadcasting Authority Act,* 1960 (*No.* 10).

European Communities — Relationship of European Communities law to domestic law — Application to High Court for interlocutory injunction — Plaintiff claiming breach of Irish law — Defendant having complained to Commission of European Communities of breach by plaintiff of community law — Investigation by Commission in progress — Whether existence of investigation should influence Irish court in deciding whether to grant injunction — Council Regulation 17 of 1962 — Treaty of Rome, 1957, *Arts.* 85, 86.] The plaintiff regularly published programme schedules and commentaries and every week published a magazine containing its television and radio schedules. The plaintiff claimed copyright in its schedules but provided a licence to newspapers and periodicals to use them subject to restrictions. From March, 1985, M.P. Ltd., an associated company of the defendant, published a weekly guide to the plaintiff's and to the British television stations' programmes called "Magill T.V. Guide." M.P. Ltd. had reluctantly accepted and complied with the terms of the plaintiff's licence. Publication of "Magill T.V. Guide" ceased due to an industrial dispute but some months later the defendant began publishing "T.V. Guide" in which the plaintiff's full programme listing was published. The plaintiff commenced proceedings for an injunction to restrain publication of the defendant's guide on the grounds that it infringed the plaintiff's copyright in its schedules and applied for an interlocutory injunction. The defendant denied that the plaintiff was entitled to copyright in its programme listings but conceded for the purposes of the motion that there was a serious question to be tried. The defendant had complained under Council Regulation 17 of 1962 to the Commission of the European Communities that the plaintiff was abusing a dominant position and was acting in concert with the B.B.C. and I.T.V. to maintain a division of the market in information, contrary to articles 85 and 86 of the Treaty of Rome. The Commission had notified the plaintiff of the complaint and had invited its comments. The defendant did not ask the court to refuse the

interlocutory injunction on the grounds that the plaintiff was in breach of the Treaty, but argued that a conflict might arise between an order of the court and an order of the Commission and that the court should make no order pending the termination of the proceedings before the Commission. **Held** by Costelo J., in granting the interlocutory injunction, 1, that the plaintiff in pursuance of its statutory duty to preserve and develop the national culture used its magazine to promote home produced programmes and programmes of national interest. The continued publication of the defendant's guide would impair this effort and would result in a loss to the plaintiff which could not be compensated by an award of damages. 2. That the public interest in the level of television licence fees, which the profits made by the plaintiff from sales of its magazine helped to reduce, was a factor which could be taken into account in determining whether to grant an injunction. 3. That any loss which might be suffered by the defendant by the granting of an interlocutory injunction could, if the defendant were successful at the trial of the action, be adequately compensated by damages. 4. That the existence of an investigation by the Commission of the European Communities into an allegation of a breach of community law was not a matter which should affect the discretion of the court in deciding an application for an interlocutory injunction arising from an alleged breach of Irish law. 5. That in the event of an order being made by the Commission or by the Court of Justice of the European Communities, either party might apply to vary or revoke the interlocutory order. *Radio Telefís Éireann* v. *Magill T.V. Guide Ltd.*

(H.C.) [1988] I.R.97

12. —— **Principles to be applied** — *Balance of convenience — Contract — Terms — Enforcement — Restraint of trade — Covenant in lease — Covenant in positive form — Solus agreement with oil company — Lessor's remedy for breach of covenant — Mandatory and prohibitory injunctions — Interlocutory relief.*] The defendants carried on a garage and petrol service business and the plaintiffs, an oil company, sold petroleum products. In the year 1969 the defendants bought a six-acre plot beside a public road and adjoining an acre plot which belonged to the plaintiffs. The plaintiffs had obtained planning permission for the development of their plot as a petrol and service station. The defendants' application for a similar permission for their plot was refused; they appealed against the refusal but withdrew the appeal after they had obtained the plaintiffs' agreement to grant the defendants a lease of the plaintiffs' plot. Subsequently, the defendants applied for and, on the 24 July, 1970, obtained

INJUNCTION—*continued.*

planning permission to develop the combined plots as a petrol and service station. By a lease dated the 30 October, 1973, the plaintiffs demised their plot to the defendants for a term of 42 years. The lease contained covenants by the defendants to use the demised plot and their plot only for the purpose of a motor garage, sales room and petrol and service station; to buy from the plaintiffs exclusively all petroleum products required by the defendants for sale or use on the combined plots; to exhibit on the combined plots the plaintiffs' signs and advertising matter and to decorate the combined plots in the plaintiff's standard colours. The defendants built a service station and installed several petrol pumps mainly, it would appear, on their own plot. On the 1 March, 1982, the defendants ceased all trading with the plaintiffs and began to buy the supplies for their business from a new supplier; the defendants removed all the plaintiffs' insignia and advertising signs from the combined plots. The plaintiffs claimed in the High Court mandatory and prohibitory injunctions compelling the defendants to comply with their covenants in the lease. By notice of motion dated the 23 March, 1982, the plaintiffs applied for interlocutory relief, in the terms of the endorsement of claim on their summons, pending the hearing of their action. **Held** by Costello J., in granting the interlocutory relief sought by the plaintiffs, 1, that where a lessee first acquires possession of premises under a lease, a negative covenant by him in the lease restricting the businesses or trades which he may conduct on the demised premises is not rendered void by the common-law doctrine of restraint of trade. *Esso Petroleum Co. Ltd.* v. *Harper's Garage (Stourport) Ltd.* [1968] A.C. 269; *Cleveland Petroleum Co. Ltd.* v. *Dartstone Ltd.* [1969] 1 W.L.R. 116 and *Amoco Australia* v. *Rocca Bros.* [1975] A.C. 562 considered. 2. That the restrictive covenants on the part of the defendants in the lease of 1973 were not rendered void by that doctrine notwithstanding the facts that those covenants were framed in a positive form, that they were expressed to apply to the defendants' adjoining lands as well as to the demised premises, and that they were expressed to apply to the source of the defendants' supplies and to the manner in which they decorated the demised premises as well as to the trades permitted thereon. 3. That there had been such a clear breach by the defendants of their covenants that it was not necessary to examine the topic of the balance of convenience. *Doherty* v. *Allman* (1878) 3 App. Cas. 709; *Dublin Port & Docks Board* v. *Brittania Dredging Co. Ltd.* [1968] I.R. 136 considered. 4. That the defendants should pay the plaintiffs' costs of the motion. The defendants, shortly after the date of the order of the High Court, complied with the terms of that

INJUNCTION—*continued.*

order by resuming their sales of the plaintiffs' products and exhibiting the plaintiffs' advertisements and insignia on the combined plots. On appeal by the defendants it was **Held** by the Supreme Court (O'Higgins C.J., Griffin and McCarthy JJ.), in affirming in part the order of the High Court, 1, that, while the plaintiffs had raised a fair question for determination at the trial of the action, the existence of breaches of covenants by the defendants had not been so clearly established in the High Court as to avoid the necessity for an enquiry about the balance of convenience involved in directing the defendants to restore the *status quo ante. Dublin Port & Docks Board* v. *Brittania Dredging Co. Ltd.* [1968] I.R. 136 and *TMG Group* v. *Al Babtain* [1982] ILRM 349 considered. 2. That at the hearing of the appeal, the balance of convenience lay in favour of preserving the position which then existed and which had existed before the alleged breaches of covenant. 3. That the judge's ruling that the defendants should pay the plaintiffs' costs of the interlocutory motion shoud be set aside and that the award of those costs should be reserved for determination by the judge at the trial of the action. *Irish Shell Ltd.* v. *Elm Motors Ltd.*

(H.C., S.C.) [1984] I.R.200 ; [1984] ILRM 595

13. —— **Principles to be applied** — *Fair question for trial — Balance of convenience — Trade dispute — Dispute between employer and employees — Employees picketing employer's premises — Employer's premises sold — Former owner's employees continuing to picket premises — Whether continued picketing in bona fide furtherance of a trade dispute — Whether sufficient connection between former owner and premises to justify continued picketing — Whether unlawful and violent picketing would justify prohibition of all picketing — Duty of plaintiff to enforce order of court — Trade Disputes Act,* 1906 (c.47).] The defendants were employed by I.M.P. at its premises in County Kildare until January, 1986, when I.M.P. ceased to trade there and made its entire workforce redundant. A trade dispute arose between I.M.P. and its former employees and the Kildare premises but not other premises owned by I.M.P. in Cork, were picketed from the 30 January, 1986. In March, 1986, the plaintiff purchased the Kildare premises with notice of the dispute and of the picket. The beneficial owners of the plaintiff were not connected with I.M.P. After completing the purchase the plaintiff sought to harvest a quantity of silage on the lands, to return to their owners a number of cattle which were grazing there and to dispose of a large quantity of frozen meat stored on the premises, of which the plaintiff was a gratuitous bailee. The plaintiff alleged, but the defendants

INJUNCTION—*continued.*

denied, that its activities were impeded by the existence of the pickets and by intimidating, threatening and violent behaviour on the part of the pickets. The plaintiff succeeded in cutting the silage and in disposing of the cattle but the frozen meat, which was destined for E.E.C. intervention and which before being removed required to be examined and certified by Department of Agriculture officials, could be neither certified nor removed as long as the pickets remained on the premises. Unless the meat was taken into intervention by December, 1986, its value would drop by £3.5m. and the plaintiff feared that a claim might be made against it by the owners of the meat. There was no dispute between the plaintiff and the defendants but two former employees of I.M.P. continued to maintain the refrigeration system in the premises and I.M.P. managers occasionally visited the premises. The plaintiff commenced proceedings claiming injunctions restraining the defendants from trespassing on or picketing at the premises and from interfering with persons attempting to work there, as well as for damages for trespass, assault, intimidation and trespass, and applied to the High Court for interlocutory injunctive relief. The President made an order restraining the defendants from trespassing on the plaintiff's premises and restraining the number of pickets to two at any one entrance at any time. The plaintiff appealed to the Supreme Court arguing that a *bona fide* question had been established as to whether the picketing was carried on in *bona fide* furtherance of a trade dispute with I.M.P.; that the balance of convenience was overwhelmingly in favour of granting an injunction and, further, that a fair question had been established as to whether the nature of the picketing would justify a prohibition on all forms of picketing. It was conceded on behalf of the defendants that there was a fair question to be tried as to whether the picketing was in *bona fide* furtherance of a trade dispute but it was argued that the balance of convenience was against granting an injunction. It was argued that the release of the meat would permanently deprive the defendants of a major weapon in the dispute and that their right to picket the Cork premises was not a proper substitute. **Held** by the Supreme Court (Finlay C.J., Henchy, Griffin and Hederman JJ.; McCarthy J. dissenting), in allowing the appeal and granting the interlocutory order, 1, that on the hearing of an application for an interlocutory injunction where damages would not be an adequate remedy, the court should enquire firstly, whether the plaintiff had raised a fair question to be tried at the hearing of the action and secondly, whether the balance of convenience is in favour of granting or refusing an interlocutory injunction. *Campus Oil* v. *Minister for Industry (No,. 2)* [1983] I.R. 88 and *Irish Shell* v. *Elm Motors* [1984] I.R. 200 applied. 2. That while the effect of an interlocutory injunction would be to deprive temporarily the defendants of a significant weapon, they could, if successful at the trial, restore the picket and paralyse the premises. The plaintiff, on the other hand, faced a real risk, if the picket continued, of a substantial loss which could not be recovered against the defendants. 3. That the defendants in order to succeed at the trial had to establish that the relationship between the plaintiff and I.M.P. was such that the plaintiff could put pressure on I.M.P. to come to a settlement with the defendants. *Per* McCarthy J. (dissenting). That the granting of an interlocutory injunction restraining an individual from doing something which it is lawful to do is primarily founded upon the desirability of preserving the *status quo ante bellum.* In this case the *status quo* to be preserved was that pertaining when the plaintiff first became involved at which time it was aware of the dispute and of the picket. *Per* McCarthy J. (dissenting). That a party calling in aid the equitable jurisdiction of the courts is required to call upon the sanction of the courts in the event of the terms of an injunction being flouted. The plaintiff ought not to be given further and more stringent orders when, although it complained of breaches of the President's order, it had taken no steps to enforce that earlier order. *Per* McCarthy J. *Semble.* That there is no principle of law to support the proposition that an individual who abuses the statutory right to picket thereby forfeits the right to picket lawfully. *Bayzana Ltd.* v. *Galligan*

(S.C.) [1987] I.R.238

14. —— **Publication** — *Criminal law — Conviction — Pending appeal to Court of Criminal Appeal — Publication of a magazine article based on material supplied by sole witness for the prosecution — Application to restrain publication — Whether article likely to prejudice the appeal — Freedom of the press — Constitution of Ireland,* 1937, *Art.* 40.6.] The plaintiff was convicted in the Central Criminal Court of murder and malicious damage to property. He appealed to the Court of Criminal Appeal against the refusal by the trial judge of a certificate of leave to appeal. The only evidence against the plaintiff in his trial was that of an alleged accomplice, Elizabeth Madden. The grounds of appeal by the plaintiff to the Court of Criminal Appeal related to the insufficiency of uncorroborated evidence of an accomplice to sustain a conviction. While the plaintiff's appeal was pending, the defendants entered into an exclusive contract to publish Elizabeth Madden's account of her relationship with the plaintiff prior to an including the events

INJUNCTION—*continued.*

which were the subject matter of his trial. The plaintiff applied for an injunction restraining publication by the defendants of the proposed article. **Held** by Barrington J., in granting the injunction, 1, the court had jurisdiction to grant such an injunction, the onus being on the plaintiff to prove on the balance of probability that publication of the article would be likely to prejudice his appeal and retrial, if ordered, even assuming this was an unlikely eventuality. 2. While the appeal would be heard by professional judges trained to exclude irrelevant material from their minds, it would be unwise to assume that they would not be affected by publication of the article. *Dicta* in *R.* v. *Davies, ex p. Delbert-Evans* [1945] K.B. 435 applied. 3. The fact that the plaintiff's trial had been discussed in other organs of the media was irrelevant as he was entitled to have his case tried in accordance with law on evidence adduced in court and not otherwise. **Held** by the Supreme Court (O'Higgins C.J., Hederman and McCarthy JJ.) in reversing the High Court, 1, the courts should only interfere with the freedom of the press and of communication guaranteed in Article 40.6 of the Constitution where this was necessary for the administration of justice. 2. Since publication of the article could not possibly prejudice the objective determination by the Court of Criminal Appeal of pure issues of law, there was no basis for the granting of the injunction in the present case. *Semble:* The refusal of the injunction would not preclude the plaintiff from seeking damages in an action for defamation. *Cullen* v. *Toibin.*

(H.C., S.C.) [1984] ILRM 577

—— Fishing rights — Interference — Whether plaintiffs entitled to order to restrain defendant's activities.
see **Real Property,** 5

—— Interlocutory — Breach of confidence — Confidential information shared between foreign government and private individual — Principles governing the protection of such information.
see **Constitution,** 14

—— Interlocutory — Breach of Constitution — Presumption — Whether fair question of law to be tried — Balance of convenience — Treaty — Ratification — effect — Status quo — Preservation — Whether injunction necessary to preserve constitutional status quo — Exceptional considerations.
see **Constitution,** 22

—— Interlocutory — Claim and counterclaim — Principles applicable — Whether serious question to be tried.
see **Copyright,** 2

—— Interlocutory — Fair question — Balance of convenience — Standard test — Application — Statutory condition — Breach by plaintiff — Criminal offence — Defendant Minister seeking to enforce compliance and to invoke section — Plaintiff applying for order restraining defendant from seeking to enforce compliance and to impose penalty.
see **Injunction,** 2

—— Interlocutory — Mandatory — Prohibitory — Lease — Covenant — Restraint of trade — Breach of covenant — Lessor's remedy — Solus agreement with oil company.
see **Injunction,** 12

—— Interlocutory — Mandatory — Unlicensed possession and use of apparatus for wireless telegraphy — Seizure of apparatus — Application for return of apparatus.
see **Broadcasting,** 1, 2

—— Interlocutory — Mareva relief — Foreign trade union — Foreign court imposing fine for union's contempt of court — Union's funds transferred to Irish bank — Foreign sequestrators seeking vesting of funds — Fine treated as penalty imposed by foreign court — Refusal of court to aid sequestrators further.
see **Conflict of Laws,** 5

—— Interlocutory — Private hospital — Public funds — Discontinuance — Executive decision — Legality — Whether fair question to be tried.
see **Statute,** 2

—— Interlocutory — Restraint of trade — Enforcement of restrictive clauses — Whether restraint reasonable.
see **Restraint of Trade,** 1

—— Interlocutory — Trade dispute — Inducement of breach of contract — Contract terminated — Whether appropriate to grant injunction in respect of continuing picketing.
see **Employer and Employee,** 24

—— Interlocutory — Trade dispute — Picketing

INJUNCTION—*continued.*

— Whether picketing entitled to statutory protection — Whether picketer an employee or independent contractor.
see **Employer and Employee,** 25

—— Planning — Application for injunction restraining continued development — Whether claim frivolous or vexatious.
see **Planning,** 4

—— Planning — S. 27 applications.
see **Planning,** 2, 20-31, 32

—— *Quia timet* injunction — Probability of further interference.
see **Landlord and Tenant,** 1

INQUEST — Verdict — Suicide — Statutory exclusions of questions of civil or criminal liability — Whether verdict available — Notice of inquest not served on next-of- kin — Whether breach of natural and constitutional justice — Certiorari.
see **Coroner**

INSANITY
see also **Mental Treatment**

—— Defence — Murder — Diminished responsibility.
see **Criminal Law,** 30

INSOLVENCY
see **Bankruptcy; Company — Winding up**

—— Industrial and provident society.
see **Industrial and Provident Societies,** 2

—— Industrial and provident society — Liquidation — Depositor receiving a dividend of only part of sum lodged — Whether Minister owed a duty of care.
see **Negligence,** 33

INSURANCE
see also **Employer's Liability**

Contract. Nos. 1-5
Contribution. No. 6
Insurer — liability. No. 7
Motor vehicle. No. 8

1. —— **Contract** — *Interpretation — Employer's liability insurance — Dispute referred to arbitration — Questions of interpretation arising — Whether the word "and" used in a conjunctive or disjunctive sense — Whether observance of claims procedure a condition precedent to the liability of the underwriters.*] The

INSURANCE—*continued.*

arbitration concerned a dispute between the underwriters and the company insured under an employer's liability insurance policy. An employee of the company had allegedly sustained injuries on two occasions in 1975, and had issued High Court proceedings against the company in respect thereof in 1977. The company notified the underwriters of the two claims, and sent to them the two plenary summonses on receipt of them from the employee. The underwriters had refused to indemnify the company under the policy on the ground that the company had failed to comply with the condition contained in clause 5 of the policy, which provided as follows: "5. Claims Procedure. The assured shall give . . . immediate notice in writing, with full particulars of the happening of any occurrence which could give rise to a claim under this insurance, or of the receipt by the assured of notice of any claim and of the institution of any proceedings against the assured." A sub-heading in relation to the conditions in that section of the policy stated 'All conditions are precedent to liability under this insurance.' The underwriters claimed to have been prejudiced by the failure of the company to give immediate notice in writing of the happening of the occurrence which gave rise to the claims of the employee. The arbitrator stated this case for the opinion of the court on (*a*) the question of the interpretation of clause 5 and whether in the circumstances the company had failed to comply with the provisions thereof; (*b*) whether clause 5 was a condition precedent to the liability of the underwriters; and (*c*) whether the underwriters would be entitled to avoid liability if it were found as a fact that they had suffered no prejudice by reason of the failure of the company to give notice to them in writing with full particulars of the happening of an occurrence which would give rise to a claim under the insurance. Submissions were made on behalf of both parties on whether the word 'or' in the relevant part of clause 5 was to be construed in a disjunctive or a conjunctive sense; that is, whether it was necessary for the insured company to give written notice of the happening of the occurrence which could give rise to a claim in addition to or in the alternative to notice of any claim received by the insured. **Held** in advising the arbitrator and for his assistance in the determination of the dispute, 1, the word 'or' in that part of clause 5 was to be read in its *prima facie* ordinary and most common sense, which was consistent with the rest of the condition. The insured was therefore obliged by clause 5 to give immediate notice in writing either of the happening of the occurrence likely to give rise to a claim or of receipt by the insured of such a claim, and was further obliged to give immediate notice in writing of the institution of proceedings

INSURANCE—*continued.*

in every case. 2. Compliance with clause 5 was a condition precedent to liability of the underwriters under the policy. 3. Unless non-compliance with clause 5 was trivial or had been waived expressly or impliedly by the underwriters they were not obliged to show that they were prejudiced by the non-compliance. *Gaelcrann Teoranta* v. *Payne*

(H.C.) [1985] ILRM 109

2. —— **Contract** — *Interpretation — Fire insurance — Destruction of premises by fire — Whether contract of insurance contained a reinstatement clause — Assessment of loss.*] The plaintiff company owned premises in Glasgow upon which policies issued by the defendants for £250,000 and £50,000 respectively were in force when the building was totally destroyed by fire. The plaintiff's director and chief shareholder, Leo O'Hara, gave evidence that he had sought £300,000 worth of fire cover to ensure full re-instatement of the property in the event of its destruction. The policies which had been issued, however, were in the standard form of an indemnity contract only: the insurance company undertook to pay the market value of destroyed property, the amount of damage, or, at its option, to reinstate or replace damaged property. The defendants gave evidence that full re-instatement cover was not lightly offered for old buildings; that pre-contractual negotiations with the plaintiff's insurance brokers did not disclose a requirement for re-instatement cover; and that the plaintiff had not expressed an unequivocal desire to rebuild the premises. In the High Court McWilliam J. held that there had been no re-instatement contract and that the plaintiff did not intend to rebuild. He awarded the plaintiff a sum of £54,000, which was designed to represent the market value of the property at the time of the fire less the value of the site. Costs were awarded against the second-named defendant on the basis that the first-named defendant had made a lodgment in excess of the award. The plaintiff appealed to the Supreme Court asserting (i) that the contract was for full re-instatement and (ii), in the alternative, if the contract were only for indemnity, that the plaintiff was entitled in any case to the cost of rebuilding. The second-named defendant cross-appealed against the order for costs. **Held** by the Supreme Court (O'Higgins C.J., Griffin and Hederman JJ.) dismissing the appeal and in allowing the cross-appeal, 1, that the evidence did not support the existence of a re-instatement contract. 2. (*Per* Griffin and Hederman JJ., O'Higgins C.J. dissenting) that the plaintiff did not intend to rebuild the premises, and that the extent of its entitlement was the market value of the property at the time of the fire, an amount increased by

INSURANCE—*continued.*

consent to £64,000. 3. (*Per* Griffin and Hederman JJ., O'Higgins C.J. dissenting) that counsel for the second-named defendant should be given an opportunity of submitting an alternative form of order in the matter of costs. *Per Curiam.* That the insured under an indemnity contract, if he desires to rebuild, and if such desire is objectively best calculated to put him in the position he was before damage occurred, may receive re-instatement damages: *Murphy* v. *Wexford County Council* [1921] 2 I.R. 230 and *Munnelly* v. *Calcon Ltd.* [1978] I.R. 387, *dicta* approved. *St.Alban's Investment Co.* v. *Sun Alliance and London Insurance Co.Ltd.*

(H.C., S.C.) [1984] ILRM 501

3. —— **Contract** — *Interpretation — Intention of parties — Professional indemnity and public liability policies — Claim of indemnity — Whether claim covered under either policy.*] Agrivest Ltd. contracted with a contractor to construct a tank for storing molasses in part of a dry dock. The plaintiffs were employed by the contractor as the main sub-contractors in respect of work to be performed under the contract. Agrivest Ltd. brought an action for negligence against the plaintiffs and for breach of contract and negligence against the contractor and another sub-contractor respectively. The action was settled for £735,000.00 plus costs and the plaintiffs agreed to pay £150,000.00 and a proportionate part of those costs. The plaintiffs had two professional indemnity policies and a public liability policy with the defendants and sought to be indemnified by the defendant against the sum of £150,000.00 and costs on foot of the said policies. The defendant repudiated the plaintiffs' claim to be indemnified and the plaintiffs instituted proceedings in the High Court. The High Court held that the defendant was not obliged to indemnify the plaintiffs under any policy ([1986] ILRM 419) and the plaintiffs appealed this decision to the Supreme Court. The only live issue in the appeal was as to whether the negligent acts of the plaintiffs occurred in the conduct and execution of the activities and duties defined in the professional indemnity policy. The defendant argued that even if the professional indemnity policy did apply the claim was still outside the scope of the policy as it was a mixed claim of negligence and breach of contract. **Held** by the Supreme Court (Finlay C.J.,Griffin and Hederman JJ.) in allowing the appeal and finding that the plaintiffs were entitled to be indemnified by the defendants under the professional indemnity policy but not under the public liability policy, 1, in construing the terms of the insurance policies the intention of the parties must prevail. In determining the intention of the parties what must be ascertained is what is to be taken as the

INSURANCE—*continued.*

intention which reasonable people would have had if placed in the situation of the parties. Such reasonable people would not have in mind that under the public liability policy the parties could expect that the events which took place would be covered. Before that policy could apply there must have been an 'accident' occurring in the course of the carrying out of the work. The plaintiffs' claim to an indemnity was covered, however, by reference to 'management of projects, contracts or works . . . and procurement of material' in the professional indemnity policy. 2. The only claim against the plaintiffs was in negligence. There was not, nor could there have been, any claim for breach of contract. *West Wake Price and Co.* v. *Ching* [1957] 1 W.L.R. 45 distinguished. *Per Curiam.* Insurers are not enabled to avoid liability under a professional indemnity policy on the basis that the same act amounts to both a tort and a breach of contract. *Finlay* v. *Murtagh* [1979] I.R. 249 referred to. *Rohan Construction Ltd.* v. *Insurance Corporation of Ireland plc.*

(S.C.) [1988] ILRM 373; (H.C.) [1986] ILRM 419

4. —— **Contract** — Uberrima fides — *Disclosure of material facts — Duty of person obtaining insurance cover — Extent of duty — Circumstances of the underwriting of a risk — Whether underwriter entitled to repudiate on ground of non-disclosure.*] On 13 July, 1981, the plaintiff company entered into a contract to have certain goods transported to Northern Ireland. The goods were to be carried at the plaintiff's own risk, and it was suggested by the carriers that the goods be insured. M., the managing director of and principal shareholder in the plaintiff, agreed to insurance being effected. The arrangements for the insurance cover were made by the carriers with the defendant. The carriers, acting throughout as agents of the defendant, completed the insurance certificates and the plaintiff was issued with an invoice for the cost of the insurance cover. The only information given to the plaintiff relating to the terms of the insurance was the extent of the cover. The identity of the underwriters was not made known to the plaintiff; the only information sought by the underwriters was the names and addresses of the consignor and consignee and the nature and value of the goods. The insurance was effected within two days of the arrangement for the transport of the goods, and no opportunity was given to the plaintiff to provide the defendant with additional information. On 20 July, 1981, one of the consignments of goods was hijacked, set on fire, and the consignment was destroyed. The plaintiff issued proceedings seeking an indemnity under the policy for the loss. The defendant sought to repudiate liability on the basis that the

INSURANCE—*continued.*

plaintiff had failed to disclose the fact that M. had been convicted of a number of offences involving dishonesty 20 years previously. That, it was alleged, was a material fact the non-disclosure of which entitled the defendant to repudiate liability under the policy. In the High Court, Carroll J. stated that she did not think that the convictions would have been material to the risk. However, she accepted the evidence on behalf of the defendant that a reasonable underwriter would have regarded the convictions as relevant to the risk, and she dismissed the plaintiff's claim. On appeal by the plaintiff it was **Held** by the Supreme Court (Walsh, Henchy, Griffin, Hederman and McCarthy JJ.) in allowing the appeal, 1, (Walsh, Hederman and McCarthy JJ.) that a contract of insurance requires the insured to disclose every matter which he might reasonably think to be material to the risk against which he is seeking indemnity. In the absence of a specific question, an insurer may not expect disclosure of a matter which he regards as material if a reasonable insured would either not advert to the matter or regard it as immaterial. *Carter* v. *Boehm* (1766) 3 Burr. 1905 applied. *Dicta* of Kenny and Keane JJ. in *Chariot Inns* v. *Assicurazioni Generali* [1981] I.R. 199 considered. 2. (Walsh, Henchy, Griffin, Hederman and McCarthy JJ.) That while it is the duty of a person seeking insurance to disclose all material facts, it is for the parties to the contract to make their own bargain. If an underwriter shows himself to be prepared to underwrite a risk without requiring full disclosure, or if the circumstances of the making of the contract are such that the insured is not afforded an opportunity to make full disclosure, then, in the absence of fraud, the underwriter cannot subsequently avoid the contract and repudiate liability on the ground of non-disclosure. *Per* McCarthy J. Good faith requires candour and disclosure, not accuracy in itself, but a genuine effort to achieve accuracy. If the duty on the insured required disclosure by him of all materials facts known to him then it might require an impossible level of performance. *Aro Road and Land Vehicles Ltd.* v. *Insurance Corporation of Ireland Ltd.*

(S.C.) [1986] I.R. 403

5. —— **Contract** — Uberrima fides — *Disclosure of material facts — Indemnity insurance — Breach of warranty — Answers given by insured on proposal form forming the basis of contract of insurance — Warranty of veracity and completeness of answers — Incomplete answer — Inaccuracy not material — Whether insurer entitled to repudiate for breach of warranty.*] The plaintiff applied to the defendant insurer for insurance cover. In reply to a question on the proposal form as to whether the plaintiff had

INSURANCE—*continued.*

ever sustained loss or damage by any of the risks he wished to insure against, the plaintiff answered 'no'. The plaintiff signed a declaration at the foot of the proposal form that the particulars therein contained were 'true and complete in every respect and that no material fact [had] been suppressed or withheld'; and agreed that the declaration and the answers given on the proposal form should be the basis of the contract between the parties. Pursuant to the plaintiff's proposal a policy of insurance issued and shortly after a fire took place in respect of which the plaintiff claimed to be indemnified by the defendant. The defendant disputed its liability to pay the plaintiff on the grounds (which was the fact) that the plaintiff had failed to disclose that he had, within the previous year, been paid £53 in respect of fire damage to a pump. The dispute was referred to arbitration where it was argued on behalf of the defendant firstly, that by virtue of the incorrect answer there had been a failure of a condition precedent; and secondly, that the plaintiff's answer had amounted to a misrepresentation or concealment of a material fact. The arbitrator found (1) that the declaration signed by the plaintiff and his agreement that the answers given should be the basis of the contract constituted a condition precedent of the contract; (2) that the plaintiff's answer was not true or complete; (3) that the inaccuracy or incompleteness did not amount to a misrepresentation or concealment of a material fact; and (4) that the defendant was under no liability to the plaintiff under the policy. The plaintiff brought proceedings to have the arbitrator's award set aside on the grounds that the arbitrator had erred in law in making an award in favour of the defendant in view of his finding that the inaccuracy or incompleteness of the plaintiff's reply was not material. **Held** by Blayney J., in giving judgment for the defendant, 1, that as a matter of construction the declaration made by the plaintiff entailed two statements: firstly, that the particulars and answers given were true and complete in every respect and secondly, that no material fact had been suppressed or withheld. It was not possible to read the two parts of the sentence together so that the first part would be qualified by the second. 2. That while at common law only a misstatement of a material fact would entitle an insurer to repudiate, the plaintiff in this case had expressly warranted the accuracy of his answers and agreed that they would be made the basis of the contract of insurance. *Chariot Inns* v. *Assicurazioni Generali* [1981] I.R. 199 distinguished. 3. That quite independently of any question of materiality, there must be strict and exact compliance with an obligation or statement which is warranted. *Keenan* v. *Shield Insurance Co. Ltd.*

INSURANCE—*continued.*

(H.C.) [1987] I.R. 113

Editor's note: For Supreme Court Judgment reported at [1988] I.R. 89, *see* **Arbitration,** 4.

6. —— **Contribution** — *Indemnity insurance — Double indemnity — Motor insurance policy — Employers' liability policy — Whether same risk covered by both policies — Subrogation — Employee injured in the course of his employment by negligence of a fellow employee driving motor car owned by employer — Action taken by injured employee against employer — Employer covered by motor insurance and by employers' liability insurance — Whether motor insurer entitled to contribution from employers' liability insurer.*] The plaintiff, by a motor insurance policy, was liable to indemnify Q. against liability in respect of the negligent driving of Q.'s motor cars and furthermore was liable to indemnify the driver of any such motor car driving with the authority of Q. The defendant, by an employers' liability policy, was liable to indemnify Q. against liability to pay compensation for injury, accident or disease sustained by any employee of Q. arising out of and in the course of his employment with Q. S., an employee of Q., was seriously injured when the motor car in which he was travelling as a passenger—which was owned by Q. and driven by D., who was also an employee of Q. — collided with a bus. At the time of the accident D. was driving and S. was travelling in the course of their employment with Q. In proceedings brought against Q. and D. for damages, S. recovered a substantial sum and Q. was held to be entitled to indemnify from D. for the full award. The plaintiff, on behalf of Q., paid the full amount of the award to S. and now claimed against the defendant to be entitled to a contribution of 50% on the grounds that Q. had enjoyed a double indemnity against its liability to S. **Held** by Gannon J., in dismissing the plaintiff's claim and affirmed by the Supreme Court (Finlay C.J., Henchy, Griffin, Hederman and McCarthy JJ.), 1, that the nature and purpose of the equitable relief of contribution was to give equality of remedy to two insurers where the rights of both were equal. *Godin et al.* v. *London Assurance Company* (1758) 1 Burr. 489 considered. 2. That the right to contribution only arose where the interest of the insured and the risk assumed by the insurer were the same under both policies. *North British and Mercantile Insurance Company* v. *London, Liverpool, and Globe Insurance Company* (1877) 5 Ch. D. 569 considered. 3. That the only liability of Q. covered by the motor policy was its vicarious liability, as the owner of the motor car, in respect of the breach by the driver of a duty owed to the public in general. That policy did not cover any breach of a duty

INSURANCE—*continued.*

owed by Q. to S. as his employer. 4. That the liability covered by the employers' liability policy — which might be direct as well as vicarious — was the liability of Q. for breach of its duty to take care for the safety of S. in the performance of the duties imposed on him by his employment. 5. That while liability to afford indemnity under each of the policies could arise on the happening of the same event, neither the interest of the insured under those policies nor the risks assumed by the plaintiff and defendant respectively, was the same. 6. That moreover, since Q. was entitled to a full indemnity from D., the defendant would be entitled to recover by subrogation from D. — and from the plaintiff as his insurer — the full amount of any sum it might pay on behalf of Q., whether directly to S. or by way of contribution to the plaintiff and would accordingly defeat the purpose of the plaintiff's claim. *Zurich Insurance Co.* v. *Shield Insurance Co. Ltd.*

(H.C., S.C.) [1988] I.R.174

7. —— **Insurer** — *Liability — Exception — Marine insurance — Insured owner of motor cruiser — Vessel laid up — Intermittent maintenance effected by owner — Vessel damaged by explosion while laid up — Explosion when authorised friend of insurer used cooker in galley in absence of insured — Defendant insurers disclaiming liability — Whether insurer exempted from liability where loss resulted from want of "due diligence" by insured — Meaning of "due diligence" — Whether exemption applicable — Warranty by insured that vessel, when laid up, would not be used for any purpose other than "customary overhauling" — Statutory duty of insured to disclose every material circumstance except matters of common notoriety — Interpretation of warranties — Whether breach of warranty by insured — Whether insurer liable — Marine Insurance Act,* 1906 (*c.* 41), *ss.* 18, 33.] Section 33, sub-s. 3 of the Marine Insurance Act, 1906, provides *inter alia* that a warranty, as defined by that section, is a condition which must be exactly complied with whether it be material to the risk or not. If a warranty is not so complied with, then the insurer may repudiate liability under the contract from the date of the breach. The plaintiff insured his motor cruiser with the defendant under a policy of marine insurance which incorporated *inter alia* a warranty as to the vessel's seaworthiness and fitness for purpose and use intended and a warranty that the vessel during the annual laid up period (from November to April) would be laid up "in a place of safety, dismantled, not fitted out or available for immediate use and not used for any purpose whatsoever other than dismantling, fitting out or customary overhauling." The policy also contained a clause confining the liability of the insurer for loss or damage to the vessel to loss or damage which did not result "from want of due diligence by the owners of the vessel or any of them, or by the managers or by the assured." The plaintiff, and a friend of his, E.T., who also owned a boat, kept their boats at a supervised mooring during the laid up period and carried out maintenance works on both boats there at intermittent times during this period. It was their custom to travel together from Dublin to the mooring and to cook meals for themselves on the boats during the maintenance works. Each had a key to the other's boat. On one occasion the plaintiff travelled alone to the mooring and removed a geyser from the gas system of his boat in order to have it repaired. Prior to doing so he removed the regulator from the gas cylinder which supplied this system. Two other gas-operated appliances on the boat were also supplied by the same system, a cooker and a refrigerator. Upon his return to Dublin, the plaintiff attempted unsuccessfully, on several occasions to contact E.T. to inform him of the works which he had carried out. Two days later, unknown to the plaintiff, E.T. travelled to the mooring to work on his own boat. While there, E.T. reconnected the regulator to the gas cylinder. This caused a gas leak from the pipe, formerly connected to the geyser but disconnected by the plaintiff and this gas accumulated in the lower part of the vessel. On his return to the plaintiff's boat at a later time that day, E.T. attempted to light the cooker. This caused an explosion of the leaked gas which injured E.T. and a companion and seriously damaged the plaintiff's boat. The plaintiff sought to be indemnified by the defendant under the policy of insurance in respect of the damage to his vessel and in respect of any claims against him for personal injuries arising from the explosion. The defendant resisted the plaintiff's claim *inter alia* on the ground that the plaintiff had been in breach of the two warranties incorporated into the policy, and in the High Court it was **Held** by O'Hanlon J. in dismissing the plaintiff's claim, 1, that as between the defendant and the plaintiff, the plaintiff had exercised due diligence in doing what he believed to be adequate to avoid danger of injury to any person arising from the disconnection of the gas supply. *Riverstone Meat Co.* v. *Lancashire Shipping Co.Ltd.* [1961] A.C. 807 and *Fraser* v. *B.N. Furman (Productions) Ltd.* [1967] 1 W.L.R. 898 applied. 2. That the use of the cooking facilities and the linking of the gas supply to the cooker on board the boat during the laid up period involved an added risk over and above the risks normally inherent in the use of the vessel during this period and accordingly, the defendant was entitled, having regard to the stringent provisions of s. 33, sub-s. 3 of the Marine Insurance Act,

INSURANCE—*continued.*

1906, to treat the risks as being outside the categories for which cover was provided. 3. That accordingly, the plaintiff was in breach of the warranty as to the limitations on use during the laid up period and the defendant was entitled to be exempted from liability under the policy of insurance. On appeal by the plaintiff it was **Held** by the Supreme Court (Finlay C.J., Walsh, Griffin, Hederman and McCarthy JJ.), in allowing the appeal, 1, that having regard to the terms of s. 33, sub-s. 3 of the Marine Insurance Act, 1906, if there had been a breach of warranty by the defendant the insured was entitled to repudiate and in such circumstances the presence or absence of an increased or additional risk was wholly immaterial. Accordingly, the trial judge had erred in considering such added risk. 2. (Finlay C.J., Walsh, Hederman, McCarthy JJ.; Griffin J. dissenting). That on the true construction of that warranty, the use of the galley was part of the customary overhaul and ancillary to it and was not a failure on the part of the plaintiff to exactly comply with the warranty. *The Cristie* [1975] 2 Lloyd's Rep. 100 considered. 3. That the terms of the warranty with respect to the seaworthiness and fitness for purpose and use intended of the vessel, construed in accordance with the *ejusdem generis* rule, did not apply during the laid up period and accordingly, no question of the breach thereof arose. *Brady* v. *Irish National Insurance Company.*

(H.C., S.C.) [1986] I.R. 698; [1986] ILRM 669

8. —— **Motor vehicle insurance** — *Obligation on insurers to keep records and to give information to members of the Garda Síochána — Request for information — Refusal to supply — Whether regulations valid — Whether natural rights of insured invaded —* Uberrima fides — *Road Traffic Act,* 1961 (*No.* 24), *s.* 75 — *Road Traffic (Compulsory Insurance) Regulations,* 1962 (*S.I. No.* 14), *arts.* 7, 9.] The Road Traffic (Compulsory Insurance) Regulations, 1962, deal with the issue by vehicle insurers of certificates of insurance (art. 7), the keeping of certain records relating to vehicle insurance (art. 9), the giving of information by the insurers when required by members of the Garda Síochána (art. 9(3)), and s. 75 of the Road Traffic Act, 1961, provides that a person who contravenes the said regulations shall be guilty of an offence. The defendant insurers were convicted in the District Court for failing to supply detailed information on demand by the complainant, an inspector in the Garda Síochána, pursuant to art. 9 of the aforesaid regulations relating to a Mr. Mallon, a member of the Garda Síochána insured with the defendant company. The defendant refused to supply the information and claimed that the information required to be made available by virtue of art.

INSURANCE—*continued.*

9(3) did not include information which the insurers were not obliged by statute to keep and which was contained in the insurers' private records. The defendant appealed by way of a case stated by the District Justice to the High Court as to whether the District Justice was wrong in law in convicting the defendant on the said charge. The complainant contended art. 9 granted him exceptional privilege to obtain the information depsite the fact that it was highly confidential information. **Held** by Doyle J. in answering the question in the case stated in terms that the defendant insurers ought to have been acquitted, 1, the contract between the insurers and the insured was one of *uberrimae fidei* and carries a corresponding obligation of confidentiality on the part of the insurers in view of the special relationship that existed between the parties and the special circumstances of this case due to the fact that the insured was a member of the Garda Síochána. 2. Art. 9(3) read in the context of the whole of the enactment and article therein does not manifest with reasonable clearness an intention to invade or limit or restrict the natural rights of the insured and to give effect to the regulation in the present case would entail an encroachment on the natural rights of the insured and also conflict with the obligation springing from a natural right which lies upon the insurers. *Murphy* v. *P.M.P.A. Insurance Company*

(H.C.) [1978] ILRM 25

—— Arbitration — Award — Finality.
see **Arbitration,** 3

—— Claim — Negligence — Unsuccessful defendant's insurers applying to be joined in appeal — Whether any issue between party and insurers.
see **Practice and Procedure,** 47

—— Claim to join insurers — Claim based on negligence of deceased driver.
see **Practice and Procedure,** 43

—— Employment insurance.
see **Social Welfare,** 1-3

—— Insurance company — Appointment of administrator — Administrator appointed receiver and manager of the property and assets of a body connected with the insurance company — Administrator's appointment ceasing upon appointment of liquidator — Administrator retaining certain funds to defray expenses — Whether certain items of expenditure be paid out of retained funds.

J

JUDGMENT—*continued.*

—— Judgment creditor — Judgment debtor obtaining bank loan on foot of solicitor's undertaking to discharge loan out of monies due to judgment debtor on foot of judgment — Judgment creditor seeking attachment of said judgment — Whether undertaking gave rise to equitable assignment or charge in favour of the bank — Whether bank had priority over judgment creditor — Whether solicitor's lien for costs had priority over judgment creditor.
see **Garnishee**

—— Precedent — *Stare decisis.*
see **Precedent**

—— Variation of interlocutory order — Powers of court.
see **Practice and Procedure,** 24

JUDGMENT MORTGAGE
—— Assent to sale of premises — Licence attached — Premises mortgaged — No reference to licence — Whether licence caught by mortgage — Whether assentor precluded from substituting hypothetical basis for sale.
see **Licensing Acts,** 1

JUDICIAL FUNCTION
see **Constitution,** 28-31

JUDICIAL INDEPENDENCE — Special Criminal Court — Appointment and removal of members.
see **Constitution,** 50

JUDICIAL NOTICE — Whether judicial notice of policies of political parties.
see **Local Government,** 4

JUDICIAL REVIEW
see also **Case Stated**

Certiorari. Nos. 1-10
Jurisdiction. Nos. 11, 12
Mandamus. Nos. 13, 14
Promissory estoppel. No. 15

CERTIORARI

1. —— **Cause** — *Extension of period for showing cause made* ex parte — *High court judge refusing to hear prosecutor — Whether prosecutor to be heard on application for extension of period for showing cause — Delay by prosecutor in appealing against refusal to hear his arguments — Whether prejudice caused to prosecutor.*] The prosecutor obtained a conditional order of certiorari quashing an order made by the respondent which had affirmed a conviction on him under the Road Traffic Act. During the 21 day period within which the respondent was directed to show cause, a successful application was made *ex parte* to the High Court for an extension for 14 days of the period fixed for showing cause. A further application was made to the court within that 14 day period for a further extension of time for showing cause. Although that application was made *ex parte,* counsel for the prosecutor was in court and sought to be heard in the matter but was refused. A further period of ten days for showing cause was allowed. The prosecutor appealed. **Held** by the Supreme Court (Henchy and Hederman JJ.) in dismissing the appeal, 1, the application for the order was properly made *ex parte* so there was no onus on the High Court judge to hear counsel for the prosecutor. 2. The fact that this was a second extension of time was of no consequence if the order was necessary for the respondent and did not work a prejudice on the prosecutor. 3. The fact that the prosecutor had allowed almost a year to pass before carrying his appeal was sufficient testimony that the ten day extension was of little or no consequence to him. *Per* McCarthy J, in refusing to entertain the appeal: the failure to bring an application to set aside the order, which was part of the inherent jurisdiction of the High Court, was fatal to any appeal. *The State (Hughes)* v. *O'Hanrahan.*
(S.C.) [1986] ILRM 218

2. —— **Delay** — *Lack of candour — Whether disentitling prosecutor to relief — Whether delay excessive — Whether certiorari would have any effect.*

Constitution — Fair procedures — Natural justice — Defence forces — Dismissal — Certiorari — Delay — Lack of candour — Whether disentitling to relief.] The prosecutor enlisted in the Irish Army for a three year period. He was a witness to an incident in the Glen of Imaal arising from which another member of the army was disciplined. Another witness to the incident was discharged from the army shortly after this incident, in July 1975, and proceedings were instituted by him for certiorari, which was granted by the High Court and Supreme Court: see *The State (Gleeson)* v. *Minister for Defence* [1976] I.R. 280. The prosecutor was discharged in August, 1975. He instituted correspondence with the army authorities and subsequently the Department of Defence and politicians in connection with his discharge and application for re-enlistment. He was informed that since his discharge had been for the reason that 'his services no longer being required' he was ineligible for re-enlistment. The prosecutor applied in October, 1979, for an order of certiorari. On showing cause the High Court discharged the

JUDICIAL REVIEW—Certiorari.

conditional order. On appeal by the prosecutor, **Held** by the Supreme Court (O'Higgins C.J. and McCarthy J.; Griffin J. dissenting) in allowing the appeal, 1, while there was a delay of just over four years in applying for certiorari, the prosecutor had attempted during that time to make representations regarding his re-enlistment, and since the respondents had not pursued the prosecutor's statement that he was, during that time, unaware of the decision in *The State (Gleeson)* v. *Minister for Defence* [1976] I.R. 280, his delay should not disentitle him to relief. *Per* Griffin J. (dissenting): the delay was inexcusable and inordinate, and in view of the widespread publicity given to the *Gleeson* decision, the prosecutor should be held disentitled to relief. 2. Delay or lack of candour should not, of itself, disentitle a prosecutor to an order of certiorari where it can de demonstrated that a public wrong has been done to him and that the wrong continues to mark his life, and in the circumstances of the case the proscutor's employment prospects and ability to re-enlist in the army were damaged by his discharge, and thus his failure to reveal on affidavit minor disciplinary offences against him should not bar him from relief. *Quaere:* whether there are circumstances in which certiorari should be refused in proceedings by a private citizen against the State, as opposed to proceedings between private parties, where lack of jurisdiction is established. *The State (Vozza)* v. *Ó Floinn* [1957] I.R. 227 applied. *The State (Cussen)* v. *Brennan* [1981] I.R. 181 discussed. *Dicta* in *R* v. *Herrod, ex p. Leeds City Council* [1976] Q.B. 540 not applied. 3. Although the three year period for which the prosecutor had enlisted had expired, an order of certiorari would not lack effect or be without advantage to the prosecutor, in view of the impact of the discharge on his employment and re-enlistment prospects. *The State (Furey)* v. *Minister for Defence*

(S.C.) [1988] ILRM 89

3. —— **Garda Síochána** — *Discipline — Inquiry — Discontinuance — Garda Commissioner directing that a new inquiry be held into same allegations — Whether appointment of new board of inquiry be quashed — Garda Síochána (Discipline) Regulations,* 1971 (*S.I. No.* 316).] On 24 September, 1985, a sworn inquiry was held at Ballyshannon Garda Station, County Donegal, to examine allegations that the applicants committed a breach of discipline under the Garda Síochána (Discipline) Regulations, 1971. Owing to certain irregularities in the documents before it, the inquiry was discontinued. On 15 January, 1987, the first named respondent directed that a sworn inquiry be held into the same allegations which has been the subject

JUDICIAL REVIEW—*continued.*

matter of the previous inquiry, and appointed the second, third and fourth named respondents to hold the inquiry. After a number of adjournments, the inquiry was fixed to take place on 29 September, 1987. On 28 September, 1987, the applicants were granted leave by the High Court (Blayney J.) to apply for an order of certiorari to quash the decision of the first named respondent appointing the second, third and fourth named respondents as a Board of Inquiry to hear and determine the allegations made against the applicants. **Held** by Gannon J. in refusing the relief sought, 1, where a sworn inquiry under the Garda Síochána (Discipline) Regulations, 1971, is discontinued before a party has an opportunity to put his case, the Commissioner of the Garda Síochána is entitled to obtain a report of the proceedings, to direct that a new inquiry be held and to appoint a new Board of Inquiry. The appointment of a second Board of Inquiry does not cause any injustice to the applicants since the nature of the investigation remains the same. 2. No inference may be drawn from the fact that the first sworn inquiry was discontinued to the effect that the case against the applicants had not been established and that they should not have to face a second sworn inquiry. *Semble:* It is undesirable that the courts should review internal investigations of this kind unless there is significant and substantial evidence of an injustice being done to an applicant. *McGowan* v. *Wren*

(H.C.) [1988] ILRM 744

4. —— **Labour Court** — *Infringement of principles of natural justice — Whether employer entitled as of right to have determination quashed — Extent of court's discretion — Whether order necessary for the protection of the employer's legal rights.*

Labour Court — Employment equality — Determination of entitlement to equal pay — Whether Labour Court acted without jurisdiction — Comparator used not named in union's original submission — Whether Labour Court acted in breach of principles of natural justice in taking legal advice on its jurisdiction in the absence of the parties — Anti-Discrimination (Pay) Act, 1974 (*No.* 15), *s.* 7.

Natural justice — Legal advice — Challenge to Labour Court's jurisdiction — Labour Court taking legal advice and proceeding with the appeal — Employer not made aware of advice and given no opportunity of commenting on it — Whether breach of natural justice — Whether, if so, employer entitled as of right to have the determination quashed.] The second named defendant (hereinafter referred to as the Union) in October, 1981, submitted a claim to the prosecutor on behalf of a number of female packers and

JUDICIAL REVIEW—Certiorari.

checkers employed by the prosecutor claiming that their work was equal in value to that performed by nine named male assistant operatives. The prosecutor rejected the claim which was referred to the Equality Officer (hereinafter referred to as the E.O.) under s. 7 of the Anti-Discrimination (Pay) Act 1974, for investigation and recommendation. In the meantime the prosecutor implemented a reorganisation plan in the printing area, whereupon the E.O. on visiting the prosecutor's premises in September, 1982, found that there was only one operative a Mr. Vaughan assisting the printer out of nine named male operatives in the original claim made by the Union. The Union in an attempt to clarify matters for the E.O. sent a written memorandum dated 11 January, 1984, to her and the Federated Union of Employers who acted for the prosecutor stating among other things that their claim was now that the work of the packers and checkers was equal in value to that of the assistant operatives' like Mr. Vaughan (as opposed to the original claim that the work was equal in value to the nine male operatives). The Federated Union of Employers replied on behalf of the prosecutor on 4 April, 1984, rejecting the Union's claim. The E.O. visited the factory again in July, 1984, and recommended that the said packers and checkers were entitled to the assistant operatives' rate of pay with effect from September, 1982. The prosecutor appealed this recommendation to the Labour Court who dismissed the appeal in September, 1985. The prosecutor now seeks to make absolute a conditional order of certiorari made on 15 April, 1986, quashing the Labour Court's determination on the following grounds: (1) the Labour Court acted without jurisdiction in holding that the E.O. was correct in law in proceeding to examine the work of Mr. Vaughan notwithstanding the fact that this amounted to a new claim by the Union in respect of the dispute between the prosecutor and the Union and that there was no dispute between the prosecutor and the Union in regard to the new claim; (2) the Labour Court had acted in breach of the principles of natural justice in that counsel for the prosecutor was not aware or given an opportunity of commenting or making submissions on the legal submissions which the court heard at the outset of the appeal on affidavit from the Registrar of the Labour Court on whether it had jurisdiction to hear the appeal. **Held** by Blayney J. in refusing to make the order sought, 1, the Equality Officer had jurisdiction to investigate the claim and make recommendations regarding it and likewise the Labour Court had jurisdiction to deal with the matter as the matter was brought to the prosecutor's attention in the form of a memorandum dated 11 January, 1984. 2. The court, in exercising its

JUDICIAL REVIEW—*continued.*

discretion to refuse to grant the order, sought relief on the ground that the granting of the said order could not protect the prosecutor's right in any way as the court has already found that the recommendation by the E.O. is binding on the prosecutor. *The State (Abenglen)* v. *Dublin Corporation* [1984] I.R. 381 applied. 3. In view of the conclusion the court has come to it is not necessary to consider whether the Labour Court did in fact breach the principles of natural justice. *Per curiam:* The procedure the Labour Court would safely follow if similar circumstances arose again was (i) inform the parties of their intention to ask the registrar for legal advice; (ii) having obtained the advice, they should at a resumed hearing inform the parties of the nature of the advice they had obtained and give the parties an opportunity of making submissions in regard to it; (iii) the members of the court having heard the submissions should on their own arrive at their own conclusion on the matter. *The State (Polymark (Ireland) Ltd.)* v. *Labour Court*

(H.C.) [1987] ILRM 357

5. —— **Prisoner** — *Natural justice* — *Temporary release* — *Expiry* — *Whether prisoner entitled to be heard on failure to renew temporary release.*] Since a temporary release is a privilege or concession in the giving of the prison governor, a prisoner has no right to be heard in accordance with natural justice on the renewal of a temporary release order which has already expired, as opposed to a revocation of a temporary release order still in being for breach of a condition attaching thereto. So **held** by Murphy J. *The State (Murphy)* v. *Governor of St. Patrick's Institution* [1985] ILRM 141 followed. *Ryan* v. *Governor of Limerick Prison*

(H.C.) [1988] I.R.198

6. —— **Remedy** — *Discretion of court* — *Alternative appellate procedure* — *Comprehensive appellate jurisdiction of special statutory tribunal* — *Local government* — *Planning* — *Decision of planning authority* — *Whether outline planning permission deemed to have been given by default* — *Whether* ultra vires *determination of application constitutes a decision* — *Local Government (Planning and Development) Regulations,* 1977 (*S,I. No.* 65), *art.* 27 — *Local Government (Planning and Development) Act,* 1963 (*No.* 28), *ss.* 26, 82 — *Local Government (Planning and Development) Act,* 1976 (*No.* 20), *s.* 14.] The prosecutors applied to the respondent planning authority for outline planning permission for the development of a site in the city of Dublin by the erection of a five-storey central block of offices flanked by three-storey residential blocks. Within the period of two months from the date of the receipt by the respondents of that appli-

JUDICIAL REVIEW—Certiorari.

cation, the respondents purported to grant to the prosecutors permission in writing in response to thesaid application. The permission was granted by the respondents subject to conditions which had the effect of making the permission apply to buildings which would be substantially different from the buildings proposed by the prosecutors in their application. Section 26, sub-s. 4, of the Act of 1963 provides that, if a planning authority does not give notice of its decision to an applicant within that period of two months, a decision by the planning authority to grant the permission sought by the applicant shall be regarded as having been given on the last day of that period. The prosecutors contended that, in giving their permission, the respondents had misinterpreted and misapplied the development plans and regulations considered by them and, by departing so radically from the proposals of the prosecutors, had failed to determine the application made by the prosecutors. Instead of appealing to the Planning Board pursuant to s. 26, sub-s. 5, of the Act of 1963, the prosecutors applied to the High Court (within the time prescribed for that purpose by s. 82 of the Act of 1963) for an order of certiorari quashing the respondents' grant of permission. The High Court made such order of certiorari and the respondents appealed to the Supreme Court. **Held** by the Supreme Court (O'Higgins C.J., Walsh, Henchy, Griffin and Hederman JJ.) in allowing the appeal, 1, — *Per* O'Higgins C.J., Henchy, Griffin and Hederman JJ. — That, even if the respondents' outline permission had been granted *ultra vires*, the court should not exercise its discretion so as to quash by certiorari the respondents' grant of permission since there had been available to the prosecutors a right of appeal to the Planning Board which right, if exercised, would have enabled the prosecutors' complaints to have been examined *de novo* by a statutory tribunal having comprehensive appellate jurisdiction to determine planning appeals, and having power to grant such permission even if the proposed development contravened materially the relevant development plan, and having power to refer questions of law to the High Court for its decision thereon. 2. *Per* Walsh, Henchy, Griffin and Hederman JJ. — That asuming that the respondents' outline permission had been granted *ultra vires,* the respondents' grant of such permission nevertheless constituted "a decision of the planning authority to grant the permission" within the meaning of s. 26, sub-s. 4, of the Act of 1963, so that, as the respondents had given the prosecutors notice of that decision within the appropriate period, the prosecutors were not entitled to claim a default permission under that sub-section. 3. *Per* Henchy, Griffin and Hederman JJ. — That the substantial

JUDICIAL REVIEW—*continued.*

reduction in the area allowed for office use in the conditional permission granted by the respondents, as compared with the area proposed for that use in the prosecutors' application for development permission, did not establish, *per se,* a failure by the respondents to determine the application that had been made by the prosecutors. *The State (Abenglen Properties Ltd.)* v. *Dublin Corporation*

(S.C.) [1984] I.R.381

7. —— **Social welfare** — *Application for old age pension refused — Whether decision of appeals officer bad in law — Whether error within jurisdiction — Social Welfare Act,* 1952 (*No.* 11), *s.* 43.] Rule 2, schedule 7 to the Social Welfare Act, 1952, provides that where a person had directly or indirectly deprived himself of any income or property in order to qualify for an old age pension, the said income or the yearly value of the said property shall be taken to be part of the means of such person. The prosecutors transferred their farm to their son, subject to a right of residence for themselves. Their subsequent application for an old age pension was refused by the local pensions sub-committee, and, on appeal, by the first named respondent who was an appeals officer. The prosecutors sought to quash the decision of the appeals officer by certiorari, and they sought also an order of mandamus directing the Minister to have their claims heard and determined by another appeals officer. The grounds on which certiorari was sought included, *inter alia,* an allegation that the appeals officer, in arriving at his decision, had taken into account matters not relevant to the question he was called upon to decide, and which had no probative value in the matter. This allegation was based on a memorandum of the appeals officer wherein he had stated that the matter should be considered in the light of the national policy objective whereby elderly landowners should be encouraged to transfer their holdings to younger persons to facilitate the workings of such holdings to the best advantage. **Held** by Gannon J. in refusing to make the orders sought, 1, one of the functions of an appeals officer on an oral hearing is that of determining the relevance and probative value of the evidence. Any errors made by him in that respect are made within jurisdiction, and do not render his decisions bad in law. 2. Even if the appeals officer had erred with regard to the relevance and probative quality of some parts of the evidence, he had before him other evidence on which he could have reached the same decision. *The State (Power)* v. *Moran*

(H.C.) [1976-7] ILRM 20

JUDICIAL REVIEW—Certiorari.

8. —— **Trial** — *Interruptions by judge — Scope of inquiry into whether lower court acted within its jurisdiction — Conduct of trial — Natural justice — Natural rights of accused — Right to cross-examine — Right to be heard in argument — Whether conduct of trial went to jurisdiction.*

Criminal law — Trial — Judge's interventions — Judge interrupting cross-examination and legal argument — Natural justice — Conduct of trial — Right of accused to test prosecution evidence by cross-examination — Right to be heard in argument before judgment given — Whether conduct of trial went to jurisdiction of trial court.] The applicant appeared before the District Court to answer a charge of driving a mechanically propelled vehicle while there was present in his body an excess quantity of alcohol contrary to s. 49 of the Road Traffic Act, 1961, as inserted. At the hearing of the prosecution before the District Court the applicant's solicitor attempted by his cross-examination of the prosecuting garda to establish that the statutory procedure for the taking of the blood sample had not been complied with but was interrupted by the respondent who said "It does not matter what you say, the Act was complied with." The applicant's solicitor submitted that he was entitled to make his argument, to which the respondent replied "You can go on and on for all the good it will do you. I am not interested in it." The applicant's solicitor persisted in his submission but the respondent interrupted saying "I do not care. I am not interested. Do you want to call any witnesses?" The applicant's solicitor decided that it would be pointless to call any witnesses and the applicant was convicted. The applicant obtained leave to seek certiorari by way of judicial review on the grounds that the respondent had failed to conduct the hearing in accordance with the principles of natural justice and had acted in excess of jurisdiction. It was argued on behalf of the respondent, in opposition to the application, that the applicant's solicitor had been given adequate opportunity to present his case and alternatively that any error on the part of the respondent (which was denied) was an error within the jurisdiction so that certiorari was not the appropriate remedy. **Held** by Lynch J., in granting the relief sought, 1, that the High Court in deciding whether or not a court of local and limited jurisdiction was acting within its jurisdiction will not only look at the statutory limits of jurisdiction but will also examine whether the accused was deprived of any of his basic rights of justice at a criminal trial. *The State (Healy)* v. *Donoghue* [1976] I.R. 325 applied. 2. That the applicant's solicitor had sought to raise an arguable point before the District Court but had not been given a proper opportunity of putting that point before the respndent for due consideration and

JUDICIAL REVIEW—*continued.*

decision. 3. That while an application for certiorari by way of judicial review could not be regarded as a readily available alternative to an appeal to the Circuit Court, in the instant case neither the facts nor the law had been adequately heard in the Distict Court. Accordingly any appeal to the Circuit Court would have been a first hearing and not a re-hearing to which the respondent would have been entitled. *The State (Roche)* v. *Delap* [1980] I.R. 170 considered. *Gill v. Connellan*

(H.C.) [1987] I.R.541; [1988] ILRM 448

9. —— **Tribunal** — *Tribunal established to award compensation to victims of fire — Claimant and his wife seeking compensation for nervous shock — Both claims arising out of similar circumstances — Tribunal awarding compensation to wife but not to claimant — Whether decision unreasonable or irrational — Test to be applied.*

Judicial review — Prohibition — Difficulties experienced by legal advisor in advising clients and obtaining medical reports — Order sought to prevent Tribunal hearing claims — Whether proper ground for issuing prohibition.] The respondent Tribunal was established by virtue of a scheme set up by the Government to award *ex gratia* compensation in respect of personal injury and loss attributable to a fire at the Stardust dancehall in Artane, County Dublin in 1981. The first prosecutor and his wife submitted claims to the Tribunal in respect of the deaths of two of their daughters in the fire (as dependants of those two people) and separate claims on their own behalf for damages for nervous shock suffered by them as a result of the deaths of their daughters and the serious injuries sustained by a third daughter in the fire. Neither the prosecutor nor his wife suffered any physical injuries in the fire. At the hearing of the claims it was agreed between the parties and accepted by the Tribunal that the nervous shock claims should be adjudicated upon in accordance with the principles enunciated by the House of Lords in *McLoughlin* v. *O'Brian* [1983] 1 A.C. 410. The first prosecutor's wife was awarded £50,000 by the Tribunal as compensation for nervous shock but the Tribunal refused to award the first prosecutor any such compensation and further refused to award him his costs of legal representation. The prosecutors obtained a conditional order of certiorari in the High Court quashing the decision of the Tribunal to refuse the first prosecutor compensation for nervous shock and his legal costs and also a conditional order of prohibition restraining the Tribunal from proceeding to deal with further claims being handled by the second prosecutor (the first prosecutor's solicitor) on the ground that as a result of the instant decision of the Tribunal he was having difficulty in advising

JUDICIAL REVIEW—Certiorari.

his clients and obtaining medical reports. On the prosecutors' motion to make the conditional orders absolute notwithstanding cause shown it was argued on their behalf that the refusal by the Tribunal to award the first prosecutor compensation for nervous shock was wrong to the point of being arbitrary and capricious; that the first prosecutor was a victim as defined by the scheme, and as such was entitled to have his claim assessed; that even if his claim was rejected, under the terms of the scheme he should be entitled to his costs and, finally, on the basis of the uncontradicted medical reports before the Tribunal, its decision clearly lacked fairness. **Held** by Blayney J., in allowing the cause shown and discharging the conditional orders, 1, that if the Tribunal had erred in refusing the first prosecutor compensation for nervous shock, it had erred within its jurisdiction and, thus, its decision could not be quashed. *Dicta* of Lord O'Brien L.C.J. in *The King (Martin)* v. *Mahony* [1910] 2 I.R. 695 at p. 707 and of Henchy J. in *The State (Abenglen Properties)* v. *Corporation of Dublin* [1984] I.R. 381 at pp. 399-400 applied. 2. That without deciding whether the refusal of compensation by the Tribunal, if characterised as arbitrary or capricious, would amount to an excess or want of jurisdiction, its decision was not arbitrary or capricious and neither did it attract the application of the principles of unfairness of procedures stated by the Supreme Court in *The State (Healy)* v. *Donoghue* [1976] I.R. 325. 3. That the first prosecutor could only be a victim within the meaning of the scheme if he had sustained injury or loss and the Tribunal had held that he had not and, furthermore, it was clear from Clause 2 of the scheme that the Tribunal was not obliged to make an award in every case that came before it. 4. That the Tribunal's refusal to award the first prosecutor costs could not be impugned since under the scheme it was only in the event of an award being made and accepted that the State was obliged to pay costs, and even if the Tribunal had a discretion to award costs in any event, the exercise of such discretion against the prosecutor here could not be criticised. 5. That the second prosecutor's difficulty in advising his clients and obtaining medical reports was not a ground for issuing an order of prohibition which only lay to a tribunal where it was purporting to usurp a jurisdiction with which it was not legally vested. Statement in Short annd Mellor on Crown Practice at p. 252 applied. On appeal by the prosecutors in relation to the Tribunal's refusal to award the first prosecutor compensation for nervous shock, it was **Held** by the Supreme Court (Finlay C.J., Hamilton P., Henchy, Griffin and Hederman JJ.) in disallowing the appeal, 1, that the test of unreasonableness or irrationality in judicial

JUDICIAL REVIEW—*continued.*

review lies in considering whether the impugned decision plainly and unambiguously flies in the face of fundamental reason and common sense. *Associated Provincial Picture Houses Ltd.* v. *Wednesbury Corporation* [1948] 1 K.B. 223 considered. *Dicta* of Lord Diplock in *Council of Civil Service Unions* v. *Minister for the Civil Service* [1985] A.C. 374 at p. 410 disapproved. 2. That on the evidence available of the proceedings before the Tribunal, it could not be said that its refusal to award compensation to the first prosecutor for nervous shock was unreasonable or irrational. *McLoughlin* v. *O'Brian* [1983] 1 A.C. 410 and *Chief Constable of the North Wales Police* v. *Evans* [1982] 1 W.L.R. 1155 considered. *Per* Finlay C.J. Even if after due debate the principles laid down in *McLoughlin* v. *O'Brian* [1983] 1 A.C. 410 or some of them were accepted as part of our law it would appear that grief even so extreme as to cause psychiatric disorder as distinct from nervous shock may not give rise to liability for damages. *The State (Keegan and Lysaght)* v. *Stardust Victims Compensation Tribunal*

(H.C., S.C.) [1986] I.R.642 ; [1987] ILRM 202

10. —— **Tribunal** — *Criminal Injuries Compensation Tribunal — Tribunal required to award compensation to dependants of persons killed in attempting to save human life — Claim by widow — Burden of proof — Primary facts not in dispute — Rejection of claim by Tribunal — Whether failure to infer from facts that deceased was attempting to save a life was at variance with reason and common sense.*] The respondent tribunal was required by virtue of rule 4 (*d*) of the Scheme of Compensation for Personal Injuries Criminally Inflicted (1974) to award compensation to the dependants of a deceased person who it was satisfied had died "because of or in the course of attempting to save human life." The applicant's husband died while attempting to stop a van containing his infant son from rolling backwards down a steep hill. In rolling down the hill, the van would have crossed another road on which children were likely to be playing. The applicant sought an award of compensation from the respondent, claiming that her husband had died while attempting to save a human life. No contrary evidence was called or given at the hearing before the respondent. The respondent rejected the applicant's claim on the grounds that it was "not satisfied that the death of [the deceased] arose because of or in the course of his attempting to save human life." By way of showing cause against conditional orders of certiorari and mandamus granted by the High Court (Keane J.) to the applicant, the respondent stated that it had acted within its jurisdiction and in accordance with

JUDICIAL REVIEW—Certiorari.

natural justice and that there had been evidence on which it was entitled to reach its decision. The High Court (Lardner J.) allowed the cause shown and discharged the conditional orders. On appeal by the applicant to the Supreme Court it was **Held** by the Supreme Court (Finlay C.J., Walsh and McCarthy JJ.) in allowing the appeal and granting the relief sought, 1, that to succeed in her application the applicant had to establish that the decision of the respondent had been at variance with reason and common sense. *The State (Keegan and Lysaght)* v. *Stardust Victims Compensation Tribunal* [1986] I.R. 642 followed. 2. That rule 4 (*d*) of the Scheme of 1974 only required that the actions of the deceased had been an attempt to save a life believed by him to have been in danger. The rule did not require a life to have been actually in danger or actually saved. 3. That the hazard to which the deceased had exposed himself was consistent only with the inference that the deceased was risking all to save the life of his child. Accordingly, the decision of the respondent had been at variance with reason and common sense. *Per* Finlay C.J.: That for a tribunal such as the respondent to reach a conclusion rejecting in full the claim of an applicant and not to give any reason for the rejection was an unacceptable and improper form of procedure. *The State (Creedon)* v. *Criminal Injuries Compensation Tribunal*

(S.C.) [1988] I.R.51

JURISDICTION

11. —— **Evidence** — *Ruling of inadmissibility — Statement of accused — Inadmissible statement accidentally given to jury — Retrial — Whether High Court entitled prior to retrial to restrain prosecution from adducing same statement — Whether such attempt an abuse of process of court.*] At a trial upon indictment in the Circuit Criminal Court on charges of rape and other offences a statement of the accused was ruled inadmissible by the trial judge, but given in error to the jury when it retired to consider its verdict. The accused applied in the High Court for orders by way of judicial review restraining the respondent from seeking to have the same statement admitted as evidence in the retrial. **Held** by Barron J., in refusing the orders sought, that the admissibility of evidence in any trial is a matter solely within the jurisdiction of the presiding trial judge and the High Court has no jurisdiction, whether by judicial review or otherwise, to make advance rulings upon matters which may or may not arise in a trial before another tribunal. *The State (O'Callaghan)* v. *Ó hUadhaigh* [1977] I.R. 42 and *Kelly* v. *Ireland* [1986] ILRM 318 considered. *Ryan* v. *D.P.P.*

(H.C.) [1988] I.R.232

JUDICIAL REVIEW—Jurisdiction.

12. —— **Prison** — *Disciplinary award against a prisoner by prison governor — Whether subject to judicial review — Observations on public policy.*] The applicant appealed against a decision of Gibson L.J. in which he held that a decision of the Governor of Her Majesty's Prison, The Maze on an adjudication was not subject to judicial review. The question for determination was whether the remedy of judicial review was available in relation to a disciplinary award made by a prison governor against a prisoner who was serving a sentence in the prison of which that governor was in charge. **Held,** allowing the appeal that, 1, the proposition that the Chief Officer of a force governed by discipline ought not to be subject to the prerogative jurisdiction is unsound in relation to the disciplinary functions of the governor of a prison when hearing charges against the inmates of that prison who do not belong to the disciplined body of which that governor is the superior officer: the analogy between prisoners (as distinct from prison officers) and military subordinates was not persuasive. 2. There was no logical distinction between a disciplinary hearing by a prison governor and one by a Board of Visitors. The administrative functions of a prison governor should be distinguished from his disciplinary functions and the latter, like decisions of a Board of Visitors, were subject to judicial review. The governor's disciplinary and judicial functions could be indentified and separated from his administrative functions by reference to his duty of hearing charges against prisoners. *R.* v. *Board of Visitors of Hull Prison, ex parte St. Germain* (No. 1) [1979] Q.B. 425 and *R.* v. *Deputy Governor of Camphill Prison, ex parte King* [1984] 1 Q.B. 735 not followed. 3. Provided that natural justice and prison rules were observed, the prison governor's procedure need not be so elaborate as that of a Board of Visitors may sometimes have to be in order to avoid the danger of quashing: justice can be summary and still remain fair and lawful. It is both reasonable and in the public interest that a prison governor, when adjudicating upon a charge against a prisoner, should be expected to proceed according to natural justice and prison rules and quite unreasonable and contrary to the public interest in a civilised state that he should, in his judicial capacity, exercise an autocratic power and enjoy a freedom from High Court supervision which are denied to the Board of Visitors and to all inferior courts. 4. A convicted prisoner in spite of his imprisonment retains all civil rights which are not taken away expressly or by necessary implication and a citizen's right of unimpeded access to the courts can only be taken away by express enactment. The fear that allowing judicial review would cause difficulty in maintaining discipline, initiate a flood of appli-

cations difficult to cope with and undermine the authority of the governor was unproven. A prisoner whose civil rights have been wrongfully infringed in exercise of a governor's judicial functions has a right to judicial review. Any restriction on the exercise of that right was a matter for express statutory enactment and was not a matter for the courts. *Per* Lord Lowry L.C.J. The existence of an alternative remedy, such as a duty to ensure compliance by prison governors with the duties set out in the Act and the rules thereunder imposed on the Secretary of State by section 4 (2) of the Prison Act, 1952, of which there was no equivalent in the Prison Act (Northern Ireland) 1953, would be no bar to certiorari; the alternative remedy was neither all-embracing nor clearly defined and the subject's recourse to the court for the determination of his rights was not to be excluded except by clear words. *In re McKieran*

(C.A., N.I.) [1985] N.I.385

MANDAMUS

13. —— **Statute** — *Instrument — Duty to state in writing grounds of decision — Grounds of decision necessary precondition to formulation of appeal — Natural justice — Fair procedures — Exercise of power — Duty to act judicially — Includes duty to furnish reasons for decision — Trade Marks Rules,* 1963 (*S.I. No.* 268), *rr. 43,* 70 — *R.S.C.,* 1986, *O.* 94, *rr.* 45, 46 — *Trade Marks Act,* 1963 (*No.* 9), *ss.* 25, 26, 34, 56, 57.] Rule 70 of the Trade Marks Rules, 1963, provides that upon an application to the respondent under s. 34 of the Act of 1963 for the expunging of an entry in the register of trade marks the provisions of rr. 36 to 46 of the Rules of 1963 shall, subject to the appropriate modifications, apply to the further proceedings thereon. Rule 43 of the Rules of 1963, with the appropriate modifications, provides that an application under s. 34 of the Act of 1963 for a written statement of the grounds of a decision of the respondent shall be made to the respondent within one month from the date of notification of the decision. Section 56, sub-s. 1 of the Act of 1963 provides that the respondent shall be given notice in writing by the applicant of any legal proceeding in which the relief sought would affect the register of trade marks including an appeal from any decision of the respondent and shall have the right to appear and be heard, and shall appear if so directed by the court, in any such legal proceeding. Sub-section 2 of that section provides that unless otherwise directed by the court, the respondent in lieu of appearing and being heard may submit to the court a statment in writing signed by him of the grounds of any decision given by him affecting the matter in

issue and the statement shall be deemed to form part of the evidence in the proceeding. Section 57 of the Trade Marks Act, 1963, provides for an appeal to the court from a decision of the respondent under any provision of that Act. Order 94, r. 45 of the Rules of the Superior Courts, 1986, provides that such an appeal shall be made by special summons and r. 46 of that order provides that such summons shall state the grounds of the appeal. The applicant applied to the respondent under s. 34 of the Act of 1963 for the expunging of a trade mark in the register on the ground of non-use. The respondent refused the application following an oral hearing at which the applicant and the registered proprietor presented their case. The applicant applied to the respondent for a written statement on the grounds of his decision, which application was refused. The applicant applied to the High Court by way of application for judicial review *inter alia* for an order of mandamus compelling the respondent to state in writing the grounds of his decision. The respondent opposed the application on the grounds *inter alia* that he was not required by s. 34 of the Act of 1963 to state the grounds of his decision. **Held** by Barron J., in granting the order sought, 1, that the respondent had a duty to state in writing the grounds of his decision by virtue of rr. 43 and 70 of the Trade Marks Rules, 1963. 2. That as the court has jurisdiction under s. 56 of the Act of 1963 to direct the respondent to state in writing the grounds of his decision once an appeal has commenced, it follows that the court has a discretion to do so in judicial review proceedings before an appeal has commenced. 3. That the respondent in exercising his power to make a decision under s. 34 of the Trade Marks Act, 1963, must guarantee fair procedures and must act judicially. 4. Accordingly, on receipt of a *bona fide* request it was the duty of the respondent to state in writing the grounds of his decision particularly as under order 94, r. 46 of the Rules of the Superior Courts, 1986, such a statement was a necessary pre-condition to the formulation of an appeal *Anheuser Busch Inc.* v. *Controller of Patents, Design and Trade Marks*

(H.C.) [1987] I.R.329; [1988] ILRM 247

14. —— **Statutory duty** — *Statutory provision effecting change in liability of road authorities — Governmental order required by that statutory provision to bring it into force — Prosecutor with no cause of action under the provision seeking such order from the Government — Whether mandamus lies against the Government — Whether Government's statutory power an unreviewable executive function — Whether statutory power conferring absolute discretion —* Locus standi *of prosecutor to seek mandamus — Civil Liability*

Act, 1961 (*No.* 41), *s.* 60.] The prosecutor instituted proceedings in the Circuit Court against Cork Corporation seeking damages for injuries sustained due to falling on a public footpath in the city of Cork. The Corporation, as road authority, would only be liable to the prosecutor in those proceedings at common law if it could be shown to have been guilty of misfeasance with regard to the construction or maintenance of the footpath and not if only guilty of non-feasance i.e. non-repair of the footpath. Section 60 of the Civil Liability Act, 1961, purports to alter the common law position in that regard by providing in sub-s. 1 that a "road authority shall be liable for damage caused as a result of their failure to maintain adequately a public road." Sub-section 7 of s. 60 provides that the section "shall come into operation on such day, not earlier than the 1st day of April, 1967, as may be fixed therefor by order made by the Government." The preceding sub-section provides that the section shall not apply to damage arising from an event which occurred before the coming into operation of the section. No order was ever made by the Government bringing s. 60 into operation and the prosecutor obtained a conditional order of mandamus in the High Court requiring it to make an order fixing a date for the coming into operation of the section. At the hearing of the prosecutor's motion to make the conditional order absolute notwithstanding the cause shown it was argued on behalf of the respondent, 1, that the order of mandamus does not lie against the Government, 2, that the exercise by the Government of its power under s. 60, sub-s. 7, was an executive function over which the courts had no jurisdiction, 3, that the statutory power conferred an open-ended discretion and, 4, that the prosecutor had no *locus standi* to seek an order of mandamus since if the Government were ordered to bring s. 60 into operation, the prosecutor could not benefit by reason of the non-restrospective effect provided for that section by sub-s. 6 thereof. **Held** by Costello J., in disallowing the cause shown and making the conditional order of mandamus absolute, 1, that the order of mandamus granted now by Irish courts was not the prerogative writ of mandamus which, before the establishment of the State, was the means by which the courts enforced observance of statutory duties and which did not lie against the Crown. Furthermore, the Government established under the Constitution is not the successor to the Crown. 2. That where a statute imposes a duty on the Government, it cannot claim immunity from a court's jurisdiction on the ground that in performing the duty it is carrying out an "executive function." *Boland* v. *An Taoiseach* [1974] I.R. 338, distinguished. 3. That from an examination

of the statutory language employed in s. 60, and having regard to the unconditional nature of sub-s. 1, whilst it appeared that the Government had some discretion as to when it should make an order under sub-s. 7, this discretion was a limited one and sub-s. 7 required the Government to make an order within a reasonable time after the 1 April, 1967. A reasonable time had elapsed since that date and the Government had accordingly failed to fulfil its statutory duty. *Padfield* v. *Minister for Agriculture, Fisheries and Food* [1968] A.C. 997, considered. 4. That the prosecutor had standing to apply for the order of mandamus; despite the fact that s. 60 would not apply to the prosecutor's Circuit Court proceedings upon it becoming operative, the prosecutor had been prejudiced to an extent greater than other members of the public by the Government's failure to make an order under s. 60, sub-s. 7, because (*a*), he might lose a substantial amount of money by reason of being unable to rest his case in the Circuit Court on the basis of non-feasance and (*b*), should he lose his case in the Circuit Court by reason of being only able to establish non-feasance against the Corporation, he might have an action for damages against the Government for breach of its statutory duty to bring s. 60 into operation. *R. (I.U.D.W. and C.)* v. *Rathmines U.D.C.* [1928] I.R. 260; *The State (Modern Homes (Ireland) Ltd.)* v. *Dublin Corporation* [1953] I.R. 202; *Cahill* v. Sutton [1980] I.R. 269 and *Reg.* v. *I.R.C., Ex. p. Fed. of Self Employed* [1982] A.C. 617, considered. On appeal by the Government, it was **Held** by the Supreme Court (Finlay C.J., Henchy, Griffin and Hederman JJ.; McCarthy J. dissenting) in allowing the appeal and discharging the order of mandamus, 1, that assuming the prosecutor had standing to apply for an order of mandamus, the Oireachtas by the manner in which it had couched the language of s. 60, sub-s. 7 and, in particular, by its choice both of the word "may" and of the Government and not a Minister in which to vest the discretion under that sub-section in, showed that the discretion to bring s. 60 into operation after 1 April, 1967, was not limited in any way, as to time or otherwise. 2. That, accordingly, the interpretation of s. 60, sub-s. 7 contended for by the prosecutor and which had found favour in the High Court could be justified only by reading into that sub-section wording beyond what was chosen by the Oireachtas. *R. (I.U.D.W. and C.)* v. *Rathmines U.D.C.* [1928] I.R. 260; *The State (Modern Homes (Ireland) Ltd.)* v. *Dublin Corporation* [1953] I.R. 202 distinguished. *Per* McCarthy J. dissenting: On the assumption that the prosecutor's action would be defeated by a finding solely of non-feasance against the Corporation, the trial judge was correct in holding that the

JUDICIAL REVIEW—Mandamus.

prosecutor had adequate *locus standi.* On the substantive issue the conclusion of the trial judge was also correct save that the Government should not now be shut out from giving evidence that a reasonable time had not elapsed since the 1 April, 1967; no factual basis with regard to that matter having been laid in the proceedings so far. Formulae used in commencement provisions of other Acts of Oireachtas for 1961 considered. *Per* Finlay C.J. and Griffin J. The issues (*a*) as to whether having regard to the separation of powers provided for in the Constitution the courts may by order direct the introduction into effect of legislation which the Oireachtas has provided should be introduced by an order made by the Government or by a Minister of the Government; and (*b*) as to whether such an order could be made in the particular case where the introduction of such legislation might impose a significant burden on the Exchequer have neither been raised nor argued in this court and fall to be decided in some future case where they have been fully argued. *The State (Sheehan)* v. *Government of Ireland*
(H.C., S.C.) [1987] I.R.550; [1988] ILRM 437

PROMISSORY ESTOPPEL

15. —— **Legitimate expectation** — *Undergraduate course — Offer of place — Acceptance — Deferral by college of place offer to next academic year — Whether enforceable by candidate — Remedies.*] The applicant was offered and accepted a place to read for Arts in University College Dublin for the academic year beginning in 1986. Shortly after paying the appropriate deposit she applied to the respondent to have that place offer deferred to the following academic year. An agent of the respondent acceded to this request but indicated that the applicant's reasons would have to be set out in writing. Some time later, and before the reasons in writing were delivered, the respondent informed the applicant's father that it was too late to consider any deferral. When the applicant failed to secure a place in the following year beginning in 1987, she brought proceedings in the High Court for judicial review seeking to quash the respondent's decision to refuse to register her for the 1987 course on the grounds that the respondent was estopped by his conduct from denying his representation that the requested deferral had been granted. Upon the respondent filing a statement of grounds of opposition it was **Held** by Barron J., in declaring the applicant entitled to be registerd for the academic year beginning in 1987, that by the doctrine of promissory estoppel the respondent was estopped from denying its grant of a deferral in that the applicant forbore to exercise her immediate entitlement upon the legitimate

JUDICIAL REVIEW—*continued.*

expectation created by the respondent's undertaking to her that the deferral of the place offer would be duly honoured. *Webb* v. *Ireland* [1988] I.R. 353 followed. *Central London Property Trust Ltd.* v. *High Trees House Ltd.* [1947] K.B. 130 approved. *Kenny* v. *Kelly*
(H.C.) [1988] I.R.457

—— Administrative act — Public Service — Staff associations — New staff association seeking negotiation recognition from Minister for the Public Service — Refusal of recognition — Nature of decision — Whether administrative or judicial — Whether refusal of recognition supported by evidence before Minister.
see **Civil Service,** 2

—— Administrative tribunal — Discretion — Whether discretion exercised *ultra vires* — Nature of judicial review — Whether court entitled to review exercise of discretion where tribunal acted honestly and reasonably.
see **Constitution,** 21

—— Appeal to Circuit Court — Correction of error.
see **District Court,** 1

—— Application — Delay — Illegality — Law applicable to facts for decision.
see **Social Welfare,** 2

—— Certiorari — Appeal to Circuit Court — Correction of error.
see **District Court,** 1

—— Certiorari and prohibition — Labour Court determination — Application to quash — Whether error of law as to jurisdiction.
see **Employer and Employee,** 14

—— Certiorari — Certificate of conviction — Circuit Court appeal — Certificate of conviction not correctly recording the orders spoken by the judge.
see **Criminal Law,** 37

—— Certiorari — Criminal law — Conviction — Accused not represented at trial — Lack of fair procedures — Conviction set aside — Failure to invoke appellate procedure unobjectionable.
see **Criminal Law,** 46

—— Certiorari — Criminal law — Conviction — Appeal pending — Election — Order of

JUDICIAL REVIEW—*continued.*

conviction made by District Court — Appeal to Circuit Court lodged by accused — Failure to establish jurisdictional incapacity of Circuit Court — Cause shown allowed.
see **District Court,** 1

—— Certiorari — Criminal law — Sentence — Consecutive sentence — Jurisdiction — Uncertainty — Felony.
see **Criminal Law,** 75

—— Certiorari — Criminal law — Sentence — Conviction — Accused already serving a sentence — Aggregate sentences exceeding 12 months — Whether District Justice acting in excess of jurisdiction.
see **Criminal Law,** 73

—— Certiorari — Criminal law — Summons — Sufficiency — Signature — Whether open to prosecutor to challenge sufficiency of summons — Prosecutor acquiescing in adjournments of his case — Validity of concept of "representation without prejudice" questioned.
see **Criminal Law,** 62

—— Certiorari — Decision of D.P.P. — Whether reviewable.
see **Criminal Law,** 74

—— Certiorari — Decision of Garda superintendent — Whether reviewable.
see **Criminal Law,** 49

—— Certiorari — Delay — Criminal law — Application to quash sentence — Out of time — Whether delay in seeking order a ground for refusal — Whether order issues *ex debito justitiae.*
see **Criminal Law,** 74

—— Certiorari — Delay — Discretion of court — Relief granted.
see **Prisons,** 3

—— Certiorari — Delay — Technical flaws — Discretion.
see **Criminal Law,** 56

—— Certiorari — Discretion — Adequacy of alternative relief.
see **District Court,** 1

—— Certiorari — Discretion — Alternative procedure available to applicant — Criminal law — Search warrant — Issue — Validity.
see **Criminal Law,** 70, 71

JUDICIAL REVIEW—*continued.*

—— Certiorari — Dismissal — Office holder — Probationer — Natural justice — Minister empowered by statute to dismiss where satisfied of certain matters — Reasons not disclosed — Whether summary dismissal permissible — Whether Minister's decision reviewable — Constitutional limitations on exercise of power.
see **Civil Service,** 1

—— Certiorari — Employment — Garda Síochána — Discipline inquiry — Reference to Appeal Board — Board deciding it had no jurisdiction — Whether jurisdictional error.
see **Garda Síochana,** 2

—— Certiorari — Extent of review.
see **Criminal Law,** 55

—— Certiorari — Grounds for granting — Distinction between a proceeding commenced without jurisdiction and one validly commenced during which jurisdiction is exceeded.
see **Criminal Law,** 53

—— Certiorari — Inquest — Verdict — Suicide — Statutory exclusions of questions of civil or criminal liability — Whether verdict available — Notice of inquest not served on next-of-kin — Whether breach of natural and constitutional justice.
see **Coroner**

—— Certiorari — Mandamus — Employment — Dismissal — Garda Síochána — Natural justice — Summary dismissal — Absence of formal inquiry — Limitations of rules of natural justice in context of certain State services — — Opportunity given to advance reasons against dismissal.
see **Employer and Employee,** 7

—— Certiorari — Mandamus — Patent Office — Arrears of work — Controller promulgating policy of accelerated acceptance of patent specifications — Refusal of increment to those examiners failing to implement this policy — Whether orders of certiorari and mandamus be granted.
see **Patents,** 2

—— Certiorari — Natural justice — Corporation flat — Notice to quit — District Court hearing — Tenant not

JUDICIAL REVIEW—*continued.*

ground proposed within 100 yards of plaintiff's premises — Whether consent in writing of plaintiff required.
see **Local Government,** 9

—— Declaration — Revenue — Information — Disclosure — Statutory notice served by Revenue Commissioners — Whether notice *ultra vires* — Whether unduly burdensome and oppressive.
see **Revenue,** 25

—— Declaration — Revenue — Whether decision of Inspector of Taxes a determination.
see **Revenue,** 1

—— Defence forces — Disability pension — Deduction — Minister — Review.
see **Defence Forces,** 2-4

—— Habeas corpus — Extradition — U.S.A. — Murder — Drug dealing — Committal warrant — Applicant arrested and imprisoned — Lawful imprisonment.
see **Constitution,** 24

—— *Locus standi* — Local authority — Estimates meeting — Whether meeting conducted in accordance with natural justice — Whether councillor having *locus standi* to seek judicial review of meeting — Form of relief — Remittal to local authority.
see **Local Government,** 5

—— Mandamus — Alternative remedy — Planning permission — Refusal appeal — Application for mandamus — Whether lodgment of appeal precludes application for mandamus — Whether mandamus more appropriate remedy where merits of case not in issue.
see **Planning,** 3

—— Mandamus — Circumstances in which mandamus will lie — Revenue Commissioners — Tax clearance certificates — No statutory jurisdiction — Revenue Commissioners acting in a public capacity and exercising lawful authority — Obligation to act judicially — Refusal of certificate subject to judicial review — Consideration by tribunal of matters outside its jurisdiction.
see **Revenue,** 2

—— Mandamus — Criminal law — Committal — Delay — Remand in custody — Whether delay unreasonable —

JUDICIAL REVIEW—*continued.*

Whether mandamus appropriate remedy.
see **Habeas Corpus**

—— Mandamus — Discretion — Lapse of time — Availability of remedies — *Locus standi* of prosecutor.
see **Education,** 2

—— Mandamus — Discretion — Statutory duty — Failure — Minister of State — Remedy appropriate in circumstances.
see **Education,** 2

—— Mandamus — Education Board — School transport — Statutory duty — Whether duty to provide transport to school actually attended.
see **Education,** 3

—— Mandamus — Minister — Power — Exercise — Enforcement of duty to repair courthouse — Minister directed to exercise his powers.
see **Courthouses**

—— Mandamus — Planning — Purchase notice — Meaning of "owner" — Date of service — Availability of alternative remedies.
see **Planning,** 39

—— Mandamus — Remedy — Discretion — Unlawful objective — Planning — Outline permission — Permission granted *ultra vires* — Developer seeking to compel grant of planning approval — Remedy refused.
see **Planning,** 35

—— Mandamus — Revenue Commissioners — Tax clearance certificate — Refusal — Prosecutor seeking to supply goods to Department of Defence — Department requiring production of certificate — Prosecutor's taxes paid — Duty of respondents to decide prosecutor's application on circumstances affecting prosecutor.
see **Revenue,** 2

—— Planning decision — Development — Waiver — Estoppel — Material change of use — Whether procedural requirement waived — Whether failure to consider material considerations.
see **Planning,** 14

—— Planning decision — Natural justice — Reasonableness of decision — Local

L

LABOUR COURT

—— Appeal — Limitation — Review by High Court of evidence before Labour Court.
see **Employer and Employee,** 13

—— Employment equality determination — Appeal — Presumption of adequate grounds for decision — Statute — Discretion — Whether Labour Court erred in law.
see **Employer and Employee,** 15

—— Employment equality determination — Judicial review — Application to quash — Whether error of law as to jurisdiction.
see **Employer and Employee,** 14

—— Equal pay appeal — Whether Labour Court entitled to allow appeal without reference to equality officer's finding of discrimination and consequent recommendation.
see **Employer and Employee,** 17

—— Equal pay — Determination of entitlement — Whether Labour Court acted without jurisdiction — Comparator used not named in union's original submission — Whether Labour Court acted in breach of principles of natural justice in taking legal advice on its jurisdiction in the absence of the parties.
see **Judicial Review,** 4

—— Member — Employment insurance — Whether employed in civil service — Whether employment under a contract of service.
see **Social Welfare,** 2, 3

—— Practice — Determination — Findings of fact to be set out.
see **Employer and Employee,** 13

LABOUR INJUNCTION

see **Employer and Employee,** 24, 25
Injunction, 13

LABOUR LAW

see **Employer and Employee**
Employer's Liability
Trade Union

LAKES AND RIVERS

—— Fishing rights — Arterial drainage scheme — Fishery — Interference — Reduction in fish stock — Compensation.
see **Real Property,** 4

—— Fishing rights — Outdoor education centre — Canoeing — Interference with fishing — Ownership of bed and soil of lake and river — Whether fishery rights of plaintiffs corporeal or incorporeal hereditaments — Whether plaintiffs entitled to order to restrain defendant's activities.
see **Real Property,** 5

LAND

see also **Adverse Possession; Arterial Drainage; Compulsory Acquisition; Landlord and Tenant; Mortgage; Rating and Valuation; Real Property; Registration of Title; Sale of Land**

1. —— **Land Acts** — *Land Commission — Sale of land — Condition of sale that contract dependent on Land Commission approval — Whether prospective purchaser has standing to object to compulsory acquisition of the land — Land Act,* 1923 (*No.* 42), *s.* 40(6).] Where a contract has been made for the sale of lands which are earmarked for compulsory acquisition, and where it is part of the conditions of sale that the contract shall be at an end if the consent of the Land Commission is not forthcoming, the prospective purchaser of such lands does not have such a special legal relationship with the lands as to allow him to object to their vesting in the Land Commission. **So Held** by the Supreme Court (Henchy J., Kenny and Parke JJ. concurring). *The State (Callaghan)* v. *Irish Land Commission* **(S.C.) [1978] ILRM 201**

2. —— **Land Acts** — *Vesting — Building ground excepted from scheme of general vesting — Application by tenant to have Land Commission acquire landlord's interest — Whether acquisition in the interest of the country — Land Act,* 1923 (*No.* 42), *s.* 24 — *Land Act,* 1939 (*No.* 26), *s.* 40(1).] The appellant, Laurence McGowan, was tenant of a five acre plot, which he farmed from his home eleven miles away. At all material times the land had been regarded as having potential as building ground. For this reason the landlord's interest appears not to have been vested in the Land Commission under the general scheme enacted by s. 24 (1) of the Land

LAND—*continued.*

Act, 1923. S. 24 (2) (*e*) of that Act excepted 'any holding or parcel of untenanted land which in the opinion of the Land Commission possesses a substantial value or utility, whether potential or actual, as building ground.' This exception in favour of building ground was subsequently much amended. S. 7 (6) of the Land Act, 1927, gave landlords five years to resume building ground and provided that, in default of their doing so, application might be made to the Judicial Commission to order that vesting take place under the 1923 Act. S. 46 of the Land Act, 1933, provided that 'tenanted lands' excepted by reason of their building potential and not resumed by 28 June, 1933, should cease to be exempted. Finally, s. 3 of the 1936 Land Act restored the exemption in favour of land which, in the opinion of the Land Commission, possessed value as building ground. The appellant wishing to realise the value of the land as building ground, sought to enlarge his tenancy into full ownership. With a view to acquiring the landlord's interest he applied to the Land Commission under s. 14 of the Land Act, 1931, for an order requiring the landlord to furnish particulars of his interest. The Lay Commissioners and the Appeal Tribunal (D'Arcy J.) successively refused to make this order on the ground (specified in s. 40 (1) of the Land Act, 1939) that purchase of the land would not be 'in the interest of the country.' From the decision of D'Arcy J. the tenant appealed to the Supreme Court, to which appeal lay on a point of law only. **Held** by the Supreme Court (*per* McCarthy J., Finaly C.J. and Hederman J. concurring), in dismissing the appeal, 1, the tenant had failed to show how the Lay Commissioners or the Appeal Tribunal had erred in law. 2. It was not 'in the interest of the country' that public monies be expended on buying out lands, the value of which was measured by their development potential. 3. The word 'holding' used in s. 24 of the Land Act, 1923, was the equivalent of the expression 'tenanted lands' used elsewhere in the Land Acts. 4. S. 23 of the Land Act, 1936, (which provides for the exemption of building ground) is applicable to tenanted land generally, and not merely to tenanted land of the type defined in s. 46 (4) of the Land Act, 1933; *In the Estate of Hanlon* 71 I.L.T.R. 160 not followed. *In re Estate of Soden*

(S.C.) [1985] ILRM 685

3. —— **Partition** — *Order for sale in lieu of partition — Whether jurisdiction to make order extant — Repeal of statutory power by statute law revision legislation — Whether power existed prior to statutory power — Effect of statute law revision — Act for Joint Tenants,* 1542 (*c.* 10) — *Statute Law Revision (Pre-Union Irish Statutes) Act,* 1962 (*No.* 29), *s.* 2(1).

Statute — Statute law revision — Effect of legislation — Partition of land — Order for sale in lieu — Act for Joint Tenants, 1542 (*c.* 10) — *Statute Law Revision (Pre-Union Irish Statutes) Act,* 1962 (*No.* 29), *s.* 2(1).] The plaintiff husband sought an order for sale of a matrimonial home which comprised a dwellinghouse which the parties held as joint tenants in equal shares under and by virtue of an indenture of lease with Dublin Corporation. The President of the Circuit Court held that he had power to make an order for sale of the matrimonial home in lieu of partition and so ordered, notwithstanding the repeal of the Act for Joint Tenants, 1542, in which the right of partition had its origin, by the Statute Law Revision (Pre-Union Irish Statutes) Act, 1962. The defendant appealed to the High Court. It was agreed by the parties that the point of law as to whether the trial judge was empowered to make an order for sale of the property, should be argued and decided by way of preliminary issue. The appellant contended that the plaintiff's right as joint tenant to an order for sale, being ancillary to the primary right to partition of the property, was dependant on the continued existence of the latter which had been swept away, albeit inadvertently by the repeal of the Act of 1542 by the Act of 1962. **Held** by Barr J., in holding that the learned trial judge had jurisdiction to make an order for sale of the matrimonial home in lieu of partition: The right of a joint tenant to partition of the property was within the meaning and intent of the phrase 'any existing principle or rule of law and equity' contained in s. 2(1) of the Act of 1962 and was a right 'derived from' the repealed Act of 1542. The safety-net provided by s. 2(1) preserved the right of a joint tenant to partition of the property, subject to the discretion of the court, notwithstanding the repeal of the statute which created it. *F.F.* v. *C.F.*

(H.C.) [1987] ILRM 1

—— Easement — Right of way.
see **Real Property,** 1-3

—— Land Acts — Compulsory purchase — Price fixed at sum payable in Land Bonds equal in nominal value to the sum fixed — Whether the statutory provisions enabling the price to be paid in such a way instead of cash ceased to be part of the law on the coming into force of the Constitution — Whether provision inconsistent with Articles 40 or 43.
see **Compulsory Acquisition,** 4

LAND—*continued.*

—— Land Acts — Sale of land — Agreement — Notice of inspection subsequent to agreement for sale — Effect of notice to require consent to sale — Purchaser obtaining consent to registration as owner — Purchaser in possession prior to conveyance — Whether consent sufficient to enable completion of sale — Delay — Whether explained — Whether specific performance should be refused.
see **Sale of Land,** 6

—— Licence — Ejectment — Waiver — Unlawful possession of dwelling by defendant — Use and occupation payments — Defendant given documents referring to tenancy — Whether a lease or licence — Whether a contractual or bare licence — Notice to quit — Payment received subsequent to notice — Whether waiver of notice — Deductions from statutory benefits — Whether an acknowledgement of subsisting licence.
see **Landlord and Tenant,** 12

—— Proprietary estoppel.
see **Real Property,** 9

—— Recovery — Limitation of actions.
see **Limitation of Actions,** 1, 5

—— Registered land — Incumbrance — Deeds of charge.
see **Real Property,** 6, 7

—— Registered land — Incumbrance — *Lis pendens.*
see **Real Property,** 8

—— Trading stock — Business of dealing in or developing land — Corporation tax — Assessment.
see **Revenue,** 22, 23

—— Transfer — Deed — Reservation of right of residence, care and support — Application to cancel transfer — Whether undue influence — Whether deed improvident.
see **Undue Influence**

—— Valuation.
see **Rating and Valuation**

LAND COMMISSION

—— Land Acts — Vesting — Building ground excepted from scheme of general vesting — Application by tenant to have Land Commission acquire landlord's interest — Whether acquisition in the interest of the country.
see **Land,** 2

—— Sale of land — Condition of sale that contract dependent on Land Commission approval — Whether prospective purchaser has standing to object to compulsory acquisition of the land.
see **Land,** 1

LAND REGISTRY
see **Registration of Title**

LANDLORD AND TENANT

Covenant. Nos. 1-5, 10
Landlord and Tenant Acts — New tenancy applications. Nos. 6-9
Lease. Nos. 10, 11
Licence. Nos. 12, 18
Rent. Nos. 13-16
Termination of tenancy. Nos. 17-19

COVENANT
see also No. 10

1. —— **Quiet and peaceable enjoyment** — *Interference by landlord — Trespass — Intimidation — Application for damages and injunction — Whether aggravated damages be awarded — Whether damages recoverable for breach of covenant to repair — Landlord and Tenant (Ireland) Act,* 1860 (*c.* 154), *ss.* 17, 41 — *Landlord and Tenant Act,* 1931 (*No.* 55), *s.* 5.] The plaintiffs are tenants of the defendant and originally signed four different letting agreements which have long since expired. As a result they now hold the flats as monthly tenants on the original terms contained in the original letting agreements. The second and fourth named plaintiffs' original tenancy agreements contained covenants by the landlord that the tenant shall have quiet and peaceable enjoyment of the premises. Evidence was adduced that the defendant became indignant about the low rents he was receiving from the plaintiffs and decided to enforce each clause in their agreements. On 5 January, 1978, he sent a letter to all the plaintiffs giving them notice that he would call and inspect the properties on 7 January, 1978. On the said date the defendant arrived at the premises and as he had no key to the main door he forced open the hall door and with a screwdriver made the three letter boxes belonging to the first, second and fourth named plaintiffs on the back of the door unusable. He did considerable damage to the second named defendant's partition wall and removed his chairs from the landing. He

LANDLORD AND TENANT—Covenant.

removed the first named plaintiff's hall door as he thought consent had not been given for its installation. On 9 January he made a number of telephone calls from a public phone box to the first named plaintiff's premises and when she lifted the speaker he said nothing. He returned on 9 January and again on 11 January with a workman with the intention of 'restoring' the premises to the condition it had been in prior to it being let to the first, second and fourth plaintiff and after an angry exchange of words he left. As a result of the defendant's behaviour the first, second and fourth named plaintiffs were frightened and the first named plaintiff was put on tranquillisers. The plaintiffs instituted proceedings, claiming an injunction restraining the defendant from interfering with their peaceable enjoyment of the properties let to them and damages for breach of the obligation to give this and for trespass and intimidation. Evidence was adduced at the hearing that the first named plaintiff was in arrears with the rent at the time of the said incidents. The defendant counterclaimed for damages for breach of the covenant to repair and complained the plaintiffs had installed certain fixtures and fittings without the consent of the landlord at the time such as the telephone, T.V. aerial and light over hall door. The second named plaintiff gave evidence that he obtained the consent of the landlord to the aforementioned fixtures and fittings. The first named plaintiff had covenanted to keep the interior of the premises in good repair, reasonable wear and tear only excepted. The second named plaintiff covenanted to keep the interior of the premises in the same order, repair and condition as they were in when the agreement was made in 1951. Evidence was adduced at the hearing that there was a crack in the return of his premises. The fourth named plaintiff covenanted to keep the interior of the premises in good repair, evidence was adduced that there were plaster cracks and a lack of proper maintenance of windows and decoration in her flat. S. 55 of the Landlord and Tenant Act, 1930, provided that damages recoverable for breach of covenant to repair in a lease shall not exceed the amount by which the value of the reversion is diminished owing to such breach. The third named plaintiff covenanted to keep the premises in good repair and evidence was adduced that the flat was full of dry rot which was caused by the absence of damp-proof course, proper ventilation into the sub-floor and the absence of concrete sub-floor. **Held** by Kenny J., 1, the first and second named plaintiffs are entitled to damages for trespass and the second and fourth named plaintiffs are entitled to damages for breach of covenant for quiet enjoyment. 2. The damages that shall be awarded to the plaintiffs shall be aggravated damages as the

LANDLORD AND TENANT—*continued.*

conduct of the defendant caused the plaintiffs considerable anxiety and nervous shock. 3. Inteference with the letter boxes is a sufficient act of interference with the plaintiffs' premises to justify an award for the breach of covenant for quiet enjoyment. 4. Where a lease does not contain a covenant for quiet enjoyment such covenant can not be implied when the tenant is in arrears in rent, therefore the first named plaintiff is not entitled to damages for breach of covenant for quiet enjoyment. 5. For the legal wrong known as intimidation to attract damages it must be successful intimidation that is if the party who is intimidated does not respond to the threat no action lies. 6. As there is a probability that the defendant will continue his campaign to get the plaintiffs out by other means of intimidation if not restrained by an injunction they are all entitled to an injunction restraining him from interfering with the quiet and peaceful enjoyment and possession of their flats. 7. The third named plaintiff is entitled to a *quia timet* injunction because in the court's view there is a probability of interference with him by the defendant. 8. No damages are recoverable for breach of covenant to repair against the first named plaintiff as the breaches come within the exception of reasonable wear and tear; or the second named plaintiff as the defendant is unable to prove that the crack was not there when the agreement was made; or against the third named plaintiff as the covenant to repair does not extend to defects caused by structural defects which were present in the premises when it was let to him. *Lister* v. *Lane & Nesham* [1893] 2 Q.B. 212; *Lurcott* v. *Wakely & Wheeler* [1911] 1 K.B. 905; *Groome* v. *Fodhla Printing Co.* [1943] I.R. 380 considered and applied. 9. S. 55 of the Landlord Act and Tenant Act, 1930, does not apply to overholding tenants such as the fourth named plaintiff and as there is evidence before the court that the plaintiff is in breach of her covenant to keep the interior of the premises in repair the defendant is entitled to succeed in his claim against her. 10. As a telephone can never become the property of the landlord it is not a fixture or fitting so the defendant's claim fails. 11. The court accepts the evidence of the second named plaintiff that he obtained the consent of the landlord at the time to install the telephone, t.v. aerial and the light over the hall door. 12. A t.v. aerial is a fixture and the defendant is entitled to insist on the removal of those belonging to the first and fourth named plaintiff as neither said they had got consent to install it. *Whelan* v. *Madigan*

(H.C.) [1978] ILRM 136

2. —— **Restrictive covenant as to user** — *Business premises — Covenant not to carry on any*

LANDLORD AND TENANT—Covenant.

business other than a supermarket — Landlord could determine that tenant should not offer an item for sale in connection with business — Whether repugnant to tenant's right to carry on business.] The respondent leased shop premises in a housing estate on standard form leases which, apart from the name of the lessee and the address of the premises, were identical save that in each covenant restrictive of use the description of the purpose for which the shop was let was different. Clause 2(i) of the appellant's lease provided that he would not without the previous consent of the respondent carry on in the shop any business other than that of a supermarket; that he would keep the shop open at all times for not less than the usual business hours and that if any difference arose as to any item to be sold in the shop in connection with the said business the decision of the respondent would be final and the appellant must, on notice from the respondent, cease to sell that item. On a complaint from a butcher and home baker in the housing estate that the appellant was selling certain items falling within the range of goods normally sold in a butcher's shop or home bakery, the respondent directed the appellant to cease dealing in certain items. The appellant took no action and the respondent obtained an injunction restraining the appellant from dealing in certain items. On the appeal the appellant argued that insofar as the covenant declared the decision of the respondent to be final it was void as attempting to oust the jurisdiction of the court and that the second sentence of clause 2(i) was repugnant to the first sentence and should be treated as a nullity. **Held,** dismissing the appeal, that, 1, an agreement declaring the decision of a private tribunal (in this case the landlord) to be final is only void as ousting the jurisdiction of the court if the decision involves a question of law. As the decision of the landlord under clause 2(i) to direct the appellant to cease trading in certain items merely determined disputes of fact, which did not involve any legal considerations, it did not effect an ouster of the jurisdiction of the court. 2. If a clause in an agreement confers a right which is not in terms restricted and is, therefore, by inference generally to be regarded as absolute, and a later clause in the same deed is so framed as to involve a limitation on the right previously given there is no repugnancy as would justify treating the later provision as void, for the right can still exist though qualified and in that way effect can be given to both provisions. As the second sentence of clause 2(1) was confined to the right to forbid the sale of certain goods which the first sentence would, if read by itself, permit then it was merely a restriction upon the right and not a negation of that right. Accordingly there was no repugnancy between the first and second sentences of clause

LANDLORD AND TENANT—*continued.*

2(i) of the lease. 3. The right of the respondent to forbid the sale of certain goods must, relying on the presumed intention of the parties, be exercised honestly and reasonably. Moreover the respondent had vested in the appellant the shop premises with the right and duty to carry on the business of a supermarket and in return exacted a substantial rent; if the range of goods he could sell were so reduced that his business was effectively destroyed it would be a repudiation of the grant and a denial of the right contractually conferred. *Northern Ireland Housing Executive* v. *Sloan*

(C.A.) [1984] N.I.29

3. —— **Restrictive covenant as to user** — *Lease of retail units in shopping centre — Subletting — Different use — No consent in writing — Proceedings to restrain breach of covenant — Whether plaintiff estopped from enforcing covenant.*] The first named defendant leased Units Nos. 45 and 46 from the plaintiff the owner of the shopping centre at Coolock, County Dublin. The said lease contained a covenant by the lessee to use the premises as a general hardware store. In June, 1978, the second named defendant leased Unit No. 48 from the plaintiff which said lease contained a similar restrictive covenant to use as a hardware store. Prior to Christmas, 1976 and 1977 the second named defendant took sublettings of a number of units in the plaintiff's centre for the sale of toys without obtaining any consent in writing and no objection was taken by any person. Prior to Christmas, 1978, the first named defendant sublet its Units No. 45 and 46 for the sale of toys to the second defendant who did not apply or obtain consent in writing. On 16 November, 1978, the second named defendant commenced selling toys in the aforementioned units and objection was taken immediately in that his posters on the shop were removed. A meeting of rival traders was then held some time prior to 23 November, 1978, at which no agreement was reached, resulting in the plaintiff commencing these proceedings herein seeking to restrain the breach of covenants of the defendants. The defendants in their defence submit that consent to the change of use was given verbally or by implication by the manager of the shopping centre and that by reason of their conduct in the previous two years in permitting subletting and change of use without consent the plaintiff is estopped from enforcing the covenants this year. The plaintiff submitted that the manager had no authority to give his consent. Further the defendant submitted that the plaintiff did not move quickly enough once breach was observed and allowed the second named defendant to incur expenditure which will cause him great hardship and that it would be inequitable now to make

LANDLORD AND TENANT—Covenant.

him cease this business. **Held** by McWilliam J. in making the order sought, 1, on the evidence before the court the court does not accept that the plaintiff was unduly dilatory in making objections to the defendants breach of covenants. *Shaw* v. *Applegate* [1977] 1 W.L.R. 970 distinguished. 2. The plaintiff is not estopped by its conduct in the previous two years from enforcing the covenants this year as all are and were temporary sub-lettings and the fact that there was a tacit consent by the plaintiff in the previous two years does not have the effect of cancelling the covenants for the future unless there had been an observed breach of covenant existing continuously for some years. *Shaw* v. *Applegate* [1977] 1 W.L.R. 970 distinguished. 3. The court accepts the evidence that the manager had no authority to give consent. *Green Property Co. Ltd.* v. *Shalaine Modes Ltd.*

(H.C.) [1978] ILRM 222

4. —— **Restrictive covenant as to user** — *Lease of retail unit in shopping centre — Covenant against change of user without consent of landlord — Refusal of landlord to consent to change — Declaration sought that refusal was unreasonable — Landlord and Tenant (Amendment) Act,* 1980 (*No.* 10), *s.* 67.] Section 67, sub-s. 2 of the Landlord and Tenant (Amendment) Act, 1980, provides *inter alia* that every lease of a tenement containing a covenant prohibiting the alteration of the user of the tenement without the consent of the lessor should be subject to a proviso to the effect that the consent should not be unreasonably withheld. The plaintiff took an assignment of a lease of a retail shop unit in a shopping centre. A covenant in the lease provided that the premises were only to be used "for the purposes of businesses of victualler, fruit, fish and vegetable merchants", and further provided that the tenant was not to use the premises or permit them to be used for any other purpose without the prior written consent of the landlord. The plaintiff used the premises as a fruit and vegetable store. Subsequently, a supermarket was opened nearby and the plaintiff found that he was unable to compete with it or to assign the lease at a reasonable price so long as the unit was operated as a fruit and vegetable shop. The plaintiff received an offer for the premises from a building society subject to the plaintiff obtaining the landlord's consent to a change of user to that of a building society. The landlord refused consent on the grounds that such a change of user would be contrary to good estate management in that there were already a large number of financial institutions in the shopping centre and the landlord did not want any more premises with dead frontages. The plaintiff sought a declaration in the Circuit Court that the landlord had

LANDLORD AND TENANT—*continued.*

unreasonably withheld its consent. The trial judge held that the landlord's refusal of consent was unreasonable. On appeal by the landlord it was **Held** by Lynch J., in allowing the appeal, 1, that in determining whether a landlord is unreasonably withholding his consent, contrary to the term implied into the covenant restricting user by s. 67 of the Landlord and Tenant (Amendment) Act, 1980, the onus rests on the tenant to establish that the landlord has unreasonably withheld his consent. 2. That in the circumstances, including the special circumstances of the tenant, the landlord's refusal to consent to a change of user was not unreasonable being based on grounds of good estate management, namely, the avoidance of an excessive number of financial institutions in the shopping centre. *O.H.S. Ltd.* v. *Green Property Co.Ltd.*

(H.C.) [1986] I.R.39 ; [1986] ILRM 451

5. —— **Restrictive covenant as to user** — *Tenant seeking permission for change of user — Landlord refusing consent — Whether refusal unreasonable — Objections from other tenants — Whether landlord likely to suffer loss.*] The appellant, a tenant of the respondent, had applied to the respondent for its consent to a change of user of the demised premises from a tailoring business to that of a confectioner. Consent was refused on the ground that other tenants of the respondent in adjoining premises, had objected that their businesses, of a similar nature, would be adversely afected. The appellant applied to the Circuit Court for an order dispensing with the respondent's consent, on the ground that it had been unreasonably withheld. He was unsuccessful in his application, and on appeal, it was **Held** by McWilliam J. in allowing the appeal, 1, a landlord may reasonably base a refusal of consent upon grounds of general policy relating to the management of his estate. 2. However, in the circumstances of the instant appeal, the landlord's decision was an arbitrary one, since there was no threat or expectation of consequential loss to the landlord. *White* v. *Carlisle Trust Ltd.*

(H.C.) [1976-7] ILRM 311

LANDLORD AND TENANT ACTS
1931-1980

see also Nos. 1, 2, 4

6. —— **New tenancy application** — *Decontrolled premises — Statutory tenancy — Death of tenant — Whether dependants entitled to tenancy — Estoppel — Whether acceptance by landlord of dependant as tenant precluded landlord from denying statutory tenancy — Landlord and Tenant Act,* 1931 (*No.* 55), *Part III — Rent Restrictions*

LANDLORD AND TENANT—*continued.*

Act, 1960 (*No.* 42), *ss.* 2(1), 31(3)—*Rent Restrictions (Amendment) Act,* 1967 (*No.* 10), *ss.* 2(4), 13(2), 13(3).] S. 13(2) of the Rent Restrictions (Amendment) Act, 1967, provides that a dwelling decontrolled by the provisions of s. 2(4) of the Act would become a tenement for the purposes of the Landlord and Tenant Act, 1931, if its rateable valuation exceeded £10 and a bachelor or spinster between the ages of 21 and 65 was the tenant thereof. A tenant as defined by s. 2(1) of the Rent Restrictions Act, 1960, includes a statutory tenant. A parol agreement was entered into in 1936 by the mother of the plaintiff (the landlord) and the father of the defendant for a weekly tenancy at the rent of £1 per week. The property the subject of the agreement was a controlled dwelling under the 1960 Act. In May, 1966, a new weekly rent was agreed between the parties, following the service of a notice of increase of rent upon the tenant, pursuant to the provisions of the 1960 Act. Some days later the tenant's solicitor forwarded to the landlord a cheque to cover eight weeks arrears of rent, but this cheque was returned. From that date, no further rent was accepted by the landlord, or by her successor, the plaintiff. In 1968, the tenant died, leaving surviving him, and residing with him at the date of his death, his widow Mrs. Eileen O'Neill and his unmarried daughter, the defendant. He died intestate, and no grant of administration of his estate was extracted. His widow died intestate in June, 1972. In July, 1972, a notice to quit was served by the plaintiff, addressed to the representatives of Mrs. O'Neill, and to the defendant. This was effective to terminate the tenancy, as there was evidence to show that Mrs. O'Neill had been accepted as a contractual tenant after the death of her husband. In August, 1972, letters of administration of Mrs. O'Neill's estate were issued to the defendant. The defendant contended that she had acquired rights under s. 13 of the Rent Restrictions (Amendment) Act, 1967, and was therefore entitled to claim relief under Part III of the Landlord and Tenant Act, 1931. On appeal by way of case stated from the Circuit Court. **Held** by the Supreme Court (O'Higgins C.J., Henchy and Kenny JJ.) in finding for the defendant, 1, the landlord, by accepting and continuing to accept the mother of the defendant as a tenant, was estopped from denying that the contractual tenancy had passed to her. 2. The dwelling the subject matter of the proceedings, which had become decontrolled by the provisions of s. 2(4) of the Rent Restrictions (Amendment) Act, 1967, became a tenement for the purposes of the Landlord and Tenant Act, 1931, by virtue of the provisions of s. 13(2) of the 1967 Act and the defendant became a statutory tenant on the termination of her mother's tenancy by virtue of s. 31(3) of the Rent Restrictions Act, 1960. 3. The defendant, having satisfied the requirement of s. 13(2) of the Rent Restrictions (Amendment) Act, 1967, was a tenant within the meaning of s. 2(1) of the 1960 Act, and could therefore claim relief under Part III of the Landlord and Tenant Act, 1931, as amended by s. 13(3) of the 1967 Act. 4. Where a non-statutory tenant dies intestate, no rights under s. 31(3) of the Rent Restrictions Act, 1960, can accrue to a member of such tenant's family, unless the tenancy has been terminated before a grant of administration has been extracted. *Byrne* v. *O'Neill*

(S.C.) [1979] ILRM 47

7. —— **New tenancy application** — *Lessor having no reversion in tenement — Notice of intention to claim relief served on superior landlord — Whether lessor served a copy of such notice on superior landlord — Amount of new rent — Landlord and Tenant (Ireland) Act,* 1860 (*c.* 154), *s.* 5 — *Landlord and Tenant Act,* 1931 (*No.* 55), *ss.* 2, 24, 25, 31, 33.] S. 31(1) of the Landlord and Tenant Act, 1931, provides that where a tenant has served notice of intention to claim relief upon a landlord who has no reversion in the tenement to which the notice relates, the landlord may serve notices on the tenant, informing him of the fact and giving him the name and address of the superior landlord, and upon the superior landlord, informing him of the intention to claim relief, and enclosing a copy of the tenant's notice. Subs. 2 of the said section provides that where a landlord has served such notices, or the tenant has served a duplicate of his notice of intention to claim relief upon the superior landlord, the claim of the tenant is deemed to have been made against the superior landlord. The appellants leased the Gaiety Theatre for a term of three years from Gaiety Theatre (Enterprises) Ltd. (the lessor). This was subsequently increased by a further term of three years, but it transpired that such estate as the lessor had at the commencement of the second term had expired before the term ended, and the landlord holding the reversion was Gaiety Theatre (Dublin) Ltd. (the respondent). Unaware of this fact, the applicants served upon the lessor a notice of intention to claim relief pursuant to s. 24 of the 1931 Act. In due course having discovered their error, the applicants served a new notice of intention to claim relief upon the respondent, who, at the hearing of the application in the Circuit Court, unsuccessfully opposed the application on the ground that the notice should not have been addressed to it, but should merely have been a duplicate of such a notice, the original of which should have been served on Gaiety Theatre (Enterprises) Ltd., pursuant to s. 31 of the 1931

LANDLORD AND TENANT—*continued.*

Act. The respondent did not adduce any evidence as to whether the lessor had served a copy of the original notice upon the respondent. On appeal from the order of the Circuit Court, and on a cross-appeal as to the amount of the new rent which had been fixed by the court, it was **Held** by Gannon J. in dismissing the appeal and in allowing the cross-appeal, 1, the provisions of s. 31(2) of the 1931 Act relied upon by the respondent apply only where the requisite notices have not been served by the landlord upon the superior landlord in conformity with s. 31(1) of the Act. Since the onus of proving that the said notices were not served rested upon the respondent, who had not discharged it, the respondent could not rely upon the alleged failure on the part of the applicant to comply with the alternative requirements of s. 31(2). 2. In view of the wish of the parties that the new lease should contain a seven year rent review clause, the amount of the rent could only be that suitable for a term of seven years. *Eamonn Andrews Productions Ltd.* v. *Gaiety Theatre (Dublin) Ltd.*

(H.C.) [1976-7] ILRM 119

8. —— **New tenancy application** — *Notice not served within statutory period — Whether time should be extended — Landlord and Tenant Act,* 1931 (*No.* 55), *ss.* 24, 31.] S. 24 of the Landlord and Tenant Act, 1931, provides that where application is being made for a new tenancy, notice of intention to claim relief must be served upon the landlord within a specified time. The appellant's lease, which it held from the respondent, having expired, and notice not having been served within the statutory period, the appellant had unsuccessfully sought in the Circuit Court to extend the time for service of such notice, pursuant to s. 45 of the 1931 Act. Evidence showed that negotiations had been in train between the parties for the purchase of the appellant's interest in the demised premises. Ultimately the respondent decided to proceed no further with the negotiations, but this fact was not communicated to the appellant company, which took the matter to be simply in temporary abeyance. **Held** by Hamilton P. in allowing the appeal and extending the time in which to serve notice of intention to claim relief, 1, in deciding whether to extend time for service of such notice, the fundamental consideration is whether justice requires that relief be granted. For this reason the appellate court may consider the matter *de novo*. *Linders (Chapelizod) Ltd.* v. *Syme* [1975] I.R. 161 applied. 2. In the circumstances of the negotiations for sale, the appellant's decision not to apply for a new tenancy was a reasonable one, since the appellant was justified, at the expiration of the tenancy and during the relevant period, in

LANDLORD AND TENANT—*continued.*

believing that the said negotiations were continuing. *Grey Door Hotel Company Ltd.* v. *Pembroke Trust Ltd.*

(H.C.) [1976-7] ILRM 14

9. —— **New tenancy application** — *Right to a new tenancy — Periodic tenancy — Tenant holding business premises under subsisting monthly tenancy — Tenant claiming to be entitled to new tenancy — Whether tenant entitled to serve notice of intention to claim relief before determination of tenancy — Whether tenant entitled to apply to court before determination of tenancy — Statute — Interpretation — "Termination" of tenancy — "Expiration" of tenancy — Landlord and Tenant Act,* 1931 (*No.* 55), *ss.* 19, 24, 25, 29 — *Landlord and Tenant (Amendment) Act,* 1980 (*No.* 10), *ss.* 13, 16, 17, 18, 20, 21, 23.] Section 16 of the Landlord and Tenant (Amendment) Act, 1980, provides *inter alia* that:— ". . . where this Part applies to a tenement, the tenant shall be entitled to a new tenancy in the tenement beginning on the termination of his previous tenancy." Section 21, sub-ss. 1 and 3 of the Act of 1980 provide:— "(1) A person who serves a notice of intention to claim relief may, at any time not less than one month thereafter, apply to the Court to determine his right to relief and (as the case may be) to fix the amount of the compensation or the terms of the new tenancy to which he is found to be entitled. (3) An application under this section may be made, heard and determined either before and in anticipation of or after the termination of the tenancy." The applicant was the tenant from month to month of business premises which she had held for upwards of three years and which were a tenement for the purposes of the Act of 1980. Her tenancy had not been determined but she was apprehensive that the landlord's interest in the property might be sold and that the purchaser might seek to determine her tenancy and resist any application for a new tenancy on the grounds that he wished to develop the property. Pursuant to s. 20 of the Act of 1980 the applicant served notice of intention to claim relief and pursuant to s. 21 applied to court to have her application heard. The Circuit Court judge dismissed the application on the grounds that the court had no jurisdiction to deal with it until notice to quit had been served. On appeal by the applicant it was **Held** by Carroll J., in dismissing the appeal, 1, that in order to deal with an application for a new tenancy the court, in order to decide whether the restrictions contained in s. 17, sub-s. 1 referable to the tenant's conduct applied, must know the reason why the tenancy was determined. In addition the court must be able to establish the rent payable by the landlord and must be able to fix the new rent; which could only be done by reference to the

LANDLORD AND TENANT—*continued.*

commencement date of the new tenancy. 2. That accordingly, while a tenant could, by virtue of s. 20, subs. 2(*c*) of the Act of 1980, give notice of intention to claim relief in advance of service of notice to quit; and while the court could, under s. 21, sub-s. 3 decide the entitlement to a new tenancy before the tenancy had expired; until notice to quit was actually served, thereby fixing a date for termination, the court could not hear and determine the matter. *Mealiffe* v. *G.N. Walsh Ltd.*

(H.C.) [1986] I.R.427; [1987] ILRM 301

LEASE

10. —— **Forfeiture** — *Covenant — Breach — Recovery of possession — Peaceable re-entry — Injunction — Interlocutory relief — Conveyancing Act,* 1881 (*c.* 41), *s.* 14.] The plaintiff had been in possession of certain business premises in a shopping centre as lessee under a lease for a term of 33 years subject to the yearly rent thereby reserved and the covenants on the part of the lessee and the conditions therein contained. The lease contained a covenant by the lessee to pay the yearly rent and certain service charges. The lease also contained a re-entry clause which empowered the lessor to re-enter the premises upon the breach by the lessee of any of the covenants to be observed or performed by the lessee. The defendant was entitled to the interest of the lessor in the demised premises. When the plaintiff was in breach of the covenants to pay the yearly rent and the service charges, the defendant lessor duly served on the plaintiff a forfeiture notice in compliance with the provisions of s. 14 of the Act of 1881. When the plaintiff still failed to pay to the defendant the arrears of the yearly rent and the service charges the defendant resumed possession of the premises by using a master key to enter upon the premises when the plaintiff was absent therefrom. The plaintiff did not claim relief against forfeiture but claimed in the High Court (*inter alia*) an order restraining the defendant from obstructing the plaintiff's right to enter and occupy the demised premises; the plaintiff obtained an interim injunction, so restraining the defendant, on the ground that the interest of the lessee in the demised premises had not been terminated. At the hearing of the plaintiff's application for an interlocutory injunction continuing such restraint until the trial of the action, it was **Held** by Carroll J., in dismissing the application, 1, that, upon the commission of admitted breaches of covenant by the plaintiff, the defendant had duly served upon the plaintiff a forfeiture notice in compliance with the provisions of s. 14, sub-s. 1, of the Act of 1881. 2. That, upon the continued failure of the plaintiff to remedy the breaches of covenant, the interest of the lessee in the premises under the lease thereof had been lawfully terminated by the peaceable re-entry of the defendant on the premises. *In re Riggs, ex p. Lovell* [1901] 2 K.B. 16 considered. *F.G. Sweeney Ltd.* v. *Powerscourt Shopping Centre Ltd.*

(H.C.) [1984] I.R.501; [1985] ILRM 442

11. —— **Option to purchase fee simple** — *Price calculation as if rent were a ground rent — Whether option enforceable — Whether refusal of county registrar to deal with matter subject to arbitration — Arbitration Act,* 1954 (*No.* 26), *s.* 18 — *Landlord and Tenant (Ground Rents) Act,* 1967 (*No.* 3), *ss.* 17, 22.] In 1969 the parties entered into a leasing agreement whereby the defendant demised premises to the plaintiff for a term of five years. Clause 19 gave the lessee an option to purchase the fee simple of the leasehold premises during the term of the lease and stated that the consideration to be paid in the event of the exercise of the option 'shall be the number of years purchase of the rent reserved by the said lease as shall be ascertained under the Landlord and Tenant (Ground Rents) Act, 1967, as if the rent reserved by the said lease was a ground rent within the meaning of that Act.' The clause stated that the condition did not operate so as to bring the lease within the Act's provisions save for the matter of ascertaining the consideration. In May, 1973, the plaintiff proposed to exercise the option contained in clause 19 and asked that the purchase money be calculated by the defendant's solicitors under the 1967 Act. The defendant refused to sell the freehold interest. In September, 1973, the plaintiff issued proceedings for specific performance. In her defence the defendant pleaded that the option to purchase was not valid or enforceable or, alternatively, that it was null and void by reason of uncertainty and that it did not provide a certain or ascertainable mode of determining the purchase price or the persons by whom same should be determined. In September, 1975, the plaintiff served a notice under the 1967 Act on the defendant, notifying her of his intention to acquire the fee simple in the premises. The plaintiff proceeded under s. 17 of the Act to apply to the county registrar to determine the purchase price by his arbitration. As the premises were not premises to which the Act applied the registrar refused the application, whereupon the plaintiff served the defendant with a notice under s. 18 of the Arbitration Act, 1954, to appoint or concur in the appointment of an arbitrator. The defendant refused, stating the question must await the result of the specific performance proceedings. The plaintiff then issued proceedings under the Arbitration Act, 1954, requesting the court to

LANDLORD AND TENANT—Lease.

appoint an arbitrator to act and make an award and determine the consideration to be paid. Both actions were heard together. **Held** by Hamilton J. in refusing the orders sought, 1, until the purchase price has been ascertained there is no contract between the parties which the court can specifically enforce. 2. The relevant clause in the leasing agreement must be construed in such a way as to give effect to the intention of the parties. It was their intention that the consideration was to be such sum as would be awarded by a county registrar acting as the arbitrator under s. 17 of the 1967 Act as if the rent reserved by the lease was a ground rent within the meaning of the Act and further that if the parties failed to agree on the sum the matter would be referred to the county registrar for determination. The county registrar correctly declined to deal with such reference by the plaintiff. 3. The Arbitration Act does not apply to the circumstances of the refusal by the county registrar to deal with the matter. The agreement does not constitute an arbitration agreement within the meaning of the Act. 4. The High Court is not empowered to appoint an arbitrator as this was not the intention of the parties. Any party aggrieved by the decision of the county registrar has a right under s. 22 of the Landlord and Tenant Act, 1967, to appeal to the Circuit Court and subsequently to the High Court but no such appeal lies under the Arbitration Act. *Carr* v. *Phelan*

(H.C.) [1976-7] ILRM 149

LICENCE

see also No. 18

12. —— **Ejectment** — *Waiver — Unlawful possession of dwelling by defendant — Use and occupation payments — Defendant given documents referring to tenancy — Whether a lease or licence — Whether a contractual or bare licence — Notice to quit — Payment received subsequent to notice — Whether waiver of notice — Deductions from statutory benefits — Whether an acknowledgement of subsisting licence — Payments for Debt (Emergency Provisions) Act (Northern Ireland),* 1971 (*c.* 30), *s.* 1.] The defendant illegally entered and went into occupation of a house owned by the plaintiff. The plaintiff, in accordance with its regular practice, required the defendant to make payments for the use and occupation of the premises. Payment books were issued to the plaintiff, one of which contained payment slips marked "use and occupation", and also contained material relating to rent and repairs and a "termination of tenancy notice." The defendant's payments fell into arrear and the plaintiff obtained direct payment from the Department of Health and Social Services of sums on account of arrears under the Payments

LANDLORD AND TENANT—*continued.*

for Debt (Emergency Provisions) Act (Northern Ireland), 1971. In June, 1983, an arrangement was made by the defendant for the payment of the arrears. The document containing this arrangement referred to rent and described the defendant as a tenant. In June, 1983, the plaintiff demanded possession of the premises and proceedings were commenced in November. In that month a housing benefit scheme came into operation under the terms of which the amounts due from illegal occupants was paid direct to the plaintiff by the Department of Health and Social Services. In May, 1984, the plaintiff was granted a decree for possession of the premises and the defendant appealed. **Held,** dismissing the appeal, that, 1, in order to determine whether the defendant was a tenant or a licensee it was necessary to ascertain the intention of the parties. At no time was it the intention of the plaintiff to offer a lawful tenancy to the defendant. While some factors on their own were consistent with an intention to create a tenancy, it was necessary to look at all the facts and to seek the true intention of the parties. One should not be over-astute to foist a tenancy on the plaintiff as a consequence of its incautious use of documents. 2. The defendant's licence was not a contractual licence as at no time did the plaintiff enter into a contract with him. The licence was a bare licence which could be revoked at any time by any unequivocal act of the plaintiff. 3. The plaintiff had not waived the revocation of the licence as it had no intention to waive the demand for possession or to grant a further licence. Obtaining payments in respect of arrears of use and occupation payments could not be regarded as a waiver and the acceptance of current payments would not be sufficient *per se* to constitute a waiver. *Northern Ireland Housing Executive* v. *Duffin*

(H.C., N.I.) [1985] N.I. 210

Notice to quit, *see* Nos. 12, 17, 19

RENT

13. —— **Fixing of rent** — *Landlord's repairing obligations not complied with — Whether rent should be fixed on the basis that the premises are in good repair — Whether allowance be made for future inflation — Housing (Private Rented Dwellings) Act,* 1982 (*No.* 6), *ss.* 12(2), 13.] The appellant was a tenant of the respondent. The tenancy was a tenancy for the purposes of the Housing (Private Rented Dwellings) Act, 1982 (the Act). The respondent had made application to the District Court for the purposes of having a rent fixed in accordance with s. 13 of the Act. Under the lease the tenant was responsible for internal repairs and the landlord responsible for

LANDLORD AND TENANT—Rent.

external repairs. No external repairs had been executed for a considerable period of time and as a result the dwellinghouse was in a considerable state of disrepair. By reason of this the tenant was unable to effect internal repairs. Notwithstanding this the District Justice fixed a new rent of £30 per week on the hypothetical basis that both landlord and tenant had complied with their respective repair covenants. Evidence had been given at the hearing that, in its present condition, the dwellinghouse had a rental value of £10 per week. The tenant appealed to the Circuit Court. **Held** by Judge Clarke in allowing the appeal, 1, given the serious state of disrepair of the dwellinghouse, the hypothetical approach followed by the District Court was wrong. 2. The fixing of a new rent should be adjourned to enable the respondent to carry out necessary external repairs. In the event of the respondent not undertaking to carry out repairs it would be proper to request the county registrar to indicate to the housing authority that the premises have been described as unfit for human habitation. *Per Curiam* The Act did not contemplate any addition to rent to compensate for inflation over a period of five years. *Dowd* v. *Pierce*

(Circ. Ct.) [1984] ILRM 653

14. —— **Fixing of rent** — *Rent Tribunal — Jurisdiction — Premises partly residential and partly used for a business — Whether a "dwelling" for the purposes of the Act of 1983 — Rent Restrictions Act,* 1960 (*No.* 42), *s.* 4 — *Housing (Private Rented Dwellings) Act,* 1982 (*No.* 6), *ss.* 2, 8 — *Housing (Private Rented Dwellings) (Amendment) Act,* 1983 (*No.* 22), *ss.* 2, 5.] Sections 2 and 5 of the Housing (Private Rented Dwellings) (Amendment) Act, 1983, established a Rent Tribunal to which a landlord of a "dwelling to which s. 8, sub-s. 1 of the Act of 1982 relates" might apply to fix the rent and other terms of the tenancy. Section 8, sub-s. 1 of the Housing (Private Rented Dwellings) Act, 1982, provides *inter alia* that it ". . . applies to every dwelling which would, at the commencement of this Act, be a controlled dwelling within the meaning of the Rent Restrictions Acts, 1960 to 1981 . . ." Section 2 of the Act of 1982 defines a "dwelling" as "a house let as a separate dwelling, or a part so let, of any house, whether or not the tenant shares with any other person any portion thereof or any accommodation, amenity or facility in connection therewith." Section 4 of the Rent Restrictions Act, 1960, provides that "the application of this Act to a dwelling shall not be excluded by reason only of the fact that part of it is used for the purposes of any business, trade or profession." The respondent landlord of a licensed premises partly used as the residence of the appellant and partly for business purposes,

LANDLORD AND TENANT—*continued.*

applied to the Tribunal to fix the rent and other terms of the tenancy. The appellant challenged the jurisdiction of the Tribunal on the grounds that the definition of a "dwelling" to which the Act of 1983 applied should be regarded as being the definition contained in s. 2 of the Act of 1982, which definition did not include premises partly used for business purposes. The Tribunal rejected this contention and fixed the rent. On appeal to the High Court pursuant to s. 13 of the Act of 1982 it was **Held** by Costello J., in dismissing the appeal, 1, that the appropriate definition of a "dwelling" for the purposes of the Act of 1983 was to be found by reference to the definition of a "controlled dwelling" contained in the Rent Restrictions Acts, 1960 to 1981. 2. That s. 4 of the Rent Restrictions Act, 1960, meant a house used as a separate dwelling was still a "controlled dwelling" even though part of it was used for business purposes. *Mullane* v. *Brosnan* [1974] I.R. 222 followed. 3. That the premises were therefore a "controlled dwelling" and consequently a "dwelling" to which s. 8, sub-s. 1 of the Act of 1982 related. Accordingly, the Rent Tribunal had jurisdiction to hear the application in relation to the premises. *Foley* v. *Johnson*

(H.C.) [1988] I.R. 7

15. —— **Fixing of rent** — *Rent Tribunal — Application to fix gross rent — Dispute over landlord's income — Tribunal refusing tenant's request for more information as to landlord's means — Whether Tribunal erred in law — Housing (Private Rented Dwellings) Act,* 1982 (*No.* 6), *s.* 13.] The Housing (Private Rented Dwellings) (Amendment) Act, 1983, established the Rent Tribunal, giving to it the same jurisdiction in relation to the fixing of rents as that formerly conferred upon the courts by the Housing (Private Rented Dwellings) Act, 1982. S. 13 of the 1982 Act provides that the gross rent should be fixed having regard to certain specified criteria, including at sub-s. 2 the means of the landlord and the tenant. The respondent landlord had applied to the Tribunal to fix a rent for a premises of which the appellant was tenant. At the hearing, the respondent's solicitor informed the Tribunal that the landlord's income was greater than that of the tenant. The Tribunal refused the appellant's demand for further information as to the means of the landlord, and proceeded to fix a rent. The appellant alleged that the Tribunal had erred in law by accepting the assurance of the respondent's solicitors, thus ruling out further enquiry, and that by so doing it had failed to take into account the means of the landlord. On a case stated to the High Court, it was held by Gannon J. that the Tribunal had not erred in law by so doing. On appeal, it was **Held** by the

LANDLORD AND TENANT—Rent.

Supreme Court (Griffin and McCarthy JJ., Hederman J. concurring) in dismissing the appeal, 1, the means of the landlord are relevant only when the landlord sought to make them so such as an argument seeking that the rent should be adjusted upwards because of some potential hardship to him. 2. The criteria set out in s. 13(2) of the 1982 Act are not in the nature of an automatic check list. They are to be considered only where relevant to the particular case then in hand. *Quirke* v. *Folio Homes Ltd.*
(S.C.) [1988] ILRM 496

16. —— **Rent review clause** — *Dispute going to arbitration — Arbitrator required to determine the rent a willing lessee not in occupation would give — Whether lessor should be excluded as a prospective lessee.*] Macey Ltd. (the lessor) had leased part of its premises to Tylers Ltd. (the lessee) at a rent which was subject to a seven-year review. The lease provided that in the event of a dispute concerning the rent payable upon review, the matter was to be determined by an arbitrator, who would determine the rent which 'a willing lessor would take and a willing lessee not already in occupation would give, in the open market, for the premises with clear vacant possession.' A dispute having arisen, the arbitrator stated a case for the decision of the High Court as to whether the lessor should be excluded as a prospective lessee for the purpose of determining the new rent. **Held** by Costello J. in finding that the lessor should be so excluded: In assessing the hypothetical situation propounded by the rent review clause, the arbitrator must consider all relevant facts. In granting a lease of the premises for a term of 21 years, the lessor had precluded himself from consideration as a willing lessee at the time of the rent review, since it was not in a position lawfully to take possession of the premises. *Macey Ltd.* v. *Tylers Ltd.*
(H.C.) [1978] ILRM 82

TERMINATION OF TENANCY

17. —— **Natural justice** — *Corporation flat — Notice to quit and Demand for Possession — District Court hearing — Tenant not represented — Tenant not invited to give evidence — Possession awarded to Corporation — Whether hearing in breach of natural justice — Housing Act,* 1966 (*No.* 21), *s.* 62.] The prosecutor, a married man, had moved with his wife and family into a flat the property of Dublin Corporation, at the invitation of the tenant, who was away on holiday. Following the death of the tenant while on holiday, the prosecutor's wife intimated to the Corporation her wish to remain in occupation of the flat, offering payment of what she considered to be rent. A receipt for this and subsequent

LANDLORD AND TENANT—*continued.*

payments was received by the prosecutor from the Corporation. The words 'in respect of rent' had been erased from the receipt, and the following words added: 'Parole Tenant £11 mesne rates.' Subsequent payments attracted similarly worded receipts up to and including 2 March, 1976. Meanwhile, in July, 1975, a combined notice to quit and demand for possession was served on the prosecutor by the Corporation, and this was followed by a summons alleging that the flat had been let to the prosecutor as tenant from week to week, and requiring him to attend at the District Court to show cause why a warrant under s. 62 of the Housing Act, 1966, should not issue for possession of the flat. At the hearing in the District Court, the prosecutor was not professionally represented. A rent collector appeared as witness for the Corporation,and he proved the service of the notice to quit and demand for possession. No other evidence, oral or documentary, was adduced. The prosecutor did not give evidence nor was he invited to do so. Possession of the flat was awarded to the Corporation. The prosecutor averred that the District Justice told him he would be 'fixed up' with alternative accommodation. Satisfied with this, he lodged no appeal against the decision. His wife continued to pay rent and receive receipts up to 9 March, 1976, on which date and thereafter her payments were not accepted. On the 26 March, the prosecutor and his family were evicted from the flat. No alternative accommodation was provided for them, and they had nowhere to go. The prosecutor obtained a conditional order of certiorari quashing the decision of the District Justice on the ground that it was made in breach of the rules of natural justice. **Held** by Doyle J. in making absolute the conditional order, 1, the prosecutor was given no opportunity to make a case at the District Court hearing. It is irrelevant to the operation of the maxim *audi alteram partem* that the prosecutor may have had no case to make. 2. In view of the fact that the decision of the District Justice was invalidated by failure to observe the maxim *audi alteram partem,* it was no necessary for the court to make any decision on the constitutionality or otherwise of s. 62 of the Housing Act, 1966. *The State (Crothers)* v. *Kelly*
(H.C.) [1978] ILRM 167

18. —— **Overholding** — *Former tenant remaining in occupation — Payment and receipt of customary payments for four months — Negotiations for new tenancy — Failure of negotiations — Demand of possession — Nature of occupant's interest during negotiations — Whether tenant at will, licensee or trespasser — Plaintiff entitled to possession — Landlord and Tenant Law Amendment Act, Ireland,* 1860 (*c.* 154), *ss.* 1, 3.] By an

LANDLORD AND TENANT—Termination.

agreement in writing dated the 14 February, 1974, the plaintiffs (*a*) hired certain motor and garage equipment to the defendants from the 1 January to the 30 June, 1974 and granted the defendants a licence to occupy the plaintiffs' premises, on which the equipment was situated, for that period. The defendants were obliged by the terms of the agreement to pay to the plaintiffs a specified monthly sum for the hire of the equipment. On the expiration on the 30 June, 1974, of the period of six months mentioned in the agreement, the parties conducted negotiations for a new agreement continuing the interest of the defendants in the said equipment and premises. Those negotiations lasted for four months, during which period the defendants continued to occupy the plaintiffs' premises and paid them four sums of money — each of which being of the same amount as the monthly hire charge specified in the agreement of 1974. The parties failed to make a new agreement and the plaintiffs, by a letter dated the 5 November, terminated the defendants' licence to occupy the premises and, on the 12 November, 1974, demanded possession of the premises from the defendants. The defendants failed to deliver possession of the premises to the plaintiffs. In their original pleadings in the action, the plaintiffs claimed in the High Court an injunction restraining the defendants from continuing to trespass upon or occupy the plaintiffs' premises. On the 10 April, 1981, the Supreme Court held that the agreement of 1974 had created the relationship of landlord and tenant between the parties; that court permitted the plaintiffs to amend their original pleadings so as to claim possession of the premises, and remitted the plaintiffs' amended claim to the High Court for the determination of the issues arising from the amended pleadings. At the trial of those issues in the High Court, the judge held that the right of the defendants to occupy the plaintiffs' premises had terminated and that the plaintiffs were entitled to recover from the defendants a sum as mesne rates from the termination of the defendants' right to occupy the premises. At the hearing of appeals by the parties it was **Held** by the Supreme Court (O'Higgins C.J. and Henchy J.; McCarthy J. dissenting), in disallowing the defendants' appeal, 1, that the plaintiffs were entitled to possession of the premises. *Per* O'Higgins C.J.: Upon the termination of the agreement of 1974 on the 30 June of that year, the defendants continued in occupation of the premises as tenants at will until that tenancy was terminated by the plaintiffs' letter of the 5 November, 1974; whereupon the defendants became trespassers. *Per* Henchy J.: Upon the termination of the agreement of 1974 on the 30 June of that year, the defendants became licensees until the demand

LANDLORD AND TENANT—*continued.*

of possession made by the plaintiffs on the 12 November; where upon the defendants became trespassers. 2. That the plaintiffs were entitled to recover from the defendants mesne rates assessed at £1,500 p.a. from the termination of the defendants' right to occupy the premises. *Irish Shell and B.P. Ltd.* v. *John Costello Ltd.*
(S.C.) [1984] I.R.511 ; [1985] ILRM 554

19. —— **Title** — *Documentary tenancy from week to week — Tenant paying no rent for 24 years — Negotiations for purchase by tenant of landlord's interest in property — Landlord's demands for payment of rent ignored by tenant — Landlord serving notice to quit — Limitation of actions — Ejectment — Accrual of right of action — Adverse possession — Abandonment of tenancy — Whether determination of tenancy could be presumed from landlord's conduct — Whether landlord's action for recovery of possession statute barred — Statute of Limitations,* 1957 (*No.* 6), *s.* 17.] In 1942 the plaintiff's predecessor in title entered a written contract of tenancy from week to week with the defendant. From 1950 onwards no rent was paid and from 1960 the defendant paid the ground rent and rates. In 1956 the defendant offered to pay rent but was dissuaded from doing so by the landlord's solicitor on the grounds that the defendant was negotiating for the purchase of the landlord's interest in the property. The plaintiff demanded payment of rent by three letters, in 1977, 1978 and 1981, but the defendant made no reply to those letters. The plaintiff took other steps to recover the rent. In 1982 the plaintiff served a notice to quit and brought District Court proceedings for possession of the premises. A decree for possession was made in the District Court and the defendant appealed to the Circuit Court. It was argued for the defendant that the landlord's failure to demand rent from 1950 to 1977 amounted to an abandonment of the landlord's interest, which was extinguished after twelve years from the last payment of rent. It was argued for the plaintiff that the failure to collect rent merely barred recovery of rent for more than six years prior to the determination of the tenancy and did not affect the plaintiff's title. On the application of the defendant, the Circuit Court judge stated a case for the determination of the Supreme Court as to whether the defendant had acquired title to the property by adverse possession. **Held** by the Supreme Court (Finlay C.J., Henchy and McCarthy JJ.), in determining that the plaintiff had not lost her title to the property, that the defendant was the original tentant under the 1942 agreement, had paid his rent until 1950 and would have resumed payment in 1956 if he had not been negotiating for the purchase of the landlord's interest. The plaintiff had shown, by

LICENSING ACTS — INTOXICATING LIQUOR

Licence. Nos. 1-12
Offence. Nos. 13, 14

LICENCE

1. —— **Alienation** — *Whether existing separately from premises to which attached — Whether capable of being sold separately — Mortgage of premises — No reference to licence — Whether licence caught by mortgage — Sale by consent of premises and licence — Estoppel — Whether assent to sale precludes substitution of hypothetical basis for sale.*

Estoppel — Assent to sale of premises — Licence attached — Premises mortgaged — No reference to licence — Whether licence caught by mortgage — Whether assentor precluded from substituting hypothetical basis for sale.] The bankrupt was owner of a house, in respect of which a number of charges plus a judgment mortgage had been registered in the Land Registry. The bankrupt was given liberty, with the assent of the official assignee, to negotiate the sale of the premises as a going concern, and the premises together with the licence was sold for £42,000. The official assignee claimed to be entitled to retain out of the proceeds of the sale the value of the licence for the benefit of the unsecured creditor, on the grounds that the licence was not captured by the charges registered against the premises, as the charges do not refer to the licence, and that a judgment mortgage itself cannot be captured by the licence. **Held** by Hamilton J. in finding for the mortgagee, 1, no right of benefit of a publican's licence can exist apart from the ownership and possession of the licensed premises, and the licence cannot be regarded as property capable of separation from the licensed premises. *Brennan* v. *Dorney* (1888) 21 L.R. Ir. 353 applied. 2. A licence is subject to the same charges and incumbrances as the said property and is therefore incapable of passing to the official assignee in priority to incumbrances registered against the property to which it is attached. **Held** by the Supreme Court (Henchy J., Hederman and McCarthy JJ.) in dismissing the appeal: Although since the charges and registered mortgages did not purport to affect the licence attaching to the premises, and so it might have been possible to take the point prior to sale, in view of the official assignee's consent to the sale of the premises together with the licence, he was estopped from overthrowing the basis for the sale and replacing it with a hypothetical and unreal sale which might never have been realised. *In re Sherry-Brennan*

(H.C., S.C.) [1979] ILRM 113

LICENSING ACTS—*continued.*

2. —— **Holder** — *Transfer* — Ad interim *transfer of publican's licence — Subsequent conviction of transferor for offences against licensing code — Effect of* ad interim *transfer — Statute — Interpretation — Licensed person — Holder of licence — Whether transferor the holder of the licence — Whether convictions endorseable on licence — Licensing (Ireland) Act,* 1833 (*c.* 68), *s.* 15 — *Licensing (Ireland) Act,* 1836 (*c.* 38), *s.* 16 — *Transfer of Licences (Ireland) Act,* 1855 (*c.* 114), *ss.* 1, 2 — *Licensing Act,* 1872 (*c.* 94), *s.* 3 — *Intoxicating Liquor Act,* 1927 (*No.* 15), *ss.* 25, 28, 29, 30, 32 — *Intoxicating Liquor Act,* 1962 (*No.* 21), *s.* 34.] The plaintiffs, who were husband and wife, were the joint owners of a public house in respect of which an intoxicating liquor licence had been issued to the first plaintiff. The first plaintiff assigned his interest in the property to the second plaintiff and, subsequently, an application was made to the District Court for an *ad interim* transfer of the licence. The District Justice transferred the licence to the second plaintiff until the next annual licensing sessions and endorsed the licence accordingly. The first plaintiff had been summoned to the same sitting of the District Court charged with a number of offences of staying open after hours and, after the licence had been transferred, was convicted of those offences and fined. Some time later the District Court clerk wrote to the plaintiffs threatening to endorse the convictions on the licence and to inform the Revenue Commissioners of the consequential forfeiture of the licence maintaining that, notwithstanding the *ad interim* transfer, the first plaintiff was the holder of the licence for the purposes of Part III of the Intoxicating Liquor Act, 1927. The plaintiffs brought proceedings for a declaration that the first plaintiff was not the holder of the licence at the time of his conviction and for a declaration that those convictions were not recordable on the licence. The claim was dismissed by the High Court (Keane J.) and the plaintiffs appealed to the Supreme Court. **Held** by the Supreme Court (Finlay C.J., Henchy, Griffin, Hederman and McCarthy JJ.), in allowing the appeal and granting the declarations sought, 1, that a licensed person could only be considered to be a person to whom the excise authorities had, pursuant to a certificate of the court, issued a licence; but the holder of a licence was the person who had the legal right to possession of the licence document itself. 2. That having regard to the manner of transfer of the licence prescribed by s. 1 of the Transfer of Licences (Ireland) Act, 1855, namely, by endorsement on the licence itself, the intention of that Act was that the licence should carry on its face the authority of the transferee to trade under it. Once the *ad interim* transfer had been granted and the licence endorsed the

LICENSING ACTS—Licence.

second plaintiff had become the holder of the licence. Judgment of Palles C.B. in *Re Deighan, a Bankrupt* 31 I.L.T.R. 45 and *Dumigan* v. *Walsh* [1904] I.R. 298 distinguished. *Fitzpatrick* v. *McCormack*

(S.C.) [1986] I.R.380

3. —— **Holder** — *Transfer — Application for certificate of transfer — Applicant company having only two shareholders — Such shareholders being sole directors of the company — Such persons having previously been convicted for licensing offences — Whether such conviction be recorded on the licence applied for — Intoxicating Liquor Act,* 1927 (*No.* 15), *s.* 30 — *Interpretation Act,* 1937 (*No.* 38), *s.* 11(*c*).] The applicant company applied to the President of the District Court on 30 September, 1982, for a certificate of transfer of a publican's on-licence pursuant to the Licensing (Ireland) Act, 1833, for a premises at Crumlin, County Dublin, for which the President had granted an interim transfer to the company on 10 March, 1982. As the President indicated an intention to grant the certificate the superintendent of Crumlin Garda Station informed the President that a conviction had been recorded against the two directors of the applicant company on 25 November, 1981, in respect of a licensed premises at Townsend Street, Dublin, of which the two directors were joint holders of an intoxicating liquor on-licence. The superintendent submitted that under the provisions of s. 30 (2) of the Intoxicating Liquor Act, 1927, such a conviction must be recorded on the licence now applied for by the company of which the directors were the sole shareholders and sole directors. The President stated this case for the opinion of the High Court on whether he was obliged to direct that the conviction of 25 November, 1981, be recorded on the applicant's licence. S. 30(2) provides that where a licence is transferred freed and discharged under subs. 1 of s. 30 of all offences then recorded on such licence under that part of the Act by reason of that transaction being to give effect to a *bona fide* sale of such licence for money or money's worth "and the person who was the holder of such licence immediately before such transfer (hereinafter called the first transfer) applies (whether in the same or another licensing area) within 5 years after such transfer for a certificate for the transfer (hereinafter called the second transfer) to him of the same or another licence (hereinafter called the second licence) the court if it grants such certificate shall in and by such certificate direct that all offences which immediately before the first transfer were recorded under this part of this Act on the first licence shall on the second transfer be recorded on the second licence and whenever such direction is so

LICENSING ACTS—*continued.*

given every such offence shall on the second transfer be recorded on the second licence and such record shall from and after the second transfer have effect as if the same had been made on the second licence at the time when it was made on the first licence . . .". It was submitted on behalf of the applicant that since the President had accepted that the present transaction was for a *bona fide* transfer within the meaning of s. 30(1) and was not therefore a device to evade the provisions of the 1927 Act, the applicant was entitled to be construed as a different legal entity from the persons holding the first licence so that the conviction against those persons should not be recorded on the second licence now applied for. The respondent submitted that the acceptance of the applicant's submissions would open the way to abuse and evasion of the provisions of the 1927 Act. **Held** by Barrington J. in answering the question stated in the negative. Section 30(2) did not apply to this case once the District Justice was satisfied that the transaction before him was for a *bona fide* sale and not a device to evade the provisions of the licensing laws. The subsection would apply where the holder of a licence made a *bona fide* transfer of his licence to a third party and later applied for a new licence in his own name. The applicant in this case was entitled to rely on the distinction between the legal entities involved. Therefore the recorded conviction of 25 November, 1981, was not to be recorded on the licence subject matter of this application and the answer to the question posed in the case stated was 'no'. *In re Hesketh Investments Ltd.*

(H.C.) [1984] ILRM 134

—— **Holder.**
see also No. 14

4. —— **New licence** — *Declaration of fitness — Objection* — Locus standi — *Applicant seeking declaration that premises when altered would be fit and convenient to be licensed — Statutory provisions requiring proof of certain matters on such an application — Objectors contending that those proofs not satisfied* — Locus standi *of those objectors to raise such objections — Whether statutory limitation on categories of person who can take objections on grounds of character, conduct and suitability of premises applicable — Fair procedures — Licensing (Ireland) Act,* 1833 (*c.* 68), *s.* 4 — *Intoxicating Liquor Act,* 1960 (*No.* 18), *ss.* 14, 15.] Section 4 of the Licensing (Ireland) Act, 1833, insofar as it provides that the grounds of objection provided therein to the grant of a certificate of entitlement to a licence can only be taken by an inhabitant of the civil parish in which the premises proposed to be licensed are situate does not extend to the particular objections

LICENSING ACTS—Licence.

which can be taken under s. 14, sub-s. 1 of the Intoxicating Liquor Act, 1960, to the grant of a certificate of the type provided under that section or to the grant of the related declaration under s. 15 of that Act. Such objections can be taken by any person provided he carries on a licensed business in any licensed premises in the neighbourhood of the premises proposed to be licensed. So **held** by the Supreme Court (Finlay C.J.; Henchy, Griffin, Hederman and McCarthy JJ.). *Per* Finlay C.J.: it would be clearly contrary to any concept of fair procedure should any person carrying on a licensed business in the neighbourhood of the premises to be licensed be prevented from being heard and represented on the hearing of an application under these statutory provisions. In so far as the interpretation of s. 14 arrived at may appear to be inconsistent with any of the provisions of the Act of 1833, that Act must, to this extent, be deemed to have been amended. *Jaggers Restaurant Ltd.* v. *Ahearne*

(S.C.) [1988] I.R.308; [1988] ILRM 553

5. —— **New licence** — *Objection — Statutory restriction on the grant of a licence in respect of premises situate within one mile of premises first licensed before 4 July 1960 — Objectors having held restricted licence prior to 4 July 1960 — Restricted licence "converted" into full licence — Effect of "conversion" — Whether "converted" licence a new licence — Whether objectors entitled to rely on restriction — Intoxicating Liquor Act,* 1960 (*No.* 18), *s.* 27 — *Intoxicating Liquor Act,* 1962 (*No.* 21), *s.* 20.] Section 27, sub-ss. 4 and 5 of the Intoxicating Liquor Act, 1960, provide: "(4) . . . the Revenue Commissioners shall, upon application within two years after the passing of this Act by a person who holds a restricted licence in respect of any premises and upon payment by that person of the sum of two hundred pounds to the Revenue Commissioners grant to that person a full licence in respect of the premises. (5) Upon the grant under subsection 4 of this section of a full licence in respect of any premises, the restricted licence in respect thereof shall be extinguished." Section 20, sub-s. 2(*a*) of the Intoxicating Liquor Act, 1962, provides: "(2)(*a*) An application to the Circuit Court under section 13 of the Act of 1960 shall not be allowed in respect of premises situate less than one mile measured by the shortest public thoroughfare from premises in respect of which there is in force a licence that was first granted on or before the 4 day of July, 1960 . . ." The applicant was the owner of a site upon which he proposed to build a public house. He applied to the Circuit Court, pursuant to s. 15 of the Act of 1960, for a declaration that he was entitled to receive a new ordinary publican's on-licence in respect of

LICENSING ACTS—*continued.*

premises proposed to be constructed and adapted by him. The objectors were the owners of licensed premises situate within one mile of the proposed premises. The licence attached to the objectors' premises prior to the 4 July, 1960, had been a restricted six day licence but on the 3 August, 1961, pursuant to s. 27 of the Act of 1960, a full seven day on-licence was granted in respect of the premises. Rather than issuing a new licence, the Revenue Commissioners had merely endorsed the existing licence. The objectors objected to the application on the grounds that the court was precluded by s. 20 of the Act of 1962 from granting the declaration sought. It was argued on behalf of the applicant that the licence attaching to the objectors' premises was a licence first granted after the 4 July, 1960, and accordingly that s. 20 did not apply. It was argued on behalf of the objectors that the procedure prescribed by s. 27 of the Act of 1960 did not constitute the granting of a new licence but only the conversion of an existing licence. The Circuit Court judge stated a case to the Supreme Court as to whether he was precluded by s. 20 of the Act of 1962 from granting the declaration sought. **Held** by the Supreme Court (Finlay C.J., Walsh, Henchy, Griffin and McCarthy JJ.), in answering the case stated in the negative, 1, that on proper construction of s. 27 of the Act of 1960, the licence held by the objectors was a licence granted by the Revenue Commissioners on the 3 August, 1961. Upon the granting of that licence the restricted licence in respect of the premises had been automatically extinguished. 2. That in view of the clear terms of s. 27 the procedure by endorsement adopted by the Revenue Commissioners was irrelevant. 3. That while it was difficult to conceive why the legislature might have treated "converted" licences differently from other licences, the Court could not depart from the clear and unambiguous meaning of the section. 4. That while s. 20 of the Act of 1962 discriminated between the holders of "converted" licences and the holders of other licences, it did not discriminate between the holders of "converted" licences themselves and so did not discriminate invidiously. *Doyle* v. *Hearne (No. 2)*

(S.C.) [1988] I.R.317

6. —— **New licence** — *Off-Licence application — Adequacy of premises in vicinity — Part of shopping centre development — Whether convenience to or reasonable requirements of public relevant — Licensing Act (Northern Ireland),* 1971 (*c.* 13), *s.* 5(2).] The appellant sought a grant of an off-licence under section 3(1)(*b*) of the Licensing Act (Northern Ireland), 1971, for premises at Connswater Shopping Centre, Belfast. The appellant adduced evidence of a

LICENSING ACTS—Licence.

market survey showing that a large number of persons would use an off-licence situate in the Centre. It was contended that the Centre and its immediate surroundings formed a distinct vicinity. The appellant submitted that in deciding the question of adequacy the court must have regard to the requirements of the public at large and the reasonable requirements of the public. This required consideration of a number of matters not merely the number of off-licence premises in a particular area but also the expectation of visitors to the Centre finding an off-licence either inside or close to the Centre. There were three existing off-licences in the area and the population of the area was declining. **Held,** dismissing the appeal, 1, while "vicinity" within the meaning of section 5(2) of the 1971 Act was not limited to premises immediately surrounding the proposed premises, it was limited to premises in the neighbourhood in the sense of which one speaks of being a neighbour of another and the successful opening of the centre had not created a new and small vicinity confined to the centre or to the centre and shops close to it. *Magill* v. *Bell* [1972] N.I. 159 applied. 2. The primary duty of the court was to apply the test stated in the statute, namely whether the number of off-licences in the vicinity was inadequate. While the evidence of the market survey conducted for the appellant had shown that an off-licence in the shopping centre would be convenient for shoppers and that such an off-licence would be commercially successful; this did not prove that the number of off-licences in the vicinity was inadequate. *Stewarts Supermarkets Ltd.* v. *Sterrit*
(H.C., N.I.) [1985] N.I.159

7. —— **New licence** — *On/off licence application — Adequacy — Extent of "vicinity" — Subsisting licence — Licence renewed after trading had been discontinued — Whether licence void — Licensing Act (Northern Ireland),* 1971 (*c.* 13), *ss.* 5(2), 5(5), *Sched. II.*] The appellant appealed from a decision of the Recorder of Belfast, refusing an application for the provisional grant of an "on/off licence" for premises situated in the basement of 42 Botanic Avenue, Belfast. The appellant sought to surrender as a "subsisting licence", a licence in respect of premises situated at 42 Thomas Street, Armagh. The Armagh premises, however, had been sold and trading on the premises had ceased on 28 July, 1984. The licence had been renewed by the Clerk of Petty Sessions on 11 September, 1984. On appeal there was argument as to whether there was an adequate number of similar licensed premises in the vicinity of the proposed licensed premises and whether the licence to be surrendered was a valid "subsisting licence" within the meaning of the Licensing Act (Northern Ireland), 1971.

LICENSING ACTS—*continued.*

Held, dismissing the appeal, that, 1, the premises were suitable for the sale of intoxicating liquor on or off the premises and, as there was a considerable and growing demand in the vicinity for licensed premises which was not met, the number of such premises in the vicinity was inadequate. 2. The court was entitled to go behind the renewal of the surrendered licence, however, and declare the same to be a nullity on the basis that trading in the relevant premises had been discontinued at the material time and for this reason, the provisional grant would be refused. *Wine Inns Ltd.* v. *Lavery Ltd.*
(Q.B.D.) [1985] N.I.427

8. —— **New licence** — *On/off licence — Suitability of premises — Extent to which court should consider locality of premises — Whether court should consider feasibility of applicant's building plans — Adequacy of premises — Extent of "vicinity" — Discretion to refuse application — Licensing Act (Northern Ireland),* 1971 (*c.* 13), *s.* 5(2).] An application for the provisional grant of a licence to sell intoxicating liquor either in or off premises at Lower Crescent, Belfast, was granted by the Recorder of Belfast despite objections by publicans in the area, owners of commercial premises, the trustees of a nearby church and the R.U.C. Some objectors appealed against the decision to grant a licence on the grounds of the unsuitability of the premises and the adequacy of licensed premises in the vicinity, and they also sought to invoke the general discretion of the court to refuse the application. A subsisting licence was surrendered at the hearing before the Recorder. Questions were raised whether the licence had to be surrendered *de novo* at the hearing of the appeal and whether it must be subsisting at the time. **Held,** dismissing the appeal, 1, the provisions of section 10 of the Licensing Act (Northern Ireland), 1971, envisage that the only surrender will take place at the county court hearing. The life of the licence surrendered is artificially kept alive under section 10(2) pending disposal of the appeal. 2. In considering the suitability of the premises, matters such as structural stability, sewage and access should be left to the relevant statutory agencies. While the court could not absolve itself of its statutory task of deciding upon suitability by placing complete reliance upon the determination of statutory agencies, it will be slow to reach a conclusion at variance with the considered decision of a competent agency acting within its own sphere. The court should focus its attention on the finished result of the submitted plans and need not be concerned with the difficulties and expense of construction. While the premises were less than ideal in a number of respects the defects were not sufficient to make

LICENSING ACTS—Licence.

the premises unsuitable for their purpose. *Quaere* whether the requirement that the premises be "suitable", within the meaning of section 5(2) of the 1971 Act, should be limited to suitability for the business being conducted in a peaceable and orderly manner and so that the premises shall be reasonably subject to such entry and inspection by the police as is authorised by law, to the exclusion of factors relating to local amenity. 3. In determining the "vicinity" for the purpose of considering under the said section 5(2) whether the number of licensed premises was inadequate, it is important to look at the physical features of an area, any natural boundaries, the established dwelling patterns and geographical allegiances of those living and working and shopping there and the habits and movements of the people in the area. Rather than drawing the boundaries of a fixed area in deciding the adequacy of the number of licensed premises in a vicinity the court should look at each set of licensed premises in turn and decide if they fell within the vicinity of the subject premises. In so doing, the court should consider not only public houses but hotels selling liquor for consumption on the premises. There was a considerable and growing demand in the vicinity which was not satisfied by the existing licensed premises. Accordingly, the applicant had discharged the onus of proving adequacy. 4. The limits of the discretion to refuse a licence notwithstanding the satisfaction of all the tests set out in the said section 5(2) are far from settled and its subject matter difficult to define. The factors put forward by the objectors, however, as grounds for exercising the discretion to refuse the grant of a licence were insufficient. *Donnelly* v. *Regency Hotel Ltd.*

(H.C., N.I.) [1985] N.I.144

9. —— **New Licence** — *Off-licence application — Extinguishment of existing on-licence — Objection by holders of existing licences — Whether on-licence may be surrendered to obtain grant of off-licence — Whether economic detriment to existing licence holders a ground for refusing grant of licence — Beer Retailers' and Spirits Grocers' Retail Licences (Ireland) Act,* 1900 (*c.* 30), *s.* 1 — *Licensing (Ireland) Act,* 1902 (*c.* 18), *s.* 2.] Section 2 of the Licensing (Ireland) Act, 1902, as amended by s. 23 of the Intoxicating Liquor Act, 1960, provides that no new licence for the sale of intoxicating liquor, whether for consumption on or off the premises, should be granted from the date of the passing of the Act. Exception to this provision is made, *inter alia,* by sub-s. 1 of s. 2 for premises which were licensed at any time during the period of five years immediately before the day on which notice of an application is given to the appropriate

LICENSING ACTS—*continued.*

District Court clerk or Circuit Court registrar. Section 1 of the Beer Retailers' and Spirit Grocers' Retail Licences (Ireland) Act, 1900, provides that the licensing justices may, in their free and unqualified discretion, either refuse a certificate for any new excise licence for sale of beer or spirits by retail to be consumed off the premises, on any grounds appearing to them sufficient, or grant the same to such persons as they deem fit and proper and, for the purposes aforesaid, shall be at liberty to hear and receive and act upon any objection and any evidence in support thereof. The applicant, the owner of a national chain of supermarkets, applied for and was granted an off-licence in lieu of a surrendered on-licence in respect of its premises in Killarney. Eight owners of on-licences in Killarney, whose businesses were confined exclusively to sale for consumption off the premises, appealed to the Circuit Court against the granting of this licence on the grounds of the economic detriment which it was proven they had suffered as a result of the local supermarket being entitled to deal in intoxicating liquor. The Circuit Court judge stated a case for the opinion of the Supreme Court as to whether s. 1 of the Act of 1900 entitled him in his discretion to refuse the grant of a licence on this ground and whether the production for extinguishment of an on-licence entitled the applicant to the grant of an off-licence under the terms of s. 2, sub-s. 1 of the Act of 1902. **Held** by the Supreme Court (Walsh J.; Finlay C.J., Griffin, Hederman and McCarthy JJ. concurring) in answering the questions set out in the case stated, 1, that s. 2, sub-s. 1 of the Act of 1902 did not require that the licence being sought be of the same character as the licence being extinguished. *R. (Collins)* v. *Donegal Justices* [1903] 2 I.R. 533 considered. 2. That the discretion vested in the court by s. 1 of the Act of 1900 was not unqualified and must be exercised in accordance with the objectives of the licensing code. *East Donegal Co-Operative Livestock Mart Limited* v. *Attorney General* [1970] I.R. 317 considered. 3. That the sheltering of existing licence-holders from competition was not an objective of the licensing code and could not be relied upon by the court, in the exercise of judicial discretion, as a ground for refusing the grant of a licence. *In re Power Supermarkets Ltd.*

(S.C.) [1988] I.R.206

10. —— **New licence** — *Restaurant certificate — Whether premises required to be in use as a restaurant at time of application — Whether licence could be granted when public bar was on the premises — Intoxicating Liquor Act,* 1927 (*No.* 15), *s.* 12A.] S. 12A of the Intoxicating Liquor Act, 1927, as inserted by s. 9 of the Intoxicating Liquor Act, 1960, provides that

LICENSING ACTS—Licence.

upon application to the District Court for a certificate that part of a premises for which an on-licence is sought is a restaurant, the court must be satisfied, *inter alia,* that the premises is '. . . structurally adapted for use and *bona fide* and mainly used as a restaurant . . .' and that 'it does not include a public bar or part of a room in which there is a public bar . . .' Ss. 16 and 17 of the 1960 Act make provision for the granting of a declaration to the effect that if certain alterations are carried out upon a premises it would be suitably adapted as a restaurant. Upon the completion of such alterations the only ground on which an on-licence can be refused is that the relevant part of the premises is not *bona fide* and mainly used as a restaurant. In a case stated from the District Court as to whether the learned District Justice had been correct in law in granting an on-licence to the respondent, the District Justice stated that he had found as a fact that the respondent did not, at the time of his application, carry on a restaurant business in the premises. The District Justice had granted the application on the basis of an undertaking by the respondent to commence immediately to carry on a restaurant business therein. The learned District Justice had also found that the relevant part of the premises contained a public bar which could, however, be separated from the proposed restaurant by means of pull-down shutters. **Held** by Finlay P. in replying to the case stated by finding that the learned District Justice had erred in law in granting an on-licence to the respondent, 1, the language of s. 12A clearly requires the premises to be in *bona fide* use as a restaurant at the time of the application. Moreover, it would be inconsistent with the provisions of ss. 16 and 17 of the 1960 Act to hold that s. 12A conferred upon the District Court jurisdiction to grant an on-licence upon mere proof of a future intention to trade. 2. The clear meaning of s. 12A is that a licence should not be granted where there is a public bar on the premises. If the legislature intended to permit a situation where there could be a bar on the premises provided it was closed at the conclusion of normal licensing hours, it would have so stated. *Whelan* v. *Tobin*

(H.C.) [1976-7] ILRM 199

11. —— **Provisional licence** — *Procedure — Notice of application for provisional licence — Notice to contain matters prescribed by County Court Rules — Notice defective — Whether dispensation power in Rules applicable — Errors held verbal or technical — Whether discretion exercised correctly — Whether application a "proceeding" — Licensing Act (Northern Ireland)* 1971 (*c.* 13), *Sched.* 1, *Part* 1, *para.* 1 — *C.C.R. (N.I.), O.* 43, *r.* 14.] The respondent applied to the County Court for the provisional grant of a

LICENSING ACTS—*continued.*

licence in respect of premises in Martinstown, County Antrim. The appellant was the owner of other licensed premises in Martinstown, County Antrim. The respondent published notice of his intended application in two newspapers at the appropriate time. In the notices published and served, however, the date of the opening of the court sitting was given as 3 May, 1984, whereas the correct date was 2 May, 1984. Furthermore, the notice published in one newspaper stated that the subsisting licence to be surrendered was for premises at Kisaboy, Charlemont, County Antrim, whereas the correct address was County Armagh. The appellant served notice of his intention to object to the application of the respondent. His notice was served too late, however, and he had no *locus standi* at the hearing. The learned County Court Judge granted the application on the basis that he was entitled to rely on his discretion under Order 43, rule 14(1) of the County Court Rules (Northern Ireland), 1981, and to treat the errors as merely verbal or technical, and not such as to invalidate the proceedings. The appellant sought an order of judicial review on the ground that the procedure contained in schedule 1 to the Licensing Act (Northern Ireland), 1971, was mandatory and that defects in the notices were fatal to the application. The application was refused and the appellants appealed. **Held,** dismissing the appeal, that the County Court Judge had jurisdiction to grant the application. While the provisions of schedule 1 to the 1971 Act are mandatory, there is a clear distinction between matters required to be performed by that schedule and the content of notices set out in the County Courts (Northern Ireland) Rules, 1981. The dispensing power in Order 43, rule 14 of the Rules applied to the latter as a licensing application came within the definition of "proceedings" in article 2 of the County Courts (Northern Ireland) Order, 1980. There was no reason for interfering with the County Court Judge's exercise of his discretion as the appellant had not been misled or prejudiced by the errors. *In re O'Loughlin*

(C.A.) [1985] N.I.421

12. —— **Renewal** — *Hotel licence — Premises licensed as a hotel after 1960 — Premises having been previously licensed as a hotel — Obligation to register premises as a hotel with Bord Fáilte Éireann — Premises not so registered — Objection by garda to renewal of licence — Licence having previously been renewed without objection — Nature of obligation to register premises as a hotel — Whether objector precluded by previous renewals from relying on non-registration — Circuit Court Rules,* 1950 (*S.I. No.* 179), *O.* 42, *r.* 3 — *Licensing (Ireland) Act,* 1902 (*c.* 18), *s.* 2,

LICENSING ACTS—Licence.

para. (2) — *Intoxicating Liquor Act,* 1927 (*No.* 15), *s.* 28 — *Intoxicating Liquor Act,* 1960 (*No.* 18), *ss.* 19, 20, 21, 23.] The applicant was the holder of an intoxicating liquor licence in respect of premises which had first been licensed in 1960 under s. 2, para. (2) of the Licensing (Ireland) Act, 1902, as a hotel. That licence had been renewed annually until 1975 when it was allowed to lapse. In 1978 application was made to the Circuit Court entitled 'In the matter of the Licensing Acts, 1833 to 1962; s. 15, sub-s. 1 of the Intoxicating Liquor Act, 1960, ss. 13 and 23 of the Act of 1960, and s. 17 of the Act of 1960 as amended by s. 32 of the Intoxicating Liquor Act, 1962.' Pursuant to the orders of the Circuit Court the County Registrar certified that the then applicant was entitled to receive an excise licence described as a hotel licence for the sale of intoxicating liquor on the premises. An *ad interim* transfer of that licence was granted to the applicant in the present proceedings in 1979 and was confirmed at the annual licensing sessions and was renewed in 1980 and 1981. At the annual licensing sessions for 1982 the Gardaí objected to the granting of a certificate for the renewal of the licence on the grounds that the applicant's premises was not registered as a hotel with Bord Fáilte Éireann, as required by s. 20 of the Act of 1960. The applicant accepted that the licence granted in 1978 was a new licence but it was submitted on his behalf, firstly, that since the premises had existed prior to the passing of the Act of 1960 as a hotel licensed under the provisions of the Act of 1902, that s. 20 did not apply to it. Secondly, it was argued that the objector could not rely on non-registration as a hotel unless he showed that the licence was one which had been granted under the Act of 1902 and that this had not been proved. Thirdly, it was argued that since the hotel had never been registered with Bord Fáilte Éireann, the granting and renewal of the licence had created an equity in the applicant so that the court could not go behind those prior orders and must presume the hotel to have been registered. The District Justice stated a case for the determination of the High Court as to whether he was precluded by s. 20 of the Act of 1960 from granting a certificate for the renewal of the licence. **Held** by Barron J., in answering the question in the affirmative, 1, that s. 20 of the Act of 1960 referred to a licence and not to a premises so that since the present licence had been granted after the passing of the Act of 1960, it was immaterial whether the premises to which the licence related had or had not been licensed prior to the passing of the Act. 2. That it was clear from the certificate of the County Registrar issued in 1978 that the court was aware that the premises in respect of which the application was brought was a hotel. There

LICENSING ACTS—*continued.*

was nothing either in the title of the application or in the certificate which indicated otherwise than that the licence was a licence under s. 2, para. (2) of the Act of 1902. 3. That while in the absence of evidence that the hotel was registered in accordance with s. 20 of the Act of 1960 the orders allowing the renewal of the licence has been made without jurisdiction, certiorari would no longer lie to quash those orders. Those orders were in effect declarations that the premises was registered at the time of each order but the vitiating element continued from year to year and could therefore be relied upon by the objector. *In re Riordan* [1981] ILRM 2 distinguished. On appeal by the applicant it was **Held** by the Supreme Court (Finlay C.J., Walsh, Henchy, Griffin and Hederman JJ.), in dismissing the appeal, 1, that while the heading of the application to the Circuit Court in 1978 did not specifically refer to s. 2, para. (2) of the Act of 1902 but did refer to s. 23 of the Act of 1960 (which allows licences to be granted in respect of premises other than hotel premises which were licensed during the period of 5 years preceding the application), it would have been clear to the Circuit Court that the certificate in 1960 had been granted in respect of hotel premises. Accordingly it was more correct to assume now that the Circuit Court in dealing with the application of 1978 had acted within jurisdiction even though the title to the application was defective, rather than to assume that that court had made a patent error. 2. That the requirement that the premises be registered as a hotel pursuant to s. 20 of the Act of 1960 arose at each annual licensing sessions so that, unlike a statutory forfeiture of a licence, an objector was not precluded by previous renewals of the licence from objecting to renewal on the grounds of non-registration. *In re Riordan* [1981] ILRM 2 distinguished. 3. That if the applicant had investigated the licensing history of the premises when he purchased it in 1979 he would clearly have seen that the premises had first been licensed in 1960 as a hotel and that that licence had been allowed to lapse. Assuming that the applicant took proper advice he must at least have suspected that the licence granted in 1978 was also a hotel licence and, being a licence granted subsequent to the passing of the Act of 1960,that therefore he would have to register the premises as a hotel if he wished to renew the licence. *In re Riordan* [1981] ILRM 2 distinguished. *In re Bannerton*

(H.C., S.C.) [1986] I.R.758; [1986] ILRM 471; [1984] ILRM 662

OFFENCE

see also Nos. 2, 3

13. —— **Conviction** — *"First conviction"* —

LICENSING ACTS—Offence.

Meaning — Convictions for two offences committed on same date — Enactment precluding endorsement of licence in respect of first conviction — Statute — Interpretation — Whether use of singular includes plural — Absence of contrary intention — Both convictions protected from endorsement — Intoxicating Liquor Act, 1927 (*No.* 15), *ss.* 25(4), 29 — *Interpretation Act,* 1937 (*No.* 38), *s.* 11(*a*) — *Intoxicating Liquor Act,* 1960 (*No.* 18), *s.* 37 — *Intoxicating Liquor Act,* 1962 (*No.* 21).] Section 25, sub-s. 4 of the Intoxicating Liquor Act, 1927, as inserted by s. 37 of the Intoxicating Liquor Act,1960, provides *inter alia* that "where a person is convicted in relation to any premises in respect of which he holds a licence for the sale of intoxicating liquor by retail of an offence . . . and the conviction is the first conviction of that person in relation to those premises . . . the conviction shall not be recorded on the licence." The prosecutor applied to the respondent District Justice for a certificate of no objection to the transfer to the prosecutor of a wine retailer's on-licence held by M. Ltd. Prior to this application M. Ltd. had been convicted of two offences relating to incidents which occurred on 23/24 November, 1982, and two further offences relating to incidents which occurred on 26/27 November, 1982, all of which were offences to which s. 25 applied. The prosecutions had all been heard together and the convictions imposed on the same day. M. Ltd. had no previous convictions and consequently three of the convictions were endorsed on the licence. The prosecutor's application was refused on the ground that as a result of the endorsements the licence had been forfeited pursuant to s. 28 of the Act of 1927 and therefore could not be transferred. The prosecutor obtained an order of certiorari in the High Court (Barron J.) quashing the order of the respondent on the ground that the word "conviction" in s. 25, sub-s. 4, should be interpreted to read "convictions" and therefore in respect of a multiple conviction of a licensee with no previous convictions, none of the convictions comprised therein should be recorded on the licence. Hence, only two of M. Ltd.'s four convictions were required to be recorded on the licence and therefore at the date of the prosecutor's application there was a valid and subsisting licence. On appeal by the respondent it was **Held** by the Supreme Court (Finlay C.J., Henchy and Hederman JJ.), in allowing the appeal, 1, that having regard to the language of s. 25, sub-s. 2, and s. 29 of the Act of 1927, the learned trial judge erred in law in construing the word "conviction" in s. 25, sub-s. 4, of the Act of 1927 as to include the plural as well as the singular. Although it might be possible to speak

LICENSING ACTS—*continued.*

of "first convictions", it was not possible to construe "second" and "third" and "every subsequent" "conviction" in s. 25, sub-s. 2 in the same manner without altering and doing violence to the meaning of the sub-section. 2. That the two offences of which M. Ltd. was convicted in respect of the two separate dates, namely the offence of permitting of persons to be on the premises at a time prohibited and the offence of permitting intoxicating liquor to be consumed on the premises at a time prohibited contrary to s. 29 of the Act of 1962 and s. 2 of the Act of 1927 respectively, were not of necessity offences which must always arise together and were not a duplication of offence and that, therefore, a separate conviction for each was not precluded. *McCarthy* v. *Murphy* [1981] ILRM 213 followed. 3. Accordingly the licence had been automatically forfeited by the endorsement of three convictions. *The State (Armstrong)* v. *Donnelly* **(S.C.) [1985] I.R.636**

14. —— **Liability** — *Licence held on behalf of limited liability company by nominee — Nominee not involved in running of business — Offences committed contrary to Licensing Acts — Whether proof of* mens rea *on the part of defendant necessary — Whether defendant liable for offences as nominal holder of licence — Whether nominee or company the "real" holder of the licence — Intoxicating Liquor (General) Act,* 1924 (*No.* 62) — *Intoxicating Liquor Act,* 1927 (*No.* 15), *s.* 2 — *Intoxicating Liquor Act,* 1960 (*No.* 18), *s.* 28.] In 1971 an order was made by the District Court transferring the intoxicating liquor licence attached to hotel premises owned by R. Ltd. to the defendant as its nominee. In1974 the defendant ceased to have any part in the running of the business but the licence was renewed annually in her name. In 1983 the defendant was convicted of three offences of selling intoxicating liquor during prohibited hours and of permitting intoxicating liquor to be consumed on the premises during prohibited hours, which resulted in a forfeiture of the licence. The defendant appealed to the Circuit Court where a case was stated for the determination of the Supreme Court as to whether, if the defendant merely held the licence as nominee and took no part in the business, her appeals should be allowed. It was argued on behalf of the defendant that although she held the licence as nominee of R. Ltd., the company remained the real holder of the licence so that the defendant could incur no liability unless she took an active part in running the premises. She could not, it was submitted, be convicted of an offence in the absence of proof of *mens rea.* It was argued on behalf of the complainant that the defendant, having accepted appointment as the

LICENSING ACTS—*continued.*

company's nominee and having permitted applications to be made annually for the renewal of the licence, had represented to the court that she was answerable for the proper and lawful running of the premises. **Held** by the Supreme Court (Finlay C.J.,Walsh and McCarthy JJ.; Griffin and Hederman JJ. dissenting), in answering the case stated in the affirmative, 1, that the defendant as nominee held the licence in relation to the company's premises entirely in trust for and under the command of the company which was the real and beneficial holder of the licence and which was liable under the Licensing Acts as the holder of the licence. *McMahon* v. *Murtagh* [1982] ILRM 342 followed. 2. That while the concept of a nominee holding a licence on behalf of a body corporate would ordinarily give the impression that the nominee was warranting to control the servants, agents or officers of the company so as to ensure compliance with the law this was not sufficient to render a person guilty of a criminal offence which the statute did not make one of strict liability. *Per* Finlay C.J.: That if a company applied for a licence in the name of a nominee rather than in its own name, the courts should ensure, by enquiry at the annual licensing sessions, that such nominee was a person taking an active part, either directly or by delegation, in the running of the premises in such manner as to be answerable to the court in the event of offences being committed. *Per* Finlay C.J.: That a nominee who was participating in the running of licensed premises could be prosecuted not only for aiding and abetting the commission of any offences which might be committed but also as a principal offender. *Dictum* of Barrington J. in *McMahon* v. *Murtagh* [1982] ILRM 342 considered. *Director of Public Prosecutions* v. *Roberts*

(S.C.) [1987] I.R.268

LIEN

—— Purchaser — Sale of land — Booking deposits — Booking deposit held not to confer on prospective purchaser a lien on building site or an equitable estate.

see **Sale of Land,** 15

—— Solicitor — Costs — Solicitor obtaining title deeds from mortgagee on accountable receipt — Particulars and conditions of sale prepared by solicitor on instructions of mortgagor — Insolvency of mortgagor — Whether solicitor entitled to lien over title deeds for costs.

see **Solicitor,** 1

—— Vendor — Sale of land — Sale by company to associated company — Vendor's lien for unpaid purchase monies —

LIEN—*continued.*

Whether lien waived, abandoned or relinquished.

see **Sale of Land,** 16

LIMITATION OF ACTIONS

1. —— **Adverse possession** — Animus possidendi — *Intended user by owner to build upon lands — Whether defendant knew intended user — Whether title of plaintiff defeated — Statute of Limitations,* 1957 (*No.* 6), *ss.* 13, 18.] Section 13, sub-s. 2 of the Statute of Limitations, 1957, provides that no action by a person to recover land "shall be brought after the expiration of 12 years from the date on which the right of action accrued to the person bringing it." Section 18, sub-s. 1, provides that "no right of action to recover land shall be deemed to accrue unless the land is in the possession (in this section referred to as adverse possession) of some person in whose favour the period of limitation can run." The defendant was a farmer with a holding adjoining certain land on which there were two sheds. The land and sheds were owned by the defendant's sister and leased to the defendant by her for the purposes respectively of grazing cattle and bottling milk for sale. The plaintiff purchased the land and sheds from the defendant's sister with the intention of building a factory premises on the land, but no use was ever made of the land or sheds by the plaintiff. The defendant's sister reserved to herself for the benefit of the defendant the right to use the two sheds for her life. Following the sale the defendant continued to use the land and sheds as before and erected a post and wire fence over a portion of the boundary of the land where necessary to prevent his cattle from straying on to the plaintiff's adjoining factory premises. From the time that the defendant erected this fence, being more than 12 years prior to the date of issue of the proceedings, the defendant had exclusive use of the land and sheds. Approximately three years prior to the date of issue of the proceedings the defendant's sister died. The plaintiff brought an action to recover the land and sheds from the defendant and the defendant claimed in his defence that the plaintiff's title to the land had been defeated by virtue of s. 13, sub-s. 2 and s. 18, sub-s. 1 of the Statute of Limitations , 1957. The plaintiff's action was dismissed by the Circuit Court and on appeal to the High Court it was **Held** by Barron J., 1, that the claimant of adverse possession of land, within the meaning of s. 18, sub-s. 1, of the Act of 1957, must prove *animus possidendi* on his part. *Leigh* v. *Jack* (1879) 5 Ex. D. 264; *Littledale* v. *Liverpool College* [1900] 1 Ch. 19; *Cork Corporation* v. *Lynch* (Unreported, High Court, Egan J., 26 July, 1985);

LIMITATION OF ACTIONS—*continued.*

Wallis's Cayton Bay Holiday Camp Ltd. v. *Shell-Mex and B.P. Ltd.* [1975] Q.B. 94; *Treloar* v. *Nute* [1976] 1 W.L.R. 1295 and *Murphy* v. *Murphy* [1980] I.R. 183 considered. *McDonnell* v. *McKinty* (1847) 10 Ir. Law Rep. 514 and *Smith* v. *Lloyd* (1854) 9 Ex. 562, distinguished. 2. That where no use is being made of land by the owner and the claimant of adverse possession knows that the owner intends to use it for a specific purpose in the future, this is a factor to be taken into account in disproving *animus possidendi*. *Leigh* v. *Jack* (1879) 5 Ex. D. 264; *Convey* v. *Regan* [1952] I.R. 56; *Cork Corporation* v. *Lynch* (Unreported, High Court, Egan J., 26 July, 1985); *Wallis's Cayton Bay Holiday Camp Ltd.* v. *Shell-Mex and B.P. Ltd.* [1975] Q.B. 94, applied. 3. That the defendant made full and exclusive use of the land for a period of 14 years and there was no evidence that the defendant intended to use the land upon a temporary basis or merely to prevent it lying idle until the owner was in a position to use it for a purpose of which the defendant was aware. Accordingly the facts supported the defendant's claim to adverse possession of the land and the plaintiff's title to the land was defeated by virtue of s. 13, sub-s. 2, of the Act of 1957. 4. That as the defendant had used the sheds with his sister's permission until her death three years previously he was not in adverse possession of the sheds during that time and the plaintiff's title to the sheds was not defeated by virtue of s. 13, sub-s. 2 of the Act of 1957. *Durack (Seamus) Manufacturing Ltd.* v. *Considine*

(H.C.) [1987] I.R.677

2. —— **Estoppel** — *Equity — Motor accident — Plaintiff passenger injured — Personal injuries — Summons not issued within limitation period — Defendant outside jurisdiction — Attempt to issue summons at end of period — Plaintiff's solicitor informed of existence of solicitor within State authorised to accept service on behalf of defendant — Representation made by defendant's insurers — Representation false but innocent — Failure to issue summons within period caused by absence of solicitor so authorised — Defendant prevented from pleading Statute — Central Office practice — Issue of proceedings when defendant resident outside the jurisdiction — Statute of Limitations,* 1957 (*No.* 6), *s.* 11 — *Rules of the Superior Courts,* 1962 (*S.I. No.* 72), *O.*11, *r.* 6.] On the 25 October, 1977, the plaintiff suffered serious injury when she was travelling, as a passenger, in a motor car being driven by J.F., who resided in Northern Ireland. The plaintiff's solicitor initiated discussions with J.F.'s, insurers, who indicated by letter of 27 March, 1979, that a firm of solicitors had been nominated within the jurisdiction to accept service of any proceedings.

LIMITATION OF ACTIONS—*continued.*

J.F.'s insurers indicated that they wished to discuss the case further. The plaintiff's solicitor wrote several letters indicating his willingness to discuss the matter. The plaintiff's solicitor then learned that J.F. had died and he wrote a further letter to J.F.'s insurers drawing this fact to their attention and he also proposed that settlement discussions be held. There was no reply from the insurance company. The plaintiff's solicitor and J.F.'s insurers agreed to nominate Elizabeth Fegan as defendant and that the insurers would honour any decree obtained in such proceedings. Order 11, r. 6 of the Rules of 1962 provides that a plaintiff wishing to obtain an order for service of proceedings on a defendant resident outside the jurisdiction should apply to the court for an order before issuing his proceedings. On the 2 October, 1980, the plaintiff's solicitor, through his town agents, attempted to issue a plenary summons out of the Central Office. The Central Office refused to issue the plenary summons as it was their practice to refuse to issue a plenary summons when the defendant was resident out of the jurisdiction unless the plaintiff had a court order authorising service out of the jurisdiction or could produce a letter from a solicitor within the jurisdiction undertaking to accept service. The solicitors nominated by J.F.'s insurers refused to accept service of the proceedings because they had no instructions. On the 24 October, 1980, the time fixed by statute expired. On the 4 December, 1980, those solicitors, having taken instructions, undertook to accept service. Proceedings were issued on the 17 December, 1980, and therefore outside the time provided for bringing actions laid down by the Statute of Limitations, 1957. The defendant raised the statute in her defence. The plaintiff pleaded that the defendant was estopped form raising the statute. At the trial of the preliminary point of law raised by the pleadings, it was **Held** by Barrington J., 1, that the defendant was estopped from pleading the statute. The representation contained in J.F.'s insurers' letter of 27 March, 1979, that they had nominated solicitors within the jurisdiction to accept service of proceedings encouraged the plaintiff's solicitor to defer taking steps to protect his client's interest. Furthermore the insurers took an inordinate amount of time in authorising solicitors to accept service of proceedings. 2. Accordingly, it would be unconscionable to allow the defendant to plead the Statute of Limitations. *O'Reilly* v. *Graville* [1971] I.R. 90; *Doran* v. *Thompson Ltd.* [1978] I.R. 223 and *Smith* v. *Ireland and ors.* [1983] ILRM 300, considered. *Traynor* v. *Fegan*

(H.C.) [1985] I.R.586

3. —— **Negligence** — *Accrual of cause of action — Economic loss — Plaintiff purchased*

LIMITATION OF ACTIONS—*continued.*

land in 1973 believing planning permission had been obtained — Permission discovered in 1977 to be a nullity — Whether proceedings statute barred.] The plaintiffs were interested in buying land for housing development. They instructed the second defendants, a firm of estate agents, to find suitable land and the second defendants found a 23 acre site near Bangor. The second defendants advised the plaintiffs that the third defendants should be engaged to apply for planning permission for the site and in August, 1973, the third defendants made such an application. In September, 1973, interim planning permission was granted and in October, 1973, the plaintiffs purchased the site for £142,871.21. In May, 1976, the first defendant, as planning authority revoked the planning permission and early in 1977 the first defendant agreed that the compensation for the revocation of planning permission would amount to £90,000. Then in July, 1977, the first defendant notified the plaintiff that it had discovered that the certificate required by section 34 of the Land Development Values (Compensation) Act (Northern Ireland), 1965, had not been lodged with the application for planning permission, with the result that the permission granted was a nullity. Consequently, the first defendant withdrew their offer of compensation. The plaintiffs instituted proceedings and in March, 1981, the writ of summons was issued alleging negligence against all the defendants and breach of contract and misrepresentations against the second and third defendants. On a preliminary issue to determine whether the plaintiffs' claims were statute-barred, **Held,** that the plaintiffs' claims were statute-barred. A cause of action accrues in negligence when the negligent act or omission occurs and damge occurs i.e. when the defect manifests itself as damage. In cases of economic loss the cause of action accrues from the moment when the plaintiff suffers a significant loss for which he can sue. In this case the plaintiffs suffered a significant loss when they bought the lands in October, 1973. From that time they could have sued the defendants in negligence if they had been aware of their predicament and in such proceedings a quantifiable loss, i.e. the difference in value between the lands with planning permission and without, could readily have been shown. The claim for breach of contract accrued either on the date in August, 1973, when the defendants failed to lodge the necessary certificate or in September, 1973, when permission was given: on either date the cause of action was clearly statute barred. *McInerney Properties Ltd.* v. *Department of the Environment*

(Q.B.D.) [1984] N.I.1

4. —— **Personal injury** — *Negligence —*

LIMITATION OF ACTIONS—*continued.*

Accrual of cause of action — Surgery performed on the plaintiff by each of the defendants — Action instituted after expiry of three years from dates of surgery — Whether action statute barred — Date on which cause of action accrued — Whether date on which act causing injury committed or date of discoverability of injury — Statute — Interpretation — Public Authorities Protection Act, 1893 (*c.* 61), *s.* 1(*a*) — *Statute of Limitations,* 1957 (*No.* 6), *s.* 11(2)(*b*).] By virtue of the provisions of s. 11, sub-s. 2 (*b*) of the Statute of Limitations, 1957, the date of accrual of a cause of action for damages for negligence in respect of personal injury is the date when the act causing the injury is committed. So **Held** by Barron J. *Morgan* v. *Park Developments* [1983] ILRM 156 distinguished; *Carroll* v. *Kildare Co. Council* [1950] I.R. 258 considered. *Per* Barron, J.: The date of accrual of a cause of action in negligence in all cases should be the date of discoverability of damage, through there should not be an unlimited period based upon discoverability. *Hegarty* v. *O'Loughran*

(H.C.) [1987] I.R.135 ; [1987] ILRM 603

5. —— **Recovery of land** — *Owner deceased — Next-of-kin in possession — Plaintiff being administrator of deceased's estate — Period of limitation applicable — Statute of Limitations,* 1957 (*No.* 6), *ss. 13,* 23, 45 — *Succession Act,* 1965 (*No.* 27), *ss.* 9, 126.] The defendant was in possession of certain freehold registered land. The registered owner of those lands had died intestate on the 1 February, 1966. Letters of administration of the estate of the registered owner were granted to the plaintiff on the 4 August, 1976. The plaintiff issued a civil bill in the Circuit Court and therein claimed, as such administrator, to be entitled to recover possession of the said lands from the defendant. In her defence the defendant pleaded that the plaintiff's action was statute barred. The defendant relied upon the present provisions of s. 45 of the Statute of Limitations, 1957, which, as substituted by the Succession Act, 1965, states that no action in respect of any claim to the estate of a deceased person shall be brought after the expiration of six years from the date when the right to receive the share or interest accrued. The plaintiff submitted that his action was an action to recover land within the meaning of s. 13, sub-s. 2 (*a*), of the Act of 1957, and that this action had been instituted within the period of 12 years from the date of the accrual of his right of action, and that his action was not statute barred pursuant to that sub-section. The Circuit Court judge gave judgment in favour of the plaintiff. On appeal by the defendant to the High Court it was **Held** by McMahon J., in disallowing the appeal, 1, that the plaintiff's action was one

LIMITATION OF ACTIONS—*continued.*

for the recovery of land within the meaning of s. 13, sub-s. 2 (*a*), of the Act of 1957, and that his action had been instituted within the period of 12 years therein specified. *Diplock* v. *Wintle* [1948] Ch. 465 and *Ministry of Health* v. *Simpson* [1951] A.C. 251 considered. 2. That, in any event, as expressly provided by s. 9 of the Act of 1965, the present provisions of s. 45 of the Act of 1957 did not apply to the estate of the deceased as he had died before the Act of 1965 came into operation on the 1 January, 1967. *Drohan* v. *Drohan*

(H.C.) [1984] I.R.311

—— Ejectment — Accrual of right of action — Adverse possession — Abandonment of tenancy — Whether determination of tenancy could be presumed from landlord's conduct — Whether landlord's action for recovery of possession statute barred.
see **Landlord and Tenant,** 19

—— Malicious injuries — Statutory construction — Accrual of cause of action — Proceedings commenced outside this period — Whether court power to extend time.
see **Criminal Injuries,** 8

—— Mode of trial — Plaintiffs alleged to be statute barred — Whether limitation issue should be tried as a preliminary issue — Whether right to jury trial of such an issue — Court's discretion to disapply limitation period — Exercise of discretion involved disputed issues of fact — Whether such issues unsuitable to be tried with a jury.
see **Practice and Procedure,** 57

—— Personal injury action — Practice — Interrogatories — Limitation period.
see **Practice and Procedure,** 45

—— Survival of cause of action — Guarantee payable on demand — Continuing security — Demand made after death of guarantor — Proceedings against estate of guarantor — Whether cause of action subsisting at time of death of deceased — Proceedings commenced 3 years after death of guarantor — Whether claim statute barred.
see **Banking,** 2

LIQUIDATION
see **Company — Winding up**
see also **under Industrial and Provident Societies**

LIQUOR LICENSING
see **Licensing Acts**

LIS PENDENS — Registration — Effect of proceedings establishing equitable interest in property on mortgage executed subsequent to registration of *lis pendens* — Whether equitable interest entitled to priority over mortgagee's interest — Whether mortgage valid.
see **Real Property,** 8

LIVELIHOOD, RIGHT TO EARN
see **Civil Service,** 3
Constitution, 42, 43
Postal Service
Statute, 3

LIVESTOCK — Excise duty — European Communities — Whether duty *ultra vires* as unreasonable.
see **European Communities,** 1

LOAN — Guarantee.
see **Guarantee**
Surety

LOCAL ELECTIONS
—— Election petition — Whether notice to be served on D.P.P. — Whether actions of returning officer an irregularity — Whether request for recount could only be made by candidate or his agent.
see **Electoral Law,** 1

—— Vacancy — County council — Standing orders providing that such vacancies be filled by co-option — Standing orders further providing that co-option be of a person from the same electoral area — Whether standing order *ultra vires.*
see **Local Government,** 7

LOCAL FINANCE
see **Rating and Valuation**

—— Service charges — Domestic dwelling.
see **Local Government,** 1, 2

LOCAL GOVERNMENT
see also **Compulsory Acquisition; Fire Services; Highway; Housing; Planning; Rating and Valuation**

Authority. Nos. 1-8
Public health — burial grounds. No. 9
Service charges. Nos. 1, 2

AUTHORITY

1. —— **Charges** — *Services* — *Charges in respect of services provided — Order of county*

LOCAL GOVERNMENT—*continued.*

manager fixing charges — Charge for water supply — Charge for water, sewage and refuse collection services — Failure of county manager's order to specify separate amounts for separate services for calendar year — Statute authorising charge coming into force on 12 July — Whether order could be interpreted as being prospective — Public Health (Ireland) Act, 1878 (*c.* 52), *s.* 65A — *County Management Act,* 1940 (*No.* 12), *s.* 19 — *Courts of Justice Act,* 1947 (*No.* 20), *s.* 16 — *City and County Management (Amendment) Act,* 1955 (*No.* 12), *s.* 20 — *Local Government (Sanitary Services) Act,* 1962 (*No.* 26), *s.* 7 — *Local Government (Financial Provisions) (No.2) Act,* 1983 (*No.* 21), *ss.* 1, 2, 3, 4, 8.] The Local Government (Financial Provisions) (No. 2) Act, 1983, came into force on the 12 July, 1983. Section 2, sub-s. 1 of that Act provides that any existing enactment which requires or enables a local authority to provide a service but which does not empower the authority to charge for the provision of the service shall be deemed so to empower the authority. Section 65A, of the Public Health (Ireland) Act, 1878, inserted by s. 7, of the Local Government (Sanitary Services) Act, 1962, and amended by s. 8 of the Act of 1983, provides that a sanitary authority may make charges for water supplied by them, whether within or outside their functional area. On the 1 September, 1983, the county manager of the plaintiff authority purported to make an order that a charge of £60 be levied on every domestic dwelling in the Athlone urban area for water, sewerage and refuse services for the year 1983. On the 2 September, 1983, the plaintiff issued the defendant with a demand for payment of this charge, which demand identified the charge as being, as to £40 a water charge and as to £20 a sewerage and refuse charge. The defendant refused to pay this charge and the plaintiff instituted proceedings in the District Court. The District Court gave a decree for £28.27 and the plaintiff appealed to the Circuit Court. On the hearing of the plaintiff's appeal evidence was given on behalf of the plaintiff that, prior to the making of the county manager's order, it had been decided that the £60 should be divided as to £40 in respect of water, £10 in respect of sewerage and £10 in respect of refuse collection. The Circuit Judge stated a case for the determination of the Supreme Court as to (*a*) whether the order was invalid because it failed to fix separate amounts in respect of each service and (*b*) whether the order was invalid by reason of the fact that it purported to fix a charge for the calendar year 1983, although the Act had not come into force until the 12 July, 1983. **Held** by the Supreme Court (Finlay C.J., Henchy, Griffin, Hederman and McCarthy JJ.) in deciding that the order of the county manager was invalid by reason of its failure to specify the amount assessed in respect of each service, 1, that the power of a local authority conferred by s. 2, sub-s. 1 of the Act of 1983 to make a charge for a service did not apply to the making of a charge for the provision of water, since that service was one for which, apart from that section, the authority could make a charge without statutory limit. 2. That s. 2, sub-s. 1 of the Act of 1983 conferred a power to make a charge for a single service and could not be interpreted as allowing a local authority to fix a single charge for a number of services. 3. That the power to make a charge for the provision of water is a separate and distinct statutory power and could not be lawfully exercised by the making of a charge of an aggregate amount for a number of services, including water. 4. That the court would not go behind the written order of the county manager and would not supply any want or deficiency in it by having regard to evidence of the process of discussion or agreement between officers of the authority which led to the making of the order. 5. That the order of the county manager was invalid by reason of its failure to specify a separate charge for each of the services provided and, accordingly, that the defendant was entitled to a dismiss of the entire of the plaintiff's claim. *Athlone Urban District Council* v. *Gavin* **(S.C.) [1985] I.R.434; [1986] ILRM 277**

2. —— **Charges** — *Services — Charges for water supply otherwise than by measure — Statute authorising charge coming into force on* 12 *July,* 1983 — *Orders of City Manager fixing amount of charges — Order made in October,* 1983, *in respect of period up to* 31 *December,* 1983 — *Order made in May,* 1984, *in respect of period* 1 *January,* 1984 *to* 31 *December,* 1984 — *Whether orders retrospective — Whether orders bad by reason of being retrospective — Manner of payment — Statute authorising charge payable by instalments — Whether authority empowered to levy charge payable at once — Public Health (Ireland) Act,* 1878 (*c.* 52), *s.* 65A — *Local Government (Sanitary Services) Act,* 1962 (*No.* 26), *s.* 7 — *Local Government (Financial Provisions) (No.2) Act,* 1983 (*No.* 2), *s.* 8.

Statute — Interpretation — "Instalments" — Whether plural includes singular — Interpretation Act, 1937 (*No.* 38) — *Local Government (Financial Provisions) (No. 2) Act,* 1983 (*No.* 21), *s.* 8.

Practice — Supreme Court — Consultative case stated — Approach of Supreme Court to case stated — Whether arguments not made before Circuit Court would be entertained — Courts of Justice Act, 1947 (*No.* 20), *s.* 16.] Section 65A of the Public Health (Ireland) Act, 1878, as inserted by s. 7 of the Local Government (Sanitary Services) Act, 1962, and amended by s. 8 of the Local Government (Financial Provisions) (No.

LOCAL GOVERNMENT—*continued.*
2) Act, 1983, which came into force on the 12 July, 1983, provides that a sanitary authority may make a charge for water supplied by them, whether within or outside their functional area. Section 65A, sub-s. 7 provides that:— "A charge under this section for water supplied otherwise than by measure shall be payable in advance by equal half-yearly instalments on the 1st day of April and on the 1st day of October or by such other instalments as the sanitary authority to whom the charge is payable shall determine, and, in default of being paid within two months after becoming payable, shall be recoverable as a simple contract debt in any court of competent jurisdiction." On the 25 October, 1983, the City Manager and Town Clerk for the City of Dublin made an order pursuant to s. 65A of the Act of 1878 fixing a charge for domestic water supply for the Dublin City and Extra Municipal areas for the period up to 31 December, 1983, payable on demand. The order was made on the recommendation and submission of the Finance Officer and Treasurer and recited that:— "the estimate of expenses for 1983 adopted by the City Council included provision for £3,100,000 to be raised by way of new charges for services." Shortly after the making of the order demands were served on the defendants for the amount of the charge. On the 25 May, 1984, the City Manager made an order pursuant to the same statutory provisions for the period up to the 31 December, 1984, fixing a charge "payable either in full or in equal instalments, the first payable not later than the 1 August and the second not later than the 1 October." That order also had been made on the submission and recommendation of the Finance Officer and recited that:— "the estimate of expenses for 1984 adopted by the City Council included provision for £4,000,000 to be raised by way of charges for domestic water supply." Shortly after that order the plaintiff served the defendants with demands for the full amount of the charge for 1984 and for the arrears due for 1983. The defendants failed to pay and were decreed for part of the sum in the District Court. The defendants appealed to the Circuit Court where evidence was given on behalf of the plaintiff that the order made in October, 1983, was for the period from the date of that order until the 31 December, 1983; and that the order made in May, 1984, was for the whole year 1984. The defendants stated that the demand notes on foot of both orders had conveyed to them the impression that the charges were for a full year. It was argued on behalf of the defendants that each of the orders was in whole or in part retrospective in effect and was therefore invalid. Counsel for the defendants relied on the recitals as indicating that what was fixed in each order was an annual charge and that the amount demanded of each defendant represented his share of the annual cost of supplying water. The learned Circuit Court judge stated a case for the determination of the Supreme Court as to whether the orders were valid and effective so as to impose a charge on the defendants. **Held** by the Supreme Court (Finlay C.J., Walsh, Griffin, Hederman and McCarthy JJ.), in answering the case stated in the negative, 1, that there was no evidence before the court to suggest either that the amounts adopted by the City Council in respect of charges was equal to the cost of supplying water for the year, or that the total amount raised by the charges would equal the cost of supplying water. 2. That the order of the 25 October, 1983, made by the City Manager on the submission and recommendation of the Finance Officer, must be interpreted as being entirely prospective. 3. That there was nothing in the Act of 1878 which made it mandatory for charges to be prospective or which prohibited them from being retrospective in relation to a period during which the Act was in force. Accordingly, that the order of 25 May, 1984, was not invalid by reason of its being partly retrospective. 4. That the power created by s. 65A of the Act of 1878 was a power to fix a charge payable by instalments and did not enable the plaintiff authority to fix a charge payable in a single amount. 5. Accordingly, that the order of 25 October, 1983, which purported to create a charge payable on demand was *ultra vires* the plaintiff and void. 6. That while the Finance Officer and Treasurer had recommended a charge for 1984 payable either in full or in two equal instalments, the City Manager and Town Clerk, in making the order of 25 May, 1984, had not clearly identified which of the two alternatives he was accepting. The order of 25 May, 1984, was bad either on the basis that it was an order for the payment of a single amount or because it was uncertain and ambiguous and failed to comply clearly with the limits of the plaintiff's statutory powers. *Semble.* That an order made under s. 65A of the Act of 1878 creating a charge payable in arrears would not be defective by reason only of the charge not being 'payable in advance.' *Per curiam.* Whereas in the case of an appeal the Supreme Court would not ordinarily hear argument on a point which had not been argued and decided in the court below, the purpose of a consultative case stated from the Circuit Court was to allow the Circuit Court judge to obtain the advice and opinion of the Supreme Court to assist him in reaching a correct legal decision. Accordingly it would be inappropriate for the Supreme Court, for any reason of procedure, to abstain from expressing a view on an issue of law which might determine the result of the case before the Circuit Court. *Dublin Corporation* v. *Ashley; Dublin Corporation* v. *Lowe*

(S.C.) [1986] I.R.781

LOCAL GOVERNMENT—*continued.*

3. —— **Declaration** — *Exclusion of councillors — Council resolved that members be required to make declaration — Applicants refused — Excluded from meeting — Whether statutory power to require declaration — Whether protective and self-defensive powers of council include power to exclude members — Whether limited to control of meeting — Whether* ultra vires — *Local Government Act (Northern Ireland),* 1972 (*c.* 9), *s.* 7(1) — *Northern Ireland Constitution Act,* 1973 (*c.* 36), *s.* 21(1).] Craigavon Borough Council resolved, by a majority, that members should not be permitted to attend or participate in meetings until they signed a declaration that they would not use their position as councillors for the purpose of advancing the aims and objects of any organisation which engaged in violence or acts of terrorism or whose aim was the subversion of the state. It was also resolved that any councillor failing to sign the declaration should be excluded from meetings and other council business. The applicants and two other councillors refused to sign the declaration and were subsequently removed from the council chamber. The applicants sought a declaration that the resolutions were invalid arguing that, by virtue of section 21(1) of the Northern Ireland Constitution Act, 1973, it was unlawful for the council to require members to make such declaration, that the council had no statutory or common law power to require such declaration or exclude members for refusing to make it, and that if the council had the power to exclude members on grounds of security it had been used for an ulterior purpose. The respondent contended that section 21(1) of the 1973 Act should be construed with the assistance of the heading to Part III of the Act and thus limited to declarations offensive to religious or political beliefs. **Held,** granting the declarations sought, that, 1, in construing section 21(1) of the 1973 Act the court could have regard to the headings forming the title of parts of the Act. While the context of section 21(1) was such that the legislature had in mind that the provisions of the subsection would be primarily aimed at declarations offensive to a person's religious or political beliefs, it did not necessarily follow that the legislature intended that only declarations specifically partaking of such characteristics should be struck down. The word "declaration" in section 21(1) bore its ordinary and natural meaning and as the declaration in this case was within that meaning it was in contravention of the section and unlawful. 2. The existence of a statutory declaration under section 7(1) of the Local Government Act (Northern Ireland), 1972, that a councillor would fulfil his duties to the best of his abilities negatived any implication of a statutory power to require other declarations. 3. The true or dominant purpose of the council was not the improvement of security, but the legally inadmissible purpose of excluding certain councillors and therefore the council's actions could not be sustained in law. *Quaere* whether the protective and self-defensive powers of a council do not go outside the sphere of control of its proceedings, and accordingly that it does not have a common law power either to expel or exclude councillors or to require a declaration on security grounds, *In re Curran and McCann's Application* [1985] N.I. 261 considered. *In re French*

(Q.B.D.) [1985] N.I.310

4. —— **Delegation of functions** — *Council delegated functions to special committee — Whether delegation for better regulation and management of council's functions — Whether a protective and self-defensive power to exclude — Whether judicial notice of party policy — Whether powers exercised reasonably — Local Government Act (Northern Ireland),* 1972 (*c.* 9), *s.* 18(1) — *European Convention for the Protection of Human Rights and Fundamental Freedoms, art.* 17.] The applicants were members of the Sinn Fein party who were elected as councillors of Craigavon Borough Council. After the applicants refused to comply with a resolution of the council that they sit at a special table apart from the main table in the council chamber, the council resolved, by a majority, to appoint a special committee of the council consisting of all members of the council except the applicants and delegated to the special committee all the functions of the council except those expressly reserved by section 18(1) of the Local Government Act (Northern Ireland), 1972, to the council. The applicants sought an order quashing the resolutions. **Held,** that the resolutions were *ultra vires* and void, 1, the power in section 18(1) of the 1972 Act to delegate to a committee was a power to appoint a committee for the better management and regulation of the council's business. It was not the intendment of the section that it be used to exclude a councillor from the work and activities of the council for protective and self-defensive purposes and a power given for one purpose cannot be exercised for another purpose. 2. The protective and self-defensive powers of a council to regulate its own proceedings implied by common law did not include a power to exclude members of a party proclaiming a particular policy. While it could be argued that a council could not properly exercise its functions if members of a particular party harnessed together its activities within the council chamber with its support outside that chamber for terrorist murder and violence, the decision whether members of the party should be prevented from sitting as councillors gave rise to an

LOCAL GOVERNMENT—*continued.*

issue of great general importance and was a decision to be made by Government and Parliament and not by individual councils. *Barton* v. *Taylor* (1886) 11 App. Cas. 197 applied. *Semble* If the protective and self-defensive power did include a power to exclude the applicants, the council would not have acted unreasonably in so exercising the power. Such exclusion would be in conformity with the intent of article 17 of the European Convention of Human Rights as Sinn Fein, by reason of its policy of supporting terrorist violence, was engaged in activities aimed at the destruction of many of the rights and freedoms set out in the Convention and, by taking part in the council, Sinn Fein councillors were seeking to advance that policy. 3. The court could take judicial notice of the policy and aims of Sinn Fein and the nature of terrorist violence in Northern Ireland. *Australian Communist Party* v. *The Commonwealth* (1951) 83 C.L.R. 1 and *Attorney General for Northern Ireland's Reference* [1976] N.I. 169 followed. *In re Curran and McCann*

(Q.B.D.) [1985] N.I.261

5. —— **Estimates meeting** — *Whether resolution adopting estimates null and void — Whether each estimate must be considered separately — Whether composite adoption sufficient — Whether motion adopting estimates and striking rate to be separate — Whether meeting conducted in accordance with natural justice — Whether councillor having legitimate expectation that meeting would consider each estimate separately — Whether councillor having* locus standi *to seek judicial review of meeting — Judicial review — Form of relief — Remittal to local authority — Rules of the Superior Courts,* 1986 (*S.I. No.* 15), *O.*84, *r.* 26(4) — *City and County Management (Amendment) Act,* 1955 (*No.* 10), *ss.* 10(1), 10(4).] The applicant was a member of the Kerry County Council. At the meeting of the Council to consider the estimates for the year 1987, held pursuant to s. 10 of the City and County Management (Amendment) Act, 1955, it was decided that one particular group of the estimates for the year should be discussed first. Many of the councillors spoke on this group, and were asked by the chairman not to speak on other aspects of the estimates as these would be dealt with later. At the end of discussing this group, however, a motion was put forward that the rate proposed by the county manager, the second respondent, should be adopted, and this motion was approved by the meeting. The applicant sought judicial review of the decision to adopt the estimates on the grounds that the meeting had not complied with the requirements of s. 10 of the 1955 Act, that the meeting had been conducted in breach of the rules of natural/constitutional justice and that the appli-

cant had a legitimate expectation that he would be afforded an opportunity to discuss, and to attempt to vary, the estimates furnished by the county manager. **Held** by Blayney J., in granting the application, 1, the appellant had the *locus standi* to bring the application because as a member of the County Council he had a special interest in ensuring that its work and resolutions were lawful and were carried out in accordance with the particular statutory requirements. *In re application of Cook and Ors* [1986] 1 N.I.J.B. 43 applied. 2. In view of the requirements of s. 10(1) of the 1955 Act that '[a]n estimate of expenses shall be considered by the local authority at . . . an estimates meeting', it could not be said that the Council had complied with this provision where only one group of expenses was considered at the estimates meeting; and it was not sufficient that each councillor had been supplied in advance of the meeting with a copy of the book of estimates as there was a great difference between a councillor considering the estimates on his own and considering them at a meeting as s. 10(1) required; nor was it relevant to the objective question of compliance with s. 10(1) that the majority at the estimates meeting had approved the estimate. *Per* Blayney J.: while every single page of the estimate need not be considered, it would seem to be at least necessary that each programme group of estimates should come up for consideration even if there might be very little discussion on some. 3. The effect of failure to comply with the requirements of s. 10(1) was to render invalid the resolution approving the estimates; and this was clear from the provisions of s. 10(4) empowering a local authority to amend or vary the estimates as proposed and also to determine the rate in the pound to be levied, since it was impossible to conceive that a local authority could do so without considering the estimate. *Per* Blayney J.: since the adoption of the estimate and the determination of the rate in the pound are dealt with in separate paragraphs in s. 10(4) of the 1955 Act, it would appear to be more correct that there should be separate resolutions for each matter. 4. Since the applicant had attended the estimates meeting it would be very difficult to say that the meeting had been conducted in breach of constitutional/natural justice. 5. While it might be that the applicant also had a legitimate expectation that he would be afforded an opportunity to discuss the estimates, this was no more than a reliance on the statutory requirements of the 1955 Act. 6. The appropriate order was to grant certiorari and, rather than grant an order of mandamus, to remit the matter to the Kerry County Council in accordance with the terms of O.84, r. 26(4) of the Rules of the Superior Courts, 1986. *Ahern* v. *Kerry County Council*

(H.C.) [1988] ILRM 392

LOCAL GOVERNMENT—*continued.*

6. —— **Member** — *Suspension* — *Standing order providing for suspension until apology — Whether power to suspend indefinitely reasonably necessary — Whether decision to suspend unreasonable.*] Standing Order 31 of the Belfast City Council provided: "In the event of any member at a meeting of the Council . . . being guilty of . . . offensive conduct, the Council may, by resolution, suspend such member for the remainder of the sitting or portion thereof and may, in addition, order the suspension to continue until submission of apology by the offending member." At a meeting of the Council on 6 December, 1984, following dissension after certain remarks by the applicant, it was resolved, "That unless Councillor McAnulty withdraws his statement referring to the Union Jack as a 'butcher's apron' he be suspended from the Council and remain suspended until he withdraws such statement." The applicant attended two subsequent meetings of the Council, but on both occasions after declining to withdraw the statement or apologise for it he was excluded from the meeting. On an application for a declaration that the resolution was null and void, **Held,** that that part of Standing Order 31 which authorised the resolution suspending the applicant indefinitely was *ultra vires* the Council. The governing principle is that the only powers relating to suspension given by the common law to an Assembly or to a Council are such powers as are necessary to the existence of such a body and the proper exercise of the functions which it is intended to execute and these powers are protective and self-defensive powers only and not punitive. *Barton* v. *Taylor* (1886) 11 App. Cas. 197 applied. The power given by Standing Order 31 to suspend a member indefinitely until he apologises was not reasonably necessary for the protection and self defence of the Council, because (i) the period between the end of the sitting and the commencement of the next sitting would give time for tempers to cool, (ii) the power seriously interfered with the rights of the local government electors who elected the member concerned and appeared to be punitive rather than defensive and, (iii) not being a graduated code, was too great and too wide and would be liable to excess or abuse. *Semble* Where a member had persistently and wilfully obstructed business, it might be necessary to require an apology from him before he was permitted to return. *Per curiam* Assuming that Standing Order 31 was *intra vires* the Council, the applicant had not shown that the decision to suspend him was so unreasonable a decision that no reasonable council could have come to it. *In re McAnulty*

(Q.B.D.) [1985] N.I.37

7. —— **Member** — *Vacancy* — *County council — Vacancy arising on death of member — Standing orders providing that such vacancies be filled by co-option — Standing orders further providing that co-option be of a person from the same electoral area — Council meetings — Whether vacancy remained unfilled — Whether standing order* ultra vires — *Electoral Act,* 1863 (*c.* 29), *s.* 82 — *Local Government Act,* 1955 (*No.* 9), *s.* 62 — *Local Government (Application of Enactments) Order,* 1898, *art.* 14 — *Local Elections Regulations,* 1965 (*S.I. No.* 128), *reg.* 87.] The Local Election Regulations, 1965, provide, at Regulation 87, that a casual vacancy arising in a local authority shall be filled by choice of the said authority, a suitable person having been proposed at a meeting of the said authority. The prior consent of such person must first be obtained in writing. A vacancy arose in the defendant County Council in November, 1977, due to the death of a member from the Glenties Electoral Area. On his death, there survived four members of the council from the same area. Standing orders adopted by the defendant council in 1976 included standing order 133, which provided that 'a vacancy on the council for an Electoral Area shall be filled by the co-option of a qualified person from that area, who shall be proposed and seconded by two of the remaining representatives of the same area.' Pursuant to the said order, the second-named defendant was proposed and seconded at a meeting held on 23 January 1978. The plaintiff, who was not from the Glenties Electoral Area, was proposed but not seconded. A vote was held on the proposal of the defendant, but it was defeated. However, the defendant subsequently claimed to have been elected, as the only properly nominated candidate at the meeting. At a meeting held on 30 January, the validity of standing order 133 was questioned. At the same meeting, the second-named defendant withdrew his consent to be nominated for the vacancy. He subsequently withdrew his withdrawal. The opinion of senior counsel to the effect that standing order 133 was *ultra vires* and void was later obtained and circularised to all council members. At a third meeting on 21 March, the plaintiff was proposed and seconded, but when a vote was taken, the proposal was defeated. To resolve the impasse thus created, the chairman of the council called a fourth meeting on 10 April. Evidence as to what occurred at this meeting was conflicting. The minute stated that the chairman requested the council to choose between the plaintiff and the defendant, and this was corroborated by the evidence of some members who had been present at the meeting. Other members alleged that the minute was incomplete, and that the chairman had canvassed for other nominations. A vote was taken, and the plaintiff was elected. He assumed office forthwith, and continued to hold office

LOCAL GOVERNMENT—*continued.*

until, on 23 June, the council passed a resolution declaring that the method of filling the vacancy had been illegal. The matter appeared anew on the agenda for a meeting on 31 July, and the plaintiff issued the instant proceedings seeking an order restraining the first-named defendant from proceeding with a proposal to fill the vacancy on the council, alleging that he had been lawfully co-opted on 10 April. **Held** by D'Arcy J., in refusing the relief sought, in ordering the council to proceed to fill its vacancy in accordance with law, and in declaring standing order 133 to be *ultra vires* and void for the purposes of the present case and as between the parties to it, 1, at the meeting of 10 April, 1978, a choice was given to the council which wrongly confined the election to two persons. Neither the plaintiff nor the second-named defendant had been co-opted to the council. 2. Standing order 133 was restrictive, in that it conferred a preferential franchise on the electors of the Glenties area. However, to declare it *ultra vires* in its entirety would deprive them of this, and it would be unconstitutional to do so without having heard what they might wish to urge. *McNelis* v. *Donegal County Council*

(H.C.) [1978] ILRM 230

8. —— **Regulations** — *County Council — County manager — "Bye-law" — Criteria — Regulations made by council resolution — Whether bye-law — Whether properly executive function exercisable by county manager or "power, function or duty" reserved to county council — County Management Act,* 1940 (*No.* 12), *ss.* 17, 19 *and 2nd Sched.*] By s. 17 of the County Management Act, 1940, every "power, function or duty" of a county council or elective body not a "reserved function" of the county council or elective body "shall . . . be an executive function" exercisable by the county manager. Paragraph 4 of the Second Schedule to the Act provided that "making, amending or revoking a bye law" was a reserved function for a county council or elective body. The prosecutor was convicted and fined by the respondent at Bantry District Court of offences under regulations adopted by resolution of Cork County Council under divers sheep dipping regulations made pursuant to the Diseases of Animals Acts, 1894-1966. He contended in the High Court that the regulations made by the county council were an executive function exercisable by the county manager only and were therefore invalid and obtained a conditional order of certiorari to quash the order of the respondent. D'Arcy J. refused the prosecutor's motion to make absolute the conditional order notwithstanding cause shown by the county council, notice party, and on the prosecutor's appeal it was **Held** by the Supreme Court (Walsh, Griffin and Hederman JJ.) in dismissing the appeal,

LOCAL GOVERNMENT—*continued.*

that upon proper construction the regulations constituted bye-laws and were therefore validly made within the "powers, functions or duties" reserved to the county council by the County Management Act, 1940. *Per curiam:* Every regulation is not a bye-law: in general a bye-law within its own sphere is something which carries an authority akin to that of a statute whereas the sanction for breach of a regulation is frequently not to be found in the regulation itself. Definition of "bye-law" of Lord Russell of Killowen C.J. in *Kruse* v. *Johnson* [1898] 2 Q.B. 91 approved. *The State (Harrington)* v. *Wallace*

(S.C.) [1988] I.R.290

PUBLIC HEALTH

9. —— **Burial ground** — *Land acquired by trustees of Church of Ireland church for use as burial ground — Land situate within 100 yards of plaintiff's premises — Whether consent in writing of plaintiff required for use of land as burial ground — Public Health (Ireland) Act,* 1878 (*c.* 52), *s.* 174 — *Local Government (Sanitary Services) Act,* 1948 (*No.* 3), *s.* 44.] Section 174 of the Public Health (Ireland) Act, 1878, provides *inter alia* that:— ". . . no ground not already used as or appropriated for a cemetery shall be appropriated as a burial ground, or as an addition to a burial ground, under this Act, nearer than one hundred yards to a dwelling-house, without the consent in writing of the owner, lessee, and occupier of such dwelling-house." The defendant was the trustee of a Church of Ireland church and lands. The defendant proposed to use part of the lands, situate within 100 yards of the plaintiff's house, as a cemetery. Pursuant to s. 44, sub-s. 2 of the Local Government (Sanitary Services) Act, 1948, the defendant obtained the approval of the Minister for the Environment to the use of the lands as a burial ground, but he did not obtain the consent of the plaintiff. The plaintiff commenced proceedings for a declaration that the defendant, by virtue of s. 174 of the Act of 1878, was not entitled to use the lands as a burial ground without his prior consent in writing. The defendant pleaded that, as the churchyard was a private cemetery, the Act of 1878 did not apply to it; and furthermore that the plaintiff had no *locus standi* to maintain the proceedings. **Held** by Hamilton P., in dismissing the plaintiff's claim, 1, that the plaintiff had sufficient *locus standi* to maintain the proceedings. *Cahill* v. *Sutton* [1980] I.R. 269 and *The State (Lynch)* v. *Cooney* [1982] I.R. 337 considered. 2. That the restriction on the appropriation or use of land as a burial ground contained in s. 174 of the Act of 1878 applied only to land appropriated or used as a burial ground by local authorities under the Act itself and did

LOCAL GOVERNMENT—*continued.*
not apply to churchyards attached to the church of a religious denomination. *Representative Church Body* v. *Crawford* 74 I.L.T.R. 49 and *Clegg* v. *Metcalfe* [1914] 1 Ch. 808 considered. *McCarthy* v. *Johnson*
(H.C.) [1988] I.R.23

—— Amusement halls — Licensing — Gaming machines.
see **Gaming and Lotteries,** 3-6

—— Authority — Breach of statutory duty — Housing authority — Loan to purchaser — Defective premises — Whether duty of care owed to purchaser.
see **Negligence,** 2, 30

—— Authority — Breach of statutory duty — Burial grounds — Duty to repair wall.
see **Negligence,** 28

—— Authority — Development — Proposed location of halting site within area of high amenity — Whether development *ultra vires* powers of Council.
see **Planning,** 18

—— Authority — Duty of care — Planning authority — Defective premises.
see **Negligence,** 3

—— Authority — Liability for contractor's negligence in carrying out work on highway authorised by local authority.
see **Negligence,** 11

—— Authority — Negligence — Duty of care — Railway bridge — Minimum clearance required by statute of railway company — Whether local authority's roadworks in reducing clearance below statutory minimum wanting in due care — Whether advance warning system agreed between railway company and local authority.
see **Negligence,** 31

—— Authority — Non-feasance — Liability — Road authority — Statutory provision effecting change in liability — Governmental order required to bring it into force — Whether mandamus lies against the Government.
see **Judicial Review,** 14

—— Burial grounds — Authority — Statutory duty — Duty to repair wall — Cattle trespassing — Cattle poisoned by eating yew leaves — Standard of care owed.
see **Negligence,** 28

LOCAL GOVERNMENT—*continued.*
—— Compulsory acquisition — Assessment of compensation.
see **Compulsory Acquisition,** 2, 3

—— Compulsory acquisition — Dispute as to value — Valuation going to arbitration — Factors to be taken into account — Sewerage facilities.
see **Arbitration,** 6

—— Compulsory acquisition — Planning application refused in view of compulsory acquisition — Whether order made in compliance with housing legislation — Effect of order.
see **Compulsory Acquisition,** 5

—— Compulsory acquisition — Residential and recreational development — County council also planning authority — Whether Council can only acquire lands for recreational purposes in its capacity as planning authority.
see **Compulsory Acquisition,** 6

—— Finance — Rating.
see **Rating and Valuation**

—— Finance — Service charges — Domestic dwelling.
see **Local Government,** 1, 2

—— Fire prevention — Fire safety notices — Terms — Description of precautions to be adopted by occupier — Occupier appealing to District Court — Subsequent compliance with requirements stated in notice — Nature of court's order — Confirmation of safety notices.
see **Fire Services**

—— Housing authority — Allocation of houses to person residing outside housing authority's functional area — Whether authority acting *ultra vires.*
see **Housing,** 2

—— Housing authority — Application for change of user — Permission refused — Applicant aggrieved — Applicant seeking declaration that refusal of housing authority void — Alternative appellate procedure available to applicant — Declaration refused.
see **Housing,** 1

—— Housing authority — Duty of care — Loan to purchaser — Defective premises.
see **Negligence,** 2, 30

—— Markets and fairs.
see **Casual Trading**

M

MEDICAL COUNCIL — Disciplinary code — Natural justice — Fair procedure.
see **Natural and Constitutional Justice,** 4

MEDICAL NEGLIGENCE
—— Accrual of cause of action — Surgery performed on the plaintiff by each of the defendants — Action instituted after expiry of three years from dates of surgery — Whether action statute barred — Date on which cause of action accrued.
see **Limitation of Actions,** 4

—— Doctor — Duty of care to patient — Test applicable — Patient having predisposition to suffer from low blood pressure — Extended period of low blood pressure — Brain damage.
see **Negligence,** 13

—— Hospital — Duty of care — Injury to patient.
see **Negligence,** 14

—— Surgeon — Emergency operation on admission to hospital — Plaintiff showing signs of improvement — New emergency — Second emergency operation — Plaintiff's injury aggravated — Whether neuro-surgical centre should have been consulted after first and/or second operation — Whether treatment in second operation was negligent
see **Negligence,** 15

MEDICAL PRACTITIONER
—— Disciplinary code — Tribunal — Fair procedures — Removal of doctor's name from register — Enquiry by inferior tribunal — Recommendation to superior tribunal — Decision of superior tribunal — Doctor entitled to appear before inferior tribunal only.
see **Natural and Constitutional Justice,** 4

—— Discipline — Tribunal — Natural justice — Fair procedures — Removal of doctor's name from register — Validity of enactment under Constitution.
see **Constitution,** 28

—— Negligence.
see under **Medical Negligence**

MEDICAL SERVICE
see **Health Services**

MENS REA — Shooting with intent to commit murder — Whether necessary to establish intention to commit murder.
see **Criminal Law,** 32

MENTAL ILLNESS
—— Defence — Murder — Insanity — Defence of diminished responsibility.
see **Criminal Law,** 30

—— Marriage — Capacity — Inability to form and sustain normal marriage relationship — Nullity petitions.
see **Family Law,** 11-13

MENTAL TREATMENT
—— **Ward of court** — *Lunacy — Petition — Inquiry as to soundness of mind — Respondent possessing no property requiring protection and management by High Court — Whether possession of property a condition precedent to exercise of wardship jurisdiction — Lunacy Regulation (Ireland) Act,* 1871 (*c.* 22) — *Courts (Supplemental Provisions) Act,* 1961 (*No.* 39), *s.* 9.] The respondent was a 20 year old woman who had been mentally retarded since birth. Until the age of eighteen, she had attended as a day pupil a special school maintained by the petitioner Health Board; thereafter, while still residing at home, she attended the petitioner's adult training centre. When officers of the Board decided that there was serious risk to the respondent's welfare in her continuing to reside at home, she was admitted to a residential institution. She possessed no property and had no independent means. Several months later the respondent's parents applied to the High Court and were granted an order under Article 40, s. 4, sub-s. 2 of the Constitution, directing the petitioner to produce the respondent before the court and to certify in writing the grounds of her detention. Upon the hearing of that return, the petitioner applied to file a petition praying that an inquiry be had as to the soundness of mind of the respondent, in order that she could be made a ward of court. The application was heard by the President of the High Court, who held that it was a condition precedent to the exercise by him of his jurisdiction to bring a person of unsound mind into wardship, that such person be entitled to property which required protection and management. On the petitioner's appeal from the President's refusal to entertain the petition it was **Held** by the Supreme Court (Finlay C.J.; Walsh, Henchy, Hederman and McCarthy JJ. concurring), that there is vested in the High Court a jurisdiction to take into wardship a person of unsound mind whose person requires protection and management but who is not entitled to any

MENTAL TREATMENT—*continued.*

property requiring such protection and management. 2. That this jurisdiction is not a jurisdiction conferred or delimited by the Lunacy Regulation (Ireland) Act, 1871, but is part of a general protective jurisdiction over persons of unsound mind which is vested in the High Court by s. 9 of the Courts (Supplemental Provisions) Act, 1961. *Per curiam* That the provisions of the Lunacy Regulation (Ireland) Act, 1871, and of the Rules of the Superior Courts relating thereto, are not practicably applicable to the exercise of wardship jurisdiction in respect of persons with no property requiring protection and management, and need not be complied with in a case such as this. *In re D. (Application of Midland Health Board)*
(S.C.) [1987] I.R.449; [1988] ILRM 251

—— Senile patient — Transfer to nursing home — Chargeability of services involved — Whether receiving more than shelter and maintenance.
see **Health Services,** 1

MINES AND MINERAL EXPLORATION

—— Nuisance — Noise and vibrations — Rural locality — Physical damage — Whether caused by defendant's activities — Whether appropriate to grant an injunction.
see **Nuisance,** 4

—— Mining profits — Corporation tax — Relief.
see **Revenue,** 16

MINIMUM NOTICE CLAIMS
see **Employer and Employee,** 19-22

MINISTER OF THE GOVERNMENT

—— Decision — Nature — Whether administrative or judicial — Staff association seeking recognition from Minister of Public Service — Refusal.
see **Civil Service,** 2

—— Duties — Enquiry — Failure — Mandamus — *Locus standi* of applicant — Teacher's employment suspended by vocational education committee — Committee reporting and giving reasons to Minister — No enquiry held promptly.
see **Education,** 2

—— Duty of care — Depositor lodging money with industrial and provident society — Society subsequently going into liquidation — Depositor receiving a dividend of only part of sum lodged — Whether Minister owed duty of care

MINISTER OF THE GOVERNMENT—*continued.*

— Whether sufficient relationship of proximity between Registrar of Friendly Societies and plaintiff.
see **Negligence,** 33

—— Function — Discharge — Review — Person aggrieved — Statutory right of appeal against ministerial order — Power of Minister to make an order for the protection and improvement of the fisheries of the State — Ministerial order revoking prohibition against taking salmon with drift net — Order annulled.
see **High Court**

—— Ministerial order — Statute — Whether in conflict — Statute incorporating Governors of Hospital — No obligation to fund imposed on Minister — Ministerial order withdrawing funds — Whether valid having regard to statute — Barrington's Hospital Act, 1830, s. 1.
see **Statute,** 2

—— Officers — Appointment — Evidence — Authorised officers of Minister for Agriculture — Whether certificate that officer had been appointed sufficient evidence of the fact of appointment.
see **Criminal Law,** 24

—— Planning permission — Exercise of statutory discretion — Plaintiff purchasing land with benefit of planning permission — Such permission granted by Minister — Supreme Court subsequently ruling such permission *ultra vires* — Whether an action in damages for breach of statutory duty or negligence lay against the Minister.
see **Planning,** 13

—— Powers — Exercise — Constitutional limitations — Dismissal — Office-holder — Probationer — Reasons for dismissal not disclosed — Whether Minister's decision reviewable.
see **Civil Service,** 1

—— Powers — Exercise — Mandamus — Enforcement of duty to repair courthouse — Minister directed to exercise his powers.
see **Courthouses**

—— Powers — Exercise — Injunction — Validity of power disputed — Interlocutory injunction granted to citizen affected.

N

NATIONAL MONUMENT

—— Application for planning permission — National monument on lands — Whether planning authority had power to grant permission by default.
see **Planning,** 17

—— Preservation order — Validity — Whether order *ultra vires* — Whether order made in accordance with principles of natural justice.
see **Constitution,** 44

—— Treasure trove — Discovery of hoard at national monument — Delivery of property to the State — Plaintiffs demanding return — State seeking to assert its own subsequently acquired title — Sovereignty — Incidents of sovereignty — Antiquities of national importance — Lost or mislaid chattels — Whether the State entitled to former royal prerogative of treasure trove.
see **Bailment**

NATIONAL PARLIAMENT

see **Dáil Éireann; Oireachtas**

NATIONALITY AND IMMIGRATION

see **Aliens**

NATURAL AND CONSTITUTIONAL JUSTICE

1. —— **Employment** — *Dismissal — Garda — Probationer — Dismissal for not being likely to become efficient and well-conducted guard — Previous breaches of discipline as basis for dismissal — Pending enquiry into breach of discipline discontinued — Whether dismissal* ultra vires — *Garda Síochána (Appointment) Regulations,* 1945 (*S.I. No.* 173), *arts.* 8, 9.] The prosecutor was a recruit member of the Garda Síochána. A recruit-guard is appointed for a probationary period of two years, pursuant to Article 8 of the Garda Síochána (Appointment) Regulations, 1945. By virtue of the provisions of Article 9 of the regulations, a Garda Commissioner may at any time dispense with the services of a member of the force who is on probation, if the Commissioner considers that such member is not likely to become 'an efficient and well-conducted guard.' The prosecutor had been found guilty and duly disciplined in respect of a breach of discipline. Disciplinary proceedings, pursuant to the Garda Síochána (Disciplinary) Regulations, 1971, were commenced against the prosecutor in respect of another alleged breach of discipline on 22 February, 1976. These proceedings were

NATURAL AND CONSTITUTIONAL JUSTICE *—continued.*

never completed. Before the expiration of the prosecutor's period of probation, the respondent, upon consideration of a report submitted by the Chief Superintendent of the prosecutor, certified that the prosecutor was not likely to become an efficient and well-conducted guard, and he dispensed with the services of the prosecutor. The prosecutor obtained from the High Court an absolute order of certiorari quashing the order of the respondent, on the grounds that the provisions of the 1971 Disciplinary Regulations had not been complied with, and that the decision had been made in breach of the rules of natural justice. The respondent appealed to the Supreme Court. **Held** by the Supreme Court (O'Higgins C.J., Griffin and Parke JJ.) in allowing the appeal, 1, the respondent, by virtue of the discretion granted to him by Article 9 of the Garda Síochána (Appointment) Regulations, 1945, was entitled to dispense with the services of the prosecutor, notwithstanding the non-completion of disciplinary proceedings under the Garda Síochána (Disciplinary) Regulations, 1971. 2. The superior officers of the prosecutor were entitled to discontinue the disciplinary proceedings, since their continuance would have extended beyond the probationary period of the prosecutor, thus effectively preventing the respondent from dispensing with the services of the prosecutor in the manner provided for by Article 9 of the 1945 Regulations. 3. There was before the respondent at the time he invoked Article 9 of the 1945 Regulations sufficient evidence to enable him to form the opinion that the prosecutor was not likely to become an efficient and well-conducted guard. *The State (Burke)* v. *Garvey* **(S.C.) [1979] ILRM 232**

2. —— **Fair procedures** — *National and international athletic bodies — Drug testing procedure — Failure of athlete to undergo test — Suspension of athlete — Judicial review* — Certiorari — *Right of athlete to be called on to make his defence before penalty imposed.*] The respondent ("B.L.E."), is a national body responsible for the development, promotion, control and management of amateur athletics in the State. It is affiliated to the International Amateur Athletics Federation ("I.A.A.F."), which controls amateur athletics at international level, and it is bound by the laws, rules and regulations of that body. A national championship meeting was held on the 25 and 26 July, 1987, at which B.L.E. introduced a drug testing procedure, in accordance with the rules of the I.A.A.F., for certain selected athletes at that meeting. The applicant

NATURAL AND CONSTITUTIONAL JUSTICE—*continued.*

was an international athlete who was a competitor at that meeting. He was asked to undergo a drug test which he agreed to do. However, prior to giving a drug control urine sample, the applicant was given permission to leave the drug control room for the purpose of collecting his clothing and valuables. The applicant failed to return to the drug control room and never gave a urine sample. A few days later the applicant telephoned a B.L.E. official to explain his failure to return and to give the required sample. The latter suggested that the applicant should write to him, setting out his explanation, which the applicant did. Some weeks later, the applicant received a letter from B.L.E. informing him that, having failed to deliver a sample for drug testing when requested to do so, he was suspended from all B.L.E. competition for an 18 month period. He was also advised that in accordance with the rules of I.A.A.F. the suspension was being notified to that body. On the applicant's motion for an order of certiorari by way of judicial review of the decision of B.L.E. it was **Held** by Barr J., in granting the relief sought, 1, that where a suspension was imposed by way of punishment, as here, it followed that the body in question had found its member guilty of significant misconduct or breach of rules. Suspending an international athlete by way of punishment from all major competition for 18 months was a substantial penalty and had moral implications even after the period of suspension had expired. 2. That it was fundamental to the concept of natural justice that no man should be condemned unheard. That principle had to be observed by all persons and bodies having the duty to act judicially. That duty rested upon, *inter alia,* committees of clubs and other voluntary organizations exercising functions of a disciplinary nature involving the imposition of substantial sanctions. 3. That as the suspension imposed by B.L.E. on the applicant amounted to a substantial penalty, he ought to have been heard in his own defence before being condemned and punished. In the circumstances, the applicant was wrongly suspended from competition at events organized by B.L.E. and I.A.A.F. 4. That this finding did not preclude the respondent from re-opening the matter and adjudicating on the complaint, provided that the applicant was given a reasonable opportunity to make his defence thereto. *Quirke* v. *Bord Lúthchleas na hÉireann*

(H.C.) [1988] I.R. 83

3. —— **Fair procedures** — *Tribunal — Evidence — Determination of remedy by tribunal not argued by parties to hearing — Whether in breach of natural justice — Whether in breach of fair procedures.*] Following an unfair dismissal hearing, the respondent Tribunal found that the employee had been unfairly dismissed and that the most appropriate remedy, having regard to all the circumstances of the case, was that the employee be re-engaged. The entire of the hearings had been confined to the circumstances of the dismissal and the financial loss arising therefrom. Neither employee nor employer, both of whom had been represented throughout the hearings by solicitor and counsel, had raised any issue as to a claim for re-instatement or re-engagement. The employer applied for and obtained a conditional order of certiorari to quash the order of the Tribunal on the grounds that, in determining that the employee should be re-engaged, the Tribunal had acted contrary to the principles of natural and constitutional justice and contrary to fair procedures, in that it failed to give the employer notice of its intention to consider this remedy and failed to give the employer any opportunity of being heard in relation to the appropriateness or feasibility of such a remedy. The High Court granted an absolute order of certiorari. The respondent appealed. **Held** by the Supreme Court (Finlay C.J., Henchy, Walsh, Hederman and McCarthy JJ.) in varying the order of the High Court, 1, whether it be identified as a principle of natural justice derived from the common law and known as *audi alteram partem* or, preferably, as the right to fair procedures under the Constitution in all judicial or quasi-judicial proceedings, it is a fundamental requirement of justice that person or property should not be at risk without the party charged being given an adequate opportunity of meeting the claim, as identified and pursued. 2. If the proceedings derive from statute, then, in the absence of any set or fixed procedure, the relevant authority must create and carry out the necessary procedures and if the set of fixed procedure is not comprehensive, the authority must supplement it in such a fashion as to ensure compliance with constitutional justice. 3. That part of the determination of the Tribunal, albeit within the terms of s. 7 of the Act of 1977, which prescribed re-engagement as the appropriate redress, was made without affording the employer any real or adequate opportunity of meeting the case and, consequently, it was made in breach of natural and constitutional justice and should be quashed. In the circumstances, the part of the Tribunal's determination which had found that the employee had been unfairly dismissed should remain intact. *The State (Irish Pharmaceutical Union)* v. *Employment Appeals Tribunal*

(S.C.) [1987] ILRM 36

4. —— **Fair procedures** — *Tribunal — Recommendation — Report to superior tribunal —*

NATURAL AND CONSTITUTIONAL JUSTICE—*continued.*

Decision — Application for cancellation — Professional disciplinary code — Doctor — Removal of name from the register — Doctor entitled to appear before inferior tribunal only — Rules of court — Absence — Rules of the Superior Courts, 1962 (*S.I. No.* 72), *O.* 95 — *Medical Practitioners Act,* 1978 (*No.* 4), *ss.* 45-7 — *Constitution of Ireland,* 1937, *Art.* 40.] Upon an allegation of professional misconduct being made against a medical practitioner, it is provided by s. 45 of the Act of 1978 that the Fitness to Practise Committee may enquire into that allegation and report its findings to the Medical Council. Section 46 provides that, having considered that report, the Council may decide, *inter alia,* that the practitioner's name should be erased from the general register of medical practitioners and, in that event, the practitioner may apply to the High Court for an order cancelling the decision of the Council; if no such application is made by the practitioner, the Council may apply to the High Court for an order affirming its decision. The petitioner, a medical practitioner, applied to the High Court pursuant to s. 46 of the Act for an order cancelling a decision of the Council that his name be erased from the register. He complained that the statutory provisions did not provide fair procedures for the determination of the relevant issues since, although he had availed of an opportunity to make submissions to the Committee before it reported to the Council, there was no opportunity for him to make submissions to the Council before it made its decision. The question of the fairness of the procedures under the Act of 1978, being thus raised, was determined by the judge as a preliminary issue. **Held** by Finlay P., in determining the issue, 1, that the hearing by the High Court of an application under s. 46 of the Act of 1978 constitutes an entire trial of the issues involved and is not a mere appeal from the combined decisions of the Committee and the Council. 2. That, at such hearing, the onus is on the Council to establish the alleged misconduct and the aptness of the penalty chosen by the Council. 3. That, in view of the first two findings and the ultimate role of the High Court, the lack of any right of the petitioner to be heard by the Council before it reached its decision on the report of the Committee did not constitute unfair procedure or want of natural justice. 4. That the further steps in the proceedings should be in accordance with the court's directions in that behalf. *In re M.* **(H.C.) [1984] I.R.479**

5. —— **Fair procedures** — *University regulations — Breach of academic discipline — Student accused of plagiarism — Disciplinary procedures — Committee of discipline — Whether committee bound to act judicially — Student's right to be informed of details of charge — Student's right to be heard in own defence — Whether disciplinary regulations adequate to ensure fair hearing.*] The applicant, a post-graduate student at the respondent College, submitted an essay the marks of which were to go towards her examination. Her lecturer considered the essay to have been plagiarised from a tape recording which had been played to the class during the year. The matter was discussed at an examiners' meeting and referred to the College Registrar as a breach of academic regulations. The applicant was summoned to appear before a committee of discipline and was informed that she could be accompanied by either her dean of residence or an official of the students' union, or both, but by no one else. At the meeting of the committee no witnesses were called. The Registrar, acting as prosecutor, read the essay and expressed his opinion that the case was a clear one. After the applicant had addressed the committee and denied any deliberate plagiarism she and her representatives were asked to retire, while the Registrar remained with the committee. The committee decided to refer the matter to an independent expert for assessment, which was agreed to by the applicant. The choice of expert was delegated by the committee to the Registrar, who did not consult the applicant when making his selection. The expert supported the views of the examiners that the essay was plagiarised. His report was sent to the applicant, with the omission of a section where he advised that the matter should have been dealt with within the Department by refusing to allow the applicant to pass her examination and requiring her to prepare and submit another essay in place of the one which was rejected. When the committee reconvened the applicant sought an adjournment, which was refused. The committee acted on the expert's report and recommended that the applicant be sent down from College for a year and be permitted to re-submit her essay towards the following year's examination. The applicant later obtained additional expert evidence on the worth of her essay, with the opinion expressed that the plagiarism was neither flagrant nor deliberate. On the applicant's application by way of judicial review for an order of certiorari quashing the decision of the committee of discipline, it was **Held** by Barron J., in allowing the application, 1, that since plagiarism was a most serious breach of academic discipline and was criminal in nature, the disciplinary procedures adopted in determining the charge should approach those of a court hearing. 2. That the applicant should have received in writing details of the precise charge being made and the basic facts alleged to constitute the offence. 3. That the applicant

NATURAL AND CONSTITUTIONAL JUSTICE—*continued.*

should have been allowed to be represented by someone of her own choice and should have been informed in sufficient time of that right and of any other rights given her by the rules governing the disciplinary procedure. 4. That the applicant should have been allowed to hear evidence of the case against her at the hearing, to challenge that evidence on cross-examination and to present her own evidence. 5. That the Registrar, as prosecutor in the case, ought not to have remained with the committee while it deliberated, made the appointment of the independent expert, or omitted a section of the expert's report from the copy sent to the applicant. 6. That the committee ought not to have delegated its disciplinary function by acting solely on the report of the independent expert.
Flanagan v. *University College Dublin*
(H.C.) [1988] I.R.724

—— Aliens — Deportation order — Constitution — Family — Whether order in conflict with rights of family — Whether order must comply with natural justice.
see **Aliens,** 1

—— *Audi alteram partem* — Corporation flat — Notice to quit — District Court hearing — Tenant not represented — Whether hearing in breach of natural justice.
see **Landlord and Tenant,** 17

—— Criminal trial — Fair procedures — Parties — Representation — Summary trial in District Court — Trial conducted in absence of legal advisers of accused — Conviction quashed on *certiorari.*
see **Criminal Law,** 46

—— Criminal trial — Judge's interventions — Judge interrupting cross-examination and legal argument — Conduct of trial — Right of accused to test prosecution evidence by cross-examination — Right to be heard in argument before judgment given — Whether conduct of trial went to jurisdiction of trial court.
see **Judicial Review,** 8

—— Employment — Disciplinary investigation — Fair procedures — Office holder — Garda Síochána — Whether member entitled to make representations on suspension.
see **Constitution,** 11

—— Employment — Dismissal — Bias — Domestic tribunal — Predisposition of tribunal to dismiss — Whether such affects validity of dismissal — Whether

NATURAL AND CONSTITUTIONAL JUSTICE—*continued.*

tribunal required only to avoid making up mind before hearing which considered dismissal.
see **Constitution,** 21

—— Employment — Dismissal — Garda Síochána — Summary dismissal by Commissioner — Absence of formal inquiry — Limitations of rules of natural justice in context of certain State services — Acquittal of dismissed Garda at trial on charge of assault on suspect — Counsel for dismissed Garda seeking admission that witness at trial committed the assault — Absence of such allegation in statement of dismissed Garda — Dismissal by Commissioner on ground that statement contained falsehood or prevarication.
see **Employer and Employee,** 7

—— Employment — Dismissal — Office-holder — Delegation of power to dismiss — Whether *ultra vires* or whether dismissal in breach of principles of natural justice.
see **Employer and Employee,** 8

—— Employment — Dismissal — Office holder — Probationer — Natural justice — Whether reasons required — Whether reasons be disclosed.
see **Civil Service,** 1

—— Employment — Dismissal — Officer in naval service — Office dependent on obtaining specified qualification — Failure to obtain qualification — Repeated warnings given — Dismissal notified but postponed to allow representations — No representations made — Whether sufficient compliance with *audi alteram partem* rule.
see **Defences Forces,** 1

—— Employment — Suspension — Civil servants — Whether suspension a breach of the constitutional right to earn a livelihood.
see **Civil Service,** 3

—— Employment — Suspension — Fair procedures — Permissible period of suspension — Criminal and civil proceedings arising out of suspension — Full hearing by employer into suspension postponed until proceedings

NATURAL AND CONSTITUTIONAL JUSTICE—*continued.*

determined — Whether such postponement reasonable — Relevant factors.
see **Employer and Employee,** 23

—— Evidence — Nullity — Non-consummation — Trial judge inferring collusion between parties — Whether inference open to judge — Whether rehearing required in view of evidence presented.
see **Family Law,** 14

—— Inquest — Verdict — Suicide — Statutory exclusions of questions of civil or criminal liability — Whether verdict available — Notice of inquest not served on next-of-kin — Whether breach of natural and constitutional justice — Certiorari.
see **Coroner**

—— Landlord and tenant — Corporation flat — Notice to quit and Demand for Possession — District Court hearing — Tenant not represented — Tenant not invited to give evidence — Possession awarded to Corporation — Whether hearing in breach of natural justice.
see **Landlord and Tenant,** 17

—— Local authority — Estimates meeting — Whether meeting conducted in accordance with natural justice — Whether councillor having *locus standi* to seek judicial review of meeting.
see **Local Government,** 5

—— Medical Bureau of Road Safety.
see **Road Traffic Offences,** 9

—— National monument — Preservation order — Validity — Whether order *ultra vires* — Whether order made in accordance with principles of natural justice.
see **Constitution,** 44

—— Planning — Appeal — Fair Procedures — Parties — Objector's rights — Requirements of constitutional justice.
see **Planning,** 1

—— Planning — Decision — Reasonableness — Local public inquiry — Rejection of application recommended — Permission granted —— Whether decision unreasonable — New material arising after inquiry — Whether breach of rules of natural justice.
see **Planning,** 15

—— Prison — Board of visitors — Preliminary hearing — Composition of Board

NATURAL AND CONSTITUTIONAL JUSTICE—*continued.*

different at substantive hearing — Third party and Governor present — Governor intervened to indicate illegality of award — Award varied.
see **Prisons,** 1

—— Prisoner — Temporary release — Expiry — Certiorari — Whether prisoner entitled to be heard on failure to renew temporary release.
see **Judicial Review,** 5

—— Trade union — Meeting — Resolution for the introduction of a compulsory retirement scheme — Plaintiff not present when vote taken — Whether resolution valid.
see **Trade Union,** 2

—— Trade union — Discipline — ICTU.
see **Trade Union,** 1

—— Tribunal — Fair procedures — Detention centre — Youth released on licence — Release conditional on youth keeping the peace — Youth arrested on charge of serious crime — Licence revoked and youth returned to detention — Governor of institution failing to hold enquiry.
see **Prisons,** 3

—— Tribunal — Fair procedures — Exercise of power — Duty to act judicially — Includes duty to furnish reasons for decision.
see **Judicial Review,** 13

—— Tribunal — Fair procedures — Professional discipline — Medical practitioner.
see **Natural and Constitutional Justice,** 4

—— Tribunal — Fair procedures — Professional discipline — Medical practitioner — Removal of doctor's name from register — Validity of enactment under Constitution.
see **Constitution,** 28

—— Tribunal — Legal advice — Labour Court — Challenge to jurisdiction — Labour Court taking legal advice and proceeding with the appeal — Employer not made aware of advice and given no opportunity of commenting on it — Whether breach of natural justice — Whether, if so, employer entitled as of right to have the determination quashed.
see **Judicial Review,** 4

NATURAL AND CONSTITUTIONAL JUSTICE—*continued.*

—— University — Whether oral hearing or legal representation required at hearing by University — Board of Visitors.
see **Education,** 5

NATURALISATION
see **Aliens; Domicile**

NAVAL SERVICE — Officer — Dismissal — Natural justice.
see **Defence Forces,** 1

NEGLIGENCE
see also **Damages**

DEFECTIVE PREMISES

1. —— **Contribution** — *Building work — Engineer's certificate as to structural stability — Architect's certificate based on such certificate — Whether builder or architect negligent — Contribution as between defendants — Damages.*] The plaintiffs had purchased a house from the first-named defendant (the builder), relying upon the builder's warranty as to structural soundness, which was supported by an architect's certificate issued by the second-named defendant, who had been consulted by the builder some time previously to examine certain internal and external defects in the house. On his advice, the third party, a firm of structural engineers, was engaged, and they reported a serious foundation problem in two areas of the house. Following the settlement of an action with the owners of an adjoining house, a condition of which was that the builder should repair certain faults in the plaintiff's premises, the third party was again retained to carry out the necessary works, including all necessary works for the general stability of the premises. Upon completion, the third party issued a certificate stating that they were now satisfied as to the structural stability of the house. Some months later, the builder requested the architect to issue a general certificate as to the stability of the house for the purpose of effecting its sale to the plaintiffs. This certificate the architect based solely on that issued by the

NEGLIGENCE—*continued.*

third party. In the course of the repairs, the third party had deviated somewhat from the method recommended in their report, but the architect, although aware of this, made no enquiries concerning it. The house was subsequently found to be so unsound structurally as to be incapable of economic repair. The plaintiffs sought damages for negligence and breach of warranty against both defendants, and the builder sought an indemnity from the architect. Proceedings against the third party were heard separately. Evidence was given during the third party proceedings that neither the architect nor the third party had instructed the deviation from the recommendations which had taken place in the method of carrying out the repairs. **Held** by Finlay P. in finding the first and second-named defendants liable in equal shares to the plaintiffs; in finding the third party liable as to 40% to the second-named defendant and in assessing damages to include the present market value of the house plus general damages for loss, inconvenience and anxiety, and an unliquidated sum for the expense of removal and disturbance and the purchase of a new house, 1, for the purpose of the issue of the architect's certificate, the architect was the agent of the builder, whose representations, supported by the said certificate, were relied upon by the plaintiffs and became an express warranty in the agreement for sale. 2. Knowing as he did that the certificate which he had issued was intended to be used in a future sale of the house, the architect was negligent in so issuing it without ascertaining the reason for the deviation which had taken place from the method recommended for the repairs, and without ascertaining from the third party firm the true meaning of their certificate. 3. Since no evidence was given by members of the third party firm in regard to the plaintiffs' claim against the architect, evidence given in the course of third party proceedings could not be used in that regard. 4. The builder, as the person to whose advantage and benefit the architect's certificate was to be used, was negligent in not making specific enquiries as to the nature and adequacy of the works which had been carried out. 5. The third party had a duty to both the builder and the architect to direct their attention to the fact that the works were not being carried out as recommended, and was negligent in issuing a certificate without specific qualifications as to the adequacy of the works undertaken. 6. The appropriate time at which to assess the market value of the house is the first time at which it could reasonably be expected that the plaintiffs would obtain alternative accommodation. *Quinn* v. *Quality Homes Ltd.*

(H.C.) [1976-7] ILRM 314

NEGLIGENCE—Defective Premises.

2. —— **Duty of care** — *Builder — Housing authority — Auctioneer — Dwelling built on land owned by builder — Whether builder owed a common law duty of care to purchaser — Whether housing authority exercising statutory power in granting loan to purchaser owed him a common law duty of care — Whether auctioneer valuing dwelling on behalf of housing authority owed the purchaser a common law duty of care — Housing Authorities (Loans for Acquisition or Construction of Houses) Regulations,* 1972 (*S.I. No.* 29) — *Housing Act,* 1966 (*No.* 21), *s.* 39.

Damages — Defective premises — Whether damages payable for defective workmanship and inconvenience as well as in respect of dangerous defects — Joint tortfeasors — Contribution or indemnity — Civil Liability Act, 1961 (*No.* 41), *s.* 21.] In 1974 the first named defendant bought a site and in 1975 built a bungalow on it for his own occupation. In July, 1980, the first named plaintiff orally agreed to purchase the bungalow from the first named defendant for the sum of £24,000 of which £3,000 was paid by way of a deposit. A contract of sale was executed on 31 March, 1981. Both before and after the agreement to purchase was concluded the bungalow was inspected by the plaintiffs, who were then engaged to be married. The plaintiffs did not have the bungalow professionally surveyed and neither had any qualification in house construction. In August, 1980, the first named plaintiff applied to the housing authority, the second named defendant, for a loan in the sum of £12,000 under the provisions of the Housing Act, 1966, and paid an application fee of £10. The second named defendant was required by the Act and by the Regulations made pursuant to the Act, before making a loan, to satisfy itself as to the value of the house. For this purpose the second named defendant retained a valuer, the third named defendant, to value the property. The third named defendant, who had no qualifications in building construction, inspected the bungalow and found no defects. He reported it to be in good repair and valued it at approximately £25,000. The plaintiffs went into occupation in December, 1981, and very soon experienced difficulty with dampness and a smoking chimney. In August, 1982, the plaintiffs had the bungalow surveyed by an engineer who reported that it was structurally unsound, a source of danger and a risk to health. The plaintiffs were advised to abandon the property which they did in October, 1982, and soon afterwards commenced these proceedings against the three defendants. **Held** by Costello J., in giving judgment for the plaintiffs against the first and second named defendants but in dismissing the claim against the third named defendant, 1, the immunity in tort of a builder who owns the land on which a house is built and who subsequently sells it to a purchaser no longer exists. Accordingly, the first named defendant when building the bungalow owed a duty of care to the person to whom he might subsequently sell it. *Siney* v. *Corporation of Dublin* [1980] I.R. 400 considered. *Dutton* v. *Bognor Regis Urban District Council* [1972] 1 Q.B. 372 and *Anns* v. *Merton London Borough* [1978] A.C. 728 followed. 2. The concept of reasonable foresight is one to be employed not only in deciding whether a duty of care exists but can also be employed in determining its scope. The first named defendant owed a duty of care to a purchaser not only to avoid dangerous defects but also to avoid defects in the quality of the work. *Colgan* v. *Connolly Construction Co. (Ireland) Limited* [1980] ILRM 33 considered. *Junior Books Ltd.* v. *Veitchi Ltd.* [1983] 1 A.C. 520 followed. 3. The first named defendant owed a duty to the purchaser and his wife to avoid hidden defects which would cause them inconvenience and discomfort. *Siney* v. *Corporation of Dublin* [1980] I.R. 400 applied. 4. It was within the reasonable contemplation of the second named defendant that carelessness on its part in carrying out the valuation of the bungalow might be likely to cause damage to the purchaser. It was consistent with the second named defendant's public law powers and just and reasonable that they should be accompanied by a private law duty of care. 5. The second named defendant was in breach of its duty to see that the valuation was carried out with reasonable care in failing to employ someone with ordinary professional qualifications in building construction. 6. The standard of care required of the third named defendant was that of an ordinary skilled auctioneer. The plaintiffs had not established a failure to conform to that standard. *Bolam* v. *Friern Hospital Management Committee* [1957] 1 W.L.R. 582 applied. 7. That, by agreement between the parties, the damages to be awarded to the plaintiff would be assessed at a later date.
Ward v. *McMaster*

(H.C.) [1985] I.R. 29; [1986] ILRM 43

Editor's note — Supreme Court judgment at No. 30 (below).

3. —— **Duty of care** — *Builder — Dwelling built on land owned by builder — Whether builder owed a common law duty of care to purchaser — Defects — Defective drainage and septic tank — Dwellinghouse built below surface of water table — Whether defects affecting health and safety of purchasers — Whether structural defects —*

NEGLIGENCE—Defective Premises.

Damages — Cost of remedial works disproportionate to value of property — Measure of damages.

Negligence — Professional — Architect — Duty of care — Architect carrying out visual inspection of property — Scope and terms of engagement — Inspection — Survey — Extent of duty of care.

Negligence — Planning authority — Duty of care — Whether local authority in granting planning permission owed a duty of care to avoid damage to purchaser of house due to defective siting and construction — Statutory functions and powers — Purpose of statutory powers — Whether sufficient relationship of proximity between local authority and purchaser of house — Local Government (Planning and Development) Act, 1963 (*No.* 28), *ss.* 26, 28, 86.] In 1979 the plaintiffs purchased from the first defendant a house which had been built by him at D., County Louth. The first defendant, who was not a builder by trade, had planning permission for the construction of a house on the site on which he built, but he built the house on a different part of the site: in a depression where the level of the water table was unusually high and was liable to flood. Furthermore, due to the level of the water table and to the first defendant's failure to provide a soak-away, the septic tank was unable to function properly. The first defendant gave the plaintiffs a six years "structural defects indemnity . . . such indemnity to include all services." Before purchasing the house the plaintiffs had engaged the second defendant, an architect, to carry out an inspection and to prepare a report. At the plaintiffs' request this was done as a matter of urgency. The second defendant inspected the property and compiled a list of relatively trivial matters for the builder to attend to. At the time of the inspection the weather was cold, the ground was frozen and there was no sign of flooding. The second defendant did not investigate whether there had been compliance with planning permission. The third defendant had granted the original planning permission for the site and after the house had been completed, had granted permission to the first defendant pursuant to s. 28 of the Local Government (Planning and Development) Act,1963, for its retention in the position where it had been built. For substantial periods of the year the plaintiffs' garden was seriously flooded; the lavatories and washing machine could not be used and sewerage escaped from the septic tank. The flooding might have been remedied by the construction of a drain to a nearby river but this would have required the consent of an adjoining landowner, which was not forthcoming. The only alternative remedy was to raise the level of the entire site, which would have been enormously expensive. The plaintiff claimed damages against the first defendant for negligence and breach of contract in the construction and siting of the house; against the second defendant for negligence and breach of contract in his inspection and report and against the third defendant for negligence and breach of its statutory duty under the Local Government (Planning and Development) Acts in granting the permission to build and/or to retain the house on a site liable to flooding. **Held** by Lardner J., ingiving judgment for the plaintiffs against the first defendant and in dismissing the claims against the second and third defendants, 1, that when the first defendant took it upon himself to build a house which was at some time likely to be sold, he was under a duty in relation to the siting and construction of the house, including the drainage system, to exercise the care and skill which a reasonably careful and skilful builder would have shown in the circumstances. *Colgan* v. *Connolly Construction Co. (Ireland) Ltd.* [1980] ILRM 33 and *Siney* v. *Corporation of Dublin* [1980] I.R. 400 followed. 2. That the first defendant had failed to exercise such care and skill in the siting and construction of the house. 3. That the first defendant's default also constituted a breach of the express structural defects indemnity. 4. That the defects in the plaintiffs' house were defects which were likely to affect the health and safety of the plaintiffs and in respect of which they were entitled to recover damages. *Colgan* v. *Connolly Construction Co. (Ireland) Ltd.* [1980] ILRM 33 considered. 5. That having regard to the disproportionately large cost of remedial work in comparison with the value of the house, the appropriate measure of damages was the amount by which the plaintiffs' house had been devalued by reason of the first defendant's negligence. 6. That, in addition, the plaintiffs would be allowed a sum for damages in respect of their own effort and labour in attempting to abate the flooding; the inconvenience of living in dampness and flooding; additional decoration and travelling expenses incurred by reason of their being unable to sell the house. 7. That the duty owed by the second defendant, as an architect, was related to and determined by the scope of his employment. 8. That the duty of the second defendant, who had been engaged to carry out a visual inspection and report, was to inspect the house with the eye of a competent architect and to draw such inferences from what he saw as a competent architect would have drawn. In particular he was not obliged to examine ordnance survey maps or the planning application or planning permission or to check whether they had been complied with or not. 9. That at the time of the second defendant's inspection there had been no physical signs either in the building or in the septic tank which would have alerted him to the problem. 10.

NEGLIGENCE—Defective Premises.

That the test to be applied in deciding whether the third defendant (as planning authority) owed a duty of care to the plaintiffs was to enquire, having regard to the statutory provisions under which the third defendant was acting, the purpose of those powers and whether the plaintiffs were within the class which the statute was designed to protect, firstly, whether there was a relationship of proximity between the parties such that it was within the reasonable contemplation of the third defendant that carelessness on their part might cause loss; and secondly, whether in all the circumstances it was reasonable to impose such a duty of care. *Ward* v. *McMaster* [1985] I.R. 29 followed. 11. That the purpose and intention of the provisions of ss. 26 and 28 of the Act of 1963 was to assist in the implementation of the proper development of the third defendant's area in accordance with the development plan and did not comprehend the subject matter of the plaintiffs' complaints. 12. That, accordingly, the third defendant did not owe the plaintiffs a common law duty of care in regard to the matters complained of. *Sunderland* v. *McGreavey*

(H.C.) [1987] I.R.372

DEFECTIVE PRODUCTS

4. —— **Masts** — *Erection of floodlighting masts — Strong wind — Mast collapsing — Whether defendant negligent — Method of installation — Relevant standard — Whether mast inherently defective.*] The appellant company had been retained to provide floodlighting for a sports pitch in Rathfarnham, Co. Dublin. The floodlighting required the erection of eight masts, which the appellant purchased from the first respondent, who was the Irish agent of the second respondent. When quoting the appellant a price for the masts, the respondents had enclosed with the written quotation their table of wind scales, with an indication of which type of mast was appropriate for a particular wind speed. Following the erection of the masts, one of them collapsed during a night of strong wind, and the other seven were found to be in a dangerous condition, and had to be taken down. The appellant sued the first respondent in contract and the second respondent in tort. At the trial of the action in the High Court, evidence was given that the appellant had not ascertained the maximum wind speed to be expected in Rathfarnham. Evidence was also given by the second respondent that they relied upon a British standard (BS 1840) for steel columns for street lighting, and further evidence disclosed that BS 1840 was the standard used by engineers all over Ireland, although the standard used in the Petitjean catalogue was a French standard, which

NEGLIGENCE—*continued.*

was more rigorous than BS 1840. Further evidence indicated that the method of installation of the masts had differed from that specified by the consulting engineer. The appellants alleged that the fact that the masts supplied by the respondents did not comply with the standard set out in their catalogue was *prima facie* evidence of negligence. **Held** by the Supreme Court (Griffin J., Finlay C.J. and McCarthy J. concurring) in dismissing the appeal, 1, the respondents were entitled to assume that they were dealing with experts who were already in possession of all their relevant data. 2. Since the masts complied with a standard recognised and used in this country by responsible authorities, there was not sufficient evidence to show on the balance of probabilities that they were inherently defective or unsuitable for use. *S.E.E.Co. Ltd.* v. *Public Lighting Services Ltd.*

(S.C.) [1988] ILRM 677

DEMOLITION WORK

5. —— **Demolition** — *Adjoining premises — Demolition work causing damage to plaintiff's premises — Whether work carried out negligently — Work being carried out by independent contractor — Whether defendant vicariously liable — Damages.*] The plaintiff and the first named defendant owned adjoining premises. The plaintiff's gable wall had been built within two inches of the first named defendant's premises and the two premises connected by means of a solid beam of concrete in 1958. In 1973 the first named defendant employed a consultant architect to draw up plans for the demolition of their premises. A tender submitted by the second named defendant, an independent contractor, was accepted and an agreement was concluded with them to carry out the demolition work in accordance with the architect's instructions. The architect advised that the demolition work should be carried out by hand. The second named defendants demolished the gable wall by cable. Following the demolition work, extensive cracking was noticed in the plaintiff's premises. **Held** by Costello J. in granting a decree against both defendants in the full amount of damages, 1, the second named defendants carried out the demolition works in a negligent manner causing injury to the plaintiff's premises, as a result of which she suffered loss and damage. 2. The architect employed by the first named defendant was not negligent in either failing to specifically provide in the contract documents that the demolition work be carried out by hand or in failing to adequately supervise the operations. 3. The first named defendant is liable for the negligence of the second named defendant. The general rule that an employer is not liable for the negligence

NEGLIGENCE—Demolition Work.

of his independent contractor does not apply due to the inherently dangerous nature of the operation. Such an employer cannot relieve himself of the duty to ensure that all reasonable precautions are taken against the inherent dangers by employing an independent contractor, if the latter does not take those precautions. *Belvedere Fish Guano Co. Ltd.* v. *Rainham Chemical Works Ltd.* [1920] 2 KB 487 followed. 4. The nature of the damage caused to the plaintiff's premises by the defendant's tortious acts does not warrant reconstruction. Consequently, the appropriate measure of damages in the circumstances is the diminution in the value of the plaintiff's premises and not the cost of the scheme of reconstruction proposed by the plaintiff. *Munnelly* v. *Calcon Ltd.* High Court (Finlay P.) 30 July 1976 applied. 5. The diminution in the value of the premises is to be calculated at the prices prevalent at the date the damage occurred *i.e.* November, 1973, and not at current prices. *Boylan* v. *Northern Bank Ltd.*

(H.C.) [1976-7] ILRM 287

EMPLOYER
see also Nos. 5, 18

6. —— **Accident at work** — *Whether employer negligent — Risk becoming manifest — Simple method of overcoming it.*] The appellant, an employee of the respondent, was injured when he fell from the platform of a lorry which he was loading at the respondent's premises. There was evidence before the court that a strip of timber was habitually nailed along the platform edges of the respondent's lorries, to indicate to the workers loading the lorries that they were standing near the edge of the platform, since the loading operation required them to look upwards at a chute through which sacks were propelled to the lorries from the respondent's premises. Evidence was also given that four of the six lorries belonging to the respondent had such a wooden strip. On the day of the accident, the lorry in use had no wooden strip, but the appellant, who was accustomed to the presence of a strip, assumed that it was there. At the trial, the learned High Court judge withdrew the case from the jury on the ground that there was no evidence to go before it. On appeal, it was **Held** by the Supreme Court (O'Higgins C.J., Kenny and Parke JJ. concurring) in allowing the appeal and ordering a retrial, when a risk or danger becomes manifest in the course of employment, and a simple means of overcoming it is available, an employer will be negligent if he permits the danger to continue. There was, therefore, evidence of negligence which should have gone to the jury. *Fortune* v. *P.E. Jacob & Co. Ltd.*

(S.C.) [1976-7] ILRM 277

NEGLIGENCE—*continued.*

7. —— **Duty of care** — *Notice given that employee fit for light work only — Employer taking no further action — Whether employer in breach of duty of care.*] The plaintiff appealed to the Supreme Court against an order made by the High Court withdrawing his claim for negligence against the defendants from the jury on the ground that a *prima facie* case had not been established by the evidence. The plaintiff contended that the defendant having been informed once that the plaintiff was fit only for light work was negligent either in not providing suitable light work for him or in permitting him to return to full work. **Held** by the Supreme Court (Finlay C.J. and Henchy J.; McCarthy J. dissenting): the trial judge had been correct in his finding that a *prima facie* case of negligence had not been established by the plaintiff. *Per* Finlay C.J.: it would be a wholly artificial and unreal standard of care to hold the defendants guilty of negligence on the basis that they reacted to a single application for light work by the plaintiff by simply informing him that they had not got any and then took no further action when he voluntarily resumed and remained at his ordinary work. *Per* Henchy J.: if the negligence alleged by the plaintiff had in fact been apparent in evidence at the trial it should have been pleaded so that the defendants could properly meet the case. *Per* McCarthy J. dissenting: there was sufficient evidence of negligence and the respondents did not complain of inadequacy in the pleadings at the hearing of the action. *Rafferty* v. *C.A. Parsons of Ireland Ltd.*

(S.C.) [1987] ILRM 98

8. —— **Injury at work** — *Action for damages — Plaintiff employed by first defendant, an independent contractor working under contract with second defendant — Employee of second defendant directing plaintiff in accordance with specifications in contract — Plaintiff injured while carrying out such directions — Whether second defendants liable.*] The Department of Posts and Telegraphs was engaged on a project of laying underground conduits and the construction of joint boxes and manholes for telephone cables at Ardcrony near Nenagh in Co. Tipperary in December, 1981. The work was being executed by the first named defendant who was an independent contractor engaged by the Minister for Posts and Telegraphs and working under contract with the Minister and in accordance with specifications and associated drawings. The plaintiff was the foreman of a gang of workmen employed by the contractor during the execution of the contract. Evidence was given by him, at the hearing of an action for damages for personal

NEGLIGENCE—Employer.

injuries in the High Court in Limerick, that he was ordered by one Michael Ryan, the clerk of works employed by the second named defendant, to lower one of the joint boxes which had been placed in the grass margin beside the public road during the course of the work. The plaintiff further stated that, as his fellow-workmen were some distance down the road he proceeded to attempt the removal of the heavy cover of the joint box himself and that he had only one key or handle available instead of two when he attempted to lift and slide back the cover. During the course of doing so he injured his back. Evidence was also given on behalf of the plaintiff by Mr. Anthony Brennan, B.E., that the cover consisted of concrete set in a steel grid and would weigh about 3 cwts. It should be lifted by two men with two keys and it amounted to an unsafe system of work if only one man with one key was engaged in the removal of the cover. Under cross-examination the witness stated that he would expect the contractor to provide the two keys. At the conclusion of the evidence for the plaintiff counsel for the first named defendant and counsel for the second named defendant each applied to the court for a direction. The court refused the application which was made on behalf of the first named defendant. **Held** by Keane J., in dismissing the action against the second named defendant, that the only allegation of negligence against that defendant was that the clerk of works allowed the plaintiff to remove the manhole cover when it was dangerous for him to do so. He had no responsibility to see that the work was carried out with safety as that was the duty of the contractor in whose employment the plaintiff was working. The clerk of works need not have been present at the time of the accident as he simply conveys the directions and does not say how they are to be carried out. Accordingly the action should be dismissed against the second named defendant. *O'Donnell* v. *Begley*

(H.C.) [1987] ILRM 105

9. —— **Occupational disease** — *Folliculitis — Whether employee's contraction of the disease reasonably foreseeable.*] The plaintiff, an employee of the defendant company, contracted folliculitis (a form of dermatitis) by inhaling chemical fumes at his workplace. A jury in the High Court had awarded the plaintiff damages of £6,266 on a finding that the defendant had been in breach of its common law duty of care but not of any statutory duty. The plaintiff appealed to the Supreme Court on the ground that the damages awarded were so inadequate as to be perverse, and that the jury's acquittal of the defendant of any breach of duty under the Factories Act was inconsistent with its finding

NEGLIGENCE—*continued.*

on the question of common law liability. The defendant appealed on the ground that the jury's findings were not supported by the evidence. The issue was whether the contraction of folliculitis by inhalation of fumes in a workplace that was well ventilated was reasonably foreseeable. **Held** by the Supreme Court (Walsh, Griffin and McCarthy JJ.) dismissing the plaintiff's appeal and allowing that of the defendant that the evidence did establish that the plaintiff contracted his disease at work; that result was so unique and improbable as not to be one which the employer could reasonably have foreseen and the trial judge should have withdrawn the case from the jury as a verdict against the defendant was not sustainable on the evidence. *Brady* v. *Beckmann Instruments (Galway) Inc.*

(S.C.) [1986] ILRM 361

10. —— **Place of work** — *Health board — Home help employed in the community — Defective condition of patient's house — Home help injured in patient's house — Responsibility of health board.*] The plaintiff, a resident of Kinsale, County Cork, provided assistance for an elderly neighbour for many years. In 1978, she was asked by the public health nurse for the area to take up employment with the Health Board as a home help to help that elderly neighbour who lived alone in a house of considerable age and dilapidation. The plaintiff's duties consisted of general housework and shopping, and she visited the neighbour four times each day over a period of seven years until she fell in the hallway of the neighbour's house in July, 1985. The plaintiff commenced Circuit Court proceedings against the Health Board arising out of her fall, alleging that the Health Board had a duty, in employing her, to ensure that the place of work where she was employed was safe, and that the Board should have, prior to the commencement of her employment, either made the premises safe, or requested the neighbour to make the premises safe. The plaintiff succeeded in the Circuit Court, and following the evidence on behalf of the plaintiff on appeal, an application was made by counsel on behalf of the defendant that the plaintiff's case be dismissed on the grounds that the defendant had no case to answer. **Held** By Murphy J., in acceding to the application, and dismissing the plaintiff's claim, that a Health Board is not bound, where a home help is employed by it to work in a patient's home, to require that those premises be brought up to modern standards. *Mulcare* v. *Southern Health Board*

(H.C.) [1988] ILRM 689

NEGLIGENCE—*continued.*

HIGHWAY

see also **Road accidents,** No. 27

11. —— **Authority** — *Duty of care — Condition of planning permission that lay-by be provided by developers — Layout agreed with defendants as planning authority — Difference in road levels — Pedestrian injured — Jury finding of negligence — Whether defendant authority liable for contractor's negligence.*] The plaintiff was injured when she tripped and fell on a public road as a result of a difference in road levels caused by work in progress on a layby for buses. A developer was constructing the layby in compliance with a condition imposed by the defendants as planning authority in relation to the planning permission for the development. The defendants knew of the carrying out of the work by the developer's contractor. The defendants were the highway authority in relation to the road. The plaintiff sued the defendants (as the highway authority) in the High Court. The trial judge refused to withdraw the case from the jury which found that the defendants had been negligent and awarded damages. The defendants appealed, submitting that the trial judge should have withdrawn the case because there was no evidence that they had authorised or permitted the interference with the roadway which had caused the plaintiff's injuries or, in the alternative, because there was no evidence of negligence. The defendants further submitted that as the highway authority under the Local Government Act of 1925 they should not be fixed with knowledge of or made liable in respect of any approval which they might have given as planning authority. **Held** *per* O'Higgins C.J. and Hederman J.; Griffin J. dissenting. The defendants had authorised and permitted the work done by the developer and they were responsible as highway authority to look after the safety of those using the roadway, who might thereby be exposed to danger if the work done caused risk of injury. There was evidence of negligence to go to the jury. The appeal would be dismissed. *Per* Griffin J. dissenting. While there had been negligence, the defendants were not liable as the work was not done by their servants or independent contractors. There was no principle or authority which warranted the imposition of liability on a highway authority for the acts of a contractor employed by a developer in doing work for which planning permission had been granted by the local authority as planning authority. *Weir* v. *Dun Laoghaire Corporation*

(S.C.) [1984] ILRM 113

NEGLIGENCE—*continued.*

12. —— **Authority** — *Street lighting — Discretionary power —* Ultra vires — *Injury to pedestrian — Plaintiff alleged accident due to non-functioning street light — Whether public authority liable for negligent exercise of discretionary powers — Whether discretion related to policy or operational matter.*] The appellant was walking along a footpath towards her home during darkness at 7.30 p.m. when she tripped on an obstacle and fell. At that time no light emanated from the street lighting standards and the darkness made it difficult for her to see. The appellant alleged that the lighting standards had not been operating for at least 4 days and claimed £5,000 damages for personal injuries. The respondent argued, as a preliminary point of law, that where a public authority, such as the respondent, exercised a discretionary power to light a public highway, the issue of negligence did not arise unless it could be shown that the authority had acted *ultra vires*. The deputy county court judge ruled in favour of the respondent's preliminary point of law and on a case stated to the Court of Appeal, **Held,** remitting the case to the county court for a hearing on the merits, that the question submitted for the court's decision was misconceived, 1, with regard to the exercise of statutory powers, the courts must draw a line between policy matters, in respect of which (if its actions are *intra vires* and not unreasonable within the meaning of *Associated Picture Houses Ltd.* v. *Wednesbury Corporation* [1948] 1 K.B. 223) a statutory authority cannot be liable for common law negligence and operational matters in respect of which the authority can be so liable. The reason for the distinction is that the considerations which may be taken into account in reaching a decision on policy matters are judicially imponderable, whereas with operational matters the court is equipped with the knowledge and the factual evidence to enable it to reach a decision as to whether there has been an invasion of the rights of private citizens. *Farrell* v. *Northern Ireland Electricity Service* [1977] N.I. 39 explained. 2. The line between policy and operational matters has not been drawn with precision, for even within the operational sphere there could be a policy element in respect of which, subject to *ultra vires* and *Wednesbury* unreasonableness, the authority remains immune. Policy includes all determinations which depend upon the weighing or assessing of general considerations and apply to the decisions of any officer or official who, in the course of the operation of the powers, has the duty to reach a decision involving the question as to what is best to be done to promote the purposes of the authority having regard to its constitution, resources and circumstances. On the other hand operational negligence need not be confined

NEGLIGENCE—Highway.

solely to the last link of the chain: subordinate officers could be badly or wrongly instructed by their superiors. 3. In respect of operational matters, in the absence of an express provision to the contrary, it is not necessary to find an *ultra vires* or *Wednesbury* unreasonable exercise of discretion before considering negligence. Negligent operational conduct, whether by act or omission is unauthorised and therefore *ultra vires,* for Parliament did not intend that a public body should exercise a discretionary power in such a way as to injure a member of the public in circumstances where, by the exercise of due care towards those who are likely to be injured thereby, the accident could be avoided. If therefore a servant of a public body acting within the operational field causes injury by reason of his lack of due care, it may be said that he acted in excess of his delegated power and therefore in an *ultra vires* manner and so the public body may be liable for his negligence. *Chambers* v. *Department of the Environment*

(C.A.) [1985] N.I.181

MEDICAL

13. —— **Doctor** — *Duty to patient — Patient not examined — Sufferer from Crohn's disease — Predisposition to low blood pressure — Intervention of second doctor — Patient suffering a stroke — Whether damage to plaintiff foreseeable — Plaintiff's action withdrawn from jury.*] During the evening of the 8 June, 1977, the plaintiff experienced very severe pains in his stomach and he vomited. The first defendant, a medical practitioner, attended the plaintiff at his home at 3 a.m. on the 9 June and injected him twice with a drug that contained morphine. He did not advise the plaintiff to go to hospital. The second defendant, also a medical practitioner, attended the plaintiff at his home at 9 a.m. on the same day and injected him with another drug. The second defendant advised the plaintiff that he needed treatment in hospital but the plaintiff refused to permit his removal to a hospital. The plaintiff suffered a stroke at 12 noon on the same day and he was admitted to hospital at 2 p.m. and an operation was performed on him. It was discovered that the plaintiff had suffered an abdominal catastrophe by a perforation of the wall of his stomach; it also appeared that the plaintiff suffered from Crohn's disease and thus had a predisposition to hypotension or low blood pressure. If untreated, a perforation of the stomach wall leads inevitably to a loss of blood pressure which eventually causes the patient to suffer brain damage. The plaintiff brought an action in the High Court in which he claimed damages from each of the defendants for his negligence in treating and advising the plaintiff

NEGLIGENCE—Medical.

and in diagnosing his illness. At the trial of the action the plaintiff adduced evidence that the first defendant had not examined the plaintiff's stomach and had injected him with an unsuitable drug at a time when he was suffering from peritonitis. The plaintiff also adduced evidence that the second defendant had injected the plaintiff with a drug which was inappropriate in the circumstances and that the second defendant had failed to realise that the plaintiff was critically ill and had failed to insist on the plaintiff's removal to a hospital. The plaintiff also adduced evidence that the damage to his brain caused by the stroke was the result of the extended period during which he had suffered from hypotension or low blood pressure. At the conclusion of the evidence adduced on behalf of the defendants, the trial judge withdrew the plaintiff's case from the jury and gave judgment for the defendants on the ground that, even if either defendant had been negligent, he could not have reasonably foreseen that his conduct would cause the stroke suffered by the plaintiff. On appeal by the plaintiff it was **Held** by the Supreme Court (O'Higgins C.J., Griffin and Hederman JJ.), in allowing the appeal and directing a retrial, 1, that at the trial, and in respect of each defendant, there had been evidence of negligence (although controverted) and that such evidence should have been left to the jury for their verdict. 2. That, if the failure to diagnose and to treat the plaintiff's abdominal perforation promptly was caused by the negligence of either of the defendants, the subsequent occurrence of the plaintiff's stroke was not an unforeseeable sequela of that negligence. *Overseas Tankship (U.K.) Ltd.* v. *Morts Dock & Engineering Co. Ltd. (The Wagon Mound)* [1961] A.C. 388 and *Burke* v. *John Paul & Co. Ltd.* [1967] I.R. 277 applied. 3. That, in respect of the possible liability of the first defendant, the intervention of the second defendant did not constitute *novus actus interveniens*. *Reeves* v. *Carthy*

(S.C.) [1984] I.R.348

14. —— **Hospital** — *Duty of care — Standard of care — In-patient subject to epileptic fits and automatism — Fall from window in toilet room — Standards of nursing or custodial care — Whether injury foreseeable — Whether hospital in breach of duty.*] The plaintiff was diagnosed in 1974 as suffering from right temporal lobe epilepsy and had been experiencing epileptic attacks and fits of a psychotic nature and some automatism, and was put on various medications. When these attacks showed no sign of decreasing, he was admitted as an in-patient on the 12 July, 1981, to the defendant's hospital under the care of a consultant for tests and observation, for which purpose he was taken off all medications. On the

NEGLIGENCE—Medical.

fifth night at 4 a.m. the plaintiff left his ward, crossed the corridor, entered a room containing two toilet cubicles, at which entry he was observed by a staff nurse, moved some bottles from the window-sill, placed a mobile commode under the window, which was open or he had opened, climbed through it and fell about twenty feet to the yard below sustaining severe injuries. He instituted proceedings against the defendants for damages for negligence in relation to his injuries. At the trial in the High Court a single question on the issue paper was put to the jury: "Were the defendants, their servants or agents negligent in not requiring that the plaintiff be attended when going to the toilet?" Evidence for the plaintiff had included that of a consultant psychiatrist and neurologist, Dr. O'Connor, who was of opinion that given the plaintiff's medical history and hospital records he should not have been allowed go to the toilet unattended and that prudence dictated that he should have been required to get prior permission so that a nurse could have attended him. The defendants' last witness, Dr. Malone, also a consultant psychiatrist and neurologist, was of the opposite opinion, namely, that close surveillance of epileptics was not required unless, exceptionally, a patient, upon careful observation, had shown a tendency to act in an untoward way, in which case attendance by a nurse with him at the toilet would be necessary. In his charge to the jury the learned trial judge said the following: ". . . if you think . . . there was a real possibility of injury to Mr. Kelly, a real possibility that he should [suffer injury] if he went to the toilet unaccompanied, you would be entitled to find the hospital guilty of negligence in that event . . ." He also set out the essence of Dr. O'Connor's evidence but made no reference to the evidence of nor did he mention Dr. Malone. The jury found the defendants negligent and awarded the plaintiff £90,000 damages. The defendants appealed to the Supreme Court against the judgment and order of the High Court on the grounds that the case ought to have been withdrawn from the jury at the close of all the evidence as the plaintiff had failed to establish that the defendants' conduct in the care and treatment of him was inconsistent with medical practice or that it was inherently defective; that the trial judge's formulation of negligence might have been interpreted by the jury so as to conclude that the defendants were negligent if their conduct gave rise to a mere possibility of the plaintiff suffering injury; that the trial judge's charge failed to put forward essential parts of the defendants' case, in particular, the evidence of Dr. Malone and despite requisitions from defence counsel; and that the damages were excessive. The plaintiff submitted that it was not a medical negligence case and

NEGLIGENCE—*continued.*

cross-appealed that the general damages were insufficient and disproportionate to the special damages awarded. **Held** by the Supreme Court (Walsh, Hederman and McCarthy JJ.; Finlay C.J. and Henchy J. dissenting) in dismissing the appeals, 1, that there was sufficient evidence of negligence on the part of the defendants and the case was properly left to the jury. 2. (Henchy J. dissenting). That the duty the defendants owed to the plaintiff was to take reasonable care to avoid permitting him to be exposed to injury which a reasonable person ought to foresee; in this case the duty of a reasonable hospital administration to provide a reasonable nursing service. *Healy* v. *Bray Urban District Council* [1962/1963] Ir. Jur. Rep. 9 considered. *Per* Henchy J. The essential question is whether the risk of injury or damage complained of was such that a reasonably careful person in the position of the defendants would have taken the precaution suggested by the plaintiff. 3. (Finlay C.J. and Henchy J. dissenting). That while the trial judge should have repeated Dr. Malone's evidence to the jury, his failure to do so did not affect the outcome of the case, since his testimony was reasonably fresh in the jury's mind and in any event his evidence as to the standard practice of a consultant in such a case did not relate to the real issue of negligence, namely, what reasonable ordinary standards of nursing or custodial care in the particular situation would be. *Per* Finlay C.J. and Henchy J. The failure of the trial judge to advert to the evidence of Dr. Malone and set out the defence to the plaintiff's case constituted a misdirection for which a re-trial on the issue of liability ought to be directed. *Per* Henchy J. The overall requirement in the charge to the jury is that the trial must essentially be, and appear to be, a fair one. 4. That while the awards upon different heads of damage were not entirely internally consistent, the total award was not so inconsistent with the evidence as to require intervention on appeal. *Kelly* v. *Board of Governors of St. Laurence's Hospital*

(S.C.) [1988] I.R.402

15. —— **Surgeon** — Novus actus interveniens — *Emergency operation on admission to hospital — Plaintiff showing signs of improvement — New emergency — Second emergency operation — Plaintiff's injury aggravated — Whether neurosurgical centre should have been consulted after first and/or second operation — Whether treatment in second operation was negligent — Whether there was negligence in prescribing hypotensive drugs to lower blood pressure after the second operation — Whether aggravation of plaintiff's injuries — Evidence — Medical records as evidence — Weight to be given to evidence based solely on records.*

NEGLIGENCE—Medical.

Damages — Personal injuries — Assessment — Loss of earnings — Care and maintenance — Actuarial evidence — Calculation of multiplier — Factors to be taken into account — Road traffic accident — Passenger in defendant's car — Contributory negligence — Failure to wear seat belt — Apportionment of fault — Civil Liability Act, 1961 (*No.* 41), *s.* 34.] On the 11 June, 1984, the plaintiff was severely injured in a road traffic accident. He was a passenger in a car owned by the first defendant and driven by the first defendant's son. The plaintiff was thrown out of the car onto the road and under the car as a result of the accident. An emergency operation was carried out on the date of the accident. On the 27 June, 1984, whilst still detained in hospital and having appeared to be recovering the plaintiff suffered a relapse and underwent a further emergency operation which was performed by the second defendant. He remained unconscious from the time of the second operation until November, 1984. When he regained consciousness the plaintiff was found to be suffering from severe disabilities. It was agreed that if the plaintiff had not suffered the setback of the 27 June, 1984, he would nonetheless have been left with serious disabilities, though not such as were comparable with the disabilities he did suffer. As a result of his injuries the plaintiff had all the characteristics of a diffuse spastic. He had a full appreciation of his state from which there would be no recovery. He was 25 years old and his life expectancy from the date of the trial was 25 years. Prior to his accident the plaintiff had been in good health and had intended going to Boston to work. The first defendant did not deny negligence but pleaded contributory negligence by the plaintiff in not wearing a seat belt. The first defendant sought a contribution from the second and third defendants on the basis that the consequences of the road traffic accident were aggravated by the negligence of the second defendant as servant or agent of the third defendant and that their alleged negligence constituted a *novus actus interveniens*. The plaintiff submitted that the second and third defendants ought to have sought advice from a neuro-surgical centre and ought to have transferred him to such a centre. It was also submitted that it was wrong to pack the plaintiff's skull with surgicell and to put a tight bandage round the same after the emergency operation performed by the second defendant on the 27 June, 1984. It was further submitted that it was wrong of the second defendant to prescribe hypotensive drugs after the same operation. The medical witnesses called on behalf of the plaintiff and the first defendant had not seen the plaintiff at any relevant time and depended on the medical records made available on discovery. **Held** by Lynch J., in giving judgment for

NEGLIGENCE—*continued.*

the plaintiff against the first defendant and in dismissing the action against the second and third defendants, 1, that as the plaintiff had been guilty of contributory negligence in not wearing a seat belt, the apportionment of fault in accordance with s. 34 of the Civil Liability Act, 1961, in the circumstances of this case would be 86% on the first defendant and 14% on the plaintiff. 2. That medical records can be outweighed by other evidence where their accuracy or interpretation is challenged. In the instant case the evidence of medical witnesses who had the plaintiff under their care regarding the seeking of advice from, or the transfer of the plaintiff to a neuro-surgical centre was preferable to that of medical witnesses whose opinions were based solely on medical records. 3. That on the evidence the allegations that the second and third defendants had been negligent in failing to seek advice from or failing to transfer the plaintiff to a neuro-surgical centre failed. 4. That the second defendant had not been negligent in using the quantitites of surgicell he deemed necessary in dealing with the emergency of the 27 June, 1984, even if it was more than would have been used by a neuro surgeon and there was no substance to the criticism of the bandage. 5. That the second defendant had been negligent in prescribing hypotensive drugs but their administration had had no adverse effects. 6. That, with regard to the asessment of damages, the reduction in the multiplier suggested by the plaintiff's actuary for future loss of earnings to take account of factors such as the dangers of redundancy, sickness, death, injury or changes in the economy should be very moderate on the facts of the case but that the discount from the multiplier suggested for the lost years (from the age of 50 to 60) to take account of such factors would be greater. 7. That, excluding accommodation costs, which would have been higher in the Boston area and which would not have affected the plaintiff because he could have shared accommodation with relatives, there was no significant difference betwen the cost of living in Ireland and the Boston area (taking into account the exchange rate between the Irish pound and the U.S. dollar on the date the evidence was given and not the date of judgment) and there would be no adjustment in loss of earnings figures on the basis of a difference in the cost of living between the two places. 8. That account must be taken of certain tax reliefs and allowances available to the plaintiff when arriving at a figure for care and attendance in the future but also of the fact that there may arise disputes between the plaintiff's advisers and the Revenue Commissioners in respect of the same. 9. That, in keeping with the interests of moderation, the figures in the plaintiff's actuary's report for certain items would not be changed, even if they were expressed in sterling. *Reddy* v. *Bates* [1983] I.R. 141, *Cooke* v. *Walsh* [1984] ILRM 208 and *Sinnott* v. *Quinnsworth* [1984] ILRM 523 considered. 10. That for the first 15 years £50 per week would be awarded in respect of paramedical attendance on the two days per week that the professional attendant would be off duty, as the family would provide for £50 what would cost £100 per week on a professional basis. 11. That the sum for full time professional domestic live-in help would be reduced from £226.70 to £50 to take account of the fact that the plaintiff's family would provide such help for a lesser sum and as the plaintiff would have had to provide himself with such help even if he had never been injured, it was only the extra cost of domestic help which would be awarded. 12. That the appropriate general damages for pain and suffering and a shortened expectation of life was £174,000 and the amount for ascertainable damages was £891,933 and when 14% was deducted from the total in respect of the plaintiff's contributory negligence, a net sum of £916,702.38 was left. *Conley* v. *Strain*

(H.C.) [1988] I.R.628

OCCUPIER

16. —— **Contribution** — *Ancient castle — Plaintiff falling down hole — Injuries — Whether plaintiff contributorily negligent — Assessment of damages.*] Donegal Castle, a national monument, was in the possession and control of the first named defendant, the Board of Works. In the castle there were two large balconies which constituted an obvious viewing point for the public. Close to one of the viewing points was an aperture in the floor, about 2 feet wide and extending almost the entire width of the balcony. The plaintiff, a 13 year old school boy, while viewing the castle with several other boys as a member of the public fell 16 feet through the said aperture and sustained severe personal injuries. At the time of the accident the said aperture was open and totally unguarded and there was no notice warning the public of any particular danger or exhorting them to take care for their own safety. The High Court found that the Board of Works was negligent and in breach of duty to the plaintiff in failing to fence or cover the aperture. The only issue on liability that remained for determination was whether the plaintiff was guilty of contributory negligence and if so how the fault was to be apportioned between the parties. There was no evidence before the court as to how the plaintiff fell down the hole, however at the hearing a number of suggestions were put forward which included that he ran towards it and attempted to jump the gap or tripped while running towards it. As a result

of the accident, the plaintiff suffered a serious head injury, a fractured leg, shoulder blade, a fractured femur and various small wounds. Evidence was adduced at the hearing that prior to the accident the plaintiff was a bright active child of at least average intelligence and ability but since the accident he had sunk to the intellectual level of 'dull normal'. The head injury allied to the sequelae of the leg injury caused the plaintiff to be clumsy and sometimes unsteady and liable to fall. The injury caused impairment in his balance and his hand movements were also affected. Evidence was given at the hearing as to the general family history of employment including the fact that his father was a principal primary teacher and that as a result of the accident in terms of working capacity the most he could expect to obtain was light menial employment. **Held** by Barr J. in finding that the plaintiff had been guilty of contributory negligence and in assessing damages, 1, the plaintiff has a duty to take reasonable care for his own safety and the court in determining what was reasonable in the circumstances should have regard to the age of the plaintiff, the nature of the premises and the fact that the plaintiff was accompanied by several boys between the ages of 10 to 17 years. 2. The plaintiff having regard to his age was 1/3 to blame as he more than likely attempted to jump the aperture which he ought to have known was dangerous and therefore failed in his duty to take reasonable care for his own safety and the defendants were 2/3 to blame as the accident would not have happened had the aperture been properly protected and further it was foreseeable that an exuberant young boy might attempt to jump it on his way to the viewing platform. 3. In the absence of specific evidence as to how the plaintiff came to fall down the hole the courts should adopt a reasonable construction of the events consistent with the established evidence which is most favourable to the defendants. 4. In view of the fact that the plaintiff will only be able to obtain light unskilled labouring work the court assessed the plaintiff's net loss of earning capacity having regard to the general family history of employment and he would have qualified in some trade if he had not been injured, and then reduced this total actuarial figure of his losses by 25% to take account of employment prospects in the future and the risk of absences from work through ill health. *Reddy* v. *Bates* [1984] ILRM 197 applied. 5. The court assessed compensation for pain, suffering and disablement to date at £30,000 and continuing disablement in the future at £70,000 compensating him for permanent sequelae of his injuries; the substantial alteration in the plaintiff's personality and way of life; his loss of sporting capacity and job satisfaction. 6. The court awarded the

NEGLIGENCE—Occupier.

plaintiff the sum of £5,000 compensation for the fact that in view of the present economic climate he will probably find great difficulty in obtaining the type of semi sheltered employment which is within his restricted physical and intellectual capacity. *Clancy* v. *Commissioners of Public Works in Ireland*

(H.C.) [1988] ILRM 268

17. —— **Contribution** — *Foreseeability — Causation* — Novus actus interveniens — *Boys playing on roof of defendant's premises — Architects' design — Absence of protective railing — Fall from roof — Injury — Defendant's prior knowledge of such games — Failure by defendant to prohibit or prevent games — Whether such foreseeable by architects — Whether sufficient nexus between architects' negligence and injury to the plaintiff — Civil Liability Act,* 1961 (*No.* 41).] The plaintiff, an infant, was one of group of boys playing tip rugby on the roof of the defendant's premises when he fell off it and sustained serious injuries. In an action for negligence in which the architects were joined as third party the High Court jury held the defendant 91% negligent and the plaintiff 9% contributorily negligent. Damages were then settled and in the issue between the defendant and third party heard without a jury Hamilton P. held the third party liable for 30% in that its design provided easy access to an unprotected roof and the accident had been a foreseeable risk. The third party appealed. **Held** by the Supreme Court (Finlay C.J., Walsh, Henchy, Hederman and Barr JJ.), in allowing the appeal, that on the jury finding that the defendant knew that boys had played and were likely to play on the unprotected roof, and in the absence of any evidence that the defendant attempted to prevent or prohibit the plaintiff and other boys from playing there, it was not open to the trial judge to hold that there was a sufficient nexus between any negligent design by the third party and the immediate causes of the accident. Principles in *Conole* v. *Redbank Oyster Co.* [1976] I.R. 191 affirmed and applied. *Crowley* v. *Allied Irish Banks Ltd.*

(S.C.) [1987] I.R.282; [1988] ILRM 225

18. —— **Invitor** — *Area of invitation — Accident outside area — Factory roof — Contractor agreeing to repair roof — Contractor engaging sub-contractor to repair gutters — Sub-contractor falling through skylight on roof — Damages claimed by plaintiff widow of sub-contractor — Liability of factory owner — Whether breach of statutory duty — Factories Act,* 1955 (*No.* 10), *s.* 37.] A contractor agreed with the defendant factory owners to repair the roof of their factory by making it weatherproof and to paint it with aluminium paint. The contractor engaged a sub-contractor to repair the gutters of the factory and

NEGLIGENCE—*continued.*

to apply the paint to so much of the roof as could be reached manually from a forklift truck; the sub-contractor was informed by the contractor that the latter would effect all repairs to the roof. On a certain Friday the contractor was informed that a skylight on the factory roof needed to be repaired and he stated his intention to effect that repair during the following week. On the following Monday the sub-contractor climbed onto the roof of the factory with the intention of repairing the defective skylight but he fell to his death through a skylight onto the floor of the factory. The plaintiff, being the sub-contractor's widow, claimed in the High Court damages from the defendants; she did so on behalf of herself and the other dependants of her husband. The plaintiff pleaded that the defendants had been negligent and had been in breach of their statutory duty under s. 37 of the Factories Act, 1955. The trial judge held that the defendants had been negligent; he attributed to the defendants 80% of the fault for the accident and he awarded the plaintiff that proportion of the damages assessed by him. On appeal by the defendants it was **Held** by the Supreme Court (Henchy, Hederman and McCarthy JJ.), in allowing the appeal, 1, that there was no evidence that the plaintiff's husband had fallen from a place at which he was required or had to work within the meaning of s. 37 of the Act of 1955 and that, accordingly, the defendants had not been in breach of their statutory duty under that section (McCarthy J. dissenting). 2. *Per* Henchy and Hederman JJ. — That the defendants' implied invitation to the sub-contractor to enter upon the defendants' factory premises extended only to those parts of the premises to which access was necessary for the purposes for which the sub-contractor had been engaged by the contractor. 3. *Per* Henchy and Hederman JJ. — That, even if the skylight through which the plaintiff's husband had fallen had been within the area of the defendants' invitation, the skylight had not been a hidden or unusual danger. *Daly* v. *Avonmore Creameries Ltd.*

(S.C.) [1984] I.R.131

19. —— **Licensor and licensee** — *Infant licensee — Roman Catholic church — Infant exhorted to visit church by parish priest — Candelabra in front of shrine — Plaintiff lighting candle as devotional exercise — Plaintiff required to lean over row of lighted candles to insert her candle — Plaintiff's clothing catching fire — Whether candelabra a danger — Whether candelabra a concealed danger — Foreseeability — Factors to be considered — Age of plaintiff — Absence of warning — Whether defendant ought to have warned plaintiff — Whether warning would have been heeded — Damages — Personal*

NEGLIGENCE—Occupier.

injuries — Burning — Scarring — Whether damages excessive.

Practice — Supreme Court — Grounds of appeal — Whether Supreme Court should hear or pronounce upon an issue not argued before and determined by the High Court.] The plaintiff, a 9 year old schoolgirl, went during the school lunch break to her local church to light a candle at a shrine. She, in common with the other children attending the local school, had been encouraged so to do by the parish priest. The candelabra in front of the shrine stood on a marble topped stand three feet two and a half inches in height and consisted of 3 rows of candles four and a half inches apart. The candelabra was three feet three inches wide and one foot two inches deep. There was a difference in height between the front and middle row of three quarter's of an inch and between the middle and back rows of one and three eighth inches. The candles supplied for the shrine were three and a quarter inches tall of which one and a quarter inches was inserted into the sprigget of the candle holder. There was some difficulty in inserting the candles fully. The plaintiff was four feet four and three quarter inches tall with a shoulder measurement of three feet and eight inches. The only vacant space for the plaintiff's candle was in the middle row. She leaned over the front row of candles to insert her candle and the sleeve of her blouse caught fire. The plaintiff was badly burned on her shoulder and arm. She required hospitalisation for treatment and skin grafts to minimise the effect of scarring. At the time of trial the plaintiff had noticeable permanent scarring which was not expected to improve. By agreement between the parties the case was tried in the High Court on the basis that the defendant as occupier of the church owed a duty to the plaintiff as a 9 year old licensee not to expose her without warning to a concealed danger of which he actually knew. Counsel on behalf of the defendant sought a non-suit arguing firstly, that there was no evidence of a concealed danger and secondly, that it was a danger of which the plaintiff had actual knowledge. The defendant's application was refused and the jury returned a verdict that the candle stand was a concealed danger; that the defendant had been negligent and that the plaintiff had not been guilty of contributory negligence. They awarded £20,000 for pain and suffering to date and £54,000 for pain and suffering into the future. The defendant appealed to the Supreme Court on the grounds firstly, that the trial judge should have withdrawn the case from the jury; secondly, that the jury ought to have found contributory negligence and thirdly, that the awards of general damages were excessive. **Held** by the Supreme Court (Finlay C.J., Henchy, Griffin, Hederman and McCarthy JJ.), in dismissing the

NEGLIGENCE—*continued.*

appeal, 1, (McCarthy J. dissenting) that having regard to the fact that it had been accepted both at the trial and before the Supreme Court that the duty owed by the defendant to the plaintiff was that of an occupier to a licensee not to expose her without warning to a danger of which he actually knew, it was unnecessary to consider what the law actually was; nor, having regard to the fact that the law had not been argued before the court, should the court pronounce upon it. 2. That the danger which caused the accident was not simply the existence of flames from lighted candles but arose from the juxtaposition of the rows of candles in the candelabra coupled with the relationship between the height of the candelabra and the height of the plaintiff, the necessity to lean over the first row of lighted candles and the difficulty in inserting them into the stand. *Boughton* v. *Bray Urban District Council* [1949] Ir. Jur. Rep. 57 and *Bohane* v. *Driscoll* [1929] I.R. 428 considered. 3. That it was open to a reasonable jury on the facts to conclude that the precise danger was one which would have been concealed from a child of the plaintiff's age. 4. That the test to be applied in determining want of reasonable care was whether a reasonable person in the position of the defendant would have anticipated the accident which happened as a natural and probable consequence of the neglect relied on by the plaintiff. 5. That while in many cases a warning given to small children was unlikely to be heeded or might even encourage children to approach the danger, in the special circumstances of this case and in particular having regard to the fact that the plaintiff had frequently been encouraged by the parish priest who was a person of considerable authority to visit the church at a time when there would be no adult supervision, it was open to the jury to hold that a warning if given would have been heeded and that the defendant was negligent in failing to give such a warning. 6. That since no application had been made to the trial judge to direct the jury to find contributory negligence on the plaintiff's part, the Supreme Court should not entertain an appeal against his failure to do so. 7. That the award of £20,000 for general damages to date was a little low and the award of £54,000 for pain and suffering into the future was high. The total sum of £74,000, though generous, was not so excessive as to warrant intervention by the court. *Per curiam.* Except in unusual circumstances dictated by the requirements of natural justice and in very rare cases the Supreme Court should not entertain a ground of appeal unless the point had been argued and decided in the High Court. *Per* Griffin J. The plaintiff is not obliged to show that the occupier realised that the facts of whose existence he was fully aware constituted a danger. If the occupier knows of the physical facts which constitute the danger and a reasonable man having that knowledge would appreciate the risk, the occupier is not excused by his own failure to appreciate the risk involved. *Per* McCarthy J. That the status distinctions of contractual invitee, invitee, licensee and trespasser which were part of the traditional approach to occupier's liability are wholly artificial and do not properly form part of the law. The liability of the occupier of premises to any person injured thereon should be tested in the same manner as any other action laid in negligence — whether or not there was a failure to take reasonable care, with such guidance as to the application of that principle as may be necessary in the circumstances of a particular case. *Rooney* v. *Connolly*

(S.C.) [1986] I.R.572 ; [1987] ILRM 768

PROFESSIONAL
see also Nos. 1-3, 13, 15, 32

Architect, *see* Nos. 1, 3, 17

20. —— **Banker** — *Customer involved in business with relative making payment by cheque to customers — Customer allowed to maintain account beyond overdraft — Customer's relative's business collapsed — Customer requesting information from bank on relative's creditworthiness — Customer's business collapsing — Whether bank liable.*] The plaintiff had a number of accounts with the defendant bank at its branch in Castlerea, County Roscommon and he was allowed overdraft facilities up to £65,000 until 1980. He was involved in cattle-dealing and throughout 1979 and 1980 had extensive dealings with his cousin whose company had a meat factory in Co. Roscommon, and who also, in his personal capacity, conducted a large scale cattle market export business between Ireland and England. The plaintiff's cousin was based in Silloth in the north-east of England and the plaintiff was paid by means of personal cheques of his cousin drawn on an Irish punt account maintained by him with the National Westminster Bank at Silloth. The plaintiff lodged these cheques at the Castlerea branch for collection, the proceeds to be credited to his account when collected. From the outset considerable delays were experienced by the defendant in collecting payment from the Silloth account. Notwithstanding measures taken to expedite the collection and payment of the cheques and the normal working of the postal system, the delays involved in collecting the sums due and crediting them to the plaintiff's account continued to give rise to persistent complaints. In the process the plaintiff was overdrawing his account far beyond the permitted limit. In the last two months of

1980 six cheques totalling a sum £252,254 were dishonoured, the business enterprise of the plaintiff's cousin collapsed, and though the plaintiff obtained judgment against his cousin in respect of this figure, it proved worthless. The plaintiff then issued proceedings claiming that he should be recouped by the defendant for the losses which he incurred by reason of the collapse of this cousin's business enterprises and the default in payments to the plaintiff which flowed from that collapse. He claimed damages for breach of contract or alternatively for negligence, saying that the defendant as his banker owed him a duty to exercise diligence in collecting payment on foot of the cheques lodged with them for collection, that they failed to do so; that he looked for advice from them as to the reliability of his cousin and as to his prospects of getting payment on cheques accepted by him and to be accepted by him from his cousin and that the bank negligently led him to believe that he had nothing to fear in this regard, when they knew or should have known that the contrary was true. As a result the plaintiff stated that he was induced to continue doing business with his cousin and to continue taking his cheques in payment for large consignments of livestock until eventually his cousin was no longer able to meet his liabilities. At the hearing the branch manager of the Castlerea branch gave evidence that the plaintiff was in constant communication with him during 1979 and 1980 about the delays in getting payment on his cousin's cheques and the nature and extent of his cousin's assets. While he insisted that the plaintiff had never addressed a specific inquiry to him about his cousin's creditworthiness, he conceded that if there was a risk, he had a duty to the customer to warn him in continuing to do business with his cousin and accepting his cheques, notwithstanding the long delays in receiving payment on foot thereof. **Held** by O'Hanlon J. in finding for the plaintiff, 1, in the circumstances the obligations of the bank towards its customer extended well beyond the conventional duty of merely presenting the cheques for payment with promptitude. 2. Consequently, the two duties, that of collecting banker and that of advising banker towards its customer tended to merge into one in the present case. The bank was in possession of a considerable body of evidence, built up over a lengthy period, which cast doubt on the reliability of the plaintiff's cousin. They knew that the plaintiff, another of its customers, was regularly staking what could have been his entire fortune on transactions confined to this single, suspect individual, and they allowed him to overdraw up to four or five times his permitted limit for that purpose, without doing anything to protect him from the dangers inherent in this course. If anything, they must be regarded as

NEGLIGENCE—Professional.

having encouraged him to persist in his dealings with his cousin. 3. In failing to advise him in a careful manner when consulted about his business dealings with his cousin and in failing in its capacity as collecting banker to take the steps necessary to protect the interest of its customer, the defendant was in breach of the duty it owed to the plaintiff. *Towey* v. *Ulster Bank Ltd.*

(H.C.) [1987] ILRM 142

Builder, *see* Nos. 1-3
Doctor, *see* Nos. 13, 15

21. —— **Solicitor** — *Duty of care — Compromise of action — Agreement — Option — Failure to exercise by solicitor on behalf of client — Failure to notify client — Whether breach of duty of care — Whether loss suffered by client attributable to breach of duty of care — Whether client entitled to damages.*] By a written agreement dated 6 July, 1963, the owner and occupier of land adjoining the plaintiff's quarry agreed to grant to the plaintiff a right of way through his said lands for five years in consideration of the sum of £100. The plaintiff sought to exercise his option of renewal in May, 1968, which was rejected by the owner of the land. The plaintiff engaged the defendant in his capacity as solicitor with regard to the renewal, and also instructed him to institute proceedings on his behalf to establish his rights concerning the renewal of the said agreement. The defendant sought counsel's opinion and explained the full position to the plaintiff on 2 July, 1973. However he did not exercise the option for renewal on the plaintiff's behalf before 6 July, 1973. In the meantime the owner of the land instituted proceedings against the plaintiff for nuisance and trespass. These proceedings were subsequently settled and a consent was entered between the parties and filed in court. The owner agreed to grant to the plaintiff a right of way for a period of 20 years at a rent of £200 for the first five years, with further subsequent increases provided for; the plaintiff was not entitled to discharge water from his lands onto his land. The plaintiff never exercised his option to execute the agreement provided for in the consent, but chose to cease working the quarry. The plaintiff claimed damages for loss and damage as a result of (1) the defendant's failure to prosecute the plaintiff's claim against the owner with regard to the plaintiff's rights under the agreement during the period 6 July, 1968, to 5 July, 1973; (2) the defendant's failure to exercise on behalf of the plaintiff his right to renew the agreement for the period of 6 July, 1973, to 5 July, 1978. **Held** by Hamilton J. in refusing to grant the plaintiff damages, 1, the defendant was not negligent or in breach of contract in the prosecution by him of the case against

NEGLIGENCE—*continued.*

the owner of the land, and the delay in the institution of the proceedings by the defendant was the sole fault of the plaintiff. 2. The defendant was negligent in failing to contact the plaintiff between 2 and 5 July, 1973, to inform him of the danger inherent in his failure to exercise the option and further that he did not intend to exercise the option on his behalf. 3. The plaintiff's loss was not attributable to the defendant's negligence but was attributable to his own decision not to avail of the agreement. 4. The plaintiff failed to establish that the loss and damage suffered by him was a consequence of a breach of duty of care owed to him by the defendant. 5. The quarry was rendered non-viable as a result of the owner of the land insisting that the plaintiff was not entitled to discharge water from the quarry on his land, and not as a result of the increase in rent. *McCarthy* v. *Moloney*

(H.C.) [1979] ILRM 39

22. —— **Solicitor** — *Duty of care — Contract for the sale of land — Purchaser successfully seeking rescission of contract — Whether vendor's solicitor negligent.*] By order dated 13 June, 1975, Hamilton J. sitting without a jury in the High Court held that the purchasers of a licensed premises, a petrol filling station and other lands situated at Rooskey, Co. Leitrim were entitled to rescind the contract with the plaintiff and to, *inter alia,* the return of their deposit money. Those proceedings were based on an allegation that the purchasers had been induced to enter into the contract by an express warranty made through their agent by the plaintiff, verbally, that the turnover derived from the property during the immediate preceding financial year was between £60,000 and £65,000 and that in his annual return of income to the Revenue Commissioners the plaintiff had returned a turnover in the region of £60,000 in respect of the property. It was further alleged, *inter alia,* that the said representation was false. The plaintiff denied the claims and counterclaimed for an order of specific performance of the contract. Hamilton J. found that the representation was made and the plaintiff appealed the decision to the Supreme Court which on 25 October, 1976, dismissed the appeal. In 1979 the plaintiff instituted proceedings against his former solicitor for negligence and breach of contract in carrying out the work concerning the sale up to the time it was repudiated by the purchasers and in the manner in which the defence of the rescission of the contract was handled by them. By order dated 9 July, 1981, McMahon J. in the High Court dismissed the plaintiff's claim having acceded to the defendant's application to withdraw the case from the jury on the basis that

NEGLIGENCE—Professional.

no *prima facie* evidence of negligence causing damage was established. The plaintiff appealed. **Held** by the Supreme Court (Finlay C.J., Griffin and Hederman JJ.) in dismissing the appeal: The trial judge correctly held that the defendants were neither negligent in connection with the carrying on of their work concerning the sale of the premises up to the time it was repudiated by the purchaser nor in the manner in which the defence of the action brought by the purchaser for rescission of the contract was handled. The duty of a solicitor with regard to the conduct of a case in court where counsel has been briefed is first to brief appropriate and competent counsel and secondly, to instruct them properly in regard to the facts of the case which he has obtained from his client, and to make provision for the attendance of appropriate witnesses and other proofs. A solicitor has not got any vicarious responsibility for the individual conduct of counsel. *Per curiam:* The basic cause of the problems of the plaintiff and his wife, as found by the High Court and affirmed by the Supreme Court, was that the plaintiff falsely represented the turnover of his business to induce the purchasers to bid for it. *Fallon* v. *Gannon*

(S.C.) [1988] ILRM 193

23. —— **Solicitor** — *Sale of land — Contract — Solicitor acting for vendor — Agreement for sale of land reached — Purchaser refusing to sign formal contract — Sale called off and new agreement for sale concluded with third party — First purchaser obtaining specific performance of his agreement — Second sale aborted — Vendor incurring losses out of both transactions — Whether vendor's solicitors liable in negligence.*] In proceedings entitled *Kelly* v. *Park Hall School* and reported in [1979] I.R. 340, K. obtained against the plaintiff school a decree of specific performance of a contract for the sale to him of certain of the school's lands. No formal contract had been entered into between the parties but the Supreme Court held that a letter written by an auctioneer, W., acting for the plaintiff to one of the plaintiff's advisers and confirming that he had agreed terms for the sale of the lands to K., constituted a sufficient note or memorandum of the agreement to sell for the purpose of the Statute of Frauds, despite the letter stating that the terms had been agreed "subject to contract". The Supreme Court further held that the circumstances of the sale justified the implication of a term requiring K. to execute a formal written contract without delay but that the plaintiff had waived that requirement by its failure to furnish that document without delay. The defendant solicitors who had been retained by the plaintiff were aware of the contents of W.'s letter. After K. had returned unsigned the formal contract

NEGLIGENCE—*continued.*

which, after some delay, had been furnished to him by the defendants, the plaintiff offered the lands for sale by tender. K., without having previously intimated to the plaintiff or the defendants that he regarded the plaintiff as contractually bound to sell the lands, then instituted the proceedings referred to above at which stage counsel were briefed by the defendants to advise and act on behalf of the plaintiff at every step in the proceedings which ensued. Pending the hearing of K.'s action the plaintiff had accepted a tender for the lands submitted by H. The plaintiff subsequently commenced these proceedings against the defendants claiming damages for negligence and breach of contract by the defendants in their handling of the sale, the damages being claimed consisting of the costs incurred in defending K.'s proceedings and of the monies and costs paid in settlement of an action that H. had brought against it for failure to complete the sale to him. It was alleged *inter alia* that the defendants had been negligent in failing to advise the plaintiff that the oral contract for sale as evidenced by W.'s letter was a valid and binding contract and failing to act with expedition in sending out a draft contract to K. At the trial of the action, on the application of the defendants to the trial judge (O'Hanlon J.) to have the plaintiff's claim dismissed upon the close of its case, it was **Held** by O'Hanlon J., in dismissing the plaintiff's claim, 1, that, having regard to the uncertain state of the law in this jurisdiction and in England in the years 1977 and 1978 concerning the ability of correspondence containing the words 'subject to contract' to constitute a note or memorandum for the purpose of the Statute of Frauds, the correct course for the defendant to have adopted in the light of the correspondence to have passed between the parties was to proceed on the assumption that whilst the position was not free from doubt by reason of the contents of that correspondence that, nevertheless, no binding contract had yet been concluded and to send on a draft contract in the conventional form for execution by K. *Kelly* v. *Park Hall School* [1979] I.R. 340; *Law* v. *Robert Roberts & Co.* [1964] I.R. 292; *Mulhall* v. *Haren* [1981] I.R. 364; *Law* v. *Jones* [1974] Ch. 112; *Tiverton Ltd.* v. *Wearwell Ltd.* [1975] Ch. 146 and *Casey* v. *Irish Intercontinental Bank* [1979] I.R. 364 considered. 2. That as the defendants had not been requested by the plaintiff to prepare a formal contract in anticipation of a sale being agreed and as the delay in producing such a contract after a sale had been agreed was fairly attributable to the necessity of procuring a map of the lands, the defendants could not be blamed for the failure to furnish a formal contract to K. without delay. 3. That after K. had returned the formal contract unsigned, the defendants had behaved properly in not enquiring of K.'s intentions in the matter lest it would have suggested to him that they detected some weakness in their client's position and thereby provoked him into pursuing the matter further. Neither was there an obligation on the defendants to bring to the notice of the plaintiff the mere possibility of a claim being made by K. or the possibility that it might be successful. 4. That upon K. instituting his proceedings against the plaintiff the defendants had chosen the only proper course open to them at that stage of instructing counsel in the matter, the views of whom regarding the litigation the plaintiff was kept duly apprised of by the defendants. 5. That, accordingly, the evidence adduced on behalf of the plaintiff failed to disclose a *prima facie* cause of action against the defendants for negligence or breach of contractual duty to use due care and skill as the plaintiff's solicitors. *Park Hall School Ltd.* v. *Overend*

(H.C.) [1987] I.R.1; [1987] ILRM 345

24. —— **Solicitor** — *Sale of land — Deposits prior to contract — Payment to vendor's solicitor — Vendor in receivership — Loss of deposits — Capacity in which deposits received by vendor's solicitor — Correspondence from purchaser's solicitor — Whether sufficient notice to vendor's solicitor to hold deposits as stakeholders — Negligence — Liability of purchasers' solicitor for loss of deposits.*] The first and second plaintiffs were interested, independently, in purchasing two flats in a proposed development. The plaintiffs were informed by the selling agent that a booking deposit of £3,000 would be required to reserve a site. The selling agent, who acted on behalf of the builder/vendor, explained that all deposits and stage payments would be paid to the builder/vendor. The plaintiffs were reluctant to pay money to the builder as there were no buildings on the site. The plaintiffs retained the services of the first defendant, a solicitor, to act on their behalf in connection with the proposed purchases. The first defendant advised each plaintiff of the risks involved in paying money to the builder/vendor. On the advice of the first defendant, each plaintiff wrote a cheque for £3,000 payable to the second, third and fourth defendants (hereinafter referred to as "the second defendants") a firm of solicitors acting for the builder/vendor. The first plaintiff paid a further sum of £5,000 balance deposit to the second defendants. The plaintiffs believed that the first defendant would arrange matters so that the deposits would be held by the second defendants until completion of the purchases. It was the intention of the first defendant that the second defendants should hold the deposits as stakeholder and not as agent of the

builder/vendor but he did not make this clear to the second defendants in correspondence or otherwise. On receipt of the cheques, the second defendants, in accordance with instructions and normal policy, endorsed them in favour of the builder/vendor. Before the contracts were signed the builder/vendor went into receivership and the plaintiffs lost the full amount of their deposits. The plaintiffs brought an action against the first and second defendants seeking to recover their losses. **Held** by Barrington J., 1, the first defendant did not exercise reasonable professional skill in that he failed to put the second defendants on notice that the deposits were being paid to them as stakeholders. 2. The plaintiffs were entitled to recover their losses against the first defendant. *Leemac Overseas Investments Ltd.* v. *Harvey* [1973] I.R. 160; *Sorrell* v. *Finch* [1977] A.C. 728 and *Burt* v. *Claude Cousins* [1971] 2 Q.B. 426 considered. *Desmond and Boyle* v. *Brophy*

(H.C.) [1985] I.R. 449; [1985] ILRM 547

25. —— **Solicitor** — *Sale of land — Licensed premises — Nature of licence attached to premises — Plaintiffs required premises with full seven days publican's licence — Vendor holding hotel licence — Plaintiffs' solicitor's failure to discover true nature of licence — Insufficient enquiries by solicitor — Damages — Inland Revenue Act,* 1880 (*c.* 20), *s.* 43(4) — *Licensing (Ireland) Act,* 1902 (*c.* 18), *s.* 2 — *Intoxicating Liquor Act,* 1960 (*No.* 18), *ss.* 19-20.] The identical form of licence is used for a publican's licence (ordinary) and certain hotel licences granted under s. 2, sub-s. 2 of the Licensing (Ireland) Act, 1902. A note on the back of each licence points this fact out. Such hotel licences are granted subject to certain restrictions which do not apply in the case of publicans' licences, namely that the premises must be operated as a hotel. In certain circumstances the holder of such a hotel licence is entitled to operate a public bar in the hotel in which case an inspection of the premises would not reveal the true nature of the licence. An examination of the Register of Licences maintained in the District Court would however reveal the nature of the licence granted. The plaintiffs wished to purchase a licensed premises to be operated as a public house. The first plaintiff saw an advertisement for the sale of premises known as "The Ivy Leaf", Rathdrum in the County of Wicklow ("the premises"). He inspected the premises which had a bar and lounge but no reception area. The premises appeared to be a public house with considerable residential accommodation. The plaintiffs duly instructed the defendant as their solicitor in and about the purchase of the premises. The defendant knew the plaintiffs intended to operate the

premises as a public house. The defendant negotiated the sale of the premises. In the requisitions on title raised by the defendant the vendor was asked to specify the exact type of licence attaching to the premises. By way of reply thereto the vendor furnished the licence to the defendant. The defendant made no inspection of the Register of Licences. The plaintiffs took possession of the premises and operated same as a public house. When the plaintiffs sought to renew the licence attaching to the premises at the Annual Licensing District Court it transpired that the licence was a hotel licence within the meaning of s. 2, sub-s. 2 of the aforesaid Act. Renewal of the licence was refused on the grounds, *inter alia,* that the premises was not operated as a hotel within the meaning of the licensing laws. The decision of the District Court was upheld on appeal. The plaintiffs instituted proceedings against the defendant for damages for negligence and breach of contract. **Held** by Murphy J., in allowing the plaintiffs' claim, 1, that the defendant, as a solicitor professing to act on behalf of the plaintiffs in an important transaction involving a licence issued under the Licensing Acts, must be deemed to be familiar with those Acts and the different types of premises in respect of which such licences could be granted. 2. That the defendant was under a duty not only to make the necessary enquiries so as to advise the plaintiffs adequately with regard to the exact nature of the licence attaching to the premises but also to make those enquiries at a time when his advice based on the replies to the enquiries would be of maximum value to his client. *Taylor* v. *Ryan and Jones* (Unreported, High Court, Finlay P. 10 March, 1983) considered. 3. That in assessing damages the plaintiffs were entitled to the difference between the purchase price of the premises and the market value of same without a publican's licence together with a sum for loss of profits but were not entitled to damages for mental distress as the same were not reasonably foreseeable. *Ford* v. *White and Co.* [1964] 1 W.L.R. 885 applied. *Kelly* v. *Crowley*

(H.C.) [1985] I.R.212

26. —— **Solicitor** — *Sale of land — Registered land — Plaintiff wishing to purchase house to be built — Sale to be effected by building company — Plaintiff consulting defendant solicitors — Building contract executed and payments by instalments by plaintiff — Title investigated by defendants on behalf of plaintiff — Investigation not made until after completion of building and making of payments — Discovery of pre-existing equitable mortgage by deposit of land certificate — Mortgage registered as charge in Companies Office prior to execution of building contract — Insolvency of building company — Refusal of*

mortgagee to release house unless paid proportion of mortgage debt — Whether defendants should have examined title before execution of building contract — No custom of solicitors — Whether defendants negligent — Companies Act, 1963 (*No.* 33), *ss.* 99, 104.] On 12 July, 1972, a building company mortgaged certain registered land by depositing the certificate of title with the mortgagee. The mortgage, being a charge on land created by the building company, was registered in the Companies Office by the company as required by s. 99 of the Companies Act, 1963. On 19 February, 1973, the building company entered into an agreement for a lease of part of the land to the plaintiffs, and also a building agreement with the plaintiffs. Under the building agreement the building company was to build a house on the land for £9,450.00 which was to be paid by the plaintiffs in instalments at certain stages in the building. The plaintiffs entered into this arrangement, and made certain stage payments, unaware of the mortgage. The defendants were engaged as solicitors by the plaintiffs. The defendants did not execute a search against the building company in the Companies Office as it was the universal conveyancing practice in Ireland not to do so. Had they done so they would have become aware of the mortgage. In October, 1974, the building company went into liquidation. The liquidator granted a lease of the lands to the plaintiffs, but the mortgagee refused to release the certificate of title to allow the registration of the lease until it was paid £6,000.00 on foot of the mortgage. The plaintiffs claimed in the High Court damages for negligence and breach of contract against the defendants. **Held** by Finlay P., in dismissing the claim, that as the defendants had followed universal conveyancing practice, they were not negligent. *O'Donovan* v. *Cork County Council* [1967] I.R. 173 considered. *Simmons* v. *Pennington & Son* [1955] 1 W.L.R. 183 approved. *Per* Finlay P., to some extent . . . the universality of a particular practice adopted by an entire profession must itself be evidence that it is not a practice which has inherent defects which ought to be obvious to any person giving the matter due consideration. On appeal by the plaintiffs it was **Held** by the Supreme Court (Walsh, Henchy, Griffin, Hederman and McCarthy JJ.), in allowing the appeal, that as the universal conveyancing practice relied upon by the defendants had inherent defects which ought to have been obvious to any person giving the matter due consideration, the defendants were negligent in failing to execute a search in the Companies Office. *O'Donovan* v. *Cork County Council* [1967] I.R. 173 considered. *Simmons* v. *Pennington & Son* [1955] 1 W.L.R. 183 distinguished. *Per* Henchy J., a person cannot be

NEGLIGENCE—Professional.

said to be acting reasonably if he automatically and mindlessly follows a practice of others when by taking thought he would have realised that the practice in question was fraught with peril for his client and was readily avoidable or remediable. *Roche* v. *Peilow*

(H.C., S.C.) [1985] I.R.232; [1986] ILRM 189

ROAD ACCIDENTS
see also Nos. 15, 31

27. —— **"Public place"** — *Accident occurring in the grounds of a country house — Plaintiff suffering personal injuries — Judgment entered against defendant — Plaintiff failing to recover — Plaintiff seeking liberty to execute judgment against defendant's motor insurance company — Whether liability for which an approved policy of insurance required — Whether accident occurred in a "public place" — Road Traffic Act,* 1961 (*No.* 24), *ss.* 3, 56, 76.] The plaintiff, having obtained a judgment for £9,000 against the defendant for personal injuries sustained in a motor-car accident in the grounds of Corduffstown House, failed subsequently to recover any portion of her damages. Relying on s. 76 of the Road Traffic Act, 1961, she brought a motion seeking liberty to enforce her award against the defendant's insurer, Messrs. Ensign Motor Policies at Lloyds. The insurer, once joined in the proceedings, defended the application on the basis that the roadway where the accident occurred was not a public place within the meaning of s. 3 of the Road Traffic Act, that there was consequently no duty on the defendant to be insured for his driving at that place under s. 56 of the Act, and that the plaintiff could therefore place no reliance on s. 76. **Held** by Hamilton J., refusing the plaintiff's application to enforce her award against the insurance company, 1, that, on the evidence, the public at large did not have access to the place where the accident happened, and that it was not therefore a 'public place': *Harrison* v. *Hill* 1932 SC (J) 13 applied. 2. That 'public' means the public generally and not any particular class of the public. *Stanbridge* v. *Healy*

(H.C.) [1985] ILRM 290

STATUTORY DUTY
see also Nos. 2, 3, 11, 12, 18

28. —— **Burial grounds** — *Cattle wandering onto cemetery — Cattle poisoned by eating yew leaves — Wall between pastureland and cemetery damaged — Whether local authority negligent or in breach of statutory duty in not having wall repaired — Public Health (Ireland) Act,* 1878 (*c.* 52), *ss.* 181, 185, 193, 234.] Part 3 of the Public Health (Ireland) Act, 1878, is a re-enactment with amendments of the greater part of the Burial

NEGLIGENCE—Statutory Duty.

Grounds (Ireland) Act, 1856, and its Amendment Act of 1860, both repealed. The declared and primary purpose of the duties imposed on a Local Authority therein are the protection of public health, the maintenance of public decency and the prevention of the violation of the remains of deceased persons. S. 193 confers power on a Local Authority to punish trespassers in a cemetery. Rule 1 of the 1888 Regulations made pursuant to s.181 of the said Act obliges the Local Authority to maintain every burial ground sufficiently fenced. Eight milch cows, the property of the plaintiff, a farmer of twenty-seven years standing, had wandered through a gap in a boundary wall between the plaintiff's pastureland and a cemetery, the responsibility of the defendant. When in the cemetery, the cattle were poisoned by eating yew leaves which grew there. During the twelve months prior to the incident, the plaintiff had noticed that the wall was damaged, but he did not think his cattle would wander through. He took no steps to prevent such an occurrence, neither did he inform the defendant of the condition of the wall. The plaintiff sought damages from the defendant on the basis either of breach of the statutory duty imposed on the defendant by s. 185 of the 1878 Act, or Regulations made on 6 July, 1888, pursuant to s. 181 of the said Act, or of negligence at common law. At the hearing, the defendant admitted that the maintenance of the wall was its responsibility and that it had since been repaired. The defendant gave evidence that the cemetery was inspected and cleaned up annually, and that at the last inspection before the incident complained of, the wall had appeared to be alright at the cemetery side. It was submitted on behalf of the defendant that the plaintiff was not a person who came within the ambit of the purposes of the statutory duty imposed by the Public Health (Ireland) Act, 1878. **Held** by Gannon J. in dismissing the plaintiff's claim, 1, not every failure to comply with the statutory duty from which damage ensues entitles the person damnified to recover compensation from the party in breach, in a claim for damages founded on that ground alone. *Monk* v. *Warbey* [1935] 1 K.B. 75 applied. 2. The Act of 1878 is an enactment for the benefit of the public at large, and the duties imposed therein are imposed for the benefit of the public at large, and not for that of any individual or class of individuals. 3. The provisions of s. 193 of the said Act which confer powers on the defendant to punish trespassers are inconsistent with the imposition upon the defendant of any duty to trespassers. 4. The circumstances of the case were such that the defendant should have foreseen as a reasonable probability that there was a risk to the plaintiff's cattle upon the defendant's property. 5. Notwithstanding the

NEGLIGENCE—Statutory Duty.

foregoing, the defendant could not reasonably have foreseen that the plaintiff's cattle would enter the area of risk, and consequently, there was no failure on the part of the defendant to take reasonable care to avoid such eventuality. 6. The standard of care owed by the defendant to the plaintiff is that due to an experienced adult farmer of twenty-seven years standing, accustomed, *inter alia,* to the care of herd of milch cows in all seasons. *Purtill* v. *Athlone U.D.C.* [1968] I.R. 205; *McNamara* v. *E.S.B.* [1975] I.R. 1 considered. *Walsh* v. *Kilkenny County Council*

(H.C.) [1978] ILRM 1

29. —— **Canal** — *Nuisance — Breach of statutory duty — Lack of maintenance — Flooding — Whether commissioners' duty to maintain canal — Whether commissioners negligent — Whether plaintiff contributorily negligent — Damages — Wexford Harbour Embankment Act,* 1852 (*c.* cli), *ss.* 25, 26, 45.] The Wexford Harbour Embankment Act, 1852, imposed responsibility upon the defendants for maintaining a catchment canal for the proper drainage of lands adjoining the Wexford North Slob, which was reclaimed land. The plaintiff, an adjoining landowner, claimed that her lands were flooded and unusable for long periods due to the negligence of the defendants in not properly maintaining the canal. Following written representations by the plaintiff to this effect, the defendants commenced work upon the canal. In this, they were hindered to some extent by the plaintiff herself, in that she refused to allow them to work on her side of the canal. The plaintiff then initiated proceedings claiming a mandatory injunction to the defendants to maintain the canal, a declaration that the defendants were under a duty to so maintain it, a declaration that, where necessary in order to discharge the said duty, the defendants were obliged to adapt and improve the canal, and damages for nuisance and breach of statutory duty. **Held** by Lynch J. in refusing the injunctions and declarations sought, in making other and more appropriate declarations and in awarding modified damages for loss suffered in respect of the letting value of the flooded lands, 1, the defendants, upon becoming aware of their statutory responsibilities, had commenced work upon the canal, and an injunction would not be appropriate. 2. The negligence of the defendants had been contributed to by the negligence of the plaintiff herself in not maintaining adequate drainage schemes on her land. Their efforts to remedy their negligence had also been hindered by the plaintiff. 3. The plaintiff could recover damages only to the extent of her own loss, and such damages would be modified by reference to

NEGLIGENCE—*continued.*

the plaintiff's hindrance and contributory negligence. *Stelzer* v. *Wexford North Slob Commissioners*

(H.C.) [1988] ILRM 279

30. —— **Housing authority** — *Duty of care — Statutory power of housing authority to make loans to persons of limited means to enable purchase of dwelling — Requirement that housing authority be satisfied as to value of house — Plaintiff applying for loan — House valued by valuer on behalf of housing authority — No structural inspection carried out by local authority — House valued at 25,000 — Loan granted to plaintiff — House seriously defective — Whether housing authority owed purchaser a common law duty of care in valuing house — Housing Authorities (Loans for Acquisition or Construction of Houses) Regulations,* 1972 (*S.I. No.* 29) — *Housing Act,* 1966 (*No.* 21), *s.* 39.

Statutory duty — Duty of care — Housing authority — Statutory power of housing authority to make loans to enable purchase of dwelling — Requirement that housing authority be satisfied as to value of dwelling — Plaintiff applying for loan — Valuation carried out on behalf of housing authority by valuer — No structural inspection carried out by housing authority — House seriously defective — Whether housing authority exercising its statutory functions owed a private law duty of care to purchaser — Housing Authorities (Loans for Acquisition or Construction of Houses) Regulations, 1972 (*S.I. No.* 29) — *Housing Act,* 1966 (*No.* 21), *s.* 39.] Section 39, sub-s. 1 of the Housing Act, 1966, provides that "(1) A housing authority may, subject to regulations made by the Minister [for Local Government] for the purposes of this section . . . lend money to a person for the purpose of acquiring or constructing a house." Regulation 12 of the Housing Authorities (Loans for Acquisition or Construction of Houses) Regulations, 1972, requires that a housing authority, before making a loan, should be satisfied, *inter alia,* that the value of the house is sufficient to provide adequate security for the loan. By reg. 4 (1) of the Regulations of 1972 the value of the house is "the amount which, in the opinion of the housing authority, the house, if sold on the open market, might reasonably be expected to realise . . ." The defendant council, in pursuance of its statutory duty under the Act of 1966 and Regulations of 1972, published a scheme for the making of loans. That scheme provided, *inter alia,* that: "6. No advance shall be made by the Council until the Council is satisfied as a result of a report by the Council's valuer, as to the actual value of an existing house . . ." As part of the scheme the Council further published an application form which provided that: "2. Applications shall be

NEGLIGENCE—Statutory Duty.

considered only from persons who are unable to obtain loans from commercial agencies . . . and whose circumstances would otherwise necessitate their being re-housed by the Council." In July, 1980, the first plaintiff agreed to purchase from the first defendant a bungalow which had been constructed by the first defendant at D., Co. Louth for the sum of £24,000, of which £3,000 was paid by way of deposit. Both before and after the agreement to purchase was concluded the bungalow was inspected by the plaintiffs but neither had any qualification in house construction and they did not have it professionally surveyed. In August, 1980, the first plaintiff applied to the defendant Council as housing authority for Co. Louth, for a loan in the sum of £12,000 under the provisions of the Act of 1966, and paid an application fee of £10. The defendant Council, in purported pursuance of its statutory duties, retained a valuer to value the premises. The valuer, who had no qualifications in building construction, inspected the bungalow and found no defects. He reported it to be in good repair and valued it at approximately £25,000. The plaintiffs went into occupation in December, 1981, but very soon began to experience difficulties with dampness and a smoking chimney. In August, 1982, the plaintiffs had the bungalow surveyed by an engineer who reported that it was structurally unsound, a source of danger and a risk to health. The plaintiffs were advised to abandon the bungalow which they did. The plaintiffs brought proceedings against the builder/vendor, the defendant Council and the valuer. In the High Court Costello J. gave judgment for the plaintiffs against the first and second defendants and dismissed the claim against the valuer. (See the report at [1985] I.R. 29). The defendant Council appealed to the Supreme Court on the grounds firstly, that it owed no private law duty of care to the plaintiffs; and secondly, that its failure to carry out a detailed structural examination was a policy decision within the discretion of the Council and which was not open to review by the courts. **Held** by the Supreme Court (Finlay C.J., Walsh, Henchy, Griffin and McCarthy JJ.), in dismissing the appeal, 1, that while the Housing Act, 1966, did not create a private duty to take care to prevent damage to purchasers under the scheme, such a duty arose from the relationship between the parties. *Donoghue* v. *Stevenson* [1932] A.C. 562, *Anns* v. *Merton London Borough* [1978] A.C. 728 and *Siney* v. *Corporation of Dublin* [1980] I.R. 400 followed. 2. That it was reasonably foreseeable by the defendant Council that purchasers under the scheme would not only lack the means of having their own expert examination of the house but would also rely, as the plaintiffs did rely, on the fact that the Council was investing its money in the house as a mark

NEGLIGENCE—*continued.*

of its value. *Anns* v. *Merton London Borough* [1978] A.C. 728 followed. 3. That the defendant Council was plainly in breach of its public duty imposed by the Regulations of 1972 to ensure by a proper valuation that the house was an adequate security for the loan which it made. 4. That contrary to the arguments made on its behalf, the carrying out of inspections by qualified engineers would not be so expensive as to substantially reduce the amount of money available to the defendant Council for the purposes of the Act. Accordingly, no question of the reviewability of policy decisions arose. *Per curiam.* That the defendant Council could have avoided the incidence of a duty of care by so providing in the preconditions of its loan. *Harris* v. *Wyne Forest D.C.* [1988] 1 All E.R. 691 considered. *Ward* v. *McMaster*

(S.C.) [1988] I.R.337

Editor's note — For High Court judgment reported at [1985] I.R. 29, *see* No. 2 (above).

31. —— **Local authority** — *Duty of care — Railway bridge — Minimum clearance required by statute of railway company — Whether local authority's roadworks in reducing clearance below statutory minimum wanting in due care — Whether advance warning system agreed between railway company and local authority — Railway Clauses Consolidation Act,* 1845 (*c.* 20), *s.* 49.] The plaintiff sued the first and second-named defendants as a result of an accident that occured when the first-named defendant while driving a low-loader transporting an excavator struck the arch of a railway bridge, tearing open the bridge and making a gap in the railway track. The High Court (Gannon J.) [1983] ILRM 173 found for the plaintiff against both defendants and apportioned the degrees of fault between both defendants on the basis of 90% to the first defendant, and 10% to the second defendant. The second-named defendant appealed the decision of Gannon J. in which he held that, 1, the second-named defendant was negligent in failing to provide advance warning signs and that they reduced the minimum clearance to less than 15 feet when they raised the surface of the road level beneath the railway bridge contrary to s. 49 of the Railway Clauses Consolidation Act, 1845. 2. That there was neither negligence nor breach of statutory duty on the part of the plaintiff. The first-named defendant did not appeal against the order of the High Court nor was he represented or present at the hearing although he was a party to it. The defendants had argued that under the 1845 Act, the plaintiff was under a duty to maintain the minimum clearance and that their own road works did not amount to negligence. **Held** by the Supreme Court (Finlay C.J., Hederman and McCarthy JJ.) in allowing

NEGLIGENCE—Statutory Duty.

the appeal and in dismissing the plaintiff's claim of negligence against the second-named defendant, 1, the trial judge was wrong in fact in deciding that there was in existence an agreement between the plaintiff and the second-named defendant for the necessity of advance warning signs at the bridge. 2. The first-named defendant was ignorant as to the height of his load and the bridge, and therefore irrespective of advance warning signs, would still have attempted to clear the bridge. 3. The first-named defendant was neither aware of nor relied on the statutory requirement of the minimum clearance of 15 feet under the Railway Clauses Consolidation Act, 1845. 4. The fact that the second-named defendant created or left a minimum clearance of 13 feet 10 inches was not an act wanting reasonable care as no evidence was adduced to the contrary. *Coras Iompair Éireann* v. *Carroll*

(S.C.) [1986] ILRM 312

32. —— **Magistrates** — *Liability* — *Jurisdiction* — *False imprisonment* — *Juvenile court made training school order in respect of plaintiff* — *Plaintiff not informed of right to legal aid* — *Order quashed* — *Action against members of juvenile court* — *Whether defendants acted "without jurisdiction or in excess of jurisdiction"* — *Whether liable in civil action for damages* — *Magistrates' Court Act (Northern Ireland),* 1964 (*c.* 21), *s.* 15.] The plaintiff, aged 14 years, was charged with offences relating to a motor vehicle. He pleaded guilty and was ordered to attend an attendance centre. The plaintiff was later charged with failing to attend the attendance centre and was ordered to attend a training school. He was not legally represented and contrary to the requirements of article 15(1) of the Treatment of Offenders (Northern Ireland) Order, 1976, he was not informed of his right to apply for legal aid. On an application for judicial review, the court quashed the order to attend a training school on the grounds that there had been a failure to comply with article 15 of the 1976 Order. The plaintiff commenced an action against the members of the juvenile court claiming damages for, *inter alia*, false imprisonment, trespass to the person and breach of statutory duty. Hutton J. **held,** on a preliminary point of law, that no cause of action lay against the magistrates as they had jurisdiction to make a training school order in respect of the plaintiff and that the failure to inform him of his right to legal aid was merely an irregularity of procedure. The plaintiff appealed. **Held,** by the Court of Appeal, that as the juvenile court had omitted a step that was a vital condition precedent to the existence of its jurisdiction to imprison, it had acted "without jurisdiction or in excess of jurisdiction" within the meaning of section 15 of the Magistrates' Courts Act (Northern Ireland), 1964. Consequently the members of the juvenile court were no longer protected by that section; and the courts were not at liberty to ignore the plain words of the statute on the grounds that it re-enacts the common law and that the court may consider that the common law should be changed in order to bring it into line with modern requirements. *Sirros* v. *Moore* [1975] Q.B. 118 not followed. The defendants appealed to the House of Lords. **Held,** dismissing the appeal, that article 15(1) of the 1976 Order was intended to ensure that a custodial sentence was not imposed for the first time on a defendant who was not legally represented unless such lack of representation was through his own choice; that, although the juvenile court had jurisdiction to try and convict the defendant, the omission to inform him of his right to legal aid amounted to a failure to fulfill a statutory condition precedent to the making of the training school order and, accordingly, the members of the court had acted "without jurisdiction or in excess of jurisdiction" within the meaning of section 15 of the 1964 Act, thus rendering them liable in a civil action for damages. *Groome* v. *Forrester* (1816) M. & S. 314, 105 E.R. 1066 and *M'Creadie* v. *Thomson* 1907 S.C. 1176 applied. *Sirros* v. *Moore* [1975] Q.B. 118 explained. *Johnston* v. *Meldon* (1890) 30 L.R. Ir. 15 considered. *Per curiam* Where magistrates have duly entered upon the summary trial of a matter within their jurisdiction, only something quite exceptional occurring in the course of their proceedings can oust their jurisdiction so as to deprive them of protection from civil liability for a subsequent trespass: the quashing of a decision or order by certiorari cannot be conclusive against the magistrates on the issue of their civil liability. *Anisminic Ltd.* v. *Foreign Compensation Commission* [1969] 2 A.C. 147 considered. *McCann* v. *Mullan*

(Q.B.D., C.A.) [1984] N.I. 186

33. —— **Minister** — *Duty to take care* — *Depositor lodging money with industrial and provident society* — *Society subsequently going into liquidation* — *Depositor receiving a dividend of only part of sum lodged* — *Whether Minister owed duty of care* — *Whether sufficient relationship of proximity between Registrar of Friendly Societies and plaintiff* — *Central Bank Act,* 1971 (*No.* 24), *s.* 7(1)(4) — Industrial and Provident Societies (Amendment) Act, 1978 (*No.* 23) — *Insurance (No. 2) Act,* 1983 (*No.* 29).] S. 5(2) of the Industrial and Provident Societies (Amendment) Act, 1978, confers wide powers upon the Registrar of Friendly Societies to investigate and control industrial and provident societies. However, a full-time Registrar was not

NEGLIGENCE—Statutory Duty.

appointed until 1980. The plaintiff had lodged a sum of money with the Private Motorists Protection Society. Following the liquidation of the said Society, the plaintiff received a dividend of part of the sum lodged, but the remainder was lost. A claim for damages for negligence, breach of duty and breach of statutory duty against the defendants was dismissed in the District Court, but on the application of the plaintiff, the District Justice stated a case for the opinion of the High Court as to whether he was correct in dismissing the action. The first and second defendants were sued as being the parties responsible for the Acts of the Minister for Industry, Trade, Commerce and Tourism and the Minister for Finance. **Held** by Blayney J. in answering the question in the affirmative, 1, neither Minister owed a duty of care towards the plaintiff. Neither was responsible for the exemption of such societies from the prohibition in the Central Bank Act, 1971, against carrying on a banking business without a licence. Neither owed a duty of care to have the 1971 Act amended. Even if either could be said to owe a duty of care, the situation was remedied by the 1978 Act and when a full time Registrar was appointed, both ceased to have any function in the matter. 2. There was not such a sufficient relationship of proximity between the Registrar of Friendly Societies and the plaintiff, as a prospective depositor, as to place the Registrar under a duty of care towards her; *Yuen Kun Yeu* v. *Attorney General of Hong Kong* [1987] 3 W.L.R. 776 followed. 3. Where a person is obliged, in the discharge of a public duty, to make a decision affecting the liberty or property of others, and he does so honestly and in good faith, he is entitled to immunity from the type of claim made by the plaintiff: *Pine Valley Developments Ltd.* v. *Minister for the Environment* [1987] ILRM 747 applied. *McMahon* v. *Ireland*

(H.C.) [1988] ILRM 610

34. —— **Prison authorities** — *Duty of care — Whether duty of care owed to prisoner — Prisoner injured by another prisoner during recreation — Whether supervision of prisoners adequate — Whether prison authorities required to conduct searches of prisoners before recreation.*] The plaintiff was serving a term of imprisonment in Arbour Hill Prison in 1985. In the course of a recreation period, he was attacked from behind by another prisoner. The plaintiff accepted in evidence that there were in the region of 40 to 50 prisoners in the recreation yard at the time, and that the attack was a sudden, unprovoked attack which it later transpired was a case of mistaken identity. The plaintiff was unable to see what instrument had been used in the attack on him, but he received 22 stitches to his neck in hospital for the wound which had been

NEGLIGENCE—*continued.*

inflicted. The Chief Officer of Arbour Hill Prison, Mr. Scannell, gave evidence that prisoners are searched on admission to the prison, and offensive weapons are removed from them. In the course of serving their sentence, he stated that both their person and their cells are checked on a regular basis. In addition, prior to going to the prison workshops, and after they leave, all the implements are checked off against a list of items to ensure that nothing is taken to or from them, and the prisoners are also given a rub down check. He stated that prisoners are issued with razor blades for shaving. He also stated that prisoners are not searched prior to going to the recreation yard, and that while the authorities aim to have total security they could not ensure absolute and total security at all times. In relation to supervision, he stated there was no absolute ratio between prison officers and prisoners during recreation periods, but that there were 16 basic grade officers plus one assistant officer on duty on the date in question to supervise recreation. He stated that, in disciplinary proceedings subsequent to the incident in question, the prisoner who had inflicted the wounds on the plaintiff had made an admission to the governor that he had used a blade in the attack. At the conclusion of the evidence from Mr. Scannell, counsel for the defendants applied to have the case withdrawn from the jury on the basis that the prison authorities had exercised reasonable care in the supervision of the prisoners in the exercise yard. Counsel for the plaintiff submitted that the authorities should have conducted a body search of the prisoners before going to the recreation yard, on the basis that similar searches took place before people entered football grounds and aeroplanes, because there was the potential for an assault taking place during recreation, particularly if there is a dispute simmering in the prison. **Held** by Hamilton P., in withdrawing the case from the jury, 1, the prison authorities are required to take all reasonable steps and reasonable care not to expose any of the prisoners to a risk of damage or injury, but the law does not expect the authorities to guarantee that prisoners do not suffer injury during the course of their imprisonment. 2. The prison authorities had not been negligent in relation to supervision, since the attack in this instance was unprovoked and took place without warning, and even if there had been more prison officers in the yard at the time the incident could not have been prevented. 3. The authorities could not be expected to take more steps than they already took in relation to searches for offensive weapons, and in view of the obligation to take reasonable care it would not be open to a jury to find them negligent. *Muldoon* v. *Ireland*

(H.C.) [1988] ILRM 367

NORTHERN IRELAND

—— Courts — Whether procedure of N.I. courts meets minimum standards applicable in the State.
see **Extradition,** 5

—— Extradition warrant issued in Northern Ireland — Warrant endorsed for execution in the Republic — Order directing delivery of plaintiff to authorities in Northern Ireland — Procedure.
see **Constitution,** 41

—— Judiciary — Impartiality.
see **Extradition,** 8

—— Local authority — Delegation of functions — Special committee — Whether delegation for better regulation and management of functions — Whether a protective and self-defensive power to exclude — Whether powers exercised reasonably.
see **Local Government,** 4

—— Local authority — Meeting — Exclusion of councillors — Whether protective and self-defensive powers of council include powers to exclude members — Whether limited to control of meeting.
see **Local Government,** 3

—— Status — Constitution of Ireland — Anglo-Irish Agreement — Whether contrary to Articles 2 and 3 of Constitution.
see **Constitution,** 23

NOTICE
see also **Judicial Notice**

—— Enforcement notice — Planning control.
see **Planning,** 19

—— Service — Date — Postal delivery — Statute authorising service of notice — Notice served on date of delivery — Delay between delivery and receipt by department of recipient addressee.
see **Planning,** 39

NOTICE TO QUIT
see **Landlord and Tenant,** 12, 17, 19

NUISANCE

1. —— **Emissions from factory** — *Whether emissions shown to be cause of injuries claimed to have been suffered — Onus of proof — Whether defendants under obligation to disprove plaintiffs' claim in nuisance — Whether plaintiffs' onus at common law amounts to failure to vindicate property rights — Whether proof of offensive smells may support claim in nuisance — Whether interference with property beyond what was reasonable — Whether on balance of probabilities medical evidence corroborated plaintiffs' claims — Injuries to animals — Whether caused by factory emissions — Damage to plant life — Whether caused by factory emissions — Constitution of Ireland,* 1937, *Art.* 40.3.

Practice — Appeal — Supreme Court — Function of Court — Primary and secondary facts — Whether Supreme Court empowered to reach different conclusions to those of trial court in relation to inferences from primary facts.] The plaintiffs farmed land which was situated about one mile from the defendants' factory, which opened in 1976. The factory engaged in the processing of pharmaceutical products, which involved the storage and use of large quantities of toxic substances as well as the disposal in the factory of toxic and dangerous chemical residues. The plaintiffs instituted proceedings claiming that by virtue of the manner in which the defendants conducted their operation from 1978 to 1983 the plaintiffs and their farm animals, as well as plant life on the farm, suffered severe injuries and damage. The plaintiffs' claim was dismissed in the High Court (Unreported, Keane J., 7 August 1985). On appeal by the plaintiffs, it was **Held** by the Supreme Court (Finlay C.J., Henchy and Hederman JJ.) in allowing the appeal, 1, although the plaintiffs had grounded their claim in negligence as well as on the rule in *Rylands* v. *Fletcher* and also in nuisance, the matter had been dealt with in the High Court as a claim in nuisance; and since it had not been contended that the trial judge had erred in this respect, the claim would be treated as one in nuisance. 2. The plaintiffs were not required to prove want of due care by the defendants in the manner in which they conducted their operation at the factory,and it was sufficient for the claim in nuisance to succeed that they establish that they had not enjoyed the comfortable and healthy use of their land to the degree that would be expected by an ordinary person whose requirements are objectively reasonable in all the particular circumstances. *Halpin and Ors.* v. *Tara Mines Ltd.* [1976-7] ILRM 28 approved. 3. The plaintiffs were required to prove that the injuries which they claimed to have suffered were caused by the emissions from the defendants' factory, and while there were difficulties of proof facing them in this regard these were not such as would require the shifting of the onus of proof to the defendants, as would be the case in circumstances where a particular matter was within the peculiar knowledge of the defendants. 4. The onus of proof placed by the common law on the plaintiffs did not amount to a failure by the State to vindicate the personal rights of the plaintiffs

NUISANCE—*continued.*

pursuant to Article 40.3 of the Constitution, since it was not alleged that the tort of nuisance was ineffective to protect their constitutional rights and it must also be noted that the guarantees contained in Article 40.3 were not absolute or unqualified and could not be taken to relieve the plaintiff in a nuisance action of the onus of proving the necessary ingredients of the tort. *Per curiam:* the tort of nuisance may be said to be an implementation of the State's duties under Article 40.3 as to the personal rights of the plaintiffs as citizens. 5. The Supreme Court was confined as an appellate court to those findings of primary facts made by a trial court, unless they cannot in all reason be supported by the evidence; but in relation to the inferences to be drawn from the findings of primary facts the Supreme Court was free to draw its own inferences where it considered that those made by the trial judge were not correct; and since the main issue in the present case was whether the plaintiffs' injuries were caused by factory emissions from the defendants' factory and since this was a matter of inference, the plaintiffs were entitled to succeed in their appeal if, on a fresh appraisal of the primary facts, the court was of opinion that the emissions were causative of the complaints. *Dicta* in *J.M. and G.M.* v. *An Bord Uchtála* [1988] ILRM 203 applied. 6. The largely uncontroverted evidence given in the High Court, from the plaintiffs and residents of the surrounding district, was to the effect that between 1978 and 1983 there were intense and frequent objectionable smells from the defendants' factory; and these were so frequent, pronounced and prolonged that each of the plaintiffs had made out a case for damages for nuisance for offensive smells from the factory. *Halpin and Ors* v. *Tara Mines Ltd.* [1976-7] ILRM 28 applied. 7. There was independent evidence to support the second plaintiff's claim that the ill-health of which he complained was due to factory emissions, other witnesses stating that where they observed emissions from the factory they felt burning sensations and other irritations; and the second plaintiff's specialist's opinion, that his ill-health could be attributed to a toxic substance if it could be shown that plant life contained chemicals and fumes and that such fumes were emanating from a source contiguous to the farm, had not been disturbed at the end of the High Court hearing. 8. The trial judge's dismissal of the second plaintiff's claim was not supported by the evidence, and the juge's view that the specialist's opinion was overborne by the absence of evidence, from the second plaintiff's general practitioner or of similar complaints from other members of the family could not properly be held to disestablish that opinion. 9. Having regard to the vague

NUISANCE—*continued.*

nature of the first plaintiff's complaints as to ill-health, and the gynaecological nature of the third plaintiff's complaints, the trial judge's dismissal of these claims should not be disturbed. 10. Because of the vagueness of the claim as to damage to plant life, the trial judge's rejection of this heading as a separate basis for an award should not be disturbed. 11. Having regard to the volume of evidence suggesting that the factory emissions were a potential cause of damage to the neighbouring environment, and that the second plaintiff had suffered ill-health as a result of toxic emissions from the factory, the defendants' scientific evidence that damage to the farm animals could not be linked directly to chemicals emanating from the defendants' factory should not be allowed to displace the proven facts; and therefore the trial judge's dismissal of the plaintiffs' claim in relation to the farm animals could not be allowed to stand; but since it had not been established that the factory emissions were the sole cause of the animal ill-health, this matter would be remitted to the High Court for the purposes of determining whether such causation could be established. 12. Since it was desirable that all the damages should, at least at first instance, be assessed by the same tribunal the matter would be remitted to the High Court for the assessment of damages, as well as the making of the findings necessary for such assessment. *Hanrahan* v. *Merck Sharp & Dohme (Ireland) Ltd.*

(S.C.) [1988] ILRM 629

2. —— **Injunction** — *24 hour shop trading at night — Nuisance caused by customers — Extent of relief — Laches.*] In 1980 M.C. acquired a premises which had been used for business closing at 7 p.m. In 1977 the previous owner began using the premises as a "24 hour shop" and M.C. continued this business unaware that there had been any complaints in relation to the use of the premises. In October, 1981, the local residents' association, of which the plaintiff was a member, complained in writing to M.C. about shouting, revving of car engines, the banging of car doors, the playing of radios and other excessive noise caused by customers of M.C. late at night. In April, 1982, M.O'K. commenced proceedings in the Circuit Court seeking an injunction and damages against M.C. The Circuit Judge granted an injunction restraining the defendant from carrying on business between the hours of 12 midnight and 8 a.m. at his premises. On appeal to the High Court by the defendant it was **Held** by Lynch J., in varying the order of the Circuit Court, 1, that the injunction granted by the Circuit Court should be varied and limited to the extent that it operate between the hours of 12 midnight and 6 a.m. and at all seasons of the

NUISANCE—*continued.*

year. 2. Although a breach of the peace might not have been committed and Garda intervention might not have been required the noise made at night by ordinary law-abiding citizens would constitute an actionable nuisance in circumstances such as those proved. 3. The defence of laches is defeated since it was shown *inter alia* that the plaintiff in conjunction with her local residents' association had been collecting signatures in support of her and other residents' complaints and that a complaint had been made in writing to the defendant prior to the institution of the proceedings. 4. The defendant could not shorten the period of prescription to 2 years in relation to the said nuisance by saying that he did not realise that there were or would be any objections when he bought and paid for the premises. 5. "In a claim for a private nuisance of this kind the judge has to act as an arbiter between the competing interests of the respective property users. He has to decide which is to prevail, the defendant's claim to use the property in the impugned manner or the plaintiff's claim to use his property free from the damage caused by the defendant." *Dictum* of Henchy J. in *Mullin* v. *Hynes* (unreported, Supreme Court 13 November, 1972) applied. 6. In cases such as this the relative position of the parties together with the fact that the plaintiff's premises were situated in an old established residential area, *inter alia,* were to be considered in deciding whether or not an actionable nuisance existed. 7. Although the plaintiff was entitled to the relief claimed the defendant was to be disturbed in the use and enjoyment of his property to the minimum extent consistent with giving the plaintiff reasonable relief. *Semble:* A night-trader is responsible for the ordinary natural conduct of people whom he attracts to the neighbourhood where such conduct causes a nuisance to the premises of other parties. *O'Kane* v. *Campbell*

(H.C.) [1985] I.R.115

3 .—— **Intended blasting operations** — *Building project delayed — Interference with cash flow — Plaintiff unable to take up all his site options — Plaintiff losing credit and discount facilities — Assessment of damages — Whether plaintiff's impecuniosity relevant.*] The plaintiff, a speculative builder, had sought an injunction in the High Court in October, 1977, restraining the defendant from carrying out intended blasting operations in the vicinity of building sites in Castlebar, Co. Mayo which the plaintiff owned and on which he had already erected two houses for sale. The plaintiff also claimed damages for nuisance, negligence and trespass, although no blasting operations had actually taken place. In

NUISANCE—*continued.*

February, 1978, the plaintiff obtained the perpetual injunction sought. The question of damages was by consent left for later determination and was the issue before the court at this instance. The plaintiff alleged that: (1) because of the defendant's intended blasting operations he was forced to release two purchasers of the houses already erected, and was compelled to pay £750 in compensation for loss of bargain to one of them; (2) although he had sold the two houses at the conclusion of the litigation at considerably higher prices than that originally expected his net gains had been converted into substantial losses (*a*) by the cost of refurbishing the houses prior to sale; (*b*) by bank interest accruing during the time of the defendant's interference; (*c*) by consequent loss of creditworthiness with the bank which deprived him of further loans to take up options to purchase nine other two-house sites before November, 1977, at £6,000 each — instead, having been unable to meet the bank's conditions on further loans (by reason of having had no returns from the houses erected) he was forced to wait until 1978 and pay £7,000 per site; (*d*) by loss of discount on materials purchased when his credit with suppliers had dried up and he was obliged to pay cash for any materials he needed to continue in business; (3) by this chain reaction of events he had eventually been forced to abandon his business and seek alternative means of living. It was submited by the defendant that on the principle contained in the case of the *Owners of Dredger Liesbosch* v. *Owners of Steamship Edison* [1933] A.C. 449 the plaintiff could not recover damages which occurred as a result of his own impecuniosity. **Held** by O'Hanlon J. in giving judgment for the sum of £8,546.76 against the defendant, 1, the plaintiff's claim for loss and damage in connection with his inability to purchase the nine sites would be allowed. Loss measured at £3,500. 2. It should have been within the contemplation of the defendant that interference with the plaintiff's cash flow and curtailment of credit would be the inevitable consequence of the litigation. The claim for bank interest of £2,573.56 and £2,100 for loss of discount on materials would therefore be allowed. 3. Credit would have to be given for the enhanced prices realised on the first two houses. 4. The claim that the plaintiff should be compensated for all the profits he might have made, had he been able to take up all the options available, would be dismissed. (*The Edison* [1933] A.C. 449 considered). *Rabbette* v *Mayo County Council*

(H.C.) [1984] ILRM 156

4. —— **Mineral exploration work** — *Noise and vibrations — Rural locality — Physical damage — Whether caused by defendant's activities —*

NUISANCE—*continued.*

Whether appropriate to grant an injunction.] The plaintiffs, residents of a rural locality, sought damages for nuisance alleged to have resulted from the defendant's prospecting operations. The nuisance complained of consisted of noise and vibrations, which the plaintiffs claimed were so strong as to have caused cracks to appear in the walls of their houses. The plaintiffs also sought an injunction to restrain the defendant's activities. In the course of the hearing of the evidence, which was interrupted by the long vacation, the defendant took steps to modify its activities. **Held** by Gannon J. in awarding damages for nuisance to each of the plaintiffs, but in refusing the injunction sought, 1, having regard to the rural nature of the locality and the standard of peace and comfort which a reasonable person might expect to enjoy therein, the activities of the defendant had given rise to such a substantial and serious disturbance as to amount to an actionable nuisance. 2. The plaintiffs had not discharged the onus of showing that on the balance of probabilities the physical damage to their properties had been caused by the defendant's activities. 3. By modifying its activities in a manner which protected the plaintiffs from further nuisance, the defendant had relieved the court of the necessity of restraining those activities by injunction. *Halpin* v. *Tara Mines Ltd.*

(H.C.) [1976-7] ILRM 28

—— Canal — Breach of statutory duty — Lack of maintenance — Flooding — Whether commissioners' duty to maintain canal — Whether commissioners negligent — Whether plaintiff contributorily negligent — Damages.
see **Negligence,** 29

—— Cattle straying onto main road — Driver colliding with cattle — Whether cattle constitute a public nuisance.
see **Animals,** 2

—— Noise — Shop — Customers — Night-time trading — Interference with plaintiff's sleep — Plaintiff's dwelling near defendant's shop — Whether any material delay in making plaintiff's complaint.
see **Nuisance,** 2

—— Quarry — Blasting operations — Heavy traffic — Dust and noise — Standard of comfort — Whether landlord liable for nuisance caused by the tenant's act — Whether plaintiffs entitled to damages and injunction — Contribution as between defendants.
see **Planning,** 27

NULLITY OF MARRIAGE
see **Family Law,** 11-22

O

P

PARKING OFFENCES
see **Road Traffic Offences,** 16

PARLIAMENT
see **Dáil Éireann**
Oireachtas

PARTIES
see **Practice and Procedure,** 12, 13, 43, 47
see also **Locus Standi**

PARTITION — Order for sale in lieu of partition — Whether jurisdiction to make order extant.
see **Land,** 3

PARTNERSHIP
see also **Agency; Company**

—— **Drug testing unit** — *Receipt of a share of the profits — Whether partnership existed — Terms of arrangement — Partnership Act,* 1890 (*c.* 39), *s.* 2(3).] Throughout the material period, 1972-1979, the plaintiff and the defendant were involved as chief biochemist and director, respectively, of a unit known as the 'Psychoendocrine Centre'. This unit, situated in the grounds of St. James's Hospital, Dublin, provided testing and analysis services to drug companies. Prior to 1972, the unit had been funded chiefly by a Swiss subsidiary of Hoffman la Roche called Biological and Medical Research Institute Inc. In 1972, in an effort to increase the revenue of the unit, the defendant, with the approval of BMRI, personally sought and negotiated a number of contracts with other pharmaceutical companies other than Hoffman la Roche. In relation to these new contracts, a special bank account in the name 'Endocrine Research Fund' was opened. All cheques drawn on the account had to be signed by the plaintiff and the defendant jointly. The plaintiff supervised the day to day running of the unit, whilst the defendant played no active part in that regard. Periodically, a sum of money in the nature of a 'dividend' was withdrawn from the account and divided equally between the plaintiff and the defendant. This practice continued until 1975, although a final disbursement was made with the closure of the account in 1979. No reference was made during this period by either the plaintiff or the defendant to the existence of a partnership. The matter came before the High Court by way of preliminary issue to determine whether a partnership existed at any time between the plaintiff and the defendant in relation to the provision of testing and analysis services to drug companies.

PARTNERSHIP—*continued.*
Held by Carroll J. answering the question in the negative, 1, the receipt by a person of a share in the profits of a business is *prima facie* evidence that he is a partner in the business but the receipt of a share or payment contingent or varying with the profits does not of itself make someone a partner in a business. The terms of the arrangement between the parties must fairly be considered as a whole. 2. Looking at the arrangement as a whole, there was not sufficient evidence to hold that the plaintiff was a partner in the enterprise. He was a key person, in the sense that he or someone with his qualifications and ability was necessary, but he was nevertheless an employee. He was entitled to be paid a share of the profits as remuneration, but not as a partner. *O'Kelly* v. *Darragh*
(H.C.) [1988] ILRM 309

—— Fisheries — Contract of service or partnership — Employer's annual obligation to provide information relating to employees — Fishing vessel owned and operated by skipper — Crew engaged prior to each voyage — Remuneration based on value of catch — Whether employment or partnership in existence — Whether skipper an employer.
see **Revenue,** 38

—— Limited partnership — Income tax — Capital expenditure — Plant — Claim by partners for initial allowances in respect of the purchase of plant — Close relationship between the partners and a hotel company to which the plant was leased — Whether partnership existed as a matter of law — Whether partnership carrying on business with a view to profit.
see **Revenue,** 28

PASSING OFF
see also **Copyright; Trade Mark**

—— Imitation of packaging — Whether product marketed in a manner calculated to deceive the public — Whether action might be maintained by a distributor or agent — Assessment of damages — Whether account of profits be directed.
see **Trade Names and Designs**

PASSPORT
—— Endorsement — Alien's passport —

PASSPORT—*continued.*

Refusal of leave to settle in the State — Fair procedures.
see **Aliens,** 5

PATENTS

see also **Copyright; Trade Mark; Trade Names and Designs**

1. —— **Patent** — *Expiry — Application for extension dismissed — Adequacy of remuneration — Research and development costs — Whether trial judge's discretion erroneously exercised — Patents Act,* 1964 (*No.* 12), *ss.* 25, 26(3), 27, 75(7).] The appellants (Fisons) were owners of the patent identified as INTAL,a large scale selling sodium cromoglycate product. Under s. 26(3) of the Patents Act, 1964, the term of the patent was for 16 years and accordingly it expired on 21 March, 1982. On a petition of Fisons for an extension of the term of the patent pursuant to s. 27 of the 1964 Act, Costello J. dismissed the application and Fisons appealed to the Supreme Court on a question of law as to whether the trial judge had correctly interpreted s. 27 of the 1964 Act, and in particular ss. 5 and 6 thereof 'by excluding from his consideration in assessing the remuneration and profit of the patentee as such under the said section a proportion of the costs to the patentee of research and development wheresoever incurred.' The appellants relied on the discretionary nature of the remedy sought as supported by the relevant authorities. **Held** by the Supreme Court in dismissing the appeal, the trial judge had found that apart from the research and development costs the appellants had been adequately remunerated in respect of the patent in Ireland; no application had been made in England for extension of the patent as remuneration in that market as well as world-wide had been adequate. The question which the trial judge had answered in the negative was whether the research and development costs should be deducted in the circumstances for Ireland alone. The right conferred by s. 25 of the 1964 Act was of daunting proportions, if, as was submitted, a proportion of the research and development costs wheresoever incurred by the patentee — a multi-national industrial giant — are to be a determining factor when applied *pro rata* to the sale of the product in a small country such as Ireland. The special relationship between the UK and Ireland was not to be overlooked in these circumstances, considering the size of the interstate traffic and unrestricted level of commerce between the two states and there was no reason to conclude that the trial judge had exercised his discretion erroneously. *In re Fisons Pharmaceuticals Ltd.*

(H.C., S.C.) [1984] ILRM 393

PATENTS—*continued.*

2. —— **Patent Office** — *Arrears of work — Controller promulgating policy of accelerated acceptance of patent specifications — Examiners refusing to carry out this policy — Whether for them so to do would involve a breach of their statutory obligations — Refusal of increment to those examiners failing to implement this policy — Application for judicial review — Whether orders of certiorari and mandamus be granted — Patents Act,* 1964 (*No.* 12), *ss.* 2, 8(6), 9, 11, 12, 13, 16(3), 77, 78(5), 79(1) — *Patent Rules, rr.* 27, 117.] A dispute arose in the Patents Office between the second-named respondent and the prosecutors, who were members of his professional staff, as to arrears of work existing in the office. Pursuant to ss. 11-13 of the Patents Act, 1964, it was the duty of the prosecutors to examine all applications made to the Patents Office for both patentability and novelty. In order to decrease the backlog of applications, the respondent directed the prosecutors to allow certain applications through with limited investigation, and in certain cases, wihtout any investigation whatsoever. The prosecutors refused to carry out these instructions, alleging that they would be in breach of their statutory obligations by so doing. Decisions were subsequently taken by the respondent to refuse to several of the prosecutors an increment in salary which would otherwise have become payable to them. The prosecutors obtained a conditional order of certiorari quashing the directions given by the respondent in so far as they required the prosecutors to waive or curtail investigations of patent applications, and quashing the decision not to authorise the payment of increments in salary due. They also obtained a conditional order of mandamus directing the respondent to withdraw such directions as purported to waive or abrogate the provisions for examination and investigation of applications pursuant to ss. 11-13 of the 1964 Act. **Held** by Barron J. in disallowing the cause shown and in making absolute the conditional orders, 1, although, by virtue of the relationship existing between professional staff and the head of their department, the prosecutors were subject to the directions of the respondent, this did not entitle the respondent to direct the prosecutors how to perform their statutory duties or to direct them to refrain from performing them. The decisions made by the prosecutors were subject to appeal to the respondent, and in the making of these decisions the prosecutors must be free from control by the person to whom the appeal lies. *McLoughlin* v. *Minister for Social Welfare* [1958] I.R. 1 considered. 2. The decision made by the respondent to refuse the increment payable to some of the prosecutors was made by reason of the failure of the prosecutors to follow the directives issued by

PATENTS—*continued.*

the respondent. Since this disciplinary action was based on an invalid directive, it must itself also be invalid. *The State (Rajan)* v. *Minister for Industry and Commerce*

(H.C.) [1988] ILRM 231

PATERNITY OF CHILD — Evidence — Admissibility — Registration of birth.
see **Family Law,** 4

PEACE COMMISSIONER
—— Search warrant — Issue — Validity.
see **Criminal Law,** 70-2

—— Summons — Whether signing of summons invalid as being an exercise of judicial power.
see **Constitution,** 2

PENSION
see also under **Social Welfare**

—— Disability pension — Defence forces — Deduction — Civil award for damages.
see **Defence Forces,** 2-4

PERSONAL INJURIES
—— Criminal injury to persons — Compensation.
see **Criminal Injuries,** 1, 2

—— Damages — Assessment.
see **Damages,** 8-13

—— Maliciously inflicted — Garda Síochána — Compensation — Assessment — Principles applicable — Future economic loss — Mitigation of loss by award of pension — Whether value of pension to be deducted from value of future economic loss proved.
see **Garda Síochána,** 4

—— Negligence — Accrual of cause of action — Surgery performed on the plaintiff by each of the defendants — Action instituted after expiry of three years from dates of surgery — Whether action statute barred — Date on which cause of action accrued.
see **Limitation of Actions,** 4

—— Trial — Mode of trial — Jury trial.
see **Practice and Procedure,** 55, 56

PERSONAL REPRESENTATIVE
see also **Administration of Estates**

—— Administration of estate — Income tax —

PERSONAL REPRESENTATIVE—*continued.*

Income accruing to estate — Liability of executor to income tax.
see **Revenue,** 27

PERSONAL RIGHTS
see **Constitution,** 10-20, 39-43
see also **Rights and Freedoms**

PICKETING
—— Trade dispute — Former employees — Injunction — Principles applicable.
see **Injunction,** 13

—— Trade dispute — Injunction to restrain.
see **Employer and Employee,** 25

PIERS AND HARBOURS
see **Harbours and Piers**

PLANNING
see also **Compulsory Acquisition; Housing**

Appeal. Nos. 1, 2
Application for permission. Nos. 3, 4, 16
Compensation. Nos. 5-9
Conditions. Nos. 10-12, 20, 21
Decision. Nos. 2, 13-16, 35, 36, 37
Development plan — Contravention. Nos. 7, 9, 15, 17, 18, 35
Enforcement. Nos. 19-31
Exempted development. Nos. 32-4
Material Change of Use. Nos. 14, 24-30
Outline Permission. Nos. 13, 35, 36
Planning Approval. Nos. 35, 36
Planning Permission. Nos. 37, 38
Purchase notice. Nos. 39, 40
Section 27 Applications. Nos. 2, 20-31, 32
Unauthorised Development or Use. Nos. 22-31

APPEAL

1. —— **Natural justice** — *Fair Procedures — Parties — Objector's rights — Prosecutrix successfully opposing grant of planning permission at first instance — Appeal by developer to An Bord Pleanála — Prosecutrix not "a party to the appeal" under the planning regulations — Written submissions furnished to Board by prosecutrix in reply to developer's grounds of appeal — Developer furnishing additional submissions in relation to its grounds of appeal — Prosecutrix not afforded opportunity to make submissions on those matters — Whether fair procedures observed — Requirements of constitutional justice — Local Government (Planning and Development) Regulations,* 1977 (*S.I. No.* 65), *arts.* 35, 38, 40 — *Local Government (Planning and Development) Act,* 1976 (*No.* 20) — *Local Government (Planning and Development) Act,* 1983 (*No.* 28), *s.*

PLANNING—Appeal.

18.] Article 38 of the Local Government (Planning and Development) Regulations, 1977, provides that on receipt of an appeal to it, An Bord Pleanála is bound to give a copy thereof to each other party to the appeal which category of person is defined in art. 35, sub-art. 2 of the Regulations. Article 40 of the Regulations provides that a person to whom a copy of an appeal has been given under art. 38 may, within such period as may at any time be specified by the Board, make in writing to the Board such observations on the appeal as he thinks fit and a copy of such observations shall be given by the Board to each other party to the appeal or, where a number of persons have made the appeal jointly, to any one of such persons. A residents' association of whom the prosecutrix was chairwoman successfully opposed an application by M.P. Ltd. to Dublin County Council for the grant of planning permission for a development immediately adjacent to the residents' association's estate in County Dublin. M.P. Ltd. appealed to An Bord Pleanála against that decision and furnished to it by letter detailed grounds of its appeal. Although the prosecutrix did not fall within the category of persons to whom An Bord Pleanála was bound under the Regulations to provide a copy of that letter, she obtained through a planning consultant acting on her association's behalf a copy of it and the planning consultant furnished the Board with a lengthy memorandum commenting on M.P. Ltd.'s grounds of appeal. The planning consultant also made short submissions in relation to a letter written by residents of another housing estate to the Board supporting M.P. Ltd's appeal. However a letter by M.P. Ltd. to the Board furnishing additional submissions with regard to its grounds of appeal was not circulated to the residents' association which only became aware of its contents after the Board had determined the appeal and reversed the decision of Dublin County Council. The prosecutrix representing the interests of the residents' association obtained a conditional order of certiorari in the High Court quashing the Board's decision to grant M.P. Ltd. planning permission on the grounds that the Board had adjudicated on the appeal, (*a*) without furnishing all of the submissions made on behalf of M.P. Ltd. to the prosecutrix so as to enable her to make submissions in relation thereto and (*b*) in purporting to adjudicate on the appeal brought by M.P. Ltd. without first ensuring that all interested parties had an opportunity of making submissions and representations relevant to their considerations including the prosecutrix. On the prosecutrix's motion to make the conditional order absolute, notwithstanding cause shown, it was **Held** by Murphy J., in allowing the cause shown and discharging the conditional order, 1, that

PLANNING—*continued.*

although the prosecutrix did not come within the category of persons to which arts. 38 and 40 of the Regulations applied and the general right of citizens to raise objections or make representations in relation to planning permission was not based on property rights, nevertheless the procedures adopted to adjudicate on contentions such as those of the prosecutrix must conform with the constitutional requirement of fairness of procedures. *The State (Stanford)* v. *Corporation of Dún Laoghaire* (Unreported, Supreme Court, 20 February, 1981); *Law* v. *Minister for Local Government* (Unreported, High Court, Deale J., 9 May, 1974) and *The State (Córas Iompair Éireann)* v. *An Bord Pleanála* (Unreported, Supreme Court, 12 December, 1984) considered. 2. That having regard to, *inter alia,* the non-proprietary interest of the prosecutrix in the matter as distinct from that of the developer and the practical fact that in any proceedings whether oral or otherwise there must be finality, the requirement of fairness of procedures had been satisfied in this case by the prosecutrix being allowed put forward a detailed professional argument before the Board even though she had not been afforded an opportunity to respond to the additional submissions of M.P. Ltd. *Per* Murphy J. There could be cases in which further communications from the developer extended the original submission so radically as to constitute a different or additional case and in that event natural justice might well require An Bord Pleanála to postpone its decision until it had afforded interested parties an opportunity of commenting upon the revised submission. *The State (Haverty)* v. *An Bord Pleanála*

(H.C.) [1987] I.R.485; [1988] ILRM 545

2. —— **Jurisdiction of An Bord Pleanála** — *Retention order — Development not in accordance with planning permission — s.* 27 *application — Application for retention permission — Application granted on appeal — Whether retention order made without jurisdiction — Local Government (Planning and Development) Act,* 1963 (*No.* 28), *s.* 26 — *Local Government (Planning and Development) Act,* 1976 (*No.* 20), *s.* 27.] In 1978, after making several unsuccessful applications for planning permission, the developers were granted permission to erect houses at Clyde Lane, Ballsbridge. Development on foot of this permission proceeded in 1980 and 1981. Early in 1981 the prosecutor, who resides in Clyde Rd., noticed that the house being built was not in accordance with the permission granted. The planning authority brought proceedings under s. 27 of the Local Government (Planning and Development) Act, 1976, for an injunction directing the removal of the unauthorised development but this was refused when the

developers gave an undertaking not to continue with the development until permission was granted. The developers made further unsuccessful attempts to obtain permission in respect of the type of house which they wished to erect. Finally, they applied for retention permission in respect of the house which they had unlawfully erected. The planning authority refused permission but, on appeal, An Bord Pleanála (the Board) permitted retention on the ground that '. . . retention . . . would be in accordance with the proper planning and development of the area. The degree of injury and departure from the original plan are not such as to warrant removal of the structure.' The prosecutor applied for and was granted a conditional order of certiorari quashing the Board's decision. The conditional order was made absolute by Carroll J. who held that the Board, in making a decision whether to grant permission, should not be concerned with the justice of the case, that while the Board could decide that the injury to amenity was not sufficient to refuse permission, it could not decide that the injury to amenity was not sufficient to warrant removal. The Board appealed to the Supreme Court. **Held** by the Supreme Court (Henchy, Griffin and Hederman JJ.) in dismissing the appeal, that in dealing with the appeal the Board was exercising a jurisdiction which was no greater than that exercised by the planning authority and was therefore restricted to considering matters specified in s. 26 of the Local Government (Planning and Development) Act, 1963, (as amended by the Local Government (Planning and Development) Act, 1976). The Board had exceeded its jurisdiction in arriving at its decision by taking into account a matter which was excluded from the range of its jurisdiction by statute *viz.* its own opinion that the degree of injury and departure from the original was not such as to warrant the removal of the structure. *The State (Fitzgerald)* v. *An Bord Pleanála*

(H.C., S.C.) [1985] ILRM 117

APPLICATION FOR PERMISSION
see also No. 16

3. —— **Advertisement** — *Description of property — Whether sufficient — Whether in compliance with planning regulations — Local Government (Planning and Development) Regulations,* 1977 (*S.I. No.* 65), *regs.* 15, 17.

Judicial review — Alternative remedy — Mandamus — Local Government — Planning permission — Refusal appeal — Application for mandamus — Whether lodgment of appeal precludes application for mandamus — Whether mandamus more appropriate remedy where merits of case not in issue.] In an application

to the respondent in 1975 for outline planning permission in respect of certain property, the application was refused but granted on appeal by the Minister on 1 May, 1975, subject to a condition. The prosecutor applied for approval of the plan on 28 November, 1978, which was received by the respondents on 1 December, 1978, and this was also advertised in the *Irish Press* on 25 November, 1978. The respondents refused the application by a notice of 11 April, 1979. On foot of the prosecutor's application of 28 November, 1978, and the respondent's notice of refusal of 11 April, 1979, the prosecutor appealed to An Bord Pleanála. He then sought a conditional order of mandamus requiring the respondent to make a formal grant of approval to the developer on the grounds that the respondents did not give their decision within the period of two months from the date of receiving the application for permission. The court granted a conditional order of mandamus to the prosecutor on 30 July, 1979. The respondent's counsel submitted in showing cause against making the order absolute (1) the notice of refusal was given within the appropriate statutory period, by virtue of their letter dated 26 January, 1979, which was a valid notice seeking further information; (2) the prosecutor's notice in the newspaper was defective in that it did not contain a statement of the location of the land pursuant to Reg. 15(b) of the Local Government (Planning and Development) Regulations, 1977; (3) the prosecutor by appealing to An Bord Pleanála had adopted an alternative remedy and therefore was not entitled to pursue the remedy of mandamus. **Held** by McMahon J in making absolute the conditional order of mandamus, 1, Reg. 15 (*b*) of the Local Government (Planning and Development) Regulations, 1977, does not require a statement of the townland or other more precise description of the location of the property. 2. The letter dated 26 January, 1979, was not a valid notice seeking further information from the developers of their plans so as to stop the period of two months running as it set out the features of the proposal the Council disliked and asked the developer to alter his proposals to meet the objections. 3. An Bord Pleanála can only give a decision on the merits of an application; therefore an appeal to An Bord Pleanála cannot be considered as another remedy equally beneficial convenient and effective as an order of mandamus. **Held** by the Supreme Court in an *ex tempore* judgment (O'Higgins C.J., Griffin and Parke JJ.) in allowing the appeal and allowing the cause shown: The application for approval of 28 November, 1978, failed to comply with Regs. 15 and 17 of the Local Government (Planning and Development) Regulations, 1977, in that 'Lucan' was an insufficient description of the

PLANNING—Application.

address; and they also failed to disclose in their application particulars of interest they held in the lands. *State (N.C.E.Ltd.)* v. *Dublin County Council*

(H.C.) [1979] ILRM 249

4. —— **Particulars** — *Interest in land — Whether requirement of stating applicant's interest in the land satisfied by a general description of the interest — Local Government (Planning and Development) Regulations,* 1977 (*S.I. No.* 65), *reg.* 17(a).

*Practice — Planning — Application for an injunction restraining continued development and declaration that the planning application was invalid — Motion to strike out — Whether claim frivolous or vexatious — Rules of the Superior Courts, O.*19, *r.*28.] In 1957 Farrell Homes Ltd. obtained planning permission pursuant to the Town and Regional Planning Act, 1934, in respect of a seven storey office development on a site between Leeson Close and Kingram Place in the City of Dublin. In 1981 Farrell Homes Ltd. were replaced as developers by the defendant. By virtue of the provisions of s. 29 of the Local Government (Planning and Development) Act, 1976, the planning permission would cease to have effect on 1 November, 1981. In November, 1980, construction of the office block began with speed and by May, 1981, it stood seven storeys high. The plaintiff who resides in Leeson Close, being satisfied that what was under construction was different in design from the plans upon which planning permission had been granted, brought a motion in the High Court under the provisions of s. 27 of the Local Government (Planning and Development) Act, 1976, for an order prohibiting the continuation of the development and directing the removal from the site of what had been constructed. The order sought was refused and, on appeal, the matter was remitted to the High Court to hear further evidence. In April, 1981, the defendant submitted a fresh planning application to the planning authority seeking planning permission to authorise what was being constructed. Such permission was granted in June, 1981, and was upheld by An Bord Pleanála in November, 1981. In this planning application the defendant failed to comply with the requirements of Regulation 17 (*a*) of the Local Government (Planning and Development) Regulations, 1977, in that it incorrectly stated its interest in the site to be a freehold interest. On this ground the plaintiff claimed a declaration that the purported grant of planning permission to the defendant was null and void and an injunction restraining the defendant from carrying out or taking the benefit of the planning permission. By notice of motion the defendant sought an order, pursuant to the provisions of R.S.C., O.19 r. 28

PLANNING—Compensation.

or alternatively, pursuant to the inherent jurisdiction of the court, striking out and dismissing the claim as being vexatious. In pursuance of the said inherent jurisdiction of the court such an order was granted dismissing the claim. The plaintiff appealed. **Held** by the Supreme Court in dismissing the plaintiff's appeal, 1, the relief claimed by the defendant could not have been granted under R.S.C., O. 19 r. 28 as for this rule to apply vexation or frivolity must appear from the pleadings alone. In the instant case it was necessary to adduce evidence in explanation of the pleadings. 2. The general description of the defendants' interest in the site was not inaccurate, wrong or misleading. They were willing purchasers of the site under a valid and subsisting contract. They had paid ⅔ of the purchase price and in these circumstances clearly had a beneficial interest which could fairly, though not precisely be described as a freehold interest. 3. Even if the description given of the defendants' interest lacked accuracy or particularity, on application of the *de minimis* rule, it was so insignificant and trivial as to be ignored. *McCabe* v. *Harding Investments Ltd.*

(S.C.) [1984] ILRM 105

COMPENSATION

5. —— **Refusal of permission** — *Exclusions — Deficiency in public sewerage facilities — Claim for compensation — Diminution in value of land — Whether compensation deniable by virtue of a deficiency in public sewerage faciliites — Whether assessment of compensation be delayed pending exhaustion of the procedure laid down in the 1878 Act — Public Health (Ireland) Act,* 1878 (*c.* 52), *s.* 24 — *Acquisition of Land (Assessment of Compensation) Act,* 1919 (*c.* 57) — *Local Government (Planning and Development) Act,* 1963 (*No.* 28), *ss.* 55, 56(1)(b).

Local Government — Public health — Application for permission to connect a sewer — No formal dispute to the claim for connection — Property arbitrator appointed — Whether developers precipitate — Whether excessive delay — Public Health (Ireland) Act, 1878 (*c.* 52), *ss.* 24, 216, 217.] In 1977 McKone Estates Ltd. obtained planning permission for a housing development at Cooldrinagh in County Dublin, a site near the river Liffey and bordering on County Kildare. The permission was subject to a requirement that the sewer from the development be brought to the sewage treatment plant at Leixlip in the adjoining county. In 1979 planning applications for the construction of the sewer were refused by the planning authorities in both counties, and the refusals were upheld by An Bord Pleanála. Permission was subsequently obtained from

PLANNING—Compensation.

Dublin County Council, but the planning authority in Kildare continued to refuse to countenance bringing the sewer to Leixlip on the ground that the capacity of the treatment plant was 'already committed' to developments projected for that county. McKone Estates Ltd. then sought compensation from Kildare County Council for the reduction in the value of its lands caused by the refusal, and the dispute was referred to the arbitration of Mr. Sean McDermott. During the arbitration it was claimed on behalf of Kildare County Council that the property affected by the decision was in County Dublin (save for a small parcel); that s. 56 (1) (*b*) of the Local Government (Planning and Development) Act, 1963, denied a claimant compensation when there was a deficiency in public sewerage facilities; and that McKone Estates Ltd. had not pursued the machinery provided in s. 24 of the Public Health (Ireland) Act, 1878, which deals with the connection of private sewers to the public system of a neighbouring area. The matters arising were set out in a consultative case stated for the opinion of the High Court, the text of the case stated being reproduced *infra* in the judgment of O'Hanlon J. **Held** by O'Hanlon J. on 24 June, 1983, 1, that s. 24 of the Public Health (Ireland) Act, 1878, confers a right, similar to that in s. 23 of the Act, to secure connection to the public sewers in an adjoining sanitary district: *The County Council of the County of Dublin* v. *Shortt* [1983] ILRM 377 applied; *Mayor of New Windsor* v. *Stovell* (1884) 27 Ch. D. 665 and *Newington Local Board* v. *Cottingham Local Board* 12 Ch. D. 725 considered. 2. That the claimant had a *prima facie* right to demand connection, and that until it had exhausted the procedure under s. 24 of the Public Health (Ireland) Act, 1878,the arbitrator could not properly deal with the question of compensation. 3. That the claimant could not sustain against Kildare County Council a claim in respect of injurious affection to its County Dublin lands: Acquisition of Land (Assessment of Compensation) Act, 1919, considered. 4. That the application for compensation under s. 55 of the Local Government (Planning and Development) Act, 1963, was premature. Following this judgment McKone Estates Ltd. applied to Kildare County Council for a connection of its sewer as provided in s. 24 of the Public Health (Ireland), Act, 1878. Failing to reach prompt agreement with the Council, the company proceeded to invoke arbitration and appointed Ronald Bergin as arbitrator. The Council responded by taking an action against McKone Estates Ltd. and the arbitrator for an injunction to postpone the arbitration until the Council had further considered the matter. **Held** by O'Hanlon J. on 19 September, 1983, granting the injunction, that the

PLANNING—*continued.*

appointment of the arbitrator had been precipitate, and that a 'dispute' within the meaning of s. 24 of the Public Health (Ireland) Act, 1878, had not arisen at the time of the arbitrator's appointment. *McKone Estates Ltd.* v. *Kildare County Council*

(H.C.) [1984] ILRM 313

6. —— **Refusal of permission** — *Exclusions — Legal interest in land — Whether applicant required to have legal interest in land affected not only at time permission refused but also at time compensation assessed — Local Government (Planning and Development) Act,* 1963 (*No.* 28), *ss.* 55, 56, 58.] S. 55 of the Local Government (Planning and Development) Act, 1963, provides for the payment of compensation in respect of a refusal of planning permission in certain circumstances. S. 56 of the Act prohibits such payment where, *inter alia,* the development consists of or includes a material change of use. S. 58 permits the Minister, notwithstanding the provisions of s. 56, to make an order declaring 'that he is satisfied that it would not be just and reasonable in the particular circumstances that payment of compensation should be prevented by the provisions of s. 56. The first and second named defendants were lessees of a dwelling-house in respect of which they sought and were refused planning permission for the development of office accommodation. The refusal was on the ground that it was envisaged that the area in which the house was situate would, in the future, be zoned for residential purposes. On appeal, the refusal was confirmed, and the defendants applied for compensation and for an order pursuant to s. 58, since a material change of use had been sought. The Minister made a s. 58 order, following which the defendants sold the property. The plaintiff challenged the right of the defendants to receive compensation, on the ground that s. 55 required an applicant to have a legal interest in the land affected not only at the time permission is refused, but also up to the time compensation is assessed, since other provisions of the Act could be construed so to mean. The plaintiff also challenged the validity of the ministerial order, on the ground that it was implied in s. 58 that a decision to make an order under that section be made within a reasonable time. **Held** by Finlay P. in refusing the reliefs sought, 1, s. 55 expressly makes the time of refusal of permission the relevant time at which the applicant must have an interest in the affected property, and the court will not imply restrictions into provisions giving a right to compensation unless forced to do so. 2. It is not sufficient that other provisions of the Act could be construed as envisaging a retention of legal interest up to the date of assessment of compensation. In order to construe them in such

PLANNING—Compensation.

a way, no other construction must be possible. 3. Many provisions of the 1963 Act contain express time limits. In the absence of such an express provision in s. 58, the court will not imply such a provision, unless it is essential to do so for the proper construction and working of the section. *Dublin Corporation* v. *Smithwick*

(H.C.) [1976-7] ILRM 280

7. —— **Refusal of permission** — *Exclusions — Legal interest in land — Whether claimant had sufficient interest in lands — Planning authority undertaking to grant permission for a residential development — Such undertaking involving a departure from the area's development plan — Whether undertaking valid — Local Government (Planning and Development) Act,* 1963 (*No.* 28), *ss.* 19(7), 55, 56, 57 — *Acquisition of Land (Assessment of Compensation) Act,* 1919 (*c.* 57) — *Property Values (Arbitrations and Appeals) Act,* 1960 (*No.* 45).] S. 55 of the Local Government (Planning and Development) Act, 1963, provides for the payment of compensation to a person whose application for planning permission has been refused, if, as a result of such refusal, the value of the lands the subject-matter of the application has been reduced. S. 57 of the said Act provides that compensation shall not be payable where the planning authority gives an undertaking to grant permission for other specified development in respect of the same lands. The claimant had applied for planning permission in respect of certain lands, stating itself to be the owner thereof. In fact, the lands were divided into several separate plots, only four of which were registered in the name of the claimant. Of the remaining three, one ('the PMPA lands') was in process of being sold to the claimant, and the sale was subsequently completed, while the second ('the Swords lands') was registered in the name of a wholly-owned subsidiary of the claimant, who had made a declaration of trust in the claimant's favour. With regard to the third plot ('the Crampton lands') the property arbitrator found that the claimant had sufficient interest therein to make the application. The application was refused and an appeal to An Bord Pleanála was dismissed, on 8 June, 1981, ('the relevant date'). The claimant applied for compensation pursuant to s. 55 of the Local Government (Planning and Development) Act, 1963. The arbitration which followed was adjourned to allow a case to be stated to the High Court. Following the resolution of this and other legal difficulties, the arbitration was resumed on 23 July, 1986. All seven plots of land were re-included in the application for compensation, but on 31 July the Crampton lands were excluded on the claimant's statement that it did not have sufficient interest therein to sustain a

PLANNING—*continued.*

claim in respect thereof. The planning authority then produced an undertaking offered without prejudice to the contention of the authority that the claimant was not entitled to compensation. This undertook to grant permission for a residential development subject to the provisions of Part V of the 1963 Act. Three earlier planning permissions in respect of the lands which were in force at the relevant date had ceased to have effect on 31 October, 1983. The arbitrator stated five questions for the opinion of the High Court, as follows: (*a*) Whether the lack of a compensatable interest in part of the lands precluded the awarding of compensation in respect of the remainder. (*b*) Whether the claimant had, at the relevant date, a compensatable interest in the Swords land. (*c*) Whether the claimant had, on the relevant date, a compensatable interest in the PMPA lands. (*d*) Whether the undertaking of 31 July, 1986, was a valid undertaking for the purposes of s. 55(2) of the 1963 Act, and whether the arbitrator should have regard to it in determining the reduction in value of the claimant's interest in the lands. (*e*) Whether the provisions of s. 57 preclude the awarding of compensation in respect of that part of the lands to which the three earlier planning permissions attached. **Held** by Murphy J. in answering the 1st, 4th and 5th questions in the negative and the 2nd and 3rd in the affirmative, 1, the references in s. 55 of the 1963 Act to 'the land' do not support the proposition that the section is necessarily speaking in all circumstances of the totality of the land. 2. The declaration of trust executed in favour of the claimant by the registered owner of the Swords lands established the claimant as full owner of the said lands with a compensatable interest therein. 3. The claimant had a compensatable interest in the PMPA lands to the extent, at the very least, of that part of the purchase money already paid at the relevant date. *Tempany* v. *Hynes* [1976] I.R. 101 applied. 4. The undertaking of 31 July, 1986, involved a significant departure from the Development Plan for the area. The provisions of the said plan, insofar as they purport to allow the planning authority to grant, in certain cases, permission for a development which contravenes the plan, constitute a breach of s. 19(7) of the 1963 Act, which makes the creating and variation of a Development Plan a reserved function. 5. Only one of the three earlier permissions was for a development to which s. 57 was capable of applying. For s. 57 to apply, the only conditions to be attached to such a permission are those specified in s. 56 sub-s. 1 (*c*). One of the conditions attached to the said permission did not comply with those requirements. *In re Grange Developments Ltd.*

(H.C.) [1987] ILRM 733

PLANNING—Compensation.

8. —— **Refusal of permission** — *Exclusions — Statutory provisions excluding compensation where refusal based on certain grounds — Whether planning authority's written reasons for refusal coming within those grounds — Principles of construction of planning documents — Local Government (Planning and Development) Act, 1963 (No.* 28), *ss.* 55, 56.] Section 55, sub-s. 1 of the Act of 1963 provides that if as a result of a decision under Part IV of that Act to refuse, *inter alia,* permission for the development of land the value of an interest of any person existing in the land to which the decision relates at the time of the decision is reduced, such person shall, subject to the provisions of Part VI of the Act, be entitled to be paid by way of compensation the amount of such reduction in value. Section 56, sub-s. 1 of the Act, contained in the said Part VI, provides that compensation shall not be payable under s. 55 where the refusal of the permission is based on certain grounds, those grounds being stated to include (at para. (*g*)) where the reason or one of the reasons for the refusal is the necessity of preserving any view or prospect of special amenity value or special interest and (at para. (*i*) (iii)) where the reason or one of the reasons for the refusal (in relation to permission sought for a development comprising any structure or any addition to or extension of a structure) is that the structure, addition or extension would seriously injure the amenities, or depreciate the value, of property in the vicinity. The claimant company purchased 24.4 acres of land in Killiney, County Dublin for £40,000 and applied to Dún Laoghaire Corporation, as the relevant planning authority, for planning permission for residential development of the lands which permission was refused by the Corporation for reasons approximating to the wording of the aforementioned statutory provisons. Both the claimant and a third party appealed that decision to An Bord Pleanála, the gravamen of the third party's ground of appeal being that the Corporation's reasons for refusal did not emphasise strongly enough the environmental objections to the proposed development. After an oral hearing the Board also refused the permission sought, giving as its written reasons (1) that the proposed development would be contrary to the zoning objective for the Corporation's planning areas in both its Development Plan 1976 and its draft Development Plan 1983 and stated that "these zoning objectives are considered reasonable and the development would therefore be contrary to the proper planning and development of the area" and (2) that the proposed development "including the access road, driveways, boundary walls, and the considerable excavation, would be seriously injuri-

PLANNING—*continued.*

ous to the overall character of the area and contrary to its proper planning and development." The claimant subsequently submitted a claim for compensation in the sum of £2,375,000 to the Corporation pursuant to s. 55 of the Act of 1963, which claim was referred to arbitration. At the request of the Corporation the property arbitrator stated a case to the High Court seeking the opinion thereof as to whether the reasons given by An Bord Pleanála for refusing the claimant permission were sufficient to deprive it of compensation by virtue of s. 56, sub-section 1 (*g*) or (*i*) (iii). The High Court (Murphy J.) held those reasons not to be so sufficient and the Corporation appealed to the Supreme Court before which it was argued, *inter alia,* on its behalf that the reference to "zoning objectives" in the first of the reasons stated by An Bord Pleanála was capable of being construed as including the preservation of amenity values in the Killiney area mentioned in both the Corporation's Development Plan 1976 and its draft plan of 1983. **Held** by the Supreme Court (Finlay C.J., Walsh, Henchy, Hederman and McCarthy JJ.) in disallowing the appeal, 1, that for the reasons stated for a refusal of permission to bar compensation pursuant to s. 56, sub-s. 1, they must follow precisely the wording of the applicable provisions of that statutory provision, particularly where as here An Bord Pleanála confirms the decision of the planning authority to refuse permission in terms differing from those used by the authority in its decision and which latter terms approximate to the statutory words. Statement in Keane: *The Law of Local Government in the Republic of Ireland* at p. 198 approved. *Grange Developments Ltd.* v. *Dublin County Council* [1986] I.R. 246 mentioned. 2. That the words "overall character" used by An Bord Pleanála in its decision could not be equated with the word "amenities" appearing in s. 56, sub-section 1 (*i*) (iii). *Quaere,* whether s. 56, sub-s. 1 (*i*) (iii) applies to a complex development as well as to a single structure. *In re X.J.S. Investments Ltd.*

(S.C.) [1986] I.R.750 ; [1987] ILRM 659

9. —— **Refusal of permission** — *Exclusions — Undertaking to grant permission — Whether statutory exception to compensation provision operative — Whether undertaking granted in time — Whether undertaking sufficiently precise and detailed — Whether development plan contravened — Local Government (Planning and Development) Act,* 1963 (*No.* 28), *ss.* 26, 55-8 — *Local Government (Planning and Development) Act,* 1976 (*No.* 20), *s.* 39.] An undertaking to grant planning permission for a development given by a planning authority under s. 57 of the Act of 1963 to a person whose own application

for a development has been refused does not deprive that person of the right to compensation under s. 55 of that Act for such refusal unless that undertaking has been given and communicated to him within the time prescribed by s. 58 of the Act for him to apply to the Minister for the Environment for a decision that the undertaking should not have the effect of precluding his entitlement to compensation. So **held** by the Supreme Court (Finlay C.J., Henchy, Griffin, Hederman and McCarthy JJ.). **Further held** by the Supreme Court (Finlay C.J., Henchy, Griffin and Hederman JJ.) that the undertaking given in this case was also not effective to bar the claimant's right to compensation because (*a*) it lacked the requisite detail as to, *inter alia,* the number density and nature of the buildings it related to so as to enable the Minister, in discharging his function under s. 58 of the Act, to reach a conclusion as to the probable value it represented to the claimant, (*b*) its lack of detail and imprecision showed that the respondents could not have had proper regard, in reaching the decision to give the undertaking, to those matters which under s. 26 of the Act they are confined to considering when deciding whether to grant planning permission and (*c*) its terms materially contravened the Development Plan for the area, which contravention would only have been permissible if the elected members of the respondent Council had pursuant to s. 26, sub-s. 3, of the Act of 1963, as amended by s. 39, para. (*d*), of the Act of 1976, concurred in the granting of the undertaking by its Assistant City and County Manager. *Quaere,* whether a further prerequisite of a valid undertaking to grant planning permission is that it be preceded by a hearing at which all the issues relating to it and which would affect interested parties have been debated and considered. *Grange Developments Ltd.* v. *Dublin County Council*

(S.C.) [1986] I.R.246; [1987] ILRM 245

CONDITIONS

see also Nos. 20, 21

10. —— **Validity** — *Adjoining land — House of architectural and historic interest owned by applicant adjacent to area of proposed development — An Bord Pleanála granting permission subject to condition that house be retained and restored — Whether condition* ultra vires *— Whether power to impose condition requiring restoration of structure outside area of development — Whether condition unreasonable or void for uncertainty — Whether condition severable from rest of permission — Local Government (Planning and Development) Act, 1963 (No.* 28), *s.*

26.] Section 26, sub-s. 1 of the Act of 1963 provides that a planning authority may grant planning permission or approval subject to, or without, conditions. Sub-section 2 of that section provides that conditions under sub-s. 1 may, without prejudice to the generality of that subsection, include (at para. (*a*)) conditions for regulating the development or use of any land adjacent to the land to be developed and which is under the control of the applicant, so far as appears to the planning authority to be expedient for the purposes of or in connection with the development authorised by the permission and (at para. (*b*)) conditions for requiring the carrying out of works (including the provision of car parks) which the planning authority consider are required for the purposes of the development authorised by the permission. The prosecutor applied for planning permission to develop certain lands. The planning authority granted permission subject, *inter alia,* to the condition that the prosecutor take certain steps in relation to the preservation of a house of historic, artistic and architectural interest adjacent to the lands and under the control of the prosecutor. On appeal, the respondents substituted a condition that the entire house "or alternatively the early eighteenth century core of the house . . ." was to be retained and restored and that the internal elements of the house were to be preserved, conserved or replaced in facsimile as their condition warranted and further that no other internal or external structural alterations were to be carried out without planning permission, and that the house was to remain in residential use. The prosecutor obtained a conditional order of certiorari in relation to the above condition on the grounds that it was *ultra vires* the powers of the respondents; that it was ambiguous and uncertain; that it did not relate to the sought or permitted development and that it was unreasonable. On the prosecutor's motion to make the conditional order absolute it was argued on its behalf that s. 26, sub-s. 2 (*a*) did not entitle the respondents to require the prosecutor to do anything positive such as carrying out development works and that there was no power in the respondents to impose a financial burden relating to lands not within the area for development. **Held** by Lynch J., in allowing the cause shown and discharging the conditional order, 1, that the effect of sub-ss. 1 and 2 (*a*) of s. 26 when read together was to give power to the planning authorities to impose a condition of the type here, provided that it was expedient for the purposes of or in connection with the development authorised. The narrow construction of s. 26 contended for by the prosecutor would entitle

PLANNING—Conditions.

developers to evade works which would obviously be required for the purposes of a development. i.e. the clearing away of eyesores and the proper landscaping of grounds surrounding the actual site of the development, by excluding such grounds and eyesores from the area of development. *Dún Laoghaire Corporation* v. *Frescati Estates Ltd.* [1982] ILRM 469 considered. 2. That the respondents could reasonably have taken the view that the preservation of the house was expedient for the purposes of and in connection with the development authorised in that it would improve the visual attractiveness of the whole area and preserve for low density residential purposes the house itself and its site. By reason of this the prosecutor's contention that the condition did not relate to the sought or permitted development also failed. 3. That the option in the condition did not render the condition void for uncertainty or ambiguity since the option was in case of the prosecutor enabling it to fulfil its obligations under the condition by retaining and restoring the house in one or other of the ways indicated. 4. That the condition was not unreasonable because the sum required for restoration work could be covered by the addition of approximately £3,000 to the price of each of the buildings in the development and the prosecutor at the end of the restoration work would have in addition a valuable house which could provide apartment accommodation and which would also add to the visual attractiveness of the whole development. On appeal by the prosecutor it was **Held** by the Supreme Court (Finlay C.J., Walsh and McCarthy JJ.) in allowing the appeal, 1, that since the requirement for planning permission constitutes an encroachment on property rights, the statutory provisions in question were to be strictly construed. The impugned condition could not be regarded as one for "regulating the development or use" of the house and neither could its imposition be regarded as "expedient for the purposes of or in connection with the development authorised by the permission." 2. That the provision in s. 26, sub-s. 2 (*b*) for conditions requiring the "carrying out of works" meant, having regard to the statutory context, works on the lands the subject of the application for permission. 3. That neither could the general opening words of sub-s. 2 be relied upon as conferring a power to impose a condition of the type here; such a power would require expression in the clearest statutory terms. 4. That as it could not be shown that the respondents, had they been advised that the impugned condition was invalid, would have granted the remainder of the permission without it, the invalid condition was not severable from the rest of the permission. *Per* McCarthy J. Without seeking to delimit the type of conditions

PLANNING—*continued.*

envisaged by s. 26, sub-s. 2 (*a*) the power under that provision would be appropriate for example to conditions which sterilise adjoining land as an integral part of the amenity of a particular development. *State (F.P.H. Properties S.A.)* v. *An Bord Pleanála*

(H.C., S.C.) [1987] I.R.698

11. —— **Validity** — *Contribution — Appeal to An Bord Pleanála — Appeal rejected — Declaration sought — Whether conditions* ultra vires *— Whether severable — Local Government (Planning and Development) Act,* 1982 (*No.* 21), *ss.* 2-3 — *Local Government (Planning and Development) Act,* 1963 (*No.* 28), *s.* 26 — *Local Government (Planning and Development) Act,* 1983 (*No.* 28), *s.* 19.] The plaintiff received a decision to grant permission for the erection of a briquette factory on the 12 January, 1983, subject to certain conditions. One of the conditions was that the plaintiff would make a 'contribution' of £300,000 towards the cost of the reconstruction of certain roads. Another condition was that this contribution should be paid in three annual instalments in the years 1983, 1984 and 1985. The plaintiff appealed to An Bord Pleanála against these conditions. The Bord rejected this appeal and directed the planning authority to attach the said conditions to the permission. The plaintiff thereupon claimed in the High Court, *inter alia,* a declaration, (*a*) that the conditions were *ultra vires* the authority and powers of the planning authority; and (*b*) that the invalid conditions were severable from the grant of permission. The plaintiff relied on the following grounds: (i) That the requirement that the contribution be paid in three annual instalments imposes an unjustifiable constraint on the plaintiff as to the time within which they are to implement the permission and restrains them in the exercise of their decision to implement the permission within a five year period from the date of granting, as provided by s. 2, sub-s. 5 (*c*), of the Act of 1982. (ii) That the conditions failed to comply with the requirements of s. 26, sub-s. 2 (*h*) of the Act of 1963, in that there was no period specified in the condition within which the works were to be commenced or the contribution returned. Further, there was no stipulation providing for the payment of interest on the contribution or on the instalments, as required by s. 26, sub-s. 2 (*h*) (ii). (iii) That the planning authority had no power to impose a condition requiring a contribution towards the costs of developments which would amount to 100% of those costs. **Held** by Keane J, in granting the plaintiff a declaration that the conditions were *ultra vires* the authority and powers of the planning authority, but denying the plaintiff any other relief, 1, that the requirement that the

PLANNING—Conditions.

contribution be paid in three annual instalments unjustifiably constrained by the plaintiff as to the time within which it might exercise the planning permission, and frustrated the intention of the legislator to afford the owner of property a period of five years from the grant of permission to implement his permission, and was, therefore, invalid. 2. That the conditions failed to comply with the requirements of s. 26, sub-s. 2 (*h*) of the Local Government (Planning and Development) Act, 1963, and were thus invalid. 3. That there is nothing in the wording of s. 26, sub-s. 2 (*h*) of the Act of 1963 to suggest that in an appropriate case the contribution required cannot amount to the total cost of the development works. 4. The effect which a finding of invalidity has on conditions imposed on the grant of permission is to render that permission a nullity in its entirety where the condition is an essential part of the permission. *Kingsway Investments (Kent) Limited* v. *Kent County Council* [1971] A.C. 72; [1970] 1 All E.R. 70 considered. *Bord na Móna* v. *An Bord Pleanála and Galway County Council*

(H.C.) [1985] I.R.205

12. —— **Validity** — *Reason for imposing condition — Whether adequate — Whether moot point — Local Government (Planning and Development) Act,* 1963 (*No.* 28), *s.* 26.] S. 26 of the Local Government (Planning and Development) Act, 1963, permits the attaching of conditions to the granting of a planning permission in certain circumstances. The section also requires that reasons be given for any conditions imposed. The second-named respondent had received permission for the construction of a number of houses on condition that no house should be built on a certain portion of the site for three years. The reason given for the imposition of this condition was 'to . . . regulate the development so as to ensure that sewage disposal facilities are satisfactory in relation to residential development on the site.' The appellants alleged that since compliance with the condition could not in itself ensure that the sewage disposal facilities would be satisfactory, the condition could not be deemed good, as it was not supported by an adequate reason. On this basis they alleged that the permission itself was invalid. At the time of the hearing, the three years specified in the condition had expired. **Held** by the Supreme Court (Henchy J., Griffin and Parke JJ. concurring) in dismissing the appeal: The validity or otherwise of the impugned condition is a moot point since the period for which it was imposed has elapsed, and the said condition can be ignored in construing the legal force and validity of the permission. *Killiney and Ballybrack*

PLANNING—*continued.*

Development Association Ltd. v. *Minister for Local Government*

(S.C.) [1978] ILRM 78

DECISION

see also Nos. 2, 35, 36, 37

13. —— **Invalidity** — *Grant of outline permission by Minister — Permission subsequently held invalid — Diminution in value of land — Whether action maintainable by the plaintiffs to recover damages for negligence, negligent misrepresentation, breach of statutory duty and for infringement of plaintiff's constitutional rights — Conveyancing and Law of Property Act,* 1881 (*c.* 41), *s.* 7 — *Local Government (Planning and Development) Act,* 1963 (*No.* 28), *s.* 26 — *Local Government (Planning and Development) Act,* 1982 (*No.* 21), *s.* 6 — *Constitution of Ireland,* 1937, *Art.* 40.] In 1977 the first defendant granted outline planning permission to P.T. for the development of certain lands situate in Clondalkin, County Dublin, for industrial buildings. The plaintiffs purchased the land from P.T. together with the benefit of the outline planning permission. In 1980, the County Council refused to grant approval for the development in the terms of the outline planning permission. The plaintiff sought an order of mandamus in the High Court. An absolute order was granted in the High Court but on appeal to the Supreme Court it was discharged on the ground that the grant of outline planning permission was *ultra vires* and was a nullity. The plaintiffs then brought an action claiming damages against the first defendant for breach of statutory duty, negligence and negligent misrepresentation. They further claimed damages against the second defendant for failure to vindicate their property rights and for failure in its laws to respect and as far as practicable to defend and vindicate their property rights. It was agreed between the parties that it should be determined as a preliminary issue whether any action for damages was maintainable in the circumstances. At the trial of the preliminary issue it was held by the High Court (McMahon J.) in dismissing the plaintiffs' claim, 1, that the first defendant in reaching his decision to grant outline planning permission had acted *bona fide* on the advice of his legal advisers and accordingly he was not guilty of negligence or negligent misrepresentation. 2. That the plaintiffs were not entitled to damages for breach of statutory duty by the first defendant because although the decision was invalid it was not unlawful. 3. That the plaintiffs' claim under Article 40, s. 3 of the Constitution could not be sustained because they had not established that any injustice had been done to their property rights, as the Minister's decision did not contain any implied representation as to its validity. On appeal by the plaintiffs it was **Held** by the

PLANNING—Decision.

Supreme Court, (Finlay C.J., Henchy, Griffin, Hederman and Lardner JJ.) in dismissing the appeal, 1, that in reaching his decision to grant outline planning permission the first defendant had acted *bona fide* in pursuance of the advice which he had been given by the department's senior legal adviser, therefore he was not guilty of negligence or negligent misrepresentation. 2. That where a minister is exercising a public statutory duty he will not be liable in damages for an *ultra vires* action unless the exercise of the power involves the commission of a tort, or is actuated by malice, or unless the authority knew that it did not possess the power which it purported to exercise. In this case the first defendant believed that he possessed the power which he purported to exercise, thus his decision to grant outline planning permission, although an *ultra vires* act, was not actionable. 3. That the grant of outline planning permission by the first defendant was not intended as a limitation of the owner's property rights but rather as an enlargement and enhancement of these rights. The purchase of the lands by the plaintiffs for development purposes must be seen as the taking by them of a speculative risk, and the subsequent invalidity of the first defendant's decision, although probably contributing towards a diminution in value of those lands, could not be seen as an unjust attack on the plaintiffs' property rights. 4. That the fact that the plaintiffs were not entitled to compensation for the diminution in value of the land was not an unjust attack on the plaintiffs' property rights as it could be seen as a requirement of the common good that immunity from claims for compensation be granted to people who exercise statutory powers of decision where they acted *bona fide* and without negligence. *Per* Henchy J. — That Article 40, s. 3, sub-s. 1 was not relevant because it was not alleged against the second defendants that they had failed to defend and vindicate a personal right but rather it was alleged that an injustice had actually been done to a personal right. *Per* Henchy J. — That the plaintiffs' claim fell to be considered under Article 40, s. 3, sub-section 2. The plaintiffs had not proved that any injustice had been done to their property rights because when the planning decision had been declared a nullity they could have sued the vendors for breach of covenant for title or they could have sued to recover so much of the purchase price as was attributable to the value of the lands with the outline planning permission annexed to it, as money paid under a common mistake. *Per* Henchy and Lardner JJ. — That even if it was accepted that the plaintiffs had suffered financial loss by reason of the invalid planning permission, no injustice had been done to them because the State had done its best to put matters right by enacting the Act of 1982

PLANNING—*continued.*

which gave validity to such planning permissions. This statute did not affect people such as the plaintiffs who had decided to exercise their constitutional right to litigate the validity of such planning permissions in the courts. This was not an unjust discrimination because the purpose of excluding such people was to avoid an invasion of the judicial domain by attempting to give validity to any planning permission which had been declared invalid by the courts. *Pine Valley Developments Ltd.* v. *Minister for the Environment*

(H.C., S.C.) [1987] I.R.23; [1987] ILRM 747

14. —— **Judicial review** — *Development — Waiver — Estoppel — Material change of use — Change from unlicensed to licensed club — Telephone inquiries as to whether permission required — Letters in reply — Whether letters a determination that permission not required — Whether procedural requirement waived — Whether failure to consider material considerations — Planning (Northern Ireland) Order,* 1972 (*S.I. No.* 1634, *N.I.*17), *art.* 30.] A sports club applied to the Department of the Environment for planning permission to demolish and rebuild its pavilion. The application stated that there would be no change of use. Permission was granted and in a note to the grant the Department advised that the premises would be unsuitable for activities involving the playing of amplified music. After the pavilion was rebuilt, the club's architects wrote to the Department enclosing drawings of proposed internal modifications to it which would adapt two rooms to a servery and lounge and asked if the modification required a planning application. The Department replied on 26 November, 1984, that: ". . . the proposed alterations to the internal layouts of the above club (which includes the provision of a bar/store and lounge) does not require the approval of the planning authority." The club then applied for a certificate of registration under the Registration of Clubs Act (Northern Ireland), 1967, which would have permitted the sale of alcoholic drinks in the club. For the purpose of that application a person speaking on behalf of the club telephoned the Department requesting that a letter be sent stating that "an unlicensed club does not require a change of use application under the Planning Order to become a licensed club." On 4 March, 1985, the Divisional Planning Officer wrote to the club's architects as follows: "I am writing to advise you that under the Planning (N.I.) Order, 1972, there is no material change in use from an unlicensed club to a licensed club and planning approval is therefore not required." The applicant, a local resident who objected to the registration of the club, sought judicial review of the

PLANNING—Decision.

Department's ruling, arguing that its replies were a determination under article 30 of the Planning (Northern Ireland) Order, 1972, and that the Department had been in error in its approach and had misdirected itself. **Held,** remitting the determination to the Department for reconsideration, that, 1, the letter of 26 November, 1984, did not amount to a determination under article 30 of the 1972 Order on change of use. The inquiry and reply related purely to the structural changes in the clubhouse and not to any possible change of use. While the planning officer could have perceived that the change of use of the rooms for the serving of drink was imminent, he was not obliged to turn his mind to that as a possible change of use until he was asked to do so or it became necessary to consider the bringing of enforcement proceedings. 2. The letter of 4 March, 1985, was a determination under article 30 of the 1972 Order. The Department, which had given a considered written response, prepared by the Divisional Planning Officer, to a clear and unequivocal request, had waived the requirement in article 30 of the 1972 Order that an application to determine whether planning permission is required be in writing. *Western Fish Products Ltd.* v. *Penwith District Council* [1981] 2 All E.R. 204 distinguished. 3. That letter expressed the conclusion that a change in use from an unlicensed to licensed club did not constitute a material change of use as a general statement. It is possible in some cases, however, that a change from unlicensed to licensed club may lead to such a difference in patterns of use involving car parking, hours of use and the numbers and types of persons coming to the clubhouse, that the neighbourhood would be materially affected and it would be proper to regard a material change as having taken place. 4. The Department was in error in ruling as it did. It ought to look at the activities in the clubhouse and grounds before the grant of a certificate of registration, then at the activities which are likely to take place after the grant. It can then form a view whether any material change of use will be involved, and rule accordingly. *In re Thompson*

(Q.B.D.) [1985] N.I.170

15. —— **Judicial review** — *Natural justice — Reasonableness of decision — Application for permission to build houses in breach of stopline — Local public inquiry — Rejection of application recommended — Permission granted — Whether duty to make formal proposals amending plan — Calculation of overzoning — Whether decision unreasonable — New material arising after inquiry — Whether breach of rules of natural justice — Planning (Northern Ireland) Order,* 1972 (*S.I. No.* 1634, *N.I.* 17), *art.* 22.] In 1982 an application was made to the Department of the Environment for planninng permission for housing development on land at Cairnshill Road, Belfast. The land was just outside a line limiting development in the Belfast urban area (the stopline). The Department caused a local public inquiry to be held by the Planning Appeals Commission under article 22(1)(*c*) of the Planning (Northern Ireland) Order, 1972. The Commission reported to the Department in 1983. In its report the Commission said that the land was suitable for housing, but that it had not been persuaded that there was sufficient evidence of need for housing that would justify such substantial development outside the stopline and it recommended that permission be refused. The Department, however, granted permission to build not more than 500 houses on the land. The applicant, who lived at Cairnshill Road, just within the stopline, applied for judicial review of the decision to grant permission. He argued that the Belfast Urban Area Plan was a development plan within the meaning of article 8 of the 1972 Order and that consequently the inquiry should have been set up under article 22(1)(*a*) of the Order; that the Department acted unreasonably in not accepting the Commission's recommendation; that the Department also acted unreasonably because, having worked out that there was a "minimum urgent need" for 1,050 or 1,100 dwellings, the Department by applying an arbitrary multiplier of 2.5, in preference to the conventional overzoning factor of 1.25, presented an unsound case that 2,500 individual sites were required which justified the inclusion of the land in the planning requirements; and that the Department had not observed the rules of natural justice because it had made use of new material which had not been before the inquiry and on which the objectors had had no opportunity to comment. The new material consisted of a reworking of the figure of "minimum urgent need" to 800, following the demonstration by the objectors of an error in the Department's calculations and the omission of 440 sites originally presented to the inquiry, which omission produced the result that the land was still required even though the site requirement had dropped to 2,000 when the multiplier of 2.5 was applied to the new figure for "minimum urgent need". **Held,** that the application be dismissed, 1, the Belfast Urban Area Plan had not been adopted as a development plan under article 8 of the 1972 Order. While it could be argued that the Department had a duty to act under article 8, the real planning point calling for decision was whether a breach of the hitherto strictly observed stopline contained in that plan was justified, and although it was at one time thought within the Department that the inquiry should have been

PLANNING—Decision.

ordered under subparagraph (*a*) of article 22(1) of the 1972 Order, no relief would be granted as the applicant could have gained no advantage by the Department's inclusion of a reference under that subparagraph. 2. The Department had not acted unreasonably. There were two conflicting policy aims, namely the preservation of the stop-line and the provision of private housing. There was room for opinion on the matter and the applicant's arguments were not conclusive in the sense that those who disagreed were to be condemned as unreasonable. Similarly, there were arguments for and against the adoption of an overzoning factor of 2.5 and that decision also was not unreasonable. 3. The applicant was not damnified by, and had no grievance concerning, any alleged post-inquiry neglect of natural justice. It was the obvious duty of the Department to rework the figures of need in the light of the Commissioner's report. The omission of 440 sites in this reworking was justified by the Department by reference to points which had been in evidence at the inquiry and that an opportunity to test or contradict evidence was one thing, while the likelihood that by cross-examination on evidence the objectors could realistically have expected to change the views of an *ex hypothesi* openminded and fair Minister about the issue was quite another. *Per curiam* A planning decision is a decision on policy and the Minister or the Department could, while acting in good faith and reasonably, reach a different decision on the same facts as those considered by the Commissioner or the Planning Appeals Commission. In order to condemn adherence to a policy, it would be necessary to show that the circumstances rendered it wholly unreasonable to persist with it, or that a wholly unwarrantable use or disregard of evidence had occurred as a means of propping up that policy. *In re Blair*

(Q.B.D.) [1985] N.I.68

16. —— **Validity** — *Time limit for questioning — Application for permission — Application not advertised — Non-compliance with mandatory requirement — Grant of permission — Whether grant a nullity — Legal proceedings instituted after expiry of time limit — Whether time limit applicable — Local Government (Planning and Development) Regulations,* 1977 (*S.I. No.* 65), *reg.* 14 — *Local Government (Planning and Development) Act,* 1963 (*No.* 28), *s.* 82(3A) — *Local Government (Planning and Development) Act,* 1976 (*No.* 20), *s.* 42.

Planning — Application for permission — Status of applicant — Application on behalf of company — Company not incorporated on date of application — Whether permission granted to non-existent person a nullity — Whether promoters of company entitled to benefit of grant —

PLANNING—*continued.*

Local Government (Planning and Development) Acts, 1963 *to* 1983.] Section 82, sub-s. 3A of the Local Government (Planning and Development) Act, 1963, as inserted by s. 42 of the Local Government (Planning and Development) Act, 1976, provides, *inter alia,* that the validity of a decision of a planning authority on an application for planning permission may not be questioned in any legal proceedings unless such proceedings are instituted within two months from the date of such decision. The first respondent, a planning authority, granted permission for the conversion of certain premises on the 4 July, 1986. The application for permission had been made in the name of a company which had not been incorporated and whose principal promoter was the second named respondent. Because the application had not been advertised in the newspaper, as required by reg. 14 of the Local Government (Planning and Development) Regulations, 1977, the applicants in these proceedings did not become aware of that planning application or of the resultant decision until the 10 September, 1986. The applicants obtained from the High Court (Barrington J.) leave to apply for judicial review of the decision to grant planning permission on the grounds that the application for planning permission had not been advertised to the public and that it had been made by a non-existent person. At the hearing of this application for judicial review they argued further that the decision of the planning authority could be quashed, notwithstanding the expiry of the two month time limit, since a permission granted to a non-existent person was a nullity, there being no one who could take its benefit. **Held** by Barron J., in refusing the application for judicial review, 1, that the validity of the decision to grant planning permission could not be attacked on the grounds of failure to advertise the application for permission, after the expiry of the two month time limit provided for in the Act of 1963. *Grehan* v. *Mount Elm Construction Limited* (*Ex tempore,* Supreme Court, 19 April, 1985) applied. 2. That the non-existence of the applicant for planning permission did not render the application itself a nullity and that the decision to grant permission was not invalid. *The State (Alf-A-Bet Promotions Limited)* v. *Bundoran U.D.C.* 112 I.L.T.R. 9 applied. 3. That the reality of the situation was that the second respondent had been the applicant for permission and that the first respondent should be directed to correct the entry in the planning register accordingly. *Inver Resources Ltd.* v. *Limerick Corporation*

(H.C.) [1987] I.R.159; [1988] ILRM 47

PLANNING—*continued.*

DEVELOPMENT PLAN
see also Nos. 7, 9, 15, 35

17. —— **Material contravention** — *Application for planning permission — National monument on lands — Postal strike — Difficulty of planning authority in replying — Whether permission obtained by default — Permission amounting to material contravention of development plan — Whether planning authority had power to grant permission by default — Local Government (Planning and Development) Act,* 1976 (*No.* 20), *s.* 39(*d*) — *Local Government (Planning and Development) Act,* 1963 (*No.* 28), *s.* 26(3).

Planning — Application — Whether validly made — Requirement that application comply with planning regulations — Extent of failure to comply — Whether de minimis *principle applicable — Whether approach different to* inter partes *litigation — Local Government (Planning and Development) Regulations,* 1977 (*S.I. No.* 65), *arts.* 18, 20.] In the first action, a motion under s. 27 of the Local Government (Planning and Development) Act, 1976, Dublin County Council sought an order restraining Mr. Marren from carrying out any unauthorised development on his land. In the second action, Mr. Marren, who had applied for planning permission, sought a declaration that he had obtained planning permission by default for a bungalow that he was building on his land. A motte and bailey stood on the applicant's land; the motte was a national monument and had been listed for preservation under the County Council's development plan. The central issue was whether the applicant had obtained planning permission by default for the erection of his proposed bungalow. The applicant, whose original application for planning permission had been refused, re-applied for planning permission during a national postal strike when on 26 March, 1977, he handed in the application to the County Council's Planning Department. Although a letter seeking further information on the application was written by the County Council before the expiration of the statutory two month period, it was not delivered until 17 June, 1979, due to the postal strike. The applicant, who heard nothing from the County Council within the two month period, subsequently obtained bye-law approval and, in the belief that he had obtained planning permission by default, commenced his development in April, 1983. When the applicant re-applied for planning permission, the application was not accompanied by house plans but the application did refer to the house plans in the previous application. **Held** by Barrington J. in deciding that the applicant had not obtained planning permission for his development, 1, it would be a material contravention of Development Plan for the County Council to grant a planning permission in total disregard of the implications of that permission for a monument listed for preservation in its own document. 2. Having regard to the elaborate procedure set out in s. 26 of the Local Government (Planning and Development) Act, 1963, as inserted by s. 39 of the Local Government (Planning and Development) Act, 1976, which a planning authority was required to adopt before it could assume power to grant a permission which materially contravened its own plan, it followed that it could not, simply by ignoring the elaborate pre-conditions prescribed by the Oireachtas, give itself power to do that which it would not otherwise have power to do, and since the County Council had made no attempt to invoke the statutory procedure, it never had authority to grant a permission and could not therefore grant a permission by default. 3. The application for planning permission had not been made in accordance with Articles 18 and 20 of the Local Government (Planning and Development) Regulations, 1977, it had not been accompanied by such plans and such other particulars as were necessary to identify the land and to describe the works or structure to which the application related as required by the regulation; that the relevant provisions of the Regulations were not merely directory but were mandatory and that although no official in the council's office was misled by such non-compliance, the matter was not simply one *inter partes,* and it was at least possible that a member of the public might be misled or incommoded by the failure to comply with the regulations. *Monaghan Urban District Council* v. *Alf-a-Bet Promotions Ltd.* [1980] ILRM 64 applied. *Dublin County Council* v. *Marren*

(H.C.) [1985] ILRM 593

18. —— **Material contravention** — *Area designated in plan as a high amenity area — Proposed location by County Council of halting site within area — Whether proposed development a material contravention of development plan — Whether proposed development* ultra vires *powers of County Council — Local Government (Planning and Development) Act,* 1963 (*No.* 28), *ss.* 4, 19, 39.] Section 4, sub-s. 1(*b*) of the Local Government (Planninng and Development) Act, 1963, provides that any "development by the council of a county in the county health district" shall be an exempted development for the purposes of the Act. However section 39, sub-s. 1, prohibits the council from effecting any development in its county health district "which contravenes materially the development plan." Paragraph 2.26 of the Dublin County Development Plan,

PLANNING—Development Plan.

1983, provides that areas of high amenity include "areas fringing waterways, both river and canal." In addition it declares that "it will generally be the policy of the council to prohibit development" in such areas, but that in certain cases the council will consider applications for development which relate to uses pertinent to coastal or riverside recreation. The respondent proposed, in March, 1986, to provide a site for the settlement of travelling people at Cherryfield Linear Park which was in close proximity to the river Dodder. The site was intended to accommodate five families at any one time. The applicants, who were residents of the areas adjoining the park, sought, by way of judicial review, a declaration that the proposed development would be a material contravention of the development plan and *ultra vires* the powers of the respondent. The respondent maintained that the proposal did not involve a material contravention of the plan because, *inter alia,* it envisaged development of only a small section of a large high amenity area. **Held** by O'Hanlon J., in making the declaration sought, 1, that, were a private developer to argue that the area involved in his project was small in relation to the area comprised in a particular high amenity area and was thus not a material contravention of a development plan, the argument would be rejected. In a case such as the instant case, the requirements of the planning law had to be applied with as much stringency against the local authority as they would be against a private developer. *O'Leary* v. *Dublin County Council*

(H.C.) [1988] I.R.150

ENFORCEMENT

19. —— **Enforcement notice** — *Application to quash by way of certiorari — Claim that development exempted — No application made to An Bord Pleanála for ruling — Whether certiorari be granted — Local Government (Planning and Development) Act,* 1963 (*No.* 28), *s.* 31.] The respondent County Council had served an enforcement notice pursuant to s. 31 of the Local Government (Planning and Development) Act, 1963, upon the applicant, requiring that structures erected by him upon his property without the requisite planning permission be removed. The applicant received leave from the High Court to apply for an order of certiorari quashing the enforcement notice on the following grounds: (*a*) that the development undertaken by him was exempted development within the meaning of the 1963 Act and Regulations; (*b*) that the service of the notice without prior warning was in breach of the rules of natural justice; (*c*) that the notice was null and void in that the council had failed to consider the proper planning and development

PLANNING—*continued.*

of the area, or to have regard to all the relevant facts; (*d*) that the notice was bad in that there was no evidence that the matter had been considered by the county manager and, (*e*) that the relief by way of enforcement notice was unreasonable and excessive having regard to the nature of the matters in respect of which it was served. **Held** by Costello J. in refusing to make the order sought, 1, where the issue of whether a development is exempt arises, application may be made to An Bord Pleanála to determine the question. The court in exercising its discretion should refuse an order of certiorari where that is the sole issue, unless it can be shown that the planning authority had no reasonable grounds for arriving at its decision. The applicant had failed to show this. 2. There was no obligation upon the respondent to give notice of its intention to serve an enforcement notice. 3. The applicant had failed to adduce evidence that the Council had disregarded the Planning Acts, or its responsibilities thereunder. 4. The enforcement notice was not bad on its face, reciting as it did that the Council had considered the planning and development of the area, and had due regard to all relevant legal factors. 5. There was no evidence to show that the Council, by its enforcement notice, had acted unreasonably. Having decided that the development was not exempt, the Council was entitled to serve the said notice. *O'Connor* v. *Kerry County Council*

(H.C.) [1988] ILRM 660

20. —— **S. 27 application** — *Breach of conditions — Respondent company in voluntary liquidation — Whether order justified against the liquidator — Whether court able to make an order against the directors of the company — Whether appropriate — Local Government (Planning and Development) Act,* 1976 (*No.* 20), *s.* 27.] Section 27(2) of the Local Government (Planning and Development) Act, 1976, empowers the High Court to order any person to do or cease to do anything necessary to ensure that the conditions of a planning permission are observed. The first-named respondent, an insolvent company in process of liquidation, had failed to observe the conditions of a planning permission granted by the applicant local authority. The second and third-named respondents were the erstwhile directors of this company. The applicant sought an order under s. 27 of the 1976 Act against both the company and its former directors. The evidence established that the directors had been guilty of no fraud. The liquidator was willing to co-operate with the applicant in seeking payment to the applicant of the balance of money due under an insurance bond that the company had taken out as a condition of the planning permission. **Held** by Barrington J., declining to

PLANNING—Enforcement.

make the order sought, 1, that in view of the insolvency of the company and of the co-operative attitude of its liquidator, it would be inappropriate to make the order against the first-named respondent. 2. In certain circumstances it would be quite proper to join the directors of a company as respondents when a s. 27 application is made. 3. But that, as the directors of the company were rendered *functus officio* by the liquidation, and as no fraud had been alleged against them, it would also be inappropriate to make the order against the second and third-named respondents. *Dublin County Council* v. *Elton Homes Ltd.*

(H.C.) [1984] ILRM 297

21. —— **S. 27 application** — *Breach of conditions — Failure to complete — Respondent director of company — Prior order in existence against company — Whether appropriate to make order against director — Local Government (Planning and Development) Act,* 1976 (*No.* 20), *s.* 27.] Section 27, sub-s. 2, of the Local Government (Planning and Development) Act, 1976, provides that where any authorised development has been commenced but has not been, or is not being, carried out in conformity with the permission because of non-compliance with the requirements of a condition attached to the permission, or for any other reason, the High Court may, on the application of a planning authority or any other person, whether or not that person has an interest in the land by order to require any person specified in the order to do or not to do, or to cease to do, anything which the Court considers necessary to ensure that the development is carried out in conformity with the permission and specifies in the order. Planning permission had been granted to one M.F.S., a director of C.E. Ltd., in respect of F.P. Estate. At all material times, the estate was owned by C.E. Ltd. By written agreement, C.E. Ltd. granted a lease of certain sites in F.P. Estate to I.R.E. Ltd. The agreement provided, *inter alia,* that I.R.E. Ltd. would erect houses on these sites. C.E. Ltd. agreed to construct and complete all roads, sewers, storm water drains and water pipes to the public cisterns, which would be necessary for the proper use and enjoyment of the houses. Certain conditions attached to the planning permission and relating primarily to the landscaping of the site and the completion of sewerage and road works, were not complied with. A mandatory order under s. 27 of the Act of 1976 was made against M.F.S., C.E. Ltd., and I.R.E. Ltd., directing them to comply with the aforesaid conditions. The applicant sought a similar order under s. 27 of the said Act against the respondent, who was at all material times a director and shareholder of I.R.E. Ltd. It was established in evidence that the affairs of I.R.E. Ltd. had not been carried on in full compliance with the provisions of the Companies Acts. **Held** by Murphy J., in refusing the order sought, 1, that on the facts of the present case including the fact that the liability of I.R.E. Ltd. to comply with the said conditions had not been established and the fact that no fraud or misapplication of monies on the part of the respondent had been established, it would not be proper to make an order against the respondent. *Dublin County Council* v. *Elton Homes Ltd.* [1984] ILRM 297 and *Ellis* v. *Nolan and Ors.* (Unreported, High Court, McWilliam J., 6 May, 1983), considered. 2. Insofar as it is alleged that a respondent has been guilty of fraud or the misappropriation of monies, the proper remedy is plenary proceedings in which the party may have knowledge of the case against him, and may have a proper opportunity to defend himself against it. 3. Where the application turns upon the relationship between a director or shareholder and a company in which he is interested, the relationship should, in most cases, be investigated in the first instance by a liquidator in accordance with the provisions of the Companies Acts. It should not be sought to establish all of the relevant facts on proceedings designed to be heard on affidavit. *Dublin County Council* v. *O'Riordan*

(H.C.) [1986] ILRM 104

22. —— **S. 27 application** — *Jurisdiction of High Court — Whether High Court authority to make a mandatory order — Local Government (Planning and Development) Act,* 1976 (*No.* 20), *s.* 27.] The applicants, as planning authority, sought to restrain the respondent from demolition of a house and tower, his property, and to require him to reinstate the house by rebuilding and protecting portions thereof pending grant of planning permission. The applicants brought a motion under s. 27 of the Local Government (Planning and Development) Act, 1976 (the 1976 Act) for that purpose. The respondent submitted that the applicants were entitled only to relief of a prohibitory nature under s. 27(1) of the 1976 Act, and as the respondent had no planninng permission for development of the property, s. 27(2) of the 1976 Act did not apply. In his submission there was a distinction between s. 27(1) and (2) in that sub-section (1) referred to cases where the court might, on an application under the section prohibit the continuance of development or unauthorised use of land where no planning permission existed and was required, but sub-section (2) referred to cases where development was being carried out in contravention of a planning permission already obtained, and in such cases the court might require the occupier to do or not to do or cease to do anything which

PLANNING—Enforcement.

the court considered necessary to ensure that the development was carried out in conformity with the permission. Therefore, the respondents were not entitled to any mandatory relief as no planning permission had been obtained by the respondent. On behalf of the applicants it was contended that notwithstanding the apparent limitation of sub-section (1) the court might make orders to include mandatory directions, and *Dublin County Council* v. *Tallaght Block Company Ltd.* (Unreported, Supreme Court, 17 May, 1983) was relied upon in support of that contention. **Held** in dismissing the applicants' claim for mandatory relief, 1, as the *Tallaght Block* case did not contain any statement of principle or ruling on the point of law at issue, s. 27 was to be construed without the benefit of authority. 2. The respondent's submission on the distinction between s. 27(1) and (2) was correct in law. The distinction between cases where a planning permission existed and where there was none was important and intended by the legislature, bearing in mind that the procedure was of a summary nature, open to members of the public as well as planning authorities, and in certain cases likely to have potentially serious effects on an occupier against whom such order was granted. In the case where no planning permission had been obtained, evidence of unauthorised use or development would probably be confined at the s. 27 application stage to the fact that no permission existed for the alleged unauthorised use or development. Such was not the case where a breach of planning permission already granted was being alleged against the occupier, as the applicants could refer to the conditions of such permission in support of their allegations; the obligations imposed on the occupier were already defined; and the court could compel the performance of those obligations in relation to the development in a summary manner. It was not, however, to be inferred from s. 27 that the court might in such summary proceedings grant mandatory relief such as should be made only after full and fair investigation in the course of plenary proceedings, which were at all times open to the applicants to institute. *Dublin County Council* v. *Kirby*

(H.C.) [1985] ILRM 325

23. —— **S. 27 application** — *Jurisdiction of High Court — Building completed — Absence of permission — Whether development being carried out — Whether court has jurisdiction to order removal of building — Use of laneway giving access to respondent's lands — Application for injunction — Local Government (Planning and Development) Act,* 1963 (*No.* 28), *ss.* 2, 3 — *Local Government (Planning and Development) Act,* 1976 (*No.* 20), *s.* 27.] Section 27, sub-s. 1

PLANNING—*continued.*

of the Act of 1976 provides that where (*a*) a development of land, being development for which permission is required under Part IV of the Act of 1963, is being carried out without permission or (*b*) an unauthorised use is being made of land, the High Court may, on the application of any person . . . by order prohibit the continuance of the development or unauthorised use. Section 3 of the Act of 1963 provides that save where the context otherwise requires "development" in relation to land means the carrying out of any works on, in, or under land or the making of any material change in the use of any structures or other land. Section 2 of the Act of 1963 provides that "works" includes any act or operation of construction, excavation, demolition, extension, alteration, repair or renewal. The applicants were the owners and occupiers of certain lands on which their dwellinghouse was situate. The garden at the rear of the applicants' dwellinghouse shared a common boundary with the respondent's lands on part of which lands the respondent's dwellinghouse was situate. A laneway running along two sides of the applicants' lands gave access to the rear of the respondent's lands. In the absence of planning permission the respondent erected a concrete building on his lands in close proximity to the applicant's garden and to where the laneway entered the respondent's lands. The building was for use in the respondent's business as a building contractor. The applicants applied to the High Court for relief under s. 27 of the Act of 1976, *inter alia* for an order directing the respondent to forthwith remove all unauthorised structures from his lands and an order restraining the respondent's use of the laneway otherwise than for the purposes incidental to the use of his dwellinghouse as a dwellinghouse. Immediately after the hearing of the application Blayney J. granted certain relief but reserved judgment in relation to the application for the orders set out above. **Held** by Blayney J. in refusing to make the orders sought, 1, that the jurisdiction of the High Court under s. 27, sub-s. 1 of the Act of 1976 is limited to prohibiting the continuance of a development or unauthorised use which has been commenced without the required planning permission. *Dublin Co. Council* v. *Kirby* [1985] ILRM 325 applied. 2. That once the building was completed there was no longer any development being carried out within the meaning of s. 27, sub-s. 1(*a*) of the Act of 1976. Accordingly, assuming without deciding that the building was an unauthorised structure, the court had no jurisdiction under s. 27, sub-s. 1(*a*) of the Act of 1976 to order its removal. *Dublin Co. Council* v. *Kirby* [1985] ILRM 325 applied. *Dublin County Council* v. *Tallaght Block Co. Ltd.* [1982] ILRM 534 (H. Ct.), Unreported, 17 May, 1983, (S. Ct.).

PLANNING—Enforcement.

considered. 3. That the court was not justified in granting an order restraining the respondent's use of the laneway in the manner sought as it was likely that the respondent was entitled to use the laneway for access to his other lands beyond those immediately adjoining the lands of the applicants. *Loughnane* v. *Hogan*

(H.C.) [1987] I.R.322

24. —— **S. 27 application** — *Material change of use — Change of user — Licensed premises with cabaret — Installation of snooker tables — Whether change of user — Local Government (Planning and Development) Act,* 1976 (*No.* 20), *s.* 27.

Planning — Locus standi — *Objection — Local member of public bringing application — Whether applicant having sufficient standing — Local Government (Planning and Development) Act,* 1976 (*No.* 20), *s.* 27.] The applicant applied to prevent the respondent from using part of the rear of its licensed premises for the purpose of installing nine snooker tables under s. 27 of the Local Government (Planning and Development) Act, 1976. The respondent had been granted planning permission for the licensed premises in May, 1976, pursuant to s. 26 (5) and (9) of the Local Government (Planning and Development) Act, 1963. In the conditions attached to the grant of planning permission there were no conditions restraining the use of the rear of the premises for cabaret only. The applicant objected to what he claimed was a change of use from cabaret to a snooker hall. **Held** by Lardner J. in refusing the application, 1, the provision of snooker tables was an activity ancillary to the main use as a premises licensed for the sale of intoxicating liquor, since in recent years many public houses provided extensive facilities, such as meals and amusement facilities for their patrons. 2. The provision of ancillary facilities such as snooker tables in part of the licensed premises was within the 'use' for which the planning permission exists. The applicant failed to discharge the onus of showing that the provisions of such ancillary activities were an unauthorised use of the premises. *Robinson* v. *Chariot Inns Ltd.*

(H.C.) [1986] ILRM 621

25. —— **S. 27 application** — *Material change of use — Change of user — Mobile ice cream van parked in driveway of residential property at night — Whether unauthorised development — Whether material change of use — Local Government (Planning and Development) Act,* 1976 (*No.* 20), *s.* 27 — *Local Government (Planning and Development) Regulations,* 1977 (*S.I. No.* 65), *3rd Sched., cl.* 16.] The defendants carried on the business of retail selling of ice cream from two large colourful vans which they used to park

PLANNING—*continued.*

in the driveway of their dwelling house. Ice cream was never sold when the vans were at the house. On some occasions the freezers in the vans were connected to the electricity supply in the house. The area was zoned residential in the Dublin Development Plan, 1980. The local authority brought proceedings under s. 27 of the Local Government (Planning and Development) Act, 1976. The High Court (McMahon J.) held that the parking of the vans was a development within the meaning of s. 3 of the 1963 Act and was not an exempted development under s. 4(1)(*h*). An order restraining the defendants from parking commercial vehicles in the curtilage of their house was made. The defendants appealed to the Supreme Court. **Held** (by Hederman and McCarthy JJ.), Griffin J. dissenting in allowing the appeal. The parking of the vans was not development within the meaning of s. 3 of the 1963 Act and they were not being parked there for the purpose of the sale of goods within the meaning of s. 3(2)(*b*)(i) because that subparagraph only included the sale of goods on the premises in question. The keeping of the vans as alleged did not constitute exempted development pursuant to s. 4(1)(*h*). Class 16 of the Third Schedule to the 1977 Regulations was not relevant because, while a caravan is a van, a van is not necessarily a caravan. Griffin J. (dissenting). The parking of the vans was a material change in the use of the premises and was therefore development within the meaning of s. 3 because the area was residential and the interest of a potential purchaser of a house beside the appellents' house would be reduced by the sight of the vans. This development was not exempted development within the meaning of s. 4(1)(*h*) because the vans were not parked 'for any purpose incidental to the enjoyment of the dwelling house as such.' *Dublin Corporation* v. *Moore*

(S.C.) [1984] ILRM 339

26. —— **S. 27 application** — *Material change of use — Facade of building formerly used to advertise business conducted thereon — Agent of new owner adapting facade for advertising generally — Application to prohibit such use — Whether unauthorised change of use — Whether such change material — Local Government (Planning and Development) Act,* 1963 (*No.* 28), *ss.* 2, 3 — *Local Government (Planning and Development) Act,* 1976 (*No.* 20), *s.* 27.] The applicant planning authority sought an order in the High Court pursuant to s. 27 of the Act of 1976 prohibiting the continuance of the unauthorised use by the first respondent of the upper part of the facade of premises owned by the second respondent for the exhibition of advertisements. Section 27 of that Act enables the High Court to grant such an order, where,

PLANNING—Enforcement.

inter alia, an unauthorised use is being made of land. By s. 2, sub-s. 1, of the Act of 1963, the term unauthorised use is defined, in relation to land, as use commenced after 1 October, 1964, such change in use being a material change and being development other than development the subject of a permission granted under s. 26 of that Act or exempted development. The second respondent purchased the premises in question in 1983 from a company which had carried on the business of commercial motor body builders therein and which had, since before 1 October, 1964, its name and the nature of the business carried on on the premises painted in large scripted letters across the premises' facade. In 1984 the first respondent entered into an arrangement with the second respondent whereby (in the form it took by April, 1985) the first respondent was permitted to fix advertisements directly to the facade of the premises, these advertisements advertising the goods and services of a variety of businesses. The issue to be determined was whether this use of the facade by the respondents constituted a material change in use from the use that had been made of it by the previous owner. **Held** by Blayney J., in granting the order sought, 1, that the present use constituted a change in use since the previous owner's advertisement was connected with the business carried on by it on the premises whereas the present advertisements were not so connected. 2. That this change of use was a material change as the facade must be regarded as a separate planning unit from the remainder of the premises and once the facade was so regarded the materiality of the change effected thereon by the respondents was clear. *Dictum* of Bridge J. in *Burdle* v. *Secretary of State for the Environment* [1972] 1 W.L.R. 1207 at p. 1213, approved. *Mills & Allen Ltd.* v. *City of Glasgow District Council* [1980] S.L.T. (Sh. Ct.) 85 distinguished. *Per* Blayney J. — The extremely wide definition of advertisement contained in s. 2, sub-s. 1, of the Act of 1963 indicates that a change from using a site for an advertisement of one kind to using it for an advertisement of a different kind can readily constitute a change in use. *Dublin Corporation* v. *Regan Advertising Ltd.*

(H.C.) [1986] I.R.171

27. —— **S. 27 application** — *Material change of use — Intensification of use — Quarry — Whether development — Whether Minister required to decide dispute — Whether permission required — Local Government (Planning and Development) Act, 1963 (No.* 28), *ss.* 3, 5(1), 24(1) — *Local Government (Planning and Development) Act,* 1976 (*No.* 20), *ss.* 27, 46(4).

PLANNING—*continued.*

Tort — Nuisance — Quarry — Blasting operations — Heavy traffic — Dust and noise — Standard of comfort — Whether landlord liable for nuisance caused by the tenant's act — Whether plaintiffs entitled to damages and injunction — Contribution as between defendants — Civil Liability Act, 1961 (*No.* 41), *ss.* 21, 34.] S. 5(1) of the Local Government (Planning and Development) Act, 1963, provides that if any question arises in any particular case as to what is or is not development, the question must be decided by the Minister. S. 27 of the Local Government (Planning and Development) Act, 1976, permits application to be made to the High Court for an order restraining unauthorised development. S. 46(4) of the said Act provides that the 1963 and 1976 Acts are to be construed together as one Act. The plaintiffs, a married couple, purchased a house from the first-named defendant in 1973. Access to the house was by means of a narrow laneway, to which, in addition to the house and surrounding land, the plaintiffs acquired a right-of-way. Prior to the purchase, the first-named plaintiff noticed that some topsoil had been scraped away from the adjoining field which was also the property of the defendant. He inspected the planning register and ascertained that no permission had been granted to use the field as a quarry. In May, 1977, an oral agreement was entered into by the son of the first-named defendant, acting on her behalf, and the managing director of the second-named defendant. The written memorandum records the fact that the second-named defendant would take a lease of the field for three years. It was expressly agreed that permission was given for the installation in the field of 'crusher screeners and conveyors and necessary equipment for the manufacture of stone.' Pursuant to this agreement blasting operations commenced on a regular and extensive basis; on one occasion causing cracks to appear in the walls of the plaintiffs' house, breaking a window and causing shock and alarm to the second-named plaintiff who was pregnant at the time. Evidence was given that dust from the operations entered the house and lay about in layers. Because of the dust, the plaintiffs were unable to sit in their garden. Lorries travelling up and down the laneway in convoys also caused noise and dust. In wet conditions the laneway became a morass, and almost impassable. The plaintiffs brought an action for damages for nuisance and seeking an injunction to restrain the defendants from committing further acts of nuisance. They also brought a motion pursuant to s. 27 of the 1976 Act. By consent, the evidence in the nuisance action was treated as the evidence in the motion, and a single judgment was given. The defendants argued that the court had no

PLANNING—Enforcement.

jurisdiction to hear the s. 27 application, contending that the work in the field was not development, and that s. 5 of the 1963 Act applied. They also argued that permission for the development was not required under Part IV of the 1963 Act, since s. 24(1) provides that permission is not required for development commenced before the appointed day, i.e. 1 October, 1964. Evidence was adduced to show that shale had been drawn from the field at intervals since 1946, but on a small scale and with primitive equipment. **Held** by Costello J. in awarding damages for nuisance, in granting the relief sought in both the nuisance action and the s. 27 motion, and in apportioning damages as follows: 75% to be borne by the second-named defendant and 25% by the first-named defendant, 1, the standard of comfort to be applied to the plaintiffs in deciding whether a nuisance had been committed was that which a reasonable person living in an area used for normal agricultural purposes would expect to enjoy. 2. The plaintiffs were entitled to damages for consequential loss resulting from the damage caused to their house by one of the blasting operations, for the shock caused to the second-named plaintiff on the same occasion and for the fact that they had been forced to leave their home and live in rented accommodation. 3. The relationship created between the defendants by the agreement of May, 1977, was that of landlord and tenant. The first-named defendant as landlord was liable for the nuisance caused by her tenant in so far as she expressly or by necessary implication authorised its commission. *Harris* v. *James* (1876) 45 L.J.Q.B. 545 followed. 4. The object of the agreement of May, 1977, was the manufacturing of stones from the field. The natural consequences of the large scale operations envisaged by the parties was nuisance arising from noise and dust in the field, and as such, was implicitly authorised by the first-named defendant. 5. The damage caused to the plaintiffs' house was not a normal consequence of the blasting operations, as evidence showed that blasting could be carried out with delayed detonators which would avoid such damage. The first-named defendant was not therefore liable for the damage, nor for the alarm caused to the second-named plaintiff on the same occasion. 6. Nuisance arising from the user of the laneway was implicitly authorised by the first-named defendant since by implication a right-of-way had been granted by her to the second-named defendant in respect of the laneway. 7. Since the nuisance was actually committed by the second-named defendant, the major share of fault must be apportioned to it. 8. The plaintiffs were *prima facie* entitled to an injunction, since the infringement of their rights was serious, and the injuries which they would suffer if the nuisance were

PLANNING—*continued.*

permitted to continue would not be adequately compensated for by damages. 9. S. 5 of the 1963 Act cannot be interpreted as meaning that the Minister is appointed to arbitrate in every possible dispute as to what constitutes development. It must be interpreted as meaning that where a question arises between a Planning Authority and another person in the course of the procedures established by the 1963 Act, as to what constitutes development, it must be referred to the Minister. S. 5 cannot therefore in any circumstances bar an application to the court under s. 27 of the 1976 Act. 10. Where present-day development differs materially from development carried on prior to the 1963 Act, it cannot be said to have been commenced prior to the appointed day. The quarrying carried on in the field following the agreement of May, 1977, was a major intensification of the drawing of shale customary in the field prior to 1963. The intensification was such as to render contemporary operations materially different from those carried on prior to the appointed day. It was, therefore, development requiring permission under Part IV of the 1963 Act. *Patterson* v. *Murphy* **(H.C.) [1978] ILRM 85**

28. —— **s. 27 application** — *Material change of use — Intensification of use — Planning permission not having been obtained — Whether unauthorised development — Quarry — Local Government (Planning and Development) Act,* 1963 (*No.* 28), *ss. 5,* 24 — *Local Government (Planning and Development) Act,* 1976 (*No.* 20), *ss.* 14(2), 27.] The applicant brought an application for an order pursuant to s. 27 of the Local Government (Planning and Development) Act, 1976, restraining the respondent from carrying out unauthorised development at its lands situate at Angliham, Menlough, in the County of Galway. The lands in question are a quarry which the applicant leased from 1950 to 1973, during which period the quarry was operated manually with mechanical loaders being used occasionally and a primary and secondary stone crusher being employed to crush stone. The only structures erected during this period were two huts used to store tools, etc. On average ten to twelve six ton lorry loads were extracted daily, reaching a maximum of 144 loads daily between 1963 and 1966. Ten people were normally employed and at peak times this number doubled. In 1976, the respondent leased this quarry and since then there has been a continuing build up of plant and machinery, ancillary buildings having been erected and the number of people employed has increased from six to fourteen. On average 300 tons of stone were extracted daily and at peak times 1,000 tons. The applicant contended that the respondent's intensified use of the quarry

PLANNING—Enforcement.

constituted a development or a material change of use within the meaning of s. 3 of the Local Government (Planning and Development) Act, 1963, for which planning permission was necessary; furthermore that the respondent's current scale of operation of the quarry was considerably in excess of the use made thereof on the appointed day (1 October, 1964), for the purposes of the Local Government (Planning and Development) Act, 1963, and that this intensified use of the quarry constituted a development within the meaning of s. 3 of the 1963 Act for which planning permission was required. The respondent denied that it had intensified the use it had made of the quarry and contended that it merely modernized its methods of quarrying and that an intensification of use would only constitute a material change of use when it was shown that the intensification gave rise to different considerations relevant to the planning code and that no evidence has been adduced nor argument made by the applicant to show that such intensification had in any way affected the proper planning and development of the area in which the quarry is situate or had adversely affected anyone living in that area. **Held** by Barron J. in dismissing the application, 1, that the respondent's present use of the quarry did not constitute a material change of use from its use on the appointed day. 2. That in determining whether or not a present use was materially different from a use being made on the appointed day one must look at the matters which a planning authority would take into consideration if a planning application were made on both dates and if these matters were materially different then the nature of the present use must be equally materially different. 3. That no evidence has been adduced to indicate that the applicant would have taken any different matters into consideration in determining an application for planning permission made now rather than on the appointed day. Hence there had been no evidence of a material change of use. *Galway County Council* v. *Lackagh Rock Ltd.*

(H.C.) [1985] I.R.120

29. —— **s.27 application** — *Material change of use — Intensification of use — Respondents slaughtering cattle prior to 1st October, 1964, for animal feed — Significant increase in numbers of cattle being killed from 1983 — Cattle being killed for use as human food — Commercial activity — Whether respondents' activity since 1983 a material change of use — Local Government (Planning and Development) Act,* 1963 (*No.* 28), *s.* 3 — *Local Government (Planning and Development) Act,* 1976 (*No.* 20), *s.* 27.] The applicant applied pursuant to s. 27 of the Local Government (Planning and Development) Act,

PLANNING—*continued.*

1976, for an order restraining the respondents from using their farm as an abattoir. The respondents had been killing cows on their farm to feed greyhounds since the 1940s but from 1983 onwards there was a significant increase in the number of cattle being killed and the respondents began to kill cattle to provide food for human consumption. The respondents did not have a licence under the Slaughter of Animals Act, 1935. It was argued on behalf of the applicant that the respondents' activity from 1983 onwards constituted a material change of use and therefore a "development" within the meaning of s. 3 of the Local Government (Planning and Development) Act, 1963, for which the respondents had not obtained planning permission. It was argued for the respondents that any intensification of use which had taken place was not a material change of use in the context of the proper planning and development of the area. It was stressed that there had been no evidence of any complaint having been made concerning the respondents' activity; nor that the applicant planning authority, had an application been made to it for permission for the current operation, would have taken into account any matters additional to those matters it would have considered had an application been made in respect of the previous operation. **Held** by Keane J., in making the order sought, 1, that in an application under s. 27 of the Act of 1976 the question whether there had been a material change of use was a matter of fact to be determined by the court. 2. There was no requirement that the applicant should adduce evidence as to the attitude the planning authority would have taken had an application been made to it for planning permission now rather than on the date of coming into effect of the Act of 1963. *Galway County Council* v. *Lackagh Rock Ltd.* [1985] I.R. 120 considered. 3. That, while the extent to which a change of use had affected other persons in the neighbourhood was a factor to be considered by the court in deciding whether the change of use was material, the absence of any evidence of complaints having been made by neighbours was not crucial. 4. That the respondents' activity since 1983, which involved slaughtering on a significantly greater scale than before and which was being carried on as part of a commercial operation. was an unauthorised material change of use of the respondents' farm. *Monaghan County Council* v. *Brogan*

(H.C.) [1987] I.R.333; [1987] ILRM 564

30. —— **s.27 application** — *Material change of use — Intensification of use — Land used for parking caravans — Increase in number of caravans — Whether unauthorised change of use — Whether intensification of use a material change of use — Local Government (Planning and*

PLANNING—Enforcement.

Development) Act, 1963 (*No.* 28) — *Local Government (Planning and Development) Act,* 1976 (*No.* 20), s. 27.] The respondent owned certain lands in County Dublin on which it operated a caravan park. The lands had been purchased by the respondent in June, 1962, at which time they were used for parking caravans and they continued to be so used. At the time of purchase approximately ten caravans used the site during the summer months, and some caravans were parked there throughout the year. No planning permission had ever been sought or obtained in respect of the use of the site as a caravan park. Since the operative date the number of caravans using the site had doubled. The applicant sought to restrain the use of the lands as a caravan park, claiming, *inter alia,* that the use had been so intensified since the operative date as to constitute a change of user. In addition it sought an order to restrain the development of the toilet facilities. **Held** by Murphy J., in refusing the application, that notwithstanding the increase in the number of caravans, the user of the lands had remained the same. The use had been intensified due to a more extensive use of the lands or a more successful operation of the business, but such intensification did not amount to a change of use. *Guildford Rural District Council* v. *Fortesque* [1959] 2 Q.B. 112 and *Glamorgan County Council* v. *Carter* [1963] 1 W.L.R. 1 considered. *Dublin County Council* v. *Carty Builders & Co. Ltd.*

(H.C.) [1987] I.R.355

31. —— **s. 27 application** — *Unauthorised use — Continuous use of premises as a garage business for period commencing before 1964 and ending in 1969 — Intermittent use of premises as garage business thereafter — Respondents' use of premises for garage business commencing in 1985 — Applicant seeking to prohibit such user — Whether such user abandoned before 1985 — Principle applicable — Local Government (Planning and Development) Act, 1963 (No.* 28), *ss.* 2, 3 — *Local Government (Planning and Development) Act,* 1976 (*No.* 20), *s.* 27.

Estoppel — Res judicata — *Applicant seeking to restrain respondents from unauthorised use of land — Previous criminal proceedings against first respondent alleging unauthorised use of the land dismissed — Whether such dismissal barring the applicant from raising issue of use in civil proceedings — Relevance of the manner in which criminal proceedings dismissed — Local Government (Planning and Development) Act,* 1963 (*No.* 28), *s.* 24 — *Local Government (Planning and Development) Act,* 1976 (*No.* 20), *ss.* 26, 27.] The applicant planning authority sought an order in the High Court pursuant to s. 27 of the Act of 1976 prohibiting the respondents from

PLANNING—*continued.*

using certain premises in County Meath for, *inter alia,* any commercial purpose unless and until planning permission therefor shall have been granted pursuant to the provisions of Part IV of the Act of 1963. Section 27 of that Act enables the High Court to grant such an order where, *inter alia,* an unauthorised use is being made of land. By s. 2, sub-s. 1 of the Act of 1963 the term unauthorised use is defined, in relation to land, as use commenced after 1 October, 1964, such change in use being a material change and being development other than development the subject of a permission granted under s. 26 of that Act or exempted development. The applicant conceded that the present use of the premises by the respondents (which had commenced in 1985) was similar to that which had been made of them prior to 1 October, 1964 — that of a garage business — but contended that his original user had been abandoned in the intervening years. The evidence showed that the use of the premises for a garage business had ceased in 1969 when the premises were acquired by a double glazing company which used them for its own business until 1975. During the latter part of this company's ownership of the premises some business in the nature of garage work was carried on followed by a short period during which the premises were used for a joinery business. Between 1975 and 1977 the premises were unused. They were then used by an individual for about a year for the manufacture of pallets. Between the years 1978 and 1982 the premises were occupied by a company and a garage business was again carried on. In 1982 the premises were again unused for a period until another company occupied them and conducted a furniture retail business therein. There was evidence of user of portion of the premises at this time for the sale and repair of motor vehicles but such user was minimal until the respondents jointly occupied the premises in 1985. The respondents contended that the pre-1964 user had not been abandoned and that in any event the issue as to whether the present user was unauthorised had already been decided in their favour and was *res judicata* by reason of the dismissal in the District Court in 1985 of criminal prosecutions under the Planning Acts against the first respondent and the landlord of the premises in respect of the user of the premises for a garage business. **Held** by Egan J., in granting the relief sought, 1, that the issue as to user was not *res judicata;* as a general proposition a finding of "not guilty"in criminal proceedings did not constitute a bar against civil proceedings being brought against an accused in respect of the same matter. The exception to this proposition — where the verdict in the criminal proceedings deals specifically with the issue sought to be

litigated in the civil action — did not apply here since the District Court dismissed the complaints without stating reasons. *Kelly* v. *Ireland* [1986] ILRM 318 distinguished. 2. That the pre-1964 user of the premises had been abandoned on a number of occasions during the intervening years, for example, during the periods of occupation by the double glazing and furniture retailing companies, with no evinced intention by any of the users to resume the lawful user. Accordingly, the subsequent resumption of the pre-1964 user by the respondents constituted an unauthorised use of the premises. *Dublin County Council* v. *Tallaght Block Co. Ltd.* [1982] ILRM 534 (H.C.); (Unreported, Supreme Court, 17 May, 1983) and *Hartley* v. *Minister of Housing and Local Government* [1970] 1 Q.B. 413 applied. *Pioneer Aggregates (U.K.) Ltd.* v. *Secretary of State for the Environment* [1985] A.C. 132 distinguished. *Meath County Council* v. *Daly*
(H.C.) [1987] I.R.391; [1988] ILRM 274

EXEMPTED DEVELOPMENT
see also Nos. 18, 19, 25

32. —— **Conversion** — *Conversion of house from use with bed-sitting rooms into two flats — Absence of permission — Whether conversion works are an exempted development — Whether carrying out of works constitute a change of user — Application for injunction — Local Government (Planning and Development) Act,* 1963 (*No.* 28), *ss.* 2(1), 4(1)(*g*) — *Local Government (Planning and Development) Act,* 1976 (*No.* 20), *ss.* 26, 27.] Section 4, sub-s. 1 (*g*), of the Local Government (Planning and Development) Act, 1963, provides that one of the categories of exempted development shall be "development consisting of the carrying out of works for the maintenance improvement or other alteration of any structure, being works . . . which do not materially affect the external appearance of the structure so as to render such appearance inconsistent with the character of the structure or of neighbouring structures." Section 2, sub-s. 1 states that, save where the context otherwise requires, "use" in relation to land does not include the use of the land by the carrying out of any works thereon. It further provides that the "works" includes any act or operation of construction, excavation, demolition, extension, alteration, repair or renewal. "Land" includes any structure. The plaintiffs, a married couple, were owners and occupiers of a three storey terraced house. The defendant owned the adjoining premises, which was used as a residence with multiple bed-sittingrooms. The defendant carried out building works on the premises in order to adapt and convert it for use as a residence with two flats. Exterior alterations were

made to the rear of the premises and consisted of insertion of a window in a side wall, replacement of a window by a door and the construction of a balcony and staircase. The defendant did not apply for planning permission for any of these works. The location of a window and the proximity of the balcony to the plaintiffs' house, resulted in their patio and downstairs rooms being overlooked. The plaintiffs applied to the High Court for an injunction pursuant to s. 27 of the Local Government (Planning and Development) Act, 1976, restraining the defendant from carrying out or continuing with the construction works. The plaintiffs argued that the works required planning permission and further that the alterations seriously interferred with the privacy of the patio and downstairs rooms. The defendant contended that the works carried out by him were an exempted development and did not require planning permission. The High Court (Barrington J.) refused the plaintiffs' application and on appeal by the plaintiffs it was **Held** by the Supreme Court (Finlay C.J., Walsh, Griffin JJ.) in disallowing the appeal, 1, that although the work materially affected the external appearance of the structure, it was not inconsistent with the character of the house itself or adjoining houses and was an exempted development pursuant to s. 4, sub-s. 1 (*g*) of the Act of 1963. 2. That the Act of 1963 provides two separate statutory schemes with regard to permission for development and permission for change of use and the carrying out of the works did not of itself, constitute a change in user within the meaning of section 2. *Cairnduff* v. *O'Connell*
(S.C.) [1986] I.R.73; [1986] ILRM 465

33. —— **Estoppel** — *Agent of planning authority representing that development exempt — Whether authority estopped from denying the development exempt — Whether representation* ultra vires — *Local Government (Planning and Development) Act,* 1963 (*No.* 28), *ss.* 5, 26.] The defendant had erected a commercial motor garage in her back garden, following representations from an inspector from the Planning Department of Dublin Corporation, who assured her husband that he could proceed with the work and that he would look after the planning permission. The inspector was subsequently dismissed from his position. The complainants brought proceedings in the District Court, alleging that the defendant had failed to comply with an enforcement notice requiring her to remove the structure. The District Justice dismissed the case on the ground that the complainants were estopped from denying that the garage was exempted development, because of the misrepresentations of their former employee. At the request of the complainants the District Justice

PLANNING—Exempted Development.

stated a case for the decision of the High Court as to whether he had been correct in law in so holding. **Held** by McMahon J. in answering the question in the negative, 1, since, pursuant to the Local Government (Planning and Development) Act, 1963, the question of whether a development is exempt must be referred to the Minister, there could be no question of an inspector from the Planning Department having ostensible authority to make representations to that effect. 2. A public authority cannot be estopped from asserting that it acted *ultra vires,* either by itself or through its agent. 3. The representation of the inspector that planning permission would be attended to was *ultra vires,* as being in breach of s. 26 of the 1963 Act, which provides that the planning authority, in dealing with applications for planning permission, must have regard to the provisions of the development plan. Such representation is not therefore binding on the planning authority. *Dublin Corporation* v. *McGrath*

(H.C.) [1978] ILRM 208

34. —— **Fried fish shop** — *Conditions implied as to opening hours — Whether violated by selling fish and chips outside opening hours — Local Government (Planning and Development) Act,* 1963 *(Exempted Development) Regulations* 1967 (*S.I. No.* 176).] Rule 4 of the Local Government (Planning and Development) Act, 1963 (Exempted Development) Regulations, 1967, combined with Part IV of the Schedule to the said Regulations, provides that a change of use from one type of shop to another is exempted development, except where the change of use is to, *inter alia,* a fried fish shop. The defendant had been granted permission by the complainant for change of use of his premises from a food-market to a fish and chip takeaway shop. No condition with regard to opening hours was attached to the permission. Upon objection and appeal by local residents to the Minister, the permission was confirmed with the addition of a condition that the premises should not open for the permitted use between the hours of 11.00 p.m. and 8.00 a.m. The permitted use was stated to be that of a fried fish and chip shop. The defendant was subsequently convicted in the District Court of having sold fish and chips after 11.00 p.m. He argued that the condition attached to the permission could only apply to the sale of fried fish, since no permission was required for a fish and chip shop, insofar as it did not sell fried fish. He submitted that the only evidence before the learned District Justice was that fish and chips had been sold, and that this could be a description of boiled or smoked fish and chips. Case stated by the learned District Justice as to whether he had been correct in law in convicting

PLANNING—*continued.*

the defendant. **Held** by Finlay P. in answering the case stated in the affirmative, 1, the defendant, having applied for permission for a fried fish and chip shop, could not be heard to assert that because the word 'chip' was unnecessarily included in the permission, the condition must be construed as prohibiting the sale of fried fish but not that of chips after 11.00 p.m. 2. Since the word 'chip' used in connection with fish and referring to a food, can only mean a fried chip of potato, the permitted use, was operated at least in part, that is, in reference to fried chips, after the prohibited hour. *Dublin Corporation* v. *Raso*

(H.C.) [1976-7] ILRM 139

Grant of permission *see* Nos. 2, 10, 15, 16, 38

Injunction applications (s.27) *see* Nos. 2, 20-31, 32

Material change of use *see* Nos. 14, 24-30

OUTLINE PERMISSION
see also No. 13

35. —— **Jurisdiction of Minister of State** — *Minister granting outline permission — Subsequent application for approval — Contravention of development plan — Application for planning approval — Whether planning authority bound by Minister's decision — Whether restricted by outline permission — Mandamus — Unlawful purpose — Local Government (Planning and Development) Act,* 1963 (*No.* 28), *ss.* 19, 26 — *Local Government (Planning and Development) Act,* 1976 (*No.* 20), *ss.* 14, 42.] In October, 1976, the prosecutor's predecessor in title appealed to the Minister for Local Government against the refusal by the respondent planning authority of his application for planning permission for a proposed industrial development in a green-belt area. The respondents refused to grant permission on the ground (*inter alia*) that the site of the proposed development was located in an area zoned on the respondents' development plan "to provide for the further development of agriculture and to preserve open space amenity." On the 10 March, 1977, the Minister allowed the developer's appeal, and granted outline permission for the development sought, subject to a condition. On the 16 July, 1980, the prosecutors applied to the respondents for planning approval of the development. The respondents, by notice dated the 15 September, 1980, notified the prosecutors of the respondents' intention to refuse the application for approval, giving (as their reasons for so refusing) the reasons which had been given in 1976 and objecting that the site for which planning approval was sought represented

PLANNING—Outline Permission.

part only of the site in respect of which the Minister had granted outline permission. On the 8 December, 1980, the prosecutors applied to the High Court for an order of mandamus, directing the respondents to grant the application for planning approval. A conditional order of mandamus was granted by the High Court. At the hearing of the prosecutors' motion for an order absolute, notwithstanding cause shown by the respondents, it was **Held** by Barrington J., in disallowing the cause shown and making an order absolute, 1, that, in determining an application for planning approval brought by an applicant who has obtained outline permission for development of the same site, a planning authority is bound to proceed on the basis that a proposal for a development of the nature indicated in the outline permission has been accepted in principle, and is inhibited from re-opening issues which have been determined by the outline permission. 2. That, as the grant of outline permission by the Minister had not been set aside, the respondents were bound to accept its validity and were not entitled to reject the prosecutors' application for planning approval on the ground that the outline permission contravened the provisions of the development plan for the area containing the prosecutors' site. 3. That the respondents were not entitled to reject the application for planning approval on the ground that it was made in respect of the development site described in the outline permission less half an acre, since the regulation made pursuant to the Planning Acts expressly authorised an applicant for planning approval to seek approval for part of the area specified in the relevant outline permission. 4. That the prosecutors' application for an order of mandamus was not precluded by the provisions of s. 82, sub-s. 3A, of the Act of 1963. On appeal by the respondents it was **Held** by the Supreme Court (Walsh, Henchy and Hederman JJ.), in allowing the appeal, 1, that the outline permission granted by the Minister for Local Government constituted a material contravention of the development plan for the area which included the prosecutors' site. 2. That, although the Minister had power under s. 26, sub-s. 3, of the Act of 1963 to authorise a planning authority to grant a permission which contravened the provisions of a development plan, where an application in that behalf has been made to him by a planning authority, nevertheless the Minister had no power under the Act of 1963 or otherwise to grant an outline permission which contravened the relevant development plan, and, accordingly,his grant of an outline permission to the prosecutors had been made *ultra vires* and was void. 3. *Per* Walsh and Hederman JJ. — That, as the respondents had not obtained permission (pursuant to s. 26,

PLANNING—*continued.*

sub-s. 3 of the Act of 1963) to approve a material contravention of the relevant development plan, the respondents were bound by that sub-section to refuse to grant planning approval of the development proposed by the prosecutors. 4. That, even if the respondents had not given to the prosecutors, within the period specified in s. 26, sub-s. 4, of the Act of 1963, notice of the respondents' rejection of the prosecutors' application for planning approval, a default approval pursuant to that sub-section could not have been deemed to have been given since such default provisions cannot be invoked where the development proposed by the applicant for planning approval is prohibited by the statute. 5. That, although the Minister's grant of outline permission had not been quashed, the court's discretion should not be exercised so as to compel the respondents to approve a development which was prohibited by statute. *The State (Pine Valley Developments Ltd.)* v. *Dublin County Council* **(H.C., S.C.) [1984] I.R.407**

36. —— **Outline permission granted** — *Subsequent application for approval — Planning authority — Jurisdiction — Consideration of application — Decision to be based on proper planning of area — Whether planning authority restricted by terms of outline permission — Whether planning authority empowered to impose condition absent from outline permission — Local Government (Planning and Development) Act,* 1963 (*No.* 28), *s.* 26.] Dublin County Council had granted the prosecutor outline planning permission for a housing development in Lucan, County Dublin, subject to certain conditions, which required the development not to be commenced until adequate sewerage should have been made available. The outline permission contained no conditions relating to the construction of access roads to and within the site of the development. Subsequent applications to the County Council both for planning approval in respect of the projected development and for full planning permission therefor, were granted by the County Council, to take effect only after certain road works to and within the boundaries of the development should have been constructed. The prosecutor was also to be required to pay a fixed sum per house erected towards the construction of those road works. The respondent Board, on appeal by the prosecutor, had confirmed the grant of full planning permission, subject substantially to the conditions imposed by the County Council, but had refused approval, alleging that the projected development would be premature, and would create a serious traffic hazard on the road then fronting its site. The prosecutor applied for and obtained a conditional order of certiorari to quash the two

orders made by the respondent refusing approval, on the ground that the outline planning permission on which the applications for approval had been based had not been circumscribed by any conditions relating to public roads. **Held** by Barron J., in allowing the cause shown and discharging the conditional order, 1, that the grant of outline planning permission in respect of a particular development implies merely a decision by the planning authority that the projected development is not inconsistent in principle with the proper planning of the area, which must be the main consideration of the authority. 2. That the authority is not precluded from granting approval for the development subject to conditions arising which had not been envisaged at the time of the granting of the outline permission. *The State (Pine Valley)* v. *Dublin County Council* [1984] I.R. 407 and *The State (Kenny)* v. *An Bord Pleanála* (Unreported, High Court, Carroll J., 23 February, 1984: Supreme Court, 20 December, 1984) considered. *The State (Tern Houses (Brennanstown) Ltd.)* v. *An Bord Pleanála*

(H.C.) [1985] I.R.725

PLANNING PERMISSION
see also Nos. 2, 15, 16

37. —— **Permission** — *Extension* — *Refusal* — *Whether* ultra vires *planning authority* — *Whether development carried out under existing permission* — *Whether completion possible within reasonable time* — *Whether irrelevant factors considered by planning authority* — *Local Government (Planning and Development) Act,* 1982 (*No.* 21), *s.* 4(1).] The prosecutor had applied for an extension to the period for which planning permission for the construction of 36 semi-detached houses would be valid. The respondent refused the extension on the ground that this permission had been superceded by permissions for 18 houses on the same site, that these houses had been constructed and that the permission for 36 houses could no longer be carried out. S. 4 (1) of the Local Government (Planning and Development) Act, 1982 provides that a local authority 'shall, as regards a particular permission, extend' the period for which permission is given to enable the development to be completed 'if, and only if' the application is in accordance with such regulations under the Act as apply to it and the authority are satisfied that development commenced before the expiration of the existing permission, that substantial works were carried out within that time pursuant to that permission and that the development will be completed within a reasonable time. The application for extension was based on the assertion

that the completion of 18 houses on the development site was part of the 36 house permission, that completion had been hampered by litigation concerning ownership and that this complied with the requirements of s. 4 (1) of the 1982 Act. Upon inspection of the planning register and the site itself, the respondent discovered that houses had been constructed pursuant to permissions granted subsequent to the permission for which an extension was now being sought. The prosecutor applied for an order of certiorari to quash the refusal. **Held** by Gannon J. in refusing to grant an absolute order, 1, s. 4 (1) of the 1982 Act, which was expressed in mandatory terms bearing both positive and negative aspects, conferred on a planning authority not merely the power but the obligation to extend a planning permission related to uncompleted development on which a developer had embarked, but only where all the conditions set out therein had been complied with. 2. In the context of s. 4 the reference to 'a particular permission' indicated that an applicant for an extension must distinguish clearly between the planning permission concerned and any other permissions which may have been granted in relation to the same structure or other lands, and the onus is on the applicant to clear the negative aspect and make way for the positive aspect of the obligation imposed on the planning authority. 3. The particularity of the provisions of s. 4 (1) precluded consideration by a planning authority of any other matters, and any decision arrived at without consideration of all the matters set out therein or on consideration of other matters would be *ultra vires*. 4. In this instance there was a remarkable disparity between the information given in the prosecutor's application form and accompanying letters and the information disclosed by inspection of the register and development site, and the planning authority would have been justified in rejecting the application on the basis that the conditions in s. 4 (1) had not been complied with. 5. While a refusal under s. 4 which simply quoted the words of the statute might have conveyed that the planning authority considered the inaccuracy of the information given as a ground of refusal and although the notice only referred to one of the conditions in s. 4, it had not been shown that in arriving at the conclusion expressed in the notice the respondent had taken account of irrelevant factors in making its decision. *The State (McCoy)* v. *Dún Laoghaire Corporation*

(H.C.) [1985] ILRM 533

38. —— **Permission** — *Grafting of part of one planning permission onto a subsequent permission* — *Adjacent plots of land fronting onto roadway* — *Planning permission granted for*

PLANNING—Permission.

development of one plot subject to condition that a common access be provided for both plots — Common entrance constructed by developer without consulting local authority — Local authority confirming compliance with condition by letter — Authority precluded from going behind letter — Revision of planning permission — Partial development — Position of partially developed site on failure to complete scheme — Whether partial development authorised — Developer not entitled to develop under mutually inconsistent permissions — Variation — Splicing of two planning permissions — Direct or implied incorporation of partial development in application for variation — Construction of planning permission — Words given natural and ordinary meaning — Whether motivation of local authority and planning policy relevant to construing permission — Builder's road — Exempted development — Permission to retain road as permanent road — Whether road would ultimately be taken in charge by local authority irrelevant to whether road an authorised development — Local Government (Planning and Development) Regulations 1977 (*S.I. No.* 65) — *Local Government (Planning and Development) Act,* 1982 (*No.* 21), *s.* 2.] The lands of F.H., part of which were owned by the plaintiff, and the adjoining lands of L.C. fronted onto a main road. Prior to 1976 each property had its own entrance from the main road but in 1981 a joint access was constructed serving separate avenues into each property. In May, 1984, a strip of land from the front of both properties was compulsorily acquired for road widening. The defendant, in carrying out the road widening operations, lowered the level of that strip of land and afterwards restored the common entrance and regraded the avenue leading into L.C. but left the avenue leading into F.H. cut off at a height of 5 feet. The plaintiff brought proceedings claiming mandatory injunctions to compel the reinstatement and regrading of the avenue into F.H. and damages for trespass. The defendant, in its defence, alleged that the joint entrance from the road had been lawfully constructed in accordance with planning permission. In 1977 the plaintiff's predecessors in title obtained planning permission for a land exchange scheme designed to achieve satisfactory joint access from the main road to both F.H. and L.C. The then owners of F.H. applied for planning permission to build a scheme of 71 houses on the lands of F.H. The application envisaged access to the development through a separate entrance where the then existing entrance was. On the 10 November, 1978, permission was granted for 68 houses on condition that access to the development should be over an access shared with L.C. On the 28 May, 1979, building bye-law approval was granted for the 68 houses. By now the then owner of F.H. had installed part of the services for the scheme but L.C., a school, decided that it needed another hockey pitch. The owner of F.H. agreed to transfer part of the lands of F.H. to L.C. for that purpose and on the 18 July, 1979, applied for revised permission for 60 houses, allowing for a change of user for a hockey pitch and providing for a joint access similar to that contemplated by the 1977 permission. This permission was granted by the defendant but was appealed by a third party. On the 10 November, 1980, the plaintiff contracted to buy the lands of F.H., less the area which was to be sold to L.C., for which the seller was to provide the services together with planning permission for building. The plaintiff refused to close this sale while the revised permission was under appeal. On the 20 November, 1981, the defendant wrote to the owner of F.H. stating that the condition in the permission of 10 November, 1978, as to joint access, had been complied with. On the 7 May, 1982, the owner of F.H. wrote to the defendant referring to the permission of 10 November, 1978, and stating that a temporary builder's road was being constructed along the line of the road in the revised permission (which was under appeal) but that it did not wish that road to be taken as part of the revised development. On the 10 August, 1982, An Bord Pleanála allowed the third party's appeal against the revised permission on the grounds that it was not satisfied that the joint access would be safe. On the 24 January, 1983, the owner of F.H. applied for planning permission for the lands of F.H. excluding the hockey pitch, the road reservation and the joint access road. This application was for a change of house type, rearrangement of sites, 12 additional sites on the already developed site and for retention of the 'as constructed' builder's road. This permission was refused by the defendant but was granted by An Bord Pleanála on the 16 March, 1984, on condition that access to the development should be located at the corner of the site at which the builder's road emerged and should be constructed in accordance with the defendant's requirements. The plaintiff, relying on the permission of the 16 March, 1984, and on the defendant's letter of 20 November, 1981, that the common access had been built to its satisfaction, closed the sale. The plaintiff now claimed to be entitled to graft the access arrangements permitted by the permission of the 10 November, 1978, onto the Board's permission of the 16 March, 1984. The defendant claimed that because the plaintiff was not the owner of the entire of the lands comprised in the permission of the 10 November, 1978, that permission was incapable of implementation and so was useless to the plaintiff; so that the access interfered with by the road works had not been a lawful access. It was further argued on behalf of the defendant that the development was unauthorised on the grounds that the joint access had been built without consultation with it; and that the avenue to F.H. was a temporary road only which might not have been constructed to a sufficiently high standard to allow it to be taken in charge. **Held** by Carroll J., in giving judgment for the plaintiff, 1, that the question of whether a partially completed development was an authorised development depended upon whether the planning permission could be regarded as severable. *Horne* v. *Freeney* (Unreported, High Court, Murphy J., 7 July, 1982) considered. 2. That while the legislature could not have intended that the purchaser of a house in a partially completed scheme should be left vulnerable if the entire scheme was not completed, it did not follow that a developer might develop part of a scheme under one permission and then develop the remainder of the site under a mutually inconsistent permission. *F. Lucas and Sons Ltd.* v. *Dorking and Horley Rural District Council* (1964) 62 L.G.R. 491 considered. 3. That the desire of a planning authority to achieve a well laid out, symmetrical and balanced housing estate was not only a matter of planning policy and motivation which operated in the mind of the authority, but was also relevant to defining the scope of the permission granted. *Dictum of* Winn J. in *F. Lucas and Sons Ltd.* v. *Dorking and Horley Rural District Council* (1964) 62 L.G.R. 491 disapproved. 4. That even if a partial development could be regarded as authorised, a developer was not entitled to draw on any other existing permission to complete the scheme but must instead apply for further permission, incorporating either directly or indirectly the partial development which had already taken place. 5. That the application for permission of the 24 January, 1983, was, as a matter of construction, an application for a variation of the permission of the 10 November, 1978, with retention of the already constructed internal road system. 6. That regardless of the circumstances in which the joint access had been constructed, the defendant could not now go behind its letter of 20 November, 1981, confirming that it had been constructed to its satisfaction; which letter had been written expressly for the benefit of third parties. 7. That because the letter of the 7 May, 1982, had been written with specific reference to the permission of the 10 November, 1978, it was irrelevant in the context of the permission of the 16 March, 1984. 8. That at the date of the granting of the permission of the 16 March, 1984, the interior roads and permanent joint access were already permitted development under the permission of the 10 November, 1978, and after that permission

was granted the builder's road became a permitted permanent road tied into a permitted permanent joint access. 9. That the question as to whether the builder's road would ultimately be taken in charge by the defendant was irrelevant to deciding whether it was a permitted development. 10. That since the plaintiff's right of access to the public road had been interfered with, the plaintiff was entitled to relief. *Holland* v. *Dublin County Council* 113 I.L.T.R. 1 applied. *Dwyer Nolan Developments Ltd.* v. *Dublin County Council*

(H.C.) [1986] I.R.130

PURCHASE NOTICE

39. —— **Mandamus** — *Meaning of "owner" — Date of service — Availability of alternative remedies — Default procedure — Local Government (Planning and Development) Act,* 1963 (*No.* 28), *s.* 29 *(as amended).*] Section 29, sub-s. 1, of the Local Government (Planning and Development) Act, 1963, provides that where planning permission to develop land has been refused or granted subject to conditions, if the owner of the land claims that the land has become incapable of reasonably beneficial use in its existing state and cannot be rendered capable of such use by any development for which permission has been granted, he may serve a "purchase notice" on the relevant planning authority, requiring it to purchase his interest in the land. Sub-section 2 of s. 29 provides that a planning authority on which a purchase notice is served shall, "before the end of the period of three months beginning on the date of the service of that notice", serve on the owner a notice either agreeing to purchase the land or refusing to do so. Thomas McInerney & Company Ltd. ("the prosecutor") entered into a contract to buy certain land, which was duly conveyed not to the prosecutor but to another company in the group of which the prosecutor was a member, the latter becoming registered owner. Planning permission in respect of the land was refused. The prosecutor served a purchase notice by registered post addressed to the County Manager at the principal office of the respondent, which was delivered on the 5 April, 1984, but not received in the Planning Department of the respondent until the 9 April, 1984. On the 6 July, 1984, the respondent served notice refusing to purchase the land. The prosecutor obtained in the High Court a conditional order of mandamus commanding the respondent to comply with the purchase notice, on the ground that it had failed to reply to it within the time limited by the Act of 1963. At the hearing of the prosecutor's motion for an order absolute, notwithstanding the cause shown, it was **Held** by Carroll J., in allowing the cause shown and discharging the

PLANNING—Purchase Notice.

conditional order, 1, that the purchase notice had not been served by the "owner" of the land within the meaning of s. 29, sub-s. 1, and, it not being a case where justice demanded that the corporate veil be lifted, was therefore invalid. 2. That the "date of service" of the purchase notice, for the purposes of s. 29, sub-s. 2, was the date the notice was delivered to the respondent's principal office, the 5 April, 1984. 3. That the prosecutor had not exhausted the statutory remedies, and was therefore not entitled to the relief sought. 4. That the Act of 1963 is not to be construed as implicitly providing that if a planning authority fails to reply to a purchase notice within the time limit it must comply with the purchase notice. *The State (McInerney & Co. Ltd.)* v. *Dublin County Council*
(H.C.) [1985] I.R.1; [1985] ILRM 513

40. —— **Property affected by road scheme** — *Underlet at comparatively low rentals — Planning permission for two years' use available — Whether "incapable of reasonably beneficial use" — Whether permission and notice referred to same premises — Whether objection not contained in counter-notice can be raised — Planning (Northern Ireland) Order,* 1972 (*S.I. No.* 1634, *N.I.* 17), *arts.* 70, 71, 73.] The claimant acquired premises in Great Victoria Street, Belfast. In July, 1980, he applied for planning permission to enlarge the premises and change their use. Permission was granted subject to a condition that the permission should be for a period of two years only. The reason given for the condition was that the site would be affected by a road scheme. The claimant then served on the Department a purchase notice under article 70 of the Planning (Northern Ireland) Order, 1972, which provides that, if permission to develop land is refused or granted subject to conditions and the owner claims that the land has become incapable of reasonably beneficial use in its existing state, the owner may serve a notice on the Department requiring it to purchase his estate in the land. The Department served a counter notice objecting to the purchase notice on the grounds that part of the land was already in reasonably beneficial use and that a planning permission existed which, if acted upon, would render the land capable of reasonably beneficial use. The Lands Tribunal, after hearing uncontradicted evidence from the claimant's valuer, found that the premises were let at rents substantially lower than rents in other parts of the street which were unaffected by the scheme and that the two year planning condition inhibited any viable economic development of the premises. The Tribunal upheld the claimant's purchase notice. On a case stated to the Court of Appeal, the Department argued that the finding that the premises were incapable of reasonably

PLANNING—*continued.*

beneficial use was wrong in law and that the Tribunal had wrongly accepted as decisive the opinion of the claimant's valuer and also sought to advance a new objection to the purchase notice, viz. that the premises subject to the planning condition were not identical to those in the notice. **Held** that, 1, the phrase "reasonably beneficial" must mean not only beneficial in the sense that a benefit of some kind is to be derived, but reasonably beneficial in the sense that a reasonable degree of benefit is to be derived. The Tribunal clearly exercised its own judgment on the evidence presented to it and the conclusion it drew from the proved facts did not support the proposition that there had been a misdirection in point of law. 2. The planning application and the purchase notice related to the entire premises. While permission was expressly sought for the ground floor and the first and second floors and the top floor of the building was not mentioned, it was unrealistic to create a vertical dichotomy by reference to the floors of a property which are mentioned in a planning application, unless one was dealing with separate units of accommodation such as self-contained flats. In any event an objection not specified in the counter-notice could not be taken into account to invalidate the purchase notice. *Essex County Council* v. *Essex Incororated Congregational Church Union* [1963] A.C. 808 applied. *Allen* v. *Department of the Environment*
(C.A.) [1985] N.I.195

Refusal of permission — compensation *see* Nos. 5-9
Retention permission *see* No. 2

Unauthorised development or use *see* Nos. 22-31
Undertaking to grant permission *see* Nos. 7, 9

—— Advertisements — Exhibition — Unauthorised change of use.
see **Planning,** 26

—— Appeal — Deposit — Requirement of lodgment of deposit — Whether arbitrary discrimination — Constitutional validity of statutory provisions.
see **Constitution,** 40

—— Appeal — Hearing — Fair procedures — Whether oral hearing required.
see **Constitution,** 40

—— Appeal — Residents' Association instituting proceedings challenging Corporation's decision to grant planning permission — Developers seeking to have these proceedings dismissed —

PLANNING—*continued.*

Whether proceedings frivolous or vexatious — Whether proceedings an abuse of the process of the courts.
see **Practice and Procedure,** 1

—— Application — Advertisement — Compliance with regulations.
see **Constitution,** 45

—— Application — Status of applicant — Application on behalf of company — Company not incorporated on date of application — Whether permission granted to non- existent person a nullity — Whether promoters of company entitled to benefit of grant.
see **Planning,** 16

—— Application — Whether validly made — Requirement that application comply with planning regulations — Extent of failure to comply — Whether *de minimis* principle applicable — Whether approach different to *inter partes* litigation.
see **Planning,** 17

—— Authority — Duty of care — Whether local authority in granting planning permission owed a duty of care to avoid damage to purchaser of house due to defective siting and construction — Statutory functions and powers — Purpose of statutory powers — Whether sufficient relationship of proximity between planning authority and purchaser of house.
see **Negligence,** 3

—— Conditions — Permission granted subject to conditions — Conditions effecting radical alteration of development proposed in application — Whether evidence of failure of planning authority to consider application made by developer.
see **Judicial Review,** 6

—— Decision of planning authority — Whether liable to be quashed by certiorari.
see **Judicial Review,** 6

—— Decision — Whether *ultra vires* determination of application constitutes a decision.
see **Judicial Review,** 6

PLANNING—*continued.*

—— Enforcement — Carrying out of development without permission — Restraining order — Retention permission subject to conditions.
see **Real Property,** 9

—— *Locus standi* — Challenge to validity of permission — Member of public affected by development.
see **Constitution,** 45

—— *Locus standi* — Objection — Local member of public bringing application — Whether applicant having sufficient standing.
see **Planning,** 24

—— Permission — Application — Advertisement — Contents inadequate — Permission invalid — Electricity supply cables — Permission invalid notwithstanding that complainant landowner purchased lands after publication of defective advertisement.
see **Constitution,** 45

—— Permission — Authorised development — Failure to comply with conditions of permission — Planning authority seeking order commanding director of company to complete development.
see **Planning,** 21

—— Permission — Construction — Words given natural and ordinary meaning — Whether motivation of local authority and planning policy relevant to construing permission.
see **Planning,** 38

—— Permission — Default permission — Whether applicable.
see **Judicial Review,** 6
Planning, 35

—— Permission — Effect — Outline permission — Subsequent application for approval — Whether planning authority restricted by terms of outline permission.
see **Planning,** 36

—— Permission — Invalidity — Default permission — Whether applicable — Material contravention of development plan — Default permission inapplicable.
see **Planning,** 35

—— Permission — Invalidity — Default permission — Whether applicable —

PLANNING—*continued.*

Decision of planning authority to grant outline permission — Notice of decision given to developer within prescribed period — Decision, even if made *ultra vires,* sufficient to exclude default permission.
see **Judicial Review,** 6

—— Permission — Invalidity — Diminution in value of land — Such permission granted by Minister — Whether action maintainable by the plaintiffs to recover damages for negligence, negligent misrepresentation, breach of statutory duty and for infringement of plaintiff's constitutional rights.
see **Planning,** 13

—— Permission — Sale of land — Contract — Condition.
see **Sale of Land,** 1, 2

—— Permission — Use — Change — Absence of permission — Land used as quarry before the appointed day — Use as quarry by respondents after that date — Whether material change of use — Test applicable.
see **Planning,** 28

—— Refusal of outline permission — Compulsory purchase order — Whether order made in compliance with housing legislation.
see **Compulsory Acquisition,** 5

—— Undertaking to grant permission.
see **Planning,** 7, 9

PLEA — Autrefois acquit.
see **Criminal Law,** 53

PLEADINGS — Particulars.
see **Practice and Procedure,** 48, 49

POINT OF LAW
see **Question of Law**

POLICE
see **Garda Síochána**
see also **Arrest and Detention**
Criminal Investigation

POLICE INFORMER
see **Criminal Law,** 47

POLITICAL OFFENCE — Extradition — Exception.
see **Extradition,** 3-8

POLITICAL PARTY
—— Local authority — Exclusion of members of party proclaiming particular policy — Whether power to exclude part of protective and self-defensive power of council.
see **Local Government,** 3, 4

—— Policies — Whether judicial notice of policies of political parties.
see **Local Government,** 4

PONTIFICAL UNIVERSITY
see **Seminary**

PORTS
see **Harbours and Piers**

POSTAL SERVICE

—— **Post office** — *Monopoly — Statutory monopoly in respect of the conveying of "letters" — Private courier service — Minister seeking an injunction — Whether defendant's trading in breach of the monopoly — Meaning of "letters" — Whether relevant provisions unconstitutional — Post Office Act,* 1908 (*c.* 48), *s.* 34.

Attorney General — Company operating in breach of a statutory monopoly — Attorney General, acting as guardian of public rights, seeking an injunction — Whether proceedings misconceived.

Constitution — Statutory monopoly in respect of the conveying of "letters" — Whether violative of personal and property rights — Right to communicate — Right to earn a livelihood — Whether such a right a personal or a property right — Whether infringed — Interpretation — Purposive or literal approach — Whether court precluded from considering the principles of social policy — Onus of proof — Constitution of Ireland, 1937, *Arts.* 38, 40.3.1, 40.3.2, 45.3.1 — *Post Office Act,* 1908.

Evidence — Challenge to the constitutionality of legislation conferring statutory monopoly on Post Office — Evidence as to the alleged inefficiency in the administration of the postal service — Whether admissible.] The Post Office Act, 1908, s. 34(2), as amended by the Ministers and Secretaries Act, 1924, gives the Minister for Posts and Telegraphs a monopoly of conveying letters and of providing related services. The defendants, a company and its directors, began to operate a courier service in Dublin in 1981. The plaintiffs sought a declaration and injunction in support of the state postal monopoly, which they contended had been breached by the defendants. The Attorney General sued as guardian of public rights. The defendants denied that they were engaged in conveying letters; alleged that their operation was a private messenger service permissible under the 1908 Act;

POSTAL SERVICE—*continued.*

and contested the right of the Attorney General to seek an injunction when the Act provided a summary criminal remedy. In a counterclaim the 2nd, 3rd and 4th-named defendants, the directors currently holding office, asserted that the 1908 Act was unconstitutional because it infringed the right of citizens to communicate freely (an alleged personal right due for protection under Article 40.3.1° or Article 40.6.1°), as well as their right to earn a livelihood (an alleged personal or property right). **Held** by Costello J., granting the injunction and declaration sought by the plaintiffs and dismissing the defendants' counterclaim, **(A) Interpreting the Post Office Act, 1908,** 1, that the defendants were not entitled to make a business of collecting letters and that they had been in breach of the Minister's monopoly. 2. That 'letter' as used in the 1908 Act included any communication written or printed by which the sender addressed himself in a personal way to the recipient, but that business communications (such as invoices or cheques) which lacked a personal salutation were not 'letters'. 3. That 'excepted letters' within the meaning of s. 34(2) of the Act were communications dealing with the private affairs of the sender or addressee delivered either by the sender's own messenger or by a contractor who so conducted his business that he obtained letters from only one sender at a time. 4. That the Attorney General was entitled to seek an injunction to restrain the breach of a statutory provision notwithstanding that the breach was also an offence: *Attorney General (O'Duffy)* v. *Mr. Appleton, Surgeon Dentist Ltd.* [1907] 1 I.R. 252 applied; *dictum* in *Attorney General* v. *Chaudry* [1971] 1 W.L.R. 1614 approved. 5. That in entertaining such a suit brought by the Attorney General, the court will act only in exceptional cases, will consider the adequacy of alternative remedies, but will not insist upon a prior criminal prosecution: *Gouriet* v. *U.P.O.W.* [1978] A.C. 435 approved. **(B) Interpreting the Constitution,** 6. That there was a 'right to communicate' to be protected under Article 40.3.1° (though not under Article 40.6.1°(i)), but it was not an absolute right and might be regulated by law. 7. That the 'right to earn a livelihood' was a personal right under Article 40.3.1°, but it was not an absolute right, and not a property right under Article 40.3.2°: *Murphy* v. *Stewart* [1973] I.R. 97 applied: *Brendan Dunne Ltd.* v. *Fitzpatrick* [1955] I.R. 29 distinguished. 8. That the State had a duty by its laws to protect from unjust attack the personal right of each of the defendants to earn a livelihood, but that the postal monopoly did not constitute such an attack. 9. That, as the Constitution was a political instrument as well as a legal document, the manner of its interpretation differed from that appropriate to the construction of a statute and should be purposive rather than literal. 10. That the court might for certain purposes have regard to the principles of social policy set out in Article 45, notwithstanding the wording of the preamble thereto: *Murtagh Properties Ltd.* v. *Cleary* [1972] I.R. 330 applied. 11. That any ideological preference for private enterprise deducible from Article 45 did not require the State in legal proceedings to justify the existence of a public monopoly, and that the onus of proving a statute unconstitutional rested with the party challenging its validity: *Norris* v. *Attorney General* [1984] I.R. 30 *dictum* applied. 12. That the inefficiency of a public service did not render the provisions of a statute unconstitutional, such inefficiency being a matter for legislative cognisance, and that evidence of inefficiency proposed to be tendered by the defendants was inadmissible as irrelevant. *Attorney General* v. *Paperlink Ltd.*

(H.C.) [1984] ILRM 373

—— Employee — Contract of service — Postal sorters — Overtime period — Break period — Whether term of contract.
see **Employer and Employee,** 5

—— Employee — Offence — Prosecution — Indictable charge against employee of Post Office — Solicitor employed by Post Office having carriage of prosecution — Whether delegation of carriage of case by D.P.P. *ultra vires* — Whether likely to create unfairness in procedure.
see **Criminal Law,** 58

—— Employee — Suspension — Act transferring plaintiff civil servant to employment of state-sponsored body — Officer suspending plaintiff — Whether officer had authority to suspend — Delegation of power — Natural justice — Permissible duration of suspension.
see **Employer and Employee,** 23

PRACTICE AND PROCEDURE
see also **Criminal Law,** 34-69

ACTION

1. —— **Abuse of process** — *Planning appeal to be conducted by way of oral hearing — Residents' Association instituting proceedings challenging Corporation's decision to grant planning permission — Developers seeking to have these proceedings dismissed — Whether proceedings frivolous or vexatious — Whether proceedings an abuse of the process of the courts — Local Government (Planning and Development) Act,* 1976 (*No.* 20), *s.* 42 — *R.S.C., O.*19, *rr.* 27, 28, *O.*84, *r.*10.] Cavern Systems Dublin Ltd. (the developers) applied to the second named defendant (the Corporation) for permission to construct an underground storage and handling facility for liquid petroleum gas at Tolka Road Extension, Dublin. On notification by the Corporation to the developers of their intention to grant the permission sought, Clontarf Residents Association appealed to An Bord Pleanála and during the first day of the hearing it was discovered that the Residents Association had instituted but not served High Court proceedings challenging the validity of the Corporation's decision. The summons named the developers and the Corporation as defendants and both issued notices of motion to stay or dismiss these proceedings (*a*) for want of prosecution; (*b*) under O. 19 r. 27 and 28 R.S.C.; and (*c*) because the proceedings were an abuse of the process of the court. By s. 42 of the Local Government (Planning and Development) Act, 1976, the Residents Association had only two months from the date of notification of an intention to grant the planning permission to institute High Court proceedings. This they had done, although they had not effected service and, on the facts, the second named defendant only became aware of the proceedings on 22 February, 1983. The hearing before An Bord Pleanála as planned was to have been extensive, and costly preparations had already been undertaken by An Bord Pleanála, the developers and by the Corporation. If the existence of these High Court proceedings had been known and had they not been determined at the time of the hearing of the appeal by the inspectors of An Bord Pleanála, an application to adjourn the appeal would have been made. **Held** by Costello J. in dismissing the Residents Association's claim, 1, the claim that the proceedings should be stayed for want of prosecution was unsustainable as the summons had not been served upon the defendants who had not therefore been required to appear thereto. 2. The court's jurisdiction under O.19 arose only when it could be shown from the pleadings themselves that the proceedings were vexatious or frivolous and it could not be said at this stage that the Residents Association had no reasonable cause of action or that their claims lacked reality or were without foundation; *McCabe* v. *Harding Investments Ltd.* Unreported, Supreme Court 1982 No. 79 (27 October, 1982); *Barry* v. *Buckley* [1981] I.R. 306. 3. An objector deciding to maintain an appeal to a planning decision under the Local Government (Planning and Development) Act, 1976, was not estopped from instituting or maintaining proceedings in the High Court to challenge the validity of a decision on a point of law. 4. The effect of s. 42 of the 1976 Act was however to require institution of proceedings at an early date in the national interest and to inform developers of a legal challenge to the validity of a decision and thereby allow the adjournment of planning appeals and the avoidance of unnecessary waste of time and money. 5. The Residents Association had instituted proceedings in accordance with the rules of court and their claim was not therefore statute barred provided they served the proceedings within twelve months, but by adopting this course of action and by deliberately not serving the summons or disclosing its existence, they were consciously rendering s. 42 useless and flouting Parliament's will. Such conduct should be regarded as an abuse of the process of the court and since there were no reasonable grounds to justify what was done the Residents Associations' claim would be dismissed. *Cavern Systems Dublin Ltd.* v. *Clontarf Residents Association*
(H.C.) [1984] ILRM 24

2. —— **Abuse of process** — *Stay of proceedings — Inherent jurisdiction of High Court — Purchaser's claim for specific performance of contract of sale by defendant — Purchaser's failure to complete sale on receipt of valid completion notice — Express terms enabling vendor to rescind and forfeit deposit — Defendant's motion for order dismissing plaintiff's action or for stay of proceedings — Motion granted and action dismissed* — Lis pendens *vacated.*

Sale of land — Contract — Rescission — Failure of purchaser to complete sale on receipt of valid completion notice — Forfeiture of deposit — Express terms enabling vendor to rescind and forfeit deposit — On defendant's motion purchaser's action for specific performance dismissed — Lis pendens *vacated.*] The plaintiff agreed to purchase and the defendant agreed to sell the defendant's stud farm. The written agreement

PRACTICE AND PROCEDURE—Action.

between the parties contained the Incorporated Law Society of Ireland's General Conditions of Sale (1978 Edition). Clause 28 of these General Conditions enables the vendor to serve a 28 day Completion Notice on the purchaser if the sale is not completed by the agreed closing date and if the vendor, at the time of service, is ready, willing and able to complete the sale. Clause 29 provides that if the purchaser fails to comply with the Completion Notice within the 28 day period his deposit shall be absolutely forfeited and the vendor at liberty to re-sell the property. The plaintiff did not complete the sale by the agreed closing date. The defendant served a 28 day Completion Notice on the plaintiff. The plaintiff failed to comply with the Completion Notice within the 28 day period and the defendant rescinded the contract and forfeited the plaintiff's deposit. The plaintiff issued a plenary summons seeking an order directing the defendant to perform her obligations under the contract of sale and for damages; the plaintiff also registered a *lis pendens* affecting the defendant's land. Before any further pleadings had been delivered the defendant applied to the court by Motion on Notice for an order staying the plaintiff's action and vacating the *lis pendens*. **Held** by Costello J., in granting the defendant's application, 1, that it was clear that the defendant has validly exercised her right of rescission and her right to forfeit the deposit under clauses 28 and 29 of the contract, and that accordingly, to allow the plaintiff's claim to proceed to trial would be to permit an abuse of the process of the court. 2. That in those circumstances the court, in the exercise of its inherent jurisdiction, should order that the plaintiff's action be struck out and that the *lis pendens* be vacated. *Goodson* v. *Grierson* [1908] 1 K.B. 761 and *Barry* v. *Buckley* [1981] I.R. 306 applied. *Stud Managers Ltd.* v. *Marshall*
(H.C.) [1985] I.R.83

Abuse of Process, *see also* No. 41

3. —— **Compromise** — *Plaintiff an infant — Action compromised by the agreement between counsel with next friend's consent — Next friend resiled before compromise approved by court — Whether a binding agreement — R.S.C. (N.I.), O.*80 *r.*8.] The plaintiff was an infant and brought proceedings against the defendants for damages. The action was compromised by agreement between counsel for the the plaintiff and the defendants with the consent of the next friend. The next friend resiled from the agreement before it was put to the court for approval. **Held,** that under Order 80 rule 8 of the Rules of the Supreme Court (Northern Ireland) the agreement was not valid without the approval of the

PRACTICE AND PROCEDURE—*continued.*

court. Accordingly there was no binding agreement and the plaintiff, through the next friend, was entitled to resile from the compromise at any time until the compromise had been approved by the court. *Duffy* v. *MacLaron*
(Q.B.D.) [1985] N.I.285

4. —— **Date listed for hearing** — *Personal injuries claim — Damages awarded less than lodgment — Question as to costs — Whether action first listed for hearing only when it appeared in a list of cases to be heard on a specified date — R.S.C.* 1986, *O.* 22 *rr.*1(2), 46.] The plaintiff claimed damages for personal injuries, loss and damage caused by the negligence of the defendant in August, 1985. Her statement of claim was delivered on 7 March, 1986, and the defence with a notice of lodgment of £5 dated 3 July, 1986, served with it was delivered on the same date. The defendant increased his lodgment by £12,996 to a total of £13,001 on 18 February, 1987. When the action came on for trial in Galway the jury found both parties to blame for the accident and they apportioned fault as to 10% against the defendant and as to 90% against the plaintiff. They assessed damages at £89,651 resulting in an award for the plaintiff of £8,965.10 and as this sum was less than the total lodgment of £13,001 a question arose as to the order to be made as to costs. The court adjourned that issue to ascertain and hear submissions as to when the case was first listed for hearing within the meaning of R.S.C. O. 22 r 1(2). Counsel on both sides had ascertained that the case appeared in the list of cases for trial in Galway in the *Legal Diary* of 22 January, 1987, and again in the *Diary* of 13 March, 1987, when it was listed eleventh last of over 150 cases. It again appeared in the *Diary* for 16 March that year which was repeated on 19 March and was listed 'not before Wednesday, 25 March'. When the case was not reached at the March sessions it was again in a list of cases for one week of sittings in Galway in June, 1987, being about 60th in that list. Finally, the case was in a list for the two weeks in Galway commencing 12 October, 1987. It was first listed at that sittings on Thursday, 15 October, for trial on 16 October but it was not reached on the latter day and was adjourned to Monday, 19 October. It was not reached on that date and was adjourned to the next day when the hearing began. The issue which the court had to decide was the meaning and effect of the phrase 'the date on which the action is first listed for hearing' in R.S.C. O. 22 r. 1(2). On 6 October, 1986, a Practice Direction stated that such date would be the date upon which a specific date was first assigned for the actual hearing of the action. **Held** by Lynch J. in deciding that the case was first listed for hearing on 15 October, 1987, 1,

PRACTICE AND PROCEDURE—Action.

the court had to interpret the Rules in their application to the facts of the case without regard to the Practice Direction by which it was not bound. 2. A case becomes listed for hearing when it is included in a list of cases to be heard on a specified day and date even though the chances of the case actually commencing on that date may be remote. 3. The date when the action was first listed for hearing within the meaning of O. 22 r. 1(2) was 15 October, 1987, and the issue of costs was therefore governed by R.S.C. O. 22 r. 6. *Donohue* v. *Dillon*

(H.C.) [1988] ILRM 654

5. —— **Delay** — *Dismissal for want of prosecution — Application to have action dismissed — Application unsuccessful — Further delay — Second application — Whether applicant estopped from raising grounds of prejudice other than those relied on first application — Whether action to be dismissed for want of prosecution — Balance of justice.*] The appellant, a widow, instituted proceedings against the respondents in 1976, claiming damages pursuant to the Civil Liability Act, 1961, for herself and other dependents of her late husband, whose death she alleged to have been caused by the negligence of the respondent. Following the filing of the respondent's defence in July, 1977, no further steps were taken by the appellant other than the filing of notices of intention to proceed in 1981 and 1984. The respondent applied at that time to have the action dismissed for want of prosecution, but the application was refused by the High Court, and again on appeal by the Supreme Court, which stated that, although the delay was inordinate, it was not satisfied that the respondent had been so prejudiced by the delay as to impede a fair trial. The ground of prejudice alleged by the respondent on that occasion was the death of an expert witness. The appellant filed a reply within six weeks, but no steps were taken to have the case set down for trial. In July, 1986, the respondent obtained in the High Court an order dismissing the appellant's action for want of prosecution. This time, an additional ground of prejudice was relied upon by the respondent, namely, that its insurance cover was limited to £100,000, and, because of the delay, the claim might exceed that figure. The appellant appealed to the Supreme Court, where she submitted that the respondent was estopped from relying on the new ground of prejudice, since it had not been raised at the earlier application. **Held** by the Supreme Court (Finlay C.J., Henchy, Griffin, Hederman and McCarthy JJ.) in allowing the appeal, 1, the respondent was not estopped from raising a ground of prejudice that had not been raised in the earlier application, since both applications were interlocutory and the appellant was not prejudiced thereby. 2. No evidence had been adduced to show that the appellant's claim might now exceed the respondent's insurance cover, or that it would not have done so had the matter been brought to trial earlier. 3. Although the appellant's delay had been inordinate, the balance of justice still lay with permitting her to prosecute her claim. *Sweeney* v. *Horan's Hotel (Tralee) Ltd.*

(S.C.) [1987] ILRM 240

6. —— **Delay** — *Dismissal for want of prosecution — Two defendants — Extent of court's inherent jurisdiction — Whether dismissal at instance of one defendant enures for benefit of other defendant — Whether defendants likely to be seriously prejudiced by delay — Judicature (Northern Ireland) Act,* 1978 (*c.* 23), *s.* 86(1) — *R.S.C. (N.I.), O.*3 *r.*6(2).] The plaintiff issued a writ of summons and later delivered a statement of claim in 1972 alleging a trespass by the defendants in 1969. The plaintiff replied to a notice for particulars in 1974 and subsequently issued two notices of change of solicitor and intention to proceed. In June 1984 the first defendant took out a summons to dismiss the action for want of prosecution. In August 1984 the plaintiff set the action down for hearing and a month later the second defendant took out a summons to dismiss the action for want of prosecution. The Master made an order on both summonses dismissing the action. The plaintiff appealed. **Held,** that the action be dismissed as against both defendants, 1, neither a notice of intention to proceed nor a notice of change of solicitor constituted a proceeding for the purpose of Order 3 rule 6(2) of the Rules of the Supreme Court (Northern Ireland), which enables the court to dismiss an action where more than two years have elapsed since the last proceeding. 2. As the first defendant took out the summons before the plaintiff set the action down for trial, the court could consider the dismissal of the action under both Order 3, rule 6(2) and also under Order 34, rule 2(2), which provides for dismissal for failure to set an action down for trial. The second defendant's summons, could not, however, be considered by the court under Order 3, rule 6(2) as the case had been set down before that summons was taken out. *Quaere* Whether there is any power under the court's inherent jurisdiction, or whether that power, if it survives, should be exercised where an application falls outside the terms of Order 3, rule 6(2). *Department of Health and Social Services* v. *Derry Construction Co. Ltd.* [1980] N.I. 187 considered. 3. At common law before the Judicature Acts, one defendant could move for a nonsuit because of want of prosecution and, unless there was some reason to the contrary, there would be a general nonsuit

PRACTICE AND PROCEDURE—Action.

which enured for the benefit of other defendants who had not joined in the application. *McMullan* v. *Wallace* [1977] N.I. 1 not followed. In equity, however, before the Judicature Acts where a defendant set a cause down for hearing and applied that the bill might be dismissed, any order dismissing the bill was limited to the defendant setting down the cause. 4. Section 86(1) of the Judicature (Northern Ireland) Act, 1978, which provides that where there is any conflict between the rules of equity and the rules of common law with reference to the same subject matter, the rules of equity are to prevail, applies to differences in law as distinct from practice. Where there is a difference of practice it is open to the court to consider which of the differing former rules of practice is to be followed. 5. In this case the court should follow the common law practice because (*a*) the equity practice was linked to a practice of setting down which is removed from the modern practice; (*b*) to do so would accord better with the wording of Order 3, rule 6(2) which is framed in terms of dismissing the action; and (*c*) it would enable the court to consider the position of each defendant at the date when the first summons to dismiss is taken out. 6. In view of the inordinate delay and the defendants' difficulties in tracing witnesses and documents, both defendants had been seriously prejudiced. *Bannon* v. *Craigavon Development Commission*

(Q.B.D.) [1984] N.I.387

7. —— **Delay** — *Request for particulars by defendant — Order to deliver same — Action to stand dismissed with costs unless particulars delivered within specified time — Inordinate and inexcusable delay — Jurisdiction to extend time where "unless" order not complied with — Discretion — Nature of action — Particulars within the knowledge of the defendant — Whether defendant unreasonably prejudiced — Balance of justice.*] The plaintiff, who was a private in the army and aged 22 years, suffered personal injuries in a road traffic accident at the Curragh Camp in Co. Kildare in 1977. In July 1979 proceedings were instituted on his behalf claiming damages against the defendant who was a military policeman. In August 1979 a Statement of Claim was delivered. The plaintiff underwent medical examinations on his own behalf and on behalf of the defendant and several medical reports were furnished. He eventually became concerned at the delay which appeared to have arisen in prosecuting his action and this concern was conveyed to his solicitors. He was assured, however, that the case would probably be listed within a short time as there was a big improvement in the listing of actions. Eventually in August 1984 for the first time he consulted his present solicitors for the

PRACTICE AND PROCEDURE—*continued.*

purpose of inquiring into the inordinate delay which appeared to have taken place. The file was received by his present solicitors only in April 1985 from which it appeared that, on 12 October, 1981, the plaintiff was ordered by the High Court to deliver within three weeks particulars of the negligence alleged against the defendant, the personal injuries suffered by the plaintiff and the age of the plaintiff and that, unless they were delivered within the said time, the action should stand dismissed with costs. The particulars were not delivered and the plaintiff became aware of the order only when he was informed of its existence in April 1985. Since that date numerous applications were made by his present solicitors to the solicitors for the defendant seeking an extension of time for their delivery but no extension was granted. By notice of motion grounded on affidavit application was made to the High Court on 13 October, 1986, for an order enlarging the time fixed by the court on 12 October, 1981. The affidavits showed *inter alia* that the witnesses to the accident were still serving in the army and were available to give evidence. During the hearing of the application it was argued on behalf of the plaintiff that, while formerly once an order had been made striking out an action unless some act was done within a specific time, there was no jurisdiction to grant an extension of time as the action was then at an end, nevertheless it had been held by the Court of Appeal in *Samuels* v. *Linzi Dresses Ltd.* [1980] 1 All E.R. 803 that the court had jurisdiction to extend the time. On the merits of the case the court ought here to extend the time because the plaintiff was not to blame for the delay, the witnesses and medical reports were available and the particulars of negligence were commonplace. It was conceded on behalf of the defendant that the court had jurisdiction and a discretion in the matter nevertheless, as there was inordinate and inexcusable delay, it was argued that it would be unreasonable to require the defendant to defend the action now. Furthermore the plaintiff clearly had an alternative remedy and, as the defendant did not contribute to the delay, it would be contrary to natural justice to extend the time. **Held** An extension of time should be granted to deliver the particulars. *Brennan* v. *Kelly.*

(H.C.) [1988] ILRM 306

Delay — dismissal for want of prosecution, *see also* No. 54

8. —— **Frivolous or vexatious** — *Motion to strike out* — Locus standi — *Claim of breach of statutory requirements — No damage or loss alleged by plaintiff — Whether plaintiff has* locus standi *to maintain action — Application to have pleadings struck out — Whether court should*

PRACTICE AND PROCEDURE—Action.

strike out at preliminary stage — Whether action requires full consideration by court — R.S.C., 1962, *O.* 19, *r.*28.

Constitution — Locus standi — *Public right — Attorney General — Intervention — Assertion of public right by private citizen — Whether common law limitations on private assertion of public right carried over from common law by the Constitution — Whether private citizen has* locus standi *to assert breach of public right without showing particular loss or damage.*] The plaintiff building society sought a declaration that the certificate of incorporation granted to the second defendant by the first defendant was null and void, as being in contravention of the Building Societies Act, 1976. The defendants applied by motion pursuant to O.19, r.28 of the Rules of the Superior Courts, 1962, for an order dismissing the plaintiff's claim on the ground of not disclosing a cause of action. The defendants argued that the plaintiff did not allege any loss arising from the decision of the first defendant to grant the certificate and that the plaintiff had, therefore, no *locus standi* to maintain the action. **Held** by Keane J. in refusing to strike out the proceedings: while the plaintiff might be found ultimately not to have standing to maintain the action, it was not appropriate where a case involved serious investigation of ancient law and questions of general importance to have the matter finally determined within the limitations imposed by an application on motion to have the pleadings struck out. *Dicta* of Cozens-Hardy M.R. in *Dyson* v. *Attorney General* [1911] 1 K.B. 410 applied: *Per curiam:* the limitations in Ireland on private citizens asserting public rights without the intervention of the Attorney General may not differ from those existing in England, and may not have been affected by the provisions of the Constitution of Saorstát Éireann. *Moore* v. *Attorney General* [1930] I.R. 471, *Kiely* v. *Minister for Social Welfare* [1977] I.R. 267 and *Gouriet* v. *Union of Post Office Workers* [1978] A.C. 435 discussed. *Irish Permanent Building Society* v. *Caldwell (Registrar of Building Societies)*

(H.C.) [1979] ILRM 273

[**Reporter's note:** this action was subsequently dismissed by Barrington J.: [1981] ILRM 242].

9. —— **Stay** — *Application based on allegation that action had been settled — Whether evidence supported the allegation — Contract — Formation — Whether agreement to settle proceedings reached.*] The plaintiff instituted proceedings against the defendant in which he claimed a partnership had existed between the defendant and himself in relation to the development of lands which they had purchased together in 1977

PRACTICE AND PROCEDURE—*continued.*

for £3,100,000; also that the terms of the partnership had been breached by the defendant. He further contended that the court should dissolve the partnership and if necessary order the partition of the lands. Having obtained an interim injunction the plaintiff then applied for interlocutory relief to prevent the defendant from doing certain acts pending the trial of the action. This motion was adjourned on consent as the parties were trying to negotiate a settlement. An outstanding point of difference between both parties referred to a down-payment of £200,000 which the plaintiff sought on signing the agreement. The defendant then applied for an order staying the procedure on the ground that the action was settled in the course of a telephone conversation between the plaintiff and the defendant on 25 January, 1979. **Held** by Costello J. in refusing to stay the action, 1, the action was not settled in the course of the telephone conversation between the plaintiff and the defendant on 25 January, 1979. 2. As confirmed by the evidence and subsequent developments that occurred after the telephone conversation, no agreement was reached in relation to the down-payment of £200,000 which was to be paid to the plaintiff on the signing of the agreement. *Tattan* v. *Cadogan*

(H.C.) [1979] ILRM 61

10. —— **Stay** — *Two actions — Separate courts — Same issues — Whether trial of first action in lower court should be stayed — No trial of civil action by jury in lower court — Rules of the Circuit Court,* 1950 (*S.I. No.* 179), *O.* 30, *r.*11 — *Courts of Justice Act,* 1924 (*No.* 10), *s.* 94 — *Civil Liability Act,* 1961 (*No.* 41), *ss.* 34, 37 — *Courts Act,* 1971 (*No.* 36), *s.* 6.] The plaintiff's motor car was damaged in a collision with the defendant's motor cycle. The plaintiff brought an action in the Circuit Court and claimed therein damages from the defendant whose negligence, as alleged, caused the collision and the damage to the plaintiff's motor car. Subsequently, the defendant claimed in a separate action in the High Court damages from the plaintiff for personal injuries sustained by the defendant in the same accident and caused, as alleged, by the plaintiff's negligence. At the start of the trial of the plaintiff's action in the Circuit Court, which occurred before the defendant's High Court action was tried, the Circuit Court judge, on the application of the defendant, ordered that the trial of the plaintiff's action be stayed pending the determination of the defendant's High Court action. The plaintiff appealed to the High Court against the order staying his action. **Held** by McWilliam J., in allowing the appeal, that the fact that the defendant was entitled to have the issues in his High Court action tried by a judge

and jury while the same issues would be determined in the plaintiff's action by a Circuit Court judge, and the fact that the determination of the issues at the trial of the plaintiff's action would govern the issues at a subsequent trial of the defendant's action, were not sufficient grounds for staying the trial of the plaintiff's action pending the conclusion of the trial of the defendant's action. *Murphy* v. *Hennessy*

(H.C.) [1984] I.R.378; [1985] ILRM 100

11. —— **Stay** — *Two actions — Separate courts — Same issues — Defendant in District Court suing plaintiff in High Court — Lodgment — Full amount of plaintiff's claim lodged by defendant in District Court — No admission of liability — Lodgment refused by plaintiff — Whether issue of liability should be determined by District Court notwithstanding lodgment by defendant — Whether trial by action in District Court should be stayed.*] The applicant, whose motor car was damaged in a collision with the notice party's motor cycle, brought an action in the District Court to recover the cost of repairing that damage. The notice party had sustained severe personal injuries in the accident and instituted proceedings against the applicant in the High Court. The full amount of the applicant's claim together with costs was lodged in the District Court, without admission of liability; this lodgment was not taken up by the applicant. At the hearing in the District Court the notice party applied for the case to be adjourned pending the outcome of his High Court action on the ground that the notice party had discharged his liability to the applicant by the lodgment, and the respondent District Justice was therefore entitled in her discretion to adjourn proceedings in order to allow the issue of liability between the parties be tried before a jury in the High Court. The respondent adjourned the action. On the applicant's application for an order of mandamus directing the respondent to hear and determine the issue of liability between the parties it was **Held** by Barr J., in refusing the application, 1, that since the full amount of the applicant's claim had been lodged in court by the notice party, it was unnecessary to try in that action any issues between the parties and accordingly the respondent had properly exercised her discretion in adjourning the matter. *Murphy* v. *Hennessy* [1984] I.R. 378 distinguished. *Gay O'Driscoll Ltd.* v. *Kotsonouris*

(H.C.) [1987] I.R.265

CONCURRENT WRONGDOERS

12. —— **Negligence** — *Negligence action against vendor and manufacturer — Jury finding defendants negligent and apportioning fault —*

Whether vendor entitled to claim contribution or indemnity against manufacturer — Civil Liability Act, 1961 (*No.* 41), *s.* 21 — *R.S.C., O.* 16, *rr.* 7, 11.] The infant plaintiff injured her thumb when the door of a mobile home, purchased from the first named defendants by her father, slammed on it. The mobile home was designed and manufactured by the second named defendants. The plaintiff having sued both defendants in negligence ([1983] ILRM 595), the jury returned a verdict against both defendants and assessed damages at £15,300. As between the defendants, the jury apportioned 12.5% of the fault to the first named defendant and 87.5% to the second named defendant. On an application by the first named defendant for contribution or indemnity from the second named defendant, the second named defendant submitted that as there was no contract of indemnity between the defendants, the issue between them could only be pursued in independent proceedings. **Held** in giving judgment against the second named defendant, under Order 16 of the Rules of the Superior Courts, it is not necessary for a defendant seeking to have resolved any issue between themselves and a co-defendant, which is substantially the same as that between themselves and the plaintiff, to rely on a contract of indemnity. *Cole* v. *Webb Caravan Services Ltd.*

(H.C.) [1985] ILRM 1

13. —— **Third party order** — *Claim for contribution — Service — Delays — Whether claim made "as soon as reasonably possible" — Limitation period — Discretion — Civil Liability Act,* 1961 (*No.* 41), *ss.* 27, 31.] Section 27, sub-s. 1 of the Civil Liability Act, 1961, provides:— "A concurrent wrongdoer who is sued for damages or for contribution and who wishes to make a claim for contribution under this part — . . . (*b*) shall, if the said person is not already a party to the action, serve a third-party notice upon such person as soon as is reasonably possible and, having served such notice, he shall not be entitled to claim contribution except under the third-party procedure. If such third-party notice is not served as aforesaid, the court may in its discretion refuse to make an order for contribution against the person from whom the contribution is claimed." Section 31 of the Act provides:— "An action may be brought for contribution within the same period as the injured person is allowed by law for bringing an action against the contributor, or within the period of two years after the liability of the claimant is ascertained or the injured person's damages are paid, whichever is the greater." The plaintiff was injured in an explosion on the 14 October, 1977, and issued a plenary summons for negligence against the defendant. By its defence delivered

on the 15 May, 1980, the defendant pleaded *inter alia* that the explosion was caused by the negligence of the third party based in England. Notice of trial was served on the 21 January, 1981, and on the 23 February, 1981, the defendant obtained liberty to issue and serve within three months a third party notice out of the jurisdiction on the third party. The defendant settled the plaintiff's claim for £46,000 and costs on the 5 May, 1981, and paid same by the 19 August, 1981. The third party notice was not served within the time specified by the High Court order of the 23 February, 1981, and the defendant obtained extension of time orders from the Master of the High Court on the 22 July, 1982, and the 21 July, 1983, and the third-party notice was then served on the 22 July, 1983. Upon close of pleadings the third party objected at a preliminary hearing on a point of law that the defendant had not served his third party notice as soon as was "reasonably possible", and that he was therefore estopped from pursuing his claim against the third party. **Held** by Blayney J., in holding with the third party and dismissing the defendant's claim for contribution, that even if the defendant's claim was within the limitation period of s. 31 of the Civil Liability Act, 1961, yet on the facts the delays in both the application for liberty to issue and the service of the third party notice were wholly unreasonable, in the absence of any explanation which might excuse them, and in addition one of the rationales for third party proceedings, *viz.* a single hearing (as opposed to a succession of actions) concluding all claims, was already excluded by the defendant's earlier settlement of the plaintiff's action, and the court would therefore refuse to exercise its discretion to order contribution under s. 27, sub-s. 1 (*b*) of the Act. *Gilmore* v. *Windle* [1967] I.R. 323 and *A. and P. (Ireland) Ltd.* v. *Golden Vale Products Ltd. t/a Golden Vale* (Unreported, High Court, McMahon J., 7 December, 1978) considered. *Neville* v. *Margan Ltd.*

(H.C.) [1988] I.R.734

CONSTITUTIONAL ISSUE

14. —— **High Court** — *Challenge to validity of pre-1937 statute — Requirement by rules of court that Attorney General be notified of proceedings challenging the validity of law having regard to the provisions of the Constitution — Whether requirement extended to challenge to validity of pre-1937 statute — Whether court would consider issue in the absence of notification — R.S.C.,* 1986 (*S.I. No.* 15), *O.* 61, *r.*1.

Infants — Custody — Protection — Court order committing infant to care of health board — Validity — Whether made in accordance with law — Whether health board had capacity to take infant

in care — Summary Jurisdiction Rules, 1909 (*S.R.O. No.* 952) — *Children Act,* 1908 (*c.* 67), *ss.* 21, 23, 24, 28, 38, 58 — *Interpretation Act,* 1937 (*No.* 38), *s.* 11 — *Children Act,* 1941 (*No.* 12), *s.* 10 — *Health Act,* 1970 (*No.* 1), *ss.* 6, 66.] Section 24, sub-s. 1 of the Children Act, 1908, provides, *inter alia,* that if it appears to a Justice that there are reasonable grounds to suspect that a child has been or is being abused, neglected or assaulted in a manner likely to be injurious to its health, the Justice may issue a warrant for the removal of the child to a place of safety and his detention there until he can be brought before a court of summary jurisdiction and such court may commit him to the care of a relative or other fit person. Section 38 provides that "unless the context otherwise requires, the expression 'fit person', in relation to the care of any child . . . includes any society or body corporate established for the reception or protection of poor children or the prevention of cruelty to children." Section 66, sub-s. 2 of the Health Act, 1970, provides that "a Health Board shall make available without charge a health examination and treatment service for pupils attending a national school . . ." By order of the District Court, pursuant to s. 24 of the Act of 1908, D.D., the child of the prosecutors, was committed to the care of the second respondent until 1995 (when the infant would reach 16 years of age), or until the order be varied or revoked. The first respondent was a social worker employed by the second respondent who dealt with the care of the infant on its behalf. The order was grounded on a finding that the infant had been a victim of sexual abuse by its father. The prosecutors denied that sexual abuse had taken place but no application was made to vary or revoke the order, nor was any appeal lodged. The prosecutors sought to recover custody of the infant by way of proceedings in the High Court under Article 40, s. 4, sub-s. 2 of the Constitution of Ireland. They alleged, *inter alia,* that s. 24 of the Children Act, 1908, was inconsistent with the Constitution; that the sections only empowered the court to make emergency and not long term orders, and that the second respondent had neither the capacity nor the statutory power to take an infant in care pursuant to the section. Furthermore it was argued that the second respondent did not come within the definition of a "fit person" contained in s. 38 of the Act of 1908. The Attorney General was not informed of the proceedings. **Held** by Carroll J., in refusing the relief sought, 1, that Order 60, r. 1 of the Superior Court Rules, 1986, required that the Attorney General be notified if a question as to the validity of any law was to be considered, including statutes enacted prior to the coming into force of the Constitution of Ireland, 1937, and, accordingly the court would decline to consider the constitutional issue raised. *The State (D.C.)* v. *Midland Health Board* (Unreported, High Court, Keane J., 31 July, 1986) and *The State (Sheerin)* v. *Kennedy* [1966] I.R. 379 considered. 2. That while the District Justice had been empowered to issue an initial warrant where he had reasonable grounds to suspect abuse or neglect such grounds would not have been sufficient grounds for a committal order, which required the prosecutors to have been notified and further required that the District Justice enter into a judicial consideration of the matter observing the requirements of natural and constitutional justice. 3. That, in addition, the District Justice would have to have been satisfied in making the order that there were compelling reasons to give the infant into the custody of a person other than its parents. *In re J.H., an infant* [1985] I.R. 375 considered. 4. That, where an allegation of sexual abuse had been made against the father alone, the District Justice would have to have considered whether the mother could safeguard the infant. 5. That, there being evidence that the above requirements had been satisfied in the District Court, the District Justice had been entitled to make the order under s. 24 and accordingly the infant was detained in accordance with law. 6. That, there being nothing in the Act of 1908 to require the meaning of "fit person" to be confined to natural persons, s. 11 of the Interpretation Act, 1937, applied and "person" accordingly included a body corporate. 7. That the health of an infant who had suffered sexual abuse was in danger and needed treatment and, accordingly, such a child fell within s. 66, sub-s. 2 of the Health Act, 1970, and a Health Board was, therefore, empowered by that section to take the child in care. *Attorney General* v. *Eastern Railway Co.* (1880) 11 Ch. D. 449, 5 App. Cas. 473 considered. *The State (D. and D.)* v. *Groarke*

(H.C.) [1988] I.R.187

COSTS

15. —— **Appeal** — *Certiorari — Appeal from the District Court — Conviction by the District Justice under the Road Traffic Act,* 1961 (*No.* 24), *s.* 53 — *Jurisdiction of the Circuit Court to award costs of appeal — Whether limitation of costs under rule 67 of the District Court Rules,* 1948 (*S.R. & O. No.* 431), *applicable — Rules of the Circuit Court,* 1950 (*S.I. No.* 179), *O.* 48, *O.* 58, *r.* 1.] Rule 67 of the District Court Rules, 1948, provides *inter alia* that a Justice who makes an order in any case of summary jurisdiction shall have power to order any party to the proceedings (other than the Attorney General or a member of the Garda Síochána acting in discharge of his

duties as a police officer) to pay the other party such costs and witnesses' expenses as he should think fit to award. A defendant to a summons was convicted in the District Court on a charge of dangerous driving under s. 53 of the Road Traffic Act, 1961. He was fined £40 and an order was made that his licence be endorsed. From this conviction he appealed to the Circuit Court. The Circuit Court Judge allowed the appeal and awarded costs of the appeal against the prosecution. The Director of Public Prosecutions obtained a conditional order of certiorari against the respondent to quash the order of the Circuit Court judge on the grounds that he had no jurisdiction to award costs on appeal against the prosecution by virtue of the aforesaid Rule 67. **Held** by Barron J. in discharging the conditional order, 1, that there is a general jurisdiction in the Circuit Court to award costs of any proceedings in that court. *The State (Minister for Lands & Fisheries)* v. *Judge Sealy* [1939] I.R. 21, applied. 2. That Order 58, Rule 1, of the Circuit Court Rules, 1950, which leaves to the discretion of the Judge the granting or withholding of the costs of any party to any proceedings in the court, save as otherwise provided, relates to proceedings of both a civil and criminal nature, thus covering the question of costs in an appeal from the District Court in a criminal matter. *The State (Minister for Lands & Fisheries)* v. *Judge Sealy* [1939] I.R. 21, applied. *The State (D.P.P.)* v. *Roe*

(H.C.) [1985] I.R.307

16. —— **Interest** — *Award of costs — Dispute as to the period in relation to which the interest thereon should be calculated — Whether interest payable from date of High Court order or from when costs were taxed — Application for directions — Regularity of procedure — Whether application could be initiated by a motion on notice.*] The plaintiff had obtained judgment in the sum of £172,614 against the defendants in a High Court action claiming damages for personal injuries. The High Court order awarded costs to the plaintiff, and, in granting a stay pending an appeal, ordered interest to be paid on the award 'or such other sum as may be found due to the plaintiff by the Supreme Court or by the judge before whom the case is ultimately disposed of from the date of the judgment herein at the rate of 11% per annum or such other rate as may be fixed by the Supreme Court or said judge.' When the appeal came before the Supreme Court in November 1985, the court was informed that a compromise had been reached. The order of the Supreme Court recited the High Court order, and varied it only by substituting the compromise sum for the sum awarded by the High Court. No order was made as to the costs of the appeal.

PRACTICE AND PROCEDURE—Costs.

The plaintiff paid the newly agreed amount plus the interest thereon before the appeal reached the Supreme Court. The costs, however, were not taxed until March 1986. The defendants paid the amount of the taxed costs in April 1986, but refused to pay any interest thereon. The plaintiff applied to the High Court upon a motion on notice for directions as to the amount and means of calculation of the interest, and for an order directing the defendants to pay such interest. The plaintiff argued that interest should be payable from the date of the High Court order, viz., February 1984, while the defendants contended that it should be payable only from the date when the costs were taxed in March 1986. **Held** by Gannon J. in expressing his opinion on the irregularity of the procedure, and in making no order, 1, a High Court judge has no function of a judicial nature in any action which has been concluded by a final order of the Supreme Court. 2. In the instant application, the court is asked to construe an earlier High Court order, subsequently affirmed by the Supreme Court. Such application is a new proceeding, which cannot be initiated by a motion on notice. [**Reporter's Note.** Although making no order, Gannon J. indicated that, had the matter come before him at first instance, he would have ordered interest to run from the date on which the costs had been taxed, following *dicta* of Fox, L.J. in *Erven Warnink B.V.* v. *Townend* [1982] 3 All E.R. 312. However, he felt that if he had been in the position of the High Court judge who having made the order, had been asked to specify whether the order for costs carried interest from the date of the judgment, he would have answered in the affirmative.] *Lambert* v. *Lambert*

(H.C.) [1987] ILRM 390

17. —— **Security for costs** — *Application by defendant for security for costs — Claim under a policy of fire insurance — Plaintiff residing outside the jurisdiction — Discretion of the Court — Special circumstances — Whether plaintiff impoverished by the defendant — Whether right of access to the courts to prosecute civil claims is fettered — Rules of the Superior Courts,* 1986 (*S.I. No.* 15), *O.* 29, *r.* 6.] Order 29, r. 6 of the Rules of the Superior Courts provides, *inter alia,* that where the court has made an order for security for costs, the amount of such security and the time or times at which, and the manner and form in which, and the person or persons to whom the same shall be given, shall be determined by the Master in every case. The plaintiff commenced proceedings against the defendant seeking, *inter alia,* a declaration that the defendant was liable to the plaintiff, under a policy of fire insurance, for loss and damage sustained by

PRACTICE AND PROCEDURE—*continued.*

the plaintiff as a result of the plaintiff's premises being damaged by a fire. The defendant brought an application for security for costs on the basis that the plaintiff was now resident outside the jurisdiction. The plaintiff resisted the claim for security on the grounds that he had been impoverished by the defendant's refusal to pay him the insurance monies and that he had a constitutional right of access to the courts and the effect of ordering him to provide security for costs would be to prevent him from exercising that right. **Held** by O'Hanlon J., in making the order sought, 1, that as the plaintiff was a person resident outside the jurisdiction, and as the defendant had complied with the requirement that it should file a satisfactory affidavit that it had a defence upon the merits, the defendant had a *prima facie* right to an order for security for costs. 2. That the order was a discretionary one and could be refused if there were special circumstances justifying the exercise of the court's discretion in the plaintiff's favour. *Heaney* v. *Malocca* [1958] I.R. 11; *Cohane* v. *Cohane* [1968] I.R. 176 and *Collins* v. *Doyle* [1982] ILRM 495 considered. 3. That although the plaintiff's current financial problems could well be attributable to the loss incurred by him as a result of the fire at his premises, the plaintiff had not been impoverished by the defendant. This was not one of the sets of circumstances which would justify the court in exercising its discretion in favour of the plaintiff. *Heaney* v. *Malocca* [1958] I.R. 111 followed. 4. That any right of access to the courts to prosecute civil claims was not an unfettered right, and the right to apply for security for costs was intended to do justice between the parties, was reasonable and was not in breach of any of the constitutional rights which the plaintiff could assert in the circumstances of this case. *Salih* v. *The General Accident Fire and Life Assurance Corporation Ltd.*

(H.C.) [1987] I.R.628

18. —— **Security for costs** — *Bankrupt — Plaintiff an undischarged bankrupt — Whether bankruptcy sufficient ground for requiring plaintiff to provide security for costs.*] The fact that a plaintiff is an undischarged bankrupt is not *per se* a sufficient reason why he should be ordered to provide security for costs. **So held** by Hamilton P. *Cook* v. *Whellock* (1890) 24 Q.B.D. 658 followed. *Tormey* v. *Economic and Social Research Institute*

(H.C.) [1986] I.R.615

19. —— **Security for costs** — *Limited company — Corporate plaintiff's action dismissed with costs — Appeal to Supreme Court — Plaintiff insolvent — Defendant seeking security of costs — Whether order discretionary — Constitution of Ireland,*

PRACTICE AND PROCEDURE—Costs.

1937, *Art.* 34.4.3 — *Companies Act,* 1963 (*No.* 33), *s.* 390.] S. 390 of the Companies Act, 1963, provides that where a limited company is a plaintiff in any action, and there is evidence that such company is unlikely to be able to pay the costs of a successful defendant, the judge having jurisdiction in the matter may require security to be given for those costs, and may stay the proceedings until such security is given. O. 58, r. 18 of the Rules of the Superior Courts gives jurisdiction to the Supreme Court to direct the security for costs to be given in the event of an appeal. The second-named defendant/respondent whose defence had succeeded in a High Court action for damages for breach of contract and negligence, sought an order pursuant to s. 390 of the 1963 Act, for security for the costs both of the appeal and of the previous High Court action. Evidence showed the plaintiff/appellant company to be insolvent, and tended to show that the insolvency stemmed mainly, if not entirely, from the events the subject-matter of the action. **Held** by the Supreme Court (Finlay C.J., Hederman and McCarthy JJ.) in refusing to make the order sought, 1, s. 390 of the 1963 Act is not mandatory. The court has a discretion which may be exercised in special circumstances. *Peppard* v. *Bogoff* [1962] I.R. 180 followed. 2. The section cannot be read as encompassing any costs other than those incurred after the demand for security has first been made. 3. Among the circumstances to be considered in the exercise of the court's discretion, the delay of the respondent in bringing the application was of particular significance. This, coupled with the fact that the inability of the appellant to pay costs stems from the subject-matter of the action was sufficient to justify the court in refusing to order security for the costs of the appeal. *S.E.E. Co. Ltd.* v. *Public Lighting Services Ltd.*

(S.C.) [1987] ILRM 255

20. —— **Security for costs** — *Limited company — Application by one defendant for security for costs in pending action — Plaintiff company unable to meet any order for costs — Whether plaintiff's impecunious state caused by wrong the subject matter of claim — Onus of proof on plaintiff — Standard of proof —* Prima facie *case — Discharge of onus — Whether bald statement sufficient — Supreme Court — Jurisdiction — Review of High Court discretion — Whether Supreme Court jurisdiction limited — Companies Act, 1963 (No.* 33), *s.* 390.] The plaintiff, a building company formed for the purpose of contracting with the second defendant to build a large number of houses, commenced proceedings for damages for breach of contract against both the first defendant, the firm of archi-

PRACTICE AND PROCEDURE—*continued.*

tects appointed by the second defendant under the contract, and the second defendant. In its statement of claim the plaintiff alleged, *inter alia,* that the first defendant knowing the plaintiff's weak financial situation, had failed and neglected to measure, quantify and adjudicate on amounts of claims submitted by the plaintiff under the contract, thereby causing the plaintiff damage and loss. On the application of the first defendant for security for costs under s. 390 of the Companies Act, 1963, it was conceded on behalf of the plaintiff that it would be unable to pay the defendants' costs should they succeed in their defences. It was further stated in an affidavit filed on behalf of the plaintiff that because of the second defendant's actions the plaintiff "had to suspend its principal activity of contractor for public works." The High Court (Barr J.) refused the application, saying that the plaintiff had established a *prima facie* case that it had been put out of business by the wrong-doing of both defendants and that its inability to give security for costs was a consequence of that wrong-doing. On appeal by the first defendant against the refusal it was contended, *inter alia,* on behalf of the plaintiff that, in the absence of an error in principle on the part of the High Court in the exercise of the discretion under s. 390, the Supreme Court should not interfere with the exercise of that discretion, even where it would have exercised the discretion differently. **Held** by the Supreme Court (Finlay C.J., Henchy, Griffin, Hederman and McCarthy JJ.) in allowing the appeal and making the order sought, 1, that no such qualification lay upon the appellate jurisdiction of the court. The court had a right and an obligation to substitute its discretion for that of the High Court, if it was satisfied it should do so. *In bonis Morelli; Vella* v. *Morelli* [1968] I.R. 11 applied. 2. That a plaintiff company which is unable to meet the costs of a successful defendant and which seeks to avoid an order for security for costs must, as a matter of onus of proof, establish a *prima facie* case that it was made insolvent and incapable of satisfying an order for costs by the wrong the subject-matter of the claim. 3. (McCarthy J. dissenting) That it was not a sufficient discharge of that onus for a plaintiff company to make as in the instant case a mere bald statement of fact that its insolvency had been caused by the wrong complained of and that in the absence of further evidence, such as financial accounts or records, the plaintiff had failed to discharge the onus of establishing such a *prima facie* case. *S.E.E. Company Ltd.* v. *Public Lighting Services Ltd.* [1987] ILRM 255 applied. *Jack O'Toole Ltd.* v. *MacEoin Kelly Associates*

(H.C., S.C.) [1986] I.R.277; [1987] ILRM 269

PRACTICE AND PROCEDURE—Costs.

21. —— **Security for costs** — *Limited company — Application by defendant for security for costs in pending action — Plaintiff company insolvent — Onus of proof — Discharge of onus — Special circumstances — Whether plaintiff's impecunious state caused by wrong the subject matter of claim — Bald statement insufficient — Whether existence of valuable asset a material consideration — Individual co-plaintiffs — Whether court's function to evaluate prospects of success — Companies Act,* 1963 (*No.* 33), *s.* 390.] The plaintiffs commenced proceedings against the defendants alleging, *inter alia,* that the first defendant had trespassed on the first plaintiff's lands and had extracted ore from the orebody situate on those lands and had sold same to third parties thus being guilty of fraud and larceny. The first fourteen defendants brought an application for security for costs pursuant to s. 390 of the Companies Act, 1963. A receiver had been appointed to the first plaintiff and the High Court had made an order for its winding up. It was accepted by the first plaintiff that it was insolvent insofar as it was unable to pay its debts as they fell due. However in an affidavit sworn by the sixth plaintiff on behalf of the first plaintiff it was alleged that "the asset worth of Bula greatly exceeds its liabilities" and it was further deposed to that the total indebtedness of the first plaintiff to its creditors did not exceed £40 million while the *in situ* value of its orebody approached £1,000 million. In addition, it was alleged by the plaintiffs that the current inability to earn and the financial difficulties of the first plaintiff, were due to the wrong acts and omissions of the defendants. On the hearing of the defendants' application it was **Held** by Murphy J., in refusing the application, 1, that in the circumstances there was reason to believe the first plaintiff would be unable to pay the defendant's costs if successful in their defence thus conferring jurisdiction on the court under s. 390 and accordingly the onus shifted onto the plaintiff to show the existence of any special circumstances which would justify the court in exercising its discretion against making the order sought. *Jack O'Toole Ltd.* v. *MacEoin Kelly Associates* [1986] I.R. 277 applied. 2. That the possibility of the plaintiffs raising further monies, to enable them to prosecute the proceedings, by way of loan on the security of the first plaintiff's valuable and substantial asset, namely the orebody, must be a material consideration, affecting the court in the exercise of its discretion. 3. That it was not part of the court's function to forecast the outcome of the litigation, or to prejudge the facts or express an interim view on the questions of law involved. Whilst the plaintiffs had to establish that they had an arguable case, it was neither necessary nor proper to evaluate the prospects of success. *Jack O'Toole Ltd.* v. *MacEoin Kelly

PRACTICE AND PROCEDURE—*continued.*

Associates* [1986] I.R. 277 and *S.E.E. Company Ltd.* v. *Public Lighting Services Ltd.* [1987] ILRM 255 considered. 4. That the facts deposed to in the affidavit of Michael Wymes referred to above and the detailed basis of that contention, which were incorporated by reference to lengthy affidavits sworn in earlier applications, whether well founded or not, amounted to more than a mere bald statement of the fact that the insolvency of the company had been caused by the wrong the subject matter of the claim. *Jack O'Toole Ltd.* v. *MacEoin Kelly Associates* [1986] I.R. 277 and *Peppard and Company Limited* v. *Bogoff* [1962] I.R. 180 followed. *Per* Murphy J., that while, in the circumstances of this case, the addition of individual plaintiffs resident within the jurisdiction, had no bearing on the question of whether a corporate co-plaintiff would be required to give security, it was nonetheless a factor to be taken into account in all other cases. *Pearson* v. *Naydler* [1977] 1 W.L.R. 899 applied.
Bula Ltd. v. *Tara Mines Ltd. (No. 3)*
(H.C.) [1987] I.R.494

22. —— **Security for costs** — *Limited company — Payment made by insolvent company — Action by liquidator for return of payment alleging fraudulent preference — Application by defendants for security for costs — Discretion of court — Special circumstances — Strength of plaintiff's case — Conduct of defendants — Defendants' response to liquidator's enquiries — Difficulty in establishing facts surrounding payment by plaintiff — Defendants having relevant documents in their possession or procurement — Companies Act,* 1963 (*No.* 33), *ss.* 286, 390.] The plaintiff company was insolvent and was in voluntary liquidation. The second defendant was a wholly owned subsidiary of the first defendant. The directors of the second defendant were the nominees of the first defendant of which they were also officers. At the time the proceedings were instituted the second defendant was in liquidation but was solvent. In investigating the affairs of the plaintiff, the liquidator discovered that it had borrowed a sum of £170,000 in January, 1982, and that those monies had been repaid in June, 1982, at a time when the plaintiff was clearly insolvent. The terms on which the loan had been made provided that it should be repayable with interest on demand but it had not been anticipated that any demand for repayment would be made before October, 1982. The monies advanced were the proceeds of two cheques drawn on the second defendant but the circumstances surrounding the making and repayment of the loan were unclear. The third defendant, an accountant, was the first defendant's agent in relation to the loan. Under the

terms of the loan he was to supervise the preparation of monthly management accounts for the plaintiff and, jointly with the plaintiff's managing director, was authorised to order payments from the plaintiff's funds. The repayment of the loan had been effected by transferring monies from the plaintiff's bank account to the third defendant's bank account. No interest had been claimed or paid on the loan but the payments out of the plaintiff's account exceeded the capital sum advanced. The surplus was used by the third defendant to pay himself a sum owed for fees and to pay "expenses" to the directors of the plaintiff. In an attempt to clarify the circumstances surrounding the loan and in particular the original source of the monies, the liquidator raised a number of queries with each of the defendants. The first and second defendants answered some of those queries but there was conflict between the answers given by the various officers. Other queries were evaded or ignored. The third defendant gave some general information but refused to deal with a series of specific queries until he was paid a sum of money for fees for co-operating with the liquidator. The liquidator commenced proceedings in the name of the plaintiff claiming the return of the monies paid by the plaintiff on the grounds that the payments were a fraudulent preference. The defendants each applied, pursuant to s. 390 of the Companies Act, 1963, for an order for security for their costs. **Held** by Costello J., in refusing the defendants' applications, 1, that the court had a discretion as to whether to order an insolvent company to give security for costs but there was an onus on the liquidator of such a company to show that special circumstances existed which would justify the court exercising that discretion in the company's favour. *Peppard & Co. Ltd.* v. *Bogoff* [1962] I.R. 180, *S.E.E. Company Ltd.* v. *Public Lighting Services Ltd.* [1987] ILRM 255 and *Jack O'Toole Ltd.* v. *MacEoin Kelly Associates* [1986] I.R. 277 applied. 2. That the court in exercising its discretion should have regard to all the circumstances of the case including the strength of the plaintiff's case and the conduct of the defendants. 3. That the conduct of the first and second defendants in offering conflicting versions of the transaction and in ignoring and evading the liquidator's attempts to resolve that conflict constituted special circumstances justifying the refusal of their applications. 4. That the third defendant's refusal to deal with the liquidator's request for information until a substantial sum for fees was paid was not reasonable and constituted special circumstances justifying the refusal of his application. 5. Furthermore, that there were clearly documents in the possession and procurement of each of the defendants which were highly relevant to the issues in the case and whose production might materially assist in establishing where, if anywhere, liability for fraudulent preference arose. In those circumstances it would be inappropriate to make an order which might have the effect of permanently staying the action. *Comhlucht Páipéar Ríomhaireachta Teo.* v. *Údarás na Gaeltachta*

(H.C.) [1987] I.R.684

23. —— **Security for costs** — *Liquidation — Liquidator instituting proceedings — Defendant seeking security for costs — Liquidator consenting to an order — Liquidator subsequently seeking to have consent order set aside — Whether consent order be set aside.*] The plaintiff companies were insolvent and in official liquidation. Proceedings against the defendants were instituted by the liquidator. The sixth named defendant in April 1984 issued a notice of motion and sought an order for security for costs against the plaintiff companies. In May, 1984, the liquidator of the plaintiff companies who had been appointed in February, 1984, consented to an order directing him to give security for costs. In November, 1985, the liquidator sought an order setting aside the consent order on the grounds that at the time he consented to the order he had limited information about the defendant's business activities and that as a result of the subsequent information he received he should be allowed to withdraw his consent. Costello J. on 29 November, 1985, made an order setting aside the consent order of May, 1984. The sixth named defendant appealed this order to the Supreme Court. Counsel for the liquidator made a number of submissions, in particular he relied on the *Peppard Rule,* namely that where the plaintiff company is unable to pay the costs of the defendant the court has a jurisdiction to refuse to make an order for security for costs against the plaintiff company if its financial position is due to the very actions of the defendant for which he is being sued. **Held** by the Supreme Court (Finlay C.J., Henchy and Hederman JJ.) in dismissing the appeal, 1, the court has an inherent equitable jurisdiction to set aside an interlocutory consent order where the party bound by it shows that he gave his consent under a misapprehension as to the true state of affairs and that the relevant facts came to light later. *Purcell* v. *F.C. Trigell Ltd.* [1971] 1 Q.B. 358 applied. 2. The facts of this case warranted the exercise of that jurisdiction in favour of the liquidator. 3. Before the liquidator can successfully invoke the *Peppard Rule* he must establish a *prima facie* case by evidence as distinct from mere assertion that the plaintiff's financial distress resulted from the defendant's conduct for which he is being sued; this he had failed to do. *Jack O'Toole Ltd.* v. *MacEoin Kelly*

PRACTICE AND PROCEDURE—Costs.

Associates and Wicklow County Council [1987] ILRM 269 cited. *Irish Commercial Society Ltd.* v. *Plunkett*
(S.C.) [1987] ILRM 504; (H.C.) [1986] ILRM 624

24. —— **Security for costs** — *Liquidation — Application by sixth defendant for security for costs in pending action — Plaintiff companies insolvent — Plaintiff companies unable to meet any order for costs — Onus on liquidator of plaintiff companies to establish existence of special circumstances — Exercise by court of discretion conferred on it — Circumstances of the case — Relevance of conduct of person or persons conducting affairs of sixth defendant — Companies Act,* 1963 (*No.* 33), *s.* 390.] On an application pursuant to s. 390 of the Companies Act, 1963, once it is shown that the plaintiff will be unable to pay the defendant's costs in full should the defence succeed, the court must consider whether the plaintiff has been able to discharge the onus on it to establish the existence of special circumstances which would justify the court in exercising the discretion under s. 390 in its favour. In considering how to exercise the discretion conferred by s. 390, the court can take into consideration all the circumstances of the case, which include the strength of the plaintiff's claim and the conduct of the applicant for security. When the court is considering the conduct of a corporate entity under s. 390, it can properly have regard to the conduct of the person or persons actually (as distinct from nominally) conducting its affairs. So **held** by Costello J. *Peppard and Company Limited* v. *Bogoff* [1962] I.R. 180, *S.E.E. Company Ltd.* v. *Public Lighting Services Ltd.* [1987] ILRM 255 and *Comhlucht Páipéar Ríomhaireachta Teo. (In voluntary liquidation)* v. *Údarás na Gaeltachta* [1987] I.R. 684 followed. *Irish Commercial Society Ltd.* v. *Plunkett*
(H.C.) [1988] I.R. 1

25. —— **Security for costs** — *Unsuccessful libel action in the Republic of Ireland — Action in Northern Ireland on same publication — Order for security for costs — Application for further security — Whether security should be ordered — Calculation of amount.*] The plaintiff commenced an action for damages for libel arising out of the publication of certain articles in the defendants' newspaper. The newspaper was published in both Northern Ireland and the Republic of Ireland and the plaintiff had earlier commenced proceedings in the Republic of Ireland where judgment had been given for the defendants. The defendants claimed costs in those proceedings of IR£94,901. In the present case the Master had ordered the plaintiff to lodge the sum

of £3,000 by way of security for the defendants' costs. No skeleton bill had been furnished to him. He then refused a subsequent application for further security. On appeal the defendants furnished a skeleton bill of costs for the action which gave a total estimate of £48,953.50. **Held,** that the plaintiff should provide further security in the sum of £20,000. The principle the court should follow in exercising its jurisdiction to vary the amount of security for costs previously ordered is one of preserving flexibility in order to meet the conditions applying at any given time. The Master had been correct in making an order for security on the first application, for the plaintiff was ordinarily resident out of the jurisdiction. The original estimates of the time required for trial and the amount for costs were wholly erroneous and further security was ordered. The plaintiff might have difficulties in putting up substantial security, but the defendants were entitled to be secured against having to spend substantial sums in defending themselves against an action where the issues were the same as those on which the plaintiff had been earlier defeated. The court had to consider what was just in all the circumstances, and the balance came down in favour of requiring the plaintiff to provide proper security for the defendants' costs. The amount of security should represent the amount of party and party costs likely to be incurred and no discounts, other than for the possibility of settlement or the case collapsing, should be made. The original estimates of the time required for trial and the amount for costs were wholly erroneous and so further security was ordered. *Deighan* v. *Sunday Newspapers Ltd.*
(Q.B.D.) [1985] N.I.9

26. —— **Taxation** — *Appeal — Counsel's fees — Several actions — Whether regard should be had to the fact that same solicitor acting in all cases — Scale fee allowed in one case and nominal fees in the others — Whether Taxing Master erred in principle — R.S.C., O.* 99, *r.* 37.] O. 99 r. 37(26) of the Rules of the Superior Courts provides: 'No fee to counsel shall be allowed on taxation unless authenticated by his signature.' Seventy-nine motions for judgment in default of defence were brought against a number of defendants and each of the plaintiffs were represented by the same solicitor. The motions were settled and counsel on behalf of the plaintiffs informed the court of the agreement and orders which were made in each case in accordance with the terms of the agreement which allowed the plaintiffs their cost in each case. Counsel never marked a fee in respect of the motions although he informed his solicitor that he would mark a fee in accordance with the Bar Council scale fees,

which he in fact never did. Eventually all the actions were disposed of and referred to the Taxing Master for taxation. The Taxing Master in taxing the motions for judgment in default of defence allowed the plaintiffs' solicitor the sum of £12.50 as an instruction fee in each case and counsel a fee of £33.60 in one case being the appropriate scale fee and a fee of £3.15 in each of the other cases. The plaintiffs appealed that decision to the High Court and submitted that each order should be taxed as if it were a separate and distinct matter and that regard should not be had to the fact that the same solicitor was acting in all the cases. **Held** by Barron J. in dismissing the appeal, 1, as the plaintiffs did not contest the order for costs in each motion and did not limit the order for costs in any way, the costs in this case must be taxed in accordance with the orders actually made which allow costs in each case. 2. The Taxing Master in deciding what is an appropriate fee for the work done in each case is entitled to take into account that once the work was done for one of these applications it was substantially done for them all as repetitive acts do not warrant the same remuneration as the first of such acts. 3. The allowance by the Taxing Master of the same fee but of a lower fee than that normally allowed in an individual case is not an error in principle. 4. The fact that the Taxing Master adopted a different approach to counsel's fee in that he allowed the solicitor the same instruction fee in each case but allowed counsel a scale fee in one case with nominal fees in the remaining ones does not indicate the application of a wrong principle as the test which he took into account was whether or not the outlay was reasonably incurred. 5. As counsel had never indicated the exact basis upon which he had accepted the brief, O. 99 r. 37(26) strictly applied and no fees should have been allowed. 6. A careful and prudent solicitor would not have offered the briefs to counsel on the basis claimed and risked the possibility that his client would have to pay all or part of the fees depending upon the nature of the order for costs made by the Court. *Ormond* v. *Ireland*

(H.C.) [1988] ILRM 490

27. —— **Taxation** — *Appeal — Solicitor and client bill paid by client — Application to Taxing Master to tax under R.S.C. O. 99, r. 15(e) — Jurisdiction to tax in absence of a court order — Attorneys and Solicitors (Ireland) Act,* 1849 (*c.* 53), *ss.* 2, 6 — *Rules of the Superior Courts,* 1962 (*S.I. No.* 72), *O.* 99, *r.* 15(*e*).] The wife in a matrimonial suit requisitioned a taxation of the prosecutors' bill of costs *after* she had paid their bill. The respondent taxing master entertained the taxation under O. 99 r. 15 (*e*) of the Rules of the Superior Courts, by which, without any

order for the purpose, he may tax solicitor and client costs upon the client's application and with his written undertaking to pay any balance which the taxing master may certify. The solicitors objected to the taxation, but submitted to it, emerging therefrom with their bill greatly reduced. They then sought from the High Court an order of certiorari against the respondent, claiming that the taxing master had no jurisdiction, without an order of the court, to tax a bill of costs which their client had already paid. The respondent showed cause against a conditional order of certiorari, and Costello J., in a judgment delivered on 9 December, 1983 [Unreported: High Court 1983 No. 493 SS], discharged the conditional order. From this judgment the prosecutor appealed to the Supreme Court, urging that Costello J. had erred in holding that O. 99 r. 15(*e*) of the Rules of the Superior Courts had conferred jurisdiction on the respondent to conduct the taxation. In the notice of appeal, the prosecutor raised for the first time the validity of s. 36 of the Courts of Justice Act, 1924, s. 68 of the Courts of Justice Act, 1936, and O. 99 r. 15(*e*) of Rules of the Superior Courts having regard to the provisions of Article 40.3 and Article 43 of the Constitution and served a notice pursuant to O. 60 purporting to raise these issues. **Held** by McCarthy J. (O'Higgins C.J., Finlay P., Henchy and Hederman JJ. concurring) allowing the appeal, that, 1, the jurisdiction of the taxing master regulated by O. 99 r. 15(*e*) derived from the Attorneys and Solicitors (Ireland) Act, 1849, and not from the Superior Courts Rules Committee acting under s. 36 of the Courts of Justice Act, 1924 or from any provision of the Courts (Supplemental Provisions) Act, 1961. 2. Ss. 2 and 6 of the Attorneys and Solicitors (Ireland) Act, 1849, govern the taxation of solicitor and client bills as follows: (*a*) The solicitor cannot lawfully sue for one month after delivery; (*b*) The client has a period of twelve months within which to demand and obtain taxation; (*c*) After the expiry of twelve months or after payment of the amount of the bill, then the court may, if the special circumstances of the case so require, refer the bill to taxation, provided the application to the court is made within twelve calendar months after payment; (*d*) After the expiry of the latter period, there is no statutory power to refer for taxation. 3. The court has an inherent right to order taxation, a right which runs parallel to the statutory jurisdiction. 4. The prosecutors, in submitting to a taxation to which they objected, were acting reasonably, and should not be held to have waived their objection. 5. In the light of all the circumstances, of some of which Costello J. had not been made aware, the prosecutors had not misled their client or failed in candour. 6. The court did not accept that the client had overpaid her solicitors: judgment of Finlay P. in *H.P.* v. *W.P.* [1985] ILRM 527 applied. 7. Whilst the prosecutors had generously offered to submit to taxation, the court did not consider it appropriate to order taxation. *The State (Gallagher Shatter & Co.)* v. *de Valera*

(S.C.) [1986] ILRM 3

Editor's note: *see also* No. 30

28. —— **Taxation** — *Review* — *Counsel's fees* — *Solicitors' disbursements for counsel's fees* — *Principles to be applied* — *Discretion of taxing master* — *R.S.C.* 1962, *O.* 31, *rr.* 12, 24, *O.* 32, *r.* 12, *O.* 52, *r.* 17(5), *O.* 99, *rr.* 11(2), 37(10), 38.

Precedent — *Principle of* stare decisis — *Whether earlier decision based on insufficient authority or incorrect submissions.*] In a motion pursuant to O. 99 r. 38 R.S.C. for a review of the taxation of a bill of costs presented by the plaintiff pursuant to an award of costs at the conclusion of its action, the defendant urged the court to depart from the ruling of Gannon J. in *Dunne* v. *O'Neill* [1974] I.R. 180, wherein the learned High Court judge laid down the principle that it is the duty of the taxing master, in assessing the amount to be allowed in respect of disbursements by solicitors for counsel's fees, to ascertain what a reasonable and prudent solicitor would consider proper to offer to a suitable counsel in order to obtain his services in the particular case in question. The items questioned in the motion related mainly to solicitors' disbursements for counsel's fees, although one item challenged related to solicitors' instructions fees. **Held** by Parke J. in allowing certain of the objections, and in applying the principle laid down in *Dunne* v. *O'Neill,* 1, the principle of *stare decisis* requires that a court should not depart from a decision of another court of equal jurisdiction unless it is established that the decision was based on insufficient authority or incorrect submissions, or that the judgment departed in some way from the proper standard to be adopted in judicial determination. 2. The discretion conferred on the taxing master is a judicial discretion and must be exercised in accordance with principles laid down by the High Court. 3. The taxation of solicitors' instruction fees is a matter peculiarly within the discretion of the taxing master and, in the absence of evidence that wrong principles have been applied, should not be interfered with by the court. *Irish Trust Bank Ltd.* v. *Central Bank of Ireland*

(H.C.) [1976-7] ILRM 50

29. —— **Taxation** — *Review* — *Counsel's fees* — *Standard applicable by taxing master* — *Whether solicitor acted reasonably and prudently in agreeing to the fees marked* — *R.S.C.*, 1962, *O.* 99, *r.* 38.] The plaintiff was awarded £37,104 and her costs at the conclusion of a fatal injuries action on 11 March, 1975. In pursuance of the said Order a Bill of Costs was prepared on behalf of the plaintiff and taxed before the Taxing Master on 29 May, 1975. The Taxing Master reduced the plaintiff's solicitor's instruction fee from £2,450 to £1,400 and the senior counsel's brief fee from £250 to £175 guineas and his refresher fees from £125 to £80 guineas and junior counsel's fees in proportion. The solicitor for the plaintiff objected to the taxation on the grounds that counsels' fees marked were fair and reasonable having regard to the nature and extent of the evidence to be considered and presented and the responsibility resting on counsel and further counsels' fees were marked after consultation with him. A hearing was heard before the Taxing Master on 28 July, 1975, who disallowed his objections. The plaintiff's solicitor brought a notice of motion pursuant to O. 99 r. 38 of the Rules of the Superior Courts to review the Taxing Master's ruling in respect of general instruction fee for the plaintiff's solicitor, and fees allowed to counsel by way of brief fee and refresher fee. Counsel for the plaintiff submitted that the Taxing Master was not entitled to decide what fees should be paid to counsel. The plaintiff called Mr. Fitzpatrick, a legal accountant who gave his opinion that £1,950 was a fair and reasonable figure by way of remuneration for the plaintiff's solicitor for work done by him. The defendant's legal accountant was called to give evidence but was not asked to and did not in fact contradict Mr. Fitzpatrick's valuation of the plaintiff's solicitor's work in the case. **Held** by Hamilton J. in directing that the matter be referred back to the Taxing Master to adjust his certificate, 1, the Taxing Master failed to have regard to the standard of the practising solicitor which is that he may only disallow solicitor's disbursements including counsel's fees if in the exercise of his discretion he is satisfied that no solicitor acting reasonably carefully and prudently would have determined such fees or made such disbursements. *Dunne* v. *O'Neill* [1974] I.R. 180; *Irish Trust Bank Ltd.* v. *Central Bank of Ireland* [1976-7] ILRM 50 approved and applied. 2. The discretion vested in the Taxing Master is of a judicial nature and should be exercised by him without any element of predetermination or rule of thumb or any arbitrary or capricious determination. 3. The solicitor for the plaintiff acted reasonably and prudently in agreeing to the fees marked by counsel after consultation with him and in paying the fees as marked and is entitled to reimbursements in respect of same. 4. The court has an obligation to review the instruction fee payable to a solicitor even where

the Taxing Master has not (as in this case) proceeded on any incorrect principles. *Lavan* v. *Walsh* [1967] I.R. 129; *Dunne* v. *O'Neill* [1974] I.R. 180 approved and applied. 5. Despite the fact that the Taxing Master in deciding the proper instruction fee payable to the plaintiff's solicitor did not err in principle the plaintiff's solicitor's instruction fee should be increased to £1,950 having regard to the gravity, complexity and difficulties of the case and the evidence of Mr. Fitzpatrick, legal accountant. *Kelly* v. *Breen*

(H.C.) [1978] ILRM 63

30. —— **Taxation** — *Review — Counsel's fees reduced on taxation — Objections to disallowance — Objections allowed in part upon review by Taxing Master — Motion to review Taxing Master's decision — Discretion of Taxing Master — Tests applicable in exercise of discretion — Taxation of fees agreed and disbursements made in the course of litigation by solicitor acting reasonably carefully and reasonably prudently — Whether counsel's fees allowed — R.S.C.*, 1962 (*S.I. No.* 72), *O.* 99, *r.* 38.] The prosecutors obtained an absolute order of certiorari and costs against the respondent in the Supreme Court in respect of a taxation of costs in certain proceedings also concerned with taxation and submitted to taxation their bill of costs in the certiorari proceedings. The respondent ruled that the prosecutors' solicitors had not acted reasonably carefully and reasonably prudently and had erred on the side of excess in accepting the fees marked by counsel for the prosecutors and declined to allow taxation of counsel's fees in full. The prosecutors objected to the disallowance under order 99, r. 38(1) of the Rules of the Superior Courts, 1962, and the respondent upon reviewing his taxation, allowed the objections in part. On the prosecutor's motion under order 99, r. 38(3) to review the decision of the respondent, it was **Held** by Barrington J., in allowing in full counsel's fees, that the respondent had erred in principle in his approach to the taxation. The respondent in the exercise of his discretion was only entitled to disallow any or any part of a solicitor's disbursement, including counsel's fees, if he was satisfied that no solicitor acting reasonably carefully and reasonably prudently based on his experiences in the course of his practice would have determined such fees or would have made such disbursements in the course of his practice. The discretion was not one to disallow any part of a solicitor's disbursement simply because the respondent considered the disbursement excessive, or because he considered that the solicitor was not reasonably careful or reasonably prudent in agreeing to so large a disbursement. *Kelly* v. *Breen* [1978] ILRM 63

applied. *The State (Gallagher Shatter & Co.)* v. *de Valera*

(H.C.) [1987] I.R.55; [1987] ILRM 555

31. —— **Taxation** — *Review — Instruction fee — Solicitor — Family law action — Instruction fee of plaintiff's solicitor — Solicitor choosing not to instruct counsel — Whether appropriate to increase fee.*] The plaintiff obtained an order for 50% of the costs of a High Court action in which she had sought orders against the defendant (her husband) for sole custody of their children, for maintenance and for the discharge of mortgage and insurance payments on the family home and a barring order. There was a motion seeking interim orders and the action itself was heard on four different days. Orders were made dealing with access to the children, the ownership of, and payments on, the family home and maintenance. The plaintiff's firm of solicitors did not instruct counsel and a solicitor in the firm conducted the case. The instruction fee in the bill of costs was £2,500.00. The Taxing Master taxed this item at £1,250.00 on the basis that the case had only involved access and maintenance and that the instruction fee should be the same as it would have been if counsel had been instructed. He also enquired about the amount and source of money paid to the plaintiff's solicitor by the plaintiff before the conclusion of the proceedings. The plaintiff applied for a review of the taxation. **Held** by Finlay P. the item in the bill of costs dealing with the instruction fee would be sent back to the Taxing Master for re-taxation. There had been errors of principle by the Taxing Master because the action had involved more than maintenance and access, with a lot of time being spent on matters relating to the family home. Also, while a solicitor acting without counsel is not entitled to a separate and specific fee, there should be an increase in the instruction fee to reflect the additional work, e.g. in advocacy, in researching and preparing legal points, and in considering the approach and pleading of the case. Finlay P. also commented that questions relating to payments, and the source thereof, by the plaintiff to her solicitors were irrelevant on a party and party taxation. *H.P.* v. *W.P.*

(H.C.) [1985] ILRM 527

32. —— **Taxation** — *Review — Town agent's charges — Whether Taxing Master entitled to disallow claim — Whether special item — Whether claimant precluded from raising an appeal point not made before Taxing Master — R.S.C.*, 1962 (*S.I. No.* 72), *O.* 99, *rr.* 13(2), 38(3).] The plaintiff had issued a motion for judgment in default. At the hearing of the motion time was extended and the plaintiff was awarded costs of the motion

PRACTICE AND PROCEDURE—Costs.

when taxed. Following the taxation of the bill of costs the plaintiff lodged an objection relating to the disallowance of an item. The Taxing Master heard the objection and disallowed it. The item related to a bill of £48 paid by the plaintiff's solicitor, a Cork practitioner, to their town agent in respect of issuance of the notice of motion and bespeaking the order. The plaintiff sought on motion an order pursuant to O. 99, r. 38 (5) of the Rules of the Superior Courts for a review of the taxation of the bill of costs. The plaintiff's counsel submitted at this stage for the first time that this was a 'special' case pursuant to O. 99, r. 13(2), and that the Taxing Master was entitled to allow a special allowance in respect of town agent's charges, as there was no item for such charges in the scale of costs in question. He further submitted that the Taxing Master ought to have disallowed another item in respect of the town agent attending in court at the hearing of the motion, and have allowed the item for issuance in full. **Held** by Blayney J. in refusing to grant the motion to review taxation, 1, the items for issuance of the orders were covered in the bill of costs, and had been duly allowed, and to allow them again would give rise to duplication. 2. A Taxing Master's certificate is final and conclusive regarding all matters which have not been objected to pursuant to O. 99, r. 38(3) of the Rules of the Superior Courts, and a party seeking a review of taxation is confined to grounds of objection made before the Taxing Master. *Walsh, In re* 96 I.L.T.R. 173 applied. 3. The fact that the plaintiff practised outside Dublin, and found it necessary to have a town agent was not abnormal or unusual and did not come within the meaning of 'special' cases pursuant to O. 99, r. 13(2) of the Rules of the Superior Courts. *O'Sullivan* v. *Hughes*

(H.C.) [1986] ILRM 555

33. —— **Taxation** — *Review — Witnesses' expenses — Appeal from decision of Taxing Master to disallow or reduce fees or expenses of professional witnesses — Principles to be observed by Taxing Master — R.S.C.*, 1962 *O.* 61 *r.* 12, *O.* 99 *r.* 37(8).] The applicant, which had successfully pursued a malicious injury claim in the Circuit Court in Cork, appealed from a decision of the Cork County Registrar (acting as Taxing Master) disallowing or reducing the amounts claimed for fees and expenses by four professional witnesses. The solicitor to the costs contended that the registrar applied to witness expenses a scale of his own devising. The registrar, in his report on the taxation, stated that he had been present at the trial of the case and was aware of the amount of work involved in it. No evidence was given at the taxation of what fees a reasonable prudent and careful solicitor would

PRACTICE AND PROCEDURE—*continued.*

have found it necessary to disburse. **Held** by Gannon J., directing re-taxation in the light of his observations in the judgment, 1, that a Taxing Master is not entitled to prescribe the standards he expects a solicitor to adopt in retaining witnesses,nor is it his duty to evaluate the nature and value of the work and evidence of witnesses. 2. That a Taxing Master is bound to apply the standards of a reasonably careful and prudent practitioner, and should keep himself informed of such standards. 3. That a Taxing Master is entitled to disallow only such sums as no prudent solicitor would have incurred. 4. That the solicitor to the costs has the onus of adducing evidence. *Crown Chemical Company (Ireland) Ltd.* v. *Cork County Council*

(H.C.) [1984] ILRM 555

DISCOVERY — Documents

34. —— **Non-party discovery** — *Scope of power of court — "Fishing" — Discretion of court — Procedure — Notice of motion — Whether parties to proceedings as well as person against whom discovery is sought should be served — Rules of the Superior Courts,* 1986 (*S.I. No.* 15), *O.* 31, *r.* 29.] 1. The power of the High Court under Order 31, r. 29 of the Rules of the Superior Courts, 1986, to make an order for discovery of documents against persons not parties to the action only arises where the court has evidence before it firstly, that documents which are relevant to an issue likely to arise at the hearing of the action exist and secondly, that it is likely that the notice party has relevant documents in his power or procurement. 2. The court has no power to make an order merely to permit a party to inspect the files of a non-party to see whether they contain any relevant document. 3. The court has a discretion as to whether or not to make an order under Order 31, r. 29. So **held** by Costello J. *Per curiam.* While Order 31, r. 29 does not specifically provide that the parties to the proceedings should be served with notice of application for discovery against a non-party, the parties may have an interest in the application and the court, before making such an order, should know their views. Accordingly, unless the parties have clearly indicated in correspondence that they do not wish to be heard, they should be served with the notice of motion. *Holloway* v. *Belenos Publications Ltd. (No. 1)*

(H.C.) [1987] I.R.405; [1987] ILRM 790

35. —— **Non-party discovery** — *Power of court to order discovery against third party — Whether* intra vires *the Superior Courts Rules Committee powers — Rules of the Superior Courts,* 1986 (*S.I. No.* 15), *O.* 31, *r.* 29 — *Courts of Justice Act,* 1924 (*No.* 10), *s.* 36.

PRACTICE AND PROCEDURE—Discovery.

Practice — Discovery — Privilege — Privilege based on public interest — Greyhound Industry Act, 1958 (*No.* 12), *s.* 26.] Order 31, r. 29 of the Rules of the Superior Courts, 1986, provides: "Any person not a party to the cause or matter before the court who appears to the court to be likely to have or to have had in his possession custody or power any documents which are relevant to an issue arising or likely to arise out of the cause or matter or is likely to be in a position to give evidence relevant to any such issue may by leave of the court upon the application of any party to the said cause or matter be directed by order of the court to answer such interrogatories or to make discovery of such documents or to permit inspection of such documents . . ." The second defendant, a journalist on the staff of the first defendant, wrote two articles for the first defendant which were highly critical of the manner in which the affairs of the Irish Coursing Club were being run. The articles contained extensive extracts from reports written by C.D., an accountant on the staff of Bord na gCon, which he had written following an investigation into the affairs of the Irish Coursing Club. The plaintiff, who was the secretary of the Club during the period the reports covered, instituted proceedings for damages for libel in respect of the articles. In their defence the defendants alleged that in so far as the words complained of consisted of allegations of fact they were true and in so far as they consisted of expressions of opinion they were fair comment. In order for the defence to succeed it was therefore necessary to establish the veracity of the facts contained in the reports of C.D. The defendants sought an order of discovery and inspection under O. 31, r. 29, against Bord na gCon, and C.D., (the notice parties) who were not parties to the action. The notice parties objected to an order being made on the ground that (*a*) O. 31, r. 29, was invalid as being *ultra vires* the rule making powers of the Superior Courts Rules Committee; (*b*) public interest privilege attached to the documents which had been prepared by C.D. for Bord na gCon in pursuit of the latter's statutory responsibilities and (*c*) the court should exercise its discretion against making the order on the basis that the documents sought had already been made available to the defendants by the plaintiff's discovery. **Held** by Costello J. in making the order sought subject to conditions, 1, that the provisions of O. 31, r. 29 were essentially procedural and did not change the substantive law and consequently were not *ultra vires* the powers of the Rules Committee. 2. That, since the production of the documents at the hearing would not be adverse to the statutory responsibilities of the notice party, and would not

PRACTICE AND PROCEDURE—*continued.*

adversely affect the public interest, the documents could be made the subject of an order under r. 29 of Order 31. 3. That, although as a general rule the court should not make an order against non parties if the documents which were sought were otherwise available to the party seeking the order, it was not certain that all the documents which the notice parties had in their possession had been discovered by the plaintiff. *Fitzpatrick* v. *Independent Newspapers plc.*

(H.C.) [1988] I.R.132; [1988] ILRM 707

36. —— **Non-party discovery** — *Superior Courts Rules Committee — Power to make rules regulating the practice and procedure of court — Rule permitting discovery to be ordered against non-parties to proceedings — Jurisdiction of High Court to order discovery — Whether discovery a matter of practice and procedure — Whether rule* intra vires *Superior Courts Rules Committee — R.S.C.,* 1986 (*S.I. No.* 15), *O.* 31, *r.* 29 — *Courts of Justice Act,* 1924 (*No.* 10), *s.* 36 — *Courts of Justice Act,* 1936 (*No.* 48), *s.* 68.] Section 36 of the Courts of Justice Act, 1924, as amended by s. 68 of the Courts of Justice Act, 1936, empowers the Superior Courts Rules Committee to make rules of court for pleading, practice and procedure generally in all civil cases. Order 31, r. 29 of the Rules of the Superior Courts, 1986, provides that the court may, on the application of any party to a cause or matter, order any person not a party to the cause or matter to answer interrogatories or to make discovery of documents. In proceedings brought by the plaintiff claiming damages for libel, the defendants applied pursuant to O. 31, r. 29 for an order for discovery against the notice parties. The notice parties opposed the application and challenged the validity of the rule on the grounds that it was *ultra vires* the Superior Courts Rules Committee. **Held** by Barron J., in declaring that O. 31, r. 29 was not *ultra vires* the Superior Courts Rules Committee, 1, that the power of the court to order discovery of documents was part of the inherent jurisdiction of the court. 2. That O. 31, r. 29 did not purport to create any new substantive rights or to modify any statutory power but was part of the procedural machinery whereby a cause of action was processed. 3. That O. 31, r. 29 was a rule of practice and procedure regulating the inherent jurisdiction of the court and, accordingly, was *intra vires* the Superior Courts Rules Committee. *The State (O'Flaherty)* v. *Ó Floinn* [1954] I.R. 295 considered. *Holloway* v. *Belenos Publications Ltd. (No. 2)*

(H.C.) [1988] I.R.494; [1988] ILRM 685

37. —— **Order of inspection** — *Whether litigant's right to inspection dependent on the strength of his cause of action — R.S.C.,* 1986

PRACTICE AND PROCEDURE—Discovery.

(*S.I. No.* 15), *O.* 50, *r.* 4.] The right of a litigant to seek and obtain an order of inspection is in no way dependent upon the court being satisfied as to the strength of his cause of action. So **held** by Murphy J. *Cooper* v. *Ince Hall Co.* [1876] W.N. 24; *Bennitt* v. *Whitehouse* (1860) 28 Beav. 119; *Montana Company* v. *St. Louis Mining and Milling Company* (1894) 152 U.S. 160; *Campus Oil Ltd.* v. *Minister for Industry and Energy* [1983] ILRM 258 and *Campus Oil Ltd.* v. *Minister for Industry (No. 2)* [1983] I.R. 88, considered. *Bula Ltd.* v. *Tara Mines Ltd. (No. 1)*

(H.C.) [1987] I.R.85; [1988] ILRM 149

38. —— **Privilege** — *Legal professional privilege — Communications in anticipation of proceedings — Privilege based on public interest — R.S.C.,* 1962 (*S.I. No.* 72), *O.* 31.] The plaintiffs brought proceedings against the defendants claiming damages for injury caused to them by the slaughter, at the direction of the first defendant, of their entire flock of ducks following an outbreak of avian influenza and for compensation pursuant to the provisions of the Diseases of Animals Act, 1966. An order for discovery of documents was made by the Master of the High Court and the affidavit of discovery filed on behalf of the defendants claimed privilege in respect of a number of documents on the grounds that they had been ". . . made in contemplation of and for the purpose of advising the Minister and his officers in relation to the plaintiffs claim" and that they were"documents of a confidential nature relating to the European Community." The plaintiffs were dissatisfied with that affidavit and moved for an order for further and better discovery. **Held** by O'Hanlon J., in making the order sought, 1, that the defendants' entitlement to claim legal professional privilege arose at the time when litigation could fairly be regarded by the defendants as apprehended or threatened. 2. That the defendants were entitled to claim professional privilege not only in respect of communications passing between the Minister and his legal advisers but in respect of all documents prepared in connection with the plaintiffs' claim for the dominant purpose of preparing for litigation. *Alfred Crompton Amusement Machines Ltd.* v. *Customs & Excise Comrs.* (No. 2) [1972] 2 Q.B. 102 (C.A.) and *Waugh* v. *British Railways Board* [1980] A.C. 521 considered. 3. That on the facts, no question of privilege based on public interest arose. *Silver Hill Duckling Ltd.* v. *Minister for Agriculture*

(H.C.) [1987] I.R.289; [1987] ILRM 516

39. —— **Privilege** — *Legal professional privilege — Communications in anticipation of proceedings — Claim by insured on foot of fire insurance policy — Report commissioned by*

PRACTICE AND PROCEDURE—*continued.*

insurers on cause of fire — Insurers repudiating liability — Whether report privileged — Whether report prepared in apprehension or anticipation of litigation.] On the 22 May, 1981, the plaintiffs' premises which was insured with the defendants, was destroyed by fire. On the 5 June,1981, the defendants were notified of the loss. The defendants immediately commissioned a report from a firm of loss adjusters which they received on the 8 June, 1981. The defendants took preliminary advices from their solicitors on the 11 June, 1981. The plaintiffs commenced proceedings on the 4 February, 1983, to recover their loss. In the course of the proceedings an order for discovery of documents was made against the defendants. The defendants disclosed the existence of the loss adjusters' report but claimed privilege in respect thereof. The plaintiffs applied for an order for further and better discovery. **Held** by O'Hanlon J., in refusing the plaintiffs' application, 1, that privilege from disclosure may be claimed by a party in respect of documents which come into existence prior to the commencement of proceedings, when it can be shown that the dominant purpose for the document coming into existence was for the purpose of preparing for litigation then apprehended or threatened. *Silver Hill Duckling Ltd.* v. *Minister for Agriculture* [1987] I.R. 289 applied. 2. That from the time the plaintiffs had claimed to be indemnified, the defendants had viewed the claim with suspicion and their motive in commissioning the report was not only to evaluate the financial value of the claim but also to gather any evidence which might justify them in repudiating liability. *P.J. Carrigan Ltd.* v. *Norwich Union Fire Society Ltd.*

(H.C.) [1987] I.R.618

40. —— **Privilege** — *State privilege — Factors to be taken into consideration — Injustice to applicant or potential damage to public service.*] The plaintiffs in pursuance of their action against the defendants brought the present application seeking an order allowing them to inspect certain documents in the possession of the defendants. The defendants pleaded state privilege for the documents. **Held** by Murphy J. in granting the plaintiffs' application, the injustice which would ensue from a refusal of the plaintiffs' application would be greater than the minimal potential damage which might result to the public service by acceding to that application. *Folens* v. *Minister for Education* [1981] ILRM 21 applied. *Incorporated Law Society of Ireland* v. *Minister for Justice.*

(H.C.) [1987] ILRM 42

ESTOPPEL

41. —— **Res judicata** — *Abuse of process — Estoppel* per rem judicatam — *Civil action for damages for assault — Criminal proceedings involving same issue finding no assault took place — Whether plaintiff estopped from bringing civil proceedings — Whether defendants estopped from denying plaintiffs ability to bring civil proceedings — Defendants not party to criminal prosecution — Additional evidence — Whether sufficient to overcome plea of estoppel.*] The plaintiff had been convicted in the Special Criminal Court of offences connected with a train robbery. During the course of his trial, he had sought to have a written statement signed by him excluded from consideration by the court, on the grounds that it had not been freely made, but was given as a result of unlawful violence used against him by members of the Gardaí. The court, having heard evidence from both sides, had rejected these allegations, ruling that the statement had been freely made and was admissible in evidence. The present proceedings were brought by the plaintiff claiming damages for alleged assault committed upon him while in custody by members of the Gardaí. These allegations were identical with those upon which he relied in seeking to have his written statement ruled inadmissible during his trial. The defendants contended that these matters were *res judicata,* and that the plaintiff was estopped from raising them anew. They also pleaded that the initiation of the civil proceedings was an abuse of the process of the court. The plaintiff alleged that the defendants were estopped by their own conduct from relying on these pleas, in that they had co-operated actively in steps taken to regularise the proceedings and to bring the matter to hearing as speedily as possible, and in that a Government statement had invited him to bring the present proceedings. The plaintiff also sought to adduce fresh evidence to defeat the pleas of the defendants. **Held** by O'Hanlon J., in dismissing the plaintiff's action, 1, the Government statement in inviting the plaintiff to commence civil proceedings, and the co-operation of the defendants regarding various stages of the proceedings, did not have the effect of inducing the plaintiff to act to his detriment, and did not preclude the defendants from relying upon a plea of issue estoppel, or upon a plea that the civil proceedings constituted an abuse of the process of the court. 2. The new evidence sought to be adduced by the plaintiff was not of such a character that, had it been adduced at the trial would have changed the entire aspect of the case. It was not, therefore, sufficient to preclude the defendants from relying on the pleas made. *Hunter* v. *Chief Constable of West Midlands* [1982] A.C. 529 followed. 3. For the purpose of issue estoppel, privity existed between the prosecutor in the criminal proceedings and the defendants in the civil proceedings. In criminal proceedings on indictment, the Director of Public Prosecutions acts on behalf of the people of Ireland, and in defending a civil claim against the State, the Attorney General also acts on behalf of the people. 4. Where a clearly identifiable issue has been decided against a party in a criminal trial, by means of a judgment explaining how the decision was reached, such decision may give rise to issue estoppel in subsequent civil proceedings in which that party is involved and in the absence of special circumstances, an effort by a party to challenge by means of civil proceedings a decision made against him by a court of competent jurisdiction is an abuse of the process of the court. *Hunter* v. *Chief Constable of West Midlands* [1982] A.C. 529 followed. *Kelly* v. *Ireland*

(H.C.) [1986] ILRM 318

42. —— **Res judicata** — *Motor accident — Personal injuries proceedings commenced in High Court — Liability for accident determined in previous litigation in District and Circuit Courts — Whether immediate High Court action barred — Whether issues in both proceedings identical — Whether parties identical — Whether action barred by Civil Liability Act — Civil Liability Act,* 1961 (*No.* 41), *ss.* 29(6), 37.

Constitution — Statute — Validity — "Full" original jurisdiction of High Court — Statute effectively barring High Court action on basis akin to issue estoppel — Whether provision valid — Civil Liability Act, 1961 (*No.* 41), *ss.* 29(6), 37 — *Constitution of Ireland,* 1937, *Art.* 34.3.] Article 34, s. 3, sub-s. 1, of the Constitution provides that the courts of first instance shall include a High Court invested with "full original jurisdiction in and power to determine all matters and questions whether of law or fact, civil or criminal." Section 37, sub-s. 1, of the Civil Liability Act, 1961, provides that where a plaintiff has his damages reduced under sub-s. 1 of s. 34 of that Act on account of contributory negligence and the defendant subsequently brings an action against the plaintiff in respect of damage arising out of the same facts, the determination of liability and apportionment of fault in the first action shall be binding between the parties in the second action. Sub-section 2 of that section provides that the foregoing provision shall apply between two parties notwithstanding that one of them is party to the two actions in different capacities. The plaintiff commenced proceedings in the High Court claiming damages against the defendants for personal injuries he alleged he had sustained in a collision between the motor cycle he was riding and a motor car, the property of the first

PRACTICE AND PROCEDURE—Estoppel.

defendant and driven with that defendant's consent by the second defendant. At the trial of an earlier action in the District Court brought by the first defendant against the plaintiff and in which she claimed damages for the damage occasioned to her motor car in that collision, the District Court found the plaintiff to have been guilty of negligence but reduced the amount of agreed damages in the first defendant's favour by half on the ground that she had been guilty of 50% contributory negligence. The first defendant appealed to the Circuit Court against that judgment and the Circuit Court varied the order of the court below by allowing the first defendant the full amount of the agreed damages, the order of the Circuit Court as drawn up reciting "AND THE COURT DOTH FIND that the defendant [*sic*] was negligent and the plaintiff [*sic*] was not negligent." The second defendant was not a party to those proceedings. In the defence filed by both defendants to the plaintiff's High Court proceedings they pleaded, *inter alia,* that his claim against them was barred by estoppel of matter *res judicata* and further by virtue of s. 37 and s. 29, sub-s. 6, of the Act of 1961, the latter statutory provision dealing with issues between claimants and contributors as those terms are defined in the Act of 1961. The issue as to whether the plaintiff's action was so barred was by order of the High Court tried as a preliminary issue by a judge without a jury and the Attorney General was joined as a notice party to the issue by reason of the plaintiff having further pleaded that if the foregoing statutory provisions were otherwise effective to bar his action, those provisions were invalid having regard to Article 34, s. 3, of the Constitution. At the trial of the preliminary issue it was argued on behalf of the plaintiff, *inter alia,* (1), that his cause of action involving a claim for damages for personal injuries was a different cause of action from that the subject matter of the determination in the courts below, namely, the damage to the first defendant's motor car, (2) that the parties were not the same in both proceedings as the second defendant was not a party to the proceedings in the courts below and could, therefore, not invoke an estoppel and (3), that the plaintiff's capacity and interest in the High Court proceedings differed from that which he had in the lower courts. **Held** by Gannon J., in holding the plaintiff's action to be barred by virtue of the doctrine of *res judicata* and by s. 37 of the Act of 1961 and that it was unnecessary to consider the constitutionality of that section, 1, that the interests of the defendants were identical in the High Court proceedings by virtue of s. 118 and s. 3, sub-s. 5, of the Road Traffic Act, 1961, and s. 34, sub-s. 1, and s. 38, sub-s. 3 of the Civil Liability Act, 1961. 2. That the only issues

PRACTICE AND PROCEDURE—*continued.*

between the parties in the previous proceedings to which the evidence related and upon which a final determination was obtained were those confined to liability for negligence, viz., the nature of the duty of care required of each party and the alleged breach thereof. 3. That whilst there was some doubt as to whether the issue of contributory negligence on the part of the first defendant by the driving of the second defendant in the previous proceedings encompassed the issue of the liability in negligence of the first defendant to all persons including the plaintiff, it was, nevertheless, clear that in those proceedings it had been determined that the plaintiff was solely and entirely liable for the negligence which caused the collision. Accordingly, the plaintiff's action in the High Court was barred by estoppel of matter *res judicata. Ord* v. *Ord* [1923] 2 K.B. 432; *Ramsay* v. *Pigram* (1968) 118 C.L.R. 271 and *Hargrave* v. *Goldman* (1963) 110 C.L.R. 40 considered. *Brunsden* v. *Humphrey* (1884) 14 Q.B.D. 141 and *Jackson* v. *Goldsmith* (1950) 81 C.L.R. 446 explained and distinguished. 4. That that conclusion also followed by virtue of the operation of s. 37 of the Civil Liability Act, 1961, which made the determination of the District Court (as revised by the Circuit Court) concerning the liability and apportionment of fault between the parties binding between them in the High Court proceedings. 5. That s. 29, sub-s. 6, of the Act of 1961 had no application to any of the parties in the High Court proceedings. 6. That the plaintiff had lost his right of recourse to the High Court by the procedural advantage obtained by the first defendant in having brought proceedings in the lower courts and having thereby established an estoppel: it was, therefore, unnecessary to consider the arguments advanced on the plaintiff's behalf, based on Article 34, s. 3, directed towards rebutting the presumption of validity attaching to the provisions of the Civil Liability Act, 1961. *Murphy* v. *Hennessy* [1984] I.R. 378 and *Troy* v. *C.I.E.* [1971] I.R. 320 considered. *Donohoe* v. *Browne*

(H.C.) [1986] I.R. 90

43. —— **Road traffic accident** — *Personal injury action — Claim made against driver of vehicle — Driver dying from injuries received in accident — Liberty sought to join insurers as defendants in place of deceased — Whether insurers estopped from opposing such an order.*] The plaintiff and the defendant were involved in a road accident in July, 1979, resulting in the death of the defendant. The plaintiff's solicitor instituted proceedings against the deceased defendant in respect of the personal injuries the plaintiff suffered. The plaintiff's solicitor issued a plenary summons on 19 October, 1981, against

PRACTICE AND PROCEDURE—Estoppel.

the defendant, despite letters they received from the defendant's insurers dated 8 July and 8 October, 1981, and headed "Peter McBride (deceased)" together with further correspondence intimating the defendant was deceased. A statement of claim was deliverd on 19 January, 1982. In January, 1983 and 1984, the plaintiff brought a notice of motion seeking liberty to join the insurers as defendants in place of the deceased defendant. Neither motion was proceeded with and in April, 1984, a third motion to the same effect was brought. The High Court ordered in February, 1985, that the insurers nominate some person to defend the action and that in default of so doing within two weeks the court would join the insurers as co-defendants. The insurers appealed this decision. **Held** by the Supreme Court (Finlay C.J., Henchy and Griffin JJ.) in allowing the appeal, 1, the insurers are not estopped from objecting to being joined as defendants as the plaintiff failed to establish that the insurers impliedly promised or assured them that they would not rely on the invalidity of the proceedings. *Doran* v. *Thompson* [1978] I.R. 223 followed. 2. Even if the court made an order allowing the insurers to be joined as defendants, such an order would be fruitless as the liability of the insurers, if any, lies in contract and not negligence as in the pending action. *Boyce* v. *McBride*

(S.C.) [1987] ILRM 95

EVIDENCE

44. —— **Privilege** — Subpoena duces tecum *issued requiring officer of the Central Bank to produce documents — Oath of secrecy — Statutory privilege — Whether summons be set aside — Central Bank Act,* 1942 (*No.* 22), *ss.* 6(1), 31.] The plaintiff, whose case against the defendant lay in the circumstances surrounding the disposal of his shareholding in the Commercial Banking Co. Ltd., issued a *subpoena duces tecum* to secure the attendance, with relevant documents, of an official of the Central Bank of Ireland. The official served with the *subpoena,* Michael Cleere, and his employer, the Central Bank, objected to the witness summons, and sought by motion to have it set aside. Michael Cleere's objection was that he had taken an oath pursuant to s. 31 of the Central Bank Act, 1942, that he would not disclose any information about the Bank's business. The Bank further contended that the disclosure of the information sought would be prejudicial to the national interest. **Held** by O'Hanlon J., accepting the objections and setting aside the witness summons, that s. 31 of the Central Bank Act, 1942, gave rise to a statutory privilege in favour of information and documents held by officers of the Central Bank.

PRACTICE AND PROCEDURE—*continued.*

Cully v. *Northern Bank Finance Corporation Ltd.*

(H.C.) [1984] ILRM 683

INTERROGATORIES

45. —— **Personal injury action** — *Bronchial condition — Limitation period — Interrogatories seeking source of plaintiff's knowledge of injury and cause — Whether interrogatories necessary for disposing fairly of matter — Statute of Limitations (Northern Ireland),* 1958 (*c.* 10), *s.* 9A, 9D — *R.S.C. (N.I.), O.* 26, *r.* 1.] In a personal injury action in which the defendant relies on section 9A of the Statute of Limitations (Northern Ireland), 1958, which provides that the limitation period runs from the date of the plaintiff's knowledge concerning the injury, or the plaintiff relies on section 9D of that Act, which gives the court a discretion to disapply the limitation period, interrogatories may be administered seeking the source of the plaintiff's first knowledge that the injury was significant and the source of his knowledge that the injury was attributable to the defendant's acts or omissions. Under these sections regard is to be had to the knowledge that the plaintiff might reasonably have been expected to acquire and the extent to which he acted promptly and reasonably and, if the plaintiff merely gave the dates on which he acquired the relevant knowledge and not the sources, the defendant could be seriously handicapped in making a case against the plaintiff. *McMullan* v. *Harland and Wolff Ltd.*

(Q.B.D.) [1985] N.I.1

JUDGMENT

46. —— **Currency** — *Contract for the sale of goods — Money of account being Dutch guilders — Whether judgment could be given in foreign currency — Conversion rate.*] The plaintiffs had applied in the Central Office of the High Court for judgment against the defendant in default of appearance to a summary summons in which the claim was for the sum of 14,740.40 Dutch guilders. The application was refused on the ground that the practice was to give judgment in Irish currency only. Upon application to the High Court it was **Held** by McMahon J. in granting the application, 1, the requirements of international commerce are more appropriately met by a rule which enables the court to give judgment in the currency to which the plaintiff is entitled by the terms of his contract with the defendant. 2. For the purpose of this rule it is not necessary that the proper law of the contract be foreign law. *Dicta* in *Barclay's Bank Ltd.* v. *Levin Bros. (Bradford) Ltd.* [1977] Q.B. 270 adopted. 3. The date to be inserted in the order for the conversion

PRACTICE AND PROCEDURE—Judgment.

of the currency into Irish currency is the date on which judgment is entered in the office. *Miliangos* v. *George Frank (Textiles) Ltd.* [1976] A.C. 443 distinguished. *Damen and Zonen* v. *O'Shea*

(H.C.) [1976-7] ILRM 275

PARTIES

see also **Nos. 12, 13, 43**

47. —— **Adding party as defendants** — *Road accident — First defendant's insurers repudiated liability — Judgment obtained against first defendant — Insurers applied to be added as defendants in order to appeal — Whether a question or issue existed between plaintiff and insurers — Whether proceedings still in being — Whether final judgment given — R.S.C. (N.I.), O.* 15, *r.* 6(2)(*b*).] A front seat passenger in the first defendant's vehicle sustained fatal injuries in a collision between that vehicle and the second defendant's vehicle. The plaintiff, the father of the deceased, brought an action against both drivers. The first defendant's insurers repudiated liability under the terms of the insurance policy on the ground that he failed to disclose material facts in his insurance proposal. The first defendant contested the action with assistance of legal aid. The jury found against the first defendant and awarded £45,000 damages. Under article 98 of the Road Traffic (Northern Ireland) Order, 1981, the plaintiff could recover the amount of the judgment and costs against the first defendant's insurers if he failed to recover it from the first defendant, even if the policy of insurance was invalid. The insurers wished to appeal against the jury's verdict on the ground that the amount of damages was excessive. The first defendant refused to bring an appeal. The insurers applied for an order under Order 15 rule 6(2)(*b*) of the Rules of the Supreme Court (Northern Ireland) that they be added as defendants in order to give them *locus standi* to appeal against the verdict. The Master allowed the application. On appeal from the Master's order the plaintiff contended that the application should have been made to the Court of Appeal rather than the High Court; that a party may not be added after final judgment consequent upon the jury's verdict being made against the defendant and that in the circumstances of the case the court should not exercise its discretion to allow the application. **Held,** dismissing the appeal that, 1, there was no procedural reason under order15 rule 6(2)(*b*) why the application of the insurers to be joined as a party should not as readily be brought in the High Court rather than the Court of Appeal. 2. There existed an issue between the plaintiff and the insurers arising out of or relating to or connected with the remedy claimed by the plaintiff and directly related to the subject matter of the action in that the insurers were bound by statute to satisfy the judgment obtained against the first defendant. The requirements of Order 15, rule 6(2)(*b*)(ii) were therefore satisfied and the court had jurisdiction to allow joinder of the insurers. 3. A person may be added as a party under Order 15, rule 6(2)(*b*)(ii) at any stage of the proceedings and the proceedings were still in being until any necessary steps had been taken to enforce judgment against the insurers under article 98 of the 1981 Order. Furthermore, where an appeal has been brought against the judgment the proceedings were still in being. *Quaere* whether where an appeal has not been brought the proceedings remain in being during the time limited for service of a notice of appeal. 4. In the circumstances it was appropriate to join the insurers as there appeared to be a proper case to be pursued on appeal concerning the amount of the award. *Millen* v. *Brown*

(Q.B.D.) [1984] N.I.328

PLEADINGS

48. —— **Particulars** — *Defence — Libel — Statement of claim reproducing alleged libel — Libel including statements of fact, opinions and comments — Defence alleging fair comment upon matters of public interest — Statement of facts alleged to be true — Statement of facts, insofar as consisting of opinion, alleged to have been made in good faith and without malice on a matter of public interest — Plaintiff entitled to further particulars of (a) what part of alleged libel consists of statements of fact (b) the facts on which defendant relies as establishing truth of alleged libel and (c) the matters relied on as supporting truth of libel — R.S.C.,* 1962 (*S.I. No.* 72), *O.* 19, *r.* 6(1).] When it is pleaded as a defence to a claim for libel that, insofar as the words complained of are a statement of fact, they are true, and insofar as they are expressions of opinion, they are fair comment on such facts, and where the facts alleged are so numerous and unspecific that it would be unfair to expect the plaintiff to present his case without notice of their true range, the plaintiff is entitled to particulars of which of the words complained of are alleged to be statements of fact, and of the facts to be relied upon in support of such factual statements. **So held** by Hamilton J. and affirmed by the Supreme Court (Finlay C.J., Henchy, Griffin, Hederman and McCarthy JJ.). *Cooney* v. *Browne*

(H.C., S.C.) [1985] I.R. 185; [1985] ILRM 673

49. —— **Particulars** — *Defence — Libel — Rolled-up plea — Further and better particulars — Compliance with court order — Whether sufficient compliance.*] In defamation proceedings the

PRACTICE AND PROCEDURE—Pleadings.

Supreme Court ordered the following particulars to be delivered by the defendants to the plaintiff: (1) which of the words complained of are facts the truth of which will be proved and which are correct, and (2) what facts are to be relied upon as supporting the actual statements made: [1985] ILRM 673. By letter the defendants purported to comply with the order of the Supreme Court. When the matter came before the High Court, Egan J. was not satisfied that the replies in the letter were adequate and the matter was adjourned to give the defendants an opportunity of furnishing more adequate replies. **Held** by Egan J. that the replies now furnished complied with the order of the Supreme Court. *Cooney* v. *Browne (No. 2)*

(H.C.) [1986] ILRM 444

SUMMONS

50. —— **Renewal** — *Plenary summons issued but not served — Limitation period expiring — Application to renew — Whether defendant prejudiced by lapse of time — R.S.C., O.* 8, *r.* 1.] The plaintiff had issued a plenary summons on 22 July, 1982, claiming damages against C.I.E. for personal injuries suffered in an accident on 20 August, 1979. An originating letter had been sent by his solicitors in February, 1980, and after correspondence C.I.E. wrote in April, 1981, denying liability. C.I.E. heard nothing further until they received a letter in April, 1984, from the plaintiff's new solicitors. The summons had not been served within twelve months of issue and applications were brought (*a*) to extend the time for applying for renewal and (*b*) to have the summons renewed. The plaintiff's claim would be statute barred if the summons were not renewed. No reason had been given for the delay. The defendants relied on the Statute of Limitations and said that they would be prejudiced by the lapse of time having regard to the poor health of their only witnesses, the crew of the bus involved, whose evidence could however be obtained on commission. **Held** by O'Hanlon J. granting the application. As the plaintiff had at an early stage made known to the defendant his intention to being proceedings and as his claim would be statute barred without a renewal the court was bound to follow the decisions of the Supreme Court in the analogous cases of *Baulk* v. *Irish National Insurance Company Ltd.* [1969] I.R. 66, and *McCooey* v. *Minister for Finance and Another* [1971] I.R. 159, in which it had been held that in such circumstances there was 'other good reason' within the meaning of R.S.C. O. 8 r. 1 for granting renewal. *Walshe* v. *Córas Iompair Éireann*

(H.C.) [1985] ILRM 180

PRACTICE AND PROCEDURE—Summons.

51. —— **Service out of the jurisdiction** — *Harbour dues in respect of ships — Whether a liability "affecting" land — Liability arising under private Act — Whether to be regarded as contractual — R.S.C. (N.I.), O.* 11, *r.* 1(1).]

Contract — Quasi-contract — Legislation — Whether rights arising under private and local Act analogous to contractual rights.] In an action by the plaintiff body, the Harbour Authority for Carlingford Lough, to recover harbour dues from the defendant, a company having its registered office in Kent, liberty was granted to the plaintiff to serve a writ of summons out of the jurisdiction. The defendant appealed arguing that the liability to pay dues was not a "liability affecting land" or a liability under a quasi-contract within the meaning of Order 11, rule 1(1), of the Rules of the Supreme Court (Northern Ireland). **Held,** allowing the appeal, that, 1, the claim for harbour dues was not a claim based on a liability or obligation affecting land as it was a mere personal obligation with no charge upon the land or remedy against any of it. 2. While an analogy may be drawn between certain private and local Acts and contracts for the purpose of the true construction of the Acts, the statutory provisions enabling the plaintiff to recover dues from a member of the public whose ship comes within the harbour cannot be regarded as creating a contractual liability. *Carlingford Lough Harbour Commissioners* v. *F.J. Everard & Sons Ltd.*

(Q.B.D.) [1985] N.I.50

52. —— **Service out of the jurisdiction** — *Negligence — Defective heart valve manufactured in foreign jurisdiction causing damage to plaintiff in this jurisdiction — Whether cause of action founded on a tort committed within the jurisdiction — Factors to be taken into consideration in exercising discretion to allow service out of the jurisdiction — R.S.C.,* 1962 (*S.I. No.* 72), *O.* 11, *r.* 1(*f*), *O.* 12, *r.* 26, *O.* 15, *r.* 14 — *Courts of Justice Act,* 1936 (*No.* 48), *s.* 27.] Order 11, r. 1(*f*) of the Rules of the Superior Courts, 1962, provides that service out of the jurisdiction of an originating summons or notice thereof may be allowed by the court when the action is founded on a tort committed within the jurisdiction. The plaintiff claimed damages for personal injuries suffered as a result of the disintegration of a heart valve which had been inserted in his heart within the jurisdiction. The valve had been manufactured in the United States by the second defendant. The plaintiff obtained an order joining the second defendant as a party to the action and authorising service of notice of the proceedings outside the jurisdiction on the said defendant. The second defendant, before entering an appearance, applied to court for an order setting aside the service and discharging the

order authorising such service on the grounds that it could not properly be sued within the jurisdiction. The application was refused by the High Court (Lynch J.). On appeal by the second defendant it was **Held** by the Supreme Court (Finlay C.J., Walsh and Griffin JJ.), in disallowing the appeal and re-affirming the order of the High Court, 1, that order 11, r. 1(*f*) required the court to determine the issue as to whether or not a tort had been committed within the State within the meaning of that rule. The issue was not merely a mechanical one; the court had to have regard to the implications for the plaintiff or the defendant if the trial were to take place within the State. The task of the court was to interpret and to apply the rule in a way designed to ensure that justice and practical common sense should prevail. The rule should be interpreted in the light of broad policy and in the light of its choice of law implications. If more than one possible interpretation of the rule was available, the one which served to encourage the operation of sensible choice of law rules should be followed, taking into account the social and economic dimensions of any particular choice of law rule. *Phillips* v. *Eyre* (1870) L.R. 6 Q.B. 1 not followed. 2. That to fulfil the requirements set out in order 11, r. 1(*f*) it is sufficient if any significant element in the commission of the tort has occurred within the jurisdiction. The court should then examine the circumstances of each case before exercising its discretion to make an order for service out of the jurisdiction. *George Monro Ltd.* v. *American Cyanimid and Chemical Corp.* [1944] K.B. 432; *Castree* v. *Squibb Ltd.* [1980] 1 W.L.R. 1248; *Distillers Co.* v. *Thompson P.C.* [1971] A.C. 458; *Dunlop* v. *Dunlop Rubber Co.* [1920] 1 I.R. 280; *Handelskwekerij G.J. Bier BV* v. *Mines de Potasse d'Alsace SA* [1976] E.C.R. 1735 considered. 3. In the instant case the appliance was fitted to the plaintiff's heart in this jurisdiction and the injury alleged occurred here. Accordingly the elements which occurred in this jurisdiction were sufficiently significant to warrant the order made. *Grehan* v. *Medical Incorporated and Valley Pines Associates*

(S.C.) [1986] I.R.528; [1986] ILRM 627

TIME LIMIT — EXTENSION

53. —— **Appeal** — *Appeal from High Court to Supreme Court — Whether Supreme Court has same powers as High Court to extend time for appeal — R.S.C.,* 1962 (*S.I. No.* 72), *O.* 58, *r.* 8, *O.* 108, *r.* 7, *O.* 111, *r.* 1.] The third and fourth-named defendants applied to the Supreme Court for leave to extend the length of time for serving a notice of appeal from an order of the High Court. O. 108, r. 7, of the Rules of the Superior

Courts provides that "the court" has power to enlarge the time "for doing any act, or taking any proceedings." The plaintiff sought to argue that "the court" in this context meant the High Court, and he based his argument on O. 111, r. 1, of the Rules which provides "that unless anything in the subject or context is repugnant thereto, 'the court' means either, as the context requires, the High Court or a judge or judges thereof . . .". The defendants contended that the jurisdiction of the Supreme Court to deal with the application was to be found in O. 58, r. 8, of the Rules which provides that the Supreme Court shall have all the powers and duties of the High Court. **Held** by the Supreme Court (Henchy J., Hederman and McCarthy JJ.) in making the order sought, 1, once a final order has been made and perfected in the High Court, the jurisdiction of that court as to the matters determined by that order is exhausted. *Per* Henchy J.: all consequent matters are outside the jurisdiction of the High Court. 2. Where a motion to enlarge time for appeal is involved, O. 111, r. 1, cannot be invoked to interpret the reference to "the court" in O. 108, r. 7, as meaning or including the High Court. It must be held to connote the Supreme Court. 3. O. 58, r. 8, refers only to appeals actually pending in the Supreme Court, and not to any intermediate matter arising between hearing and appeal, and over which the High Court has no jurisdiction. *Hughes* v. *O'Rourke*

(S.C.) [1986] ILRM 538

54. —— **Delivery of statement of claim** — *Inordinate delay — Infant plaintiff — Period of* 21 *years after accident — Four years after second action — Action dismissed — R.S.C.,* 1962 (*S.I. No.* 72), *O.* 20, *r.* 2, *O.* 27, *r.* 1, *O.* 108, *rr.* 7, 11.] On the 5 March, 1961, when she was three years old, the plaintiff suffered severe personal injuries when a motor car, allegedly driven by the defendant, collided with the plaintiff. On the 26 March, 1965, the plaintiff (suing by her next friend) claimed damages from the owner of the car in a High Court action in which she alleged that her injuries had been caused by the negligence of the owner, his servants or agents. In the year 1968 that action was dismissed for want of prosecution at the hearing of the owner's uncontested motion in that behalf. At that time the relevant legislation appeared to provide that an infant's right of action for damages arising from personal injuries was barred on the expiry of three years from the accrual of the cause of action, if the infant was in the custody of a parent at the date of such accrual. In the year 1972 the Supreme Court held that such legislation was invalid having regard to the provisions of the Constitution of Ireland, 1937. For the purposes

of the plaintiff's present action the relevant limitation period was accepted as expiring on the 28 November, 1981, being 24 years after the birth of the plaintiff. In the plaintiff's present action, which was commenced by plenary summons in the High Court on the 9 September, 1977, she claimed damages from the defendant and alleged that the defendant had driven the car negligently at the time of the collision and thus had caused the plaintiff's injuries. The plaintiff did not deliver a statement of claim. On the 7 May, 1982, the Master of the High Court made an order extending for two weeks the period for delivery of a statement of claim. On appeal by the defendant to the High Court, the order of the Master was discharged and the plaintiff's action was dismissed for want of prosecution. On appeal by the plantiff it was **Held** by the Supreme Court (Henchy and Griffin JJ., McCarthy J. dissenting), in disallowing the appeal, that the plaintiff's delay was inordinate and inexcusable and that it would not be reasonable to compel the defendant to defend the action after such delay. *Ó Domhnaill* v. *Merrick*

(S.C.) [1984] I.R.151; [1985] ILRM 40

TRIAL

55. —— **Mode of trial** — *Jury trial — Personal injuries — Proceedings commenced in the High Court — Motion to remit case to District or Circuit Court — Damages likely to be within District Court jurisdiction — Whether plaintiff right to a jury trial — Courts of Justice Act,* 1924 (*No.* 10), *s.* 94 — *Courts Act,* 1971 (*No.* 36), *s.* 6.] The combined effect of s. 94 of the Courts of Justice Act, 1924, as amended by s. 20 of the Courts of Justice Act, 1928, and s. 6 of the Courts Act, 1971, is that a plaintiff has a right to a jury in all cases in which he had such a right prior to 1924, except in claims for breach of contract, for liquidated sums, for the recovery of land or for any claim in the Circuit Court. In a High Court action for damages for personal injuries arising from an assault, the defendant moved to have the case remitted to either the District or Circuit Court on the ground that the statement of claim disclosed no injuries, and any award in excess of the Circuit Court's jurisdiction must be set aside as excessive. The plaintiff claimed, in substance, that, in a claim in tort, he had a right to have his case tried by a jury, and that this right flowed from his constitutional right of access to the court. **Held** by McWilliam J. in allowing the motion and in remitting the case to the Circuit Court, although the plaintiff was entitled as of right to a jury in the High Court, this was not an absolute right which could be enforced by commencing proceedings in the High Court. Instead, he would have such a right only in the

event of his case actually going to trial in the High Court. *McDonald* v. *Galvin*

(H.C.) [1976-7] ILRM 41

56. —— **Mode of trial** — *Jury trial — Personal injuries — Damage to plaintiff's eye — Liability denied — Application for hearing before judge sitting alone — Whether a jury unlikely to be able to comprehend evidence — Judicature (Northern Ireland) Act,* 1978 (*c.* 23), *s.* 62(2).] The plaintiff was admitted to hospital for treatment and tests for high blood pressure. He claimed that in the course of treatment his previous drug treatment was withdrawn causing his blood pressure to rise which resulted in the destruction of the macula of the left eye and loss of sight in that eye. He brought an action alleging that the defendant was negligent in the manner of his treatment. The plaintiff set down the action for hearing before a judge and jury. The defendant, who denied negligence, applied to have the issue of liability tried by a judge sitting without a jury on the ground of the nature of the scientific evidence to be given on the aetiology of the deterioration of the plaintiff's vision. **Held,** that the issue of liability be tried by a judge sitting without a jury. The trial of the action would require a technical or scientific investigation, within the meaning of section 62(2)(*b*) of the Judicature (Northern Ireland) Act, 1978, and the court was satisfied that the nature of the evidence to be given was such that a jury would be unlikely to be able to comprehend it. The likely inability of the jury to understand the evidence sufficiently would also constitute a special reason, within the meaning of section 62(2)(*d*) of the 1978 Act, which made the issue unsuitable for jury trial. *Monteith* v. *Western Health and Social Services Board*

(Q.B.D.) [1984] N.I.257

57. —— **Mode of trial** — *Limitation of action — Plaintiffs alleged to be statute barred — Whether limitation issue should be tried as a preliminary issue — Whether right to jury trial of such an issue — Court's discretion to disapply limitation period — Exercise of discretion involved disputed issues of fact — Whether such issues unsuitable to be tried with a jury — Statute of Limitations (Northern Ireland),* 1958 (*c.* 10), *s.* 9A, 9D — *Judicature (Northern Ireland) Act,* 1978 (*c.* 23), *s.* 62 — *R.S.C. (N.I.), O.* 32, *r.* 12A, *O.* 33, *rr.* 3, 4.] The plaintiff issued a writ of summons in May, 1980, claiming damages for negligence and breach of statutory duty of the defendants whereby she contracted dermatitis while employed by the defendants as a hairdresser from September, 1976, to January, 1980. The action was set down for trial by a judge and jury. The defendants pleaded that the action was statute barred by virtue of section 9A of the Statute of Limitations (Northern Ireland), 1958

PRACTICE AND PROCEDURE—Trial.

and applied by summons under Order 33 rule 3 of the Rules of the Supreme Court for an order that the limitation issue be tried by a judge alone as a preliminary issue. The plaintiff denied that the action was statute barred and invited the court to exercise the discretion under section 9D of the 1958 Act to disapply the provisions of section 9A of that Act. The Master ordered that the limitation issue be tried by a judge and jury as a preliminary issue. The defendants appealed against the part of the Master's order directing that the issue be tried by a judge and jury. They also issued a notice of motion seeking an order under order 33 rule 4(4) that the limitation issue under section 9A should be tried by judge alone and under order 32 r. 12(A) that the issue as to the exercise of the court's discretion under section 9D should be heard by the same judge alone. The parties agreed that there should be a pre-trial determination of the issues arising under the 1958 Act. The plaintiff argued that the limitation issue should be tried by judge and jury. The defendants contended that the questions of fact on the limitation issue were so complicated that they were not suitable for a jury. **Held,** 1, that whether the pre-trial determination should be by way of an interlocutory application or by trial of a preliminary issue depended on the particular circumstances of the case. Because of the nature of the matters in dispute and as much of the evidence on the issues arising under sections 9A and 9D of the 1958 Act would be common to both, there should be a preliminary trial of both those issues. Such a preliminary trial would not result in unnecessary duplication of effort and evidence. 2. The questions of fact connected with the issue under section 9A of the 1958 Act were not so complicated as to justify depriving the plaintiff of her right to trial of that issue by a judge and jury, consequently the trial of that issue under section 9A should be by a judge and jury. 3. The Master on the application under Order 33, rule 3 was limited to making an order for the preliminary trial of the issue and his order should not have specified any mode of trial. 4. The procedure under section 9D of the 1958 Act is designed for determination of the issue by a judge alone. It is inappropriate to involve a jury in the process as there may be difficulties in obtaining satisfactory special verdicts from a jury on questions of fact which have to be resolved and some of the matters under that section can only be decided by a judge alone. Accordingly there were special reasons under section 62(2) of the Judicature (Northern Ireland) Act, 1978, that the trial of the issue under section 9D of the 1958 Act should be by judge alone being the judge who heard the issue under section 9A. *Moane* v. *Reilly*

(Q.B.D.) [1984] N.I.269

PRACTICE AND PROCEDURE—*continued.*

58. —— **Preliminary point of law** — *Trial of issue of constitutional law as preliminary point of law — Moot — Reluctance of Supreme Court to decide any question of law not strictly necessary for the determination of rights of parties — Court to dispose first of issues of law before deciding issues of constitutional law — Overriding requirement that justice be done* inter partes — *R.S.C.,* 1962 (*S.I. No.* 72), *O.* 25.] The plaintiff was a member of an unincorporated members' club. While attending a dance at the club premises, to which he had paid an admission fee, he was injured as a result of a fall which, he alleged, was caused by the negligence of the organisers of the dance and he commenced proceedings for damages. The defendants filed a defence containing a full denial and specifically pleaded that the plaintiff, as a member of the club, was estopped from maintaining proceedings against the club or against the defendants as trustees of the club. The plaintiff, by way of special reply, denied that he was so estopped and further contended that any estoppel as alleged by the defendants was a matter of law repugnant to the Constitution of Ireland. The plaintiff applied under order 25 of the Rules of the Superior Courts to have the points of law raised by the defence and reply determined as preliminary issues and, since a matter of constitutional law was raised, served notice on the Attorney General. The defendants were satisfied to have the issues determined as preliminary issues but the Attorney General objected on the grounds that, as the question of negligence was in issue, it was inappropriate to have a question of constitutional law determined in the form of what might ultimately prove to be a moot. Hamilton J. ordered the trial of a preliminary issue whether a member of an unincorporated members' club could maintain an action for negligence against the representatives of the club. The Attorney General appealed to the Supreme Court. **Held** by the Supreme Court (Finlay C.J., Henchy and Griffin JJ.), in allowing the appeal and varying the order of the High Court, 1, that the Supreme Court, in general, must decline to decide any question of law which is in the form of a moot and the decision of which is not necessary for the determination of the rights of the parties before it. 2. That where the issues between the parties can be finally disposed of by the resolution of an issue of law other than constitutional law, the court should consider that issue first and, if it determines the case, should decline to express any view on the constitutional issue which may have been raised. 3. That these principles, however, must be subject to the overriding consideration of doing justice between the parties. 4. That the balance of justice, convenience and economy in the instant case was in favour of the deter-

PRACTICE AND PROCEDURE—Trial.

mination of the legal issues as a preliminary issue rather than subsequent to a jury trial. 5. That having regard to the difficulty and unnecessary expense which might arise from the trial of the legal and constitutional issues together, the appropriate order was to direct the trial of the issue of club law alone and to adjourn the constitutional issue until such time as that issue had been finally determined. *Murphy* v. *Roche (No. 1)*

(S.C.) [1987] I.R.106

Editor's note: for judgment in club law issue, *see* **Club,** 1.

—— Absence of rules — Directions of court — Professional discipline — Medical practitioners — Removal of doctor's name from register.
see **Natural and Constitutional Justice,** 4

—— Action — Abuse of process.
see **Criminal Law,** 40
Extradition, 4
Judicial Review, 11
Practice and Procedure, 1, 2, 41

—— Action — Cause — Confidence — Breach — Equitable principles — Absence of Contractual liability — Proposals for commercial partnership — Plaintiff divulging to defendant details of design of body armour.
see **Contract,** 3

—— Action — Cause — Settlement of action — Sale of land part of settlement agreement — Absence of note or memorandum — Sale of land unenforceable — Whether original action discharged.
see **Contract,** 5

—— Action — Compromise — Claim under contract discharged by settlement of action although settlement unenforceable.
see **Contract,** 5

—— Action — Compromise — Conflicting evidence of experts on liability — Whether settlement permitted.
see **Insurance,** 3

—— Action — Compromise — Mutual mistake — Document authenticated by signatures of counsel — Lack of consensus *ad idem* — Whether compromise

PRACTICE AND PROCEDURE—*continued.*

enforceable — Whether agreement a nullity.
see **Contract,** 9

—— Action — Settlement — Sale of land part of settlement agreement — Absence of note or memorandum — Sale of land unenforceable — Whether original action discharged.
see **Contract,** 5

—— Action — Stay.
see **Stay on Proceedings** *(below).*

—— Action — Transfer — Power of High Court to transfer action to Circuit Court — Whether power of transfer inconsistent with provisions of Constitution.
see **Constitution,** 33

—— Agreement — Arbitration clause — Disputes — Injunctions to enforce compliance — Appearance — Interlocutory order — Plaintiff subsequently seeking to refer all disputes to arbitration — Whether "taking any other steps in the proceedings" — Whether plaintiff estopped from staying proceedings.
see **Arbitration,** 13

—— Agreement — Arbitration clause — Proceedings to enforce an agreement — Application to stay proceedings pending arbitration — Whether court should stay proceedings.
see **Arbitration,** 12

—— Appeal — Grounds — Appeal to Supreme Court — Sole ground — Ground not argued or decided in trial court — Refusal of appellate court to decide issue raised in sole ground.
see **Conflict of Laws,** 6

—— Appeal — Supreme Court — Function of Court — Primary and secondary facts — Whether Supreme Court empowered to reach different conclusions to those of trial court in relation to inferences from primary facts.
see **Nuisance,** 1

—— Appeal — Supreme Court — Grounds of appeal — Whether Supreme Court should hear or pronounce upon an issue not argued before and determined by the High Court.
see **Negligence,** 19

PRACTICE AND PROCEDURE—*continued.*

PRACTICE AND PROCEDURE—*continued.*

PRACTICE AND PROCEDURE—*continued.*

Motion to strike out — Whether claim frivolous or vexatious.
see **Planning,** 4

—— Interest — Statutory jurisdiction to award interest — Case stated by Appeal Commissioners — Decision by High Court on interpretation of Income Tax Acts — Consequential order for repayment of overpaid tax — Order for payment of a sum of money — Whether court had jurisdiction to order payment of interest.
see **Revenue,** 39

—— Judgment — Currency — Whether a judgment for a sterling debt obtained at a time when the currencies of the State and of the U.K. were of equal value — Whether amount should be payable in Irish pounds or in sterling.
see **Conflict of Laws,** 2

—— Judgment — Enforcement.
see under **Judgment**

—— Judgment — Evidence — Nullity — Non-consummation — Evidence indicating marriage was not consummated — Trial judge inferring collusion between parties — Whether inference open to judge — Whether in accordance with natural justice — Whether rehearing required in view of evidence presented.
see **Family Law,** 14

—— Judicial review.
see under **Judicial Review**

—— Parties — Absence — Local Government — Planning — Minister of State — Minister granting outline permission — Minister acting *ultra vires* — Developer applying for planning approval — Planning authority relying upon invalidity of outline permission — Minister not party to developer's action.
see **Planning,** 35

—— Parties — Estoppel — Road traffic accident — Personal injury action — Claim made against driver of vehicle — Driver dying from injuries received in accident — Liberty sought to join insurers as defendants in place of deceased — Whether insurers estopped from opposing such an order.
see **Practice and Procedure,** 43

—— Parties — *Locus standi.*

PRACTICE AND PROCEDURE—*continued.*

see **Locus Standi**

Parties — Representation — Criminal trial — Fair procedures — Trial conducted in absence of legal advisers of accused — Conviction quashed on certiorari.
see **Criminal Law,** 46

—— Parties — Sufficiency — Planning permission — Invalidity — Permission given to statutory undertaking — Complainant landowner not prevented from relying upon invalidity of permission by reason of planning authority not being a party to action.
see **Constitution,** 45

—— Parties — Third party — Claim for contribution — Service — Delays — Whether claim made "as soon as possible" — Limitation period — Discretion.
see **Practice and Procedure,** 13

—— Plea — Autrefois acquit.
see **Criminal Law,** 53

—— Pleadings — Application to amend pleadings for purpose of appeal hearing.
see **Assault**

—— Point of law — Revenue case — Statutory provision requiring person to express dissatisfaction with the determination of a point of law "immediately after the determination" — Whether "immediately" to be interpreted strictly — Whether provision directory or mandatory.
see **Revenue,** 4

—— Relator proceedings — *Locus standi* of relator — Whether constitutional provisions self-executing in the absence of legislation.
see **Constitution,** 20

—— Set off — Building contract — Architect's certificate of sum due to contractor — Interim certificate — Final certificate — Set off — Employer claiming damages for negligence and delay — Whether employer entitled to withold sums certified as payable and due to contractor pending determination of cross-claim.
see **Building Contract,** 4

—— Set off — Summary judgment — Building contract — Whether defendant entitled

PRELIMINARY EXAMINATION
see **Criminal Law,** 54-6

PRESS
see also **Broadcasting**

—— Advertisement in newspaper.
see **Advertisement**

—— Freedom of the press — Application for attachment for contempt of court — Newspaper publication — Article stating that Director of Public Prosecutions intended to bring charges against a local authority councillor — Political party to which councillor belonged referred to — Name of councillor not given — Whether publication could tend to prejudice the trial of proceedings that were pending.
see **Contempt of Court,** 3

—— Freedom of the press — Criminal law — Conviction — Pending appeal — Publication of a magazine article based on material supplied by sole witness for the prosecution — Injunction application to restrain publication — Whether article likely to prejudice the appeal — Freedom of the press.
see **Injunction,** 14

—— Newspaper — Defamation — Libel — Ordinary meaning of words — Whether words published capable of bearing other than a defamatory meaning.
see **Defamation,** 1

PRICES
—— Consumer subsidies — Standard bread subsidy scheme — Whether retailer in breach of terms.
see **Contract,** 1

—— Regulation — Restrictive practices — Retail prices — Prohibition on advertising goods at cost less than net invoice price — Whether meaning of prohibition clear — Whether injunction appropriate remedy to seek.
see **Restrictive Practices**

PRINCIPAL AND AGENT
see **Agency**

PRINCIPAL AND SURETY
see **Surety**

PRIOR MORTGAGE
see under **Mortgage**

PRISONS

1. —— **Board of visitors** — *Award — Natural justice — Preliminary hearing — Composition of Board different at substantive hearing — Third party and Governor present — Governor intervened to indicate illegality of award — Award varied — Whether contrary to natural justice.*] The applicant, a prisoner, was charged with assaulting a prison officer. A prison governor considered the matter and referred it to the Secretary of State who delegated the hearing to the Board of Visitors. At the commencement of the hearing before a Board of two members, the applicant requested legal representation. The Board then took evidence relating to the extent of the prison officer's injuries and, taking into account the seriousness of the offence, granted the application and adjourned the hearing. At the resumed hearing, held before a Board which included a third additional member, counsel for the applicant objected to his presence and also to that of a prison governor. The Board rejected these objections and proceeded to find the applicant guilty of assault. The Board awarded the applicant 50 days cellular confinement, of which 30 were suspended for 6 months, and 100 days loss of remission, including 50 days suspended for 6 months. The governor then brought to the attention of the Board a letter from the Northern Ireland Office indicating that there was no power to suspend part of an award. After an adjournment, the Board revised its award to 30 days cellular confinement suspended for 6 months and 140 days loss of remission. The applicant applied for judicial review arguing that there had been a breach of the rules of natural justice in that (*a*) the membership of the Board which determined the matter differed from that which first dealt with it; (*b*) the Board had permitted a representative of the Prison Officers Association to be present; (*c*) a governor had been permitted to attend and intervene in the proceedings and (*d*) the award had been altered without giving the applicant an opportunity to make representations. **Held,** dismissing the application, that, 1, there is no rule of law that in all circumstances the same and only the same persons may sit throughout an inquiry; if, however, a person participates in a decision without having heard all the evidence and arguments, that decision may be set aside. Here the earlier sitting merely determined a preliminary issue; the later hearing was a complete hearing of every aspect of the substantive issue and it was fantasy to suggest that because the two members at the earlier hearing heard part of the evidence, which was later repeated, they might have conceived a bias against the applicant. 2. The Board can regulate its own proceedings and, subject to the Prison Rules and the general requirement to secure justice and the appearance of justice,

PRISONS—*continued.*

admit a person not directly connected with the case if it sees fit. 3. The objection that a governor, who originally determined that the offence was of such a gravity that it should be referred to the Secretary of State, should not be present at the hearing was not relevant to this case, as at no stage was the person who acted in the capacity of governor the same as the person who so acted at any other stage. 4. The governor who attended the hearing would have failed in his duty if he had not acted to obviate a breach of the law by the Board. 5. The variation of the award originally made by the Board was not a breach of natural justice because the original award was a nullity, the variation was made in the presence of the applicant and his counsel after an indication that the Board was going to make an alternative award and the intention of the Board was to make the substituted award harmonious with the original. *R* v. *May* [1981] 3 Crim. App. R.(S.) 165 and *R* v. *Cleere* [1983] 5 Crim. App. R.(S.) 465 distinguished. *In re McNally*

(Q.B.D.) [1985] N.I.17

2. —— **Prison regulations** — *Prisoners' access to legal advisers and legal advice — Certain solicitors excluded — Whether regulations unconstitutional — Whether specific regulations* ultra vires — *General Prisons (Ireland) Act,* 1877 (*c.* 49), *ss.* 12, 13(2) — *Rules of the Government of Prisons,* 1976.] The General Prisons (Ireland) Act, 1877, s. 12 provides that the General Prison Board may from time to time subject to the approval of the Lord Lieutenant and the Privy Council repeal and alter the bye laws for the regulation of any prison and the duties and conduct of the governor and the officers and may make new rules instead thereof. S.13 provides that special rules should be made with respect to communications between an unconvicted prisoner and his solicitor which was done by r.210 of the Rules of the Government of Prisons, 1947. The Rules of the Government of Prisons, 1976, r.2 provides ". . . the Minister for Justice may, where he considers it necessary in the interests of the security of a prison or of the State and for the reasons related to the particular person, direct that a person (including a prisoner's legal adviser) shall not be admitted or be admitted only on conditions to a specified prison." Rule 3 provides "The powers conferred by Rule 2 of these Rules shall not be so exercised as to prohibit or restrict visits from so many members of the legal profession as to deny to a prisoner a reasonable choice of legal adviser and legal advice given by such adviser in the sight but not in the hearing of a prison officer." The plaintiff sought a declaration that the Rules of the Government of Prisons, 1976, were invalid on the grounds that they were made in excess of

PRISONS—*continued.*

powers of ss. 12 and 13 of the General Prisons (Ireland) Act, 1877, and were unconstitutional. The plaintiffs made a number of submissions in support of their claim: (1) S.13(2) of the Act gives a prisoner an absolute right to consult with a solicitor of his choice and any rule which deprives a solicitor of this right is invalid; (2) that the 1976 Rules enable the Minister to draw up a list of solicitors who are different from the rest of the profession in that they can not be trusted to visit prisoners and that this can be done without establishing any impropriety, breach of professional etiquette or other offence on the part of such solicitor; (3) that the 1877 Act did not give the Minister power to give directions in the interest of the security of the State as apart from the regulation of the prison. **Held** by McWilliam J. in making an order declaring r.2 of the 1976 Rules to be *ultra vires* ss. 12 and 13 of the 1877 Act, 1, s. 12 of the 1877 Act does not give power to make rules in the interest of the security of the State unless such interest effect the security of the prison or the rules are required for the regulation of the prison. 2. Provided a prisoner is given adequate facilities to engage and employ a solicitor and communicate with him, the exclusion of a particular solicitor does not offend against the wording or spirit of s. 13(2) of the 1877 Act. 3. The method adopted by the Minister for dealing with the problem of solicitors who can not be trusted to visit prisoners is invidious from the aspect of the solicitors' profession but does not render the provisions *ultra vires* the Act of 1877 or unconstitutional from the aspect of the prison. *Incorporated Law Society* v. *Minister for Justice*

(H.C.) [1978] ILRM 112

3. —— **Temporary release scheme** — *Detention — Release on licence — Revocation of licence — Legality — Youthful offender released conditionally from detention — Condition that youth keep the peace — Youth arrested on charge of serious crime during period of release — Licence revoked and accused returned to detention — Absence of enquiry — Natural justice — Certiorari — Delay — Prisoners (Temporary Release) Rules,* 1960 (*S.I. No.* 167), *rr.* 3, 5, 7 — *Criminal Justice Act,* 1960 (*No.* 27), *ss.* 4, 6.] The prosecutor, a youthful offender, was convicted in the District Court of a certain offence and he was sentenced to 12 months detention in St. Patrick's Institution. Having served part of that sentence, the prosecutor was granted by the respondent, who was the governor of that Institution, a conditional release from detention. One of the conditions was that, during the period of his release, the prosecutor should keep the peace and be of good behaviour. During that period, the prosecutor was arrested by the police and charged in

PRISONS—*continued.*

the District Court with attempted murder; he denied the charge and was remanded in custody to St. Patrick's Institution where, on his re-admission, he was treated initially as an accused person on remand. However, on the next day the respondent, because of the gravity of the offence with which the prosecutor had been charged, revoked the prosecutor's conditional release, whereupon he was treated as a detainee who was serving his sentence. The prosecutor obtained in the High Court a conditional order of certiorari quashing the revocation of this release, unless cause were shown to the contrary. He then applied for an order absolute, notwithstanding the cause shown by the respondent. **Held** by Barron J. and affirmed by the Supreme Court (O'Higgins C.J., Griffin and McCarthy JJ.), in disallowing the cause shown and making an order absolute, 1, that the only issue to be determined was whether or not there had been a breach of one of the conditions, subject to which the prosecutor's release had been granted, prior to the purported revocation of that release by the respondent. 2. That the facts that the prosecutor had been charged in the District Court with the commission of an act of attempted murder and had been remanded in custody pending his trial on that charge were not sufficient to rebut the presumption of his innocence with regard to the crime so charged or to establish that he had acted in breach of his said condition of release. 3. That, accordingly, the revocation of the prosecutor's release by the respondent had been unlawful. *Semble:* If, to the knowledge of the respondent, there had been any significant indication that the prosecutor had acted during the period of his release in breach of a condition of that release, the requirements of natural justice would have obliged the respondent to have instituted, before considering whether to revoke such release, an informal enquiry for the purpose of determining whether or not there was any evidence of such breach and, if so, to have given the prosecutor an opportunity to be heard at that enquiry. *The State (Murphy)* v. *Kielt (Governor of St. Patrick's Institution)*
(H.C., S.C.) [1984] I.R.458; [1985] ILRM 141

4. —— **Temporary release scheme** — *Order for re-arrest of released prisoner following breach of a condition of his release — Failure to make arrest until after the expiry of the prisoner's sentence — Whether subsequent imprisonment lawful or fair — Criminal Justice Act,* 1960 (*No.* 27), *s.* 2.] The prosecutor, who had been sent to prison for a term of six months, was released after only five weeks under the scheme established pursuant to s. 2 of the Criminal Justice Act, 1960. His release was conditional on his reporting to a probation officer. He broke this condition and

PRISONS—*continued.*

the respondent prison governor duly requested the man's re-arrest. Because the subsequent re-arrest was not made until seven months later, and after the expiry of the original term of imprisonment, the prosecutor sought an order of certiorari on the basis that his return to prison at that stage was unlawful. Because he also alleged that it was an infringement of his constitutional rights, notice of the proceeding was served on the Attorney General. **Held** by Egan J. in granting an absolute order of certiorari, 1, a sentence of imprisonment may be re-activated after its original currency has expired but fairness of the procedure is a requirement when such a sentence is re-activated: *The State (Murphy)* v. *Kielt* [1984] I.R. 458 applied. 2. In the present case the authorities had without explanation delayed the prosecutor's re-arrest, and that fact, in the circumstances of the present case, was unfair. *Cunningham* v. *Governor of Mountjoy Prison*
(H.C.) [1987] ILRM 33

—— Illtreatment allegation — Whether established.
see **Extradition,** 8

—— Prison authority — Duty of care — Whether duty of care owed to prisoner — Prisoner injured by another prisoner during recreation — Whether supervision of prisoners adequate — Whether prison authorities required to conduct searches of prisoners before recreation.
see **Negligence,** 34

—— Prisoner — Disciplinary award against a prisoner by prison governor — Whether subject to judicial review — Observations on public policy.
see **Judicial Review,** 12

—— Prisoner — Personal rights — Communication — Prison Rules — Inspection and censorship of plaintiff's mail — Whether breach of constitutional right to communicate — Whether plaintiff entitled to damages for non-delivery of letters addressed to him.
see **Constitution,** 10

—— Prisoner — Personal rights — Procreation — Opportunity to beget children — Deprivation — Husband and wife each serving sentence of imprisonment for life — No children of marriage — Basis for restriction on prisoners' rights by State — Constitutional rights of prisoners not infringed by conditions of imprisonment.

Q

R

RADIO BROADCASTING
see **Broadcasting**

RAILWAY BRIDGE — Damage — Struck by low-loader transporting excavator — Minimum clearance required by statute of railway company — Whether local authority's roadworks in reducing clearance below statutory minimum wanting in due care — Whether advance warning system agreed between railway company and local authority.
see **Negligence,** 31

RAPE
see under **Sexual Offences**

RATING AND VALUATION

1. —— **Agricultural land** — *Valuation — Valuation carried out between* 1852 *and* 1866 — *No revaluation ever taking place — Valuation unrelated to present day circumstances — Valuation determining the extent of liability in respect of certain taxes and the extent of eligibility for certain benefits — Whether unjust attack on property rights — Whether arbitrary and unjust discrimination — Whether constitutional challenge includes a challenge to the validity of a section of a post-constitutional statute — Constitution of Ireland,* 1937, *Arts.* 40.1, 40.3 — *Valuation (Ireland) Act,* 1852 (*c.* 63), *ss.* 5, 11, 32, 33, 34 — *Local Government Act,* 1946 (*No.* 24), *ss.* 11, 12.] The plaintiffs were farmers in County Wexford who, on 23 July, 1982, obtained in the High Court from Barrington J. declarations *inter alia* that ss. 11 and 34 of the Valuation Act, 1852, were invalid (see [1983] ILRM 449).These sections provided for a valuation of agricultural land in accordance with agricultural prices obtaining in the 1850s; and for a discretionary (and never-employed) review of valuations at fourteen-year intervals. Barrington J., having heard evidence for fourteen days, found that the valuation system was inconsistent, anomalous and failed to reflect changing patterns of agriculture. Appealing to the Supreme Court, the Attorney General argued that the State's position in regard to taxation and fiscal policy was a special one, with which the courts should not lightly interfere; that the valuation system, while inconsistent, significantly reflected real values; that the system did not discriminate as among persons contrary to Article 40.1 of the Constitution; that inequity inhered in any system of taxation; that it had not been established that anomalies and inconsistencies were widespread; and that failure of a review procedure could not on its own lead to a finding of unconstitutionality.

RATING AND VALUATION—*continued.*
Counsel for the farmers contended *inter alia* that the citizen's personal rights included a right to a rational, consistent and non-arbitrary system of taxation; and that failure to reform longstanding inconsistencies was a failure to protect property from unjust attack. **Held** by the Supreme Court (O'Higgins C.J., Finlay P., Walsh, Henchy and Griffin JJ.) in varying the declaration made by Barrington J., 1, that what concerned the plaintiffs was not an improper system of valuation but the use to which the valuation was put by the State. 2. That s. 11 of the Local Government Act, 1946 (which provided for the collection of County Rate on the basis of the 1852 system of valuation) was to be impugned in place of the Valuation Act. 3. That it was unnecessary, given Barrington J.'s finding that the valuation system was "shot through with unnecessary anomalies and inconsistencies", to say whether the finding of a significant relationship between valuations and land values could justify the system. 4. That Article 40.1 of the Constitution was inapplicable: *Quinn's Supermarket* v. *Attorney General* [1972] I.R. 11 considered. 5. That the valuation system constituted an unjust attack on the property rights of persons, such as the plaintiffs, who found themselves with poor land paying more than their neighbours with better land: Article 40.3 of the Constitution considered. 6. That, in place of the declarations made by Barrington J., the court would substitute a declaration that s. 11 of the Local Government Act, 1946, was invalid to the extent that it authorised the collection of County Rate on land independently of buildings. *Brennan* v. *Attorney General*
(S.C.) [1984] ILRM 355

2. —— **Annual value** — *Calculation of valuation — Hotel — Decrease in profitability — Reduction of valuation sought — Valuation (Ireland) Act,* 1852 (*c.* 63).] The determination of valuation of premises is a question of fact which may be decided by considering the rent which a hypothetical tenant would pay for the premises; and in determining this rent it is appropriate to consider any matters likely to affect it including matters not directly connected with the subject premises. So **held** by Barron J. *Roadstone Ltd.* v. *Commissioner of Valuation* [1961] I.R. 239 and *Reg.* v. *Guardians of the North Aylesford Union* (1872) 37 J.P. 148 applied. *Rosses Point Hotel Co. Ltd.* v. *Commissioner of Valuation*
(H.C.) [1987] I.R.143 ; [1987] ILRM 512

3. —— **Assessment** — *Valuation — Whether owner of premises entitled to be furnished with evidence of valuation of similar premises in locality — Whether finding of fact that premises*

RATING AND VALUATION—*continued.*
were separately valued previously — Review of findings of fact on appeal.] The appellant, owner of a premises in Cork city which had been valued by the respondent at £450, appealed from this decision to the Circuit Court, and at its request the Circuit Court judge stated a case to the High Court. The appellant contended in argument that: (*a*) the valuation should have been reduced on the ground that the property included part of a tenement which previously had been separately valued; (*b*) the respondent ought to have been required by the court to furnish the appellant with a breakdown of the valuations of certain other premises in Cork city; and (*c*) the Circuit Court judge ought to have taken into consideration the valuations of certain other premises in Cork city, evidence as to which had been tendered by the appellant. **Held** by McMahon J. in affirming the order of the Circuit Court judge, 1, since it was a finding of fact made on evidence that the premises of the appellant did not include part of a tenement which previously had been separately valued, this could not be reviewed on the hearing of the case stated. 2. The appellant had not shown any legal right to be furnished with a breakdown of the valuations of certain other premises in Cork city. 3. The evidence tendered with regard to the valuations of other premises in Cork city was not relevant, in that the said other premises were not similar to the property under appeal, and therefore such evidence had been properly rejected by the Circuit Court judge. *Munster and Leinster Bank Ltd.* v. *Commissioner of Valuation*

(H.C.) [1979] ILRM 246

4. —— **Exemption** — *Private fee paying school — Charitable purposes — Whether school of a public nature — Basis of exemption — Poor Relief (Ireland) Act,* 1838 (*c.* 56), *s.* 63 — *Valuation (Ireland) Act,* 1854 (*c.* 8), *s.* 2.] Wesley College is an educational institution which provides education of a general character for pupils. One of the conditions for the admission of most of the pupils is the payment of a sizeable fee. Under its Constitution the Governors are required to provide education for Methodist and other children and for such children of Methodist Ministers as may be designated by the Conference of the Methodist Church in Ireland subject to charges determined by the Governors. In 1973, 19.3% of the pupils were Methodist, 59.3% were members of the Church of Ireland and the remaining 12.54% were other Protestants, Roman Catholics, Jews and Muslims. The school makes a profit, within its terms of reference, from the fees, which are paid in respect of the vast majority of the pupils. The question of rateability essentially depends on whether Wesley College is an institution altogether of a public nature and used exclusively for public purposes.

RATING AND VALUATION—*continued.*
The Circuit Court stated a case for the Supreme Court which contained the following questions: (1) Are the said tenements or hereditaments or is any part thereof used exclusively for charitable purposes within the meaning of s. 63 of the Poor Relief Act, 1838, and ss. 12 and 16 of the Valuation (Ireland) Act, 1852, and s. 2 of the Valuation (Ireland) Act, 1854. (2) Are the said tenements or hereditaments or is any part thereof of a public nature and dedicated to or used for public purposes within the meaning of the Poor Relief (Ireland) Act, 1838, and ss. 12 and 16 of the Valuation (Ireland) Act, 1852, and s. 2 of the Valuation (Ireland) Act, 1854. (3) Should the said tenements or hereditaments or any part thereof be distinguished pursuant to s. 2 of the Valuation (Ireland) Act, 1854, in the Valuation Lists mentioned in the Valuation (Ireland) Act, 1852, as tenements or hereditaments of a public nature or used for charitable purposes? **Held** (O'Higgins C.J., Walsh, Henchy, Griffin and Hederman JJ.). As the college enures overwhelmingly for the benefit of non Methodists and is essentially a private fee paying school which makes a profit from fees it is occupied and used, at least partly, for beneficial or private purposes, as distinct from public or charitable purposes. The case for an exemption fell to be decided exclusively by reference to the proviso to s. 63 of the Poor Relief (Ireland) Act, 1838, counsel for Wesley College having withdrawn his suggestion that the exemption was to be sought in s. 2 of the Valuation (Ireland) Act, 1854. All three questions should be answered no. *Pembroke U.D.C.* v. *Commissioner of Valuation* [1904] 2 I.R. 429 and *University College Cork* v. *Commissioner of Valuation* [1911] 2 I.R. 593 distinguished. *Governors of Wesley College* v. *Commissioner of Valuation*

(S.C.) [1984] ILRM 117

5. —— **Relief** — *Relief against municipal rate — Whether relief extends only to hereditaments occupied by rate-payer at time statute enacted — Whether relief extends to hereditaments subsequently acquired by rate-payer — Interpretation of legislation — Local Government (Dublin) Act,* 1930 (*No.* 27), *s.* 69 *and 2nd Schedule.*] Trinity College Dublin had enjoyed various partial reliefs and exemptions from rates prior to the enactment of the Local Government (Dublin) Act, 1930, s. 69 and the second schedule of which provided that the college should henceforth pay only 34/100ths of the municipal rate otherwise due on "the hereditaments and tenements" it occupied. The College took the view that the relief provided by the 1930 Act was applicable to all premises in its occupation and in particular to numerous houses on Pearse Street and Westland Row on the periphery of its historic site,

RATING AND VALUATION—*continued.*

which houses had been acquired since 1960. The Corporation held that the relief applied only to premises in the occupation of the college in 1930. The College reduced to 34/100ths the amounts due for rates on the peripheral properties, and the Corporation proceeded to sue for payment of the withheld balances. Hamilton J. on 20 April, 1983, [1984] ILRM 84 found in favour of the College in its interpretation of the 1930 statute, and, in a second judgment delivered on 16 February, 1984, permitted the College to set off overpayments made to the Corporation in the six years preceding the commencement of the action. From both judgments the Corporation appealed to the Supreme Court. **Held** (by Henchy J., Griffin and Hederman JJ. concurring) reversing the first judgment of Hamilton J. and consequently not proceeding to deal with the second judgment, 1, that the form of words used to define the premises occupied by Trinity College was most likely influenced by the difficulty of listing a plurality of valuation units. 2. That the absence of a formula according relief to premises "for the time being" in the occupation of the defendant, a formula used in the case of another ratepayer mentioned in the Act, and the absence of any requirement that premises qualifying for the relief should be used only "for the purposes of the university", a qualification also employed elsewhere in the Act, bore significance. 3. That the use of the definite article ("*the* hereditaments and tenements") had a demonstrative and specific effect. 4. That the plaintiff should have judgment for £100,051.74 and the costs of the appeal. *Dublin Corporation* v. *Trinity College Dublin*

(H.C., S.C.) [1985] ILRM 283; [1984] ILRM 84

—— Valuation list — Alteration — Date at which alteration to list takes effect.
see **Gaming and Lotteries,** 2

REAL PROPERTY

see also **Adverse Possession; Joint Tenancy; Land; Landlord and Tenant; Mortgage; Registration of Title; Sale of Land**

Easement — Right of way. Nos. 1-3
Fishing Rights. Nos. 4, 5
Incumbrance. Nos. 6-8
Proprietary Estoppel. No. 9

1. —— **Easement** — *Right of way — Absence of defined path — Evidence of user — Lack of defined* terminus a quo *and* terminus ad quem — *Whether use of the way over the land sufficient in extent and regularity — Whether knowledge of such user to be imputed to the owner of the land.*] In the Circuit Court the plaintiff, suing as the personal representative of the registered owner of certain lands in County Offaly, sought an

REAL PROPERTY—*continued.*

injunction restraining the defendant who was the personal representative of the registered owner of adjoining lands from entering upon or trespassing on the plaintiff's said lands. The plaintiff also sought a mandatory injunction compelling the defendant to remove a water pipe laid by her, the defendant's predecessor in title across the plaintiff's lands and damages for trespass. In her defence the defendant denied the alleged trespass and counterclaimed that she was entitled to a right of way over the plaintiff's lands. At the hearing of the action in the Circuit Court, the Circuit Court judge decided at the preliminary stage that the only basis which the defendant could defend the proceedings was to establish some entitlement to enter upon the lands and accordingly the issue as to whether the defendant was entitled to a right of way would determine whether the defendant was guilty of trespass. The defendant therefore went into evidence first on her counterclaim and on an application by the plaintiff for a direction it was held that the defendant was not entitled to a right of way over the said lands of the plaintiff and had wrongfully trespassed over the said lands. The Circuit Court judge accordingly dismissed the defendant's counterclaim and granted the plaintiff liberty to apply to the court for any necessary injunction. The court also awarded the plaintiff the sum of £1 damages for trespass and the costs of the proceedings. The defendant appealed to the High Court against this order. **Held** by O'Hanlon J. in dismissing the appeal, that the defendant had failed to establish an entitlement to the alleged right of way and the court therefore affirmed the order of the Circuit Court. *Flanagan* v. *Mulhall*

(H.C.) [1985] ILRM 134

2. —— **Easement** — *Right of way — Estoppel by conduct — Whether evidence of any detrimental act done with the knowledge or encouragement of the defendant.*] The plaintiff had unsuccessfully sought in the Circuit Court to assert a right of way over the defendant's land. On appeal, the evidence before the court failed to establish acquisition of a right of way either by prescription or by presumed lost grant. The plaintiff therefore submitted that the principle of estoppel by conduct applied, and that the defendant should not now be permitted to deprive the plaintiff of a right exercised by him over the defendant's land with the knowledge of the defendant. **Held** by Gannon J. in dismissing the appeal and affirming the order of the Circuit Court, 1, to establish the principle of estoppel by conduct, a plaintiff must show that the defendant encouraged him either directly or indirectly to act to his detriment in reliance upon the right claimed. *Crabb* v. *Arun District Council* [1976

REAL PROPERTY—*continued.*

Ch. 179 followed. 2. There was no evidence of any detrimental act done by the plaintiff with either the encouragement or knowledge of the defendant. *Dunne* v. *Molloy*

(H.C.) [1976-7] ILRM 266

3. —— **Easement** — *Right of way — Overgrown and little-used path — Whether intention to abandon right.*] The plaintiffs owned land abutting on an ancient path a mile in length linking two public roads. The path was overgrown, and it was no longer practicable to travel along it from end to end. The defendants, owners of land at one end of the lane, asserted that any right of way which may formerly have existed in favour of the plaintiffs' land had been extinguished by non-user. The plaintiffs sought a declaration that they were entitled to a right of way over the length of the lane. Failing to obtain such in the Circuit Court, they appealed to the High Court on Circuit. Twenty witnesses were heard, whose evidence is summarised in the judgment of O'Hanlon J. and is of local historical interest. **Held** by O'Hanlon J., granting the appellants/plaintiffs a declaration that they were entitled to a right of way, 1, that the evidence established that there was from time immemorial a road or lane as claimed, and that the owners of the soil had dedicated the way to the use of the abutting landowners if not to the public in general. 2. That the plaintiffs had not included in their Civil Bill a claim that the path was a public right of way, and would not be permitted upon appeal to amend their pleadings. 3. That public rights over highways cannot be lost by disuse. 4. That mere evidence of non-user is not sufficient to bring about the extinguishment of private rights of way. 5. That a presumption of abandonment, which is not lightly to be inferred, required to be supported by evidence of conduct or intention adverse to the exercise of the right. *Carroll* v. *Sheridan*

(H.C.) [1984] ILRM 451

4. —— **Fishing rights** — *Corporeal hereditament — Drainage scheme — Statutory powers — Compulsory interference — Spawning beds upstream beyond fishery area — Interference — Reduction in fish stock — Whether injury to fishery — Compensation — Assessment — Rules — Acquisition of Land (Assessment of Compensation) Act,* 1919 (*c.* 57), *s.* 1 — *Arterial Drainage Act,* 1945 (*No.* 3).] The Arterial Drainage Act, 1945, authorised the Commissioners of Public Works in Ireland to prepare, undertake and execute schemes subject to confirmation by the Minister for Finance. Section 9, paras. (*c*) and (*e*)conferred on the Commissioners powers "to acquire compulsorily" and "to restrict, terminate, or otherwise interfere with any easements, fisheries, water-rights, navigation rights, or other rights proposed in the scheme to be compulsorily restricted, terminated, or interfered with . . . before any ascertainment of compensation in respect thereof . . ." Special precautions for the protection of fisheries were enacted by section 10. Sections 14 to 17 provided generally for payment of compensation upon injury to property and its assessment, to be fixed, in default of agreement, in accordance with the rules for assessment of compensation set out in the Acquisition of Land (Assessment of Compensation) Act, 1919, by an arbitrator nominated by the reference committee from the panel of drainage arbitrators. The claimant owned land and exclusive fishery rights to a seven and a half mile stretch of the Bonet river at Dromahaire, Co. Leitrim. By the Bonet catchment drainage scheme prepared by the respondents the works to be undertaken involved *inter alia* channel excavations of the upper reaches of the river on land not owned by the claimant but affecting the spawning beds of the river's fish stock. A claim for compensation for interference with his fishery pursuant to s. 14 of the Act was submitted by the claimant. The respondents contended before the arbitrator that the claimant was not entitled to compensation for loss caused by their drainage scheme works outside his property which did not cause direct physical damage to his lands or water but which might merely cause a reduction in future numbers of fish in the claimant's fishery. By his final award the arbitrator stated a special case on that issue for the High Court where it was **Held** by Gannon J., in holding that the claimant was entitled to compensation, that, on construction of its general scheme and specific compensation provisions, the Arterial Drainage Act, 1945, recognised fisheries as distinct interests in real property and that injury to such interests was distinct from and independent of direct physical damage to the claimant's lands and waters and entitled him to compensation under the Act. Observations in *Metropolitan Bord of Works* v. *McCarthy* (1874) L.R. 7 H.L. 243 considered. *Uyttewaal* v. *Commissioners of Public Works*

(H.C.) [1987] I.R. 439

5. —— **Fishing rights** — *Injunction — Interference with plaintiffs' fishing rights by canoes — Rights of riparian owner — Whether fishery rights of plaintiffs corporeal or incorporeal hereditaments — Whether plaintiffs entitled to order to restrain defendant's activities.*] The plaintiffs and defendant owned separate portions of what had once been the same estate in Connemara. The defendant's property adjoined a river and two lakes (Lough Inagh and Derryclare Lough);

REAL PROPERTY—*continued.*

the plaintiffs' property also adjoined those waters and they had certain fishing rights in and over them. The defendant ran an outdoor education centre on his property from which canoeing was carried out during the year both on the river and on the lakes. The use of the canoes interfered with the plaintiffs' fishing rights, both affecting the angling being carried on and the spawning of fish. The defendant maintained that the plaintiffs' fishing rights had been severed from the bed and soil of the river and lakes and that the plaintiffs' rights were merely an incorporeal hereditament in the nature of a profit à prendre; that he, as riparian owner, owned the bed and soil of the portion of the river and lakes contiguous to his holding and that his activities merely constituted a reasonable user of his rights as riparian owner and were not actionable at the suit of the plaintiffs. The plaintiffs sought an injunction to restrain the defendant's activities. **Held** by Costello J., in granting the relief sought, that the title adduced by the plaintiffs expressly established that the plaintiffs owned the bed and soil of the lakes and river, and, in consequence, enjoyed a corporeal right to fishing. Such title defeated the defendant's claim and entitled the plaintiffs to an order restraining the defendant's activities absolutely. *Dictum* of Lord Maxwell in *Will's Trustees* v. *Cairngorm Canoeing and Sailing School Ltd.* 1976 S.C. 30 at p. 63 applied. *Per* Costello J., it is well established that even where a riparian owner owns the bed and soil of a river or lake to a median line out from his lands he cannot act so as to interfere substantially with the incorporeal fishing rights on the river or lake. Thus if the defendant had been able to establish the title he claimed he would still have been restrained from committing the substantial interference with the plaintiffs' incorporeal hereditament (if that had been all they had owned) which the evidence had established had occurred. *Rawson* v. *Peters* (1972) 116 S.J. 884 considered. *Tennent* v. *Clancy*

(H.C.) [1987] I.R.15; [1988] ILRM 214

6. —— **Incumbrance** — *Deed of charge — Possession — Entitlement — Peaceable entry — Registered land — Charge created by registered owner — Deed of charge registered as burden — Charge securing repayment to chargeant of monies advanced to owner — Express term of charge permitting chargeant to enter into possession of land during continuance of security — Proviso precluding entry unless owner in default in repayments of advance — Default of owner — Peaceable entry of chargeant into possession of land without court order — Whether chargeant entitled to take possession in the absence of court order — Registration of Title Act,* 1964 (*No.* 16).] The first plaintiff was the registered owner of certain

REAL PROPERTY—*continued.*

registered lands in County Wicklow. To secure a loan from the defendant, the plaintiffs, by deed, created a charge over the property in favour of the defendant. It was provided in the deed that if the plaintiffs failed to pay the instalments due on the loan over a certain period of time, then the defendant could enter into possession of the premises without any further consent or notice to the plaintiffs. The plaintiffs defaulted in the instalments payable. The defendant entered and took possession peaceably of the property. The plaintiffs sought an injunction to restrain the defendant from continuing in possession of the property. **Held** by Costello J., in dismissing the plaintiffs' claim, 1, that an express provision in a deed of charge of registered land permitting the registered owner of the charge to take possession in the event of certain defaults by the chargor creates a contractual licence between the parties under which the registered owner of the charge may, upon such default, take possession of the property without the necessity of obtaining a court order. 2. That a provision in a deed of charge permitting the registered owner of a charge to take possession in the event of certain defaults by the chargor need not be registered on the folio separately from the deed of charge. *Gale* v. *First National Building Society*

(H.C.) [1985] I.R.609; [1987] ILRM 30

7. —— **Incumbrance** — *Deeds of charge — Registered land — Charges created by registered owners to secure repayment to chargeant of monies advanced — Default of registered owner — Appointment by chargeant of receiver of income and/or rents and profits of property charged — Receiver attempting to claim or receive proceeds of sale of chattels on owners' property — Chattels not part of property charged — Chattels not subject of any chattel mortgage in favour of chargeant — Owners seeking injunction restraining receiver from attempting so to claim or receive — Conveyancing and Law of Property Act,* 1881 (*c.* 41), *ss.* 2, *para.* (*iii*), 19(1)(*iii*), 24(3), 24(8) — *Registration of Title Act,* 1964 (*No.* 16), *s.* 62(6).] The plaintiffs were the registered owners of certain registered lands comprising approximately 304 acres on which they maintained a dairy herd. To secure advances from the defendant the plaintiffs, by deed, created two charges over certain of those lands comprising approximately 124 acres and the defendant was duly registered as the owner of those charges. The plaintiffs defaulted in the repayments of the advances payable to the defendant under the deeds and the entire of the monies charged by the deeds became due to the defendant. The defendant, in pursuance of its

REAL PROPERTY—*continued.*

right under s. 19, sub-s. 1(iii), of the Conveyancing and Law of Property Act, 1881 (incorporated into the deeds of charge by s. 62, sub-s. 6, of the Registration of Title Act, 1964) appointed a receiver of the income and/or rents and profits of the lands charged. The receiver, in purported exercise of the powers vested in him by s. 24, sub-s. 3, of the Act of 1881, requested the creameries to which the plaintiffs supplied the produce of the dairy herd maintained by them on the entire of their lands to forward to the receiver a proportion of the payment due to the plaintiffs for such produce. The proportion requested by the receiver was to represent the proportion of the plaintiffs' lands comprised in the deed of charge. The plaintiffs disputed the defendant's right by its receiver to divert any of the proceeds of sale of the plaintiffs' dairy produce. The plaintiffs sought an injunction permanently to restrain the defendant by its receiver from claiming or receiving any of the proceeds of sale of the plaintiffs' chattels arising in the course of the plaintiffs' business. **Held** by Keane J., in granting the injunction sought, that as the dairy herd which the plaintiffs maintained on the entire of the lands owned by them was not part of the property comprised in the deeds of charge and was not made the subject of any chattel mortgage in favour of the defendant, it followed that the defendant by its receiver was not entitled to appropriate any of the proceeds of sale of the chattels in the purported exercise of the receiver's powers under s. 24, sub-s. 3, of the Act of 1881. *Salmon* v. *Matthews* (1841) 8 M. & W. 827 and *Charles Hoare & Co.* v. *Hove Bungalows Ltd.* (1912) 56 Sol. Jo. 686 applied. *Quaere:* whether the effect of s. 24, sub-s. 8, of the Act of 1881, is to prescribe an order of payments by the receiver of all the monies received by him in the exercise of his powers under s. 24, sub-s. 3 of that Act. *Donohoe* v. *Agricultural Credit Corporation*

(H.C.) [1986] I.R.165; [1987] ILRM 26

8. —— **Incumbrance** — Lis pendens — *Registration — Effect of proceedings establishing equitable interest in property on mortgage executed subsequent to registration of* lis pendens — *Whether equitable interest entitled to priority over mortgagee's interest — Whether mortgage valid.*] In September, 1981, the liquidator of Kelly's Carpetdrome Ltd. issued proceedings claiming that eight specified properties and "all other properties standing in the name" of Monck Properties Ltd. were held by Monck in trust for Kelly's Carpetdrome Ltd. and that the two companies constituted a single business whose assets fell to be aggregated in the latter's winding up. These proceedings were registered as a *lis pendens* one month before UDT Bank Ltd. provided finance to Monck for the purchase of certain property, not one of the properties specified in the September, 1981, proceedings, at which time the property was also conveyed to Monck and the bank received a first legal mortgage over the property. The mortgage had been requested by the Bank in November, 1980, as a condition of providing finance. A deposit was then paid by Monck on the property in March, 1981, through money provided by Kelly's Carpetdrome Ltd. and a contract of sale executed in April. No search was made by the bank prior to the execution of the mortgage to discover whether any proceedings had been registered as a *lis pendens.* In April, 1982, a consent order was made by the High Court in the September, 1981, proceedings, in the terms sought by the liquidator. The liquidator then applied to the High Court for directions as to whether Kelly's Carpetdrome Ltd. enjoyed an equitable estate in the property in priority to the Bank's mortgage and also whether the mortgage itself was valid. **Held** by Costello J. in ruling the application, 1, while there was no specific reference to the property in the September, 1981, proceedings, by virtue of the April, 1981, contract of sale Monck had an equitable interest in the property, that this constituted one of its assets mentioned in those proceedings and that the order made in those proceedings recognised that Monck held its property as constructive trustee for the company. 2. While Monck may have been in breach of its duty to the Bank in failing to disclose its position as trustee, this did not invalidate the mortgage. 3. The effect of registering the *lis pendens* was that, while the Bank had no knowledge of it, it was bound by the prior equitable interest of the company when the mortgage was executed since the requirements of s. 10 of the Registration of Judgments (Ire.) Act, 1844, had been fully complied with. *Giles* v. *Brady* [1974] I.R. 462 applied. *In re Kelly's Carpetdrome Ltd.; Byrne* v. *UDT Bank Ltd.*

(H.C.) [1984] ILRM 418

9. —— **Proprietary estoppel** — *Lease — Agreement for lease — Licence — Conditions to be satisfied before equity can be enforced against the owner of the land — Claimant acting to his detriment — Claimant's belief or expectation that he had interest in the land — Encouragement or acquiescence of landowner — Onus of proof on claimant — Special circumstances — Land Act,* 1965 (*No.* 2), *s.* 12.

Planning — Carrying out of development without permission — Restraining order — Retention permission subject to conditions — Local Government (Planning and Development) Act, 1976 (*No.* 20), *s.* 27.] The plaintiffs, who were the trustees of an association which promotes and

REAL PROPERTY—*continued.*

governs harness racing, sought to lease the defendant's land for the purpose of holding trotting races. The defendant agreed to let a field for a trial period in 1984 at a rent of £2,000. It was further agreed that the plaintiffs were to carry out certain works in the field including the construction of a racetrack. If the plaintiffs left the defendant's property at the end of the trial period they would pay no rent and the defendant would retain the benefit of the work done. There was no agreement as to the terms on which the plaintiffs would remain on the property if they wished to stay. After the plaintiffs began to construct the racetrack the agreement was altered insofar as a larger portion of the defendant's land was covered and the field was levelled to support a more permanent type of track than was originally intended. Before the track was completed the County Council obtained an order under s. 27 of the Local Government (Planning and Development) Act, 1976, restraining the defendant from continuing the development on his land and the construction of the racetrack without planning permission. The plaintiffs subsequently sought retention permission with respect to the track and this was granted subject to certain conditions. The plaintiffs had not been in possession of the track from the time the s. 27 order was made against the defendant and the defendant refused to allow them back into possession until they executed a formal licence agreement. This was duly agreed between the parties at a rent of £8,000 for one year from the 30 April, 1985. No formal agreement was executed with respect to 1986 and the plaintiffs continued to use the track on the same terms. During 1986 a number of problems arose relating to the plaintiffs' failure to pay arrears of licence fees, rates and water rates and the plaintiffs' breach of a condition of the planning permission. As a result, the defendant served notice on the plaintiffs and re-took possession of the lands. The plaintiffs commenced proceedings seeking specific performance of the alleged agreement to grant a lease of the lands or alternatively requiring the defendant to let the plaintiffs into possession of the lands. **Held** by Blayney J., in dismissing the plaintiffs' claim, 1, that in order for the plaintiffs to establish an equitable interest in the lands which could be enforced against the defendant by way of proprietary estoppel, they had to show that they had acted to their detriment in the belief that they owned, or in the expectation that they would own, a sufficient interest in the lands to justify such action, which belief was encouraged by the owner of the property and that there was no bar to the equity. *Ramsden* v. *Dyson* (1866) L.R. 1 H.L. 129 applied. 2. That the plaintiffs had not discharged the onus of proof on them to show that they had built the track in the belief that they would obtain a lease of the lands. 3. That if such a belief had existed, there was no evidence to show that the defendant had encouraged or acquiesced in it. 4. That there were no special circumstances in the case to take it out of the rule of law as stated in *Ramsden* v. *Dyson* (1866) L.R. 1 H.L. 129. *Haughan* v. *Rutledge*

(H.C.) [1988] I.R. 295

—— Lease — Covenant — Restraint of trade — Positive covenant — Enforcement — Injunction — Solus agreement with oil company.
see **Injunction,** 12

—— Possession — Recovery — Limitation of actions.
see **Limitation of Actions,** 1, 5

—— Registered land — Inhibition — Whether affected parties must be given notice of entry of inhibition — Whether power to be exercised in judicial manner.
see **Registration of Title**

—— Transfer of land — Deed — Reservation of right of residence, care and support — Application to cancel transfer — Whether undue influence — Whether deed improvident.
see **Undue Influence**

REASONABLE EXPECTATION
see **Legitimate Expectation**

RECEIVERSHIP
see **Company,** 4, 10

—— Distribution — Whether receiver administrator.
see **Company,** 1

—— Liability — Receiver — Corporation tax — Monies placed on deposit in name of receiver — Interest accruing on monies deposited — Whether receiver liable to pay corporation tax.
see **Revenue,** 19

—— Receiver appointed by foreign court — Whether order designed to give effect to penal order.
see **Conflict of Laws,** 5

—— Receiver appointed by mortgagee of land — Receiver attempting to claim or receive proceeds of sale of chattels on owners' property — Chattels not part of property charged — Dairy produce.

REGISTRATION OF TITLE
—— **Inhibition** — *Entry of inhibition in register of freeholds — Whether affected parties must be given notice of entry of inhibition — Whether power to be exercised in judicial manner — Registration of Title Act,* 1964 (*No.* 16), *s.* 121.

Statute — Discretion — Exercise — Notice — Registered land — Registration of inhibition — Whether affected parties be given notice — Whether registration must be made in judicial manner — Opportunity to object to registration of inhibition — Registration of Title Act, 1964 (*No.* 16), *s.* 121.] S. 121 of the Registration of Title Act, 1964, provides that the Registrar of Titles may enter in the register of freeholds an inhibition against dealings with any land where it appears to him than an error capable of rectification has been made in registration, and that this inhibition is for the purpose of protecting the Central Fund against claims for compensation made by parties affected by the error. The section further provides that the Registrar shall give notice of the inhibition to all persons who appear to be affected by it. The prosecutor entered into a contract for sale of certain lands of which he was the registered owner. Before the closing of the sale, the respondent, without prior notice to the prosecutor, entered an inhibition pursuant to s. 121 above, on the folio of the prosecutor in the Land Registry. The prosecutor obtained from the High Court a conditional order of certiorari quashing the decision of the respondent to enter the inhibition on the grounds that the respondent had failed to adhere to the procedure laid down by s. 121, and that he had failed to exercise the power granted him in accordance with the requirements of natural and constitutional justice. **Held** by Gannon J. in disallowing the cause shown, and making absolute the conditional order: the power entrusted to the Registrar of Titles by virtue of s. 121 of the Registration of Title Act, 1964, must be exercised by him in a judicial manner, and unless the urgency of the situation requires otherwise, prior notice should be given to any person whose rights may be affected thereby, of the intention to enter an inhibition, and an opportunity should be given to such person to show cause why such inhibition should not be entered. *The State (Philpott)* v. *Registrar of Titles*

(H.C.) [1986] ILRM 499

RESTRAINT OF TRADE

1. —— **Contract for the sale of a business** — *Restrictive covenant — Enforceability of restraint clauses — Whether restraint reasonable.*] The first plaintiff which manufactured and sold upholstery fabrics and garment fabrics was established by the defendant in 1971 but early in 1977 it was insolvent and to revitalise the company an agreement was entered into in March of that year by which the second plaintiff would purchase its business and invest £50,000 in it. This was achieved by purchasing the shares of its two members, the defendant and J.L. for a nominal sum and as a result of the agreement the first plaintiff became a wholly owned subsidiary of the second plaintiff. The share transfer agreement also contained provisions for the future role of the defendant and J.L. requiring both to enter into service agreements, in addition to containing restraint of trade clauses and restraint on soliciting customers. The defendant took up his duties under the service agreement but decided to resign in 1985 and his resignation became effective from 31 October of that year from which date the restraints which were of one year's duration began to run. Unknown to the plaintiffs the defendant had established in England a company called Rossbrae Ltd. which traded in upholstery fabrics. The plaintiffs ascertained that Rossbrae Ltd. was doing business with one of the most important customers in England of the first plaintiff and also that the defendant had been visiting some of its most valuable customers in the U.S. soliciting business for his new company. The plaintiffs instituted proceedings and then sought an injunction to restrain breaches of the restraint clauses. The court decided that the main issue was whether these clauses were enforceable and it decided to

RESTRAINT OF TRADE—*continued.*

try this point as a preliminary issue, adjourning the motion until the issue had been determined. **Held** by Costello J. in granting the plaintiffs an injunction effective until 31 October, 1986, 1, the reasonableness of the restraints imposed on the defendant was to be tested by reference to the commercial realities of the situation which existed when they were imposed in 1977. What was in the reasonable contemplation of the parties for the future development of the first plaintiff was also relevant. 2. The non-solicitation clauses were enforceable subject to the deletion of certain specific words through application of the severance rule. 3. (*a*) The range of goods subjected to the restraints in the non-competition clauses of the share-purchase agreement was unreasonably wide. It was also excessively restrictive for another reason: a blanket world wide restraint based merely on the possibility that markets in other parts of the world might be entered by the first plaintiff was unreasonable as it was not reasonably required for the protection of the second plaintiff's investment in the first plaintiff. (*b*) The restrictions contained in another clause of the service agreement were also unenforceable because the protection of the first plaintiff's trade connections could be assured without prohibiting the defendant from manufacturing or selling upholstery fabrics in any part of the world. 4. In light of the preliminary issue, the plaintiff's claim to interlocutory relief would not be considered by the principles established in *American Cyanamid Co.* v. *Ethicon Ltd.* [1975] A.C. 296 but rather on the basis that the plaintiff's right to an injunction had in fact been established. 5. The injunction would restrain the defendant either personally or by means of Rossbrae Ltd. or any other company or firm with which he may be associated directly or indirectly from soliciting or seeking orders from or interfering with or endeavouring to entice away any person, firm or company which were customers of the first plaintiff or were in the habit of dealing with the first plaintiff at any time within the period of twelve months ending 31 October, 1986. *John Orr Ltd.* v. *Orr*

(H.C.) [1987] ILRM 702

2. —— **Maximum wage** — *Second defendant's regulations limited wage payable by first defendant to plaintiff — Whether in restraint of trade — Whether reasonable.*] The plaintiff was a part-time professional footballer who was playing football as goalkeeper for the first defendant, the Cliftonville Football and Athletic Club Limited. On 12 August, 1983, the plaintiff signed a contract with the first defendant for the 1983/84 season. The contract provided that the plaintiff be paid a "signing on" bonus of £120 and a weekly wage of £12. These sums were the

RESTRAINT OF TRADE—*continued.*

maximum permitted in regulations made by the second defendant, the Irish Football League Limited, who conducted the Irish League's senior championship and with whom all professional footballers playing in the Irish League had to be registered. However, under a separate agreement, which was in breach of the second defendant's regulations, a higher signing on bonus of £400 was payable by the first defendant to the plaintiff. The plaintiff, who was dissatisfied with his contract, had earlier asked the first defendant for a weekly wage of £15 but the first defendant refused because it would conflict with the second defendant's maximum wage regulations. The plaintiff commenced an action for declarations that the maxima prescribed by the second defendant's regulations were unreasonable restraints of trade. The defendants argued that the regulations were not restraints of trade and, in any event, that the regulations were reasonable because they prevented the wealthiest clubs from capturing all the best players and that a free-for-all on wages would lead to serious financial difficulties for some of the clubs. **Held,** that the maximum signing on bonus and maximum weekly wage provided for in the defendant's regulations were void as in restraint of trade and not binding on the plaintiff because, 1, they constituted a restraint of trade in that they interfered with the plaintiff's liberty of action in trading, viz his liberty to negotiate the basic matter of the payment he was to receive for his service to his employer. 2. Such restraint was unreasonable, the evidence was that the wealthy clubs would not be able to capture all the good players and the evidence of the effect on the financial position of the clubs of removing the maxima was inadequate to sustain the defendant's case. *Johnston* v. *Cliftonville Football and Athletic Club Ltd.*

(Ch.D.) [1984] N.I. 9

—— Contract — Terms — Enforcement — Covenant in lease — Covenant in positive form — Solus agreement with oil company — Lessor's remedy for breach of covenant — Mandatory and prohibitory injunctions — Interlocutory relief — Balance of convenience.
see **Injunction,** 12

—— Rule-making body — Prohibition on use of non-Irish horses by Irish showjumpers in international competition — Whether unreasonable restraint on individual showjumper's trade — Whether contrary to public policy — Protection of Irish half-bred horse industry.
see **European Communities,** 2

RESTRICTIVE COVENANT — Lease.
see **Injunction,** 12
Landlord and Tenant, 2-5

RESTRICTIVE PRACTICES

—— **Prices regulation** — *Retail prices — Prohibition on advertising goods at cost less than net invoice price — Whether meaning of prohibition clear — Whether injunction appropriate remedy to seek — Restrictive Practices Act,* 1972 (*No.* 11), *s.* 19 — *Restrictive Practices (Groceries) (Amendment) (No.2) Order,* 1978 (*S.I. No.* 336), *art.* 5.

Words and phrases — "Net invoice price".] Article 5 of the Restrictive Practices (Groceries) (Amendment) (No. 2) Order, 1978, provides that a retailer shall not advertise goods to which the order applies at a price (after deduction of the cost to him of any discount given on a sale of the goods) which is less than the net invoice price of the goods, inclusive of VAT, at which the retailer purchased the goods. The defendants advertised goods for sale at a price less than that stated on the document accompanying the goods. The plaintiffs contended that this document was an invoice for the purpose of the order, while the defendant argued that the net invoice price ought to be equated to the real purchase price of the goods. The plaintiffs sought an injunction restraining the defendant from advertising goods for sale at a price lower than the net invoice price. **Held** by Keane J., in granting the injunction sought, 1, the expression "net invoice price" had a clear and ascertainable meaning, which was the price appearing on the document accompanying the goods, after deduction of any credits, and inclusive of value-added tax, and to equate the net invoice price with the real purchase price would be to create a situation where it would be impossible to say at any given time whether or not a crime was being committed. 2. The ability of the defendant to buy in bulk enabled it to reduce its prices in a manner denied to its competitiors who have not the same resources; the 1978 order could be construed as applying in such circumstances; and the defendant was in breach of Article 5 of the order. 3. Where regulations under the Restrictive Practices Act, 1972, are broken, the proper remedy is an injunction pursuant to s. 19 of the Act. *Irish Association of Distributive Trades Ltd.* v. *3 Guys Ltd.*

(H.C.) [1979] ILRM 269

RETENTION OF TITLE
see **Company,** 10
Sale of Goods, 3-5

RETURN FOR TRIAL

—— Delay — Error — Return to wrong Circuit Court — Whether a ground for setting aside proceeding.
see **Criminal Law,** 60

—— Rule of court directing that order be transmitted to trial court within specified period — Document transmitted after expiry of period.
see **District Court,** 3

—— Special Criminal Court.
see **Criminal Law,** 65

REVENUE
see also **Rating and Valuation**

Administration. Nos. 1, 2
Appellate procedure. Nos. 3, 4
Capital acquisitions tax. No. 5
Capital gains tax. Nos. 6, 7
Corporation tax. Nos. 3, 4, 8-24
Disclosure of information. Nos. 25, 26
Income tax. Nos. 1, 27-41
Stamp duty. No. 42
Value added tax. Nos. 43, 44

ADMINISTRATION

1. —— **Advance rulings** — *Application by taxpayer to Revenue Commissioners — Application setting out proposed course of action and requesting Revenue Commissioners' ruling on applicability of certain fiscal legislation to the course of action proposed — Information relating to course of action proposed supplied in general terms — Revenue Commissioners expressing views on tax implications of proposals — Whether views expressed constituted binding advance rulings — Whether views expressed binding on Inspector of Taxes — Income Tax Act, 1967 (No.* 6), *s.* 161.

Judicial review — Declaration — Whether decision of Inspector of Taxes a determination — Rules of the Superior Courts, 1986 (*S.I. No.* 15), *O.*84, *r.* 18 — *Income Tax Act,* 1967 (*No.* 6), *s.* 432.

Tax avoidance — Commercial transaction — Whether steps inserted having no commercial purpose — Whether steps inserted to avoid a tax liability — Whether Furniss v. Dawson *principle applicable.*

Income tax — Income from qualifying patents — Payment of royalties under licence — Whether of revenue nature — Finance Act, 1973 (*No.* 19), *s.* 34.] T.O'D., P.O'D. and M.F. invented a hot car wash system. Patent applications were filed in respect of the invention in Ireland, the United Kingdom and Belgium. The third applicant, "O.S.D.L.", was incorporated in July, 1982, its shares being issued to T.O'D., P.O'D., M.F. and M.McG. The first and second applicants, "Pandion" and "Ospreycare", were incorporated in December, 1982. The shareholders in Pandion were the same as O.S.D.L., and Ospreycare was a wholly-owned subsidiary of O.S.D.L. In April, 1983, T.O'D. wrote to the respondents seeking their rulings on certain propositions outlined by him, in particular, concerning the interpretation of s. 34 of the Finance Act, 1973, (which provides for exemption from tax for income derived from qualifying patents). The respondents replied in July, 1983, setting out their views on the application of s. 34 to the patents. Further correspondence took place in April and May of 1984 when T.O'D. sought and received further rulings on the interpretation of s. 34; on whether payment of royalties under a licence would be of a revenue nature and on whether such royalty payments would be treated as a charge on the income of a licensee pursuant to s. 10 of the Corporation Tax Act, 1976. Pandion, the owner of the patents, granted non-exclusive licences in respect of them to Cobes and Langtry in August and September, 1984. In each case the licence was granted in consideration of the payment by the licensee of an advance royalty of £540,000. Each licence provided for a royalty of five per cent of net revenue; the advance royalty was to be deducted from the annual royalties accruing, and further payments would arise only where the total of royalties payable exceeded the advance royalty paid. Following the grant of the licences the licensees in turn granted sub-licences to the second applicant, Ospreycare. Under the terms of the sub-licences, Cobes and Langtry were each paid an advance royalty of £415,462.50, and a royalty of six per cent of net revenues was provided for, otherwise the terms of the sub-licences were identical with those of the licences. In March, 1985, further correspondence was initiated by T.O'D. Having considered some further proposals of the applicant the respondents took the view that the proposals might involve a tax avoidance scheme and refused to comment on them. Pandion applied for a refund of the standard rate tax which had been withheld by the licensees when paying the advance royalties. The Inspector of Taxes advised the applicant that the claim for the refund was appropriate in view of the provisions of s. 34 of the Act of 1973, but that, in his opinion, a claim could not be made by Cobes and Langtry to have the payments allowed charges under s. 10 of the Corporation Tax Act, 1976. The first applicant's accountant replied acknowledging the s. 34 relief and stating that the application of s. 10 was a matter for the other companies and that it did not concern the first applicant. The monies claimed by the first

applicant were refunded in part only and an assessment to corporation tax was raised on the second applicant. The applicants commenced proceedings in the High Court seeking, *inter alia,* a declaration that the monies withheld by the licensees and paid to the respondents were due and payable to the first applicant; an order of certiorari to quash the assessment raised on the second applicant and further orders to compel the respondents to allow a claim by the second applicant arising from the provisions of s. 10 of the Act of 1976. **Held** by Blayney J., in granting the declaration sought but disallowing the other claims for relief, 1, that the monies were properly payable to the first applicant by virtue of the Inspector of Taxes' determination that the royalties received constituted income from a qualifying patent within the meaning of s. 34. 2. That the term "advance ruling" was not a term of art. It was simply a label attached to the opinions expressed by the Revenue Commissioners. In order to determine whether the opinions were binding on the revenue authorities it was necessary to look at the transactions entered into by the applicants to see whether, prior to the transactions being entered into, the respondents had committed themselves to take a particular view of the tax implications involved in the transactions. Since the respondents did not have clear details of the scheme, the views they expressed did not relate to it and, accordingly, they did not commit themselves to any binding view concerning the scheme. 3. That the Revenue Commissioners were not the agents of the Inspector of Taxes, if anything, the Inspector of Taxes was the agent of the Revenue Commissioners by virtue of s. 161 of the Income Tax Act, 1967. Neither could be identified with the other and accordingly an Inspector was not bound by a prior opinion expressed to the taxpayer by the Revenue Commissioners. 4. That the decision of the Inspector that s. 34 applied to the income received from the patents was a determination in respect of which an order could be made under order 84 of the Rules of the Superior Courts. Accordingly, the court could make a declaration that the monies withheld were due and payable to the first applicant. 5. That the transactions entered into by the applicants did not amount to a tax avoidance scheme to which the principle in *Furniss* v. *Dawson* [1984] A.C. 474 could be applied. The grant of the licences to Cobes and Langtry had the commercial purpose of financing the commercialisation of the patent, and no step was inserted to avoid a tax liability since no such liability existed prior to the scheme being set in train. *Furniss* v. *Dawson* [1984] A.C. 474 not applied. *Pandion Haliaetus Ltd.* v. *Revenue Commissioners*

REVENUE—Administration.

(H.C.) [1987] I.R.309 ; [1988] ILRM 419

2. —— **Tax clearance certificate** — *Government contracts — Administrative requirement — Certificate that Collector General has no objection to award of contract — Production of tax clearance certificate a pre-requisite to award of Government contract — Prosecutor applying for certificate — Prosecutor having discharged all his liabilities to Revenue Commissioners — Refusal of certificate on grounds of default in connected case — Prosecutor having directors, shareholders and employees in common with separate company in default — Prosecutor incorporated after demise of company in default to carry on same business — Revenue Commissioners not entitled to take account of default of separate company.*

Judicial review — Mandamus — Circumstances in which mandamus will lie — Revenue Commissioners — Function of granting tax clearance certificates conferred by executive — No statutory jurisdiction — Revenue Commissioners acting in a public capacity and exercising lawful authority — Obligation to act judicially — Refusal of certificate subject to judicial review — Consideration by tribunal of matters outside its jurisdiction — Revenue Commissioners taken to have declined jurisdiction.] In 1984, the Government decided that any person tendering for public contracts would be required, before the contract was awarded, to produce a tax clearance certificate from the Revenue Commissioners to the effect that the Collector General would have no objection to the award of the contract. The object of the requirement was to prevent persons in default with their tax liabilities from benefiting from contracts financed from public funds. The procedure for the issue of such certificates was not put on any statutory basis but was a matter of administrative arrangement between Government departments. The prosecutor was incorporated in 1983, very soon after a company, (J.M. & Co. Ltd.) had gone into liquidation owing a substantial sum of money to the respondents. The prosecutor had the same directors and shareholders and many of the same employees as J.M. & Co. Ltd. had had, and carried on the business which that company had carried on. The prosecutor, having tendered for a Government contract, applied to the respondents for a tax clearance certificate. Its liabilities had been paid up to date but the certificate was refused on the grounds that the Collector General "must have regard to tax default in any connected case." The respondents took the view that the directors and shareholders of J.M. & Co. Ltd. had ordered their affairs in such a manner as to avoid meeting that company's tax liabilities in full and, very soon after its insolvent demise, were back in business under the name of the prosecutor. The

REVENUE—*continued.*

prosecutor obtained a conditional order of mandamus directed to the respondents to forthwith issue a tax clearance certificate in relation to the contract for which the prosecutor had tendered. The respondents, in showing cause, argued that in all the circumstances they had had valid grounds for refusing the certificate; and that, in any event, the issue of the certificate was not a statutory function or obligation but merely a matter of contract between the prosecutor and the relevant Government department and that their decision, therefore, was not susceptible to review by state side order. On the prosecutor's motion to make absolute the conditional order notwithstanding cause shown it was **Held** by Hamilton P., in disallowing the cause shown and in substituting an order commanding the respondents to consider and deal with the prosecutor's application for a tax clearance certificate in accordance with law, 1, that while the issue of tax clearance certificates was not a statutory function, the respondents were a public tribunal upon whom a public or official jurisdiction to grant such certificates had been conferred by the lawful authority of the executive. Accordingly, the repondents in considering applications for certificates, were obliged to act judicially and were amenable to mandamus. *Reg.* v. *Criminal Injuries Compensation Board, ex parte Lain* [1967] 2 Q.B. 864 followed. 2. That where a tribunal whose duty it was to hear and determine a question according to law took into consideration or allowed its determination to be affected by matters outside its jurisdiction, it might be held to have declined jurisdiction and might be required on mandamus to hear and determine the issue properly in accordance with law. *The State (Keller)* v. *Galway County Council and Another* [1958] I.R. 142 applied. 3. That the prosecutor in applying for a tax clearance certificate had a legal right to have its application considered. 4. That the respondents, in considering the prosecutor's application for a certificate were not entitled to take into account any factors other than the prosecutor's own liability for tax payments. 5. That it was clear in this case that the certificate had been refused not because of any default by the prosecutor with regard to its tax but because of the liabilities of a separate company, two of the directors of which were also directors of the prosecutor and which had gone into liquidation owing money to the respondents; and therefore that the respondents must be taken to have declined to carry out their duty according to law. *The State (Melbarien Enterprises Ltd.)* v. *Revenue Commissioners*

(H.C.) [1985] I.R. 706; [1986] ILRM 476

REVENUE—*continued.*

APPELLATE PROCEDURE

3. —— **Case stated** — *Corporation tax — Trade or adventure in the nature of trade — Finding of fact by Circuit Court — Inferences drawn from facts — Case stated — Jurisdiction of High Court — Function of High Court in hearing revenue cases stated — Income Tax Act,* 1967 (*No.* 6), *s.* 428.] The respondent was required by the Central Bank to hold certain minimum quantities of government stocks. Because of the low yield on such stocks the respondent would not have purchased them in the ordinary course of its business. The respondent purchased and retained quantities of short-dated low interest rate stock. On maturity gains were realised by the respondent. The appellant assessed the respondents in respect of the gains, alleging that they arose from a trade or adventure in the nature of a trade. On appeal the Circuit Court discharged the assessments, holding that since the reason for the purchase of the stocks was the respondent's obligation to fulfil the requirements of the Bank the gains were not trading receipts and were not part of the respondent's profits for tax purposes. On appeal by way of case stated it was **Held** by Blayney J., in affirming the decision of the Circuit Court, 1, that the manner in which the jurisdiction of the High Court is to be exercised on hearing a case stated in revenue matters was settled by the Supreme Court in *Mara* v. *Hummingbird Ltd.* [1982] ILRM 421, where the court had explained that a case stated consisted of findings of fact and inferences drawn from those facts, and held that such inferences should not be rejected unless they were such that a reasonable tribunal of fact could not draw them or they were based on a mistaken view of the law. *Mara* v. *Hummingbird Ltd.* [1982] ILRM 421 and *Edwards (Inspector of Taxes)* v. *Bairstow* [1956] A.C. 14 applied. 2. That the inferences drawn by the Circuit Court judge, namely, that the respondent was not dealing in securities and that the transactions involving the stocks were not part of a trade or adventure in the nature of trade, were entirely justified on the facts of the case; the court should not adopt an alternative conclusion unless satisfied that that alternative conclusion was the true and only reasonable conclusion. *Browne* v. *Bank of Ireland Finance Ltd.*
(H.C.) [1987] I.R.346

4. —— **Questions of law** — *Corporation tax — Questions of law arising before Circuit Court — Prosecutor not expressing dissatisfaction with the judge's determination at the end of the hearing — Prosecutor subsequently wishing to express dissatisfaction — Judge refusing to state case to the High Court on the basis that dissatisfaction had not been expressed "immediately" after the determination — Meaning of "immediately" — Whether mandatory requirement — Income Tax Act,* 1967 (*No.* 6), *ss.* 428, 430.

Practice — Revenue case — Statutory provision requiring person to express dissatisfaction with the determination of a point of law "immediately after the determination" — Whether "immediately" to be interpreted strictly — Whether provision directory or mandatory.] The prosecutor appealed to the Circuit Court against a determination for corporation tax made by the Appeal Commissioners. The appeal was heard and dismissed by the respondent. The prosecutor's representative did not express dissatisfaction with the respondent's determination as being erroneous in point of law at the end of the hearing. On the same day this omission was discovered and on the next morning a letter was delivered to the county registrar and addressed to the respondent expressing dissatisfaction with his determination and requesting him in accordance with s. 430 of the Income Tax Act, 1967, to state a case to the High Court on the issues involved in the case. The respondent replied that the terms of s. 430 must be strictly complied with and that he had no discretion in the matter. He refused to state a case to the High Court. S. 430 of the 1967 Act (adapting s. 428 of the Act) provides that dissatisfaction with the decision of the Circuit Court is to be made known to the judge "immediately after the determination of an appeal" and also that within 21 days a request be made in writing for a case stated to the High Court. The practice in cases of this kind was to require dissatisfaction to be made known at the conclusion of the hearing and not later. The prosecutor applied for an order of mandamus directing the respondent to state a case pursuant to s. 430 of the 1967 Act. **Held** by Finlay P in refusing to make an order of mandamus, 1, since s. 430 provided for notice within 21 days of intention to appeal the Circuit Court decision, the requirement of expressing dissatisfaction "immediately" should not be construed so strictly as to involve an expression of dissatisfaction at the conclusion of the actual hearing, or alternatively the requirement should be construed as directory and not mandatory, its purpose being to ensure that a taxpayer would not be obliged to pay more tax than is legally due by him, nor on the other hand to obtain an illegal relief from tax by reason of an error on a point of law occurring before the Appeal Commissioners or the Circuit Court. *Dicta* of Fletcher-Moulton L.J. in *In re Coleman's Depositories Ltd.* [1907] 2 K.B. 798, and *Reg.* v. *Inspector of Taxes, ex p. Clarke* [1974] Q.B. 220 applied. 2. Although the prosecutor was entitled to state a case to the High Court, it would be

REVENUE—Appellate Procedure.

inappropriate to direct mandamus to the respondent since his refusal to state a case to the High Court was in accordance with what had been considered the correct practice and that accordingly the proper course would be to have the case stated approved in the normal way between the parties and submitted to the respondent. *State (Multiprint Label Systems Ltd.)* v. *Neylon*

(H.C.) [1984] ILRM 545

CAPITAL ACQUISITIONS TAX

5. —— **Relief** — *Nephew or niece — Gift of farm to niece — Whether niece worked substantially full time on the farm — Whether supervision of another's cattle under a letting agreement constituted a business — Capital Acquisitions Tax Act,* 1976 (*No.* 8), *2nd Sched., part* 1, *para.* 9.] Paragraph 9 of Part 1 of the 2nd Schedule to the Capital Acquisitions Tax Act, 1976, permits a nephew or niece to take a gift or inheritance of certain property on which he or she "has worked substantially on a full-time basis" for the preceding five years, subject to the scale of capital taxation applicable to a transaction between parent and child. The appellant, Mrs. A.E., was the niece of B., a farmer of advancing years, B.'s farm, the subject of a gift made in 1979, was situated close to where Mrs. A.E. lived with her husband and children. In evidence Mrs. A.E. said that she visited the farm every day to herd the cattle and to examine the fences. The cattle were the property of a third party, to whom grazing rights were let under an oral customary agreement whereby the landowner was responsible for herding and for the reporting of eventualities. The revenue authorities contended that Mrs. A.E.'s work was not "substantially on a full-time basis" and that B.'s letting agreement did not constitute a "business". **Held** by Judge Sheridan, finding for the appellant, 1, that "substantially full-time" could be construed to imply "the continued presence of a niece or nephew on a day to day basis whereby their labour (including expertise) is put at the disposal of the disponer whereby material benefit is conferred or is attempted to be conferred on the disponer's business." 2. That the attention given to B.'s lands jointly by B. and Mrs. A.E. was sufficient to indicate that a farming business was being carried on. 3. That it was not essential for a nephew or niece claiming under the relevant provision to show that he or she had taken over the entire running of the business. *A.E.* v. *Revenue Commissioners*

(Circ.Ct.) [1984] ILRM 301

REVENUE—*continued.*

CAPITAL GAINS TAX

6. —— **Rollover relief** — *Postponement of liability to tax where assets used for the purpose of trade sold and the proceeds used to acquire further assets for the purpose of trade — Farming — Land purchased by taxpayer and let on conacre — Land sold and proceeds used by taxpayer to purchase other land — Whether taxpayer entitled to postponement of liability to capital gains tax — Finance Act,* 1974 (*No.* 27), *ss.* 13, 17 — *Finance Act,* 1975 (*No.* 6), *s.* 12 — *Capital Gains Tax Act,* 1975 (*No.* 20), *s.* 28.] Section 28 of the Capital Gains Tax Act, 1975, provides *inter alia:*— "(1) If the consideration which a person carrying on a trade obtains for the disposal of . . . assets . . . used . . . for the purposes of the trade . . . is applied by him in acquiring other assets . . . which on the acquisition are taken into use . . . for the purposes of the trade . . . then the person carrying on the trade shall, on making a claim in that behalf, be treated for the purposes of this Act as if the chargeable gain accruing on the old assets did not accrue until he ceases to use the new assets for the purposes of the trade: (5) The following are assets for the purpose of this section— (*b*) (ii) any land occupied (as well as used) only for the purposes of the trade . . . (9) This section shall apply with the necessary modifications— (*g*) In relation to farming." Section 17 of the Finance Act, 1974, provides *inter alia:*— "(1) For the purposes of this Chapter, farm land shall be deemed to be occupied by an individual where . . . it is farm land of which he or his wife is the beneficial owner . . . and which is occupied by any other person." In 1975 the respondent and his wife bought a farm in County Westmeath. Immediately after the purchase they moved to Canada for 3 years during which time the lands were let on conacre. Upon their return to Ireland in 1978 the farm was sold at a profit and the proceeds used to buy another farm in County Galway which the respondent farmed himself. The respondent claimed, and the Circuit Court judge decided, that by virtue of s. 17 of the Act of 1974 he was deemed to have been in occupation of the farm while he was in Canada and, accordingly, that he was entitled to the rollover relief provided for by s. 28 of the Act of 1975. On a case stated by the Circuit Court judge as to whether he had been correct in point of law it was **Held** by Carroll J., in answering the case stated in the negative, 1, that the artificial meaning given to "occupation" by s. 17 of the Act of 1974 was only given for the purposes of Chapter II of that Act, that was, the taxation of farming profits and not for the purposes of capital gains tax. 2. That the relief provided for by s. 28 of the Act of 1975 was confined to assets used and land occupied as

REVENUE—Capital Gains Tax.

well as used for the purposes of the trade carried on by the person making the claim. 3. That the respondent was not carrying on the trade of farming at any time during which he owned the farm at Westmeath. 4. That the Westmeath farm was neither occupied by the respondent nor used by him for the purpose of his trade. *O Coindealbhain* v. *Price*

(H.C.) [1988] I.R. 14

7. —— **Tax avoidance** — *Capital gains realised by taxpayers — Further transactions carried out by taxpayers for the purpose of creating capital losses — Doctrine of "fiscal nullity" — Whether losses so arising capable of being set against gains — Capital Gains Tax Act,* 1975 (*No.* 20).

Statute — Interpretation — Revenue — Interpretation of taxing statutes — Principles applicable.] In the fiscal year 1981/82 the appellants realised certain gains on the disposal of assets. In order to offset the capital gains tax that would otherwise have been payable, the appellants carried out a series of transactions which were designed to create losses, and claimed to set off the gains against the losses so created. The transactions carried out by each of the appellants were substantially the same. PMcG. purchased the issued preference share capital of P. Ltd. By virtue of the application of s. 102 of the Corporation Tax Act, 1976, PMcG. was deemed to control P. Ltd. and was therefore "connected" with it for capital gains tax purposes. He then purchased the entire issued ordinary share capital from G. Ltd. at a price of £1 per share. These ordinary shares were subject to an option vested in the owners of the preference shares in G. Ltd. (P. Ltd.). whereby the option holder could purchase the ordinary share capital at a price of £2 per share. By virtue of s. 33 of the Capital Gains Tax Act, 1975, since the shares in G. Ltd. were purchased from a connected person they were deemed to have been purchased at a price which was undiminished by the option applicable to them. Accordingly, the deemed cost of shares in G. Ltd. was considerably in excess of the price actually paid by PMcG. PMcG. then disposed of the shareholdings in G. Ltd. and P. Ltd. at their market value, *viz.* £900 and £100 respectively. The purchasers of these shares were not connected with PMcG. The appellant then claimed to have suffered a loss on the disposal of the shares, being the difference between the deemed cost and the actual sale proceeds. Similar loss claims were made by the other appellants. The Inspector of Taxes refused to allow the appellants' claims on the basis that no loss had in fact arisen. On appeal, the Appeal Commissioners upheld the Inspector's decision on the basis that a transaction (or series of transactions viewed as a whole) which had no purpose other than the

REVENUE—*continued.*

avoidance of tax, and which did not involve a real loss, should be disregarded. On appeal by the appellants by way of case stated it was **Held** by Carroll J., in allowing the appeal, 1, that in determining whether a liability to tax arose from a transaction it was necessary to look, not at the substance or financial results, but at the actual legal effect of the transaction and the legal rights of the parties to the transaction according to legal ideas and concepts and not solely according to the words used by the parties themselves. *O'Sullivan* v. *P. Ltd.* (1962) 3 I.T.C. 355 and *Inland Revenue Commissioners* v. *Duke of Westminister* [1936] A.C. 1 followed. 2. That an exemption from tax is governed by the same considerations as a liability to tax. *Revenue Commissioners* v. *Doorley* [1933] I.R. 750 applied. 3. That the courts in the United Kingodm had developed a doctrine of "fiscal nullity". This provided that if steps were inserted in a pre-ordained series of transactions, and if the steps had no commercial purpose other than the avoidance of tax, they could be disregarded for fiscal purposes and the scheme viewed as a whole. The doctrine represented a new approach to tax avoidance which had not been accepted by the Irish courts. *W.T. Ramsay Ltd.* v. *Inland Revenue Comrs.* [1982] A.C. 300 and *Furniss* v. *Dawson* [1984] A.C. 474; *Inland Revenue Commissioners* v. *Duke of Westminister* [1936] A.C. 1 and *O'Sullivan* v. *P. Ltd.* (1962) 3 I.T.C. 355 considered. 4. That the imposition of tax and the granting relief from tax was solely a matter for the legislature. If parliament had failed to legislate against a tax avoidance scheme in advance or to confer on the courts the power to determine that a scheme was devised primarily for the avoidance of tax and to disallow it accordingly, then it was not the function of the courts to intervene. Accordingly the appellants were entitled to the reliefs claimed. *W.T. Ramsay Ltd.* v. *Inland Revenue Comrs.* [1982] A.C. 300 and *Furniss* v. *Dawson* [1984] A.C. 474 not followed. On appeal by the respondent it was **Held** by the Supreme Court (Finlay C.J., Henchy, Griffin, Hederman and McCarthy JJ.) in disallowing the appeal, 1, that the doctrine of "fiscal nullity" which represented a new approach to tax avoidance schemes on the part of the courts in the United Kingdom and the United States did not form part of Irish law. *W.T. Ramsay Ltd.* v. *Inland Revenue Comrs.* [1982] A.C. 300 and *Furniss* v. *Dawson* [1984] A.C. 474; *Knetsch* v. *U.S.* (1960) 364 U.S. 361 and *Goldstein* v. *C.I.R.* (1966) 364 F. 2nd 735 not followed. 2. That the function of the courts in interpreting a statute is limited to ascertaining the true meaning of each statutory provision. The courts may not add to or delete from express statutory provisions so as to condemn tax avoidance schemes which are not prohibited by statute

REVENUE—Capital Gains Tax.

law. To do so would constitute an invasion of the legislative powers of the Oireachtas. *Revenue Commissioners.* v. *Doorley* [1933] I.R. 750 and *Inspector of Taxes* v. *Kiernan* [1981] I.R. 117 approved. *Per* McCarthy J.; where an earlier decision of a superior court is based on case law which has been reviewed and made subject to a new approach, this new approach cannot be taken into consideration by a lower tribunal to conclude that the earlier decision would have been different. *McGrath* v. *McDermott*

(H.C., S.C.) [1988] I.R.258 ;[1988] ILRM 181, 647

CORPORATION TAX

8. —— **Capital or revenue transaction** — *Settlement of action for nuisance — Whether expenditure on settling the claim to be regarded as capital or revenue transaction.*] A company manufacturing building materials, was sued in the High Court by the owner of adjacent property, who complained that the company's operations produced noise and dust. The suit and a planning objection based on related facts were withdrawn when the company agreed to buy the objector's lands, to provide him with building materials, and to pay him £8,000 and costs. The company accepted that the cost of purchasing the land was an item of capital expenditure, but sought to treat the remaining outlay as deductible from Corporation Tax. The Inspector of Taxes disallowed the deduction, and argued that the entire transaction was of a capital nature. The company appealed to the Circuit Court. **Held** by Judge Sheridan, dismissing the appeal, 1, that the expenditure was of a capital nature. 2. That, where a transaction involves elements both of capital and revenue, and separation is practicable, the elements may lawfully be separated. 3. That, where expenditure has been made once and for all with a view to bringing into existence an asset or advantage for the enduring benefit of a trade, such expenditure is *prima facie* capital in nature: *British Insulated and Helsby Cables* v. *Atherton* [1926] A.C. 205 applied. 4. That "buying off" a sustainable legal claim, if it results in the alteration of the original character of an asset, is a capital transaction: *dicta* in *Davis* v. *'M'* [1947] I.R. 145 considered. *Insulation Products Ltd.* v. *Inspector of Taxes*

(Circ. Ct.) [1984] ILRM 610

9. —— **Distributions** — *Company in voluntary liquidation — Distributable income exceeding amount of distributions — Whether additional surcharge of tax payable — Definition of distributions of a company — Whether literal interpretation would lead to absurd or unjust results — Income Tax Act,* 1967 (No. 6), *s.* 428 — *Corporation Tax Act,* 1976 (*No.* 7), *ss.* 84, 100,

REVENUE—Corporation Tax.

101, 146.] The combined effect of ss. 100 and 101 of the Corporation Tax Act, 1976, is that where the available distributable income of a close company during a given accounting period exceeds the amount of distributions made by the company during the said period, an additional surcharge of tax is imposed on the company, amounting to 20% of the excess. Sub-s. 1 (*a*) of s. 100 provides that distributions of a company for an accounting period include not only dividends declared and paid during the relevant period, but also such dividends as were declared and payable during that period, and paid within eighteen months of the end of the said period. S. 84 (1) of the Act provides that any references in the Act to distributions of a company shall not apply to distributions made in respect of share capital in a winding up. Finally, s. 100 (7) provides that where a company is subject to any restriction imposed by law in the making of distributions, regard is to be had to such restrictions in determining the amount of income on which a surcharge is to be imposed in accordance with s. 101. The instant proceedings were an appeal by way of case stated from a decision of the Appeals Commissioner. The appellant was a close company within the meaning of the 1976 Act. The excess distributable income of the appellant for its final accounting period from 6 April, 1977, to the commencement of winding up on 24 October, 1977, amounted to £772, and for the penultimate period, to £1,129. The Revenue sought to impose a surcharge at the rate of 20% on each sum. The appellant alleged that it was unfairly penalised by the operation of s. 84 (1), in that the eighteen-month period provided for by s. 100 (1) (*a*) was reduced in respect of its final accounting period, and submitted that the provisions of s. 101 imposing a surchage should therefore have no application. In the High Court, although not before the Appeals Commissioner, the appellant further claimed that s. 100, sub-s. 7 could be applied in its favour. **Held** by Murphy J. in dismissing the appeal, in finding that s. 84 (1) of the Corporation Tax Act, 1976, did not prevent the application of s. 101 (1) of the said Act in the circumstances of the case, and in making no finding in respect of the application of s. 100 (7), 1, it is not appropriate for the court to decide questions raised in a case stated by reference to matters of fact or law not dealt with by the tribunal stating the case. 2. Where it is not contended that a particular provision of legislation is unconstitutional, effect should be given to it unless it would lead to a result so manifestly absurd or unjust that there is good reason to seek an alternative interpretation. *Rahinstown Estates Co.* v. *Hughes*

(H.C.) [1987] ILRM 599

REVENUE—Corporation Tax.

10. —— **Dividends** — *Company receiving dividends — Dividend derived from sale of capital assets — Whether dividend liable to be assessed for tax — Finance Act,* 1920 (*c.* 18), *ss.* 52, 53(2) — *Corporation Tax Act,* 1976 (*No.* 7), *s.* 164, *3rd Sched.*

Statute — Interpretation — Literal interpretation giving result plainly contrary to the legislative intent — Finance Act, 1920 (*c.* 18), *s.* 53(2).] This case concerns the interpretation of ss. 52 and 53 of the Finance Act, 1920, relating to the charge of corporation tax. Although Part V of that Act is repealed by s. 164 and the Third Schedule of the Corporation Tax Act, 1976, the liability for accounting periods prior to 5 April, 1976, is not affected. The appellant company made profits for the accounting period ending 31 March, 1974, consisting of two dividends received from companies which arose out of the sale by those companies of certain capital assets. No assessments to corporation profits tax in respect of the sales were made on either of these two companies. It was argued *inter alia* on behalf of the plaintiff that since it did not carry on any trade or business, it was not liable to corporation profits tax in respect of the holding of investments on the grounds that s. 52 (2) (*a*) of the Finance Act, 1920, which imposed a charge to corporation profits tax on an Irish company, only applied to a company "carrying on any trade or business or any undertaking of a similar character, including the holding of investments', that the plaintiff's sole activity was the holding of investments and that the carrying on of a trade or business has implications of commercial transactions totally different from the mere holding of investments. It was held by the Circuit Court that the plaintiff was liable to corporation profits tax as where the holding of investments was the whole or part of the business of the company, that activity of itself was sufficient to bring it within the charge to corporation profits tax. The opinion of the High Court was sought by case stated as to whether the Circuit Court was correct in law in so holding. It was **held** by McWilliam J. that the Circuit Court judge was correct in holding that the plaintiff was chargeable to corporation profits tax in respect of the said dividends. A taxpayer was not entitled to arrange his affairs on the basis of the practice of the Revenue Commissioners and a provision in a statute does not become obsolete because it has not been operated for a number of years. S. 53 (2) of the Finance Act, 1920, was not of an ambiguous or doubtful meaning when applied to the facts of the case. Even if the two companies in question had received some element of profit on the sale of the capital assets and so subject to corporation profits tax in the hands of those companies, s. 53 (2) does not operate to relieve

REVENUE—*continued.*

the taxpayer from liability on its dividends. Appealed to the Supreme Court. **Held** by the Supreme Court (Henchy J. and Griffin J.; Hederman J. dissenting) that the dividends were liable to corporation profits tax and that the appeal should be dismissed. The clear purpose of the proviso in s. 53 (2) (*a*) of the Finance Act, 1920, "not being interest, dividends or income received directly or indirectly from a company liable to be assessed to corporation profits tax in respect thereof" was to ensure, in case of the company receiving the dividend, that the company will not be chargeable to the tax if the paying company has already paid or is liable to be assessed to corporation profits tax or in other words, to ensure that the same money would not be subject to double taxation in the hands of the paying company and again in the hands of the receiving company. The words "in respect thereof" in the proviso only refer to the particular dividend received by the receiving, and it is necessary to look to the source of that income to ascertain whether corporation profits tax has been paid out of it or if it has a liability to assessment for the tax — since in the instant case there was no payment of or liability for assessment to corporation profits tax on the part of the paying companies, there was a liability to tax on the part of the appellant, the recipient of the dividend. *Per* Henchy J.; while it is not the function of the courts to extend artificially the ambiguous words of a statutory provision so as to produce a liability to taxation, where the words used are reasonably capable of a meaning which is in accord with the essence of the provision, it is that interpretation that should prevail. *Kellystown Co.* v. *Hogan*

(S.C.) [1985] ILRM 200

11. —— **Export sales relief** — *Calculation — "Total income brought into the charge to corporation tax" — Meaning — Surrender of loss of associate company — Corporation Tax Act,* 1976 (*No.* 7), *Parts IV, XI.*] Part IV of the Corporation Tax Act, 1976 ("the Act") provides for relief from corporation tax ("export sales relief") in respect of profits arising from the sale of goods by export. Part XI of the Act provides certain reliefs for companies which are members of the same group. Under this part, where a company suffers a trading loss it may transfer that loss to an associate company. The associate company may set the loss received against its own income and thereby reduce that income and accordingly its liability to corporation tax. In the accounting period for the twelve months ending on the 31 December, 1985, the taxpayer company earned certain profits from the sale of goods. A large

REVENUE—Corporation Tax.

proportion of these sales qualified for export sales relief, which entitled the company to reduce the corporation tax payable proportionately. In the same accounting period an associate company suffered a loss which it surrendered to the taxpayer. In order to ascertain the exact amount of export sales relief available to the company it was necessary to calculate the income from the sale of goods exported (this figure was agreed) and to compare this figure with the "total income brought into the charge to corporation tax." This latter amount was in dispute. The Inspector of Taxes assessed the taxpayer on the basis that this amount was calculated without any allowance being made for the loss surrendered by the associate company. The taxpayer contended that the loss should be taken into account in calculating the "total income", and that its export sales relief should therefore be greater than the Inspector had allowed for, and that accordingly the assessment for the accounting period ending 31 December, 1978, was excessive. The Appeal Commissioner rejected the taxpayer's contention and affirmed the assessment. The taxpayer appealed to the Circuit Court. The Circuit Court judge reversed the decision of the Appeal Commissioner, but, at the request of the Inspector, agreed to state a case to the High Court. **Held** by O'Hanlon J., in confirming the opinion of the Circuit Court that the phrase "total income brought into charge to corporation tax" can be construed in *pari materia* with the phrase used in income tax legislation "profits or gains brought into charge" which has been construed in a number of cases as meaning the taxable, and not the actual profits or gains in the year of assessment. On appeal by the Inspector of Taxes it was **Held** by the Supreme Court (Finlay C.J., Griffin and Henchy JJ.), in disallowing the appeal, 1, that s. 11, sub-s 1, of the Act applies income tax principles, law and practice in very broad terms to the computation of income for the purposes of corporation tax. The long accepted meaning of the income tax phrase "brought into the charge to tax" is of taxable income and not actual income. The expression "total income" must be read with the qualifying words "brought into charge." 2. Accordingly the phrase "total income brought into the charge to corporation tax" should be interpreted in this case to be the income of the company after the deduction of the loss surrendered to the company. *Per curiam,* where a word or expression in an Act has received clear judicial interpretation, then there is a presumption that a subsequent Act which incorporates the same word or expression in a similar context should be construed so that the word or expression is interpreted according to the meaning that has previously been ascribed to it, unless a contrary intention appears. *Cronin* v. *Youghal Carpets (Yarns) Ltd.*

REVENUE—*continued.*

(H.C., S.C.) [1985] I.R.312 ; [1985] ILRM 666

12. —— **Export sales relief** — *Goods manufactured within the State — Process of ripening bananas — Whether process constitutes manufacturing — Statute — Interpretation — Manufacture — Corporation Tax Act,* 1976 (*No.* 7), *Part IV.*] Part IV of the Corporation Tax Act, 1976, provides for relief from corporation tax for profits derived from the sale by export of goods manufactured within the State. The appellant imported unripened bananas into the State and subjected them to an artificial ripening process. This process was carried out in specially constructed and equipped rooms, and it was supervised by employees of the appellant who had special skills and expertise. The appellant sought relief pursuant to Part IV of the Act of 1976. The relief was refused, and, on appeal, the Circuit Court judge upheld the refusal but agreed, following the request of the appellant, to state a case for the opinion of the High Court. Carroll J., in the High Court (in a decision reported at [1985] I.R. 298) confirmed the decision of the Circuit Court and held that the process carried out by the appellant did not constitute a "manufacture" within the meaning of Part IV of the Act of 1976. On appeal by the appellant it was **Held** by the Supreme Court (Finlay C.J., Hederman and McCarthy JJ.). in allowing the appeal, 1, that Part IV of the Act of 1976 is addressed to the public at large, accordingly, in the absence of internal evidence suggesting the contrary, the word used in the Act should be given its ordinary or colloquial meaning. In order to determine whether the goods were "manufactured" within the meaning of the Act, a court should consider whether a person, properly informed as to the nature of the goods and the extent to which the process in question contributed to the characteristics of the goods, would attribute the word "manufacture" to the process. This question is, to a certain extent, one of degree, and, in determining the question, a judge should have regard to his own experience. *Dictum* of Henchy J. in *Inspector of Taxes* v. *Kiernan* [1981] I.R. 117 and *dictum* of Murphy J. in *Cronin (Inspector of Taxes)* v. *Strand Dairies* (Unreported, High Court, 18 December, 1985) applied. *McCausland* v. *Ministry of Commerce* [1956] N.I. 36 considered. 2. That in construing the particular words used in a statute, it is necessary, in the case of doubt or ambiguity, to look to the scheme and purpose of the statute as disclosed in the statute. In the instant case the purpose of Part IV of the Act of 1976 was to encourage the creation of employment within the State and the promotion of exports. The

REVENUE—Corporation Tax.

process in question clearly came within both categories, and, since the process converted the raw materials into a commercially different product, it amounted to manufacturing. Decision of the High Court (Carroll J.) in *Charles McCann Ltd.* v. *Ó Culacháin* [1985] I.R. 298 reversed. *McCann (Charles) Ltd.* v. *Ó Cúlacháin*

(S.C.) [1986] I.R.196; (H.C.) [1985] I.R.298; [1986] ILRM 229

13. —— **Export sales relief** — *Income from the sale of goods — Monies regularly paid in advance by customers — Monies placed on deposit — Whether interest accruing was income from the sale of goods — Corporation Tax Act,* 1976 (*No.* 7), *s.* 58.] The respondent manufactured ambulances, a large number of which were regularly supplied to customers in the U.K. These customers had adopted a practice of paying the respondent sums of money in advance of ordering ambulances. If the ambulances were not ordered the monies paid were refunded. The monies advanced were placed on deposit with a bank by the respondent. This procedure was carried out at the respondent's own initiative and was not part of its agreement with the customers. Interest accrued on the monies deposited and the respondent argued that the interest was not liable to tax being income from the sale of goods by export within the meaning of the provisions of Part IV of the Corporation Tax Act, 1976. On the application of the appellant the Circuit Court judge agreed to state a case for the opinion of the High Court as to whether the interest was such income. **Held** by Murphy J., in answering the case stated, 1, that to establish its claim to relief from tax the respondent would have to show that the interest received was received from or attributable to the sale of goods. 2. That the interest received by the respondent did not derive from the carrying on of the trade. The interest was payable by virtue of a contractual obligation between the respondent and the bank and it did not constitute income from the sale of goods. *Bucks* v. *Bowers* [1970] Ch. 431 and *Northend* v. *White & Leonard* [1975] 1 W.L.R. 1037 considered. *Kerrane* v. *Hanlon (N.) (Ireland) Ltd.*

(H.C.) [1987] I.R.259

14. —— **Group of companies** — *Parent company providing services to subsidiaries — Services supplied free of charge — Cost of services borne by parent company — Whether loss suffered by parent company — Whether services provided in ordinary course of trade — Corporation Tax Act,* 1976 (*No.* 7), *ss.* 2, 25, 28.] The appellant, a holding company, also carried on the trade of

REVENUE—*continued.*

managing several of its subsidiary companies and providing them with finance. It provided services free of charge to some of its subsidiaries. The cost of providing these services was borne by the appellant, and it suffered losses as a result. Section 2 of the Corporation Tax Act, 1976, provides that corporation tax is not to be chargeable on dividends and other distributions of a company resident in the State, and that such dividends or distributions are not to be treated as income for the purposes of assessing corporation tax on the recipient. By virtue of s. 88 of the Act of 1976, where a company resident in the State makes a distribution, and the person receiving the distribution is also resident in the State, the recipient is generally entitled to a tax credit. Section 25 of the Act of 1976 enables an Irish resident company to elect to have such payments treated as income for corporation tax purposes. Two of the appellant's subsidiaries paid dividends (to which tax credits attached) to the appellant. The appellant made an election under s. 25 to have the dividends treated as income. Since the appellant had suffered trading losses, no tax liability arose in respect of the income from the dividends, and the appellant in accordance with s. 25, sub-s. 1, sought to claim the value of the tax credits attached to the dividends the subject matter of the s. 25 election. The respondent, an Inspector of Taxes, did not accept that the appellant had, in fact, suffered a trading loss. The decision of the respondent was appealed to an Appeal Commissioner. The Appeal Commissioner agreed that the losses which the appellant had suffered were not losses occurring in the ordinary course of trade. He estimated a notional fee which the appellant could have expected to receive from its subsidiaries for the services provided and he determined the appeal accordingly. The appellant appealed to the High Court by way of case stated against the decision of the Appeal Commissioner. **Held** by Carroll J., in allowing the appeal, 1, that the Appeal Commissioner was entitled to find that the transactions between the appellant and its subsidiaries were not carried out in the course of trade, as they were far outside the course of business of any trader. *Petrotim Securities Ltd.* v. *Ayres* [1964] 1 W.L.R. 190, applied. 2. That the accounts of the appellant must be adjusted by the inclusion of a figure for notional fees representing the market value of the services provided. 3. That the figure for the notional fees is a question of fact to be decided by the Appeal Commissioner on the basis of evidence before him. 4. That in estimating the value of the services provided by the appellant, the Appeal Commissioner made a finding which he was not entitled to do as it was not based on

REVENUE—Corporation Tax.

any evidence before him. *Belville Holdings Ltd.* v. *Cronin*

(H.C.) [1985] I.R.465

15. —— **Loss relief** — *Change of ownership of company which ceased to slaughter and to manufacture meat products and continued to distribute products of new owner — Whether permanent cessation — Whether change in nature or conduct of trade — Whether scale of activities became small or negligible — Corporation Tax Act, 1976 (No.* 7), *ss.* 16(1), 27, 182, 184.]

Statute — Interpretation — Ejusdem generis *rule — Ordinary and natural meaning of words — Revenue — Corporation Tax Act,* 1976 (*No.* 7), *s.* 27.] S. 27 of the Corporation Tax Act, 1976, disallows relief for past losses on a change in ownership of a company when there is a major change in the nature or conduct of its trade, or when the scale of activities carried on has become small or negligible. During a sixteen month period the taxpayer company changed ownership, temporarily ceased to slaughter and to manufacture meat products, and continued to distribute the products of its new owner. The Inspector of Taxes disallowed relief for past losses under ss. 16 (1), 182 and 184 Corporation Tax Act, 1976, on the grounds that there had been a permanent cessation of the trade, and that s. 27 applied. The Circuit Court judge held that the company was entitled to relief. The inspector appealed by case stated on the grounds that the judge had misdirected himself in law. **Held** by Carroll J. in dismissing the appeal, 1, there were ample grounds for the judge's finding of fact that there had been no permanent cessation of the trade. 2. Having regard to the ordinary and natural meaning of the words, a major change in the nature and conduct of the trade could not be said to have taken place where the company, during a temporary cessation of the slaughtering and manufacturing side of its business, continued in the business of selling the same type of goods supplied to it by another supplier to the same customers. Accordingly the inspector had not shown that the judge had disregarded the ordinary and natural meaning of the words. 3. There were grounds for the judge's finding that the activities of the trade had not become small or negligible. *Per* Carroll J.: The *ejusdem generis* rule as applied to the interpretation of statutes means that where a general word follows particular and specific words of the same nature as itself, it takes its meaning from them and is presumed to be restricted to the same genus as those words. The rule applies to general words following words which are less general. *Cronin* v. *Lunham Brothers Ltd.*

(H.C.) [1986] ILRM 415

16. —— **Mines** — *Profits on mining operations*

REVENUE—*continued.*

— Relief from taxation — Option to have tax assessed by relation to income — Period to which calculation relates — Avoidance of retrospective imposition of tax — Intentions of legislators — Finance (Taxation of Profits of Certain Mines) Act, 1974 (*No.* 17), *ss.* 15, 16 *— Income Tax Act,* 1967 (*No.* 6), *s.* 386 *— Corporation Tax Act,* 1976 (*No.* 7), *s.* 174.] The appellant appealed against an assessment to income tax under Case 1 of Schedule D for the year 1974-75. The Appeal Commissioner stated a case to the High Court under s. 428 of the Income Tax Act. The question of law for determination was how to calculate the amount of the deduction for corporation profits tax in computing the amount of profits or gains to be charged to income tax. The appellant is a mining company and carried on the trade of operating a qualifying mine as defined in s. 1 of the Finance (Taxation of Profits of Certain Mines) Act, 1974. The appellant was relieved from income tax in its mining profits for all years up to and including the year 1973-74 by virtue of the provisions of s. 386 of the Income Tax Act, 1967. Relief under s. 386 was terminated by s. 15 of the Act of 1974 for all years subsequent to 1973-74. Consequent on such termination the appellant for the first time became liable to tax for the year 1974-75 on all mining profits. The appellant elected to be charged to income tax for the year 1974-75 by reference to the amount of its actual profits of that year. This was done by notice in writing given to the Inspector of Taxes in accordance with s. 16 (1) of the Act of 1974. The appellant claimed that it was entitled to have its profits from April, 1974, to April, 1975, added together and sought to have the corporation profits tax that had been paid for the year ended 30 December, 1973, to be set against the above income tax due and to be deducted as an expense. **Held** by McWilliam J. in finding for the respondent inspector, 1, the corporation profits tax deductible must be related to profits which are to be deducted as it is possible that the tax paid in respect of the year 1973-74 might bear no relation to the profits in the year 1974-75 and could conceivably exceed those profits. 2. The calculations in respect of the income tax of the appellant company should be made on the basis that corporation profits tax was notionally payable on the profits for the entire period to 30 December, 1975, and therefore deductible as an expense. 3. The learned High Court Judge declined to address himself to the third question which related to the interpretation of the above relevant statutes. *Semble:* the option to the appellant provided for by the 1974 Act may have been intended to avoid retrospective imposition of tax under the Corporation Tax Act, 1976. *Mogul of Ireland Ltd.* v. *Ó Riain*

(H.C.) [1979] ILRM 75

REVENUE—Corporation Tax.

17. —— **Non-resident company** — *Company incorporated within the State but resident outside the State — Branch or agency carrying on business within the State — Monies transferred by Irish branch to company — Monies invested abroad by company — Part of investment fund retransferred to Irish branch — Whether income from investment fund liable to Irish corporation tax — Whether fund "used by or held by or for" Irish branch — Corporation Tax Act,* 1976 (*No.* 7), *s.* 8.] Section 8, sub-s. 2 of the Corporation Tax Act, 1976, provides:— "For the purposes of corporation tax the chargeable profits of a company not resident in the State but carrying on a trade there through a branch or agency shall be— (*a*) any trading income arising directly or indirectly through or form the branch or agency, and any income from property or rights used by, or held by or for, the branch or agency. . ." D. Ltd. was incorporated within the State and carried on a manufacturing business within the State but was resident in the Netherlands. A sum of money earned by the Irish branch of the company was transferred to Switzerland where it was invested and managed by the company in accordance with directions given by the United States based parent. The management of the Irish branch had no control over those monies or over their investment or disposal. Due to an unforeseen operational shortfall some of the monies were re-transferred to Dublin and were used by the Irish branch. The interest earned on these monies was declared for Irish tax and the tax paid but the appellant sought to charge the income from the entire investment fund to corporation tax under s. 8 of the Act of 1976. The Circuit Court judge held that the investment fund was not property used by or held by or for the Irish branch but, on the application of the Inspector of Taxes, stated a case for the opinion of the High Court. **Held** by Carroll J., in affirming the decision of the Circuit Court, that the investment fund, other than that part which had been retransferred to the Irish branch, was held by and for and used by the company and not the Irish branch and, accordingly, that the income deriving from the fund was not chargeable to Irish corporation tax. *Murphy* v. *Dataproducts (Dublin) Ltd.*

(H.C.) [1988] I.R. 10

18. —— **Profits or gains** — *Manufacturing company — Stock in hand — Accountancy — Computation of profits — Historical Cost Accounting — Current Cost Accounting — Whether estimated future loss can be taken into account — Correct accounting system to be used — Role of the principles of commercial accountancy — Whether different accounting methods can be used in different circumstances — Income Tax*

REVENUE—*continued.*

Act, 1967 (*No.* 6), *s.* 428 — *Finance Act,* 1975 (*No.* 6), *s.* 31(2) — *Corporation Tax Act,* 1976 (*No.* 7), *s.* 146.] The appellants, who were cigarette and tobacco manufacturers, held their tobacco purchases in stock for 15 to 30 months. For this reason, they changed their method of accountancy from Historic Cost Accounting (H.C.A.) to Current Cost Accounting (C.C.A.) in 1975 (although accounts based on H.C.A. were also included). Under C.C.A. costs could be related to current costs at the time of sale (replacement cost) and not to the cost of stock purchased a considerable time previously, which was the case with H.C.A. The appellants felt that C.C.A. was the only way to judge the real performance of the company. The respondent refused to accept the changed system of accountancy. The question for the determination of the High Court was whether the Appeal Commissioners were correct in determining that the profits of the appellants should be determined in accordance with H.C.A. The appellants argued that profits should be ascertained in accordance with the correct principles of commercial accountancy; that there were several methods of accountancy which were appropriate in different circumstances; that C.C.A. was accepted by accountants as being the only means by which a fair view of profits can be ascertained; that profits were to be ascertained in accordance with the correct principles of commercial accountancy whether or not this was the prevailing system. The respondent submitted that the overall structure of the tax code presupposed the use of H.C.A.; that the correct principles of commercial accounting should be those prevailing and generally accepted; that the usefulness of a particular method of accountancy for a business did not establish it as a principle of commercial accountancy for tax purposes. **Held** by Carroll J., in answering the case stated in the affirmative, 1, that profits and gains were not defined by statute but had been interpreted judicially as the difference between receipts and the expenditure laid out to earn them ascertained by accounts framed consistently with the ordinary principles of commercial accounting as modified by relevant statutory provisions and, accordingly, methods which reflected expected future profits or expected future losses for tax purposes were contrary to principle. *Whimster & Co.* v. *The Inland Revenue* [1926] S.C. 20; *Minister of National Revenue* v. *Anaconda American Brass Ltd.* [1956] A.C. 85; *Patrick* v. *Broadstone Mills Ltd.* [1954] 1 W.L.R. 158; *B.S.C. Footwear* v. *Ridgway* [1972] A.C. 544; *Lowe & Others* v. *Inland Revenue Commissioners* [1983] S.T.C. 816; *Secretan* v. *Hart* [1969] 1 W.L.R. 1599 and *Heather* v. *P-E Consulting Group Ltd.* [1973] Ch. 189 approved. *Dicta* of Pennycuick V.C. in

REVENUE—Corporation Tax.

Odeon Assoc. Theatres v. *Jones* [1971] 1 W.L.R. 442 considered. 2. That the correct test for a system of accountancy for tax purposes was not whether that system was the prevailing system or whether the system was in accordance with sound commercial practice but rather it was whether a system was appropriate to the company involved and ascertained the full profits for the year of assessment and no one system could be described as the proper system. *Minister for National Revenue* v. *Anaconda American Brass Ltd.* [1956] A.C. 85; *Patrick* v. *Broadstone Mills Ltd.* [1954] 1 W.L.R. 158 and *B.S.C. Footwear Ltd.* v. *Ridgway* [1972] A.C. 544 approved. 3. That C.A.A., which did not show the expenditure laid out to earn receipts as it substituted current replacement costs for actual cost against current sales even though the stock had not yet been replaced, was not applicable. *Carroll Industries plc* v. *Ó Cúlacháin*

(H.C.) [1988] I.R.705

19. —— **Receiver** — *Liability — Debentures executed to secure loans received by company — Receiver appointed under terms of debenture — Appointment of receiver as agent of company — Monies placed on deposit in name of receiver — Interest accruing on monies deposited — Whether receiver chargeable to corporation tax — Whether receiver liable to pay corporation tax — Income Tax Act,* 1967 (*No.* 6), *ss.* 105, 207, 212 — *Corporation Tax Act,* 1976 (*No.* 7), *ss.* 1, 6, 11, 141-5.] The applicant was appointed receiver and agent of W. Ltd. under a deed of debenture. Certain monies accruing to the company were placed on deposit in an interest-bearing account in the name of the applicant. Interest accrued on those monies and the applicant sought the directions of the High Court as to whether he would be liable to pay corporation tax which might be chargeable in respect of the interest accruing. Section 105 of the Income Tax Act, 1967, imposes a charge to tax under Schedule D on a person receiving or entitled to income which is assessable under schedule D. The respondent argued that s. 11, sub-s. 6 of the Corporation Tax Act, 1976, which provides that the provisions of the Act of 1967 shall "except as otherwise provided" have the same effect for the purposes of corporation tax, adopted s. 105 into the corporation tax code. Accordingly, the respondent submitted that the combined effect of the two Acts was to render the applicant liable to pay corporation tax on the interest accruing. **Held** by Costello J., in giving directions, 1, that where a receiver is the person receiving or entitled to income in respect of which tax is chargeable under Schedule D, then, by virtue of s. 105 of the Income Tax Act, 1967, he can be personally assessed for the tax and become personally liable

REVENUE—*continued.*

to pay the tax on the income which arises during his receivership. *Inland Revenue Commissioners* v. *Thompson* [1937] 1 K.B. 290; [1936] 2 All E.R. 651; (1936) T.C. 422 applied. 2. That s. 11, sub-s, 6 of the Corporation Tax Act, 1976, adopts charging provisions of the income tax code into the corporation tax code. However, that subsection only applies where other provision has not been made. Section 6 of the Act of 1976 makes clear and unambiguous provision for charging and assessing companies; therefore s. 11, sub-s. 6 does not operate to adopt into the corporation tax code an entirely different provision of the income tax code which renders a person who "receives" income assessable and liable to pay the tax. Accordingly, s. 105 of the Act of 1967 has not been made part of the corporation tax code. 3. That s. 105 of the Act of 1967 imposes liability to pay income tax only on those on whom it is charged according to the assessment procedures contained in that Act. It would not be permissible to adopt for the purposes of corporation tax that part of s. 105 which imposes a liability to pay tax when the part which imposes the charge was not adopted. Accordingly, since the receiver was not chargeable to corporation tax he was not liable to pay it. *Quaere:* Whether a receiver can be regarded as an officer of a company "performing the duties of secretary" within the meaning of s. 207, sub-s. 2 of the Income Tax Act, 1967, and therefore bound by the duties imposed on secretaries by that sub-section.*In re Wayte (Holdings) Ltd.; Burns* v. *Hearne*

(H.C.) [1986] I.R.448

20. —— **Small companies relief** — *Whether non-resident company associated company — Statute — Interpretation — Context of words — "Associated company" — Corporation Tax Act,* 1976 (*No.* 7), *ss.* 1(5), 28(4).] S. 28 Corporation Tax Act, 1976, provides for a reduced rate of corporation tax on company profits below a certain limit. The normal limit is reduced if the company has "associated companies" as defined in s. 28(4). The taxpayer company was registered and traded in the Republic of Ireland. A second company under the control of the same persons as the taxpayer company was registered and traded in Northern Ireland. The profits of the taxpayer company were below the normal limit for the relevant accounting period. The Inspector of Taxes refused to allow the reduced rate of tax on the basis that the Northern Ireland company was an associated company. The appeal commissioners held that s. 28(3) did not apply to non-resident companies under common control. The inspector appealed by way of case stated. **Held** by Carroll J., in dismissing the appeal: having regard to the context of the words of s.

28, an associated company was a body corporate wherever incorporated within the meaning of s. 1(5) of the Act. This definition included non-resident companies. Accordingly the Northern Ireland company was an associated company of the taxpayer company so that the reduced rate of tax did not apply. *Bairead* v. *Maxwells of Donegal Ltd.*

(H.C.) [1986] ILRM 508

21. —— **Stock relief** — *Relief confined to profits derived from certain trades — Trades defined to include both manufacture of goods and sale to particular trades of machinery, plant or goods — Statute — Interpretation — Manufacture — Sale — Finance Act,* 1975 (*No.* 6), *ss.* 31, 31A.] The Finance Act, 1975 (as amended), provided for a reduction in profits chargeable to tax by reference to increases in the value of trading stock held at the beginning and end of an accounting period. The relief was granted to companies engaged in certain trades, and those trades were limited, *inter alia,* to those consisting, wholly or mainly, of the manufacture of goods or of farming or of sale of machinery, plant or goods to persons engaged in those trades. The appellant's business consisted of the assembly and sale of farm machinery. A proportion of the sales were made directly to farmers, but a far greater proportion were made to finance houses and dealers. They in turn sold the machinery to farmers in deals procured or arranged by the company. The company claimed an entitlement to stock relief on the basis that it was carrying on a trade within the meaning of s. 31 of the Act of 1975, *viz.* that not less than 75 per cent of its receipts came from the manufacture of goods or alternatively from the sale of machinery to qualifying persons. The company's claim was disallowed by the Inspector of Taxes and his decision was upheld by the Circuit Court. On the application of the company, the Circuit Court judge agreed to state a case for the opinion of the High Court. **Held** by Murphy J., in answering the case stated and affirming the decision of the Circuit Court, 1, that the operations carried out by the company were processes which merely assembled the components of the machinery. The processes did not bring about any significant change in the components themselves. Any process properly described as assembly would not be understood by the ordinary well-informed layman to be a manufacturing process. *Cronin (Inspector of Taxes)* v. *Strand Dairies Limited* (Unreported, High Court, Murphy J., 18 December, 1986) and *Charles McCann Ltd.* v. *Ó Culacháin (Inspector of Taxes)* [1986] I.R. 196 applied. 2. That an arrangement whereby one person sold goods to another as a result of the activities of a third party was not a "sale" by the third party within

the ordinary legal meaning of the term. In the absence of an indication in the relevant legislation that the term was to be interpreted in a broad commercial sense the court was obliged to apply the traditional legal meaning. Therefore, only the sales by the company directly to farmers could be said to be qualifying sales. Since these sales were only a small portion of the company's total sales it was not carrying on a qualifying trade and was not entitled to the relief provided by section 31. *Fraser* v. *London Sports Car Centre* [1985] S.T.C. 688 distinguished. *Per* Murphy J. A court hearing a case stated may not consider facts and form a view on those facts which might be in conflict with the view which the court of first instance would have taken if it had found it necessary to form a view. Nor does it seem appropriate for a tribunal or court to incorporate into the case stated a detailed note or transcript of the evidence given orally before it. Such a practice is unnecessary for resolving a disputed point of law. *Irish Agricultural Machinery Ltd.* v. *Ó Culacháin*

(H.C.) [1987] I.R.458

22. —— **Trade of dealing in or developing land** — *Cost of acquiring interest in land — Merger of interests — Date for valuing land held as trading stock — Finance (Miscellaneous Provisions) Act,* 1968 (*No.* 7), *s.* 18.] C.D. Ltd. had two wholly owned subsidiaries, B.E. Ltd. and M.I. Ltd. In December of 1974 C.D. Ltd. acquired certain lands in fee simple. On the 23 May, 1975, it granted a 99 year lease of a portion of the lands (the "Corduff plot") to M.I. Ltd. at an annual rent of £30,000. The market value of the rent reserved on that plot had been estimated to be £250,000. On the 28 May, 1975, M.I. Ltd. assigned the Corduff plot to B.E. Ltd. for £1,000. The day after that assignment C.D. Ltd. transferred the fee simple reversion to B.E. Ltd. for £75,000 with a declaration of merger. Purporting to rely on the provisions of s. 18 of the Finance (Miscellaneous Provisions) Act, 1968, B.E. Ltd. valued the Corduff plot at £326,000 in its accounts for the year ending 31 May, 1975. At all material times B.E. Ltd. carried on the trade of dealing in or developing land. The Appeal Commissioners held that it was permissible for the company to include the aggregate of the market value of the rent reserved (as estimated) the consideration paid for the assignment of the lease and the consideration paid for the transfer of the fee simple reversion as being the cost of the acquisition of the interest held by B.E. Ltd. at the 31 May, 1975. On appeal by the appellant it was **Held** by Carroll J., in allowing the appeal, 1, that the Appeal Commissioners had erred in law in holding that the value of the lands at Corduff included the estimated market value of

REVENUE—Corporation Tax.

the rent reserved under the lease. 2. That the formula in s. 18 of the Act for valuing interests in land is relevant only for the purpose of computing the profits and gains of a business of dealing in or developing land. It is applied to any interest in land held by a trader on the date on which the calculations of profits and gains fall to be made. In this case the relevant date was the 31 May, 1975, and the formula could only be applied to interests which actually existed on that date. 3. That the only interest in land held by the trader on the relevant date was the unencumbered fee simple. The cost of acquiring this was the aggregate of the cost of acquiring the fee simple reversion and the cost of acquiring the term of years. *O'Connlain* v. *Belvedere Estates Ltd.*

(H.C.) [1985] I.R.22

23. —— **Trade of dealing in or developing land** — *Profits or gains — Leasehold interest acquired without payment of fine — Interest assigned during accounting period — Calculation of profit or loss — Ordinary principles of commercial accounting — Whether ordinary principles superseded by statutory provisions — Finance (Miscellaneous Provisions) Act,* 1968 (*No.* 7), *s.* 18.] Section 18 of the Finance (Miscellaneous Provisions) Act, 1968, provides for the calculation of profits or gains for the purpose of Case 1 of Schedule D for a trade of dealing in or developing land. The respondent was engaged in a trade of dealing in or developing land. During the accounting period for the 12 months ended 31 December, 1975, the respondent acquired a 34 year lease of certain property which it then assigned for £100. No fine was payable on the acquisition of the lease. The rent reserved under the lease was the sum of £2,500 per annum. Purporting to rely on the provisions of s. 18 of the Act of 1968, the respondent valued the cost of acquisition of the lease at £25,000 (being ten times the rent reserved) and, having deducted the assignment proceeds of £100, claimed to have suffered a loss of £24,900. The appellant rejected the respondent's calculation of profits and argued that the ordinary principles of commercial accounting applied and, accordingly, that no loss had been suffered in the transaction. The matter came before the Circuit Court and the court adopted the respondent's calculation and held that the loss claimed was provided for by s. 18 of the Act of 1968. On the application of the appellant the Circuit Court judge stated a case for the opinion of the High Court as to whether he was correct in his finding. **Held** by Finlay P. in answering the case stated and reversing the finding of the Circuit Court, 1, that the ordinary principles of commercial accounting demanded that the profits of an accounting period consisted

REVENUE—*continued.*

of the difference between the receipts of the accounting period and the expenditure laid out to earn those receipts. These principles were applicable to calculate the profits of a trade for tax purposes subject to the express prohibitions contained in the relevant statutes. *Dicta* of Lord President Clyde in *Whimster and Co.* v. *Commissioners of Inland Revenue* (1925) 12 T.C. 813 and Pennycuick V.C. in *Odeon Assoc. Theatres* v. *Jones* [1971] 1 W.L.R. 442 applied. 2. That the valuation method laid down in s. 18 of the Act of 1968 only applied to circumstances specified in the section. Those circumstances did not arise in relation to the dealings of the taxpayer, and, accordingly, the ordinary principles of commercial accounting applied. On appeal by the respondent it was **Held** by the Supreme Court, in dismissing the appeal, 1, that the profits of a trade or business for tax purposes are those calculated by means of ordinary methods of commercial accounting as modified by legislation. *Dicta* of Lord President Clyde in *Whimster and Co.* v. *Commissioners of Inland Revenue* (1925) 12 T.C. 813 and Pennycuick V.C.in *Odeon Assoc. Theatres* v. *Jones* [1971] 1 W.L.R. 442 applied. 2. That where stock is bought and sold within an accounting period there is no question of valuing the stock within the period. In order to arrive at a true assessment of the profits gained by the trading in land it is therefore not necessary to have regard to the method of valuation provided for by section 18. *Per curiam* the court cannot construe a statute in the light of amendments subsequently made. Such amendments can, at best, only be neutral as they may have been made for any one of a variety of reasons. It is for the courts to construe a statute and that construction cannot be influenced by the subsequent interpretation by the Oireachtas. *Cronin* v. *Cork and County Property Company Ltd.*

(H.C., S.C.) [1986] I.R.559

24. —— **Training grants** — *Whether capital or revenue receipts — Industrial Development Act,* 1969 (*No.* 32), *s.* 39.] The appellant company, an international engineering business, had obtained grants from the Industrial Development Authority under a scheme established by s. 39 of the Industrial Development Act, 1969. The grants were for "the training . . . of persons in the process of an industrial undertaking." The company regarded these grants as capital payments in aid of its establishing a venture in Ireland. The respondent inspector of taxes contended that the payments should have appeared in the trading accounts, where their inclusion would have increased the profits subject to corporation tax. In the High Court, to which the matter came by way of case stated, Keane J. found in favour of

the company. From this judgment the respondent inspector appealed to the Supreme Court. **Held** by the Supreme Court (*per* Hederman J., Henchy and McCarthy JJ. concurring), allowing the appeal and restoring the assessments made by the inspector that, 1, the training grants were revenue payments. 2. The status of a payment is determined by its true nature, regardless of the intention of the payor or the mode of application by the payee. 3. The grants did not influence the capital position of the company but affected its trading position palpably and directly. *Jacob International Ltd. Inc.* v. *Ó Cléirigh*
(S.C.) [1985] ILRM 651

DISCLOSURE OF INFORMATION

25. —— **Accountants** — *Statutory notice served on firm of accountants — Obligation to supply information sought — Transactions occurring before enactment of legislation authorising notice — Validity of notice — Whether notice unduly burdensome and oppressive — Finance Act,* 1974 (*No.* 27), *ss.* 57-60.] Chapter IV of the first part of the Finance Act, 1974, contains certain provisions designed to deal with attempts to avoid liability to taxation. In particular, ss. 59-60 of the Act contain measures designed to deal with the transferring by individuals of assets out of the jurisdiction for the purposes of avoiding taxation. Section 59 empowers the Revenue Commissioners to seek information concerning transactions carried out in connection with the transfer of assets abroad. In August, 1976, a duly authorised officer of the Revenue Commissioners served a notice on the plaintiffs pursuant to s. 59, requiring the plaintiffs, a large accountancy firm, to provide details of all transactions which they had advised on or been involved in between 1970 and 1976, inclusive, which concerned the transfer by individuals of assets out of the jurisdiction to ten specified territories. The plaintiffs sought a declaration that the notice issued by the defendants was invalid on the grounds that it was *ultra vires* the legislation in seeking details of transactions occurring before the Act of 1974 came into force and that it was unduly burdensome and oppressive. **Held** by Costello J., in dismissing the plaintiffs' claim, 1, that s. 57 of the Act of 1974 imposed taxation from 6 April, 1974, onwards in connection with the transfer of assets and associated operations irrespective of whether these transactions took place before or after that date. The defendants were empowered by s. 59 to seek information regarding all transactions affected by section 57. That information could be sought from any person, including a taxpayer's accountant. Accordingly, the notice was not *ultra vires*. 2. That s. 88 of the Act of 1974, which

provided that the Act came into force in 1974, did not exclude the right of the defendants to do what they were expressly empowered to do by ss. 57 to 60. *Dictum* of O'Higgins C.J. in *Dunne* v. *Hamilton* [1982] I.R. 466 applied. 3. That the court had jurisdiction to declare such a notice invalid if it sought particulars which went substantially beyond those required for the purposes of the legislation and the notice as a result could properly be regarded as oppressive and burdensome. 4. That since the transactions referred to in the notice were ones which could give rise to liability to taxation under s. 57, the information sought was necessary for the purposes of the legislation. 5. That once it was established that the notice was not *ultra vires* and that the information sought was reasonably necessary for the purposes of the legislation, the notice was not rendered invalid by virtue of the fact that, as a large firm of accountants, the plaintiffs would incur more trouble and expense than a smaller firm would. *Warnock* v. *Revenue Commissioners*
(H.C.) [1985] I.R.663; [1986] ILRM 37

26. —— **Banker** — *Order directing financial institution to furnish information concerning taxpayer's accounts — Statutory condition precedent — Demand that taxpayer deliver a statement of profits or gains or a return of income — Burden of proving compliance with condition precedent — Failure to prove demand — Extent of information properly the subject of an order — Statute — Interpretation — "Full particulars of accounts" — "Bankers' books" — Bankers' Books Evidence Act,* 1879 (*c.* 11), *s.* 9 — *Bankers' Books Evidence (Amendment) Act,* 1959 (*No.* 21), *s.* 2 — *Income Tax Act,* 1967 (*No.* 6), *ss.* 169, 172, 174 — *Finance Act,* 1983 (*No.* 15), *s.* 18.] The applicant inspector of taxes applied to the High Court for an order pursuant to s. 18 of the Finance Act, 1983, directing the second respondent ("the bank") to furnish full particulars of all accounts maintained with the bank by the first respondent ("the taxpayer") as well as other information relating to the financial transactions of the taxpayer. The uncontroverted evidence of the applicant was that the taxpayer had failed to make returns of income for over 10 years, had failed to keep proper accounting records, had mislaid his banking records and had been very uncooperative with the revenue authorities. The taxpayer resisted the application arguing that it was a condition precedent to the right to relief under s. 18, that he should have been duly required by an inspector of taxes to deliver either a statement of profits or gains or a return of income and that the applicant had not shown that this had been fulfilled. **Held** by Murphy J., in refusing the relief sought, 1, that it was a condition precedent to the right to apply for an order that the taxpayer

should have been duly required to deliver either a statement of profits or gains or a return of income and that he should have failed to do so; alternatively, that a statement of profits or gains or a return of income should have been delivered, with which the inspector of taxes was not satisfied. 2. That the burden of proof on the applicant was no greater than that applicable in an ordinary civil case. 3. That a request to submit accounts, pursuant to s. 174 of the Income Tax Act, 1967, could not be interpreted as a request to deliver a statement of profits or gains or a return of income. 4. That, there being no evidence of compliance with the statutory condition precedent, the application should be refused. *Semble,* that the words "full particulars of all accounts" cover only the name of the account holder, the nature of the account and the dates upon which it was opened or closed and in particular do not cover particulars of transactions of any account. *Semble,* that the information that may be specified in an order is confined to information which is both recorded in the books of the financial institution and which would be material in determining the correctness or otherwise of any statement or returns made. *Semble,* that the words "bankers' books" do not extend to files of correspondence or to documents which are in no sense books, either in their present method of presentation or in the form in which they originally evolved. *Reg.* v. *Jones* [1978] 1 W.L.R. 195, considered. On appeal by the applicant it was **Held** by the Supreme Court (Finlay C.J., Henchy, Griffin, Hederman and McCarthy JJ.), in disallowing the appeal, 1, that the section must be construed as containing a precondition that the taxpayer has been duly required to deliver a statement of profits or gains or a return of income and that this requirement applies both in the case of a failure to deliver and to the delivery of a statement or return with which the inspector of taxes is not satisfied. 2. That the burden of proof on the applicant was that appropriate in a civil case, proof as a matter of probability. 3. That it could not be inferred, either from the fact that a notice requiring accounts had been served, or from the taxpayer's general conduct, that he had been duly requested to make a statement or return. 4. That the applicant had failed to establish, according to a proper standard of proof, that the precondition had been satisfied. *O'C.(J.B.)* v. *D.(P.C.).*

(H.C., S.C.) [1985] I.R.265; [1985] ILRM 123

INCOME TAX

27. —— **Assessment** — *Estate of deceased person — Income accruing to the estate — Liability of executor to income tax — Whether executor the person "receiving or entitled to the income" —*

Income Tax Act, 1967 (*No.* 6), *ss.* 105, 208, 211, 213 — *Succession Act,* 1965 (*No.* 27), *s.* 10(3).] Section 105 of the Income Tax Act, 1967, provides that tax under Schedule D of the income tax code is assessable on and payable by the "person or body of persons receiving or entitled to the income" which is taxable under Schedule D. The respondent was the executor of the estate of the late F.D. from June, 1974 to January, 1981. The appellant raised assessments on the respondent for the years 1974/75 to 1980/81 in respect of income accruing to the estate in the administration period. The assessments were appealed to an Appeal Commissioner and he upheld them. The respondent appealed that decision to the Circuit Court. The Circuit Court judge reversed the Commissioner's ruling, and held that the Income Tax Act, 1967, did not impose a charge to tax on the executor in respect of the income it received during the administration. On appeal to the High Court, it was **Held** by Keane J., in allowing the appeal, 1, that while the estate of a deceased person is being administered the income of the estate is that of the personal representatives. *Dictum* of Viscount Finlay in *Barnardo's Homes* v. *Special Income Tax Commrs.* [1921] 2 A.C. 1 applied. 2. That neither the Administration of Estates Act, 1959, nor the Succession Act, 1965, had altered the law under which the executor of the estate of a deceased person was, during the administration period, the person "receiving or entitled to the income" of the estate within the meaning of s. 105 of the Income Tax Act, 1967, and its statutory predecessors. 3. That accordingly, by virtue of s. 105 of the Income Tax Act ,1967, the respondent, as executor of the estate of a deceased person, was chargeable to tax in respect of the income accruing to the estate received by it in the course of the administration. *Dictum* of Viscount Cave in *Williams* v. *Singer* [1921] 1 A.C. 65 approved. *Reid's Trustees* v. *C.I.R.* (1929) 14 T.C. 512 approved. *Moloney* v. *Allied Irish Banks Ltd.*

(H.C.) [1986] I.R.67

28. —— **Capital expenditure** — *Plant — Allowance for wear and tear — Lease by partnership of plant to hotel — Burden of wear and tear falling upon lessor — Allowance exceeding leading income — Partner claiming share of allowance — Whether partnership existed as a matter of law — Whether partnership carrying on business with a view to profit — Whether court bound by findings of fact of Appeal Commissioner — Limited Partnerships Act,* 1907 (*c.* 24), *ss.* 4, 5, 8 — *Income Tax Act,* 1967 (*No.* 6), *ss.* 241(5), 252, 282, 296, 307, 428.] Section 241, sub-s. 5, of the Income Tax Act, 1967, provides *inter alia* that where machinery or plant is let

REVENUE—Income Tax.

upon such terms that the burden of the wear and tear thereof falls directly on the lessor, he should be entitled to an allowance on account of the wear and tear equal to the amount which might have been allowed if, during the period of the letting, the machinery or plant were in use for the purposes of a trade, profession, employment or office carried on or held by him. The respondent tax-payer, a practising solicitor, was a partner in a partnership which was registered under the Limited Partnerships Act, 1907. The partnership business, *inter alia,* consisted of the leasing and providing of plant and equipment of all sorts. Plant was let to SMHC Limited, which company owned and operated an hotel, under a written leasing agreement in which the burden of wear and tear fell upon the lessor. The respondent was a director of SMHC Limited. The sum which could be claimed by the partnership as an initial allowance or under the heading of "wear and tear" exceeded the leasing income enuring for the benefit of the partnership. The respondent claimed a 15% share of the loss for the purpose of computing his own personal liability for tax and claimed to set off this sum against his income as a solicitor. The respondent appealed against a determination of the appellant, an inspector of taxes, refusing to allow relief in respect of the said loss. The Appeal Commissioner, however held that the loss was available to be set off by way of relief against the other income of the respondent but on the application of the appellant stated a case for the opinion of the High Court. **Held** by O'Hanlon J., in deciding that the determination of the Appeal Commissioner was correct in point of law, 1, the High Court was bound by the finding of the Appeal Commissioner that the respondent and his associates carried on business in partnership from the month of December, 1977, which involved a finding of fact by implication by the Appeal Commissioner that the parties carried on a business with a view to profit. This was a finding of primary fact and it could not be said that there was no evidence to support it or that the evidence was patently inadequate for this purpose. *Mara (Inspector of Taxes)* v. *Hummingbird Limited* [1982] ILRM 421, applied. 2. The scheme of the partnership was not of such extreme character as to convince the court that it should be regarded as having no commercial reality. The leasing of the plant could fairly be regarded as a trading transaction which qualified for the tax relief claimed by the respondent pursuant to s. 241, sub-s. 5, of the Income Tax Act, 1967. *Petrotim Securities Ltd.* v. *Ayres* [1964] 1 W.L.R. 190, considered. *MacCarthaigh* v. *Daly*

(H.C.) [1985] I.R.73; [1986] ILRM 116

29. —— **Capital expenditure** — *Plant — Allowance for wear and tear — Barrister's purchase of law books — Whether plant includes law books — Whether barrister entitled to such allowance — Statute — Interpretation — Plant — Income Tax Act,* 1967 (*No.* 6), *s.* 241.] Section 241, sub-s. 1, of the Income Tax Act, 1967, provides *inter alia* that, subject to the provisions of that Act, where a person carrying on a trade in any chargeable period has incurred capital expenditure on the provision of "machinery or plant" for the purposes of the trade, an allowance shall be made to him for that chargeable period on account of the wear and tear of any of the "machinery or plant" which belongs to him and is in use for the purposes of the trade at the end of that chargeable period or its basis period. Subsection 10 of s. 241 states that the preceding provisions of that section shall apply, with any necessary modifications, in relation to professions, employments and offices as they apply to trades. The respondent taxpayer was a barrister who had bought law books, consisting mainly of a complete set of Irish and English law reports, for the purposes of his practice and profession. The books had been kept in his private residence and had been used by him continually in his practice as a barrister since he had bought them. On appeal to the Appeal Commissioners, they decided that the law books bought by the respondent were "plant" within the meaning of s. 241, sub-s. 1, of the Act of 1967 and qualified for wear-and-tear allowance pursuant to that sub-section. At the request of the appellant, an inspector of taxes, the Appeal Commissioner stated a case for the opinion of the High Court asking whether they had been entitled so to decide. **Held** by McWilliam J. that the Appeal Commissioners were entitled to decide that the law books described in the case stated were "plant" used by the respondent in the practice of his profession as a barrister. *Daphne* v. *Shaw* (1926) 11 T.C. 256; *Munby* v. *Furlong* [1977] Ch. 359 and *Inspector of Taxes* v. *Kiernan* [1981] I.R. 117 considered. *Breathnach* v. *McC.*

(H.C.) [1984] I.R.340; [1984] ILRM 679

30. —— **Cessation of profession** — *Outstanding fees paid after cessation — Fees remitted to an unconnected company at taxpayer's request — No consideration received by taxpayer in connection with fees paid to the company — Whether fees "received" by taxpayer — Finance Act,* 1970 (*No.* 14), *ss.* 20, 21.] The respondent practised as a barrister until he was appointed to the High Court Bench in January, 1973. In February, 1973, a company was incorporated, and all issued shares were held by relatives of the respondent. Following the cessation of practice, the respondent wrote to solicitors for whom he had done

REVENUE—Income Tax.

work and indicated that he did not wish to receive any fees in respect of that work, but that if the solicitors wished, they could pay the fees to the company; he returned cheques received and indicated that the solicitors might wish to pay the fees to the company instead; he retained some fees for State work and some small fees. Fees were paid to the company in accordance with the respondent's direction. The sums received by the company were treated as part of its capital reserve. The respondent held no interest in the company whatsoever. No consideration was received by him or on his behalf in connection with the receipt by the company of the fees. It was the respondent's intention that the company should receive the sums for its absolute use and benefit and should not hold them on any trust on his behalf. The respondent was assessed to income tax pursuant to s. 20 of the Finance Act, 1970, in respect of the fees received by the company. Section 20 provides, *inter alia,* that sums payable in respect of professional services which are "received" after the permanent discontinuance of a profession shall be charged to tax under Case IV. The assessment was discharged by the Appeal Commissioner and his decision was upheld by the Circuit Court. On appeal by way of case stated, it was **Held** by Barrington J., in allowing the appeal, 1, that the mere fact that a taxpayer does not apply his income for his own benefit does not excuse him from paying tax on it. When sums are placed at a taxpayer's disposal and they are in fact disposed of by him they are to be treated for the purposes of the Income Tax Acts as having been received by him. *Dictum* of Lord Hanworth M.R., in *Dewar* v. *C.I.R.* [1935] 2 K.B. 351 applied. *Dolan* v. *"K."* [1944] I.R. 470 followed. 2. That where a solicitor has been put in funds to pay counsel's fees, it is the duty of the solicitor to discharge those fees unless counsel waives them, in which case it would be the solicitor's duty to return the fees. Where a solicitor has discharged counsel's fees without being put in funds by the client, the solicitor looks to the client to reimburse him. The respondent did not waive his fees, but gave the solicitors a general licence to dispose of fees which would otherwise be payable to him together with a reference to a specific method of disposition which the respondent would find acceptable. Under these circumstances, notwithstanding the strict canons of literal interpretation applicable to revenue statutes, it would be unreal to suggest that the sums at issue were not "received" by the respondent within the meaning of section 20. *Per* Barrington J., it is a general principle in the construction of revenue statutes that to be liable to tax the citizen must come clearly within the words of the charge to tax. On the other hand,

REVENUE—*continued.*

once within the scope and terms of the charge to tax, he cannot escape unless clearly within the terms of an exemption. There is no rule of law against the citizen making genuine and lawful arrangements of his affairs by which the incidence of tax on his property is lessened. In the construction of a Taxing Act the court has primary regard to the statutory words themselves and to their proper judicial construction. Particular words must be construed in their context. Taxing Acts are to be construed strictly, in the sense that one has to look merely at what was clearly said, there being no room for any intendment, but a fair and reasonable construction must be given to the language without leaning to one side or the other. Whether applying the terms of the charge or the terms of the exemption, no considerations of equity or hardship affect the construction of the Act. *Ó Coindealbháin* v. *Gannon*

(H.C.) [1986] I.R.154

31. —— **Deductions** — *Expenses of management — Auctioneer's commission and solicitor's costs — Whether expense of a capital nature — Income Tax Act,* 1967 (*No.* 6), *ss.* 81(5)(*d*), 81(6)(*a*)(*i*) — *Finance Act,* 1969 (*No.* 21), *s.* 22.] In calculating the appellant's liability to tax under case V of schedule D in respect of rental income received by them under a lease, the Revenue did not allow as deductions, auctioneer's commission and solicitor's costs incurred by the appellant in negotiating the lease, on the ground that they were expenses of a capital nature. The Circuit Court held in favour of the Revenue on the ground that, the expenditure could not be said to constitute costs of management within the meaning of s. 81(5)(*d*) of the Income Tax Act, 1967 (as substituted by s. 22 of the Finance Act, 1969) and was not therefore an authorised deduction. The premises in question had been built and were owned by the appellant. A case was stated for the opinion of the High Court as to whether the determination of the President of the Circuit Court was correct. **Held** by McWilliam J. in deciding that the President of the Circuit Court was not correct. The capital asset of the appellant consisted of the premises known as Stephen Court and the business of the company was both the letting of the premises and the collection of the rent reserved under the lease. The auctioneer's commission and the solicitor's costs could not be said to be expenses of a capital nature in that they were incurred for the creation of a capital asset, namely the lease, since this would in effect mean that the capital asset of the appellant was some sort of landlord's interest in the lease divorced from the ownership of the premises. Similarly it was correct for the respondent to argue

REVENUE—Income Tax.

that the business of the appellant consisted solely in the collection of the rent. It followed that the expenses of negotiating the lease and preparing the necessary documents were expenses of management within the meaning of s. 81(5)(*d*) of the Income Tax Act, 1967, and so were an authorised deduction in calculating the appellant's profits. *Stephen Court Ltd.* v. *Browne*

(H.C.) [1984] ILRM 231

32. —— **Deductions** — *Travelling expenses — Holder of an office — Tax payer incurring incidental expenses — Whether deduction could be allowed — Whether necessary for taxpayer to establish that he was necessarily obliged to incur these expenses — Income Tax Act,* 1967 (*No.* 6), *2nd Sched., para.* 3.] Par. (3) of the second schedule to the Income Tax Act, 1967, provides: "If a holder of an office or employment of profits is necessarily obliged to incur and defray out of the emoluments thereof the expenses of travelling in the performance of the duties of the office or employment, or of keeping and maintaining a horse to enable him to perform the same, or otherwise to expend money wholly, exclusively, and necessarily in the performance of the said duties, there may be deducted from the emoluments to be assessed the expenses so necessarily incurred and defrayed." The respondent was a director of nine companies for which he travelled extensively. Of these nine companies this case was only concerned with the emoluments from five Irish companies. All the companies paid his expenses except minor additional expenses which he estimated came to the sum of £750 which he did not claim for from the companies due to the difficulty he alleged of keeping records and apportioning the amounts between the companies. The Appeal Commissioner estimated that one third of these incidental expenses would have been incurred on behalf of the five companies in question and allowed a deduction of £250. The Appeal Commissioner then at the request of the Inspector of Taxes, the appellant, stated a case to the High Court to determine whether a deduction of £250 in respect of expenses could be allowed under par. (3) of the second schedule of the Income Tax Act, 1967. **Held** by McWilliam J. in answering the question in the case stated in the negative: There was insufficient evidence before the Appeal Commissioner by which he could make a deduction of any of these incidental expenses as the respondent has failed to establish that he was necessarily obliged to incur these expenses out of his emoluments in accordance with par. (3) of the second schedule of the Income Tax Act, 1967. *MacDaibheid* v. *Carroll*

(H.C.) [1978] ILRM 14

33. —— **Double taxation relief** — *Interest paid*

REVENUE—*continued.*

by Irish company on loan from Japanese parent company — Assessment to income tax on interest payments — Whether chargeable under Schedule D or Schedule F — "Distribution" — Double taxation relief convention — Whether conflict between convention and subsequent domestic statute — Double Taxation Relief (Taxes on Income) (Japan) Order, 1974 (*S.I. No.* 259) — *Corporation Tax Act,* 1976 (*No.* 7), *ss.* 83, 84, 151.] In the year of assessment 1979/80 the respondent, an Irish company, paid to its Japanese parent a sum of money in respect of interest on a loan from the parent. The appellant Inspector of Taxes sought to charge the respondent to income tax on those payments under Schedule D of the Income Tax Act, 1967, at the rate of 10% prescribed by art. 12, para. 2 of the Double Taxation Relief (Taxes on Income) (Japan) Order, 1974. The respondent argued, and the Appeal Commissioners decided, that the interest payment was not chargeable under Schedule D but was a distribution within the meaning of s. 84, sub-s. 2, para. (*d*)(iv) of the Corporation Tax Act, 1976, and accordingly, was chargeable under Schedule F. On the application of the appellant the Appeal Commissioners stated a case to the High Court as to whether they had been correct in so deciding. O'Hanlon J. affirmed the decision of the Appeal Commissioners (see [1985] I.R. 509) and the appellant appealed to the Supreme Court. The appellant argued that ss. 83 and 84 of the Act of 1976, relating to Schedule F and company distributions, were in conflict with the provisions of the Convention between Ireland and Japan for the Avoidance of Double Taxation, 1974; and, accordingly (it having been conceded on behalf of the respondent that in case of any such conflict the provisions of the Convention must prevail) that the payments by the respondent were chargeable under the law as it had stood prior to the passing of the Act of 1976. **Held** by the Supreme Court (Henchy, Griffin and Hederman JJ.), in dismissing the appeal, 1, that the payment of interest by the respondent to its Japanese parent was a "distribution" within the meaning of s. 84, sub-s. 2, para. (*d*)(iv) of the Act of 1976 and fell to be dealt with under art. 12 of the Convention. 2. That art. 12 of the Convention between Ireland and Japan for the Avoidance of Double Taxation did not impose a tax on payments of interest but merely set an upper limit on the tax which might be charged by either of the contracting states. Accordingly there was no conflict between the Convention and the Act of 1976. Decision of the High Court (O'Hanlon J.) [1985] I.R. 509 upheld. *Murphy* v. *Asahi Synthetic Fibres (Ireland) Ltd.*

(S.C.) [1986] I.R.777; (H.C.) [1985] I.R. 509; [1986] ILRM 24

REVENUE—Income Tax.

34. —— **Exemption** — *Artistic work — Exemption from tax for income arising from certain artistic work — Work to be "original and creative" — Appellant granted exemptions in respect of earlier works — Other works of similar nature subsequently published — Exemption not granted for later works — Whether later works "original and creative" — Finance Act,* 1969 (*No.* 21), *s.* 2.] Section 2 of the Finance Act, 1969, provides that the earnings of an individual arising from original and creative works produced by the individual which are, in the opinion of the Revenue Commissioners, of cultural or artistic merit, are exempt from tax. The appellant was a journalist who wrote a series of articles which were published in a daily newspaper and subsequently collected together and published as a book. In 1970 the appellant was exempted from income tax under the provisions of s. 2 on the profits arising to him from the sale of the book. Further exemptions were granted to him for earnings from the articles published in the newspaper. In March, 1976, the respondent advised the appellant that the exemption for the earnings from the newspaper articles would not be granted for the tax years 1974/75 and 1975/76. The appellant appealed against the determination of the respondent but his appeal was dismissed by the Appeal Commissioners and, upon his further appeal, by the Circuit Court. On the application of the appellant, the Circuit Court judge stated a case for the opinion of the High Court. **Held** by Barrington J., in dismissing the appeal by way of case stated, 1, that a work could be "original and creative", being the work of the author's brain or imagination and not a copy, and still not be within the meaning of s. 2 of the Finance Act, 1969. 2. That in determining whether a work is "original and creative" within the meaning of s. 2 of the Act of 1969, it might be helpful to enquire whether the work is recognisable as a work of art; however this test did not necessarily apply in all cases. 3. That, notwithstanding the fact that the case stated concerned the nature and quality of the appellant's work, the High Court was not in a position to reconsider the appellant's works and come to findings of fact which differed from those of the Circuit Court since that court, in addition to seeing the works of the appellant, had heard evidence from expert witnesses concerning the works. Accordingly the findings of fact of the Circuit Court were binding on the High Court. *Mara* v. *Hummingbird Limited* [1982] ILRM 421 followed. *Healy* v. *Breathnach*

(H.C.) [1986] I.R.105

35. —— **Exemption** — *Club to promote athletic sport — Whether legitimate avoidance of*

REVENUE—*continued.*

payment of tax — Funds provided by one person — Total control in two trustees — Whether two persons can constitute a "body of persons" — Income Tax Act, 1967 (*No.* 6), *ss.* 1(1), 349.] The defendants, a solicitor and an accountant, founded an athletic club, the membership of which they controlled. Vaunting the name "Club 349", the club was designed to reap the benefits of s. 349 of the Income Tax Act, 1967, which provides that "exemption shall be granted from income tax in respect of so much of the income of any 'body of persons' established for the sole purpose of promoting athletic or amateur games or sports as is shown to the satisfaction of the Revenue Commissioners to be income which has been or will be applied to that purpose." The defendants asserted that they had lent £30,000 to Club 349 (of which they were the trustees) to the intent that the club would have income from the interest on that money. The Revenue Comissioners denied that Club 349 was *bona fide* an athletic club and sought to tax the interest. The Appeal Commissioners ruled in favour of the defendants, but their finding was upset in the High Court by McWilliam J., whose judgment is reported at [1983] ILRM 34. McWilliam J., interpreting s. 1(1) of the Income Tax Act, 1967, ruled that the members of Club 349 did not constitute a "body of persons" within the language of s. 349. The term "body of persons" is defined in the Act as "any body politic, corporate or collegiate, and any company, fraternity, fellowship and society of persons, whether corporate or not corporate." The defendants appealed. **Held** by the Supreme Court upholding the decision of McWilliam J. (by Henchy and Griffin JJ.) that a club of two effective persons did not have the degree of plurality encompassed by the term "body of persons." A summary of the facts and a survey of the history of tax exemption for athletic clubs are contained in the dissenting judgment of McCarthy J. *Revenue Commissioners* v. *O'R.*

(S.C.) [1984] ILRM 406

36. —— **Exemption** — *Farming — Animal husbandry — Partnership — Fattening of pigs in purpose-built housing — Whether constitutes farming — Whether exempt from taxation — Whether trade or profession — Finance Act,* 1974 (*No.* 27), *s.* 13(1), (3) — *Finance Act,* 1969 (*No.* 21), *s.* 18(1).] The second to fourth appellants were a partnership which carried on the business of pig farming on nine acres of land and appealed against determinations of partnership profits and against assessments under Case 1 Schedule D of the Income Tax Act, 1967. The pigs were fattened in piggeries which had been erected on the

REVENUE—Income Tax.

land and supplied to a bacon factory owned by a limited liability company in which the appellants held 87% of the issued share capital. They argued that the business carried on by the partnership was farming as defined in s. 13(1) of the Finance Act, 1974 (incorporating s. 18(1) of the Finance Act, 1969) and accordingly that the profits were exempt from taxation. The respondent contended that the trade carried on by the partnership was a trade for the purpose of Schedule D and not exempt from taxation. The Appeal Commissioners held, *inter alia,* that the definition of "husbandry" in s. 13(1) of the Finance Act, 1974, could not reasonably be applied to the enterprise carried on by the partnership and, in the absence of accounts, confirmed the determinations made by the respondent but stated a case for the opinion of the High Court as to whether their decision was correct in law. **Held** by Barrington J. in holding that the determination of the Appeal Commissioners was not correct in law, 1, since the tillage of the soil and rearing and management of livestock for food came within the primary meaning of the word "husbandry", which presupposes a connection with land and production of crops or food in some shape, the activity in which the appellants were engaged was husbandry within s. 13(1) of the 1974 Act. *Dicta* in *In re Cavan Central Co-Operative Society Ltd.* [1917] 2 I.R. 594 applied; *Revenue Commissioners* v. *N.* 101 I.L.T.R. 196 discussed; *Jones* v. *Nuttall* (1926) 10 T.C. 346 not followed. 2. The appellants, in using the land for the purposes of rearing and fattening pigs and generally looking after their health and welfare, were farming the lands within the meaning of s. 13(1) and if it was sought to capture the profits from this farm as farming under Schedule D of the 1967 Act, this should be done by appropriate legislation. 3. The enterprise carried on by the appellants could not be excluded from the category of "farming" merely because one third of the land was covered by buildings purposely built by them for their enterprise, since the proviso in s. 13(3) of the Finance Act, 1974, providing that the rateable valuation of buildings on the land was to be excluded in calculating the rateable valuation of farm land for the purposes of that Chapter meant that the buildings would be included for purposes other than the calculation of the rateable valuation. *Knockhall Piggeries* v. *Kerrane*

(H.C.) [1985] ILRM 655

37. —— **Penalties** — *Employer — Failure to make returns — Prosecution by Director of Public Prosecutions* — Vires — *Whether D.P.P. empowered to bring proceedings — Whether civil liability or criminal offence — Income Tax Act,* 1967 (*No.* 6), *s.* 128.] Section128 of the Income Tax Act, 1967, in imposing a fixed penalty for non-compliance with statutory obligations creates a civil liability enforceable by civil proceedings and accordingly is not an offence capable of being prosecuted by the Director of Public Prosecutions. So **held** by Barr J. *McLoughlin* v. *Tuite* [1986] I.R. 235 applied. *Downes* v. *Director of Public Prosecutions*

(H.C.) [1987] I.R.139; [1987] ILRM 665

38. —— **Returns** — *Employer's annual obligation to provide information relating to employees — Social welfare and income tax codes — Fishing vessel owned and operated by skipper — Crew engaged prior to each voyage — Remuneration based on value of catch — Whether employment or partnership in existence — Whether skipper an employer — Income Tax (Employments) Regulations,* 1960 (*S.I. No.* 28) — *Social Welfare (Collection of Employment Contributions by The Collector General) Regulations,* 1979 (*S.I. No.* 77) — *Partnership Act,* 1890 (*c.* 39) — *Finance Act* (*No.* 2), 1959 (*No.* 42) — *Income Tax Act,* 1967 (*No.* 6).] Employers are required under the social welfare and income tax codes to make annual returns to the Revenue Commissioners. The returns provide details of emoluments paid to and deductions withheld from employees. Failure to make the requisite returns is an offence. The defendant was the owner and skipper of a fishing trawler. The vessel normally carried a crew of five. The members were engaged by the defendant prior to each expedition. Crew members tended to turn up regularly, but there was no contract between the defendant and the other crew members that they would be engaged after the end of an expedition. No member of the crew was paid a wage for the services he rendered on any voyage. Remuneration was agreed after the end of each voyage and was based solely on the value of the catch; the rate of remuneration of each crew member was determined by custom and by the crew members in consultation with the defendant. The defendant was prosecuted by the complainants for failing to make the requisite returns. Having heard the evidence, the District Justice stated a case for the opinion of the High Court as to whether a contract of employment existed between the defendant and the other members of the crew. **Held** by Costello J., in answering the case stated, 1, that a partnership relationship rather than an employer-employee relationship existed between the defendant and the other members of the crew. 2. That, accordingly, the defendant was not guilty of the offence charged. *Director of Public Prosecutions* v. *McLoughlin*

(H.C.) [1986] I.R.355; [1986] ILRM 493

39. —— **Trading losses** — *Relief — Relief for*

REVENUE—Income Tax.

interest paid on loans to acquire shares — Income — Meaning of "income" — Income Tax Act, 1967 (*No.* 6) — *Finance Act,* 1976 (*No.* 27), *ss.* 33, 35.

Practice — Interest — Statutory jurisdiction to award interest — Case stated by Appeal Commissioners — Decision by High Court on interpretation of Income Tax Acts — Consequential order for repayment of overpaid tax — Order for payment of a sum of money — Whether court had jurisdiction to order payment of interest — Courts Act, 1981 (*No.* 11), *s.* 22.] Section 307 of the Income Tax Act, 1967, provides that a person may set off trading losses against other income and reduce the tax which would otherwise have been payable on that income or recover tax which has already been paid in respect thereof. Sections 33 and 35 of the Finance Act, 1974, provide relief to companies for interest on loans used to acquire shares in a connected company. The qualifying interest is treated as a charge on income and reduces the taxable income of the borrower. In the tax year 1975/76 the taxpayer suffered trading losses. It received a large dividend from a subsidiary from which tax at the standard rate was deducted on payment by the subsidiary. It paid interest to a Dutch company on money it had borrowed and applied to the purchase of shares in the subsidiary. Part of the interest paid was eligible for relief as a charge on income under ss. 33 and 35 of the Act of 1974. In calculating the taxpayer's relief under s. 307 of the Act of 1967, the inspector of taxes first deducted the charge from the income represented by the dividend, and allowed relief only in respect of that income reduced by the charge. On appeal, the Appeal Commissioners upheld the inspector's finding but agreed to state a case for the opinion of the High Court as to whether or not the word "income" in s. 307 of the Act of 1967 was to be interpreted as "income reduced by charges". **Held** by Costello J. in answering the question in the negative, 1, that there is nothing in the wording of s. 307 of the Income Tax Act, 1967, to show that the word "income" as used in the section should be interpreted as income after deductions. 2. The "income" in the sections of the income tax code dealing with assessment to tax means "gross income" except where express statutory authority exists to the contrary. *Commissioners of Inland Revenue* v. *Dalgety & Co.* [1930] 1 K.B. 1; *Inland Revenue Commissioners* v. *Frere* [1965] A.C. 402; *Lord Chetwode* v. *Inland Revenue Commissioners* [1977] 1 W.L.R. 248 considered. 3. That, accordingly, the word "income" in s. 307, sub-s. 1, of the Act of 1967 does not mean income after deduction of charges. Having determined the case stated in the taxpayer's favour, Costello J. went on to order

REVENUE—*continued.*

the repayment of the tax overpaid by the taxpayer and to order the payment of interest on that sum pursuant to s. 22 of the Courts Act, 1981. The inspector appealed against the order for payment of interest on the ground that the jurisdiction to award interest under s. 22 of the Act of 1981 was predicated upon the existence of a cause of action *inter partes,* which did not exist in the instant case. **Held** by the Supreme Court (Walsh, Henchy and McCarthy JJ.), in dismissing the appeal, 1, that the case stated was a proceeding to which a state authority was a party and in which a court ordered the payment by a person of a sum of money, within the meaning of s. 22 of the Act of 1981. 2. Accordingly, that the High Court was entitled to order the payment of interest pursuant to s. 22 of the Courts Act, 1981. 3. That it was mere semantics to say that a claim by a taxpayer that he had been overcharged and had overpaid tax, however it was procedurally promoted, was not an action *inter partes. Navan Carpets Ltd.* v. *O Culachain*
(H.C., S.C.) [1988] I.R.164

40. —— **Trading profits** — *Deduction — Increase in stock values — Company having a number of activities — If all activities taken together, company not entitled to relief — Whether activities can be assessed separately — Whether decision one of fact — Finance Act,* 1975 (*No.* 6), *ss.* 31 (1), 31 (9) — *Finance Act,* 1977 (*No.* 18), *s.* 43.] The company carried on the business of millers, farm fertilisers, grinding corn, animal feed sales, hardware, furniture, furnishings, fancy goods, toys, china, wholesale grocers and publicans. Each of these activities was located in a separate place with separate entrances. Separate accounts were prepared for each activity and interdepartmental sales were invoiced from one department to another. Some of these activities were carried on in separate buildings and some, those of millers and hardware would, if taken on their own, each qualify for relief under s. 31 (1) and (9) of the Finance Act, 1975. If all the activities were taken together the company would not qualify for relief. The Circuit Court judge held that the company was carrying on one trade rather than several different trades and refused the relief sought. In a case stated to the High Court by the Circuit Court judge it was argued on behalf of the Revenue Commissioners: (i) that although a company may carry on two or more trades, the defendant company was carrying on one business which had been acquired when the company was formed; (ii) that there can only be a separate trade or business when a company takes on a new business; (iii) that the business of the company was one of selling goods as general merchants and that none of its activities could be segregated

REVENUE—Income Tax.

from the others; (iv) that the decision of the Circuit Court judge was one of fact which could not be disturbed on appeal. **Held** by McWilliam J. that the milling and public house operations constituted separate trades but in remitting the question of whether the hardware business was a separate trade, 1, a company may be held to carry on different trades for the purpose of tax. 2. It is a question of fact for the Circuit Court judge to decide whether a company is carrying on one or more than one trade, but the judge should have considered whether the company was carrying on a number of separate trades rather than whether one company was carrying on trade or business. *In re P. McElligott & Sons Ltd.*

(H.C.) [1985] ILRM 210

41. —— **Trading stock** — *Farm land — Formation of company — Company letting land to partners on conacre — Land zoned for development — Whether land trading stock of company — Finance (Miscellaneous Provisions) Act,* 1968 (*No.* 7), *s.* 17.] P.N. and J.M. entered into partnership in 1954 to purchase some acres of Scaldswood Farm in Blanchardstown for the purpose of development. At about the same time, they purchased two acres of land at Castleknock for the same purpose. A year later, they were afforded the opportunity of purchasing the remainder of Scaldswood Farm for the sum of £10,000, the vendor reserving for himself a right of residence. Upon advice, the partners formed a company in June, 1955, to own the land. The partners were equal shareholders in this company. In July the shareholders transferred the property at Castleknock to the company, which acquired adjoining lands in December and proceeded to develop both properties. In the same month, that part of Scaldswood Farm first acquired was transferred to the company, which developed part of it. The remainder was reconveyed to the shareholders in 1960. That portion of Scaldswood Farm which had been purchased for £10,000 was not conveyed to the company until 1956. The company's memorandum of association contained, as well as objects which might be described as building objects, a reference to farming and cultivating land. Although no farming was carried on directly by the company, the land was let to the two partners in conacre, and an uncle of one of them was hired to manage the farm. After a year, this activity was carried on at a loss. Up to 1966, the farm lands were unsuitable for development, due to a lack of services in the area, but in that year, following the publication of the Myles Wright Report, forty acres of Scaldswood Farm were zoned for development. In 1966, the company decided to exploit the development potential of the farm. Following advice, it went into voluntary liquidation, and the farm was sold to a new company formed for that purpose by P.N. and one other shareholder. The Appeal Commissioner stated a case to the High Court for a decision whether they were entitled to hold that Scaldswood Farm was never trading stock of a trade of dealing in or developing land carried on by the first company, or trading stock of a business which was deemed by s. 12 of the Finance (Miscellaneous Provisions) Act, 1968, to be such a trade. **Held** by McWilliam J. in finding that the Commissioners were not entitled so to hold, 1, the decision of the company in 1966 to exploit the development potential of Scaldswood Farm was consistent with the conclusion that the farm was appropriated as trading stock of the company at that date. 2. The decision to put the company into liquidation and form another company to carry out the work of development was merely the manner in which the company chose to carry out its development. *O hArgain* v. *Beechpark Estates Ltd.*

(H.C.) [1979] ILRM 57

STAMP DUTY

42. —— **Conveyance or transfer** — *Transferor entitled to residue of deceased's estate — Administration incomplete — Deed purported to make gift of lands, part of residue — Whether a "conveyance or transfer" of "any property" — Whether deed implemented disposition — Stamp Duty Act,* 1891, (*c.* 39), *ss.* 54, 62 — *Finance* (1909-1910) *Act,* 1910, (*c.* 8), *s.* 74.] By his will the testator, who died in 1981, left the residue of his estate to his son, George Berkeley. A very substantial portion of the residue consisted of lands, which had a market value of £100,000. Mrs. Berkeley, George's wife, took no benefit under the will. In 1982, before the administration of the testator's estate had been completed, a deed was executed, the operative part of which contained the following provisions: "1. The said [George Berkeley] hereby agrees to release an undivided one half share in the lands . . . to the said [Mrs. Berkeley]. 2. To fully effect the agreement contained in paragraph (*a*) herein [sic] the said [George Berkeley] hereby agrees to consent to any appropriation, effected by the personal representatives to fulfil the agreement contained in paragraph (*a*) herein. 3. It is hereby agreed and declared that the settlement under the will of the [testator] shall be read and construed as though the lands . . . had been devised equally to the said [George Berkeley] and [Mrs. Berkeley] as tenants in common share and share alike and not solely to the said [George Berkeley] . . . ." No assent, conveyance or transfer by the personal representatives to Mrs. Berkeley

REVENUE—Stamp Duty.

was made because the lands were sold to a third party in 1983. The Commissioners of Inland Revenue assessed stamp duty on the deed on the basis that it operated as a voluntary disposition of property worth £50,000. The appellants argued that the deed was not a conveyance or transfer within the meaning of section 74 of the Finance (1909-1910) Act, 1910. **Held,** that the deed executed in 1982 was not liable to stamp duty. In order for an instrument to be a conveyance or transfer within the meaning of section 74 of the 1910 Act, it must implement the disposition i.e. be the instrument chosen by the donor to complete the disposition in such a way as to show that he did not intend any other document to be executed. While the deed did transfer a property right to Mrs. Berkeley, viz. a chose in action consisting of the right to have the testator's estate properly administered, it was clear that the parties contemplated that a further document or documents would be executed by the personal representatives in order to achieve the object of the deed, namely to give Mrs. Berkeley a half share of the legal fee simple in the land. *Per curiam* If, instead of selling the lands, the personal representatives had assented to a half share in the lands being vested in Mrs. Berkeley, duty would have been payable on that assent. *Berkeley* v *Commissioners of Inland Revenue*

(Ch.D.) [1984] N.I.341

VALUE-ADDED TAX

43. —— **Exempted activities** — *"Credit card, charge card or similar card scheme" — Applicant's card scheme formally expressed to be applicant's purchase of cardholder's consumer debts to retailer — Debt factoring — Whether overall scheme a service supplied by applicant — Value-Added Tax (Exempted Activities) (No.* 1) *Order,* 1985 (*S.I. No.* 430) — *Value-Added Tax Act,* 1972 (*No.* 22), 1*st schedule.*] By ministerial order made under powers conferred by s. 6, sub-s. 2 of the Value-Added Tax Act, 1972, the second respondent inserted into the first schedule to the Act, specifying activities exempted from value-added tax ("V.A.T.") accountability, the following amendment:— "(xia) services supplied to a person under arrangements which provide for the reimbursement of the person in respect of the supply by him of goods or services in accordance with a credit card, charge card or similar card scheme." The first respondent by letter notified the applicant of its decision, in accordance with the said ministerial order, to deregister the applicant from V.A.T. accountability from the 19 December, 1985. The applicant objected that its scheme differed from a "credit card or charge

REVENUE—*continued.*

card" scheme in that it merely factored the consumer debts due to its associate retailers and did not extend credit or banking facilites to its cardholding club members and obtained in the High Court leave to apply for orders of judicial review against the respondents. The respondents filed grounds of opposition and on full hearing of the matter, it was **Held** by Johnson J., in refusing the orders sought, that upon construction of the particular scheme in practice, while each single agreement between the applicant and its associate retailer might be formally expressed to be the applicant's purchase of the cardholding consumer's debt to the retailer, the overall continuous effect was the applicant's supply of services under arrangements for payment to the retailer for supply by him of goods or services to cardholders in accordance with a card scheme, and the arrangements were accordingly exempted from V.A.T. by the ministerial order. *In re Charge Card Services Ltd.* [1987] 1 Ch. 150 considered. *Diners Club Ltd.* v. *Revenue Commissioners*

(H.C.) [1988] I.R.158

44. —— **"Fixtures"** — *Television aerials installed on the roofs of private houses — Value-Added Tax Act,* 1972 (*No.* 22), *s.* 10(8).] The applicant/appellant, whose trade was the erection of television aerials, sought from the Revenue Commissioners a determination that his work entailed the 'installation of fixtures' within the meaning of s. 10(8) of the Value Added Tax Act, 1972, and was, as such, liable to V.A.T. at the lower rate of 3% rather than at the higher rate of 16%. The matter came to the High Court by way of case stated from the President of the Circuit Court. **Held** by O'Hanlon J. that: the television aerials were fixtures (*a*) by reason of the substantial means used to secure them to premises, and (*b*) having regard to their purpose — that of ensuring successful reception on any television sets brought into the premises by their occupants. *Maye* v. *Revenue Commissioners*

(H.C.) [1986] ILRM 377

—— Arrears of tax — Collection after tax deduction unconstitutional.
see **Constitution,** 38

—— Capital gains tax — Compulsory acquisition — Compensation — Assessment — Lands — Tax on chargeable gain accruing on disposal of assets — Compensation assessable without regard to liability of landowner for tax on chargeable gain.
see **Compulsory Acquisition,** 1

—— Corporation tax — Appellate procedure —

RIGHTS AND FREEDOMS—*continued.*
see **Equality before the Law**

—— Right to fair procedures.
see **Fair Procedures**

—— Right to free legal aid.
see **Criminal Law,** 50

—— Right to free primary education.
see **Damages,** 1

—— Right to liberty.
see **Aliens,** 3, 4
Constitution, 15-17, 41
Special Criminal Court

—— Right to life of unborn — Pregnancy counselling services.
see **Constitution,** 20

—— Right to privacy.
see **Constitution,** 18, 39

—— Right to procreate.
see **Constitution,** 19

—— Right to property.
see **Constitution,** 13, 44-8, *and cross-references following* **Constitution**

—— Right to vote.
see **Constitution,** 36

—— Right to work.
see **Trade Union,** 2

RIVERS
see **Lakes and Rivers**

ROAD AUTHORITY — Non-feasance — Statutory provision effecting change in liability — Governmental order required to bring it into force — Whether mandamus lies against the Government.
see **Judicial Review,** 14

ROAD TRAFFIC
see also **Highway; Motor Insurance; Motor Vehicle; Road Traffic Accidents; Road Traffic Offences; Safety Belts**

—— Cattle straying onto main road — Whether cattle constituted a public nuisance — Whether owner had duty to prevent cattle straying onto public road.
see **Animals,** 2

ROAD TRAFFIC ACCIDENTS
see **Negligence,** 15, 27, 31

—— Contributory negligence — Failure to wear seat belt — Apportionment of fault.
see **Negligence,** 15

—— Personal injuries — Damages — Failure to wear seat belt — Proportion of fault appropriate — Factors to be considered in compensating victim.
see **Damages,** 11

—— Personal injuries — Damages.
see **Damages,** 8-12

—— Personal injuries — Regulations rendering victims of road accidents ineligible for free medical services — Validity.
see **Damages,** 9

ROAD TRAFFIC OFFENCES

Arrest. Nos. 1-6
Disqualification. No. 7
Driving while drunk. Nos. 1-6, 8-14
Motor vehicle — definition. No. 15
Parking. No. 16

ARREST — Legality

1. —— **Drunken driving** — *Conviction — Appeal — Whether gardai entitled to require accused to take a breath test, and subsequently arrest accused in a place that was not a public place — Road Traffic (Amendment) Act,* 1978 (*No.* 19), *ss.* 12, 49 (2), 49 (4) (*a*).] Two members of the Gardaí who were on foot patrol entered a private yard owned by the defendant for the purpose of examining a motor vehicle. While examining the vehicle they were approached by the defendant. Garda C. alleged that an offence had been committed in relation to the motor vehicle approximately 30 minutes earlier. The defendant admitted having driven the car at the relevant time. Garda C. noticed a strong smell of intoxicating liquor from the defendant's breath, that he was unsteady on his feet and incoherent. He formed the opinion that the defendant was unfit to drive a mechanically propelled vehicle due to having consumed an intoxicant and required him to take a breath test. It proved positive and they then arrested him. The defendant subsequently provided the Gardaí with a blood sample which showed a concentration of 197 milligrams of alcohol per 100 millitres of blood. The defendant was convicted in the District Court of an offence contrary to s. 49 (2) of Road Traffic Act, 1961, as amended by s. 10 of Road Traffic (Amendment) Act, 1978, fined £175, disqualified from driving for twelve months and his licence endorsed. The defendant

ROAD TRAFFIC OFFENCES—Arrest.

appealed against conviction and sentence to the Circuit Court which permitted a case stated to the Supreme Court on the question whether the Circuit Court judge was correct in deciding that he would dismiss the prosecution and allow the appeal on the ground that the Gardaí did not have power (i) to require the defendant to take a breath test on his private property and (ii) to arrest him on his private property. **Held** by the Supreme Court (O'Higgins C.J., Henchy and Hederman JJ.) in answering the questions in the affirmative, 1, a request by a member of the Gardaí to require any person to provide a specimen of his breath must be in a public place and that person must then be in charge of a mechanically propelled vehicle in such public place. S. 12 is limited to these powers. 2. The yard was private property and was not a public place. 3. At the time the request to take a breath test was made the defendant could not be said to be "in charge" of a motor vehicle in a public place. 4. The evidence on which the Gardaí relied for the purpose of arresting the accused was improperly obtained and tainted with illegality everything the Gardaí did thereafter, including arresting the accused. *Director of Public Prosecutions* v. *Joyce*

(S.C.) [1985] ILRM 206

2. —— **Drunken driving** — *Whether accused lawfully arrested — Whether necessary that accused be brought to Garda station as an arrested person — Road Traffic Act,* 1961 (*No.* 24), *ss.* 12, 49 (2), 49 (4) (*a*), 49 (6) — *Road Traffic (Amendment) Act,* 1978 (*No.* 19), *ss.* 10, 12 (3), 13 (1), 17 (1), 17 (4), 21, 23.] The defendant was apprehended by a Garda Síochána, who, having observed the defendant's driving and demeanour suspected that he had consumed excess alcohol. The defendant submitted to a breath alcoholiser test at the scene of driving, which proved positive. He agreed to accompany the garda to the police station voluntarily, where he was arrested under s. 49 (6) of the Road Traffic Act, 1961-1978. A blood sample was taken and the certificate of the Medical Bureau which issued showed a concentration of 183 milligrams per millilitre of blood. In the District Court it was contended on behalf of the defendant that since the defendant had not been arrested at the scene of driving, and brought under arrest to the garda station, the subsequent procedure under s. 13 (1) of the Road Traffic (Amendment) Act, 1978, was rendered invalid and illegal, and therefore the certificate of the Medical Bureau was not admissible in evidence. The relevant part of s. 13 (1) of the 1978 Act provides: "Where a person arrested under s. 49 (6) of the principal Act or s. 12 (3) has been brought to a garda station a member of the Garda Síochána may at his

ROAD TRAFFIC OFFENCES—*continued.*

discretion do either or both of the following: (*a*) Require the person to provide . . . a specimen of his breath; (*b*) Require the person either to permit a designated registered medical practitioner to take from the person a specimen of his blood or . . . urine." The submission on behalf of the defendant was that before a garda could lawfully make such a requirement, the case must be brought within the opening words of s. 13 (1). This submission was contested by the prosecution on the ground that even if there had been no arrest or an invalid procedure had been followed at the scene of driving, such invalidity had been cured at the garda station by formal arrest and because the remainder of the procedure leading to the issue of the certificate had been correctly followed. The District Justice, on his own motion, stated a case for the determination by the High Court on this issue. **Held** by Barrington J. that the certificate of the Medical Bureau was not admissible, 1, s. 13, in contrast with s. 17 of the 1978 Act (the procedure in the case of a person suspected of being drunk in charge of a mechanically propelled vehicle) specifically refers only to persons who have been brought to a garda station having been arrested either under s. 49 (6) or s. 13 (3). Under s. 17 a person may be required by a garda to accompany him to a garda station, but there is no statutory requirement for a preliminary arrest. 2. There was no question in this case of evidence having been obtained in breach of the defendant's constitutional or legal rights, but as s. 23 of the 1978 Act make *prima facie* evidence a certificate which without that express statutory requirement would not be evidence at all, the system presupposed that the appropriate legal procedure culminating in the issue of the certificate had been followed. Once it was shown that the correct procedure had not been followed, and that there was no power to require the defendant to furnish a blood specimen, then that certificate was not of a kind contemplated by s. 23 of the 1978 Act, and had no status as evidence in a court of law. *Director of Public Prosecutions* v. *Greeley*

(H.C.) [1985] ILRM 320

3. —— **Drunken driving** — *Arrest under statutory power — Whether removal to a second Garda station made arrest unlawful — Reason for removal — Carrying out of statutory procedures — Offences Against the State Act,* 1939 (*No.* 13) — *Interpretation Act,* 1937 (*No.* 38), *s. 11 (a)* — *Road Traffic (Amendment) Act,* 1978 (*No.* 19), *s.* 13.] The defendant was driving a motor car when he was stopped by a member of the Garda Síochána who formed the opinion that the defendant was incapable of having proper control

of the vehicle due to consumption of an intoxicant. The Garda arrested the defendant under s. 49 of the Road Traffic Act, 1961, and brought him to Rathkeale garda station to carry out the statutory tests and procedures but could not do so because the necessary equipment was unavailable at that time. The Garda then contacted the Askeaton Garda patrol car which conveyed both the defendant and arresting Garda to another garda station where procedures set out in the Road Traffic (Amendment) Act, 1978, were followed. The certificate from the medical bureau showed the defendant to be in excess of the lawful limit of blood alcohol. Following legal argument, the District Justice dismissed the summons on the ground that the defendant had been informed when arrested that he was being brought to a particular garda station and was in fact brought there and that there was no power to carry out the procedures in any other garda station. The Director of Public Prosecutions (D.P.P.) appealed by way of case stated to the High Court. **Held** by Lynch J. in holding that the District Justice was wrong in dismissing the summons, 1, if the defendant had been brought from one garda station to another in order to defeat his rights the detention would become unlawful. *In the Emergency Powers Bill,* 1976 [1977] I.R. 159 applied. 2. S. 11 of the Interpretation Act, 1937, applied in that unless the contrary intention appeared, every word importing the plural be construed as importing the singular and vice versa so that detention in more than one station was not unlawful as such. 3. That there was no irregularity in carrying out the procedures under the Road Traffic (Amendment) Act, 1978, and the matter should be referred back to the District Justice to enter continuances. *Director of Public Prosecutions* v. *Sheehy*

(H.C.) [1987] ILRM 138

4. —— **Excessive concentration of alcohol** — *Opinion of member of Garda Síochána that accused person had committed offence — Whether statement that accused person was being arrested for offence under relevant section sufficient to support conviction — Road Traffic Act,* 1961 (*No.* 24), *s.* 49 — *Road Traffic (Amendment) Act,* 1978 (*No.* 19), *s.* 10.] The defendant was charged with having driven a bus on a public road when the concentration of alcohol in his blood was in excess of that permitted by s. 49 of the Road Traffic Act, 1961, as inserted by s. 10 of the Road Traffic (Amendment) Act, 1978. In evidence, a member of the Garda Síochána stated that he saw the defendant's bus swerving on the road, and that when it stopped he noticed the smell of alcohol from the defendant's breath and that his speech was slurred. An alcolyser test proved

positive. The garda told the defendant he was being arrested under s. 49 (6) of the 1961 Act for offences under s. 49 (2) and (3). In the District Court, it was submitted that the evidence was merely to the effect that the garda had formed the opinion that the defendant may have committed an offence under s. 49, not, as required, that he had committed an offence. The Justice acquitted the defendant and on a case stated to the High Court this was upheld. On appeal by the Director of Public Prosecutions: **Held** by the Supreme Court (Henchy, Griffin and Hederman JJ.) in allowing the appeal: when the garda stated he was arresting the defendant under s. 49 (6), he was by necessary implication invoking the terms of the section and it would be to ignore the realities and to fail to give plain words their ordinary meaning if they were not taken to mean that he had formed the required opinion that the defendant had committed an offence under the section. *Director of Public Prosecutions* v. *O'Connor*

(S.C.) [1985] ILRM 333

5. —— **Excessive concentration of alcohol** — *No breath test — Whether breath test essential for formation of opinion — Whether observation may suffice — Honest opinion reasonably arrived at — Road Traffic Act,* 1961 (*No.* 24), *s.* 49.] In forming the opinion that an offence has been committed under s. 49, sub-ss. 2 or 3 of the Road Traffic Act, 1961, (as inserted by s. 10 of the Road Traffic (Amendment) Act, 1978) such as is sufficient to ground the power of arrest provided for in s. 49, sub-s. 6, it is not necessary for a breath test to be administered, or that the arresting garda forms the opinion that an offence under s. 49, sub-s. 1 has been committed. It is sufficient that the opinion formed is reasonably arrived at and honestly held, and such opinion can be arrived at by observation alone. So **Held** by Barron J. *The Director of Public Prosecutions* v. *Gilmore* [1981] ILRM 102 and *Hobbs* v. *Hurley* (Unreported, High Court, Costello, J., 10 June, 1980) applied. *The Director of Public Prosecutions* v. *O'Connor* [1985] ILRM 333 considered. *Director of Public Prosecutions* v. *Donoghue*

(H.C.) [1986] I.R.188; [1987] ILRM 129

6. —— **Gardaí trespassers on private property** — *Arrest affected through non-violent trespass not unlawful per se — Road Traffic Act,* 1961 (*No.* 24), *s.* 49 — *Road Traffic (Amendment) Act,* 1978 (*No.* 19), *s.* 13 — *Constitution of Ireland,* 1937, *Art.* 40.] Where in exercising their power of arrest under s. 49 of the Road Traffic Act, 1961, Gardaí do so while trespassing on private property the arrest is nonetheless lawful. An arrest, otherwise lawful, is lawful though

effected through a non-violent trespass. So **Held** by Blayney J. *People* (*Attorney General*) v. *O'Brien* [1965] I.R. 142 explained. *Launock* v. *Brown* (1819) 2 B. & Ald. 592 considered. *Burdett* v. *Abbott* (1811) 14 East 1 applied. *Director of Public Prosecutions* v. *Corrigan*

(H.C.) [1986] I.R.290; [1987] ILRM 575

DISQUALIFICATION

7. —— **Disqualification from driving** — *Appeal — Whether applicant should be refused permission to drive pending appeal — Road Traffic (Northern Ireland) Order,* 1981 (*S.I. No.* 154, *N.I.*), *art.* 194 (3).] It is only in the rarest of cases that a court of summary jurisdiction can properly refuse permission to drive pending appeal against a disqualification from driving. While there will be exceptional cases, that course ought to be adopted only where disqualification is mandatory and the accused pleads guilty or makes a very clearly unsustainable defence or where the circumstances of the offence and the offender virtually demand that, in the interests of safety, he be forthwith prevented from driving. *In re Hamill*

(Q.B.D.) [1985] N.I.255

DRIVING WHILE DRUNK

see also Nos. 1-6

8. —— **Blood sample** — *Certificate of Medical Bureau of Road Safety showing an excessive concentration of alcohol — Whether certificate evidence of concentration of alcohol at any time other than when the sample was analysed — Road Traffic Act,* 1961 (*No.* 24), *s.* 49 — *Road Traffic (Amendment) Act,* 1978 (*No.* 19), *ss.* 2, 23 (2).] The defendant had been arrested and charged with having committed an offence under s. 49 of the Road Traffic Act, 1961. He provided a specimen of his blood, which was forwarded to the Medical Bureau of Road Safety. A certificate, purporting on its face to have been issued by the said Bureau pursuant to the provisions of s. 2 of the Road Traffic (Amendment) Act, 1978 showed a concentration of 163 milligrams of alcohol per 100 millilitres of blood. At the hearing in the District Court, counsel for the defendant submitted that the offence with which the defendant was charged was that he was driving a mechanically propelled vehicle while there was present in his body a quantity of alcohol such that within three hours of so driving it exceeded the statutory limit, and that the certificate was not evidence of the concentration of alcohol at any time other than when the blood sample was analysed, which was four days later. Counsel submitted further that there was accordingly no

evidence of what the concentration of alcohol was at the relevant time. The learned District Justice stated a case for the opinion of the High Court as to whether the complainant had discharged the onus of proof resting upon him. **Held** by Blayney J. in answering the question posed in the case stated in the affirmative, 1, there is no onus on the prosecution to prove that no change had taken place in the specimen between the time it was taken and the time it was analysed. 2. The prosecution has discharged its burden of proof once it has established a *prima facie* case, i.e., when it has proved facts on the strength of which a jury would be entitlted to convict. *Director of Public Prosecutions* v. *Collins* [1981] ILRM 447 applied. 3. In determining whether a *prima facie* case has been established, all the evidence must be looked at, and not merely the certificate in isolation. *Director of Public Prosecutions* v. *Smyth*

(H.C.) [1987] ILRM 570

9. —— **Blood sample** — *Certificate of Medical Bureau of Road Safety — Accused not receiving copy of certificate of analysis of a blood specimen until just before the trial — Conviction — Whether District Court order be quashed — Road Traffic Act,* 1961 (*No.* 24), *s.* 49 (2) — *Road Traffic (Amendment) Act,* 1978 (*No.* 19), *s.* 10.] The prosecutor (O'Regan) in August, 1982, was arrested under s. 49 (6) of the Road Traffic Act, 1961, as amended, gave a specimen of his blood and received a corresponding specimen. In early September the Gardaí became aware that the copy certificate of the analysis of the specimen carried out by the Medical Bureau had been returned to the Bureau by the Post Office without reaching O'Reagan. In late October, 1982, the Gardaí served a summons on O'Regan charging him with the offence to which the certificate related. On 21 December, 1982, a District Justice granted a Garda request for an adjournment on being informed by the Gardaí that the copy certificate had not been delivered. The District Justice refused an application to have the charge for a dismissal for want of delivery of the certificate. On 25 January, 1983, the date to which the hearing had been adjourned, the prosecuting Garda handed the copy certificate to O'Regan immediately before the hearing began. The District Justice ruled against a defence submission that the copy certificate had not been forwarded by the Medical Bureau as soon as practicable after analysis of the blood specimen and convicted O'Regan. A conditional order of certiorari for the quashing of the conviction was obtained. **Held,** making the order of certiorari absolute, the copy certificate, which was an essential proof in a s. 49 case, had been deliberately withheld until the last minute even though it was known

ROAD TRAFFIC OFFENCES—Drunk Driving.

that delivery of it was required. Therefore there had been a failure of natural justice. *The State* (*Walshe*) v. *Murphy* [1981] I.R. 275 applied. *The State (O'Regan)* v. *Plunkett*

(H.C.) [1984] ILRM 347

10. —— **Blood sample** — *Certificate of Medical Bureau of Road Safety — Copy sent to accused but returned "uncollected" — Whether Bureau under an obligation to ensure accused receives a copy — Road Traffic (Amendment) Act,* 1978 (*No.* 19), *s.* 22 (3).] The defendant was charged with having driven a mechanically propelled vehicle on a public road when the concentration of alcohol in his blood was in excess of that permitted by s. 49 (2) of the Road Traffic Act, 1961, as inserted by s. 10 of the Road Traffic (Amendment) Act, 1978. In the District Court it was submitted that the defendant should not be convicted since he had not received a copy of the certificate of blood-alcohol level from the Medical Bureau of Road Safety. The evidence given was that the Bureau had forwarded a copy certificate to the defendant's address but it had been returned "not collected". S. 22 (3) of the 1978 Act provided that the Bureau "shall forward a copy of the completed certificate to the person . . . from whom the specimen was taken." The District Justice held that the steps taken in this case did not comply with the requirements of s. 22 (3) and he acquitted the defendant. Case stated to the High Court. **Held** by Gannon J.: interpreting the words of s. 22 (3) in their ordinary meaning, and so far as they involved any ambiguity considering them in the context of the related provisions of the 1978 Act, there was no absolute obligation imposed on the Bureau to forward a copy certificate to a person from whom a specimen was taken; and that, having regard to the presumption of compliance with statutory requirements on the part of the prosecution (of which the Bureau did not form part), the onus lay on the defendant to establish that there was some default of procedure but that the non-delivery of a copy certificate would not be such a default standing on its own as to avoid conviction. *Per* Gannon J.: a standard form case stated expressing a Justice's conclusion upon all issues of law and fact as a verdict of conviction or dismissal of a criminal charge together with an absence of the statement of the submissions of law made to the Justice leaves room for doubt as to the particular question of law upon which the guidance of the High Court is required. *Director of Public Prosecutions* v. *Walsh*

(H.C.) [1985] ILRM 243

11. —— **Certificate of Medical Bureau of Road Safety** — *Whether statutory requirements to*

ROAD TRAFFIC OFFENCES—*continued.*

be strictly complied with — Road Traffic (Amendment) Act, 1978 (*No.* 19), *ss.* 22, 23 (2).] To comply with the requirements of ss. 22 (3) and 23 (2) of the Road Traffic (Amendment) Act, 1978, it is not necessary that the certificate of the Medical Bureau of Road Safety contain a specific statement to the effect that it has been issued pursuant to s. 22 of the said Act. It is sufficient if the certificate as a whole makes it clear that it has been so issued. **Held** by the Supreme Court (Griffin and McCarthy JJ., Finlay C.J. concurring) in allowing an appeal from the decision of Barr J. reported at [1988] ILRM 35. *Connolly* v. *Sweeney*

(S.C.) [1988] ILRM 483; (H.C.) [1988] ILRM 35

12. —— **Certificate of Medical Bureau of Road Safety** — *Typographical error — Whether affects the certificate — Road Traffic (Amendment) Act,* 1978 (*No.* 19), *s.* 23 (2).] The respondent, who had been charged with an offence contrary to s. 49 (3) and 4 (*a*) of the Road Traffic Act, 1961, as amended, had her case dismissed in the District Court on the ground that the certificate of the Medical Bureau of Road Safety was defective, because the date on which the seal of the Bureau was given was stated to be "6 May 1992'. The appellant stated a case for the opinion of the High Court as to whether the learned District Justice had been correct in law in so holding. The High Court having replied in the affirmative, the appellant appealed to the Supreme Court. Some argument was heard in the Supreme Court on the subject of alleged delay by the appellant in prosecuting the appeal. **Held** by the Supreme Court (Finlay C.J., Hederman and Henchy JJ.) in allowing the appeal and answering the case stated in the negative: As there is no inherent defect in the certificate, an obvious typographical error of the kind in question does not affect the certificate itself, and cannot render the seal of the Medical Bureau of Road Safety invalid. *Obiter* Any party seeking a case stated to the High Court has an obligation to prosecute the appeal diligently. Where there is undue delay, the High Court, and on appeal, the Supreme Court, should refuse to entertain the case where the court is of opinion that such delay is prejudicial or unjust to the other party. *Director of Public Prosecutions* v. *Flahive*

(S.C.) [1988] ILRM 133

13. —— **Refusal to provide blood sample** — *Caution — Whether caution prescribed by the regulation fell short of what was required by statute — Whether requirement that caution be given as to the possible consequences of such a refusal — Road Traffic Act,* 1968 (*No.* 25), *s.* 36 (1) (*b*) *— Road Traffic Act,* 1968 (*Part V*) *Regulations,*

1969 (*S.I. No.* 196).] The defendant was convicted in the District Court of an offence under s. 30 (3) of the Road Traffic Act, 1968 (as amended). The defendant had been arrested pursuant to s. 49 (4) of the said Act and brought to the garda station. Having declined the offer of having a doctor of his own choice examine him at his own expense, the defendant had then refused to permit the garda doctor to take a blood sample unless his own doctor was present. The defendant had been duly cautioned by the station sergeant in accordance with regulation 7 of the Road Traffic Act, 1968 (Part V) Regulations, 1969. The defendant appealed his conviction and submitted that the caution prescribed by regulation 7 fell short of what was required by s. 36 (1) (*b*) of the 1968 Act in that it did not convey to the accused that a failure to allow a blood specimen to be taken would leave the accused open to prosecution under s. 30 (3) of the 1968 Act and mandatory disqualification if convicted of an offence under that section. The Circuit Court judge stated a case to the Supreme Court as to whether the caution laid down by regulation 7 met the requirements of s. 36 (1) (*b*) of the Road Traffic Act, 1968. **Held** by the Supreme Court (Henchy J., Griffin and Kenny JJ.) in answering the question in the affirmative: The caution laid down by regulation 7 of the 1969 Regulations gives, as is required by s. 36 (1) (*b*) of the 1968 Act, a caution as to the "possible effects" of a refusal or failure to permit a blood sample to be taken. The words "possible effects" refer to the immediate legal result of a refusal *i.e.* liability to prosecution under s. 30 (3). S. 36 (1) (*b*) does not require that a caution be given as to the possible consequences of such a refusal. A mandatory disqualification following conviction under s. 30 (3) is a possible consequence and not a possible effect of a failure or refusal to give a blood sample in the circumstances. *Attorney General* (*O'Connor*) v. *Jordan* 107 I.L.T.R. 113 overruled in part. *Grogan* v. *Byrne*

(S.C.) [1976-7] ILRM 68

14. —— **Refusal to provide blood or urine specimen** — *Whether proof of time of driving or time of requirement to provide specimen required — Road Traffic (Amendment) Act,* 1978 (*No.* 19), *s.* 13 (3).

Statute — Interpretation — Clear and unambiguous language — Whether liberal interpretation produces unjust results — Road Traffic (Amendment) Act, 1978 (*No.*19), *s.* 13 (3).] The defendant's car was involved in a road traffic accident involving two other cars. On arrival at the scene the garda formed the opinion that the defendant was unfit to drive his vehicle due to the consumption of intoxicating liquor and arrested him under s. 49 (6) of the Road Traffic Act,

1961, and conveyed the defendant to a garda station. Whilst at the garda station a medical practitioner arrived. The defendant was requested to supply a specimen of either blood or urine and the consequences of a refusal so to do were explained to him. The defendant said he understood but refused to give any type of specimen. The defendant was charged with refusing to provide a specimen of blood or urine contrary to s. 13 (3) of the Road Traffic (Amendment) Act, 1978. The District Justice stated a case as to whether, in a prosecution under s. 13 (3) of the Road Traffic (Amendment) Act, 1978, proof of time of driving or proof of time of the requirement to provide a specimen was necessary. **Held** by Gannon J. in answering the questions in the case stated in the negative. There was nothing in the wording of s. 13 as expressed, nor in its apparent purpose which required proof of time of driving or time of the requirement to provide a specimen. *Director of Public Prosecutions* v. *Clinton*

(H.C.) [1984] ILRM 127

MOTOR VEHICLE — DEFINITION

15. —— **Motor vehicle** — *Motorised tricycle known as a fun bike — Whether "intended or adapted for use on roads" — Road Traffic (Northern Ireland) Order,* 1981 (*S.I. No.* 154, *N.I.* 1), *art.* 2.] The defendant was charged with driving a motor vehicle carelessly. He argued that the vehicle, a motorised tricycle known as a fun bike, was intended and designed for sport or amusement on rough terrain and was not suitable for road use, as it lacked a horn and traffic indicators. No evidence was given as to whether the vehicle was equipped for use on roads; but the resident magistrate concluded that as the tricycle was capable of being used on a road, it was a vehicle. On a case stated to the Court of Appeal, **Held,** that there was no evidence before the court which could justify the conclusion that the fun bike was intended (by anyone) or adapted (in any sense of that word) for use on roads and accordingly it did not come within the definition, in article 2 of the Road Traffic (Northern Ireland) Order, 1981, of a motor vehicle as "a mechanically propelled vehicle . . . which is intended or adapted for use on roads." *Per curiam* The word "intended" might be paraphrased as "suitable or apt". But, when "adapted" is coupled disjunctively with another word, the former must be contrasted with the latter. "Apt" or "suitable" are given as dictionary meanings of "adapted" although, by derivation, it is not a synonym for them and the natural meaning of "adapted" is "rendered suitable". If the word or phrase is ambiguous, it cannot arbitrarily be

ROAD TRAFFIC OFFENCES—*continued.*

given a meaning that will prejudice a defendant. *Symington* v. *McMaster*

(C.A.) [1985] N.I.293

PARKING

16. —— **Parking regulations** — *Statutory authority for regulations — Statute authorising regulations making parking in a particular manner a criminal offence — General regulations prohibiting parking in contravention of parking sign — Parking sign prohibiting parking by reference to weight of vehicle — No particular regulations prohibiting parking by reference to weight — Whether offence created by parking sign — Limerick Traffic and Parking Bye-laws,* 1978 (*S.I. No.* 262), *reg.* 18 — *Road Traffic Act,* 1961 (*No.* 24), *ss.* 89 (2) (*m*), 89 (7), 90 (2), 90 (9).] The defendant was summoned before the District Court to answer the charge that he had driven a motor lorry, the unladen weight of which acceeded two tons in contravention of an authorised road traffic sign, contrary to Reg. 18 of the Limerick Traffic and Parking Bye-Laws, 1975, made under ss. 89 and 90 of the Road Traffic Acts, 1961 to 68. Reg. 18 provided that "a driver shall comply with a prohibition, restriction or requirement indicated by means of a traffic sign." The District Justice was of the opinion that Reg. 18 had to be construed not as an omnibus or "catch-all" article but as a provision requiring a driver to comply with traffic signs that were erected for the purposes of endorsing the bye-laws enacted by the 1975 Regulations and in particular the bye-laws enacted by Regs. 5 to 17. Since there was no provision in the 1975 Regulations dealing with the prohibition or restrictions of traffic by reference to the weight of the vehicles, the District Justice found that the defendant was not obliged to obey the traffic sign in question and he accordingly dismissed the complaint. On appeal by case stated at the request of the Director of Public Prosecutions. **Held** by Gannon J. in holding that the District Justice was correct in law, 1, Reg. 18 did not itself create an offence as it was not within the competence of the Commissioner of the Garda Síochána to create an offence and as both s. 89 and s. 90 of the Act of 1961, under which the bye-laws in question had been made, provided that it was an offence to contravene a bye-law or rule made under the particular section. 2. The mere placing, at the request of the Commissioner, of a traffic sign of a nature in force by virtue of regulations made under s. 95 of the Act of 1961 was not the making of a bye-law under s. 89 (2) (*m*) or under s. 90 (2) of the Act of 1961. 3. If Reg. 18 was to have any meaning it must relate to some traffic sign designated and prescribed in some bye-law, the contravention of which would be recognised as an offence under s. 89 (7) or s. 90 (9) of the Act of 1961. Whatever offence (if any) the defendant might have been guilty of, it was not the offence of contravening a prohibition created by a traffic sign. The charge would have to be a charge of contravention of a bye-law contrary to either s. 89 (7) or s. 90 (9) of the Act of 1961. *Director of Public Prosecutions* v. *Clancy*

(H.C.) [1986] ILRM 268

—— Arrest — Legality — Dwelling — Inviolability — Garda Síochána entering dwelling house — Whether Gardaí trespassing.
see **Criminal Law,** 7

—— Disqualification — Whether factors to be considered taken into account in judicial manner — Whether necessary to reconsider evidence presented to convict.
see **Constitution,** 2

RULES OF COURT — Whether *ultra vires.*
see **Criminal Law,** 36, 44
Practice and Procedure, 35, 36

S

SAFETY
see **Accidents; Health and Safety**

—— At work.
see **Negligence,** 6-10, 18

—— Fire safety notice.
see **Fire Services**

SAFETY BELTS
—— Car — Failure to wear seat belts — Road traffic accident — Personal injuries — Damages.
see **Damages,** 11

—— Car — Failure to wear seat belts — Road traffic accident — Passenger in defendant's car — Contributory negligence — Apportionment of fault.
see **Negligence,** 15

SALE OF GOODS
see also **Defective Products; Hire Purchase; Prices**

1. —— **Contract** — *Term — Implied term — Test applicable — Payment — Letter of credit — Payment on specified day within shipment period — Whether buyer to provide letter before start of period — Whether contract enforceable — Memorandum — Sale of Goods Act,* 1893 (*c.* 71), *s.* 4.] By an oral agreement made on the 23 March, 1978, by the respective agents of the plaintiffs and defendants, the defendants agreed to sell to the plaintiffs 25,000 metric tonnes of feed barley in two lots at a specified price for each lot, making an aggregate price of £2.4 million. The parties expressly agreed that the contract barley would be available for delivery to the plaintiffs during the three months April-June, 1978, and that the plaintiffs would pay for the entire contract barley by a letter of credit "maturing" on the 1 May, 1978. The agents of the parties had no experience in the use of letters of credit. The identity of the bank which was to issue the letter of credit, notification of the opening of the credit, the relationship between the opening of the credit and deliveries of consignments of barley, and the documents to be presented by the defendants in order to obtain payment were not topics discussed or settled by the parties. The plaintiffs arranged for and received deliveries of barley from the defendants from the 7 April until the 21 April, 1978, when the defendants refused to make further deliveries on the ground that the plaintiffs, having failed to furnish a letter of credit, were in breach of their contract with the

defendants. By a letter dated the 21 April, 1978, and signed by the secretary of the defendant company, the defendants referred to the terms of the contract of sale and repudiated that contract. On the 24 April, 1978, the plaintiffs' bank issued two letters of credit in favour of the defendants, which letters would have enabled the defendants to obtain on the 1 May, 1978, payment from that bank of the price of each lot of barley upon presentation to the bank of the appropriate invoice. On the same day the defendants were informed that such credit arrangements had been made. The plaintiffs claimed in the High Court damages from the defendants for breach of contract. At the hearing of the action the defendants submitted that there should be implied in the contract of sale a term requiring the plaintiffs to furnish an appropriate letter or letters of credit before the start of the shipment period for the goods. In giving judgment for the plaintiffs, the trial judge **Held** (*a*) that the circumstances of the agreement between the parties did not justify the implication of the term sought by the defendants and (*b*) that the provisions of s. 4 of the Sale of Goods Act, 1893, were satisfied by the defendants' letter dated the 21 April, 1978. On appeal by the defendants it was **Held** by the Supreme Court (O'Higgins C.J., Henchy, Griffin, Hederman and McCarthy JJ.) in disallowing the appeal, 1, that, as the parties had expressly agreed upon the date and method of payment of the contract price, the implied term sought by the defendants was not required in order to implement the intention of the parties (McCarthy J. dissenting). *The Moorcock* (1889) 14 P.D. 64 considered; *Pavia & Co. S.P.A.* v. *Thurmann-Nielson* [1952] 2 Q.B. 84 distinguished. 2. *Per* O'Higgins C.J., Henchy, Griffin and Hederman JJ. — That the provisions of s. 4 of the Act of 1893 were satisfied by the defendants' letter dated the 21 April, 1978. *Tradax (Ireland) Ltd.* v. *Irish Grain Board Ltd.*

(S.C.) [1984] I.R. 1; [1984] ILRM 471

2. —— **Dealing as a consumer** — *Drink dispensing machine — Defects manifesting themselves — Whether purchaser entitled to refund of monies paid and damages for loss of profits — Whether purchaser "dealing as a consumer" — Sale of Goods and Supply of Services Act,* 1980 (*No.* 16), *s.* 3(1).] The plaintiff owned and operated a Take Away Food Shop known as The Magnet Take Away Foods at Main Street, Dunleer, County Louth. The shop sold chips, hamburgers, ice-cream, minerals and other similar types of food. There was a cigarette vending machine

SALE OF GOODS—*continued.*

in the premises. In March, 1982, the plaintiff purchased from the second-named defendant (Access Refrigeration) a machine known as a "Slush Puppy Iced Drink Dispensing Machine" for use in his shop. The machine produced fruit drinks containing crushed ice. The plaintiff himself dispensed them from the machine before serving them to his customers. The purchase was financed on foot of a leasing agreement concluded between the plaintiff and the first-named defendant (Hamilton Leasing) dated 12 March, 1982. The plaintiff signed this agreement "T/A The Magnet". On foot of the agreement, the plaintiff leased from the first-named defendant for a period of sixty months the said machine at a quarterly rent of £210.00 plus VAT. The machine proved to be defective and after the plaintiff had made the first two quarterly payments he instituted proceedings in the Circuit Court claiming a refund of the monies paid by him to the first-named defendant, as well as damages for loss of profits. The second-named defendant was later joined as a co-defendant and on 7 July, 1983, Judge Roe held that the plaintiff was entitled to succeed and entered judgment, against both defendants in the sum of £1,112.50. He also ordered that the first-named defendant be indemnified against the decree by the second-named defendant. The first-named defendant appealed the decision but no appeal was filed by the second-named defendant. At the hearing of the appeal, the first-named defendant did not contest the Circuit Court finding that the machine was defective or the damages decree. It disputed the Circuit Court finding against it, solely on the basis that the plaintiff, in entering into the said leasing agreement, was not dealing as a consumer within the meaning of s. 3 of the Sale of Goods and Supply of Services Act, 1980, and that, in consequence, was not entitled to succeed against the first-named defendant, either under ss. 14 or 38 of the said Act. McWilliam J. heard evidence from the plaintiff as to the nature of his business and the circumstances surrounding the conclusion of the leasing agreement. He also heard evidence from a representative of the first-named defendant, to the effect that it was its policy to only conclude leasing agreements with firms, companies or persons carrying on business. S.3 of the Sale of Goods and Supply of Services Act, 1980, provides as follows: (1) In the Act of 1893 and this Act the party to a contract is said to deal as consumer in relation to another party if: (*a*) he neither makes the contract in the course of a business nor holds himself out as doing so, and (*b*) the other party does not make the contract in the course of a business, and (*c*) the goods or services supplied under or in pursuance of the contract are of a type ordinarily supplied for

SALE OF GOODS—*continued.*

private use or consumption. (2) On: (*a*) a sale by competitive tender, or (*b*) a sale by auction: (i) of goods of a type, or (ii) by or on behalf of a person of a class defined by the Minister by order, the buyer is not in any circumstances to be regarded as dealing as consumer. (3) Subject to this, it is for those claiming that a party does not deal as consumer to show that he does not. **Held** by McWilliam J. in allowing the appeal by the first named defendant, the contract was made in the course of the plaintiff's business and accordingly he did not "deal as consumer" within the meaning of the Act. *O'Callaghan* v. *Hamilton Leasing (Ireland) Ltd.*

(H.C.) [1984] ILRM 146

3. —— **Retention of title clause** — *Conditional contract — Terms of contract — Goods sold and delivered but not paid for — Whether passing of property in goods can be postponed — Effect of phrase "in trust" — Whether property passed coupled with charge in favour of seller — Whether retention of equitable interest creates a charge — Sale of Goods Act,* 1893 (*c.* 71), *ss.* 1, 17 — *Companies Act,* 1963 (*No.* 33), *s.* 316.] Section 1, sub-s. 2 of the Sale of Goods Act, 1893, provides for conditional contracts of sale. Subsection 3 thereof provides *inter alia* for contracts of sale, called agreements to sell, where the transfer of the property in the goods is to take place at a future time or subject to some condition. Section 17, sub-s. 1 of the Act of 1893 states that in a contract for the sale of specific or ascertained goods the property in them in transferred to the buyer at such time as the parties to the contract intend it to be transferred. The applicant as receiver of the company applied to the High Court for directions concerning the ownership of goods sold and delivered by the respondent to the company but not paid for. The contract of sale had a reservation of title clause which stated that no property in the goods would pass until full payment had been received. Until then the buyer was obliged to hold the goods in trust for the respondent in a manner which enabled them to be identified and to return the goods to the respondent on demand. The buyer was permitted to sell the goods to a third party but the proceeds of such sale were to be held by the buyer in trust for the respondent in a manner which enabled them to be identified as such. The applicant argued that the words "in trust" indicated that the legal estate in the goods passed to the buyer and that the respondent retained a beneficial interest by way of charge only. **Held** by Barron J., in giving directions, 1, that the creation of a charge would require that all the property in the goods be passed to the buyer so that an assignment back to the respondent of an equitable interest by way of charge could take

SALE OF GOODS—*continued.*

place. *Clough Mill Ltd.* v. *Martin* [1985] 1 W.L.R. 111 approved. *In re Interview Ltd.* [1975] I.R. 382 and *Kruppstahl A. G.* v. *Quitmann Products Ltd.* [1982] ILRM 551 distinguished. 2. That the goods had been delivered under a conditional contract of sale which was an agreement to sell within the meaning of s. 1 of the Act of 1893 and the respondent was entitled to postpone the date of the passing of the property in the goods. *Frigoscandia (Contracting) Ltd.* v. *Continental Irish Meat Ltd.* [1982] ILRM 396 followed. 3. That the use of the expression "in trust" indicated that an equitable interest was retained which was not a charge. *In re Bond Worth Ltd.* [1980] Ch. 228 distinguished. *Henry* v. *Hammond* [1913] 2 K.B. 515 applied. 4. That the property in the goods remained in the respondents and that transfer never took place. *In re W.J. Hickey Ltd.; Uniacke* v. *Cassidy Electrical Supply Co. Ltd.*

(H.C.) [1988] I.R.126

4. —— **Retention of title clause** — *Passing of property — Personal chattels — Power of settlor to take possession — Retention of title clause appearing on seller's invoices — Whether clause effective to reserve title — Whether a bill of sale — Whether void for non-registration — Price of goods unpaid at date of appointment of receiver — Seller not holder or grantee of bill of sale — Receiver without claim to goods — Bills of Sale (Ireland) Act,* 1879 (*c.* 50) — *Bills of Sale (Ireland) Act* (1879) *Amendment Act,* 1883 (*c.* 7), *s.* 8 — *Sale of Goods Act,* 1893 (*c.* 71), *ss.* 1, 17 — *Agricultural Credit Act,* 1978 (*No.* 2), *ss.* 23 (1), 36(1).] The applicant was appointed receiver over the property of a company which had manufactured animal feed products. The respondent was a supplier to the company of certain component products. The respondent company supplied these goods subject to conditions of sale which were set out on the back of their invoice and which included a retention of title clause ("the clause"). This clause provided that the title of goods would not pass until the invoice had been paid in full. At the time of the appointment of the applicant, the company was in possession of a quantity of goods which had been supplied by the respondent. These goods were still indentifiable and had not been subjected to any manufacturing process. The applicant sought directions from the High Court in relation to the effect of the clause and the obligations arising therefrom. Four propositions were advanced by the applicant. Firstly, that there was a conflict between the clause and another clause in the contract which must be construed *contra proferentes.* Secondly, that a seller of goods to a manufacturer, who knows his goods are to be used in manufacturing, cannot rely on a simple retention of title clause. Thirdly, that the clause creates a charge registrable under the Bills of Sale (Ireland) Act, 1879 and 1883, and fails for lack of registration. Fourthly, if the contract is registrable as a bill of sale, it is void having regard to the provisions of the Agricultural Credit Act, 1978. **Held** by Carroll J., 1, that there was no conflict between the retention of title clause and the earlier clause. 2. The simplicity of the clause did not *per se* prevent it being effective to reserve to the respondent the title of the goods as supplied to the company and still existing in that state. Title in the goods has not been extinguished by manufacture and since payment had not been made, that title had not been transferred. *Borden (U.K.) Limited* v. *Scottish Timber Products Ltd.* [1981] Ch. 25, considered. 3. A contract which deals with the future title of the buyer in the goods to be manufactured from the goods supplied would, as regards that future title, constitute a bill of sale. The instant contract dealt only with the present title to the goods sold and did not create a charge requiring registration under the Bills of Sale (Ireland) Acts 1879 and 1883. 4. Accordingly, the applicant must account to the respondent for the goods. The applicant appealed to the Supreme Court, confining his argument to the contention that the retention of title clause constituted a bill of sale and was thus void by virtue of s. 36 of the Agricultural Credit Act, 1978. **Held** by the Supreme Court (Henchy, Griffin and McCarthy JJ.) that the clause did not constitute a bill of sale of stock and accordingly, s. 36 of the Agricultural Credit Act, 1978, did not apply. *Per* McCarthy J., s. 36 of the Agricultural Credit Act, 1978, was intended only to apply to a bill of sale given to secure the payment of money. *Somers* v. *James Allen (Ireland) Ltd; In re Charles Dougherty & Co. Ltd.*

(H.C., S.C.) [1985] I.R. 340; [1985] ILRM 624; [1984] ILRM 437

5. —— **Retention of title clause** — *Whether clause waived.*] The plaintiff, a Belgian company, manufactured cookers and stoves which were imported to Ireland by John R. Taylor Ltd. The defendant was a company which had obtained possession of the plaintiff's goods as factors for John R. Taylor Ltd. The plaintiff supplied its wares under conditions of sale which included a retention of title clause. The present action hinged on whether the plaintiff had, during an exchange of telex messages, waived its retention of title clause. **Held** by Barrington J. that the plaintiff had not waived its retention of title clause and that the defendant was liable to account to the plaintiff for the goods or the

SALE OF GOODS—*continued.*

proceeds of their sale. *S.A.Foundries du Lion MV* v. *International Factors (Ire.) Ltd.*
(H.C.) [1985] ILRM 66

6. —— **Title** — *Mercantile agent — Third party sold business with equipment to defendant — Equipment property of plaintiff — Whether third party a mercantile agent for plaintiff — Factor's Act,* 1889 (*c.* 45), *s.* 9 — *Sale of Goods Act,* 1979 (*c.* 54), *s.* 25(1).] The plaintiff sold and delivered catering equipment to the third party who carried on a restaurant business. It was a term of the sale that the property in the equipment would not pass to the third party until they were paid for in full. At the time of the action no payment had been made for the equipment. The third party purported to sell the restaurant business together with the catering equipment to the defendant. The plaintiff commenced proceedings against the defendant claiming delivery of the goods or their value and damages. The defendant's sole defence was that he received the goods in good faith and without notice of any title or other right of the plaintiff in respect of them and he relied on section 9 of the Factors Act, 1889, and section 25(1) of the Sale of Goods Act, 1979. The defendants served notice on the third party who took no part in the proceedings. **Held** giving judgment against the defendant and the third party, that the meaning of section 9 of the 1889 Act was that innocent purchasers can be protected not only when dealing with mercantile agents acting in the ordinary course of a mercantile agent's business but also with ordinary persons acting in a way in which a mercantile agent would be expected to act in the ordinary course of business. *Newtons of Wembley Ltd.* v. *Williams* [1965] 1 Q.B. 560 followed. The re-enactment of section 9 in section 25(1) of the 1979 Act indicated that Parliament had endorsed this meaning. Here the entire business had been transferred by the third party to the defendant with no separate value attributed to the catering equipment; a transaction which did not bear the slightest resemblance to the sale of goods by a mercantile agent. *R.F. Martin Ltd.* v. *Duffy*
(Q.B.D.) [1985] N.I.417

—— Contract — Breach — Claim for damages — Whether contract void for illegality — Onus of proof.
see **Contract,** 2

—— Contract — Mistake — Both parties contracting on assumption which proved false — Supply of seed potatoes — Crop failure — Whether contract rendered void — Whether implied obligations remaining.
see **Contract,** 8

SALE OF GOODS—*continued.*

—— Reservation of title — Company — Receivership — Suppliers claiming to be entitled to trace the proceeds of their goods — Whether reservation of title clause effective.
see **Company,** 10

SALE OF INTOXICATING LIQUOR
see **Licensing Acts**

SALE OF LAND
see also **Auctioneers and Estate Agents**

Condition. Nos. 1-3
Contract. Nos. 4-14
Lien. Nos. 15, 16
Requisitions on title. No. 17

CONDITION

1. —— **Planning permission** — *Agreement subject to obtaining planning permission — Vendor requiring sale within specified period — Non-refundable deposit paid by purchaser — Contract not completed within specified time — Vendor waiving completion date — Vendor specifying new completion date — Time agreed to be of the essence — Planning permission not obtained — Purchaser not waiving permission requirement — Vendor treating contract as repudiated — Whether refusal of purchaser to complete on specified dates constituted repudiation — Whether vendor entitled to rescind — Whether vendor entitled to retain deposits.*] The plaintiffs were property developers who had entered into a contract with the defendants on 16 May, 1974, for the sale to the plaintiffs of a block of houses. A contract for the sale of a second block of houses was made between the same parties on 16 May, 1975, and this also amended the first contract. The first contract was expressed to be subject to obtaining planning permission, but it also contained a condition that in the event of planning permission not having been obtained by the closing date, the contract would be at an end, and the defendants would be entitled to retain the deposit of £30,000 which was payable. Subsequently, delays arose with respect to the purchase of the freehold of some of the properties, but the evidence disclosed that this delay was not attributable to any fault of the defendants. Further delays occurred with respect to obtaining planning permission. The second contract provided that the closing date for both sales would be 30 June, 1976, or alternatively 31 December, 1976, but that if the latter date were chosen, the consideration would be increased to cover the financial loss of the defendants in the face of higher interest rates. A non-refundable deposit was expressed to be payable with respect

SALE OF LAND—Condition.

to the second contract. On 16 July, 1976, the plaintiffs' solicitor sought an extension of the time for the completion of the two sales. This was refused by letter of the defendants' solicitor dated 6 September. A delay occurred on the part of the defendants in furnishing satisfactory title to the property the subject of the second contract, but this had been remedied by 9 December, 1976. The sales were not completed by the specified closing date. By letter dated 1 April, 1977, the plaintiff's' solicitor made it clear that his clients made completion conditional upon a grant of planning permission, which had not yet been obtained. By notice in writing of 7 April the defendants required the completion of both sales by 7 July, 1977, and time was declared to be of the essence of the contracts. On 26 July the defendants informed the plaintiffs that they were in breach of contract, which breach would be treated as a repudiation of the contracts. They further informed the plaintiffs that they were retaining both deposits. The plaintiffs sought a decree of specific performance, and, *inter alia*, declarations that the defendants were not entitled to retain the deposits. **Held** by Costello J. in refusing the order and declarations sought, 1, the condition relating to planning permission in the first contract was inserted for the exclusive benefit of the plaintiffs, and accordingly could have been waived by them. *Heron Garage Properties Ltd.* v. *Moss* [1974] 1 W.L.R. 148 discussed. 2. Failure on the part of the plaintiffs to waive the condition relating to planning permission, and to complete the contract, caused the contract to terminate. 3. In the light of the length of time that had elapsed since the making of the first contract, and of the fact that the defendants had refused on 7 September, 1976, to agree to an extension of the completion date, the three months' notice to complete the sales given by the defendants was not unreasonable. 4. The refusal of the plaintiffs to complete the two sales on the specified date was not in accordance with their contractual rights, and worked inequity to the defendants. This refusal constituted a repudiation of the contracts. *Sepia Ltd.* v. *M. & P. Hanlon Ltd.*

(H.C.) [1979] ILRM 11

2. —— **Planning permission** — *Requirement that purchaser obtain permission by specified date — Purchaser not obtaining permission — Vendor withdrawing from sale — Purchaser purporting to waive requirement — Whether waiver effective — Whether vendor obliged to complete sale — Whether contract discharged by failure to obtain permission — Whether term to be implied for discharge — Whether for mutual benefit of parties — Whether capable of unilateral waiver.*] By an agreement in writing dated 16 March, 1978, the

SALE OF LAND—*continued.*

plaintiff agreed to sell certain lands in County Clare to the defendant for £39,500 and the closing date was expressed to be "20 days after full planning permission and Land Commission consent received or 10/7/78 whichever be later." Special condition No. 1 included in the agreement drawn up on the 1976 edition of the Incorporated Law Society Form stated that the sale was subject to the purchaser getting full planning permission before 31 July, 1978. If the permission was not forthcoming before the latter date the purchaser was to be refunded his deposit. Planning permission was not obtained until November, 1978, and the Land Commission consent to subdivision was obtained on 11 September, 1978. The solicitors for the plaintiff wrote to the solicitors for the defendant stating that as the closing date had passed, they wished to withdraw from the sale. The solicitors for the defendant replied that their client was quite happy about the planning position and, in the circumstances, waived special condition No. 1 in the contract. Following further correspondence the plaintiff issued proceedings claiming a declaration that the contract terminated on 31 July, 1978, because full planning permission had not been forthcoming by that date. **Held** by McWilliam J. in granting the declaration sought, on the facts of the case the defendant was not entitled to waive the condition without the consent of the plaintiff, since the term as to permission was for the mutual benefit of the parties and was not capable of unilateral waiver by one party to the agreement. *Maloney* v. *Elf Investments Ltd.*

(H.C.) [1979] ILRM 253

3. —— **Subject to option to purchase** — *Pre-condition to contract — Option exercised by third party — Whether purchaser can maintain action against vendor.*] The first-named defendant purchased certain lands from one P.H. By written contract dated 7 December, 1972, it was agreed between the parties that the vendor would have the right to re-acquire certain premises on the land in order to destroy the messuages thereon, if it were not otherwise reasonably practicable for him or the actual developer to develop adjoining lands the property of the vendor. The sale was completed by a conveyance dated 8 October, 1973. On 5 June, 1973, 70 acres adjoining the lands purchased by the first-named defendant were conveyed by P.H. to one L.D. He in turn conveyed the lands to the second-named defendant, of which company he was a director. By deed dated 31 December, 1974, P.H. assigned his rights in relation to the reserved premises to the second-named defendant. In 1974, the first-named defendant agreed to sell part of the lands included in the deed of 8 October, 1973, to the plaintiff, who was on notice of the right of P.H.

SALE OF LAND—Condition.

to re-acquire the reserved lands. The sale to the plaintiff was made subject to the clause to that effect in the contract of 7 December, 1972. The lands purchased by the plaintiff included the reserved lands. The sale was not completed. On 18 July, 1975, the reserved lands were conveyed by the first-named defendant to the second-named defendant. The plaintiff sought an injunction restraining the second-named defendant from demolishing or damaging any of the buildings on the said lands. The injunction was refused in the High Court, and the plaintiff appealed to the Supreme Court. **Held** by the Supreme Court (Griffin, Kenny and Parke JJ.) in disallowing the appeal, 1, the plaintiff, notwithstanding that the sale had not been completed, could maintain the proceeding against the first-named defendant. *Echliff* v. *Baldwin* (1809) 16 Ves. Junior 267; *Curtis* v. *The Marquis of Buckinhgam* (1814) 3 Ves. & B. 168; *Spiller* v. *Spiller* (1819) 3 Swan. 556, applied. 2. Since the right of the second-named defendant to re-acquire the reserved lands was prior in creation to the right of the plaintiff, and since the former right had been perfected by the conveyance of 18 July, 1975, the plaintiff could not maintain a claim against the second-named defendant. 3. The clause relating to the re-acquisition of the reserved lands in the agreement of 7 December, 1972, related to the land, and did not create a right personal to the vendor only, so as to prevent him from assigning it to the second-named defendant and the clause was not void for uncertainty. *O'Hara* v. *Flint*

(S.C.) [1979] ILRM 156

CONTRACT
see also Nos. 1-3

4. —— **Damages for failure to complete** — *Vendor obtaining income from property while contract completed — Whether purchaser entitled to damages in addition to decree for specific performance.*] The plaintiff had obtained a decree of specific performance against the defendants for completion of a sale to him of a substantial property. It was agreed upon between the parties that the completion of the sale had been delayed by reason of the default of the defendants. The plaintiff sought damages in addition to specific performance, and the defendants contended that these must be set off against the amount of interest which the plaintiff had saved or earned during the year's delay. Since this greatly exceeded the amount of the rental value of the property, which would be the normal measure of damages, the defendants further contended that the plaintiff was not entitled to any damages. **Held** by McWilliam J. in finding against the plaintiff, 1, where a sale has been delayed by the vendor, and where the interest exceeds the rents and profits, the vendor cannot take the interest, but only the rents and profits. He must not, however, lose both, and this principle applied equally to a situation in which there has been a deliberate and unjustifiable breach of the contract. *Esdaile* v. *Stephenson* (1822) 1 Sim. & St. 122 applied. 2. That, on the evidence, no circumstances existed which could give rise to punitive, exemplary or liquidated damages. *O'Brien* v. *White-Spunner*

(H.C.) [1979] ILRM 240

5. —— **Damages in lieu of specific performance** — *Sale of licensed premises — Memorandum containing no express terms as to licence — Whether enforceable agreement that existing licence was to pass with premises — Whether vendor lacked capacity to enter into such agreement — Laches — Whether decree of specific performance be granted — Statute of Frauds,* 1695 (*c.* 12).] The plaintiff brought an action for specific performance of a verbal agreement with the defendant for the sale of a licensed premises. The agreement was evidenced by a subsequent informal written document, signed by both parties. The plaintiff understood, although it was not an express term of the agreement, that the existing seven day licence was to pass with the premises. The defendant disputed the plaintiff's claim on the grounds that there was no agreement, that he, the defendant, lacked the capacity to enter into an agreement due to intoxication, that if an agreement was made, it was unfair and unenforceable and that that plaintiff was barred from relief by delay in bringing the proceedings. **Held** by Gannon J. in awarding the plaintiff £4,500 in damages in lieu of specific performance, 1, on 1 September, 1972, the defendant agreed to the sale of the licensed premises with furniture to the plaintiff for the sum of £6,000. 2. A memorandum in writing of the contract was made after the agreement was reached and signed by the defendant. The memorandum satisfied the requirements of the Statute of Frauds. The omission of a term relating to the seven day licence did not alter the contract nor entitle the defendant to invoke the Statute simply to deprive the plaintiff of the benefit of such agreement. The defendant has no separate property in the seven day licence capable of being sold or withheld independently of the sale of the premises. 3. The defendant failed to establish that he was incapable through drunkeness of entering into a binding agreement such as has been proved. The plaintiff neither knew, nor had he reason to suppose, that the defendant was so affected. 4. There was not such disparity between the price which the defendant might reasonably have expected from any other buyer as would

SALE OF LAND—Contract.

suggest unfairness about the contract. 5. There was neither evidence from which to infer an intention on the part of the plaintiff to abandon his claim, nor evidence of injurious effect upon the defendant's position by such delay as did occur. 6. Having regard to the difficulties which might be encountered with the transfer of the licence and contractual relations between the defendant and his tenants, damages provide the more appropriate remedy. The measure is such sum of money as now would enable him with the £6,500 he was prepared to spend in 1972, to purchase the property if it still be available today, at a reasonable estimate of its present value. *White* v. *McCooey*

(H.C.) [1976-7] ILRM 72

6. —— **Delay in completion** — *Land Acts — Notice of inspection subsequent to agreement for sale — Effect of notice to require consent to sale — Purchaser obtaining consent to registration as owner — Purchaser in possession prior to conveyance — Whether consent sufficient to enable completion of sale — Delay — Whether explained — Whether specific performance should be refused — Land Act,* 1965 (*No.* 2), *s.* 13.] The plaintiff entered into a contract for the sale of land to the defendant. The date fixed for the completion was 21 March, 1972. The Land Commission became interested in the lands and served a notice of inspection dated 29 March, 1972, under s. 40 of the Land Act, 1923. The effect of this notice was to prevent the sale or transfer of the lands without the consent in writing of the Land Commission during the three months from the date of service of the notice under s. 13 of the Land Act, 1965. The plaintiff's solicitor wrote to the defendant on 1 May, 1972, stating that the plaintiff had executed the transfer and other appropriate documents necessary to complete the transaction. The Land Commission certified on the 16 June, 1972, that the lands were required for relief of congestion, and published a notice to that effect in *Iris Oifigiúil* on 27 June, 1972. The plaintiff lodged an objection to the acquisition of the lands by the Land Commission but this objection was disallowed on 14 June, 1973. The defendant's solicitor, by letter of 19 July, 1973, wrote to the Land Commissioner asking if they would agree that the defendant was entitled to complete the contract. They replied by letter of 7 September, 1973, stating that they had no objection to the registration of the defendant as owner of the lands and further that the letter could be produced to the Land Registry as evidence of such consent. The plaintiff sought a declaration that the contract between himself and the defendant was null and void on the basis that they were prohibited from dealing with the lands pursuant to the provisions

SALE OF LAND—*continued.*

of the Land Acts. The defendant counterclaimed for specific performance and the plaintiff defended this claim by saying that the defendant was guilty of laches. **Held** by McWilliam J. in dismissing the plaintiff's claim and in making an order for specific performance, 1, the contract between the parties was binding as neither party took any steps to rescind it. 2. The letter of 7 September, 1973, from the Land Commission was sufficient consent to enable the lands to be transferred within the meaning of s. 13 of the Land Act, 1965. 3. On the facts of the case the alleged delay has been explained and so is not a ground for refusing the decree of specific performance. *Horgan* v. *Deasy*

(H.C.) [1979] ILRM 71

7. —— **Formation** — *"Subject to contract' — Negotiations between vendor and purchaser — Written agreement on terms of contract — Subsequent correspondence describing negotiations as subject to contract — Whether such correspondence deprives previous agreement of binding effect — Whether previous correspondence amounts to sufficient note or memorandum of agreement — Statute of Frauds,* 1695 (*c.* 12), *s.* 2.] The plaintiff claims against the defendant specific performance of an agreement alleged to have been reached on 13 and 21 March, 1978, for the sale by the defendant to the plaintiff of certain lands and premises. The lands and premises were to be sold for the sum of £650,000 and a note and memorandum in writing to that effect was contained in the correspondence between the defendant's agent and the plaintiff's solicitor in the letters of 23 March, 1978, 7 April, 1978, and a draft contract, also in a letter from the plaintiff's solicitor to the defendant's agent dated 7 April, 1978, and a draft contract. The defendant submitted that an agreement had not been reached at the meetings held on 13 and 21 March, 1978, and further that the letters of 23 March, 1978, and 17 April, 1978, could not be regarded as a note or memorandum sufficient to satisfy the requirements of the Statute of Frauds as both letters were headed "subject to contract". **Held** by Hamilton J. in making an order for specific performance, 1, a final agreement not "subject to contract" was reached on all material terms of the agreement by the defendant's agent to sell to the plaintiff company the lands and premises for the sum of £650,000 at a meeeting held on 13 March, 1978, which was confirmed at a further meeting on 21 March, 1978. 2. The letters contained a recognition and acknowledgement that agreement had been reached between the defendant and plaintiff, and all the essential terms of the agreement are contained in the letters, draft contract, and amendments of the contract, pursuant to the

requirements of the Statute of Frauds. 3. Neither a principal nor his solicitor having entered into a binding contract can thereafter deprive the said contract of its binding effect by unilaterally treating the transaction as "subject to contract". *McInerney Properties Ltd.* v. *Roper*

(H.C.) [1979] ILRM 119

8. —— **Mistake** — *Deposit paid — Purchaser seeking to withdraw — Whether vendor entitled to forfeit deposit — Whether deposit paid under mistake of fact.*] The plaintiffs, German nationals with little knowledge of the English language, had come to Ireland with the intention of purchasing land. With the assistance of an interpreter, they entered into negotiations with the defendant, who had a farm and some 117 acres of land for sale. Having agreed upon a purchase price, the plaintiffs were informed that the consent of the Land Commission would have to be obtained before the sale could be completed; and the auctioneer who had carriage of the sale was especially concerned that the plaintiffs be made aware that, should the Land Commission's consent not be forthcoming, the transaction would have to be cancelled. The parties then signed a memorandum of agreement and the plaintiffs paid a small deposit. At the same time, they agreed to pay within three weeks the balance of one quarter of the deposit, which was duly done. The plaintiffs then returned to Germany. Some time later, one of the plaintiffs wrote to the solicitor who was acting on his behalf in Ireland informing him that on careful consideration of the political climate in Ireland, both plaintiffs wished to cancel the arrangements and recover the monies paid. When the first-named plaintiff received no reply to this letter, he returned to Ireland. In the interim, the consent of the Land Commission to the proposed sale had been obtained. The defendant issued a formal note of forfeiture of the deposit to the plaintiffs, who thereupon instituted proceedings against him, alleging that the monies had been paid upon a mistake of fact, since they believed they were entering only into a "brokers contract", and that no complete contract had been signed. The defendant asserted his right to forfeit the deposit upon the terms of the conditions attached to the contract for sale. These conditions had not been read out to the plaintiffs, not was their attention drawn to the fact that the conditions of sale contained such a term. **Held** by Finlay P. in allowing the plaintiffs' claim, 1, notwithstanding the general principle that a person of full capacity who signs an unread contract does so at his own risk and is bound by its terms, the plaintiffs, with whom there was significant difficulty in communicating, did not appear on the evidence to have understood that the general conditions of

sale formed part of the contract which they had signed. 2. Notwithstanding the principle that if monies are paid by way of deposit on a purchase price they fall to be forfeited should the purchaser fail to complete the purchase, the plaintiffs did not appear to have understood that the monies they had advanced were indeed a deposit on a binding agreement to purchase the land, especially since they understood that for the contract to be binding, it would have to be entered into before a notary or other state official. *Siebel* v. *Kent*

(H.C.) [1976-7] ILRM 129

9. —— **Rescission** — *Damage to premises after execution of contract — Duty of vendor pending completion of the sale — Whether vendor entitled to rescind contract — Whether purchaser entitled to damages — Whether contributory negligence of purchaser — Civil Liability Act,* 1961 (*No.* 41).] By contract executed in January, 1983, the vendor and the purchaser agreed on the sale of a premises. The contract was subject to the general conditions of sale contained in the Incorporated Law Society of Ireland (1978 Edition) contract. There was delay in completing the transaction and in October, 1983, the purchaser requested a reduction in the sale price because of damage occasioned to the property subsequent to the execution of the contract. The vendor did not accede to this request and by notice fixed the 31 August, 1984, as the date for completion of the contract, making time of the essence. Before this completion date the vendor offered to close the sale and to reserve £10,000 out of the proceeds pending litigation on the question of damage to the property. The purchaser did not agree to this and in October, 1984, issued a plenary summons claiming specific performance of the contract. On the 14 November, 1984, the vendor gave notice to the purchaser of intention to rescind the contract in pursuance of clause 10 of the general conditions of sale, and on 26 November, 1984, returned the deposit paid by the purchaser with notification that the contract had been rescinded. On 7 March, 1985, the vendor issued a special summons under s. 9 of the Vendor and Purchaser Act, 1874, claiming a declaration that the contract had been validly rescinded. The two issues were tried together. **Held** by Murphy J., in allowing the claim for specific performance, 1, that the vendor was not justified in rescinding the contract. 2. That the purchaser was entitled to be paid compensation for the damage to the property; the vendor could not escape liability for this compensation by rescinding the contract. 3. That subsequent to the execution of a contract for sale the vendor has a duty to use reasonable care to maintain the property in a reasonable state of preservation.

SALE OF LAND—Contract.

Tempany v. *Hynes* [1976] I.R. 101 and *Clarke* v. *Ramuz* [1891] 2 Q.B. 456 followed. 4. The vendor was guilty of wilful default in allowing damage to the property. 5. The purchaser, being a frequent visitor to the premises, was guilty of contributory negligence in that he took no steps to secure the premises or to inform the vendor of his visits and the condition of the property as he found it. Accordingly ten per cent of the blame should be apportioned to him. *Lyons* v. *Thomas*

(H.C.) [1986] I.R.666

10. —— **Rescission** — *Illegality — Auction — Licensed premises — Whether representation as to turnover — Agent for vendor bidding — Whether contract rendered illegal — Sale of Land by Auction Act,* 1867 (*c.* 48), *s.* 3.] The Sale of Land by Auction Act, 1867, provides in s. 3 that where land sold at auction is stated to be sold without reserve, it shall not be lawful for the vendor to employ any person to bid at such sale. The plaintiffs had contracted to purchase a licensed premises from the defendant at a public auction. The plaintiffs subsequently sought to repudiate the contract on the ground that the defendant had told them in the course of the auction that the annual turnover was much higher than in fact it was, and they had thus been induced to enter into the contract. The defendant denied having made any such representation, and submitted that in any event the contract had been ratified subsequent to the auction by the payment of the balance of the deposit. Other evidence adduced by the plaintiffs' solicitors tended to show that the plaintiffs had been concerned, from the commencement of negotiations, to ascertain the amount of the annual turnover. At the auction, an agent representing the vendor was the only other bidder. Although the premises had initially been subject to a reserved price, this was lifted during the course of the bidding, and the property was put on the market. **Held** by Hamilton J. in finding that the plaintiffs were entitled to rescind the contract, and to obtain a return of the deposit, together with the auction fees paid by them and interest by way of damages, 1, on the balance of probabilities, the conflict of evidence as to the representation relating to annual turnover must be resolved in favour of the plaintiffs. This representation had been such as to induce them to enter into the contract at a price which they would otherwise have been unprepared to pay. 2. The contract had, in any event, been rendered illegal, pursuant to the provisions of the 1867 Act, by the presence of the defendant's agent who was actively bidding at the auction after the reserve price had been lifted. *Airlie* v. *Fallon*

SALE OF LAND—*continued.*

(H.C.) [1976-7] ILRM 1

11. —— **Rescission** — *Property in fee simple subject to lease — Lease originally subject to a trust — Condition that any objections or requisitions on title should be sent within ten days after delivery of title deeds — Time made of the essence — Plaintiff seeking to rely upon this condition and rescind the sale and retain the deposit — Whether defendant's objection went to the root of title — Whether trust disclosed on the conveyance of the freehold — Freehold interest purchased by trustee of trusts of the leasehold interest — Whether fee simple interest taken upon same trusts.*] The plaintiff was the owner of a property in fee simple, subject to and with the benefit of a lease. The leasehold interest had originally been the subject of a trust. The persons appointed by order of the court as trustees for the purpose of the Settled Land Acts had acquired, prior to their appointment as trustees, the fee simple interest in the property. They had been purported to convey the property to the plaintiff in fee simple, subject to and with the benefit of the lease. The leasehold interest was assigned to the plaintiff by the tenant for life, who was not a party to the other transaction. The plaintiff subsequently agreed to sell the property to the defendant. It was a condition of the agreement that any objections or requisitions on title should be sent to the vendor's solicitor within ten days after the delivery to the purchaser of the title deeds. Any objections or requisitions not made within that time and not going to the root of the title would be deemed to have been waived, time was made of the essence of this condition. It was also a condition of the contract that the purchaser should forfeit his deposit and the vendor should be at liberty to resell the property if the purchaser failed to comply with any of the said conditions. Copy documents of title were furnished to the defendant on 7 June, 1978. On 21 July, the plaintiff notified the defendant that she required completion within days; failure to comply would result in forfeiture of the deposit and rescission of the contract. No requisitions were furnished until 9 August, and these were answered without prejudice by the plaintiff on 11 August. The said requisitions included one which stated that the freehold interest should have been brought into the application on foot of which the trustees of the settlement had been appointed by the court, and that the conveyance of the fee simple to the plaintiff should have included the joinder of the tenant for life. The plaintiff replied that the trustees had not acquired the freehold in a trust capacity. On 17 August, the plaintiff notified the defendant that she was relying on the notice of 21 July and the conditions of the contract, and was retaining the deposit. After some further

correspondence, the present proceedings were instituted. **Held** by McWilliam J. in finding that the defendant's objection went to the root of the title, and that the plaintiff could not therefore rely on the conditions of the contract so as to rescind the sale and retain the deposit, 1, since both the freehold and the leasehold interests were being sold together to the same purchaser as one transaction, the purchaser was bound to look at the documents relating to both interests together. 2. Since the freehold interest was purchased by a trustee of the trust of the leasehold interest, he is bound by the equitable rule which forbids him from entering into engagements which conflict with the interests of the tenant for life. He is therefore prevented from taking any beneficial interest in the property the subject of the trust. *Keech* v. *Sandford* (1726) Sel. Cas. Ch. 61 followed. 3. The trustees of the settlement took the fee simple interest upon the same trusts as those on which they held the leasehold interest. The property could only be sold by the tenant for life or by all beneficiaries if of full age. *Coyle* v. *Central Trust Investment Society Ltd.*
(H.C.) [1978] ILRM 211

12. —— **Specific performance** — *Agreement by receiver in possession to sell factory — Performance of agreement delayed by the court — Allegation that the agreed price an undervalue — Whether contract enforceable.*] In 1977 the first-named defendant, a receiver in possession of the property of the second-named defendant, agreed to sell the latter's factory to the plaintiff for £21,000. The plaintiff paid a deposit, went into occupation of the factory as a tenant, and incurred expenditure on improvements. The second-named defendant objected to the sale on the ground that the price was insufficient. In other proceedings heard in 1977 the sale was ordered to be postponed pending an independent valuation. These proceedings were not pursued, and the sale remained uncompleted. This action for specific performance was brought in 1983, as the matter remained unresolved. In resisting the claim the second-named defendant alleged that the original agreement was insufficiently evidenced to be enforceable; that it had been discharged by a subsequent agreement to increase the price; and that the court had the power to set aside a contract made by a receiver if it were shown that he had not exercised reasonable care in obtaining the best price. **Held** by McWilliam J., granting a decree of specific performance, that, 1, there was a valid and enforceable contract for the sale of the factory to the plaintiff. 2. It would be inequitable to deny to the plaintiff the remedy it sought. 3. The receiver did not act reasonably in that he did not obtain a proper valuation prior to the sale and did not advertise

the property. 4. The second-named defendant would be left to pursue a claim for damages against the receiver. *W.P. McCarter & Co. Ltd.* v. *Roughan*
(H.C.) [1986] ILRM 447

13. —— **Specific performance** — *Contract — Completion — Interest — Dispute as to whether contract was completed on certain date — Basis on which interest to be awarded — Contract price placed on deposit — Interest gained on deposit.*] By agreement in writing of 6 September, 1977, between the defendant and the plaintiff, the defendant agreed to build and complete a house for the plaintiff by 29 September, 1977. The agreement provided that in the event of a dispute arising between the parties the defendant's architect's decision would be final. The defendant informed the plaintiff that the house was completed on 27 October, 1977. The plaintiff alleged that it was not completed and listed a number of defects that existed, which the defendant remedied in early December, 1977. Despite this the plaintiff continued to claim that the house was defective until May, 1978, when the defendant furnished him with the architect's certificate. The plaintiff then agreed to complete the sale and put the balance of the purchase money on deposit on 25 June, 1978. The defendant then refused to complete as the plaintiff would only pay interest on the purchase price from May, 1978, and not from November, 1977, as he sought. The plaintiff sought a decree of specific performance. **Held** by McWilliam J. in making a decree of specific performance on consent, 1, the defendant was entitled to interest from 1 January, 1978, to 25 June, 1978, at the rate of 20% per annum, and after 25 June, 1978, he was only entitled to interest which accrued on the deposit. 2. The plaintiff was not entitled to any damages for being deprived of the use of the house from 1 January, 1978, to the date of judgment. 3. The defendant was responsible for damage caused to the house by the severe winter in early 1979 insofar as this was due to his want of reasonable care. *Treacy* v. *Dwyer Nolan Developments Ltd.*
(H.C.) [1979] ILRM 163

14. —— **Specific performance** — *Contract subject to planning permission being obtained — Contract further providing that if permission obtained purchaser might pay a higher price at his own discretion — Whether void for uncertainty — Subsequent agreement as to wayleave — Whether material part of contract — Whether sufficient note or memorandum — Statute of Frauds,* 1695 (*c.* 12), *s.* 2.] The plaintiff entered into a contract to buy some acres of land from the defendant. The contract, which was drawn up by the plaintiff's solicitor, provided for the

SALE OF LAND—Contract.

sale of the land at £1,500 per acre, subject to outline planning permission being obtained. The contract further provided that in the event of planning permission being obtained, the purchaser might pay a higher price, at his own discretion. On the day on which the contract was signed by both parties, a further agreement was drawn up and signed by the plaintiff alone — although witnessed by the defendant's wife. This provided that a wayleave would be granted to the defendant for the connection of water and sewage. When the plaintiff sought to enforce the contract, the defendant (who meantime had received a higher offer) refused to furnish the title deeds on the grounds that the contract was unenforceable until planning permission had been obtained, and on the further ground of uncertainty as to the amount of the consideration. The plaintiff subsequently received planning permission. His claim for specific performance was resisted by the defendant on the grounds that the contract was void for uncertainty, planning permission had not been obtained within a reasonable time, the sale was at a gross undervalue due to the fact that the defendant did not have the benefit of independent advice, and the agreement relating to the wayleave was a material part of the contract, and that there was no memorandum in writing signed by the defendant. **Held** by McWilliam J. in awarding a decree of specific performance, the plaintiff submitting to the agreement which had been signed by him alone, 1, although a contract subject to a condition is unenforceable until the condition is fulfilled, it is nevertheless a contract from the beginning. The time therefore at which the value of the land should be assessed is the time of the making of the contract. *Aberfoyle Plantations Ltd.* v. *Khaw Bien Cheng* [1960] A.C. 115 distinguished. 2. The defendant did not appear, on the evidence, to have attempted to rescind the contract on the ground of delay at any stage in the negotiations. 3. There is no uncertainty attached to the amount of the consideration. The contract clearly gave the plaintiff a discretion to increase the price or not. 4. The wayleave agreement since it was not referred to in the principal agreement, could not be incorporated with it so as to constitute a sufficient memorandum for the purpose of the Statute of Frauds. *Timmins* v. *Moreland Street Property Co. Ltd.* [1958] Ch. 110 applied. 5. Nevertheless, since the wayleave agreement was to the benefit of the defendant, the plaintiff could concede it so as to cure its omission from the memorandum. *Scott* v. *Bradley* [1971] Ch. 850 approved and followed. *O'Mullane* v. *Riordan*

(H.C.) [1978] ILRM 73

Deposit, *see* Nos. 1, 8, 11, 15

SALE OF LAND—*continued.*

Depositor's lien, *see* No. 15

LIEN

15. —— **Purchaser** — *Deposit — Building company intending to build apartment block — "Booking" deposits paid — Neither building agreements nor contracts for the sale of land executed — Winding up of company — Company insolvent — Depositors claiming lien over site of proposed development — Depositors claiming to rank as secured creditors.*

Company law — Registration of charges — Purchaser's lien — Lien arising by operation of law — Companies Act, 1963 (*No.* 33), *s.* 99.] On various dates prior to September, 1980, Barrett Apartments Limited, a building company which proposed to build a block of flats on a site at Clontarf, County Dublin, received deposits of between £1,000 and £10,000 from 14 persons interested in purchasing the proposed apartments. In two cases only building agreements were signed but in the other 12 there was no binding contract, either to sell or to build and the deposits were described as "booking deposits". On 26 September, 1980, the company created an equitable mortgage of the site of the proposed development by deposit of the title deeds with Northern Bank Limited. On 1 October, 1980, Northern Bank Limited, exercising a power contained in a debenture dated 20 December, 1979, which created a floating charge over the assets of the company in favour of the Bank, appointed a receiver over its assets. On 25 May, 1981, the High Court ordered that the company be compulsorily wound up. The assets of the company, which consisted only of the site at Clontarf, were insufficient to meet the claims of unsecured creditors and the liquidator applied to the High Court for directions as to whether the persons who had paid the deposits were entitled to rank as secured creditors. **Held** by Keane J., in directing that the depositors were secured creditors, 1, that the lien claimed by the depositors arose not from the existence of any contract but from the uncontestable right of each prospective purchaser to recover his deposit in circumstances where it would be unjust for the prospective vendor to retain it. *Whitbread & Co. Limited* v. *Watt* [1902] 1 Ch. 835, considered. 2. The liens of the depositors arose by operation of law and were not created by the company. Accordingly the fact that particulars of charge had not been delivered to the registrar of companies, pursuant to s. 99 of the Companies Act, 1963, did not affect their validity. 3. The liens of the depositors had priority over the equitable interests of the Bank created by the deposit of the title deeds and the appointment of the receiver. On appeal by the receiver it was **Held**

SALE OF LAND—Lien.

by the Supreme Court (Henchy, Hederman and McCarthy JJ.), in allowing the appeal, 1, that the rationale behind allowing a purchaser a lien on the purchased property in respect of a deposit paid to the vendor is that, by paying the deposit in pursuance of the contract, the purchaser acquires an equitable estate or interest in the property and therefore should be allowed to follow that estate or interest by being awarded a lien on it. *Rose and others* v. *Watson* (1864) 10 H.L.C. 672; *Whitbread & Co. Limited* v. *Watt* [1902] 1 Ch. 835 and *Tempany* v. *Hynes* [1976] I.R. 101, considered. 2. That where, as was the case here, no contract to purchase was entered and the only payment made was a booking deposit, returnable upon notification by either party, and it had been expressly accepted that the proposed purchase would be the subject of a written contract, the payer acquired no estate or interest, legal or equitable, in the property. 3. That the depositors ranked in the liquidation as unsecured creditors. *Per* McCarthy J.: Justice does not demand that those who pay advances in respect of an anticipated contract should be put in a position better than that of trading creditors or professional creditors who have put their goods or their services at the disposal of the self same debtor without payment and whose claims can only rank as those of unsecured creditors. *In re Barrett Apartments Ltd.*

(H.C., S.C.) [1985] I.R.350; [1985] ILRM 679

16. —— **Vendor** — *Sale by company to associated company — Vendor's lien for unpaid purchase monies — Whether lien waived, abandoned or relinquished.*

Company — Liquidation — Application for directions by liquidator of vendor company — Companies Act, 1963 (*No.* 33), *s.* 280.] Under the terms of an agreement with Dublin Corporation A. Ltd. became entitled to the grant of a Corporation lease in respect of factory premises erected by A. Ltd. on Corporation property. Prior to the grant of the lease the directors and shareholders of A. Ltd. resolved to sell to S.F. Ltd. (of which company they were also the sole directors and shareholders) the interest of A. Ltd. in the premises for the sum of £65,000. The Corporation was informed of the arrangement and, on the direction of A. Ltd., subsequently granted a lease of the premises to S.F. Ltd. A. Ltd. was a party to the lease, which recited, *inter alia,* that A. Ltd. had resolved to waive its rights under the earlier agreement in favour of S.F. Ltd. In addition, A. Ltd. requested its bank, I.C.C. to restructure and transfer to S.F. Ltd. certain loan facilities made available by I.C.C. to A. Ltd. in connection with the building of the premises. No written contract was entered into between A. Ltd. and S.F. Ltd. in respect of the sale, the only written evidence of which remained the resolution of A. Ltd. The evidence was that, of the purchase price of £65,000, only £29,338 had been paid by S.F. Ltd. to A. Ltd. On the application of the liquidator of both companies for directions under s. 280 of the Companies Act, 1963, as to whether A. Ltd. was entitled to an unpaid vendor's lien over the premises in respect of the unpaid balance of the purchase price, it was **Held** by Murphy J., that to the extent that there were monies payable by S.F. Ltd. to A. Ltd. in connection with the sale, A. Ltd., as vendor, had on the facts waived, abandoned or relinquished any lien to which it was entitled. The implementation of the financial restructuring arrangement was ample consideration for the abandonment of the lien. *In re Aluminium Shop Fronts Ltd.*

(H.C.) [1987] I.R.419

Rescission of contract, *see* Nos. 9-11

REQUISITIONS ON TITLE

17. —— **Contract for the sale of land** — *No special condition relating to planning permission — Standard form warranty — Purchaser put an enquiry as to unauthorised use — Whether purchaser entitled to raise the matter by way of requisition — Whether certificate of discharge of capital acquisitions tax required to be furnished.*] By contract dated 1 December, 1981, the defendants agreed to purchase a house and premises from the plaintiff for the sum of £35,000.00. The closing date, as extended, was 2 February, 1982. The contract was in standard form and contained a standard warranty that planning permission had been obtained for any development in the property since 1 October, 1964. The defendants did not insert any special condition relating to planning permission. On 20 November, 1981, the defendants asked the plaintiff to confirm that planning permission had been obtained in respect of two self-contained flats adjoining the main bungalow and in requisitions on title stated that evidence of user of the premises at 1 October, 1964, and of use since that date must be given by a competent independent person and by the vendor. The reply to this requisition was the word "noted", and the plaintiff refused to comply with it until after proceedings had been issued by her. The plaintiff sued the defendants for interest on the unpaid balance of the purchase money from the closing date, contending that the defendants/purchasers were obliged to rely on the warranty given and to sue for any breach thereof and were not entitled to raise the matter by way of requisition. The question also arose as to whether the vendor's solicitor's undertaking to pay the capital acquisitions tax when assessed

SALE OF LAND—*continued.*

and to furnish a certificate of discharge therefrom as quickly as possible was sufficient to discharge the vendor from an obligation to hand over such certificate on closing. **Held** by Judge Sheridan in denying relief to the plaintiff, at the time of the issue of proceedings herein a valid requisition on title in respect of planning permission was outstanding. The defendants were therefore not in default in refusing to complete and the plaintiff was not entitled to interest on the unpaid balance of the purchase monies. Also, the vendor's solicitor's undertaking to pay the capital acquisitions tax when assessed and to furnish a certificate of discharge therefrom as quickly as possible was sufficient to discharge him from an obligation to hand over that certificate on closing. *Meagher* v. *Blount*

(Circ. Ct.) [1984] ILRM 671

Specific performance, *see* Nos. 4-6, 12-14

—— Condition of sale that contract dependent on Land Commission approval — Whether prospective purchaser has standing to object to compulsory acquisition of the land.
see **Land,** 1

—— Contract — Conditions — Particulars — Misdescription — Materiality — Registered land — Recorded folio acreage greater than acreage actually held in possession — Land Registry practice — Registration of Title Act, 1964, ss. 31, 85.
see **Arbitration,** 8

—— Contract — Negligence — Solicitor acting for vendor — Agreement for sale of land reached — Purchaser refusing to sign formal contract — Sale called off and new agreement for sale concluded with third party — First purchaser obtaining specific performance of his agreement — Second sale aborted — Vendor incurring losses out of both transactions — Whether vendor's solicitors liable in negligence.
see **Negligence,** 23

—— Contract — Negligence — Solicitor — Licensed premises — Nature of licence attached to premises — Plaintiffs required premises with full seven days publican's licence — Vendor holding hotel licence — Plaintiffs' solicitor's failure to discover true nature of licence — Insufficient enquiries by solicitor.
see **Negligence,** 25

SALE OF LAND—*continued.*

—— Contract — Rescission — Failure of purchaser to complete sale on receipt of valid completion notice — Forfeiture of deposit — Express terms enabling vendor to rescind and forfeit deposit — On defendant's motion purchaser's action for specific performance dismissed — *Lis pendens* vacated.
see **Practice and Procedure,** 2

—— Deposits — Booking deposits — Anticipatory payment — Payment made by plaintiff before house built by developer — House not built — Insolvency of developer — Depositors claiming lien over site of proposed development.
see **Sale of Land,** 15

—— Deposits — Booking deposits — Payments made to vendor's solicitor — Vendor in receivership — Loss of deposits — Capacity in which deposits received by vendor's solicitor — Correspondence from purchaser's solicitor — Whether sufficient notice to vendor's solicitor to hold deposits as stakeholders — Negligence — Liability of purchasers' solicitor for loss of deposits.
see **Negligence,** 24

—— Family home — Consent — Spouse not informed of sale — Purchaser making no inquiries — Vendor spouse making statutory declaration that house not a family home — Whether purchaser deemed to have notice — Whether desertion avoids necessity to obtain consent to sale.
see **Family Law,** 29

—— Negligence — Solicitor — Building contract followed by lease — Investigation of title not made until after completion of building and making of payments — Discovery of pre-existing equitable mortgage by deposit of land certificate — Insolvency of building company — Refusal of mortgagee to release house unless paid proportion of mortgage debt — Whether defendants should have examined title before execution of building contract — No custom of solicitors — Whether defendants negligent.
see **Negligence,** 26

—— Solicitor — Negligence — Conveyancing — Duty of care.
see **Negligence,** 22-6

SOCIAL WELFARE

1. —— **Employment insurance** — *Insurability of employment — Rate of contribution — Whether ordinary or special rate of contribution applied — Whether board a public authority — Health Act,* 1970 (*No.* 1), *ss.* 11, 18, 20, 27, 28, 31(1), 33, 58(1), 59(1) — *Social Welfare (Modification of Insurance) Regulations,* 1956 (*S.I. No.* 236), *art.* 5(1)(*c*) — *General Medical Services (Payments) Board (Establishment) Order,* 1973 (*S.I. No.* 184), *arts.* 3, 4, 5, 6, 11, 18, 19.] McC., an employee of the plaintiff board, had applied to a deciding officer of the Department of Social Welfare for a decision as to whether his employment was insurable for the purposes of the Social Welfare Act, 1952, at the ordinary rate of contribution, or at the special rate applicable to employment by a public authority pursuant to article 5(1)(*c*) of the Social Welfare (Modification of Insurance) Regulations, 1956. The decision of the deciding officer that the employee was insurable at the ordinary rate having been upheld by an appeals officer, the plaintiff appealed to the High Court pursuant to s. 45 of the 1952 Act. Since it was conceded that the employee fulfilled all other conditions, the only issue before the court was whether the plaintiff board was a public authority. **Held** by Hamilton J. in allowing the appeal and declaring that the employee was employed in the service of a public authority, viz., the plaintiff board, 1, a public authority is a body which has public or statutory duties to perform for the benefit of the public, and not for private profit. 2. The services provided by the plaintiff were delegated to it by the health board in pursuance of statutory obligations placed upon it by the Health Act, 1970. The said obligations are imposed for the benefit of the public in the administration of the health services. *General Medical Services (Payments) Board* v. *The Minister for Social Welfare*
(H.C.) [1976-7] ILRM 210

2. —— **Employment insurance** — *Insurability of employment — Ordinary member of the Labour Court — Whether employed in civil service — Whether employed under a contract of service — Employment contribution — Submission to deciding officer — Decision on issues not submitted — Upheld by appeals officer — Judicial review — Application — Delay — Illegality — Law applicable to facts for decision — Social Welfare (Consolidation) Act,* 1981 (*No.* 1), *s.* 111 *and* 1*st Sched.*] The applicant, an ordinary member of the Labour Court, submitted for decision the question of what rate of contribution was payable by his employer to a deciding officer under the Social Welfare (Consolidation) Act, 1981. The deciding officer determined that since the applicant was not employed under a contract of service or in the civil service

SOCIAL WELFARE—*continued.*

of the Government or of the State, that the applicant's employment was not insurable at all. That decision was affirmed by his appeals officer. The applicant sought and obtained in the High Court leave to apply for orders of judicial review quashing those decisions and declaring that he was in insurable employment under the Act. Upon the respondent filing grounds of opposition it was **Held** by Blayney J., in granting the orders of judicial review sought, 1, that the deciding officer had jurisdiction to decide only those questions actually submitted to him. 2. That the decisions of both the deciding officer and appeals officer were vulnerable on the ground of illegality in that they arose from a misunderstanding of the law applicable to the established facts. *Council of Civil Service Unions* v. *Minister for Civil Service* [1985] A.C. 374 considered. 3. That the applicant was a civil as opposed to a combatant servant of the State and was engaged in the civil service of the State and accordingly his employment was insurable under the Social Welfare (Consolidation) Act, 1981. *McLoughlin* v. *Minister for Social Welfare* [1958] I.R. 1 applied. *Murphy* v. *Minister for Social Welfare*

(H.C.) [1987] I.R.295

3. —— **Employment insurance** — *Estoppel — Minister — Statutory authority — Whether extendable by estoppel — Social Welfare (Consolidation) Act,* 1981 (*No.* 1).] *Power* v. *Minister for Social Welfare*

(H.C.) [1987] I.R.307

Editor's note: This case was heard immediately after *Murphy* v. *Minister for Social Welfare* (see No.2 — above), in which the legal submissions were substantially the same.

4. —— **European directive** — *Equal treatment in matters of social security — Failure to fully implement directive — Whether directive has direct effect — Whether directive sufficiently unconditional and precise — Whether in the absence of implementing measures, women entitled to the benefits under the same conditions as men — Council Directive* 79/7/*EEC, Art.* 4(1) — *Social Welfare* (*No.* 2) *Act,* 1985 (*No.* 14), *ss.* 2, 6(*c*).] Article 117 of the EEC Treaty of Rome confers jurisdiction on the European Court of Justice to give preliminary rulings on questions referred to it by national courts, concerning, *inter alia,* the validity and interpretation of acts of the institutions of the Community. Article 189 of the Treaty provides that a Directive of the European Council shall be binding, as to the results to be achieved, upon each member state to which it is addressed. Article 4(1) of Directive 79/7/EEC, on the progressive implementation of the principle of equal treatment for men and women in

SOCIAL WELFARE—*continued.*

matters of social security, provides that in such matters there shall be no discrimination whatsoever on grounds of sex, either directly, or indirectly by reference, in particular, to marital or family status, in particular as concerns the scope of social security schemes, and the conditions of access thereto. Member states should have taken the necessary steps to implement the Directive by 23 December, 1984. Ireland had not done so. Under the provisions of Chapters 4 and 6 of Part 2 of the Social Welfare (Consolidation) Act, 1981, the unemployment benefit payable to married women is less and of shorter duration than that payable to married men and single persons. These provisions were repealed by ss. 2 and 6(*c*) of the Social Welfare (No. 2) Act, 1985, which afford equality of treatment to married women in relation to unemployment benefit. The sections have limited retroactive effect. The prosecutrices, two married women, had had their unemployment benefit terminated in accordance with the provisions of the 1981 Act. They did not come within the retroactive effect of the 1985 legislation. They argued that if they had not been married women, they would have been entitled to receive unemployment benefit for a further period. They therefore made application to the High Court in Dublin for an order quashing the decisions which terminated their benefit on the ground that these decisions infringed their rights under Article 4 of Directive 79/7/EEC. The respondents submitted that Article 4 could not be relied upon in the Irish courts, as it did not impose clear and precise obligations upon Ireland, and that Ireland consequently had considerable discretion in determining the manner of implementation. The High Court stayed the proceedings and submitted the following questions to the Court of Justice for a preliminary ruling: (1) Do the provisions of Directive 79/7/EEC, and in particular Article 4 thereof, have direct effect in the Republic of Ireland as and from the 23 December, 1984, so as to confer enforceable Community rights upon married women such as the prosecutrices in the circumstances of the present case? (2) If the answer to question 1 is in the affirmative, does this mean that national provisions such as those contained in Chapters 4 and 6 of Part 2 of the Social Welfare (Consolidation) Act, 1981, as amended, are inactable, and that the prosecutrices as married women living in a Member State which had failed to repeal or adapt such provisions are entitled to equal treatment in relation to the relevant social welfare benefits as and from the 23 December, 1984, and have rights of action in that regard which are enforceable by them against such Member States? **Held** by the Court of Justice of European Communities in answering both questions in the affirmative, 1, where the provisions of a Directive appear, as far as their subject-matter is concerned, to be unconditional and precise, individuals may rely on those provisions in the absence of implementing measures adopted within the prescribed period as against a national provision incompatible with the Directive, or insofar as the Directive defines rights assertable against the State. *Becker* v. *Finanzamt Munster-Innenstadt* [1982] E.C.R. 53, followed. 2. Article 4(1) is sufficiently precise to be relied upon in legal proceedings, and the said article does not permit a Member State to restrict or place conditions on the application of the principle of equal treatment in its particular area of application. 3. The fact that Directives leave to the national authorities the choice of form and method for achieving the required result cannot constitute a ground for denying all effect to those provisions which may be relied upon before a court. *Becker* v. *Finanzamt Munster-Innenstadt* [1982] E.C.R. 53, applied. 4. Where national measures have not been implemented, women are entitled to have the same rules applied to them as men in the same circumstances, since these rules are the only valid points of reference. *Netherlands* v. *FNV* [1987] 3 C.M.L.R. 767. *McDermott and Cotter* v. *Minister for Social Welfare*

(E.C.J.) [1987] ILRM 324

5. —— **Invalidity pension** — *Non-contributory invalidity pension — Respondent incapable of work throughout qualifying period before her sixtieth birthday — No claim for benefit until after birthday — Whether respondent "entitled" to invalidity pension before her sixtieth birthday — Social Security (Northern Ireland) Act,* 1975 (*c.* 14), *ss.* 36, 79.] The respondent was born on 15 April, 1920, and reached pensionable age on 15 April, 1980, being her sixtieth birthday. On 10 April, 1981, she claimed a non-contributory invalidity pension under section 36(1) of the Social Security (Northern Ireland) Act, 1975, having been incapable of work for the required minimum period of 196 days before 15 April, 1980. The appellant refused the claim on the ground that section 36(4) of the 1975 Act provided that a person who had attained pensionable age shall not be entitled to a pension under the section unless he was entitled to a pension immediately before he attained pensionable age and that the respondent had failed to show she was so entitled. From that decision the respondent appealed to a local tribunal which upheld her appeal. The appellant appealed to the Social Security Commissioner who dismissed the appeal. The appellant appealed by way of case stated to the Court of Appeal contending that the making of a claim for a pension under section 79(1) of the 1975 Act was essential and as the respondent had not made a claim before her sixtieth birthday she was not entitled to a pension. **Held,** dismissing the appeal that, 1, the only relevant provision limiting entitlement to a pension conferred by section 36(1) was subsection (4) which excluded from entitlement a person of pensionable age unless so entitled immediately before attaining that age. The respondent was entitled to a pension as she fulfilled the qualifications of sub-section (1) in that she had been incapable of work for the required minimum period of 196 days before her sixtieth year. 2. The entitlement conferred by section 36 was not subject to the condition, imposed by section 79, of making a claim which was concerned only with administration of the benefit. On appeal by the appellant to the House of Lords **Held,** dismissing the appeal that, 1, the respondent's entitlement was governed by section 36 which did not define entitlement by reference to the making of a claim or require a claim as a condition precedent to entitlement and section 79(1) had to be construed so as to be consistent with the entitlement created by section 36. 2. The effect of section 79(1) was that a claimant not only had to show the existence of an entitlement but also had to make a claim in the prescribed manner and within the prescribed time in order that he may be paid and the subsection did not govern a claimant's entitlement to a benefit. *Insurance Officer* v. *McCarthy*

(C.A., H.L.) [1984] N.I. 108

6. —— **Supplementary benefit** — *Entitlement to benefit — Applicant an unpaid solicitor's apprentice — Whether exempt from requirement to be "available for employment" — Whether in receipt of a "training allowance" — Whether in analogous circumstances — Supplementary Benefits (Conditions of Entitlement) Regulations (Northern Ireland)* 1981 (*S.R. No.* 28), *reg.* 6(1), 6(*u*).] The appellant was in receipt of supplementary benefit until he began a period of full-time training as a solicitor's apprentice. He was not paid any remuneration during this period. He was subsequently refused supplementary benefit by the Supplementary Benefits Officer on the ground that he was not longer available for employment as required by article 7 of the Supplementary Benefits (Northern Ireland) Order, 1977. This refusal was reversed on appeal by the Belfast Supplementary Benefit Appeals Tribunal. On a further appeal the Social Security Commissioner reversed the Appeals Tribunal finding and decided against the appellant's entitlement to benefit. The appellant argued that he was exempt from the requirement of being available for employment by virtue of regulation 6(*u*) of the Supplementary Benefits

(Conditions of Entitlement) Regulations (Northern Ireland), 1981, as his circumstances were analogous to those of a recipient of a training allowance under regulation 6(1) on further appeal by the appellant. **Held,** dismissing the appeal, that the effect of regulation 6(1) is to prescribe the receipt of an allowance from public funds as the basic circumstance in the exempted case. Although the appellant was following a course of training he was unpaid and therefore his circumstances were not analogous to regulation 6(1). *Semble,* it is doubtful as to whether a purely private course of training could be said to be analogous to a government or government approved course. *Smith* v. *Supplementary Benefit Officer*

(C.A.) [1984] N.I. 24

7. —— **Supplementary welfare allowance** — *Fuel allowance — Regulations providing for payment of allowance on means test — Departmental circular excluding from scheme persons on short term social welfare — Whether circular* ultra vires *the Minister for Social Welfare — Whether decision based on guidelines in circular valid — Social Welfare (Consolidation) Act,* 1981 (*No.* 1), *ss.* 209, 312 — *Social Welfare (Supplementary Welfare Allowances) Act,* 1975 (*No.* 28), *s.* 11 — *Social Welfare (Supplementary Welfare Allowances) Regulations,* 1977 (*S.I. No.* 168 *of* 1977), *art.* 6.] The prosecutrix was a married woman with one child whose husband had deserted her. She was in receipt of unemployment benefit. She applied for supplementary welfare allowance for fuel under the National Fuel Scheme operated by the health board pursuant to the Social Welfare (Consolidation) Act, 1981. The Department of Social Welfare had issued a circular excluding from the Scheme persons on short term social welfare payments such as unemployment disability benefit or assistance. The prosecutrix was refused a fuel allowance on the basis of the circular and this decision was affirmed by an appeals officer on the same ground. S. 11 of the Social Welfare (Supplementary Welfare Allowances) Act, 1975, which was replaced by similar provisions in s. 209 of the 1981 Act, empowered the Minister for Social Welfare to make regulations to grant a person a weekly supplementary allowance or increase an existing one where the person's income or existing allowance "is not sufficient to meet that person's needs." The Minister made regulations, the Social Welfare (Supplementary Welfare Allowances) Regulations, 1977, which were carried over by s. 312 of the 1981 Act. Art. 6 of the Regulations provided that a payment, including a payment in kind for heating needs, may be made by a health board "of such amount as . . . is determined by the health board to be appropriate to meet such

SOCIAL WELFARE—*continued.*

needs." The prosecutrix applied for certiorari to quash the refusal. **Held** by Finlay P. in granting the order: while the circular was a valid administrative act so far as it formed advice and guidance to the health boards, it was *ultra vires* the Minister to the extent that it purported to exclude absolutely from the National Fuel Scheme persons in receipt of unemployment disability benefit or assistance, and since the prosecutrix's means had not been considered in her application for an allowance the refusals must be quashed. *The State (Kershaw)* v. *Eastern Health Board*

(H.C.) [1985] ILRM 235

8. —— **Supplementary welfare allowance** — *Fuel allowance — Statutory right to supplementary welfare allowance — Power of Minister for Social Welfare to prescribe circumstances in which fuel allowance might be paid — Regulations providing for payment of fuel allowance — Regulation excluding persons from eligibility for fuel allowance by reference to type of social welfare payment which they received — Whether regulation* ultra vires.

Statute — Statutory instrument — Severance — Minister for Social Welfare making regulations with consent of Minister for Finance — Part of regulations ultra vires — *Whether void provisions severable — Effect of severance of void provisions on scheme created by statutory instrument — Social Welfare (Supplementary Welfare Allowances) Regulations,* 1977 (*S.I. No.* 168), *art.* 6, *sub-art.* 7(*a*) — *Social Welfare (Supplementary Welfare Allowances) Amendment Regulations,* 1985 (*S.I. No.* 49) — *Social Welfare (Supplementary Welfare Allowances) Amendment* (*No.* 2) *Regulations,* 1985 (*S.I. No.* 334) — *Social Welfare (Consolidation) Act,* 1981 (*No.* 1), *ss.* 3, 199, 200, 207, 208, 209 — *Constitution of Ireland,* 1937, *Arts.* 15.4, 50.] Section 200 of the Social Welfare (Consolidation) Act, 1981, provides: "Subject to this Chapter, every person in the State whose means are insufficient to meet his needs and the needs of any adult or child dependant of his shall be entitled to supplementary welfare allowance." Section 209, sub-ss. 1 and 2 of the Act of 1981 provide: "(1) Where the weekly amount of supplementary welfare allowance, if any, payable to a person . . . and any other income, including any payment under this Act or under any other statute, of that person, is not sufficient to meet his needs, then— (*a*) in any case where that person is in receipt of supplementary welfare allowance, the weekly amount of such allowance payable to that person may, subject to this section,be increased, or (*b*) in any other case, a weekly payment of supplementary welfare allowance may be made, subject to this section, to supplement that person's other income. (2) The Minister may prescribe—

SOCIAL WELFARE—*continued.*

(*a*) the circumstances under which a payment may be made to any person pursuant to *subsection* (1), and (*b*) the amounts of payments to be made either generally or in relation to a particular class of persons." Section 3, sub-ss. 1 and 2 of the Act of 1981 provide that: "(1) The Minister may [*with the consent of the Minister for Finance*] make regulations— (*a*) for any purpose in relation to which regulations are provided for by any of the provisions of this Act, and (*b*) for prescribing any matter or thing referred to in this Act as prescribed or to be prescribed. (2) Except in so far as this Act otherwise provides, any power conferred thereby to make regulations may be exercised— (*a*) either in relation to all cases to which that power extends, or in relation to all those cases subject to specified exceptions, or in relation to any specified cases or classes of case . . ." Article 6, sub-art. 7(*a*) of the Social Welfare (Supplementary Welfare Allowances) Regulations, 1977, as inserted by art. 3 of the Social Welfare (Supplementary Welfare Allowances) Amendment Regulations, 1985, provided that an increase in supplementary welfare allowance or a supplementary welfare allowance, to be known as a "fuel allowance", might be paid for the period commencing on the first Monday of October of each year to a person whose means were insufficient for his needs and who was in receipt of one of 15 listed social welfare payments. In November, 1985, the prosecutor, who was a person in receipt of unemployment assistance, applied to the first respondent for a fuel allowance. His application was refused on the sole ground that he did not fall within one of the 15 categories listed at art. 6, sub-art. 7(*a*) of the Regulations of 1977. The prosecutor's means were insufficient to meet his needs and the amount of unemployment assistance he received was less than some of the 15 listed payments. The prosecutor obtained a conditional order of certiorari in the High Court quashing the decision of the first respondent on the grounds, *inter alia,* that the Regulations of 1985 were *ultra vires* the Minister for Social Welfare. Barron J. made the conditional order absolute notwithstanding cause shown and declared that art. 6, sub-art. 7(*a*) of the Regulations of 1977, as inserted by the Regulations of 1985, was *ultra vires* the Minister. The respondents appealed to the Supreme Court on the grounds firstly, that Barron J. had erred in law in holding that art. 6, sub-art. 7(*a*) was void; and secondly, if art. 6, sub-art. 7(*a*) was *ultra vires,* then Barron J. ought to have struck down the entire of S.I. No. 49 of 1985 and S.I. No. 334 of 1985 — which increased the amount of the fuel allowance — and not just the impugned provision. **Held** by the Supreme Court (Finlay C.J., Henchy, Griffin, Hederman and McCarthy JJ.), in varying the order of the

SOCIAL WELFARE—*continued.*

High Court, 1, that the combined effect of ss. 199, 200 and 209 of the Act of 1981, was to give to any person whose means were insufficient to meet his needs a vested right to a supplementary welfare allowance. *The State (Kershaw)* v. *Eastern Health Board* [1985] ILRM 235 followed. 2. That the power given to the Minister for Social Welfare by s. 209 of the Act of 1981 to prescribe the circumstances in which such payments might be made did not, either on its own or read in conjunction with the general power to make regulations given to the Minister by s. 3 of the Act, entitle him to exclude persons from consideration for fuel allowance merely on the basis that such person was in receipt of unemployment assistance. To do so would be to use a power given to allow the statutory right to be implemented, to cut down that right. 3. Accordingly, art. 6, sub-art. 7(*a*) of the Regulations of 1977, as inserted by art. 3 of the Regulations of 1985, was *ultra vires* the Minister for Social Welfare. 4. That to condemn only art. 6, sub-art. 7(*a*) of the Regulations of 1977 would be to impose on the State a scheme which was never intended and to impose on the exchequer a burden to which the Minister for Finance had never consented; and, accordingly, would amount to an amendment rather than an interpretation of the scheme. In the circumstances, the entire of S.I. No.49 as well as S.I. No. 334 of 1985 should be declared void. *Maher* v. *The Attorney General* [1973] I.R. 140 considered. *Per* McCarthy J. *Quaere* where any material part of a statutory instrument is found to be *ultra vires,* whether in principle, having regard to the fact that statutory instruments do not enjoy the restorative protection which is afforded to statutes by Art. 15, s. 4, sub-s. 2 of the Constitution, the remainder can be allowed to stand. *The State (McLoughlin)* v. *Eastern Health Board*

(S.C.) [1986] I.R.416

9. —— **Unmarried mother's allowance** — *Entitlement — Statutory regulations defining unmarried mother for purposes of entitlement — Whether exclusion of mother who is a divorced woman is* ultra vires *the Act of* 1981 — *Social Welfare (Social Assistance (Allowance) Regulations,* 1973 (*S.I. No.* 190) — *Social Welfare (Consolidation) Act,* 1981 (*No.* 1), *s.* 197.] Section 197 of the Social Welfare (Consolidation) Act, 1981, provides that a social assistance allowance shall be paid to an unmarried mother in certain circumstances. Article 4 of the Social Welfare (Social Assistance Allowance) Regulations, 1973, provides that a "woman is to be regarded for the purposes of [*the Act of 1981*] as being an unmarried mother if, not being or having been a married woman, she is the mother of a child who has not been adopted."

SOCIAL WELFARE—*continued.*

The prosecutrix, a divorced woman with one child born outside the marriage, was held by the relevant social welfare officers to be ineligible for social assistance allowance because she was excluded under the above definition of unmarried mother. The prosecutrix obtained a conditional order of certiorari quashing the above decision on the grounds that (*a*) art. 4 of the Regulations of 1973 was void and of no legal effect as the power to make same was *ultra vires* the powers of the first respondent pursuant to s. 8 of the Social Welfare Act, 1973, which section corresponds with s. 197 of the Social Welfare (Consolidation) Act, 1981 and (*b*) the decision was made without and in excess of jurisdiction in that if art. 4 of the Regulations of 1973 was made *ultra vires* the powers of the first respondent, then s. 8 of the Act of 1973 and s. 197, sub-s. 4A of the Act of 1981 were unconstitutional in that they purported to vest power to legislate in the first respondent. **Held** by Egan J., in making absolute the order of certiorari notwithstanding cause shown, that it would be oppressive and unfair if one class of mother were excluded from such benefits as those to which other classes of mother were entitled and such exclusion was never intended by the legislature. Accordingly, art. 4 of the Regulations of 1973 was invalid as being *ultra vires* the Act of 1981. *Dicta* of Henchy J. in *Cassidy* v. *Minister for Industry and Commerce* [1978] I.R. 297 applied. *The State (Kenny)* v. *Minister for Social Welfare*

(H.C.) [1986] I.R.693

—— Disability benefit — Pay-related benefit — Road accident — Damages — Whether possible future social welfare payments deductible from damages.
see **Damages,** 8

—— Employment contributions — Employer's annual obligation to provide information relating to employees — Whether employment or partnership in existence.
see **Revenue,** 38

—— Offence — Making false statements to obtain unemployment benefit — Number of similar offences charged in the one summons — District Court — Jurisdiction.
see **District Court,** 1

—— Old age pension — Refusal — Certiorari — Whether decision of appeals officer bad in law.
see **Judicial Review,** 7

—— Payments by Health Boards — Disabled

SOCIAL WELFARE—*continued.*

person's maintenance allowance — Provision requiring account to be taken of income of spouse — Whether account could be taken of social welfare benefits or allowances received by first applicant's spouse in his own right.
see **Statute,** 1

—— Unemployment benefit — Compensation payment for period of notice — Whether payment should be reduced by reference to social welfare benefits received.
see **Employer and Employee,** 20

SOLDIER

see **Defence Forces**

SOLICITOR

1. —— **Costs** — *Lien — Solicitor obtaining title deeds from mortgagee on accountable receipt — Particulars and conditions of sale prepared by solicitor on instructions of mortgagor — Insolvency of mortgagor — Whether solicitor entitled to lien over title deeds for costs.*] G. Ltd. was the owner of premises which were mortgaged to I.C.C. who had possession of the title deeds. G. Ltd. instructed H., a firm of solicitors, to prepare particulars and conditions of sale for an auction. For that purpose H. obtained the title deeds from I.C.C. on accountable receipt "to hold the . . . documents on trust for" I.C.C. H. did the work but the property did not sell and soon after G. Ltd. went into liquidation. The title deeds were returned to I.C.C. but H., in a covering letter, claimed to be entitled to a lien over the deeds for their fees. The liquidator applied to the High Court for directions and Carroll J. held that no lien had been created in favour of H. On appeal by H. it was **Held** by the Supreme Court (Finlay C.J., Hederman and McCarthy JJ.) in dismissing the appeal, that the solicitors had held the title deeds not on behalf of their client but, by the terms of the accountable receipt, expressly as trustee for I.C.C. Such possession was inconsistent with the existence of any lien over the deeds. *Semble:* That the owner of a lien who is compelled through force of circumstance to part with possession of the subject matter will not lose his rights by reason only of the mere physical parting. *Caldwell* v. *Sumpters* [1972] Ch. 478 considered. *In re Galdan Properties Ltd.*

(S.C.) [1988] I.R. 213; [1988] ILRM 559

2. —— **Misconduct** — *Bank loan to solicitor — Loan for private purposes — Undertakings from solicitor's firm required by bank — Undertakings forged by solicitor — Default in repayment*

SOLICITOR—*continued.*

of loan — Solicitor struck off roll — Claim by bank for compensation — Compensation Fund maintained by Law Society — Compensation payable where loss sustained in consequence of dishonesty on part of solicitor "in connection with that solicitor's practice as a solicitor" — Whether forged undertakings were furnished by solicitor in connection with his practice — Whether compensation payable only to clients of solicitors — Solicitors (Amendment) Act, 1960 (*No.* 37), *s.* 21(4).] The Solicitors Acts, 1954 and 1960, provide, *inter alia,* for the maintenance by the Incorporated Law Society of Ireland of a fund for the purpose of providing compensation to persons who have suffered loss in consequence of dishonesty on the part of solicitors. Section 21, sub-s. 4 of the Act of 1960 provides as follows: "Where it is proved to the satisfaction of the Society that any person has sustained loss in consequence of dishonesty on the part of any solicitor or any clerk or servant of a solicitor in connection with that solicitor's practice as a solicitor or in connection with any trust of which that solicitor is a trustee, then, subject to the provisions of this section, the Society shall make a grant to that person out of the Fund and the amount of the grant shall be such as represents in the opinion of the Society full indemnity for that loss." M., a partner in a firm of solicitors, applied to the plaintiff for a loan which was expressed to be for the purpose of purchasing a house. The bank agreed to make the loan on condition that it received certain undertakings from the applicant's firm. A letter, which contained the required undertakings and which purported to be signed by another partner on behalf of the firm, was forged by M. and presented to the plaintiff and monies were advanced by the plaintiff to the firm's account. When called upon to do so, both M. and his firm failed to repay that loan. M. was subsequently struck off the roll of solicitors. The plaintiff applied to the defendant for compensation in respect of its loss from the Fund maintained by the defendant. The defendant refused on the grounds that the plaintiff had not been a client of the solicitor and therefore did not fall within the class of persons which the Solicitors Acts were intended to protect. On the plaintiff's application to the High Court for a declaration that it was entitled to be paid compensation by the defendant out of the said fund, and for an order for payment as aforesaid, it was **Held** by Johnson J., in granting the orders sought, that, in writing a false undertaking in the name of his firm and forging the signature of his partner thereto, M. had held himself out as acting on behalf of his firm and was therefore acting in connection with his practice as a solicitor. *Per* Johnson J. That the protection provided by s. 21 of the Act of 1960 was not restricted

SOLICITOR—*continued.*

to clients of solicitors, and to beneficiaries of trusts of which solicitors are trustees. *Trustee Savings Bank* v. *Incorporated Law Society*
(H.C.) [1987] I.R. 430; [1988] ILRM 541

—— Appearance — Presumption that counsel and solicitor appear on express instruction of the client.
see **Constitution,** 42

—— Apprentice — Unpaid solicitor's apprentice — Supplementary benefit — Entitlement — Whether in receipt of a "training allowance"—Whether "available for employment".
see **Social Welfare,** 6

—— Costs — Lien — Solicitor claiming against proceeds of judgment for costs — Judgment creditor obtaining conditional order of garnishee against proceeds — Judgment creditor applying for absolute order before solicitor had applied for charging order — Whether solicitor entitled to priority over judgment creditor.
see **Garnishee**

—— Costs — Taxation.
see **Practice and Procedure,** 26-33

—— Negligence — Duty of care — Compromise of action — Agreement — Option — Failure to exercise by solicitor on behalf of client — Failure to notify client — Whether breach of duty of care — Whether loss suffered by client attributable to breach of duty of care — Whether client entitled to damages.
see **Negligence,** 21

—— Negligence — Duty of care — Contract for the sale of land — Purchaser successfully seeking rescission of contract — Whether vendor's solicitor negligent.
see **Negligence,** 22

—— Negligence — Sale of land — Deposits prior to contract — Payment to vendor's solicitor — Vendor in receivership — Loss of deposits — Capacity in which deposits received by vendor's solicitor — Correspondence from purchaser's solicitor — Whether sufficient notice to vendor's solicitor to hold deposits as stakeholders — Liability of purchasers' solicitor for loss of deposits.
see **Negligence,** 24

SOLICITOR—*continued.*

—— Negligence — Sale of land — Licensed premises — Nature of licence attached to premises — Plaintiffs required premises with full seven days publican's licence — Vendor holding hotel licence — Plaintiffs' solicitor's failure to discover true nature of licence — Insufficient enquiries by solicitor — Damages.
see **Negligence,** 25

—— Negligence — Sale of land — Registered land — Building contract followed by lease — Stage payments — Investigation of title not made until after completion of building and making of payments — Discovery of pre-existing equitable mortgage by deposit of land certificate — Mortgage registered as charge in Companies Office prior to execution of building contract — Insolvency of building company — Refusal of mortgagee to release house unless paid proportion of mortgage debt — Whether defendants should have examined title before execution of building contract — No custom of solicitors — Whether defendants negligent.
see **Negligence,** 26

—— Negligence — Sale of land — Solicitor acting for vendor — Agreement for sale of land reached — Purchaser refusing to sign formal contract — Sale called off and new agreement for sale concluded with third party — First purchaser obtaining specific performance of his agreement — Second sale aborted — Vendor incurring losses out of both transactions — Whether vendor's solicitors liable in negligence.
see **Negligence,** 23

—— Prisoner's access to solicitor — Prison regulations excluding certain solicitors — Whether unconstitutional.
see **Prisons,** 2

—— Representation "without prejudice" — "Watching brief"—Validity of concept.
see **Criminal Law,** 62

—— Undertaking — Effect — Solicitor undertaking to pay proceeds of judgment to bank — Judgment creditor seeking to attach proceeds — Whether undertaking created equitable assignment of proceeds of judgment — Whether bank entitled to priority over judgment creditor.

SOLICITOR—*continued.*

see **Garnishee**

SPECIAL CRIMINAL COURT

—— **Establishment** — *Validity — Appointment of members — Qualification for membership — Removal and registration of members — Whether Government empowered to establish Special Criminal Court — Whether judges appointed to Special Criminal Court ceased to be members on ceasing to be judges — Offences Against the State Act,* 1939 (*No.* 13), *Part V.*

Habeas Corpus — Detention — Grounds — Certificate — Special Criminal Court — Appointment and composition — Conviction — Whether detention vitiated by events prior to charge of applicant — District Court Rules, 1948 (*S.I. No.* 431 *of* 1947) — *Offences Against the State Acts,* 1939 to 1972 *(Special Criminal Court) Rules,* 1975 (*S.I. No.* 234) — *Offences Against the State Act,* 1939 (*No.* 13), *Part V — Constitution of Ireland,* 1937, *Art.* 40(4).] The applicant was arrested by gardaí after a shoot-out at Newmarket-on-Fergus on the 17 March, 1984, and extradited to Northern Ireland on foot of a warrant issued there and backed for execution in the Republic of Ireland. While in Northern Ireland a warrant for the applicant's arrest on foot of offences arising out of the shoot-out was issued from Ennis District Court on the 19 May, 1984. The applicant stood trial and was acquitted in Northern Ireland and was then extradited to the Republic of Ireland, where he was arrested at Carrickarnon on the 11 October, 1985, on foot of the Ennis warrant and immediately conveyed to Ennis District Court. He was returned for trial to the Special Criminal Court and there convicted on the 11 March, 1986, of possession of firearms and shooting with intent to resist arrest and sentenced to ten years imprisonment and penal servitude respectively. Pending an appeal against conviction to the Court of Criminal Appeal, the applicant unsuccessfully applied *ex parte* to the High Court for a determination that he was being unlawfully detained. Upon his *ex parte* appeal the Supreme Court (Finlay C.J., Walsh and McCarthy JJ.) directed that the High Court hold an enquiry, pursuant to Article 40 of the Constitution, into the legality of the applicant's detention. The respondent in his certificate justified the detention by reference to the order of the Special Criminal Court. At the hearing the applicant challenged the appointment, selection and composition procedures of the Special Criminal Court and the propriety of certain aspects of the information leading to the issue and execution of the Ennis warrant. **Held** by the High Court (Gannon, Carroll and Lynch JJ.) and affirmed by the Supreme Court (Finlay C.J., Henchy, Griffin, Hederman and McCarthy JJ.), in refusing to order release, 1, that although Part

V of the Offences Against the State Act, 1939, did not expressly confer power on the Government to establish a Special Criminal Court, such a power must be inferred from the power to appoint the members of such court and to determine their number and from the express power of the Government to establish additional Special Criminal Courts. 2. That so long as a person appointed to be a member of a Special Criminal Court was qualified at the date of his appointment, his membership of that court would not be affected if he ceased to hold that qualification. 3. That, in any event, the judicial members of the court, even if they ceased after appointment to hold judicial office, were nevertheless qualified as barristers or solicitors of at least 7 years standing. 4. That by producing the order of the Special Criminal Court, a court duly established by law and exercising lawful authority, the respondent had justified the applicant's detention. 5. That decisions of the Special Criminal Court as to which of its members will sit to hear particular applications or trials are merely administrative procedures. It was not necessary that such matters be debated or decided in public or that formal orders be drawn up or authenticated. 6. That an enquiry under Article 40 of the Constitution could not properly be used to resolve disputed questions of law or of fact previously ruled upon by other courts or which were already pending determination under regular court procedure. Principles in *The State (McDonagh)* v. *Frawley* [1978] I.R. 131 affirmed. 7. That in any event there was no substance in any of the points raised by the applicant as to validity of his arrest, preliminary examination or return for trial. *McGlinchey* v. *Governor of Portlaoise Prison*

(H.C., S.C.) [1988] I.R.671

—— Evidence — Effect of admission of prejudicial evidence.
see **Criminal Law,** 23

—— Establishment — Validity — Judicial independence — Trial in due course of law — Whether s. 39 of Offences Against the State Act, 1939 inconsistent with Constitution.
see **Constitution,** 50

—— Jurisdiction — Trial — Commencement — Accused before the court — Manner in which accused was brought before court — Arrest — Second arrest — Whether manner in which attendance of accused before court was procured was relevant to jurisdiction to commence trial.
see **Criminal Law,** 8

—— Return for trial — D.P.P. directing trial in Special Criminal Court — Whether power unconstitutional — Opinion of D.P.P. that ordinary courts inadequate — Whether reviewable by the courts.
see **Criminal Law,** 66

SPECIAL POWERS
see **Emergency Powers**

SPECIFIC PERFORMANCE
—— Building contract.
see **Injunction,** 1

—— Contract — Sale of land.
see **Sale of Land,** 4-6, 12-14

—— Lease — Option to purchase fee simple — Price calculated as if rent were a ground rent — Whether option enforceable.
see **Landlord and Tenant,** 11

SPORTING ACTIVITIES
—— Athlete — Suspension — B.L.E. — Drug testing procedure — Judicial review — Certiorari.
see **Natural and Constitutional Justice,** 2

—— Club — Football club — Limitation on wages payable to professional footballer.
see **Restraint of Trade,** 2

—— Club — Income tax — Exemption — Whether legitimate avoidance of payment of tax.
see **Revenue,** 35

SPOUSE
see also **Husband and Wife; Widower**

—— Meaning of "spouse" — Maintenance provisions.
see **Family Law,** 9

—— Spouse of disabled person — Disabled person's maintenance allowance — Provision requiring account to be taken of income of spouse.
see **Statute,** 1

—— Surviving spouse — Legal right.
see **Succession,** 1, 7, 11

STAMP DUTY
see **Company,** 27
Revenue, 42

STARE DECISIS
see under **Precedent**

1. —— **Interpretation** — *Statutory instrument — Ambiguous provision — Choice of more logical interpretation — Choice of interpretation in accordance with provisions of Constitution — Disabled Persons (Maintenance Allowances) Regulations,* 1984 (*S.I. No.* 71) — *Health Act,* 1970 (*No.* 1), *s.* 69 — *Social Welfare (No.*2) *Act,* 1985 (*No.* 14), *s.* 3.

Social welfare — Payments by Health Boards — Disabled person's maintenance allowance — Provision requiring account to be taken of income of spouse — Whether account could be taken of social welfare benefits or allowances received by first applicant's spouse in his own right — Disabled Persons (Maintenance Allowances) Regulations, 1984 (*S.I. No.* 71), *art.* 4 — *Health Act,* 1970 (*No.* 1), *s.* 69 — *Social Welfare* (*No.* 2) *Act,* 1985 (*No.* 14), *s.* 3.

Constitution — Family — Married persons — Right of married persons to be treated no less favourably than unmarried persons in similar circumstances — Social welfare payments — Disabled person's maintenance allowance — Provision requiring account to be taken of income of spouse — Whether requirement extended to social welfare income of spouse in his own right — Validity of provision — Disabled Persons (Maintenance Allowances) Regulations, 1984 (*S.I. No.* 71), *art.* 4 — *Health Act,* 1970 (*No.* 1), *s.* 69 — *Social Welfare* (*No.*2) *Act,* 1985 (*No.* 14), *s.* 3 — *Constitution of Ireland,* 1937, *Art.* 41.3.] Section 69 of the Health Act, 1970, and the Disabled Persons (Maintenance Allowances) Regulations, 1984, provide for the payment by health boards of a disabled person's maintenance allowance to persons who are handicapped in undertaking work. Article 4 of the Regulations of 1984 provides, *inter alia,* that:— "In determining the amount of a maintenance allowance . . .a health board shall have regard to the income of that person, the spouse of that person, and of all persons [dependant upon] that person . . . In this regard full account shall be taken of all income arising by way of benefit or assistance or any increase thereof in respect of a dependant . . ." By s. 3 of the Social Welfare (No. 2)

STATUTE—*continued.*

Act, 1985, "adult dependant" does not include a spouse who is in receipt of disabled person's maintenance allowance. The applicants were a married couple with two dependent children. Prior to November, 1986, the husband had been unemployed for some years and had been in receipt of unemployment assistance in respect of himself, his wife and their two children. During some of that time the wife, who was ill, had been in receipt of a disabled person's maintenance allowance (D.P.M.A.). Neither applicant had any other source of income. On the 14 November, 1986, on the coming into force of the Social Welfare (No. 2) Act, 1986, implementing the principle of equal treatment for men and women as required by E.C. Council Directive 79/7, the wife ceased to be dependent on her husband. On the 9 June, 1987, the wife was informed by the first respondent that payment of her D.P.M.A. would cease and that she would again be treated as dependent on her husband. The applicants obtained leave to apply for an order of certiorari by way of judicial review of the first respondent's decision on the grounds that it was *ultra vires* the legislation, in breach of the wife's constitutional rights and in breach of Council Directive 79/7. On the hearing of the application it was conceded on behalf of the respondents that the husband was entitled to unemployment assistance at the maximum personal rate plus half the allowance in respect of the two children and that the wife was entitled to D.P.M.A. at the maximum personal rate plus half the allowance in respect of the children. However, since the total of these sums exceeded the total sum of D.P.M.A. which might have been payable to the wife in respect of herself, her husband and the children, the first respondent, in reliance on art. 4 of the Regulations of 1984, reduced the amount of D.P.M.A. payable so that the combined income of the applicants should not exceed the maximum amount of D.P.M.A. It was argued on behalf of the applicants that this calculation, like the earlier decision, was *ultra vires* the legislation, unconstitutional and contrary to Directive 79/7. **Held** by Keane J., in finding for the applicants, 1, that it would be illogical in calculating the wife's entitlement to disabled person's maintenance allowance to take account of the husband's income from unemployment assistance, no part of which was attributable to the wife's dependency on him. 2. That since in the case of an unmarried couple living together no account could be taken under art. 4 of the Regulations of 1984 of the income of the man, the construction of art. 4 contended for by the respondents would result in it being invalid having regard to Article 43, s. 3, sub-s. 1 of the Constitution. *Murphy* v. *Attorney General* [1982] I.R. 241 and *Hyland* v. *Minister for Social Welfare* (Unreported, High Court, Barrington J., 18 January, 1988) considered. 3. That art. 4 of the Regulations of 1984 must be construed to allow account to be taken only of the income by way of benefit or assistance of an applicant for D.P.M.A. himself, or payable to another but attributable to such applicant's dependency. 4. That in the circumstances the appropriate relief was a declaratory order and an enquiry into damages. *J.H.* v. *Eastern Health Board*

(H.C.) [1988] I.R.747

2. —— **Ministerial order** — *Statute — Whether in conflict — Statute incorporating Governors of Hospital — No obligation to fund imposed on Minister — Ministerial order withdrawing funds — Whether valid having regard to statute — Barrington's Hospital Act,* 1830 (*c.* lxxii), *s.* 1.

Injunction — Interlocutory — Private hospital — Public funds — Discontinuance — Executive decision — Legality — Whether fair question to be tried.] In the absence of a statutory provision imposing a duty upon a Minister to fund a hospital, the withdrawal of funds from that hospital by the Minister could not be a legal wrong. So **Held** by Costello J. *Governors of Barrington's Hospital* v. *Minister for Health*

(H.C.) [1988] I.R. 56

3. —— **Powers** — *Construction — Statutory duty — Harbour Commissioners — Pier vested in Commissioners — Powers — Duty to maintain pier — Power to make bye-laws — Power to appoint officer — Restriction on user of pier — Whether harbour master empowered to restrict user permanently — Whether Commissioners in breach of statutory duty —* Locus standi — *Whether plaintiffs members of class specifically benefited by statutes — Action for damages — Pecuniary loss — Harbours, Docks and Piers Clauses Act,* 1847 (*c.* 127) — *Londonderry Port and Harbour Acts,* 1854 (*c.* 177), 1874 (*c.* 144) and 1882 (*c.* 162).

Constitution — Personal rights — Right to earn a livelihood — Breach of statutory duty — Whether amounts to breach of constitutional rights — Constitution of Ireland, 1937, *Art.* 40.3.1.] The Harbours, Docks, and Piers Clauses Act, 1847, regulates the establishment and management of harbour commissioners generally and defines their powers and duties. Section 33 provides that the public, subject to defined conditions, shall have access to docks and piers maintained by the harbour commissioners. By the Londonderry Port and Harbour Acts, 1854, 1874 and 1882, being special private Acts subject to the general Act of 1847, the defendants were conferred with duties, *inter alia,* to maintain the docks and pier at Carrickarory, County Donegal.

STATUTE—*continued.*

The defendants were empowered to restrict user of the pier through bye-laws subject to judicial approval. In addition, the harbour master, an officer appointed by the defendants, was empowered to give directions restricting user of the pier. The plaintiffs were coal distributors and imported their coal through Carickarory pier, vested by the special Acts in the defendants. By letter dated the 24 February, 1977, the defendants' harbour master gave notice that the pier "is now closed for discharging and loading of vessels until further notice." On the 22 August, 1980, the harbour master wrote to one of the plaintiffs announcing that the pier would be open from the 25 August to the 24 September, 1980, as a trial period, but that the type and manner of vessels loading and unloading would be restricted by four specified conditions. Use of the pier was extended beyond the trial period by further direction of the harbour master, but subject to the same restrictive conditions. The plaintiffs instituted proceedings in the High Court seeking a declaration that the closure of the pier and restriction on user was *ultra vires* the powers of the defendants, void and of no legal effect. They also claimed damages for breach of statutory duty, compensation for loss of income and sought further a declaration that the defendants were in breach of the plaintiffs' constitutional property rights and claimed damages for such breach. On the preliminary hearing on agreed questions of law, it was **Held** by Costello J., 1, that the defendants were under a statutory duty to keep the pier open for vessels reasonably suitable for berthing at the pier as it was originally constructed or subsequently improved, save for such periods as were necessary for carrying out repairs or improvements to the pier. 2. That the defendants were entitled to restrict user through bye-laws made and approved but not through mere administrative decision. *London & North Eastern Ry. Co.* v. *British Trawlers Federation Ltd.* [1934] A.C. 279 approved. 3. That in the absence of validly adopted bye-laws neither the defendants nor their harbour master could permanently restrict user of the pier. *The Guelder Rose* [1927] P. 1 and *Pearn* v. *Sargent* [1973] 2 Lloyds Rep. 141 considered. 4. That the plaintiffs had sufficient standing to maintain an action for damages for breach of statutory duty in so far as they belonged to a definable class apart from the public with interests materially affected by the defendants' breach and, upon construction of the relevant statutes, in the absence of other remedies enacted to protect those interests, the legislature had envisaged that an action for damages would lie. *Waterford Harbour Commissioners* v. *British Railway Board* [1979] ILRM 296. 5. That the damages to be awarded at the trial would depend on the damage by way of pecuniary loss actually suffered by the plaintiffs. 6. That the defendants' breach of statutory duty did not amount to a breach of constitutional obligation not to infringe the plaintiff's right to earn a livelihood. *Moyne* v. *The Londonderry Port and Harbour Commissioners*
(H.C.) [1986] I.R.299

—— Conclusive evidence clause.
see **Company,** 6

—— Construction — Conflict between provisions in articles and schedule — Whether words should be read into schedule.
see **Education,** 4

—— Construction — Extradition treaty — Incorporation into domestic law — State not bound by treaty — Whether statutory sub-section automatically incorporating treaty into domestic law — Legislative powers — Delegation — Whether delegation constitutional — Presumption of constitutionality of sub-section.
see **Constitution,** 25

—— Declaration of invalidity — Effect on assessment of compensation for compulsory purchase.
see **Compulsory Acquisition,** 3

—— Delegated legislation — Interpretation.
see **Road Traffic Offences,** 13
Statute, 1

—— Delegated legislation — Retrospectivity.
see **Constitution,** 35

—— Delegated legislation — Statutory instrument — Presumption of constitutionality.
see **Injunction,** 4

—— Delegated legislation — Statutory instrument — Severance — Minister for Social Welfare making regulations with consent of Minister for Finance — Part of regulations *ultra vires* — Whether void provisions severable — Effect of severance of void provisions on scheme created by statutory instrument.
see **Social Welfare,** 8

—— Delegated legislation — Statutory instrument — *Ultra vires* — Social welfare — Fuel allowance — Minister making regulations — Department circular excluding persons on short term social

SUCCESSION

ADMINISTRATION

1. —— **Appropriation** — *Dwelling — Widow's legal right — Application to appropriate dwelling in part satisfaction — Whether 5-acre field "occupied with the dwelling" — Widow dying after application — Whether her executor could enforce appropriation — Succession Act,* 1965 (*No.* 27), *s.* 56.] The plaintiff was the widow of the deceased. During the last ten years of his life, the deceased, who had retired, lived with the widow in a bungalow in a 5 acre field, which he owned, beside a road. Beside the bungalow a small part of the field had been fenced off as a small garden with a hedge in it. A small wooden gate gave access from the garden to the field and a full-sized gate gave access from the road to the field. The deceased used to fatten a few cattle which he looked after himself, every year in the field. The widow elected to take her legal right under s. 115 of the Succession Act, 1965, and, under s. 56, she called on the deceased's executor to appropriate the bungalow and the field in satisfaction of her claim. She died shortly after commencing these proceedings in which she asked the court to declare her entitlement to the bungalow and the field. Her executor was then substituted as plaintiff. S. 56(14) provides "In this section — 'dwelling' . . . includes any garden or portion of ground attached to and usually occupied with the dwelling or otherwise required for the amenity or convenience of the dwelling." **Held** by O'Hanlon J. assessing the value of the property and making the orders sought. The field outside the hedge and fence was not a "garden" and was not

SUCCESSION—Administration.

"required for the amenity or convenience of the dwelling." It was a "portion of ground attached to" the dwelling. If s. 56(14) read "occupied with a dwelling" rather than "the dwelling" then the definition would not include the field. But in this case the field was occupied with the dwelling because the deceased, rather than letting or developing it as a building land, occupied it constantly with the dwelling for the particular purpose which appealed to him. Therefore the field could be appropriated under s. 56. Furthermore once the widow had applied for appropriation of the dwelling an equity arose which her personal representative could enforce. This entitlement was subject herein to the obligation which might arise to pay any balance that might be necessary to make up the difference in value between her share of the estate and the value of the dwelling which is to be appropriated. *In re Hamilton; Hamilton v. Armstrong*

(H.C.) [1984] ILRM 306

2. —— **Ascertainment of next-of-kin** — *Insufficiency of evidence — Refusal of examiner's certificate — Application for order presuming the deaths of certain persons and giving administrator leave to distribute assets — Benjamin order.*] The late Dora Mieth, an elderly spinster, died having survived the persons she had appointed in her will to be her executors and beneficiaries. A native of Dresden, the child of deaf mutes, the deceased appeared to have lost all her immediate family and many of her wider kin in concentration camps and otherwise during the war. The plaintiff, the attorney of a distant relative, obtained a grant of administration with will annexed. The defendant, one of the next-of-kin, was appointed to represent the interests of all. A special summons taken out by the administrator sought an enquiry into the next-of-kin under the auspices of the court. The assistant-examiner, who assembled the available evidence in a report to the court dated 12 November, 1979, concluded that because of the lack of proper evidence and of the large number of assumptions involved an examiner's certificate could not be issued. There the matter rested until 10 June, 1985, when, upon motion brought by the plaintiff, it was: **Held** by Barrington J., dispensing with the need for further advertisements and enquiries, 1, that *it was to be presumed* that the deceased had survived numerous persons and classes of her relatives. 2. That the plaintiff was entitled to distribute the estate among three third cousins identified on the deceased's maternal side. *In re Benjamin, Neville* v. *Benjamin* [1902] 1 Ch. 723 applied. *In the estate of Mieth; Baker v. Cohn-Vossen*

(H.C.) [1986] ILRM 175

SUCCESSION—*continued.*

FAMILY PROVISION

3. —— **Testator** — *Application by deceased's son — Deceased made no provision for applicant in will — Applicant had succeeded to family business in deceased's lifetime — Business later closed — Whether reasonable financial provision for applicant's maintenance — Inheritance (Provision for Family and Dependants) (Northern Ireland) Order,* 1979 (*S.I. No.* 924, *N.I.* 8), *arts.* 2, 5.] The plaintiff was the son of the deceased who died in 1982. The plaintiff had for many years worked for low pay in the deceased's shoe shop in the expectation that he would succeed to the business and, in 1968 the deceased retired from it and left its management to the plaintiff. The business did not prosper, however, and, in 1972, after he had quarrelled with the deceased over the disposal of the proceeds of the sale of a house, which the plaintiff expected would come to him, the plaintiff abandoned the business and wen to live in England. By his will, the deceased left all his property to his daughter, the defendant. On an application by the plaintiff under the Inheritance (Provision for Family and Dependants) (Northern Ireland) Order, 1979, **Held,** that the disposition of the deceased's estate effected by the will did not make reasonable financial provision for the plaintiff and that a lump sum representing one third of the value of the net estate should be paid to him. Article 2(2) of the 1979 Order defines reasonable financial provision in cases where an application is made by a person other than the spouse of the deceased, as "such financial provision as it would be reasonable in all the circumstances of the case for the applicant to receive for his maintenance." Article 5(1), which sets out the matters to which the court should have regard, applies to all cases under the Order with the consequence that the court is bound to have regard to factors which might appear to have more relevance in the case of an application on the part of a spouse, where the provision made can go beyond maintenance. It is necessary, however, in order to give proper effect to the definition in article 2(2), to limit financial provision for an adult son to what still can be regarded as maintenance. The paramount consideration is to pay attention to the terms of the Order and the matters to which the court is enjoined to have regard. It is not necessary to find a moral claim in favour of an applicant and reference to a need to find such a claim may be regarded as a convenient shorthand reference to the need to take into account the factors set out in article 5(1). *In re Coventry* [1980] Ch. 461 and *In re McGarrell* [1983] 8 N.I.J.B. considered. *In re Creeney; Creeney v. Smith*

(Ch.D.) [1984] N.I.397

SUCCESSION—Family Provision.

4. —— **Testator** — *Moral duty — Duty to provide for children — Testator failing to make provision for three of his children — Children having independent incomes — Factors to be considered — Succession Act,* 1965 (*No.* 27), *s.* 117.] S. 117 of the Succession Act, 1965, permits the court, upon application of a child of a testator, to make provision for such child out of the estate, where the court is satisfied that the testator has failed in his moral duty to make provision for such child either during his lifetime or by his will. The plaintiffs were three children of one N. MacN., who had died, leaving a large estate. The estate was subject to a large claim for estate duty. The three children all of whom were adults, had independent substantial incomes of their own. The testator had divorced his first wife, and had remarried, making provision by his will for his second wife. The will made no provision for the first-named applicant, with whom the testator had quarelled neither did it provide for the second and third-named applicants, clause 7 reading: "I have made no provision for my daughters as they are already provided for out of other funds." No provision had been made for any of the applicants during the testator's lifetime. Previously, in a scheme entered into by the testator to reduce liability for estate duty he had signed a memorial to the effect that he would make provision for his two daughters in his will. It was submitted by the respondents that the applicants had been so well provided for by other relatives, that there was no moral obligation to provide for them resting upon the testator. It was also submitted that a testator has no moral obligation towards a married daughter to make provision for her from his estate. **Held** by Kenny J. in granting the application, 1, the existence of a moral duty to make proper provision by will for a child must depend upon the amount left to the surviving spouse, or the value of that spouse's legal right, the number and ages of the other children and their position in life, the means of the testator, the age and position in life of the applicant and whether the testator had provided for the applicant during his lifetime. 2. The first-named applicant had been induced to believe that he would ultimately inherit a large stud owned by the testator, and he had shaped his life accordingly. The third-named applicant had been persuaded by the testator to settle her property in a manner which prevented her from leaving it to her husband or children. 3. The testator had failed to make provision in accordance with his means for the second-named applicant, since her education was paid for by money to which she was contingently entitled, and which would have been hers absolutely when she attained the age of 25, if it had accumulated. 4. The court, in making provision for the applicants, must give

SUCCESSION—*continued.*

an amount which, after the deduction of estate duty, would be a just legacy. *MacNaughton* v. *Walker*

(H.C.) [1976-7] ILRM 106

5. —— **Testator** — *Moral duty — Bulk of estate left to testator's grandchild — Whether testator failed in his moral duty to make proper provision for his children — Whether court empowered to create a discretionary trust — Succession Act,* 1965 (*No.* 27), *ss.* 90, 117.] The plaintiffs applied for an order pursuant to section 117 of the Succession Act, 1965. The evidence showed that during his lifetime the conduct of the testator had been such as to drive first his wife, and successively, each of his children, from the family home. None of the plaintiffs received a proper education, notwithstanding the considerable wealth enjoyed by their father. Upon leaving home, they were fitted only for the most menial work. The eldest child suffered from a serious mental illness requiring specialised medical care which the testator refused to provide. Another child injured her back at the age of fifteen and again her father refused to provide the appropriate medical attention. This refusal resulted ultimately in a permanent disability. A third child, having been forced to leave home at an early age was later convicted of a criminal offence and spent some years in prison. By his will, the testator made certain pecuniary bequests to the plaintiffs, but left the bulk of his estate to his grandchild, the daughter of a deceased son of the testator. **Held** by Costello J. in making the orders sought, and in particular, in creating a discretionary trust to provide for the care of the testator's eldest son, 1, in approaching the division of the estate from the viewpoint of a just and prudent parent, the court must have special regard to those of the testator's children who are in need of medical attention. 2. Since the creation of a discretionary trust appeared to be the most fitting way of making provision for the testator's eldest son, the court was empowered to create such a trust by virtue of the provisions of s. 117 of the Succession Act, 1965. 3. The testator had a moral duty which he had failed to perform to help the rehabilitation of his son who had been convicted of a criminal offence by making proper provision for his future. *H. L.* v. *Bank of Ireland*

(H.C.) [1978] ILRM 160

6. —— **Testator** — *Moral duty — Estate valued at £40,000 — Legacies of £1,000 to each of testator's two children — Whether testator failed to make proper provision for his children — Succession Act,* 1965 (*No.* 27), *s.* 117.] This is an application pursuant to s. 117 of the Succession Act, 1965, for a declaration that the testator failed in his moral duty to make proper provision

SUCCESSION—Family Provision.

for his children and for an order making provision for them out of his estate. The testator left an estate valued at approximately £40,000 including the family home which is worth approximately £25,000. He left one third of his real and personal estate to his wife and legacies of £1,000 to each of his two children, with the residue of his estate going to his sister and his nephew in equal shares. The testator had been separated from his wife for six years prior to his death. His daughter has some educational qualifications and is presently employed in a secretarial capacity. His son is educated to intermediate certificate standard with no training for any special job and presently has a poorly paid job in a clothing firm. **Held** by McWilliam J., 1, that the testator had a moral duty to make provision for his children in accordance with his means however neglected, thwarted or aggrieved he may have felt. *F.M.* v. *T.A.M.* 106 I.L.T.R. 82 followed. 2. That the testator failed in that moral duty and that a prudent and just parent would take such steps as were open to him to preserve the health and provide for the advancement in life of his children. The testator had not done so in the case of his son and had done so partially in the case of his daughter. *M.L. & A.W.* v. *M.L.* [1978] I.R. 288 applied. 3. Accordingly, the greater part of the estate after deducting the third given to his wife should have been made available to provide for his two children. *J.H.* v. *Allied Irish Banks Ltd.*

(H.C.) [1978] ILRM 203

7. —— **Testator** — *Moral duty — Objective nature of factors to be considered — Effect on legal right share of widow — Whether court precluded from reviving will which would interfere with legal right share — Succession Act,* 1965 (*No.* 27), *ss.* 111, 117.] The plaintiff's father the testator made his first will on 19 March, 1976, leaving his property to the defendant (the plaintiff's step-mother) for her life with the remainder to the plaintiff, his only son, absolutely. A few weeks later the testator made a second will revoking the first will leaving all his property to the defendant solely. On the death of the testator the plaintiff instituted proceedings under s. 117 of the Succession Act, 1965, on the basis that the testator had failed in his moral duty to make proper provision for the plaintiff in accordance with the testator's means. **Held** by Keane J. in allowing the plaintiff to succeed and ordering the sale of the farm, 1, the question of whether a moral duty existed within the meaning of s. 117 of the Succession Act, 1965, must be decided by objective considerations, as distinct from subjective considerations. 2. Having regard to the objective considerations the testator has failed in his moral duty to make proper provision for

SUCCESSION—*continued.*

the plaintiff in accordance with his means. 3. An order made under s. 117 of the Succession Act, 1965, must not affect the legal right of the defendant to one-third of the estate and so the court is precluded from reviving the first will. 4. Pursuant to s. 117 of the Succession Act, 1965, the plaintiff is entitled to two fifths of the testator's estate. *J.R.* v. *J.R.*

(H.C.) [1979] ILRM 236

8. —— **Testator** — *Moral duty of father — Testator's home left to wife for life with remainder to grandson — Farm left to one son — No provision made for other children — Succession Act,* 1965 (*No.* 27), *s.* 117.] A testator, who died on the 30 May, 1980, was survived by the nine children of his first marriage and by his second wife. The defendant, one of his sons, had assisted the testator in his farming and agricultural business from 1974. On his second marriage the testator ceased to reside in the family home on the farm but lived in a bungalow with his second wife. The farm was occupied by the plaintiffs; the testator's two unmarried sons M.F.H. and J.M.H. and his unmarried daughters, B.C.H. and M.F. M.F.H. suffered from a disability and was not, together with J.M.H. in steady secure employment. B.C.H. did have steady employment and also looked after M.F., who required care and supervision and was not in steady employment. By his last will dated 8 May, 1980, the testator appointed the defendant his sole executor and left the bungalow to his widow for life and after her death to a grandson, the son of one of his married sons. The residue of his estate including the farm was left to the defendant and the testator made no provision for any of the plaintiffs. The plaintiffs brought an application under s. 117 Succession Act, 1965, claiming that the testator had failed in his moral duty to make proper provision for them in accordance with his means, and asked for such provision to be made for them out of the testator's estate as the court thought just. The remaining five children made no claim against the testator's estate. **Held** by Barron J., in granting the relief sought by the plaintiffs, 1, that, being required by s. 117 of the Succession Act, 1965, to approach the matter from the point of view of a prudent and just parent and to take into account the position of each of the children and any other circumstances which it might consider to be of assistance, the court must reach a decision as fair as possible in the circumstances to the applicants and, where there are other children who may be affected by the exercise of the court's powers, to those too. Accordingly, in reaching a decision, the position of the applicants cannot be taken in isolation, as the quantum of what is proper provision in any particular case is not an absolute but is dependent

SUCCESSION—Family Provision.

on all the matters which the court must take into account and the standard which is applied depends on the means of the testator. 2. Although the court has very wide powers both as to when to make provision for an applicant child and as to the nature of such provision, these must not be construed as giving the court power to make a new will for the testator but only power to remedy a failure on the testator's part to fulfil the moral duty owed to his child. In general, this will arise where the child has a particular need which the means of the testator can satisfy in whole or in part. If no such need exists, even where no provision has been made by the testator whether by his will or otherwise, the court has no power to intervene. 3. The testator had failed to make proper provision for the plaintiffs. Although a prudent parent would not have divided up the lands but bequeathed them to an appropriate beneficiary — in this case the defendant — the testator ought to have made some provision for the plaintiffs. 4. Accordingly J.M.H. and M.F.H. would be granted a licence to reside in the family home until such time as each might marry in which case each would be provided with a site on the testator's lands upon which to build a home at his own expense. B.C.H. and M.F. would also be granted a licence to reside in the family home until each should marry. If B.C.H. continued to look after M.F. after her marriage both she and her husband should be entitled to remain in the family home during M.F.'s lifetime. In addition, the defendant should make reasonable provision for M.F. during any period she might be unemployed and should stock the land with a limited number of young cattle for the benefit of M.F. and any member of the family who was looking after her. The plaintiffs should be entitled to certain lands the subject matter of a recent planning application as tenants in common in equal one fifth shares with the defendant subject to the latter's right to use the land for agricultural purposes. *In the goods of J.H., H.* v. *H.*

(H.C.) [1984] I.R.599

9. —— **Testator** — *Moral duty — Devise of farm to nephew — Charges in favour of daughter and testator's sister — Moral duty to daughter — Other moral obligations of the testator — Succession Act,* 1965 (*No.* 27), *s.* 117.] The plaintiff's mother married the deceased in 1942 and the plaintiff was the only issue of the marriage. From the date of her birth in 1944 the plaintiff was reared by her mother and her mother's sister on the mother's home farm as the parties to the marriage had become estranged. No financial assistance had been provided by the deceased towards the maintenance or education of the plaintiff although the plaintiff occasionally

SUCCESSION—*continued.*

visited her father at his home. She married in 1967. The defendant, who is a nephew of the deceased, was born in 1933 and was reared on the deceased's farm since the death of his mother in 1934. When he completed his secondary school education in 1951 he began working on the said farm in County Limerick and, since 1973, he managed the farm and received 75% of the profits. By his will dated 19 September, 1977, the deceased appointed his nephew, the defendant, as his sole executor and he devised the dwelling house and farm to him, together with the stock and effects thereon, absolutely "in consideration of the help and assistance he has given me and the kindness he has shown me for the last twenty years." The deceased charged the said dwelling house and lands with the rights of residence, support and maintenance in favour of his unmarried sister for her life. He also charged his lands with the payment of the sum of £2,000 to his daughter, the plaintiff, to be paid to her by his executor within three years of the date of his death. The deceased died in 1981 without having altered his will and probate of same was granted to the defendant in 1982. The plaintiff's mother had died in 1979 and, prior to her death, she transferred 22 acres of land to her said daughter. The plaintiff's husband was an employee earning approximately £90 net per week. The aforesaid farm of the deceased, which he devised to the defendant, had a value of between £60,000 and £77,000, while the defendant was the owner of other separate lands of in or about the same value. The plaintiff, as the only child of the deceased, claimed a declaration in the High Court, pursuant to s. 117 of the Succession Act, 1965, and the testator had failed in his moral duty to make proper provision for her in accordance with his means and she asked the court to make such provision from the estate of the testator. The plaintiff's claim was contested by the defendant, as the executor of the deceased testator, and affidavits were filed on behalf of both parties. **Held** in making the declaration sought. The deceased testator had a clear moral duty to make proper provision for his daughter, the plaintiff. During his lifetime the testator had ignored this duty which still subsisted even if his wife had deserted him. The deceased was *in loco parentis* to the defendant and the obligations towards him and towards his own sister must also be considered. The court awarded £20,000 to the plaintiff out of the estate of the deceased as it considered that such sum would have amounted to a proper provision for the plaintiff in accordance with the means of the testator. The said sum of money was to be paid over a period of five years from the taking out of the grant of probate on 24 May, 1982, together with interest at the Bank of Ireland deposit rate, the same to

SUCCESSION—Family Provision.

be charged on the aforesaid lands of the deceased. *L.* v. *L.*

(H.C.) [1984] ILRM 607

10. —— **Testator** — *Moral duty — Claim by son abandoned by mother/testatrix at birth — Succession Act,* 1965 (*No.* 27), *s.* 117.] The plaintiff, a 45-year-old man, applied unders s. 117 of the Succession Act, 1965, for provision to be made for him out of the estate of his mother, who had abandoned him at birth and whose identity he had first ascertained 37 years later. The mother had purported to leave the whole of her small estate to two friends. The plaintiff had seen his mother only once. He had left school at the age of 13 and made his own way in life. He had never been well off, and was the father of five children. **Held** by Costello J. that, 1, the testatrix had failed in her moral duty to her son in his early years and subsequently, the moral duty of parents to make proper provision for their children may continue to the end of their lives. 2. In the circumstances her moral duty to her son outweighed any obligations to the friends mentioned in the will, and (with the concurrence of the beneficiaries and of the husband, who waived his legal right share) the entire estate should pass to the plaintiff. *N. O'H.* v. *G.R.*

(H.C.) [1986] ILRM 563

LEGAL RIGHT

see also Nos. 1, 7

11. —— **Surviving spouse** — *Surviving spouse unaware of will made by husband — Death of surviving spouse — Whether knowledge of will essential prerequisite to imputed exercise of legal right by surviving spouse — Whether exercise personal to surviving spouse — Whether legal right becomes exerciseable by surviving spouse's executor in default of exercise — Succession Act,* 1965 (*No.* 27), *s.* 115.] A testator died in 1971, survived only by his spouse. On the assumption that the testator had died intestate, the surviving spouse sought and obtained letters of administration intestate and went into possession of the testator's property. The surviving spouse died in 1979. Unknown to her the testator had in fact made a will. An application to have his will admitted to probate was begun in 1972 but no further steps were taken to process this until 1980 (after the surviving spouse's death) and probate was ultimately granted in 1981. Under the will, the testator bequeathed to his spouse all stock on his lands for her sole use as well as his land to her for life, and after her death to his nephew absolutely. S. 115 of the Succession Act, 1965, provides that where a testator makes a devise or bequest in favour of a spouse, the spouse must elect to take either that devise or

SUCCESSION—*continued.*

bequest or the share to which he or she is entitled under the Act as a legal right, being in the present instance one-half of the estate. The surviving spouse was unaware either of the existence of the will or of her legal right of election. The issues before the court were: whether the surviving spouse had become, prior to her death, entitled to the legal right in place of the testamentary bequest or, whether the right of election survived for the benefit of her estate. **Held** by Murphy J., 1, since the surviving spouse had at no stage been made aware of the existence of the will, she could not be deemed to have exercised her right of election in procuring herself to be registered as owner of her husband's lands. 2. Where death takes place before an election is made, the legal right share does not form part of the spouse's estate. *Dicta* of Walsh J. in *In re Urquhart* [1974] I.R. 201 applied. 3. The right of election, being a personal discretion conferred by the 1965 Act on the surviving spouse and whose exercise might be influenced by factors quite different from those of a hypothetical outsider, did not survive the spouse's death for the benefit of her estate. *Reilly* v. *McEntee*

(H.C.) [1984] ILRM 572

WILL

see also **Charities — Cy-près**
Trusts

Condition. Nos. 12, 13, 16
Construction. Nos. 14-18
Validity. Nos. 19-24

12. —— **Condition** — *Bequest of leasehold property — Settled Land Acts — Condition as to residence — Whether void for uncertainty — Whether inconsistent with widow's power of sale and lease — Construction of will — Testator's intention — Whether fee tail created — Whether widow's estate extinguished by running of time — Conveyancing Act,* 1881 (*c.* 41), *s.* 65 — *Settled Land Act,* 1882 (*c.* 38), *ss.* 51, 58 (1) — *Statute of Limitations,* 1957 (*No.* 6), *ss.* 13(2), 18.] A testator had bequeathed his leasehold property to the use of his wife during her widowhood and so long as she desired to reside therein, but upon her death, or her ceasing to reside therein, to the use of the first-named plaintiff (the testator's nephew) and his male issue "to be tenant for life without impeachment of waste with remainder to his first and other sons successively by seniority in tail male . . ." In a codicil to the will, the testator made residence a condition for the plaintiff also, failure to comply with which was to determine the plaintiff's interest in the property, which was then to pass to the second-named defendant. The widow resided in the property from 1941 to 1956 when she moved away. The

SUCCESSION—Will.

plaintiff then took up residence therein. In a summons to determine the proper construction of the will, it was **Held** by Kenny J., 1, the conditions as to residence were not void for uncertainty, since the place of residence was clearly indicated. *Perpetual Trustees, Executors and Agency Co. of Tasmania* v. *Walker* (1953) 90 C.L.R. 270 followed. *Sifton* v. *Sifton* [1938] A.C. 656 distinguished. 2. Since the later part of the will prevails over the earlier, the testator's clear intention to make the plaintiff a tenant for life prevailed over his attempt to create a fee tail. 3. Since the testator's widow was also a tenant for life within the meaning of the Settled Land Acts, the condition as to residence was void in her regard under s. 51 of the Settled Land Act, 1882, as imposing upon her an obligation inconsistent with her powers of sale and lease under that Act. 4. The plaintiff's possession of the property from 1956 was inconsistent with the widow's estate, which thus became barred in 1968 pursuant to s. 13 (2) (*a*) of the Statute of Limitations, 1957. At that date, the plaintiff became the new tenant for life and the condition as to residence was also void in his regard. *Atkins* v. *Atkins*

(H.C.) [1976-7] ILRM 62

13. —— **Conditional gift** — *Freehold land — Partial restriction on alienation of land — Whether condition valid — Whether condition registrable — Public policy — Uncertainty.*] The deceased left his freehold property to the applicant and the applicant's wife, subject to the condition that the house and lands should not be transferred by the beneficiaries or their successors or assigns to any member of the Meredith families of O'Moore's Forest, Mountmellick. The applicant who was also the executor, sought a determination as to whether the condition was valid and therefore registrable on the folio of the Register of Freeholders. **Held** by O'Hanlon J., in declaring the said condition invalid and void, 1, that it is a general principle that freehold land should be freely alienable and that any restriction on its alienability is void. The courts must decide if a given partial restriction is so restrictive as to be void. Statement in Wylie on *Irish Land Law* (2nd ed.) at p. 186 approved. 2. That it is against public policy to allow a restrictive condition the purpose of which is to perpetuate old family resentments, particularly where the condition purports to apply indefinitely into the future. *Billing* v. *Welch* (1871) I.R. 6 C.L. 88, distinguished. 3. That the description of the persons intended to be covered by the condition was too vague and uncertain to be effective. 4. That, accordingly, the applicant's title should be registered without including in the registration any

SUCCESSION—*continued.*

reference to the condition in question. *In re Dunne*

(H.C.) [1988] I.R.155

Condition, *see also* No. 16

14. —— **Construction** — *Admissibility of extrinsic evidence — Testator making elaborate provisions in the event of his wife surviving him — No provision made for the case of the wife predeceasing husband — Wife predeceasing husband — Whether intestacy — Whether court power to transpose words within a will — Whether extrinsic evidence admissible — Succession Act,* 1965 (*No.* 27), *s.* 90.] The plaintiff, the administrator of the will of John Collins (the testator) who died on 2 October, 1973, brought proceedings for the determination of a number of questions arising upon the interpretation of the said will. The testator had made in his will provisions for the spiritual welfare of his wife and himself and both their parents in the event of the wife surviving him and or dying within two months of the testator's death but made no provision for the case of his wife predeceasing him which she in fact did by a period of eight years approximately. The plaintiff pointed out that the literal interpretation of the will produced the incongruous result that the testator in effect died intestate by failing to make provision for his wife predeceasing him and suggested principles which he considered should be applied so as to avoid this situation. The plaintiff submitted that the court had power to transpose certain words within a clause or expression which are senseless and contradictory and referred to the clause which deals with the case of the testator's wife surviving the testator and dying within two months of his death. Further he submitted that evidence from the solicitor who drew up the will should be admitted by the court pursuant to s. 90 of the Succession Act, 1965, which provides that extrinsic evidence should be admissible to show the intention of the testator and to assist in the construction of or to explain any contradiction in the will. **Held** by McWilliam J. in determining that there was an intestacy, 1, the clause which deals with the testator's wife surviving the testator and dying within two months of his death is neither senseless or contradictory but put in deliberately and is correctly phrased. *Macandrew's Will Trusts* [1963] 3 W.L.R. 822 considered. 2. The court is only entitled to consider extrinsic evidence in order to explain some ambiguity or contradiction in the will and although there is an inconsistency in the will there is no ambiguity or contradiction in it and therefore the court shall not admit the evidence tendered. *Rowe* v. *Law* [1978] I.R. 55 applied. 3. The court is not entitled to make a will for a testator to

SUCCESSION—Will.

cover circumstances which he has overlooked as in this case where he did not advert to the possibility of his wife predeceasing him, he therefore died intestate in this respect. *Fitzpatrick* v. *Collins*

(H.C.) [1978] ILRM 244

15. —— **Construction** — *Admissibility of extrinsic evidence to show testator's intention — Whether will sufficiently certain to enable effect to be given to it.*] The first named plaintiff and the first and second named defendants are the executors of the will of Joseph Clinton who died on 10 February, 1983. The testator in his will directed that the lands let to the third named defendant for over 20 years and the lands let to the fourth and fifth named defendants for over 25 years (hereinafter called the purchasers) be sold to them at a price to be agreed between them and the executors and the purchase monies to be paid by the purchasers over a period of ten years from the date of his death. The will further provided that the plaintiffs would receive the residue of his property including the proceeds of the aforesaid sale. The plaintiffs claimed against the first and second named defendants for the administration of the testator's estate and against all the defendants for the construction of the will. The court had to decide whether the evidence of the second named defendant, an executor and solicitor who had known the testator all his life was admissible to show the intention of the testator and further it had to answer questions both as to the construction of the directions to the executors and as to whether it was sufficiently certain to enable effect to be given to it. The second named defendant submitted that he took instructions for the testator's will on 30 January, 1983, while the testator was in hospital though not in expectation of death. He further submitted that the testator had said that when he came home he would sell the lands to the purchasers at a fair and reasonable price that would not impose any burden on them and that he made no distinction between the purchasers regarding the provision for payment over ten years and there was no mention of any interest payable thereon. **Held** by Blayney J. in construing the said will, 1, the evidence of the second named defendant should be admitted to show the intention of the testator as there is a legitimate dispute as to the meaning or effect of the language used in the will. *Rowe* v. *Law* [1978] I.R. 55 applied. 2. The direction to the executors did not involve an agreement to agree, but imposed an absolute obligation on them to make an offer of sale to the purchasers named in the will. *Smith* v. *Morgan* [1971] 1 W.L.R. 803 considered and applied. 3. The purchasers have a right in equity to have the lands offered for sale to them by the executors at a price which is fair and reasonable. 4. Although the testator intended the executors to fix the price, as they have been unable to agree the court must intervene and shall hear evidence from a valuer as to what is fair and reasonable and in so doing shall take upon itself the execution of the directions of the testator. 5. As the testator did not wish the purchase of the lands to impose a burden on the purchasers the provision in regard to the spreading of the purchase price over ten years after the testator's death shall not be taken into account in considering the figure at which the price should be fixed nor shall interest be payable thereon. *In re Clinton; O'Sullivan* v. *Dunne*

(H.C.) [1988] ILRM 80

16. —— **Construction** — *Devise subject to a condition — Whether words imperative — Whether subject certain — Whether trust created.*] In his will, dated 9 August, 1974, the testator gave, devised and bequeathed all his assets of every nature and description to his wife (the first named defendant) for her own absolute use and benefit subject to the express wish that she made provision for payment of certain legacies after her death to the second, third and fourth named defendants. The testator appointed the plaintiffs as his executors. In June, 1975, the testator's wife expressed her right of election under the Succession Act, 1965. The plaintiffs applied to the High Court for the determination of several questions turning on the construction of the said will. The principal question was whether the above provision was an absolute devise and bequest of all the deceased's assets and not subject to any trust or condition. **Held** by Hamilton J. in answering the question in the affirmative, 1, in order to create a trust or make a gift or devise subject to a condition, the words must be imperative and the subject and the object must be certain. Although capable of being imperative, in the context of the clear words of the gift, devise and bequest of all the testator's assets of every nature and description to his wife for her own absolute use, the words "subject to the express wish" are not imperative. 2. The testator did not state that such provision for payment should be made out of his assets already bequeathed to his wife and consequently the requirement that the subject must be certain is not satisfied. 3. There is no gift or bequest of any legacies contained in the will to the second, third or fourth named defendants. The testator did not intend to create a trust in favour of the said defendants or to impose a legal obligation on the first named defendant, his wife, but merely expressed a wish for the guidance of his wife as to the manner, in which she should dispose of

SUCCESSION—Will.

her assets after her death. *In re Sweeney; Hillary* v. *Sweeney*

(H.C.) [1976-7] ILRM 88

17. —— **Construction** — *Remainder interest given to testator's child and grandchild — Provision in event of failure to survive widow — Whether substitutional gift — Whether interests vested or subject to condition precedent.*] A testator who died in 1968 was survived by his widow, the first defendant, and a married daughter who died in 1981 and one grand-daughter who died in 1984 without issue. By his will the testator gave his widow a life interest in his residuary estate and then provided; "From and after the decease of my said wife the Bank shall hold my trust estate and the income thereon for my daughter . . . and my grand-daughter . . .in equal shares absolutely. Should either of them . . . die before the death of the survivor of myself and my said wife leaving issue living at the decease of the survivor of myself and my said wife then such issue shall take . . . the share in my trust estate which . . . his parent would have taken if living . . .and attained a vested interest." There was no possibility of there being issue of the daughter and grand-daughter alive at the death of the widow. The plaintiff executor brought a construction summons to determine whether since neither the daughter or grand-daughter survived the widow and there was no issue to survive the widow there was an intestacy in respect of the residuary estate. The second and third defendants were the executors of the grand-daughter's will. **Held,** that on the death of the testator the daughter and grand-daughter took vested remainder interests subject to being divested by the substitutional gift in favour of their issue if they died in the lifetime of the widow leaving issue. As there were no living issue capable of taking there was nothing in the will to disturb the gift made to the daughter and grand-daughter and accordingly no intestacy occurred. The words "from and after the decease" did not impose a condition precedent but merely meant the gift was subject to the interest of the widow as life-tenant and the reference to attaining a vested interest at the end of the clause should be read as referring to attaining an interest vested in possession. *Ulster Bank Ltd.* v. *McCullough*

(Ch.D.) [1985] N.I.288

18. —— **Construction** — *Trust — Power of appointment — No disposition in default of appointment — Executor unable to carry out the trusts in the manner directed by the testator — Direction of the court as to the proper application of the proceeds — Whether should pass under the residuary clause.*] The plaintiff, as executor of

SUCCESSION—*continued.*

his uncle's will, brought proceedings for the determination of questions arising from a particular disposition in the said will. The disposition bequeathed the lands, and effects of the testator, a farmer, to the plaintiff in trust for "such child of his as he my nephew shall in his absolute discretion consider best suited to possess the lands and pursue the occupation of farmer." The provision gave power to the plaintiff to appoint in favour of such child when such child should reach the age of 25 years. No disposition was made in default of appointment, and the residue of the estate was bequeathed to the plaintiff, a second nephew and two nieces of the testator. Following the testator's death, the lands were compulsorily acquired by the Land Commission. The plaintiff had five children, all sons, none of whom had yet reached the age of 25. As he was unable to carry out the trust in the manner directed by the testator, he sought the direction of the court as to the proper application of the money acquired from the sale of the lands. **Held** by McWilliam J. in directing that the proceeds of sale should pass under the residuary clause in the will, 1, in ascertaining the intention of the testator, the correct approach is to enquire whether there is any clear indication that the testator intended the object of the power to take even if the donee failed or neglected to execute the power. *Robinson* v. *Moore* [1962-3] Ir. Jur. Rep. 29, applied. 2. The intention of the testator in this case showed no such indication; on the contrary, he appeared more anxious to benefit the older generation, to whom he gave the residue of his estate. *Tuite* v. *Tuite*

(H.C.) [1978] ILRM 197

19. —— **Validity** — *Capacity — Onus of proof — Testator suffering serious illness — Whether testator of sound disposing mind — Whether testator knew and approved of contents of the will — Succession Act,* 1965 (*No.* 27).] The deceased Michael O'Connor, a bachelor, had continued to reside in the family home, a licensed premises, with his parents after his two sisters left to get married and his brother to work as a lorry helper. Not being interested in the licensed business he spent his time working his lands of about 60 acres. In December, 1968, his father transferred the licensed premises to him subject to a right of support and maintenance for his life and that of his wife and on 10 September, 1970, the deceased transferred the licensed premises to his brother, the first defendant, subject to the right of support and maintenance for his mother and a similar right to himself for life in consideration of the extinguishment of a debt of £1,000, his father having died on 3 November, 1969. On the transfer, the first defendant, his wife and children resided in the premises. In the Autumn of 1973

SUCCESSION—Will.

after becoming ill the deceased was admitted to hospital where he was found to be suffering from viral meningitis and encephalitis with inflammation of the brain. He had a tumour on the brain and suffered epileptic seizures. He was in a coma for a number of weeks and although he was discharged on 7 January, 1974, it was common case that he never made a complete recovery. While he was in the hospital some of his cattle had to be sold and the proceeds were loged in a joint bank account in the names of his mother and his sister, the plaintiff. In March, 1974, the deceased left the licensed premises and resided with the plaintiff in her home. A week or two later by arrangement between the deceased and the plaintiff his lands were let and his stock cleared, the proceeds of which were lodged in a bank account in the joint names of the deceased and the plaintiff. Both of these events led to objections by other members of the family, including by the deceased's mother. On 29 May, 1974, the deceased was admitted to hospital suffering from orchitis and on his discharge about three weeks later he returned to live with the plaintiff. His mother died on 24 August, 1974, and on 10 December, 1974, he made his first will, bequeathing £3,000 each to his three nieces and leaving all his property to the plaintiff. On or about 2 May, 1975, he transferred his land, subject to certain rights and money payments reserved to himself and to a charge of £1,000 each in favour of his three nieces, to the plaintiff. On 5 May, 1975, the deceased made his last will, bequeathing all his property to the plaintiff. He died of lung cancer on 16 May, 1975. The plaintiff sought to have the will dated 5 May, 1975, established in solemn form and the defendants, his brother and sister, entered caveats claiming, *inter alia,* that execution of the wills was secured by the undue influence of the plaintiff. The questions set for the trial judge were: (*a*) whether the will dated 5 May, 1975, was executed pursuant to the Succession Act, 1965; (*b*) whether the deceased at the time of the execution of the alleged will was of sound disposing mind; (*c*) whether the deceased at the time of the said execution knew and approved of the contents. Similar questions were left regarding the alleged will dated 10 December, 1974. The pleas of undue influence were withdrawn. **Held** by D'Arcy J. in granting letters of administration with the will dated 5 May, 1975, to the plaintiff, 1, the onus of proof lay on the plaintiff propounding a will. 2. The evidence of the plaintiff under whose "protection" the deceased lived must be approached with suspicion and the court must be vigilant and zealous in examining it. Principles in *Corboy* v. *Leahy* [1969] I.R. 148 and *Fulton* v. *Andrews* (1875) L.R. 7 H.L. 448 applied. 3. The evidence of five solicitors and two doctors convinced the court that the deceased had the mental capacity to make a will on both dates. 4. The court was not prepared to accept the evidence of the plaintiff in full. 5. The true position regarding the mental incapacity of the deceased was that he was not as well as the plaintiff and her lay witnesses suggested nor was it as bad as the defendants' witnesses stated. 6. It was unnecessary to consider the other questions fixed by the Master. *In the goods of O'Connor; O'Connor* v.*O'Connor*
(H.C.) [1978] ILRM 247

20. —— **Validity** — *Capacity — Application to condemn a will — Deceased suffering a stroke — Subsequent to attack deceased executing a document — Whether document purporting to be a will represented the testamentary wishes of the deceased — Whether deceased had capacity to know and appreciate contents of executed document — Succession Act,* 1965 (*No.* 27), *s.* 78.] The plaintiff a sister of the deceased William Glynn who died on 14 February, 1982, brought an action to condemn what she alleged was a pretended or purported will of the deceased dated 20 October, 1981, and sought an order giving her liberty to apply for and obtain a grant of letters of administration to the estate of the deceased. The defendant, a cousin of the deceased, counter-claimed in his defence that the court should admit the said will of the deceased to probate in solemn form of law. Evidence was adduced by two independent witnesses that approximately a year before the deceased's death he had discussed on a number of occasions the making of the will and disposing of all his property to the defendant. The deceased had expressed a wish not to go to a solicitor and asked the two witnesses to promise to witness his will. On one occasion one of the witnesses gave evidence of suggesting to the deceased that the deceased leave £20,000 to the plaintiff, and £1,000 to the local priest. The deceased confirmed to one of the witnesses on 5 October, 1981, and a week before that to the other witness that he had drawn up a will and that he had decided to give £20,000 to the plaintiff, £1,000 to the local priest and the remainder to the defendant. Later that day the deceased suffered a massive stroke and thereafter was unable to communicate verbally with anyone. The said two witnesses gave evidence of visiting the deceased in hospital on 20 October, 1981, and after being satisfied that he recognised them they produced the will and told him that they were there to do what they had promised to do. They gave further evidence that they read the will slowly and distinctly to him and were satisfied that he knew what was being said. He then made an "X" at the end of the document with difficulty in the

SUCCESSION—Will.

presence of two witnesses. Evidence was also given by Dr. O'Gorman who was of the opinion that the deceased was not fit to make a will or able to communicate his intentions. **Held** By Hamilton P. in making an order that the will be admitted to probate in solemn form, 1, the two witnesses had no interest in the manner in which the testator disposed of his property and their sole concern was to give effect to his wishes. 2. The contents of the document represented what had been agreed and approved recently by the testator, and the two witnesses satisfied themselves on 20 October, 1981, that the testator knew what he was doing and that he approved the contents of the will. *Glynn* v. *Glynn*

(H.C.) [1987] ILRM 589

21. —— **Validity** — *Revocation — Subsequent marriage — Will executed in* 1951 — *Whether will revoked by subsequent marriage — Whether will made in contemplation of marriage — Whether will valid and effective within scope of Succession Act,* 1965 — *Wills Act,* 1837 (*c.* 26), *s. XVIII — Succession Act,* 1965 (*No.* 27), *s.* 9.] In 1951 the deceased executed a will in which he devised and bequeathed all his real and personal estate to M.G. In 1954 the deceased married M.G. He died in 1983, solely survived by his wife, M.G., and not having executed any other will. The executor named in the will of 1951 applied for an order that the deceased's will was not revoked by his subsequent marriage, in accordance with the provisions of s. 85, sub-s. 1, of the Succession Act, 1965; or, alternatively, that the will was revoked by the subsequent marriage and that the deceased died intestate. **Held** by Gannon J. in dismissing the application, 1, that the will executed by the deceased in 1951 was governed by the Wills Act, 1837, and was revoked by his subsequent marriage, whereupon it became invalid and ineffective and accordingly it could not come within the scope of s. 9, sub.-s. 4, of the Succession Act, 1965. 2. Accordingly, the applicant could not competently call upon the court to make any order within the scope of the provisions of the Succession Act, 1965, or the rules of the court in probate matters. *In the goods of Baker*

(H.C.) [1985] I.R.101

22. —— **Validity** — *Revocation — Subsequent marriage — Will made in* 1971 — *Deceased going through ceremony of marriage in* 1977 — *Whether will revoked by this marriage — Whether deceased free to marry in* 1977 — *Previous marriage annulled in* 1968 — *Whether such order would be recognised — Domicile of deceased — Succession Act,* 1965 (*No.* 27), *ss.* 27(4), 85.] S. 85(1) of the Succession Act, 1965, provides that "A will shall be revoked by the subsequent marriage of the testator except a will made in contemplation of that marriage, whether so expressed in the will or not." The deceased was born in Ireland in 1912 and moved to England in 1928 where he lived all his working life until 1977. During his life time he entered into the contract of marriage on five occasions. His fourth marriage to a Virginia McWatters took place in Nevada, U.S.A. on 16 September, 1967, and no place of residence for the deceased was mentioned. This marriage was annulled on 26 January, 1968, by the Nevada courts. On 19 May, 1971, he made and executed a will in London in which he described himself as residing in London and domiciled in England. On 23 October, 1977, he retired from work and sold his flat and all his furniture and went to live in the U.S.A. He went through a ceremony of marriage on 28 November, 1977, to Virginia McWatters for the second time. This marriage came to an end by virtue of a property settlement agreement dated 4 August, 1980, on foot of which the Superior Court of California made an interlocutory judgment of dissolution of the marriage. The deceased returned to Ireland in August, 1980, and remained there until his death on 8 March, 1983. The applicant, the deceased's sister, issued a notice of motion seeking a number of declaratory orders and in particular an order pursuant to s. 27(4) of the Succession Act, 1965, that she be at liberty to apply for letters of administration (intestate) of the estate of the deceased. The applicant submitted that the deceased had died intestate as although he had executed a will in 1971 that will was revoked by the subsequent marriage of the deceased in Nevada on 28 November, 1977, pursuant to s. 85 of the Succession Act, 1965. Therefore the issue arose as to whether the marriage of 28 November, 1977, was a valid marriage for the purposes of s. 85, and as a consequence of that in order to ascertain whether s. 85 applied the court had to determine the domicile of the deceased in order to make a decision as to whether the deceased, subsequent to the making of his will, was free to marry in November, 1977. A brother of the deceased Jarlath Fleming opposed application and submitted that the deceased's will of 19 May, 1971, was not revoked. **Held** by Gannon J. in refusing to grant the applicaion, 1, on the evidence submitted the presumption that the deceased retained his domicile of origin is rebutted by his conduct and the general course of events during the whole period of his continued employment and up to the date of his second marriage. 2. The evidence supports the inference that the deceased up to his retirement in 1977 had intentionally chosen England as his domicile and thereafter on moving to America and marrying Virginia McWatters he had chosen America as his domicile prior to the

SUCCESSION—Will.

break-up of that marriage. 3. The deceased's marriage to Virginia McWatters on 16 September, 1967, was a valid marriage and it was not lawfully dissolved nor annulled on 26 January, 1968, as there was insufficient evidence before the court to infer that the deceased was domiciled in Nevada on 26 January, 1968, and as a consequence the parties were not free to marry in 1977. 4. The deceased's purported marriage to Virginia McWatters on 28 November, 1977, was in law and in effect a nullity and therefore did not have the effect of revoking the will made on 19 May, 1971. 5. A motion to the probate court in the form mentioned above herein is not appropriate or suitable as a means for having a trial of an issue as to the domicile of the deceased person or as to the validity of the marriage of the deceased. *In the estate of Fleming*

(H.C.) [1987] ILRM 638

23. —— **Validity** — *Revocation — Later will — Will executed in* 1956 — *Later will executed in* 1970 — *Later will contained expressions "on the eve of going to Malta . . . if I should not return" — Whether later will conditional — Whether earlier will revoked.*] The testatrix, who died in 1982, made a will in 1956 and a codicil thereto in 1960. In or about 1970 she made an undated will which commenced: "On the eve of going to Malta, and in view of recent happenings I think it wise to say how I should like my goods disposed of if I should not return. . . ." The later will contained dispositions which differed widely from those of the 1956 will and the 1960 codicil. In an action to determine whether probate should be granted to the 1956 will and 1960 codicil or the 1970 will, **Held,** that, on the true construction of the 1970 will, the testatrix's failure to return from Malta was unequivocally made the condition on which her goods were to be disposed of in accordance with the 1970 will. Consequently the 1956 will and 1960 codicil ought to be admitted to probate as they represented, in law, the testatrix's testamentary intentions. *Robinson* v. *Napier.*

(Fam. Div.) [1984] N.I.235

24. —— **Validity** — *Undue influence claim — Person instrumental in having will prepared taking a benefit under it — Allegation of undue influence — Whether will be condemned — Whether testator knew and approved of its contents.*] The plaintiff had lived for many years with her cousin, one Patrick Kavanagh deceased, a bachelor, and had acted as his housekeeper. A strong bond of affection existed between them. By his will dated 23 February, 1971, the deceased had left a valuable property, his residence and only asset, to the defendant, subject to a life interest in the plaintiff. He made some other pecuniary bequests, and left the residue of his

SUCCESSION—*continued.*

estate to the plaintiff. The defendant had been a friend of the deceased since the early nineteen sixties. The plaintiff alleged that the defendant had exercised undue influence over the deceased in the making of his will, and sought an order condemning the said will. Evidence was given by friends and acquaintances of the deceased as to the apparent inability of the deceased to resist any suggestions of the defendant, who frequently adopted a bullying manner towards him. Evidence was also given as to the high regard in which the deceased held the plaintiff, and his oft-expressed intention of leaving her all his property. He had in fact made a will in 1965 in which the plaintiff was the executor and legatee universal. Evidence given by the defendant himself as to monies borrowed from the deceased was contradictory. Evidence was then given as to the circumstances surrounding the making of the will of 1971. The deceased was brought by the defendant to see the defendant's own solicitor. The deceased was at this time in a poor state of health, both physical and mental. The solicitor did not caution the deceased or urge him to take precipitate action. The will was witnessed by a friend of the defendant. **Held** by Costello J. in granting the order sought, as a person instrumental in framing the will under which he received a benefit, the defendant had not discharged the onus of proving that the testator knew and approved of its contents. *Re Corboy, Leahy* v. *Corboy* [1969] I.R. 148 applied. *In the goods of Kavanagh; Healy* v. *MacGillicuddy*

(H.C.) [1978] ILRM 175

—— Administration — Income tax — Assessment — Estate of deceased person — Income accruing to the estate — Liability of executor to income tax — Whether executor the person "receiving or entitled to the income".
see **Revenue,** 27

—— Administration — Intestacy — Recovery of land — Limitation of actions — Period applicable — Plaintiff administrator — Widow of son of intestate in possession.
see **Limitation of Actions,** 5

—— Administration — Joint tenants — Next-of-kin of deceased owner remaining in possession — Whether interest of other next-of-kin defeated by adverse possession.
see **Adverse Possession**

—— Inheritance rights — Separated wife — Separation agreement — Subsequent proceedings by husband for divorce *a*

SUMMONS—*continued.*

plaintiff to serve notice of summons outside jurisdiction.
see **Injunction,** 9

—— Sufficiency — Signature — District Court Clerk affixing signature to the summons by use of a rubber stamp — Conviction — Certiorari — Whether open to prosecutor to challenge sufficiency of summons.
see **Criminal Law,** 62

SUPERIOR COURTS RULES COMMITTEE — Rules of court — Discovery of documents — Whether *ultra vires.*
see **Practice and Procedure,** 35, 36

SUPPLEMENTARY WELFARE ALLOWANCES
see **Social Welfare,** 6-8

SUPREME COURT

—— Cases stated — Consultative case stated — Approach of Supreme Court to case stated — Whether arguments not made before Circuit Court would be entertained.
see **Local Government,** 2

—— Jurisdiction — Appellate jurisdiction — Appeal — Grounds — Sole ground — Ground not argued or decided in trial court — Refusal of appellate court to decide issue raised in sole ground.
see **Conflict of Laws,** 6

—— Jurisdiction — Appellate jurisdiction — Damages — Personal injuries — Appeal — Substitution of award for that of High Court — Whether Court has jurisdiction in absence of consent from parties — Whether jurisdiction limited by legislation — Court empowered in lieu of ordering re-trial to enter such judgment as it considers proper.
see **Constitution,** 6

—— Jurisdiction — Review of High Court discretion — Whether Supreme Court jurisdiction limited.
see **Practice and Procedure,** 20

—— Practice — Appeal — Function of Court — Primary and secondary facts — Whether Supreme Court empowered to reach different conclusions to those of trial court in relation to inferences from primary facts.
see **Nuisance,** 1

—— Practice — Appeal — Issue not argued

SUPREME COURT—*continued.*

before High Court — Issue as to jurisdiction of High Court to have entertained proceedings — Whether Supreme Court will decide issue not argued in court below.
see **Arbitration,** 3

—— Practice — Appeal — Time limit — Extension — Appeal from High Court to Supreme Court — Whether Supreme Court has same powers as High Court to extend time for appeal.
see **Practice and Procedure,** 53

—— Practice — Grounds of appeal — Whether Supreme Court should hear or pronounce upon an issue not argued before and determined by the High Court.
see **Negligence,** 19

—— Precedent — *Stare decisis* — Decision not followed.
see **Constitution,** 26

—— Precedent — *Stare decisis* — Previous decisions of Supreme Court — Jurisdiction of Supreme Court to review its previous decisions.
see **Case Stated,** 2

—— Reference to European Court of Justice — Issue arising for first time.
see **European Communities,** 2

SURETY

—— **Principal and surety** — *Deed of bond — Deferred payment of excise duty — Whether necessary for creditor to have resort to securities received by the creditor from the principal before proceeding against the surety — Excise Collection and Management Act,* 1841 (*c.* 20), *s.* 24.] The plaintiff, suing on behalf of the Minister for Finance and the Revenue Commissioners, recovered the sum of £504,416.37 together with interest against the defendant in an order of the High Court made by McWilliam J. The defendant, an insurance company, by deed of bond dated 2 December, 1981, had held and bound itself to pay to the Minister for Finance on behalf of the Revenue Commissioners the penalty sum of £1,400,000 conditional upon the failure of J.J. Murphy and Company Ltd. (the company), a company engaged in the warehousing of spirits and beers, to pay the duties of excise chargeable in respect of spirits delivered from bonded warehouses. Excise duty in an amount of £458,909.72 became due by the company to the Revenue Commissioners on the delivery of spirits from the warehouses in the months of June and July, 1982, the payment of which was deferred to

SURETY—*continued.*

31 August, 1982. The defendant had agreed to undertake the suretyship to a general bond in respect of the deferred payment of excise duty on beer imported by the company in a penalty of £90,000. Excise duty in an amount of £45,506.65 became due by the company to the Revenue Commissioners on the importation of beer in the months of June and July, 1982. The agreed period of deferral for the payment of all the excise duty on the beer expired before 15 August, 1982, so that by the end of August, 1982, the total of £504,416.37 was due by the defendant to the Revenue Commissioners in respect of excise duties on spirits and beer. The defendant appealed the order of the High Court to the Supreme Court and argued that by virtue of s. 24 of the Excise Collection and Management Act, 1841, the Revenue Commissioners had a statutory lien which they should have enforced against the goods specified in the section in the possession of the company. It was contended on behalf of the defendant that the Revenue Commissioners should have realised such goods as assets of the company and applied the sum realised in the lessening of the excise duty payable. **Held** by the Supreme Court (Finlay C.J., Griffin and McCarthy JJ.) in dismissing the appeal, 1, it was well settled that it is not necessary for the creditor, before proceeding against the surety, to request the principal debtor to pay, or to sue him, though solvent, unless this be expressly stipulated in the surety document. 2. There was authority for the proposition that the creditor did not have to resort to securities received by the creditor from the principal debtor. *Ranelaugh (Earl)* v. *Hayes* (1683) 1 Vern. 189; *Wilks* v. *Heeley* (1832) 1 Cr. & M. 249; *Re Howe, ex parte Brett* (1871) 6 Ch. App. 838, 841 referred. 3. There was no provision in the terms of the bond obliging the Revenue Commissioners to engage upon the exercise con-

SURETY—*continued.*

templated by s. 24 of the Excise Collection and Management Act, 1841, before proceeding against the surety. 4. The law would not infer an additional term to the contract nor call in aid some alleged equity which would delay, if not defeat, in whole or in part, the remedy expressly provided for in the contract, in the absence of a mistake or some impropriety, neither of which were applicable. *Attorney General* v. *Sun Alliance and London Insurances Ltd.*

(S.C.) [1985] ILRM 522

—— Charge to bank to secure loan to company — Associated company acting as surety — Directors also guaranteeing loan and charging property — Default in repayments — Proceedings against corporate surety — Decree for possession of property — Appeal to Supreme Court pending — Proceedings also instituted against directors — Whether bank entitled to exercise its rights to possession of directors' property until they have exercised their rights against the principal debtor and co-surety — Whether doctrine of marshalling applicable.
see **Banking,** 3

SURGEON — Negligence claim.
see **Negligence,** 15

SUSPENSION

—— Athlete.
see **Natural and Constitutional Justice,** 2

—— Employment.
see **Civil Service,** 3
Constitution, 11
Education, 2
Employer and Employee, 23

T

TORTS—*continued.*

—— Passing off.
see **Trade Names and Designs**

—— Unlawful interference with economic interest.
see **Injunction,** 7

TOUR OPERATOR — Licence — Breach of a condition — Decision to revoke — Appeal to High Court — Whether applicant fit and proper to carry on business — Power of High Court on appeal.
see **Transport**

TOWN AND COUNTRY PLANNING
see **Planning**

TRADE AND INDUSTRY
see **Casual Trading; Company; Consumer Protection; Copyright; Customs and Excise; Hire Purchase; Monopoly; Patents; Restraint of Trade; Revenue; Sale of Goods; Trade Mark; Trade Names and Designs**

—— Nuisance — Noise — Shop — Customers — Night-time trading — Interference with plaintiff's sleep — Plaintiff's dwelling near defendant's shop — Whether any material delay in making plaintiff's complaint — Defendant restrained from trading between midnight and 6 a.m.
see **Nuisance,** 2

—— Restrictive practices — Prices regulation — Retail prices — Prohibition on advertising goods at cost less than net invoice price — Whether meaning of prohibition clear — Whether injunction appropriate remedy to seek.
see **Restrictive Practices**

—— Revenue — Corporation tax.
see **Revenue,** 3, 4, 8-24

—— Revenue — Income tax.
see **Revenue,** 28, 29, 33, 39-41

TRADE DISPUTE
see **Employer and Employee,** 24, 25
Injunction, 13

—— Constitutional right — Interference — Right to free primary education — Primary school teachers' dispute — Damages — Whether such claim a claim in tort.

TRADE DISPUTE—*continued.*
see **Damages,** 1

TRADE MARK
see also **Copyright; Patents; Trade Names and Designs**

Infringement. Nos. 1, 2
Registration. Nos. 3-7

1. —— **Infringement** — *Similar goods with similar marks — Whether likelihood of direct confusion — Trade Marks Act,* 1963 (*No.* 9), *ss.* 12(1), 20(1).] The plaintiff is seeking an injunction to restrain the defendant from infringing the plaintiff's trade mark "Trex" by the use of a mark "Pastrex". The commodity sold under the name "Trex" is a cooking fat intended to be used for making pastry. The defendant's commodity "Pastrex" is also a cooking fat intended specifically for use in making pastry. The question the court had to decide was whether the registration of the defendant's mark complied with the requirements of the Trade Marks Act, 1963, and in so doing had to adopt the following specific heads of inquiry: (1) the look and sound of the registered mark and the mark complained of; (2) the goods to which they are to be applied; (3) the nature and kind of customers likely to buy the goods; (4) all the surrounding circumstances. The plaintiffs argued that the word "Pastrex" is likely to deceive or cause confusion with their product "Trex" on the grounds that the prefix added to the plaintiff's mark refers to the purpose for which the plaintiff's product is used and is likely to provide the belief that the defendant's product is a variation of the plaintiff's product. **Held** by McWilliam J. in granting the order sought, 1, the goods of each party are an almost identical form of cooking fat although each manufacturer would undoubtedly claim special properties for its product. 2. 90% of the customers likely to buy the goods are expected to be housewives shopping in supermarkets or grocery shops and no evidence of confusion on the part of the customers had been given as such evidence is not available as opposed to not existing. 3. There is little likelihood of direct confusion between the two words in the present case when spoken as the first syllable in a trade mark is the one which is usually emphasised and remains in the memory of the public. *Mediline A.G., Application of* [1970] I.R. 169 approved. 4. The look of the two words is likely to cause confusion as their appearance would suggest a business connection between them, as the prefix added by the defendant indicates the very purpose for which the plaintiff's goods are intended to be used. *Industrie Buitoni Perugina S.P.A.* v. *Dowdall O'Mahoney & Co. Manufacturing Ltd.*

TRADE MARK—*continued.*

(H.C.) [1978] ILRM 116

2. —— **Infringement** — *Soft drink — "Tango" — Marketing of product ceasing — Application for removal of mark from register — Use resumed shortly before application — Whether resumed user* bona fide — *Trade Marks Act,* 1963 (*No.* 9), *s.* 34(1)(3) — *Trade Mark Rules,* 1963 (*S.I. No.* 268), *Sched.* 2, *class* 32.] S. 34 of the Trade Marks Act, 1963, provides that a registered trade mark may be removed from the register on the application to the Court or to the Controller of Patents Designs and Trademarks of a person aggrieved on the ground, *inter alia,* that up to the date one month before the date of the application a continuous period of five years or longer elapsed during which there was no *bona fide* use of the said trade mark by the proprietor thereof. The plaintiff was the registered proprietor of the trade mark "Tango", in respect of an aereated soft drink produced in two flavours, orange and lemon. The marketing of this product ceased around the year 1968. In 1974, the reintroduction of the product was under consideration, but various problems created a difficulty in so doing over the next three years. In June, 1977, the defendant introduced onto the market a concentrated orange drink under the name "Tang". Before the end of July of the same year, the plaintiff had once again distributed its product "Tango" throughout the country. The defendant lodged an application pursuant to s. 34 of the Act. The plaintiff issued the instant proceedings claiming relief on the ground that its trademark had been infringed by the use of the word "Tang" by the defendant — a word so closely resembling the plaintiff's trademark that it was likely to deceive or cause confusion in the course of trade. The defendant emphasised the difference in the dictionary meaning of the two words. The defendant also claimed in the alternative that the plaintiff's trademark should be confined to aereated drinks, thus allowing the defendant to use the name "Tang" in respect of concentrated fruit juices. **Held** by McWilliam J. in finding for the plaintiff, 1, where purchasers of a product are concerned, the appearance of a word, or its sound when spoken, are more important than its dictionary definition. The name used by the defendant would, in such circumstances, be likely to deceive or cause confusion with the plaintiff's trademark. 2. The use of the plaintiff's trademark which recommenced in July, 1977, was a genuine use for the purpose of marketing the plaintiff's goods, and was thus a *bona fide* use within the meaning of the 1963 Act, notwithstanding that the time of recommencement was expressly chosen for the purpose of protecting the mark and of causing disadvantage to the defendant. *Electrolux Ltd.* v. *Electrix Ltd.* [1959] R.P.C. 283 followed. 3. In exercising its discretion as to whether to exclude from the protection of a trademark goods in respect of which it has not been used, the court must first decide whether the goods are of the same description as those in respect of which the trademark is being used. It would be unreal to differentiate between aereated mineral drinks and fruit juices of a concentrated variety, so as to exclude the latter from the protection of the trademark attaching to the former. *Beecham Group Ltd.* v. *Goodalls of Ireland Ltd.*

(H.C.) [1978] ILRM 106

3. —— **Registration** — *Refusal — "Crocodile" — Distinctiveness — Whether mark distinctive — Whether mark inherently capable of distinguishing the goods — Whether mark likely to deceive — Trade Marks Act,* 1963 (*No.* 9), *ss.* 17, 18, 19.] S. 17 of the Trade Marks Act, 1963, provides that, for a trade mark to be registrable in Part A of the Register of Trade Marks, it must "contain or consist of at least . . . any . . . distinctive mark." The word "distinctive" is defined in the section as "adapted . . . to distinguish goods with which the proprietor of the trade mark is or may be connected in the course of trade from goods in the case of which no such connection subsists." S. 18 of the Act provides that to be registrable in Part B of the register, the trade mark must be capable of so distinguishing the goods of its proprietor, and that in determining whether it is so capable, the court or the Controller "may have regard to the extent to which — (*a*) the trade mark is inherently capable of distinguishing as aforesaid; and (*b*) by reason of the trade mark or of any other circumstances, the trade mark is in fact capable of distinguishing as aforesaid." The appellant applied to register in Part A of the register a trade mark consisting of a crococile. The application was in respect of clothing, including leather footwear. In the alternative, the appellant sought registration in Part B, and amended the specification of the goods by adding the words: "none being goods made of crocodile skin or of material in imitation of crocodile skin." The Controller objected to registration on the grounds that the trade mark was neither adapted to distinguish nor capable of distinguishing the goods of the appellant, and that it was prohibited under s. 19 of the 1963 Act as being likely to deceive. **Held** by the Supreme Court (Parke J., Henchy and Griffin JJ. concurring) in dismissing the appeal, 1, the crocodile in the proposed trade mark was not so different from other crocodiles as to make it adapted to distinguish the goods of the appellant. 2. A drawing of a well-known creature is not any more capable of distinguishing than it is adapted to distinguish the goods of the

TRADE MARK—*continued.*

appellant. 3. The appearance of a crocodile on leather goods is likely to mislead purchasers into believing that the goods are made of crocodile skin. 4. Notwithstanding that all prospective purchasers may not be deceived by the trade mark, it is sufficient for the purposes of s. 19 of the Act that any substantial body of the public, even a minority, is likely to be deceived. *La Chemise Lacoste S.A.* v. *Controller of Patents, Designs and Trade Marks*

(S.C.) [1978] ILRM 8

4. —— **Registration** — *Refusal — "Dent" — Rare surname — Whether evidence of distinctiveness — Whether mark inherently capable of distinguishing the goods — Trade Marks Act,* 1963 (*No.* 9), *ss.* 17, 18.] Ss. 17 and 18 of the Trade Marks Act, 1963, set out the conditions governing registration of a trade mark in Part "A" and "B" respectively. Briefly, distinctiveness of the proposed trade mark is a requisite for registration in part "A" and capability of distinguishing the goods of the applicants from the goods of others is a requisite for registration in part "B". The plaintiff appealed a decision of the defendant who refused an application by the plaintiff for registration of the word "Dent" in either part "A" or part "B" of the register of trade marks in connection with clocks and watches. **Held** by McWilliam J. in dismissing the appeal, 1, the application for registration in part "A" must be refused due to the absence of any evidence of distinctiveness within the meaning of s. 17 of the Act as the vast majority of people in this country would assume that the word "Dent" when used as a trade mark in connection with clocks and watches was a name. 2. Where there are no special circumstances of use or otherwise a surname is only capable of distinguishing the goods of the proprietor of the trade mark within the meaning of s. 18 when it is unusual to the eye and ear of those Irish people likely to be concerned in dealing with the goods which is not the situation with regard to the name "Dent". *Kreuzer* v. *Controller of Patents* [1978] F.S.R. 239 considered and distinguished. *Dent (A.) & Co. Ltd.* v. *Controller of Patents*

(H.C.) [1978] ILRM 172

5. —— **Registration** — *Refusal — "Durex" — Extent to which controller entitled to seek information from applicant — Whether mark's use would be deceptive or confusing — Trade Marks Act,* 1963 (*No.* 9), *ss.* 2, 17, 19, 25, 27, 57(2) — *Criminal Law Amendment Act,* 1935 (*No.* 6), *s.* 17.] The plaintiff had applied for the registration of the trademark "Durex" in respect of surgeons' gloves and diagnostic finger cots and finger stalls. The defendant sought, and was refused, all relevant information in the plaintiff's possession on matters such as the derivation and origin of the trade mark, the nature and purpose of the goods in question, the plaintiff's intention as to the use of the mark, and how the mark would appear in use in the course of trade in the State. The plaintiff contended that the defendant was not entitled to such information, or to any information other than that required by the trade mark rules. Following a hearing requested by the plaintiff, the application for registration was refused on the grounds, *inter alia,* that the mark had become identified in the State with contraceptive articles to such an extent that its use in relation to other goods would be deceptive or confusing within the meaning of s. 19 of the Trade Marks Act, 1963, and that contraceptives were goods in respect of which a trade mark could not be registered. The plaintiff appealed to the High Court. **Held** by Hamilton J. in allowing the appeal, 1, the Controller of Patents was entitled to such information as he might reasonably require in order to enable him to fulfil his functions under the Act and to exercise the discretion which it conferred upon him. In particular, he was in the instant case entitled to take into consideration the use made of the trademark in places outside the State. 2. If the proposed trade mark were to be used in respect of the specified goods, the public as a whole would be likely to appreciate that the said goods were manufactured by the maker of "Durex" contraceptives. 3. The registration of the trademark would not in any circumstances appear to be an authorisation from a competent authority for the legal importation, sale, or any illegal use of contraceptives, since the public must be presumed to be aware of the law in this regard. 4. The trade mark "Durex" was an invented word of which the plaintiff was proprietor, and there was at the time at which the application was filed a genuine present intention to use the mark for the purpose of indicating a connection in the course of trade between the goods and the proprietors. *LRC International Ltd.* v. *Controller of Patents, Designs and Trade Marks*

(H.C.) [1976-7] ILRM 164

6. —— **Registration** — *Refusal — "Golden Pages" — Classified telephone directories — Whether directories constitute goods — Whether "connection in the course of trade" necessitates sale — Whether words descriptive of the goods produced — Trade Marks Act,* 1963 (*No.* 9), *ss.* 2(1), 17.] I.T.T. were the publishers of the classified telephone directory of businesses known as The Golden Pages. The company obtained permission from the Minister for Posts and Telegraphs for publication, as well as to obtain and insert advertisements in the directory. The directory was distributed by the Minister to

TRADE MARK—*continued.*

all telephone subscribers; I.T.T. obtained no revenue from direct sales of the directory. The company applied for registration as a trade mark the words "Golden Pages" together with associated devices, but this was refused by the Controller. On appeal to the High Court, McWilliam J. remitted the matter to the Controller to proceed with registration, but he granted leave to appeal to the Supreme Court on specified points of law. S. 2(1) of the Trade Marks Act, 1963, defines trade mark as "a mark used . . . in relation to goods . . . indicating . . . a connection in the course of trade between the goods and some person having the right . . . to use the mark." **Held** by the Supreme Court (Walsh, Henchy, Griffin, Hederman and McCarthy JJ.) in dismissing the appeal, 1, the directories were goods within the meaning fo the Act and the fact that I.T.T. was not paid directly by the Minister did not affect this. 2. The goods were dealt with in the course of trade, since although it was not essential to a trade that a profit should be made, this was the only reason for production in this case; that while I.T.T. did not distribute the directories, it would be unreal to suggest that they did not put them on the market; and that it was not necessary to effect a sale for there to be a connection in the course of trade. *Dicta* of Kenny J. in *Bank of America National Trust & Savings Association's Trade Mark* [1977] F.S.R. 7 disapproved. 3. Both marks, that without and that with the words "Golden Pages", were entitled to be registered, the latter because the words were descriptive of the directories produced by I.T.T. Decision of McWilliam J. in the High Court (22 June, 1982) affirmed. *I.T.T. World Directories Inc.* v. *Controller of Patents, Designs and Trade Marks*

(S.C.) [1985] ILRM 30

7. —— **Registration**—*Refusal*—*"High life"*—*Distinctiveness — Application to register words "high life" as a trade mark for beer — Whether any direct reference to the character or quality of the goods — Whether proposed mark capable of distinguishing the goods — Trade Marks Act,* 1963 (*No.* 9), *ss.* 17, 18.] Section 18 of the Trade Marks Act, 1963, provides that to qualify as a trade mark capable of registration in Part B of the register of trade marks a mark must be capable of distinguishing the goods in respect of which it is sought to be registered from other goods. Subsection 2 of s. 18 provides that in determining whether a mark is so capable the Controller or court may have regard to the extent to which (*a*) the mark is inherently capable of distinguishing the goods; and (*b*) the trade mark is in fact capable of distinguishing the goods by reason of its use or of any other circumstances. The plaintiff was a manufacturer of beer. In 1977 it applied

TRADE MARK—*continued.*

to register the words "High Life" as a trade mark. The application was refused by the defendant who held that the words could not be registered in Part B of the register on the ground that the words conveyed a reference to the goods which was so direct as to be likely to interfere with or restrict the legitimate rights of other manufacturers of beer to use the words in describing their products. The plaintiff appealed to the High Court against the ruling of the defendant. The High Court (Costello J.) reversed the ruling of the defendant and held that the proposed trade mark should be registered in Part B of the register. On appeal by the defendant it was **Held** by the Supreme Court (Finlay C.J., Henchy and McCarthy JJ.), in dismissing the appeal, that the phrase "High Life" had connotations applicable to a vast range of activities and goods and was not such a direct description of the quality and character of the product as would restrict the legitimate rights of other manufacturers of beer to use the words in describing their products. *Application of Mothercare Ltd.* [1968] I.R. 359 applied. *Miller Brewing Co.* v. *Controller of Patents, Designs and Trade Marks*

[1987] I.R.434; [1988] ILRM 259

8. —— **Registration** — *Refusal — "Kiku" — Perfumes and toiletries — Whether mark direct reference to character of the goods — Foreign words — Whether word apt to distinguish — Trade Marks Act,* 1963 (*No.* 9), *s.* 17 — *Trade Mark Rules,* 1963 (*S.I. No.* 268), *r.* 19(4).] S. 17 of the Trade Marks Act, 1963, provides that, for a proposed trade mark to be registrable in Part A of the Register of Trade Marks, it must, *inter alia,* have no "direct reference to the character or quality of the goods." The applicant had appealed to the High Court from a decision of the Controller refusing to register the word "Kiku" as a trade mark for perfumes and toiletries. Evidence was adduced to show that "Kiku" was a Japanese word meaning "chrysanthemum", and it was to be used in conjunction with a distinctive type of oriental design. The Controller stated that foreign words proposed for registration must be considered by reference to their English translation, and the word "chrysanthemum" could not be registered because of a practice whereby names of flowers and plants were not registered in connection with perfumes and soaps. Kenny J., in finding for the applicant, held that a foreign word could be registered where it was apt to distinguish the goods in question, unless, *inter alia,* it was known to be a translation of an English or Irish word which could not be registered. He held further that the word "Kiku" was apt to distinguish and would not commonly be known as a translation of the

TRADE MARK—*continued.*

word "chrysanthemum". On appeal by the Controller on a question of law as to whether, where a word for which registration is sought is one in a foreign language, the Controller and the court must treat the application as one for the registration of the corresponding English or Irish word, it was **Held** by the Supreme Court (O'Higgins C.J., Griffin and Parke JJ. concurring) in answering the question in the negative and in dismissing the appeal: In order to have a "direct reference" to the character and quality of the goods within the meaning of s. 17 of the 1963 Act, a proposed trade mark must, as it stands, so refer. Where a word has to be translated in order for the reference to become clear, the word itself does not have a direct reference, and may be registered. *Faberge Incorporated* v. *Controller of Patents, Designs and Trade Marks*

(H.C., S.C.) [1976-7] ILRM 335

9. —— **Registration** — *Refusal* — *"Waterford" — Distinctiveness — Geographical name — Mark factually distinctive of goods — Whether "inherently capable of distinguishing" — Trade Marks Act,* 1963 (*No.* 9), *ss.* 17, 18(2)(*b*), 58(3).] Waterford Glass Ltd. sought registration of the word "Waterford" as a trade mark for its crystal. The Controller of Patents, Designs and Trade Marks refused registration on the ground that the word "Waterford" lacked an inherent capacity to distinguish glassware. The company appealed to the High Court, where Hamilton J. (whose judgment is reported at [1982] ILRM 91) allowed the appeal. The Controller of Patents, Designs and Trade Marks thereupon appealed to the Supreme Court. Argument hinged on whether the words "capable of distinguishing" used in s. 18 of the Trade Marks Act, 1963, should be construed as meaning "capable in law of distinguishing." **Held** by the Supreme Court (*per* O'Higgins C.J. and McCarthy, J.: Henchy J. dissenting) in dismissing the appeal that the mark "Waterford" had achieved one hundred per cent factual distinctiveness in relation to the products of Waterford Glass Ltd., and that the company was entitled to have the mark registered; and that the words "capable of distinguishing" were to be understood in their plain sense: *York Trailer Holdings Ltd.* v. *Registrar of Trade Marks* [1982] 1 All E.R. 257 not followed. *Waterford Glass Ltd.* v. *Controller of Patents, Designs and Trade Marks.*

(S.C.) [1984] ILRM 565

—— Application to remove trade mark from register — Application refused — Whether controller required to give reasons — Natural justice.

see **Judicial Review,** 13

TRADE NAMES AND DESIGNS

—— **Passing off** — *Imitation of packaging — Whether product marketed in a manner calculated to deceive the public — Whether action might be maintained by a distributor or agent — Assessment of damages — Whether account of profits be directed.*] The plaintiff was sole distributor and handling agent in Ireland for a piece of exercising equipment known as the "body shaper." The defendant subsequently introduced its brand of equipment, known as "slimliner" into the market. The packaging of the two products was very similar, and evidence was given to show that the defendant had used the plaintiff's packaging as a model in designing its own. The defendant's advertising slogan was identical to that of the plaintiff, although the evidence of the defendant's advertising company was that its slogan had been independently created. The plaintiff sought damages and an injunction to restrain the defendant from advertising their product or packaging it in a form identical to that of the plaintiff. The defendant argued that the plaintiff could not sue as mere distributors or sole agents. **Held** by McWilliam J. in granting the relief sought and in assessing damages at £1,500, 1, in appropriate circumstances, such as the present, an action for passing-off may be maintained by a sole agent. *Dental Manufacturing Co. Ltd.* v. *De Troy* [1912] 3 K.B. 76 distinguished. 2. The defendant's product was marketed in a manner calculated to deceive the public because of the many similarities between its packaging and that of the plaintiff's product. *Grange Marketing Ltd.* v. *M & Q Plastic Products Ltd.*

(H.C) [1976-7] ILRM 144

TRADE UNION

1. —— **Irish Congress of Trade Unions** — *Disciplinary powers — Complaint to ICTU executive council — Whether injunction be granted restraining executive council from considering a resolution to impose any sanction on union — ICTU Constitution, Ch.* 41.] On 17 January, 1987, an interview with Mr. John Mitchell, General Secretary of the plaintiff union, appeared in the *Andersonstown News,* a newspaper circulating in the Belfast area under the heading,"An Unusual Union?" In the course of this interview, Mr. Mitchell, whilst speaking "about his union's attitude to the 'acquiescent' trade unions in the North", attacked certain of the trade unions operating in Northern Ireland as "Uncle Tom" and "reactionary." He also made reference to "the trade union mafia here, which leads to a comfortable sort of existence." A complaint was made to the executive council of the Irish Congress of Trade Unions which decided, *inter alia,* to seek from the plaintiff a public retraction and repudiation of the statements attributed to its general secretary. The

TRADE UNION—*continued.*

executive council informed the plaintiff that unless such a repudiation were forthcoming, action would be initiated by the executive council against the plaintiff under Clause 41(*a*) of the Constitution of the Irish Congress of Trade Unions, which provided in relevant part: "The executive council shall be empowered to investigate on its own initiative, or on complaint made by an affiliated organisation, the conduct or action of any affiliated organisation which is alleged to be detrimental to the interests of Congress or affiliated organisations." The plaintiff responded by stating that the views expressed by Mr. Mitchell did not represent IDATU policy and were merely personal opinions. The plaintiff was not prepared to publicly disassociate itself from the remarks made by Mr. Mitchell and, on 15 April, 1987, the executive council decided that the plaintiff's response was unsatisfactory and inadequate. That decision, together with a statement that unless the plaintiff publicly disassociated itself from Mr. Mitchell's remarks it would be required to show why it should not be suspended from the Irish Congress of Trade Unions, was communicated to the plaintiff on 16 April, 1987. Before the meeting could again be considered by the executive council at its next meeting, the plaintiff issued proceedings seeking an injunction to restrain the executive council from passing or considering any resolution to impose any sanction on the plaintiff for failing to comply with the previously expressed views of the executive council. On 19 May, 1987, the High Court (Blayney J.) granted an interim injunction to the plaintiff. **Held** by Lardner J. in refusing the relief sought, 1, the disciplinary powers contained in Clause 41 must be exercised in good faith for the benefit of the Irish Congress of Trade Unions, and in strict conformity with the provisions of the Constitution of the Irish Congress of Trade Unions. Such exercise must also observe the principles of natural and constitutional justice and basic fairness of procedures. 2. Whilst Mr. Mitchell's remarks may have been his personal opinions only, by virtue of the context in which they appeared, the plaintiff was associated with those views and could thus be called upon to disassociate itself from them. 3. By allowing Mr. Mitchell's views to be identified as those of the plaintiff union, and by subsequently failing to put the matter right by publicly disassociating itself from those views, the plaintiff had given grounds for a complaint to be made against it to the executive council. 4. The executive council afforded the plaintiff every opportunity to put forward any submissions it wished to make at every stage in the matter. 5. The trade unions associated in the Irish Congress of Trade Unions have freely accepted its Constitution by affiliation. There was no inequality

TRADE UNION—*continued.*

between the member trade unions and the Irish Congress of Trade Unions. Thus the plaintiff could not allege that Clause 41 offended against natural justice. 6. Although the matter lies entirely within the authority of the executive council to determine, the remarks made could reasonably be construed as capable of being detrimental to the interests of Congress and its affiliates. Accordingly the executive council may invoke Clause 41 and hold a meeting to consider and determine any resolution it deems to be appropriate. *Irish Distributive and Administrative Trade Union* v. *Carroll*

(H.C.) [1988] ILRM 713

2. —— **Meeting** — *Resolution for the introduction of a compulsory retirement scheme — Resolution passed — Plaintiff not present when vote taken — Whether resolution valid — Whether natural justice infringed — Whether infringement of plaintiff's right to work — Constitution of Ireland,* 1937, *Arts.* 40.3.1, 45.] The plaintiff, a member of the Dockers Section of the defendant Trade Union, had been employed as a casual foreman docker for approximately 34 years. Some days prior to 25 June, 1976, the first-named defendant posted notices on notice-boards at the docks, advertising a meeting of the Docker's Section on the aforementioned date. This was the usual method of advertising such meetings. On the face of the notices were the words "Re vote on nat. wage ag." No other subject for discussion was mentioned. It was, however, accepted in evidence that the other named defendants, who were members of the Docker's Section Committee, *bona fide* believed that a meeting on the national wage agreement was one that was likely to be well attended. Unknown to the plaintiff, the defendants had, prior to the meeting, decided to recommend a resolution of a compulsory retirement pension scheme which would oblige its members to retire at the age of 65 years. The resolution was duly recommended, members spoke for and against it and a vote was taken by show of hands, resulting in the carrying of the resolution by a substantial majority. The plaintiff arrived late at the meeting, and was informed of the decision which had been reached. Since he was due to reach the age of 65 on the following month, the defendants subsequently asked him to submit a birth certificate. Understanding this correctly to mean that he was to be compulsorily retired, he objected, and subsequently protested again through his solicitor, threatening legal proceedings. Another meeting was summoned for the 3 August, and was advertised in the usual way, but in addition was advertised in the evening paper. The business of the meeting was stated to be "pension

TRADE UNION—*continued.*

scheme". The plaintiff did not attend this meeting. In evidence he stated firstly that he did not think it had to do with the compulsory retirement scheme, and secondly, that his solicitor had advised him not to attend. At the meeting a ballot was held for the purpose of confirming the resolution of 25 June. The vote was carried by an overwhelming majority. The plaintiff sought, *inter alia,* a declaration that the decision was invalid, on two grounds: (*a*) that, since a penalty had been imposed upon him thereby, the proceedings were of a quasi-judicial nature, and fair procedures and natural justice had been infringed in that he did not have explicit notice of the meetings, or an opportunity to speak and cast his vote, and (*b*) that, even if the procedures were fair, the decision infringed his constitutional right to work. **Held** by Finlay P. in refusing the relief sought, 1, the concept of a penalty involves a charge and verdict of misconduct, and the imposition of a consequent punishment. The disadvantage suffered by the plaintiff as a result of the decision of 25 June and 3 August, 1976, cannot be construed as a penalty, nor can the proceedings during which the decisions were reached be classed as quasi-judicial in nature. 2. The constitutional right to join or to abstain from joining a trade union involves as a corollary the right to take part in its democratic and decision-making processes, within the limits of its rules. The plaintiff had not been afforded this right, with regard to the meeting of 25 June, but he had been given fair and reasonable notice of the meeting of 3 August. 3. The introduction of a compulsory retirement age with pension rights is not an infringement of the constitutional right to work enjoyed by persons who may reach that age of retirement. *Murphy* v. *Stewart* [1973] I.R. 97 applied. *Rodgers* v. *Irish Transport and General Workers' Union*

(H.C.) [1978] ILRM 51

—— Civil service — Staff association — Recognition — Refusal.
see **Civil Service,** 2

—— Constitution — Personal rights — Freedom of association — Plaintiff offered position as principal of a primary school — Plaintiff not being a member of trade union — Pressure exerted on manager to cancel appointment — Whether defendants engaged in actionable conspiracy to cause plaintiff to abandon his constitutional right to dissociate.
see **Employer and Employee,** 1

—— Foreign trade union — Foreign court imposing fine for union's contempt of court — Union's funds transferred to Irish bank — Foreign sequestrators seeking vesting of funds — Injunction — Interlocutory — Mareva relief.
see **Conflict of Laws,** 5

—— Freedom of association.
see **Freedom of Association**

TRAFFIC ACCIDENTS
see **Road Traffic Accidents**

TRAFFIC OFFENCES
see **Road Traffic Offences**

TRANSPORT
see also **Highway; Motor Vehicle; Road Traffic**

—— **Tour operator** — *Licence — Breach of a condition — Decision to revoke — Appeal to High Court — Whether applicant fit and proper to carry on business — Power of High Court on appeal — Transport (Tour Operators and Travel Agents) Act,* 1982 (*No.* 3), *ss.* 8(2)(*b*), 9(2),(3),(4) — *Rules of the Superior Courts, O.* 102.] The plaintiff company held a tour operator's licence and travel agent's licence in 1985/86 pursuant to the Transport (Tour Operators & Travel Agents) Act, 1982. In respect of the former licence they breached a number of conditions which necessitated a series of correspondence which culminated in the plaintiff eventually complying with the conditions. The defendant issued the plaintiff with 1986/87 licences on 10 December, 1986. On that occasion the plaintiff was warned of the necessity to observe the conditions of the licences and that a serious view would be taken of any breaches in the future. Condition no. (8) of the tour operator's licence required that the said licence be reproduced in the same form exactly in the plaintiff's brochure. Evidence was adduced at the hearing in the High Court that the printer acting on his own initiative without instruction from or knowledge of the plaintiff, used a third party's licence for the purpose of setting up print for the 1986/87 licence with the intention of making it conformable to the 1986/87 licence but failed to do so. Once the brochures were printed they were immediately dispatched without checking the accuracy of the copies as they were already late for circulation. The defendant discovered that the purported true copy of the tour operator's licence printed in the brochure was not a true copy of the tour operator's licence issued to the plaintiffs either for 1986/87 or 1985/86 and the defendant's offices complained to the plaintiff, indicating their intention to revoke the licence and inviting representations. The plaintiff replied by letter of 3

TRANSPORT—*continued.*

January, 1987, in which it dealt only with the wrong date of commencement on the licence and by telex of 8 January, 1987, in which it suggested that the printed copy was in reality a copy of the 1985/86 licence, which it was not. These representations were not satisfactory to the defendant who revoked the licences and the plaintiff appealed his decision to the High Court pursuant to s. 9(2) of the 1982 Act. **Held** by Lynch J. in allowing the appeal subject to a number of terms being complied with, 1, the High Court on appeal from the Minister's decision by virtue of s. 9 of the 1982 Act must ascertain all the relevant facts of the case whether they were before the Minister or not and then give effect to them. 2. The revocation of the licence would cause damage to the plaintiff disproportionate to its fault as the publication of a falsified tour operator's licence in the brochure was done without positive intention as distinct from carelessness and negligence on the part of the plaintiff. 3. The information contained in the letter and telex from the plaintiff to the defendant in January, 1987, entitled the defendant to believe that there was no satisfactory explanation for the discrepancies in the brochures and the fact that the plaintiff had circulated them all entitled the defendant to revoke the licence. 4. The defendant was entitled to revoke the breaches of the conditions and the misconduct he relied on as a serious matter in view of the plaintiffs' previous record. 5. On the evidence before the court the defendant in revoking the plaintiffs' licences did not act in a discriminatory manner. *Balkan Tours Ltd.* v. *Minister for Communications*

(H.C.) [1988] ILRM 101

—— Canal — Lack of maintenance — Flooding — Breach of statutory duty — Nuisance.
see **Negligence,** 29

—— Ferry service — Enactment of Parliament of Great Britain and Ireland — Provision of ferry service from Ireland to Wales — Suspension of service by decision of English government minister — Whether statutory obligation suspended by Oireachtas — Constitution — Adaptation of enactments.
see **Contract,** 12

—— Piers and harbours — Pier vested in Harbour Commissioners — Duty to maintain pier — Restriction on user — Whether harbour master empowered to restrict user permanently.
see **Statute,** 3

TRANSPORT—*continued.*

—— School transport.
see **Education,** 3

TRAVEL AGENTS — Tour operator — Licence — Breach of a condition — Decision to revoke — Appeal to High Court — Whether applicant fit and proper to carry on business — Power of High Court on appeal.
see **Transport**

TRAVELLING COMMUNITY — Halting site.
see **Planning,** 18

TREASURE TROVE — State — Prerogative — Constitution — Whether the State entitled to former royal prerogative of treasure trove.
see **Bailment**

TREATY
see **International Treaty**

TREATY OF ROME
see **European Communities,** 2
Injunction, 10

TRESPASS

—— Animals — Cattle wandering into cemetery — Cattle poisoned by eating yew leaves — Wall between pastureland and cemetery damaged — Whether local authority negligent.
see **Negligence,** 28

—— Landlord — Intimidation — Breach of covenant as to quiet and peaceable enjoyment — Damages — Aggravated damages.
see **Landlord and Tenant,** 1

—— Offence — Entering premises as trespasser and stealing therein — Evidence of owner of premises — Whether offence established — Whether accused entered as trespasser — Distinction between breaking and entering.
see **Criminal Law,** 33

—— Trespasser — Injury — Occupier's liability — Contribution — Foreseeability.
see **Negligence,** 17

—— Trespasser claiming right of way — Absence of defined path — Whether use of the way over the land sufficient in extent and regularity.
see **Real Property,** 1

TRIAL OF OFFENCES—*continued.*

—— Jury — Whether jury must try issues of fact — Whether court of trial may be precluded from assessing issues relating to guilt or innocence of accused.
see **Constitution,** 53

—— Minor offence — Whether minor offence triable summarily.
see **Minor Offence**

—— Procedure — Defect in book of evidence — Whether trial unsatisfactory.
see **Criminal Law,** 10

—— Retrial — Whether judge in retrial should have access to judgment quashing conviction.
see **Criminal Law,** 38

—— Right to trial in due course of law — Special Criminal Court — Establishment — Validity — Judicial independence — Whether s. 39 of Offences Against the State Act, 1939 inconsistent with Constitution.
see **Constitution,** 50

—— Special Criminal Court — D.P.P. directing trial in Special Criminal Court — Whether power unconstitutional — Opinion of D.P.P. that ordinary courts inadequate — Whether reviewable by the courts.
see **Criminal Law,** 66

—— Special Criminal Court — Jurisdiction — Manner in which accused was brought before court — Arrest — Second arrest — Whether manner in which attendance of accused before court was procured was relevant to jurisdiction.
see **Criminal Law,** 8

—— Transfer — Circuit Court — Jurisdiction — Statutory provision for exercise of jurisdiction in circuit where offence committed or where accused resided or was arrested — Provision allowing for transfer of trial to Dublin Circuit Court — Transfer of trial mandatory if 7 days notice given by prosecution or defence — Whether criminal jurisdiction of Circuit Court a local and limited jurisdiction — Whether mandatory transfer of trial contrary to natural justice.
see **Constitution,** 3

—— Venue — Indictable offence — Accused sent forward for trial in Circuit Court — Accused formerly entitled to obtain order transferring trial to High Court — Abolition of that right — Whether lawful exclusion of High Court jurisdiction.
see **Constitution,** 32

—— *Voir dire* — Evidence — Admissibility — Whether issue to be tried on *voir dire* by judge or by jury — Whether accused prejudiced by having issue determined by jury on *voir dire* — Function of jury under the Constitution — Whether jury impartiality on ultimate issue likely to be affected.
see **Criminal Law,** 17

—— *Voir dire* — Witnesses — Accused requested presence of jury during *voir dire* — Whether trial judge erred in refusing request — Whether trial judge failed to consider accused's request that other witnesses be excluded while one witness giving evidence — Whether new trial should be ordered.
see **Criminal Law,** 67

—— Young offender — Juvenile court — Jurisdiction — Summons signed before defendant was 17 — Served afterwards — Whether juvenile court had jurisdiction — Whether proceedings had commenced.
see **Criminal Law,** 68

TRIBUNAL
see also **Employment Appeals Tribunal**
Judicial Review
Labour Court
Natural and Constitutional Justice

—— Criminal Injuries Compensation Tribunal — Tribunal required to award compensation to dependants of persons killed in attempting to save human life — Claim by widow — Burden of proof — Primary facts not in dispute — Rejection of claim by Tribunal — Whether failure to infer from facts that deceased was attempting to save a life was at variance with reason and common sense.
see **Judicial Review,** 10

—— Decision — Tribunal established to award compensation to victims of fire — Claimant and his wife seeking compensation for nervous shock — Both

TRIBUNAL—*continued.*

claims arising out of similar circumstances — Tribunal awarding compensation to wife but not to claimant — Whether decision unreasonable or irrational.
see **Judicial Review,** 9

—— Disciplinary — Garda Síochána.
see **Constitution,** 11
Garda Síochána, 1, 2
Judicial Review, 3

—— Disciplinary — Medical practitioner — Fair procedures.
see **Constitution,** 28
Natural and Constitutional Justice, 4

—— Disciplinary — Trade unions — Irish Congress of Trade Unions — Disciplinary powers — Exercise — Natural justice.
see **Trade Unions,** 1

—— Disciplinary — University student.
see **Natural and Constitutional Justice,** 5

—— Natural justice — Evidence — Determination of remedy by tribunal not argued by parties to hearing — Whether in breach of natural justice — Whether in breach of fair procedures.
see **Natural and Constitutional Justice,** 3

—— Natural justice — Fair procedures — Detention centre — Youth released on licence — Release conditional on youth keeping the peace — Youth arrested on charge of serious crime — Licence revoked and youth returned to detention — Governor of institution failing to hold enquiry.
see **Prisons,** 3

—— Natural justice — Fair procedures — Exercise of power — Duty to act judicially — Includes duty to furnish reasons for decision.
see **Judicial Review,** 13

—— Natural justice — Fair procedures — Professional discipline — Medical practitioner — Removal of doctor's name from register — Validity of enactment under Constitution.
see **Constitution,** 28

—— Natural justice — Fair procedures — Professional discipline — Medical practitioner — Removal of doctor's name from register.
see **Natural and Constitutional Justice,** 4

TRIBUNAL—*continued.*

—— Rent tribunal — Fixing of rent.
see **Landlord and Tenant,** 13, 14, 15

—— University.
see under **University**

TRUSTS
see also **Charities**

1. —— **Condition** — *Residence — Maintenance of building — Whether condition subsequent — Certainty — Building to be maintained unless "impracticable" — Whether in financial or structural sense — Condition that house "is used as his home" — Whether conditions uncertain.*] The testatrix devised and bequeathed the residue of her real and personal estate, which included Waringstown House, to trustees on trust for the plaintiff, ". . .until he attain the age of thirty years provided that Waringstown House become and is used as his home and on attaining the age of thirty years to the [plaintiff] for his own use and benefit absolutely provided he continues to reside in and maintain Waringstown House unless the state and structure of the building shall make proper maintenance impossible . . ." On an originating summons to determine whether the proviso relating to residence in and maintenance of the house was a condition subsequent and whether it was void for uncertainty, **Held,** that, 1, the proviso created a condition subsequent and that it was void for uncertainty. The condition required maintenance unless it was impracticable. Impracticable could mean financially impractical or impractical in an engineering or architectural sense. While the will provided some support for each construction, the arguments in favour of impractical meaning impracticable in financial terms were stronger, but there was no indication as to the standard to be applied in determining at what point maintenance would become financially impractical and whether the financial position of the plaintiff was to be taken into account. On further hearing to determine the validity of the condition attaching to the gift to the plaintiff until he attained the age of thirty years, **Held,** that, 1, the condition constituted two conditions, namely a condition precedent that the plaintiff makes the house his home and a condition subsequent that he thereafter should continue to use the house as his home. The condition precedent was not void for uncertainty and the plaintiff had satisfied it by living in the house as his home after the death of the testatrix. 2. The condition subsequent was not void for uncertainty because a judge of fact would on any given state of facts be able to decide whether the house was used as the plaintiff's home and the use of the term "reside" in the next condition

TRUSTS—*continued.*

did not cause the phrase "used as his home" to be void for uncertainty. *In re Waring's Will Trusts; Harnett* v. *Calvert*

(Ch.D.) [1985] N.I.105

2. —— **Construction** — *Marriage settlement — Original deed of settlement destroyed by fire — Whether secondary evidence of the contents of the deed admissible — Construction of admitted document — Whether parties take trust property in equal shares or whether they enjoy life interests only.*] The above entitled parties are sisters and the only children of the late Patrick Doran and Elizabeth White nee Doran. The plaintiffs allege that at the time of their parents' marriage, a marriage settlement dated 26 July, 1921, was executed. They submit that their grandparents were the settlors who transferred the trust property to the trustees and after making provision for certain life interests decided that the trust property should be held by the trustees upon trust "for the children of the said intended marriage as the said Patrick Doran and Elizabeth White shall by deed jointly appoint and in default of such appointment upon trust for the children of the said intended marriage in equal shares." The plaintiffs say that no deed of joint appointment was executed and accordingly they and the defendant are each entitled absolutely to an undivided one-third share in the trust property. The defendant denies that there was any marriage settlement and claims that under the will of her parents she became entitled to the land and property. The original deed of settlement was destroyed by the Fourt Courts fire on 30 June, 1922, and the plaintiffs are seeking to advance secondary evidence of the contents of the deed in the form of two documents. The court had to determine initially the admissibility of the secondary evidence and, if such evidence was admissible, whether on the true construction of the admitted document the parties take the trust property in equal shares or merely enjoy life interests only in the property. Evidence was adduced that the Doran's family solicitor had in its "value file" a document which appeared to be the final draft from which the original deed was prepared and not a copy. Evidence was further adduced that it was the hand writing of the solicitor at the time who filled in the date and made corrections on the typescript. Independent evidence also corroborated the contents of part of this document such as excerpts from the original deed abstracted from the Land Registry Folios which corresponded with the terms of the document. The defendant submitted that if the document is admitted that they as children of the marriage only took life interests as there were no words of limitation used in the deed, and relied on the rule in *Bostock's* case; that in the

TRUSTS—*continued.*

absence of words of limitation the court as a general rule is precluded from considering the intention of the settlor. The plaintiff submitted that the settlor intended that the children of the marriage would take an absolute interest and that the exception to the rule in *Bostock's* case applied here as the children of the intended marriage were within the consideration of the marriage and accordingly the settlement constitutes an agreement which was enforceable by them. **Held** by Hamilton J. in admitting the secondary evidence and finding for the plaintiff, 1, in the circumstances of this case and on the balance of probabilities the document represents the contents of the lost deed and as there is no rule of law which prohibits the court from reaching that conclusion or admitting it, the court proposes to accept it as secondary evidence. 2. Although the settlors did not use any words of limitation to the effect that the children of the marriage were to take the property in fee simple it is clear from an examination of the settlement that the settlor intended that the said children would take the trust property in equal shares absolutely if no joint appointment was made. 3. Because the children of the intended marriage are within the consideration of the marriage and a marriage settlement constitutes an agreement enforceable by them, this constitutes an exception to the rule in *Bostock's* case and allows the court to give effect to the intention of the settlor. *Jameson* v. *McGovern* [1934] I.R. 758 explained and applied. *Savage* v. *Nolan*

(H.C.) [1978] ILRM 151

3. —— **Powers** — *Alteration of objects of association — Whether* ultra vires *the deed of trust — Whether application by trustees of certain monies a breach of trust.*] On 27 June, 1974, the members of the Presbyterian Association met in special general meeting and purported, by a three quarter majority, to pass a resolution declaring that the objects of the association, as set out in the trust deed dated 31 October, 1961, be added to by the insertion of a clause to establish a charitable organisation in the form of a limited company, to be known as the P.A. Foundation and further, to transfer or assign to that foundation such portion or portions of the association's property or assets as might be decided by a two thirds resolution of the members in general meeting. The plaintiff sought a determination as to whether the members of the association, having regard to the terms of the 1961 deed of trust, had acted *ultra vires* and secondly, as to whether, even if the resolution and subsequent alteration of the objects were valid, the trustees, without a breach of their trust and without exceeding their powers, could comply with a resolution of the members asking to transfer and

TRUSTS—*continued.*

lend funds to the P.A. Foundation. **Held** by Finlay P. in answering these questions in the negative, 1, having regard to the objects of the Presbyterian Association as derived from its history and the trust deed of 1961, and also to the objects of the P.A. Foundation as set out in its draft memorandum of association, the amendment to the objects of the Presbyterian Association is not inconsistent with its fundamental objects as stated in the 1961 deed. 2. The 1961 deed refers to two classes of persons, the members of the association and associates. The trust upon which the trustees, including the plaintiff, hold all property coming into their hands in respect of the Presbyterian Association is a trust for the members and not for the associates, nor are the associates in any way beneficiaries of that trust. The application of the trust fund for the benefit of the Presbyterian Foundation whose membership is the same as and confined to members of the association is not a breach of trust. 3. Clause 2 of the trust deed which provides for the investment of capital monies coming into the hands of the trustees and requiring investment, does not form an impediment to the proposal which may now be brought before a special meeting of the association. *McMillan* v. *McMillan*

(H.C.) [1976-7] ILRM 45

4. —— **Variation** — *Mitigation of tax liability — Insurance — Adult beneficiaries entitled under remote contingencies not parties to application — Whether court should approve arrangement — Trustee Act (Northern Ireland),* 1958 (*c.* 23), *s.* 57 (1) (*b*).] A testator left his estate on the following trusts: (i) a life interest to his elder son (R.), determinable on the event of his joining any religious order or brotherhood or entering any monastery in connection with the Roman Catholic Church which would require him to be celibate or surrender any part of his property, with remainder to his son's children or remoter issue as he might by deed or will appoint; (ii) in the even of the elder son dying without issue, or the operation of the cesser clause, a determinable life interest with a similar power of appointment to the testator's younger son; (iii) in the event of the latter's death without issue, or the operation of the cesser clause, determinable life interests with similar powers of appointment to each of the testator's daughters successively; and (iv) in the event of the failure or determination of the above trusts, for the testator's sister, or if she be then dead for her children subject to certain contingencies. The will did not contain any ultimate unconditional interest. In order to minimise liability to Capital Transfer Tax it was proposed that R. should appoint immediately part of the estate to his son M. (an adult), and then to make further appointments of capital to M. to enable him to pay the tax chargeable on the first appointment. It was envisaged that after 10 years when R. would again be entitled to an exemption on the first £64,000 to be transferred, he would appoint the bulk of the remaining estate to M. It was also proposed that the trustees should take out term assurance to provide sufficient funds to meet the tax liability if R. should die within 10 years and commence a special investment plan to provide a sum sufficient to meet the anticipated tax liability on the second proposed appointment. As the trustees did not have the power to make payments for the proposed term assurance and the special investment plan, an application was made for the court's approval of the arrangement under section 57 of the Trustees Act (Northern Ireland), 1958. **Held,** that in certain events the cesser clause could result in the testator's daughters, or the children of his deceased sister, becoming entitled to benefit from the testator's estate and, because of the effect of the proviso to section 57 (1) (*b*) of the 1958 Act, the court would be unable to approve the arrangement on their behalf with the result that an order approving it would not bind them. These events, however, were extremely unlikely and the trustees were willing to take the risks involved, consequently the arrangement was approved on behalf of the minors and other persons party to the application as the court was satisfied that, subject to certain minor amendments, it was for their benefit. *In re Hall's Will Trusts; Hall* v. *Mullan*

(Ch.D.) [1985] N.I.118

—— Charitable trusts — Cy-près.
see **Charities,** 1-3

—— Constructive trust — Money paid in error — Claim for repayment — Mixed fund — Whether money held in trust — Purpose of constructive trust.
see **Company,** 17

—— Trust — Creation — Family home — Wife's contributions.
see **Family Law,** 27, 28

—— Trust — Creation — Will — Devise subject to a condition — Whether words imperative — Whether subject certain — Whether trust created.
see **Succession,** 16

—— Will — Construction — Power of appointment — No disposition in default of appointment — Executor unable to carry out the trust in the manner directed by the testator.
see **Succession,** 18

U

ULTRA VIRES—*continued.*

—— Statutory notice — Revenue Commissioners.
see **Revenue,** 25

UNAUTHORISED DEVELOPMENT
see **Planning,** 22-31

UNBORN, RIGHT TO LIFE OF — Pregnancy counselling services — Abortion considered as an option — Referral to medical clinic in Great Britain — Whether the giving of such assistance unlawful — Whether admitted activities of defendants amounted to conspiracy to corrupt public morals.
see **Constitution,** 20

UNDUE INFLUENCE
see also **Duress; Fraud**

—— **Deed** — *Transfer of land — Reservation of right of residence, care and support — Application to cancel transfer — Whether undue influence — Whether deed improvident.*] The plaintiff by a deed entered into in March, 1985, transferred to her son, the first named defendant, her lands and reserved for herself a right of residence, support, care and maintenance from him. In 1986 the plaintiff instituted proceedings in the Circuit Court to set aside and cancel the said transfer of lands on the grounds that the defendants exercised undue influence over her and that she did not understand what she was doing and that she did not have proper legal advice. Judge Grattan Esmonde allowed the plaintiff's claim which said decision was appealed to the High Court. At the hearing in the High Court evidence was adduced that in 1985 the plaintiff, an elderly lady, was living alone and afraid because of the appalling actions and murder that were at that time being carried out on the elderly in the west of Ireland and further was afraid the Land Commission might take her lands as she was unable to work them entered into discussions with the defendants and the defendants' solicitor who referred her to a Mr. Carr, a practising solicitor in another office in the town. Evidence was adduced that Mr. Carr very prudently and carefully explained everything to the plaintiff in particular revocation clauses, taking the line that a revocation clause should be included and further recommending that she should get another opinion. The plaintiff instructed him that there was to be no revocation clause as she knew her son would not accept it. The court had to decide if the deed was valid and in order for it to so decide it had to be satisfied that the plaintiff was mentally able to understand her action, her will had been free and spontaneous, she had proper legal advice

UNDUE INFLUENCE—*continued.*

and the act itself had not been improvident. **Held** by MacKenzie J. in allowing the appeal, 1, having regard to the circumstances of the case namely that the plaintiff was alone, elderly, unable to work the land, afraid and in need of company and support which she got with the deed, there was no undue influence on her on the part of the first named defendant, as the coercion was because of her situation and not her son's making. 2. The plaintiff was acting spontaneously and was free and was acting without undue influence, she had independent legal advice and the court did not consider that the deed was improvident. 3. The court was satisfied that in March, 1985, the plaintiff's mental capacity was clear and coherent. *Leonard* v. *Leonard*
(H.C.) [1988] ILRM 245

—— Marriage — Duress — Nullity petition.
see **Family Law,** 18

—— Will — Validity — Person instrumental in having will prepared taking a benefit under it — Allegation of undue influence — Whether will be condemned — Whether testator knew and approved of its contents.
see **Succession,** 24

UNEMPLOYMENT BENEFIT
see also **Social Welfare**

—— Compensation payment for period of notice — Whether payment should be reduced by reference to social welfare benefits received.
see **Employer and Employee,** 20

—— Offence — False statements to obtain benefits.
see **District Court,** 1

UNFAIR COMPETITION
see **Restraint of Trade; Restrictive Practices**

UNFAIR DISMISSALS
see **Employer and Employee,** 9-12, 19

UNIONS
see **Trade Union**

UNIVERSITY
—— Disciplinary procedures — Breach of academic discipline — Natural justice — Fair procedures — Whether disciplinary regulations adequate to ensure fair hearing.
see **Natural and Constitutional Justice,** 5

V

W

STOCHASTIC PROCESSES

Selected Papers of Hiroshi Tanaka

STOCHASTIC PROCESSES

Selected Papers of Hiroshi Tanaka

Edited by

Makoto Maejima
Keio University, Japan

Tokuzo Shiga
Tokyo Institute of Technology, Japan

World Scientific
New Jersey • London • Singapore • Hong Kong

Published by

World Scientific Publishing Co. Pte. Ltd.
P O Box 128, Farrer Road, Singapore 912805
USA office: Suite 1B, 1060 Main Street, River Edge, NJ 07661
UK office: 57 Shelton Street, Covent Garden, London WC2H 9HE

British Library Cataloguing-in-Publication Data
A catalogue record for this book is available from the British Library.

STOCHASTIC PROCESSES
Selected Papers of Hiroshi Tanaka

ISBN 981-02-4591-2

Printed in Singapore by Uto-Print

Hiroshi Tanaka

Contents

---

†Numbers in brackets refer to the Bibliography of Hiroshi Tanaka (see pages 425–428)

H. Tanaka: An Appreciation

by Henry McKean

It is a pleasant thing for me to write this little note to accompany the selected papers of H. Tanaka collected in this volume.

When I was young and fresh out of school, I visited Kyôto for a year (1957/58) at the invitation of K. Itô. My great-grandfather (whom I never knew) was an amateur of Japanese art, generally, and of Okyô in particular. Part of his collection came down to my family, so even when I was quite little, I was fascinated by Japan and things Japanese. The double chance to see Japan and to work with Itô was an irresistible piece of luck and I was pretty well prepared for that.

What I was not prepared for, but happily surprised by, was the enthusiastic crowd of young Japanese probabilists under Itô's wing who came faithfully, once a week, to hear the new developments in Brownian motion and diffusion stemming from the ideas of W. Feller and E.B. Dynkin — "sowing the seeds of diffusion in the mathematical fields of Japan" as Itô put it. H. Tanaka stood out in this company for the quickness of his understanding, for his mathematical taste, and for his quiet but strong personality. That was our first acquaintance. Later he visited me at MIT in Cambridge; in between, we collaborated on additive functions of the Brownian path ([5] †, 1961).

Tanaka's mathematical production is marked by the elegant use of common ideas employed in novel ways and with uncommon skill. No better example can be found than his 1963 paper ([7]) in which Itô's lemma is used with a bit of extra audacity to prove a wonderful formula, simple but highly effective, for the Brownian local time. I would like particularly to cite the deep series of papers ([15], [16], [19], [27]) on Boltzmann's equation for the Maxwellian gas and the Markov process that underlies it, a subject dear to my heart. This had been initiated by Kaç and studied somewhat by me, but it was Tanaka who really understood it correctly, and everything of Tanaka's shows like elegance, simplicity, depth.

This note is to express to Tanaka my admiration and friendship and to wish him health and happy productive years still to come.

†Numbers in brackets refer to the Bibliography of Hiroshi Tanaka (see pages 425–428)

From Local Times to Random Environments...

by Marc Yor

It is both a pleasure and an honor to have been asked to write a few words about the works of Professor H. Tanaka.

At least two aspects of Professor Tanaka's works have been of much interest to me and, more generally to many probabilists in France, for quite some time :

a) The celebrated Tanaka formula, expressing the local time at 0 *of linear Brownian motion as the last term of an extended Itô formula.*

Not only does this formula extend to Brownian local time taken at every level $a(\in \mathbb{R})$, which makes it a very powerful tool to deduce the Markovian properties of these local times with respect to a, i.e. the Ray-Knight theorems ([1], [2]), but as shown by P.A. Meyer in his "Cours sur les intégrales stochastiques" (Lecture Notes in Math., 511, Séminaire de Probabilités X, 1976), it extends easily to the framework of continuous semi-martingale local times.

The works of P. Mc Gill ([3]) and T. Jeulin ([4]) for instance, and later those of L.C.G. Rogers and J. Walsh ([5], [6]), concerning the spatially indexed filtration of Brownian excursions, give ample evidence of the power of Tanaka formula.

It is an interesting fact that Tanaka formula appears as a "personal communication" in H.P. McKean's "Stochastic Integrals" (1969) whilst more general discussions describing every additive functional of (possibly multidimensional) Brownian motion appeared earlier, e.g., in Professor Tanaka's paper (Zeitschrift für Wahr.,1963), and a number of papers by probabilists in the then Soviet Union.

There, I see some similarity with the role Problem 1 on p. 72 of Itô-McKean's book (1965), which establishes the existence of principal values of Brownian local times, has taken in the later development of these principal values (see, e.g. the discussion by T. Yamada [7], p. 414).

In the study of intersections of 2 - or 3 - dimensional Brownian motion, variants of Tanaka formula - the Tanaka-Rosen formulae - have also played some part in understanding Varadhan type renormalizations (see, e.g., [8]).

b) The study of many properties - most of them asymptotic - of diffusions in random, especially white noise, environments.

There are at least sixteen papers by Professor Tanaka, which have been devoted to this topic ; through his perseverance, many facts about these diffusions have been exposed in great clarity, in particular via the study of the so called "valleys".

For quite some time, I wished to establish some relationship between the $(\log t)^2$ normalization in the asymptotics of these diffusions, and the following radial version of Spitzer's theorem for the windings of two dimensional Brownian motion $(Z_t)_{t\geq 0}$:

$$\frac{4}{(\log t)^2}\int_0^t \frac{ds}{|Z_s|^2} \xrightarrow[t\to\infty]{(law)} T$$

where T denotes a stable $\left(\frac{1}{2}\right)$ variable.

More generally, I thought some link might exist between the one-dimensional diffusions in random environment (: RED) and some two-dimensional diffusions; a careful analysis of the scale and speed changes involved in the construction of these RED processes, together with a skew-product representation for a pair of independent Bessel processes led the authors of [9] to the recovery of some of Professor Tanaka's results via the asymptotics of local time functionals. A synthetic discussion of Sinaï's walk via stochastic calculus is presented by Z. Shi ([10]).

To conclude, let me convey the admiration of a number of collegues in France for the remarkable homogeneity of the works of Professor Tanaka which led him from the asymptotics of one-dimensional diffusions to those of the RED processes.

References

[1] Ray, D. : Sojourn times of a diffusion process. Illinois J. Math. **7** (1963), 615-630.

[2] Knight, F. : Random walks and a sojourn density process of Brownian motion. Trans. Amer. Math. Soc. **107** (1963), 56-86.

[3] McGill, P. : Markov properties of diffusion local time : a martingale approach. Adv. Appl. Prob. **14** (1982), 789-810.

[4] Jeulin, T. : Ray-Knight's theorems on Brownian local times and Tanaka formula. Seminar on Stoch. Proc. 1983, Birkhäuser (1984), 131-142.

[5] Rogers, L.C.G. and J. Walsh : The intrinsic local time sheet of Brownian motion. Prob. Th. Rel. Fileds. **88** (1991), 363-379.

[6] Rogers, L.C.G. and J. Walsh : Local time and stochastic area integrals. Ann. Prob. **19** (1991), 457-482.

[7] Yamada, T. : Principal values of Brownian local times and their related topics. In : N. Ikeda, S. Watanabe, M. Fukushima, H. Kunita (eds). Itô's stochastic calculus and probability theory. Springer (1996), 413-422.

[8] Rosen, J. and M. Yor : Tanaka formulae and renormalization for triple intersections of Brownian motion in the plane. Ann. Prob. **19** (1991), 142-159.

[9] Hu, Y., Z. Shi and M. Yor : Rates of convergence of diffusions in drifted Brownian potentials. Trans. Amer. Math. Soc. **351** (1999), 3915-3934.

[10] Shi, Z. : Sinaï's random walk via stochastic calculus. To appear in "Milieux Aléatoires", Collection : Panorama et Synthèse (Soc. Math. France).

Contributions and Influences of Professor Tanaka in Stochastic Analysis

by Shinzo Watanabe

The aim of this note is to express my hearty admiration and respect to Professor Hiroshi Tanaka for his works in probability theory which have influenced much and are playing important roles in its modern developments. As we can see by his great contributions collected in this volume, his works have been widely ranged in the field of stochastic analysis with two high peaks around main themes; stochastic models associated with nonlinear equations, particularly Boltzmann equations, and diffusion models in random environment. For me it is difficult and also, I think I am not well qualified, to make comments on his works in these main themes. I would rather give some historical account, combined with my own experience, of his contributions and influences in the area of stochastic analysis and the theory of stochastic differential equations (SDE's) in general. I should say, however, that motivations of Professor Tanaka must have been always to challenge new and unsolved problems; developing or organizing general theories may not have been his major concern.

Around 1960, when I started studying the theory of stochastic processes as a graduate student at Kyoto University, Professor Tanaka was a Research Associate at Kyushu University and was just making his debut as a young researcher in this area. At that time, people were interested in and studied extensively the theory of Markov processes, as was initiated and developed by Kolmogorov and Feller, among others. For example, my teacher, Professor K. Itô had been working jointly with H. P. McKean on sample paths description and construction of one-dimensional diffusion processes which attracted much attention of a group of young probabilists in Japan. Certainly, Itô-McKean's theory is a really important and beautiful achievement in probability theory. On the other hand, we know now well that the essential part of Itô's theory of SDE's had been established by that time and his AMS Memoir on the SDE theory was already published in 1951. However, students of Itô at that time could have had few occasions of learning the SDE theory directly from him at Kyoto University. Rather, I came to know Itô's theory through the guidance of several members in the group of Japanese probabilists like N. Ikeda, M. Nisio and Tanaka.

Tanaka's formula for the local time of one-dimensional Brownian motion was my first exciting experience of usefulness of Ito's stochastic calculus. As a graduate student, I read, in a seminar of Professor Itô, Trotter's paper [T] which established for the first time the existence of Brownian local time. Also, he kindly showed me a part of the manuscript which he was jointly preparing with McKean (this now appeared as famous Itô-McKean's book [IM]) in which was given a proof of Trotter's theorem. Both Trotter's paper and Itô-McKean's manuscript were very difficult for me. However, Brownian local time plays a key role in the Itô-McKean construction of sample functions for one-dimensional diffusion processes so that it was necessary to have some deep understanding of Trotter's theorem. A few years later, when I was still a graduate student, Professor Itô was abroad and Professor Ikeda was our adviser and sometimes our joint collaborator, Ikeda got a letter from Tanaka who was then visiting McKean at MIT, and Ikeda informed us that Tanaka found a nice proof of Trotter's theorem by applying the notion of Itô's stochastic integrals. Of course, we could not completely understand what exactly it was judging from the little information. On the other hand, Ikeda and I knew and read a paper by Skorohod [S] for reflecting Brownian motion on a one-dimensional interval in which local times at boundary points play an important role so that we could immediately have a vague idea what it might be. Later, McKean's book [M] appeared and I could then finally and completely understand the splendid idea of Tanaka. Skorohod's paper regarded Tanaka's formula as a stochastic equation and established its uniqueness of solutions. This is the origin of *Skorohod equations* to which, we know, Tanaka has also made an essential contribution ([24] in this volume).

Now Tanaka's formula is an indispensable content in every standard text book of stochastic analysis. It is now defined most generally for any continuous semimartingale. I have to confess that, at first, I could not well see the importance of such a generalization. Gradually, however, through the work of Le Gall [L] who applied generalized Tanaka's formula to the pathwise uniqueness problem for solutions of SDE's and also through more recent works in [BEKSY] and [EY] which discuss Tsirelson's discovery that the natural filtration of Walsh's Brownian motion on $n \geq 3$ rays cannot be a Brownian filtration, for example, I came to recognize that such a generalization (as treated nicely in the text books by Revuz-Yor [RY] or Rogers-Williams [RW], among others) is really important and useful.

Tanaka's formula may be considered an extension of Itô's formula so that it may be reasonably called Itô-Tanaka's formula, as well. An important and interesting aspect of this formula is that it *produces a new process*, namely, the local time: If we consider a similar extension of Itô's formula, we may obtain another interesting new process. An important idea to extend Itô's formula along the line of Tanaka's formula was given by M. Fukushima in his theory of Dirichlet forms and symmetric Markov processes associated with them. He introduced a class of stochastic processes *with zero energy* and extended Itô's formula by using this notion. Important examples of new processes thereby obtained contain the Cauchy principal value of the Brownian local times introduced and studied by T. Yamada and M. Yor, among others (cf. [Ya], [Yo]).

As I remarked above, Itô's theory on SDE's has already been established around 1960 but the only books available to study this theory at that time were those by Doob [D] and Itô [I 1], [I 2]. These are most valuable books which still keep high values at present. Fortunately in Japan, there was still another valuable research monograph written by Tanaka jointly with M. Hasegawa ([TH]) in 1964. It was one volume (Vol.19) in the series of research monographs written in Japanese, printed mimeographically and published by Seminar on Probability, an organization formed voluntarily by younger members of probabilists in Japan. It was a time when the communications and circulations were much less convenient than the present and these research monographs, some of which contained top class results at the world research level, have not been known to the world outside Japan. These promoted so much the progress of the probability theory in Japan, particularly, they helped those who just began to study in this field. For me, it was really lucky that I came across this monograph by Tanaka right after I had learned, from books by Doob and Itô, the basic elements of Itô's theory such as stochastic integrals, Itô's formula, SDE's with Lipschitz continuous coefficients and diffusion processes associated with them, and so on. It taught me, among others, the importance of *studying separately* the uniqueness problem and the existence problem for solutions of SDE's. In this monograph, Tanaka discussed SDE's with continuous coefficients; the existence of solutions was established by following Skorohod's method; for the uniqueness problem, he only wrote that it is an interesting open problem whether the solutions are unique or whether there exist solutions which define a Markov process. However, he could immediately solve ([8] in this volume) the question concerning the existence of Markovian solutions in the nondegenerate case. This Tanaka's result was further improved by D. W. Stroock and S. R. S. Varadhan who established the law uniqueness of solutions in the nondegenerate case, and by N. V. Krylov who obtained a Markov selection theorem for solutions in the general case (cf. [SV] for these results).

As far as the theory of Markov processes is concerned, what is necessary is only the existence of weak solutions and their uniqueness in law which is also equivalent to the existence of solutions and the well-posedness of martingale problems. However, in the study of stochastic flows generated by SDE's and in the innovation problems (the problems concerning filtrations and noises) associated with solutions, for example, the notion of strong solutions and relevant notion of pathwise uniqueness are also important. The terms like *strong solutions, weak solutions* and *pathwise uniqueness* did not appear explicitly in this monograph but I think that Tanaka might have been the first in Japan who recognized the importance of these notions. Actually, Tanaka is the first to give a simple and most understandable example (known as *Tanaka's example*, cf. e.g., [IW], [RW]) of SDE which enjoys uniqueness in law but *no* pathwise unique solutions. In this monograph, the pathwise uniqueness of one-dimensional SDE's with Hölder continuous coefficients of order $\alpha > 1/2$ was obtained. Later, when I was working on continuous state branching processes, I needed some uniqueness result for SDE's with Hölder continuous coefficients of order $\alpha = 1/2$ and I suddenly remembered the proof of Tanaka in this monograph. By modifying his proof, I could manage to obtain the necessary result. The proof of pathwise uniqueness I gave was still not general enough but Yamada found a nice improvement of Tanaka's proof so that an almost best possible condition for the pathwise uniqueness was obtained. However, it was not obvious for us that the pathwise uniqueness implies the law uniqueness so that it can define a strong Markov process, and we could not find any existing literature concerning this problem. Such were our main motivations of joint work [YW] and we owe much to Tanaka in this joint work.

Among many important contributions and influences of Tanaka in connection with SDE's, I would choose one more topic. This is concerned with his SDE based on a Poisson point process, which he introduced to describe a stochastic model associated with Boltzmann's equation of Maxwellian gas without cutoff ([16] in this volume). The notion of Poisson random measures (Poisson point processes) has been established by Itô, among others, in the study of the Lévy-Itô theorem for the paths structure of additive processes and a general theory of SDE's based on them has been discussed by Itô, Gihman and Skorohod, among others. It seems to me, however, that there had not been any significant application of the theory before Tanaka: I believe that Tanaka's equation is the first truly significant example of SDE's based on Poisson point processes. I remember well when Tanaka visited us and gave a series of lectures on this topic at Kyoto University around 1970. I was really fascinated by his splendid way of defining and applying a SDE based on a cleverly chosen Poisson point process. Later, I discussed with S. Takanobu on some application of SDE's based on Poisson point processes of Brownian excursions to solve SDE's for diffusion processes in a domain satisfying the most general Wentzell's boundary conditions. The idea was motivated by the work of Tanaka and I remember I was always wishing to imitate Tanaka's method, even in a small way, in this problem.

References

[BEKSY] M. T. Barlow, M. Émery, F. B. Knight, S. Song et M. Yor, Autour d'un théorème de Tsirelson sur des filtrations browniennes et non browniennes, *Sém. Prob. XXXII*, Lecture Notes in Math., **1686**, Springer, Berlin (1998), 264-305

[D] J. L. Doob, *Stochastic Processes*, John Wiley & Sons, New York, 1953

[EY] M. Émery et M. Yor, Sur un théorème de Tsirelson relatif à des mouvements browniens corrélés et à la nullité de certains temps locaux, *Sém. Prob. XXXII*, Lecture Notes in Math., **1686**, Springer, Berlin (1998), 306-312

[IW] N. Ikeda and S. Watanabe, *Stochastic Differential Equations and Diffusion Processes*, Second Edition, North-Holland/Kodansha, Amsterdam/Tokyo, 1988

[I 1] K. Itô, *Kakuritsuron* (*Probability Theory*), in Japanese, Iwanami-Shoten, Tokyo, 1955

[I 2] K. Itô, *Lectures on Stochastic Processes*, Tata Institute of Fundamental Research, Bombay, 1961

[IM] K. Itô and H. P. McKean, *Diffusion Processes and their Sample Paths*, Springer, Berlin, 1965, 1974-Printing in *Classics in Mathematics*, 1996

[L] J. F. Le Gall, Applications du temps local aux équations différentielles stochastiques unidimensionnelles, *Sém. Prob. XVII*, Lecture Notes in Math., **986**, Springer, Berlin (1983), 15-31

[M] H. P. McKean, *Stochastic Integrals*, Academic Press, New York,1969

[RY] D. Revuz and M. Yor, *Continuous Martingales and Brownian Motion,* Third Edition, Springer, Berlin, 1999

[RW] L.C.G. Rogers and D. Williams, *Diffusions, Markov Processes and Martingales, Vol. 2: Itô's Calculus*, John Wiley & Sons, New York, 1987

[S] A. V. Skorohod, Stochastic equations for diffusion processes in a bounded region, Theor. Prob. Appl., **6** (1961), 264-274

[SV] D. W. Stroock and S. R. S. Varadhan, *Multidimensional Diffusion Processes*, Springer, Berlin, 1979

[TH] H. Tanaka and M. Hasegawa, *Kakuritsu Bibun Hōteishiki,* (*Stochastic Differential Equations*), in Japanese, Seminar on Prob. **17**, 1964

[T] H. F. Trotter, A properties of Brownian motion paths, Illinois J. Math. **2** (1958), 425-433

[Ya] T. Yamada, Principal values of Brownian local times and their related topics, in *Itô's Stochastic Calculus and Probability Theory, ed. N. Ikeda et al.*, Springer, Tokyo (1996), 413-422

[YW] T. Yamada and S. Watanabe, On the uniqueness of solutions of stochastic differential equations, Jour. Math. Kyoto Univ. **11** (1971), 155-167

[Yo] M. Yor, *Some Aspects of Brownian Motion,* Part II, Some Recent Martingale Problems, Lectures in Math. ETH Zürich, Birkhäuser, Basel, 1997

Some Comments on My Mathematical Works in Retrospect

by Hiroshi Tanaka

In this short note I would like to give some comments on my works on probability theory, first by mentioning briefly the initial stage of my mathematical development and then by concentrating on those works which are related mainly to Boltzmann's equation and diffusion processes in random environments.

When I was a graduate student at Kyushu University (1955–1958), the theory of Markov processes with related potential theory went through much development. As a student of Professor Gisiro Maruyama I began to study probability theory toward the above field by reading papers on Markov processes by A.N. Kolmogorov, W. Feller, J.L. Doob, K. Itô and E.B. Dynkin. I also learned many things from N. Ikeda, T. Watanabe and T. Ueno, who also began to work in this field and were taking the initiative in research activities of young probabilists in Japan, in particular, in the Probability and Statistics Summer Seminar, the April Probability Symposium and the publication of Seminar on Probability (in Japanese). I was encouraged by Ikeda through frequent conversation; I owed much to Watanabe for the problem of the paper [1] † ; the motivation of the paper [4] was to realize Ueno's idea on invariant measures of recurrent Markov processes ([U1]).

In 1957–1958 H.P. McKean visited Kyoto University, where K. Itô was at the time. He gave interesting lectures there, sometimes in other places as well, and inspired young probabilists in Japan. Itô and McKean were developing their theory on one-dimensional diffusion processes which is now found in the book [IM]. I learned some of the essential points directly by listening to their lectures and also through Itô's seminar which I sometimes attended. By analogy with their results in one-dimension Itô and McKean introduced a class of multi-dimensional diffusion processes $X(t)$ admitting the same system of harmonic measures as Brownian motion $B(t)$ and anticipated the construction of such $X(t)$ by means of time-change from $B(t)$. I carried out the actual construction but under some condition on mean exit times of $X(t)$ from bounded domains (I arrived at additive functionals of Brownian motion as a multi-dimensional substitute, though less explicit, of one-dimensional local time integrals due to Itô-McKean). McKean also obtained almost the same result. The final result was published as the

†Numbers in brackets refer to the Bibliography of Hiroshi Tanaka (see pages 425–428)

joint paper [5] which was written up while I was visiting MIT (1960–1962) at the invitation of McKean. I was much influenced by him and afterward became interested in Boltzmann's equation through his paper [M].

After writing the paper [8] on the existence of diffusion processes with continuous coefficients, I was interested in the approach from stochastic differential equations (SDEs). The uniqueness result which was lacking in my paper [8] was given later by D.W. Stroock and S.R.S. Varadhan [SV] in a clear way by introducing martingale problems. I had some misunderstanding on (or expected too much from) the pathwise uniqueness in SDEs and thus obtained no results, but from the works of A.V. Skorohod (Chapter 3 of the book [Sk]) and I.V. Girsanov ([G]) I was able to acquire some knowledge on strong and weak solutions of SDEs and often used SDEs in my later works.

In the research of probability theory in Japan around the mid 1960s there was a trend of taking up some nonlinear problems from the view-point of probability theory; in particular, N. Ikeda, M. Nagasawa and S. Watanabe were discussing nonlinear problems in connection with branching processes in a series of interesting papers (e.g. [INW]). I myself attempted to treat quasilinear parabolic equations making use of SDEs ([10]) but it had no connection with concrete problems. In 1966 McKean ([M]) introduced a class of Markov processes (with nonconstant transition mechanism) that can be associated with certain nonlinear parabolic equations such as Burgers' equation and Boltzmann's equation. I soon became interested in [M]. Probably the willingness to study Boltzmann's equation had also come from my experience of reading R. Kubo's book "Statistical Mechanics" (published in 1952, Japanese) when I was a sophomore at Kyushu University. By reading [M] carefully and comparing it with Kac's earlier paper [K], I could understand its main part: The spatially homogeneous Boltzmann's equation (nonlinear) can be derived from the master equation (linear) through the propagation of chaos and this idea is applicable to certain nonlinear parabolic equations. But the rigorous verification had been carried out only in few cases such as Boltzmann's equation of Maxwellian and cutoff type by using an analytic method. I wanted to discuss the problem by a more probabilistic method. It was easy to write down the SDE (based on a Poisson random measure) describing the Markov process associated with spatially homogeneous Boltzmann's equation but the actual proof of the existence and uniqueness of solutions was usually hard and interesting particularly when the total scattering cross section (t.s.c.s. for short) is infinite. The papers [16] and [22] treated the case of Maxwellian and non-cutoff type. The idea behind was in an extension of the previous work[15] on Kac's one-dimensional model of Maxwellian molecules in which a sort of mean square deviation from the Gaussian distribution was effectively used. In solving the SDE there was a difficulty due to the infiniteness of t.s.c.s. but the Maxwellian type provided a special method, so to say, an iteration method in the sense of law in solving the SDE (this was not applicable to Boltzmann's equation in general).

Since the argument of [22] seemed technically complicated, I tried to simplify it with some improvement on the SDE in [38]. Let (Ω_1, P_1) be a *copy* of the basic probability space (Ω, P) on which a solution $X(t,\omega)$ is to be constructed. Then the SDE (written in the form of an integral equation) was improved to

$$X(t,\omega) = X(0,\omega) + \int_{(0,t]\times\Lambda\times\Omega_1} b(X(s-,\omega), X(s-,\omega_1),\lambda)N(dsd\lambda d\omega_1),$$

where $N(\cdot)$ is a Poisson random measure on $(0,\infty)\times\Lambda\times\Omega_1$ with intensity measure $ds\mu(d\lambda)P_1(d\omega_1)$, (Λ,μ) being a suitable measure space. The presence of the copy $X(s-,\omega_1)$ of an unknown $X(s-,\omega)$ matches the *nonlinearity* of the problem.

I thought that there was a gap between the uniqueness of solutions to the SDE of [16] and the uniqueness of solutions to the Boltzmann equation itself, so I wrote the paper [19] to fill this gap but later was able to obtain a better result, namely the uniqueness of probability measure solutions of the Boltzmann equation itself (unpublished) by making use of Varadhan's result ([V]) concerning the uniqueness of probability measure solutions of certain parabolic equations.

When writing the paper [6] with K. Sato, in 1962, which was motivated by Ueno's idea on Markov processes on boundaries ([U2]), I became aware that a reflecting Brownian motion $X(t)$ for a multi-dimensional domain can be expressed as $B(t) + \Phi(t)$ where $B(t)$ is a standard Brownian motion and $\Phi(t)$ is an integral with respect to the local time on the boundary for $X(t)$. However, I could not regard this expression as an equation in which $X(t)$ and $\Phi(t)$ are considered as unknown, because I did not anticipate the uniqueness of solutions at that time. Later I noticed that the uniqueness can be obtained easily from the convexity assumption on the domain, and so I could formulate Skorohod's problem for convex domains ([24]). The convexity assumption was soon removed by P.L. Lions and A.S. Sznitman ([LS]). Thanks to their result I was able to construct the motion of a finite number of mutually reflecting Brownian balls as a solution to Skorohod's problem in [34] (the infinite case was discussed later by H. Tanemura [T]).

In 1984 I stayed in Zürich for three months at the invitation of H. Föllmer and Nagasawa. I attended the probability seminar organized jointly by Föllmer (ETH Zürich) and Nagasawa (the University of Zürich), which was fresh and active, with many young probabilists. This visit gave much influence to my later works. A series of joint works with Nagasawa ([31][33][39][42]) began around this time; there we discussed some types of many particle systems with mean field interaction which arose from Nagasawa's idea on the Schrödinger equation.

At that time T. Brox, a postdoctral fellow at the University of Zürich, was working on a diffusion analogue (appeared in [B]) of Ya.G. Sinai's random walk in a random environment ([S]). I came to know the results of Sinai and Brox for the first time (as I knew later there is also S. Schumacher's work [Sch] on a similar subject) and was much impressed by their works since it seemed to me that the results gave a new type of limit theorems involving a scaling quite different from those I had ever encountered. I thus became interested in stochastic processes in random environments.

A diffusion process in a Brownian environment or Brox's diffusion for simplicity is a continuous time version of Sinai's random walk in a random environment and described by the (symbolic) SDE

$$dX(t) = dB(t) - \frac{1}{2}w'(X(t))dt, \qquad X(0) = 0,$$

where $B(t), t \geq 0$, is a one-dimensional Brownian motion independent of a Brownian environment $w(x)$, $x \in \mathbb{R}$. For a precise definition, e.g. see [B] or [41]. Brox's diffusion is sometimes called a Brownian motion in a white noise environment. The arguments of Brox were based on many of Sinai's ideas ([S]), among which the notion of a valley — a depression in English translation ([S]) — played an essential role together with the self-similarity of the random environment. Reading Brox's preprints I was able to obtain a better understanding of Sinai's result. Since I preferred to work with Brownian motion rather than with random walks, I considered most of the problems in the framework of diffusion processes. Most of the results obtained for diffusions in random environments were preceded by the corresponding ones for random walks; however, working with diffusion processes was more fun for me; it often seemed to clarify methods and results since one could use a lot of fine properties of Brownian motion.

I give some comments on my works concerning the following problems.

(A) Some refinements of the results of [S][B][Sch] (localization).
(B) A generalization of the problem (A) to a wider class of random environments.
(C) A Brownian motion with drift in a white noise environment.
(D) A multi-dimensional problem.

(A): When I heard from Brox that $(\log t)^{-2}X(t) - b(t)$ tends to 0 in probability as $t \to \infty$ (where $b(t)$, for each fixed t, is defined as the bottom of a suitable valley and admits a probability distribution independent of t), I got interested in the limit theorem of the next stage: Can one obtain a non-degenerate limit distribution by a suitable rescaling of $(\log t)^{-2}X(t) - b(t)$? I could not immediately anticipate that the multiplication by $(\log t)^2$ simply is enough to have a limit distribution. The paper [41] discusses this problem. The result is that $X(t) - (\log t)^2 b(t)$ admits a non-degenerate limit distribution as $t \to \infty$ which can be expressed in terms of independent Bessel processes β_+ and β_- appearing in (ii) below. This result seemed interesting particularly when compared with the fact that an individual diffusion process with frozen environment w is null-recurrent (a.s.). I must remark that there is also an earlier work [Go] by A.O. Golosov on the same subject for random walks. Following [Go] and also for terminological convenience I call a result of this type *localization* (in some occasions the term *localization* is used in a wider sense). The key points of the argument in [41] were (i) to refine Brox's method and (ii) to describe the local behavior (law) of the environment around the bottom $b(e)$ in terms of two independent Bessel processes β_+ and β_- of index 3. This part, (ii), was most interesting for me, in which I used the construction of a reflecting Brownian motion on $[0, \infty)$ by means of the associated Poisson point process of excursions ([I][IW:pp.123–125]) and then a certain reversal of time. Theorems of D. Williams [W] and J.W. Pitman [P] were also used. The same problem as [41] was again discussed in [52], in which the part (i) was replaced by a use of a theorem of Y. Ogura ([O], see also p.756 of [52]) and consequently the whole story of the proof became transparent.

(B): In [47] we proved that the localization of the type discussed in [41] holds for a certain class of random environments that are asymptotically strictly stable. But after having written [52] I began to anticipate that the localization will hold if we take for the random environment $\{w(x), x \in \mathbb{R}\}$ any Lévy process satisfying the following condition: There exists $\alpha\,(0 < \alpha < 2)$ such that every positive sequence $\{\lambda_k\}$ tending to ∞ contains a subsequence $\{\lambda'_k\}$ along which $\{\lambda^{-1}w(\lambda^\alpha x), x \in \mathbb{R}\}$ converges in law to some nice non-degenerate process *that may depend on* $\{\lambda'_k\}$. So I wanted to find a *good* class of Lévy random environments for which the localization of the type discussed in [41] holds. For this purpose I was often led to the study of some properties of Lévy processes themselves and this was also fun for me. For instance, I studied superharmonic transforms of absorbing Lévy processes in the half line $(0, \infty)$ in order to grasp the asymptotic law of a certain part of the environment around some bottom (a summary in Japanese is in Cooperative Research Report 51, The Institute of Statist. Math.; what I had for the proof of (ii) of Theorem 7 therein is incomplete).

(C): The limiting behavior of the process $X(t)$ described by

$$dX(t) = dB(t) + \frac{\kappa}{2}dt - \frac{1}{2}w'(X(t))dt$$

can not be treated by the method of Sinai-Brox-Schumacher. In 1986 when I was at Minnesota, B. Tóth pointed out to me that this would correspond to the random walk model discussed in an earlier work [KKS] by H. Kesten M.V. Kozlov and F. Spitzer. However, an adaptation of their method to our case seemed very hard to me. On the other hand, it was already recognized that Krein's spectral theory of strings (e.g. see [KK]) provides a powerful method in the study of various problems on one-dimensional diffusion processes (in non-random environments); for example, see S. Kotani-S. Watanabe [KW] and the references therein. In 1989 K. Kawazu and I had a chance, at a small symposium, to discuss with Kotani on the problem of limiting behavior of the above $X(t)$ from the view point of the applicability of Krein's theory and learned the method of Laplace transform of a hitting time, i.e., Kotani's formula (unpublished, see [56]), which he had obtained previously in finding the limit distribution of the maximum of the Brox-Schumacher diffusion. We thus became interested in using Kotani's formula and Krein's theory for our problem and were able to obtain the first result [56].

But it gave only a partial answer; namely, the case $1 \leq \kappa \leq 2$ was not discussed, in which the limit distribution was expected to have the whole real line for the support. So I was misled, for a good while, to a false conclusion that the method of Laplace transform (i.e., Kotani's formula) would not work. However, luckily it worked as was discussed later in the second paper [57] where, in addition to [KK], I also used Krein's more specific result [Kr] (see also [DM:p.266] [KW:p.239]). The same result was obtained also by Y. Hu, Z. Shi and M. Yor ([HSY]) by a method quite different from ours. Finally I remark that an environment-wise central limit theorem was proved in the case $\kappa > 2$ (see [55]); the proof needed a series of detailed computations in spite of the easy-looking problem. I do not know whether a similar result holds for $\kappa = 2$. (The right hand side of the equality in the 13th line of p.1809 of [57] should be

$$(2^7\pi)^{-1/2} \int_{-\infty}^{t} \exp\{-2^{-7}s^2\}ds.$$

I remark also that the formula at the top of p.201 of [36] is not correct; it was corrected in [35].)

(D): P. Mathieu ([Ma]) considered a diffusion process in a multi-dimensional Brownian environment. The paper [51] proved its recurrent property. The process $X(t)$ corresponds to one of random walk models in R. Durrett [D], but is not a diffusion analogue of the random walk of J. Bricmont and A. Kupiainen [BK], a multi-dimensional random walk corresponding to Sinai's one. From [Ma] and [D] we see that the process $X(t)$ has the localization property of the type discussed in [S] but the existence problem of a limit distribution of $(\log t)^{-2}X(t)$ seemed unsettled. In this connection I studied some properties of sample functions of a Lévy's Brownian motion with a multi-dimensional time (e.g. [61]).

References

[BK] J. Bricmont and A. Kupiainen, Random walks in asymmetric random environments, Comm. Math. Phys. **142** (1991), 345-420.

[B] T. Brox, A one-dimensional diffusion process in Wiener medium, Ann. Probab. **14** (1986), 1206-1218.

[D] R. Durrett, Multidimensional random walks in random environments with subclassical limiting behavior, Comm. Math. Phys. **104** (1986), 87-102.

[DM] H. Dym and H.P. McKean, Gaussian Processes, Function Theory, and the Inverse Spectral Problem, Academic Press, 1976.

[G] I.V. Girsanov, An example of nonuniqueness for solutions of K. Itô's stochastic integral equations, Theor. Probab. Appl. **7** (1962), 336-342.

[Go] A.O. Golosov, Localization of random walks in one-dimensional random environments, Comm. Math. Phys. **92** (1984), 491-506.

[HSY] Y. Hu, Z. Shi and M. Yor, Rate of Convergence of diffusions with drifted Brownian potentials, Trans. Amer. Math. Soc. **351** (1999), 3915-3934.

[I] K. Itô, Poisson point processes attached to Markov processes, Proc. 6th Berkeley Symp. Math. Statist. Probab. **III**, 1970, 225–239.

[IM] K. Itô and H.P. McKean, Diffusion Processes and Their Sample Paths, Springer, 1965.

[INW] N. Ikeda, M. Nagasawa and S. Watanabe, Branching Markov processes I, II, III, J. Math. Kyoto Univ. **8** (1968), 233–278, 365–410; **9** (1969), 95–160.

[IW] N. Ikeda and S. Watanabe, Stochastic Differential Equations and Diffusion Processes, North-Holland, 1981.

[K] M. Kac, Foundations of kinetic theory, Proc. 3rd Berkeley Symp. Math. Statist. Probab., 3, 1955, 171–197.

[Kr] M.G. Krein, On some cases of the effective determination of the density of a non-homogeneous string from its spectral function, Dokl. Akad. Nauk SSSR **93** (1953), 617–620.

[KK] I.S. Kac and M.G. Krein, On the spectral functions of the string, Amer. Math. Soc. Transl. (2), **103** (1974), 19–102.

[KKS] H. Kesten, V. Kozlov and F. Spitzer, A limit law for random walk in a random environment, Compositio Math. **30** (1975), 145-168.

[KW] S. Kotani and S. Watanabe, Krein's spectral theory of strings and generalized diffusion processes, 235-259 in Lecture Notes in Math. **923**, Springer, 1982.

[LS] P.L. Lions and A.S. Sznitman, Stochastic differential equations with reflecting boundary conditions, Comm. Pure Appl. Math. **37** (1984), 511–537.

[Ma] P. Mathieu, Zero white noise limit through Dirichlet forms, Application to diffusions in a random medium, Probab. Theory Related Fields **99** (1994), pp. 549-580.

[M] H.P. McKean, A class of Markov processes associated with nonlinear parabolic equations, Proc. Nat. Acad. Sci. U.S.A. **56** (1966), 1907-1911.

[O] Y. Ogura, One-dimensional bigeneralized diffusion processes, J. Math. Soc. Japan **41** (1989), 213-242.

[P] J.W. Pitman, One-dimensional Brownian motion and three-dimensional Bessel process, Adv. Appl. Probab. **7** (1975), 511-526.

[Sch] S. Schumacher, Diffusions with random coefficients, pp.351-356 in: Particle Systems, Random Media and Large Deviations, R. Durrett, ed., Contemporary Math. **41**, 1985.

[S] Y.G. Sinai, The limiting behavior of a one-dimensional random walk in a random medium, Theory Probab. Appl. **27** (1982), 256-268.

[Sk] A.V. Skorokhod, Studies in the Theory of Random Processes, Addison-Wesley, 1965.

[SV] D.W. Stroock and S.R.S. Varadhan, Diffusion processes with continuous coefficients, I, II, Comm. Pure Appl. Math. **22** (1969), 345–400, 479–530.

[T] H. Tanemura, A system of infinitely many mutually reflecting Brownian balls in $\mathbb{R}^d$, Probab. Th. Rel. Fields **104** (1996), 399–426.

[U1] T. Ueno, On recurrent Markov processes, Kōdai Math. Sem. Rep. **12** (1960), 109-142.

[U2] T. Ueno, The diffusion satisfying Wentzell's boundary condition and the Markov process on the boundary I, II, Proc. Japan Acad. **36** (1960), 533–538, 625–629.

[V] S.R.S. Varadhan, Invariant measures of Markov processes, Lecture at Kyoto Univ., 1980; A brief summary of it taken and written up by S. Kotani in Japanese is in Sugaku Vol.**33**, No.3, 1981, p.276.

[Wi] D. Williams, Path decomposition and continuity of local time for one-dimensional diffusions, I, Proc. London Math. Soc. (3) **28** (1974), 738-768.

MEMOIRS OF THE COLLEGE OF SCIENCE, UNIVERSITY OF KYOTO, SERIES A
Vol. XXXIII, Mathematics No. 3, 1961.

Additive functionals of the Brownian path

By

H. P. McKEAN, JR. and Hiroshi TANAKA

(Communicated by Prof. K. Itô, March 14, 1961)

1. INTRODUCTION.

A functional $\mathfrak{f}(t)=\mathfrak{f}(t, w)$ of $t(\geq 0)$ and a several-dimensional Brownian path $w: t \to x(t)$ is said to be *additive* if

1.1 $\mathfrak{f}(t, w)$ *depends upon* t *and* $x(s): s \leq t$ *alone.*

1.2 $0=\mathfrak{f}(0) \leq \mathfrak{f} < +\infty$

1.3 $\mathfrak{f}(t\pm)=\mathfrak{f}(t)$

1.4 $\mathfrak{f}(t)=\mathfrak{f}(s)+\mathfrak{f}(t-s, w_s^+) \qquad t \geq s,$

where w_s^+ is the shifted path $w_s^+: t \to x(t+s)$; for example, $\mathfrak{f}(t)=\int_0^t f(x(s))ds$ is an additive functional if $f \geq 0$ is bounded and Borel.

K. Itô and H. P. McKean, Jr. [13] proved that in the 1-dimensional case such an additive functional is an *integral*

1.5 $\mathfrak{f}(t)=\int \mathfrak{t}(t, b)e(db)$

of the *standard Brownian local times*

1.6 $\mathfrak{t}(t, a)=\lim_{b \downarrow a} \dfrac{\text{measure } (s: a \leq x(s) < b, s \leq t)}{b-a}$

with respect to a non-negative measure e, finite on bounded intervals.

Brownian local times are not available in $d \geq 2$ dimensions, but $\mathfrak{f}$ can still be expressed as a (*formal*) Hellinger *integral*

1.7 $\mathfrak{f}(t)=\int \dfrac{\text{measure } (s: x(s) \in db, s \leq t)e(db)}{db}$

with a non-negative measure e which is *smooth* in the sense that *each bounded open D is the union of an increasing series of sets* $B_n(n \geq 1)$, *closed in D, such that*

1.8a *the charge distributions* $e|B_n$ *have bounded potentials* $\int_{B_n} Gde \leq n (n \geq 1)$, *where G is the Green function of D;*

1.8b *for large n, depending upon the path, the Brownian particle lies in* B_n *until it leaves D, i.e.,*

$$P_\cdot[x(t) \in B_n,\ t < \min(s: x(s) \notin D),\ n \uparrow +\infty] = 1,$$

where $P_\cdot(B)$ *is the probability of the event B as a function of the starting point of the Brownian motion.*

The correspondence embodied in 1.7 *between the class of smooth measures e and the class of additive functionals* $\mathfrak{f}$ *is one to one and onto.*

1.8a implies that $e(B)=0$ unless B has positive logarithmic capacity in the 2-dimensional case or has positive Newtonian capacity in the $d \geq 3$ dimensional case; thus, a smooth measure cannot attach positive mass to a line in 3 dimensions, nor, in 4 dimensions, to a surface. But it can be singular relative to Lebesgue measure; the simplest example in 3 dimensions is the uniform distribution on the spherical surface $|a|=1$.

Choose $d=3$, $e(db)=|b|^\alpha db$, and let G be the Green function of D: $|a|<1$; then

$$\text{1.9a} \quad \begin{aligned} p = \int Gde & \\ \leq \text{constant } (2+\alpha)^{-1} & \qquad \alpha > -2 \\ < +\infty \text{ except at } 0 & \qquad -3 < \alpha \leq -2 \\ \equiv +\infty & \qquad \alpha \leq -3, \end{aligned}$$

$$\text{1.9b} \quad \mathfrak{G}(e) \equiv \iint Gdede < +\infty \qquad \alpha > -5/2,$$

and it follows that e is smooth for $\alpha > -2$. *e is not smooth for* $\alpha \leq -2$; in fact, choosing $B_n \uparrow D$ as needed for 1.8,

$$\text{1.10} \quad \begin{aligned} & E_0\left[\int_0^\varepsilon |x(s)|^\alpha ds,\ x(t) \in B_n,\ t < \varepsilon\right] \\ & \leq \int_0^{+\infty} ds \int_{B_n} P_0[x(s) \in db,\ \max_{t \leq s} |x(t)| < 1]|b|^\alpha \\ & \leq \int_{B_n} G(0, b)de < +\infty, \end{aligned}$$

thanks to 1.8a, and

1.11 $\lim_{\varepsilon\downarrow 0}\lim_{n\uparrow+\infty} P_0[x(t)\in B_n,\ t<\varepsilon]=1$

thanks to 1.8b, while, as is not hard to prove,

1.12 $P_0\left[\int_0^\varepsilon |x(s)|^\alpha ds \equiv +\infty\ ,\ \varepsilon>0\right]=1\,,$

contradicting 1.10.

V. A. Volkonskii [15, 16] also studied additive functionals, establishing a special case of the above for a wider class of motions; the method used below is similar to his.

Given a 1-dimensional diffusion with the same hitting probabilities as the standard Brownian motion:

1.13 $$P_\xi[\min(t:\ x(t)=a)<\min(t:\ x(t)=b)] = \frac{b-\xi}{b-a} \qquad a<\xi<b\,,$$

W. Feller [8] explained how to express the associated generator $\mathfrak{G}$ as a *differential opearator* based upon a *speed measure e*, positive on open intervals:

1.14 $$\mathfrak{G}u=\frac{u^+(da)}{e(da)}=\lim_{b\downarrow a}\frac{u^+(b)-u^+(a)}{e(a,b)}$$
$$u^+(a)=\lim_{b\downarrow a}\frac{u(b)-u(a)}{b-a}\,,$$

and K. Itô and H. P. McKean, Jr. [13] found that its sample paths could be expressed as standard Brownian sample paths run with the *stochastic clock* $\mathfrak{f}^{-1}$ which is the inverse function of the additive functional (local time integral) $\mathfrak{f}=\int \mathfrak{t}\,de$ associated with the speed measure.

V. A. Volkonskiî [15] also studied such time substitutions; his method is less explicit because it does not use local times but has the advantage that it can be applied in higher dimensions.

As will be explained below, a $d\geq 2$ dimensional *diffusion with Brownian hitting probabilities* has as its generator *the closure of a differential operator*

1.15 $\quad \mathfrak{G}u = -\dfrac{e^{u}(db)}{e(db)}$

based upon a (smooth) *speed measure* e, positive on the neighborhoods of H. Cartan's *fine topology* [2]; moreover, the associated motion is the standard Brownian motion run with the inverse function $\mathfrak{f}^{-1}$ of the additive functional $\mathfrak{f}$ associated with e, and *this correspondence between the class of diffusions with Brownian hitting probabilities and the class of smooth measures e positive on fine neighborhoods is one to one and onto.*

2. BROWNIAN MOTION.

Choose $d \geq 2$, let $E^d = R^d$ it $d=2$, let it be the one-point compactification $R^d + \infty$ if $d \geq 3$, introduce the space of continuous *sample paths* $w: [0, +\infty) \to E^d$ with

2.1 $\quad \begin{aligned} w(t) &\in R^d \qquad t < \mathfrak{m}_\infty \\ &= \infty \qquad t \geq \mathfrak{m}_\infty, \end{aligned}$

where $\mathfrak{m}_\infty = \mathfrak{m}_\infty(w) \leq +\infty$ and $\mathfrak{m}_\infty \equiv +\infty$ in case $d=2$, let $w(t) = x(t, w) = x(t)$ as need be, note that $x(+\infty) \equiv \infty$ even if $d=2$, and, introducing the corresponding *coordiante fields* $\boldsymbol{B}_t = \boldsymbol{B}[x(s): s \leq t]$ and $\boldsymbol{B} = \boldsymbol{B}_{\infty+}$, let $P_\cdot(B)$ be the *probability* (*Wiener measure*) of the event $B \in \boldsymbol{B}$ as a function of the starting point of the *d-dimentional Brownian motion* with *generator* $\mathfrak{G} = \dfrac{\partial^2}{\partial b_1^2} + \dfrac{\partial^2}{\partial b_2^2} + \cdots + \dfrac{\partial^2}{\partial b_d^2}$.[1]

Brownian motion enthusiasts are familiar with the fact that the Brownian traveller *starts afresh* at a passage time; the full significance of this was explained by E. B. Dynkin [6] and G. Hunt [9] as follows.

An instant of time $0 \leq \mathfrak{m} \leq +\infty$ depending upon the path is said to be a *Markov time* if

2.2 $\quad (w: \mathfrak{m} < t) \in \boldsymbol{B}_t \qquad t \geq 0;$

for example, the passage time $\mathfrak{m}_Q = \inf(t: x(t) \in Q)$ to a closed or

---

[1] $\mathfrak{G}/2$ is often used as the generator of the Brownian motion, but for our purpose it is simpler to omit the factor 1/2.

open d-dimensional figure Q is a Markov time and so is $\mathfrak{m}=\min\left(t:\int_0^t f(x(s))ds=1\right)$ if $0<f\leq 1$ is a Borel function.

Given such a Markov time $\mathfrak{m}$, if $w_{\mathfrak{m}}^+$ is the *shifted path*

2.3 $\quad w_{\mathfrak{m}}^+: t\to x(t+\mathfrak{m})$

and if $\boldsymbol{B}_{\mathfrak{m}+}$ is the *field* of events $B\in\boldsymbol{B}$ such that

2.4 $\quad B\cap(w:\mathfrak{m}<t)\in\boldsymbol{B}_t \qquad t\geq 0,$

then the Brownian particle *starts afresh* at time $t=\mathfrak{m}$, i.e.,

2.5 $\quad P_a[w_{\mathfrak{m}}^+\in B\,|\,\boldsymbol{B}_{\mathfrak{m}+}]=P_b(B) \qquad a\in E^d,\ B\in\boldsymbol{B},\ b\equiv x(\mathfrak{m})$ [2].

Blumenthal's 01 law [1]:

2.6 $\quad P_\cdot(B)=\begin{matrix}0\\1\end{matrix} \qquad B\in\boldsymbol{B}_{0+}=\bigcap_{\varepsilon>0}\boldsymbol{B}_\varepsilon$

is a special case of 2.5.

A. R. Galmarino[3] has pointed out that a *non-negative* Borel *function* $\mathfrak{m}$ *of the sample path is a Markov time if and only if*

2.7a $\quad \mathfrak{m}(u)<t$

2.7b $\quad x(u,u)=x(s,v) \qquad s\leq t$

imply $\mathfrak{m}(u)=\mathfrak{m}(v)$ and that *an event* $B\in\boldsymbol{B}$ *is a member of* $\boldsymbol{B}_{\mathfrak{m}+}$ *if and only if* 2.7 *coupled with* $u\in B$ *implies* $v\in B$. As a simple application of this test, note that $B_{\mathfrak{m}+}$ measures both $\mathfrak{m}$ and the *past* $x(\theta\wedge\mathfrak{m})$ $(\theta\geq 0)$[4] because 2.7 implies $\theta\wedge\mathfrak{m}(u)=\theta\wedge\mathfrak{m}(v)<t$ and hence $x(\theta\wedge\mathfrak{m}(u),u)=x(\theta\wedge\mathfrak{m}(v),v)$.

Given bounded open $D\subset R^d$ with boundary ∂D, if $\mathfrak{m}_{\partial D}$ is the *exit time* $\min(t: x(t)\in\partial D)$, then the *hitting probability*

2.8 $\quad h_{\partial D}(a,db)=P_a[x(\mathfrak{m}_{\partial D})\in db] \qquad a\in D,\ db\in\partial D$

is the *classical harmonic measure* of db as viewed from the point a, and, if $G_D(a,b)$ is the *classical Green function* of D, then

2.9 $\quad E_a[\text{measure}(t: x(t)\in db,\ t<\mathfrak{m}_{\partial D}]=G_D(a,b)db$ [5] $\quad a,b\in D;$

---

[2] $x(\mathfrak{m})\equiv\infty$ in case $\mathfrak{m}=+\infty$; it is understood that $P_\infty[x(t)\equiv\infty,\ t\geq 0]=1$.

[3] private communication.

[4] $a\wedge b$ is the smaller of a and b.

[5] $E_\cdot(f)=\int f dP_\cdot$.

for the proofs, see J. Doob [5] and G. Hunt [9].

G. Hunt [10] has called a non-negative Borel function p *excessive* on D if

2.10 $\quad E_a[p(x(t)), t < \mathfrak{m}_{\partial D}] \uparrow p(a) \qquad t \downarrow 0,\ a \in D.$

An excessive function can be split into its *greatest harmonic minorant* h plus the *potential* $\int G_D de$ of a non-negative (Riesz) measure e, indeed, Hunt's excessive functions are the same as the *superharmonic* functions of F. Riesz [14]. J. Doob [5] proved that *an excessive function is continuous on the Brownian path* $(t < \mathfrak{m}_{\partial D})$ and that *a potential tends to* 0 *along the Brownian path* $(t \uparrow \mathfrak{m}_{\partial D})$.

3. THE ASSOCIATED MEASURE OF AN ADDITIVE FUNCTIONAL.

Consider an additive functional $\mathfrak{f}$ of the Brownian sample path as described in seition 1, interpreting 1.1 to mean

3.1 $\quad \mathfrak{f}(t, w)$ *is measurable* $\boldsymbol{B}_t$ *for each* $t \geq 0$.

The purpose of this section is *to associate with* $\mathfrak{f}$ *a unique non-negative measure* e *such that, for each bounded open* $D \subset R^d$,

3.2 $\quad 1 - p_\alpha = \alpha \int G p_\alpha de \qquad p_\alpha = E.[e^{-\alpha \mathfrak{f}(\mathfrak{m}_{\partial D})}],\ \alpha > 0,$

where G is the Green funetion of D and the integral is extended over D; *it will follow from* 3.2 *that* e *is smooth.*

Ccnsider, for this purpose, the additive functional

3.3 $\quad \mathfrak{f}_\alpha(t) = \int_0^{t \wedge \mathfrak{m}_{\partial D}} p_\alpha(x(s)) \mathfrak{f}(ds) \qquad t \geq 0,$

and let us begin with the following simple lemmas:

a) $1 - p_\alpha$ *is the potential of a non-negative measure* αe_α.

b) $E.[\mathfrak{f}_\alpha(\mathfrak{m}_{\partial D})] < +\infty$.

c) $\mathfrak{f}_\alpha \uparrow \mathfrak{f}$ *as* $\alpha \downarrow 0$.

d) $1 - p_\alpha = \alpha E.[\mathfrak{f}(\mathfrak{m}_{\partial D})] = \alpha \int G de_\alpha$.

e) $E.\left[\int_0^{\mathfrak{m}_{\partial D}} f(x(s)) \mathfrak{f}_\alpha(ds)\right] = \int G f de_\alpha$ *if* $f \geq 0$ *is a Borel function.*

f) *$p_\alpha^{-1}e_\alpha(db) = e(db)$ is independent of α and of D.*
g) *e is unique.*

Because

3.3 $$E_\cdot(1-p_\alpha(x(t)), t<\mathfrak{m}_{\partial D}) = E_\cdot(1-e^{-\alpha[\mathfrak{f}(\mathfrak{m}_{\partial D})-\mathfrak{f}(t)]}, t<\mathfrak{m}_{\partial D}) \\ \uparrow 1-p_\alpha \qquad t\downarrow 0,$$

$1-p_\alpha$ is excessive; it is, in fact, a potential thanks to

3.4 $$\int_{\partial \dot D} h_{\partial \dot D}(a, db)[1-p_\alpha] = E_a(1-e^{-\alpha[\mathfrak{f}(\mathfrak{m}_{\partial D})-\mathfrak{f}(\mathfrak{m}_{\partial \dot D})]})\downarrow 0 \qquad \dot D\uparrow D,$$

and this completes the proof of a). As to b), p_α is continuous on the Brownian path because of 1, and, since $\mathfrak{f}$ is continuous, b) follows on letting $n\uparrow +\infty$ in

3.5 $$1-p_\alpha = E_\cdot\Big[\int_0^{\mathfrak{m}_{\partial D}} e^{-\alpha[\mathfrak{f}(\mathfrak{m}_{\partial D})-\mathfrak{f}(t)]}\mathfrak{f}(dt)\Big] \\ \geq \alpha E_\cdot\Big[\sum_{k2^{-n}<\mathfrak{m}_{\partial D}} e^{-\alpha\mathfrak{f}(\mathfrak{m}_{\partial D}(w_{k2^{-n}}^+), w_{k2^{-n}}^+)}e^{-\alpha\mathfrak{f}(I_k)}\mathfrak{f}(I_k)\Big] \\ I_k = [(k-1)2^{-n}, k2^{-n}) \\ = \alpha E_\cdot\Big[\sum_{k2^{-n}<\mathfrak{m}_{\partial D}} p_\alpha(x(k2^{-n}))e^{-\alpha\mathfrak{f}(I_k)}\mathfrak{f}(I_k)\Big].$$

Because of c), which is obvious,

3.6 $$\alpha^{-1}(1-p_\alpha) = \lim_{\varepsilon\downarrow 0} E_\cdot\Big[\int_0^{\mathfrak{m}_{\partial D}} e^{-\alpha[\mathfrak{f}(\mathfrak{m}_{\partial D})-\mathfrak{f}(t)]}\mathfrak{f}_\varepsilon(dt)\Big],$$

and, using the method of 3.5 and $E_\cdot[\mathfrak{f}_\varepsilon(\mathfrak{m}_{\partial D})]<+\infty$, it appears that

3.7 $$\alpha^{-1}(1-p_\alpha) = \lim_{\varepsilon\downarrow 0} E_\cdot\Big[\int_0^{\mathfrak{m}_{\partial D}} p_\alpha(x(t))\mathfrak{f}_\varepsilon(dt)\Big] = E_\cdot\Big[\int_0^{\mathfrak{m}_{\partial D}} p_\alpha d\mathfrak{f}\Big]$$

proving d).

K. Itô (private communication) pointed out the following neat method for proving e). Choose closed $B\subset D$ such that $e_\alpha(\partial B)=0$ and let e_1 and e_2 be the charge distributions of the potentials $p_1=E_\cdot\Big[\int_0^{\mathfrak{m}_{\partial D}} f d\mathfrak{f}_\alpha\Big]$ and $p_2=E_\cdot\Big[\int_0^{\mathfrak{m}_{\partial D}}(1-f)d\mathfrak{f}_\alpha\Big]$, in which f is the indicator function of B. Because p_1 is harmonic *outside* B and differs from $\alpha^{-1}(1-p_\alpha)=E_\cdot[\mathfrak{f}_\alpha(\mathfrak{m}_{\partial D})]$ by a harmonic function *inside* B, e_1 is not smaller than the restriction of e_α to B, and, for the same reasons, e_2 is not smaller than the restriction of e_α to $D-B$. But $p_1+p_2=\alpha^{-1}(1-p_\alpha)$, whence

3.8 $$p_1 = E.\left[\int_0^{\mathfrak{m}_{\partial D}} f d\mathfrak{f}_\alpha\right] = \int_B G de_\alpha ,$$

and since such figures B generate the class of Borel subsets of D, e) follows.

As to f), $p_\alpha > 0$ because $\mathfrak{f}(\mathfrak{m}_{\partial D}) < +\infty$, and, choosing $0<\beta<\alpha$, e) implies

3.9 $$\int G de_\alpha = E.\left[\int_0^{\mathfrak{m}_{\partial D}} p_\alpha / p_\beta d\mathfrak{f}_\beta\right] = \int G p_\alpha / p_\beta de_\beta ,$$

i.e., $de \equiv p_\alpha^{-1} de_\alpha$ is indeqendent of α; it is also independent of D because if $\dot{D} \supset D$ and if $p_\alpha \equiv 0$ outside D, then, with an obvious notation,

3.10 $$\begin{aligned}\int G p_\alpha \dot{p}_\beta de &= E.\left[\int_0^{\mathfrak{m}_{\partial D}} p_\alpha d\dot{\mathfrak{f}}_\beta\right] \\ &= E.\left[\int_0^{\mathfrak{m}_{\partial \dot{D}}} p_\alpha d\dot{\mathfrak{f}}_\beta\right] - E.\left[\int_{\mathfrak{m}_{\partial D}}^{\mathfrak{m}_{\partial \dot{D}}} p_\alpha d\dot{\mathfrak{f}}_\beta\right] \\ &= \int \dot{G} p_\alpha \dot{p}_\beta d\dot{e} - \int dh_{\partial D} \int \dot{G} p_\alpha \dot{p}_\beta d\dot{e} \\ &= \int G \dot{p}_\alpha p_\beta d\dot{e} .\end{aligned}$$

g) is immediate from 3.2.

To establish the *smoothness* of e, take bounded open D and put $B_n = D \cap (p_1 \geq n^{-1})$. Because $1-p_1$ is a potential, B_n is closed in D and increases to D as $n \uparrow +\infty$; moreover, according to 3.2,

3.11 $$\int_{B_n} G de \leq n \int G p_1 de = n(1-p_1) \leq n ,$$

which is 1.8a, and, since, along the Brownian path, $0<p_1$ is continuous and tends to 1 ($t \uparrow \mathfrak{m}_{\partial D}$),

3.12 $$\begin{aligned}&P.[\inf (t: x(t) \notin B_n) < \mathfrak{m}_{\partial D}] \\ &= P.[\inf_{t<\mathfrak{m}_{\partial D}} p_1(x(t)) < n^{-1}] \downarrow 0 \qquad n \uparrow +\infty ,\end{aligned}$$

which verifies 1.8b.

4. UNIQUENESS.

The following simple lemma is useful in later sections: *two additive functionals* $\mathfrak{f}_1$ and $\mathfrak{f}_2$ *with the same bounded mean*

4.1 $$p = E_{\cdot}[\mathfrak{f}(\mathfrak{m}_{\partial D})] = \lim_{\varepsilon \downarrow 0} \varepsilon^{-1}(1-p_\varepsilon) = \int G de \qquad \mathfrak{f} = \mathfrak{f}_1, \mathfrak{f}_2$$

are the same for $t \leq \mathfrak{m}_{\partial D}$.

An argument similar to 3.5 implies

4.2 $$E_{\cdot}\left(\int_0^{\mathfrak{m}_{\partial D}} [\mathfrak{f}_i(\mathfrak{m}_{\partial D}) - \mathfrak{f}_i(t)]\mathfrak{f}_k(dt)\right) = E_{\cdot}\left(\int_0^{\mathfrak{m}_{\partial D}} p d\mathfrak{f}_k\right) = \int G p de \leq \|p\|_\infty^2 < +\infty;$$

thus, putting $\mathfrak{f} = \mathfrak{f}_2 - \mathfrak{f}_1$,

4.3 $$E_{\cdot}[\mathfrak{f}(\mathfrak{m}_{\partial D})^2] = 2E_{\cdot}\left[\int_0^{\mathfrak{m}_{\partial D}} [\mathfrak{f}(\mathfrak{m}_{\partial D}) - \mathfrak{f}(t)]\mathfrak{f}(dt)\right] = 0,$$

and hence

4.4 $$0 = E_{\cdot}[\mathfrak{f}(\mathfrak{m}_{\partial D}) \mid \boldsymbol{B}_{t \wedge \mathfrak{m}_{\partial D}+}] = E_{\cdot}[\mathfrak{f}(\mathfrak{m}_{\partial D}) - \mathfrak{f}(t) \mid \boldsymbol{B}_{t \wedge \mathfrak{m}_{\partial D}+}] + \mathfrak{f}(t) = \mathfrak{f}(t) \qquad t \leq \mathfrak{m}_{\partial D}$$

as desired.

It is a simple matter to deduce from this that *two additive functionals with the same associated measure are the same*; indeed, the difference p of two solutions of 3.2 satisfies $-p = \alpha \int G p de$, which implies

4.5 $$0 \geq -\int p^2 de = \mathfrak{E}(pde) = \int G p de p de,$$

and it follows that two additive functionals with the same associated measure have the same p_α, hence the same $\alpha^{-1}(1-p_\alpha) = E_{\cdot}[\mathfrak{f}_\alpha(\mathfrak{m}_{\partial D})]$ ($< \alpha^{-1} < +\infty$), and hence the same $\mathfrak{f}_\alpha$. But this means that the two functionals are the same up to time $\mathfrak{m}_{\partial D}$, and, to finish the proof, it is enough to make D swell out to R^d.

5. CONSTRUCTION OF AN ADDITIVE FUNCTIONAL FROM ITS ASSOCIATED MEASURE.

Given a *smooth* non-negative measure e, *our task is to find an additive functional* $\mathfrak{f}$ *with* e *as its associated measure.*

Consider, for this purpose, a non-negative measure e on a bounded open figure D with *bounded potential* $p=\int Gde$ and *finite energy* $\mathfrak{E}(e)=\int Gdede$, let p_n be the potential $\int Gf_n db$ of

5.1 $\qquad f_n = n(p-E.[p(x(n^{-1})), n^{-1}<\mathfrak{m}_{\partial D}])$,

let

5.2 $\qquad \mathfrak{f}_n(t) = \int_0^{t\wedge\mathfrak{m}_{\partial D}} f_n(x(s))ds$,

and let us construct a functional $\mathfrak{f}$ associated with e as a limit of $\mathfrak{f}_n$ with the aid of the following simple lemmas:

a) p *is a Brownian excessive function*; *esp.* $0\leq f_n$.

b) $E.[p(x(t)), t<\mathfrak{m}_{\partial D}]\downarrow 0$ *inside* D *as* $t\uparrow+\infty$.

c) $p_n = n\int_0^{n^{-1}} E.[p(x(t)), t<\mathfrak{m}_{\partial D}]dt$ *increases to* p *inside* D *as* $n\uparrow+\infty$.

d) $\lim_{n\uparrow+\infty}\mathfrak{E}(e-f_n db) = 0$, *where* $\mathfrak{E}$ *is the energy* $\mathfrak{E}(e)\equiv\int Gdede$.

e) $E.[\mathfrak{f}_n(+\infty)\,|\,\boldsymbol{B}_{t\wedge\mathfrak{m}_{\partial D}+}]\equiv\mathfrak{l}_n(t)$
$= p_n(x(t))+\mathfrak{f}_n(t) \qquad \mathfrak{m}_{\partial D}>t\geq 0$
$= \mathfrak{f}_n(\mathfrak{m}_{\partial D}) \qquad \mathfrak{m}_{\partial D}\leq t$,
i.e., $\mathfrak{l}_n$ *is a martingate with respect to the fields* $\boldsymbol{B}_{t\wedge\mathfrak{m}_{\partial D}+}$; *moreover*, $\mathfrak{l}_n$ *is continuous in* t.

f) $P.[\max_{t\geq 0}|\mathfrak{l}_n(t, w_s^+)-\mathfrak{l}_m(t, w_s^+)|>\varepsilon]$
$\leq \textit{constant}\times\varepsilon^{-2}s^{-d/2}\sqrt{\mathfrak{E}(f_n db-f_m db)}$.

g) $P.[\lim_{n\uparrow+\infty}\mathfrak{f}_n(t, w_s^+) = \mathfrak{f}(t, w_s^+), t\geq s>0] = 1$.
where the limit is taken as $n\uparrow+\infty$ *via suitable* $n_1<n_2<$ *etc.*, $\mathfrak{f}(t)$ *is continuous*, $\mathfrak{f}(0)\equiv\mathfrak{f}(0+)=0$, *and* $\mathfrak{f}(t)=\mathfrak{f}(s)+\mathfrak{f}(t-s, w_s^+)$ $(\mathfrak{m}_{\partial D}\geq t\geq s)$.

h) $E.[\mathfrak{f}(\mathfrak{m}_{\partial D})]=p$.

Because p is a potential, it is excessive; a) is obvious from this, b) is obvious from the bound

5.3 $E_\cdot[p(x(t)), t < \mathfrak{m}_{\partial D}] \leq \|p\|_\infty P_\cdot(t < \mathfrak{m}_{\partial D}) \downarrow 0 \qquad t \uparrow +\infty,$

and c) follows from b):

5.4 $$p_n = E_\cdot\left[\int_0^{\mathfrak{m}_{\partial D}} f_n(x(s))ds\right]$$
$$= n\int_0^{+\infty} dsE_\cdot[p(x(s)) - E_{x(s)}[p(x(n^{-1})), n^{-1} < m_{\partial D}], s < \mathfrak{m}_{\partial D}]$$
$$= n\int_0^{+\infty} ds[E_\cdot[p(x(s)), s < \mathfrak{m}_{\partial D}] - E_\cdot[p(x(s+n^{-1})), s+n^{-1} < \mathfrak{m}_{\partial D}]]$$
$$= n\int_0^{n^{-1}} E_\cdot[p(x(s)), s < \mathfrak{m}_{\partial D}]ds \uparrow p \qquad n \uparrow +\infty.$$

An application of c) establishes

5.5 $$\mathfrak{E}(e) = \int pde \geq \int p_n de = \int pf_n db \geq \mathfrak{E}(f_n db) \uparrow \mathfrak{E}(e) \qquad n \uparrow +\infty,$$

and this implies d):

5.6 $$\lim_{n\uparrow+\infty} \mathfrak{E}(e - f_n db) = \lim_{n\uparrow+\infty} [\mathfrak{E}(e) - 2\int p_n de + \mathfrak{E}(f_n db)] = 0.$$

Because $t \wedge \mathfrak{m}_{\partial D}$ is a Markov time,

5.7 $$E_\cdot[\mathfrak{f}_n(\mathfrak{m}_{\partial D}) \mid B_{t\wedge \mathfrak{m}_{\partial D}+}] = E_\cdot\left[\int_{t\wedge\mathfrak{m}_{\partial D}}^{\mathfrak{m}_{\partial D}} f_n(x(s))ds \mid B_{t\wedge\mathfrak{m}_{\partial D}+}\right] + \mathfrak{f}_n(t)$$
$$= E_{x(t\wedge\mathfrak{m}_{\partial D})}\left[\int_0^{\mathfrak{m}_{\partial D}} f_n ds\right] + \mathfrak{f}_n(t) = p_n(x(t)) + \mathfrak{f}_n(t) \equiv \mathfrak{l}_n(t) \quad t < \mathfrak{m}_{\partial D},$$

i.e., $\mathfrak{l}_n$ is martingale, and since p_n is continuous and tends to 0 along the Brownian path $(t \uparrow \mathfrak{m}_{\partial D})$, $\mathfrak{l}_n$ is continuous. e) is now established, and f) follows from Doob's submartingale extension of Kolmogorov's inequality [4], the Schwarz inequality

5.8 $$\left(\int G de_1 de_2\right)^2 \leq \mathfrak{E}(e_1)\mathfrak{E}(e_2)$$

(see H. Cartan [2]), and the resulting

5.9 $$E_\cdot[\,|\mathfrak{l}_n(+\infty, w_s^+) - \mathfrak{l}_m(+\infty, w_s^+)|^2, s < \mathfrak{m}_{\partial D}]$$
$$\leq E_\cdot[E_{x(s)}[\,|\mathfrak{f}_n(\mathfrak{m}_{\partial D}) - \mathfrak{f}_m(\mathfrak{m}_{\partial D})|^2], s < \mathfrak{m}_{\partial D}]$$
$$\leq E_\cdot\left[\int G(x(s), b)(f_n - f_m)(p_n - p_m)db, s < \mathfrak{m}_{\partial D}\right]$$

$$= \iint G(a, b) e_{nm}(da) E_\bullet[G(x(s), b), s < \mathfrak{m}_{\partial D}] e_{nm}(db)$$

$$e_{nm}(db) = (f_n - f_m) db$$

$$\leq \mathfrak{E}(e_{nm})^{1/2} \mathfrak{E}(E_\bullet[G(x(s), b), s < \mathfrak{m}_{\partial D}] de_{nm})^{1/2}$$

$$\leq \mathfrak{E}(e_{nm})^{1/2} \textit{ constant } \times s^{-d/2} \mathfrak{E}(e_{nm})^{1/2}.$$

Choose $n_1 < n_2 <$ etc. so as to make $P_\bullet[\max_{t \geq 0} |\mathfrak{l}_n(t, w_s^+) - \mathfrak{l}_s(t)| \downarrow 0, s > 0] = 1$, where $\mathfrak{l}_s$ is a continuous function of t. Because $p = \lim_{n \uparrow \infty +} p_n$ is continuous and tends to 0 along the Brownian path ($t \uparrow \mathfrak{m}_{\partial D}$), it follows that $\mathfrak{f}_s(t) = \lim_{n \uparrow +\infty} \mathfrak{f}_n(t, w_s^+)$ is continuous ($t \geq 0$) and additive ($t \leq \mathfrak{m}_{\partial D}(w_s^+)$); moreover

5.10 $$E_\bullet[\mathfrak{f}_n(+\infty)^2] = 2 \int G p_n f_n db \leq 2 \|p\|_\infty^2 < +\infty$$

implies

5.11 $$E_\bullet[\mathfrak{f}_s(t-s)] = \lim_{n \uparrow +\infty} E_\bullet[\mathfrak{f}_n(+\infty, w_s^+) - \mathfrak{f}_n(+\infty, w_t^+)]$$
$$= \lim_{n \uparrow +\infty} [E_\bullet(p_n(x(s)), s < \mathfrak{m}_{\partial D}) - E_\bullet(p_n(x(t)), t < \mathfrak{m}_{\partial D})]$$
$$= E_\bullet(p(x(s)), s < \mathfrak{m}_{\partial D}) - E_\bullet(p(x(t)), t < \mathfrak{m}_{\partial D}),$$

and, to finish the proof of g) and h), it is enough to define

5.12 $$\mathfrak{f}(t) = \lim_{s \downarrow 0} \mathfrak{f}_s(t)$$

and to make $s \downarrow 0$ and $t \uparrow +\infty$ in 5.11.

Now take a smooth measure e, choose $B_n \uparrow D$ as needed for 1.8 with the additional property that $e|B_n$ has *finite energy* $\mathfrak{E}(e|B_n) = \int_{B_n \times B_n} G de de$[6], let $\mathfrak{f}_n$ be the additive functional associated with $e|B_n$ as in 5.12 above, and note that

5.13 $$E_\bullet\left[\int_0^{\mathfrak{m}_{\partial D}} f d\mathfrak{f}_n\right] = \int_{B_n} G f de \qquad f \geq 0$$

as in e) of section 3. It follows that if f is the indicator function

---

6 $\mathfrak{E}(e|B_n) < +\infty$ is achieved as follows: take $\dot{D} \supset D$ with $\partial \dot{D}$ at a positive distance from ∂D, choose $\dot{B}_n \uparrow \dot{D}$ as needed for 1.8, and let $B_n = \dot{B}_n \cap D$; then $\mathfrak{E}(e|B_n) \leq \int_{B_n} de \int_{B_n} \dot{G} de \leq n e(B_n) \leq n (\inf_{D \times D} \dot{G})^{-1} \sup_D \int_{B_n} \dot{G} de \leq n^2 (\inf_{D \times D} \dot{G})^{-1} < +\infty$.

of B_m, then the functionals $\int_0^t f d\mathfrak{f}_n$ $(n>m)$ and $\int_0^t f d\mathfrak{f}_m$ have the same (bounded) mean:

5. 14 $$E_{\cdot}\left[\int_0^{\mathfrak{m}_{\partial D}} f d\mathfrak{f}_n\right] = E_{\cdot}\left[\int_0^{\mathfrak{m}_{\partial D}} f d\mathfrak{f}_m\right] = \int_{B_m} G d e$$

and are therefore identical up to time $\mathfrak{m}_{\partial D}$ according to the first uniqueness lemma for additive functionals of section 4. But this means that $\mathfrak{f}_n = \mathfrak{f}_m$ up to the exit time from B_m, and since this exit time $= \mathfrak{m}_{\partial D}$ for large m, it is legitimate to define a functional $\mathfrak{f}$ for $t \leq \mathfrak{m}_{\partial D}$ by means of

5. 15 $$\mathfrak{f}(t) = \mathfrak{f}_n(t) \qquad t \leq \inf(t: x(t) \notin B_n), \; n \geq 1.$$

Introducing $p_\alpha = E_{\cdot}[e^{-\alpha \mathfrak{f}(\mathfrak{m}_{\partial D})}]$ and using the method of 3. 5, 5. 13 implies

5. 16 $$1 - p_\alpha = \lim_{n \uparrow +\infty} \alpha E_{\cdot}\left[\int_0^{\mathfrak{m}_{\partial D}} e^{-\alpha[\mathfrak{f}(\mathfrak{m}_{\partial D}) - \mathfrak{f}(t)]} \mathfrak{f}_n(dt)\right]$$
$$= \lim_{n \uparrow +\infty} \alpha E_{\cdot}\left[\int_0^{\mathfrak{m}_{\partial D}} p_\alpha d\mathfrak{f}_n\right] = \lim_{n \uparrow +\infty} \alpha \int_{B_n} G p_\alpha d e = \alpha \int G p_\alpha d e;$$

in brief, e is the measure associated with $\mathfrak{f}$ as in 3. 2.

Because two additive functionals with same associated measure are the same, it follows that if e is smooth and if $D_1 \subset D_2 \subset$ *etc.* swell out to R^d, then the functionals $\mathfrak{f}_n$ associated with $e_n = e \mid D_n$ as in 5. 15 above determine an additive functional

5. 17 $$\mathfrak{f}(t) = \mathfrak{f}_n(t) \qquad t < \mathfrak{m}_{\partial D_n}, \; n \geq 1$$

depending upon e alone, for which 3. 2 holds for each D.

$\mathfrak{f}$ is additive for *almost all* Brownian paths, but of course it can be modified on a negligeable class of paths so as to be Borel in the pair (t, w) and to satisfy 1. 1, 1. 2, 1. 3, 1. 4, as *identities*; with *this modification, $\mathfrak{f}$ is the additive functional associated with e.*

6. DIFFUSIONS WITH BROWNIAN HITTING PROBABILITIES.

To avoid confusion, let w, x, $\mathfrak{m}$, B, $\boldsymbol{B}$, $\boldsymbol{B}_{\mathfrak{m}+}$, *etc.* be used to describe the Brownian motion, introduce the same paths, times, events, and fields with the new names $\dot{w}$, $\dot{x}$, $\dot{\mathfrak{m}}$, $\dot{B}$, $\dot{\boldsymbol{B}}$, $\dot{\boldsymbol{B}}_{\dot{\mathfrak{m}}+}$, *etc.*, and take a *new motion* $\dot{\boldsymbol{D}}$ with probabilities $\dot{P}_a(\dot{B})$.

$\dot{D}$ is said to be a *diffusion* if it *starts afresh* at each Markov time $\dot{\mathfrak{m}}$:

6.1 $\dot{P}_a[\dot{w}^+_{\dot{\mathfrak{m}}} \in \dot{B} \mid \dot{\boldsymbol{B}}_{\dot{\mathfrak{m}}+}] = \dot{P}_b(\dot{B}) \qquad a \in E^d,\ \dot{B} \in \dot{\boldsymbol{B}},\ b \equiv \dot{x}(\dot{\mathfrak{m}})$;

it is said to have Brownian *hitting probabilities* if, for each bounded open D,

6.2 $\dot{P}_a[\dot{x}(\dot{m}_{\partial D}) \in db] = P_a[x(\mathfrak{m}_{\partial D}) \in db] = h_{\partial D}(a, db)$

$a \in D,\ db \subset \partial D$.

Given such a diffusion with Brownian hitting probabilities

6.3a $\dot{p}_\alpha \equiv \dot{E}_\bullet[e^{-\alpha \dot{\mathfrak{m}}_{\partial D}}]$ [7]

solves

6.3b $1 - \dot{p}_\alpha = \alpha \int G \dot{p}_\alpha de$,

where $e \geq 0$ is independent of α and of D. e is the so-called *speed measure* of the diffusion; the speed measure of the Brownian motion is the Lebesgue measure db. Because of 6.2, $\dot{P}_\bullet[\dot{\mathfrak{m}}_{\partial D} < +\infty] = 1$ and $\dot{p}_\alpha > 0$, which implies that *e is smooth, i.e., that it is the associated measure of some additive functional $\mathfrak{f}$* of the Brownian path; moreover, *e is positive on the neighborhoods of H. Cartan's fine topology, and this implies that its associated additive functional satisfies*

6.4 $P_\bullet[\mathfrak{f}(s) < \mathfrak{f}(t),\ 0 \leq s < t] = 1$.

Introducing the *inverse function* $\mathfrak{f}^{-1}$ of $\mathfrak{f}$, it turns out that

6.5 $\dot{P}_\bullet(\dot{B}) = P_\bullet[x(\mathfrak{f}^{-1}) \in \dot{B}] \qquad \dot{B} \in \dot{\boldsymbol{B}}$;

in brief, $\dot{D}$ is identical in law to the Brownian motion run with the stochastic clock $\mathfrak{f}^{-1}$; moreover, *each smooth measure e, positive on fine neighborhoods, is the speed measure of a diffusion with Brownian hits.*

The proofs are carried out in the next few sections.

---

[7] $\dot{E}_\bullet(f) = \int f d\dot{P}_\bullet$.

7. SPEED MEASURES

Beginning with the speed measure e of 6.3b, if a $a \in R^d$ and if $\mathfrak{m}_\varepsilon = \min(t : |\dot{x}(t) - a| \geq \varepsilon)$, then $\mathfrak{m}_{0+} = \lim_{\varepsilon \downarrow 0} \mathfrak{m}_\varepsilon$ satisfies

$$7.1 \qquad \dot{E}_a(e^{-\mathfrak{m}_{0+}}) = \dot{E}_a[e^{-\mathfrak{m} - \mathfrak{m}(w^+_{\mathfrak{m}})}] = \dot{E}_a(e^{-\mathfrak{m}_{0+}})^2, \qquad \mathfrak{m} = \mathfrak{m}_{0+}$$

and since $\dot{E}_a(e^{-\mathfrak{m}_{0+}}) = 0$ implies $\dot{P}_a[\mathfrak{m}_{0+} = +\infty] = 1$, violating the fact that the dot motion has Brownian hitting probabilities, it follows that $\dot{P}_a[\mathfrak{m}_{0+} = 0] = 1$.

Because

$$7.2 \qquad 1 - \dot{p}_\alpha = \alpha \dot{E}.\left[\int_0^{\mathfrak{m}_{\partial D}} e^{-\alpha(\mathfrak{m}_{\partial D} - t)}\, dt\right] = \alpha \dot{E}.\left[\int_0^{\mathfrak{m}_{\partial D}} \dot{p}_\alpha(x(t))dt\right],$$

$1 - \dot{p}_\alpha$ satisfies

$$7.3 \qquad 1 - \dot{p}_\alpha(a) \geq \alpha \dot{E}_a\left[\int_{\mathfrak{m}_{\partial \dot{D}}}^{\mathfrak{m}_{\partial D}} \dot{p}_\alpha dt\right] = \int h_{\partial \dot{D}}(a, db)(1 - \dot{p}_\alpha) \qquad a \in \dot{D} \subset D,$$

and, using 7.3 and $\dot{P}_a[\mathfrak{m}_{0+} = 0] = 1$ to establish

$$7.4\text{a} \qquad \int h_{\partial \dot{D}}(a, db)(1 - \dot{p}_\alpha) \downarrow 0 \qquad \dot{D} \uparrow D$$

$$7.4\text{b} \qquad \int h_{|b-a|=\varepsilon}(a, db)(1 - \dot{p}_\alpha) \uparrow 1 - \dot{p}_\alpha \qquad \varepsilon \downarrow 0,$$

it appears that $1 - \dot{p}_\alpha$ is the potential $\alpha \int G de_\alpha$ of a non-negative charge distribution αe_α

It remains to verify that $\dot{p}_\alpha^{-1} de_\alpha \equiv de$ is independent of α and of D, which is done with the aid of the additive functional $\dot{\mathfrak{f}}_\alpha(t) = \int_0^t \dot{p}_\alpha(\dot{x}(s))ds \ (t < \mathfrak{m}_{\partial D})$ and the method of section 3; in outline,

$$7.5 \qquad 1 - \dot{p}_\alpha = \alpha \dot{E}_\alpha[\dot{\mathfrak{f}}_\alpha(\mathfrak{m}_{\partial D})] = \alpha \int G de_\alpha$$

implies

$$7.6 \qquad \dot{E}\left[\int_0^{\mathfrak{m}_{\partial D}} f(\dot{x}(s))\dot{\mathfrak{f}}_\alpha(ds)\right] = \int G f de_\alpha$$

as in e) of section 3, and 3.9 follows as before, *etc.*.

8. TWO DIFFUSIONS WITH BROWNIAN HITS AND THE SAME SPEED MEASURE ARE THE SAME.

Consider a pair of diffusions with Brownian hitting probabilities and the *same* speed measure.

Because 6.3b=3.2 has unique solutions as noted in section 4, both diffusions have the same $\dot{p}_\alpha = \dot{E}_\cdot[e^{-\alpha \mathfrak{m}_{\partial D}}]$ and hence the same

8.1 $$\dot{G}_{0+}: f \to \dot{E}_\cdot\left[\int_0^{\mathfrak{m}_{\partial D}} f(\dot{x})\dot{\mathfrak{f}}_\varepsilon(dt)\right] = \int G f \dot{p}_\varepsilon de$$

$$\dot{\mathfrak{f}}_\varepsilon(t) \equiv \int_0^t \dot{p}_\varepsilon(\dot{x}(s))ds \qquad t \leq \mathfrak{m}_{\partial D}.$$

Choose $\varepsilon > 0$ and introduce the Green operators

8.2 $$\dot{G}_\alpha: f \to \dot{E}_\cdot\left[\int_0^{\mathfrak{m}_{\partial D}} e^{-\alpha \dot{\mathfrak{f}}_\varepsilon(t)} f(\dot{x})\dot{\mathfrak{f}}_\varepsilon(dt)\right] \qquad \alpha > 0;$$

then

8.3 $$\alpha \dot{G}_{0+}\dot{G}_\alpha f = \alpha \dot{E}_\cdot\left[\int_0^{\mathfrak{m}_{\partial D}} \dot{\mathfrak{f}}_\varepsilon(dt)(\dot{G}_\alpha f)(\dot{x})\right]$$

$$= \alpha \dot{E}_\cdot\left[\int_0^{\mathfrak{m}_{\partial D}} \dot{\mathfrak{f}}_\varepsilon(dt)\int_t^{\mathfrak{m}_{\partial D}} e^{-\alpha[\dot{\mathfrak{f}}_\varepsilon(s)-\dot{\mathfrak{f}}_\varepsilon(t)]} f(\dot{x}(s))\dot{\mathfrak{f}}_\varepsilon(ds)\right]$$

$$= \alpha \dot{E}_\cdot\left[\int_0^{\mathfrak{m}_{\partial D}} e^{-\alpha \dot{\mathfrak{f}}_\varepsilon(s)} f(\dot{x})\dot{\mathfrak{f}}_\varepsilon(ds)\int_0^s e^{\alpha \dot{\mathfrak{f}}_\varepsilon} d\dot{\mathfrak{f}}_\varepsilon\right]$$

$$= \dot{E}_\cdot\left[\int_0^{\mathfrak{m}_{\partial D}} (1-e^{-\alpha \dot{\mathfrak{f}}_\varepsilon}) f d\dot{\mathfrak{f}}_\varepsilon\right] = \dot{G}_{0+}f - \dot{G}_\alpha f,$$

i.e.,

8.4 $$\dot{G}_\alpha = \dot{G}_{0+} - \alpha \dot{G}_{0+}\dot{G}_\alpha,$$

and, using the bound

8.5 $$\dot{G}_{0+}1 = \int G\dot{p}_\varepsilon de = \varepsilon^{-1}(1-\dot{p}_\varepsilon) \leq \varepsilon^{-1} < +\infty,$$

the obvious iteration of 8.4 implies

8.6 $$\dot{G}_\alpha = \sum_{n \geq 0} (-)^n \alpha^n \dot{G}_{0+}^{n+1} \qquad \alpha < \varepsilon.$$

Because $\dot{G}_\alpha$ is a Laplace transform in its dependence on α, 8.6 implies that both diffusions have the same Green operators ($\alpha \geq 0$) and hence the same

8.7 $$\dot{E}_\cdot\left[\int_0^{\mathfrak{m}_\infty} e^{-\alpha t} f(\dot{x})dt\right] = \lim_{D \uparrow R^d} \lim_{\varepsilon \downarrow 0} \dot{G}_\alpha f.$$

But this implies that both diffusions have the same

8.8 $$\dot{P}_a[\dot{x}(t) \in db,\, t < \mathfrak{m}_\infty] \qquad (t, a, b) \in (0, +\infty) \times R^{2d}$$

and hence are the same in all respects as stated in the section title.

9. SPEED MEASURES ARE POSITIVE ON FINE NEIGHBORHOODS.

Given a point a of bounded open D and a (Brownian) excessive function p on D, the set of points $b \in D$ at which $|p(b)-p(a)|<n^{-1}$ is said to be a *fine neighborhood* of a; the corresponding topology is called the *fine topology of H. Cartan* [2]. E. B. Dynkin [7] has pointed out that a point a is in the fine interior of $B \subset R^d$ if and only if almost all Brownian paths starting at a remain in B for some positive time. Because an excessive function in 1-dimension is concave and hence continuous, the 1-dimensional *fine* topology is the same as the usual one; in higher dimensions it is different.

Given a diffusion with Brownian hitting probabilities, *its speed measure e has to be positive on fine neighborhoods*; for the proof, it is enough to verify that if $Z \subset R^d$ is bounded and Borel and if $e(Z)=0$, then Z has no fine interior.

Choose an open ball D and a decreasing series of open figures D_n so as to have

9.1a $\quad D \supset D_1 \supset D_2 \supset etc. \supset Z$

9.1b $\quad \int_{D_n} G_D \dot{p}_1 de \downarrow 0 \qquad n \uparrow +\infty, \ \dot{p}_1 = \dot{E}.[e^{-\mathfrak{m}_{\partial D}}],$

and let

9.2 $\quad \mathfrak{f}_1(t) = \int_0^t \dot{p}_1(\dot{x}(s))ds \qquad t \leq \mathfrak{m}_{\partial D}.$

Because of

9.3a $\quad 1-\dot{E}_a[e^{-\mathfrak{f}_1(\partial \mathfrak{m}_{D_n})}] = \int_{D_n} G_{D_n} \dot{p}_1 de \leq \int_{D_n} G_D \dot{p}_1 de \downarrow 0$

$$n \uparrow +\infty, \ a \in Z$$

9.3b $\quad \dot{p}_1 > 0,$

it is apparent that

9.4a
$$\begin{aligned} 1 &= \dot{P}_a[\mathfrak{m}_{\partial D_n} \downarrow 0, n \uparrow +\infty] \\ &= \dot{P}_a[\lim_{n\uparrow+\infty} \dot{x}(\mathfrak{m}_{\partial D_n}) = a] \\ &= \lim_{n\uparrow+\infty} \int h_{\partial D_n}(a, db)e^{-|b-a|} \qquad a \in Z. \end{aligned}$$

But this final expression depends upon the (Brownian) hitting probabilities $h_{\partial D}$ alone; thus,

9.4b $\quad P_a[\lim_{n\uparrow+\infty} x(\mathfrak{m}_{\partial D}) = a] = 1 \qquad a \in Z$

for the Brownian motion also, and since almost no Brownian path meets its starting point at a *positive* time, it follows that

9.5 $\quad P_a[\mathfrak{m}_{\partial D_n} \downarrow 0,\ n \uparrow +\infty] = 1 \qquad a \in Z$;

an application of Dynkin's description of fine neighborhoods completes the proof.

10. SPEED MEASURES GIVE RISE TO INCREASING ADDITIVE FUNCTIONALS.

Because the speed measure of a diffusion with Brownian hits is smooth, it has associated with it an additive functional $\mathfrak{f}$ of the Brownian path; moreover, e is positive on fine neighborhoods, and this is reflected in the fact that $\mathfrak{f}$ *is increasing as in* 6.4: $\mathfrak{f}(s) < \mathfrak{f}(t) (s < t)$.

It will be enough to verify that the set A of points a at which

10.1 $\quad P_a(\mathfrak{m} > 0) = P_a[\mathfrak{f}(t) = 0 \text{ for some } t > 0] = 1$
$\qquad \mathfrak{m} = \inf(t: f(t) > 0)$

is vaccuous; note that A is Borel and that $P_\cdot(\mathfrak{m} > 0) = 0$ or 1 according to Blumenthal's 01 law.

Because A is either *void* or *fine open* and e is positive on fine neighborhoods, it is enough to show that $e(A) = 0$, and, for this, it is enough to show that for each bounded open D, the points of D at which $P_\cdot[\mathfrak{f}(\mathfrak{m}_{\partial D}) > 0] < 1$ have e-mass 0. But this is immediate on letting $\alpha \uparrow +\infty$ in

10.2 $\quad \alpha^{-1}(1 - p_\alpha) = \int G p_\alpha de \qquad p_\alpha = E_\cdot[e^{-\alpha \mathfrak{f}(\mathfrak{m}_{\partial D})}]$.

11. WHEN IS $\mathfrak{f}(+\infty) = +\infty$?

In making up the stochastic clock $\mathfrak{f}^{-1}$ for use in 6.5, two cases arise according as $\mathfrak{f}(+\infty) = +\infty$ or not, and it is desirable to have a test for this.

Because $p \equiv P_\cdot[\mathfrak{f}(+\infty) < +\infty]$ satisfies

11. 1 $$p(a) = P_a[\mathfrak{f}(\mathfrak{m}_{\partial D}) < +\infty,\ \mathfrak{f}(+\infty, w^+_{\mathfrak{m}_{\partial D}}) < +\infty]$$
$$= E_a[p(x(\mathfrak{m}_{\partial D}))] = \int h_{\partial D}(a, db)p(b) \qquad a \in D$$

for bounded open D, it is harmonic and since $p \geq 0$, it must be constant; moreover, letting first t and then $n \uparrow +\infty$ in

11. 2 $$P.[\mathfrak{f}(+\infty) < n] \leq E.[\mathfrak{f}(t) < n,\ p(x(t))] \leq P.[\mathfrak{f}(t) < n]p\,,$$

it appears that $p \leq p^2$ and hence that $p = 0$ or 1.

Our test states that $p = 1$ *if and only if one of the following conditions is met*:

a) $d \geq 3$ *and* $1 - p_1 = \int G p_1 de$ *admits a solution* $0 < p_1 \leq 1$ *on the whole of* R^d, *where* G *is the function of* R^d.

b) $\mathfrak{G} p_1 = p_1$ *admits a solution* $0 < p_1 \leq 1$ *on the whole of* R^d, *where* $\mathfrak{G} p_1$ *is the negative of the Radon-Nikodym derivative of the Riesz measure of* p_1 *with respect to* e (see section 13 for the meaning of $\mathfrak{G}$).

c) $d \geq 3$ *and* $R^d = A \cup B$, *where* A *is thin at* ∞ *in the sense that* $P.[x(t) \in A$ *for some* $t > n] \downarrow 0$ $(n \uparrow \infty)$, *and* $\int_B G de < +\infty$.[8]

Beginning with $p = 1$, $p_1 \equiv E.[e^{-\mathfrak{f}(+\infty)}]$ is positive and ≤ 1, and, since $G_D \uparrow G$ as $D \uparrow R^d$,

11. 3 $$1 - p_1 = \lim_{D \uparrow R^d} E.[e^{-\mathfrak{f}(+\infty,\ w^+_{\mathfrak{m}_{\partial D}})}] - p_1$$
$$= \lim_{D \uparrow R^d} \int G_D p_1 de = \int G p_1 de\,.$$

Because $G \equiv +\infty$ in case $d = 2$, it follows that $p = 1$ implies a), that a) implies b) is clear, that c) implies $p = 1$ is evident from

11. 4 $$E.\left[\int_0^{+\infty} f d\mathfrak{f}\right] = \int_B G de < +\infty\,,$$

where f is the indicator function of B, and now it remains to verify that b) implies c).

But, if $0 < p_1 \leq 1$ is a solution of $\mathfrak{G} p_1 = p_1$ and if h_1 is its

---

[8] $A \subset R^d (d \geq 3)$ is thin at ∞ if and only if (Wiener's test) $\sum_{n \geq 1} 2^{-n(d-2)} C(A_n) < +\infty$, where A_n is the meet of A with the spherical $2^{n-1} \leq |b| < 2^n$ and C is the d-dimensional Newtonian capacity; for the proof in the case of the d-dimensional random walk, see K. Itô and H. P. McKean, Jr. [12].

harmonic part $E_\cdot[p_1(x(\mathfrak{m}_{\partial D}))]$ inside D, then $h_1 - p_1 = \int G_D p_1 de$ inside D, and, as $D \uparrow R^d$, h_1 decreases to a non-negative (and hence constant) harmonic function $p_1(\infty)$ such that $p_1(\infty) - p_1 = \int G p_1 de$. R^d is now split into $A = (p_1 < \frac{1}{2} p_1(\infty))$ and $B = (p_1 \geq \frac{1}{2} p_1(\infty))$ and the fact that $p_1(\infty) - p_1$ excessive is used to ensure that p_1 has a limit along the Brownian path as $t \uparrow +\infty$, permitting us to conclude from

11.4a $p_1 \leq p_1(\infty)$

11.4b $p_1(\infty) = \lim_{D \uparrow R^d} E_\cdot[p_1(x(\mathfrak{m}_{\partial D}))] = E_\cdot[\lim_{t \uparrow +\infty} p_1(x(t))]$

that A is thin at ∞. Because $0 < p_1(\infty)$,

11.5 $\int_B G de \leq 2 p_1(\infty)^{-1} \int G p_1 de < +\infty$,

and this completes the verification of c).

12. PERFORMING THE TIME SUBSTITUTION.

Coming to the actual time substitution $t \to \mathfrak{f}^{-1}$ which is supposed to send the Brownian motion into the diffusion $\dot{\boldsymbol{D}}$, let $\mathfrak{f}$ be modified on a negligeable class of Brownian paths so as to have

12.1 $0 = \mathfrak{f}(0) \leq \mathfrak{f}(t\pm) = \mathfrak{f}(t) < +\infty$

12.2 $\mathfrak{f}(t) = \mathfrak{f}(s) + \mathfrak{f}(t-s, w_s^+) \qquad t \geq s$

12.3 $\mathfrak{f}(t) > \mathfrak{f}(s) \qquad t > s$

as *identities*, let x^{-1} denote the sample path

12.4 $w^{-1}: t \to x^{-1}(t) \equiv x^{-1}(t, w^{-1}) \equiv x[\mathfrak{f}^{-1}(t, w), w]$,

note that this path is continuous even if $\mathfrak{f}(+\infty) < +\infty (d \geq 3)$, and let us check that *the motion* $\dot{\boldsymbol{D}}$ *with sample paths*

12.5a $\dot{w}: t \to \dot{x}(t)$

and probabilities

12.5b $\dot{P}_a(\dot{B}) \equiv P_a(w^{-1} \in \dot{B})$

is the diffusion with Brownian hitting probabilities and speed measure e.

Beginning with the proof of the *diffusive character* 6.1 of this motion, the problem is to check that if $\dot{\mathfrak{m}}$ is a Markov time and if$\dot{B} \in \dot{\boldsymbol{B}}$, then

12.6 $\dot{P}_a[\dot{w}^+_{\dot{\mathfrak{m}}} \in \dot{B} \mid \dot{\boldsymbol{B}}_{\dot{\mathfrak{m}}+}] = \dot{P}_b(\dot{B}) \qquad b \equiv \dot{x}(\dot{\mathfrak{m}})$.

Given such a Markov time $\dot{\mathfrak{m}}$,

12.7 $\mathfrak{m}(w) \equiv \mathfrak{f}^{-1}(\dot{\mathfrak{m}}(w^{-1}), w)$

is a Markov time for the Brownian path; indeed, using Galmarino's test, if

12.8a $\mathfrak{m}(u) < t$

12.8b $x(s, u) = x(s, v) \qquad s \leq t$,

then

12.9a $\mathfrak{f}(s, u) = \mathfrak{f}(s, v) \qquad s \leq t$

12.9b $\mathfrak{f}^{-1}(s, u) = \mathfrak{f}^{-1}(s, v) \leq t \qquad s \leq \dot{t} = \mathfrak{f}(t, u) = \mathfrak{f}(t, v)$,

and it follows that

12.10a $\dot{\mathfrak{m}}(u^{-1}) = \mathfrak{f}(\mathfrak{m}(u), u) < \mathfrak{f}(t, u) = \dot{t}$

12.10b $x^{-1}(s, u^{-1}) = x[\mathfrak{f}^{-1}(s, u), u] = x[\mathfrak{f}^{-1}(s, v), v]$

$= x^{-1}(s, v^{-1}) \qquad s \leq \dot{t}$.

Because $\dot{\mathfrak{m}}$ was a Markov time for the dot motion, 12.10 implies

12.11a $\dot{\mathfrak{m}}(u^{-1}) = \dot{\mathfrak{m}}(v^{-1}) < \dot{t}$,

and an application of 12.9b implies

12.11b $\mathfrak{m}(u) = \mathfrak{f}^{-1}(\dot{\mathfrak{m}}(u^{-1}), u) = \mathfrak{f}^{-1}(\mathfrak{m}(v^{-1}), v) = \mathfrak{m}(v)$;

in brief, 12.8 *implies*, 12.11b, as needed to conclude by Galmarino's test that $\mathfrak{m}$ is a Markov time.

Given $\dot{A} \in \dot{\boldsymbol{B}}_{\dot{\mathfrak{m}}+}$, if $A = (w: w^{-1} \in \dot{A})$ and if

12.12a $\mathfrak{m}(u) < t$

12.12b $x(s, u) = x(s, v) \qquad s \leq t$

12.12c $u \in A$,

then, using 12.10,

12.13a $\dot{\mathfrak{m}}(u^{-1}) < \dot{t}$

12.13b $x^{-1}(s, u^{-1}) = x^{-1}(x, v^{-1}) \qquad s \leq \dot{t}$

12.13c $u^{-1} \in A$,

and it follows that $v^{-1}\in\dot{A}$, or, what is the same, that $v\in A$; thus, by Galmarino's test, $A\in\boldsymbol{B}_{\mathfrak{m}+}$, and now it appears that

$$
\begin{aligned}
12.14\quad & \dot{P}_a[\dot{A},\ \dot{w}^+_{\dot{\mathfrak{m}}}\in\dot{B}] \\
&= P_a[w^{-1}\in\dot{A},\ (w^+_{\mathfrak{m}})^{-1}\in\dot{B}] \\
&= P_a[w\in A,\ (w^+_{\mathfrak{m}})^{-1}\in\dot{B}] \\
&= E_a[A,\ P_b(w^{-1}\in\dot{B})] \qquad b\equiv x(\mathfrak{m}) = x^{-1}(\dot{\mathfrak{m}}(w^{-1}),\ w^{-1}) \\
&= E_a[w^{-1}\in\dot{A},\ \dot{P}_b(\dot{B})] \\
&= \dot{E}_a[\dot{A},\ \dot{P}_b(\dot{B})] \qquad b = \dot{x}(\dot{\mathfrak{m}}),
\end{aligned}
$$

completing the proof of 12.6.

$\dot{\boldsymbol{D}}$ is now identified as a *diffusion*; that it has *Brownian hitting probabilities* is clear, and to complete the discussion, it suffices to verify that *it has e as its speed measure.* But this is clear because

$$12.15\qquad \mathfrak{m}^{-1}_{\partial D}\equiv\min(t: x^{-1}(t)\in\partial D) = \mathfrak{f}(\mathfrak{m}_{\partial D}),$$

and $\mathfrak{f}$ has e as its associated measure.

13. GENERATORS.

Given a diffusion with Brownian hitting probabilities, the *Green operators*

$$13.1\qquad \dot{G}_\alpha: f\to\dot{E}_\cdot\Big[\int_0^{+\infty}e^{-\alpha t}f(\dot{x})dt\Big]\qquad \alpha>0$$

map into itself the space $\dot{C}(E^d)$ of real, bounded, fine-continuous functions having ordinary limits at ∞ in case $d\geq 3$; in fact, if $d\geq 3$, then $\dot{P}_\cdot[\min_{t\geq 0}|\dot{x}(t)|\geq n] = P_\cdot[\min_{t\geq 0}|x(t)|\geq n]$ tends to 1 at ∞, so that $\dot{G}_\alpha f$ tends to $\alpha^{-1}f(\infty)$, and, if $a\in R^d$ $(d\geq 2)$ and if the ball $D\ni a$ is so small that $1-\dot{p}_\alpha(a) = 1-\dot{E}_\cdot[e^{-\alpha\dot{\mathfrak{m}}_{\partial D}}]<n^{-1}$, then, inside the *fine neighborhood* $B=D\cap(\dot{p}_\alpha>1-n^{-1})$, the difference between

$$
\begin{aligned}
13.2a\quad u &= \dot{G}_\alpha f \\
&= \dot{E}_\cdot\Big[\int_0^{\dot{\mathfrak{m}}_{\partial D}}e^{-\alpha t}f(\dot{x})dt + e^{-\alpha\dot{\mathfrak{m}}_{\partial D}}\int_0^{+\infty}e^{-\alpha t}f(\dot{x}(t,\ \dot{w}^+_{\dot{\mathfrak{m}}_{\partial D}}))dt\Big] \\
&= \dot{E}_\cdot\Big[\int_0^{\dot{\mathfrak{m}}_{\partial D}}e^{-\alpha t}f(\dot{x})dt + e^{-\alpha\dot{\mathfrak{m}}_{\partial D}}u(\dot{x}(\dot{\mathfrak{m}}_{\partial D}))\Big]
\end{aligned}
$$

and the harmonic (and hence continuous) function

13.2b $\quad h = \dot{E}_\cdot[u(\dot{x}(\mathfrak{m}_{\partial D}))]$

is not greater than

13.3 $\quad constant \times (1-\dot{p}_\alpha) < constant \times n^{-1}$.

Because

13.4 $\quad \dot{G}_\alpha - \dot{G}_\beta + (\alpha-\beta)\dot{G}_\alpha\dot{G}_\beta = 0 \qquad \alpha, \beta > 0$,

it is evident that $\dot{G}_\alpha$ maps our space of fine continuous functions onto some subspace $D(\dot{\mathfrak{G}})$ independent of α and that its null-space $\dot{G}_\alpha^{-1}(0)$ is likewise independent of α. But, for fine-continuous $f \in \dot{G}_\alpha^{-1}(0)$,

13.5 $\quad 0 = \lim_{\beta \uparrow +\infty} \beta \dot{G}_\beta f = \dot{E}_\cdot\left[\lim_{\beta\uparrow+\infty} \beta \int_0^{+\infty} e^{-\beta t} f(\dot{x})\,dt\right] = f$

according to E. B. Dynkin's description of fine neighborhoods; thus the null-space is trivial, $\dot{G}_\alpha$ is invertable, and another application of 13.4 verifies that $\dot{\mathfrak{G}} \equiv \alpha - \dot{G}_\alpha^{-1}$ acting on $D(\dot{\mathfrak{G}})$ is independent of α.

$\dot{\mathfrak{G}}$ is the so-called generator; it is *closed* in the sense that if $u_n \in D(\dot{\mathfrak{G}})$ and $\dot{\mathfrak{G}}u_n = f_n$ converge pointwise under fixed bounds to u and $f \in \dot{C}(E^d)$, then $u \in D(\dot{\mathfrak{G}})$ and $\dot{\mathfrak{G}}u = f$.

Consider the *differential operator*

13.6 $\quad \mathfrak{D}u = \dfrac{-e^u(db)}{e(db)} \qquad |b| < +\infty$

$\quad\quad = 0 \qquad b = \infty,\ d \geq 3$

acting on the class $D(\mathfrak{D})$ of functions $u \in \dot{C}(E^d)$ such that

a) *inside each D, u is the sum of the harmonic function* $h = \int h_{\partial D}(a, db)u(b)$ *and the potential* $\int G_D de^u$ *of its Riesz measure* e^u.

b) $\int G_D |de^u|$ *is bounded.*

c) $\mathfrak{D}u$, *as described in* 13.6, *exists and belongs to* $\dot{C}(E^d)$.

$\dot{\mathfrak{G}}$ *is the closure* $\overline{\mathfrak{D}}$ *of* $\mathfrak{D}$ *in the topology of bounded pointwise convergence* as will now be explained.

Choose a fine-continuous function $0 < p_n \leq 1$ tending to 0 at ∞ in the ordinary topology such that $\int G_D p_n de$ is bounded for each bounded open D and $p_n \uparrow 1$ as $n \uparrow +\infty$, and introduce the additive functional $\dot{\mathfrak{f}}_n = \int_0^t p_n(\dot{x})ds \ (t \geq 0)$.

$\dot{x}(\dot{\mathfrak{f}}_n^{-1})$ *is a diffusion with Brownian hitting probabilities and speed measure* $de_n = p_n \times de$,

$$13.7 \qquad \dot{E}_\cdot[\min(t : \dot{x}(\dot{\mathfrak{f}}_n^{-1}) \in \partial D)] = \dot{E}_\cdot[\dot{\mathfrak{f}}_n(\dot{\mathfrak{m}}_{\partial D})] = \int G_D p_n de < +\infty ,$$

and it follows from 13.2a that if u is in the domain of its generator $\dot{\mathfrak{G}}_n$, then

$$13.8 \qquad u = -\dot{E}_\cdot\left[\int_0^{\dot{\mathfrak{m}}_{\partial D}} (\dot{\mathfrak{G}}_n u)(\dot{x}(t))\dot{\mathfrak{f}}_n(dt)\right] + E_\cdot[u(\dot{x}\mathfrak{m}_{\partial D}))]$$

$$= -\int G_D(\dot{\mathfrak{G}}_n u) p_n de + \textit{a harmonic function},$$

which is a special case of a formula of E. B. Dynkin [6]; *in brief,*

$$13.9 \qquad -e^u(db) = (\dot{\mathfrak{G}}_n u) p_n de \qquad u \in D(\dot{\mathfrak{G}}_n) .$$

Choose $u = \dot{G}_1 f \in D(\dot{\mathfrak{G}})$, then

$$13.10 \qquad u_n \equiv \dot{E}_\cdot\left[\int_0^{+\infty} e^{-t} f(\dot{x}(\dot{\mathfrak{f}}_n^{-1}))dt\right]$$

tends pointwise under the bound $\|f\|_\infty$ to u. Because $u_n \in D(\dot{\mathfrak{G}}_n)$,

$$13.11 \qquad \mathfrak{D} u_n = \frac{-e^u(db)}{e(db)} = p_n \dot{\mathfrak{G}}_n u_n = p_n(u_n - f)$$

satisfies all the conditions for u_n to belong to $D(\mathfrak{D})$, and, what is more, $\mathfrak{D} u_n$ converges pointwise under the bound $2\|f\|_\infty$ to $u - f = \dot{\mathfrak{G}} u$; thus, $u \in D(\bar{\mathfrak{D}})$ and $\bar{\mathfrak{D}} u = \dot{G} u$, i.e.,

$$13.12 \qquad \bar{\mathfrak{D}} \supset \dot{\mathfrak{G}} .$$

As to the proof of $\bar{\mathfrak{D}} \subset \dot{\mathfrak{G}}$, it is enough to show that if $u \in D(\bar{\mathfrak{D}})$, then $\dot{G}_1(1 - \bar{\mathfrak{D}})u = u$, and, for this, it is enough to deduce from $u \in D(\bar{\mathfrak{D}})$ and $\bar{\mathfrak{D}} u = u$ that $u \equiv 0$.

Given such a $u \in D(\bar{\mathfrak{D}})$ with $\bar{\mathfrak{D}} u = u$ and choosing $u_n \in D(\mathfrak{D})$ so as to make u_n and $\mathfrak{D} u_n$ converge pointwise and boundedly to u and $\bar{\mathfrak{D}} u = u$,

$$13.13 \qquad u_n - h_n = -\int G_D \mathfrak{D} u de = -\dot{E}_\cdot\left[\int_0^{\dot{\mathfrak{m}}_{\partial D}} (\mathfrak{D} u_n)(\dot{x}) ds\right]$$

$$h_n = \int h_{\partial D}(0, db) u_n(b)$$

implies

13.14 $$\dot{E}_{\bullet}[(u_n-h_n)(\dot{x}(t)),\ t<\dot{\mathfrak{m}}_{\partial D}]-(u_n-h_n) = \dot{E}_{\bullet}\left[\int_0^{t\wedge \dot{\mathfrak{m}}_{\partial D}}(\mathfrak{D}u_n)(\dot{x})ds\right] \qquad t\geq 0,$$

which, in turn, implies

13.15 $$\dot{E}_{\bullet}[(u-h)(\dot{x}(t)),\ t<\dot{\mathfrak{m}}_{\partial D}]-(u-h) = \dot{E}_{\bullet}\left[\int_0^{t\wedge \dot{\mathfrak{m}}_{\partial D}}(\overline{\mathfrak{D}}u)(\dot{x})ds\right] \qquad t\geq 0$$

$$h=\int h_{\partial D}(\cdot,\ db)u(b),$$

and, letting $D\uparrow R^d$ so as to make h tend to a bounded (and hence constant) harmonic function $h(\infty)$,

13.16a $\dot{P}_{\bullet}[\dot{\mathfrak{m}}_{\infty}<+\infty]=P_{\bullet}[\mathfrak{f}(\mathfrak{m}_{\infty})<+\infty]=0 \qquad d=2$

13.16b $u(\infty)=h(\infty)=0 \qquad d\geq 3$

implies

13.17 $$\dot{E}_{\bullet}[u(\dot{x}(t)]-u=\dot{E}_{\bullet}\left[\int_0^t u(\dot{x})ds\right] \qquad t\geq 0,$$

and the desired $u\equiv 0$ follows.

The Green operators leave invariant the space $C(E^d)$ of bounded functions continuous in the ordinary topology of E^d if and only if, for each D, the mean exit time

13.18 $$\dot{p}=\dot{E}_{\bullet}[\dot{\mathfrak{m}}_{\partial D}]=\int G_D de$$

is continuous inside D and tends to 0 on ∂D; in this case, the generator $\dot{\mathfrak{G}}$ coincides with the differential operator $\mathfrak{D}$ acting on the class of functions $u\in C(E^d)$ such that $\mathfrak{D}u\in C(E^d)$; the reader will easily supply the details of the proof.

Here is an example in which the Green operators *do not map $C(E^d)$ into itself.*

Choose $d=3$ and $e=f\times db$, where $f=1+\sum_{n\geq 1}f_n$ and the f_n are the indicators of little non-overlapping open balls D_n converging to as $n\uparrow+\infty$ but not covering 0 itself and so small that

13.19 $P_0[\mathfrak{m}_{\partial D} < -\infty] < 2^{-n} \qquad n \geq 1.$

Because of the first Borel-Cantelli lemma, $p \equiv P.[\mathfrak{m}_{\partial D_n} < +\infty, i.o.] = 0$ at the origin, and it is also clear that $p \equiv 0$ on the rest of R^3. But then $\mathfrak{f} = \int_0^t f(x(s))ds$ is a continuous additive functional, $\mathfrak{f}(s) < \mathfrak{f}(t)$ $(s < t)$, and $x(\mathfrak{f}^{-1})$ is a diffusion with Brownian hitting probabilities and speed measure e.

Given a neighborhood D of 0,

13.20
$$\begin{aligned} &E_0[\min(t: x(\mathfrak{f}^{-1}) \in \partial D)] \\ &= E_0[\mathfrak{f}(\mathfrak{m}_{\partial D})] \\ &\geq \sum_{n \geq 1} E_0\left[\int_0^{\mathfrak{m}_{\partial D}} f_n(x(s))ds\right] \\ &= \sum_{n \geq 1} \int_{D_n} G_D(0, b)db/\text{volume}(D_n) \\ &= +\infty. \end{aligned}$$

But, as E. B. Dynkin [6] has pointed out, this cannot happen for all small neighborhoods if the Green operators map $C(E^d)$ into itself.

14. DISCONTINUOUS ADDITIVE FUNCTIONALS.

V. A. Volkonskii [16] has studied *discontinuous* additive functionals; in the present Brownian case their structure is very simple.

A functional $\mathfrak{t}$ *of the Brownian path which satisfies*

14.1 $\mathfrak{t}(t, w)$ is measurable $\boldsymbol{B}_t$ for each $t \geq 0$.

14.2 $0 \leq \mathfrak{t} < +\infty$

14.3 $\mathfrak{t}(t-) = \mathfrak{t}(t)$

14.4 $\mathfrak{t}(t) = \mathfrak{t}(s) + \mathfrak{t}(t-s, w_s^+) \qquad t \geq s$

is the sum of a continuous additive functional $\mathfrak{f}$ *and a discontinuous additive functional* $\mathfrak{j}$ *with*

14.5 $P.[\mathfrak{j}(t) = \mathfrak{j}(0+), t > 0] = 1$

14.6a $P.[\mathfrak{j}(0+) > 0] = 0$ *or* 1

14.6b $C(E) = 0$, *where* E *is the set of points at which*

$P_\bullet[\mathfrak{j}(0+)>0]=1$ and C is the Newtonian (logarithmic) capacity in $d\geq 3$ $(=2)$ dimensions.[9]

Consider the (discontinuous) additive functional $\mathfrak{j}_n(t)=$ *the sum of the jumps of* $\mathfrak{t}$ *of magnitude* $\geq n^{-1}$ *taking place before time* t, note that $\mathfrak{j}_n(0+)>0)\in \boldsymbol{B}_{0+}$ so that $P_\bullet[\mathfrak{j}_n(0+)>0]=0$ or 1 according to Blumenthal's 01 law, let E_n be the (Borel) set on which $P_\bullet[\mathfrak{j}_n(0+)>0]=1$, and introduce the least *positive* jumping time $\mathfrak{m}$ of $\mathfrak{j}_n$.

If $P_\bullet(\mathfrak{m}<+\infty)>0$ at some point, then

14.7 $$0<P_\bullet[0<\mathfrak{m}<+\infty,\ \mathfrak{j}_n(\mathfrak{m})<\mathfrak{j}_n(\mathfrak{m}+)] = P_\bullet[0<\mathfrak{m}<+\infty,\ x(\mathfrak{m})\in E_n];$$

this implies $C(E_n)>0$[10], and it follows that E_n contains a subcompact A of positive capacity, having a (regular) point at which $P_\bullet[x(t)\in A,\ \text{i.o.},\ t\downarrow 0]=1.$[11] But then $P_\bullet[\mathfrak{j}_n(t)\equiv+\infty,\ t>0]=1$ at that point, contradicting $\mathfrak{j}_n\leq\mathfrak{t}<+\infty$, and it follows that

14.8a $$P_\bullet[\mathfrak{j}_n(t)\equiv\mathfrak{j}_n(0+),\ t>0]\equiv 1$$

14.8b $$C(E_n)=0.$$

The rest is clear: $\mathfrak{j}=\lim_{n\uparrow+\infty}\mathfrak{j}_n$ satisfies 14.5, the remainder $\mathfrak{f}=\mathfrak{t}-\mathfrak{j}$ is a continuous additive functional, 14.6a is immediate from Blumenthal's 01 law, and $C(E)=\lim_{n\uparrow+\infty}C(E_n)=0.$

Massachusetts Institute
of Technology
Kyushu University

---

9 G. Choquet [3] found that if $E\subset R^d$ is Borel, then
$$\inf C(B):B \text{ open},\ B\supset E$$
$$=\sup C(A):A \text{ compact},\ A\subset E;$$
this common value is the *capacity* of E.

10 $P_\bullet[x(t)\in E$ *at some positive time*$]$ is positive or $\equiv 0$ according as $C(E)>0$ or not; see, for example, G. Hunt [9].

11 See O. D. Kellogg [11] for the classical significance of regular points and J. Doob [5] for the probabilistic interpretation.

REFERENCES

[1] R. Blumenthal: An extended Markov property. Trans. Am. Math. Soc. 85 (1957), 52–72.

[2] H. Cartan: Théorie générale du balayage en potentiel newtonien. Ann. Univ. Grenoble 22 (1946), 221–280.

[3] G. Choquet: Theory of capacities. Ann. Inst. Fourier Grenoble, 5 (1953–1956), 131–295.

[4] J. Doob: Stochastic Processes. J. Wiley and Sons. New York (1953).

[5] ———: Semimartingales and subharmonic functions. Trans. Am. Math. Soc. 77 (1954), 86–121.

[6] E. B. Dynkin: Infinitesimal operators of Markov processes. Teor. Veroyat. i Primenen. 1 (1956), 38–60.

[7] ———: Natural topology and excessive functions connected with a Markov process. Doklady Akademii Nayk CCCP, 127 (1959), 17–19.

[8] W. Feller: The general diffusion operator and positivity preserving semi-groups in one dimension. Ann. Math. 60 (1954), 417–436.

[9] G. Hunt: Some theorems concerning Brownian motion. Trans. Am. Math. Soc. 81 (1956), 294–319.

[10] ———: Markov processes and potentials (1). Illinois J. Math. 1 (1957), 44–93.

[11] O. D. Kellogg: Foundations of Potential Theory. J. Springer. Berlin (1929).

[12] K. Itô and H. P. McKean, Jr.: Potentials and the random walk. Illinois J. Math. 4 (1960), 119–132.

[13] ———: Diffusion. to appear.

[14] F. Riesz: Sur les fonctions subharmoniques et leur rapport a la théorie du potentiel. Acta Math. 48 (1926), 329–343.

[15] A. Volkonskiĭ: Random substitution of time in strong Markov process. Teor. Veroyat. i Primenen. 3 (1958), 332–350.

[16] ———: Additive functionals of Markov processes. Doklady Akademii Nayk CCCP. 127 (1959), 735–738.

Note added in proof. The authors came to know that A. D. Ventsel' [19] obtained almost the same result as in sect. 3–5 of the present paper and that A. Meyer [18] studied the same problem for a more general class of Markov processes. As for signed additive functionals, E. B. Dynkin [17] constructed them using stochastic integrals in case of a Brownian motion.

[17] E. B. Dynkin: Additive functionals of a Wiener process determined by stochastic integrals. Teor. Veroyat. i Primenen. 5 (1960), 441–452.

[18] A. Meyer: Representations integrales des potentiels. C. R. Paris 251 (1960), 22 79–2280.

[19] A. D. Ventsel': Non-negative additive functionals of Markov processes. Doklady Akademii Nayk CCCP 137 (1961), 17–20

Z. Wahrscheinlichkeitstheorie 1, 251—257 (1963)

Note on Continuous Additive Functionals of the 1-Dimensional Brownian Path

By

HIROSHI TANAKA

1. Introduction

A functional $\mathfrak{a}(t) = \mathfrak{a}(t, w)$ of $t \geqq 0$ and a Brownian path $w : t \to x(t)$ is called *additive* if

1.1 a $\qquad \mathfrak{a}(t, w)$ *depends on* t *and* $x(s) : 0 \leqq s \leqq t$ *only,*

1.1 b $\qquad \mathfrak{a}(t, w) = \mathfrak{a}(s, w) + \mathfrak{a}(t - s, w_s^+), \quad 0 \leqq s \leqq t,$

where w_s^+ is the *shifted* path $w_s^+ : t \to x(t + s)$.

Additive functionals play an important rôle in transforming a Markov process, such as the substitution of time by the inverse functional of a non-negative additive functional (K. ITÔ and H. P. MCKEAN [7], V. A. VOLKONSKII [10]) and the transformation of a Brownian motion to a diffusion with a drift (E. B. DYNKIN [2], M. MOTOO [8]). As for the structure of additive functionals of the several dimensional Brownian motion, A. D. VENTSEL [9] proved that such a functional $\mathfrak{a}$ can be written in the form:

1.2 $$\mathfrak{a}(t, w) = f(x(t)) - f(x(0)) + \int_0^t g(x(s)) \cdot dx(s),$$

under the assumption that $\mathfrak{a}(t, w)$ has a finite expectation for each $t < \infty$. Here, f and g are Borel functions on the state space, g satisfies $\int_0^t g(x(s))^2\, ds < \infty$ $(t < \infty)$ with probability one and the integral in 1.2 is a stochastic integral of K. ITÔ [5].

In this note, it will be proved that, for *every continuous* additive functional $\mathfrak{a}$ of the 1-dimensional Brownian path, $\mathfrak{a}(\tau, w) : \tau = \min(t, \mathfrak{m})$ has finite moments of all orders $\geqq 0$, where $\mathfrak{m}$ is the first time $\mathrm{x}(\cdot)$ hits the complement of a bounded interval. This result combined with a slight modification of A. D. VENTSEL's proof implies that *any continuous additive functional of the* 1*-dimensional Brownian path has the representation* 1.2 *with continuous* f.

I wish to thank Professor H. P. MCKEAN for helpful suggestions.

2. Existence of moments

Given the space W of continuous sample paths $w : t \in [0, \infty) \to w_t \in R^1$, write $w_t = x(t, w)$ (or $= x(t) = x_t$ for short), and introducing the corresponding coordinate fields $\boldsymbol{B}_t = \boldsymbol{B}[x(s) : s \leqq t]$ and $\boldsymbol{B} = \boldsymbol{B}[x(s) : s < \infty]$, let $P_a(\cdot)$ be the *Wiener measure* on $\boldsymbol{B}$ with initial position $a \in R^1$. $[x, \boldsymbol{B}, P.]$ is the so-called (standard) 1-dimensional *Brownian motion*. We use the notation $E_a(f, B)$ for the integral over $B \in \boldsymbol{B}$ of a $\boldsymbol{B}$-measurable function f with respect to P_a and write $E_a(f, B) = E_a(f)$ when $B = W$. The *first passage time* $\inf\{t : x(t) = r\}$ through r and the *first exit time* $\inf\{t : x(t) \notin I\}$ for an interval I are denoted respectively by $\mathfrak{m}_r$ and $\mathfrak{m}_I$. The following *strong Markov property** will be used often: if $\mathfrak{m}$ is a *Markov time***, then for $a \in R^1$ and $B \in \boldsymbol{B}$

2.1 $$P_a[(P_a(w_{\mathfrak{m}}^+ \in B \mid \boldsymbol{B}_{\mathfrak{m}+}) = P_{x(\mathfrak{m})}(B), \mathfrak{m} < \infty] = P_a(\mathfrak{m} < \infty),$$

where $w_{\mathfrak{m}}^+$ is the *shifted* path $w_{\mathfrak{m}}^+ : t \to x(t + \mathfrak{m})$ and $\boldsymbol{B}_{\mathfrak{m}+}$ is the field generated by the events $B \in \boldsymbol{B}$ such that $B \cap (w : \mathfrak{m} < t) \in \boldsymbol{B}_t$, $t \geqq 0$. By definition, a *continuous additive functional* is a functional $\mathfrak{a}(t, w)$ of t and w which satisfies the following conditions 2.2a—2.2c:

2.2a $$\mathfrak{a}(t, w) \text{ is } \boldsymbol{B}_t\text{-measurable for each } t \geqq 0,$$

2.2b $$|\mathfrak{a}(t, w)| < \infty \text{ and } \mathfrak{a}(t, w) \text{ is continuous in } t \text{ (a.e.)},$$

2.2c $$\mathfrak{a}(t, w) = \mathfrak{a}(s, w) + \mathfrak{a}(t - s, w_s^+), \quad 0 \leqq s \leqq t \text{ (a.e.)},$$

where (a.e.) means (for every w outside a certain set which has P_a-measure zero for all $a \in R^1$).

Now, consider a continuous additive functional $\mathfrak{a}$ of the 1-dimensional Brownian path, and put

$$\bar{\mathfrak{a}}(t, w) = \max_{0 \leqq s \leqq t} |\mathfrak{a}(s, w)|.$$

Then, we have the following

Theorem 1. *For any bounded interval* $I = [r_1, r_2]$ *we have*

2.3 $$P_a[\bar{\mathfrak{a}}(\mathfrak{m}) > t] < c_1 e^{-c_2 t}, \quad a \in I,$$

where $\mathfrak{m} = \mathfrak{m}_I$, *and* c_1, c_2 *are some positive constants depending on* r_1 *and* r_2 *but not on* $a \in I$. *In particular,* $\mathfrak{a}(t \wedge \mathfrak{m})$*** *has finite moments of all orders* $\geqq 0$.

Proof. First we note that

2.4 $$-\bar{\mathfrak{a}}(t, w) + \bar{\mathfrak{a}}(s, w_t^+) \leqq \bar{\mathfrak{a}}(t + s, w) \leqq \bar{\mathfrak{a}}(t, w) + \bar{\mathfrak{a}}(s, w_t^+), \quad s, t \geqq 0 \text{ (a.e.)},$$

which follows from the additivity 2.2c of $\mathfrak{a}$. Let $\dot{I}$ be a bounded open interval containing I, and, for each $a \in \dot{I}$, choose a constant $t_a < \infty$ such that $P_a[\bar{\mathfrak{a}}(\dot{\mathfrak{m}}) > t_a] < 1/2$, where $\dot{\mathfrak{m}} = \mathfrak{m}_{\dot{I}}$. Then, using 2.4 and the strong Markov property 2.1, we have

$$\begin{aligned} 1/2 &\geqq P_a[\bar{\mathfrak{a}}(\dot{\mathfrak{m}}) > t_a] \\ &\geqq P_a[\bar{\mathfrak{a}}(\dot{\mathfrak{m}}) > t_a, \mathfrak{m}_b < \dot{\mathfrak{m}}], \qquad b \in \dot{I} \\ &\geqq P_a[\bar{\mathfrak{a}}(\dot{\mathfrak{m}}(w_{\mathfrak{m}_b}^+), w_{\mathfrak{m}_b}^+) - \bar{\mathfrak{a}}(\mathfrak{m}_b, w) > t_a, \mathfrak{m}_b < \dot{\mathfrak{m}}] \\ &\geqq P_a[\bar{\mathfrak{a}}(\dot{\mathfrak{m}}(w_{\mathfrak{m}_b}^+), w_{\mathfrak{m}_b}^+) > 2t_a, \mathfrak{m}_b < \dot{\mathfrak{m}}, \bar{\mathfrak{a}}(\mathfrak{m}_b) < t_a] \\ &= P_a[\mathfrak{m}_b < \dot{\mathfrak{m}}, \bar{\mathfrak{a}}(\mathfrak{m}_b) < t_a] P_b[\bar{\mathfrak{a}}(\dot{\mathfrak{m}}) > 2t_a]. \end{aligned}$$

---

* See G. A. HUNT [4] or R. BLUMENTHAL [1].

** $\mathfrak{m}$ is called a Markov time if $\mathfrak{m} \geqq 0$ and $(w : \mathfrak{m} < t) \in \boldsymbol{B}_t$ for each $t \geqq 0$.

*** $a \wedge b$ $(a \vee b)$ is the smaller (larger) of a and b.

Now, choosing a neighborhood U_a of a such that for all $b \in U_a$

$$P_a[\mathfrak{m}_b < \dot{\mathfrak{m}}, \bar{\mathfrak{a}}(\mathfrak{m}_b) < t_a] > 3/4,$$

it follows that

2.5 $$P_b[\bar{\mathfrak{a}}(\dot{\mathfrak{m}}) > 2t_a] < 2/3, \quad b \in U_a.$$

Because $\bar{\mathfrak{a}}(\mathfrak{m}) \leqq \bar{\mathfrak{a}}(\dot{\mathfrak{m}})$, 2.5 is true for $a \in I$ and $b \in U_a \cap I$ when $\dot{\mathfrak{m}}$ is replaced by $\mathfrak{m}$. Therefore, using Heine-Borel's covering theorem, it is clear that

2.6 $$P_a[\bar{\mathfrak{a}}(\mathfrak{m}) > T] < 2/3, \quad a \in I,$$

for some constant $T < \infty$ independent of a.

Next, put $\sigma_n = \inf\{t : \bar{\mathfrak{a}}(t) \geqq nT\}$ if $\bar{\mathfrak{a}}(t) \geqq nT$ for some $t < \infty$, and $= \infty$ if there is no such t ($n \geqq 1$). Because σ_n ($n \geqq 1$) is a Markov time and

$$\sigma_n \geqq \sigma_{n-1} + \sigma_1(w^+{\sigma_{n-1}}), \text{ (a.e.)}, \ n \geqq 2,$$

by 2.4, it follows from 2.6 and by induction that

$$\begin{aligned} P_a[\bar{\mathfrak{a}}(\mathfrak{m}) > nT] &= P_a[\sigma_n < \mathfrak{m}] \\ &\leqq P_a[\sigma_{n-1} + \sigma_1(w^+{\sigma_{n-1}}) < \mathfrak{m}] \\ &= E_a[P_{x(\sigma_{n-1})}(\sigma_1 < \mathfrak{m}), \ \sigma_{n-1} < \mathfrak{m}] \\ &\leqq (2/3)\, P_a(\sigma_{n-1} < \mathfrak{m}) \leqq (2/3)^n, \end{aligned}$$

and this implies 2.3.

3. Representation

Let g be a Borel function on R^1 such that

3.1 $$P_a[\int_0^t g^2(x_s)\,ds < \infty, \ 0 \leqq t < \infty] = 1, \qquad a \in R^1.$$

Then, the stochastic integral $\int_0^t g(x_s)\,dx_s$ is defined (K. Itô [5]).

We first remark that a version of this stochastic integral can be chosen so that it gives a continuous additive functional. When g is bounded, such a version exists, as was discussed by E. B. Dynkin [3]. When g is unbounded, we use the following simple lemma, which corresponds to lemma 1 in [3] and can be proved similarly.

Lemma. *Suppose the stochastic integral* $\int_0^t g_n(x_s)\,dx_s$ *has a version of continuous additive functional* ($n = 1, 2, \ldots$). *Under the notation* $e(a, h) = E_a[\int_0^{\mathfrak{m}_I} h^2(x_s)\,ds]$, *suppose, for each compact interval* I, *that* $e(a, g)$ *and* $e(a, g_n)$ *are finite for* $a \in I$ *and that* $e(a, g - g_n)$ *converges to zero uniformly in* $a \in I$ *as* $n \to \infty$. *Then, the stochastic integral* $\int_0^t g(x_s)\,dx_s$ *has a version of continuous additive functional.*

Given g satisfying 3.1, putting $g_n(b) = g(b)$ for $|g(b)| < n$ and $= 0$ for $|g(b)| \geqq n$, we show that the assumptions of the lemma are satisfied. Theorem 1 applied to the additive functional $\mathfrak{f}(t) = \int_0^t g^2(x_s)\,ds$ implies that $e(a, g)$ is finite, and using the additivity of $\mathfrak{f} \geqq 0$ and the strong Markov property, we see that e is concave and hence continuous on I. By the same reason $e(a, g_n)$ is continuous on I, and since $e(a, g_n)$ increases to $e(a, g)$ as $n \uparrow \infty$ on I, $e(a, g - g_n) = e(a, g) - e(a, g_n)$ tends to zero uniformly on I as $n \to \infty$ Thus the lemma is applicable.

From now on, we take a version of continuous additive functional for a stochastic integral.

Theorem 2. *A continuous additive functional* $\mathfrak{a}$ *of the* 1*-dimensional Brownian path can be written in the following form:*

3.2 $$\mathfrak{a}(t, w) = f(x_t) - f(x_0) + \int_0^t g(x_s)\, dx_s, \quad 0 \leqq t < \infty \qquad \text{(a.e.)},$$

where f is a continuous function on R^1 and g satisfies 3.1.

Because of theorem 1, the method of A. D. VENTSEL is applicable, but here we will give a proof which is different from A. D. VENTSEL's except as regards 3.12. Our method of obtaining the function g in 3.2 seems to be simpler.

Proof. Take $I = [r_1, r_2]$ as before, let $\mathfrak{m} = \mathfrak{m}_I$, and put

3.3a $$\mathfrak{s}(t, w) = \mathfrak{a}(t, w) - [f(x_t) - f(x_0)], \quad t \leqq \mathfrak{m},$$

3.3b $$f = f_I = -E_\cdot[\mathfrak{a}(\mathfrak{m})].$$

Denote by $G(a, b)$ the Green function:

$$G(a, b) = 2(a \wedge b - r_1)(r_2 - a \vee b)/(r_2 - r_1),$$

and by $L_2(a)$ $(r_1 < a < r_2)$ the space of those functions on I which are square integrable with respect to the measure $G(a, b)db$. $L_2(a)$ is a Hilbert space with inner product $(\Phi_1, \Phi_2)_a = \int_{r_1}^{r_2} G(a, b)\Phi_1(b)\Phi_2(b)db$ for each a; it is independent of $a \in (r_1, r_2)$ as a set. For each $\Phi \in L_2(a)$ let $\mathfrak{s}_\Phi(t \wedge \mathfrak{m})$ be the stochastic integral $\int_0^{t \wedge \mathfrak{m}} \Phi(x_s)dx_s$ and note that (see K. ITÔ [5])

3.4a $$E_a[\mathfrak{s}(t \wedge \mathfrak{m})] = E_a[\mathfrak{s}_\Phi(t \wedge \mathfrak{m})] = 0$$

3.4b $$E_a[\mathfrak{s}_{\Phi_1}(\mathfrak{m})\, \mathfrak{s}_{\Phi_2}(\mathfrak{m})] = E_a[\int_0^{\mathfrak{m}} \Phi_1(x_s)\Phi_2(x_s)\, ds] = (\Phi_1, \Phi_2)_a.$$

Now, consider the functions $p_\pm(a, \Phi) = E_a[|\mathfrak{s}(\mathfrak{m}) \pm \mathfrak{s}_\Phi(\mathfrak{m})|^2]$ and $p(a, \Phi) = E_a[\mathfrak{s}(\mathfrak{m})\mathfrak{s}_\Phi(\mathfrak{m})] = (1/4)(p_+ - p_-)$. Because $\mathfrak{s}$ and $\mathfrak{s}_\Phi$ satisfy 2.2 for $t \leqq \mathfrak{m}$, it follows, using 3.4a and the strong Markov property, that for any compact subinterval $J = [\varrho_1, \varrho_2]$ in (r_1, r_2)

3.5 $$p_\pm(a, \Phi) = E_a[|\mathfrak{s}(\mathfrak{n}) \pm \mathfrak{s}_\Phi(\mathfrak{n})|^2] + E_a[p_+(x(\mathfrak{n}), \Phi)]$$
$$\geqq \frac{\varrho_2 - a}{\varrho_2 - \varrho_1} p_\pm(\varrho_1, \Phi) + \frac{a - \varrho_1}{\varrho_2 - \varrho_1} p_\pm(\varrho_2, \Phi), \quad a \in (\varrho_1, \varrho_2), \quad \mathfrak{n} = \mathfrak{m}_I,$$

and hence $p_\pm$ is concave in (r_1, r_2) and $p_\pm(a, \Phi) \downarrow 0$ as $a \downarrow r_1$ or $a \uparrow r_2$. Therefore, there exists a non-negative measure $\mu_\Phi^\pm$ finite on compact subsets in (r_1, r_2) such that

3.6 $$p_\pm(a, \Phi) = \int_{r_1}^{r_2} G(a, b)\, \mu_\Phi^\pm(db), \quad a \in (r_1, r_2);$$

this $\mu_\Phi^\pm$ is uniquely determined by $p_\pm$; in fact $d\mu_\Phi^\pm = d(-D^+p_\pm)$*. Hence we have**

3.7
$$p(a, \Phi) = \int_{r_1}^{r_2} G(a, b)\,\mu_\Phi(db), \quad a \in (r_1, r_2)$$
$$d\mu_\Phi = (1/4)\,(d\mu_\Phi^+ - d\mu_\Phi^-) = d(-D^+p);$$

μ_Φ is the unique signed measure finite on compact subsets in (r_1, r_2) and satisfying 3.7.

Next, we prove that there exists a unique function $g(b)$ independent of a and belonging to $L_2(a)$ such that

3.8
$$p(a, \Phi) = (\Phi, g)_a, \quad \Phi \in L_2(a), \quad a \in (r_1, r_2).$$

This results from the following three steps ((1)—(3)).

(1) If Φ vanishes identically in $J = (\varrho_1, \varrho_2) \subset I$, then μ_Φ has no mass inside J. In fact, in this case $\mathfrak{s}_\Phi = 0$ up to the exist time $\mathfrak{m}_J$ and hence from 3.5

$$p(a, \Phi) = \frac{\varrho_2 - a}{\varrho_2 - \varrho_1}\,p(\varrho_1, \Phi) + \frac{a - \varrho_1}{\varrho_2 - \varrho_1}\,p(\varrho_2, \Phi),$$

i.e., p is linear inside J, proving $d\mu_\Phi = d(-D^+p) = 0$ there.

(2) If χ_E is the indicator function of a Borel set $E \subset I$, then

3.9
$$p(a, \chi_E) = \int_E G(a, b)\,\mu_{\mathbf{1}}(db),$$

where $\mathbf{1}$ is the function identically equal to one on I. First, from 3.4 b we note that

$$p_+(a, \Phi) + p_-(a, \Phi) = 2p_+(a, \mathbf{0}) + 2\int G(a, b)\,\Phi^2(b)\,db$$

and hence from 3.6 that

3.10
$$d\mu_\Phi^+ + d\mu_\Phi^- = 2\,d\mu_{\mathbf{0}}^+ + 2\,\Phi^2\,db.$$

Now, if E is an open interval with $\mu_{\mathbf{0}}^+(\partial E) = 0$ and if $\Phi = \chi_E$, then from (1) and 3.10 $d\mu_\Phi = 0$ on $I - E$ and $d\mu_{\mathbf{1}-\Phi} = 0$ on $\bar{E}$ and hence $d\mu_\Phi = \Phi\,d\mu_{\mathbf{1}}$ follows from the identity $d\mu_\Phi + d\mu_{\mathbf{1}-\Phi} = d\mu_{\mathbf{1}}$. Thus we have 3.9 for such an E. But, because $|p(a, \chi_E)| \leqq \sqrt{E_a[\mathfrak{s}(\mathfrak{m})^2]} \cdot \|\chi_E\|_a$*** by Schwarz's inequality and 3.4b, $p(a, \chi_E)$ is a signed measure in E. Hence 3.9 must hold for any Borel set E in I because it holds for open intervals E with $\mu_0^+(\partial E) = 0$ and these intervals generate all Borel sets in I.

(3) From (2) we have

3.11
$$p(a, \Phi) = \int G(a, b)\,\Phi(b)\,\mu_{\mathbf{1}}(db), \quad a \in (r_1, r_2),$$

if Φ is a linear combination of finite numbers of indicator functions. On the other hand, for each a, $p(a, \Phi)$ is a linear functional on $L_2(a)$ because of the bound $|p(a, \Phi)| \leqq \sqrt{E_a[\mathfrak{s}(\mathfrak{m})^2]} \cdot \|\Phi\|_a$, and hence by Riesz's theorem there is a unique

* D^+ means the right derivative, and $d(-D^+p_\pm)$ is the measure induced by the function $-D^+p_\pm$ of bounded variation.

** I owe this reasoning to H. P. McKean.

*** $\|\Phi\|_a = \sqrt{(\Phi, \Phi)_a}$.

$g_a \in L_2(a)$ such that $p(a, \Phi) = (\Phi, g_a)_a$ for $\Phi \in L_2(a)$. Comparing this with 3.11, it follows that $d\mu_1 = g_a db$ and that g_a must be independent of a, which we denote by g. Thus we have 3.8 with a unique $g \in L_2(a)$.

Next, we sketch the proof that $\mathfrak{s}(t) = \mathfrak{s}_g(t)$ for $t \leqq \mathfrak{m}$ (a.e.), following A. D. VENTSEL [9]. Putting $\bar{\mathfrak{s}} = \mathfrak{s} - \mathfrak{s}_g$, it is sufficient to show that

$$E_a[F_1(x(t_1 \wedge \mathfrak{m})) \cdots F_n(x(t_n \wedge \mathfrak{m}))\bar{\mathfrak{s}}(t \wedge \mathfrak{m})] = 0,$$
$$0 \leqq t_1 < \cdots < t_n < \infty, \quad 0 \leqq t < \infty,$$

for any bounded Borel functions $F_1, \ldots, F_n$, and by the additive property of $\bar{\mathfrak{s}}$ and the Markovian property of Brownian motion, it is also enough to prove that

3.12 $$E_a[F(x(t \wedge \mathfrak{m}))\bar{\mathfrak{s}}(t \wedge \mathfrak{m})] = 0$$

for any continuous function F on I. From 3.4b and 3.8 we note that $E_a[\mathfrak{s}_\Phi(\mathfrak{m})\bar{\mathfrak{s}}(\mathfrak{m})] = 0$ and hence by the additive property and 3.4a that

3.13 $$E_a[\mathfrak{s}_\Phi(t \wedge \mathfrak{m})\bar{\mathfrak{s}}(t \wedge \mathfrak{m})] = 0, \quad \Phi \in L_2(a).$$

Now, if F is continuous on I, writing $F = F_0 + h$ where $F_0(r_1) = F_0(r_2) = 0$ and h is a linear function, we have $E_a[h(x(t \wedge \mathfrak{m}))\bar{\mathfrak{s}}(t \wedge \mathfrak{m})] = 0$ by 3.13 and 3.4a. On the other hand, if q is an eigenfunction for the problem $(1/2)q'' = \lambda q$ with $q(r_1) = q(r_2) = 0$, then applying the formula of stochastic integrals (K. ITÔ [6]) to $q(x_t)$ and using 3.13, we have

$$E_a[q(x(t \wedge \mathfrak{m}))\bar{\mathfrak{s}}(t \wedge \mathfrak{m})] = \tfrac{1}{2}\int_0^t E_a[q''(x(\mathfrak{s} \wedge \mathfrak{m}))\bar{\mathfrak{s}}(\mathfrak{s} \wedge \mathfrak{m})]\,ds$$
$$= \lambda \int_0^t E_a[q(x(s \wedge \mathfrak{m}))\bar{\mathfrak{s}}(\mathfrak{s} \wedge \mathfrak{m})]\,ds,$$

and hence $E_a[q(x(t \wedge \mathfrak{m}))\bar{\mathfrak{s}}(t \wedge \mathfrak{m})] = 0$. Now, $E_a[F_0(x(t \wedge \mathfrak{m}))\bar{\mathfrak{s}}(t \wedge \mathfrak{m})] = 0$ follows by approximating F_0 uniformly by a linear combination of q's. Thus 3.12 holds.

Finally, to obtain 3.2, take an increasing sequence of bounded intervals $I_n = [r_{n1}, r_{n2}]$, $n \geqq 1$, with union R^1. We have obtained already

3.14a $$\mathfrak{a}(t, w) = f_n(x_t) - f_n(x_0) + \int_0^t g_n(x_s)\,dx_s, \quad t \leqq \mathfrak{n}_n \qquad \text{(a.e.)},$$

3.14b $$f_n = -E.[\mathfrak{a}(\mathfrak{n}_n)], \quad \mathfrak{n}_n = \mathfrak{m}_{I_n}.$$

Put $l_1(a) = 0$ and for $n \geqq 2$

$$l_n(a) = \sum_{k=1}^{n-1} (r_{k2} - r_{k1})^{-1}[(r_{k2} - a) f_{k+1}(r_{k1}) + (a - r_{k1}) f_{k+1}(r_{k2})].$$

Then, because $l_n(x_t) - l_n(x_0)$ can be written as the stochastic integral $\int_0^t l'(x_s)\,dx_s$, 3.14a remains valid when f_n and g_n are replaced respectively by $\bar{f}_n \equiv f_n - l_n$ and $\bar{g}_n \equiv g_n + l_n'$. On the other hand, from 3.14b, it follows that $\bar{f}_n = \bar{f}_{n+1}$ inside I_n and hence $\bar{g}_n = \bar{g}_{n+1}$ inside I_n. Thus, defining $f = \bar{f}_n$ and $g = \bar{g}_n$ inside I_n, we obtain 3.2. 3.1 is clear from the construction of g. Because $\mathfrak{a}$ and the stochastic integral term are continuous in t (a.e.), f must be continuous on R^1. Thus the theorem is completely proved.

Note added in proof. As for the multidimensional case, the author found, in the course of proof reading, A. B. SKOROHOD's paper (Teor. Verojatn. Primen **6**, 430–439 (1961)) and A. D. VENTSEL's paper (Doklady Akad. Nauk SSSR n. Ser. **142**, 1223–1226 (1962)). These papers treats the same representation as 3.2 for continuous additive functionals, and especially the latter paper treats the most general continuous addive functionals of a Brownian motion, but the proof given here is different from theirs. The multidimensional version of Theorem 1 was obtained also by H. P. McKEAN (private communication) where I (in the theorem) must be replaced by a suitable *fine* open set.

References

[1] BLUMENTHAL, R.: An extended Markoff property. Trans. Amer. math. Soc. **85**, 52—72 (1957).
[2] DYNKIN, E. B.: Some transformations of Markov processes. Doklady Akad. Nauk SSSR n. Ser. **133**, 269—272 (1960).
[3] — Additive functionals of a Wiener process determined by stochastic integrals. Teor. Verojatn. Primen. **5**, 441—452 (1960).
[4] HUNT, G. A.: Some theorems concerning Brownian motion. Trans. Amer. math. Soc. **81**, 294—319 (1956).
[5] ITÔ, K.: On stochastic differential equations. Mem. Amer. math. Soc. No. 4.
[6] — On a formula concerning stochastic differentials. Nagoya math. J. **3**, 55—65 (1951).
[7] —, and H. P. McKEAN: Diffusion. (Forthcoming.)
[8] MOTOO, M.: Diffusion process corresponding to $\frac{1}{2} \sum \partial^2/\partial x^{i^2} + \sum b^i(x)\, \partial/\partial x^i$. Ann. Inst. statist. Math. **12**, 37—61 (1960).
[9] VENTSEL, A. D.: Additive functionals of several dimensional Wiener process. Doklady Akad. Nauk SSSR n. Ser. **139**, 13—16 (1961).
[10] VOLKONSKII, V. A.: Random substitution of time in strong Markov process. Teor. Verojatn. Primen. **3**, 332—350 (1958).

Mathematicae Institute
Kyusyu University
Fukuoka, Japan

(Received February 15, 1962)

Memoirs of the Faculty of Science, Kyushu University
Ser. A, Vol. 18, No. 1, 1964

EXISTENCE OF DIFFUSIONS WITH CONTINUOUS COEFFICIENTS

By
Hiroshi TANAKA

(Received Nov. 30, 1963)

Introduction. The object of this paper is to prove the following theorem. Let a^{ij}, b^i for $1\leq i,\ j\leq d$ be real-valued continuous functions on Euclidean d-space R^d $(d\geq 2)$, such that for each $x=(x^1, \cdots, x^d)$ in R^d $a^{ij}(x)$ is a positive definite symmetric matrix. Let $B(R^d)$ be the Banach space of all real-valued bounded Borel functions on R^d, with the supremum norm. Then, (1) *there exists a family of linear transformations T^t acting on $B(R^d)$, $0\leq t<+\infty$, such that*

0·1
$$T^tT^s=T^{t+s}, \qquad \|T^t\|\leq 1$$
$$T^tf\geq 0 \quad \text{if} \quad f\geq 0$$
$$\lim_{t\downarrow 0} T^tf(x)=f(x), \qquad x\in R^d,\ f\in C(R^d),$$

and, such that whenever f is of class C^2 with compact support in R^d,

0·2
$$\lim_{t\downarrow 0} t^{-1}\|T^tf(x)-f(x)\|$$
$$=\sum_{i,j=1}^{d} a^{ij}(x)\frac{\partial^2 f(x)}{\partial x^i\partial x^j}+\sum_{i=1}^{d} b^i(x)\frac{\partial f(x)}{\partial x^i}$$

uniformly for x in R^d. (2) *There exists a diffusion process on R^d with semigroup $\{T^t\}$.*

We also consider the case when b^i $(1\leq i\leq d)$ is bounded measurable. In general, there is no uniqueness for the semigroups satisfying 0.1 and 0.2, and the semigroup constructed here seems to be the smallest one among such semigroups.

If the coefficients a^{ij} and b^i are more smooth, the essentially same problem has been treated in various ways and in somewhat more precise form, such as the (probabilistic) construction of a diffusion based on Ito's stochastic integral equations (b^i and the positive square root of (a^{ij}) are assumed to be

Lipschitz continuous), and the construction of fundamental solutions for parabolic differential equations (the coefficients are assumed to be Hölder continuous). Recently, Ito's stochastic integral equation with coefficients merely continuous or having certain discontinuity was treated by Skorohod [10] and Girsanov [3].

Our construction is based on Hille-Yosida theorem in semigroup theory, and relies heavily on the followings:

(1) A result of Morrey [6] in elliptic differential equations.

(2) McKean's estimate of an a priori kind concerning the continuity of sample paths (4.2 in section 4).

(1) plays an important rôle in the present application of Hille-Yosida theorem. As for the construction of diffusions, we first construct diffusions inside balls, and then obtain a (global) diffusion in R^d connecting these local ones. (2) will be used for proving some properties of local diffusions which will be needed for the later constructions. The present result extends Nelson's result [7] to the case of continuous coefficients.

I wish to thank Professor McKean for helpful talks and for communicating the result (2).

§1. Notations and preliminaries.

All functions we consider are real-valued. We shall use the following notations. If D is a bounded domain in Euclidean d-space $R^d (d \geq 2)$, $\rho(x, \partial D)$ denotes the distance between x and the boundary ∂D of D, and

$$C(D) = \{f: \ f \text{ is bounded continuous in } D\},$$
$$C(\bar{D}) = \{f: \ f \text{ is continuous on the closure } \bar{D} \text{ of } D\},$$
$$C_0(D) = \{f: \ f \in C(D) \text{ and } f(x) \to 0 \text{ as } \rho(x, \partial D) \to 0\},$$
$$C_0(\bar{D}) = \{f: \ f \in C(\bar{D}) \text{ and } f = 0 \text{ on } \partial D\}.$$

The supremum norm of a bounded function f on D (or $\bar{D}$) is denoted by $\|f\|_D$ (or $\|f\|_{\bar{D}}$). If n is a positive integer, $C^n(D) = \{f: \ f$ and all its partial derivatives of order $\leq n$ are defined and belong to $C(D)\}$. The first and the second partial derivatives of u is denoted by $u_{,\alpha}$ and $u_{,\alpha\beta}$ respectively ($1 \leq \alpha, \beta \leq d$). $L_2(D)$ is the real Hilbert space of square summable functions on D. The inner product in $L_2(D)$ is denoted by $(*, *')_{2,D}$ and the norm is by $\|*\|_{2,D}$.

Suppose a second-order elliptic differential operator A:

1·1 $$A=\sum_{i,j=1}^{d} a^{ij}(x)\frac{\partial^2}{\partial x^i \partial x^j}+\sum_{i=1}^{d} b^i(x)\frac{\partial}{\partial x^i},$$

is given in R^d, $x=(x^1, \cdots, x^d)\in R^d$; here we assume that

1·2a a^{ij} is continuous in R^d $(1\leq i, j\leq d)$,

1·2b b^i is measurable and bounded on each compact set in R^d $(1\leq i\leq d)$,

1·2c (a^{ij}) is symmetric positive definite:

$$\sum_{i,j=1}^{d} a^{ij}(x)\lambda_i\lambda_j>0, \qquad (\lambda_1, \cdots, \lambda_d)\neq 0, x\in R^d.$$

Let D be a bounded domain, and denote by $k(s, D)$ the modulus of continuity of (a^{ij}) on D:

1·3 $$k(s, D)=\max_{\substack{|x_1-x_2|\leq s\\ x_1, x_2\in \bar{D}}}\left[\sum_{i,j=1}^{d}|a^{ij}(x_1)-a^{ij}(x_2)|^2\right]^{\frac{1}{2}}, \qquad s>0.$$

We say, for convenience, that

$$A_n=\sum_{i,j=1}^{d} a_n^{ij}(x)\frac{\partial^2}{\partial x^i \partial x^j}+\sum_{i=1}^{d} b_n^i(x)\frac{\partial}{\partial x^i}, \qquad n=1, 2, \cdots,$$

are *approximating operators* of A on D, if the coefficients are defined in some domain $\dot{D}$ containing $\bar{D}$ and satisfy the following conditions 1·4a–d.

1·4a $a_n^{ij}\in C^3(\dot{D})$ and $\|a_n^{ij}-a^{ij}\|_{\bar{D}}\to 0$ as $n\to+\infty$ $(1\leq i, j\leq d)$.

1·4b $b_n^i\in C^3(\dot{D})$, $\|b_n^i\|_{\bar{D}}$ is bounded in $n\geq 1$ and $\|b_n^i-b^i\|_{2,D}\to 0$ as $n\to+\infty$ $(1\leq i\leq d)$.

1·4c If $k_n(s, D)$ is the modulus of continuity of (a_n^{ij}) on D defined in the same way as 1·3, then

$$k_n(s, D)\leq k(s), \quad s>0, \quad n=1, 2, \cdots,$$

with some function $k(s)$ such that $k(s)\downarrow 0$ $(s\downarrow 0)$.

1·4d (a_n^{ij}) is symmetric and for some constant M

$$0<\left[\sum_{i,j=1}^{d} a_n^{ij}(x)\lambda_i\lambda_j\right]^{-1}\leq M, \qquad |\lambda|=1, \quad x\in \bar{D}.$$

Such operators A_n can be obtained as follows. Let φ be *a* C^∞-function with bounded support such that $\varphi\geq 0$ and $\int_{R^d}\varphi(x)dx=1$ and put

1·5a $\varphi_n(x)=n^d\varphi(nx)$,

1·5b $a_n^{ij}(x)=(a^{ij}*\varphi_n)(x)=\int a^{ij}(x-y)\varphi_n(y)dy$, $b_n^i(x)=(b^i*\varphi_n)(x)$.

Then, if the support of φ is contained in a sphere of sufficiently small radius with center the origin, the a_n^{ij} and b_n^i have all the properties required for the coefficients of approximating operators. The function $k(s)$ in 1·4c can be taken as $k(s, \dot{D})$.

The following is a result of Morrey [6: Theorem 4.7], and is quoted here in a simple and restricted form for the convenience of the present applications.

Let D be a bounded domain, A an elliptic differential operator in D with the form 1·1, and assume that

1·6a $a^{ij}\in C(\bar{D})$ and b^i is bounded measurable $(1\leq i, j\leq d)$,

1·6b there exist constants M, M_1 and M_2 such that

$$\|a^{ij}\|_{\bar{D}}\leq M_1, \qquad \|b^i\|_{\bar{D}}\leq M_2, \qquad (1\leq i, j\leq d),$$
$$0<[\sum_{i,j}^{d} a^{ij}(x)\lambda_i\lambda_j]\leq M, \qquad |\lambda|=1, x\in\bar{D}.$$

Then, 1) *if u has continuous partial derivatives up to the second order, and if u and Au belong to $L_2(D)$, then*

1·7 $$[\sum_{\alpha,\beta=1}^{d}\|u,_{\alpha\beta}\|_{2,D_0}^2]^{\frac{1}{2}}\leq L_1, \qquad \bar{D}_0\subset D,$$

where the constant L_1 depends only on

1·8
the dimension d, M, M_1, M_2, D_0, $\|u\|_{2,D}$, $\|Au\|_{2,D}$,
the modulus of continuity $k(s, D)$ of (a^{ij}) on D, and
the distance of D_0 from ∂D.

2) *If, in addition to the hopotheses in* 1), *Au satisfies*

1·9 $$\|Au\|_{2,B(x,r)}\leq L(r/\rho)^{\lambda}, \qquad 0\leq r\leq\rho=\rho(x, \partial D),$$

with $\lambda=(d/2)-1+\mu$, $0<\mu<1$, for all $B(x, r)\equiv\{y:|y-x|<r\}\subset D$, $x\in D$, then

1·10
$$\|u\|_{\bar{D}_0}\leq L_2, \quad \|u,_\alpha\|_{\bar{D}_0}\leq L_3 \qquad (1\leq\alpha\leq d),$$
$$|u,_\alpha(x)-u,_\alpha(y)|\leq L_4|x-y|^\mu, \qquad x, y\in\bar{D}_0\subset D,$$

where the constants L_2, L_3 and L_4 depend only on the quantities 1·8 *and on*

μ and L.

In particular, if Au is bounded, 1·9 is satisfied with $L=\omega^{1/2}\rho_0{}^{d/2}\|Au\|_D$ and $\mu=1/2$ where ω is the volume of the unit ball in R^d and $\rho_0=$(diameter of D)/2.

§ 2. Extension of A.

Given A with the coefficients satisfying 1·2, we shall define an extension $\bar{A}$ of A. First, for each $x_0 \in R^d$, we denote by $\mathfrak{D}_{x_0}(\bar{A})$ the collection of all functions u defined in some neighborhoods (which may depend on each u) of x_0 with the following property: for each $u \in \mathfrak{D}_{x_0}(\bar{A})$, there exist a bounded domain U containing x_0, approximating operators A_n of A on U and a sequence of functions $u_n \in C^2(U)$ such that u_n and $A_n u_n \equiv f_n$ converges uniformly in U to u and a certain limit $f \in C(U)$ respectively. We want to define $\bar{A}$ by $\bar{A}u(x_0)=f(x_0)$ for $u \in \mathfrak{D}_{x_0}(\bar{A})$. But, for this, we must prove that the above limit f does not depend on the choice of (U, A_n, u_n).

To prove this, suppose there exist two (U, A_n, u_n) and (U', A'_n, u'_n) with the property in the definition of $\mathfrak{D}_{x_0}(\bar{A})$. In U we consider the equation

2·1 $$A_n u_n = f_n\,.$$

For this equation, as is easily verified, all the conditions assumed in Morrey's theorem are satisfied; in fact, the corresponding quantities 1·8, L and μ can be chosen to be independent of n, because the coefficients of A_n satisfy 1·4 and $\|u_n\|_D$ and $\|f_n\|_D$ are bounded in $n \geq 1$. Thus, if D_0 is a domain such that $D_0 \ni x_0$ and $\bar{D}_0 \subset U \cap U'$, Morrey's theorem applied to the equation 2·1 implies the existence of constants L_1, L_2, L_3 and L_4 independent of n such that 1·7 and 1·10 hold for $u=u_n$, $n \geq 1$. Hence, we have

2·2 $$\sup_{n\geq 1}\Big[\|u_n\|_{2,D_0}^2+\sum_{\alpha=1}^{d}\|u_{n,\alpha}\|_{2,D_0}^2+\sum_{\alpha,\beta=1}^{d}\|u_{n,\alpha\beta}\|_{2,D_0}^2\Big]^{\frac{1}{2}}<+\infty\,.$$

By the same reason, 2·2 remains true when all the u_n are replaced by u'_n. Now, introduce in $C^2(D_0)$ the inner product:

$$\langle u, v\rangle=(u, v)_{2,D_0}+\sum_{\alpha}(u_{,\alpha}, v_{,\alpha})_{2,D_0}+\sum_{\alpha,\beta}(u_{,\alpha\beta}, v_{,\alpha\beta})_{2,D_0}\,,$$

and denote by $\mathbf{H}$ the real Hilbert space obtained by the completion of $C^2(D_0)$ with respect to the metric $|||u-v||| \equiv \langle u-v, u-v\rangle^{\frac{1}{2}}$. Then, 2·2 means that

$\{u_n, n\geq 1\}$ is a bounded set in $\mathbf{H}$, and therefore contains a subsequence converging weakly. By Banach-Saks theorem, one can choose a sequence of certain convex combinations v_k of elements in that subsequence so that v_k converges strongly in $\mathbf{H}$. v_k can be written as follows:

$$v_k=\sum_{l=k}^{l_k} c_{kl}u_l, \qquad c_{kl}\geq 0, \qquad \sum_{l=1}^{l_k} c_{kl}=1 .$$

By the same argument, there exist some convex combinations v_k':

$$v_k'=\sum_{l=k}^{l_k'} c_{kl}'u_l' , \qquad c_{kl}'\geq 0, \qquad \sum_{l=k}^{l_k'} c_{kl}'=1 ,$$

converging strongly. Put $\tilde{v}_k=v_k-v_k'$. Then, each of $\tilde{v}_k$, $\tilde{v}_{k,\alpha}$ and $\tilde{v}_{k,\alpha\beta}$ $(1\leq\alpha, \beta\leq d)$ converges in the norm of $L_2(D_0)$. But, because by the assumption u_n and u_n' have the same uniform limit u on D_0, the $L_2(D_0)$-limit of $\tilde{v}_k$ is zero, and hence the same holds for $\tilde{v}_{k,\alpha}$ and $\tilde{v}_{k,\alpha\beta}$ as is verified by taking Fourier transform. Hence one has $\|A\tilde{v}_k\|_{2,D_0}\to 0$ as $k\to+\infty$. On the other hand, using the assumptions on u_n and u_n' and on the approximating operators it follows that

$$A\tilde{v}_k=\sum_{l=k}^{l_k} c_{kl}A_lu_l-\sum_{l=k}^{l_k'} c_{kl}'A_l'\,u_l' +\sum_{l=k}^{l_k} c_{kl}(A-A_l)u_l-\sum_{l=k}^{l_k'} c_{kl}'(A-A_l')u_l'$$

converges to $f-f'$ $(f'=\lim A_n'u_n')$ in the norm of $L_2(D_0)$. Thus $f=f'$ almost everywhere on D_0, and hence $f(x)=f'(x)$ for $x\in D_0$ by the continuity.

We now define $\bar{A}$ by $\bar{A}u(x)=f(x)$, $x\in U$ for $u\in\mathfrak{D}_{x_0}(\bar{A})$ where U and f are the same ones in the definition of $\mathfrak{D}_{x_0}(\bar{A})$. $\mathfrak{D}_{x_0}(\bar{A})$ is the local domain at x_0 of $\bar{A}$. Note that if u is defined on a domain D and $u\in\mathfrak{D}_x(\bar{A})$ for every $x\in D$, then $\bar{A}u(x)$ is continuous in D.

LEMMA 2·1. *If* $u\in\mathfrak{D}_{x_0}(\bar{A})$ *and has a local maximum at* x_0 *then* $\bar{A}u(x_0)\leq 0$.

Proof. The proof is similar to that of Lemma 1 of Ventsel [13]. Suppose, on the contrary, that $\bar{A}u(x_0)>0$. By the definition of $\mathfrak{D}_{x_0}(\bar{A})$, there exist a bounded domain U containing x_0, $u_n\in C^2(U)$ $(n\geq 1)$ and approximating operators A_n such that u_n and A_nu_n converge to u and $\bar{A}u$ uniformly on U respectively. Then, there exist ε, $\delta>0$ such that $A_nu_n(x)>\varepsilon$ for $|x-x_0|\leq\delta$ for all sufficiently large n. Put

$$\bar{u}_n(x)=u_n(x)-\varepsilon[\max_{|x-x_0|\leq\delta} A_n|x-x_0|^2]^{-1}|x-x_0|^2.$$

Then for all sufficiently large n, $A_n\bar{u}_n(x)>0$ for $|x-x_0|\leq\delta$, and hence, $\bar{u}_n$ can not have a local maximum inside $|x-x_0|<\delta$. Thus

$$\begin{aligned}u_n(x_0)=\bar{u}_n(x_0)&<\max_{|x-x_0|=\delta}\bar{u}_n(x)\\&=\max_{|x-x_0|=\delta}u_n(x)-\varepsilon\delta^2[\max_{|x-x_0|\leq\delta}A_n|x-x_0|^2]^{-1},\end{aligned}$$

and hence

$$u(x_0)\leq\max_{|x-x_0|\leq\delta}u(x)-2\varepsilon\delta^2[\sum_{i=1}^{d}\{\|a_n^{ij}\|_{B(x_0,\delta)}+\delta\|b_n^i\|_{B(x_0,\delta)}\}]^{-1}.$$

This is true for all sufficiently small $\delta>0$, and therefore contradicts the hypothesis, proving $\bar{A}u(x_0)\leq 0$.

§ 3. The equation $(\lambda-\bar{A})u=f$ and the semigroup on $C_0(\bar{D})$.

In this and later sections, D denotes an open ball $B(a, r)$ with center a and radius r. Take approximating operators $\{A_n\}$ of A on D, and let us prepare a simple lemma.

LEMMA 3·1. *Let $0<r_0\leq r$ and $D_0=\{x:|x-a|<r_0\}$. Let u_n, $n\geq 1$, be the solution of*

3·1
$$\begin{cases}A_nu_n=-f & \text{in } D_0,\ f\in C(\bar{D}_0)\\ u_n=0 & \text{on } \partial D_0\,.\end{cases}$$

Then, there exists a function $\omega(s)$ $(s>0)$, independent of $n\geq 1$ and r_0, such that $\omega(s)\downarrow 0$ as $s\downarrow 0$ and $|u_n(x)|\leq\|f_n\|_{\bar{D}_0}\cdot\omega(\rho)$, $\rho=\rho(x, \partial D)$.

Proof. It is sufficient to prove the lemma in the case $f=1$, because $|u_n(x)|\leq\|f\|_{\bar{D}_0}\cdot|u_n'(x)|$ where u_n' is the solution of 3·1 corresponding to $f_n=1$. Take any $x_0\in\partial D_0$, and let $l=(l_{pq})$ be an orthogonal transformation which sends the vector $r_0^{-1}(a-x_0)$ to the unit vector $(1, 0, \cdots, 0)$. Let M be the constant in 1·4d and $M_2=\sup\|b_n^i\|_{\bar{D}}$, and consider the function

$$v_{x_0}(x)=c_1^2c_2e^{2c_1r_0}\{1-e^{-2c_1l_1(x-x_0)}\}-c_1^{-1}c_2l_1(x-x_0),$$

$$l_1(x-x_0)=\sum_{p=1}^{d}l_{1p}(x^p-x_0^p)\,,\qquad c_1=\sqrt{d}\cdot M\cdot M_2,\qquad c_2=2M\,.$$

Then, using the orthogonality of l and 1·4d, it follows that

3·2
$$v_{x_0}(x)\geq 0\quad\text{and}\quad A_nv_{x_0}(x)\leq -2\,,$$

for x in $\{y:0\leq l_1(y-x_0)\leq 2r_0\}$ and hence in D_0. Thus

3·3 $$A_n(v_{x_0}-u_n)\leq -1$$

in D_0. We now prove that $u_n\leq v_{x_0}$ on $\bar{D}$. Suppose it were not true, and let x_1 be a point at which $v_{x_0}-u_n$ attains its negative minimum on $\bar{D}_0$. Then x_1 must be inside D_0, because $v_{x_0}-u_n\geq 0$ on ∂D_0 by 3·1 and 3·2. Therefore, $A_n(v_{x_0}-u_n)(x_1)\geq 0$ and this contradicts 3·3. Since $u_n\geq 0$, one has $0\leq u_n\leq v_{x_0}$. Thus the lemma holds with

$$\omega(s)=c_1^{-2}c_2e^{2c_1r}(1-e^{-2c_1s})+c_1^{-1}c_2s\,.$$

THEOREM 3·1. *For any $\lambda>0$ and $f\in C(\bar{D})$ the equation*

3·4 $$(\lambda-\bar{A})u=f \text{ in } D,\quad u=0 \quad on \quad \partial D\,,$$

is uniquely solvable in $C_0(\bar{D})$, and the solution u satisfies

3·5 $$\|u\|_{\bar{D}}\leq\lambda^{-1}\|f\|_{\bar{D}},\quad and \quad u\geq 0 \quad if \quad f\geq 0\,,$$

and is the uniform limit of the sequence of the solutions u_n of

3·6 $$(\lambda-\bar{A}_n)u=f \quad in\ D,\quad u=0 \quad on \quad \partial D.$$[1]

Proof. We first notice that any solution of 3·4 or 3·6 satisfies 3·5, which, in fact, follows from Lemma 2·1. If f is of class C^1 on $\bar{D}$, then it is well-known that the solution $\in C^2(D)$ of $(\lambda-A_n)u=f$ in D and $u=0$ on ∂D exists uniquely (for example, see [5: p. 84]). For general $f\in C(\bar{D})$, it follows from the bound 3·5 that the solution u_n of 3·6 is the uniform limit (on $\bar{D}$ and in $n\geq 1$), as $k\uparrow +\infty$, of the solutions $u_{n,k}$ of $(\lambda-A_n)u=f_k$ in D and $u=0$ on ∂D, where f_k is a sequence of functions of class C^1 on $\bar{D}$ converging to f uniformly on $\bar{D}$. We now prove that $u_{n,n}$ converges to the solution 3·4 uniformly as $n\uparrow +\infty$. Because of the bound 3·5 for $u_{n,n}$, 1·9 with Au replaced by $\lambda u_{n,n}-f_n$ holds with constants L and μ independent of n, while A_n satisfies 1·4. Therefore, the Morrey's theorem applied to the equation $A_nu_{n,n}=\lambda u_{n,n}-f_n$ implies that $u_{n,n}$ and its all first derivatives are bounded, on each subdomain D_0 with $\bar{D}_0\subset D$, by certain constants independent of n; in particular, $\{u_{n,n}\}$ constitutes a family of equicontinuous functions on $\bar{D}_0$. Using Lemma 3·1 and noting that D_0 is arbitrary under the condition $\bar{D}_0\subset D$, $\{u_{n,n}\}$ turns out to be an equicontinuous family on $\bar{D}$. Thus, there exists a subsequence of

1) $\bar{A}_n$ is related to A_n as $\bar{A}$ is to A. Similar notations with suffix n will be used throughout.

$\{u_{n,n}\}$ which converges to a certain limit u uniformly on $\bar{D}$. This limit u solves 3·5 because $u \in C_0(\bar{D}) \cap \{\bigcap_{x \in D} \mathfrak{D}_x(\bar{A})\}$, and the uniqueness of the solution follows from Lemma 2·1. Finally, because $u_{n,k}$ converges to u_n uniformly on $\bar{D}$ and in $n \geq 1$ as $k \uparrow +\infty$, and because every (uniform) limit function in the (compact) set $\{u_{n,n}\}$ is the unique solution of 3·4, u_n converges to u uniformly on $\bar{D}$ as $n \uparrow +\infty$. Q.E.D.

Denote by $\mathfrak{D}(\bar{A}_D)$ the space of functions $u \in C_0(D)$ such that $u \in \mathfrak{D}_x(\bar{A})$ for each $x \in D$ and $\bar{A}u \in C_0(D)$. We define $\bar{A}_D$ by $\bar{A}_D u(x) = \bar{A}u(x)$, $x \in D$, for $u \in \mathfrak{D}(\bar{A}_D)$.

THEOREM 3·2. *If $\mathfrak{D}(\bar{A}_D)$ is dense in $C_0(D)$, then* (1) *there exists a unique semigroup of operators $\{T_D^t, t>0\}$ acting on $C_0(D)$ with generator $\bar{A}_D$ such that*

3·7 $$\lim_{t \downarrow 0} \|T_D^t f - f\|_D = 0, \qquad f \in C_0(D)$$

3·8 $$T_D^t f \geq 0 \quad \textit{if} \quad f \geq 0, \quad \textit{and} \quad \|T_D^t 1\|_D \leq 1 .$$

(2) *Let $\{T_{n,D}^t\}$ denote the semigroup with generator $\bar{A}_{n,D}$. Then*

3·9 $$\lim_{n \uparrow +\infty} \|T_D^t f - T_{n,D}^t f\|_D = 0, \qquad f \in C_0(D), \quad t>0 .$$

Proof. Under the assumption, Theorem 3·1 means that, for each $\lambda>0$, $(\lambda - \bar{A}_D)$ maps the dense subset $\mathfrak{D}(\bar{A}_D)$ of $C_0(D)$ onto $C_0(D)$ in one to one way, and the inverse $(\lambda - \bar{A}_D)^{-1}$ is a positive operator with norm $\leq \lambda^{-1}$. Thus, (1) follows from Hille-Yosida's theorem. (2) results from Theorem 3·1 using Trotter [12: Theorem 5·1]. Q.E.D.

Remark. If b^i is continuous ($1 \leq i \leq d$), then $\mathfrak{D}(\bar{A}_D)$ is dense in $C_0(D)$, because $\mathfrak{D}(\bar{A}_D)$ contains functions in $C^2(D)$ with compact supports $\subset D$. Without the continuity of b^i, this dense property of $\mathfrak{D}(\bar{A}_D)$ will be proved in the next section.

§ 4. $\{T_{n,D}^t\}$ and the corresponding diffusion.

To the semigroup $\{T_{n,D}^t\}$ there corresponds a unique system of transition measures $\{P_{n,D}(t, x, \cdot), t>0, x \in D\}$ on D with total mass ≤ 1 such that

$$T_{n,D}^t f(x) = \int f(y) P_{n,D}(t, x, dy), \qquad f \in C_0(D) .$$

These transition measures give rise to a diffusion on $\tilde{D}$. To be precise, let $\tilde{D}$

be the one-point compactification $D\cup\{\infty\}$ of D (∞ is an extra point), and introduce the sample space $\mathbf{W}_D$ of continuous paths w: $t\in[0,+\infty)\to x(t,w)=x(t)=x_t\in D$ such that $x(t,w)\in D$ for $t<\sigma_\infty$ and $=\infty$ for $t\geq\sigma_\infty$ where $0\leq\sigma_\infty(w)\leq+\infty$, and the corresponding coordinate field $\mathbf{B}_D$. Then, probability measures $\mathbf{P}^x_{n,D}(\cdot)$, $x\in D$, on $\mathbf{B}_D$ can be introduced by

$$\mathbf{P}^x_{n,D}[x(t)\in A]=\mathbf{P}_{n,D}(t,x,A),\quad x\in D,\ A\subset D,$$
$$\mathbf{P}^\infty_{n,D}[x(t)=\infty,\quad t\geq 0]=1.$$

$[\mathbf{W}_D, \mathbf{B}_D, \mathbf{P}^x_{n,D}, x\in D]$ is a strong Markov process[2], which is called $\bar{A}_{n,D}$-diffusion.

$\bar{A}_{n,D}$-diffusion can also be constructed using the stochastic integral equation of K. Ito [4] as follows. Let $\alpha^{ij}_n(x)$ be the positive definite square root of the matrix $\{2a^{ij}_n(x)\}$, extend $\alpha^{ij}_n(x)$ and $b^i_n(x)$ $(1\leq i,j\leq d)$ to the whole of R^d so that they satisfy the Lipschitz condition, and let $y^{(x)}_t$ be the solution of the stochastic integral equation:

4·1 $$y^{(x)i}_t=x^i+\sum_{j=1}^d\int_0^t\alpha^{ij}_n(y^{(x)}_s)d\xi^j_s+\int_0^t b^i_n(y^{(x)}_s)ds,$$

where $\xi_t=(\xi^1_t,\cdots,\xi^d_t)$ is a Brownian motion in R^d. Then

$$\mathbf{P}^x_{n,D}(x_t\in A)=\mathbf{P}(y^{(x)}_t\in A,\quad \tau<t),\qquad x\in D,\quad A\subset D;\quad \tau=\inf\{t\geq 0:y^{(x)}_t\notin D\}.$$

Using the above stochastic integral representation of the sample path, H. P. McKean[3] showed that for any open set U and compact set $F\subset U$

4·2a $$\mathbf{P}^x_{n,D}(x_t\in U^c)=o(t),\qquad t\downarrow 0,$$

$o(t)$ being uniform in $x\in F$ and in $n\geq 1$, and that for any $\varepsilon>0$ there exists a constant $\delta>0$ independent of n such that

2) Strong Markov property results from the fact that the corresponding semigroup maps $C_0(D)$ into itself.

3) 4.2 are the consequences of the following McKean's sharper estimate concerning stochastic integrals: if $(\alpha^{ij}(t))$ is a positive definite $d\times d$-matrix with eigenvalues bounded above and below by positive constants, and each component is a measurable function of the sample path $\{\xi^i(s);s\leq t\}$ of the d-dimensional Brownian motion (ξ^i), and if $\boldsymbol{a}(t)$ is the d-dimensional vector with components $\sum_{j=1}^d\int_0^t\alpha^{ij}(s)\xi^j(ds)$ (stochastic integrals), then

$$P[|\boldsymbol{a}(t)|>\varepsilon]\leq K\cdot e^{-\frac{c}{t}}$$

where K, $c>0$ depend only on the bounds of eigenvalues, $\varepsilon>0$ and d.

4·2b $$\mathbf{P}^x_{n,D}[\sup_{\substack{0<t_1,t_2<\sigma_\infty \\ |t_2-t_1|\leq\delta}} |x(t_2)-x(t_1)|<\varepsilon]>1-\varepsilon\,.$$

Let $G^\lambda_{n,D}$ be the Green operator:

4·3 $$G^\lambda_{n,D}f(x)=\mathbf{E}^x_{n,D}\Big[\int_0^{\sigma_\infty} e^{-\lambda t}f(x_t)dt\Big], \qquad \lambda>0^{4)},$$
$$=\int_0^{+\infty} e^{-\lambda t}T^t_{n,D}f(x)dt, \qquad \text{if } f\in C_0(D)\,.$$

Then, $u=G^\lambda_{n,D}f$ $(f\in C_0(D))$ is the solution of 3·6. 4·1 implies that

4·4 $$\|\lambda G^\lambda_{n,D}f-f\|_D\to 0, \qquad f\in C_0(D)\,,$$

uniformly in $n\geq 1$ as $\lambda\uparrow+\infty$. But, because by Theorem 3·1 for each $\lambda>0$ $G^\lambda_{n,D}f$ converges uniformly on D to the solution u_λ of 3·4, 4·4 holds when $G^\lambda_{n,D}f$ is replaced by u_λ, and in particular, *$\mathfrak{D}(\bar{A}_D)$ is dense in $C_0(D)$*. Thus, Theorem 3·2 *is valid without the continuity assumption of b^i*.

§ 5. Construction of the diffusion with generator $\bar{A}$.

Let $\{T^t_D\}$ be the semigroup constructed in Theorem 3·2. By the Riesz-Markoff theorem, for each $x\in D$ and $t>0$ there is a unique regular positive measure $P_D(t, x, \cdot)$ with total mass ≤ 1 such that

$$T^t_D f(x)=\int f(y)P_D(t, x, dy), \qquad f\in C_0(D)\,,$$
$$P_D(t+s, x, \cdot)=\int P_D(s, x, dy)P_D(t, y, \cdot)\,.$$

Defining

$$P_D(t, x, \infty)=1-P_D(t, x, D), \qquad x\in D$$
$$P_D(t, \infty, A)=1 \quad , \quad \text{if } A\ni\infty$$
$$=0 \quad , \quad \text{otherwise,}$$

$\{P_D(t, x, \cdot),\ x\in\tilde{D}\}$ turns out to be a transition probability on $\tilde{D}$.

LEMMA 5·1. *$P_D(t, x, \cdot)$ has a uniform local character: if U is open in $\tilde{D}$ and F is a closed subset of U then $t^{-1}P_D(t, x, U^c)\to 0$ uniformly in $x\in F$ as $t\downarrow 0$.*

---

4) $\mathbf{E}^x_{n,D}[f\,;B]=\int_B f(w)\mathbf{P}^x_{n,D}(dw)$ and $\mathbf{E}^x_{n,D}[f]=\mathbf{E}^x_{n,D}[f\,;\mathbf{W}_D]$. We also use the similar notations without suffix n.

Proof. If $U \not\ni \infty$, take another open set U_1 such that $F \subset U_1$ and $\bar{U}_1 \subset U$, and choose $f \geq 0$ in $C_0(D)$ such that $f=1$ in U_1 and $=0$ outside U. Then, from 3·9 and 4·2a,

$$\begin{aligned} P_D(t, x, U^c) &\leq 1 - T_D^t f = 1 - \lim_{n \to +\infty} T_{n,D}^t f \\ &\leq 1 - \varliminf_{n \to +\infty} P_{n,D}(t, x, U_1) \\ &\leq \varlimsup_{n \to +\infty} P_{n,D}^x[x(t) \in U_1^c] = o(t), \end{aligned}$$

$o(t)$ being uniform in $x \in F$. The case when $U \ni \infty$ is treated similarly.

By this lemma, using Ray's theorem[5)], one can introduce a family of probability measures $\{\mathbf{P}_D^x(\cdot),\ x \in \tilde{D}\}$ on $\mathbf{B}_D$ so that $[\mathbf{W}_D, \mathbf{B}_D, \mathbf{P}_D^x, x \in \tilde{D}]$ is a diffusion process[5)] with transition probability $P_D(t, x, \cdot)$. We call this process $\bar{A}_D$-diffusion. Of course, $G_D^\lambda f$ $(f \in C_0(D))$ defined similarly to 4·3 is the solution of 3·4.

Next, take an open ball D_1 such that $D_1 \supset \bar{D}$. Then, if $\{A_n\}$ are approximating operators on D_1, they are also approximating operators on D and $\bar{A}_{n,D}$-diffusion up to σ_∞ is identical in law to $\bar{A}_{n,D_1}$-diffusion up to the exit time $\sigma_D = \inf\{t : x(t) \notin D\}$, because for $f \in C_0(D)$

5·1 $$u_n(x) = \mathbf{E}_{n,D_1}^x\left[\int_0^{\sigma_D} e^{-\lambda t} f(x_t)\,dt\right], \qquad \lambda > 0, \quad n \geq 1$$

solves the (resolvent) equation 3·6 for $\bar{A}_{n,D}$-diffusion. But, this identity in law is not obvius for $\bar{A}_D$- and $\bar{A}_{D_1}$-diffusions. Let $\tilde{W}_{D_1}$ be the space of continuous paths

$$w : [0, +\infty) \to x(t, w) = x(t) = x_t \in \tilde{D}_1 = D_1 \cup \{\infty\}$$

such that $\lim_{t \to +\infty} x(t, w) = \infty$. $\tilde{W}_{D_1}$ endowed with the metric

$$\rho(w, w') = \sup_{0 \leq t < +\infty} \tilde{\rho}(x(t, w), x(t, w'))$$

is a complete metric space, where $\tilde{\rho}$ is the metric of the compact set $\tilde{D}_1$. Each of $\mathbf{P}_{n,D_1}^n(\cdot)$ and $\mathbf{P}_{D_1}^x(\cdot)$ is a probability measure on the topological Borel field of $\tilde{W}_{D_1}$, and because of 3·9 and 4·2b an application of Prohorov's theorem [8:p. 181] yields, for any bounded continuous function F on $\tilde{W}_{D_1}$,

5) See [9] or [2:Chap. 6].

5·2 $$\lim \mathbf{E}^x_{n,D_1}(F)=\mathbf{E}^x_{D_1}(F).$$

LEMMA 5·2. *For any $\varepsilon>0$ and $x\in D$ there exist continuous functions h_1 and h_2 on $\tilde{W}_{D_1}$ such that $0\leq h_1\leq \sigma_D\leq h_2$ and $\mathbf{E}^x_{n,D_1}(h_2-h_1)<\varepsilon$.*

Proof. Take $D_2=B(a, r_2)$ and $D_0=B(a, r_0)$ so that $x\in D_2$, $\bar{D}_2\subset D$, $\bar{D}\subset D_0$, $\bar{D}_0\subset D_1$; put $\sigma_0=\sigma_{D_0}$, $\sigma_2=\sigma_{D_2}$. Because $\mathbf{E}^x_{n,D_1}(\sigma_0)$ is equal to

$$\mathbf{E}^x_{n,D_1}(\sigma_2)+\mathbf{E}^x_{n,D_1}[\mathbf{E}^{x(\sigma_2)}_{n,D}(\sigma_0)]$$

and is the solution of 3·1 with $f=1$, using Lemma 3·1 one sees that there exist r_0 and r_2 such that $\mathbf{E}^x_{n,D}(\sigma_0-\sigma_2)<\varepsilon$, $n\leq 1$. Let g_1 and g_2 be continuous functions on $[0, +\infty)$ such that $0\leq g_1$, $g_2\leq 1$, $g_1=1$ on $[0, r_2]$ and $g_1=0$ on $[r, +\infty)$, $g_2=1$ on $[0, r]$ and $g_2=0$ on $[r_0, +\infty)$. Then the following functions have the desired properties.

$$h_i(w)=\int_0^{+\infty} g_i(\max_{0\leq s\leq t}|x_s-a|)ds, \qquad i=1, 2.$$

LEMMA 5·3. *$\bar{A}_D$-diffusion up to σ_∞ is identical in law to $\bar{A}_{D_1}$-diffusion up to σ_D.*

Proof. It is enough to prove that for $f\geq 0$ in $C_0(D_1)$

$$u(x)=\mathbf{E}^x_{D_1}\left[\int_0^{\sigma_D} e^{-\lambda t}f(x_t)dt\right], \qquad \lambda>0, \quad x\in D,$$

is the limit of $u_n(x)$ defined by 5.1 as $n\uparrow +\infty$, because u_n is the solution of 3·6 and hence by Theorem 3·1 converges to the solution $G^\lambda_D f$ of 3·4. Fix $x\in D$, and for given $\varepsilon>0$ choose h_1 and h_2 as in Lemma 5·2. Then

$$F_i(w)=\int_0^{h_i(w)} e^{-\lambda t}f(x_t)dt, \qquad i=1, 2,$$

is bounded continuous on $\tilde{W}_{D_1}$ and hence by 5·2 $\mathbf{E}^x_{n,D_1}(F_i)\to\mathbf{E}^x_{D_1}(F_i)$, $i=1, 2$, as $n\to+\infty$. But, because

$$F_1(w)\leq \int_0^{\sigma_D} e^{-\lambda t}f(x_t)dt\leq F_2(w), \qquad \mathbf{E}^x_{n,D_1}(F_2-F_1)<\varepsilon\|f\|_{D_1},$$

one sees that $\lim u_n(x)=u(x)$. Q.E.D.

---

6) a is the center, and r is the radius of D.

Let E^d be the one-point compactification $R^d \cup \{\infty\}$ of R^d, **W** the space of continuous paths $w: t \in [0, +\infty) \to x(t, w) = x(t) = x_t \in E^d$ such that $x(t, w) \in R^d$ for $t < \tau_\infty$ and $= \infty$ for $t \geq \tau_\infty$, where $0 \leq \tau_\infty(w) \leq +\infty$, and **B** the corresponding coordinate Borel field. From Lemma 5·3, one can construct a family of probability measures $\{\mathbf{P}^x(\cdot),\ x \in R^d\}$ on **B** such that $[\mathbf{W}, \mathbf{B}, \mathbf{P}^x]$ is a diffusion and that $\mathbf{P}^x(x_t \in A, t < \sigma_D) = \mathbf{P}^x_D(x_t \in A)$, $x \in D$, $A \subset D$, for each open ball D (for example, by Bochner's projective limit construction of stochastic processes [1:p. 120] [11]). Denote by $\{T^t\}$ and $\{G^\lambda\}$ the corresponding semigroup and Green operators, and by $H_{\partial D}$ the harmonic measure:

$$H_{\partial D}(x, A) = \mathbf{E}^x[x(\sigma_D) \in A], \qquad x \in D, \quad A \subset \partial D.$$

LEMMA 5·4. i) *G^λ, $\lambda > 0$, maps $B(R^d)$ into $C(R^d)$, and if $f \in C(R^d)$, $u \equiv G^\lambda f$ is a solution of $(\lambda - \tilde{A})u = f$ in R^d.* ii) *$H_{\partial D}$ maps $B(\partial D)$ into $C(D)$.*

Proof. i) For each D, let $A_{n,D}$ be the approximating operators on D obtained by the method of 1.5 with φ (may depend on D) having sufficiently small support in $\{|x| < 1\}$. If $f \in C(R^d)$, then by the proof of Lemma 5·3,

$$u_{n,D}(x) = \mathbf{E}^x_{n,D}\left[\int_0^{+\infty} e^{-\lambda t} f(x_t) dt\right]$$

converges, as $n \uparrow +\infty$, to the function

$$u_D(x) = \mathbf{E}^x_D\left[\int_0^{\sigma_\infty} e^{-\lambda t} f(x_t) dt\right] = \mathbf{E}^x\left[\int_0^{\sigma_D} e^{-\lambda t} f(x_t) dt\right],$$

and, if $f \geq 0$, $u_D(x)$ increases to $u(x)$ as $D \uparrow R^d$. On the other hand, if in addition, $f \in C^1(R^d)$, $u_{n,D}$ is a bounded ($\|u_{n,D}\|_D \leq \lambda^{-1} \|f\|_D$) solution of $(\lambda - A_n)u = f$ in D, and hence applying the estimate in § 1 to the quation $(\lambda - A_n)u_{n,D} = f$ in a fixed domain D_0 $\{u_{n,D};\ n \geq 1, D \supset D_0, f \in C^1(R^d)$ and $\|f\|_{R^d} \leq 1\}$ turns out to be equicontinuous in D_0. Therefore $\{G^\lambda f;\ f \in C^1(R^d)$ and $\|f\|_{R^d} \leq 1\}$ is equicontinuous on each compact set, and hence the same for $\{G^\lambda f;\ f \in B(R^d)$ and $\|f\|_{R^d} \leq 1\}$. This implies that G^λ maps $B(R^d)$ into $C(R^d)$, and the rest is clear. The proof of ii) is much the same as above and is omitted.

We see easily that the range $G^\lambda(C(R^d))$ is independent of $\lambda > 0$, G^λ is one to one from $C(R^d)$ onto the common range and that $\lambda - (G^\lambda)^{-1}$ acting on the on the common range is also independent of $\lambda > 0$. $\lambda - (G^\lambda)^{-1}$ is called the generator of the diffusion $[\mathbf{W}, \mathbf{B}, \mathbf{P}^x]$. Summarizing the results in this section, we have

THEOREM 5·1. *There exists a diffusion* $[\mathbf{W}, \mathbf{B}, \mathbf{P}^x]$ *on* R^d *such that the Green opertor maps* $C(R^d)$ *into itself and the generator is a contraction of* $\bar{A}$.

If b^i is continuous $(1 \leq i \leq d)$, and if f is a C^2-function with compact support, then f restricted on D belongs to $\mathfrak{D}(\bar{A}_D)$ provided D contains the support of f. Noting the uniform local character of the transition function of $\bar{A}$-diffusion, we have the following

THEOREM 5·2. *If* b^i *is continuous* $(1 \leq i \leq d)$, *there exists a diffusion on* R^d *such that the corresponding semigroup* T^t *(acting on the space* $B(R^d)$) *satisfies*

$$\lim_{t \downarrow 0} \left\| \frac{T^t f - f}{t} - \sum_{i,j=1}^{d} a^{ij} \frac{\partial^2 f}{\partial x^i \partial x^j} - \sum_{i=1}^{d} b^i \frac{\partial f}{\partial x^i} \right\|_{R^d} = 0$$

for any C^2*-function* f *with compact support.*

References.

[1] S. BOCHNER, *Harmonic analysis and the theory of probability*, 1955.
[2] E. B. DYNKIN, *Theory of Markov processes* (English translation). Pergamon Press. 1961.
[3] I. B. GIRSANOV, *On stochastic integral equations of Ito*. D. A. H. CCCP. **138** (1961), 18–21.
[4] K. ITO, *On stochastic differential equations in a differentiable manifold.* Nagoya Math. J. **1** (1950), 35–47.
[5] S. ITO, *Fundamental solutions of parabolic differential equations and boundary value problems*. Jap. J. Math. 27 (1957), 55–102.
[6] C. B. MORREY, JR, *Second order elliptic system of differential equations.* Contribution to the theory of partial differential equations. Ann. Math. Studies. **33**, 101–159.
[7] E. NELSON, *An existence theorem for second order parabolic equations.* 88 (1958), 414–429.
[8] YU. V. PROHOROV, *Convergence of random processes and limit theorems in probability theory* (English translation). Theory of prob. and its appl. **1** (1956), 157–214.
[9] D. RAY, *Stationary Markov processes with continuous paths.* 82 (1956), 452–493.
[10] A. B. SKOROHOD, Исследования по теории случайных процессов, (1961).
[11] H. TOTOKI, *A Method of construction of measures on function spaces and its applications to stochastic processes.* Mem. Fac. Sci., Kyushu Univ. A. **15**, (1962), 178–190.
[12] H. TROTTER, *Approximation of semigroups of operators.* Pacific J. Math. **8** (1958), 887–919.
[13] A. D. VENTSEL, *On lateral conditions for multidimensional diffusion processes.*

Propagation of chaos for certain purely discontinuous Markov processes with interactions

Dedicated to Professor Kôsaku Yosida on his 60th birthday

By Hiroshi TANAKA

§1. Introduction.

Given a measurable space $(Q, \mathfrak{F})$ such that each single point set is in $\mathfrak{F}$, we consider a nonlinear equation for probability measures on Q:

$$\frac{du(t)}{dt}=\sum_{n=1}^{\infty}\int_Q q_n(x)\{\Pi_n(x, u(t), \cdot)-\delta(x, \cdot)\}u(t, dx)\ , \tag{1.1}$$

with the initial data f in $\mathfrak{M}$, the set of all probability measures on $(Q, \mathfrak{F})$. We assume that each $q_n(x)$ is a nonnegative $\mathfrak{F}$-measurable function on Q, $q(x)\equiv \sum_{n=1}^{\infty} q_n(x)<\infty$ and

$$\Pi_n(x,f,\Gamma)=\int\cdots\int\Pi_n(x, x_1, \cdots, x_n, \Gamma)f(dx_1)\cdots f(dx_n)\ , \tag{1.2}$$
$$(f\in\mathfrak{M}, \Gamma\in\mathfrak{F})$$

where (i) $\Pi_n(x, x_1, \cdots, x_n, \cdot)\in\mathfrak{M}$ for each fixed $n, x_1, \cdots, x_n$, and (ii) $\Pi_n(x, x_1, \cdots, x_n, \Gamma)$ is measurable in $(x, x_1, \cdots, x_n)$ for each $\Gamma\in\mathfrak{F}$ and symmetric in $(x_1, \cdots, x_n)$ for each x and Γ. The precise meaning that $u(t)$ is a solution of (1.1) with $u(0)=f$ in $\mathfrak{M}$ is understood as follows. $u(t)$ is in $\mathfrak{M}$ for each $t\geq 0$ and satisfies

$$\begin{aligned} u(t, \Gamma)=&\int_\Gamma e^{-q(x)t}f(dx)\\ &+\int_0^t ds\int_Q u(s, dy)\sum_{n=1}^{\infty}q_n(y)\int_\Gamma e^{-(t-s)q(z)}\Pi_n(y, u(s), dz), \Gamma\in\mathfrak{F}, t\geq 0\ . \end{aligned} \tag{1.3}$$

The usual method of successive approximation provides us with the smallest solution of (1.3) among substochastic solutions, but of course, this smallest solution is not necessarily stochastic. We denote by $\mathfrak{U}$ the set of those $f\in\mathfrak{M}$ for which the smallest solutions of (1.3) belong to $\mathfrak{M}$ for each $t\geq 0$; it can happen that the class $\mathfrak{U}$ becomes empty.

Probabilistic significance is that the equation (1.1) corresponds to a Markov process describing the motion of one particle under the interactions with infinite number of similar particles. This class of Markov processes was first introduced and the explanation was given in the works of McKean [2] [3] through the so-called propagation of chaos, the notion which Kac [1] discovered for his 1-dimensional model of Maxwellian gas. In this direction, there are also works of D. P. Johnson [4] and T. Ueno [8], in which the propagation of chaos for the equation (1.1) were proved under a certain growth condition on $\{q_n(x)\}_{n\geq 1}$ when each $q_n(x)$ is bounded. The purpose of this paper is to prove that the propagation of chaos for (1.1) holds in the sense described below if the initial distribution f is taken from the class $\mathfrak{U}$. The method is similar to that of H. Tanaka [7] in its outline.

For each $n\geq 2$, we consider a Markov process $X(t)$ of n particles under motion. If each $q_k(x)$ is bounded, it is the Markov process on the state space $Q^n=Q\times\cdots\times Q$ with generator A_n given by

$$(1.4)\qquad (A_n\varphi)(x_1,\cdots,x_n)=\sum_{N=1}^{n-1} n^{-N}\sum{}' q_n(x_i)\{\varphi_N(x_i, x_{i_1},\cdots,x_{i_N})-\varphi\},$$

where $\varphi_N(x_i, x_{i_1},\cdots,x_{i_N})$ denotes the integral of $\varphi(\cdots,x_{i-1},x,x_{i+1},\cdots)$ viewed as a function of x alone with respect to the measure $\Pi_N(x_i, x_{i_1},\cdots,x_{i_N}, dx)$, and $\sum{}'$ means the summation over all ordered $(N+1)$-tuples $(i, i_1,\cdots,i_N)$ of different integers taken from $\{1,\cdots,n\}$. But, if $q_k(x)$ is unbounded, the minimal Markov process corresponding to (1.4) is not necessarily conservative, that is, it can happen that the life time ζ is finite with positive probability. If this is the case, possibly some particles have jumped only finite number of times before ζ, and in our definition of the process $X(t)$ each of such particles continues the motion without dying until it performs infinite number of jumps. The precise definition of the process $X(t)$ will be given in §4. Now our main result is stated as follows. For each $f\in\mathfrak{U}$ and $1\leq m<\infty$, the probability distribution at time t of m particles with arbitrary fixed coordinate numbers among n particles starting from the initial distribution $f^n=f\otimes\cdots\otimes f$ and performing the Markovian motion $X(\cdot)$ tends as $n\uparrow\infty$ to the m-fold outer product $u(t)^m=u(t)\otimes\cdots\otimes u(t)$ of the solution $u(t)$ of (1.3).

§2. Preliminaries.

In this paper we shall be concerned with several spaces such as the n-fold product space Q^n, the direct sum spaces $\boldsymbol{Q}_n=Q^1+\cdots+Q^n$ and $\boldsymbol{Q}=Q^1+Q^2+\cdots$; since Q is a measurable space, these spaces can also be considered as measurable spaces by the usual way. All functions we consider in this paper are real-valued and measurable, and so the words *real-valued* and *measurable* are often omitted for functions; the latter omission is the same for sets. The supremum norm of a bounded function φ is denoted by $\|\varphi\|$, and the integral over a set Γ of a function φ with respect to a (signed) measure f is denoted by $\langle f, \varphi\rangle_\Gamma$ or simply by $\langle f, \varphi\rangle$ if Γ is the whole space.

1°. *$\{q, \Pi\}$-minimal transition function.* Given a measurable space $(R, \mathfrak{G})$, we consider a kernel $A(x, \Gamma)$ over $(R, \mathfrak{G})$ expressed in the form:

$$A(x, \Gamma)=q(x)\{\Pi(x, \Gamma)-\delta(x, \Gamma)\}, \qquad x\in R,\ \Gamma\in\mathfrak{G},$$

where $0\leq q(x)<\infty$, and $\Pi(x, \Gamma)$ is a substochastic measure on R for each x and $\mathfrak{G}$-measurable in x for each Γ. The minimal solution $p(t, x, \Gamma)$ of the backward equation associated with $A(x, \Gamma)$:

$$u(t, x, \Gamma)=e^{-q(x)t}\delta(x, \Gamma)+\int_0^t ds\int_R q(x)e^{-q(x)s}u(t-s, y, \Gamma)\Pi(x, dy) \tag{2.1}$$

is obtained by the usual successive approximation as follows. Set

$$p_0(t, x, \Gamma)=e^{-q(x)t}\delta(x, \Gamma) \tag{2.2a}$$

$$p_{k+1}(t, x, \Gamma)=p_0(t, x, \Gamma)+\int_0^t ds\int_R q(x)e^{-q(x)s}p_k(t-s, y, \Gamma)\Pi(x, dy)\ . \tag{2.2b}$$

Then, $p_k(t, x, \Gamma)$ increases to $p(t, x, \Gamma)$ as $k\uparrow\infty$; the p_k's are also obtained by

$$p_0(t, x, \Gamma)=e^{-q(x)t}\delta(x, \Gamma) \tag{2.3a}$$

$$p_{k+1}(t, x, \Gamma)=p_0(t, x, \Gamma)+\int_0^t ds\int_R p_k(s, x, dy)q(y)\int_\Gamma e^{-q(z)(t-s)}\Pi(y, dz)\ , \tag{2.3b}$$

and hence $p(t, x, \Gamma)$ is the minimal solution of the forward equation:

$$u(t, x, \Gamma)=e^{-q(x)t}\delta(x, \Gamma)+\int_0^t ds\int_R u(s, x, dy)q(y)\int_\Gamma e^{-q(z)(t-s)}\Pi(y, dz)\ . \tag{2.4}$$

$p(t, x, \Gamma)$ is called the $\{q, \Pi\}$-minimal transition function; it is a substochastic measure for each t and x.

We now prepare a simple convergence lemma for a sequence of $\{q_n, \Pi_n\}$-minimal transition functions. Let $0\leq q_n(x)<\infty$ and $\Pi_n(x, \Gamma)=r_n(x)\Pi(x, \Gamma)$, and assume that (i) $\Pi(x, \cdot)$ and $\Pi_n(x, \cdot)$ are substochastic measures for each x and (ii) $q_n(x)$ and $r_n(x)$ converge respectively to finite limits $q(x)$ and $r(x)\equiv 1$ as $n\uparrow\infty$. Define $p_{k,n}(t, x, \Gamma)$ by (2.2) with q and Π replaced by q_n and Π_n respectively, and let $p_{\cdot,n}(t, x, \Gamma)$ be the $\{q_n, \Pi_n\}$-minimal transition function. Then, $p_{k,n}(t, x, \Gamma)$ *tends to $p_k(t, x, \Gamma)$ as $n\uparrow\infty$ for each t, x and k, and therefore if at a point x there exists an integer $m\geq 1$ such that*

$$p_{k,n}(t, x, \cdot)=p_{m,n}(t, x, \cdot) \text{ for all } k\geq m \text{ and } n\geq 1,$$

then $p_{\cdot,n}(t, x, \cdot)$ *tends to* $p(t, x, \cdot)$ *as* $n\uparrow\infty$.

2°. *A formula solving the equation* (1.3). S. Tanaka [7] and T. Ueno [9] expressed the (minimal) solution of the equation (1.3) in an explicit form; a part of their results is sketched here as a preparation for the next section. First we introduce the set $T=\bigcup_{n=1}^{\infty} T_n$, each set T_n being defined inductively as follows. (a) T_1 consists of single element θ. (b) If T_m is defined for $m<n$, then T_n is defined as the set consisting of all objects τ's of the form $\tau=[\tau_0, \tau_1, \cdots, \tau_k]$ where $\tau_j\in T_{n_j}$, $n_0+n_1\cdots+n_k=n$, $k\geq 1$. Next, we introduce the following notation for measure-valued t-functions $f_0(t), \cdots, f_k(t)$.

$$[f_0, f_1, \cdots, f_k](t, \Gamma)=\int_0^t ds\int_Q f_0(s, dx)q_k(x)\int_{Q^k} f_1(s, dx_1)$$

$$\cdots f_k(s, dx_k)\int_\Gamma e^{-q(y)(t-s)}\Pi_k(x, x_1, \cdots, x_k, dy).$$

Given the equation (1.3), we now define the measure-valued t-function $u_\tau=u_\tau(t)$ indexed by $\tau\in T$ inductively as follows.

(i) $u_\theta=u_\theta(t, \Gamma)=\langle f, e^{-q(\cdot)t}\rangle_\Gamma$.

(ii) $u_\tau=[u_{\tau_0}, u_{\tau_1}, \cdots, u_{\tau_k}]$ for $\tau=[\tau_0, \tau_1, \cdots, \tau_k]$.

Then the (minimal) solution $u(t)$ of (1.3) is expressed as

$$u(t)=\sum_{\tau\in T} u_\tau(t)=\sum_{n=1} u_n(t)\ ;$$

here $u_n(t)=\sum_{\tau\in T_n} u_\tau(t)$ is defined inductively by

$$u_n=\sum_{k=1}^{n-1}\sum_{\substack{n_0+\cdots+n_k=n\\ n_0,\cdots,n_k\geq 1}}[u_{n_0}, u_{n_1}, \cdots, u_{n_k}]\,, \qquad u_1=u_\theta\,. \tag{2.5}$$

§ 3. A formula concerning the minimal solution of (1.3).

In this section the formula given in the second half of the preceding section is discussed from another point of view; the resulting formula (3.2) will be the basis for the proof of the propagation of chaos.

Let φ_m be a function on Q^m. Writing $\Pi_N(x_i, x_{i_1}, \cdots, x_{i_N}, \varphi_m)$ for the integral

$$\int_Q \Pi_N(x_i, x_{i_1}, \cdots, x_{i_N}, dx)\varphi_m(\cdots, x_{i-1}, x, x_{i+1}, \cdots)\ (i_1, \cdots, i_N>m)$$

and regarding it as a functions of $\max_{1\leq k\leq N} i_k$ variables, we collect the functions of k variables in the formal series:

$$\sum_{m=1}^{\infty}\sum_{N=1}^{\infty}\sum_{i=1}^{m} q_N(x_i)\{\Pi_N(x_i, x_{m+1}, \cdots, x_{m+N}, \varphi_m)-\varphi_m\} .$$

The result is

$$\sum_{m=1}^{k-1}\sum_{i=1}^{m} q_{k-m}(x_i)\Pi_{k-m}(x_i, x_{m+1}, \cdots, x_k, \varphi_m)-\sum_{i=1}^{k} q(x_i)\varphi_m$$

for $k\geq 2$ and $-q(x_1)\varphi_1(x_1)$ for $k=1$. On the basis of this result, we introduce a $\{q, \Pi\}$-function on $\boldsymbol{Q}$ as follows. For $\boldsymbol{x}=(x_1, \cdots, x_k)\in Q^k$

$$\boldsymbol{q}(\boldsymbol{x})=q(x_1)+\cdots+q(x_k) , \tag{3.1a}$$

$$\begin{aligned}\boldsymbol{\Pi}(x, \Gamma)&=\boldsymbol{q}(\boldsymbol{x})^{-1}\sum_{i=1}^{m} q_{k-m}(x_i)\Pi_{k-m}(x_i, x_{m+1}, \cdots, x_k, \chi_{\Gamma}) \\ &\qquad \text{for } \Gamma\subset Q^m \text{ with } 1\leq m\leq k-1 \\ &=0 \quad \text{for } \Gamma\subset Q^m \text{ with } m\geq k \\ &=0 \quad \text{for all } \Gamma \text{ if } k=1 .\end{aligned} \tag{3.1b}$$

An easy calculation shows that $\boldsymbol{\Pi}$ is substochastic, and so the $\{\boldsymbol{q}, \boldsymbol{\Pi}\}$-minimal transition function $P(t, x, \cdot)$ is substochastic.

Denote by Φ_k the space of bounded measurable functions on Q^k, and by Φ the space of those functions on $\boldsymbol{Q}$ whose restrictions on each Q^k belong to Φ_k. The restriction of $\boldsymbol{\varphi}\in\Phi$ on Q^k is denoted by φ_k or $(\boldsymbol{\varphi})_k$. Then Φ is a Fréchet space with seminorms $\|\boldsymbol{\varphi}\|_k=\sum_{1\leq j\leq k}\|\varphi_j\|$. The transition function $P(t, x, \cdot)$ induces in the usual way a semigroup $\{T^t\}$ on Φ which is positive and $T^t1\leq 1$. Our task in this section is to prove the following theorem.

THEOREM 1. *For any* $\varphi\in\Phi_k$,

$$\langle u(t)^k, \varphi\rangle=\sum_{m=k}^{\infty}\langle f^m, (T^t\boldsymbol{\varphi})_m\rangle \tag{3.2}$$

where $u(t)$ *is the minimal solution of* (1.3), *and* $(\boldsymbol{\varphi})_m=\varphi$ (*for* $m=k$), $=0$ (*for* $m\neq k$).

Before giving the proof of this theorem, we introduce some notations. Denote by Ξ_k the space of functions ξ's on $\mathfrak{M}$ which are expressed as $\xi(f)=\langle f^k, \varphi\rangle$ for some $\varphi\in\Phi_k$; here φ can be chosen to be symmetric. By setting $\|\xi\|_k=\|\varphi\|$ for $\xi(f)=\langle f^k, \varphi\rangle$ with symmetric $\varphi\in\Phi_k$, Ξ_k becomes a Banach space with the norm $\|\xi\|_k$, since a bounded symmetric function φ on Q^k is recovered by the value $\xi(f)=\langle f^k, \varphi\rangle$ for f running on $\mathfrak{M}$ as the following formula indicates:

$$\varphi(x_1, \cdots, x_k)=\frac{1}{k!}\sum_{m=1}^{k}(-1)^{k-m}\sum_{J\in\mathfrak{J}_m} m^k\langle f_J^k, \varphi\rangle , \tag{3.3}$$

where $\mathfrak{J}_m$ is the family of all subsets of $\{1, \cdots, k\}$ with m elements, and f_J^k denotes the k-fold outer product of f_J defined by $f_J(\Gamma)=\frac{1}{m}\sum_{j\in J}\delta(x_j, \Gamma)$ for $J\in\mathfrak{J}_m$ (see [6]). Let Ξ be the space of all sequences $\boldsymbol{\xi}=(\xi_1, \xi_2, \cdots)$ with each ξ_j in Ξ_j, and define a multiplication $\boldsymbol{\xi}\otimes\boldsymbol{\eta}$ by $(\boldsymbol{\xi}\otimes\boldsymbol{\eta})_k=\sum_{i+j=k}\xi_i\eta_j$. Then, Ξ is a Fréchet space with the seminorms $\|\boldsymbol{\xi}\|_k=\sum_{1\le j\le k}\|\xi_j\|_j$, and $\|\boldsymbol{\xi}\otimes\boldsymbol{\eta}\|_k\le\|\boldsymbol{\xi}\|_k\|\boldsymbol{\eta}\|_k$ holds for all k. The mapping $\mathfrak{S}:\Phi\to\Xi$ defined by

$$(\mathfrak{S}\boldsymbol{\varphi})_k(f)=\langle f^k, \varphi_k\rangle \quad \text{for} \quad \boldsymbol{\varphi}=(\varphi_k)_{k\ge1}$$

satisfies $\|\mathfrak{S}\boldsymbol{\varphi}\|_k\le\|\boldsymbol{\varphi}\|_k$ for all k.

Now the proof of Theorem 1 is carried out in 3 steps.

Step 1. Suppose $q(x)$ is bounded. In this case, the linear operator $A:\Phi\to\Phi$ defined by

$$(A\boldsymbol{\varphi})_k(x_1, \cdots, x_k)=\sum_{m=1}^{k-1}\sum_{i=1}^{m}q_{k-m}(x_i)\Pi_{k-m}(x_i, x_{m+1}, \cdots, x_k, \varphi_m)$$
$$-\sum_{m=1}^{k}q(x_m)\varphi_k(x_1, \cdots, x_k)$$
(the first term vanishes for $k=1$)

is bounded, and the semigroup with generator A is nothing but $\{T^t\}$. Since one can easily prove that $\langle f^m, \varphi\rangle=0$ for all $f\in\mathfrak{M}$ implies

$$\int\cdots\int\sum_{i=1}^{m}q_{k-m}(x_i)\Pi_{k-m}(x_i, x_{m+1}, \cdots, x_k, \varphi)f(dx_1)\cdots f(dx_k)=0\ ,$$

one can define a linear operator $\mathfrak{A}:\Xi\to\Xi$ by $\mathfrak{A}\mathfrak{S}\boldsymbol{\varphi}=\mathfrak{S}A\boldsymbol{\varphi}$. Then obviously the semigroup $\{\mathfrak{T}^t\}$ with generator $\mathfrak{A}$ satisfies $\mathfrak{T}^t\mathfrak{S}\boldsymbol{\varphi}=\mathfrak{S}T^t\boldsymbol{\varphi}$. Moreover, by direct computations one can show that $\mathfrak{A}$ is a derivation of the algebra Ξ, that is $\mathfrak{A}(\boldsymbol{\xi}\otimes\boldsymbol{\eta})=(\mathfrak{A}\boldsymbol{\xi})\otimes\boldsymbol{\eta}+\boldsymbol{\xi}\otimes(\mathfrak{A}\boldsymbol{\eta})$, and this fact is reflected to the multiplicative property of $\{\mathfrak{T}^t\}$:

$$\mathfrak{T}^t(\boldsymbol{\xi}\otimes\boldsymbol{\eta})=(\mathfrak{T}^t\boldsymbol{\xi})\otimes(\mathfrak{T}^t\boldsymbol{\eta})\ . \tag{3.4}$$

Step 2. If $q(x)$ is unbounded, we set $q_k^{(n)}(x)=q_k(x)\wedge n$ (for $k\le n$), $=0$ (for $k>n$) and $q^{(n)}(x)=\sum_{k=1}^{n}q_k^{(n)}(x)$. Let $P_n(t, x, \Gamma)$ be the $\{\boldsymbol{q}_n, \boldsymbol{\Pi}_n\}$-minimal transition function and $\{\mathfrak{T}_n^t\}$ the associated semigroup on Ξ, where $\boldsymbol{q}_n$ and $\boldsymbol{\Pi}_n$ are defined by (3.1) with $q_k(x)$ and $q(x)$ replaced by $q_k^{(n)}(x)$ and $q^{(n)}(x)$ respectively. Since $q^{(n)}(x)$ is bounded for each n, the semigroup $\{\mathfrak{T}_n^t\}$ is multiplicative by Step 1. On the other hand, by the convergence lemma mentioned in 1° of §2, the transition function $P_n(t, x, \Gamma)$ tends to $P(t, x, \Gamma)$ as $n\uparrow\infty$ for each $\Gamma\subset Q^k$ and hence

$$(\mathfrak{S}T^t\varphi)_k(f)=\langle f^k, \sum_{j\le k}\int_{Q^j} P(t,\cdot,d\boldsymbol{y})\varphi_j(\boldsymbol{y})\rangle_{Q^k}$$
$$=\lim_{n\to\infty}\langle f^k, \sum_{j\le k}\int_{Q^j} P_n(t,\cdot,d\boldsymbol{y})\varphi_j(\boldsymbol{y})\rangle_{Q^k}$$
$$=\lim_{n\to\infty}(\mathfrak{T}_n^t\mathfrak{S}\varphi)_k(f)\,.$$

Therefore, one can define $\mathfrak{T}^t$ on Ξ by $\mathfrak{T}^t\mathfrak{S}\varphi=\mathfrak{S}T^t\varphi$ and so-defined $\{\mathfrak{T}^t\}$ becomes a *multiplicative* semigroup as the limit of such ones.

Step 3. For each $t\ge 0$ and integers k, n with $1\le k\le n$ we define a measure $f_{n,k}(t)$ on Q^k by $f_{n,k}(t,\Gamma)=\langle f^n, P(t,\cdot,\Gamma)\rangle_{Q^n}$, $\Gamma\subset Q^k$. If $\varphi(x_1,\cdots,x_k)=\varphi_1(x_1)\cdots\varphi_k(x_k)$, then

$$\langle f_{n,k}(t),\varphi\rangle=(\mathfrak{T}^t\xi_1\otimes\cdots\otimes\xi_k)_n(f)$$

where $\xi_j(f)=(\langle f,\varphi_j\rangle,0,0,\cdots)$, and hence by the multiplicative property (3.4) of $\{\mathfrak{T}^t\}$ we have

$$f_{n,k}(t)=\sum_{n_1+\cdots+n_k=n} f_{n_1,1}(t)\otimes\cdots\otimes f_{n_k,1}(t)\,. \tag{3.5}$$

On the other hand, by the forward equation for $P(t,\cdot,\cdot)$ we have for $\Gamma\subset Q^1$

$$P(t,x,\Gamma)=e^{-q(x_1)t}\delta(x_1,\Gamma) \qquad \text{if} \quad x\in Q^1$$
$$=\int_0^t ds\sum_{m=2}^n\int_{Q^m}P(s,x,dy)q_{m-1}(y_1)\int_\Gamma e^{-q(z)(t-s)}\Pi_{m-1}(y_1,y_2,\cdots,y_m,dz)$$
$$\text{if} \quad x\in Q^n,\ n\ge 2\,.$$

Integrating both sides of the above by f^n and then using (3.5),

$$f_{1,1}(t,\Gamma)=\langle f, e^{-q(\cdot)t}\delta(\cdot,\Gamma)\rangle=u_0(t,\Gamma)$$
$$f_{n,1}(t,\Gamma)=\int_0^t ds\sum_{m=2}^n\int_{Q^m}f_{n,m}(s,d\boldsymbol{y})q_{m-1}(y_1)\int_\Gamma e^{-q(z)(t-s)}\Pi_{m-1}(y_1,y_2,\cdots,y_m,dz)$$
$$=\int_0^t ds\sum_{m=2}^n\sum_{n_1+\cdots+n_m=n}\int_{Q^m}f_{n_1,1}(s,dy_1)\cdots f_{n_m,1}(s,dy_m)q_{m-1}(y_1)$$
$$\times\int_\Gamma e^{-q(z)(t-s)}\Pi_{m-1}(y_1,y_2,\cdots,y_m,dz)$$
$$=\sum_{m=2}^n\sum_{n_1+\cdots+n_m=n}[f_{n_1,1},\cdots,f_{n_m,1}] \qquad \text{for} \quad n\ge 2\,.$$

Comparing this with (2.5), we conclude that $u(t)=\sum_{n=1}^\infty f_{n,1}(t)$, and this means that (3.2) holds for $k=1$. For $k\ge 2$, using (3.5) again, we have

$$\sum_{n=k}^\infty f_{n,k}(t)=\sum_{n=k}^\infty\sum_{n_1+\cdots+n_k=n}f_{n_1,1}(t)\otimes\cdots\otimes f_{n_k,1}(t)=(\sum_{n=1}^\infty f_{n,1}(t))^k=u(t)^k\,,$$

completing the proof of the theorem.

§ 4. The motion of n particles.

Let $\bar{Q}$ be the adjoined space $Q\smile\{\Delta\}$, Δ being an extra point $\notin Q$. In this section let $n\geq 2$ be fixed. The motion of n particles we consider in this section is a Markov process $X(t)=(X_1(t), \cdots, X_n(t))$ with state space $\bar{Q}^n=\bar{Q}\times\cdots\times\bar{Q}$ whose probabilistic development is determined in the following way. Suppose the process starts at $\boldsymbol{x}=(x_1, \cdots, x_n)\in\bar{Q}^n$ and set $I=\{i: x_i\in Q\}$, $I'=\{i; x_i=\Delta\}$. Then,

(1)
$$X_i(t)=\Delta \quad \text{for} \quad i\in I' \quad \text{and all} \quad t\geq 0\,,$$
$$X_i(t)=x_i \quad \text{for} \quad i\in I,\ t<S_1\,,$$

where S_1 is a random variable with

$$\boldsymbol{P}_x\{S_1>t\}=\exp\{-t\sum_{i\in I} r(x_i)\} \qquad (t\geq 0)$$

$$r(x_i)=\sum_{N=1}^{n-1} n^{-N}\frac{(n-1)!}{(n-1-N)!}q_N(x_i)\,.$$

(2) At time S_1, one of the particles with index in I jumps according to the following probability law. For each $i\in I$

$$\boldsymbol{P}_x\{X_i(S_1)\in\Gamma, X_j(S_1)=x_j, j\neq i\}$$
$$=\sum_{N=1}^{n-1} n^{-N}\sum' q_N(x_i)\Pi_N(x_i, x_{i_1}, \cdots, x_{i_N}, \Gamma)/\sum_{j\in I} r(x_j),\ \Gamma\subset Q\,.$$

For $\Gamma=\{\Delta\}$, the left hand side of the above is replaced by

$$\{r(x_i)-\sum_{N=1}^{n-1} n^{-N}\sum' q_N(x_i)\Pi_N(x_i, x_{i_1}, \cdots, x_{i_N}, Q\}/\sum_{j\in I} r(x_j)\,.$$

Here, we set $\Pi_N(x_i, x_{i_1}, \cdots, x_{i_N}, \Gamma)=0$ for $\Gamma\subset Q$ if at least one of $x_i, x_{i_1}, \cdots, x_{i_N}$ is Δ, and $\sum'$ is taken over all ordered N-tuples $(i_1, \cdots, i_N)$ such that $i\leq i_1, \cdots, i_N\leq n$ and $i_1, \cdots, i_N$ $(\neq i)$ are all different.

(3) After the time S_1, we define the process $X(t)$ up to the second jumping time S_2 so that the process $X(S_1+t)$ conditional to the σ-field generated by $\{X_1(t_1\wedge S_1)\in\Gamma_1, \cdots, X_n(t_n\wedge S_1)\in\Gamma_n\}$ is exactly the same in law as the one defined by (1) and (2) with initial state $X(S_1)$. We proceed in the same way after the second jumping time S_2, the third jumping time S_3 and so on. Thus we obtain the process $X(t)$ for $t<S=\lim_{n\to\infty} S_n$.

(4) If $S(\omega)<\infty$, then each component process $X_i(t)$ has performed either infinitely many jumps or finitely many (including no) jumps. In the former case we set $X_i(S)=\Delta$ and in the latter case $X_i(S)=X_i(S-)$, and then start afresh

at time S as in (1) (2) and (3). Repeated arguments of this now leads to the process $X(t)$ defined for all $t\geq 0$.

The following explicit construction of the process $X(t)$ will be used later. For each $\boldsymbol{x}=(x_1, \cdots, x_n)\in \bar{Q}^n$ we set

$$\alpha(t, \boldsymbol{x})=\exp\{-t\sum_{i=1}^{n} r(x_i)\}, \qquad r(\Delta)=0$$

$$\beta(\boldsymbol{i}, \boldsymbol{x})=n^{-N}q_N(x_i)/\sum_{j=1}^{n} r(x_j),\ \boldsymbol{i}=(i, i_1, \cdots, i_N),\ q_N(\Delta)=0$$

$$\gamma(\boldsymbol{i}, \boldsymbol{x}, \Gamma)=\begin{cases} \Pi_N(x_i, x_{i_1}, \cdots, x_{i_N}, \Gamma), & \text{for } \Gamma\subset Q \\ 0, & \text{for } \Gamma=\{\Delta\} \text{ if all } x_i, x_{i_1}, \cdots, x_{i_N} \text{ are in } Q \\ 1, & \text{for } \Gamma=\{\Delta\} \text{ if at least one of } x_i, x_{i_1}, \cdots, x_{i_N} \text{ is } \Delta, \end{cases}$$

and then construct a discrete parameter Markov process $U_k=(R_k, Y_k, Z_k)$, $k\geq 1$, over a suitable probability space $(\Omega, \boldsymbol{P}_x)$ with the following properties.

(i)
$$0<R_k\leq\infty,\ Y_k\in\mathfrak{J},\ Z_{k,m}(\boldsymbol{i})\in\bar{Q},$$
$$Z_k=\{Z_k(\boldsymbol{i}), \boldsymbol{i}\in\mathfrak{J}\}=\{(Z_{k,1}(\boldsymbol{i}), \cdots, Z_{k,n}(\boldsymbol{i})), \boldsymbol{i}\in\mathfrak{J}\};$$

here $\mathfrak{J}$ denotes the set of all $\boldsymbol{i}=(i, i_1, \cdots, i_N)$ such that $i, i_1, \cdots, i_N$ are different integers taken from $1, \cdots, n$.

(ii) The initial distribution is given by

$$\begin{aligned} \boldsymbol{P}_x\{R_1>t,\ Y_1=\boldsymbol{i},\ Z_{1,m}(\boldsymbol{l})\in\Gamma_{m,\boldsymbol{l}}, 1\leq m\leq n, \boldsymbol{l}\in\mathfrak{J}\} \\ =\alpha(t, \boldsymbol{x})\beta(\boldsymbol{i}, \boldsymbol{x})\prod_{\substack{(m,\boldsymbol{l})\\ m=|\boldsymbol{l}|}}\gamma(\boldsymbol{l}, x, \Gamma_{m,\boldsymbol{l}})\prod_{\substack{(m,\boldsymbol{l})\\ m\neq|\boldsymbol{l}|}}\delta(x_m, \Gamma_{m,\boldsymbol{l}}) \end{aligned} \tag{4.1}$$

where $|\boldsymbol{l}|=l$ for $\boldsymbol{l}=(l, l_1, \cdots, l_N)$.

(iii) For $\Lambda=\{R_{k+1}>t,\ Y_{k+1}=i,\ Z_{k+1,m}(\boldsymbol{l})\in\Gamma_{m,\boldsymbol{l}}, 1\leq m\leq n, \boldsymbol{l}\in\mathfrak{J}\}$, the conditional probability $\boldsymbol{P}_x\{\Lambda| U_1, \cdots, U_k\}=\boldsymbol{P}_x\{\Lambda| U_k\}$ is given by the right hand side of (4.1) with $\boldsymbol{x}$ replaced by $Z_k(Y_k)$ almost surely on the set $\{\sum_{m=1}^{n} r(Z_{k,m}(Y_k))>0\}$, while we set $U_j=\Delta'$ for $j\geq k+1$ on the set $\{\sum_{m=1}^{n} r(Z_{k,m}(Y_k))=0\}$, Δ' being an extra point (death point).

In order to construct the process $X(t)$ by means of $\{U_k\}$, we need to extend the scope of the time parameter of $\{U_k\}$ further to

$$\infty+1, \infty+2, \cdots, 2\infty+1, 2\infty+2, \cdots, (n-1)\infty+1, (n-1)\infty+2, \cdots.$$

We set

$$(4.2)\qquad x_i(\infty)=\begin{cases}\Delta & \text{if } \#\{k: |Y_k|=i\}=\infty \\ Z_{k(i),i}(Y_{k(i)}) & \text{if } k(i)=\sup\{1\le k<\infty;\ |Y_k|=i\}<\infty\ ,\end{cases}$$

and then construct $\{U_{\infty+k}\}_{k=1,2,\cdots}$ so that its distribution conditional to $\{U_1, U_2, \cdots\}$ coincides with that of the process obtained exactly by the same way as in (i) (ii) and (iii) but with the replacement of $\boldsymbol{x}$ by $\boldsymbol{x}(\infty)=(x_1(\infty), \cdots, x_n(\infty))$. Repeating this kind of construction again and again, we obtain a Markov process $\{U_k\}$ with time parameters

$$1, 2, \cdots, \infty+1, \infty+2, \cdots, 2\infty+1, 2\infty+2, \cdots, (n-1)\infty+1, (n-1)\infty+2, \cdots .$$

Now the process $X(t)$ is constructed over $(\Omega, \boldsymbol{P}_x)$ by

$$X(t)=Z_{k-1}(Y_{k-1}) \quad \text{if} \quad \sum_{j<k} R_j\le t<\sum_{j\le k} R_j\ ^{1)}$$

$$=(\Delta, \cdots, \Delta) \quad \text{if} \quad \sum_{j<n\infty} R_j\le t<+\infty\ .$$

For a subset I of $\{1, \cdots, n\}$, we define the first jumping time $T(I)$ of the particles with index in I by

$$(4.3)\qquad T(I)=\sum_{j\le k(I)} R_j \quad \text{if} \quad k(I)=\min\{k: |Y_k|\in I\}<n\infty$$

$$=+\infty \qquad \text{if} \quad |Y_k|\notin I \quad \text{for all} \quad k<n\infty\ ;$$

it is distributed according to the exponential distribution with mean $1/\sum_{i\in I} r(x_i)$.

Next, we introduce a (q, Π)-function on the space $\boldsymbol{Q}_n$ as follows: for $\boldsymbol{x}=(x_1, \cdots, x_k)\in Q^k$

$$\boldsymbol{q}_n(\boldsymbol{x})=\sum_{i=1}^{k} r(x_i)$$

$$\boldsymbol{\Pi}_n(x, \Gamma)=\boldsymbol{q}_n(\boldsymbol{x})^{-1}n^{-(k-m)}\frac{(n-m)!}{(n-k)!}\sum_{i=1}^{m} q_{k-m}(x_i)\Pi_{k-m}(x_i, x_{m+1}, \cdots, x_k, \chi_\Gamma)$$
$$\text{for } \Gamma\subset Q^m \text{ with } 1\le m\le k-1$$
$$=0 \qquad \text{for } \Gamma\subset Q^m \text{ with } k\le m\le n$$
$$=0 \qquad \text{for all } \Gamma \text{ if } k=1\ ,$$

and denote by $P_n(t, \boldsymbol{x}, \Gamma)$ the $\{\boldsymbol{q}_n, \boldsymbol{\Pi}_n\}$-minimal transition function.

PROPOSITION 2. *If φ is a nonnegative bounded function on Q^m $(m\le n)$, then for any $f\in\mathfrak{M}$*

---

1) We set $R_0=0$, $Z_0(Y_0)=\boldsymbol{x}$ and $Z_{k-1}(Y_{k-1})=\boldsymbol{x}(j\infty)$ if $k=j\infty+1$, where $\boldsymbol{x}(j\infty)$ is defined similarly to (4.2).

$$\sum_{k=m}^{n} \langle f^k, \int_{Q^m} P_n(t, \cdot, d\boldsymbol{y})\varphi(\boldsymbol{y})\rangle_{Q^k}$$
$$\leq \int_{Q^n} \boldsymbol{E}_{(x_1,\dots,x_n)}\{\varphi(X_1(t), \cdots, X_m(t))\} f(dx_1)\cdots f(dx_n)^{2)} .$$

PROOF. Taking a family $\sigma=\{I_0, \cdots, I_p\}$ of subsets of $\{1, \cdots, n\}$ such that

$$I_0=\{1, \cdots, m\}, \ I_{j-1}\subsetneqq I_j \ (1\leq j\leq p) \tag{4.4}$$

and recalling (4.3), we set inductively

$$T(I_p, I_{p-1}, \cdots, I_{p'})= \sum_{j\leq k(I_p, I_{p-1}, \cdots, I_{p'})} R_j$$

if $k(I_p, \cdots, I_{p'})=\min\{k>k(I_p, \cdots, I_{p'+1}): |Y_k|\in I_{p'}\}<n\infty$,

$$T(I_p, I_{p-1}, \cdots, I_{p'})=+\infty$$

if $T(I_p, \cdots, I_{p'+1})=+\infty$ or if $|Y_k|\notin I_{p'}$ for $k(I_p, \cdots, I_{p'+1})<k<n\infty$,

and then

$$\Lambda_\sigma=\{T(I_p)\leq t, Y_{k(I_p)}\in \tilde{I}_p, T(I_p, I_{p-1})\leq t, Y_{k(I_p, I_{p-1})}\in \tilde{I}_{p-1}$$
$$\cdots, T(I_p, \cdots, I_1)\leq t, Y_{k(I_p, \cdots, I_1)}\in \tilde{I}_1, T(I_p, \cdots, I_0)>t\} ,$$

where $\tilde{I}_j$ denotes the set of all ordered $(p'+1)$-tuples $(i, i_1, \cdots, i_{p'})$ such that $i\in I_{j-1}$ and $\{i_1, \cdots, i_{p'}\}=I_j-I_{j-1}$ $(p'=\#(I_j-I_{j-1}))$. If we set

$$\varphi(t, \sigma)=\int_{\Lambda_\sigma} \varphi(X_1(t), \cdots, X_m(t))\boldsymbol{P}_{(x_1, \cdots, x_n)}(d\omega) ,$$

then $\varphi(t, \sigma)$ is a function of $x(I_p)=(x_j, j\in I_p)$ alone for each t and σ, and

$$\varphi(t, \sigma)=\int_0^t e^{-sr(I_p)}n^{-N}N! \sum_{i\in I_p} q_N(x_i)\Pi_N(x_i, x(I_p-I_{p-1}), \varphi(t-s, \sigma_1))ds \tag{4.5}$$

where $\qquad N=\#(I_p-I_{p-1}), \sigma_1=\{I_0, \cdots, I_{p-1}\}$ and $r(I_p)=\sum_{i\in I_p} r(x_i)$.

Two $\sigma=\{I_0, \cdots, I_p\}$ and $\sigma'=\{I_0, I'_1, \cdots, I'_{p'}\}$ both satisfying (4.4) are said to be similar, if $p=p'$ and $\# I_j=\# I'_j$ for $1\leq j\leq p$. Using (4.5) we can easily prove by induction on p that $\langle f^n, \varphi(t, \sigma)\rangle=\langle f^n, \varphi(t, \sigma')\rangle$ for similar σ and σ', and so, if σ is of the form:

$$\{\{1, 2, \cdots, m\}, \{1, 2, \cdots, l\}, \cdots, \{1, 2, \cdots, j\}, \{1, 2, \cdots, k\}\} \quad (m<l<\cdots<j<k) \tag{4.6}$$

then the function $\tilde{\varphi}(t, \sigma)=$(the number of σ' similar to $\sigma)\varphi(t, \sigma)$ satisfies

2) We set $\varphi(x_1, \cdots, x_m)=0$ if at least one of $x_1, \cdots, x_m$ is Δ.

$$\langle f^n, \tilde{\varphi}(t,\sigma)\rangle = \langle f^n, \sum_{\sigma': \text{ similar to } \sigma} \varphi(t,\sigma')\rangle \tag{4.7}$$

$$\tilde{\varphi}(t,I)=\int_0^t e^{-sr(I_p)}n^{-(k-j)}\frac{(n-j)!}{(n-k)!}\sum_{i=1}^{j} q_{k-j}(x_i)\Pi_N(x_i, x_{j+1}, \cdots, x_k, \tilde{\varphi}(t-s,\sigma_1))ds \tag{4.8a}$$

$$(\sigma_1=\{\{1,\cdots,m\},\{1,\cdots,l\},\cdots,\{1,\cdots,j\}\}, p>1)$$

$$\tilde{\varphi}(t,\sigma)=e^{-tr(I_0)}\varphi(x_1,\cdots,x_m),\quad \sigma=\{\{1,\cdots,m\}\}\ . \tag{4.8b}$$

Therefore, the function $\varphi_k(t,(x_1,\cdots,x_k))$ defined by

$$\varphi_k(t,(x_1,\cdots,x_k))=\begin{cases}\displaystyle\sum_{\substack{\sigma \text{ is of the form (4.6)}\\ \text{with fixed } k}} \tilde{\varphi}(t,\sigma), & \text{for } m<k\\ \tilde{\varphi}(t,\sigma), \text{ for } m=k & (\sigma=\{\{1,\cdots,m\}\}\ ,\end{cases}$$

satisfies

$$\varphi_k(t,(x_1,\cdots,x_k))=\int_0^t e^{-sq_n(x_1,\cdots,x_k)}\sum_{j=1}^{k-1} n^{-(k-j)}\frac{(n-j)!}{(n-k)!} \tag{4.9}$$

$$\times\sum_{i=1}^{j} q_{k-j}(x_i)\Pi_N(x_i, x_{j+1},\cdots,x_k,\varphi_j(t-s))ds,\ k>m$$

which is nothing but the backward equation associated with $\{\boldsymbol{q}_n, \boldsymbol{\Pi}_n\}$, and hence $\varphi_k(t,(x_1,\cdots,x_k))$ coincides with $\langle P_n(t,(x_1,\cdots,x_k),\cdot),\varphi\rangle_{Q^m}$. On the other hand, by the definition of Λ_σ two events Λ_σ and $\Lambda_{\sigma'}$ are mutually exclusive unless σ and σ' are the same, and so we have

$$\int_{Q^n}\boldsymbol{E}_{(x_1,\cdots,x_n)}\{\varphi(X_1(t),\cdots,X_m(t))\}f(dx_1)\cdots f(dx_n)$$

$$\geq\sum_{\sigma}\langle f^n,\varphi(t,\sigma)\rangle=\langle f^n,\sum_{\sigma \text{ is of the form (4.6)}}\tilde{\varphi}(t,\sigma)\rangle$$

$$=\sum_{k=m}^{n}\langle f^k,\varphi_k(t)\rangle=\sum_{k=m}^{n}\langle f^k,\int_{Q^m}P_n(t,\cdot,d\boldsymbol{y})\varphi(\boldsymbol{y})\rangle\ ,$$

completing the proof of the proposition.

§ 5. Propagation of chaos.

In the preceding section we fixed n, the number of particles under motion, but here we let $n\uparrow\infty$ and prove that the propagation of chaos holds if the initial distribution f of (1.3) belongs to the class $\mathfrak{U}$. Let $u_n(t)$ be the probability distribution at time t of n particles under motion starting with the initial distribution f^n, that is

$$u_n(t,\Gamma)=\int_{Q^n}\boldsymbol{P}_{(x_1,\cdots,x_n)}\{X(t)\in\Gamma\}f(dx_1)\cdots f(dx_n)\ ,$$

where $\{X(t), \boldsymbol{P}_{(x_1,\cdots,x_n)}\}$ is the Markov process on $\bar{Q}^n$ introduced in §4.

THEOREM 3. *For each* $m\geq 1$, $f\in\mathfrak{U}$ *and a bounded function* φ *on* Q^m,

$$\int_{Q^m\times\bar{Q}^{n-m}}\varphi(x_1,\cdots,x_m)u_n(t,dx_1,\cdots,dx_n)\to\langle u(t)^m,\varphi\rangle \text{ as } n\uparrow\infty, \tag{5.1}$$

where $u(t)$ *is the solution of* (1.3).

PROOF. By the convergence lemma in 1° of §2, $P_n(t,\boldsymbol{x},\Gamma)$ tends to $P(t,\boldsymbol{x},\Gamma)$ as $n\uparrow\infty$ for each t, $\boldsymbol{x}$ and $\Gamma\subset Q^m$, and so if we set for $\Gamma\subset Q^m$

$$F_{n,k}(t,\Gamma)=\langle f^k, P_n(t,\cdot,\Gamma)\rangle_{Q^k}, \quad F_k(t,\Gamma)=\langle f^k, P(t,\cdot,\Gamma)\rangle_{Q^k},$$

then $F_{n,k}(t,\Gamma)$ tends to $F_k(t,\Gamma)$ as $n\uparrow\infty$. Therefore, by Theorem 1 and Proposition 2 and using Fatou's lemma, we have

$$1\geq\underline{\lim}_{n\to\infty}\sum_{k=1}^{n}F_{n,k}(t,\Gamma)\geq\sum_{k=1}^{\infty}F_k(t,\Gamma)=u(t)^m(\Gamma).$$

Since $f\in\mathfrak{U}$ implies $u(t)^m(Q^m)=1$, we have the equality if $\Gamma=Q^m$ in the above, and therefore

$$\sup_n\sum_{k>l}F_{n,k}(t,\Gamma)\leq\sup_n\sum_{k>l}F_{n,k}(t,Q^m)\to 0,\ l\to\infty,\ \Gamma\subset Q^m.$$

Thus we have by Proposition 2

$$\underline{\lim}_{n\to\infty}v_n(t,\Gamma)\geq\underline{\lim}_{n\to\infty}\sum_{k=1}^{n}F_{n,k}(t,\Gamma)=u(t)^m(\Gamma),\ \Gamma\subset Q^m,$$

where $v_n(t,\Gamma)$ denotes the left hand side of (5.1) with $\varphi=\chi_\Gamma(x_1,\cdots,x_m)$. On the other hand,

$$\begin{aligned}\overline{\lim}_{n\to\infty}v_n(t,\Gamma)&=\overline{\lim}_{n\to\infty}\{v_n(t,Q^m)-v_n(t,Q^m-\Gamma)\}\\&=1-\underline{\lim}_{n\to\infty}v_n(t,Q^m-\Gamma)\leq 1-u(t)^m(Q^m-\Gamma)=u(t)^m(\Gamma),\end{aligned}$$

and so we must have $\lim_{n\to\infty}v_n(t,\Gamma)=u(t)^m(\Gamma)$, which was to be proved.

References

[1] Kac, M., Foundation of kinetic theory, Proc. Third Berkely Symp. on Math. Stat. and Prob. **3**, 171-197.

[2] McKean, H. P. Jr., A class of Markov processes associated with nonlinear parabolic equations, Proc. Nat. Acad. Sci. **56** (1966), 1907-1911.

[3] McKean, H. P. Jr., An exponential formula for solving Boltzmann's equation for a Maxwellian gas, J. Combinatorial Theory **2** (1967), 358-382.

[4] Johnson, D.P., On a class of stochastic processes and its relationship to infinite particle gases, Trans. Amer. Math. Soc. **132** (1968), 275-295.

[5] Tanaka, H., Propagation of chaos for certain Markov processes of jump type with nonlinear generators, I, II. Proc. Japan Acad. **45** (1969), 449-452, 598-600.

[6] Tanaka, H., Purely discontinuous Markov processes with nonlinear generators and their propagation of chaos, to appear in Теория Вероят. и ее Примен.

[7] Tanaka, S., An extension of Wild's sum for solving certain non-linear equation of measures, Proc. Japan Acad. **44** (1968), 884-889.

[8] Ueno, T., A class of Markov processes with bounded, non-linear generators, Japan. J. Math. **38** (1969), 19-38.

[9] Ueno, T., A class of purely discontinuous Markov processes with interactions, I, II. Proc. Japan Acad. **45** (1969), 348-353, 437-440.

(Received December 11, 1969)

Department of Mathematics
Faculty of Science
University of Tokyo
Hongo, Tokyo
113 Japan

Z. Wahrscheinlichkeitstheorie verw. Geb. 27, 47–52 (1973)

An Inequality for a Functional of Probability Distributions and Its Application to Kac's One-Dimensional Model of a Maxwellian Gas

Hiroshi Tanaka

1. Introduction

Let $\mathscr{P}$ be the class of 1-dimensional probability distributions f with

$$0<\alpha_2(f)<\infty,$$

where $\alpha_2(f)$ denotes the second moment of f. Taking a probability space (Ω, P) which is big enough to carry Gaussian random variables, we introduce a functional $\mathfrak{e}$ defined for $f\in\mathscr{P}$ by

$$\mathfrak{e}[f]=\inf E\{|X-Y|^2\},$$

where the infimum is taken over all pairs of random variables X and Y defined on (Ω, P) and distributed according to f and g respectively; here g is the Gaussian distribution with mean 0 and variance $\sigma^2=\alpha_2(f)$. $\mathfrak{e}[f]$ is sometimes denoted by $\mathfrak{e}[X]$ when X is a random variable with distribution f. It should be noticed that the value of $\mathfrak{e}[f]$ does not depend upon a choice of the probability space (Ω, P). The purpose of this paper is to present some basic properties of $\mathfrak{e}$ (especially, the inequality (2.2)) together with an application to the central limit theorem and then to show that the functional $\mathfrak{e}$ is monotone decreasing along Boltzmann solutions of Kac's one-dimensional model of a Maxwellian gas. Some of our results can be generalized to the case of R^3; for example, the functional $\mathfrak{e}$ similarly defined in R^3 decreases along solutions of Boltzmann's problem for the 3-dimensional Maxwellian gas, but this will be discussed in another occasion.

2. Basic Properties of $\mathfrak{e}$ and a Proof of the Central Limit Theorem

Theorem 1. *Let $f\in\mathscr{P}$, and denote by g the Gaussian distribution with mean* 0 *and variance $\sigma^2=\alpha_2(f)$. Let X and Y be random variables with distributions f and g, respectively. Then, $\mathfrak{e}[f]=E\{|X-Y|^2\}$ if and only if $X=F^{-1}(G(Y))$ almost surely, where F^{-1} is the right continuous inverse function of the distribution function F corresponding to f, and G is the distribution function corresponding to g.*

In the proof of this theorem the probability space is chosen as follows: Ω is the unit interval $[0, 1)$ and P is the Lebesgue measure in Ω. The proof is carried out in 3 steps.

Step 1. $(X(\omega)-X(\omega'))\,(Y(\omega)-Y(\omega'))\geqq 0$ for almost all (ω, ω') $(P\otimes P)$. Suppose the contrary holds. Then for some $\varepsilon>0$ at least one of the following events has positive $P\otimes P$-probability:

$$\{(\omega,\omega')\in\Omega\times\Omega:\ X(\omega)-X(\omega')<-3\varepsilon \text{ and } Y(\omega)-Y(\omega')>3\varepsilon\} \tag{1}$$

$$\{(\omega,\omega')\in\Omega\times\Omega:\ X(\omega)-X(\omega')>3\varepsilon \text{ and } Y(\omega)-Y(\omega')<-3\varepsilon\}. \tag{2}$$

We assume that the event (1) has positive probability for simplicity. Then, for some integers j_1, j_2, k_1, k_2 with $j_1+1<j_2$ and $k_1+1<k_2$, the event

$$\tilde{A}=\left\{(\omega,\omega'):\ \begin{matrix} j_1\varepsilon<X(\omega)\leqq(j_1+1)\varepsilon,\ j_2\varepsilon<X(\omega')\leqq(j_2+1)\varepsilon \\ k_1\varepsilon<Y(\omega')\leqq(k_1+1)\varepsilon,\ k_2\varepsilon<Y(\omega)\leqq(k_2+1)\varepsilon \end{matrix}\right\}$$

has positive $P\otimes P$-probability. If we set

$$A=\{\omega:\ j_1\varepsilon<X(\omega)\leqq(j_1+1)\varepsilon,\ k_2\varepsilon<Y(\omega)\leqq(k_2+1)\varepsilon\}$$

$$A'=\{\omega:\ j_2\varepsilon<X(\omega)\leqq(j_2+1)\varepsilon,\ k_1\varepsilon<Y(\omega)\leqq(k_1+1)\varepsilon\},$$

then $\tilde{A}=A\times A'$ and hence $P(A)>0$, $P(A')>0$. Next, we take an irrational number λ and denote by T the Weyl automorphism: $\omega\in\Omega\to\omega+\lambda \pmod 1$. Then there exists an integer $n\geqq 0$ such that $P(A\cap T^{-n}A')>0$. If we set $B=A\cap T^{-n}A'$, $B'=T^nB$, $\varphi=T^n$, then $P(B)=P(B')>0$ and $B\cap B'=\emptyset$. We now define

$$X^{\#}(\omega)=\begin{cases} X(\varphi(\omega)) & \text{for } \omega\in B \\ X(\varphi^{-1}(\omega)) & \text{for } \omega\in B' \\ X(\omega) & \text{for } \omega\notin B\cup B'. \end{cases}$$

Since φ: $B\to B'$ is measure-preserving[1], $X^{\#}$ has still distribution f, and we have

$$\begin{aligned} E\{|X^{\#}-Y|^2\} &= \int_B |X(\varphi(\omega))-Y(\omega)|^2 P(d\omega)+\int_{B'} |X(\varphi^{-1}(\omega))-Y(\omega)|^2 P(d\omega) \\ &\quad+\int_{(B\cup B')^c} |X(\omega)-Y(\omega)|^2 P(d\omega) \\ &= \int_B \{|X(\varphi(\omega))-Y(\omega)|^2+|X(\omega)-Y(\varphi(\omega))|^2\} P(d\omega) \\ &\quad+\int_{(B\cup B')^c} |X(\omega)-Y(\omega)|^2 P(d\omega) \\ &< \int_B \{|X(\omega)-Y(\omega)|^2+|X(\varphi(\omega))-Y(\varphi(\omega))|^2\} P(d\omega) \\ &\quad+\int_{(B\cup B')^c} |X(\omega)-Y(\omega)|^2 P(d\omega)=E\{|X(\omega)-Y(\omega)|^2\}; \end{aligned}$$

the inequality part in the above employs the following elementary fact: if $a_1<a_2$ and $b_1<b_2$, then $(a_1-b_1)^2+(a_2-b_2)^2<(a_1-b_2)^2+(a_2-b_1)^2$. We thus arrive at a contradiction.

Step 2. Let $P(y,\cdot)$ be a regular conditional probability distribution of X given $Y=y$, and denote by S_y the smallest closed interval such that $P(y,S_y)=1$. We claim that

S_y and $S_{y'}$ are non-overlapping for almost all (y,y') with respect to $g\otimes g$. (2.1)

[1] I owe the use of the Weyl automorphism for constructing φ to Y. Takahashi.

Since $P(y,\cdot)\otimes P(y',\cdot)$ is a regular conditional probability distribution of $(X(\omega), X(\omega'))$ given $(Y(\omega), Y(\omega'))=(y,y')$, we have from Step 1

$$\iint g(dy)\,g(dy')\iint \chi(x,x',y,y')\,P(y,dx)\,P(y',dx') = E\{\chi(X(\omega),X(\omega'),Y(\omega),Y(\omega'))\}=1$$

where χ is the indicator function of the set

$$\Gamma=\{(x,x',y,y')\in R^4\colon\ (x-x')(y-y')\geqq 0\}.$$

Therefore, for almost all (y,y') with respect to $g\otimes g$, we have

$$\iint \chi(x,x',y,y')\,P(y,dx)\,P(y',dx')=1.$$

So, if we set $\Gamma_1=\{(x,x')\in R^2\colon x\geqq x'\}$, then $P(y,\cdot)\otimes P(y',\cdot)$ is supported by Γ_1 for almost all $(y,y')\in\Gamma_1$; but this is a complicated way of saying that (2.1) holds.

Step 3. From Step 2 one can prove easily that S_y is a single point for almost all y with respect to g. Now, this fact combined with the inequality of Step 1 implies that X is an increasing function of Y (a.s.); this is possible only when $X=F^{-1}(G(Y))$ almost surely. The "if" part is obvious, since the infimum in the definition of $\mathfrak{e}[f]$ is actually attained by some pair.

Theorem 2. *Let X and Y be independent random variables with distributions f_1 and $f_2\in\mathscr{P}$, respectively, and assume that $E\{X\}=E\{Y\}=0$. Then, for any real constants a, b such that $a\neq 0$, $b\neq 0$,*

$$\mathfrak{e}[aX+bY]<a^2\,\mathfrak{e}[X]+b^2\,\mathfrak{e}[Y], \tag{2.2}$$

unless both X and Y are Gaussian.

The proof of this theorem is based upon Theorem 1. It is obvious that

$$\mathfrak{e}[aX+bY]\leqq a^2\,\mathfrak{e}[X]+b^2\,\mathfrak{e}[Y]$$

holds, and so assuming the equality holds in the above, we will prove $f_i=g_i$, where g_i is the Gaussian distribution with mean 0 and variance $\sigma_i^2=\alpha_2(f_i)$, $i=1,2$. If X_1 and X_2 are independent random variables with distributions g_1 and g_2, respectively, then with the obvious notation it follows from Theorem 1 that

$$\begin{aligned} a^2\,\mathfrak{e}[X]+b^2\,\mathfrak{e}[Y]&=a^2\,E\{|F_1^{-1}(G_1(X_1))-X_1|^2\}+b^2\,E\{|F_2^{-1}(G_2(X_2))-X_2|^2\}\\ &=E\{|aF_1^{-1}(G_1(X_1))+bF_2^{-1}(G_2(X_2))-(aX_1+bX_2)|^2\}.\end{aligned}$$

Since aX_1+bX_2 is also G-distributed, we have again from Theorem 1

$$aF_1^{-1}(G_1(X_1))+bF_2^{-1}(G_2(X_2))=F^{-1}(G(aX_1+bX_2))\ \text{a.s.}, \tag{2.3}$$

where F is the distribution function of $aX+bY$. By the right continuity of the functions involved, (2.3) yields

$$aF_1^{-1}(G_1(x))+bF_2^{-1}(G_2(y))=F^{-1}(G(a\,x+b\,y))$$

for all $x,y\in R^1$. This functional equation for unknown F_1, F_2, F can easily be solved; the result is $F_1=G_1$, $F_2=G_2$, completing the proof.

We next list some simple properties of $\mathfrak{e}$ for later use.

1. If f_n converges to some $f \in \mathscr{P}$ as $n \uparrow \infty$ in such a way that

$$\lim_{N\to\infty} \sup_{n\geq 1} \int_{|x|>N} x^2 f_n(dx) = 0, \tag{2.4}$$

then $\lim_{n\to\infty} \mathfrak{e}[f_n] = \mathfrak{e}[f]$. The condition (2.4) is satisfied if for some $p>2$ the absolute p-th moments of f_n are bounded in n.

2. Let $f_\theta \in \mathscr{P}$ and $\alpha_2(f_\theta) = \sigma^2$ for $0 \leqq \theta < 1$, and assume that $\int \varphi(x) f_\theta(dx)$ is Borel measureable in θ for any bounded continuous function φ. Then for any probability measure μ on $[0, 1)$ we have

$$\mathfrak{e}[\int f_\theta\, \mu(d\theta)] \leqq \int \mathfrak{e}[f_\theta]\, \mu(d\theta).$$

3. By Theorem 1, $\mathfrak{e}$ admits the expression

$$\mathfrak{e}[f] = 2\int \{x^2 - x G^{-1}(F(x))\} f(dx)$$

for a continuous probability distribution f in $\mathscr{P}$.

The inequality (2.2) will now be applied to give a simple proof of the central limit theorem. Let $\{X_n\}_{n=1,2,\dots}$ be a sequence of independent identically distributed random variables with mean 0 and variance 1. Then the so-called central limit theorem states that the distribution of $\xi_n = n^{-\frac{1}{2}}(X_1 + \cdots + X_n)$ tends to a Gaussian distribution as $n \uparrow \infty$. *Here we prove that* $\mathfrak{e}[\xi_n] \to 0$ *as* $n \to \infty$ *assuming* $E\{X_1^4\} < \infty$[2]. This condition implies that

$$E\{\xi_n^4\} = \frac{1}{n} E\{X_1^4\} + 3\left(1 - \frac{1}{n}\right) < \text{const.} \quad (\text{independent of } n). \tag{2.5}$$

Putting $\eta_k = \xi_{2^k}$, we first prove that $\mathfrak{e}[\eta_k] \downarrow 0$ as $k \uparrow \infty$. The decreasing property of $\mathfrak{e}[\eta_k]$ is obvious by the inequality (2.2), and so we denote by l the limit of $\mathfrak{e}[\eta_k]$ as $k \to \infty$. If f is a limit distribution of η_k as $k \to \infty$ via some subsequence $k_1 < k_2 < \cdots$, and if η and ζ are independent random variables with distribution f, then it follows from (2.5) and 1 of § 2 that

$$\mathfrak{e}[\eta] = \lim_{p\to\infty} \mathfrak{e}[\eta_{k_p}] = l \quad \text{and} \quad \mathfrak{e}\left[\frac{\eta+\zeta}{2}\right] = \lim_{p\to\infty} \mathfrak{e}[\eta_{2^{k_p}}] = l,$$

therefore by Theorem 2 the limit l must be 0. Next, we write an integer $n \geqq 1$ as $n = \sum_{k=0}^{m} n_k$ where $n_k = \varepsilon_k 2^k$ with $\varepsilon_k = 0$ or 1. Then, using the inequality (2.2) we have $\mathfrak{e}[\xi_n] \leqq \frac{1}{n} \sum_{k=0}^{m} n_k\, \mathfrak{e}[\eta_k]$, and hence $\mathfrak{e}[\xi_n] \to 0$ as was to be proved.

3. $\mathfrak{e}$ Decreases along Solutions of Boltzmann's Problem for Kac's Model of a Maxwellian Gas

Given $f_1, f_2 \in \mathscr{P}$ and $\theta \in [0, 2\pi)$, we denote by $B_\theta(f_1, f_2)$ the probability distribution of $X_1 \cos\theta + X_2 \sin\theta$, where X_1 and X_2 are random variables with distri-

[2] This condition is assumed just to simplify the proof. Without this $\mathfrak{e}[\xi_n]$ still tends to 0.

butions f_1 and f_2 respectively. We also put

$$B(f_1, f_2) = \frac{1}{2\pi} \int_0^{2\pi} B_\theta(f_1, f_2)\, d\theta.$$

In Kac's one-dimensional model of a Maxwellian gas, the distribution $u(t, dx)$ of molecular speeds at time $t > 0$ is determined by the solution of Boltzmann's problem

$$\frac{\partial u(t, \cdot)}{\partial t} = B\big(u(t), u(t)\big) - u(t, \cdot). \tag{3.1}$$

The solutions of this equation can be obtained by Wild's sum [2]. If the initial distribution has a density, then so does the solution, and it is known that the entropy increases along the solution with time, while the solution itself tends to a Gaussian distribution as $t \uparrow \infty$. McKean [1] gave detailed discussions on this subject; he gave also other functionals which are (or, at least are expected to be) monotone along the solutions of (3.1) together with an interesting conjecture about them. But, among these functionals, the entropy and Linnik's functional are the only ones which were used effectively in the investigation of the asymptotic properties of the solutions of (3.1). In this section, we prove that the functional $\mathfrak{e}$ decreases monotonically to zero along the solutions of (3.1); this statement itself implies automatically that the solutions of (3.1) tend to Gaussian distributions as $t \uparrow \infty$.

Theorem 3. *Let $u(t)$ be the solution of* (3.1) *with initial distribution $f \in \mathscr{P}$. Then,* (i) $\mathfrak{e}[u(t)]$ *is decreasing in* t, *and* (ii) *if f has finite fourth moment,* $\mathfrak{e}[u(t)]$ *decreases to* 0 *as* $t \uparrow \infty$.

The following corollary is an immediate consequence of the above theorem and 3 of § 2.

Corollary. *Let $\mathscr{P}_0$ be the subclass of $\mathscr{P}$ consisting of continuous probability distributions, and put $\mathfrak{e}_0[f] = \int x G^{-1}[F(x)] f(dx)$. Then the functional $\mathfrak{e}_0$ is increasing along the solutions of* (3.1) *with initial distributions* $\in \mathscr{P}_0$.

The proof of Theorem 3 will be given in several steps.

Proof. 1. Let $\mathscr{P}_n(f)$, $n \geqq 1$, be the (finite) set of probability measures from $\mathscr{P}$ defined inductively as follows: (i) $\mathscr{P}_1(f)$ consists of a single element f, and (ii) $\mathscr{P}_n(f)$ is the set of all probability measures of the form $B(f_1, f_2)$ with $f_1 \in \mathscr{P}_{n_1}(f)$, $f_2 \in \mathscr{P}_{n_2}(f)$, $n_1 + n_2 = n$. Then, the solution $u(t)$ of (3.1) with initial distribution f can be expressed as Wild's sum

$$u(t) = e^{-t} \sum_{n=1}^{\infty} (1 - e^{-t})^{n-1}\, p_n(f), \tag{3.2}$$

where $p_n(f)$ stands for a convex combination of elements in $\mathscr{P}_n(f)$, $n \geqq 1$ ([2], see also [1]).

2. If $\tilde{f}$ denotes the even part of f, say $\tilde{f}(dx) = \frac{1}{2}(f(dx) + f(-dx))$, then it is easy to see that $B(f_1, f_2) = B(\tilde{f}_1, \tilde{f}_2)$. Therefore, if f_1 and f_2 have the same second

moment, it follows from 2 of § 2 and Theorem 2 that

$$\mathfrak{e}[B(f_1,f_2)]=\mathfrak{e}[B(\tilde{f}_1,\tilde{f}_2)]\leqq\frac{1}{2\pi}\int_0^{2\pi}\mathfrak{e}[B_\theta(\tilde{f}_1,\tilde{f}_2)]\,d\theta$$

$$\leqq\frac{1}{2\pi}\int_0^{2\pi}\{\mathfrak{e}[\tilde{f}_1]\cos^2\theta+\mathfrak{e}[\tilde{f}_2]\sin^2\theta\}\,d\theta\leqq\frac{\mathfrak{e}[f_1]+\mathfrak{e}[f_2]}{2},$$

because $\mathfrak{e}[\tilde{f}]\leqq\mathfrak{e}[f]$. Therefore we have $\mathfrak{e}[p_n(f)]\leqq\mathfrak{e}[f]$, and hence by Wild's sum (3.2) and 2 of § 2 we see that

$$\mathfrak{e}[u(t)]\leqq\mathfrak{e}[f]\qquad(t>0); \tag{3.3}$$

the equality holds if and only if f is a Gaussian distribution. (3.3) implies the part (i) of the theorem.

3. If $\int x^4 f(dx)<\infty$, then by (3.1) the function $\alpha(t)=\int x^4\,u(t,dx)$ satisfies the differential equation

$$\frac{d\alpha(t)}{dt}=\frac{3}{4}\sigma^4-\frac{1}{4}\alpha(t),\qquad\sigma^2=\alpha_2(f),$$

which implies that $\alpha(t)\to3\sigma^4$ as $t\to\infty$, and hence $\alpha(t)$ is bounded. Next, let u_∞ be a limit distribution of $u(t)$ as $t\uparrow\infty$ via some subsequence $t_1<t_2<\cdots$. Since $\alpha(t)$ is bounded, we have $\mathfrak{e}[u_\infty]=\lim_{n\to\infty}\mathfrak{e}[u(t_n)]=\lim_{t\to\infty}\mathfrak{e}[u(t)]$ by 1 of § 2. If $u_\infty(t)$ denotes the solution of (3.1) with initial distribution u_∞, then an application of Wild's sum shows that $u_\infty(t)=\lim_{n\to\infty}u(t_n+t)$ and hence $\mathfrak{e}[u_\infty(t)]=\lim_{t\to\infty}\mathfrak{e}[u(t_n+t)]=\mathfrak{e}[u_\infty]$. Therefore u_∞ must be a Gaussian distribution from the preceding step, as was to be proved.

Note. After sending the manuscript to the editor, I was informed from T. Yanagimoto of a simple proof of Theorem 1 based upon the following Hoeffding's formula: if F denotes the joint and F_X and F_Y the marginal distribution functions of X and Y, then

$$E(XY)-E(X)\,E(Y)=\int_{-\infty}^{\infty}\int_{-\infty}^{\infty}[F(x,y)-F_X(x)\,F_Y(y)]\,dx\,dy$$

provided the expectations on the left hand side exist.

References

1. McKean, H. P.: Speed of approach to equilibrium for Kac's caricature of a Maxwellian gas. Arch. Rat. Mech. Analysis **21**, 343–367 (1966)
2. Wild, E.: On Boltzmann's equation in the kinetic theory of gases. Proc. Cambridge Philos. Soc. **47**, 602–609 (1951)

Hiroshi Tanaka
Department of Mathematics
Hiroshima University
Hiroshima, Japan

(Received January 10, 1973)

ON MARKOV PROCESS CORRESPONDING TO BOLTZMANN'S EQUATION OF MAXWELLIAN GAS

Hiroshi Tanaka

§1. Introduction. The basic equation in the kinetic theory of dilute monoatomic gases is the famous Boltzmann's equation. In the spatially homogeneous case, the initial value problem of this equation was solved for a gas of hard balls by Carleman [1], for Maxwellian gas with cutoff by Wild [14], and for bounded total collision cross-section by Povzner [8] (in modified spatially inhomogeneous case), but it seems that no results (for existence and uniqueness) have been obtained for Maxwellian gas without cutoff. On the other hand, H. P. McKean [5] introduced a class of Markov processes associated with certain nonlinear (parabolic) equations such as Boltzmann's equation, and brought a new light in the field of investigation of such equations by probabilistic methods (see also [6]). Then, there appeared works by D. P. Johnson [3], T. Ueno [11] [12], Y. Takahashi [9] and H. Tanaka [10], mostly concerned with Boltzmann's equation of cutoff type and certain nonlinear equations with similar structure. Especially, Ueno [12] constructed Markov processes which describe motions of infinitely many interacting particles, while Takahashi [9] introduced interaction semigroups and discussed their relationship to branching semigroups. In this paper we are exclusively concerned with non-cutoff Maxwellian gas ; our purpose is to construct a Markov process in the sense of McKean [5] corresponding to the 3-dimensional Maxwellian gas without cutoff by solving appropriate stochastic differential equation (the equation (2.10) in §2). The theory of stochastic differential equations was initiated by K. Itô [2] and, in the case of diffusions, equations similar to (2.10) were considered by McKean [7] in connection with certain nonlinear parabolic equations. The results are only summarized ; full proofs will be published elsewhere.

We consider a monoatomic dilute gas composed of a large number of molecules moving in the space and assume that there are no outside forces. Let $Nu(t,x)dx$ be the number of molecules with velocities x within the differential element dx at time t, where N is the total number of molecules. Then under the assumption of spatial homogeneity, $u(t,x)$ satisfies the following Boltzmann's equation :

$$(1.1) \quad \frac{\partial u(t,x)}{\partial t} = \int_{S_o \times R^3} \{u(t,x^*)u(t,y^*)-u(t,x)u(t,y)\}|x-y|Q(|x-y|,\theta)\sin\theta d\theta d\psi dy,$$

where $S_o=(0,\pi)\times[0,2\pi)$ and θ,ψ are points in $(0,\pi)$ and $[0,2\pi)$ respectively. Denote by $S_{x,y}$ the sphere with center $\frac{x+y}{2}$ and diameter $|x-y|$, and on this sphere we consider a spherical coordinate system with polar axis defined by the relative velocity $x-y$. x^* and y^* are the post-collisional velocities. Let θ and ψ be the colatitude of x^*(the angle between two vectors $x-y$ and x^*-y^*) and the logitude of x^*, respectively. By the conservation laws of momentum and energy x^* and y^* are always situated on $S_{x,y}$ and constitute a diameter of $S_{x,y}$, and so y^* is also determined by θ and ψ. For each x and y the origin of the longitude ψ may be arbitrary chosen within the requirement that x^* and y^* as functions of (x,y,θ,ψ) should be Borel measurable. A nonnegative function Q is determined by the intermolecular force and is called the differential collision cross-section. In the model of gas of hard balls Q is a positive constant, while in the Maxwellian model in which molecules repel each other with a force inversely proportional to the fifth power of their distance, $|x-y|Q(|x-y|,\theta)$ turns out to be a function $Q_M(\theta)$ of θ alone ; in the latter case $Q_M(\theta)$ is a decreasing function of θ with $Q_M(\theta) \sim \text{const.}\ \theta^{-\frac{5}{2}}$, $\theta\downarrow 0$, and so the total collision cross-section is infinite (non cutoff) (see [13]). This is the case we consider in this paper.

§2. Markov processes and stochastic differential equation

In order to indicate our problem clearly, we first explain how a Markov process in the sense of McKean [5] is associated with Boltzmann's equation, taking gas of hard balls by example. The equation (1.1) for gas of hard balls is usually treated in the following form :

$$\frac{\partial u(t,x)}{\partial t} = \int_{S^2\times R^3} \{u(t,x^*)u(t,y^*)-u(t,x)u(t,y)\}|(y-x),\ell)|d\ell dy, \tag{2.1}$$

where $x^*=x+(y-x,\ell)\ell$, $y^*=y-(y-x,\ell)\ell$, $\ell \in S^2$, and $d\ell$ is the uniform distribution on S^2. We set

$$\begin{cases} u(t,\Gamma) = \int_\Gamma u(t,x)\,dx , & \Gamma\in \mathcal{B}(R^3) \\ u(t,\varphi) = \int \varphi(x)u(t,dx) , & \varphi\in C_b(R^3) \end{cases} \tag{2.2}$$

where $C_b(R^3)$ denotes the space of real valued bounded continuous functions on R^3 (the notation (2.2) will be used throughout in this paper). Then, from (2.1) we have

$$\frac{\partial u(t,\varphi)}{\partial t} = \int_{S^2\times R^3\times R^3} \{\varphi(x^*)-\varphi(x)\}|(y-x,\ell)|d\ell u(t,dx)u(t,dy),\ \varphi\in C_b(R^3). \tag{2.3}$$

Povzner's result [8] may be stated as follows : given an initial data f (probability measure on R^3) such that $\int|x|^4 f(dx)<\infty$, there exists a unique solution $u(t,\cdot)$ (probability measure) of (2.3) such that $\mu(t)=\int|x|^4u(t,dx)$ is locally bounded. Now, keeping f and $u(t,\cdot)$ as above, we consider the following equation for $v(t,\cdot)$:

$$(2.4)\quad \begin{cases} \dfrac{\partial v(t,\varphi)}{\partial t} = \displaystyle\int_{S^2\times R^3\times R^3} \{\varphi(x^*)-\varphi(x)\}\,|(y-x,\ell)|\,d\ell\, v(t,dx)\,u(t,dy) \\ v(0,\cdot) = \delta(z,\cdot), \qquad \varphi\in C_b(R^3) \,, \end{cases}$$

where $\delta(z,\cdot)$ denotes the unit distribution with mass at z. Then, using the result of [8] it is not hard to prove that (2.4) has a unique solution, which we denote by $P_f(t,z,\cdot)$. We can also prove that

(2.5a) $\quad P_f(t,z,\cdot)$ is a probability measure on R^3,

$$(2.5b)\quad u(t,\Gamma) = \int_{R^3} P_f(t,z,\Gamma)f(dz), \quad \Gamma\in\mathcal{B}(R^3) \,,$$

$$(2.5c)\quad P_f(t+s,z,\Gamma) = \int_{R^3} P_f(t,z,dy)P_{u(t)}(s,y,\Gamma).$$

The above properties of $P_f(t,z,\cdot)$ enable us to construct a Markov process as follows. Let Ω be the space of step functions $z(t)$ defined on $[0,\infty)$ and taking values in R^3, and $\mathcal{B}$ the σ-field generated by (measurable) cylinder sets in Ω. For each probability measure f on R^3 such that $\int |x|^4 f(dx)<\infty$, we can construct a probability measure $P_f(\cdot)$ on $(\Omega,\mathcal{B})$ so that $\{\Omega,z(t),P_f\}$ is a Markov process in the following sense.

$$(2.6a)\quad P_f\{z(0)\in dx\} = f(dx) \,,$$

$$(2.6b)\quad P_f\{z(t+s)\in\Gamma\,|\,z(\tau):0\leqq\tau\leqq t\}=P_{u(t)}(s,z(t),\Gamma), \text{ a.s. } (P_f).$$

This is the Markov process in the sense of [5] associated with the gas of hard balls (2.1).

Now, our problem can be stated as follows : construct a Markov process $x(t)$ in the sense of [5] which is related to the Maxwellian gas without cutoff as $z(t)$ is to (2.1). So we take up the equation (1.1) with Q_M specified as in §1 and rewrite it as in the form (2.3). A formal but careful calculation yields

$$\frac{\partial u(t,\varphi)}{\partial t} = \int_{S_0\times R^3\times R^3} \{\varphi(x^*)-\varphi(x)\}Q_M(\theta)\sin\theta d\theta d\psi u(t,dx)u(t,dy). \tag{2.7}$$

Considering the singularity of $Q_M(\theta)$ at $\theta=0$, it may be natural to take φ (test function) from the space $C_0^1(R^3)$ of C^1-functions with compact supports. However, we do not treat (2.7) directly ; instead we consider a suitable stochastic differential equation as will be described below.

Let $S=(0,1)\times(0,\pi)\times[0,2\pi)$ and λ the measure on S defined by $d\lambda = d\alpha\otimes Q(d\theta)\otimes d\psi$, where $Q(d\theta)=Q_M(\theta)\sin\theta d\theta$. Although we have thus specified $Q(d\theta)$, we remark that the only property of $Q(d\theta)$ we need later is

$$\int_{(0,\pi)} \theta Q(d\theta) < \infty, \tag{2.8}$$

and so our results remain valid for arbitrary measure $Q(d\theta)$ subject to the condition (2.8). Let $\tilde{\lambda}$ be the product measure $dt\otimes d\lambda$ on the space $(0,\infty)\times S$ and denote by $\mathfrak{F}$ the class of Borel sets in $(0,\infty)\times S$ which have finite $\tilde{\lambda}$-measure. A family of random variables $\{p(A,\omega)\}_{A\in\mathfrak{F}}$ defined on a probability space $(\Omega,\mathfrak{B},P)$ is called a <u>Poisson random measure</u> on $(0,\infty)\times S$ associated with the measure $\tilde{\lambda}$, if the following two conditions are satisfied.

(i) Each $p(A,\omega)$ is distributed according to the Poisson distribution with mean $\tilde{\lambda}(A)$.

(ii) If $A_1, A_2, \cdots \in \mathcal{F}$, $A_j \cap A_K = \phi \ (j \neq k)$ and $A = \bigcup_{k=1}^{\infty} A_k \in \mathcal{F}$,

then the family $\{p(A_k,\omega)\}_{k=1,2,\cdots}$ is independent and

(2.9) $$p(A,\omega) = \sum_{k=1}^{\infty} p(A_k,\omega) \quad \text{(a.s.)}.$$

Since a Poisson random measure always admits a suitable modification for which (2.9) holds for all ω, we may suppose, if necessary, that $\{p(A,\omega)\}$ satisfies this stronger version of (2.9). For a Poisson random measure $\{p(A,\omega)\}_{A\in\mathcal{F}}$ we set

$$\mathcal{B}_\infty^t = \sigma\{p(A,\omega) : A \subset (t,\infty)\times S\},$$

where the notation $\sigma\{ \text{——} \}$ stands for the smallest σ-field that makes all the random variables in $\{ \text{——} \}$ measurable. Next, we regard the unit interval (0,1) as a probability space by considering the Lebesgue measure (precisely, its restriction) on the Borel field of (0,1), and on this probability space we sometimes consider an R^3-valued stochastic process $\{y(t,\alpha),\ 0\leqq t<\infty\}$ with path functions which are right continuous and have left hand limits. Such a process is called an α-process for simplicity ; similarly a random variable defined on the probability space (0,1) is called an α-random variable. Now our stochastic differential equation associated with (2.7) can be written as follows :

(2.10a) $$x(t,\omega) = x(0,\omega) + \int_{(0,t]\times S} a(x(s,\omega), y(s,\alpha), \theta, \psi)\, p(ds d\sigma,\omega).$$

(2.10b) $\{y(t,\alpha),\ 0\leqq t<\infty\}$ is an α-process which is equivalent in law to $\{x(t,\omega),\ 0\leqq t<\infty\}$.

(2.10c) For each $t\geqq 0$, the σ-field

$$\sigma\{x(s,\omega),\ p(A,\omega) : 0\leqq s\leqq t,\ A\subset(0,t]\times S\}$$

is independent of $\mathcal{B}_\infty^t$

Here $a(x,y,\theta,\psi)=x^*(x,y,\theta,\psi)-x$, $d\sigma=d\alpha d\theta d\psi$, and of course $\{p(A,\omega)\}$ is a Poisson random measure associated with $\tilde{\lambda}$ defined over a (basic) probability space $(\Omega,\mathcal{B},P)$. $\{x(t,\omega),\ 0\leq t\leq\infty\}$ is unknown process to be determined by the equation (2.10a) under the additional conditions (2.10b) and (2.10c). Solving (2.10) gives rise to an answer to the problem of finding Markov process associated with the Maxwellian gas, as will be seen in the next section.

§3. Solving the stochastic differential equation. Main results

Let f be a probability measure on R^3. By a solution of (2.10) with initial distribution f, we mean an R^3-valued stochastic process $\{x(t,\omega),\ 0\leq t\leq\infty\}$ defined over a suitable probability space $(\Omega,\mathcal{B},P)$ and satisfying the following conditions:

(i) $x(t,\omega)$ is right continuous and has left hand limits with probability 1,

(ii) $P\{x(0,\omega)\in dx\} = f(dx)$,

(iii) the relations (2.10a), (2.10b) and (2.10c) hold for some Poisson random measure $\{p(A,\omega)\}$ associated with $\tilde{\lambda}$ and defined over the probability space $(\Omega,\mathcal{B},P)$.

In solving the existence problem, the usual method of successive approximation can not be applied directly, since the function $a(x,y,\theta,\psi)$ is not smooth. However, it can be shown that $a(x,y,\theta,\psi)$ has a nice property similar to the Lipschitz continuity (Lemma 1). Owing to this property a kind of successive approximation method works, but in the results the usual pathwise uniqueness will be replaced by weaker one, the uniqueness in law. Here, we say that the uniqueness in law holds for initial distribution f, if any two solutions of (2.10) with initial distribution f (which may be defined on different probability spaces) are identical in law as stochastic processes.

In what follows, $a(x,y,\theta,\psi)$ viewed as function of ψ alone is regarded as a periodic function on R^1 with period 2π.

<u>Lemma 1</u>. <u>There exists a Borel function</u> $\psi_o(x,y,\tilde{x},\tilde{y},)$ of $x,y,\tilde{x},\tilde{y} \in R^3$ <u>such that</u>

$$|a(x,y,\theta,\psi)-a(\tilde{x},\tilde{y},\theta,\psi+\psi_o(x,y,\tilde{x},\tilde{y}))| \leqq K\{|x-\tilde{x}|+|y-\tilde{y}|\}\cdot\theta,$$

<u>where</u> K <u>is an absolute constant</u>.

In fact, ψ_o can be defined as follows. If $x=y$ or $\tilde{x}=\tilde{y}$, we set $\psi_o(x,y,\tilde{x},\tilde{y}) =0$. If $x\neq y$ and $\tilde{x}\neq\tilde{y}$, we set

$$x^o = \frac{|x-y|}{|\tilde{x}-\tilde{y}|}\ \frac{\tilde{x}-\tilde{y}}{2} + \frac{x+y}{2}$$

and denote by ρ the rotation around ℓ such that $\rho x = x^o$, where ℓ is the straight line passing through the point $\frac{x+y}{2}$ and perpendicular to the plane determined by the three points $\frac{x+y}{2}$, x, x^o (when $x^o=y$, we define ρ by $\rho z = x+y-z$). Now we set

$$x^{\#}(x,y,\theta,0)= \frac{|\tilde{x}-\tilde{y}|}{|x-y|}\ (\rho x^*(x,y,\theta,0)- \frac{x+y}{2}\ ) + \frac{\tilde{x}+\tilde{y}}{2}\ .$$

Then $x^{\#}$ lies on the sphere $S_{\tilde{x},\tilde{y}}$ and hence we can define ψ_o $(0\leqq\psi_o<2\pi)$ by the formula

$$x^{\#}(x,y,\theta,0) = x^*(\tilde{x},\tilde{y},\theta,\psi_o(x,y,\tilde{x},\tilde{y})).$$

One of our main results is

<u>Theorem A</u>. <u>Assume that</u> $\int|x|f(dx)<\infty$. <u>Then</u>,

(i) <u>there exists a solution</u> $\{x(t,\omega),\ 0\leqq t<\infty\}$ <u>of</u> (2.10) <u>with initial distribution</u> f,

(ii) <u>the uniqueness in law holds for initial distribution</u> f,

(iii) <u>the probability distribution</u> $u(t,\cdot)$ <u>of</u> $x(t,\omega)$ <u>satisfies</u> (2.7) <u>for any</u> $\varphi \in C_o^1(R^3)$,

(iv) (a) (<u>conservation of momentum</u>) $E\{x(t,\omega)\}$ <u>is independent of</u> t,

(b) (<u>conservation of energy</u>) $E\{|x(t,\omega)|^2\}$ <u>is independent of</u> t, <u>provided</u> $\int|x|^2 f(dx)<\infty$.

Here is an outline of the proof of the existence part (i). Choose a sequence $\{\xi_n(\alpha)\}_{n=o,1,\cdots}$ of independent α-random variables with the uniform distribution on $(0,1)$, and set $\mathcal{F}_n = \sigma\{\xi_k(\alpha),\ 0\leq k\leq n\}$. Over a suitable probability space $(\Omega,\mathcal{B},P)$ we take an R^3-valued random variable $x(0,\omega)$ with distribution f and a Poisson random measure $\{\tilde{p}(A,\omega)\}$ associated with $\tilde{\lambda}$ so that $x(0,\omega)$ is independent of $\{\tilde{p}(A,\omega)\}$, and set $x_o(t,\omega)=x(0,\omega)$ for all $t\geq 0$. Then, taking arbitrary $\mathcal{F}_o$--measurable α-process $\{y_o(t,\alpha),\ 0\leq t<\infty\}$ which is equivalent in law to the process $\{x_o(t,\omega),\ 0\leq t<\infty\}$, we put

$$x_1(t,\omega)=x(0,\omega)+\int_{(0,t]\times S} a(x_o(s,\omega),y_o(s,\alpha),\theta,\psi)\tilde{p}(dsd\sigma,\omega).$$

In general, for $n\geq 1$ we put

$$x_{n+1}(t,\omega)=x(0,\omega)+\int_{(0,t]\times S} a(x_n(s,\omega),y_n(s,\omega),\theta,\psi+\tilde{\psi}_n)\tilde{p}(dsd\sigma,\omega),$$

where $\{y_n(t,\alpha),\ 0\leq t<\infty\}$ is an $\mathcal{F}_n$-measurable *) α-process such that the process $\{(y_{n-1}(t,\alpha),y_n(t,\alpha)),\ 0\leq t<\infty\}$ is equivalent in law to the process $\{(x_{n-1}(t,\omega), x_n(t,\omega)),\ 0\leq t<\infty\}$, and $\tilde{\psi}_n=\tilde{\psi}_{n-1}+\psi_o(x_{n-1}(s,\omega),y_{n-1}(s,\alpha),x_n(s,\omega),y_n(s,\alpha))$, $\tilde{\psi}_o=0$.

Then by Lemma 1

$$\text{(3.1)}\qquad |a(x_{n-1}(s),y_{n-1}(s),\theta,\psi+\tilde{\psi}_{n-1})-a(x_n(s),y_n(s),\theta,\psi+\tilde{\psi}_n)|$$
$$\leq K\{|x_n(s)-x_{n-1}(s)|+|y_n(s)-y_{n-1}(s)|\}\theta,$$

and hence

$$E|x_{n+1}(t)-x_n(t)|\leq \text{const.}\int_o^t E|x_n(s)-x_{n-1}(s)|ds,$$

which implies

$$\sum_{n=1}^{\infty} E|x_n(t)-x_{n-1}(t)|<\infty.$$

---

*) $\mathcal{F}_n$-measurability is imposed only to make the construction of $\{y_n(t,\alpha)\}$ easier.

Therefore, $x(t)=\lim_{n\to\infty} x_n(t)$ exists (a.s.), and hence the same for $y(t)=\lim_{n\to\infty} y_n(t)$. Again using (3.1), it can be shown that $\lim_{n\to\infty} a(x_n(t),y_n(t),\theta,\psi+\tilde{\psi}_n)$ exists and is equal to $a(x(t),y(t),\theta,\psi+\tilde{\psi}_\infty)$ with some $\tilde{\psi}_\infty=\tilde{\psi}_\infty(t,\alpha,\omega)$ except on a negligible set. Now setting

$$p(A,\omega)=\int_{(0,\infty)\times S} \chi_A(t,\alpha,\theta,\psi+\tilde{\psi}_\infty)\tilde{p}(dtd\sigma,\omega),$$

we obtain (2.10).

The uniqueness part (ii) follows from the following

Lemma 2. Let f be the same as in the theorem and $\{x(t,\omega),\ 0\leq t<\infty\}$ any solution of (2.10) with initial distribution f. Take arbitrary finite interval $[0,T]$ and let Δ be a partition of $[0,T]$: $0=t_o<t_1<\cdots<t_n=T$. Choosing an R^3-valued random variable $X(0)$ independent of $\{p(A)\}$ and with distribution f, we define a process $\{X_\Delta(t),\ 0\leq t\leq T\}$ as follows :

$$\begin{cases} X_\Delta(t)=X(0)+\displaystyle\int_{(0,t]\times S} a(X(0),Y_o(\alpha),\theta,\psi)p(dsd\sigma), & 0\leq t\leq t_1 \\ X_\Delta(t)=X_\Delta(t_1)+\displaystyle\int_{(t_1,t)\times S} a(X_\Delta(t_1),Y_1(\alpha),\theta,\psi)p(dsd\sigma), & t_1<t\leq t_2 \\ \quad\vdots & \\ X_\Delta(t)=X_\Delta(t_{n-1})+\displaystyle\int_{(t_{n-1},t]\times S} a(X_\Delta(t_{n-1}),Y_{n-1}(\alpha),\theta,\psi)p(dsd\sigma), & t_{n-1}<t\leq T, \end{cases}$$

where $Y_o(\alpha),\cdots,Y_{n-1}(\alpha)$ are α-random variables defined successively so that each $Y_k(\alpha)$ has the same distribution as $X_\Delta(t_k)$. Then, any finite dimensional distribution of $\{X_\Delta(t),\ 0\leq t\leq T\}$ converges to the corresponding finite dimensional distribution of $\{x(t),\ 0\leq t\leq T\}$ as $|\Delta|=\max_{1\leq k\leq n}|t_k-t_{k-1}|$ tends to 0.

The following theorem shows that the process $\{x(t,\omega),\ 0\leq t<\infty\}$ is the Markov process we were looking for. The proof is almost the same as that of Theorem A.

Theorem B. (i) *Let* $\{y(t,\alpha),\ 0\leq t<\infty\}$ *be any* α*-process equivalent in law to the process* $\{x(t,\omega),\ 0\leq t<\infty\}$ *constructed in Theorem A. Then, for each* $x\in R^3$ *there exists a solution* $z(t,\omega)$ *for the stochastic differential equation*

$$z(t,\omega)=x+\int_{(0,t]\times S} a(z(s,\omega),y(s,\alpha)\theta,\psi)p(dsd\sigma,\omega),$$

and the uniqueness in law holds for this equation.

(ii) *Set*

$$P_f(t,x,\Gamma)=P\{z(t,\omega)\in\Gamma\}\ ,\quad \Gamma\in\mathcal{B}(R^3)\ ,$$

and let $\{x(t,\omega),\ 0\leq t<\infty\}$ *be the solution of* (2.10). *Then*

$$P\{x(t+s,\omega)\in\Gamma\,|\,\mathcal{B}_t\}=P_{u(t)}(s,x(t,\omega),\Gamma)\quad a.s.,$$

where $\mathcal{B}_t=\sigma\{x(s,\omega),p(A,\omega)\ :\ 0\leq s\leq t,\ \ A\subset(0,t]\times S\}.$

References

[1] T. Carleman, Problèmes Mathematiques dans la Théorie Cinétique des Gaz, Uppsala, 1957.

[2] K. Itô, On stochastic differential equations, Mem. Amer. Math. Soc. No. 4 (1951).

[3] D. P. Johnson, On a class of stochastic processes and its relationship to infinite particle gases, Trans. Amer. Math. Soc. 132(1968),275-295.

[4] M. Kac, Foundation of Kinetic theory, Proc. Third Berkeley Symp. on Math. Stat. and Prob. 3, 171-197.

[5] H. P. McKean, Jr., A class of Markov processes associated with nonlinear parabolic equations, Proc. Nat. Acad. Sci. 56(1966), 1907-1911.

[6] H. P. McKean, Jr., An exponential formula for solving Boltzmann's equation for a Maxwellian gas, J. Combinatorial Theory 2(1967), 358-382.

[7] H. P. McKean, Jr., Propagation of chaos for a class of non-linear parabolic equations, Lecture series in Differential Equations, session 7, Catholic Univ. (1967).

[8] A. Ya. Povzner, On Boltzmann's equation in the kinetic theory of gases, Mat. Sb. 58(1962), 63-86.

[9] Y. Takahashi, Markov semigroups with simplest interactions I, II (to appear in Proc. Japan Acad.).

[10] H. Tanaka, Propagation of chaos for certain purely discontinuous Markov processes with interactions, J. Fac. Sci., Univ. of Tokyo, Sec. I 17(1970), 259-272.

[11] T. Ueno, A class of Markov processes with interactions I, Proc. Japan Acad. 45(1969), 641-646 ; II, ibd., 995-1000.

[12] T. Ueno, A path space and the propagation of chaos for a Boltzmann's gas model, Proc. Japan Acad., 47(1971), 529-533.

[13] G. E. Uhlenbeck and G. W. Ford, Lectures in Statistical Mechanics, Amer. Math. Soc. Providence 1963.

[14] E. Wild, On Boltzmann's equation in the kinetic theory of gases, Proc. Camb. Phil. Soc. 47(1951), 602-609.

Department of Mathematics
Hiroshima University.

Reprinted from
Proc. 2nd Japan-USSR Symp. on Probab. Th., 478–489,
Lecture Notes in Math., **330**, Springer-Verlag, 1973.

Proc. of Intern. Symp. SDE
Kyoto 1976, pp. 409–425

On the Uniqueness of Markov Process Associated with the Boltzmann Equation of Maxwellian Molecules

Hiroshi TANAKA

§1. Introduction

The spatially homogeneous Boltzmann equation of Maxwellian molecules takes the following form:

$$(1.1)\qquad \frac{\partial u(t,x)}{\partial t} = \int (u'u_1' - uu_1)Q(d\theta)d\varepsilon dx_1 ,$$

where $Q(d\theta) = Q_M(\theta)\sin\theta d\theta$ with a positive decreasing function $Q_M(\theta)$ such that $Q_M(\theta) \sim$ const. $\times\ \theta^{-5/2}$, $\theta \downarrow 0$, and the integration is carried out over $(0,\pi)\times(0,2\pi)\times R^3$. In this paper we consider the following weak version of (1.1):

$$(1.2)\qquad \frac{d}{dt}\langle u,\varphi\rangle = \langle u\otimes u, K\varphi\rangle , \qquad \varphi\in C_0^\infty(R^3) ,$$

where $C_0^\infty(R^3)$ is the space of real valued C^∞-functions on R^3 with compact supports and $(K\varphi)(x,x_1) = \int \{\varphi(x') - \varphi(x)\}Q(d\theta)d\varepsilon$; x' is on the sphere S_{x,x_1} with center $(x+x_1)/2$ and diameter $|x-x_1|$; θ and ε are the colatitude and the longitude of x', respectively, with respect to a spherical coordinate system on S_{x,x_1} having $x-x_1$ for the polar axis, and finally $u = u(t,\cdot)$ is a probability measure solution to be found.

McKean [3] introduced a class of Markov processes associated with certain nonlinear parabolic equations. The existence problem for (1.1) or (1.2) is almost equivalent to the problem of constructing an associated Markov process of the type introduced by McKean, but it seems that no rigorous results on the existence problem for (1.1) or (1.2), from (non-probabilistic) analysis, have been obtained. The difficulty lies in that $\int_0^\pi Q(d\theta)$ diverges. In [4] I have constructed a Markov process associated with (1.2) by solving the stochastic differential equation:

$$(1.3a)\qquad X_t = X_0 + \int_{(0,t]\times S} a(X_s, Y_s(\alpha),\theta,\varepsilon)\hat{p}(dsd\theta d\varepsilon d\alpha) ,$$

where $S = (0, \pi) \times (0, 2\pi) \times (0, 1)$, $a(x, x_1, \theta, \varepsilon) = x' - x$ and

(i) $\hat{p}(dsd\theta d\varepsilon d\alpha)$ is a Poisson random measure on $(0, \infty) \times S$ associated with $dsQ(d\theta)d\varepsilon d\alpha$,

(ii) $\{Y_t(\alpha),\ t \geq 0\}$ is a stochastic process defined on the probability space $\{(0, 1), d\alpha\}$, and is equivalent in law to the process $\{X_t, t \geq 0\}$ to be found.

An alternative form of (1.3a) is

$$X_t = X_0 + \sum_{s \leq t} a(s, X_s, \hat{Z}_s)\ , \tag{1.3b}$$

where $a(s, x, \sigma) = a(x, Y_s(\alpha), \theta, \varepsilon)$ for $\sigma = (\theta, \varepsilon, \alpha)$ and $\{\hat{Z}_t, t > 0\}$ is the Poisson point process on S corresponding to the Poisson random measure $\hat{p}$, i.e., defined by the relation $\hat{p}(A) = \sum \chi_A(s, \hat{Z}_s)$ for $A \in \mathscr{B}(R_+ \times S)$. It has been also proved in [4] that the uniqueness in the law sense for solutions of (1.3) holds, however this uniqueness does not mean the uniqueness of the associated Markov process.

The purpose of this paper is to fill this gap by showing that *path functions of any Markov process associated with* (1.2) *can be represented as solutions of* (1.3) *after a suitable extension of basic probability space.* Our task is to find a Poisson point process $\{\hat{Z}_t,\ t > 0\}$ on S with characteristic measure $Q(d\theta)d\varepsilon d\alpha$ such that (1.3b) holds. For this we have to find the compensator of the point process $\{Z_t,\ t > 0\}$ on $R^3 - \{0\}$ defined by $Z_t = X_t - X_{t-}$; this will be done in § 3 and it will follow that $X_t = X_0 + \sum_{s \leq t} Z_s$. Once the compensator of $\{Z_t\}$ is found, a Poisson point process $\{\hat{Z}_t\}$ will be obtained by an application of general results on point processes due to Grigelionis [1] and Karoui-Lepeltier [2]; we will give a construction of $\{\hat{Z}_t\}$ in a simplified form adapted to the present situation.

§ 2. Markov process associated with (1.2)

We begin with the definition of transition function associated with (1.2). Denote by $\mathscr{P}$ the family of probability distributions f on R^3 satisfying $\int_{R^3} |x| f(dx) < \infty$, and for $f \in \mathscr{P}$ we put

$$(K_f\varphi)(x) = \int_{R^3} (K\varphi)(x, x_1) f(dx_1)\ .$$

Definition. $\{e_f(t, x, \cdot) : f \in \mathscr{P},\ t \geq 0,\ x \in R^3\}$ is called a *transition function associated with* (1.2), if the following five conditions are satisfied.

(e.1) For fixed $f \in \mathscr{P}$, $t \geq 0$ and $x \in R^3$, $e_f(t, x, \cdot)$ is a probability measure on R^3.

(e.2) For fixed $A \in \mathscr{B}(R^3)$, $e_f(t, x, A)$ is jointly measurable in $(f, t, x) \in \mathscr{P} \times R_+ \times R^3$.

(e.3) For each $t \geq 0$ and $f \in \mathscr{P}$, there exists a constant c depending only upon t and f such that

$$\int_{R^3} |y|\, e_f(s, x, dy) \leq c(1 + |x|)\,, \qquad 0 \leq s \leq t\,, \quad x \in R^3\,.$$

(e.4) If we set $u(t, \cdot) = \int_{R^3} f(dx) e_f(t, x, \cdot)$, then

$$\langle e_f(t, x, \cdot), \varphi\rangle = \varphi(x) + \int_0^t \langle e_f(s, x, \cdot),\, K_{u(s)}\varphi\rangle ds\,, \qquad \varphi \in C_0^\infty(R^3)\,.$$

(e.5) (Kolmogorov-Chapman equation)

$$e_f(t, x, \cdot) = \int_{R^3} e_f(s, x, dy) e_{u(s)}(t - s, y, \cdot)\,, \qquad 0 \leq s \leq t\,,$$

where u is the same as in (e.4).

Given a transition function $\{e_f(t, x, \cdot)\}$ associated with (1.2), we can construct a Markov process on R^3. To be precise, let Ω be the space of R^3-valued functions on R_+, and denote the value $\omega(t)$ of $\omega(\in \Omega)$ at t by $X_t(\omega)$ or X_t. We put $\mathscr{B} = \sigma\{X_t : t < \infty\}$ and $\mathscr{B}_t = \sigma\{X_s : s \leq t\}$, where $\sigma\{—\}$ denotes the smallest σ-field on Ω that makes $\{—\}$ measurable. Then there exists a unique family $\{P_f^x : x \in R^3, f \in \mathscr{P}\}$ of probability measures on $(\Omega, \mathscr{B})$ with the following properties (i) and (ii).

(i) For fixed $A \in \mathscr{B}$, $P_f^x(A)$ is jointly measurable in $(x, f) \in R^3 \times \mathscr{P}$.

(ii) For $0 < t_1 < \cdots < t_n$ and $A_k \in \mathscr{B}(R^3)$, $0 \leq k \leq n$,

$$\begin{aligned} P_f^x\{X_0 \in A_0, X_{t_1} \in A_1, \cdots, X_{t_n} \in A_n\} \\ = \delta_x(A_0) \int_{A_1} e_f(t_1, x, dx_1) \int_{A_2} e_{u(t_1)}(t_2 - t_1, x_1, dx_2) \\ \cdots \int_{A_n} e_{u(t_{n-1})}(t_n - t_{n-1}, x_{n-1}, dx_n)\,. \end{aligned}$$

We put $P_f(\cdot) = \int_{R^3} f(dx) P_f^x(\cdot)$, and denote by E_f (or E_f^x) the expectation with respect to P_f (or P_f^x). Then the following Markov property is proved by a routine method. For a nonegative $\mathscr{B}$-measurable function Φ on Ω we have

(2.1a) $$E_f^x\{\Phi(\Theta_t\omega)\,|\,\mathscr{B}_t\} = E_{u(t)}^{X_t}\{\Phi\}\,, \qquad P_f^x\text{-a.s.}\,,$$

(2.1b) $$E_f\{\Phi(\Theta_t\omega)\,|\,\mathscr{B}_t\} = E_{u(t)}^{X_t}\{\Phi\}\,, \qquad P_f\text{-a.s.}\,,$$

where $\Theta_t: \Omega \to \Omega$ is the shift operator defined by $X_s(\Theta_t\omega) = X_{t+s}(\omega)$ for $0 \leq s < \infty$.

Lemma 1. *If $\varphi: R^3 \to R$ is Lipschitz continuous, then*

(i) *there exists a constant c_1 depending only upon the Lipschitz constant of φ such that $|(K\varphi)(x, x_1)| \leq c_1|x - x_1|$,*

(ii) *for each $t \geq 0$ and $f \in \mathscr{P}$, there exists a constant c_2 depending only upon t, f and the Lipschitz constant of φ such that*

$$|(K_{u(s)}\varphi)(x)| \leq c_2(1 + |x|)\,, \qquad 0 \leq {}^\forall s \leq t\,,$$

where $u(s) = \int_{R^3} f(dx)e_f(s, x, \cdot)\,.$

Proof. From $|x' - x| \leq \theta|x - x_1|/2$, we have $|\varphi(x') - \varphi(x)| \leq \text{const.}\,|x - x_1|\theta$ and hence

$$|(K\varphi)(x, x_1)| \leq \text{const.}\,|x - x_1| \int_{(0,\pi)\times(0,2\pi)} \theta Q(d\theta)d\varepsilon = c_1|x - x_1|\,,$$

proving (i). (ii) follows from (i) and (e.3).

The following lemma is an immediate consequence of the above lemma and (e.4),

Lemma 2. *If $\varphi: R^3 \to R$ is Lipschitz continuous, then*

$$\langle e_f(t, x, \cdot), \varphi\rangle = \varphi(x) + \int_0^t \langle e_f(s, x, \cdot), K_{u(s)}\varphi\rangle ds\,.$$

Lemma 3. $E_f^x\{|X_t - X_s|\} \leq \text{const.}\,(1 + |x|)\,|t - s|$ *for* $0 \leq s, t \leq T$, *where* const. *may depend upon f and T but not upon x.*

Proof. For $0 < s < t$ we have

$$E_f^x\{|x_t - x_s|\} = \int_{R^3} e_f(s, x, dy) \int_{R^3} e_{u(s)}(t - s, y, dz)\,|z - y|\,.$$

We now put $\varphi(z) = |z - y|$ for fixed y and apply Lemma 2:

$$\int_{R^3} e_{u(s)}(t - s, y, dz)\,|z - y|$$
$$= \varphi(y) + \int_0^{t-s} \langle e_{u(s)}(\tau, y, \cdot), K_{u(s+\tau)}\varphi\rangle d\tau$$

$$\leq \int_0^{t-s} \langle e_{u(s)}(\tau, y, \cdot), |K_{u(s+\tau)}\varphi|\rangle d\tau$$

$$\leq c_2 \int_0^{t-s} d\tau \int_{R^3} e_{u(s)}(\tau, y, dz)(1 + |z|) .$$

Therefore we have

$$E_f^x\{|X_t - X_s|\} \leq c_2 \int_0^{t-s} d\tau \int_{R^3} e_f(s, x, dy) \int_{R^3} e_{u(s)}(\tau, y, dz)(1 + |z|)$$

$$= c_2 \int_0^{t-s} d\tau \int_{R^3} e_f(s + \tau, x, dz)(1 + |z|)$$

$$\leq \text{const. } (1 + |x|)(t - s) .$$

Theorem 1. *The stochastic process $\{X_t, P_f^x\}$ has a modification which is right continuous and of bounded variation on each finite t-interval.*

Proof. Let Y_t be any component of X_t. Let $Q_+ = \{r_k\}_{k\geq 1}$ be the set of nonnegative rational numbers, and for any partition of $[0, t]$:

$$\Delta : 0 = t_0 < t_1 < \cdots < t_n = t , \qquad t_j \in Q_+ \quad (0 \leq j \leq n) ,$$

we put

$$V_t^\Delta = \sum_{j=1}^n |Y_{t_j} - Y_{t_{j-1}}| ,$$

$$U_t^\Delta = V_t^\Delta - (Y_t - Y_0) = 2 \sum_{k=1}^n (Y_{t_j} - Y_{t_{j-1}})^- ,$$

and then

$$V_t = \sup V_t^\Delta , \quad U_t = \sup_\Delta U_t^\Delta , \quad t \in Q_+ ,$$

where the supremum is taken over all such partitions Δ. For each $t \in Q_+$ and $k \geq 1$ we write $\{r_1, \cdots, r_k\} \cap [0, t] = \{\tau_j\}_{1\leq j\leq n}$ with $0 = \tau_0 < \cdots < \tau_n = t$ and then denote by Δ_k the partition of $[0, t]$ with partitioning points $\{\tau_j\}_{1\leq j\leq n}$. Then V_t is clearly the increasing limit of $V_t^{\Delta_k}$ as $k \uparrow \infty$, and hence

$$E_f^x\{V_t\} = \lim_{k\to\infty} E_f^x\{V_t^{\Delta_k}\} = \lim_{k\to\infty} \sum_{j=1}^n E_f^x\{|Y_{\tau_j} - Y_{\tau_{j-1}}|\}$$

$$\leq \text{const. } (1 + |x|)t < \infty , \qquad t \in Q_+ ,$$

and similarly $E_f^x\{U_t\} < \infty$, $t \in Q_+$. On the other hand, since V_t and U_t

are non-decreasing in $t \in Q_+$, $Y_t = Y_0 + V_t - U_t$, $t \in Q_+$, has right hand limits. Therefore the limit

$$\tilde{X}_t = \lim_{\substack{s \downarrow t \\ s \in Q+}} X_s , \qquad t \in R_+$$

exists and gives a desired modification of X_t.

By virtue of Theorem 1, the probability measures P_f^x and P_f can be constructed on *the space of R^3-valued right continuous functions on R_+ having bounded variation on each finite t-interval*. From now on, Ω denotes this restricted space and so the σ-fields $\mathscr{B}$ and $\mathscr{B}_t$ are the ones on this new Ω. We call $\{\Omega, \mathscr{B}, X_t, P_f : f \in \mathscr{P}\}$ *a Markov process associated with* (1.2).

§ 3. Point process $\{Z_t\}$

3.1. In general suppose we are given a probability space $(\Omega, \mathscr{F}, P)$, a Borel subset S of R^d and an extra point ∂ not belonging to S. An $S \cup \{\partial\}$-valued process $\{Z_t(\omega),\ t > 0\}$ defined on $(\Omega, \mathscr{F}, P)$ is called *a point process on* S, if i) $Z_t(\omega)$ is jointly measurable in (t, ω), and ii) $\{t : Z_t(\omega) \in S\}$ is a countable set.

Given a point process $\{Z_t,\ t > 0\}$ on S, we put

$$p(A) = \sum_t \chi_A(t, Z_t) , \qquad A \in \mathscr{B}((0, \infty) \times S) ,$$

$$p_t(B) = \sum_{0<s\le t} \chi_B(Z_s) , \qquad B \in \mathscr{B}(S) , \quad t \ge 0 .$$

Given also a σ-finite Borel measure λ on S, we introduce the following definition. A point process $\{Z_t, t > 0\}$ is called a *Poisson point process on S with characteristic measure* λ, if for any *disjoint* family $A_1, \cdots, A_n$ of Borel sets in $(0, \infty) \times S$ such that $\bar{\lambda}(A_k) = \int_{A_k} dt d\lambda < \infty$ $(1 \le k \le n)$ we have

$$P\{p(A_k) = m_k, k = 1, \cdots, n\} = \prod_{k=1}^{n} \left\{ e^{-\bar{\lambda}(A_k)} \frac{(\bar{\lambda}(A_k))^{m_k}}{m_k !} \right\}$$

$$\text{for } m_1, \cdots, m_n \in N .$$

Then the following characterization of Poisson point processes is well-known.

Theorem 2. *Suppose we are given a point process $\{Z_t,\ t > 0\}$ on S, a σ-finite Borel measure λ on S and an increasing family $\{\mathscr{F}_t\}$ of sub-σ-fields of $\mathscr{F}$. If, for each $B \in \mathscr{B}(S)$ with $\lambda(B) < \infty$, $\{p_t(B) - \lambda(B)t$,*

$t \geq 0\}$ is an $\{\mathscr{F}_t\}$-martingale, then $\{Z_t, t > 0\}$ is a Poisson point process on S with characteristic measure λ.

In the above case, we also call $\{Z_t, t > 0\}$ an $\{\mathscr{F}_t\}$-adapted Poisson point process.

3.2. Suppose we are given a Markov process $\{\Omega, \mathscr{B}, X_t, P_f : f \in \mathscr{P}\}$ introduced in § 2, and put $Z_t = X_t - X_{t-}$. Then $\{Z_t, t > 0\}$ is a point process on $R_0^3 = R^3 - \{0\}$. The purpose of this subsection is to find the compensator of $\{Z_t\}$.

Fixing $f \in \mathscr{P}$, we introduce the following notations.

$$\mathscr{F} = \text{the completion of } \mathscr{B} \text{ with respect to } P_f ,$$
$$\mathscr{F}_t^0 = \{A \in \mathscr{F} : P_f(A \ominus B) = 0 \text{ for some } B \in \mathscr{B}_t\} ,$$
$$\mathscr{F}_t = \textstyle\bigcap_{\varepsilon>0} \mathscr{F}_{t+\varepsilon}^0 .$$

We now think of the unit interval $(0, 1)$ as a probability space by considering the Lebesgue measure on $\mathscr{B}((0, 1))$, and we take an R^3-valued stochastic process $\{Y_t(\alpha), t \geq 0\}$ defined on this probability space $(0, 1)$ with the following properties: (a) Sample paths of $\{Y_t\}$ are right continuous and have bounded variation on each finite t-interval, and (b) $\{Y_t, t \geq 0\}$ is equivalent in law to the process $\{X_t, t \geq 0, P_f\}$. Next, we put $S = (0, \pi) \times (0, 2\pi) \times (0, 1)$ and denote by $\sigma = (\theta, \varepsilon, \alpha)$ a generic element of S. On S we consider the Borel measure λ defined by $d\lambda = Q(d\theta) \otimes d\varepsilon \otimes d\alpha$. We also put

$$a(x, x_1, \theta, \theta, \varepsilon) = x' - x ,$$
$$a(t, x, \sigma) = a(x, Y_t(\alpha), \theta, \varepsilon) \qquad \text{for } \sigma = (\theta, \varepsilon, \alpha) ,$$
$$n(x, x_1, A) = \int_{(0,\pi)\times(0,2\pi)} \delta_{x'-x}(A) Q(d\theta) d\varepsilon , \qquad A \in \mathscr{B}(R_0^3) ,$$
$$n_u(x, A) = \int_{R^3} n(x, x_1, A) u(dx_1) , \qquad A \in \mathscr{B}(R_0^3) .$$

Then, $\langle n_{u(t)}(y, \cdot), \psi \rangle = \langle \lambda, \psi(a(t, y, \cdot)) \rangle$ holds for any non-negative Borel function ψ on R^3 with $\psi(0) = 0$, where $u(t, \cdot) = \int_{R^3} f(dx) e_f(t, x, \cdot)$. Finally we put

$$p_t(\varphi) = \sum_{s \leq t} \varphi(s, X_{s-}, Z_s)$$

for a real valued Borel function φ on $R_+ \times R^3 \times R^3$ with $\varphi(t, y, 0) = 0$.

Theorem 3. *Let $\varphi: R_+ \times R^3 \times R^3 \to R$ be a Borel function with $\varphi(t, y, 0) = 0$ and assume that*

$$\int_0^t ds \int_{R^3} u(s, dy) \int_{R_0^3} n_{u(s)}(y, dz) \, |\varphi(s, y, z)| < \infty \tag{3.1}$$

for each $t \in R_+$. *Then*

$$p_t(\varphi) - \int_0^t \langle \lambda, \varphi(s, X_s, a(s, X_s, \cdot)) \rangle ds$$

is an $\{\mathscr{F}_t\}$*-martingale with respect to* P_f. *In other words*

$$\int_0^t \langle \lambda, \varphi(s, X_s, a(s, X_s, \cdot)) \rangle ds$$

is the compensator of $p_t(\varphi)$.

Remark. The condition (3.1) is satisfied, if $|\varphi(t, y, z)| \leq \text{const.}\ |z|$.

Before going to the proof of this theorem, we prepare some lemmas. First we assume that $\varphi \in C_0^\infty(R_+ \times R^3 \times R_0^3)$. For fixed $t > 0$ we consider a partition of $[0, t]$:

$$\Delta : 0 = t_0 < t_1 < \cdots < t_n = t ,$$

and put

$$I_\Delta = E_f^x \left\{ \sum_{k=1}^n \varphi(t_{k-1}, X_{t_{k-1}}, X_{t_k} - X_{t_{k-1}}) \right\} .$$

Then, with the notation $\varphi^{k,y}(z) = \varphi(t_{k-1}, y, z - y)$ we have

$$\begin{aligned} I_\Delta &= \sum_{k=1}^n \int_{R^3} e_f(t_{k-1}, x, dy) \int_{R^3} e_{u(t_{k-1})}(t_k - t_{k-1}, y, dz) \varphi^{k,y}(z) \\ &= \sum_{k=1}^n \int_{R^3} e_f(t_{k-1}, x, dy) \int_0^{t_k - t_{k-1}} ds \int_{R^3} e_{u(t_{k-1})}(s, y, dz) K_{u(t_{k-1}+s)} \varphi^{k,y}(z) , \\ &= I'_\Delta + I''_\Delta , \end{aligned}$$

where

$$\begin{aligned} I'_\Delta = \sum_{k=1}^n \int_{R^3} e_f(t_{k-1}, x, dy) \int_0^{t_k - t_{k-1}} ds \int_{R^3} e_{u(t_{k-1})}(s, y, dz) \\ \times \chi_\varepsilon(z - y) K_{u(t_{k-1}+s)} \varphi^{k,y}(z) , \end{aligned}$$

and I''_Δ denotes a similar formula obtained from I'_Δ with the replacement of

$$\chi_\varepsilon(z - y) = \begin{cases} 1 & \text{for } |z - y| > \varepsilon \\ 0 & \text{for } |z - y| \leq \varepsilon \end{cases}$$

by $\bar{\chi}_\varepsilon(z-y) = 1 - \chi_\varepsilon(z-y)$.

Lemma 4. *If $\varphi \in C_0^\infty(R_+ \times R^3 \times R_0^3)$, then for any $\varepsilon > 0$*

$$I'_\Delta \to 0 \quad as \quad |\Delta| = \max_{1\le k\le n}(t_k - t_{k-1}) \to 0 \, .$$

Proof. By Lemma 1 there exists a constant c independent of y, z, k and s such that

$$|K_{u(t_{k-1}+s)}\varphi^{k,y}(z)| \le c(1+|z|) \, .$$

If we put

$$\rho(z) = \begin{cases} 0 & \text{for } |z| \le \varepsilon/2 \\ 2|z|/\varepsilon - 1 & \text{for } \varepsilon/2 < |z| < \varepsilon \\ 1 & \text{for } |z| \ge \varepsilon \, , \end{cases}$$

$$\xi^y(z) = c\rho(y-z)(1+|z|) \, ,$$

then we have

$$\chi_\varepsilon(z) \le \rho(z) \, ,$$

$$|I'_\Delta| \le \sum_{k=1}^n \int_{R^3} e_f(t_{k-1}, x, dy) \int_0^{t_k - t_{k-1}} ds \int_{R^3} e_{u(t_{k-1})}(s, y, dz)\xi^y(z) \, .$$

Since the support of φ is compact, the integral with respect to $e_{u(t_{k-1})}(s, y, dz)$ in the above may be performed only on some compact set B of R^3. Moreover, $\xi^y(z)$ is Lipschitz continuous as a function of z for each fixed y, and the Lipschitz constant is bounded as far as y is on B. Therefore, by Lemma 2 we have

$$\begin{aligned} \int_{R^3} e_{u(t_{k-1})}(s, y, dz)\xi^y(z) &= \int_0^s d\tau \int_{R^3} e_{u(t_{k-1})}(\tau, y, dz) K_{u(t_{k-1}+\tau)}\xi^y(z) \\ &\le \text{const.} \int_0^s d\tau \int_{R^3} e_{u(t_{k-1})}(\tau, y, dz)(1+|z|) \, , \end{aligned}$$

and hence

$$\begin{aligned} |I'_\Delta| &\le \text{const.} \sum_{k=1}^n \int_{R^3} e_f(t_{k-1}, x, dy) \int_0^{t_k - t_{k-1}} ds \int_0^s d\tau \\ &\qquad \times \int_{R^3} e_{u(t_{k-1})}(\tau, y, dz)(1+|z|) \\ &= \text{const.} \sum_{k=1}^n \int_0^{t_k - t_{k-1}} ds \int_0^s d\tau \int_{R^3} e_f(t_{k-1}+\tau, x, dz)(1+|z|) \end{aligned}$$

$$\leq \text{const.} \sum_{k=1}^{n} (t_k - t_{k-1})^2 \to 0 , \qquad \text{as } |\Delta| \to 0 .$$

Lemma 5. *If* $\varphi \in C_0^\infty(R_+ \times R^3 \times R_0^3)$, *then*

$$\lim_{|\Delta|\to 0} I_\Delta = E_f^x\left\{\int_0^t \langle n_{u(s)}(X_s, \cdot), \varphi(s, X_s, \cdot)\rangle ds\right\} .$$

Proof. Define $\Delta(s)$, $0 \leq s \leq t$, by

$$\Delta(0) = 0 , \quad \Delta(s) = t_{k-1} \qquad \text{for } t_{k-1} < s \leq t_k \ (1 \leq k \leq n) ,$$

and for $\varepsilon > 0$ (small enough) put

$$\begin{aligned} \Phi(s, y, z, z_1) &= (K\varphi^{k,y})(z, z_1)\bar{\chi}_\varepsilon(z - y) \\ &= \int_{R_0^3} \varphi(s, y, z - y + w)\bar{\chi}_\varepsilon(z - y)n(z, z_1, dw) . \end{aligned}$$

Then

$$\begin{aligned} I''_\Delta &= \sum_{k=1}^{n} \int_{R^3} e_f(t_{k-1}, x, dy) \int_0^{t_k - t_{k-1}} ds \int_{R^3} e_{u(t_{k-1})}(s, y, dz) \\ &\qquad \times \int_{R^3} u(t_{k-1} + s, dz_1)\Phi(t_{k-1}, y, z, z_1) \\ &= \sum_{k=1}^{n} \int_0^{t_k - t_{k-1}} ds \int_0^1 d\alpha E_f^x\{\Phi(t_{k-1}, X_{t_{k-1}}, X_{t_{k-1}+s}, Y_{t_{k-1}+s}(\alpha))\} \\ &= \int_0^1 d\alpha E_f^x\left\{\int_0^t \Phi(\Delta(s), X_{\Delta(s)}, X_s, Y_s(\alpha))ds\right\} \\ &= \int_0^1 d\alpha E_f^x\left\{\int_{[0,t]\times R_0^3} dsn(x_s, Y_s(\alpha), dz) \right. \\ &\qquad \left. \times \varphi(\Delta(s), X_{\Delta(s)}, X_s - X_{\Delta(s)} + z)\bar{\chi}_\varepsilon(X_s - X_{\Delta(s)})\right\} \\ &\to \int_0^1 d\alpha E_f^x\left\{\int_{[0,t]\times R_0^3} dsn(X_{s-}, Y_s(\alpha), dz)\varphi(s, X_{s-}, z)\right\} , \quad \text{as } |\Delta| \to 0 \\ &= E_f^x\left\{\int_0^t \langle n_{u(s)}(X_s, \cdot), \varphi(s, X_s, \cdot)\rangle ds\right\} . \end{aligned}$$

This combined with Lemma 4 completes the proof.

Lemma 6. *Let* $\varphi: R_+ \times R^3 \times R^3 \to R_+$ *be a Borel function with* $\varphi(t, y, 0) = 0$. *Then*

$$E_f^x\{p_t(\varphi)\} = E_f^x\left\{\int_0^t \langle \lambda, \varphi(s, X_s, a(s, X_s, \cdot))\rangle ds\right\} . \tag{3.2}$$

Proof. We first consider the case $\varphi \in C_0^\infty(R_+ \times R^3 \times R_0^3)$. In this case we have

$$p_t^\Delta(\varphi) \equiv \sum_{k=1}^{n} \varphi(t_{k-1}, X_{t_{k-1}}, X_{t_k} - X_{t_{k-1}}) \to p_t(\varphi) ,$$

as $|\Delta| \to 0$. Since $|\varphi(s, y, z)| \leq \text{const.}\ |z|$, we have also

$$|p_t^\Delta(\varphi)| \leq \text{const.} \sum_{k=1}^{n} |X_{t_k} - X_{t_{k-1}}| \leq V ,$$

where V is some P_f^x-integrable random variable. Therefore by Lebesgue's dominated convergence theorem,

$$\begin{aligned} E_f^x\{p_t(\varphi)\} &= \lim_{|\Delta|\to 0} E_f^x\{p_t^\Delta(\varphi)\} \\ &= E_f^x\left\{\int_0^t \langle n_{u(s)}(X_s, \cdot), \varphi(s, X_s, \cdot)\rangle ds\right\} \\ &= E_f^x\left\{\int_0^t \langle \lambda, \varphi(s, X_s, a(s, X_s, \cdot))\rangle ds\right\} , \end{aligned}$$

and this proves (3.2) for smooth φ. Finally, it is easy to remove the smoothness condition of φ in (3.2).

We now come to the proof of Theorem 3. For $0 \leq s \leq t$ we have

$$\begin{aligned} & p_t(\varphi) = p_s(\varphi) + p_{t-s}(\varphi^s) \circ \Theta_s , \\ & \int_0^t \langle \lambda, \varphi(\tau, X_\tau, a(\tau, X_\tau, \cdot))\rangle d\tau \\ & \quad = \int_0^s \langle \lambda, \varphi(\tau, X_\tau, a(\tau, X_\tau, \cdot))\rangle d\tau \\ & \qquad + \int_0^{t-s} \langle n_{u(s+\tau)}(X_\tau(\Theta_s\omega), \cdot), \varphi^s(\tau, X_\tau(\Theta_s\omega), a(\tau, X_\tau(\Theta_s\omega), \cdot))\rangle d\tau , \end{aligned}$$

where $\varphi^s(\tau, y, z) = \varphi(s + \tau, y, z)$. Therefore, if we put

$$q_t(\varphi) = p_t(\varphi) - \int_0^t \langle \lambda, \varphi(\tau, X_\tau, a(\tau, X_\tau, \cdot))\rangle d\tau ,$$

then we have $q_t(\varphi) = q_s(\varphi) + q_{t-s}(\varphi^s) \circ \Theta_s$, and hence by using the Markov property (2.1a)

$$\begin{aligned} E_f\{q_t(\varphi) \,|\, \mathscr{B}_s\} &= q_s(\varphi) + E_f\{q_{t-s}(\varphi^s) \circ \Theta_s \,|\, \mathscr{B}_s\} \\ &= q_s(\varphi) + E_{u(s)}^{x_s}\{q_{t-s}(\varphi^s)\} \\ &= q_s(\varphi) , \qquad\qquad P_f\text{-a.s.} \,. \end{aligned}$$

Thus $\{q_t(\varphi)\}$ is a $\{\mathscr{B}_t\}$-martingale, and hence an $\{\mathscr{F}_t\}$-martingale.

Corollary. $X_t = X_0 + \sum_{s\le t} Z_s$, P_f-a.s. .

Proof. For $\varphi(z) = z$ we have $\sum_{s\le t} Z_s = p_t(\varphi)$, and $E_f\{p_t(\varphi)\} = E_f\{X_t - X_0\}$ by making use of Theorem 3 and Lemma 2. Therefore $X_t - X_0 - \sum_{s\le t} Z_s$ is a martingale with respect to P_f; also it is continuous and has bounded variation on each finite t-interval. But, such a martingale must be 0, and so the corollary is proved.

§ 4. Derivation of stochastic differential equation

Notations are the same as in the subsection 3.2. We now know the compensator of the point process $\{Z_t\}$, and so the representation (1.3b) of $\{Z_t\}$ by means of certain Poisson point process $\{\hat{Z}_t\}$ might be a consequence of general works due to Grigelionis [1] and Karoui-Lepeltier [2]. However we give the construction of $\{\hat{Z}_t\}$ in detail, because we wish the whole proof to be self-contained. The construction given here seems to be simpler.

Theorem 4. *For each fixed $f \in \mathscr{P}$ we can find a probability space $\{\hat{\Omega}, \hat{\mathscr{F}}, \hat{P}\}$, an increasing family $\{\hat{\mathscr{F}}_t\}$, a mapping π from $\hat{\Omega}$ onto Ω and an $\{\hat{\mathscr{F}}_t\}$-adapted Poisson point process $\{\hat{Z}_t, t > 0\}$ on S with characteristic measure λ, having the following properties.*

(i) $\pi^{-1}(\mathscr{F}_t) \subset \hat{\mathscr{F}}_t$, $\pi^{-1}(\mathscr{F}) \subset \hat{\mathscr{F}}$ *and* $\hat{P}\{\pi^{-1}(A)\} = P_f\{A\}$ *for* $A \in \mathscr{F}$.

(ii) $X_t \circ \pi = X_0 \circ \pi + \sum_{s\le t} a(s, X_{s-} \circ \pi, \hat{Z}_s)$, $\hat{P}$*-a.s.,*

or what is the same

$$X_t \circ \pi = X_0 \circ \pi + \int_{(0,t]\times S} a(X_{s\text{-}} \circ \pi, Y_s(\alpha), \theta, \varepsilon)\hat{p}(dsd\sigma) , \qquad \hat{P}\text{-a.s.} ,$$

where $\hat{p}(A) = \sum \chi_A(t, \hat{Z}_t)$ *for* $A \in \mathscr{B}((0, \infty) \times S)$.

Lemma 7. *There exists $Q(t, y, z, A)$ such that*

(i) *for fixed $t \ge 0$, $y \in R^3$ and $z \in R_0^3$, $Q(t, y, z, \cdot)$ is a probability measure on S,*

(ii) *for fixed $A \in \mathscr{B}(S)$, $Q(t, y, z, A)$ is jointly measurable in (t, y, z),*

(iii) *for any nonnegative Borel function φ on $R^3 \times S$ with $\varphi(0, \sigma) = 0$ and for any $t \ge 0$, $y \in R^3$,*

$$\int_S \lambda(d\sigma)\varphi(a(t, y, \sigma), \sigma) = \int_{R_0^3\times S} n_{u(t)}(y, dz)Q(t, y, z, d\sigma)\varphi(z, \sigma) .$$

Proof of the lemma. For fixed $t \ge 0$, $y \in R^3$ and $A \in \mathscr{B}(S)$ we put

$$n^A_{u(t)}(y, B) = \int_A \chi_B(a(t, y, \sigma))\lambda(d\sigma) , \qquad B \in \mathscr{B}(R^3_0) .$$

Then $Q(t, y, z, A)$, as a function of z, should be the Radon-Nikodym derivative of $n^A_{u(t)}(y, \cdot)$ with respect to $n_{u(t)}(y, \cdot)$. A nice version of $Q(t, y, z, A)$ as stated in the lemma can be obtained by making use of the convergence theorem of martingales.

In order to prove Theorem 4 we must prepare some probability spaces together with various quantities defined on them.

1°. $\{\Omega, \mathscr{F}, P\}$: This is, of course, the basic probability space on which our Markov process $\{X_t\}$ has been given. Let

$$B_0 = \{z \in R^3 : |z| > 1\} , \qquad B_n = \left\{z \in R^3 : \frac{1}{n+1} < |z| \leq \frac{1}{n}\right\} \qquad n \geq 1 ,$$

and define $\{\mathscr{F}_t\}$-stopping times T_{nk}, $n \geq 0$, $k \geq 1$, by

$$T_{n0}(\omega) = \inf\{t > 0 : Z_t(\omega) \in B_n\} , \qquad n \geq 0$$
$$T_{nk}(\omega) = \inf\{t > T_{n,k-1}(\omega) : Z_t(\omega) \in B_n\} , \qquad n \geq 0 , k \geq 1 .$$

2°. $\{\Omega', \mathscr{F}', P'\}$: This is the probability space obtained by taking $\Omega' = (0, 1)$, $\mathscr{F}' = \mathscr{B}((0, 1))$ and P' = the Lebesgue measure (restricted on $\mathscr{F}'$). On this probability space we choose a sequence of independent random variables $\{\xi_{nk}(\omega') : n \geq 0,\ k \geq 1\}$, each being uniformly distributed on (0, 1). Moreover we choose a jointly measurable function $Y(t, y, z, \omega')$ on $R_+ \times R^3 \times R^3_0 \times \Omega'$ such that, for each $t \geq 0$, $y \in R^3$ and $z \in R^3_0$, $Y(t, y, z, \cdot)$ is an S-valued random variable defined on $\{\Omega', \mathscr{F}', P'\}$ and with probability distribution $Q(t, y, z, \cdot)$.

3°. $\{\tilde{\Omega}, \tilde{\mathscr{F}}, \tilde{P}\}$: We choose an arbitrary probability space $\{\tilde{\Omega}, \tilde{\mathscr{F}}, \tilde{P}\}$ on which there is defined a Poisson point process $\{\tilde{Z}_t, t > 0\}$ on S with characteristic measure λ, and put $\tilde{\mathscr{F}}_t = \sigma\{\tilde{Z}_s : s \leq t\}$.

Now we can construct all that we need.

(a) $\hat{\Omega} = \Omega \times \Omega' \times \tilde{\Omega}$, $\hat{\mathscr{F}} = \mathscr{F} \otimes \mathscr{F}' \otimes \tilde{\mathscr{F}}$, $\hat{P} = P_f \otimes P' \otimes \tilde{P}$.

(b) $\hat{\mathscr{F}}_t$ = the σ-field on $\hat{\Omega}$ generated by all sets of the form

$$(A \cap B) \times A' \times \tilde{A} , \tag{4.1}$$

where $B \in \mathscr{F}_t$, $\tilde{A} \in \tilde{\mathscr{F}}_t$ and

$$A = \{T_{nk} \leq t \text{ for } \forall(n, k) \in M\} ,$$
$$A' = \{\xi_{nk} \in B_{nk} \text{ for } \forall(n, k) \in M\} ,$$

for some $M \subset N \times N$ and $B_{nk} \in \mathscr{B}((0,1))$.

(c) $$Z'_t = \begin{cases} Y(T_{nk}, X_{nk}, Z_{nk}, \xi_{nk}) & \text{if } t = T_{nk} \\ 0 & \text{if } t \neq T_{nk} \quad \text{for } \forall (n,k) , \end{cases}$$

where $X_{nk} = X_{T_{nk}-}$ and $Z_{nk} = X_{T_{nk}} - X_{T_{nk}-}$.

(d) $$Z''_t = \begin{cases} \tilde{Z}_t & \text{if } a(t, X_{t-}, \tilde{Z}_t) = 0 \\ 0 & \text{otherwise} . \end{cases}$$

(e) $$\hat{Z}_t = Z'_t + Z''_t .$$

Then, (i) of Theorem 4 is obvious with the self-evident notation π (projection), and the rest will be proved in the following two lemmas.

Lemma 8. *$\{\hat{Z}_t, t > 0\}$ is an $\{\hat{\mathscr{F}}_t\}$-adapted Poisson point process on S with characteristic measure λ.*

Proof. Since the $\{\hat{\mathscr{F}}_t\}$-adaptedness of $\{\hat{Z}_t, t > 0\}$ is clear from the definition of $\hat{Z}_t$, it is enough to prove that

$$\hat{E}\{\hat{p}_t(\varphi) - \hat{p}_s(\varphi) \mid \hat{\mathscr{F}}_s\} = (t-s)\langle \lambda, \varphi \rangle , \qquad \hat{P}\text{-a.s.}$$

for any λ-integrable Borel function φ on S and $s \leq t$, where $\hat{p}_t(\varphi) = \sum_{s \leq t} \varphi(\hat{Z}_s)$. For this, it is also enough to prove that

$$\int_{\hat{A}} \{\hat{p}_t(\varphi) - \hat{p}_s(\varphi)\} d\hat{P} = (t-s)\langle \lambda, \varphi \rangle \hat{P}\{\hat{A}\}$$

for any set $\hat{A}$ of the form (4.1). Since

$$p'_t(\varphi) - p'_s(\varphi) = \sum_{n,k} \chi_{(s,t]}(T_{nk}) \varphi(Y(T_{nk}, X_{nk}, Z_{nk}, \xi_{nk})) ,$$

we have

$$\begin{aligned} (4.2) \quad & \int_{(A \cap B) \times A'} \{p'_t(\varphi) - p_s(\varphi)\} d(P_f \otimes P') \\ &= \int_{(A \cap B) \times A'} \sum_{(n,k) \notin M} \chi_{(s,t]}(T_{nk}) \varphi(Y(T_{nk}, X_{nk}, Z_{nk}, \xi_{nk})) d(P_f \otimes P') \\ &= P'\{A'\} \sum_{(n,k) \notin M} \int_{(A \cap B) \times \Omega'} \chi_{(s,t]}(T_{nk}) \varphi(Y_{nk}, X_{nk}, Z_{nk}, \xi_{nk})) d(P_f \otimes P') \\ &= P'\{A'\} \int_0^1 d\alpha \int_{A \cap B} \sum_{s < \tau \leq t} \chi(Z_\tau) \varphi(Y(\tau, X_{\tau-}, Z_\tau, \alpha)) dP_f {}^{*)} \\ &= P'\{A'\} \int_0^1 d\alpha \int_{(A \cap B) \times (s,t] \times R_0^3} dP_f d\tau n_{u(\tau)}(X_{\tau-}, dz) \varphi(Y(\tau, X_{\tau-}, z, \alpha)) \end{aligned}$$

---

*) $\chi(z) \neq 1$ for $z \neq 0$, and $=0$ for $z = 0$.

$$= \int_{(A\cap B)\times A'} d(P_f \otimes P') \int_{(s,t]\times R_0^3\times S} d\tau n_{u(\tau)}(X_{\tau-}, dz) Q(\tau, X_{\tau-}, z, d\sigma)\chi(z)\varphi(\sigma)$$

$$= \int_{(A\cap B)\times A'} d(P_f \otimes P') \int_{(s,t]\times S} d\tau\lambda(d\sigma)\chi(a(\tau, X_{\tau-}, \sigma))\varphi(\sigma)\,;$$

in the above we used Theorem 3 and Lemma 7. We have also

$$(4.3) \qquad \int_{\hat{A}} \{p_t''(\varphi) - p_s''(\varphi)\} d\hat{P}$$

$$= \int_{(A\cap B)\times A'} d(P_f \otimes P') \int_{\tilde{A}} \{p_t''(\varphi) - p_s''(\varphi)\} d\tilde{P}$$

$$= \int_{(A\cap B)\times A'} d(P_f \otimes P') \int_{\tilde{A}} d\tilde{P} \int_{(s,t]\times S} d\tau\lambda(d\sigma) \times \{1 - \chi(a(\tau, X_{\tau-}, \sigma))\}\varphi(\sigma)$$

$$= \int_{\hat{A}} d\hat{P} \int_{(s,t]\times S} d\tau\lambda(d\sigma)\{1 - \chi(a(\tau, X_{\tau-}, \sigma))\}\varphi(\sigma)\,.$$

Combining (4.2) with (4.3), we obtain

$$\int_{\hat{A}} \{\hat{p}_t(\varphi) - \hat{p}_s(\varphi)\} d\hat{P} = \tilde{P}\{\tilde{A}\} \int_{(A\cap B)\times A'} \{p_t'(\varphi) - p_s'(\varphi)\} d(P_f \otimes P') + \int_{\hat{A}} \{p_t''(\varphi) - p_s''(\varphi)\} d\hat{P} = (t - s)\langle\lambda, \varphi\rangle \hat{P}\{\hat{A}\}\,,$$

as was to be proved.

Lemma 9. *$Z_t \circ \pi = a(t, X_{t-}, \hat{Z}_t)$, $\hat{P}$-a.s., in which we have put $a(t, y, 0) = 0$.*

Proof. Since the sets $\{t: Z_t' \in S\}$ and $\{t: Z_t'' \in S\}$ are disjoint with $\hat{P}$-probability 1, we have $a(t, X_{t-}, \hat{Z}_t) = a(t, X_{t-}, Z_t') + a(t, X_{t-}, Z_t'') = a(t, X_{t-}, Z_t')$ with $\hat{P}$-probability 1, and hence it is enough to prove that for each fixed n and k

$$Z_{nk} = a(T_{nk}, X_{nk}, Y(T_{nk}, X_{nk}, Z_{nk}, \xi_{nk}))\,, \qquad \hat{P}\text{-a.s.}\,.$$

Putting

$$\Phi^{\omega'}(t, y, z) = \chi_{B_n}(z)\,|z - a(t, y, Y(t, y, z, \xi_{nk}(\omega')))|\,,$$

and then applying Theorem 3 and Lemma 7, we have

$$\hat{E}\{\chi_{(0,t]}(T_{nk})\,|Z_{nk}-a(T_{nk},X_{nk},Y(T_{nk},X_{nk},Z_{nk},\xi_{nk}))|\}$$
$$\le \hat{E}\Big\{\sum_{s\le T_{nk}\wedge t}\Phi^{\omega'}(s,X_{s-},Z_s)\Big\}$$
$$\le E'\Big\{\int_{[0,t]\times R^3\times R_0^3} ds u(s,dy) n_{u(s)}(y,dz)\Phi^{\omega'}(s,y,z)\Big\}$$
$$=\int_{[0,t]\times R^3\times R_0^3\times S} ds u(s,dy) n_{u(s)}(y,dz) Q(s,y,z,d\sigma)\chi_{B_n}(z)\,|z-a(s,y,\sigma)|$$
$$=\int_{[0,t]\times R^3\times S} ds u(s,dy)\lambda(d\sigma)\chi_{B_n}(a(s,y,\sigma))\,|a(s,y,\sigma)-a(s,y,\sigma)|=0\ ,$$

as required.

Combining the above two lemmas with the corollary to Theorem 3, we now complete the proof of Theorem 4.

§ 5. Concluding remark

The existence and uniqueness of solutions for the stochastic differential equation (1.3) were discussed by Tanaka [4]. The main results of [4] read as follows.

(A) Let $f\in\mathscr{P}$ be fixed. Then, on a suitable probability space $\{\hat{\Omega},\hat{\mathscr{F}},\hat{P}\}$ with an increasing family $\{\hat{\mathscr{F}}_t\}$ of sub-σ-fields we can construct an $\{\hat{\mathscr{F}}_t\}$-adapted Poisson point process $\{\hat{Z}_t,\ t>0\}$ on S with characteristic measure λ and an $\{\hat{\mathscr{F}}_t\}$-adapted right continuous process $\{X_t,\ t\ge 0\}$ on R^3 with initial distribution f such that

(i) $\int_0^t \hat{E}\{|X_s|\}ds<\infty$ for each $t<\infty$,

(ii) (1.3b) holds with probability 1,

where $\{Y_t(\alpha),\ t\ge 0\}$ is some right continuous process defined on the probability space $\{(0,1),\ d\alpha\}$ and is equivalent in law to the solution process $\{X_t,\ t\ge 0\}$. Moreover, the probability measure on the path space induced by $\{X_t,\ t\ge 0\}$ is uniquely determined from f.

(B) Let $f\in\mathscr{P}$ and $x\in R^3$ be fixed. Then, we can construct a Poisson point process $\{\hat{Z}_t,\ t>0\}$ on S with characteristic measure λ and an $\{\hat{\mathscr{F}}_t\}$-adapted right continuous process $\{X_t^x,\ t\ge 0\}$ on R^3 such that

(iii) $\int_0^t \hat{E}\{|X_s^x|\}ds<\infty$ for each $t<\infty$,

(iv) $X_t^x = x+\sum_{s\le t} a(s,X_{s-}^x,\hat{Z}_s)$, a.s.,

where $a(s,y,\sigma)$ is the same as used in (1.3b). Moreover, the probability measure on the path space induced by $\{X_t^x,\ t\ge 0\}$ is uniquely determined by f and x, and

$$e_f(t,x,A)=\hat{P}\{X_t^x\in A\}\ ,\qquad A\in\mathscr{B}(R^3)\ ,$$

gives a transition function associated with (1.2) in the sense of § 2.

Combining these results with Theorem 4, we obtain the existence and *uniqueness* of Markov process associated with (1.2).

References

[1] Grigelionis, B., On representation of integer-valued random measures by means of stochastic integrals with respect to the Poisson measure, Liet. Mat. Sb., **XI** (1971), 93–108, (Russian).

[2] Karoui, N. E. and Lepeltier, J. P., Représentation des processus ponctuels multivariés à l'aide d'un processus de Poisson, Z. Wahrscheinlichkeits-theorie verw. Gebiete **39** (1977), 111–133.

[3] McKean, H. P., A class of Markov processes associated with non-linear parabolic equations, Proc. Nat. Acad. Sci. U.S.A., **56** (1966), 1907–1911.

[4] Tanaka, H., On Markov process corresponding to Boltzmann's equation of Maxwellian gas, Proc. 2nd Japan-USSR Symp. Prob. Th., Lecture Notes in Mathematics, **330**, Springer, 478–489.

[5] Uhlenbeck, G. E. and Ford, G. W., Lectures in statistical mechanics, Lectures in Appl. Math., vol. **1**, Amer. Math. Soc., Providence, 1963.

DEPARTMENT OF MATHEMATICS
HIROSHIMA UNIVERSITY
HIROSHIMA 730, JAPAN

Z. Wahrscheinlichkeitstheorie verw. Gebiete
46, 67 – 105 (1978)

Zeitschrift für
Wahrscheinlichkeitstheorie
und verwandte Gebiete

Probabilistic Treatment of the Boltzmann Equation of Maxwellian Molecules

Hiroshi Tanaka

Department of Mathematics, Faculty of Science, Hiroshima University,
J-730 Hiroshima, Japan

Introduction

The Boltzmann equation in the kinetic theory of dilute gases is the equation that governs the time evolution of the number density $u(t,x)$ given by

$$u(t,x)\,dx = \frac{\text{the number of molecules with velocities} \in dx \text{ at time } t}{\text{the total number of molecules}}$$

for a gas composed of a very large number of molecules moving in space according to the law of classical mechanics and colliding in pairs. Here we assume spatial homogeneity. When there is no outside force, the equation is

$$\frac{\partial u}{\partial t} = \int_{(0,\infty)\times(0,2\pi)\times\mathbf{R}^3} (u'u'_1 - u u_1)\,|x-x_1|\,r\,dr\,d\varphi\,dx_1, \qquad t \geqq 0,\ x \in \mathbf{R}^3$$

where $u=u(t,x)$, $u_1=u(t,x_1)$, $u'=u(t,x')$ and $u'_1=u(t,x'_1)$. If we denote by S_{x,x_1} the sphere with center $(x+x_1)/2$ and diameter $|x-x_1|$, then x' and x'_1 (the velocities of molecules after "collision") are always on the sphere S_{x,x_1} or more precisely $S_{x,x_1}=S_{x',x'_1}$ according to the conservation laws of momentum and energy. We consider a spherical coordinate system with polar axis defined by the relative velocity $x-x_1$, and put

θ = the colatitude of x'

φ = the longitude of x'.

The Maxwellian gas is the case in which molecules repel each other with a force inversely proportional to the fifth power of their distance, and in this case the colatitude θ is determined from the impact parameter r by the following relation:

$$\frac{\pi-\theta}{2} = \int_0^{\rho_0} \frac{d\rho}{\sqrt{1-\rho^2-\dfrac{4}{|x-x_1|^2}\,U\!\left(\dfrac{r}{\rho}\right)}}, \tag{0.1}$$

where $U(\rho)=\text{const}\cdot\rho^{-4}$ and ρ_0 is the positive root of

$$1-\rho^2-\frac{4}{|x-x_1|^2}U\left(\frac{r}{\rho}\right)=0.$$

From the relation (0.1) we have $|x-x_1|\,r\,dr=Q_M(\theta)\sin\theta\,d\theta$ with some positive decreasing function $Q_M(\theta)$ of θ such that $Q_M(\theta)\sim\text{const}\cdot\theta^{-5/2}$ as $\theta\downarrow 0$. Thus we have the following Boltzmann equation of Maxwellian molecules

$$\frac{\partial u}{\partial t}=\int_{(0,\pi)\times(0,2\pi)\times\mathbf{R}^3}(u'u'_1-uu_1)\,Q(d\theta)\,d\varphi\,dx_1, \tag{0.2}$$

where $Q(d\theta)=Q_M(\theta)\sin\theta\,d\theta$. For these matters, see Uhlenbeck and Ford [20]. The fact that $Q(d\theta)$ does not involve $|x-x_1|$ is a consequence of the inverse fifth power force, and in this sense the situation is simplified. But difficulties arise from the non-cutoff type $\left(\int_0^\pi Q(d\theta)=\infty\right)$ especially when we deal with the existence of solution for (0.2), and it seems that rigorous results on the existence of (global) solutions to Boltzmann equation have been obtained only for the cutoff type ([2, 15, 1]).

McKean [9] introduced a class of Markov processes associated with certain nonlinear parabolic equations. The initial value problem for (0.2) is *nearly* the same as the existence problem of the associated Markov process of the type introduced by McKean. In this paper, instead of (0.2) we study its weak version by probabilistic methods:

$$\frac{d}{dt}\langle u,\xi\rangle=\langle u\otimes u,K\xi\rangle,\qquad \xi\in C_0^\infty(\mathbf{R}^3); \tag{0.3}$$

here $C_0^\infty(\mathbf{R}^3)$ is the space of real valued C^∞-functions on R^3 with compact support,

$$(K\xi)(x,x_1)=\int_{(0,\pi)\times(0,2\pi)}\{\xi(x')-\xi(x)\}\,Q(d\theta)\,d\varphi, \tag{0.4}$$

and $\langle u,\xi\rangle$ denotes the integral of ξ with respect to a probability measure solution $u=u(t,\cdot)$ to be sought.

The main objectives of this paper are the followings:

(I) The construction of the Markov process associated with (0.3) by solving certain stochastic differential equation.

(II) The trend to the equilibrium for (0.3).

Chapter I is devoted to the construction of the associated Markov process. A part of the present results was summarized in [18]; here we will give full proofs. The idea is to use the following stochastic differential equation

$$X(t)=X(0)+\int_{(0,t]\times S}a(X(s-),Y(s-,\alpha),\theta,\varphi)\,N(ds\,d\theta\,d\varphi\,d\alpha), \tag{0.5a}$$

or what is the same thing,

$$X(t)=X(0)+\sum_{s\leqq t} a(X(s-), Y(s-), p(s)); \tag{0.5b}$$

here $S=(0,\pi)\times(0,2\pi)\times(0,1)$ and

(i) $\{p(t), t>0\}$ is a Poisson point process on S with characteristic measure $Q(d\theta)\,d\varphi\,d\alpha$, and $N(ds\,d\theta\,d\varphi\,d\alpha)$ is the corresponding Poisson random measure defined by $N(A)=\sum \mathbb{1}_A(s, p(s))$ [1] for $A\in\mathscr{B}(\mathbf{R}_+\times S)$,

(ii) $\{Y(t,\alpha), t\geqq 0\}$ is a right continuous $\mathbf{R}^3$-valued stochastic process defined on the probability space $\{(0,1), d\alpha\}$ and is equivalent in law to the solution process $\{X(t), t\geqq 0\}$,

(iii) $a(x, x_1, \theta, \varphi)=x'-x$ and $a(X(s-), Y(s-), \sigma)=a(X(s-), Y(s-, \alpha), \theta, \varphi)$ for $\sigma=(\theta,\varphi,\alpha)\in S$.

Because of the nonlinearity of (0.3), the right hand side of (0.5) involves not only the solution $X(s)$ but also its copy $Y(s)$; in this sense the equation (0.5) is similar to the one considered by McKean [11] in the diffusion case. It will be proved that the equation (0.5) has a solution $\{X(t)\}$ provided the initial distribution has finite expectation, and that the uniqueness in the law sense holds. Also, the solutions to (0.5) will give a Markov process associated with (0.3), the precise definition of which will be given in §1. On the other hand, it was proved in [19] that path functions of any Markov process associated with (0.3) can be represented as solutions to (0.5) after a suitable extension of the basic probability space. Thus we shall obtain the existence and the uniqueness of the associated Markov process.

The existence of the associated Markov process implies that of the associated nonlinear semigroup. Let $\{X(t)\}$ be the associated Markov process (solution of (0.5)) with initial distribution f satisfying $\int |x| f(dx)<\infty$, and denote by $T_t f$ the probability distribution of $X(t)$. Then $u(t)=T_t f$ solves (0.3) and $\{T_t\}$ becomes a nonlinear semigroup. Denote by $\mathscr{P}_2$ the space of probability distributions f on $\mathbf{R}^3$ satisfying $\int |x|^2 f(dx)<\infty$. In Chapter II of this paper, we study $\{T_t\}$ on the space $\mathscr{P}_2$ by making use of the functional $\mathfrak{e}$ and the metric ρ defined on $\mathscr{P}_2$ as follows. For $f_1, f_2\in\mathscr{P}_2$ we put

$$\mathfrak{e}(f_1,f_2)=\inf \int_{\mathbf{R}^3\times\mathbf{R}^3} |x-y|^2\, F(dx\,dy),$$

$$\rho(f_1,f_2)=\sqrt{\mathfrak{e}(f_1,f_2)},$$

where the infimum is taken over all probability measures F in $\mathbf{R}^6$ satisfying $F(A\times\mathbf{R}^3)=f_1(A)$ and $F(\mathbf{R}^3\times A)=f_2(A)$ for any $A\in\mathscr{B}(\mathbf{R}^3)$. For $f\in\mathscr{P}_2$ satisfying $\int |x-m|^2 f(dx)\equiv 3v>0$ where m is the mean vector of f, we put

$$\mathfrak{g}_f(dx)=(2\pi v)^{-3/2}\exp\{-|x-m|^2/2v\}\,dx,$$

$$\mathfrak{e}(f)=\mathfrak{e}(f,\mathfrak{g}_f).$$

It will be seen that ρ gives a metric in $\mathscr{P}_2$. In the one-dimensional case the functional $\mathfrak{e}$ was introduced in connection with the study of Kac's one-dimen-

[1] $\mathbb{1}_A$ denotes the indicator function of A throughout

sional model of Maxwellian molecules by Tanaka [17], and a part of the results in [17] (concerning some basic properties of $\mathfrak{e}$ itself) was then extended to the several dimensional case by Murata and Tanaka [12] and to the case of Hilbert spaces by Kondô and Negoro [8].

The main results of Chapter II are as follows:

(A) *The nonlinear semigroup* $\{T_t\}$ *on* $\mathscr{P}_2$ *is non-expansive with respect to the metric* ρ:

$$\rho(T_t f_1, T_t f_2) \leqq \rho(f_1, f_2), \qquad t \geqq 0,\ f_1, f_2 \in \mathscr{P}_2.$$

(B) *If* $f \in \mathscr{P}_2$ *satisfies* $\int |x-m|^2 f(dx) \equiv 3v > 0$ *where* m *is the mean vector of* f, *then* $\mathfrak{e}(T_t f)$ *decreases to* 0 *as* $t \uparrow \infty$, *and hence in particular* $T_t f$ *converges to* $\mathfrak{g}_f$ *as* $t \uparrow \infty$.

The (rigorous) entropy arguments in dealing with the trend to equilibrium require the existence of initial densities with finite entropy. According to our method, though it works only for Maxwellian type, we need less restrictions on initial distributions for proving the trend to equilibrium. Also, the result (A) will provide a typical example of a semigroup of nonlinear operators which are non-expansive with respect to certain metric.

I wish to thank T. Ueno; I came to be interested in Maxwellian molecules through conversations with him.

Chapter I. Associated Markov Process

§ 1. Definition of Markov Process Associated with (0.3)

Let us denote by $\mathscr{P}_1$ the family of probability distributions f on $\mathbf{R}^3$ satisfying $\int_{\mathbf{R}^3} |x| f(dx) < \infty$, and introduce the following

Definition. $\{e_f(t,x,\cdot): f \in \mathscr{P}_1, t \geqq 0, x \in \mathbf{R}^3\}$ is called a transition function associated with (0.3), if the following five conditions are satisfied.

(e.1) For fixed $f \in \mathscr{P}_1$, $t \geqq 0$ and $x \in \mathbf{R}^3$, $e_f(t,x,\cdot)$ is a probability measure on $\mathbf{R}^3$.

(e.2) For fixed $A \in \mathscr{B}(\mathbf{R}^3)$, $e_f(t,x,A)$ is jointly measurable in $(f,t,x) \in \mathscr{P}_1 \times \mathbf{R}_+ \times \mathbf{R}^3$, the Borel structure on $\mathscr{P}_1$ being the one induced by the usual vague topology on $\mathscr{P}_1$.

(e.3) For each $t \geqq 0$ and $f \in \mathscr{P}_1$, there exists a constant c depending only upon t and f such that

$$\int_{\mathbf{R}^3} |y|\, e_f(s,x,dy) \leqq c(1+|x|), \qquad 0 \leqq s \leqq t,\ x \in \mathbf{R}^3.$$

(e.4) If we put

$$u(t,\cdot) = \int_{\mathbf{R}^3} f(dx)\, e_f(t,x,\cdot),$$

$$(K_{u(t)}\xi)(x) = \int_{\mathbf{R}^3} (K\xi)(x,x_1)\, u(t,dx_1),$$

then for $\xi \in C_0^\infty(\mathbf{R}^3)$

$$\langle e_f(t,x,\cdot), \xi\rangle = \xi(x) + \int_0^t \langle e_f(s,x,\cdot), K_{u(s)}\xi\rangle \, ds.$$

(e.5) (Kolmogorov-Chapman equation)

$$e_f(t,x,\cdot) = \int_{\mathbf{R}^3} e_f(s,x,dy)\, e_{u(s)}(t-s,y,\cdot), \qquad 0 \leqq s \leqq t,$$

where u is the same as in (e.4).

In the cutoff case $\left(\int_0^\pi Q(d\theta) < \infty\right)$, solutions to (0.3) can easily be obtained from Wild's formula ([21, 10]); a similar formula can also be used to obtain $e_f(t,x,\cdot)$ defined for *all* probability distributions f on $\mathbf{R}^3$. In the non-cutoff case with which we are concerned in this paper, the restriction $f \in \mathscr{P}_1$ is imposed in the above definition since our present method works only under this restriction.

To proceed, let Ω be the space of $\mathbf{R}^3$-valued function on R_+, and denote by $X_t(\omega)$ (or X_t, for short) the value $\omega(t)$ of $\omega(\in\Omega)$ at t. We put $\mathscr{B} = \sigma\{X_t : t < \infty\}$ and $\mathscr{B}_t = \sigma\{X_s : s \leqq t\}$, where $\sigma\{$——$\}$ denotes the smallest σ-field on Ω that makes $\{$——$\}$ measurable. Now suppose we are given a transition function $\{e_f(t,x,\cdot)\}$ associated with (0.4). Then there exists a unique family $\{P_f, f \in \mathscr{P}_1\}$ of probability measures on $(\Omega, \mathscr{B})$ such that for $A \in \mathscr{B}(\mathbf{R}^3)$

$$P_f\{X_0 \in A\} = f(A),$$

$$P_f\{X_t \in A \mid \mathscr{B}_s\} = e_{u(s)}(t-s, X_s, A), \qquad P_f\text{-a.s.}, \ 0 \leqq s \leqq t.$$

Thus we obtain a (temporally inhomogeneous) Markov process $\{X_t, P_f, f \in \mathscr{P}_1\}$. This is a Markov process which is associated with (0.3).

In the above we have assumed the existence of $\{e_f(t,x,\cdot)\}$, but we do not know its existence in advance; the analytical proof of the existence seems to be difficult. What we are going to do in Chapter I is, as stated in the introduction, to employ the method of stochastic differential equations in order to obtain an associated Markov process.

§ 2. Preliminaries from Poisson Point Process

Suppose we are given a complete probability space $(\Omega, \mathscr{F}, P)$, a Borel subset S of $\mathbf{R}^d$ and an extra point ∂ not belonging to S. An $S \cup \{\partial\}$-valued process $\{p(t,\omega), t > 0\}$ defined on $(\Omega, \mathscr{F}, P)$ is called a *point process* on S, if i) $p(t,\omega)$ is jointly measurable in (t,ω), and ii) the set $\{t : p(t,\omega) \in S\}$ is countable.

Given a point process $\{p(t), t > 0\}$ on S, we put

$$N(A) = \sum_t \mathbb{1}_A(t, p(t)), \qquad A \in \mathscr{B}((0,\infty) \times S)$$

$$N_t(B) = \sum_{0 < s \leqq t} \mathbb{1}_B(p(s)), \quad B \in \mathscr{B}(S), \ t \geqq 0;$$

$N(\cdot)$ is the associated random measure. Let λ be a given σ-finite Borel measure on S. Then, a point process $\{p(t), t>0\}$ is called a *Poisson point process on S with characteristic measure* λ, if for any *disjoint* family $\{A_1, \ldots, A_n\}$ of Borel sets in $(0, \infty) \times S$ such that $\bar{\lambda}(A_k) = \int_{A_k} dt\, d\lambda < \infty$ $(1 \leqq k \leqq n)$ we have

$$P\{N(A_k)=m_k,\ 1 \leqq k \leqq n\} = \prod_{k=1}^{n} \left\{ e^{-\bar{\lambda}(A_k)} \frac{(\bar{\lambda}(A_k))^{m_k}}{m_k!} \right\}$$

for $m_1, \ldots, m_n \in \mathbf{N}$. The following characterization of Poisson point processes is well-known.

Theorem 2.1. *Suppose we are given a point process* $\{p(t), t>0\}$ *on* S, *a* σ-*finite Borel measure* λ *on* S *and an increasing family* $\{\mathscr{F}_t\}$ *of sub-*σ*-fields of* $\mathscr{F}$. *If, for each* $B \in \mathscr{B}(S)$ *with* $\lambda(B) < \infty$, $\{N_t(B) - \lambda(B)t, t \geqq 0\}$ *is an* $\{\mathscr{F}_t\}$-*martingale, then* $\{p(t), t>0\}$ *is a Poisson point process on* S *with characteristic measure* λ. *In this case,* $\{p(t), t>0\}$ *is said to be* $\{\mathscr{F}_t\}$-*adapted.*

We often deal with integrals of the form

$$\sum_{s \leqq t} A(s, p(s), \omega) = \int_{(0,t] \times S} A(s, \sigma, \omega)\, N(ds\, d\sigma),$$

where $\{p(t), t>0\}$ is a given $\{\mathscr{F}_t\}$-adapted Poisson point process on S with characteristic measure λ and $N(\cdot)$ is the associated Poisson random measure. When $A(t, \sigma, \omega)$ is predictable[2] satisfying the integrability condition $\int_{(0,t] \times S} E|A(s, \sigma, \omega)|\, ds\, \lambda(d\sigma) < \infty$, then

$$E\{\sum_{s \leqq t} A(s, p(s), \omega)\} = E\{\int_{(0,t] \times S} A(s, \sigma, \omega)\, ds\, \lambda(d\sigma)\}, \tag{2.1}$$

and if in addition $A(s, \sigma, \omega)$, $\tau \leqq s \leqq t$, are $\mathscr{F}_\tau$-measurable in ω for some τ, then

$$\begin{aligned} &E\{\exp(i\zeta \sum_{\tau < s \leqq t} A(s, p(s), \omega)) | \mathscr{F}_\tau\} \\ &\quad = \exp\{\int_{(\tau, t] \times S} (e^{i\zeta A(s, \sigma, \omega)} - 1)\, ds\, \lambda(d\sigma)\}, \qquad \zeta \in \mathbf{R}. \end{aligned} \tag{2.2}$$

For $X(t) = X(0) + \sum_{s \leqq t} A(s, p(s), \omega)$ and $\xi \in C^1(\mathbf{R})$ we have

$$\xi(X(t)) = \xi(X(0)) + \sum_{s \leqq t} \{\xi(X(s-) + A(s, p(s), \omega)) - \xi(X(s-))\}. \tag{2.3}$$

The following lemma is also elementary, but we give the proof for completeness.

---

[2] A real valued function $A(t, \sigma, \omega)$ on $\mathbf{R}_+ \times S \times \Omega$ is said to be predictable, if it is measurable with respect to the predictable σ-field; the latter is defined as the smallest σ-field on $\mathbf{R}_+ \times S \times \Omega$ with respect to which all real valued functions $a(t, \sigma, \omega)$ with the following properties (i) and (ii) are measurable.

(i) For each fixed $t \geqq 0$, $a(t, \sigma, \omega)$ is $\mathscr{B}(S) \otimes \mathscr{F}_t$-measurable.

(ii) For each fixed σ and ω, $a(t, \sigma, \omega)$ is left continuous in t.

Lemma 2.1. *Let $A(t,\sigma,\omega)$ be real valued and predictable. Let $T>0$ and assume that there exists $A(\sigma,\omega)$ such that*

$$|A(t,\sigma,\omega)| \leqq A(\sigma,\omega) \quad \text{for } 0 \leqq t \leqq T,$$
$$E\{\int_S A(\sigma,\omega)\,\lambda(d\sigma)\} < \infty. \tag{2.4}$$

Then, for any $\varepsilon>0$ there exists a partition Δ of $[0,T]$:

$$\Delta: 0=t_0<t_1<\cdots<t_n=T$$

such that $|\Delta|=\max(t_k-t_{k-1})<\varepsilon$ and

$$E\{\int_{(0,T]\times S} |A(t,\sigma,\omega)-A(\Delta(t),\sigma,\omega)|\,dt\,\lambda(d\sigma)\}<\varepsilon,$$

where $\Delta(t)$ is defined by $\Delta(0)=0$ and

$$\Delta(t)=t_{k-1} \quad \text{for } t_{k-1}<t\leqq t_k \ (1\leqq k\leqq n).$$

Proof. For convenience we redefine $A(t,\sigma,\omega)$ for $t>T$ by putting $A(t,\sigma,\omega)=0$ there, and then extend it to $-\infty<t<\infty$ by putting $A(t,\sigma,\omega)=0$ for $t<0$. For an integer $n\geqq 1$ we put

$$\delta_n(t)=k2^{-n} \quad \text{for } k2^{-n}<t\leqq(k+1)2^{-n} \ (k=0,\pm 1,\ldots).$$

Then by (2.4) we have for each t

$$\lim_{n\to\infty}\int_0^1 |A(t+s,\sigma,\omega)-A(\delta_n(t)+s,\sigma,\omega)|\,ds=0$$

almost everywhere with respect to $\lambda\otimes P$, and hence

$$\lim_{n\to\infty}\int_{(0,1)\times\mathbf{R}\times S\times\Omega} |A(t+s,\sigma,\omega)-A(\delta_n(t)+s,\sigma,\omega)|\,ds\,dt\,\lambda(d\sigma)\,P(d\omega)=0.$$

Therefore, there exist $s\in(0,1)$ and $n_1<n_2<\cdots$ such that

$$\lim_{k\to\infty}\int_{\mathbf{R}\times S\times\Omega} |A(t+s,\sigma,\omega)-A(\delta_{n_k}(t)+s,\sigma,\omega)|\,dt\,\lambda(d\sigma)\,P(d\omega)=0,$$

or equivalently

$$\lim_{k\to\infty} E\{\int_{\mathbf{R}\times S} |A(t,\sigma,\omega)-A(\delta_{n_k}(t-s)+s,\sigma,\omega)|\,dt\,\lambda(d\sigma)\}=0.$$

But this formula clearly implies the existence of a partition Δ as stated in the lemma.

§ 3. Two Lemmas

We state two lemmas. The first one is of particular importance.

3.1. We set

$$a(x,x_1,\theta,\varphi)=x'-x,$$

and as a function of φ we extend it to the periodic function on $\mathbf{R}$ with period 2π. This function depends upon the choice of the origin $\varphi=0$ in a spherical coordinate system on the sphere S_{x,x_1}. We can easily see that no choices of the origin $\varphi=0$ imply the smoothness of $a(x,x_1,\theta,\varphi)$ in the variables x and x_1, but we can prove that $a(x,x_1,\theta,\varphi)$ has *a sort of* Lipschitz continuity which is enough for our later developments.

Lemma 3.1. *There exist a constant c and a Borel function* $\varphi_0(x,x_1,y,y_1)$ *on* $\mathbf{R}^{12}$ *such that*

$$|a(x,x_1,\theta,\varphi)-a(y,y_1,\theta,\varphi+\varphi_0(x,x_1,y,y_1))| \leqq c\{|x-y|+|x_1-y_1|\}\,\theta.$$

Proof. (i) When $x=x_1$, we put $\varphi_0(x,x,y,y_1)=0$. Since $a(x,x,\theta,\varphi)=0$, we have

$$\begin{aligned}&|a(x,x,\theta,\varphi)-a(y,y_1,\theta,\varphi+\varphi_0)|\\&\quad=|a(y,y_1,\theta,\varphi)|\leqq\frac{|y-y_1|}{2}\theta\\&\quad\leqq\tfrac{1}{2}\{|x-y|+|x_1-y_1|\}\,\theta.\end{aligned}$$

(ii) When $y=y_1$, we obtain a similar result with $\varphi_0(x,x_1,y,y)=0$.
(iii) We assume that $x\neq x_1$ and $y\neq y_1$. Let l be the straight line which passes through the point $(x+x_1)/2$ and is perpendicular to the plane determined by the three points $(x+x_1)/2$, x and x^*, where

$$x^*=\frac{|x-x_1|}{|y-y_1|}\cdot\frac{y-y_1}{2}+\frac{x+x_1}{2}.$$

We denote by ρ the rotation around l sending x to x^*. Also we define the transformations τ and $\tilde{\tau}$ from $\mathbf{R}^3$ to itself by

$$\tau z=\frac{|y-y_1|}{|x-x_1|}\left(z-\frac{x+x_1}{2}\right)+\frac{x+x_1}{2},$$

$$\tilde{\tau} z=z+\frac{y+y_1}{2}-\frac{x+x_1}{2}.$$

Then we have

$$\rho x=x^*,\qquad \tau x^*=x_*\equiv\frac{y-y_1}{2}+\frac{x+x_1}{2},\qquad \tilde{\tau}x_*=y,$$

and $\tilde{\tau}\tau\rho$ sends the sphere S_{x,x_1} to the sphere S_{y,y_1}. So, if we put

$$A(x,x_1,\theta,\varphi)=a(x,x_1,\theta,\varphi)+x\,(=x'),$$

$\tilde{\tau}\tau\rho A(x,x_1,\theta,0)$ lies on S_{y,y_1} and its longitude is independent of the colatitude θ. Therefore, there exists a function $\varphi_0(x,x_1,y,y_1)$ taking values in $[0,2\pi)$ such that

$$\tilde{\tau}\tau\rho A(x,x_1,\theta,0)=A(y,y_1,\theta,\varphi_0(x,x_1,y,y_1)).$$

We then have the following formula.

$$\tilde{\tau}\tau\rho A(x,x_1,\theta,\varphi)=A(y,y_1,\theta,\varphi+\varphi_0(x,x_1,y,y_1)).$$

We now claim that

$$|a(x,x_1,\theta,\varphi)-a(y,y_1,\theta,\varphi+\varphi_0(x,x_1,y,y_1))| \\ \leqq(\pi+\tfrac{1}{2})\{|x-y|+|x_1-y_1|\}\,\theta. \tag{3.1}$$

To show this, we first notice that

$$|a(x,x_1,\theta,\varphi)-(\rho A(x,x_1,\theta,\varphi)-x^*)| \\ \leqq|a(x,x_1,\theta,\varphi)|\times(\text{the rotation angle of }\rho) \\ \leqq\frac{\pi}{2}|x-x^*|\,\theta, \tag{3.2}$$

$$|(\rho A(x,x_1,\theta,\varphi)-x^*)-(\tau\rho A(x,x_1,\theta,\varphi)-\tau x^*)| \\ \leqq\tfrac{1}{2}\{|x-x_1|-|y-y_1|\}\,\theta\leqq\tfrac{1}{2}\{|x-y|+|x_1-y_1\}\theta, \tag{3.3}$$

$$\begin{aligned}\tau\rho A(x,x_1,\theta,\varphi)-\tau x^*&=\tilde{\tau}\tau\rho A(x,x_1,\theta,\varphi)-\tilde{\tau}\tau x^*\\ &=A(y,y_1,\theta,\varphi+\varphi_0(x,x_1,y,y_1))-y\\ &=a(y,y_1,\theta,\varphi+\varphi_0(x,x_1,y,y_1)).\end{aligned} \tag{3.4}$$

From (3.2), (3.3) and (3.4) we then have

$$|a(x,x_1,\theta,\varphi)-a(y,y_1,\theta,\varphi+\varphi_0(x,x_1,y,y_1))| \\ \leqq\frac{\pi}{2}|x-x^*|\,\theta+\tfrac{1}{2}\{|x-y|+|x_1-y_1|\}\,\theta,$$

which combined with the following inequalities proves (3.1):

$$\begin{aligned}|x-x^*|&\leqq|x-y|+|y-x_*|+|x_*-x^*|\\ &\leqq|x-y|+\left|\frac{x+x_1}{2}-\frac{y+y_1}{2}\right|+\left|\frac{|x-x_1|}{|y-y_1|}-1\right|\cdot\frac{|y-y_1|}{2}\\ &\leqq|x-y|+|x-y|+|x_1-y_1|.\end{aligned}$$

3.2. In this paper we often consider stochastic processes having sample paths in the following space W:

W = the space of R^3-valued right continuous functions on $\mathbf{R}_+$ having left limits.

In W we consider the Skorohod topology. Then it is well known that W is a completely metrizable and separable space (see [7, 14]) and that the topological Borel field $\mathscr{B}_W$ on W coincides with the usual coordinate σ-field. We think of the unit interval $(0,1)$ as a probability space by considering the Lebesgue measure (strictly speaking, its restriction to $\mathscr{B}(0,1)$, the σ-field of Borel sets in

(0, 1)). A stochastic process defined on this probability space and having sample paths in W is called an α-process for simplicity; similarly a random variable on this probability space is called an α-random variable. We sometimes want to have α-processes constructed as in the following way.

Lemma 3.2. *Suppose we are given two processes* $\mathbf{X}_1=\{X_1(t), t\geqq 0\}$ *and* $\mathbf{X}_2=\{X_2(t), t\geqq 0\}$ *defined on a common probability space* $(\Omega, \mathscr{F}, P)$ *and having sample paths in* W. *Let* $\mathbf{Y}_1=\{Y_1(t,\alpha), t\geqq 0\}$ *be an* α*-process which is equivalent in law to* $\mathbf{X}_1$. *We assume that there exists an* α*-random variable* η *which is independent of* $\mathbf{Y}_1$ *and uniformly distributed on the interval* (0, 1). *Then we can construct an* α*-process* $\mathbf{Y}_2=\{Y_2(t,\alpha), t\geqq 0\}$ *in such a way that* (i) *the joint process* $(\mathbf{Y}_1, \mathbf{Y}_2)$ *is equivalent in law to* $(\mathbf{X}_1, \mathbf{X}_2)$ *and* (ii) *there still exists an* α*-random variable which is independent of* $\mathbf{Y}_2$ *and uniformly distributed on* (0, 1).

Proof. Denote by U the probability measure on $W\times W$ induced by the joint process $(\mathbf{X}_1, \mathbf{X}_2)$, and by U_1 the one on W induced by $\mathbf{X}_1$. Since W is a complete metric separable space, there exists a transition function $P(w, A)$ of $\mathbf{X}_2$ given $\mathbf{X}_1$ with the following three properties:

For each fixed $w\in W$, $P(w,\cdot)$ is a probability measure on W. (3.5)

For each fixed $A\in\mathscr{B}_W$, $P(\cdot, A)$ is a Borel function on W. (3.6)

For any $A_1, A_2\in\mathscr{B}_W$

$$U(A_1\times A_2)=\int_{A_1} P(w, A_2)\, U_1(dw). \tag{3.7}$$

Since any complete metric separable space having the same cardinality as $\mathbf{R}$ is Borel isomorphic to $\mathbf{R}$ (see [14]), there exists a Borel isomorphism Φ from W into $\mathbf{R}$. We fix such a Φ and put

$$\tilde{Y}(w,\alpha)=\sup\{x: P(w, \Phi^{-1}((-\infty, x]))\leqq\alpha\},$$
$$\mathbf{Y}(w,\alpha)=\Phi^{-1}(\tilde{Y}(w,\alpha)), \qquad \alpha\in(0,1).$$

Then $\mathbf{Y}(w,\alpha)$ is jointly measurable, and for each fixed $w\in W$ the distribution of $Y(w,\cdot)$ on W is $P(w,\cdot)$. Taking two (arbitrary) independent α-random variables η_1 and η_2 with the uniform distribution on (0, 1), and regarding $\mathbf{Y}_1(\alpha)=\{Y_1(t,\alpha), t\geqq 0\}$ as an element of W, we can define a W-valued α-random variable $\mathbf{Y}_2$ by $\mathbf{Y}_2(\alpha)=\mathbf{Y}(\mathbf{Y}_1(\alpha), \eta_1(\eta(\alpha)))$. Then the joint process $(\mathbf{Y}_1, \mathbf{Y}_2)$ is clearly U-distributed, and $\eta_2(\eta(\alpha))$ is a uniformly distributed α-random variable independent of $\mathbf{Y}_2$.

§ 4. Stochastic Differential Equation

We use the notations introduced in § 3, such as the function $a(x, x_1, \theta, \varphi)$, the probability space (0, 1) and the space W. In this section the probability space (0, 1) is of an auxiliary character, and the basic complete probability space is $(\Omega, \mathscr{F}, P)$ which is chosen suitably. Let $S=(0,\pi)\times(0,2\pi)\times(0,1)$ and λ be the measure on S defined by $d\lambda = Q(d\theta)\, d\varphi\, d\alpha$, where $Q(d\theta)$ is a given probability measure on $(0, \pi)$ satisfying $\int_0^{\pi} \theta Q(d\theta) < \infty$.

On a probability space $(\Omega, \mathscr{F}, P)$ suppose we are given (i) an increasing family $\{\mathscr{F}_t\}_{t \geqq 0}$ of sub-σ-fields of $\mathscr{F}$, (ii) an $\{\mathscr{F}_t\}$-adapted Poisson point process $\{p(t), t > 0\}$ on S with characteristic measure λ and (iii) an $\mathscr{F}_0$-measurable $\mathbf{R}^3$-valued random variable X. Let $N(ds\, d\theta\, d\varphi\, d\alpha)$ be the Poisson random measure corresponding to $\{p(t), t > 0\}$. Then X and $\{p(t), t > 0\}$ $(N(ds\, d\theta\, d\varphi\, d\alpha))$ are independent. We now consider the stochastic differential equation

$$dX(t) = a(X(t-), Y(t-), \theta, \varphi)\, dN, \qquad X(0) = X, \tag{4.1}$$

whose precise meaning is

$$X(t) = X + \int_{(0, t] \times S} a(X(s-), Y(s-, \alpha), \theta, \varphi)\, N(ds\, d\theta\, d\varphi\, d\alpha), \qquad \text{a.s.,} \tag{4.2a}$$

or equivalently

$$X(t) = X + \sum_{s \leqq t} a(X(s-), Y(s-), p(s)), \qquad \text{a.s.,} \tag{4.2b}$$

where $\{X(t), t \geqq 0\}$ is to be sought as an $\{\mathscr{F}_t\}$-adapted process with sample paths in W under the condition that $\{Y(t, \alpha), t \geqq 0\}$ is an α-process equivalent in law to $\{X(t), t \geqq 0\}$; the notation $a(x, Y, \sigma)$ for an $\mathbf{R}^3$-valued α-random variable Y is defined by

$$a(x, Y, \sigma) = a(x, Y(\alpha), \theta, \varphi) \qquad \text{for } \sigma = (\theta, \varphi, \alpha) \in S. \tag{4.3}$$

In the right hand sides of (4.2a) and (4.2b) we may (and sometimes do) replace the left limits $X(s-)$ and $Y(s-)$ by $X(s)$ and $Y(s)$, respectively. However, the use of the left limits seems to be suited for the intuitive meaning of the motion: *a particle changes its velocity by the interaction with another similar independent particle.*

We use the following notation. For $f_1, f_2 \in \mathscr{P}_1$ we put

$$\rho_1(f_1, f_2) = \inf_{F \in \mathbf{F}} \int_{\mathbf{R}^3 \times \mathbf{R}^3} |x - y|\, F(dx\, dy), \tag{4.4}$$

where $\mathbf{F} = \mathbf{F}(f_1, f_2)$ is the class of probability measures F on R^6 satisfying $F(A \times \mathbf{R}^3) = f_1(A)$ and $F(\mathbf{R}^3 \times A) = f_2(A)$ for any $A \in \mathscr{B}(\mathbf{R}^3)$. Then it is clear that the infimum in (4.4) is attained at some $F \in \mathbf{F}(f_1, f_2)$. Also, it can be proved that ρ_1 gives a metric in $\mathscr{P}_1$; in fact the triangle inequality can be proved as follows. Given $f_1, f_2, f_3 \in \mathscr{P}_1$, we take $F_1 \in \mathbf{F}(f_1, f_2)$ and $F_2 \in \mathbf{F}(f_2, f_3)$ such that

$$\rho_1(f_1, f_2) = \int |x - y|\, F_1(dx\, dy), \qquad \rho_1(f_2, f_3) = \int |x - y|\, F_2(dx\, dy).$$

We can easily construct a probability measure F on $\mathbf{R}^9$ satisfying $F(\tilde{A} \times \mathbf{R}^3) = F_1(\tilde{A})$ and $F(\mathbf{R}^3 \times \tilde{A}) = F_2(\tilde{A})$ for any $\tilde{A} \in \mathscr{B}(R^6)$, and we have

$$\begin{aligned} \rho_1(f_1, f_2) + \rho_1(f_2, f_3) &= \int |x - y|\, F(dx\, dy\, dz) + \int |y - z|\, F(dx\, dy\, dz) \\ &\geqq \int |x - z|\, F(dx\, dy\, dz) \geqq \rho_1(f_1, f_3). \end{aligned}$$

The existence and uniqueness of the solution to (4.1) are now our objectives. We begin with the uniqueness part. Denote by f the probability distribution of the initial value X.

Lemma 4.1. *Assume that* $E\{|X|\}<\infty$, *that is,* $f\in\mathscr{P}_1$. *Let* T *be any positive constant,* Δ *a partition of the interval* $[0,T]$:

$$\Delta: 0=t_0<t_1<\cdots<t_n=T, \tag{4.5}$$

and define a process $\{X_\Delta(t), 0\leqq t\leqq T\}$ *by*

$$X_\Delta(0)=X$$
$$X_\Delta(t)=X_\Delta(t_k)+\sum_{t_k<s\leqq t} a(X_\Delta(t_k), Y_k, p(s)) \text{ for } t_k<t\leqq t_{k+1} \ (0\leqq k\leqq n-1), \tag{4.6}$$

where $Y_0,\ldots,Y_{n-1}$ *are* α*-random variables defined in each step so that* Y_k *has the same probability law as* $X_\Delta(t_k)$. *Then we have the following assertions.*

(i) *The probability law of the process* $\{X_\Delta(t), 0\leqq t\leqq T\}$ *is uniquely determined by* f *(and so does not depend upon the choice of* $Y_0,\ldots,Y_{n-1}$).

(ii) *Let* $X^\#$ *be another* $\mathscr{F}_0$*-measurable random variable with probability distribution* $f^\#$ *in* $\mathscr{P}_1$, *and define* $\{X^\#(t), 0\leqq t\leqq T\}$ *by a rule similar to* (4.6) *replacing* X *by* $X^\#$. *Then, enlarging the probability space if necessary, we can construct two processes* $\{X(t), 0\leqq t\leqq T\}$ *and* $\{\tilde{X}(t), 0\leqq t\leqq T\}$ *which are equivalent in law to* $\{X_\Delta(t), 0\leqq t\leqq T\}$ *and* $\{X_\Delta^\#(t), 0\leqq t\leqq T\}$, *respectively, and satisfying*

$$E|X(t)-\tilde{X}(t)|\leqq e^{c_0 t}\rho_1(f,f^\#) \tag{4.7}$$

with $c_0=4\pi c\int_0^\pi \theta Q(d\theta)$, *where* c *is the constant appearing in Lemma* 3.1.

Proof. (i) By (2.2) we have

$$E\{e^{i\zeta\cdot X_\Delta(t)}|\mathscr{F}_{t_k}\}$$
$$=\exp\{i\zeta\cdot X_\Delta(t_k)+(t-t_k)\int_S(e^{i\zeta\cdot a(X_\Delta(t_k),y,\theta,\varphi)}-1)\,u_k(dy)\,Q(d\theta)\,d\varphi\}$$
$$t_k\leqq t\leqq t_{k+1},\ \zeta\in\mathbf{R}^3,$$

where $u_k(dy)$ is the probability distribution of $X_\Delta(t_k)$. Then (i) is clear from this formula.

(ii) Enlarging the probability space if necessary, we can assume that there exists an $f^\#$-distributed random variable $\tilde{X}$ such that $E|X-\tilde{X}|=\rho_1(f,f^\#)$. For each k $(0\leqq k<n)$, denote by u_k and $u_k^\#$ the probability distributions of $X_\Delta(t_k)$ and $X_\Delta^\#(t_k)$, respectively, and then take α-random variables Y_k and $\tilde{Y}_k$ with distributions u_k and $u_k^\#$, respectively, in such a way that $E_\alpha|Y_k-\tilde{Y}_k|=\rho_1(u_k,u_k^\#)$ holds. We now put $X(0)=X$ and $\tilde{X}(0)=\tilde{X}$, and assume that $\{X(t)\}$ and $\{\tilde{X}(t)\}$ are defined for $0\leqq t\leqq t_k$. We first define $\tilde{a}(x,\tilde{Y}_k,\sigma)$ for $\sigma=(\theta,\varphi,\alpha)$ by

$$\tilde{a}(x,\tilde{Y}_k,\sigma)=a(x,\tilde{Y}_k(\alpha),\varphi+\varphi_0),$$
$$\varphi_0=\varphi_0(X(t_k),Y_k(\alpha),\tilde{X}(t_k),\tilde{Y}_k(\alpha)),$$

using the function φ_0 of Lemma 3.1, and then put

$$X(t)=X(t_k)+\sum_{t_k<s\leqq t} a(X(t_k), Y_k, p(s)),$$
$$\tilde{X}(t)=\tilde{X}(t_k)+\sum_{t_k<s\leqq t} \tilde{a}(\tilde{X}(t_k), \tilde{Y}_k, p(s)),$$

for $t_k<t\leqq t_{k+1}$. By virtue of (2.1) and Lemma 3.1 we have for $t_k<t\leqq t_{k+1}$

$$\begin{aligned} E|X(t)-\tilde{X}(t)| &\leqq E|X(t_k)-\tilde{X}(t_k)| \\ &\quad +c_1(t-t_k)\{E|X(t_k)-\tilde{X}(t_k)|+\rho_1(u_k, u_k^{\#})\} \\ &\leqq \{1+2c_1(t-t_k)\}\, E|X(t_k)-\tilde{X}(t_k)|, \end{aligned} \tag{4.8}$$

where $c_1=2\pi c\int_0^\pi \theta Q(d\theta)$. Now (4.7) follows from (4.8). The proof is finished.

Lemma 4.2. *Let T be any positive constant and Δ a partition of the interval $[0, T]$ given by (4.5). Let Y_k, $0\leqq k<n$, be α-random variables with probability distributions u_k in $\mathscr{P}_1$, $0\leqq k<n$. Given an $\mathscr{F}_0$-measurable random variable X with probability distribution f in $\mathscr{P}_1$, we define a process $\{X_\Delta(t), 0\leqq t\leqq T\}$ by*

$$\begin{aligned} &X_\Delta(0)=X \\ &X_\Delta(t) =X_\Delta(t_k)+\sum_{t_k<s\leqq t} a(X_\Delta(t_k), Y_k, p(s)), \qquad t_k<t\leqq t_{k+1}. \end{aligned} \tag{4.9}$$

Then we have the following assertions.

(i) *The probability law of $\{X_\Delta(t), 0\leqq t\leqq T\}$ is uniquely determined by f and u_k, $0\leqq k<n$.*

(ii) *Take another $\mathscr{F}_0$-measurable random variable $X^{\#}$ with probability distribution $f^{\#}$ in $\mathscr{P}_1$ and also α-random variables $Y_k^{\#}$, $0\leqq k<n$, with probability distributions $u_k^{\#}$ in $\mathscr{P}_1$. We define a process $\{X_\Delta^{\#}(t), 0\leqq t\leqq T\}$ by a rule similar to (4.9) making use of $X^{\#}$ and $Y_k^{\#}$. Then, enlarging the probability space if necessary, we can construct two processes $\{\mathring{X}(t), 0\leqq t\leqq T\}$ and $\{\mathring{X}^{\#}(t), 0\leqq t\leqq T\}$ which are equivalent in law to the processes $\{X_\Delta(t), 0\leqq t\leqq T\}$ and $\{X_\Delta^{\#}(t), 0\leqq t\leqq T\}$, respectively, and satisfying*

$$\begin{aligned} &E|\mathring{X}(t)-\mathring{X}^{\#}(t)| \\ &\quad\leqq \{1+c_1(t-t_k)\}\, E|\mathring{X}(t_k)-\mathring{X}^{\#}(t_k)|+c_1(t-t_k)\,\rho_1(u_k, u_k^{\#}), \\ &\qquad t_k<t\leqq t_{k+1} \quad (0\leqq k<n), \end{aligned} \tag{4.10}$$

where $c_1=2\pi c\int_0^\pi \theta Q(d\theta)$. In particular, if $\rho_1(u_k, u_k^{\#})<\varepsilon$ for $0\leqq k<n$, then

$$E|\mathring{X}(t)-\mathring{X}^{\#}(t)|\leqq e^{c_1 t}\{\rho_1(f, f^{\#})+\varepsilon\}. \tag{4.11}$$

The proof of this lemma is similar to that of Lemma 4.1 and so is omitted.

Lemma 4.3. *Let $\{X_\Delta(t), 0\leqq t\leqq T\}$ be the same as in Lemma 4.1. Then, any finite dimensional probability law of $\{X_\Delta(t), 0\leqq t\leqq T\}$ is convergent as $|\Delta|\to 0$. More* *precisely, if* $\square$: $0=s_0<s_1<\cdots<s_m=T$ *is another partition of* $[0,T]$, *then we can construct two processes* $\{X(t), 0\leqq t\leqq T\}$ *and* $\{\tilde{X}(t), 0\leqq t\leqq T\}$ *which are equivalent in law to* $\{X_\Delta(t), 0\leqq t\leqq T\}$ *and* $\{X_\square(t), 0\leqq t\leqq T\}$, *respectively, and satisfying*

$$E|X(t)-\tilde{X}(t)|\leqq c_2(|\Delta|+|\square|), \qquad 0\leqq t\leqq T, \tag{4.12}$$

where

$$c_2=2\pi\int_0^\pi \theta Q(d\theta)\exp\left\{2\pi(1+2c)\,T\int_0^\pi \theta Q(d\theta)\right\}E|X|. \tag{4.13}$$

Proof. We may assume that $\square$ is a sub-partition of Δ without loss of generality. First we construct $\{X_\Delta(t), 0\leqq t\leqq T\}$ as in (4.6) using auxiliary α-random variables $Y_0,\ldots,Y_{n-1}$, and then put $X(t)=X_\Delta(t)$, $0\leqq t\leqq T$. Each Y_k can be arbitrarily chosen under the restriction that it is equivalent in law to $X_\Delta(t_k)$. Now we require, in addition, that each Y_k satisfies the following condition:

There exists an α-random variable which is independent of Y_k and uniformly distibuted on $(0,1)$. (4.14)

The process $\{\tilde{X}(t), 0\leqq t\leqq T\}$ must be constructed more carefully. We put

$$\tilde{X}(t)=X+\sum_{s\leqq t} a(X, Y_0, p(s)), \qquad 0\leqq t\leqq s_1.$$

Assuming that $\tilde{X}(t)$ is defined for $0\leqq t\leqq s_k$, we define $\tilde{X}(t)$ for $s_k<t\leqq s_{k+1}$ as follows. Define k' by $t_{k'}=\max\{t_j: t_j\leqq s_k\}$, and then choose an α-random variable $\tilde{Y}_k$ so that the joint distribution of $(Y_{k'}, \tilde{Y}_k)$ coincides with that of $(X(t_{k'}), \tilde{X}(s_k))$; this is possible by virtue of (4.14). Putting

$$\tilde{a}(\tilde{X}(s_k), \tilde{Y}_k, \sigma)=a(\tilde{X}(s_k), \tilde{Y}_k(\alpha), \theta, \varphi+\varphi_0), \qquad \sigma=(\theta,\varphi,\alpha),$$
$$\varphi_0=\varphi_0(X(t_{k'}), Y_{k'}(\alpha), \tilde{X}(s_k), \tilde{Y}_k(\alpha)),$$

we define $\tilde{X}(t)$ for $s_k<t\leqq s_{k+1}$ by

$$\tilde{X}(t)=\tilde{X}(s_k)+\sum_{s_k<s\leqq t}\tilde{a}(\tilde{X}(s_k), \tilde{Y}_k, p(s)).$$

In this way we can construct $\tilde{X}(t)$ for $0\leqq t\leqq T$, and it is not hard to see that thus constructed $\{\tilde{X}(t), 0\leqq t\leqq T\}$ is equivalent in law to $\{X_\square(t), 0\leqq t\leqq T\}$.

We assume that $s_k\leqq t\leqq s_{k+1}$ for a moment. Since

$$X(t)=X(s_k)+\sum_{s_k<s\leqq t} a(X(t_{k'}), Y_{k'}, p(s)),$$

using Lemma 3.1 we have

$$\begin{aligned} &E|X(t)-\tilde{X}(t)| \\ &\quad\leqq E|X(s_k)-\tilde{X}(s_k)|+E\Big\{\int_{(s_k,t]\times S}|a(X(t_{k'}), Y_{k'},\sigma)-\tilde{a}(\tilde{X}(s_k), \tilde{Y}_k,\sigma)|\,ds\,\lambda(d\sigma)\Big\} \\ &\quad\leqq E|X(s_k)-\tilde{X}(s_k)|+(t-s_k)\,2\pi c\int_0^\pi \theta Q(d\theta)\{E|X(t_{k'})-\tilde{X}(s_k)|+E_\alpha|Y_{k'}-\tilde{Y}_k|\} \\ &\quad=E|X(s_k)-\tilde{X}(s_k)|+c_0(t-s_k)\,E|X(t_{k'})-\tilde{X}(s_k)|, \end{aligned} \tag{4.15}$$

where $c_0 = 4\pi c \int_0^\pi \theta Q(d\theta)$. On the other and

$$\begin{aligned}E|X(t)| &\leqq E|X(t_k)| + (t-t_k)\, E\int_S |a(X(t_k), Y_k, \sigma)|\,\lambda(d\sigma)\\ &\leqq E|X(t_k)| + (t-t_k)\, E\int_S (|X(t_k)-Y_k|/2)\,\theta\lambda(d\sigma)\\ &\leqq E|X(t_k)| + c'(t-t_k)\, E|X(t_k)|, \qquad t_k < t \leqq t_{k+1},\end{aligned}$$

where $c' = 2\pi \int_0^\pi \theta Q(d\theta)$, and hence by Gronwall's inequality

$$E|X(t)| \leqq E|X|\, e^{c't}, \qquad 0 \leqq t \leqq T.$$

Therefore

$$\begin{aligned}E|X(s_k) - X(t_{k'})| &\leqq c'(s_k - t_{k'})\, E|X(t_{k'})|\\ &\leqq c''(s_k - t_{k'}), \qquad c'' = E|X|\, c'\, e^{c'T},\end{aligned}$$

and hence

$$\begin{aligned}&E|X(t) - \tilde{X}(t)| + c''|\Delta|\\ &\quad \leqq \{E|X(s_k) - \tilde{X}(s_k)| + c''|\Delta|\}\, e^{c_0(t-s_k)}, \qquad s_k < t \leqq s_{k+1},\end{aligned}$$

which implies that

$$E|X(t) - \tilde{X}(t)| \leqq c''|\Delta|(e^{c_0 t} - 1), \qquad 0 \leqq t \leqq T, \tag{4.16}$$

as was to be proved.

In what follows, a process $\{X(t)\}$ is said to be *integrable* for simplicity, if $E\{\sup_{0\leqq s\leqq t} |X(s)|\} < \infty$ for each $t \in \mathbf{R}_+$.

Lemma 4.4. *Given an $\mathscr{F}_0$-measurable random variable X with $E\{|X|\} < \infty$, we assume that there exists an integrable solution $\{X(t), t \geqq 0\}$ of* (4.2). *Let T be any positive constant, Δ a partition of $[0, T]$ and $\{X_\Delta(t), 0 \leqq t \leqq T\}$ a process of Lemma* 4.1. *Then, any finite dimensional probability law of $\{X_\Delta(t), 0 \leqq t \leqq T\}$ converges to the corresponding one of $\{X(t), 0 \leqq t \leqq T\}$ as $|\Delta| \to 0$. More precisely, on a suitable probability space $(\tilde{\Omega}, \tilde{\mathscr{F}}, \tilde{P})$ we can construct two processes $\{\tilde{X}(t), 0 \leqq t \leqq T\}$ and $\{\tilde{X}_\Delta(t), 0 \leqq t \leqq T\}$, which are equivalent in law to $\{X(t), 0 \leqq t \leqq T\}$ and $\{X_\Delta(t), 0 \leqq t \leqq T\}$, respectively, and satisfying*

$$\tilde{E}|\tilde{X}(t) - \tilde{X}_\Delta(t)| \leqq c_2|\Delta|, \qquad 0 \leqq t \leqq T, \tag{4.17}$$

with the constant c_2 given by (4.13).

Proof. Define $\Delta(t)$, $0 \leqq t \leqq T$, by

$$\Delta(0) = 0, \ \Delta(t) = t_k \quad \text{for } t_k < t \leqq t_{k+1} \ (0 \leqq k < n), \tag{4.18}$$

and put

$$\mathrm{X}^{\Delta}(t)=X+\sum_{s\leqq t} a(X(\Delta(s)), Y(\Delta(s)), p(s)).$$

Also, we define $\{X^{\#}(t), 0\leqq t\leqq T\}$ by

$$X^{\#}(0)=X,$$

$$X^{\#}(t)=X^{\#}(t_k)+\sum_{t_k<s\leqq t} \tilde{a}(X^{\#}(t_k), Y(t_k), p(s))$$

$$\text{for } t_k<t\leqq t_{k+1} \ (0\leqq k<n), \tag{4.19}$$

where, in each step, $\tilde{a}(X^{\#}(t_k), Y(t_k), \sigma)$ is defined to be equal to $a(X^{\#}(t_k), Y(t_k, \alpha), \sigma, \varphi+\varphi_0)$ for $\sigma=(\theta, \varphi, \alpha)$ with $\varphi_0=\varphi_0(X(t_k), Y(t_k), X^{\#}(t_k), Y(t_k))$. Then we have for $t_k<t\leqq t_{k+1}$

$$\begin{aligned} &E|X^{\Delta}(t)-X^{\#}(t)| \\ &\leqq E|X^{\Delta}(t_k)-X^{\#}(t_k)|+c_1(t-t_k)E|X(t_k)-X^{\#}(t_k)| \\ &\leqq \{1+c_1(t-t_k)\}E|X^{\Delta}(t_k)-X^{\#}(t_k)|+c_1(t-t_k)E|X(t_k)-X^{\Delta}(t_k)|, \end{aligned} \tag{4.20}$$

where c_1 is the same as in (4.10). Now, if we put

$$\varepsilon(\Delta)=E\int_{(0,T]\times S} |a(X(t), Y(t), \sigma)-a(X(\Delta(t)), Y(\Delta(t)), \sigma)|\,dt\,\lambda(d\sigma),$$

then $E|X(t)-X^{\Delta}(t)|\leqq\varepsilon(\Delta)$ for $0\leqq t\leqq T$, and hence (4.20) yields

$$E|X^{\Delta}(t)-X^{\#}(t)|\leqq\varepsilon(\Delta)(e^{c_1T}-1), \tag{4.21}$$

$$E|X(t)-X^{\#}(t)|\leqq\varepsilon(\Delta)\,e^{c_1T}. \tag{4.22}$$

Since $\{X^{\#}(t)\}$ is equivalent in law to $\{X_{\Delta}^{\#}(t)\}$ which is defined by a rule similar to (4.19) with $\varphi_0\equiv 0$, we can apply Lemma 4.2 to obtain two processes $\{\mathring{X}(t)\}$ and $\{\mathring{X}^{\#}(t)\}$ which are equivalent in law to $\{X_{\Delta}(t)\}$ and $\{X^{\#}(t)\}$, respectively, and satisfying (4.10). Since u_k and $u_k^{\#}$ are the probability distributions of $\mathring{X}(t_k)$ and $X(t_k)$, the uses of the triangle inequality for ρ_1 and the estimate (4.22) result in

$$\begin{aligned} \rho_1(u_k, u_k^{\#}) &\leqq E|\mathring{X}(t_k)-\mathring{X}^{\#}(t_k)|+E|X^{\#}(t_k)-X(t_k)| \\ &\leqq E|\mathring{X}(t_k)-\mathring{X}^{\#}(t_k)|+\varepsilon(\Delta)\,e^{c_1T}. \end{aligned}$$

Therefore, (4.10) yields

$$\begin{aligned} E|\mathring{X}(t)-\mathring{X}^{\#}(t)| &\leqq \{1+c_0(t-t_k)\}E|\mathring{X}(t_k)-\mathring{X}^{\#}(t_k)| \\ &\quad +c_1(t-t_k)\,\varepsilon(\Delta)e^{c_1T}, \qquad t_k<t\leqq t_{k+1}, \end{aligned}$$

which implies that

$$E|\mathring{X}(t)-\mathring{X}^{\#}(t)|\leqq\varepsilon(\Delta)\,e^{c_1T}(e^{c_0T}-1), \qquad 0\leqq t\leqq T. \tag{4.23}$$

By virtue of (4.22) and (4.23), on a suitable probability space $(\tilde{\Omega}, \tilde{\mathscr{F}}, \tilde{P})$ we can construct two porcesses $\{\tilde{X}(t), 0\leqq t\leqq T\}$ and $\{\tilde{X}_{\Delta}(t), 0\leqq t\leqq T\}$ equivalent in law to

$\{X(t),\ 0 \leqq t \leqq T\}$ and $\{X_\Delta(t),\ 0 \leqq t \leqq T\}$, respectively, so that they satisfy

$$\begin{aligned}\tilde{E}|\tilde{X}(t)-\tilde{X}_\Delta(t)| &\leqq E|X(t)-X^{\#}(t)|+E|\mathring{X}^{\#}(t)-\mathring{X}(t)| \\ &\leqq \varepsilon(\Delta)\, e^{3c_1 T}, \quad 0 \leqq t \leqq T. \end{aligned} \tag{4.24}$$

Now by an application of Lemma 2.1 we can make both $\varepsilon(\Delta)$ and $|\Delta|$ arbitrary small, and hence the right hand side of (4.24) tends to 0 as $|\Delta| \to 0$ via some subsequence $\{\Delta_m\}$. Combining this fact with Lemma 4.3, especially with the estimate (4.12), we can easily prove the assertion of the lemma. The proof is finished.

Making use of methods similar to those employed in Lemma 4.3 and 4.4, we obtain the following lemma in which $\{Y(t)\}$ is an α-process given in advance (we do not require that it is equivalent in law to the solution process).

Lemma 4.5. *Given an $\mathscr{F}_0$-measurable random variable X with $E|X|<\infty$ and also an integrable α-process $\{Y(t)\}$ which is continuous in the mean, we assume that there exists an integrable solution $\{X(t)\}$ of*

$$X(t)=X+\sum_{s \leqq t} a(X(s-),\ Y(s-),\ p(s)).$$

Let T be any positive constant, Δ a partition of $[0, T]$ and $\{X_\Delta(t),\ 0 \leqq t \leqq T\}$ the process obtained by (4.9) with $Y_k = Y(t_k)$. Then, any finite dimensional probability law of $\{X_\Delta(t), 0 \leqq t \leqq T\}$ converges to the corresponding one of $\{X(t), 0 \leqq t \leqq T\}$ as $|\Delta| \to 0$. More precisely, on a suitable probability space $(\tilde{\Omega}, \tilde{\mathscr{F}}, \tilde{P})$ we can construct two processes $\{\tilde{X}(t),\ 0 \leqq t \leqq T\}$ and $\{\tilde{X}_\Delta(t),\ 0 \leqq t \leqq T\}$ in such a way that they are equivalent in law to $\{X(t), 0 \leqq t \leqq T\}$ and $\{X_\Delta(t), 0 \leqq t \leqq T\}$, respectively, and satisfy

$$\tilde{E}|\tilde{X}(t)-\tilde{X}_\Delta(t)| \leqq c_3|\Delta|+\varepsilon_Y(\Delta) e^{c_1 T}, \quad 0 \leqq t \leqq T, \tag{4.25}$$

where

$$\begin{aligned} c_3 &= \pi \int_0^\pi \theta Q(d\theta) \exp\left\{\pi(1+2c)\, T \int_0^\pi \theta Q(d\theta)\right\}(E|X|+M), \\ M &= \sup_{0 \leqq t \leqq T} E_\alpha |Y(t)|, \\ \varepsilon_Y(\Delta) &= \max_{0 \leqq k < n} E_\alpha |Y(t_{k+1})-Y(t_k)|. \end{aligned}$$

The following uniqueness theorem follows immediately from Lemma 4.1 and 4.4.

Theorem 4.1. *The uniqueness in the law sense holds for integrable solutions of (4.1), that is, the probability law on W of any integrable solution of (4.1) is uniquely determined by its initial distribution f if $f \in \mathscr{P}_1$. More precisely, if $\{X(t)\}$ and $\{X^{\#}(t)\}$ are any integrable solutions of (4.1) with initial distributions f and $f^{\#}$ $(\in \mathscr{P}_1)$, respectively, then on a suitable probability space $(\tilde{\Omega}, \tilde{\mathscr{F}}, \tilde{P})$ we can construct two processes $\{\tilde{X}(t)\}$ and $\{\tilde{X}^{\#}(t)\}$ in such a way that they are equivalent in law to $\{X(t)\}$ and $\{X^{\#}(t)\}$, respectively, and satisfy*

$$\tilde{E}|\tilde{X}(t)-\tilde{X}^{\#}(t)| \leqq e^{c_0 t} \rho_1(f, f^{\#}), \quad t \geqq 0. \tag{4.26}$$

Next we deal with the existence theorem concerning (4.1); the precise statement of this is given as follows.

Theorem 4.2. *Let* $f \in \mathscr{P}_1$ *be given. Then, on a suitable probability space* $\{\Omega, \mathscr{F}, P\}$ *with an increasing family* $\{\mathscr{F}_t\}$ *of sub-σ-fields we can construct an* $\{\mathscr{F}_t\}$*-adapted Poisson point process* $\{p(t)\}$ *on S with characteristic measure* λ *so that* (4.1) *has an integrable solution with initial distribution f.*

In order to prove this theorem it is convenient to introduce another stochastic differential equation which will turn out to be essentially the same as (4.1). It is expressed as

$$dX(t) = a(X(t-), Y(t-), \theta, \varphi + \varphi^*)\, dN, \qquad X(0) = X, \tag{4.1*}$$

and a solution $\{X(t)\}$ of this equation should be found as an $\{\mathscr{F}_t\}$-adapted process with sample paths in W under the conditions that $\{Y(t)\}$ is an α-process equivalent in law to $\{X(t)\}$ and that $\varphi^* = \varphi^*(t, \alpha, \omega)$ is an $\{\mathscr{F}_t\}$-predictable process. Always, $\varphi + \varphi^*$ should be interpreted mod 2π. Now, for φ^* appearing in (4.1*) we put

$$N^*(A) = \int_{(0,\infty)\times S} 1\!\!1_A(t, \theta, \varphi + \varphi^*(t, \alpha, \omega), \alpha)\, N(dt\, d\sigma), \qquad A \in \mathscr{B}((0,\infty)\times S).$$

Then by Theorem 2.1 $\{N^*(dt\, d\sigma)\}$ is again an $\{\mathscr{F}_t\}$-adapted Poisson random measure corresponding to λ, and (4.1*) is nothing but (4.1) with N replaced by N^*. Therefore, for the proof of Theorem 4.2 it is enough to prove the following theorem.

Theorem 4.3. *Let* $\{p(t)\}$ *be an* $\{\mathscr{F}_t\}$*-adapted Poisson point process on S with characteristic measure* λ*, and* $\{N(dt\, d\sigma)\}$ *the associated Poisson random measure. Then, for any* $\mathscr{F}_0$*-measurable* R^3*-valued random variable X with* $E|X| < \infty$*, there exists an integrable solution of* (4.1*).

Proof. We prove this by iteration. First we take an α-random variable Y with the same distribution as X and also with the property that

there exists an α-random variable which is independent of Y and uniformly distributed on (0.1). (4.27)

We then define $\{X_1(t)\}$ by

$$X_1(t) = X + \sum_{s \leq t} a_1(X_0(s-), Y_0(s-), p(s)),$$

where $X_0(s) \equiv X$, $Y_0(s) \equiv Y$, $\varphi_0^* \equiv 0$ and $a_1(x, Y, \sigma) = a(x, Y(\alpha), \varphi + \varphi_0^*)\ (= a(x, Y, \sigma))$ for $\sigma = (\theta, \varphi, \alpha)$. Next, assuming that $\{X_k(t)\}$, $1 \leq k \leq n$, are defined together with auxiliary α-processes $\{Y_k(t)\}$ and $\{\mathscr{F}_t\}$-predictable processes $\{\varphi_k^*(t, \alpha, \omega)\}$, $0 \leq k < n$, we choose an α-process $\{Y_n(t)\}$ in such a way that the joint process $\{(Y_{n-1}(t), Y_n(t))\}$ is equivalent in law to $\{(X_{n-1}(t), X_n(t))\}$ and that (4.27) holds with Y replaced by $\{Y_n(t)\}$; this is possible by virtue of Lemma 3.2. Using the function φ_0 of Lemma 3.1, we then put

$$\varphi_n^*(t, \alpha, \omega) = \varphi_{n-1}^*(t, \alpha, \omega) + \varphi_0(X_{n-1}(t-), Y_{n-1}(t-), X_n(t-), Y_n(t-)),$$
$$a_{n+1}(X_n(t-), Y_n(t-), \sigma) = a(X_n(t-), Y_n(t-, \alpha), \theta, \varphi + \varphi_n^*(t, \alpha, \omega)),$$

for $\sigma=(\theta,\varphi,\alpha)$, and define $\{X_{n+1}(t)\}$ by

$$X_{n+1}(t)=X+\sum_{s\leqq t} a_{n+1}(X_n(s-),Y_n(s-),p(s)). \tag{4.28}$$

Thus we obtain a sequence of processes $\{X_n(t)\}$, $n\geqq 1$. By Lemma 3.1 we have

$$\begin{aligned}&|a_{n+1}(X_n(s-),Y_n(s-),\sigma)-a_n(X_{n-1}(s-),Y_{n-1}(s-),\sigma)|\\ &\quad\leqq c\{|X_n(s-)-X_{n-1}(s-)|+|Y_n(s-)-Y_{n-1}(s-)|\}\,\theta.\end{aligned} \tag{4.29}$$

and hence

$$\begin{aligned}&E|X_{n+1}(t)-X_n(t)|\\ &\quad\leqq cE\int_{(0,t]\times S}\{|X_n(s-)-X_{n-1}(s-)|+|Y_n(s-)-Y_{n-1}(s-)|\}\,\theta\,ds\,\lambda(d\sigma)\\ &\quad=c_0\int_0^t E|X_n(s)-X_{n-1}(s)|\,ds.\end{aligned}$$

Since $E|X_1(t)-X|\leqq c_0 E|X|\,t$ we have

$$E|X_{n+1}(t)-X_n(t)|\leqq E|X|(c_0 t)^{n+1}/(n+1)!$$

and hence

$$\begin{aligned}&E\{\sup_{0\leqq s\leqq t}|X_{n+1}(s)-X_n(s)|\}\\ &\quad\leqq E\{\sum_{s\leqq t}|a_{n+1}(X_n(s-),Y_n(s-),p(s))-a_n(X_{n-1}(s-),Y_{n-1}(s-),p(s))|\}\\ &\quad\leqq E|X|(c_0 t)^{n+1}/(n+1)!.\end{aligned}$$

Therefore, $X_n(t)$ converges almost surely to some limit $X(t)$ as $n\to\infty$ uniformly on each finite t-interval, and hence $Y_n(t)$ also converges almost surely to some α-process $\{Y(t)\}$ which is obviously equivalent in law to $\{X(t)\}$. These convergences together with the inequality (4.29) imply the almost sure convergence of $a_n(X_{n-1}(t-),$ $Y_{n-1}(t-),\sigma)$ to some $\{\mathcal{F}_t\}$-predictable limit $a_\infty(t,\sigma,\omega)$. It is then clear that $X(t-)$ $+a_\infty(t,\sigma,\omega)$ lies on the sphere $S_{X(t-),Y(t-)}$ and has the colatitude θ (almost surely). Consequently, there exists an $\{\mathcal{F}_t\}$-predictable process $\varphi^*=\varphi^*(t,\alpha,\omega)$ such that $a_\infty(t,\sigma,\omega)=a(X(t-),Y(t-),\theta,\varphi+\varphi^*)$. Now letting $n\uparrow\infty$ in (4.28), we see that (4.1*) is satisfied by the triple $(X(t),Y(t),\varphi^*)$, or equivalently, that $\{X(t)\}$ is a solution of (4.1*).

As the final task of this section we prove some moment estimates concerning solutions of (4.1).

Theorem 4.4. *Let $\{X(t)\}$ be any integrable solution of* (4.1) *with initial value X satisfying $E\{|X|^\nu\}<\infty$ for some positive integer ν. Then we have*

$$E\{|X(t)|^\nu\}\leqq e^{c'_\nu t}E\{|X|^\nu\},\qquad t\geqq 0, \tag{4.30}$$

where $c'_\nu = 3^\nu \nu\pi \int_0^\pi \theta Q(d\theta)$. *When* $\nu = 1, 2$, *we have*

$$E\{X(t)\} = E\{X\}, \qquad t \geqq 0, \tag{4.31}$$

$$E\{|X(t)|^2\} = E\{|X|^2\}, \qquad t \geqq 0. \tag{4.32}$$

Proof. Let $\{X_\Delta(t), 0 \leqq t \leqq T\}$ be the same as in Lemma 4.1. Then, by Lemma 4.4, in order to prove (4.30) it is enough to show

$$E\{|X_\Delta(t)|^\nu\} \leqq e^{c'_\nu t} E\{|X|^\nu\}, \qquad 0 \leqq t \leqq T. \tag{4.33}$$

We first notice that $E\{|X_\Delta(t)|^\nu\}$ is bounded in $t \in [0, T]$; in fact this follows from the fact that the ν-th moment of

$$\sum_{t_k < s \leqq t} |a(X_\Delta(t_k), Y_k, p(s))|, \qquad t_k < t \leqq t_{k+1}$$

conditioned on the σ-field $\mathscr{F}_{t_k}$ is given by

$$\sum_{j=1}^{\nu} \frac{1}{j!} \sum_{\substack{\nu_1 + \cdots + \nu_j = \nu \\ \nu_1, \cdots, \nu_j \geqq 1}} \frac{\nu!}{\nu_1! \ldots \nu_j!} \prod_{l=1}^{j} ((t - t_k) \int_S |a(X_\Delta(t_k), Y_k, \sigma)|^{\nu_l} \lambda(d\sigma)).$$

We next write $a_k = a(X_\Delta(t_k), Y_k, p(s))$, $\tilde{a}_k = a(X_\Delta(t_k), Y_k, \sigma)$ and then apply (2.3) to (4.6); the result is

$$\begin{aligned} |X_\Delta(t)|^\nu &= |X_\Delta(t_k)|^\nu + \sum_{t_k < s \leqq t} \{|X_\Delta(s-) + a_k|^\nu - |X_\Delta(s-)|^\nu\} \\ &\leqq |X_\Delta(t_k)|^\nu + \nu \sum_{t_k < s \leqq t} |a_k| \{|X_\Delta(s-)| + |a_k|\}^{\nu-1}, \qquad t_k < t \leqq t_{k+1}. \end{aligned}$$

Therefore, we have for $t_k < t \leqq t_{k+1}$

$$E\{|X_\Delta(t)|^\nu\} \leqq E\{|X_\Delta(t_k)|^\nu\} + \nu E \int_{(t_k, t] \times S} |\tilde{a}_k| \{|X_\Delta(s)| + |\tilde{a}_k|\}^{\nu-1} ds\, \lambda(d\sigma).$$

On the other hand, since $|\tilde{a}_k| \{|X_\Delta(s)| + |\tilde{a}_k|\}^{\nu-1}$ is dominated by

$$\begin{aligned} &(\theta/2) \{|X_\Delta(t_k)| + |Y_k|\} \{|X_\Delta(s)| + |X_\Delta(t_k)| + |Y_k|\}^{\nu-1} \\ &\qquad \leqq 3^{\nu-1} (\theta/2) \{|X_\Delta(s)|^\nu + |X_\Delta(t_k)|^\nu + |Y_k|^\nu\}, \end{aligned}$$

we have for $t_k < t \leqq t_{k+1}$

$$\begin{aligned} &E\{|X_\Delta(t)|^\nu\} \\ &\quad \leqq E\{|X_\Delta(t_k)|^\nu\} + \bar{c}_\nu \int_{(t_k, t] \times (0,1)} E\{|X_\Delta(s)|^\nu + |X_\Delta(t_k)|^\nu + |Y_k|^\nu\} ds\, d\alpha \\ &\quad = \{1 + 2\bar{c}_\nu(t - t_k)\} E\{|X_\Delta(t_k)|^\nu\} + \bar{c}_\nu \int_{t_k}^{t} E\{|X_\Delta(s)|^\nu\} ds, \\ &\bar{c}_\nu = 3^{\nu-1} \nu\pi \int_0^\pi \theta Q(d\theta). \end{aligned}$$

Now an application of Gronwall's inequality yields (4.33).

When $E\{|X|^2\}<\infty$, we take the expectation in

$$|X(t)|^2=|X|^2+\sum_{s\leqq t}\{|X(s-)+a(X(s-),Y(s-),p(s))|^2-|X(s-)|^2\}$$

to obtain

$$\begin{aligned}
&E\{|X(t)|^2\}\\
&=E\{|X|^2\}+\int_{(0,t]\times S}E\{|X(s)+a(X(s),Y(s),\sigma)|^2-|X(s)|^2\}\,ds\,\lambda(d\sigma)\\
&=E\{|X|^2\}+\int(|x'|^2-|x|^2)\,Q(d\theta)\,d\varphi\,u(s,dx)\,u(s,dx_1)\,ds\\
&=E\{|X|^2\}+\int\frac{|x'|^2+|x_1'|^2-|x|^2-|x_1|^2}{2}Q(d\theta)\,d\varphi\,u(s,dx)\,u(s,dx_1)\,ds\\
&=E\{|X|^2\},
\end{aligned}$$

proving (4.32), where $u(s,\cdot)$ denotes the probability distribution of $X(s)$ and the last two inegrals are performed on $(0,\pi)\times(0,2\pi)\times\mathbf{R}^3\times\mathbf{R}^3\times(0,t]$. The equality (4.31) can also be proved by a method similar to the above. The proof is finished.

§ 5. The Transition Function and the Markov Process Associated with (0.3)

In this section we show that the solutions of (4.1) give rise to a Markov process which is associated with (0.3) in the sense of § 1. As in the preceeding section, $\{p(t)\}$ and $\{N(dt\,d\sigma)\}$ stand for an $\{\mathscr{F}_t\}$-adapted Poisson point process on S with characteristic measure λ and the associated Poisson random measure, respectively. By virtue of the uniqueness in the law sense for solutions of (4.1) we may write P_f for the probability distribution on $(W,\mathscr{B}_W)$ induced by any integrable solution of (4.1) with initial distribution $f\in\mathscr{P}_1$. Given $f\in\mathscr{P}_1$, we take a P_f-distributed α-process $\{Y(t)\}$ and consider the stochastic differential equation

$$dX(t)=a(X(t-),Y(t-),\theta,\varphi)\,dN,\qquad X(0)=x. \tag{5.1}$$

Although this equation has the same expression as (4.1) (except for the initial value), it should be noticed that $\{Y(t)\}$ of (5.1) is a given α-process and so, of course, is not required to be equivalent in law to the solution of (5.1). As in the case of (4.1), the stochastic differential equation (5.1) is essentially equivalent to

$$dX(t)=a(X(t-),Y(t-),\theta,\varphi+\varphi^*)\,dN,\qquad X(0)=x, \tag{5.1*}$$

in which $\varphi^*=\varphi^*(t,\alpha,\omega)$ is an $\{\mathscr{F}_t\}$-predictable process.

The existence of a solution of (5.1*) can be proved by a method of iteration similar to that used in solving (4.1*), and from Lemma 4.5 and (i) of Lemma 4.2 it follows that the probability distribution on $(W,\mathscr{B}_W)$ of any integrable solution of (5.1) (or (5.1*)) is uniquely determined by f and x; we denote this probability distribution on $(W,\mathscr{B}_W)$ by P_f^x. Also we denote by $X_t(w)$, or X_t for short, the value $w(t)$ of $w\in W$ at time t, and put $\mathscr{B}_t=\sigma\{X_s: s\leqq t\}$, $\mathscr{B}=\vee\,\mathscr{B}_t(=\mathscr{B}_W)$. Here the notation X_t should not be confused with $X(t)$; the former is defined on W while the latter is on Ω. Combining (4.11) with (4.26) and then using Lemma 4.5, we have the following assertion: For any $x, y \in \mathbf{R}^3$ and $f, g \in \mathscr{P}_1$ we can construct two processes $\{\tilde{X}(t)\}$ and $\{\tilde{X}^{\#}(t)\}$ on a suitable probability space $(\tilde{\Omega}, \tilde{\mathscr{F}}, \tilde{P})$ in such a way that their probability distributions on the path space W are P_f^x and P_g^y respectively, and that

$$\tilde{E}|\tilde{X}(t)-\tilde{X}^{\#}(t)| \leqq e^{c_1 t}\{|x-y|+e^{c_0 t}\rho_1(f,g)\}, \quad t \geqq 0.$$

This assertion immediately implies the following lemma, in which we put

$$e_f(t,x,A)=P_f^x\{X_t \in A\}, \qquad A \in \mathscr{B}(R^3). \tag{5.2}$$

Lemma 5.1. (i) *For any $B \in \mathscr{B}_W$, $P_f^x(B)$ is jointly measurable in $(f,x) \in \mathscr{P}_1 \times \mathbf{R}^3$.*

(ii) *For each $A \in \mathscr{B}(R^3)$, $e_f(t,x,A)$ is jointly measurable in $(f,t,x) \in \mathscr{P}_1 \times \mathbf{R}_+ \times \mathbf{R}^3$.*

It can be easily verified that the function $e_f(t,x,A)$ of (5.2) satisfies (e.3) of § 1. (e.4) can also be verified by first applying (2.3) to a solution $X(t)$ of (5.1) and then taking the expectation.

Theorem 5.1. *For any $x \in \mathbf{R}^3, f \in \mathscr{P}_1$, $A \in \mathscr{B}(\mathbf{R}^3)$ and $0 \leqq t_0 < t_1$, we have*

$$P_f^x\{X_{t_1} \in A \mid \mathscr{B}_{t_0}\}=e_{u(t_0)}(t_1-t_0, X_{t_0}, A), \qquad P_f^x\text{-a.s.}, \tag{5.3}$$

$$P_f\{X_{t_1} \in A \mid \mathscr{B}_{t_0}\}=e_{u(t_0)}(t_1-t_0, X_{t_0}, A), \qquad P_f\text{-a.s.}, \tag{5.4}$$

where $u(t_0)=u(t_0,\cdot)=P_f\{X_{t_0} \in \cdot\}$.

Proof. For a fixed $t_0 \geqq 0$, if we put

$$p^{\#}(t)=p(t_0+t), \qquad t>0,$$
$$\mathscr{F}_0^{\#}=\{\phi, \Omega\}, \qquad \mathscr{F}_t^{\#}=\sigma\{p^{\#}(s), 0<s \leqq t\},$$

then $\{p^{\#}(t)\}$ is also an $\{\mathscr{F}_t^{\#}\}$-adapted Poisson point process on S with characteristic measure λ. Let $N^{\#}(dt\,d\sigma)$ be the associated Poisson random measure. Taking a P_f-distributed α-process $\{Y(t)\}$, we define a $P_{u(t_0)}$-distributed α-process $\{Y^{\#}(t)\}$ by $Y^{\#}(t)=Y(t_0+t)$, $t \geqq 0$, and then consider the stochastic differential equation

$$dX^{\#}(t)=a(X^{\#}(t-), Y^{\#}(t-), \varphi+\varphi^{\#})\,dN^{\#}, \qquad X^{\#}(0)=y, \tag{5.5}$$

where $\varphi^{\#}=\varphi^{\#}(t,\alpha,\omega)$ is a suitable $\{\mathscr{F}_t^{\#}\}$-predictable process. By a method of iteration similar to that used in solving (4.1*), we can construct a family $\{X_y^{\#}(t), y \in \mathbf{R}^3\}$ of integrable solutions of (5.5) together with $\{\mathscr{F}_t^{\#}\}$-predictable processes $\varphi_y^{\#}=\varphi_y^{\#}(t,\alpha,\omega)$, $y \in \mathbf{R}^3$, in such a way that

(i) $X_y^{\#}(t,\omega)$ is $\mathscr{B}(\mathbf{R}^3) \times \mathscr{F}_t^{\#}$-measurable for each fixed $t \geqq 0$,

(ii) $\varphi_y^{\#}(t,\alpha,\omega)$ is $\mathscr{B}(\mathbf{R}^3) \times \mathfrak{F}^{\#}$-measurable where $\mathfrak{F}^{\#}$ is the predictable σ-field on $\mathbf{R}_+ \times (0,1) \times \Omega$ corresponding to $\{\mathscr{F}_t^{\#}\}$.

We now take an integrable solution $\{X(t)\}$ of (5.1*) and put

$$X^0(t)=\begin{cases} X(t) & \text{for } 0 \leqq t < t_0 \\ X_{X(t_0)}^{\#}(t-t_0) & \text{for } t \geqq t_0. \end{cases}$$

$$\varphi^0(t,\alpha,\omega)=\begin{cases} \varphi^*(t,\alpha,\omega) & \text{for } 0 \leqq t < t_0 \\ \varphi_{X(t_0)}^{\#}(t-t_0,\alpha,\omega) & \text{for } t \geqq t_0. \end{cases}$$

Since $\mathscr{F}_{t_0}$ and $\{\mathscr{F}_t^{\#}\}$ are independent and the process $\{X_y^{\#}(t)\}$ is $P_{u(t_0)}^y$-distributed, we have for $t_1 > t_0$

$$\begin{aligned} P\{X^0(t_1)\in A\,|\,\mathscr{F}_{t_0}\} &= P\{X_{X(t_0)}^{\#}(t_1-t_0)\in A\,|\,\mathscr{F}_{t_0}\} \\ &= P\{X_y^{\#}(t_1-t_0)\in A\}, \qquad y=X(t_0), \text{ a.s.} \\ &= P_{u(t_0)}^{X(t_0)}\{X_{t-t_0}\in A\}=e_{u(t_0)}(t-t_0, X(t_0), A), \qquad \text{a.s.} \end{aligned} \tag{5.6}$$

On the other hand, from (i) and (ii) it follows that $\{X^0(t)\}$ is $\{\mathscr{F}_t\}$-adapted, φ^0 is $\{\mathscr{F}_t\}$-predictable and that $\{X^0(t)\}$ is a solution of (5.1*) with $\varphi^* = \varphi^0$. Thus $\{X^0(t)\}$ is P_f^x-distributed and hence (5.6) implies (5.3). (5.4) can also be proved in a similar manner. The proof is finished.

From what we have proved, it is now clear that $e_f(t, x, A)$ is a transition function associated with (0.3) and so the corresponding Markov process $\{X_t, P_f, f\in\mathscr{P}_1\}$ is also associated with (0.3). As stated in the introduction, it was proved in [19] that this Markov process is the unique one which is associated with (0.3) in the sense of §1.

Chapter II. Trend to Equilibrium

§6. Some Lemmas Concerning ρ-metric on $\mathscr{P}_2$

The purpose of this section is to prepare some lemmas concerning $\mathfrak{e}$ and ρ, defined below, for the use in later sections. We denote by $\mathscr{P}_2$ the space of probability distributions on $\mathbf{R}^3$ with finite second moments. For f and g in $\mathscr{P}_2$ we put

$$\mathfrak{E}(F) = \int_{R^3\times R^3} |x-y|^2\, F(dx\,dy),$$

$$\mathfrak{e}(f,g) = \inf_{F\in\mathbf{F}(f,g)} \mathfrak{E}(F), \qquad \rho(f,g)=\sqrt{\mathfrak{e}(f,g)},$$

where $\mathbf{F}(f,g)$ denotes the family of probability distributions F on $\mathbf{R}^6$ satisfying $F(A\times\mathbf{R}^3)=f(A)$ and $F(\mathbf{R}^3\times A)=g(A)$ for any $A\in\mathscr{B}(R^3)$. Since $\mathbf{F}(f,g)$ is compact with respect to the topology induced by the usual convergence as probability distributions on $\mathbf{R}^6$ and since $\mathfrak{E}(F)$ is continuous on $\mathbf{F}(f,g)$, the infimum value $\mathfrak{e}(f,g)$ is attained at some $F\in\mathbf{F}(f,g)$. As in the case of ρ_1 of §4, it can be proved that ρ gives a metric on $\mathscr{P}_2$. However, when we speak of a convergence in $\mathscr{P}_2$, we always mean that it is the usual one as probability distributions unless ρ-convergence is explicitly stated.

The proof of the following lemma is elementary and so is omitted.

Lemma 6.1. (i) *The ρ-convergence implies the usual convergence in $\mathscr{P}_2$.*

(ii) *If $f_n\to f$ in $\mathscr{P}_2$ and if*

$$\lim_{N\to\infty}\sup_{n\geq 1}\int_{|x|>N}|x|^2 f_n(dx)=0, \tag{6.1}$$

then $\{f_n\}$ is also ρ-convergent to f. In general, $f_n\to f$ and $g_n\to g$ in $\mathscr{P}_2$ imply $\mathfrak{e}(f,g)\leq \lim_{n\to\infty}\mathfrak{e}(f_n,g_n)$.

Let $\varepsilon>0$ be fixed. We denote by $\mathfrak{g}_\varepsilon$ the Gaussian distribution $(2\pi\varepsilon)^{-3/2}$ $\exp(-|x|^2 2\varepsilon)\,dx$ on $\mathbf{R}^3$ and put

$$\mathscr{P}_{(\varepsilon)}=\{f*\mathfrak{g}_\varepsilon|f\in\mathscr{P}_2 \text{ and } f(\{|x|>1/\varepsilon\})=0\}.$$

Then we have the following lemma.

Lemma 6.2. *For each pair $(f,g)\in\mathscr{P}_{(\varepsilon)}\times\mathscr{P}_{(\varepsilon)}$, there exists a unique $F_{f,g}\in\mathbf{F}(f,g)$ such that $\mathfrak{E}(F_{f,g})=\mathfrak{e}(f,g)$. Moreover, the mapping Φ from $\mathscr{P}_{(\varepsilon)}\times\mathscr{P}_{(\varepsilon)}$ into the space $\mathscr{P}(\mathbf{R}^6)$ of probability distributions on $\mathbf{R}^6$, defined by $\Phi(f,g)=F_{f,g}$, is continuous.*

Proof. First we remark that

if $F\in\mathbf{F}(f,g)$ and $\mathfrak{E}(F)=\mathfrak{e}(f,g)$, then
$F(A\times B)=\int_B \delta_{\psi(x)}(A)\,g(dx)$ for any $A,B\in\mathscr{B}(R^3)$ with a
suitable Borel mapping ψ from $\mathbf{R}^3$ into itself, (6.2)

where $\delta_{\psi(x)}(\cdot)$ denotes the δ-distribution at $\psi(x)$. In fact, (6.2) was proved in [12: Theorem 1] in the special case when g is the Gaussian distribution with the same mean vector and variance matrix as those of f, and the proof in [12] is also adapted, without any change, to the more general case when g has a strictly positive density with respect to the Lebesgue measure. Next, assume that F_1 and F_2 are in $\mathbf{F}(f,g)$ and satisfy $\mathfrak{E}(F_1)=\mathfrak{E}(F_2)=\mathfrak{e}(f,g)$. Then, $F=(F_1+F_2)/2$ also belongs to $\mathbf{F}(f,g)$ and satisfies $\mathfrak{E}(F)=\mathfrak{e}(f,g)$, and so by (6.2)

$$\delta_{\psi(x)}(A)=\{\delta_{\psi_1(x)}(A)+\delta_{\psi_2(x)}(A)\}/2, \qquad g\text{-a.s.}$$

with some Borel mappings ψ, ψ_1 and ψ_2. But this formula clearly implies that $\psi=\psi_1=\psi_2$, g-a.s., and hence $F_1=F_2$. This proves the first half of the lemma. Finally, to prove the second half, we assume that $f_n\to f$ and $g_n\to g$ in $\mathscr{P}_{(\varepsilon)}$, and write $F_n=F_{f_n,g_n}$. Obviously $\{F_n\}$ is relatively compact in $\mathscr{P}(\mathbf{R}^6)$. Let F be any limit point of $\{F_n\}$. Then by (ii) of Lemma 6.1 we have

$$\mathfrak{e}(f,g)=\lim_{n\to\infty}\mathfrak{e}(f_n,g_n)=\lim_{n\to\infty}\mathfrak{E}(F_n)=\mathfrak{E}(F),$$

which implies that $F=F_{f,g}$ by the uniqueness part of the lemma, proving the continuity of Φ. Thus the proof of the lemma is finished.

Lemma 6.3. *Let $(\Omega,\mathscr{F},P)$ be an arbitrary probability space and suppose that we are given sub-families $\{f^\omega,\omega\in\Omega\}$ and $\{g^\omega,\omega\in\Omega\}$ of $\mathscr{P}_2$ satisfying the following conditions.*

(i) *For each $A\in\mathscr{B}(R^3)$, $f^\omega(A)$ and $g^\omega(A)$ are $\mathscr{F}$-measurable in ω.*

(ii) *The probability distributions $f=\int_\Omega f^\omega P(d\omega)$ and $g=\int_\Omega g^\omega P(d\omega)$ belong to $\mathscr{P}_2$.*

Then we have

$$\mathfrak{e}(f,g)\leqq E\{\mathfrak{e}(f^\omega,g^\omega)\}. \qquad (6.3)$$

Proof. For each $\varepsilon>0$ and $f\in\mathscr{P}_2$ let f_ε stand for the probability distribution $\tilde{f}*\mathfrak{g}_\varepsilon$, where $*$ denotes convolution and

$$\tilde{f}(A)=f(A\cap\{|x|\leqq 1/\varepsilon\})+f(\{|x|>1/\varepsilon\})\,\delta_0(A), \qquad A\in\mathscr{B}(\mathbf{R}^3).$$

Then we have $f_\varepsilon\to f$ as $\varepsilon\downarrow 0$, $\lim_{N\to\infty}\sup_{0<\varepsilon<1}\int_{|x|>N}|x|^2 f_\varepsilon(dx)=0$, and hence $\mathfrak{e}(f_\varepsilon,g_\varepsilon)\to\mathfrak{e}(f,g)$ as $\varepsilon\downarrow 0$ for any $f,g\in\mathscr{P}_2$ by (ii) of Lemma 6.1. Next, denote by F_ε^ω the unique probability distribution on $\mathbf{R}^6$ such that $F_\varepsilon^\omega\in\mathbf{F}(f_\varepsilon^\omega,g_\varepsilon^\omega)$ and $\mathfrak{E}(F_\varepsilon^\omega)=\mathfrak{e}(f_\varepsilon^\omega,g_\varepsilon^\omega)$. Since each mapping in

$$\omega\in\Omega\to(f^\omega,g^\omega)\in\mathscr{P}_2\times\mathscr{P}_2\to(f_\varepsilon^\omega,g_\varepsilon^\omega)\in\mathscr{P}_{(\varepsilon)}\times\mathscr{P}_{(\varepsilon)}\to F_\varepsilon^\omega\in\mathscr{P}(\mathbf{R}^6)$$

is measurable (the last mapping is continuous and hence Borel measurable according to the preceeding lemma), F_ε^ω is also measurable in ω. Therefore $\mathfrak{E}(F_\varepsilon^\omega)\equiv\mathfrak{e}(f_\varepsilon^\omega,g_\varepsilon^\omega)$ is $\mathscr{F}$-measurable in ω, and it follows that

$$\lim_{\varepsilon\downarrow 0}E\{\mathfrak{e}(f_\varepsilon^\omega,g_\varepsilon^\omega)\}=E\{\mathfrak{e}(f^\omega,g^\omega)\}, \tag{6.4}$$

because the integrand $\mathfrak{e}(f_\varepsilon^\omega,g_\varepsilon^\omega)$ is dominated by $2\int|x|^2 f^\omega(dx)+2\int|x|^2 g^\omega(dx)$ which is P-integrable by the assumption (ii) of the lemma. On the other hand, $F_\varepsilon=\int_\Omega F_\varepsilon^\omega\,P(d\omega)$ clearly belongs to $\mathbf{F}(f_\varepsilon,g_\varepsilon)$ and hence we have

$$\mathfrak{e}(f_\varepsilon,g_\varepsilon)\leqq\mathfrak{E}(F_\varepsilon)=\int_\Omega\mathfrak{E}(F_\varepsilon^\omega)\,P(d\omega)=E\{\mathfrak{e}(f_\varepsilon^\omega,g_\varepsilon^\omega)\}.$$

Now letting $\varepsilon\downarrow 0$ in the above and then noting (6.4), we obtain (6.3).

To state the last lemma of this section, let us denote by $C_{x,r,l}$ the circle with center $x\,(\in\mathbf{R}^3)$, of radius r and lying on a plane which is perpendicular to a unit vector l. Also we denote by $U_{x,r,l}$ the uniform distribution on $C_{x,r,l}$; this can be regarded as a probability distribution on $\mathbf{R}^3$ and so $U_{x,r,l}\in\mathscr{P}_2$.

Lemma 6.4. *For any $x,y\in\mathbf{R}^3$, $r,s>0$ and unit vectors l and m, we have*

$$\mathfrak{e}(U_{x,r,l},U_{y,s,m})\leqq|x-y|^2+r^2+s^2-rs\{1+|(l,m)|\}.$$

Proof. In proving the lemma, without loss of generality we may assume that $x=0$, $l=(0,0,1)$ and $m=(0,-\sin\gamma,\cos\gamma)$ with $0\leqq\gamma\leqq\pi/2$. Let $\Omega=[0,2\pi)$, P be the Lebesgue measure in $[0,2\pi)$ multiplied by $1/2\pi$ and put

$$X(\omega)=(r\cos\omega,\ r\sin\omega,\ 0),$$

$$Y(\omega)=y+(s\cos\omega,\ s\sin\omega\cos\gamma,\ s\sin\omega\sin\gamma), \qquad \omega\in\Omega.$$

Then X and Y are random variables that are uniformly distributed on $C_{x,r,l}$ and $C_{y,s,m}$, respectively. Therefore,

$$\mathfrak{e}(U_{x,r,l},U_{y,s,m})\leqq E\{|X-Y|^2\}=\frac{1}{2\pi}\int_0^{2\pi}|X(\omega)-Y(\omega)|^2\,d\omega.$$

By elementary calculations we see that the last term is equal to

$$|y|^2+r^2+s^2-rs(1+\cos\gamma),$$

completing the proof.

§ 7. Non-expansive Property of the Associated Nonlinear Semigroup with Respect to the Metric ρ

Let $\mathbf{X}=\{X_t, P_f, f\in\mathscr{P}_1\}$ be the Markov process associated with (0.3). We associate with each $t\geqq 0$ and $f\in\mathscr{P}_1$ the probability distribution $T_t f$ on $\mathbf{R}^3$ defined by

$$(T_t f)(A)=P_f\{X_t\in A\}, \qquad A\in\mathscr{B}(\mathbf{R}^3).$$

Then, the Markovian property of $\mathbf{X}$ implies the semigroup property of $\{T_t\}$, that is,

$$T_{t+s}f=T_t T_s f, \qquad t,s\geqq 0,\ f\in\mathscr{P}_1.$$

Since $f\in\mathscr{P}_2$ implies $T_t f\in\mathscr{P}_2$ by Theorem 4.4, $\{T_t\}$ is also a nonlinear semigroup on $\mathscr{P}_2$. The purpose of this section is to prove that T_t is non-expansive with respect to the metric ρ on $\mathscr{P}_2$.

First we prepare a lemma of an approximation type. Namely, we prove that the Markov process associated with (0.3) can be approximated in an appropriate sense by the one associated with

$$\frac{d}{dt}\langle u,\xi\rangle=\langle u\otimes u, K_\varepsilon\xi\rangle, \qquad \xi\in C_0^\infty(\mathbf{R}^3) \tag{7.1}$$

for small $\varepsilon>0$, where $K_\varepsilon\xi$ is defined by (0.4) with the replacement of $Q(d\theta)$ by $Q_\varepsilon(d\theta)\equiv\mathbb{1}_{(\varepsilon,\pi)}(\theta)\,Q(d\theta)$. As in § 4, we take an $\{\mathscr{F}_t\}$-adapted Poisson random measure $\{N(dt\,d\sigma)\}$ corresponding to the measure λ. Then the Markov process associated with (7.1) can be obtained by the family of solutions of

$$dX(t)=a_\varepsilon(X(t-), Y(t-), \theta, \varphi)\,dN, \tag{7.2}$$

where $a_\varepsilon(x,x_1,\theta,\varphi)=\mathbb{1}_{(\varepsilon,\pi)}(\theta)\,a(x,x_1,\theta,\varphi)$ and $\{Y(t)\}$ is an α-process which is required to be equivalent in law to the $\{\mathscr{F}_t\}$-adapted solution $\{X(t)\}$ as in the case of (4.1). We denote by $T_t^{(\varepsilon)}f$ the probability distribution of the solution, at time t, of (7.2) with initial distribution $f\in\mathscr{P}_1$.

The proof of the following lemma is slightly complicated, but it can be done in a manner similar to that of Lemma 4.1 and so is omitted.

Lemma 7.1. *Let T be any positive number, Δ a partition of the interval $[0,T]$ given by (4.5) and define a process $\{X_\Delta(t), 0\leqq t\leqq T\}$ by (4.6). Also for a given $\varepsilon\in(0,\pi)$ define a process $\{X_\Delta^\varepsilon(t), 0\leqq t\leqq T\}$ by*

$$X_\Delta^\varepsilon(0)=X$$

$$X_\Delta^\varepsilon(t)=X_\Delta^\varepsilon(t_k)+\sum_{t_k<s\leqq t} a_\varepsilon(X_\Delta^\varepsilon(t_k), Y_k^\varepsilon, p(s)) \quad \text{for } t_k<t<t_{k+1}\ (0\leqq k<n),$$

where $Y_0^\varepsilon, \ldots, Y_{n-1}^\varepsilon$ *are* α*-random variables defined in each step so that* Y_k^ε *has the same probability law as* $X_\Delta^\varepsilon(t_k)$. *Then, if* $E\{|X|^2\} < \infty$, *we can construct two processes* $\{\tilde{X}_\Delta(t), 0 \leqq t \leqq T\}$ *and* $\{\tilde{X}_\Delta^\varepsilon(t), 0 \leqq t \leqq T\}$ *in such a way that they are equivalent in law to* $\{X_\Delta(t), 0 \leqq t \leqq T\}$ *and* $\{X_\Delta^\varepsilon(t), 0 \leqq t \leqq T\}$ *respectively and satisfy*

$$E\{|\tilde{X}_\Delta(t) - \tilde{X}_\Delta^\varepsilon(t)|^2\} \leqq const \int_0^\varepsilon \theta Q(d\theta).$$

Here, const depends on T but neither on ε *nor on* Δ.

The following approximation lemma is an immediate consequence of the above and Lemma 4.4

Lemma 7.2. (i) *Let T be a positive number,* $\varepsilon \in (0, \pi)$ *and* $f \in \mathscr{P}_2$. *Then, on a suitable probability space* $(\tilde{\Omega}, \tilde{\mathscr{F}}, \tilde{P})$ *we can construct two processes* $\{\tilde{X}(t), 0 \leqq t \leqq T\}$ *and* $\{\tilde{X}^\varepsilon(t), 0 \leqq t \leqq T\}$ *in such a way that they are equivalent in law to solutions of* (4.1) *and* (7.2), *respectively, with initial distribution f and satisfy*

$$\tilde{E}\{|\tilde{X}(t) - \tilde{X}^\varepsilon(t)|^2\} \leqq const \int_0^\varepsilon \theta Q(d\theta)$$

with const depending on T but not on ε.

(ii) $\rho(T_t f, T_t^{(\varepsilon)} f) \to 0$ *as* $\varepsilon \downarrow 0$ *for each* $t \geqq 0$ *and* $f \in \mathscr{P}_2$.

Before stating the theorem of this section, we introduce some notations. For each $\theta \in (0, \pi)$ and $x, x_1 \in \mathbf{R}^3$, we put

$$\Pi_{x, x_1, \theta} = U_{z, r, l} = \text{the uniform distribution on } C_{z, r, l},$$

where $z = \{x + x_1 + (x - x_1)\cos\theta\}/2$, $r = |x - x_1|(\sin\theta)/2$ and $l = (x - x_1)/|x - x_1|$, and regard $\Pi_{x, x_1, \theta}$ as a probability distribution on $\mathbf{R}^3$. For any probability distributions f, g on $\mathbf{R}^3$ and $\theta \in (0, \pi)$, we define another probability distribution $(f \circ g)_\theta$ on $\mathbf{R}^3$ by

$$(f \circ g)_\theta(A) = \int_{\mathbf{R}^3 \times \mathbf{R}^3} \Pi_{x, x_1, \theta}(A) f(dx) g(dx_1), \qquad A \in \mathscr{B}(\mathbf{R}^3).$$

Obviously

$$\langle (f \circ g)_\theta, \xi \rangle = \int_{(0, 2\pi) \times \mathbf{R}^3 \times \mathbf{R}^3} \xi(x') d\varphi f(dx) g(dx_1), \qquad \xi \in C_0^\infty(\mathbf{R}^3),$$

and hence $(f \circ g)_\theta \in \mathscr{P}_2$ provided $f, g \in \mathscr{P}_2$. We write $[f]_\theta = (f \circ f)_\theta$ for short, and put

$$\bar{\mathfrak{e}}_\theta(f, g) = \mathfrak{e}(f, g) - \mathfrak{e}([f]_\theta, [g]_\theta).$$

Theorem 7.1. *For each* $t \geqq 0$ T_t *is non-expansive on* $\mathscr{P}_2$ *with respect to the metric* ρ, *that is,*

$$\rho(T_t f, T_t g) \leqq \rho(f, g), \qquad f, g \in \mathscr{P}_2.$$

More precisely, for any $f, g \in \mathscr{P}_2$ we have

$$\bar{\mathrm{e}}_\theta(f, g) \geqq 0, \tag{7.3}$$

$$\mathrm{e}(T_t f, T_t g) \leqq \mathrm{e}(f, g) - 2\pi \int_0^t ds \int_0^\pi \bar{\mathrm{e}}_\theta(T_s f, T_s g)\, Q(d\theta). \tag{7.4}$$

Our discussions are devided into two cases according whether

$$\int_0^\pi Q(d\theta) < \infty \qquad \text{or} \quad = \infty.$$

Case I. First we discuss the special case in which $q \equiv 2\pi \int_0^\pi Q(d\theta) < \infty$. In this case, for each pair of probability distributions f and g on $\mathbf{R}^3$ we can define a probability distribution $f \circ g$ on $\mathbf{R}^3$ by

$$f \circ g = (2\pi/q) \int_0^\pi (f \circ g)_\theta\, Q(d\theta).$$

With this notation the equation (0.3) is equivalent to

$$\frac{d}{dt}\langle u, \xi\rangle = \langle q(u \circ u - u), \xi\rangle, \qquad \xi \in C_0^\infty(\mathbf{R}^3). \tag{7.5}$$

A unique (probability) solution $u(t)$ of (7.5) for any given initial distribution f can be obtained by a method of iteration, and the solution is explicitly expressed by the so-called Wild sum ([21]):

$$u(t) = e^{-qt} \sum_{n=1}^\infty (1 - e^{-qt})^{n-1} f^{(n)}.$$

Here $f^{(n)}$, $n \geqq 1$, are probability measures on $\mathbf{R}^3$ defined inductively by

$$f^{(1)} = f,$$

$$f^{(n)} = \frac{1}{n-1} \sum_{k=1}^{n-1} f^{(k)} \circ f^{(n-k)}, \qquad n > 1.$$

On the other hand, from what we have proved in Chapter I we know that $T_t f$ is also a solution of (7.5) with initial distribution f, at least if $f \in \mathscr{P}_1$. Therefore, we have

$$T_t f = e^{-qt} \sum_{n=1}^\infty (1 - e^{-qt})^{n-1} f^{(n)}, \qquad f \in \mathscr{P}_1.$$

The proof of the theorem in Case I will be based on the above Wild sum and the following three lemmas.

Lemma 7.3.

$$\mathrm{e}(\Pi_{x, x_1, \theta}, \Pi_{y, y_1, \theta}) \leqq \Phi_\theta(x, x_1, y, y_1),$$

where

$$\Phi_\theta(x,x_1,y,y_1)=\left|\frac{1+\cos\theta}{2}(x-y)+\frac{1-\cos\theta}{2}(x_1-y_1)\right|^2$$
$$+\frac{\sin^2\theta}{4}\{|x-x_1|^2+|y-y_1|^2-|x-x_1||y-y_1|-|(x-x_1,y-y_1)|\}.$$

Proof. It is enough to apply Lemma 6.4 with the replacements:

$$x\to\{x+x_1+(x-x_1)\cos\theta\}/2,\qquad y\to\{y+y_1+(y-y_1)\cos\theta\}/2,$$
$$r\to|x-x_1|(\sin\theta)/2,\qquad s\to|y-y_1|(\sin\theta)/2,$$
$$l\to(x-x_1)/|x-x_1|,\qquad m\to(y-y_1)/|y-y_1|.$$

Lemma 7.4. *Let f_1, f_2, g_1 and g_2 belong to $\mathscr{P}_2$. Then we have the following inequalities.*

(i) $\mathfrak{e}[(f_1\circ f_2)_\theta,(g_1\circ g_2)_\theta]\leqq\frac{1+\cos\theta}{2}\mathfrak{e}(f_1,g_1)+\frac{1-\cos\theta}{2}\mathfrak{e}(f_2,g_2),\qquad \theta\in(0,\pi).$

(ii) $\mathfrak{e}(f_1\circ f_2,g_1\circ g_2)\leqq\gamma\,\mathfrak{e}(f_1,g_1)+(1-\gamma)\,\mathfrak{e}(f_2,g_2),$ *where*

$$\gamma=(2\pi/q)\int_0^\pi 2^{-1}(1+\cos\theta)\,Q(d\theta).$$

Proof. We choose two pairs $\{X_1, Y_1\}$ and $\{X_2, Y_2\}$ of random variables so that they satisfy the following three conditions.

(a) $E\{|X_1-Y_1|^2\}=\mathfrak{e}(f_1,g_1),\quad E\{|X_2-Y_2|^2\}=\mathfrak{e}(f_2,g_2).$

(b) For $i=1,2$, X_i is f_i-distributed while Y_i is g_i-distributed.

(c) $\{X_1, Y_1\}$ and $\{X_2, Y_2\}$ are independent.

Then we have

$$(f_1\circ f_2)_\theta=E\{\Pi_{X_1,X_2,\theta}\},\qquad (g_1\circ g_2)_\theta=E\{\Pi_{Y_1,Y_2,\theta}\},$$

and hence by Lemma 6.3 and 7.3

$$\begin{aligned}&\mathfrak{e}[(f_1\circ f_2)_\theta,(g_1\circ g_2)_\theta]\\&\quad\leqq E\{\mathfrak{e}(\Pi_{X_1,X_2,\theta},\Pi_{Y_1,Y_2,\theta})\}\leqq E\{\Phi_\theta(X_1,X_2,Y_1,Y_2)\}\\&\quad=E\left\{\left|\frac{1+\cos\theta}{2}(X_1-Y_1)+\frac{1-\cos\theta}{2}(X_2-Y_2)\right|^2\right\}\\&\quad\quad+\frac{\sin^2\theta}{4}E\{|X_1-X_2|^2+|Y_1-Y_2|^2-|X_1-X_2||Y_1-Y_2|\\&\quad\quad\quad-|(X_1-X_2,Y_1-Y_2)|\}.\end{aligned}$$

We now use the inequality

$$(X_1-X_2,Y_1-Y_2)\leqq|X_1-X_2||Y_1-Y_2| \tag{7.6}$$

to obtain

$$\begin{aligned}
&\mathrm{e}[(f_1\circ f_2)_\theta,(g_1\circ g_2)_\theta]\\
&\leqq E\left\{\left|\frac{1+\cos\theta}{2}(X_1-Y_1)+\frac{1-\cos\theta}{2}(X_2-Y_2)\right|^2\right\}\\
&\quad+\frac{\sin^2\theta}{4}E\{|X_1-X_2|^2+|Y_1-Y_2|^2-2(X_1-X_2,Y_1-Y_2)\}\\
&=\frac{(1+\cos\theta)^2}{4}E\{|X_1-Y_1|^2\}+\frac{(1-\cos\theta)^2}{4}E\{|X_2-Y_2|^2\}\\
&\quad+\frac{\sin^2\theta}{4}E\{|X_1-Y_1|^2\}+\frac{\sin^2\theta}{4}E\{|X_2-Y_2|^2\}\\
&=\frac{1+\cos\theta}{2}\mathrm{e}(f_1,g_1)+\frac{1-\cos\theta}{2}\mathrm{e}(f_2,g_2).
\end{aligned}$$

This proves (i), and (ii) follows from (i) and Lemma 6.3. The proof of the lemma is finished.

Lemma 7.5. *For any f and g in $\mathscr{P}_2$, we have*

$$\mathrm{e}(f^{(n)},g^{(n)})\leqq \mathrm{e}(f,g),\qquad n\geqq 1. \tag{7.7}$$

Proof. Since (7.7) is evident for $n=1$, it is enough to prove that (7.7) holds for $n=m$ assuming that it holds for $n<m$. Making use of Lemma 6.3 first and then (ii) of Lemma 7.4, we have

$$\begin{aligned}
\mathrm{e}(f^{(m)},g^{(m)})&=\mathrm{e}\left(\frac{1}{m-1}\sum_{k=1}^{m-1}f^{(k)}\circ f^{(m-k)},\frac{1}{m-1}\sum_{k=1}^{m-1}g^{(k)}\circ g^{(m-k)}\right)\\
&\leqq\frac{1}{m-1}\sum_{k=1}^{m-1}\mathrm{e}(f^{(k)}\circ f^{(m-k)},g^{(k)}\circ g^{(m-k)})\\
&\leqq\frac{1}{m-1}\sum_{k=1}^{m-1}\{\gamma\,\mathrm{e}(f^{(k)},g^{(k)})+(1-\gamma)\,\mathrm{e}(f^{(m-k)},g^{(m-k)})\}\\
&\leqq\mathrm{e}(f,g),
\end{aligned}$$

as was to be proved.

Now the proof of the theorem in *Case I* is completed as follows. (7.3) is immediate from (i) of Lemma 7.4. To prove (7.4), we notice that

$$T_{t+s}f=e^{-qs}\sum_{n=1}^{\infty}(1-e^{-qs})^{n-1}(T_tf)^{(n)},$$

$$T_{t+s}g=e^{-qs}\sum_{n=1}^{\infty}(1-e^{-qs})^{n-1}(T_tg)^{(n)},$$

and then apply Lemma 6.3 and 7.5. The result is

$$\begin{aligned}&\mathfrak{e}(T_{t+s}f, T_{t+s}g)\\&\quad\leqq e^{-qs}\,\mathfrak{e}(T_t f, T_t g)+e^{-qs}(1-e^{-qs})\,\mathfrak{e}[(T_t f)^{(2)}, (T_t g)^{(2)}]\\&\qquad+(1-2e^{-qs}+e^{-2qs})\,\mathfrak{e}(T_t f, T_t g),\end{aligned}$$

and hence

$$\begin{aligned}&\overline{\lim_{s\downarrow 0}}\,\{\mathfrak{e}(T_{t+s}f, T_{t+s}g)-\mathfrak{e}(T_t f, T_t g)\}/s\\&\quad\leqq -q\,\{\mathfrak{e}(T_t f, T_t g)-\mathfrak{e}[(T_t f)^{(2)}, (T_t g)^{(2)}]\}\\&\quad\leqq -q(2\pi/q)\int_0^\pi \{\mathfrak{e}(T_t f, T_t g)-\mathfrak{e}[[T_t f]_\theta, [T_t g]_\theta]\}\,Q(d\theta)\\&\quad= -2\pi\int_0^\pi \bar{\mathfrak{e}}_\theta(T_t f, T_t g)\,Q(d\theta).\end{aligned}$$

The inequality (7.4) now follows from the above, since $\mathfrak{e}(T_t f, T_t g)$ is continuous in t. The proof in *Case I* is finished.

Case II. We deal with the case when $\int_0^\pi Q(d\theta)=\infty$. For each $\varepsilon\in(0,\pi)$, the result in *Case I* is applicable to the semigroup $\{T_t^{(\varepsilon)}\}$ which is associated with $Q_\varepsilon(d\theta)$, and hence

$$\mathfrak{e}(T_t^{(\varepsilon)}f, T_t^{(\varepsilon)}g)\leqq \mathfrak{e}(f,g)-2\pi\int_0^t ds\int_\varepsilon^\pi \bar{\mathfrak{e}}_\theta(T_s^{(\varepsilon)}f, T_s^{(\varepsilon)}g)\,Q(d\theta). \tag{7.8}$$

On the other hand, making use of (i) of Lemma 7.4 and (ii) of Lemma 7.2, we have $\rho[[T_s^{(\varepsilon)}f]_\theta, [T_s f]_\theta]\leqq\rho(T_s^{(\varepsilon)}f, T_s f)\to 0$ as $\varepsilon\downarrow 0$ and hence

$$\rho[[T_s^{(\varepsilon)}f]_\theta, [T_s^{(\varepsilon)}g]_\theta]\to\rho[[T_s f]_\theta, [T_s g]_\theta], \qquad \varepsilon\downarrow 0.$$

Therefore we have $\bar{\mathfrak{e}}_\theta(T_s^{(\varepsilon)}f, T_s^{(\varepsilon)}g)\to\bar{\mathfrak{e}}_\theta(T_s f, T_s g)$ as $\varepsilon\downarrow 0$, the convergence being bounded. Now, letting $\varepsilon\downarrow 0$ in (7.8) we obtain (7.4). Thus the proof of the theorem is completed.

§ 8. Theorem of Ikenberry and Truesdell on Time Evolution of Moments

The result on the time evolution of the moments for solutions to Boltzmann's equation of Maxwellian molecules goes back to Ikenberry and Truesdell [4]. In [4], however, the existence of solutions of the Boltzmann equation is not discussed rigorously. Here we state and prove the theorem of Ikenberry and Truesdell in our setting, for completeness. We state also a corollary; this will be useful in the next section where a more precise result on the trend to equilibrium will be obtained in connection with our metric ρ.

The method of [4] is to use harmonic polynomials. For each $k\geqq 0$ we choose $2k+1$ linearly independent (homogeneous) harmonic polynomials $\{\xi_k^l(x)\}_{|l|\leqq k}$ of degree k in $\mathbf{R}^3$ and put

$$\xi_{\mathbf{n}}(x)=|x|^{2r}\,\xi_k^l(x) \qquad \text{for } \mathbf{n}=(r,k,l),$$
$$\xi_{(0,0,0)}(x)=1,$$

where $r=0,1,\ldots,k=0,1,\ldots$, and $|l|\leqq k$. The degree of $\xi_{\mathbf{n}}$ is $|\mathbf{n}|=2r+k$. Then it is well-known that any homogeneous polynomial of x with degree n can be expressed by a linear combination of $\xi_{\mathbf{n}}(x)$ with $|\mathbf{n}|=n$, and therefore when dealing with moments of a probability distribution f on $\mathbf{R}^3$ it is sufficient to consider only the (harmonic) moments $\mu_{\mathbf{n}}(f)\equiv\langle f,\xi_{\mathbf{n}}\rangle$.

Lemma 8.1. (i) *Let $h(x)$, $|x|=1$, be a spherical harmonic of degree k and y be a unit vector in $\mathbf{R}^3$. On the unit sphere $S^2=\{|x|=1\}$ we take a spherical coordinate system with polar axis y, and denote by γ and ψ the colatitude and the longitude, respectively, of a point $x\in S^2$. Then*

$$\int_0^{2\pi} h(x)\,d\psi=2\pi\,P_k(\cos\gamma)\,h(y), \tag{8.1}$$

where P_k denotes the Legendre polynomial of degree k.

(ii) *If $\xi(x)$ is a (homogeneous) harmonic polynomial of degree k, then*

$$\langle \Pi_{x,-x,\theta},\xi\rangle=P_k(\cos\theta)\,\xi(x).$$

Proof. (i) is known as the mean value theorem for spherical harmonics; for the proof it is enough to check (8.1) for each h in the list

$$\begin{aligned}&P_k(\cos\gamma)\\&P_k^{(m)}(\cos\gamma)\sin^m\gamma\cos m\psi\\&P_k^{(m)}(\cos\gamma)\sin^m\gamma\sin m\psi, \qquad m=1,\ldots,k,\end{aligned} \tag{8.2}$$

because (8.2) forms a basis for the vector space of spherical harmonics of degree k ([3]). (ii) follows from (i), since ξ can be expressed as $\xi(x)=|x|^k h(x/|x|)$, $x\in\mathbf{R}^3$, with some spherical harmonic h of degree k.

Theorem 8.1 (Ikenberry and Truesdell [4]). *Given a probability distribution f on $\mathbf{R}^3$ with $\int|x|^\nu f(dx)<\infty$ for some integer $\nu\geqq 1$, we put $\mu_{\mathbf{n}}(t)=\mu_{\mathbf{n}}(T_t f)$ for $\mathbf{n}$ such that $|\mathbf{n}|\leqq\nu$. Then, for any $\mathbf{n}$ with $|\mathbf{n}|\leqq\nu$ we have*

$$\frac{d}{dt}\mu_{\mathbf{n}}(t)=\sum{}'\,\beta^{\mathbf{n}}_{\mathbf{n}_1,\mathbf{n}_2}\,\mu_{\mathbf{n}_1}(t)\,\mu_{\mathbf{n}_2}(t)-\beta_{\mathbf{n}}\mu_{\mathbf{n}}(t), \tag{8.3}$$

where $\sum'$ means the summation taken over all pairs $(\mathbf{n}_1,\mathbf{n}_2)$ satisfying $|\mathbf{n}_1|+|\mathbf{n}_2|=|\mathbf{n}|$ and $|\mathbf{n}_1|,|\mathbf{n}_2|\geqq 1$. $\beta_{\mathbf{n}}$ is given by

$$\beta_{\mathbf{n}}=2\pi\int_0^{\pi}\left\{1-\left(\cos\frac{\theta}{2}\right)^{|\mathbf{n}|}P_k\left(\cos\frac{\theta}{2}\right)-\left(\sin\frac{\theta}{2}\right)^{|\mathbf{n}|}P_k\left(\sin\frac{\theta}{2}\right)\right\}Q(d\theta)>0,$$

and $\beta^{\mathbf{n}}_{\mathbf{n}_1,\mathbf{n}_2}$ are also some constants.

Proof. The proof will be given in four steps.

Step 1. We prove that

$$\langle \Pi_{x,\,0,\,\theta}, \xi_{\mathbf{n}} \rangle = \left(\cos\frac{\theta}{2}\right)^{|\mathbf{n}|} P_k\left(\cos\frac{\theta}{2}\right)\xi_{\mathbf{n}}(x), \qquad \mathbf{n} = (r, k, l).$$

In fact, from the relation $\Pi_{x,0,\theta} = \Pi_{x\cos(\theta/2),\, -x\cos(\theta/2),\, \theta/2}$ it follows that

$$\begin{aligned}\langle \Pi_{x,0,\theta}, \xi_{\mathbf{n}} \rangle &= \langle \Pi_{x\cos(\theta/2),\, -x\cos(\theta/2),\, \theta/2}, \xi_{\mathbf{n}} \rangle \\ &= |x|^{2r}\left(\cos\frac{\theta}{2}\right)^{2r} \langle \Pi_{x\cos(\theta/2),\, -x\cos(\theta/2),\, \theta/2}, \xi_k^l \rangle \\ &= \left(\cos\frac{\theta}{2}\right)^{|\mathbf{n}|} P_k\left(\cos\frac{\theta}{2}\right)\xi_{\mathbf{n}}(x).\end{aligned}$$

Step 2 is to prove that

$$\begin{aligned}K_{\mathbf{n}}(x, y) &\equiv 2\pi \int_0^\pi \{\langle \Pi_{x,\,y,\,\theta}, \xi_{\mathbf{n}} \rangle - \xi_{\mathbf{n}}(x)\}\, Q(d\theta) \\ &= (K\xi_{\mathbf{n}})(x, y)\end{aligned}$$

is a homogeneous polynomial in x and y of degree $|\mathbf{n}|$. Since we can write $\xi_{\mathbf{n}}(y+x) = \sum_i \eta_i(x)\,\zeta_i\, y)$, where η_i and ζ_i are homogeneous polynomials of degree m_i and n_i, respectively, with $m_i + n_i = |\mathbf{n}|$, we have

$$\begin{aligned}\langle \Pi_{x,y,\theta}, \xi_{\mathbf{n}} \rangle &= \langle \Pi_{x-y,\,0,\,\theta}, \xi_{\mathbf{n}}(y+\cdot) \rangle \\ &= \sum_i \zeta_i(y) \langle \Pi_{x-y,\,0,\,\theta}, \eta_i \rangle.\end{aligned}$$

On the other hand, η_i can be expressed as

$$\eta_i = \sum_{|\mathbf{m}| = m_i} c^i_{\mathbf{m}}\, \xi_{\mathbf{m}}, \qquad \mathbf{m} = (s, j, l'),$$

and hence from Step 1 we have

$$\langle \Pi_{x,\,y,\,\theta}, \xi_{\mathbf{n}} \rangle = \sum_i \zeta_i(y) \sum_{|\mathbf{m}| = m_i} c^i_{\mathbf{m}} \left(\cos\frac{\theta}{2}\right)^{m_i} P_j\left(\cos\frac{\theta}{2}\right)\xi_{\mathbf{m}}(x-y).$$

Therefore

$$\begin{aligned}&\langle \Pi_{x,\,y,\,\theta}, \xi_{\mathbf{n}} \rangle - \xi_{\mathbf{n}}(x) \\ &\quad = \sum_i \sum_{|\mathbf{m}| = m_i} \left\{\left(\cos\frac{\theta}{2}\right)^{m_i} P_j\left(\cos\frac{\theta}{2}\right) - 1\right\} c^i_{\mathbf{m}}\, \zeta_i(y)\, \xi_{\mathbf{m}}(x-y).\end{aligned}$$

This is a homogeneous polynomial in x and y of degree $|\mathbf{n}|$ with coefficients depending upon θ in such a way that they are $O(\theta)$ as $\theta \downarrow 0$. Thus $K_{\mathbf{n}}(x, y)$ is a homogeneous polynomial in x and y of degree $|\mathbf{n}|$.

Step 3 is to prove that

$$K_{\mathbf{n}}(x,0)=-\beta'_{\mathbf{n}}\,\xi_{\mathbf{n}}(x),\qquad K_{\mathbf{n}}(0,y)=-\beta''_{\mathbf{n}}\,\xi_{\mathbf{n}}(y) \tag{8.4}$$

where

$$\beta'_{\mathbf{n}}=2\pi\int_0^\pi\left\{1-\left(\cos\frac{\theta}{2}\right)^{|\mathbf{n}|}P_k\left(\cos\frac{\theta}{2}\right)\right\}Q(d\theta),$$

$$\beta''_{\mathbf{n}}=-2\pi\int_0^\pi\left(\sin\frac{\theta}{2}\right)^{|\mathbf{n}|}P_k\left(\sin\frac{\theta}{2}\right)Q(d\theta),\qquad \mathbf{n}=(r,k,l).$$

In fact, the first expression of (8.4) follows immediately from Step 1. As for the second, noting $\Pi_{0,y,\theta}=\Pi_{y,0,\pi-\theta}$ and then using the result of Step 1 we have

$$\begin{aligned}\langle\Pi_{0,y,\theta},\xi_{\mathbf{n}}\rangle&=\langle\Pi_{y,0,\pi-\theta},\xi_{\mathbf{n}}\rangle\\&=\left(\cos\frac{\pi-\theta}{2}\right)^{|\mathbf{n}|}P_k\left(\cos\frac{\pi-\theta}{2}\right)\xi_{\mathbf{n}}(y)\\&=\left(\sin\frac{\theta}{2}\right)^{|\mathbf{n}|}P_k\left(\sin\frac{\theta}{2}\right)\xi_{\mathbf{n}}(y).\end{aligned}$$

This implies the second expression of (8.4).

Step 4. If we set $J_{\mathbf{n}}(x,y)=K_{\mathbf{n}}(x,y)-K_{\mathbf{n}}(x,0)-K_{\mathbf{n}}(0,y)$, then by Step 2 the polynomial $J_{\mathbf{n}}(x,y)$ consists only of those terms which have at least degree 1 in x as well as in y, and therefore it can be expressed as

$$J_{\mathbf{n}}(x,y)=\sum{}'\,\beta^{\mathbf{n}}_{\mathbf{n}_1,\mathbf{n}_2}\,\xi_{\mathbf{n}_1}(x)\,\xi_{\mathbf{n}_2}(y).$$

Now, keeping in mind the moment estimate (4.30), we obtain

$$\begin{aligned}\frac{d}{dt}\mu_{\mathbf{n}}(t)&=\langle(T_tf)\otimes(T_tf),K_{\mathbf{n}}(x,y)\rangle\\&=\langle(T_tf)\otimes(T_tf),J_{\mathbf{n}}(x,y)\rangle\\&\quad+\langle(T_tf)\otimes(T_tf),K_{\mathbf{n}}(x,0)+K_{\mathbf{n}}(0,y)\rangle\\&=\sum{}'\,\beta^{\mathbf{n}}_{\mathbf{n}_1,\mathbf{n}_2}\mu_{\mathbf{n}_1}(t)\,\mu_{\mathbf{n}_2}(t)-\beta_{\mathbf{n}}\mu_{\mathbf{n}}(t),\end{aligned}$$

where $\beta_{\mathbf{n}}=\beta'_{\mathbf{n}}+\beta''_{\mathbf{n}}$. This completes the proof of the theorem.

It should be noticed that, in the right hand side of (8.3), there appear only the moments of degree less than $|\mathbf{n}|$ except for $\mu_{\mathbf{n}}(t)$ and that the coefficient $\beta_{\mathbf{n}}$ of $\mu_{\mathbf{n}}(t)$ is positive (we exclude the trivial case $Q\equiv 0$). As a consequence we have the following corollary which is also found in [4].

Corollary. *Let f be a probability distribution on $\mathbf{R}^3$ with finite absolute moments of all degrees, and assume that*

$$\int|x-m|^2f(dx)=3v>0,\qquad m=\int xf(dx). \tag{8.5}$$

Let $\mathfrak{g}$ be the Gaussian distribution

$$(2\pi v)^{-3/2}\exp(-|x-m|^2/2v)\,dx \tag{8.6}$$

and put $\mu_{\mathbf{n}} = \mu_{\mathbf{n}}(\mathfrak{g})$. *Then, for each* $\mathbf{n}$

$$\mu_{\mathbf{n}}(t) \text{ converges to } \mu_{\mathbf{n}} \text{ exponentially fast as } t \to \infty. \tag{8.7}$$

In particular, $T_t f$ *converges to* $\mathfrak{g}$ *as* $t \to \infty$.

Proof. Clearly (8.7) holds for $|\mathbf{n}|=0$ and 1 (the case of $|\mathbf{n}|=1$ is nothing but (4.31)). So we assume that (8.7) holds for $0 \leqq |\mathbf{n}| < k$ and prove it for $|\mathbf{n}|=k$. First we notice that $\mathfrak{g}$ is invariant under T_t (see **2** of Appendix). This implies

$$\sum{}' \beta^{\mathbf{n}}_{\mathbf{n}_1, \mathbf{n}_2} \mu_{\mathbf{n}_1} \mu_{\mathbf{n}_2} - \beta_{\mathbf{n}} \mu_{\mathbf{n}} = 0. \tag{8.8}$$

For any $\mathbf{n}$ with $|\mathbf{n}|=k$ we put $\bar{\mu}_{\mathbf{n}}(t) = \sum' \beta^{\mathbf{n}}_{\mathbf{n}_1, \mathbf{n}_2} \mu_{\mathbf{n}_1}(t) \mu_{\mathbf{n}_2}(t)$. Then the induction hypothesis implies that $\bar{\mu}_{\mathbf{n}}(t)$ converges, exponentially fast as $t \to \infty$, to $\sum' \beta^{\mathbf{n}}_{\mathbf{n}_1, \mathbf{n}_2} \mu_{\mathbf{n}_1} \mu_{\mathbf{n}_2}$ which is equal to $\beta_{\mathbf{n}} \mu_{\mathbf{n}}$ by (8.8). This fact combined with (8.3) implies that

$$\mu_{\mathbf{n}}(t) = e^{-\beta_{\mathbf{n}} t} \mu_{\mathbf{n}}(0) + \int_0^t e^{-\beta_{\mathbf{n}}(t-s)} \bar{\mu}_{\mathbf{n}}(s)\, ds \to \mu_{\mathbf{n}}, \qquad \text{exponentially fast as } t \to \infty.$$

So the proof is finished.

§ 9. Proof of the Trend to Equilibrium

In this section we make use of the results of § 7 to prove the trend to equilibrium without assuming the existence of higher absolute moments. Fundamentally, our theorem is an extension of the result [17] in Kac's one-dimensional model to the case of Boltzmann's equation of Maxwellian molecules.

Theorem 9.1. *Let* $f \in \mathscr{P}_2$ *and assume that* (8.5) *is satisfied. Let* $\mathfrak{g}$ *be the Gaussian distribution* (8.6) *and put* $\mathfrak{e}(f) = \mathfrak{e}(f, \mathfrak{g})$. *Then,* $\mathfrak{e}(T_t f)$ *decreases to* 0 *as* $t \uparrow \infty$. *In particular,* $T_t f$ *converges to* $\mathfrak{g}$ *as* $t \uparrow \infty$.

The proof is based on the following lemma.

Lemma 9.1. *Let* f *and* $\mathfrak{g}$ *be the same as in the theorem and put* $\bar{\mathfrak{e}}_\theta(f) = \bar{\mathfrak{e}}_\theta(f, \mathfrak{g})$. *Then,* $\bar{\mathfrak{e}}_\theta(f) > 0$ *for* $0 < \theta < \pi$ *if* $f \neq \mathfrak{g}$.

Proof of the Lemma. Since $(\mathfrak{g} \circ \mathfrak{g})_\theta = \mathfrak{g}$ by **2** of Appendix, what we have to prove is $\mathfrak{e}[(f \circ f)_\theta, (\mathfrak{g} \circ \mathfrak{g})_\theta] < \mathfrak{e}(f, \mathfrak{g})$ for $0 < \theta < \pi$ provided $f \neq \mathfrak{g}$. By (i) of Lemma 7.4 we have

$$\mathfrak{e}[(f \circ f)_\theta, (\mathfrak{g} \circ \mathfrak{g})_\theta] \leqq \mathfrak{e}(f, \mathfrak{g}). \tag{9.1}$$

So, assuming the equality holds in the above, we prove that $f = \mathfrak{g}$. We now recall the proof of (i) of Lemma 7.4. Then, in order to have the equality in (9.1), the inequality (7.6) must be the equality

$$(X_1 - X_2, Y_1 - Y_2) = |X_1 - X_2| |Y_1 - Y_2|, \qquad \text{a.s.,}$$

which is equivalent to

$$\frac{X_1 - X_2}{|X_1 - X_2|} = \frac{Y_1 - Y_2}{|Y_1 - Y_2|}, \qquad \text{a.s.,} \tag{9.2}$$

On the other hand, both Y_1 and Y_2 are $\mathfrak{g}$-distributed in the present case, by Theorem 1 of [12] (or by (6.2)) there exists a unique Borel mapping ψ from $\mathbf{R}^3$ into itself such that $X_i=\psi(Y_i)$, $i=1,2$, almost surely (the uniqueness of ψ was remarked in the proof of Lemma 6.2). Therefore, (9.2) yields

$$\frac{\psi(y_1)-\psi(y_2)}{|\psi(y_1)-\psi(y_2)|}=\frac{y_1-y_2}{|y_1-y_2|}$$

for almost all $y_1, y_2 \in \mathbf{R}^3$ with respect to the Lebesgue measure. Thus for some $y_0 \in \mathbf{R}^3$

$$\psi(y)=\psi(y_0)+\frac{|\psi(y)-\psi(y_0)|}{|y-y_0|}(y-y_0) \tag{9.3}$$

must hold for almost all y. Therefore,

$$\frac{|\psi(y_1)-\psi(y_0)|}{|y_1-y_0|}(y_1-y_0)-\frac{|\psi(y_2)-\psi(y_0)|}{|y_2-y_0|}(y_2-y_0)$$
$$=\psi(y_1)-\psi(y_2)=\frac{|\psi(y_1)-\psi(y_2)|}{|y_1-y_2|}(y_1-y_2), \quad \text{a.e.,}$$

and hence

$$\frac{|\psi(y_1)-\psi(y_0)|}{|y_1-y_0|}=\frac{|\psi(y_2)-\psi(y_0)|}{|y_2-y_0|}, \quad \text{a.e.}$$

This combined with (9.3) implies that $\psi(y)=\psi(y_0)+const\,(y-y_0)$, a.e., and hence $\psi(y)=y$ because $E\{X_1\}=E\{Y_1\}$ and $E\{|X_1|^2\}=E\{|Y_1|^2\}$. Thus we obtain $f=\mathfrak{g}$, as was to be proved.

Proof of the Theorem. Since $\mathfrak{e}(T_tf, T_t\mathfrak{g})=\mathfrak{e}(T_tf,\mathfrak{g})=\mathfrak{e}(T_tf)$, the decreasing property of $\mathfrak{e}(T_tf)$ in t follows from Theorem 7.1. To prove that $\mathfrak{e}(T_tf)$ tends to 0 as $t\uparrow\infty$, we first assume that $\int|x|^4 f(dx)<\infty$. Then by the corollary to Theorem 8.1 $\int|x|^4(T_tf)(dx)$ is bounded in t, say, by M. We denote by $\tilde{\mathscr{P}}$ the family of probability distributions $\tilde{f}$ on $\mathbf{R}^3$ satisfying

$$\int x\tilde{f}(dx)=m, \quad \int|x-m|^2\tilde{f}(dx)=3v, \quad \int|x|^4\tilde{f}(dx)\leqq M,$$

and put $\tilde{\mathscr{P}}_\varepsilon=\{\tilde{f}\in\tilde{\mathscr{P}}: \mathfrak{e}(\tilde{f})\geqq\varepsilon\}$ for $\varepsilon>0$. Then $\tilde{\mathscr{P}}_\varepsilon$ is compact with respect to the metric ρ. Moreover, using the triangle inequality for ρ and (i) of Lemma 7.4 we can see that $|\bar{\mathfrak{e}}_\theta(\tilde{f})-\bar{\mathfrak{e}}_\theta(\tilde{g})|\leqq 2\mathfrak{e}(\tilde{f},\tilde{g})$ for $\tilde{f},\tilde{g}\in\tilde{\mathscr{P}}_\varepsilon$ and hence $\bar{\mathfrak{e}}_\theta$ is ρ-continuous on $\tilde{\mathscr{P}}_\varepsilon$ for each $\theta\in(0,\pi)$. Since $\bar{\mathfrak{e}}_\theta$ is strictly positive on $\tilde{\mathscr{P}}_\varepsilon$ by Lemma 9.1, we have

$$\inf_{\tilde{f}\in\tilde{\mathscr{P}}_\varepsilon}\bar{\mathfrak{e}}_\theta(\tilde{f})>0, \qquad \theta\in(0,\pi),$$

and hence

$$\Phi(\varepsilon)\equiv\inf_{\tilde{f}\in\tilde{\mathscr{P}}_\varepsilon}2\pi\int_0^\pi\bar{\mathfrak{e}}_\theta(\tilde{f})\,Q(d\theta)>0. \tag{9.4}$$

On the other hand, from (7.4) we have

$$\mathrm{e}(T_t f) \leqq \mathrm{e}(f) - 2\pi \int_0^t ds \int_0^\pi \bar{\mathrm{e}}_\theta(T_s f)\, Q(d\theta).$$

Because $T_t f \in \tilde{\mathscr{P}}_\varepsilon$ with $\varepsilon = \mathrm{e}(T_t f)$ if $\mathrm{e}(T_t f) > 0$, the above inequality combined with (9.4) implies

$$\mathrm{e}(T_t f) \leqq \mathrm{e}(f) - \int_0^t \Phi[\mathrm{e}(T_s f)]\, ds \tag{9.5}$$

for t such that $\mathrm{e}(T_t f) > 0$. But, this inequality clearly implies that $\mathrm{e}(T_t f) \to 0$ as $t \to \infty$.

Finally we remove the restriction $\int |x|^4 f(dx) < \infty$. For each $\varepsilon > 0$ and $f \in \mathscr{P}_2$ satisfying (8.5) we can choose f_ε in such a way that

$$\int x f_\varepsilon(dx) = m, \quad \int |x-m|^2 f_\varepsilon(dx) = 3v, \quad \int |x|^4 f_\varepsilon(dx) < \infty,$$

and $\rho(f, f_\varepsilon) < \varepsilon$ hold. Then, using Theorem 8.1 we have

$$\begin{aligned} \mathrm{e}(T_t f) &\leqq \{\rho(T_t f, T_t f_\varepsilon) + \rho(T_t f_\varepsilon, \mathrm{g})\}^2 \\ &\leqq \{\varepsilon + \sqrt{\mathrm{e}(T_t f_\varepsilon)}\}^2 \end{aligned}$$

and hence $\overline{\lim\limits_{t\to\infty}}\, \mathrm{e}(T_t f) \leqq \varepsilon^2$. The proof of the theorem is completed.

Remark. Making use of the corollary to Theorem 8.1 in full, we obtain a much simpler proof of Theorem 9.1. If f has finite absolute moments of all degrees, then $\mu_{\mathbf{n}}(T_t f) \to \mu_{\mathbf{n}}$ as $t \to \infty$ for every $\mathbf{n}$ and hence $\mathrm{e}(T_t f) \to 0$ as $t \to \infty$. The general case when f belongs to $\mathscr{P}_2$ and satisfies (8.5) can be treated by choosing f_ε with finite absolute moments of all degrees in such a way that $\int x f_\varepsilon(dx) = m$, $\int |x-m|^2 f_\varepsilon(dx) = 3v$ and $\rho(f, f_\varepsilon) < \varepsilon$ hold. However, our first proof based upon the inequality (9.5) seems to be interesting.

Appendix

1. In the introduction we regarded the equation (0.3) as a weak version of (0.2). This is justified by the formula

$$\begin{aligned} &\int_{(0,\pi)\times(0,2\pi)\times\mathbf{R}^6} \xi(x)(u' u_1' - u u_1)\, Q(d\theta)\, d\varphi\, dx\, dx_1 \\ &\quad = \int_{\mathbf{R}^6} (K\xi)(x, x_1)\, u(x)\, u(x_1)\, dx\, dx_1, \qquad \xi \in C_0^\infty(\mathbf{R}^3), \end{aligned}$$

which holds, at least if $u(x)$ is smooth enough, according to the following lemma.

Lemma. *Let $\xi(x, x_1, y, y_1)$ be a continuous function on R^{12} with compact support. Then, for each* $0 \in (0, \pi)$

$$\int_{(0,2\pi)\times\mathbf{R}^6} \xi(x, x_1, x', x_1')\, d\varphi\, dx\, dx_1 = \int_{(0,2\pi)\times\mathbf{R}^6} \xi(x', x_1', x, x_1)\, d\varphi\, dx\, dx_1. \tag{1}$$

Proof. We denote by $\Phi(\theta)$ and $\Psi(\theta)$ the left and right hand sides of (1), respectively. Since Φ and Ψ are continuous in θ, for the proof of (1) it is enough to show

$$\int_0^\pi \Phi(\theta)\,Q_0(\theta)\,\sin\theta\,d\theta=\int_0^\pi \Psi(\theta)\,Q_0(\theta)\sin\theta\,d\theta \tag{2}$$

for any continuous function $Q_0(\theta)$ with compact support in $(0,\pi)$. For $x\neq x_1$ we put $l=(x'-x)/|x'-x|$ and define $\gamma\in(0,\pi/2)$ by $\cos\gamma=(x_1-x,l)/|x_1-x|$. Since $\theta=\pi-2\gamma$, $Q_0(\theta)\cos\gamma$ becomes a function of $|(x_1-x,l)|$ and $|x_1-x|$. Thus we can write $Q_0(\theta)\cos\gamma=F(x,x_1,l)$ with some function F on $\mathbf{R}^3\times\mathbf{R}^3\times S^2$ satisfying

$$F(x,x_1,l)=F(x',x_1',l)=F(x,x_1,-l). \tag{3}$$

We then have

$$\begin{aligned}\int_0^\pi \Phi(\theta)\,Q_0(\theta)\sin\theta\,d\theta\\ &=4\int_{(0,\,\pi/2)\times(0,\,2\pi)\times\mathbf{R}^6}\xi(x,x_1,x',x_1')\,Q_0(\theta)\cos\gamma\sin\gamma\,d\gamma\,d\varphi\,dx\,dx_1\\ &=4\int_{\mathbf{R}^6}dx\,dx_1\int_{\{l\in S^2:\,(x_1-x,\,l)>0\}}\xi(x,x_1,x',x_1')\,F(x,x_1,l)\,dl\\ &=2\int_{\mathbf{R}^6\times S^2}\xi(x,x_1,x',x_1')\,F(x,x_1,l)\,dx\,dx_1\,dl;\end{aligned} \tag{4}$$

in the last line of the above x' and x_1' are defined by

$$\begin{aligned}x'&=x+(x_1-x,l)\,l\\ x_1'&=x_1-(x_1-x,l)\,l.\end{aligned} \tag{5}$$

Since $dx\,dx_1=dx'\,dx_1'$ for each fixed $l\in S^2$, the last integral in (4) is equal to

$$\int_{\mathbf{R}^6\times S^2}\xi(x,x_1,x',x_1')\,F(x,x_1,l)\,dx'\,dx_1'\,dl, \tag{6}$$

where x and x_1 are defined by the same rule as (5):

$$\begin{aligned}x&=x'+(x_1'-x',l)\,l\\ x_1&=x_1'-(x_1'-x',l)\,l.\end{aligned}$$

Now, from (3) it is clear that (6) is equal to

$$\int_{\mathbf{R}^6\times S^2}\xi(x',x_1',x,x_1)\,F(x,x_1,l)\,dx\,dx_1\,dl.$$

But this is equal to the right hand side of (2) by the same reason as (4) holds. The proof is finished.

2. Let $\mathfrak{g}$ be the Gaussian distribution (8.6). Then $\mathfrak{g}$ is invariant under T_t. For the proof, we first notice that the density function g satisfies $g'g_1'=g\,g_1$ and hence by the above lemma

$$\langle \mathfrak{g}\otimes\mathfrak{g},K\xi\rangle=0,\qquad \xi\in C_0^\infty(\mathbf{R}^3).$$

This implies $T_t\mathfrak{g}=\mathfrak{g}$ at least if $\int_0^\pi Q(d\theta)<\infty$, because the uniqueness of the solution for (0.3) clearly holds in that case. Therefore, in general, we have $T_t\,\mathfrak{g}=\lim_{\varepsilon\downarrow 0} T_t^{(\varepsilon)}\mathfrak{g}=\mathfrak{g}$, proving the invariance of $\mathfrak{g}$ under T_t. Moreover, $(\mathfrak{g}\circ\mathfrak{g})_\theta=\mathfrak{g}$ also follows from $g'g'_1=gg_1$ and the above lemma.

References

1. Arkeryd, L.: On the Bolztmann equation, Part I: Existence, Part II: The full initial value problem. Arch Rational Mech. Anal. **45,** 1–16, 17–34 (1972)
2. Carleman, T.: Problèmes Mathématiques dans la Théorie Cinétique des Gaz. Uppsala 1957.
3. Erdélyi, A. (Editor): Higher Transcendental Functions, Vol. II, New York-Toronto-London: McGraw-Hill 1953
4. Ikenberry, E., Truesdell, C.: On the pressure and the flux of energy in a gas according to Maxwell's kinetic theory I. J. Rational Mech. Anal. **5**, 1–54 (1956)
5. Itô, K.: On stochastic differential eqations. Mem. Amer. Math. Soc. No. 4, 1951.
6. Kac, M.: Probability and Related Topics in the Physical Sciences, New York-London: Interscience 1959.
7. Kolmogorov, A.N.: On Skorohod convergence. Theor. Probability Appl. **1**, 215–222 (1956)
8. Kondô, R., Negoro, A.: Certain functional of probability mesures on Hilbert spaces. Hiroshima Math. J. **6**, 421–428 (1976)
9. McKean, H.P.: A class of Markov processes associated with nonlinear parabolic equations. Proc. Nat. Acad. Sci. **56**, 1907–1911 (1966)
10. McKean, H.P.: An exponential formula for solving Boltzmann's equation for a Maxwellian gas. J. Combinatorial Theory **2**, 358–382 (1967)
11. McKean, H.P.: Propagation of chaos for a class of nonlinear parabolic equation. Lecture series in Differential Equtions, session 7: Catholic Univ. 1967
12. Murata, H., Tanaka, H.: An inequality for certain functional of multidimensional probability distributions. Hiroshima Math. J. **4**, 75–81 (1974)
13. Murata, H.: Propagation of chaos for Boltzmann-like equation of non-cutoff type in the plane. Hiroshima Math. J. **7**, 479–515 (1977)
14. Parthasarathy, K.R.: Probability Measures on Metric Spaces, New York-London: Academic Press 1967
15. Povzner, A.Ya.: The Boltzmann equation the kinetic theory of gases. Mat. Sb. **58**, 65–86 (1962). (English Transl.) Amer. Math. Soc. Transl. **(2)47**, 193–216 (1965)
16. Skorohod, A.V.: Limit theorems for stochastic processes, Theor. Probability Appl. **1**, 261–290 (1956)
17. Tanaka, H.: An inequality for a functional of probability distributions and its application to Kac's one-dimensional model of a Maxwellian gas. Z. Wahrscheinlichkeitstheorie verw. Gebiete **27**, 47–52 (1973)
18. Tanaka, H.: On Markov process corresponding to Boltzmann's equation of Maxwellian gas. In: Proc. 2nd Japan-USSR Sympos. on Probab. Theory, Lecture Notes in Math., **330**, 478–489. Berlin-Heidelberg-New York: Springer-Verlag 1973
19. Tanaka, H.: On the uniqueness of Markov process associated with the Boltzmann equation of Maxwellian molecules. In: Proc. Intern. Sympos. on Stochastic Differential Equations, Kyoto, 1976
20. Uhlenbeck, G.E., Ford, G.W.: Lectures in Statistical Mechanics. Amer. Math. Soc., Providence, Rhode Island, 1963
21. Wild, E.: On Boltzmann's equation in the kinetic theory of gases. Proc. Cambridge Philos. Soc. **47**, 602–609 (1951)

Received December 19, 1977

HIROSHIMA MATH. J.
9 (1979), 163–177

Stochastic Differential Equations with Reflecting Boundary Condition in Convex Regions

Hiroshi TANAKA

(Received September 16, 1978)

§ 1. Introduction

A. V. Skorohod [4] considered a stochastic differential equation for a reflecting diffusion process on $\bar{D}=[0, \infty)$ (see also McKean [2] [3]). This is the simplest case among stochastic differential equations subject to boundary conditions and can be solved easily. The purpose of this paper is to show that the multi-dimensional version of Skorohod's equation is still easy to solve if we assume that the domain D is convex.

Skorohod's equation describing a reflecting Brownian path ξ on $\bar{D}=[0, \infty)$ is

$$(1.1) \qquad \xi = w + \varphi,$$

where w is a standard Brownian path and ξ is to be found as a $\bar{D}$-valued continuous function under the condition that $\varphi(t)$ increases only when $\xi(t)=0$. The equation (1.1) has a unique solution not only for almost all Brownian paths but also for *all* continuous functions w with $w(0) \in \bar{D}$, and the solution is given by

$$(1.2) \qquad \xi(t) = \begin{cases} w(t) & \text{for} \quad 0 \le t \le T, \\ w(t) - \inf\{w(s)\colon T \le s \le t\} & \text{for} \quad t > T, \end{cases}$$

where $T=\inf\{t>0\colon w(t)<0\}$. Our first problem is to consider a multi-dimensional version of the equation (1.1) assuming that D is a *convex* domain. Although we can not obtain an explicit formula for the solution like (1.2), we are able to construct the unique solution ξ for any $\mathbf{R}^d$-valued continuous function w with $w(0) \in \bar{D}$ and to prove that ξ depends continuously on w, *if* D is a convex domain in $\mathbf{R}^d$ satisfying certain condition (Theorem 2.1). This additional condition is automatically satisfied if D is bounded or $d=2$. This result will lead to a simple solution to our second problem which is concerned with a stochastic differential equation with (normal) reflection having variable coefficients similar to Skorohod's. The following may be stressed.

(i) The boundary does not need to be smooth as far as the domain is assumed to be convex.

(ii) The diffusion coefficients may degenerate (however, in this case the path of

the solution might not behave like an ordinary reflection).
Our results are roughly stated as follows. The convexity assumption for the domain makes the situation quite similar to that in the whole space; in fact, the existence of solutions will be obtained assuming only the bounded continuity of the coefficients (Theorem 4.2), and the pathwise uniqueness of solutions will be proved under the same regularity assumption on the coefficients as found in the work of Watanabe and Yamada [9] for the case of whole space (Theorem 4.3).

However, it is noted that our methods and results are restricted to the case of reflecting boundary condition; the convexity assumption will not simplify the situation in the case of general boundary conditions such as discussed by Ikeda [1], Watanabe [8], Stroock and Varadhan [6] and Tsuchiya [7].

§2. A deterministic problem

An $\mathbf{R}^d$-valued function $\varphi(t)=(\varphi^1(t),\ldots, \varphi^d(t))$ defined on $\mathbf{R}_+=[0, \infty)$ is said to be of bounded variation for simplicity if the component functions are of bounded variation on each finite t-interval. Given such a function $\varphi(t)$ which is right continuous and $\varphi(0)=0$, we put

$$|\varphi|(t) = \text{the total variation of } \varphi \text{ on } [0, t]$$

$$= \sup \sum_k |\varphi(t_k) - \varphi(t_{k-1})|,$$

where the supremum is taken over all partitions: $0=t_0<t_1<\cdots<t_n=t$. $\varphi(t)$ can be expressed as

$$\varphi(t) = \int_0^t \boldsymbol{n}(s) d|\varphi|(s) = \int_{[0,t]} \boldsymbol{n}(s)\,|\varphi|(ds) \tag{2.1}$$

with a unit vector valued function $\boldsymbol{n}(t)$; $\boldsymbol{n}(t)$ is uniquely determined almost everywhere with respect to the measure $d|\varphi|$.

Let D be a convex domain in $\mathbf{R}^d$ and $\bar{D}$ its closure; D will be fixed throughout. For $x\in\partial D$ we denote by $\mathscr{H}_x(D)$ the set of all supporting hyperplanes of D at x. By (an inward) normal vector at $x\in\partial D$ we mean *any* inward unit vector perpendicular to some $H\in\mathscr{H}_x(D)$, and denote by $\mathscr{N}_x(D)$ the set of all inward normal vectors at $x\in\partial D$. Of course, it can happen that $\sharp\mathscr{N}_x(D)=\infty$ unless ∂D is smooth near x. We shall also consider the following spaces of functions.

$\mathbf{C}(\mathbf{R}_+, \mathbf{R}^d)$ (resp. $\mathbf{C}(\mathbf{R}_+, \bar{D})$)=the space of $\mathbf{R}^d$-valued (resp. $\bar{D}$-valued) continuous functions on $\mathbf{R}_+$.

$\mathbf{D}(\mathbf{R}_+, \mathbf{R}^d)$ (resp. $\mathbf{D}(\mathbf{R}_+, \bar{D})$)=the space of $\mathbf{R}^d$-valued (resp. $\bar{D}$-valued) right continuous functions on $\mathbf{R}_+$ with left limits.

On $\mathbf{C}(\mathbf{R}_+, \mathbf{R}^d)$ and $\mathbf{C}(\mathbf{R}_+, \bar{D})$ we consider the compact uniform topology. Given a function ξ in $\mathbf{D}(\mathbf{R}_+, \bar{D})$, a function φ is said to be *associated* with ξ if the following three conditions are satisfied.

(2.2) φ is a function in $\mathbf{D}(\mathbf{R}_+, \mathbf{R}^d)$ with bounded variation and $\varphi(0)=0$.

(2.3) The set $\{t \in \mathbf{R}_+ : \xi(t) \in D\}$ has $d|\varphi|$-measure zero.

(2.4) The function $\boldsymbol{n}(t)$ appearing in the expression (2.1) is a normal vector at $\xi(t)$ for almost all t with respect to the measure $d|\varphi|$.

REMARK 2.1. The condition (2.4) can be replaced by the following one.

(2.4′) For any $\eta \in \mathbf{C}(\mathbf{R}_+, \bar{D})$, $(\eta(t) - \xi(t), \varphi(dt)) \geq 0$.

EXAMPLE. Let ∂D be *smooth*, $\boldsymbol{n}(x)$ the inward normal vector at $x \in \partial D$ and $\xi \in \mathbf{D}(\mathbf{R}_+, \bar{D})$. Then, for any right continuous non-decreasing function $\rho(t)$ on $\mathbf{R}_+$ with $\rho(0)=0$

$$\varphi(t) = \int_0^t \mathbf{1}_{\partial D}(\xi(s))\boldsymbol{n}(\xi(s))d\rho(s)$$

is clearly an associated function of ξ.

Our first problem stated in the introduction can now be formulated as follows.

PROBLEM. Given $w \in \mathbf{D}(\mathbf{R}_+, \mathbf{R}^d)$ with $w(0) \in \bar{D}$, find a solution ξ of

$$\xi = w + \varphi. \tag{2.5}$$

When we speak of the equation (2.5), it is always understood that $\xi \in \mathbf{D}(\mathbf{R}_+, \bar{D})$ and φ is associated with ξ.

As stated in the introduction, in the simplest case $\bar{D}=[0, \infty)$ the solution of (2.5) is given by (1.2). However, in the general multi-dimensional case the existence of a solution of (2.5) is not trivial. An example in which a solution of (2.5) can easily be found is the case when w is a step function as will be seen in the lemma below. For a given point $x \in \mathbf{R}^d - \bar{D}$ we denote by $[x]_\partial$ the (unique) point on ∂D which gives the minimum distance between x and $\bar{D}$.

LEMMA 2.1. *If w is a step function with $w(0) \in \bar{D}$, then a solution of* (2.5) *exists.*

PROOF. Put $T_1 = \inf\{t>0: w(t) \notin \bar{D}\}$ and define $\xi(t)$, $0 \leq t \leq T_1$, by $\xi(t) = w(t)$ for $t < T_1$ and $\xi(T_1) = [w(T_1)]_\partial$. Then, $T_1 > 0$ and $\xi(t)$ solves (2.5) for $0 \leq t \leq T_1$. Next, suppose a solution $\xi(t)$ of (2.5) is obtained for $0 \leq t \leq T_{n-1}$ and put

$$T_n = \inf\{t > T_{n-1}\colon w(t) + \varphi(T_{n-1}) \notin \bar{D}\},$$

$$\xi(t) = \begin{cases} w(t) + \varphi(T_{n-1}) & \text{for } T_{n-1} < t < T_n, \\ [w(T_n) + \varphi(T_{n-1})]_\partial & \text{for } t = T_n. \end{cases}$$

Then, $\xi(t)$ solves (2.5) for $0 \le t \le T_n$. Repeating this argument, we can obtain a solution of (2.5) for $0 \le t < \infty$ because $T_n \uparrow \infty$ as $n \uparrow \infty$.

Lemma 2.2. (i) *Let* $w, \tilde{w} \in \mathbf{D}(\mathbf{R}_+, \mathbf{R}^d)$ *with* $w(0), \tilde{w}(0) \in \bar{D}$, *and* $\xi, \tilde{\xi}$ *be any solutions of*

$$\xi = w + \varphi, \quad \tilde{\xi} = \tilde{w} + \tilde{\varphi},$$

respectively. Then we have

$$|\xi(t) - \tilde{\xi}(t)|^2 \le |w(t) - \tilde{w}(t)|^2$$
$$+ 2\int_0^t (w(t) - \tilde{w}(t) - w(s) + \tilde{w}(s), \varphi(ds) - \tilde{\varphi}(ds)).$$

(ii) *If* ξ *is a solution of* (2.5), *then*

$$|\xi(t) - \xi(s)|^2 \le |w(t) - w(s)|^2$$
$$+ 2\int_{(s,t]} (w(t) - w(\tau), \varphi(d\tau)), \qquad 0 \le s \le t.$$

Proof. (i) We have

$$|\varphi(t) - \tilde{\varphi}(t)|^2 = \int_0^t \int_0^t (\varphi(dt_1) - \tilde{\varphi}(dt_1), \varphi(dt_2) - \tilde{\varphi}(dt_2))$$
$$= 2\iint_{0 \le t_1 \le t_2 \le t} (\varphi(dt_1) - \tilde{\varphi}(dt_1), \varphi(dt_2) - \tilde{\varphi}(dt_2))$$
$$- \sum_{0 \le s \le t} |\varphi(s) - \tilde{\varphi}(s) - \varphi(s-) + \tilde{\varphi}(s-)|^2$$
$$\le 2\int_0^t (\varphi(s) - \tilde{\varphi}(s), \varphi(ds) - \tilde{\varphi}(ds)),$$

$$(w(t) - \tilde{w}(t), \varphi(t) - \tilde{\varphi}(t)) = \int_0^t (w(t) - \tilde{w}(t), \varphi(ds) - \tilde{\varphi}(ds))$$
$$= \int_0^t (w(t) - \tilde{w}(t) - w(s) + \tilde{w}(s), \varphi(ds) - \tilde{\varphi}(ds))$$
$$+ \int_0^t (w(s) - \tilde{w}(s), \varphi(ds) - \tilde{\varphi}(ds)).$$

Therefore

$$|\xi(t)-\tilde{\xi}(t)|^2 = |w(t)-\tilde{w}(t)|^2 + 2(w(t)-\tilde{w}(t), \varphi(t)-\tilde{\varphi}(t)) + |\varphi(t)-\tilde{\varphi}(t)|^2$$
$$\leq |w(t)-\tilde{w}(t)|^2 + 2\int_0^t (\xi(s)-\tilde{\xi}(s), \varphi(ds)-\tilde{\varphi}(ds))$$
$$+ 2\int_0^t (w(t)-\tilde{w}(t)-w(s)+\tilde{w}(s), \varphi(ds)-\tilde{\varphi}(ds)).$$

But the second term is non-positive by (2.4′) of Remark 2.1.

(ii) By a method similar to the case (i), we have

$$|\xi(t)-\xi(s)|^2 = |w(t)-w(s)|^2 + |\varphi(t)-\varphi(s)|^2 + 2(w(t)-w(s), \varphi(t)-\varphi(s))$$
$$\leq |w(t)-w(s)|^2 + 2\int_{(s,t]} (\xi(\tau)-\xi(s), \varphi(d\tau))$$
$$+ 2\int_{(s,t]} (w(t)-w(\tau), \varphi(d\tau)).$$

But the second term is non-positive by (2.4′); the proof is finished.

REMARK 2.2. By a method similar to the above, we can prove the following: If w and $\tilde{w}$ of (i) of Lemma 2.2 are replaced by $w+a$ and $\tilde{w}+\tilde{a}$, respectively, where a and $\tilde{a}$ are $\mathbf{R}^d$-valued right continuous functions of bounded variation with $a(0)=\tilde{a}(0)=0$, then

$$|\xi(t)-\tilde{\xi}(t)|^2 \leq |w(t)-\tilde{w}(t)|^2 + 2\int_0^t (\xi(s)-\tilde{\xi}(s), a(ds)-\tilde{a}(ds))$$
$$+ 2\int_0^t (w(t)-\tilde{w}(t)-w(s)+\tilde{w}(s), a(ds)+\varphi(ds)-\tilde{a}(ds)-\tilde{\varphi}(ds)).$$

By a similar replacement of w in (ii) by $w+a$, the inequality in (ii) becomes

$$|\xi(t)-\xi(s)|^2 \leq |w(t)-w(s)|^2 + 2\int_{(s,t]} (\xi(\tau)-\xi(s), a(d\tau))$$
$$+ 2\int_{(s,t]} (w(t)-w(\tau), a(d\tau)+\varphi(d\tau)).$$

LEMMA 2.3. *(2.5) has at most one solution.*

PROOF. Let ξ and $\tilde{\xi}$ be solutions of (2.5). Then, putting $w=\tilde{w}$ in (i) of Lemma 2.2 we obtain $|\xi(t)-\tilde{\xi}(t)|^2 \leq 0$.

LEMMA 2.4. *If w is continuous, then the solution of (2.5) is also continuous.*

PROOF. From (ii) of Lemma 2.2 we have

$$|\xi(t)-\xi(s)|^2 \le |w(t)-w(s)|^2 + 2\int_{(s,t]} |w(t)-w(\tau)|\,|\varphi|(d\tau),$$

from which the continuity of ξ follows.

LEMMA 2.5. *Let $\{w_n\}_{n\ge 1}$ be a sequence in $\mathbf{D}(\mathbf{R}_+, \mathbf{R}^d)$ such that for each n the equation $\xi_n = w_n + \varphi_n$ has a solution for $0\le t\le T$, T being a positive constant. If w_n converges uniformly on $[0, T]$ to some $w\in\mathbf{C}(\mathbf{R}_+, \mathbf{R}^d)$ as $n\to\infty$ and if $\{|\varphi_n|(T)\}_{n\ge 1}$ is bounded, then ξ_n converges uniformly on $[0, T]$ as $n\to\infty$ to the solution ξ of $\xi = w+\varphi$ for $0\le t\le T$.*

PROOF. Let K be the bound of $\{|\varphi_n|(T)\}_{n\ge 1}$. Then applying Lemma 2.2, we have

$$\text{(2.6a)} \qquad |\xi_n(t)-\xi_m(t)|^2 \le |w_n(t)-w_m(t)|^2 + 8K \sup_{0\le s\le t} |w_n(s)-w_m(s)|,$$

$$\text{(2.6b)} \qquad |\xi_n(t)-\xi_n(s)|^2 \le |w_n(t)-w_n(s)|^2 + 2K \sup_{s\le t_1\le t_2\le t} |w_n(t_2)-w_n(t_1)|.$$

From the first inequality it follows that $\{\xi_n\}_{n\ge 1}$ is uniformly convergent on $[0, T]$ and hence the same for $\{\varphi_n\}_{n\ge 1}$. Letting $n\uparrow\infty$ in the second inequality, we obtain the inequality concerning the limit functions ξ and φ:

$$|\xi(t)-\xi(s)|^2 \le |w(t)-w(s)|^2 + 2K \sup_{s\le t_1\le t_2\le t} |w(t_2)-w(t_1)|.$$

This implies the continuity of ξ. We now prove that ξ is a solution of (2.5) for $0\le t\le T$. For this it is enough to prove that φ is associated with ξ. First, $|\varphi_n|(T)\le K$ implies $|\varphi|(T)\le K$ and hence φ is of bounded variation. The condition (2.3) is also verified easily. To verify (2.4), let $\eta\in\mathbf{C}(\mathbf{R}_+, \bar{D})$ and notice that for $0\le t_1<t_2\le T$

$$\left|\int_{t_1}^{t_2}(\eta(t)-\xi_n(t), \varphi_n(dt)) - \int_{t_1}^{t_2}(\eta(t)-\xi(t), \varphi(dt))\right|$$

$$\le \left|\int_{t_1}^{t_2}(\xi(t)-\xi_n(t), \varphi_n(dt))\right| + \left|\int_{t_1}^{t_2}(\eta(t)-\xi(t), \varphi_n(dt)-\varphi(dt))\right|.$$

The first is dominated by $K \sup_{t_1\le t\le t_2} |\xi(t)-\xi_n(t)|$ and hence tends to 0 as $n\to\infty$; the second term also does as can be seen by approximating the integral by the Riemann sum. Therefore

$$\int_{t_1}^{t_2}(\eta(t)-\xi(t), \varphi(dt)) = \lim_{n\to\infty}\int_{t_1}^{t_2}(\eta(t)-\xi_n(t), \varphi_n(dt)) \ge 0,$$

and the proof is finished.

We proceed to the existence problem for (2.5) assuming that $w \in \mathbf{C}(\mathbf{R}_+, \mathbf{R}^d)$. We begin with the special case when D satisfies the following condition.

CONDITION (A). There exist a unit vector $\mathfrak{e}$ and a constant $c>0$ such that $(\mathfrak{e}, \boldsymbol{n}) \geq c$ for any $\boldsymbol{n} \in \bigcup_{y \in \partial D} \mathcal{N}_y(D)$.

LEMMA 2.6. *Assume that D satisfies the condition (A). Then, there exists a solution ξ of* (2.5) *for any $w \in \mathbf{C}(\mathbf{R}_+, \mathbf{R}^d)$, and for $0 \leq s < t$*

(2.7a) $$|\xi(t) - \xi(s)| \leq K\Delta_{s,t},$$

(2.7b) $$|\varphi|(t) - |\varphi|(s) \leq K'\Delta_{s,t},$$

where K and K' are constants depending only upon the constant c in the condition (A); $\Delta_{s,t} = \sup_{s \leq t_1 < t_2 \leq t} |w(t_2) - w(t_1)|$.

PROOF. For each integer $n \geq 1$ we define $w_n \in \mathbf{D}(\mathbf{R}_+, \mathbf{R}^d)$ by $w_n(t) = w\left(\frac{k}{n}\right)$ for $\frac{k-1}{n} \leq t < \frac{k}{n}$, $k \geq 1$. Then w_n converges to w uniformly on compacts as $n \to \infty$, and by Lemma 2.1 there exists a solution ξ_n of $\xi_n = w_n + \varphi_n$. We put

$$\Delta_{n,s,t} = \sup_{s \leq t_1 < t_2 \leq t} |w_n(t_2) - w_n(t_1)|,$$

$$K_{n,s,t} = |\varphi_n|(t) - |\varphi_n|(s),$$

and notice that

$$(\mathfrak{e}, \xi_n(t) - \xi_n(s)) = (\mathfrak{e}, w_n(t) - w_n(s)) + (\mathfrak{e}, \varphi_n(t) - \varphi_n(s))$$
$$\geq (\mathfrak{e}, w_n(t) - w_n(s)) + cK_{n,s,t},$$

that is,

(2.8) $$K_{n,s,t} \leq \{|\xi_n(t) - \xi_n(s)| + \Delta_{n,s,t}\}/c.$$

On the other hand, (2.6b) yields

$$|\xi_n(t) - \xi_n(s)|^2 \leq \Delta_{n,s,t}^2 + 2K_{n,s,t}\Delta_{n,s,t}$$
$$\leq \Delta_{n,s,t}^2 + \varepsilon^2 K_{n,s,t}^2 + \Delta_{n,s,t}^2/\varepsilon^2,$$

that is,

$$|\xi_n(t) - \xi_n(s)| \leq \left(1 + \frac{1}{\varepsilon}\right)\Delta_{n,s,t} + \varepsilon K_{n,s,t}, \qquad \varepsilon > 0.$$

This combined with (2.8) implies

$$|\xi_n(t) - \xi_n(s)| \leq \left(1 + \frac{1}{\varepsilon} + \frac{\varepsilon}{c}\right)\Delta_{n,s,t} + \frac{\varepsilon}{c}|\xi_n(t) - \xi_n(s)|,$$

and therefore

$$(2.9)\qquad |\xi_n(t)-\xi_n(s)|\le K\Delta_{n,s,t},\quad K_{n,s,t}\le K'\Delta_{n,s,t},$$

where K is the minimum of $\left(1+\frac{1}{\varepsilon}+\frac{\varepsilon}{c}\right)\left(1-\frac{\varepsilon}{c}\right)^{-1}$ as ε ranges over the interval $(0, c)$ and $K'=(1+K)/c$. In particular, $|\varphi_n|(T)$ $(=K_{n,0,T})$ is bounded and so by Lemma 2.5 ξ_n converges uniformly on compacts to the solution ξ of (2.5) as $n\to\infty$. This proves the existence part. The estimates (2.7a) and (2.7b) are also immediate from (2.9). The proof is finished.

Next, we introduce the condition (B) for a convex domain D.

CONDITION (B). There exist $\varepsilon>0$ and $\delta>0$ such that for any $x\in\partial D$ we can find an open ball $B_\varepsilon(x_0)=\{y\in\mathbf{R}^d: |y-x_0|<\varepsilon\}$ satisfying $B_\varepsilon(x_0)\subset D$ and $|x-x_0|\le\delta$.

We can easily see that the condition (B) is always satisfied if D is bounded or if $d=2$. We now assume that D satisfies the condition (B) and for a point $x\in\partial D$ put

$$B(x)=\{y\in\mathbf{R}^d: |y-x|<\varepsilon/2\},$$

$$D_x=\bigcap_{y\in\partial D\cap\overline{B(x)}}\ \bigcap_{H\in\mathscr{H}_y(D)} H(D),$$

where $H(D)$ denotes the open half space bounded by a supporting hyperplane H and containing D. Then D_x is a convex domain satisfying the condition (A) with

$$\mathfrak{e}=(x_0-x)/|x_0-x|,\quad c=\varepsilon/2\delta.$$

THEOREM 2.1. (i) *Assume that D satisfies the condition (B). Then there exists a unique solution of* (2.5) *if $w\in\mathbf{C}(\mathbf{R}_+,\mathbf{R}^d)$, and the solution depends continuously upon w with respect to the compact uniform topology.* (ii) *Let D be a general convex domain and $\{w_n\}_{n\ge1}$ be a sequence in $\mathbf{C}(\mathbf{R}_+,\mathbf{R}^d)$ such that $\xi_n=w_n+\varphi_n$ has a solution for each n. Assume that w_n and ξ_n converge to w and ξ uniformly on compacts as $n\to\infty$, respectively. Then ξ is a solution of* (2.5).

PROOF. (i) If we put $T_0=\inf\{t\ge0: w(t)\notin\overline{D}\}$, then $\xi_0(t)\equiv w(t)$ $(0\le t\le T_0)$ is the solution of (2.5) for $0\le t\le T_0$. Assuming that the solution ξ_{n-1} of (2.5) is constructed for $0\le t\le T_{n-1}$ $(n\ge1)$, we now extend it beyond T_{n-1} as follows. Put $w^{(n)}(t)=w(T_{n-1}+t)$, $t\ge0$, let $\xi^{(n)}$ be the solution of $\xi^{(n)}=w^{(n)}+\varphi^{(n)}$ on $\overline{D}_{\xi_{n-1}(T_{n-1})}$ and again put

$$t_n=\inf\{t\ge T_{n-1}: |\xi^{(n)}(t-T_{n-1})-\xi^{(n)}(0)|=\varepsilon/2\},$$

$$T_n=\inf\{t\ge t_n: \xi^{(n)}(t_n-T_{n-1})+w(t)-w(t_n)\notin\overline{D}\},$$

$$\xi_n(t) = \begin{cases} \xi_{n-1}(t) & , \quad 0 \le t \le T_{n-1}, \\ \xi^{(n)}(t - T_{n-1}) & , \quad T_{n-1} \le t \le t_n, \\ \xi^{(n)}(t_n - T_{n-1}) + w(t) - w(t_n), & \quad t_n \le t \le T_n. \end{cases}$$

Then ξ_n is the solution of (2.5) on $\bar{D}$ for $0 \le t \le T_n$. Repeating this argument, we obtain an increasing sequence $\{T_n\}$ and a continuous function ξ defined for $t < T_\infty = \lim T_n$ such that ξ is the solution of (2.5) for $0 \le t < T_\infty$. The associated function φ is flat on each interval (t_n, T_n) and (2.7) holds for $s, t \in [T_{n-1}, t_n]$. Therefore, (2.7) holds for $s, t \in [T_{n-1}, T_n]$ with constants K and K' depending only on $c = \varepsilon/2\delta$. But, (2.7a) with $s = T_{n-1}$ and $t = t_n$ implies

$$\varepsilon/2K \le \Delta_{T_{n-1},t_n} \le \Delta_{T_{n-1},T_n},$$

from which we can claim as follows: If $h > 0$ is so small that $\Delta_T(h) < \varepsilon/2K$ where

$$\Delta_T(h) = \max\{|w(t) - w(s)| : 0 \le s, t \le T \text{ and } |t - s| \le h\},$$

T being an arbitrarily fixed positive constant, then $T_n \le T$ implies $T_n - T_{n-1} > h$. In other words, $T_n > T$ for all $n > T/h$. This fact implies the followings:

(2.10) $T_n = \infty$, that is, there exists a solution of (2.5) for $0 \le t < \infty$.

(2.11) For $0 \le s < t \le T$ the solution satisfies

(a) $|\xi(t) - \xi(s)| \le \left(\frac{T}{h} + 1\right) K \Delta_{s,t}$,

(b) $|\varphi|(t) - |\varphi|(s) \le \left(\frac{T}{h} + 1\right) K' \Delta_{s,t}$.

Next, let $\{w_n\}_{n \ge 1}$ be a sequence in $\mathbf{C}(\mathbf{R}_+, \mathbf{R}^d)$ converging to w uniformly on compacts and let $\xi_n = w_n + \varphi_n$. Then (b) of (2.11) applied to φ_n yields

$$|\varphi_n|(t) - |\varphi_n|(s) \le \left(\frac{T}{h_n} + 1\right) K' \Delta_{n,s,t}, \qquad 0 \le s < t \le T.$$

Here h_n depends upon w_n, but it can be chosen to be independent of w_n for all sufficiently large n because $w_n \to w$. Therefore the above inequality on $|\varphi_n|$ implies that $\{|\varphi_n|(T)\}$ is bounded and hence by Lemma 2.5 $\xi_n \to \xi$ uniformly on $[0, T]$.

(ii) Let $T > 0$ be any fixed constant. Then there exists N such that

$$\sup_n \max_{0 \le t \le T} |\xi_n(t)| < N.$$

For such an N both ξ_n and ξ are the solutions of $\xi_n = w_n + \varphi_n$ and $\xi = w + \varphi$, $0 \le t \le T$, for the domain $D_N = D \cap \{|x| < N\}$. Since D_N satisfies the condition (*B*), we can apply the result of (i) to conclude that ξ is the solution of (2.5) ($0 \le t \le T$) for D_N and hence for D. The proof is finished.

REMARK 2.3. Even if D does not satisfy the condition (B) (so $d \ge 3$ and D is unbounded), for each $x \in \partial D$ we can find an open ball $B_\varepsilon(x_0) = \{y \in \mathbf{R}^d: |y - x_0| < \varepsilon\}$ inside D (but now ε or $|x - x_0|^{-1}$ is not bounded away from zero as x moves on ∂D). Therefore, in a manner similar to the proof of Theorem 2.1, (i), we can construct the solution of (2.5) for $t < T_\infty = \lim T_n$. I can neither prove that $T_\infty = \infty$ in general nor give an example in which $T_\infty < \infty$.

§3. A stochastic version of (2.5)

The purpose of this section is to remove the condition (B) in the existence of global solutions of (2.5) by taking w from sample paths of a continuous semi-martingale.

Let $(\Omega, \mathscr{F}, P)$ be a complete probability space with an increasing family $\{\mathscr{F}_t\}_{t \ge 0}$ of sub-σ-fields of $\mathscr{F}$; it is assumed that each $\mathscr{F}_t$ contains all P-negligible sets and $\mathscr{F}_t = \bigcap_{\varepsilon > 0} \mathscr{F}_{t+\varepsilon}$. Let D be a convex domain as before.

THEOREM 3.1. *Let $\{M(t)\}$ be an $\mathbf{R}^d$-valued process with $M(0) \in \bar{D}$ such that each component is a continuous local $\mathscr{F}_t$-martingale and $\{A(t)\}$ be an $\mathbf{R}^d$-valued, continuous and $\mathscr{F}_t$-adapted process of bounded variation with $A(0) = 0$. Then there exists a unique $\mathscr{F}_t$-adapted solution $\{X(t)\}$ of*

$$X(t) = M(t) + A(t) + \Phi(t). \tag{3.1}$$

Moreover, for $f \in \mathbf{C}^2(\mathbf{R})$ with $f' \ge 0$ on $\mathbf{R}_+$ and $0 \le s \le t$ we have

$$\begin{aligned} f(|X(t) - X(s)|^2) &\le f(0) + 2\int_s^t f' \sum_i (X^i(\tau) - X^i(s))(M^i(d\tau) + A^i(d\tau)) \\ &+ 2\int_s^t f'' \sum_{i,j} (X^i(\tau) - X^i(s))(X^j(\tau) - X^j(s)) d[M^i, M^j] \\ &+ \int_s^t f' \sum_i d[M^i, M^i], \end{aligned} \tag{3.2}$$

where f', f'' are evaluated at $|X(\tau) - X(s)|^2$ and $[M^i, M^j]$ denotes the quadratic variation process.

REMARK 3.1. By a solution of (3.1), we mean a $\bar{D}$-valued process $\{X(t)\}$ which satisfies (3.1) almost surely, under the condition that almost all sample paths of $\{\Phi(t)\}$ are associated with those of $\{X(t)\}$.

PROOF. Let $\tau(t)$ be the inverse function of

$$\theta(t) = t + \sum_{i=1}^{d} [M^i, M^i] + |A|(t),$$

and put

$$\mathscr{F}_t^* = \mathscr{F}_{\tau(t)}, \; M^*(t) = M(\tau(t)), \quad A^*(t) = A(\tau(t)).$$

Then $\{M^*(t)\}$ is a continuous $\mathscr{F}_t^*$-martingale and $\{A^*(t)\}$ is a continuous $\mathscr{F}_t^*$-adapted process of bounded variation, satisfying

$$(3.3a) \qquad 0 \le \sum_{i,j=1}^{d} x^i x^j d[M^{*i}, M^{*j}] \le |x|^2 dt, \qquad x \in \mathbf{R}^d,$$

$$(3.3b) \qquad A^*(t) = \int_0^t a^*(s)ds, \qquad |a^*(t)| \le 1.$$

Moreover, once we obtain the $\mathscr{F}_t^*$-adapted solution of $X^*(t) = M^*(t) + A^*(t) + \Phi^*(t)$, the $\mathscr{F}_t$-adapted solution of (3.1) can be obtained by $X(t) = X^*(\theta(t))$. Therefore, in proving the theorem we may assume that $\{M(t)\}$ and $\{A(t)\}$ themselves satisfy (3.3) (without the symbol $*$).

First we prove (3.2) assuming the existence of the $\mathscr{F}_t$-adapted solution $\{X(t)\}$. An application of Itô's formula yields

$$f(|X(t) - X(s)|^2) = \text{the right hand side of } (3.2)$$
$$+ \int_s^t f' \cdot (X(\tau) - X(s), \Phi(d\tau)).$$

But the last term is non-positive by (2.4′).

In order to prove the existence of the solution, we first consider the equation for $D_n = D \cap \{|x| < n\}$. Taking a point x^* in D_n (we may consider only those n for which $D_n \neq \emptyset$), we put

$$M_n(t) = \mathbf{1}_{D_n}(M(0))M(t) + \mathbf{1}_{\mathbf{R}^d - D_n}(M(0))x^*,$$

$$A_n(t) = \mathbf{1}_{D_n}(M(0))A(t).$$

Since D_n is bounded and hence satisfies the condition (B), by Theorem 2.1 there exists a unique $\mathscr{F}_t$-adapted solution $\{X_n(t)\}$ of $X_n(t) = M_n(t) + A_n(t) + \Phi_n(t)$ for D_n. If we put

$$T_n = \inf\{t \ge 0: |X_n(t)| = n\},$$

then $\{X_n(t \wedge T_n)\}$ is again the solution of $X_n(t \wedge T_n) = M_n(t \wedge T_n) + A_n(t \wedge T_n) + \Phi_n(t \wedge T_n)$ for D_n, and so (3.2) can be applied to $|X_n(t \wedge T_n) - X_n(0)|^2$. Thus, by taking the expectation we have

$$E\{|X_n(t \wedge T_n) - X_n(0)|^2\} \leq 2\int_0^t E\{|X_n(s \wedge T_n) - X_n(0)|\}ds + t$$

$$\leq \int_0^t E\{|X_n(s \wedge T_n) - X_n(0)|^2\}ds + 2t,$$

and hence

$$E\{|X_n(t \wedge T_n) - X_n(0)|^2\} \leq 2te^t,$$

that is, $E\{|X_n(t \wedge T_n)|^2\}$ is bounded in n for each fixed t. Therefore, for each t

$$P\{T_n \leq t\} \leq E\{|X_n(t \wedge T_n)|^2\}/n^2 \to 0 \quad \text{as} \quad n \to \infty. \tag{3.4}$$

On the other hand, the uniqueness lemma in § 2 implies that

$$T_n \leq T_m \quad \text{and} \quad X_n(t) = X_m(t) \qquad \text{for} \quad t \leq T_n$$

hold on the set $\{M(0) \in \bar{D}_n\}$ if $n<m$. This fact combined with (3.4) enables us to define $\{X(t)\}$ almost surely by

$$X(t) = X_n(t) \quad \text{on} \quad \{M(0) \in \bar{D}_n\} \cap \{t \leq T_n\}.$$

Thus defined $\{X(t)\}$ is clearly the $\mathscr{F}_t$-adapted solution of (3.1).

§ 4. Stochastic differential equation with reflection

Let D be a convex domain in $\mathbf{R}^d$ and $\{\Omega, \mathscr{F}, P; \mathscr{F}_t\}$ satisfy the same condition as in § 3. We suppose that an $\mathscr{F}_t$-adapted r-dimensional Brownian motion $B(t)=(B^1(t),\dots, B^r(t))$ with $B(0)=0$ is given; that is, $\{B(t)\}$ is an $\mathscr{F}_t$-adapted continuous process and for $0 \leq s \leq t$, $\xi \in \mathbf{R}^d$

$$E\{e^{i(\xi, B(t)-B(s))}|\mathscr{F}_s\} = e^{-(t-s)|\xi|^2/2}, \quad \text{a.s.}$$

Given an $\mathbf{R}^d \otimes \mathbf{R}^r$-valued function $\sigma(t, x)=\{\sigma_k^i(t, x)\}$ and an $\mathbf{R}^d$-valued function $b(t, x)=\{b^i(t, x)\}$, both being defined on $\mathbf{R}_+ \times \bar{D}$, we consider the stochastic differential equation with reflection

$$dX = \sigma(t, X)dB + b(t, X)dt + d\Phi, \quad X(0) = x, \tag{4.1}$$

or equivalently

$$X^i(t) = x^i + \sum_{k=1}^r \int_0^t \sigma_k^i(s, X(s))dB^k(s) + \int_0^t b^i(s, X(s))ds + \Phi^i(t), \tag{4.1$'$}$$

where $x=(x^1,\dots, x^d) \in \bar{D}$. Our problem is to find an $\mathscr{F}_t$-adapted $\bar{D}$-process $\{X(t)\}$ under the condition that $\{\Phi(t)\}$ is an associated process of $\{X(t)\}$. It is always assumed that $\sigma(t, x)$ and $b(t, x)$ are Borel measurable in (t, x).

THEOREM 4.1. *If there exists a constant $K>0$ such that*

$$\|\sigma(t, x) - \sigma(t, y)\| \leq K|x - y|, \ |b(t, x) - b(t, y)| \leq K|x - y|, \tag{4.2}$$

$$\|\sigma(t, x)\| \leq K(1 + |x|^2)^{1/2}, \ \|b(t, x)\| \leq K(1 + |x|^2)^{1/2}, \tag{4.3}$$

then there exists a (pathwise) unique $\mathscr{F}_t$-adapted solution of (4.1) *for any $x \in \bar{D}$.*

PROOF. First we prove the pathwise uniqueness of the solution. Let $\{X(t)\}$ and $\{Y(t)\}$ be $\mathscr{F}_t$-adapted solutions of (4.1). Then by the first inequality in Remark 2.2

$$|X(t) - Y(t)|^2 \leq \left|\int_0^t \sigma(s, X)dB - \int_0^t \sigma(s, Y)dB\right|^2$$

$$+ 2\int_0^t (X(s) - Y(s), b(s, X) - b(s, Y))ds$$

$$+ \text{the remainder.}$$

Writing the remainder term explicitly, we can see that it has zero expectation[1] and hence

$$E\{|X(t) - Y(t)|^2\} \leq E\int_0^t \|\sigma(s, X) - \sigma(s, Y)\|^2 ds \tag{4.4}$$

$$+ E\int_0^t |X(s) - Y(s)|^2 ds + E\int_0^t |b(s, X) - b(s, Y)|^2 ds$$

$$\leq (2K^2 + 1)\int_0^t E\{|X(s) - Y(s)|^2\}ds.$$

Therefore, $E\{|X(t) - Y(t)|^2\} = 0$.

We give the existence proof, first assuming that D is bounded. By Theorem 2.1, we can define a sequence $\{X^{(n)}(t)\}$ of $\bar{D}$-processes by

$$X^{(0)}(t) = x$$

$$X^{(n)}(t) = x + \int_0^t \sigma(s, X^{(n-1)})dB + \int_0^t b(s, X^{(n-1)})ds + \Phi^{(n)}, \ n \geq 1.$$

Then, as in (4.4) we have

---

1) Because we do not know beforehand that $|X(t) - Y(t)|^2$ and the remainder term are integrable, we must employ the following truncation argument. Let T_n be the infimum of $t \geq 0$ at which

$$\int_0^t \left|X(s) - Y(s)\right|^2 ds + |\Phi|(t) + |\Psi|(t) = n,$$

and derive (4.4) for $X(\cdot \wedge T_n)$ and $Y(\cdot \wedge T_n)$; it then follows that $E\{|X(t \wedge T_n) - Y(t \wedge T_n)|^2\} = 0$; now let $n \uparrow \infty$.

$$E\{|X^{(n+1)}(t) - X^{(n)}(t)|^2\} \le (2K^2 + 1)\int_0^t E\{|X^{(n)}(s) - X^{(n-1)}(s)|^2\}ds.$$

Therefore, by a routine argument we see that

$$\int_0^t \sigma(s, X^{(n)})dB + \int_0^t b(s, X^{(n)})ds$$

is convergent uniformly on compacts as $n\to\infty$ (a. s.). Consequently, from Theorem 2.1, (i), it follows that $\{X^{(n)}(t)\}$ is also convergent uniformly on compacts as $n\to\infty$ (a. s.) and the limit process $\{X(t)\}$ is an $\mathscr{F}_t$-adapted solution of (4.1). When D is unbounded, we put $D_n = D \cap \{|x| < n\}$ and consider the solution $\{X_n(t)\}$ of (4.1) on $\bar{D}_n$. Let T_n be the infimum of $t \ge 0$ at which $|X_n(t)| = n$. Then, applying (3.2) to $|X_n(t\wedge T_n) - x|^2$ and taking the expectation, we have

$$E\{|X_n(t\wedge T_n - x|^2) \le 2E\int_0^{t\wedge T_n}(X_n(s) - x, b(s, X_n))ds$$

$$+ E\int_0^{t\wedge T_n}\sum_{i,k}\sigma_k^i(s, X_n)^2 ds,$$

and hence by making use of (4.3)

$$E\{|X_n(t\wedge T_n) - x|^2\} \le \int_0^t E\{|X_n(s\wedge T_n) - x|^2\}ds$$

$$+ 2K^2\int_0^t E\{1 + |X_n(s\wedge T_n)|^2\}ds.$$

Therefore, by Gronwall's inequality we see that $E\{|X_n(t\wedge T_n)|^2\}$ is bounded in n for each fixed t and hence $P\{T_n \le t\} \le E\{|X_n(t\wedge T_n)|^2\}/n^2 \to 0$ as $n\to\infty$. On the other hand, by the uniqueness already proved we have $T_n \le T_m$ and $X_n(t) = X_m(t)$ for $t \le T_m$ (a. s.) provided $n < m$, and therefore we can construct an $\mathscr{F}_t$-adapted solution $\{X(t)\}$ of (4.1) for D by $X(t) = X_n(t)$, $0 \le t \le T_n$. This completes the proof.

THEOREM 4.2. *If $\sigma(t, x)$ and $b(t, x)$ are bounded continuous on $\mathbf{R}_+ \times \bar{D}$, then on some probability space $(\Omega, \mathscr{F}, P)$ we can find an r-dimensional Brownian motion $\{B(t)\}$ in such a way that* (4.1) *has a solution.*

PROOF. We choose sequences $\{\sigma_n(t, x)\}$ and $\{b_n(t, x)\}$ such that (i) $\sigma_n \to \sigma$ and $b_n \to b$ boundedly and uniformly on compacts as $n\to\infty$, and (ii) σ_n and b_n satisfy the Lipschitz condition. Then there exists a solution $\{X_n(t)\}$ of (4.1) with coefficients σ_n and b_n, for each n. Making use of (3.2) with $f(u) = u^p$, $p \ge 1$,

$$E\{|X_n(t) - X_n(s)|^{2p}\} \le c_p\Big\{E\int_s^t |X_n(\tau) - X_n(s)|^{2p-1}d\tau$$

$$+ E\int_s^t |X_n(\tau) - X_n(s)|^{2p-2}d\tau\Big\},$$

where c_p is some constant depending on p but not on n. Therefore $E\{|X_n(t) - X_n(s)|^4\} \leq c|t-s|^2$ for $0 \leq s$, $t \leq T$, where c is some constant depending on T but not on n, T being an arbitrary positive constant. This implies that the family of probability measures on $\mathbf{C}(\mathbf{R}_+, \bar{D}) \times \mathbf{C}(\mathbf{R}_+, \mathbf{R}^d)$ induced by $\{(X_n(t), B(t))\}$ is tight. Therefore, noticing the result (ii) of Theorem 2.1 we can fill the rest of our proof exactly in the same way as in the case of the whole space $\mathbf{R}^d$ (see [5]). The proof is finished.

The following theorem, due to O. Tanbara (unpublished), can be proved in the same way as in [9] making use of the estimate (3.2).

THEOREM 4.3. *Let ρ and $\bar{\rho}$ satisfy*

$$\int_{0+} \{\rho^2(u)u^{-1} + \bar{\rho}(u)\}^{-1} du = \infty, \tag{4.5}$$

$$\rho^2(u)u^{-1} + \bar{\rho}(u) \quad \text{is concave.} \tag{4.6}$$

Then, for any $\sigma(t, x)$ and $b(t, x)$ satisfying

$$\|\sigma(t, x) - \sigma(t, y)\| \leq \rho(|x-y|), \quad |b(t, x) - b(t, y)| \leq \bar{\rho}(|x-y|),$$

the pathwise uniqueness of solutions holds for (4.1).

References

[1] N. Ikeda, On the construction of two-dimensional diffusion processes satisfying Wentzell's boundary conditions and its application to boundary value problems, Mem. Coll. Sci. Univ. Kyôto, **33** (1961), 367–427.

[2] H. P. McKean, A. Skorohod's integral equation for a reflecting barrier diffusion, J. Math. Kyôto Univ., **3** (1963), 86–88.

[3] H. P. McKean, Stochastic Integrals, Academic Press, 1969.

[4] A. V. Skorohod, Stochastic equations for diffusion processes in a bounded region 1, 2, Theor. Veroyatnost. i Primenen. **6** (1961), 264–274; **7** (1962), 3–23.

[5] A. V. Skorohod, Studies in the Theory of Random Processes, Addison Wesley, 1965.

[6] D. W. Stroock and S. R. S. Varadhan, Diffusion processes with boundary conditions, Comm. Pure Appl. Math., **24** (1971), 147–225.

[7] M. Tsuchiya, On the stochastic differential equation for a two-dimensional Brownian motion with boundary condition, to appear.

[8] S. Watanabe, On stochastic differential equations for multi-dimensional diffusion processes with boundary conditions, J. Math Kyôto Univ., **11** (1971), 169–180.

[9] S. Watanabe and T. Yamada, On the uniqueness of solutions of stochastic differential equations II, J. Math. Kyôto Univ., **11** (1971), 553–563.

Department of Mathematics,
Faculty of Science,
Hiroshima University

SOME PROBABILISTIC PROBLEMS IN THE SPATIALLY HOMOGENEOUS BOLTZMANN EQUATION

Hiroshi Tanaka

Department of Mathematics
Faculty of Science and Technology
Keio University, Yokohama, Japan

1. Introduction

1.1. The master equation approach to the spatially homogeneous Boltzmann equation initiated by Kac [1] and continued by McKean [3], Grünbaum [5] and others is briefly reviewed together with some new results on

(I) propagation of chaos (law of large numbers),

(II) fluctuation (central limit theorem).

We are interested in the time evolution of the velocities $X_1^{(n)}(t), \dots, X_n^{(n)}(t)$ of n particles moving in the space R^3 under certain binary interaction (collision). We assume that $(X_1^{(n)}(t), \dots, X_n^{(n)}(t))$ is a Markov process on R^{3n} with generator

$$(K_n\varphi)(x_1,\dots,x_n)$$

$$= \frac{1}{n} \sum_{1\le i<j\le n} \int_{(0,\pi)\times(0,2\pi)} \{\varphi(\dots,x_i',\dots,x_j',\dots) - \varphi(x_1,\dots,x_n)\} Q(x_i,x_j,\theta)\,d\theta\,d\epsilon ,$$

where x_i' and x_j' are the post-collision velocities of the i-th and j-th particles with velocities x_i and x_j. If $S(x,y)$ denotes the 2-dimensional sphere with center $(x+y)/2$ and diameter $|x-y|$, the x_i' and x_j' are always on $S(x_i,x_j)$ or more precisely $S(x_i',x_j')=S(x_i,x_j)$. We now take a spherical coordinate system on $S(x_i,x_j)$ with north pole x_i and denote by θ (resp. ϵ) the colatitude (resp. longitude) of x_i'. The function $Q(x,y,\theta)$, which is determined by the interparticle (binary) potential, is assumed to be nonnegative and depend only on $|x-y|$, $x+y$ and θ. The forward equation

$$\frac{d}{dt}\langle u(t),\varphi\rangle = \langle u(t),K_n\varphi\rangle, \quad \varphi = \text{(test) function on } R^{3n} \tag{1}$$

describing the Markov process $X^{(n)}(t)$ is called the n-particle <u>master equation</u> corresponding to the following spatially homogeneous <u>Boltzmann equation</u>

(2) $$\frac{\partial u}{\partial t} = \int_{(0,\pi)\times(0,2\pi)\times R^3} (u'u_1' - uu_1)Q(x,x_1,\theta)\,d\theta\, d\epsilon\, dx_1 ,$$

where $u = u(t,x)$, $u_1=u(t,x_1)$, $u'=u(t,x')$, $u_1'=u(t,x_1')$; x' and x_1' are the post-collision velocities, i.e., $(x,x_1) \to (x',x_1')$ by "collision"; the notation $\langle u,\varphi\rangle$ in general stands for the integral of a function φ with respect to a measure u. As in [7] we consider a weak version of (2);

(3) $$\frac{d}{dt}\langle u(t),\varphi\rangle = \langle u(t)\otimes u(t),K\varphi\rangle ,$$

or equivalently

(3#) $$\frac{d}{dt}\langle u(t),\varphi\rangle = \langle u(t)\otimes u(t),K^{\#}\varphi\rangle ,$$

where φ is a (test) function R^3 and

(4) $$(K\varphi)(x,x_1) = \int_{(0,\pi)\times(0,2\pi)} \{\varphi(x') - \varphi(x)\}Q(x,x_1,\theta)\,d\theta\, d\epsilon ,$$

$$(K^{\#}\varphi)(x,x_1) = \{(K\varphi)(x,x_1) + (K\varphi)(x_1,x)\}/2 .$$

By a weak solution of (2) we mean a probability measure solution of (3) ($=(3^{\#})$) .

1.2. <u>Propagation of chaos</u>. Let $\{u_n,\ n>1\}$ be a sequence of probability measures, each u_n being a symmetric probability measure on the n-fold product space $R^{3n} = R^3\times\ldots\times R^3$. Let u be a probability measure on R^3 . Then a sequence $\{u_n\}$ is said to be u-chaotic if

$$\langle u_n,\varphi_1\otimes\cdots\otimes\varphi_m\otimes 1\otimes\cdots\otimes 1\rangle \to \prod_{k=1}^{m}\langle u,\varphi_k\rangle \quad \text{as } n\to\infty \text{ for any } \varphi_1,\ldots,$$

$\varphi_m\in C_0(R^3)$, $m\geq 1$. The relation between the master equation (1) and the corresponding Boltzmann equation (2) was made clear by Kac [1] through the following propagation of chaos : <u>Let</u> $u_n(t)$ <u>be the solution of</u> (1) <u>with initial value</u> u_n <u>and assume that</u> $\{u_n,\ n>1\}$ <u>is</u> u-<u>chaotic</u>. <u>Then</u> $\{u_n(t),\ n>1\}$ <u>is also</u> u(t)-<u>chaotic where</u> $u(t)$ <u>is the</u> (<u>weak</u>) <u>solution</u> <u>of</u> (2) <u>with initial value</u> u . We next introduce the normalized occupation number

$$\bar{X}_n(t) = \frac{1}{n}\sum_{k=1}^{n}\delta_{X_k^{(n)}(t)}$$

where δ_x denotes the δ-distribution at x . We can easily show that

$\{u_n\}$ is u-chaotic if and only if the law of large numbers holds for $\{u_n\}$ in the following sense:

$$\frac{1}{n}\sum_{k=1}^{n} \delta_{X_k^{(n)}} \longrightarrow u\ , \qquad n \to \infty \text{ (in probability)}$$

where $X^{(n)} = (X_1^{(n)},\dots,X_n^{(n)})$ is a u_n-distributed random vector. Therefore, since $X^{(n)}(t)$ is $u_n(t)$-distributed provided that $X^{(n)}(0)$ is u_n-distributed, the propagation of chaos is equivalent to the following <u>law of large numbers</u>:

(5) $\quad \overline{X}_n(0) \to u,\ \ n \to \infty$ (in prob.) $\Rightarrow \overline{X}_n(t) \to u(t),\ \ n \to \infty$ (in prob.)

where $u(t)$ is the same as before.

The proof of the propagation of chaos was first given by Kac [1] for the case of 1-dimensional Kac's model of Maxwellian molecules; McKean [3] gave a beautiful proof for some special case including cutoff model of the Boltzmann equation of Maxwellian molecules. Murata [6] treated the 2-dimensional non-cutoff Maxwellian model. Grünbaum [5] discussed the case of a considerably wide (cutoff) class; his discussions covered the gas of hard spheres but under some assumption which was unverified though very believable. In §2 of this article the propagation of chaos will be proved in the following two cases.

(i) $\displaystyle\int_0^{\pi} Q(x,y,\theta)d\theta \le \text{const.}(1+|x|^2+|y|^2)$.

(ii) (Maxwellian type) $Q(x,y,\theta)$ is a function $Q(\theta)$ of θ alone satisfying $\displaystyle\int_0^{\pi} \theta^2 Q(\theta)d\theta < \infty$.

It is to be noted that the case (i) includes the gas of hard spheres ($Q(x,y,\theta) = \text{const.}|x-y|\sin\theta$) while the case (ii) includes the 3-dimensional Maxwellian molecules with the inverse 5-th power interparticle repulsive force (in such a case $Q(\theta) \sim \text{const.}\,\theta^{-3/2}$, $\theta \downarrow 0$) .

1.3. <u>Fluctuation</u>. Since the normalized occupation number $\overline{X}_n(t)$ is fluctuating about a solution $u(t)$ of the Boltzmann equation (2), the next problem is to study the asymptotic behavior of

(6) $$Y_n(t) = \sqrt{n}(\overline{X}_n(t) - u(t))$$

as $n \to \infty$. The case of McKean's 2-state model of Maxwellian moleclues was first discussed by Kac [2] and then by McKean [4] in detail. As found in heuristic discussion by [4] for the case of gas of hard spheres, the limit process of $Y_n(t)$ must be, in general, an infinite dimensional Ornstein-Uhlenbeck process. Rigorous discussions in the case of Kac's 1-dimensional model of Maxwellian molecules were given by Tanaka [7] (equilibrium case) from the point of view of a limit theorem on Markov processes taking values of tempered distributions. Non-equilibrium case was then treated by Uchiyama [8]. Recently, Uchiyama [9] discussed the equilibrium case of cutoff type including gas of hard spheres. In §3 of this article the fluctuation theory (=central limit theorem) will be discussed in the case (ii) (Maxwellian type) along the same lines as in [7]. The emphasis here is on the non-cutoff property.

Fundamentally our method is to derive appropriate convergences of Markov processes $\overline{X}_n(t)$ and $Y_n(t)$ knowing the convergence of their generators (a martingale problem approach will then be useful), except for the treatment of chaos propagation in the case (ii) where the cutoff approximation will be used. Proofs are only outlined; details will appear elsewhere.

2. Propagation of chaos

2.1. Case (i). Let $\xi_0=1$, $\xi_1=x$ and $\xi_k=|x|^k$ for $k\geq 2$ $(x\in R^3)$.

Theorem 1. The function $Q(x,y,\theta)$, depending only on $|x-y|$, $x+y$ and θ, is assumed to satisfy the condition (i) of §1. In addition, we assume that

(7) $K\varphi$ is continuous provided that φ is bounded and continuous.

Let u_n be the initial distribution of $X^{(n)}(\cdot)$ and assume that $\{u_n\}$ is a u-chaotic sequence satisfying

$$\langle u,\xi_6\rangle<\infty, \quad \sup_{n\geq 1}\langle u_n,\xi_6\otimes 1\otimes\cdots\otimes 1\rangle<\infty .$$

Then for any $\varepsilon>0$ and T $(0<T<\infty)$

(8) $$P\left\{\sup_{0\leq t\leq T}\rho(\overline{X}_n(t),\ u(t))>\varepsilon\right\}\to 0$$

as $n\to\infty$, where ρ is any metric on $\mathcal{M}$ (the space of probability measures on R^3) which gives the usual vague topology on $\mathcal{M}$.

Remark. $u(t)$ in (8) is the solution of (3) (with $u(0)=u$) whose existence and uniquencess are guaranteed by the following Arkeryd's result [10]: Under the same assumption on $Q(x,y,\theta)$ as in Theorem 1 except for (7) (which is unnecessary here), for any initial value $u(o) = u$ satisfying $\langle u, \xi_4\rangle < \infty$ there exists a unique solution $u(t)$ of (3) such that $\langle u(t), \xi_4\rangle$ is bounded on each finite t-interval. The solution $u(t)$ also satisfies $\langle u(t), \xi_k\rangle = \langle u, \xi_k\rangle$, $k = 0,1,2$.

The proof of the theorem is sketched here. Choose a sequence $\{f_k, k\geq 1\}$ in $C_0(R^3)$ such that $\|f_k\|_\infty \leq 1$ and the set of all (finite) linear combinations of f_k's is dense in $C_0(R^3)$, and set $\rho(u, \tilde{u}) = \sum_{k=1}^{\infty} 2^{-k}|\langle u-\tilde{u}, f_k\rangle|$ for $u, \tilde{u}\in\mathcal{M}$. We first consider the special case in which $u_n(\mathcal{X}_n) = 1$, $n>1$, where $\mathcal{X}_n$ is the ball in R^{3n} of radius cn, the constant c being independent of n. Let $\mathcal{M}_0$ be the set of $u\in\mathcal{M}$ such that $\langle u, \xi_2\rangle \leq c$ and W be the space (endowed with the Skorohod topology) of $\mathcal{M}_0$-valued right continuous paths with left limits. Then $\overline{X}_n(t)$ is regarded as a Markov process with sample path in W. Denote by P_n the probability measure on W induced by the process $\overline{X}_n(t)$. We can prove the following lemmas (1°-3°) in which T is an arbitrary positive constant.

1°. $E_n\{\rho(w(t_1),w(t_2))^2\rho(w(t_2),w(t_3))^2\}\leq \text{const.}|t_3-t_1|^2$ for $0\leq t_1<t_2<t_3\leq T$, where const. may depend on T. Therefore, $\{P_n\}$ is tight.

2°. $\sup_n P_n\{\sup_{0\leq t\leq T}\langle w(t), \xi_4\rangle > N\} \longrightarrow 0$ as $N\to\infty$.

3°. If P_∞ is any limit point of $\{P_n\}$, then

a) $\sup_{0\leq t\leq T}\langle w(t), \xi_4\rangle < \infty$, P_∞-a.s.,

b) $\langle w(t),\varphi\rangle - \langle w(0),\varphi\rangle - \int_0^t \langle w(s)\otimes w(s), K^{\#}\varphi\rangle ds = 0$, P_∞-as, $\varphi\in C_0(R^3)$.

Since $\overline{X}_n(0)\to u$ in probability, $w(0)=u$ (P_∞-a.s.). Therefore, Arkeryd's uniqueness result applied to 3° implies that $w(t)=u(t)$, $t\geq 0$, P_∞-a.s., i.e., $P_\infty = \delta_{u(\cdot)}$. This implies (8).

General case can be reduced to the spacial case by noticing that $u_n(\mathcal{X}_n)\to 1$ as $n\to\infty$ where $\mathcal{X}_n$ is defined as before choosing a constant $c>\langle u,\xi_2\rangle$.

2.2. Case (ii). We deal with this case by approximating $Q(x,y,\theta)$ by cutoff one. Let $Q_\varepsilon(\theta)=Q(\theta)$ (for $\varepsilon<\theta<\pi$) and $=0$ (for $0<\theta\leq\varepsilon$), and define $K^{(\varepsilon)}$ with $Q(\theta)$ replaced by $Q_\varepsilon(\theta)$ (cutoff) in the definition (4) of K. Let $u_\varepsilon(t)$ be the solution of

$$(3\varepsilon) \qquad \frac{d}{dt}\langle u(t),\varphi\rangle = \langle u(t)\otimes u(t), K^{(\varepsilon)}\varphi\rangle$$

with initial value u .

Theorem 2. (i) If $\langle u,\xi_2\rangle<\infty$, then $u_\varepsilon(t)$ converges weakly to some $u(t)$ (as $\varepsilon\downarrow 0$) which is a solution of (3) with initial value u . (ii) If $\langle u,\xi_2\rangle<\infty$ and if $\{u_n\}$ is a u-chaotic sequence satisfying

$$\lim_{n\to\infty}\langle u_n, \xi_2\otimes 1\otimes\ldots\otimes 1\rangle = \langle u,\xi_2\rangle ,$$

then $\{u_n(t)\}$ is also u(t)-chaotic and

$$\lim_{n\to\infty}\langle u_n(t), \xi_2\otimes 1\otimes\ldots\otimes 1\rangle = \langle u(t),\xi_2\rangle ,$$

where u(t) is the solution of (3) constructed in (i).

3. Fluctuation

We consider only the case of non-cutoff Maxwellian type. Thus we assume that a function $Q(\theta)$ satisfying (ii) of §1 is given. We set

$$g(x)=(2\pi)^{-3/2}e^{-|x|^2/2} , \quad g=g(x)dx , \quad e_0(x)=\sqrt{g(x)} .$$

We also assume that the initial distribution of $X^{(n)}(\cdot)$ is the n-fold product $g^{n\otimes}$. In this case we have $u_n(t)=g^{n\otimes}$ and $u(t)=g$, and (for notational convention) it is better to modify the definition (6) of $Y_n(t)$ as follows.

$$Y_n(t) = \sqrt{n}\{\overline{X}_n(t) - g\}/e_0(\cdot) ,$$

i.e.,
$$\langle Y_n(t),\varphi\rangle = n^{-1/2}\sum_{k=1}^{n}\left\{\frac{\varphi(X_k^{(n)}(t))}{e_0(X_k^{(n)}(t))} - \langle e_0,\varphi\rangle\right\} .$$

The fluctuation theory is to study the asymptotic behavior of $Y_n(t)$ as $n\to\infty$. Note that $Y_n(t)$ is a Markov process on the state space

$$\left\{\eta\in\mathcal{S}'(R^3) : \eta=\sqrt{n}(\overline{x}-g)/e_0(\cdot) , \quad \overline{x} = \frac{1}{n}\sum_{1}^{n}\delta_{x_k}, x_1,\ldots,x_n\in R^3\right\} .$$

We introduce some notation.

$$\hat{\varphi}(x,y) = \varphi(x') + \varphi(y') - \varphi(x) - \varphi(y) ,$$

$$Q[\varphi,\psi] = \frac{1}{4}\int_{(0,\pi)\times(0,2\pi)} \hat{\varphi}(x,y)\hat{\psi}(x,y)Q(x,y,\theta)\,d\theta\, d\epsilon \ ,$$

$$\varphi^{\#}(x) = \varphi(x)/e_0(x), \quad \tilde{\varphi}(x,y) = \widehat{\varphi^{\#}}(x,y) \ .$$

Let $F(\eta)$ be a function of the form

$$F(\eta) = f(\langle\eta,\varphi_1\rangle,\dots,\langle\eta,\varphi_m\rangle), \quad f\in C_0^{\infty}(R^3), \quad \varphi_1,\dots,\varphi_m\in\mathcal{S} ,$$

where $\mathcal{S} = \mathcal{S}(R^3)$, the space of rapidly decreasing C^{∞}-functions. Then the generator L_n of the Markov process $Y_n(t)$ is given by

$$L_nF(\eta) = \sum_{\alpha=1}^{m}\left\langle e_0\eta\otimes\left(\frac{e_0\eta}{\sqrt{n}} + 2g\right) , K^{\#}\varphi_{\alpha}^{\#}(x,y)\right\rangle\partial_{\alpha}f$$

$$+ \sum_{\alpha,\beta=1}^{m}\left\langle\left(\frac{e_0\eta}{\sqrt{n}} + g\right)^{2\otimes}, Q[\varphi_{\alpha}^{\#},\varphi_{\beta}^{\#}]\right\rangle\partial_{\alpha\beta}^2 f + R_n ,$$

$$R_n = \frac{1}{6n^2\sqrt{n}}\sum_{\alpha,\beta,\gamma=1}^{m}\ \sum_{1\le i<j\le n}\int_{(0,\pi)\times(0,2\pi)}(\tilde{\varphi}_{\alpha}\tilde{\varphi}_{\beta}\tilde{\varphi}_{\gamma})(x_i,x_j)\partial_{\alpha\beta\gamma}^3 fQ\,d\theta\, d\epsilon \ ,$$

where the argument in $\partial_{\alpha\beta\gamma}^3 f$ is

$$(\langle\eta,\varphi_1\rangle + \frac{\kappa\tilde{\varphi}_1(x_i,x_j)}{\sqrt{n}},\dots,\langle\eta,\varphi_m\rangle + \frac{\kappa\tilde{\varphi}_m(x_i,x_j)}{\sqrt{n}}) , \quad 0<\kappa<1 ,$$

and hence the limiting generator $L=\lim_{n\to\infty}L_n$ is given (at least formally) by

$$LF(\eta) = 2\sum_{\alpha=1}^{m}\langle e_0\eta\otimes g, K^{\#}\varphi_{\alpha}^{\#}\rangle\partial_{\alpha}f + \sum_{\alpha,\beta=1}^{m}\langle g\otimes g, Q[\varphi_{\alpha}^{\#},\varphi_{\beta}^{\#}]\rangle\partial_{\alpha\beta}^2 f \ .$$

Now the problem may be stated as follows: (a) Find a diffusion process $Y(t)$ with generator L on a suitable space of distributions. (b) Prove the convergence in the law sense of $Y_n(t)$ to $Y(t)$.

Linearized collision operator: If we introduce l.c.o. $\mathcal{L}$ by

$$\mathcal{L}\varphi(x) = e_0(x)\int_{(0,\pi)\times(0,2\pi)\times R^3} g(y)\tilde{\varphi}(x,y)Q(x,y,\theta)\,d\theta\, d\epsilon\, dy \ ,$$

L can be expressed as

(9) $$LF(\eta) = -\sum_{\alpha,\beta=1}^{m} (\mathcal{L}\varphi_\alpha, \varphi_\beta)_0 \partial^2_{\alpha\beta} f + \sum_{\alpha=1}^{m} \langle \eta, \mathcal{L}\varphi_\alpha \rangle \partial_\alpha f ,$$

where (,) denotes the usual inner product in $L^2(R^3)$.

Eigenfunctions of $\mathcal{L}$: For each integer $\ell \geq 0$ we choose $2\ell+1$ harmonic polynomials H^m_ℓ, $m=0, \pm1,\dots,\pm\ell$ of degree ℓ so that the family

$$\left\{ S^m_\ell \equiv H^m_\ell \big|_{S^2} \text{(spherical harmonics)}: \quad m=0, \pm1,\dots,\pm\ell \right\}$$

forms an ONS in $L^2(S^2)$, and set

$$e_{\underline{n}}(x) = c_{\underline{n}} e_0(x) L_n^{\ell+\frac{1}{2}}(|x|^2/2) H^m_\ell(x) ,$$

$$\underline{n} = (n,\ell,m), \quad n,\ell = 0,1,\dots, \quad m = 0,\pm1,\dots,\pm\ell ,$$

where

$L_n^{\ell+\frac{1}{2}}(t)$ = the associated Laguerre polynomial of degree n and order $\ell + \frac{1}{2}$,

$$c_{\underline{n}} = \left\{ \frac{n!\pi^{3/2}}{2^{\ell-1}\,\Gamma(n+\ell+\frac{3}{2})} \right\}^{1/2} .$$

Then $\left\{ e_{\underline{n}} : \underline{n} = (n,\ell,m) \right\}$ is a CONS in $L^2(R^3)$. It is known that $e_{\underline{n}}$'s are eigenfunctions of $\mathcal{L}$ ([11] [12]), i.e.,

$$e_{\underline{n}} = -\lambda_{\underline{n}} e_{\underline{n}} ,$$

where

$$\lambda_{\underline{n}} = 2\pi \int_0^\pi \left\{ 1 - (\cos\tfrac{\theta}{2})^{2n+\ell} P_\ell(\cos\tfrac{\theta}{2}) - (\sin\tfrac{\theta}{2})^{2n+\ell} P_\ell(\sin\tfrac{\theta}{2}) \right\} Q(\theta)\, d\theta$$

$$\geq 0 \qquad \text{if} \quad 2n + \ell > 0 ,$$

$$\lambda_{(0,0,0)} = \lambda_{(0,1,m)} = \lambda_{(1,0,0)} = 0 \quad \text{for} \quad m = 0, \pm1 ,$$

$P_\ell(t)$ being the Legendre polynomial of degree ℓ . We can prove that

(10) $$\lambda_{\underline{n}} \leq \text{const.}(2n + \ell)^2 .$$

Moreover, $e_{\underline{\underline{n}}}$'s are also eigenfunctions of $\frac{|x|^2}{4} - \Delta$, i.e.,

$$(11) \qquad (\frac{|x|^2}{4} - \Delta)e_{\underline{\underline{n}}} = (2n + \ell + \frac{3}{2})e_{\underline{\underline{n}}} .$$

Spaces of distributions:

$$\|\varphi\|_\alpha = \|(\frac{|x|^2}{4} - \Delta)^{\alpha/2}\varphi\|_0 , \quad \alpha \in R$$

$$(= \left\{\sum_{\underline{\underline{n}}} a_{\underline{\underline{n}}}^2 (2n + \ell + \tfrac{3}{2})^\alpha\right\}^{1/2} \quad \text{for } \varphi = \sum a_{\underline{\underline{n}}} e_{\underline{\underline{n}}} \quad \text{by (11)}),$$

$\mathcal{S}_\alpha$ = the Hilbert space obtained by completing $\mathcal{S}$ with respect to $\|\cdot\|_\alpha$,

$\mathcal{S}'_\alpha$ = the dual space of $\mathcal{S}_\alpha$ $(\cong \mathcal{S}_{-\alpha})$.

Stochastic differential equation: Let $B(t)$ be a Brownian motion on $\mathcal{S}'$ determined by

$$E\left\{e^{i\langle B(t),\varphi\rangle}\right\} = e^{-t\|\varphi\|_0^2/2} , \quad \varphi \in \mathcal{S} , \quad B(0) = 0;$$

in fact $B(t)$ exists as an $\mathcal{S}'_{3+\varepsilon}$-Brownian motion $(\forall \varepsilon > 0)$. From the expression (9) of $\mathcal{L}$ it follows that the Markov process $Y(t)$ with generator L should satisfy the stochastic differential equation

$$(12) \qquad dY(t) = \sqrt{-2\mathcal{L}}\, dB(t) + \mathcal{L}\, Y(t)dt .$$

If we set $Y_{\underline{\underline{n}}}(t) = \langle Y(t), e_{\underline{\underline{n}}}\rangle$, then (12) yields

$$dY_{\underline{\underline{n}}}(t) = \sqrt{2\lambda_{\underline{\underline{n}}}}\, dB_{\underline{\underline{n}}}(t) - \lambda_{\underline{\underline{n}}} Y_{\underline{\underline{n}}}(t)dt ,$$

where $B_{\underline{\underline{n}}}(t)$'s are independent copies of 1-dimensional Brownian motion. Making use of the bound (10) for $\lambda_{\underline{\underline{n}}}$ it can be proved that

$$\sum_{2n+\ell \leq k} Y_{\underline{\underline{n}}}(t) e_{\underline{\underline{n}}} \to Y(t) \quad \text{as} \quad k \to \infty$$

uniformly on each finite t-interval in the space $\mathcal{S}'_{3+\varepsilon}$ almost surely for any $\varepsilon > 0$, and we can finally prove the following theorem.

Theorem 3. The Markov process $Y(t)$ with generator L and satisfying

$$E\left\{e^{i\langle Y(0),\varphi\rangle}\right\} = e^{-\left\{\|\varphi\|_0^2-(e_0,\varphi)_0^2\right\}/2}, \quad \varphi\in\mathcal{S}$$

exists as a diffusion process on $\mathcal{S}'_{3+\varepsilon}$ for any $\varepsilon>0$, and any finite dimensional distribution of $Y_n(t)$ as a process on $\mathcal{S}'_{3+\varepsilon}$ converges to the corresponding finite dimensional distribution of $Y(t)$ as $n\to\infty$.

It is to be noted that the SDE (12) has a solution $Y(t)$ which is continuous in $\mathcal{S}'_{3+\varepsilon}$, while the process $\sqrt{-2\mathcal{L}}\,B(t)$ is not always continuous in $\mathcal{S}'_{3+\varepsilon}$.

References

1. M. Kac, Foundations of kinetic theory, Proc. Third Berkeley Symp. on Math. Stat. and Prob., 3(1956), 171-197.
2. M. Kac, Some probabilistic aspects of the Boltzmann-equation, Acta Physica Austriaca, Suppl. X(1973), 379-400.
3. H. P. McKean, An exponential formula for solving Boltzmann's equation for a Maxwellian gas, J. Combinatorial Theory, 2(1967), 358-382.
4. H. P. McKean, Fluctuations in the kinetic theory of gases, Comm. Pure Appl. Math., 28(1975), 435-455.
5. F. A. Grünbaum, Propagation of chaos for the Boltzmann equation, Arch. Rational Mech. Anal., 42(1971), 323-345.
6. H. Murata, Propagation of chaos for Boltzmann-like equation of non-cutoff type in the plane, Hiroshima Math. J., 7(1977), 479-515.
7. H. Tanaka, Fluctuation theory for Kac's one-dimensional model of Maxwellian molecules, to appear in Sankhyā, 44, Series A, Part I (1982).
8. K. Uchiyama, Fluctuations of Markovian systems in Kac's caricature of a Maxwellian gas, to appear in J. Math. Soc. Japan.
9. K. Uchiyama, A Fluctuation problem associated with the Boltzmann equation for a gas of molecules with a cut-off potential, to appear.
10. L. Arkeryd, On the Boltzmann equation, Part I, II, Archive for Rational Mech. Anal., 45(1972), 1-16, 17-34.
11. C. S. Wang Chang and G. E. Uhlenbeck (1952), In "The Kinetic Theory of Gases", Studies in Statistical Mechanics, Vol. V, North-Holland, Amsterdam (1970).
12. C. Cercignani, Mathematical Methods in Kinetic Theory, Plenum Press, New York (1969).

Reprinted from

Theory and Application of Random Fields, 258–267, Lecture Notes in Control and Information Sciences, **49**, Springer-Verlag, 1983.

Taniguchi Symp. SA
Katata 1982, pp. 469–488

Limit Theorems for Certain Diffusion Processes with Interaction

Hiroshi TANAKA

Introduction

Given smooth functions $\sigma(x, y)$ and $b(x, y)$, we write

$$\sigma[x, u] = \int_R \sigma(x, y)u(y)dy \quad \left(= \int_R \sigma(x, y)u(dy)\right)$$

$$b[x, u] = \int_R b(x, y)u(y)dy \quad \left(= \int_R b(x, y)u(dy)\right)$$

for a function $u(y)$ (or a measure $u(dy)$). On the analogy of Kac's master equation approach [5] to the Boltzmann equation, McKean [9] considered the n-particle diffusion process $\xi^{(n)}(t) = (\xi_1^{(n)}(t), \cdots, \xi_n^{(n)}(t))$ described by the stochastic differential equation (abbreviated: SDE)

$$\text{(1)} \qquad \begin{aligned} d\xi_i^{(n)}(t) &= \frac{1}{n-1} \sum_{j=1(\neq i)}^{n} \sigma(\xi_i^{(n)}(t), \xi_j^{(n)}(t))dw_j(t) \\ &\quad + \frac{1}{n-1} \sum_{j=1(\neq i)}^{n} b(\xi_i^{(n)}(t), \xi_j^{(n)}(t))dt, \quad 1 \leq i \leq n, \end{aligned}$$

($w_j(t)$'s are independent copies of a 1-dimensional Brownian motion) and proved the following: If the initial values $\xi_1^{(n)}(0), \cdots, \xi_n^{(n)}(0)$ are independent random variables with the same distribution u, then for each m the process $(\xi_1^{(n)}(t), \cdots, \xi_m^{(n)}(t))$ converges in law to $(\xi_1(t), \cdots, \xi_m(t))$ as $n \to \infty$ where $\xi_1(t), \xi_2(t), \cdots$ are independent copies of the diffusion process $\xi(t)$ obtained by solving the stochastic differential equation

$$\text{(2.a)} \qquad d\xi(t) = \sigma[\xi(t), u(t)]dw(t) + b[\xi(t), u(t)]dt$$

(2.b) $\qquad \xi(0)$ is independent of $w(t)$ and u-distributed

subject to the condition "$u(t)$ = the probability distribution of $\xi(t)$", $w(t)$ being a 1-dimensional Brownian motion. Moreover, $u(t)$ is the weak solution of the nonlinear parabolic equation

(3) $$\frac{\partial u}{\partial t} = \frac{1}{2}\cdot\frac{\partial^2}{\partial x^2}(\sigma[x, u]^2 u) - \frac{\partial}{\partial x}(b[x, u]u)$$

with $u(0) = u$. Let W be the space of real valued continuous paths. Then each process $\xi_i^{(n)}(t)$ is regarded as a W-valued random variable $\xi_i^{(n)}$ and McKean's result implies the following law of large numbers:

(4) $$U_n = \frac{1}{n}\sum_{i=1}^{n}\delta_{\xi_i^{(n)}} \longrightarrow \mu, \quad n \to \infty \quad \text{(in prob.)};$$

where μ is the probability measure on W induced by the process $\xi(t)$ and the notation δ_x stands for the δ-distribution at x. The next stage is the central limit theorem in which the asymptotic behavior of

(5) $$Y_n = \sqrt{n}(U_n - \mu),$$

as $n \to \infty$, is studied. The special case when $\sigma = 1$ and $b(x, y) = -\lambda(x - y)$, $\lambda > 0$, was discussed by Tanaka and Hitsuda [14]. We shall discuss, in this paper, the case when $\sigma = 1$ with general $b(x, y)$ but the SDE (1) will be slightly modified as follows:

(6) $$d\xi_i^{(n)}(t) = dw_i(t) + \frac{1}{n}\sum_{j=1}^{n} b(\xi_i^{(n)}(t), \xi_j^{(n)}(t))dt.$$

Braun and Hepp [1] studied similar limit theorems in the case of modified Vlasov equation starting from a (deterministic) n-body problem. Their result on the law of large numbers is covered by McKean's result, since σ may be assumed to vanish in (1). However, the work of Braun and Hepp is very interesting because of their method used in the discussion of the central limit theorem. The purpose of this paper is to study the central limit theorem and the large deviation problem for U_n in the case when $b(x, y)$ is general but $\sigma = 1$, by amplifying the method of Braun and Hepp. The central limit theorem in the time evolution, which studies the asymptotic behavior of Markov processes

(7) $$Y_n(t) = \sqrt{n}\left(\frac{1}{n}\sum_{i=1}^{n}\delta_{\xi_i^{(n)}(t)} - u(t)\right)$$

as $n \to \infty$, may also be discussed by employing the method of martingale problem as in the works [12] [13] [15] for Boltzmann's equation; however, the result in the time evolution does not automatically imply the result in the path space. The advantage of the present method is that we can easily arrive at the result in the path space and also can find the I-functional governing the large deviation for U_n. This result for the large deviation problem of U_n will lead to a conjecture for a similar problem in the case of Boltzmann's equation.

§ 1. A method of Braun and Hepp

We state a general theorem which is an abstraction of the method used by Braun and Hepp in the proof of Theorem 3.5 of [1].

Let S be a Polish space and $\mathfrak{M}$ be the Banach space of bounded signed measures on S with total variation norm $\|\cdot\|$. Let $\mathfrak{M}_1$ be the subset of $\mathfrak{M}$ consisting of substochastic measures on S. Suppose we are given a function

$$f\colon S \times \mathfrak{M} \longrightarrow \boldsymbol{R}$$

satisfying the following assumption.

Assumption. There exists a (Borel) function

$$f'\colon S \times S \times \mathfrak{M}_1 \longrightarrow \boldsymbol{R}$$

satisfying the following conditions (A.1)–(A.4).

(A.1) f' is bounded.

(A.2) $\|f'(x, y, \rho) - f'(x, y, \rho')\|_\infty \leq \text{const.}\ \|\rho - \rho'\|$ for any $\rho, \rho' \in \mathfrak{M}_1$.

(A.3) If $\rho_n, \rho \in \mathfrak{M}_1$ and if $\rho_n \to \rho$ weakly as $n \to \infty$, then

$$\lim_{n\to\infty} f'(x, y, \rho_n) = f'(x, y, \rho)\,.$$

(A.4) $f(x, \rho+\nu) = f(x, \rho) + f'(x, \nu, \rho) + \int_0^1 \{f'(x, \nu, \rho + t\nu) - f'(x, \nu, \rho)\}dt$

for any $\rho \in \mathfrak{M}_1$ and $\nu \in \mathfrak{M}$ such that $\rho + \nu \in \mathfrak{M}_1$, where

$$f'(x, \nu, \rho) = \int_S f'(x, y, \rho)\nu(dy)\,.$$

Notation. For $\rho, \rho' \in \mathfrak{M}$ we use the notation

$$f(\rho', \rho) = \int_S f(x, \rho)\rho'(dx)\,.$$

Theorem 1.1. *Let f be a bounded function satisfying the above assumption and $X_1, X_2, \cdots$ be a sequence of independent S-valued random variables with the same distribution λ. We set*

$$\lambda_n = \frac{1}{n}\sum_{i=1}^{n} \delta_{X_i}\,,$$

$$Y_n = \sqrt{n}\{f(\lambda_n, \lambda_n) - f(\lambda, \lambda)\} = \frac{1}{\sqrt{n}} \sum_{i=1}^{n} \{f(X_i, \lambda_n) - f(\lambda, \lambda)\}.$$

Then the probability distribution of Y_n converges to the Gaussian distribution with mean 0 and variance σ^2 as $n \to \infty$, where

$$\sigma^2 = \int_S \{f(x, \lambda) + f'(\lambda, x, \lambda) - m\}^2 \lambda(dx),$$

$$m = \int_S \{f(x, \lambda) + f'(\lambda, x, \lambda)\} \lambda(dx).$$

Proof. First we consider the *special case* when $f(x, \rho)$ is given by

$$f(x, \rho) = \int_S f(x, y) \rho(dy)$$

with a bounded function $f(x, y)$ on $S \times S$ (for simplicity we use the same notation with confusion). In this case $f'(x, y, \rho) = f(x, y)$ and hence the variance σ^2 is equal to

$$\int_S \{f(x, \lambda) + f(\lambda, x) - 2f(\lambda, \lambda)\}^2 \lambda(dx).$$

If we set

$$\tilde{Y}_n = \sqrt{n}\{f(\lambda_n, \lambda) + f(\lambda, \lambda_n) - 2f(\lambda, \lambda)\}$$
$$= \frac{1}{\sqrt{n}} \sum_{i=1}^{n} \{f(X_i, \lambda) + f(\lambda, X_i) - 2f(\lambda, \lambda)\},$$

then the probability distribution of $\tilde{Y}_n$ converges to $N(0, \sigma^2)$ as $n \to \infty$, and hence it is enough to prove that

$$E\{|Y_n - \tilde{Y}_n|^2\} \longrightarrow 0, \quad n \to \infty.$$

Setting $Z_{ni} = f(X_i, \lambda_n) - f(X_i, \lambda) - f(\lambda, \lambda_n) + f(\lambda, \lambda)$, we have

$$Y_n - \tilde{Y}_n = \sqrt{n}\{f(\lambda_n, \lambda_n) - f(\lambda, \lambda_n) - f(\lambda, \lambda_n) + f(\lambda, \lambda)\}$$
$$= \frac{1}{\sqrt{n}} \sum_{i=1}^{n} Z_{ni}.$$

We now claim

(i) $E\{Z_{ni}^2\} = o(1), \quad n \to \infty,$

(ii) $E\{Z_{ni}Z_{nj}\} = O(n^{-2}), \quad n \to \infty \quad (i \neq j).$

(i) is immediate from the law of large numbers. As for (ii), setting

$$\lambda_n^{ij} = \frac{1}{n} \sum_{k=1(\neq i,j)}^{n} \delta_{X_k},$$

$$Z_{nij} = f(X_i, \lambda_n^{ij}) - f(X_i, \lambda) - f(\lambda, \lambda_n^{ij}) + f(\lambda, \lambda),$$
$$R_{nij} = f(X_i, X_i) + f(X_i, X_j) - f(\lambda, X_i) - f(\lambda, X_j),$$

we have $Z_{ni} = Z_{nij} + n^{-1}R_{nij}$ $(i \neq j)$, and hence

$$E\{Z_{ni}Z_{nj}\} = E\{Z_{nij}Z_{nji}\} + n^{-1}E\{Z_{nij}R_{nji}\} + n^{-1}E\{Z_{nji}R_{nij}\} + 0(n^{-2}).$$

The first term on the right hand side of the above vanishes because

$$E\{Z_{nij}Z_{nji} \mid X_k, k \neq i, j\} = 0,$$

while the second and the third terms are $O(n^{-2})$ because

$$\begin{aligned} E\{Z_{nij}R_{nji} \mid X_i, X_j\} &= E[R_{nji}E\{Z_{nij} \mid X_i, X_j\}] \\ &= E[R_{nji}\{n^{-1}(n-2)f(X_i, \lambda) - f(x_i, \lambda) \\ &\qquad - n^{-1}(n-2)f(\lambda, \lambda) + f(\lambda, \lambda)\}] \\ &= E[R_{nji} \cdot 2n^{-1}\{f(\lambda, \lambda) - f(X_i, \lambda)\}] = O(n^{-1}). \end{aligned}$$

Since $E\{Z_{ni}^2\}$ and $E\{Z_{ni}Z_{nj}\}$ are independent of i and j $(i \neq j)$, (i) and (ii) imply

$$\lim_{n\to\infty} E\{|Y_n - \tilde{Y}_n|^2\} = \lim_{n\to\infty} n^{-1} \sum_{i,j=1}^{n} E\{Z_{ni}Z_{nj}\} = 0.$$

Next we consider the *general case*. If we set

$$\tilde{Y}_n = \sqrt{n}\{f(\lambda_n, \lambda) + f(\lambda, \lambda_n) - 2f(\lambda, \lambda)\}$$
$$Z_{ni} = f(X_i, \lambda_n) - f(X_i, \lambda) - f(\lambda, \lambda_n) + f(\lambda, \lambda),$$

then

$$\begin{aligned} Y_n - \tilde{Y}_n &= \sqrt{n}\{f(\lambda_n, \lambda_n) - f(\lambda_n, \lambda) - f(\lambda, \lambda_n) + f(\lambda, \lambda)\} \\ &= \frac{1}{\sqrt{n}} \sum_{i=1}^{n} Z_{ni}. \end{aligned}$$

Step 1. $E\{|Y_n - \tilde{Y}_n|^2\} \to 0$, $n \to \infty$. For this it is enough to prove the followings:

(iii) $E\{Z_{ni}^2\} = o(1), \quad n \to \infty,$

(iv) $E\{Z_{ni}Z_{nj}\} = O(n^{-2}), \quad n \to \infty \quad (i \neq j).$

Setting $\rho = \lambda$ and $\nu = \lambda_n - \lambda$ in (A.4), we have

$$f(x, \lambda_n) = f(x, \lambda) + f'(x, \lambda_n - \lambda, \lambda) + \int_0^1 \{f'(x, \lambda_n - \lambda, \lambda + t(\lambda_n - \lambda)) - f'(x, \lambda_n - \lambda, \lambda)\}dt\,,$$

and hence

$$\begin{aligned} f(x, \lambda_n) - f(x, \lambda) &= \varphi(x, \lambda_n - \lambda) + \varphi_n(x, \lambda_n - \lambda, \omega) \\ &= n^{-1}\sum_{j=1}^{n} \varphi(x, X_j) + n^{-1}\sum_{j=1}^{n} \varphi_n(x, X_j, \omega)\,, \end{aligned}$$

where

$$\begin{aligned} \varphi(x, y) &= f'(x, y, \lambda) - f'(x, \lambda, \lambda) \\ \varphi_n(x, y, \omega) &= \int_0^1 \{f'(x, y, \lambda + t(\lambda_n - \lambda)) - f'(x, y, \lambda)\}dt \\ &\quad - \int_0^1 \{f'(x, \lambda, \lambda + t(\lambda_n - \lambda)) - f'(x, \lambda, \lambda)\}dt\,. \end{aligned}$$

Therefore

$$\begin{aligned} &E\{|f(X_i, \lambda_n) - f(X_i, \lambda)|^2\} \\ &\quad \le 2n^{-2}\sum_{j,k=1}^{n} E\{\varphi(X_i, X_j)\varphi(X_i, X_k)\} \\ &\qquad + 2n^{-2}\sum_{j,k=1}^{n} E\{\varphi_n(X_i, X_j, \omega)\varphi_n(X_i, X_k, \omega)\} \\ &\quad = 2n^{-2}\sum{}' E\{\varphi(X_i, X_j)\varphi(X_i, X_k)\} \\ &\qquad + 2n^{-2}\sum{}' E\{\varphi_n(X_i, X_j, \omega)\varphi_n(X_i, X_k, \omega)\} + O(n^{-1})\,, \end{aligned}$$

where $\sum'$ is the summation over all pairs (j, k) such that $1 \le j, k \le n$ and $j \ne i, k \ne i, j \ne k$. Since the first term in the above vanishes and since the number of such pairs (j, k) is $(n-1)(n-2)$, we have

$$\begin{aligned} &E\{|f(X_i, \lambda_n) - f(X_i, \lambda)|^2\} \\ &\quad \le 2n^{-2}(n-1)(n-2)E\{\varphi_n(X_1, X_2, \omega)\varphi_n(X_1, X_3, \omega)\} + O(n^{-1}) \\ &\quad \longrightarrow 0\,, \quad n \to \infty\,, \end{aligned}$$

because $\varphi_n(x, y, \omega) \to 0$ as $n \to \infty$ (a.s.) for each fixed $x, y \in S$ by (A.3). Similarly

$$E\{|f(\lambda, \lambda_n) - f(\lambda, \lambda)|^2\} \longrightarrow 0\,, \quad n \to \infty\,,$$

and hence we obtain (iii). For the proof of (iv) let $i \ne j$. Noticing that

$$f(X_i, \lambda_n) = f(X_i, \lambda_n^{ij}) + n^{-1}\{f'(X_i, X_i, \lambda_n^{ij}) + f'(X_i, X_j, \lambda_n^{ij})\} + O(n^{-2})$$

and also a similar formula for $f(\lambda, \lambda_n)$, we have

$$Z_{ni} = Z_{nij} + n^{-1}R_{nij} ,$$

where

$$\begin{aligned} Z_{nij} &= f(X_i, \lambda_n^{ij}) - f(X_i, \lambda) - f(\lambda, \lambda_n^{ij}) + f(\lambda, \lambda) , \\ R_{nij} &= f'(X_i, X_i, \lambda_n^{ij}) + f'(X_i, X_j, \lambda_n^{ij}) \\ &\qquad - f'(\lambda, X_i, \lambda_n^{ij}) - f'(\lambda, X_j\, \lambda_n^{ij}) . \end{aligned}$$

Therefore

$$E\{Z_{ni}Z_{nj}\} = E\{Z_{nij}Z_{nji}\} + n^{-1}E\{Z_{nij}R_{nji} + Z_{nji}R_{nij}\} + O(n^{-2})$$

which is still $O(n^{-2})$ as $n \to \infty$, because the first and the second terms on the right hand side of the above vanish as will be verified below:

$$\begin{aligned} E\{Z_{nij}Z_{nji}\} &= E[E\{Z_{nij}Z_{nji} \,|\, X_k, k \neq i, j\}] = 0 , \\ E\{Z_{nij}R_{nji}\} &= E[Z_{nij}\{f'(X_j, X_i, \lambda_n^{ij}) - f'(\lambda, X_i, \lambda_n^{ij})\}] \\ &\quad + E[Z_{nij}\{f'(X_j, X_j, \lambda_n^{ij}) - f'(\lambda, X_j, \lambda_n^{ij})\}] \\ &= E[Z_{nij}E\{f'(X_j, X_i, \lambda_n^{ij}) - f'(\lambda, X_i, \lambda_n^{ij}) \,|\, X_k, k \neq j\}] \\ &\quad + E[\{f'(X_j, X_j, \lambda_n^{ij}) - f'(\lambda, X_j, \lambda_n^{ij})\}E\{Z_{nij} \,|\, X_k, k \neq i\}] \\ &= 0 . \end{aligned}$$

Step 2. *The distribution of $\tilde{Y}_n$ converges to $N(0, \sigma^2)$.* Using the notation $\varphi_n(x, y, \omega)$ in the proof of Step 1, we can write

$$f(\lambda, \lambda_n) - f(\lambda, \lambda) = f'(\lambda, \lambda_n - \lambda, \lambda) + \varphi_n(\lambda, \lambda_n, \omega) ,$$

and hence

$$\begin{aligned} \tilde{Y}_n &= \frac{1}{\sqrt{n}} \sum_{i=1}^{n} \{f(X_i, \lambda) - f(\lambda, \lambda) + f(\lambda, \lambda_n) - f(\lambda, \lambda)\} \\ &= \sqrt{n}\, \varphi(\lambda_n - \lambda) + \sqrt{n}\, \varphi_n(\lambda, \lambda_n, \omega) , \end{aligned}$$

where $\varphi(x) = f(x, \lambda) + f'(\lambda, x, \lambda)$. Since the distribution of $\sqrt{n}\, \varphi(\lambda_n - \lambda)$ converges to $N(0, \sigma^2)$, it is enough to prove that

$$E\{|\sqrt{n}\, \varphi_n(\lambda, \lambda_n, \omega)|^2\} = o(1) , \quad n \to \infty .$$

The left hand side of the above equals

$$E\left\{\left|\frac{1}{\sqrt{n}}\sum_{i=1}^{n}\varphi_n(\lambda, X_i, \omega)\right|^2\right\}$$
$$= E\left\{\left|\varphi_n(\lambda, X_1, \omega)\right|^2\right\} + \frac{n^2-n}{n}E\{\varphi_n(\lambda, X_1, \omega)\varphi_n(\lambda, X_2, \omega)\}.$$

The first term of the above tends to 0 as $n \to \infty$, because $\varphi_n(\lambda, X_1, \omega) \to 0$ boundedly (a.s.) by (A.3). As for the second term we first write

$$\varphi_n(\lambda, y, \omega) = \psi_n(\lambda, y, \omega) + O(n^{-1}) \quad \text{(by (A.2))},$$
$$\psi_n(\lambda, y, \omega) = \int_0^1 \{f'(\lambda, y, \lambda + t(\lambda_n^{12} - \lambda)) - f'(\lambda, y, \lambda)\}dt$$
$$+ \int_0^1 \{f'(\lambda, \lambda, \lambda + t(\lambda_n^{12} - \lambda)) - f'(\lambda, \lambda, \lambda)\}dt,$$

and then notice that

$$E\{\psi_n(\lambda, X_1, \omega)\psi_n(\lambda, X_2, \omega) \mid X_k,\ k \neq 1, 2\} = 0.$$

Thus the second term also tends to 0 as $n \to \infty$, because

$$E\{\varphi_n(\lambda, X_1, \omega)\varphi_n(\lambda, X_2, \omega)\}$$
$$= E\{\psi_n(\lambda, X_1, \omega)\psi_n(\lambda, X_2, \omega)\}$$
$$+ \frac{\text{const.}}{n}E\{|\psi_n(\lambda, X_1, \omega)| + |\psi_n(\lambda, X_2, \omega)|\} + O(n^{-2})$$
$$= o(n^{-1}) \quad \text{(by (A.3))}.$$

§ 2. Central limit theorem

In this section we explain how Theorem 1.1 can be applied to the central limit theorem for Y_n of (5) when the coefficient $\sigma = 1$.

2.1. Let W be the space of continuous paths $w: t \in [0, 1] \to R$. For simplicity the time parameter t is restricted to $0 \leq t \leq 1$. W is a Banach space with the maximum norm $\|\cdot\|_\infty$ and will stands for the Polish space S of § 1. Let $\mathfrak{M}$ be the Banach space of finite signed measures on W with total variation norm $\|\cdot\|$, $\mathfrak{M}_1$ be the subset of $\mathfrak{M}$ consisting of sub-stochastic measures on W and $C_b^2(\boldsymbol{R}^2)$ be the space of C^2-functions which are bounded together with their first and second partial derivatives. Given a coefficient $b = b(x, y) \in C_b^2(\boldsymbol{R}^2)$ and a signed measure $\rho \in \mathfrak{M}$, we consider the equation

(2.1) $$\xi(t, w) = w(t) + \int_0^t b_\rho(\xi(s, w), \xi(s))ds, \quad 0 \leq t \leq 1,$$

where $\xi(s)$ is the map: $w \in W \to \xi(s, w) \in \boldsymbol{R}$ and the notation

$$b_\rho(x, \alpha) = \int_W b(x, \alpha(w))\rho(dw)$$

is used for a map $\alpha: W \to \boldsymbol{R}$. The equation (2.1) can be solved easily by iteration. We denote by $\xi(t, w, \rho)$ the solution of (2.1). When we regard $\xi(t, w, \rho)$ as a function of t alone by fixing w and ρ, we denote it by $\xi(w, \rho)$. Then $\xi(w, \rho) \in W$, because

$$(2.2) \quad |\xi(t, w, \rho) - \xi(s, w, \rho)| \leq |w(t) - w(s)| + \|\rho\| \cdot \|b\|_\infty \cdot |t - s| .$$

Lemma 2.1. *$\xi(w, \rho)$ has the following properties.*

(i) $\|\xi(w, \rho) - \xi(w', \rho)\|_\infty \leq c_1 \|w - w'\|_\infty$, *where c_1 is a constant depending only on $\|\rho\|$ and $\|b_x\|_\infty$* ($b_x = \partial b/\partial x$, etc.).

(ii) $\|\xi(w, \rho) - \xi(w, \rho')\|_\infty \leq c_2 \|\rho - \rho'\|$, *where c_2 is a constant depending only on $\|\rho\|$, $\|\rho'\|$, $\|b\|_\infty$, $\|b_x\|_\infty$ and $\|b_y\|_\infty$.*

(iii) *Let $\rho_n, \rho \in \mathfrak{M}_1$ and $\rho_n \to \rho$ weakly as $n \to \infty$. Then*

$$\xi(w, \rho_n) \to \xi(w, \rho) \quad (\textit{in } W), \quad n \to \infty$$

uniformly on each compact subset K of W.

Proof. We give only the proof of (iii). By (2.2) and (i) the family of functions $\xi(t, w, \rho_n)$, $n = 1, 2, \cdots$, on $[0, 1] \times K$ is uniformly bounded and equicontinuous provided that K is a compact subset of W. Therefore, for any subsequence $n_1 < n_2 < \cdots$ we can choose a further subsequence $\{n'_k\}$ of $\{n_k\}$ such that

(2.3a) $\xi(t, w, \rho_{n'_k})$ converges to some $\xi(t, w)$ as $k \to \infty$ for any (t, w),

(2.3b) the above convergence is uniform on $[0, 1] \times K$ for each compact subset K of W.

The assertion (iii) follows once we identify $\xi(t, w)$ as $\xi(t, w, \rho)$. This can be done as follows. Letting $n \to \infty$ via $\{n'_k\}$ in

$$\xi(t, w, \rho_n) = w(t) + \int_0^t ds \int_W \rho_n(dw') b(\xi(s, w, \rho_n), \xi(s, w', \rho_n)) ,$$

we have

$$\xi(t, w) = w(t) + \int_0^t ds \int_W \rho(dw') b(\xi(s, w), \xi(s, w')) ,$$

and hence the uniqueness of the solution implies $\xi(t, w) = \xi(t, w, \rho)$.

For $\rho, \nu \in \mathfrak{M}$ we set

$$\eta(t, w, \nu, \rho) = \lim_{h \to 0} \frac{1}{h} \{\xi(t, w, \rho + h\nu) - \xi(t, w, \rho)\} .$$

Under the assumption $b \in C_b^2(\boldsymbol{R}^2)$ it can be proved that the above convergence is uniform in $(t, w) \in [0, 1] \times W$, and hence

$$\eta(w, \nu, \rho) = \lim_{h \to 0} \frac{1}{h} \{\xi(w, \rho + h\nu) - \xi(w, \rho)\}$$

also exists as the strong limit in the Banach space W. Moreover, for fixed ρ and ν, $\eta(t) \equiv \eta(t, w) \equiv \eta(t, w, \nu, \rho)$ can be regarded as a W-valued function of t and satisfies

$$\begin{aligned}\dot{\eta}(t, w) = \int_W \rho(dw')\{&b_x(\xi(t, w, \rho), \xi(t, w', \rho))\eta(t, w) \\ &+ b_y(\xi(t, w, \rho), \xi(t, w', \rho))\eta(t, w')\} \\ + \int_W &\nu(dw')b(\xi(t, w, \rho), \xi(t, w', \rho))\end{aligned}$$

with initial condition $\eta(0) = 0$ (the dot $= d/dt$). Setting

$$\eta(t, w, \tilde{w}, \rho) = \eta(t, w, \delta_{\tilde{w}}, \rho) , \qquad \eta(w, \tilde{w}, \rho) = \eta(w, \delta_{\tilde{w}}, \rho) ,$$

we have

$$\begin{aligned}\dot{\eta}(t, w, \tilde{w}, \rho) = \int_W \rho(dw')\{&b_x(\xi(t, w, \rho), \xi(t, w', \rho))\eta(t, w, \tilde{w}, \rho) \\ &+ b_y(\xi(t, w, \rho), \xi(t, w', \rho))\eta(t, w', \tilde{w}, \rho)\} \\ + b(&\xi(t, w, \rho), \xi(t, \tilde{w}, \rho)) ,\end{aligned} \tag{2.4}$$

$$\eta(t, w, \nu, \rho) = \int_W \nu(d\tilde{w})\eta(t, w, \tilde{w}, \rho) . \tag{2.5}$$

Now looking carefully at (2.4) which is a differential equation in the Banach space W (for fixed $\tilde{w}$ and ρ), we see that $\eta(t, w, \tilde{w}, \rho)$ can be expressed as

$$\eta(t, w, \tilde{w}, \rho) = \zeta(t, \xi(w, \rho), \xi(\tilde{w}, \rho), \rho \circ \xi(\rho)^{-1}) , \tag{2.6}$$

where $\zeta(t, w, \tilde{w}, \rho)$ is the solution of

$$\begin{aligned}\dot{\zeta}(t, w, \tilde{w}, \rho) = \int_W &\rho(dw')\{b_x(w(t), w'(t))\zeta(t, w, \tilde{w}, \rho) \\ &+ b_y(w(t), w'(t))\zeta(t, w', \tilde{w}, \rho)\} + b(w(t), \tilde{w}(t))\end{aligned} \tag{2.7}$$

with the initial condition $\zeta(0, w, \tilde{w}, \rho) = 0$ and $\rho \circ \xi(\rho)^{-1}$ is the image measure of ρ under the map $\xi(\rho)\colon w \in W \to \xi(w, \rho) \in W$.

When we regard $\zeta(t, w, \tilde{w}, \rho)$ as a function of t alone by fixing w, $\tilde{w}$ and ρ, we denote it by $\zeta(w, \tilde{w}, \rho)$. The proof of the following lemma is easy (especially, the proof of (viii) is similar to that of (iii)), so is omitted.

Lemma 2.2. *$\zeta(w, \tilde{w}, \rho)$ has the following properties.*

(iv) $\|\zeta(w, \tilde{w}, \rho)\|_\infty \le c_3$ *with a constant c_3 depending only on $\|\rho\|$, $\|b\|_\infty$, $\|b_x\|_\infty$ and $\|b_y\|_\infty$.*

(v) $\|\zeta(w, \tilde{w}, \rho) - \zeta(w', \tilde{w}, \rho)\|_\infty \le c_4\|w - w'\|_\infty$ *with a constant c_4 depending only on $\|\rho\|$ and the supremum norms of b and its first and second partial derivatives.*

(vi) $\|\zeta(w, \tilde{w}, \rho) - \zeta(w, \hat{w}, \rho)\|_\infty \le c_5\|\tilde{w} - \hat{w}\|_\infty$ *with a constant c_5 depending only on $\|\rho\|$, $\|b_x\|_\infty$ and $\|b_y\|_\infty$.*

(vii) $\|\zeta(w, \tilde{w}, \rho) - \zeta(w, \tilde{w}, \rho')\|_\infty \le c_6\|\rho - \rho'\|$ *with a constant c_6 depending only on $\|\rho\|$, $\|\rho'\|$, $\|b\|_\infty$, $\|b_x\|_\infty$ and $\|b_y\|_\infty$.*

(viii) *Let $\rho_n, \rho \in \mathfrak{M}_1$ and $\rho_n \to \rho$ weakly as $n \to \infty$. Then*

$$\zeta(w, \tilde{w}, \rho_n) \longrightarrow \zeta(w, \tilde{w}, \rho) \quad (\text{in } W), \quad n \to \infty$$

uniformly on each compact subset of $W \times W$.

Lemma 2.3. *$\eta(w, \tilde{w}, \rho)$ has the following properties.*

(ix) $\|\eta(w, \tilde{w}, \rho) - \eta(w, \tilde{w}, \rho')\|_\infty \le c_7\|\rho - \rho'\|$ *with a constant c_7 depending only on $\|\rho\|$, $\|\rho'\|$ and the supremum norms of b and its first and second partial derviatives.*

(x) *Let $\rho_n, \rho \in \mathfrak{M}$ and $\rho_n \to \rho$ weakly as $n \to \infty$. Then*

$$\eta(w, \tilde{w}, \rho_n) \to \eta(w, \tilde{w}, \rho_n) \quad (\text{in } W), \quad n \to \infty$$

uniformly on each compact subset of $W \times W$.

Proof. (ix) can be proved directly from (2.4), and (x) follows from (2.6), (iii) and (viii).

2.2. Given a probability measure u in $\boldsymbol{R}$, we denote by λ the Wiener measure on W such that $\lambda\{w(0) \in \cdot\} = u(\cdot)$. Then the solution $\xi(t)$ of (2) with $\sigma = 1$ is expressed as

$$\xi(t) = \xi(t, w, \lambda). \tag{2.8}$$

To describe the solution of (6) let $\Omega = W \times W \times \cdots$ and P be the product measure $\lambda \otimes \lambda \otimes \cdots$. Then, the solution process $\xi^{(n)}(t) = (\xi_1^{(n)}(t), \cdots, \xi_n^{(n)}(t))$ of (6) with the initial condition

(2.9) $\xi_1^{(n)}(0), \cdots, \xi_n^{(n)}(0)$ are independent random variables with the same distribution u

is realized on the probability space (Ω, P) by

$$(2.10)\qquad \xi_i^{(n)}(t, \omega) = \xi(t, w_i, \lambda_n), \quad 1 \leq i \leq n,$$

where $\lambda_n = n^{-1} \sum_{k=1}^n \delta_{w_k}$ and $\omega = (w_1, w_2, \cdots)$. Therefore, Y_n of (5) is expressed as

$$(2.11)\qquad Y_n = \sqrt{n}\left\{\frac{1}{n} \sum_{k=1}^n \delta_{\xi(w_k, \lambda_n)} - \mu\right\}, \quad \mu = \lambda \circ \xi(\lambda)^{-1},$$

and hence for a (nice) function φ on W we have

$$(2.12)\qquad Y_n(\varphi) = \sqrt{n}\left\{\frac{1}{n} \sum_{k=1}^n \varphi(\xi(w_k, \lambda_n)) - \langle \mu, \varphi \rangle\right\},$$

to which Theorem 1.1 can now be applied with $f(w, \rho) = \varphi(\xi(w, \rho))$. A real valued function φ on W is said to be in the class $C_b^1(W)$ if there exists a bounded continuous map $\varphi'\colon W \to W^*$ (the dual space) such that

$$|\varphi(w + w') - \varphi(w) - \varphi'(w)(w')| = o(\|w'\|_\infty), \quad w' \to 0.$$

For $\varphi \in C_b^1(W)$ we set

$$(2.13)\qquad \Lambda\varphi(\tilde{w}) = E_\mu\{\varphi'(w)(\zeta(w, \tilde{w}, \mu))\}, \quad \tilde{w} \in W,$$

$$(2.14)\qquad Q(\varphi) = E_\mu\{|(I + \Lambda)\varphi|^2\} - |E_\mu\{(I + \Lambda)\varphi\}|^2,$$

where E_μ denotes the expectation with respect to $\mu(dw)$. If $f(w, \rho) = \varphi(\xi(w, \rho))$, then $f(w, \rho)$ satisfies (A.1)–(A.4) of § 1 with $f'(w, \tilde{w}, \lambda) = \varphi'(\xi(w, \lambda))(\zeta(\xi(w, \lambda), \xi(\tilde{w}, \lambda), \mu))$ and hence by Theorem 1.1 we have the following theorem.

Theorem 2.1. *Let $\xi^{(n)}(t) = (\xi_1^{(n)}(t), \cdots, \xi_n^{(n)}(t))$ be the solution of* (6) *with the initial condition* (2.9) *and let Y_n be defined by* (5) *in the introduction. Then*

$$(2.15)\qquad \lim_{n\to\infty} E\{e^{iY_n(\varphi)}\} = e^{-Q(\varphi)/2}, \quad \varphi \in C_b^1(W),$$

that is, the distribution of $Y_n(\varphi)$ converges to $N(0, Q(\varphi))$.

§ 3. Another expression of Λ

The soluution $\xi(t)$ of (2) ($\sigma = 1$) is a temporally inhomogeneous Markov process. This Markov process is called the diffusion process associated with the nonlinear parabolic equation (3) ($\sigma = 1$) ([8]). Similarly, for each fixed $w \in W$ we can consider the diffusion process $\tilde{\xi}(t)$ associated with the nonlinear parabolic equation

$$\frac{\partial \tilde{u}(t)}{\partial t} = \frac{1}{2} \cdot \frac{\partial^2 \tilde{u}(t)}{\partial x^2} - \frac{\partial}{\partial x}[\{b[x, \tilde{u}(t)] + \varepsilon b(x, w(t))\}\tilde{u}(t)] . \tag{3.1}$$

This diffsion process $\tilde{\xi}(t)$ with initial distribution u is described by

$$\tilde{\xi}(t, w') = w'(t) + \int_0^t b_\lambda(\tilde{\xi}(s, w'), \tilde{\xi}(s))ds + \varepsilon \int_0^t b(\tilde{\xi}(s, w'), w(s))ds , \tag{3.2}$$

where $\{w'(t), 0 \leq t \leq 1, \lambda\}$ is a Brownian motion with initial distribution u as before. Noting that $\tilde{\xi}(t) = \xi(t)$ when $\varepsilon = 0$, we can prove by a routine argument in differential equations that

$$\lim_{\varepsilon \to 0} \frac{1}{\varepsilon} \{\tilde{\xi}(t, w') - \xi(t, w')\} = \tilde{\eta}(t, w') \tag{3.3}$$

exists as a uniform limit on $[0, 1] \times W$ and that $\tilde{\eta}(t, w')$ satisfies

$$\begin{aligned} \tilde{\eta}(t, w') = \int_0^t ds \int_W \lambda(d\tilde{w})\{b_x(\xi(s, w')\xi(s, \tilde{w}))\tilde{\eta}(s, w') \\ + b_y(\xi(s, w'), \xi(s, \tilde{w}))\tilde{\eta}(s, \tilde{w})\} \\ + \int_0^t b(\xi(s, w'), w(s))ds . \end{aligned} \tag{3.4}$$

Comparing (3.4) with (2.7) we see that

$$\tilde{\eta}(t, w') = \zeta(t, \xi(w'), w, \mu) , \quad \mu = \lambda \circ \xi(\lambda)^{-1} . \tag{3.5}$$

Theorem 3.1. *For each fixed $w \in W$ let $\mu_{w,\varepsilon}$ be the probability measure on W induced by the diffusion process associated with* (3.1) *having initial distribution u and denote by $E_{\mu,w,\varepsilon}$ the expectation with respect to $\mu_{w,\varepsilon}$. Then for $\varphi \in C_b^1(W)$*

$$\Lambda\varphi(w) = \lim_{\varepsilon \to 0} \frac{1}{\varepsilon} \{E_{\mu,w,\varepsilon}(\varphi) - E_\mu(\varphi)\} . \tag{3.6}$$

Proof. From (2.13), (3.5) and (3.3) we have

$$\begin{aligned} \Lambda\varphi(w) &= \int_W \mu(dw')\varphi'(w')(\zeta(w', w, \mu)) \\ &= \int_W \lambda(dw')\varphi'(\xi(w'))(\tilde{\eta}(w')) \end{aligned}$$

$$= \lim_{\varepsilon \to 0} \frac{1}{\varepsilon} \int_W \lambda(dw')\{\varphi(\tilde{\xi}(w')) - \varphi(\xi(w'))\}$$

$$= \lim_{\varepsilon \to 0} \frac{1}{\varepsilon} \{E_{\mu,w,\varepsilon}(\varphi) - E_\mu(\varphi)\} .$$

§ 4. An infinite dimensional SDE

Let $\{Y(\varphi), \varphi \in C_b^1(W)\}$ be a Gaussian system defined on a probability space $(\Omega, \mathscr{F}, P)$ such that

$$E\{e^{iY(\varphi)}\} = e^{-Q(\varphi)/2}, \tag{4.1}$$

$$Y(c_1\varphi_1 + c_2\varphi_2) = c_1 Y(\varphi_1) + c_2 Y(\varphi_2) \quad \text{a.s.}, \tag{4.2}$$

and define $Y(t)$ by $\langle Y(t), f\rangle = Y(f(w(t)))$ for f in the space $\mathscr{S}$ of rapidly decreasing C^∞-functions on $\boldsymbol{R}$. We also define $Y_n(t)$ by (7) or equivalently by $\langle Y_n(t), f\rangle = Y_n(f(w(t))), f \in \mathscr{S}$, where Y_n is given by (5). Then Theorem 2.1 implies the following *central limit theorem in the time evolution scheme*: For any $0 \le t_1 < \cdots < t_m$ and $f_1, \cdots, f_m \in \mathscr{S}$ the joint distribution of $\langle Y_n(t_1), f_1\rangle, \cdots, \langle Y_n(t_m), f_m\rangle$ converges to that of $\langle Y(t_1), f_1\rangle, \cdots, \langle Y(t_m), f_m\rangle$ as $n \to \infty$.

SDE for $Y(t)$: Once we know (2.15), we can derive the SDE for $Y(t)$ as in Itô [4]. Let $u(t)$ be the (probability measure) solution of (3) with $\sigma = 1$ and with initial distribution u. We set

$$(K_{u(t)}f)(x) = \frac{1}{2}f''(x) + b[x, u(t)]f'(x),$$

$$(L_{u(t)}f)(x) = \int b(y, x)f'(y)u(t, dy),$$

$$M_f(t) = f(w(t)) - f(w(0)) - \int_0^t (K_{u(s)}f)(w(s))ds,$$

$$N_f(t) = M_f(t) - \int_0^t (L_{u(s)}f)(w(s))ds.$$

Then $M_f(t)$ is a μ-martingale and it is not hard to prove that

$$E_\mu\{|M_f(t) - M_f(s)|^2 | \mathscr{B}_s\} = \int_s^t \|f'\|^2_{u(\tau)} d\tau, \quad \text{a.s.} \quad (0 \le s \le t), \tag{4.3}$$

where $\mathscr{B}_s = \sigma\{w(\tau): 0 \le \tau \le s\}$ and $\|\cdot\|_{u(\tau)}$ is the norm in $L^2(R, u(\tau))$.

Lemma 4.1. $(I + \Lambda)N_f(t) = M_f(t), \quad f \in \mathscr{S}.$

Proof. It is enough to prove that

$$
\begin{aligned}
&-\int_0^t (L_{u(s)}f)(w(s))ds + E_\mu\{f'(w(t))\zeta(t, w)\} \\
(4.4)\qquad &-\int_0^t E_\mu\{(K_{u(s)}f)'(w(s))\zeta(s, w)\}ds \\
&-\int_0^t E_\mu\{(L_{u(s)}f)'(w(s))\zeta(s, w)\}ds = 0
\end{aligned}
$$

for each fixed $\tilde{w} \in W$, where $\zeta(t, w) = \zeta(t, w, \tilde{w}, \mu)$. Since $w(t)$ (as a process defined on the probability space (W, μ)) can be expressed as

$$\textit{a Brownian motion} + \int_0^t b[w(s), u(s)]ds\,,$$

an application of Itô's formula yields

$$E_\mu\{f'(w(t))\,\zeta(t, w)\} = E_\mu\left\{\int_0^t F(s)ds\right\},$$

where $F(s)$ is equal to

$$
\begin{aligned}
&f''(w(s))\zeta(s, w)b[w(s), u(s)] + f'(w(s))\dot{\zeta}(s, w) + \frac{1}{2}f'''(w(s))\zeta(s, w) \\
&\quad = b[w(s), u(s)]f''(w(s))\zeta(s, w) + \frac{1}{2}f'''(w(s))\zeta(s, w) \\
&\quad\quad + f'(w(s))\Big[\int \mu(dw')\{b_x(w(s), w'(s))\zeta(s, w) \\
&\quad\quad + b_y(w(s), w'(s))\zeta(s, w')\} + b(w(s), \tilde{w}(s))\Big] \quad (\textit{by } (2.7))\,.
\end{aligned}
$$

Therefore, writing down $(K_{u(s)}f)'$ and $(L_{u(s)}f)'$ explicitly, we see that the left hand side of (4.4) is equal to $\int_0^t E_\mu\{G(s)\}ds$ where

$$
\begin{aligned}
G(s) = &-b(w(s), \tilde{w}(s))f'(w(s)) + b[w(s), u(s)]f''(w(s))\zeta(s, w) \\
&+ \frac{1}{2}f'''(w(s))\zeta(s, w) + f'(w(s))\Big[\int \mu(dw')\{b_x(w(s), w'(s))\zeta(s, w) \\
&\quad + b_y(w(s), w'(s))\zeta(s, w')\} + b(w(s), \tilde{w}(s))\Big] \\
&- \frac{1}{2}f'''(w(s))\zeta(s, w) - f'(w(s))\zeta(s, w)\int b_x(w(s), y)u(s, dy) \\
&- b[w(s), u(s)]f''(w(s))\zeta(s, w) - \zeta(s, w)\int b_y(z, w(s))f'(z)u(s, dz)
\end{aligned}
$$

$$= \int \mu(dw')\{b_y(w(s), w'(s))f'(w(s))\zeta(s, w') - b_y(w'(s), w(s))f'(w'(s))\zeta(s, w)\}.$$

But from the last expression of $G(s)$ it follows that $E_\mu\{G(s)\} = 0$ and so the lemma is proved.

We now write

$$\langle Y(t), f\rangle - \langle Y(0), f\rangle = \langle Y, f(w(t)) - f(w(0))\rangle$$
$$= \langle Y, N_f(t)\rangle + \int_0^t \langle Y(s), K_{u(s)}f\rangle ds + \int_0^t \langle Y(s), L_{u(s)}f\rangle ds.$$

If we set

$$B_f(t) = \langle Y, N_f(t)\rangle,$$

then by (4.1), (2.14), Lemma 4.1 and (4.3) we have

$$E\{e^{i\{B_f(t)-B_f(s)\}} \mid \mathscr{F}_s\} = \exp\left\{-\int_s^t \|f'\|^2_{u(\tau)} d\tau/2\right\}, \quad 0 \le s \le t,$$

where $\mathscr{F}_s$ is the smallest σ-field on Ω that makes $\{B_f(\tau), 0 \le \tau \le s, f \in \mathscr{S}\}$ measurable. Let $\{B(t)\}$ be a (distribution-valued) Brownian motion such that

$$\langle B(t), f\rangle = B_f(t) \quad \text{a.s.} \quad \text{(regularization)}.$$

Then

$$d\langle Y(t), f\rangle = d\langle B(t), f\rangle + \langle Y(t), K_{u(t)}f + L_{u(t)}f\rangle dt,$$

or symbolically we have the infinite dimensional SDE

$$dY(t) = dB(t) + (K^*_{u(t)} + L^*_{u(t)})Y(t)dt,$$

where $*$ means the dual operator. This is, of course, consistent with the following formal computation about the generator of the Markov process $Y(t)$.

Generators: $Y_n(t)$ is a (temporally inhomogeneous) Markov process and its generator $L_t^{(n)}$ "at time t" is given as follows. Let

$$\Phi(\eta) = \varphi(\langle\eta, f_1\rangle, \cdots, \langle\eta, f_m\rangle), \qquad f_1, \cdots, f_m \in \mathscr{S}, \quad \varphi \in C_0^\infty(\boldsymbol{R}^m).$$

Then for $\eta = \sqrt{n}(\bar{x} - u(t))$ ($\bar{x} = n^{-1}\sum \delta_{x_k}$) we have

$$(L_t^{(n)}\Phi)(\eta) = \sum_{\alpha,\beta=1}^m \left\langle \bar{x}, \frac{1}{2} f'_\alpha f'_\beta \right\rangle \partial^2_{\alpha\beta}\varphi + \sum_{\alpha=1}^m \langle \eta, K_{u(t)} f_\alpha\rangle \partial_\alpha \varphi$$
$$+ \sum_{\alpha=1}^m \langle \bar{x}, b[\cdot, \eta] f'_\alpha\rangle \partial_\alpha\varphi,$$

and hence the generator L_t of $Y(t)$ "at time t" is given (at least formally) by

$$(L_t\Phi)(\eta) = \lim_{n\to\infty} (L_t^{(n)}\Phi)(\eta) = \sum_{\alpha,\beta=1}^{m} \left\langle u(t), \frac{1}{2} f'_\alpha f'_\beta \right\rangle \partial^2_{\alpha\beta}\varphi$$

$$+ \sum_{\alpha=1}^{m} \langle \eta, K_{u(t)} f_\alpha \rangle \partial_\alpha \varphi + \sum_{\alpha=1}^{m} \langle \eta, L_{u(t)} f_\alpha \rangle \partial_\alpha \varphi .$$

§ 5. Large deviation

Let U_n be defined by (4) and let Q_n be its probability distribution, i.e.,

$$Q_n(A) = P\{U_n \in A\}, \quad A \subset \mathscr{P},$$

where $\mathscr{P}$ is the set of probability measures on W. For $\nu \in \mathscr{P}$ we set $v(t) = v(t, \cdot) = \nu\{w(t) \in \cdot\}$ and denote by $\tilde{\nu}$ the probability measure on W induced by the diffusion process (initial distribution $= u$) associated with the linear equation

$$\frac{\partial \tilde{u}}{\partial t} = \frac{1}{2} \cdot \frac{\partial^2 \tilde{u}}{\partial x^2} - \frac{\partial}{\partial x} \{b[x, v(t)]\tilde{u}\} .$$

We then define

$$(5.1) \qquad I_\mu(\nu) = \begin{cases} \int_W \log (d\nu/d\tilde{\nu}) d\nu , & \text{if } \nu \prec \mu \text{ and } \log (d\nu/d\tilde{\nu}) \in L^1(\nu) \\ \infty, & \text{otherwise.} \end{cases}$$

Theorem 5.1. (i) *For any closed set $C \subset \mathscr{P}$ and open set $G \subset \mathscr{P}$ (weak topology on $\mathscr{P}$)*

$$\overline{\lim_{n\to\infty}} \frac{1}{n} \log Q_n(C) \leq - \inf_{\nu \in C} I_\mu(\nu) ,$$

$$\underline{\lim_{n\to\infty}} \frac{1}{n} \log Q_n(G) \geq - \inf_{\nu \in G} I_\mu(\nu) .$$

(ii) *For any bounded weakly continuous function F on $\mathscr{P}$*

$$\lim_{n\to\infty} \frac{1}{n} \log E\{e^{nF(U_n)}\} = \sup_{\nu \in \mathscr{P}} \{F(\nu) - I_\mu(\nu)\} .$$

Proof. If we define a mapping $\theta: \mathscr{P} \to \mathscr{P}$ by $\theta(\rho) = \rho \circ \xi(\rho)^{-1}$, then $U_n = \theta(U_n^0)$ where $U_n^0 = n^{-1} \sum \delta_{w_k}$. Moreover, it is easy to see that θ is a homeomorphism from $\mathscr{P}$ onto itself and hence by a result of Donsker and Varadhan [3] for independent identically distributed random variables

$$\varlimsup_{n\to\infty}\frac{1}{n}\log Q_n(C)=\varlimsup_{n\to\infty}\log P\{U_n^0\in\theta^{-1}(C)\}$$
$$\leq -\inf_{\rho\in\theta^{-1}(C)} I_\lambda^0(\rho)\,,$$

where

$$I_\lambda^0(\rho)=\begin{cases}\int_W \log(d\rho/d\lambda)d\rho\,, & \text{if } \rho\prec\lambda \text{ and } \log(d\rho/d\lambda)\in L^1(\rho)\\ \infty\,, & \text{otherwise}.\end{cases}$$

We now set $\mu=\theta(\lambda)$ and $\nu=\theta(\rho)$. Since $\rho\prec\lambda\Leftrightarrow\nu\prec\tilde{\nu}\equiv\lambda\circ\xi(\rho)^{-1}$ $\Leftrightarrow\nu\prec\mu$ and $d\rho/d\lambda=g(\xi(w,\rho))$ where $g=d\nu/d\tilde{\nu}$, we have

$$I_\lambda^0(\rho)=I_\mu(\nu)\,,\qquad \inf_{\rho\in\theta^{-1}(C)} I_\lambda^0(\rho)=\inf_{\nu\in C} I_\mu(\nu)\,,$$

proving the first inequality. The second inequality of (i) and the equality of (ii) can also be proved by the same method.

§ 6. The case of Boltzmann's equation

Kac's master equation approach to Boltzmann's equation goes back to 1956. The central limit theorem (fluctuation theory) in the time evolution scheme as in § 4 was discussed in [6], [10], [12], [13] and [15]. Although the methods in the preceding sections can not be applied in a straightforward way to the case of Boltzmann's equation, one may give some conjectures about fluctuations in the path space and large deviation problem for U_n. Here we consider McKean's 2-state model of Maxwellian molecules.

Let $\xi^{(n)}(t)=(\xi_1^{(n)}(t),\cdots,\xi_n^{(n)}(t))$ be a Markov process on the n-fold product space $\{\pm1\}^n$ with generator

$$(K_nf)(x_1,\cdots,x_n)$$
$$=\frac{1}{n}\sum_{1\leq i<j\leq n}\sum{}'\{f(\cdots,x_i',\cdots,x_j',\cdots)-f(x_1,\cdots,x_n)\}\,,$$

where $\sum'$ is the sum with respect to the two types of collisions

$$\begin{pmatrix}x_i'\\x_j'\end{pmatrix}=\begin{pmatrix}x_ix_j\\x_j\end{pmatrix}\quad\text{or}\quad\begin{pmatrix}x_i\\x_ix_j\end{pmatrix}.$$

Let u be a given probability measure on $\{\pm1\}$ and assume that the initial distribution of $\xi^{(n)}(t)$ is $u \otimes \cdots \otimes u$. Sample paths of each component process $\xi_k^{(n)}(t)$ are in the space W of right continuous step functions taking values of ± 1 (the time is restricted to $0 \leq t \leq 1$ as before). Define U_n and Y_n as in (4) and (5). For each fixed $w \in W$ and $\varepsilon > 0$ we denote by $\mu_{w,\varepsilon}$ the probability measure on W induced by the Markov process associated with the nonlinear equation

$$\text{(6.1)} \qquad \frac{d}{dt}\langle \tilde{u}(t), f\rangle = \langle \tilde{u}(t) \otimes (\tilde{u}(t) + \varepsilon\delta_{w(t)}), Kf\rangle$$

having initial distribution u, where $(Kf)(x, y) = f(xy) - f(x)$. $\mu = \mu_{w,0}$ is nothing but the probability law of the Markov process associated with the Boltzmann equation

$$\frac{d}{dt}\langle u(t), f\rangle = \langle u(t) \otimes u(t), Kf\rangle$$

of McKean's 2-state fictitious gas. We now define Q-functional by

$$Q(\varphi) = E_\mu\{|(I + \Lambda)\varphi|^2\} - |E_\mu\{(I + \Lambda)\varphi\}|^2$$

on the class of functions φ of the form

$$\varphi(w) = f(w(t_1), \cdots, w(t_m)), \quad f \in C_0^\infty(\boldsymbol{R}^m), \quad 0 \leq t_1 < \cdots < t_m,$$

where

$$\Lambda\varphi(w) = \lim_{\varepsilon \downarrow 0} \frac{1}{\varepsilon}\{E_{\mu, w, \varepsilon}(\varphi) - E_\mu(\varphi)\},$$

and also define I-functional by

$$I_\mu(\nu) = \begin{cases} \log(d\nu/d\tilde{\nu})d\nu, & \text{if } \nu \prec \tilde{\nu} \text{ and } \log(d\nu/d\tilde{\nu}) \in L^1(\nu) \\ \infty, & \text{otherwise}, \end{cases}$$

where $\tilde{\nu}$ is the probability measure induced by the Markov process (initial distribution $= u$) associated with the linear equation

$$\frac{d}{dt}\langle \tilde{u}(t), f\rangle = \langle \tilde{u}(t) \otimes v(t), Kf\rangle,$$

$v(t)$ being defined by $v(t, \cdot) = \nu\{w(t) \in \cdot\}$. Then from the results in the diffusion case one may conjecture as follows.

$$\text{(6.2)} \qquad \lim_{n \to \infty} E\{e^{iY_n(\varphi)}\} = e^{-Q(\varphi)/2}.$$

(6.3) The large deviation for U_n will be governed by the functional $I_\mu(\nu)$ as in Theorem 5.1.

Notes added in proof. Recently, making use of a method of Sznitman [11], T. Shiga and the author proved that (6.2) is correct.

References

[1] W. Braun and K. Hepp, The Vlasov dynamics and its fluctuations in the 1/N limit of interacting classical particles, Comm. Math. Phys., **56** (1977), 101–113.
[2] D. A. Dawson, Critical dynamics and fluctuations for a mean field model of cooperative behavior, J. Statistical Physics, **31** (1978), 29–85.
[3] M. D. Donsker and S. R. S. Varadhan, Asymptotic evaluation of certain Markov process expectations for large time–III, Comm. Pure Appl. Math., **29** (1976), 389–461.
[4] K. Itô, Motions of infinite particles (in Japanese), Kokyuroku RIMS, Kyoto Univ., **367** (1979), 1–33.
[5] M. Kac, Foundation of kinetic theory, Proceedings of 3rd Berkeley Symposium on Math. Stat. and Prob., vol. **3** (1956), 171–197.
[6] ——, Some probabilistic aspects of the Boltzmann equation, Acta Phys. Austriaca Supp. X, Springer Verlag, (1973), 379–400.
[7] S. Kusuoka and Y. Tamura, The convergence of Gibbs measures associated with mean field potentials, to appear in J. Fac. Sci., Univ. of Tokyo.
[8] H. P. McKean, A class of Markov processes associated with nonlinear parabolic equations, Proc. Nat. Acad. Sci., **56** (1966), 1907–1911.
[9] ——, Propagation of chaos for a class of non-linear parabolic equations, Lecture Series in Differential Equations **7**, Catholic Univ. (1967), 41–57.
[10] ——, Fluctuations in the kinetic theory of gases, Comm. Pure Appl. Math., **28** (1975), 435–455.
[11] A. S. Sznitman, An example of non-linear diffusion process with normal reflecting boundary condition and some related limit theorems, preprints, 1983.
[12] H. Tanaka, Fluctuation theory for Kac's one dimensional model of Maxwellian molecules, Sankhyā: The Indian Journal of Statistics, **44** (1982), Series A. Pt. I, 23–26.
[13] ——, Some probabilistic problems in the spatially homogeneous Boltzmann equation, Proc. IFIP-WG 7/1 Working Conference on Theory and Applications of Random Fields held in Bangalore, January 1982, Lecture Notes in Control and Information Sciences **49**, Springer-Verlag.
[14] H. Tanaka and M. Hitsuda, Central limit theorem for a simple diffusion model of interacting particles, Hiroshima Math. J., **11** (1981), 415–423.
[15] K. Uchiyama, Fluctuations of Markovian systems in Kac's caricature of a Maxwellian gas, J. Math. Soc. Japan, **35** (1983), 477–499.

DEPARTMENT OF MATHEMATICS
FACULTY OF SCIENCE AND TECHNOLOGY
KEIO UNIVERSITY,
YOKOHAMA 223, JAPAN

Z. Wahrscheinlichkeitstheorie verw. Gebiete
69, 439–459 (1985)

Zeitschrift für
Wahrscheinlichkeitstheorie
und verwandte Gebiete

Central Limit Theorem for a System of Markovian Particles with Mean Field Interactions

Tokuzo Shiga[1] and Hiroshi Tanaka[2]

[1] Department of Applied Physics, Faculty of Science, Tokyo Institute of Technology, Oh-okayama, Tokyo, Japan
[2] Department of Mathematics, Faculty of Science and Technology, Keio University, Yokohama, Japan

§ 0. Introduction

Let S be a measurable space and $\mathscr{P}(S)$ be the totality of probability measures on S. Suppose that to each $v \in \mathscr{P}(S)$ there corresponds a generator Q_v of a Markov process on S. Starting from the family we can consider an interacting n-particle system $X^{(n)}(t) = (X_1^{(n)}(t), \ldots, X_n^{(n)}(t))$, which is a Markov process on $S^{\otimes n} = S \times \ldots \times S$ with generator

$$Q^{(n)} \phi(x_1, \ldots, x_n) = \sum_{i=1}^{n} Q_{v_n}^{(i)} \phi(x_1, \ldots, x_n), \qquad v_n = \frac{1}{n} \sum_{j=1}^{n} \delta_{x_j}, \tag{0.1}$$

where δ_x stands for the δ-distribution at x, and $Q_v^{(i)}$ is used instead of Q_v when it acts on the i-th variable of $\phi(x_1, \ldots, x_n)$.

Denoting by W the path space on S, let us consider an empirical distribution U_n of the n-particle system:

$$U_n = \frac{1}{n} \sum_{i=1}^{n} \delta_{X_i^{(n)}(\cdot)}, \tag{0.2}$$

which is a random measure on W.

Our problem is described as follows. Assume that $(X_1^{(n)}(0), \ldots, X_n^{(n)}(0))$ is independent and identically distributed with common distribution $u \in \mathscr{P}(S)$ for any $n \geq 1$. It is known that there exists a probability distribution μ on the path space W such that U_n converges to μ as $n \to \infty$ in the sense that $\langle U_n, \Phi \rangle$ converges to $\langle \mu, \Phi \rangle$ in probability for any bounded measurable function Φ on W (the law of large numbers). Then the marginal distribution $u(t)$ of μ solves the following non-linear equation

$$\frac{d}{dt} \langle u(t), \phi \rangle = \langle u(t), Q_{u(t)} \phi \rangle, \qquad (\phi\text{: test function}). \tag{0.3}$$

As the next stage we consider the central limit theorem on the path space, that is to show that

(0.4) $$\xi_n = \sqrt{n}(U_n - \mu)$$

converges as $n \to \infty$ to a Gaussian field.

In the case of diffusion processes there have been many works concerning these problems (cf. Dawson [1], Kusuoka-Tamura [7], McKean [9], Sznitman [13], [14], Tanaka [15], Tanaka-Hitsuda [16]). Above all, Sznitman recently proved the central limit theorem on the path space for a general class of diffusion processes on $\boldsymbol{R}^d$ associated with $\{Q_v;\, v \in \mathscr{P}(\boldsymbol{R}^d)\}$ where

(0.5) $$Q_v = \frac{1}{2}\sum_{i=1}^{d}\sum_{j=1}^{d} a_{ij}[x, v]\frac{\partial^2}{\partial x_i \partial x_j} + \sum_{i=1}^{d} b_i[x, v]\frac{\partial}{\partial x_i},$$

$\{\alpha_{ij}(x, y)\}_{1 \leq i,j \leq d}$ and $\{b_i(x, y)\}_{1 \leq i \leq d}$ being uniformly bounded and Lipschitz continuous functions on $\boldsymbol{R}^d \times \boldsymbol{R}^d$ and

$$a_{ij}[x, v] = \sum_{k=1}^{d} \int \alpha_{ik}(x, y)\, v(dy) \int \alpha_{jk}(x, y)\, v(dy),$$

$$b_i[x, v] = \int b_i(x, y)\, v(dy).$$

In the present paper we study the central limit theorem mainly for pure jump type Markov processes. More precisely, let $(S, \mathscr{B}_S)$ be a measurable space and let $Q(x, x'; dy)$ be a bounded measurable kernel on $S \times S \times \mathscr{B}_S$. Then to each $v \in \mathscr{P}(S)$ there corresponds a generator Q_v of a Markov process on S by

(0.6) $$Q_v \phi(x) = \int v(dx') \int Q(x, x'; dy)(\phi(y) - \phi(x)).$$

Under a certain condition of non-degeneracy we obtain the central limit theorem for (0.4) (see § 2).

Furthermore, we remark in § 3 that our proof is valid for McKean's 2-state model of Boltzmann's equation with a slight modification and we have the central limit theorem as conjectured in [15]. We also give some remarks in § 4 to the case of diffusion processes as discussed in [13], [14] and [15]; here we assume the diffusion matrix $\alpha(x, y)$ is the identity matrix but the drift vector $b(x, y)$ is bounded measurable.

Our method of the proof is essentially based on Sznitman's paper [13], which treats the case of diffusion processes with $\alpha(x, y) =$ identity matrix. There he calculates a limiting quantities of Cameron-Martin-Maruyama-Girsanov density by making use of symmetric statistics and multiple Wiener integrals. His method is also applicable to our case. However we emphasize that once we obtain formulae on multiple Wiener integrals (the two lemmas in § 1) the proof turns out to be more transparent.

§ 1. Symmetric Statistics and Multiple Wiener Integrals

For the later use we summarize some facts on symmetric statistics and multiple Wiener integrals according to Dynkin and Mandelbaum [3], and present two formulae on multiple Wiener integrals.

Let $(\mathfrak{X}, \mathscr{B})$ be a separable Borel space, and let $\{X_n\}_{n=1}^{\infty}$ be a sequence of independent and identically distributed $\mathfrak{X}$-valued random variables with a distribution ν. For each $k=1,2,\dots$ let $L^2(\nu^{\otimes k})(L_c^2(\nu^{\otimes k}))$ be the space of all real-valued (complex-valued) square integrable functions on $\mathfrak{X}^{\otimes k}=\mathfrak{X}\times\dots\times\mathfrak{X}$ (k-fold) with respect to $\nu^{\otimes k}=\nu\times\dots\times\nu$ (k-fold). Denote by $L^2_{\text{symm}}(\nu^{\otimes k})$ the space of all symmetric functions of $L^2(\nu^{\otimes k})$. Then all of these spaces are separable Hilbert spaces. To $h_k\in L^2_{\text{symm}}(\nu^{\otimes k})$ there corresponds a symmetric statistic $\sigma_k^n(h_k)$ defined by

$$\begin{aligned}(1.1)\qquad \sigma_k^n(h_k) &= \sum_{1\leqq i_1<\dots<i_k\leqq n} h_k(X_{i_1},\dots,X_{i_k}) \qquad \text{for } n\geqq k\\ &=0 \qquad\qquad \text{for } n<k.\end{aligned}$$

Let $\{I_1(\phi);\phi\in L^2(\nu)\}$ be a centered Gaussian field satisfying

$$(1.2)\qquad E\{I_1(\phi)I_1(\psi)\}=(\phi,\psi)_{L^2(\nu)}.$$

For each $\phi\in L^2(\nu)$ set

$$(1.3)\qquad h_0^\phi=1,\quad h_k^\phi(x_1,\dots,x_k)=\phi(x_1)\dots\phi(x_k)\quad k=1,2,\dots.$$

A multiple Wiener integral $I_k(h_k^\phi)$ is defined by the following relation,

$$(1.4)\qquad \sum_{k=0}^{\infty}\frac{t^k}{k!}I_k(h_k^\phi)=\exp\left(tI_1(\phi)-\frac{t^2}{2}\|\phi\|^2_{L^2(\nu)}\right).$$

For a general $h_k\in L^2_{\text{symm}}(\nu^{\otimes k})$ $I_k(h_k)$ is defined by a standard procedure making use of the fact that the linear hull of $\{h_k^\phi:\phi\in L^2(\nu)\}$ is dense in $L^2_{\text{symm}}(\nu^{\otimes k})$. Then we have

Theorem 1.1 (Dynkin-Mandelbaum [3]). *Suppose $\{h_k\}_{k=1}^{\infty}$ satisfies the following: for each $k\geqq 1$ $h_k\in L^2_{\text{symm}}(\nu^{\otimes k})$, and*

$$(1.5)\qquad \int h_k(x_1,\dots,x_{k-1},x)\,\nu(dx)=0 \quad \textit{for } \nu^{\otimes k-1}\textit{-a.e. } (x_1,\dots,x_{k-1}).$$

Then

$$\{n^{-\frac{k}{2}}\sigma_k^n(h_k);k\geqq 1\} \textit{ converges to } \left\{\frac{1}{k!}I_k(h_k);k\geqq 1\right\} \quad \textit{as } n\to\infty$$

in the sense of convergence of finite dimensional distributions.

Let $a(x,y)\in L^2(\nu\otimes\nu)$ and denote by A the integral operator on $L_c^2(\nu)$ associated with $a(x,y)$,

$$(1.6)\qquad A\phi(x)=\int a(x,y)\,\phi(y)\,\nu(dy)\qquad (\phi\in L_c^2(\nu)).$$

Then A is a Hilbert-Schmidt operator, and A^n $(n\geqq 2)$ and AA^* are trace class operators. It is easy to see

$$(1.7)\qquad \operatorname{Trace} A^n=\int\dots\int a(x_1,x_2)\,a(x_2,x_3)\dots a(x_n,x_1)\,\nu(dx_1)\dots\nu(dx_n)$$

for any $n \geqq 2$, and

$$\text{Trace}\, A A^* = \|a\|^2_{L^2(\nu \otimes \nu)}. \tag{1.8}$$

The following lemmas will be used effectively in proving central limit theorems in the following sections.

Lemma 1.2. *Suppose that* $\text{Trace}\, A^n = 0$ *for all* $n \geqq 2$. *Then*

$$E[e^{\frac{1}{2} I_2(f)}] = e^{\frac{1}{2} \text{Trace}\, A A^*} \tag{1.9}$$

where

$$f(x,y) = a(x,y) + a(y,x) - \int a(x,z)\, a(y,z)\, \nu(dz). \tag{1.10}$$

Proof. Theorem 9.3 of Simon [12] implies that $\text{Trace}\, A^n = 0$ for all $n \geqq 2$ if and only if

$$\det{}_2(I + \mu A) = 1 \quad \text{for any complex number } \mu, \tag{1.11}$$

where $\det_2(I + \mu A)$ stands for the regularized determinant. In particular we have

$$\det{}_2(I - A) = \det{}_2(I - A^*) = 1. \tag{1.12}$$

Hence it follows from Theorem 9.2 of [12] that $I - A^*$ is invertible. Denoting by F the integral operator on $L^2_c(\nu)$ associated with $f(x,y)$, $I - F = (I - A)(I - A^*)$ is strictly positive definite because of the invertibility of $I - A^*$. Accordingly any eigen-value of F is real and less than one.

Let $\lambda_1, \lambda_2, \ldots$ be all eigen-values of F and $\{e_1, e_2, \ldots\}$ be the orthonormal base of the corresponding eigen-vectors of F on $L^2(\nu)$. Then f is represented as follows:

$$f = \sum_{k=1}^{\infty} \lambda_k e_k \otimes e_k.$$

Since $\sum_{k=1}^{\infty} \lambda_k^2 < \infty$ and $\lambda_k < 1$ for any $k \geqq 1$, we get using the relation (1.4) and the independence of $\{I_1(e_k)\}_{k=1}^{\infty}$

$$\begin{aligned} E[e^{\frac{1}{2} I_2(f)}] &= E\left[\exp \sum_{k=1}^{\infty} \frac{\lambda_k}{2} (I_1(e_k)^2 - 1)\right] \\ &= \prod_{n=1}^{\infty} E\left[\exp \frac{\lambda_k}{2} (I_1(e_k)^2 - 1)\right] \\ &= \prod_{k=1}^{\infty} \frac{e^{-\frac{\lambda_k}{2}}}{\sqrt{1 - \lambda_k}}. \end{aligned} \tag{1.13}$$

On the other hand the following formulae are known (cf. Simon [12], p. 107):

$$\det{}_2(I - F) = \prod_{k=1}^{\infty} (1 - \lambda_k) e^{\lambda_k} \tag{1.14}$$

$$\det{}_2(I - A)(I - A^*) = \det{}_2(I - A) \det{}_2(I - A^*) e^{-\text{Trace}\, A A^*}. \tag{1.15}$$

Thus we have by (1.12)

$$\det_2(I-F)=\det_2(I-A)(I-A^*)=e^{-\operatorname{Trace}AA^*}. \tag{1.16}$$

Therefore (1.9) follows immediately from (1.13)–(1.16).

Lemma 1.3. *Assume the same condition as in Lemma* 1.2. *Then* $I-A$ *is invertible and for any* $\phi\in L^2(\nu)$

$$\begin{aligned} &E[\exp\{\sqrt{-1}I_1(\phi)+\tfrac{1}{2}I_2(f)\}] \\ &\quad=\exp-\tfrac{1}{2}\{\|(I-A)^{-1}\phi\|^2_{L^2(\nu)}-\operatorname{Trace}AA^*\}. \end{aligned} \tag{1.17}$$

Proof. It follows from (1.12) that $I-A$ is invertible. Also using the same $\{e_k\}$ of the proof of Lemma 1.2 we have

$$\begin{aligned} &E[\exp\{\sqrt{-1}I_1(\phi)+\tfrac{1}{2}I_2(f)\}] \\ &=\prod_{k=1}^{\infty}E\left[\exp\left\{\sqrt{-1}(\phi,e_k)I_1(e_k)+\frac{\lambda_k}{2}(I_1(e_k)^2-1)\right\}\right] \\ &=\prod_{k=1}^{\infty}\frac{e^{-\frac{\lambda_k}{2}}}{\sqrt{1-\lambda_k}}\exp\left\{-\frac{1}{2}\sum_{k=1}^{\infty}(1-\lambda_k)^{-1}(\phi,e_k)^2\right\} \\ &=\{\det_2(I-F)\}^{-\frac{1}{2}}\exp\{-\tfrac{1}{2}((I-F)^{-1}\phi,\phi)_{L^2(\nu)}\} \\ &=e^{\frac{1}{2}\operatorname{Trace}AA^*}\exp\{-\tfrac{1}{2}\|(I-A)^{-1}\phi\|^2_{L^2(\nu)}\}. \end{aligned} \tag{1.18}$$

§ 2. The Case of Pure Jump Type Markov Processes

Let S be a standard Borel space, i.e., $(S,\mathscr{B}_S)$ is Borel isomorphic with a complete separable metric space. Denote by $\mathbb{B}(S)$ the Banach space of all bounded measurable functions on S equipped with the supremum norm $\|\cdot\|_\infty$.

Let $Q(x,x';dy)$ be a measure kernel satisfying the following conditions:

(2.1) for any fixed $(x,x')\in S\times S$ $Q(x,x';dy)$ is a bounded measure on $(S,\mathscr{B}_S)$ and $Q(x,x';\{x\})=0$;

(2.2) for any fixed $E\in\mathscr{B}_S$ $Q(x,x';E)$ is measurable in (x,x') with respect to $\mathscr{B}_S\otimes\mathscr{B}_S$;

(2.3) $q(x,x')=Q(x,x';S\setminus\{x\})$ is bounded in $(x,x')\in S\times S$;

(2.4) there exist constants $c_1>0$ and $c_2>0$ such that $c_1Q(x,x';dy)\leqq Q(x,x'';dy)\leqq c_2Q(x,x';dy)$ for any x, x' and x'' of S.

For each finite measure u on S, we write

$$Q_u(x;dy)=\int_S Q(x,x';dy)\,u(dx'), \tag{2.5}$$

and define a bounded operator Q_u on $\mathbb{B}(S)$ by

$$Q_u\phi(x)=\int_S Q_u(x;dy)(\phi(y)-\phi(x))\qquad\text{for } \phi\in\mathbb{B}(S). \tag{2.6}$$

Let W be the set of all S-valued step functions, i.e. for each $w \in W$ there exist $0=t_1<t_2<\ldots<t_n<\ldots$ with $t_n \to \infty$ such that

$$w(t)=w(t_i) \quad \text{for } t_i \leqq t < t_{i+1}. \tag{2.7}$$

Denote by $\mathscr{F}$ and $\mathscr{F}_t$ the usual σ-field of W. For any $T>0$ $(W_T, \mathscr{F}_T)$ denotes the restriction of $(W, \mathscr{F})$ to $[0,T]$. Then these are separable Borel spaces. Let $\mu \in \mathscr{P}(W)$, the set of probability measures on $(W, \mathscr{F})$. μ is called a McKean measure (or a McKean process) corresponding to $\{Q_v; v \in \mathscr{P}(S)\}$ if

$$\phi(w(t)) - \int_0^t Q_{u(s)} \phi(w(s))\, ds \quad \text{is a } \mu\text{-martingale for any } \phi \in \mathbb{B}(S), \tag{2.8}$$

$$\mathscr{L}(w(t); \mu) = u(t). \tag{2.9}$$

Here $\mathscr{L}(w(t); \mu)$ stands for the probability distribution of $w(t)$ under μ.

For any fixed $u \in \mathscr{P}(S)$, the set of probability measures on $(S, \mathscr{B}_S)$, there exists a unique McKean measure μ corresponding to $\{Q_v; v \in \mathscr{P}(S)\}$ with $\mathscr{L}(w(0); \mu) = u$, which will be shown in Lemma 2.3.

Now, let us consider an n-particle system, which is a Markov process $(X_1^n(t), \ldots, X_n^n(t))$ on $S^{\otimes n} = S \times \ldots \times S$ generated by the following operator:

$$Q^{(n)} \phi(x_1, \ldots, x_n) = \frac{1}{n} \sum_{i=1}^n \sum_{j=1}^n \int_S Q(x_i, x_j; dy)\, \Delta_i^y \phi(x_1, \ldots, x_n) \tag{2.10}$$

where $\Delta_i^y \phi(x_1, \ldots, x_n) = \phi(x_1, \ldots, \underset{\text{the } i\text{-th}}{y}, \ldots, x_n) - \phi(x_1, \ldots, x_n)$.

We assume the initial distribution is $u^{\otimes n} = u \otimes \ldots \otimes u$, the n-fold product measure of u. Let us introduce an empirical distribution U_n of the n-particle system,

$$U_n = \frac{1}{n} \sum_{i=1}^n \delta_{X^n_i(\cdot)}. \tag{2.11}$$

Then U_n is a random variable with values in $\mathscr{P}(W)$, and we can show that U_n converges as $n \to \infty$ to the McKean measure μ.

In order to discuss a central limit theorem for U_n let us introduce some notations. From now on, we fix $T>0$. For any $w \in W_T$, $0 \leqq t \leqq T$ and $E \in \mathscr{B}_S$ set

$$N(t, w; E) = \sum_{s \leqq t} I(w(s) \in E,\, w(s) \neq w(s-)), \tag{2.12}$$

and

$$\tilde{N}(t, w; E) = N(t, w, E) - \int_0^t Q_{u(s)}(w(s); E)\, ds, \tag{2.13}$$

where $I(B)$ stands for the indicator function of B. For each $(w, w') \in W_T \times W_T$ set

$$a(w, w') = \int_S \int_{[0,T]} (q_t(w'(s-), w(s-); y) - 1)\, \tilde{N}(ds, dy; w') \tag{2.14}$$

where

$$q_t(x, x'; y) = Q(x, x'; dy) / Q_{u(t)}(x; dy),$$

$$u(t) = \mathscr{L}(w(t); \mu).$$

We note $q_t(x, x'; y)$ is bounded by (2.4). Furthermore since $a(w, w')$ is square integrable with respect to $\mu \otimes \mu$, there corresponds a Hilbert-Schmidt operator A on $L_c^2(W_T, \mu)$,

$$A\phi(w) = \int_{W_T} a(w, w')\,\phi(w')\,\mu(dw'). \tag{2.15}$$

Note that $L_c^2(W_T, \mu)$ is a separable complex Hilbert space. Then it is shown that $I - A$ is an invertible operator.

Let us describe our main results. Let

$$\xi_n(\Phi) = \sqrt{n}\,\langle U_n - \mu, \Phi\rangle = \frac{1}{\sqrt{n}} \sum_{i=1}^{n} \tilde{\Phi}(w_i) \quad \text{for } \Phi \in L^2(W_T, \mu) \tag{2.16}$$

where $\tilde{\Phi} = \Phi - \langle \mu, \Phi \rangle$.

Theorem 2.1. *$\{\xi_n(\Phi): \Phi \in L^2(W_T, \mu)\}$ converges as $n \to \infty$ to a centered Gaussian field $\{\xi(\Phi): \Phi \in L^2(W_T, \mu)\}$ satisfying*

$$E[\xi(\Phi)\,\xi(\Psi)] = ((I - A)^{-1}\tilde{\Phi}, (I - A)^{-1}\tilde{\Psi})_{L^2(W_T, \mu)} \tag{2.17}$$

in the sense of convergence of finite dimensional distributions.

Next let us consider another interpretation of the operator $(I - A)^{-1}$ as in Tanaka [15] and Sznitman [13]. For any fixed $\zeta \in W$ and $\varepsilon > 0$ there exists a unique $\mu_\varepsilon^\zeta \in \mathscr{P}(W)$ such that

$$\phi(w(t)) - \int_0^t Q_{(u_\varepsilon^\zeta(s) + \varepsilon\delta_{\zeta(s)})}\,\phi(w(s))\,ds \tag{2.18}$$

is a μ_ε^ζ-martingale for any $\phi \in \mathbb{B}(S)$, and

$$\mathscr{L}(w(t); \mu_\varepsilon^\zeta) = u_\varepsilon^\zeta(t), \qquad \mathscr{L}(w(0); \mu_\varepsilon^\zeta) = u. \tag{2.19}$$

For any $\Phi \in L^2(W_T, \mu)$ and $\varepsilon > 0$

$$\Pi_\varepsilon \Phi(\zeta) = \frac{1}{\varepsilon}\langle \mu_\varepsilon^\zeta - \mu, \Phi \rangle \tag{2.20}$$

is well-defined, and we can show

$$\Pi\Phi = \operatorname*{s\text{-}lim}_{\varepsilon \to 0} \Pi_\varepsilon \Phi \quad \text{exists in } L^2(W_T, \mu). \tag{2.21}$$

Furthermore the following identity holds.

Theorem 2.2

$$I + \Pi = (I - A)^{-1}. \tag{2.22}$$

We will prove these theorems by a series of lemmas.

Lemma 2.3. *Assume* (2.1)–(2.3). *Then for any $u \in \mathscr{P}(S)$ there exists a unique McKean measure μ corresponding to $\{Q_v; v \in \mathscr{P}(S)\}$ with $\mathscr{L}(w(0); \mu) = u$.*

Proof. Let $v(t)$ be a $\mathscr{P}(S)$-valued function defined on $[0,\infty)$ such that $\langle v(t),\phi\rangle$ is Borel measurable in t for any $\phi\in\mathbb{B}(S)$. We first claim that there exists a unique solution $v\in\mathscr{P}(W)$ of the following martingale problem:

(2.23) $$\phi(w(t))-\int_0^t Q_{v(s)}\phi(w(s))\,ds$$

is a v-martingale for any $\phi\in\mathbb{B}(S)$, *and*

(2.24) $$\mathscr{L}(w(0);v)=v(0).$$

For a $c>\|q\|_\infty=\sup_{x,x'}q(x,x')$ define a probability kernel P_t by

(2.25) $$P_t(x;E)=\frac{1}{c}Q_{v(t)}(x;E\setminus\{x\})+\left(1-\frac{q[x,v(t)]}{c}\right)\delta_{\{x\}}(E)$$

where $x\in S$, $E\in\mathscr{B}_S$ and $q[x,v]=\int_S q(x,y)\,v(dy)$. Then

(2.26) $$Q_{v(t)}\phi(x)=c\left[\int P_t(x;dy)\,\phi(y)-\phi(x)\right].$$

Let $X(0)$ be an S-valued randon variable with the distribution $v(0)$, and N_t be a Poisson process on $\{0,1,2,\ldots\}$ with the intensity c independent of $X(0)$. Denote by σ_n the n-th jumping time of N_t. Let us construct an S-valued process $X(t)$. Set $X(t)=X(0)$ for $0\leqq t<\sigma_1$. At $t=\sigma_1$, $X(\sigma_1)$ is a randomly chosen point of S according to the transition law $P_{\sigma_1}(X(\sigma_1-);dy)$, and set $X(t)=X(\sigma_1)$ for $\sigma_1\leqq t<\sigma_2$. Repeating this procedure we get an S-valued process $X(t)$. It is a routine work to see the distribution μ on W induced by $X(t)$ is a unique solution of the above martingale problem (2.23) and (2.24).

Next we note for any $u\in\mathscr{P}(S)$ the following equation has a unique $\mathscr{P}(S)$-valued solution

(2.27) $$\langle u(t),\phi\rangle-\langle u,\phi\rangle=\int_0^t\langle u(s),Q_{u(s)}\phi\rangle\,ds\quad \textit{for any } \phi\in\mathbb{B}(S).$$

Let $u^0(t)=u$. If $u^{n-1}(t)$ is defined we have a unique solution μ^n of (2.23) and (2.24) with $v(t)=u^{n-1}(t)$, and set $u^n(t)=\mathscr{L}(w(t);\mu^n)$. Then we have

(2.28) $$\langle u^n(t),\phi\rangle-\langle u,\phi\rangle=\int_0^t\langle u^n(s),Q_{u^{n-1}(s)}\phi\rangle\,ds$$

for any $\phi\in\mathbb{B}(S)$. Noting (2.3) it follows

(2.29) $$\|u^{n+1}(t)-u^n(t)\|_{\mathrm{var}}\leqq 2\|q\|_\infty\int_0^t(\|u^{n+1}(s)-u^n(s)\|_{\mathrm{var}}+\|u^n(s)-u^{n-1}(s)\|_{\mathrm{var}})\,ds,$$

where $\|\cdot\|_{\mathrm{var}}$ stands for the total variation norm. This yields that there exists $u(t)\in\mathscr{P}(S)$ such that

(2.30) $$\lim_{n\to\infty}\sup_{0\leqq t\leqq T}\|u^n(t)-u(t)\|_{\mathrm{var}}=0\quad \textit{for any } T>0.$$

Thus we get a solution $u(t)$ of (2.27), and the uniqueness also is obvious.

Finally, let μ be a unique solution of (2.23) with $v(t)=u(t)$. Then $\tilde{u}(t) = \mathscr{L}(w(t);\mu)$ is a solution of

(2.31) $$\langle \tilde{u}(t), \phi \rangle - \langle u, \phi \rangle = \int_0^t \langle u(s), Q_{u(s)} \phi \rangle \, ds \qquad \phi \in \mathbb{B}(S).$$

Since the uniqueness of solutions to the linear equation (2.31) can also be proved easily, $\tilde{u}(t)$ coincides with $u(t)$ which is also a solution of (2.27). Therefore μ is a McKean measure corresponding to $\{Q_v; v \in \mathscr{P}(S)\}$ with $\mathscr{L}(w(0);\mu)=u$ which is also unique by virtue of the uniqueness result for (2.27) and (2.23).

From now on, we fix the McKean measure μ obtained in Lemma 2.3.

Lemma 2.4 (i). *For any* $E \in \mathscr{B}_S$

(2.32) $$\tilde{N}(t, E; w) \text{ is a } \mu\text{-martingale, and}$$

(ii) *for any* E_1 *and* E_2 *of* $\mathscr{B}_S$

(2.33) $$\tilde{N}(t, E_1; w)\tilde{N}(t, E_2; w) - \int_0^t Q_{u(s)}(w(s); E_1 \cap E_2) \, ds$$

is a μ*-martingale.*

Proof. Noting that for any $\phi \in \mathbb{B}(S)$

(2.34) $$\phi(w(t)) - \phi(w(0)) = \int_{[0,t] \times S} (\phi(y) - \phi(w(s-)))N(ds, dy; w), \quad \text{and}$$

(2.35) $$\phi(w(t)) - \int_0^t Q_{u(s)} \phi(w(s)) \, ds \quad \text{is a } \mu\text{-martingale},$$

we have

(2.36) $$\int_{[0,t] \times S} (\phi(y) - \phi(w(s-)))\tilde{N}(ds, dy; w) \quad \text{is a } \mu\text{-martingale}.$$

Also it is easily seen that for $\psi \in \mathbb{B}(S)$

(2.37) $$\int_{[0,t] \times S} \psi(w(s-))(\phi(y) - \phi(w(s-)))\tilde{N}(ds, dy; w) \quad \text{is a } \mu\text{-martingale}.$$

In particular, if $\phi(x)\psi(x)=0$ for all $x \in S$ then

(2.38) $$\int_{[0,t] \times S} \phi(y)\psi(w(s-))\tilde{N}(ds, dy; w) \quad \text{is a } \mu\text{-martingale}.$$

Furthermore noticing $\tilde{N}((s, y); w(s-)=y, 0 \leqq s \leqq t)=0$ for any $t>0$ it is easy to see that for any $f \in \mathbb{B}(S \times S)$

(2.39) $$\int_{[0,t] \times S} f(y, w(s-))\tilde{N}(ds, dy; w) \quad \text{is a } \mu\text{-martingale},$$

from which (i) follows. (ii) is immediate from (i) combined with the following identity obtained by integration by parts,

$$(2.40)\quad \tilde{N}(t,E_1;w)\tilde{N}(t,E_2;w)-N(t,E_1\cap E_2;w) = \int_0^t \tilde{N}(s-,E_1;w)\,d\tilde{N}(s,E_2;w)+\int_0^t \tilde{N}(s-,E_2;w)\,d\tilde{N}(s,E_1;w).$$

Let $(X^n(t)=(X_1^n(t),\ldots,X_n^n(t)))$ be the Markov process on $S^{\otimes n}$ with the initial distribution $u^{\otimes n}$, generated by $Q^{(n)}$ of (2.10). Let us denote by P^n the probability distribution induced by $\{X^{(n)}(t)\}_{0\leqq t\leqq T}$ on the path space $(W_T^n,\mathscr{F}_T^n)$, where $W_T^n = W_T\times\ldots\times W_T$ and $\mathscr{F}_t^n=\mathscr{F}_t\times\ldots\times\mathscr{F}_t$ for $0\leqq t\leqq T$.

Lemma 2.5. *For each $n\geqq 1$ P^n and $\mu^{\otimes n}$ are mutually absolutely continuous and*

$$(2.41)\quad \frac{dP^n}{d\mu^{\otimes n}}(\mathbf{w})=\exp H_T^n(\mathbf{w}),$$

$$(2.42)\quad H_t^n(\mathbf{w})=\sum_{i=1}^n \int_{[0,t]\times S}\left\{\log\frac{1}{n}\sum_{j=1}^n q_s(w_i(s-),w_j(s-);y)\right\}N(ds,dy;w_i) - \int_0^t\left(\frac{1}{n}\sum_{i=1}^n\sum_{j=1}^n q(w_i(s),w_j(s))-\sum_{i=1}^n q[w_i(s),u(s)]\right)ds$$

for $\mathbf{w}=(w_1,\ldots,w_n)\in W_T^n$ and $t>0$.

Proof. Let $M_t^n(\mathbf{w})=\exp H_t^n(\mathbf{w})$. Since $\{w_i(t)\}_{1\leqq i\leqq n}$ have no common jumps almost surely $(\mu^{\otimes n})$, it follows from Itô's formula (cf. Ikeda-Watanabe [4], p. 66)

$$(2.43)\quad M_t^n(\mathbf{w})-1=\sum_{i=1}^n\int_{[0,t]\times S} M_{s-}^n\left(\frac{1}{n}\sum_{j=1}^n q_s(w_i(s-),w_j(s-);y)-1\right)\tilde{N}(ds,dy;w_i).$$

Hence $M_t^n(\mathbf{w})$ is a $\mu^{\otimes n}$-martingale.

Next, for $\phi\in\mathbb{B}(S^{\otimes n})$, set

$$(2.44)\quad K_\phi(t)=\phi(\mathbf{w}(t))-\int_0^t Q^{(n)}\phi(\mathbf{w}(s))\,ds$$

$$(2.45)\quad \tilde{K}_\phi(t)=\phi(\mathbf{w}(t))-\sum_{i=1}^n\int_0^t\int_S Q_{u(s)}(w_i(s);dy)\,\Delta_i^y\phi(\mathbf{w}(s))\,ds.$$

It is obvious that $\tilde{K}_\phi(t)$ is a $\mu^{\otimes n}$-martingale. We will show

$$(2.46)\quad M_t^n K_\phi(t)\quad \text{is also a } \mu^{\otimes n}\text{-martingale.}$$

By integration by parts

$$(2.47)\quad M_t^n K_\phi(t)=\int_0^t K_\phi(s-)\,dM_s^n+\int_0^t M_{s-}^n\,d\tilde{K}_\phi(s) +\int_0^t M_{s-}^n(dK_\phi(s)-d\tilde{K}_\phi(s))+\sum_{s\leqq t}(M_s^n-M_{s-}^n)(K_\phi(s)-K_\phi(s-)).$$

Also,

$$(2.48)\qquad \sum_{s\leq t}(M_s^n - M_{s-}^n)(K_\phi(s) - K_\phi(s-))$$
$$= \sum_{s\leq t}(M_s^n - M_{s-}^n)(\phi(\mathbf{w}(s)) - \phi(\mathbf{w}(s-)))$$
$$= \sum_{i=1}^{n}\int M_{s-}^n\left(\frac{M_s^n}{M_{s-}^n} - 1\right)\Delta_i^y\phi(\mathbf{w}(s-))N(ds,dy;w_i)$$
$$= \sum_{i=1}^{n}\int_{[0,t]\times S} M_{s-}^n\left(\frac{1}{n}\sum_{j=1}^{n} q_s(w_i(s-),w_j(s-);y) - 1\right)$$
$$\cdot\Delta_i^y\phi(\mathbf{w}(s))N(ds,dy;w_i).$$

On the other hand noting that

$$(2.49)\qquad \int_0^t M_{s-}^n(dK_\phi(s) - d\tilde{K}_\phi(s))$$
$$= -\sum_{i=1}^{n}\int_0^t\int_S M_{s-}^n\left(\frac{1}{n}\sum_{j=1}^{n} q_s(w_i(s),w_j(s);y) - 1\right)Q_{u(s)}(w_i(s);dy)\Delta_i^y\phi(\mathbf{w}(s))\,ds,$$

we have

$$(2.50)\qquad M_t^n K_\phi(t) = \int_0^t K_\phi(s-)\,dM_s^n + \int_0^t M_{s-}^n\,d\tilde{K}_\phi(s)$$
$$+\sum_{i=1}^{n}\int_{[0,t]\times S} M_{s-}^n\left(\frac{1}{n}\sum_{j=1}^{n} q_s(w_i(s-),w_j(s-);y) - 1\right)$$
$$\cdot\Delta_i^y\phi(\mathbf{w}(s))\tilde{N}(ds,dy;w_i).$$

Hence $M_t^n K_\phi(t)$ is a $\mu^{\otimes n}$-martingale.

Finally for each $A\in\mathscr{F}_T^n$ we set

$$(2.51)\qquad \tilde{P}^n(A) = \int_A M_T^n(\mathbf{w})\,\mu^{\otimes n}(dw).$$

Then $\tilde{P}^n$ is well-defined as a probability measure on $(W_T^n, \mathscr{F}_T^n)$. Moreover it is easily seen that for any $\phi\in\mathbb{B}(S^{\otimes n})$

$$(2.52)\qquad K_\phi(t) \text{ is a } \tilde{P}^n\text{-martingale}$$

since $M_t^n K_\phi(t)$ is a $\mu^{\otimes n}$-martingale. Therefore $\tilde{P}^n = P^n$, because of the uniqueness of the martingale problem (2.52) with $\mathscr{L}(\mathbf{w}(0);\tilde{P}^n) = u^{\otimes n}$, which completes the proof of Lemma 2.5.

Next we discuss a limit of a functional $H_T^n(w_1,\ldots,w_n)$. Since $H_T^n(w_1,\ldots,w_n)$ can be regarded as a symmetric statistic of $\{w_n\}_{n=1}^\infty$, which is a sequence of $(W_T,\mathscr{F}_T)$-valued independent random variables with common distribution μ, Dynkin-Mandelbaum's theorem of § 1 is applicable.

Lemma 2.6

$$(2.53)\qquad \lim_{n\to\infty} H_T^n(w_1,\ldots,w_n) = \tfrac{1}{2}I_2(f) - \tfrac{1}{2}\mathrm{Trace}\,AA^*$$

in the sense of convergence of probability distributions, where

(2.54) $$f(w,w')=a(w,w')+a(w',w)-\int a(w,w'')\,a(w',w'')\,\mu(dw'')$$

and $I_2(f)$ *is a multiple Wiener integral associated with* (W_T,μ).

Proof. Using Taylor's expansion of $\log x$ we have

(2.55) $$\begin{aligned} H_T^n(w_1,\dots,w_n) &= \sum_{i=1}^n \int_{[0,T]\times S} \left(\frac{1}{n}\sum_{j=1}^n q_s(w_i(s-),w_j(s-);y)-1\right)\tilde N(dt,dy;w_i) \\ &\quad -\tfrac{1}{2}\sum_{i=1}^n \int_{[0,T]\times S} \left(\frac{1}{n}\sum_{j=1}^n q_s(w_i(s-),w_j(s-);y)-1\right)^2 N(dt,dy;w_i) \\ &\quad +\tfrac{1}{3}\sum_{i=1}^n \int_{[0,T]\times S} \left(\frac{1}{n}\sum_{j=1}^n q_s(w_i(s-),w_j(s-);y)-1\right)^3 N(dt,dy;w_i) \\ &\quad -\tfrac{1}{4}\sum_{i=1}^n \int_{[0,T]\times S} R_i(t)\,N(dt,dy;w_i) \\ &= I_1^n+I_2^n+I_3^n+I_4^n, \end{aligned}$$

where

(2.56) $$|R_i(t)|\leqq \text{const.}\left(\frac{1}{n}\sum_{j=1}^n q_s(w_i(s-),w_j(s-),y)-1\right)^4.$$

We first note

(2.57) $$I_1^n=\frac{1}{n}\sum_{i=1}^n\sum_{j=1}^n a(w_j,w_i).$$

Since it is easily seen that

(2.58) $$a(w,w')\in L^2(\mu\otimes\mu),\quad \text{and}$$

(2.59) $$\int a(w,w')\,\mu(dw')=\int a(w',w)\,\mu(dw)=0 \qquad \mu\text{-a.s.},$$

it follows immediately from Theorem 1.1

(2.60) $$\lim_{n\to\infty} I_1^n=\tfrac{1}{2}I_2(a+a^*).$$

where a^* is defined by $a^*(w,w')=a(w',w)$.

Let

(2.61) $$\begin{aligned} b(w;w',w'') &= \int_{[0,T]\times S} (q_s(w(s-),w'(s-);y)-1)(q_s(w(s-),w''(s-);y)-1)\,N(ds,dy;w). \end{aligned}$$

Then

$$(2.62)\qquad I_2^n = -\frac{1}{2n^2}\sum_{i=1}^{n}\sum_{j=1}^{n}\sum_{k=1}^{n} b(w_i; w_j, w_k)$$
$$= -\frac{1}{2n^2}\sum_{\substack{(i,j,k)\\ \text{distinct}}} (b(w_i; w_j, w_k) - b[\mu; w_j, w_k])$$
$$-\frac{n-2}{2n^2}\sum_{j\neq k} b[\mu; w_j, w_k] - \frac{1}{2n^2}\sum_{i\neq j} b(w_i; w_j, w_j)$$
$$-\frac{1}{n^2}\sum_{i\neq j} b(w_i; w_i, w_j) - \frac{1}{2n^2}\sum_{i=1}^{n} b(w_i; w_i, w_i)$$
$$= I_{2,1}^n + I_{2,2}^n + I_{2,3}^n + I_{2,4}^n + I_{2,5}^n,$$

where $b[\mu; w', w''] = \int b(w; w', w'')\,\mu(dw)$. Note that

$$(2.63)\qquad b(w; w', w'') = b(w; w'', w') \quad \textit{and} \quad \int b(w; w', w'')\,d\mu(w'') = 0.$$

Also it follows from Lemma 2.4

$$(2.64)\qquad b[\mu; w', w''] = \int a(w', w)\,a(w'', w)\,\mu(dw).$$

Accordingly, by virtue of Theorem 1.1 we see $I_{2,1}^n\, I_{2,4}^n$ and $I_{2,5}^n$ vanish as $n\to\infty$, and furthermore we get by (2.64)

$$(2.65)\qquad \lim_{n\to\infty} I_{2,2}^n = -\tfrac{1}{2} I_2(b[\mu; \cdot, \cdot])$$

$$(2.66)\qquad \lim_{n\to\infty} I_{2,3}^n = -\tfrac{1}{2}\int_{W_T} b[\mu; w', w']\,\mu(dw')$$
$$= -\tfrac{1}{2}\int_{W_T\times W_T} a(w, w')^2\,\mu(dw)\,\mu(dw')$$
$$= -\tfrac{1}{2}\operatorname{Trace} AA^*.$$

Consequently we obtain

$$(2.67)\qquad \lim_{n\to\infty} I_2^n = \tfrac{1}{2} I_2 - \tfrac{1}{2} b[\mu; \cdot, \cdot] - \tfrac{1}{2}\operatorname{Trace} AA^*.$$

As for I_3^n and I_4^n, by making use of Theorem 1.1 repeatedly we can show that they both vanish as $n\to\infty$, and the proof of Lemma 2.6 is completed.

Lemma 2.7. Trace $A^n = 0$ *for all* $n \geqq 2$.

Proof. By (1.7) it suffices to show that for any $n \geqq 2$

$$(2.68)\qquad \int_{W_T^n} a(w_1, w_2)\,a(w_2, w_3)\ldots a(w_n, w_1)\,\mu(dw_1)\ldots\mu(dw_n) = 0.$$

Let

$$(2.69)\qquad a(t; w, w') = \int_{[0,t]\times S} (q_s(w'(s-), w(s-); y) - 1)\,\tilde{N}(ds, dy; w').$$

Since $a(t;w_1,w_2)$, $a(t;w_2,w_3),\dots,a(t;w_n,w_1)$ are square integrable $\mu^{\otimes n}$ martingales of bounded variation, and any two of them have no common discontinuities with respect to $\mu^{\otimes n}$, Theorem d) of [2] p. 367 implies that $a(t;w_1,w_2)\,a(t;w_2,w_3)\dots a(t;w_n,w_1)$ is a $\mu^{\otimes n}$-martingale, which yields (2.68).

Now we are in position to prove Theorem 2.1. Let any $\Phi\in L^2(W_T,\mu)$ be fixed. By Lemma 2.5

$$E^{P^n}[\exp\sqrt{-1}\langle\sqrt{n}(U_n-\mu),\Phi\rangle] \tag{2.70}$$
$$=E^{\mu^{\otimes n}}\left[\exp\left\{\sqrt{-1}\frac{1}{\sqrt{n}}\sum_{i=1}^{n}\tilde{\Phi}(w_i)+H_T^n(w_1,\dots,w_n)\right\}\right].$$

It follows from Lemma 2.6 that $\exp H_T^n(w)$ converges as $n\to\infty$ to $\exp\frac{1}{2}(I_2(f)-\operatorname{Trace}AA^*)$ in the law sense. Noting Lemma 2.7 we can apply Lemma 1.2, and we get

$$E[\exp\tfrac{1}{2}(I_2(f)-\operatorname{Trace}AA^*)]=1. \tag{2.71}$$

Hence $\{\exp H_T^n(w)\}$ *is uniformly integrable.* Also, using Theorem 1.1 again

$$\exp\left\{\sqrt{-1}\frac{1}{\sqrt{n}}\sum_{i=1}^{n}\tilde{\Phi}(w_i)+H_T^n(w)\right\}_{n=1}^{\infty}$$

is uniformly integrable and converges as $n\to\infty$ to

$$\exp\{\sqrt{-1}I_1(\tilde{\Phi})+\tfrac{1}{2}I_2(f)-\tfrac{1}{2}\operatorname{Trace}AA^*\}$$

in the law sense. Therefore we have by Lemma 1.3

$$\lim_{n\to\infty}E^{\mu^{\otimes n}}\left[\exp\left\{\sqrt{-1}\frac{1}{\sqrt{n}}\sum_{i=1}^{n}\tilde{\Phi}(w_i)+H_T^n(w)\right\}\right] \tag{2.72}$$
$$=E[\exp\{\sqrt{-1}I_1(\tilde{\Phi})+\tfrac{1}{2}I_2(f)-\tfrac{1}{2}\operatorname{Trace}AA^*\}]$$
$$=\exp\{-\tfrac{1}{2}\|(I-A)^{-1}\tilde{\Phi}\|^2_{L^2(W_T,\mu)}\},$$

which completes Theorem 2.1.

Next we proceed to prove Theorem 2.2. We can show in the same way as Lemma 2.3 that for any fixed $\zeta\in W_T$ and $\varepsilon>0$ there exists a unique solution of the martingale problem (2.18) and (2.19), which we denote by μ_ε^ζ. Moreover the proof of Lemma 2.5 implies that $\mu_\varepsilon^\zeta\in\mathscr{P}(W_T)$ and $\mu\in\mathscr{P}(W_T)$ are mutually absolutely continuous and

$$\frac{d\mu_\varepsilon^\zeta}{d\mu}(w)=\exp H_T^{\varepsilon,\zeta}(w), \tag{2.73}$$

where

$$H_T^{\varepsilon,\zeta}(w)=\int_{[0,T]\times S}\{\log q_s[w(s-),u_\varepsilon^\zeta(s)+\varepsilon\delta_{\zeta(s)};y]\}\,N(ds,dy;w) \tag{2.74}$$
$$-\int_0^T q[w(s),u_\varepsilon^\zeta(s)+\varepsilon\delta_{\zeta(s)}-u(s)]\,ds$$

where $u_\varepsilon^\zeta(s)=\mathscr{L}(w(s);\mu_\varepsilon^\zeta)$, $u(s)=\mathscr{L}(w(s);\mu)$ and $q_s[x,v;y]$ is defined similarly to $q[x,v]$.

Lemma 2.8. *There exists $C>0$ independent of $\zeta\in W$ and $\varepsilon>0$ such that*

$$\|u_\varepsilon^\zeta(t)-u(t)\|_{\mathrm{var}}\leqq C\varepsilon t \quad \textit{for } 0\leqq t\leqq T, \tag{2.75}$$

and

$$|H_T^{\varepsilon,\zeta}(w)|\leqq C\varepsilon(1+N(T,S;w)) \quad \textit{for any } w\in W_T. \tag{2.76}$$

Proof. For any $\phi\in\mathbb{B}(S)$

$$\begin{aligned}
(2.77)\quad &|\langle u_\varepsilon^\zeta(t)-u(t),\phi\rangle|\\
&=\left|\int_0^t\langle u_\varepsilon^\zeta(s), Q_{u_\varepsilon^\zeta(s)+\varepsilon\delta_{\zeta(s)}}\phi\rangle\,ds-\int_0^t\langle u(s),Q_{u(s)}\phi\rangle\,ds\right|\\
&=\left|\int_0^t\langle u_\varepsilon^\zeta(s)-u(s),Q_{u(s)}\phi\rangle\,ds+\int_0^t\langle u_\varepsilon^\zeta(s),Q_{u_\varepsilon^\zeta(s)+\varepsilon\delta_{\zeta(s)}-u(s)}\phi\rangle\,ds\right|\\
&\leqq\int_0^t\|u_\varepsilon^\zeta(s)-u(s)\|_{\mathrm{var}}\|Q_{u(s)}\phi\|_\infty\,ds+\int_0^t\|Q_{u_\varepsilon^\zeta(s)+\varepsilon\delta_{\zeta(s)}-u(s)}\phi\|_\infty\,ds\\
&\leqq\mathrm{Const.}\,\|\phi\|_\infty\left(\int_0^t\|u_\varepsilon^\zeta(s)-u(s)\|_{\mathrm{var}}\,ds+\varepsilon t\right).
\end{aligned}$$

Thus we see

$$\|u_\varepsilon^\zeta(t)-u(t)\|_{\mathrm{var}}\leqq\mathrm{Const.}\left(\int_0^t\|u_\varepsilon^\zeta(s)-u(s)\|_{\mathrm{var}}+\varepsilon t\right), \tag{2.78}$$

which yields (2.75). (2.76) follows immediately from (2.75), noting that $q_s(x,x';y)$ is bounded from above and from zero and that a trivial identity $q_s[x,u(s);y]=1$ holds.

We give the proof of Theorem 2.2. We have for any $\Phi\in L^2(W_T,\mu)$

$$\begin{aligned}
(2.79)\quad \Pi^\varepsilon\Phi(\zeta)&=\frac{1}{\varepsilon}\langle\mu_\varepsilon^\zeta-\mu,\Phi\rangle\\
&=\frac{1}{\varepsilon}\langle\mu,(e^{H_T^{\varepsilon,\zeta}}-1)\Phi\rangle\\
&=\frac{1}{\varepsilon}\langle\mu,H_T^{\varepsilon,\zeta}\Phi\rangle+\frac{1}{\varepsilon}\langle\mu,(e^{H_T^{\varepsilon,\zeta}}-1-H_T^{\varepsilon,\zeta})\Phi\rangle.
\end{aligned}$$

Using Taylor's expansion $H_T^{\varepsilon,\zeta}$ is represented as follows:

$$\begin{aligned}
(2.80)\quad H_T^{\varepsilon,\zeta}(w)&=\int_{[0,T]\times S}(q_s[w(s-),u_\varepsilon^\zeta(s);y]-1)\,\tilde N(ds,dy;w)\\
&\quad+\varepsilon\int_{[0,T]\times S}(q_s(w(s-),\zeta(s);y)-1)\,\tilde N(ds,dy;w)+J_T^{\varepsilon,\zeta}(w)
\end{aligned}$$

$$(2.81)\quad |J_T^{\varepsilon,\zeta}(w)|\leqq\mathrm{Const.}\int_{[0,T]\times S}(q_s[w(s-),u_\varepsilon^\zeta(s)+\varepsilon\delta_{\zeta(s)};y]-1)^2\,N(ds,dy;w).$$

Since

(2.82)
$$\begin{aligned}&|q_s[w(s-), u_\varepsilon^\zeta(s)+\varepsilon\delta_{\zeta(s)}; y]-1|\\&=|q_s[w(s-), u_\varepsilon^\zeta(s)-u(s); y]-\varepsilon q_s(w(s-), \zeta(s); y)|\\&\leqq \|q_s\|_\infty(\|u_\varepsilon^\zeta(s)-u(s)\|_{\mathrm{var}}+\varepsilon)\end{aligned}$$

it follows from Lemma 2.8 that

(2.83)
$$|J_T^{\varepsilon,\zeta}(w)|\leqq \mathrm{Const.}\,\varepsilon^2 N(T, S; w).$$

Furthermore we note by (2.14) and (2.80)

(2.84)
$$H_T^{\varepsilon,\zeta}(w)=\int a(w', w)(\mu_\varepsilon^\zeta-\mu)(dw')+\varepsilon a(\zeta, w)+J_T^{\varepsilon,\zeta}.$$

Hence combining these it is easily checked

(2.85)
$$\lim_{\varepsilon\downarrow 0}\left(\frac{1}{\varepsilon}\langle\mu, H_T^{\varepsilon,\zeta}\Phi\rangle-\Pi_\varepsilon A\Phi(\zeta)-A\Phi(\zeta)\right)=0$$

uniformly in $\zeta\in W_T$. Also, using an inequality $|e^x-1-x|\leqq\frac{x^2}{2}e^{|x|}$ and (2.76), we have

(2.86)
$$\begin{aligned}&\frac{1}{\varepsilon}|\langle\mu, (e^{H_T^{\varepsilon,\zeta}}-1-H_T^{\varepsilon,\zeta})\Phi\rangle|\\&\leqq\frac{1}{2\varepsilon}\langle\mu, e^{|H_T^{\varepsilon,\zeta}|}|H_T^{\varepsilon,\zeta}|^2|\Phi|\rangle\\&\leqq\frac{1}{2\varepsilon}\|\Phi\|_{L^2(W_T,\mu)}\langle\mu, e^{2|H_T^{\varepsilon,\zeta}|}|H_T^{\varepsilon,\zeta}|^4\rangle^{\frac{1}{2}}\\&\leqq\mathrm{Const.}\,\|\Phi\|_{L^2(W_T,\mu)}\varepsilon\langle\mu, e^{CN(T,S;w)}(1+N(T,S;w))^4\rangle^{\frac{1}{2}},\end{aligned}$$

which tends to 0 as $\varepsilon\downarrow 0$, since $\langle\mu, e^{aN(T,S;w)}\rangle<+\infty$ holds for any $a>0$. Consequently we obtain by (2.79), (2.85) and (2.86)

(2.87)
$$\lim_{\varepsilon\downarrow 0}(\Pi_\varepsilon(I-A)\Phi(\zeta)-A\Phi(\zeta))=0$$

uniformly in $\zeta\in W_T$. Noting that $I-A$ is invertible and $(I-A)^{-1}$ is a bounded operator on $L^2(W_T, \mu)$,

(2.88)
$$s\text{-}\lim_{\varepsilon\downarrow 0}\Pi_\varepsilon\Phi=A(I-A)^{-1}\Phi$$

which completes the proof of Theorem 2.2.

§3. The Case of McKean's Model of Boltzmann's Equation

Let us consider McKean's 2-velocity model of Maxwellian gases. For each $v\in\mathscr{P}(\{\pm 1\})$ set

(3.1)
$$Q_v\phi(x)=v(-1)(\phi(-x)-\phi(x))\qquad x=\pm 1.$$

Let any $T>0$ be fixed. W_T denotes the set of all right continuous step functions defined on $[0,T]$ taking values in $\{\pm 1\}$. Let any $u\in\mathscr{P}(\{\pm 1\})$ be given. Then by Lemma 2.3 there exists a unique McKean's measure μ on W_T corresponding to $\{Q_v; v\in\mathscr{P}(\{\pm 1\})\}$, and $u(t)=\mathscr{L}(w(t);\mu)$ is a solution of the following Boltzmann's equation:

$$(3.2)\qquad \frac{d}{dt}\langle u(t),\phi\rangle=\langle u(t)\otimes u(t), Q\phi\rangle,\qquad \phi\in\mathbb{B}(\{\pm 1\}),$$

where $Q\phi(x,y)=\phi(xy)-\phi(x)$.

To avoid triviality we henceforth assume $0\leqq u(+1)<1$. The n-particle system $X^{(n)}(t)=(X_1^n(t),\dots,X_n^n(t))$ is defined as a Markov process on the n-fold product space $\{\pm 1\}^n$ with generator

$$(3.3)\qquad Q^{(n)}\phi(x_1,\dots,x_n)=\frac{1}{n}\sum_{1\leqq i<j\leqq n}\sum_c\{\phi(\dots,x_i',\dots,x_j',\dots)-\phi(x_1,\dots,x_n)\}$$

where $\sum_c$ is the sum with respect to the two types of collisions

$$\begin{pmatrix}x_i'\\ x_j'\end{pmatrix}=\begin{pmatrix}x_ix_j\\ x_j\end{pmatrix}\quad\text{or}\quad\begin{pmatrix}x_i\\ x_ix_j\end{pmatrix}.$$

It is assumed the initial distribution of $X^{(n)}(t)$ is $u^{\otimes n}$.

Noting

$$(3.4)\qquad Q^{(n)}\phi(\mathbf{x})=\sum_{i=1}^n u_i^{(n)}(\mathbf{x})\{\phi(x_1,\dots,-x_i,\dots,x_n)-\phi(\mathbf{x})\}\qquad(\mathbf{x}=(x_1,\dots,x_n))$$

with $u_i^{(n)}(\mathbf{x})=\frac{1}{n}\sum_{\substack{j=1\\ j\neq i}}^n i_{\{-1\}}(x_j)$, we see that this model is essentially contained in the framework of the preceding section although the condition (2.4) fails. If we set for each $w\in W_T$

$$N_t(w)=\sum_{s\leqq t} I(w(s)\neq w(s-))$$

$$\tilde{N}_t(w)=N_t(w)-\int_0^t u(s,-1)\,ds$$

$\tilde{N}_t(w)$ and $\tilde{N}_t(w)^2-\int_0^t u(s,-1)\,ds$ are μ-martingales as in Lemma 2.4. We note that Lemma 2.5 should be modified in the following way:

Lemma 2.5′. *Let any* $T>0$ *be fixed, and let* P^n *be the probability measure on* $W_T^n=W_T\times\dots\times W_T$ *induced by* $\{X^{(n)}(t)\}_{0\leqq t\leqq T}$. *Then* P^n *is absolutely continuous with respect to* $\mu^{\otimes n}$, *and*

$$(3.5)\qquad \frac{dP^n}{d\mu^{\otimes n}}(\mathbf{w})=\exp H_T^n(\mathbf{w})$$

where

$$H_T^n(\mathbf{w})=\sum_{i=1}^{n}\int_0^T \log\frac{u_i^{(n)}(\mathbf{w}(s-))}{u(s,-1)}\,dN_s(w_i) - \sum_{i=1}^{n}\int_0^T (u_i^{(n)}(\mathbf{w}(s))-u(s,-1))\,ds.$$

We notice that $-\infty \leqq H_T^n(\mathbf{w}) < +\infty$.

For $(w,w')\in W_T\times W_T$ we set

$$a(w,w')=\int_0^T I_{\{-1\}}(w(s-))\,d\tilde{N}_s(w'), \tag{3.6}$$

and

$$f(w,w')=a(w,w')+a(w',w)-\int_W a(w,w'')\,a(w' w'')\,\mu(dw''). \tag{3.7}$$

Then we have

Lemma 2.6′

$$\lim_{n\to\infty}\exp H_T^n(\mathbf{w})=\exp\{\tfrac{1}{2}I_2(f)-\tfrac{1}{2}\operatorname{Trace}AA^*\} \tag{3.8}$$

in the sense of convergence of probability distributions where $I_2(f)$ is a multiple Wiener integral associated with (W_T,μ).

Outline of the proof of the lemma. Let

$$\overline{W}_n=\left\{\mathbf{w}=(w_1,\dots,w_n);\ \sup_{0\leqq t\leqq T}\left|\frac{u^{(n)}(\mathbf{w}(t))}{u(s,-1)}-1\right|<\frac{1}{2}\right\}.$$

Then we claim

$$\lim_{n\to\infty}\mu^{\otimes n}(\overline{W}_n)=1. \tag{3.9}$$

Note

$$\sum_{i=1}^{n}\left\{\phi(w_i(t))-\langle u(t),\phi\rangle-\int_0^t u(s,-1)(\phi(w_i(s))-\langle u(s),\phi\rangle)\,ds\right\}$$

is a $\mu^{\otimes n}$-martingale for any $\phi\in\mathbb{B}(\{\pm 1\})$. Making use of the law of large numbers and a maximal inequality for martingales, it is easy to check

$$\sup_{0\leqq t\leqq T}\left|\frac{1}{n}\sum_{i=1}^{n}\phi(w_i(t))-\langle u(t),\phi\rangle\right|$$

vanishes as $n\to\infty$ in probability w.r.t. $\mu^{\otimes n}$, and (3.9) follows immediately from this. Accordingly we obtain Lemma 2.6′ combining the proof of Lemma 2.6 with (3.9).

Thus we see that Theorem 2.1 and Theorem 2.2 are valid in the case of McKean's 2-velocity model of Maxwellian gases since the remaining parts of the proof are quite same as the preceding section.

§ 4. The Case of Diffusion Processes

Let $b(x, y)$ be an $\boldsymbol{R}^d$-valued bounded measurable function on $\boldsymbol{R}^d \times \boldsymbol{R}^d$. For each $v \in \mathscr{P}(\boldsymbol{R}^d)$ set

$$Q_v \phi(x) = \frac{1}{2} \sum_{i=1}^{d} \frac{\partial^2}{\partial x_i^2} \phi(x) + \sum_{i=1}^{d} b_i[x, v] \frac{\partial}{\partial x_i} \phi(x) \tag{4.1}$$

where $b_i[x, v] = \int b_i(x, y)\, v(dy)\, (i = 1, \ldots, d)$.

Let any $T > 0$ be fixed. Denote by W_T the set of all $\boldsymbol{R}^d$-valued continuous functions defined on $[0, T]$, equipped with the usual σ-fields $\mathscr{F}_t$.

Let any $u \in \mathscr{P}(\boldsymbol{R}^d)$ be given. Then we have

Lemma 2.3″. *There exists a McKean measure μ on W_T corresponding to $\{Q_v; v \in \mathscr{P}(\boldsymbol{R}^d)\}$ with $\mathscr{L}(w(0); \mu) = u$. Namely μ is a solution of the following martingale problem:*

$$\phi(w(t)) - \int_0^t Q_{u(s)} \phi(w(s))\, ds \tag{4.2}$$

is a μ-martingale for any bounded C^2-function ϕ, and

$$\mathscr{L}(w(t); \mu) = u(t) \quad (0 \leqq t \leqq T) \quad \textit{and} \quad u(0) = u. \tag{4.3}$$

We omit the proof since it can be shown easily along the same line as in Krylov [5] concerning the existence theorem of SDE. But we think it is not easy to prove the uniqueness of the above martingale problem by some direct methods. However, the method of Sznitman [13] for proving the central limit theorem works even if we do not know the uniqueness in advance and we can easily obtain the uniqueness as a consequence of the central limit theorem.

Now we take a solution μ of the above martingale problem. Then

$$B(t, w) = w(t) - w(0) - \int_0^t b[w(s), u(s)]\, ds, \tag{4.4}$$

is a d-dimensional Brownian motion with respect to μ. The corresponding n-particle system $X^{(n)}(t) = (X_1^n(t), \ldots, X_n^n(t))$ is an $(\boldsymbol{R}^d)^n$-valued diffusion process having the initial distribution $u^{\otimes n}$ with generator

$$\begin{aligned} Q^{(n)} \phi(x_1, \ldots, x_n) = \tfrac{1}{2} \sum_{i=1}^{n} \Delta_{x_i} \phi(x_1, \ldots, x_n) \\ + \frac{1}{n} \sum_{i=1}^{n} \sum_{j=1}^{n} b(x_i, x_j) \cdot \nabla_{x_i} \phi(x_1, \ldots, x_n) \end{aligned} \tag{4.5}$$

where Δ_{x_i} and ∇_{x_i} act on the i-th variable of $\phi(x_1, \ldots, x_n)$. Let P_n be the probability measure on $W_T^n = W_T \times \ldots \times W_T$ induced by $\{X^{(n)}(t)\}_{0 \leqq t \leqq T}$.

Lemma 2.5″. *P^n and $\mu^{\otimes n}$ are mutually absolutely continuous, and*

$$\frac{dP^n}{d\mu^{\otimes n}}(\mathbf{w}) = \exp H_T^n(\mathbf{w}) \tag{4.6}$$

where

$$H_T^n(\mathbf{w}) = \sum_{i=1}^{n} \int_0^T \left(\frac{1}{n}\sum_{j=1}^{n} b(w_i(s), w_j(s)) - b[w_i(s), u(s)]\right) dB(s, w_i)$$
$$-\frac{1}{2}\sum_{i=1}^{n}\int_0^T \left\|\frac{1}{n}\sum_{j=1}^{n} b(w_i(s), w_j(s)) - b[w_i(s), u(s)]\right\|^2 ds.$$

For $(w, w') \in W_T \times W_T$ let

(4.7) $$a(w, w') = \int_0^T (b(w'(s), w(s)) - b[w'(s), u(s)])\, dB(s, w')$$

and

(4.8) $$f(w, w') = a(w, w') + a(w', w) - \int_{W_T} a(w, w'')\, a(w', w'')\, \mu(dw'').$$

Then we see that Theorem 2.1 also holds in the present case. In particular, for any bounded measurable function Φ on W_T

$$\lim_{n\to\infty} E^{P^n}[\exp\{\sqrt{-1}\langle U_n, \Phi\rangle\}] = \lim_{n\to\infty} E^{\mu^{\otimes n}}\left[\exp\left\{\frac{\sqrt{-1}}{n}\sum_{i=1}^{n}\Phi(w_i) + H_T^n(\mathbf{w})\right\}\right]$$
$$= \exp\{\sqrt{-1}\langle \mu, \Phi\rangle\},$$

and hence $\left\langle P^n, \frac{1}{n}\sum_{i=1}^{n}\Phi(w_i)\right\rangle \to \langle \mu, \Phi\rangle$ as $n\to\infty$. Since P^n is unique, this implies that $\langle \Phi, \mu\rangle$ is uniquely determined by the initial distribution u. Thus μ is the *unique* solution of the martingale problem (4.2) and (4.3).

Furthermore, by the same reason, for any $\zeta \in W_T$ and $\varepsilon > 0$ there exists a unique probability measure μ_ε^ζ on W_T such that

(4.9) $$\phi(w(t)) - \int_0^t Q_{(u_\varepsilon^\zeta(s) + \delta_{\zeta(s)})}\phi(w(s))\, ds \quad \textit{is a } \mu_\varepsilon^\zeta\text{-martingale}$$

and

(4.10) $$\mathscr{L}(w(t); \mu_\varepsilon^\zeta) = u_\varepsilon^\zeta(t) \quad \text{and} \quad u_\varepsilon^\zeta(0) = u.$$

Noting that μ_ε^ζ and μ are mutually absolutely continuous Π_ε of (2.20) is well-defined, and by a similar argument to § 2 we see that Theorem 2.2 is also valid for the diffusion case.

References

1. Dawson, D.A.: Critical dynamics and fluctuations for a mean-field model of cooperative behavior. J. Statist. Phys. **31**, 29–85 (1983)
2. Dellacherie, C., Meyer, P.A.: Probabilities et potentiel, Chapitres V a VIII. Herman: Paris 1980
3. Dynkin, E.B., Mandelbaum, A.: Symmetric statistics, Poisson point processes and multiple Wiener integrals. Ann. Statist. **11**, 739–745 (1983)
4. Ikeda, N., Watanabe, S.: Stochastic differential equations and diffusion processes. Amsterdam: North-Holland/Kodansha 1981

5. Krylov, N.V.: On Ito's stochastic differential equations. Theory Probab. Appl. **14**, 330–336 (1969)
6. Kunita, H., Watanabe, S.: On square integrable martingales. Nagoya Math. J. **30**, 209–245 (1967)
7. Kusuoka, S., Tamura, Y.: Gibbs measures for mean field potentials. J. Fac. Sci. Univ. Tokyo **31**, 223–245 (1984)
8. Maruyama, G.: On the transition probability functions of the Markov processes. Nat. Sci. Rep. Ochanomizu Univ. **5**, 10–20 (1954)
9. McKean, H.P.: Propagation of chaos for a class of non-linear parabolic equations. Lecture Series in Differential Equations, 7 Catholic Univ. 41–57 (1967)
10. McKean, H.P.: Fluctuations in the kinetic theory of gases. Commun. Pure Appl. Math., **28**, 435–455 (1975)
11. Parthasarathy, K.R.: Probability measures on metric spaces. New York: Academic Press 1967
12. Simon, B.: Trace ideals and their applications. London Math. Soc. Lecture Note Series, **35**. Cambridge: Univ. Press 1979
13. Sznitman, A.S.: Nonlinear reflecting diffusion process, and the propagation of chaos and fluctuations associated. J. Funct. Anal. **56**, 311–336 (1984)
14. Sznitman, A.S.: A fluctuation result for non-linear diffusions. [Preprint]
15. Tanaka, H.: Limit theorems for certain diffusion processes with interaction. Proceeding of the Taniguchi International Symposium on Stochastic Analysis (K. Itô ed.), pp. 469–488. Tokyo: Kinokuniya 1984
16. Tanaka, H., Hitsuda, M.: Central limit theorem for a simple diffusion model of interacting particles. Hiroshima Math. J. **11**, 415–423 (1981)

Received October 16, 1984

Probab. Th. Rel. Fields 71, 69-83 (1986)

Probability Theory and Related Fields

Propagation of Chaos for Diffusing Particles of Two Types with Singular Mean Field Interaction

Massao Nagasawa and Hiroshi Tanaka

Institut für Angewandte Mathematik der Universität Zürich, Rämistrasse 74, CH-8001 Zürich, Switzerland

Department of Mathematics, Faculty of Science and Technology, Keio University, Yokohama, 223 Japan

Introduction

In a system of diffusion processes with a pair interaction $b(x, y)$ described by

$$X_i(t)=B_i(t)+\frac{1}{n}\sum_{j=1}^{n}\int_0^t ds\, b(X_i(s), X_j(s)), \qquad i=1,2,\ldots,n,$$

where $\{B_i(t): i=1,2,\ldots,n\}$ is a family of mutually independent Brownian motions, if the number n of particles tends to infinity, then the distribution of $(X_1, X_2, \ldots, X_m)$, for fixed $m \leqq n$, converges to that of a collection of independent copies of a (non-linear) diffusion process $X(\cdot)$ with the so called mean field drift

$$b[x, u(t)]=\int b(x, y)\, u(t, dy)$$

induced by the distribution $u(t,\cdot)$ of $X(t)$ itself. Limit theorems of this kind were called "propagation of chaos" by McKean [4]. One can regard it as a law of large numbers: $u_n=\frac{1}{n}\sum_{i=1}^{n}\delta_{X_i}\to u$. The propagation of chaos for a system of diffusion processes was proved by McKean [5] for Lipschitz continuous interaction $b(x, y)$. Besides this Tanaka [13] discussed an associated fluctuation problem (central limit theorem) modifying a method of Braun and Hepp [1] for Vlasov equation. The same problem has been treated also by Kusuoka and Tamura [2] as a limit theorem of Gibbs measures for mean field potentials, and by Sznitman [11] with the help of (Cameron-Martin) Maruyama formula [3], which enabled him to handle the case of bounded measurable interaction $b(x, y)$ (cf. also Shiga and Tanaka [10]).

The present paper is concerned with the propagation of chaos for a system $\{(X_i, Y_i): i=1,2,\ldots,n\}$ of particles of two types with a singular pair-interaction, which arises in a statistical model for segregation of interacting random motion (cf. Nagasawa [6, 7], Nagasawa-Yasue [8] and Nagasawa-Tanaka [9]). It can be described by a system of stochastic differential equations:

$$(1)\quad \begin{aligned} X_i(t) &= X_i(0)+B_i(t)+\int_0^t ds\left\{\frac{1}{n}\sum_{l=1}^{n} f(X_i(s)-Y_l(s))+v(X_i(s))\right\}+\Phi_i(t), \\ & i=1,2,\ldots,n, \\ Y_j(t) &= Y_j(0)+B'_j(t)+\int_0^t ds\left\{-\frac{1}{n}\sum_{l=1}^{n} f(X_l(s)-Y_j(s))+v(Y_j(s))\right\}-\Psi_j(t), \\ & j=1,2,\ldots,n, \end{aligned}$$

where $\{B_i(t), B'_j(t); i,j=1,2,\ldots,n\}$ is a family of mutually independent Brownian motions, $X_i(0)$ (resp. $-Y_j(0)$) has a common distribution $\nu^{(+)}$ (resp. $\nu^{(-)}$) whose support is in $[0,\infty)$, $f(x)$ is a non-increasing continuous function on $(0,\infty)$ which may diverge at the origin, an example of which is

$$f(x)=\frac{\alpha}{x^4}, \qquad \alpha>0,$$

$v(x)$ is an odd function which is continuous and nonincreasing in $\mathbb{R}-\{0\}$, and $\Phi_i(t)$ (resp. $\Psi_j(t)$) is a non-decreasing continuous function which makes the origin a reflecting boundary for $X_i(t)$ (resp. $Y_j(t)$). That is, $X_i(t)$ (resp. $Y_j(t)$) is a reflecting diffusion process on $[0,\infty)$ (resp. $(-\infty,0]$) repelled by $Y_l(t)$ with the interaction $\frac{1}{n}f(X_i-Y_l)$ $\left(\text{resp. } -\frac{1}{n}f(X_l-Y_j)\right)$ under the influence of an environment potential $v(X_i)$ (resp. $v(Y_j)$).

The propagation of chaos implies that (X_i, Y_j) converges in law, as $n\to\infty$, to (X, Y) which is a solution of a system of (non-linear) stochastic differential equations

$$(2)\quad \begin{aligned} X(t) &= X(0)+B(t)+\int_0^t ds\{\int_{(-\infty,0]} f(X(s)-y)\,u_Y(s,dy)+v(X(s))\}+\Phi(t), \\ Y(t) &= Y(0)+B'(t)+\int_0^t ds\{-\int_{[0,\infty)} f(x-Y(s))\,u_X(s,dx)+v(Y(s))\}-\Psi(t), \end{aligned}$$

where $u_X(s,\cdot)$ and $u_Y(s,\cdot)$ stand for the distributions of $X(s)$ and $Y(s)$, respectively, $B(t)$ and $B'(t)$ are Brownian motions, and $X(0)$ and $Y(0)$ are distributed by $\nu^{(+)}$ and $\nu^{(-)}$, respectively.

Because of singularity of $f(x)$ (and possibly of $v(x)$) at the origin, it seems that the methods of [2, 5, 11] and [13] can not be immediately applied to the present case. However, thanks to the monotonicity of $f(x)$ and $v(x)$, one can find a rather direct way of proving the propagation of chaos based on the construction of unique solutions of Eqs. (1) and (2) by iteration (Theorem 1 in §1). In Sect. 2, preparing several lemmas, we will prove a limit theorem (Theorem 2). The propagation of chaos, which is a direct corollary of the limit theorem, will be discussed in Sect. 3.

In the original model (cf. [8, 9]) the interaction $f(x)$ (e.g. $f(x)=1/x^4$) diverges at the origin so rapidly that the Y-particles lie always left to the X-particles even without the additional terms Φ_i and $-\Psi_j$, or in other words Y-

particles are separated from the X-particles by a moving boundary. The terms Φ_i and $-\Psi_j$ are added in (1) artificially in order to avoid mathematical difficulties of handling the moving boundary. The propagation of chaos for the unmodified model (i.e. without Φ_i and $-\Psi_j$) is an open problem.

1. Existence and Uniqueness of Solutions

In this section we will prove the existence and uniqueness of solutions of a system of equations

$$(3)\quad \begin{aligned} \xi(t,w) &= w(t)+\int_0^t ds \int_W b(\xi(s,w),\eta(s,\tilde{z}))\,\mu^{(-)}(d\tilde{z})+\phi(t,w),\\ \eta(t,z) &= z(t)+\int_0^t ds \int_W b\eta(s,z),\xi(s,\tilde{w}))\,\mu^{(+)}(d\tilde{w})+\psi(t,z), \end{aligned}$$

where $b(x,y)$ is the sum

$$(4)\qquad b(x,y)=f(x+y)+v(x),$$

of f and v with the properties

(5) $f(x)$ is a non-increasing continuous function on $(0,\infty)$ which may diverge at the origin, and $v(x)$ is an odd function which is nonincreasing and continuous in $\mathbb{R}-\{0\}$.

As will be seen in §3, solutions of the system of Eqs. (3) will provide those for the Eqs. (1) and (2) at the same time.

In Eq. (3), w and z are elements of $W=C([0,\infty)\to\mathbb{R}\cap\{w: w(0)\geqq 0\}$, $\mu^{(+)}$ and $\mu^{(-)}$ are probability measures on W, ξ and η are elements of $W^+ = C([0,\infty)\to\mathbb{R}^+)$, $\phi\in\Phi_\xi = C([0,\infty)\to\mathbb{R}^+)\cap\{\phi$: nondecreasing, $\phi(0)=0$ and constant on each connected component of $\{t>0;\ \xi(t)>0\}\}$, and $\psi\in\Phi_\eta$ (cf. [9]).

A dominating process $\zeta(t,w)$ is defined to be the solution of a Skorokhod equation on $[1,\infty)$:

$$(6)\qquad \zeta(t,w)=w(0)\vee 1+(w(t)-w(0))+ct+\phi(t,w),$$

where $c\geqq f(1)+v(1)$. The solution (ζ,ϕ) can be given explicitly (cf. §1 of [9]). Because $c\geqq f(x+y)+v(x)$ for $x\geqq 1$ and $y\geqq 0$, Lemma 5 of [9] implies that for any (ξ,η) satisfying (3)

$$(8)\qquad 0\leqq\xi(t,w)\leqq\zeta(t,w),\qquad 0\leqq\eta(t,z)\leqq\zeta(t,z).$$

We impose, in addition, integrability conditions on $\mu^{(+)}$, $\mu^{(-)}$, f and v:

$$(9)\qquad \int_W |w(t)|\,\mu(dw)<\infty,\qquad \mu=\mu^{(+)},\mu^{(-)};$$

$$(10)\qquad \int_W\int_W f^-(\zeta(s,w)+\zeta(s,z))\,\mu^{(+)}(dw)\,\mu^{(-)}(dz),$$

and

$$\int_W v^-(\zeta(s,w))\,\mu(dw), \qquad \mu=\mu^{(+)},\mu^{(-)}, \tag{11}$$

are bounded on each finite time interval, where $f^-=(-f)\vee 0$ and $v^-=(-v)\vee 0$.

Theorem 1.[1] *Under the conditions* (5), (9), (10) *and* (11) *on* f, v, $\mu^{(+)}$ *and* $\mu^{(-)}$, *there exists a unique solution* $\{(\xi(t,w),\phi(t,w)),(\eta(t,z),\psi(t,z))\}$ *of the system of Eq.* (3), *where* $\xi\in W^+$, $\phi\in\Phi_\xi$, $\eta\in W^+$ *and* $\psi\in\Phi_\eta$.

Proof. Denoting $b^-=(-b)\vee 0$ and

$$\begin{aligned} a^{(+)}(s,x)&=-\int_W b^-(x,\zeta(s,\tilde z))\,\mu^{(-)}(d\tilde z),\\ a^{(-)}(s,x)&=-\int_W b^-(x,\zeta(s,\tilde w))\,\mu^{(+)}(d\tilde w), \end{aligned} \tag{12}$$

we define $(\xi^{(k)}(t,w),\eta^{(k)}(t,z))$, $k\geqq 0$, to be the solutions of Skorokhod equations on $[0,\infty)$

$$\begin{aligned} \xi^{(0)}(t,w)&=w(t)+\int_0^t ds\,a^{(+)}(s,\xi^{(0)}(s,w))+\phi^{(0)}(t,w),\\ \eta^{(0)}(t,z)&=z(t)+\int_0^t ds\,a^{(-)}(s,\eta^{(0)}(s,z))+\psi^{(0)}(t,z), \end{aligned} \tag{13}$$

$$\begin{aligned} \xi^{(k)}(t,w)&=w(t)+\int_0^t ds\int_W b(\xi^{(k)}(s,w),\eta^{(k-1)}(s,\tilde z))\,\mu^{(-)}(d\tilde z)\\ &\quad+\phi^{(k)}(t,w),\\ \eta^{(k)}(t,z)&=z(t)+\int_0^t ds\int_W b(\eta^{(k)}(s,z),\xi^{(k-1)}(s,\tilde w))\,\mu^{(+)}(d\tilde w)\\ &\quad+\psi^{(k)}(t,z). \end{aligned} \tag{14}$$

Theorem 1 of [9] implies the existence of unique solutions $(\xi^{(k)},\phi^{(k)})$ and $(\eta^{(k)},\psi^{(k)})$ which satisfy

$$0\leqq\xi^{(0)}(t,w)\leqq\xi^{(k)}(t,w)\leqq\zeta(t,w), \qquad \text{for all } k\geqq 0, \tag{15}$$

$$\begin{aligned} &0\leqq\xi^{(0)}\leqq\xi^{(2)}\leqq\xi^{(4)}\leqq\ldots\leqq\xi^{(5)}\leqq\xi^{(3)}\leqq\xi^{(1)}\leqq\zeta,\\ &\phi^{(1)}\leqq\phi^{(3)}\leqq\phi^{(5)}\leqq\ldots\leqq\phi^{(4)}\leqq\phi^{(2)}\leqq\phi^{(0)}, \end{aligned} \tag{16}$$

and the same inequalities for $(\eta^{(k)},\psi^{(k)})$. Therefore there exist monotone limits

$$\begin{aligned} \underline{\xi}(t,w)&=\lim_{k\to\infty}\xi^{(2k)}(t,w), & \underline{\phi}(t,w)&=\lim_{k\to\infty}\phi^{(2k)}(t,w),\\ \bar\xi(t,w)&=\lim_{k\to\infty}\xi^{(2k+1)}(t,w), & \bar\phi(t,w)&=\lim_{k\to\infty}\phi^{(2k+1)}(t,w), \end{aligned}$$

[1] This is a reformulation of Theorem 2 of [9]

and correspondingly $\underline{\eta}$, $\underline{\psi}$, $\bar{\eta}$ and $\bar{\psi}$. They satisfy

(17)
$$\underline{\xi}(t,w) \leqq \bar{\xi}(t,w), \qquad \phi(t,w) \geqq \bar{\phi}(t,w),$$
$$\underline{\eta}(t,z) \leqq \bar{\eta}(t,z), \qquad \underline{\psi}(t,z) \geqq \bar{\psi}(t,z),$$

(18)
$$0 \leqq \mu^{(+)}[\underline{\xi}(t,\cdot)] \leqq \mu^{(+)}[\bar{\xi}(t,\cdot)] \leqq \mu^{(+)}[\zeta(t,\cdot)] < \infty,$$
$$0 \leqq \mu^{(-)}[\underline{\eta}(t,\cdot)] \leqq \mu^{(-)}[\bar{\eta}(t,\cdot)] \leqq \mu^{(-)}[\zeta(t,\cdot)] < \infty,$$

(19)
$$\underline{\xi}(t,w) = w(t) + \int_0^t ds \int_W b(\bar{\xi}(s,w), \underline{\eta}(s,\tilde{z}))\, \mu^{(-)}(d\tilde{z}) + \bar{\phi}(t,w),$$
$$\bar{\xi}(t,w) = w(t) + \int_0^t ds \int_W b(\underline{\xi}(s,w), \bar{\eta}(s,\tilde{z}))\, \mu^{(-)}(d\tilde{z}) + \underline{\phi}(t,w),$$

(20)
$$\bar{\eta}(t,z) = z(t) + \int_0^t ds \int_W b(\bar{\eta}(s,z), \underline{\xi}(s,\tilde{w}))\, \mu^{(+)}(d\tilde{w}) + \bar{\psi}(t,z),$$
$$\underline{\eta}(t,z) = z(t) + \int_0^t ds \int_W b(\underline{\eta}(s,z), \bar{\xi}(s,\tilde{w}))\, \mu^{(+)}(d\tilde{w}) + \underline{\psi}(t,z).$$

To get (19) and (20) from (14) notice, for example, $b(\xi^{(2k+1)}, \underline{\eta}) \leqq b(\xi^{(2k+1)}, \eta^{(2k)}) \leqq b(\bar{\xi}, \eta^{(2k)})$, where the first term (resp. the third) is monotone nondecreasing (resp. nonincreasing).

Then, Lemma 1 below completes the proof of the existence of solutions.

Lemma 1. *If* (17–19) *and* (20) *are fulfilled, then* $\bar{\xi} = \underline{\xi}$, $\bar{\phi} = \underline{\phi}$, $\bar{\eta} = \underline{\eta}$ *and* $\bar{\psi} = \underline{\psi}$.

Proof. Because of the assumptions (5), (10) and (11) it holds that

$$\int_0^t ds \int_W \int_W f^-(\bar{\xi}(s,w) + \underline{\eta}(s,z))\, \mu^{(-)}(dz)\, \mu^{(+)}(dw)$$
$$\leqq \int_0^t ds \int_W \int_W f^-(\zeta(s,w) + \zeta(s,z))\, \mu^{(-)}(dz)\, \mu^{(+)}(dw) < \infty,$$
$$\int_0^t ds \int_W v^-(\bar{\xi}(s,w))\, \mu^{(+)}(dw) \leqq \int_0^t ds \int_W v^-(\zeta(s,w))\, \mu^{(+)}(dw) < \infty$$

and corresponding inequalities for $\bar{\eta}$. Therefore, each term of the right hand side of (19) (resp. (20)) is $\mu^{(+)}$ (resp. $\mu^{(-)}$) integrable because (9) is assumed, and

$$0 \leqq \mu^{(+)}[\bar{\xi}(t,\cdot) - \underline{\xi}(t,\cdot)] + \mu^{(-)}[\bar{\eta}(t,\cdot) - \underline{\eta}(t,\cdot)]$$
$$\leqq \int_0^t ds \int_W \{v(\bar{\xi}(s,w)) - v(\underline{\xi}(s,w))\}\, \mu^{(+)}(dw) + \mu^{(+)}[\bar{\phi}(t,\cdot) - \underline{\phi}(t,\cdot)]$$
$$+ \int_0^t ds \int_W \{v(\bar{\eta}(s,z)) - v(\underline{\eta}(s,z))\}\, \mu^{(-)}(dz) + \mu^{(-)}[\bar{\psi}(t,\cdot) - \underline{\psi}(t,\cdot)],$$
$$\leqq \mu^{(+)}[\bar{\phi}(t,\cdot) - \underline{\phi}(t,\cdot)] + \mu^{(-)}[\bar{\psi}(t,\cdot) - \underline{\psi}(t,\cdot)] < \infty.$$

The inequality above combined with $\bar{\phi}-\underline{\phi}\leqq 0$ and $\bar{\psi}-\underline{\psi}\leqq 0$ implies that $\bar{\phi}(t,w)=\underline{\phi}(t,w)$ for $\mu^{(+)}$-a.e. $w\in W$ (resp. $\bar{\psi}(t,z)=\underline{\psi}(t,z)$ for $\mu^{(-)}$-a.e. $z\in W$) and hence $\bar{\xi}(t,w)=\underline{\xi}(t,w)$ for $\mu^{(+)}$-a.e. $w\in W$ (resp. $\bar{\eta}(t,z)=\underline{\eta}(t,z)$ for $\mu^{(-)}$-a.e. $z\in W$). To show the equalities for all $w, z\in W$, denoting

$$c(s,x)=\int_W b(x,\bar{\eta}(s,z))\,\mu^{(-)}(dz)$$

we consider a Skorokhod equation on $[0,\infty)$

$$\xi(t)=w(t)+\int_0^t ds\,c(s,\xi(s))+\phi(t).$$

Since the solution of the equation is unique by Theorem 1 of [9], $\xi(t,w)=\underline{\xi}(t,w)=\bar{\xi}(t,w)$ and $\phi(t,w)=\underline{\phi}(t,w)=\bar{\phi}(t,w)$ for all $w\in W$. The same argument applies to showing $\eta(t,z)=\underline{\eta}(t,z)=\bar{\eta}(t,z)$ for all $z\in W$. This completes the proof of Lemma 1.

To prove the uniqueness let $(\xi_1,\phi_1,\eta_1,\psi_1)$ and $(\xi_2,\phi_2,\eta_2,\psi_2)$ be solutions of Eq. (3) and define sequences $\{\xi^{(k)}\}$ and $\{\eta^{(k)}\}$ by

$$\xi^{(0)}=\xi_1\wedge\xi_2 \qquad \eta^{(0)}=\eta_1\wedge\eta_2,$$

and

$$\xi^{(k)}(t,w)=w(t)+\int_0^t ds\int_W b(\xi^{(k)}(s,w),\eta^{(k-1)}(s,\tilde{z}))\,\mu^{(-)}(d\tilde{z})$$
$$+\phi^{(k)}(t,w),$$

$$\eta^{(k)}(t,z)=z(t)+\int_0^t ds\int_W b(\eta^{(k)}(s,z),\xi^{(k-1)}(s,\tilde{w}))\,\mu^{(+)}(d\tilde{w})$$
$$+\psi^{(k)}(t,z),$$

for $k\geqq 1$. Then it is easy to see that

$$\xi^{(2k)}\leqq\xi_1,\xi_2\leqq\xi^{(2k+1)}, \qquad \text{for } k\geqq 0,$$
$$\xi^{(0)}\geqq\xi^{(2)}\geqq\xi^{(4)}\geqq\ldots, \qquad \phi^{(2)}\leqq\phi^{(4)}\leqq\phi^{(6)}\leqq\ldots,$$
$$\xi^{(1)}\leqq\xi^{(3)}\leqq\xi^{(5)}\leqq\ldots, \qquad \phi^{(1)}\geqq\phi^{(3)}\geqq\phi^{(5)}\geqq\ldots,$$

and the same inequalities for $(\eta^{(k)},\psi^{(k)})$, which imply the existence of monotone limits

$$\bar{\xi}(t,w)=\lim_{k\to\infty}\xi^{(2k+1)}(t,w), \qquad \bar{\phi}(t,w)=\lim_{k\to\infty}\phi^{(2k+1)}(t,w),$$
$$\underline{\xi}(t,w)=\lim_{k\to\infty}\xi^{(2k)}(t,w), \qquad \underline{\phi}(t,w)=\lim_{k\to\infty}\phi^{(2k)}(t,w),$$

and correspondingly $(\bar{\eta},\bar{\psi},\underline{\eta},\underline{\psi})$. It is clear that they satisfy (17–19) and (20). Therefore, Lemma 1 implies $\bar{\xi}=\underline{\xi}$, $\bar{\phi}=\underline{\phi}$, $\bar{\eta}=\underline{\eta}$, $\bar{\psi}=\underline{\psi}$, and hence $\xi_1=\xi_2$, $\phi_1=\phi_2$, $\eta_1=\eta_2$ and $\psi_1=\psi_2$, completing the proof of Theorem 1.

2. A Limit Theorem

Given a function $b(t,x)$ defined on $[0,\infty)\times(0,\infty)$ with the property

(21) $b(t,x)$ is continuous in $(t,x)\in[0,\infty)\times(0,\infty)$ and nonincreasing in x for each $t\geqq 0$,

we consider a Skorokhod equation on $[0,\infty)$

$$\xi(t,w)=w(t)+\int_0^t ds\, b(s,\xi(s,w))+\phi(t,w). \tag{22}$$

Theorem 1 of [9] guarantees the existence of a unique solution $(\xi(t,w),\phi(t,w))$ for $w\in W$, where $\xi\in W^+$ and $\phi\in\Phi_\xi$. We will denote it as $(\xi(t),\phi(t))$ without w, if there will be no confusion.

Lemma 2. *Let $b(t,x)$ satisfy the condition* (21) *and let (ξ^a,ϕ^a), $a>0$, be the solution of a Skorokhod equation on $[a,\infty)$:*

$$\xi^a(t)=a+w(t)+\int_0^t ds\, b(s,\xi^a(s))+\phi^a(t). \tag{23}$$

Then

$$\xi^a(t)\searrow\xi(t), \quad \text{as} \quad a\searrow 0.$$

Proof. See Lemma 5 and what follows in Sect. 3 of [9].

Lemma 3. *Under the assumption* (21) *define for $a>0$*

$$b_a(t,x)=b(t,x\vee a), \qquad \text{for } (t,x)\in[0,\infty)\times(0,\infty). \tag{24}$$

Let (ξ_a,ϕ_a) be the solution of (22) *with $b_a(t,x)$ in place of $b(t,x)$. Then*

$$\xi_\alpha(t)\nearrow\xi(t), \quad \text{as} \quad a\searrow 0.$$

Proof. Theorem 1 of [9] implies that $\xi_a(t)\nearrow$ and $\phi_a(t)\searrow$, as $a\searrow 0$. Therefore

$$\int_0^t ds\, b_a(s,\xi_a(s))=\xi_a(t)-w(t)-\phi_a(t)\nearrow, \quad \text{as} \quad a\searrow 0,$$

and hence the limit

$$\lim_{a\searrow 0}\int_0^t ds\, b_a(s,\xi_a(s))$$

exists. Denote

$$\tilde{\xi}(t)=\lim_{a\searrow 0}\xi_a(t).$$

Since $b_a(s,\xi_a(s))\,1_{(\varepsilon,\infty)}(\xi_a(s))$ decreases to $b(s,\tilde{\xi}(s))\,1_{(\varepsilon,\infty)}(\tilde{\xi}(s))$, as $a\searrow 0$, for $\varepsilon>0$, we have

$$\lim_{a\searrow 0}\int_0^t ds\, b_a(s, \xi_a(s))$$
$$=\int_0^t ds\, b(s, \tilde{\xi}(s))\, 1_{(\varepsilon,\infty)}(\tilde{\xi}(s)) + \lim_{a\searrow 0}\int_0^t ds\, b_a(s, \xi_a(s))\, 1_{[0,\varepsilon]}(\xi_a(s))$$
$$=\int_0^t ds\, b(s, \tilde{\xi}(s))\, 1_{(0,\infty)}(\tilde{\xi}(s)) + \lim_{\varepsilon\searrow 0}\lim_{a\searrow 0}\int_0^t ds\, b_a(s, \xi_a(s))\, 1_{[0,\varepsilon]}(\xi_a(s)).$$

Therefore $\tilde{\xi}(t)$ satisfies

$$\tilde{\xi}(t) = w(t) - ct + \int_0^t ds\{b(s, \tilde{\xi}(s)) + c\} + \tilde{\phi}(t), \tag{25}$$

where a constant c is chosen to be $b(t,1)+c>0$, for $\forall t\in[0,T]$, and $\tilde{\phi}$ is defined by

$$\tilde{\phi}(t) = \lim_{\varepsilon\searrow 0}\lim_{a\searrow 0}\int_0^t ds\{b_a(s, \xi_a(s)) + c\}\, 1_{[0,\varepsilon]}(\xi_a(s)) + \lim_{a\searrow 0}\phi_a(t).$$

It is easy to see that $\tilde{\xi}(t)$ is continuous in t (cf. §3 of [9]), and hence $\tilde{\phi}(t)$ is also continuous in t by (25). Moreover, $\tilde{\phi}(t)$ is monotone nondecreasing and stays constant on each connected open interval in which $\tilde{\xi}(t)>0$. Because of the uniqueness of solutions for a Skorokhod equation (22) which is the same as (25), the $(\tilde{\xi}, \tilde{\phi})$ must coincide with (ξ, ϕ), completing the proof.

We consider W and W^+ as metric spaces with the metric of the uniform convergence on each finite time interval.

Lemma 4. *Let $b(t,x)$ be bounded and Lipschitz continuous: $|b(t,x) - b(t,y)| \leqq c(T)\cdot|x-y|$, for $\forall t\in[0,T]$, and $\forall x, y\in[0,\infty)$. Then the solution $\xi(t,w)$ of Eq.* (22) *is continuous in $(t,w)\in[0,T]\times W$.*

Proof. The lemma is an easy consequence of Lemma 2 of [9]. In fact, as is shown there, the solution $\xi(t,w)$ is given as the limit of $\{\xi^{(k)}(t,w)\}$ defined by

$$\begin{aligned}\xi^{(0)}(t,w) &= w(t) + \phi^{(0)}(t,w),\\ \xi^{(k)}(t,w) &= w(t) + \int_0^t ds\, b(s, \xi^{(k-1)}(s,w)) + \phi^{(k)}(t,w),\end{aligned} \tag{26}$$

and the convergence is uniform in $(t,w)\in[0,T]\times W$. Since it is easy to see by induction that $\xi^{(k)}(t,w)$ is continuous in $(t,w)\in[0,T]\times W$, so is $\xi(t,w)$, completing the proof.

Lemma 5. *Under the condition* (21) *on $b(t,x)$, the solution $\xi(t,w)$ of Eq.* (22) *is continuous in $(t,w)\in[0,T]\times W$, for any $\forall T>0$.*

Proof. Let K be an arbitrary compact subset of W and denote $M = \sup_{w\in K}\sup_{t\in[0,T]}\xi(t,w) < \infty$, where ζ is a dominating process which is the solution of a Skorokhod equation on $[1,\infty)$

$$\zeta(t,w) = w(0)\vee 1 + (w(t) - w(0)) + ct + \psi(t,w)$$

with $c \geqq \sup_{t\in[0,T]} b(t,1)$. It is to be noted that $b_a(t,x)$ (resp. $b(t,x)$) can be approximated from below (resp. from above) on $[0, M+1]$ (resp. $[a, M+1]$) by Lipschitz continuous ones. Therefore, $\xi_a(t,w)$ (resp. $\xi^a(t,w)$) is the increasing (resp. decreasing) limit of continuous functions on $[0,T]\times K$, and hence lower (resp. upper) semi-continuous in $(t,w)\in[0,T]\times K$. Now, let $a\searrow 0$. Then $\xi_a(t,w)$ (resp. $\xi^a(t,w)$) increases (resp. decreases) to $\xi(t,w)$ by Lemma 2 and 3. Therefore $\xi(t,w)$ is lower and upper semi-continuous, and hence continuous in $(t,w)\in[0,T]\times K$. This completes the proof of Lemma 5.

Lemma 6. *Let $b(t,x)$ and $b_n(t,x)$, $n=1,2,3,\ldots$, satisfy the condition* (21), *and for $\forall a>0$ and $\forall T>0$*

$$(27)\qquad \lim_{n\to\infty} b_n(t,x)=b(t,x),\ \textit{uniformly in}\ (t,x)\in[0,T]\times\left[a,\frac{1}{a}\right],\qquad \sup_{n\geqq 1}\max_{t\in[0,T]} b_n(t,a)<\infty.$$

Let $\xi_n(t,w)$ denote the solution of Eq. (22) *with $b_n(t,x)$ in place of $b(t,x)$. Then for any compact subset K of W*

$$(28)\qquad \lim_{n\to\infty}\xi_n(t,w)=\xi(t,w),\quad \textit{uniformly in}\quad (t,w)\in[0,T]\times K.$$

Proof. We first prove the assertion assuming that $b(t,x)$ is bounded above and $b_n(t,x)$ converges uniformly on $[0,T]\times\left[0,\frac{1}{a}\right]$. With the help of Lemma 1 of [9] we have

$$|\xi_n(t)-\xi(t)|^2 \leqq 2\int_0^t ds(\xi_n(s)-\xi(s))\{b_n(s,\xi_n(s))-b_n(s,\xi(s))\}$$
$$+2\int_0^t ds(\xi_n(s)-\xi(s))\{b_n(s,\xi(s))-b(s,\xi(s))\},$$

where the first integral is nonpositive and the second is, by Schwartz inequality, dominated by

$$\int_0^t ds|\xi_n(s)-\xi(s)|^2+\int_0^t ds|b_n(s,\xi(s))-b(s,\xi(s))|^2.$$

Therefore, applying Gronwall's lemma, we have

$$(29)\qquad |\xi_n(t,w)-\xi(t,w)|^2 \leqq e^T\int_0^T ds|b_n(s,\xi(s,w))-b(s,\xi(s,w))|^2.$$

Since

$$\sup_{w\in K}\sup_{s\in[0,T]}\xi(s,w)\leqq \sup_{w\in K}\sup_{s\in[0,T]}\zeta(s,w)<\infty,$$

for any compact subset K of W, the integrand of the right hand side of (29) is bounded and converges to zero uniformly in $(s,w)\in[0,T]\times K$, as $n\to\infty$. Therefore (29) implies that $\xi_n(t,w)$ converges to $\xi(t,w)$ uniformly on $[0,\mathrm{T}]\times\mathrm{K}$.

We apply what we have proved above to $b_a(t,x)$ and $(b_n)_a(t,x)$ defined by (24) (resp. $b(t,x)$ and $b_n(t,x)$ for $x \geqq a$) and obtain, using the notations in Lemma 2 and 3,

$$(30) \qquad (\xi_n)_a(t,w) \to \xi_a(t,w), \quad (\xi_n)^a(t,w) \to \xi^a(t,w), \quad \text{as} \quad n\to\infty,$$

uniformly on $[0,T]\times K$. On the other hand $\xi_a(t,w) \nearrow \xi(t,w)$ and $\xi^a(t,w) \searrow \xi(t,w)$ as $a \searrow 0$ uniformy on $[0,T]\times K$ by Lemma 2 and Dini's theorem, and hence there exists $a>0$ such that

$$0 \leqq \xi^a(t,w) - \xi_a(t,w) < \varepsilon, \quad \text{uniformly in} \quad (t,w)\in[0,T]\times K.$$

Because of (30) it holds that for this $a>0$

$$|(\xi_n)_a(t,w) - \xi_a(t,w)| < \varepsilon, \qquad |(\xi_n)^a(t,w) - \xi^a(t,w)| < \varepsilon,$$

uniformly on $[0,T]\times K$, for sufficiently large n. Therefore we have

$$|\xi(t,w) - \xi_n(t,w)| \leqq 3\varepsilon, \quad \text{uniformly in} \quad (t,w)\in[0,T]\times K,$$

where made is use of the inequality $(\xi_n)_a \leqq \xi_n \leqq (\xi_n)^a$. This completes the proof of Lemma 6.

Theorem 2. *Besides* (5) *assume that* f *is bounded below.*[2] *Let* $\mu^{(+)}, \mu^{(-)}, \mu_n^{(+)}, \mu_n^{(-)}$, $n=1,2,\ldots$, *be probability measures on* W *satisfying conditions* (9) *and* (11) *for given* v. *Let* (ξ,η) *(resp.* (ξ_n,η_n)*) be solution of* (3) *with* $(\mu^{(+)},\mu^{(-)})$ *(resp.* $(\mu_n^{(+)},\mu_n^{(-)})$*). If* $\mu_n^{(+)}$ *(resp.* $\mu_n^{(-)}$*) converges to* $\mu^{(+)}$ *(resp.* $\mu^{(-)}$*) weakly, then for any compact subsets* K_1, K_2 *of* W *and* $\forall\, T>0$

$$(31) \qquad \lim_{n\to\infty} \xi_n(t,w) = \xi(t,w), \qquad \lim_{n\to\infty} \eta_n(t,z) = \eta(t,z)$$

uniformly in $(t,w,z)\in[0,T]\times K_1\times K_2$.

Proof. Let $(\xi^{(k)},\eta^{(k)})$ and $(\xi_n^{(k)},\eta_n^{(k)})$, $k\geqq 0$, be defined by (12), (13) and (14) with $(\mu^{(+)},\mu^{(-)})$ and $(\mu_n^{(+)},\mu_n^{(-)})$, respectively. We will prove first of all that $\xi_n^{(k)}(t,w)$ (resp. $\eta_n^{(k)}(t,z)$) converges to $\xi^{(k)}(t,w)$ (resp. $\eta^{(k)}(t,z)$), as $n\to\infty$, uniformly on $[0,T]\times K$, where K is a compact subset of W. We show it by induction in k. Since $\mu_n^{(+)}$ (resp. $\mu_n^{(-)}$) converges weakly to $\mu^{(+)}$ (resp. $\mu^{(-)}$) by the assumption, $(a^{(+)}(s,x), a^{(-)}(s,x))$ and $(a_n^{(+)}(s,x), a_n^{(-)}(s,x))$ defined by (12) with $(\mu^{(+)},\mu^{(-)})$ and $(\mu_n^{(+)},\mu_n^{(-)})$, respectively, satisfy the conditions of Lemma 6. Therefore, $\xi_n^{(0)}(t,w)$ (resp. $\eta_n^{(0)}(t,z)$) converges to $\xi^{(0)}(t,w)$ (resp. $\eta^{(0)}(t,z)$) uniformly on $[0,T]\times K$.

Assume that $\xi_n^{(k)}(t,w)$ (resp. $\eta_n^{(k)}(t,z)$) converges to $\xi^{(k)}(t,w)$ (resp. $\eta^{(k)}(t,z)$), as $n\to\infty$, uniformly on $[0,T]\times K$. We will only prove that $\xi_n^{(k+1)}(t,w)$ converges to $\xi^{(k+1)}(t,w)$ uniformly in $(t,w)\in[0,T]\times K$, since the same argument can be applied to $\eta_n^{(k+1)}(t,z)$ and $\eta^{(k+1)}(t,z)$. Define

$$b^{(k+1)}(s,x) = \int_W f(x+\eta^{(k)}(s,\tilde z))\,\mu^{(-)}(d\tilde z) + v(x),$$

$$b_n^{(k+1)}(s,x) = \int_W f(x+\eta_n^{(k)}(s,\tilde z))\,\mu_n^{(-)}(d\tilde z) + v(x).$$

---

[2] Then f satisfies the condition (10) automatically

It is clear that $\xi^{(k+1)}$ and $\xi_n^{(k+1)}$ satisfy Skorokhod equations

$$\xi^{(k+1)}(t,w)=w(t)+\int_0^t ds\, b^{(k+1)}(s,\xi^{(k+1)}(s,w))+\phi^{(k+1)}(t,w),$$

$$\xi_n^{(k+1)}(t,w)=w(t)+\int_0^t ds\, b_n^{(k+1)}(s,\xi_n^{(k+1)}(s,w))+\phi_n^{(k+1)}(t,w),$$

respectively. If we prove that $b^{(k+1)}(t,x)$ and $b_n^{(k+1)}(t,x)$ satisfy the conditions of Lemma 6, it implies that $\xi_n^{(k+1)}(t,w)$ converges to $\xi^{(k+1)}(t,w)$ uniformly on $[0,T]\times K$, *as* $n\to\infty$.

The condition (21) is clearly satisfied. The condition (27) can be verified as follows:

(32)
$$\begin{aligned}&|b_n^{(k+1)}(s,x)-b^{(k+1)}(s,x)|\\ &\leqq \int_W |f(x+\eta_n^{(k)}(s,z))-f(x+\eta^{(k)}(s,z))|\,\mu_n^{(-)}(dz)\\ &+|\int_W f(x+\eta^{(k)}(s,z))(\mu_n^{(-)}(dz)-\mu^{(-)}(dz))|.\end{aligned}$$

Since $\mu_n^{(-)}$ converges weakly to $\mu^{(-)}$ by the assumption, there exists a compact subset K_0 of W such that

$$\mu_n^{(-)}(K_0^c)\leqq\frac{\varepsilon}{2f(a)}.$$

Keeping this in mind, we estimate

(33) The first term of the right hand side of (32)

$$\leqq \int_{K_0} |f(x+\eta_n^{(k)}(s,z))-f(x+\eta^{(k)}(s,z))|\,\mu_n^{(-)}(dz)+\varepsilon,$$

where the integral is smaller than ε for sufficiently large n uniformly in $(s,x)\in[0,T]\times\left[a,\frac{1}{a}\right]$, because the integrand converges to zero uniformly in $(s,x,z)\in[0,T]\times\left[a,\frac{1}{a}\right]\times K_0$; and

(34) The second term of the right hand side of (32)

$$\leqq|\int_{K_0} f(x+\eta^{(k)}(s,z))(\mu_n^{(-)}(dz)-\mu^{(-)}(dz))|+\varepsilon,$$

where $f(x+\eta^{(k)}(s,z))$ is uniformly continuous in $(s,x,z)\in[0,T]\times\left[a,\frac{1}{a}\right]\times K_0$, and the integral is smaller than 3ε uniformly in $(s,x)\in[0,T]\times\left[a,\frac{1}{a}\right]$ for sufficiently large n. In fact,[3] let $\left\{U(s,x)\colon (s,x)\in[0,T]\times\left[a,\frac{1}{a}\right]\right\}$ be a covering of

[3] Thanks to a referee's remark one can invoke Theorem 6.8 (p. 51) in *Probability measures on metric spaces* by Parthasarathy

$[0, T] \times \left[a, \frac{1}{a}\right]$, where

$$U(s, x) = \{(t, y) : \sup_{z \in K_0} |f(x + \eta^{(k)}(s, z)) - f(y + \eta^{(k)}(t, z))| < \varepsilon\}.$$

Then, there exists a finite subcovering $\{U(s_i, x_i) : i = 1, 2, \ldots, l\}$. Let n be sufficiently large so that

$$\left| \int_{K_0} f(x_i + \eta^{(k)}(s_i, z)) (\mu_n^{(-)}(dz) - \mu^{(-)}(dz)) \right| < \varepsilon$$

for $i = 1, 2, \ldots, l$. For any $(s, x) \in [0, T] \times \left[a, \frac{1}{a}\right]$ we can find $U(s_i, x_i)$ such that $(s, x) \in U(s_i, x_i)$, and hence

$$\begin{aligned} &\left| \int_{K_0} f(x + \eta^{(k)}(s, z)) (\mu_n^{(-)}(dz) - \mu^{(-)}(dz)) \right| \\ &\quad < 2\varepsilon + \left| \int_{K_0} f(x_i + \eta^{(k)}(s_i, z)) (\mu_n^{(-)}(dz) - \mu^{(-)}(dz)) \right| \\ &\quad < 3\varepsilon, \end{aligned}$$

for sufficiently large n. Thus we have finally

$$\sup_{(s, x) \in [0, T] \times \left[a, \frac{1}{a}\right]} |b_n^{(k+1)}(s, x) - b^{(k+1)}(s, x)| \leqq 6\varepsilon$$

for sufficiently large n. Hence $b^{(k+1)}(s, x)$ and $b_n^{(k+1)}(s, x)$ satisfy the condition (27), the second condition of (27) being trivial.

Now, the proof can be completed as follows: Because of Theorem 1, especially inequality (16), Lemma 5 and Dini's theorem we can find k_0 for any $\varepsilon > 0$ such that

$$(35) \qquad 0 \leqq \xi^{(2k+1)}(t, w) - \xi^{(2k)}(t, w) \leqq \varepsilon, \quad \text{for } k \geqq k_0,$$

uniformly in $(t, w) \in [0, T] \times K$. On the other hand there exists n_0 such that for $n \geqq n_0$

$$(36) \qquad \begin{aligned} &|\xi_n^{(2k)}(t, w) - \xi^{(2k)}(t, w)| \leqq \varepsilon, \\ &|\xi_n^{(2k+1)}(t, w) - \xi^{(2k+1)}(t, w)| \leqq \varepsilon, \end{aligned}$$

uniformly in $(t, w) \in [0, T] \times K$ as is proved above. Therefore, combining (35) and (36) with

$$(37) \qquad \begin{aligned} &\xi^{(2k)}(t, w) \leqq \xi(t, w) \leqq \xi^{(2k+1)}(t, w), \\ &\xi_n^{(2k)}(t, w) \leqq \xi_n(t, w) \leqq \xi_n^{(2k+1)}(t, w), \end{aligned}$$

we obtain

$$\sup_{(t, w) \in [0, T] \times K} |\xi(t, w) - \xi_n(t, w)| \leqq 3\varepsilon, \quad \text{for } n \geqq n_0.$$

Thus $\xi_n(t,w)$ converges to $\xi(t,w)$, as $n\to\infty$, uniformly on $[0,T]\times K$ for any $T>0$ and compact subset K of W. This completes the proof of Theorem 2.

3. Propagation of Chaos

We consider a system of Eq. (3) with f and v satisfying the condition (5). Moreover we assume that f is bounded below. Let P_x be the Wiener measure on W starting from $x\in\mathbb{R}$, $\nu^{(+)}$ and $\nu^{(-)}$ be probability measures on $\mathbb{R}^+$ with

$$\int_{\mathbb{R}^+} x\,\nu(dx)<\infty, \qquad \nu=\nu^{(+)},\nu^{(-)}, \tag{38}$$

and define probability measures $\mu^{(+)}$ and $\mu^{(-)}$ on W by

$$\mu^{(+)}(\cdot)=\int_{\mathbb{R}^+}\nu^{(+)}(dx)\,P_x(\cdot), \qquad \mu^{(-)}(\cdot)=\int_{\mathbb{R}^+}\nu^{(-)}(dx)\,P_x(\cdot). \tag{39}$$

Because of (38), the probability measures $\mu^{(+)}$ and $\mu^{(-)}$ satisfy the condition (9). In addition we assume the condition (11).[4] Then there exists a unique solution $(\xi(t,w),\eta(t,z))$ of (3) with $(\mu^{(+)},\mu^{(-)})$ for all $(w,z)\in W\times W$ by Theorem 1. A stochastic process (X,Y) on $(W\times W,\mu^{(+)}\otimes\mu^{(-)})$ defined by

$$(X(t),Y(t))=(\xi(t),-\eta(t)), \tag{40}$$

coincides clearly with the process described by Eq. (2).

Let (Ω,P) be the infinite product of $(W\times W,\mu^{(+)}\otimes\mu^{(-)})$ i.e.

$$\begin{aligned}&\Omega=W^2\times W^2\times\ldots, && W^2=W\times W,\\ &P=\mu\otimes\mu\otimes\ldots, && \mu=\mu^{(+)}\otimes\mu^{(-)}.\end{aligned} \tag{41}$$

For $\omega=((w_1,z_1),(w_2,z_2),\ldots)\in\Omega$ define $\mathbf{X}(t,\omega)$ by

$$\begin{aligned}&X_i(t,\omega)=\xi(t,w_i),\\ &Y_i(t,\omega)=-\eta(t,z_i), \qquad i=1,2,3,\ldots,\end{aligned} \tag{42}$$

and

$$\mathbf{X}(t)=((X_1(t),Y_1(t)),(X_2(t),Y_2(t)),\ldots). \tag{43}$$

By definition $\{(X_i(t),Y_i(t)):\ i=1,2,3,\ldots\}$ is a family of independent copies of the process described by (2).

Now, define for $\omega=((w_1,z_1),(w_2,z_2),\ldots)\in\Omega$ sequences $\{\mu_n^{(+)}(\omega)\}$ and $\{\mu_n^{(-)}(\omega)\}$ of probability measures on W by

$$\begin{aligned}\mu_n^{(+)}(\omega,\cdot)&=\frac{1}{n}\sum_{i=1}^{n}\delta_{w_i}(\cdot),\\ \mu_n^{(-)}(\omega,\cdot)&=\frac{1}{n}\sum_{i=1}^{n}\delta_{z_i}(\cdot).\end{aligned} \tag{44}$$

[4] A sufficient condition for (11) is given in Proposition 1 of [9], i.e. if v^- satisfies (i) $v^-(x)\leqq c(1+|x|^\alpha)$ for some nonnegative constants c and α, and if $\nu=\nu^{(+)},\nu^{(-)}$ satisfy (ii) $\int_{\mathbb{R}^+} x^\alpha\nu(dx)<\infty$, then the condition (11) is fullfilled

They satisfy trivially the conditions (9) and (11). Therefore, by Theorem 1, there exists for each $(w,z)\in W\times W$ a unique solution $(\xi_n(t,w,\omega),\eta_n(t,z,\omega))$ of (3) with $(\mu_n^{(+)}(\omega),\mu_n^{(-)}(\omega))$. Define, for $\omega=((w_1,z_1),(w_2,z_2),\dots)\in\Omega$, processes $(X_i^{(n)},Y_i^{(n)})$, $i=1,2,\dots,n$, on (Ω,P) by

$$X_i^{(n)}(t,\omega)=\xi_n(t,w_i,\omega),\qquad (45)$$
$$Y_i^{(n)}(t,\omega)=-\eta_n(t,z_i,\omega),$$

and put

$$\mathbf{X}^{(n)}(t)=((X_1^{(n)}(t),Y_1^{(n)}(t)),\dots,(X_n^{(n)}(t),Y_n^{(n)}(t))).\qquad (46)$$

Clearly $\{(X_i^{(n)}(t),Y_i^{(n)}(t)):\ i=1,2,\dots,n\}$ is a family of particles of two types described by (1).

Since $\mu_n^{(+)}(\omega)$ (resp. $\mu_n^{(-)}(\omega)$) converges to $\mu^{(+)}$ (resp. $\mu^{(-)}$) weakly for P-a.e. $\omega\in\Omega$ by the strong law of large numbers, Theorem 2 implies that for P-a.e. $\omega\in\Omega$ the sequence $(\xi_n(t,w,\omega),\ \eta_n(t,z,\omega))$ converges to $(\xi(t,w),\eta(t,z))$ uniformly in $(t,w,z)\in[0,T]\times K_1\times K_2$, for $\forall T>0$ and $\forall$ compact $K_1,K_2\subset W$. In other words, the propagation of chaos (of Kac-McKean) holds for a family of diffusing particles of two types with singular interaction described by (1).

Theorem 3. (Propagation of chaos.) *Under the stated conditions*[5] *let* $((X_1^{(n)}(t,\omega),Y_1^{(n)}(t,\omega)),\dots,(X_n^{(n)}(t,\omega),Y_n^{(n)}(t,\omega)))$ *be the system of 2n-particles of two types defined on* (Ω,P) *by* (45) *and* (46). *Then, for* P-a.e. $\omega\in\Omega$, $((X_1^{(n)}(t,\omega),Y_1^{(n)}(t,\omega)),\dots,(X_m^{(n)}(t,\omega),\ Y_m^{(n)}(t,\omega)))$, *for fixed* $m\leqq n$, *converges uniformly in* $t\in[0,T]$ *for* $\forall T>0$, *as* $n\to\infty$, *to* $((X_1(t,\omega),Y_1(t,\omega)),\dots,X_m(t,\omega),Y_m(t,\omega)))$ *which is a family of independent copies of the non-linear diffusion process of two types defined by* (42). *That is, the diffusion process on* $(\mathbb{R}^2)^n$ *described by equation* (1) *converges in law to the infinite direct product of the diffusion process described by* (2) *as n tends to infinity.*

Remark. P_x in (39) is not necessarily to be the Wiener measure, and Theorem 3 remains valid for arbitrary Markov processes on W, since our treatment of the problem is purely pathwise and does not depend on a special choice of probability measures on W.

---

5 See the first paragraph of this section

References

1. Braun, W., K. Hepp: The Vlasov dynamics and its fluctuations in $1/N$ limit of interacting classical particles. Commun. Math. Phys. **56**, 101–113 (1977)
2. Kusuoka, S., Y. Tamura: Gibbs measures for mean field potentials. J. Fac. Sci. Univ. Tokyo Sect. 1A Math. **31**, 223–245 (1984)
3. Maruyama, G.: On the transition probability functions of the Markov processes. Nat. Sci. Rep. Ochanomizu Univ. **5**, 10–20 (1954)
4. McKean, H.P.: A class of Markov processes associated with non-linear parabolic equations. Proc. Natl. Acad. Sci. **56**, 1907–1911 (1966)
5. McKean, H.P.: Propagation of chaos for a class of non-linear parabolic equations. Lecture Series in Differential Equations. Catholic Univ. 41–57 (1967), Washington D.C.

6. Nagasawa, M.: Segregation of a population in an environment. J. Math. Biol. **9**, 213-235 (1980)
7. Nagasawa, M.: An application of segregation model for septation of *Escherichia coli*. J. Theor. Biol. **90**, 445-455 (1981)
8. Nagasawa, M., K. Yasue: A statistical model of mesons. Publication de l'Institute recherche Mathematique Avanceé (CNRS) **33**, 1-48. Université Louis Pasteur (Strasbourg) (1982/83)
9. Nagasawa, M., H. Tanaka: A diffusion process in a singular mean-drift-field. Z. Wahrscheinlichkeitstheor. Verw. Geb. **68**, 247-269 (1985)
10. Shiga, T., H. Tanaka: Central limit theorem for a system of Markovian particles with mean field interaction. Z. Wahrscheinlichkeitstheor. Verw. Geb. **69**, 439-459 (1985)
11. Sznitman, A.S.: Non-linear reflecting diffusion processes, and propagation of chaos, and fluctuations associated. J. Funct. Anal. **56**, 311-336 (1984)
12. Tanaka, H.: Stochastic differential equations with reflecting boundary condition in convex regions. Hiroshima Math. J. **9**, 163-177 (1979)
13. Tanaka, H.: Limit theorems for certain diffusion processes with interaction. In: Stochastic Analysis, pp. 469-488. Itô, K. (ed.). Tokyo: Kinokuniya Co. Ltd., Amsterdam-Oxford-New York: North-Holland Pub. Co. 1984

Received November 29, 1984

Saisho, Y. and Tanaka, H.
Osaka J. Math.
23 (1986), 725–740

STOCHASTIC DIFFERENTIAL EQUATIONS FOR MUTUALLY REFLECTING BROWNIAN BALLS

YASUMASA SAISHO AND HIROSHI TANAKA

(Received August 1, 1985)

Introduction

In this paper we construct a random motion of mutually reflecting hard balls of diameter ρ in $\boldsymbol{R}^d$ by solving certain stochastic differential equation (abbreviated: SDE) with a kind of singular drift. For simplicity we first consider the motion of mutually reflecting Brownian balls of diameter ρ. In order to construct such a motion we pose the following problem. Let W denote the space of continuous paths in $\boldsymbol{R}^d$. *Given* $w_1, \cdots, w_n \in W$ *satisfying*

(1) $$|w_i(0)-w_j(0)| \geqq \rho, \quad 1 \leqq i < j \leqq n,$$

solve the equation

(2) $$\xi_i(t) = w_i(t) + \sum_{j=1(\neq i)}^{n} \int_0^t (\xi_i(s)-\xi_j(s))\, d\phi_{ij}(s), \quad 1 \leqq i \leqq n,$$

under the following conditions (3) *and* (4).

(3) $\xi_i \in W$, $1 \leqq i \leqq n$, and $|\xi_i(t)-\xi_j(t)| \geqq \rho$, $1 \leqq i < j \leqq n$, $t \geqq 0$.

(4) ϕ_{ij}'s are continuous non-decreasing functions with $\phi_{ij}(0)=0$, $\phi_{ij}(t)=\phi_{ji}(t)$ and

$$\phi_{ij}(t) = \int_0^t \mathbf{1}_\rho(|\xi_i(s)-\xi_j(s)|)\, d\phi_{ij}(s),$$

where $\mathbf{1}_\rho(r) = 1$ if $r = \rho$, and $=0$ if $r \neq \rho$.

A pair (ξ, ϕ) of functions or simply a function ξ is called a solution of (2) provided that (2), (3) and (4) are satisfied. One of the main results in this paper is that *there exists a unique solution of* (2) for given $w_1, \cdots, w_n$. By taking $w_1, \cdots, w_n$ to be independent d-dimensional Brownian motions satisfying (1), we obtain a process $(\xi_1(t), \cdots, \xi_n(t))$. This is what we call the motion of mutually reflecting Brownian balls. $\xi_i(t)$ denotes the center of the i-th Brownian ball at time t. In analogy with Skorohod's equation for a 1-dimensional reflecting Brownian motion ([3] [5] [7]), the equation (2) may be regarded as Skorohod's equation for the motion of mutually reflecting Brownian balls.

We next consider the SDE on a probability space $(\Omega, \mathcal{F}, P)$:

$$(5) \qquad dX_i(t) = \sigma(X_i(t))\, dB_i(t) + b(X_i(t))\, dt + \sum_{j=1(\neq i)}^{n} (X_i(t) - X_j(t))\, d\phi_{ij}(t), \quad 1 \leqq i \leqq n,$$

where

$$\sigma: \boldsymbol{R}^d \to \boldsymbol{R}^d \otimes \boldsymbol{R}^d, \quad b: \boldsymbol{R}^d \to \boldsymbol{R}^d$$

are given, $X_i(0)$'s are $\mathcal{F}_0$-measurable initial values satisfying $|X_i(0) - X_j(0)| \geqq \rho$, $1 \leqq i < j \leqq n$, and $B_i(t)$, $1 \leqq i \leqq n$, are independent d-dimensional $\mathcal{F}_t$-adapted Brownian motion with $B_i(0) = 0$. Here $\{\mathcal{F}_t\}_{t \geqq 0}$ is a right continuous filtration on $(\Omega, \mathcal{F}, P)$ such that each $\mathcal{F}_t$ contains all P-negligible sets. As in (2), $X_i(t)$ and $\Phi_{ij}(t)$ should be found under the following conditions (6) and (7).

(6) $X_i(t)$'s are $\mathcal{F}_t$-adapted continuous processes with $|X_i(t) - X_j(t)| \geqq \rho$, $1 \leqq i < j \leqq n$, $t \geqq 0$.

(7) $\Phi_{ij}(t)$'s are $\mathcal{F}_t$-adapted continuous non-decreasing processes with $\Phi_{ij}(0) = 0$, $\Phi_{ij}(t) = \Phi_{ji}(t)$ and

$$\Phi_{ij}(t) = \int_0^t \mathbf{1}_\rho(|X_i(s) - X_j(s)|)\, d\Phi_{ij}(s).$$

The equation (5) may be considered as Skorohod's SDE for mutually reflecting diffusion balls with coefficients σ and b. Another main result of this paper is that *there exists a unique solution of* (5) *provided that* σ *and* b *are bounded and Lipschitz continuous.*

Our method for solving (2) and (5) is to make use of the results of [6] concerning Skorohod's equation for general domain. Skorohod's equation for a multi-dimensional domain D with reflecting boundary (a precise formulation is explained in **1**) was discussed by Tanaka [8] when D is a convex domain and then by Lions and Sznitman [4] when D is a general domain satisfying Conditions (A) and (B) (see **1**) together with the additional condition that D is *admissible*, which means roughly that D can be approximated in some sense by smooth domains. Recently, Frankowska [2] and Saisho [6] amplified Lions and Sznitman's result by removing the additional condition. Now the present discussion is based on the fact that Skorohod's equation (2) (or SDE (5)) is equivalent to Skorohod's equation (or SDE) for the domain

$$(8) \qquad D = \{(x_1, \cdots, x_n) \in \boldsymbol{R}^{nd}: |x_i - x_j| > \rho,\ 1 \leqq i < j \leqq n\}.$$

So the crucial point of our discussions is to prove that the domain D of (8) satisfies Conditions (A) and (B). In solving Skorohod's SDE for D we make use of Theorem 5.1 of Saisho [6].

In **1** we state briefly the results of Lions and Sznitman [4] and Saisho [6] concerning Skorohod's equation for a general domain. We prove that the domain D of (8) satisfies Condition (B) in **2** and (A) in **3**. We solve Skorohod's equation (2) in **4** and SDE (5) in **5**.

1. Some known results on Skorohod's equation for an N-dimensional domain with reflecting boundary

Let D be a domain in $\boldsymbol{R}^N$ and define the set $\mathcal{N}_x$ of inward normal unit vectors at $\boldsymbol{x}\in\partial D$ by

$$\mathcal{N}_x = \bigcup_{r>0} \mathcal{N}_{x,r},$$
$$\mathcal{N}_{x,r} = \{\boldsymbol{n}\in\boldsymbol{R}^N : |\boldsymbol{n}|=1, B(\boldsymbol{x}-r\boldsymbol{n}, r)\cap D=\phi\},$$

where $B(\boldsymbol{z}, r)=\{\boldsymbol{y}\in\boldsymbol{R}^N: |\boldsymbol{y}-\boldsymbol{z}|<r\}$, $\boldsymbol{z}\in\boldsymbol{R}^N$. In general it can happen that $\mathcal{N}_x=\phi$. In what follows $\langle\cdot,\cdot\rangle$ denotes the usual inner product in $\boldsymbol{R}^N$. We introduce two conditions on the domain D.

Condition (A) (uniform exterior sphere condition). There exists a constant $r_0>0$ such that

$$\mathcal{N}_x = \mathcal{N}_{x,r_0}\neq\phi \quad \text{for any} \quad \boldsymbol{x}\in\partial D.$$

Condition (B). There exist constants $\delta>0$ and $\beta(1\leqq\beta<\infty)$ with the following property: for any $\boldsymbol{x}\in\partial D$ there exists a unit vector $\boldsymbol{l}_x$ such that

$$\langle\boldsymbol{l}_x, \boldsymbol{n}\rangle\geqq 1/\beta \quad \text{for any} \quad \boldsymbol{n}\in \bigcup_{\boldsymbol{y}\in B(\boldsymbol{x},\delta)\cap\partial D} \mathcal{N}_y.$$

REMARK 1.1. For any fixed $r>0$ and a unit vector $\boldsymbol{n}$ the following two statements are equivalent.

(i) $B(\boldsymbol{x}-r\boldsymbol{n}, r)\cap D=\phi$.

(ii) $\langle\boldsymbol{y}-\boldsymbol{x}, \boldsymbol{n}\rangle+\dfrac{1}{2r}|\boldsymbol{y}-\boldsymbol{x}|^2\geqq 0$ for any $\boldsymbol{y}\in\bar{D}$.

REMARK 1.2. D satisfies Condition (B) if it satisfies the following condition.

Condition (B'). There exist $\delta>0$ and $\alpha(0\leqq\alpha<1)$ with the following property: for any $\boldsymbol{x}\in\partial D$ there exists a unit vector $\boldsymbol{l}_x$ such that

$$C(\boldsymbol{y}, \boldsymbol{l}_x, \alpha)\cap B(\boldsymbol{x}, \delta)\subset\bar{D}, \quad \forall\boldsymbol{y}\in B(\boldsymbol{x}, \delta)\cap\partial D,$$

where $C(\boldsymbol{y}, \boldsymbol{l}_x, \alpha)$ is the convex cone with vertex $\boldsymbol{y}$, defined by

$$C(\boldsymbol{y}, \boldsymbol{l}_x, \alpha) = \{z \in \boldsymbol{R}^N : \langle z-y, \boldsymbol{l}_x \rangle \geqq \alpha |z-y|\} .$$

Denote by $W(\boldsymbol{R}^N)$ (resp. $W(\bar{D})$) the space of continuous paths in $\boldsymbol{R}^N$ (resp. $\bar{D}$). Skorohod's equation for D with reflecting boundary is written in the form

$$\xi(t) = w(t) + \int_0^t \boldsymbol{n}(s)\, d\phi(s) , \tag{1.1}$$

where $w \in W(\boldsymbol{R}^N)$ is given and satisfies $w(0) \in \bar{D}$; a solution (ξ, ϕ) of (1.1) should be found under the following conditions.

(1.2) $\xi \in W(\bar{D})$.

(1.3) ϕ is a continuous non-decreasing function such that $\phi(0) = 0$ and

$$\phi(t) = \int_0^t \mathbf{1}_{\partial D}(\xi(s))\, d\phi(s) .$$

(1.4) $\boldsymbol{n}(s) \in \mathcal{N}_{\xi(s)}$ if $\xi(s) \in \partial D$.

The following theorem was proved by Lions and Sznitman [4] under the additional condition that D is admissible. Frankowska [2] and Saisho [6] removed this additional condition. Frankowska's result is of a general type but contains what we need only in a less explicit form, so we state the theorem in the form of Saisho [6].

Theorem 1.1. *If the domain D satisfies Conditions (A) and (B), then there exists a unique solution of* (1.1) *for any given $w \in W(\boldsymbol{R}^N)$ with $w(0) \in \bar{D}$.*

Next, given

$$\sigma: \bar{D} \to \boldsymbol{R}^N \otimes \boldsymbol{R}^N, \quad b: \bar{D} \to \boldsymbol{R}^N ,$$

we consider Skorohod's SDE

$$dX(t) = \sigma(X(t))\, dB(t) + b(X(t))\, dt + \boldsymbol{n}(t)\, d\Phi(t) , \tag{1.5}$$

where the initial value $X(0) \in \bar{D}$ is assumed to be $\mathcal{F}_0$-measurable and $B(t)$ is an $\boldsymbol{N}$-dimensional $\mathcal{F}_t$-adapted Brownian motion with $B(0)=0$. Here $\{\mathcal{F}_t\}$ is a right continuous filtration on $(\Omega, \mathcal{F}, P)$ such that $\mathcal{F}_0$ contains all P-negligible sets. A solution $(X(t), \Phi(t))$ should be found under the following conditions (1.6)–(1.8).

(1.6) $X(t)$ is a $\bar{D}$-valued $\mathcal{F}_t$-adapted continuous process.

(1.7) $\Phi(t)$ is a continuous non-decreasing process with $\Phi(0)=0$ and

$$\Phi(t) = \int_0^t \mathbf{1}_{\partial D}(X(s))\, d\Phi(s) .$$

(1.8) $\boldsymbol{n}(s) \in \mathcal{N}_{X(s)}$ if $X(s) \in \partial D$.

In addition to Conditions (A) and (B), Lions and Sznitman [4] introduced the following Condition (C) and discussed the existence and uniqueness of the solution of (1.5).

Condition (*C*). There exists a function f in $C^2(\boldsymbol{R}^N)$ which is bounded together with its first and second partial derivatives such that $\exists \gamma > 0$, $\forall \boldsymbol{x} \in \partial D$, $\forall \boldsymbol{y} \in \bar{D}$, $\forall \boldsymbol{n} \in \mathcal{N}_{\boldsymbol{x}}$

$$\langle \boldsymbol{y}-\boldsymbol{x}, \boldsymbol{n} \rangle + \frac{1}{\gamma} \langle \nabla f(\boldsymbol{x}), \boldsymbol{n} \rangle |\boldsymbol{y}-\boldsymbol{x}|^2 \geqq 0 .$$

The following theorem was proved by Lions and Sznitman ([4: Theorem 3.1]) under Condition (C) and the admissibility of D; however, recently Saisho ([6: Theorem 5.1]) removed these additional conditions.

Theorem 1.2 ([6]). *Let D satisfy Conditions* (*A*), (*B*) *and assume that σ and b are bounded and Lipschitz continuous. Then for any initial value $X(0) \in \bar{D}$ there exists a unique* (*strong*) *solution of* (1.5).

2. $\boldsymbol{D}$ satisfies Condition ($\boldsymbol{B}'$)

Let D be the domain in $\boldsymbol{R}^{nd}$ defined by (8). We are going to prove the following proposition.

Proposition 2.1. *The domain D satisfies Condition* (B'), *that is, there exist constants $\delta > 0$ and $\alpha (0 \leqq \alpha < 1)$ with the following property: for any $\boldsymbol{x} \in \partial D$ there exists a unit vector $\boldsymbol{l}_{\boldsymbol{x}}$ such that*

(2.1) $$C(\boldsymbol{y}, \boldsymbol{l}_{\boldsymbol{x}}, \alpha) \cap B(\boldsymbol{x}, \delta) \subset \bar{D}$$

holds for any $\boldsymbol{y} \in B(\boldsymbol{x}, \delta) \cap \partial D$.

For a non-empty subset I of $\{1, 2, \cdots, n\}$ and $\boldsymbol{x} = (x_1, \cdots, x_n) \in \bar{D}$ we set

$$\boldsymbol{x}(I) = \{x_i : i \in I\} .$$

DEFINITION 2.1. Let I, I' be non-empty subsets of $\{1, 2, \cdots, n\}$.

(i) $\boldsymbol{x}(I)$ and $\boldsymbol{x}(I')$ are said to be *separated* if

(2.2) $$I \cap I' = \phi \quad \text{and} \quad |x_i - x_j| \geqq 2\rho, \ \forall i \in I, \ \forall j \in I' .$$

(ii) $\boldsymbol{x}(I)$ is called a *cluster* if

(2.3) for any $i, j \in I$ with $i \neq j$ there exist $i_0 (= i)$, $i_1, \cdots, i_{p-1}, i_p (= j)$ in I such that $|x_{i_{k-1}} - x_{i_k}| < 2\rho$, $1 \leqq k \leqq p$.

REMARK 2.1. If $\boldsymbol{x}(I)$ is a cluster, then

$$|x_i - x_j| < 2(n-1)\rho, \quad \forall i, j \in I, \tag{2.4}$$

$$\begin{aligned} |x_i - x_I| &= \frac{1}{\# I} |\sum_{j\in I}(x_i - x_j)| \\ &< 2(n-1)\rho, \quad \forall i \in I, \end{aligned} \tag{2.5}$$

where $x_I = (\# I)^{-1} \sum_{j\in I} x_j$ and $\# I$ is the number of elements in I.

Let $\boldsymbol{x} = (x_1, \cdots, x_n)$. Then $\{x_1, \cdots, x_n\}$ can be represented as the sum of mutually separated clusters:

$$\{x_1, \cdots, x_n\} = \bigcup_{k=1}^{m} \boldsymbol{x}(I_k). \tag{2.6}$$

Here $1 \leqq m \leqq n$. In what follows we assume that $\boldsymbol{x} \in \partial D$ and keep it fixed, so $I_1, \cdots, I_m$ appearing in (2.6) are also fixed. Let $c > 1$ be a constant which will be determined later and set

$$\begin{cases} u_i = x_{I_k} + c(x_i - x_{I_k}), & i \in I_k, \ 1 \leqq k \leqq m, \\ \boldsymbol{u} = (u_1, \cdots, u_n) \in \boldsymbol{R}^{nd}. \end{cases}$$

Also we set for $\boldsymbol{y} = (y_1, \cdots, y_n) \in \boldsymbol{R}^{nd}$

$$\begin{cases} v_i = y_{I_k} + c(y_i - y_{I_k}), & i \in I_k, \ 1 \leqq k \leqq m, \\ \boldsymbol{v} = (v_1, \cdots, v_n) \in \boldsymbol{R}^{nd}. \end{cases}$$

We are going to prove Proposition 2.1 with

$$\begin{cases} \boldsymbol{l}_x = \dfrac{\boldsymbol{u} - \boldsymbol{x}}{|\boldsymbol{u} - \boldsymbol{x}|}, \\ \delta = \dfrac{\varepsilon}{4(c-1)+2}, \\ \alpha = \cos\theta, \end{cases} \tag{2.7}$$

where c, ε and θ are constants determined by

$$\begin{cases} (c-1)(n-1) = 1/8, \\ \varepsilon = (c-1)\rho/4, \end{cases} \tag{2.8}$$

$$\sin\frac{\theta}{2} = \frac{\varepsilon}{8(c-1)\sqrt{n}\,(n-1)\rho}, \quad 0 < \theta \leqq \pi/2. \tag{2.9}$$

From now on let c, ε, δ be constants determined by (2.7) and (2.8). Let $\boldsymbol{y} \in B(\boldsymbol{x}, \delta) \cap \partial D$ and set

$$\boldsymbol{z} = \boldsymbol{y} + (\boldsymbol{u} - \boldsymbol{x}).$$

Lemma 2.1. $|\boldsymbol{u}-\boldsymbol{x}|=|\boldsymbol{z}-\boldsymbol{y}|<2(c-1)\sqrt{n}(n-1)\rho$.

Proof. Since $i\in I_k$ for some k, we have

(2.10) $$|u_i-x_i| = (c-1)|x_i-x_{I_k}|<2(c-1)(n-1)\rho$$

by (2.5), and hence we obtain the lemma.

Lemma 2.2. (i) *For any* $\boldsymbol{u}'\in B(\boldsymbol{u}, \varepsilon)$, $\boldsymbol{v}'\in B(\boldsymbol{v}, \varepsilon)$ *and* $0<t\leqq 1$,

$$\boldsymbol{u}'' = (1-t)\boldsymbol{x}+t\boldsymbol{u}'\in D, \quad \boldsymbol{v}'' = (1-t)\boldsymbol{y}+t\boldsymbol{v}'\in D.$$

(ii) $B(\boldsymbol{u}, \varepsilon)\subset D$, $B(\boldsymbol{v}, \varepsilon)\subset D$.

Proof. Since (ii) can be proved by setting $t=1$ in (i), it is enough to prove (i), that is,

$$|u_i''-u_j''|>\rho, \quad |v_i''-v_j''|>\rho, \quad 1\leqq i<j\leqq n.$$

Case (I): $i, j\in I_k$ *for some* k. Since

$$\begin{aligned} u_i''-u_j'' &= (1-t)(x_i-x_j)+t\{(u_i-u_j)+(u_i'-u_i)-(u_j'-u_j)\} \\ &= \{1+(c-1)t\}(x_i-x_j)+t\{(u_i'-u_i)-(u_j'-u_j)\}, \end{aligned}$$

we have

$$|u_i''-u_j''|\geqq\{1+(c-1)t\}\rho-2\varepsilon t>\rho,$$

and a similar inequality for $|v_i''-v_j''|$.
Case (II): $i\in I_k$, $j\in I_l$ $(k\neq l)$. Since

$$u_i''-x_i = t(u_i'-x_i) = t(u_i-x_i)+t(u_i'-u_i),$$

we have

$$\begin{aligned} |u_i''-x_i| &\leqq |u_i-x_i|+|u_i'-u_i| \quad (\text{setting } t=1) \\ &<2(c-1)(n-1)\rho+\varepsilon \quad (\text{by (2.10)}), \end{aligned}$$

and hence, making use of the inequality $|x_i-x_j|\geqq 2\rho$ which is a consequence of the assumption that $\boldsymbol{x}(I_k)$ and $\boldsymbol{x}(I_l)$ are separated, we have

$$\begin{aligned} |u_i''-u_j''| &\geqq |x_i-x_j|-|u_i''-x_i|-|u_j''-x_j| \\ &>2\rho-4(c-1)(n-1)\rho-2\varepsilon>\rho. \end{aligned}$$

Next, to prove the inequality for $|v_i''-v_j''|$, we notice that

$$\begin{aligned} |(y_i-y_{I_k})-(x_i-x_{I_k})| &= |(y_i-x_i)-\frac{1}{\# I_k}\sum_{p\in I_k}(y_p-x_p)| \\ &\leqq 2\max_{1\leqq p\leqq n}|y_p-x_p|\leqq 2|\boldsymbol{y}-\boldsymbol{x}|<2\delta, \end{aligned}$$

from which it follows that

$$|y_i-y_{I_k}|<|x_i-x_{I_k}|+2\delta<2(n-1)\rho+2\delta \quad \text{(use (2.5))}.$$

Therefore

$$|v_i-y_i|=(c-1)|y_i-y_{I_k}|<2(c-1)(n-1)\rho+2(c-1)\delta,$$

and hence

$$|v_i''-y_i|\leqq t|v_i-y_i|+t|v_i'-v_i|<2(c-1)(n-1)\rho+2(c-1)\delta+\varepsilon.$$

Thus we have

$$\begin{aligned}|v_i''-v_j''|&\geqq|y_i-y_j|-|v_i''-y_i|-|v_j''-y_j|\\ &\geqq|x_i-x_j|-|y_i-x_i|-|y_j-x_j|-|v_i''-y_i|-|v_j''-y_j|\\ &>2\rho-2\delta-4(c-1)(n-1)\rho-4(c-1)\delta-2\varepsilon\\ &>\rho.\end{aligned}$$

The proof of the lemma is finished.

Lemma 2.3. $|z-v|<\varepsilon/2$.

Proof. Taking I_k such that $i\in I_k$, we have

$$\begin{aligned}|z_i-v_i|&=|(c-1)(x_i-y_i)-(c-1)(x_{I_k}-y_{I_k})|\\ &\leqq(c-1)|x_i-y_i|+(c-1)|x_{I_k}-y_{I_k}|,\end{aligned}$$

and hence

$$\begin{aligned}(2.11)\qquad |\boldsymbol{z}-\boldsymbol{v}|^2&=\sum_{i=1}^{n}|z_i-v_i|^2\\ &\leqq 2(c-1)^2|\boldsymbol{x}-\boldsymbol{y}|^2+2(c-1)^2\sum_{k=1}^{m}\#I_k|x_{I_k}-y_{I_k}|^2.\end{aligned}$$

Because $|x_{I_k}-y_{I_k}|^2\leqq(\#I_k)^{-1}\sum_{j\in I_k}|x_j-y_j|^2$, we have

$$\sum_{k=1}^{m}\#I_k|x_{I_k}-y_{I_k}|^2\leqq|\boldsymbol{x}-\boldsymbol{y}|^2,$$

and (2.11) yields

$$|\boldsymbol{z}-\boldsymbol{v}|\leqq 2(c-1)|\boldsymbol{x}-\boldsymbol{y}|<2(c-1)\delta<\varepsilon/2.$$

The proof of the lemma is finished.

Proof of Proposition 2.1. By (ii) of Lemma 2.2 and Lemma 2.3 we have

$$B(\boldsymbol{z},\varepsilon/2)\subset B(\boldsymbol{v},\varepsilon)\subset D,$$

and hence by (i) of Lemma 2.2

$$\bar{D} \supset \text{the convex hull } \Gamma \text{ of the set } B(z, \varepsilon/2) \cup \{y\} . \tag{2.12}$$

We have also

$$|z-y| = |u-x| \geqq \varepsilon > 2\delta , \tag{2.13}$$

because $x \notin B(u, \varepsilon)$ by (ii) of Lemma 2.2. Therefore, if θ is defined by (2.9), then (2.12) combined with Lemma 2.1 and (2.13) implies that

$$C(y, l_x, \cos\theta) \cap B(y, 2\delta) \subset \bar{\Gamma} \subset \bar{D} . \tag{2.14}$$

Since $B(x, \delta) \subset B(y, 2\delta)$, (2.14) implies (2.1) with $\alpha = \cos\theta$. The proof of Proposition 2.1 is finished.

3. *D* satisfies Condition (A)

For $1 \leqq i < j \leqq n$ let D_{ij} be the domain defined by

$$D_{ij} = \{x = (x_1, \cdots, x_n) \in \mathbf{R}^{nd} : |x_i - x_j| > \rho\} .$$

The domain D of (8) is expressed as

$$D = \bigcap_{1 \leqq i < j \leqq n} D_{ij}$$

and $x \in \partial D$ implies $x \in \bigcap_{(i,j) \in L} \partial D_{ij}$, where

$$L = L_x = \{(i,j) : 1 \leqq i < j \leqq n, \ |x_i - x_j| = \rho\} .$$

Obviously, if $x \in \bar{D}$ then $x \in \partial D$ is equivalent to $L_x \neq \phi$. For $(i,j) \in L_x$ we define a unit vector n_{ij} in $\mathbf{R}^{nd}$ by

$$n_{ij} = \{0, \cdots, 0, \underset{(i\text{—th})}{\frac{x_i - x_j}{\sqrt{2}\rho}}, 0, \cdots, 0, \underset{(j\text{—th})}{\frac{x_j - x_i}{\sqrt{2}\rho}}, 0, \cdots, 0\} ,$$

let $\alpha (0 \leqq \alpha < 1)$ be the constant appearing in Proposition 2.1 and set

$$r_0 = \rho \sqrt{\frac{1-\alpha^2}{2}} .$$

Proposition 3.1. *The domain D satisfies Condition (A) with* $r_0 = \rho \sqrt{\frac{1-\alpha^2}{2}}$, *and for any* $x \in \partial D$

$$\mathcal{N}_x = \{n = \sum_{(i,j) \in L} c_{ij} n_{ij} : c_{ij} \geqq 0, \ |n| = 1\} . \tag{3.1}$$

Lemma 3.1. (i) $B(x - 2^{-1/2} \rho n_{ij}, 2^{-1/2} \rho) \cap D_{ij} = \phi$, $x \in \partial D_{ij}$.
(ii) $B(x - 2^{-1/2} \rho n_{ij}, 2^{-1/2} \rho) \cap D = \phi$ *for any* $(i,j) \in L_x$, $x \in \partial D$, *that is,* $n_{ij} \in$

$\mathcal{N}_{x,2^{-1/2}\rho}$ *for any* $(i,j)\in L_x$.

Proof. Since (ii) follows immediately from (i), it is enough to prove (i). We set

$$\boldsymbol{y}=\boldsymbol{x}-2^{-1/2}\rho\boldsymbol{n}_{ij}\,,$$

that is,

$$y_k=\begin{cases}(x_i+x_j)/2 & \text{for}\quad k=i,j\,,\\ x_k & \text{for}\quad k\neq i,j\,.\end{cases}$$

Then for any $\boldsymbol{z}\in B(\boldsymbol{y},2^{-1/2}\rho)$ we have

$$\begin{aligned}|z_i-z_j|&\leqq|z_i-y_i|+|y_i-y_j|+|y_j-z_j|\\&=|z_i-y_i|+|z_j-y_j|\leqq\sqrt{2}\,|\boldsymbol{z}-\boldsymbol{y}|<\rho\,,\end{aligned}$$

and hence $\boldsymbol{z}\notin D_{ij}$, completing the proof.

Lemma 3.2. *Let* $\mathcal{N}'_x$ *be the right-hand side of* (3.1). *Then*

$$\mathcal{N}'_x\subset\mathcal{N}_{x,r_0},\quad \boldsymbol{x}\in\partial D\,.$$

Proof. By Remark 1.1 it is enough to prove that for any $\boldsymbol{n}\in\mathcal{N}'_x$

$$\langle\boldsymbol{y}-\boldsymbol{x},\boldsymbol{n}\rangle+\frac{1}{2r_0}|\boldsymbol{x}-\boldsymbol{y}|^2\geqq0,\quad \forall\boldsymbol{y}\in\bar{D}\,.$$

Let $\boldsymbol{l}=\boldsymbol{l}_x$ be the unit vector appearing in Proposition 2.1. Then by Proposition 2.1

$$C(\boldsymbol{x},\boldsymbol{l},\alpha)\cap B(\boldsymbol{x},\delta)\subset\bar{D}$$

from which it follows that

$$\boldsymbol{x}-\mathcal{N}_x\subset C(\boldsymbol{x},\boldsymbol{l},\alpha)^*\,, \tag{3.2}$$

where $C(\boldsymbol{x},\boldsymbol{l},\alpha)^*$ is the *dual cone* of $C(\boldsymbol{x},\boldsymbol{l},\alpha)$, that is,

$$\begin{aligned}C(\boldsymbol{x},\boldsymbol{l},\alpha)^*&=\{\boldsymbol{z}\in\boldsymbol{R}^{nd}:\langle\boldsymbol{z}-\boldsymbol{x},\boldsymbol{y}-\boldsymbol{x}\rangle\leqq0,\ \forall\boldsymbol{y}\in C(\boldsymbol{x},\boldsymbol{l},\alpha)\}\\&=\{\boldsymbol{z}\in\boldsymbol{R}^{nd}:\langle\boldsymbol{z}-\boldsymbol{x},-\boldsymbol{l}\rangle\geqq\sqrt{1-\alpha^2}\,|\boldsymbol{z}-\boldsymbol{x}|\}\,.\end{aligned}$$

From (ii) of Lemma 3.1 and (3.2)

$$\boldsymbol{x}-\boldsymbol{n}_{ij}\in C(\boldsymbol{x},\boldsymbol{l},\alpha)^*,\quad \forall(i,j)\in L_x\,,$$

and hence

$$\langle\boldsymbol{n}_{ij},\boldsymbol{l}\rangle\geqq\sqrt{1-\alpha^2},\quad \forall(i,j)\in L_x\,. \tag{3.3}$$

Now let $\boldsymbol{n}\in\mathcal{N}'_{\boldsymbol{x}}$ be expressed as

$$\boldsymbol{n}=\sum_{(i,j)\in L} c_{ij}\,\boldsymbol{n}_{ij}, \quad c_{ij}\geqq 0 .$$

Then by (3.3)

$$1\geqq\langle\boldsymbol{n},\boldsymbol{l}\rangle=\sum_{(i,j)\in L} c_{ij}\langle\boldsymbol{n}_{ij},\boldsymbol{l}\rangle\geqq\sqrt{1-\alpha^2}\sum_{(i,j)\in L} c_{ij}$$

and hence

$$\frac{1}{2r_0}=\frac{1}{\sqrt{2}\,\rho\sqrt{1-\alpha^2}}\geqq\frac{1}{\sqrt{2}\,\rho}\sum_{(i,j)\in L} c_{ij} .$$

Therefore, for any $\boldsymbol{y}\in\bar{D}$

$$\begin{aligned}&\langle\boldsymbol{y}-\boldsymbol{x},\boldsymbol{n}\rangle+\frac{1}{2r_0}|\boldsymbol{x}-\boldsymbol{y}|^2\\ &\geqq\sum_{(i,j)\in L} c_{ij}\langle\boldsymbol{y}-\boldsymbol{x},\boldsymbol{n}_{ij}\rangle+\frac{1}{\sqrt{2}\,\rho}\sum_{(i,j)\in L} c_{ij}|\boldsymbol{x}-\boldsymbol{y}|^2\\ &=\sum_{(i,j)\in L} c_{ij}\{\langle\boldsymbol{y}-\boldsymbol{x},\boldsymbol{n}_{ij}\rangle+\frac{1}{\sqrt{2}\,\rho}|\boldsymbol{x}-\boldsymbol{y}|^2\}\geqq 0\end{aligned}$$

by (ii) of Lemma 3.1 and Remark 1.1. The proof of Lemma 3.2 is finished.

Lemma 3.3. *For any* $\varepsilon(0<\varepsilon<1)$ *and* $\boldsymbol{x}\in\partial D$ *there exists* $\delta'>0$ *such that*

$$\{\bigcap_{(i,j)\in L} C_{ij}(\boldsymbol{x},\varepsilon)\}\cap B(\boldsymbol{x},\delta')\subset D\cup\{\boldsymbol{x}\} ,$$

where

$$C_{ij}(\boldsymbol{x},\varepsilon)=\{\boldsymbol{y}\in\boldsymbol{R}^{nd}\colon\langle\boldsymbol{y}-\boldsymbol{x},\boldsymbol{n}_{ij}\rangle\geqq\varepsilon|\boldsymbol{y}-\boldsymbol{x}|\},\ (i,j)\in L .$$

Proof. Let $\boldsymbol{y}\in C_{ij}(\boldsymbol{y},\varepsilon)$, $\boldsymbol{y}\neq\boldsymbol{x}$. Then $\boldsymbol{y}$ can be expressed as

$$\boldsymbol{y}=\boldsymbol{x}+\boldsymbol{z},\quad\langle\boldsymbol{z},\boldsymbol{n}_{ij}\rangle\geqq\varepsilon|\boldsymbol{z}|>0 ,$$

and hence

$$\begin{aligned}|y_i-y_j|^2&=|x_i-x_j|^2+2\langle x_i-x_j,z_i-z_j\rangle+|z_i-z_j|^2\\ &\geqq\rho^2+2\langle z_i-z_j,x_i-x_j\rangle>\rho^2 ,\end{aligned}$$

because

$$\begin{aligned}0<\langle\boldsymbol{z},\boldsymbol{n}_{ij}\rangle&=\frac{1}{\sqrt{2}\,\rho}\langle z_i,x_i-x_j\rangle+\frac{1}{\sqrt{2}\,\rho}\langle z_j,x_j-x_i\rangle\\ &=\frac{1}{\sqrt{2}\,\rho}\langle z_i-z_j,x_i-x_j\rangle .\end{aligned}$$

Therefore $C_{ij}(\boldsymbol{x}, \varepsilon) \subset D_{ij} \cup \{\boldsymbol{x}\}$, and hence

$$\bigcap_{(i,j)\in L} C_{ij}(\boldsymbol{x}, \varepsilon) \subset \{\bigcap_{(i,j)\in L} D_{ij}\} \cup \{\boldsymbol{x}\} . \tag{3.4}$$

Since $|x_i - x_j| > \rho$ for any $(i, j) \notin L_x$, there exists $\delta' > 0$ such that for any $\boldsymbol{y} \in B(\boldsymbol{x}, \delta')$

$$|y_i - y_j| > \rho \quad \text{for any} \quad (i, j) \notin L_x .$$

This combined with (3.4) implies

$$\{\bigcap_{(i,j)\in L} C_{ij}(\boldsymbol{x}, \varepsilon)\} \cap B(\boldsymbol{x}, \delta') \subset D \cup \{\boldsymbol{x}\} .$$

The proof of the lemma is finished.

Proof of Proposition 3.1. We make use of Lemma 3.3 and then Corollary in [1: p. 11] to obtain

$$\boldsymbol{x} - \mathcal{N}_x \subset \{\bigcap_{(i,j)\in L} C_{ij}(\boldsymbol{x}, \varepsilon)\}^* = \overline{\sum_{(i,j)\in L} C_{ij}(\boldsymbol{x}, \varepsilon)^*} ,$$

where Σ means the vector sum. Thus

$$\boldsymbol{x} - \mathcal{N}_x \subset \bigcap_{0<\varepsilon<1} \{\overline{\sum_{(i,j)\in L} C_{ij}(\boldsymbol{x}, \varepsilon)^*}\} .$$

But the right-hand side of the above is the convex cone with vertex $\boldsymbol{x}$ spanned by $\{\boldsymbol{x} - \boldsymbol{n}_{ij}, (i, j) \in L_x\}$, so we have

$$\mathcal{N}_x \subset \mathcal{N}'_x ,$$

which combined with Lemma 3.2 implies

$$\mathcal{N}_x = \mathcal{N}_{x,r_0} = \mathcal{N}'_x .$$

This means that Proposition 3.1 holds.

4. Mutually reflecting Brownian balls

Since the domain D satisfies Conditions (A) and (B′) (and hence (B) by Remark 1.2), Theorem 1.1 guarantees the existence and uniqueness of the solution of Skorohod's equation for D:

$$\xi(t) = w(t) + \int_0^t \boldsymbol{n}(s)\, d\phi(s) , \tag{4.1}$$

where $w = (w_1, \cdots, w_n)$, $w_k \in W$, $1 \leqq k \leqq n$, and $|w_i(0) - w_j(0)| \geqq \rho$, $1 \leqq i < j \leqq n$. A solution of (4.1) is a pair (ξ, ϕ) of functions satisfying (4.1), (1.2), (1.3) and (1.4). The component-wise expression of (4.1) is

(4.2) $$\xi_k(t)=w_k(t)+\int_0^t n_k(s)\,d\phi(s),\quad 1\leqq k\leqq n\,.$$

In this section we prove the following theorem by showing that (4.2) is equivalent to the equation

(2) $$\xi_k(t)=w_k(t)+\sum_{j=1(\neq k)}^{n}\int_0^t(\xi_k(s)-\xi_j(s))\,d\phi_{kj}(s),\quad 1\leqq k\leqq n\,.$$

Theorem 4.1. *There exists a unique solution of Skorohod's equation* (2) *for the motion of mutually reflecting Brownian balls.*

Proof. By Proposition 3.1 we have

(4.3a) $$\boldsymbol{n}(s)=\sum_{1\leqq i<j\leqq n}c_{ij}(s)\,\boldsymbol{n}_{ij}(\xi(s))\,,$$

(4.3b) $$\boldsymbol{n}_{ij}(\xi(s))=(0,\cdots,0,\underset{(i\text{—th})}{\frac{\xi_i(s)-\xi_j(s)}{\sqrt{2}\rho}},0,\cdots,0,\underset{(j\text{—th})}{\frac{\xi_j(s)-\xi_i(s)}{\sqrt{2}\rho}},0,\cdots,0)\,,$$

(4.3c) $$c_{ij}(s)\geqq 0,\quad 1\leqq i<j\leqq n\,,$$

(4.3d) $$c_{ij}(s)=0\quad\text{for}\quad (i,j)\notin L_{\xi(s)}\,.$$

The component-wise expression of $\boldsymbol{n}(s)$ is

$$n_k(s)=\sum_{j:j>k}c_{kj}(s)\frac{\xi_k(s)-\xi_j(s)}{\sqrt{2}\rho}+\sum_{i:i<k}c_{ik}(s)\frac{\xi_k(s)-\xi_i(s)}{\sqrt{2}\rho}\,.$$

Therefore if we define $c_{ij}(s)$ for $i>j$ by $c_{ij}(s)=c_{ji}(s)$, then we have

$$n_k(s)=\sum_{j:j\neq k}c_{kj}(s)\frac{\xi_k(s)-\xi_j(s)}{\sqrt{2}\rho}\,,$$

and hence

$$\xi_k(t)=w_k(t)+\sum_{j:j\neq k}\int_0^t c_{kj}(s)\frac{\xi_k(s)-\xi_j(s)}{\sqrt{2}\rho}\,d\phi(s)\,.$$

So if we set

$$\phi_{kj}(t)=\frac{1}{\sqrt{2}\rho}\int_0^t c_{kj}(s)\,d\phi(s)\,,$$

we have

(4.4) $$\phi_{kj}(t)=\phi_{jk}(t)\,,$$

$$\phi_{kj}(t) = \int_0^t \mathbf{1}_\rho(|\xi_k(s)-\xi_j(s)|)\, d\phi_{kj}(s)\,, \tag{4.5}$$

because $\phi_{kj}(t)$ can increase only when $|\xi_k(t)-\xi_j(t)|=\rho$ by (4.3d). Thus (4.1) finally yields (2). Recalling (3.1), we see easily that (2) also implies (4.1) with

$$\boldsymbol{n}(t) = \sum_{1\leqq i<j\leqq n} a_{ij}(t)\, \boldsymbol{n}_{ij}(\xi(t))/|\sum_{1\leqq i<j\leqq n} a_{ij}(t)\, \boldsymbol{n}_{ij}(\xi(t))|\,,$$

$$d\phi(t) = \sqrt{2}\,\rho\,|\sum_{1\leqq i<j\leqq n} a_{ij}(t)\, \boldsymbol{n}_{ij}(\xi(t))|\, d\bar{\phi}(t)\,,$$

where $\bar{\phi}(t)=\sum_{1\leqq i<j\leqq n} \phi_{ij}(t)$ and $a_{ij}(t)$ is the Radon-Nikodym derivative of $d\phi_{ij}(t)$ with respect to $d\bar{\phi}(t)$. The proof of Theorem 4.1 is finished.

5. Skorohod's SDE for mutually reflecting diffusion balls

Let $B_i(t)$, $1\leqq i\leqq n$, be independent d-dimensional $\mathcal{F}_t$-Brownian motions with $B_i(0)=0$ defined on a probability space $(\Omega, \mathcal{F}, P)$ with a filtration $\{\mathcal{F}_t\}_{t\geqq 0}$. We assume that each $\mathcal{F}_t$ contains all P-null sets and $\mathcal{F}_t=\bigcap_{\varepsilon>0}\mathcal{F}_{t+\varepsilon}$. Given the coefficients

$$\sigma\colon \boldsymbol{R}^d \to \boldsymbol{R}^d\otimes\boldsymbol{R}^d, \quad b\colon \boldsymbol{R}^d \to \boldsymbol{R}^d\,,$$

we consider the following Skorohod's SDE for mutually reflecting diffusion balls:

$$\begin{aligned} dX_i(t) &= \sigma(X_i(t))\, dB_i(t)+b(X_i(t))\, dt \\ &\quad + \sum_{j=1(\neq i)}^{n} (X_i(t)-X_j(t))\, d\Phi_{ij}(t), \quad 1\leqq i\leqq n\,, \end{aligned} \tag{5.1}$$

where the initial values are assumed to be $\mathcal{F}_0$-measurable random variables satisfying $|X_i(0)-X_j(0)|>\rho$, $1\leqq i<j\leqq n$. The solution $X_i(t)$, $1\leqq i\leqq n$, should be found under the following conditions.

(5.2) $X_i(t)$'s are $\mathcal{F}_t$-adapted continuous processes with $|X_i(t)-X_j(t)|\geqq\rho$, $1\leqq i<j\leqq n$, $t\geqq 0$.

(5.3) $\Phi_{ij}(t)$'s are $\mathcal{F}_t$-adapted continuous non-decreasing processes with $\Phi_{ij}(0) = 0$, $\Phi_{ij}(t) = \Phi_{ji}(t)$ and

$$\Phi_{ij}(t) = \int_0^t \mathbf{1}_\rho(|X_i(s)-X_j(s)|)\, d\Phi_{ij}(s)\,.$$

In this section we prove the following theorem.

Theorem 5.1. *Suppose σ and b are bounded and Lipschitz continuous. Then there exists a unique strong solution of* (5.1).

Proof. Let

$$D=\{\boldsymbol{x}=(x_1,\cdots,x_n)\in\boldsymbol{R}^{nd}:\ |x_i-x_j|>\rho,\ 1\leqq i<j\leqq n\}\,,$$

and for $\boldsymbol{x}=(x_1,\cdots,x_n)\in\boldsymbol{R}^{nd}$ set

$$\boldsymbol{\sigma}(\boldsymbol{x})=\begin{bmatrix}\sigma(x_1) & & & 0\\ & \sigma(x_2) & & \\ & & \ddots & \\ 0 & & & \sigma(x_n)\end{bmatrix},\quad \boldsymbol{b}(\boldsymbol{x})=\begin{bmatrix}b(x_1)\\ \vdots\\ b(x_n)\end{bmatrix}.$$

Then as in **4** the SDE (5.1) can be regarded as Skorohod's SDE for D

(5.4) $$d\boldsymbol{X}(t)=\boldsymbol{\sigma}(\boldsymbol{X}(t))\,d\boldsymbol{B}(t)+\boldsymbol{b}(\boldsymbol{X}(t))\,dt+\boldsymbol{n}(t)\,d\Phi(t)\,,$$

where $\boldsymbol{B}(t)$ is an nd-dimensional $\mathcal{F}_t$-Brownian motion. The solution $\boldsymbol{X}(t)$ is to be found under the following conditions.

(5.5) $\boldsymbol{X}(t)$ is a $\bar{D}$-valued continuous process.

(5.6) $\boldsymbol{n}(t)\in\mathcal{N}_{\boldsymbol{X}(t)}$ if $\boldsymbol{X}(t)\in\partial D$.

(5.7) $\Phi(t)$ is a continuous non-decreasing process and

$$\Phi(t)=\int_0^t \mathbf{1}_{\partial D}(\boldsymbol{X}(s))\,d\Phi(s)\,.$$

But since D satisfies Conditions (A) and (B), it follows immediately from Theorem 5.1 in [6] that the Skorohod's SDE (5.4) has a unique strong solution. The proof is finished.

References

[1] W. Fenchel: Convex cones, sets, and functions, Lecture notes, Princeton Univ., 1953.

[2] H. Frankowska: *A viability approach to the Skorohod problem,* Stochastics **14** (1985), 227–244.

[3] N. Ikeda and S. Watanabe: Stochastic differential equations and diffusion processes, North Holland-Kodansha, Amsterdam-Tokyo, 1981.

[4] P.L. Lions and A.S. Sznitman: *Stochastic differential equations with reflecting boundary conditions,* Comm. Pure Appl. Math. **37** (1984), 511–537.

[5] H.P. McKean: Stochastic integrals, Academic Press, New York, 1969.

[6] Y. Saisho: *Stochastic differential equations for multi-dimensional domain with reflecting boundary,* to appear in Probab. Th. Rel. Fields.

[7] A.V. Skorohod: *Stochastic equations for diffusion processes in a bounded region* 1, 2, Theor. Veroyatnost. i Primenen. **6** (1961), 264–274; **7** (1962), 3–23.

[8] H. Tanaka: *Stochastic differential equations with reflecting boundary condition in*

convex regions, Hiroshima Math. J. **9** (1979), 163–177.

Department of Mathematics
Faculty of Science and Technology
Keio University
Kohokuku, Yokohama 223
Japan

LIMIT DISTRIBUTION FOR 1-DIMENSIONAL DIFFUSION IN A REFLECTED BROWNIAN MEDIUM

By H. Tanaka

Introduction

In analogy with Sinai's problem [8] on a random walk in a random medium, Brox [1] considered the diffusion process $X(t)$ described by the stochastic differential equation

$$(1) \qquad dX(t) = dB(t) - \frac{1}{2} W'(X(t))dt , \quad X(0) = 0 ,$$

where $\{W(x), x \in \mathbb{R}\}$ is a Brownian medium independent of another Brownian motion $B(t)$, and proved that $(\log t)^{-2}X(t)$ converges in distribution as $t \to \infty$. Similar results in the case of a considerably wider class of self-similar random media were obtained by Schumacher [7]. Recently Kesten [5] obtained the exact form of the limit distribution for Sinai's random walk as well as for a diffusion in a Brownian medium. See also [2] for a related problem.

In this paper we substitute $W(x)$ in (1) by a nonnegative reflected Brownian medium and find the corresponding limit distribution. The result was already anounced in [9] without proof but the Laplace transform of the limit distribution given in [9: §3] is not correct. We give here a full proof to the whole result of [9: §3] with a correction (see Theorem 1 and 2 below). Our method is similar to that of [1].

Theorem 1. Let $X(t)$ be a solution of (1) where $W_+ = \{W(x), x \geq 0\}$ and $W_- = \{W(-x), x \geq 0\}$ are independent reflected Brownian motions on the half line $[0, \infty)$ starting from 0 which are also independent of the Brownian motion $B(t)$. Then the distribution of $(\log t)^{-2}X(t)$ converges as $t \to \infty$ to the distribution μ defined by

$$(2) \qquad \mu = \int m_W Q(dW)$$

where m_W is the probability measure on $\mathbb{R}$ defined by (3.1) and Q is the probability measure on the space of media $\mathbb{W} = C(\mathbb{R} \to [0,\infty)) \cap \{W: W(0)=0\}$ such that $W_\pm$ are independent reflected Brownian motions on $[0, \infty)$.

Theorem 2. μ has a symmetric density and for $\lambda > 0$

$$(3) \qquad \int_0^\infty e^{-\lambda x} \mu(dx) = \int_0^\infty \frac{\sinh\sqrt{2\lambda}}{\sqrt{2\lambda}\cosh\sqrt{2\lambda} + t\sinh\sqrt{2\lambda}} \cdot \frac{dt}{(1+t)^2} .$$

The present case is not contained in the framework of [7] since the nonnegative reflected medium $W(x)$ has (uncountably) many points giving its minimum. The case of a nonpositive reflected Brownian medium was discussed in [9]. Some generalizations will be discussed in [5].

Acknowledgment. I wish to thank Professor H.Kesten for pointing out mistakes of the first version of this paper.

§1. Preliminaries and exit times from valleys

Let $\mathbb{W}$ and Q be defined as in Theorem 1. For each $W \in \mathbb{W}$ solutions of the stochastic differential equation (1) define a diffusion process in $\mathbb{R}$ with generator

$$(1.1) \qquad \frac{1}{2} e^{W(x)} \frac{d}{dx}\left(e^{-W(x)} \frac{d}{dx}\right) .$$

Such a diffusion can be constructed from a Brownian motion $B(t)$[1] as follows ([4]). Let Ω be the space of continuous functions $\omega : [0, \infty) \to \mathbb{R}$ with $\omega(0) = 0$, and denote by P the Wiener measure on Ω. Denote the value of ω at time t by $\omega(t)$ or by $B(t)$ and put

$$L(t,x) = \lim_{\varepsilon \downarrow 0} \frac{1}{\varepsilon} \int_0^t \mathbb{I}_{[x,x+\varepsilon)}(B(s))ds \qquad \text{(local time)},$$

$$S(x) = \int_0^x e^{W(y)} dy ,$$

$$A(t) = \int_0^t e^{-2W(S^{-1}(B(s)))} ds = \int_{\mathbb{R}} e^{-2W(S^{-1}(x))} L(t,x)dx , \quad t \geq 0 ,$$

S^{-1}, A^{-1} = the inverse functions .

Then the process $X(t, W) = S^{-1}(B(A^{-1}(t)))$ defined on the probability space (Ω, P) is a diffusion process with generator (1.1) starting at 0. If we set $(W^x)(\cdot) = W(\cdot + x)$, then $X^x(t, W) = x + X(t, W^x)$ is a diffusion process with generator (1.1) starting at x. Let

$$T(x_1, x_2) = \inf \{t \geq 0 : B(t) \notin (x_1, x_2)\} ,$$

1) The Brownian motion here is not the same as the one in (1) but we use the same notation $B(t)$.

$$L(x_1, x_2, x) = L(T(x_1, x_2), x) , \quad x \in \mathbb{R} ,$$

$$S_\lambda(x) = \int_0^x e^{\lambda W(y)} dy ,$$

$$X_\lambda(t) = X(t, \lambda W) , \quad X_\lambda^x(t) = x + X(t, \lambda W^x) .$$

Next we define a valley. Given $W \in \mathbb{W}$, a quartet $V = (a, b_1, b_2, c)$ is called a valley of W if

(i) $a < b_1 < 0 < b_2 < c$,

(ii) $W(b_1) = W(b_2) = 0$, $W(a) = W(c) = D$,

(iii) $0 < W(x) < W(a)$ for $a < x < b_1$,

$0 < W(x) < W(c)$ for $b_2 < x < c$,

(iv) $A_- = \sup \{W(y) - W(x) : a < x < y < b_2\} < D$,

$A_+ = \sup \{W(x) - W(y) : b_1 < x < y < c\} < D$.

We call D (resp. $A = A_- \vee A_+$ [2)]) the depth (resp. the inner directed ascent) of V. It is clear that there exist valleys of W with $A < 1 < D$ for almost all reflected Brownian media W .

In what follows let $W \in \mathbb{W}$ be given and $V = (a, b_1, b_2, c)$ be a valley of W with the depth D and the inner directed ascent A . We put

$$T_\lambda^x = T_\lambda^x(a, c) = \inf \{t \geq 0 : X_\lambda^x(t) \notin (a, c)\} .$$

The following three lemmas were proved in [1] .

Lemma 1. For $a < x < c$

$$T_\lambda^x(a, c) \overset{d}{=} \int_a^c L(\hat{S}_\lambda(a), \hat{S}_\lambda(c), \hat{S}_\lambda(y)) e^{-\lambda W(y)} dy ,$$

where

$$\hat{S}_\lambda(y) = \int_x^y e^{\lambda W(z)} dz$$

and $\overset{d}{=}$ means the equality in distribution.

Lemma 2. For each $\lambda > 0$

$$\{L(\lambda x_1, \lambda x_2, \lambda x), x \in \mathbb{R}\} \overset{d}{=} \{\lambda L(x_1, x_2, x), x \in \mathbb{R}\}.$$

2) $a \vee b = \max \{a, b\}$, $a \wedge b = \min \{a, b\}$.

Lemma 3. For $\lambda > 0$ and $W \in \mathbb{W}$

$$\{X(t, \lambda W_\lambda), t \geq 0\} \overset{d}{=} \{\lambda^{-2} X(\lambda^4 t, W), t \geq 0\} , \tag{1.2}$$

where W_λ ($\in \mathbb{W}$) is defined by

$$W_\lambda(x) = \lambda^{-1} W(\lambda^2 x) , \quad x \in \mathbb{R} .$$

The following lemma plays an essential role in our discussions.

Lemma 4. For any $\lambda > 0$ and $[u, v] \subset (a, c)$

$$\inf_{u \leq x \leq v} P\left\{e^{\lambda(D-\delta)} < T_\lambda^x < e^{\lambda(D+\delta)}\right\} \to 1 , \quad \lambda \to \infty .$$

Proof. The proof is similar to that of the corresponding lemma of [1] but even much simpler. Let $x \in [u, v]$ be fixed. Setting

$$s_\lambda(y) = \hat{S}_\lambda(y)/\hat{S}_\lambda(c) = \int_x^y e^{\lambda W(z)} dz \Big/ \!\! \Big/ \int_x^c e^{\lambda W(z)} dz$$

and applying Lemma 1 and 2, we have

$$T_\lambda^x \overset{d}{=} \hat{S}_\lambda(c) \int_a^c L(s_\lambda(a), 1, s_\lambda(y)) e^{-\lambda W(y)} dy .$$

Since

$$\hat{S}_\lambda(c) \leq (c - x) \exp\left\{\lambda \max_{[x,c]} W\right\} \quad {}^{3)}$$

$$T_\lambda^x \overset{d}{\leq} (c - x)(c - a) \exp\left\{\lambda \max_{[x,c]} W - \lambda \min_{[a,c]} W\right\} L' \leq (c - a)^2 L' e^{\lambda D},$$

$$L' = \max_{y \leq 1} L(-\infty, 1, y) ,$$

we have

$$\begin{aligned} & P\left\{T_\lambda^x > e^{\lambda(D+\delta)}\right\} \\ & \leq P\left\{(c - a)^2 L' e^{\lambda D} > e^{\lambda(D+\delta)}\right\} \\ & = P\left\{L' > e^{\lambda\delta}/(c - a)^2\right\} \to 0 , \quad \lambda \to \infty . \end{aligned}$$

To obtain an estimate from below first we notice that

$$\lim_{\lambda \to \infty} \lambda^{-1} \log C_\lambda = D , \tag{1.3}$$

3) $\max_I W = \max\{W(x), x \in I\}$, $\min_I W = \min\{W(x), x \in I\}$.

where

$$C_\lambda = |\hat{S}_\lambda(a)| \wedge |\hat{S}_\lambda(c)| ,$$

and the convergence is uniform in $x \in [u, v]$. Next, for given $\delta > 0$ we set

$$a_1 = \sup\{x < b_1 : W(x) = \delta/4\} ,$$
$$\hat{s}_\lambda(y) = \hat{S}_\lambda(y)/C_\lambda ,$$
$$L_\lambda = \min\{L(-1, 1, y) : \hat{s}_\lambda(a_1) \le y \le \hat{s}_\lambda(b_1)\} .$$

Then applying Lemma 1 and 2 we have

$$T_\lambda^x \overset{d}{=} C_\lambda \int_a^c L(\hat{s}_\lambda(a), \hat{s}_\lambda(c), \hat{s}_\lambda(y)) e^{-\lambda W(y)} dy$$

$$\ge C_\lambda \int_{a_1}^{b_1} L(-1, 1, \hat{s}_\lambda(y)) e^{-\lambda W(y)} dy$$

$$\ge e^{\lambda(D-\frac{\delta}{4})} (b_1 - a_1) L_\lambda \exp\left\{-\lambda \max_{[a_1, b_1]} W\right\}$$

$$= (b_1 - a_1) L_\lambda e^{\lambda(D-\frac{\delta}{2})} .$$

Since $\lambda^{-1}\log|\hat{s}_\lambda(a_1)|$ and $\lambda^{-1}\log|\hat{s}_\lambda(b_1)|$ converges to $\max\limits_{[x\wedge a_1, x\vee a_1]} W - D$, $\max\limits_{[x\wedge b_1, x\vee b_1]} W - D$, respectively, which are both negative, we have

$$\lim_{\lambda\to\infty} \hat{s}_\lambda(a_1) = \lim_{\lambda\to\infty} \hat{s}_\lambda(b_1) = 0 ,$$

the convergence being uniform in $x \in [u, v]$. Therefore

$$P\left\{T_\lambda^x < e^{\lambda(D-\delta)}\right\} \le P\left\{L_\lambda < (b_1 - a_1)^{-1} e^{-\lambda\delta/2}\right\} \to 0 , \quad \lambda \to \infty$$

uniformly in $x \in [u, v]$, because $\lim\limits_{\lambda\to\infty} L_\lambda = L(-1, 1, 0) > 0$.

§2. The limit distribution of $X(e^{\lambda r}, \lambda W)$

In this section we change the notation slightly. Given $W \in \mathbb{W}$ and a valley $V = (a, b_1, b_2, c)$ of W , we set

$$\Omega = C([0, \infty) \to \mathbb{R}) ,$$
$$\hat{\Omega} = C([0, \infty) \to [a, c]) ,$$

and denote by P_λ^x , $x \in \mathbb{R}$ (resp. $\hat{P}_\lambda^y$, $y \in [a, c]$) the probability measure on Ω (resp. $\hat{\Omega}$) induced by the diffusion process with generator

$$\frac{1}{2}e^{\lambda W(x)}\frac{d}{dx}(e^{-\lambda W(x)}\frac{d}{dx}) \tag{2.1}$$

(resp. the diffusion process on $[a, c]$ with (local) generator (2.1) and with reflecting barriers at a and c). The latter diffusion has the invariant probability measure m_λ given by

$$m_\lambda(dy) = e^{-\lambda W(y)}dy \Big/ \int_a^c e^{-\lambda W(z)}dz .$$

For any interval $[u, v] \subset [a, c]$

$$m_\lambda([u, v]) = \frac{\int_0^\infty e^{-\lambda\xi} K([u, v], \xi)d\xi}{\int_0^\infty e^{-\lambda\xi} K([a, c], \xi)d\xi}$$

where, for an interval I in $\mathbb{R}$, $K(I, \xi)$ is the local time at ξ for the reflected Brownian medium, i.e.,

$$K(I, \xi) = \lim_{\varepsilon\downarrow 0}\frac{1}{\varepsilon}\int_I \mathbb{1}_{[\xi,\xi+\varepsilon)}(W(s))ds . \tag{2.2}$$

Therefore

$$m_\lambda([u, v]) = \frac{\int_0^\infty e^{-\xi} K([u, v], \lambda^{-1}\xi)d\xi}{\int_0^\infty e^{-\xi} K([a, c], \lambda^{-1}\xi)d\xi} \tag{2.3}$$

$$\longrightarrow \frac{K([u, v], 0)}{K([a, c], 0)} \equiv m([u, v]) , \quad \lambda \to \infty .$$

Next we set

$$\hat{P}_\lambda = \int_a^b m_\lambda(dy)\hat{P}^y_\lambda , \quad \mathbb{P}^{x,y}_\lambda = P^x_\lambda \otimes \hat{P}^y_\lambda , \quad \mathbb{P}^x_\lambda = P^x_\lambda \otimes \hat{P}_\lambda .$$

$$R = R(\omega, \hat{\omega}) = \inf\{t \geq 0 : \omega(t) = \hat{\omega}(t)\} .$$

Lemma 5. For any $\delta > 0$

$$\lim_{\lambda\to\infty} \mathbb{P}^0_\lambda\left\{R < e^{\lambda(A+\delta)}\right\} = 1 .$$

Proof. First we prove that

$$\lim_{\lambda\to\infty} \mathbb{P}^x_\lambda\left\{R < e^{\lambda(A+\delta)}\right\} = 1 \quad \text{holds for } x = b_1 \text{ and } b_2 . \tag{2.4}$$

Without loss of generality we may consider the case $x = b_2$. We write b instead of b_2 for simplicity. For any $\delta > 0$ such that $A + \delta < D$ we define $a_1 \in (a, b_1)$, $a_2 \in (a, b_1)$, $c_2 \in (b_2, c)$ by

$$a_1 = \max\left\{x < b_1 : W(x) = A + \frac{\delta}{4}\right\},$$

$$a_2 = \max\left\{x < b_1 : W(x) = A + \frac{\delta}{2}\right\},$$

$$c_2 = \min\left\{x > b_2 : W(x) = A + \frac{\delta}{2}\right\},$$

and set

$$T_0 = T_0(\omega) = \inf\left\{t \geq 0 : w(t) = a_1\right\},$$

$$T_1 = T_1(\omega) = \inf\left\{t \geq 0 : w(t) \notin (a_1, c_2)\right\},$$

$$T_2 = T_2(\omega) = \inf\left\{t \geq 0 : w(t) \notin (a_2, c_2)\right\}.$$

Then we can prove easily that

$$(2.5) \qquad P_\lambda^b\left\{T_0 < \infty\right\} \geq P_\lambda^b\left\{T_0 = T_1\right\} = \frac{S_\lambda(c_2) - S_\lambda(b)}{S_\lambda(c_2) - S_\lambda(a_1)} \to 1, \quad \lambda \to \infty,$$

and hence

$$(2.6) \qquad \mathbb{P}_\lambda^b\left\{R \leq T_0\right\}$$
$$\geq \mathbb{P}_\lambda^b\left\{\hat{\omega}(0) \in [a, b], \hat{\omega}(T_0) \in [a_1, c]\right\}$$
$$\geq \mathbb{P}_\lambda^b\left\{\hat{\omega}(0) \in [a, b]\right\} + P_\lambda^b\left\{\hat{\omega}(T_0) \in [a_1, c]\right\} - 1$$
$$= m_\lambda([a, b]) + \int_0^\infty \hat{P}_\lambda\left\{\hat{\omega}(t) \in [a_1, c]\right\} P_\lambda^b\left\{T_0 \in dt\right\} - 1$$
$$\to 1, \quad \lambda \to \infty,$$

by (2.3) because $m(\{x \in (a, c) : W(x) = 0\}) = 1$. On the other hand Lemma 4 applied to the valley (a_2, b_1, b_2, c_2) whose depth is $A + (\delta/2)$ implies

$$(2.7) \qquad P_\lambda^b\left\{T_1 < e^{\lambda(A+\delta)}\right\} \geq P_\lambda^b\left\{T_2 < e^{\lambda(A+\delta)}\right\} \to 1, \quad \lambda \to \infty,$$

and so

$$\mathbb{P}_\lambda^x\left\{R < e^{\lambda(A+\delta)}\right\}$$
$$\geq P_\lambda^x\left\{T_0 < e^{\lambda(A+\delta)}\right\} - o(1) \qquad \text{(by (2.6))}$$
$$\geq P_\lambda^x\left\{T_1 < e^{\lambda(A+\delta)}, T_1 = T_0\right\} - o(1)$$

$$\geq P_{\lambda}^{x}\left\{T_1 < e^{\lambda(A+\delta)}\right\} - o(1) \qquad \text{(by (2.5))}$$

$$\longrightarrow 1 , \quad \text{as } \lambda \to \infty \qquad \text{(by (2.7))} .$$

Next , to consider the case where the diffusion starts at 0 we shall consider three diffusion processes starting at 0 , b_1 and b_2 , respectively. By making use of the comparison theorem in one-dimensional diffusion processes (for example, see [3: p.352]) we can construct, on a suitable probability space $(\widetilde{\Omega}_\lambda, \widetilde{P}_\lambda)$, three processes $\widetilde{X}_0(t)$, $\widetilde{X}_1(t)$ and $\widetilde{X}_2(t)$ such that the probability measure on Ω induced by $\widetilde{X}_0(t)$ (resp. $\widetilde{X}_1(t)$, $\widetilde{X}_2(t)$) coincides with P_λ^0 (resp. $P_\lambda^{b_1}$, $P_\lambda^{b_2}$) and

$$\text{(2.8)} \qquad \widetilde{X}_1(t) \leq \widetilde{X}_0(t) \leq \widetilde{X}_2(t) , \qquad \forall t \geq 0 , \quad \widetilde{P}_\lambda\text{-a.s.}$$

Put

$$\widetilde{\mathbb{P}}_\lambda = \widetilde{P}_\lambda \otimes \widehat{P}_\lambda ,$$

$$\widetilde{R}_i = \inf\left\{t \geq 0 : \widetilde{X}_i(t) = \widehat{\omega}(t)\right\} , \quad i = 0, 1, 2 .$$

Since $\widetilde{R}_0 \leq \widetilde{R}_1 \vee \widetilde{R}_2$ by (2.8), we have

$$\begin{aligned} P_\lambda^0\left\{R < e^{\lambda(A+\delta)}\right\} &= \widetilde{\mathbb{P}}_\lambda\left\{\widetilde{R}_0 < e^{\lambda(A+\delta)}\right\} \\ &\geq \widetilde{\mathbb{P}}_\lambda\left\{\widetilde{R}_1 \vee \widetilde{R}_2 < e^{\lambda(A+\delta)}\right\} \\ &\geq \mathbb{P}_\lambda^{b_1}\left\{R < e^{\lambda(A+\delta)}\right\} + \mathbb{P}^{b_2}\left\{R < e^{\lambda(A+\delta)}\right\} - 1 \\ &\longrightarrow 1 , \quad \lambda \to \infty \end{aligned}$$

by (2.4), completing the proof of Lemma 5.

<u>Lemma 6</u>. For any r_1 , r_2 with $A < r_1 < r_2 < D$ and for any interval $[u, v]$ in $\mathbb{R}$

$$\lim_{\lambda \to \infty} P_\lambda^0\left\{\omega(e^{\lambda r}) \in [u, v]\right\} = m([u, v] \cap [b_1, b_2])$$

uniformly in $r \in [r_1, r_2]$, where m is defined in (2.3).

Proof. Denote by T (resp. $\widehat{T}$) the exit time of (a, c) for $\omega(t)$ (resp. $\widehat{\omega}(t)$), and by T_R (resp. $\widehat{T}_R$) the exit time of (a, c) for $\omega(t)$ (resp. $\widehat{\omega}(t)$) after the collision time R . Since $m_\lambda(U) \to 1$ as $\lambda \to \infty$ for any open set U containing $\{x \in (a, c) : W(x) = 0\}$, it follows from Lemma 4 that

$$\widehat{P}_\lambda\left\{e^{\lambda(D-\delta)} < \widehat{T} < e^{\lambda(D+\delta)}\right\}$$

$$= \int_a^c m_\lambda(dx) P_\lambda^x \left\{ e^{\lambda(D-\delta)} < T < e^{\lambda(D+\delta)} \right\}$$

$$\longrightarrow 1 \ , \ \lambda \to \infty \ .$$

This combined with Lemma 5 implies

$$p_\lambda \ := \mathbb{P}_\lambda^0 \left\{ R < e^{\lambda r_1} < e^{\lambda r_2} < \widehat{T}_R \right\}$$

$$\geq \mathbb{P}_\lambda^0 \left\{ R < e^{\lambda r_1} < e^{\lambda r_2} < \widehat{T} \right\} \quad (\because \widehat{T} \leq \widehat{T}_R)$$

$$\longrightarrow 1 \ , \ \lambda \to \infty \ .$$

Therefore for $r \in [r_1, r_2]$

(2.9) $$P_\lambda^0 \left\{ \omega(e^{\lambda r}) \in [u, v] \right\}$$

$$\geq \mathbb{P}_\lambda^0 \left\{ R < e^{\lambda r_1}, \omega(e^{\lambda r}) \in [u, v], e^{\lambda r_2} < \widetilde{T}_R \right\}$$

$$= \mathbb{P}_\lambda^0 \left\{ R < e^{\lambda r_1}, \widehat{\omega}(e^{\lambda r}) \in [u, v], e^{\lambda r_2} < \widehat{T}_R \right\}$$

$$\geq p_\lambda + m_\lambda([u, v]) - 1$$

$$\longrightarrow m([u, v] \cap [b_1, b_2]) \ , \lambda \to \infty \ ;$$

as for the above equality we used the strong Markov property. Similarly we have

$$\varliminf_{\lambda \to \infty} P_\lambda^0 \left\{ \omega(e^{\lambda r}) \in [u, v]^c \right\} \geq m([u, v]^c \cap [b_1, b_2]) \ ,$$

which combined with (2.9) implies

$$P_\lambda^0 \left\{ \omega(e^{\lambda r}) \in [u, v] \right\} \to m([u, v] \cap [b_1, b_2]) \ , \lambda \to \infty \ .$$

The uniform convergence in $r \in [r_1, r_2]$ is also clear.

§3. Proof of Theorem 1

Let $V = (a, b_1, b_2, c)$ be a valley of W such that $A < 1 < D$. Such a valley exists with Q-probability 1. In fact, b_1 and b_2 are taken as

b_1 = the smallest root of $W(x) = 0$ in $(a', 0)$

b_2 = the largest root of $W(x) = 0$ in $(0, c')$

where $a' = \sup\{x < 0 : W(x) = 1\}$ and $c' = \inf\{x > 0 : W(x) = 1\}$. The endpoints a and c can be chosen suitably so that $a < a'$, $c > c'$ and

$V = (a, b_1, b_2, c)$ is a valley with $A<1<D$. In what follows $V = (a, b_1, b_2, c)$ denotes such a valley of W. We denote by m_W the probability measure on $\mathbb{R}$ defined by

$$(3.1) \qquad m_W([u, v]) = \frac{K([u', v'], 0)}{K([b_1, b_2], 0)}$$

where $[u', v'] = [u, v]\cap[b_1, b_2]$. Then, in the notation of §1 Lemma 6 reads as follows: For any interval I in $\mathbb{R}$ and for any family $\{r(\lambda), \lambda>0\}$ satisfying $\lim_{\lambda\to\infty} r(\lambda) = 1$,

$$(3.2) \qquad \lim_{\lambda\to\infty} P\{X(e^{\lambda r(\lambda)}, \lambda W) \in I\} = m_W(I)$$

for almost all W with respect to Q. Now we define $\mathbb{P} = P\otimes Q$ and $\mu = \int m_W Q(dW)$. Integrating both sides of (3.2) with respect to Q we have

$$(3.3) \qquad \lim_{\lambda\to\infty} \mathbb{P}\left\{X(e^{\lambda r(\lambda)}, \lambda W)\in I\right\} = \mu(I) .$$

Next, define W_λ as in Lemma 3. Then $\{W_\lambda(x), x\in\mathbb{R}\}$ is again a reflected Brownian medium. Therefore (3.3) yields

$$(3.4) \qquad \lim_{\lambda\to\infty} \mathbb{P}\left\{X(e^{\lambda r(\lambda)}, \lambda W_\lambda) \in I\right\} = \mu(I) .$$

We now apply the scaling relation (1.2) to (3.4); the result is

$$\lim_{\lambda\to\infty} \mathbb{P}\left\{\lambda^{-2}X(\lambda^4 e^{\lambda r(\lambda)}, W) \in I\right\} = \mu(I) .$$

Taking $r(\lambda) = 1 - 4\lambda^{-1}\cdot\log\lambda$ in the above, we obtain

$$\lim_{\lambda\to\infty} \mathbb{P}\left\{\lambda^{-2}X(e^{\lambda}, W) \in I\right\} = \mu(I) .$$

This completes the proof of Theorem 1.

§4. Proof of Theorem 2

The absolute continuity of μ can be proved easily. In fact, if μ_n is the measure in $\mathbb{R}$ defined by

$$\mu_n(I) = E^Q\left\{\frac{K(I\cap[b_1, b_2])}{K([b_1, b_2])} ; K([b_1, b_2])>\frac{1}{n}\right\},$$

then μ_n is absolutely continuous because

$$\mu_n(I) \le nE^Q\left\{K(I\cap[b_1, b_2])\right\}$$
$$= 2n\int_I p(|x|, 0, 0)dx ,$$

where $p(t, \xi, \eta)$ is the transition density of the Brownian motion with absorbing barriers at ± 1. Thus μ is absolutely continuous because $\mu_n \uparrow \mu$ as $n \uparrow \infty$.

We proceed to the proof of (3). Let $K(I) = K(I, 0)$ be the local time at 0 for the reflected Brownian medium as defined by (2.2) with $\xi = 0$ and consider the number of times $d_\varepsilon(t)$ that the reflected Brownian path $\{W(u) : u \geq 0\}$ crosses down from $\varepsilon > 0$ to 0 before time t. Then as found in [4: p.48]

$$Q\left\{\lim_{\varepsilon \downarrow 0} 2\varepsilon d_\varepsilon(t) = K([0, t]),\ t \geq 0\right\} = 1 . \tag{4.1}$$

Let a', c', b_1 and b_2 be defined as in the beginning of §3.

Lemma 7. For $\alpha, \beta > 0$

$$E^Q\left\{e^{-\alpha K([0,b_2]) - \beta c'}\right\} = \frac{1}{2\alpha + c(\beta)} \cdot \frac{2\sqrt{2\beta}}{e^{\sqrt{2\beta}} - e^{-\sqrt{2\beta}}} , \tag{4.2}$$

where

$$c(\beta) = \frac{e^{\sqrt{2\beta}} + e^{-\sqrt{2\beta}}}{e^{\sqrt{2\beta}} - e^{-\sqrt{2\beta}}} \cdot \sqrt{2\beta} .$$

In Particular, $K([0, b_2])$ is exponentially distributed:

$$E^Q\left\{e^{-\alpha K([0,b_2])}\right\} = \frac{1}{2\alpha + 1} . \tag{4.3}$$

Proof. Since $c(\beta) \sim 1$ as $\beta \downarrow 0$, (4.3) follows from (4.2) by letting $\beta \downarrow 0$. To prove (4.2) we first apply (4.1) to write down

$$\begin{aligned} &E^Q\left\{e^{-\alpha K([0,b_2]) - \beta c'}\right\} \quad (4.4)\\ &= E^Q\left\{e^{-\alpha K([0,c']) - \beta c'}\right\} \\ &= \lim_{\varepsilon \downarrow 0} E^Q\left\{e^{-2\alpha\varepsilon d_\varepsilon(c') - \beta c'}\right\} \\ &= \lim_{\varepsilon \downarrow 0} \sum_{n=0}^{\infty} e^{-2\alpha\varepsilon n}\, E^Q\left\{e^{-\beta T_\varepsilon}\right\}^{n+1} E^Q_\varepsilon\left\{e^{-\beta T_0} ; T_0 < T_1\right\}^n E^Q_\varepsilon\left\{e^{-\beta T_1} ; T_1 < T_0\right\} , \end{aligned}$$

where E^Q_ε denotes the expectation with respect to the probability measure of the reflected Brownian motion starting at ε and

$$T_x = \inf\{u \geq 0 : W(u) = x\} .$$

If we set

$$A_\varepsilon = e^{-2\alpha\varepsilon} E^Q\left\{e^{-\beta T_\varepsilon}\right\} E^Q_\varepsilon\left\{e^{-\beta T_0};\ T_0 < T_1\right\},$$

$$B_\varepsilon = E^Q\left\{e^{-\beta T_\varepsilon}\right\} E^Q_\varepsilon\left\{e^{-\beta T_1};\ T_1 < T_0\right\},$$

then (4.4) yields

$$(4.5)\qquad E^Q\left\{e^{-\alpha K([0,b_2])-\beta c'}\right\} = \lim_{\varepsilon\downarrow 0} B_\varepsilon \sum_{n=0}^{\infty} A_\varepsilon^n = \lim_{\varepsilon\downarrow 0} \frac{B_\varepsilon}{1 - A_\varepsilon}\ .$$

Next we make use of the well-known formula

$$E_x\left\{e^{-\alpha T_a}; T_a < T_b\right\} = \frac{e^{\sqrt{2\alpha}(b-x)} - e^{-\sqrt{2\alpha}(b-x)}}{e^{\sqrt{2\alpha}(b-a)} - e^{-\sqrt{2\alpha}(b-a)}}\ , \quad a \le x \le b\ ,$$

where E_x denotes the expectation with respect to the probability measure of a standard Brownian motion starting at x . We then have

$$(4.6)\qquad E^Q\left\{e^{-\beta T_\varepsilon}\right\} = 2E_0\left\{e^{-\beta T_\varepsilon};\ T_\varepsilon < T_{-\varepsilon}\right\}$$

$$= \frac{2(e^{\varepsilon\sqrt{2\beta}} - e^{-\varepsilon\sqrt{2\beta}})}{e^{2\varepsilon\sqrt{2\beta}} - e^{-2\varepsilon\sqrt{2\beta}}}$$

$$= 1 + o(\varepsilon^2)\ ,\quad \varepsilon\downarrow 0\ ;$$

$$(4.7)\qquad E^Q_\varepsilon\left\{e^{-\beta T_0}; T_0 < T_1\right\} = \frac{e^{\sqrt{2\beta}(1-\varepsilon)} - e^{-\sqrt{2\beta}(1-\varepsilon)}}{e^{\sqrt{2\beta}} - e^{-\sqrt{2\beta}}}$$

$$= 1 - \frac{\sqrt{2\beta}(e^{\sqrt{2\beta}} + e^{-\sqrt{2\beta}})}{e^{\sqrt{2\beta}} - e^{-\sqrt{2\beta}}}\cdot\varepsilon + o(\varepsilon),\quad \varepsilon\downarrow 0\ ;$$

$$(4.8)\qquad E^Q_\varepsilon\left\{e^{-\beta T_1};\ T_1 < T_0\right\} = \frac{e^{\sqrt{2\beta}\,\varepsilon} - e^{-\sqrt{2\beta}\,\varepsilon}}{e^{\sqrt{2\beta}} - e^{-\sqrt{2\beta}}}$$

$$\sim \frac{2\sqrt{2\beta}}{e^{\sqrt{2\beta}} - e^{-\sqrt{2\beta}}}\cdot\varepsilon\ ,\quad \varepsilon\downarrow 0\ .$$

From (4.6), (4.7) and (4.8) we obtain

$$\frac{B_\varepsilon}{1 - A_\varepsilon} \sim \frac{1}{2\alpha + c(\beta)} \cdot \frac{2\sqrt{2\beta}}{e^{\sqrt{2\beta}} - e^{-\sqrt{2\beta}}} , \quad \varepsilon \downarrow 0 ,$$

which combined with (4.5) proves the lemma.

Given $x > 0$ we set

$$K_1 = K([b_1, 0]), \quad K_2 = K([0, x]), \quad K_3 = K([x, b_2]) .$$

Lemma 8. For $x > 0$ and $t > 0$

$$\text{(4.9)} \qquad E^Q\left\{K_3 e^{-t(K_1+K_2+K_3)} ; \; x < b_2\right\}$$
$$= \frac{2}{(2t+1)^3} E^Q\left\{(1 - W(x)) e^{-tK([0,x])} ; \; x < c'\right\} .$$

Proof. The left hand side of (4.9) equals

$$E^Q\left\{e^{-tK_1}\right\} E^Q\left\{K_3 e^{-t(K_2+K_3)} ; \; x < b_2\right\} .$$

Since $E^Q\left\{e^{-tK_1}\right\} = (2t+1)^{-1}$ by Lemma 7, for the proof of the lemma it is enough to show

$$\text{(4.10)} \qquad E^Q\left\{K_3 e^{-t(K_2+K_3)} : \; x < b_2\right\}$$
$$= \frac{2}{(2t+1)^2} E^Q\left\{(1 - W(x)) e^{-tK_2} ; \; x < c'\right\} .$$

To prove this we introduce the smallest σ-field $\mathcal{F}_x$ on $\mathbb{W}$ which makes $W(s)$, $0 \le s \le x$, measurable and consider the event Γ that the shifted trajectory $W(\cdot + x)$ hits 0 before it hits 1. Then first using the strong Markov property of the reflected Brownian motion and then (4.3), we have

$$E^Q\left\{K_3 e^{-tK_3} \mathbb{1}_\Gamma / \mathcal{F}_x\right\}$$
$$= \left\{1 - W(x)\right\} E^Q\left\{K([0, b_2]) e^{-tK([0,b_2])}\right\}$$
$$= \frac{2}{(2t+1)^2}\left\{1 - W(x)\right\} , \quad \text{a.s.}$$

Since $\left\{x < b_2\right\} = \left\{x < c'\right\} \cap \Gamma$ and $\left\{x < c'\right\} \in \mathcal{F}_x$, we have

$$E^Q\left\{K_3 e^{-t(K_2+K_3)} ; \; x < b_2\right\}$$
$$= E^Q\left(e^{-tK_2} \mathbb{1}_{\{x<c'\}} E^Q\left\{K_3 e^{-tK_3} \mathbb{1}_\Gamma / \mathcal{F}_x\right\}\right)$$

$$= \frac{2}{(2t+1)^2} E^Q\left\{(1 - W(x))e^{-tK_2};\ x < c'\right\} ,$$

proving (4.10) and hence the lemma.

Lemma 9. For $\lambda > 0$ and $t > 0$

$$\int_0^\infty e^{-\lambda x} E^Q\left\{(1 - W(x))e^{-tK([0,x])};\ x < c'\right\} dx \tag{4.11}$$

$$= \frac{1}{\lambda}\left\{1 - \frac{(2t+1)S}{C + 2tS}\right\},$$

where

$$C = \cosh\sqrt{2\lambda} \quad , \quad S = \frac{\sinh\sqrt{2\lambda}}{\sqrt{2\lambda}} .$$

Proof. Let $\varphi(x) = 1 - |x|$. Consulting with [4: Chapter 5] , we see that the left hand side of (4.11) equals $f_\lambda(0)$ where f_λ is the continuous solution of

$$\begin{cases} \lambda f - \frac{1}{2}f'' = \varphi & \text{in } (-1, 0)\cup(0, 1) \\ \frac{1}{2}\{f'(0+) - f'(0-)\} = 2tf(0) \\ f(-1) = f(1) = 0 . \end{cases} \tag{4.12}$$

To solve (4.12) we first find the solution g_λ of $\lambda f - \frac{1}{2}f'' = \varphi$ in (-1,1) with boundary condition $f(-1) = f(1) = 0$ and then express f_λ as follows:

$$f_\lambda(x) = \begin{cases} g_\lambda(x) + c\sinh\sqrt{2\lambda}\,(1+x) & \text{for } x \in (-1, 0) \\ g_\lambda(x) + c\sinh\sqrt{2\lambda}\,(1-x) & \text{for } x \in (0, 1) \end{cases} .$$

If we determine c so that the above f_λ satisfies the second condition of (4.12), then the f_λ is a solution of (4.12). Thus $f_\lambda(0)$ can be computed and we obtain (4.11).

Now Theorem 2 can be proved as follows. By Lemma 8 we have

$$\mu((x,\infty)) = E^Q\left\{\frac{K((x,\ x\vee b_2])}{K([b_1,\ b_2])}\right\}$$

$$= E^Q\left\{\frac{K_3}{K_1 + K_2 + K_3} ;\ x < b_2\right\}$$

$$= \int_0^\infty E^Q\left\{K_3 e^{-t(K_1+K_2+K_3)};\ \ x < b_2\right\}dt$$

$$= \int_0^\infty \frac{2}{(2t+1)^3} E^Q\left\{(1 - W(x))e^{-tK([0,x])} \; ; \; x < c'\right\}dt$$

and hence by Lemma 9

$$\int_0^\infty e^{-\lambda x} \mu((x,\infty))dx = \int_0^\infty \frac{2}{(2t+1)^3}\cdot\frac{1}{\lambda}\left\{1 - \frac{(2t+1)S}{C+2tS}\right\}dt$$

$$= \frac{1}{2\lambda} - \frac{1}{\lambda}\int_0^\infty \frac{2}{(2t+1)^2}\cdot\frac{S}{C+2tS}\,dt \; .$$

Thus integration by parts yields

$$\int_0^\infty e^{-\lambda x}\mu(dx) = \frac{1}{2} - \lambda\int_0^\infty e^{-\lambda x}\mu((x,\infty))dx \qquad (\text{notice that } \mu((0,\infty)) = \tfrac{1}{2})$$

$$= \int_0^\infty \frac{2S}{(2t+1)^2(C+2tS)}\,dt$$

$$= \int_0^\infty \frac{Sdt}{(t+1)^2(C+tS)} \; ,$$

and this proves (3).

REFERENCES

[1] T.Brox, A one-dimensional diffusion process in a Wiener medium, to appear in Ann. Probab.

[2] A.O.Golosov, The limit distributions for random walks in random environments, Soviet Math. Dokl., 28(1983), 18-22.

[3] N.Ikeda and S.Watanabe, Stochastic Differential Equations and Diffusion Processes, North-Holland, 1981.

[4] K.Itô and H.P.McKean, Diffusion Processes and Their Sample Paths, Springer-Verlag, 1965.

[5] K.Kawazu, Y.Tamura and H.Tanaka, One-dimensional diffusions and random walks in random environments, in preparation.

[6] H.Kesten, The limit distribution of Sinai's random walk in random environment, to appear in Physica.

[7] S.Schumacher, Diffusions with random coefficients, Contemporary Math. (Particle Systems, Random Media and Large Deviations, ed. by R. Durrett), 41(1985), 351-356.

[8] Y.G.Sinai, The limiting behavior of a one-dimensional random walk in a random medium, Theory of Probab. and its Appl. 27(1982), 256-268.

[9] H.Tanaka, Limit distributions for one-dimensional diffusion processes in self-similar random environments, to appear in the Proc. of the workshop on Hydrodynamic behavior and interacting particle systems and applications held at IMA, University of Minnesota, March 1986.

Department of Mathematics
Faculty of Science and Technology
Keio University
Yokohama, Japan

Reprinted from
Seminaire de Probabilites XXI, 246–261,
Lecture Notes in Math., **1247**, Springer-Verlag, 1987.

LIMIT DISTRIBUTIONS FOR ONE-DIMENSIONAL DIFFUSION PROCESSES IN SELF-SIMILAR RANDOM ENVIRONMENTS

H. Tanaka

Department of Mathematics
Faculty of Science and Technology
Keio University, Yokohama, JAPAN

Introduction

Let $X(t)$ be the one-dimensional diffusion process described by the stochastic differential equation

$$(1) \qquad dX(t) = dB(t) - \frac{1}{2} W'(X(t))dt, \qquad X(0) = 0,$$

where $B(t)$ is a one-dimensional Brownian motion starting at 0 and $\{W(x), x \in \mathbb{R}\}$ is a random environment which is independent of the Brownian motion $B(t)$. We are interested in the asymptotic behavior of $X(t)$ as $t \to \infty$: Under what scaling does $X(t)$ have a limit distribution? Similar problems for random walks were considered by Kesten, Kozlov and Spitzer [5] and Sinai [8]. The problem we discuss here is a diffusion analogue of Sinai's random walk problem [8]. In the case of a Brownian environment Brox [1] proved that the distribution of $(\log t)^{-2}X(t)$ is convergent as $t \to \infty$. Similar results were obtained by Schumacher [7] for a considerably wider class of self-similar random environments. As was seen by these works the assumption of the self-similarity of the random environment is important and the notion of suitably defined valleys of the environment plays a central role in the proof. However, it was assumed that the environment has only one point which gives the same value of local minima or maxima (the bottom of a valley consists of a single point), and the explicit form of the limit distribution was unknown until a recent discovery by Kesten ([6]) for Sinai's random walk which corresponds to the case of a Brownian environment in our diffusion setup (Golosov also obtained the same result as Kesten's; see also Golosov [2] for the corresponding result in another different model).

In this paper we discuss the following three typical examples of random environments with emphasis on finding the limit distributions:

(i) Nonpositive reflected Brownian environment.

(ii) Nonnegative reflected Brownian environment.

(iii) Symmetric stable environment.

In the first two examples the environment has (uncountably) many points giving the same value of local maxima or minima. The proof in (ii) is only sketched. For details see [9]. The result in (iii) on the limit distribution is an extension of Kesten's result [6].

In [4] a unified definition of valleys of an environment is given in a general setup containing the above examples and some results similar to Brox's and Schumacher's are obtained, but here we limit ourselves to the above examples because we are interested mainly in the form of the limit distributions and we have explicit results concerning this only in some special cases.

The author wishes to thank K. Kawazu and Y. Tamura; his frequent discussions with them were very valuable.

1. Preliminaries and the Result of Brox

1.1. Given a real valued right continuous function $W(x)$ defined on the real line $\mathbb{R}$ and having left limits, we consider the stochastic differential equation (1) with environment $W(x)$. Since $W(x)$ is not differentiable in general, what is meant by a solution of (1) will need explanation. However, without considering a solution itself for a given Brownian motion $B(t)$, we just interprete the diffusion described by (1) as a diffusion process starting at 0 with generator

$$\frac{1}{2}\, e^{W(x)} \frac{d}{dx} \left(e^{-W(x)} \frac{d}{dx}\right). \tag{1.1}$$

Such a diffusion can be obtained from a Brownian motion through a scale change and a time change ([3]). To be precise let

$$\Omega = C([0,\infty) \to \mathbb{R})^{1)} \cap \{\omega(0) = 0\},$$

$$P = \text{the Wiener measure on } \Omega,$$

$$B(t) = \omega(t) = \text{the value of } \omega \text{ at time } t,$$

$$L(t,x) = \lim_{\varepsilon \downarrow 0} \frac{1}{\varepsilon} \int_0^t 1_{[x,x+\varepsilon)}(B(s))ds \qquad \text{(local time)},$$

$$S(x) = \int_0^x e^{W(y)}dy ,$$

$$A(t) = \int_0^t e^{-2W(S^{-1}(B(s)))}ds = \int_{\mathbb{R}} e^{-2W(S^{-1}(x))}L(t,x)dx, \ t \geq 0,$$

S^{-1}, A^{-1} = the inverse functions.

Then the process $X(t,W) = S^{-1}(B(A^{-1}(t)))$ defined on the probability space (Ω,P) is a diffusion process with generator (1.1) starting at 0. The Brownian motion $B(t)$ used here is not the same as the one in (1) but we use the same notation. Let $(W^x)(\cdot) = W(\cdot+x)$. For a fixed $x \in \mathbb{R}$ we replace W in $X(t,W)$ by W^x and then consider

$$X^x(t,W) = x + X(t,W^x).$$

Then $X^x(t,W)$ is a diffusion process with generator (1.1) starting at x. In this paper we shall deal with $X(t) = X(t,W)$ and $X^x(t) = X^x(t,W)$ and the following notation will be used throughout.

$$S_\lambda(x) = \int_0^x e^{\lambda W(u)}du,$$

W_λ: a function (environment) defined by $W_\lambda(x) = \lambda^{-1}W(\lambda^2 x)$ for $\forall\, x \in \mathbb{R}$, $\lambda > 0$ being fixed.

In the following lemma due to Brox the medium W is fixed. For the proof see [1].

Lemma 1.1 ([1]). For each $\lambda > 0$

$$\{X(t,\lambda W_\lambda),\ t \geq 0\} \overset{d}{=} \{\lambda^{-2}X(\lambda^4 t,\ W),\ t \geq 0\}$$

where $\overset{d}{=}$ means the equality in distribution.

---

1) For a topological space R the notation $C([0,\infty) \to R)$ stands for the space of R-valued continuous functions defined on $[0,\infty)$.

When we consider the environment to be random, we denote by Q the probability distribution (on the space of environments) of the random environment. Since we are assuming that the random environment and the Brownian motion $B(t)$ are independent, the full distribution is $\mathcal{P} = P \times Q$. Thus, when the environment is fixed $X(t)$ is governed by P, and when the environment is random $X(t)$ is governed by $\mathcal{P}$.

1.2. In this subsection we limit ourselves to the case of continuous environment and state a result of Brox [1] in a form which is convenient for our use in §2.

Given a continuous function W on $\mathbb{R}$ which is supposed to be the environment in (1), we define a valley of W following [1]. For $x \neq y$ we put

$$H_{x,y} = \sup \{W(y') - W(x')\} \tag{1.2}$$

where the supremum is taken over all pairs of x' and y' such that $x < x' < y' < y$ or $y < y' < x' < x$ according as $x < y$ or $y < x$. A triple $V = (a,b,c)$ is called a <u>valley</u> of W if

(i) $a < b < c$,

(ii) $W(b) < W(x) < W(a)$ for every $x \in (a,b)$,

$W(b) < W(x) < W(c)$ for every $x \in (b,c)$,

(iii) $H_{a,b} < W(c) - W(b)$, $H_{c,b} < W(a) - W(b)$.

For a valley $V = (a,b,c)$, $D = (W(a) - W(b)) \wedge (W(c) - W(b))$ and $A = H_{a,b} \vee H_{c,b}$ are called the <u>depth</u> of V and the <u>inner directed ascent</u> of V, where $u \wedge v$ (resp. $u \vee v$) denotes $\min\{u,v\}$ (resp. $\max\{u,v\}$). It is obvious that $A < D$.

<u>Theorem 1.1 (Brox [1])</u>. (i) Let $V = (a,b,c)$ be a valley of W with the depth D and the inner directed ascent A.

(i) Let T_λ^x be the exit time of (a,c) for the process $X_\lambda^x(t) = x + X(t,\lambda W^x)$. Then for any $\delta > 0$ and any closed interval $I \subset (a,c)$

$$\lim_{\lambda\to\infty} \inf_{x\in I} P\{e^{\lambda(D-\delta)} < T_\lambda^x < e^{\lambda(D+\delta)}\} = 1.$$

(ii) For any $\varepsilon>0$, any closed interval $I \subset (a,c)$ and for any closed interval $J \subset (A,D)$

$$\lim_{\lambda\to\infty} \sup_{\substack{x\in I \\ r\in J}} P\{|X^x(e^{\lambda r}, \lambda W) - b| > \varepsilon\} = 0.$$

First proving the above result and then making use of the scaling relation (Lemma 1.1), Brox derived his main theorem:

Theorem 1.2 (Brox [1]). For any $\varepsilon>0$

$$P\{|\lambda^{-2}X(e^{-\lambda}, W) - b_\lambda| > \varepsilon\} \to 0, \quad \lambda\to\infty$$

in probability with respect to the probability measure Q of the Brownian environment, where b_λ is the unique bottom of a valley $V_\lambda = (a_\lambda, b_\lambda, c_\lambda)$ of W_λ such that

(1.3) $$a_\lambda < 0 < c_\lambda \ , \quad A_\lambda < 1 < D_\lambda.$$

2. Nonpositive Reflected Brownian Environment

As a simple example in which the environment has (uncountably) many points giving the same value of local maxima we consider the case of a nonpositive reflected Brownian environment. Main ideas of this section grew out from the conversation with Y. Tamura.

We first introduce the space $\underline{\underline{W}} = C(\mathbb{R}\to(-\infty, 0]) \cap \{W(0) = 0\}$ and denote by Q the probability measure on $\underline{\underline{W}}$ with respect to which $\{W(u) : u\geq 0\}$ and $\{W(-u) : u\geq 0\}$ are independent reflected Brownian motions on $(-\infty,0]$. An essential difference between the present case and Brox's one is that there is no valley of W_λ satisfying (1.3) in the present case. For $W \in \underline{\underline{W}}$ we put

$$W^*(u) = W(u) - \inf_{[0,u]} W, \quad u \geq 0 ,$$

$$= W(u) - \inf_{[u,0]} W, \quad u \leq 0 ,$$

and define $a_\pm = a_\pm(W)$, $b_\pm = b_\pm(W)$ and $c_\pm = c_\pm(W)$ as follows.

1. $d_\pm = \pm \min \{u > 0 : W^*(\pm u) = 1\}$,

2. $b_\pm = \pm \min \{u > 0 : W(\pm u) = M_\pm\}$

   where $M_+ = \min_{[0,d_+]} W$ and $M_- = \min_{[d_-,0]} W$,

3. $c_- = \min \{u > b_- : W(u) = 0\}$,

   $a_+ = \max \{u < b_+ : W(u) = 0\}$,

4. $e_\pm = \pm \min \{u > d_\pm : W(\pm u) = W(b_\pm)\}$,

5. $a_- = \max \{u < b_- : W(u) = \max_{[e_-,b_-]} W\}$,

   $c_+ = \min \{u > b_+ : W(u) = \max_{[b_+,e_+]} W\}$.

Then $V_\pm = (a_\pm , b_\pm , c_\pm)$ are valleys of W with $a_- < b_- < c_- < 0 < a_+ < b_+ < c_+$, Q-a.s. As for the depth and the inner directed ascent we have $A_\pm < 1 < D_\pm$, Q-a.s., because $W(a_-) > W(d_-)$ and $W(c_+) > W(d_+)$, Q-a.s. Substracting a suitable null set from $\underline{\underline{W}}$ we may assume that the statements hold for all W in the subtracted space and so we often omit the phrase "Q-a.s."

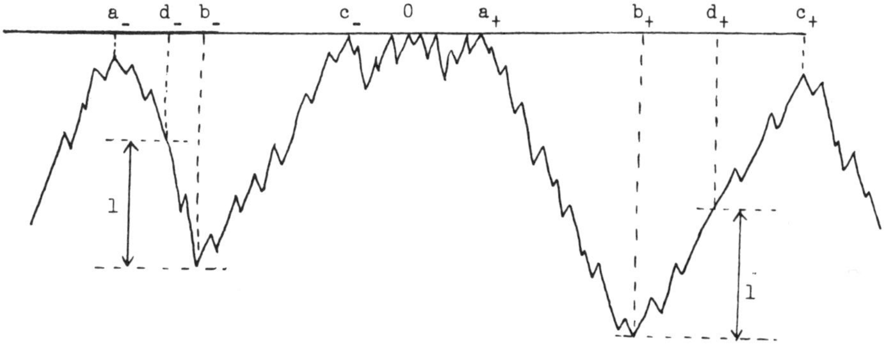

Our aim is to know the asymptotic behavior of $X(t,W)$ as $t\to\infty$, or more precisely, to find the limit distribution of $(\log t)^{-2}X(t,W)$ as $t\to\infty$. First we observe the process $X(t,\lambda W)$. If λ becomes large and time goes on, the process eventually falls into one of the valleys $V_\pm$ and thereafter Theorem 1.1 will tell about the asymptotic behavior of $X(e^{\lambda r}, \lambda W)$, $\lambda\to\infty$, $r\sim 1$. Then a use of the scaling relation (Lemma 1.1) will give the result for the limit distribution of $\lambda^{-2}X(e^{\lambda},W)$ as $\lambda\to\infty$.

To be precise choose α such that

(2.1) $$-\min_{[c_-,a_+]} W < \alpha < 1$$

and put

$$x_\pm = \pm \min\{u > 0:\ W(\pm u) = -\alpha\},$$
$$T^\pm_\lambda = \min\{t > 0:\ X(t,\lambda W) = x_\pm\},\quad \hat{T}_\lambda = T^-_\lambda \quad T^+_\lambda .$$

Denote by $L_-(I,\xi)$ the local time at ξ for the reflected Brownian environment $\{W(u),\ u\in\mathbb{R}\}$, i.e.,

$$L_-(I,\xi) = \lim_{\varepsilon\downarrow 0}\frac{1}{\varepsilon}\int_I 1_{(\xi-\varepsilon,\xi]}(W(u))du,\quad I = \text{interval in } \mathbb{R}.$$

Lemma 2.1. (i) There exists $\delta = \delta(W) > 0$ such that

$$\lim_{\lambda\to\infty} P\{\hat{T}_\lambda < e^{\lambda(1-\delta)}\} = 1.$$

(ii) $$\lim_{\lambda\to\infty} P\{T^-_\lambda < T^+_\lambda\} = L_-([0,a_+],\ 0)/L_-([c_-,a_+],\ 0).$$

Proof. The condition (2.1) implies the existence of a modification $W^\#$ of W with the following properties (2.2) and (2.3).

(2.2) $W^\#\in C(\mathbb{R}\to\mathbb{R})$ and $W^\#(x) = W(x)$ for $\forall x\in[x_-,x_+]$.

(2.3) There exists a valley $V^\# = (a^\#,\ b^\#,\ c^\#)$ of $W^\#$ with depth $D^\# < 1$ and $a^\# < x_- < x_+ < c^\#$.

Let $T^\#_\lambda = \min\{t > 0:\ X(t,\lambda W^\#)\notin (x_-,\ x_+)\}$. Then for any $\delta>0$ such that $D^\# + 2\delta < 1$ we have

$$P\{\hat{T}_\lambda < e^{\lambda(1-\delta)}\} = P\{T_\lambda^\# < e^{\lambda(1-\delta)}\} \geq P\{T_\lambda^\# < e^{\lambda(D^\#+\delta)}\} \to 1, \ \lambda\to\infty$$

by (i) of Theorem 1.1. The proof of (ii) is easy; in fact

$$P\{T_\lambda^- < T_\lambda^+\} = \frac{S_\lambda(x_+) - S_\lambda(0)}{S_\lambda(x_+) - S_\lambda(x_-)}$$

$$= \frac{\int_{-\infty}^0 e^{\lambda\xi} L_-([0, x_-], \xi)d\xi}{\int_{-\infty}^0 e^{\lambda\xi} L_-([x_-, x_+], \xi)d\xi}$$

$$= \frac{\int_{-\infty}^0 e^{\xi} L_-([0,x_+], \lambda^{-1}\xi)d\xi}{\int_{-\infty}^0 e^{\xi} L_-([x_-,x_+], \lambda^{-1}\xi)d\xi}$$

$$\to L_-([0,x_+], 0)/L_-([x_-,x_+], 0), \ \lambda \to \infty$$

$$= L_-([0,a_+], 0)/L_-([c_-, a_+], 0).$$

Lemma 2.2. There exist r_1 and r_2 with $r_1 < 1 < r_2$ such that for any $\varepsilon > 0$ and $r \in [r_1,r_2]$

$$\lim_{\lambda\to\infty} P\{X(e^{\lambda r}, \lambda W) \in U_\varepsilon(b)\} = p$$

holds with $b = b_\pm$ and $p = p_\pm$ where $p_+ = L_-([c_-,0],0)/L_-([c_-,a_+],0)$, $p_- = 1 - p_+$ and $U_\varepsilon(b)$ denotes the ε-neighborhood of b. The above convergence is uniform with respect to r on $[r_1, r_2]$.

Proof. It is easy to see that there exist valleys $\tilde{V}_\pm = (\tilde{a}_\pm, \tilde{b}_\pm, \tilde{c}_\pm)$ of W with depth $\tilde{D}_\pm > 1$ and satisfying $a_- < \tilde{a}_- < b_- < x_- < \tilde{c}_- < c_-$ and $a_+ < \tilde{a}_+ < x_+ < b_+ < \tilde{c}_+ < c_+$, respectively. Denote by $\tilde{T}_\lambda^{x+}$ the exit time of $\tilde{I}_+ = (\tilde{a}_+, \tilde{c}_+)$ for the process $X^{x_+}(t, \lambda W)$ and by $\tilde{T}_\lambda^{x-}$ the exit time of $\tilde{I}_- = (\tilde{a}_-, \tilde{c}_-)$ for the process $X^{x_-}(t,\lambda W)$. Then using the strong Markov property of $X(t,\lambda W)$ we have

$$P\{X(e^{\lambda(1-\delta)}, \lambda W) \in \tilde{I}_+\}$$

(2.2)
$$\geq P\{T_\lambda^+ = \hat{T}_\lambda < e^{\lambda(1-\delta)}\} \, P\{\tilde{T}_\lambda^{x+} > e^{\lambda(1-\delta)}\}$$

and a similar inequality with $+$ replaced by $-$. We now take $\delta = \delta(W)$ of Lemma 2.1 and then let $\lambda\uparrow\infty$ in (2.2). Then the assertion (i) of Theorem 1.1 combined with Lemma 2.1 implies

(2.3a) $$\varliminf_{\lambda\to\infty} P\{X(e^{\lambda(1-\delta)}, \lambda W) \in \Upsilon_+\} \geq p_+$$

and a similar inequality (= (2.3b)) with $+$ replaced by $-$. (2.3a) and (2.3b) clearly imply that

(2.4) $$\lim_{\lambda\to\infty} P\{X(e^{\lambda(1-\delta)}, \lambda W) \in \Upsilon_\pm\} = p_\pm .$$

We now take r_1 and r_2 such that

$$A_- \vee A_+ \vee (1-\delta) < r_1 < 1 < r_2 < D_- \wedge D_+$$

and prove the lemma with these r_1 and r_2. Let $r_1 \leq r \leq r_2$ and $t = e^{\lambda r} - e^{\lambda(1-\delta)}$. Then we have

$$P\{X(e^{\lambda r}, \lambda W) \in U_\varepsilon(b_+)\}$$
$$= \int_{\Upsilon_+} P\{X(e^{\lambda(1-\delta)}, \lambda W) \in dx\} P\{X^x(t, \lambda W) \in U_\varepsilon(b_+)\} + o(1)$$

which tends to p_+ uniformly in r as $\lambda\to\infty$ by Theorem 1.1 as applied to the valley V_+ because t can be expressed as $t = e^{\lambda r'}$ with $r' \to r$ as $\lambda\to\infty$. The other case $(b = b_-, p = p_-)$ can be proved similarly and so the proof is finished.

Since $b_\pm$ and $p_\pm$ are Borel functions of W we can define a probability measure μ_- on R by

$$\int \phi(x)\mu_-(dx) = \int\{p_- \phi(b_-) + p_+\phi(b_+)\}Q(dW), \quad \phi \in C_b(\mathbb{R}).$$

<u>Theorem 2.1</u>. The full distribution of $(\log t)^{-2}X(t)$ converges to μ_- as $t \to \infty$.

Proof. Lemma 2.2 implies that the full distribution of $X(e^{\lambda r(\lambda)}, \lambda W)$ converges to μ_- as $\lambda\to\infty$ provided that $r(\lambda)\to 1$ as $\lambda\to\infty$. Since our reflected Brownian environment is self-similar, i.e., $\{W_\lambda(x), x \in \mathbb{R}\}$ is again a reflected

Brownian environment, we see that the full distribution of $X(e^{\lambda r(\lambda)}, \lambda W_\lambda)$ also converges to μ_-. Applying the scaling relation (Lemma 1.1) we see that the full distribution of $\lambda^{-2}X(\lambda^4 e^{\lambda r(\lambda)}, W)$ converges to μ_-. If we take $r(\lambda) = 1 - 4\lambda^{-1}\log\lambda$, the last statement is nothing but the assertion of the theorem.

Theorem 2.2. μ_- has a symmetric density and

$$(2.5)\qquad \int_0^\infty e^{-\lambda x}\mu_-(dx) = \int_0^\infty \frac{d\sigma}{(\sigma+1)^2(\sigma + \sqrt{2\lambda}\coth\sqrt{2\lambda})\cosh\sqrt{2\lambda}}, \quad \lambda > 0.$$

Proof. If $d_\varepsilon(t)$ denotes the number of times that the reflected Brownian path $\{W(u) : u \geq 0\}$ crosses down from 0 to $-\varepsilon$ before t, then $\lim_{\varepsilon \downarrow 0} 2\varepsilon d_\varepsilon(t) = L_-([0,t],0)$, $t \geq 0$, Q-a.s. (see [3]). Therefore, putting $f_+ = \min\{u>0 : W(u) = -1\}$ and $L_2 = L([0,a_+],0)$ we can write for $\sigma, \lambda > 0$

$$(2.6)\qquad E^Q\{e^{-\sigma L_2 - \lambda f_+}\}$$

$$= \lim_{\varepsilon\downarrow 0}\sum_{n=0} e^{-\sigma(2\varepsilon n)} E_0^Q\{e^{-\lambda H_{-\varepsilon}}\}^n E_{-\varepsilon}^Q\{e^{-\lambda H_0}; H_0 < H_{-1}\}^{n-1}$$

$$\cdot E_{-\varepsilon}^Q\{e^{-\lambda H_{-1}}; H_{-1} < H_0\},$$

where H_a denotes the hitting time to a for the reflected Brownian motion on $(-\infty,0]$ and the suffix x in E_x^Q indicates that the initial position is x. Using the explicit form of $E^Q\{e^{-\lambda H_{-\varepsilon}}\}$, etc., the right hand side of (2.6) can be computed. The result is

$$(2.7)\qquad E^Q\{e^{-\sigma L_2 - \lambda f_+}\} = \frac{2\sqrt{2\lambda}}{e^{\sqrt{2\lambda}} - e^{-\sqrt{2\lambda}}} \cdot \frac{1}{2\sigma + c(\lambda)},$$

where $c(\lambda) = (e^{\sqrt{2\lambda}} + e^{-\sqrt{2\lambda}})(e^{\sqrt{2\lambda}} - e^{-\sqrt{2\lambda}})^{-1}\sqrt{2\lambda}$. In particular L_2 is exponentially distributed with mean 2. In a similar spirit we see easily that

$$(2.8)\qquad E^Q\{e^{-\lambda g_+}\} = \frac{e^{\sqrt{2\lambda}} - e^{-\sqrt{2\lambda}}}{\sqrt{2\lambda}(e^{\sqrt{2\lambda}} + e^{-\sqrt{2\lambda}})},$$

where $g_+ = b_+ - f_+$. Let $L_1 = L_-([c_-, 0], 0)$. Then

$$\int_0^\infty e^{-\lambda x}\, \mu_-(dx) = E^Q\{ \frac{L_1}{L_1 + L_2} \cdot e^{-\lambda b_+} \}$$

$$= \int_0^\infty E^Q \{L_1 e^{-\sigma(L_1 + L_2) - \lambda f_+ - \lambda g_+}\} d\sigma ,$$

and making use of (2.7), (2.8) and the fact that L_1 , g_+ and $\{L_2 , f_+\}$ are independent we can compute the right hand side of the above. We thus obtain (2.5).

3. Nonnegative Reflected Brownian Environment

In this section we consider the case of a nonnegative reflected Brownian environment. This is a typical case where the bottom of a valley consists of (uncountably) many points.

Let $\underline{\underline{W}}$ be the space $C(\mathbb{R} \to [0,\infty)) \cap \{W(0) = 0\}$ and consider the probability measure Q on $\underline{\underline{W}}$ with respect to which $\{W(u):u > 0\}$ and $\{W(-u):u > 0\}$ are independent reflected Brownian motions on $[0,\infty)$. The study of asymptotic behaviors of $X(t,W)$ as $t \to \infty$ can be done by a method similar to that of Brox [1] as will be sketched here.

The definition of a valley given in 1.2 must be slightly modified. Given $W \in \underline{\underline{W}}$, a quartet $V = (a, b_1, b_2, c)$ is called a <u>valley</u> of W if

(i) $a < b_1 < 0 < b_2 < c$,

(ii) $W(b_1) = W(b_2) = 0$, $W(a) = W(b) = D > 0$,

(iii) $0 < W(x) < W(a)$ for $0 < x < b_1$,

$0 < W(x) < W(c)$ for $b_2 < x < c$,

(iv) $A = H_{a,b_2} \vee H_{c,b_1} < D$.

D and A are called the <u>depth</u> and the <u>inner directed ascent</u> of V , respectively. There exists a valley of W such that $A < 1 < D$ with Q-probability 1. In fact, let

$$a' = \max \{u < 0 : W(u) = 1\} , \quad c' = \min \{u > 0 : W(u) = 1\} ,$$

$$b_1 = \min \{u > a': W(u) = 0\} , \quad b_2 = \max \{u < c': W(u) = 0\} .$$

Then with a suitable choice of a and c with $a < a'$, $c' < c$, the quartet $V = (a, b_1, b_2, c)$ becomes a valley of W with $A < 1 < D$, Q-a.s. In what follows $V = (a, b_1, b_2, c)$ denotes such a valley of W. We first observe $X(t, \lambda W)$. As in [1] we can prove that $X(e^{\lambda r}, \lambda W)$ falls into an ε-neighborhood of $[b_1, b_2]$ as $\lambda \to \infty$, $r \sim 1$. Then how is $X(e^{\lambda r}, \lambda W)$ distributed on $[b_1, b_2]$ in the limit? This limit distribution can be identified with the limit, as $\lambda \to \infty$, of the invariant probability measure m_λ of the diffusion process on $[a,c]$ with (local) generator $\frac{1}{2} e^{\lambda W(x)} \frac{d}{dx} (e^{-\lambda W(x)} \frac{d}{dx})$ and with reflecting barriers at a and c. If $L_+(I, \xi)$ denotes the local time at ξ for the reflected Brownian environment $\{W(x), x \in \mathbb{R}\}$, then for an interval $I \subset [a,c]$

$$m_\lambda(I) = \int_I e^{-\lambda W(y)} dy \Big/ \int_a^c e^{-\lambda W(y)} dy$$

$$= \int_0^\infty e^{-\lambda\xi} L_+(I,\xi) d\xi \Big/ \int_0^\infty e^{-\lambda\xi} L_+([a,c], \xi) d\xi.$$

$$\to L_+(I \cap [b_1, b_2], 0) / L_+([b_1, b_2], 0).$$

Define a probability measure m_W in $\mathbb{R}$ by

$$m_W([u,v]) = L_+(I', 0)/L_+([b_1, b_2], 0)$$

where $I' = [u,v] \cap [b_1, b_2]$. Then for any interval I in $\mathbb{R}$ and for any family $\{r(\lambda), \lambda > 0\}$ satisfying $\lim_{\lambda \to \infty} r(\lambda) = 1$ we have

$$\lim_{\lambda \to \infty} P\{X(e^{\lambda r(\lambda)}, \lambda W) \in I\} = m_W(I)$$

for almost all W with respect to Q. Now we define $\mu_+ = \int m_W Q(dW)$. Then

$$\lim_{\lambda \to \infty} \mathcal{P}\{X(e^{\lambda r(\lambda)}, \lambda W) \in I\} = \mu_+(I).$$

Substituting W in the above by the scaled W_λ and then using Lemma 1.1 we obtain the following result.

<u>Theorem 3.1 ([9]).</u> (i) The full distribution of $(\log t)^{-2} X(t)$ converges to μ_+ as $t \to \infty$. (ii) μ_+ has a symmetric density and for $\lambda > 0$

$$\int_0^\infty e^{-\lambda x}\,\mu_+(dx) = \int_0^\infty \frac{\cosh\sqrt{2\lambda}-1}{(\sigma+1)^3\{\cosh\sqrt{2\lambda}+\sigma\frac{\sinh\sqrt{2\lambda}}{\sqrt{2\lambda}}\}\lambda}\,d\sigma\ ,\ \lambda > 0.$$

4. Symmetric Stable Environment

In this section the space $\underline{\underline{W}}$ of the environments is $D(\mathbb{R}\to\mathbb{R})$[1] $\cap\ \{W(0) = 0\}$ and Q is the probability measure on $\underline{\underline{W}}$ with respect to which $\{W(u) : u>0\}$ and $\{W(-u) : u>0\}$ are independent and symmetric stable processes with exponent $\alpha(0 < \alpha < 2)$ such that

$$E^Q\{e^{\sqrt{-1}\xi W(u)}\} = e^{-|u||\tau|^\alpha}\ ,\ u\in\mathbb{R},\quad \xi\ \ \mathbb{R}.$$

This case is contained in the frame of Schumacher's work [7] (see also Kawazu-Tamura-Tanaka [4] for additional information) and so the full distribution of $(\log t)^{-\alpha}X(t,W)$ is convergent as $t\to\infty$. The purpose this section is to give a simple probabilistic description of the limit distribution. In the case of a Brownian environment Kesten [6] proved that the density of the limit distribution is given by

$$(4.1)\qquad \frac{2}{\pi}\sum_{k=0}^{\infty}\frac{(-1)^k}{2k+1}\,e^{-(2k+1)^2\pi^2|x|/8}\ ,\ x\in\mathbb{R}.$$

We begin by stating some known results (see [7], [4]). First we give the definition of a valley, which is a slight modification of the one given in §1. Let $W\in\underline{\underline{W}}$. By definition W is said to be <u>oscillating</u> at x $(\in\mathbb{R})$ if

$$\sup_{I_\pm} W > W(x\pm)\ ,\ \inf_{I_\pm} W < W(x\pm)$$

for any $\varepsilon > 0$, where $I_+ = (x, x+\varepsilon)$ and $I_- = (x-\varepsilon, x)$. W is said to have a local minimum at x if $\inf_I W = W(x)\wedge W(x-)$ for some $\varepsilon>0$ where $I = (x-\varepsilon, x+\varepsilon)$. A local maximum is defined similarly. Denote by $\underline{\underline{W}}^\#$ the set of $W\in\underline{\underline{W}}$ with the following four properties.

1) This is the space of $\mathbb{R}$-valued right continuous functions on $\mathbb{R}$ with left limits.

(4.2a) $$\overline{\lim_{x\to\infty}}\ \{W(x) - \inf_{[0,x]} W\} = \overline{\lim_{x\to-\infty}}\ \{W(x) - \inf_{[x,0]} W\} = \infty .$$

(4.2b) If W is discontinuous at x, then W is oscillating at x.

(4.2c) For any open set G in $\mathbb{R}$ both the sets

$$\{x \in G : W(x) = \sup_G W\},\ \{x \in G : W(x) = \inf_G W\}$$

contain at most one point.

(4.2d) W does not have a local maximum at $x = 0$.

Let $W \in \underline{\underline{W}}^{\#}$. Then $V = (a,b,c)$ is called a <u>valley</u> of W if

(i) $a < b < c$,

(ii) W is continuous at a, b and c,

(iii) $W(b) < W(x) < W(a)$ for every $x \in (a,b)$,

$W(b) < W(x) < W(c)$ for every $x \in (b,c)$,

(iv) $H_{a,b} < W(c) - W(b)$, $H_{c,b} < W(a) - W(b)$.

Here the notation $H_{x,y}$ is defined as in (1.2). The depth D and the inner directed ascent A are defined as in §1. Notice that (ii) implies that W is continuous at x if W has a local minimum (or maximum) at x. It can be proved that $Q(W^{\#}) = 1$. Moreover, making use of the self-similarity of a symmetric stable environment we can prove the following: There exists a valley $V = (a,b,c)$ of W such that $a < 0 < c$ and $A < 1 < D$, Q-a.s. The bottom of such a valley is uniquely determined by W and so is denoted by $b = b(W)$. For $\lambda > 0$ we define the scaled environment W_λ^α by $W_\lambda^\alpha(x) = \lambda^{-1}W(\lambda^\alpha x)$, $x \in \mathbb{R}$. Then as a special case of [6] (see also [4]) we have the following result: For any $\varepsilon>0$

$$P\{|\lambda^{-\alpha}X(e^\lambda, W) - b(W_\lambda^\alpha)| > \varepsilon\} \to 0$$

in probability with respect to Q as $\lambda\to\infty$ and consequently the full distribution of $(\log t)^{-\alpha}X(t)$ converges to the distribution of $b = b(W)$ as $t \to \infty$.

Our task is now to compute the distribution of $b = b(W)$. Although we are unable to give an analytic representation like (4.1), we have the following simple probabilistic representation of the limit distribution.

Theorem 4.1. The full distribution of $(\log t)^{-\alpha} X(t)$ converges, as $t \to \infty$, to the distribution with density

$$\phi(x) = \{ \frac{\Gamma(\alpha+1)}{\Gamma(\frac{\alpha}{2})} \}^2 \cdot Q\{ \sup_{[0,|x|]} W^* < 1\} , x \in \mathbb{R},$$

where

$$W^*(u) = W(u) - \inf_{[0,u]} W, \ u \geq 0.$$

The proof will be based on the following description of $b(W)$ due to Kesten. For $W \in \underline{\underline{W}}^{\#}$ we set

$$d_\pm = \pm \inf\{u > 0 : W^*(\pm u) \geq 1\}$$

where $W^*(-u)$, $u \geq 0$, is defined in a way similar to $W^*(u)$, and define $b_\pm$ by

$$W(b_+) = \inf_{[0,d_+]} W, \quad W(b_-) = \inf_{[d_-,0]} W.$$

We also set

$$V_\pm = W(b_\pm), \quad M_+ = \sup_{[0,b_+]} W, \quad M_- = \sup_{[b_-,0]} W.$$

Lemma 4.1 (Kesten [6]). Let (a, b, c) be a valley of W such that $a < 0 < c$ and $A < 1 < D$. Then

$$b = b_+ \text{ or } b_-$$

and the equality $b = b_+$ holds if and only if one of the following conditions holds:

(i) $V_- > V_+$ and $M_+ < (V_- + 1) \vee M_-$,

(ii) $V_- < V_+$ and $M_- > (V_+ + 1) \vee M_+$.

Since we deal only with the probability measure Q in the sequel, we write simply $E\{\cdot\}$ instead of $E^Q\{\cdot\}$ for the expectation with respect to Q. Again we introduce notation:

$$F_\lambda(x) = E\{e^{-\lambda b_+} ; V_+ < x - 1, M_+ < x\}$$
$$= E\{e^{-\lambda b_-} ; V_- < x - 1, M_- < x\} .$$

Clearly $F_\lambda(x)$ vanishes identically on $(-\infty, 0]$ and equals $E\{e^{-\lambda b_+}\}$ on $[1,\infty)$.

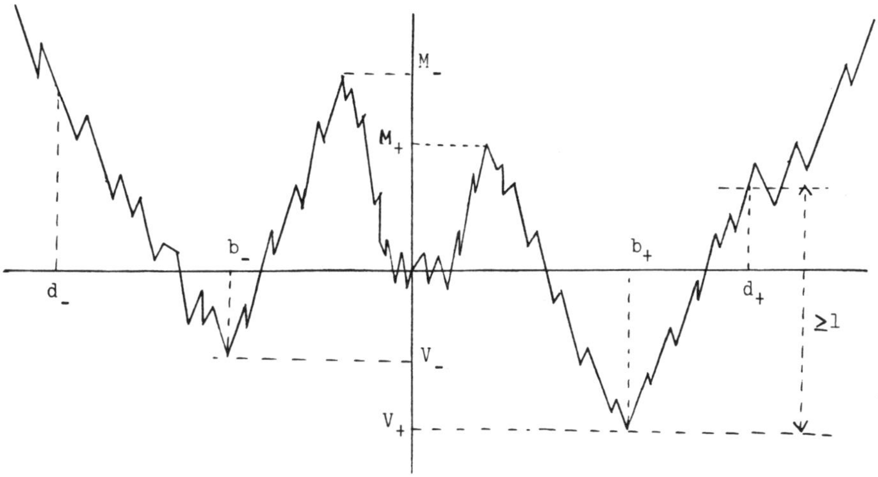

Lemma 4.2. $E\{e^{-\lambda b}; b > 0\} = \int_0^1 F_\lambda(x)dF_0(x)$, $\lambda > 0$.

Proof. Let

$$E_1 = \{V_- > V_+ , M_+ < (V_- + 1)\vee M_-\} ,$$
$$E_2 = \{V_1 < V_+ , M_- > (V_+ + 1)\vee M_+\} .$$

Then it is easy to see that

$$(E_1 \cup E_2)^c = \{V_- < V_+\vee(M_+ - 1), M_- < (V_+ + 1)\vee M_+\},$$

and hence

$$E\{e^{-\lambda b} ; b > 0\}$$
$$= E\{e^{-\lambda b_+} ; V_- > V_+ , M_+ < (V_- + 1)\vee M_-\}$$
$$+ E\{e^{-\lambda b_+} ; V_- < V_+ , M_- > (V_+ + 1)\vee M_+\}$$
$$= E\{e^{-\lambda b_+} ; E_1 \cup E_2\}$$

$= E\{e^{-\lambda b_+}\} - E\{e^{-\lambda b_+} ; (E_1 \cup E_2)^c\}$

$= E\{e^{-\lambda b_+}\} - E\{e^{-\lambda b_+} ; V_- < V_+ \vee (M_+ - 1), M_- < (V_+ + 1) \vee M_+\}$

$= F_\lambda(1) - E\{e^{-\lambda b_+} \cdot F_0((V_+ + 1) \vee M_+)\}$

$= F_\lambda(1) - \int_0^1 F_0(x) dF_\lambda(x)$

$= \int_0^1 F_\lambda(x) dF_0(x).$

Now the rest of the proof of Theorem 4.1 is divided into two parts.

1. Properties of a symmetric stable process. We deal with the symmetric stable process $\{x + W(t), t \geq 0, x \in \mathbb{R}, Q\}$ and prepare some of its properties for our later use. For the proof omitted here, see [10]. For $x, a \in \mathbb{R}$ we set

$$S_a^x = \inf\{t > 0 : x + W(t) > a\},$$

$$T_a^x = \inf\{t > 0 : x + W(t) < a\},$$

$$T^x = S_1^x \wedge T_0^x .$$

Let $g_\lambda(x,y)$ be the Green function of order $\lambda > 0$ of the symmetric stable process with absorbing barriers at 0 and 1. We thus have

$$E\{ \int_0^{T^x} e^{-\lambda t} f(x + W(t)) dt\} = \int_0^1 g_\lambda(x,y) f(y) dy, \quad 0 < x < 1.$$

It is known that $g_\lambda(x,y)$ is symmetric in x and y. We still need the following notation:

$$p_\lambda^+(x) = E\{e^{-\lambda S_1^x} ; S_1^x < T_0^x\} , \; p_\lambda^-(x) = E\{e^{-\lambda T_0^x} ; T_0^x < S_1^x\} ,$$

$$p_\lambda(x) = p_\lambda^+(x) + p_\lambda^-(x) = E\{e^{-\lambda T^x}\} ,$$

$$q^+(x) = 2\alpha^{-1}\{\Gamma(\alpha/2)\}^{-2} x^{\frac{\alpha}{2}} (1-x)^{\frac{\alpha}{2}-1},$$

$$q^-(x) = 2\alpha^{-1}\{\Gamma(\alpha/2)\}^{-2} (1-x)^{\frac{\alpha}{2}} x^{\frac{\alpha}{2}-1},$$

$$q_\lambda^{\pm}(x) = q^{\pm}(x) - \lambda \int_0^1 g_\lambda(x,y)q^{\pm}(y)dy,$$

$$r(x) = x^{\frac{\alpha}{2}-1}(1-x)^{\frac{\alpha}{2}-1}.$$

Notice that

$$g_\lambda(x,y) = g_\lambda(1-x, 1-y),$$

$$p_\lambda^+(x) = p_\lambda^-(1-x), \; p_\lambda(x) = p_\lambda(1-x),$$

$$q^+(x) = q^-(1-x), \; q_\lambda^+(x) = q_\lambda^-(1-x).$$

We also use the notation:

$$c(\alpha) = \Gamma(\alpha+1)\pi^{-1}\sin(\alpha\pi/2),$$
$$\langle p, q\rangle = \int_0^1 p(x)q(x)dx .$$

Lemma 4.3. $\alpha\{\Gamma(\alpha/2)\}^2 \langle p_\lambda, q^+\rangle = \langle p_\lambda, r\rangle$.

Proof. The left hand side equals

$$2\langle p_\lambda, xr\rangle = 2\langle p_\lambda, (1-x)r\rangle = \text{the right hand side;}$$

the second equality is obtained by adding the preceding two terms and then dividing the sum by 2.

Lemma 4.4 (Watanabe [10]). (i) For any $f \in C([0,1])$

$$\lim_{x\downarrow 0} x^{-\alpha/2} \int_0^1 g_\lambda(x,y)f(y)dy = \langle f, q_\lambda^-\rangle,$$

$$\lim_{x\downarrow 0} x^{-\alpha/2} \int_0^1 g_\lambda(1-x, y)f(y)dy = \langle f, q_\lambda^+\rangle .$$

(ii) $$p_\lambda^+(x) = \alpha^{-1}c(\alpha) \int_0^1 g_\lambda(x,y)(1-y)^{-\alpha} dy,$$

$$p_\lambda^-(x) = \alpha^{-1}c(\alpha) \int_0^1 g_\lambda(x,y)y^{-\alpha} dy ,$$

$$p_0^+(x) = 2^{1-\alpha}\Gamma(\alpha)\{\Gamma(\alpha/2)\}^{-2} \int_{-1}^{-1+2x} (1-y^2)^{\frac{\alpha}{2}-1} dy .$$

Lemma 4.5. We have

(i) $\lim_{x\downarrow 0} p_\lambda^+(x)x^{-\alpha/2} = \lim_{x\downarrow 0} p_\lambda^-(1-x)x^{-\alpha/2} = K - \lambda\langle p_\lambda^-, q^+\rangle$,

(ii) $\lim_{x\downarrow 0}\{1 - p_\lambda^-(x)\}x^{-\alpha/2} = \lim_{x\downarrow 0}\{1 - p_\lambda^+(1-x)\}x^{-\alpha/2} = K + \lambda\langle p_\lambda^+, q^+\rangle$

where

$$K = \alpha^{-1}c(\alpha)\int_0^1 q^+(x)x^{-\alpha}dx = 2\Gamma(1-\tfrac{\alpha}{2})c(\alpha)/\Gamma(\alpha/2).$$

Proof. We give the proof of (ii). Since

$$\int_0^1 g_\lambda(x,y)dy = \lambda^{-1}\{1 - p_\lambda(x)\}$$

we have

$$\begin{aligned}
\lim_{x\downarrow 0}\{1 - p_\lambda^-(x)\}x^{-\alpha/2} &= \lim_{x\downarrow 0}\{1 - p_\lambda(x)\}x^{-\alpha/2} + \lim_{x\downarrow 0} p_\lambda^+(x)x^{-\alpha/2} \\
&= \lambda\lim_{x\downarrow 0} x^{-\alpha/2}\int_0^1 g_\lambda(x,y)dy + \lim_{x\downarrow 0} p_\lambda^+(x)x^{-\alpha/2} \\
&= \langle \lambda + \alpha^{-1}c(\alpha)\cdot x^{-\alpha}, q_\lambda^+\rangle \\
&= K + \lambda\langle p_\lambda, q^+\rangle - \lambda\langle p_\lambda^-, q^+\rangle \\
&= K + \lambda\langle p_\lambda^+, q^+\rangle .
\end{aligned}$$

2. Computation of $E\{e^{-\lambda b}; b > 0\}$.

Lemma 4.6. For $\lambda, \mu > 0$

$$E\{e^{-\lambda b_+ - \mu(d_+ - b_+)}\} = \{K - \mu\langle p_\mu^-, q^+\rangle\}\{K + \lambda\langle p_\lambda^+, q^+\rangle\}^{-1}.$$

In particular

$$E\{e^{-\lambda b_+}\} = K\{K + \lambda\langle p_\lambda^+, q^+\rangle\}^{-1},$$

$$E\{e^{-\lambda d_+}\} = \{K - \lambda\langle p_\lambda^-, q^+\rangle\}\{K + \lambda\langle p_\lambda^+, q^+\rangle\}^{-1}.$$

Proof. The proof is similar to that in [6]. For $\varepsilon > 0$ we set

$$T^{(0)} = T_\varepsilon^{(0)} = 0,$$

$$T^{(n)} = T_\varepsilon^{(n)} = \inf\{t > T^{(n-1)} : W(t) - W(T^{(n-1)}) < -\varepsilon\}$$

$$S^{(n)} = S_\varepsilon^{(n)} = \inf\{t > T^{(n-1)} : W(t) - W(T^{(n-1)}) > 1-\varepsilon\},\ n = 1,2,\ldots$$

Then

$$E\{e^{-\lambda b_+ - \mu(d_+ - b_+)}\}$$

$$= \lim_{\varepsilon\downarrow 0} \sum_{n=1}^{\infty} E\{e^{-\lambda T^{(n)} - \mu(S^{(n+1)} - T^{(n)})};\ T^{(k)} < S^{(k)} \text{ for } 1 \leq \forall k \leq n \text{ and } S^{(n+1)} < T^{(n+1)}\}$$

$$= \lim_{\varepsilon\downarrow 0} \sum_{n=1}^{\infty} \{E\{e^{-\lambda T^0_{-\varepsilon}};\ T^0_{-\varepsilon} < S^0_{1-\varepsilon}\}\}^n E\{e^{-\mu S^0_{1-\varepsilon}};\ S^0_{1-\varepsilon} < T^0_{-\varepsilon}\}$$

$$= \lim_{\varepsilon\downarrow 0} \sum_{n=1}^{\infty} \{p_\lambda^-(\varepsilon)\}^n \cdot p_\lambda^+(\varepsilon).$$

If we set

$$K_1 = K + \lambda\langle p_\lambda^+, q^+\rangle,\quad K_2 = K - \lambda\langle p_\lambda^-, q^+\rangle,$$

then

$$1 - p_\lambda^-(\varepsilon) \sim K_1\varepsilon^{\alpha/2},\quad p_\lambda^+(\varepsilon) \sim K_2\varepsilon^{\alpha/2} \quad \text{as} \quad \varepsilon\downarrow 0 .$$

Therefore we have

$$E\{e^{-\lambda b_+ - \mu(d_+ - b_-)}\} = \lim_{\varepsilon\downarrow 0} \sum_{n=1}^{\infty} (1 - K_1\varepsilon^{\alpha/2})^n K_2\varepsilon^{\alpha/2}$$

$$= K_2/K_1 = \{K - \lambda\langle p_\lambda^-, q^+\rangle\}\{K + \lambda\langle p_\lambda^+, q^+\rangle\}^{-1},$$

completing the proof of the lemma.

For the proof of the theorem it is enough to prove the following lemma.

Lemma 4.7. For $\lambda > 0$

$$E\{e^{-\lambda b};\ b>0\} = \{\Gamma(\alpha+1)/\Gamma(\alpha/2)\}^2 \int_0^\infty e^{-\lambda t} Q\{d_+ > t\}dt.$$

Proof. We first notice that

$$F_\lambda(x) = E\{e^{-\lambda b_+} ; V_+ < x - 1, M_+ < x\}$$

$$= E\{e^{-\lambda T^0_{x-1}} ; T^0_{x-1} < T^0_x\}E\{e^{-\lambda b_+}\} = p^+_\lambda(x)E\{e^{-\lambda b_+}\} ,$$

$$F_0(x) = p^+_0(x) = 2^{1-\alpha}\Gamma(\alpha)\{\Gamma(\alpha/2)\}^{-2} \int_{-1}^{-1+2x} (1 - y^2)^{\frac{\alpha}{2}-1} dy,$$

$$dF_0(x) = \Gamma(\alpha)\{\Gamma(\alpha/2)\}^{-2}r(x)dx .$$

We thus have

(4.3) $$E\{e^{-\lambda b} ; b > 0\} = \int_0^1 F_\lambda(x)dF_0(x)$$

$$= E\{e^{-\lambda b_+}\} \int_0^1 p^+_\lambda(x)\, dF_0(x) = \Gamma(\alpha)\{\Gamma(\alpha/2)\}^{-2} E\{e^{-\lambda b_+}\}\langle p^+_\lambda , r\rangle$$

$$= 2^{-1}\Gamma(\alpha)\{\Gamma(\alpha/2)\}^{-2}E\{e^{-\lambda b_+}\}\langle p_\lambda, r\rangle .$$

On the other hand, using Lemma 4.3 we have

$$\int_0^\infty e^{-\lambda t}Q\{d_+ > t\}dt = \lambda^{-1}\{1 - E(e^{-\lambda d_+})\} = \langle p_\lambda, q^+\rangle\{K + \lambda\langle p^+_\lambda, q^+\rangle\}^{-1}$$

$$= \alpha^{-1}\{\Gamma(\alpha/2)\}^{-2} \langle p_\lambda, r\rangle\{K + \lambda\langle p^+_\lambda, q^+\rangle\}^{-1}$$

$$= (\alpha K)^{-1}\{\Gamma(\alpha/2)\}^{-2} E\{e^{-\lambda b_+}\}\langle p_\lambda,r\rangle .$$

Combining this with (4.3) we obtain Lemma 4.7. This completes also the proof of Theorem 4.1.

Remark. The density ϕ in Theorem 4.1 is symmetric and

$$\int_0^\infty e^{-\lambda x}\phi(x)dx = \frac{\alpha\{\Gamma(\alpha)\}^2}{\{\Gamma(\alpha/2)\}^4} \cdot \frac{\langle p_\lambda , r\rangle}{K + \lambda\langle p^+_\lambda, q^+\rangle} , \lambda > 0.$$

References

[1] T. Brox, A one-dimensional diffusion process in a Wiener medium, to appear in Ann. Probab.

[2] A.O. Golosov, The limit distributions for random walks in random environments, Soviet Math. Dokl., 28 (1983), 19-22.

[3] K. Itô and H.P. McKean, Diffusion Processes and Their Sample Paths, Springer-Verlag, Berlin, 1965.

[4] K. Kawazu, Y. Tamura and H. Tanaka, One-dimensional diffusions and random walks in random media, in preparation.

[5] H. Kesten, M.V. Kozlov and F. Spitzer, A limit law for random walk in a random environment, Compositio Math., 30 (1975), 145-168.

[6] H. Kesten, The limit distribution of Sinai's random walk in random environment, to appear in Physica.

[7] S. Schumacher, Diffusions with random coefficients, Contemporary Mathematics (Particle Systems, Random Media and Large Deviations, ed. by R. Durrett), 41 (1985), 351-356.

[8] Y.G. Sinai, The limiting behavior of a one-dimensional random walk in a random medium, Theory of Probab. and its Appl., 27 (1982), 256-268.

[9] H. Tanaka, Limit distribution for 1-dimensional diffusion in a reflected Brownian medium, preprint, 1986.

[10] S. Watanabe, On stable processes with boundary conditions, J. Math. Soc. Japan, 14(1962), 170-198.

J. Fac. Sci. Univ. Tokyo
Sect. IA, Math.
34 (1987), 351-369.

Stochastic differential equation corresponding to the spatially homogeneous Boltzmann equation of Maxwellian and non-cutoff type

Dedicated to Professor Seizô Itô on his 60th birthday

By Hiroshi TANAKA

Introduction

It is known that a Markov process can be associated with a certain nonlinear equation of Boltzmann type ([2][3][4][5][7]). In the case of the spatially homogeneous Boltzmann equation of Maxwellian molecules, the associated Markov process was constructed by solving certain stochastic differential equation (abbreviated: SDE) based on a Poisson random measure ([7], see also [5][6]). The purposes of this paper are to simplify the proof of existence of solutions of the SDE of [7] by modifying the form of the SDE and also to give some remarks concerning the uniqueness of solutions.

We consider the Boltzmann equation of Maxwellian molecules:

$$(1)\qquad \frac{\partial u}{\partial t}=\int_{(0,\pi)\times(0,2\pi)\times \boldsymbol{R}^3}(u'u_1'-uu_1)Q(\theta)d\theta\hat{d}\epsilon dx_1,\ t\geq 0,\ x\in \boldsymbol{R}^3,$$

where $u=u(t, x)$, $u_1=u(t, x_1)$, $u'=u(t, x')$, $u_1'=u(t, x_1')$ and $\hat{d}\epsilon=d\epsilon/2\pi$. $Q(\theta)$, $0<\theta<\pi$, is a positive function determined by the intermolecular repulsive force which is inversely proportional to the fifth power of their distance and has the property: $Q(\theta)\sim const.\,\theta^{-3/2}$, $\theta\downarrow 0$; so $\int_0^\pi Q(\theta)d\theta=\infty$ (non-cut-off) but

$$(\mathrm{I})\qquad \int_0^\pi \theta Q(\theta)d\theta<\infty.$$

However, the special form of $Q(\theta)$ is not important in our methods and hence in this paper we assume that $Q(\theta)$ is an arbitrary nonnegative function satisfying only the condition (I) or even the following weaker one:

(II) $$\int_0^\pi \theta^2 Q(\theta)d\theta<\infty.$$

The two cases (I) and (II) are discussed separately.

A molecule with velocity x collides with a similar test molecule with velocity x_1; the post-collision velocities are denoted by x' and x_1', respectively. If $S(x, x_1)$ denotes the 2-dimensional sphere with center $(x+x_1)/2$ and radius $|x-x_1|/2$, then x' and x_1' are always on $S(x, x_1)$, or more precisely, $S(x', x_1')=S(x, x_1)$. Taking a spherical coordinate system on $S(x, x_1)$ with north pole x, denote by θ (resp. ϵ) the colatitude (resp. longitude) of x'. Then x' and x_1' can be regarded as functions of x, x_1, θ and ϵ. We set

$$a(x, x_1, \theta, \epsilon)=x'-x.$$

A probability measure valued function $u(t)$, $t>0$, is called a weak solution of (1) if

$$\frac{d}{dt}\langle u(t), \varphi\rangle=\langle u(t)\otimes u(t), K\varphi\rangle, \quad \varphi\in C_0^\infty(\boldsymbol{R}^3),$$

where $(K\varphi)(x, x_1)=\int_{(0,\pi)\times(0,2\pi)}\{\varphi(x')-\varphi(x)\}Q(\theta)d\theta\hat{d}\epsilon$ (see Appendix of [7]).

In [7] the following SDE was considered in connection with the Boltzmann equation (1) under the assumption (I):

$$(2) \quad X(t, \omega)=X(0, \omega) + \int_{(0,t]\times(0,\pi)\times(0,2\pi)\times(0,1)} a(X(s-, \omega), Y(s-, \alpha), \theta, \epsilon)N(dsd\theta d\epsilon d\alpha).$$

Here, $N(\cdot)$ is a Poisson random measure on $(0, \infty)\times(0, \pi)\times(0, 2\pi)\times(0, 1)$ with intensity measure $dsQ(\theta)\hat{d}\epsilon d\alpha$, and the solution process $\{X(t, \omega), t\geq 0\}$ is to be found on a basic probability space $\{\Omega, P\}$ under the condition that the process $\{Y(t, \alpha), t\geq 0\}$, defined on the probability space $\{(0, 1), d\alpha\}$ and describing the motion of a test molecule, is equivalent in law to $\{X(t, \omega), t\geq 0\}$. The relation between the Boltzmann equation (1) and the SDE (2) is that the probability distribution of $X(t)$ is a weak solution of (1) (general theory of SDE's including jump parts goes back to K. Itô [1]).

The modification we are making for the SDE (2) in proving existence theorem is as follows:

(i) $N(\cdot)$ is replaced by a Poisson random measure (again denoted by $N(\cdot)$) on $(0, \infty)\times(0, \pi)\times S^2\times\Omega_1$ with intensity measure $dsQ(\theta)d\theta\hat{d}\sigma dP_1$, where $\{\Omega_1, P_1\}$ is a copy of the basic probability space $\{\Omega, P\}$ and $\hat{d}\sigma$ is the uniform probability distribution on the 2-dimensional unit sphere S^2.

(ii) $Y(s-, \alpha)$ is replaced by $X(s-, \omega_1)$.

(iii) $a(x, x_1, \theta, \epsilon)$ is replaced by $b(x, x_1, \theta, \sigma)$ (the definition is given in § 1).

Thus in the case (I) the modified SDE can be written as

$$X(t, \omega)=X(0, \omega)+\int_{S_t} b(X(s-, \omega), X(s-, \omega_1), \theta, \sigma)N(dsd\theta d\sigma d\omega_1), \tag{3}$$

where $S_t=(0, t]\times(0, \pi)\times S^2\times\Omega_1$ (in the case (II) the modified SDE is given by (3.3) in § 3). Advantage of the modified SDE (3) is that the new coefficient $b(x, x_1, \theta, \sigma)$ is Lipschitz continuous in (x, x_1) as an $L^1(\hat{d}\sigma)$-valued function for each fixed θ (see Lemma 1) and that the process describing the motion of a test molecule is exactly a copy of the solution process $X(t, \omega)$, and in fact, by virtue of these, (3) can be solved easily by using a routine iteration method. The proof of pathwise uniqueness for (3) is also easy.

Most of the discussions on the uniqueness in the law sense are essentially the same as the proof of Theorem 4.1 of [7] but they are somewhat simplified. In formulating the uniqueness in the law sense we further modify the SDE (3) as follows:

(i′) $\{\Omega_1, P_1\}$ is replaced by a probability space $\{\tilde{\Omega}, \tilde{P}\}$ which need not be a copy of $\{\Omega, P\}$.

(ii′) $X(s-, \omega_1)$ is replaced by $\tilde{X}(s, \tilde{\omega})$ which is an arbitrary measurable process defined on $\{\tilde{\Omega}, \tilde{P}\}$ such that it has the same distribution as the solution $X(s, \omega)$ for each s.

The uniqueness in the law sense is proved for this modified SDE so (in the case (I)) the solution process has the same law as the solution process of (3) (and also (2)).

Similar discussions in the case (II) are also given.

§ 1. L^1-Lipschitz continuity of $b(x, x_1, \theta, \sigma)$

Think of $S(x, x_1)$ as a celestial globe with north pole x and let $C(x, x_1, \theta)$ denote the circle on $S(x, x_1)$ with constant colatitude θ. Given

$\sigma \in S^2$, let $s(x, x_1, \sigma)=2^{-1}|x-x_1|\sigma+2^{-1}(x+x_1)$, let $M(x, x_1, \sigma)$ denote the meridian on $S(x, x_1)$ passing through $s(x, x_1, \sigma)$ and set

$$b_0(x, x_1, \theta, \sigma)=C(x, x_1, \theta)\cap M(x, x_1, \theta)=\text{a point on } S(x, x_1),$$
$$b(x, x_1, \theta, \sigma)=b_0(x, x_1, \theta, \sigma)-x.$$

Then for fixed $x, x_1 \in \boldsymbol{R}^3$, $x \neq x_1$ and $\theta \in (0, \pi)$, $b_0(x, x_1, \theta, \sigma)$ is uniformly distributed on $C(x, x_1, \theta)$ as a random variable defined on the probability space $\{S^2, \hat{d}\sigma\}$. When $x=x_1$, we set $b(x, x_1, \theta, \sigma)=0$.

LEMMA 1. *For any $x, x_1, y, y_1 \in \boldsymbol{R}^3$ and $\theta \in (0, \pi)$,*

$$\int_{S^2}|b(x, x_1, \theta, \sigma)-b(y, y_1, \theta, \sigma)|\hat{d}\sigma \leq const.\,\{|x-y|+|x_1-y_1|\}\theta, \tag{1.1}$$

where const. is independent of x, x_1, y, y_1 and θ.

PROOF. First we consider a special case.

(i) Special case: $S(x, x_1)=S(y, y_1)=S^2$.

In this case the integral on the left in (1.1) depends only on θ and the angle ξ $(0\leq \xi \leq \pi)$ between x and y. Therefore, it is enough to consider the case

$$x=(0, 0, 1),\ y=(0, \sin\xi, \cos\xi),\ x_1=-x,\ y_1=-y, \tag{1.2}$$

and prove that the integral on the left in (1.1) is dominated by const. $\theta\xi$. Let A be the rotation in $\boldsymbol{R}^3$ around the x^1-axis by the angle ξ. Then in the case (1.2) we have

$$b(y, y_1, \theta, \sigma)=A^{-1}b(x, x_1, \theta, A\sigma). \tag{1.3}$$

A point $\sigma \in S^2$ is expressed as $\sigma=(r, \sqrt{1-r^2}\cos\varphi, \sqrt{1-r^2}\sin\varphi)$ where $-1\leq r\leq 1$, $0\leq\varphi<2\pi$. We assume $0\leq r\leq 1$ for simplicity. We notice that $A\sigma=(r, \sqrt{1-r^2}\cos(\varphi+\xi), \sqrt{1-r^2}\sin(\varphi+\xi))$. Next, we define α and $\tilde{\alpha}$, respectively, by

$$\cos\alpha=\frac{r}{\sqrt{r^2+(1-r^2)\cos^2\varphi}}, \qquad \sin\alpha=\frac{\sqrt{1-r^2}\cos\varphi}{\sqrt{r^2+(1-r^2)\cos^2\varphi}}$$
$$\cos\tilde{\alpha}=\frac{r}{\sqrt{r^2+(1-r^2)\cos^2(\varphi+\xi)}}, \quad \sin\tilde{\alpha}=\frac{\sqrt{1-r^2}\cos(\varphi+\xi)}{\sqrt{r^2+(1-r^2)\cos^2(\varphi+\xi)}}.$$

Then

$$b(x, x_1, \theta, \sigma) = (\sin\theta\cos\alpha, \sin\theta\sin\alpha, \cos\theta - 1)$$
$$b(x, x_1, \theta, A\sigma) = (\sin\theta\cos\tilde{\alpha}, \sin\theta\sin\tilde{\alpha}, \cos\theta - 1),$$

and hence from (1.3)

$$b(y, y_1, \theta, \sigma) = (\sin\theta\cos\tilde{\alpha}, \sin\theta\sin\tilde{\alpha}\cos\xi + (\cos\theta - 1)\sin\xi, \\ -\sin\theta\sin\tilde{\alpha}\sin\xi + (\cos\theta - 1)\cos\xi).$$

Therefore

$$\begin{aligned} (1.4)\qquad & b(x, x_1, \theta, \sigma) - b(y, y_1, \theta, \sigma) \\ &= (\sin\theta(\cos\alpha - \cos\tilde{\alpha}), \sin\theta(\sin\alpha - \sin\tilde{\alpha}\cos\xi) + (1 - \cos\theta)\sin\xi, \\ &\qquad \sin\theta\sin\tilde{\alpha}\sin\xi - (1 - \cos\theta)(1 - \cos\xi)), \end{aligned}$$

and hence

$$\begin{aligned} &\int_{S^2} |b(x, x_1, \theta, \sigma) - b(y, y_1, \theta, \sigma)|\hat{d}\sigma \\ &= \frac{1}{2\pi}\int_0^1\int_0^{2\pi} |b(x, x_1, \theta, \sigma) - b(y, y_1, \theta, \sigma)|\,dr\,d\varphi \leq \text{const.}\,\theta\xi \end{aligned}$$

follows from (1.4) once we prove the following estimates.

$$(1.5)\qquad \int_0^1\int_0^{2\pi} |\cos\alpha - \cos\tilde{\alpha}|\,dr\,d\varphi \leq \text{const.}\,\xi.$$

$$(1.6)\qquad \int_0^1\int_0^{2\pi} |\sin\alpha - \sin\tilde{\alpha}\cos\xi|\,dr\,d\varphi \leq \text{const.}\,\xi.$$

The proof of (1.5) is as follows. Setting $f(r, \varphi, \xi) = \cos\alpha - \cos\tilde{\alpha}$ and $f_\xi(r, \varphi, \xi) = \partial f/\partial\xi$, we have

$$\begin{aligned} \int_0^1\int_0^{2\pi} |\cos\alpha - \cos\tilde{\alpha}|\,dr\,d\varphi &= \int_0^1\int_0^{2\pi} \left|\int_0^\xi f_\xi(r, \varphi, \eta)\,d\eta\right| dr\,d\varphi \\ &\leq \int_0^\xi d\eta \int_0^1\int_0^{2\pi} |f_\xi(r, \varphi, \eta)|\,dr\,d\varphi \leq \text{const.}\,\xi, \end{aligned}$$

because

$$\begin{aligned} \int_0^1\int_0^{2\pi} |f_\xi(r, \varphi, \eta)|\,dr\,d\varphi &= \int_0^1\int_0^{2\pi} r(1 - r^2)\{r^2 + (1 - r^2)\cos^2\varphi\}^{-3/2}|\cos\varphi\sin\varphi|\,dr\,d\varphi \\ &= 4\int_0^1\int_0^1 r(1 - r^2)\{r^2 + (1 - r^2)x^2\}^{-3/2}x\,dr\,dx \\ &\leq 4\int_0^1\int_0^1 rx(rx)^{-3/2}\,dr\,dx < \infty \quad (\text{use } r^2 + (1 - r^2)x^2 \geq rx). \end{aligned}$$

As for (1.6), it is enough to prove

$$\int_0^1\int_0^{2\pi}|\sin\alpha-\sin\tilde{\alpha}|drd\varphi\leq\text{const.}\,\xi,$$

and for this it is also enough to prove that

$$\int_0^1\int_0^{2\pi}|g_\xi(r,\varphi,\xi)|drd\varphi=\text{indep. of }\xi<\infty, \tag{1.7}$$

where $g(r,\varphi,\xi)=\sin\alpha-\sin\tilde{\alpha}$ and $g_\xi(r,\varphi,\xi)=\partial g/\partial\xi$. But the left hand side of (1.7) is dominated by I_1+I_2, where

$$\begin{aligned}
I_1&=\int_0^1\int_0^{2\pi}\sqrt{1-r^2}\{r^2+(1-r^2)\cos^2\varphi\}^{-1/2}|\sin\varphi|drd\varphi\\
&\leq 4\int_0^1\int_0^1\{r^2+(1-r^2)x^2\}^{-1/2}drdx<\infty\quad(\text{because } r^2+(1-r^2)x^2\geq rx).\\
I_2&=\int_0^1\int_0^{2\pi}(1-r^2)^{3/2}\{r^2+(1-r^2)\cos^2\varphi\}^{-3/2}\cos^2\varphi|\sin\varphi|drd\varphi\\
&\leq 4\int_0^1\int_0^1\{r^2+(1-r^2)x^2\}^{-3/2}x^2drdx<\infty.
\end{aligned}$$

(ii) General case: Since

$$b(x,x_1,\theta,\sigma)=b\left(\frac{x-x_1}{2},-\frac{x-x_1}{2},\theta,\sigma\right)=\frac{|x-x_1|}{2}b(e_1,-e_1,\theta,\sigma),$$

$$e_1=\frac{x-x_1}{|x-x_1|},\quad e_2=\frac{y-y_1}{|y-y_1|},$$

we have

$$\begin{aligned}
&\int_{S^2}|b(x,x_1,\theta,\sigma)-b(y,y_1,\theta,\sigma)|\hat{d}\sigma\\
&\leq\int_{S^2}\frac{|x-x_1|}{2}\cdot|b(e_1,-e_1,\theta,\sigma)-b(e_2,-e_2,\theta,\sigma)|\hat{d}\sigma\\
&\quad+\left|\frac{|x-x_1|}{2}-\frac{|y-y_1|}{2}\right|\cdot\int_{S^2}|b(e_2,-e_2,\theta,\sigma)|\hat{d}\sigma\\
&\leq\text{const.}\frac{|x-x_1|}{2}\cdot|e_1-e_2|\theta+\left|\frac{|x-x_1|}{2}-\frac{|y-y_1|}{2}\right|\theta\\
&\leq\text{const.}\left\{\left|(x-x_1)-\frac{|x-x_1|}{|y-y_1|}(y-y_1)\right|+\Big||x-x_1|-|y-y_1|\Big|\right\}\theta,
\end{aligned}$$

where we have used the result of case (i). Now (1.1) follows from the following trivial inequalities.

$$\Big| |x-x_1|-|y-y_1| \Big| \leq |x-y|+|x_1-y_1| .$$

$$\Big| (x-x_1)-\frac{|x-x_1|}{|y-y_1|}(y-y_1) \Big| \leq 2(|x-y|+|x_1-y_1|) .$$

§ 2. Stochastic differential equation—I

In this section we assume that $Q(\theta)$ satisfies the condition (I).

2.1. Existence theorem

We assume that a basic probability space $\{\Omega, \mathcal{F}, P\}$, equipped with a filtration $\{\mathcal{F}_t\}$ of increasing sub-σ-fields of $\mathcal{F}$, satisfies the following conditions.

(2.1) The σ-field $\mathcal{F}_0$ contains all P-negligible sets and is rich enough in the sense that, for any probability distribution μ in $\boldsymbol{R}^3$, there exists an $\mathcal{F}_0$-measurable $\boldsymbol{R}^3$-valued random variable with distribution μ.

(2.2) There exists an $\mathcal{F}_t$-adapted Poisson random measure $N(\cdot)$ on $(0, \infty)\times(0, \pi)\times S^2\times\Omega_1$ with intensity measure $dsQ(\theta)d\theta\hat{d}\sigma dP_1$ where $\{\Omega_1, P_1\}$ is a copy of $\{\Omega, P\}$.

A Poisson random measure $N(\cdot)$ on $(0, \infty)\times(0, \pi)\times S^2\times\Omega_1$ is said to be $\mathcal{F}_t$-adapted if, for each $t\geq 0$, $\mathcal{F}_t^0\subset\mathcal{F}_t$ and $\mathcal{F}_t$ is indepedent of $\mathcal{F}_\infty^t$, where $\mathcal{F}_t^0$ (resp. $\mathcal{F}_\infty^t$) is the smallest σ-field on Ω with respect to which the random variables $N(A)$, $A\in\mathcal{A}_t^0$ (resp. $A\in\mathcal{A}_\infty^t$), are measurable; here $\mathcal{A}_t^0$ (resp. $\mathcal{A}_\infty^t$) denotes the class of measurable subsets of $S_t=(0, t]\times(0, \pi)\times S^2\times\Omega_1$ (resp. $S_\infty^t=(t, \infty)\times(0, \pi)\times S^2\times\Omega_1$).

REMARK 1. The conditions (2.1) and (2.2) are not severe restrictions on $\{\Omega, \mathcal{F}, P\}$; in fact, it is easy to see that even the unit interval (0, 1) with the Lebesgue measure satisfies these conditions.

The SDE we are going to discuss is the following (=(3)):

$$X(t, \omega)=X(0, \omega)+\int_{S_t} b(X(s-, \omega), X(s-, \omega_1), \theta, \sigma)N(dsd\theta d\sigma d\omega_1). \tag{2.3}$$

By a solution of (2.3) we mean an $\mathcal{F}_t$-adapted process $X(t, \omega)$, $t\geq 0$, which is right continuous and has left limits for almost all ω. $X(t, \omega)$, $t\geq 0$, is said to be integrable if $\int_0^T E|X(t, \omega)|dt<\infty$, $0<{}^\forall T<\infty$.

THEOREM 1. *Let the condition* (I) *be satisfied and let* $X(0, \omega)$ *be a given* $\mathcal{F}_0$*-measurable random variable with* $E|X(0, \omega)|<\infty$. *Then there exists a unique integrable solution of* (2.3).

PROOF. We set $X_0(t, \omega)=X(0, \omega)$, $t\geq 0$, and define $X_n(t, \omega)$, $n\geq 1$, successively by

$$(2.4)\quad X_n(t, \omega)=X(0, \omega)+\int_{S_t} b(X_{n-1}(s-, \omega), X_{n-1}(s-, \omega_1), \theta, \sigma)N(dsd\theta d\sigma d\omega_1).$$

The stochastic integral is well-defined for each n by virtue of the estimate $|b(x, x_1, \theta, \sigma)|\leq|x-x_1|\theta/2$. By Lemma 1 we have

$$\begin{aligned}
&E\Big\{\sup_{0\leq s\leq t}|X_{n+1}(s)-X_n(s)|\Big\}\\
&\leq E\Big\{\int_{S_t}|b(X_n(s-, \omega), X_n(s-, \omega_1), \theta, \sigma)\\
&\qquad\qquad -b(X_{n-1}(s-, \omega), X_{n-1}(s-, \omega_1), \theta, \sigma)|N(dsd\theta d\sigma d\omega_1)\Big\}\\
&\leq \text{const.}\, E\Big[\int_{S_t}\{|X_n(s-, \omega)-X_{n-1}(s-, \omega)|\\
&\qquad\qquad +|X_n(s-, \omega_1)-X_{n-1}(s-, \omega_1)|\}\theta dsQ(\theta)d\theta P_1(d\omega_1)\Big]\\
&\leq \text{const.}\int_0^t E|X_n(s, \omega)-X_{n-1}(s, \omega)|ds,
\end{aligned}$$

and hence

$$\sum_{n=0}^{\infty} E\Big\{\sup_{0\leq s\leq t}|X_{n+1}(s)-X_n(s)|\Big\}\leq \sum_{n=0}^{\infty}\frac{c(c't)^n}{n!}<\infty$$

with some constants c and c'. Therefore

$$X(t, \omega)=\lim_{n\to\infty}X_n(t, \omega)$$

exists as a uniform convergence on each finite t-interval (a.s.); clearly $X(t, \omega)$ is an integrable solution of (2.3). To prove the uniqueness, let $X(t, \omega)$ and $Y(t, \omega)$ be any integrable solutions of (2.3). Then we have $E|X(t)-Y(t)|\leq$ const. $\int_0^t E|X(s)-Y(s)|ds$ and hence $X(t)=Y(t)$, $t\geq 0$, a.s.

2.2. Uniqueness in the law sense

The uniqueness in Theorem 1 asserts that there is only one solution of (2.3) so far as the basic probability space, the initial value and the Poisson random measure are fixed. Different choices of the basic probability space etc. yield different solutions, but we can prove that their probability laws in the path space are the same provided that their initial distributions are the same. We prove this uniqueness in the law sense for a slightly modified SDE (Theorem 2).

Let $\{\Omega, \mathcal{F}, P\}$ be a probability space with a filtration $\{\mathcal{F}_t\}$ satisfying (2.1) and (2.2) as before. But now we replace $\{\Omega_1, P_1\}$ by $\{\tilde{\Omega}, \tilde{P}\}$ which need not be a copy of $\{\Omega, P\}$. A process $Y(t, \tilde{\omega})$ defined on $\{\tilde{\Omega}, \tilde{P}\}$ is said to be integrable if it is jointly measurable and if

$$\int_0^T \int_{\tilde{\Omega}} |Y(t, \tilde{\omega})| dt d\tilde{P} < \infty, \quad 0 < {}^\forall T < \infty.$$

Let W denote the space of $\boldsymbol{R}^3$-valued right continuous paths with left limits.

Given an integrable process $Y(t, \tilde{\omega})$ defined on $\{\tilde{\Omega}, \tilde{P}\}$, we consider the SDE

$$X(t, \omega) = X(0, \omega) + \int_{S_t} b(X(s-, \omega), Y(s, \tilde{\omega}), \theta, \sigma) N(ds d\theta d\sigma d\tilde{\omega}) \tag{2.5}$$

where $S_t = (0, t] \times (0, \pi) \times S^2 \times \tilde{\Omega}$.

PROPOSITION 1. *Let the condition* (I) *be satisfied and let* $X(0, \omega)$ *be a given* $\mathcal{F}_0$*-measurable random variable with* $E|X(0, \omega)| < \infty$. *Then for any given integrable process* $Y(t, \tilde{\omega})$ *there exists an integrable solution of* (2.5). *Also the law uniqueness holds in the following sense: The probability measure on* W *induced by a solution of* (2.5) *is uniquely determined by* u_0 *and* $\tilde{u}(t)$, $t \geq 0$, *where* u_0 *is the probability distribution of* $X(0, \omega)$ *and* $\tilde{u}(t)$ *is that of* $Y(\cdot, \tilde{\omega})$ *at time* t.

PROOF. The existence of a solution is proved by a routine iteration method as in the proof of Theorem 1. The law uniqueness is proved as follows. First we choose a sequence $\{h_n(t), t \geq 0\}$ of step functions such that

(2.6) each $h_n(t)$ is expressed as

$$h_n(t) = \begin{cases} 0 & \text{for} \quad t = 0 \\ t_{nk} & \text{for} \quad t_{nk} < t \leq t_{nk+1} \ (k = 0, 1, \cdots), \end{cases}$$

where $\{t_{nk}\}$ satisfies
$0=t_{n0}<t_{n1}<\cdots$, $\lim_{k\to\infty} t_{nk}=\infty$, $\lim_{n\to\infty}\sup_k(t_{nk+1}-t_{nk})=0$;

$$\lim_{n\to\infty}\int_0^t\int_{\tilde\Omega}|Y(s,\tilde\omega)-Y(h_n(s),\tilde\omega)|dsd\tilde P=0,\quad 0<{}^\forall t<\infty. \tag{2.7}$$

Let $X(t)$ be the solution of (2.5) and let $X_n(t)$ be the solution of

$$X_n(t)=X(0)+\int_{S_t} b(X_n(h_n(s)),\, Y(h_n(s),\tilde\omega),\theta,\sigma)N(dsd\theta d\sigma d\tilde\omega). \tag{2.8}$$

Then $X_n(t)$ is obtained as follows:

$$X_n(t)=X_n(t_{nk})+\int_{S_t-S_{t_{nk}}} b(X_n(t_{nk}),\, Y(t_{nk},\tilde\omega),\theta,\sigma)dN,\quad t_{nk}<t\le t_{nk+1}\quad (k\ge 0). \tag{2.9}$$

Making use of the estimate

$$|b(x,x_1,\theta,\sigma)|\le|x-x_1|\theta/2, \tag{2.10}$$

and also (2.7), we can easily prove that

$$E|X_n(s)|\le \text{const.},\quad 0\le s\le t, \tag{2.11}$$

$$\sup\{E|X_n(t_1)-X_n(t_2)| : 0\le t_1,t_2\le t,\ |t_1-t_2|\le\varepsilon,\ n\ge 1\}\to 0\quad\text{as } \varepsilon\downarrow 0, \tag{2.12}$$

where const. may depend on t but not on n. Then, making use of Lemma 1 and then (2.7), (2.12), we have

$$\begin{aligned}E|X_n(t)-X(t)|&\le \text{const.}\int_0^t E|X_n(h_n(s))-X(s)|ds\\&\quad+\text{const.}\int_0^t\int_{\tilde\Omega}|Y(h_n(s))-Y(s)|dsd\tilde P\\&\le \text{const.}\int_0^t E|X_n(s)-X(s)|ds+o(1),\end{aligned}$$

and hence by Gronwall's inequality

$$\lim_{n\to\infty} E|X_n(t)-X(t)|=0. \tag{2.13}$$

On the other hand, by (2.9) we have for any $\xi\in\mathbf{R}^3$ and $t_{nk}<t\le t_{nk+1}$

$$E\Big[\exp\Big\{\sqrt{-1}\xi\cdot X_n(t)\Big\}\Big|\mathcal{F}_{t_{nk}}\Big]$$

$$= \exp\left[\sqrt{-1}\xi\cdot x+(t-t_{nk})\int_{(0,\pi)\times S^2\times\tilde{\Omega}}\left\{e^{\sqrt{-1}\xi\cdot b(x,\,Y(t_{nk},\tilde{\omega}),\theta,\sigma)}-1\right\}Q(\theta)d\theta\hat{d}\sigma d\tilde{P}\right]$$
$$= \exp\left[\sqrt{-1}\xi\cdot x+(t-t_{nk})\int_{(0,\pi)\times S^2\times R^3}\left\{e^{\sqrt{-1}\xi\cdot b(x,y,\theta,\sigma)}-1\right\}Q(\theta)d\theta\hat{d}\sigma\tilde{u}(t_{nk},dy)\right]$$

where we put $x=X_n(t_{nk})$. This conditional expectation formula implies that the probability measure on W induced by the process $X_n(t)$ is uniquely determined by u_0 and $\tilde{u}(t)$, $t\geq 0$. Therefore, by (2.13) the probability measure on W induced by $X(t)$ is also uniquely determined by u_0 and $\tilde{u}(t)$, $t\geq 0$. This completes the proof of the proposition.

Now we consider the following SDE for which we are going to prove the law uniqueness:

$$X(t)=X(0)+\int_{S_t} b(X(s-),\tilde{X}(s,\tilde{\omega}),\theta,\sigma)N(dsd\theta d\sigma d\tilde{\omega}). \tag{2.14a}$$

Here, an $\mathfrak{F}_t$-adapted integrable solution $X(t)$ is found under the condition that

(2.14b) $\tilde{X}(t,\tilde{\omega})$ is a measurable process defined on the probability space $\{\tilde{\Omega},\tilde{P}\}$ such that $\tilde{X}(t,\tilde{\omega})$ has the same distribution as $X(t)$ for each t.

REMARK 2. When $\{\tilde{\Omega},\tilde{P}\}=\{\Omega_1,P_1\}$, a solution of (2.3) is also a solution of (2.14).

THEOREM 2. *Let the condition* (I) *be satisfied and let* $X(0,\omega)$ *be any* R^3*-valued and* $\mathfrak{F}_0$*-measurable random variable with* $E|X(0,\omega)|<\infty$. *Then the probability measure on* W *induced by any integrable solution of* (2.14) *is uniquely determined by the probability distribution* u_0 *of the initial value* $X(0,\omega)$.

PROOF. Let $\hat{\Omega}=[0,1]$, $\hat{\mathfrak{F}}=$the σ-field of Borel subsets of $[0,1]$, $\hat{P}(A)=$ the Lebesgue measure of A $(\in\hat{\mathfrak{F}})$ and let $\{\Omega_1,P_1\}$ be a copy of $\{\hat{\Omega},\hat{P}\}$. As in 2.1 we construct, on the probability space $\{\hat{\Omega},\hat{P}\}$, a u_0-distributed random variable $\hat{X}$ and a Poisson random measure $\hat{N}(\cdot)$ on $(0,\infty)\times(0,\pi)\times S^2\times\Omega_1$ with intensity measure $dtQ(\theta)d\theta\hat{d}\sigma dP_1$ so that $\hat{X}$ and $\hat{N}(\cdot)$ are independent. We then consider the SDE of the type (2.3)

$$\hat{X}(t)=\hat{X}+\int_{\hat{S}_t} b(\hat{X}(s-),\hat{X}(s-,\omega_1),\theta,\sigma)d\hat{N}, \tag{2.15}$$

where $\hat{S}_t=(0, t]\times(0, \pi)\times S^2\times\Omega_1$. We are going to prove that for any solution $X(t)$ of (2.14) there exists a solution of (2.15) which (as a process) is equivalent in law to $X(t)$. Once this has been proved, the law uniqueness of solutions of (2.14) follows immediately from the pathwise uniqueness of solutions of (2.15).

On the probability space $\{\Omega_1, P_1\}$ we can find an $\boldsymbol{R}^3$-valued right continuous process $\hat{X}_0(t, \omega_1)$ having left limits which is equivalent in law to a solution $X(t)$ of (2.14). Given such a process $\hat{X}_0(t, \omega_1)$, we consider the SDE

$$(2.16) \qquad \hat{X}(t)=\hat{X}+\int_{\hat{S}_t} b(\hat{X}(s-), \hat{X}_0(s-, \omega_1), \theta, \sigma)d\hat{N}.$$

Since the both (test) processes $\tilde{X}(t, \tilde{\omega})$ and $\hat{X}_0(t-, \omega_1)$ in (2.14) and (2.16) have the same marginal distribution at each time t, Proposition 1 implies that the unique solution $\hat{X}_1(t)$ of (2.16) is equivalent in law to a solution process $X(t)$ of (2.14). Next we construct $\hat{X}_n(t)$ for $n\geq 2$ by $\hat{X}_n(t)=$the solution of (2.16) with $\hat{X}_0(s-, \omega_1)$ replaced by $\hat{X}_{n-1}(s-, \omega_1)$. Then as in the proof of Theorem 1 we can prove that $\hat{X}_n(t)$ converges to a solution $\hat{X}(t)$ of (2.15) as $n\to\infty$. Since each process $\hat{X}_n(t)$ is equivalent in law to $X(t)$, so is $\hat{X}(t)$. This completes the proof of Theorem 2.

§ 3. Stochastic differential equation—II

In this section we assume

$$(3.1) \qquad \int_0^\pi \theta Q(\theta)d\theta=\infty, \qquad \int_0^\pi \theta^2 Q(\theta)d\theta<\infty.$$

Let $\{\Omega, P\}$, $\{\Omega_1, P_1\}$ and $N(\cdot)$ be the same as in 2.1 and set $M(A)=N(A)-\lambda(A)$ for a measurable subset A of $(0, \infty)\times(0, \pi)\times S^2\times\Omega_1$ with $\lambda(A)=\int_A dtQ(\theta)d\theta\hat{d}\sigma dP_1<\infty$. Then the stochastic integral on the right of (2.3) can be written as

$$\int_{S_t} b(X(s-, \omega), X(s-, \omega_1), \theta, \sigma)dM+\int_{S_t} b(X(s-, \omega), X(s-, \omega_1), \theta, \sigma)d\lambda.$$

The first integral in the above will make sense under the condition (3.1) while the second integral equals

$$-c\int_0^t \{X(s, \omega)-\overline{X(s, \omega)}\}ds$$

where $\overline{X(s,\omega)}=E\{X(s,\omega)\}$ and $c=\int_0^{\pi}2^{-1}(1-\cos\theta)Q(\theta)d\theta$. So we are led to the following SDE:

$$(3.2)\qquad X(t,\omega)=X(0,\omega)+\int_{S_t}b(X(s-,\omega),X(s-,\omega_1),\theta,\sigma)dM \\ -c\int_0^t\{X(s,\omega)-\overline{X(s,\omega)}\}ds.$$

If $\int_{S^2}|b(x,x_1,\theta,\sigma)-b(y,y_1,\theta,\sigma)|^2\hat{d}\sigma$ were dominated by a constant multiple of $\{|x-y|^2+|x_1-y_1|^2\}\theta^2$, we could solve (3.2) easily. But this is not likely to be true. So we further modify the SDE (3.2) so that it can be solved in an easier way. First we introduce the predictable σ-field $\mathcal{P}$ on $[0,\infty)\times\Omega\times\Omega_1$; it is defined as the smallest σ-field on $[0,\infty)\times\Omega\times\Omega_1$ with respect to which all functions $a(t,\omega,\omega_1)$ satisfying the following conditions (i) and (ii) are measurable.

(i) For each fixed $t\geq 0$, $a(t,\omega,\omega_1)$ is $\mathcal{F}_t\otimes\hat{\mathcal{F}}$-measurable where $\{\Omega_1,\hat{\mathcal{F}},P_1\}$ is a copy of $\{\Omega,\mathcal{F},P\}$.

(ii) For fixed ω and ω_1, $a(t,\omega,\omega_1)$ is left continuous in t.

Let $\mathcal{R}$ denote the class of predictable processes (i.e., $\mathcal{P}$-measurable functions on $[0,\infty)\times\Omega\times\Omega_1$) with values in the space $0(3)$ of orthogonal matrices of degree 3. Then our modified SDE can be written as

$$(3.3)\quad X(t,\omega)=X(0,\omega)+\int_{S_t}b(X(s-,\omega),X(s-,\omega_1),\theta,R(s,\omega,\omega_1)\sigma)dM \\ -c\int_0^t\{X(s,\omega)-\overline{X(s,\omega)}\}ds.$$

By a solution of (3.3) we mean an $\mathcal{F}_t$-adapted process $X(t,\omega)$, $t\geq 0$, which is right continuous in t, has left limits for almost all ω and satisfies (3.3) with some $R=R(t,\omega,\omega_1)\in\mathcal{R}$. $X(t,\omega)$ is said to be square integrable if $\int_0^T E\{|X(t,\omega)|^2\}dt<\infty$, $0<\forall T<\infty$.

REMARK 3. If we set

$$\tilde{N}(A)=\int_{S_\infty}\mathbf{1}_A(s,\theta,R(s,\omega,\omega_1)\sigma)N(dsd\theta d\sigma d\omega_1),$$
$$\tilde{M}(A)=\tilde{N}(A)-\lambda(A),$$

then $\tilde{N}(\cdot)$ is also an $\mathcal{F}_t$-adapted Poisson random measure with the same intensity measure λ and (3.3) becomes (3.2) with M replaced by $\tilde{M}$. In this sense (3.2) and (3.3) may be regarded as equivalent. The corresponding martingale problems are the same.

For $\sigma, \sigma' \in S^2$ we denote by $R(\sigma, \sigma')$ the rotation (orthogonal matrix) in $\boldsymbol{R}^3$ which sends σ to σ' along the geodesic connecting σ with σ', and set $R(x, x_1, y, y_1)=R((x-x_1)|x-x_1|^{-1}, (y-y_1)|y-y_1|^{-1})$ (for $x\neq x_1, y\neq y_1$), $=$the identity matrix (otherwise). Then we have the following lemma (see Lemma 3.1 of [7]).

LEMMA 2. *For any* $x, x_1, y, y_1 \in \boldsymbol{R}^3$

$$|b(x, x_1, \theta, \sigma)-b(y, y_1, \theta, R(x, x_1, y, y_1)\sigma)| \leq \text{const.}\{|x-y|+|x_1-y_1|\}\theta.$$

THEOREM 3. *Let the condition* (II) *be satisfied and let* $X(0, \omega)$ *be a given* $\mathcal{F}_0$*-measurable random variable with* $E\{|X(0, \omega)|^2\}<\infty$. *Then there exists a square integrable solution of* (3.3). *Moreover, the law uniqueness holds for* (3.3) *in the sense that the probability measure on* W *induced by any square integrable solution of* (3.3) *is uniquely determined by the probability distribution* u_0 *of* $X(0, \omega)$.

PROOF. Define $X_n(t, \omega)$, $n\geq 0$, by

$$\begin{aligned} X_0(t, \omega) &= X(0, \omega), \\ X_n(t, \omega) &= X(0, \omega)+\int_{S_t} b(X_{n-1}(s-, \omega), X_{n-1}(s-, \omega_1), \theta, R_{n-1}\sigma)dM \\ &\quad -c\int_0^t \{X_{n-1}(s, \omega)-\overline{X_{n-1}(s, \omega)}\}ds, \qquad n\geq 1, \end{aligned}$$

where $R_n=R_n(s, \omega, \omega_1)=\prod_{k=1}^{n} R(X_{k-1}(s-, \omega), X_{k-1}(s-, \omega_1), X_k(s-, \omega), X_k(s-, \omega_1))$. Then, making use of Lemma 2 and the convergence of the second integral of (3.1) we have

$$\begin{aligned} &E\Big\{\sup_{0\leq s\leq t} |X_{n+1}(s)-X_n(s)|^2\Big\} \\ &\leq 8E\Big\{\int_{S_t} |b(X_n(s-, \omega), X_n(s-, \omega_1), \theta, R_n\sigma)-b(X_{n-1}(s-, \omega), X_{n-1}(s-, \omega_1), \\ &\qquad\qquad \theta, R_{n-1}\sigma)|^2 d\lambda\Big\} \\ &\quad +2c^2 t\int_0^t E\{|X_n(s, \omega)-\overline{X_n(s, \omega)}-X_{n-1}(s, \omega)+\overline{X_{n-1}(s, \omega)}|^2\}ds \\ &\leq \text{const.}\,(1+t)\int_0^t E\{|X_n(s)-X_{n-1}(s)|^2\}ds, \end{aligned}$$

and hence by a routine argument we can prove that

$$(3.4) \qquad \sum_{n=1}^{\infty} \sup_{0\le s\le t} |X_n(s, \omega) - X_{n-1}(s, \omega)|$$

is convergent for all $t\ge 0$ with probability 1. We denote by $\tilde{\Omega}$ the set of ω for which (3.4) is convergent for all $t\ge 0$ and also by $\tilde{\Omega}_1$ $(\subset\Omega_1)$ the copy of $\tilde{\Omega}$. We set

$$X(t, \omega) = \begin{cases} \lim_{n\to\infty} X(t, \omega), & \omega\in\tilde{\Omega} \\ 0 \quad , & \text{otherwise,} \end{cases}$$

$$\Gamma = \{(t, \omega, \omega_1) \in [0, \infty) \times \tilde{\Omega} \times \tilde{\Omega}_1 \,:\, X(t-, \omega) \ne X(t-, \omega_1)\}.$$

Then $\Gamma \in \mathcal{P}$. We first claim that $R_n(t, \omega, \omega_1)$ is convergent as $n\to\infty$ for each fixed $(t, \omega, \omega_1) \in \Gamma$. Using the notation $\|A\| = \sup\{|Ax| : |x| = 1\}$ for a matrix A, we have

$$\begin{aligned}
&\|R_n(t, \omega, \omega_1) - R_{n-1}(t, \omega, \omega_1)\| \\
&= \|\{R(X_{n-1}(t-, \omega), X_{n-1}(t-, \omega_1), X_n(t-, \omega), X_n(t-, \omega_1)) - I\} R_{n-1}(t, \omega, \omega_1)\| \\
&\le \sqrt{3}\, \|R(X_{n-1}(t-, \omega), X_{n-1}(t-, \omega_1), X_n(t-, \omega), X_n(t-, \omega_1)) - I\| \\
&\le \sqrt{3} \left| \frac{X_{n-1}(t-, \omega) - X_{n-1}(t-, \omega_1)}{|X_{n-1}(t-, \omega) - X_{n-1}(t-, \omega_1)|} - \frac{X_n(t-, \omega) - X_n(t-, \omega_1)}{|X_n(t-, \omega) - X_n(t-, \omega_1)|} \right| \\
&\le \frac{2\sqrt{3}\,\{|X_{n-1}(t-, \omega) - X_n(t-, \omega) + X_{n-1}(t-, \omega_1) - X_n(t-, \omega_1)|\}}{|X_n(t-, \omega) - X_n(t-, \omega_1)|}.
\end{aligned}$$

If $(t, \omega, \omega_1) \in \Gamma$, then $|X_n(t-, \omega) - X_n(t-, \omega_1)| \ge \varepsilon$ for some $\varepsilon > 0$, and for all sufficiently large n (say, for $n \ge n_0$) and hence

$$\begin{aligned}
&\sum_{n=n_0}^{\infty} \|R_n(t, \omega, \omega_1) - R_{n-1}(t, \omega, \omega_1)\| \\
&\le \frac{2\sqrt{3}}{\varepsilon} \sum_{n=n_0}^{\infty} \{|X_n(t-, \omega) - X_{n-1}(t-, \omega)| + |X_n(t-, \omega_1) - X_{n-1}(t-, \omega_1)|\} < \infty.
\end{aligned}$$

Next we define $R \in \mathcal{R}$ by

$$R(t, \omega, \omega_1) = \begin{cases} \lim_{n\to\infty} R_n(t, \omega, \omega_1), & (t, \omega, \omega_1) \in \Gamma \\ \text{identity}, & \text{otherwise,} \end{cases}$$

and claim that $\{X(t, \omega), R\}$ is a solution of (3.3). For this it is enough to prove that

$$(3.5) \qquad E\left[\left|\int_{S_t} \{b(X_n(s-, \omega), X_n(s-, \omega_1), \theta, R_n\sigma) - b(X(s-, \omega), X(s-, \omega_1), \theta, R\sigma)\} dM\right|^2\right]$$

tends to 0 as $n\to\infty$. If $\tilde{R}_n=R(X_n(s-,\omega), X_n(s-,\omega_1), X(s-,\omega), X(s-,\omega_1))$, then (3.5) is dominated by

$$2E\left\{\int_{S_t}|b(X_n(s-,\omega), X_n(s-,\omega_1), \theta, R_n\sigma) - b(X(s-,\omega), X(s-,\omega_1), \theta, \tilde{R}_nR_n\sigma)|^2 d\lambda\right\}$$

$$+2E\left\{\int_{S_t}|b(X(s-,\omega)-X(s-,\omega_1), \theta, \tilde{R}_nR_n\sigma) - b(X(s-,\omega), X(s-,\omega_1), \theta, R\sigma)|^2 d\lambda\right\}$$

$$\leq \text{const.}\int_0^t E\{|X_n(s)-X(s)|^2\}ds+2E\left\{\int_{S_t} b_n(s,\omega,\omega_1,\theta,\sigma)d\lambda\right\},$$

where

$$b_n(s,\omega,\omega_1,\theta,\sigma)=|b(X(s-,\omega), X(s-,\omega_1), \theta, R_n'\sigma) - b(X(s-,\omega), X(s-,\omega_1), \theta, \sigma)|^2, \quad R_n'=\tilde{R}_nR_nR^{-1}.$$

Moreover, we can easily prove that $R_n'(s,\omega,\omega_1)\to I$ as $n\to\infty$ for each fixed $(s,\omega,\omega_1)\in\Gamma$, and hence for each fixed $(s,\omega,\omega_1,\theta)\in(0,\infty)\times\tilde{\Omega}\times\tilde{\Omega}_1\times(0,\pi)$ we have

$$\lim_{n\to\infty} b_n(s,\omega,\omega_1,\theta,\sigma)=0$$

for almost all σ with respect to $\hat{d}\sigma$. Since we also have the bound $b_n(s,\omega,\omega_1,\theta,\sigma)\leq|X(s-,\omega)-X(s-,\omega_1)|^2\cdot\theta^2$, an application of Lebesgue's dominated convergence theorem yields

$$\lim_{n\to\infty} E\left\{\int_{S_t} b_n(s,\omega,\omega_1,\theta,\sigma)d\lambda\right\}=0,$$

which implies that (3.5) tends to 0 as $n\to\infty$. Thus the existence proof is finished.

To prove the law uniqueness let $h_n(t)=k2^{-n}$ for $k2^{-n}<t\leq(k+1)2^{-n}$ and $h(0)=0$. Let $X(t,\omega)$ be any square integrable solution of (3.3) with auxiliary process $R=R(t,\omega,\omega_1)\in\mathcal{R}$ and consider the SDE

$$(3.6)\qquad Y_n(t,\omega)=X(0,\omega)+\int_{S_t} b(Y_n(h_n(s),\omega), Y_n(h_n(s),\omega_1), \theta, R_n\sigma)dM - c\int_0^t \{Y_n(h_n(s))-\overline{Y_n(h_n(s))}\}ds,$$

where

$$R_n=R_n(s,\omega,\omega_1) = R(X(s-,\omega), X(s-,\omega_1), Y_n(h_n(s),\omega), Y_n(h_n(s),\omega_1))R(s,\omega,\omega_1).$$

(3.6) can be solved easily; in fact, once we know $Y_n(t,\omega)$ for $0\leq t\leq k2^{-n}$, we can define $Y_n(t,\omega)$ for $k2^{-n}<t\leq(k+1)2^{-n}$ by the right hand side of (3.6). We can prove that

$$E\{|Y_n(t)-Y_n(s)|^2\}\leq \text{const.}\,|t-s|,\quad 0\leq s<t\leq T,$$

and also, by making use of Lemma 2, that

$$E\{|Y_n(t)-X(t)|^2\}\leq \text{const.}\int_0^t E\{|Y_n(s)-X(s)|^2\}ds+\text{const.}\,\varDelta_n(t),$$

where

$$\varDelta_n(t)=\sup\{E(|Y_n(u)-Y_n(s)|^2):0\leq s<u\leq t,\ u-s\leq 2^{-n}\}\leq \text{const.}\,2^{-n},$$

const. being independent of n. Therefore

$$E\{|Y_n(t)-X(t)|^2\}\longrightarrow 0,\qquad n\to\infty. \tag{3.7}$$

On the other hand, let $k2^{-n}<t\leq(k+1)2^{-n}$, $x\in \boldsymbol{R}^3$ and set

$$\begin{aligned}\Phi_n(t)=ix\cdot Y_n(k2^{-n},\omega)&+\int_{S_t-S_{k2^{-n}}}(e^{ix\cdot b}-1-ix\cdot b)d\lambda\\ &-ic(t-k2^{-n})x\cdot\{Y_n(k2^{-n},\omega)-\overline{Y_n(k2^{-n},\omega)}\}\\ &\qquad(\text{where } b=b(Y_n(k2^{-n},\omega),\ Y_n(k2^{-n},\omega_1),\theta,\sigma)).\end{aligned}$$

Then, for $k2^{-n}<t\leq(k+1)2^{-n}$ we have

$$E\{e^{ix\cdot Y_n(t)}|\mathcal{F}_{k2^{-n}}\}=e^{\Phi_n(t)},\qquad \text{a.s.},$$

and hence the probability measure on W induced by the process $Y_n(t,\omega)$, $t\geq 0$, is uniquely determined by u_0. This combined with (3.7) proves the law uniqueness of square integrable solutions of (3.3).

In the rest of this section let $\{\Omega,P\}$ and $\{\tilde\Omega,\tilde P\}$ be the same as in 2.2 and consider the SDE

$$\begin{aligned}X(t)=X(0)&+\int_{S_t}b(X(s-),\ Y(s,\tilde\omega),\theta,R(s,\omega,\tilde\omega)\sigma)dM\\ &-c\int_0^t\{X(s)-\overline{Y(s,\tilde\omega)}\}ds\end{aligned}\tag{3.8}$$

where $Y(t,\tilde\omega)$ is a given square integrable process defined on $\{\tilde\Omega,\tilde P\}$ and $R=R(t,\omega,\tilde\omega)$ is similar to one in (3.3).

PROPOSITION 2. *Let the condition* (II) *be satisfied and* $X(0,\omega)$ *be a given* $\mathcal{F}_0$*-measurable random variable with* $E\{|X(0,\omega)|^2\}<\infty$. *Then for* *any given square integrable process* $Y(t, \tilde{\omega})$ *there exists a square integrable solution of* (3.8). *Also the law uniqueness holds in the same sense as in Proposition* 1.

The above proposition can be proved by a method similar to Proposition 1. Only point one has to be careful is that the SDE (2.8) is now replaced by

$$X_n(t)=X(0)+\int_{S_t} b(X_n(h_n(s)),\ Y(h_n(s),\tilde{\omega}),\theta,R_n\sigma)dM \\ -c\int_0^t \{X_n(h_n(s))-\overline{Y(h_n(s))}\}ds,$$

where

$$R_n=R_n(s,\omega,\tilde{\omega}) \\ =R(X(s-,\omega),\ Y(s,\tilde{\omega}),\ X_n(h_n(s),\omega),\ Y(h_n(s),\tilde{\omega}))R(s,\omega,\tilde{\omega}).$$

Next we consider the SDE

$$X(t)=X(0)+\int_{S_t} b(X(s-),\ \tilde{X}(s,\tilde{\omega}),\theta,R(s,\omega,\tilde{\omega})\sigma)dM-c\int_0^t\{X(s)-\overline{X(s)}\}ds, \tag{3.9}$$

where $\tilde{X}(t,\tilde{\omega})$ satisfies the same conditions as stated in (2.14b). Then the following theorem can be proved in the same spirit as in Theorem 2.

THEOREM 4. *Under the condition* (II) *the probability measure on* W *induced by any square integrable solution of* (3.9) *is uniquely determined by the probability distribution* u_0 *of* $X(0,\omega)$.

REMARK 4. The martingale problems corresponding to the SDE's (2), (3), (2.14), (3.2), (3.3) and (3.9) have the same form and the probability distribution $u(t)$, at time t, of a solution to any one of these SDE's is a weak solution of the Boltzmann equation (1).

References

[1] Itô, K., On stochastic differential equations, Mem. Amer. Math. Soc. **4** (1951).

[2] McKean, H. P., A class of Markov processes associated with nonlinear parabolic equations, Proc. Nat. Acad. Sci. USA **56** (1966), 1907-1911.

[3] Murata, H., Propagation of chaos for Boltzmann-like equation of non-cutoff type in the plane, Hiroshima Math. J. **7** (1977), 479-515.

[4] Sznitman, A. S., Équations de type de Boltzmann, spatialement homogènes, Z. Wahrsch. Verw. Gebiete **66** (1984), 559-592.

[5] Tanaka, H., On Markov process corresponding to Boltzmann's equation of Maxwellian gas, Proc. 2nd Japan-USSR Symp. on Probab. Theory, Lecture Notes in Math. vol. 330, Springer-Verlag, Berlin-Heidelberg-New York, 1973, 478–489.
[6] Tanaka, H., Stochastic differential equation associated with the Boltzmann equation of Maxwellian molecules in several dimensions, Proc. of Conf. on Stochastic Analysis (edited by A. Friedman and M. Pinsky), Academic Press, New York-San Fancisco-London, 1978, 301–314.
[7] Tanaka, H., Probabilistic treatment of the Boltzmann equation of Maxwellian molecules, Z. Wahrsch. Verw. Gebiete **46** (1978), 67–105.

(Received September 19, 1986)

Department of Mathematics
Faculty of Science and Technology
Keio University
Yokohama
223 Japan

LIMIT THEOREM FOR ONE-DIMENSIONAL DIFFUSION PROCESS IN BROWNIAN ENVIRONMENT

Hiroshi TANAKA
Department of Mathematics. Faculty of Science and Technology
Keio University, Yokohama, 223 (Japan)

INTRODUCTION

Let $\mathbb{W}$ be the space of continuous functions $W: \mathbb{R} \to \mathbb{R}$ with $W(0) = 0$. In this paper an element of $\mathbb{W}$ is called an environment. Given an environment W, Brox[1] considered a diffusion process starting at 0 with generator

$$(1) \qquad \mathcal{L}_W = \frac{1}{2} e^{W(x)} \frac{d}{dx}\left(e^{-W(x)} \frac{d}{dx}\right) .$$

Such a diffusion, denoted by $X(t, W)$, is constructed from a one-dimensional Brownian motion $B(t)$ by a scale-change and a time-change. The probability measure governing $B(t)$ is denoted by P. We consider the Wiener measure Q on $\mathbb{W}$. Thus $\{W(x), x \geq 0, Q\}$ and $\{W(-x), x \geq 0, Q\}$ are independent one-dimensional Brownian motions starting at 0. We assume that $B(t)$ and $W(x)$ are independent so the full distribution governing $X(t, W)$ is $\mathcal{P} = P \otimes Q$. If $W(\cdot)$ were smooth, $X(t, W)$ would satisfy

$$X(t) = \text{a Brownian motion} - \frac{1}{2}\int_0^t W'(X(s))ds .$$

Although our $W(\cdot)$ is never smooth, the above remark will explain that $X(t, W)$ is regarded as a diffusion analogue of Sinai's random walk in a random environment([11]). $X(t, W)$ is called a diffusion process in a Brownian environment. The problem is to study the limiting behavior of $X(t, W)$ as $t \to \infty$. Brox[1] obtained the following result which is analogous to that of Sinai[11]: For any $\varepsilon > 0$

$$P\{(\log t)^{-2} X(t, W) \in U_\varepsilon(t, W)\} ,$$

which is regarded as a W-random variable, converges to 1 in probability as $t \to \infty$, where $U_\varepsilon(t, W)$ is the ε-neighborhood of $b_t(W)$ which is defined suitably in terms of "valleys" of the environment. The distribution of $b_t(W)$ is independent of t so the full distribution of $(\log t)^{-2}X(t, W)$ converges to that of $b_1(W)$. Kesten[7] obtained the exact form of the limit distribution. Kesten's result was then extended to the case of symmetric stable environments([12]).

The purpose of this paper is to elaborate Brox's result. We prove that, without scaling but only by centering, $X(t,\cdot)$ has a limit distribution as $t \to \infty$. To state the result more precisely, put $b(t, W) = (\log t)^2 b_t(W)$ and let $\tilde{Q}$ be the probability measure on $\mathbb{W}$ such that $\{W(x), x \geq 0, \tilde{Q}\}$ and $\{W(-x), x \geq 0, \tilde{Q}\}$ are independent Bessel processes of index 3 starting at 0. Note that $e^{-W} \in L^1(\mathbb{R})$ with $\tilde{Q}$-measure 1. Let Ω be the space of continuous paths $\omega: [0, \infty) \to \mathbb{R}$ and, for each W with $e^{-W} \in L^1(\mathbb{R})$, denote by $\tilde{P}_W$ the probability measure on Ω such that $\{\omega(t), t \geq 0, \tilde{P}_W\}$ is a diffusion process with generator (1) and with initial distribution

$$\tilde{\mu}_W(dx) = e^{-W(x)}dx \Big/ \int_{-\infty}^{\infty} e^{-W(y)}dy .$$

Finally put $\tilde{\mu} = \int \tilde{\mu}_W \tilde{Q}(dW)$ and $\tilde{P} = \int \tilde{P}_W \tilde{Q}(dW)$. Then our result is stated as follows.

Theorem. *The process* $\{X(t_0 + t, W) - b(t_0, W), t \geq 0, \mathcal{P}\}$ *converges as* $t_0 \to \infty$ *to the stationary process* $\{\omega(t), t \geq 0, \tilde{P}\}$ *in the sense of weak convergence of probability measures on* Ω. *In particular the distribution of* $X(t,\cdot) - b(t,\cdot)$ *converges to* $\tilde{\mu}$ *as* $t \to \infty$.

Similar results were also obtained by Golosov[2] for a reflecting random walk in random environment. Our method is on the extension line of Brox's and uses fine results on one-dimensional Brownian motion obtained by Lévy[8], Itô and McKean[4] and others.

§1. OUTLINE OF BROX'S METHOD

1.1. Let Ω_0 be the space of continuous paths $\omega: [0, \infty) \to \mathbb{R}$ with $\omega(0) = 0$ and let P be the Wiener measure on Ω_0. We write $B(t)$ for $\omega(t)$, the value of ω at time t. Thus $\{B(t), t \geq 0, P\}$ is a Brownian motion starting at 0. For a fixed $W \in \mathbb{W}$ we set

$$S(x) = \int_0^x e^{W(y)}dy ,$$

$$S^{-1}(y) = \text{the inverse function of } S(x),$$

$$A(s) = \int_0^s e^{-2W(S^{-1}(B(r)))}dr,$$

$$A^{-1}(t) = \text{the inverse function of } A(s).$$

Then $X(t, W) = S^{-1}(B(A^{-1}(t)))$ is a diffusion process with generator (1) starting at 0. If we set $(W^{x_0})(\cdot) = W(\cdot + x_0) - W(x_0)$, then

$X^{x_0}(t, W) = x_0 + X(t, W^{x_0})$ is a diffusion process with generator (1) starting at x_0.

Regarding W as a random element as well as ω, we have a process $X(t,\cdot)$ defined on the product probability space $\{\Omega \times \mathbb{W}, \mathcal{P} = P \otimes Q\}$. This full process is denoted by $\{X(t,\cdot)\}$ to distinguish it from the diffusion process $\{X(t, W), t \geq 0, P\}$ with a fixed W.

For $\lambda > 0$ and $W \in \mathbb{W}$ we define $W_\lambda \in \mathbb{W}$ by $W_\lambda(x) = \lambda^{-1}W(\lambda^2 x)$, $x \in \mathbb{R}$. The following scaling relation is important([1]): For any fixed $\lambda > 0$ and $W \in \mathbb{W}$

(1.1) $$\{X(t, \lambda W_\lambda), t \geq 0, P\} \overset{d}{=} \{\lambda^{-2}X(\lambda^4 t, W), t \geq 0, P\}$$

where $\overset{d}{=}$ means the equality in distribution.

1.2. We give the definition of a valley. Let $W \in \mathbb{W}$. A part $\{W(x), a \leq x \leq c\}$ of W is called a *valley* of W if

(i) $a < c$,

(ii) there exists $b \in (a, c)$ such that

$$W(a) > W(x) > W(b) \quad \text{for every } x \in (a, b),$$
$$W(c) > W(x) > W(b) \quad \text{for every } x \in (b, c),$$

(iii) for the same b as above

$$H_- \equiv \sup\{W(y) - W(x) : a \leq x < y \leq b\} < W(c) - W(b),$$
$$H_+ \equiv \sup\{W(x) - W(y) : b \leq x < y \leq c\} < W(a) - W(b).$$

The value b in the above definition is particularly important and so, to stress b and also for simplicity, we write (a, b, c) instead of $\{W(x), a \leq x \leq c\}$. $A = H_+ \vee H_-$ is called the *inner directed ascent* (abbreviated to i.d.a.) and $D = (W(a) - W(b)) \wedge (W(c) - W(b))$ is the *depth* of the valley. When the letters A and D are used for notation they always mean the i.d.a. and the depth of (a,b,c). A valley (a,b,c) is said to contain 0 if $a < 0 < c$. It is easy to see that if (a, b, c) and (a', b', c') are valleys of W both containing 0 and satisfying $A < r < D$, $A' < r < D'$ (r is a positive constant), then $b = b'$. It is known that for any $r > 0$ and for any W in *some subset* $\tilde{\mathbb{W}}$ ($\subset \mathbb{W}$) with Q-measure 1 there exists a valley (a, b, c) of W with $A < r < D$ and containing 0 (see[1]). We denote by $b(W)$ the unique b of such a valley (a, b, c) for $r = 1$.

To give another description of $b(W)$ we put

$$W^\#(x) = \begin{cases} W(x) - \min_{[0,x]} W & \text{for } x \geq 0, \\ W(x) - \min_{[x,0]} W & \text{for } x < 0, \end{cases}$$

$$d_+ = \inf\{x > 0 : W^\#(x) = 1\} ,$$
$$d_- = \sup\{x < 0 : W^\#(x) = 1\} ,$$
$$V_+ = \min_{[0,d_+]} W, \quad V_- = \min_{[d_-,0]} W ,$$

and define b_+ and b_- by $W(b_\pm) = V_\pm$ (such $b_\pm$ are uniquely determined with Q-measure 1). We also set

$$M_+ = \max_{[0,b_+]} W, \quad M_- = \max_{[b_-,0]} W.$$

Then another description of $b(W)$ is given as follows(see[7]):

$$(1.2) \qquad b(W) = \begin{cases} b_+ & \text{if } M_+ \vee (V_+ + 1) < M_- \vee (V_- + 1), \\ b_- & \text{if } M_+ \vee (V_+ + 1) > M_- \vee (V_- + 1). \end{cases}$$

Moreover, if we define $a(W)$ and $c(W)$ by

$a(W)$ = the infimum of the set of a's $(a < b(W))$ such that

$$\begin{cases} W(a) > W(x) > W(b(W)) & \text{for every } x \in (a, b(W)), \\ \sup\{W(y) - W(x) : a \leq x < y \leq b(W)\} < 1, \end{cases}$$

$c(W)$ = the supremun of the set of c's $(c > b(W))$ such that

$$\begin{cases} W(c) > W(x) > W(b(W)) & \text{for every } x \in (b(W), c), \\ \sup\{W(x) - W(y) : b(W) \leq x < y \leq c\} < 1. \end{cases}$$

Then $(a(W), b(W), c(W))$ is the maximum valley of W containing 0 and satisfying $A(W) < 1 < D(W)$, and is called the *standard valley* of W. Note that $a(W)$, $b(W)$, etc., are Borel functions on $\tilde{W}$.

1.3. Let (a, b, c) be a valley of W and, for $\lambda > 0$, let T_λ^x be the exit time from (a, c) for the diffusion process $X^x(t, \lambda W)$. The following lemma is due to Brox[1].

Lemma 1 *([1]). For any $\delta > 0$ and a closed interval $I \subset (a, c)$*

$$(1.3) \qquad \liminf_{\lambda\to\infty} \inf_{x \in I} P\{e^{\lambda(D - \delta)} < T_\lambda^x < e^{\lambda(D + \delta)}\} = 1 .$$

1.4. Brox([1]) employs a coupling technique. To explain it we had better adopt the path space representation of $X(t, \lambda W)$. So let $\Omega = C([0, \infty) \to \mathbb{R})$ and denote by $P_{\lambda W}$ the probability measure on Ω induced by the diffusion process $X(t, \lambda W)$. Moreover, we use the following notation. For an arbitrary interval $[a, c]$ and an environment W we denote by $P^\lambda_{W[a,c]}$ the probability measure on the path space $\Omega_{[a,c]} = C([0, \infty) \to [a, c])$ induced by the diffusion process on $[a, c]$ with (local) generator $\mathcal{L}_{\lambda W}$, with reflecting barriers at a and c and with initial distribution

$$\mu^{\lambda}_{W[a,c]}(dx) = e^{-\lambda W(x)}dx \Big/ \int_a^c e^{-\lambda W(y)}dy \ .$$

This reflecting diffusion is stationary since $\mu^{\lambda}_{W[a,c]}$ is its invariant measure. In particular, in case (a, b, c) is the standard valley of W, $P^{\lambda}_{W[a,c]}$, $\mu^{\lambda}_{W[a,c]}$ and $\Omega_{[a,c]}$ are abbreviated to P^{λ}_{W}, μ^{λ}_{W} and $\hat{\Omega}$, respectively.

We now assume that (a, b, c) is the standard valley of W. Let ω and $\hat{\omega}$ stand for generic elements of Ω and $\hat{\Omega}$ with values $\omega(t)$ and $\hat{\omega}(t)$ at time t, respectively, and consider two processes $\{\omega(t),\ t \geqq 0\}$ and $\{\hat{\omega}(t),\ t \geqq 0\}$ defined on the product probability space $\{\Omega^{\lambda}\times \hat{\Omega},\ \mathbb{P}^{\lambda}_{W}\}$ where $\mathbb{P}^{\lambda}_{W} = P_{\lambda W} \otimes P^{\lambda}_{W}$. Thus the two processes are independent. Put

$$R = \inf\{t \geqq 0 : \omega(t) = \hat{\omega}(t)\} ,$$
$$T_R = \inf\{t \geqq R : \omega(t) \notin (a,\ c)\} ,$$
$$\hat{T}_R = \inf\{t \geqq R : \hat{\omega}(t) \notin (a,\ c)\} .$$

Notice that these are random variables defined on $\{\Omega \times \hat{\Omega},\ \mathbb{P}^{\lambda}_{W}\}$. If we define a process $\{\omega'(t),\ t \geqq 0\}$ by

$$\omega'(t) = \begin{cases} \omega(t) & \text{for } 0 \leqq t \leqq R , \\ \hat{\omega}(t) & \text{for } t > R , \end{cases}$$

then

$$(1.4) \qquad \{\omega(t),\ 0 \leqq t \leqq T_R,\ \mathbb{P}^{\lambda}_{W}\} \overset{d}{=} \{\omega'(t),\ 0 \leqq t \leqq \hat{T}_R,\ \mathbb{P}^{\lambda}_{W}\} .$$

The following lemma is also due to Brox[1]; the equality is a consequence of (1.4).

Lemma 2 ([1]). For any r_1 and r_2 such that $A < r_1 < r_2 < D$

$$(1.5) \qquad \mathbb{P}^{\lambda}_{W}\{R < e^{\lambda r_1} < e^{\lambda r_2} < T_R\}$$
$$= \mathbb{P}^{\lambda}_{W}\{R < e^{\lambda r_1} < e^{\lambda r_2} < \hat{T}_R\} \to 1, \quad \lambda \to \infty .$$

Using Lemma 2 and the scaling relation (1.1), Brox([1]) obtained his main results: For any $\varepsilon > 0$

$$(1.6) \qquad P\{|\lambda^{-2}X(e^{\lambda},\ W) - b(W_{\lambda})| > \varepsilon\} \to 0$$

in probability with respect to Q as $\lambda \to \infty$.

By the same argument as Brox's we can obtain a refinement of his result as will be discussed in the next subsection.

1.5. We keep the notation of 1.4 and, in addition, we denote by θ_t (resp. $\hat{\theta}_t$) the shift on Ω (resp. $\hat{\Omega}$) defined by $(\theta_t\omega)(\cdot) = \omega(t+\cdot)$ (resp. $(\hat{\theta}_t\hat{\omega})(\cdot) = \hat{\omega}(t+\cdot)$). For $\lambda > 0$, γ_λ denotes the map: $\Omega \to \Omega$ defined by $(\gamma_\lambda\omega)(t) = \lambda^2\omega(\lambda^{-4}t)$, $t \geq 0$. $\mathcal{B}_t$ denotes the σ-field on Ω generated by the sets of the form $\{\omega: \omega(s) \leq x\}$, $0 \leq s \leq t$, $x \in \mathbb{R}$, and $\mathcal{B} = \bigvee \mathcal{B}_t$. For $\omega \in \Omega$ and $x \in \mathbb{R}$, $\omega - x$ denotes the path whose value at time t is $\omega(t) - x$; $\hat{\omega} - x$ (for $\hat{\omega} \in \Omega$) also denotes a similar path. The following notational convention is used:

$$(1.7a) \qquad P^\lambda_{W[a,c]}\{\Gamma\} = P^\lambda_{W[a,c]}\{\Gamma \cap \Omega_{[a,c]}\}, \quad \Gamma \in \mathcal{B},$$

$$(1.7b) \qquad P^\lambda_W\{\hat{\omega} \in \Gamma\} = P^\lambda_W\{\Gamma \cap \hat{\Omega}\}, \quad \Gamma \in \mathcal{B}.$$

Note that the right hand sides of the above make sense since both $\Omega_{[a,c]}$ and $\hat{\Omega}$ are measurable subsets of Ω.

For any family $\{r(\lambda)\}$ such that $r(\lambda) \to 1$ $(\lambda \to \infty)$ Lemma 2 implies

$$(1.8) \qquad \varepsilon_\lambda(W) \equiv 1 - \mathbb{P}^\lambda_W\{R < s(\lambda) < s(\lambda) + t(\lambda) < T_R\} \to 0$$

as $\lambda \to \infty$ for any $W \in \hat{\mathbb{W}}$ and the same is true with T_R replaced by $\hat{T}_R$, where

$$(1.9) \qquad s(\lambda) = \lambda^{-4}e^\lambda, \quad t(\lambda) = \lambda^{-4}e^{\lambda r(\lambda)}.$$

We are now in position to state

Refinement of Brox's result. For $\{r(\lambda)\}$ *as above and for any* $\Gamma_\lambda \in \mathcal{B}_{u(\lambda)}$, $u(\lambda) = e^{\lambda r(\lambda)}$, $\lambda > 0$, *we have*

$$(1.10) \qquad P_W\{\theta_{\exp\lambda}\omega - \lambda^2 b(W_\lambda) \in \Gamma_\lambda\}$$
$$\stackrel{d}{=} P^\lambda_W\{\hat{\omega} - b(W) \in \gamma_\lambda^{-1}(\Gamma_\lambda)\}^{*)} + \varepsilon_\lambda(W, \Gamma_\lambda),$$

where $b(\cdot)$ *is defined by* (1.2) *and* $\varepsilon_\lambda(\cdot, \Gamma_\lambda)$ *is a suitable random variable defined on* $(\tilde{W}, Q)$ *satisfying*

$$(1.11) \qquad |\varepsilon_\lambda(W, \Gamma_\lambda)| \leq \varepsilon_\lambda(W).$$

The proof is as follows. Since the scaling relation (1.1) implies

---

*) The convention (1.7b) is used.

$$\{(\theta_{\exp\lambda}\omega)(t),\ t \geq 0,\ P_W\} \overset{d}{=} \{(\gamma_\lambda \theta_{s(\lambda)}\omega)(t),\ t \geq 0,\ P_{\lambda W_\lambda}\},$$

using the notation (1.9) we have

$$\begin{aligned}
&P_W\{\theta_{\exp\lambda}\omega - \lambda^2 b(W_\lambda) \in \Gamma_\lambda\} \\
&= P_{\lambda W_\lambda}\{\gamma_\lambda \theta_{s(\lambda)}\omega - \lambda^2 b(W_\lambda) \in \Gamma_\lambda\} \\
&\overset{d}{=} P_{\lambda W}\{\gamma_\lambda \theta_{s(\lambda)}\omega - \lambda^2 b(W) \in \Gamma_\lambda\} \qquad (\text{since } W_\lambda \overset{d}{=} W) \\
&= \mathbb{P}^\lambda_W\{R < s(\lambda),\ \theta_{s(\lambda)}\omega - b(W) \in \gamma_\lambda^{-1}(\Gamma_\lambda),\ s(\lambda)+t(\lambda) < T_R\} + \varepsilon^0_\lambda \\
&\qquad\qquad (\text{by } (1.8)) \\
&= \mathbb{P}^\lambda_W\{R < s(\lambda),\ \hat{\theta}_{s(\lambda)}\omega - b(W) \in \gamma_\lambda^{-1}(\Gamma_\lambda),\ s(\lambda)+t(\lambda) < \hat{T}_R\} + \varepsilon^0_\lambda \\
&\qquad\qquad (\text{by } (1.4)) \\
&= P^\lambda_W\{\hat{\theta}_{s(\lambda)}\ \hat{\omega} - b(W) \in \gamma_\lambda^{-1}(\Gamma_\lambda)\} + \varepsilon_\lambda \qquad (\text{by } (1.8) \text{ for } \hat{T}_R) \\
&= P^\lambda_W\{\hat{\omega} - b(W) \in \gamma_\lambda^{-1}(\Gamma_\lambda)\} + \varepsilon_\lambda,
\end{aligned}$$

where $\varepsilon^0_\lambda = \varepsilon^0_\lambda(W, \Gamma_\lambda)$ and $\varepsilon_\lambda = \varepsilon_\lambda(W, \Gamma_\lambda)$ are suitable random variables satisfying (1.11).

Before ending this section we state one more lemma.

Lemma 3. *Let (a, b, c) be the standard valley of W $(\in \tilde{\mathbb{W}})$. If $\rho(\lambda)$, $\lambda > 0$, satisfies*

(1.12) $\quad \rho(\lambda) \geq 0$ *and* $\rho(\lambda) = o(e^{\varepsilon\lambda})$ *as* $\lambda \to \infty$ *for* $\forall\varepsilon > 0$,

then for any Γ_λ, $\lambda > 0$, *satisfying*

(1.13) $\quad \Gamma_\lambda \in \mathcal{B}_{\rho(\lambda)}$, $\lambda > 0$,

and for any a' *and* c' *with* $a < a' < b < c' < c$ *we have*

(1.14) $\quad P^\lambda_W\{\hat{\omega} - b \in \Gamma_\lambda\} = P^\lambda_{W^b[a'-b,c'-b]}\{\Gamma_\lambda\} + o(1)$, $\lambda \to \infty$,

where $o(1)$ *is uniform with respect to the choice of* Γ_λ *under the condition (1.13) and* $W^b(\cdot) = W(\cdot + b) - W(b)$.

Proof. Since for any $\delta > 0$ both $\mu^\lambda_W\{(b - \delta, b - \delta)\}$ and $\mu^\lambda_{W^b[a'-b,c'-b]}\{(-\delta,-\delta)\}$ tend to 1 as $\lambda \to \infty$, it follows from Lemma 1 and (1.12) that

(1.15) $\quad P^\lambda_W\{\hat{T} > \rho(\lambda)\} \to 1$, $P^\lambda_{W^b[a'-b,c'-b]}\{T' > \rho(\lambda)\} \to 1$ $(\lambda \to \infty)$, where $\hat{T}$ and T' are the exit times of (a', c') and $(a'-b, c'-b)$, respectively, for the processes under consideration. Moreover, we see that

(1.16a) $\mu_W^\lambda(dx) = \kappa(\lambda)\mu^\lambda_{W[a',c']}(dx)$ on $[a', c']$,

(1.16b) $\kappa(\lambda) = \int_{a'}^{c'} e^{-\lambda W(x)}dx \Big/ \int_a^c e^{-\lambda W(x)}dx \to 1, \quad \lambda \to \infty$.

Therefore, we have as $\lambda \to \infty$

$$P_W^\lambda\{\hat{\omega} - b \in \Gamma_\lambda\}$$

$$= P_W^\lambda\{\hat{\omega} - b \in \Gamma_\lambda, \hat{T} > \rho(\lambda)\} + o(1) \qquad \text{(by (1.15))}$$

$$= \kappa(\lambda)P^\lambda_{W^b[a'-b,c'-b]}[\Gamma_\lambda \cap \{T' > \rho(\lambda)\}] + o(1) \qquad \text{(by 1.16a))}$$

$$= P^\lambda_{W^b[a'-b,c'-b]}[\Gamma_\lambda \cap \{T' > \rho(\lambda)\}] + o(1) \qquad \text{(by 1.16b))}$$

$$= P^\lambda_{W^b[a'-b,c'-b]}\{\Gamma_\lambda\} + o(1) \qquad \text{(by (1.15))} ,$$

completing the proof of the lemma.

§2. THE LAW OF THE STANDARD VALLEY.

Recalling the notation of 1.2 we put

$$W_+ = \{W(b_+ + t) - W(b_+), \ -b_+ \le t \le d_+ - b_+, \ Q\} ,$$
$$W_- = \{W(b_- - t) - W(b_-), \ b_- \le t \le -(d_- - b_-), \ Q\} .$$

On a suitable probability space we consider a process $\{x_+(t), t \in \mathbb{R}\}$ such that $\{x_+(t), t \ge 0\}$ and $\{x_+(-t), t \ge 0\}$ are independent reflecting Brownian motions on $[0, \infty)$ starting at 0 (abbreviation: RBM^0). Let $\{\ell_+(t), t \in \mathbb{R}\}$ be the local timeat 0 of $x_+(t)$, that is,

$$\ell_+(t) = \lim_{\varepsilon \downarrow 0} \frac{1}{2\varepsilon} \int_I \mathbf{1}_{[0,\varepsilon]}(x_+(s))ds ,$$

where $I = [0, t]$ or $[t, 0]$ according as $t \ge 0$ or $t < 0$. Also put $\beta_+(t) = x_+(t) + \ell_+(t)$. Then by Pitman's theorem([9]) $\{\beta_+(t), t \ge 0\}$ is a Bessel process of index 3 starting at 0 (abbreviation: $BES^0(3)$). We put

(2.1a) σ_+ = the smallest zero of $x_+(t)$ in $(z, 0]$ where z is the maximum of $t < 0$ with $x_+(t) = 1$,

(2.1b) $\tau_+ = \min\{t > 0 : \beta_+(t) = 1\}$.

Proposition. W_- *and* W_+ *are independent and*

(2.2) $$W_- \overset{d}{=} W_+ \overset{d}{=} \{\beta_+(t),\ \sigma_+ \leq t \leq \tau_+\} .$$

Proof. The independence of W_- and W_+ and the first law equality in (2.2) are obvious. For the proof of the second law equality it is convenient to use the construction of an equivalent of W_+ by means of the excursions of a RBM^0 ([4][5][3]). Denote by $\mathcal{W}^+$ the space of $w:[0, \infty) \to \mathbb{R}^+$ satisfying

(i) $w(t) > 0$ for $0 < t < \zeta(w) = \min\{s > 0 : w(s) = 0\}$,

(ii) $w(0) = w(t) = 0$ for $t \geq \zeta(w)$.

We consider a σ-finite measure n^+ on $\mathcal{W}^+$ defined by

$$n^+\left[\{w(t_1) \in A_1,\ w(t_2) \in A_2, \cdots,\ w(t_n) \in A_n\}\right]$$

$$= \int_{A_1} K^+(t_1,\ x_1)dx_1 \int_{A_2} p^0(t_2-t_1, x_1, x_2)dx_2 \int_{A_3} \cdots$$

$$\cdots \int_{A_n} p^0(t_n-t_{n-1}, x_{n-1}, x_n)dx_n$$

where $0 < t_1 < t_2 < \cdots < t_n$, $A_i \in \mathcal{B}(\mathbb{R}^+)$, $1 \leq i \leq n$, and

$$K^+(t,\ x) = \sqrt{\frac{2}{\pi t^3}}\, e^{-x^2/2t} ,\quad t > 0,\quad x \in \mathbb{R}^+,$$

$$p^0(t,x,y) = \frac{1}{\sqrt{2\pi t}}\{e^{-(x-y)^2/2t} - e^{-(x+y)^2/2t}\} ,$$

$$t > 0,\quad x,\ y \in \mathbb{R}^+.$$

Let $p(t)$ be a stationary Poisson point process on $\mathcal{W}^+$ with characteristic measure n^+ and set

$$a(t) = \sum_{0<s\leq t} \zeta(p(s)) ,$$

$$\ell(t) = \text{the inverse function of } a(\cdot) .$$

We define $x(t)$ by

$$x(t) = \begin{cases} p(s)(t - a(s-)) & \text{if } a(s-) \leq t \leq a(s) \\ 0 & \text{if } a(s-) = t = a(s) , \end{cases}$$

where $s = \ell(t)$. Then $x(t)$ is a RBM^0 and $\ell(t)$ is its local time at 0 ([3]). For $w \in \mathcal{W}^+$ we denote by $h(w)$ the maximum value of $w(t)$ and put

$$\xi = \min\{s > 0 : h(p(s)) > 1\} .$$

$$\tau = \min\{t > 0 : p(\xi)(t) = 1\} .$$

Note that $\xi < \infty$ a.s. because $n^+[\{h(w) > 1\}] = 1 < \infty$. We also put

$$W_+^- = \{W(b_+ + t) - W(b_+),\ -b_+ \leq t \leq 0,\ Q\},$$

$$W_+^+ = \{W(b_+ + t) - W(b_+),\ 0 \leq t \leq d_+ - b_+,\ Q\},$$

$$W_+^0 = \{W(t),\ 0 \leq t \leq b_+,\ Q\}.$$

Since $\{W^\#(t),\ t \geq 0,\ Q\}$ is a RBM^0 and $-\min\{W(s): 0 \leq s \leq t\}$ is its local time at 0, we see that the joint distribution of W_+^0 and W_+^+ is the same as the joint distribution of the following processes (2.3) and (2.4):

(2.3) $\{x(t) - \ell(t),\ 0 \leq t \leq a(\xi-)\}$,

(2.4) $\{p(\xi)(t),\ 0 \leq t \leq \tau\}$.

On the other hand, $\{p(s),\ 0 \leq s < \xi\}$ and $\{p(\xi)(t),\ 0 \leq t \leq \tau\}$ are independent and hence the processes (2.3) and (2.4) are also independent. Therefore, W_+^+ is independent of W_+^0 and consequently of W_+^-. Moreover, since $\{p(\xi)(t),\ 0 \leq t \leq \tau\}$ is a part of a $BES^0(3)$ ([13], see also [10]), it follows that

$$W_+^+ \stackrel{d}{=} \{\beta_+(t),\ 0 \leq t \leq \tau_+\}.$$

It remains to prove

(2.5) $W_+^- \stackrel{d}{=} \{\beta_+(t),\ \sigma_+ \leq t \leq 0\}$.

To prove this we must consider the time reversal of (2.3), or more precisely, of

(2.6) $\{x(t) - \ell(t) + \xi,\ 0 \leq t \leq a(\xi-)\}$.

Put

$$\mathcal{W}_0^+ = \{w \in \mathcal{W}^+ : h(w) < 1\},$$

$$\mathcal{W}_1^+ = \{w \in \mathcal{W}^+ : h(w) \geq 1\},$$

and define two point processes p_0 and p_1 by

$$p_i(t) = p(t) \qquad \text{for } t \in D_{p_i},\quad i = 0, 1,$$

where D_{p_i} (the domain of definition of p_i) is given by

$$D_{p_i} = \{t \in (0, \infty) : p(t) \in \mathcal{W}_i^+\},\quad i = 0, 1.$$

Then p_0 and p_1 are independent stationary Poisson point processes on $\mathcal{W}_0^+$ and $\mathcal{W}_1^+$ with characteristic measures $n_i^+ =$ the restriction of n^+ to $\mathcal{W}_i^+$, i = 0, 1, respectively. For $w \in \mathcal{W}_0^+$ we define $\hat{w} \in \mathcal{W}_0^+$ by

$$\hat{w}(s) = \begin{cases} w(\zeta(w) - s) & \text{for } 0 \leq s \leq \zeta(w) \\ 0 & \text{for } s > \zeta(w) . \end{cases}$$

Then the measure n_0^+ is invariant under the map: $w \to \hat{w}$. We define $\tilde{p}_0$ by

$$\tilde{p}_0(t) = \begin{cases} \widehat{p_0(\xi - t)} & \text{for } t < \xi \\ p_0(t) & \text{for } t \geq \xi . \end{cases}$$

It can be proved that $\tilde{p}_0$ is again a stationary Poisson point process on $\mathcal{W}_0^+$ with characteristic measure n_0^+ and is independent of p_1. Therefore, the point process $\tilde{p}$ defined by

$$\tilde{p}(t) = \begin{cases} \tilde{p}_0(t) & \text{for } t \in D_{\tilde{p}_0} \\ p_1(t) & \text{for } t \in D_{p_1} \end{cases}$$

is equivalent in law to p. Therefore, if we set

$$\tilde{a}(t) = \sum_{0<s\leq t} \zeta(\tilde{p}(t)) ,$$

$$\tilde{\ell}(t) = \text{the inverse function of } \tilde{a}(\cdot) ,$$

and if we define $\tilde{x}(t)$ by

$$\tilde{x}(t) = \begin{cases} \tilde{p}(s)(t - \tilde{a}(s-)) & \text{if } \tilde{a}(s-) \leq t \leq \tilde{a}(s) \\ 0 & \text{if } \tilde{a}(s-) = t = \tilde{a}(s) \end{cases}$$

where $s = \tilde{\ell}(t)$, then $\tilde{x}(t)$ is a RBM^0 and $\tilde{\ell}(t)$ is its local time at 0. Also we have $\tilde{a}(\xi-) = a(\xi-)$. Moreover, it is seen that (drawing a picture is helpful)

$$\begin{aligned} \tilde{x}(t) &= x(a(\xi-) - t) , & 0 \leq t \leq a(\xi-) , \\ \tilde{\ell}(t) &= \ell(a(\xi-)) - \ell(a(\xi-) - t) \\ &= \xi - \ell(a(\xi-) - t) , & 0 \leq t \leq a(\xi-) . \end{aligned}$$

Therefore, the time reversal of (2.6) is

$$\text{(2.7)} \qquad \{x(a(\xi-) - t) - \ell(a(\xi-) - t) + \xi,\ 0 \leq t \leq a(\xi-)\}$$
$$\stackrel{d}{=} \{\tilde{x}(t) + \tilde{\ell}(t),\ 0 \leq t \leq \tilde{a}(\xi-)\} .$$

Since W_+^- is equivalent in law to

$$\{x(a(\xi-) + t) - \ell(a(\xi-) + t) + \xi,\ -a(\xi-) \leq t \leq 0\} ,$$

(2.7) implies (2.5) as was to be proved.

§3. PROOF OF THE THEOREM

We are going to prove the theorem announced in the introduction with

$$b(t,W) = (\log t)^2 b(W_{\log t}), \quad t > 1 . \tag{3.1}$$

Let $\mathbb{P}$ be the probability measure on $\Omega \times \mathbb{W}$ defined by $\mathbb{P}(d\omega dW) = P_W(d\omega)Q(dW)$. Then the theorem is rephased as follows: The process

$$\{\omega(e^\lambda + t) - \lambda^2 b(W_\lambda), \quad t \geq 0, \quad \mathbb{P}\}$$

converges in law to the process $\{\omega(t), t \geq 0, \tilde{P}\}$ as $\lambda \to \infty$.

In addition to the process $x_+(t)$ of §2, we need another process $\{x_-(t), t \in \mathbb{R}\}$ which is equivalent in law to $\{x_+(t), t \in \mathbb{R}\}$. We assume that $x_+(t)$ and $x_-(t)$ are defined on a common probability space $\{\bar{\Omega}, \bar{P}\}$ and that they are independent. Denote by $\ell_-(t)$ the local time at 0 of $x_-(t)$, put $\beta_-(t) = x_-(t) + \ell_-(t)$ and define σ_- and τ_- in a way similar to (2.1). The expectation with respect to $\bar{P}$ is denote by $\bar{E}$.

Let $\rho(\lambda)$, $\lambda > 0$, be a given function satisfying the condition (1.12) and let $\Gamma_\lambda \in \mathcal{B}_{\rho(\lambda)}$, $\lambda > 0$. Then the condition for Γ_λ in the refinement of Brox's result is automatically satisfied. Therefore, by (1.10) and (1.2) we have

$$\begin{aligned} (3.2) \qquad & E_Q[P_W\{\theta_{\exp\lambda}\omega - \lambda^2 b(W_\lambda) \in \Gamma_\lambda\}] \\ &= E_Q[P_W^\lambda\{\hat{\omega} - b(W) \in \gamma_\lambda^{-1}(\Gamma_\lambda)\}] + o(1) \\ &= I_\lambda + II_\lambda + o(1) , \end{aligned}$$

where

$$I_\lambda = E_Q[P_W^\lambda\{\hat{\omega} - b_+ \in \gamma_\lambda^{-1}(\Gamma_\lambda)\}; \ b = b_+]$$

$$II_\lambda = E_Q[P_W^\lambda\{\hat{\omega} - b_- \in \gamma_\lambda^{-1}(\Gamma_\lambda)\}; \ b = b_-] ,$$

and E_Q denotes the expectation with respect to Q while $E_Q\{—; b = b_+\}$ denotes the integral over the set $\{b = b_+\}$. It is to be noted that in the above (and also in what follows) $o(1)$ means a term which tends to 0 as $\lambda \to \infty$ uniformly with respect to the choice of $\{\Gamma_\lambda\}$ so far as it satisfies the condition (1.13). We are going to use (2.2) to compute I_λ and II_λ.

We put

$$\bar{b}_+ = -\sigma_+, \quad \bar{b}_- = \sigma_- ,$$

$$\bar{d}_+ = \tau_+ - \sigma_+, \quad \bar{d}_- = -(\tau_- - \sigma_-),$$

$$\bar{M}_+ = \max_{[\sigma_+,0]} \beta_+ - \beta_+(\sigma_+), \quad \bar{M}_- = \max_{[\sigma_-,0]} \beta_- - \beta_-(\sigma_-),$$

$$\bar{V}_+ = -\beta_+(\sigma_+), \quad \bar{V}_- = -\beta_-(\sigma_-),$$

$$\beta(t) = \begin{cases} \beta_+(\sigma_+ + t) - \beta_+(\sigma_+) & \text{for } t \geq 0, \\ \beta_-(\sigma_- - t) - \beta_-(\sigma_-) & \text{for } t < 0, \end{cases}$$

Then the proposition of §2 implies

$$(3.3) \qquad \{W(t),\ d_- \leq t \leq d_+\} \stackrel{d}{=} \{\beta(t),\ \bar{d}_- \leq t \leq \bar{d}_+\}.$$

As in (1.2) we define $\bar{b}$ by

$$\bar{b} = \begin{cases} \bar{b}_+ & \text{if } \bar{M}_+ \vee (\bar{V}_+ + 1) < \bar{M}_- \vee (\bar{V}_- + 1), \\ \bar{b}_- & \text{if } \bar{M}_+ \vee (\bar{V}_+ + 1) > \bar{M}_- \vee (\bar{V}_- + 1). \end{cases}$$

Using Lemma 3 and then (3.3) we have

$$(3.4) \qquad I_\lambda = E_Q[P^\lambda_{W^{b+}[-b_+,\ d_+-b_+]}\{\gamma_\lambda^{-1}(\Gamma_\lambda)\};\ b = b_+] + o(1)$$

$$= \bar{E}[P^\lambda_{\beta_+[\sigma_+,\ \tau_+]}\{\gamma_\lambda^{-1}(\Gamma_\lambda)\};\ b = b_+] + o(1),$$

where $P^\lambda_{\beta_+[\cdot,\cdot]}$ is the probability measure defined in a way similar to $P^\lambda_{W[\cdot,\cdot]}$.

For $\varepsilon > 0$ put

$$\sigma_\varepsilon = \max\{t < 0 : x_+(t) = 0 \text{ and } t < \exists s < 0 \text{ s.t. } x_+(s) = \varepsilon\},$$

$$P^\lambda_{\beta_+,\varepsilon} = P^\lambda_{\beta_+[\sigma_\varepsilon,\tau_+]}.$$

Also let $\tilde{\mu}_{\lambda\beta_+}$ be the probability measure on $\mathbb{R}$:

$$\tilde{\mu}_{\lambda\beta_+}(dx) = e^{-\lambda\beta_+(x)}dx \Big/ \int_{-\infty}^{\infty} e^{-\lambda\beta_+(t)}dt,$$

and let $\tilde{P}_{\lambda\beta_+}$ be the probability measure on Ω defined in a way similar to $\tilde{P}_{\lambda W}$ (see the introduction). Then the scaling relation

$$(3.5) \qquad \{\lambda^{-1}\beta_+(\lambda^2 t),\ t \in \mathbb{R}\} \stackrel{d}{=} \{\beta_+(t),\ t \in \mathbb{R}\}$$

implies that for any $\delta > 0$

$$\tilde{\mu}_{\lambda\beta_+}\{(-\delta,\delta)\} \stackrel{d}{=} \int_{-\lambda^2\delta}^{\lambda^2\delta} e^{-\beta_+(x)}dx \Big/ \int_{-\infty}^{\infty} e^{-\beta_+(t)}dt \to 1, \quad \lambda \to \infty,$$

and hence $E[\tilde{\mu}_{\lambda\beta_+}\{(-\delta,\delta)\}] \to 1$. Similarly $E[\mu^{\lambda}_{\beta_+[\sigma_+,\tau_+]}\{(-\delta,\delta)\}] \to 1$ and $E[\mu^{\lambda}_{\beta_+[\sigma_\varepsilon,\tau_+]}\{(-\delta,\delta)\}] \to 1$ as $\lambda \to \infty$. Therefore, just as in the case of Lemma 3, we can prove the following: Let Γ_λ, $\lambda > 0$, be the same as before. Then

$$(3.6) \qquad \bar{E}[\tilde{P}_{\lambda\beta_+}\{\gamma_\lambda^{-1}(\Gamma_\lambda)\}] = \bar{E}[P^{\lambda}_{\beta_+[\sigma_+,\tau_+]}\{\gamma_\lambda^{-1}(\Gamma_\lambda)\}] + o(1)$$
$$= \bar{E}[P^{\lambda}_{\beta_+,\varepsilon}\{\gamma_\lambda^{-1}(\Gamma_\lambda)\}] + o(1), \quad \lambda \to \infty .$$

From (3.4) and (3.6) we have for any $\varepsilon > 0$

$$(3.7) \qquad I_\lambda = \bar{E}[P^{\lambda}_{\beta_+,\varepsilon}\{\gamma_\lambda^{-1}(\Gamma_\lambda)\};\ \bar{b} = \bar{b}_+] + o(1), \quad \lambda \to \infty ,$$

and a similar formula for II_λ.

We put

$$\tilde{x}_+(t) = x_+(\sigma_\varepsilon + t) - x_+(\sigma_\varepsilon) ,$$
$$\tilde{\beta}_+(t) = \beta_+(\sigma_\varepsilon + t) - \beta_+(\sigma_\varepsilon) ,$$

$\tilde{\sigma}_+$ = the smallest zero of $\tilde{x}_+(t)$ in $(z, 0]$ where z is the maximum of $t < 0$ such that $\tilde{x}_+(t) = 1$,

$$\tilde{M}_+ = \max_{[\tilde{\sigma}_+,0]} \tilde{\beta}_+ - \tilde{\beta}_+(\tilde{\sigma}_+) ,$$

$$m_+ = \max_{[\sigma_+,0]} \beta_+, \qquad m_\varepsilon = \max_{[\sigma_\varepsilon,0]} \beta_+ .$$

Then $m_\varepsilon < m_+$ for all sufficiently small $\varepsilon > 0$ ($\bar{P}$-a.s.) and

$$m_\varepsilon < m_+ \Longrightarrow \sigma_+ < \sigma_\varepsilon$$
$$\Longrightarrow \beta_+(\sigma_+) = \tilde{\beta}_+(\tilde{\sigma}_+) + \beta_+(\sigma_\varepsilon), \quad \bar{M}_+ = \tilde{M}_+ .$$

Therefore

$$\{\bar{b} = \bar{b}_+\} \cap \{m_\varepsilon < m_+\}$$
$$= \{\tilde{M}_+ \vee (1 - \tilde{\beta}_+(\tilde{\sigma}_+) - \beta_+(\sigma_\varepsilon)) < \bar{M}_- \vee (1 - \beta_-(\sigma_-))\} \cap \{m_\varepsilon < m_+\} ,$$

and hence

$$(3.8) \qquad \bar{E}[P^{\lambda}_{\beta_+,\varepsilon}\{\gamma_\lambda^{-1}(\Gamma_\lambda)\};\ \bar{b} = \bar{b}_+]$$
$$= \bar{E}[P^{\lambda}_{\beta_+,\varepsilon}\{\gamma_\lambda^{-1}(\Gamma_\lambda)\};\ \tilde{M}_+ \vee (1-\tilde{\beta}_+(\tilde{\sigma}_+)-\beta_+(\sigma_\varepsilon)) < \bar{M}_- \vee (1-\beta_-(\sigma_-))]$$
$$+ \Delta(\varepsilon,\lambda) ,$$

where $\Delta(\varepsilon,\lambda)$ tends to 0 as $\varepsilon\downarrow 0$ uniformly in λ. Since $P^{\lambda}_{\beta_+,\varepsilon}\{\gamma_\lambda^{-1}(\Gamma_\lambda)\}$ is a measurable function of $\{x_+(t),\ \sigma_\varepsilon\leqq t\leqq\tau_+\}$ and since the process $\{\tilde\beta_+(t),\ \tilde\sigma_+\leqq t\leqq 0\}$ conditioned by $\{x_+(t),\ \sigma_\varepsilon\leqq t\leqq\tau_+\}$ is equivalent in law to $\{\beta_+(t),\ \sigma_+\leqq t\leqq 0\}$, by using the strong Markov property of $x_+(t)$ we see that the right hand side of (3.8) equals

$$\bar{E}[P^{\lambda}_{\beta_+,\varepsilon}\{\gamma_\lambda^{-1}(\Gamma_\lambda)\}\Psi(\beta_+(\sigma_\varepsilon))] + \Delta(\varepsilon,\lambda)\ , \tag{3.9}$$

where $\psi(x) = \bar{P}\{\bar{M}_+^{\vee}(1-\beta_+(\sigma_+)-x) < \bar{M}_-^{\vee}(1-\beta_-(\sigma_-))\}$. Since $\beta_+(\sigma_\varepsilon)\to 0$ as $\varepsilon\downarrow 0$ and $\psi(x)\to 1/2$ as $x\to 0$, (3.9) is equal to

$$\frac{1}{2}\,\bar{E}[P^{\lambda}_{\beta_+,\varepsilon}\{\gamma_\lambda^{-1}(\Gamma_\lambda)\}] + \Delta'(\varepsilon,\lambda)$$

which, by (3.6), is again equal to

$$\frac{1}{2}\,\bar{E}[\tilde{P}_{\lambda\beta_+}\{\gamma_\lambda^{-1}(\Gamma_\lambda)\}] + \Delta'(\varepsilon,\lambda) + \Delta''(\varepsilon,\lambda)\ , \tag{3.10}$$

where $\Delta'(\varepsilon,\lambda)\to 0$ as $\varepsilon\downarrow 0$ uniformly in λ and $\Delta''(\varepsilon,\lambda)\to 0$ as $\lambda\to\infty$ for each fixed $\varepsilon > 0$. Therefore, from (3.7) $\sim$ (3.10) we have

$$I_\lambda = \frac{1}{2}\,\bar{E}[\tilde{P}_{\lambda\beta_+}\{\gamma_\lambda^{-1}(\Gamma_\lambda)\}] + o(1),\quad \lambda\to\infty\ , \tag{3.11}$$

and a similar formula for II_λ.

To complete the proof of the theorem we need the following simple lemma.

<u>*Lemma 4*</u>. *For any $\lambda > 0$ and $\Gamma\in\mathcal{B}$ we have*

$$\tilde{P}_{\lambda\beta_+}\{\gamma_\lambda^{-1}(\Gamma)\} \stackrel{d}{=} \tilde{P}_{\beta_+}\{\Gamma\}\ .$$

Proof. For each W with $e^{-W}\in L^1(\mathbb{R})$, $\tilde{X}(t,W)$ denotes the stationary $\mathcal{L}_W$-diffusion process with initial distribution $\tilde\mu_W$. Fixing a sample path $\beta_+(\cdot)$, we put $\tilde{X}(t) = \tilde{X}(t,\beta_+(\cdot))$ and $\tilde{X}_\lambda(t) = \tilde{X}(t,\beta_+(\lambda^2\cdot))$. Since the scaling relation (3.5) implies

$$\tilde{P}_{\lambda\beta_+}\{\gamma_\lambda^{-1}(\Gamma)\} \stackrel{d}{=} \tilde{P}_{\beta_+(\lambda^2\cdot)}\{\gamma_\lambda^{-1}(\Gamma)\}\ ,$$

for the proof of the lemma it is enough to show

$$\{\gamma_\lambda\tilde{X}_\lambda(t),\ t\geqq 0\} \stackrel{d}{=} \{\tilde{X}(t),\ t\geqq 0\}$$

for each fixed sample path $\beta_+(\cdot)$. In what follows the notation $\hat\mu$

stands for the image measure of $\tilde{\mu}_{\beta_+(\cdot)}$ under the map $\hat{S}: \mathbb{R} \to \mathbb{R}$, where $\hat{S}(x) = \int_0^x e^{\beta_+(y)} dy$. Similarly $\hat{\mu}_\lambda$ stands for the image measure obtained by replacing $\beta_+(\cdot)$ by $\beta_+(\lambda^2 \cdot)$. The following fact can be easily verified:

(3.12) If $B(0)$ is a random variable with distribution $\hat{\mu}_\lambda$, then $\lambda^2 B(0)$ is distributed according to $\hat{\mu}$.

As in 1.1, $\tilde{X}_\lambda(t)$ can be constructed from a Brownian motion $B(t)$ with initial distribution $\hat{\mu}_\lambda$. Write $B(t) = B(0) + \tilde{B}(t)$ and put $B_\lambda(t) = B(0) + \lambda^{-2}\tilde{B}(\lambda^4 t)$. Then $B_\lambda(t)$ is again a Brownian motion with initial distribution $\hat{\mu}_\lambda$. Therefore if, in the construction of $\tilde{X}_\lambda(t)$, we use $B_\lambda(t)$ instead of $B(t)$, we still have a diffusion process $\hat{X}_\lambda(t)$ which is equivalent in law to $\tilde{X}_\lambda(t)$. By an easy calculation we see that

$$\hat{X}_\lambda(t) = \lambda^{-2}\hat{S}^{-1}(\lambda^2 B(0) + \tilde{B}(\hat{A}^{-1}(\lambda^4 t))) ,$$

$$= \lambda^{-2}\hat{S}^{-1}(\hat{B}(\hat{A}^{-1}(\lambda^4 t))) ,$$

where $\hat{B}(t) = \lambda^2 B(0) + \tilde{B}(t)$ is a Brownian motion with initial distribution $\hat{\mu}$ (by (3.12)) and $\hat{A}^{-1}(t)$ is the inverse function of

$$\hat{A}(s) = \int_0^s e^{-2\beta_+(\hat{S}^{-1}(\hat{B}(u)))} du .$$

Therefore, $\{\gamma_\lambda \hat{X}_\lambda(t)\}$ and consequently $\{\gamma_\lambda \tilde{X}_\lambda(t)\}$ is equivalent in law to $\{\tilde{X}(t)\}$.

The proof of the theorem is now completed as follows. Take an arbitrary $\Gamma \in \mathcal{B}_t$, $t > 0$ being arbitrarily fixed, and put $\Gamma_\lambda = \Gamma$ in (3.2). Then from (3.2), (3.11) and Lemma 4 we have

$$\lim_{\lambda\to\infty} E_Q[P_W\{\theta_{\exp\lambda}\omega - \lambda^2 b(W_\lambda) \in \Gamma\}] = \bar{E}[\tilde{P}_{\beta_+}\{\Gamma\}] ,$$

and this prove the theorem.

<u>REFERENCES</u>

[1] Th. Brox, A one-dimensional diffusion process in a Wiener medium, Ann. Probab., 14(1986), 1206-1218.

[2] A. O. Golosov, Localization of random walks in one-dimensional random environments, Commun. Math Phys., 92(1984), 491-506.

[3] N. Ikeda and S. Watanabe, Stochastic Differential Equations and Diffusion Processes, North-Holland, 1981.

4] K. Itô and H. P. McKean, Diffusion Processes and Their Sample Paths, Springer-Verlag, 1965.

5] K. Itô, Poisson point processes attached to Markov Processes, Proc. 6th Berkeley Symp. Math. Statist. Probab. III, 225-239, Univ. California Press, Berkeley, 1972.

6] K. Kawazu, Y. Tamura and H. Tanaka, One-dimensional diffusions and random walks in random environments, to appear in Proc. 5th Japan-USSR Symp. Probab. Th.

7] H. Kesten, The limit distribution of Sinai's random walk in random environment, Physica, 138A(1986), 299-309.

8] P. Lévy, Processus stochastiques et mouvement brownien, Gauthier-Villars, Paris, 1948.

9] J. W. Pitman, One-dimensional Brownian motion and the three-dimensional Bessel process, Adv. Appl. Probab., 7(1975), 511-526.

10] J. W. Pitman and M. Yor, A decomposition of Bessel bridges, Z. Wahrscheinlichkeitstheorie verw. Gebiete, 59(1982), 425-457.

11] Y. G. Sinai, The limiting behavior of a one-dimensional random walk in a random medium, Theory of Probab. Appl., 27(1982), 256-268.

12] H. Tanaka, Limit distributions for one-dimensional diffusion processes in self-similar random environments, to appear in Hydrodynamic Behavior and Interacting Particle Systems, the IMA Volumes in Math. and its Appl., Vol. 9, 1987, Springer-Verlag.

13] D. Williams, Path decomposition and continuity of local time for one-dimensional diffusions, I, Proc. London Math. Soc., (3)28(1974), 738-768.

Reprinted from
Stochastic Analysis, 156–172,
Lecture Notes in Math., **1322**, Springer-Verlag, 1988.

On the maximum of a diffusion process in a drifted Brownian environment

KIYOSHI KAWAZU AND HIROSHI TANAKA

1. Introduction

In this paper we investigate asymptotic behavior of the tail of the distribution of the maximum of a diffusion process in a drifted Brownian environment. This problem is a diffusion analogue of the Afanas'ev problem([1]). Our result is naturally compatible with that of Afanas'ev[1].

Let $\{W(x), x \in \mathbf{R}, P\}$ be a Brownian environment, namely, let $\{W(t), t \geq 0, P\}$ and $\{W(-t), t \geq 0, P\}$ be independent Brownian motions in one-dimension with $W(0) = 0$. We consider a diffusion process $X(t, W)$ defined formally by

$$X(t, W) = \text{Brownian motion} - \frac{1}{2}\int_0^t \{W'(X(s, W)) + c\}ds,$$

where c is a positive constant. The precise meaning of $X(t, W)$ is simply a diffusion process with generator

$$\frac{1}{2}e^{W(x)+cx}\frac{d}{dx}(e^{-W(x)-cx}\frac{d}{dx}),$$

starting at 0. Such a diffusion process can be constructed from a Brownian motion through changes of scale and time. For a fixed environment $W = (W(x), x \in \mathbf{R})$ we denote by P_W the probability law of the process $\{X(t, W)\}$ and put

$$\mathcal{P} = \int P(dW)P_W.$$

Thus $\mathcal{P}$ is the full law of $\{X(t, \cdot)\}$. We often write $X(t) = X(t, \cdot)$. Since $c > 0$, $\max_{t\geq 0} X(t)$ is finite ($\mathcal{P}$-a.s.). The problem is the following : How fast does $\mathcal{P}\{\max_{t\geq 0} X(t) > x\}$ decay as $x \to \infty$? Since

$$\mathcal{P}\{\max_{t\geq 0} X(t) > x\} = E\{A(A+B)^{-1}\}, \tag{1.1}$$

where

$$(1.2)\qquad A=\int_{-\infty}^{0} e^{W(t)+ct}\,dt,\quad B=\int_{0}^{x} e^{W(t)+ct}\,dt,$$

the problem is nothing but to find the asymptotics of $E\{A(A+B)^{-1}\}$ as $x\to\infty$. The result varies according as $c>1$, $c=1$, $0<c<1$, as will be stated in the following theorem.

THEOREM. (i)*If* $c>1$ *, then*

$$\mathcal{P}\{\max_{t\geq 0} X(t)>x\}\sim\frac{2c-2}{2c-1}\exp\{-(c-\frac{1}{2})x\},\quad x\to\infty.$$

(ii) If $c=1$ *, then*

$$\mathcal{P}\{\max_{t\geq 0} X(t)>x\}\sim(2/\pi)^{1/2}x^{-1/2}\exp\{-x/2\},\quad x\to\infty.$$

(iii) If $0<c<1$ *, then*

$$\mathcal{P}\{\max_{t\geq 0} X(t)>x\}\sim const.x^{-3/2}\exp\{-c^2x/2\},\quad x\to\infty,$$

where

$$const.=2^{5/2-2c}\Gamma(2c)^{-1}\int_0^\infty\int_0^\infty\int_0^\infty\int_0^\infty z(a+z)^{-1}a^{2c-1}e^{-a/2}y^{2c}e^{-\lambda z}u\sinh u\,da\,dy\,dz\,du\,,$$

$\lambda=(1+y^2)/2+y\cosh u$.

2. Proof of the theorem

Since A and B are independent, the right hand side of (1.1) equals $E\{Af(A)\}$ where $f(a)=E\{(a+B)^{-1}\}, a\geq 0$. Fixing $x>0$, we consider the time reversal $\widehat{W}(t)=W(x-t)-W(x), 0\leq t\leq x$. Since $\{\widehat{W}(t), 0\leq t\leq x\}$ is also a Brownian motion, we have

$$(2.1)\qquad \begin{aligned} f(a) &= E\{(a+\int_0^x \exp\{\widehat{W}(t)+ct\}\,dt)^{-1}\}\\ &= E\{(a+e^{-W(x)}\int_0^x \exp\{W(x-t)+ct\}\,dt)^{-1}\}\\ &= E\{(ae^{W(x)-cx}+\int_0^x e^{W(t)-ct}\,dt)^{-1}e^{W(x)-cx}\}\\ &= e^{(1/2-c)x}E\{(ae^{W(x)-cx}+\int_0^x e^{W(t)-ct}\,dt)^{-1}e^{W(x)-x/2}\}\\ &= e^{(1/2-c)x}E\{(ae^{W(x)-(c-1)x}+\int_0^x e^{W(t)-(c-1)t}\,dt)^{-1}\}\\ &= e^{(1/2-c)x}E\{(a+\int_0^x e^{W(t)+(c-1)t}\,dt)^{-1}e^{W(x)+(c-1)x}\}. \end{aligned}$$

In deriving the fifth equality in the above we used the formula of Cameron-Martin-Maruyama-Girsanov; the last equality was derived by using $\widehat{W}(t)$ as in the case of the first equality. From the fifth equality of (2.1) we obtain the following lemma.

LEMMA 1. *For any $c > 0$ and $x > 0$*

$$\mathcal{P}\{\max_{t\geq 0} X(t) > x\} = e^{(1/2-c)x} E\{A(Ae^{W(x)-(c-1)x} + \int_0^x e^{W(t)-(c-1)t} dt)^{-1}\}, \tag{2.2}$$

where A is given by (1.2).

The following lemma due to Yor will also be used.

LEMMA 2(Yor[2]). *For any $\nu > 0$ we have*

$$\int_0^\infty \exp(W(t) - \frac{\nu t}{2}) dt \stackrel{d}{=} 2/Z_\nu, \tag{2.3}$$

where $\stackrel{d}{=}$ means equality in distribution and Z_ν is a gamma variable of index ν, that is,

$$P\{Z_\nu \in dt\} = \Gamma(\nu)^{-1} t^{\nu-1} e^{-t} dt \qquad (t > 0).$$

2.1. Proof of (i)

When $c > 1$, Lemma 1 implies

$$\lim_{x\to\infty} e^{-(1/2-c)x} \mathcal{P}\{\max_{t\geq 0} X(t) > x\} = E\{A(\int_0^\infty e^{W(t)-(c-1)t} dt)^{-1}\} \quad .$$

It is easy to see that the above expectation is finite. To obtain its exact value we use Lemma 2. We thus obtain (i).

2.2. Proof of (ii)

For $x > 0$ we put

$$\varphi(x) = E\{\log \int_0^x e^{W(t)} dt\}, \quad \psi(x) = \frac{d}{dx}\varphi(x).$$

Then it is easy to see that

$$\psi(x) = E\{(\int_0^x e^{W(t)} dt)^{-1} e^{W(x)}\} = E\{(\int_0^x e^{W(t)} dt)^{-1}\} \ ;$$

in fact, the second equality is a consequence of the last equality of (2.1) with $a = 0$ and $c = 1$. Thus $\psi(x)$ is monotone decreasing in x.

LEMMA 3. *When $c = 1$, we have*

$$E\{A(\int_0^x e^{W(t)+t} dt)^{-1}\} \sim \sqrt{2/\pi}\, x^{-1/2} e^{-x/2} \quad \text{as } x \to \infty \quad . \tag{2.4}$$

Proof. Since $E\{A\} = 2$ in case $c = 1$, the left hand side of (2.4) equals $2E\{(\int_0^x e^{W(t)+t} dt)^{-}$ which also equals $2e^{-x/2} E\{(\int_0^x e^{W(t)} dt)^{-1} e^{W(x)}\}$ by virtue of (2.1) with $a = 0$ and $c = 1$. Thus we have

$$E\{A(\int_0^x e^{W(t)+t} dt)^{-1}\} = 2e^{-x/2}\psi(x). \tag{2.5}$$

On the other hand, using the scaling property $\{W(t)\} \stackrel{d}{=} \{\sqrt{x}\, W(t/x)\}$ we have

$$\varphi(x) = E\{\log \int_0^1 e^{\sqrt{x} W(t)}\, dt\} + \log x\,,$$

and hence

$$\begin{aligned} \lim_{x\to\infty} x^{-1/2}\varphi(x) &= \lim_{x\to\infty} E\{\frac{1}{\sqrt{x}}\log \int_0^1 e^{\sqrt{x}W(t)}\, dt\} \\ &= E\{\max_{0\le t\le 1} W(t)\} = \sqrt{2/\pi}\,, \end{aligned}$$

which combined with the monotonicity of $\psi(x) = \varphi'(x)$ implies

$$\psi(x) \sim (2\pi x)^{-1/2} \quad \text{as } x \to \infty \quad . \tag{2.6}$$

This together with (2.5) proves the lemma.

LEMMA 4. *For $x > 0$ we have*

$$E\{(\int_0^x e^{W(t)}\, dt)^{-2} e^{W(x)}\} \le \psi(x/2)^2 \quad . \tag{2.7}$$

Proof. The left hand side of (2.7) is dominated by

$$\begin{aligned} & E\{(\int_0^{x/2} e^{W(t)}\, dt)^{-1}(\int_{x/2}^{x} e^{W(t)}\, dt)^{-1} e^{W(x)}\} \\ = \;& E\{(\int_0^{x/2} e^{W(t)}\, dt)^{-1}(\int_{x/2}^{x} e^{W(t)-W(x/2)}\, dt)^{-1} e^{W(x)-W(x/2)}\} \\ = \;& E\{(\int_0^{x/2} e^{W(t)}\, dt)^{-1}\} E\{(\int_0^{x/2} e^{W(t)}\, dt)^{-1} e^{W(x/2)}\} \\ = \;& \psi(x/2)^2\ ; \end{aligned}$$

in deriving the second equality in the above we used the fact that $\{W(t+\frac{x}{2})) - W(\frac{x}{2}), t \ge 0\}$ is a Brownian motion independent of $\{W(t), 0 \le t \le x/2\}$.

The proof of (ii) is now given as follows. By (1.1) we have

$$\begin{aligned} 0 \;&\le E\{A(\int_0^x e^{W(t)+t}\, dt)^{-1}\} - \mathcal{P}\{\max_{t\ge 0} X(t) > x\} \\ &= E\{AB^{-1} - A(A+B)^{-1}\} \\ &\le E\{2^{-1}A^{3/2}B^{-3/2}\} = 2^{-1}E\{A^{3/2}\}E\{B^{-3/2}\}. \end{aligned} \tag{2.8}$$

We prove

$$E\{A^{3/2}\} < \infty\,, \tag{2.9}$$

$$E\{B^{-3/2}\} < \text{const.}\, x^{-3/4}e^{-x/2}\,. \tag{2.10}$$

(2.9) follows immediately from Lemma 2 ; a direct proof can also be given as follows. Using Hölder's inequality we have

$$\begin{aligned} E\{A^{3/2}\} &= E\{(\int_0^\infty e^{W(t)-4t/5}e^{-t/5}\,dt)^{3/2}\} \\ &\le (5/3)^{1/2}E\{\int_0^\infty \exp\{\frac{3}{2}(W(t)-\frac{4t}{5})\}dt\} = (5/3)^{1/2}\cdot(40/3)\,. \end{aligned}$$

(2.10) can be proved by making use of the CMMG formula, the Schwarz inequality, Lemma 4 and then (2.6) ; in fact, putting $B_0 = \int_0^x e^{W(t)}dt$ we have

$$\begin{aligned} E\{B^{-3/2}\} &= E\{B_0^{-3/2}e^{W(x)-x/2}\} \\ &\le e^{-x/2}E\{B_0^{-1}e^{W(x)}\}^{1/2}E\{B_0^{-2}e^{W(x)}\}^{1/2} \\ &\le e^{-x/2}\psi(x)^{1/2}\psi(x/2) \\ &\le \text{const.}\,e^{-x/2}x^{-1/4}\cdot x^{-1/2}\,. \end{aligned}$$

The assertion (ii) of our theorem follows from Lemma 3, (2.8), (2.9) and (2.10).

2.3. Proof of (iii)

The proof of (iii) relies essentially on the following Yor's formula.

Yor's formula([3: the formula(6.e)]). *For any bounded Borel functions f and g we have*

$$\begin{aligned} &E\{f(\int_0^t e^{2W(s)}\,ds)g(e^{W(t)})\} \\ &= c_t\int_0^\infty dy\int_0^\infty dz\, g(y)f(1/z)\exp\{-z(1+y^2)/2\}\psi_{yz}(t), \end{aligned}$$

where

$$\begin{aligned} c_t &= (2\pi^2 t)^{-1/2}\exp\{\pi^2/2t\}, \\ \psi_r(t) &= \int_0^\infty \exp\{-u^2/2t\}e^{-r(\cosh u)}(\sinh u)\sin(\pi u/t)\,du\,. \end{aligned}$$

To proceed to the proof of (iii) we put

$$f(a,z) = a(a+4z)^{-1}, \quad g(y) = y^{2c},$$

$$B^{(\nu)}(t) = \int_0^t e^{2(W(s)+\nu s)}\,ds\,.$$

Using first the CMMG formula and then Yor's formula we have

$$\begin{aligned} &E\{a(a+\int_0^x e^{W(t)+ct}\,dt)^{-1}\} = E\{a(a+4B^{(2c)}(x/4))^{-1}\} \\ &= E\{a(a+4B^{(0)}(x/4))^{-1}\exp(2cW(x/4)-\tfrac{c^2x}{2})\} \\ &= \exp(-c^2x/2)E\{f(a,B^{(0)}(x/4))g(e^{W(x/4)})\} \\ &= \exp(-c^2x/2)c_{x/4}\int_0^\infty dy\int_0^\infty dz\, g(y)f(a,1/z)\exp\{-z(1+y^2)/2\}\psi_{yz}(x/4)\,. \end{aligned}$$

Since Lemma 2 implies

$$P\{A \in da\} = 2^{2c}\Gamma(2c)^{-1}a^{-2c-1}e^{-2/a}da \quad (a > 0),$$

we have

$$\begin{aligned} &\mathcal{P}\{\max_{t\geq 0} X(t) > x\} \\ (2.11) \quad &= 2^{2c+1/2}\Gamma(2c)^{-1}\pi^{-1}\exp(2\pi^2/x)x^{-1/2}\exp(-c^2x/2) \\ &\times \int_0^\infty dy \int_0^\infty dz \int_0^\infty du\, y^{2c}h(z)e^{-\lambda z}\exp(-2u^2/x)(\sinh u)\sin(4\pi u/x), \end{aligned}$$

where

$$\begin{aligned} h(z) &= \int_0^\infty az(az+4)^{-1}a^{-2c-1}e^{-2/a}\,da, \\ \lambda &= (1+y^2)/2 + y\cosh u. \end{aligned}$$

LEMMA 5. *Let* $0 < c < 1$ *and put*

$$F(y,z,u) = y^{2c}h(z)e^{-\lambda z}u\sinh u.$$

Then we have

$$M = \int_0^\infty \int_0^\infty \int_0^\infty F(y,z,u)\,dy\,dz\,du < \infty,$$

Proof. By a change of variable $\cosh u = v$, we have

$$M = \int_0^\infty dy \int_0^\infty dz \int_1^\infty dv\, y^{2c}h(z)e^{-\lambda z}\log(v+\sqrt{v^2-1}),$$

where $\lambda = (1+y^2)/2 + yv$. Since

$$h(z) = 2^{-2c-1}z\int_0^\infty u^{2c-1}e^{-u}(u+\frac{z}{2})^{-1}du,$$

it is easy to see that

$$(2.12) \qquad h(z) \longrightarrow 2^{-2c}\Gamma(2c) \qquad \text{as } z \to \infty \quad ,$$

$$(2.13) \qquad h(z) \sim_{\text{as } z\downarrow 0} \begin{cases} 2^{-2c-1}\Gamma(2c-1)z & \text{if } c > 1/2, \\ 2^{-2}z\log 1/z & \text{if } c = 1/2, \\ 2^{-4c}\int_0^\infty a^{2c-1}(a+1)^{-1}da \cdot z^{2c} & \text{if } 0 < c < 1/2. \end{cases}$$

Therefore for any $\varepsilon > 0$ and $\alpha > 0$ we have

$$\begin{aligned} M_1 &= \int_0^\infty dy \int_1^\infty dz \int_1^\infty dv\, y^{2c}h(z)e^{-\lambda z}\log(v+\sqrt{v^2-1}) \\ &\leq \text{const.} \int_0^\infty \int_1^\infty y^{2c}v^{\varepsilon}\lambda^{-1}e^{-\lambda}\,dydv \\ &\leq \text{const.} \int_0^\infty \int_1^\infty y^{2c}v^{\varepsilon}\lambda^{-\alpha}\,dydv \\ &\leq \text{const.} \int_0^\infty \int_0^\infty y^{2c-\varepsilon-1}(1+y^2)^{-\alpha+1+\varepsilon}z^{\varepsilon}(1+z)^{-\alpha}\,dy\,dz \end{aligned}$$

(by putting $v = (2y)^{-1}(1+y^2)z$ with y fixed),

which is finite if $\varepsilon > 0$ is sufficiently small and $\alpha > 0$ sufficiently large. Note that const. in the above may vary from place to place and depend on ε and α . Next we prove that

$$(2.14)\qquad M_2 = \int_0^\infty dy \int_0^1 dz \int_1^\infty dv\, y^{2c} h(z) e^{-\lambda z} \log(v + \sqrt{v^2-1}) < \infty \quad .$$

Assume $1/2 < c < 1$. Then by (2.13)

$$\begin{aligned} M_2 &\le \text{const.} \int_0^\infty dy \int_0^1 dz \int_1^\infty dv\, y^{2c} z e^{-\lambda z} v^{\varepsilon} \\ &\le \text{const.} \int_0^\infty \int_1^\infty \lambda^{-2} y^{2c} v^{\varepsilon}\, dy\, dv \qquad (\text{ we used } \int_0^1 z e^{-\lambda z} dz \le \lambda^{-2}\ ) \\ &\le \text{const.} \int_0^\infty \int_0^\infty y^{2c-1-\varepsilon}(1+y^2)^{-1+\varepsilon} z^{\varepsilon}(1+z)^{-2}\, dy\, dz \end{aligned}$$

(by putting $v = (2y)^{-1}(1+y^2)z$ with y fixed)

which is finite for sufficiently small $\varepsilon > 0$ by virtue of $1/2 < c < 1$. When $c = 1/2$, (2.13) implies

$$M_2 \le \text{const.} \int_0^\infty dy \int_0^1 dz \int_1^\infty dv\, y z^{1-\varepsilon} e^{-\lambda z} v^{\varepsilon}$$

for $0 < \varepsilon < 1$. Since $\int_0^1 z^{1-\varepsilon} e^{-\lambda z}\, dz \le \text{const.}\lambda^{-2+\varepsilon}$, we have

$$\begin{aligned} M_2 &\le \text{const.} \int_0^\infty \int_1^\infty \lambda^{-2+\varepsilon} y v^{\varepsilon}\, dy\, dv \\ &\le \text{const.} \int_0^\infty \int_0^\infty y^{-\varepsilon}(1+y^2)^{-1+2\varepsilon} z^{\varepsilon}(1+z)^{-2+\varepsilon}\, dy\, dz < \infty \end{aligned}$$

provided that $\varepsilon > 0$ is small enough. Finally assume $0 < c < 1/2$. Then by (2.13)

$$\begin{aligned} M_2 &\le \text{const.} \int_0^\infty dy \int_0^1 dz \int_1^\infty dv\, y^{2c} z^{2c} e^{-\lambda z} v^{\varepsilon} \\ &\le \text{const.} \int_0^\infty \int_1^\infty \lambda^{-1-2c} y^{2c} v^{\varepsilon}\, dy\, dv \\ &\le \text{const.} \int_0^\infty \int_0^\infty y^{2c-\varepsilon-1}(1+y^2)^{-2c+\varepsilon} z^{\varepsilon}(1+z)^{-1-2c}\, dy\, dz < \infty \end{aligned}$$

provided that $\varepsilon > 0$ is small enough. Thus (2.14) is proved.

We can now complete the proof of (iii) as follows. From (2.11) we have

$$(2.15)\qquad \mathcal{P}\{\max_{t\ge 0} X(t) > x\} = 2^{2c+5/2}\Gamma(2c)^{-1} \exp(2\pi^2/x) x^{-3/2} \exp(-c^2 x/2) M(x),$$

where

$$M(x) = \int_0^\infty \int_0^\infty \int_0^\infty F(y,z,u) \sin(4\pi u/x)/(4\pi u/x) \exp(-2u^2/x)\, dy\, dz\, du\,.$$

By Lemma 5 we have $\lim_{x\to\infty} M(x) = M$ which equals

$$2^{-4c}\int_0^\infty\int_0^\infty\int_0^\infty\int_0^\infty z(a+z)^{-1}a^{2c-1}e^{-a/2}y^{2c}e^{-\lambda z}u\sinh u\,da\,dy\,dz\,du\,.$$

Thus the assertion (iii) follows from (2.15).

Acknowledgment. We wish to thank Prof. S.Kotani and Prof. M.Yor for giving us valuable information ; Prof. M.Yor kindly sent us preprints including [2] and [3], without which the result (iii) would not have been obtained.

References

[1] V.I.Afanas'ev, On a maximum of a transient random walk in random environment, Theor.Probab.Appl.**35**(1990), 205 - 215.

[2] M.Yor, Sur certaines fonctionelles exponentielles du mouvement brownien réel, J.Appl.Probab.**29**(1992) , 202 - 208.

[3] M.Yor, On some exponential functionals of Brownian motion, to appear in Adv.Appl. Probab. (September 1992).

Kiyoshi Kawazu
Department of Mathematics
Faculty of Education
Yamaguchi University
Yosida, Yamaguchi 753
Japan

Hiroshi Tanaka
Department of Mathematics
Faculty of Science and Technology
Keio University
Hiyoshi, Yokohama 223
Japan

Reprinted from
Seminaire de Probabilites XXVII, 78–85,
Lecture Notes in Math., **1557**, Springer-Verlag, 1993.

86. *Recurrence of a Diffusion Process in a Multidimensional Brownian Environment**)

By Hiroshi TANAKA

Department of Mathematics, Faculty of Science and Technology, Keio University

(Communicated by Kiyosi ITÔ, M. J. A., Nov. 12, 1993)

Introduction. Let $\boldsymbol{W}$ be the space of continuous functions on $\boldsymbol{R}^d$ vanishing at the origin. In this paper an element of $\boldsymbol{W}$ is called an environment. Given an environment W, we consider a diffusion process $\boldsymbol{X}_W = \{X(t), t \geq 0, P_W^x, x \in \boldsymbol{R}^d\}$ with generator

$$\frac{1}{2}(\Delta - \nabla W \cdot \nabla) = \frac{1}{2} e^W \sum_{k=1}^{d} \frac{\partial}{\partial x_k}\left(e^{-W}\frac{\partial}{\partial x_k}\right).$$

When W is bounded, the result of Nash [8] for fundamental solutions of parabolic equations guarantees the existence of a diffusion process $\boldsymbol{X}_W^0$ with generator

$$\sum_{k=1}^{d} \frac{\partial}{\partial x_k}\left(e^{-W}\frac{\partial}{\partial x_k}\right).$$

For a general W we still have a nice diffusion process $\boldsymbol{X}_W^0$ (e.g. see [4]) and hence $\boldsymbol{X}_W$ can be constructed from $\boldsymbol{X}_W^0$ through a random time change. Without any assumption on the behavior of $W(x)$ for large $|x|$ the process $\boldsymbol{X}_W$ may explode within a finite time, but such a case is excluded automatically since we are interested in the recurrence of $\boldsymbol{X}_W$. We consider the probability measure P on $\boldsymbol{W}$ with respect to which $\{W(x), x \in \boldsymbol{R}^d, P\}$ is a Lévy's Brownian motion with a d-dimensional time. The collection of diffusion processes $\boldsymbol{X} = \{\boldsymbol{X}_W\}$ in which W is allowed to vary as a random element in $(\boldsymbol{W}, P)$ is called a diffusion in a d-dimensional Brownian environment. When $d = 1$ this was considered by Brox [1] and Schumacher [9] as a diffusion model exhibiting the same asymptotic behavior as Sinai's random walk in a random environment ([10]); see also [11] for some refined results. Recently Mathieu [7] obtained some very interesting results concerning a long time asymptotic problem for $\boldsymbol{X}$ in the case $d \geq 2$. Motivated by [7] the present paper was written.

In this paper we prove that $\boldsymbol{X}_W$ is recurrent for almost all Brownian environments W in any dimension d, namely, for any nonnegative Borel function f on $\boldsymbol{R}^d$ such that $f > 0$ on a set of positive Lebesgue measure the equality

$$P_W^x\left\{\int_0^\infty f(X(t))\,dt = \infty\right\} = 1,\ x \in \boldsymbol{R}^d,$$

holds for almost all W with respect to P. In [3] Fukushima, Nakao and Takeda discussed the same problem but with the replacement of $W(x)$ by $\tilde{W}(|x|)$,

*) This research was partially supported by Grant-in-Aid for Science Research No. 04452011, the Ministry of Education, Science and Culture, Japan.

where $\tilde{W}(t)$ is a Brownian motion with a 1-dimensional time.

To obtain our result we employ Ichihara's recurrence criterion ([4]) which, in the present special case, asserts that $\boldsymbol{X}_W^0$ (W is fixed) is recurrent if

$$\int_1^{\infty}\left\{\int_{S^{d-1}} e^{-W(r\theta)}d\theta\right\}^{-1} r^{-d+1}dr = \infty,$$

where $d\theta$ is the uniform distribution on S^{d-1}. We can also employ Fukushima's recurrence criterion ([2]) which, in the present special case, asserts that $\boldsymbol{X}_W$ (W is fixed) is recurrent if there exists a sequence $\{u_n\}$ such that $0 \leq u_n \leq 1$, $\lim u_n = 1$ a.e. and $\lim \mathscr{E}(u_n, u_n) = 0$, where $\mathscr{E}(u, v)$ is the Dirichlet form associated with $\boldsymbol{X}_W$, namely,

$$\mathscr{E}(u, v) = \frac{1}{2}\int_{\boldsymbol{R}^d} \nabla u\cdot \nabla u\, e^{-W}dx.$$

Since it is obvious that $\boldsymbol{X}_W$ is recurrent if and only if $\boldsymbol{X}_W^0$ is recurrent, either criterion yields our result. But for the verification of these criteria we need some information on the asymptotic behavior of $W(x)$ for large $|x|$. A key point in obtaining this informaiton is to consider the one-parameter family $\{T_t,\ t \in \boldsymbol{R}\}$ of measure preserving transformations on $(\boldsymbol{W}, P)$ defined by (1. 3) and then to use its ergodicity.

§1. Brownian motion with a d-dimensional time. Let $d \geq 2$ and as before let P be the probability measure on $\boldsymbol{W}$ such that $\{W(x),\ x \in \boldsymbol{R}^d,\ P\}$ is a Brownian motion with a d-dimensional time ([6: p. 277]), that is, a Gaussian system with

(1.1) $$E\{W(x)\} = 0,\ W(0) = 0,$$

(1.2) $$E\{W(x)\,W(y)\} = \frac{1}{2}\{|x|+|y|-|x-y|\}.$$

For each $t \in \boldsymbol{R}$ and $W \in \boldsymbol{W}$ we define an element T_tW of $\boldsymbol{W}$ by

(1.3) $$(T_tW)(x) = e^{-t/2}W(e^tx), \quad x \in \boldsymbol{R}^d.$$

Then $\{T_t,\ t \in \boldsymbol{R}\}$ is a one-parameter family of measure preserving transformations on the probalility space $(\boldsymbol{W}, P)$. Using (1. 2) we can easily compute the covariance matrix of

$$e^{-t/2}W(e^tx_1),\ e^{-t/2}W(e^tx_2),\cdots,e^{-t/2}W(e^tx_m),\ W(x_1'),\ W(x_2'),\cdots,W(x_n')$$

for fixed $t \in \boldsymbol{R}$ and $x_1,\ldots,x_m,\ x_1',\ldots,x_n' \in \boldsymbol{R}^d$, and the following lemma can be proved in the same way as in Itô [5].

Lemma 1. $\{T_t,\ t \in \boldsymbol{R}\}$ *is mixing and hence ergodic.*

Next let $0 < a < b$, put $K = \{x \in \boldsymbol{R}^d : a \leq |x| \leq b\}$ and consider the Banach space $B = C(K)$, the space of real valued continuous functions on K, and the real Hilbert space $H = L^2(K, dx)$. The inner product in H is denoted by $\langle\cdot\,,\cdot\rangle$. Regarding $W_K = \{W(x),\ x \in K\}$ as an H-valued random variable, we denote by γ the probability distribution of W_K. Since every Borel set in the space B is also a Borel set in the space H and since W_K is regarded as a B-valued random variable, we have $\gamma(B) = 1$. γ is a Gaussian measure on H with

(1.4a) $$\int_H e^{\langle f,g\rangle}\,\gamma(dg) = E\left\{\exp\int_K f(x)\,W(x)dx\right\} = \exp\left\{\frac{1}{2}\langle Af, f\rangle\right\},\ f \in H,$$

$$(1.4b)\qquad Af(x) = \int_K \frac{1}{2}\{|x| + |y| - |x-y|\} f(y)dy.$$

For $\phi = Af_0$ with $f_0 \in H$ we define the ϕ-transform γ_ϕ by $\gamma_\phi(\Gamma) = \gamma(\{g : g + \phi \in \Gamma\})$. Then the following Cameron-Martin formula is easily verified by using (1. 4).

$$(1.5)\qquad \gamma_\phi(dg) = \exp\left\{\langle f_0, g\rangle - \frac{1}{2}\langle Af_0, f_0\rangle\right\}\gamma(dg).$$

Lemma 2. *Any nonempty open set in the space B has a positive γ*-measure.

Proof. We first prove that the range $R = \{Af : f \in H\}$ is dense in B. If this were not true, there exists a finite signed measure $\mu \neq 0$ on K such that

$$(1.6)\qquad \int_K Af(x)\mu(dx) = 0 \quad \text{for all} \quad f \in H.$$

Since the left hand side of (1. 6) equals $\langle f, g\rangle$ where

$$g(x) = \int_K \frac{1}{2}\{|x| + |y| - |x-y|\}\mu(dy) \in H,$$

(1.6) implies $g = 0$. Therefore, regarding μ as a signed measure in $\boldsymbol{R}^d$ we have

$$(1.7)\qquad \int_{\boldsymbol{R}^d}\int_{\boldsymbol{R}^d} \frac{1}{2}\{|x| + |y| - |x-y|\}\mu(dy)\mu(dy) = 0.$$

In the same way as in the proof of Théorème 58 of [6: p. 276] we can prove that the left hand side of (1. 7) equals

$$\text{const.} \int_{\boldsymbol{R}^d} |\xi|^{-d-1} |\hat{\mu}(\xi) - \hat{\mu}(0)|^2 d\xi,$$

where $\hat{\mu}(\xi)$ is the Fourier transform of μ. Therefore μ must be concentrated on $\{0\}$. But this is impossible because $0 \notin K$ and hence R must be dense in B. Next we notice that the whole space B, which has γ-measure 1, can be expresses as a union of a countable number of open balls of the form $B_\varepsilon(\phi) = \{\psi \in B : \|\psi - \phi\|_\infty < \varepsilon\}$, $\phi \in R$, $\varepsilon > 0$ being arbitrary but fixed. On the other hand by the Cameron-Martin formula (1.5) $\gamma(B_\varepsilon(\phi)) = \gamma_{-\phi}(B_\varepsilon(0)) > 0$ if and only if $\gamma(B_\varepsilon(0)) > 0$ provided that $\phi \in R$. Therefore we must have $\gamma(B_\varepsilon(\phi)) > 0$ for all $\phi \in R$. This implies the assertion of the lemma.

§2. Recurrence of X_W. Since our result in the 1-dimensional case is easily obtained from a general theory of 1-dimensional diffusion processes, we assume $d \geq 2$.

Theorem 1. *X_W is recurrent for almost all Brownian environments W.*

Proof. It is enough to prove that X_W^0 is recurrent for almost all Brownian environments W and, according to Ichihara's criterion ([4: Theorem A]) it is also enough to prove that

$$(2.1)\qquad \int_1^\infty \left\{\int_{S^{d-1}} e^{-W(r\theta)}d\theta\right\}^{-1} r^{-d+1}dr = \infty,\ P\text{-}a.s.$$

If we put $M(t) = \min\{(T_tW)(\theta) : \theta \in S^{d-1}\}$, then

(2.2) the left hand side of (2. 1)

$$= \int_0^\infty e^{(2-d)t} \left\{ \int_{S^{d-1}} \exp(-e^{t/2}(T_tW)(\theta))d\theta \right\}^{-1} dt$$

$$\geq \int_0^\infty e^{(2-d)t} \exp\{e^{t/2} M(t)\} dt \geq \int_0^\infty \mathbf{1}_{(a,\infty)}(M(t))dt,$$

provided that $a > 0$ is chosen so that $(2-d)t + ae^{t/2} \geq 0$ holds for all $t \geq 0$. Next take $K = \{x \in \boldsymbol{R}^d : 1 \leq |x| \leq 2\}$ and consider B, H and γ as in the preceeding section. Since $\Gamma = \{\phi \in B : \min(\phi(x) : |x| = 1) > a\}$ is an open set in B, we have $\gamma(\Gamma) > 0$ by Lemma 2. The ergodicity of $\{T_t, t \in \boldsymbol{R}\}$ now implies

$$\lim_{T\to\infty} T^{-1} \int_0^T \mathbf{1}_{(a,\infty)}(M(t))dt = E\{\mathbf{1}_{(a,\infty)}(M(0))\} = \gamma(\Gamma) > 0, \ P\text{-}a,s.,$$

and hence $\int_0^\infty \mathbf{1}_{(a,\infty)}(M(t))dt = \infty$, P-$a.s.$, which combined with (2.2) proves (2. 1).

Remark 1. $\boldsymbol{X}_W$ is null-recurrent (P-$a.s.$) in the sense that $m_W(dx) = e^{-W}dx$ is an invariant measure for $\boldsymbol{X}_W$ with $m_W(\boldsymbol{R}^d) = \infty$.

Remark 2. Fukushima's criterion can also be used for proving Theorem 1; in fact, by virtue of Lemmas 1, 2 it is still easy to prove the existence of a sequence of radial functions u_n in $C_0^\infty(\boldsymbol{R}^d)$ such that $0 \leq u_n \leq 1$, $\lim u_n = 1$ a.e. and $\mathscr{E}(u_n, u_n) = 0$. This argument also proves the recurrence of $\boldsymbol{X}_{|W|}$ for almost all Brownian environments W.

Remark 3. $\boldsymbol{X}_{-|W|}$ is recurrent for $d = 1$ and transient for $d \geq 2$ for almost all Brownian environments W. The proof in the case $d \geq 2$ is as follows. According to Theorem B of [4] the transience of $\boldsymbol{X}^0_{-|W|}$ (and consequently of $\boldsymbol{X}_{-|W|}$) follows if one proves that, for almost all Brownian environments W,

$$\int_0^\infty e^{-|W(r\theta)|} r^{-d+1} dr < \infty \tag{2.3}$$

for θ belonging to some subset (which may depend on W) of S^{d-1} with a positive uniform measure. But this can be proved by showing that the expectation (with respect to P) of the left hand side of (2. 3) is finite for each fixed θ.

References

[1] Th. Brox: A one-dimensional diffusion process in a Wiener medium. Ann. Probab., **14**, 1206–1218 (1986).

[2] M. Fukushima: On recurrence criteria in the Dirichlet space theory. Local Times to Global Geometry, Control and Physics (ed. Elworthy). Research Notes in Math., Series 150, Longman (1987).

[3] M. Fukushima, S. Nakao and M. Takeda: On Dirichlet forms with random data - recurrence and homogenization. Stochastic Processes - Mathematics and Physics II (eds. S. Albeverio, Ph. Blanchard and L. Streit). Lect. Notes in Math., vol. 1250, Springer-Verlag (1987).

[4] K. Ichihara: Some global properties of symmetric diffusion processes. Publ. RIMS, Kyoto Univ., **14**, 441–486 (1978).

[5] K. Itô: On the ergodicity of a certain stationary process. Proc. Imp. Acad., **20**, 54–55 (1944).

[6] P. Lévy: Processus Stochastiques et Mouvement Brownien. Gauthier-Villars, Paris (1948).

[7] P. Mathieu: Zero white noise limit through Dirichlet forms. Application to diffusions in a random medium (1992) (preprint).

[8] J. Nash: Continuity of solutions of parabolic and elliptic equations. Amer. J. Math., **80**, 931–953 (1958).

[9] S. Schumacher: Diffusions with random coefficients. Contemporary Math. Particle Systems, Random Media and Large Deviations (ed. Durrett). vol. 41, pp. 351–356 (1985).

[10] Y. G. Sinai: The limiting behavior of a one-dimensional random walk in a random medium. Theor. Probab. Appl., **27**, 256–268 (1982).

[11] H. Tanaka: Limit theorem for one-dimensional diffusion process in Brownian environment. Stochastic Analysis (Proc. Japanese-French Seminar, Paris 1987). Lect. Notes in Math., vol. 1322, Springer-Verlag, pp. 156–172.

Localization of a Diffusion Process in a One-Dimensional Brownian Environment

HIROSHI TANAKA
Keio University

Dedicated to H. P. McKean.

1. Introduction

Let $\mathbb{W}$ be the space of continuous functions $W : \mathbb{R} \to \mathbb{R}$ with $W(0) = 0$ and Q be the Wiener measure on $\mathbb{W}$, namely, let $\{W(x), x \geqq 0, Q\}$ and $\{W(-x), x \geqq 0, Q\}$ be independent one-dimensional Brownian motions starting at 0. An element of $\mathbb{W}$ is called an environment. Given an environment W we consider a diffusion process $X(t, W)$ starting at 0 and with generator

$$L_W = \frac{1}{2} e^{W(x)} \frac{d}{dx} \left(e^{-W(x)} \frac{d}{dx} \right). \tag{1.1}$$

$X(t, W)$ can be constructed from a one-dimensional Brownian motion $B(t)$ by a scale change and a time change; see [3]. We denote by (Ω, P) the probability space on which $B(t)$ is defined and put $\mathcal{P} = P \otimes Q$. Thus $B(t)$ and $W(x)$ are independent. $X(t, W)$ is then called a diffusion process in a Brownian environment. Sinai presented this model as a diffusion analogue of his random walk in a random environment; see [10], page 268. Brox (see [1]) and Schumacher (see [9]) proved that $X(t, \cdot)$ exhibits an asymptotic behavior as $t \to \infty$ which is similar to that of Sinai's random walk of [10]. We consider another probability measure $\widetilde{Q}$ on $\mathbb{W}$ such that $\{W(x), x \geqq 0, \widetilde{Q}\}$ and $\{W(-x), x \geqq 0, \widetilde{Q}\}$ are independent Bessel processes of index 3 starting at 0. Then $e^{-W} \in L^1(\mathbb{R})$, $\widetilde{Q}$-a.s. For each W with $e^{-W} \in L^1(\mathbb{R})$ let μ_W be the probability measure in $\mathbb{R}$ of the form

$$\mu_W(dx) = \text{const. } e^{-W(x)}\, dx\,. \tag{1.2}$$

For each $\lambda > 0$ we define $b_\lambda(W)$, a function of the environment W alone, by (3.1). Then it was proved in [11] that the distribution of $X(e^\lambda, \cdot) - b_\lambda(\cdot)$ converges to μ as $\lambda \to \infty$, where $\mu = \int \mu_W \widetilde{Q}(dW)$. A similar localization theorem had already been obtained by Golosov (see [2]) for reflecting random walks on $\mathbb{Z}^+$. In the present paper we restate the above localization theorem for $X(t, \cdot)$ in a modified form and prove it by a method different from that of [11].

THEOREM 1.1. *For any $t_j, 1 \leqq j \leqq k$, with $0 < t_1 < \cdots < t_k$ the joint distribution of $X(e^\lambda t_j, \cdot) - b_\lambda(\cdot)$, $1 \leqq j \leqq k$, with respect to $\mathcal{P}$ converges to the mixture $\int \mu_W^k \widetilde{Q}(dW)$ as $\lambda \to \infty$ where μ_W^k is the k-fold product distribution of μ_W.*

Communications on Pure and Applied Mathematics, Vol. XLVII, 755–766 (1994)

CCC 0010–3640/94/050755–12

Ogura (see [7], Example 7.2) gave another proof to Brox's Theorem 1.4 (see [1]) from which the present method was suggested. The notion of valleys of environments still plays an essential role as before. The main difference between the present proof and that of [11] is as follows: In [11] we used Brox's estimates for exit times from valleys and a coupling technique, but now, instead of these, we use a theorem of Ogura (see [7]) concerning the convergence of a sequence of one-dimensional (generalized) diffusion processes.

2. Convergence Theorem for Diffusion Processes in One-Dimension

It is well known that the generator of a diffusion process in $\mathbb{R}$ can be expressed as a diffusion operator $d/\{m(dx)\}\, d/\{dS(x)\}$. The measure $m(dx)$, called the speed measure, is finite on compact subsets and positive on open subsets ($\neq \emptyset$) of $\mathbb{R}$, and the function $S(x)$, called the canonical scale, is continuous and strictly increasing. Ogura (see [7]) discussed a more general case, namely, the case of "bi-generalized diffusion processes," but for our present purpose it is enough to consider a sequence of diffusion processes. Thus, suppose we are given a sequence of diffusion operators L_n with speed measure $m_n(dx)$ and canonical scale $S_n(x), n = 1, 2, \ldots$, and denote by $X_n^x(t)$ the diffusion process with generator L_n starting at x. We assume that the following conditions (2.1), (2.2), and (2.3) are satisfied:

(2.1) For each n $S_n(0) = 0$ and $S_n(x)$ tends to ∞ or $-\infty$ accordingly as $x \to \infty$ or $x \to -\infty$; for each x the canonical scale $S_n(x)$ tends to 0 as $n \to \infty$.

(2.2) For any $f \in C_0(\mathbb{R})$, the space of continuous functions with compact supports,

$$\lim_{n\to\infty} \int f\, dm_n = \int f\, dm\,,$$

where m is a nontrivial finite measure (namely, m_n converges vaguely to m as $n \to \infty$).

(2.3) The measure $\widetilde{m}_n = m_n \circ S_n^{-1}$ converges vaguely to $c\delta_0$ as $n \to \infty$, where S_n^{-1} is the inverse function of $S_n, c = m(\mathbb{R}) > 0$ and δ_0 denotes the δ-measure at 0.

The author learned the following theorem through the kindness of Y. Ogura.

OGURA'S THEOREM. (SEE [7]) *Let ε be an arbitrary constant such that $0 < \varepsilon < 1$, put*

$$T_{k,\varepsilon} = \{(t_1, \ldots, t_k) \in \mathbb{R}^k : \varepsilon \leqq t_1 < t_k \leqq 1/\varepsilon\,, \quad t_j - t_{j-1} \geqq \varepsilon (1 \leqq \forall j \leqq k)\Big\} \tag{2.4}$$

and consider a sequence $\{x_n\}$ satisfying

$$|S_n(x_n)| \leqq \frac{1}{\varepsilon} \quad \textit{for } n = 1, 2, \ldots\,. \tag{2.5}$$

Then for any $f_j \in C_0(\mathbb{R})$, $1 \leqq j \leqq k$,

$$E\left\{\prod_{j=1}^{k} f_j\left(X_n^{x_n}(t_j)\right)\right\} \to \prod_{j=1}^{k}\int c^{-1} f_j\, dm$$

as $n \to \infty$ *uniformly in* $\{x_n\}$ *satisfying condition* (2.5) *and in* $(t_1, \cdots, t_k) \in T_{k,\varepsilon}$.

Proof: Since the case of $\lim S_n(x) = 0$ is excluded in Theorem 5.1 of [7], strictly speaking the above theorem is not a straightforward consequence of Theorem 5.1 of [7]. The proof can be done, however, in the same way. Denote by $q_n(t, x, y)$ the transition density with respect to $\widetilde{m}_n$ of the diffusion process with speed measure $\widetilde{m}_n$ and canonical scale x. It is defined through formula (5.6) of [7] by taking $\widetilde{m} = \widetilde{m}_n$ and $\widetilde{Q} = \mathbb{R}$. It is known that $q_n(t, x, y)$ is continuous in $(t, x, y) \in (0, \infty) \times \mathbb{R} \times \mathbb{R}$ and symmetric in x and y. Also we define $q(t, x, y)$ through formula (5.6) of [7] by taking $\widetilde{m} = c\delta_0$ and $\widetilde{Q} = \mathbb{R}$. By an easy computation we see that $q(t, x, y) = 1/c$ for any $(t, x, y) \in (0, \infty) \times \mathbb{R} \times \mathbb{R}$. Probabilistically (and formally) $q(t, x, y)$ is the transition density with respect to $c\delta_0$ of the "generalized diffusion process" which jumps to 0 immediately at $t = 0$ and remains there for any $t > 0$. Now Proposition 5.1 of [7] implies that $q_n(t, x, y)$ converges to $q(t, x, y)$ uniformly on each compact subset of $(0, \infty) \times \mathbb{R} \times \mathbb{R}$ as $n \to \infty$. Therefore, if $p_n(t, x, y)$ denotes the transition density with respect to m_n of $X_n(t)$, then for any $f \in C_0(\mathbb{R})$

$$\begin{aligned}&\int p_n(t, x_n, y) f(y) m_n(dy)\\ &= \int q_n(t, S_n(x_n), S_n(y)) f(y) m_n(dy) \to \int c^{-1} f\, dm\end{aligned}$$

as $n \to \infty$ uniformly in $t \geqq \varepsilon$ and in $\{x_n\}$ satisfying condition (2.5), $\varepsilon > 0$ being an arbitrary constant. This implies the theorem.

3. Valleys

3.1. We give the definition of a valley of an environment W following [1]. A part $\{W(x), x_1 \leqq x \leqq x_2\}$ of W is called a *valley* of W if:

(i) $x_1 < x_2$;

(ii) there exists $x_0 \in (x_1, x_2)$ such that

$$W(x_1) > W(x) > W(x_0) \quad \text{for any } x \in (x_1, x_0)\,,$$
$$W(x_2) > W(x) > W(x_0) \quad \text{for any } x \in (x_0, x_2)\,;$$

(iii) for the same x_0 as above

$$H_- = \sup\{W(y) - W(x) : x_1 \leqq x < y \leqq x_0\} < W(x_2) - W(x_0)\,,$$
$$H_+ = \sup\{W(x) - W(y) : x_0 \leqq x < y \leqq x_2\} < W(x_1) - W(x_0)\,.$$

For simplicity we write (x_1, x_0, x_2) instead of $\{W(x), x_1 \leqq x \leqq x_2\}$ and call x_0 the *bottom* of the valley. $A = H_+ \vee H_-$ is called the *inner directed ascent* (abbreviated to *i.d.a.*) and $D = (W(x_1) - W(x_0)) \wedge (W(x_2) - W(x_0))$ is the *depth* of the valley. A valley (x_1, x_0, x_2) is said to contain 0 if $x_1 < 0 < x_2$. For any fixed $r > 0$, with Q-measure 1, there exists a valley of W with *i.d.a.* $< r <$ *depth* and containing 0 (see [1]); moreover, there are many such valleys for fixed W but it can be easily seen that their bottoms are the same. We denote by $b = b(W)$ the unique (common) bottom of such valleys for $r = 1$.

To give another description of a valley due to Kesten (see [6]) let $\lambda > 0$, $W \in \mathbb{W}$ and put

$$W^{\#}(x) = \begin{cases} W(x) - \min\limits_{[0,x]} W & \text{for } x \geqq 0 , \\ W(x) - \min\limits_{[x,0]} W & \text{for } x < 0 , \end{cases}$$

$$d_\lambda^+ = \min\{x > 0 : W^{\#}(x) = \lambda\} , \qquad V_\lambda^+ = \min_{[0,d_\lambda^+]} W ,$$

$$d_\lambda^- = \max\{x < 0 : W^{\#}(x) = \lambda\} , \qquad V_\lambda^- = \min_{[d_\lambda^-,0]} W .$$

We define b_λ^+ and b_λ^- by $W(b_\lambda^\pm) = V_\lambda^\pm$ (such $b_\lambda^\pm$ are uniquely determined with Q-measure 1 for each fixed $\lambda > 0$). Let

$$M_\lambda^+ = \max_{[0,b_\lambda^+]} W , \qquad J_\lambda^+ = M_\lambda^+ \vee (V_\lambda^+ + \lambda) ,$$

$$M_\lambda^- = \max_{[b_\lambda^-,0]} W , \qquad J_\lambda^- = M_\lambda^- \vee (V_\lambda^- + \lambda) ,$$

and define $b_\lambda = b_\lambda(W)$ by

$$b_\lambda(W) = \begin{cases} b_\lambda^+ & \text{if } J_\lambda^+ < J_\lambda^- , \\ b_\lambda^- & \text{if } J_\lambda^+ > J_\lambda^- . \end{cases} \tag{3.1}$$

Moreover, we define $a_\lambda = a_\lambda(W)$ and $c_\lambda = c_\lambda(W)$ by

(3.2) $a_\lambda(W) =$ the infimum of the set of a's ($a < b_\lambda$) such that

$$\begin{cases} W(a) > W(x) > W(b_\lambda) & \text{for any } x \in (a, b_\lambda) , \\ \sup\{W(y) - W(x) : a \leqq x < y \leqq b_\lambda\} < \lambda , \end{cases}$$

(3.3) $c_\lambda(W) =$ the supremum of the set of c's ($c > b_\lambda$) such that

$$\begin{cases} W(c) > W(x) > W(b_\lambda) & \text{for any } x \in (b_\lambda, c) , \\ \sup\{W(x) - W(y) : b_\lambda \leqq x < y \leqq c\} < \lambda . \end{cases}$$

Then we see that, with Q-measure $1, (a_\lambda, b_\lambda, c_\lambda)$ is the maximum valley of W containing 0 and satisfying $A_\lambda < \lambda < D_\lambda$, where A_λ and D_λ are, respectively, the i.d.a. and the depth of the valley. Thus b_1 coincides with b of the preceding paragraph. From now on we suppress the suffix 1 in $a_1, b_1, c_1, D_1, d_1^+, d_1^-$, etc.

3.2. For $\lambda > 0$ and $W \in \mathbb{W}$ we define $W_\lambda \in \mathbb{W}$ by $W_\lambda(x) = \lambda^{-1}W(\lambda^2 x), x \in \mathbb{R}$. Then for each fixed $\lambda > 0$ $\{W_\lambda, Q\}$ is equivalent in law to $\{W, Q\}$ and $a_\lambda(W) = \lambda^2 a(W_\lambda), b_\lambda(W) = \lambda^2 b(W_\lambda), c_\lambda(W) = \lambda^2 c(W_\lambda), D_\lambda(W) = \lambda D(W_\lambda)$. As stated in the Introduction we denote by $X(t, W)$ the diffusion process with generator L_W and starting at 0. Then the following scaling relation holds (see [1], Lemma 1.3): For any fixed $\lambda > 0$ and $W \in \mathbb{W}$

$$\{X(t, \lambda W_\lambda), t \geqq 0, P\} \overset{\text{d}}{=} \{\lambda^{-2}X(\lambda^4 t, W), t \geqq 0, P\} \tag{3.4}$$

where $\overset{\text{d}}{=}$ means the equality in distribution (W is fixed).

3.3. The following is a result of Brox, proved in [1], Proposition 4.1 (see also [4], Theorem I-A-1): *If (x_1, x_0, x_2) is a valley of W with i.d.a. $< r <$ depth and containing* 0, *then $X(e^{\lambda r}, \lambda W)$ converges to x_0 in probability as $\lambda \to \infty$* (W *is fixed*).

3.4. On a suitable probability space we consider a process $\{w^+(x), x \in \mathbb{R}\}$ such that $\{w^+(x), x \geqq 0\}$ and $\{w^+(-x), x \geqq 0\}$ are independent reflecting Brownian motions on $[0, \infty)$ starting at 0. Let $\{\ell^+(x), x \in \mathbb{R}\}$ be the local time at 0 of $w^+(x)$, namely,

$$\ell^+(x) = \lim_{\varepsilon \downarrow 0} \left(\frac{1}{2\varepsilon}\right) \int_I \mathbf{1}_{[0,\varepsilon]}(w^+(y))\, dy \ ,$$

where $I = [0, x]$ or $[x, 0]$ accordingly as $x \geqq 0$ or $x < 0$. Now we put $\beta^+(x) = w^+(x) + \ell^+(x)$. Then by Pitman's theorem (see [8]) $\{\beta^+(x),\ x \geqq 0\}$ and $\{\beta^+(-x),\ x \geqq 0\}$ are independent Bessel processes of index 3 starting at 0. For $\lambda > 0$ we put

(3.5a) σ_λ^+ = the smallest zero of $w^+(x)$ in $(z, 0]$ where z is the maximum of

$$x < 0 \quad \text{with } w^+(x) = \lambda \ .$$

(3.5b) $\tau_\lambda^+ = \min\{x > 0 : \beta^+(x) = \lambda\}$.

We next introduce another process $\{w^-(x), x \in \mathbb{R}\}$ which is equivalent in law to $\{w^+(x), x \in \mathbb{R}\}$. We assume that $w^+(x)$ and $w^-(x)$ are defined on a common probability space $(\bar{\Omega}, \bar{P})$ and that they are independent. Denote by $\ell^-(x)$ the local time at 0 of $w^-(x)$, put $\beta^-(x) = w^-(x) + \ell^-(x)$ and define σ_λ^- and τ_λ^- in a way similar to equation (3.5). We put

$$
\begin{aligned}
\bar{b}_\lambda^+ &= -\sigma_\lambda^+ , & \bar{b}_\lambda^- &= \sigma_\lambda^- , \\
\bar{d}_\lambda^+ &= \tau_\lambda^+ - \sigma_\lambda^+ , & \bar{d}_\lambda^- &= -(\tau_\lambda^- - \sigma_\lambda^-) , \\
\bar{V}_\lambda^+ &= -\beta^+(\sigma_\lambda^+) , & \bar{V}_\lambda^- &= -\beta^-(\sigma_\lambda^-) , \\
\bar{M}_\lambda^+ &= \max_{[\sigma_\lambda^+,0]} \beta^+ - \beta^+(\sigma_\lambda^+) , & \bar{M}_\lambda^- &= \max_{[\sigma_\lambda^-,0]} \beta^- - \beta^-(\sigma_\lambda^-) , \\
\bar{J}_\lambda^+ &= \bar{M}_\lambda^+ \vee (\bar{V}_\lambda^+ + \lambda) , & \bar{J}_\lambda^- &= \bar{M}_\lambda^- \vee (\bar{V}_\lambda^- + \lambda) .
\end{aligned}
$$

The following lemma for $\lambda = 1$ was proved in [11]. The proof for a general $\lambda > 0$ can be done in the same way.

LEMMA 3.1. (SEE [11]) *Let $\lambda > 0$ and put*

$$
\begin{aligned}
W_\lambda^+ &= \{W(x + b_\lambda^+) - W(b_\lambda^+) , & -b_\lambda^+ &\leqq x \leqq d_\lambda^+ - b_\lambda^+\} , \\
W_\lambda^- &= \{W(-x + b_\lambda^-) - W(b_\lambda^-) , & b_\lambda^- &\leqq x \leqq -(d_\lambda^- - b_\lambda^-)\} .
\end{aligned}
$$

Then, under the law Q $(W_\lambda^+, J_\lambda^+)$ and $(W_\lambda^-, J_\lambda^-)$ are independent and have the same distribution which is equal to the joint distribution of $\{\beta^+(x), \sigma_\lambda^+ \leqq x \leqq \tau_\lambda^+\}$ and $\bar{J}_\lambda^+$.

LEMMA 3.2. *Let $\widetilde{W}_\lambda(x) = \lambda\{W(\lambda^{-2}x + b) - W(b)\}, x \in \mathbb{R}$. Then $\{\widetilde{W}_\lambda, Q\}$ converges in law to $\{W, \widetilde{Q}\}$ as $\lambda \to \infty$.*

Proof: It is enough to prove that, for any positive constant K and for any bounded continuous function F on $\mathbb{W}$ depending only on $\{W(x), |x| \leqq K\}$,

$$
\lim_{\lambda\to\infty} \int F\left(\widetilde{W}_\lambda\right) Q(dW) = \int F \, d\widetilde{Q} . \tag{3.6}
$$

From now on we suppress the suffix 1 in J_1^+, J_1^+, W_1^+, etc. We put $\Gamma_\lambda = \{J^+ < J^-\} \cap \{\lambda^{-2}K < b^+ \wedge (d^+ - b^+)\}$ and notice that $Q(\Gamma_\lambda)$ increases to $Q\{J^+ < J^-\} = 1/2$ as $\lambda \uparrow \infty$. Moreover, if $W \in \Gamma_\lambda$ then the value of $F(\widetilde{W}_\lambda)$ is determined by W^+, namely, we can write

$$
F\left(\widetilde{W}_\lambda\right) = G_\lambda(W^+) \quad \text{on } \Gamma_\lambda
$$

with a suitable function G_λ. Thus, using the notation $E_Q\{F;\Gamma\} = \int_\Gamma F dQ$ and applying Lemma 3.1, we can write

$$
\begin{aligned}
&E_Q\left\{F\left(\widetilde{W}_\lambda\right);\ J^+ < J^-\right\}\\
&= E_Q\left\{F\left(\widetilde{W}_\lambda\right);\ \Gamma_\lambda\right\} + o(1)\\
&= E_Q\{G_\lambda(W^+);\ \Gamma_\lambda\} + o(1)\\
&= \bar{E}\{G_\lambda(\beta^+(x), \sigma^+ \leqq x \leqq \tau^+);\ \bar{\Gamma}_\lambda\} + o(1)\\
&= \bar{E}\{F(\lambda\beta^+(\lambda^{-2}\cdot));\ \bar{\Gamma}_\lambda\} + o(1)\\
&= \bar{E}\{F(\lambda\beta^+(\lambda^{-2}\cdot));\ \bar{J}^+ < \bar{J}^-\} + o(1)\,,
\end{aligned}
\tag{3.7}
$$

where $\bar{\Gamma}_\lambda = \{\bar{J}^+ < \bar{J}^-\} \cap \{\lambda^{-2}K < \bar{b}^+ \wedge (\bar{d}^+ - \bar{b}^+)\}$, and $o(1)$ represents a term which tends to 0 as $\lambda \to \infty$. By an argument similar to that used for arriving at expression (3.9) of [11" we can prove that the last term in equation (3.7) is asymptotically equal to

$$\bar{E}\{F(\lambda\beta^+(\lambda^{-2}\cdot))\}/2 \tag{3.8}$$

as $\lambda \to \infty$. Since $\{\lambda\beta^+(\lambda^{-2}\cdot), \bar{P}\}$ is equivalent in law to $\{\beta^+(\cdot), \bar{P}\}$, (3.8) is equal to

$$\bar{E}\{F(\beta^+(\cdot))\}/2 = \int F d\widetilde{Q}/2\,, \tag{3.9}$$

and hence the first term of equation (3.7) tends to (3.9) as $\lambda \to \infty$. Since $E_Q\{F(\widetilde{W}_\lambda); J^+ > J^-\}$ can be treated similarly, we obtain equality (3.6).

4. Proof of Theorem 1.1

The idea of the proof is to apply Ogura's theorem to study the limiting behavior of $X(e^\lambda t, \cdot) - b_\lambda(\cdot)$ as $\lambda \to \infty$.

4.1. We consider the diffusion processes

$$X_\lambda^W(t) = X(e^\lambda t, W) - b_\lambda(W)\,, \qquad t \geqq 0\,, \tag{4.1}$$

$$Y_\lambda^W(t) = \lambda^2\{X(\lambda^{-4}e^\lambda t, \lambda W) - b(W)\}\,, \quad t \geqq 0\,. \tag{4.2}$$

The scaling relation (3.4) implies that, for each fixed $\lambda > 0$ and W,

$$\left\{X_\lambda^W(t), t \geqq 0\right\} \stackrel{\mathrm{d}}{=} \left\{Y_\lambda^{W_\lambda}(t), t \geqq 0\right\}.$$

Since the distributions of W and W_λ under Q are the same,

$$\left\{Y_\lambda^{W_\lambda}(t), t \geqq 0\right\} \stackrel{\mathscr{D}}{=} \left\{Y_\lambda^{W}(t), t \geqq 0\right\},$$

where $\stackrel{\mathscr{D}}{=}$ means the equality in distribution (W is random). Thus the processes (4.1) and (4.2) are equivalent in law under $\mathscr{P}$. For a fixed W the generator of the diffusion process $Y_\lambda^W(t)$ is expressed as the diffusion operator L_λ^W with the following canonical scale and speed measure:

$$S_\lambda^W(x) = 2e^{-\lambda} \int_0^x \exp\left\{\lambda\left(W\left(\lambda^{-2}y + b\right) - W(b)\right)\right\} dy\,. \tag{4.3}$$

$$m_\lambda^W(dx) = \exp\left\{-\lambda\left(W\left(\lambda^{-2}x + b\right) - W(b)\right)\right\} dx\,. \tag{4.4}$$

LEMMA 4.1. (i) *For any x the canonical scale $S_\lambda^W(x)$ tends to 0 as $\lambda \to \infty$ with Q-measure* 1.

(ii) *We regard m_λ^W and $\widetilde{m}_\lambda^W = m_\lambda^W \circ (S_\lambda^W)^{-1}$ as random variable taking values in the space of non-negative Radon measures in $\mathbb{R}$ equipped with the topology of vague convergence. Then the joint distribution (under Q) of m_λ^W and $\widetilde{m}_\lambda^W$ converges to the joint distribution (under $\widetilde{Q}$) of $e^{-W(x)}dx$ and const.δ_0(const. $= \int e^{-W}dx$) as $\lambda \to \infty$.*

Proof: The assertion (i) is obvious. To prove (ii) we first put

$$x_1 = \max\{x < 0 : W(x+b) - W(b) = 1\}\,,$$
$$x_2 = \min\{x > 0 : W(x+b) - W(b) = 1\}\,,$$

and observe that, with Q-measure 1, for any $\varepsilon > 0$ there exist $x' \in (x_1 - \varepsilon, x_1)$ and $x'' \in (x_2, x_2 + \varepsilon)$ such that $W(x'+b) - W(b) > 1$ and $W(x''+b) - W(b) > 1$. Thus, if x varies with λ in such a way that $x > \lambda^2(x_2+\varepsilon)$ or $x < \lambda^2(x_1 - \varepsilon)$, then $|S_\lambda^W(x)| \to \infty$ as $\lambda \to \infty$. On the other hand, if x varies with λ in such a way that $\lambda^2(x_1+\varepsilon) < x < \lambda^2(x_2 - \varepsilon)$, then $S_\lambda^W(x) \to 0$ as $\lambda \to \infty$, where $\varepsilon > 0$ can be chosen arbitrarily under the condition $\varepsilon < (-x_1) \wedge x_2$. Therefore, for each fixed $y \neq 0$ $\lambda^{-2}(S_\lambda^W)^{-1}(y)$ tends as $\lambda \to \infty$ to x_1 or x_2 accordingly as $y < 0$ or $y > 0$. Thus, putting $z_i = (S_\lambda^W)^{-1}(y_i)$, $i = 1, 2$, for any given y_1 and y_2 with $y_1 < 0 < y_2$, we see that $\lambda^{-2}z_1 \to x_1$ and $\lambda^{-2}z_2 \to x_2$ as $\lambda \to \infty$. Now we write

$$\begin{aligned}\widetilde{m}_\lambda^W([y_1, y_2]) &= m_\lambda^W([z_1, z_2]) \\ &= \int_{z_1}^{z_2} \exp\left\{-\lambda\left(W\left(\lambda^{-2}x + b\right) - W(b)\right)\right\} dx \\ &= I_1 + I_2 + I_3\,,\end{aligned}$$

where

$$I_1 = \int_{-1/\varepsilon}^{1/\varepsilon}, \quad I_2 = \int_{-\lambda^2\varepsilon}^{-1/\varepsilon} + \int_{1/\varepsilon}^{\lambda^2\varepsilon}, \quad I_3 = \int_{z_1}^{-\lambda^2\varepsilon} + \int_{\lambda^2\varepsilon}^{z_2},$$

and prove the following:

(4.5) $\{m_\lambda^W, Q\}$ converges in law to $\{e^{-W(x)}dx, \widetilde{Q}\}$ as $\lambda \to \infty$. In particular, for each $\varepsilon > 0\,\{I_1, Q\}$ converges in law to $\{\int_{|x|<1/\varepsilon} \exp\{-W\}dx, \widetilde{Q}\}$ as $\lambda \to \infty$.

(4.6) For any $\gamma > 0$ $\lim_{\varepsilon\downarrow 0} \overline{\lim}_{\lambda\to\infty} Q\{I_i > \gamma\} = 0$, $i = 2, 3$.

(4.5) is an immediate consequence of Lemma 3.2. For the proof of (4.6) with $i = 3$ it is enough to note that

$$\begin{aligned} I_3 &= \lambda^2 \left(\int_{\lambda^{-2}z_1}^{-\varepsilon} + \int_{\varepsilon}^{\lambda^{-2}z_2} \right) \exp\{-\lambda(W(x+b) - W(b))\}\, dx \\ &\sim \lambda^2 \left(\int_{x_1}^{-\varepsilon} + \int_{\varepsilon}^{x_2} \right) \exp\{-\lambda(W(x+b) - W(b))\}\, dx \\ &\to 0\,, \quad \lambda \to \infty\,, \end{aligned}$$

provided that W is in the event $\{(-x_1) \wedge x_2 > \varepsilon\}$ whose Q-measure tends to 1 as $\varepsilon \downarrow 0$. As for (4.6) with $i = 2$, by replacing W by W_λ we see that I_2 is equivalent in law to

$$\left(\int_{-\lambda^2\varepsilon}^{-1/\varepsilon} + \int_{1/\varepsilon}^{\lambda^2\varepsilon} \right) \exp\{-(W(x+b_\lambda) - W(b_\lambda))\}\, dx\,,$$

which is dominated by

$$\begin{aligned} &\left(\int_{-b_\lambda^+}^{-1/\varepsilon} + \int_{1/\varepsilon}^{d_\lambda^+ - b_\lambda^+} \right) \exp\{-(W(x+b_\lambda^+) - W(b_\lambda^+))\}\, dx \\ &+ \left(\int_{b_\lambda^-}^{-1/\varepsilon} + \int_{1/\varepsilon}^{-(d_\lambda^- - b_\lambda^-)} \right) \exp\{-(W(-x+b_\lambda^-) - W(b_\lambda^-))\}\, dx\,, \end{aligned} \tag{4.7}$$

provided that W is in the event

$$\begin{aligned} &\{d_\lambda^+ - b_\lambda^+ > \lambda^2\varepsilon > 1/\varepsilon,\ -b_\lambda^+ < -\lambda^2\varepsilon, \\ &-(d_\lambda^- - b_\lambda^-) > \lambda^2\varepsilon,\ b_\lambda^- < -\lambda^2\varepsilon\}\,. \end{aligned} \tag{4.8}$$

But by virtue of Lemma 3.1, (4.7) is equivalent in law to

$$\begin{aligned} &\left(\int_{\sigma_\lambda^+}^{-1/\varepsilon} + \int_{1/\varepsilon}^{\tau_\lambda^+} \right) \exp\{-\beta^+(x)\}\, dx \\ &+ \left(\int_{\sigma_\lambda^-}^{-1/\varepsilon} + \int_{1/\varepsilon}^{\tau_\lambda^-} \right) \exp\{-\beta^-(x)\}\, dx\,, \end{aligned}$$

which is dominated by

$$\int_{|x|>1/\varepsilon} \exp\{-\beta^+(x)\}\, dx + \int_{|x|>1/\varepsilon} \exp\{-\beta^-(x)\}\, dx\,. \tag{4.9}$$

It is known (see [3], Lemma 1.3) that, for fixed W, the process $\{\omega(\lambda^4 t), t \geq 0, P_W\}$ is equivalent in law to $\{\lambda^2\omega(t), t \geq 0, P_{\lambda W_\lambda}\}$. This combined with the fact that $b_\lambda(W) = \lambda^2 b(W_\lambda)$ implies that the process $\{\omega(e^\lambda t) - b_\lambda(W), t \geq 0, P_W\}$ is equivalent in law to $\{\lambda^2(\omega(\lambda^{-4}e^\lambda t) - b(W_\lambda)), t \geq 0, P_{\lambda W_\lambda}\}$; in addition, W_λ and W are identical in law. Therefore, for the proof of Theorem 1 it is enough to show

$$\int E_{\lambda W}\left\{\prod_{j=1}^k f_j(\lambda^2(\omega(\lambda^{-4}e^\lambda t_j) - b(W)))\right\} P(dW)$$
$$\longrightarrow \int \left\{\prod_{j=1}^k \int f_j \, d\mu_W\right\} Q(dW), \quad \lambda \to \infty. \tag{3.4}$$

For fixed W the generator of the diffusion process $\{\lambda^2(\omega(\lambda^{-4}e^\lambda t) - b(W)), t \geq 0, P_{\lambda W}\}$ is given by $\{d/m_\lambda^W(dx)\}\{d/dS_\lambda^W(x)\}$, where

$$S_\lambda^W(x) = 2e^{-\lambda}\int_0^x \exp\{\lambda(W(\lambda^{-2}y + b) - W(b))\} \, dy,$$
$$m_\lambda^W(dx) = \exp\{-\lambda(W(\lambda^{-2}x + b) - W(b))\}dx.$$

LEMMA 1 ([28]). (i) *$S_\lambda^W(x)$ tends to 0 as $\lambda \to \infty$ with P-measure 1.*
(ii) *If we regard m_λ^W and $\widetilde{m}_\lambda^W = m_\lambda^W \circ (S_\lambda^W)^{-1}$ as random variables taking values in the space of Radon measures in* **R** *equipped with the topology of vague convergence, then the joint distribution (under P) of m_λ^W and $\widetilde{m}_\lambda^W$ converges to the joint distribution (under Q) of $\exp\{-W(x)\}dx$ and $c_W\delta_0$ as $\lambda \to \infty$ where $c_W = \int \exp\{-W(x)\} \, dx$.*

Making use of Lemma 1 and Ogura's theorem we can prove (3.4) and hence Theorem 1. For details see [28].

A similar localization problem was discussed in [11] when $\{W(x)\}$ is a step process arising from a random walk that is assumed to converge in law, under a suitable scaling, to a strictly stable process.

4 Limit theorems in the case $\kappa \neq 0$

Let $\mathbf{X} = \{\omega(t), t \geq 0, \mathcal{P}\}$ denote the diffusion in a Brownian environment with drift ($\kappa \neq 0$), and set $T_x = \inf\{t > 0 : \omega(t) = x\}, \overline{\omega}(t) = \max\{\omega(s) : 0 \leq s \leq t\}$ and $\underline{\omega}(t) = \inf\{\omega(s) : s \geq t\}$.

THEOREM 2 ([13]). (i) *If $\kappa > 1$, then*

$$\lim_{x\to\infty} T_x/x = \frac{4}{\kappa - 1}, \quad \mathcal{P} - a.s.,$$
$$\lim_{t\to\infty} \omega(t)/t = \frac{\kappa - 1}{4}, \quad \mathcal{P} - a.s.$$

(ii) *If $\kappa = 1$, then $(x\log x)^{-1}T_x$ converges to 4 in probability (w.r.t. $\mathcal{P}$) as $x \to \infty$ and each of*

$$t^{-1}(\log t)\overline{\omega}(t), \quad t^{-1}(\log t)\omega(t) \quad \text{and} \quad t^{-1}(\log t)\underline{\omega}(t)$$

converges to 1/4 in probability (w.r.t. $\mathcal{P}$) as $t \to \infty$.

(iii) *If* $0 < \kappa < 1$, *then*

$$\lim_{x\to\infty} \mathcal{P}\{x^{-1/\kappa}T_x \le t\} = F_\kappa(t), \quad t > 0,$$

$$\lim_{t\to\infty} \mathcal{P}\{t^{-\kappa}\overline{\omega}(t) \le x\} = \lim_{t\to\infty} \mathcal{P}\{t^{-\kappa}\omega(t) \le x\}$$

$$= \lim_{t\to\infty} \mathcal{P}\{t^{-\kappa}\underline{\omega}(t) \le x\} = 1 - F_\kappa(x^{-1/\kappa}), \quad x > 0,$$

where F_κ *is the distribution function of a one-sided stable distribution with Laplace transform* $\exp(-c\lambda^\kappa)$.

REMARK. *The constant* c *in the Laplace transform* $\exp(-c\lambda^\kappa)$ *is given by*

$$c = \left\{2^{1-\kappa}\Gamma(\kappa)\int_0^\infty \phi(x)^{-2}dx\right\}^{-1},$$

where $\phi(x)$ *is the solution of* $\frac{d}{dM(x)} \cdot \frac{d\phi}{dx} = 2\phi, \phi(0) = 1, \phi'(0) = 0; M(x)$ *is given by* $M(x) = 2\gamma(\rho^{-1}(x))$, *where* $\gamma(x) = \int_0^x z^{-\kappa}e^{-4z}dz$ *and* $\rho^{-1}(x)$ *is the inverse function of* $\rho(y) = \int_0^y z^{\kappa-1}e^{4z}\,dz$.

Theorem 2 is a diffusion analogue of (a part of) the results for random walks due to Kesten et al. [15]. We do not give a detailed proof here but we remark that our method of the proof, in particular, of (ii) and (iii) is different from that of [14] and is based on the following lemma due to Kotani.

KOTANI'S LEMMA (1988, unpublished; see [13]). *Let* $\lambda > 0$. *Then for* $t \ge 0$

$$E_W\left\{e^{-\lambda T_t}\right\} = \exp\left\{-\int_0^t U_\lambda(s)\,ds\right\}, \quad \mathcal{P}-a.s.,$$

where $U_\lambda(t)$ *is the unique stationary positive solution of*

$$dU_\lambda(t) = U_\lambda(t)dW(t) + \left\{2\lambda + \frac{1-\kappa}{2}U_\lambda(t) - U_\lambda(t)^2\right\}dt.$$

By virtue of Kotani's lemma, for the proof of (iii) it is enough to show that, with $\lambda = \xi x^{-1/\kappa}$,

$$\lim_{x\to\infty} \mathcal{E}\left\{\exp(-\xi T_x/x^{1/\kappa})\right\}$$

$$= \lim_{\lambda\downarrow 0} E\left\{\exp\left(-\int_0^{\lambda^{-\kappa}\xi^\kappa} U_\lambda(s)\,ds\right)\right\} = \exp(-c\xi^\kappa),$$

and the key point in proving the last equality is the use of Kasahara's continuity theorem [9] concerning Krein's correspondence (e.g. see [16]). A full proof is given in [13].

The following theorem is a diffusion analogue of the result of Afanas'ev [1].

THEOREM 3 ([12]). (i) *If* $-2 < \kappa < 0$, *then*

$$\mathcal{P}\{T_x < \infty\} \sim const.x^{-3/2}\exp(-\kappa^2 x/8), \quad x \to \infty,$$

where

$$const. = 2^{\frac{5}{2}+\kappa}\Gamma(-\kappa)^{-1}\int_0^\infty\int_0^\infty\int_0^\infty\int_0^\infty z(a+z)^{-1}a^{-\kappa-1}e^{-a/2}y^{-\kappa}e^{-\lambda z}u\sinh u\,da\,dy\,dz\,du,$$

$(\lambda = 2^{-1}(1+y^2) + y\cosh u)$.

(ii) *If* $\kappa = -2$, *then*

$$\mathcal{P}\{T_x < \infty\} \sim (2/\pi)^{1/2}x^{-1/2}\exp(-x/2), \quad x \to \infty.$$

(iii) *If* $\kappa < -2$, *then*

$$\mathcal{P}\{T_x < \infty\} \sim \frac{-\kappa-2}{-\kappa-1}\cdot\exp\{(\kappa+1)x/2\}, \quad x \to \infty.$$

The proof of (i) relies on an explicit representation of the distribution of a certain Brownian functional due to Yor ([29], see the formula (6.e)).

5 A diffusion in a multidimensional Brownian environment

One generalization of the model discussed in Section **3** to a multidimensional case is to take a Lévy's Brownian motion with a multidimensional time as an environment. Let $\{W(x), x \in \mathbf{R}^d, P\}$ be a Lévy's Brownian motion with a d-dimensional time that is supposed to be an environment. For a frozen Brownian environment W let $\mathbf{X}_W = \{\omega(t), t \geq 0, P_W\}$ be a diffusion process with generator $2^{-1}(\Delta - \nabla W \cdot \nabla)$ starting at 0. Existence of such a diffusion is guaranteed by the result of Nash ([20]). As in a one-dimensional case we call $\mathbf{X} = \{\omega(t), t \geq 0, \mathcal{P}\}$ a diffusion in a d-dimensional Brownian environment, where $\mathcal{P}(dW d\omega) = P(dW)P_W(d\omega)$. A similar diffusion model appeared in a heuristic argument of [18]. Durrett [4] obtained rigorous results on recurrence and localization for random walks on $\mathbf{Z}^d$ described by a certain random potential having asymptotic self-similarity and stationary increments. The diffusion $\mathbf{X}$ may be regarded as the continuous time analogue of what was discussed in Example 2 ($\beta = 1$) of [4]. Recently Mathieu [19] considered the diffusion $\mathbf{X}$ itself and discussed its long time asymptotic behavior.

THEOREM 4 ([27]; see also [4] for random walks). $\mathbf{X}_W$ *is recurrent for almost all Brownian environments* W *for any dimension* d.

This theorem can easily be proved by making use of Ichihara's recurrence test ([8], see Theorem A) concerning symmetric diffusions. We can also use Fukushima's recurrence criterion [5] in terms of the associated Dirichlet form. $\mathbf{X}_{|W|}$ is also recurrent, P-a.s.; however, $\mathbf{X}_{-|W|}$ is transient, P-a.s., for any $d \geq 2$ as can be proved by using Ichihara's transience test ([8], see Theorem B). From the argument of [27] it is also easy to see that Theorem 4 remains valid when $\{W(x)\}$ is replaced by any continuous random field $\{V(x)\}$ in $\mathbf{R}^d$ satisfying the following conditions (i), (ii), and (iii).

(i) Self-similarity: there exists $\alpha > 0$ such that the law of $\{\lambda^{-1}V(\lambda^\alpha x)\}$ equals that of $\{V(x)\}$, denoted by P, for each $\lambda > 0$.

(ii) $\{T_t, t \in \mathbf{R}\}$ is ergodic, where T_t is a P-preserving transformation from $C(\mathbf{R}^d)$ onto itself defined by $(T_tV)(x) = e^{-t/\alpha}V(e^t x), x \in \mathbf{R}^d$.

(iii) $\min\{V(x) : |x| = 1\} > 0$ with positive probability.

The argument of [19] entails the following theorem.

THEOREM 5 ([19]; see also [4] for random walks). *Localization takes place for* $\mathbf{X}$ *in the sense that*

$$\lim_{N\to\infty} \overline{\lim_{\lambda\to\infty}} \mathcal{P}\{\lambda^{-2}\max(|\omega(t)| : 0 \le t \le e^\lambda) \ge N\} = 0.$$

It seems that there is no proof of the existence of the limiting distribution of $\lambda^{-2}\omega(e^\lambda)$ as $\lambda \to \infty$. It is to be noted, however, that Mathieu [19] gave the existence proof together with an explicit representation of the limiting distribution of $\lambda^{-2}\omega(e^\lambda)$ in terms of the local time of $|W|$ at level 0 *when* W *is replaced by* $|W|$.

The above results on recurrence and localization rely heavily on the (asymptotic) self-similarity of W as well as the symmetry of $\mathbf{X}_W$. Without these conditions the situation will change much. In the case of random walks there is a profound work by Bricmont and Kupiainen [2].

References

[1] V. I. Afanas'ev, *On a maximum of a transient random walk in random environment*, Theor. Probab. Appl. **35** (1990), 205–215.

[2] J. Bricmont and A. Kupiainen, *Random walks in asymmetric random environments*, Comm. Math. Phys. **142** (1991), 345–420.

[3] T. Brox, *A one-dimensional diffusion process in Wiener medium*, Ann. Probab. **14** (1986), 1206–1218.

[4] R. Durrett, *Multidimensional random walks in random environments with subclassical limiting behavior*, Comm. Math. Phys. **104** (1986), 87–102.

[5] M. Fukushima, *On recurrence criteria in the Dirichlet space theory*, in Local Times to Global Geometry, Control and Physics (ed. Elworthy), Research Notes in Math., Longman Scientific & Technical, Essex **150** (1986), 100–110.

[6] A. O. Golosov, *Localization of random walks in one-dimensional random environments*, Comm. Math. Phys. **92** (1984), 491–506.

[7] A. O. Golosov, *On limiting distributions for a random walk in a critical one-dimensional random environment*, Russian Math. Surveys **41** (1986), 199–200.

[8] K. Ichihara, *Some global properties of symmetric diffusion processes*, Publ. Res. Inst. Math. Sci., Kyoto Univ. **14** (1978), 441–486.

[9] Y. Kasahara, *Spectral theory of generalized second order differential operators and its applications to Markov processes*, Japan. J. Math. (New Ser.) **1** (1975), 67–84.

[10] K. Kawazu, Y. Tamura, and H. Tanaka, *One-dimensional diffusions and random walks in random environments*, Lecture Notes in Math., Springer-Verlag, Berlin and New York, **1299** (1988), 170–184.

[11] K. Kawazu, Y. Tamura and H. Tanaka, *Localization of diffusion processes in one-dimensional random environment*, J. Math. Soc. Japan **44** (1992), 515–550.

[12] K. Kawazu and H. Tanaka, *On the maximum of a diffusion process in a drifted Brownian environment*, Lecture Notes in Math. (Séminaire de Probabilités XXVII), Springer-Verlag, Berlin and New York, **1557** (1993), 78–85.
[13] K. Kawazu and H. Tanaka, *A diffusion process in a Brownian environment with drift*, to appear in J. Math. Soc. Japan.
[14] H. Kesten, *The limit distribution of Sinai's random walk on random environment*, Phys. A **138** (1986), 299–309.
[15] H. Kesten, M. V. Kozlov and F. Spitzer, *A limit law for random walk in a random environment*, Compositio Math. **30** (1975), 145–168.
[16] S. Kotani and S. Watanabe, *Krein's spectral theory of strings and generalized diffusion processes*, Lecture Notes in Math., Springer-Verlag, Berlin and New York, **923** (1982), 235–259.
[17] A. V. Letchikov, *Localization of one-dimensional random walks in random environments*, Soviet Sci. Rev. Sect. C: Math. Phys. Rev. **8** (1989), 173–220.
[18] E. Marinari, G. Parisi, D. Ruelle, and P. Windey, *On the interpretation of* $1/f$ *noise*, Comm. Math. Phys. **89** (1983), 1–12.
[19] P. Mathieu, *Zero white noise limit through Dirichlet forms, with application to diffusions in a random medium*, Probab. Theory Related Fields **99** (1994), 549–580.
[20] J. Nash, *Continuity of solutions of parabolic and elliptic equations*, Amer. J. Math. **80** (1958), 931–953.
[21] Y. Ogura, *One-dimensional bi-generalized diffusion processes*, J. Math. Soc. Japan **41** (1989), 213–242.
[22] S. Schumacher, *Diffusions with random coefficients*, Contemp. Math. **41** (1985), 351–356.
[23] Ya. G. Sinai, *The limiting behavior of a one-dimensional random walk in a random medium*, Theor. Probab. Appl. **27** (1982), 256–268.
[24] F. Solomon, *Random walks in a random environment*, Ann. Probab. **3** (1975), 1–31.
[25] H. Tanaka, *Limit distribution for* 1*-dimensional diffusion in a reflected Brownian medium*, Lecture Notes in Math. (Séminaire de Probabilités XXI), Springer-Verlag, Berlin and New York, **1247** (1987), 246–261.
[26] H. Tanaka, *Limit theorem for one-dimensional diffusion process in Brownian environment*, Lecture Notes in Math., Springer-Verlag, Berlin and New York, **1322** (1988), 156–172.
[27] H. Tanaka, *Recurrence of a diffusion process in a multidimensional Brownian environment*, Proc. Japan Acad. Ser. A Math. Sci. **69** (1993), 377–381.
[28] H. Tanaka, *Localization of a diffusion process in a one-dimensional Brownian environment*, Comm. Pure Appl. Math. **47** (1994), 755–766.
[29] M. Yor, *On some exponential functionals of Brownian motion*, Adv. Appl. Probab. **24** (1992), 509–531.

Environment-wise central limit theorem for a diffusion in a Brownian environment with large drift

Hiroshi Tanaka

Department of Mathematics, Faculty of Science and Technology, Keio University, Hiyoshi, Yokohama, Kanagawa 223, Japan

Introduction

General theory of one-dimensional diffusion process was established by Itô and McKean ([1]) more than thirty years ago. In this paper we discuss the central limit theorem concerning a diffusion process in one-dimensional Brownian environment with large drift. Many of our methods benefit from the theory by Itô and McKean.

By a diffusion process in a Brownian environment with drift we mean a process $\mathbf{X}^{x_0} = \{\omega(t), t \geq 0, \mathcal{P}^{x_0}\}$ which is defined in the following way.
(i) W is the space of continuous functions on $\mathbb{R}$ vanishing at 0 and is endowed with the Wiener measure P. For an element w of W, w_κ denotes an element of W defined by $w_\kappa(x) = w(x) - \kappa x/2$ where κ is a given positive constant.
(ii) For $w \in W$ and $x_0 \in \mathbb{R}$, $P_w^{x_0}$ denotes the probability measure on $\Omega = C[0, \infty)$ such that $\mathbf{X}_w^{x_0} = \{\omega(t), t \geq 0, P_w^{x_0}\}$ is a diffusion process with generator

$$\mathcal{L}_w = \frac{1}{2} e^{w_\kappa(x)} \frac{d}{dx}\left(e^{-w_\kappa(x)} \frac{d}{dx}\right)$$

starting from x_0; $\omega(t)$ denotes the value of a trajectory $\omega (\in \Omega)$ at time t.
(iii) $\{\omega(t), t \geq 0\}$ is regarded as a process defined on the probability space $(W \times \Omega, \mathcal{P}^{x_0})$ where $\mathcal{P}^{x_0}(dw d\omega) = P(dw) P_w^{x_0}(d\omega)$. This process is what we denote by $\mathbf{X}^{x_0} = \{\omega(t), t \geq 0, \mathcal{P}^{x_0}\}$; x_0 indicates the starting point of our process.

The process $\mathbf{X}^{x_0}$ is a diffusion analogue of what was considered by Kesten-Kozlov-Spitzer [4] and Solomon [6] as a random walk in a random environment. Asymptotic behavior of the process $\mathbf{X}^0$ as t becomes large was investigated by Kawazu-Tanaka [3]. The results are analogous to those of [4][6] and vary with κ. In particular, when $\kappa > 1$, it was proved that

$$\lim_{x \to \infty} T_x / x = m, \quad \lim_{t \to \infty} \omega(t)/t = 1/m, \qquad \mathcal{P}^0\text{-a.s.},$$

where $m = 4(\kappa - 1)^{-1}$ and T_x is the hitting time: $T_x = \inf\{t > 0 : \omega(t) = x\}$.

The next problem is then to study a fluctuation. In this paper we assume $\kappa > 2$ and discuss central limit theorems concerning T_x and $\omega(t)$. We put

$$M_x = 2\int_0^x dy \int_{-\infty}^y e^{w_\kappa(y)-w_\kappa(z)}dz,$$

$$\mu(t) = \text{ the inverse function of } M_x,$$

$$\overline{\omega}(t) = \max\{\omega(s) : 0 \le s \le t\},\ \underline{\omega}(t) = \inf\{\omega(s) : s \ge t\},$$

$$A = 64(\kappa-1)^{-2}(\kappa-2)^{-1}.$$

Then it will be seen that $E_w^0\{T_x\} = M_x$, $E\{M_x\} = mx$ and $E\{\mathrm{Var}_w^0(T_x)\} = Ax$ for $x \ge 0$ where E_w^0 and Var_w^0 denotes the expectation and variance under P_w^0, respectively.

Our results are the following where $\kappa > 2$ is assumed.

Environment-wise central limit theorem

(I) *For almost all w with respect to P the process*

$$\left\{\frac{T_{\lambda x} - M_{\lambda x}}{\sqrt{A\lambda}}, x \ge 0, P_w^0\right\}$$

converges in law to a Brownian motion as $\lambda \to \infty$ (in the sense of convergence of probability measures on the Skorohod space).

(II) *For almost all w the process*

$$\left\{\frac{\omega(\lambda t) - \mu(\lambda t)}{\sqrt{m^{-3}A\lambda}}, t \ge 0, P_w^0\right\}$$

converges in law to a Brownian motion as $\lambda \to \infty$. The same is true when $\omega(\lambda t)$ is replaced by either of $\overline{\omega}(\lambda t)$ and $\underline{\omega}(\lambda t)$.

Central limit theorem in random environment, namely CLT under $\mathcal{P}^0$ will be discussed in another occasion.

§1. Some preliminaries

1.1. We compute the first and the second moments of various quantities related to hitting times for $\mathbf{X}^0$. Let $T_{a,b} = \inf\{t > 0 : \omega(t) = a \text{ or } b\}, b < a$. Then it is well-known that

$$u(x) = E_w^x\{\exp(-\lambda \int_0^{T_{a,b}} f(\omega(t))dt)\}$$

satisfies (e.g. see [1])

$$(1.1) \qquad \begin{cases} (\lambda f - \mathcal{L}_w)u = 0 & \text{in } (b,a), \\ u(a) = u(b) = 1. \end{cases}$$

For $n \ge 0$ we put $u_n(x) = E_w^x\{(\int_0^{T_{a,b}} f(\omega(t))dt)^n\}$. Then $u(x) = \sum_{n=0}^\infty u_n(x) \times (-\lambda)^n/n!$ and (1.1) imply $\sum_{n=0}^\infty (\lambda f - \mathcal{L}_w)u_n(-\lambda)^n/n! = 0$. Therefore we have $u_0 \equiv 1$ and for $n \ge 1$

$$(1.2)\qquad \begin{cases} \mathcal{L}_w u_n = -n u_{n-1} f & \text{in } (b,a), \\ u_n(a) = u_n(b) = 0. \end{cases}$$

Let $S_w(x) = \int_0^x \exp\{w_\kappa(y)\}dy$, the canonical scale of $\mathcal{L}_w$. Then

$$(1.3)\qquad S_w(-\infty) = -\infty, \quad P\text{-a.s., if } \kappa > 0.$$

The following formulas (1.4) and (1.5), which hold for almost all w, can be proved under the assumption $\kappa > 0$ by making use of (1.2) and (1.3): For $x < a$,

$$(1.4)\qquad E_w^x\{T_a\} = 2\int_x^a e^{w_\kappa(y)}dy \int_{-\infty}^y e^{-w_\kappa(z)}dz;$$

$$(1.5)\quad E_w^x\{T_a^2\} = 8\int_x^a e^{w_\kappa(y)}dy \int_{-\infty}^y e^{-w_\kappa(z)}dz \int_z^a e^{w_\kappa(u)}du \int_{-\infty}^u e^{-w_\kappa(v)}dv.$$

Making use of the above formulas we can compute $\mathrm{Var}_w^0\{T_x\}$ for $x > 0$; the result is

$$(1.6)\quad \mathrm{Var}_w^0\{T_x\} = 8\int_0^x dy \int_{-\infty}^y e^{w_\kappa(y)-w_\kappa(z)}dz \int_z^y dy \int_{-\infty}^u e^{w_\kappa(u)-w_\kappa(v)}dv.$$

It will be useful for our later discussions to introduce a one-parameter family of measure preserving transformations $\theta_t, t \in \mathbb{R}$, on (W,P) defined by $(\theta_t w)(x) = w(x+t) - w(t), x \in \mathbb{R}$. It is easy to see that $\theta_t\theta_s = \theta_{t+s}$ and $\{\theta_t\}$ is ergodic. If $\kappa > 0$, then

$$(1.7)\qquad f_0(w) = \int_{-\infty}^0 e^{-w_\kappa(t)}dt$$

is finite (P-a.s.) and $\theta_t f_0 \equiv f_0(\theta_t w) = \int_{-\infty}^t e^{w_\kappa(t)-w_\kappa(s)}ds$. From (1.4) and (1.6) we have for $x > 0$

$$(1.8)\qquad E_w^0\{T_x\} = M_x = 2\int_0^x \theta_y f_0 dy,$$

$$\begin{aligned}(1.9)\quad \mathrm{Var}_w^0\{T_x\} &= 8\int_0^x dy \int_{-\infty}^y e^{w_\kappa(y)-w_\kappa(z)}(\theta_z f_0)^2 dz \\ &= 8\int_0^x \theta_y g dy, \quad \left(g(w) = \int_{-\infty}^0 e^{-w_\kappa(t)}(\theta_t f_0)^2 dt\right).\end{aligned}$$

Making use of $E\{\exp(w_\kappa(x) - w_\kappa(y))\} = \exp\{-\gamma(x-y)\}$ for $x > y$ where

$$\gamma = (\kappa - 1)/2,$$

we have $E\{f_0\} = 1/\gamma$ and hence $E\{M_x\} = mx$, $x \geq 0$, if $\kappa > 1$ (note that $E\{f_0\} < \infty$ iff $\kappa > 1$ and $E\{{f_0}^2\} < \infty$ iff $\kappa > 2$). From now on we assume $\kappa > 2$. The constant A given in the introduction is expressed as $A = 16\gamma^{-2}(2\gamma - 1)^{-1}$. We put $f = f_0 - \gamma^{-1}$. Then we have the following:

$$E\{f_0{}^2\} = 2\gamma^{-1}(2\gamma - 1)^{-1}; \tag{1.10}$$

$$E\{f\theta_x f\} = \gamma^{-2}(2\gamma - 1)^{-1}e^{-\gamma x} \quad \text{for } x \geq 0; \tag{1.11}$$

$$E\{\mathrm{Var}_w^0(T_x)\} = Ax \quad \text{for } x \geq 0. \tag{1.12}$$

1.2. The process $\{\theta_x f_0, x \in \mathbb{R}, P\}$ will often play an important role in our discussions. We make use of habitual notation t (instead of x) to indicate time. By an application of Itô's formula we have

$$d\theta_t f_0 = \theta_t f_0 dw(t) - (\gamma\theta_t f_0 - 1)dt, \tag{1.13}$$

and hence $\theta_t f_0$ is a stationary diffusion process obtained as the unique stationary positive solution of the stochastic differential equation. It can be also written as

$$\theta_t f_0 - f_0 = \int_0^t \theta_s f_0 dw(s) - \gamma \int_0^t \theta_s f ds. \tag{1.14}$$

From now on we assume $\kappa > 2$. Then we can easily prove that $E\{f_0{}^{2\delta}\} < \infty$ if $0 \leq \delta < \kappa/2$. Therefore by the Burkholder-Davis-Gundy inequalities we have

$$E\left\{\max_{0\leq s\leq t}\left|\int_0^s \theta_s f_0 dw(s)\right|^{2\delta}\right\} \leq \text{const.}t^\delta, \quad (t \geq 0, 1 \leq \delta < \kappa/2), \tag{1.15}$$

where const. means a constant that may depend on δ but not on t; such const. will also appear in later discussions and may vary from place to place.

Lemma 1. *$t^{-1/2}\max\{\theta_s f_0 : |s| \leq t\} \to 0$ as $t \to \infty$, P-a.s.*

Proof. Since the stationary diffusion $\theta_t f_0$ is reversible, it is enough to prove that $t^{-1/2}\max\{\theta_s f_0 : 0 \leq s \leq t\} \to 0$ as $t \to \infty$, P-a.s. Define stopping times σ_n, $n \geq 0$, by $\sigma_0 = \inf\{t > 0 : \theta_t f_0 = 2\}$ and $\sigma_n =$ the time of first return of $\theta_t f_0$ to 2 visiting 1 after σ_{n-1} $(n \geq 1)$ and then consider the random variables $X_n = \max\{\theta_t f_0 : \sigma_{n-1} \leq t \leq \sigma_n\}, n \geq 1$. Then $X_n, n \geq 1$, are i.i.d. random variables. Since $\sigma_n/n \to$ const.> 0 (a.s.),

$$\begin{aligned} \varlimsup_{t\to\infty} t^{-1/2}\max_{0\leq s\leq t}\theta_s f_0 &= \varlimsup_{n\to\infty}\sigma_n{}^{-1/2}\max_{1\leq k\leq n} X_k \\ &= \text{const.}\varlimsup_{n\to\infty} n^{-1/2}\max_{1\leq k\leq n} X_k, \quad \text{a.s.,} \end{aligned}$$

and the rightmost hand of the above equals to 0, a.s., because

$$P\{X_1 > x\} = \{S(2) - S(1)\}\{S(x) - S(1)\}^{-1} \sim \text{const.}x^{-\kappa}, x \to \infty,$$

(here $S(x)$ is the canonical scale of the diffusion $\theta_t f_0$; it is given by $S'(x) = x^{\kappa-1}\exp(2/x), x > 0$). This proves the lemma.

Lemma 2. *For any* $c_1 > 0$

$$M_{t+u} - M_t = mu(1 + o(1)) + o(\sqrt{\lambda}), \quad |t| \le c_1\lambda, \ u \in \mathbb{R},$$

where $o(1)$ *represents a general term that tends to* 0 *as* $\lambda \to \infty$ *uniformly in* (t, u) *such that* $|t| \le c_1\lambda$ *and* $u \in \mathbb{R}$, *for almost all* w; $o(\sqrt{\lambda})$ *is a term that can be expressed as* $o(1)\sqrt{\lambda}$.

Proof. Step1. For any positive constants c_1 and c_2

$$(1.16) \qquad \sup \left\{ \left| \frac{M_{t+u} - M_t}{u} - m \right| : |t| \le c_1\lambda, |u| \ge c_2\sqrt{\lambda} \right\} \to 0 \quad \text{as } \lambda \to \infty, \ P\text{-a.s.}$$

We give a proof in the case $c_1 = c_2 = 1$ since the case of general c_1 and c_2 can be treated without any essential change in the proof. We use the notation $\sup_{(\lambda)}$ to denote supremum taken over all t, u satisfying $|t| \le \lambda$ and $u \ge \sqrt{\lambda}$. Since $M_t'/2 = \theta_t f_0$ is a stationary reversible process, it is enough to prove that

$$(1.17) \qquad \sup_{(\lambda)} \left| \frac{1}{u} \int_t^{t+u} \theta_s f \, ds \right| \to 0 \text{ as } \lambda \to \infty, \text{ a.s.}$$

By Lemma 1 we have $\sup_{(\lambda)} u^{-1} |\theta_t f_0 - \theta_{t+u} f_0| \to 0$ as $\lambda \to \infty$, a.s. Combining this fact with (1.14) we see that, for the proof of (1.17), it is enough to show that

$$(1.18) \qquad \sup_{(\lambda)} \left| \frac{1}{u} \int_t^{t+u} \theta_s f_0 dw(s) \right| \to 0 \text{ as } \lambda \to \infty, \text{ a.s.}$$

To prove (1.18) we take δ and α such that

$$(1.19) \qquad 1 < \delta < \kappa/2, \quad 0 < \alpha < 1/2, \quad \delta/2 + \alpha - 1 > 0,$$

and prepare the estimate

$$(1.20) \qquad E\{R(\lambda)^{2\delta}\} \le \text{const.}\lambda^{-\delta_1},$$

where $\delta_1 = \delta/2 + \alpha - 1$ and

$$R(t, u) = \frac{1}{u} \int_t^{t+u} \theta_s f_0 dw(s), \quad R(\lambda) = \sup_{(\lambda)} |R(t, u)|.$$

Putting $I_k = [k\lambda^\alpha, (k+1)\lambda^\alpha]$ for an integer k and denoting by $\sup_{(k,\lambda)}$ the supremum over all $t \in I_k$ and $u \ge \sqrt{\lambda}$, we write

$$\begin{aligned} &\sup_{(k,\lambda)} |R(t, u) - R(k\lambda^\alpha, u)| \\ = \ &\sup_{(k,\lambda)} \frac{1}{u} \left| - \int_{k\lambda^\alpha}^t \theta_s f_0 dw(s) + \int_{k\lambda^\alpha + u}^{t+u} \theta_s f_0 dw(s) \right| \le U + V, \end{aligned}$$

where

$$U = \lambda^{-1/2} \max_{0 \le r \le \lambda^\alpha} \left| \int_{k\lambda^\alpha}^{k\lambda^\alpha + r} \theta_s f_0 dw(s) \right|,$$

$$V = \sup_{u \ge \sqrt{\lambda}} \max_{0 \le r \le \lambda^\alpha} \left| \frac{1}{u} \int_{k\lambda^\alpha + u}^{k\lambda^\alpha + u + r} \theta_s f_0 dw(s) \right|.$$

Making use of (1.15) we have

(1.21) $$E\{U^{2\delta}\} \le \text{const.}\lambda^{-(1-\alpha)\delta},$$

and $E\{V^{2\delta}\}$ is dominated by

$$\sum_{n=1}^{\infty} E\left\{ \sup_{\sqrt{\lambda}n \le u \le \sqrt{\lambda}(n+1)} \max_{0 \le r \le \lambda^\alpha} \left| \frac{1}{u} \int_{k\lambda^\alpha + u}^{k\lambda^\alpha + u + r} \theta_s f_0 dw(s) \right|^{2\delta} \right\}$$

$$\le \lambda^{-\delta} \sum_{n=1}^{\infty} n^{-2\delta} E\{R_\lambda^{2\delta}\} = \text{const.}\lambda^{-\delta} E\{R_\lambda^{2\delta}\},$$

where

$$R_\lambda = \sup_{0 \le u \le \sqrt{\lambda}} \max_{0 \le r \le \lambda^\alpha} \left| \int_u^{u+r} \theta_s f_0 dw(s) \right|.$$

If $0 \le u \le \sqrt{\lambda}$ and $0 \le r \le \lambda^\alpha$, then u and $u+r$ are simultaneously contained in one of the intervals $[l\lambda^\alpha, l\lambda^\alpha + 2\lambda^\alpha]$, $l = 0, 1, \dots, l_\lambda$, where $l_\lambda = [\lambda^{\frac{1}{2}-\alpha}]$. Therefore

$$R_\lambda \le 2 \max_{0 \le l \le l_\lambda} \max_{0 \le r \le 2\lambda^\alpha} \left| \int_{l\lambda^\alpha}^{l\lambda^\alpha + r} \theta_s f_0 dw(s) \right|,$$

and hence $E\{V^{2\delta}\}$ is dominated by

$$\text{const.}\lambda^{-\delta}(l_\lambda + 1) E\left\{ \max_{0 \le r \le 2\lambda^\alpha} \left| \int_0^r \theta_s f_0 dw(s) \right|^{2\delta} \right\}$$

$$\le \text{const.}\lambda^{-(1-\alpha)(\delta-1)-\frac{1}{2}} \ (\text{use}(1.15)).$$

This combined with (1.21) implies

(1.22) $$E\left\{ \sup{}_{(k,\lambda)} |R(t,u) - R(k\lambda^\alpha, u)|^{2\delta} \right\} \le \text{const.}\lambda^{-(1-\alpha)(\delta-1)-\frac{1}{2}},$$

because $(1-\alpha)\delta > (1-\alpha)(\delta-1) + \frac{1}{2}$. Let $k(t)$ be the integer determined from t by $k(t)\lambda^\alpha < t \le (k(t)+1)\lambda^\alpha$ and put $K_\lambda = \{k(t) : |t| \le \lambda\}$. Then $\# K_\lambda \le \text{const.}\lambda^{1-\alpha}$ and (1.22) implies

(1.23) $$E\left\{ \sup{}_{(\lambda)} |R(t,u) - R(k(t)\lambda^\alpha, u)|^{2\delta} \right\} \le \text{const.}\# K_\lambda \cdot \lambda^{-(1-\alpha)(\delta-1)-\frac{1}{2}} \le \text{const.}\lambda^{-\delta_1},$$

because $(1-\alpha)(\delta-2)+\frac{1}{2}>\delta_1$. By a similar method we can prove that

$$(1.24)\qquad E\left\{\sup_{(\lambda)}|R(k(t)\lambda^{\alpha},u)|^{2\delta}\right\}\le \text{const.}\lambda^{-\delta_1}$$

and hence (1.20) follows from (1.23) and (1.24).

We finally prove (1.18). If β is a constant such that $\beta\delta_1>1$, then $E\{R(n^{\beta})^{2\delta}\}\le \text{const.}n^{-\beta\delta_1}$ by (1.20) so by using the Chebyschev inequality and the Borel-Cantelli lemma we see that $R(n^{\beta})\to 0$ as $n\to\infty$, a.s. Likewise

$$R_c(n^{\beta})\equiv \sup\left\{|R(t,u)|:|t|\le cn^{\beta},u\ge n^{\beta/2}\right\}\to 0,\ \text{a.s.},$$

for any constant $c>0$. The assertion (1.18) now follows from $R(\lambda)\le R_c(n(\lambda)^{\beta})$ with $c=2^{\beta}$ where $n(\lambda)$ is the integer satisfying $n(\lambda)^{\beta}<\lambda\le (n(\lambda)+1)^{\beta}$.

Step 2 is to complete the proof of the lemma. The result (1.16) implies that

$$(1.25)\qquad M_{t+u}-M_t=(m+o(1))u,\quad \text{if } |t|\le c_1\lambda \text{ and } |u|\ge\sqrt{\lambda}/2.$$

When t and u are restricted to $|t|\le c_1\lambda$ and $|u|<\sqrt{\lambda}/2$, we write $M_{t+u}-M_t=M'+M''$ where

$$M'=M_{t-\sqrt{\lambda}+(\sqrt{\lambda}+u)}-M_{t-\sqrt{\lambda}},\quad M''=M_{t-\sqrt{\lambda}}-M_t.$$

Then applying (1.16) we have $M'=(m+o(1))(\sqrt{\lambda}+u)$ and $M''=-(m+o(1))\sqrt{\lambda}$. Therefore $M_{t+u}-M_t=mu(1+o(1))+o(\sqrt{\lambda})$ if $|t|\le c_1\lambda$ and $|u|<\sqrt{\lambda}/2$. This combined with (1.25) proves the lemma.

§2. Environment-wise central limit theorem

2.1. Proof of (I). We put $\tau_k=T_k-T_{k-1},k\ge 1$. Then $\tau_k,k\ge 1$, are independent under the probability measure P_w^0. Since $T_n=\sum_1^n\tau_k$, the central limit theorem for T_n with fixed w can be obtained by verifying the Lindeberg condition. We have

$$\text{Var}_w^0\{T_n\}=\sum_{k=1}^{n}\text{Var}_w^0\{\tau_k\}=\sum_{k=1}^{n}V(\theta_{k-1}w)$$

where $V(w)=\text{Var}_w^0\{\tau_1\}$. We now assume $\kappa>2$ to ensure the existence of $E\{V\}$, which is equal to A by (1.3). Since $\{\theta_t\}$ is ergodic, we have

$$(2.1)\qquad \lim_{n\to\infty}\frac{\text{Var}_w^0\{T_n\}}{n}=A,\ P\text{-a.s.}$$

Putting $\tilde{\tau}_k = \tau_k - E_w^0\{\tau_k\}$ and $V_N(w) = E_w^0\{|\tilde{\tau}_1|^2; |\tilde{\tau}_1| > N\}$ (the integral of $|\tilde{\tau}_1|^2$ over $\{|\tilde{\tau}_1| > N\}$ with respect to P_w^0), we have for any $\varepsilon > 0$ and for almost all w

$$\begin{aligned}
(2.2) \quad & \frac{1}{\mathrm{Var}_w^0\{T_n\}} \sum_{k=1}^{n} E_w^0 \left\{ |\tilde{\tau}_k|^2; |\tilde{\tau}_k| > \varepsilon\sqrt{\mathrm{Var}_w^0\{T_n\}} \right\} \\
\le\ & \frac{\text{const.}}{n} \sum_{k=1}^{n} E_w^0 \left\{ |\tilde{\tau}_k|^2; |\tilde{\tau}_k| > N \right\} \ \text{(by (2.1))} \\
=\ & \frac{\text{const.}}{n} \sum_{k=1}^{n} V_N(\theta_{k-1}w) \to \text{const.} E\{V_N\}, \quad n \to \infty.
\end{aligned}$$

Since $E\{V_N\} \downarrow 0$ as $N \uparrow \infty$ because of $E\{V\} < \infty$, the left hand side of (2.2) tends to 0 as $n \uparrow \infty$ (P-a.s.), which shows that the Lindeberg condition is satisfied for $\{\tilde{\tau}_k\}$. Therefore for almost all w the central limit theorem holds for T_n with respect to P_w^0. By (1.4) $E_w^0\{T_n\} = M_n$ and by (2.1) $\mathrm{Var}_w^0\{T_n\} \sim An, n \to \infty$ (P-a.s.). Therefore the Lindeberg condition together with an application of Theorem 3.1 of [5] implies the assertion of (I). Further details will be given in a joint paper with K. Kawazu.

2.2. Proof of (II). The probability measure we consider in this proof is P_w^0 where w is taken from some subset of W that has P-measure 1. Thus events we consider here can be regarded as subsets of $\Omega_0 = \{\omega \in \Omega : \omega(0) = 0\}$. For any $s > 0$, $\rho \in \mathbb{R}$ and $\nu > 0$ we have, with convention $\underline{\omega}(\infty) = \infty$,

$$\begin{aligned}
(2.3) \quad \{T_{\rho^+} < s\} &= \{\overline{\omega}(s) > \rho\} \supset \{\omega(s) > \rho\} \supset \{\underline{\omega}(s) > \rho\} \\
&\supset \{T_{(\rho+\nu)^+} < s\} \cap \{\underline{\omega}(T_{\rho+\nu}) > \rho\},
\end{aligned}$$

where $\rho^+ = \max\{\rho, 0\}$ and T_x denotes the hitting time to $x \in \mathbb{R}$. Similarly

$$\begin{aligned}
(2.4) \quad \{T_{\rho^+} > s\} &= \{\overline{\omega}(s) < \rho\} \subset \{\omega(s) < \rho\} \subset \{\underline{\omega}(s) < \rho\} \\
&\subset \{T_{(\rho+\nu)^+} > s\} \cup \{\underline{\omega}(T_{\rho+\nu}) < \rho\}.
\end{aligned}$$

Lemma 3. *For any fixed $t_1 > 0$ let (φ, ψ) be a pair of continuous functions on $[0, t_1]$ such that*

$$(2.5) \quad \begin{array}{l} \varphi \text{ and } \psi \text{ are absolutely continuous, } \varphi', \psi' \in L^2[0, t_1], \\ \varphi(t) < \psi(t) \text{ for all } t \in [0, t_1] \text{ and } \varphi(0) \neq 0, \psi(0) \neq 0. \end{array}$$

Then for almost all w

$$\begin{aligned}
(2.6) \quad \lim\nolimits_{\lambda \to \infty} \quad & P_w^0 \left\{ \varphi(t) < \frac{\omega(\lambda t) - \mu(\lambda t)}{\sqrt{m^{-3} A \lambda}} < \psi(t) \text{ for all } t \in [t_0, t_1] \right\} \\
= \quad & P\{\varphi(t) < w(t) < \psi(t) \text{ for all } t \in [t_0, t_1]\}.
\end{aligned}$$

Proof. For the proof it is enough to consider the case $\varphi(0) < 0 < \psi(0)$. We put $\rho(t) = \mu(\lambda t) + \varphi(t)\sqrt{m^{-3}A\lambda}$ and $\rho_1(t) = \mu(\lambda t) + \psi(t)\sqrt{m^{-3}A\lambda}$. Then $\rho_1(t) > 0$ for all $t \in [0, t_1]$ if λ is sufficiently large, but $\rho(t) < 0$ if t is sufficiently small for each fixed λ. Since $\{\varphi(t) < (m^{-3}A\lambda)^{-1/2}(\omega(\lambda t) - \mu(\lambda t)) < \psi(t)\} = \{\rho(t) < \omega(\lambda t) < \rho_1(t)\}$, an application of (2.3) and (2.4) yields

$$\begin{aligned}&\{T_{(\rho(t)+\nu)^+} < \lambda t, T_{\rho_1(t)} > \lambda t, \underline{\omega}(T_{\rho(t)+\nu}) > \rho(t)\}\\ &\subset \{\varphi(t) < (m^{-3}A\lambda)^{-1/2}(\omega(\lambda t) - \mu(\lambda t)) < \psi(t)\}\\ &\subset \{T_{\rho(t)^+} < \lambda t\} \cap [\{T_{\rho_1(t)+\nu} > \lambda t\} \cup \{\underline{\omega}(T_{\rho_1(t)+\nu}) < \rho_1(t)\}].\end{aligned}$$

Therefore if we put

$$\begin{aligned}\Gamma_\lambda &= \{\varphi(t) < (m^{-3}A\lambda)^{-1/2}(\omega(\lambda t) - \mu(\lambda t)) < \psi(t) \text{ for all } t \in [0, t_1]\},\\ \Gamma_\lambda^- &= \{T_{(\rho(t)+\nu)^+} < \lambda t, T_{\rho_1(t)} > \lambda t \text{ for all } t \in [0, t_1]\},\\ \Gamma_\lambda^+ &= \{T_{\rho(t)^+} < \lambda t, T_{\rho_1(t)+\nu} > \lambda t \text{ for all } t \in [0, t_1]\},\\ A_\lambda &= \{\underline{\omega}(T_{\rho(t)+\nu}) > \rho(t) \text{ for all } t \in [0, t_1]\},\\ B_\lambda &= \{\underline{\omega}(T_{\rho_1(t)+\nu}) < \rho_1(t) \text{ for some } t \in [0, t_1]\},\end{aligned}$$

then

(2.7) $$\Gamma_\lambda^- \cap A_\lambda \subset \Gamma_\lambda \subset \Gamma_\lambda^+ \cup B_\lambda.$$

Put $\nu = 6\log\lambda$ and let us prove

(2.8) $$\lim_{\lambda\to\infty} P_w^0\{A_\lambda^c\} = \lim_{\lambda\to\infty} P_w^0\{B_\lambda\} = 0, \quad P\text{-a.s.}$$

Since $\{\underline{\omega}(T_{\rho(t)+\nu}) \leq \rho(t)\} \subset \{\underline{\omega}(T_{[\rho(t)+\nu]}) < [\rho(t)+\nu] - (\nu - 1)\}$, we have

$$A_\lambda^c \subset \bigcup_{k=\rho_\lambda^-}^{\rho_\lambda^+} \{\underline{\omega}(T_k) < k - (\nu - 1)\},$$

where $\rho_\lambda^- = \min\{[\rho(t)+\nu] : 0 \leq t \leq t_1\}$ and $\rho_\lambda^+ = \max\{[\rho(t)+\nu] : 0 \leq t \leq t_1\}$. Therefore

$$P_w^0\{A_\lambda^c\} \leq \sum_{k=\rho_\lambda^-}^{\rho_\lambda^+} P_w^0\{\underline{\omega}(T_k) < k - (\nu - 1)\}.$$

By an ergodic theorem $M_x/x \to m$ as $x \to \infty$ (P-a.s.) and hence $\mu(t)/t \to m^{-1}$ as $t \to \infty$ (P-a.s.), which implies $\rho_\lambda^+ \sim \lambda m^{-1} t_1$ and $\rho_\lambda^- = o(\lambda)$ as $\lambda \to \infty$ (P-a.s.). Therefore for the proof of (2.8) it is enough to show that for any constant $c > 0$

$$\lim_{\lambda\to\infty} \sum_{|k|<c\lambda} P_w^0\{\underline{\omega}(T_k) < k - (\nu - 1)\} = 0, \quad P\text{-a.s.}$$

Taking the expectation we have

$$E\left\{\sum_{|k|<c\lambda} P_w^0\{\underline{\omega}(T_k) < k-(\nu-1)\}\right\}$$
$$= \sum_{|k|<c\lambda} \mathcal{P}^0\{\underline{\omega}(0) < -(\nu-1)\}$$
$$< \text{const.}\lambda \exp\{-(\kappa-1)(\nu-1)/2\} \le \text{const.}\lambda^{-2},$$

where we used the result of [2]. The above estimate holds for $\nu = 6\log\lambda + O(1)$. Therefore an application of Borel-Cantelli lemma implies

$$\lim_{n\to\infty} \sum_{|k|<cn} P_w^0\{\underline{\omega}(T_k) < k-(\nu_n-1)\} = 0, \quad P\text{-a.s.},$$

for any given sequence $\{\nu_n\}$ such that $\nu_n = 6\log n + O(1)$ as $n \to \infty$. We thus have

$$\sum_{|k|<c\lambda} P_w^0\{\underline{\omega}(T_k) < k-(\nu-1)\}$$
$$\le \sum_{|k|<c([\lambda]+1)} P_w^0\{\underline{\omega}(T_k) < k-(\nu-1)\}$$
$$\to 0 \quad \text{as } \lambda \to 0 \ (P\text{-a.s.}),$$

which implies the assertion (2.8) concerning A_λ^c. The assertion for B_λ can be proved similarly.

To proceed let $\xi = \lambda m^{-1}$ and put

$$\alpha(t) = \xi^{-1}\rho(t) = \lambda^{-1}m\left\{\mu(\lambda t) + \varphi(t)\sqrt{m^{-3}A\lambda}\right\},$$

$$\beta(t) = \xi^{-1}\rho_1(t) = \lambda^{-1}m\left\{\mu(\lambda t) + \psi(t)\sqrt{m^{-3}A\lambda}\right\}.$$

Then for almost all w both $\alpha(t)$ and $\beta(t)$ tend to t as $\lambda \to \infty$, the convergence being uniform on each finite t-interval. From now on we write $T(x)$ and $M(x)$ for T_x and M_x, respectively. Since $\mu(\lambda t) = \xi\alpha(t) - \varphi(t)\sqrt{m^{-3}A\lambda}$, an application of Lemma 2 yields

$$\text{(2.9)}\quad \lambda t = M(\xi\alpha(t) - \varphi(t)\sqrt{m^{-3}A\lambda}) = M(\xi\alpha(t)) - \varphi(t)\sqrt{m^{-1}A\lambda} + o(\sqrt{\lambda}),$$

where $o(\sqrt{\lambda})$ is a term that, when divided by $\sqrt{\lambda}$, tends to 0 uniformly in $t \in [0, t_1]$ as $\lambda \to \infty$ for almost all w. Similarly

$$\text{(2.10)}\qquad \lambda t = M(\xi\beta(t)) - \psi(t)\sqrt{m^{-1}A\lambda} + o(\sqrt{\lambda}).$$

In what follows the notation $o(1)$ represents a term that tends to 0 uniformly in $t \in [0, t_1]$ as $\lambda \to \infty$ for almost all w. Using (2.9) and (2.10) we can obtain the following (2.11) $\sim$ (2.14) that hold for almost all w:

$$(2.11)\quad T(\rho(t)^+) < \lambda t \Leftrightarrow \frac{T(\xi\alpha(t)^+) - M(\xi\alpha(t)^+)}{\sqrt{A\xi}} < -\varphi(t) + o(1);$$

$$(2.12)\quad T(\rho_1(t)) > \lambda t \Leftrightarrow \frac{T(\xi\beta(t)) - M(\xi\beta(t))}{\sqrt{A\xi}} > -\psi(t) + o(1);$$

$$\begin{aligned}(2.13)\quad T\left((\rho(t)+\nu)^+\right) &< \lambda t \Leftrightarrow T\left((\rho(t)+\nu)^+\right) - M(\xi\alpha(t)) \\ &\qquad < -\varphi(t)\sqrt{m^{-1}A\lambda} + o(\sqrt{\lambda}) \\ &\Leftrightarrow \frac{T\left(\xi(\alpha(t)+\frac{\nu}{\xi})^+\right) - M\left(\xi(\alpha(t)+\frac{\nu}{\xi})^+\right)}{\sqrt{A\xi}} \\ &\qquad < -\varphi(t) + o(1);\end{aligned}$$

$$\begin{aligned}(2.14)\quad & T\left((\rho_1(t)+\nu)\right) > \lambda t \Leftrightarrow \\ & \frac{T\left(\xi(\beta(t)+\frac{\nu}{\xi})\right) - M\left(\xi(\beta(t)+\frac{\nu}{\xi})\right)}{\sqrt{A\xi}} > -\psi(t) + o(1).\end{aligned}$$

In deriving the second equivalence in (2.13) as well as the equivalence (2.14) we again used Lemma 2. From (2.11) $\sim$ (2.14) we have the following: For *almost all* w, $P^0_w\{\Gamma^+_\lambda\}$ is equal to $p_w(\xi)$ where $p_w(\xi)$ is the probability, evaluated by P^0_w, of the event

$$\left\{ \begin{array}{l} (A\xi)^{-1/2}\left\{T(\xi\alpha(t)^+) - M(\xi\alpha(t))^+\right\} < -\varphi(t) + o(1), \\ (A\xi)^{-1/2}\left\{T(\xi(\beta(t)+\nu\xi^{-1})) - M(\xi(\beta(t)+\nu\xi^{-1}))\right\} > -\psi(t) + o(1), \\ \qquad\qquad \text{for all } t \in [0, t_1] \end{array} \right\}.$$

But by (I), for almost all w, $p_w(\xi)$ tends to

$$\begin{aligned} & P\{-\psi(t) < w(t) < -\varphi(t) \text{ for all } t \in [0, t_1]\} \\ = \; & P\{\varphi(t) < w(t) < \psi(t) \text{ for all } t \in [0, t_1]\} \end{aligned}$$

as $\xi \to \infty$ (here we used the assumption (2.5)). We also have a similar statement for $P^0_w\{\Gamma^-_\lambda\}$. Therefore from (2.7) and (2.8) we finally obtain Lemma 3. It is also to be noted that, by virtue of (2.3) and (2.4), Lemma 3 remains valid when $\omega(\cdot)$ is replaced by either of $\overline{\omega}(\cdot)$ and $\underline{\omega}(\cdot)$.

For fixed $t_1 > 0$ we denote by $\mathbb{F}$ the set of all pairs (φ, ψ) of functions on $[0, t_1]$ of the form $\varphi = p_1 \vee p_2 \vee \cdots \vee p_n$(maximum) and $\psi = q_1 \wedge q_2 \wedge \cdots \wedge q_n$ (minimum) where p_j and q_j are polynomials with rational coefficients satisfying $p_j(t) < q_j(t)$ for all $t \in [0, t_1], p_j(0) \neq 0, q_j(0) \neq 0 (1 \leq j \leq n)$. Since $\mathbb{F}$ is countable, Lemma 3 implies that for almost all w (2.6) holds for all $(\varphi, \psi) \in \mathbb{F}$. Fixing an arbitrary w for which (2.6) holds for all $(\varphi, \psi) \in \mathbb{F}$, we denote by Q_λ the probability law of the process $\{(m^{-3}A\lambda)^{-1/2}(\omega(\lambda t) - \mu(\lambda t)), 0 \leq t \leq t_1, P^0_w\}$; we also denote by Q the Wiener measure on $C[0, t_1]$ with $Q\{\tilde{w}(0) = 0\} = 1$. A Borel set in the Banach space $C[0, t_1]$ is said to be admissible if $Q_\lambda(A) \to Q(A)$ as $\lambda \to \infty$. Then for each pair $(\varphi, \psi) \in \mathbb{F}$ the open set $U(\varphi, \psi) \equiv \{\tilde{w} \in C[0, t_1] : \varphi(t) < \tilde{w}(t) < \psi(t)$ for all $t \in [0, t_1]\}$ is admissible. On the other hand any open set G in $C[0, t_1]$ can be expressed as $\cup_{n=1}^{\infty} U_n$ where each U_n is of the form $U(\varphi, \psi)$ with $(\varphi, \psi) \in \mathbb{F}$. The intersection of any finite number of U_k's is admissible because it is still of the form $U(\varphi, \psi)$, so $G_n \equiv \cup_{k=1}^{n} U_k$ is admissible because of the inclusion-exclusion formula

$$Q_\lambda(G_n) = \sum_{k=1}^{n} (-1)^{k-1} \sum_{1 \le i_1 < \cdots < i_k \le n} Q_\lambda(U_{i_1} \cap U_{i_2} \cap \cdots \cap U_{i_k}).$$

Since $G_n \uparrow G$ we have $\underline{\lim}_{\lambda \to \infty} Q_\lambda(G) \ge Q(G)$, which implies that $Q_\lambda \to Q$ as $\lambda \to \infty$. Since $t_1 > 0$ is arbitrary, this completes the proof of (II).

References

[1] Itô, K., and McKean, H.P., Diffusion Processes and Their Sample Paths, Springer-Verlag, New York, 1965.
[2] Kawazu, K., and Tanaka,H., On the maximum of a diffusion process in a drifted Brownian environment, Séminaire de Probabilités, LMN 1557, 78–85.
[3] Kawazu, K., and Tanaka,H., A diffusion process in a Brownian environment with drift, to appear in J.Math.Soc.Japan.
[4] Kesten, H., Kozlov, M. V., and Spitzer, F., A limit law for random walk in a random environment, Composito Math. **30** (1975), 145–168.
[5] Prohorov, Yu. V., Convergence of random processes and limit theorems in probability theory, Theor. Probab. Appl. **1** (1956), 157–214.
[6] Solomon, F., Random walks in a random environment, Ann. Probab. **3** (1975),1–31.

Reprinted from
Itô's Stochastic Calculus and Probability Theory,
373–384, Springer-Verlag, 1996.

J. Math. Soc. Japan
Vol. 49, No. 2, 1997

A diffusion process in a Brownian environment with drift*

By Kiyoshi KAWAZU and Hiroshi TANAKA

(Received Feb. 8, 1995)

Introduction.

Let $\boldsymbol{W}$ be the space of continuous functions W defined in $\boldsymbol{R}$ and vanishing at the origin. Let P be the Wiener measure on $\boldsymbol{W}$, namely, the probability measure on $\boldsymbol{W}$ such that $\{W(t), t\geqq 0, P\}$ and $\{W(-t), t\geqq 0, P\}$ are independent one-dimensional Brownian motions. Let $\Omega=C[0, \infty)$ and denote by $\omega(t)$ the value of a function ω $(\in\Omega)$ at time t. Given a sample function W $(\in\boldsymbol{W})$ and a nonnegative constant κ we consider a probability measure P_W^x on Ω such that $\{\omega(t), t\geqq 0, P_W^x\}$ is a diffusion process with generator

$$(1)\qquad \mathcal{L}_W=\frac{1}{2}e^{W_\kappa(x)}\frac{d}{dx}\left(e^{-W_\kappa(x)}\frac{d}{dx}\right)=\frac{d x}{m_W(dx)}\cdot\frac{d x}{dS_W(x)}$$

starting from x, where

$$(2)\qquad W_\kappa(x)=W(x)-\frac{1}{2}\kappa x,$$

$$(3)\qquad S_W(x)=\int_0^x e^{W_\kappa(y)}dy,\quad m_W(dx)=2e^{-W_\kappa(x)}dx.$$

It is well-known that a version of $\{\omega(t), t\geqq 0, P_W^x\}$ can be constructed from a Brownian motion by a scale-change and a time-change. When W is considered *random*, $\{\omega(t), t\geqq 0\}$ is regarded as a process defined on the probability space $(\boldsymbol{W}\times\Omega, \mathcal{P}^x)$ where $\mathcal{P}^x(dWd\omega)=P(dW)P_W^x(d\omega)$. We thus have a process $\boldsymbol{X}^x=\{\omega(t), t\geqq 0, \mathcal{P}^x\}$ which, in this paper, is called a *diffusion process in a Brownian environment with drift*. The following intuitive description may suggest the name. The process $\boldsymbol{X}^x$ is obtained as a formal solution of the symbolic equation

$$(4)\qquad dX(t)=dB(t)-\frac{1}{2}W_\kappa'(X(t))dt,$$

* This work was partially supported by Grant-in Aid for Science (No. 07454034), Ministry of Education of Japan.

where $B(t)$ is a Brownian motion independent of $W(\cdot)$ (however, note that (4) has no rigorous meaning).

When $\kappa>0$ X^0 may be regarded as a diffusion model of a random walk in a random environment discussed by Kozlov [**14**], Solomon [**18**] and Kesten-Kozlov-Spitzer [**10**]. When $\kappa=0$ X^0 is a diffusion model of Sinai's random walk in a random environment ([**17**]). The asymptotic behavior of $\{\omega(t), \mathcal{P}^0\}$ as $t\to\infty$ when $\kappa=0$ was discussed by Schumacher [**16**] and Brox [**1**]. They showed that $\{\omega(t), \mathcal{P}^0\}$ exhibits the same asymptotic behavior as Sinai's random walk, namely, that the limiting distribution of $(\log t)^{-2}\omega(t)$ as $t\to\infty$ exists (see also [**2**], [**3**], [**8**], [**11**], [**19**] for related works). When $\kappa>0$ (in particular when $0<\kappa<1$) it was an open problem to obtain results for X^0 which are (or at least expected to be) similar to those of Kesten-Kozlov-Spitzer [**10**]. The purpose of the present paper is to give some answer to this problem.

Let $T_x=\inf\{t>0: \omega(t)=x\}$, $\bar{\omega}(t)=\max\{\omega(s): 0\leqq s\leqq t\}$ and $\underline{\omega}(t)=\inf\{\omega(s): s\geqq t\}$. Then our result in the case $\kappa>0$ is the following.

THEOREM 1. (i) *If* $0<\kappa<1$, *then*

$$\lim_{x\to\infty}\mathcal{P}^0\{x^{-1/\kappa}T_x\leqq t\} = F_\kappa(t), \quad t>0, \tag{5}$$

$$\lim_{t\to\infty}\mathcal{P}^0\{t^{-\kappa}\bar{\omega}(t)\leqq x\} = \lim_{t\to\infty}\mathcal{P}^0\{t^{-\kappa}\omega(t)\leqq x\} = \lim_{t\to\infty}\mathcal{P}^0\{t^{-\kappa}\underline{\omega}(t)\leqq x\} = 1-F_\kappa(x^{-1/\kappa}), \quad x>0, \tag{6}$$

where F_κ *is the distribution function of a one-sided stable distribution with Laplace transform* $\exp(-c\lambda^\kappa)$; *the constant* c *is given by*

$$c=\left\{2^{1-\kappa}\Gamma(\kappa)\int_0^\infty \frac{dx}{u(x)^2}\right\}^{-1}$$

where $u(x)$ *is the solution of*

$$\frac{d}{dM(x)}\frac{d}{dx}u=2u, \quad u(0)=1, \quad u'(0)=0,$$

the function $M(x)$ *being given in Lemma* 1.

(ii) *If* $\kappa=1$, *then*

(7) $(x\log x)^{-1}T_x$ *converges to* 4 *in probability with respect to* $\mathcal{P}^0$ *as* $x\to\infty$;

(8) *each of* $t^{-1}(\log t)\bar{\omega}(t)$, $t^{-1}(\log t)\omega(t)$ *and* $t^{-1}(\log t)\underline{\omega}(t)$ *converges to* 1/4 *in probability with respect to* $\mathcal{P}^0$ *as* $t\to\infty$.

(iii) *If* $\kappa>1$, *then*

$$\lim_{x\to\infty}T_x/x=\frac{4}{\kappa-1}, \quad \mathcal{P}^0\text{-a.s.}, \tag{9}$$

$$\lim_{t\to\infty} \omega(t)/t = \frac{\kappa-1}{4}, \quad \mathcal{P}^0\text{-a.s.}. \tag{10}$$

The assertion (i) can be slightly strengthened as follows.

THEOREM 2. *Let* $0<\kappa<1$.

(i) *The process* $\{\lambda^{-1/\kappa}T_{\lambda x},\ x\geqq 0,\ \mathcal{P}^0\}$ *converges to* $\{L(x),\ x\geqq 0\}$ *as* $\lambda\to\infty$ *in the sense of convergence of finite dimensional distributions, where* $\{L(x),\ x\geqq 0\}$ *is an increasing stable process with Laplace transform*

$$E\{\exp(-\xi L(1))\} = \exp(-c\xi^\kappa), \quad \xi \geqq 0.$$

(ii) *The process* $\{\lambda^{-\kappa}\omega(\lambda t),\ t\geqq 0,\ \mathcal{P}^0\}$ *converges to* $\{L^{-1}(t),\ t\geqq 0\}$ *as* $\lambda\to\infty$ *in the sense of convergence of finite dimensional distributions, where*

$$L^{-1}(t) = \inf\{x>0 : L(x)>t\}.$$

In the case of random walks, results similar to (5) and (6) were obtained by Kesten-Kozlov-Spitzer [**10**] and results similar to (7), (8), (9) and (10) by Solomon [**18**]. Our method of proving (9) and (10) is similar to that of [**18**] but as for (5), (6), (7) and (8) our method is different from either of [**10**] and [**18**]; it is based on Kotani's formula (see § 1) which reduces our problem to the study of limiting behavior of another diffusion process described by a certain stochastic differential equation with non-random coefficients. In proving (5) and (6) we must also use Kasahara's continuity theorem ([**7**]) concerning Krein's correspondence ([**6**]) between the m-measure and the spectral measure (or more precisely the h-function) of a one-dimensional diffusion operator.

ACKNOWLEDGMENT. The authors wish to thank S. Kotani for valuable discussions on the subject and for permitting us to contain his formula (1.1) here.

§ 1. Kotani's formula.

The following formula was obtained by S. Kotani in 1988 in his study of the limiting distribution of $(\log t)^{-2}\bar{\omega}(t)$ in the case $\kappa=0$ (unpublished).

KOTANI'S FORMULA. *Let* $\lambda>0$. *Then for* $t\geqq 0$

$$E_W^0\{e^{-\lambda T_t}\} = \exp\left\{-\int_0^t U_\lambda(s)ds\right\}, \quad P\text{-a.s.}, \tag{1.1}$$

where $U_\lambda(t)$ *is the unique stationary positive solution of*

$$dU_\lambda(t) = U_\lambda(t)dW(t) + \left\{2\lambda + \frac{1-\kappa}{2}U_\lambda(t) - U_\lambda(t)^2\right\}dt. \tag{1.2}$$

PROOF. Taking an arbitrary but fixed $a>0$ we put for $0<t<a$

$$u(t)=1/E_W^0\{e^{-\lambda T_t}\}, \quad v(t)=E_W^t\{e^{-\lambda T_a}\}.$$

Then

$$\begin{aligned} E_W^0\{e^{-\lambda T_a}\} &= E_W^0\{e^{-\lambda T_t}\}E_W^t\{e^{-\lambda T_a}\} \\ &= v(t)/u(t), \quad P\text{-a.s.}. \end{aligned}$$

Since $\mathcal{L}_W v(t)=\lambda v(t)$, $t<a$, $u(t)$ also satisfies $\mathcal{L}_W u(t)=\lambda u(t)$, $t>0$, or equivalently

$$d\{e^{-W_\kappa(t)}u'(t)\} = 2\lambda e^{-W_\kappa(t)}u(t)dt, \quad t>0. \tag{1.3}$$

If we put $U_\lambda(t)=\{\log u(t)\}'=u'(t)/u(t)$, then $U_\lambda(t)>0$, P-a.s.. Since $u(t)$ and $U_\lambda(t)$ are adapted to the filtration generated by $\{W(t)\}$, we can apply Itô's formula to compute the stochastic differential $dU_\lambda(t)$. Using (1.3) we have

$$\begin{aligned} dU_\lambda(t) &= d(u'(t)u(t)^{-1}) \\ &= d(e^{-W_\kappa(t)}u'(t)e^{W_\kappa(t)}u(t)^{-1}) \\ &= e^{W_\kappa(t)}u(t)^{-1}d(e^{-W_\kappa(t)}u'(t)) \\ &\quad + e^{-W_\kappa(t)}u'(t)u(t)^{-1}de^{W_\kappa(t)} - e^{-W_\kappa(t)}u'(t)e^{W_\kappa(t)}u(t)^{-2}du(t) \\ &= 2\lambda dt + u'(t)u(t)^{-1}dW_\kappa(t) + 2^{-1}u'(t)u(t)^{-1}dt - \{u'(t)u(t)^{-1}\}^2dt \\ &= U_\lambda(t)dW(t) + \left\{2\lambda + \frac{1-\kappa}{2}U_\lambda(t) - U_\lambda(t)^2\right\}dt. \end{aligned}$$

For $h>0$ we can write $u(t+h)=u(t)\tilde{u}(h)$ where

$$\tilde{u}(h) = 1/E_W^t\{e^{-\lambda T_{t+h}}\} \stackrel{d}{=} u(h);$$

in the above "$\stackrel{d}{=}$" means the equality in distribution. Therefore

$$\begin{aligned} U_\lambda(t) = u'(t)u(t)^{-1} &= \lim_{h\downarrow 0}\frac{\tilde{u}(h)-1}{h} \\ &\stackrel{d}{=} \lim_{h\downarrow 0}\frac{u(h)-1}{h} = u'(0) \\ &= u'(0)u(0)^{-1} = U_\lambda(0). \end{aligned}$$

This implies that $U_\lambda(t)$ is a stationary solution of (1.2). The uniqueness of such a solution follows from Theorem 18 of Itô-Nisio [5].

§ 2. Kasahara's continuity theorem for Krein's correspondence.

Krein's theory of strings ([6]) has many applications to diffusion processes (e.g., see [12], [13], [20]). In this section we do not give the general theory but list some of the results of Kasahara [7] on Krein's correspondence that will be useful for our later discussions. For a general statement of Krein's correspondence theory it is convenient to consider inextensible measures (e.g., see [20]). From the view point of its application to the present paper, however, it is enough to consider simply Radon measures in $[0, \infty)$. Thus suppose we are given a Radon measure $m(dx)$ in $[0, \infty)$. We exclude the trivial case where $m(dx)=0$. The associated function $M(x)$ is defined by $M(x)=m([0, x))$ for $x>0$ and $M(0)=0$. Consider the generalized differential operator $\mathcal{L}=d/m(dx)\cdot d/dx$ and let $\varphi(x, \alpha)$ and $\psi(x, \alpha)$ be the solutions of $\mathcal{L}u=\alpha u$ with the initial conditions

(2.1) $$u(0)=1, \quad u'(0)=0,$$

(2.2) $$u(0)=0, \quad u'(0)=1,$$

respectively. For $x>0$ $\varphi(x, \alpha)$ and $\psi(x, \alpha)$ satisfy

(2.3) $$\varphi(x, \alpha)=1+\alpha\iint_{0\leq z<y<x}\varphi(z, \alpha)m(dz)dy,$$

(2.4) $$\psi(x, \alpha)=x+\alpha\iint_{0\leq z<y<x}\psi(z, \alpha)m(dz)dy.$$

The pair $\{\varphi(x, \alpha), \psi(x, \alpha)\}$ is called the system of fundamental solutions associated with $m(dx)$. It is known that for $\alpha>0$

(2.5) $$h(\alpha)=\lim_{x\to\infty}\psi(x, \alpha)/\varphi(x, \alpha)=\int_0^\infty\frac{dx}{\varphi(x, \alpha)^2}<\infty$$

exists. The function $h(\alpha)$ is called the characteristic function of $m(dx)$ or of $M(x)$. The following (2.6), (2.7) and (2.8) are also known.

(2.6) The correspondence between $m(dx)$ and $h(\alpha)$ is one to one ([6], see also [13]).

(2.7) $a^{-1}h(c\alpha)$ is the characteristic function of $acM(ax)$ for arbitrary positive constants a and c ([7]).

(2.8) Assume that ∞ is not regular for $\mathcal{L}$, namely, that at least one of the integrals $\iint_{0<y<x<\infty}m(dy)dx$, $\iint_{0<y<x<\infty}dy\,m(dx)$ diverges. Then for each $\alpha>0$ a positive decreasing solution u of $\mathcal{L}u=\alpha u$ with $u(0)=1$ is unique and expressed as $u(x)=\varphi(x, \alpha)-\psi(x, \alpha)/h(\alpha)$ ([4]).

We now state

KASAHARA'S CONTINUITY THEOREM ([7]). *Let $m_n(dx)$, $n=0, 1, \cdots$, be Radon measures in $[0, \infty)$ with associated functions $M_n(x)$, characteristic functions $h_n(\alpha)$ and systems of fundamental solutions $\{\varphi_n(x, \alpha), \psi_n(x, \alpha)\}$. Then the following statements are equivalent to each other.*

(i) *$M_n(x) \to M_0(x)$ as $n \to \infty$ at each continuity point x of $M_0(\cdot)$.*

(ii) *For $x \geqq 0$ and $\alpha > 0$ $\varphi_n(x, \alpha) \to \varphi_0(x, \alpha)$ as $n \to \infty$.*

(iii) *For $\alpha > 0$ $h_n(\alpha) \to h(\alpha)$ as $n \to \infty$.*

§3. Proof of Theorem 1 in the case $0<\kappa<1$.

Let $U_\lambda(t)$ be the diffusion process appearing in Kotani's formula and put

$$V_\lambda(t) = \frac{1}{2\lambda} U_\lambda(t).$$

Since $V_\lambda(t)$ satisfies the stochastic differential equation

$$dV_\lambda(t) = V_\lambda(t)dW(t) + \Big(1 + \frac{1-\kappa}{2} V_\lambda(t) - 2\lambda V_\lambda(t)^2\Big)dt,$$

the generator of the diffusion process $V_\lambda(t)$ is $\mathcal{L}_\lambda = d/m_\lambda(dx) \cdot d/dS_\lambda(x)$ where

$$S_\lambda(x) = \int_1^x y^{\kappa-1} \exp\Big(\frac{2}{y} + 4\lambda y\Big) dy, \tag{3.1}$$

$$m_\lambda(dx) = 2x^{-\kappa-1} \exp\Big(-\frac{2}{x} - 4\lambda x\Big) dx. \tag{3.2}$$

We also put

$$\tilde{V}_\lambda(t) = V_\lambda(A_\lambda^{-1}(t)), \quad Y_\lambda(t) = S_\lambda(\tilde{V}_\lambda(t)),$$

where $A_\lambda^{-1}(t)$ is the inverse function of $A_\lambda(s) = \int_0^s V_\lambda(u) du$. The generators of $\tilde{V}_\lambda(t)$ and $Y_\lambda(t)$ are denoted by $\tilde{\mathcal{L}}_\lambda$ and $\mathcal{L}_\lambda^0$ respectively. $\mathcal{L}_\lambda^0$ is then given by $\mathcal{L}_\lambda^0 = d/m_\lambda^0(dx) \cdot d/dx$ with

$$m_\lambda^0(dx) = 2\theta_\lambda(x)^{-2\kappa+1} \exp\Big\{-\frac{4}{\theta_\lambda(x)} - 8\lambda\theta_\lambda(x)\Big\} dx, \tag{3.3}$$

where $\theta_\lambda(x)$ is the inverse function of $S_\lambda(\cdot)$. The path space representations of the diffusion processes with generators $\mathcal{L}_\lambda$, $\tilde{\mathcal{L}}_\lambda$ and $\mathcal{L}_\lambda^0$ are denoted by $\{\omega(t), t \geqq 0, P_\lambda^x\}$, $\{\omega(t), t \geqq 0, \tilde{P}_\lambda^x\}$ and $\{\omega(t), t \geqq 0, P_\lambda^{0,x}\}$, respectively. The expectations with respect to P_λ^x, $\tilde{P}_\lambda^x$ and $P_\lambda^{0,x}$ will be denoted by E_λ^x, $\tilde{E}_\lambda^x$ and $E_\lambda^{0,x}$, respectively. We begin by proving the following lemma.

LEMMA 1. *For any $x > 0$*

(3.4) $$\lim_{\lambda\downarrow 0}\lambda^{1-\kappa}M_\lambda(\lambda^{-\kappa}x)=M(x),$$

where $M_\lambda(x)$ *is the associated function of* $m_\lambda^0(dx)$ *and*

$$M(x)=2\gamma(\rho^{-1}(x)),$$

$$\gamma(x)=\int_0^x y^{-\kappa}e^{-4y}dy,$$

$\rho^{-1}(x)$ *is the inverse function of* $\rho(x)=\int_0^x y^{\kappa-1}e^{4y}dy.$

PROOF. By an easy computation we have for $x>\lambda$

$$S_\lambda(\lambda^{-1}x)=\lambda^{-\kappa}\rho_\lambda(x),$$

where

$$\rho_\lambda(x)=\int_\lambda^x y^{\kappa-1}\exp\Big(\frac{2\lambda}{y}+4y\Big)dy.$$

It is also easy to see that $\rho_\lambda(x)\to\rho(x)$ as $\lambda\downarrow 0$ and hence $S_\lambda(\lambda^{-1}x)\sim\lambda^{-\kappa}\rho(x)$ as $\lambda\downarrow 0$. Therefore for any $\varepsilon\in(0, x)$ $S_\lambda(\lambda^{-1}(x-\varepsilon))<\lambda^{-\kappa}\rho(x)$ holds for all sufficiently small $\lambda>0$. In other words

(3.5) $$\lambda^{-1}(x-\varepsilon)<\theta_\lambda(\lambda^{-\kappa}\rho(x)) \text{ for all sufficiently small } \lambda>0.$$

Similarly

(3.6) $$\lambda^{-1}(x+\varepsilon)>\theta_\lambda(\lambda^{-\kappa}\rho(x)) \text{ for all sufficiently small } \lambda>0.$$

Next we note that

$$M_\lambda(x)=2\int_1^{\theta_\lambda(x)} z^{-2\kappa+1}\exp\Big(-\frac{4}{z}-8\lambda z\Big)S_\lambda'(z)dz,$$

and hence

$$M_\lambda(\lambda^{-\kappa}\rho(x))=2\int_1^{\theta_\lambda(\lambda^{-\kappa}\rho(x))} z^{-\kappa}\exp\Big(-\frac{2}{z}-4\lambda z\Big)dz.$$

This combined with (3.5) and (3.6) yields

(3.7) $$2\int_1^{\lambda^{-1}(x-\varepsilon)} z^{-\kappa}\exp\Big(-\frac{2}{z}-4\lambda z\Big)dz<M_\lambda(\lambda^{-\kappa}\rho(x))$$
$$<2\int_1^{\lambda^{-1}(x+\varepsilon)} z^{-\kappa}\exp\Big(-\frac{2}{z}-4\lambda z\Big)dz$$

for all sufficiently small $\lambda>0$. Since

$$2\int_1^{\lambda^{-1}x} z^{-\kappa}\exp\Big(-\frac{2}{z}-4\lambda z\Big)dz=2\lambda^{\kappa-1}\gamma_\lambda(x)$$

where

$$\gamma_\lambda(x)=\int_\lambda^x y^{-\kappa}\exp\Big(-\frac{2\lambda}{y}-4y\Big)dy,$$

(3.7) yields

$$\gamma_{\lambda}(x-\varepsilon) < M_{\lambda}(\lambda^{-\kappa}\rho(x))/(2\lambda^{\kappa-1}) < \gamma_{\lambda}(x+\varepsilon),$$

which again yields

$$\lim_{\lambda\downarrow 0} M_{\lambda}(\lambda^{-\kappa}\rho(x))/(2\lambda^{\kappa-1}) = \gamma(x),$$

because $\gamma_{\lambda}(x)\to\gamma(x)$ as $\lambda\downarrow 0$. Taking $\rho^{-1}(x)$ instead of x we obtain

$$\lim_{\lambda\downarrow 0} M_{\lambda}(\lambda^{-\kappa}x)/(2\lambda^{\kappa-1}) = \gamma(\rho^{-1}(x)),$$

which proves Lemma 1.

By virtue of Kasahara's continuity theorem and (2.7) Lemma 1 yields the following lemma concerning the characteristic functions $h_{\lambda}(\alpha)$ and $h(\alpha)$ of $M_{\lambda}(x)$ and $M(x)$ respectively.

LEMMA 2. $\lim_{\lambda\downarrow 0} \lambda^{\kappa}h_{\lambda}(\lambda\alpha)=h(\alpha)$, $\alpha>0$.

Let $\tau=\inf\{t>0: \omega(t)=1\}$. Then for $x>0$ and $\alpha\geqq 0$

$$E_{\lambda}^{x}\left\{\exp\left(-\alpha\lambda\int_{0}^{\tau}\omega(s)ds\right)\right\} = \tilde{E}_{\lambda}^{x}\{e^{-\alpha\lambda\tau}\} = E_{\lambda}^{0,S_{\lambda}(x)}\{e^{-\alpha\lambda\sigma}\}, \tag{3.8}$$

where $\sigma=\inf\{t>0: \omega(t)=0\}$. For a given $a>0$ determine $a_{\lambda}(>1)$ by $S_{\lambda}(a_{\lambda})=a$. Also let

$$S(x) = \int_{1}^{x} y^{\kappa-1}\exp\left(\frac{2}{y}\right)dy,$$

and determine $a_0(>1)$ by $S(a_0)=a$. Then $a_{\lambda}\uparrow a_0$ as $\lambda\downarrow 0$.

LEMMA 3. *If* $0<\kappa<1$, *then for* $\alpha>0$

$$1-E_{\lambda}^{a_{\lambda}}\left\{\exp\left(-\alpha\lambda\int_{0}^{\tau}\omega(s)ds\right)\right\} \sim c(a,\alpha)\lambda^{\kappa} \quad \text{as } \lambda\downarrow 0, \tag{3.9}$$

where

$$c(a,\alpha) = a/h(\alpha). \tag{3.10}$$

PROOF. Since ∞ is not regular for $\mathcal{L}_{\lambda}^{0}$, (2.8) implies that for each $\alpha>0$ a positive decreasing solution $u_{\lambda}(\cdot,\alpha)$ of $\mathcal{L}_{\lambda}^{0}u=\alpha u$ with $u(0)=1$ is unique and expressed as

$$u_{\lambda}(x,\alpha) = \varphi_{\lambda}(x,\alpha)-\psi_{\lambda}(x,\alpha)/h_{\lambda}(\alpha), \tag{3.11}$$

where the pair $\{\varphi_{\lambda}(x,\alpha), \psi_{\lambda}(x,\alpha)\}$ is the system of fundamental solutions associated with $m_{\lambda}^{0}(dx)$. By (3.8) we have

$$E_{\lambda}^{a_{\lambda}}\left\{\exp\left(-\alpha\lambda\int_{0}^{\tau}\omega(s)ds\right)\right\} = u_{\lambda}(a,\alpha\lambda). \tag{3.12}$$

By making use of (2.3) and (2.4) with $m(dz)$ replaced by $m_\lambda^0(dz)$ we can easily prove that

$$\varphi_\lambda(a,\ \alpha\lambda)-1 = 2\alpha\lambda\int_0^a dx\int_1^{\theta_\lambda(x)} y^{-\kappa}\exp\left(-\frac{2}{y}-4\lambda y\right)dy+o(\lambda), \tag{3.13}$$

$$\psi_\lambda(a,\ \alpha\lambda) = a+O(\lambda), \tag{3.14}$$

as $\lambda\downarrow 0$. Denoting by $\theta(x)$ the inverse function of $S(\cdot)$, we have

$$\lim_{\lambda\downarrow 0}\frac{\varphi_\lambda(a,\ \alpha\lambda)-1}{\alpha\lambda} = 2\int_0^a dx\int_1^{\theta(x)} y^{-\kappa}\exp\left(-\frac{2}{y}\right)dy = const.. \tag{3.15}$$

From (3.12) and (3.11) we have

$$1-E_\lambda^{a_\lambda}\left\{\exp\left(-\alpha\lambda\int_0^\tau \omega(s)ds\right)\right\} = 1-\varphi_\lambda(a,\ \alpha\lambda)+\psi_\lambda(a,\ \alpha\lambda)/h_\lambda(\alpha\lambda),$$

which combined with (3.15), (3.14) and Lemma 2 finally implies (3.9).

The idea of the proof of (5) of Theorem 1 is as follows. We want to compute

$$\lim_{\lambda\downarrow 0}\mathcal{E}^0\{\exp(-\lambda T_{\lambda^{-\kappa}t})\}$$

which, by virtue of Kotani's formula, equals

$$\begin{aligned}\tag{3.16} &\lim_{\lambda\downarrow 0} E\left\{\exp\left(-\int_0^{\lambda^{-\kappa}t} U_\lambda(s)ds\right)\right\}\\ &= \lim_{\lambda\downarrow 0} E\left\{\exp\left(-2\lambda\int_0^{\lambda^{-\kappa}t} V_\lambda(s)ds\right)\right\}\\ &= \lim_{\lambda\downarrow 0} E_\lambda^{\mu_\lambda}\left\{\exp\left(-2\lambda\int_0^{\lambda^{-\kappa}t}\omega(s)ds\right)\right\},\end{aligned}$$

where $E_\lambda^{\mu_\lambda}$ denotes the expectation with respect to $P_\lambda^{\mu_\lambda}=\int\mu_\lambda(dx)P_\lambda^x$, μ_λ being the invariant probability measure of the diffusion process with generator $\mathcal{L}_\lambda$. We first compute

$$\lim_{\lambda\downarrow 0} E_\lambda^{a_\lambda}\left\{\exp\left(-2\lambda\int_0^{\lambda^{-\kappa}t}\omega(s)ds\right)\right\},$$

with the starting point a_λ defined by $S_\lambda(a_\lambda)=a$, by showing that $\int_0^{\lambda^{-\kappa}t}\omega(s)ds$ can be approximated by $\sum\int_{\sigma_{k-1}}^{\tau_k}\omega(s)ds$ where σ_k and τ_k are defined as follows:

$$\sigma_0 = 0,\quad \tau_k = \inf\{t>\sigma_{k-1} : \omega(t)=1\},\quad k\geqq 1,$$

$$\sigma_k = \inf\{t>\tau_k : \omega(t)=a_\lambda\},\qquad k\geqq 1.$$

Note that $\sigma_k-\sigma_{k-1}$, $k\geqq 1$, are i.i.d. random variables.

LEMMA 4. (i) $m_\lambda = E_{\lambda,1}^{a_\lambda}\{\sigma_1\} = am_\lambda(\boldsymbol{R}^+) < \infty$, $\lambda \geqq 0$, *where* $\boldsymbol{R}^+ = (0, \infty)$.
(ii) *For any* $\varepsilon > 0$ *and* $\lambda \geqq 0$

$$P_\lambda^{a_\lambda}\left\{\left|\frac{\sigma_n}{n} - m_\lambda\right| > \varepsilon\right\} \to 0 \quad as\ n \to \infty, \tag{3.17}$$

and the convergence is uniform in $\lambda \in [0, 1]$.

PROOF. For $b > 0$ and $x > 0$ let $I = (x, b)$ and $J = (0, y)$ or $I = (b, x)$ and $J = (y, \infty)$ according as $0 < x < b$ or $0 < b < x$. Let $\sigma = \inf\{t > 0 : \omega(t) = b\}$. Then it is well-known that

$$E_\lambda^x\{\sigma\} = \int_I dS_\lambda(y) \int_J m_\lambda(dz) \tag{3.18}$$

holds (note that $-S_\lambda(0) = S_\lambda(\infty) = \infty$ is also taken into account in deriving the above formula). By virtue of (3.18) we can easily compute $m_\lambda = E_\lambda^{a_\lambda}\{\tau_1\} + E_\lambda^{a_\lambda}\{\sigma_1 - \tau_1\}$, obtaining (i). The assertion (3.17) is nothing but the law of large numbers for i.i.d. random variables. Only the uniform convergence needs proof for which it is enough to verify the uniform integrability of $\{\sigma_1, P_\lambda^{a_\lambda}, 0 \leqq \lambda \leqq 1\}$, namely,

$$\lim_{N\to\infty} \sup_{0 \leq \lambda \leq 1} \int_{\{\sigma_1 > N\}} \sigma_1 dP_\lambda^{a_\lambda} = 0. \tag{3.19}$$

We use the fact that the diffusion process $\{\omega(t), t \geqq 0, P_\lambda^{a_\lambda}\}$ can also be realized as a solution of the stochastic differential equation

$$dV(t) = V(t)dW(t) + \left\{1 + \frac{1-\kappa}{2}V(t) - 2\lambda V(t)^2\right\}dt \tag{3.20}$$

with $V(0) = a_\lambda$. Then a comparison theorem in stochastic differential equations implies that the solution of (3.20) lies below the solution of (3.20) with $\lambda = 0$. From this observation we see that

$$P_\lambda^{a_\lambda}\{\tau_1 > N\} \leqq P_0^{a_0}\{\tau_1 > N\}, \tag{3.21}$$

and by a similar argument

$$P_\lambda^{a_\lambda}\{\sigma_1 - \tau_1 > N\} \leqq P_1^1\{\sigma > N\}, \tag{3.22}$$

where $\sigma = \inf\{t > 0 : \omega(t) = a_0\}$. Thus (3.19) follows from (3.21) and (3.22). The proof of the lemma is finished.

We are now in the final stage of the proof of Theorem 1 in the case $0 < \kappa < 1$. For fixed $t > 0$ and small $\varepsilon > 0$ we put

$$n_1(\lambda) = [\lambda^{-\kappa}t(1-\varepsilon)/m_0], \quad n_2(\lambda) = [\lambda^{-\kappa}t(1+\varepsilon)/m_0].$$

Then the uniform convergence of (3.17) implies

$$\lim_{\lambda \downarrow 0} P_\lambda^{a\lambda}\left\{\left|\frac{\sigma_{n_i(\lambda)}}{n_i(\lambda)}-m_\lambda\right|>m_0\varepsilon\right\}=0, \quad i=1, 2.$$

Since $m_\lambda \to m_0$ as $\lambda \downarrow 0$ we have

$$\lim_{\lambda \downarrow 0} P_\lambda^{a\lambda}\left\{\left|\frac{\sigma_{n_i(\lambda)}}{n_i(\lambda)}-m_0\right|>m_0\varepsilon\right\}=0, \quad i=1, 2, \tag{3.23}$$

and in particular

$$\lim_{\lambda \downarrow 0} P_\lambda^{a\lambda}\{\sigma_{n_1(\lambda)}<n_1(\lambda)m_0(1+\varepsilon)\}=1.$$

But $n_1(\lambda)m_0(1+\varepsilon)<\lambda^{-\kappa}t$ for all sufficiently small $\lambda>0$ and hence

$$\lim_{\lambda \downarrow 0} P_\lambda^{a\lambda}\{\sigma_{n_1(\lambda)}<\lambda^{-\kappa}t\}=1. \tag{3.24}$$

Similarly we have

$$\lim_{\lambda \downarrow 0} P_\lambda^{a\lambda}\{\sigma_{n_2(\lambda)}>\lambda^{-\kappa}t\}=1. \tag{3.25}$$

Next we put

$$Y_k=\int_{\sigma_{k-1}}^{\tau_k}\omega(s)ds, \quad Z_k=\int_{\tau_k}^{\sigma_k}\omega(s)ds, \quad k \geqq 1.$$

Then on the event $A_\lambda=\{\sigma_{n_1(\lambda)}<\lambda^{-\kappa}t<\sigma_{n_2(\lambda)}\}$

$$\sum_{k=1}^{n_1(\lambda)}(Y_k+Z_k)<\int_0^{\lambda^{-\kappa}t}\omega(s)ds<\sum_{k=1}^{n_2(\lambda)}(Y_k+Z_k)$$

holds and hence

$$\begin{aligned} &E_\lambda^{a\lambda}\left\{\exp\left(-2\lambda\sum_{k=1}^{n_2(\lambda)}(Y_k+Z_k)\right); A_\lambda\right\} \\ &\leqq E_\lambda^{a\lambda}\left\{\exp\left(-2\lambda\int_0^{\lambda^{-\kappa}t}\omega(s)ds\right); A_\lambda\right\} \\ &\leqq E_\lambda^{a\lambda}\left\{\exp\left(-2\lambda\sum_{k=1}^{n_1(\lambda)}(Y_k+Z_k)\right); A_\lambda\right\}, \end{aligned}$$

where the notation $E_\lambda^{a\lambda}\{X; A\}$ stands for the integral of X over A with respect to $P_\lambda^{a\lambda}$. Since $P_\lambda^{a\lambda}\{A_\lambda\}\to 1$ by (3.24) and (3.25),

$$\begin{aligned} &E_\lambda^{a\lambda}\left\{\exp\left(-2\lambda\sum_{k=1}^{n_2(\lambda)}(Y_k+Z_k)\right)\right\} \\ &\leqq E_\lambda^{a\lambda}\left\{\exp\left(-2\lambda\int_0^{\lambda^{-\kappa}t}\omega(s)ds\right)\right\}+o(1) \\ &\leqq E_\lambda^{a\lambda}\left\{\exp\left(-2\lambda\sum_{k=1}^{n_1(\lambda)}(Y_k+Z_k)\right)\right\}+o(1), \end{aligned} \tag{3.26}$$

where $o(1)$ indicates a term which tends to 0 as $\lambda \downarrow 0$. We now compute

$$\lim_{\lambda \downarrow 0} E_\lambda^{a\lambda}\left\{\exp\left(-2\lambda \sum_{k=1}^{n_i(\lambda)} (Y_k+Z_k)\right)\right\}$$

$$= \lim_{\lambda \downarrow 0} E_\lambda^{a\lambda}\{\exp(-2\lambda Y_1)\}^{n_i(\lambda)} \cdot E_\lambda^{a\lambda}\{\exp(-2\lambda Z_1)\}^{n_i(\lambda)}.$$

By Lemma 3 we have

$$\lim_{\lambda \downarrow 0}[E_\lambda^{a\lambda}\{\exp(-2\lambda Y_1)\}]^{n_1(\lambda)} = \lim_{\lambda \downarrow 0}\{1-c(a,\, 2)\lambda^\kappa\}^{n_1(\lambda)} \tag{3.27}$$

$$= \exp\{-c(a,\, 2)t(1-\varepsilon)/m_0\}.$$

Similarly we have

$$\lim_{\lambda \downarrow 0} E_\lambda^{a\lambda}\left\{\exp\left(-2\lambda \sum_{k=1}^{n_2(\lambda)} Y_k\right)\right\} = \exp\{-c(a,\, 2)t(1+\varepsilon)/m_0\}. \tag{3.28}$$

On the other hand, we have

$$2\lambda \sum_{k=1}^{n_i(\lambda)} Z_k < 2\lambda a_\lambda \sigma_{n_i(\lambda)} < 2a_\lambda \lambda^{1-\kappa} t(1+\varepsilon)m_0^{-1}\sigma_{n_i(\lambda)}/n_i(\lambda)$$

which tends to 0 in probability as $\lambda \downarrow 0$ by virtue of $0<\kappa<1$ and (3.23). Therefore

$$\lim_{\lambda \downarrow 0} E_\lambda^{a\lambda}\left\{\exp\left(-2\lambda \sum_{k=1}^{n_i(\lambda)} Z_k\right)\right\} = 1. \tag{3.29}$$

From (3.26), (3.27), (3.28) and (3.29) we have for any $\varepsilon>0$

$$\exp\{-c(a,\, 2)t(1+\varepsilon)/m_0\} \leqq \liminf_{\lambda \downarrow 0} E_\lambda^{a\lambda}\left\{\exp\left(-2\lambda\int_0^{\lambda^{-\kappa}t} \omega(s)ds\right)\right\}$$

$$\leqq \limsup_{\lambda \downarrow 0} E_\lambda^{a\lambda}\left\{\exp\left(-2\lambda\int_0^{\lambda^{-\kappa}t} \omega(s)ds\right)\right\}$$

$$\leqq \exp\{-c(a,\, 2)t(1-\varepsilon)/m_0\},$$

which implies

$$\lim_{\lambda \downarrow 0} E_\lambda^{a\lambda}\left\{\exp\left(-2\lambda\int_0^{\lambda^{-\kappa}t} \omega(s)ds\right)\right\} = \exp\{-c(a,\, 2)t/m_0\}. \tag{3.30}$$

LEMMA 5. *For any* $t>0$

$$\lim_{\lambda \downarrow 0} E\left\{\exp\left(-\int_0^{\lambda^{-\kappa}t} U_\lambda(s)ds\right)\right\} = \exp\{-c(a,\, 2)t/m_0\}. \tag{3.31}$$

PROOF. Note that by (3.16) the left hand side of (3.31) equals

$$\lim_{\lambda \downarrow 0} E_\lambda^{\mu\lambda}\left\{\exp\left(-2\lambda\int_0^{\lambda^{-\kappa}t} \omega(s)ds\right)\right\}.$$

Let $\sigma_0=\inf\{t>0: \omega(t)=a_\lambda\}$ and put $\Gamma_u=\{\sigma_0<u\}$. Then using the strong Markov property we see that

$$E_\lambda^{\mu\lambda}\left\{\exp\left(-2\lambda\int_0^{\lambda^{-\kappa}t}\omega(s)ds\right);\,\Gamma_u\right\}$$

is bounded from below by

$$E_\lambda^{\mu\lambda}\left\{\exp\left(-2\lambda\int_0^{\sigma_0}\omega(s)ds\right);\,\Gamma_u\right\}\cdot E_\lambda^{a\lambda}\left\{\exp\left(-2\lambda\int_0^{\lambda^{-\kappa}t}\omega(s)ds\right)\right\}$$

and is bounded from above by

$$E_\lambda^{a\lambda}\left\{\exp\left(-2\lambda\int_0^{\lambda^{-\kappa}(t-\lambda^\kappa u)}\omega(s)ds\right)\right\}.$$

Taking into account of the fact that $P_\lambda^{\mu\lambda}\{\Gamma_u\}\to 1$ as $u\to\infty$ uniformly in $\lambda\in(0,1)$ and also of (3.30), we first left $\lambda\downarrow 0$ and then $u\uparrow\infty$. As a result we obtain (3.31).

The proof of (5) in Theorem 1 is now completed as follows. By Kotani's formula we have for $\xi>0$

$$\begin{aligned}\mathcal{E}^0\{\exp(-\xi T_x/x^{1/\kappa})\} &= E\left\{\exp\left(-\int_0^x U_{\xi x^{-1/\kappa}}(s)ds\right)\right\}\\ &= E\left\{\exp\left(-\int_0^{\lambda^{-\kappa}t}U_\lambda(s)ds\right)\right\},\end{aligned}$$

where we put $t=\xi^\kappa$ and $\lambda=\xi x^{-1/\kappa}$. Letting $x\to\infty$ (so $\lambda\downarrow 0$) we obtain

$$\lim_{x\to\infty}\mathcal{E}^0\{\exp(-\xi T_x/x^{1/\kappa})\} = \exp\{-c(a,2)t/m_0\} = e^{-ct} = e^{-c\xi^\kappa},$$

where $c=\{2^{1-\kappa}\Gamma(\kappa)h(2)\}^{-1}$, because $c(a,2)=a/h(2)$ and

$$m_0 = am_0(\boldsymbol{R}^+) = 2a\int_0^\infty x^{-\kappa-1}e^{-2/x}dx = 2^{1-\kappa}\Gamma(\kappa)a$$

by (3.10) and (i) of Lemma 4.

Finally we prove (6). Clearly we see that for any $u>0$, $y>0$ and $t>0$

$$\begin{aligned}\{T_u\geqq t\} &\subset \{\overline{\omega}(t)\leqq u\}\subset\{\omega(t)\leqq u\}\subset\{\underline{\omega}(t)\leqq u\}\\ &\subset \{T_{u+y}\geqq t\}\cup\left\{\inf_{s\geqq T_{u+y}}\omega(s)-(u+y)\leqq -y\right\}.\end{aligned}$$

We notice that

$$\lim_{y\to\infty}\mathcal{P}^0\left\{\inf_{s\geqq T_{u+y}}\omega(s)-(u+y)\leqq -y\right\} = \lim_{y\to\infty}\mathcal{P}^0\left\{\inf_{s\geqq 0}\omega(s)\leqq -y\right\} = 0 \tag{3.32}$$

since $\omega(s)\to\infty$ as $s\uparrow\infty$, $\mathcal{P}^0$-*a.s.*. Therefore we have for all $x>0$

$$\begin{aligned}\mathcal{P}^0\{T_{t^\kappa x}\geqq t\} &\leqq \mathcal{P}^0\{\overline{\omega}(t)\leqq t^\kappa x\}\leqq\mathcal{P}^0\{\omega(t)\leqq t^\kappa x\}\\ &\leqq \mathcal{P}^0\{\underline{\omega}(t)\leqq t^\kappa u\}\leqq\mathcal{P}^0\{T_{t^\kappa x+y}\geqq t\}+\mathcal{P}^0\left\{\inf_{s\geqq 0}\omega(s)\leqq -y\right\}.\end{aligned} \tag{3.33}$$

For any sufficiently large fixed y, the result (5) ensures

$$\lim_{t\to\infty} \mathcal{P}^0\{T_{t^\kappa x}\geqq t\} = \lim_{t\to\infty} \mathcal{P}^0\{T_{t^\kappa x+y}\geqq t\}$$
$$= \lim_{v\to\infty} \mathcal{P}^0\{v^{-1/\kappa}T_v\geqq x^{-1/\kappa}\} = 1-F_\kappa(x^{-1/\kappa}),$$

which combined with (3.32) and (3.33) proves (6).

§4. Proof of Theorem 2.

For the proof of (i) it is enough to show that

$$\lim_{\lambda\to\infty} \mathcal{P}^0\Big\{\exp\Big(-\sum_{k=1}^n \xi_k\lambda^{-1/\kappa}(T_{\lambda x_k}-T_{\lambda x_{k-1}})\Big)\Big\} = \exp\Big\{-c\sum_{k=1}^n (x_k-x_{k-1})\xi_k^\kappa\Big\} \tag{4.1}$$

for any $\xi_1, \xi_2, \cdots, \xi_n\geqq 0$ and $0=x_0<x_1<\cdots<x_n$. Take an ε such that $0<\varepsilon<\min\{x_k-x_{k-1}: 1\leqq k\leqq n\}$ and let us prove first that

$$\lim_{\lambda\to\infty} \mathcal{E}^0\Big\{\exp\Big(-\sum_{k=1}^n \xi_k\lambda^{-1/\kappa}(T_{\lambda(x_k-\varepsilon)}-T_{\lambda x_{k-1}})\Big)\Big\} = \exp\Big\{-c\sum_{k=1}^n (x_k-x_{k-1}-\varepsilon)\xi_k^\kappa\Big\}. \tag{4.2}$$

In what follows $T_x=T_x(\omega)$ denotes the first passage time $\inf\{t>0: \omega(t)=x\}$ where x may lie either to the right or to the left of $\omega(0)$. If we put

$$F_{\lambda,k} = E_W^{\lambda x_{k-1}}\{\exp(-\xi_k\lambda^{-1/\kappa}T_{\lambda(x_k-\varepsilon)}); T_{\lambda(x_k-\varepsilon)}<T_{\lambda(x_{k-1}-\varepsilon)}\},$$
$$G_{\lambda,k} = E_W^{\lambda x_{k-1}}\{\exp(-\xi_k\lambda^{-1/\kappa}T_{\lambda(x_k-\varepsilon)}); T_{\lambda(x_k-\varepsilon)}>T_{\lambda(x_{k-1}-\varepsilon)}\},$$

then

$$\begin{aligned} &E_W^0\Big\{\exp\Big(-\sum_{k=1}^n \xi_k\lambda^{-1/\kappa}(T_{\lambda(x_k-\varepsilon)}-T_{\lambda x_{k-1}})\Big)\Big\} \\ &= \prod_{k=1}^n E_W^{\lambda x_{k-1}}\{\exp(-\xi_k\lambda^{-1/\kappa}T_{\lambda(x_k-\varepsilon)})\} \\ &= \prod_{k=1}^n (F_{\lambda,k}+G_{\lambda,k}). \end{aligned} \tag{4.3}$$

Making use of a trivial inequality $0\leqq\prod_{k=1}^n(a_k+b_k)-\prod_{k=1}^n a_k\leqq\sum_{k=1}^n b_k$ which holds under the assumption that $a_k, b_k\geqq 0$ and $a_k+b_k\leqq 1$ $(1\leqq k\leqq n)$, we have

$$\begin{aligned} 0 &\leqq E\Big\{\prod_{k=1}^n (F_{\lambda,k}+G_{\lambda,k})\Big\}-E\Big\{\prod_{k=1}^n F_{\lambda,k}\Big\} \\ &\leqq \sum_{k=1}^n E\{G_{\lambda,k}\} \leqq \sum_{k=1}^n \mathcal{P}^{\lambda x_{k-1}}\{T_{\lambda(x_k-\varepsilon)}>T_{\lambda(x_{k-1}-\varepsilon)}\} \\ &= \sum_{k=1}^n E\Big\{\int_{\lambda x_{k-1}}^{\lambda(x_k-\varepsilon)} e^{W_\kappa(x)}dx\Big/\int_{\lambda(x_{k-1}-\varepsilon)}^{\lambda(x_k-\varepsilon)} e^{W_\kappa(x)}dx\Big\} \end{aligned} \tag{4.4}$$

$$= \sum_{k=1}^{n} E\left\{\int_0^{\lambda(x_k - x_{k-1} - \varepsilon)} e^{W_\kappa(y+\lambda x_{k-1})} dy \Big/ \int_{-\lambda\varepsilon}^{\lambda(x_k - x_{k-1} - \varepsilon)} e^{W_\kappa(y+\lambda x_{k-1})} dy\right\}$$

$$= \sum_{k=1}^{n} E\left\{\int_0^{\lambda(x_k - x_{k-1} - \varepsilon)} e^{W_\kappa(y)} dy \Big/ \int_{-\lambda\varepsilon}^{\lambda(x_k - x_{k-1} - \varepsilon)} e^{W_\kappa(y)} dy\right\}$$

(since W_κ has stationary increments)

$$\leqq nE\left\{\int_0^{\infty} e^{W_\kappa(y)} dy \Big/ \int_{-\lambda\varepsilon}^{\infty} e^{W_\kappa(y)} dy\right\} \to 0, \quad \lambda \to \infty.$$

On the other hand it is easy to see that

$$E\left\{\prod_{k=1}^{n} F_{\lambda,k}\right\} = \prod_{k=1}^{n} E\{F_{\lambda,k}\}, \tag{4.5}$$

$$\begin{aligned} \lim_{\lambda\to\infty} E\{F_{\lambda,k}\} &= \lim_{\lambda\to\infty} E\{F_{\lambda,k} + G_{\lambda,k}\} \\ &= \lim_{\lambda\to\infty} \mathcal{E}^0\{\exp(-\xi_k \lambda^{-1/\kappa} T_{\lambda(x_k - x_{k-1} - \varepsilon)})\} \\ &= \exp\{-c(x_k - x_{k-1} - \varepsilon)\xi_k^\kappa\}, \end{aligned} \tag{4.6}$$

the last equality being a consequence of (5). From (4.3)$\sim$(4.6) we obtain (4.2). To derive (4.1) from (4.2) it is enough to notice that

$$\begin{aligned} 0 &\leqq \mathcal{E}^0\left\{\exp\left(-\sum_{k=1}^{n} \xi_k \lambda^{-1/\kappa}(T_{\lambda(x_k-\varepsilon)} - T_{\lambda x_{k-1}})\right)\right\} \\ &\quad - \mathcal{E}^0\left\{\exp\left(-\sum_{k=1}^{n} \xi_k \lambda^{-1/\kappa}(T_{\lambda x_k} - T_{\lambda x_{k-1}})\right)\right\} \\ &\leqq \mathcal{E}^0\left\{1 - \exp\left(-\sum_{k=1}^{n} \xi_k \lambda^{-1/\kappa}(T_{\lambda x_k} - T_{\lambda(x_k-\varepsilon)})\right)\right\} \\ &\leqq \sum_{k=1}^{n} \mathcal{E}^0\{1 - \exp(-\xi_k \lambda^{-1/\kappa}(T_{\lambda x_k} - T_{\lambda(x_k-\varepsilon)}))\} \\ &= \sum_{k=1}^{n} \mathcal{E}^0\{1 - \exp(-\xi_k \lambda^{-1/\kappa} T_{\lambda\varepsilon})\} \\ &\to \sum_{k=1}^{n} \{1 - \exp(-c\varepsilon\xi_k^\kappa)\} \quad \text{as } \lambda \to \infty \\ &\to 0 \quad \text{as } \varepsilon \downarrow 0. \end{aligned}$$

The proof of (ii) can be done in a way similar to (6). In fact, as in (3.33) we have for any $t_k > 0$, $x_k > 0$ $(1 \leqq k \leqq n)$ and $y > 0$

$$\begin{aligned} &\mathcal{P}^0\{T_{\lambda^\kappa x_k} \geqq \lambda t_k,\ 1 \leqq k \leqq n\} \\ &\leqq \mathcal{P}^0\{\lambda^{-\kappa}\omega(\lambda t_k) \leqq x_k,\ 1 \leqq k \leqq n\} \\ &\leqq \mathcal{P}^0\{T_{\lambda^\kappa x_k + y} \geqq \lambda t_k,\ 1 \leqq k \leqq n\} + n\mathcal{P}^0\left\{\inf_{s\geqq 0} \omega(s) \leqq -y\right\}. \end{aligned}$$

Letting $\lambda\uparrow\infty$ in the above we obtain

$$\lim_{\lambda\to\infty}\mathcal{P}^0\{\lambda^{-\kappa}\omega(\lambda t_k)\leqq x_k,\ 1\leqq k\leqq n\}$$
$$=P\{L(x_k)\geqq t_k,\ 1\leqq k\leqq n\}=P\{L^{-1}(t_k)\leqq x_k,\ 1\leqq k\leqq n\}.$$

§5. Proof of Theorem 1 in the case $\kappa=1$.

Assume $\kappa=1$ and recall

$$E_W^0\{e^{-\lambda T_t}\}=\exp\left\{-2\lambda\int_0^t V_\lambda(s)ds\right\},\quad a.s., \tag{5.1}$$

where $V_\lambda(t)=(2\lambda)^{-1}U_\lambda(t)$ is a stationary diffusion process with generator

$$\mathcal{L}_\lambda=\frac{d}{m_\lambda(dx)}\cdot\frac{d}{dS_\lambda(x)},$$

wherein

$$S_\lambda(x)=\int_0^x\exp\left(\frac{2}{y}+4\lambda y\right)dy,\quad m_\lambda(dx)=2x^{-2}\exp\left(-\frac{2}{x}-4\lambda x\right)dx.$$

Once the following proposition is proved, (7) of Theorem 1 follows immediately from (5.1).

PROPOSITION 1. *For any* $\lambda>0$

$$(x\log x)^{-1}\int_0^x V_{\lambda(x\log x)^{-1}}(t)dt\to 2\quad \text{in probability as } x\to\infty. \tag{5.2}$$

Before proving this proposition we prepare three lemmas. We put for $\xi>0$

$$a_\xi=m_\xi(\boldsymbol{R}^+)^{-1}\int_0^\infty x\,m_\xi(dx),$$

$$u_\xi(x)=\int_0^x dS_\xi(y)\int_0^y(z-a_\xi)m_\xi(dz).$$

LEMMA 6. $a_\xi\sim-2\log\xi$ *as* $\xi\downarrow 0$.

PROOF. a_ξ can be expressed as $a_\xi=2m_\xi(\boldsymbol{R}^+)^{-1}(I_\xi+II_\xi)$ where

$$I_\xi=\int_0^N x^{-1}\exp\{-2x^{-1}-4\xi x\}\,dx,\quad II_\xi=\int_N^\infty x^{-1}\exp\{-2x^{-1}-4\xi x\}\,dx.$$

For fixed $N>0$ I_ξ remains bounded as $\xi\downarrow 0$ and $e^{-2/N}II'_\xi\leqq II_\xi\leqq II'_\xi$ where

$$II'_\xi=\int_N^\infty x^{-1}e^{-4\xi x}dx=\int_{4\xi N}^\infty y^{-1}e^{-y}dy\sim-\log\xi$$

as $\xi \downarrow 0$. Thus the lemma is proved since $m_\xi(\boldsymbol{R}^+)^{-1} \to 1$ as $\xi \downarrow 0$.

LEMMA 7. *$\xi^2 \int_0^\infty u_\xi(x)^2 m_\xi(dx) \to 0$ as $\xi \downarrow 0$.*

PROOF. In what follows *const.* means a constant which is independent of ξ but may vary from place to place. First we prove

$$0 < -u_\xi(x) \leqq const.\, x \log \frac{1}{\xi} \quad \text{for } 0 < x \leqq a_\xi. \tag{5.3}$$

The restriction $0 < x \leqq a_\xi$ implies

$$\begin{aligned} 0 < -u_\xi(x) &= 2\int_0^x \exp\{2y^{-1} + 4\xi y\}\, dy \int_0^y (a_\xi - z) z^{-2} \exp\{-2z^{-1} - 4\xi z\}\, dz \\ &\leqq 2a_\xi \int_0^x \exp\{2y^{-1} + 4\xi y\}\, dy \int_0^y z^{-2} \exp\{-2z^{-1} - 4\xi z\}\, dz. \end{aligned}$$

Since $0 < y < x < a_\xi \sim -2 \log \xi$ as $\xi \downarrow 0$, we have $0 < \xi y < \xi a_\xi \to 0$ as $\xi \downarrow 0$. Therefore

$$-u_\xi(x) \leqq const.\, \log \frac{1}{\xi} \int_0^x \exp\{2y^{-1}\}\, dy \int_0^y z^{-2} \exp\{-2z^{-1}\}\, dz \leqq const.\, x \log \frac{1}{\xi}$$

as was to be proved. Next we prove

$$0 < -u_\xi(x) \leqq const.\, x \log \frac{1}{\xi} + const.\, \frac{1}{\xi} \log \frac{x}{a_\xi} \quad \text{for } x > a_\xi. \tag{5.4}$$

Since

$$-\int_0^y (z - a_\xi) m_\xi(dz) = \int_y^\infty (z - a_\xi) m_\xi(dz),$$

$-u_\xi(x)$ can be expressed as $-u_\xi(x) = 2(I + II)$, where

$$\begin{aligned} 0 < I &= 2\int_0^{a_\xi} \exp\{2y^{-1} + 4\xi y\}\, dy \int_0^y (a_\xi - z) z^{-2} \exp\{-2z^{-1} - 4\xi z\}\, dz \\ &\leqq const.\, x \log \frac{1}{\xi} \quad \text{(by (5.3))}, \end{aligned}$$

$$\begin{aligned} 0 < II &= 2\int_{a_\xi}^x \exp\{2y^{-1} + 4\xi y\}\, dy \int_y^\infty (z - a_\xi) z^{-2} \exp\{-2z^{-1} - 4\xi z\}\, dz \\ &\leqq 2\int_{a_\xi}^x \exp\{2y^{-1} + 4\xi y\}\, dy \int_y^\infty z^{-1} \exp\{-4\xi z\}\, dz. \end{aligned}$$

If we put $g(y) = \int_y^\infty z^{-1} e^{-4\xi z}\, dz$, then

$$g(y)=\int_{4\xi y}^{\infty}u^{-1}e^{-u}du\leqq(4\xi y)^{-1}e^{-4\xi y},$$

and hence

$$II\leqq 2\int_{a_\xi}^{x}\exp\{2y^{-1}+4\xi y\}\cdot(4\xi y)^{-1}e^{-4\xi y}dy$$
$$\leqq const.\frac{1}{\xi}\int_{a_\xi}^{x}\frac{dy}{y}=const.\frac{1}{\xi}\log\frac{x}{a_\xi}.$$

This proves (5.4). We can now complete the proof of Lemma 7 as follows. From (5.3) and (5.4) we have

$$\xi^2\int_0^\infty u_\xi(x)^2 m_\xi(dx)\leq const.\Big(\xi\log\frac{1}{\xi}\Big)^2\int_0^{a_\xi}\exp\{-2x^{-1}-4\xi x\}dx$$
$$+const.\Big(\xi\log\frac{1}{\xi}\Big)^2\int_{a_\xi}^{\infty}\exp\{-2x^{-1}-4\xi x\}dx$$
$$+const.\int_{a_\xi}^{\infty}\Big(\log\frac{x}{a_\xi}\Big)^2x^{-2}\exp\{-2x^{-2}-4\xi x\}dx$$
$$\leq const.\Big(\xi\log\frac{1}{\xi}\Big)^2\int_0^\infty e^{-4\xi x}dx$$
$$+const.\int_{a_\xi}^{\infty}\Big(\log\frac{x}{a_\xi}\Big)^2x^{-2}dx$$
$$=const.\,\xi\Big(\log\frac{1}{\xi}\Big)^2+\frac{const.}{a_\xi}\int_1^\infty(\log y)^2y^{-2}dy$$
$$\to 0 \quad \text{as } \xi\downarrow 0.$$

LEMMA 8. $\Big(\log\frac{1}{\xi}\Big)^{-1}\xi\int_0^\infty|u_\xi'(x)|^2x^2m_\xi(dx)\to 0$ as $\xi\downarrow 0$.

PROOF. First we prove

(5.5) $$0<-u_\xi'(x)\leqq const.\log\frac{1}{\xi}\quad\text{for } 0<x\leqq a_\xi.$$

Under the restriction $0<x\leqq a_\xi$ we have

$$0<-u_\xi'(x)=2\exp\{2x^{-1}+4\xi x\}\int_0^x(a_\xi-y)y^{-2}\exp\{-2y^{-1}-4\xi y\}dy$$
$$<2a_\xi\exp\{2x^{-1}+4\xi x\}\int_0^x y^{-2}\exp\{-2y^{-1}-4\xi y\}dy$$
$$\leqq const.\log\frac{1}{\xi}e^{2/x}\int_0^x y^{-2}e^{-2/y}dy=const.\log\frac{1}{\xi}.$$

Next we prove

(5.6) $$0 < -u'_\xi(x) \leqq const.\, e^{4\xi x}\varphi(4\xi x) \quad \text{for } x > a_\xi,$$

where

$$\varphi(x) = \int_x^\infty y^{-1}e^{-y}dy.$$

In fact, if $x > a_\xi$ then

$$\begin{aligned} 0 < -u'_\xi(x) &= 2\exp\{2x^{-1}+4\xi x\}\int_x^\infty (y-a_\xi)y^{-2}\exp\{-2y^{-1}-4\xi y\}\,dy \\ &\leqq const.\, e^{4\xi x}\int_x^\infty y^{-1}e^{-4\xi y}dy \\ &= const.\, e^{4\xi x}\varphi(4\xi x). \end{aligned}$$

Now the proof of Lemma 8 is completed as follows.

$$\begin{aligned} &\left(\log\frac{1}{\xi}\right)^{-1}\xi\int_0^{a_\xi} |u'_\xi(x)|^2 x^2 m_\xi(dx) \\ &\leqq const.\, \xi \log\frac{1}{\xi}\int_0^{a_\xi} \exp\{-2x^{-1}-4\xi x\}\,dx \quad \text{(by (5.5))} \\ &\leqq const.\, \xi \log\frac{1}{\xi}\cdot a_\xi \to 0 \quad \text{as } \xi \downarrow 0. \end{aligned}$$

To estimate the integral over (a_ξ, ∞) we notice that

$$\varphi(x) \sim \begin{cases} e^{-x}/x & \text{as } x \to \infty, \\ \log\dfrac{1}{x} & \text{as } x \downarrow 0, \end{cases}$$

and hence $e^x\varphi(x)^2 \in L^1(0, \infty)$. Therefore

$$\begin{aligned} &\left(\log\frac{1}{\xi}\right)^{-1}\xi\int_{a_\xi}^\infty |u'_\xi(x)|^2 x^2 m_\xi(dx) \\ &\leqq const.\, \xi\left(\log\frac{1}{\xi}\right)^{-1}\int_{a_\xi}^\infty e^{4\xi x}\varphi(4\xi x)^2 dx \quad \text{(by (5.6))} \\ &= const. \left(\log\frac{1}{\xi}\right)^{-1}\int_{4\xi a_\xi}^\infty e^x\varphi(x)^2 dx \\ &\to 0 \quad \text{as } \xi \downarrow 0. \end{aligned}$$

We now proceed to the proof of Proposition 1. Since $\mathcal{L}_\xi u_\xi = x - a_\xi$, an application of Itô's formula yields

$$u_\xi(V_\xi(t)) - u_\xi(V_\xi(0)) = \int_0^t u'_\xi(V_\xi(s))V_\xi(s)dW(s) + \int_0^t (V_\xi(s)-a_\xi)ds.$$

Putting $t=x$, $\xi=\lambda(x\log x)^{-1}$ and multiplying the both sides of the above by $(x\log x)^{-1}$ we have

$$(5.7)\qquad (x\log x)^{-1}\int_0^x (V_\xi(s)-a_\xi)ds$$
$$=(x\log x)^{-1}\{u_\xi(V_\xi(x))-u_\xi(V_\xi(0))\}-(x\log x)^{-1}\int_0^x u'_\xi(V_\xi(s))V_\xi(s)dW(s).$$

The distribution of $V_\xi(s)$ is $c_\xi m_\xi(dx)$ where c_ξ is the normalizing constant which tends to a finite value as $\xi\downarrow 0$. Therefore the second moment of the left hand side of (5.7) is dominated by

$$const.(x\log x)^{-2}\int_0^\infty u_\xi(y)^2 m_\xi(dy)+const.(x\log x)^{-2}x\int_0^\infty |u'_\xi(y)|^2 y^2 m_\xi(dy),$$

which tends to 0 as $x\to\infty$ by virtue of Lemma 7 and Lemma 8 because

$$(x\log x)^{-2}x\sim\frac{1}{\lambda}\left(\log\frac{1}{\xi}\right)^{-1}\xi\quad\text{as } x\to\infty.$$

This combined with

$$(x\log x)^{-1}\int_0^x a_\xi ds\to 2\quad\text{as } x\to\infty$$

proves Proposition 1.

The assertion of (7) of Theorem 1 follows immediately from Proposition 1. The assertion (8) can be derived from (7) by a method similar to that used for deriving (6) in § 3.

§ 6. Proof of Theorem 1 in the case $\kappa>1$.

For any integer $k\geq 1$ we put $\tau_k=T_k-T_{k-1}$. Then for any $\lambda_1,\lambda_2,\cdots,\lambda_n\geq 0$ we have

$$(6.1)\qquad E_W^0\left\{\exp\left(-\sum_{k=1}^n\lambda_k\tau_k\right)\right\}=\prod_{k=1}^n E_W^{k-1}\{\exp(-\lambda_k\tau_k)\}$$
$$=\prod_{k=1}^n f(\Gamma_{k-1}W,\lambda_k),$$

where $f(W,\lambda)=E_W^0\{\exp(-\lambda T_1)\}$ and $\Gamma_x:\boldsymbol{W}\to\boldsymbol{W}$ (for fixed x) is defined by $(\Gamma_x W)(y)=W(x+y)-W(x)$ for any $y\in\boldsymbol{R}$. From (6.1) and the ergodicity of $\{\Gamma_x\}$ it follows that $\{\tau_k, k\geq 1, \mathcal{P}^0\}$ is stationary and ergodic. Therefore

$$(6.2)\qquad \lim_{n\to\infty}\frac{T_n}{n}=\lim_{n\to\infty}\frac{\tau_1+\cdots+\tau_n}{n}=\mathcal{E}^0\{\tau_1\},\quad \mathcal{P}^0\text{-}a.s..$$

The condition $\kappa>1$ is equivalent to the finiteness of $\mathcal{E}^0\{\tau_1\}$ as will be seen below. First we compute $E_W^0\{T_1\}$; the result is

$$E_W^0\{T_1\} = \int_0^1 dS_W(x)\int_{-\infty}^x m_W(dy).$$

Therefore

$$\begin{aligned}\mathcal{E}^0\{\tau_1\} &= E\{W_W^0(T_1)\}\\ &= 2\int_0^1 dx\int_{-\infty}^x E\{\exp\{W_\kappa(x)-W_\kappa(y)\}\}\,dy = \frac{4}{\kappa-1}.\end{aligned}$$

Thus (9) follows from (6.2). Next we prove (10). Clearly $\bar{\omega}(t)\to\infty$ as $t\uparrow\infty$ ($\mathcal{P}^0$-*a.s.*) and for any $\varepsilon>0$

$$\frac{T_{\bar{\omega}(t)}}{\bar{\omega}(t)} \leqq \frac{t}{\bar{\omega}(t)} < \frac{T_{\bar{\omega}(t)+\varepsilon}}{\bar{\omega}(t)}.$$

Letting $t\uparrow\infty$ in the above we obtain

$$\lim_{t\to\infty}\frac{t}{\bar{\omega}(t)} = \frac{4}{\kappa-1}, \quad \mathcal{P}^0\text{-}a.s.,$$

which means that the left hand side of (10) equals $(\kappa-1)/4$, a.s.. To prove that the second and the third terms of (10) equal $(\kappa-1)/4$, a.s., we put $\theta(n)=(1-\varepsilon)\cdot(\kappa-1)n/4$ for an integer $n\geqq 1$ and for $0<\varepsilon<1$. Then

$$\begin{aligned}&\mathcal{P}^0\Big\{\inf_{s\geq T_{\theta(n)}}\omega(s)-\theta(n)<-\sqrt{n}\Big\}\\ &= E\Big\{P_W^{\theta(n)}\Big(\inf_{s\geq 0}\omega(s)-\theta(n)<-\sqrt{n}\Big)\Big\}\\ &= \mathcal{P}^0\Big\{\inf_{s\geq 0}\omega(s)<-\sqrt{n}\Big\}.\end{aligned}$$

The last term in the above is a general term of a convergent series by the result of [**9**]. Therefore an application of Borel-Cantelli's lemma yields

$$\inf_{s\geq T_{\theta(n)}}\omega(s)-\theta(n)\geqq -\sqrt{n} \tag{6.3}$$

for all sufficiently large n, $\mathcal{P}^0$-*a.s.*. Since $T_{\theta(n)}/n\to 1-\varepsilon$ as $n\to\infty$ ($\mathcal{P}^0$-*a.s.*), (6.3) implies

$$\inf_{s\geq n}\omega(s)-\theta(n)\geqq -\sqrt{n} \tag{6.4}$$

for all sufficiently large n, $\mathcal{P}^0$-*a.s.*. For $t>0$ we now take $n=n(t)$ such that $n\leqq t<n+1$. Then (6.4) implies

(6.5) $$\theta(n)-\sqrt{n} \leqq \underline{\omega}(n) \leqq \underline{\omega}(t) \leqq \omega(t) \leqq \bar{\omega}(t)$$

for all sufficiently large t, $\mathcal{P}^0$-*a.s.*. Dividing (6.5) by t and then letting $t \uparrow \infty$ we finally see that the second and the third terms of (10) equal $(\kappa-1)/4$, $\mathcal{P}^0$-*a.s.*.

§7. Remark to the case $\kappa=0$.

A limit theorem concerning $\bar{\omega}(t)=\max\{\omega(s): 0\leqq s\leqq t\}$ was obtained by Kotani (1988), Ogura (1989) and Kawazu-Tanaka (1989) independently and by different methods (proofs were unpublished). The result is as follows. Let $t>0$ and put

$$W^{\#}(x)=W(x)-\min_{[x\wedge 0,\, x\vee 0]} W, \quad x\in \boldsymbol{R},$$
$$d_t^+=\min\{x>0: W^{\#}(x)=t\}, \quad V_t^+=\min_{[0,\, d_t^+]} W,$$
$$d_t^-=\max\{x<0: W^{\#}(x)=t\}, \quad V_t^-=\min_{[d_t^-,\, 0]} W,$$

and define b_t^+ and b_t^- by $W(b_t^{\pm})=V_t^{\pm}$ (such $b_t^{\pm}$ are uniquely determined P-a.s. for each fixed $t>0$). Let

$$M_t^+=\max_{[0,\, b_t^+]} W, \quad J_t^+=M_t^+\vee(V_t^++t),$$
$$M_t^-=\max_{[b_t^-,\, 0]} W, \quad J_t^-=M_t^-\vee(V_t^-+t),$$

and finally define $b_t^{\#}$ by

$$b_t^{\#}=\begin{cases}\min\{x>0: W^{\#}(x)=t\} & \text{if } J_t^+<J_t^-,\\ \min\{x>0: W(x)=J_t^-\} & \text{if } J_t^+>J_t^-.\end{cases}$$

Then the process $\{\lambda^{-2}\bar{\omega}(e^{\lambda t}),\ t>0,\ \mathcal{P}^0\}$ converges to $\{b_t^{\#},\ t>0,\ P\}$ as $\lambda\to\infty$ in the sense of convergence of finite dimensional distributions. In particular, $(\log t)^{-2}\bar{\omega}(t)$ converges in law to $b_1^{\#}$ as $t\to\infty$ and

$$E\{e^{-\xi b_1^{\#}}\}=\int_0^1 E_+^x\{e^{-\xi T_1}\}\,dx, \quad \xi\geqq 0,$$

where E_+^x and T_1 denote the expectation and the first hitting time to 1, respectively, for the reflecting Brownian motion on $[0, \infty)$ starting at x.

The corresponding result in the case of random walks on $\{0, 1, 2, \cdots\}$ with reflecting barrier at 0 was obtained by Golosov [**2**].

References

[1] T. Brox, A one-dimensional diffusion process in a Wiener medium, Ann. Probab., 14 (1986), 1206-1218.

[2] A.O. Golosov, Limit distributions for random walks in random environments, Soviet Math. Dokl., **28** (1983), 18-22.
[3] A.O. Golosov, Localization of random walks in one-dimensional random environments, Comm. Math. Phys., **92** (1984), 491-506.
[4] K. Itô, Stochastic Processes II, Iwanami, 1958, (in Japanese).
[5] K. Itô and M. Nisio, On stationary solutions of a stochastic differential equation, J. Math. Kyoto Univ., **4-1** (1964), 1-75.
[6] I.S. Kac and M.G. Krein, On the spectral functions of the string, Amer. Math. Soc. Transl. (2), **103** (1974), 19-102.
[7] Y. Kasahara, Spectral theory of generalized second order differential operators and its applications to Markov processes, Japan J. Math., **1** (1975), 67-84.
[8] K. Kawazu, Y. Tamura and H. Tanaka, Localization of diffusion processes in one-dimensional random environment, J. Math. Soc. Japan, **44** (1992), 515-550.
[9] K. Kawazu and H. Tanaka, On the maximum of a diffusion process in a drifted Brownian environment, In Séminaire de Probabilités, (eds. J. Azéma et al.), Lecture Notes in Math., **1557**, Springer-Verlag, 1993, 78-85.
[10] H. Kesten, M.V. Kozlov and F. Spitzer, A limit law for random walk in a random environment, Compositio Math., **30** (1975), 145-168.
[11] H. Kesten, The limit distribution of Sinai's random walk in random environment, Physica, **138A** (1986), 299-309.
[12] F.B. Knight, Characterization of the Lévy measure of inverse local times of gap diffusions, In Seminar on Stochastic Processes, Birkhäuser, 1981, 53-78.
[13] S. Kotani and S. Watanabe, Krein's spectral theory of strings and generalized diffusion processes, In Functional Analysis in Markov Processes, (ed. M. Fukushima), Lecture Notes in Math., **923**, Springer-Verlag, 1982, 235-259.
[14] M.V. Kozlov, A random walk on the line with stochastic structure, Theory Probab. Appl., **18** (1973), 406-408.
[15] Y. Ogura, One-dimensional bi-generalized diffusion processes, J. Math. Soc. Japan, **41** (1989), 213-242.
[16] S. Schumacher, Diffusions with random coefficients, Particle Systems, Random Media and Large Deviations, Contemp. Math., **41** (1985), 351-356.
[17] Ya.G. Sinai, The limiting behavior of a one-dimensional random walk in a random medium, Theory Probab. Appl., **27** (1982), 256-268.
[18] F. Solomon, Random walks in a random environment, Ann. Probab., **3** (1975), 1-31.
[19] H. Tanaka, Localization of a diffusion process in a one-dimensional Brownian environment, Comm. Pure Appl. Math., **XLVII** (1994), 755-766.
[20] S. Watanabe, On time inversion of one-dimensional diffusion processes, Z. Wahrscheinlichtkeitstheorie verw. Gebiete, **31** (1975), 115-124.

Kiyoshi KAWAZU
Department of Mathematics
Faculty of Education
Yamaguchi University
Yoshida, Yamaguchi 753
Japan

Hiroshi TANAKA
Department of Mathematics
Faculty of Science and Technology
Keio University
Hiyoshi, Yokohama 223
Japan

Pergamon

Chaos, Solitons & Fractals, Vol. 8, No. 11, pp. 1807–1816, 1997

0960-0779/97 $17.00 + 0.00

PII: S0960-0779(97)00029-5

Limit Theorems for a Brownian Motion with Drift in a White Noise Environment

HIROSHI TANAKA

Department of Mathematics, Faculty of Science and Technology, Keio University, 3-14-1 Hiyoshi, Kohoku-ku, Yokohama 233, Japan

Abstract—This paper discusses limit theorems for a diffusion analogue of Kesten–Kozlov–Spitzer's random walk in a random environment. The results obtained are similar to theirs but can be presented in a more explicit form by the use of Krein's spectral theory for one-dimensional generalized second-order differential operators of the form $\mathrm{d}/\mathrm{d}M\mathrm{d}/\mathrm{d}x$. © 1997 Elsevier Science Ltd

1. INTRODUCTION

The model of a random process in a random environment that we discuss in this paper has its origin on physical grounds in the works by Chernov [1] and Temkin [2]. Mathematical investigation of this model was then done by Kozlov [3], Kesten–Kozlov–Spitzer [4], Solomon [5] and Sinai [6], all in the framework of random walks. A diffusion analogue of Sinai's random walk was discussed by Brox [7] and Schumacher [8]. In this paper we discuss a diffusion model, namely, a model continuous in time and space (still in one dimension), which corresponds to what was discussed by Kesten–Kozlov–Spitzer in the framework of random walks. A rough description of our model is the following. Consider the heat or electric flow on a one-dimensional conductor such as a thin wire. Suppose the flow has a drift (or a bias) so that the movement takes place more likely to the right than to the left. In addition, the conductor contains some impurities located irregularly that cause fluctuation of the drift. We thus consider a particle performing Brownian motion with its own constant drift plus a random drift caused by impurities, or in a more mathematically idealized form, we consider the random process $X(t)$ described by the stochastic differential equation

$$\mathrm{d}X(t) = \mathrm{d}B(t) + \frac{\kappa}{4}\,\mathrm{d}t - \tfrac{1}{2}w'(X(t))\,\mathrm{d}t, \quad X(0) = 0, \tag{1}$$

where $B(t)$ is a standard one-dimensional Brownian motion, $\{w'(x),\ x \in \mathrm{R}\}$ is a white noise independent of $B(t)$ and κ is a non-negative constant. The problem is to know how the long-time behavior of $X(t)$ changes under the perturbation of the white noise term. The answer for this will vary with κ as in Kesten–Kozlov–Spitzer [4].

The case $\kappa = 0$ was treated by Brox [7] and Schumacher [8]; the limiting behavior of $X(t)$ as $t \to \infty$ is the same as that of Sinai's random walk, namely, the limit distribution of $(\log t)^{-2}X(t)$ as $t \to \infty$ exists. Kesten [9] proved that the limit distribution has a density

$$\frac{2}{\pi}\sum_{k=0}^{\infty}\frac{(-1)^k}{2k+1}\exp\{-(2k+1)^2\pi^2\,|x|/8\}.$$

The purpose of this paper is to report detailed results in the case $\kappa > 0$. In this case one may anticipate the result for $X(t)$ from that of Kesten–Kozlov–Spitzer. However, to obtain exact and more elaborated results such as the determination of constants appearing in the limit, we need rigorous arguments. The result for $0 < \kappa < 1$ and part of the results for $\kappa > 2$ were obtained by Kawazu–Tanaka [10, 11]. For the case $\kappa = 0$, cf. Tanaka [12] and references therein. The proof of the results for $1 \le \kappa \le 2$ is new but only its outline will be given (see Section 3). Full proof will appear elsewhere. It is to be noted that, our problem being formulated in the framework of diffusion processes, we can make much use of methods in differential equations, in particular, Krein's spectral theory. Our results (see Section 1) naturally correspond to those of Kesten–Kozlov–Spitzer, but some new light is shed from the viewpoint of methods. In Section 4 we give an explicit (but complicated) representation of the constant $c(\kappa)$ appearing in the limit distributions.

2. MAIN RESULTS

We begin with giving a precise definition of $X(t)$ since the stochastic differential eqn (1) has no rigorous meaning because of the term $w'(X(t))\mathrm{d}t$. By a formal argument we see that a "symbolic solution $X(t)$ of eqn (1)" is a diffusion process with the generator

$$\mathscr{L}_w = \frac{1}{2}\frac{\mathrm{d}^2}{\mathrm{d}x^2} + \frac{\kappa}{4}\frac{\mathrm{d}}{\mathrm{d}x} - \tfrac{1}{2}w'(x)\frac{\mathrm{d}}{\mathrm{d}x} = \tfrac{1}{2}\mathrm{e}^{w(x)-(\kappa x)/2}\frac{\mathrm{d}}{\mathrm{d}x}\left(\mathrm{e}^{-w(x)+(\kappa x)/2}\frac{\mathrm{d}}{\mathrm{d}x}\right).$$

The latter expression of $\mathscr{L}_w$ has a rigorous meaning since it is of the form of Feller's canonical representation of a generator (for a quick view cf., for example, Section 2.10 of Nagasawa [13]). The process $X(t)$ is therefore defined as the diffusion process with generator $\mathscr{L}_w$ (defined by the latter expression)—a Markov process with transition probability $\exp(t\mathscr{L}_w)(x,\mathrm{d}y)$. To be more precise we introduce the space $W = \{w \in C(\mathrm{R})\colon w(0) = 0\}$ and the Wiener measure P on W. Then the formal derivative $w'(x)$, $x \in \mathrm{R}$, is a white noise defined on the probability space (W,P). For each $w \in W$ we denote by P_w the probability law of the diffusion process with generator $\mathscr{L}_w$ starting from 0. Therefore, if $\Omega = C[0,\infty)$ and if $w(t)$ denotes the value of $w(\in \Omega)$ at time $t \ge 0$, then $\{w(t), t \ge 0, P_w\}$ is a diffusion process with generator $\mathscr{L}_w$ starting from 0. Let $\mathscr{P}(\mathrm{d}w\mathrm{d}w) = P(\mathrm{d}w)P_w(\mathrm{d}w)$. We then regard the process $\{w(t), t \ge 0\}$ as defined on the probability space $(W \times \Omega, \mathscr{P})$. This is the process $X(t)$ in the introduction and is called a Brownian motion with drift in a white noise environment in this paper.

We are interested in the long-time behavior of $w(t)$ as $t \to \infty$, or more precisely speaking, the limit distributions of $\tau(x)$ and $w(t)$ under the suitable centering and scaling as $x, t \to \infty$, where

$$\tau(x) = \inf\{s > 0 \colon \omega(s) = x\}, \quad x \ge 0,$$

Our main results are the following in which $c(\kappa)$ denotes a suitable constant depending on κ.

(I) (Kawazu–Tanaka [10]) If $0 < \kappa < 1$, then

$$\lim_{x\to\infty} \mathscr{P}\left\{\frac{\tau(x)}{x^{1/\kappa}} \le t\right\} = F_\kappa(t), \quad t > 0,$$

$$\lim_{t\to\infty} \mathscr{P}\left\{\frac{\omega(t)}{t^\kappa} \le x\right\} = 1 - F_\kappa(x^{-1/\kappa}), \quad x > 0,$$

where

$$\int_0^\infty \mathrm{e}^{-\xi t}\,\mathrm{d}F_\kappa(t) = \exp\{-c(\kappa)\xi^\kappa\}, \quad \xi \ge 0.$$

(II) If $\kappa = 1$, then

$$\lim_{x\to\infty} \mathscr{P}\left\{\frac{\tau(x) - 4x\log x}{x} \le t\right\} = F_1(t), \quad t \in \mathbb{R},$$

$$\lim_{t\to\infty} \mathscr{P}\left\{\frac{\omega(t) - \bar{\mu}(t)}{t(\log t)^{-2}} \le x\right\} = 1 - F_1(-16x), \quad x \in \mathbb{R},$$

where

$$\bar{\mu}(t) = t(4\log t)^{-1}\left(1 + \frac{\log\log t + \log 4}{\log t}\right),$$

$$\int_{-\infty}^{\infty} e^{-\xi t}\, dF_1(t) = \exp\{c(1)\xi + 4\xi\log\xi\}, \quad \xi \ge 0.$$

(III) If $1 < \kappa < 2$, then

$$\lim_{x\to\infty} \mathscr{P}\left\{\frac{\tau(x) - mx}{x^{1/\kappa}} \le t\right\} = F_\kappa(t), \quad t \in \mathbb{R},$$

$$\lim_{t\to\infty} \mathscr{P}\left\{\frac{\omega(t) - m^{-1}t}{t^{1/\kappa}} \le x\right\} = 1 - F_\kappa(-m^{1+1/\kappa}x), \quad x \in \mathbb{R},$$

where $m = 4(\kappa - 1)^{-1}$ and

$$\int_{-\infty}^{\infty} e^{-\xi t}\, dF_\kappa(t) = \exp\{c(\kappa)\xi^\kappa\}, \quad \xi \ge 0.$$

(IV) If $\kappa = 2$, then

$$\lim_{x\to\infty} \mathscr{P}\left\{\frac{\tau(x) - 4x}{\sqrt{x\log x}} \le t\right\} = (2^8\pi)^{1/2}\int_{-\infty}^{t} e^{-2^{-8}s^2}\, ds, \quad t \in \mathbb{R},$$

$$\lim_{t\to\infty} \mathscr{P}\left\{\frac{\omega(t) - (t/4)}{\sqrt{t\log t}} \le x\right\} = (2\pi)^{-1/2}\int_{-\infty}^{x} e^{-y^2/2}\, dy, \quad x \in \mathbb{R}.$$

(V) Assume $\kappa > 2$.

(i) Environment-wise invariance principle [14].
(a) For almost all w (with respect to P) the process

$$\left\{\frac{\tau(\lambda x) - M(\lambda x)}{\sqrt{A\lambda}}, \ x \ge 0, \ P_w\right\}$$

converges in law to a Brownian motion as $\lambda \to \infty$ (in the sense of convergence of probability measures on the Skorohod space) where $A = 64(\kappa - 1)^{-2}(\kappa - 2)^{-1}$ and

$$M(x) = E_w\{\tau(x)\}$$
$$= 2\int_0^x dy \int_{-\infty}^{y} \exp\left\{w(y) - w(z) - \frac{\kappa(y - z)}{2}\right\} dz, \quad x \ge 0.$$

(In this theorem the definition of $\tau(x)$ is modified slightly so that $\tau(x)$ becomes right continuous in x, namely, $\tau(x) = \inf\{s > 0: \omega(s) > x\}$).

(b) For almost all w the process

$$\left\{\frac{\omega(\lambda t)-\mu(\lambda t)}{\sqrt{m^{-3}A\lambda}},\ t\geq 0,\ P_w\right\}$$

converges in law to a Brownian motion as $\lambda \to \infty$ where A is the same as in (a), $m=4(\kappa-1)^{-1}$ and $\mu(t)$ is the inverse function of $M(x)$.

(ii) Invariance principle in random environment [11]. Each of the processes

$$\left\{\frac{\tau(\lambda x)-\lambda m x}{\sqrt{C\lambda}},\ x\geq 0, \mathcal{P}\right\},\ \left\{\frac{\omega(\lambda t)-\lambda m^{-1}t}{\sqrt{m^{-3}C\lambda}},\ t>0, \mathcal{P}\right\}$$

converges in law to a Brownian motion as $\lambda \to \infty$ where m is the same as in (i) and $C=64\kappa(\kappa-1)^{-3}(\kappa-2)^{-1}>A$.

Let E denote the expectation with respect to $\mathcal{P}$. Then it is easy to see that $E\{\tau(x)\}<\infty$ iff $\kappa>1$ and $E\{\tau(x)^2\}<\infty$ iff $\kappa>2$ for $x>0$. This is a simple reason why the result is divided into the five cases (I)–(V).

3. KEY METHODS

Here are two key methods in our arguments. One is to use Kotani's formula which reduces our problem to the study of another diffusion process $X_\lambda(t)$ described by a certain stochastic differential equation with non-random coefficients. The other is to use Krein's spectral theory with which we can obtain some asymptotic properties of the Laplace transform of a certain hitting time of $X_\lambda(t)$.

3.1. Kotani's formula (unpublished; see Ref. [10] for a proof)

For $\lambda \geq 0$ and $t\geq 0$ (we use t instead of x)

$$E_w\{e^{-\lambda\tau(t)}\}=\exp\left\{-\int_0^t U_\lambda(s)\,ds\right\},\ P-\text{a.s.,} \tag{2}$$

where $U_\lambda(t)$ is the unique stationary positive solution of

$$dU_\lambda(t)=U_\lambda(t)\,dw(t)+\left\{2\lambda+\frac{1-\kappa}{2}U_\lambda(t)-U_\lambda(t)^2\right\}dt.$$

For our later arguments it is convenient to consider $X_\lambda(t)=(2\lambda)^{-1}U_\lambda(t)$, $\lambda>0$. Kotani's formula eqn (2) then yields

$$E_w\{e^{-\lambda\tau(t)}\}=\exp\left\{-2\lambda\int_0^t X_\lambda(s)\,ds\right\},\ P-\text{a.s.,} \tag{3}$$

and $X_\lambda(t)$ is a stationary diffusion process on $\mathbb{R}^+=(0,\infty)$ obtained as the unique stationary positive solution of

$$dX_\lambda(t)=X_\lambda(t)\,dw(t)+\left(1+\frac{1-\kappa}{2}X_\lambda(t)-2\lambda X_\lambda(t)^2\right)dt. \tag{4}$$

Note that eqns (3) and (4) hold for $\lambda\geq 0$. The generator $\mathcal{L}_\lambda$ of $X_\lambda(t)$ is given by

$$\mathcal{L}_\lambda=\frac{d}{m_\lambda(dx)}\frac{d}{ds_\lambda(x)},$$

where

$$s_\lambda(x) = \int_1^x y^{\kappa-1} \exp\left(\frac{2}{y} + 4\lambda y\right) dy, \tag{5}$$

$$m_\lambda(dx) = 2x^{-\kappa-1} \exp\left(-\frac{2}{x} - 4\lambda x\right) dx, \; x > 0. \tag{6}$$

3.2. Krein's spectral theory (Ref. [15], see also Refs [16–18])

Here we sketch its main part. Let $\mathcal{M}$ be the class of functions $M:[0,\infty) \to [0,\infty]$ that are right continuous and non-decreasing. Note that $\mathcal{M}$ contains the function $\equiv\infty$. We put $M(0-) = 0$ and $l = l_M = \sup\{x: M(x) < \infty\}$. When $l > 0$ (i.e. $\mathcal{M}(x) \not\equiv \infty$) we consider

$$\varphi(x,\alpha) = 1 + \alpha \int_0^x dy \int_{0-}^y \varphi(z,\alpha)\, dM(z), \; 0 \le x < l,$$

$$h(\alpha) = \int_0^l \frac{dx}{\varphi(x,\alpha)^2}, \; \alpha > 0, \; (< \infty \text{ if } M(x) \not\equiv 0).$$

When $l = 0$ (i.e. $M(x) \equiv \infty$) we put $h(\alpha) \equiv 0$. The function $h(\alpha)$ is called the characteristic function of $M(x)$ and the correspondence $M(x) \leftrightarrow h(\alpha)$ is called Krein's correspondence. When $M(x) \not\equiv 0$, $h(\alpha)$ can be represented as

$$h(\alpha) = c + \int_{0-}^\infty \frac{\sigma(d\xi)}{\alpha + \xi}, \; \alpha > 0, \tag{7}$$

where $c \ge 0$ and $\sigma(d\xi)$ is a measure on $[0,\infty)$ such that

$$0 < c + \int_{0-}^\infty \frac{\sigma(d\xi)}{1 + \xi} < \infty.$$

Let $\mathcal{H}$ be the class of functions h of the form of eqn (7) augmented by the functions that are identically equal to 0 or to ∞. Then one of the main results in Krein's theory is that the correspondence

$$M \in \mathcal{M} \leftrightarrow h \in \mathcal{H}$$

is one-to-one, onto and induces a homeomorphism under suitable topologies on $\mathcal{M}$ and $\mathcal{H}$. We now list up some facts that will be used in our arguments.

(i) For positive constants a and

$$\mathrm{acM(ax)} \leftrightarrow \frac{1}{\mathrm{a}} \mathrm{h}(\mathrm{c}\alpha).$$

(ii) When $l = \infty$, $\lim_{\alpha \downarrow 0} 1/\{\alpha h(\alpha)\} = M(\infty -) = 1/\sigma(\{0\})$ (when $l < \infty$, the limit $= \infty$).
(iii) (Krein [19], see also [16]: p. 266, [18]: p. 239). Let $l = \infty$ and put

$$h^*(\alpha) = h(\alpha) - \frac{\sigma(\{0\})}{\alpha} = c + \int_{0+}^\infty \frac{\sigma(d\xi)}{\alpha + \xi} \in \mathcal{H}.$$

Then

$$h^*(\alpha) \leftrightarrow M^*(x)$$

where

$$M^*(x) = M(\gamma^{-1}(x)) \Big/ \left(1 - \frac{M(\gamma^{-1}(x))}{M(\infty -)}\right),$$

$\gamma^{-1}(x)$ is the inverse function of

$$\gamma(t)=\int_0^t\left(1-\frac{M(s)}{M(\infty-)}\right)^2 \mathrm{d}s,\ l^*=\int_0^\infty\left(1-\frac{M(s)}{M(\infty-)}\right)^2 \mathrm{d}s.$$

4. OUTLINE OF PROOF

We give here an outline of the proof of (II) since (III) and (IV) can be proved in the same spirit as (II). The key points in the proof are to make use of Kotani's formula and fact (iii) in Section 2. From a technical viewpoint of our proof, it is convenient to regard x in the first limit theorem of (II) *as time* so we use habitual notation t instead of x.

From now on we assume $\kappa=1$ and put $\lambda=\xi t^{-1}$ where $\xi>0$ and $t>0$; ξ is fixed but later we let $t\to\infty$ so $\lambda\downarrow 0$. By Kotani's formula we have

$$\mathcal{E}\left\{\exp\left(-\xi\frac{\tau(t)-4t\log t}{t}\right);A\right\}=E\{\mathrm{e}^{-V(t)};A\}\mathrm{e}^{4\xi\log t} \tag{8}$$

for any event A in the probability space (W,P), where

$$V(t)=2\lambda\int_0^t X_\lambda(s)\,\mathrm{d}s$$

and the notation $\mathcal{E}\{X;A\}$ (resp. $E\{X;A\}$) stands for the integral of X over A with respect to $\mathcal{P}$ (resp. P). Given $a>0$ we define a_λ by $s_\lambda(a_\lambda)=a$ where $s_\lambda(x)$ is given by eqn (5) with $\kappa=1$. Obviously $a_\lambda>1$ and $a_\lambda\uparrow a_0$ as $\lambda\downarrow 0$. We define stopping times T_n, T_n', $n=0,1,\ldots$, based on the process $X_\lambda(s)$ as follows:

$$T_0=\inf\{s>0:X_\lambda(s)=a_\lambda\},\quad T_0'=\inf\{s>T_0:X_\lambda(s)=1\},$$

$$T_n=\inf\{s>T_{n-1}':X_\lambda(s)=a_\lambda\},\quad T_n'=\inf\{s>T_n:X_\lambda(s)=1\},\quad n\geq 1.$$

Then T_n-T_{n-1}, $n=1,2,\ldots$, are i.i.d. random variables with

$$E\{T_n-T_{n-1}\}=am_\lambda,$$

$$\mathrm{Var}\{T_n-T_{n-1}\}\leq\text{const.},\quad 0\leq\lambda\leq 1,$$

where m_λ is the total mass $m_\lambda(\mathbb{R}^+)$ of the measure defined by eqn (6) with $\kappa=1$ and const. is independent of λ. Therefore

$$P\left\{\left|\frac{T_n-T_0}{n}-am_\lambda\right|>\varepsilon\right\}\leq\frac{\text{const.}}{\varepsilon^2 n},\quad(\varepsilon>0). \tag{9}$$

Let $\varepsilon(t)=t^{-1/2}(\log t)^{1/4}$ and put

$$n_1(t)=\left[\frac{t(1-\varepsilon(t))}{am_\lambda}\right],\quad n_2(t)=\left[\frac{t(1+\varepsilon(t))}{am_\lambda}\right].$$

Then $n_i(t)\sim t(am_0)^{-1}$ as $t\to\infty$ because $m_\lambda\to m_0$ as $\lambda\downarrow 0$. Therefore inequality (9) implies, for $i=1$ and 2,

$$P\left\{\left|\frac{T_{n_i(t)}-T_0}{n_i(t)}-am_\lambda\right|>\varepsilon(t)\right\}\to 0\text{ as }t\to\infty. \tag{10}$$

We now put $A_t(\xi)=\{T_{n_1(t)}<t<T_{n_2(t)}\}$. Then, by making use of fact (10) we can prove that

$P\{A_t(\xi)\} \to 1$ as $t \to \infty$ for each fixed $\xi > 0$. On the other hand, by the definition of $A_t(\xi)$, writing $T(n)$ instead of T_n we have

$$E\{e^{-V(T(n_2(t)))}; A(\xi)\} e^{4\xi \log t} \le E\{e^{-V(t)}; A_t(\xi)\} e^{4\xi \log t}$$
$$\le E\{e^{-V(T(n_1(t)))}; A_t(\xi)\} e^{4\xi \log t}. \quad (11)$$

Next we are going to prove, for $i = 1$ and 2, that

$$\lim_{t \to \infty} E\{e^{-\alpha V(T(n_i(t)))}\} e^{4\alpha\xi \log t} = \exp\{2\alpha k(\alpha)\xi + 4\alpha\xi \log \xi\}, \ \alpha > 0, \quad (12)$$

with some constant $k(\alpha) > 0$. Making use of the strong Markov property of $X_\lambda(s)$ we see that

$$E\{e^{-\alpha V(T(n(t)))}\} = E_0(E_1 E_2)^{n(t)},$$

where

$$E_0 = E\left\{\exp\left(-2\lambda\alpha \int_0^{T_0} X_\lambda(s)\, ds\right)\right\}, \ E_1 = E\left\{\exp\left(-2\lambda\alpha \int_{T_0}^{T_0'} X_\lambda(s)\, ds\right)\right\},$$

$$E_2 = E\left\{\exp\left(-2\lambda\alpha \int_{T_0'}^{T_1} X_\lambda(s)\, ds\right)\right\},$$

and the suffix i in $n_i(t)$ is suppressed to simplify the notation. Let $\tilde{X}_\lambda(s) = s_\lambda(X_\lambda(\Phi_\lambda^{-1}(s)))$ where $\Phi^{-1}{}_\lambda(s)$ is the inverse function of $\Phi_\lambda(\mathrm{r}) = \int_0^{\mathrm{r}} X_\lambda(u)\, du$. Then $X_\lambda(s)$ is a stationary diffusion process in $\mathbb{R}$ with generator

$$\tilde{\mathscr{L}}_\lambda = \frac{\mathrm{d}}{\mu_\lambda(\mathrm{d}x)} \frac{d}{\mathrm{d}x}$$

where

$$\mu_\lambda(\mathrm{d}x) = 2\theta_\lambda(x)^{-1} \exp\left\{-\frac{4}{\theta_\lambda(x)} - 8\lambda\theta_\lambda(x)\right\} \mathrm{d}x,$$

$$\theta_\lambda(x) = \text{the inverse function of } s_\lambda(\cdot).$$

Denote by $\left\{\omega(t), t \ge 0, \tilde{P}_\lambda^x\right\}$ the path-space representation of the diffusion process with generator $\tilde{\mathscr{L}}_\lambda$ starting from x. Then we can prove that

$$E_1 = \tilde{E}_\lambda^a\{e^{-2\lambda\alpha\tilde{\tau}}\} = u_\lambda(a, 2\lambda\alpha),$$

where $\tilde{\tau} = \inf\{s > 0: \omega(s) = 0\}$ and $u_\lambda(x,\alpha) \equiv \tilde{E}_\lambda^x\{e^{-\alpha\tilde{\tau}}\}$ is the unique positive decreasing solution of $\tilde{\mathscr{L}}_\lambda u = \alpha u$, $x \ge 0$ with $u(0) = 1$. The solution $u_\lambda(x,\alpha)$ can be expressed as

$$u_\lambda(x,\alpha) = \varphi_\lambda(x,\alpha) - \frac{\psi_\lambda(x,\alpha)}{h_\lambda(\alpha)}, \quad \alpha > 0,$$

where $\varphi_\lambda(x,\alpha)$ and $\psi_\lambda(x,\alpha)$ are the solutions of

$$\varphi_\lambda(x,\alpha) = 1 + \alpha \int_0^x \mathrm{d}y \int_0^y \varphi_\lambda(z,\alpha)\mu_\lambda(\mathrm{d}z),$$

$$\psi_\lambda(x,\alpha) = x + \alpha \int_0^x \mathrm{d}y \int_0^y \psi_\lambda(z,\alpha)\mu_\lambda(\mathrm{d}z),$$

respectively, and $h_\lambda(\alpha) \leftrightarrow M_\lambda(x) \equiv \mu_\lambda([0,x])$. What we want to know is the behavior of

$1-E_1$, namely, of $1-u_\lambda(a,2\lambda\alpha)$ as $\lambda\downarrow 0$. For this it is enough to know the behavior of $h_\lambda(2\lambda\alpha)$ as $\lambda\downarrow 0$. By fact (iii) of Section 2 we see that

$$h_\lambda^*(\alpha)\equiv h_\lambda(\alpha)-\frac{1}{\alpha\mu_\lambda([0,\infty))}\leftrightarrow M_\lambda^*(x)$$

where the explicit form of $M_\lambda^*(x)$ is given in terms of $M_\lambda(x)\equiv\mu_\lambda([0,x])$. Now an essential step is the following Lemma 1, which is stated in general $(1\le\kappa\le 2)$. We put

$$\mathrm{e}_\kappa(x)=\int_x^\infty y^{-\kappa}\,\mathrm{e}^{-4y}\,\mathrm{d}y,\ f_\kappa(x)=\int_0^x y^{\kappa-1}\,\mathrm{e}^{4y}\,\mathrm{d}y, \tag{13}$$

$$g_\kappa(x)=4\int_0^x\{\mathrm{e}_\kappa(f_\kappa^{-1}(y))\}^2\,\mathrm{d}y,\ f_\kappa^{-1}=\text{the inverse function}, \tag{14}$$

$$M_\lambda=\mu_\lambda([0,\infty))=2\int_1^\infty x^{-\kappa}\exp\left(-\frac{2}{x}-4\lambda x\right)\mathrm{d}x. \tag{15}$$

4.1. Lemma 1

(i) If $1\le\kappa<2$, then

$$\lim_{\lambda\downarrow 0}M_\lambda^{-2}\lambda^{\kappa-1}M_\lambda^*(M_\lambda^{-2}\lambda^{\kappa-2}x)=M^*(x),\ x>0,\ x\ne l^*,$$

where

$$M^*(x)=\begin{cases}\dfrac{1}{2(\mathrm{e}_\kappa\circ f_\kappa^{-1}\circ g_\kappa^{-1})(x)} & \text{for } 0<x<l^*,\\ \infty & \text{for } x\ge l^*,\end{cases} \tag{16}$$

$$l^*=g_\kappa(\infty)<\infty.$$

Therefore

$$\lim_{\lambda\downarrow 0}M_\lambda^{-2}\lambda^{-(\kappa-2)}h_\lambda^*(\lambda\alpha)=h^*(\alpha),\ \alpha>0, \tag{17}$$

where $h^*(\alpha)\leftrightarrow M^*(x)$.

(ii) If $\kappa=2$, then

$$\lim_{\lambda\downarrow 0}\lambda\log\frac{1}{\lambda}M_\lambda^*\left(x\log\frac{1}{\lambda}\right)=M^*(x),\ x>0,\ x\ne l^*,$$

where $l^*=4/M_0^2$, and $M^*(x)=0$ for $0\le x<l^*$ and $=\infty$ for $x\ge l^*$. Therefore

$$\lim_{\lambda\downarrow 0}\left(\log\frac{1}{\lambda}\right)^{-1}h_\lambda^*(\lambda\alpha)=h^*(\alpha),\ \alpha>0,$$

where $h^*(\alpha)\equiv l^*\leftrightarrow M^*(x)$.

Coming back to the case $\kappa=1$, we now know the behavior of $h_\lambda^*(2\lambda\alpha)$ as $\lambda\downarrow 0$ from eqn (17) with $\kappa=1$. Therefore we know the behavior of $1-E_1$ as $\lambda\downarrow 0$ and similarly of $1-E_2$. Thus we can obtain the following result:

$$E_1E_2=1-4a\alpha\lambda\log\frac{1}{\lambda}+2a\alpha k(\alpha)\lambda(1+o(1))\quad\text{as } \lambda\downarrow 0; \tag{18}$$

$$k(\alpha)=2\int_0^1(2-\mathrm{e}^{-4x}-\mathrm{e}^{-2x}-\mathrm{e}^{-4/x}-\mathrm{e}^{-2/x})\frac{\mathrm{d}x}{x}+2\alpha h^*(2\alpha). \tag{19}$$

Noting that $E_0 \to 1$ as $t \to \infty$, we finally obtain

$$E\{e^{-\alpha V(T(n(t)))}\}\, e^{4\alpha\xi \log t} \sim (E_1 E_2)^{n(t)}\, e^{4\alpha\xi \log t}$$
$$\sim (1 + 2a\alpha k(\alpha)\lambda)^{n(t)}\, e^{4\alpha\xi \log t - 4a\alpha n(t)\lambda \log 1/\lambda}$$
$$\to \exp\{2\alpha k(\alpha)\xi + 4\alpha\xi \log \xi\} \quad \text{as } t \to \infty,$$

proving eqn (12). Combining eqn (12) with the fact that $P\{A_t(\xi)\} \to 1$ as $t \to \infty$, we have

$$\lim_{t\to\infty} E\{e^{-V(t)}; A_t(\xi)\} = \lim_{t\to\infty} E\{e^{-V(t)}; A_t(\xi) \cap A_t(\xi+1)\}$$
$$= \exp\{2k(1)\xi + 4\xi \log \xi\},$$

which again combined with eqn (8) and inequality (11) implies

$$\lim_{t\to\infty} E\left\{\exp\left(-\xi\frac{\tau(t) - 4t\log t}{t}\right); A_t(\xi)\right\} = \lim_{t\to\infty} E\left\{\exp\left(-\xi\frac{\tau(t) - 4t\log t}{t}\right); A_t(\xi) \cap A_t(\xi+1)\right\}$$
$$= \exp\{2k(1)\xi + 4\xi \log \xi\}.$$

This proves the first limit theorem of (II) with $c(\kappa) = 2k(1)$ in virtue of the following technical lemma.

4.2. Lemma 2

Suppose we are given a sequence of random variables $\{X_n, n = 1, 2, ...\}$ and a sequence of events $\{A_n(\xi), n = 1, 2, ...\}$ for each $\xi \ge 0$. We put

$$\varphi_n(\xi) = E\{e^{-\xi X_n}; A_n(\xi)\},$$
$$\psi_n(\xi) = E\{e^{-\xi X_n}; A_n(\xi) \cap A_n(\xi+1)\},$$

and assume that the following conditions are satisfied:

(i) $\lim_{n\to\infty} P\{A_n(\xi)\} = 1$ *for* $\xi \ge 0$.
(ii) There exists a continuous function $\varphi(\xi)$ on $[0,\infty)$ such that

$$\lim_{n\to\infty} \varphi_n(\xi) = \lim_{n\to\infty} \psi_n(\xi) = \varphi(\xi) \quad \text{for } \xi \ge 0.$$

Then X_n converges in law as $n \to \infty$ to some random variable X whose law is uniquely determined by $E\{e^{-\xi X}\} = \varphi(\xi)$, $\xi \ge 0$.

To close this section we remark that the second limit theorem of (II) can be obtained from the first one with a small amount of effort.

5. REMARKS

1. The limit distribution dF_κ is strictly stable if $\kappa \ne 1$ and stable if $\kappa = 1$. The limit distribution concerning $\omega(t)$ is also strictly stable except for the case $0 < \kappa \le 1$. It is the Mittag–Leffler distribution if $0 < \kappa < 1$ and a stable distribution if $\kappa = 1$.
2. The constant $c(\kappa)$ appearing in dF_κ is given as follows.
 (I) If $0 < \kappa < 1$, then

$$c(\kappa) = \{2^{1-\kappa}\Gamma(\kappa)h(2)\}^{-1},$$

 where $h(\alpha)$ is the characteristic function of $M(x) = 2\gamma(f_\kappa^{-1}(x))$, $f_\kappa(x)$ is given by eqn (13) and $\gamma(x) = \int_0^x y^{-\kappa} e^{-4y}\, dy$ (see Ref. [10]).

(II) If $\kappa = 1$, then

$$c(1) = 4\int_0^1 (2 - e^{-4x} - e^{-2x} - e^{-4/x} - e^{-2/x})\frac{dx}{x} + 4h^*(2).$$

(III) If $1 < \kappa < 2$, then

$$c(\kappa) = 2\left\{\frac{8}{\kappa - 1}\int_0^\infty x^{-\kappa+1}e^{-4x}\,dx + 2h^*(2)\right\}/m_0$$

$$= \left\{\frac{2^{2\kappa}}{\kappa - 1}\Gamma(2-\kappa) + 4h^*(2)\right\}/\{2^{1-\kappa}\Gamma(\kappa)\}.$$

In (II) and (III) $h^*(\alpha)$ is the characteristic function of $M^*(x)$ defined by eqn (16).

REFERENCES

1. Chernov, A. A., Replication of a multicomponent chain by the lightning mechanism. *Biofizika*, 1967, **12,** 297–301.
2. Temkin, D. E., One-dimensional random walks in a two-component chain. *Dokl. Akad. Nauk SSSR*, 1972, **206,** 27–30.
3. Kozlov, M. V., Random walk on the line with stochastic structure. *Theor. Probab. Appl.*, 1973, **18,** 406–408.
4. Kesten, H., Kozlov, M. V. and Spitzer, F., A limit law for random walk in a random environment. *Composito Math.*, 1975, **30,** 145–168.
5. Solomon, F., Random walks in a random environment. *Ann. Probab.*, 1975, **3,** 1–31.
6. Sinai, Ya. G., The limiting behavior of a one-dimensional random walk in a random medium. *Theor. Probab. Appl.*, 1982, **27,** 256–268.
7. Brox, T., A one-dimensional diffusion process in a Wiener medium. *Ann. Probab.*, 1986, **14,** 1206–1218.
8. Schumacher, S., Diffusions with random coefficients. In *Contemporally Math, Particle Systems, Random Media and Large Deviations,* ed. R. Durrett. American Mathematical Society, New York, 1985, Vol. 41, pp. 351–356.
9. Kesten, H., The limit distribution of Sinai's random walk in random environment. *Physica*, 1986, **138A,** 299–309.
10. Kawazu, K., and Tanaka, H., A diffusion process in a Brownian environment with drift. *J. Math. Soc. Japan*, 1997, **49,** 189–211.
11. Kawazu, K. and Tanaka, H., Invariance principle for a Brownian motion with large drift in a white noise environment (preprint).
12. Tanaka, H., Diffusion processes in random environments. In *Proc. International Congress of Mathematicians*, Zürich, 1994, Switzerland. Birkhäuser, Basel, 1995, pp. 1047–1054.
13. Nagasawa, M., *Schrödinger Equations and Diffusion Theory*. Birkhäuser, Berlin, 1993.
14. Tanaka, H., Environment-wise central limit theorem for a diffusion in a Brownian environment with large drift. In *Itô's Stochastic Calculus and Probability Theory,* eds N. Ikeda *et al*. Springer, Berlin, 1996, pp. 373–384.
15. Krein, M. G., On a generalization of an investigation of Stieltjes. *Dokl. Akad. Nauk SSR*, 1952, **87,** 881–884.
16. Dym, H. and McKean, H. P., *Gaussian Processes, Function Theory, and the Inverse Spectral Problem*. Academic Press, New York, 1976.
17. Kasahara, Y., Spectral theory of generalized second order differential operators and its applications to Markov processes. *Japanese J. Math.*, 1975, **1,** 67–84.
18. Kotani, S. and Watanabe, S., Krein's spectral theory of strings and generalized diffusion processes. In *Functional Analysis in Markov Processes, Lecture Notes in Math,* ed. M. Fukushima. Springer, Berlin, 1982, Vol. 923, pp. 235–259.
19. Krein, M. G., On some cases of the effective determination of the density of a non-homogeneous string from its spectral function. *Dokl. Akad. Nauk SSSR*, 1953, **93,** 617–620.

Hiroshima Math. J.
28 (1998), 129–137

Invariance principle for a Brownian motion with large drift in a white noise environment

Kiyoshi Kawazu and Hiroshi Tanaka

(Received November 14, 1996)

Abstract. This paper discusses an invariance principle for a Brownian motion with drift coefficient $\kappa/4$ in a white noise environment under the assumption that κ is large. Our method clarifies the relation between the environment-wise invariance principle discussed in [7] and the present result (the invariance principle in random environment).

Introduction

Let W be the space of continuous functions on $\mathbf{R}$ vanishing at 0 that is equipped with the Wiener measure P. For an element $w \in W$ let us denote by w_κ the element of W defined by $w_\kappa(x) = w(x) - (\kappa x/2)$ where κ is a given positive constant. For $w \in W$, P_w denotes the probability measure on $\Omega = C[0, \infty)$ such that $\mathbf{X}_x = \{\omega(t), t \geq 0, P_w\}$ is a diffusion process with generator

$$\mathscr{L}_w = \frac{1}{2} e^{w_\kappa}(x) \frac{d}{dx}\left(e^{-w_\kappa}(x)\frac{d}{dx}\right)$$

starting at 0, where $\omega(t)$ is the value of a function $\omega(\in \Omega)$ at time t. We regard $\omega(t)$ as a process defined on the probability space $\{W \times \Omega, \mathscr{P}\}$ where $\mathscr{P}(dw\, d\omega) = P(dw)P_w(d\omega)$. Then symbolically

$$d\omega(t) = dB(t) + \frac{\kappa}{4}\, dt - \frac{1}{2} w'(\omega(t))\, dt,$$

where $B(t)$ is a standard Brownian motion independent of the white noise $\{w'(x)\}$. We call the process $\mathbf{X} = \{\omega(t), t \geq 0, \mathscr{P}\}$ a Brownian motion with drift in a white noise environment; in [2] [6] [7] it is called a diffusion process in a Brownian environment with drift. The present authors obtained some limit theorems for $\mathbf{X}$ in [2] (see [8] for further results; see also [6] for a brief survey on related problems), which are analogous to those of [3] and [5]; however, some problems remain open. The present paper is a continuation of [7] and

---

1991 *Mathematics Subject Classification.* 60J60

Key words and phrases. Invariance principle, Brownian motion, Random environment.

discusses the central limit theorem, or more precisely speaking, invariance principle *in random environment* in the case $\kappa > 2$.

We set

$$M_x(= M(x)) = 2\int_0^x dy \int_{-\infty}^y e^{w_\kappa(y)-w_\kappa(z)}\,dz, x \in \mathbf{R},$$

$$\mu(t) = \text{the inverse function of } \{M_x, x \in \mathbf{R}\}, t \in \mathbf{R},$$

$$T_x(= T(x)) = \inf\{t > 0 : \omega(t) > x\}, x \geq 0.$$

We use also the following notation:

$$\bar{\omega}(t) = \max\{\omega(s) : 0 \leq s \leq t\}, \underline{\omega}(t) = \inf\{\omega(s) : s \geq t\}, (\omega \in \Omega),$$

$$\gamma = (\kappa - 1)/2, m = 4/(\kappa - 1) = 2/\gamma,$$

$$A = 64(\kappa - 1)^{-2}(\kappa - 2)^{-1} = 16\gamma^{-2}(2\gamma - 1)^{-1},$$

$$B = 64(\kappa - 1)^{-3}(\kappa - 2)^{-1} = 8\gamma^{-3}(2\gamma - 1)^{-1},$$

$$C = A + B = 64\kappa(\kappa - 1)^{-3}(\kappa - 2)^{-1} = 8(2\gamma + 1)\gamma^{-3}(2\gamma - 1)^{-1}.$$

The following theorem was proved in [7].

THEOREM A (*Environment-wise invariance principle, see* [7]). *When* $\kappa > 2$, *we have the following*:

(i) *For almost all* $w \in W$ *with respect to* P, *the process*

$$\left\{\frac{T_{\lambda x} - M_{\lambda x}}{\sqrt{A\lambda}}, x \geq 0, P_w\right\}$$

converges in law to a Brownian motion as $\lambda \to \infty$ (*in the sense of convergence of probability measures on the Skorohod space*).

(ii) *For almost all* w, *the process*

$$\left\{\frac{\omega(\lambda t) - \mu(\lambda t)}{\sqrt{m^{-3}A\lambda}}, t \geq 0, P_w\right\}$$

converges in law to a Brownian motion as $\lambda \to \infty$ (*in the sense of convergence of probability measures on* $C[0, \infty)$). *The same is true when* $\omega(\lambda t)$ *is replaced by either of* $\bar{\omega}(\lambda t)$ *and* $\underline{\omega}(\lambda t)$.

Our main theorems are the following ($\kappa > 2$ is assumed throughout).

THEOREM 1. (i) *The process*

$$\left\{\frac{M_{\lambda x} - \lambda m x}{\sqrt{B\lambda}}, x \in \mathbf{R}, P\right\}$$

converges in law to a Brownian motion as $\lambda \to \infty$.

(ii) *The process*

$$\left\{\frac{\mu(\lambda t)-\lambda m^{-1}t}{\sqrt{m^{-3}B\lambda}}, t\in\mathbf{R}, P\right\}$$

converges in law to a Brownian motion as $\lambda\to\infty$.

THEOREM 2 (*Invariance principle in random environment*). (i) *The process*

$$\left\{\frac{T_{\lambda x}-\lambda mx}{\sqrt{C\lambda}}, x\geq 0, \mathscr{P}\right\}$$

converges in law to a Brownian motion as $\lambda\to\infty$.

(ii) *The process*

$$\left\{\frac{\omega(\lambda t)-\lambda m^{-1}t}{m^{-3}C\lambda}, t\geq 0, \mathscr{P}\right\}$$

converges in law to a Brownian motion as $\lambda\to\infty$. *The same is true when* $\omega(\lambda t)$ *is replaced by either of* $\bar{\omega}(\lambda t)$ *and* $\underline{\omega}(\lambda t)$.

As in [7] we introduce a one parameter family of measure preserving transformations θ_t, $t\in\mathbf{R}$, on (W,P) defined by $(\theta_t w)(x)=w(x+t)-w(t)$, $x\in\mathbf{R}$. Clearly $\theta_t\theta_s=\theta_{t+s}$ and $\{\theta_t\}$ is ergodic. Set

$$f_0(w)=\int_{-\infty}^{0} e^{-w_\kappa(t)}\,dt. \tag{0.1}$$

Then $\theta_t f_0\equiv f_0(\theta_t w)=\int_{-\infty}^{t} e^{w_\kappa(t)-w_\kappa(s)}\,ds$ and we have the following (see [7]):

$$E_w\{T_x\}=M_x=2\int_0^x \theta_y f_0\,dy; \tag{0.2}$$

the first equality of (0.2) holds for $x\geq 0$ and the second one holds for $x\in\mathbf{R}$.

$$\mathrm{Var}_w\{T_x\}=8\int_0^x \theta_y g\,dy \text{ for } x\geq 0 \quad \left(g(w)=\int_{-\infty}^{0} e^{-w_\kappa(t)}(\theta_t f_0)^2\,dt\right). \tag{0.3}$$

$$E\{f_0\}=\gamma^{-1}, E\{f_0^2\}=2\gamma^{-1}(2\gamma-1)^{-1}. \tag{0.4}$$

$$E\{\mathrm{Var}_w(T_x)\}=Ax \text{ for } x\geq 0. \tag{0.5}$$

$$\mathrm{Var}\{M_x\}=Bx+O(1), x\to\infty, (\mathrm{Var}=\text{variance}). \tag{0.6}$$

It was also observed in [7] that

$$d\theta_t f_0=\theta_t f_0\,dw(t)-(\gamma\theta_t f_0-1)\,dt, \tag{0.7}$$

so $\theta_t f_0$ is a stationary diffusion process obtained as the unique stationary positive solution of the stochastic differential equation (0.7). Therefore

$$\theta_t f_0 - f_0 = \int_0^t \theta_s f_0 \, dw(s) - \lambda \int_0^t \theta_s f \, ds, \tag{0.8}$$

where $f = f_0 - \gamma^{-1}$.

1. Proof of Theorem 1

For the proof of Theorem 1 we need some lemmas.

LEMMA 1 ([7]). $t^{-1/2} \max\{\theta_s f_0 : |s| \leq t\} \to 0$ as $t \to \infty$.

LEMMA 2 ([7]). *For any positive constants* c_1,

$$M_{t+u} - M_t = mu(1 + o(1)) + o(\sqrt{\lambda}), \quad |t| \leq c_1 \lambda, \quad u \in \mathbf{R},$$

where $o(1)$ *represents a general term that tends to* 0 *as* $\lambda \to \infty$ *uniformly in* (t, u) *such that* $|t| \leq c_1 \lambda$ *and* $u \in \mathbf{R}$, *for almost all* w; $o(\sqrt{\lambda})$ *is a term that can be expressed as* $o(1)\sqrt{\lambda}$.

To prove (i) of Theorem 1 it is enough to consider $\int_0^x \theta_y f \, dy$ by virtue of (0.2). Making habitual use of t to indicate time we write

$$\frac{1}{\sqrt{\lambda}} \int_0^{\lambda t} \theta_s f \, ds = \frac{1}{\gamma\sqrt{\lambda}} \int_0^{\lambda t} \theta_s f_0 \, dw(s) - \frac{1}{\gamma\sqrt{\lambda}} (\theta_{\lambda t} f_0 - f_0). \tag{1.1}$$

By the ergodicity of $\{\theta_t\}$ and also by (0.4) we see that the quadratic variation of the stochastic integral term in (1.1) tends to $Bt/4$ as $\lambda \to \infty$, a.s., so the stochastic integral term itself converges in law to $\{(B/4)^{1/2} w(t), t \geq 0, P\}$ as $\lambda \to \infty$. The second term of the right hand side of (1.1) is negligible by Lemma 1. Therefore $X_\lambda^+ = \{\lambda^{-1/2} \int_0^{\lambda t} \theta_s f \, ds, t \geq 0\}$ converges in law to $\{(B/4)^{1/2} w(t), t \geq 0\}$, so does $X_\lambda^- = \{\lambda^{-1/2} \int_0^{-\lambda t} \theta_s f \, ds, t \geq 0\}$ because of the reversibility of the diffusion $\theta_t f$. Now the assertion (i) of Theorem 1 follows from the fact that X_λ^+ and X_λ^- are asymptotically independent as $\lambda \to \infty$.

To proceed let $\xi = \lambda m$ and put

$$\beta_\lambda(t) = (B\lambda)^{-1/2}(M_{\lambda t} - \lambda m t), \quad \tilde{\beta}_\lambda(t) = (m^{-3} B \xi)^{-1/2}(\mu(\xi t) - \xi m^{-1} t). \tag{1.2}$$

Then the assertion of (ii) of Theorem 1 follows immediately from the following Lemma.

LEMMA 3. *For any* $t_0 > 0$ *and* $\varepsilon > 0$

$$\lim_{\lambda \to \infty} P\left\{ \sup_{|t| \leq t_0} |\beta_\lambda(t) + \tilde{\beta}_\lambda(t)| > \varepsilon \right\} = 0.$$

Proof. From the second equality of (1.2) we have $\lambda mt = M(\lambda t + \tilde{\beta}_\lambda(t)m^{-1}\sqrt{B\lambda})$ and hence

$$(B\lambda)^{-1/2}\{M(\lambda t + \tilde{\beta}_\lambda(t)m^{-1}\sqrt{B\lambda}) - M(\lambda t)\} = -\beta_\lambda(t),$$

so an application of Lemma 2 yields $\tilde{\beta}_\lambda(t)(1 + o(1)) + o(1) = -\beta_\lambda(t)$, where $o(1)$ is a term tending to 0 uniformly on each finite t-interval as $\lambda \to \infty$, a.s. This implies the lemma.

The following observation will lead to another proof of (ii) of Theorem 1. If $v(t)$ denotes the inverse function of $\int_0^x \theta_y f_0\,dy$, then $v(t) = \mu(2t)$ and the derivative $v'(t)$, which equals to $1/\theta_{v(t)}f_0$, is a stationary diffusion process obtained from $\theta_t f_0$ by changing time and scale.

2. The proof of Theorem 2

We give the proof of the part (i). Taking an arbitrary positive sequence $\{\lambda_n, n = 1, 2, \ldots\}$ tending to ∞, we denote by $P^{(n)}$ the probability law of the process $\{\lambda_n^{-1/2}(T_{\lambda_n x} - \lambda_n mx), x \geq 0, \mathscr{P}\}$. Note that $P^{(n)}$ is a probability measure on the Skorohod space $D = D[0, \infty)$. For the proof of the part (i) it is enough to show that $P^{(n)}$ converges to the probability law of the process $\{\sqrt{C}w(x), x \geq 0, P\}$ as $n \to \infty$. We first prove that the sequence $\{P^{(n)}, n \geq 1\}$ is tight. If $Q_w^{(n)}$ denotes the probability law of the process $\{\lambda_n^{-1/2}(T_{\lambda_n x} - M_{\lambda_n x}), x \geq 0, P_w\}$, then $Q_w^{(n)} \to Q_1$ (P-a.s.) by Theorem A and hence $Q^{(n)} = \int Q_w^{(n)} P(dw)$ also converges to Q_1 as $n \to \infty$ where Q_1 is the probability law (on D) of the process $\{\sqrt{A}w(x), x \geq 0, P\}$. All the convergence here is to be understood as the convergence of probability measures on D. Therefore for any $\varepsilon > 0$ there exists a compact set $K_1 \subset D$ such that $Q^{(n)}(K_1^c) < \varepsilon^2$ for all $n \geq 1$. We then have $P\{L_n\} < \varepsilon$ where $L_n = \{w : Q_w^{(n)}(K_1^c) > \varepsilon\} = \{w : Q_w^{(n)}(K_1) \leq 1 - \varepsilon\}$. We also introduce, for each fixed w, an element $\varphi_n(w)$ of Ω which is defined to be the function $\lambda_n^{1/2}(M_{\lambda_n x} - \lambda_n mx)$ of x. Then $P \circ \varphi_n^{-1} \to Q_2$ as $n \to \infty$ by Theorem 1 where Q_2 is the probability law (on Ω) of the process $\{\sqrt{B}w(x), x \geq 0, P\}$. We can thus find a compact set $K_2 \subset \Omega$ such that $P \circ \varphi_n^{-1}(K_2^c) < \varepsilon$ for all $n \geq 1$. We now put $K = \{w_1 + w_2 : w_1 \in K_1, w_2 \in K_2\}$. Then K is a compact subset of D. Since

$$\frac{T_{\lambda_n x} - \lambda_n mx}{\sqrt{\lambda_n}} = \frac{T_{\lambda_n x} - M_{\lambda_n x}}{\sqrt{\lambda_n}} + \frac{M_{\lambda_n x} - \lambda_n mx}{\sqrt{\lambda_n}},$$

we have

$$\begin{aligned} P^{(n)}(K) &= \iint 1_K(w_1 + \varphi_n(w)) Q_w^{(n)}(dw_1) P(dw) \\ &\geq \iint 1_{K_1}(w_1) 1_{K_2}(\varphi_n(w)) Q_w^{(n)}(dw_1) P(dw) \\ &= \int_{\varphi_n^{-1}(K_2)} Q_w^{(n)}(K_1) P(dw) \\ &\geq \int_{\varphi_n^{-1}(K_2) \cap L_n^c} (1-\varepsilon) P(dw) \geq (1-\varepsilon)(1-2\varepsilon), \end{aligned}$$

which proves that $\{P^{(n)}, n \geq 1\}$ is tight. Therefore, for the proof of Theorem 2 it is enough to show that

$$\text{(2.1)} \qquad \lim_{n\to\infty} \int f(w) P^{(n)}(dw) = \iint f(w_1 + w_2) Q_1(dw_1) Q_2(dw_2),$$

for any function f of the form

$$f(w) = \exp\left\{ \sqrt{-1} \sum_{j=1}^{k} \alpha_j w(t_j) \right\},$$

where $\alpha_j \in \mathbf{R}$ and $t_j \geq 0$, $1 \leq j \leq k$. For such an f the left hand side of (2.1) equals

$$\begin{aligned} &\lim_{n\to\infty} \iint f(w_1 + \varphi_n(w)) Q_w^{(n)}(dw_1) P(dw) \\ &= \lim_{n\to\infty} \int_W \left\{ \int_D f(w_1) Q_w^{(n)}(dw_1) \right\} f(\varphi_n(w)) P(dw) \\ &= \int f(w_1) Q_1(dw_1) \int f(w_2) Q_2(dw_2) \end{aligned}$$

which also equals the right hand side of (2.1). This completes the proof of (i) of Theorem 2.

The part (ii) of Theorem 2 can be proved in a way similar to the above by making use of Theorem A and Theorem 1.

3. Supplement to the proof of (i) of Theorem A

The proof of Theorem A was given in [7]; however, some details in the proof of the part (i) were omitted. It will be worth supplementing them.

The proof of Theorem A given in [7] proceeds as follows. Let $\tau_k =$

$T_k - T_{k-1}$, $\tilde{\tau}_k = \tau_k - E_w\{\tau_k\}$, $k \geq 1$. Then it was proved that, for almost all w, $\{\tilde{\tau}_k, k \geq 1, P_w\}$ is a sequence of independent random variables satisfying the Lindeberg condition. Therefore the central limit theorem holds for T_n with respect to P_w, for almost all w. Note that $E_w\{T_n\} = M_n$ and $\mathrm{Var}_w\{T_n\} \sim An$ as $n \to \infty$ (P-a.s.). Now the rest of the proof, whose detail was omitted in [7], is given as follows.

Let $t_{nk} = \mathrm{Var}_w\{\tau_k\}/\mathrm{Var}_w\{T_n\}$, $\zeta_{nk} = (An)^{-1/2}\{T_k - M_k\}$, $1 \leq k \leq n$, and $t_{n0} = \zeta_{n0} = 0$. For each fixed w we construct a piece-wise linear function $\xi_n(x)$, $0 \leq x \leq 1$, with vertexes $(\sum_{j=0}^{k} t_{nj}, \zeta_{nk})$, $0 \leq k \leq n$. We regard $\{\xi_n(x), 0 \leq x \leq 1, P_w\}$ as a process with time parameter x. Then by Theorem 3.1 of [5], for almost all w, the process $\{\xi_n(x), 0 \leq x \leq 1, P_w\}$ converges in law to a Brownian motion as $n \to \infty$. We now modify $\xi_n(x)$ slightly, namely, we consider a piece-wise linear function $\eta_n(x)$ with vertexes $(k/n, \zeta_{nk})$, $0 \leq k \leq n$. Then $\eta_n(x)$ can be represented as $\eta_n(x) = \xi_n(\varphi_n(x))$ where $\varphi_n(x)$ is the piece-wise linear function with vertexes $\left(k/n, \sum_{j=0}^{k} t_{nj}\right)$, $0 \leq k \leq n$. On the other hand it is easy to see that, for each fixed x, $\varphi_n \to x$ as $n \to \infty$ for almost all w. This combined with the fact that φ is increasing implies that $\varphi_n \to x$ uniformly as $n \to \infty$ (P-a.s.). Therefore

(3.1) the process $\{\eta_n(x), 0 \leq x \leq 1, P_w\}$ converges in law to a Brownian motion as $n \to \infty$ for almost all w.

We finally prove that the process $\{(A\lambda)^{-1/2}(T_{\lambda x} - M_{\lambda x}), x \in [0,1], P_w\}$ converges in law to a Brownian motion as $\lambda \to \infty$ for almost all w; the time interval $[0,1]$ can be replaced by an arbitrary interval $[0, t_0]$ with a minor modification of the proof. Given $x \in (0,1]$ and an integer $n \geq 1$ we take the integer k such that $(k-1)/n < x \leq k/n$. Then $T_{nx} - M_{nx} > T_{k-1} - M_k > \sqrt{An}\eta_n(x) - \tau_k - m_k$ where $m_k = M_k - M_{k-1}$. Similarly $T_{nx} - M_{nx} < \sqrt{An}\eta_n(x) + \tau_k + m_k$ and hence

$$\sqrt{An}\eta_n(x) - (\tau_k + m_k) < T_{nx} - M_{nx} < \sqrt{An}\eta_n(x) + (\tau_k + m_k).$$

This implies that for $x \in [0,1]$

$$\sqrt{An}\eta_n(x) - (\hat{\tau}_n + \hat{m}_n) < T_{nx} - M_{nx} < \sqrt{An}\eta_n(x) + (\hat{\tau}_n + \hat{m}_n), \tag{3.2}$$

where $\hat{\tau}_n = \max\{\tau_k : 1 \leq k \leq n\}$ and $\hat{m}_n = \max\{m_k : 1 \leq k \leq n\}$. Next, given $\lambda > 0$ let $n = n(\lambda)$ be the integer such that $n - 1 < \lambda \leq n$. Then $T_{(n-1)x} - M_{\lambda x} < T_{\lambda x} - M_{\lambda x} \leq T_{nx} - M_{\lambda x}$, which combined with (3.2) implies

$$\sqrt{A(n-1)}\eta_{n-1}(x) - (\hat{\tau}_{n-1} + \hat{m}_{n-1}) - (M_{\lambda x} - M_{(n-1)x})$$
$$< T_{\lambda x} - M_{\lambda x} < \sqrt{An}\eta_n(x) + (\hat{\tau}_n + \hat{m}_n) + (M_{nx} - M_{\lambda x}).$$

Since $M_{\lambda x} - M_{(n-1)x}$ and $M_{nx} - M_{\lambda x}$ are dominated by $2\hat{m}_n$, we obtain

$$(3.3) \quad \left(\frac{n-1}{\lambda}\right)^{1/2} \eta_{n-1}(x) - (A\lambda)^{-1/2}(\hat{\tau}_n + 3\hat{m}_n) < (A\lambda)^{-1/2}(T_{\lambda x} - M_{\lambda x})$$
$$< \left(\frac{n}{\lambda}\right)^{1/2} \eta_n(x) + (A\lambda)^{-1/2}(\hat{\tau}_n + 3\hat{m}_n).$$

On the other hand we can prove that for almost all w

$$(3.4) \quad P_w\left\{\lim_{n\to\infty} \hat{\tau}_n/\sqrt{n} = 0\right\} = 1,$$

$$(3.5) \quad \lim_{n\to\infty} \hat{m}_n/\sqrt{n} = 0.$$

In fact, it is easy to see that $\{\tau_k, k \geq 1, \mathscr{P}\}$ is stationary and ergodic. Since τ_k^2 is integrable we have $n^{-1}\sum_1^n \tau_k^2 \to \text{const.}$ as $n \to \infty$ ($\mathscr{P}$-a.s.) and hence $n^{-1}\tau_n^2 \to 0$, namely, $n^{-1/2}\tau_n \to 0$ ($\mathscr{P}$-a.s.). This implies $n^{-1/2}\hat{\tau}_n \to 0$ ($\mathscr{P}$-a.s.) and hence (3.4). (3.5) can be proved in a similar manner. By virtue of (3.1), (3.4) and (3.5) the processes of the leftmost and rightmost hands of (3.3) converge in law to a Brownian motion as $\lambda \to \infty$. Therefore (3.3) implies the assertion for $(A\lambda)^{-1/2}(T_{\lambda x} - M_{\lambda x})$ that we wanted to prove.

References

[1] K. Itô and H. P. McKean, Diffusion Processes and Their Sample Paths, Springer-Verlag, New York, 1965.

[2] K. Kawazu and H. Tanaka, A diffusion process in a Brownian environment with drift, J. Math. Soc. Japan **49** (1997), 189–211.

[3] H. Kesten, M. V. Kozlov and F. Spitzer, A limit law for random walk in a random environment, Composito Math. **30** (1975), 145–168.

[4] Yu. V. Prohorov, Convergence of random processes and limit theorems in probability theory, Theor. Probab. Appl. **1** (1956), 157–214.

[5] F. Solomon, Random walks in a random environment, Ann. Probab. **3** (1975), 1–131.

[6] H. Tanaka, Diffusion processes in random environments, Proc. International Congress of Mathematicians, Zürich, 1994, 1047–1054, Birkhäuser Verlag, Basel, 1995.

[7] H. Tanaka, Environment-wise central limit theorem for a diffusion in a Brownian environment with large drift, Itô's Stochastic Calculus and Probability Theory, ed. by N. Ikeda et al., pp. 373–384, Springer, 1996.

[8] H. Tanaka, Limit theorems for a Brownian motion with drift in a white noise environment, Chaos, Solitons & Fractals, **8** (1997), 1807–1816.

K. Kawazu
Department of Mathematics
Faculty of Education
Yamaguchi University
Yosida, Yamaguchi 753-8513
Japan

H. Tanaka
Department of Mathematics
Faculty of Science and Technology
Keio University
Yokohama 223-0061
Japan

Tanaka, H.
Osaka J. Math.
38 (2001), 369–377

SOME THEOREMS CONCERNING EXTREMA OF BROWNIAN MOTION WITH *d*-DIMENSIONAL TIME

Dedicated to Professor N. Ikeda on his 70th birthday

HIROSHI TANAKA

(Received October 16, 1999)

Introduction

Let $X = \{X(x), x \in \mathbf{R}^d\}$ be a Lévy's Brownian motion with d-dimensional time ([2]) defined on a certain probability space (Ω, P); thus X is a centered Gaussian system with continuous sample functions satisfying $X(0) = 0$ and $E\{X(x)X(y)\} = (|x| + |y| - |x - y|)/2$. For a nonempty subset A of $\mathbf{R}^d$ we put

$$\underline{X}(A) = \inf\{X(x) : x \in A\}, \quad \overline{X}(A) = \sup\{X(x) : x \in A\}.$$

We often use the notation $X(A)$ to denote either $\underline{X}(A)$ or $\overline{X}(A)$. For example, $X(A) - X(B)$ denotes any one of $\underline{X}(A) - \underline{X}(B)$, $\underline{X}(A) - \overline{X}(B)$, $\overline{X}(A) - \underline{X}(B)$ and $\overline{X}(A) - \overline{X}(B)$. A point x in $\mathbf{R}^d$ is called a point of local minimum (resp. local maximum) of a sample function X if there exists a neighborhood U of x such that $X(x) = \underline{X}(U)$ (resp. $X(x) = \overline{X}(U)$). A point of either local minimum or local maximum is called an extreme-point.

The following are typical of those problems and theorems we discuss in this paper.

(I) Under what condition on A does the probability distribution of $X(A)$ admit a strictly positive C^∞-density?

(II) Under what condition on A and B does the joint probability distribution of $X(A)$ and $X(B)$ admit a strictly positive C^∞-density?

(III) Almost all sample functions X have the following property: There are no distinct extreme-points x and y with $X(x) = X(y)$.

We give some sufficient conditions that will give positive answers to the problems (I) and (II) and then give a proof of (III). Formulating the problems somewhat generally we state our main results in the following theorems.

Theorem 1. *Let A_k, $1 \le k \le n$, be nonempty bounded closed sets not containing the origin* 0. *Then for any constants c_k, $1 \le k \le n$, such that $c_1 + c_2 + \cdots + c_n \neq 0$, the probability distribution of*

$$c_1 X(A_1) + c_2 X(A_2) + \cdots + c_n X(A_n)$$

can be expressed as a convolution $\gamma * \mu$ where γ is a nondegenerate Gaussian distribution with mean 0 and μ is some probability distribution in $\boldsymbol{R}$. In particular, the distribution of each of $\underline{X}(A)$ and $\overline{X}(A)$ has a strictly positive C^∞-density provided that A is a nonempty bounded closed set not containing 0.

Theorem 2. *Let A_j, B_k, $1 \le j \le m$, $1 \le k \le n$, be nonempty bounded closed sets such that $\cup_{j=1}^m A_j$ is separated from $\cup_{k=1}^n B_k$ by a certain $(d-1)$-dimensional hyperplane Π passing through the origin 0. Then for any constants c_j, c'_k, $1 \le j \le m$, $1 \le k \le n$, such that $\sum_{j=1}^m c_j \ne 0$ and $\sum_{k=1}^n c'_k \ne 0$, the joint distribution of*

$$f_1(X) = \sum_{j=1}^m c_j X(A_j), \qquad f_2(X) = \sum_{k=1}^n c'_k X(B_k) \tag{1}$$

has a form $(\gamma_1 \otimes \gamma_2) * \nu$ where each γ_i is a nondegenerate Gaussian distribution with mean 0 and ν is some 2-dimensional probability distribution. In particular, the joint distribution of $X(A)$ and $X(B)$ has a strictly positive C^∞-density provided that A and B are nonempty bounded closed sets separated from each other by a certain $(d-1)$-dimensional hyperplane passing through 0.

Theorem 3. *Let A_j, B_k, $1 \le j \le m$, $1 \le k \le n$, be nonempty bounded closed sets such that $\cup_{j=1}^m A_j$ is separated from $\cup_{k=1}^n B_k$ by a certain $(d-1)$-dimensional hyperplane. Then for any constants c_j, c'_k, $1 \le j \le m$, $1 \le k \le n$, such that $\sum_{j=1}^m c_j = \sum_{k=1}^n c'_k \ne 0$, the probability distribution of $f_1(X) - f_2(X)$, with f_1 and f_2 given by (1), has a form $\gamma * \mu$ where γ is a nondegenerate Gaussian distribution with mean 0 and μ is some distribution in R. In particular, the distribution of each of $\underline{X}(A) - \underline{X}(B)$, $\underline{X}(A) - \overline{X}(B)$ and $\overline{X}(A) - \overline{X}(B)$ has a strictly positive C^∞-density provided that A and B are nonempty bounded closed sets separated from each other by a certain $(d-1)$-dimensional hyperplane.*

Theorem 4. *Almost all sample functions X have the following property: There. are no distinct extreme-points x and y of X such that $X(x) = X(y)$.*

An example of the applicability (or our motivation) of Theorem 4 will be given in the final section.

1. A lemma

Given a centered Gaussian system $\{X_\lambda,\ \lambda \in \Lambda\}$ defined on a certain probability space (Ω, P), we denote by H the real Hilbert space spanned by $\{X_\lambda,\ \lambda \in \Lambda\}$ and by H_0 the closed linear span (abbreviation: c.l.s.) of $\{X_\lambda - X_\mu,\ \lambda,\ \mu \in \Lambda\}$. Clearly $H_0 \subset H \subset L^2(\Omega, P)$. We now introduce the following conditions.

Condition (A). There exists a nondegenerate Gaussian random variable Y_0 independent of $\{X_\lambda - Y_0,\ \lambda \in \Lambda\}$.

Condition (B). There exists $\lambda \in \Lambda$ such that $X_\lambda \notin H_0$.
It is easy to see that the condition (B) implies that $X_\lambda \notin H_0$ for all $\lambda \in \Lambda$. Denote by $\mathbf{R}^\Lambda$ the space of real valued functions on Λ; it has a Borel structure defined in a natural way. Then we can regard $X_\Lambda = \{X_\lambda,\ \lambda \in \Lambda\}$ as a random variable taking values in $\mathbf{R}^\Lambda$. The following lemma is rather trivial; nevertheless, it plays a fundamental role in this paper.

Lemma 1. (i) *Let f be a Borel function from $\mathbf{R}^\Lambda$ to* R *such that*

$$f(w + t\mathbf{1}) = f(w) + ct \tag{1.1}$$

for any $w \in \mathbf{R}^\Lambda$ and $t \in$ R where c is some nonzero constant and $\mathbf{1}$ denotes the function on Λ that identically equals 1. *Then under the condition* (A) *we have $f(X_\Lambda) = cY_0 + Y$ with a suitable random variable Y independent of Y_0; in particular, the probability distribution of $f(X_\Lambda)$ has a strictly positive C^∞-density.*
(ii) *Suppose Λ is a locally compact space with a countable open base and assume that X_λ is continuous in λ with probability* 1. *We regard $X_\Lambda = \{X_\lambda,\ \lambda \in \Lambda\}$ as a random variable taking values in the space $C(\Lambda)$ of continuous functions on Λ, which is equipped with the compact uniform topology. Then, under the condition* (A), *the conclusion of* (i) *remains valid for any Borel function f from $C(\Lambda)$ to* R *satisfying* (1.1) *for $w \in C(\Lambda)$ and $t \in$* R.
(iii) *The condition* (B) *implies the condition* (A).

REMARK 1. Let Λ_k, $1 \le k \le n$, be subsets of Λ and let c_k, $1 \le k \le n$, be constants such that $c_1 + \cdots + c_n \ne 0$. Let $w(\Lambda_k)$ indicate either $\inf\{w(\lambda) : \lambda \in \Lambda_k\}$ or $\sup\{w(\lambda) : \lambda \in \Lambda_k\}$; the choice may depend on k but not on w. Then

$$f(w) = c_1 w(\Lambda_1) + \cdots + c_n w(\Lambda_n) \tag{1.2}$$

is a typical example of f satisfying (1.1) with $c = c_1 + \cdots + c_n$ provided that f can be defined to be a Borel function.

REMARK 2. Let F be a class of functions defined on $[0, 1]$ and taking values in Λ (an example of such an F is the space of continuous paths in Λ connecting two given points of Λ). Then the function f defined by $f(w) = \inf\{g(w, u) : u \in F\}$ with $g(w, u) = \sup\{w(u(t)) : 0 \le t \le 1\}$ satisfies (1.1).

REMARK 3. If $\{X_\lambda,\ \lambda \in \Lambda\}$ satisfies (A) (resp. (B)) and if Λ_1 is a nonempty subset of Λ, then the sub-system $\{X_\lambda,\ \lambda \in \Lambda_1\}$ also satisfies (A) (resp. (B)).

Proof of Lemma 1. (i) Under the condition (A) $X_\Lambda - Y_0\mathbf{1}$ and Y_0 are independent so $f(X_\Lambda) - cY_0 = f(X_\Lambda - Y_0\mathbf{1})$ and Y_0 are independent. If we put $Y = f(X_\Lambda) - cY_0$,

then we have the expression $f(X_\Lambda) = cY_0 + Y$ in which Y_0 and Y are independent and Y_0 is a nondegenerate Gaussian random variable. The assertion (ii) follows from (i).
(iii) It is easy to see that $X_\lambda + H_0 = \{X_\lambda + Y : Y \in H_0\}$ does not depend on λ. The condition (B) means that $X_\lambda + H_0 \not\ni 0$. Since $X_\lambda + H_0$ is a closed convex set, there exists a unique $Y_0 \in X_\lambda + H_0$ such that

$$\sqrt{E\{Y_0^2\}} = \min\left\{\sqrt{E\{|X_\lambda + Y|^2\}} : Y \in H_0\right\} > 0.$$

Then clearly $Y_0 \perp H_0$. Since $X_\lambda - Y_0 \in H_0$, $X_\lambda - Y_0 \perp Y_0$ for all λ. This implies that Y_0 is independent of $\{X_\lambda - Y_0, \lambda \in \Lambda\}$. □

2. Proof of Theorem 1

As stated in Introduction let $X = \{X(x),\ x \in \mathrm{R}^d\}$ be a Brownian motion with d-dimensional time. For any fixed pair of real numbers t_1 and t_2 such that $0 < t_1 < t_2$ we put $\Lambda = \{x \in \mathrm{R}^d : t_1 \le |x| \le t_2\}$, $H = \text{c.l.s.}\{X(x),\ x \in \Lambda\}$ and $H_0 = \text{c.l.s.}\{X(x) - X(y), x, y \in \Lambda\}$. First we prepare the following lemma.

Lemma 2. *The condition* (B) *is satisfied for* $\{X(x),\ x \in \Lambda\}$, *namely, there exists* $x \in \Lambda$ *such that* $X(x) \notin H_0$.

Proof. (i) We consider the case where the dimension d is odd and $d \ge 3$. Denoting by $\hat{d}\theta$ the uniform distribution on $S^{d-1} = \{\theta \in \mathrm{R}^d : |\theta| = 1\}$, we put

$$\begin{aligned} R(t) &= \int_{S^{d-1}} X(t\theta)\hat{d}\theta, \qquad t \ge 0, \\ H_1 &= \text{c.l.s.}\{R(t),\quad t_1 \le t \le t_2\}, \\ H_1^\perp &= \text{the orthogonal complement of } H_1 \text{ in } H. \end{aligned}$$

Then we have

$$X(x) - R(|x|) \in H_1^\perp \qquad \text{for any } x \in \Lambda. \tag{2.1}$$

In fact, it is easy to see that, for each fixed $t \ge 0$, $E\{(X(x) - R(|x|))R(t)\}$ depends only on $|x|$ and hence it must vanish, which implies (2.1). We are going to prove that $X(t_1\theta) \notin H_0$ for $\theta \in S^{d-1}$. The relation (2.1) implies that $X(t_1\theta) = R(t_1) + X'$ with $X' \in H_1^\perp$ and that $H_0 \subset H_{10} \oplus H_1^\perp$ where $H_{10} = \text{c.l.s.}\{R(t) - R(s), t, s \in [t_1, t_2]\}$. Therefore, for the proof of $X(t_1\theta) \notin H_0$ it is enough to show that $R(t_1) \notin H_{10}$. We now make use of the canonical representation of the Gaussian process $\{R(t),\ t \ge 0\}$ due to McKean [5], which means that

$$R(t) = \int_0^t f(t, r)\,dB(r), \quad t \ge 0,$$

where $\{B(r),\ r \geq 0\}$ is a one-dimensional standard Brownian motion and

$$f(t,r) = k(d) \int_{r/t}^{1} (1-u^2)^{(d-3)/2}\, du, \qquad 0 \leq r \leq t, \tag{2.2}$$

$k(d)$ being a suitable constant depending only on d. For any s and t with $t_1 \leq s < t \leq t_2$ we have

$$R(t) - R(s) = \int_0^{t_1} f_{ts}(r)\, dB(r) + \int_{t_1}^{t} g_{ts}(r) dB(r),$$
$$R(t_1) = \int_0^{t_1} f(r)\, dB(r),$$

where $f_{ts}(r) = f(t,r) - f(s,r)$, $f(r) = f(t_1, r)$ and $g_{ts}(r)$ is a suitable function. Therefore, if we put

$$\tilde{H}_0 = \text{c.l.s.} \left\{ \int_0^{t_1} f_{ts}(r)\, dB(r), t, s \in [t_1, t_2] \right\},$$
$$\tilde{H}_+ = \text{c.l.s.} \left\{ B(u) - B(r), r, u \in [t_1, t_2] \right\},$$

then $\tilde{H}_0 \perp \tilde{H}_+$, $H_{10} \subset \tilde{H}_0 \oplus \tilde{H}_+$ and $R(t_1) \perp \tilde{H}_+$. From these observations we see that for the proof of $R(t_1) \notin H_{10}$, it is enough to show

$$\int_0^{t_1} f(r) dB(r) \notin \tilde{H}_0. \tag{2.3}$$

Let L_0^2 be the subspace of $L^2[0, t_1]$ spanned by the functions $f_{ts}(\cdot), t, s \in [t_1, t_2]$. Then the Hilbert space $\tilde{H}_0$ is isomorphic to L_0^2 and (2.3) is equivalent to $f \notin L_0^2$. Now the assumption that d is an odd integer ≥ 3 implies that $f_{ts}(r), t, s, \in [t_1, t_2]$, are polynomials of degree $d-2$ vanishing at $r = 0$ (use (2.2)). Therefore all the functions in L_0^2 are also polynomials of degree at most $d-2$ vanishing at $r = 0$. On the other hand it is easy to see that f is a polynomial of degree $d-2$ with $f(0) > 0$. Therefore $f \notin L_0^2$, which finally implies $X(t_1\theta) \notin H_0$. This completes the proof in the case where d is odd and $d \geq 3$.

(ii) The proof in the case where d is even can be obtained by the method of descent in which a Brownian motion with d-dimensional time is viewed as the restriction of a Brownian motion with $(d+1)$-dimensional time to $\mathrm{R}^d \times \{0\} \subset \mathrm{R}^{d+1}$ and also by using Remark 3. The proof in the case $d = 1$ is easy. The proof of Lemma 2 is finished. □

We are now able to prove Theorem 1. From the assumption on A_k, $1 \leq k \leq n$, there exist t_1 and t_2 with $0 < t_1 < t_2$ such that $\Lambda = \{x \in \mathrm{R}^d : t_1 \leq |x| \leq t_2\}$ includes all A_k. Then, by Lemma 2 the condition (B) is satisfied for $X_\Lambda = \{X(x), x \in \Lambda\}$

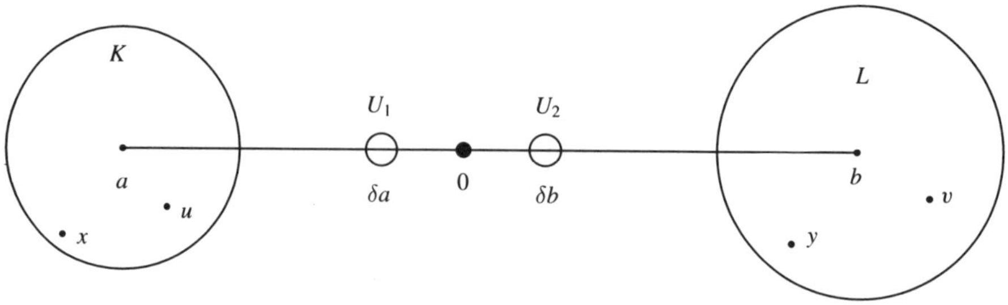

and by Remark 1 the condition (1.1) is satisfied for the function $f(w) = c_1 w(A_1) + c_2 w(A_1) + \cdots + c_n W(A_n)$, $w \in C(\Lambda)$, with $c = c_1 + \cdots + c_n$. Therefore by Lemma 1 the probability distribution of the random variable $f(X_\Lambda) = c_1 X(A_1) + c_2 X(A_2) + \cdots + c_n X(A_n)$ has a form $\gamma * \mu$. This completes the proof of Theorem 1.

3. Proof of Theorem 2

Under the assumption on A_j and B_k in Theorem 2 we can take disjoint closed balls K and L with the following properties:

(3.1) $K \supset \cup_{j=1}^m A_j$, $\quad L \supset \cup_{k=1}^n B_k$.

(3.2) K is separated from L by the hyperplane Π.

(3.3) The center a of K and the center b of L are on the straight line that passes through the origin 0 and is perpendicular to Π.

We consider open balls U_1 and U_2 with a common radius ε and with centers δa and δb, respectively, where $\delta > 0$ is chosen so that $\delta a \notin K$ and $\delta b \notin L$ (see the figure). We now make use of the Chentsov representation of $X(x)$ ([1]), which asserts that

$$X(x) = W(D_x), \tag{3.4}$$

where D_x is the open ball with center $x/2$ and radius $|x|/2$, and $\{W(d\xi)\}$ is a suitable white noise in R^d associated with the measure $c_d|\xi|^{-d+1}d\xi$ (c_d is a suitable constant), namely, a Gaussian random measure in R^d such that $E\{W(d\xi)\} = 0$ and $E\{W(d\xi)^2\} = c_d|\xi|^{-d+1}d\xi$. By taking $\varepsilon > 0$ small enough, we can assume

$$U_1 \subset \left\{\bigcap_{x\in K} D_x\right\} \cap \left\{\bigcup_{y\in L} D_y\right\}^c, \qquad U_2 \subset \left\{\bigcap_{y\in L} D_y\right\} \cap \left\{\bigcup_{x\in K} D_x\right\}^c. \tag{3.5}$$

If we write $X(x) = W(D_x) = W(U_1) + \tilde{X}_x$ and $X(y) = W(D_y) = W(U_2) + \tilde{X}_y$, then (3.5) implies that the 2-dimensional random vector $(W(U_1), W(U_2))$ is independent of the Gaussian family $\{(\tilde{X}_x, \tilde{X}_y) : x \in K, y \in L\}$. Therefore we have

$$f_1(X) = cW(U_1) + \tilde{f}_1, \qquad f_2(X) = c'W(U_2) + \tilde{f}_2,$$

with $c = \sum_{j=1}^{m} c_j$, $c' = \sum_{k=1}^{n} c'_k$ and $(W(U_1), W(U_2))$ is independent of $(\tilde{f}_1, \tilde{f}_2)$. Since $W(U_1)$ and $W(U_2)$ are independent and each of them is a nondegenerate Gaussian random variable with mean 0, the joint distribution of $f_1(X)$ and $f_2(X)$ has a form $(\gamma_1 \otimes \gamma_2) * \nu$.

4. Proof of Theorem 3 and Theorem 4

By using the fact that $\{X(x) - X(x_0), x \in \mathrm{R}^d\}$ is identical in law to $\{X(x - x_0), x \in \mathrm{R}^d\}$ for each $x_0 \in \mathrm{R}^d$ and also by using the assumption $\sum_{j=1}^{m} c_j = \sum_{k=1}^{n} c'_k$, we see that the probability distribution of $f_1(X) - f_2(X)$ is invariant under any simultaneous shift of A_j and B_k. Therefore, in proving Theorem 3 we may assume that A_j. and B_k satisfy the same assumption as in Theorem 2. Then the joint distribution of $f_1(X)$ and $f_2(X)$ has a form $(\gamma_1 \otimes \gamma_2) * \nu$ by Theorem 2 and this implies the conclusion of Theorem 3.

Before going to the proof of Theorem 4 we introduce some notation. Denote by $\mathcal{K}$ the set of all pairs (K_1, K_2) of disjoint closed balls K_1 and K_2 with rational centers and rational radii. We put $f(K_1, K_2; \sigma_1, \sigma_2) = X(K_1; \sigma_1) - X(K_2; \sigma_2)$ where each σ_i is either 0 or 1 and $X(K_i; \sigma_i)$ denotes either $\underline{X}(K_i)$ or $\overline{X}(K_i)$ according as $\sigma_i = 0$ or 1. We also denote by $\mathcal{E}(K_1, K_2; \sigma_1, \sigma_2)$ the event $\{f(K_1, K_2; \sigma_1, \sigma_2) = 0\}$ and then put $\mathcal{E}' = \cup \mathcal{E}(K_1, K_2; \sigma_1, \sigma_2)$ where the union is taken over all $(K_1, K_2) \in \mathcal{K}$ and all $(\sigma_1, \sigma_2) \in \{0, 1\}^2$. Finally let $\mathcal{E}$ be the event such that there exist distinct extreme-points x and y with $X(x) = X(y)$. It is then easy to see that $\mathcal{E} \subset \mathcal{E}'$. On the other hand Theorem 3 implies $P\{\mathcal{E}(K_1, K_2; \sigma_1, \sigma_2)\} = 0$ and hence $P\{\mathcal{E}'\} = 0$. This implies $P\{\mathcal{E}\} = 0$ as was to be proved.

5. Remarks on a diffusion process in a d-dimensional Brownian environment

This section is to supply an example for the applicability of Theorem 4. We change the notation for a Brownian motion with a d-dimensional time since we want to use $X(t)$ for a diffusion process. Let $\mathbf{W}$ be the space of continuous functions on R^d vanishing at 0. In this section an element W of $\mathbf{W}$ is called an environment. We consider the probability measure P on W such that $\{W(x), \ x \in \mathrm{R}^d, P\}$ is a Lévy's Brownian motion with a d-dimensional time. Let Ω be the space of continuous functions on $[0, \infty)$ taking values in R^d. The value of $\omega (\in \Omega)$ at time t is denoted by $X(t) = X(t, \omega) = \omega(t)$. For each fixed environment W we consider the probability measure P_W on Ω such that $\{X(t), t \geq 0, P_W\}$ is a diffusion process in R^d with generator

$$\frac{1}{2}(\Delta - \nabla W \cdot \nabla) = \frac{1}{2} e^W \sum_{k=1}^{d} \frac{\partial}{\partial x_k} \left(e^{-W} \frac{\partial}{\partial x_k} \right)$$

and starting from 0. Let $\mathcal{P}$ be the probability measure on $W \times \Omega$ defined by $\mathcal{P}(dW d\omega) = P(dW) P_W(d\omega)$. Then $\{X(t), t \geq 0, \mathcal{P}\}$ can be regarded as a process defined on the probability space $(W \times \Omega, \mathcal{P})$, which we call a diffusion process in a d-dimensional Brownian environment. When $d = 1$, this model is a diffusion analogue of well-known Sinai's random walk in a random environment(1982) and much is known about the long-term behavior of X(t) such as localization. When $d \geq 2$, a similar diffusion model appeared in [3]. Now our interest is the long-term behavior of $\{X(t), t \geq 0, \mathcal{P}\}$ in the case $d \geq 2$. Tanaka [6](see also [7]) proved that, for any dimension d, $\{X(t), t \geq 0, P_W\}$ is *recurrent* for almost all Brownian sample environments W. Mathieu[4] proved that *localization* takes place for $\{X(t), t \geq 0, \mathcal{P}\}$, in the sense that

$$\lim_{N\to\infty} \overline{\lim_{\lambda\to\infty}}\, \mathcal{P}\left(\lambda^{-2}\max\{|X(t)| : 0 \leq t \leq e^{\lambda}\} > N\right) = 0.$$

However, in the case $d \geq 2$, it seems that the existence of the limiting distribution of $\{\lambda^{-2}X(e^{\lambda}), \mathcal{P}\}$ as $\lambda \to \infty$ is still an open problem. We give a remark on this problem. We notice the scaling relation

$$\{X(t),\ t \geq 0,\ P_{\lambda W_\lambda}\} \overset{d}{=} \{\lambda^{-2}X(\lambda^4 t),\ t \geq 0,\ P_W\},$$

where $\lambda > 0$ and $W \in \mathbf{W}$ are fixed, W_λ denotes an element of W defined by $W_\lambda(x) = \lambda^{-1}W(\lambda^2 x)$, $x \in \mathrm{R}^d$, and $\overset{d}{=}$ means the equality in distribution. This scaling relation combined with $W_\lambda \overset{d}{=} W$ imply the following: If we can prove that $\{X(e^{r\lambda}),\ P_{\lambda W}\}$ has the limiting distribution as $\lambda \to \infty$ under the condition $r = r(\lambda) \to 1$, then so does $\{\lambda^{-2}X(e^{\lambda}), \mathcal{P}\}$. From now on we are interested in $\{X(t), P_{\lambda W}\}$. For $W \in \mathbf{W}$ we define the sub-level domain D as the connected component of the open set $\{x \in \mathrm{R}^d : W(x) < 1\}$ containing 0. Then it is easy to see that D is bounded, P-a.s. *By making use of* Theorem 4 we see that for W not belonging to some P-negligible subset of $\mathbf{W}$, there exists a point $\tilde{b}$ of local (strict) minimum of W with depth > 1 inside D. Such a point $\tilde{b}$ is characterized by (i) $W(\tilde{b}) < W(x)$ for $x \in U - \{\tilde{b}\}$ and (ii) $U \subset D$, where U denotes the connected component of the open set $\{x \in \mathrm{R}^d : W(x) - W(\tilde{b}) < 1\}$ containing $\tilde{b}$. It is obvious that the totality of such points $\tilde{b}$ is a finite set, which is denoted by $\{b_k(W),\ 1 \leq k \leq l(W)\}$. Now suppose $l(W) = 1$ and put $b = b_1(W)$. Then from the argument of [4] we see that

$$X(e^{r\lambda}) \to b \text{ (in probability with respect to } P_{\lambda W}) \tag{5.1}$$

as $\lambda \to \infty$ provided $r = r(\lambda)$(non-random) tends to 1. If $l(W) \geq 2$, we do not know whether the limiting distribution of $X(e^{r\lambda})$ exists. Hoping for the best, we think it might be possible to define b, in one way or another, as *a single point* among $b_k(W)$, $1 \leq k \leq l(W)$, and to prove (5.1) even in the case $l(W) \geq 2$, for almost all w.

References

[1] N.N. Chentsov: *Lévy Brownian motion for several parameters and generalized white noise*, Theory Probab. Appl. **2** (1957), 265–266 (English translation).
[2] P. Lévy: Processus Stochastiques et Mouvement Brownien, Gauthier-Villars, Paris, 1948.
[3] E. Marinari, G. Parisi, D. Ruelle and P. Windy: *On the interpretation of $1/f$ noise*, Comm. Math. Phys. **89** (1983), 1–12.
[4] P. Mathieu: *Zero white noise limit through Dirichet forms, with application to diffusions in a random medium*, Probab. Theory Related Fields, **99** (1994), 549–580.
[5] H.P. McKean: *Brownian motion with a several-dimensional time*, Theory Probab. Appl. **8** (1963), 335–354.
[6] H. Tanaka: *Recurrence of a diffusion process in a multidimensional Brownian environment*, Proc. Japan Acad. Math. Sci. **69** (1993), 377–381.
[7] H. Tanaka: *Diffusion processes in random environments*, Proc. International Congress of Mathematicians, Zürich, 1994, Birkhäuser, Basel, 1995, 1047–1054.

Department of Mathematical and Physical Sciences
Japan Women's University
2-8-1 Mejirodai Bunkyo-ku, Tokyo 112-8681
Japan

Present address: 1-4-17-104 Miyamaedaira
Miyamae-ku, Kawasaki 216-0006
Japan

Bibliography of Hiroshi Tanaka

All of $*$ are contained in this volume.

[1] On limiting distributions for one-dimensional diffusion processes, Bull. Math. Statist., **7** (1957), 84–91.

[2] Some properties of one-dimensional diffusion processes (with G. Maruyama), Mem. Fac. Sci., Kyushu Univ., Ser. A, **11** (1957), 117–141.

[3] Certain limit theorems concerning one-dimensional diffusion processes, Mem. Fac. Sci., Kyushu Univ., Ser. A, **12** (1958), 1–11.

[4] Ergodic property of N-dimensional recurrent Markov processes (with G. Maruyama), Mem. Fac. Sci., Kyushu Univ., Ser. A, **13** (1959), 157–172.

[5]* Additive functionals of the Brownian path (with H.P. McKean), Mem. Coll. Sci., Kyoto Univ., Ser. A, **33** (1961), 479–506.

[6] Local times on the boundary for multi-dimensional diffusion (with K. Sato), Proc. Japan Acad., **38** (1962), 699–702.

[7]* Note on continuous additive functionals of the 1-dimensional Brownian path, Z. Wahrscheinlichkeitstheorie verw. Gebiete, **1** (1963), 251–257.

[8]* Existence of diffusions with continuous coefficients, Mem. Fac. Sci., Kyushu Univ., Ser. A, **18** (1964), 89–103.

[9] Note on additive functionals of the class (U) of Meyer of Markov processes, Mem. Fac. Sci., Kyushu Univ., Ser. A, **18** (1964), 154–165.

[10] Local solutions of stochastic differential equations associated with certain quasilinear parabolic equations, J. Fac. Sci., Univ. Tokyo, Sec. I, **14** (1967), 313–326.

[11] On the pre-closedness of the potential operator (with K. Yosida and T. Watanabe), J. Math. Soc. Japan, **20** (1968), 419–421.

[12] Propagation of chaos for certain Markov processes of jump type with non-linear generators I, II, Proc. Japan Acad., **45** (1969), 449-452; 598–600.

[13] Purely discontinuous Markov processes with nonlinear generators and their propagation of chaos, Teor. Verojatnost. Primenen., **15** (1970), 599–621.

[14]* Propagation of chaos for certain purely discontinuous Markov processes with interactions, J. Fac. Sci., Univ. Tokyo, Sec. I, **17** (1970), 259–272.

[15]* An inequality for a functional of probability distributions and its application to Kac's one-dimensional model of a Maxwellian gas, Z. Wahrscheinlichkeitstheorie verw. Gebiete, **27** (1973), 47–52.

[16]* On Markov process corresponding to Boltzmann's equation of Maxwellian gas, Proc. Second Japan-USSR Symp. on Probab. Th., 478–489, Lecture Notes in Math., **330**, Springer-Verlag, 1973.

[17] An inequality for certain functional of multidimensional probability distributions (with H. Murata), Hiroshima Math. J., **4** (1974), 75–81.

[18] Perturbation of drift-type for Lévy processes (with M. Tsuchiya and S. Watanabe), J. Math. Kyoto Univ., **14** (1974), 73–92.

[19]* On the uniqueness of Markov process associated with the Boltzmann equation of Maxwellian molecules, Proc. Intern. Symp. on Stochastic Differential Equations, 1976, 409–425, Kinokuniya, 1978.

[20] On the growing up problem for semilinear heat equations (with K. Kobayashi and T. Sirao), J. Math. Soc. Japan, **29** (1977), 407–424.

[21] Homogenization of certain one-dimensional discontinuous Markov processes (with M. Horie and T. Inuzuka), Hiroshima Math. J., **7** (1977), 629–641.

[22]* Probabilistic treatment of the Boltzmann equation of Maxwellian molecules, Z. Wahrscheinlichkeitstheorie verw. Gebiete, **46** (1978), 67–105.

[23] Stochastic differential equation associated with the Boltzmann equation of Maxwellian molecules in several dimensions, Stochastic Analysis, Proc. Intern. Conf. held at Northwestern Univ., 1978, 301–314, Academic Press, 1978.

[24]* Stochastic differential equations with reflecting boundary condition in convex regions, Hiroshima Math. J., **9** (1979), 163–177.

[25] Central limit theorem for a simple diffusion model of interacting particles (with M. Hitsuda), Hiroshima Math. J., **11** (1981), 415–423.

[26] Fluctuation theory for Kac's one-dimensional model of Maxwellian molecules, Sankhyā, Ser. A, Part I, **44** (1982), 23–46.

[27]* Some probabilistic problems in the spatially homogeneous Boltzmann equation, Theory and Application of Random Fields, 258–267, Lecture Notes in Control and Information Sciences, **49**, Springer-Verlag, 1983.

[28] Limit distribution of the minimum distance between independent and identically distributed d-dimensional random variables (with T. Onoyama and M. Sibuya), Statistical Extremes and Applications, 549–562, Reidel, 1984.

[29]* Limit theorem for certain diffusion processes with interaction, Stochastic Analysis : Proceedings of the Taniguchi Intern. Symp. on Stochastic Analysis, Katata and Kyoto, 1982, 469–488, Kinokuniya, 1984.

[30] Homogenization of diffusion processes with boundary conditions, Advances in Probab., 411–437, Marcel Dekker, 1984.

[31] A diffusion process in a singular mean-drift-field (with M. Nagasawa), Z. Wahrscheinlichkeitstheorie verw. Gebiete, **68** (1985), 247–269.

[32]* Central limit theorem for a system of Markovian particles with mean field interaction (with T. Shiga), Z. Wahrscheinlichkeitstheorie verw. Gebiete, **69** (1985), 439–459.

[33]* Propagation of chaos for diffusing particles of two types with singular mean field interaction (with M. Nagasawa), Probab. Th. Rel. Fields, **71** (1986), 69–83.

[34]* Stochastic differential equations for mutually reflecting Brownian balls (with Y. Saisho), Osaka J. Math., **23** (1986), 725–740.

[35]* Limit distribution for 1-dimensional diffusion in a reflected Brownian medium, Seminaire de Probabilites XXI, 246–261, Lecture Notes in Math., **1247**, Springer-Verlag, 1987.

[36]* Limit distributions for one-dimensional diffusion processes in self-similar random environments, Hydrodynamic Behavior and Interacting Particle Systems, 189–210, IMA Volumes, **9**, Springer-Verlag, 1987.

[37] On the symmetry of a reflecting Brownian motion defined by Skorohod's equation for multi-dimensional domain (with Y. Saisho), Tokyo J. Math., **10** (1987), 419–435.

[38]* Stochastic differential equation corresponding to the spatially homogeneous Boltzmann equation of Maxwellian and non-cutoff type, J. Fac. Sci., Univ. Tokyo, Sec. IA, **34** (1987), 351–369.

[39] Diffusion with interaction and collisions between coloured particles and the propagation of chaos (with M. Nagasawa), Probab. Th. Rel. Fields, **74** (1987), 161–198.

[40] One-dimensional diffusions and random walks in random environments (with K. Kawazu and Y. Tamura), Probability Theory and Mathematical Statistics, Fifth Japan-USSR Symposium Proceedings, 1986, 170–184, Lecture Notes in Math., **1299**, Springer-Verlag, 1988.

[41]* Limit theorem for one-dimensional diffusion process in Brownian environment, Stochastic Analysis, 156–172, Lecture Notes in Math., **1322**, Springer-Verlag, 1988.

[42] On the propagation of chaos for diffusion processes with drift coefficients not of average form (with M. Nagasawa), Tokyo J. Math., **10** (1989), 403–418.

[43] Time reversal of random walks in one-dimension, Tokyo J. Math., **12** (1989), 159–174.

[44] A theorem of Pitman type for simple random walks on $\boldsymbol{Z}^d$ (with H. Miyazaki), Tokyo J. Math., **12** (1989), 235–240.

[45] Limit theorems for one-dimensional diffusions and random walks in random environments (with K. Kawazu and Y. Tamura), Probab. Th. Rel. Fields, **80** (1989), 501–541.

[46] Time reversal of random walks in $\boldsymbol{R}^d$ Tokyo J. Math., **13** (1990), 375–389.

[47] Localization of diffusion processes in one-dimensional random environment (with K. Kawazu and Y. Tamura), J. Math. Soc. Japan, **44** (1992), 515–550.

[48] Limit theorems of the minimum interpoint distance between any pair of i.i.d. random points in $\boldsymbol{R}^d$ (with S. Kanagawa and Y. Mochizuki), Ann. Inst. Statist. Math., **44** (1992), 121–131.

[49]* On the maximum of a diffusion process in a drifted Brownian environment (with K. Kawazu), Seminaire de Probabilites XXVII, 78–85, Lecture Notes in Math., **1557**, Springer-Verlag, 1993.

[50] Green operators of absorbing Lévy processes on the half line, Stochastic Processes, A Festschrift in honour of G. Kallianpur, 313–319, Springer-Verlag, 1993.

[51]* Recurrence of a diffusion process in a multidimensional Brownian environment, Proc. Japan Acad., **69**, Ser. A (1993), 377–381.

[52]* Localization of a diffusion process in a one-dimensional Brownian environment, Comm. Pure Appl. Math., **47** (1994), 755–766.

[53] Localization of one-dimensional random walks in random environment (with K. Kawazu and Y. Tamura), Proc. Intern. Conf. on "Stochastic Processes, Physics and Geometry II", 1991, 444–452, World Scientific, 1995.

[54]* Diffusion processes in random environments, Proc. Intern. Congress of Mathematicians, Zürich, Switzerland 1994, 1047–1054, Birkhäuser, 1995.

[55]* Environment-wise central limit theorem for a diffusion in a Brownian environment with large drift, Itô's Stochastic Calculus and Probability Theory, 373–384, Springer-Verlag, 1996.

[56]* A diffusion process in a Brownian environment with drift (with K. Kawazu), J. Math. Soc. Japan, **49** (1997), 189–211.

[57]* Limit theorems for a Brownian motion with drift in a white noise environment, Chaos, Solitons & Fractals, **8** (1997), 1807–1816.

[58]* Invariance principle for a Brownian motion with large drift in a white noise environment (with K. Kawazu), Hiroshima Math. J., **28** (1998), 129–137.

[59] Stochastic differential equations of pure-jumps in relativistic quantum theory (with M. Nagasawa), Chaos, Solitons & Fractals, **10** (1999), 1265–1280.

[60] Time dependent subordination and Markov processes with jumps (with M. Nagasawa), Seminaire de Probabilités XXXIV, 257-288, Lecture Notes in Math., **1729**, Springer-Verlag, 2000.

[61] The principle of variation for relativistic quantum particles (with M. Nagasawa), Seminaire de Probabilités XXXV, 1-27, Lecture Notes in Math., **1755**, Springer-Verlag, 2001.

[62] A diffusion process with a one-sided Brownian potential (with K. Kawazu, and Y. Suzuki), Tokyo J. Math., **24** (2001), 211-229.

[63]* Some theorems concerning extrema of Brownian motion with d-dimensional time, Osaka J. Math., **38** (2001), 369-377.

Permissions

The editors and World Scientific Publishing Co. Pte. Ltd. would like to thank the original publishers of Tanaka's papers for granting permissions to reprint specific papers in this volume. The following list contains the credit lines for those articles.

[5] Reprint from Mem. Coll. Sci., Kyoto Univ., Ser. A, **12**, © 1961 by Kyoto University.

[7] Reprint from Z. Wahrscheilichkeitstheorie verw. Gebiete, **1**, © 1963 by Springer-Verlag.

[8] Reprint from Mem. Fac. Sci., Kyushu Univ., Ser. A, **18**, © 1964 by Kyushu University.

[14] Reprint from J. Fac. Sci., Univ. Tokyo, Sec. I, **17**, © 1970 by the University of Tokyo.

[15] Reprint from Z. Wahrscheilichkeitstheorie verw. Gebiete, **27**, © 1973 by Springer-Verlag.

[16] Reprint from Lecture Notes in Mathematics, **330**, © 1973 by Springer-Verlag.

[19] Reprint from Proc. Intern. Symp. on Stochastic Differential Equations, © 1978 by Kinokuniya Co. Ltd.

[22] Reprint from Z. Wahrscheilichkeitstheorie verw. Gebiete, **46**, © 1978 by Springer-Verlag.

[24] Reprint from Hiroshima Math. J., **9**, © 1979 by Hiroshima University.

[27] Reprint from Lecture Note in Control and Information Sciences, **49**, © 1983 by Springer-Verlag.

[29] Reprint from Stochastic Analysis : Proceedings of the Taniguchi Intern. Symp. on Stochastic Analysis, Katata and Kyoto, 1982, © 1984 by Kinokuniya Co. Ltd.

[32] Reprint from Z. Wahrscheilichkeitstheorie verw. Gebiete, **69**, © 1985 by Springer-Verlag.

[33] Reprint from Probab. Th. Rel. Fields, **71**, © 1986 by Springer-Verlag.

[34] Reprint from Osaka J. Math., **23**, © 1986 by Osaka University.

[35] Reprint from Lecture Notes in Mathematics, **1247**, © 1987 by Springer-Verlag.

[36] Reprint from Hydrodynamic Behavior and Interacting Particle Systems, (ed. G. Papanicolaou), IMA Volumes in Mathematics and Its Applications, **9**, © 1987 by Springer-Verlag.

[38] Reprint from J. Fac. Sci., Univ. Tokyo, Sec. IA, **34**, © 1987 by the University of Tokyo.